W9-BUO-020

europe
on a shoestring

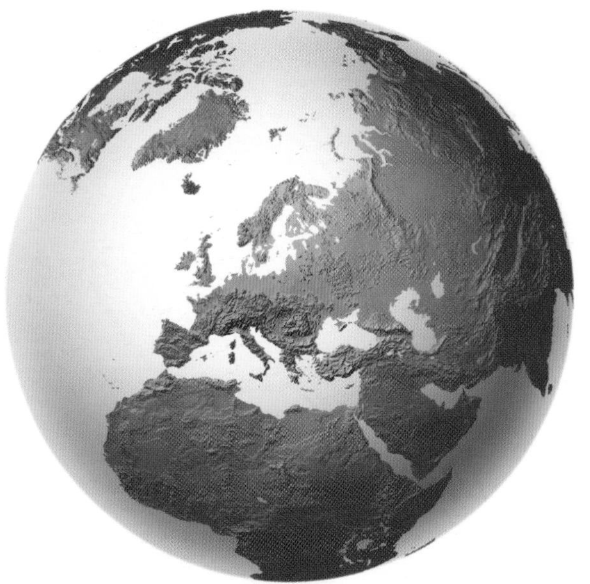

Tom Masters

Brett Atkinson, Carolyn Bain, James Bainbridge, Neal Bedford, Oliver Berry, Paul Clammer, Geert Cole, Jayne D'Arcy, Chris Deliso, Peter Dragicevich, Lisa Dunford, Mark Elliott, David Else, Steve Fallon, Duncan Garwood, Leanne Logan, Vesna Maric, Marika McAdam, Craig McLachlan, Becky Ohlsen, Fran Parnell, Leif Pettersen, Brandon Presser, Robert Reid, Tim Richards, Simon Richmond, Miles Roddis, Damien Simonis, John Spelman, Regis St Louis, Andrew Stone, Andy Symington, Ryan Ver Berkmoes, Nicola Williams, Neil Wilson

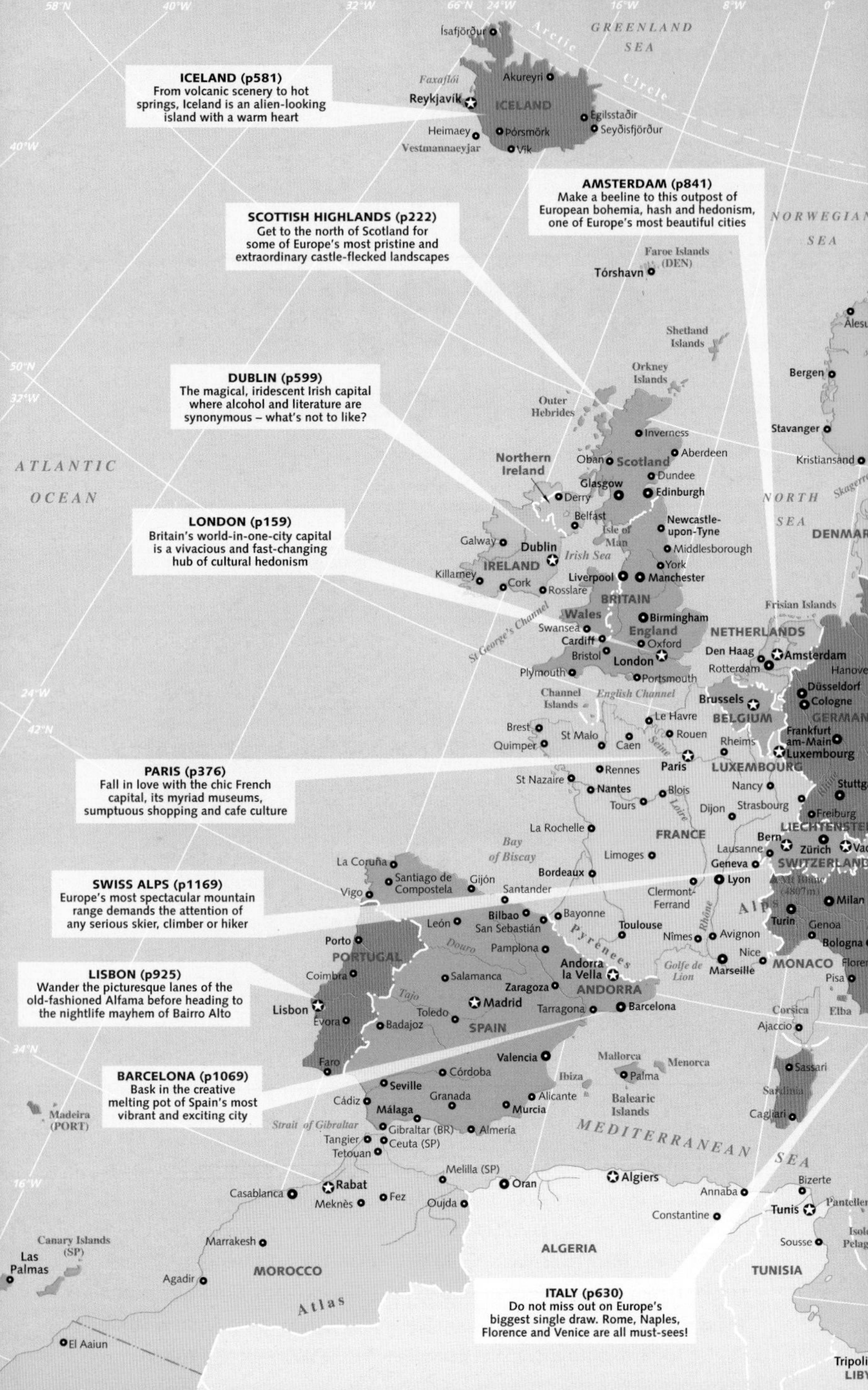

ICELAND (p581)
From volcanic scenery to hot springs, Iceland is an alien-looking island with a warm heart
AMSTERDAM (p841)
Make a beeline to this outpost of European bohemia, hash and hedonism, one of Europe's most beautiful cities
SCOTTISH HIGHLANDS (p222)
Get to the north of Scotland for some of Europe's most pristine and extraordinary castle-flecked landscapes
DUBLIN (p599)
The magical, iridescent Irish capital where alcohol and literature are synonymous – what's not to like?
LONDON (p159)
Britain's world-in-one-city capital is a vivacious and fast-changing hub of cultural hedonism
PARIS (p376)
Fall in love with the chic French capital, its myriad museums, sumptuous shopping and cafe culture
SWISS ALPS (p1169)
Europe's most spectacular mountain range demands the attention of any serious skier, climber or hiker
LISBON (p925)
Wander the picturesque lanes of the old-fashioned Alfama before heading to the nightlife mayhem of Bairro Alto
BARCELONA (p1069)
Bask in the creative melting pot of Spain's most vibrant and exciting city
ITALY (p630)
Do not miss out on Europe's biggest single draw. Rome, Naples, Florence and Venice are all must-sees!
GREENLAND SEA
NORWEGIAN SEA
ATLANTIC OCEAN
NORTH SEA
MEDITERRANEAN SEA
ICELAND
IRELAND
BRITAIN
NETHERLANDS
BELGIUM
LUXEMBOURG
FRANCE
SWITZERLAND
LIECHTENSTEIN
PORTUGAL
SPAIN
ANDORRA
MONACO
MOROCCO
ALGERIA
TUNISIA

NORWAY (p861)
Prepare to be blown away by Europe's most spectacular coastline on the train ride from Oslo to Bergen
STOCKHOLM (p1123)
Tour the waterways, explore top-notch museums and wander the backstreets of Sweden's graceful capital
MOSCOW (p979) & ST PETERSBURG (p986)
Discover two of Russia's many faces – first in consumerist, irrepressible Moscow, then in grand imperial St Petersburg
BERLIN (p452)
Europe's coolest city? Have fun deciding yourself in the bars and clubs of the reborn German capital
BRAŞOV (p964)
Scale castles and mountains in haunting Transylvania using this Gothic, medieval centrefold as a base
BAY OF KOTOR (p800)
Explore Montenegro's charming historic towns hemmed in between majestic limestone cliffs
İSTANBUL (p1179)
The glorious one-time Byzantine and Ottoman capital is one of the world's truly great cities
CROATIA (p249)
Word may now be out about this Adriatic gem, but don't miss its gorgeous coastline and unspoiled islands
GREECE (p517)
Embark on your own odyssey across the sun-drenched isles of this ancient civilisation
BARENTS SEA
White Sea
Gulf of Bothnia
Gulf of Finland
Gulf of Riga
BALTIC SEA
Lake Ladoga
SWEDEN
FINLAND
NORWAY
ESTONIA
LATVIA
LITHUANIA
Russia
RUSSIA
BELARUS
POLAND
UKRAINE
CZECH REPUBLIC
SLOVAKIA
AUSTRIA
HUNGARY
MOLDOVA
ROMANIA
SLOVENIA
CROATIA
BOSNIA & HERCEGOVINA
SERBIA
MONTENEGRO
Kosovo
MACEDONIA
ALBANIA
BULGARIA
GREECE
TURKEY
ITALY
SAN MARINO
MALTA
GEORGIA
AZERBAIJAN
ARMENIA
IRAN
IRAQ
SYRIA
LEBANON
ISRAEL & the Palestinian Territories
JORDAN
SAUDI ARABIA
EGYPT
LIBYA
KAZAKHSTAN
NORTH CYPRUS
REPUBLIC OF CYPRUS
Carpathian Mountains
Sea of Azov
Crimea
BLACK SEA
CASPIAN SEA
ADRIATIC SEA
TYRRHENIAN SEA
IONIAN SEA
AEGEAN SEA
Sea of Crete
MEDITERRANEAN SEA
Cyclades Islands
Dodecanese Islands
Ionian Islands
Volga
Don
Dnipro
Dnestr
Pripet
Danube
Tigris
Nordkapp
Tromsø
Ivalo
Murmansk
Narvik
Kiruna
Bodø
Mo i Rana
Kemi
Luleå
Oulu
Arkhangelsk
Trondheim
Umeå
Vaasa
Jyväskylä
Tampere
Petrozavodsk
Lillehammer
Bollnäs
Turku
Helsinki
Vyborg
St Petersburg
Oslo
Uppsala
Åland
Stockholm
Tallinn
Örebro
Vänern
Norrköping
Linköping
Saaremaa
Tartu
Novgorod
Pskov
Yaroslavl
Nizhny Novgorod
Kazan
Kattegat
Jönköping
Gotland
Gothenburg
Ventspils
Rīga
Moscow
Samara
Aalborg
Öland
Liepāja
Daugavpils
Århus
Helsingborg
Copenhagen
Malmö
Odense
Zealand
Bornholm
Klaipėda
Kaunas
Vitsebsk
Smolensk
Tula
Kaliningrad
Vilnius
Lübeck
Stralsund
Gdańsk
Minsk
Mahileu
Schwerin
Szczecin
Hrodna
Hamburg
Białystok
Voronezh
Poznań
Homel
Berlin
Warsaw
Brest
Łódź
Leipzig
Lublin
Volgograd
Dresden
Wrocław
Zhytomyr
Kyiv
Kharkiv
Katowice
Plzeň
Prague
Kraków
Lviv
Ostrava
Dnipropetrovsk
Donetsk
Brno
Rostov-on-Don
Munich
Košice
Vienna
Linz
Bratislava
Salzburg
Chişinău
Győr
Budapest
Odesa
Cluj-Napoca
Szeged
Krasnodar
Ljubljana
Trieste
Timişoara
Simferopol
Grozny
Zagreb
Bran
Braşov
Sevastopol
Belgrade
Sukhumi
Tbilisi
Bucharest
Constanta
Craiova
Yerevan
Zadar
Sarajevo
Split
Varna
Ancona
Pescara
Dubrovnik
Pristina
Sofia
Burgas
Trabzon
Samsun
Rome
Podgorica
Plovdiv
Erzurum
Skopje
Zonguldak
İstanbul
Tirana
Van
Sivas
Naples
Bari
Ankara
Salerno
Taranto
Thessaloniki
Bursa
Golfo di Taranto
Vlore
Diyarbakır
Larisa
Kayseri
Corfu
Lesvos
Palermo
Reggio di Calabria
Evia
İzmir
Adana
Patra
Athens
Aleppo
Sicily
Piraeus
Catania
Kuşadası
Antalya
Kaş
Lefkosia (Nicosia)
Kalamata
Rhodes
Valletta
Cyprus
Homs
Hania
Iraklio
Lemesos
Crete
Beirut
Damascus
Jerusalem
8°E
16°E
32°E
40°E
48°E
24°E

Europe Highlights

How can you possibly sum up a continent as diverse, rich and surprising as Europe? You may have come for its iconic landmarks, extraordinary museums and breathtaking architecture, but we'll wager that the memories you take home with you will be even more wide-ranging and less predictable than a list of monuments. From exciting train journeys and amazing views to meals you'll remember for years to come, and nights out in all corners of the continent with newly found friends, Europe will quickly prove itself to be far more than the sum of its parts.

MARTIN MO

1 TRAIN TRAVEL

Travelling by train (p1242) and chatting with locals who shared our train compartments throughout Eastern Europe was a major highlight. One Bulgarian chap was so excited to speak to Australians he gave us a huge jar of homemade honey from his father's farm in the countryside.

Trent Paton, Lonely Planet staff

HISTORY

'I grew up in Europe, where the history comes from' – Eddie Izzard.

From Ancient Greece and the Renaissance, to 19th-century empires and 20th-century conflicts, Europe's complicated, violent but fascinating history (p37) provides a great backstory to any trip around the continent.

Clifton Wilkinson, Lonely Planet staff

2

JON DAVISON

ITALY

Other countries might have great food, spectacular landscapes, history, art, culture, but nowhere offers them with as much verve as Italy (p630), Europe's sexy southern boot. Mired in myth, the *bel paese* (beautiful country) is a mesmerising mix of natural wonders and artistic glories, of cultural icons, revered traditions and unexpected treats.

Duncan Garwood, Lonely Planet author, Italy

3

JULIET COOMBE

OLIVIER CIREND

4 PARIS

The French capital (p376) has drawn artists from around the world for centuries, from Leonardo da Vinci to Picasso. Today the city's galleries and museums mean that visitors can enjoy the fruits of these artistic labours.

Oliver Berry, Lonely Planet author, UK

DALLAS STRIB

5 FOOD

My fondest travel memories revolve around food (p41). Finishing a huge portion of cassoulet in Paris, to the joy of the bistro owner; perfect ham and fresh fish ordered through mutual sign language in Spain; local goat's cheese and olives on the train to Athens – my Europe trips are all punctuated by moments of foodie bliss.

Jo Potts, Lonely Planet staff

GOING UNDERGROUND

Tube, Métro, U-Bahn – Europe's underground systems are an experience in themselves. There's some great people-watching to be had and some fascinating architecture, in Paris and Moscow for example. Mind the gap!

Chris Girdler, Lonely Planet staff

6

TOM COCKREM

CAFE CULTURE

When your trip becomes a bewildering 'if it's Tuesday it must be Paris' blur, take a leaf out of the locals' book and spend a day enjoying some cafe culture. Unwind with the papers, indulge yourself with a huge piece of cake, people-watch, or decide on your next destination.

Caroline Sieg, Lonely Planet staff

7

DALLAS STRIBLEY

DAVID TOMLIN

8 ANDALUCÍA

Other Spaniards might disagree but for many visitors Andalucía (p1088) is quintessential Spain. The sun beating down on white hill-hugging villages, an impromptu flamenco performance in a backstreet bar, and the Islamic architecture of Granada, Córdoba and Seville are all experiences worth seeking out and not easily forgotten.

Lucy Monie, Lonely Planet staff

GARETH McCORM

9 THE ALPS

Awe-inspiring but accessible, Europe's most famous mountain range offers beauty and outdoor activities in every season. Want to try some summer glacier skiing or make like Julie Andrews in *The Sound of Music*? This is the place to do it.

Sue Holmes, traveller, UK

MARTIN MOOS

10 ART

From prehistoric rock paintings to the latest in performance art, Europe has a long history of putting on its smock and waiting for the muse to arrive (p38). The major capitals are famous for their breathtaking collections of Old Masters, while many provincial cities have becomes home to cutting-edge contemporary galleries – Newcastle in the UK and Graz in Austria are just two where the buildings are artworks in themselves.

Imogen Hall, Lonely Planet staff

11 FESTIVALS & EVENTS

Travel around Europe at whatever time of year and you're likely to coincide with at least one local or national celebration (p45). Keep your distance from the fireworks mayhem during Valencia's Las Fallas, get down and dirty at Glastonbury, mess up your body clock during St Petersburg's White Nights, or enjoy the weird and wonderful at the Edinburgh Festival.

Katrina Browning, traveller, UK

GARETH McCORMACK

IZZET KERIBAR

12 İSTANBUL

Europe comes to a glorious full-stop in exotic, historic İstanbul (p1179). Turkey's biggest urban centre offers fantastic food, amazing sights and the chance to sail backwards and forwards from Asia to Europe on a Bosphorus ferry. One of the world's truly great cities.

James Bainbridge, Lonely Planet author, UK

MARTIN M

13 BEACHES

Chill out at cool French resorts, dance till dawn in Ibiza, discover your own secluded Greek cove or skinny dip along Croatia's coast – Europe has plenty of beach options (p33) whether you want to party, get off the beaten track or just top up your (all-over) tan.

Paula Hardy, Lonely Planet staff

ORIEN HA

14 LONDON

Huge, magnificent, expensive and dynamic, London (p159) is just too diverse to easily classify and too important to ignore. More than just the capital of the UK, it's also Europe's centre for nightlife, culture, eating and drinking. Expect to stay longer and spend more than you planned.

Clifton Wilkinson, Lonely Planet staff

THE GAMES PEOPLE PLAY

Europe has an idiosyncratic sport for every occasion. Caber tossing in Scotland, *baby foot* (table football) in France and *kiiking* (a giant swing) in Estonia. Finns enjoy *eukonkanto* (wife-carrying) while English cheese-rolling finds new uses for a Double Gloucester. The Netherlands has chess-boxing and the Greeks have *rouketopolemos* (rocket wars) which light up the skies and your itinerary.

Debra Herrmann, Lonely Planet staff

JONATHAN SMITH

15 ST PETERSBURG

Peter the Great's extraordinary city was Russia's 'window on Europe' – and what a window. Picking and mixing the most glorious European architectural and artistic styles, from the facade of the Winter Palace to the fountains of Peterhof, St Petersburg (p86) is a jaw-dropping place that more than deserves its nickname 'Venice of the North'.

Tom Masters, Lonely Planet author, UK

16

JAMES BRAUND

ANDREW BURKE

17 NIGHTLIFE

There's nowhere like London for diversity of nightlife and nowhere like Madrid for infectious 'kill the night' enthusiasm, but Berlin's reinvention as the continental clubbing capital (p462) and the burgeoning scenes in places like Belgrade (p1006) mean you can party your way from one side of Europe to the other.

Owen Eszeki, traveller, Australia

WILL SA

18 GET LOST

The most memorable highlights of any trip are often those unexpected little treasures you discover on your own: a beautiful hidden church, a tranquil hike through the hills for the most amazing views, or a friendly local bar you stumble upon in the backstreets.

David Else, Lonely Planet author, UK

DAVID TOMLI

19 FOOTBALL

Football (p43) is a religion in Europe. Top stadiums like London's Wembley and Barcelona's Camp Nou do tours, but nothing beats a fan's eye view during a game. A local derby is the ultimate experience – big ones include Glasgow's 'Old Firm Derby' (Rangers v Celtic) and the 'Derby della Madonnina' with Milan's two clubs battling it out in the San Siro.

Matt Bowell, Lonely Planet staff

Contents

Europe Highlights	**4**
Destination Europe	**20**
Getting Started	**25**
Itineraries	**31**
Snapshot	**36**
A Year in Europe	**45**
Albania	**50**
TRANSPORT	53
TIRANA	54
CENTRAL ALBANIA	58
Kruja	58
Durrës	58
Apollonia	58
Berat	59
SOUTHERN ALBANIA	59
Dhërmi & Drymades Beaches	59
Saranda	59
ALBANIA DIRECTORY	60
Andorra	**62**
TRANSPORT	64
ANDORRA LA VELLA	64
AROUND ANDORRA	66
Canillo & Soldeu	
Ordino & Around	68
Arinsal & Pal	69
Sant Julià de Lòria	69
ANDORRA DIRECTORY	69
Austria	**71**
TRANSPORT	74
VIENNA	76
THE DANUBE VALLEY	86
Krems an der Donau	87
Melk	87
Linz	87
THE SOUTH	88
Graz	88
Klagenfurt	91
SALZBURG	91
AROUND SALZBURG	95
Werfen	95
SALZKAMMERGUT	95
Hellbrunn	95
Hallstatt	95
TIROL	96
Innsbruck	96
Kitzbühel	99
Lienz	100
Hohe Tauern National Park	100
VORARLBERG	100
AUSTRIA DIRECTORY	101
Belarus	**103**
TRANSPORT	105
MINSK	105
BREST	109
BELARUS DIRECTORY	110
Belgium	**112**
TRANSPORT	115
BRUSSELS	116
AROUND BRUSSELS	120
Waterloo	120
FLANDERS	120
Antwerp	120
Ghent (Gent, Gand)	124
Bruges (Brugge)	126
Ypres (Ieper)	128
WALLONIA	129
Liège (Luik)	129
Around Liège	130
Namur (Namen)	130
Rochefort & Han-sur-Lesse	131
Bastogne (Bastenaken)	131
BELGIUM DIRECTORY	132
Bosnia & Hercegovina	**134**
TRANSPORT	136
SARAJEVO	137
AROUND BOSNIA & HERCEGOVINA	143
Jajce	143
Mostar	144
Around Mostar	146
BOSNIA & HERCEGOVINA DIRECTORY	147

Britain 149

TRANSPORT 154
LONDON 159
AROUND LONDON 179
Windsor & Eton 179
SOUTHEAST ENGLAND 179
Canterbury 179
Dover 180
Brighton 181
Portsmouth 183
Winchester 184
SOUTHWEST ENGLAND 185
Salisbury 185
Stonehenge 186
Avebury 186
Bath 187
Bristol 189
Glastonbury 191
Exmoor National Park 191
Dartmoor National Park 191
Newquay 192
St Ives 192
Penzance 193
Land's End 193
CENTRAL ENGLAND 193
Oxford 193
The Cotswolds 196
Stratford-Upon-Avon 197
Peak District National Park 198
EASTERN ENGLAND 198
Cambridge 198
NORTHWEST ENGLAND 200
Manchester 200
Liverpool 202
Lake District National Park 203
NORTHEAST ENGLAND 204
York 204
Durham 207
Newcastle-Upon-Tyne 207
Hadrian's Wall 209
CARDIFF 209
SOUTHERN & WESTERN WALES 211
Brecon Beacons National Park 211
Brecon 211
Pembrokeshire Coast National Park 213
St Davids 213
Fishguard 213
NORTHERN WALES 213
Snowdonia National Park 213
EDINBURGH & GLASGOW 214
Edinburgh 214
Glasgow 218
CENTRAL & EASTERN SCOTLAND 221
Stirling 221
St Andrews 221
WESTERN & NORTHERN SCOTLAND 222
Loch Lomond 222
Oban 222
Isle of Mull 223
Fort William 223
Isle of Skye 224
Inverness 224
John O'Groats 225
BRITAIN DIRECTORY 225

Bulgaria 229

TRANSPORT 231
SOFIA 233
SOUTHERN BULGARIA 238
Rila Monastery 238
Plovdiv 238
CENTRAL BULGARIA 240
Veliko Târnovo 240
BLACK SEA COAST 243
Varna 243
North Coast 246
Nesebâr 246
Burgas 246
South Coast 247
BULGARIA DIRECTORY 247

Croatia 249

TRANSPORT 253
ZAGREB 254
ISTRIA (ISTRA) 260
Pula 260
DALMATIA (DALMACIJA) 261
Split (Spalato) 261
Hvar Island 263
Korčula Island 264
Dubrovnik 266
CROATIA DIRECTORY 269

Cyprus 272

TRANSPORT 274
REPUBLIC OF CYPRUS 275
Lefkosia (South Nicosia) 275
Larnaka 277
Lemesos (Limasol) 277
Troodos Massif 278
Pafos 278
Polis 279
NORTH CYPRUS 279
Lefkoşa (North Nicosia) 279
Girne (Kyrenia) 280
Around North Cyprus 280
CYPRUS DIRECTORY 281

Czech Republic 283

TRANSPORT 284
PRAGUE 287
AROUND PRAGUE 296
Karlštejn 296
Kutná Hora 296
BOHEMIA 297
Karlovy Vary 297
Plzeň 298
České Budějovice 299
Český Krumlov 300
MORAVIA 302
Brno 302
Telč 303
CZECH REPUBLIC DIRECTORY 303

Denmark 306

TRANSPORT 309
COPENHAGEN 311
ZEALAND 318
Helsingør (Elsinore) 318
Roskilde 318
BORNHOLM 319
FUNEN 320
Odense 320
JUTLAND 321
Århus 321
Aalborg 324
Frederikshavn 325
Skagen 325
Hirtshals 326
Ribe 326
DENMARK DIRECTORY 326

Estonia 329

TRANSPORT 331
TALLINN 332
AROUND TALLINN 339
Lahemaa National Park 339
SOUTHEASTERN ESTONIA 339
Tartu 339
SOUTHWESTERN ESTONIA 342
Pärnu 342
ESTONIA DIRECTORY 343

Finland 345
TRANSPORT 348
HELSINKI 350
AROUND HELSINKI 358
Porvoo 358
SOUTHWESTERN FINLAND 358
Turku 358
Tampere 360
ÅLAND 361
Mariehamn 361
The Islands 362
SOUTHEASTERN FINLAND 362
Savonlinna 362
Kuopio 363
NORTHERN FINLAND 364
Oulu 364
Rovaniemi 366
Inari 367
FINLAND DIRECTORY 367

France 370
TRANSPORT 374
PARIS 376
AROUND PARIS 396
Versailles 396
Chartres 396
FAR NORTHERN FRANCE 397
Lille 397
Calais 398
NORMANDY 399
Rouen 399
Bayeux 400
Mont St-Michel 401
BRITTANY 402
Quimper 402
St-Malo 403
ALSACE & LORRAINE 404
Strasbourg 404
LOIRE VALLEY 408
Blois 408
Around Blois 409
Tours 410
Around Tours 411
Amboise 412
BURGUNDY & THE RHÔNE VALLEY 413
Dijon 413
Beaune 414
Lyon 415
FRENCH ALPS 419
Chamonix 419
DORDOGNE & QUERCY 420
Sarlat-la-Canéda 420
ATLANTIC COAST & FRENCH BASQUE COUNTRY 421
Bordeaux 421
Biarritz 423
Lourdes 424
LANGUEDOC-ROUSSILLON 425
Carcassonne 425
Nîmes 425
Pont du Gard 426
Toulouse 426
PROVENCE 428
Marseille 428
Aix-en-Provence 431
Avignon 431
CÔTE D'AZUR & MONACO 434
Nice 434
Cannes 438
Monaco 439
CORSICA 440
Ajaccio 440
Bonifacio 441
Bastia 442
FRANCE DIRECTORY 443

Germany 447
TRANSPORT 450
BERLIN 452
AROUND BERLIN 463
Potsdam 463
Sachsenhausen Concentration Camp 464
EASTERN GERMANY 465
Dresden 465
Around Dresden 467
Leipzig 467
Erfurt 469
Around Erfurt 470
Weimar & Around 470
BAVARIA 472
Munich 472
Romantic Road 478
Würzburg 478
Bamberg 479
Rothenburg ob der Tauber 480
Nuremberg 480
Regensburg 481
Füssen 482
BAVARIAN ALPS 482
Berchtesgaden 482
BADEN-WÜRTTEMBERG 483
Stuttgart 483
Around Stuttgart 485
Heidelberg 485
Black Forest 486
Freiburg 488
LAKE CONSTANCE 489
WESTERN GERMANY 490
Moselle Valley 490
Trier 491
Rhine Valley – Koblenz to Mainz 491
Frankfurt-am-Main 492
Cologne 496
Bonn 499
Düsseldorf 499
Aachen 500
LOWER SAXONY 502
Hanover 502
Around Hanover 503
BREMEN 504
NORTHERN GERMANY 505
Hamburg 506
Lübeck 511
GERMANY DIRECTORY 512

Greece 517
TRANSPORT 519
ATHENS 524
AROUND ATHENS 531
Piraeus 531
THE PELOPONNESE 532
Patra 532
Corinth 532
Nafplio 533
Mycenae 533
Sparta 533
Mystras 533
Gefyra & Monemvasia 534
Gythio 534
The Mani 534
Olympia 535
NORTHERN GREECE 535
Thessaloniki 535
Mt Olympus 537
Meteora 537
Ioannina 538
Zagorohoria & Vikos Gorge 538
Igoumenitsa 538
SARONIC GULF ISLANDS 539
Aegina 539
Hydra 539
Spetses 539
CYCLADES 540
Mykonos 540
Paros 541
Naxos 542
Ios 543

Santorini (Thira) 544
CRETE 546
Iraklio 546
Knossos 547
Rethymno 547
Hania 548
Samaria Gorge 549
DODECANESE 550
Rhodes 550
Kos 551
Patmos 552
NORTHEASTERN AEGEAN ISLANDS 553
Samos 553
Lesvos (Mytilini) 553
SPORADES 555
Skiathos 555
Skopelos 555
Alonnisos 556
IONIAN ISLANDS 556
Corfu 556
Kefallonia 557
GREECE DIRECTORY 557

Hungary 560

TRANSPORT 563
BUDAPEST 564
AROUND BUDAPEST 573
Szentendre 573
Visegrád 574
Esztergom 574
WESTERN HUNGARY 574
Sopron 574
Keszthely 575
Siófok 575
SOUTHERN HUNGARY 576
Pécs 576
GREAT PLAIN 577
Kecskemét 577
Szeged 578
NORTHEASTERN HUNGARY 578
Eger 578
HUNGARY DIRECTORY 579

Iceland 581

TRANSPORT 583
REYKJAVÍK 584
AROUND REYKJAVÍK 591
Blue Lagoon (Bláa Lónið) 591
The Golden Circle 592
Þórsmörk 592
ICELAND DIRECTORY 592

Ireland 594

TRANSPORT 598
DUBLIN 599
AROUND DUBLIN 609
Brú na Bóinne 609
SOUTHEASTERN IRELAND 609
Kilkenny 609
SOUTHWESTERN IRELAND 610
Cork 610
Around Cork 613
Killarney 614
The Ring of Kerry 615
THE WEST COAST 615
The Burren 615
Galway 616
Aran Islands 618
NORTHWESTERN IRELAND 619
Sligo 619
Bundoran 620
NORTHERN IRELAND 620
Belfast 620
The Causeway Coast 625
Derry 625
IRELAND DIRECTORY 627

Italy 630

TRANSPORT 634
ROME 636
AROUND ROME 654
Ostia Antica 654
Tivoli 654
Tarquinia 655
Cerveteri 655
NORTHERN ITALY 655
Genoa 655
Cinque Terre 657
Turin 658
Milan 659
Verona 662
Padua 664
Venice 665
Ferrara 673
Bologna 674
Ravenna 676
THE DOLOMITES 676
Canazei 677
Val Gardena 677
San Martino di Castrozza 677
CENTRAL ITALY 677
Florence 677
Pisa 684
Siena 685
Lucca 687
Perugia 688
Assisi 689
Urbino 690
SOUTHERN ITALY 690
Naples 690
Pompeii 695
Capri 696
Sorrento 697
Amalfi Coast 697
Matera 698
Bari 699
Lecce 699
SICILY 700
Getting There & Away 700
Palermo 700
Aeolian Islands 702
Taormina 703
Mt Etna 704
Syracuse 704
Agrigento 705
SARDINIA 705
Getting There & Away 706
Cagliari 706
Alghero 707
ITALY DIRECTORY 708

Kosovo 712

TRANSPORT 713
PRISTINA 714
AROUND PRISTINA 716
Peja (Peć) 716
Prizren 716
KOSOVO DIRECTORY 716

Latvia 717

TRANSPORT 719
RĪGA 720
AROUND RĪGA 727
Jūrmala 727
WESTERN LATVIA 727
EASTERN LATVIA 728
Sigulda 728
LATVIA DIRECTORY 729

Liechtenstein 731

TRANSPORT 732
VADUZ 732
AROUND VADUZ 734
Malbun 735

Lithuania 736

TRANSPORT 737
VILNIUS 740

AROUND VILNIUS 747
Paneriai 747
Trakai 747
CENTRAL LITHUANIA 748
Kaunas 748
Šiauliai 749
WESTERN LITHUANIA 749
Klaipėda 749
Curonian Spit 749
LITHUANIA DIRECTORY 750

Luxembourg 752

TRANSPORT 754
LUXEMBOURG CITY 754
AROUND LUXEMBOURG 758
Vianden 758
Clervaux 758
Château de Bourscheid 759
Echternach 759
Diekirch 759
LUXEMBOURG DIRECTORY 760

Macedonia 761

TRANSPORT 763
SKOPJE 764
WESTERN MACEDONIA 767
Ohrid 767
Bitola 770
MACEDONIA DIRECTORY 771

Malta 773

TRANSPORT 775
VALLETTA 776
AROUND MALTA 778
Sliema, St Julian's & Paceville 778
Mdina & Rabat 781
GOZO 781
Victoria (Rabat) 781
Marsalforn 781
Xagħra 782
COMINO 782
MALTA DIRECTORY 782

Moldova 785

TRANSPORT 788
CHIŞINĂU 788
AROUND CHIŞINĂU 792
Cricova 792
Mileştii Mici 793
Cojuşna 793
Orheiul Vechi 793
TRANSDNIESTR 793
Tiraspol 793
MOLDOVA DIRECTORY 794

Montenegro 797

TRANSPORT 799
COASTAL MONTENEGRO 800
Kotor 800
Budva 802
Bar 802
Ulcinj 803
CENTRAL MONTENEGRO 803
Cetinje 803
Durmitor National Park 804
MONTENEGRO DIRECTORY 805

Morocco 807

TRANSPORT 810
MEDITERRANEAN COAST & THE RIF 811
Tangier 811
Ceuta 814
Chefchaouen 815
ATLANTIC COAST 816
Casablanca 816
Rabat 819
Essaouira 820
IMPERIAL CITIES 821
Fez 821
Meknès 826
Around Meknès 827
Marrakesh 827
HIGH ATLAS MOUNTAINS & DESERT 832
High Atlas 832
Drâa Valley 833
MOROCCO DIRECTORY 833

The Netherlands 837

TRANSPORT 839
AMSTERDAM 841
RANDSTAD 848
Leiden 848
Den Haag (The Hague) 849
Delft 850
Rotterdam 851
Utrecht City 854
NORTHERN NETHERLANDS 855
Groningen City 855
Texel 856
SOUTHERN NETHERLANDS 856
Maastricht 856
THE NETHERLANDS DIRECTORY 857

Norway 861

TRANSPORT 864
OSLO 866
SOUTHERN NORWAY 875
Stavanger & Around 875
Kristiansand 876
BERGEN & THE WESTERN FJORDS 877
Oslo to Bergen 877
Bergen 877
Sognefjorden 881
Åndalsnes 882
Ålesund 882
NORTHERN NORWAY 883
Røros 883
Trondheim 883
Bodø 885
Lofoten 885
Tromsø 886
Nordkapp 887
NORWAY DIRECTORY 887

Poland 891

TRANSPORT 893
WARSAW (WARSZAWA) 895
MAŁOPOLSKA 901
Kraków 901
Oświęcim 905
Lublin 906
Zamość 907
CARPATHIAN MOUNTAINS 908
Zakopane 908
Tatra Mountains 909
SILESIA (ŚLĄSK) 909
Wrocław 909
WIELKOPOLSKA 912
Poznań 912
POMERANIA (POMORZE) 913
Gdańsk 913
Toruń 916
WARMIA & MASURIA 918
Great Masurian Lakes 918
POLAND DIRECTORY 919

Portugal 921

TRANSPORT 924
LISBON 925
AROUND LISBON 935

Sintra 935
Cascais 936
Setúbal 936
THE ALGARVE 937
Faro 937
Tavira 938
Lagos 938
Silves 939
Sagres 939
CENTRAL PORTUGAL 939
Évora 940
Monsaraz 941
Óbidos 941
Nazaré & Around 942
Tomar 942
Coimbra 942
Luso & the Buçaco Forest 943
Serra da Estrela 944
NORTHERN PORTUGAL 944
Porto 944
Along the Douro 948
Viana do Castelo 949
Braga 949
Parque Nacional da Peneda-Gerês 950
PORTUGAL DIRECTORY 951

Romania 953

TRANSPORT 956
BUCHAREST 957
TRANSYLVANIA 963
Sinaia 963
Braşov 964
Bran & Râşnov 967
Sighişoara 967
Sibiu 968
Cluj-Napoca 969
CRIŞANA & BANAT 971
Timişoara 971
ROMANIA DIRECTORY 972

Russia 975

TRANSPORT 978
MOSCOW 979
ST PETERSBURG 986
KALININGRAD REGION 992
Kaliningrad 992
RUSSIA DIRECTORY 995

Serbia 998

TRANSPORT 1000
BELGRADE 1001
VOJVODINA 1007
Novi Sad 1007
Subotica 1008
SERBIA DIRECTORY 1009

Slovakia 1011

TRANSPORT 1013
BRATISLAVA 1015
WESTERN & CENTRAL SLOVAKIA 1019
Trenčín 1019
Malá Fatra National Park 1020
EASTERN SLOVAKIA 1020
High Tatras 1020
Belá Tatras 1022
Poprad 1022
Levoča 1022
Spišské Podhradie 1023
Košice 1023
Bardejov 1024
SLOVAKIA DIRECTORY 1024

Slovenia 1027

TRANSPORT 1028
LJUBLJANA 1031
JULIAN ALPS 1037
Bled 1037
Bohinj 1039
SOČA VALLEY 1040
Bovec 1040
KARST & COAST 1040
Postojna & Škocjan Caves 1040
Koper 1041
Piran 1042
SLOVENIA DIRECTORY 1043

Spain 1046

TRANSPORT 1049
MADRID 1051
CASTILLA Y LEÓN 1062
Ávila 1062
Salamanca 1063
Segovia 1065
León 1066
Burgos 1066
CASTILLA-LA MANCHA 1067
Toledo 1067
Cuenca 1069
CATALONIA 1069
Barcelona 1069
Girona 1079
Figueres 1079
Tarragona 1080
BALEARIC ISLANDS 1080
Getting There & Away 1080
Mallorca 1082
Ibiza 1083
Formentera 1084
Menorca 1085
VALENCIA & MURCIA 1086
Valencia 1086
Alicante 1087
Murcia 1088
ANDALUCÍA 1088
Seville 1088
Córdoba 1092
Granada 1094
Costa de Almería 1098
Málaga 1099
Algeciras 1100
Cádiz 1100
Tarifa 1101
GIBRALTAR 1102
EXTREMADURA 1103
Trujillo 1103
Cáceres 1103
Mérida 1104
ARAGÓN, BASQUE COUNTRY & NAVARRA 1105
Aragón 1105
Basque Country 1106
Navarra 1109
CANTABRIA, ASTURIAS & GALICIA 1110
Santander 1110
Around Santander 1111
Santiago de Compostela 1111
SPAIN DIRECTORY 1112

Sweden 1116

TRANSPORT 1119
STOCKHOLM 1123
AROUND STOCKHOLM 1134
Stockholm Archipelago 1134
Uppsala 1135
GOTLAND 1135
Visby 1136
SOUTHERN SWEDEN 1136
Malmö 1136
Lund 1139
Helsingborg 1139
Göteborg (Gothenburg) 1140
NORTHERN SWEDEN 1144
Östersund 1144
Umeå 1144
Kiruna 1144
SWEDEN DIRECTORY 1145

Switzerland 1148

LAKE GENEVA REGION 1152
Geneva 1152
Lausanne 1156
Montreux 1157
FRIBOURG, NEUCHÂTEL & THE JURA 1157
VALAIS 1158
Zermatt 1158
BERN 1159
TICINO 1162
Locarno 1162
Lugano 1162
GRAUBÜNDEN 1163
St Moritz 1163
Flims-Laax 1163
ZÜRICH 1163
CENTRAL SWITZERLAND & BERNER OBERLAND 1167
Lucerne 1167
Interlaken 1168
Jungfrau Region 1169
NORTHERN SWITZERLAND 1171
Basel 1171
SWITZERLAND DIRECTORY 1172

Turkey 1174

TRANSPORT 1177
İSTANBUL 1179
AEGEAN COAST 1187
Gallipoli (Gelibolu) 1187
Çanakkale 1188
Troy 1188
Bergama 1188
İzmir 1189
Selçuk 1189
Kuşadasi 1190
Bodrum 1191
MEDITERRANEAN COAST 1192
Marmaris 1192
Dalyan 1193
Fethiye 1193
Patara 1194
Kaş 1194
Olympos 1195
Antalya 1195
CENTRAL ANATOLIA 1196
Ankara 1196
Konya 1197
CAPPADOCIA 1198
Göreme 1198
Ihlara Valley 1199
Kayseri 1200
EASTERN TURKEY 1200
Mt Nemrut National Park 1200
Van 1200
Kars 1201
TURKEY DIRECTORY 1201

Ukraine 1204

TRANSPORT 1205
KYIV 1206
LVIV 1211
UKRAINE DIRECTORY 1212

Europe Directory 1214

Transport 1232

Health 1246

Language 1251

The Authors 1287

Behind the Scenes 1294

Index 1304

Destination Europe

WILL SALTER

An art nouveau building with Westerkerk in the background, Amsterdam (p841), the Netherlands

Few places pack the punch of Europe – a historical, cultural and geographical heavyweight that squares up confidently to any other continent on earth. From its northern lights to its southern shores, this drama queen keeps on thrilling, surprising and confusing with her extraordinary wealth of sights, sounds, peoples and parties. Whatever your connection to Europe – whether descendent of one or more of its peoples, a current inhabitant or future visitor – be prepared for sensory overload as your eyes, ears and taste buds take the trip of a lifetime through a part of planet earth that never fails to dazzle.

Europe today is a continent more united than ever, with the European Union (EU) stretching from the frozen Arctic to the tip of Africa, and a single currency now used in the majority of European states. But don't let these facts fool you – with centuries of parochial development bringing about unique cultural values and traditions, the globalising sheen of the EU has little day-to-day effect on the continent's myriad nationalities, all of whom retain their idiosyncrasies and fiercely guard their independence. Indeed, there are few places in the world where you can pass through so many countries in such a short span of time and witness the striking differences between each one so markedly. Beyond the EU, this is even more noticeable of course, whether in old-timer refusenik Switzerland, for whom neutrality remains sacrosanct, or the pariah state of Belarus – 'Europe's last dictatorship' and a place where time has seemingly stood still since the end of communism.

Wherever you go on the continent you'll find that the subject of the EU comes up again and again – whether from the arch-federalist Benelux countries that passionately support the growth of the union, to your more cautious Brits, Danes and Swedes who, while in the club, still can't bear to give up their centuries-old currencies and hand over economic decisions to Brussels.

Of course, for many Europe is all about history, and oh, what a history! Even buffs will be astonished to find the layer cake of ancient and modern that Europe presents visitors with at every turn. As well as the birthplace of democracy in Athens, the Forum of Rome, the Renaissance buildings and art of Florence, the graceful canals of Venice and the Napoleonic grandeur of Paris, there's always the less expected sites such as the Moorish palaces of Andalucía, the remains of one of the Seven Wonders of the World in Turkey, the majesty of a second Venice in St Petersburg and the haunting buildings of Auschwitz in Poland.

While Europe revels and takes pride in its extraordinary heritage, it is certainly not one to be limited by it. Indeed, the continent leads the world in fashion, art, music, architecture and design; just see the street styles and music scenes of London and Berlin, the ground-breaking design in Antwerp, Copenhagen and Stockholm or the amazing displays of contemporary art, well, just about everywhere, to confirm that.

If glorious scenery is your thing, you'll not be disappointed either – check out the awesome fjords of Norway, the stunning scenery of the Scottish Highlands, the volcanic dramatics of Iceland, the breathtaking Alps of France, Switzerland and Italy, and the lesser-known mountains of Spain, Slovenia, southern Poland and Slovakia. For beach life you can fight for some sand on France's Côte d'Azur, Spain's Costa Brava or Portugal's Algarve, or – far more enjoyably – discover your own pristine beach in Albania, Bulgaria or on the gemlike islands of Greece and Croatia.

'While Europe revels and takes pride in its extraordinary heritage, it is certainly not one to be limited by it'

Of course, travel in Europe is not always about the dazzling sights and world-famous museums. Perhaps the single biggest pleasure of travelling around this incredible continent is the range of different people of all nationalities you'll meet along the way – whether fellow travellers or locals. However cosmopolitan your background may be, there's nothing quite like strolling the streets of Venice with a Venetian, taking a *banya* (steam bath) and being beaten with birch twigs by a Russian, or just kicking back, watching live music and drinking Guinness in a pub with a Dubliner.

Hassles? There'll be a few, inevitably. While Europe has to be one of the easiest and safest places on earth to travel, you'll find your money won't always go very far (especially in London, Paris and much of Switzerland – ouch!) and that in the summer months hostels can be booked up weeks ahead, making creative bed finding and flexibility key. A sense of humour is needed for many places. Whether it's another strike by French railway workers when you *really* need to get somewhere, or the greediness of petty bureaucrats on the make in Belarus or Moldova, just remember that it can be these challenges and dramas that end up making the best stories of the trip.

So don't delay – get planning your own European odyssey as soon as you can. With more than 45 extraordinary destinations offering incredible things to see and do, your only problem should be where to start…

IZZET KERIBAR

The door to the Circumcision Room, part of impressive Topkapı Palace (p1183), İstanbul

HIGHLIGHTS

BEST CLASSIC CITIES

Rome – have a divine time at the Vatican, the Colosseum and the Sistine Chapel in Italy's Eternal City (p636)

İstanbul – the glorious one-time Byzantine and Ottoman capital is one of the world's truly great cities (p1179)

Venice – forget anything you've ever heard about this glorious city on water and come to see it with your own eyes (p665)

Paris – marvel at the style, romance and pure *joie de vivre* of the iconic French capital (p376)

London – dive into the extraordinary British capital – this world in one city has culture, history, shopping and nightlife to rival anywhere else on earth (p159)

BEST MUSIC FESTIVALS

Roskilde – book your tickets, pack your tent and make for the ultimate musical line-up at Scandinavia's very best rock festival (p327)

Exit Festival – see the modern face of Serbia as big names play in the grounds of the Petrovaradin Citadel in the country's second city (p1008)

Iceland Airwaves – join the Reykjavik crowds for this great festival each October when international bands play super-intimate venues, and cheery, beery partygoers whirl from gig to gig (p588)

Glastonbury – come for the fantastic line-ups and endure the mudslides at Britain's most famous and notorious summer festival (p191)

Fête de la Musique – roam the streets of Paris and see live music performed for free as bands and buskers take to the streets for this celebration of music (p445)

BEST OUTDOOR EXPERIENCES

Pembrokeshire – discover this sparkling corner of Wales, with soaring cliffs and golden beaches, where you can hike, bike, surf and kayak, or learn the wacky art of coasteering (p213)

Crete's southern coast – hike out to Crete's southern coast through the spectacular Samaria Gorge, then recover with a cold beer in Agia Roumeli and a swim in the crystal-clear Libyan Sea (p549)

Durmitor National Park – the Tara Canyon's kilometre-plus walls provide a sublime backdrop to a rafting trip through paradise (p804)

Sognefjorden – trek from fjord-head to glacier and witness nature at its most sublime in one of Norway's most spectacular regions (p881)

Chamonix – world-class slopes are matched by world-class après-ski in France's legendary Alpine centre, near Mont Blanc (p419)

BEST UP-&-COMING PLACES

Pristina – Europe's newest capital fizzes with energy and ambition in the wake of Kosovo's 2008 declaration of independence (p714)

Sibiu – this classic Saxon town gleams after careful restoration for its 2007 turn as an EU 'Capital of Culture' (p968)

Lviv – explore Ukraine's most gorgeous city, awash with Armenian, Austro-Hungarian, Italian, Jewish and Polish influences almost perfectly preserved in its Unesco-listed old town (p1211)

Ghent – with its historic architecture, fab restaurants and sublime chocolate shops, Flanders' best-kept secret is at its happiest during the good-time Gentse Feesten (p124)

Kaliningrad – discover this compact island of Russia with its youthful, Western vibe, beautiful beaches, languid countryside and fascinating Prussian heritage (p992)

JONATHAN SMITH

Relaxing along the Leie River and Graslei (p124), Ghent, Belgium

JULIETE COOMBE

Masked woman during the famous Carnevale (p671), Venice, Italy

BEST FESTIVALS & CELEBRATIONS

Las Fallas – fireworks, music, festive bonfires and all-night partying make the week-long festivities of Valencia's Las Fallas (12–19 March) one of the most spectacular parties in Spain (p1087)

St Patrick's Day – party town Dublin sees a cacophony of parades, fireworks and light shows (not to mention the limitless supply of Guinness) for three inebriated days around 17 March (p628)

Oktoberfest – held in Munich over the 15 days before the first Sunday in October, this extraordinary assembly of beer lovers in Bavaria is the world's largest and most raucous (p475)

Venice Carnevale – see La Serenissima at its sybaritic best by joining the crowds for some masked ribaldry in the 10 days before Ash Wednesday (p671)

Sanfermines – famous worldwide for acts of bravery-cum-foolhardiness, the Sanfermines festival is held in Pamplona, Spain on 6–14 July, when the city is overrun with thrill-seekers, curious onlookers and, oh yeah, bulls (p1109)

BEST ARCHITECTURAL ICONS

Museo Guggenheim, Bilbao – a postmodern symphony in stainless steel, this gallery has become a global byword for urban regeneration (p1108)

Centre Pompidou, Paris – decide for yourself whether this hi-tech '70s icon retains high style before spending half a day exploring its fantastic museums and seeing the view from the top floor (p385)

Reichstag Dome, Berlin – Sir Norman Foster's millennial addition to the top of the German parliament is a stunning glass dome that sheds light on the politicians below and affords wonderful views of the city (p453)

La Sagrada Família, Barcelona – Anton Gaudí's unfinished masterpiece is testament to his eccentric imagination and style (p1075)

St Basil's Cathedral, Moscow – famously, the architect of this flamboyantly colourful, onion-domed church had his eyes put out by the Tsar so he could never again create anything so beautiful (p980)

Getting Started

Whether you'll be spending just a couple of weeks or several months travelling through Europe, all trips can be made a little more enjoyable and somewhat easier by a little advance planning. That said, it would be a big mistake to over-plan your itinerary – much of the joy of backpacking through Europe comes from the unexpected, so don't punish yourself by setting unrealistic targets or by trying to see too much – make sure you hang back, absorb the towns and cities and have the freedom to do things you never imagined you'd do.

This chapter gives information for the region as a whole; refer to the country chapters or the Europe Directory (p1214) for more specific information.

WHEN TO GO

Europe has a high season in summer and another in winter. Crowding is the main difficulty in the warmest months of June, July and particularly August. In some countries, such as France and Italy, many shops and restaurants close in August while locals take their own holidays, meaning that some cities can feel rather dead.

See Climate Charts (p1218) for more information.

Global warming has meant a later start to the skiing season; often, decent snowfalls aren't recorded until January (or even February). December is always busy in locations such as Paris, Prague and any Austrian or German city with a quaint Christmas market. Easter is another busy time.

You can find bargains by visiting traditionally 'summer' destinations such as Greece in winter, but be aware that public transport might be less frequent. In some northern locations such as Scotland and Scandinavia, it might not run at all as heavy snow and ice mean services are seasonal.

For all the above reasons, by far the best months to travel in Europe are May, June and September.

COSTS & MONEY

Excluding transport costs, you can get by on about €40 to €80 a day in Western Europe. You might be able to squeak by on less in smaller towns and in Mediterranean Europe, but Switzerland costs at the upper end of the range. Scandinavia is slightly dearer than Western Europe (especially when it comes to alcohol). Eastern Europe is the cheapest region, costing a daily total of €30 to €50, although Ukraine and Russia can be more expensive than that.

The quickest way to get cash these days is to withdraw it directly from ATMs in each new place. The best way to track such spending is to set up your account for online banking. Do this before you leave home, and on the road remember to log off properly in internet cafes. International transactions might take a few days to register on your statement.

For more information, see Money (p1225) in the Europe Directory.

TRAVELLING RESPONSIBLY

Lonely Planet has long been a supporter of responsible tourism, believing that when travellers consider carefully the impact their trips can have on other people, communities and the world in general, travel can be enormously beneficial and mutually advantageous.

First of all, consider the environmental impact of your travel plans. Flights produce large carbon dioxide emissions and so while you may be forced to take a plane to reach Europe, it's always best to try to avoid flying between European countries and take a train, bus or boat instead. As well as being more environmentally friendly, these journeys are often spectacular and ensure you'll see far more of the continent than you would from an aeroplane window. When you do take flights, you might like to offset the emissions (a far-from-perfect method, but one worth doing anyway) by using a company such as Climate Care (see www.climatecare.org).

Before you travel do as much research as you can into the countries you're planning to visit. Try to learn a few words of the various languages that will be spoken on your route – they'll more than repay the effort to learn them and locals will be delighted to hear your attempts, however stumbling!

When planning where to stay, choose carefully as the tourist dollar can make or break ecologically sound and sustainable options. If you have the option of staying in a progressively run 'green' hotel, check it out in detail before you book to be sure that its green credentials are not just lip service, but reflect a well thought through and sound environmental and sustainability policy. Questions to ask include: how are they dealing with the main environmental issues facing them? Do they employ local guides, leaders and staff and provide training opportunities? And do they have a 'green' purchasing policy?

When on the road remember that you are a guest in the countries you pass through and behave accordingly. This means behaving just as well as you do at home – if not even better. Cultural sensitivity is key. Part of this can be learned by research – learning about the different cultural norms in each country – but it's most usefully learned on the spot: go with the flow and don't stress out if people you meet do things that would be considered

WHAT TO TAKE?

Packing light is the (often elusive) goal. A backpack that won't fit in luggage racks or hostel lockers is a drag, literally, and everyday essentials are widely available in most European cities. Still, it's sensible to make space for some of these:

- Earplugs – Necessary unless you're a very heavy sleeper; a snoring dorm mate, loud music nearby and traffic noise are almost inevitable at some point.
- First-aid kit – Just the basics: some aspirin, sticking plasters, antiseptic cream, sun block and perhaps, if you have a delicate stomach, antidiarrhoea pills.
- Mobile phone – Get your mobile unlocked so that you can buy a cheap local SIM card in Europe to make inexpensive calls. For technical specifications, see p1229.
- Padlock – For hostel lockers and train luggage racks.
- Photocopies – An absolute essential. Make two copies of your passport title page, visas, travellers cheque serial numbers and tickets, leaving one copy at home and packing the other separately from the originals. Make a note of your credit card numbers and keep it somewhere safe.
- Plastic bags – Just a couple to line your bag and keep the contents dry or to isolate dirty laundry.
- Power adapter – Preferably with both a chunky UK plug and a continental plug with two round prongs.
- Rain gear – It *always* rains in some parts of Europe.
- Small torch (flashlight) – To prevent painful bumps in the night.
- Swiss Army knife – Handy if opening tins and beer bottles; less handy if you accidentally leave it in your carry-on airline luggage – so don't.
- Memory stick – Put any documents you might need on here. You can also store photos on here when your camera gets full.

TEN TIPS TO STAY ON A BUDGET

- Buddy up – Finding a travel partner slashes accommodation costs.
- Spend more time East – Things still cost less in Poland, Romania, Bulgaria and Albania.
- Head for the countryside – Where the living is also cheaper.
- Investigate buying a rail pass – If you're travelling extensively in expensive Western countries, it will save money. Local fares and deals are cheaper for quick trips and in Eastern Europe. See p1243.
- Take overnight trains – Sleeping in your seat or couchette on longer trips saves on a night's lodging.
- Hand wash clothes – Do your laundry in hostel and hotel sinks; even hostels that forbid it don't notice the odd item or two.
- Invest in a phonecard – The cheaper alternative for calling home or within Europe.
- Eat cheap – Buy food from street stalls or eat at informal, self-service places, where tipping doesn't even enter the equation.
- Look up old mates – And don't be shy about being a (gracious) guest of friends of friends living in the countries you're visiting.
- Become a couch surfer – Join www.couchsurfing.com, where residents let travellers stay with them for free (see p1216).

rude or highly bizarre in your home country; this is just one of the many reasons that travel can be so rewarding. Try to adopt local standards of dress wherever you are, but most obviously in conservative and religious areas where it may be considered disrespectful to flaunt your flesh or to wear those short shorts.

Buy local wherever possible – go for the locally made crafts in the market rather than something factory-made elsewhere, and likewise, try the local beers or soft drinks rather than giving more money to global corporations – you never know what you'll discover!

Be especially vigilant when you're out in the countryside. When hiking stick to the trails, so as not to contribute to soil erosion, and bring a plastic bag with you so that you can collect and responsibly dispose of any litter you come across. When going to the toilet, make sure you're at least 100m from the nearest watercourse.

When bathing or washing your clothes, be sparing with the water and the amount of detergent you use – remember that water can be a very precious commodity, especially in southern Europe during the long, dry summer months.

When watching wildlife, keep a good distance so that the animals aren't nervous about your presence. In the same spirit, don't buy any local crafts made from wild animal products, including skins, ivory or bone. Not only is it illegal to import or export them in most cases, you're likely to be supporting poaching practices that have had devastating impacts on animal populations. Similar principles apply to wooden products: check you're not purchasing a chunk of old-growth rainforest.

HOW MUCH FOR WESTERN EUROPE?

Camping €10-15

Hostel €15-25

Budget restaurant meal €10-20

Local transport (single fare) €2-3.50

Museum fees €3-12

One beer (500mL) €3-5

LIFE ON THE ROAD

Generally, travel goes smoothly in orderly Europe. Dusty roads, buses that constantly break down and general chaos are only really found on the continent's outer fringes. Which is why Europe can make an ideal destination for a first-time trip.

READING UP

Rev up your wanderlust with witty travelogues such as Bill Bryson's *Neither Here nor There: Travels in Europe,* Tim Moore's *Continental Drifter* and Peter Moore's *The Wrong Way Home*. For travel-literature classics, try Mark Twain's *A Tramp Abroad* and Patrick Leigh Fermor's *A Time of Gifts*. See p1218 for further details on each. Alternatively, mull over the meaning of it all with pop philosopher Alain de Botton's *The Art of Travel.*

HOW MUCH FOR SCANDINAVIAN EUROPE?

Camping €7.50-20

Hostel €15-35

Budget restaurant meal €10-20

Local transport (single fare) €0.60-2

Museum fees €5-12

One beer (500mL) €6-10

More often than not, you'll roll into town on a train that's not too late and easily find a train-station locker to store your backpack until you can check into your hostel at 5pm. A nearby tourist office will usually be on hand to help with anything this book can't provide.

More than in other parts of the world, sightseeing is dominated by churches and museums. But there are also spooky catacombs, cobblestoned streets and quaint houses in Europe's compact cities. And there are also places where being a visitor is all about hiking, cycling or perhaps even skiing.

It sounds relatively effortless, but even in Europe a month-long holiday can start to feel like…work. So pace yourself. Of course, it's great to spend lots of time in hostels drinking with dorm mates. But you might want to try to treat yourself to your own room and a little privacy every two weeks or so.

There's a lot to see in Europe, but try to avoid the 'if-it's-Friday-it-must-be-Rome' syndrome. Rest up in one of your fantasy cities. Spending several days in one hostel also makes it easier to get to know people.

Concerns about the effects flying has on global warming have made train travel and cycling more fashionable with some travellers in recent years. It's nice to know that going slowly is not only an ethical way of getting around, but frequently more interesting and less stressful too.

CONDUCT

One of the great delights of travelling in Europe is the way so many cultures live shoulder to shoulder. The differences can make your head spin – especially as you enter countries such as Bulgaria, where people nod their heads up and down to say 'no'.

Introductions

Don't assume everyone speaks English or will suddenly get it if you speak very loudly. Learn a few local phrases instead. 'Hello' and 'goodbye' are particularly useful in the many countries where it's customary to greet the proprietor when entering and leaving a place. 'Thank you', 'please', 'sorry' and 'do you speak English?' are always good to know, too.

Watch the local customs for hand and body gestures. Be careful, for example, about raising your fingers to order two beers, even with your palm facing the bar staff; it's rude in some countries.

Public etiquette is helpful to know. If on foot, stay out of the bicycle-only paths in northern Europe. In Eastern Europe be prepared to give up your seat to the elderly or infirm.

If introduced to locals, follow their cues. In some northern European countries, say Denmark or Germany, it's still common to shake hands with a stranger. In charming France, Spain or Italy, it doesn't matter if people don't know you from Adam, they'll still kiss you.

Dress

Europeans are among the planet's most dedicated followers of fashion, and in uberchic Paris, Rome and Milan scruffy clothing will give you away as a tourist. But equally, as long as you're not trying to get into trendy clubs, upmarket hotels or the opera, few will bat an eyelid at anything you wear in northern Europe. Away from the larger northern cities – and even in some of them, such as Berlin – attitudes are more relaxed.

Snobbery can be more acute in southern and Eastern Europe. In the latter region, that's partly a result of nouveau-riche attitudes and partly to do with old-fashioned pride in one's appearance.

All this said, the universal uniform of jeans, T-shirt and trainers will do for most daywear. If you're going clubbing or somewhere posh, you can dress up a pair of everyday trousers with a funky top/formal shirt and shoes.

If you're hiking or cycling, obviously you'll need the appropriate gear. Otherwise, hard-and-fast rules really only apply in places of worship; see p30.

HOW MUCH FOR EASTERN EUROPE?

Camping €5-12

Hostel €10-20

Budget restaurant meal €7-15

Local transport (single fare) €0.50-1.50

Museum fees €2-5

One beer (500mL) €2-4

Meals

Habits are changing, but lunch, rather than dinner, remains the main meal in many parts of the Continent. With such rich and varied gastronomic traditions (see p41), Continental Europeans do tend to turn every sit-down meal into a social ritual. However, it's just as common to eat on the run – devouring everything from chips and mayonnaise in paper cones to hot dogs with mustard, pizza slices, spicy kebabs and gelati.

Giving Gifts

If you are invited to someone's home, bring them a gift, perhaps a bouquet of flowers or a bottle of wine. One of the hallmarks of a great trip is meeting kind people who help just when you've missed the last train or can't find a room for the night. Bring along a few region-specific gifts –

TEN MUST-SEE MOVIES

- *All about My Mother* (Spain, 1999) Pedro Almodóvar's tribute to Barcelona, mothers and transvestites.
- *Amélie* (France, 2001) An utterly charming Parisian fairy tale.
- *The Beat That My Heart Skipped* (France, 2005) A dodgy, violent real-estate agent finds taking up the piano interferes with doing the job.
- *Bicycle Thieves* (Italy, 1948) Haunting catch-22 situation in postwar Rome.
- *Lilja 4-ever* (Sweden/Denmark 2002) Lukas Moodysson's take on sex trafficking, this is the sad story of Estonian Lilja, lured to Sweden in search of a better life.
- *Festen* (Denmark, 1998) Hand-held cameras and dark family secrets – the ultimate in naturalistic Dogme movies.
- *Good Bye Lenin!* (Germany, 2003) Heart-warming comedy where Berliners pretend the wall never fell.
- *The Seventh Seal* (Sweden, 1957) Death plays chess for a man's life in this Bergman classic.
- *Trainspotting* (UK, 1996) Scrappy heroin junkie eventually chooses life. Great soundtrack.
- *Vera Drake* (UK, 2004) Uneasy but Oscar-nominated tale of a 1950s working-class woman leading a double life as an abortionist.
- *La Dolce Vita* (Italy, 1960) Fellini's classic early art film paeon to Rome, in which a young journalist explores the meaning of the decadent world around him through a series of erotic encounters.

like a magnet, key chain or postcard of your hometown – to give to people on the road.

HOW MUCH FOR MEDITERRANEAN EUROPE?

Camping €8-12

Hostel €12-20

Budget restaurant meal €6-10

Local transport (single fare) €2-3

Museum fees €3-10

One beer €2-4

Taking Photographs

Use common sense when taking photographs. Ask permission before you take a photo of a stranger and if they ask you to send them a copy, do so if you say you will (or take their email address for a rather easier way of photosharing). Don't take photos of sensitive objects such as military installations in any country, and be aware that the Cold War isn't dead in places such as Belarus and Russia, where you should avoid taking pictures of police posts or government buildings as well.

Religion

Be respectful in churches or other religious buildings. Refrain from using flash photography and keep your voice to a whisper, especially during Mass or other services. In mosques, women will be required to cover their heads with a scarf or similar; everyone has to remove their shoes. It's often a requirement in Christian churches in Eastern Europe for women to cover their heads too – look to see what locals are doing and follow suit.

Itineraries

FIRST TIME EUROPE

This is the ultimate introduction to fabulous Europe. It includes many of the continent's absolute highlights and is a good way to discover which parts of Europe you want to come back to and explore in greater detail.

Start in **London** (p159), a place both familiar and strange, with enough history, culture and nights out for an entire continent. Jump on the Eurostar to **Paris** (p376), where you'll need several days to take in the seductive City of Lights. Side trips from here could include decadent, canalside **Amsterdam** (p841) or Eurocapital **Brussels** (p116) for beer and chocolate.

From Paris take the superfast TGV to **Nice** (p434) for some stylish hobnobbing on the Côte d'Azur, before paying a visit to decadent **Monaco** en route to fashionable **Milan** (p659). Take the train to **Florence** (p677), where you'll fall in love with the art and architecture, and continue to **Rome** (p636), where the remains of the Roman Empire await you, not to mention the **Vatican** (p641).

Turn north from Rome and take the train to **Venice** (p665), which despite the hype does not disappoint. Head north to baroque **Salzburg** (p91) before waltzing into opulent **Vienna** (p76).

From Vienna, make for Hungary's stunner of a capital **Budapest** (p564) and then **Braşov** (p964), to explore Transylvania for a few days. Catch the train to **Prague** (p287) and spend a long weekend south in **Český Krumlov** (p300). Visit the ancient Polish city of **Kraków** (p901) and make a sombre side trip to **Auschwitz** (p905). From here, your last stop is the buzzing German capital, **Berlin** (p452).

HOW LONG?
4-6 weeks

WHEN TO GO?
Mar-Dec, but shoulder seasons (Apr-May, Sep-Oct) are best

BUDGET?
€30-70 per day

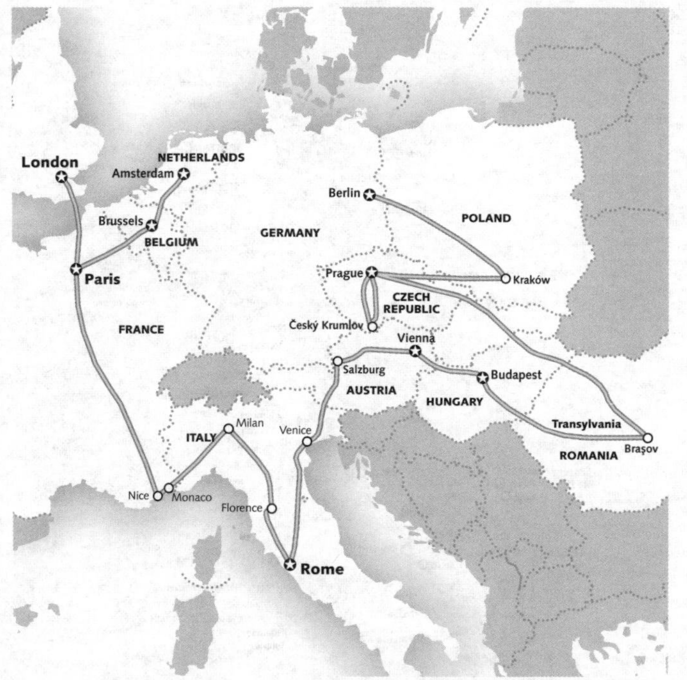

About 7950km; balance your budget by offsetting the more expensive first half of your journey against the cheaper second stretch, but save a small amount for a final blow-out in Berlin. Make sure you give Paris, Rome and Venice plenty of time – in fact you may well not want to leave!

FROM LONDON TO THE SUN

Spin around Britain and Ireland, before escaping across the channel to France, Spain and Portugal.

Enjoy **London** (p159), then head to **Cambridge** (p198) and **Edinburgh** (p214). Continue north to **Inverness** (p224), where you can look for monsters in Loch Ness. The next stop is **Glasgow** (p218). Go via Stranraer for the ferry to **Belfast** (p620). Afterwards, bus to **Galway** (p616) and take a ferry to the windswept **Aran Islands** (p618). Rejoin the modern world in **Dublin** (p599).

Take the Dublin ferry to Holyhead, **Wales** (p209), or take a cheap Dublin–Bristol flight, visiting **Bath** (p187) on your return train trip to London.

Take the Eurostar to romantic **Paris** (p376) with side trips to **Versailles** (p396), the **D-Day Beaches** (p402) and **Mont St-Michel** (p401).

Rail south to **Barcelona** (p1069), possibly stopping at Limoges for the **Dordogne Valley** (p420) en route. From Barcelona, it's possible to make a longish round trip to the **Balearic Islands** (p1080) and **Valencia** (p1086). Or, zip up to the Basque seaside resort of **San Sebastián** (p1106) and the Museo Guggenheim in **Bilbao** (p1108). Turn south for **Madrid** (p1051), making day trips to Moorish **Toledo** (p1067) and enchanting **Segovia** (p1065). Then board a bus to the Islamic fortress, the Alhambra in **Granada** (p1094).

Dance the flamenco in pricey **Seville** (p1088) before getting back on the bus to **Lisbon** (p925). Relax and eat custard tarts in Portugal's breezy capital. Sidestep to **Sintra** (p935), before thoroughly exploring this gorgeous but cheap country. North lies **Porto** (p944), and the **Parque Natural da Peneda-Gerês** (p950), with lots of hiking opportunities. The southern **Algarve** (p937) is very touristy, but the train journey along the coast is beautiful.

HOW LONG?

1-2 months

WHEN TO GO?

Jun-Aug; Sep-May (high/low season)

BUDGET?

€50-70 per day

About 6500km; omit the British Isles if you're short on funds or time. Linger in the Spanish or French countryside, and don't under-estimate the amount of time you're likely to want to spend in Paris, Barcelona, Madrid and Lisbon – all great cities!

BEACHCOMBING ALONG THE MED

Think Europe doesn't do beaches? It does, but with lashings of culture on the side, as you'll find during this romp along its southern shores. While the famous beaches of Europe – those on the Côte d'Azur and the Italian Riviera for example – are usually crowded and very expensive places to spend time, this trip lets you in on some of Europe's least-known gems, from the up-and-coming islands of Croatia to the blissful virgin beaches of Albania.

HOW LONG?
1-2 months

WHEN TO GO?
Jun-Aug; Sep-May (high/low season)

BUDGET?
€50-70 per day

Head to **Nîmes** (p425), **Marseille** (p428) or **Nice** (p434), and spend time exploring the Côte d'Azur stretch between them. From Nice, take the train to **Rome** (p636) and continue south to energetic **Naples** (p690), peer into ill-fated **Pompeii** (p695) and explore the **Amalfi Coast** (p697).

Cross Italy from Naples to **Bari** (p699), from where you head across the Adriatic by ferry to the Croatian pearl of **Dubrovnik** (p266), bussing it south through Montenegro and Albania – two of Europe's least-known gems – and onwards to Corfu and Patra.

Docking in **Patra** (p532), do a loop of the Peloponnese: bus to Byzantine pin-up city **Mystras** (p533), the ancient heavyweight **Mycenae** (p533) and onwards to Venetian **Nafplio** (p533). Take the train to the ruins of Apollo's temple in **Corinth** (p532), and bus to venerable **Athens** (p524). Bus south to **Piraeus** (p531) for an island-hopping expedition to **Mykonos** (p540), **Naxos** (p542), **Paros** (p541) and volcanic **Santorini** (p544).

Continue to island-hop until you've had your fill, then set sail for Turkey from Piraeus, via **Lesvos** (p553). Bus north along the Aegean coast to the ruins of Troy and **Çanakkale** (p1188) and to throbbing, chaotic **İstanbul** (p1179).

About 5500km to 6000km; weeks will slip away in this idyllic region. Allow at least a week in each, to savour the atmosphere in Italy and to explore Greece and Turkey.

EASTERN EUROPE TODAY

HOW LONG?

2-3 months

WHEN TO GO?

Mar-Dec, but shoulder seasons (Apr-May, Sep-Oct) are best

BUDGET?

€30-50 per day

Forget the stereotypes of the grim and grey 'Eastern Bloc' of the early 1990s – this half of Europe is one of the most dynamic and fast-changing places in the world.

Pick a cheap flight to **Berlin** (p452), a city once straddling the East–West divide but now a veritable music, art and nightlife mecca for the whole of Europe. Then travel to vibrant **Warsaw** (p895) and on into the Baltic region to see the cutting edge of Eastern Europe – take in the old town in Lithuania's ancient capital **Vilnius** (p740), wander the streets of gorgeous art nouveau **Rīga** (p720) and party in technophile **Tallinn** (p332). When in Vilnius, don't miss side trips to the Hill of Crosses at **Šiauliai** (p749) and the **Curonian Spit** (p749).

From the Baltics head into Russia and gasp at the sheer scale of monolithic **Moscow** (p979) before passing through the time capsule of Belarus where **Minsk** (p105) presents the perfect opportunity to see how things were under communism. Head south into Ukraine and spend a few days in its bustling Soviet capital **Kyiv** (p1206), then contrast it with the very Ukrainian city of **Lviv** (p1211).

Head through Moldova, stopping in charming **Chişunău** (p788) before heading into Romania where you should make a beeline for Transylvania. Sharpen your fangs at 'Dracula's' castle in **Bran** (p967) and enjoy the gorgeous old towns nearby before enjoying some urban renewal in Romania's capital **Bucharest** (p957).

From Bucharest the train zips you through the mountains to Bulgaria's loveliest town, **Veliko Târnovo** (p240), from where it's an easy journey to historic **Plovdiv** (p238) and the amazing monastery at **Rila** (p238). Head to the relaxed capital **Sofia** (p233) and then by train to Serbia's vibrant capital **Belgrade** (p1001), which is showing itself to be far more mainstream these days. Head back to Berlin via sumptuous **Budapest** (p564) and romantic **Prague** (p287).

About 6950km; lower costs mean your budget will stretch further here so you can linger longer. Remember to sort out visas for Russia, Belarus (and Ukraine if you're from Down Under) in advance.

a remarkably successful force in fostering economic growth and political stability, there remains an uneasy discord about what exactly the union's role should be. Expansion cannot be infinite, and the concentration of power in Brussels has arguably created a political entity that is self-perpetuating, seeking an ever-growing role as an overall European government, one that has been repeatedly rejected by nation states from France and Ireland to the Netherlands when put to a referendum. Whatever the next few decades hold for Europe, it's easy to predict that the role of the EU will remain absolutely central to events.

HISTORY

'In the beginning, there was no Europe,' writes Professor Norman Davies in *Europe: A History*. In the beginning all that existed was an unpopulated peninsula attached to the western edge of the world's largest landmass (Asia). But after humanoid settlers arrived between 850,000 and 700,000 BC, Europe's temperate climate and unthreatening environment would make it ripe for agricultural exploitation and the birthplace of great civilisations.

It was in Greece and Rome that the continent's two great ancient societies arose. Greece (first emerging around 2000 BC) was renowned for its philosophers (Aristotle, Plato, Socrates) and democratic principles. Rome – boasting brilliant politicians, and writers like Cicero, Ovid and Virgil – spread its influence by military might. At its peak, the Roman Empire stretched from England to the Sahara and from Spain to Persia.

The name Europa, a mythological Phoenician aristocrat who was ravished by Zeus, was first used to describe the continent by Ancient Greek geographers. There's no single explanation as to why this name was chosen.

By the 4th century AD both empires were in terminal decline. Greece had been swallowed by Macedonia under Alexander the Great, then by Rome itself in AD 146. Although Roman emperors in Constantinople (İstanbul) hung on for another 1000 years, the empire's western half fell to Germanic tribes in 476.

This marked the start of the Dark Ages in Western Europe. From 768 Charlemagne, King of the Franks, brought together much of Western Europe under his rule into what would later be known as the 'Holy Roman Empire'. After this territory passed into the hands of Austrian Habsburgs in the 13th century, it became the continent's dominant political power. Elsewhere, an alliance of Christian nations repeatedly sent troops to reclaim the Holy Land from Islamic control. These unsuccessful 'Crusades' (1096–1291) unfortunately set the stage for centuries of skirmishes with the neighbouring Ottoman Empire as it took control of Asia Minor and parts of the Balkans from 1453 onwards.

Europe's grand reawakening also began in the mid-15th century, and the subsequent Renaissance, Reformation and French Revolution ushered in enormous social upheaval.

Mt Elbrus, on the border between Russia and Georgia, is Europe's tallest mountain at 5642m, followed by Mont Blanc (France) at 4807m and the Matterhorn (Switzerland) at 4478m.

The Renaissance fomented mainly artistic expression and ideas. The Reformation was a question of religion. Challenging Catholic 'corruption' in 1517, German theologian Martin Luther established a breakaway branch of Christianity, Protestantism. Struggles between Catholics and Protestants for supremacy were behind the bloody Thirty Years War (1618–48).

The French Revolution in 1789 was about the populace's attempt to wrest political power from the monarchy. But in the ensuing vacuum, plucky general Napoleon Bonaparte (1769–1821) crowned himself emperor. Napoleon's efforts to colonise all Europe ended in defeat by the British at Waterloo in 1815, but the civil laws he introduced in France in 1804 would spread the revolutionary ideas of liberty and equality across the globe.

Having vanquished Napoleon, Britain became a major world player itself. With the invention of the steam engine, railways and factories, it unleashed the Industrial Revolution. Needing markets for goods, it and other European powers accelerated their colonisation of countries around the world, bringing new and exotic riches back to Europe.

Meanwhile the death throes of the Habsburg Empire, or the Austro-Hungarian Empire, were about to rock the continent. Serbia was accused of backing the assassination of the heir to the Austro-Hungarian throne in 1914 and the battle between the two states developed into WWI, as allies lined up on each side (Germany and the Ottoman Empire on the Austro-Hungarian side; Britain, France, Russia, Italy and the USA with Serbia).

Crippled by a huge bill for reparations imposed at the war's end in 1918, Austria's humbled ally, Germany, proved susceptible to politician Adolf Hitler's nationalist rhetoric during the 1930s. Other nations watched as Nazi Germany annexed Austria and parts of Czechoslovakia, but its invasion of Poland in 1939 sparked WWII. During the final liberation of Europe in 1945, Allied troops from Britain, France, the USA and the USSR uncovered the full extent of the genocide that had occurred in Hitler's concentration camps for Jews, Roma, the disabled, homosexuals, communists and other 'degenerates'.

The coldest place in Europe is Vorkuta, Russia (average low -20°C), and the warmest is Seville, Spain (average high 29°C).

The Allies carved out spheres of influence, and Germany was divided to avoid its rising up again militarily. Differences in ideology between the Western powers and the communist USSR soon led to a stand-off. The USSR closed off its assigned sectors – East Germany, East Berlin and much of Eastern Europe – behind the figurative Iron Curtain. With the Stasi, Stalinist purges and more, many Eastern European citizens have appalling tales of political repression to relate from these times.

The 'Cold War' lasted until 1989 when the Berlin Wall fell. Germany was unified in 1990. A year later the USSR was dissolved. Czechoslovakia, Hungary, Poland, Romania, Bulgaria and Albania all grasped multiparty democracy shortly afterwards.

The downfall of communism had a terrible effect in Yugoslavia, where nationalist leaders seized the chance to stir up political unrest and war: some of the young independent nations there are still recovering. For the most part, however, the end of the Cold War has brought a sense of peace to Europe. A sense of cooperation is proving slightly trickier to locate. The EU was formed in 1957 as a trade alliance and has developed fitfully into a political entity since. At this stage, while 16 members have adopted a common currency, governments are having difficulty pushing through the European Constitution needed.

THE CULTURE

Europe is the cradle of Western civilisation and the continent's legacy to the world unquestionably includes some touchstones of world art and literature.

Art

After the prolific creativity of ancient Greek and Roman culture, the continent went through a fallow period – a kind of communal artistic block – during the Middle Ages. Times were hard, mere survival was difficult enough and the church, the leading patron of the arts, wanted religious icons not realism.

But then in the 15th century a sea change occurred and European art came storming back with the Renaissance. The movement began slowly in the Italian city-states of Florence and Venice, with the rediscovery of Greco-Roman culture. Then it spread further afield over the next few centuries.

Leonardo da Vinci (1452–1519) and Michelangelo Buonarroti (1474–1564) led the Italian Renaissance, spurred on by Jan van Eyck (1390–1441) and other Flemish masters who led the Northern Renaissance in art.

THE AGE OF REASON

Forced to pick just one defining era and philosophy to sum up modern Europe, it would be hard to pass over the Enlightenment, or the so-called 'Age of Reason'. This was the period in the 18th century when science and human logic for the first time took supremacy over religious belief. Heavily intertwined with the rapid scientific advances of the time (see p41), it ushered in the modern age with its move away from the church and its emphasis on logic, education, individualism and liberal social values.

Whole university courses are taught on the Enlightenment, its factions (eg rationalism versus empiricism), and its pros and cons. However, two thinkers closely associated with it were the antimonarchist, antireligious liberal Voltaire (1694–1778) and Immanuel Kant (1724–1804), who believed humans are rational and autonomous beings, so universal moral laws are possible. Kant was also intensely interested in how humans made sense of the surrounding world.

René Descartes (1596–1650), who famously declared 'I think, therefore I am', was one of the rationalist forerunners of the Enlightenment. Jean Jacques Rousseau (1712–78) started off as a believer but later fell out with the movement – whose main social consequence was the French Revolution.

The baroque period of the 17th century was defined by Rembrandt and Peter Paul Rubens' ornate portraits. During the 18th century, Romantic painters (such as Eugène Delacroix and Francisco Goya) chose exultant political themes of liberty and great battles.

The late-19th-century Impressionists (including Edgar Degas, Edouard Manet, Claude Monet and Pierre-Auguste Renoir) progressively moved away from realism, using small disjointed brushstrokes to create an 'impression' of subject and light, and depicting ordinary people (instead of royalty) engaged in everyday pursuits. Their work segued into that of their successors, like Vincent van Gogh and Paul Gauguin.

In the 20th century came the Fauvists and the cubists. The Fauvists used colour to suggest figures and motion, and are probably best represented by Henri Matisse. Among the cubists was one Pablo Picasso, who went on to become a one-man art movement, abandoning perspective and drawing heavily on African and other native art to forge a style of wholly modernist painting. Following generations stripped away more elements of reality. In the 1930s René Magritte, Joan Miró, Max Ernst, Salvador Dalí and Alberto Giacometti visually explored the subconscious. Sculpture was escorted into modernity by Auguste Rodin and later by Constantin Brancusi.

Music

Of course music is another art form in which Europe has excelled. Baroque music in the 17th and early 18th centuries was developed in Italy by the likes of Vivaldi and Scarlatti, but it reached its zenith in Germany with the genius of Bach and Handel. Germany remained the cradle of European music during the classical era as both Beethoven and Mozart worked to raise music to unsurpassed heights. The romantic era produced Poland's Chopin, Italy's Puccini, Russia's Tchaikovsky and Rimsky-Korsakov, Norway's Grieg, Hungary's Bartók, the Czech Dvořák, Austria's Schubert and Britain's Elgar, to name but a few of the dazzling cast of 19th-century masters. Orchestral music continued to follow artistic fashions into the 20th century, with modernist composers such as Russians Prokofiev and Shostakovich and the English Britten pioneering new works that kept European music an essential art form recognised around the world.

'Ode to Joy', the choral finale to Beethoven's Ninth Symphony, uses words by poet Friedrich Schiller to espouse universal brotherhood and has been adopted as the official EU anthem.

Rock and roll may have been pioneered in the United States, but it was arguably changed forever by the likes of the Beatles, Small Faces, the Rolling

Stones, the Who and the Kinks, all of whom emerged from Britain in the 1960s. The 1970s were just as extraordinary for British music – where to begin between Led Zeppelin, David Bowie, T.Rex, Queen, the Sex Pistols and the punk movement that conquered the world? Irish bands have similarly had massive influence beyond Ireland's borders – Van Morrison, the Undertones, U2 and the Pogues are just a few of them. Of course no account of Europe's pop prowess would be complete without name-checking Sweden's ABBA, one of the most successful pop groups of all time, still packing the aisles with their smash hit musical Mamma Mia.

The Eurovision Song Contest, the annual extravaganza of European cultural brotherhood that has become something of a camp icon over its five decades of existence, is watched by over 300 million viewers.

Literature

In the pantheon of European storytellers, the Greek epic poets (including Homer), dramatists (Aeschylus, Sophocles, Euripides) and philosophers (Plato, Aristotle) occupy revered positions. Rome's dominance of the continent impressed Latin as the voice of learning and literature (namely Virgil's *Aenid* and Plutarch's histories) until Geoffrey Chaucer *(The Canterbury Tales),* Miguel de Cervantes *(Don Quixote)* and Dante Alighieri *(La Divina Commedia),* among others, fashioned their native tongues into epics.

Johannes Gutenberg pioneered printing in Europe with his invention of moveable type printing in the mid-15th century, which was to contribute to the spread of ideas during the Renaissance and the following Enlightenment (see the boxed text, p39). The period building up to the Enlightenment was also a time of unbridled creativity in theatre and poetry (William Shakespeare, Molière, John Milton) and political theory (Niccolo Machiavelli).

With the advent of the machine age, the Romantics (eg Johann Wolfgang von Goethe, Alexander Pushkin, Lord Byron, John Keats, Percy Bysshe Shelley) bemoaned the severed ties with nature and looked to ancient Greece. Henrik Ibsen and Charles Baudelaire were also eminent literary figures in the 19th century. Here, too, at the door of modernity, philosophers including Friedrich Nietzsche dismantled the absolutes of morality and reality, and Sigmund Freud's theories opened a lid on the subconscious.

The modern age saw the rise of the novel from the character-driven stories of George Eliot, Jane Austen, the Brontë sisters, Charles Dickens, Thomas Hardy, Fyodor Dostoevsky, Leo Tolstoy and Thomas Mann among others to the literary experiments of celebrated Irish novelist James Joyce. In 1960s France, Jean-Paul Sartre and Albert Camus were the two leading lights of the existentialist movement. Many contemporary European writers (such as VS Naipul, Salman Rushdie, Milan Kundera, Michel Houellebecq and Hanif

TEN CLASSIC EUROPEAN NOVELS

- *Anna Karenina* by Leo Tolstoy (1877)
- *Crime and Punishment* by Fyodor Dostoevsky (1866)
- *Death in Venice* by Thomas Mann (1912)
- *Don Quixote* by Miguel de Cervantes (1605)
- *Madame Bovary* by Gustave Flaubert (1857)
- *Oliver Twist* by Charles Dickens (1838)
- *Remembrance of Things Past* by Marcel Proust (1913)
- *The Outsider* by Albert Camus (1942)
- *The Trial* by Franz Kafka (1925)
- *Ulysses* by James Joyce (1904)

Kureishi to name but a few) wrestle with such modern problems as the pressures and conflicts of straddling two cultures, escaping political persecution, and balancing love and desire.

Norman Davies' international bestseller *Europe: A History* is impressive in size, scope and balance, giving the Continent's east and west an equal hearing.

SCIENCE & MEDICINE

Scientific reason and method are central planks of European identity, and much science has its roots here. The Ancient Greeks were keen investigators of the physical world and many of their theories reigned for centuries, including the notion of four elements – earth, water, air and fire. Aristotle thought the universe was a system of concentric spheres. Astronomer Ptolemy backed this with his contention that the earth was the centre of the universe.

Most Greek publications were lost to the world for centuries, thanks to a paucity of translations. Arab scholars resurrected them and during Islamic rule in Spain the texts reached medieval Europe.

The 16th and 17th centuries marked what would later be called 'the scientific revolution'. Humankind's knowledge of the world changed swiftly and radically, while 'science' came to mean a strict discipline of systemic, empirical observation and experimentation.

Nicolaus Copernicus (1473–1543) and his notion that the earth revolved around the sun was a forerunner. His work was rapidly expanded by Johannes Kepler (1571–1630), who discovered that planetary orbits were elliptical not circular, and Galileo Galilei (1564–1642), who honed the primitive telescope and was the first to record the phases of Venus and the moons of Jupiter. Galileo's formulations most famously include the universal speed of falling bodies (irrespective of weight), although he also crucially introduced maths into physics.

Isaac Newton (1642–1727) continued that mathematical application, developing calculus and advancing the theory of universal gravitation. Its aim was to describe the whole world in one mathematical system. This was also what Albert Einstein (1879–1955) was attempting when formulating his theory of relativity – $E=mc^2$ – in the early 20th century.

There are hundreds of languages spoken in Europe, with 73 currently recognised by the United Nations as endangered, seriously endangered and almost extinct. Endangered languages include Cornish and Breton.

Without mathematicians and philosophers, such as René Descartes (1596–1650), Blaise Pascal (1623–62) and Francis Bacon (1561–1626), who contributed to geometry, probability and inductive reasoning, none of the earlier advances in physics and astronomy would have been possible.

Great strides in medicine also began during the scientific revolution, with works by Andreas Vesalius (1514–64) and William Harvey (1578–1657) unveiling the mysteries of blood circulation. However, the real boom in biological knowledge came in the 19th century, led by Louis Pasteur (1822–95) and Robert Koch (1843–1910), who discovered that bacteria, or germs, cause disease.

Around the same time, Charles Darwin (1809–92) made a watershed contribution to the understanding of the natural world, publishing *On the Origin of Species* (1859) and *The Descent of Man* (1871), thus launching the science of evolution by natural selection.

FOOD & DRINK

European cuisine often represents variations on a theme. Where Italians have ravioli (stuffed pasta), Polish have similar *pierogi* and Ukrainians *vareniki*. Spaniards tuck into rice-based *paella* dishes; Italians are keen on risotto. Turks dish out kebabs and tangy haloumi cheese, while Greeks serve *gyros* and feta.

Italy and France are the Continent's two top gourmet destinations, where the love of good food is seemingly inculcated in every citizen. The first boasts homemade pizza and pasta, polenta, truffles, fresh herbs and wonderful gelati (ice cream). The second is the home of classic haute cuisine. Yet there's more to traditional French food than rich creamy sauces, steak tartare, coq au vin, duck confit and goose-liver pâté. Rustic French cooking features simple, satisfying dishes, such as ratatouille (vegetable stew), cassoulet (grain-based stew) or bouillabaisse (a seafood stew from Marseille).

Serving food in courses was a Russian tradition that was widely adopted throughout Europe in the 19th century.

Spain and Portugal follow closely behind these two culinary giants, with tapas, ham and grilled sardines on the menu. Along the North and Baltic Sea coastlines, fish is understandably popular, where Scandinavians, for example, find salty 'roll mop' herrings a particular delicacy, and northern Germans are keen on smoked varieties.

Otherwise, German cuisine has much in common with hearty central European fare. The country shares a love of *Wurst* (sausage) and smoked pork with the Czech Republic and Austria (which also makes a mean apple strudel). And both Germans and Slavic countries are fond of cooked cabbage (*Sauerkraut* to the Germans). The latter consume plenty of borscht (beet soup) and vodka.

Like its language, Hungary's cuisine is unique and unusual. Always open to outside influences (especially Ottoman), it makes ample use of spices, such as the paprika found in the national goulash stew. Other European regions have their own specialities: the Swiss are known for fondue, *rösti* (fried, buttery, shredded potatoes), chocolate and cheese, while Belgians favour mussels and chips.

While British cuisine has improved immeasurably in the past decade and a half, you can always order curry if in doubt, thanks to the country's links to the Indian subcontinent.

RELIGION

Ironically, although the Romans weren't particularly fond of Christianity at the outset and fed early believers to the lions, they did much to spread the faith. Not only did this minority religion go with the Roman Empire as it spread across Europe, eventually Rome performed an about face; in AD 313 Emperor Constantine converted to Christianity and made it Rome's official religion.

When the Roman Empire fell in the west, the church's existing independent hierarchy of popes often assumed state power. In 1054 the church split over a theological debate on the Roman Catholic Church, which spread through most of Western Europe, as well as the Eastern Orthodox Church in Asia Minor. The Roman Catholic Church dominated political, artistic and cultural life in Europe for nearly 500 years until the Protestant Reformation in the 1520s. Inspired by the teachings of Martin Luther, parts of Germany, Switzerland, Scotland, Hungary and England broke away from Rome, adopting Protestant tenets that assumed a variety of subgroups (Lutherans, Evangelicals, Episcopalians etc).

Today traditionally Catholic countries such as France have a large Muslim minority thanks to immigration from former African colonies. However, Islam (emerging in Saudi Arabia in the 7th century) has had a permanent presence in Europe and North Africa since the 12th century. That's due largely to military conquest, particularly of Spain and the Balkans.

All said, it's worth remembering Europe's history of scientific rationalism. It still has the largest number and proportion of atheists and agnostics in the world.

SPORT

An immediate word of warning: don't call it soccer. The 'beautiful game' that is Europe's number-one spectator sport – by far – is called football. And if anything, the Continent seems to have gone more football-mad following Germany's successful hosting of the 2006 World Cup and Italy's win (despite a match-fixing scandal at home). The Euro 2008 (European Championship), that also gripped the continent, was won by Spain.

In the interim there's always the annual UEFA Champions League and UEFA Cup (both www.uefa.com) where you can watch some of the world's most famous teams, like Arsenal, Real Madrid, Chelsea and Manchester United, do battle. National leagues play the same October to May season.

If you prefer your ball elliptical, England, France, Scotland and Wales are all rugby heavyweights. If you prefer your ball to be a puck, you'll find fast-paced ice hockey has a huge following in Eastern Europe and in Scandinavia.

Otherwise you have a wide choice of sports. Two of the four global tennis Grand Slams are held on European soil. The French Open, Roland Garros (www.rolandgarros.org) is held on clay in Paris at the end of May. Grass courts and genteel manners are the order of the day at Wimbledon (www.wimbledon.org) in London every June.

Similarly, Formula One (www.formula1.com) motor races take place in Europe, including in England, Germany, Hungary, Italy and Monaco. In summer cricket is the English speciality, while across the Channel the annual Tour de France (www.letour.fr) cycling race in July draws huge crowds. A list of wintertime skiing and snowboarding competitions can be found at FIS-Ski (www.fis-ski.com).

Parts of Iceland look so out of this world, NASA sent Apollo astronauts to train there. The space agency is still studying the country in an effort to better understand Mars.

ENVIRONMENT

Europe is often referred to as a continent, when it is more accurately a peninsula, surrounded on three sides by the Mediterranean Sea, Atlantic Ocean and the North Sea. Coastal Europe is much more temperate than it should be at this northerly latitude, thanks to moist warm air brought in on the Gulf Stream. Southern Europe is dry and sunny, while central Europe is more variable.

In between the Baltic Sea and the spine of the Alps lies the European Plain, one of the greatest uninterrupted expanses on earth, stretching from the Pyrenees and the Atlantic coast to the Ural Mountains in Russia. This arable region of grassland and dense forests contains the Rhine, Danube and Main Rivers.

Belting the centre of Europe, the Alps were carved by the retreating glaciers during past ice ages, and the mountain range stretches from France to the significantly shorter Carpathian Mountains in Eastern Europe. Below the Alps is the warm Mediterranean region, running along a volcanic range that was most active between 1628 BC (Thera) and AD 79 (Vesuvius) – although Mt Etna in Sicily remains active today, with its last eruption in 2008. The Mediterranean land is rocky and exhausted from mismanagement, although olive trees, cypress and grape vines thrive. Along the Dalmatian coast, karst shimmers like a jewel.

Europe has experienced 17 ice ages through its geologic history. The next one is due to reach its peak in about 80,000 years.

In the far north, the arctic fingers of Scandinavia dip into the northern Atlantic and the shallow North Sea. Fjords, steep cliffs and mud flats all prepare the Continent to meet water. Glaciers, formed by layers of snow accumulating year after year, are also found here as well as in the Alps.

The Carpathians are considered one of the last refuges of wilderness, with healthy populations of brown bear, wolf and lynx, imperial eagle and Ural owl, species that have all but disappeared elsewhere. The last population of Iberian lynx lives in the southwestern corner of Spain and Portugal.

The world's largest reed-bed welcomes the Danube River into the Black Sea near Romania and Ukraine. More than half of the world's population of white pelicans, pygmy cormorants and red-breasted geese live in this Danube Delta. The northern Atlantic Ocean and North Sea provide unique habitats for sharks, seals and migratory birds.

Despite this, Europe suffers from a vast array of environmental problems. Air and water pollution from industry are high in many regions, and approximately 56% of Europe has been deforested. Rivers have been dammed or straightened, resulting in destruction of wetlands and loss of wildlife habitat. The once-abundant Mediterranean Sea has been overfished and its role as a popular tourist destination puts additional stress on limited resources, like fresh water and open space. Homes and hotels crowd more than half the Mediterranean coast, clawing over each other for a water view.

One Swiss ski resort, Andermatt, has taken drastic steps to protect its main glacier. It now wraps 3000 to 4000 sq m of foil blanket around the Gurschen Glacier in summer to reflect the sun's rays and slow melting.

Since the International Commission for the Protection of the Danube River (www.icpdr.org) was established in the mid-1990s, pollution in the Danube River has returned to 1980s' levels. However, concerns remain about the building of a shipping canal in the Danube Delta region and its impact on rare wildlife.

Global warming is taking its toll, with unsettled weather bringing extreme heat and drought to some parts of the continent and flooding to others. During a 2007 heatwave, for example, forest fires in Greece wiped out 2700 sq km of forest and caused enormous damage to the south of the country. Two years before that Europe saw its worst floods in decades with inundations stretching from Switzerland to Romania.

In fact, Switzerland seems to have been particularly hit hard, with its glaciers retreating at an alarming rate, causing unstable ground and excess melt water. Scientists at the University of Zürich believe 70% of Alpine glaciers will disappear in the next 30 years.

In addition to global problems, Europe has had at least one unique issue to deal with. The world's worst nuclear disaster occurred at the Chornobyl reactor in 1986, and parts of Belarus and Ukraine around the reactor remain off limits, although are accessible on day tours from Kyiv.

More information on these and other topics is available from the European Environment Agency (www.eea.europa.eu), which continually monitors and assesses the state of the environment across the Continent.

A Year in Europe

The weather is certainly more hospitable in summer, but Europe can keep you occupied all year round with its intoxicating mix of pagan and religious celebrations, its broad range of sporting activities and quirky festivals that border on the downright weird!

This chapter attempts to highlight a few events that are at least worth considering, if not making a detour for.

January

See in New Year in Edinburgh (29 December to 1 January; Scotland; www.edinburghshogmanay.org) Croon 'Auld Lang Syne' and go 'first footing' (popping into strangers' homes with a lump of coal and receiving a drink) during four days of revelry.

Celebrate Orthodox Christmas (7 January; Belarus, Russia and Ukraine) Missed Christmas at home through travelling, or just want to celebrate two? Then join in these countries' wonderful celebrations and feastlike meals.

Ski the Carpathians (January and February; Romania and Slovakia) Everyone knows about the Alps, but you get more for your money skiing the slopes in Romania (p973 and p964) or the Slovakian Tatras, the highest part of the Carpathians (p1020).

Compete in the Inferno Race (third weekend in January; Mürren, Switzerland; www.inferno-muerren.ch) Test your skills in Europe's biggest and most challenging amateur ski race. There's a cross-country course, slalom and downhill event, plus the burning of a devil's effigy, obviously!

February

Commemorate Sami Day (6 February; Sweden, Norway and Finland; www.sametinget.se) Get to know the native Sami people, with exhibitions and events in their homeland across the entire Arctic region. In mid-July, there's also the Riddu Riddu (www.riddu.com) festival near Tromsø, Norway.

Cheer on Europe's top dogs (first week of February; from Tarvisio, Udine, Italy, to Kranjska Gora, Slovenia; www.tarvisiano.org) Watch more than 1000 huskies and 200 humans as they race 22km, bound for the Slovenian border in the European Dog-Sledding Championships.

Enjoy Valentine's Day in Paris (14 February; Paris, France; www.paris.fr) Declare your undying devotion in the world's most romantic city, when even official public announcement boards are used to say 'I love you' and propose marriage.

March

Get fired up at Las Fallas (mid-March; Valencia, Spain) Spain's noisiest festival celebrates St Joseph by making huge, satirical papier-mâché figures, burning them on a pyre and letting off fireworks. Burn baby, burn.

Toast St Patrick's Day (17 March; Dublin, Ireland; www.stpatricksday.ie) Raise a pint of Guinness to mark the 'falling asleep' (death) of Ireland's patron saint, while also partaking of the accompanying revelry.

April

Spend Easter in the Med (mid-April; Spain, Portugal and Italy) Strong Catholic traditions mean atmospheric Easter celebrations. In Seville up to 3000 penitents in dark robes and hoods shuffle slowly through the town during the week of Semana Santa (p1113). Similar events include Braga's Ecce Homo (p952) and various penitent processions in Italy (p710).

Party royally on Queen's Day (Koninginnedag; 30 April; Amsterdam, the Netherlands) Join a million revellers marking the Dutch Queen's birthday in the wildest of fashions, with street performers, bands, markets, booze and more.

Feel the magic of Walpurgis Night (Walpurgisnacht; 30 April; Harz Mountains, Germany) Merrymakers dressed as witches, warlocks, devils and imps invade the summit of the Brocken Mountain (p504) for a little pagan bacchanalia. Similar celebrations are held in the Czech Republic, Sweden and Finland.

May

Discover your favourite beach island (Greece and Croatia) Intending to party or to chill out? What you're looking for is always just a boat ride away in these two countries (see p540 and p261).

Listen to Sacred Music in Fez (late May to mid-June; Fez, Morocco; www.fesfestival.com) 'Cleanse your soul' with moving performances of spiritual and religious music from around the world over 10 uplifting days.

Meet the Roma at 'Khamoro' (late May; Prague, Czech Republic; www.khamoro.cz) Learn through music and dance about the little-known and much-maligned Roma culture. The Khamoro Festival culminates in a richly orchestrated parade through Prague's Old Town.

June

Experience White Nights (mid-June to mid-July; St Petersburg, Russia) The sun doesn't set on the imperial Russian capital until very late in sum-

GOODBYE WINTER!

Think Rio de Janeiro has the only Carnival? Europeans are quite good at it, too. Every year, just before Lent, they take to the streets in a wild array of masks and costumes, tooting loudly and practising their dance moves. Historians believe Carnival has its roots in pagan rituals marking the passage of winter into spring. As so often happened, the Christian church then coopted and modified it.

Today it kicks off in the week before Ash Wednesday (the start of Lent), culminating on 'Fat Tuesday' or *Mardi Gras* – in late February or early March.

Most famous is the **Venice Carnevale** (www.carnivalofvenice.com), which centres on St Mark's Sq and features elegant 18th-century masked balls and costumes. However, northwest Germans also hold their **Karneval** rituals dear, particularly in Cologne (see p497), Düsseldorf and Mainz.

In Bavaria and Austria, it goes by the name **Fasching** (after fasting). In Switzerland, it's called **Fasnacht**, when it's celebrated particularly exuberantly in Lucerne and staged with aplomb in Basel. Other Carnivals worth making a detour for are in Aalborg in Denmark, Rijeka in Croatia and Maastricht in the Netherlands.

Many other spring pagan rituals run in parallel with Carnival. In Poland, for example, they have **Drowning Marzanna** on 21 March, when they immerse the straw effigy of a witch in Warsaw's Vistula and other rivers, to mark winter's end. Cautious Zürich citizens wait until the third Monday of April for **Sechseläuten**, when they ignite a fireworks-filled 'snowman' (the Böögg) to acknowledge the passage of the seasons.

SUMMER SOLSTICE

William Shakespeare knew what a rich seam he was mining when he wrote the play *A Midsummer's Night Dream*. Even in the modern age the days around 21 June, the longest day of the year, are marked with wild pagan rituals in northern Europe. This was an important time in the Viking calendar, and the Scandinavians particularly have a huge bash, with bonfires and all-night music festivals.

The same is true in Scotland, the very northwest of Germany and the Baltics. Take Estonia, for example, where bonfires are lit for all-nighters along the beach during **Jaanipäev** (St John's Eve; June 23).

A slightly different tradition exists in Belarus, Russia and Ukraine, where the summer solstice was seen as a good time for young people to choose a marriage partner. Christianisation has shifted **Ivan Kupalo** to 6 or 7 July, but the evening still begins with folk singing and maypole-style dancing by young women, who then float wreaths (symbolising virginity) down a nearby river. Later, a bonfire is lit, over which couples will jump, holding hands, to test whether – if they maintain their grip – their love will last.

mer, casting a bewitching glow over the city. The same effect can be observed in northern Scandinavia and Iceland (where the sun never really sets at all).

Go to Glastonbury (late June; Pilton in Somerset, England; www.glastonburyfestivals.co.uk) Get knee-deep in pop culture, celebrity and inevitably, given the English weather, mud at the world's most famous festival where top global acts headline and the cream of Britain's indie and rock scene play on a variety of stages.

Rock at Roskilde (late June/early July; Roskilde, Denmark; www.roskildefestival.dk) Glastonbury with a slightly more grungy feel, Roskilde has big-name alternative bands, folk, soul and reggae.

July

Race to Il Palio (2 July and 16 August; Siena, Italy) Bareback riders urge their horses on for three laps around the city's main piazza, Il Campo, in this incredible 'everything-goes' race.

Run with the bulls (San Fermines; early July; Pamplona, Navarra, Spain; www.sanfermin.com) Exercise your adventurous Hemingway-esque streak running before a herd of bulls through 800m of narrow streets. Seriously dangerous and much better enjoyed as a spectator 'sport'!

Get into the Exit Festival (early July; Novi Sad, Serbia; www.exitfest.org) Virtually 19 rock festivals in one and arguably Europe's coolest, Exit has different stages connected through the labyrinth of tunnels and ramparts of an amazing hilltop fortress overlooking the Danube River (p1008).

B-Parade (July; Berlin, Germany; www.b-parade.eu) Held each July, Berlin's huge techno street parade is the successor to the world-famous Love Parade. Party to screaming techno between the Brandenburg Gate and the Siegessäule victory column, and beyond.

Raise a glass to Õllesummer (Beer Summer; early July; Tallinn, Estonia; www.ollesummer.ee) The Baltics' largest beer festival mixes Estonian folk culture, local bands and international beers.

Revolt on Bastille Day (14 July; Paris, France; www.paris.fr) *Vive la révolution!* Fireworks, parties and a military parade on the Champs-Élysées mark the French national day (p445).

Marvel at the Mostar Bridge Dive (last weekend in July; Mostar, Bosnia and Hercegovina) Carrying on the tradition of the world's oldest high-diving competition, young Mostar men plunge 21m from this famously rebuilt arched bridge (p144).

August

Go wild at Street Parade (early August; Zürich, Switzerland; www.streetparade.ch) Join Switzerland's supposedly uptight bankers as they cut massively loose on street floats and pavements, at one of Europe's largest techno parties.

Be outrageous at Amsterdam Pride (early August; The Netherlands; www.amsterdamgaypride.nl) The Continent's largest annual gay and lesbian pride march is also known as the 'canal parade', as outlandishly dressed participants literally float down the canals on floats and boats.

Attend the Edinburgh Fringe Festival (three weeks in August; Edinburgh, Scotland; www.edfringe.com) Join the crowds for Europe's largest and best arts festival, where the creative juices never stop flowing. Here you'll catch the stand ups, theatre and music that will shape the year to come before anyone else.

Toss your food at La Tomatina (last Wednesday of August; Buñol, Spain) Throw 'em if you've got 'em at the world's largest food fight. More than 20,000 revellers pelt each other with tomatoes for two free-for-all hours in the tiny town of Buñol, near Valencia.

Revel in the Notting Hill Carnival (last weekend in August; London, England; www.thecarnival.tv) Be dazzled by the colourful floats, the steel bands and the fantastic Jamaican food stalls of this enormous Caribbean-flavoured affair.

September

Arrange a late-year beach party (first half of September; Bulgaria, Croatia, Cyprus, France, Greece, Italy, Malta, Portugal, Spain and Turkey) The high season has just finished, so now is a perfect time to hit the remarkably less crowded beaches. But don't dally; it swiftly gets too cold.

Chase the Northern Lights (September to October, also March to April; northern Finland, Norway and Sweden) Nature's most beautiful light show, the *aurora borealis* can be elusive. So give yourself at least a week to spot this quick-changing succession of colours and patterns, created by electrical charges in the upper atmosphere.

Have a rollicking Oktoberfest (mid-September to start of October; Munich, Germany; www.oktoberfest.de) Germans are so keen to start this annual beer orgy – consuming five million litres of beer and 400,000 pork sausages – that they kick off two weeks before October (see p475).

October

Watch the cows come home (early October; Switzerland and Austria) Decorated with bells and ribbons, local herds are led down from high

HIGHLAND FLINGS

Many Scots still consider themselves cut from the *Braveheart* tartan cloth, particularly those you find at the numerous Highland Games across the country from May to September. Originally a test of strength and skill for potential clan warriors, such games were revived in the 19th century, with all their caber-tossing (a caber is a tree trunk), hammer-throwing and stone-putting. Bagpipers, Scottish dancers and haggis are all in evidence too.

At the **Lonach Games** (last weekend of August; Strathdon, Aberdeenshire; www.lonach.org) local resident Billy Connolly is wont to bring along celebrity friends, which in the past have included Robin Williams, Ewan McGregor and Dame Judi Dench to name a few. The royal family, by contrast, turn out for the traditional **Braemar Gathering** (early September; Braemar, Deeside; www.braemargathering.org).

A good list can be found at www.albagames.co.uk, or ask Visit Scotland (www.visitscotland.com).

pastures to winter barns, cheered on by locals in a ritual variously called *dèsalpe, Alpabfahrt* and *Almabtrieb*.

Take a hot bath (all month; Budapest, Hungary) Stave off the autumn chill by taking to the thermal waters of Budapest's many spas (see p567), just in time for the city's Autumn Festival of classical music, too.

November

Celebrate Guy Fawkes Night (5 November; across England) Bonfires, fireworks, sparklers and the burning of 'the Guy' recall a foiled attempt to blow up parliament in 1605.

Ice skate in London (late November to late January; London, England) The British capital can't get enough of urban ice-skating rinks, the best being at Somerset House (www.somerset-house.org.uk), Kew Gardens (www.rbgkew.org.uk), the Natural History Museum (www.nhm.ac.uk) and the Tower of London (www.hrp.org.uk).

Shop 'til you drop at Christmas markets (late November to late December; across Austria, Germany and Poland) Quaint stalls sell mulled wine, sausages, tree ornaments, Christmas cards and other presents in some thousands of markets heralding the arrival of the festive season.

December

Admire Kraków's Nativity Cribs (first Thursday of December to end February; Kraków, Poland) Crafting ornate nativity scenes *(szopka)* is an ancient Polish art and Krakow's best annual efforts are displayed in the Museum of History (www.mhk.pl).

Ski around Lake Bled (all month; Lake Bled, Slovenia) Avoid the summer crowds that swarm to Slovenia's most beautiful lake by visiting it and the Julian Alps in winter.

Have your head turned at Mevlâna (mid-December; Konya, Turkey) The ancient town where the mystical Islamic order of the whirling dervishes was established, Konya pays tribute to the Sufi saint Mevlâna with an annual festival of spectacular dances.

Albania

HIGHLIGHTS

- **Berat** Clamber past white Ottoman houses, then look back at the distant mountains hiding behind this Unesco-listed town's minarets (p59)
- **Gjirokastra** Hunt down strange souvenirs in Ottoman shop fronts while negotiating its slate roofs that melt into the narrow cobblestone streets (p60)
- **Dhërmi** Join the beach-brigade heading down to Dhërmi's busy beach, or pop next door to Drymades for a more peaceful experience (p59)
- **Butrint** Find peace and tranquillity in the natural setting of these jungly, ancient ruins south of Saranda (p59)

FAST FACTS

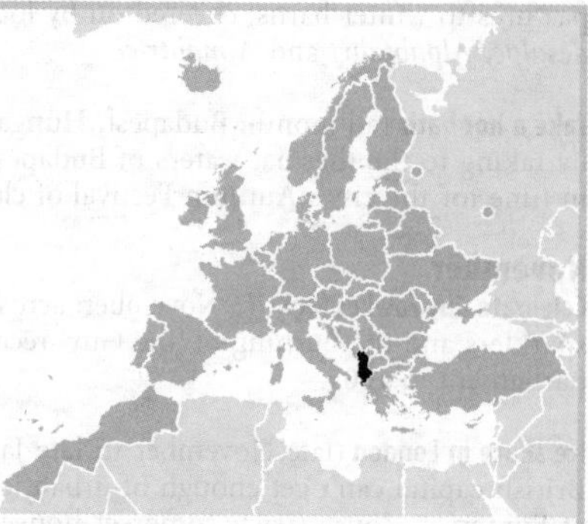

- **Area** 28,748 sq km
- **Budget** €40 per day
- **Capital** Tirana
- **Country code** ☎ 355
- **Famous for** cool flag, concrete bunkers, international diaspora
- **Language** Albanian
- **Money** lekë; A$1 = 72 lekë; C$1 = 82 lekë; €1 = 130 lekë; ¥100 = 103 lekë; NZ$1 = 57 lekë; UK£1 = 147 lekë; US$1= 97 lekë
- **Phrases** *miredita* (hello/good day), *lamtumirë* (goodbye), *ju lutem* (please), *ju falem nderit* (thank you), *më fal* (excuse me/sorry)
- **Population** 3.62 million
- **Visas** no visa needed for citizens of the EU, Australia, New Zealand, the US and Canada; see p61

TRAVEL HINTS

Aim for early-morning departures as few buses run after midday. Torches come in handy during blackouts, at historical sights and for evening pothole-spotting. Toilets rarely have paper: BYO.

ROAMING ALBANIA

Start in Saranda, check out Butrint and Gjirokastra, then head up the coastal route via Dhërmi to Tirana.

It's been nearly twenty years since Albania opened up to the world and she's almost an adult, although reaching this milestone hasn't been challenge-free. Her childhood, featuring one massive financial collapse and resulting rioting, wasn't ideal. There are plenty of stretch marks. Her streets, car-free until 1991, are now clogged; sections of her picturesque landscape are strewn with rampant development and in places her beaches can't be seen for the hotels.

Yet, after years of government-enforced isolation and the ensuing growing pains of freedom, there's evidence of prosperity in the upgraded roads that swirl past new houses and bar/restaurant/hotel developments, though blackouts and water shortages are nagging signs that

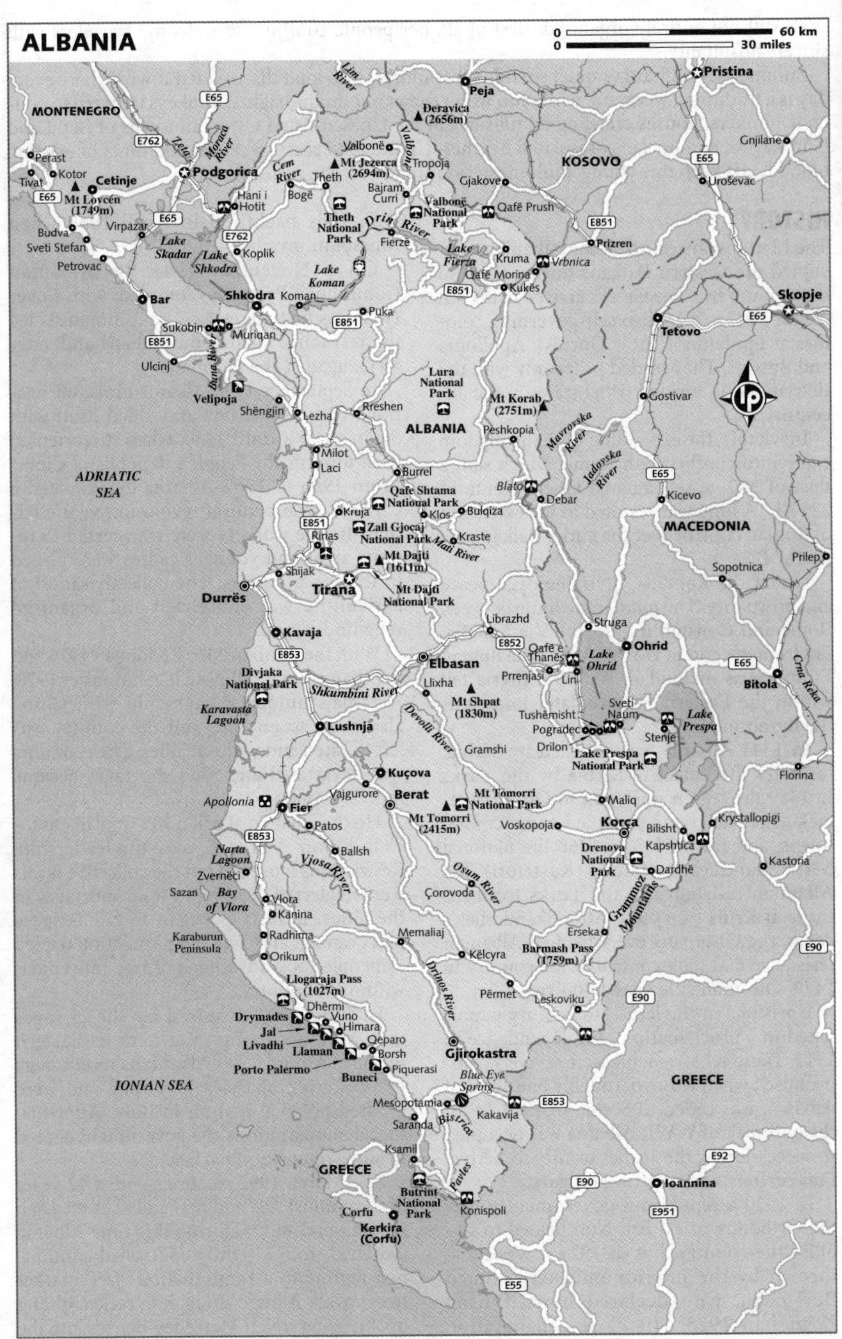
ALBANIA
0 60 km
0 30 miles
MONTENEGRO
KOSOVO
ALBANIA
MACEDONIA
GREECE
ADRIATIC SEA
IONIAN SEA
Pristina
Peja
Podgorica
Cetinje
Shkodra
Tirana
Durrës
Elbasan
Berat
Fier
Korça
Gjirokastra
Saranda
Vlora
Skopje
Tetovo
Ohrid
Bitola
Ioannina
Kerkira (Corfu)
Mt Jezerca (2694m)
Mt Korab (2751m)
Mt Dajti (1611m)
Mt Shpat (1830m)
Mt Tomorri (2415m)
Llogaraja Pass (1027m)
Barmash Pass (1759m)
Lake Ohrid
Lake Prespa
Lake Shkodra
Butrint National Park
Blue Eye Spring

she's still not entirely organised. Best of all, her people continue to welcome travellers with sincere hospitality.

Summer sees Albania's quiet seaside spots morph into loud disco-laden towns where every day is a thumping weekend, while you won't forget her unique sights: donkeys tethered to concrete bunkers, houses crawling up hillsides in the Unesco-listed Ottoman towns of Berat and Gjirokastra, and pockets of isolated beaches. Unfettered access to castles and hints of existing blood feuds keep this young adult mysterious (and yes, she's cheap).

HISTORY

The Illyrians, ancestors of the Albanians, occupied the western Balkans during the 2nd millennium BC. The Greeks arrived in the 7th century BC to establish self-governing colonies at Epidamnos (now Durrës), Apollonia and Butrint. They traded peacefully with the Illyrians, who formed tribal states in the 4th century BC.

Inevitably, the expanding Illyrian kingdom came into conflict with Rome, which sent a fleet of 200 vessels against Queen Teuta in 229 BC. A long war resulted in the extension of Roman control over the entire Balkan area by 167 BC.

Under the Romans, Illyria enjoyed peace and prosperity. The main trade route between Rome and Constantinople, the Via Egnatia, ran from the port at Durrës. When the Roman Empire was divided in AD 395, Illyria fell within the Eastern Empire, later known as the Byzantine Empire.

In 1344 Albania was annexed by Serbia, but after the defeat of Serbia by the Turks in 1389 the region was open to Ottoman attack. The Venetians occupied some coastal towns, and from 1443 to 1468 the national hero Skanderbeg (Gjergj Kastrioti) led Albanian resistance to the Turks from his castle at Kruja (see p58). After Skanderbeg's death, the Ottomans overwhelmed Albanian resistance and took control of the country in 1479. Ottoman rule lasted 400 years.

Uprisings in the late 19th century culminated in a proclamation of independence in 1912. These achievements were severely compromised when Kosovo, roughly one-third of Albania, was ceded to Serbia in 1913. With the outbreak of WWI, Albania was occupied in succession by the armies of Greece, Serbia, France, Italy and Austria-Hungary.

In 1920 a republican government under the Orthodox priest Fan Noli helped to stabilise the country, but in 1924 it was overthrown by the interior minister, Ahmed Bey Zogu, who declared himself King Zogu I in 1928. His close collaboration with Italy backfired in April 1939 when Mussolini invaded.

On 8 November 1941 the Albanian Communist Party was founded, with Enver Hoxha as first secretary. The communists led the resistance against the Italians and, after 1943, against the Germans.

In September 1948 Albania broke off relations with Yugoslavia and allied itself with Stalin's USSR until 1960, when it reoriented itself towards the People's Republic of China. From 1966 to 1967 Albania experienced a Chinese-style cultural revolution where administrative workers were transferred to remote areas and younger cadres were placed in leading positions. The collectivisation of agriculture was completed and organised religion banned.

With the death of Mao Zedong in 1976 and the changes that followed in China after 1978, Albania's unique relationship with China also came to an end, and the country was left isolated and without allies. The economy was devastated and food shortages became more common.

Hoxha died in April 1985 and his associate Ramiz Alia took over the leadership. Restrictions loosened but the collective farms were neglected, leading to food shortages in the cities. Industries began to fail as spare parts ran out and Tirana's population tripled as people took advantage of free movement within the country.

In June 1990, inspired by the changes that were occurring elsewhere in Eastern Europe, around 4500 Albanians took refuge in Western embassies in Tirana and were granted political asylum in Italy. After further demonstrations the government agreed to allow opposition parties.

The March 1992 elections ended 47 years of communist rule and parliament elected Sali Berisha president. During this time Albania switched from a tightly controlled communist regime to a rambunctious free-market free-for-all. A huge smuggling racket sprang up, bringing stolen Mercedes-Benzes into the

BUNKER LOVE

On the hillsides, beaches, people's front gardens and generally most surfaces in Albania, you will notice small concrete domes with rectangular slits. Meet the bunkers: Enver Hoxha's concrete legacy, built from 1950 to 1985. Weighing in at 5 tonnes of concrete and iron, these little mushrooms are almost impossible to destroy. They were built to repel an invasion and can resist full tank assault – a fact proved by their chief engineer. He vouched for his creation's strength by standing inside one while it was bombarded. The shell-shocked engineer emerged unscathed and tens of thousands were built. Quite a few Albanians will admit to losing their virginity in the security of a bunker and they seem to make handy public toilets.

country, and the port of Vlora became a major crossing point for illegal immigrants.

In 1996, 70% of Albanians lost their savings when private pyramid-investment schemes collapsed. Riots ensued, elections were called, and the victorious Socialist Party under Fatos Nano was able to restore some degree of security and investor confidence.

In 1999 Albania housed 465,000 fleeing Kosovars (ethnic Albanians) during the Serbian ethnic-cleansing campaign and in 2008 Albanians celebrated Kosovo's independence.

The general election of 2005 saw a return of Berisha's Democratic Party to government. Albanian politics and the economy have been stable, but infrastructure deficiencies plague the country.

Albania became a member of NATO in 2009 and whilst the IMF predicts low growth for Albania's economy, both income per capita and revenue from tourism was up 9% and 20% respectively in 2009.

THE CULTURE

In July 2008 the population was estimated to be 3,619,778, of which approximately 95% are Albanian, 3% Greek and 2% 'other' – comprising Vlachs, Roma, Serbs, Macedonians and Bulgarians. The Ghegs in the north and the Tosks in the south have different dialects, music and dress, and the usual jokes about each other's weaknesses.

Albanians are generally kind, helpful and generous, and shake their heads for yes *(po)* and nod to say no *(jo)*. Albania is a safe country for women travellers, but outside Tirana you'll find few women in the bars – it's mainly men who go out. Staring seems to be a national pastime, and all travellers will find themselves on the receiving end.

ENVIRONMENT

Albania is comprised of 30% vast interior plains, a 300km coastal region and a mountainous spine that runs the length of the country. Mt Korab, at 2764m, is Albania's highest peak.

Albania borders beautiful lakes including the Balkan's largest – Lake Shkodra – in the north, and the ancient Lake Ohrid in the east. National park numbers have risen from six to 15 since 1966 and include Mt Dajti, Butrint, Mt Tomorri and Valbonë. Most are protected only by their remoteness, and tree felling and hunting still take place.

Environmentally, Lake Ohrid's trout is endangered (but still eaten), badly maintained oil fields around Fier leak sludge into the surrounding environment and several coastal regions discharge raw sewage into seas and rivers. Rubbish is an issue; it's everywhere. The **Organic Agriculture Association** (www.organic.org.al) is one group trying to make a difference.

TRANSPORT

GETTING THERE & AWAY

Air

Albania's international airport is **Nënë Tereza International Airport** (www.tirana-airport.com.al), aka Mother Teresa/Rinas, 26km northwest of Tirana. There are flights to Italy, London Gatwick and Athens, Belgrade, Budapest, İstanbul, Frankfurt, Pristina, Sofia, Vienna and Zurich.

READING UP

Anything by Man Booker International prizewinner Ismail Kadare gives great insight into Albania's history, and don't miss the excellent *Chronicle in Stone* (1987) if you're Gjirokastra-bound. New Zealander Lloyd Jones wrote the excellent *Biografi* (1993) about Albania's transition from communism.

Land

Buses to Pristina (€30, 10 hours) depart every evening from beside the Tirana International Hotel on Sheshi Skënderbej at 6pm. Macedonia-bound buses leave Tirana's train station at 9am and 9pm for Skopje (€25, eight hours). Buy tickets at **Pollogu travel agency** (☎ 04-2235 000; Pall 103 Blvd Zogu I), upstairs in a modern apartment building near the station. **Drita Travel and Tours** (☎ 04-2251 277; www.dritatravel.com) sells tickets for its evening service to Skopje from the train station and National Museum of History. *Furgons* (shared minibuses) leave Shkodra for Ulcinj in Montenegro at 9am and 3pm (€5, 40 minutes).

Sea

Finikas (☎ 0852-6057; finikaslines@yahoo.com; Rr Mithat Hoxha) and **Ionian Cruises** (www.ionian-cruises.com) have daily ferries departing Saranda for Corfu at 10.30am, 4pm and 4.15pm. A one-way ticket is €17.50. Regular services to Italy depart from Vlora (to Brindisi) and Durrës (Ancona, Bari and Trieste). One-way fares cost around €30 to €75.

GETTING AROUND

Bus

Private *furgons* compete with cheap buses to transport Albanians around, though they're often a distant memory by 2pm. Municipal buses operate in larger towns and charge 30 lekë per trip. They can get crowded; watch your stuff.

Car & Motorcycle

If you're keen to drive, sample conditions in a taxi first. Driving at night is particularly hazardous; watch for open drains. **Avis** (☎ 04-2235 011; Rogner Hotel Europapark Tirana, Blvd Dëshmorët e Kombit) and **Hertz** (☎ 04-2255 028; Tirana International Hotel, Sheshi Skënderbej) have hire cars.

Hitching

The Albanian sense of hospitality certainly shines if you've got your thumb out, though with transport so cheap it's an unnecessary risk.

Train

Albanians who cannot afford buses or *furgons* use the dilapidated trains, and they're certainly an interesting, albeit slow, way to see Albania. Trains run from Tirana north to Shkodra, west to Durrës, south to Vlora, and east to Pogradec.

BORDER CROSSINGS

The main crossings to Kosovo are Qafë Morina and Qafë Prush. Buses to/from Macedonia use the Qafë e Thanës crossing, while the Tushëmisht–Sveti Naum crossing is a quieter walk-through followed by a 4km walk into town. Cross into Montenegro at Han i Hotit or Muriqan. For Greece most people use Kakavia in the south and Kapshtica to the east.

CONNECTIONS

Albania is a mere hop from Greece's Corfu (see left), but it's a longer sea journey to Italy from Vlora and Durrës. Mainland Greece is easily reached via bus throughout Albania. Travel via the Koman River ferry to Kosovo is a wonderful experience. Shkodra has daily buses to Bar, in Montenegro.

TIRANA

☎ 04 / pop 600,000

Lively, colourful Tirana has changed beyond belief from the dull, grey city it once was. It's amazing what a lick of paint can do – covering one ugly tower block with horizontal orange and red stripes, another with concentric pink and purple circles, and planting perspective-fooling cubes on its neighbour.

Trendy Blloku buzzes with the well-dressed nouvelle bourgeoisie hanging out in bars. Quite where their money comes from is the subject of much speculation, but thankfully you don't need much of it to have a fun night out in the city's many bars and clubs.

Tirana's grand central boulevards are lined with fascinating relics of the city's Ottoman, Italian and communist past, from delicate minarets to socialist murals. The traffic does daily battle with both itself and pedestrians in a constant scene of unmitigated chaos.

Loud, crazy, colourful, dusty – Tirana is simply fascinating.

ORIENTATION

Running through Tirana is Blvd Zogu I, which changes its name to Dëshmorët e Kombit as it crosses the Lana River. At its northern end is Tirana train station, and the southern section ends at Tirana University. The main sites of interest are on or very close to this large boulevard, including, roughly halfway along, Sheshi Skënderbej (Skanderbeg Square).

Most of the eating and drinking action is at Blloku, a square of shops, restaurants, cafes and hotels situated one block west of Dëshmorët and along the Lana River in south Tirana. Mt Dajti (1611m) rises in the distant east.

INFORMATION

Tirana in Your Pocket (www.inyourpocket.com) knows what's going on and can be downloaded free, or bought at bookshops and hotels for 400 lekë.

There are plenty of ATMs linked to international networks. Cash travellers cheques before heading out of Tirana at **American Bank of Albania** (☎ 2276 000; Rr Ismail Qemali 27; 9.30am-3.30pm Mon-Fri).

ABC Family Healthy Center (☎ 2234 105; Rr Qemal Stafa 260; 9am-1pm Mon-Fri) English-speaking Christian doctors; services include regular (€50) and emergency (€80) consultations.

Albanian Experience (☎ 2266 389; Sheraton Hotel, Sheshi Italia) Organises tours.

Outdoor Albania (☎ 069 218 8845, 2227 121; www.outdooralbania.com; Rr Sami Frasheri Metropol Bldg; 8am-8pm Mon-Fri) Excellent adventure-tour agency offering trekking, rafting, sea and white-water kayaking.

Top Net (Rr Vaso Pasha; per hr 100 lekë; 8.30am-11pm;) Internet access.

SIGHTS

Sheshi Skënderbej is the best place to start witnessing Tirana's daily goings-on. Until it was pulled down by an angry mob in 1991, a 10m-high statue of Enver Hoxha stood here, watching over a mainly car-less square. Now only the **equestrian statue of Skanderbeg** remains, deaf to the cacophony of screeching horns as cars four lanes deep try to shove their way through the battlefield below.

Close by is the minaret of the 1789–1823 **Et'hem Bey Mosque**. The small and elegant mosque is one of the oldest buildings left in the city, spared from destruction during the atheism campaign of the late 1960s because of its status as a cultural monument. Inside is a 'shoes off' zone.

Behind the mosque is the **Clock Tower** (admission 50 lekë) which you can climb up on Mondays and Thursdays to watch the square. Further on, the socialist-realist **Statue of the Unknown Partisan** attracts day-labourers waiting for work, some with their own jackhammers.

To the east is the white stone **Theatre of Opera and Ballet** (Palace of Culture, Pallate Kulturës; Sheshi Skënderbej), which has a theatre and shops. Construction of the palace began as a gift from the Soviet people in 1960 and was completed in 1966, years after the 1961 Soviet–Albanian split.

On the northwestern side of the square is the **National Museum of History** (Muzeu Historik Kombëtar; Sheshi Skënderbej; admission 300 lekë; 9am-1pm & 4-7pm Tue-Sat, 9am-noon Sun). This museum holds most of the country's archaeological treasures and a replica of Skanderbeg's massive sword. A sombre gallery devoted to the Hoxha era's miseries is on the top floor. There's no entry half an hour before closing time.

Stroll down the spacious tree-lined Blvd Dëshmorët e Kombit to Tirana's **National Art Gallery** (Galeria Kombëtare e Arteve; Blvd Dëshmorët e Kombit; admission 100 lekë; 9am-1pm & 5-8pm Tue-Sun). If you're lucky you'll catch some modern work by Albanian artists in the temporary exhibition space.

South of the river is the sloping white-marble and glass walls of the 1988 **Pyramid**

EMERGENCY NUMBERS

- Ambulance ☎ 127
- Fire ☎ 128
- Police ☎ 129

GETTING INTO TOWN

Rinas Express (250 lekë; 6am-6pm) is an hourly shuttle bus between the airport and the National Museum of History. A taxi costs €25. Buses drop you off at the train station at the north end of Blvd Zogu I, a five-minute walk north from Sheshi Skënderbej. *Furgons* (minibuses) drop you at various points around the city, and it's often worth catching a waiting taxi to your final destination.

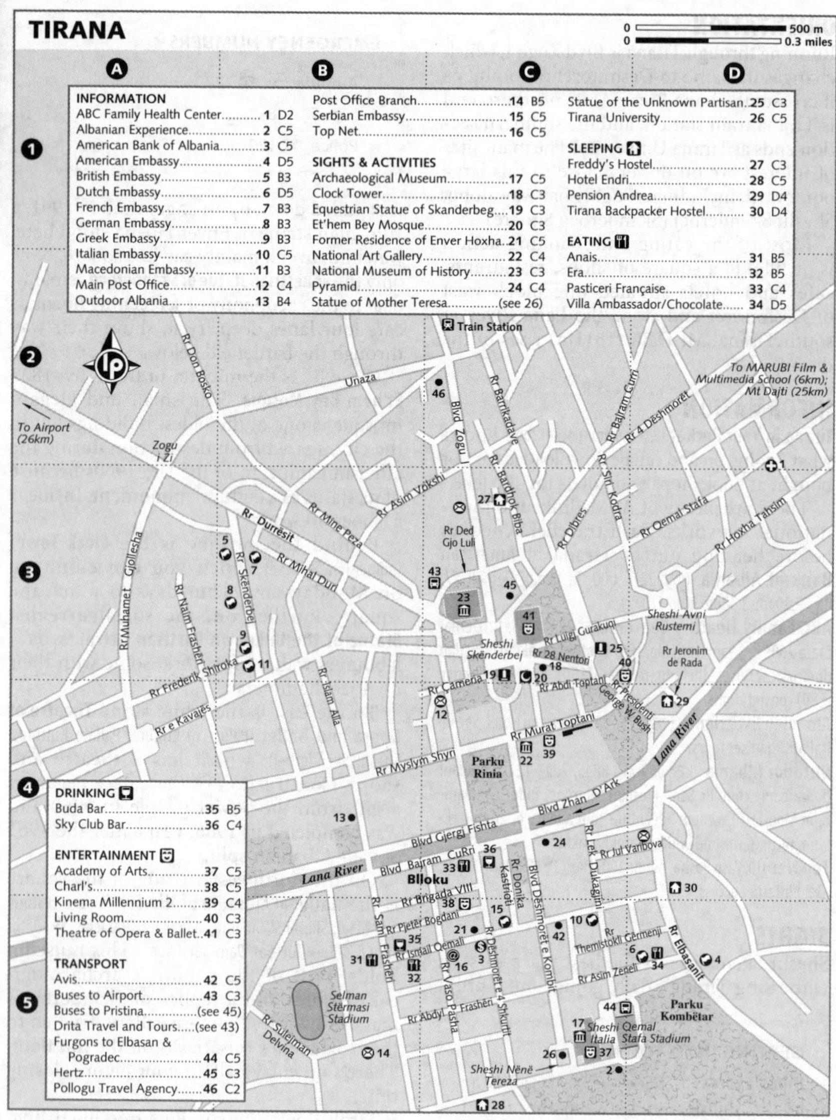

(former Enver Hoxha Museum; Blvd Dëshmorët e Kombit). Its uses have varied from disco to conference centre and it is undergoing change once again.

Head south and follow Rr Ismal Qemali west to enter the once totally forbidden but now totally trendy **Blloku** area. This former communist party–elite hang-out was opened to the general public for the first time in 1991. Security still guards the **former residence of Enver Hoxha** (cnr Rr Dëshmorët e 4 Shkurtit & Rr Ismail Qemali).

The **Archaeological Museum** (Muzeu Arkeologik; Sheshi Nënë Tereza; admission 200 lekë; 10.30am-2.30pm Mon-Fri) houses an extensive collection close to Mother Teresa University.

ALBANIA FOR FREE

- Hunt down the last house standing by the Lana River (protected by a blood feud), a few kilometres west of central Tirana
- On Thursdays during term see free art-house movies at MARUBI (p57)
- Stroll with the masses on the evening *xhiro* (walk)
- Admire the innovative artwork on Tirana's apartment blocks

SLEEPING

our pick **Tirana Backpacker Hostel** (☎ 068 216 7357; www.tiranahostel.com; Rr Elbasanit 85; dm €12) Albania's first hostel opened in 2005 in a 70-year-old villa close to the city centre. The 25 beds are spread over four rooms with shared bathrooms. It has big balconies, a great garden with a cosy outdoor kitchen, a summer cinema in the basement and friendly, helpful young managers. Head east along Rr Ismail Qemali until it meets Rr Elbasanit; it's over the road on your left.

Freddy's Hostel (☎ 068 203 5261; www.freddyshostel.com; Rr Bardhok Biba 75; dm/r €12/30) A bunch of clean, basic rooms in different configurations and in two different buildings in the same area. To find the main apartment block, walk north of Tirana International Hotel and look for the suburban street parallel to Blvd Zogu I. The hostel is on the left.

Pension Andrea (☎ 069 290 4915; Rr Jeronim de Rada 103; s/d €20/30; ❄) Gina runs this homey, quiet pension. All rooms have TVs and a couple have aircon. On Rr Jeronim de Rada, take the first right down the court; it's on your right.

Hotel Endri (☎ 2244 168, 2229 334; Rr Vaso Pasha 27; r €30; ❄) South of Blloku, where all the action is, this 'hotel' is basically a couple of clean rooms in a building next to owner Petrit Alikaj's apartment. It's on the left at the end of Rr Vaso Pasha; call Petrit for directions.

EATING

With 30 lekë *burek* stands, you won't go hungry on a small budget.

Pasticeri Française (☎ 2251 336; Rr Dëshmorët e 4 Shkurtit 1; breakfast 300 lekë; ⏲ 8am-10pm) One of the few breakfast spots in Tirana, this French-owned cafe has red walls, high ceilings and a huge selection of sweet pastries.

Era (☎ 2266 662; Rr Ismail Qemali; mains 400 lekë; ⏲ 11am-midnight) Serves traditional Albanian and Italian fare in the heart of Blloku. Be warned: it's hard to move on once you've eaten here.

Villa Ambassador/Chocolate (☎ 069 206 6257; Rr Asim Zeneli 2; meals 1000 lekë; ⏲ 8am-midnight) Located in the former Romanian Ambassador's residence, this well-regarded restaurant has a great team creating and serving up tasty Albanian dishes for both carnivores and vegetarians. Crepes and pastries make it a good spot for breakfast.

Anais (☎ 2246 624; Rr Sami Frashëri 20; meals from 2500 lekë; ⏲ 11am-11pm) Quite expensive by local standards, the Ottoman cuisine served here is utterly superb. The selection of mezes is tremendous: puréed eggplant, spicy beans and mushrooms, and rich kebabs. Main courses cost around 1000 to 1200 lekë, starters around 400 lekë.

DRINKING & CLUBBING

Sky Club Bar (☎ 2221 666; Sky Tower, Rr Dëshmorët e 4 Shkurtit; ⏲ 8am-midnight) Start your night here for spectacular city views from the revolving bar. If you're just going up for a look, it's cheaper to buy a beer up there than pay the 250 lekë 'entry fee'.

Living Room (☎ 2274 837; Rr Presidenti George W Bush 16; ⏲ 7.30pm-late) This is the hippest place to drink and dance in Tirana – with eclectic DJs, a good crowd, cool lampshades and '70s sofas for you to lounge on when you're danced (or drunk) off your feet. The terrace is airy and fun.

Charl's (☎ 2253 754; Rr Pjetër Bogdani 36; ⏲ 8am-late) Charl's is a consistently popular bar with Tirana's students because of its ever-varying live music, with bands coming from places as diverse as Cuba and Serbia. Charl's relaxed vibe is cemented by its open-air garden.

Buda Bar (☎ 068 205 8825; Rr Ismail Qemali; ⏲ 4.30pm-late) Buda has a relaxed atmosphere with subdued lighting, incense burning, chaise longues and armchairs abounding with cushions.

ENTERTAINMENT

MARUBI Film & Multimedia School (www.afmm.edu.al; Rr Aleksander Moisiu 76; admission free; ⏲ 7pm Thu) shows free art-house movies during the semester. It's located near the last Kino Studio bus stop. For current releases, try **Kinema Millennium 2** (☎ 2253 654; www.ida-millennium.com; Rr Murat Toptani; film 200-500 lekë).

Classical music lovers head to **Theatre of Opera & Ballet** (☎ 2224 753; Sheshi Skënderbej; admission from 300 lekë; ⏲ performances from 7pm, from 6pm winter) and **Academy of Arts** (☎ 2257 237; Sheshi Nënë Tereza).

GETTING THERE & AWAY

Air

Nënë Tereza International Airport (www.tirana-airport.com.al) is at Rinas, 26km northwest of Tirana (see p53).

Bus

You have the option of buses or *furgons* (see p54), but as there are few actual bus stations in Tirana it's impossible to pin down where buses or *furgons* actually leave from. Taxi drivers can usually take you to the latest departure point.

Buses to Berat take 2½ hours and tickets are 400 lekë; *furgons* to Elbasan (300 lekë, 1½ hours) leave from near Qemal Stafa Stadium. Other destinations include Durrës (100 lekë, one hour), Fier (300 lekë, two hours), Gjirokastra (1000 lekë, seven hours) and Saranda (1200 lekë, eight hours).

Train

The rundown train station is at the northern end of Blvd Zogu I. Albania's trains range from sort-of OK to very decrepit. Destinations include Durrës (70 lekë, one hour, six daily) and Vlora (250 lekë, 5½ hours). Check timetables at the station.

GETTING AROUND

Taxi stands dot the city. Taxis charge 400 lekë for a ride inside Tirana and 600 lekë at night and to destinations outside the first 'ring'. A municipal bus charges 30 lekë.

CENTRAL ALBANIA

KRUJA

☎ 0511 / pop 20,000

From the road below, Kruja's houses appear to sit in the lap of a mountain. An ancient castle juts out to one side, and the massive Skanderbeg Museum juts out of the castle itself. The local plaster industry is going strong, so expect visibility-reducing plumes of smoke to cloud views.

Kruja is Skanderbeg's town. Yes, Albania's hero was born here, and although it was over 500 years ago, there's still a great deal of pride in the fact that he and his forces defended Kruja until his death. As soon as you get off the *furgon* you're face to knee with a statue of Skanderbeg wielding his mighty sword with one hand.

Kruja's sights can be covered in a few hours, making this an ideal town to visit en route to Tirana's international airport, which is only 16km away. The main sight in Kruja is the **castle** (admission 100 lekë) and its peculiar **Skanderbeg Museum** (admission 200 lekë; ⏲ 9am-1pm & 4-7pm Tue-Sun). The **Ethnographic Museum** (admission 100 lekë; ⏲ 9am-7pm) in the castle complex below the Skanderbeg Museum is one of the best in the country. The **bazaar** is the best place for souvenir shopping in the country.

Kruja is 32km from Tirana. A *furgon* from Tirana costs 200 lekë.

DURRËS

☎ 052 / pop 114,000

Durrës is an ancient city with a 10km-long beach, an **Archaeological Museum** (Muzeu Arkeologik; Rr Taulantia; admission 200 lekë; ⏲ 9am-3pm Tue-Sun) on the waterfront, some great 6th-century **Byzantine city walls** and an impressive, central **Amphitheatre** (Rr e Kalasë; admission 500 lekë; ⏲ 8am-7pm).

Durrës is connected to Italy by ferry; **Dea Lines** (☎ 30 386; dealines@dealines.com; Rr Tregtare 102; ⏲ 8.30am-8pm) has ferry information. Albania's railway network centres on Durrës and there are regular *furgons* (150 lekë, one hour) to Tirana from the train station.

APOLLONIA

The ruined city of ancient **Apollonia** (admission 700 lekë; ⏲ 9am-5pm) is 90km south of Durrës. There is less to see at Apollonia than at Butrint (opposite), but picturesque ruins include a small original theatre and the elegant pillars on the restored facade of the city's 2nd-century AD administrative centre.

Inside the Museum of Apollonia complex is the Byzantine monastery and church of St Mary, which has fascinating gargoyles on the outside pillars.

Apollonia is easily a day trip from Tirana, Durrës, Vlora or Berat. There's no public transport from Fier to the site, and it's around 2500 lekë for a return taxi journey (15 minutes each way, including an hour's waiting time).

BERAT

☎ 032 / pop 45,500

Berat is a highlight of any trip to Albania. The collection of white Ottoman houses climbing up the hill to its castle earned it the title of 'town of a thousand windows' and helped it join Gjirokastra in the Unesco ranks in 2008. Its rugged mountain setting is particularly evocative when the clouds swirl around the tops of the minarets, or break up to show the icy top of Mt Tomorri.

Sights

Berat is in the middle of a tourism transformation: audio guides to the sights are available for hire from the medieval centre.

Begin by taking a walk up to the impressive 14th-century **Kalasa** (Citadel; admission 100 lekë; 24hr). The quarter's biggest church, **Church of the Dormition of St Mary** (Kisha Fjetja e Shën Mërisë), is the site of the **Onufri Museum** (Muzeu Onufri; ☎ 32 248; admission 200 lekë; 9am-1pm & 4-7pm Tue-Sun Apr-Oct, 9am-4pm Tue-Sun Nov-Mar).

Berat's **Ethnographic Museum** (Muzeu Etnografik; ☎ 32 224; admission 200 lekë; 9am-1pm & 4-7pm Tue-Sat & 9am-2pm Sun Apr-Oct, 9am-4pm Tue-Sat & 9am-2pm Sun Nov-Mar) is based in a wonderful 18th-century Ottoman house.

Down in the traditionally Muslim Mangalem quarter is the 16th-century **Sultan's Mosque** (Xhamia e Mbretit), one of the oldest in Albania. The 19th-century **Bachelors' Mosque** (Xhamia e Beqarëvet) is on the river; look for the enchanting paintings on its external walls. It's perched between some fine Ottoman-era shop fronts.

Sleeping & Eating

Berat Backpackers (☎ 069 306 4429; www.beratbackpackers.com; Gorica; dm €12; Apr-Oct) This newly opened English-run backpackers has dorm rooms and camping spots on the other side of the Osum River.

Hotel Mangalemi (Hotel Tomi; ☎ 32 093, 068 242 9803; Rr e Kalasë; s/d €17/25) Tomi runs a sprawling hotel in an Ottoman house with a restaurant on the ground floor and a clutch of warm, cosy rooms upstairs. The terrace has great views of Mt Tomorri. It's on the street up to Kala from the main square.

Getting There & Away

Buses and *furgons* run between Tirana and Berat (400 lekë, 2½ hours) hourly until 4pm.

SOUTHERN ALBANIA

DHËRMI & DRYMADES BEACHES

Dhërmi (Dhërmiu) is under the tourist trance and ferryloads of Italians arrive almost daily in summer, while Tirana-based Albanians and expats descend on weekends. The white-wedge beach is an easy 10-minute walk downhill from the Vlora–Saranda road.

The best place to stay and eat is **Hotel Luciano** (☎ 069 209 1431; Dhërmi Beach; per person 1000 lekë;). The water is metres away and the views are sublime. The waterfront restaurant serves great wood-fired pizzas (300 lekë).

If you take a quick right on the road down to Dhërmi, you'll find yourself amongst olive groves en route to Drymades beach. This quieter option has a white virgin beach (albeit with bunkers) and **Drymades Hotel** (☎ 068 228 5637; camp sites 500 lekë, cabins 4000 lekë), a constellation of cabins and rooms under the shade of pine trees just a step away from the blue sea.

SARANDA

☎ 0852 / pop 32,000

Despite massive development, Saranda is a really pleasant town with spectacular views and a daily stream of Corfu day trippers.

The mesmerising ancient archaeological site of Butrint is a bus or taxi trip out of the town and you'll pass the lovely beaches and islands of Ksamil, perfect for a dip after a day of exploring.

Sights & Activities

The ancient ruins of **Butrint** (www.butrint.org; admission 700 lekë; 8am-dusk), 18km south of Saranda, are renowned for their size, beauty and tranquillity. Their fantastic natural setting is part of a 29-sq-km national park. Set aside three hours to explore this fascinating place.

Ksamil, 17km south of Saranda, has three small, dreamy islands within swimming distance and dozens of beachside bars and restaurants that open in the summer.

Sleeping & Eating

Hairy Lemon (☎ 069 355 9317; www.hairylemonhostel.com; dm €13) This new backpackers is in an orange and yellow apartment block. It's a 10-minute walk from the port (turn left as you exit).

Castle of Lekursi (Kalaja e Lëkurësit; ☎ 55 55; mains 250-1200 lekë; 11am-midnight) Great views, a castle

WORTH THE TRIP

Bats gobble up fireflies on narrow cobblestone streets that lead past Ottoman shop fronts in the creepy yet incredibly beautiful stone city of **Gjirokastra**. Above it all, a gloomy dark castle with a blood-chilling history watches over everything. It's the sort of place where dictators are raised (Enver Hoxha) and young boys dream up dramatic stories and become famous writers (Ismail Kadare).

our pick **Hotel Kalemi** (☎ 84-263 724; http://hotelkalemi.tripod.com; r 4000 lekë) offers an authentic experience of Ottoman Albania. Gjirokastra (300 lekë, 1½ hours) is 70km northeast of Saranda.

atmosphere and traditional Albanian cuisine make it worth the taxi trip (1000 lekë return).

Getting There & Away

The helpful **information centre** (ZIT; Rr Skënderbeu; 🕑 8am-4pm Mon-Fri) has bus timetables. Buses to Tirana (1200 lekë, eight hours) and *furgons* to Gjirokastra (one hour, 300 lekë) and Vlora (six hours, 600 lekë) via Himara usually leave between 5am and 10.30am.

A taxi to the Greek border at Kakavija costs 4000 lekë; to the border near Konispoli it's 5000 lekë.

ALBANIA DIRECTORY

ACCOMMODATION

Albania's budget accommodation (singles €15 to €30) is usually decent and clean; breakfast is sometimes included in the price. Free camping is possible.

ACTIVITIES

Head south for the best swimming. Adventure sports are in their infancy in Albania, and the national leaders are the enthusiastic Outdoor Albania team (p55) in Tirana. Mountain biking is becoming popular.

BUSINESS HOURS

Usual business hours in Albania:

Banks 🕑 9am-2.30pm
Bars 🕑 8.30am-midnight, or later
Restaurants 🕑 8.30am-11pm
Shops 🕑 8am-7pm, some close for a siesta at noon

DANGERS & ANNOYANCES

Albania is a safe country to travel around, although travel with a local guide in the alpine area north of Shkodra. The most serious risk is on the roads – Albania has a high traffic accident rate.

Beware of pickpockets on crowded city buses and packs of dogs in castles and towns. Stick to bottled water and UHT milk.

EMBASSIES & CONSULATES

There are no Australian, New Zealand or Irish embassies in Albania.

The following embassies and consulates are in Tirana:

France (☎ 042-2234 054; ambafrance.tr@adanet.com.al; Rr Skënderbej 14)
Germany (☎ 042-2274 505; www.tirana.diplo.de; Rr Skënderbej 8)
Greece (☎ 042-2274 670; gremb.tir@mfa.gr; Rr Frederik Shiroka 3)
Italy (☎ 042-2275 900; www.ambtirana.esteri.it; Rr Lek Dukagjini 2)
Macedonia (☎ 042-2230 909; makambas@albnet.net; Rr Kavajës 116)
Netherlands (☎ 042-2240 828; www.mfa.nl/tir; Rr Asim Zeneli 10)
Serbia (☎ 042-2232 091; www.tirana.mfa.gov.yu; Rr Donika Kastrioti 9/1)
UK (☎ 042-2234 973; www.uk.al; Rr Skënderbej 12)
USA (☎ 042-2247 285; Rr Elbasanit 103)

GAY & LESBIAN TRAVELLERS

Gay and lesbian life in Albania is alive and well but is not yet organised into out clubs or NGOs. For gay and lesbian visitors, your gaydar will serve you well; ask anyone who looks funky on the street where the parties are – the alternative music and party scene is queer friendly.

HOLIDAYS

New Year's Day 1 January
Summer Day 14 March
Nevruz 22 March
Catholic Easter March/April
Orthodox Easter April/May
May Day 1 May
Bajram i Madh September
Mother Teresa Day 19 October
Bajram i Vogël November
Independence Day 28 November
Liberation Day 29 November
Christmas Day 25 December

MONEY

Albanian banknotes come in denominations of 100, 200, 500, 1000 and 5000 lekë. There are five, 10, 20, 50 and 100 lekë coins.

Everything in Albania can be paid for with lekë but most of the hotel prices are quoted in euros. A variety of ATMs can be found in most towns and cities, and frequently offer currency in euros or lekë. Credit cards are accepted only in the larger hotels and travel agencies, and in only a handful of establishments outside Tirana. Major banks can offer credit-card advances. You will not be able to change Albanian lekë outside of the country, so exchange them or spend them before you leave.

It's usual to round up the bill for a tip.

POST

Post offices are springing up, though few post boxes exist. Sending a postcard overseas costs around 60 lekë and a letter costs 80 to 160 lekë, though both take their time.

TELEPHONE

Long-distance phone calls made from post offices (Albtelecom) are cheap, costing about 90 lekë a minute to Italy. Calls to the US are 230 lekë per minute. Albania's country code is ☎ 355. For domestic directory enquiries call ☎ 124; international directory assistance is ☎ 12. It's 100 lekë for a SIM with some credit.

VISAS

No visa is required for citizens of EU countries or nationals of Australia, Canada, New Zealand, Japan, South Korea, Norway, South Africa or the US. Travellers from other countries should check www.mfa.gov.al. Citizens of all countries are required to pay €1 to enter the country. Those arriving at Tirana's international airport pay €10.

Andorra

HIGHLIGHTS

- **Grandvalira** Slip-slide your way over the most extensive snowfields in the Pyrenees (p66)
- **Caldea** Steep yourself in the warm mineral waters of this space-age spa complex (p68)
- **Off-the-beaten track** Tramp a sample of the walking trails that thread through the principality, especially above Ordino (p68) and Soldeu (p66)

FAST FACTS

- **Area** 468 sq km (that's 2½ times smaller than Paris)
- **Budget** €50 to €70 per day
- **Capital** Andorra la Vella
- **Country code** ☎ 376
- **Famous for** skiing, shopping, smuggling
- **Languages** Catalan (but nearly everyone knows Spanish)
- **Money** euro (€); A$1 = €0.55; C$1 = 0.60; ¥100 = €0.78; NZ$1 = €0.43; UK£1 = €1.12; US$1 = €0.74
- **Phrases** *hola* (hello), *adéu* (goodbye), *si us plau* (please), *gràcies* (thanks)

- **Population** 81,200
- **Visas** none required

TRAVEL HINT

Skiing and summer walking packages (eg offered by UK tour operators, usually including flights) are cheaper than going solo. Once here, use Andorra as a springboard for Mediterranean travels.

ROAMING ANDORRA

To really savour Andorra, put on your walking boots and get out of Andorra la Vella, hub for all bus routes.

People may tell you Andorra's all skiing and shopping. They might add that Andorra la Vella, its capital and only town, is a fuming traffic jam bordered by palaces of consumerism (fact: Andorra has more than 2000 shops – roughly one for every 40 inhabitants).

They're partly right but also very wrong. Shake yourself from Andorra la Vella's tawdry embrace, take one of the state's only three secondary roads and discover some of the most dramatic scenery in all the Pyrenees. Go soon, though; it may not be the same in a few years. Greed and uncontrolled development risk spoiling those side valleys. Already the pounding of piledrivers drowns out the winter thrum of ski lifts and threatens the silence of summer.

What's sure is that this minicountry, wedged between France and Spain, offers by far the best skiing in the Pyrenees (tourism, mainly skiing, accounts for around 60% of the country's GDP). In the last few years, Andorra has invested well over €100 million in mountain cafes and restaurants, lifts, car parks, snowmaking machines and hotels. And once the snows have melted, there's great walking in abundance, ranging from hands-in-pockets strolling to demanding day hikes in the principality's higher, more remote reaches.

EMERGENCY NUMBER

Ambulance, fire, police ☎ 112

Hospital Nostra Senyora de Meritxell (☎ 871 000; Avinguda Fiter i Rossell)

National tourist office (☎ 820 214; sindicatdiniciativa@andorra.ad; Edificio Davi, Local C, Carrer Doctor Vilanova 13; 9am-1pm & 3-7pm Mon-Sat, 10am-1pm Sun Jul-Sep; 10am-1.30pm & 3-7pm Mon-Sat Oct-Jun)

Town tourist office (☎ 827 117; turisme@comuandorra.ad; Plaça de la Rotonda; 9am-9pm Jul & Aug, 9am-1pm & 3-7pm Mon-Sat, 9am-1pm Sun Sep-Jun) Also carries pan-Andorra information.

SIGHTS & ACTIVITIES

The tiny **historic quarter** (Barri Antic) was the heart of Andorra la Vella until well after WWII, when the principality's capital was still little more than a village. Within it is the **Casa de la Vall** (House of the Valley), built in 1580 as a private home and Andorra's parliament building since 1702.

Rooftop **Plaça del Poble**, a popular gathering place, especially in the evening, gives good views of the valley.

If you've spare cash for **shopping**, you'll save on things like sports gear, photographic equipment, shoes and clothing, where prices are around 25% less than in Spain or France. Stock up on rock-bottom priced booze and cigs too.

SLEEPING

Camping Valira (☎ 722 384; campingvalira@Andorra.ad; Avinguda de Salou; camp sites per person/tent/car €5.75/5.75/5.75; year-round;) Just west of town and overlooking the valley, Camping Valira, with a small indoor swimming pool, is the town's only camping option. You'll have to hunt to find a space between the resident caravans.

Hotel Pyrénées (☎ 879 879; www.hotelpyrenees.com; Avinguda Príncep Benlloch 20; s €37-52, d €50-84; P) Built in 1940, it's one of Andorra's very few venerable buildings. Cosily furnished rooms have plenty of appealing dark woodwork. Haunting black-and-white photos of a long-lost Andorra flank the walls of its excellent restaurant (set menu €16, mains €13 to €18), with its sparkling chandeliers and crisp linen.

Hotel Residencia Paris (☎ 820 843; edumol@andorra.ad; Avinguda Meritxell 65; r €40) In a town where most economical lodgings have closed their shutters for good, the Paris still hangs in there. Its 12 rooms are fairly bare and clinical but double glazing filters out all traffic noise from the busy street.

Hôtel de L'Isard (☎ 876 800; www.hotelisard.com, in French & Spanish; Avinguda Meritxell 36; s €40-52, d €67-87; P) Behind the attractive stone facade, you'll find a comfortable, family-run hotel. Rear rooms overlook the valley and mountain beyond. There are also six split-level rooms, ideal for friends travelling together. Breakfast is included and it runs a good restaurant (set menu €16.10, mains €9.50 to €13).

Hotel Florida (☎ 820 105; www.hotelflorida.ad; Carrer Llacuna 15; s €41-63, d €56-90) This welcoming modern hotel sits on a quiet side street. Its 27 rooms vary in size; ask for one of the larger ones, which cost no more. After a day in the fresh air, relax in the hotel's sauna, free for guests. Breakfast included.

EATING & DRINKING

Pans y Company (Plaça de Rebés 2 & Avinguda de Meritxell 91; baguettes €3.50-4.75) This Spanish chain, with a couple of branches, does crunchy baguettes and salads.

Pyrénées department store (Avinguda de Meritxell 21) At this megastore's top-floor self-service cafeteria, pile your salad plate (€4.95) high at the buffet, then tuck into the dish of the day (€4.90) or pick from one of the seven varieties of *plato combinado* (mixed plate; €7.25). Beside it, the gourmet restaurant does a good-value midday menu (€17), while one floor down there's a particularly well-stocked supermarket, great for self-caterers.

Papanico (☎ 867 333; Avinguda Príncep Benlloch 4; mains €12.50-20.50) It's quick service at Papanico, where you can snack on tapas and sandwiches (around €5) or tuck into a full meal. Sit at the bar or retreat to the rear restaurant with its vast collection of beer bottles ranged around the walls.

La Borsa (The Stock Exchange; ☎ 827 657; Avinguda de Tarragona 36; 11pm-3am Tue-Sun) Like a little flutter while you drink and dance? The price of each drink varies according to the night's consumption so far, so keep an eye on the electronic, computer-controlled screen.

Cervesería l'Albadia (☎ 820825; Cap del Carrer 2) Here's a place for serious beerophiles, with lots of classics on draught and many more in the bottle.

Sala Apolo (☎ 828 260; www.apoloandorra.com; Carrer de la Borda 5; 10.30pm-3am Fri & Sat) There's weekly live music and disco dancing at this

ANDORRA

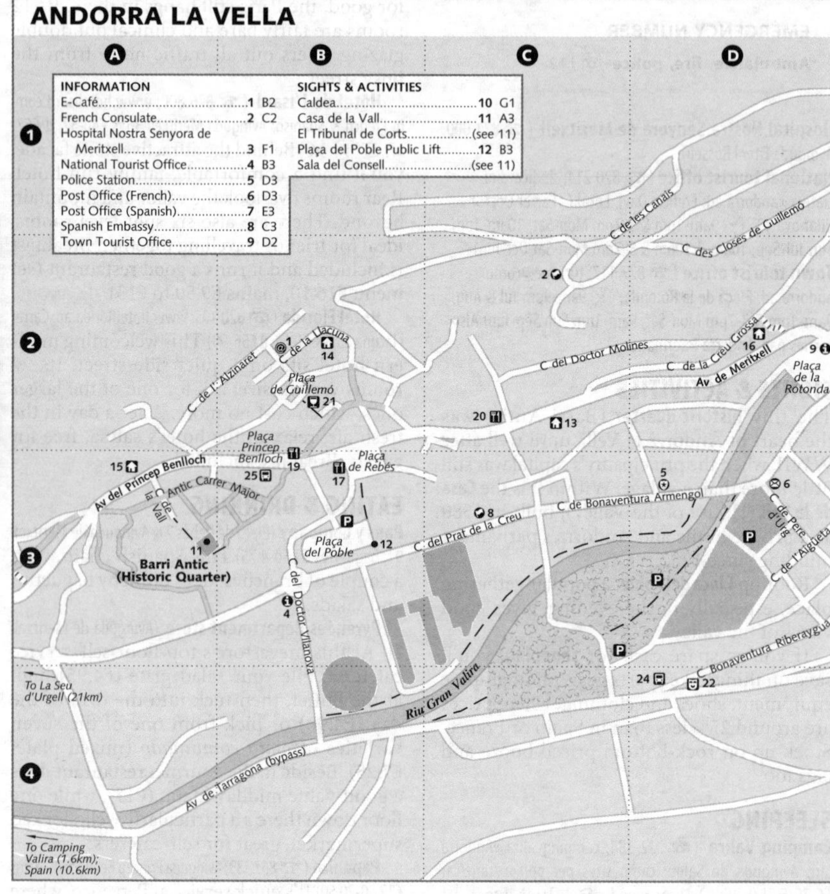

recently opened sister to Barcelona's famous club of the same name.

GETTING THERE & AWAY

Long-distance buses for France and Spain pull in at the main **bus station** (Avinguda de Tarragona).

Andorra la Vella is a traffic nightmare. If you're driving, stick your vehicle in the huge open-air car park just north of the bus station.

> **AGELESS ANDORRA**
>
> Could it be that fresh mountain air? Or regular doses of retail therapy? Whatever, life expectancy in Andorra, at 83.5 years, is the world's highest.

AROUND ANDORRA

CANILLO & SOLDEU

Canillo, 11km northeast of Andorra la Vella, and Soldeu, a further 7km up the valley along the CG2, share a helpful **tourist office** (☎ 751 090; www.vdc.ad; 🕓 9am-1pm & 3-7pm Mon-Sat, 8am-4pm Sun), beside the main road at the eastern end of Canillo.

The two villages are at the heart of the combined snowfields of **Grandvalira** (☎ 808 900; www.grandvalira.com; 1/3-day lift pass €41/107), the vastest ski playground in the Pyrenees with 193km of runs and a combined lift system that can shift over 100,000 skiers every hour.

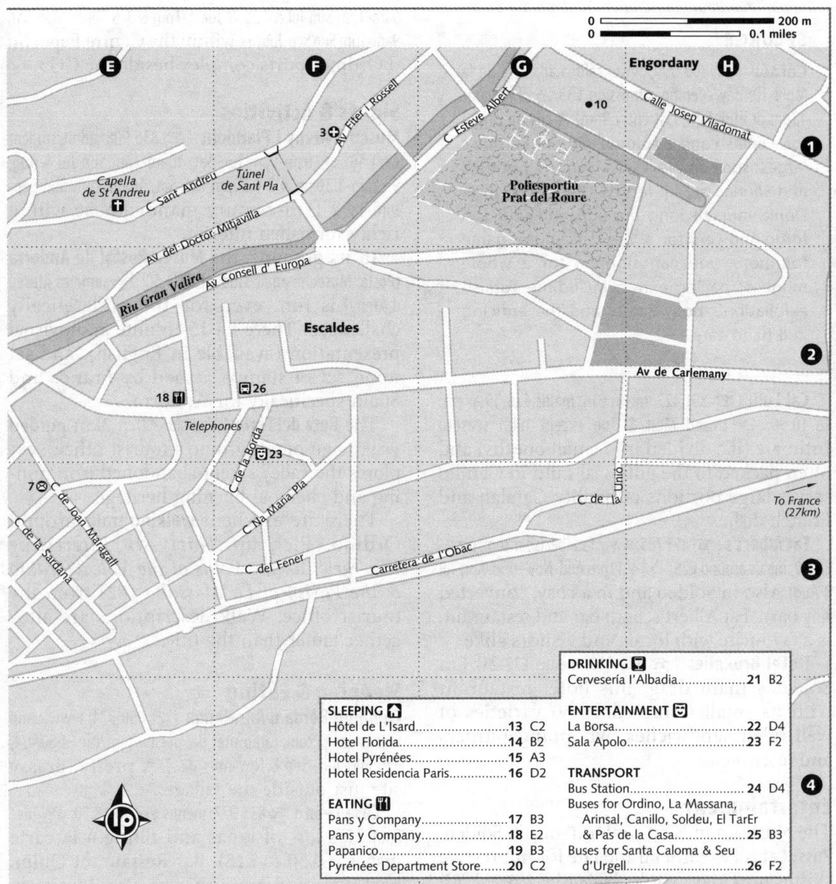

In summer, **Canillo** (1500m) has canyon clambering, four *via ferrata* (iron way) climbing gullies, a climbing wall; the year-round **Palau de Gel** with ice rink and pool (plus a good restaurant and a bar with internet access and free wi-fi); guided walks and endless hiking options. Grab the comprehensive *Mountain, Nature and Sports Guide* (€2) from its tourist office.

Sleeping & Eating

Camping Santa Creu (☎ 851 462; camping_santacreu@yahoo.com; camp sites per person/tent/car €3.50/3.50/3.50; ⏰ mid-Jun–Sep) The greenest and quietest of Canillo's five camp grounds.

Aina (☎ 851 434; colonies.aina@andorra.ad; dm €18, half-board €24; ⏰ Sep–mid-Jun) Just east of Canillo, friendly, riverside Aina functions as a youth hostel outside high summer. Dormitories sleep six, you need your own sleeping bag and it's important to reserve.

Hotel Roc de Sant Miquel (☎ 851 079; www.hotel-roc.com; half-board per person winter €30-70, summer €33-43; ⏰ closed May & Oct) This relaxed Soldeu hotel, run by a young Anglo-Andorran couple – the owner plays lead guitar in a local band – rents mountain bikes to guests for a small fee. Half-board is compulsory in winter; in summer you can simply rent a room (per person €18 to €28).

Slim Jim's (☎ 852 567; ⏰ 8am-10pm mid-Nov–mid-Apr) In winter, this British-run place, one block from Soldeu's main street, does sandwiches, snacks and sizzling English breakfasts (€8) with all the trimmings. It has wi-fi.

Book your stay at lonelyplanet.com/hotels

SPLURGE

Caldea (☎ 800 999; www.caldea.ad; Parc de la Mola 10; day/evening admission €33/25; 9am-11pm or midnight, last entry 9pm) A great place for a splash and a splurge. One of Europe's largest spa complexes, its lagoons, hot tubs and saunas are all fed by thermal springs. Dunk yourself long enough and you can forgo showers for a week! If you're game for more, you can sign on for a whole range of paying extras, including 'Turkish exfoliation', 'body scrub' and the enticing 'full hand care'.

Cal Lulu (☎ 851 427; menú €14, mains €16-19, pizzas €8-10.50; closed Mon & Tue except high season) Intimate (it's divided into small booths) and often packed to the gills, Cal Lulu in Canillo serves large portions of quality Catalan and French dishes.

Fat Albert's (☎ 851 765; www.fatalbertsbar.com; pizzas €8-10, meals around €25; 4-11pm mid-Nov–mid-Apr, Jul & Aug) Also in Soldeu and in a cosy, converted hay barn, Fat Albert's, both bar and restaurant, is a favourite with locals and visitors alike.

Hotel Bruxelles (☎ 851 010; menus €12-21) On Soldeu's main drag, this hotel restaurant with its small terrace does 50 varieties of well-filled sandwiches, whopping burgers and tasty *menús*.

Entertainment

The music pounds on winter nights in Soldeu. **Pussy Cat** rocks until far too late for impressive skiing next day, while **Avalanche** (☎ 852 282) and, three doors away, **Aspen** (☎ 851 974), have regular live bands. Also on the main drag, **The Stone Bar** has table football and occasional live music.

Getting There & Around

Buses run from Andorra la Vella to Soldeu (€2.40) via Canillo (€1.20) every half-hour until 8.45pm. In winter, hourly ski buses (free if you flash your ski pass) also cover the same route.

ORDINO & AROUND

Ordino, on highway CG3 8km north of Andorra la Vella, is Andorra's most attractive village. At 1300m, it's a good starting point for summer activity holidays. The **tourist office** (☎ 878 173; www.ordino.ad; 8am-6pm Mon-Sat, 9am-1pm Sun Jul & Aug, 8.30am-1pm & 3-6.30pm Mon-Sat, 9am-1pm Sun Sep-Jun) is within the Centre Esportiu d'Ordino sports complex beside the CG3.

Sights & Activities

Museu d'Areny i Plandolit (☎ 836 908; adult/student €3/1.50; 9am-9pm Tue-Sat, 10am-2pm Sun Jul & Aug; 9.30am-1.30pm & 3-6.30pm Tue-Sat, 10am-2pm Sun Sep-Jun) is a 17th-century manor house with a richly furnished interior.

In its grounds, the **Museo Postal de Andorra** (Postal Museum; adult/student €3/1.50; same as Museu d'Areny) is fun, even for the philatelically challenged. There's a 15-minute audiovisual presentation (available in English), and set upon set of stamps, issued by France and Spain specifically for Andorra.

The **Ruta del Ferro** (admission €3), a 3km guided walk (sign on at Ordino's tourist office), explores the valley's long-abandoned iron mining and charcoal burning heritage.

There are excellent **walking trails** around Ordino. Pick up *Thirty-six Interesting Itineraries on the Paths of the Vall d'Ordino & the Parish of La Massana* (€2) from the tourist office. Walk descriptions are altogether tauter than the title.

Sleeping & Eating

Camping Borda d'Ansalonga (☎ 850 374; www.campingansalonga.com; camp sites per person/tent/car €4.80/4/4; mid-Jun–Sep & Nov-Apr;) A pretty, grassy site just outside the village.

Casa León (☎ 835 977; menus €12.50-18.50; Tue-Sun) Has lots of tapas and filling à la carte dishes (€9.50 to €15). Bar Restaurant Quim, next door and more snacky, also does tasty tapas and a filling midday *menú* (€10).

Getting There & Away

Buses to/from Andorra la Vella run every half-hour from 7am to 9pm.

FREE AND NEARLY FREE IN ANDORRA

- walk the mountains
- window-shop
- visit Casa de la Vall, Andorra's parliament building
- get a dab of free scent at the perfume counter of big stores
- hire snowshoes and stride out, off-piste

ARINSAL & PAL

In winter, Arinsal, 10km northwest of Andorra la Vella, has good skiing and snowboarding and a lively après-ski scene. It's linked with the smaller ski station of Pal, in turn part of the **Vallnord complex** (☎ 878 000; www.vallnord.com; 1-day lift pass low/high season €29/34.50). The combined slopes have 63km of pistes with a vertical drop of 1010m.

In summer, the **Vallnord Bike Park** (☎ 878 000; www.vallnordbikepark.com; per day €20) has a pulse-racing choice of downhill and cross-country mountain bike tracks. From Arinsal, a good departure point for many a mountain walk, a trail leads to **Estany de les Truites** (2260m), a natural lake and a staffed mountain hut. A further two hours brings you to **Pic de Coma Pedrosa** (2942m), Andorra's highest point.

Sleeping & Eating

Xixerella Parc (☎ 738 613; www.campingxixerella.com, in Spanish; camp sites per person/tent/car €6.20/6.20/6.20; Nov-Sep;) Between Pal and Arinsal, this large, well-equipped camping ground has plenty of shade and greenness.

Hostal Pobladó (☎ 835 122; www.hotpoblado.com; r €57-65, with shared bathroom €30-40; closed Nov;) Right beside the cabin lift, it's a great, friendly place to make contact with other skiers or walkers. The small restaurant serves pizzas, Tex-Mex and à la carte (€6 to €9.50) and an evening *menú* (€15), and there's a lively bar with an internet point, free for guests.

Café Everest (☎ 839 599; from 8pm) Run by Brit Ian Woodall, twice conqueror of Everest, and bedecked with Himalayan posters and magazine covers, this chalet restaurant offers meat, cheese and even chocolate fondues, together with tasty bistro fare.

Entertainment

In winter, Arinsal fairly throbs after sunset. In summer, it can be almost mournful. When the snow's around, call by **Surf** (☎ 838 069), near the base of the cabin lift. It's pub, dance venue and restaurant (sink your teeth into the juicy Argentine grilled meat dishes) all in one.

Getting There & Away

Eight daily buses (€2.50) leave Andorra la Vella for Arinsal via La Massana. There are also at least 12 local buses (€1) daily between La Massana and Arinsal.

SANT JULIÀ DE LÒRIA

Here, 6km south of Andorra la Vella, is the splendid **Museu del Tabac** (☎ 741 545; Carrer Doctor Palau 17; admission €5; 10am-6.30pm Tue-Sat, 10am-1pm Sun). Occupying a one-time tobacco factory, it recalls the pleasurable sins of tobacco and smuggling. Allow at least an hour.

ANDORRA DIRECTORY

ACCOMMODATION

Tourist offices stock a free booklet, *Guia d'Allotjaments Turístics* (Guide to Tourist Accommodation). Inexpensive accommodation is as rare as edelweiss. At the most modest end, expect to pay about €25 per person in a shared double. There are no youth hostels, but there are plenty of camp sites, many in beautiful surroundings. Most hotels hike their prices by a good 20% throughout the ski season, in August and during major Spanish and French public holidays. Others don't take in independent travellers and may insist upon half-board at these times.

If you're trekking, ask at tourist offices for the free *Mapa de Refugis i Grans Recorreguts*, which marks and describes Andorra's 26 remote *refugis* (mountain refuges).

ACTIVITIES

Above the main valleys, you'll find attractive lake-dotted mountain country, great for skiing in winter and walking in summer. The largest and best ski stations are those of the Grandvalira complex (p66). Those of Vallnord (left) are cheaper but can be colder and windier.

Downhill ski-gear hire costs between €10 and €18 per day, while snowboards go for €16 to €22.

Naturlandia-La Rabassa (☎ 759 798; www.naturlandia.ad), nudged up against the frontier with Spain, is a great little cross-country skiing centre with 15km of marked forest trails and – the big innovation of 2008 – Tobotronc, a 4km toboggan run through the woods that's the world's longest.

In summer, you can hire mountain bikes in some resorts for around €15 per day.

But Andorra is, above all, for walkers. Ordino (opposite), Canillo and Soldeu (p66) make great bases and the trails, once you head out of the valley, will be all for you.

BUSINESS HOURS

Banks (🕑 9am-1pm & 3-5pm Mon-Fri, 9am-noon Sat)
Restaurants (🕑 1-3.30pm & 8-10.30pm)
Shops (🕑 generally 9.30am-1pm & 3.30-8pm Mon-Sat, 9.30am-1pm Sun)

EMBASSIES & CONSULATES

France (☎ 736 730; Carrer Sobrevia 7, Andorra la Vella)
Spain (☎ 800 030; Carrer Prat de la Creu 34a, Andorra la Vella)

FESTIVALS & EVENTS

On 8 September, the Dia de Meritxell, in honour of the patron saint of Andorra, is celebrated throughout the country.

INTERNET RESOURCES

www.andorra.ad Website of the Ministry of Tourism and Environment.
www.andorramania.com Has a host of worthwhile links.
www.skiandorra.ad For skiing and practical wintertime information.
www.turismeandorra.com Maintained by the local hotel association.

POST

Andorra has no postal system of its own; France and Spain operate separate services with their own Andorran stamps and their own post boxes. Tourist offices sell stamps.

TELEPHONE

Buy a *teletarja* (phonecard; €3 and €6 from tourist offices and kiosks). Off-peak times are 9pm to 8am, plus all day Sunday.

WORKING

You'll be up against strong competition from Chileans and Argentines, but you might pick up a ski-season bar or table-waiting job.

Austria

HIGHLIGHTS

- **Vienna's Innere Stadt** Explore the twisting cobbled alleyways and wide boulevards of an Old Town that dates back to the Roman age (p76)
- **Salzburg** Wander a town where baroque beauty and fabulously kitsch tours of the *Sound of Music* go hand in hand (p91)
- **Hohe Tauern National Park** Road-trip along one of the world's most scenic highways, where 3000m peaks are a dime a dozen (p100)
- **Salzkammergut** Cruise from one lakeside town to the next, then catch a cable car to salt mines and ice caves (p95)
- **Innsbruck** Experience Tirolean hospitality and glorious alpine scenery in this westerly city (p96)

FAST FACTS

- **Area** 83,870 sq km
- **Budget** €45 to €60 per day
- **Capital** Vienna
- **Country code** ☎ 43
- **Famous for** apple strudel, Wiener schnitzel, Arnold Schwarzenegger and Freudian psychoanalysis
- **Languages** German (Slovene, Croat and Hungarian are also official languages in some southern states)
- **Money** euro (€); A$1 = €0.55; C$1 = 0.60; ¥100 = €0.78; NZ$1 = €0.43; UK£1 = €1.12; US$1 = €0.74
- **Phrases** *Grüss Gott* (hello), *servus* (hello and goodbye), *ba ba* (bye bye), *danke* (thank you)

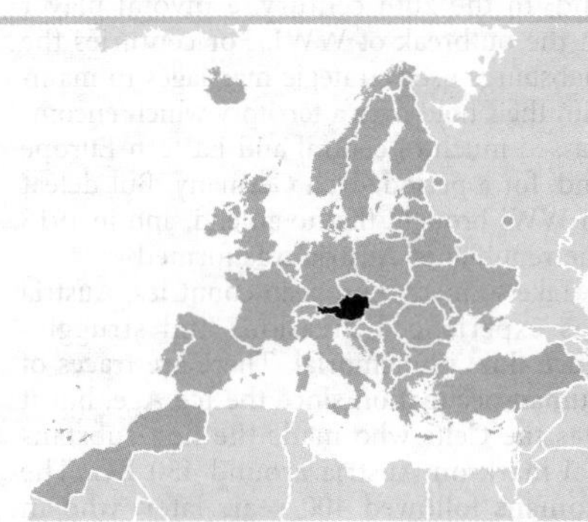

- **Population** 8.3 million
- **Visas** no visa needed for citizens of the EU, Australia, New Zealand, the US and Canada; see p102

TRAVEL HINTS

Make lunch your main meal, when there are cheap *Tagesmenus* (daily specials/menus). Make sure to have a shot of schnapps, just for the hell of it (and it helps digestion).

ROAMING AUSTRIA

Many backpackers arrive on a train from Zürich or Munich, stop at Salzburg, move on to Vienna and head straight to Eastern Europe. With more time, stop first in Innsbruck and later visit the Salzkammergut lakes district south of Salzburg. Graz makes a good budget stopover en route to Hungary or Slovenia.

There's no need to tell people Austria is an alpine country. Everyone's seen Julie spinning around in *The Sound of Music*, with one snowcapped mountain spilling out behind her after the next, all sloped in thick forests of pine. And it's all true – this small land in central Europe

is an outdoor purist's dream, with some of the best skiing and snowboarding in the Northern Alps and a largely untapped network of hiking and mountain-biking trails.

But Austria has more to offer than its plethora of peaks. Vienna, the capital and heart of the country, is an architectural extravaganza where past and present mix and mingle with ease. Salzburg, guarded by a powerful hilltop fortress, is baroque beyond belief. Lesser-known drawcards wait in the wings. Graz, a student town with drive and energy, hides contemporary architectural gems, while Innsbruck, a city with an intact medieval centre, proudly sits among towering alpine ranges. Then there are the lakes and peaks of the Salzkammergut, meadows and mountains of Vorarlberg, and sunshine and wine of the Wachau.

Whether you can spare a day or a month for Austria on your European travels, you certainly won't be disappointed.

HISTORY

Austria is a small nation with a big past. It may be hard to believe that this diminutive, landlocked Alpine country was once the epicentre of the mighty Habsburg empire and, in the 20th century, a pivotal player in the outbreak of WWI. For centuries the Habsburgs used strategic marriages to maintain their hold over a territory which encompassed much of central and Eastern Europe and, for a period, even Germany. But defeat in WWI brought that to an end, and in 1918 the republic of Austria was formed.

Like so many European countries, Austria has experienced invasions and struggles since time immemorial. There are traces of human occupation since the Ice Age, but it was the Celts who made the first substantial mark on Austria around 450 BC. The Romans followed 400 years later, who in turn were followed by Bavarians, and, in 1278, the House of Habsburg took control of the country by defeating the head of the Bavarian royalty.

The 16th and 17th centuries saw the Ottoman threat reach the gates of Vienna, and in 1805 Napoleon defeated Austria at Austerlitz. Austrian chancellor Metternich cleverly reconsolidated Austria's power in 1815 after Waterloo, but the loss of the 1866 Austro-Prussian War, and creation of the Austrian-Hungarian empire in 1867, diminished the Habsburg's influence in Europe.

However, these setbacks pale beside Archduke Franz Ferdinand's assassination by Slavic separatists in Sarajevo on 28 June 1914. When his uncle, the Austro-Hungarian emperor Franz Josef, declared war on Serbia in response, the ensuing 'Great War' (WWI) would prove the Habsburgs' downfall.

During the 1930s Nazis began to influence Austrian politics and by 1938 the recession-hit country was ripe for picking. German troops met little resistance and Hitler was greeted on Heldenplatz as a hero by 200,000 Viennese.

Austria was heavily bombed during WWII, but the country recovered well, largely through the Marshall Plan and sound political and economic decisions. Austria has maintained a neutral stance since 1955, been home to a number of international organisations, including the UN since 1979, and joined the EU in 1995. In recent history, Austria's biggest impact on the international scene was its political foray in the '90s with the far-right Freedom Party – FPÖ – and its former controversial leader, Jörg Haider (Haider died in a car accident in October 2008). FPÖ's current leader, HC Strache, has used his good looks and populist propaganda to win over many young voters in the last years, and ranks high in Austrian poles.

THE CULTURE

At first Austrians seem reserved and even slightly suspicious of strangers, and are not generally regarded for outward displays of friendliness. However, when you get to know them better, most are friendly and exhibit genuine interest in sharing a multifaceted culture with the rest of the world. Politeness and formality are highly esteemed and expected, especially among the older generation.

Vienna has always been a paradox, mixing Austrian conservatism with a large dollop of decadence. The scene you might find at Viennese balls – grand old society dames flirting with drag queens – aptly reflects this. The capital's pervading humour, *Wiener Schmäh,* is quite ironic and cutting, but is also meant to be charming.

ARTS

Beethoven, Brahms, Haydn, Mozart, Schubert and other European composers were

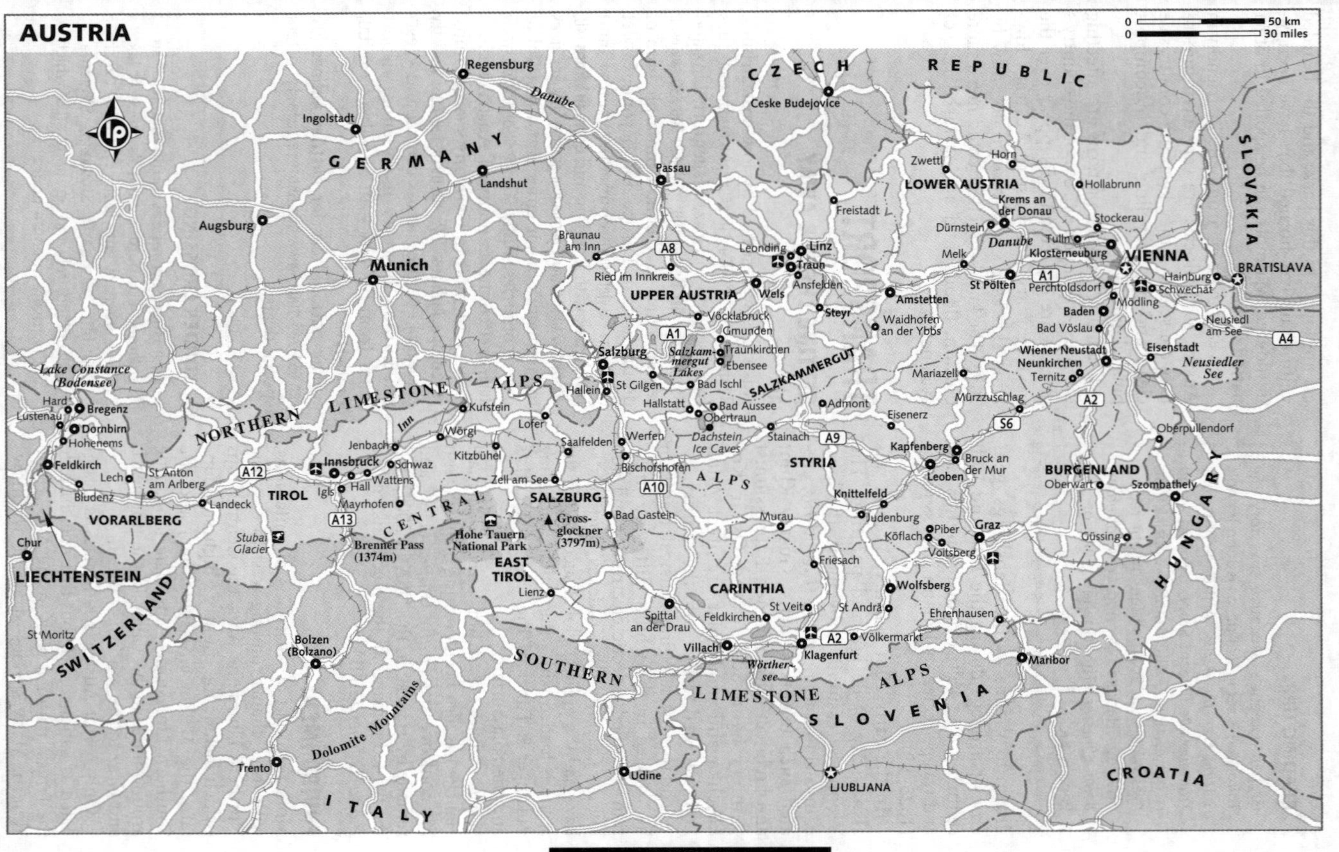
AUSTRIA
0 50 km
0 30 miles
CZECH REPUBLIC
SLOVAKIA
HUNGARY
CROATIA
SLOVENIA
ITALY
SWITZERLAND
LIECHTENSTEIN
GERMANY
VIENNA
BRATISLAVA
LOWER AUSTRIA
UPPER AUSTRIA
BURGENLAND
STYRIA
CARINTHIA
SALZBURG
SALZKAMMERGUT
TIROL
EAST TIROL
VORARLBERG
NORTHERN LIMESTONE ALPS
CENTRAL ALPS
SOUTHERN LIMESTONE ALPS
Dolomite Mountains
Danube
Inn
Neusiedler See
Wörther-see
Lake Constance (Bodensee)
Salzkam-mergut Lakes
Dachstein Ice Caves
Hohe Tauern National Park
Gross-glockner (3797m)
Brenner Pass (1374m)
Stubai Glacier
A1
A2
A4
A8
A9
A10
A12
A13
S6
Regensburg
Ceske Budejovice
Ingolstadt
Landshut
Passau
Augsburg
Munich
Braunau am Inn
Ried im Innkreis
Freistadt
Leonding
Linz
Traun
Ansfelden
Wels
Steyr
Amstetten
Waidhofen an der Ybbs
Zwettl
Horn
Hollabrunn
Krems an der Donau
Dürnstein
Stockerau
Melk
Tulln
Klosterneuburg
St Pölten
Perchtoldsdorf
Mödling
Hainburg
Schwechat
Baden
Bad Vöslau
Neusiedl am See
Eisenstadt
Wiener Neustadt
Neunkirchen
Ternitz
Mariazell
Mürzzuschlag
Oberpullendorf
Vöcklabruck
Gmunden
Traunkirchen
Ebensee
Salzburg
St Gilgen
Bad Ischl
Hallein
Hallstatt
Bad Aussee
Obertraun
Admont
Eisenerz
Stainach
Kapfenberg
Bruck an der Mur
Leoben
Oberwart
Szombathely
Lustenau
Hard
Bregenz
Dornbirn
Hohenems
Feldkirch
Lech
Bludenz
St Anton am Arlberg
Landeck
Kufstein
Lofer
Wörgl
Jenbach
Kitzbühel
Saalfelden
Werfen
Bischofshofen
Innsbruck
Schwaz
Hall
Wattens
Igls
Zell am See
Mayrhofen
Bad Gastein
Knittelfeld
Judenburg
Murau
Piber
Köflach
Graz
Voitsberg
Güssing
Chur
Lienz
Friesach
Wolfsberg
St Veit
St Andrä
Ehrenhausen
Spittal an der Drau
Feldkirchen
Völkermarkt
St Moritz
Bolzen (Bolzano)
Villach
Klagenfurt
Maribor
Trento
Udine
LJUBLJANA

AUSTRIA

READING UP

Graham Greene's evocative spy story *The Third Man* is set in Vienna, as is John Irving's *Setting Free the Bears.* Arthur Schnitzler's *Traumnovelle* (Dream Story) inspired – and is better than – the Stanley Kubrick film *Eyes Wide Shut.* Football fans might recognise Peter Handke's *Der Angst des Tormanns beim Elfmeter* (The Goalie's Fear of the Penalty Kick).

drawn to Vienna by the Habsburgs' generous patronage during the 18th and 19th centuries. The waltz originated in this city, and was perfected by Johann Strauss junior (1825–99).

In the early 20th century, Vienna was also a city of design and painting. The Vienna Secessionist movement, the local equivalent of art nouveau *(Jugendstil),* created such talents as artist Gustav Klimt and architect Otto Wagner. Expressionist painters Egon Schiele and Oskar Kokoschka and modernist architect Adolf Loos followed further into the century.

Today Austria's fine musical tradition has moved in the wholly different direction of chilled, eclectic electronica and dub lounge. Celebrity DJs Kruder & Dorfmeister have had the greatest global success, but the scene is loaded with other talent, including Pulsinger & Tunakan, the Vienna Scientists and the Sofa Surfers.

Meanwhile, expert film director Michael Haneke has also been creating a splash with his controversial *Funny Games* (1997 and remade by Haneke in the USA in 2007) and the twisted romance of the much-lauded *The Piano Teacher* (2001).

ENVIRONMENT

More than half of Austria is mountainous, with three chains running west to east: the Northern Limestone Alps, the Central Alps (which include the country's highest mountain, the 3797m Grossglockner) and the Southern Limestone Alps. The landscape around the Danube Valley in the northeast, and Graz to the southeast, is flat.

Only 3% of Austria's landmass is designated as national park, but that does include the largest national park in the Alps, Hohe Tauern. Many species of alpine wildflowers are found in this park, and the bearded vulture and lyre-horned ibex have been reintroduced. Marmots can be spotted in other national parks.

It's easy to be environmentally friendly in Austria as the locals are very environmentally conscious – they keep the countryside clean and use recycling and biocompost bins religiously.

Changing weather patterns are affecting the Alps – as much as 75% of the country's glaciers are expected to disappear over the next 45 years and most of Austria's low-lying ski resorts will receive no snow by 2030. The knock-on effect could mean more erosion, floods, and an increased risk of avalanches.

TRANSPORT

GETTING THERE & AWAY

Air

Austria is well served by low-cost airlines. **Ryanair** (FR; ☎ 0900-210 240; www.ryanair.com) flies from London to Graz, Klagenfurt, Linz and Salzburg; **Air Berlin** (AB; ☎ 0820-600 830; www.airberlin.com) flies to Vienna from a plethora of destinations in Europe and beyond; **EasyJet** (U2; www.easyjet.com) connects Vienna and Innsbruck with London; and **German Wings** (4U; ☎ 0820-240 554; www.germanwings.com) has services to Germany's major cities and a handful of other countries. **TUIfly** (X3; ☎ 0820 820 033; www.tuifly.com) connects many of Austria's cities (except Vienna) to Germany's larger hubs. **SkyEurope Airlines** (5P; ☎ 0910-160 696; www.skyeurope.com) operates across central and Western Europe, however its 'Vienna' airport is far from the city – in Slovakia's capital, Bratislava.

The national carrier **Austrian Airlines** (OS; ☎ 051 766 1000; www.aua.com) regularly offers special deals.

BORDER CROSSINGS

As Austria now resides in the middle of an enlarged EU, border controls are very lax. There are many entry points from the Czech Republic, Hungary, Slovakia, Slovenia, Switzerland, Italy and Germany, all of which are normally open 24 hours.

CONNECTIONS

Due to its central location, Austria has plenty of connections to all parts of Europe. Trains from Vienna (p86) run to many Eastern European destinations, including Bratislava, Budapest, Prague and Warsaw; there are also connections south to Italy via Klagenfurt (p91) and north to Berlin. Salzburg is within sight of the Bavarian border, and there are many trains (p94) Munich-bound and beyond from the baroque city. Innsbruck is on the main trunk line connecting Austria to Switzerland, and there are a handful of trains from Bregenz to the bigger Swiss cities.

Boat
Hydrofoils run to Bratislava and Budapest from Vienna (see p86). Other boats go from Linz to Passau in Germany (see p87).

Bus
There are comprehensive bus services to Eastern European cities small and large, from the likes of Belgrade, Sofia and Warsaw, to Banja Luka, Mostar and Sarajevo. Other services go as far afield as England, the Baltic States, Germany, the Netherlands and Switzerland.

Vienna (see p86) is the main departure point for services operated by **Eurolines** (www.eurolines.at), although some also leave from Salzburg and Graz as well as other provincial cities.

Car & Motorcycle
Austria levies fees for its entire motorway network. Tourists must buy a 10-day pass (€7.70/4.40 per car/motorcycle), a two-month pass (€22.20/11.10) or a yearly pass (€73.80/29.50) and clearly display the toll label *(Vignette)* on their vehicle. Passes are available at borders or from petrol stations. Otherwise, there's an on-the-spot fine of up to €300. For details, see www.oesag.at (in German).

Train
The main rail services in and out of the country from the west normally pass through Bregenz, Innsbruck or Salzburg on their way to Vienna's Westbahnhof. Trains to Eastern Europe invariably leave from Südbahnhof in Vienna. Express services to Italy go via Innsbruck or Villach; trains to Slovenia are routed through Graz.

GETTING AROUND

Air
Austrian Airlines and its subsidiary, Tyrolean Airlines, operate regular internal flights, but train, bus or car suffices in such a small country.

Bicycle
There are many national cycling paths. Private operators and hostels rent bikes; be prepared to pay anything from €7 to €10 a day. Vienna has cheap city bikes.

You can pay separately to take your bike on slow trains (€2.90/7.50/22.50 per day/week/month); on fast trains, it costs €6.80 a day, if space allows. Booking is advisable.

Boat
Services along the Danube (see p86) are mainly pleasure cruises, but provide a leisurely, scenic way of getting from A to B.

Bus
Both Postbus and Bahnbus are now operated by the railways, ÖBB. Bus services are generally limited to less-accessible regions, such as the Salzkammergut or Hohe Tauern National Park. Between major cities in environmentally friendly Austria, only train services exist. Call ☎ 01-711 01 (between 7am and 8pm) for inquiries or consult www.postbus.at.

Car & Motorcycle
All the multinational hire firms are here, but ask tourist offices about local agencies, which are usually cheaper. The minimum age for renting small cars is 19 years, and 25 for larger 'prestige' cars. Customers must have held a licence for at least a year. Many firms charge an additional fee for taking cars into Eastern Europe.

Whether you hire a vehicle or bring your own, you must pay a tax to drive on motorways and affix a *Vignette* to your windscreen.

Motorcyclists must switch their headlights on at all times, and crash helmets are compulsory.

Train
The efficient state network **ÖBB** (☎ 05-17 17; www.oebb.at) is supplemented by a few private lines. Eurail and Inter-Rail passes are valid

EMERGENCY NUMBERS

- Alpine Rescue ☎ 140
- Ambulance ☎ 144
- Doctor ☎ 141 (after hours)
- Fire ☎ 122
- Police ☎ 133
- Roadside Assistance ☎ 120

on the former, but only sometimes on the latter. There is no supplement on Eurail and Inter-Rail passes for national travel on faster Eurocity (EC) and Intercity (IC) trains. Tickets purchased on the train cost about €3 extra. Within Austria, anyone can buy a Vorteilscard (adult/under 26 years/senior €99.90/19.90/26.90), which reduces fares by at least 45% and is valid for a year. At €19.90/99.90 per person aged under 26/over 26, it's of most interest to under 26s.

VIENNA

☎ 01 / pop 1.66 million

Vienna is a city that straddles the past and present with ease. No other city effortlessly combines a rich history that has left behind such remarkable gifts as gothic Stephansdom or baroque Schönbrunn palace with contemporary gems like the Leopold Museum or MuseumsQuartier. Here you can spend your days marvelling at one historical building after the next and evenings clubbing to electronic beats. And that's to mention nothing of the musical history that abounds from this city the Turks once called the 'golden apple'.

Culture is the mainstay of the city, but it's not the only thing on offer. Coffee houses, wine taverns, markets, the Vienna Woods, and even swimming in the Danube are here, all within easy reach of Vienna's marvellous medieval centre.

ORIENTATION

Many sights are in the Innere Stadt (inner city), which is encircled by the Danube Canal (Donaukanal) to the northeast and broad boulevards called the Ring or Ringstrasse.

In addresses, the number of a building follows the street name. Any number before the street name denotes the district, of which there are 23. District 01 (the Innere Stadt) is the most central. Generally, the higher the district number, the further out it is.

INFORMATION

Internet Access

Bignet (Map pp82-3; ☎ 533 29 39; 01, Hoher Markt 8-9; per hr €5.90)
Speednet Café (Map pp82-3; ☎ 532 57 50; 01 Morzinplatz 4; per hr €4.60)
Surfland Internetcafé (Map pp82-3; ☎ 512 77 01; 01, Krugerstrasse 10; initial charge €1.50, per extra min €0.10)

Medical Services

Allgemeines Krankenhaus (General Hospital; Map pp78-9; ☎ 40 400-0; 09, Währinger Gürtel 18-20; 24hr)
Dental Treatment (☎ 512 20 78; 24hr) German-speaking only.

Tourist Information

Tourist offices and hotels sell the Vienna Card (€18.50), which provides admission discounts and a free 72-hour travel pass.

Jugend-Info Wien (Vienna Youth Information; Map pp82-3; ☎ 17 99; www.wienxtra.at; 01, Babenbergerstrasse 1; noon-7pm Mon-Sat) Offers various reduced-price tickets for 14- to 26-year-olds.
Tourist-Info Wien (Map pp82-3; ☎ 24 555; www.wien.info; 01, cnr Am Albertinaplatz & Maysedergasse; 9am-7pm)

SIGHTS & ACTIVITIES

Vienna's ostentatious buildings and beautiful parks make it a lovely city for strolling. Catch tram 1 or 2 around the Ringstrasse (the road circling the centre) to acquire a taste of the city. It passes the neo-Gothic **Rathaus** (Town Hall; Map pp82–3), the Greek Revival–style **Parlament** (Map pp82–3), and the 19th-century **Burgtheater** (Map pp82–3) – you can even glimpse the baroque **Karlskirche** (St Charles' Church; Map pp82–3) from the tram.

Heading into the Innere Stadt (Inner City) will take you to a different age. Designated a Unesco World Heritage site, the heart of the city is blessed with a plethora of architectural wonders that hint at Vienna's long love affair with history. Begin by strolling along the pedestrian-only Kärntner Strasse past its plush shops, cafes and street entertainers and into Graben, where the knobbly **Petsäule** (Plague Column; Map pp82–3), designed by Fischer von Erlach, was built to commemorate the end of the Plague. Turning left into Kohlmarkt brings the impressive Hofburg

(Imperial Palace), the Habsburgs' city-centre base, into view. Walk towards it and wander around this large complex's nooks and crannies. There are several museums inside, including the **Kaiserappartements & 'Sissi' Museum** (Map pp82-3; ☎ 535 75 70; Hofburg; admission €9.90; 🕒 9am-5pm), which relates the unusual life story of Empress Elisabeth (Sissi), and the **Schatzkammer** (Treasury; Map pp82-3; ☎ 525 24-0; Schweizerhof; admission €10; 🕒 10am-6pm Wed-Mon), where all manner of wonders, including the 10th-century Imperial Crown, a 2860-carat Columbian emerald, and even a thorn from Christ's crown, are on display.

Not far from the Hofburg is the **Kaisergruft** (Imperial Vault; Map pp82-3; ☎ 512 68 53; 01, Tegetthofstrasse/Neuer Markt; admission €4; 🕒 10am-6pm), the final resting place of most of the Habsburg elite (their hearts and organs reside elsewhere).

Stephansdom

The prominent latticework spire of **Stephansdom** (St Stephen's Cathedral; Map pp82-3; ☎ 515 52-0; www.stephanskirche.at; 01, Stephansplatz; admission free; 🕒 6am-10pm Mon-Sat, 7am-10pm Sun), along with the geometric pattern of its roof tiles, make this 13th-century Gothic masterpiece one of the city's key points of orientation. The interior is nothing to scoff at either, complete with a 16th-century stone pulpit and gigantic baroque high altar. Inside, you can take the lift up the **north tower** (admission €4.50; 🕒 8.30am-5.30pm), tackle the 343 steps to the top of the **south tower** (admission €3.50; 🕒 9am-5.30pm), and explore the church's **Katakomben** (catacombs; admission €4.50; 🕒 10-11.30am & 1.30-4.30pm Mon-Sat, 1.30-4.30pm Sun), which contains some of the internal organs of the former Habsburgs rulers. Guided tours (€4.50) are also available, as are audio guides (€3.50).

Museums & Galleries

When it comes to classical works of art, nothing comes close to the **Museum of Fine Arts** (Kunsthistorisches Museum; Map pp82-3; ☎ 52 524-0; www.khm.at; 01, Maria Theresien Platz; adult/student €10/7.50; 🕒 10am-6pm Tue-Sun, to 9pm Thu). It houses a huge range of art amassed by the Habsburgs and includes works by Rubens, van Dyck, Holbein and Caravaggio.

The **MuseumsQuartier** (Map pp82-3; ☎ 523 04 31; www.mqw.at; 07, Museumsplatz 1), a public and exhibition space unrivalled in the capital, contains both contemporary and baroque architectural splendour. Its highpoint is the **Leopold Museum** (Map pp82-3; ☎ 525 700; www.leopoldmuseum.org; adult/student/senior €10/6.50/9; 🕒 10am-6pm Fri-Wed, to 9pm Thu), which houses the world's largest collection of Egon Schiele paintings, with some minor Klimts and Kokoschkas.

Belvedere Palace (Schloss Belvedere; Map pp82-3; ☎ 79 557-0; www.belvedere.at; combined ticket adult/senior/student €12.50/9.50/8.50) consists of two main buildings. One is the **Oberes Belvedere & Österreichische Galerie** (Upper Belvedere & Austrian Gallery; Map pp78-9; 03, Prinz Eugen Strasse 37; adult/senior/student €9.50/7.50/6; 🕒 10am-6pm), where you'll find instantly recognisable works, such as Gustav Klimt's *The Kiss*, accompanied by other late-19th to early-20th-century Austrian works. The other is the **Unteres Belvedere** (Lower Belvedere; Map pp82-3; 03, Rennweg 6A; adult/senior/student €9.50/7.50/6; 🕒 10am-6pm Thu-Tue, 10am-9pm Wed), which contains a baroque museum. The buildings sit at opposite ends of a manicured garden.

Built in 1898, the **Secession** (Map pp82-3; ☎ 587 53 07; www.secession.at; 01, Friedrichstrasse 12; adult/student €6/3.50; 🕒 10am-6pm Tue-Sun, to 8pm Thu) is a popular art nouveau 'temple of art'. It bears an intricately woven gilt dome, and inside the highlight is the 34m-long *Beethoven Frieze* by Klimt.

Albrecht Dürer's *Hare* and a few Michelangelos are joined by superbly curated modern exhibitions at the **Albertina** (Map pp82-3; ☎ 53 483-0; www.albertina.at; 01, Albertinaplatz 1a; adult/student/senior €9.50/7/8; 🕒 10am-6pm Thu-Tue, to 9pm Wed).

At **Haus der Musik** (House of Music; Map pp82-3; ☎ 51 648; www.haus-der-musik-wien.at; 01, Seilerstätte 30; adult/student €10/8.50; 🕒 10am-10pm) make your own music in this mind-blowing array of interactive exhibits.

Sigmund Freud Museum (Map pp82-3; ☎ 319 15 96; www.freud-museum.at; 09, Berggasse 19; adult/student €7/4.50; 🕒 9am-6pm Jul-Sep, to 5pm Oct-Jun) is the former home of the father of psychoanalysis, while the **Wien Museum** (Map pp82-3; ☎ 505 87 47-0; www.wienmuseum.at; 04, Karlsplatz 5; adult/student/senior €6/3/4, permanent exhibition free Sun; 🕒 9am-6pm Tue-Sun) provides a snapshot of the city's history, and contains a handsome art collection.

Schloss Schönbrunn

The Habsburgs' 1441-room summer palace, **Schloss Schönbrunn** (Map pp78-9; ☎ 81 113-0; www.schoenbrunn.at; 13, Schönbrunner Schlossstrasse 47; self-guided 22-/40-room tour €9.50/12.90; 🕒 8.30am-5pm Apr-Oct, to 6pm Jul-Aug, to 4.30pm Nov-Mar) is a grand display of baroque imperialism. Inside is one luxurious

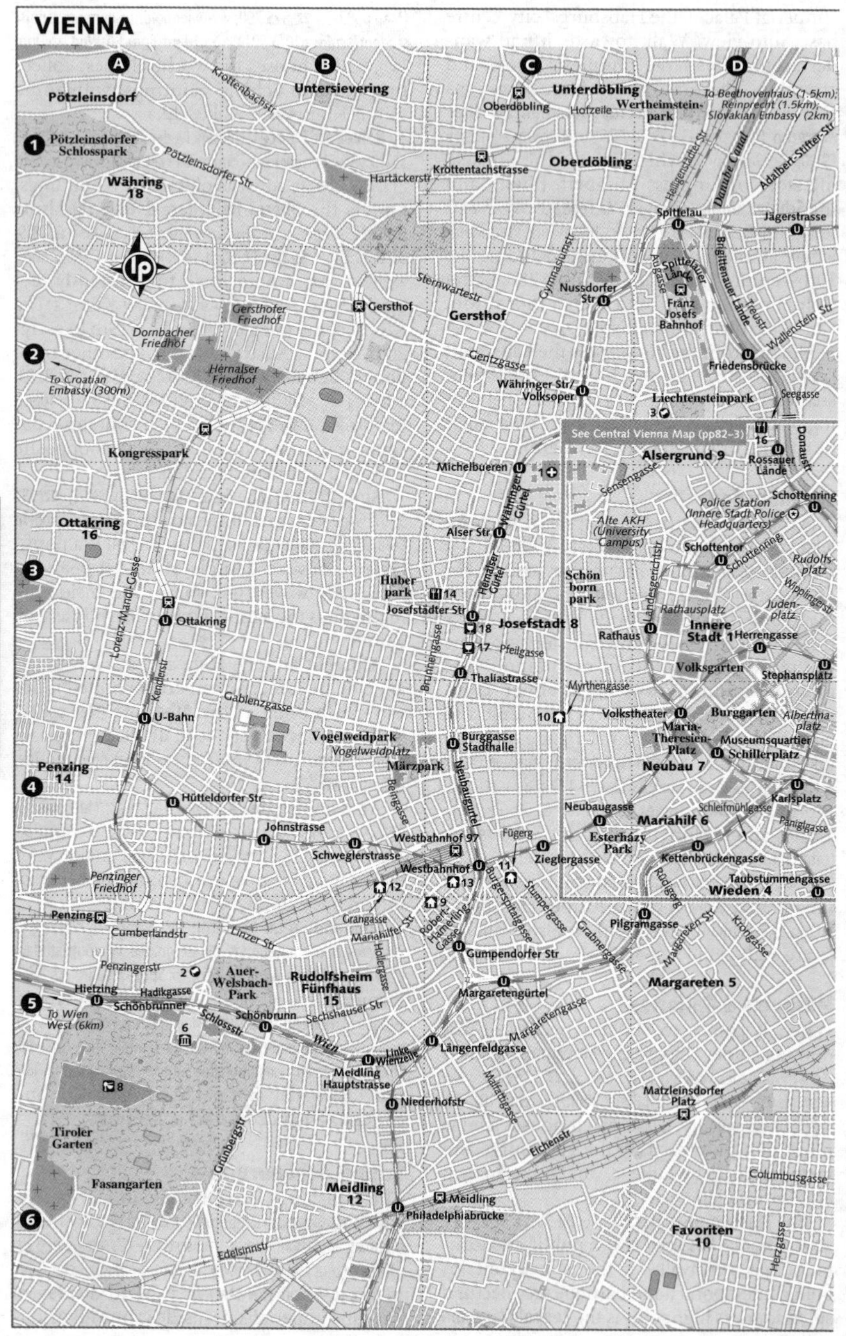
VIENNA
Pötzleinsdorf
Untersievering
Unterdöbling
Oberdöbling
Hofzeile
Wertheimstein-park
To Beethovenhaus (1.5km); Reinprecht (1.5km); Slovakian Embassy (2km)
Pötzleinsdorfer Schlosspark
Pötzleinsdorfer Str
Krottenbachstr
Krottenbachstrasse
Hartäckerstr
Oberdöbling
Währing 18
Danube Canal
Adalbert-Stifter-Str
Heiligenstädter Str
Spittelau
Jägerstrasse
Brigittenauer Lände
Spittelauer Lände
Augasse
Franz Josefs Bahnhof
Gymnasiumstr
Nussdorfer Str
Sternwartestr
Gersthof
Gersthofer Friedhof
Dornbacher Friedhof
Hernalser Friedhof
To Croatian Embassy (300m)
Gentzgasse
Währinger Str/ Volksoper
Friedensbrücke
Wallensteinstr
Treustr
Liechtensteinpark
Seegasse
Kongresspark
See Central Vienna Map (pp82-3)
Alsergrund 9
Rossauer Lände
Donaustr
Michelbeuern
Währinger Gürtel
Sensengasse
Schottenring
Police Station (Innere Stadt Police Headquarters)
Alte AKH (University Campus)
Alser Str
Ottakring 16
Schottentor
Rudolfsplatz
Wipplingerstr
Judenplatz
Huber park
Hernalser Gürtel
Schönborn park
Landesgerichtstr
Rathausplatz
Josefstädter Str
Josefstadt 8
Rathaus
Innere Stadt 1
Herrengasse
Ottakring
Lorenz-Mandl-Gasse
Pfeilgasse
Volksgarten
Stephansplatz
Thaliastrasse
Brunnengasse
Kendlerstr
Myrthengasse
Gablenzgasse
U-Bahn
Volkstheater
Burggarten
Albertinaplatz
Maria-Theresien-Platz
Museumsquartier
Schillerplatz
Vogelweidpark
Vogelweidplatz
Burggasse Stadthalle
Märzpark
Neubau 7
Penzing 14
Neubaugürtel
Beingasse
Hütteldorfer Str
Karlsplatz
Neubaugasse
Mariahilf 6
Schleifmühlgasse
Paniglgasse
Johnstrasse
Westbahnhof 97
Fügerg
Esterházy Park
Schweglerstrasse
Westbahnhof
Zieglergasse
Kettenbrückengasse
Penzinger Friedhof
Taubstummengasse
Wieden 4
Burgerspitalgasse
Stumpergasse
Rüdigerg
Penzing
Grangasse
Mariahilfer Str
Robert-Hamerling-Gasse
Pilgramgasse
Cumberlandstr
Linzer Str
Hollergasse
Grabnergasse
Margaretenstr
Krongasse
Gumpendorfer Str
Penzingerstr
Auer-Welsbach-Park
Rudolfsheim Fünfhaus 15
Margaretengürtel
Margareten 5
Hietzing
Hadikgasse
Schönbrunner Schlossstr
Schönbrunn
Sechshauser Str
To Wien West (6km)
Margaretengasse
Wien
Linke Wienzeile
Längenfeldgasse
Meidling Hauptstrasse
Niederhofstr
Malfattigasse
Matzleinsdorfer Platz
Tiroler Garten
Grünbergstr
Eichenstr
Fasangarten
Columbusgasse
Meidling 12
Meidling
Philadelphiabrücke
Favoriten 10
Edelsinnstr
Herzgasse
A
B
C
D
1
2
3
4
5
6

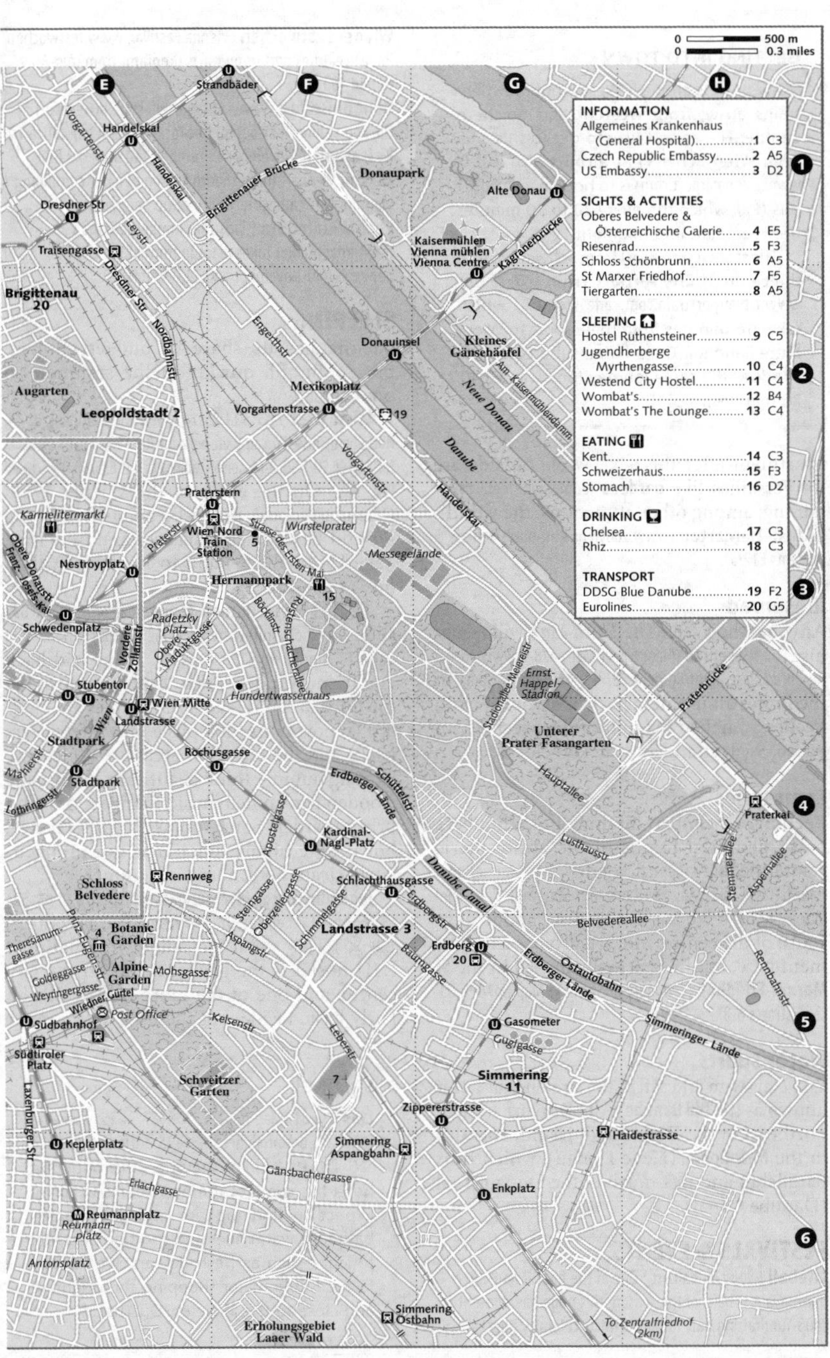
0 500 m
0 0.3 miles
E
F
G
H
1
2
3
4
5
6
INFORMATION
Allgemeines Krankenhaus (General Hospital) 1 C3
Czech Republic Embassy 2 A5
US Embassy 3 D2
SIGHTS & ACTIVITIES
Oberes Belvedere & Österreichische Galerie 4 E5
Riesenrad 5 F3
Schloss Schönbrunn 6 A5
St Marxer Friedhof 7 F5
Tiergarten 8 A5
SLEEPING
Hostel Ruthensteiner 9 C5
Jugendherberge Myrthengasse 10 C4
Westend City Hostel 11 C4
Wombat's 12 B4
Wombat's The Lounge 13 C4
EATING
Kent 14 C3
Schweizerhaus 15 F3
Stomach 16 D2
DRINKING
Chelsea 17 C3
Rhiz 18 C3
TRANSPORT
DDSG Blue Danube 19 F2
Eurolines 20 G5
Strandbäder
Handelskai
Vorgartenstr
Brigittenauer Brücke
Donaupark
Alte Donau
Dresdner Str
Leystr
Traisengasse
Kaisermühlen Vienna mühlen Vienna Centre
Kagranerbrücke
Brigittenau 20
Nordbahnstr
Engerthstr
Donauinsel
Kleines Gänsehäufel
Am Kaisermühlendamm
Neue Donau
Augarten
Mexikoplatz
Leopoldstadt 2
Vorgartenstrasse
Danube
Praterstern
Karmelitermarkt
Wien Nord Train Station
Strasse des Ersten Mai
Wurstelprater
Praterstr
Messegelände
Obere Donaustr
Franz-Josefs-Kai
Nestroyplatz
Hermannpark
Schwedenplatz
Böcklinstr
Rustenschacherallee
Radetzky platz
Obere Viaduktgasse
Vordere Zollamtsstr
Stadionallee
Meiereistr
Ernst-Happel-Stadion
Praterbrücke
Stubentor
Hundertwasserhaus
Wien Mitte
Landstrasse
Wien
Unterer Prater Fasangarten
Stadtpark
Rochusgasse
Hauptallee
Schüttelstr
Erdberger Lände
Lothringerstr
Apostelgasse
Praterkai
Kardinal-Nagl-Platz
Lusthausstr
Stemmerallee
Aspernallee
Danube Canal
Schloss Belvedere
Rennweg
Schlachthausgasse
Erdbergstr
Steingasse
Oberzellergasse
Schimmelgasse
Belvederealle
Theresianumgasse
Botanic Garden
Landstrasse 3
Aspangstr
Erdberg
Baumgasse
Prinz-Eugen-Str
Ostautobahn
Goldeggasse
Alpine Garden
Mohsgasse
Weyringergasse
Wiedner Gürtel
Post Office
Rennbahnstr
Südbahnhof
Kelsenstr
Gasometer
Simmeringer Lände
Guglgasse
Südtiroler Platz
Leberstr
Schweitzer Garten
Simmering 11
Laxenburger Str
Zippererstrasse
Haidestrasse
Keplerplatz
Simmering Aspangbahn
Gänsbachergasse
Erlachgasse
Enkplatz
Reumannplatz
Antonsplatz
Simmering Ostbahn
Erholungsgebiet Laaer Wald
To Zentralfriedhof (2km)

Book your stay at lonelyplanet.com/hotels

GETTING INTO TOWN

Many hostels are near Westbahnhof, where trains arrive from Western and northern Europe. The easiest way to get to this area from **Wien Schwechat airport** (☎ 7007-0; www.viennaairport.com) is to hop on an airport bus (€7), which run every 20 to 30 minutes between 5am and midnight.

The fastest transport from Schwechat into the centre is **City Airport Train** (☎ 25 250; www.cityairporttrain.com; one way €9), which takes 16 minutes from the airport to Wien-Mitte Bahnhof. The S-bahn (suburban train; S7) does the same journey (one way €3.40, 26 minutes).

apartment after the next, while outside are its Versailles-like **gardens** (admission free), containing, among other attractions, the world's oldest **Tiergarten** (www.zoovienna.at; adult/seniors & students €12/5).

Riesenrad

Anyone who's seen *The Third Man* will recognise the **Riesenrad** (Giant Wheel; Map pp78-9; www.wienerriesenrad.com; adult/student €8/7; 10am-7.45pm) in the Prater amusement park; it's where Orson Welles ad libbed his immortal speech about peace, Switzerland and cuckoo clocks.

Cemeteries

Beethoven, Schubert, Brahms and Schönberg have memorial tombs in the atmospheric **Zentralfriedhof** (Central Cemetery; 11, Simmeringer Hauptstrasse 232-244; 7am-7pm May-Aug, 7am-6pm Mar, Apr, Sep & Oct, 8am-5pm Nov-Feb), about 4km south of the centre. Mozart also has a monument here, but he is actually buried in the **St Marxer Friedhof** (Cemetery of St Mark; Map pp78-9; 03, Leberstrasse 6-8).

Water Sports

You can swim and sail in the stretches of water known as the **Old Danube** (Alte Donau), located northeast of the Donaustadt island, and also in the **New Donau** (Neue Donau), which runs parallel to and just north of the Donaukanal (Danube Canal).

FESTIVALS & EVENTS

Lifeball (www.lifeball.org) One of the final – and flamboyant – balls of the season, this huge gay/straight AIDS-fundraising gala in May attracts celebrity guests.

Wiener Festwochen (Vienna Festival; www.festwochen.or.at) Features performing-arts programs from mid-May to mid-June.

Donauinselfest (www.donauinselfest.at, in German) At the end of June, look out for free rock, jazz and folk concerts.

Kaiserball In November/December, the Imperial Ball kicks off Vienna's three-month season of balls, combining glamour and high society with camp decadence.

Christkindlmarkt (Christmas market) Vienna's traditional market takes place in front of the city hall between mid-November and 24 December.

SLEEPING

Vienna has its share of budget choices, but rooms fill quickly in the summer, so book ahead.

Wien West (☎ 914 23 14; www.wiencamping.at; 14, Hüttelbergstrasse 80; camp site per adult/tent Sep-Jun €5.90/4.50, Jul-Aug €6.90/5.50, 2-/4-person cabins Apr-Oct €35/50; closed Feb;) On the edges of the Wiener Wald (Vienna Woods), this well-equipped camping ground has modern facilities and bike hire. Take U4 or the S-Bahn to Hütteldorf, then bus 148 or 152.

our pick **Hostel Ruthensteiner** (Map pp78-9; ☎ 893 42 02; www.hostelruthensteiner.com; 15, Robert Hamerling Gasse 24; dm/d from €16/50;) This laid-back and friendly independent hostel is one of the top finds in central Europe. Facilities are modern (renovations took place only a few years back) and the common areas are a pleasure to hang out in – think beautifully handmade wooden bar, chilled music/lounge room, and private garden. Some rooms are a little pokey, but they're highly functional and immaculately clean. Book ahead in summer.

Jugendherberge Myrthengasse (Map pp78-9; ☎ 523 63 16; hostel@chello.at; 07, Myrthengasse 7; dm from €17;) This small Hostelling International (HI) hostel is the closest hostel to the city centre, and one of the more chilled. It's all fairly basic inside, but there's a lovely inner

SPLURGE

Das Tyrol (Map pp82-3; ☎ 587 54 15; www.das-tyrol.at; 06, Mariahilfer Strasse 15; s/d from €109/149;) For the price, this boutique hotel has some of the best rooms in town. Expect to find modern and cosy rooms bathed in warm hues and sporting personal touches such as fresh flowers. It's handily located on a major shopping thoroughfare and close to the MuseumsQuartier.

AUSTRIA

courtyard to enjoy. Breakfast is included; towels aren't.

Westend City Hostel (Map pp78-9; ☎ 597 67 29; www.westendhostel.at; 6, Fügergasse 3; dm/s/d from €19.50/52/62; 💻 ⊠) The pale purple facade of this former bordello fronts a spick-and-span hostel suitable for families and backpackers looking for a quiet night's rest. Rooms are pretty bland, but each has an en suite bathroom and lockers for every guest. Prices include breakfast.

Wombat's (Map pp78-9; ☎ 897 23 36; www.wombats.at; 15, Grangasse 6; dm/d €21/25; 💻 ⊠) Top-flight cleanliness and comfort fuse with a gregarious party bar to make Wombat's immensely popular. The mixed-gender dorms have secured entry, wooden bunk beds and modern bathrooms. There's a second location just around the corner, Wombat's The Lounge (Map pp78–9; 15, Mariahilfer Strasse 137; internet access).

Schweizer Pension (Map pp82-3; ☎ 533 81 56; www.schwiezerpension.com; 01, Heinrichsgasse 2; s/d with shared bathroom from €42/62; Ⓟ ⊠) The Schweizer isn't overly modern but who cares when the beds are still comfy and you're paying a pittance for such a great location. And they're big on the environment too – energy-saving bulbs are employed throughout and organic produce is used for breakfasts. Book ahead as there's only 11 rooms.

EATING

Der Wiener Deewan (Map pp82-3; 09, Liechtensteinstrasse 10; 🕑 Mon-Sat) Pakistani curries – three vegetarian and two meat – are prepared daily and served buffet-style at this easy-going eatery. There's no set price here, just eat at much as you like and pay as much as you like, although the food's so good you'll want to fork over a decent amount of cash.

Kent (Map pp78-9; 16, Brunnengasse 67; mains €4-9) Authentic Turkish cuisine and one of the largest gardens in the city make Kent a hugely popular choice with locals of all ethnic backgrounds. After your meal, take a wander along the nearby Brunnen market and pick up some fresh fruit for dessert.

Zu den 2 Leiserln (Map pp82-3; 07, Burggasse 63; schnitzel from €6) A classic *Beisl* (traditional Viennese pub serving solid Viennese fare) if ever there was one. Leiserln has been serving enormous schnitzels for over 100 years to politicians, blue-collar workers, and everyone in between. Take a seat and appreciate a true Viennese institution.

SPLURGE

DO & CO (Map pp82-3; ☎ 535 39 69; 01, Haas Haus, Stephansplatz 12; mains €15-30) The food and the views from seven floors above Stephansplatz keep this elegant restaurant in business. Contemporary Viennese dishes are highlighted, but it also serves Austrian classics, Uruguayan beef and Asian specialities. The service is flawless. Book ahead.

St Josef (Map pp82-3; 07, Mondscheingasse 10; mains €6-7.20; 🕑 Mon-Sat) St Josef is the choice of the healthy diner. It only serves wholly organic and vegetarian cuisine, and the menu changes daily.

our pick **Stomach** (Map pp78-9; ☎ 310 20 99; 09, Seegasse 26; mains €10-18; 🕑 dinner Wed-Sat, lunch & dinner Sun) Many vegetarian dishes have dropped off the menu at Styrian-style Stomach, but some remain, and the quaint, ramshackle rooms and the courtyard create a rustic outpost in the big city.

Schweizerhaus (Map pp78-9; 02, Strasse des Ersten Mai 116; mains €10-20; 🕑 mid-Mar–Oct) In the Prater park, this place serves *Hintere Schweinsstelze* (roasted pork hocks) and the like to a rowdy crowd of international travellers who wash it all down with huge mugs of Czech beer fresh from the barrel.

Sausages are the fast-food choice of many Viennese (especially at the end of a night out), and sausage stands dot the city. For fresh fruit and cheap kebabs, head for the colour **Naschmarkt** (Map pp82-3; 06, Linke Wienzeile; 🕑 6am-6pm Mon-Sat), which also has a string of fine Asian diners.

Cheap student cafeterias include **Technical University Mensa** (Map pp82-3; 04, Resselgasse 7-9; mains €3.50-5; 🕑 11am-2pm Mon-Fri) and **University Mensa** (Map pp82-3; 7th fl, 01, Universitätsstrasse 7; mains €4.50-5; 🕑 11am-2pm Mon-Fri Sep-Jun).

DRINKING

Bars

The area near Schwedenplatz, dubbed the Bermudadreieck (Bermuda Triangle; Map pp82–3), may still attract plenty of drinkers (mainly drunk teenagers and out-of-towners), but the real scene has moved out of the centre to the likes of the Naschmarkt, along the Danube Canal (summer only), Schleifmühlgasse area (Map pp78–9), and along the Gürtel (Map pp78–9), an outer ring

AUSTRIA

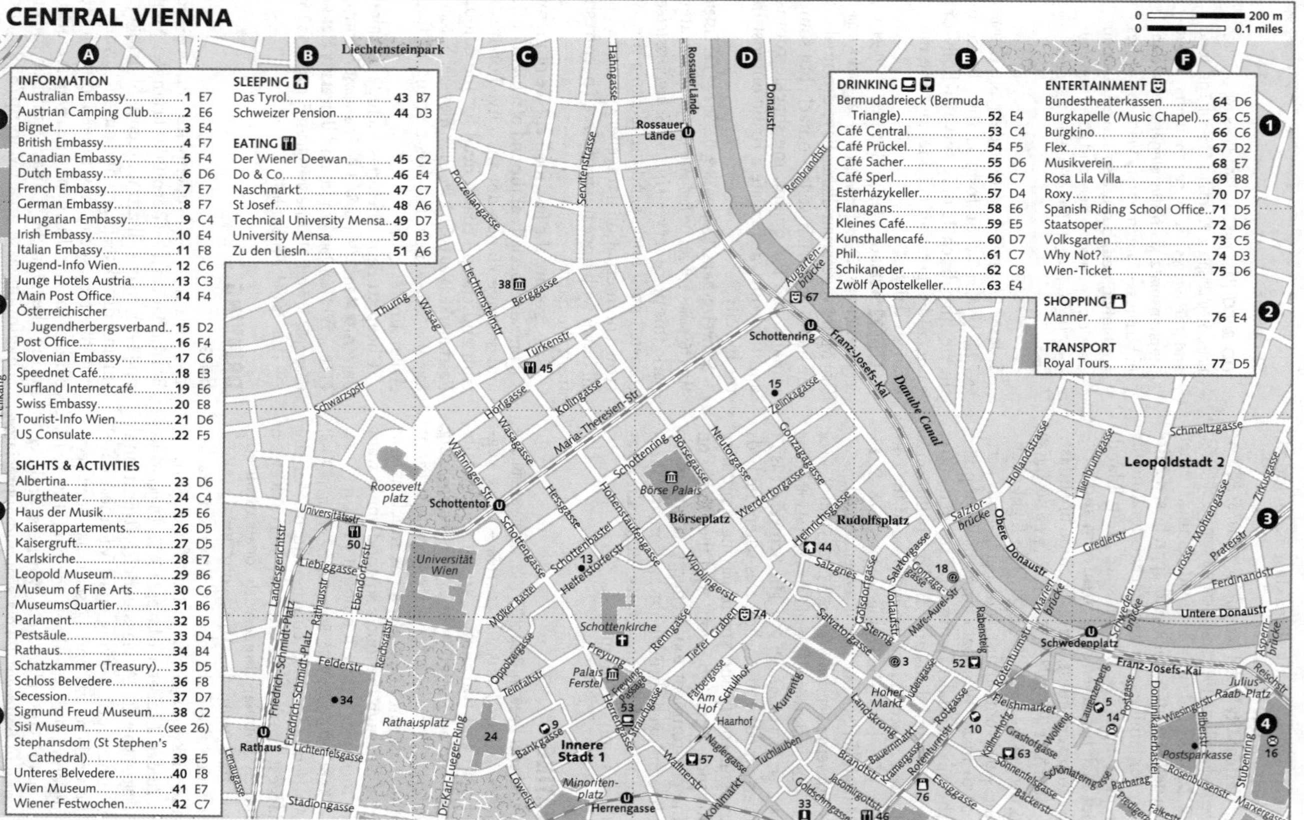
CENTRAL VIENNA
0 200 m
0 0.1 miles
INFORMATION
Australian Embassy 1 E7
Austrian Camping Club 2 E6
Bignet 3 E4
British Embassy 4 F7
Canadian Embassy 5 F4
Dutch Embassy 6 D6
French Embassy 7 E7
German Embassy 8 F7
Hungarian Embassy 9 C4
Irish Embassy 10 E4
Italian Embassy 11 F8
Jugend-Info Wien 12 C6
Junge Hotels Austria 13 C3
Main Post Office 14 F4
Österreichischer Jugendherbergsverband 15 D2
Post Office 16 F4
Slovenian Embassy 17 C6
Speednet Café 18 E3
Surfland Internetcafé 19 E6
Swiss Embassy 20 E8
Tourist-Info Wien 21 D6
US Consulate 22 F5
SIGHTS & ACTIVITIES
Albertina 23 D6
Burgtheater 24 C4
Haus der Musik 25 E6
Kaiserappartements 26 D5
Kaisergruft 27 D5
Karlskirche 28 E7
Leopold Museum 29 B6
Museum of Fine Arts 30 C6
MuseumsQuartier 31 B6
Parlament 32 B5
Pestsäule 33 D4
Rathaus 34 B4
Schatzkammer (Treasury) 35 D5
Schloss Belvedere 36 F8
Secession 37 D7
Sigmund Freud Museum 38 C2
Sisi Museum (see 26)
Stephansdom (St Stephen's Cathedral) 39 E5
Unteres Belvedere 40 F8
Wien Museum 41 E7
Wiener Festwochen 42 C7
SLEEPING
Das Tyrol 43 B7
Schweizer Pension 44 D3
EATING
Der Wiener Deewan 45 C2
Do & Co 46 E4
Naschmarkt 47 C7
St Josef 48 A6
Technical University Mensa 49 D7
University Mensa 50 B3
Zu den Liesln 51 A6
DRINKING
Bermudadreieck (Bermuda Triangle) 52 E4
Café Central 53 C4
Café Prückel 54 F5
Café Sacher 55 D6
Café Sperl 56 C7
Esterházykeller 57 D4
Flanagans 58 E6
Kleines Café 59 E5
Kunsthallencafé 60 D7
Phil 61 C7
Schikaneder 62 C8
Zwölf Apostelkeller 63 E4
ENTERTAINMENT
Bundestheaterkassen 64 D6
Burgkapelle (Music Chapel) 65 C5
Burgkino 66 C6
Flex 67 D2
Musikverein 68 E7
Rosa Lila Villa 69 B8
Roxy 70 D7
Spanish Riding School Office 71 D5
Staatsoper 72 D6
Volksgarten 73 C5
Why Not? 74 D3
Wien-Ticket 75 D6
SHOPPING
Manner 76 E4
TRANSPORT
Royal Tours 77 D5
Liechtensteinpark
Rossauer Lände
Donaustr
Danube Canal
Franz-Josefs-Kai
Schottenring
Schottentor
Leopoldstadt 2
Börseplatz
Rudolfsplatz
Universität Wien
Rathausplatz
Rathaus
Innere Stadt 1
Herrengasse
Schwedenplatz
Schottenkirche
Hoher Markt
Postsparkasse
Untere Donaustr
Obere Donaustr

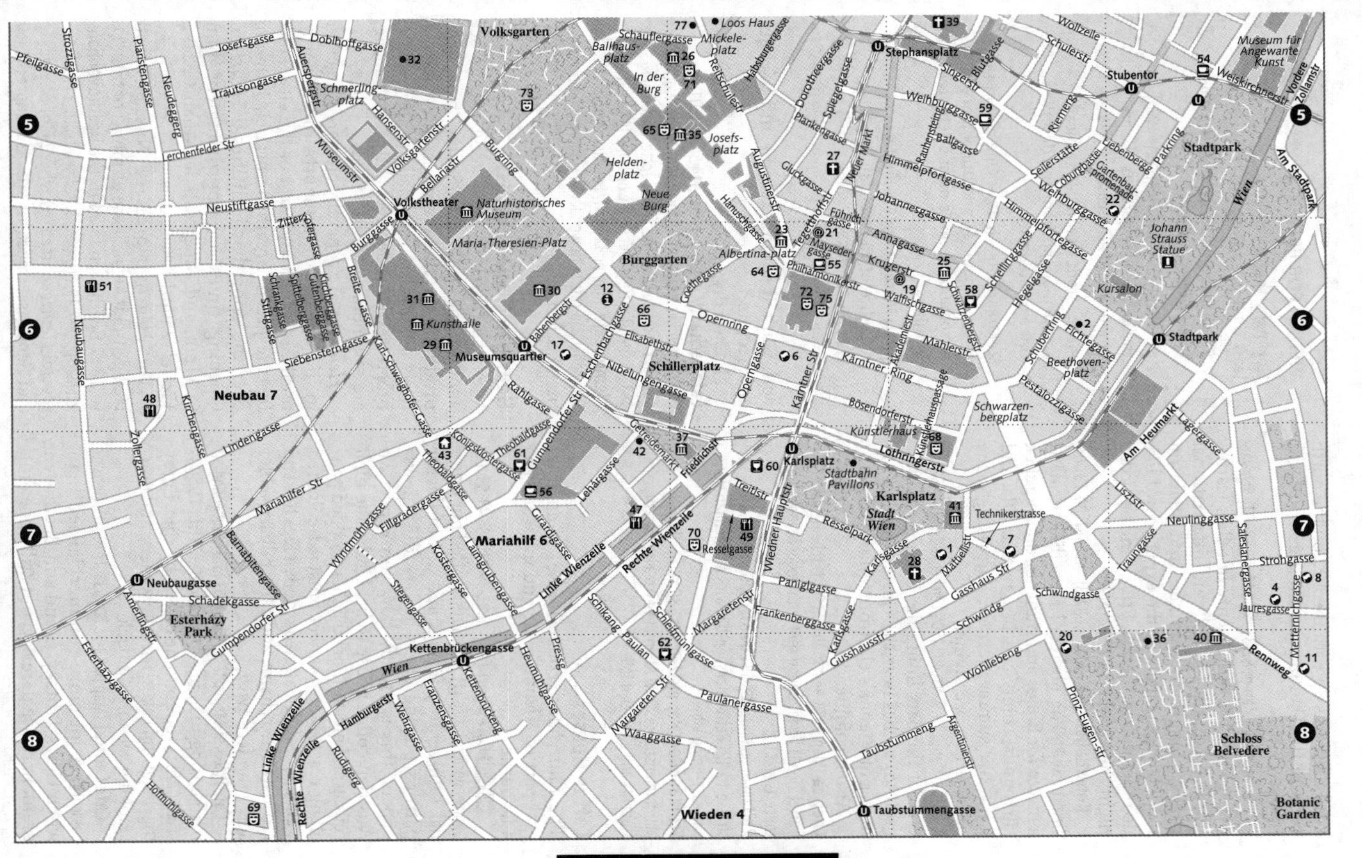
Volksgarten
Loos Haus
Michaelerplatz
Schauflergasse
Ballhausplatz
In der Burg
Reitschulestr
Habsburgergasse
Dorotheergasse
Spiegelgasse
Stephansplatz
Blutgasse
Singerstr
Wollzeile
Schulerstr
Stubentor
Museum für Angewante Kunst
Weiskirchnerstr
Vordere Zollamtstr
Stadtpark
Am Stadtpark
Wien
Johann Strauss Statue
Kursalon
Parkring
Liebenberg
Gartenbaupromenade
Coburgbastei
Seilerstätte
Riemerg
Weihburggasse
Rauhensteing
Ballgasse
Plankengasse
Neuer Markt
Himmelpfortgasse
Johannesgasse
Annagasse
Krugerstr
Walfischgasse
Schwarzenbergstr
Schellinggasse
Hegelgasse
Schubertring
Fichtegasse
Beethovenplatz
Pestalozzigasse
Schwarzenbergplatz
Am Heumarkt
Lagergasse
Mahlerstr
Akademiestr
Kärntner Ring
Bösendorferstr
Künstlerhaus
Künstlerhauspassage
Lothringerstr
Josefsplatz
Heldenplatz
Neue Burg
Burggarten
Augustinerstr
Gluckgasse
Tegetthoffstr
Führichgasse
Maysedergasse
Hanuschgasse
Albertina-platz
Philharmonikerstr
Goethegasse
Opernring
Operngasse
Kärntner Str
Elisabethstr
Eschenbachgasse
Schillerplatz
Nibelungengasse
Babenbergerstr
Museumsquartier
Kunsthalle
Naturhistorisches Museum
Maria-Theresien-Platz
Volkstheater
Burgring
Bellariastr
Volksgartenstr
Hansenstr
Schmerlingplatz
Museumstr
Auerspergstr
Doblhoffgasse
Josefsgasse
Trautsongasse
Pfeilgasse
Strozzigasse
Piaristengasse
Neudeggerg
Lerchenfelder Str
Neustiftgasse
Zitterhofergasse
Burggasse
Breite Gasse
Kirchberggasse
Gutenberggasse
Spittelberggasse
Schrankgasse
Stiftgasse
Siebensterngasse
Karl-Schweighofer-Gasse
Neubaugasse
Neubau 7
Kirchengasse
Zollergasse
Lindengasse
Mariahilfer Str
Rahlgasse
Königsklostergasse
Theobaldgasse
Gumpendorfer Str
Getreidemarkt
Friedrichstr
Lehargasse
Girardigasse
Mariahilf 6
Fillgradergasse
Windmühlgasse
Köstergasse
Laimgrubengasse
Stiegengasse
Barnabitengasse
Neubaugasse
Schadekgasse
Esterházy Park
Amerlingstr
Gumpendorfer Str
Esterházygasse
Hofmühlgasse
Linke Wienzeile
Rechte Wienzeile
Kettenbrückengasse
Kettenbrückeng
Wien
Hamburgerstr
Wehrgasse
Franzensgasse
Rüdigerg
Heumühlgasse
Pressg
Schikang
Paulan
Schleifmühlgasse
Margaretenstr
Margareten Str
Waaggasse
Paulanergasse
Wieden 4
Karlsplatz
Stadtbahn Pavillons
Treitlstr
Wiedner Hauptstr
Resselgasse
Resselpark
Stadt Wien
Karlsgasse
Mattiellistr
Technikerstrasse
Paniglgasse
Frankenberggasse
Karlsgasse
Gusshausstr
Gasshaus Str
Schwindgasse
Schwindg
Wohllebeng
Taubstummeng
Argentinierstr
Taubstummengasse
Prinz-Eugen-str
Lisztstr
Traungasse
Neulinggasse
Salesianergasse
Strohgasse
Jauresgasse
Metternichgasse
Rennweg
Schloss Belvedere
Botanic Garden

road that joins up with the A22 on the north bank of the Danube and the A23 southeast of town.

Flanagans (Map pp82-3; ☎ 513 73 78; 01, Schwarzenberg Strasse 1-3) With plenty of tellies featuring live English football and international rugby, along with Guinness and Stella on tap, Flanagans pulls in the expat crowd like no other pub in Vienna. Friday and Saturday nights here can be a spectacle.

Kunsthallencafé (Map pp82-3; ☎ 587 00 73; 04, Treitlstrasse 2) The ubercool Kunsthallencafé is a mecca for BoBos and students, offering slick surrounds, comfy couches, regular DJs, and a massive summer terrace. Surprisingly, the desserts here are divine.

Rhiz (Map pp78-9; ☎ 409 25 05; Lerchenfelder Gürtel 37-38) One of the bars lining the U-Bahn (underground) arches near the Gürtel, this is a hip mecca of Vienna's electronic music scene.

Also recommended:

Chelsea (Map pp78-9; ☎ 407 93 09; Lerchenfelder Gürtel 29-31) Underground spot with frequent indie band concerts and DJs.

Phil (Map pp82-3; ☎ 581 04 89; 06, Gumpendorferstrasse 10-12) Retro bookshop-bar with a bohemian slant and easy-going vibe.

Schikaneder (Map pp82-3; ☎ 585 58 88; 04, Margaretenstrasse 22-4) Alternative bar-cinema attracting students and black-clad folk.

AUSTRIA

Coffee Houses

The *Kaffeehaus* (coffee house) is an integral part of Viennese life and everyone has a favourite.

our pick Café Sperl (Map pp82-3; ☎ 586 41 58; 06, Gumpendorfer Strasse 11) With its scuffed but original 19th-century fittings and cast of slacker patrons playing chess and reading newspapers, this is exactly how you expect an Austrian coffee house to be. Under the high ceiling and old-fashioned lights, wooden panelling reaches up to meet mustard-coloured wallpaper, while battered wooden legs hold up red-patterned chairs, and a few billiard tables add a modern twist.

Café Prückel (Map pp82-3; ☎ 512 61 15; 01, Stubenring 24) Juxtaposing Vienna's formal cafes, this 1950s-style cafe is the epitome of shabby chic. Enjoy the delightful cakes, friendly waiters, and non-smoking section out back.

Café Central (Map pp82-3; ☎ 533 37 63; 01, Herrengasse 14) A lot more commercialised than when Herrs Trotsky, Freud and Beethoven drank here, we dare say, but still appealing with vaulted ceilings, palms and baroque architecture.

Noteworthy:

Café Sacher (Map pp82-3; ☎ 514 56-661; 01, Philharmoniker strasse 4) An institution for its world-famous chocolate cake, the Sacher Torte, baked here since 1832. Expensive treat, but well worth the little extra.

Kleines Café (Map pp82-3; 01, Franziskanerplatz 3) Tiny bohemian cafe with wonderful summer seating on Franziskanerplatz.

VIENNA FOR FREE

Not many things in Vienna are free, but at least there are some:

- Stephansdom (p77) – Only the nave is free, but what a nave!
- Schönbrunn Gardens (p77) – Wander the immaculate gardens like an emperor and empress.
- Innere Stadt (centre) – Practically an open-air museum and deserved Unesco-listed site.
- Zentralfriedhof (p80) – One of Europe's finest cemeteries, and burial place to some of Vienna's most celebrated burghers.
- Wien Museum (p77) – Perfect snapshot of Vienna in all its guises; free on Sunday.

Heurigen (Wine Taverns)

Vienna's *Heurigen* are a good way to see another side of the city. Selling 'new' wine produced on the premises, they have a lively atmosphere, especially as the evening progresses. Outside tables and picnic benches are common, as is buffet food.

Heurigen are generally clustered together in the wine-growing suburbs to the north, northeast, south and west of the city. Look for the green wreath or branch hanging over the door that identifies a *Heuriger*. Opening times are approximately 4pm to 11pm, and wine costs less than €2.50 a *Viertel* (250mL).

The *Heurigen* areas of Nussdorf and Heiligenstadt are near the terminus of tram D. In 1817 Beethoven lived in the **Beethovenhaus** (off Map pp78-9; 19, Pfarrplatz 3, Heiligenstadt). There are several *Heurigen* in a row where Cobenzlgasse and Sandgasse meet, of which **Reinprecht** (off

Map pp78-9; ☎ 320 14 71; 19, Cobenzlgasse 22) is the best, even if still rather touristy.

If you don't have time to venture out into the suburbs, you can get a taste of the *Heurigen* experience at **Esterházykeller** (Map pp82-3; ☎ 533 34 82; Haarhof 1; 11am-11pm Mon-Fri, 4-11pm Sat & Sun), a cellar *Heurigen* dating from 1683. Alternatively, try **Zwölf Apostelkeller** (Map pp82-3; ☎ 512 67 77; 01, Sonnenfelsgasse 3), another atmospheric cellar haunt with as many levels as *Dante's Inferno*.

CLUBBING

our pick **Flex** (Map pp82-3; ☎ 533 75 25; www.flex.at; 01, Danube Canal/Augartenbrücke) Time after time this uninhibited shrine to music (it has one of the best sound systems in Europe) puts on great live shows and features the top DJs from Vienna and abroad. Each night is a different theme, with Crazy on Tuesday and London Calling on Wednesday among the most popular.

Roxy (Map pp82-3; www.roxyclub.at; 04, Operngasse 24; Wed-Sun) Often leading the way, or at least keeping pace, with Vienna's progressive clubbing scene. Its tiny dance floor is therefore regularly bursting at the seams. The sounds range from jazz to world music.

Volksgarten (Map pp82-3; ☎ 532 42 41; www.volksgarten.at; 01, Burgring 1) In the middle of the park of the same name, this place is very popular. There's modern dance and an atmospheric 1950s-style salon that was once a former *Walzer Dancing* venue. Friday and Saturday are the big nights, although it's open other evenings, too.

Gay & Lesbian Venues

Rosa Lila Villa (Map pp82-3; ☎ 586 81 50; 06, Linke Wienzeile 102) The leading venue of Vienna's gay scene is this pink-and-purple information centre with a popular bar and restaurant.

Why Not? (Map pp82-3; ☎ 535 11 58; www.why-not.at; 01, Tiefer Graben 22; Fri & Sat) A popular gay bar/disco for like-minded people.

ENTERTAINMENT

Falter (€2.40, in German) and the tourist office's *Vienna Scene* have up-to-date listings.

Cinemas

Burgkino (Map pp82-3; ☎ 587 84 06; 01, Opernring 19) Screens *The Third Man* every Friday evening and Sunday, Tuesday, Wednesday and Thursday afternoons. Seats are cheapest on Monday.

Classical Music

There are no performances in July and August. Ask the tourist office for details of free concerts at the Rathaus or in churches.

The state ticket office, **Bundestheaterkassen** (Map pp82-3; ☎ 514 44-7880; www.bundestheater.at; 01, Goethegasse 1), sells tickets without commission for the Staatsoper and Volksoper. In the hut by the Staatsoper, **Wien Ticket** (Map pp82-3; ☎ 58 885; www.wien-ticket.at, in German; 01, Kärtner Strasse 40) also charges little or no commission for cash sales.

The cheapest deals are the standing-room tickets that go on sale at each venue around an hour before performances. However, you may need to queue three hours before that for major productions.

Staatsoper (State Opera; Map pp82-3; ☎ 513 15 13; www.staatsoper.at; 01, Opernring 2; standing room €2-3.50, seats €7-254) Performances are lavish, formal affairs, where people dress up.

Musikverein (Map pp82-3; ☎ 505 18 90; www.musikverein.at; 01, Bösendorferstrasse 12; standing room €4-6, seats €17-118) The opulent and acoustically perfect (unofficial) home of the Vienna Philharmonic Orchestra. You can buy standing tickets three weeks in advance at the box office to hear this world-class orchestra.

Lipizzaner Museum & Spanish Riding School

The famous Lipizzaner stallions strut their stuff in the **Spanish Riding School** (Map pp82-3; ☎ 533 90 31-0; www.srs.at; 01, Michaelerplatz 1; standing room €20-28, seats €35-165) near the Hofburg. Ask in the adjacent museum about seats. Same-day tickets can be bought for **training sessions** (tickets €12; 10am-noon Tue-Sat Feb-Jun & Sep-Dec).

Vienna Boys' Choir

The Wiener Sängerknaben perform weekly at the **Burgkapelle** (Music Chapel; Map pp82-3; ☎ 533 99 27; whmk@chello.at; 01, Hofburg, Rennweg 1; standing free, seats €5-29; performances 9.15am Sun mid-Sep–Jun). Tickets are available on Friday and from 8.15am Sunday before performances. The group also performs regularly in the Musikverein (above); check www.wsk.at for more information.

SHOPPING

Vienna's main shopping street is **Mariahilfer Strasse** (Map pp82–3), near the MuseumsQuartier, but the best window-shopping to be had is in the back alleyways of the Innere Stadt, where stores selling designer labels and overpriced jewellery are a dime a dozen.

A perfect souvenir from Vienna, which unfortunately won't last long, is the city's favourite sweet, the *Manner Schnitten* (wafers filled with hazelnut cream). Get the real thing from **Manner** (Map pp82-3; ☎ 513 70 18; 01, Stephansplatz 7).

GETTING THERE & AWAY

Air

Vienna is a major hub between Western and Eastern Europe, with flight connections to many major European cities. Check with **Austrian Airlines** (OS; ☎ 051 766 1000; www.aua.com; Vienna Schwechat airport) for schedules.

Boat

Between April and October, fast hydrofoils travel eastwards to Bratislava (one way €16 to €28, return €32 to €48, bike extra €6, 1¼ hours, also Saturday and Sunday March) and Budapest (one way/return €89/109, bike extra €20, 5½ hours) daily. Bookings can be made through **DDSG Blue Danube** (Map pp78-9; ☎ 58 880-0; www.ddsg-blue-danube.at; 02, Handelskai 265).

AUSTRIA

Bus

Eurolines (Map pp78-9; ☎ 798 29 00; 03, Erdbergstrasse 202; 🕑 6.30am-9pm) is the main bus company operating out of Vienna. Most buses, including those destined for Bratislava (one way/return €5/10, one hour), Budapest (one way/return €23/36, three hours), Prague (one way/return €19/35, 4¼ hours) Split (one way/return €41/74, 12½ hours) and Warsaw (one way/return €35/63, 12 hours), leave from Erdbergstrasse, but some buses can be picked up at Südbahnhof train station, or Schwedenplatz or Praterstern underground stations.

Car & Motorcycle

The Gürtel is an outer ring road that joins up with the A22 on the north bank of the Danube and the A23 southeast of town. All the main road routes intersect with this system, including the A1 from Linz and Salzburg, and the A2 from Graz.

Train

International trains leave from Westbahnhof (Map pp78–9) or Südbahnhof (Map pp78–9); Wien-Mitte Bahnhof handles local trains only, and Franz Josefs Bahnhof has local and regional trains.

Westbahnhof has trains to northern and Western Europe, and western Austria. Services to Salzburg (€44, three hours) leave roughly hourly, where a change is normally required if travelling onto Munich (€77, 5½ hours). To Zürich there are two trains during the day (€91, 8¾ hours) and one night train (€91, plus charge for fold-down seat/couchette); Paris is served by two daytime (€216, 12 hours) and three overnight trains (€174, 13 to 15½ hours); all require a change in either Germany or Switzerland. Ten direct trains daily go to Budapest (€34.20, three hours).

Südbahnhof has trains to Italy (including to Rome, via Venice and Florence), Slovakia, the Czech Republic, Hungary, Poland, and southern Austria. Trains go hourly to Bratislava (€14.40, one hour), while five daily head to Prague (from €52, four hours), with two of those continuing to Berlin (€108, nine hours).

For train information, call ☎ 05-17 17.

GETTING AROUND

Underground (U-Bahn), tram, suburban train (S-Bahn) and bus routes are outlined in the free tourist office map.

All advance-purchase tickets must be slotted into the validation machines at the entrance to U-Bahn stations or on trams and buses. Singles cost €1.70 from automatic machines before you board, or €2.20 on board.

Stunden-Netzkarte (daily passes) cost €5.70 (valid 24 hours from first use); three-day passes €14 (valid for 72 hours); weekly passes €14 (valid Monday to Sunday).

You'll need a Visa, MasterCard or JCB credit card, or a Tourist Card available from **Royal Tours** (Map pp82-3; ☎ 710 4606; 01, Herrengasse 1-3; card €2; 🕑 9am-11.30am & 1-6pm) to use Vienna's cheap **city bikes** (☎ 0810-500 500; www.citybikewien.at; 1st hr free, 2nd hr €1, 3rd hr €2, per hr thereafter €4). Check the website for locations.

THE DANUBE VALLEY

Terraced vineyards, ruined castles and medieval towns line the Danube River's most picturesque stretch between Krems and Melk, known locally as the Wachau.

Boats operate from April to October between Krems and Melk, with a handful of services originating in Vienna. Two respectable operators are **DDSG Blue Danube** (Map pp78-9; ☎ 01-58 880-0; www.ddsg-blue-danube.at; 02, Handelskai

265) and **Brandner** (☎ 07433-25 90; www.brandner.at; Ufer 50, Wallsee); both charge around €11 one way for a trip from Krems to Melk. For trips into Germany, contact **Donauschiffahrt Wurk + Köck** (☎ 0732-783607; www.donauschiffahrt.de; Untere Donaulände 1, Linz).

Most operators carry bicycles without charge along these routes.

KREMS AN DER DONAU

☎ 02732 / pop 24,000

Quaint as it is, Krems is unlikely to be more than a stopover on a boat or bike trip through the Danube Valley. The **tourist office** (☎ 82 676; www.tiscover.com/krems; Kloster Und, Undstrasse 6; 9am-6pm Mon-Fri, to 5pm Sat, to 4pm Sun May-Oct, 9am-5pm Mon-Fri Nov-Apr) has information on the region. Riverside camping is available at **ÖAMTC Camping Krems** (☎ 84 455; Wiedengasse 7; camp sites per person & tent €5.50; Easter-Oct) and the central HI **Jugendherberge** (☎ 83 452; Ringstrasse 77; dm from €18.20; Apr-Oct) has basic facilities.

The *Schiffsstation* (boat station) is a 20-minute walk west from the train station along Donaulände. Three buses leave daily from outside the train station to Melk (€6.50, 56 minutes), and frequent trains head in the opposite direction to Vienna (€14, one hour).

MELK

☎ 02752 / pop 5200

Melk's impressive Benedictine monastery, which towers over river and town, is an enduring Wachau landmark of international acclaim.

Walk straight ahead from the train station along Bahnhofstrasse and turn right into Rathausplatz at the bottom of the hill, following the signs to the **tourist office** (☎ 52 307-410; www.tiscover.com/melk; Babenbergerstrasse 1; 9am-noon & 2-6pm Mon-Fri, 10am-noon Sat Apr, 9am-noon & 2-6pm Mon-Fri, 10am-noon & 4-6pm Sat & Sun May, Jun & Sep, 9am-7pm Mon-Sat, 10am-noon & 5-7pm Sun Jul-Aug, 9am-noon & 2-5pm Mon-Fri, 10am-noon Sat Oct).

On a hill overlooking the town is the ornate golden abbey **Stift Melk** (☎ 555 232; www.stiftmelk.at; adult/student €7.70/4.50, with guided tour €9.50/6.30; 9am-5.30pm May-Sep, 9am-4.30pm mid-Mar–Apr & Oct, guided tours only Nov-Mar). Home to monks since the 11th century, the current building was erected in the 18th century after a devastating fire. It's an elaborate example of baroque architecture, most often lauded for its imposing marble hall and beautiful library, but just as unforgettable for the curved terrace connecting these two rooms.

> **GETTING INTO TOWN**
>
> There's a shuttle bus (€2.50, 20 minutes) from the airport to the train station. From here, take tram 3 (€1.70) to the main square, Hauptplatz.

Melk has a good range of accommodation, including tranquil **Camping Melk** (☎ 53 291; Kolomaniau 3; camp sites per person/tent/car €3/3.50/2; Mar-Oct) on the west bank of the town's canal, and the modern HI **Jugendherberge** (☎ 52 681; melk@noejhw.at; Karl Strasse 42; dm €19.90; check-in 4-9pm) 10 minutes' walk from the train station.

For a little more luxury, try **Gasthof Goldener Stern** (☎ 52 214; www.sternmelk.at; Sterngasse 17; s/d from €35/42; P), which sports individually decorated rooms with more than a touch of romance about them.

Pasta e Pizza (☎ 53 686; Jakob Prandtauerstrasse 4; pizzas €7-10) offers heaps of pizza and pasta dishes in cheerful environs. Self-caterers should stock up at the **Spar supermarket** (Rathausplatz 9).

Boats leave from the canal by Pionierstrasse, 400m behind the monastery. There are hourly direct trains to Vienna's Westbahnhof (€16.10, 1¼ hours) daily.

LINZ

☎ 0732 / pop 189,000

In Linz beginnt's (it begins in Linz) goes the Austrian saying, but at first glance it's hard to know what began here. On closer inspection, however, it soon becomes clear. Linz is blessed with a leading-edge cyber centre and world-class contemporary-art gallery, both signs that the country's technological industry got its kick-start in the Upper Austrian capital. And even though Linz is essentially industrial by nature, there's plenty of culture to contend with, so much so that it gained the title of European Capital of Culture 2009.

Information

Ars Electronica Center (☎ 72 720; www.aec.at; Hauptstrasse 2; 9am-5pm Wed-Fri, 10am-6pm Sat & Sun) Offers free internet access.

Tourist office (☎ 7070-1777; www.linz.at; Hauptplatz 1; 8am-7pm Mon-Fri, 10am-7pm Sat & Sun May-Oct, 8am-6pm Mon-Fri, 10am-6pm Sat & Sun Nov-Apr) Has the Linz City Ticket Premium (€20), which offers free public transport, sightseeing discounts and a meal valued at €10.

Book your stay at lonelyplanet.com/hotels

Sights & Activities

Architecturally eye-catching and artistically impressive, the riverside **Lentos Kunstmuseum Linz** (☎ 7070 3614; www.lentos.at, in German; Ernst Koref Promenade 1; adult/concession €6.50/4.50; ⏰ 10am-6pm, till 9pm Thu) is a must-see. Built a little like an asymmetric tray table, with legs on either side, the building looks particularly spectacular at night when it's lit up. Behind its partially reflective glass facade lie works by artists such as Klimt, Schiele, Picasso, Kokoschka, Matisse, Haring and Warhol.

Across the Danube is the **Ars Electronica Center** (☎ 72 72-0; www.aec.at; Hauptstrasse 2; adult/student €6/3; ⏰ 9am-5pm Wed-Fri, 10am-6pm Sat & Sun), the city's centre for technological wizardry. Spend the afternoon strapped into a flight simulator over Linz, or use 'Gulliver's World' to rearrange the world a mountain range at a time.

Festivals & Events

Linz has several famous festivals, held in September:

Ars Electronica Festival (www.aec.at) This is a celebration of weird and wonderful technological art and computer music.

Bruckner Fest (www.brucknerhaus.at) This highbrow classical music festival pays homage to native Linz son Bruckner.

Sleeping

Camping Linz (☎ 305 314; www.camping-linz.at; Wiener Bundesstrasse 937; per adult/camp site €5/10; ⏰ Apr-Oct) Camping ground southeast of town near the Pichlinger lake.

Jugendgästehaus (☎ 664 434; www.oejhv.or.at; Stanglhofweg 3; dm/s/d €19.50/29.50/44; P ⊠) This modern and comfortable hostel offers half- and full-board options. Its only drawback is its location 1.5km west of the city centre; board bus 17, 19 or 27 to get there.

Wilder Mann (☎ 656 078; wilder-mann@aon.at; Goethestrasse 14; s/d with shared bathroom €25/42, with private bathroom €30/50; P ⊠) Despite first impressions, rooms at this simple place are reasonably comfy and the bathrooms clean. Try to avoid the top floor, where frosted-glass door panels let in hall light. Breakfast is an extra €6.

Eating & Drinking

Café Traximayr (☎ 773 353; Promenadestrasse 16; snacks from €5; ⏰ 8am-10pm Mon-Fri, 8am-8pm Sat, 9am-6pm Sun) An elegant coffee house, with only a few snooker tables breaking up the formal environment of white walls, marble, mirrors and chandeliers. Try the Linzer torte – this heavy, nutty-tasting sponge filled with strawberry jam isn't on the menu but it is on the cake trolley, so just ask.

p'aa (☎ 776 461; Altstadt 28; mains €8-12; ⏰ Mon-Sat) The menu here is an eclectic mix of Tibetan, Indian and Mexican cuisine, most of which is vegetarian. Sit on the cobblestones outside or inside under low arched ceilings.

Stiegelbräu zum Klosterhof (Landstrasse 30; mains €10-18) Klosterhof has earned a fine gastronomic reputation with its Austrian classics and seasonal specialities. In summer the huge beer garden is a favourite of half the town.

Getting There & Around

Ryanair (www.ryanair.com) flies daily from London Stansted to **Linz airport** (www.flughafen-linz.at). Linz is halfway between Salzburg (€20.70 by train) and Vienna (€29.10), both between 1¼ and two hours away.

Around the city, it's €0.80 per bus journey up to four stops, €1.70 for anything over that, and €3.40 for a day card, or €3 for a day card for the train. Some bus services stop early evening.

THE SOUTH

Austria's two main southern states, Styria (Steiermark) and Carinthia (Kärnten), often feel worlds apart from the rest of the country, both in climate and attitude. Styria is a blissful amalgamation of genteel architecture, rolling green hills, vine-covered slopes and soaring mountains. Its capital, Graz, is one of Austria's most attractive cities.

A jet-setting, fashion-conscious crowd heads to sun-drenched Carinthia for summer holidays. The region (right on the border with Italy) exudes an atmosphere that's as close to Mediterranean as this staunch country gets.

GRAZ

☎ 0316 / pop 248,000

The Styrian capital of Graz wins the hearts and minds of locals and tourists alike for a plethora of reasons. It exudes a laid-back, almost Mediterranean, atmosphere, sports a thumping, student-fuelled nightlife, contains a mix of modern architectural gems

AUSTRIA

GETTING INTO TOWN

An hourly train (€1.70) runs between the airport and the train station. Trams 3 and 6 connect the train station with the Hauptplatz.

and Renaissance flourishes, and has a long list of captivating museums. Pop in for a visit and Graz is sure to leave an indelible impression.

Orientation

Graz is dominated by its *Schlossberg* (castle hill) looming above the city centre. The River Mur runs in a north–south path in front (west) of the hill, separating the city centre from the main train station (Hauptbahnhof), 1km west of the central Hauptplatz (square). Several streets radiate from Hauptplaz, including cafe-lined Sporgasse and the primary pedestrian thoroughfare, Herrengasse. The latter leads to Jakominiplatz, a major transport hub.

Information

Graz Tourismus (☎ 80 75-0; www.graztourismus.at; Herrengasse 16; ⏲ 10am-5pm Mon-Fri, 10am-4pm Sat & Sun Jan-Mar & Nov, 10am-6pm Mon-Sat, 10am-4pm Sun Apr-Jun, Sep-Oct & Dec, 10am-7pm Mon-Fri, 10am-6pm Sat & Sun Jul-Aug) Also has an information stand and terminal in the train station (open 8.30am to 5pm Monday to Saturday), which has a free hotline to the main tourist office.

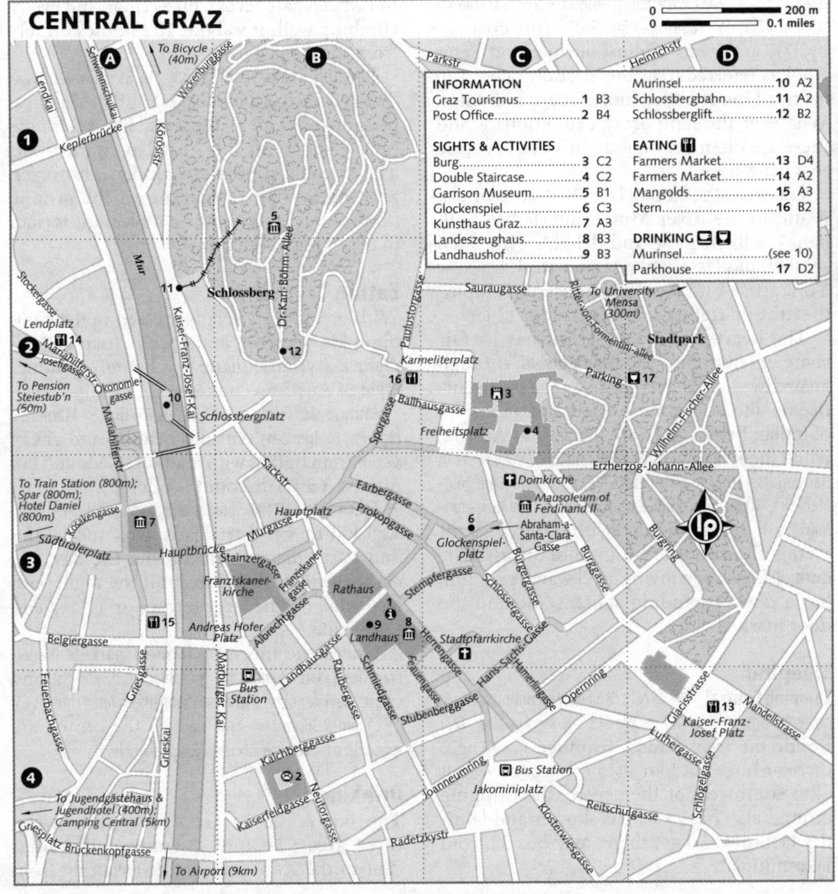

 Book your stay at lonelyplanet.com/hotels

High Speed Internet-Selfstore (Herrengasse 3; per hr €3; 7am-1pm) Also offers wi-fi connection.

Sights & Activities

Graz is a city easily enjoyed by simply wandering aimlessly, discovering its plethora of museums, galleries, grandiose architecture, churches and unusual surprises. Climb the 260 steps up the **Schlossberg** for an overview of the city and explore what remains of its fortress. This includes the medieval **clock tower**, plus a **bell tower**, **bastion** and **garrison museum** (827 348; admission €1; 10am-4pm Tue-Sun). Alternatively, take the glass **Schlossberglift** (€0.60), hewn through the hill, or the **Schlossbergbahn** funicular railway (€1.70; free with 24-hour public ticket).

From this vantage point, you can't help but notice the striking bubble-shaped **Kunsthaus Graz** (8017 9200; www.kunsthausgraz.at; Lendkai 1; adult/student €7/3; 10am-6pm Tue-Sun). This creation by UK architects Colin Fournier and Peter Cook is referred to as the 'friendly alien' and is one of Europe's leading modern buildings. Whatever the temporary exhibitions – and these are often very good – it's the structure that's the star.

Likewise, the **Murinsel** (24hr), an artificial island in the River Mur connected to both banks, will surprise and delight. This open seashell of glass, concrete and steel, by New York artist Vito Acconic, houses an amphitheatre and trendy cafe-bar in aqua blue.

The heart of the Old Town has its fair share of triumphs. The **Landhaushof**, through an archway on Herrengasse by the tourist office, is one of the most celebrated examples of Italian Renaissance architecture in Austria, while the nearby **Landeszeughaus** (8017 9810; Herrengasse 16; adult/student €7/3; 10am-6pm mid-Mar–Oct, 10am-5pm Mon-Sat, 10am-4pm Sun Nov–mid-Mar) will leave anyone with even a slight medieval-armour fetish in pure ecstasy. The **Burg** (Hofgasse), occupying an elevated position, has a double-winding staircase behind the door marked 'Stiege III'.

Sleeping

Camping Central (0676-378 51 02; Martinhofstrasse 3; powered camp sites for 1/2 people €13/20; Apr-Nov;) Beside the tree-shaded, trimmed lawn here there's a huge outdoor swimming pool. About 6km southwest of the centre, the camping ground also has excellent shower and laundry facilities. To get there, take bus 32 from Jakominiplatz.

SPLURGE

our pick **Hotel Daniel** (711 080; www.hoteldaniel.com; Europlatz 1; r €59-79; P) Daniel may look like just another ugly train-station hotel from the outside, but inside it's an immaculate shrine to modern design and living. Rooms come in 'Smart' and 'Loggia': both are bedecked with clean, minimalist furniture and fittings; however, the latter are larger and come with balcony. Vespas are available to guests for €15 per day.

Jugendgästehaus & Jugendhotel (708 3-210; www.jfgh.at; Idlhofgasse 74; dm/s/d €22/33/52) Ultra-modern and comfortable, with en suite rooms, spacious reception/restaurant areas, full wheelchair access, bike rental, and even a climbing wall. It's about 10 minutes on foot from the train station.

Pension Steierstub'n (716 855; www.pension-graz.at; Lendplatz 8; s/d/tr from €41/74/111) This neat pension looks for all the world like a *Gästhaus* (guest house) in the Austrian countryside. The sizeable rooms are modern, however, and the Styrian restaurant on the ground floor serves tasty food on a pleasant terrace overlooking Lendplatz.

Eating

With green, leafy salads dressed in delicious pumpkin-seed oil, and *Pfand'l* (pan-grilled) dishes, Styrian cuisine is a lighter, healthier style of Austrian cooking.

Mangolds (Griesgasse 11; meals €5-10; 11am-7pm Mon-Fri, to 4pm Sat) An ultrahealthy and cheap vegetarian buffet, with loads of salads and hot dishes. A 30% discount is offered after 5pm.

Stern (818 400; Sporgasse 38; mains €5-14; 9am-3am) Fill up on fine salads, wok specialities and pasta dishes here during the day and early evening, then finish off the night with a cocktail on the large terrace or a boogie to DJs inside.

Graz's two morning **farmers markets** (Kaiser-Franz-Josef Platz & Lendplatz; 4.30am-1pm Mon-Sat) and main university's **Mensa** (Sonnenfelsplatz 1; menus €5; 11am-2.30pm Mon-Fri), east of the centre, are excellent choices for cheap meals.

Drinking

The bar scene in Graz is split between three areas; around the university; adjacent to the Kunsthaus; and stretching from

Karmeliterplatz to Prokopgasse in the Old Town.

Murinsel (☎ 818 669) You'll never again drink anywhere quite like the Murinsel, so at least start the evening in this shimmering, fluorescent-lit platform in the middle of the river. There are DJs some evenings.

Parkhouse (☎ 827 434; Stadtpark 2; 11am-4am) Join the crowd at this atmospheric and friendly place in the city park if you're looking to party minus any type of pretentious vibe.

Getting There & Around

Ryanair (www.ryanair.com) has regular flights from London Stansted and Barcelona to **Graz airport** (☎ 290 20; www.flughafen-graz.at), while **Intersky** (www.intersky.biz) connects the city with Berlin and Friedrichshafen (in Germany) six times a week, and **TUIfly** (www.tuifly.com) with Cologne five times. Direct IC trains to destination include Salzburg (€44.20, four hours), Vienna (€31.40, 2¾ hours), Ljubljana (€34, four hours) and Budapest via Szombathely (€47, 5¾ hours).

Public transport tickets (single/daily passes €1.70/3.70) cover trams, buses and the Schlossbergbahn.

KLAGENFURT

☎ 0463 / pop 92,000

This sunny provincial capital on the water makes a handy base for exploring the Wörthersee's lakeside villages and elegant medieval towns to the north.

The **tourist office** (☎ 537 22 23; www.klagenfurt-tourismus.at; Rathaus, Neuer Platz; 8am-6pm Mon-Fri, 10am-5pm Sat, 10am-3pm Sun) is in the centre, about 1km north of the train station. Walk down Bahnhofstrasse and turn left into Paradiesergasse to get there, or take bus 40 or 41 to Heiligengeistplatz, just around the corner from Neuer Platz. For the Wörthersee, take bus 10, 11, 12, 20, 21 or 22, all of which depart from Heiligengeistplatz.

The **Wörthersee**, 4km west of the city centre, is one of the region's warmer lakes, thanks to subterranean thermal springs: the average water temperature between June and September is 21°C (69°F). Events from go-cart rallies to avant-garde festivals of tattoo and body painting ensure you'll never be left without something to see. The 50km **cycle path** around the lake is a fabulous way to explore the area. There is a *Fahrad Verleih* (bike hire) scheme from May to September; hire a standard bicycle at one of several outlets around the lake or the tourist office and return it at any other outlet (three hours/24 hours/one week €6/10/40). Mountain bikes (€12/19/85) are also available.

Hotels in the city centre are unexpectedly expensive, so budget travellers usually stay near the lake. When you check into your accommodation in Klagenfurt, ask for a copy of your *Gästekarte* (guest card), which entitles you to a range of discounts on local attractions and on public transport. The **Jugendherberge** (☎ 230 020; jgh.klagenfurt@oejhv.or.at; Neckheimgasse 6; dm/r €19.90/27.90; P) is a large, modern salmon-shaded hostel close to the university and within walking distance to the lake.

There's a **University Mensa** (Universitätsstrasse 90; mains from €5; 11am-2.30pm Mon-Fri) near the hostel. In town, you can get hot meals from the stalls in the **Benediktinerplatz market** (meals from €4) or **Zum Augustin** (☎ 513 992; Pfarrhofgasse 2; mains €8-18), a smoky brewery that makes its own beer. It is popular with the after-work crowd, serves a decent range of regional food and has a pleasant cobblestone patio.

Klagenfurt airport (☎ 41 500; www.klagenfurt-airport.com) is served by **Ryanair** (www.ryanair.com) from London Stansted and Frankfurt am Main, and **TUIfly** (www.tuifly.com) from Berlin, Cologne, Hamburg and Hannover. Trains to Graz (€33, 2½ to 3½ hours) go via Bruck an der Mur, departing roughly every two hours. Trains to western Austria, Italy and Germany go via Villach (€7.80, 30 minutes).

Bus drivers sell single tickets (€1.70), while daily/weekly passes cost €4/13. To the airport, take bus 40 to Annabichl and change to bus 45. Bikes can be hired from **Zweirad Impulse** (☎ 516 310; 24hr hire €10).

SALZBURG

☎ 0662 / pop 149,000

The joke 'if it's baroque, don't fix it' is a perfect maxim for Salzburg; the tranquil Old Town burrowed in below steep hills looks as much as it did when Mozart lived here 250 years ago. Its cobbled streets are overshadowed by ornate 17th-century buildings, which are in turn dominated by the medieval Hohensalzburg fortress from high above. Across the fast-flowing Salzach River rests the baroque Schloss Mirabell, surrounded by gorgeous manicured gardens.

If this doesn't whet your appetite, then bypass the grandeur and head straight for kitsch-country by joining a tour of *The Sound of Music* film locations.

ORIENTATION

The pedestrianised Old Town, with most attractions, is south of the Salzach River. On the north bank is the new town plus Mozart's Wohnhaus and Schloss Mirabell.

INFORMATION

Salzburg Internet Café (Gstättengasse 3; per hr €2; ⌚ 10am-10pm) Cheap internet access and calls.

> **GETTING INTO TOWN**
>
> Bus 2 will get you from Salzburg airport to the train station. It's about a 10-minute walk from the train station into town; buses 3 and 5 make the journey in five minutes.

Main Tourist Office (☎ information 88-987 330, hotel reservations 88-987 314; www.salzburg.info; Mozartplatz 5; ⌚ 9am-6pm Mon-Sat Jan-Apr & mid-Oct–Nov, 9am-7pm May–mid-Oct & Dec) Sells the Salzburg Card (€21/29/34 for 24/48/72 hours), which provides free museum entry and public transport, and offers various reductions. Also has a counter at the train station.

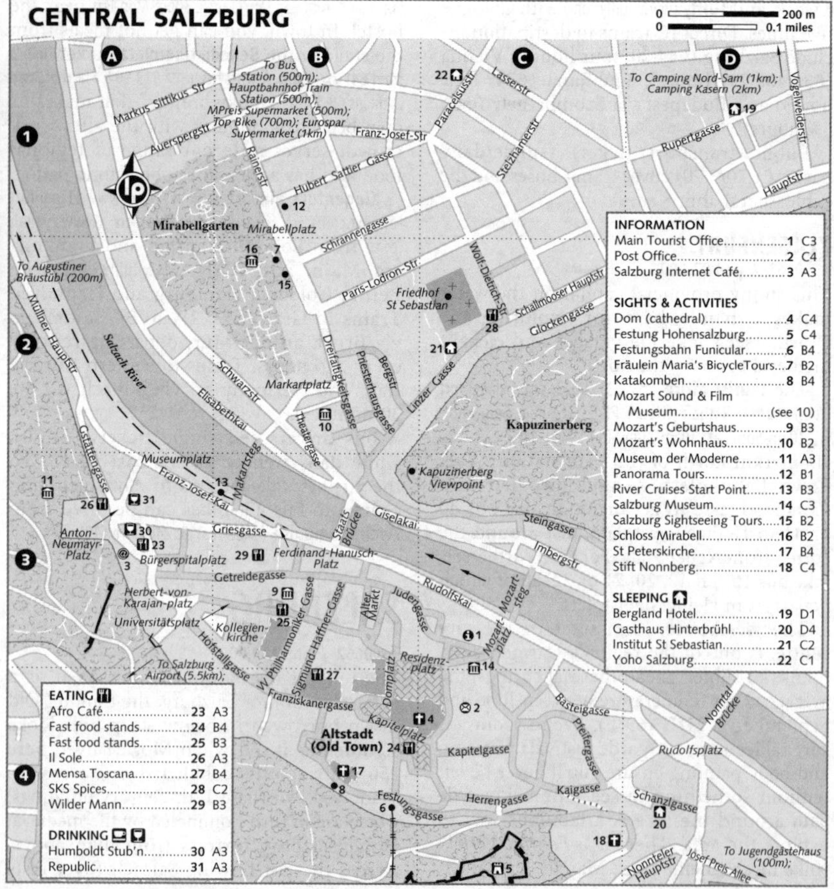

SIGHTS & ACTIVITIES

A Unesco World Heritage site, Salzburg's Old Town is entrancing both at ground level and from the hills above.

Residenzplatz is a good starting point for exploration. The **Dom** (cathedral; Domplatz; admission free; 6.30am-5pm Mon-Sat, 8am-5pm Sun), just to the south, has bronze doors symbolising faith, hope and charity, and excavations of a medieval cathedral and Roman remains (adult/student €2.50/1.50; open 9am to 5pm). From the cathedral, head west along Franziskanergasse and turn left into a courtyard for **St Peterskirche** (St Peter Bezirk 1/2; admission free; 8am-noon & 2.30-6.30pm). Among the lovingly tended graves in this abbey's grounds is the entrance to the **Katakomben** (Catacombs; adult/student €1/0.60; 10.30am-5pm May-Sep, 10.30am-3.30pm Wed & Thu, 10.30am-4pm Fri-Sun Oct-Apr). The **Stift Nonnberg** (Nonnberg Abbey) is back east of the Festung Hohensalzburg and where *The Sound of Music* first finds Maria.

Festung Hohensalzburg

Castle-fortress **Festung Hohensalzburg** (☎ 842430-11; www.salzburg-burgen.at; Mönchsberg 34; adult/student €10/9.10; 9am-7pm May-Sep, to 5pm Oct-Apr), built in 1077, was home to many archbishop-princes (who ruled Salzburg from AD 798). Inside are the impressively ornate staterooms, torture chambers and two museums.

It takes 15 minutes to walk up the hill to the fortress, or you can catch the funicular **Festungsbahn** (Festungsgasse 4; included in castle ticket, otherwise 1 way/return €2.10/3.40; 9am-10pm May-Aug, to 9pm Sep, to 5pm Oct-Apr).

Schloss Mirabell

The formal gardens, with their tulips, crocuses and Greek statues, are the main drawcard at this palace, built by the prince-archbishop Wolf Dietrich for his mistress in 1606. Standing at the western end and looking east towards the fortress gives you an iconic Salzburg view. Having featured in *The Sound of Music*, the gardens are now popular for weddings and open-air concerts (normally at 10.30am and 8.30pm May to August).

Museums

Although Mozart is a major Salzburg attraction, the man himself couldn't wait to leave. Consequently, **Mozart's Geburtshaus** (birthplace; ☎ 844 313; www.mozarteum.at; Getreidegasse 9; adult/student €6.50/5.50; 9am-6pm Sep-Jun, to 7pm Jul & Aug, last entry 30min before closing) and his **Wohnhaus** (residence; ☎ 874 227; Makartplatz 8; adult/student €6.50/5.50; 9am-6pm Sep-Jun, to 7pm Jul & Aug, last entry 30min before closing) cover only his early years before he left town in 1780 at 24 years of age. A combined ticket to both houses is €10 (students and seniors €8). The more extensive Wohnhaus houses the **Mozart Sound and Film Museum** (admission free; 9am-1pm Mon, Tue & Fri, 1-5pm Wed & Thu).

The **Salzburg Museum** (☎ 620 808-700; www.salzburgmuseum.at, in German; Mozartplatz 1; Tue-Sat adult/student €7/6, Sun €5.50/4.50; 9am-5pm Tue-Sun, 9am-8pm Thu, also 9am-5pm Mon Jul, Aug & Dec) covers the city and its favourite citizens in an interactive way, while the **Museum der Moderne** (☎ 842 220-403; www.museumdermoderne.at; Mönchsberg; adult/student €8/6; 10am-6pm Tue-Sun, to 9pm Wed) adds a further contemporary touch to historic Salzburg with rotating modern art shows.

TOURS

Sound of Music Tours

How much fun you have on these depends on entering into the kitsch attitude necessary. Tours take three to four hours, mostly in neighbouring Salzkammergut.

Fräulein Maria's Bicycle Tours (☎ 0650 342 62 97; www.mariasbicycletours.com; Mirabellplatz; adult €22; 9.30am May-Sep) Near main entrance to Schloss Mirabell.

Panorama Tours (☎ 874 029; www.panoramatours.com; Mirabellplatz; adult €37; 9.30am & 2pm)

Salzburg Sightseeing Tours (☎ 881 616; www.salzburg-sightseeingtours.at; Mirabellplatz; adult €37; 9.30am & 2pm)

Boat Tours

In summer, **Salzburg Schiffahrt** (☎ 825 769-12; www.salzburgschifffahrt.at) operates 40-minute round-trip river cruises (€13) and trips to **Schloss Hellbrunn** (€16; 12.45pm Apr-Sep, 10.45am & 12.45pm Jul & Aug). Boats leave from the city side of the Makart Bridge at the Salzach Insel boat landing.

FESTIVALS & EVENTS

The famous **Salzburg Festival** (www.salzburgfestival.at) of classical music is held from late July to late August. Book online well in advance if you want cheap tickets.

SLEEPING

Camping Kasern (☎ 450 576; www.camping-kasern-salzburg.com; Carl Zuckmayer Strasse 4; camp sites per adult/

car/tent €6/5/5, bungalow tents per person €10; Apr-Oct;) Just north of the A1 Nord exit.

Camping Nord-Sam (660 494; www.camping-nord-sam.com; Samstrasse 22a; camp sites per adult/car & tent €7.50/10; Easter & mid-Apr–Sep) Slightly closer to the city. Has a pool, shop and bike rental.

International Youth Hotel (YoHo; 879 649; www.yoho.at; Paracelsusstrasse 9; dm with shared bathroom from €17, s/d/tr €29/44/60;) YoHo appeals for its lively bar scene, cheap beer, friendly staff, regular events, and daily screenings of *The Sound of Music*. Book ahead on its website; phone reservations are accepted only one day in advance. Rooms were undergoing renovation at the time of research, but expect them to be clean and spartan.

Jugendgästehaus (842 670; salzburg@jfgh.at; Josef Preis Allee 18; dm/d from €18.90/30.90; check-in from 11am, access to rooms from 1pm;) Lots of Austrians, families and backpackers stay at this comfy HI hostel. The eight-bed dorms feel a bit like boarding school, but the en suite four-bed dorms and doubles on the floors above could belong to a nice budget hotel. There's a small cafe on site and bike rental for €9.50 per day.

Institut St Sebastian (871 386; www.st-sebastian-salzburg.at; Linzer Gasse 41; dm €19, s/d with shared bathroom €32/51, with private bathroom €39.50/64;) Just a few minutes' walk from the bridge, through the gate marked 'Feuerwache Bruderhof', on Linzer Gasse. Don't expect much of a social atmosphere, but (aside from the church bells) you'll be guaranteed of some peace and quiet. There is a roof terrace and kitchen for guest use.

Gasthaus Hinterbrühl (846 798; www.fam-wagner.at; Schanzlgasse 12; s/d €42/58) This small guest house may be a bit frayed around the edges, but it's central, cheap, and can trace its history back to the 14th century. Room 14, with private bathroom and balcony, is the best.

Bergland Hotel (872 318; www.berglandhotel.at; Rupertgasse 15; s/d/tr/f €65/95/125/140;) Bergland is an excellent midrange hotel with comfy rooms coloured in warm hues. It's about a 15-minute walk from the Old Town, or hire a bike for €6.

EATING

Mensa Toscana (Sigmund-Haffner-Gasse 11; meals €4.10-4.80; 8.30am-5pm Mon-Thu, to 3pm Fri) University *Mensa* in the heart of the Old Town.

SKS Spices (Wolf-Dietrich-Strasse 1; mains €6) If you're into healthy eating, don't pass over this tiny eatery that specialises in vegan and vegetarian food from the Indian subcontinent.

Wilder Mann (841 787; Getreidegasse 20; mains €8-11; Mon-Sat) Traditional Austrian food in a friendly, bustling environment, located in the passageway off Getreidegasse. Tables, both inside and out, are often so packed it's almost impossible not to get chatting with fellow diners.

Il Sole (Gstättengasse 15; mains €6-15) Fill up on tasty pasta dishes and wood-fired pizzas at Il Sole, a small trattoria with a lively buzz and superfriendly staff.

our pick **Afro Cafe** (844 888; Bürgerspitalplatz 5; mains €10-20; Mon-Sat) This vibrant, multicoloured restaurant-cafe-bar is bedecked with retro furniture, palm trees and junk art, and its full menu features the likes of Pemba Island prawns and ostrich kebabs. A delightful, unpretentious eatery.

There are market stalls and fast-food stands on Universitätsplatz and Kapitelplatz. A **Eurospar supermarket** (Mon-Sat) is opposite the train station.

DRINKING

On weekend evenings, the crowds stream along Rudolfskai, Salzburg's most famous stretch of bars, clubs, Irish pubs and discos. However, most punters are barely out of, or still in, their teens.

Augustiner Bräustübl (431 246; Augustinergasse 4-6; 3-11pm Mon-Fri, 2.30-11pm Sat & Sun) Known locally as Müllnerbräu (after its neighbourhood), this hillside complex of beer halls and gardens is not to be missed. The local monks' brew keeps the huge crowd of up to 2800 humming.

Humboldt Stub'n (843 171; Gstättengasse 4-6) Perennial favourite with students – particularly on Wednesday nights when beers are €2.50. The decor is particularly wacky, featuring cartoons and purple antelope horns.

Republic (841 613; Anton Neumayr Platz 2) A hip, American bar-brasserie which features regular club nights.

GETTING THERE & AWAY

Salzburg's **airport** (85 80-0; www.salzburg-airport.com) receives **Ryanair** (www.ryanair.com) flights from London Stansted and Dublin.

Fast trains leave for Vienna (€44, three hours) via Linz (€20.70, 1¼ hours) hourly. The express service to Klagenfurt (€33, 3¼ hours) goes via Villach. The quickest way to

AUSTRIA

Innsbruck (€35.20, two hours) is by the 'corridor' train through Germany via Kufstein. There are trains every hour or so to Munich (€28, two hours).

Services to the Salzkammergut region leave from just to the left of the main train-station exit. Destinations include Bad Ischl (€8.70, 1½ hours) and St Wolfgang (€7.90, 1½ hours; change normally required at Strobl). There are timetable boards at each departure point and a bus information office in the train station.

GETTING AROUND

Bus drivers sell singles for €1.70. Other tickets, including day passes (€4.20), must be bought from the automatic machines at major stops or *Tabak* (tobacco) shops.

Top Bike (☎ 0676-476 72 59; www.topbike.at; 2hr/4hr/day €6/10/15, 20% discount with all train tickets) rents bikes from just outside the train station.

AROUND SALZBURG

HELLBRUNN

Ingenious trick fountains are the highlight at the 17th-century **Schloss Hellbrunn** (☎ 820 372-0; www.hellbrunn.at; Fürstenweg 37; adult/student €8.50/6; 9am-10pm Jul-Aug, to 5.30pm May, Jun & Sep, to 4.30pm Mar, Apr & Oct), so expect to get wet! Admission includes a palace tour; other parts of the garden (without fountains) are open year-round and free to visit.

City bus 25 runs to Hellbrunn every 30 minutes from Salzburg's main train station, via Rudolfskai in the Old Town. Salzburg tickets are valid. You can also catch a boat (see p93).

WERFEN

☎ 06468 / pop 3000

The world's largest accessible ice caves, the **Eisriesenwelt Höhle** (Giant Ice Caves; ☎ 56 48; www.eisriesenwelt.at; adult/concession with cable car ride up €19/17, without cable car €8.50/7.50; 9am-4.30pm Jul-Aug, to 3.30pm May-Jun & Sep-Oct) houses elaborate and beautiful ice formations. Take warm clothes as it gets cold during the 75-minute tour. Well below the caves is the **Hohenwerfen Fortress** (☎ 76 03; adult/student €13/7; 9am-6pm Jul-Aug, 9am-5pm May-Jun & Sep, 9.30am-4.30pm Apr, Oct & Nov, closed Mon Apr), a formidable edifice originally dating from 1077.

The **tourist office** (☎ 53 88; www.werfen.at; Markt 24; 9am-7pm Mon-Fri, 5-7pm Sat mid-Jul–mid-Aug, 9am-5pm Mon-Fri mid-Aug–mid-Jul) can provide further details.

Werfen can be reached from Salzburg by Hwy 10 or by train (€8.60, 50 minutes). A minibus (return €5.80) from the train station leads to the cave car park, where you can walk to the cable car (return €10.50).

SALZKAMMERGUT

The Salzkammergut is Austria's Lakes District. An idyllic spot for hiking, water sports and even winter skiing, it boasts salt mines (for which it's named), ice caves, mountains and more than 80 lakes.

Bad Ischl is the region's transport hub, but Hallstatt is its true jewel. For info, visit **Salzkammergut Touristik** (☎ 24 000-0; www.salzkammergut.co.at; Götzstrasse 12, Bad Ischl; 9am-8pm); enquire about the Salzkammergut Card (€4.90, available May to October), which provides a 25% discount on sights, ferries, cable cars and some buses.

HALLSTATT

☎ 06134 / pop 900

The somewhat touristy village of Hallstatt, now a Unesco World Heritage site, has been inhabited for millennia. Its pastel-hued homes cling precariously to a tiny bit of land between mountain and shore, and make perfect photo fodder.

Orientation & Information

Seestrasse is the main street. Turn left from the ferry to reach the **tourist office** (☎ 82 08; www.hallstatt.net; Seestrasse 169; 9am-noon & 2-5pm Mon-Fri year-round, 9am-5pm Mon-Fri, 10am-5pm Sat Jul-Aug). The **post office** (Seestrasse 160), a couple of doors away, exchanges money.

Sights & Activities

Unmissable is the macabre **Beinhaus** (Bone House; ☎ 82 79; Kirchenweg 40; admission €1.50; 10am-6pm 1 May-27 Oct) near the village parish church; it contains rows of neatly stacked skulls painted with flowery designs and the names of their former owners. These human remains have been exhumed from the too-small graveyard since 1600 in a practice that recalls the old Celtic pagan custom of mass burial. The last skull in the collection was added as recently as 1995.

Salt mining was Hallstatt's principal activity for millennia, and a **funicular** (one way/

Book your stay at lonelyplanet.com/hotels

return adult €6/10, student €4/6) goes uphill to the **Salzbergwerk** (Saltworks; ☎ 06132-200 2400; adult/student €16/10; 9am-4.30pm late Apr–mid-Sep, 9am-3.30pm mid-Sep–end Sep, 9.30am-3pm Oct). There are two scenic hiking trails from here; ask the tourist office for details.

At nearby **Obertraun** are the intriguing **Dachstein Rieseneishöhle** (Giant Ice Caves; ☎ 06131-53 10; www.dachsteinwelterbe.at; cable car return plus 2 caves €29.30, cable car return plus 1 cave €24.20, 2 caves only €14.90, 1 cave only €9.80; May-late Oct, tours 9.20am-4pm), including the arch-ceiling, stone **Mammoth Cave**.

Sleeping & Eating

Some private rooms are available during the busiest months of July and August only; others require a minimum three-night stay. The tourist office will telephone around for you without charge.

Campingplatz Krausner-Höll (☎ 83 22; www.camping.hallstatt.net, in German; Lahnstrasse 7; per adult/car/tent €7/3/4; 15 Apr-15 Oct;) This camping ground is conveniently located south of the town centre.

Gasthaus zur Mühle (☎ 83 18; toeroe.f@magnet.at; Kirchenweg 36; dm €13) On the Hallstatt hillside and overlooking the lake, this place is popular with independent travellers. Dorms are rather basic.

Gasthof Hallberg (☎ 82 86; www.pension-hallberg.at.tf; Seestrasse 113; s/d from €40/70;) Hallberg is an excellent-value guest house. The best rooms are light and airy, furnished with pale wood and boast superb lake views on both sides.

Gasthaus zur Mühle (mains €6-12) does a fine take on pastas, pizzas and Austrian dishes, while **Bräu Gasthof** (☎ 82 21; Seestrasse 120; mains €8-15; May-Oct) serves hearty local fare in vaulted rooms or on tables by the lake.

Getting There & Away

There are five buses per day between Hallstatt and Bad Ischl (€4.50, 30 minutes); you get off at 'Lahn', just south of the road tunnel. Up to 12 trains a day service the village from Bad Ischl (€4.50, 30 minutes). The train station is across the lake from the village, but the ferry captain is nice enough to wait for trains to arrive before making the short crossing (€2). Though trains run later, the last ferry departs the train station at 6.29pm (leaving Hallstatt at 6.15pm).

TIROL

With converging mountain ranges behind lofty pastures and tranquil meadows, Tirol (also Tyrol) captures a quintessential Alpine panoramic view. Occupying a central position is Innsbruck, the region's jewel, while in the northeast and southwest are superb ski resorts. In the southeast, separated somewhat from the main state since part of South Tirol was ceded to Italy at the end of WWI, lies the protected natural landscape of the Hohe Tauern National Park. The latter is home to 30 peaks over 3000m, including the country's highest, the Grossglockner (3797m).

INNSBRUCK

☎ 0512 / pop 118,000

Tirol's capital is a sight to behold. Majestic snowcapped mountains dominate your view everywhere you look and its centre is graced with an authentic medieval *Altstadt* (Old Town) made up of narrow, cobbled streets. Add to this inventive, contemporary architecture and a vibrant, student-driven nightlife, and you have a city well worth visiting.

Orientation

Innsbruck lies in the valley of the River Inn, scenically squeezed between the northern chain of the Alps and the Tuxer mountain range to the south. The town centre is compact, with the Hauptbahnhof only a 10-minute walk from the pedestrian-only, Old Town centre.

Information

Bubble Point Waschsalon (☎ 565 007; Brixner Strasse 1; per load €4, internet access per hr €6) Internet cafe and laundrette combined.

Innsbruck Information (☎ 53 56, hotel reservations 562 00; www.innsbruck.info; Burggraben 3; 9am-6pm Apr-Oct, 8am-6pm Nov-Mar) Main tourist information office.

Tourist counter (Train station lower concourse, 9am-7pm) At the Hauptbahnhof.

Sights

OLD TOWN

The best thing to do among the warren of streets and covered walkways in Innsbruck's medieval town is simply to wander around

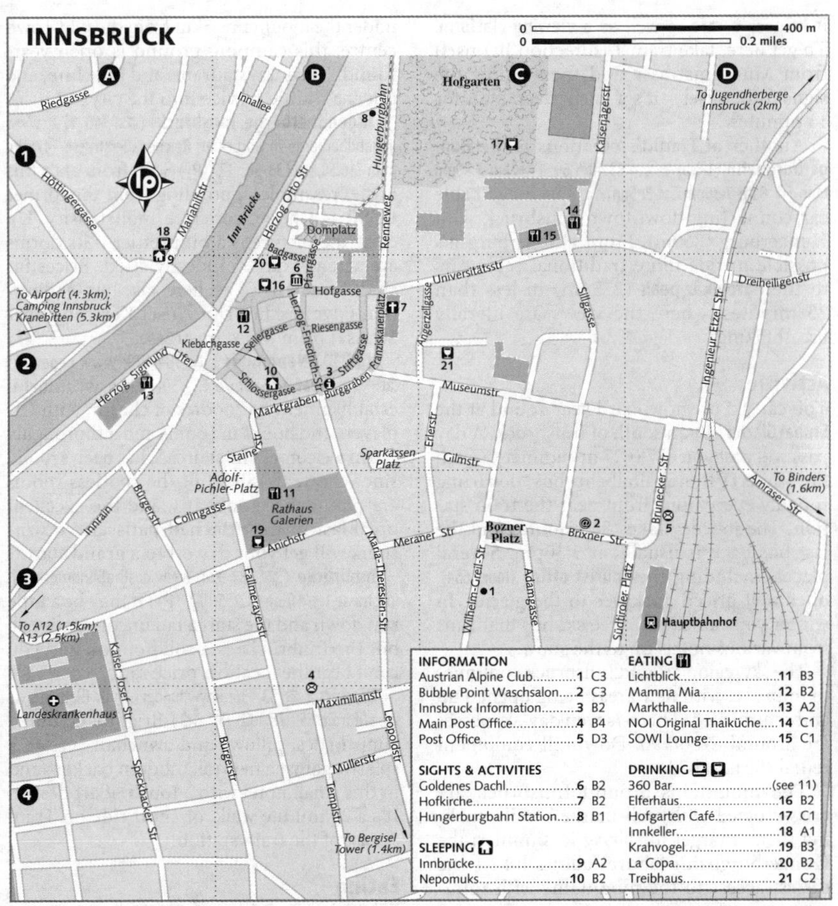

and soak up the atmosphere. Most people usually start at the famous **Goldenes Dachl** (Golden Roof; Herzog Friedrich Strasse). Built by Emperor Maximilian I in the 16th century as a display of wealth, it comprises 2657 gilded copper tiles.

The **Hofkirche** (Imperial Church; Universitätsstrasse 2; admission €4; 9am-5pm Mon-Sat, 10am-5pm Sun) contains a memorial to Maximilian, and although his 'sarcophagus' has been restored, it's actually empty. Perhaps more memorable are the 28 giant statues of Habsburgs lining either side of the cask. You're now forbidden to touch the statues, but numerous inquisitive hands have already polished parts of the dull bronze, including Kaiser Rudolf's codpiece!

While in this neighbourhood, wander north through the pleasant **Hofgarten** city-centre park.

ROOFTOP VIEWS

Views across the city can be enjoyed from the futuristic **Bergisel tower** (☎ 589 259; admission €8.30; 10am-6.30pm), south of the city. The tower was designed by Iraqi-born, British-based Zaha Hadid and sits atop Innsbruck's refurbished Winter Olympics ski-jump stadium –

GETTING INTO TOWN

Bus F leaves from outside the airport terminal for the train station.

it houses a **cafe** as well as a **viewing platform**. To get here, take tram 1 (direction Bergisel) from Museumstrasse and then follow the signs to Bergisel – it's a fairly steep path for 15 minutes.

Another of Hadid's creations is the **Hungerburgbahn** (1-way/return €3.40/5.60; 7am-7.30pm Mon-Fri, 8am-7.30pm Sat & Sun), a space-age cable car connecting downtown Innsbruck with Hungerburg (860m). From Hungerburg it's possible to ride more traditional cable cars to the **Hafelekar peak** (2256m) in less than 25 minutes, where the views are literally breathtaking.

Activities

You can ski or snowboard year-round at the **Stubai Glacier**, 40km south of Innsbruck. A day pass will cost you €37 (€27 in summer). Catch the white IVB Stubaltalbahn bus, departing roughly every hour from near the train station. The journey takes 80 minutes and the last bus back is usually at 5.30pm. Several places, including the **tourist office** (tours €54), offer well-priced packages to the glacier. In winter you can catch a free ski bus that runs from various hotels up to the snow.

The ski region around Innsbruck continues to improve, with new areas being opened up and refurbished. Three-/seven day-ski passes are around €100/190. Downhill equipment rental starts at €20.

The mountains around Innsbruck are criss-crossed with well-marked trails, making them a target for **hiking** in summer; the Hungerburgbahn (above) allows hikers the easiest access to the mountains with minimum fuss. Those staying in Innsbruck are entitled to the Club Innsbruck Card, which gives discounts on transport, admission fees, and includes **free guided mountain hikes**. The hiking program runs from June to the beginning of October, and includes day hikes, sunrise hikes and night-time lantern walks. For more information, contact the tourist office.

AUSTRIA

Sleeping

The tourist office has lists of private rooms in Innsbruck from €35 per person. If you're staying at a hostel or hotel, ask for the complimentary Club Innsbruck card, which provides various discounts and benefits.

Camping Innsbruck Kranebitten (☎ 284 180; www.campinginnsbruck.com; Kranebitter Allee 214; adult/tent/car €5.40/3.40/3.40;) In an idyllic location under the mountains 5km from the Old Town centre, this camping ground is open year-round. It has a restaurant, and bike hire, and offers a shuttle service into the city.

Jugendherberge Innsbruck (☎ 346 179; www.jugendherberge-innsbruck.at; Reichenauerstrasse 147; dm from €16.50, s/d €33/50;) Seen from afar, this hostel resembles a building from the former USSR – a huge, concrete monstrosity. Up close the picture is a bit prettier – its dorms are actually quite modestly sized. Prices include breakfast. To get here, take bus O (direction Olympisches Dorf/Josef Kerschbaumer Strasse) from Museumstrasse.

our pick **Nepomuks** (☎ 584 118; www.nepomuks.at; Kiebachgasse 16; dm/d €20/50) This wonderful establishment has oodles of charm, with CD players and books in rooms and a thoroughly warm welcome. The staircase has been around since the year 1800, but the spotless rooms are remodelled (only 10), and the excellent breakfast in the attached patisserie downstairs will get your day off to a grand start.

Innbrücke (☎ 281 934; www.gasthofinnbruecke.at; Innstrasse 1; s/d from €32/55;) It may be a little run down and the staff a tad unconventional, but the Innbrücke is a solid option and you can't beat the location/price ratio.

Binders (☎ 33 436; www.binders.at; Dr Glatz Strasse 20; s/d from €59/78;) Brightly coloured lampshades, pillows and armchairs create a splash against a neutral, modern background in this small hotel with a touch of art design. It's a 20 minute walk, or short ride on Tram 3, east of the train station.

Eating

NOI Original Thaiküche (☎ 589 777; Kaiserjägerstrasse 1; mains €4-11, midday menu €8; Mon-Fri, dinner Sat) The whiff of Thai spices – and the reasonable prices – attracts both students and business lunchers to this tiny eatery. Expect delicious

SPLURGE

Lichtblick (☎ 566 550; 7th fl, Maria Theresien Strasse 18; daytime snacks €7-11, evening menu €35-45; Mon-Sat) This is the city's hot ticket, and little wonder, given both the fabulous views of the surrounding mountains and the delicious modern international food from seven floors up. It's a romantic setting at night. After dinner grab a drink across the foyer in the 360 Bar.

DETOUR: AROUND INNSBRUCK

Within a 30-minute radius of the Tirolean capital is an unusual world of crystals, a gruesome collection of saintly bones, and a town with an intact medieval centre.

Crystal Worlds (☎ 05224-51 080; www.swarovski.com/kristallwelten; Kristallweltenstrasse 1; admission €9.50; ⌚ 9am-5.30pm), located in **Wattens**, is the work of crystal-makers Swarovski. The centre features elaborate installations by – or based on – leading artists, including Eno, Warhol and Dali, but the giant cranium at the entrance, complete with sparkling crystalline eyes and waterfall-spewing mouth, steals the show. Juxtaposing such sparkling beauty is the 13th-century **Pfarrkirche** (Oberer Stadtplatz; admission free; ⌚ dawn-dusk) in **Hall in Tirol**. It's home to a collection of 45 skulls and 12 bones, removed from the skeletons of minor saints by Florian Waldauf, advisor to Maximilian I. The spectacle is sure to repulse and fascinate. **Schwaz**, some 18km east of Innsbruck, was, in the 15th century, Austria's second-largest city after Vienna. Now it's a sleepy town, but the labyrinth of pretty cobbled streets at its medieval heart is testament to the wealth it accumulated from silver mines over the centuries.

Wattens is best reached by bus (€3.90 return, 20 minutes) from Innsbruck, as is Hall in Tirol (€2.80, 30 minutes). The train to Schwaz (€5.20, 20 minutes) is the quickest option.

Thai staples, such as soups, noodle dishes and curries, and outdoor tables in summer.

SOWI Lounge (Universitätstrasse 15; meals around €5; ⌚ 8am-9pm Mon-Thu, to 6pm Fri) University *Mensa* with an ever-changing menu but always a good selection of dishes.

Mamma Mia (☎ 562 902; Kiebachgasse 2; mains €6.40-7) This cheap and cheerful Italian serves generous helpings of pizza and pasta in the heart of the Old Town. It's sunny terrace is perfect in summer.

There is an **MPreis Supermarket** (⌚ 6am-9pm) in the main train station and a large indoor food market by the river in **Markthalle** (Herzog-Siegmund-Ufer; ⌚ 7am-6.30pm Mon-Fri, to 1pm Sat). Otherwise, if you're looking for cheap eats, pop across the river to Innstrasse, which is lined with kebab shops, takeaway pizzerias and cut-price Indian restaurants.

Drinking

Elferhaus (☎ 582 875; Herzog-Friedrich Strasse 11) Tunnelling into a slab of rock, this cool *Bierhaus* (beer house) has a vibe that gets lively late when the mostly college crowd shows up.

Hofgarten Café (☎ 588 871; Rennweg 6a) If you're looking for a green, tree-shaded spot outdoors in which to enjoy a drink while DJs spin tunes in the background, then Hofgarten will more than suffice.

Treibhaus (☎ 572 000; Angerzellgasse 8) The arty, community-minded Treibhaus hosts live music ranging from urban groove to ska, short-film festivals and the like. Attracts students and those with an alternative bent.

Krahvogel (☎ 5801 4971; Anichstrasse 12) This student haunt gets busy after 10pm.

Innkeller (☎ 291 508; Innstrasse 1) Innkeller offers a party spot, electronic tunes, and an outdoor terrace on busy Innstrasse.

Getting There & Away

EasyJet (www.easyjet.com) flies twice a week from London Gatwick to **Innsbruck airport** (☎ 22 525-0; www.innsbruck-airport.com).

Fast trains depart eight times daily to Bregenz (€29.20, 2½ hours) and every two hours to Salzburg (€35.20, two hours) and Kitzbühel (€17.90, one hour). On many trains to Lienz (€30.10, 3¼ hours), people travelling on Austrian rail passes must pay a surcharge for travelling through Italy; check before boarding.

Heading south by car through the Brenner Pass to Italy, you'll hit the A13 toll road (€8). Toll-free Hwy 182 follows the same route, although it is less scenic.

Getting Around

Single bus tickets cost €1.70; a 24-hour pass €3.80.

KITZBÜHEL

☎ 05356 / pop 8500

Once a silver- and copper-mining town in the 16th century, present-day Kitzbühel is a fashionable and prosperous winter resort. It's renowned for its excellent slopes, white-knuckled Hahnenkamm downhill ski race in January, and charming medieval centre.

The **tourist office** (☎ 777; www.kitzbuehel.com; Hinterstadt 18; ⌚ 8.30am-6pm Mon-Fri, 9am-6pm Sat,

10am-noon & 4-6pm Sun Jul-Sep & Christmas-Easter, 8.30am-6pm Mon-Fri, 9am-1pm Sat rest of year) is in the centre, about 1km from the train station (follow the signs). Ask here about homestays and skiing and hiking options.

Snow Bunnys (☎ 0676 794 0233; www.snowbunnys.co.uk; Bichstrasse 30; dm/d from €28/70) is a friendly, relaxed hostel with tiny communal lounge, spacious and bright rooms, DIY breakfast, and two cats. **Pension Mühlbergerhof** (☎ 628 35; muehlbergerhof@tirol.com; Schwarzseestrasse 6; s/d from €38/76) provides large rooms with balconies and views of the Hahenhkamm.

Huberbräu Stüberl (Vorderstadt 18; mains €7-13) is a Kitzbühel 'must' for Austrian food, while **La Fonda** (Hinterstadt 13; mains €8-13) dishes out nachos, burritos and enchiladas.

For self-caterers, there's a **Spar supermarket** (Mon-Sat) at Bichlstrasse 22.

Direct trains to Innsbruck (€17.90, one to 1½ hours) leave Kitzbühel every two hours, but there are hourly services to Wörgl (€7.80, 30 minutes), where you can change for Innsbruck. Trains to Salzburg (€25, two to 2½ hours) leave roughly hourly and normally require a change in Wörgl. Slower trains stop at Kitzbühel-Hahnenkamm, which is closer to the town centre than the main Kitzbühel stop.

The train connection to Lienz is terrible; bus (€13.20, two hours) is the way to go. Six run Monday to Friday and four Saturday and Sunday.

AUSTRIA

LIENZ

☎ 04852 / pop 12,000

With the jagged Dolomite mountain ranges crowding its southern skyline, the capital of East Tirol is a scenic staging point for travels through the Hohe Tauern National Park.

Staff at the **tourist office** (☎ 652 65; www.lienz-tourismus.at; Europaplatz 1; 8am-6pm Mon-Fri, 9am-noon & 5-7pm Sat Jul–mid-Sep, 10.30am-noon Sun Jul-Aug) will find rooms free of charge, or you can use the hotel board (with free telephone) outside.

There is downhill skiing nearby, but the area is more renowned for its cross-country skiing; Lienz fills up for the annual Dolomitenlauf cross-country skiing race in mid-January. In summer hiking is good in the mountains. The cable cars are closed in April, May, October and November.

Lienz has an excellent camping ground, **Comfort-Camping Falken** (☎ 64 022; www.camping-falken.com, in German; Eichholz 7; camp sites per adult/tent €5.50/9; mid-Dec–Oct), with good washing facilities, a restaurant and marvellous mountain views. Check with the tourist office for B&B options.

There is an ADEG supermarket at Hauptplatz 12 and a few sausage and kebab stands scattered around town; for a fuller meal, try **Adlerstüberl** (☎ 625 50; Andrä Kranz Gasse 5; mains €8-14, midday-menu €9-11).

Except for the 'corridor' route through Italy to Innsbruck, trains to the rest of Austria connect via Spittal Millstättersee station (in Spittal an der Drau) to the east. Trains to Salzburg (€31.40) take at least 3½ hours. Villach, between Spittal and Klagenfurt (€22.60, two hours), is a main junction for rail routes to the south. To head south by car, you must first divert west or east along Hwy 100.

HOHE TAUERN NATIONAL PARK

The largest national park in the Alps, Hohe Tauern (1786 sq km) is a hiking paradise where the flora and fauna are protected. The park contains the **Grossglockner** (3797m), Austria's highest mountain, which towers over the 10km-long Pasterze Glacier. The best viewing point is **Franz Josefs Höhe** (2369m), reached from Lienz by bus between late June and late September (€4.10, 30 minutes).

Buses go via Heiligenblut, where there's a **tourist office** (☎ 04824-20 01; www.heiligenblut.at), HI **Jugendherberge** (☎ 04824-22 59; Hof 36; dm/r €19/26), and other accommodation available.

The **Grossglockner Hochalpenstrasse** (Hwy 107; www.grossglockner.at; per car/motorcycle €28/18; May–mid-Sep) through the park is considered one of the world's most scenic. The road winds upwards for 2000m past waterfalls, glaciers and Alpine meadows.

VORARLBERG

Alluringly beautiful, Austria's most westerly region is an aesthetic mix of mountains, hills and valleys. Angling down from the Alps to the shores of Lake Constance (Bodensee), it provides a convenient gateway to Germany, Liechtenstein or Switzerland.

Vorarlberg's capital, **Bregenz**, occupies a pretty spot on shores of Lake Constance – and holds the **Bregenzer Festspiele** (www.bregenzerfestspiele.com) in July/August, when opera is performed on a floating stage on the lake – but the real action here is in the Arlberg region, shared by Vorarlberg and neighbouring Tirol. Some of the best skiing in Austria can be found at **St Anton am Arlberg**, where good medium-to-advanced runs, as well as nursery slopes on Gampen and Kapall, criss-cross the Alberg range. The **tourist office** (☎ 05446-226 90; www.stantonamarlberg.com), on the main street, has details. Head diagonally left from the train station to find it.

A ski pass valid for St Anton and neighbouring St Christoph, Lech, Zürs and Stuben costs €42.50/224 for one day/week; a summer lift pass for seven days will set you back €32.

Accommodation is mainly in small B&Bs. Many budget places (prices from €30 per person in the winter high season) are booked months or even years in advance.

St Anton is on the main railway route between Bregenz (€16.90, 1½ hours) and Innsbruck (€20, 1¼ hours). It's close to the eastern entrance of the Arlberg Tunnel, the toll road connecting Vorarlberg and Tirol (€8.50 one-way).

AUSTRIA DIRECTORY

ACCOMMODATION

Reservations are recommended at Christmas and Easter, during summer in cities, and winter at alpine resorts.

If you pitch a tent outside an established camping ground, you need the property owner's approval; on public land it's illegal. Outside Vienna, Tirol and protected areas, free camping is allowed in a campervan, but only if you don't set up equipment outside the van.

Hostels generally cost from €15 to €20. If you want a break from dorms, some householders rent out rooms in their homes (€18 to €40 per person). Ask the tourist office or look out for *Zimmer frei* (rooms vacant) signs. Prices quoted in this chapter are for the high summer season (or winter in ski resorts) and include all taxes and breakfast, unless otherwise stated.

Some useful organisations:

Austrian Camping Club (Österreichischer Camping Club; Map pp82-3; ☎ 01-713 6151; www.campingclub.at; 01, Schubertring 1-3, A-1010 Vienna)

Junge Hostels Austria (Map pp82-3; ☎ 01-533 18 33; www.jungehotels.at; 01, Helferstorferstrasse 4, Vienna)

Österreichischer Jugendherbergsverband (Map pp82-3; ☎ 01-533 53 53; www.oejhv.or.at; 01, Gonzagagasse 22, A-1010 Vienna)

ACTIVITIES

Austria has some of the world's best skiing and snowboarding, particularly in Tirol and Vorarlberg. You'll pay €20 to €40 for a daily ski pass (to ride the ski lifts). Rental generally starts at €20 for downhill equipment or €15 for cross-country skis; rates drop for multiple days.

Most tourist offices sell hiking maps. Mountain paths have direction indicators and often markers indicating the level of difficulty. Paths marked with a red-white-red marker require sturdy hiking boots and a pole; a blue-white-blue marker indicates the need for mountaineering equipment. The **Austrian Alpine Club** (Österreichischer Alpenverein, ÖAV; Map p97; ☎ 0512-59 547; www.alpenverein-ibk.at, in German; Wilhelm Greil Strasse 15, Innsbruck) has a list of huts, for overnight stays.

Cycling is also popular, as are swimming and spa resorts.

BUSINESS HOURS

Banks (🕑 usually 9am-12.30pm & 1.30-3pm Mon-Fri, to 5.30pm Thu)

Post office (🕑 8am-noon & 2-6pm Mon-Fri, 8-11am Sat) Money exchange tends to be open until 5pm Monday to Friday. A few main post offices in big cities are open daily till late, or even 24 hours.

Restaurants (🕑 11am-3pm & 6pm-midnight)

Shops (🕑 9am-6pm Mon-Fri, 9am-1pm or 5pm Sat) However, grocery stores may open at 6am, and other shops don't close their doors until 7.30pm. In smaller cities, there's sometimes a two-hour lunch break.

DANGERS & ANNOYANCES

Pickpockets work Vienna's two main train stations and pedestrian centre.

Take care in the mountains; helicopter rescue is expensive unless you are covered by insurance (assuming they find you in the first place).

EMBASSIES & CONSULATES

Only *Botschaften* (embassies) and *Konsulate* (consulates) in Vienna issue visas. In an emergency, you may be redirected to a limited-hours consulate in a nearer city.

Australia (Map pp82-3; ☎ 01-506 740; www.australian-embassy.at; 04, Mattiellistrasse 2-4)

Canada (Map pp82-3; ☎ 01-53 138-3000; www.kanada.at; 01, Laurenzerberg 2)

Croatia (off Map pp78-9; ☎ 01-484 87 83-0; 17, Heuberggasse 10)

Czech Republic (Map pp78-9; ☎ 01-899 58-111; www.mzv.cz/vienna; 14, Penzingerstrasse 11-13)

France (Map pp82-3; ☎ 01-50 275-0; www.ambafrance-at.org; 04, Technikerstrasse 2)

Germany (Map pp82-3; ☎ 01-71 154-0; www.wien.diplo.de; 03, Metternichgasse 3)
Hungary (Map pp82-3; ☎ 01-53 780-300; 01, Bankgasse 4-6)
Ireland (Map pp82-3; ☎ 01-715 42 46-0; 01, Rotenturmstrasse16-18)
Italy (Map pp82-3; ☎ 01-712 51 21; www.ambvienna.esteri.it; 03, Rennweg 27)
Netherlands (Map pp82-3; ☎ 01-58 939; www.mfa.nl/wen; 01, Opernring 5)
New Zealand (☎ 49-30 20 621-0; www.nzembassy.com; Friedrichstrasse 60, D-10117 Berlin, Germany)
Slovakia (off Map pp78-9; ☎ 01-318 90 55-200; www.vienna.mfa.sk; 19, Armbrustergasse 24)
Slovenia (Map pp82-3; ☎ 01-586 13 09; 01, Niebelungengasse 13)
Switzerland (Map pp82-3; ☎ 01-79 505-0; www.eda.admin.ch/wien; 03, Prinz Eugen Strasse 7)
UK (Map pp82-3; ☎ 01-71 613-0; www.britishembassy.at; 03, Jauresgasse 12)
USA Consulate (Map pp82-3; ☎ 512 58 35; 01, Parkring 12a); Embassy (Map pp78-9; ☎ 01-31 339-0; www.usembassy.at; 09, Boltzmanngasse 16) Visas at the consulate only.

AUSTRIA

FESTIVALS & EVENTS

The **Austrian National Tourist Office Vienna** (ANTO; www.austria.info) has a list of annual and one-off events on its website; click on 'Themed Holidays' and then 'Events'. Following is a list of major festivals.

Fasching (February) This Shrovetide carnival before Lent involves parties, waltzes and a parade; celebrated countrywide.
Christmas Markets (November/December; particularly Vienna and Salzburg) Quaint stalls selling traditional decorations, foodstuffs, mulled wine and all manner of presents heralding the arrival of the festive season.
Krampus (December; Innsbruck and elsewhere) St Nicholas, his friend Krampus (Black Peter) and an array of masked creatures cause merriment and mischief in a parade that harks back to pagan celebrations.

HOLIDAYS

New Year's Day 1 January
Epiphany 6 January
Easter Monday March/April
May Day 1 May
Ascension Five and a half weeks after Easter
Whit Monday Seven weeks after Easter
Corpus Christi 10 days after Whit Monday
Assumption of the Virgin Mary 15 August
National Day 26 October
All Saints' Day 1 November
Immaculate Conception 8 December
Christmas Day 25 December
St Stephen's Day 26 December

INTERNET RESOURCES

Austrian National Tourist Office (www.austria.info) Official tourist office website; in a number of languages.
Tiscover (www.tiscover.com) Information on Austria's provinces, and includes online booking.

LANGUAGE

Although they understand 'High' or received German, Austrians use different words and speak a dialect. In some parts of the country dialects are so strong that even other Austrians have trouble understanding their compatriots. English is generally widely spoken, especially by the younger generation.

MONEY

The euro is the currency of Austria. An approximate 10% tip is expected in restaurants. Pay it directly to the server; don't leave it on the table.

POST

Postcards and letters (up to 20g) cost €0.55 within Austria and €0.65 to Europe. Stamps are also available in *Tabak* (tobacco) shops.

TELEPHONE

Telekom Austria (☎ 0800-100 100; www.aon.at, in German) is Austria's main telecommunications provider. It maintains the public phones throughout the country, which take either coins or phonecards and cost a minimum of €0.20 for a local call. Some boxes only accept *Telefon-Wertkarte* (phonecards), which can be bought from post offices, train stations, and newsstands.

Handy (mobile phones) in Austria operate on GSM 900/1800, which is compatible with other European countries and Australia, but not with the North American GSM 1900 system or the system used in Japan. Prepaid Austrian SIM cards can be purchased for €30 or €39 in phone stores. Mobile numbers start with 0699, 0676, 0650, 0644 or 0660.

VISAS

Visas are not required for stays up to three months for US, Canadian, Australian or New Zealand citizens. There are no time limits for EU and Swiss nationals, but they should register with the police before taking up residency. Most African and Arab nationals require a visa.

Seasonal work in ski resorts is the most obvious and readily available work option; non-EU nationals will need their prospective employer to apply for a work permit for them.

Belarus Беларусь

HIGHLIGHTS

- **Minsk** Enjoy 'communism with cappuccino' in the trendy cafes of contradictory Minsk (p105).
- **Brest Fortress** Stroll through the mellow pedestrian streets of cosmopolitan Brest to the epic WWII memorial (p109).
- **Best journey** Drink beer and eat sausage with friendly locals on the train from Minsk (p105) to Brest (p109).

FAST FACTS

- **Area** 207,600 sq km (slightly smaller than the UK)
- **Budget** BR135,000/US$50 per day
- **Capital** Minsk
- **Country code** ☎ 375
- **Famous for** Being a Soviet time capsule, dictatorial president Lukashenko, bearing the brunt of Chornobyl
- **Languages** Russian, Belarusian
- **Money** Belarusian rouble (BR); A$1 = BR2069; C$1 = 2348; €1 = BR3722; ¥100 = BR2924; NZ$1 = BR1619; UK£1 = BR4193; US$1 = BR2770
- **Phrases** *dobry dzyen* (hello), *kalee laska* (please), *dzyahkooee* (thanks)

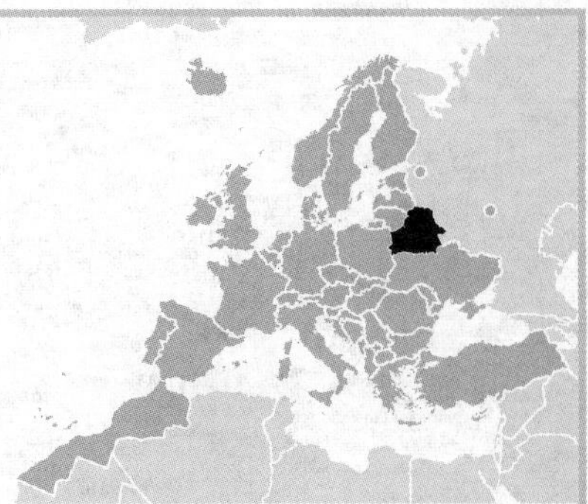

- **Population** 10 million
- **Visas** Almost everybody needs one, including those transiting through to Russia. Best arranged in advance (see p111).

TRAVEL HINTS

Keep your Lonely Planet guide hidden from customs officers when you arrive – they aren't fans of our Belarus politics coverage!

ROAMING BELARUS

Give Minsk two days; if you have a couple of days more, get to Brest to see the WWII memorial.

Europe's outcast, Belarus lies at the edge of Eastern Europe and looks far more to the Soviet Union than the European Union. Yet this lies at the heart of its appeal – while the rest of the former communist countries have charged headlong into capitalism, Belarus offers a chance to visit a Europe with almost no advertising, litter or graffiti. Far more than just the 'last dictatorship in Europe' – the phrase that has come to haunt Alexander Lukashenko's democratically challenged fiefdom – Belarus is a land of earthy humour, friendly people and courage in the face of bleak political adversity.

Ever wonder what life would be like if the Cold War had never ended? Here's your chance to find out. But you'd better be quick – surrounded by capitalist democracies whose influence is creeping more and more into daily life, Belarus can't stay this way forever.

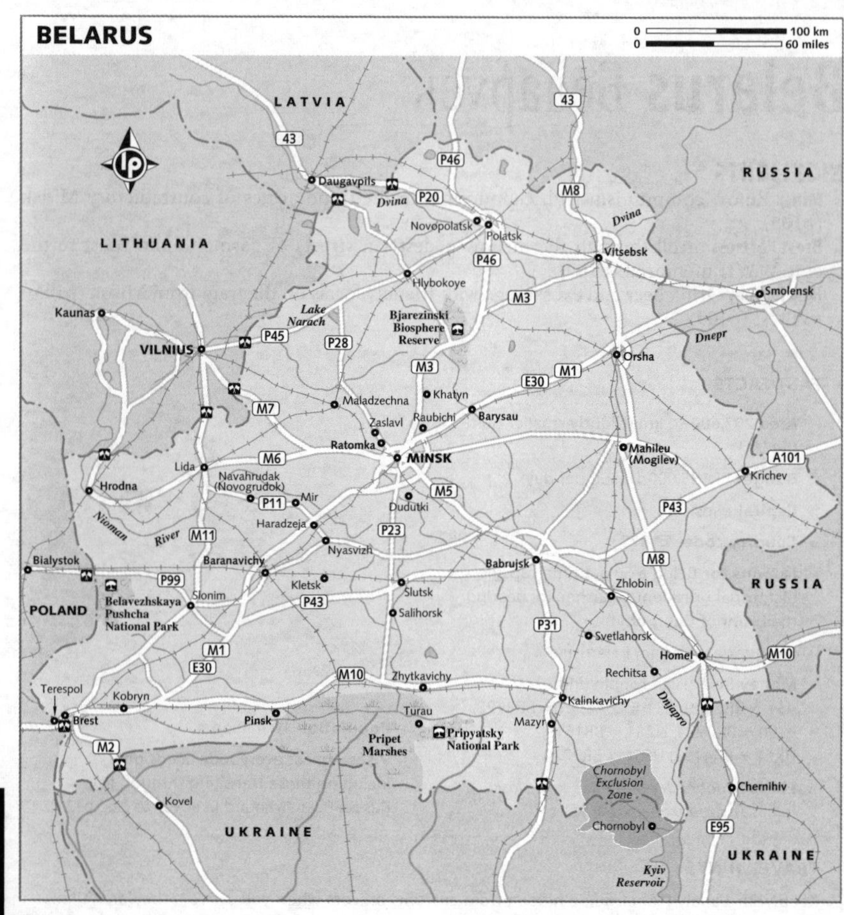

HISTORY

Belarus has an unhappy history. In the 1930s, under Stalin, hundreds of thousands of people were executed in purges here. The savage Nazi occupation during WWII was ended in 1944 by the Red Army, with massive destruction on both sides. At least 25% of the Belarusian population died between 1939 and 1945, most in the 200-plus concentration camps.

The 1986 nuclear accident at Chornobyl, just over the border in Ukraine, left about a quarter of the country seriously contaminated, and its effects are still felt today. On 25 August 1991 Belarus declared independence from the USSR. Since 1994, Belarus has been governed by Alexander Lukashenko, whose presidential style has been seen by many as autocratic and authoritarian. In March 2006, Lukashenko won another five-year term in presidential elections that were widely regarded as corrupt, and which were followed by peaceful protests hoping to emulate the success of Ukraine's Orange Revolution on Minsk's main square. Eventually, the police cleared the square with no government climb down.

Since then it's been business as usual for Lukashenko, and, despite the president paying some very slight lip service to reform, Belarus remains an isolated and backwards land on the edge of the EU. Amnesty International reports that democracy activists continue to be harassed and arrested.

READING UP

For a startlingly neutral and extremely detailed history of the past two decades of Belarus' history read *The Last Soviet Republic: Alexander Lukashenko's Belarus* by Stewart Parker. And for something completely different, check out Lee Hogan's bizarre sci-fi novel, *Belarus*.

THE CULTURE

The Belarusian population is 81.2% Belarusian, 11.4% Russian, 4% Polish and 2.4% Ukrainian, with the remaining 1% consisting of other groups. Prior to WWII, 10% of the population was Jewish. They now make up less than 1%.

The Belarussian character makes for a refreshing change from that of their Russian cousins. Here, you can usually expect people to be more open and friendly when they meet you.

ENVIRONMENT

Belarus is, for the most part, completely flat, with marshes and swamps in the south and lakes in the north. The 1986 disaster at Chornobyl (see p1205) has been the defining event for the Belarusian environment, if not for the republic as a whole.

TRANSPORT

GETTING THERE & AWAY

Air

International flights use **Minsk-2 airport** (☎ 006, 279 1300), 40km east of Minsk. Domestic flights and those to/from Kyiv, Kaliningrad and Moscow use the smaller **Minsk-1 airport** (☎ 006; vul Chkalova 38), a few kilometres from the centre.

Belarus' national airline is **Belavia** (B2; ☎ 210 4100; www.belavia.by; vul Nyamiha 14) with flights to London, Paris, Frankfurt, Berlin, Vienna, Rome and Milan.

The main international airlines with offices in Minsk:

Aeroflot (SU; ☎ 017-227 2887; www.aeroflot.com/eng)
Austrian Airlines (OS; ☎ 017-288 2535/55; www.aua.com)
El Al (LY; ☎ 017-211 2606; www.elal.co.il)
LOT Polish Airlines (LO; ☎ 017-226 6628; www.lot.com)
Lufthansa (LH; ☎ 017-284 7129; www.lufthansa.com)

CONNECTIONS

Belarus has excellent overland rail links to all its neighbours; daily trains from Minsk serve Moscow, St Petersburg, Vilnius, Warsaw (via Terespol) and Kyiv. Bus services, which tend to be less comfortable, connect Minsk to Moscow, St Petersburg, Kyiv, Warsaw and Vilnius and Brest to Terespol in Poland.

Bus

Minsk is connected by daily buses to Moscow, Rīga, St Petersburg and Vilnius. Brest has daily buses to/from Warsaw and Lviv and weekly buses to/from Prague.

Car

International driving permits are recognised in Belarus. The Brest–Minsk highway is very well sealed, but there are several points at which cars with foreign licence plates are charged US$1.

Train

There are dozens of trains between Moscow and Minsk and once-daily trains connecting Minsk with Kaliningrad and Kyiv. Other destinations include Lviv, St Petersburg, Vilnius and Warsaw. Brest is well connected to Moscow, Warsaw and Prague, with trains at least once daily.

GETTING AROUND

Trains between major cities are moderately frequent and inexpensive – and the views are lovely. Buses are slightly cheaper but more uncomfortable and more likely to break down.

MINSK МІНСК

☎ 017 / pop 1.73 million

Minsk will almost certainly surprise you. The capital of the tractor factory republic of Belarus is in fact, despite its thoroughly dreary sounding name, an amazingly progressive and modern place. Here, fashionable cafes, restaurants with wi-fi and crowded bars and night clubs vie for your attention, and sushi bars and art galleries have taken up residence in a city centre totally remodelled to the tastes of Stalin. Despite the strong police presence and obedient citizenry, scrape the surface and you'll find that there's more than a whiff of rebellion in the air.

ORIENTATION

Minsk's main thoroughfare, pr Nezalezhnastsi, extends over 11km from the train station to the outer city limits. The main drag is a vivid testament to Stalin's vision of grandeur.

INFORMATION

There are no tourist information centres and while travel agencies can provide information they are also keen to book tours. Check out In Your Pocket's free online Minsk guide (www.inyourpocket.com)

Downstairs at the train station is a 24-hour left-luggage place, as well as self-service lockers that employ a fiendishly difficult system involving old Soviet kopecks (ask the staff for help).

ATMs abound, but there's often a small queue. Hotels all have exchange bureaus, and some cash traveller's cheques, but an ATM is the smartest way to go.

Most hotels offer cheap laundry services.

24-hour Pharmacy (☎ 227 4844; pr Nezalezhnastsi 16)

Central post office (☎ 227 8492; pr Nezalezhnastsi 10; 🕑 7am-11pm) There's an express mail office on the 2nd floor. There's also a phone office.

EcoMedservices (☎ 207 7474; vul Tolstoho 4; 🕑 8am-9pm) The closest thing to a reliable, Western-style clinic. Dental services are here too.

Prachechnaya (vul Berestyanskaya 1; 🕑 9am-5.30pm Mon-Fri; M Pl Peremoni) Offers cheaper laundry service than hotels.

Soyuz Online (☎ 226 0279; www.soyuzoline.by; 2nd fl, vul Krasnaarmeyskaya 3; 🕑 24hr) Go up the steps to the Dom Ofitserov; enter the far door, near the tank monument.

Tsentralnaya Kniharnya (☎ 227 4918; pr Nezalezhnastsi 19) Bookshop with large selection, including some books in English.

SIGHTS

The post-WWII rebuilding of Minsk has given the city a victorious, fiercely proud Soviet flair. The eerily litter- and graffiti-free streets are also unique for a European capital.

The city's main square, Pl Nezalezhnastsi (Independence Square) is dominated by the **Belarusian Government Building** (behind the Lenin statue) on its northern side and the **Belarusian State University** on the southern side.

An entire block at No 17 pr Nezalezhnastsi is occupied by a yellow neoclassical building with an ominous, temple-like Corinthian portal – this is the all-too-fully functioning **KGB headquarters**. Opposite is a **bust of Felix Dzerzhinsky**, the founder of the KGB's predecessor (the Cheka) and a native of Belarus.

> **EMERGENCY NUMBERS**
>
> - Ambulance ☎ 03
> - Fire ☎ 01
> - Police ☎ 02

Between vul Enhelsa and vul Yanki Kupaly is Kastrychnitskaya pl (October Square) where the attempted Denim Revolution of March 2006 and other opposition protests take place. On the square is the impressive, severe **Palats Respubliki** (Palace of the Republic), a concert hall and the multicolumned **Trade Unions' Culture Palace**. Next door is the harrowing **Museum of the Great Patriotic War** (☎ 277 7635; pr Nezalezhnastsi 25a; admission BR5000; 🕑 10am-6pm Tue-Sun).

Across the street and up the stairs is **Dom Ofitserov** (Officer's Building), which has a tank memorial devoted to the soldiers who freed Minsk from the Nazis. Southeastward is the seriously guarded **Presidential Administrative Building**, from where Lukashenko runs the country. Every day, an armoured-car procession slams through the city to take him to lunch; hang out around the McDonald's on pr Nezalezhnastsi around 1pm.

Further north on pr Nezalezhnastsi is Pl Peramohi, marked by a giant **Victory Obelisk** and its eternal flame.

SLEEPING

For apartments, try www.belarusrent.com or www.belarusapartment.com. Rates range from €40 to €90 a day.

Moskovsky Bus Station Dorms (☎ 219 3651; vul Filimonava 63; s/d BR17,720/35,440) In the back of the station about 5km from the centre, these clean, quiet rooms are the cheapest in town. We challenge you to make the serious babushka in charge smile.

40 Let Pobedy (☎ 294 7963; vul Azgura 3; s/d from BR80,000/160,000, dm from BR51,000) The women on staff are kind and motherly, and the hotel is a good deal for its old but clean and thoroughly Soviet rooms.

Hotel Turist (☎ 295 4031; Partizansky Pr 81; s/d from BR110,000/165,000) Out of the city centre, but handily located near the Partizanskaya metro station, this old Soviet place has been

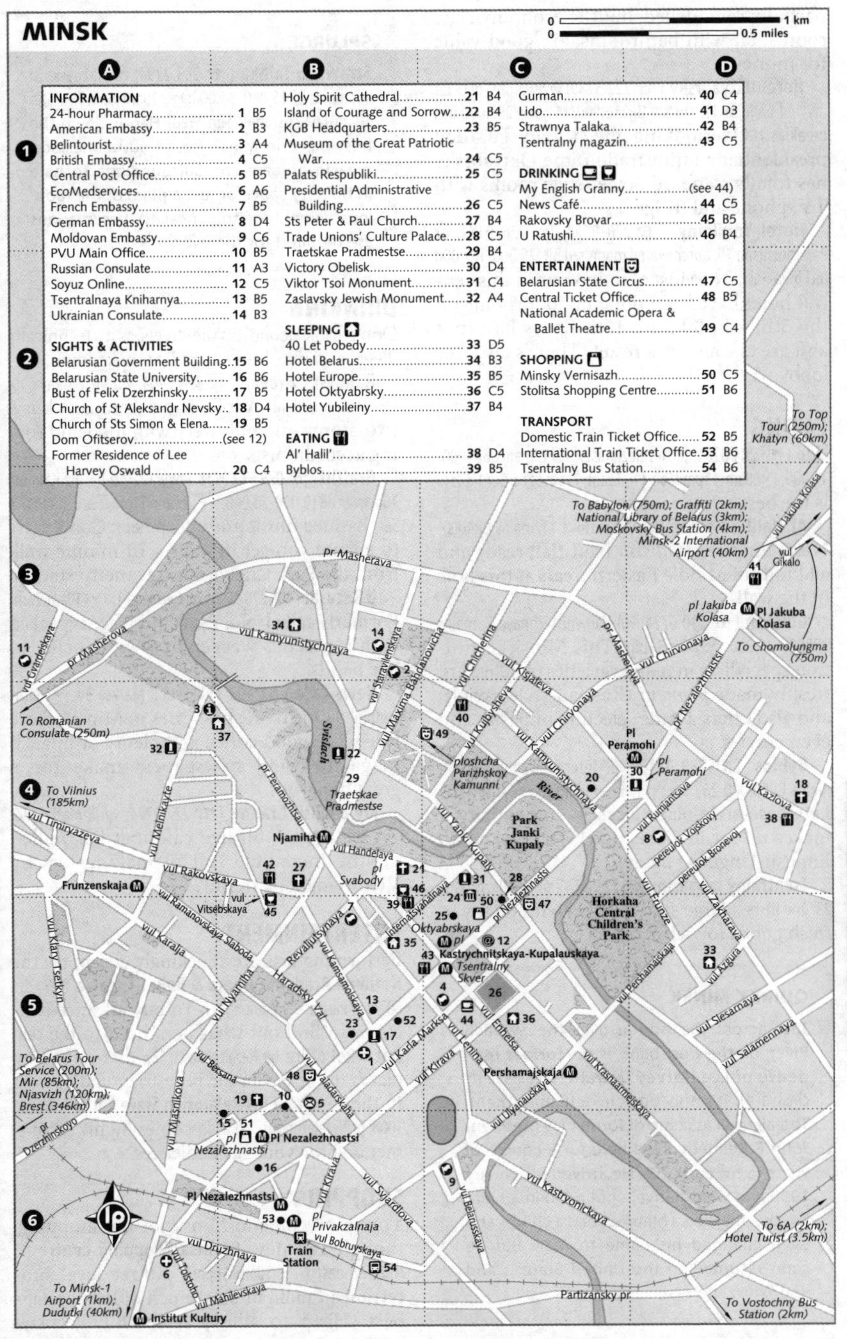
MINSK
0 1 km
0 0.5 miles
INFORMATION
24-hour Pharmacy 1 B5
American Embassy 2 B3
Belintourist 3 A4
British Embassy 4 C5
Central Post Office 5 B5
EcoMedservices 6 A6
French Embassy 7 B5
German Embassy 8 D4
Moldovan Embassy 9 C6
PVU Main Office 10 B5
Russian Consulate 11 A3
Soyuz Online 12 C5
Tsentralnaya Kniharnya 13 B5
Ukrainian Consulate 14 B3
SIGHTS & ACTIVITIES
Belarusian Government Building 15 B6
Belarusian State University 16 B6
Bust of Felix Dzerzhinsky 17 B5
Church of St Aleksandr Nevsky 18 D4
Church of Sts Simon & Elena 19 B5
Dom Ofitserov (see 12)
Former Residence of Lee Harvey Oswald 20 C4
Holy Spirit Cathedral 21 B4
Island of Courage and Sorrow 22 B4
KGB Headquarters 23 B5
Museum of the Great Patriotic War 24 C5
Palats Respubliki 25 C5
Presidential Administrative Building 26 C5
Sts Peter & Paul Church 27 B4
Trade Unions' Culture Palace 28 C5
Traetskae Pradmestse 29 B4
Victory Obelisk 30 D4
Viktor Tsoi Monument 31 C4
Zaslavsky Jewish Monument 32 A4
SLEEPING
40 Let Pobedy 33 D5
Hotel Belarus 34 B3
Hotel Europe 35 B5
Hotel Oktyabrsky 36 C5
Hotel Yubileiny 37 B4
EATING
Al' Halil' 38 D4
Byblos 39 B5
Gurman 40 C4
Lido 41 D3
Strawnya Talaka 42 B4
Tsentralny magazin 43 C5
DRINKING
My English Granny (see 44)
News Café 44 C5
Rakovsky Brovar 45 B5
U Ratushi 46 B4
ENTERTAINMENT
Belarusian State Circus 47 C5
Central Ticket Office 48 B5
National Academic Opera & Ballet Theatre 49 C4
SHOPPING
Minsky Vernisazh 50 C5
Stolitsa Shopping Centre 51 B6
TRANSPORT
Domestic Train Ticket Office 52 B5
International Train Ticket Office 53 B6
Tsentralny Bus Station 54 B6
To Top Tour (250m); Khatyn (60km)
To Babylon (750m); Graffiti (2km); National Library of Belarus (3km); Moskovsky Bus Station (4km); Minsk-2 International Airport (40km)
To Chomolungma (750m)
To Romanian Consulate (250m)
To Vilnius (185km)
To Belarus Tour Service (200m); Mir (85km); Njasvizh (120km); Brest (346km)
To Minsk-1 Airport (1km); Dudutki (40km)
To 6A (2km); Hotel Turist (3.5km)
To Vostochny Bus Station (2km)
pr Masherava
vul Kamyunistychnaya
Svislach River
Park Janki Kupaly
Horkaha Central Children's Park
Njamiha
Frunzenskaja
Kastrychnitskaya-Kupalauskaya
Pershamajskaja
Pl Nezalezhnastsi
Pl Jakuba Kolasa
Pl Peramohi
Institut Kultury
Train Station
Partizansky pr

partially remodelled, but the economy class rooms, all with bathrooms, are good value for money.

Hotel Oktyabrsky (☎ 222 3289; www.hotel-oktyabr.by; vul Enhelsa 13; s/d/ste BR116,500/144,000/260,000 incl breakfast) Overlooking the heavily guarded presidential administration, the Oktyabrsky has totally standard Soviet-style rooms with TV, phone and fridge.

Hotel Yubileiny (☎ 226 9024; fax 226 9171; pr Peramozhtsau 19; unrenovated rooms s/d BR125,000/167,000 incl breakfast;) Most of the rooms in this central hotel have been done up, but rooms on the 5th, 7th, 8th and 13th floors have not and are cheaper as a result. There's also free lobby wi-fi.

EATING

Lido (☎ 284 8264; pr Nezalezhnastsi 49/1; mains BR4000-10,000; 8am-11pm Mon-Fri, 11am-11pm Sat & Sun) This is the best cafeteria in town.

Al' Halil' (☎ 285 2780; vul Kazlova 14; mains BR4000-14,000) Find fresh *lavash* (soft flatbread) and all kinds of Middle Eastern treats at this hole in the wall.

Gurman (☎ 290 6774; vul Kamynistychnaya 7; mains BR8000-25,000; 8am-11pm) This Minsk institution specialises in many varieties of delicious, freshly made *pelmeni* (Russian-style ravioli) and also offers a wide selection of pastas and even curries.

Byblos (☎ 289 1218; vul Internatsyanalnaya 21; mains BR10,000-25,000; noon-midnight) What this Lebanese-style place lacks in authenticity it makes up for in value, quick service and an English-language menu.

Tsentralny magazin (☎ 227 8876; pr Nezalezhnastsi 23, 2nd fl) is a large supermarket with plenty of fresh goods for self-caterers.

QUIRKY MINSK

Just across the bridge over the Svislach River, on the west bank, is the **former residence of Lee Harvey Oswald** (vul Kamunistychnaya 4); it's the bottom left apartment. The alleged assassin of former US president John F Kennedy lived here for a couple of years in his early 20s. He arrived in January 1960 and went native – got a job in a radio factory, married a Minsker, had a child – and even changed his name to Alek. But he soon returned to the United States…and you know the rest.

BELARUS

SPLURGE

Strawnya Talaka (☎ 203 2794; vul Rakovskaya 18; mains BR15,000-30,000; 10am-6am Thu-Sat, 10am-last customer Sun-Wed) Hands down the best place in Minsk for an authentic local meal in intimate, cosy surroundings. Try hare in bilberry sauce or just a plate of the fabulous *deruni* (potato pancakes). Reservations are required for the evenings.

DRINKING

Don't drink alcohol on the streets, as it's technically illegal and may lead to a police shakedown.

Rakovsky Brovar (☎ 328 6404; vul Vitsebskaya 10; noon-midnight) A jolly and perennially busy, two-storey microbrewery with food and roving accordionists.

Graffiti (☎ 029 179 9918; www.graffiti.by; per Kalinina 16; cover BR10,000-20,000; 11am-11pm, until 1am Fri & Sat) Banned music and cheap beer. Come early to ensure you get in – it's a 10-minute walk from the Park Chelyuskintsev metro station.

U Ratushi (☎ 226 0643; vul Gertsena 1; 10am-2am) Formerly called 'Nul Pyat', this place is packed with a raucous weekend crowd dancing to live bands.

News Café (☎ 103 1111; vul K Marksa 34; 8am-midnight) One of the best cafes in Minsk where free wi-fi, good coffee and plenty of English magazines and newspapers make for a great hang-out.

My English Granny (☎ 227 2224; vul K Marksa 36; 9am-11pm) A bizarre cafe that has pulled off the incredible feat of making kitschy Victoriana look trendy.

ENTERTAINMENT

Performing arts are shockingly cheap; try the **National Academic Opera & Ballet Theatre** (☎ 234 8074; pl Parizhskoy Kamunni 1). To buy advance tickets or to find out what's on, head to the **central ticket office** (pr Nezalezhnastsi 18); there are more places for tickets in the pedestrian underpasses in the centre. The **Belarusian State Circus** (☎ 226 1008; pr Nezalezhnastsi 32) also comes highly recommended for younger audiences.

SHOPPING

You don't come to Minsk for the shopping, though the new **Stolitsa Shopping Centre** (Pl Nezalezhnastsi; 10am-10pm), a three-level subterranean mall, houses much of the capital's best. Head to **Minsky Vernisazh** (Oktyabrskaya

Pl; ⏰ 8am-6pm), next to the Museum of the Great Patriotic War for local art, folk crafts and other traditional items.

GETTING THERE & AWAY

Air

International flights entering and departing Belarus do so at the **Minsk-2 international airport** (☎ 006, 279 1300; www.airport.by), about 40km east of Minsk. Some domestic flights as well as those to Kyiv, Kaliningrad and Moscow depart from the smaller **Minsk-1 airport** (☎ 006; vul Chkalova 38), only a few kilometres from the city centre.

Bus

There are three main bus stations, and you can buy tickets for anywhere at any of them. At the time of writing the Tsentralny bus station next to the train station was being rebuilt and all the Tsentralny routes were being run from the Vostochny Bus Station. The excellent MinskTrans website (www.minsktrans.by) also gives full timetable information in English.

Moskovsky (☎ 219 3622; vul Filimonava 63) Near Maskovskaya metro station.

Tsentralny (☎ international 225 2256, CIS destinations 227 3725; vul Bobruyskaya 6; Ⓜ Pl Lenina) By the train station, though under reconstruction at the time of writing.

Vostochny (☎ 248 5821; vul Vaneeva 34) To get here from the train station (or metro Pl Lenina), take bus 8 or trolley 20 or 30; get off at 'Avtovokzal Vostochny'.

Public Transport

Minsk's metro operates until midnight. One token *(zheton)* costs BR600; buses, trams and trolleybuses cost the same (minibuses BR1200). Bus 100 plies pr Nezalezhnastsi.

Taxi

For taxis, call ☎ 081 for the state service that almost always has cars available. A cheaper and more reliable (less likely to rip off foreigners) private service (call ☎ 007) sometimes doesn't have any cars available during peak times. You can also hail a taxi from the street. Unlike in Russia, private cars don't usually stop for passengers.

> **GETTING INTO TOWN**
>
> From Minsk-2, a 40-minute taxi ride into town should cost US$25, but you'll be lucky to get it for under US$40. Buses (BR3000, 90 minutes, hourly) will bring you to the Tsentralny bus station, which is next to the train station and on the metro. There are also regular minibuses that make the trip in under an hour (BR5000). If you arrive by train, you're already in the centre of the city.

Train

Domestic train ticket office (☎ 225 6271; pr Nezalezhnastsi 18; ⏰ 9am-8pm Mon-Fri, 9am-7pm Sat & Sun) Tickets for domestic and CIS destinations.

International train ticket office (☎ 213 1719; vul Babruyskaya 4; ⏰ 9am-8pm) Advance tickets for non-CIS destinations; located to the right of the train station.

Minsk train station (☎ 005, 596 5410) Domestic and CIS tickets.

BREST БРЭСТ

☎ **0162 / pop 290,000**

After visiting Minsk you'd be forgiven for thinking you've arrived in another country when you get off the train in Brest. This prosperous and cosmopolitan border town looks far more to the neighbouring EU than to Minsk or Moscow, and is a pleasant place to pass a day or two. The city's main site is the remains of the Brest Fortress, an astounding WWII memorial.

ORIENTATION

Central Brest fans out southeast from the train station to the Mukhavets River. Vul Savetskaya is the main drag and has several pedestrian sections. Brest Fortress lies where the Buh and Mukhavets Rivers meet, about 2km southwest of the centre down pr Masherava.

INFORMATION

Belarusbank (pl Lenina) Currency exchange, Western Union and a nearby ATM.

Beltelekom (☎ 22 13 15; pr Masherava 21; ⏰ 7am-10.30pm) You can make long-distance calls here, as well as use the internet cafe. There's also a free wi-fi zone for those with laptops

Cyber Brest (☎ 20 03 00; 3rd fl, vul Kamsamolskaya 36; ⏰ 9am-11pm) Internet access from one of 50 computers costs BR2000 per hour **City Emergency Hospital** (☎ 23 58 38; vul Lenina 15)

Post office (pl Lenina)

SIGHTS

If you are going to see only one Soviet WWII memorial in your life, make it **Brest Fortress** (Brestskaya krepost; ☎ 20 03 65; pr Masherava; admission

BELARUS

free; 9am-6pm). Epic monuments, solemn re-enactments and sombre music played over loudspeakers pay tribute to the regiments who defended the fort for an astonishing month when the Germans invaded in 1941. It's at the western end of pr Masherava, about a 20-minute walk from the centre.

The **Museum of Confiscated Art** (☎ 20 41 95; vul Lenina 39; admission BR2500; 10am-5.15pm Tue-Sun), displays art pieces – mostly breathtaking icons – seized by border guards as smugglers attempted to sneak them out to the West.

Anyone interested in trains will love the excellent outdoor **Museum of Railway Technology** (☎ 27 47 64; pr Masherava 2; admission BR6000; 9am-6pm May-Oct, 9am-5pm Wed-Sun Nov-April).

SLEEPING

Hotel Buh (☎ 23 64 17; vul Lenina 2; s/d/ste BR60,000/95,000/120,000) It's a bit old, but the rooms are spacious and the women who run it are a scream, though they speak not a word of English.

Hotel Belarus (☎ 22 16 48; bresttourist@tut.by; bul Shevchenko 6; s/d BR102,000/126,000 incl breakfast) Simple but clean rooms with basic bathrooms contain TV, fridge and phone. Rooms at the back are much quieter.

Vesta Hotel (☎ 23 71 69; hotelvesta@tut.by; vul Krupskoi 16; s/d BR108,000/156,000, ste BR210,000-430,000) Identical to its sister Soviet hotels in town, the Vesta does, however, boast a side-street location making it far more peaceful than other options.

EATING & DRINKING

For self-caterers, there is a decent **grocery store** (vul Savetskaya 48; 8am-8pm Mon-Sat, 10am-8pm Sun) in the centre. There are lots of little cafes along the pedestrian-only part of vul Savetskaya.

Pizzeria (vul Pushkinskaya 20; pizzas BR9000-15,000) It's not well signed, but you can pretty much follow your nose into the building and down the stairs. The pizzas are great; salads and fries are available too.

Jules Verne (☎ 23 67 17; vul Hoholya 29; mains BR18,000-26,000; noon-midnight) This superb gentleman's club-style restaurant is the best in town, with a delicious international menu that's worth every penny.

Pub House (☎ 21 93 46; vul Hoholya; 9am-11pm) This friendly and rustic old-style wooden bar offers beers from all over Europe.

Matritsa (☎ 23 82 39; vul Savetskaya 73; 9pm-5am) Bowling, billiards and bars – it's all here. There's dancing too.

BELARUS

GETTING THERE & AWAY

The **train station** (☎ 005) has on-site customs. When taking a train from Brest, note the platform nearest the city centre is for east-bound trains; the other is for westbound trains. The **bus station** (☎ 004) is in the centre of town.

BELARUS DIRECTORY

ACCOMMODATION

Standards here tend to be lower than in the West, but they are still generally acceptable. Most places are old Soviet hotels that, while frumpy, are generally clean. Hotels don't have cooking facilities, but some have in-room fridges.

BUSINESS HOURS

Offices are generally open 9am to 6pm during the week, with banks closing at 5pm. Shops are open from about 9am or 10am to about 9pm Monday to Saturday; some are open Sunday until around 6pm. Restaurants and bars open around 10am and close around 10pm to midnight.

Lunch is for an hour sometime between noon and 2pm.

EMBASSIES & CONSULATES

There is no representation for Canada, Australia or New Zealand in Belarus. Unless otherwise indicated, the listed missions are in Minsk.

France (☎ 017-210 2868; www.ambafrance-by.org; pl Svabody 11)

Germany (☎ 017-217 5900; www.minsk.diplo.de; vul Zakharava 26)

Moldova (☎ 017-289 1441; vul Belarusskaya 2)

Romania (☎ 017-203 8097; per Moskvina 4)

Russia Minsk (☎ 017-222 4985; fax 222 4980; vul Gvardeiskaya 5a); Brest (☎ 0162-23 78 42; fax 0162-21 0473; brestcons@brest.by; vul Pushkinskaya 10)

UK (☎ 017-210 5920; www.ukinbelarus.fco.gov.uk; vul Karla Marksa 37)

Ukraine Minsk (☎/fax 017-283 1990; vul Staravilenskaya 51); Brest (☎ 0162-22 04 55; vul Vorovskogo 19)

USA (☎ 017-210 1283; http://minsk.usembassy.gov; vul Staravilenskaya 46)

FESTIVALS & EVENTS

The night of 6 July is a celebration with pagan roots called **Kupalye**, when young girls gather flowers and throw them into a river as a method of fortune-telling, and everyone else sits by lake- or riverside fires drinking beer.

HOLIDAYS

New Year's Day 1 January
Orthodox Christmas 7 January
International Women's Day 8 March
Constitution Day 15 March
Catholic & Orthodox Easter March/April
Labour Day (May Day) 1 May
Victory Day 9 May
Independence Day 3 July
Dzyady (Day of the Dead) 2 November
Day of the October Revolution 7 November
Catholic Christmas 25 December

MONEY

There is no coinage in Belarus, but notes range from five to 100,000 roubles – quite a span. ATMs are easy to find, and exchange offices are in hotels. Cashing traveller's cheques is possible at a few hotels (primarily in Minsk), but ATMs are an easier and more dependable method of getting cash.

TELEPHONE

Use a Beltelekom office for calls, not a phone booth. To call, pay in advance, go to your assigned booth and hit ответ (the answer button) when the person you're calling answers.

To dial within Belarus, dial ☎ 8 (wait for tone) + city code + number. To dial abroad, dial ☎ 8 (wait for tone) + 10 + country code + city code + number. To make an intercity call, dial ☎ 375, followed by the city code (without the first zero) and number.

To dial a Belarusian mobile number from Belarus, dial ☎ 8029 or ☎ 8025 and then the number. Anyone with an unlocked mobile phone handset can buy a SIM card for next to nothing, although some vendors will be wary of selling a SIM card to foreigners.

For operator inquiries, call ☎ 085; a few of the staff speak English.

VISAS

Belarusian visa regulations *change frequently,* so check with your nearest Belarus embassy for the latest details (most embassies have visa information on their websites, although be aware that they too are not always up to date). All Western visitors need a visa, and arranging one before you arrive is essential.

AT YOUR OWN RISK

There is effectively no border between Russia and Belarus. In theory, by train, it's possible to enter Belarus and return to Russia – or go to Russia and back from Belarus – without going through passport control, and therefore without needing a visa for the country you're sneaking into. However, a hotel won't take you without a visa, so you'd have to stay with friends or rent an apartment, and if your visa-less passport is checked on the street, you will be deported.

To get a visa, you will need a photograph, an invitation from a private person or a business, or a confirmation of reservation from a hotel, and your passport. There are three main visas: tourist, issued if you have a tourist invitation or hotel reservation voucher; visitor (guest), if your invitation comes from an individual in Belarus; and business, if your invitation is from a business. There are also transit visas, if you are passing through and won't be in the country for more than 48 hours, for which no invite or voucher is necessary. Visitor and tourist visas are issued for 30 days (tourist visas can be multi-entry); business visas are for 90 days and can also be multi-entry. Visa costs vary depending on the embassy you apply at and your citizenship. Americans pay more, but typically single-entry visas cost about €90 for five working-days' service and €160 for next-day service; double-entry visas usually cost double that.

Your visa must be registered if you are in the country for more than 72 hours. Hotels do this automatically, sometimes for a fee. Keep the small pieces of stamped paper for immigration agents upon departure. In theory, you'll be fined if you don't provide proof of registration for every day of your stay; in practice, proof of one day is good enough if you're asked.

Transit Visas

All persons passing through Belarusian territory are required to possess a transit visa, which can be obtained at any Belarusian consulate upon presentation of travel tickets clearly showing the final destination as being outside Belarus. The possession of a valid Russian visa is not enough to serve as a transit visa. Transit visas are not available at the border.

Belgium

HIGHLIGHTS

- **Brussels** Be seduced by its surrealist art, art nouveau architecture, strange breweries, cafe culture, and galleries and restaurants galore (p116)
- **Bruges** Cycle this quaint medieval city's beautiful bridges and cobblestone streets (p126)
- **Chocolates** Pick and choose pralines from either supermarket delicatessens or expensive *chocolateries* such as Pierre Marcolini (p120)

FAST FACTS

- **Area** 30,278 sq km (about one third of Portugal)
- **Budget** €50 to €60 per day
- **Capital** Brussels
- **Country code** ☎ 32
- **Famous for** chocolate, beer and Bruges
- **Languages** Dutch, French, German
- **Money** Euro (€); A$1 = €0.55; C$1 = 0.60; ¥100 = €0.78; NZ$1 = €0.43; UK£1 = €1.12; US$1 = €0.74
- **Phrases** *Dag/bonjour* (hello in Dutch/French), *dag/au revoir* (goodbye), *dank U/merci* (thanks), *hoeveel kost het?/c'est combien?* (how much is it?)

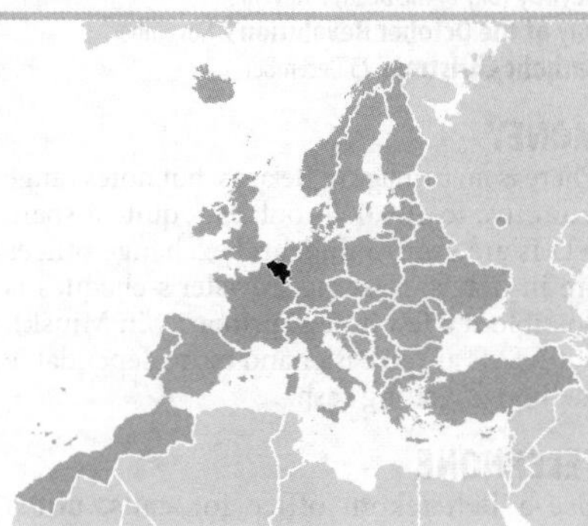

- **Population** 10.6 million
- **Visas** Citizens of many countries don't need visas for stays up to three months (p133)

TRAVEL HINTS

Buy pralines from supermarkets rather than expensive *chocolateries,* and in restaurants order the good-value lunchtime 'dish of the day' (*dagschotel* in Dutch, *plat du jour* in French).

ROAMING BELGIUM

Belgium's big three – Brussels, Bruges and Antwerp – are essential stops. Day trip it to Ypres and Ghent, then burrow down in the Ardennes.

Stir the pot of Europe, and Belgium's not likely to bubble up in your face. This slow cooker has spent centuries simmering on the back burner, producing more history, art, architecture and varieties of beer than many of its bigger, bossier neighbours. And all that without boiling over – yet. Political crisis in recent times has left many speculating whether Belgium will split in two. You see België to Dutch speakers and La Belgique to the nation's French speakers is an eccentric little country with deep cultural division. On the surface it's all fine food, beer and chocolate, but underneath these apt stereotypes is a longstanding division between the nation's Dutch and French speakers. As a traveller you'll probably witness little or none of this conflict and only time will tell whether Belgium breaks up or remains united. But what goes without question is its ageless appeal and ease of travel. Start with Brussels, the capital of Belgium and the EU, and then move effortlessly on to the myriad other cities and sights that this little country has to offer. You'll quickly find nothing in Belgium is far far away.

HISTORY

Bruges, Ghent and Ypres were the first major cities in Belgium, with their economies booming in the 13th and 14th centuries on the manufacturing and trading of cloth. Their craftspeople established several powerful guilds (organisations to stringently control arts and crafts), whose elaborate guildhalls you'll see in many cities – the most famous are those on Brussels' Grand Place (see p118).

As Belgium is sandwiched between the major European powers, its history from the 15th to 19th centuries is a battle tale. The subsequent years saw the start of Flemish nationalism, creating tension between Dutch and French speakers that has continued to this day (see p114).

For details on King Léopold II's shocking rule of the Congo, see the boxed text, p121.

The Germans invaded in WWI and the town of Ypres was wiped off the map – tours of the Ypres Salient (p129) offer poignant reminders.

Following WWII, Belgium underwent an economic boom, later accentuated by Brussels' appointment as the headquarters of the EU and NATO.

In 1999, sick of mismanagement and political scandals, Belgians booted out the Christian Democrat party after 40 years in power. In came Liberal prime minister Guy Verhofstadt, best remembered for robust foreign policies and new moral freedoms (legalising gay marriage and euthanasia).

But political crisis was looming. Following the 2007 federal election the country was without a government for nine months. Finally, in March 2008, Yves Leterme, a Flemish Christian Democrat, took the helm. Four months later, he resigned after failing to get agreement between the Dutch-speaking and French-speaking political parties on constitutional reform. King Albert II rejected Leterme's resignation, and only time will tell whether consensus can be reached, or whether talk of Belgium splitting in two becomes reality.

THE CULTURE

'National' character is elusive – many Belgians think of themselves first as Flemish or Walloon, and then as Belgian. This state of affairs was made official in 1962 when the government drew an invisible line – known as the linguistic divide – across the country, cutting it almost equally in half in a bid to ease long-standing tension between the Flemish and Walloon communities. To the north of the divide lies Flanders (Vlaanderen), whose Dutch speakers make up 60% of Belgium's 10.6 million population. South of the divide is Wallonia (La Wallonie), where French-speaking Walloons make up most – but not all – of the remainder: there's also a German-speaking enclave in the Eastern Cantons. For more on Belgium's language situation, see p133.

On top of all this there's Brussels. The only area in Belgium to be officially bilingual, the capital is predominantly French-speaking and lies within Flanders, but is governed separately. Brussels' population includes more than 100 nationalities, from Europeans through to Moroccans, Turks and Africans, the latter largely from the former Belgian colony of Congo.

BELGIUM FOR FREE

- Swoon at the Grand Place/Grote Markt in many cities – start with Brussels (p118), Antwerp (p121) or Bruges (p126).
- Watch out for museums offering a free day or half-day, such as Ghent's art museums (p124) .
- Go into galleries like Brussels' Galeries St Hubert (p118).
- Take in one of the country's many beautiful *begijnhof* (see p126).
- Time a visit for free events like the Brussels Jazz Marathon or the Gentse Feesten (see p132).

READING UP

King Léopold's Ghost by Adam Hochschild investigates the atrocities committed in the Congo during Léopold II's reign and chronicles the small band of activists who fought his rule. *A Tall Man in a Low Land* is Harry Pearson's tale of family travel in Belgium, spotlighting the country's many idiosyncrasies. Belgium warrants two chapters in Bill Bryson's European sojourn, *Neither Here nor There*.

ARTS

Belgium's rich artistic heritage began in Bruges in the late Middle Ages with the painters known as the Flemish Primitives. Their works greatly influenced the course of European art and, centuries later, they still astonish viewers. Key players included Jan van Eyck and Hans Memling; their paintings are best viewed at Bruges' Groeningemuseum (p126) and Hospitaalmuseum Memling in St Jan (p126), and also at Ghent's St Baafskathedraal (p124).

Antwerp held the cultural high ground during the 17th century, mainly due to Flemish baroque painter Pieter Paul Rubens. His famous altarpieces can be seen in the city's Onze Lieve Vrouwkathedraal (see p121).

Surrealism, a movement that developed in Paris in the 1920s, found fertile ground here. Works by René Magritte, the movement's best known Belgian artist, are displayed at Brussels' new Magritte Museum (p118).

Also not to be missed is Brussels' art nouveau architecture. Check out the Musée Horta (p118) and the Old England building (p118).

Inspector Maigret fans would know that Belgium's the birthplace of Liège novelist Georges Simenon.

Comic strips are a Belgian forte. *Tintin* by Georges Remi, aka Hergé, is unquestionably the best known internationally, but all comic art is high-profile here (see p118).

ENVIRONMENT

Belgium's northern half is flat ol' Flanders. Here only church steeples break the monoto-

BELGIUM

nous topography. Sitting in stark contrast is the Ardennes in the southeast, a region of high plateaus and deep wooded valleys.

Belgium's environmental picture is ugly and the scene is not getting rosier – the country's two green parties were catapulted out of federal government in 2003 and both have failed to gain ground since. The only nationally protected reserves are the Hautes Fagnes Nature Reserve (see p130) in Wallonia and the Hoge Kempen in Limburg province. When hiking, remember to stay on marked paths, take litter with you, and obey signs restricting access to forests during fauna breeding seasons.

Water and noise pollution, urbanisation and waste management are the most pressing environmental issues.

TRANSPORT

GETTING THERE & AWAY

Air

Brussels Airlines (SN; ☎ 02 754 19 00; www.brusselsairlines.com) has flights from Brussels National Airport to European and African destinations. **VLM Airlines** (VG; ☎ 03 287 80 80; www.flyvlm.com) flies from Brussels National and Antwerp airport to London.

Belgium's main international airports:

Antwerp (ANR; ☎ 03 285 65 00; www.antwerpairport.be)
Brussels National Airport (BRU; ☎ 0900 70 000; www.brusselsairport.be)
Charleroi (CRL; ☎ 071 25 12 11; www.charleroi-airport.com)
Liège (LGG; ☎ 04 234 84 11; www.liegeairport.com)

Check the following budget airlines flying into Belgium: **Wizz Air** (www.wizzair.com), **Welcome Air** (www.welcomeair.com), **Sky Europe** (www.skyeurope.com), **Condor** (www.condor.de) and **Aer Arann** (www.aerarann.com).

Boat

The following car-ferry services operate to/from Belgium:

P&O (☎ in Belgium 070 70 07 74, in the UK 0871 664 5645; www.poferries.com) Sails overnight from Zeebrugge in Belgium to Hull in the UK (14 hours).
Superfast Ferries (☎ in Belgium 05 025 22 52, in the UK 0870 234 0870; www.superfast.com) Sails three times per week between Zeebrugge in Belgium and Rosyth in Scotland (18 hours).

CONNECTIONS

Belgium is well connected by train (below) to many neighbouring cities including Amsterdam, Paris, Cologne, Luxembourg City and London.

Transeuropa Ferries (☎ in Belgium 059 34 02 60, in the UK 01843 59 55 22; www.transeuropaferries.com) Eight sailings daily between Ostend in Belgium and Ramsgate in the UK (four hours).

Bus

Eurolines (www.eurolines.com; Brussels ☎ 02 274 13 50; Rue du Progrès 80; Antwerp ☎ 03 233 86 62; Van Stralenstraat 8; Ghent ☎ 09 220 90 24; Koningin Elisabethlaan 73; Liège ☎ 04 222 36 18; Rue des Guillemins 94) operates several international bus services to and from Belgium. Services from Brussels (one way) include Amsterdam (from €7, 3¾ hours, six daily), Frankfurt (€34, 5¼ hours, one daily), London (€29, 8½ hours, five daily), Luxembourg City (€15, 3¼ hours, one or two daily) and Paris (€20, 3¾ hours, 16 daily).

Car & Motorcycle

The main motorways into Belgium are the E19 from the Netherlands, the E40 from Germany, the E411 from Luxembourg, and the E17 and E19 from France. There are no controls at border crossings on any of these motorways.

Hitching

TaxiStop (☎ 070 22 22 92; www.taxistop.be; Rue du Fossé aux Loups 28, Brussels) is an agency that matches long-distance travellers with drivers who are headed for the same destination for a reasonable fee.

Train

Eurostar (☎ 02 528 28 28; www.eurostar.com) operates trains between Brussels' Gare du Midi station and London's St Pancras station (one hour 50 minutes, 10 trains Monday to Friday, eight trains Saturday and Sunday) through the Channel Tunnel.

Thalys (☎ 070 66 77 88; www.thalys.com) fast trains link various Belgian cities with destinations in France, the Netherlands and Germany. In Brussels, Thalys trains depart only from Gare du Midi. Thalys fares are cheaper on weekends and for trips booked well in advance. People aged 12 to 26 get a 50% discount.

GETTING INTO TOWN

From Brussels National airport, take the Airport City Express train to Gare Centrale (€2.90, 20 minutes), Brussels' most central train station, from where it's five minutes by hoof to the Grand Place.

Travellers on Eurostar and Thalys trains arrive at Gare du Midi, which is located 2.5km southwest of the Grand Place. You do not need to buy another train ticket to journey on to Gare Centrale – simply hop on a local train.

Eurolines buses deposit travellers at Gare du Nord, 1.5km north of the Grand Place; walk into town via Rue Neuve, or jump on a train to Gare Centrale.

Belgische Spoorwegen/Société National des Chemins de Fer Belges (Belgian Railways; ☎ 02 528 28 28; www.b-rail.be) operates services to Luxembourg City (one-way 2nd-class ticket €29, 2¾ hours, hourly).

GETTING AROUND

Bicycle

For details on cycling, see p132.

Car & Motorcycle

Foreign drivers do not need an international licence to drive in Belgium: your licence from home will suffice. Road rules are easy to understand, though the peculiar 'give way to the right' law takes some getting used to. Motorways are toll-free. The speed limit is 30km/h or 50km/h in towns, 90km/h outside towns and 120km/h on motorways. The blood alcohol limit is 0.05%.

Train

Train is the best way to get around. Belgium built Continental Europe's first railway line in the 1830s and has since developed an extremely dense network. Trains are run by the **Belgische Spoorwegen/Société National des Chemins de Fer Belges** (Belgian Railways; ☎ 02 528 28 28; www.b-rail.be).

At weekends (starting 7pm Friday), return tickets to anywhere within Belgium are 50% cheaper than on weekdays. For day excursions, find discounted packages called B-Excursions. A rail pass to consider is Go Pass (€46), which gives 10 one-way trips anywhere in Belgium for those under 26.

BRUSSELS (BRUSSEL, BRUXELLES)

pop 1,030,000

For some, Brussels' enduring image is of Manneken Pis, a fountain of a little boy peeing. Thank goodness, though, the city offers much more than that. You'll find art nouveau architecture, comic-strip art, sublime chocolate shops and mouth-watering menus. French versus Flemish, historic versus hip, bizarre versus boring – if you're into quirky, secretive or surreal, Brussels will seduce.

ORIENTATION

The Grand Place, the imposing 15th-century market square, sits in the centre of Petit Ring, a pentagon of boulevards enclosing central Brussels. The centre is divided into the Lower Town, with its medieval core and atmospheric quarters such as Ste Catherine, St Géry and the Marolles; and the Upper Town, home to museums and chic shopping areas based around the Sablon and Ave Louise. East of the Petit Ring is the EU's headquarters, looking like a real-life Gotham City.

INFORMATION

Internet Access

Concepts Telecom (Gare du Midi; 🕑 9am-8.30pm Mon-Fri, 10am-7.30pm Sat; per hr €4; Ⓜ Gare du Midi) Inside the main international train station.

Medical Services

Hôpital St Pierre (☎ 02 535 31 11, emergency 02 535 40 51; cnr Rue Haute & Rue de l'Abricotier; 🕑 24hr; Ⓜ Hôtel des Monnaies) Central hospital offering emergency assistance.

Money

ATMs and exchange facilities are both found on and around the Grand Place, at Gare du Midi and Brussels National Airport.

EMERGENCY NUMBERS

- Ambulance/fire brigade ☎ 100
- EU-wide emergency hotline ☎ 112
- Police ☎ 101
- Roadside assistance ☎ 070 34 47 77 (Touring Secours 24-hour assistance)

BELGIUM

BRUSSELS
0 500 m
0 0.3 miles
To 2GO4 (100m)
To Eurolines (400m); Gare du Nord (700m)
To Atomium (6km)
To Hôtel George V (300m)
To Brussels National Airport (10km)
To Irish Embassy (1km); Luxembourg Embassy (1.5km); Canadian Embassy (2km); German Embassy (3km)
To British Embassy (200m)
To Gare du Midi Train Station; Concepts Telecom (600m); Brussels International – Tourism (650m); Musée Bruxellois de la Gueuze (1.4km)
To Bruxelles Europe à Ciel Ouvert (100m); Dutch Embassy (4km); Koninklijk Museum voor Midden-Afrika (10km)
To Musée Horta (800m)
Ste Catherine
St Géry
Grand Place
Sablon
Upper Town
Royal Quarter
Marolles
Matonge
L'Étoile D'or
Parc de Bruxelles
Palais Royal
Palais de Justice
Cathédrale des Sts Michel & Gudule
Botanique
De Brouckère
Bourse
Gare Centrale
Parc
Arts-Loi
Madou
Trône
Porte de Namur
Louise
Porte de Hal
Anneessens
Hotel des Monnaies
Horta
Barrière de St-Gilles
INFORMATION
Australian Embassy 1 D3
Brussels International 2 B2
French Embassy 3 D2
Hôpital St Pierre 4 A4
Les Auberges de Jeunesse 5 D1
Main Post Office 6 B1
New Zealand Embassy 7 D4
USA Embassy 8 D3
SIGHTS & ACTIVITIES
Centre Belge de la Bande Dessinée 9 C1
Galeries St Hubert (see 39)
Grand Place 10 B2
Hôtel de Ville 11 B2
Manneken Pis Fountain 12 A3
Musee Magritte 13 C3
Musée des Instruments de Musique 14 C3
Musées Royaux des Beaux-Arts 15 B3
Neuhaus (see 39)
Old England Building (see 14)
SLEEPING
Bruegel 16 B3
Centre Vincent van Gogh 17 D1
Hôtel Métropole 18 B1
Sleep Well 19 B1
EATING
AD Delhaize 20 A2
African Eateries 21 D4
Belgo Belge 22 C4
Fritland 23 A2
Hong Kong Delight 24 A1
Jacques 25 A1
Le Perroquet 26 B4
Pita Places 27 B2
Vincent 28 B2
DRINKING
À la Bécasse 29 A2
À la Mort Subite 30 B2
Delirium Café 31 B2
Tels Quels 32 A2
ENTERTAINMENT
AB 33 A2
Fuse 34 A4
La Monnaie/De Munt 35 B2
Musée du Cinéma 36 C3
SHOPPING
De Biertempel 37 B2
Galerie d'Ixelles 38 C4
Galeries St Hubert 39 B2
Pierre Marcolini 40 B3
Place du Jeu-de-Balle Fleamarket 41 A4
Stijl 42 A1
TRANSPORT
Taxi Stop 43 B1

BELGIUM

Tourist Offices

Brussels International (☎ 02 513 89 40; www.brusselsinternational.be; Grand Place; ⌚ 9am-6pm Easter-Oct, 9am-6pm Mon-Sat, 10am-2pm Sun Nov-Dec, 9am-6pm Mon-Sat Jan-Easter; Ⓜ Gare Centrale, 🚊 Bourse) Tiny tourist office located inside the town hall and usually crammed.

Brussels International – Tourism (Gare du Midi; ⌚ 8am-8pm Sat-Thu, 8am-9pm Fri May-Sep, 8am-5pm Mon-Thu, 8am-8pm Fri, 9am-6pm Sat, 9am-2pm Sun Oct-Apr; Ⓜ Gare du Midi) For visitors arriving by Eurostar or Thalys.

SIGHTS

Brussels' magnificent central square, **Grand Place** (Ⓜ Gare Centrale), tops the itinerary. Here the splendid Gothic-style **Hôtel de Ville** was the only building to escape bombardment by the French in 1695 – ironic, considering it was the target. The square's splendour is due largely to its antique frame of **guildhalls**, erected by merchant guilds and adorned with gilded statues and symbols.

Galeries St Hubert (Rue du Marché aux Herbes; Ⓜ Gare Centrale), one block northeast of Grand Place, is a European first and a must visit. Opened in 1847, this *grande dame* of Brussels' shopping arcades contains an eclectic mix of cafes and traders, including **Neuhaus** (☎ 02 512 63 59; Galerie de la Reine 25; Ⓜ Gare Centrale), a gorgeous chocolate shop established in 1857 (it was thanks to Neuhaus' grandson that pralines were invented). Off one of the arcades is **Rue des Bouchers**, the capital's famous dining street – worth a wander for its barking hawkers and dancing lobsters (but dine elsewhere).

The **Musées Royaux des Beaux-Arts** (☎ 02 508 32 11; www.fine-arts-museum.be; Rue de la Régence 3; adult/concession €6/3.50, admission free 1-5pm 1st Wed of month; ⌚ 9.30am-5pm Tue-Fri, 10am-5pm Sat & Sun; Ⓜ Gare Centrale) has Belgium's premier collection of ancient and modern art; walk from the Lower Town.

Next door is the new **Musée Magritte** (☎ tickets 02 508 33 33; www.musee-magritte-museum.be; Place Royale; admission €8; ⌚ 10am-5pm Tue-Sun, till 8pm Wed; Ⓜ Gare Centrale or Parc, 🚊 92, 93 or 94). It houses 150 works by Belgium's most famous surrealist artist, René Magritte.

The nearby **Musée des Instruments de Musique** (☎ 02 545 01 30; www.mim.fgov.be; Rue Montagne de la Cour 2; adult/concession €5/4; ⌚ 9.30am-5pm Tue-Fri, 10am-5pm Sat & Sun; Ⓜ Gare Centrale) boasts one of the world's biggest collections of musical instruments. It's housed in the **Old England building**, an art nouveau showpiece and worth a look in itself.

A superb introduction to art nouveau is the **Musée Horta** (☎ 02 543 04 90; www.hortamuseum.be; Rue Américaine 25; adult/concession €7/5; ⌚ 2-5.30pm Tue-Sun; Ⓜ Horta, 🚊 91 or 92). It occupies two adjoining houses in St Gilles that Horta designed in 1898. It's 2.5km south of the Grand Place.

If you are into national symbols, consider visiting the **Manneken Pis fountain** (cnr Rue de l'Étuve & Rue du Chêne; Ⓜ Gare Centrale), a little boy cheerfully taking a leak into a pool near the Grand Place, and the **Atomium** (☎ 02 475 47 77; www.atomium.be; Sq de l'Atomium; adult/concession €9/6; ⌚ 10am-7pm May-Sep, 10am-6pm Oct-Apr; Ⓜ Heyzel, 🚊 81), a space-age leftover from the 1958 World Fair, 5km north of the city centre.

Dedicated beer buffs must not miss the excellent **Musée Bruxellois de la Gueuze** (☎ 02 521 49 28; www.cantillon.be; Rue Gheude 56; admission €5; ⌚ 9am-5pm Mon-Fri, 10am-5pm Sat; Ⓜ Gare du Midi). This working brewery is 800m from Gare du Midi – head to Place Bara, take Rue Limnander, and then cross into Rue Gheude.

The **Centre Belge de la Bande Dessinée** (☎ 02 219 19 80; www.cbbd.be, in Dutch & French; Rue des Sables 20; adult/concession €7.50/6; ⌚ 10am-6pm Tue-Sun; Ⓜ Botanique or Rogier) tours the country's vibrant comic-strip culture. It's 10 minutes' walk from the Grand Place.

SLEEPING

Brussels has all bases covered where sleeping is concerned. Most of the city's B&B accommodation is organised by **Bed & Brussels** (☎ 02 646 07 37; www.bnb-brussels.be).

Bruxelles Europe à Ciel Ouvert (☎ 02 640 79 67; www.cielouvertcamping.world/word/workpress.com; Chaussée de Wavre 203; camp sites per adult/tent €6/6; ⌚ Jul & Aug; 🚌 34 or 80) Summer-only camping ground (no caravans or campervans) at the back of an imposing building.

Centre Vincent Van Gogh (☎ 02 217 01 58; www.chab.be; Rue Traversière 8; dm/s/d/q €15/30/44/70, bed sheets €4; 💻 ⊠; Ⓜ Botanique) Brussels' cheapest and grooviest hostel has clean, basic rooms and a laid-back vibe. It's strictly 17 to 35ers only and is located 1.2km uphill from Gare Centrale.

Bruegel (☎ 02 511 04 36; www.jeugdherbergen.be; Rue du St Esprit 2; dm/s/d €19/33/62; 💻 ⊠; Ⓜ Gare Centrale) The most central of Brussels' three HI hostels.

Sleep Well (☎ 02 218 50 50; www.sleepwell.be; Rue du Damier 23; dm/s/d/tr with shared bathroom €22/30/54/72; 💻 ⊠; Ⓜ Rogier) This is a bright, modern

SPLURGE

Hôtel Métropole (☎ 02 217 23 00, reservations 02 214 24 24; www.metropolehotel.com; Pl de Brouckère 31; s/d/ste weekday from €330/360/500, s/d weekend from €130/155; P 💻 ⊠ ❄; M De Brouckère) For a weekend in luxury, book into the *grande dame* of Brussels' accommodation scene, the Métropole. The soberly furnished rooms contrast sharply with the lavish French Renaissance-style foyer, but the buffet breakfast is regal enough for all tastes.

hostel-cum-hotel close to brash Rue Neuve, Brussels' main shopping thoroughfare.

2G04 (☎ 02 219 30 19; www.2G04.be; Blvd Émile Jacqmain 99; dm/d/q €25/65/110; 💻 ⊠; M Rogier) Brussels' newest and trendiest hostel occupies a bright-red terrace house at the slightly sleazy end of town. The location makes it an excellent base for those wanting to pub crawl the night away. Breakfast is not included, but a morning coffee is.

Hôtel George V (☎ 02 513 50 93; www.george5.com; Rue t' Kint 23; s/d/tr/q €65/75/90/100; 🚋 Bourse) This presentable, family-run hotel on the edge of St Géry has prices that are a snip for this funky part of town.

EATING

As the capital of a nation of foodies, Brussels is over-endowed with quality eateries.

Fritland (☎ 02 514 06 27; Rue Henri Maus 49; snacks from €1.80; 🕑 11am-1am Sun-Thu, 11am-dawn Fri & Sat; 🚋 Bourse) Fill up fast on a cone of *frites* (chips or fries) or a stuffed baguette sandwich at this corner snack bar. It's been around for more than 30 years.

Hong Kong Delight (☎ 02 503 2628; Rue Ste Catherine 33; plat du jour €5; mains €8-14; 🕑 noon-2am; 🚋 Bourse) Several nondescript restaurants compete for customers in Brussels' little Chinatown area. This place does good food, and it's open 'til late.

Le Perroquet (☎ 02 512 99 22; Rue Watteeu 31; light meals €8-10; 🕑 noon-1am; ⊠; M Porte de Namur) Art nouveau cafe in the affluent Sablon. Salads and stuffed pitas, including vegetarian options, are the mainstay.

our pick **Belgo Belge** (☎ 02 511 11 21; Rue de la Paix 20; mains from €15; 🕑 noon-midnight; ⊠; M Porte de Namur) Just one of many great eateries in this Ixelles back street (check out the options in Rue St Boniface too). An eclectic crowd keeps this restaurant buzzing day and night, and the lunchtime *menu du jour* (€10) is well priced.

Jacques (☎ 02 513 27 62; Quai aux Briques 44; mains €17-25, mussels €23; 🕑 lunch & dinner Mon-Sat; M Ste Catherine) One of many seafood restaurants in Ste Catherine. This one's down to earth and has been around for more than 60 years.

Vincent (☎ 02 511 26 07; Rue des Dominicains 8; mains €18-29; 🕑 lunch & dinner; ⊠; M Gare Centrale) Over a century old, and still drawing in the locals, this Brussels' institution combines classic Belgian cuisine with good-natured waiters and historic decor.

Also recommended:

AD Delhaize (☎ 02 512 80 87; cnr Rue du Marché aux Poulets & Blvd Anspach; 🕑 9am-8pm Mon-Thu & Sat, 9am-9pm Fri, 9am-6pm Sun; 🚋 Bourse) Supermarket.

African eateries (Rue Longue Vie; M Porte de Namur) Casual Congolese cafes line up on this pedestrianised street in the Matonge quarter. Best at night and definitely off-the-beaten track.

Pita places (M Gare Centrale) For pita, pick from the swarm of places along Rue du Marché aux Fromages, just south of Grand Place.

DRINKING

Pub and cafe culture is ingrained in Brussels. Most streets in the city centre have at least one pub – Place St Géry is particularly well endowed.

Delirium Café (www.deliriumcafe.be; Impasse de la Fidélité 4A; 🕑 10am-4am, until 2am Sun; M Gare Centrale) This cellar pub guarantees to stock at least 2004 beers – the lion's share are Belgian, of course. When we visited there were 2851 brews on hand, and not an empty stool. Cheers!

À la Mort Subite (☎ 02 513 13 18; Rue Montagne aux Herbes Potagères 7; 🕑 10.30am-midnight; ⊠; M Gare Centrale) Long cafe with wood panelling, mirrored walls and brusque service. A must to get the vibe of Brussels.

À La Bécasse (☎ 02 511 00 06; Rue de Tabora 11; 🕑 10am-1am; 🚋 Bourse) Try a jug of draught *lambic*, a beer unique to the Brussels region, at this little institution.

Tels Quels (☎ 02 512 45 87; www.telsquels.be, in French; Rue du Marché-au-Charbon 81; 🕑 5pm-late Thu, Fri & Sun-Tue, 2pm-late Wed & Sat; M Anneessens) Cafe-cum-information centre catering to both lesbians and gay men. Located on one of the city's nightlife streets.

Fuse (☎ 02 511 97 89; www.fuse.be; Rue Blaes 208; depending on DJs admission €3-12; 🕑 11pm-7am Sat; M Porte de Hal) The Marolles house club that put Brussels on the international circuit.

ENTERTAINMENT

The weekly English-language magazine *The Bulletin* has entertainment coverage. Also check *Le Soir* on Wednesday.

Musée du Cinéma (☎ 02 551 19 19; Rue Baron Horta 9; admission €2.50; from 5pm; Ⓜ Gare Centrale) One to make cinema buffs swoon. It houses two auditoriums: silent movies with live piano accompaniment are screened every night of the year in one; the other is devoted to classic talkies.

AB (☎ 02 548 24 24; www.abconcerts.be; Blvd Anspach 110; Bourse) Great venue smack in the heart of the city. AB, or Ancienne Belgique, has two auditoriums accommodating international and home-grown bands.

La Monnaie/De Munt (☎ 02 229 12 00; www.demunt.be; Pl de la Monnaie; Ⓜ De Brouckère) Brussels' premier venue for opera, theatre and contemporary dance.

SHOPPING

Browse **Place du Jeu-de-Balle fleamarket** (Pl du Jeu-de-Balle; 7am-2pm; Ⓜ Porte de Hal), the Marolles' famous *brocante* (second-hand) market; a stately *galerie* such as **Galeries St Hubert** (p118); or **Galerie d'Ixelles** (off Chaussée de Wavre; Ⓜ Porte de Namur), the pulse of Brussels' African community.

De Biertempel (☎ 02 502 19 06; Rue du Marché aux Herbes 56; Ⓜ Bourse) stocks 550 Belgian brews plus matching glasses.

For Belgium's most expensive pralines (€70 per kg) there's **Pierre Marcolini** (☎ 02 514 12 06; Pl du Grand Sablon 39; Ⓜ Porte de Namur).

Rue Antoine Dansaert is Brussels' avant-garde fashion hub – head to **Stijl** (☎ 02 512 03 13; Rue Antoine Dansaert 74; Ⓜ Ste Catherine).

GETTING THERE & AWAY

Brussels is Belgium's international transport hub. For information on air services to Brussels, see p115. Details on rail services, including Eurostar and Thalys, are on p115. For information on Eurolines buses, see p115.

GETTING AROUND

Brussels' efficient public transport system is operated by **Société des Transports Intercommunaux de Bruxelles** (☎ 070 23 20 00; www.stib.be); buses, trams, the metro and prémetro (trams that dive underground) run from about 6am to midnight. Single tickets/day cards cost €1.70/€4.

AROUND BRUSSELS

For details on the Koninklijk Museum voor Midden-Afrika (Royal Museum for Central Africa), see the boxed text, opposite.

WATERLOO

pop 31,000

Waterloo's enough to defeat anyone. The battleground where Napoleon fell and European history changed course in 1815 is staid in essence and tedious to get around on public transport. You've got to be a war or history buff to make the pilgrimage 18km south of Brussels. Catch TEC bus W from Ave Fosny at Brussels' Gare du Midi train station (buy a €6.50 day card) and start at the **Office du Tourisme** (☎ 02 352 09 10; www.waterloo-tourisme.be; Chaussée de Bruxelles 218; 9.30am-6.30pm Apr-Sep, 10.30am-5pm Oct-Mar) in the village of Waterloo; bus W stops out the front.

FLANDERS

The only thing flat about Flanders is topography. Belgium's Dutch-speaking northern region is the country's powerhouse. Economically, this is the wealthy half of Belgium. The region's financial boom in the last 50 years is quickly evident in historic art cities like Bruges, Antwerp and Ghent, where modern – whether it be art, architecture or fashion – sits successfully beside historic treasures. And then there's Ypres, a little town with a big place in wartime history.

ANTWERP (ANTWERPEN, ANVERS)

pop 457,000

Attitude with a capital A – that's Antwerp. As an avant-garde fashion capital snapping at the heels of Milan and New York and the top spot on the clubbing circuit between Amsterdam and Paris, Belgium's second-biggest city's a magnet for fashionistas, foodies and party queens alike. And that's without even mentioning history, architecture or cafe culture, or its new position on the high-speed train network.

Orientation & Information

Antwerp's impressive train station, Centraal Station, is 1km east of the historic centre, which is based around the Grote Markt and

KING LÉOPOLD II & THE CONGO

In 1885 Belgium's King Léopold II personally acquired the Congo in Africa, an area almost 100 times the size of his homeland. Between then and 1908, when the Belgian state stripped the king of his possession, it is estimated up to 10 million Africans died from starvation or overwork, or were murdered, in Léopold's quest for rubber.

We'll never know for sure the number of people who died. On Léopold's orders, the Congo archives were destroyed. But what is certain is that the booty from this barbarity was enormous. Brussels' landmarks – such as the Arcade du Cinquantenaire – were built on these proceeds. So, too, was the **Koninklijk Museum voor Midden-Afrika** (Royal Museum for Central Africa; ☎ 02 769 52 30; www.africamuseum.be; Leuvensesteenweg 13, Tervuren; adult/concession €4/1.50; 10am-5pm Tue-Fri, 10am-6pm Sat & Sun; M Montgomèry then 44). This monumental museum, located 14km east of the capital, makes for a half-day excursion that won't be readily forgotten. The museum houses the world's most impressive array of African artefacts, all of which will be dusted and polished for the museum's centennial celebrations in 2010.

Groenplaats. To get to the centre walk along the Meir (pronounced 'mare'), a bustling shopping thoroughfare, or take tram 2 or 15 from prémetro station Diamant below Centraal Station.

2Zones (☎ 03 232 24 00; Wolstraat 15; per hr €4.40; 11am-8pm Mon-Sat; Groenplaats) Internet bar.

KBC Bank (Eiermarkt; Meir) ATM; also at the post offices.

Tourism Antwerp (☎ 03 232 01 03; www.antwerpen.be; Grote Markt 13; 9am-5.45pm Mon-Sat, 9am-4.45pm Sun; Groenplaats) Main tourist office.

Tourist Office (Level 0, Centraal Station; 9am-5.45pm Mon-Sat, 9am-4.45pm Sun; Diamant) For travellers arriving by train.

Sights

Antwerp's epicentre is the **Grote Markt** (Groenplaats), a pedestrianised market square presided over by the impressive Renaissance-style **Stadhuis** and lined by **guildhalls**, most of which were reconstructed in the 19th century.

The splendid **Onze Lieve Vrouwkathedraal** (☎ 03 213 99 51; www.dekathedraal.be; Handschoenmarkt; adult/concession €4/2; 10am-5pm Mon-Fri, 10am-3pm Sat, 10am-4pm Sun; Groenplaats) is Belgium's largest and finest Gothic cathedral (built 1352–1521). Its light interior houses four canvasses by Rubens.

Antwerp's prestigious **Rubenshuis** (☎ 03 201 15 55; www.museum.antwerpen.be; Wapper 9-11; adult/concession €6/4, admission free last Wed of month; 10am-5pm Tue-Sun; Meir) was the home and studio of Pieter Paul Rubens, northern Europe's greatest baroque artist.

The **Koninklijk Museum voor Schone Kunsten** (☎ 03 238 78 09; www.kmska.be; Leopold De Waelplaats, 't Zuid; adult/concession €6/4, admission free last Wed of month; 10am-5pm Tue-Sat, 10am-6pm Sun; 8, 1 or 23 direction Zuid) houses paintings dating from the Flemish Primitives to contemporary times. It's 1.25km south of the Grote Markt.

Fashion followers must start with Antwerp's mode museum, **MoMu** (☎ 03 470 27 70; www.momu.be; Nationalestraat 28; adult/concession €6/4; 10am-6pm Tue-Sun; Groenplaats). To see what local designers are up to, visit **Walter** (☎ 03 213 26 44; St-Antoniusstraat 12; 10am-6pm Mon-Sat; Groenplaats), the shop of fashion guru Walter Van Beirendonck.

The raised riverside promenade known as **Zuiderterras** (Groenplaats) offers a great skyline view plus an essential pit stop (see Drinking, p123). Nearby is the entry to **St Annatunnel** (Groenplaats). This 570m-long pedestrian tunnel, dug under the Scheldt in the 1930s, links the city centre with the **Linkeroever**, or Left Bank, from where there's another fab city panorama.

Zurenborg, about 2km southeast of Centraal Station, is famed for the eclectic architecture found in a handful of streets. The showcase is **Cogels-Osylei** (11 direction Eksterlaar), a street where affluent citizens went wild a century ago.

Sleeping

To explore the city's burgeoning B&B scene, check out the **Association of Antwerp Guestrooms** (www.bedandbreakfast-antwerp.com).

Camping De Molen (☎ 03 219 81 79; info.sport@stad.antwerpen.be; Thonetlaan; camp sites per adult/car/tent €2.50/1/1.25; Apr-Sep; 36, direction Linkeroever) The pick of the city's two camping grounds; across the river on the Linkeroever.

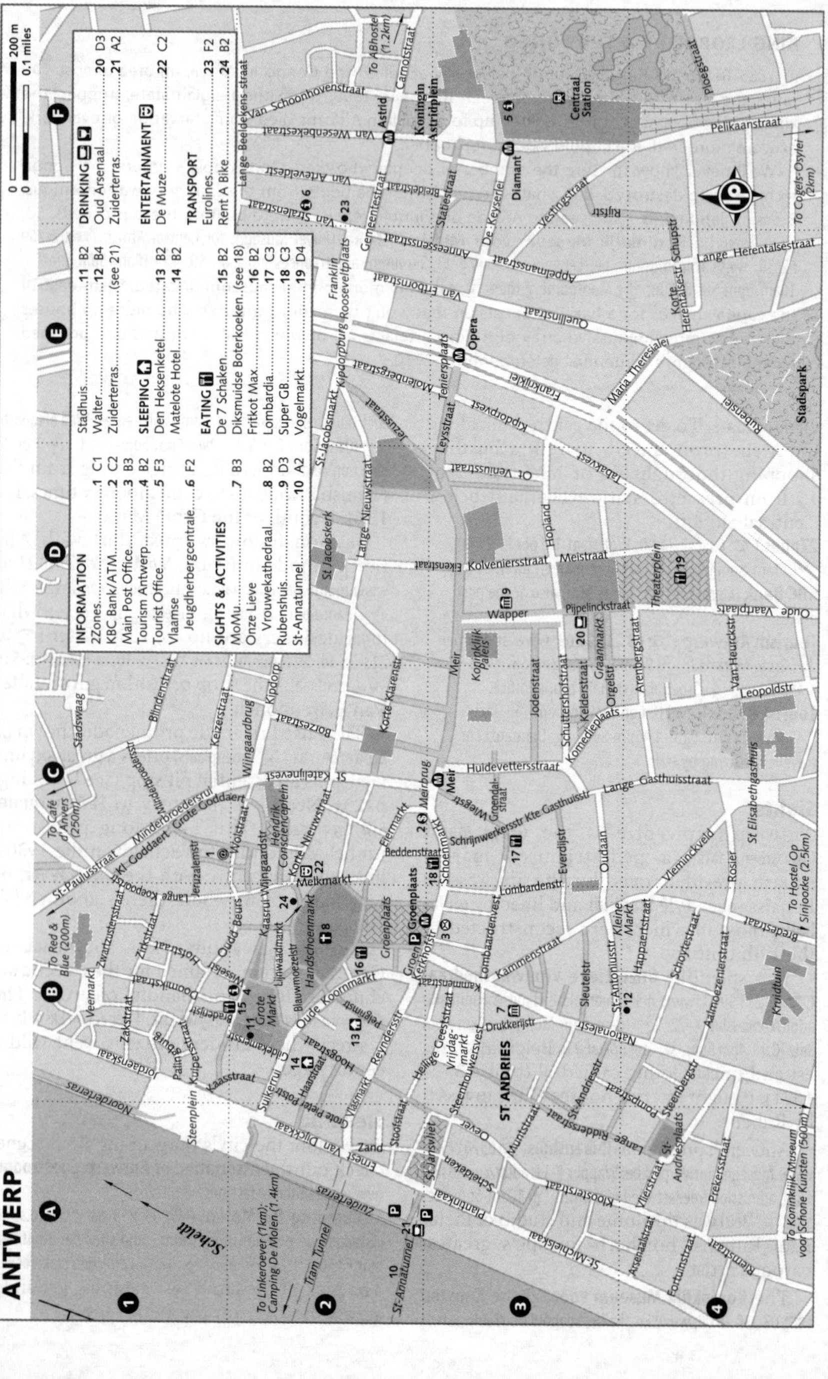

ANTWERP

0 — 200 m
0 — 0.1 miles

INFORMATION
2Zones....1 C1
KBC Bank/ATM....2 C2
Main Post Office....3 B3
Tourism Antwerp....4 B2
Tourist Office....5 F3
Vlaamse Jeugdherbergcentrale....6 F2

SIGHTS & ACTIVITIES
MoMu....7 B3
Onze Lieve Vrouwekathedraal....8 B2
Rubenshuis....9 D3
St-Annatunnel....10 A2
Stadhuis....11 B2
Walter....12 B4
Zuiderterras....(see 21)

SLEEPING
Den Heksenketel....13 B2
Matelote Hotel....14 B2

EATING
De 7 Schaken....15 B2
Diksmuidse Boterkoeken....(see 18)
Fritkot Max....16 B2
Lombardia....17 C3
Super GB....18 C3
Vogelmarkt....19 D4

DRINKING
Oud Arsenaal....20 D3
Zuiderterras....21 A2

ENTERTAINMENT
De Muze....22 C2

TRANSPORT
Eurolines....23 F2
Rent A Bike....24 B2

To Red & Blue (200m)
To Café d'Anvers (250m)
To Linkeroever (1km); Camping De Molen (1.4km)
To ABhostel (1.2km)
To Koninklijk Museum voor Schone Kunsten (500m)
To Hostel Op Sinjoorke (2.5km)
To Cogels-Osylei (2km)

Hostel Op Sinjoorke (☎ 03 238 02 73; www.jeugdherbergen.be; Eric Sasselaan 2; dm/s/d €16.40/36/52; Jan-Nov; P; ; 2, direction Hoboken) HI-affiliated hostel 3km south of the city centre.

our pick **ABhostel** (☎ 0473 57 01 66; www.abhostel.com; Langstraat 83; dm/d €17/50, sheets €2; ; 11, direction Eksterlaar stop Ploegstraat) Probably Belgium's smallest hostel, and a gem to boot. Avid traveller Bridget runs this eight-bed hostel in Borgerhout, Antwerp's Moroccan neighbourhood east of Centraal Station. Guests have the run of two floors (kitchen included), and lots of little added extras make it comfy and cosy. If only more hostels were like this.

Den Heksenketel (☎ 03 226 71 64; www.heksenketel.org; Pelgrimstraat 22; dm €17, sheets €2; ; Groenplaats) The only cheap accommodation in the city heart and located on a street with an unbeatable cathedral view. Three simple but fresh dorms are situated above a small folk-music club. There's a small kitchen.

Matelote Hotel (☎ 03 201 88 00; www.matelote.be; Haarstraat 11; r from €120, breakfast €10; ; Groenplaats) Discreet new design hotel on a pedestrianised backstreet in the city heart. It offers nine contemporary rooms tastefully arranged throughout a 16th-century building.

Eating

Foodies love Antwerp. Dining out is a favourite local pastime, evident by the number of eateries of all persuasions that compete in this vibrant city.

Fritkot Max (Groenplaats 12; chips €2.35, sauce €0.65; 11.30am-midnight Mon-Fri, 11.30am-3am Sat & Sun; Groenplaats) Join the queue and don't expect service with a smile at this most authentic Belgian *fritkot* (chip shop).

Diksmuidse Boterkoeken (☎ 03 227 40 26; Groenplaats; filled bread roll €3; 8.30am-7.30pm Mon-Sat; Groenplaats) *The* place in town to buy a sandwich – ask for a 'Smos' and you'll soon find out why. Located in the basement of the Grand Bazar shopping centre.

De 7 Schaken (☎ 03 232 52 44; Braderijstraat 24; snacks €7-10, mains €11-17; 11am-11pm; ; Groenplaats) Tucked away on a corner of the Grote Markt, this smooth relatively new bistro/bar beautifully blends the old with the new. Prices for the well-presented meals are a snip.

our pick **Lombardia** (☎ 03 233 68 19; Lombaardenvest 78; light meals €8-12; 7.45am-6pm Mon-Sat; ; Meir) Legendary health-food-shop-cum-cafe that has been around for nearly four decades. The food's all *bio* (organic) and the decor's bizarre. Try Alain's new sensation, Ginger Love tea (€3).

Also recommended:

Super GB (Groenplaats; 8.30am-8pm; Groenplaats) Basement supermarket in the Grand Bazar shopping centre.

Vogelmarkt (Theaterplein; 6am-3pm Sat & Sun; Meir) Food market.

Drinking

The only thing better in Antwerp than eating is drinking. Het Zuid (The South), commonly abbreviated as 't Zuid, is a popular nightlife quarter.

Oud Arsenaal (☎ 03 232 97 45; Pijpelinckstraat 4; 7.30am-7.30pm Sat & Sun, from 9am Wed-Fri & Mon; Meir) Catch the city's most congenial brown cafe while it lasts. Beers are among the cheapest in town – you'll pay just €2.70 for a Duvel.

Zuiderterras (☎ 03 234 12 75; Ernest van Dijckkaai 37; 9am-midnight; Groenplaats) Modern landmark cafe-restaurant at the southern end of the riverside promenade and designed by the city's eminent contemporary architect, bOb Van Reeth.

Red & Blue (☎ 03 213 05 55; www.redandblue.be; Lange Schipperskapelstraat 11; 11pm-7am Sat; 7) The biggest nightclub in this corner of Europe, drawing party queens from outside Belgium's borders to house, techno, rap and soul. It's men only on Saturday nights but goes mixed on Friday.

Café d'Anvers (☎ 03 226 38 70; www.café-d-anvers.com; Verversrui 15; 11pm-7.30am Fri & Sat; 7). This legendary club does funk and house, disco and soul in a refurbished church in the city's red-light district. Many of Belgium's top DJs started here.

De Muze (☎ 03 226 01 26; Melkmarkt 15; noon-4am) Listen to free live jazz from 10pm Friday and Saturday.

Getting There & Around

From **Centraal Station** (☎ 02 528 28 28), train connections include Brussels (€6.30, 35 minutes), Ghent (€8.20, 45 minutes) and Bruges (€12.90, 70 minutes).

For details on Eurolines buses, see p115.

De Lijn Antwerpen (☎ 070 22 02 00; www.delijn.be) runs a good network of buses, trams and a prémetro (trams that run underground).

Hire bikes from **Rent A Bike** (☎ 03 290 49 62; Lijnwaadmarkt 6; per half/full day from €6/8.50, 2 days €13; 9am-6pm; Groenplaats).

GHENT (GENT, GAND)

pop 235,000

Ghent is Flanders' unsung city. Right in the middle of Brussels, Bruges and Antwerp, it's often overlooked on the hop between Belgium's big three. With historic architecture, fab restaurants and sublime chocolate shops, it's a great place to give crowds the flick (but don't expect to have it all to yourself during the Gentse Feesten, see p132).

Orientation & Information

Central Ghent is based around the Korenmarkt (🚊 1), 2km north of the main train station, St Pietersstation.

Tourist office (☎ 09 266 52 32; www.visitgent.be; Botermarkt 17; 🕒 9.30am-6.30pm Apr-Oct, 9.30am-4.30pm Nov-Mar; 🚊 1)

Use-it (☎ 09 324 39 06; www.use-it.be; St Pietersnieuwstraat 21; 🕒 1-6pm Mon-Fri; 🚊 1) Tourist office for under 26ers.

Sights

Leave the Korenmarkt behind to reach one of Belgium's most picturesque shots – the view from **St Michielsbrug** (🚊 1), the bridge over the Leie River. Stretching before you is the **Graslei**, the city's favoured waterfront promenade.

Join the queues at **St Baafskathedraal** (☎ 09 269 20 45; St Baafsplein; 🕒 8.30am-6pm Apr-Oct, 8.30am-5pm Nov-Mar; 🚊 1) to see the **Adoration of the Mystic Lamb** (admission €3; 🕒 9.30am-4.30pm Mon-Sat, 1-4.30pm Sun Apr-Oct, 10.30am-3.30pm Mon-Sat, 1-3.30pm Sun Nov-Mar). This lavish representation of medieval religious thinking is one of the earliest-known oil paintings, executed in 1432 by Flemish Primitive artist Jan van Eyck and not to be missed.

The 14th-century **Belfort** (☎ 09 233 39 54; Botermarkt; admission €3; 🕒 10am-6pm Easter–mid-Nov; 🚊 1) affords spectacular views of the city; there's a lift or stairs.

The **Gravensteen** (☎ 09 225 93 06; St Veerleplein; adult/concession €6/1.20; 🕒 9am-6pm Apr-Sep, 9am-5pm Oct-Mar; 🚊 1), smack in the heart of the city, belonged to the 12th-century counts of Flanders and is the quintessential castle.

Ghent's highly regarded **SMAK** (Stedelijk Museum voor Actuele Kunst; ☎ 09 221 17 03; www.smak.be; Citadelpark; adult/concession €5/3.80, 10am-1pm Sun free; 🕒 10am-6pm Tue-Sun; 🚊 4) contains works by Karel Appel, Pierre Alechinsky and Panamarenko – three of Belgium's best-known modern artists.

Nearby is the newly-renovated **Museum voor Schone Kunsten** (Fine Arts Museum; ☎ 09 240 07 00; www.mskgent.be; Citadelpark; adult/concession €4/2.50, 10am-1pm Sun free; 🕒 10am-6pm Tue-Sun; 🚊 4).

Sleeping & Eating

The old Patershol quarter is awash with ambient restaurants and pubs. The Vrijdagmarkt is another good nightlife spot. B&B bookings are organised by **Bed & Breakfast Ghent** (www.bedandbreakfast-gent.be).

Camping Blaarmeersen (☎ 09 266 81 60; camping.blaarmeersen@gent.be; Zuiderlaan 12; camp sites per adult/tent/car €4.50/4.50/2.50; 🕒 Mar–mid-Oct) Way west of town – take bus 9 (direction Mariakerke) from St Pietersstation to the Europabrug stop, then bus 38 or 39.

De Draecke (☎ 09 233 70 50; www.vjh.be; St Widostraat 11; dm/tw €17.5/44; ⊠; 🚊 1) This is one of Belgium's best HI-affiliated hostels, housed in a renovated warehouse in the city heart.

Brooderie (☎ 09 225 06 23; www.brooderie.be; Jan Breydelstraat 8; s/d/t €45/65/85; ⊠; 🚊 1) Three simple rooms (shared bathroom facilities) located above a bakery-cum-tearoom. Unpolished wooden floors, earthy furniture, and a fabulous location are the salient features.

our pick **Fritkot Jozef** (Vrijdagmarkt; chips & sauce €2.50; 🕒 11.30am-10pm Mon-Fri, until 8pm Sat; 🚊 1) *Frieten* (chips) have been served from this traditional *frituur* since 1898.

Slagerij Hooiaard (Hooiaard 2; 🕒 8am-6pm Mon-Fri, closed mid-Jul–mid-Aug; 🚊 1) Where else but meat-loving Belgium would a butcher's double as a take-away shop? The *belegde broodjes* (filled bread rolls; €1) are the cheapest in town.

't Hoekske (☎ 09 224 24 70; Kortrijksepoortstraat 1; snacks & light meals €2.65-10; 🕒 24hr; 🚊 1) This modern little brasserie is an institution in Ghent, and is open anytime of the day or night.

Also recommended:

Food market (Vrijdagmarkt; 🕒 8am-2pm Fri; 🚊 1) Weekly food market.

Souplounge (☎ 09 223 62 03; Zuivelbrugstraat 6; small/large soup €3.50/4.50; 🕒 10am-7pm; 🚊 1) Modern soup kitchen. The new branch (Overpoortstraat 1) in the student hub is closed Sunday.

Getting There & Around

From **St Pietersstation** (☎ 02 528 28 28) trains run half-hourly to Antwerp (€8.20, 45 minutes), Bruges (€5.60, 20 minutes) and Brussels (€8.20, 45 minutes), and hourly to Ypres (€9.90, one hour).

For details about Eurolines buses, see p115.

Public transport is operated by **De Lijn** (☎ 070 22 02 00).

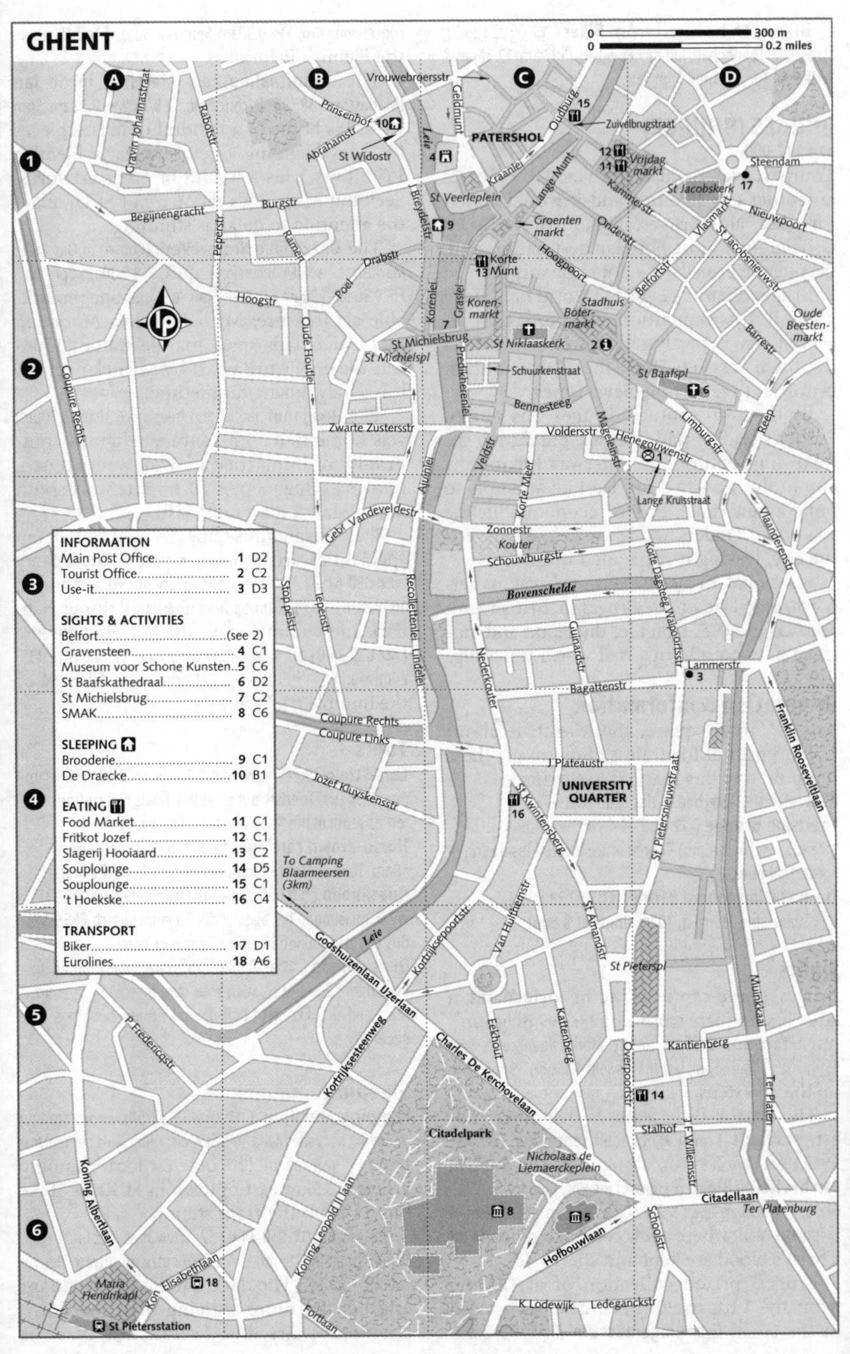
GHENT
0 300 m
0 0.2 miles
INFORMATION
Main Post Office 1 D2
Tourist Office 2 C2
Use-it 3 D3
SIGHTS & ACTIVITIES
Belfort (see 2)
Gravensteen 4 C1
Museum voor Schone Kunsten 5 C6
St Baafskathedraal 6 D2
St Michielsbrug 7 C2
SMAK 8 C6
SLEEPING
Brooderie 9 C1
De Draecke 10 B1
EATING
Food Market 11 C1
Fritkot Jozef 12 C1
Slagerij Hooiaard 13 C2
Souplounge 14 D5
Souplounge 15 C1
't Hoekske 16 C4
TRANSPORT
Biker 17 D1
Eurolines 18 A6
PATERSHOL
UNIVERSITY QUARTER
Citadelpark
To Camping Blaarmeersen (3km)
St Pietersstation
BELGIUM

Bikes can be hired from **Biker** (☎ 09 224 29 03; Steendam 16; per half/full day €6.50/9; 9am-12.30pm & 1.30-6pm Tue-Fri, until 5pm Sat).

BRUGES (BRUGGE)

pop 117,000

Touristy, overcrowded and a tad fake: preface any other city like this and it would be left for dead. Not Bruges. This medieval town is Belgium's most popular destination and, despite the crowds, it's not to be missed.

Bruges dreamily evokes a world long since gone. But its reputation as a perfectly preserved city is partly fabrication – much of the town was rebuilt in the 19th and 20th centuries to reflect medieval times.

By the 14th century, Bruges was one of Europe's leading trade centres. But during the following century, the waterway linking the city to the sea silted up. Despite attempts to build a new canal, Bruges' economic lifeline was gone. Traders and townsfolk abandoned the city, leaving it suspended in time.

For a modern take on this medieval masterpiece, track down *In Bruges,* a British film released in 2008. Don't let the blood and violence put you off – it's well worth watching.

Orientation & Information

Bruges' main square, the Markt, is about 1.5km north of the train station; to get there jump on any bus marked 'Centrum'.

ATM (Markt 5) Attached to the main post office.

Toerisme Brugge (☎ 050 44 46 46; www.brugge.be; 't Zand; 10am-6pm) Tourist office located inside the Concertgebouw.

Train station tourist office (☎ 050 38 80 83; 10am-5pm Mon-Fri, 10am-2pm Sat & Sun)

Sights

Bruges' nerve centre is the historic **Markt**, a large open square from which rises Belgium's most famous **Belfort** (Belfry; Markt; adult/concession €5/4; 9.30am-5pm, last tickets sold 4.15pm). Squeeze up the 366 steps.

The nearby Burg features Belgium's oldest **stadhuis** (Town Hall; adult/concession €2.50/2; 9.30am-5pm Tue-Sun), along with the **Basiliek van het Heilig Bloed** (Basilica of the Holy Blood; admission €1.50; 9.30am-noon & 2-5.50pm Apr-Sep, 10am-noon & 2-4pm Oct-Mar), where a few coagulated drops of Christ's blood are kept and cherished.

Bruges' prized collection of art dating from the 14th to 20th centuries is housed in the small **Groeningemuseum** (Dijver 12; adult/concession €8/6; 9.30am-5pm Tue-Sun). Don't miss the Flemish Primitives.

The **Hospitaalmuseum Memling in St Jan** (Mariastraat 38; adult/concession €8/6; 9.30am-5pm Tue-Sun) is home to a handful of masterpieces by Hans Memling, one of the early Flemish Primitives, plus a wealth of other artworks. Seek out Memling's reliquary of St Ursula – the attention to detail is stunning.

The **Onze Lieve Vrouwekerk** (Church of Our Lady; Mariastraat; adult/concession €2.50/2; 9.30am-5pm Tue-Fri, 9.30am-4.20pm Sat, 1.30-5pm Sun) has one remarkable art treasure: Michelangelo's *Madonna and Child.* This small marble statue (1504) was the only work of art by Michelangelo to leave Italy during his lifetime.

The **Begijnhof** (admission free; 6.30am-6.30pm) was home to a 13th-century religious community of unmarried or widowed women, known as Begijnen. A 10-minute walk south of the Markt, it's a must visit.

Two private museums devoted to Belgian specialities are worth a squiz – **Choco-Story** (☎ 050 61 22 37; www.choco-story.be; Wijnzakstraat 2; admission €6; 10am-5pm) is about all things rich, dark and yummy, while the new **Frietmuseum** (☎ 050 34 01 50; www.frietmuseum.be; Vlamingstraat33; admission €6; 10am-5pm) traces the history of the humble *friet* (chip).

Tours

Canal tours (Steenhouwersdijk & Dijver; €6.50; 10am-6pm Mar-Oct) Touristy but essential. Boats depart from jetties south of the Burg, and tours last 30 minutes.

Horse-drawn carriages (Markt; 5 passengers €34; 10am-10pm) Trips (35 minutes) depart from the Markt.

Quasimodo (☎ 050 37 04 70; freephone 0800 975 25; www.quasimodo.be; over/under 26 yr incl lunch €55/45) Bus day trips taking in either Bruges or Ypres.

Quasimundo (☎ 050 33 07 75; www.quasimundo.eu; over/under 26 €24/22, with your own bike €15; mid-Mar–mid-Oct) Excellent half-day bike tours; bookings necessary.

Sleeping

Camping Memling (☎ 050 35 72 50; www.camping-memling.be; Veltemweg 109, St Kruis; camp sites per tent/car €12/5; year-round) The quietest local camping ground, 2.5km east of town in St Kruis. Take bus 11 from the train station.

Passage (☎ 050 34 02 32; www.passagebruges.com, Dweersstraat 26-28; dm €14, d without/with private shower €50/65;) The dark, candle-lit restaurant and bar are more enticing than the dorm rooms upstairs, but overall this place is

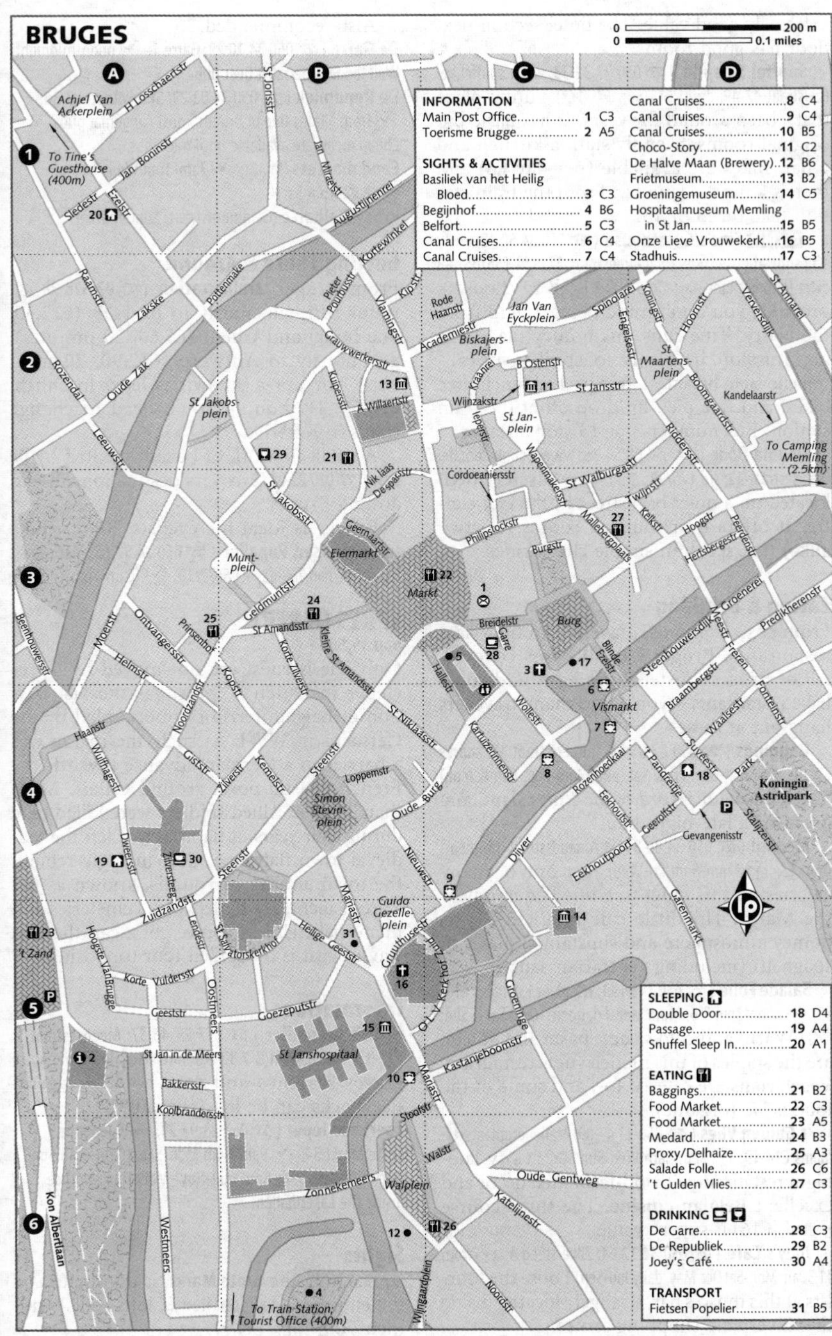
BRUGES
0 200 m
0 0.1 miles
A
B
C
D
1
2
3
4
5
6
INFORMATION
Main Post Office 1 C3
Toerisme Brugge 2 A5
SIGHTS & ACTIVITIES
Basiliek van het Heilig Bloed 3 C3
Begijnhof 4 B6
Belfort 5 C3
Canal Cruises 6 C4
Canal Cruises 7 C4
Canal Cruises 8 C4
Canal Cruises 9 C4
Canal Cruises 10 B5
Choco-Story 11 C2
De Halve Maan (Brewery) 12 B6
Frietmuseum 13 B2
Groeningemuseum 14 C5
Hospitaalmuseum Memling in St Jan 15 B5
Onze Lieve Vrouwekerk 16 B5
Stadhuis 17 C3
SLEEPING
Double Door 18 D4
Passage 19 A4
Snuffel Sleep In 20 A1
EATING
Baggings 21 B2
Food Market 22 C3
Food Market 23 A5
Medard 24 B3
Proxy/Delhaize 25 A3
Salade Folle 26 C6
't Gulden Vlies 27 C3
DRINKING
De Garre 28 C3
De Republiek 29 B2
Joey's Café 30 A4
TRANSPORT
Fietsen Popelier 31 B5
Achjel Van Ackerplein
To Tine's Guesthouse (400m)
To Camping Memling (2.5km)
To Train Station; Tourist Office (400m)
St Jakobsplein
Muntplein
Eiermarkt
Markt
Burg
Vismarkt
Jan Van Eyckplein
Biskajersplein
St Janplein
St Maartensplein
Simon Stevinplein
Guido Gezelleplein
St Janshospitaal
Walplein
't Zand
Koningin Astridpark
Kon Albertlaan
Oude Gentweg
Oude Burg
Westmeers
Oostmeers
Wijngaardplein

extremely good value. The hotel section next door has good rooms.

Snuffel Sleep In (☎ 050 33 31 33; www.snuffel.be; Ezelstraat 47-49; dm/d €15/36; ☐ ☒) Funky place that's been around for years. It has basic but original rooms, friendly staff, a kitchen and a bar. Bikes are available (per day €6) and there's a nearby laundry. From the train station take bus 3 or 13.

our pick Tine's Guesthouse (☎ 050 34 50 18; www.tinesguesthouse.com; Zwaluwenstraat 11; s/d €55/65, €5 extra for one-night stay; ☒) *The* B&B to choose – provided you don't mind being 1.5km from the belfry. Tine runs this homey place and her mission in life is to spoil visitors – unbelievable breakfast, free packed lunch, free bikes, and free pick-up/drop off at the train station! Bus number 3 or 13 stops nearby.

Double Door (☎ 050 68 51 76; www.doubledoor.be; Waalsestraat 12; s/d €75/90; ☒) Very discreet B&B located on a quiet backstreet in the city centre. It offers four modern rooms (no two alike) that speak in simple clean tones.

Eating & Drinking

From cosy *estaminets* (taverns) to first-class restaurants, Bruges has all bases covered. All of Bruges' hostels have bars, and some have restaurants – you'll find many travellers hang out at these.

Baggings (☎ 050 67 95 94; Kuipersstraat 17; snacks €2-10; ⏲ noon-6am Fri & Sat, until 4am Thu, Sun & Mon) Snack bar with a *Lord of the Rings* slant, and great for a late-night bite.

Medard (☎ 050 34 86 84; St Amandsstraat 18; mains from €3; ⏲ 11am-8pm Fri-Wed) Just one of many eateries on this quiet tree-lined square near the Markt. This little cafe is noted for its homey atmosphere and substantial plates of spaghetti (including vegetarian sauces).

Salade Folle (☎ 050 34 94 43; Walplein 13; mains €10-15; ⏲ noon-3pm & 6-10pm Mon-Fri, noon-10pm Sat & Sun; ☒) Warm and cold salads, pasta and quiche are the staples of this modern new restaurant. Vegetarians are catered for, and some of the food is *bio* (organic).

't Gulden Vlies (☎ 050 33 47 09; Mallebergplaats 17; mains €14-19; ⏲ 7pm-3am Wed-Sun; ☒) Cosy late-night restaurant with old-fashioned decor and excellent Belgian cuisine. The three-course *menú* (€16) is superb value.

Joey's Café (☎ 050 34 12 64; Zilversteeg 4; ⏲ from 11.30am Mon-Sat Oct-May, daily Jun-Sep) Loose the tourists at this muso's bar, strangely located inside the Zilverpand shopping centre.

Also recommended:

De Garre (☎ 050 34 10 29; Garre 1; ⏲ noon-midnight) Well hidden specialist beer pub.

De Republiek (☎ 050 34 02 29; St Jakobsstraat 36; ⏲ from 11am) One of Bruges' most congenial pubs. Cheap meals are available until midnight.

Food markets (Markt; ⏲ 7am-1pm Wed; 't Zand; ⏲ 8am-1pm Sat)

Proxy/Delhaize (Geldmuntstraat) Supermarket.

Getting There & Around

From Bruges' **train station** (☎ 02 528 28 28), trains run half-hourly to Brussels (€12.30, one hour) and Ghent (€5.60, 20 minutes), and hourly to Antwerp (€12.90, 70 minutes). For Ypres (known as Ieper in Dutch; €10.50, 1¼ hours), you'll need to change trains in Kortrijk.

A small network of buses operated by **De Lijn** (☎ 070 22 02 00) covers destinations in and around Bruges.

Bruges is ideal for cyclists. Rent a bike from **Fietsen Popelier** (☎ 050 34 32 62; Mariastraat 26; per hr/half/full day €3.50/7/10; ⏲ 10am-7pm).

YPRES (IEPER)

pop 35,500

Only the hardest are not moved by Ypres (Ieper in Dutch). Ypres was the last bastion of Belgian territory unoccupied by the Germans in WWI. As such, the region was a barrier to a German advance towards the French coastal ports around Calais. More than 300,000 Allied soldiers were killed here during four years of fighting that left the medieval town flattened. Convincingly rebuilt, the town and its surrounds, known as the Ypres Salient, are dotted with cemeteries and memorials. Unless you've got a car, the best way to visit is by guided tour (opposite).

Information

British Grenadier (☎ 057 21 46 57; Meensestraat 5; ⏲ 9.30am-5.30pm & 7.30-8.30pm) Bookshop, war graves searches and tour-booking agent. Backpacks can be left (per day €3).

Toerisme Ieper (☎ 057 23 92 20; www.ieper.be; Grote Markt 34; ⏲ 9am-6pm Mon-Sat, 10am-6pm Sun Apr–mid-Nov, 9am-5pm mid-Nov–Mar) Tourist office inside the Lakenhallen.

Sights

Ypres' hub, the **Grote Markt**, is dominated by the enormous **Lakenhallen** (Cloth Halls) with their 70m-high belfry.

On the 1st floor of the Lakenhallen is **In Flanders Fields Museum** (☎ 057 23 92 20; www.inflandersfields.be; Grote Markt 34; admission €8; 🕑 10am-6pm Apr–mid-Nov, 10am-5pm Tue-Sun mid-Nov–Mar), a moving testament to the wartime horrors experienced by ordinary people.

The **Menin Gate** (Meensestraat) is perhaps the saddest reminder of the town's tragic past. The huge white gate is inscribed with the names of 54,896 British and Commonwealth troops whose lives were lost in the quagmire of the trenches and who have no graves. Every evening at 8pm, traffic is halted while buglers sound the **Last Post** (www.lastpost.be).

Tyne Cot Cemetery, the largest British Commonwealth war cemetery in the world, sits on a plateau about 8km northeast of Ypres. A total of 11,956 soldiers are buried here, and the names of a further 35,000 missing soldiers are engraved on the rear wall. A new visitor centre, discreetly located behind the cemetery, opened in 2007 and uses simple means to honour the war dead. The cemetery can be visited by guided tour, or take bus 94 (hourly, 20 minutes) from Ypres and walk the last 300m.

The **Memorial Museum Passchendaele 1917** (☎ 051 77 04 41; www.passchendaele.be; Ieperstraat 5, Zonnebeke; admission €5; 🕑 10am-6pm Feb-Nov), in the village of Zonnebeke, 3km south of Tyne Cot Cemetery, provides a chilling dugout experience. Bus 94 stops nearby.

Tours

Several companies offer good bus tours of the Ypres Salient. Book in advance:

Quasimodo (☎ 050 37 04 70, freephone 0800 975 25; www.quasimodo.be; adult/under 26 €55/45; 🕑 mid-Mar–mid-Oct) Located in Bruges (see p126).

Salient Tours (☎ 057 21 46 57; www.salienttours.com; 2½/4hr tours €28/35; 🕑 Thu-Tue Mar-Nov) Run by an Englishman based in Ypres. Book at the British Grenadier (see opposite)

Sleeping & Eating

Jeugdstadion (☎ 057 21 72 82; www.jeugdstadion.be; Bolwerkstraat 1; camp sites per adult/car €5/5; 🕑 Easter-Sep) Basic camping ground attached to a youth centre, 900m southeast of Grote Markt.

B&B Nooit Gedacht (☎ 057 20 84 00; erna.tant@telenet.be; Ligywijk 129; s/d/t with shared bathroom €30/50/70) If you've ever wanted to stay in a typical red-brick suburban Belgian home, this is your chance! It's 900m northeast of the Menin Gate, very old-fashioned, and decidedly friendly.

B&B Ter Thuyne (☎ 057 36 00 42; www.terthuyne.be; Gustave de Stuersstraat 19; s/d/f €55/70/120; 💻) Delightful B&B smack in the heart of town with three modern rooms – the light-blue room at the front is the pick.

In 't Klein Stadhuis (☎ 057 21 55 42; Grote Markt 32; mains €13-21; 🕑 closed Sun Oct-May; ⊠) Split-level cafe tucked away in a quaint guildhall next to the Stadhuis. Offers good-value meals day and night.

Getting There & Around

From Ypres **train station** (☎ 02 528 28 28) hourly trains go direct to Kortrijk (€4.50, 30 minutes) and Ghent (€9.90, one hour). For Brussels (€15.20, 1½ hours), Bruges (€10.50, 1¼ hours) and Antwerp (€17, two hours), change in Kortrijk.

WALLONIA

Parlez-vous français? You'll need to in Wallonia, Belgium's French-speaking southern half. Step across the linguistic divide to enter a seemingly different country. Gone are the flat fields and affluence of the north – here it's forested hillsides, intimate villages and industrial decay. Then burrow down in the Ardennes, Wallonia's southeastern corner, where ancient castles loom over tranquil hamlets.

LIÈGE (LUIK)

pop 189,000

Love or loathe it, Liège always leaves an impression. This gritty city, sprawled along the Meuse River about 90km east of Brussels, takes time to know. Stay a while and explore its excellent museums devoted to Walloon life, and it may win you over. For Simenon fans, this is Georges' birthplace and his primary place of homage.

The main tourist office is **Maison du Tourisme** (☎ 04 237 92 92; www.ftpl.be; Pl St Lambert 32-35; 🕑 9am-6pm Jun-Sep, 9.30am-5.30pm Oct-May). There's also a tourist office at the main train station, Gare Guillemins.

Sights

For an overview of the life of Belgium's most prolific writer, pick up the English-language

 Book your stay at lonelyplanet.com/hotels

brochure, the **Simenon Route**, which describes a walking tour around Outremeuse where Georges spent his youth.

The **Musée Tchantchès** (☎ 04 342 75 75; www.tchantches.be, in French; Rue Surlet 56; admission €1; 🕑 2-4pm Tue & Thu, puppet shows 2.30pm Wed & 10.30am Sun Jun-Sep) honours Liège's mascot and oldest 'citizen', Tchantchès, a wooden puppet with a big nose and bad behaviour.

The excellent **Musée d'Art Réligieux et d'Art Mosan** (Museum of Religious Art & Art from the Meuse Valley; ☎ 04 221 42 25; Rue Mêre Dieu; admission €3.80; 🕑 11am-6pm Tue-Sat, 11am-4pm Sun) is chock-full of well-preserved regional religious relics.

Sleeping & Eating

Auberge de Jeunesse (☎ 04 344 56 89; www.laj.be; Rue Georges Simenon 2; dm/s/d €17.50/31/44; 💻 ⊠) To get to this modern HI-affiliated hostel on Outremeuse take bus 4 from Gare Guillemins to Pl St Lambert and change to bus 18.

Hors Château (☎ 04 250 60 68; www.hors-chateau.be; Rue Hors Château 62; s/d €78/95, breakfast €12; 💻) Ordinary, small, functional rooms are the trademark of this hotel, but the excellent central location in the city's historic quarter make up for the dearth of atmosphere.

Le Grain de Sel (☎ 04 232 03 23; En Bergerue 15; mains €12-17, salads €10; 🕑 lunch Tue-Sat, dinner Mon-Sat; ⊠) Cheery informal eatery set up in three connecting rooms, and a good respite for vegetarians.

Getting There & Away

Liège's newly renovated train station, **Gare Guillemins** (☎ 02 528 28 28), is 2km south of Place St Lambert, the city's heart and main bus hub – to get there simply catch another train to the city's most central station, Gare du Palais.

From Gare Guillemins, trains connect with Brussels (€12.90, one hour), Namur (€7.70, 50 minutes), Spa (€4.50, 50 minutes) and Luxembourg City (€33, 2½ hours, every two hours).

For info on Eurolines buses, see p115.

AROUND LIÈGE

Hautes Fagnes Nature Reserve

The Hautes Fagnes, or High Fens, is a plateau of swampy heath, woods and windy moors that sweeps over to Germany's Eifel hills. The area is popular with walkers and cyclists. Start a visit at the **Botrange Nature Centre** (☎ 080 44 03 00; www.centrenaturebotrange.be; Route de Botrange 131; 🕑 10am-6pm).

DETOUR: SPA

There's no bursting its bubble. **Spa,** Europe's oldest health resort, has for centuries embraced royalty and the wealthy who came to drink, bathe and cure themselves in the mineral-rich waters that bubble forth here. These days a new generation interested in well-being is taking to the town's palatial hilltop complex, the **Thermes de Spa** (☎ 087 77 25 60; www.thermesdespa.com; 3hr session €17; 🕑 10am-9pm).

Spa is 40km southeast of Liège and connected by regular trains (€4.30, 50 minutes).

It takes at least 1¼ hours to arrive here on public transport from Liège – take the train to Verviers (€3.80, 20 minutes, hourly) and then bus 390 (€3.80, 30 minutes, five daily) to Rocherath.

NAMUR (NAMEN)

pop 108,000

Namur is a great jumping-off point for exploring Wallonia's forested Ardennes. Some 60km southeast of Brussels, it's a picturesque town built at the confluence of the Meuse and Sambre Rivers and presided over by a citadel that, in times gone by, ranked as one of Europe's mightiest.

The **Office du Tourisme** (☎ 081 24 64 49; www.namurtourisme.be; Sq Léopold; 🕑 9.30am-6pm) is near the train station.

Sights

Don't miss the **Trésor du Prieuré d'Oignies** (☎ 081 25 43 00; Rue Julie Billiart 17; admission €2; 🕑 10am-noon & 2-5pm Tue-Sat, 2-5pm Sun), a one-room hoard of exquisite Gothic treasures housed in a modern convent. Ring the bell to be taken on a guided tour by one of the nuns.

What remains of the once-mighty **Citadelle de Namur** (☎ 081 65 45 00; www.citadelle.namur.be; Route Merveilleuse) is slung high above the town on a rocky outcrop. For easy access take the **shuttle minibus** (☎ 081 24 64 49; tickets €1; 🕑 10am-5pm daily Jun–mid-Sep, Sat & Sun Apr, May & mid-Sep–Oct), which departs hourly from the tourist office. Alternatively, walk up (trail distances vary; the shortest walk is 1km).

The **Musée Félicien Rops** (☎ 081 22 01 10; www.ciger.be/rops; Rue Fumal 12; admission €3; 🕑 10am-6pm Tue-Sun) devotes itself to Namur-born artist

Félicien Rops (1833–98) who fondly illustrated the erotic and macabre.

Sleeping & Eating

Camping Les 4 Fils Aymon (☎ 081 58 02 94; Chaussée de Liège 989, Lives-sur-Meuse; camp sites per tent, car & 2 people €8; ⏰ Apr-Sep) Pleasant camping ground 6km east of Namur; take bus 12 (hourly) from the bus station.

Auberge de Jeunesse (☎ 081 22 36 88; www.laj.be; Ave F Rops 8; dm/s/d €17.50/31/43.60; 💻 🅿 ⊠) Attractive riverfront hostel 3km southwest of the train station. Buses 3 and 4 from Pl de la Station stop nearby.

Hôtel Les Tanneurs (☎ 081 24 00 24; www.tanneurs.com; Rue des Tanneries 13; s €50-210, d €65-225; ❄ 💻 🅿) Unique hotel situated in the heart of town. Unites modern comfort with 17th-century charm. Book well ahead.

Brasserie Henry (☎ 081 22 02 04; Pl St Aubain 3; mains €8-20; ⏰ noon-midnight Mon-Thu, noon-1am Fri & Sat; ⊠) Sociable brasserie and an institution among Namur's late-night diners.

Self-caterers can stock up at **Match** (☎ 081 23 40 80; Rue des Fossés Fleuris; ⏰ 9am-7pm Mon-Sat) supermarket.

Getting There & Away

Namur **train station** (☎ 025 28 28 28) is a major rail hub. Regional connections include Brussels (€7.70, one hour, half-hourly), Jemelle (€7.70, 40 minutes, hourly), Liège (€7.70, one hour, half-hourly) and Marloie (€7, 35 minutes, hourly).

Regional and local buses are operated by **TEC** (☎ 081 25 35 55; Place de la Station; ⏰ 7am-7pm).

ROCHEFORT & HAN-SUR-LESSE

pop 16,000

As a base in the Ardennes, Rochefort is hard to beat. Together with its neighbour Han-sur-Lesse, 6km away, Rochefort is famed for the millennia-old underground limestone grottoes that attract visitors from all over Belgium. The caves at Han are the more spectacular of the two, but Han itself is a tourist trap; stay in Rochefort and commute between the towns.

Rochefort's **tourist office** (☎ 084 34 51 72; www.valdelesse.be; Rue de Behogne 5; ⏰ 8am-6pm Mon-Fri, 9.30am-5pm Sat & Sun Jul & Aug, 8am-5pm Mon-Fri, 10am-5pm Sat & Sun Sep-Jun) is in the centre of town.

Sights & Activities

The impressive **Grottes de Han** (☎ 084 37 72 13; www.grotte-de-han.be; Rue Lamotte 2; admission €9.50; ⏰ 10am-noon & 1-5pm Apr-Oct, 11.30am-4pm Nov, Dec & Mar) is a series of caves dripping with stalactites and stalagmites a little way out of Han. Excursions here start with a toy-train ride, followed by a long walk through cold tunnels and finally a boat trip on an underground lake. Rochefort's cave, **Grotte de Lorette** (☎ 084 21 20 80; Drève de Lorette; admission €7.25; ⏰ 10.30am-4.30pm Mar-Oct), is smaller but also worth seeing.

The area is a great base for **walking** and cycling. One trail for cyclists is **RAVeL**, a stretch of disused train line linking Rochefort and the villages of Jemelle and Houyet. Rent a bike from **Cycle Sport** (☎ 084 21 32 55; Rue de Behogne 59; per morning/afternoon/full day €10/15/20; ⏰ 9.30am-noon & 1.30-6.30pm Tue-Sat, 9.30am-noon Sun).

Sleeping & Eating

The following options are all in Rochefort.

Camping Les Roches (☎ 084 21 19 00; Rue du Hableau; camp sites per adult plus tent €14, extra adult €4; ⏰ Easter-Oct) Next to the Lomme River, immediately below the main part of town.

Le Vieux Moulin (☎ 084 21 46 04; www.giterochefort.be; Rue du Hableau 25; under/over 26 yr €11.10/13.90; ⏰ year-round) Pleasant *gîte d'étape* (basic hostel-style accommodation) in the heart of town. The price includes breakfast.

Hôtel La Malle Poste (☎ 084 21 09 86; www.malleposte.be; Rue de Behogne 46; s/d Maison du Cocher €85/120, Les Thermes from €95/140; 🏊 🅿) Opt for a night in the quaint old stagecoach quarter, Maison du Cocher, or choose a more stylish room (complete with spa bath) in the Les Thermes section.

Figaro (☎ 084 21 13 22; Rue de Behogne 43; mains €13-18; ⏰ lunch & dinner Wed-Sun; ⊠) Big new brasserie doing modern Belgian cuisine. The elevated terrace out back is great for a quiet Rochefort beer.

Getting There & Away

To get to Rochefort from Namur, take the train to Jemelle (€7.70, 40 minutes, hourly) then bus 29 to Rochefort (€1.40, seven minutes, hourly), which continues on to Han (€1.40, seven minutes).

BASTOGNE (BASTENAKEN)

pop 14,200

It was in Bastogne, close to the Luxembourg border, that thousands of soldiers and civilians died during WWII's Battle of the Bulge. Testament to these events is a huge, star-shaped **American memorial** on a hill 2km from

Bastogne. The neighbouring **Bastogne Historical Centre** (☎ 061 21 14 13; www.bastognehistoricalcenter.be; Colline du Mardasson; admission €8.50; 9.30am-5pm May-Sep, 10am-4.30pm Oct-Apr) recounts the battle.

The **Maison du Tourisme** (☎ 061 21 27 11; www.paysdebastogne.be; Pl McAuliffe 60; 9am-6pm mid-Jun–mid-Sep, 9.30am-12.30pm & 1-5.30pm mid-Sep–mid-Jun) is in a conspicuous building in the heart of town.

Hôtel Collin (☎ 061 21 43 58; www.hotel-collin.com; Place McAuliffe 8; s/d/tr €67/85/105; P) has carpeted rooms fitted out in warm, rustic tones.

To get to Bastogne, the closest rail junction is Libramont, from where bus 163B departs every two hours (€3.80, 45 minutes).

BELGIUM DIRECTORY

ACCOMMODATION

Camping grounds are plentiful throughout the country and at their best in Wallonia's hilly Ardennes region. Check www.campingbelgique.be for listings.

Hostels (*jeugdherberg* in Dutch, *auberge de jeunesse* in French) affiliated with Hostelling International (HI) are easily found in Belgium. Contact **Vlaamse Jeugdherbergcentrale** (☎ 03 232 72 18; www.jeugdherbergen.be; Van Stralenstraat 40, B-2060 Antwerp) for hostels in Flanders and **Les Auberges de Jeunesse** (☎ 02 219 56 76; www.laj.be; Rue de la Sablonnière 28, B-1000 Brussels) for Wallonia. There are also a few private hostels.

In rural areas, you'll occasionally come across *gîtes d'étapes,* basic hostel-style dwellings that welcome individual travellers.

B&Bs *(gastenkamers/chambres d'hôtes)* normally represent excellent value, with prices starting at €40/50 a single/double. Hotels start at similar rates, but at this price you'll get communal bathroom facilities.

ACTIVITIES

Cycling

Cycling is one of Belgium's national passions. In flat Flanders, many roads have dedicated cycle lanes. In Wallonia, the hilly terrain is favoured by mountain bike (VTT, or *vèlo tout-terrain* in French, *terreinfiets* in Dutch) enthusiasts.

Bikes can be hired from private operators or from about 20 train stations for around €6.50/9.50 per half/full day. You may have to pay a deposit (€12 to €20) and show your passport. Bikes can also be taken on trains (one way/return €5/8 to anywhere in Belgium).

Hiking

Hiking ranges from the easy terrain in Flanders to the more inspiring hills of the Ardennes. Local tourist offices have copious information about hiking paths and they sell regional hiking maps.

BUSINESS HOURS

Standard opening hours:

Banks 9am-5pm Mon-Fri
Clubs 11pm-6am Fri-Sun
Pubs & cafes 10am or 11am-1am or 2am (some stay open till dawn)
Restaurants 11.30am-2pm or 3pm & 6.30-11pm, brasseries 11am to 1am
Shops 9am-6pm Mon-Sat, 10am-4pm Sun in major cities; most supermarkets stay open until 9pm. Shops in smaller towns often close for lunch (noon to 2pm).

EMBASSIES & CONSULATES

The following diplomatic missions are located in Brussels.

Australia (☎ 02 286 05 00; www.austemb.be; Rue Guimard 6, B-1040)
Canada (☎ 02 741 06 11; www.belgium.gc.ca; Ave de Tervuren 2, B-1040)
France (☎ 02 548 87 11; www.ambafrance-be.org; Rue Ducale 65, B-1000)
Germany (☎ 02 787 18 00; fax 02 787 28 00; Rue Jacques de Lalaing 8-14, B-1040)
Ireland (☎ 02 235 66 76; fax 02 235 66 71; Rue Wiertz 50, B-1050)
Luxembourg (☎ 02 735 20 60; http://bruxelles.mae.lu; Ave de Cortenbergh 75, B-1000)
Netherlands (☎ 02 679 17 11; www.nederlandseambassade.be; Ave Herrmann-Debroux 48, B-1160)
New Zealand (☎ 02 512 10 40; www.nzembassy.com; 7th fl, Sq de Meeus 1, B-1100)
UK (☎ 02 287 62 11; http://ukinbelgium.fco.gov.uk; Rue d'Arlon 85, B-1040)
USA (☎ 02 508 21 11; http://belgium.usembassy.gov; Blvd du Régent 27, B-1000)

FESTIVALS & EVENTS

Belgium buzzes with music, pageantry and parades including:

Brussels Jazz Marathon (www.brusselsjazzmarathon.be) The second-last weekend in May brings free nonstop jazz to Brussels.
Rock Werchter (www.rockwerchter.be) Held near Leuven, a Flemish town near Brussels, for four days over the first weekend of July. Together with Glastonbury (England), this is one of Europe's biggest 'field' rock festivals.
De Gentse Feesten (www.gentsefeesten.be) Ghent's annual 10-day shindig in mid-July transforms the city into

a free party of music and theatre. It includes 10 Days Off (www.10daysoff.be), one of Europe's main techno parties.

FOOD & DRINK

Belgians love food. They are reputed to dine out, on average, more than any other people in the world. Expect to pay €14 or less for a main course in budget eateries; midrange restaurants charge between €15 and €35; anything over €35 is top end.

The national dish is *mosselen/moules,* mussels cooked in white wine and served in steaming cauldrons with a mountain of *frieten/frites* (chips or fries). Meat and seafood are abundantly consumed, as are offal and *filet américain.* Don't be deceived, the latter is not a succulent American steak but a blob of minced beef served raw. A *belegd broodje/sandwich garni* (half a baguette with a prepared filling) is an immensely popular snack food. At lunchtime many restaurants offer a *dagschotel/plat du jour* (dish of the day), which often represents excellent value.

Brussels' dining scene is eminently international, reflecting its status as the EU capital, but around the countryside things are less diverse. Many cafes and brasseries these days cater to vegetarian tastes (but not to vegans).

On the drinking scene, beer rules. No country in the world boasts a brewing tradition as rich and diverse as Belgium's. And nowhere will you find the quantity of quality beers – literally hundreds exist. Try a dark Trappist beer made by monks, golden nectars like Duvel (named after the devil himself) or the acquired taste of tangy, fruity *lambics* (beer unique to the Brussels region). For the latter, don't miss Brussels' Musée Bruxellois de la Gueuze (p118).

HOLIDAYS

New Year's Day 1 January
Easter Monday March/April
Labour Day 1 May
Ascension Day 40th day after Easter
Whit Monday 7th Monday after Easter
Flemish Community Festival 11 July (Flanders only)
National Day 21 July
Assumption 15 August
Walloon Community Festival 27 September (Wallonia only)
All Saints' Day 1 November
Armistice Day 11 November
German Community Festival 15 November (Eastern Cantons only)
Christmas Day 25 December
School Holidays July and August; one week in November; two weeks at Christmas; one week around Carnival; two weeks at Easter; one week in May

LANGUAGE

Belgium has three official languages – Dutch, French and German. To find out what lingo is spoken where, see the Culture section (p114) and take a look at the inset on the Belgium map (p113).

Many Flemish prefer to call their language Vlaams (Flemish) rather than Nederlands (Dutch) due to historical and cultural reasons.

MONEY

Banks are the best place to exchange money. Outside banking hours, exchange bureaus (*wisselkantoren* in Dutch; *bureaux d'échange* in French) operate at Brussels National airport and at main train stations. ATMs are widespread. Tipping is optional as service and VAT are included in prices.

POST

Letters under 50g cost €0.80 within the EU, or €0.90 anywhere else.

TELEPHONE

To call abroad, the international access code is ☎ 00. Belgium's country code is ☎ 32. Mobile codes are 0472 to 0479, 0482 to 0489 and 0492 to 0499. Numbers prefixed with 0900 or 070 are expensive pay-per-minute numbers. Numbers prefixed with 0800 are free calls. For an international operator, call ☎ 1324.

VISAS

There are no entry requirements or restrictions on EU nationals visiting Belgium. Citizens of Australia, Canada, Israel, Japan, New Zealand and the USA do not need visas to visit as tourists for up to three months. Except for people from a few other European countries (such as Switzerland), everyone else must have a visa issued by a Belgian embassy or consulate.

For up-to-date visa information, check **Federal Public Service Foreign Affairs Belgium** (www.diplomatie.be).

Bosnia & Hercegovina

HIGHLIGHTS

- **Sarajevo** Explore the vibrant cafe-filled heart of this very 'human' capital (p137)
- **Mostar** Survey the picturesque Ottoman old town from the iconic bridge (p144)
- **Adrenalin overload** Raft from Foča (p147), go canyoning beyond historic Jajce (p143), ski at Jahorina (p139) or quad-bike at Bjelašnica (p139)
- **Off-the-beaten track** Trailblaze the 'alternative route' to Dubrovnik from Mostar or Sarajevo via Trebinje (p146)

FAST FACTS

- **Area** 51,129 sq km
- **Budget** 65KM per day
- **Capital** Sarajevo
- **Country code** ☎ 387
- **Famous for** Mostar's Stari Most, Franz Ferdinand's 1914 assassination, U2's 'Miss Sarajevo'
- **Languages** Bosnian, Croatian, Serbian
- **Money** convertible mark (KM); A$1 = 1.08KM; C$1 = 1.23KM; €1 = 1.95KM; ¥100 = 1.54KM; NZ$1 = 0.85KM; UK£1 = 2.20KM; US$1 = 1.45KM
- **Phrases** *zdravo* (hello), *doviđenja* (see you later), *molim* (please), *hvala* (thanks)

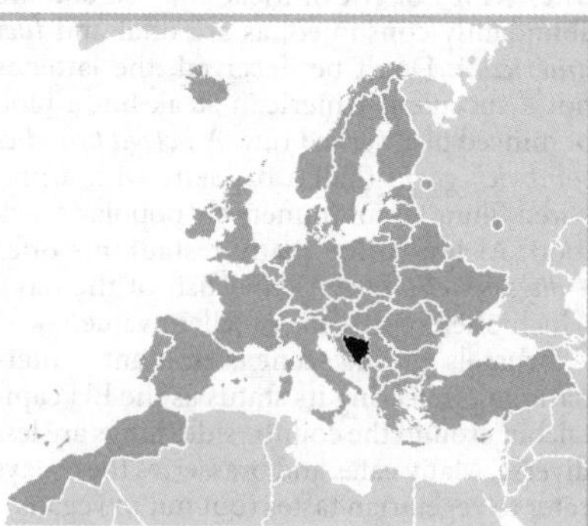

- **Population** 4.59 million
- **Visas** no visa needed for citizens of the EU, Australia, New Zealand, the US and Canada; see p148

TRAVEL HINTS

Try BiH's under-appreciated wines (www.wineroute.ba), especially Hercegovina's rich red Blatina. Some restaurants' *domaći* (house) wine costs only 12KM per litre carafe.

ROAMING BOSNIA & HERCEGOVINA

Visit Mostar then Sarajevo from coastal Croatia, cross to Jajce and consider summer rafting between there and Banja Luka.

Undiscovered Bosnia and Hercegovina (BiH) is a land of seemingly endless mountains etched with canyons whose rivers provide world-class rafting. Around fascinating Sarajevo Olympic-quality slopes offer some of Europe's best-value skiing. Lively cafes fill Ottoman-era old town and add to the super-quaint atmosphere of Mostar, one of Eastern Europe's delights. Though there are some post-Soviet monstrosities, the majority of Bosnian towns are lovably small affairs wrapped around medieval castle ruins. A few lingering scars remain from the heartbreaking societal haemorrhaging of the '90s but BiH has largely regained its once-famed religious tolerance. Rebuilt churches, mosques and synagogues once again huddle together, rekindling an intriguing East-meets-West atmosphere born of Bosnia's fascinating Ottoman and Austro-Hungarian histories. BiH offers a great sense of discovery, of real personal interaction and of very fair value-for-money that's all too rare in 21st-century Europe. Many visitors stay longer than they'd planned.

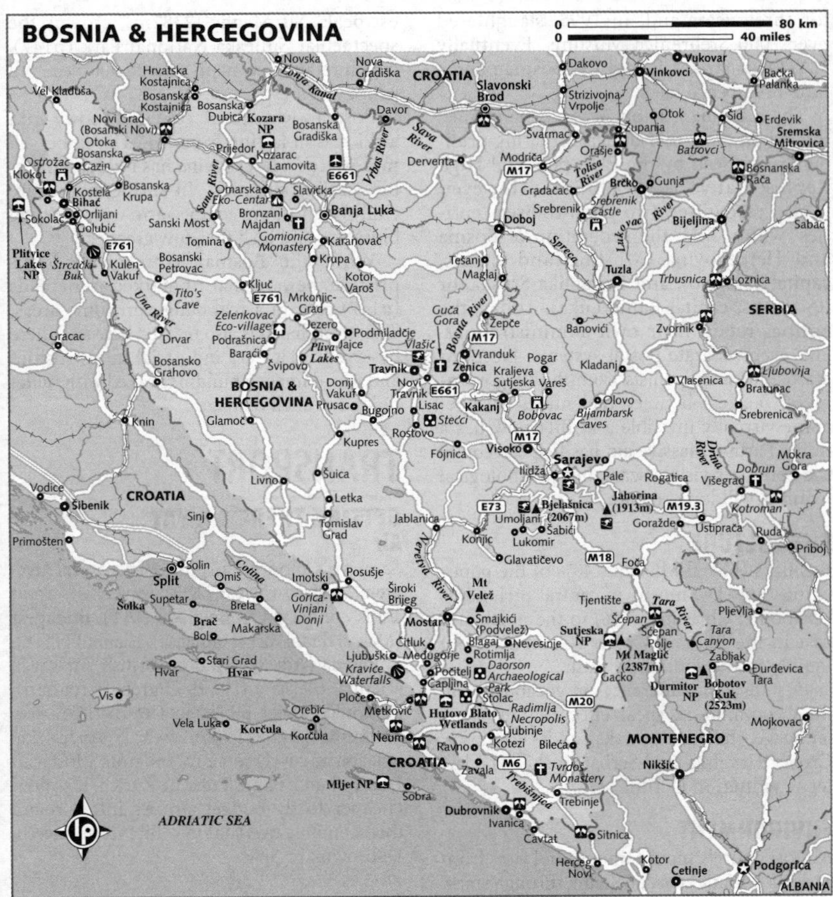

HISTORY

Ancient Illyrians, followed by Romans from AD 9 and Slavs from the late 6th century were Bosnia's early arrivals. The medieval Bosnian kingdom had its own rather mysterious Christian Church and reached several cultural zeniths between 1180 and 1463. Thereafter the area was absorbed by the Turkish Ottoman Empire. Islam rapidly became the predominant religion of Bosnia's elite, though much of the peasantry remained Christian.

After 1878, BiH became controlled by predominantly Catholic Austria-Hungary. This alienated Muslim Bosniaks and Orthodox Serbs, and in 1914 a Bosnian Serb assassinated Austria-Hungary's imperial heir, Franz Ferdinand, in Sarajevo. This ultimately ignited WWI, which killed an astonishing 15% of the Bosnian population. Postwar BiH joined proto-Yugoslavia and in WWII its mountains were the scene of numerous battles between Nazi occupiers and Tito's Communist Partizans.

In 1991 BiH's Croats and Bosniaks united to declare independence from Serb-dominated Yugoslavia. In reply Bosnian-Serb nationalists started seizing territory and 'ethnic cleansing' Muslims from the north and east. By 1992 a three-way war was raging between Serbs, Croats and Bosniaks. Atrocities were committed by all sides. Most infamously, Croats senselessly destroyed Mostar's Old Bridge while Bosnian Serbs besieged Sarajevo for three years and, in 1995, slaughtered over 7000 Srebrenica Muslims. Eventually NATO air strikes forced the Bosnian Serbs into 1995 peace talks.

The resulting Dayton Accords maintained the existence of BiH under a rotating presidency overseen by the EU's powerful High Representative (www.ohr.int). However, it also recognised two decentralised 'entities' within BiH: the Federation of Bosnia and Hercegovina (Muslims and Croats, capital Sarajevo), and Republika Srpska, or RS (Serbs, capital Banja Luka). Today, the entities retain their own administrations, and even separate postal systems. Elections ejected ultranationalists from the RS government, 'borders' between the entities have become virtually invisible and BiH now has a unified army. Massive aid has helped rebuild the country's visible scars, but psychological wounds will long remain.

THE CULTURE

Bosniaks (liberal Muslims, 48% of the population) now live mostly in central BiH, Serbs (Orthodox Christian, 37%) to the north and east in the RS, and Croats (Catholic, 14%) mainly in the south and west.

Despite some differences in vocabulary, all three communities speak effectively the same language, though Bosniaks call it 'Bosanski', Croats 'Hrvatski' and Serbs 'Srpski'. The latter is written in Cyrillic script.

ENVIRONMENT

Almost entirely mountainous, BiH rises from a toe of Adriatic coast at Neum, through stark, arid Hercegovina towards the dramatically canyon-diced central highlands before descending northwards through green rolling hills towards the flat Hungarian plain. On the Montenegrin border, BiH's highest peak, Mt Maglić (2387m), crowns the spectacular Sutjeska National Park (p147), which retains remnants of a 20,000-year-old primeval forest.

Bosnia's winters are cold and snowy with a ski season lasting from mid-December till mid-March. Hercegovina has milder winters but sizzling summers. In spring, nights are chilly but days are gently warm with dazzling blossoms and lush meadow greenery.

While the Bosnian countryside looks pristine, beware that unmarked minefields (p147) remain a real danger in some areas. The rural charm is also marred here and there by eyesore Tito-era industrial monstrosities and war-damaged buildings raked with bullet holes and shell damage.

> **READING UP**
>
> Noel Malcolm's very readable *Bosnia: A Short History* is a great introduction to the complexities of Bosnian history and helpful at deconstructing many commonly held myths. Nobel Prize–winning Ivo Andrić's epic historical-fictions *Bridge over the Drina* and *Travnik Chronicles* offer especially vivid portrayals of life in Bosnia under the Turks and Austria-Hungarians.

TRANSPORT

GETTING THERE & AWAY

Air

Sarajevo's modern airport, **Međunarodni Aerodrom Sarajevo** (☎ 033-289100; www.sarajevo-airport.ba) is connected to Belgrade (JAT), Budapest (Malev), Frankfurt (Lufthansa), İstanbul (THY), Ljubljana (Adria), London (British Airways), Vienna (Austrian) and Zagreb (Croatian). National carrier **BH Airlines** (☎ 033-218605; www.bhairlines.ba; 15 Branilaca Sarajeva, Sarajevo; 🕑 9am-5pm Mon-Fri, to 2pm Sat) covers more routes, from Mostar to İstanbul and Banja Luka to Zürich. It's often cheaper to fly budget airlines into Croatia then continue overland into BiH from Zagreb, Dubrovnik or Split.

Bus

Many Federation towns have buses to Zagreb, Split and/or Dubrovnik (Croatia). Sarajevo plus most RS towns have various links to Serbia and Montenegro. Sarajevo has daily connections to Vienna ('Beč', 92KM), Munich ('Minhen', 190KM) and Stockholm (280KM) but there's no bus to Budapest.

Car & Motorcycle

Drivers need Green Card insurance for their vehicle and an EU or International Driving Permit. Driving is on the right, seat belts are compulsory, headlights must be kept on day and night, and speed limits are low with police spot-checks common. Parking (typically 1KM per hour) is fairly easy except in Mostar and Sarajevo.

> **CONNECTIONS**
>
> Regular buses link Mostar and Sarajevo to the Croatian coast, plus there's one little-publicised Trebinje–Dubrovnik bus (p146). Sarajevo–Zagreb is more comfy by sleeper train. Links to Serbia and Montenegro are easiest from the RS. There's one Sarajevo–Budapest day train.

Train

From Sarajevo trains depart for Zagreb (56.60KM, 9½ hours) at 10.27am and 9.20pm. The latter has some six-berth couchettes (19.60KM supplement). For Belgrade (46KM, nine hours) take the 9.20pm and change at Doboj or the 7.14am train bound for Budapest (96KM, 12 hours), changing at Strizivojna-Vrpolje, Croatia.

GETTING AROUND

Bus

BiH's buses are punctual but slow and relatively infrequent, with shorter-hop routes drastically reduced at weekends and often stopping altogether on Sundays. Advance reservations are rarely needed except in peak holiday season. Fares average around 7KM per hour travelled plus 2KM per stowed bag. Return tickets are cheaper but limit you to returning with the same bus company (often inconvenient).

Car & Motorcycle

Bosnian roads are winding, lightly trafficked and almost unanimously beautiful: delightful if you aren't in a hurry. Car hire is available in most cities, and costs from around €43/245 per day/week with unlimited mileage and basic insurance.

Train

Trains are even less frequent than buses but around 30% cheaper. **RS Railways** (www.zrs-rs.com/red_voznje.php) has up-to-date timetables.

SARAJEVO

☎ 033 / pop 737,000

The nation's cosy, vibrant capital has a central core that's manageably human in scale and ambience with a wonderful cafe scene and unique East-meets-West architecture. This is emphasised by the city's attractive enfolding contours, polka-dotted with red-roofed homes, church towers and endless minarets. The centre's distinctive Ottoman-era bazaars and cobbled lanes date from the city's 16th-century glory days as a Turkic silk-trading entrepôt. After 1878 the Austro-Hungarians added grandeur by erecting many sturdy central-European buildings. It was here in 1914 that Gavrilo Princip assassinated Austro-Hungary's Archduke Franz Ferdinand, plunging the world into WWI.

Around Sarajevo, a pair of mountain resorts that still offer some of Europe's best-value skiing (p139), hosted the Winter Olympics in 1984. But just eight years later the city was devastated by an appalling three-year siege. Over 10,500 Sarajevans died and six centuries of heritage was pounded into rubble by Bosnian-Serb shelling. The city's only access to the outside world was via a metre-wide, 800m-long tunnel under the airport. You can still visit an entrance of that tunnel (p138) and some bullet-pocked buildings are still visible in the southern suburbs. But otherwise today's visitor would be hard-pressed to notice any signs of the conflict in what is now an enticing, low-key city that brims over with a very personal warmth and charm.

ORIENTATION

Sarajevo is tightly wedged into a narrow mountain valley of the modest Miljacka River. Flanking the very atmospheric 'Turkish' old town (Baščaršija), the valley sides are attractively fuzzed with red-roofed Bosnian houses and uncountable minarets. Westward, however, Sarajevo sprawls for over 10km past contrastingly dismal bullet-scarred apartment blocks, improving somewhat beyond the airport with park-filled Ilidža, where the city's tramway spine terminates.

INFORMATION

Bookshops

Maps, guidebooks and English-language books:

BuyBook (☎ 716450; www.buybook.ba; Radićeva 4; 🕑 9am-10pm Mon-Sat, 10am-6pm Sun)
Šahinpašić Bookshop (☎ 667210; www.btcsahinpasic.com; Vladislava Skarića 8; 🕑 9am-8pm Mon-Sat)

Internet Access

Click (Kundurdžiluk 1a; per hr 3KM; 🕑 9am-11pm)
Internet Caffe Baščaršija (Aščiluk; per hr 1.5KM; 🕑 24hr)

EMERGENCY NUMBERS

- Ambulance ☎ 124
- Fire ☎ 123
- Police ☎ 122
- Roadside Assistance ☎ 1282/1288

Laundry

Askos Laundry (Halilbašića 2; 🕑 9am-5pm Mon-Fri, 9am-3pm Sat)

Left Luggage

Main bus station (Put Života 8; 1st hr 2KM, then per hr 1KM)

Medical Services

Check the useful health listings website: www.sarajevo-tourism.com/eng/health.wbsp.

Baščaršija Pharmacy (Obala Kulina Bana 40; 🕑 24hr)

Centar Urgente Medicine (☎ 297330; Stepana Tomića bb; 🕑 24hr) Emergency assistance section of Koševo Hospital; take bus 14 from Dom Armije to Hotel Belvedere then walk 300m northwest.

Money

ATMs are widely sprinkled, with one outside the bus station, but oddly there are no money-changing facilities at the stations.

Turkish Ziraat Bank (www.ziraatbosnia.com; Ferhadija 10) Cashes travellers cheques if you show original receipts.

Tourist Information

Tourist information centre (☎ 220724; www.sarajevo-tourism.com; Zelenih Beretki 22a; 🕑 9am-6pm Mon-Fri, to 9pm in summer, 9am-3pm Sat & Sun) Remarkably helpful with maps, bus timetables, brochures etc.

Travel Agencies

Centrotrans-Eurolines (☎ 205481; www.centrotrans.com; Ferhadija 16; 🕑 8.30am-8.30pm Mon-Fri, 9am-3pm Sat) Sells international bus, train and ferry tickets.

Relax Tours (☎/fax 263330; www.relaxtours.com; Zelenih Beretki 22)

SIGHTS

Central Sarajevo

Fanning out from the distinctive 1891 **Sebilj Drinking Fountain** (Pigeon Square) is **Baščaršija**, old Sarajevo's delightful warren of marble-flagged pedestrian lanes and open courtyards. Cafes, souvenir shops, mosques, copper workshops and charming little restaurants surround Ottoman-era architectural gems, including the six-domed 1551 **Bursa Bezistan** (☎ 239590; www.muzejsarajeva.ba; Abadžiluk 10; admission 2KM), a former silk bazaar, the one-block **covered bazaar** and the imposing **Gazi-Husrevbey Mosque** (☎ 534375; www.vakuf-gazi.ba; Sarači 18). Both the 1740 **orthodox church** (☎ 571065; Mula Mustafe Başeskije 59; admission 1KM; 🕑 8am-8pm summer, to 4pm winter) and the 1581 **Sephardic Synagogue** (☎ 535688; Mula Mustafe Başeskije 40; admission 2KM; 🕑 10am-6pm Mon-Fri, to 1pm Sun) host interesting religiously relevant museums.

Climb the grassy-topped **Yellow Bastion** (Žuta Tabija; Jekovac) of the once-vast 1720s Vratnik Citadel for great city views. Seek out the brilliantly restored 18th-century **Svrzo House** (Svrzina Kuća; ☎ 535264; Glođina 8; admission 2KM) for a taste of a traditional Sarajevan home, then take a wander along cafe-filled Ferhadija to sample Sarajevo's Austro-Hungarian-era architecture. There are more impressive buildings along the riverbank, including the splendid Gothic-revival **Academy of Arts** (www.unsa.ba/eng/pregled.php; Obala Maka Dizdara). Facing the **Latin Bridge** (Map pp140–1) and **Sarajevo 1878–1918 Museum** (☎ 533288; Zelenih Beretki 2; admission 2KM) is the point where Austrian crown-prince Franz Ferdinand was assassinated in 1914, ultimately triggering WWI.

Novo Sarajevo

Hop off tram 3 just beyond the startling pudding coloured **Holiday Inn** (wartime home to besieged international journalists) to find the palatial, wide-ranging **National Museum** (☎ 668026; www.zemaljskimuzej.ba; Zmaja od Bosne 3; adult/concession 5/1KM; 🕑 10am-5pm Tue-Fri, to 2pm Sat & Sun). Its archaeological collections are especially impressive. Peep through the locked, high-security glass door of room 37 to glimpse the world-famous **Sarajevo Haggadah**, a priceless 14th-century Jewish codex said to be the world's most valuable book.

Next door, the small but engrossing **History Museum** (☎ 210418; Zmaja od Bosne 5; admission 2KM; 🕑 9am-4pm Mon-Fri, to 1pm Sat & Sun) 'non-ideologically' charts the course of the 1990s conflict with affectingly personal exhibits. Tucked behind is an amusingly tongue-in-cheek Tito-themed cafe.

Ilidža Area

Way out in Butmir, the unmissable **Tunnel Museum** (☎ 061 213760; Tuneli 1, Butmir; admission 5KM; 🕑 9am-4pm) gives visitors a glimpse of the makeshift tunnel hand-dug beneath Sarajevo's airport during the 1992–95 siege.

Without the food and armaments that passed through it the besieged city would probably have capitulated. Photos and construction equipment are displayed and there's a 20-minute video of the wartime tunnel experience. By public transport take tram 3 to the Ilidža terminus (around 25 minutes) then switch to bus 68A. From the last bus stop cross the small bridge, turn immediately left and walk down Tuneli for 600m.

ACTIVITIES

For superb-value **skiing** (day passes 30KM, equipment rental 24-50KM) consider taking a day trip to the 1984 Winter Olympic centres of Jahorina (30KM by taxi from Pale) or much smaller Bjelašnica (9am bus from National Museum on ski weekends only; bus returns at 4pm). In summer, Bjelašnica's **EkoPlanet** (www.touristbiro.ba) offers quad-biking expeditions. Rafting is possible near Konjic with **Badžo-Raft** (www.badzoraft.com).

TOURS

Various city tours are available through the tourist information centre (opposite), travel agents (opposite), budget accommodation agencies including **Sartour** (☎ 238680; www.sartour-hostel-sarajevo.ba; Mula Mustafe Baševskije 63/3) and Ljubičica (see right), and through eco-tourism specialists **Green Visions** (☎ 717290; www.greenvisions.ba; opposite Radnićka 66; 9am-5pm Mon-Fri), which also runs regular hike-and-explore day trips to rural getaways.

FESTIVALS & EVENTS

Baščaršijske Noći (Baščaršija Nights; www.bascarsijskenoci.ba) Dance, music and street theatre at open-air stages around town in July.

Sarajevo Film Festival (☎ 209411; www.sff.ba; Zelenih Beretki 12/1; tickets 3-6KM) Globally acclaimed film festival held in August.

Futura Electronic music fest in October.

International Jazz Festival (www.jazzfest.ba) November's world-class jazz festival.

SLEEPING

Agencies and hostel-booking sites offer homestays and essentially similar but more crowded 'hostels'. Check if sheets are included. Beware that hostels often have much less central 'overflow' locations.

AutoKamp Oaza (☎ 636141; www.hoteliilidza.ba/site/oaza; tent/car/campervan 7/8/12KM plus per person 10KM) Sarajevo's main camping ground is 1.5km west of Ilidža tram terminus.

Sartour Hotel (☎ office 238680; www.sartour-hostel-sarajevo.ba; Hadžišabanovića 15; camping from €5, dm €7-13, tw €24-30, linen €3) Obliging Sartour (see left) arranges homestays and has its own house-hostel with a pleasant if sloping garden for camping. Lock-out is 11am to 5pm.

Ljubičica Hostel (☎ 232109; www.hostelljubicica.com; Mula Mustafe Baševskije 65; dm/homestay/apt from €10/15/20) The dingy, tight-packed hostel has battered old bathrooms but it's superbly central and free station-transfers ensure a steady clientele. Homestay rooms can be better value.

our pick **Hostel City Center** (☎ 503294; www.hcc.ba; 3rd fl, Saliha Muvekita 2; dm/s/d/tr/q €12/18/32/45/54) Sarajevo's only 'real' hostel, the brand-new HCC has airy wooden bunk rooms leading off an appealing chill-out space with kitchen and free internet. No sign; book ahead.

Hostel Sebilj (☎ 573500; www.pansionsebilj.com.ba; Bravadžiluk; dm/s/d/tr from €15/15/30/45) Around a decent sized if unsophisticated barnlike sitting area, most rooms share his-or-hers bathrooms. The €20 four-bed dorms have en-suite facilities.

Kod Keme (☎ 531140; www.hostel.co.ba; Mali Ćurčiluk 15; s/d from €20/40) Run by a charming Bosnian-Aussie, Kod Keme's neat, unfussy rooms mostly share bathrooms. Great location.

Pansion Lion (☎ 236137, 61 268150; www.lion.co.ba; Bravadžiluk 30; s/d/tr/q €25/50/60/80; P) The cheaper five- and eight-bed dorms are windowless but better rooms are appealingly cutesy. There's no real lounge area.

SPLURGE

Hotel Michele (☎ 560310; www.hotelmichele.ba; Ivana Cankara 27; d/apt €100/150) Behind a banally suburban exterior lies a marvellously off-beat boutique hotel whose vast, exotically furnished apartments have housed celebrity guests including Bono and Richard Gere.

EATING

Bosanska Kuća (Bravadžiluk 3; mains 6-9KM; 24hr) Colour-picture menus make choosing easy and among the Bosnian standards are a couple of vegie options.

Karuzo (☎ 444647; Dženetića Čikma 2; mains 6-18KM; noon-3pm & 6-11pm Mon-Fri, 6-11pm Sat) Tiny, friendly one-man (ie slow-service) restaurant styled

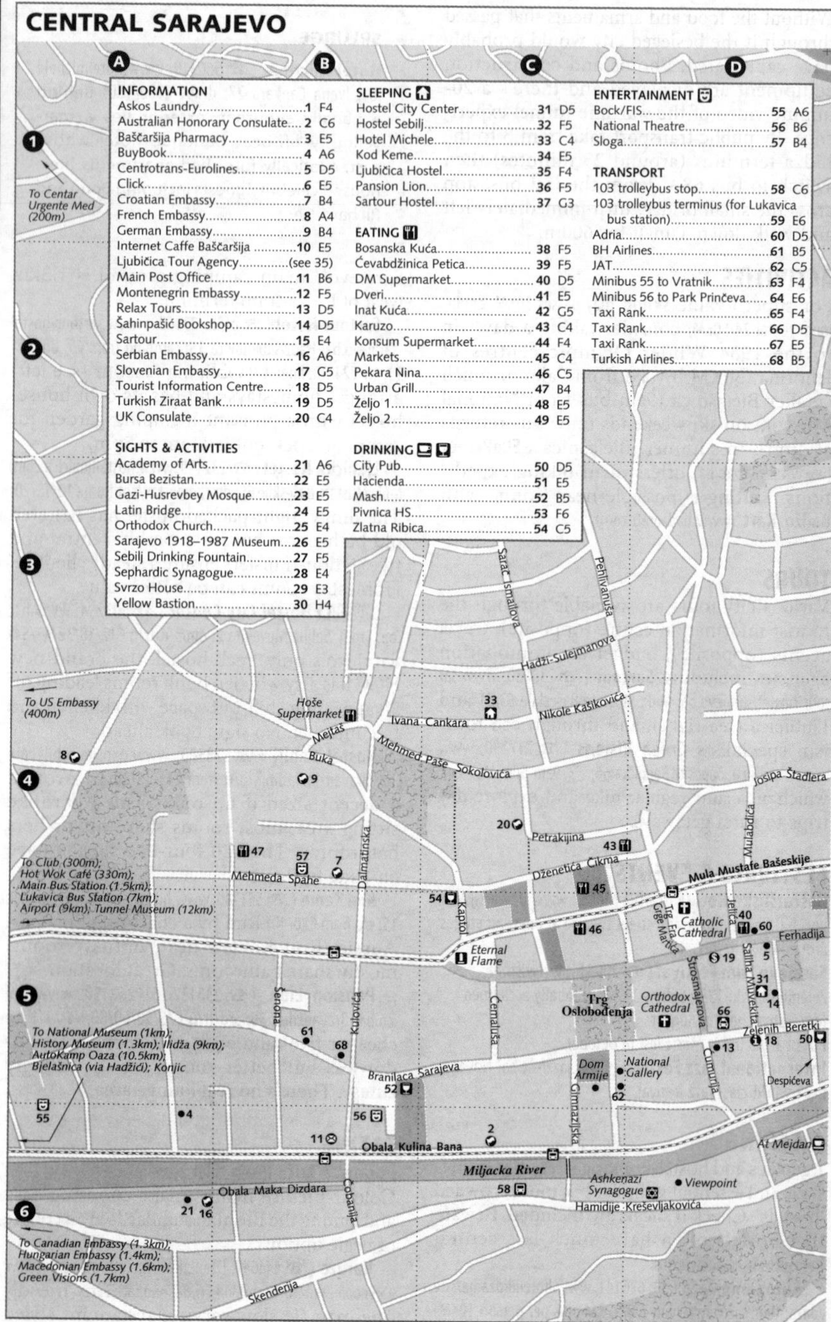
CENTRAL SARAJEVO
INFORMATION
Askos Laundry 1 F4
Australian Honorary Consulate 2 C6
Baščaršija Pharmacy 3 E5
BuyBook 4 A6
Centrotrans-Eurolines 5 D5
Click 6 E5
Croatian Embassy 7 B4
French Embassy 8 A4
German Embassy 9 B4
Internet Caffe Baščaršija 10 E5
Ljubičica Tour Agency (see 35)
Main Post Office 11 B6
Montenegrin Embassy 12 F5
Relax Tours 13 D5
Šahinpašić Bookshop 14 D5
Sartour 15 E4
Serbian Embassy 16 A6
Slovenian Embassy 17 G5
Tourist Information Centre 18 D5
Turkish Ziraat Bank 19 D5
UK Consulate 20 C4
SIGHTS & ACTIVITIES
Academy of Arts 21 A6
Bursa Bezistan 22 E5
Gazi-Husrevbey Mosque 23 E5
Latin Bridge 24 E5
Orthodox Church 25 E4
Sarajevo 1918–1987 Museum 26 E5
Sebilj Drinking Fountain 27 F5
Sephardic Synagogue 28 E4
Svrzo House 29 E3
Yellow Bastion 30 H4
SLEEPING
Hostel City Center 31 D5
Hostel Sebilj 32 F5
Hotel Michele 33 C4
Kod Keme 34 E5
Ljubičica Hostel 35 F4
Pansion Lion 36 F5
Sartour Hostel 37 G3
EATING
Bosanska Kuća 38 F5
Ćevabdžinica Petica 39 F5
DM Supermarket 40 D5
Dveri 41 E5
Inat Kuća 42 G5
Karuzo 43 C4
Konsum Supermarket 44 F4
Markets 45 C4
Pekara Nina 46 C5
Urban Grill 47 B4
Željo 1 48 E5
Željo 2 49 E5
DRINKING
City Pub 50 D5
Hacienda 51 E5
Mash 52 B5
Pivnica HS 53 F6
Zlatna Ribica 54 C5
ENTERTAINMENT
Bock/FIS 55 A6
National Theatre 56 B6
Sloga 57 B4
TRANSPORT
103 trolleybus stop 58 C6
103 trolleybus terminus (for Lukavica bus station) 59 E6
Adria 60 D5
BH Airlines 61 B5
JAT 62 C5
Minibus 55 to Vratnik 63 F4
Minibus 56 to Park Prinčeva 64 E6
Taxi Rank 65 F4
Taxi Rank 66 D5
Taxi Rank 67 E5
Turkish Airlines 68 B5
To Centar Urgente Med (200m)
To US Embassy (400m)
To Club (300m); Hot Wok Café (330m); Main Bus Station (1.5km); Lukavica Bus Station (7km); Airport (9km); Tunnel Museum (12km)
To National Museum (1km); History Museum (1.3km); Ilidža (9km); AutoKamp Oaza (10.5km); Bjelašnica (via Hadžići); Konjic
To Canadian Embassy (1.3km); Hungarian Embassy (1.4km); Macedonian Embassy (1.6km); Green Visions (1.7km)
Hoše Supermarket
Šarač Ismailova
Pehlivanuša
Hadži-Sulejmanova
Nikole Kašikovića
Ivana Cankara
Mejtaš
Buka
Mehmed Paše Sokolovića
Josipa Štadlera
Petrakijina
Mulabdića
Dalmatinska
Mehmeda Spahe
Dženetića Čikma
Mula Mustafe Baševskije
Kaptol
Trg Fra Grge Martića
Catholic Cathedral
Jelića
Ferhadija
Eternal Flame
Saliha Muvekita
Štrosmajerova
Šenoina
Kulovića
Čemaluša
Trg Oslobođenja
Orthodox Cathedral
Zelenih Beretki
Despićeva
Cumurija
Branilaca Sarajeva
Dom Armije
National Gallery
Gimnazijska
Obala Kulina Bana
At Mejdan
Miljacka River
Ashkenazi Synagogue
Viewpoint
Obala Maka Dizdara
Čobanija
Hamidije Kreševljakovića
Skenderija

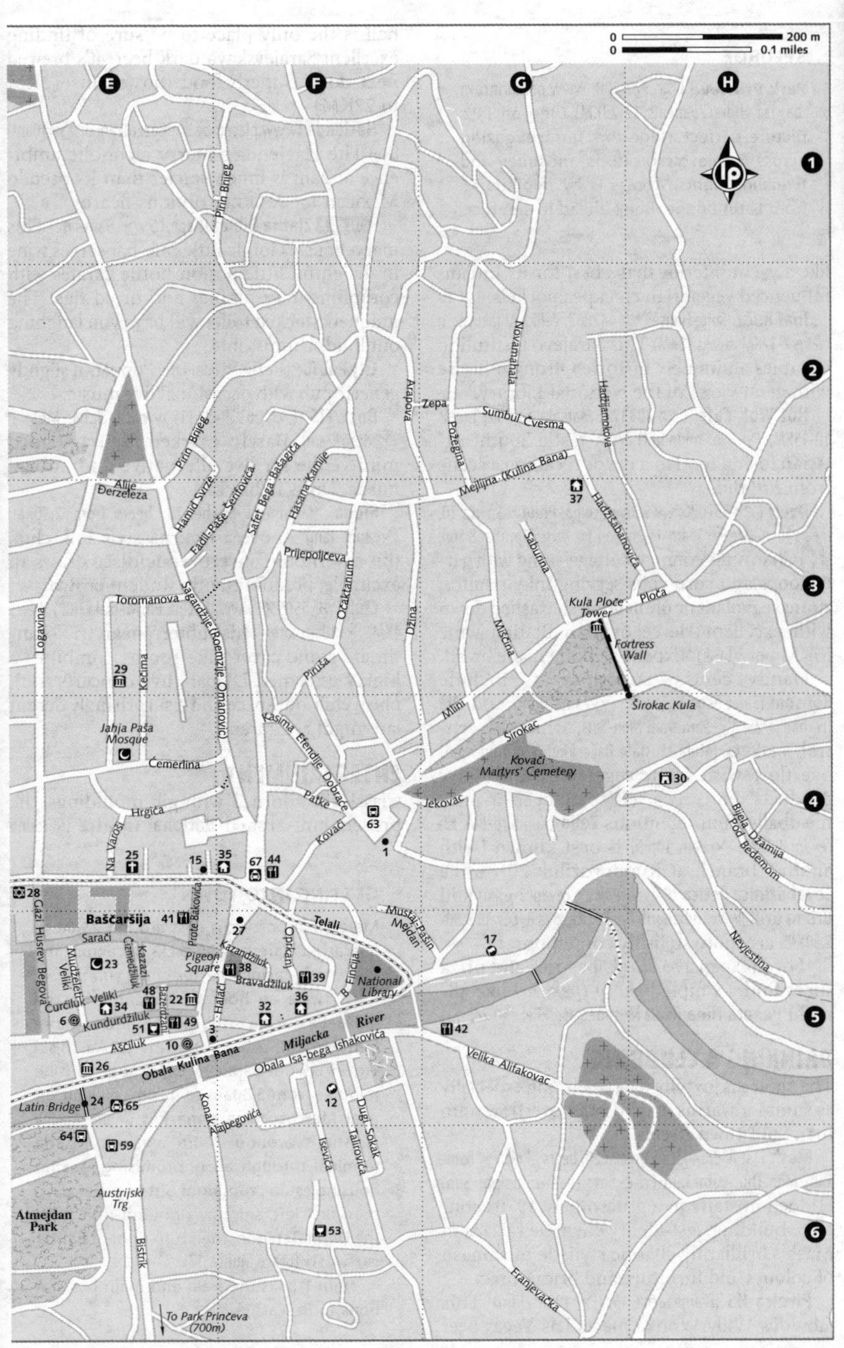
0 200 m
0 0.1 miles
E
F
G
H
1
2
3
4
5
6
Pirin Brijeg
Novamahala
Hadžijamokova
Arapova
Zepa
Sumbul Čvesma
Požegina
Mejlijna (Kulina Bana)
37
Alije Đerzeleza
Hamid Svrze
Fadil-Paše Šerifovića
Safet Bega Bašagića
Hasana Kamije
Prijepoljčeva
Očaktanum
Džina
Saburina
Hadžisabanovića
Kula Ploče Tower
Ploča
Fortress Wall
Mištčina
Toromanova
Sagardžije (Roemzije Omanović)
Logavina
Kečina
29
Jahja Paša Mosque
Piruša
Kasima Efendije Dobrače
Mimi
Širokac
Širokac Kula
Kovači Martyrs' Cemetery
30
Čemerlina
Hrgiča
Patke
Jekovac
Bijela Džamija
Pod Bedemom
Na Varoši
25
15
35
67
44
63
1
Kovači
28
Gazi Husrev Begova
Baščaršija
41
Prote Bakovića
27
Telali
Mustaj-Pašin Mejdan
17
Sarači
Mudželeti Veliki
Kazazi
Čizmedžiluk
Pigeon Square
Kazandžiluk
38
Oprkanj
B. Fincija
National Library
Nevjestina
23
Bravadžiluk
39
Čurčiluk Veliki
34
48
22
Bazerdžani
32
36
6
Kundurdžiluk
49
51
Halači
River
Miljacka
42
3
Aščiluk
10
Obala Kulina Bana
Obala Isa-bega Ishakovića
Velika Alifakovac
26
Latin Bridge
24
65
Konak
Alajbegovića
12
Dugi Sokak
Tahirovića
Isevića
64
59
Austrijski Trg
Atmejdan Park
53
Bistrik
Franjevačka
To Park Prinčeva (700m)

SPLURGE

Park Prinčeva (☎ 222 708; www.parkprinceva.ba; Iza Hidra 7; meals 12-23KM) Dine on PP's picture-perfect ridge-top terrace gazing across Sarajevo's rooftops, mosques and twinkling lights. Access is by minibus 56 from Latin Bridge. Book ahead in summer.

like a yacht interior that's best for its Indian-influenced vegetarian chickpea pockets.

Inat Kuća (Spite House; ☎ 447867; Velika Alifakovac 1; mains 7-12KM, steaks 18KM) This Sarajevo institution occupies a uniquely historic Ottoman house with great views of the National Library.

Hot Wok Café (☎ 203322; Maršala Tita 12; meals 10-15KM; 🕑 8am-midnight) Pun-tastic Southeast-Asian fusion food in a decor recalling a scene from *Kill Bill*.

Dveri (☎ 537020; www.dveri.co.ba; Prote Bakovića 10; meals 10-16KM; 🕑 11am-11pm Mon-Fri, 8am-11pm Sat & Sun; ⊠) Charming 'country-cottage' hung with garlic loops and corn cobs serving inky risottos, stuffed eggplant or plum goulash washed down with excellent Hercegovinian Blatina wine (5KM per glass). Expensive homemade bread.

Handy central supermarkets include **Konsum** (Safet Bega Bašagiča; 🕑 7am-10pm) and **DM** (Ferhadija 25; 🕑 9am-9pm Mon-Sat), while the central **markets** (Mula Mustafe Bašeskije; 🕑 7am-4pm) overflow with fruit, vegetables and dairy products. For *ćevapčići* (spicy beef or pork meatballs), unpretentious **Željo** (Kundurdžiluk 17; ćevapi 3-7KM; 🕑 8am-10pm) is best known (with another branch at Kundurdžiluk 20), while **Ćevabdžinica Petica** (Bravadžiluk 29; ćevapi 3-6KM) and **Urban Grill** (www.urbangrill.ba; Pruščakova 8; ćevapi 3.50-5.50KM) are more stylishly contemporary.

For inexpensive *burek*, pastries and pizza slices find a simple bakery *(pekara)* like all-night **Pekara Nina** (Mula Mustafe Bašeskije; 🕑 24hr).

DRINKING & CLUBBING

The choice is joyfully overwhelming especially as summer warms up and cafes overflow onto many old-town streets.

Mash (1st fl, Branilaca Sarajeva 20; beers 2KM; 🕑 8am-1am Mon-Thu, 9am-3am Fri & Sat, 10am-midnight Sun) Hidden upstairs in a gruesomely 1970s concrete building, a studenty clientele buzzes in Mash's brilliantly chaotic stylistic mishmash of colours, old furniture and bric-a-brac.

Pivnica HS (Franjevačka 15; 🕑 10am-1am) This fabulous Willy Wonka meets Las Vegas beer hall is the only place to be sure of finding excellent Sarajevskaya dark beer: it's brewed next door! Superb food too (mains 12KM to 22KM).

Hacienda (www.placetobe.ba; Bazerdzani 3; 🕑 10am-late) The Hacienda's merry alcoholic ambience at 2am is much spicier than its pseudo Mexican food. Other options nearby.

our pick **Zlatna Ribica** (Kaptol 5; 🕑 9am-late) This marvellously Gothic little cafe-bar serves wine in delightful little potion-bottle carafes with complimentary nibbles and dried figs. The uniquely stocked toilet will have you laughing out loud. Unmissable.

City Pub (Despićeva; 🕑 8am-late) Popular if slightly generic pub with occasional live music.

Bock/FIS (☎ 063 943431; www.bock.ba; Musala; 🕑 6pm-2am) Barely marked, zebra-striped mini-venue for live alternative and 'urban' music. Dress in black.

Sloga (Mehmeda Spahe 20; beers from 2.50KM; 🕑 8pm-4am) Above a taverna-style folk club, this cavernous concert venue/disco draws an excitable, predominantly student crowd.

Club (☎ 550550; www.theclub.ba; Maršala Tita 7; beers 4KM; 🕑 10am-late) This subterranean trio of intimate stone cavernlike rooms combines a highly esteemed DJ bar (live concerts too), plush chill-out space and a surprisingly decent late-night restaurant.

ENTERTAINMENT

Classically adorned with gilt mouldings, the proscenium-arched **National Theatre** (Narodno

GETTING INTO TOWN

Metered airport taxis cost around 25KM to Baščaršija. Rare bus 36 picks up across the main road facing the terminal, running at most twice an hour to Nedžarići on the Ilidža–Baščaršija tram 3 line. Much more frequent trolleybus 103 runs to Austrijski Trg in central Sarajevo every four to nine minutes from 5.30am to 11pm, picking up near **Mercator Hypermarket** (Mimar Sinana 1). That's around 700m away from the terminal through an unpromising-looking housing estate: turn right out of the airport, then first left, shimmy right-left-right past the Hotel Octagon, then turn right at **Panda car-wash** (Brače Mulića 17).

Tram 1 links the train and main bus stations to Baščaršija.

Pozorište; ☎ 221682; www.nps.ba; Obala Kulina Bana 9; ⏰ mid-September–mid-Jun) hosts ballet, opera, plays and philharmonic concerts.

SHOPPING

Pedestrianised Baščaršija's wooden-shuttered souvenir shops flog jewellery, oriental slippers, Bosnian kilims, imported carpets, BiH flags, wooden spoons and metalwork including archetypal coffee-pot sets and pens made from bullet casings. However, if you're heading to Mostar you might find prices better there.

GETTING THERE & AWAY

Bus

Sarajevo has two bus stations. The tourist office keeps current timetables.

MAIN BUS STATION

From this **bus station** (☎ 213100; Put Života 8) near the train station, buses serve Banja Luka (29KM, five hours via Jajce and Travnik), Bihać (41KM, 6½ hours, 7.30am, 1.30pm and 10pm), Mostar (16KM, 2½ hours, 15 daily) plus several destinations in Western Europe (p136) and Croatia including Dubrovnik (from 30KM, five to seven hours), Split (41KM, 6¾ to eight hours, five daily) and Zagreb (54KM, 9½ hours, 6.30am, 12.30pm and 10pm). The 10pm bus to Novi Pasar, Serbia (€15, seven hours, five daily), continues to Pristina, Kosovo.

LUKAVICA BUS STATION

This **station** (Autobuska Stanica Istočno Sarajevo; ☎ 057 317377; Nikole Tesle), about 10km south of town, is 300m beyond the final stop of frequent trolleybus 103 from Austrijski Trg. Buses run to Pale (3.50KM, 45 minutes, 14 services weekdays, 3.15pm only weekends), Foča (9KM, 11.10am and 4.35pm), Belgrade (55KM, eight hours, seven daily via Zvornik), Podgorica in Montenegro (31KM, eight hours, 8.15am and 2pm) and Novi Sad, Serbia (28KM, nine hours, 6.40am, 1.30pm and 11.15pm).

Train

The best trains for Mostar (9.90KM, three hours) and Banja Luka (23.30KM, five hours) depart at 6.45am and 10.27am respectively. See p137 for international services.

GETTING AROUND

Frequent tram 3 links Ilidža to Baščaršija (from 6am to 11pm) along the north bank. Rarer tram 1 connects the stations and Baščaršija. Frequent trolleybus 103 runs along the south bank almost to Lukovica Bus Station.

Buy bus, tram and trolleybus tickets from a kiosk (1.60KM) or the driver (1.80KM) and validate them in the machines on board. One-day passes cost 5.30KM from major kiosks including one at the tram stop near the Catholic Cathedral.

Full timetables are available in Bosnian on www.gras.co.ba. Click 'Redove Voznje' then select mode of transport.

Metered taxis, including **Žuti** (Yellow Cab; ☎ 663555), charge from 2KM plus around 1KM per kilometre.

AROUND BOSNIA & HERCEGOVINA

JAJCE

☎ **030 / pop 30,000**

Jajce's compact **old town** is topped by a powerful if ruined castle where Bosnia's medieval kings were once crowned. Viewed across the River Vrbas from the Banja Luka road, the city ensemble is especially photogenic, fronted by Jajce's signature 21m **waterfall**.

The helpful summer **tourist information kiosk** (⏰ 9am-8pm May-Sep) sits at the riverbank near the very sparse **AVNOJ-a Museum** (☎ 657712; admission 2KM; ⏰ 8am-6pm), which commemorates the 1943 proclamation of Yugoslavia's postwar socialist constitution with an oversized Tito statue in gold-painted polystyrene. Helpful **Alida** (☎ 065 323782) at the tourist kiosk can arrange keys for visiting the **castle** (Tvrđava; admission 1KM), the small but intriguing 600-year-old **catacombs** (Svetog Luke; admission 1KM) and the hidden 4th-century **Mithras sculpture** (Mitrasova 12; admission 1KM).

For an idyllic off-season stroll, take a Jezero-bound bus (nine daily) 5km west to **Plaža Motel** (☎ 647200; M5 hwy km93) then walk back 1km alongside **Plivsko Jezero**, a picture-perfect lake reflecting the prettily wooded mountains. Notice the quaint collection of 17 miniature **watermills**.

Based at a rural riverside camping ground-cafe on the dramatic Banja Luka road (an hour's drive from Jajce), **Kanjon Rafting** (☎ 065 420000; www.kanjonraft.com) is a well-organised adventure-sports outfit offering rafting (from €25 per person) and guided canyoning.

Book your stay at lonelyplanet.com/hotels

Sleeping & Eating

Autokamp (camp site with/without electricity 12/8KM plus per person 10KM; mid-Apr–Sep) This camping ground is near Plivsko Jezero.

Hotel Stari Grad (654006; hotel.stari.grad@tel.net.ba; Svetog Luke 3; s/d/apt 55/80/160KM; P) Comfortable, unbeatably central little old-town hotel with a good lobby-restaurant (mains 9KM to 14KM; open 7am to 9pm) beneath whose glass floor are the excavations of an Ottoman-era *hamam* (Turkish bath).

Hotel Tourist 98 (658151; Kraljice Katerine; s/d/tr/q/apt 57/84/106/135/120KM; P) Very straightforward, new rooms in a bright-red box hotel beside the big hypermarket directly west of the old town, down a short-cut stairway from the catacombs.

The tourist kiosk can arrange old-city **homestays** (s/d 30/50KM). Half a kilometre west of old Jajce, **Eko Kuća** (654100; www.plivatourism.ba; Pijavice; 8am-3pm Mon-Fri, to 1pm Sat) organises rural homestays (from 30KM).

Getting There & Away

The **bus station** (659202; II-Zasjedanja AVNOJ-a) is hidden behind a small hill, less than five minutes' walk from the tourist kiosk. Useful destinations include Bihać (23.50KM, 3½ hours, four daily), Mostar (18.50KM, three hours, 2.20pm) and Sarajevo (23.50KM, 3½ hours) at 7am, 9.15am, 10.20am and 5.20pm via modestly historic Travnik. It's a beautiful drive to Banja Luka (9.50KM, 1½ hours, five daily), whence trains connect to Zagreb and Belgrade.

MOSTAR

036 / pop 94,000

Set in a deep valley flanked by arid mountains, Mostar's splendidly rebuilt Ottoman-era core forms one of Eastern Europe's most photogenic scenes. Arcing majestically between Neretva River's rugged banks, Mostar's world-famous 1566 **Stari Most** (Old Bridge) was infamously destroyed in the 1990s conflict but has since been meticulously reconstructed as a powerful and very beautiful symbol of BiH's reconciliations.

In summer Mostar's unique breed of **divers** plunge 21m off the bridge's parapet into the icy waters below…at least, once enough photo-money has been collected from the watching tourists. Directly west lies the historic **Tabahana** (an enclosed courtyard with numerous bars and restaurants), the **tourist information centre** (397350; www.hercegovina.ba; Onešćukova; 9am-9pm) and the helpfully well-stocked **BuyBook** (558810; Onešćukova 24; 9am-9pm Mon-Sat, 10am-6pm Sun) bookshop.

Directly east of Stari Most, a five-storey defence tower houses the **Old Bridge Museum** (admission 5KM; 11am-2pm, 10am-6pm May-Sep). Colourful tourist-oriented, stone-fronted stores line **Kujundžiluk**, Mostar's very appealing Turkish-era bazaar-lane, which leads north becoming Mala Tepe then Braće Fejića. The latter is Mostar's main commercial thoroughfare lined with numerous ATMs, eateries, rebuilt historic **mosques** plus a post office and **Barbados** (Braće Fejića 26; internet per hr 2KM; 9am-11pm). At Braće Fejića's north end, if you turn left and cross the bridge on Mostarskog Bataljona, after five minutes' walk you'll come to the **Bulevar**. Today it's a fairly ordinary main road but from 1992 to 1995 this was an intercommunal frontline across which Croats and Bosniaks shelled and fired at each other almost endlessly. In places shockingly war-ravaged buildings still lie in bullet-peppered ruins awaiting reconstruction.

Learn more at the little **Museum of Hercegovina** (551602; Bajatova 4; admission 1.5KM; 9am-2pm Mon-Fri, 10am-noon Sat), which screens a well-paced 10-minute film featuring bridge-diving and showing the very moment that Stari Most was blown apart.

WORTH THE TRIP

Overlooked by spooky ridge-top **Ostrožac Fortress** (www.ostrozac.com) in the northwest corner of BiH, the beautiful emerald-green **Una Valley** is popular for climbing, canyoning, kayaking and a full grade-range of white-water rafting. Useful contacts include **Una Kiro** (037-223760, www.una-kiro-rafting.com; Golubić), **Sport Bjeli** (037-388555; www.una-rafting.ba; Klokot) and **Limit** (061 144248; www.limit.co.ba), based in regional transport-hub Bihać.

Sleeping

Booking ahead is wise, especially in summer when prices can rise significantly.

Hostel Nina (061 382743; www.hostelnina.ba; Čelebica 18; dm/s/d €10/15/20; P) Good-value, English-speaking homestay-style accommodation with three rooms per neat bathroom. Turn third left off Maršala Tita walking south from Lučki bridge. No sign.

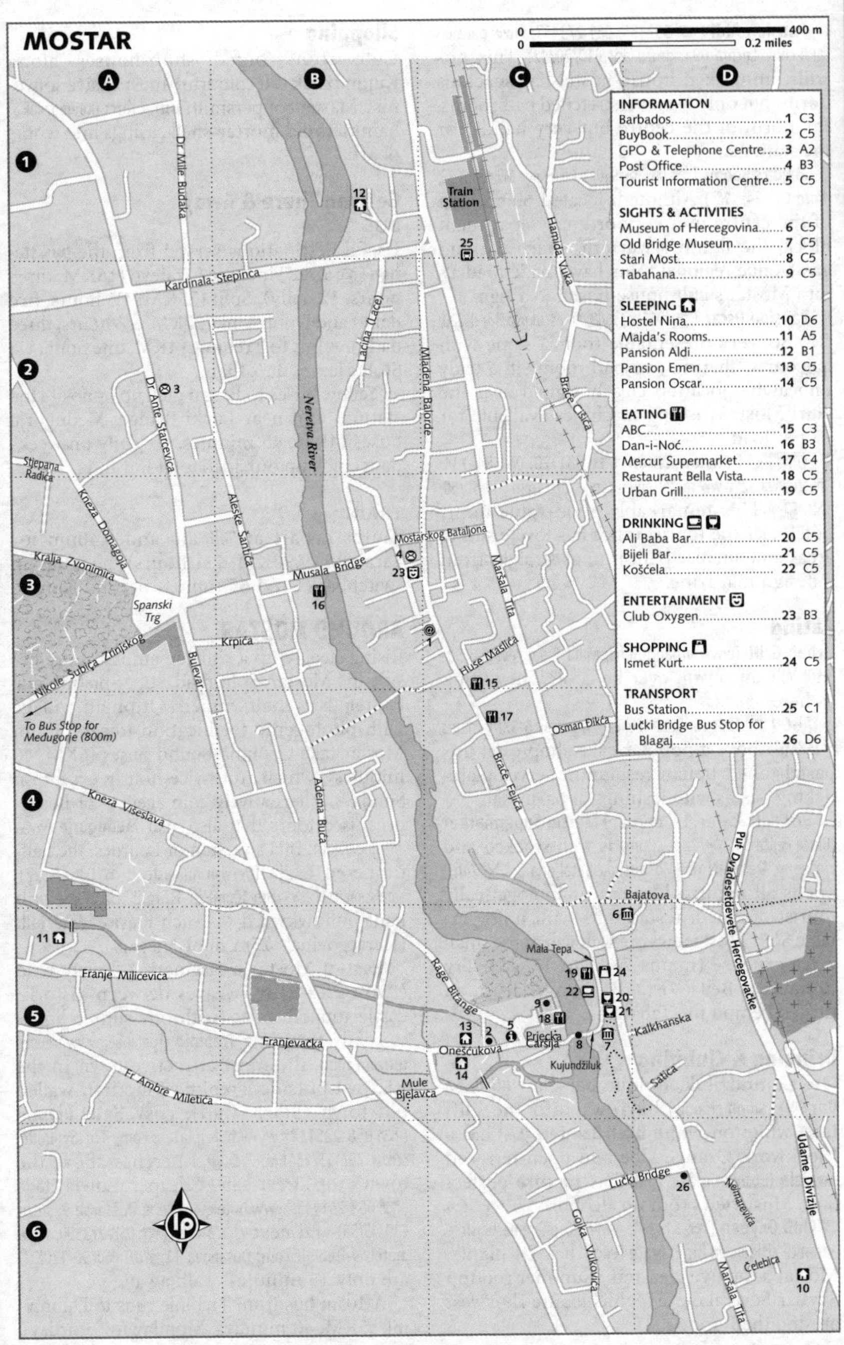
MOSTAR
0 400 m
0 0.2 miles
INFORMATION
Barbados 1 C3
BuyBook 2 C5
GPO & Telephone Centre 3 A2
Post Office 4 B3
Tourist Information Centre 5 C5
SIGHTS & ACTIVITIES
Museum of Hercegovina 6 C5
Old Bridge Museum 7 C5
Stari Most 8 C5
Tabahana 9 C5
SLEEPING
Hostel Nina 10 D6
Majda's Rooms 11 A5
Pansion Aldi 12 B1
Pansion Emen 13 C5
Pansion Oscar 14 C5
EATING
ABC 15 C3
Dan-i-Noć 16 B3
Mercur Supermarket 17 C4
Restaurant Bella Vista 18 C5
Urban Grill 19 C5
DRINKING
Ali Baba Bar 20 C5
Bijeli Bar 21 C5
Košćela 22 C5
ENTERTAINMENT
Club Oxygen 23 B3
SHOPPING
Ismet Kurt 24 C5
TRANSPORT
Bus Station 25 C1
Lučki Bridge Bus Stop for Blagaj 26 D6
Train Station
Dr Mile Budaka
Kardinala Stepinca
Lacina (Laće)
Mladena Balorde
Hamida Vuka
Braće Ćišića
Dr Ante Starčevića
Neretva River
Stjepana Radića
Kneza Domagoja
Aleske Šantića
Mostarskog Bataljona
Kralja Zvonimira
Musala Bridge
Spanski Trg
Krpića
Nikole Šubića Zrinjskog
Bulevar
Maršala Tita
Huse Maslića
To Bus Stop for Međugorje (800m)
Osman Đikća
Braće Fejića
Adema Buća
Kneza Višeslava
Bajatova
Put Dvadesetdevete Hercegovačke
Mala Tepa
Franje Milicevića
Rage Bitange
Prječka Čaršija
Kalkhanska
Franjevačka
Onešćukova
Kujundžiluk
Fr Ambre Miletića
Mule Bjelavca
Šatića
Udarne Divizije
Lučki Bridge
Nelmarevića
Gojka Vukovića
Čelebića

Pansion Aldi (☎ 552185, 061 273457; www.pansion-aldi.com; Laćina 69a; dm/d/apt €10/20/42) This no-frills, unmarked house-hostel has spacious dorms but only two overstretched bathrooms. It's north of the centre but very handy for the stations.

Majda's Rooms (☎ 061 382940; 1st fl, Franje Milicevica 39; dm/d €11/24;) Although located 600m west of the centre in a very ordinary apartment block, the family's warmth, sharp wit and great-value regional tours have made Madja's into Mostar's cult house-hostel. No sign.

Pansion Oscar (☎ 061 823649; Onešćukova 33; d €20;) Six very presentable rooms, some with balconies, sharing two bathrooms in a truly unbeatable location clearly signed near the Stari Most. Washing machines available for €5 per load.

our pick Pansion Emen (☎ 581120, 061 848734; Onešćukova 32; www.motel-emen.com; s/d/tr from €30/50/60;) This remarkably good-value mini-hotel near the tourist office has lovely sitting areas and angular bath fittings straight from a design magazine.

Eating

Urban Grill (www.urbangrill.ba; Mala Tepa; ćevapi 3.50-5.50KM) Can *ćevapi* ever be cool? They think so here.

ABC (☎ 194656; Braće Fejića 45; pizzas 6-9KM, mains 6-15KM) Above a popular cake shop/cafe, this pastel-toned Italian restaurant serves plate-licking pastas with lashings of parmesan.

For self-caterers, central **Mercur Supermarket** (Braće Fejića 51; 7am-10pm) is well stocked and bakery **Dan-i-Noć** (Mostarskog Bataljona 8; 24hr) opens all night. Although unapologetically tourist-oriented, restaurants with unforgettable Stari Most views are well worth the small extra expense (mains 7KM to 17KM). Try Restaurant Bella Vista, Babilon or Teatr, all tucked behind the Tabahana.

Drinking & Clubbing

Off Kujundžiluk, unique bar-club **Ali Baba Bar** (summer only) burrows into the cliff face, white-on-white **Bijeli Bar** (beer 4KM) has a Clockwork Orange vibe and open-terraced **Košćela** (Bosnian coffee 2KM) has picture-perfect Stari Most views (but no alcohol).

Club Oxygen (☎ 512244; www.biosphere.ba/biosfere-stranice-oxigen-en.html; Braće Fejića) has DJ nights, Mostar's top live gigs and a summer rooftop SkyBar. Several more nightclubs are 1km west around the Rondo.

Shopping

Cute stone-roofed shop-houses along Kujundžiluk sell colourful, inexpensive souvenirs. Master coppersmith **Ismet Kurt** (Kujundžiluk 5) hammers old mortar-shell casings into works of art.

Getting There & Away

BUS

Useful destinations served from the **bus station** (☎ 552025) include Sarajevo (16KM, three hours, 12 daily), Split (25KM, 4½ hours, five daily) and Dubrovnik (27KM, 3½ hours, three daily). A bus to Trebinje (4KM, one hour) via Stolac leaves at 6.15am.

Yellow buses to Blagaj pick up opposite the stations and near Lučki Bridge. Međugorje buses (4KM, 45 minutes, six daily on weekdays) pick up outside Hotel Bevanda.

TRAIN

Trains depart at 7.38am and 6.40pm for Sarajevo (9.90KM, 2¾ hours), negotiating switchbacks and 65 tunnels beyond Konjic.

AROUND MOSTAR

Rising steeply up a cliffside amphitheatre beside the Mostar–Split road, super-picturesque **Počitelj** is a half-ruined Ottoman village with photogenic fortification towers. From Mostar take Čapljina-bound buses (6KM, 40 minutes), which run twice hourly except on Sundays. Alternatively, join agency- or hostel-organised tours that also visit **Međugorje** (www.medjugorje.hr), BiH's version of Lourdes, the half-timbered **Tekija** (Dervish monastery; ☎ 036-573221; admission 3KM; 8am-10pm) at Blagaj, plus the brilliant but awkward-to-reach **Kravice Waterfalls** (Hercegovina's 25m mini-Niagara).

East of Mostar a fascinating, lonely road (two buses daily) weaves between historic, castle-topped **Stolac** (with one simple hotel) to gently appealing **Trebinje** (Требиње; www.trebinjeturizam.com), the most attractive town in the RS. Just outside Trebinje's modest, walled old town (Stari Grad), cosy **Hotel Platani** (☎ 058-225134; www.hotelplatani.com; Trg Svobode; s/d/tr 79/115/135KM; P) perches above the town's top street-cafe. Cheaper motels **Etage** (☎ 058-261443; www.hoteletage.com; Dušanova 9; s/d/tr €30/45/55) and next-door **Viv** (☎ 058-273500; www.hotelviv-trebinje.com; Dušanova 11; s/d/tr 60/90/120KM) are only 15 minutes' walk away.

A 10am bus from Trebinje runs to Dubrovnik (5KM, 40 minutes, Monday to Saturday), returning at 1.30pm. The 6am bus to Herceg Novi, Montenegro (13KM, 1¾ hours), runs via Risan, handy for Perast and Kotor (p800). Three daily buses run to Podgorica in Montenegro via Nikšič. Sarajevo buses (20KM, four hours, three daily) and the 8am Belgrade bus (40KM, 11 hours) travel via the glorious **Sutjeska National Park** (www.npsutjeska .srbinje.net) and war-battered **Foča** (Фоча), a centre for world-class rafting organised through professional extreme-sports outfit **Encijan** (☎ 058-211220; www.pkencijan.com; Kraljapetra-I 1).

BOSNIA & HERCEGOVINA DIRECTORY

ACCOMMODATION

Sarajevo and Mostar offer numerous no-frills house-hotels. Being glorified homestays, few have any sign. Some, especially in Mostar, are virtually dormant and unheated off season. In midsummer occupancy and prices rise noticeably but touts helpfully appear at Mostar and Sarajevo stations. Agencies and tourist offices can often organise homestays. Backpacker accommodation is scarce in the provinces.

Decent-value motels and *pansions* (typically singles/doubles from 60/90KM) are usually less expensive and better than hotels, many of which inhabit old Tito-era concrete monster-buildings.

ACTIVITIES

BiH is an outdoor wonderland. The 1984 Olympic skiing pistes at Jahorina and Bjelašnica outside Sarajevo (p139) open from December to March. Rafting around Foča (above), Jajce (p143) and parts of the Una Valley (see boxed text, p144) reaches ferocious grade 5 in April/May but is more suitable for beginners in summer (€25 to €40 per person, minimum group six). Persistent landmine dangers mean that trekkers and off-road mountain-bikers should always follow a reliable guide.

BUSINESS HOURS

Typical business hours in Bosnia and Hercegovina:

Banks 8am-8pm Mon-Fri, 8am-1pm Sat
Cafes 9am-midnight
Restaurants 11am-11pm
Shops 9am-8pm

DANGERS & ANNOYANCES

Be aware that an estimated million mines and fragments of unexploded ordnance remain from the 1990s conflicts (see www.bhmac .org). These cause around 40 casualties a year (barely a 20th of annual casualties in Cambodia), but many mine locations remain unmarked, so play safe: stick to worn paths, asphalt or concrete surfaces, and don't enter abandoned or war-damaged buildings.

EMBASSIES & CONSULATES

The following embassies and consulates are in Sarajevo:

Australia (Map pp140-1; ☎ 033-206167; Obala Kulina Bana 15/1) Honorary consulate.
Canada (off Map pp140-1; ☎ 033-222033; Grbavička 4/2)
Croatia (Map pp140-1; ☎ 033-444331; Mehmeda Spahe 16)
France (Map pp140-1; ☎ 033-282050; Mehmed-bega Kapetanovica Ljubusaka 18)
Germany (Map pp140-1; ☎ 033-275000; Buka)
Hungary (off Map pp140-1; ☎ 033-208353; www.hungemb.ba; Splitska 2)
Macedonia (off Map pp140-1; ☎ 033-206004; Splitska 57)
Montenegro (Map pp140-1; ☎ 033-239925; Talirovića 4)
Serbia (Map pp140-1; ☎ 033-260080; Obala Maka Dizdara 3a)
Slovenia (Map pp140-1; ☎ 033-271251; Bentbaša 7)
UK (Map pp140-1; ☎ 033-208229; Petrakijina 11)
USA (off Map pp140-1; ☎ 033-445700; Alipašina 43)

FOOD & DRINK

Archetypal *ćevapčići* comprise several sausage-shaped kebabs in spongy *somun* bread…perfect with an added 1KM dollop of *kajmak* (sour cream). Ubiquitous *pekara* (bakeries) sell inexpensive *burek*, *sirnica* (cheese pie) and *zeljanica* (spinach pie). For dessert try *tufahije* (baked apple stuffed with walnut paste).

Traditional Bosnian coffee comes Turkish style with the grinds, decanted from a long-handled copper pot (*lđezva*). Most tap water is drinkable.

GAY & LESBIAN TRAVELLERS

Although homosexuality was decriminalised per se in 1998 (2000 in the RS), attitudes are very conservative. Any gay and lesbian scene is underground without any public presence. Logos (www.logos.org.ba/cont/) focuses on combating discrimination against sexual minorities while Association Q attempts to empower the self-reliance of the gay community in BiH. The English language chat website www.gayromeo.com reportedly has around 400 Sarajevo members and www.queer.ba (in Bosnian) organises occasional local meet-ups.

HOLIDAYS

Some holidays are celebrated only in the Federation or RS.

Serbian Orthodox Christmas 7 January (RS)
New Year's Day 1 January
Independence Day 1 March
Catholic Easter (Federation) March/April
Orthodox Easter (RS) April/May
May Day 1 May
National Statehood Day 25 November
Catholic Christmas 25 December (Federation)
Kurban Bajram Islamic feast of sacrifice (Federation); dates vary
Ramazanski Bajram End of Ramadan celebration (Federation); dates vary

INTERNET RESOURCES

Embassies & Visas www.mvp.gov.ba
Events www.insidebosnia.com and www.sarajevoarts.ba
Sarajevo information www.sarajevo.ba
Tourist information www.bhtourism.ba, www.hiddenbosnia.com

MONEY

Pronounced *kai-em* or maraka, the convertible mark (KM or BAM) is tied to the euro at around €1 = 1.95KM. Many tourist-oriented places accept euros. Some in Mostar also take Croatian kuna. ATMs are widespread. Changing travellers cheques often requires the original purchase receipt.

Tipping in restaurants usually means rounding up the bill, or leaving one or two maraka extra.

POST & TELEPHONE

BiH is a philatelic curiosity with three parallel stamp-issuing postal systems (see www.post.ba, www.bhp.ba and www.filatelija.rs.ba). Post offices and telephone offices are often co-located.

RS and Federation payphones use mutually incompatible prepaid cards but BiH's three mobile phone networks have cross-regional coverage. Useful phone numbers include ☎ 00 (international access code), ☎ 1201 (international operator) and ☎ 1182 (directory information).

VISAS

Australian, Canadian, EU, ex-Yugoslav, Japanese, Malaysian, New Zealand, Norwegian, Swiss, Turkish and US citizens don't need visas. Other nationalities should consult www.mvp.gov.ba.

Britain

HIGHLIGHTS

- **London's South Bank** Stroll beside the River Thames to get grandstand views of the city's iconic bridges and buildings (p168)
- **Brighton** Party hard in lively bars and top-class clubs, or shop for vintage skater gear in back-alley boutiques (p181)
- **Pembrokeshire** Find solitude in quiet coves or surf wild waves in this corner of Wales (p213)
- **Best journey** Ride the train on the scenic West Highland Line through the glens of Scotland from Glasgow (p218) to Fort William (p223) and Mallaig, and catch a ferry on to Skye (p224)
- **Off the beaten track** Hike the hills and valleys of the Lake District (p203)

FAST FACTS

- **Area** 88,500 sq miles/229,000 sq km
- **Budget** £30-60 per day
- **Capital** London
- **Country code** ☎ 44
- **Famous for** tea, football, Shakespeare
- **Languages** English, Welsh, Gaelic
- **Money** pound sterling (£); A$1 = £0.49; C$ = £0.56; €1 = £0.88; ¥100 = £0.70; NZ$1 = £0.39; US$1 = £0.66
- **Population** 60 million
- **Visas** none required for most tourists (p228)

TRAVEL HINTS

Check out lunch or early evening special menus in restaurants, and try no-frills pubs for cheap grub. Travel by coach and train at 'off-peak' times, and buy your tickets in advance.

ROAMING BRITAIN

From London, head west via historic Winchester, Salisbury and Bath, dropping into Bristol's nightlife, to reach Cardiff or the Cotswolds.

Visitors to Britain often arrive expecting a genteel country of warm beer and double-decker buses, with red telephone boxes on every street corner. Instead they discover a nation that has dramatically moved on from such stereotypes – but this doesn't mean that Britain has abandoned the qualities that still make it great for travellers.

Cosmopolitan London remains one of the most exciting cities in the world, with rising postindustrial challengers like Manchester, Bristol and Glasgow jostling for the mantle of Britain's second-most vibrant metropolis.

For outdoor addicts, there are remote or rural areas of jaw-dropping beauty, including the picture-postcard Cotswolds, the stunning coasts of Cornwall and west Wales, and the craggy Scottish Highlands.

And for history fans, there's Britain's roll-call of grand cathedrals, royal castles, stately homes, Roman remains and mystic stone circles, while almost every town in the country has an ancient market square, a centuries-old church and a clutch of pubs little changed since medieval days.

So be it history, nature or contemporary culture that attracts you to Britain, it's clearly a good idea to leave your preconceptions at the border.

HISTORY

It may be a small island on the edge of Western Europe, but Britain was never on the sidelines of history. For thousands of years, invaders and incomers have arrived, settled and made their mark. The result is Britain's fascinating mix of landscape and culture – a dynamic pattern that shaped the nation and continues to evolve today.

Going back to prehistoric times, the island now called Britain was populated by bands of hunter-gatherers, and changed significantly around 4000 BC when a group of migrants wielding new-fangled stone tools crossed the land-bridge from the European mainland. (Sea levels were lower then – and it was long before the Channel Tunnel). Perhaps the most enduring legacy left by these nascent Britons are the great stone circles of Avebury and Stonehenge (p186), still clearly visible today.

The next important migration was the Celts from central Europe, whose smelting skills launched a mini cultural revolution. London's British Museum (p166), along with many city museums across the country, display artefacts from this period.

Even more numerous are the excavated discoveries from Britain's colourful Roman era. The main invasion was in AD 43, and the legions quickly overcame local resistance to rule much of the province they called Britannia for the next 350 years. The Romans built villas, forts and bath-houses that can still be seen in cities like Bath (p187), and at Hadrian's Wall (p209).

The Romans abandoned Britain in AD 410, and the province entered a period known by some historians as the Dark Ages. Rural areas became no-go zones as local warlords fought over fiefdoms, but the vacuum didn't go unnoticed and once again invaders crossed from the European mainland – this time Germanic tribes called Angles and Saxons.

By the late 6th century much of southern and central Britain was predominantly Anglo-Saxon, divided into separate kingdoms dominated by Wessex (today's southern England), Mercia (central England) and Northumbria (northern England and southern Scotland), with the Celts pushed to the western and northern edges (today's Wales and northern Scotland).

Anglo-Saxon expansion forced the disparate tribes of Wales to band together and sow the seeds of nationhood. They called themselves cymry (fellow countrymen), and today Cymru is the Welsh word for Wales. Meanwhile, in the north of Britain, the local people, called the Picts, were invaded from the south by the Anglo-Saxons, and from the west by the Scotti tribe from Ireland – the latter group eventually became dominant and gave their name to the region we call Scotland.

While the tribal kingdoms of Britain ebbed and flowed, yet again the island was invaded by a bunch of pesky Continentals – the Vikings (from modern-day Scandinavia) – and by the end of the first millennium they occupied large parts of northern and eastern England, making York their capital. The sights, sounds and smells of the settlement are colourfully evoked today at the city's Jorvik Centre (p205).

In the 9th century, the king of the Scotti declared himself ruler of both the Scotti and the Picts, and therefore of all Scotland. The Stone of Destiny, now at Edinburgh Castle (p214), was launched into legend as a symbol of nascent Scottish nationhood, but back in England things remained unsettled until the Battle of Hastings of 1066, when King William of Normandy landed his army on England's southern coast, and defeated the Saxons. Their king, Harold, was killed – according to legend by an arrow in the eye.

England's new Norman rulers built an imposing network of hulking castles and astonishing cathedrals, and many architectural landmarks you'll see on your travels in Britain date from this period, such as Windsor Castle (p179) and Durham Cathedral (p207) – although of course they've undergone additions over the centuries.

The centuries after the Norman invasion saw England racked with conspiracy as aristocratic families competed to influence the royal

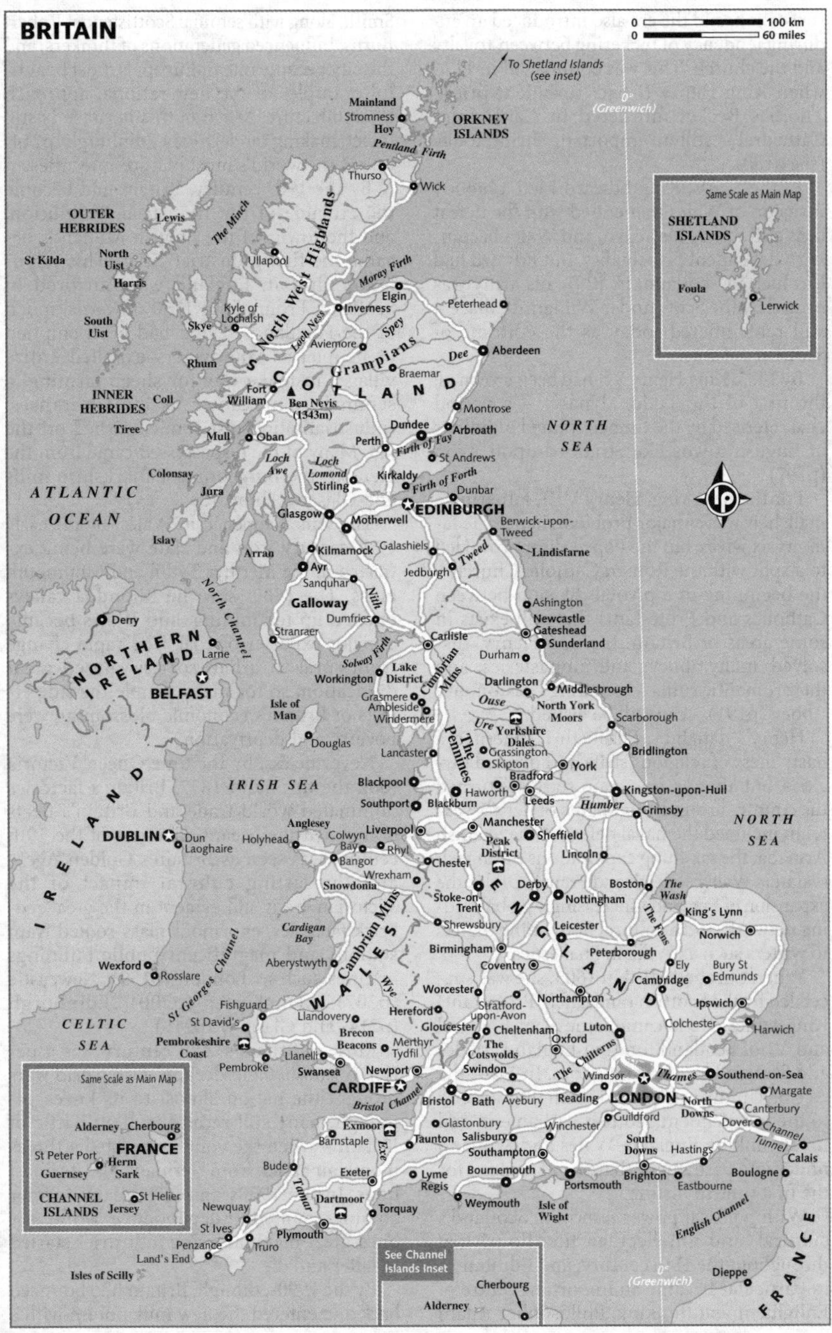
BRITAIN
0 100 km
0 60 miles
To Shetland Islands (see inset)
Same Scale as Main Map
SHETLAND ISLANDS
Foula
Lerwick
0° (Greenwich)
Mainland
Stromness
Hoy
ORKNEY ISLANDS
Pentland Firth
Thurso
Wick
OUTER HEBRIDES
Lewis
The Minch
North West Highlands
St Kilda
North Uist
Harris
Ullapool
Moray Firth
Elgin
Peterhead
Inverness
South Uist
Kyle of Lochalsh
Skye
Loch Ness
Spey
Aviemore
Grampians
Aberdeen
Dee
Rhum
Braemar
SCOTLAND
INNER HEBRIDES
Coll
Fort William
Ben Nevis (1343m)
Montrose
Tiree
Dundee
Arbroath
NORTH SEA
Mull
Oban
Perth
Firth of Tay
St Andrews
Loch Awe
Loch Lomond
Colonsay
Kirkaldy
Stirling
Firth of Forth
Dunbar
ATLANTIC OCEAN
Jura
Glasgow
EDINBURGH
Motherwell
Berwick-upon-Tweed
Islay
Arran
Kilmarnock
Galashiels
Lindisfarne
Ayr
Tweed
Jedburgh
Sanquhar
North Channel
Galloway
Nith
Ashington
Derry
Dumfries
Newcastle
Gateshead
Stranraer
Carlisle
Sunderland
NORTHERN IRELAND
Larne
Solway Firth
Durham
BELFAST
Workington
Lake District
Cumbrian Mtns
Darlington
Middlesbrough
Grasmere
Ambleside
Windermere
Ouse
North York Moors
Isle of Man
Scarborough
Ure
Yorkshire Dales
The Pennines
Douglas
Grassington
Bridlington
Lancaster
Skipton
York
IRISH SEA
Bradford
Blackpool
Haworth
Kingston-upon-Hull
Leeds
Southport
Blackburn
Humber
Grimsby
NORTH SEA
Anglesey
Liverpool
Manchester
DUBLIN
Dun Laoghaire
Holyhead
Colwyn Bay
Rhyl
Peak District
Sheffield
Lincoln
Bangor
Chester
IRELAND
Wrexham
Boston
The Wash
Snowdonia
Derby
Nottingham
ENGLAND
Stoke-on-Trent
The Fens
King's Lynn
Cardigan Bay
Shrewsbury
Leicester
Norwich
Cambrian Mtns
WALES
Birmingham
Peterborough
Wexford
Rosslare
Aberystwyth
Coventry
Ely
Bury St Edmunds
St Georges Channel
Wye
Worcester
Cambridge
Northampton
Fishguard
Stratford-upon-Avon
Ipswich
CELTIC SEA
St David's
Llandovery
Hereford
Colchester
Harwich
Gloucester
Cheltenham
Luton
Pembrokeshire Coast
Brecon Beacons
Merthyr Tydfil
Oxford
The Cotswolds
The Chilterns
Llanelli
Pembroke
Swansea
Newport
Swindon
Windsor
Thames
Southend-on-Sea
CARDIFF
Bristol Channel
Bristol
Bath
Avebury
Reading
LONDON
Margate
North Downs
Canterbury
Same Scale as Main Map
Alderney
Cherbourg
FRANCE
St Peter Port
Herm
Guernsey
Sark
CHANNEL ISLANDS
Jersey
St Helier
Exmoor
Glastonbury
Winchester
Guildford
Dover
Channel Tunnel
Barnstaple
Taunton
Salisbury
South Downs
Hastings
Calais
Exe
Southampton
Bude
Exeter
Lyme Regis
Bournemouth
Brighton
Boulogne
Portsmouth
Eastbourne
Tamar
Weymouth
Isle of Wight
Newquay
Dartmoor
Torquay
English Channel
St Ives
Plymouth
Penzance
Truro
FRANCE
Land's End
See Channel Islands Inset
Isles of Scilly
Cherbourg
Dieppe
Alderney
0° (Greenwich)
BRITAIN

succession, and the era also introduced an enduring tendency of bickering between royalty and the church. This was epitomised in 1170 when King Henry II had 'turbulent priest' Thomas Becket murdered in Canterbury Cathedral – still an important shrine today (see p180).

In the 1270s, King Edward I led a bloody invasion of Wales that ended with the defeat of Welsh Prince Llewellyn, and Wales becoming a dependent principality. But Edward had less luck in Scotland; in 1297, his army was routed by the Scots under William Wallace – still remembered today as the epitome of Scottish patriots.

By 1485, King Henry VII had been crowned, the first of the Tudor dynasty – a period characterised by the timber-framed buildings of English towns like Stratford-upon-Avon (p197).

For the next king, Henry VIII, fathering a male heir was a major problem, hence the famous six wives, but the Pope's disapproval led to a split with the Roman Catholic Church – the beginning of a pivotal division between Catholics and Protestants that still exists in some areas of Britain. In 1536 Henry 'dissolved' many abbeys and monasteries, and their romantic ruins – including Glastonbury Abbey (p191) – can still be visited.

Henry's daughter, Elizabeth I, inherited a nasty mess of religious strife and divided loyalties, but after an uncertain start she turned the country around. Highlights of her 45-year reign included the naval defeat of the Spanish Armada, the far-flung explorations of English seafarers Walter Raleigh and Francis Drake, the expansion of England's increasingly global trading network, and a cultural flourishing thanks to writers such as William Shakespeare.

When Elizabeth died in 1603, she was succeeded by the Scottish (and safely Protestant) King James. He became James I of England and VI of Scotland, uniting England, Wales and Scotland into one kingdom. In 1707, the Act of Union was passed, bringing an end to the independent Scottish Parliament, and finally linking England, Wales and Scotland under one parliament (based in London) for the first time in history.

With political power removed, Scotland's cultural and intellectual life flourished throughout the 18th century, and Edinburgh in particular became an important centre of Enlightenment thinking. Philosopher Adam Smith, along with seminal Scottish poet Robert Burns, influenced generations of thinkers, and the city became one of Europe's most beautiful examples of the new rational approach to architecture. Much of this heritage is still intact, making modern-day Edinburgh (p214) one of the world's most picturesque cities.

By the 19th century, Britain had become the crucible of the Industrial Revolution, and the towns of the English Midlands became the first industrial cities. This population shift in England was mirrored in Scotland. From about 1750 onwards, much of the Highlands region had been emptied of people, as landowners expelled entire villages to make way for sheep farming, a seminal event known as the Clearances. Industrialisation just about finished off the job. Many of the dispossessed came from the glens to the burgeoning Lanarkshire mills and Glasgow shipyards.

The same happened in Wales. By the early 19th century iron and slate were being extracted in the Merthyr Tydfil and Monmouth areas. The 1860s saw the Rhondda valleys opened up for mining, and Wales became a major exporter of coal. The rapid change from rural to urban society caused great dislocation, so for many people the side effects of Britain's economic blossoming were poverty and deprivation.

Nevertheless, by the time Queen Victoria took the throne in 1837, Britain's factories dominated world trade and Britain's fleets dominated the oceans. The rest of the 19th century was seen as Britain's Golden Age – and the lasting cultural impact of the Victorian era is still evident in the great red-brick factories, enormous glass-roofed train stations and magnificent public buildings in cities such as London (p159), Newcastle (p207), Manchester (p200), Edinburgh (p214) and Glasgow (p218).

Most of Britain's 20th century was a period of conflict and decline. Two world wars brought the nation almost to its knees, although many still recall the 1940 Battle of Britain – when the country resisted a three-month air attack from Germany – as its finest hour. In the 1950s and '60s, many former colonies gained independence while the once-great manufacturing industries started to falter and die.

By the 1990s, though, Britain had bounced back and entered the new millennium with a strong economy and a cultural scene dubbed (briefly) 'Cool Britannia'. In the general election of 1997, after nearly 18 years of Conservative rule, 'New' Labour swept to power under a fresh-faced leader called Tony Blair.

Britain's role on the world stage was exemplified by its relationship with the USA and military campaigns in Afghanistan and Iraq – not that everyone agreed with such moves. Meanwhile, on the home front, history turned full circle as the state of Britain began to devolve into its three constituent nations. The new Scottish Parliament came into being in 1999 and its new home in Edinburgh (p216) is one of the city's main sights. Concurrently, the people of Wales voted for a Welsh Assembly, which now meets in a fantastic new building in Cardiff (p210).

June 2007 saw the resignation of Tony Blair, allowing Gordon Brown to become Britain's Prime Minister. His first year in office was initially deemed a disappointment, but his handling of the global economic crisis towards the end of 2008 earned many plaudits and restored public support. With the next election expected in 2009, it remains to be seen if the voters will award Labour yet another term in office, or if the political pendulum finally swings back the other way.

THE CULTURE

With a population of around 60 million, Britain is one of the world's most densely populated countries. Despite this, there are many different cultural identities, the obvious ones being the distinct English, Welsh and Scottish nationalities. Within each of the three 'home nations' are definite north-south divides derived from ancient Saxon, Norman, Celtic or Viking origins, and then even stronger local identities that may be based on a county (eg Yorkshire), a clan (in Scotland) or a valley (in Wales).

Several British towns and cities have sizable South Asian and Afro-Caribbean communities, with many families here for three or more generations. In recent years large numbers of people from Eastern Europe have also come to Britain for work.

Historically the three nations that make up Britain have long been dominated by England – which is why many visitors confuse 'Britain' with 'England', and 'British' with 'English', but of course you should take care you use the right term – especially in Wales and Scotland. Calling a Scot 'English' is like calling a New Zealander 'Australian' or – horrors – a Canadian 'American'.

READING UP

To get under the skin of Britain, and to while away the waiting time at dreary coach stations, nothing beats losing yourself in a novel. Britain's best-known contemporary writer is probably JK Rowling, author of the Harry Potter stories, closely followed in a similar genre by Philip Pullman's *His Dark Materials* trilogy. But away from parallel worlds, some novels based in Britain to sample might include Muriel Spark's *The Prime of Miss Jean Brodie*, Irvine Welsh's *Trainspotting*, Zadie Smith's *White Teeth* or Monica Ali's *Brick Lane*. In the travelogue genre, try Bill Bryson's classic but still on-the-button *Notes from a Small Island*, or Josie Dew's *Slow Coast Home*.

SPORT

If you want to take a shortcut into the heart of British culture, watch the British at play. They're fierce and proud about their sport, whether participating or spectating, and the mood of the nation is more closely aligned to the success of its international teams than budget announcements from the government, or even the weather – no more clearly evidenced than the massive support for Team GB, especially the phenomenal cyclists and swimmers, in the 2008 Beijing Olympics.

Sometimes, though, it's the success of the nations that matters; the separate rugby teams of England, Wales and Scotland, and the English and Scottish national football sides have supporters with passion that borders on the insane. Elsewhere, sporting highlights such as tennis at Wimbledon or the Grand National horse race keep everyone enthralled. And Team GB will have a chance to shine again, this time on home soil, when the next Olympics come to London in 2012.

ARTS

Britain has a colourful artistic history (notably in the realms of theatre and literature) that stretches back centuries, while modern popular cultural movements (notably music and conceptual art) resonate throughout the world.

Travelling in the footsteps of English, Scottish or Welsh writers can be the highlight of any trip to Britain. Ambling through the cobbled streets of Canterbury recalls Chaucer's ribald comedy, a trip to Bath evokes Jane Austen, while strolling in the Scottish glens might summon up the spirit of Robbie Burns. Spirits of a different variety should be sampled in the pubs of Wales, some of which inspired the poetry of Dylan Thomas.

Britain's home-grown film industry's worldwide hits include *Shakespeare in Love* and *Bend it Like Beckham*. For more grit, try *The Full Monty, Secrets and Lies, Billy Elliot, East is East* or *Atonement*. For a great laugh, go for *Hot Fuzz*.

There's a great depth of classical music performance in Britain, with several cities hosting their own renowned symphony orchestras, but the music this country is best known for is pop and rock, with venerable juggernauts like Elton John and the Rolling Stones routinely topping lists of high-grossing concert tours around the world. The '90s was notable for the rise of British 'indie' bands, with the likes of Blur, Supergrass, Manic Street Preachers, Pulp, Travis, Feeder, Stereophonics, Catatonia, Radiohead and, above all, Oasis reviving the guitar-based format. Heralded as the 'Britpop revolution', it was over almost as soon as it started, but a host of bands like Coldplay, Franz Ferdinand, Snow Patrol and Razorlight play on.

As the first decade of the 21st century draws to a close, British pop and rock have divided into a host of genres mixing a wide range of influences including glam, punk, electronica and folk (while British folk itself, thanks largely to the rise of world music, enjoys its biggest revival since the 1960s). Worth a listen are atmospheric and eclectic British Sea Power; energetic and nostalgic Go! Team; the rousing rock- country-psychedelia mix that is The Coral; popular Yorkshire rockers Arctic Monkeys; Dundee's indie darlings The View; and jazz-soul diva Amy Winehouse.

On the visual arts side, cities like Glasgow, Cardiff, Manchester and London boast some of Europe's finest galleries, with works by well-known British artists such as Turner, Constable, Francis Bacon and Lucian Freud.

In recent years, contemporary art has undergone a transformation, with new galleries such as the capital's Tate Modern (p168) and Newcastle's Baltic (p208) and boundary-pushing installations creating feverish debate in tabloid newspapers.

Public art has also taken on a new role, epitomised by the Angel of the North (p208) becoming a symbol of northern pride. In a different genre, guerrilla graffiti artist Banksy regularly stokes the fires of controversy by smuggling his works onto the walls of august galleries.

ENVIRONMENT

The island of Britain sits on the eastern edge of the North Atlantic and consists of England in the south and centre, Scotland to the north and Wales to the west – together making up the state of Great Britain. Further west lies the island of Ireland. Looking southeast, France is just 20 miles away, while to the northeast lie the countries of Scandinavia. Measuring around 600 miles (around 1000km) north to south, and about half that at its widest point, Britain is roughly the same size as New Zealand and half the size of France. When it comes to topology, Britain is not a place of extremes – there are no Himalayas or Lake Baikals – but even a short journey can take you through a surprising mix of landscapes, from the flatlands of eastern England (p198), or rolling moors of Devon (p191) to the craggy peaks of Snowdonia (p213) and windswept islands off the west coast of Scotland (p222).

TRANSPORT

GETTING THERE & AWAY

Air

You can fly to Britain from just about anywhere in the world. London is a global hub, but major regional airports such as Manchester and Glasgow also handle many international flights, and in recent years many other airports around Britain have increased their choice – especially on budget (no-frills) airlines to/from mainland Europe – which can be very handy for travels around the continent. Avoiding busy London airports also means you're less likely to be delayed.

LONDON AIRPORTS

London is served by five airports, with Heathrow and Gatwick being the busiest:

CONNECTIONS

As an island on the edge of Western Europe, Britain's overland options to neighbouring countries are pretty much limited to ferries (yes, OK, we know that's over sea). If time is tight, ferry rides eat into schedules, but if you're relaxed they're a great part of a trip. Many Brits, for example, take ferries to northern Spain as a 'mini-cruise', for sea-air or a bit of partying, and may not even get off at the other end. For pan-European travels, other options include ferries from southern England across to the Netherlands or France (also possible via the Channel Tunnel), from eastern England to Germany, from northern England to Scandinavia, from southwest Scotland to Northern Ireland and from Wales to the Republic of Ireland. For details, see below.

London City (LCY; ☎ 020-7646 0088; www.londoncityairport.com)
London Gatwick (LGW; ☎ 0870 000 2468; www.gatwickairport.com)
London Heathrow (LHR; ☎ 0870 000 0123; www.heathrowairport.com)
Luton (LTN; ☎ 01582-405100; www.london-luton.co.uk)
Stansted (STN; ☎ 0870 000 0303; www.stanstedairport.com)

For more details on reaching central London from these airports, see the Getting into Town box (p165).

REGIONAL AIRPORTS

Regional airports with international flights:
Bristol (BRS; ☎ 0870 121 2747; www.bristolairport.co.uk)
Cardiff (CWL; ☎ 01446-711111; www.cwlfly.com)
Edinburgh (EDI; ☎ 0870 040 0007; www.edinburghairport.com)
Glasgow (GGW; ☎ 0870 040 0008; www.glasgowairport.com)
Liverpool (LPL; ☎ 0870 129 8484; www.liverpooljohnlennonairport.com)
Manchester (MAN; ☎ 0161 489 3000; www.manchesterairport.co.uk)
Newcastle (NCL; ☎ 0870 122 1488; www.newcastleairport.com)

AIRLINES FLYING TO/FROM BRITAIN

Following are some airlines (with UK phone contact details) flying to/from Britain:
Aer Lingus (EI; ☎ 0845 876 5000; www.flyaerlingus.com)
Air Canada (AC; ☎ 0871 220 1111; www.aircanada.com)
Air France (AF; ☎ 0870 142 4343; www.airfrance.com)
American Airlines (AA; ☎ 0845 778 9789; www.aa.com)
British Airways (BA; ☎ 0870 850 9850; www.ba.com)
BMI (BD; ☎ 0870 6070 555; www.flybmi.com)
Cathay Pacific (CX; ☎ 020-8834 8888; www.cathaypacific.com)
easyJet (EZY; ☎ 0870 600 0000; www.easyjet.com)
KLM (KLM; ☎ 0870 507 4074; www.klm.com)
Lufthansa (LH; ☎ 0870 833 7747; www.lufthansa.com)
Qantas (QF; ☎ 0845 774 7767; www.qantas.com.au)
Ryanair (FR; ☎ 0871 246 0000; www.ryanair.com)
United (UA; ☎ 0845 844 4777; www.united.com)
Virgin Atlantic (VS; ☎ 0870 574 7747; www.virgin-atlantic.com)

Boat

Britain has many ferries serving Ireland and mainland Europe. The shortest crossing is between Dover (southeast England) and Calais (France). Others include Harwich to Hoek van Holland (Netherlands), Portsmouth to Santander (Spain), and Newcastle to Bergen (Norway) or Göteborg (Sweden). There are many more. Shorter routes have many services daily. On longer routes there may be only one per day each way.

Competition from Eurotunnel and budget airlines forces ferry operators to offer great bargains at quiet times of the day or year. Short cross-channel routes such as Dover to Calais can be £20 for a car plus passengers, although £50 is more likely. If you're a foot passenger, or cycling, there's often less need to book ahead, and cheap fares on the short crossings start from about £10 each way.

Main ferry operators include the following. Some operators take only online bookings; others charge a supplement (up to £20) for booking by phone.
Brittany Ferries (www.brittany-ferries.com)
DFDS Seaways (☎ 0871 522 9955; www.dfds.co.uk)
Irish Ferries (☎ 08705 171717; www.irishferries.com)
Norfolkline (☎ 08701 450603; www.norfolkline.com)
P&O Ferries (☎ 08716 645 645; www.poferries.com)
Speedferries (☎ 0871 222 7456; www.speedferries.com)
Stena Line (www.stenaline.com)
Superfast Ferries (☎ 0870 420 1267; www.superfast.ferries.org)
Transmanche (☎ 0800 917 1201; www.transmancheferries.com)

A great portal site is www.ferrybooker.com, selling tickets for all sea-ferry routes, plus Eurotunnel, and with a handy map showing who goes where.

Bus

With a vast network of international long-distance routes, **Eurolines** (www.eurolines.com) is an umbrella company of around 30 bus/coach operators. The website is full of information on routes and options, and you can buy tickets online. Services to/from Britain are operated by **National Express** (www.nationalexpress.com) and most arrive/leave from the giant Victoria Coach Station in central London. Some sample journey times to/from London are: Amsterdam (12 hours), Paris (eight or nine hours), Dublin (12 hours) and Barcelona (24 hours). Fares vary enormously: if you book early and can be flexible with timings you'll get some good deals. For example, London to Paris or Amsterdam one-way starts at just £18, although nearer £25 is more usual. If you book late and/or travel at a busy time, you'll pay around £40 or more on the same route.

Car & Motorcycle

Visitors can bring vehicles to Britain from Europe via ferry services or the Channel Tunnel. If you're hiring, check with the rental company regarding insurance for travelling between Britain and mainland Europe.

Train

The Channel Tunnel allows direct train travel between Britain and continental Europe. High-speed **Eurostar** (☎ 08705 186186; www.eurostar.com) passenger services hurtle at least 10 times daily between London St Pancras and Paris (2½ hours) or Brussels (two hours). You can buy tickets from travel agencies, major train stations or the Eurostar website. The normal single fare between London and Paris/Brussels is around £150, but if you buy in advance and travel at a quiet period, deals drop to around £45. Look out for train-and-hotel combo deals – bizarrely sometimes cheaper than train fare only.

If you're travelling by car, use **Eurotunnel** (☎ 08705 353535; www.eurotunnel.com). At Folkestone (England) or Calais (France) you drive onto a train, go through the tunnel, and drive off at the other end. The trains run four times hourly from 6am to 10pm, then hourly. You can book in advance or pay on the spot. The one-way cost for car and passengers is £90 to £150 (less busy times are cheaper), and promotional fares often bring this down to nearer £50.

As well as Eurostar, many 'normal' trains run between Britain and mainland Europe. You buy one ticket, but get off the train at the port, walk onto a ferry, then get another train on the other side. Routes include Amsterdam–London (via Hoek van Holland and Harwich). Travelling between Britain and Ireland the main train–ferry–train route is London to Dublin via Holyhead and Dun Laoghaire. Ferries also run between Fishguard or Pembroke (southwest Wales) to Rosslare (southeast Ireland) with train connections on either side. For details and ideas, see www.raileurope.co.uk and www.raileurope.com.

GETTING AROUND

For getting around Britain, a car makes the best use of your time and helps reach remote places, but rental and fuel can be expensive for budget travellers so public transport is often a better way to go – and using a mix of train, coach, local bus, taxi, walking or hiring a bike, you can get almost anywhere. You'll certainly see more of the countryside than you will slogging along motorways, and in the serene knowledge you're doing less environmental damage.

The best portal site is **Traveline** (☎ 0871 200 2233; www.traveline.org.uk) covering bus, coach, taxi and train services nationwide, with numerous links to help plan your journey.

Air

If you're pushed for time, flights on longer routes across Britain (eg Exeter or Southampton to Edinburgh or Inverness) are handy. On shorter or direct routes (eg London to Newcastle) train durations compare favourably with planes – once airport downtime is factored in. With advance booking, domestic flights start as low as £20 one-way, but up to £100 is more likely.

AIRLINES IN BRITAIN

Airlines operating domestic flights within Britain:

Air Southwest (WOW; ☎ 0870 241 8202; www.airsouthwest.com) Serving Bristol, Cardiff, Leeds-Bradford, Gatwick, Manchester, Newquay and Plymouth.

bmibaby (WW; ☎ 0870 224 0224; www.bmibaby.com) Serving Cardiff, Edinburgh, Glasgow, Manchester and Newquay.
Eastern Airways (☎ 08703 669100; www.easternairways.com) Routes between Newcastle, Norwich, Cardiff, Southampton and more.
easyJet (EZY; ☎ 0870 600 0000; www.easyjet.com) Serving Bristol, Edinburgh, Glasgow, Inverness, Liverpool, Luton, Stansted and Newcastle.
Flybe (BE; ☎ 0871 700 2000; www.flybe.com) Airports served include Bristol, Edinburgh, Exeter, Glasgow, Liverpool, Manchester, Newcastle and Newquay.
Ryanair (FR; ☎ 0871 246 0000; www.ryanair.com) Serving Edinburgh, Glasgow, Inverness, Liverpool, Stansted and Newquay.

Bicycle

A bike is a great way to explore back-road Britain, or simply reach places a few miles out of town. Details on bike hire are given throughout this chapter; for more pedal-powered info, see p226.

Bus

Long-distance bus is nearly always the cheapest way to get around, although also the slowest. In Britain, long-distance buses are called coaches, and many towns have separate bus and coach stations. Make sure you go to the right place!

National Express (☎ 08717 818181; www.nationalexpress.com) is Britain's biggest coach operator, with a wide network and frequent services between main centres. North of the border, **Scottish Citylink** (☎ 08705 505050; www.citylink.co.uk) is the leading coach company. As a guide, a 200-mile trip (eg London to York) will cost around £15 to £20 if you book a few days in advance, but special off-peak 'fun fares' can go as low as £1.

Also offering fares from £1 is **Megabus** (www.megabus.com), a budget coach service between about 30 destinations in Britain. Go at a quiet time, book early, and your ticket will be very cheap. Book last-minute, for a busy time and… you get the picture.

BUS PASSES

National Express discount passes for full-time students and under-26s, called Young Persons Coachcards, cost £10 and get 30% off standard adult fares. For touring the country, Brit Xplorer passes allow unlimited travel for 7/14/28 days (£79/139/219). You don't need to book in advance; if the coach has a spare seat, you can take it.

HOW MUCH TO…?

When travelling long-distance by train or coach in Britain, or by plane and boat to/from the rest of Europe, it's important to note that there's no such thing as a standard fare. On pretty much every form of transport (except local buses), prices vary according to demand and when you buy your ticket. Book long in advance and travel on Tuesday mid-morning, and it's cheap. Buy at the station to travel on the next train, late afternoon on Friday, and it'll be a lot more expensive. Throughout this Britain chapter, to give you an idea, we have quoted sample fares somewhere in between the very cheapest and most expensive options. The price you pay will almost certainly be different.

Car & Motorcycle

Often the quickest way to tour Britain is by motorbike or car – particularly in remote areas – but petrol costs around £1 per litre, and parking in cities can be troublesome and expensive. Hiring is costly compared to many countries (especially the USA); you'll pay around £250 per week for a small car (including insurance and unlimited mileage) but rates rise at busy times. In Britain, there are the following main players:

1car1 (☎ 0113 263 6675; www.1car1.com)
Avis (☎ 0844 581 0147; www.avis.co.uk)
Budget (☎ 0844 581 9998; www.budget.co.uk)
Europcar (☎ 0870 607 5000; www.europcar.co.uk)
Sixt (☎ 08701 567567; www.sixt.co.uk)
Thrifty (☎ 01494-751540; www.thrifty.co.uk)

You might get a better deal if you arrange car hire (through a real or virtual travel agent) at the same time as buying your air ticket. Your other option is to use an internet search engine to find small local car-hire companies who can undercut the big boys, or see a rental-broker site such as www.ukcarhire.net.

ROAD RULES

The Highway Code, available in bookshops (or at www.direct.gov.uk/en/TravelAndTransport/Highwaycode), contains everything you need to know about Britain's road rules. The main ones:

- drive on the left
- wear fitted seat belts
- give way to your right at junctions and roundabouts
- always use the left-side lane on motorways and dual-carriageways, unless overtaking (although so many people ignore this rule, you'd think it didn't exist)
- don't use a mobile phone while driving unless it's fully hands-free (another rule frequently flouted)

Speed limits are 30mph in built-up areas, 60mph on main roads and 70mph on motorways and most (but not all) dual carriageways. Drinking and driving is taken very seriously; the maximum blood-alcohol level allowed is 80mg/100mL.

Train

For long-distance travel around Britain, trains are faster than coaches but can be more expensive – although with discount tickets they're competitive – and often take you through beautiful countryside.

About 20 companies operate train services in Britain (for example: First Great Western runs from London to Bristol; Virgin Trains run the 'west coast' route from London to Glasgow), while Network Rail operates track and stations. This system can seem confusing, but information and ticket-buying are mostly centralised. If you have to change trains, or use two train operators, you usually still buy one ticket – valid for the whole journey. The main railcards are also accepted by all operators.

Your first stop should be **National Rail Enquiries** (☎ 08457 484950; www.nationalrail.co.uk). Punch in your start and end destinations, and the site will offer a range of routes, times and fares. Once you've found the journey you need, links take you to the relevant train operator or centralised ticketing services (www.thetrainline.com, www.qjump.co.uk, www.raileasy.co.uk) to buy the ticket. Train travel websites can be confusing at first (you always have to state an approximate preferred time and day of travel, even if you don't mind when you go), but with a little delving they offer some real bargains.

For planning your trip, handy maps of the UK's rail network can be downloaded from www.nationalrail.co.uk/tocs_maps/maps/network_rail_maps.html.

NO PASSPORTS REQUIRED

Travelling between England, Scotland and Wales is easy. The bus and train systems are fully integrated and often you won't even know you've crossed the border. Passports are not required – although some independent-minded Scots and Welsh may think they should be!

CLASSES, COSTS & RESERVATIONS

There are two classes of rail travel: first and standard. First class costs around 50% more than standard – except on crowded trains, it's not worth it. At weekends some train operators offer 'upgrades' for an extra £10 to £15.

For short journeys (under about 50 miles), it's usually fine to buy tickets on the spot at stations. For longer journeys, on-the-spot fares are always available, but fares are much cheaper if bought in advance (you'll get a reserved seat too). Basically, the earlier you book, the cheaper it gets. You also save if you travel 'off-peak' – ie avoiding commuter times, Fridays and Sundays. The cheapest fares are nonrefundable though, so if you miss your train you'll have to buy a new ticket.

If you buy online, you can have the ticket posted to you (UK addresses only), or collect it at the station on the day of travel, either at the ticket desk (leave time to spare, as queues can be long) or via automatic machines.

Whichever operator you travel with and wherever you buy tickets, the three main fare types are: Advance (buy ticket in advance, travel only on specific trains); Off-peak (buy ticket any time, travel off-peak); and Anytime (buy anytime, travel anytime).

For an idea of the price difference, an Anytime single ticket from London to York will cost around £100, an Off-peak around £80, and an Advance around £20, or even less if you book early enough or don't mind arriving at midnight.

Advance tickets are subject to availability, and usually available as singles only, but if you're coming back you just buy two singles. Off-peak and Anytime tickets are available as returns and the price varies from just under double the single fare to just a pound more than the single fare.

If the train doesn't get you all the way to your destination, a **PlusBus** supplement (usually around £2) validates your train ticket for onwards travel by bus – more convenient and usually cheaper than buying a separate bus ticket.

And finally, it's worth a look at **Megatrain** (www.megatrain.com) – ultra-low train fares on ultra off-peak services between London and a few destinations in southwest England and the east Midlands.

TRAIN PASSES

If you're staying in Britain for a while, passes known as 'railcards' are available. There's a 16-25 Railcard – for those aged 16 to 25, or a full-time UK student. These cost around £25 (valid for one year, available from major stations or online) and get you a 33% discount on most train fares, except those already heavily discounted. For details see www.railcard.co.uk.

A **Disabled Person's Railcard** costs £18. You can get an application from stations or from the railcard website. Call ☎0191-281 8103 for more details.

For country-wide travel, **BritRail Passes** (www.britrail.com) are good value, but only for visitors from overseas and not for sale in Britain. There are many BritRail variants; the following is an outline of the main options, quoting high-season adult prices:

BritRail Consecutive Unlimited travel on all trains in England for four/eight/15/22/30 days, for US$259/375/559/709/839. Anyone getting their money's worth out of the last pass should earn some sort of endurance award.

BritRail Flexipass You don't have to get on a train every day to get full value. Your options are four days of unlimited travel in England within a 60-day period for US$329, eight in 60 days for US$479, or 15 in 60 days for US$725.

Of the other international passes, Eurail cards are not accepted in Britain, and InterRail cards are only valid if bought in another mainland European country.

LONDON

☎020 / pop 7.5 million

One of the world's greatest cities, London has enough history, vitality and cultural drive to keep you occupied for weeks. In recent years this most cosmopolitan of capitals has led international trends in music, fashion and the arts, a 21st-century renaissance that's breathed new life into established neighbourhoods like Westminster and Knightsbridge, and reinvented areas like the East End. With the Olympic Games rolling into town in 2012, and even despite the little matter of a global economic downturn, London's landscape will continue to alter and thrive.

The downside of this renaissance, of course, is increasing cost: London is now Europe's most expensive city for visitors – whatever their budget. But with some careful planning and a bit of common sense (and a few pointers from this book), you can find great bargains and freebies among the popular attractions.

And don't forget that the greatest show of all is simply wandering the streets, strolling through London's wonderful parks, or admiring the world-famous buildings from the embankments beside the Thames – that costs nothing but shoe-leather.

> **EMERGENCY NUMBERS**
>
> For almost any type of emergency dial ☎999. You will reach an operator, who will then connect you to the police, ambulance, fire service, mountain rescue or coast guard.

HISTORY

London first came into being as a Celtic village, possibly called Lundyn, near a ford across the River Thames. In the Roman era the settlement – now called Londinium – became properly established, enclosed in protective walls with four main entrances still remembered today by the areas of Ludgate, Aldgate, Bishopsgate and Newgate.

By the end of the 3rd century AD, Londinium was almost as multicultural as it is now, home to 30,000 people of many ethnic groups, with temples dedicated to various cults and religions. But the Romans abandoned Britain in the early 5th century, reducing Londinium to a backwater. Then came the Saxons, and the town – now called Lundenwic – prospered again, eventually becoming capital in 1016.

After the Battle of Hastings in 1066, William the Conqueror's first moves included ordering

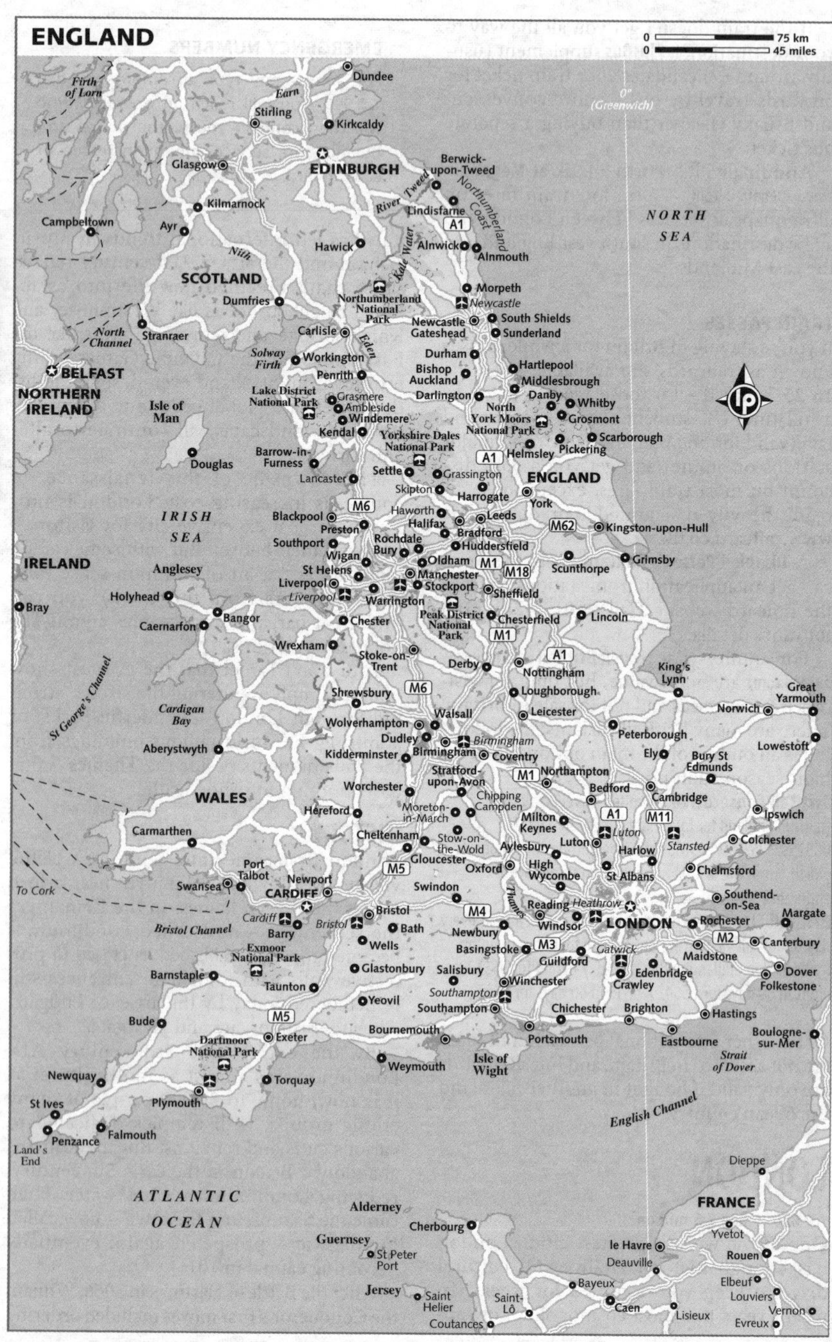
ENGLAND
0 75 km
0 45 miles
0° (Greenwich)
NORTH SEA
IRISH SEA
ATLANTIC OCEAN
English Channel
Bristol Channel
St George's Channel
Cardigan Bay
Strait of Dover
SCOTLAND
ENGLAND
WALES
NORTHERN IRELAND
IRELAND
FRANCE
EDINBURGH
BELFAST
LONDON
CARDIFF
Dundee
Stirling
Kirkcaldy
Glasgow
Berwick-upon-Tweed
Lindisfarne
Kilmarnock
Campbeltown
Ayr
Hawick
Alnwick
Alnmouth
Morpeth
Newcastle
Northumberland National Park
Dumfries
Newcastle
Gateshead
South Shields
Sunderland
Carlisle
Stranraer
Workington
Durham
Hartlepool
Penrith
Bishop Auckland
Middlesbrough
Lake District National Park
Grasmere
Ambleside
Windemere
Darlington
Danby
Whitby
Grosmont
North York Moors National Park
Kendal
Yorkshire Dales National Park
Helmsley
Pickering
Scarborough
Isle of Man
Douglas
Barrow-in-Furness
Lancaster
Settle
Grassington
Skipton
Harrogate
York
Haworth
Blackpool
Preston
Halifax
Leeds
Bradford
Kingston-upon-Hull
Southport
Rochdale
Bury
Huddersfield
Wigan
Oldham
Manchester
Grimsby
Scunthorpe
St Helens
Anglesey
Liverpool
Stockport
Warrington
Sheffield
Holyhead
Bray
Bangor
Caernarfon
Chester
Peak District National Park
Chesterfield
Lincoln
Wrexham
Stoke-on-Trent
Derby
Nottingham
King's Lynn
Shrewsbury
Loughborough
Great Yarmouth
Walsall
Leicester
Norwich
Wolverhampton
Dudley
Birmingham
Peterborough
Lowestoft
Aberystwyth
Kidderminster
Coventry
Ely
Bury St Edmunds
Stratford-upon-Avon
Northampton
Worchester
Chipping Campden
Bedford
Cambridge
Hereford
Moreton-in-March
Milton Keynes
Ipswich
Carmarthen
Cheltenham
Stow-on-the-Wold
Luton
Stansted
Colchester
Aylesbury
Harlow
Gloucester
Port Talbot
High Wycombe
Oxford
St Albans
Chelmsford
Swansea
Newport
To Cork
Swindon
Southend-on-Sea
Reading
Heathrow
Bristol
Windsor
Rochester
Margate
Cardiff
Barry
Bath
Newbury
Wells
Basingstoke
Guildford
Gatwick
Maidstone
Canterbury
Exmoor National Park
Glastonbury
Salisbury
Edenbridge
Dover
Barnstaple
Taunton
Winchester
Crawley
Folkestone
Southampton
Yeovil
Chichester
Brighton
Hastings
Bude
Exeter
Bournemouth
Portsmouth
Eastbourne
Boulogne-sur-Mer
Dartmoor National Park
Isle of Wight
Weymouth
Newquay
Torquay
Plymouth
St Ives
Penzance
Falmouth
Land's End
Dieppe
Alderney
Cherbourg
Yvetot
Guernsey
le Havre
St Peter Port
Deauville
Rouen
Elbeuf
Jersey
Saint Helier
Bayeux
Louviers
Saint-Lô
Caen
Lisieux
Vernon
Coutances
Evreux
Firth of Lorn
Earn
River Tweed
Northumberland Coast
Kale Water
Nith
North Channel
Solway Firth
Eden
Thames
A1
M6
M62
M1
M18
M5
M4
M3
M2
M11

the construction of the White Tower (the core of today's Tower of London) and affirming the city's right to self-government. With this foundation, London prospered and increased in global importance throughout the medieval period, surviving devastating challenges like the 1666 Great Fire.

By 1720 London had 750,000 inhabitants and was the centre of a growing world empire. Building on this mercantile wealth, the Victorian era of the 19th century was a golden age. In contrast, WWII was London's darkest hour, with the city on the edge of destruction after relentless bombing – still fresh in the memory of many locals.

The ugly postwar rebuilding of the 1950s gave way to the cultural renaissance of the 1960s when London was the planet's swinging capital. Things dipped again in the 1970s, while the 1980s was a time of great plenty for some Londoners and hardship for others. The pendulum swung again in the 1990s, and London was the focus of the Cool Britannia phenomenon of new politics, arts and music.

In 2000 the modern metropolis of London got its first elected Mayor (as opposed to the Lord Mayor of the City of London – a largely ceremonial role) and through the early years of the 21st century the city rediscovered a self-confidence that fuelled its selection as 2012 Olympic Games host.

But for every period of success, tragedy has never been far away. The day after winning its Olympic bid, four terrorist bombs killed dozens of people on buses and underground trains around the city. While deep anxiety initially gripped many Londoners, most soon returned to their daily routines – a response mirrored throughout the capital's turbulent history.

ORIENTATION

The M25 circular motorway encompasses the area broadly regarded as Greater London. Cutting the circle in two is the city's main geographical feature – the River Thames – while near the centre of the circle are many of London's best-known attractions, including Buckingham Palace and Big Ben, in the Westminster area. East of Westminster, The City (note the big 'C') is the capital's financial district, covering roughly a square mile bordered by long-gone city walls; well-known features here include the Tower of London. The areas to the east of the City are collectively known as the East End. The West End, on the city's other flank, is effectively the centre of London nowadays, and where you'll find iconic landmarks such as Trafalgar Sq.

INFORMATION

Internet Access

You'll find free wi-fi at many bars, cafes and hotels. Internet cafes cost about £1 to £2 per hour:

BTR (Map pp162-3; ☎ 7209 0984; 39 Whitfield St W1; ⊖ Goodge St)

easyInternetcafé (www.easy.com) Oxford St (Map pp162-3; 358 Oxford St W1; ⊖ Bond St); Trafalgar Sq (Map pp162-3; 456 The Strand WC2; ⊖ Charing Cross); Kensington (Map pp172-3; 160 Kensington High St W8; ⊖ High St Kensington) Attached to Subway outlets.

Internet Resources

The Lonely Planet website (www.lonelyplanet.com) has lots of London information. You can also try the following news, transport and listings sites:

BBC London (www.bbc.co.uk/london)

Evening Standard (www.thisislondon.co.uk)

Time Out (www.timeout.com/london)

View London (www.viewlondon.co.uk)

Media

Evening Standard London's daily evening newspaper.

Metro Best of the free newspapers.

Time Out (£2.95) Excellent weekly listings guide.

Medical Services

Hospitals with 24-hour accident and emergency units:

Royal Free Hospital (off Map pp162-3; ☎ 7794 0500; Pond St NW3; ⊖ Belsize Park)

University College Hospital (Map pp162-3; ☎ 0845-155 5000; 235 Euston Rd WC1; ⊖ Euston Sq)

Money

ATMs are two-a-penny in central London. You can also change money at banks, *bureaux de changes* and post offices (where rates are usually fair). The following are reliable (both have many other branches):

American Express (Amex; Map pp162-3; ☎ 7484 9610; 30-31 Haymarket SW1; 🕒 9am-6pm Mon-Sat, 10am-4pm Sun; ⊖ Piccadilly Circus)

Thomas Cook (Map pp162-3; ☎ 0845-308 9570; 30 St James's St SW1; 🕒 9am-5.30pm Mon, Tue, Thu & Fri, 10am-5.30pm Wed; ⊖ Green Park)

BRITAIN

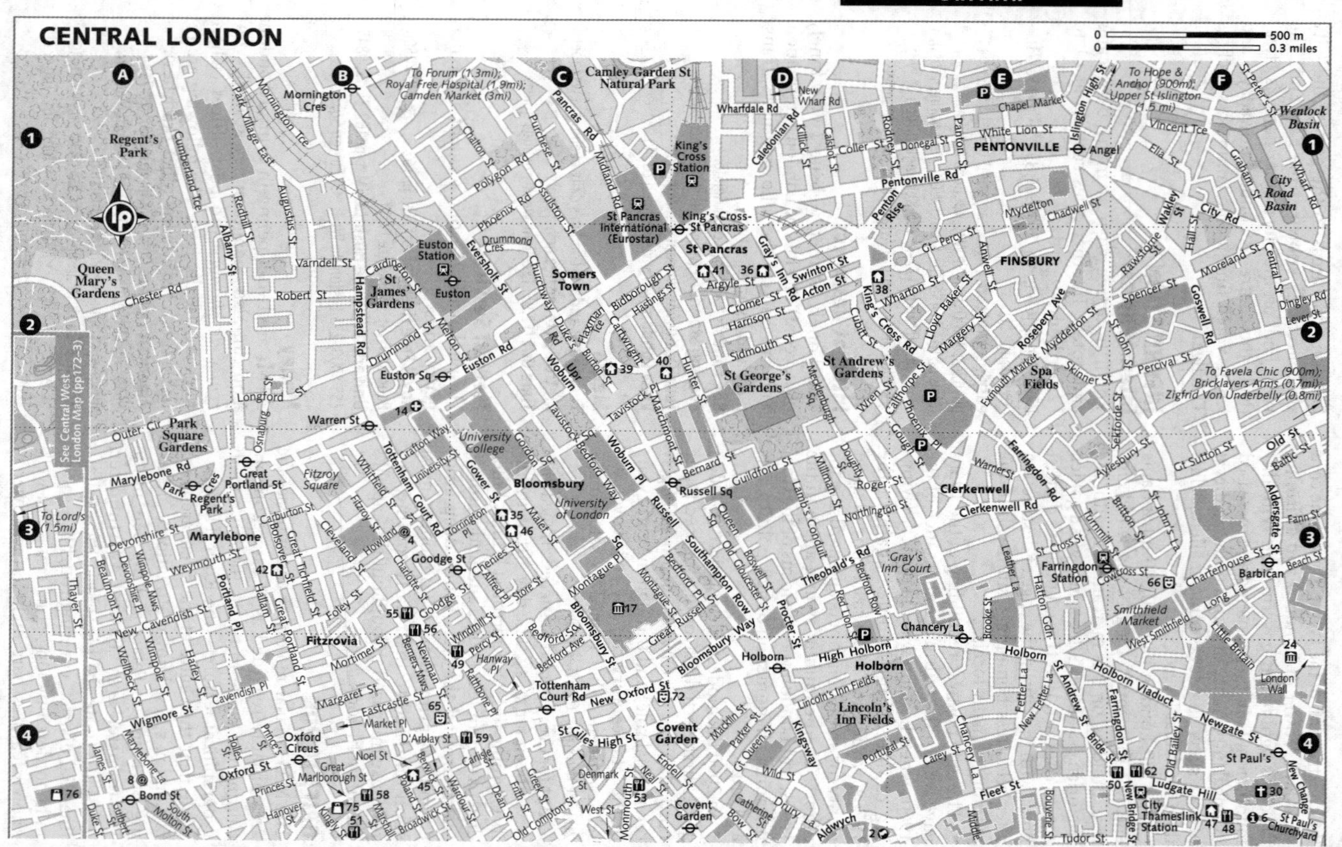

CENTRAL LONDON
0 500 m
0 0.3 miles
Regent's Park
Queen Mary's Gardens
Park Square Gardens
See Central West London Map (pp172-3)
To Lord's (1.5mi)
To Forum (1.3mi); Royal Free Hospital (1.9mi); Camden Market (3mi)
To Hope & Anchor (900m); Upper St Islington (1.5 mi)
To Favela Chic (900m); Bricklayers Arms (0.7mi); Zigfrid Von Underbelly (0.8mi)
Camley Garden St Natural Park
King's Cross Station
St Pancras International (Eurostar)
King's Cross-St Pancras
St Pancras
Euston Station
Euston
Euston Sq
St James' Gardens
Somers Town
Upr Woburn
Bloomsbury
University of London
University College
Russell Sq
St George's Gardens
St Andrew's Gardens
Spa Fields
Clerkenwell
Farringdon Station
Barbican
Smithfield Market
Finsbury
Pentonville
Angel
City Road Basin
Wenlock Basin
Gray's Inn Court
Lincoln's Inn Fields
Holborn
Chancery La
Covent Garden
Tottenham Court Rd
Oxford Circus
Bond St
Fitzrovia
Fitzroy Square
Goodge St
Warren St
Great Portland St
Regent's Park
Marylebone
Mornington Cres
City Thameslink Station
St Paul's
St Paul's Churchyard
London Wall

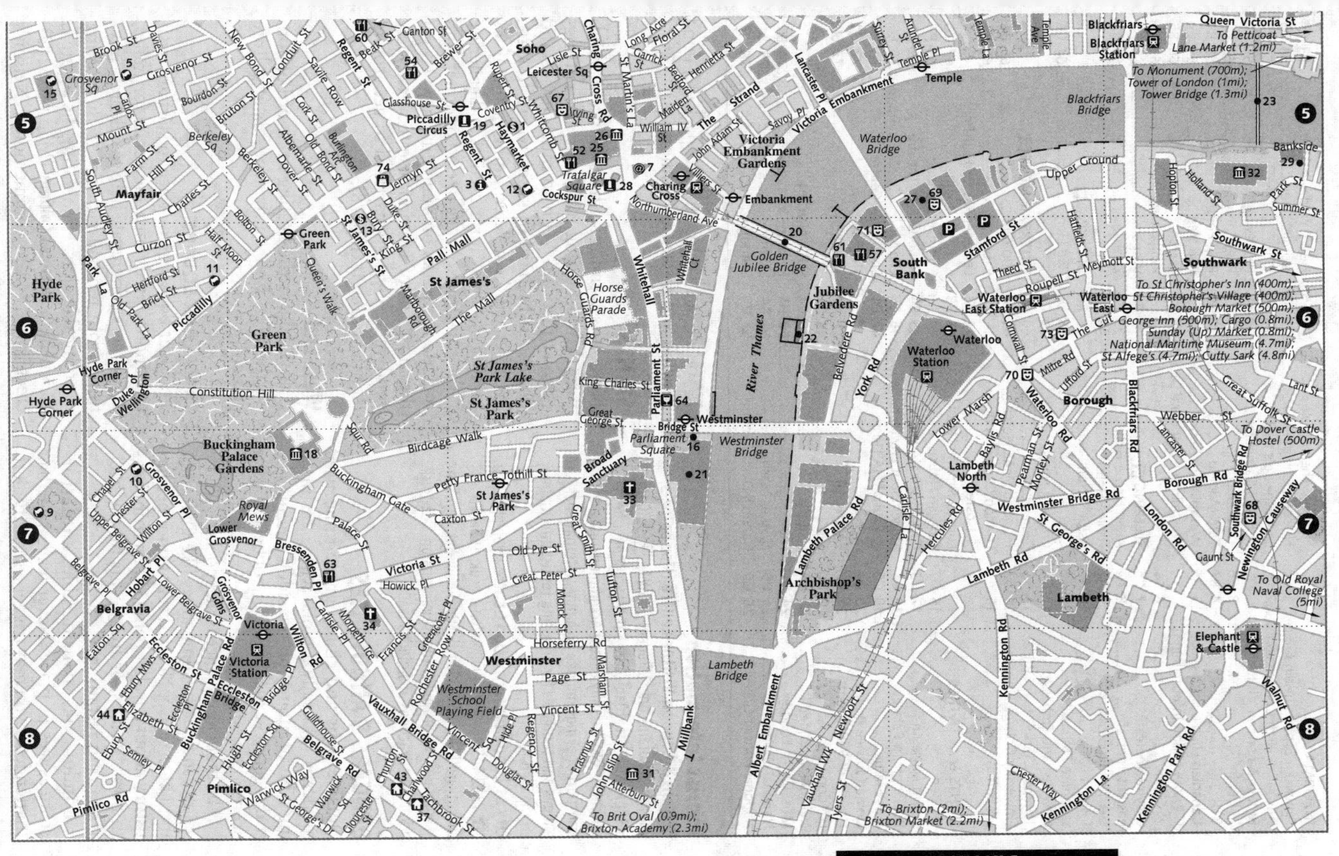

River Thames
Waterloo Bridge
Blackfriars Bridge
Westminster Bridge
Lambeth Bridge
Golden Jubilee Bridge
Victoria Embankment
Victoria Embankment Gardens
Albert Embankment
Jubilee Gardens
South Bank
Waterloo
Waterloo Station
Waterloo East Station
Southwark
Borough
Lambeth
Lambeth North
Archbishop's Park
Elephant & Castle
Blackfriars
Blackfriars Station
Temple
Embankment
Charing Cross
Trafalgar Square
Leicester Sq
Piccadilly Circus
Soho
Mayfair
St James's
St James's Park
St James's Park Lake
Green Park
Buckingham Palace Gardens
Royal Mews
Horse Guards Parade
Westminster
Westminster School Playing Field
Victoria Station
Victoria
Belgravia
Pimlico
Hyde Park
Hyde Park Corner
Whitehall
Parliament St
Parliament Square
Broad Sanctuary
Horse Guards Rd
The Mall
Birdcage Walk
Constitution Hill
Piccadilly
Pall Mall
Haymarket
Regent St
Strand
Charing Cross Rd
Park La
Victoria St
Vauxhall Bridge Rd
Buckingham Palace Rd
Millbank
Kennington Rd
Kennington La
Kennington Park Rd
Lambeth Rd
Lambeth Palace Rd
Westminster Bridge Rd
St George's Rd
Waterloo Rd
Blackfriars Rd
Borough Rd
London Rd
Newington Causeway
Southwark Bridge Rd
Southwark St
Stamford St
York Rd
Belvedere Rd
Carlisle La
Hercules Rd
Walnut Rd
To Monument (700m); Tower of London (1mi); Tower Bridge (1.3mi)
To Petticoat Lane Market (1.2mi)
To St Christopher's Inn (400m); St Christopher's Village (400m); Borough Market (500m); George Inn (500m); Cargo (0.8mi); Sunday (Up) Market (0.8mi); National Maritime Museum (4.7mi); St Alfege's (4.7mi); Cutty Sark (4.8mi)
To Dover Castle Hostel (500m)
To Old Royal Naval College (5mi)
To Brixton (2mi); Brixton Market (2.2mi)
To Brit Oval (0.9mi); Brixton Academy (2.3mi)

BRITAIN

INFORMATION
American Express (Main Office)..1 C5
Australian High Commission.......2 D4
Britain & London Visitor Centre.......3 C5
BTR.......4 B3
Canadian High Commission........5 A5
City of London Information Centre.......6 F4
easyInternetcafé.......7 C5
easyInternetcafé.......8 A4
German Embassy.......9 A7
Irish Embassy.......10 A7
Japanese Embassy.......11 A6
New Zealand Embassy.......12 C5
Thomas Cook (Main Office).....13 B6
University College Hospital........14 B2
US Embassy.......15 A5

SIGHTS & ACTIVITIES
Big Ben.......16 D7
British Museum.......17 C3
Buckingham Palace.......18 B7
Eros Statue.......19 C5
Golden Jubilee Bridge.......20 D6
Houses of Parliament.......21 D7
London Eye.......22 D6
Millennium Bridge.......23 F5
Museum of London.......24 F4
National Gallery.......25 C5
National Portrait Gallery.......26 C5
National Theatre.......27 E5
Nelson's Column.......28 C5
Shakespeare's Globe.......29 F5
St Paul's Cathedral.......30 F4
Tate Britain.......31 C8
Tate Modern.......32 F5
Westminister Abbey.......33 C7
Westminster Cathedral.......34 B7

SLEEPING
Arran House Hotel.......35 C3
Ashlee House.......36 D2
Astor Victoria Hostel.......37 B8
Clink.......38 D2
Crescent Hotel.......39 C2
Generator.......40 C2
Jesmond Dene Hotel.......41 D2
London Central YHA Hostel.......42 B3
Luna & Simone Hotel.......43 B8
Morgan House.......44 A8
Oxford St YHA Hostel.......45 B4
Ridgemount Private Hotel.......46 C3
St Paul's YHA Hostel.......47 F4

EATING
GBK.......48 F4
La Perla.......49 C4
Leon.......50 F4
Mother Mash.......51 B4
National Dining Rooms.......52 C5
Neal's Yard Salad Bar.......53 C4
Nordic Bakery.......54 B5
Ooze.......55 B3
Ping Pong.......56 B3
Ping Pong.......57 D6
Ping Pong.......58 B4
Red Veg.......59 C4
Sacred.......60 B5
Wagamama.......61 D6
Wagamama.......62 F4
Zizzi.......63 B7

DRINKING
Red Lion.......64 C6

ENTERTAINMENT
100 Club.......65 B4
Fabric.......66 F3
Leicester Square Half-Price Ticket Booth.......67 C5
Ministry of Sound.......68 F7
National Film Theatre.......69 E5
Old Vic.......70 E6
Southbank Centre.......71 D6
The End.......72 C4
Young Vic.......73 E6

SHOPPING
Fortnum & Mason.......74 B5
Liberty.......75 B4
Selfridges.......76 A4

Tourist Information

Britain & London Visitor Centre (Map pp162-3; www.visitbritain.com; 1 Regent St SW1; 9.30am-6.30pm Mon-Fri, 10am-4pm Sat & Sun, longer hr in summer; Piccadilly Circus) Accommodation and transport bookings, money exchange, international phones and terminals for accessing tourist information on the web.

City of London Information Centre (Map pp162-3; 7332 1456; www.cityoflondon.gov.uk; St Paul's Churchyard EC4; 9.30am-5.30pm Mon-Sat, also Sun in summer; St Paul's) Tourist information, fast-track tickets to attractions and guided walks.

DANGERS & ANNOYANCES

Outside pubs and clubs, ignore unlicensed minicabs (basically a bloke with a car making a bit of money on the side); you may be at danger of sexual attack or robbery. Take a licensed taxi instead.

The main annoyance is pickpockets, whose haunts include bustling areas like Oxford St and Leicester Sq. Nearly every Londoner has a story about a wallet being stolen from bags on floors in bars, or from coats on the back of chairs in restaurants.

London has considerable antiterrorist measures in place. Never leave your bag unattended – you may trigger a security alert. If you do see an unattended package, don't touch it and inform the authorities.

SIGHTS

London is teeming with magnificent buildings, world-leading museums and cutting-edge attractions. With so much to see and do, it can be hard to know where to start. Weather will be a determining factor: if it's raining, it's a day for museums and galleries; if the sun shines, make like a Londoner, and include the parks on your itinerary. To get the most out of London, use the extremely good-value Oyster smartcard to get around (see the boxed text, p178).

West End

If anywhere is the beating heart of London, it's the West End – a strident mix of culture and consumerism.

TRAFALGAR SQUARE

Trafalgar Sq is a great place to start any visit to London. Frequently the venue for rallies, Londoners congregate here to celebrate anything from football victories to the ousting of political leaders. Dominating the square is 43.5m-high **Nelson's Column** (Map pp162–3), erected in 1843 to commemorate Nelson's

1805 victory over Napoleon. At the edges of the square are four plinths, three of which have permanent statues while the fourth has temporary modern installations.

NATIONAL GALLERY

Gazing grandly over Trafalgar Sq, the **National Gallery** (Map pp162-3; ☎ 7747 2885; www.nationalgallery.org.uk; Trafalgar Sq WC2; admission free; 10am-6pm Sat-Thu, 10am-9pm Fri; ⊖ Charing Cross) is the nation's most important art repository, with seminal paintings from every epoch, including works by Giotto, Leonardo da Vinci, Michelangelo and Van Gogh. It can be daunting; arrive early and take your time, or target your visit.

NATIONAL PORTRAIT GALLERY

The excellent **National Portrait Gallery** (Map pp162-3; ☎ 7312 2463; www.npg.org.uk; St Martin's Pl WC2; admission free; 10am-6pm Sat-Wed, to 9pm Thu-Fri; ⊖ Charing Cross) is like stepping into a picture book of English history or, depending on how you see things, an *OK* magazine spread on history's celebrities.

GETTING INTO TOWN

If you come to London by train, you'll arrive in one of the main rail terminals that form a ring around the city centre. Most long-distance buses arrive at London Victoria coach station, also central. The rest of this box covers getting into town from the airports:

Heathrow

Heathrow airport is 15 miles west of central London. The cheapest option to the city centre is the Piccadilly line of the Underground (£4, one hour, every five minutes 5am to 11.30pm). For first-timers, buying a ticket can be confusing – there are few signs, and the Underground staff seem to delight in using impenetrable West London accents. If there are queues at the ticket office, use the self-service machines instead; it helps to have the correct coins, although some machines give change and/or accept credit cards. The easiest option is the **Heathrow Express** (☎ 0845 600 1515; www.heathrowexpress.co.uk) train to London Paddington station (£15, 15 minutes, four per hour 5am to 11.25pm); purchase tickets online, from self-service machines (cash and credit cards accepted) or on-board (£2 extra).

Gatwick

Gatwick airport is 30 miles south of central London. There are regular train services from Gatwick's South Terminal to London Victoria train station (£9.50, 37 minutes, four per hour, hourly at night). The **Gatwick Express** (☎ 0845 850 1530; www.gatwickexpress.co.uk) also heads to Victoria (one-way/return £18/31, 30 minutes, four per hour 5am to 1am).

Your other option is the **EasyBus** (www.easybus.co.uk) minibus service between Gatwick and Victoria (return from £11, allow 1½ hours, every 30 minutes from 3am to 1am). Prices start very low, depending when you book. You'll be charged extra if you have more than one carry-on and one check-in bag.

Stansted

Stansted airport is 35 miles northeast of central London. The **Stansted Express** (☎ 0845-600 7245; www.stanstedexpress.com) runs to/from London Liverpool St train station (one way/return £17/26, 46 minutes, four per hour 5am to 11pm).

EasyBus (www.easybus.co.uk) has services between Stansted and Victoria coach station (return from £13, allow 1¾ hours, two per hour 3am to 1am). The **Airbus A6** (☎ 0870 580 8080; www.nationalexpress.com/airports) also runs to/from Victoria coach station (one way/return £10/16, allow 1¾ hours, departing at least every 30 minutes).

Luton

There are regular train services between Luton Airport Parkway train station and London St Pancras (£14, 28 to 48 minutes). A shuttle bus (£1) runs between the airport and the train station. **EasyBus** (www.easybus.co.uk) minibuses run to/from Victoria (return from £12, allow 1¼ hours, two per hour).

BRITISH MUSEUM

London's most visited attraction, the **British Museum** (Map pp162-3; ☎ 7323 8000; www.thebritishmuseum.org; Great Russell St WC1; admission free; 10am-5.30pm Sat-Wed, 10am-8.30pm Thu & Fri; Tottenham Court Rd or Russell Sq) is one of the finest in the world, boasting vast Egyptian, Greek, Oriental and Roman galleries – among many others – the result of judicious acquisition and controversial plundering. A latter-day wonder is the museum's spectacular **Great Court**, the largest covered public square in Europe.

PICCADILLY CIRCUS

Neon-lit, turbo-charged Piccadilly Circus is home to the popular but unremarkable **Eros statue** (Map pp162–3). Ironically the love god looks over an area long linked to prostitution, both male and female, although it's less conspicuous these days.

COVENT GARDEN

As well as being home of the esteemed Royal Opera House, **Covent Garden** (Map pp162–3) is one of London's biggest tourist traps, where chain restaurants, souvenir shops, balconied bars and street entertainers vie for the punters' pound. It was once a garden, and then a famous fruit and flower market, immortalised in the film *My Fair Lady*.

Westminster, St James's & Pimlico

Purposefully positioned outside the old City (to keep monarch and parliament at arm's length), Westminster has been the centre of political power for a millennium.

HOUSES OF PARLIAMENT

Coming face-to-face with one of the world's most recognisable landmarks is always a surreal moment, but for the **Houses of Parliament** (Map pp162-3; ☎ 0870-906 3773; www.parliament.uk; Parliament Sq SW1; Westminster), it's a revelation. Officially called the Palace of Westminster, the oldest part dates from 1097, but much of the visible building today was built in the mid-19th century. Its most famous feature is its clock tower, known as **Big Ben** – actually it's the name of the 13-ton bell inside the tower, named after Benjamin Hall, commissioner of works in 1858. The best views are from nearby **Westminster Bridge**.

WESTMINSTER ABBEY

Not merely a beautiful place of worship, **Westminster Abbey** (Map pp162-3; ☎ 7222 5152; www.westminster-abbey.org; 20 Dean's Yard SW1; adult £12; 9.15am-4.30pm Mon, Tue, Thu & Fri, 9.15am-6pm Wed, 9.15am-2.30pm Sat; Westminster) serves up England's history on slabs of stone. This is where most British monarchs have been crowned since 1066, and for centuries the great and the good have been interred here.

WESTMINSTER CATHEDRAL

Not to be confused with the eponymous abbey, the neo-Byzantine **Westminster Cathedral** (Map pp162-3; ☎ 7798 9055; www.westminstercathedral.org.uk; Victoria St SW1; admission free; 7am-7pm; Victoria)

EXCUSE ME, WHERE'S THE NEAREST LOO?

Many foreign visitors are surprised at London's lack of public toilets, or 'loos' (also called 'public conveniences' on signs). They're available at most museums and sights, but in limited supply on the streets. If you're caught short, here are some tips: very few tube stations have loos but bigger rail stations usually do (although they're often coin-operated, so yes, it's 20p to pee). Smarter department stores are a good bet, if you can handle five floors by escalator, as are fast food outlets. In a busy pub, you might be able to use the loo, but it's polite to order a drink afterwards – which kinda defeats the purpose.

LONDON FOR FREE

London may be an expensive place to eat, drink and sleep, but when it comes to sights, most of the very best things are free. First off, there are the wonderful parks, then of course you can admire the breathtaking historic buildings from the outside without paying a penny. And it won't cost any more to go into the following: National Gallery (p165), National Portrait Gallery (p165), Tate Britain (opposite), Tate Modern (p168), British Museum (above), Victoria & Albert Museum (p168), Natural History Museum (p169), Science Museum (p169), several other museums and galleries listed in this London section – and many more that we haven't got room to mention.

dates from 1895, and is the headquarters of Britain's Roman Catholic Church. It's still a work in progress, the vast interior part dazzling marble and mosaic and part bare brick; new sections are completed as funds allow.

TATE BRITAIN

Unlike at the National Gallery, it's Britannia that rules the walls of **Tate Britain** (Map pp162-3; ☎ 7887 8008; www.tate.org.uk; Millbank SW1; admission free; 10am-5.50pm; ⊖ Pimlico). Reaching from 1500 to the present, it's crammed with local heavyweights like Blake, Hogarth, Gainsborough, Whistler, Spencer and, especially, Turner, whose 'interrupted visions' – unfinished canvasses of moody skies – wouldn't look out of place in the contemporary section, alongside works by David Hockney, Francis Bacon, Tracey Emin and Damien Hirst. There are free hour-long guided tours, daily at midday and 3pm, plus 11am and 2pm on weekdays.

BUCKINGHAM PALACE

With so many imposing buildings in the capital, the Queen's well-proportioned but relatively plain city pad, **Buckingham Palace** (Map pp162-3; ☎ 7766 7302; www.royalcollection.org.uk; The Mall SW1; adult £16; 9.45am-6pm late Jul-late Sep; ⊖ St James's Park), is an anticlimax for some. Queen Elizabeth II splits her time between here, Windsor (p179) and Balmoral. A handy way of telling whether she's home is to check for the 'royal standard' flag flying on the roof. The gaudily furnished **State Rooms** are open in summer, but it's more fun outside watching the **changing of the guard** (11.30am daily May-Jul, alternate days for rest of year, weather permitting).

The City

Once, the City of London was London. Its boundaries have changed little from the Roman walls built here two millennia ago. Today it's the central business district and on Sundays it becomes a virtual ghost-town, which is a good time to walk around. There are enough interesting churches, intriguing architecture, hidden gardens and atmospheric laneways to spend weeks exploring – though you will miss the smell of fear as the planet's leading bankers cope with the global credit crunch.

ST PAUL'S CATHEDRAL

Dominating the City with its giant dome, **St Paul's Cathedral** (Map pp162-3; ☎ 7236 4128; www.stpauls.co.uk; adult £10; 8.30am-4pm Mon-Sat; ⊖ St Paul's) was built by 'London's architect' Christopher Wren between 1675 and 1710. The dome is renowned for somehow dodging the bombs during the Blitz and became an icon of the capital's resilience during WWII. Outside the cathedral is a **monument to the people of London**, a simple and elegant memorial to the 32,000 Londoners who weren't so lucky. Inside, attractions include the **Whispering Gallery** – if you talk close to the wall it carries your words around to the opposite side – and the **Golden Gallery** at the very top, with an unforgettable view of London.

TOWER OF LONDON

If you pay only one admission fee while you're in London, make it the **Tower of London** (off Map pp162-3; ☎ 0844-482 7777; www.hrp.org.uk; Tower Hill EC3; adult £17; 10am-5.30pm Sun-Mon, 9am-5.30pm Tue-Sat Mar-Oct, 10am-4.30pm Sun-Mon, 9am-4.30pm Tue-Sat Nov-Feb; ⊖ Tower Hill), one of the city's three World Heritage sites. After the obligatory **Crown Jewels** visit, leave plenty of time to explore the walls, dungeons and museum rooms – a window on a gruesome and fascinating history, from London's Roman era to the present day.

TOWER BRIDGE

The south bank of the Thames was a thriving port in 1894 when elegant **Tower Bridge** (off Map pp162–3) was built. So ships could reach the port, the bridge was designed so the roadway could be raised. It still goes up most days, although electricity has replaced the original steam engines. Walking across is free. For more insights, the **Tower Bridge Exhibition** (☎ 7403 3761; www.towerbridge.org.uk; adult £6; 10am-6.30pm Apr-Sep, 9.30am-6pm Oct-Mar; ⊖ Tower Hill) recounts the story with videos and animatronics.

MUSEUM OF LONDON

A visit to the fascinating **Museum of London** (Map pp162-3; ☎ 0870 444 3851; www.museumoflondon.org.uk; 150 London Wall EC2; admission free; 10am-5.50pm Mon-Sat, noon-5.50pm Sun; ⊖ Barbican) early in your stay helps make sense of the layers of history that make up this great city.

THE MONUMENT

Built to commemorate the 1666 Great Fire of London, the **Monument** (off Map pp162-3; ☎ 7626 2717; www.themonument.info; Monument St; adult/concession £3/2; 9.30am-5.30pm; ⊖ Monument) is

THAMES FOOTBRIDGES

The River Thames in central London is crossed by several bridges, including the famous Tower Bridge and the surprisingly unremarkable London Bridge. To get away from the cars and enjoy views up or down river, take one of the bridges for walkers only:

The **Millennium Bridge** (Map pp162-3; ⊖ St Paul's or Blackfriars) is recently built but already iconic – billed as a 'blade of light' – usefully linking the key sights of St Paul's Cathedral and the Tate Modern.

On the **Golden Jubilee Bridge** (Map pp162-3; ⊖ Embankment or Waterloo), two hi-tech pedestrian walkways cross between Embankment tube station and the South Bank.

60.6m high, the exact distance from its base to the bakery on Pudding Lane where the blaze began. Climb the 311 tight spiral steps for an eye-watering view from beneath the golden vase of flames.

South of the Thames

Outside the walls (and rules) of the city, Londoners once crossed the river to the south bank for a wide range of diversions. This was the perfect spot to drink yourself silly, hook up with a prostitute, watch a bear being tortured for your amusement, then head to the theatre. The area is much more seemly now.

TATE MODERN

It's hard to miss this surprisingly elegant former power station, which is the tremendous **Tate Modern** (Map pp162-3; ☎ 7887 8888; www.tate.org.uk; Queen's Walk SE1; admission free; ⏰ 10am-6pm Sun-Thu, 10am-10pm Fri & Sat; ⊖ Southwark). Focusing on modern art in all its wonderful permutations, it's been extraordinarily successful in bringing challenging work to the masses, becoming one of London's most popular attractions.

SHAKESPEARE'S GLOBE

An authentic rebuild of the original open-roofed theatre where many Shakespeare plays were performed, the **Globe** (Map pp162-3; ☎ 7401 9919; www.shakespeares-globe.org; 21 New Globe Walk SE1; adult £9; ⏰ 10am-5pm; ⊖ London Bridge) is a pilgrimage destination for fans of the Bard. Admission includes a guided tour and extensive exhibition. Plays – by Shakespeare and his contemporaries, plus modern works – are still performed here (seats £15 to £35). As in Elizabethan times, 'groundlings' can stand (£5) but there's no protection from the elements.

LONDON EYE

Originally designed as a temporary structure to celebrate the year 2000, the giant revolving wheel that is the **London Eye** (Map pp162-3; ☎ 0870 5000 600; www.londoneye.com; adult £15.50; ⏰ 10am-8pm Jan-May & Oct-Dec, 10am-9pm Jun & Sep, 10am-9.30pm Jul & Aug; ⊖ Waterloo) is now a permanent addition to the cityscape, joining the tower of Big Ben as one of London's most distinctive landmarks. For budget travellers it's not cheap, but on a clear day the views are spectacular, and give you a real feel for London's size and the delightfully random layout of the city's historic streets. Rides take 30 minutes. Queues can be long, but you can book a slot online (also gaining a 10% discount).

Chelsea, Kensington & Knightsbridge

Knightsbridge is where you'll find some of London's best-known department stores, while Kensington High St has a lively mix of chains and boutiques. Away from mammon, south Kensington boasts some of London's most beautiful and interesting museums.

VICTORIA & ALBERT MUSEUM

A vast, rambling and wonderful museum of decorative art and design, the **Victoria & Albert** (V&A; Map pp172-3; ☎ 7942 2000; www.vam.ac.uk; Cromwell Rd SW7; admission free; ⏰ 10am-5.45pm Sat-Thu, 10am-10pm Fri; ⊖ South Kensington) is a bit like the nation's attic, comprising four million objects collected from Britain and around the globe. Spread over nearly 150 galleries, it houses the world's greatest collection of decorative arts. Yes, you'll need to plan.

TATE-A-TATE

To get between London's two Tate galleries in style, the **Tate Boat** – which sports a Damien Hirst dot painting – will ferry you across the Thames, stopping en route at the London Eye. Services run from 10am to 6pm daily at 40-minute intervals. A River Roamer hop-on hop-off ticket (purchased on board) costs £8; single tickets cost £4.

NATURAL HISTORY MUSEUM

Crammed full of interesting stuff, starting with the giant dinosaur skeleton that greets you in the main hall, the **Natural History Museum** (Map pp172-3; ☎ 7942 5725; www.nhm.ac.uk; Cromwell Rd SW7; admission free; 🕙 10am-5.50pm; ⊖ South Kensington) is a sure-fire hit with kids of all ages.

SCIENCE MUSEUM

With seven floors of interactive and educational exhibits, the **Science Museum** (Map pp172-3; ☎ 0870-870 4868; www.sciencemuseum.org.uk; Exhibition Rd SW7; admission free; 🕙 10am-6pm; ⊖ South Kensington) covers everything from the Industrial Revolution to the exploration of space.

HYDE PARK

At 145 hectares, **Hyde Park** (Map pp172-3; 🕙 5.30am-midnight; ⊖ Marble Arch, Hyde Park Corner or Queensway) is central London's largest open space. Henry VIII expropriated it from the Church in 1536, when it became a hunting ground and later a venue for executions and horse racing. The 1851 Great Exhibition was held here and during WWII the park became an enormous potato field. These days, it serves as an occasional concert venue and a full-time green space for fun and relaxation – the perfect place for a stroll away from the hustle and bustle.

Greenwich

Simultaneously the first and last place on earth, Greenwich (pronounced gren-itch) straddles the hemispheres as well as the ages, with splendid architecture and strong connections with the sea and science. Southeast of the centre, Greenwich is easily reached from the City via the Docklands Light Railway (DLR; a great trip in its own right for birds-eye views of London) or by boat with **Thames River Services** (☎ 7930 4097; www.westminsterpier.co.uk) departing half-hourly from Westminster Pier.

OLD ROYAL NAVAL COLLEGE

Designed by Christopher Wren, the **Old Royal Naval College** (☎ 8269 4747; www.oldroyalnavalcollege.org; 2 Cutty Sark Gardens SE10; admission free; 🕙 10am-5pm Mon-Sat; DLR Cutty Sark) is a magnificent example of monumental classical architecture. Parts are now used by the University of Greenwich and Trinity College of Music, but you can visit the extraordinary **Painted Hall**, which took artist Sir James Thornhill 19 years of hard graft to complete.

NATIONAL MARITIME MUSEUM & ROYAL OBSERVATORY

Behind the old college, the **National Maritime Museum** (off Map pp162-3; ☎ 8858 4422; www.nmm.ac.uk; Romney Rd SE10; admission free; 🕙 10am-5pm, last entry 4.30pm; DLR Cutty Sark) houses a massive collection of paraphernalia recounting Britain's seafaring history. Highlights include Nelson's uniform complete with a hole from the bullet that killed him.

Nearby, **Greenwich Park** climbs up the hill, affording great views of London, capped by the Royal Observatory, built in 1675 to help solve the riddle of longitude. Success was confirmed in 1884, and Greenwich became the prime meridian of the world, and Greenwich Mean Time (GMT) the universal measurement. Most popular is the line where you can stand in both western and eastern hemispheres.

CUTTY SARK

A famous Greenwich landmark, the **Cutty Sark** (off Map pp162-3; ☎ 8858 3445; www.cuttysark.org.uk; King William Walk; DLR Cutty Sark) was the fastest sailing ship in the world when launched in 1869. Damaged by fire in 2007, it should have re-opened by 2010. Watch the website for details.

TOURS

One of the best ways to get orientated when you first arrive in London is with a 24-hour hop-on-hop-off pass for the double-decker bus **Original London Sightseeing Tour** (☎ 8877 1722; www.theoriginaltour.com; adult £22) or the **Big Bus Company** (☎ 7233 9533; www.bigbustours.com; adult £24). The buses provide a commentary as they go, and the price includes a river cruise and three walking tours. You'll save a couple of pounds by booking online.

There are loads of walking tours, including the following:

Citisights (☎ 8806 3742; www.chr.org.uk/cswalks.htm) Focusing on academic and literary tours.

London Walks (☎ 7624 3978; www.walks.com) Including Harry Potter tours, ghost walks and the ever-popular Jack The Ripper tours.

FESTIVALS & EVENTS

Although not renowned as a festival city, London has a few events that might sway your plans.

University Boat Race (www.theboatrace.org) The traditional Oxford-versus-Cambridge row-off along the Thames in March.

Trooping the Colour (www.royal.gov.uk) The Queen's 'other birthday' is celebrated with pomp and pageantry in mid-June.

Meltdown (www.southbankcentre.co.uk/festivals-series/meltdown) The Southbank Centre hands over curatorial reigns to a legend (eg David Bowie, Morrissey or Patti Smith) to pull together a full program of concerts, talks and films; late June.

Pride (www.pridelondon.org) The big event on the gay and lesbian calendar, a technicolour West End street parade and Trafalgar Sq concert; June/July.

Notting Hill Carnival (www.nottinghillcarnival.biz) Held over two days in August, this is Europe's largest and London's most vibrant outdoor carnival, where London's Caribbean community shows the city how to party.

BRITAIN

SLEEPING

London can be a horribly pricey city to sleep in, but if all you need is a place to lay your head there are plenty of relatively cheap hostel options. For hotels, it's well worth checking the official **Visit London hotel bookings service** (☎ 0845 644 3010; www.visitlondonoffers.com) for up-to-date bargains throughout the city. If your hotel charges for breakfast, anything over £5 just isn't worth it when there are so many eateries to explore.

West End

This is the heart of the action, so most accommodation comes at a price, but there's one good budget option.

Oxford St YHA Hostel (Map pp162-3; ☎ 7734 1618; www.yha.org.uk; 14 Noel St W1; dm/tw £25/64; ⊖ Oxford Circus; 💻) This standard YHA has all the usual facilities (kitchen, TV room, laundry), plus a terrific (albeit noisy) location and decent views over London's rooftops. Wi-fi available.

Westminster & Pimlico

Handy for the big sights, the streets get prettier the further you stray from Victoria station.

Astor Victoria Hostel (Map pp162-3; ☎ 7834 3077; www.astorhostels.com; 71 Belgrave Rd SW1; dm £16-19, d & tw £60; ⊖ Pimlico; 💻) This cheap and cheerful hostel has plenty of dorms and a few private rooms, plus comfortable lounges, a fully equipped kitchen and wi-fi.

Morgan House (Map pp162-3; ☎ 7730 2384; www.morganhouse.co.uk; 120 Ebury St SW1; s/d with shared bathroom £52/72, with private bathroom £86/92; ⊖ Victoria) More homely than swanky, this place offers romantic iron beds, chandeliers, sparkling bathrooms and a full English breakfast.

Luna & Simone Hotel (Map pp162-3; ☎ 7834 5897; www.lunasimonehotel.com; 47-49 Belgrave Rd SW1; s £45-65, d/tw/tr/q £95/95/115/140; ⊖ Pimlico; 💻) The ensign of Luna (the moon) and Simone (the owner) is etched into the glass porch and this personal touch continues inside with the friendly service. Full English breakfast and wi-fi included.

Bloomsbury & Fitzrovia

One step removed from the West End, these neighbourhoods are much more affordable.

London Central YHA Hostel (Map pp162-3; ☎ 0870 770 6144; www.yha.org.uk; 104-108 Bolsover St W1; dm £19-32; ⊖ Great Portland St; 💻) The newest and best London YHA; everything's got that just-out-of-the-wrapper look and most of the four- to six-bed rooms have en suites. Wi-fi available.

Generator (Map pp162-3; ☎ 7388 7666; www.generatorhostels.com/London; Compton Pl, 37 Tavistock Pl WC1; dm £20-25, s/tw/tr/q £70/70/75/100; ⊖ Russell Sq; 💻) Lashings of primary colours and shiny metal are the hallmarks of this futuristic but fun hostel boasting 850 beds, a late bar, safe-deposit boxes, wi-fi and a large eating area (but no kitchen). Come to party.

Ridgemount Private Hotel (Map pp162-3; ☎ 7636 1141; www.ridgemounthotel.co.uk; 65-7 Gower St WC1; s/d with shared bathroom £42/58; ⊖ Goodge St; 💻) There's a comfortable, welcoming feel at this old-fashioned, slightly chintzy place. Wi-fi available.

Crescent Hotel (Map pp162-3; ☎ 7387 1515; www.crescenthoteloflondon.com; 49-50 Cartwright Gardens WC1; s £49-81, d/tw/tr/q £97/97/110/120; ⊖ Russell Sq; 💻) There's a homely feel to this humble hotel, one of the cheaper options on this street.

Arran House Hotel (Map pp162-3; ☎ 7636 2186; www.arranhotel-london.com; 77-79 Gower St WC1; s/d with shared bathroom £50/77, with private bathroom £60/100; ⊖ Goodge St; 💻) Period features and a comfy lounge lift this hotel from average to attractive. Squashed en suites or shared bathrooms are the trade-off for reasonable rates. Wi-fi available.

The City

Bristling with bankers during the week, this is not the most obvious spot for budget digs, but the exception is a gem.

St Paul's YHA Hostel (Map pp162-3; ☎ 0870 770 5764; www.yha.org.uk; 36 Carter Lane EC4; dm £27; ⊖ Blackfriars; 💻) Located in a lovely building near the cathedral itself, this place has small dorms (with

TVs and lockers) and licensed cafe but no kitchen. Wi-fi available.

South of the Thames

Just south of the river is good if you want to immerse yourself in workaday London and still be central.

Dover Castle Hostel (☎ 7403 7773; www.dovercastlehostel.com; 6a Great Dover St; dm £10-16; ⊖ Borough; 💻) If living in a pub is your fantasy, this is your chance. It's a modest affair (what do you expect for a tenner?), but the dorms are neat and tidy and there's wi-fi. If you fancy a sound sleep, bring earplugs, or drink yourself into oblivion downstairs.

St Christopher's Village (off Map pp162-3; ☎ 7407 1856; www.st-christophers.co.uk; 163 Borough High St SE1; dm £16-24, d £52; ⊖ London Bridge; 💻) With three locations on the same street, there's a range of experiences here. The main hub is the **Village**, a huge amp-up party hostel, with a club that opens until 4am on the weekends and a spa pool on the roof terrace. It's heaven or hell, depending on your tastes. The others are much smaller and quieter: **St Christopher's Inn** (121 Borough High St), situated above a very nice pub; and the **Orient** (59 Borough High St), above a cafe, with a separate women's floor.

Chelsea, Kensington & Knightsbridge

Classy Chelsea and Kensington offer easy access to the museums and fashion retailers. It's all a bit sweetie-darling, along with the prices.

Holland House YHA Hostel (Map pp172-3; ☎ 7937 0748; www.yha.org.uk; Holland Walk W8; dm £15-25; ⊖ High St Kensington; 💻) There's a school-camp vibe in the large dorms, but this place is well looked after, the setting unforgettable, and the cheapest option for miles around. Wi-fi available.

Vicarage Private Hotel (Map pp172-3; ☎ 7229 4030; www.londonvicaragehotel.com; 10 Vicarage Gate W8; s/d with shared bathroom £52/88, with private bathroom £88/114; ⊖ High St Kensington) This grand Victorian townhouse has simply furnished rooms and wi-fi. The cheaper ones are on the upper floors, so you get a view as well as a workout.

Euston & King's Cross

While hardly a salubrious location, King's Cross is handy and has some excellent budget options.

Ashlee House (Map pp162-3; ☎ 7833 9400; www.ashleehouse.co.uk; 261-265 Grays Inn Rd; dm £21-24, s/tw/tr £57/76/76; ⊖ Kings Cross; 💻) This hostel is a cheery surprise in a gritty but central location.

Clink (Map pp162-3; ☎ 7183 9400; www.clinkhostel.com; 78 Kings Cross Rd; dm £21-28, d £70; ⊖ Kings Cross; 💻) The former courthouse where The Clash went on trial now has custom-built and comfortable rooms. Also has wi-fi.

Jesmond Dene Hotel (Map pp162-3; ☎ 7837 4654; www.jesmonddenehostel.co.uk; 27 Argyle St; s/d from £50/60; ⊖ King's Cross; 💻) A surprisingly pleasant option in this location, with full English breakfast and wi-fi included.

Greenwich

If you'd rather keep the bustle of central London at arm's length, Greenwich offers a villagey ambience.

St Christopher's Inn (off Map pp162-3; ☎ 8858 3591; www.st-christophers.co.uk; 189 Greenwich High Rd SE10; dm £18-22, tw £44-50; 🚆/DLR Greenwich; 💻) The nicest of the St Christopher's chain, right by the station, with bright six- to eight-bed dorms and bunk-style twins. Downstairs there's a pub and claustrophobic basement lounge. Wi-fi, too.

St Alfege's (off Map pp162-3; ☎ 8853 4337; www.st-alfeges.co.uk; 16 St Alfege Passage SE10; s/d £60/90; DLR Cutty Sark) House and host have personality plus, and the two double rooms are elegant, while the single would suit the vertically challenged. Also has wi-fi.

Earl's Court

Earl's Court is cosmopolitan and so popular with travelling Antipodeans it's been nicknamed Kangaroo Valley. There are no real sights but it does have inexpensive places to crash – and an infectious holiday atmosphere.

Barmy Badger Backpackers (Map pp172-3; ☎ 7370 5213; www.barmybadger.com; 17 Longridge Rd SW5; dm £18, d £38; ⊖ Earl's Court; 💻) A humble but friendly hostel in a big old house, with a kitchen and small garden out the back. Also has wi-fi.

our pick **Globetrotter Inn** (☎ 8746 3112; www.globetrotterinns.com; Ashlar Ct, Ravenscourt Gardens W6; dm £24, d £60; ⊖ Stamford Brook; 💻) Further from the centre than most (but still relatively central) this former nurses' home is an attractive art deco building in a leafy suburb, with nearly 400 beds. Reading lights and curtains in the dorms allow extra privacy.

Barclay House (off Map pp172-3; ☎ 7384 3390; www.barclayhouselondon.co.uk; 21 Barclay Rd SW6; s/d £68/88; ⊖ Fulham Broadway) At this proper homestay

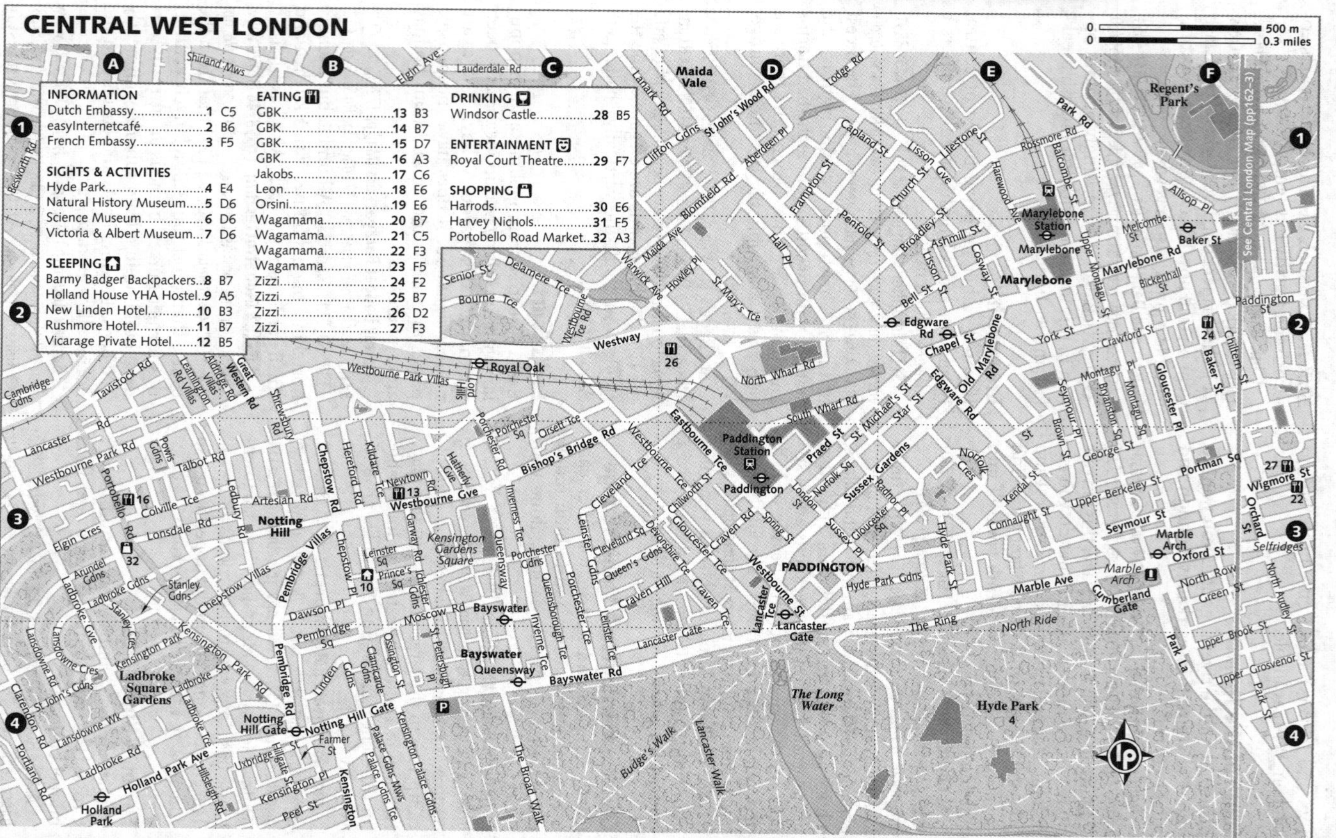
CENTRAL WEST LONDON
INFORMATION
Dutch Embassy 1 C5
easyInternetcafé 2 B6
French Embassy 3 F5
SIGHTS & ACTIVITIES
Hyde Park 4 E4
Natural History Museum 5 D6
Science Museum 6 D6
Victoria & Albert Museum 7 D6
SLEEPING
Barmy Badger Backpackers 8 B7
Holland House YHA Hostel 9 A5
New Linden Hotel 10 B3
Rushmore Hotel 11 B7
Vicarage Private Hotel 12 B5
EATING
GBK 13 B3
GBK 14 B7
GBK 15 D7
GBK 16 A3
Jakobs 17 C6
Leon 18 E6
Orsini 19 E6
Wagamama 20 B7
Wagamama 21 C5
Wagamama 22 F3
Wagamama 23 F5
Zizzi 24 F2
Zizzi 25 B7
Zizzi 26 D2
Zizzi 27 F3
DRINKING
Windsor Castle 28 B5
ENTERTAINMENT
Royal Court Theatre 29 F7
SHOPPING
Harrods 30 E6
Harvey Nichols 31 F5
Portobello Road Market 32 A3
500 m
0.3 miles
See Central London Map (pp162-3)
Regent's Park
Maida Vale
Marylebone Station
Marylebone
Baker St
Edgware Rd
Royal Oak
Westway
Paddington Station
Paddington
PADDINGTON
Lancaster Gate
Marble Arch
Oxford St
Selfridges
Notting Hill
Kensington Gardens Square
Bayswater
Queensway
Bayswater Rd
Notting Hill Gate
Ladbroke Square Gardens
Holland Park
Holland Park Ave
Kensington
The Long Water
Hyde Park
The Broad Walk
Lancaster Walk
North Ride
The Ring
Park La
Westbourne Gve
Bishop's Bridge Rd
Praed St
Sussex Gardens
Edgware Rd
Marylebone Rd
Pembridge Rd
Portobello Rd

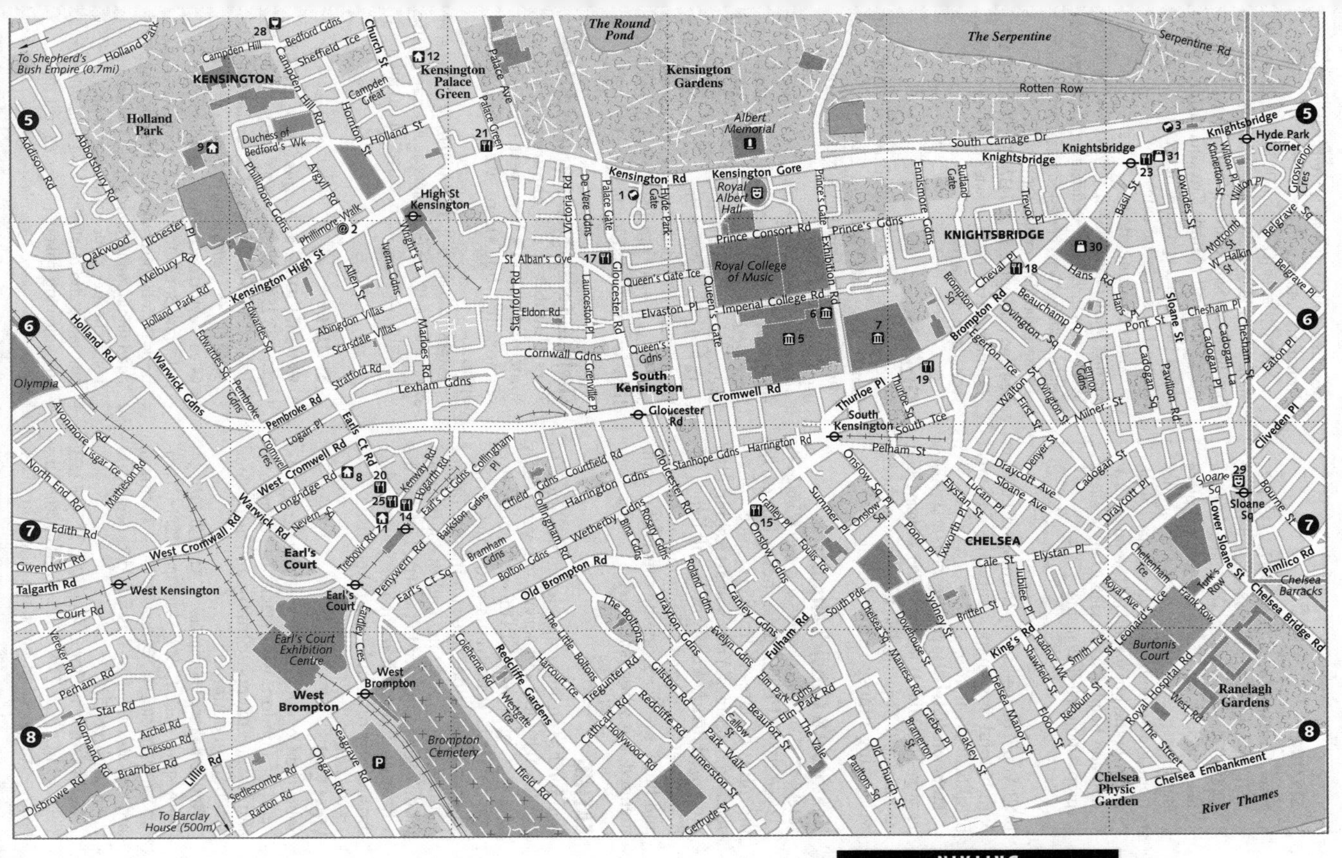
To Shepherd's Bush Empire (0.7mi)
KENSINGTON
Holland Park
Kensington Palace Green
The Round Pond
Kensington Gardens
The Serpentine
Serpentine Rd
Rotten Row
Albert Memorial
South Carriage Dr
Knightsbridge
Hyde Park Corner
Kensington Rd
Kensington Gore
Royal Albert Hall
High St Kensington
Kensington High St
Prince Consort Rd
Royal College of Music
Imperial College Rd
Exhibition Rd
Queen's Gate
Gloucester Rd
KNIGHTSBRIDGE
Brompton Rd
Sloane St
Cromwell Rd
South Kensington
Thurloe Pl
Pelham St
Olympia
Holland Rd
Warwick Gdns
Earls Ct Rd
West Cromwell Rd
Warwick Rd
Earl's Court
West Kensington
Talgarth Rd
Old Brompton Rd
Earl's Court Exhibition Centre
West Brompton
Brompton Cemetery
Redcliffe Gardens
Fulham Rd
CHELSEA
King's Rd
Lower Sloane St
Sloane Sq
Pimlico Rd
Chelsea Barracks
Chelsea Bridge Rd
Burton's Court
Ranelagh Gardens
Royal Hospital Rd
Chelsea Physic Garden
Chelsea Embankment
River Thames
Lillie Rd
To Barclay House (500m)

SPLURGE

New Linden Hotel (Map pp172-3; ☎ 7221 4321; www.newlinden.co.uk; 58-60 Leinster Sq W2; s/d £95/130; ⊖ Bayswater; 💻) Cramming in a fair whack of style for the price, this place has modern art in the rooms and carvings from India combined with elegant wallpaper in the guest lounge. The quiet location and helpful staff make it an excellent proposition. Wi-fi available.

B&B, you'll be well set up to conquer London with helpful tips, maps, umbrellas and great breakfast. Wi-fi, too.

Rushmore Hotel (Map pp172-3; ☎ 7370 3839; www.rushmore-hotel.co.uk; 11 Trebovir Rd SW5; s/d from £70/90; ⊖ Earl's Court) This modest hotel has a cheery, welcoming atmosphere and wi-fi.

Heathrow & Gatwick Airports

Yotel (☎ 7100 1100; www.yotel.com; r per 4/5/6/7-24hr £38/45/53/59; 💻) The best news for early-morning or late-night flyers since coffee-vending machines, Yotel's smart 'cabins' offer pint-sized luxury: comfy beds, soft lights, wi-fi, internet-connected TVs, monsoon showers and fluffy towels. Swinging cats isn't recommended, but when is it ever?

EATING

London has an amazing selection of places to eat, though food and service can vary wildly regardless of price tag. In this section, we steer you towards restaurants and cafes distinguished by location, value for money, unique features, original settings and, of course, good food. Vegetarians needn't worry; London has a host of dedicated meat-free joints, while most others offer at least a token dish.

West End

Soho and Covent Garden are the gastronomic heart of London, with stacks of restaurants and cuisines to choose from – and many good low-budget options.

Nordic Bakery (Map pp162-3; ☎ 3230 1077; 14a Golden Sq W1; snacks £3-5; 🕑 8am-8pm Mon-Fri, 11am-7pm Sat, 11am-6pm Sun; ⊖ Piccadilly Circus) A simple and stylish cafe – just as you'd expect from the Scandinavians.

Neal's Yard Salad Bar (Map pp162-3; ☎ 7836 3233; Neal's Yard WC2; mains £3-11.50; ⊖ Covent Garden) This bright-orange salad bar has waiters in black bowties serving fresh leafy meals and moist Brazilian cakes.

Sacred (Map pp162-3; ☎ 7734 1415; 13 Ganton St W1; mains £3.60-5.30; 🕑 7.30am-8.30pm Mon-Fri, 9.30am-8pm Sat, 10am-7pm Sun; ⊖ Oxford Circus) Spiritual paraphernalia and blatant Kiwiana don't seem to deter the smart Carnaby St set from lounging around this eclectic cafe.

Also recommended:

Mother Mash (Map pp162-3; ☎ 7494 9644; 26 Ganton St W1; mains £6.95-7.10; ⊖ Oxford Circus) Comfort food Central, with four types of mashed potato, eight varieties of sausage (including a vegetarian). Lovely.

Red Veg (Map pp162-3; ☎ 7437 3109; 95 Dean St W1; ⊖ Tottenham Court Rd) Everyone's favourite communist vegetarian burger bar.

Fitzrovia

Tucked away behind busy Tottenham Court Rd, Charlotte and Goodge Sts form one of central London's most vibrant eating precincts.

Ooze (Map pp162-3; ☎ 7436 9444; 62 Goodge St W1; mains £6.95-14.50; ⊖ Goodge St) The humble risotto gets its moment on the catwalk in this breezy Italian restaurant.

La Perla (Map pp162-3; ☎ 7436 1744; 11 Charlotte St W1; mains £9-17; 🕑 closed Sun lunch; ⊖ Goodge St) The service is lovely, but it's the street tacos that have us infatuated at this great place.

Chelsea, Kensington & Knightsbridge

These highbrow neighbourhoods harbour some of London's very best (and priciest) restaurants, but there are a few budget options.

Jakobs (Map pp172-3; ☎ 7581 9292; 20 Gloucester Rd SW7; mains £4-10; ⊖ Gloucester Rd) A charismatic deli-cafe serving a mixture of Armenian,

SPLURGE

National Dining Rooms (Map pp162-3; ☎ 7747 2525; Sainsbury Wing, National Gallery, Trafalgar Sq WC2; 2 courses £25; 🕑 lunch daily, dinner Fri; ⊖ Charing Cross) It's fitting that chef Oliver Peyton's acclaimed restaurant should celebrate British food, such as smoked haddock, Suffolk cob chicken and 'Farmer Shep's aged sirloin', while overlooking Trafalgar Sq. For a cheaper option with the same views, ambience and quality try a pie and salad at the adjoining bakery (mains £5 to £10).

BRITAIN

CHAIN GANG

It's an unnerving but not uncommon experience to discover that the idiosyncratic cafe or pub you were so proud of finding on your first day in London then pops up on every other high street. But among the endless Caffe Neros, Pizza Expresses and All-Bar-Ones are some gems or, at least, great fallback options:

- **GBK** (www.gbkinfo.com) Creative burger constructions.
- **Leon** (www.leonrestaurants.co.uk) Fresh salads, wraps and the like.
- **Ping Pong** (www.pingpongdimsum.com) Stylish Chinese dumplings.
- **Wagamama** (www.wagamama.com) Japanese noodles taking over the world.
- **Zizzi** (www.zizzi.co.uk) Wood-fired pizza.

Persian and Mediterranean dishes, including salads, falafel and quiches.

Orsini (Map pp172-3; ☎ 7581 5553; 8a Thurloe Pl SW3; mains £7.50-12; ⊖ South Kensington) This is a tiny family-run eatery, marinated in authentic Italian charm.

DRINKING

As long as there's been a city, Londoners have loved to drink – and, as history shows, often immoderately. Soho is undoubtedly the heart of bar culture, with enough variety to cater to all tastes. For up-and-coming bohemian-cool, try some of the venues in the East End neighbourhoods of Hoxton and Shoreditch. Elsewhere, you'll find plenty of pub-crawl potential in places like Islington, Clerkenwell, Southwark, Notting Hill, Earl's Court… Hell, it's just not that difficult. The following reviews are the tip of the ice cube, simply to make sure you don't miss out on some of London's best drinkeries.

West End

Coach & Horses (Map pp162-3; 29 Greek St W1; ⊖ Leicester Sq) This Soho institution has been patronised by Francis Bacon, Dylan Thomas, Peter Cooke and Peter O'Toole. Wednesday night singalong is tops.

Queen Mary (Map pp162-3; Waterloo Pier WC2; ⊖ Embankment) All aboard this steamer for a welcoming pub-like atmosphere with great views of the London Eye.

South of the Thames

George Inn (Talbot Yard, 77 Borough High St SE1; ⊖ London Bridge or Borough) Tucked away in a cobbled courtyard is London's last surviving galleried coaching inn, dating from 1677. Charles Dickens and Shakespeare used to prop up the bar here (but not together, obviously).

Notting Hill

Windsor Castle (Map pp172-3; 114 Campden Hill Rd W11; ⊖ Notting Hill Gate) A memorable pub with oak partitions separating the original bars, and one of the loveliest gardens of any London pub.

East End

The following are all good stops on a Hoxton hop:

Bricklayer's Arms (off Map pp162-3; 63 Charlotte Rd EC2; ⊖ Old St) Back-street pub with an interesting crowd.

Favela Chic (off Map pp162-3; ☎ 7613 4228; 91-93 Great Eastern St EC2; entry after 9pm £5-10; 🕓 5pm-1am Tue-Thu, 5pm-2am Fri, 6pm-2am Sat; ⊖ Old St) Hip young things, crazy theme nights, fun and funky music.

Red Lion (Map pp162-3; 41 Hoxton St N1; ⊖ Old St) Old corner pub with eclectic furniture and cheap drinks.

Zigfrid Von Underbelly (off Map pp162-3; 11 Hoxton Sq N1; ⊖ Old St) Furnished like an oversized lounge – it's cool and fun.

CLUBBING

London's had a lot of practice perfecting the art of clubbing – Samuel Pepys used the term in 1660! The volume and variety today is staggering; you'll find clubs wherever there's a venue big enough, cheap enough or quirky enough. The big nights are Friday and Saturday, although you'll find some of the most cutting-edge sessions midweek. Admission prices vary widely; it's often cheaper to arrive early or pre-book tickets.

Cargo (off Map pp162-3; ☎ 7739 3440; www.cargo-london.com; 83 Rivington St EC2; admission free-£16; ⊖ Old St) Hugely popular, local and international DJs, plus courtyard to enjoy big sounds and the great outdoors.

our pick **The End** (Map pp162-3; ☎ 7419 9199; www.endclub.com; 18 West Central St WC1; admission £6-16; 🕓 from around 10.30pm Mon-Sat, 5.30am-midday Sun; ⊖ Tottenham Court Rd) Eclectic range of cutting-edge nights.

Fabric (Map pp162-3; ☎ 7336 8898; www.fabriclondon.com; 77A Charterhouse St EC1; admission £13-16; 🕓 10pm-6am Fri, 11pm-8am Sat; ⊖ Farringdon) In 2008, once again voted the world's best club by *DJ* magazine.

Ministry of Sound (Map pp162-3; ☎ 0870-060 0010; http://club.ministryofsound.com/club; 103 Gaunt St SE1; admission £12-20; ⏰ 10pm-6am Fri, 11pm-7am Sat; ⊖ Elephant & Castle) London's most famous club, where the global brand started; it still packs in a diverse crew.

ENTERTAINMENT

London is a world capital for theatre and there's a lot more than mammoth musicals to tempt you into the West End, including heavyweights like the **Royal Court Theatre** (Map pp172-3; ☎ 7565 5000; www.royalcourttheatre.com; Sloane Sq SW1; ⊖ Sloane Sq), the **National Theatre** (Map pp162-3; ☎ 7452 3000; www.nationaltheatre.org.uk; South Bank SE1; ⊖ Waterloo), and the **Royal Shakespeare Company** (RSC; ☎ 0870 609 1110; www.rsc.org.uk).

On performance days you can buy half-price tickets for West End productions (cash only) from the official **Leicester Square Half-Price Ticket Booth** (Map pp162-3; Leicester Sq; ⏰ 10am-7pm Mon-Sat, noon-3pm Sun; ⊖ Leicester Sq). The booth is the one with the clock tower; beware of touts elsewhere selling dodgy tickets. For more on what's being staged where, visit www.officiallondontheatre.co.uk or www.theatremonkey.com.

Sport

For information on fixtures, times, venues and ticket prices for all spectator sports, the entertainment listings weekly *Time Out* is the best source.

FOOTBALL

London is home to some of the best-known clubs in the world, but tickets for Premier League football (soccer) matches are ridiculously hard to come by for casual fans these days. Rather than contact the clubs direct, try your luck at www.premierleague.com or a general ticketing website.

The spiritual home of English football is **Wembley Stadium** (www.wembleystadium.com), in northwest London. It's been the national team's home turf since it was built in 1923, and it's where the FA Cup final is contested every May. Controversially, the great stadium and its two landmark towers were demolished in 2001, and replaced (even more controversially) with a new 90,000-capacity, state-of-the-art complex, which hosted its first game in 2007 – four years later than planned.

RUGBY

Twickenham (☎ 0870-405 2000; www.rfu.com; Rugby Rd, Twickenham; tickets £10-45, more for internationals; 🚉 Twickenham) is the home of English rugby union, but tickets for big games are difficult to get. Once again, try the ticketing agencies.

CRICKET

Cricket is as popular as ever in the land of its origin. Test matches take place at two venerable grounds: **Lord's** (☎ 7616 8500; www.lords.org; St John's Wood Rd NW8; ⊖ St John's Wood) and the **Brit Oval** (off Map pp162-3; ☎ 08712 461100; www.surreycricket

LONDON CALLING

London was swinging in the '60s, and every subsequent generation has enjoyed new flavours of pop, rock, indie and countless other genres along with the city's energetic live-music scene. There are numerous smaller venues, and several large famous ones, too. We've listed just a few here. Big name gigs sell out quickly, so agencies like www.seetickets.com are your best bet.

- **100 Club** (Map pp162-3; ☎ 7636 0933; www.the100club.co.uk; 100 Oxford St W1; ⊖ Oxford Circus) Legendary London venue, once the centre of the punk revolution, now dividing time between jazz, rock and even a little swing.
- **Brixton Academy** (off Map pp162-3; ☎ 0844-477 2000; www.brixton-academy.co.uk; 211 Stockwell Rd SW9; ⊖ Brixton) Always winning awards for 'best live venue', hosting big name acts in a relatively intimate setting.
- **Forum** (off Map pp162-3; ☎ 0844-847 2405; www.kentishtownforum.com; 9-17 Highgate Rd NW5; ⊖ Kentish Town) Grand old theatre and one of London's best large venues.
- **Hope & Anchor** (off Map pp162-3; ☎ 7700 0550; 207 Upper St; admission free-£6; ⊖ Angel) Live music's still the focus of the pub that hosted the first London gigs of Joy Division and U2.
- **Shepherd's Bush Empire** (off Map pp172-3; ☎ 8354 3300; www.shepherds-bush-empire.co.uk; Shepherd's Bush Green W12; ⊖ Shepherd's Bush) Slightly dishevelled, midsize theatre that hosts terrific bands.

GAY & LESBIAN LONDON

The West End, particularly Soho, remains the visible centre of gay and lesbian London, with numerous venues clustered around Old Compton St and its surrounds, but one of the nice things about London is the local gay bars in many neighbourhoods.

South of the river, Vauxhall has taken off as a hub for the hirsute, hefty and generally harder-edged sections of the community. The railway arches are now filled with dance clubs, leather bars and a sauna. In southwest London, Clapham's got some of the friendliest gay bars in the city, while Earl's Court (West London), Islington (North London) and Limehouse (East End) have their own scenes.

The easiest way to find out what's going on is to pick up the free press *(Pink Paper, Boyz, QX)* from a venue, but be warned: the mags can be somewhat...confronting. The gay section of *Time Out* is useful, as are www.gaydarnation.com (for men) and www.gingerbeer.co.uk (for women).

.com; Kennington SE11; ⊖ Oval). Tickets are £24 to £80, but if you're a fan it's worth it. If not, it's an expensive and protracted form of torture.

SHOPPING

From world-famous department stores to quirky backstreet markets, London is a mecca for shoppers. If you're looking for something distinctly British, eschew the Union Jack–emblazoned kitsch of the tourist thoroughfares and fill your bags with Twinings tea, Paul Smith shirts, Royal Doulton china and Marmite. London's famous department stores are a tourist attraction in themselves, even if you don't intend to contribute to the orgy of consumption:

Fortnum & Mason (Map pp162-3; ☎ 7734 8040; 181 Piccadilly W1; ⊖ Piccadilly Circus) The byword for quality and service from a bygone era.

Harrods (Map pp172-3; ☎ 7730 1234; 87 Brompton Rd SW1; ⊖ Knightsbridge) Overpriced theme park for fans of Britannia.

Harvey Nichols (Map pp172-3; ☎ 7235 5000; 109-125 Knightsbridge SW1; ⊖ Knightsbridge) Temple of fashion, jewellery and perfume.

Liberty (Map pp162-3; ☎ 7734 1234; 214-220 Regent St W1; ⊖ Oxford Circus) Irresistible blend of contemporary styles and indulgent pampering.

Selfridges (Map pp162-3; ☎ 0870 837 7377; 400 Oxford St W1; ⊖ Bond St) Funkiest and most vital of London's one-stop shops.

GETTING THERE & AWAY

London is the country's major gateway, and transport information (including airlines flying to/from Britain) can be found on p154. For details on transport to/from the airports, see the box on p165.

GETTING AROUND

Although locals love to complain, London's public transport is excellent, with frequent buses, boats and trains (overground and underground – the latter called the Tube) to get you pretty much anywhere. The system is divided into six concentric zones, with nearly all the places covered by this book in Zones 1 and 2, and **Transport for London** (www.tfl.gov.uk) is the glue that keeps it all together. The only downside: the crush at peak rush-hours (roughly 7.30am to 9am, and 5pm to 6.30pm), but as a tourist you can easily avoid these periods by travelling 'off-peak'.

Bus

Travelling around London by bus is an enjoyable way to get a feel for the city, especially if you're on a double-decker. Buses run regularly during the day, while less-frequent night buses (number prefixed with 'N') run after about 11pm. Single-journey bus tickets (valid for two hours) cost £2 (90p on Oyster, capped at £3 per day); day-passes are £3.50 and books of six tickets are £6. At stops with yellow signs you have to buy your ticket from the automatic machine before boarding. Buses stop on request, so clearly signal with an outstretched arm.

If you want a classic old 'Routemaster' double-decker, these operate only on route 9 (Aldwych to Royal Albert Hall) and 15 (Trafalgar Sq to Tower Hill).

London Underground & DLR

The Underground (or Tube) extends its subterranean tentacles throughout London and into the surrounding suburbs, with services

MARKET FEVER

London has more than 350 markets selling everything from antiques and curios to flowers and fish. Some, such as Camden and Portobello Rd, cater for tourists, while others exist just for the locals and sell everything from lunch to underwear. Here's a sample:

- **Borough Market** (off Map pp162-3; cnr Borough High & Stoney Sts SE1; 11am-5pm Thu, noon-6pm Fri, 9am-4pm Sat; London Bridge) Wonderfully atmospheric, with everything from organic falafel to boar's heads.
- **Brixton Market** (Electric Ave; 10am-dusk Mon-Sat, closes 1pm Wed; Brixton) Immortalised by the Eddie Grant song, Electric Ave is a cosmopolitan treat mixing everything from reggae to exotic spices.
- **Camden Market** (off Map pp162-3; 10am-5.30pm; Camden Town) A series of markets, with the **Lock** and **Stables** markets still the place for punk fashion, hippy shit and cheap food.
- **Petticoat Lane Market** (off Map pp162-3; Wentworth St & Middlesex St E1; 9am-2pm Mon-Fri & Sun; Aldgate) Cherished East End institution overflowing with cheap consumer durables.
- **Portobello Rd Market** (Map pp172-3; Portobello Rd W10; 8am-6.30pm Mon-Sat, closes 1pm Thu; Ladbroke Grove) One of London's most famous (and crowded) street markets, selling new and vintage clothes, antiques and food.
- **Sunday (Up)market** (off Map pp162-3; The Old Truman Brewery, Brick Lane E1; 10am-5pm Sun; Liverpool St) Handmade handbags, jewellery, new and vintage clothes and shoes, plus food if you need refuelling.

running every few minutes from 5.30am (7am on Sunday) to roughly 12.30am. Tickets can be purchased from counters or machines at each station using cash or credit card. Included within the tube network is the Docklands Light Railway (DLR), linking the City to Greenwich.

Train

Particularly south of the Thames, where tube lines are in short supply, the various local 'overground' train lines are an important part of the public transport network. Some, but not all, are shown on the tube map (see opposite); for a complete picture you can get larger maps showing all overground and underground lines. Especially as you get further into the suburbs, not all stations are fitted with Oyster readers, so check before travelling in case you need to purchase a separate ticket.

Waterbus

The public-service boats plying the Thames are ideal for avoiding traffic jams and getting great views. **Thames Clippers** (☎ 0871 781 5049; www.thamesclippers.com) runs regular commuter services between Embankment, Waterloo, Bankside, London Bridge, Tower, Canary Wharf, Greenwich and Woolwich piers (adult £2.50 to £6.50, from 7am to midnight weekdays, from 9am weekends). Another service runs from Putney to Blackfriars

LONDON'S YOUR OYSTER

To get the most out of London you need to be able to jump on and off public transport like a local, not scramble to buy a ticket each time. If you're here just a few days, get an off-peak daily Travelcard (£5.30 per day for Zones 1 and 2), which covers all tubes, buses and local trains. For five days or more, the best option is a reusable Oyster smartcard on which you can load either a season ticket (weekly/monthly £24/93) or pre-paid credit. The card itself is £3 (free with a season ticket). This gives unlimited travel on tubes, buses and most suburban train services. If you opt for pre-paid credit, the fare will be deducted from your card at a much lower rate than if you were buying a one-off paper ticket. Even better, in any single day your fares will be capped at the equivalent Oyster day-pass rate (Zones 1-2 off-peak £4.80).

LONDON'S TUBE MAP

For getting around on the tube, pick up a copy of the Tube Map (free at underground stations) and don't worry if you take a wrong turn: it's always easy to retrace. Many of the city's main attractions lie within the loop of the Circle Line (colour-coded yellow). Note though that the map is an iconic piece of graphic design but highly systematic and not remotely to scale; the distance between stations is much greater the further you get from central London.

during the morning and evening rush hours. Passengers with daily, weekly or monthly travelcards (Oyster or otherwise) get one-third off all fares.

AROUND LONDON

'When you're tired of London, you're tired of life' opined 18th-century Londoner Samuel Johnson, although he wasn't living in an age when too many days on the tube can leave you grouchy. But escape is easy. Well-known day-trip haunts like Brighton (p181) and Oxford (p193) are covered in the Southeast England and Central England sections. Some other gems an easy train-ride from the capital are covered here.

WINDSOR & ETON

☎ 01753 / pop 31,000

One of Britain's largest and most imposing medieval palaces, **Windsor Castle** (☎ 020-7766 7304; www.royalcollection.org.uk; adult £15; 9.45am-4pm Mar-Oct, 9.45am-3pm Nov-Feb) is still one of the Queen's residences, but that doesn't mean visitors have to content themselves with peering through the gates. Instead, you can enter large sections of the castle complex to see highlights including Queen Mary's giant dolls' house, and St George's Chapel, containing the tombs of several monarchs, including Henry VIII. The surrounding Victorian town of Windsor is also worth checking out, particularly for its traditional tea rooms.

A short walk through Windsor and across the River Thames brings you to **Eton College** (☎ 671177; www.etoncollege.com; adult £4.20; 10.30am-4.30pm Mar-Apr & Jul-Sep [school holidays], 2-4.30pm [term-time]), the famous public school – which in Britain means a private school – that educated 18 prime ministers and many royals. Several buildings date from the mid-15th century. Entry includes the **Museum of Eton Life**, about the world of the public schoolboy past and present. As you wander around you may recognise some of the buildings; *Chariots of Fire*, *Mrs Brown* and *Shakespeare in Love* are just some of the classics filmed here.

To get here, Windsor and Eton have two train stations, both easily reached from London: trains from London Paddington run to Central station (30 to 45 minutes); trains from London Waterloo go to Riverside station (55 minutes). Services run half hourly on both lines and tickets cost £8.

SOUTHEAST ENGLAND

Traditionally a day-trip playground for Londoners escaping overcrowded streets, England's southeast (often dubbed the 'Home Counties') offers fascinating historic towns, sweeping greenbelt vistas and some vibrant seaside resorts – most less than an hour by train from the capital. This section covers the counties of Kent, Sussex and Hampshire, with places listed roughly east to west. For visitor information, see www.visitsoutheastengland.com.

CANTERBURY

☎ 01227 / pop 43,600

With its jaw-dropping, multispired cathedral surrounded by medieval cobbled streets, this Unesco World Heritage city has been a popular pilgrimage site for Christians and tourists for centuries. Today's visitors overwhelm the area during summer, coming to immerse themselves in religious and secular history, including Thomas Becket's murder and the bawdy works of Geoffrey Chaucer. But this is no mothballed outdoor museum: Canterbury is surprisingly vibrant, and a good base for exploring the wider region.

Orientation & Information

Almost enclosed by a medieval wall and fully surrounded by a modern ring road, the historic centre of Canterbury is compact enough to explore on foot, which is just as well since many of its ancient streets are closed to cars. The bus station is within the old city walls, but

BRITAIN

the two train stations – Canterbury East and Canterbury West – are a few minutes' walk from the ancient perimeter.

The **TIC** (☎ 378100; www.canterbury.co.uk; 12-13 Sun St; 🕑 9.30am-5pm Mon-Sat, 10am-4pm Sun Easter-Oct, 10am-4pm Mon-Sat Nov-Easter) is opposite the cathedral. Internet access is available at **Dotcafe** (☎ 478778; 19-21 St Dunstan's St; per hr £3; 🕑 10am-7pm) near the train station.

BRITAIN

Sights

The Church of England could not have a more imposing mother ship than extraordinary **Canterbury Cathedral** (☎ 762862; www.canterbury-cathedral.org; adult/concession £7/5.50; 🕑 9am-6.30pm Mon-Sat Easter-Sep, 9am-4.30pm Mon-Sat Oct-Easter, plus 12.30-2.30pm & 4.30-5.30pm Sun year-round). It's easy to spend a couple of hours marvelling at the Early English architecture, but to hear the stories behind the stonework, it's worth taking a one-hour **tour** (£5).

Illuminating earlier history, Canterbury's **Roman Museum** (☎ 785575; Butchery Lane; adult £3; 🕑 10am-5pm Mon-Sat year-round, plus 1.30-5pm Sun Jun-Oct) is a fascinating mix of excavated artefacts and clever reconstructions – check out the mosaic remains and the smells in the Roman kitchen.

Sleeping

Like many popular tourist towns, Canterbury is ultracrowded in summer, so book a bed ahead if you can.

Kipp's Independent Hostel (☎ 786121; www.kipps-hostel.com; 40 Nunnery Fields; dm/s/d £15/20/35; ⊠ 💻) This place is popular for its homely atmosphere, friendly hosts, lots of communal areas, clean though cramped dorms, bike hire and garden.

Canterbury YHA Hostel (☎ 462911; canterbury@yha.org.uk; 54 New Dover Rd; dm £20.95; ⊠ 💻) This grand villa is out of town, but spacious and organised, with a garden and some single rooms, plus cheaper tent accommodation.

Cathedral Gate Hotel (☎ 464381; www.cathgate.co.uk; 36 Burgate; s/d from £41/72; ⊠) This much-photographed 15th-century hotel is older than the next-door eponymous gate, hence labyrinthine passageways where few rooms escape an angled floor, low door or wonky walls.

Eating & Drinking

The streets of Canterbury are full of coffee bars and sandwich shops offering cheap eats, and with history on their side, olde-worlde pubs are satisfyingly plentiful.

Tiny Tim's Tearoom (34 St Margaret's St; mains £7-13; 🕑 9.30am-5pm Tue-Sat, 10.30am-4pm Sun) Not a hint of chintz in this English tearoom – just pure 1930s elegance. The place to enjoy big breakfasts, tiers of cakes, crumpets and sandwiches.

Goods Shed (☎ 459153; Station Rd West; lunch £8-12, dinner £10-16; 🕑 market 10am-7pm Tue-Sat & 10am-4pm Sun, restaurant lunch & dinner Tue-Sun) Farmers market, food hall and fabulous restaurant all rolled into one, this converted station warehouse is a hit with everyone from self-caterers to sit-down gourmets.

Our favourite pubs include the **Old Brewery Tavern** (High St) with soft leather sofas, a great choice of beers and good bar food; and the **Thomas Beckett** (21 Best Lane), a classic pub with traditional decor, quality ales and decent grub (mains £6 to £9).

Getting There & Away

Hourly buses run to/from London Victoria (£12.70, two hours) and Dover (35 minutes). There are two train stations: Canterbury East, accessible from London Victoria; and Canterbury West, accessible from London's Charing Cross. On both routes, trains run frequently (£20, 1½ hours, two to three hourly).

DOVER

☎ **01305 / pop 34,100**

The brightest things about Dover are its sprawling hilltop castle and the world-famous White Cliffs. The rest is a grey melange of access routes to the ferry port.

Orientation & Information

Dover Priory train station is a short walk west of the city centre. The bus station is more central. The city centre **TIC** (☎ 205108; www.whitecliffscountry.org.uk; Biggin St; 🕑 9am-5.30pm daily Jun-Aug, 9am-5.30pm Mon-Fri & 10am-4pm Sat & Sun Sep-May) provides booking services for accommodation, ferry and bus.

Sights

One of England's mightiest fortresses, **Dover Castle** ☎ 211067; admission £10.30; 🕑 10am-6pm Apr-Sep, 10am-5pm Oct, 10am-4pm Thu-Mon Nov-Jan, 10am-4pm Feb-Mar) occupies a spectacular hilltop promontory dripping with history. There are Roman, Saxon and Norman remains, while the secret Napoleonic tunnels were expanded during WWII, and used as a command post.

Immortalised in song, film and literature, the iconic **White Cliffs of Dover** are embedded in

DETOUR: LEEDS CASTLE

One of Britain's most-visited historic attractions, **Leeds Castle** (☎ 01622-765400; www.leeds-castle.com; adult £11; ⏲ 10.30am-6pm Apr-Oct, to 4pm Nov-Mar) never fails to impress. Near Maidstone in Kent (not the northern city of the same name) it's situated on two islands surrounded by woodlands, and began life as a Norman stronghold before housing six of England's medieval queens. Save time for the elaborate maze – if you solve it, you're rewarded with panoramic views. National Express runs one direct coach daily from London Victoria, leaving at 9am, returning at 3pm (£12.30, 1½ hours, must be prebooked). To save a bit, a combined entrance and coach ticket is £22.

the national consciousness – a big welcome-home sign to generations of travellers and soldiers. The Langdon Cliffs (their proper name) are managed by the National Trust, which has a **visitor centre** (☎ 01304-202756; admission free; ⏲ 10am-5pm Mar-Oct, 11am-4pm Nov-Feb) 2 miles east of Dover, from where you can take a stroll along a 5-mile stretch of marked coastal trail.

Sleeping

Castle St and Maison Dieu Rd are B&B hotspots but there are many other options in town.

East Lee Guest House (☎ 210176; www.eastlee.co.uk; 108 Maison Dieu Rd; d from £50, with breakfast from £55; ⊠) This lovely house has elegantly decorated communal areas, energetic hosts, comfy beds and excellent breakfasts.

Number One Guest House (☎ 202007; www.number1guesthouse.co.uk; 1 Castle Street; d from £45; ⊠) At the foot of Dover Castle, rooms are decorated in traditional Victorian style. There's also a pretty walled garden with lovely views.

Hubert House (☎ 202253; www.huberthouse.co.uk; 9 Castle Hill Rd; s/d incl breakfast from £40/55; ⊠ 🖳) The comfortable bedrooms may be flowery but the welcome is warm, and there's a nice little bistro downstairs. This hotel also has wi-fi.

Eating & Drinking

La Salle Verte (14-15 Cannon St; ⏲ 9am-4.30pm Mon-Sun) This funky little cafe serves great coffee and snacks – inside or in a little suntrap patio garden.

Cullins Yard (☎ 211666; 11 Cambridge Rd; ⏲ 10am-midnight) This bar-restaurant has a nautical theme and a great location down by Wellington Docks.

Getting There & Away

For details of ferries to/from mainland Europe, and the Channel Tunnel, see p155.

National Express runs 20 daily coaches to/from London Victoria (£12, 2¾ hours), and there are more than 40 trains daily to/from London Victoria and Charing Cross (£26, two hours). Dover will be a stop on the UK's first high-speed rail line, with trains leaving London St Pancras from late 2009.

BRIGHTON

☎ 01273 / pop 247,800

While some British seaside resorts are paint-peeled reminders of an earlier era, Brighton and Hove – two towns combined to form a new city in 2000 – moved on big time, and now boasts a bohemian spirit, exuberant gay community, dynamic student population and a healthy number of ageing and new-age hippies. There's also traditional candy-floss fun – although the beach has never been the main attraction, mainly because it's stones not sand. But Brighton rocks all year round, and really comes to life in summer, when tourists, language students and revellers from London pour in, keen to explore the city's legendary nightlife, summer festivals and shops.

Orientation & Information

The train station is half a mile north of the beach, while the bus station is tucked away close to Brighton Pier. Old Steine (pronounced 'steen') is the major thoroughfare linking pier and centre. The gay scene flourishes in Kemptown – known of course as Camptown.

At the **TIC** (☎ 0906-711 2255; www.visitbrighton.com; Royal Pavilion; ⏲ 9.30am-5.30pm), overworked staff and a 50p-per-minute telephone line provide local information. You may find the website and on-site 24-hour accessible computer more helpful. For internet, go to **Netpama** (☎ 227188; 37 Preston St; per hr £2) or **Internet Junction** (109 Western Rd; per hr £2.50; ⏲ 10am-9pm Mon-Fri, 10am-8pm Sat, 11am-6pm Sun).

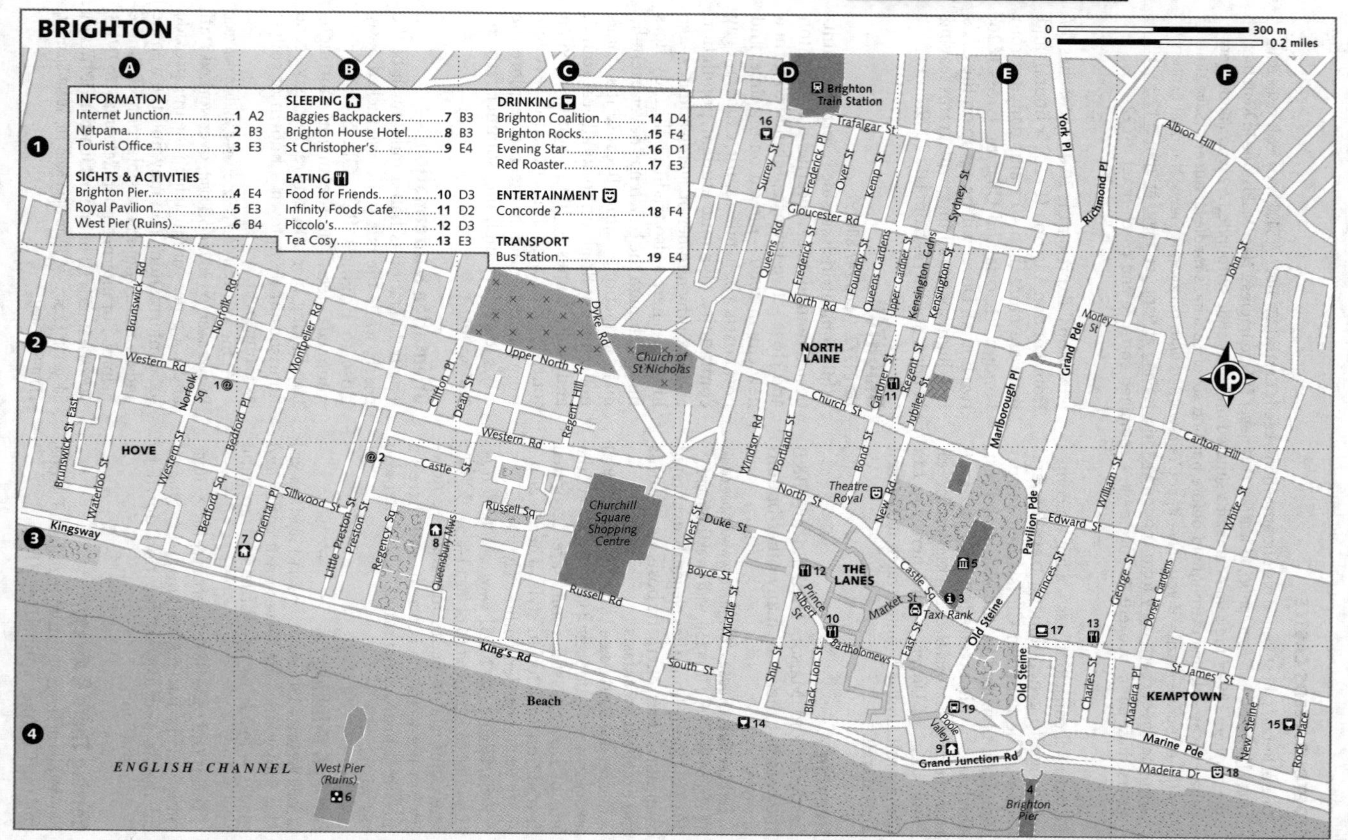
BRIGHTON
0 300 m
0 0.2 miles
INFORMATION
Internet Junction....1 A2
Netpama....2 B3
Tourist Office....3 E3
SIGHTS & ACTIVITIES
Brighton Pier....4 E4
Royal Pavilion....5 E3
West Pier (Ruins)....6 B4
SLEEPING
Baggies Backpackers....7 B3
Brighton House Hotel....8 B3
St Christopher's....9 E4
EATING
Food for Friends....10 D3
Infinity Foods Cafe....11 D2
Piccolo's....12 D3
Tea Cosy....13 E3
DRINKING
Brighton Coalition....14 D4
Brighton Rocks....15 F4
Evening Star....16 D1
Red Roaster....17 E3
ENTERTAINMENT
Concorde 2....18 F4
TRANSPORT
Bus Station....19 E4
Brighton Train Station
HOVE
NORTH LAINE
THE LANES
KEMPTOWN
Church of St Nicholas
Churchill Square Shopping Centre
Theatre Royal
Taxi Rank
Beach
ENGLISH CHANNEL
West Pier (Ruins)
Brighton Pier
Kingsway
King's Rd
Grand Junction Rd
Madeira Dr
Marine Pde
Western Rd
Upper North St
Dyke Rd
Church St
North St
North Rd
Gloucester Rd
Trafalgar St
Queens Rd
York Pl
Richmond Pl
Grand Pde
Marlborough Pl
Pavilion Pde
Old Steine
Edward St
Carlton Hill
Albion Hill
John St
St James' St

Sights

An absolute must is the **Royal Pavilion** (☎ 290900; www.royalpavilion.org.uk; admission £8.50; 🕑 10am-4.30pm Oct-Mar, 9.30am-5pm Apr-Sep), the exotic palace and party-pad of Prince George, later King George IV. The flamboyant Indian-style domes are a prelude to the lavish oriental-themed interior, where no colour is deemed too strong, while dragons swoop from gilt-smothered ceilings and gem-encrusted snakes slither down pillars.

Brighton's original fishing-village heart is **The Lanes**, a cobblestone web of 17th-century cottages housing a gentrified cornucopia of independent shops, pubs and one-of-a-kind eateries. The adjacent **North Laine** has a funkier, alternative vibe with multicoloured shops, secondhand record stores and vegetarian cafes for local hipsters.

Formerly named Palace Pier, the landmark **Brighton Pier** (www.brightonpier.co.uk; admission free) is a suitably brash reminder of England's seaside-loving past, with noisy amusement arcades, greasy-food stands, and a clutch of thrill rides and traditional attractions, including a helter-skelter. Nearby, the skeletal remains of the **West Pier** shimmer in the haze.

Sleeping

Traditional B&Bs line the streets radiating from Brighton Pier, along with some boutique properties and a good selection of backpacker joints – several catering to raucous stag and hen nights. Peaceful nights are not guaranteed, which may or may not be a plus for you.

Baggies Backpackers (☎ 733740; 33 Oriental Pl; dm/d £13/35) A warm atmosphere, worn-in charm, motherly owner and clean dorms have made this long-established hostel something of an institution.

St Christopher's (☎ 202035; www.palacebrighton.co.uk; Palace Hotel, 10/12 Grand Junction Rd; dm £16-19.50, s/d £25/50; 💻) This basic seafront hostel is a magnet for party people, thanks to its heart-of-the-action location.

Brighton House Hotel (☎ 323282; www.brighton-house.co.uk; 52 Regency Sq; s/d from £45/85; ⊠ 💻) You'll get honest value at this welcoming B&B; rooms are immaculate and traditionally styled. Wi-fi, too.

Eating

Unlike many British seaside resorts, Brighton has more to offer than limp fish and chips. The Lanes is a good area for foodie exploring. Here are our favourites:

Piccolo's (☎ 203701; 56 Ship St; mains £3.60-8.50; 🕑 11.30am-11.30pm) Cheap, tasty pizza served in a friendly and bustling restaurant.

Tea Cosy (☎ 677055; 3 George St; 🕑 noon-5pm Wed, 11am-6pm Thu-Sat, noon-6pm Sun) Barmy tearoom full of strict etiquette rules and royal family memorabilia.

Red Roaster (1D St James' St; mains £4-5; 🕑 7am-7pm Mon-Fri, 8am-7pm Sat, 9am-6.30pm Sun) You can smell the great coffee from across the street.

Infinity Foods Cafe (☎ 670743; 11a Kensington Gardens; mains £5-8; 🕑 9.30am-5pm Mon-Sat) Serving up a wide variety of vegetarian, vegan and organic food.

Food For Friends (☎ 202310; www.foodforfriends.com; 17a Prince Albert St; mains £8-13; 🕑 lunch & dinner) Airy glass-sided restaurant with ever-inventive choice of vegetarian and vegan food.

Drinking & Clubbing

It would be criminal to come to Brighton and not sample the ever-happening nightlife, which ranges from some of the region's best pubs to a wide array of live music and clubbing options – although the tacky scene on West Street is avoided by aficionados.

Evening Star (55 Surrey St) This unpretentious pub is a beer drinkers' nirvana, with a wonderful selection of award-winning real ales.

Brighton Rocks (6 Rock Pl; 🕑 4pm-late) This cocktail bar is firmly on the Kemptown gay scene but welcomes all-comers.

Brighton Coalition (171-181 Kings Rd Arches) On a summer's day, sit and watch the world go by at this popular beach bar, diner and club.

Concorde 2 (☎ 673311; www.concorde2.co.uk; Madeira Dr, Kemptown; admission £8-20) Brighton's best-known and best-loved club is a disarmingly unpretentious den where Fatboy Slim still occasionally graces the decks.

For more ideas, visit www.drinkinbrighton.co.uk.

Getting There & Away

National Express coaches run hourly to/from London Victoria (£11, two hours 20 minutes) and regularly to all London airports. There are trains to/from London Victoria and King's Cross stations (£19, 1¼ hours, four per hour).

PORTSMOUTH

☎ 023 / pop 187,100

Prepare to splice the main brace and potter around the poop deck – Portsmouth is the principal port of Britain's Royal Navy, ranking alongside Greenwich as Britain's most fascinating centre of maritime history.

The city is not noted for its beauty, though, so you're better off heading straight for the waterfront.

Orientation & Information

The Historic Dockyard, tourist office, train station and passenger-ferry terminal for the Isle of Wight are all conveniently grouped together. Just southeast in Old Portsmouth, ancient buildings survive amid the postwar rebuild. Two miles away is Southsea, with many good restaurants, pubs and hotels. The main **TIC** (☎ 9282 6722; www.visitportsmouth.co.uk; The Hard; 🕑 9.30am-5pm) has an accommodation booking service (£2). For internet access, try **Online Café** (☎ 9283 1106; 163 Elm, Southsea; per hr £2.60; 🕑 9am-9pm Mon-Fri, 10am-9pm Sat & Sun) in Southsea.

Sights

Dripping with seafaring heritage, Portsmouth's **Historic Dockyard** (☎ 9283 9766; www.historicdockyard.co.uk; single attraction £10, all-inclusive £18.50; 🕑 10am-5.30pm) is the final resting place for a gaggle of prized vessels, including the **Mary Rose**, Henry VIII's favourite warship; **HMS Victory**, Lord Nelson's Battle of Trafalgar flagship; and **HMS Warrior**, the world's first all-iron battleship.

And representing the modern era, Portsmouth's unmistakeable new landmark is the **Spinnaker Tower** (☎ 9285 7520; www.spinnakertower.co.uk; adult £7; 🕑 10am-6pm Sun-Fri, 10am-10pm Sat Sep-Jul, 10am-10pm daily Aug), soaring 170m above Gunwharf Quays, with two sweeping white arcs resembling a billowing sail, and offering truly extraordinary views.

A short waterside walk from Gunwharf Quays, but a world apart in atmosphere, **The Point** has characterful cobbled streets dotted with salty sea-dog pubs – a top spot to gaze at the Spinnaker Tower and the passing parade of ferries and navy ships.

Sleeping

Most B&Bs are in Southsea, but there's a few good options on The Point. To get you started:

Southsea Backpackers Lodge (☎ 9283 2495; www.portsmouthbackpackers.co.uk; 4 Florence Rd, Southsea; dm £15, d £33-38; 💻) Old-fashioned hostel, with low shower-to-people ratio.

Fortitude Cottage (☎ 9282 3748; www.fortitudecottage.co.uk; 51 Broad St, The Point; s from £45, d £70-80) Airy B&B with ferry-port views.

Eating & Drinking

Sallyport Tea Rooms (35 Broad St, The Point; breakfast £4, lunch £3-5; 🕑 10am-5pm Tue-Sun) Just as a traditional teashop should be: serving speciality teas and old-fashioned delights to the strains of 1940s jazz.

Custom House (Gunwharf Quays; mains £8; 🕑 lunch & dinner) This traditional-style pub offers better than average bar food.

Still & West (2 Bath Sq) Relaxed old pub with great waterside terrace.

Getting There & Away

A wide array of ferries go to/from France and Spain (for details, see p155). Regular ferries to the nearby Isle of Wight (30 minutes) are provided by **Wightlink** (☎ 0870 582 7744; www.wightlink.co.uk).

National Express buses go to/from London (£14, 2½ hours, at least hourly). Trains run every 15 minutes to/from London Victoria (£24, two hours 20 minutes) and Waterloo stations (£24, one hour 40 minutes).

WINCHESTER

☎ 01962 / pop 41,400

Dripping with attractions, the ancient capital of Saxon England is a dream for history-lovers, with a grand cathedral, links to King Arthur (of the round table) and dozens of centuries-old buildings lining its streets. Far from being a sleepy museum piece, though, Winchester has a busy city centre, plenty of shops and some great old pubs.

Orientation & Information

Winchester's compact centre is easy to explore on foot, but make sure you duck down the backstreets to find the historic gems. The train station is a 10-minute walk west of the centre, and the bus station is opposite the **TIC** (☎ 840500; www.visitwinchester.co.uk; High St; 🕑 9.30am-5.30pm Mon-Sat, 11am-4pm Sun May-Sep, 10am-5pm Mon-Sat Oct-Apr). The **Discovery Centre** (☎ 0845-603 5631; Jewry St; 🕑 9am-7pm Mon-Fri, 9am-5pm Sat, 10am-4pm Sun) has free internet access.

Sights

Glorious **Winchester Cathedral** (☎ 857200; www.winchester-cathedral.org.uk; adult £5; 🕑 8.30am-5.30pm) is the city's star attraction and one of southern England's most inspirational buildings. A magnificent melange of architectural styles, it's also the final resting place of Jane Austen, whose discreet gravestone resides in the nave.

In contrast, a modern Antony Gormley sculpture stands in the crypt, spookily reflected in several inches of water during the basement's regular floods.

Winchester's other showpiece is the cavernous **Great Hall** (☎ 846476; ⌚ 10am-5pm/dusk), all that remains of a gargantuan castle destroyed by Oliver Cromwell in 1651. Crowning the wall like a giant dartboard is **King Arthur's Round Table**. It's actually a 700-year-old fake, but it's still fascinating.

Sleeping

There's no hostel in town, and B&B space is often at a premium in summer.

12 Christchurch Rd (☎ 854272; 12 Christchurch Rd; s/d £35/50) This traditional B&B has lace doilies, feather beds and a flower-filled conservatory.

Wolvesey View (☎ 852082; www.wintonian.com; 10 Colebrook Pl; s/d £40/68; 💻 ⊠) A simply furnished place, hidden away in a quiet cul-de-sac in the middle of town.

Dolphin House (☎ 853284; www.dolphinhousestudios.co.uk; 3 Compton Rd; s/d £55/70; ⊠) A kind of B&B-plus, this charming townhouse offers two en-suite rooms, which share a compact kitchen and a terrace overlooking the lawn.

Eating & Drinking

Black Boy (1 Wharf Hill; ⌚ noon-11pm) This adorable old pub dishes up decent grub in a quaintly whacky environment filled with freaky collections.

Bishop on the Bridge (1 High St; ⌚ noon-11pm) The riverside garden of this contemporary pub makes a great spot for a meal or drink.

Winchester isn't big on late-night revelry, though the students head for cheap pubs along Jewry St.

Getting There & Away

National Express has several direct coaches to/from London Victoria (£13, 2¼ hours). Trains run every 20 minutes to/from London Waterloo (£24, one hour) and hourly to/from Portsmouth (£8.60, one hour).

SOUTHWEST ENGLAND

Southwest England offers the pick of Britain's cities, coast and countryside – all on one verdant, sea-fringed platter. Here you'll find the golden sands and surging waves of Cornwall, your very own fossil on Dorset's Jurassic Coast, Wiltshire's prehistoric sites, Bath's exquisite cityscape, Bristol's buzzing nightlife, Somerset's hippy-chic ambience and Devon's beguiling blend of moors and shores.

The places in this section are listed roughly east to west. For information, see www.visitsouthwest.co.uk.

SALISBURY

☎ 01722 / pop 43,400

Centred around a majestic cathedral topped by the tallest spire in England, gracious Salisbury has been an important provincial city for more than 1000 years, and its streets form an architectural timeline of medieval walls, Tudor houses, Georgian mansions and Victorian villas. Salisbury is also a lively place, boasting plenty of bars, restaurants and cafes, as well as a concentrated cluster of excellent museums.

Orientation & Information

The compact centre is easy to get around on foot, with Market Sq the focal point and the train station a 10-minute walk away. Behind the hulking Guildhall is the **TIC** (☎ 334956; www.visitsalisbury.com; Fish Row; ⌚ 9am-5pm Mon-Sat year-round, 10.30am-4.30pm Sun May-Sep). There's free internet at the **library** (☎ 324145; Market Pl; ⌚ 10am-7pm Mon, 9am-7pm Tue, Wed & Fri, 9am-5pm Thu & Sat).

Sights & Activities

Beneath its soaring spire, **Salisbury Cathedral** (☎ 555120; www.salisburycathedral.org.uk; adult £5; ⌚ 7.15am-6.15pm) is one of Britain's finest 13th-century Gothic churches. Free tours run throughout the day and illuminate the intricate stonework interior of flying buttresses and arching vaulted ceilings. Restore the crick in your neck in the octagonal **chapter house**, where one of only four original Magna Carta documents is displayed, before admiring **Cathedral Close**, an impressive medieval perimeter of small museums and restored period houses.

A 2-mile walk or 10-minute bus ride (bus 3, 5, 6, 8 or 9) from the centre is **Old Sarum** (☎ 335398; adult £3; ⌚ 9am-6pm Jul & Aug, 10am-5pm Apr-Jun & Sep, 10am-4pm Oct & Mar, 11am-3pm Nov-Feb), an Iron Age hill fort, later occupied by Romans and Saxons, and by the mid-11th century one of the most important towns in western England, with the first cathedral being built

Book your stay at lonelyplanet.com/hotels

in 1092. But within 30 years the cathedral was moved, founding the new city of Salisbury, and by 1331 Old Sarum was abandoned. Today, it's a grassy knoll perfect for a summer stroll or picnic.

Sleeping

Salisbury has a good batch of characterful hotels and heritage-hugging B&Bs.

Salisbury YHA Hostel (☎ 0870-770 6018; salisbury@yha.org.uk; Milford Hill; dm £17.50; ⊠) A welcoming hostel in a 19th-century building, with doubles, dorms, cafe-bar, laundry and dappled gardens.

Rokeby Guesthouse (☎ 329800; www.rokebyguesthouse.co.uk; 3 Wain-a-long Rd; s/d from £45/55; ⊠ 💻) Fancy furnishing and lovely bay windows make this cheerful B&B stand out from the crowd. Also has wi-fi.

Old Rectory (☎ 502702; www.theoldrectory-bb.co.uk; 75 Belle Vue Rd; s £35-50, d £55-80; ⊠) This serene B&B has spick-and-span rooms and a delightful enclosed garden.

Websters (☎ 339779; www.websters-bed-breakfast.com; 11 Hartington Rd; s/d £40/58; ⊠ 💻) Exterior charms include quaint blue shutters and dinky arched windows. Inside it's flowery wallpaper and a genuinely warm welcome.

Eating & Drinking

There are plenty of budget cafes and sandwich bars in central Salisbury.

our pick **Bird & Carter** (3 Fish Row; snacks from £4; ⏲ 8.30am-6pm Mon-Sat, 10am-4pm Sun) Nestling amid 15th-century beams, this deli-cafe blends old world charm with a tempting array of antipasti, charcuterie and local goodies.

Lemon Tree (☎ 333471; 92 Crane St; mains £8-13; ⏲ lunch & dinner Mon-Sat) The menu at this tiny bistro is packed with character and the patio-garden makes warm-weather dining a delight.

One (☎ 411313; 1-5 Minster St; mains £8-15; ⏲ lunch & dinner) Sloping floors, slanting beams and fake pony-hide chairs surround you in the quirky restaurant above the historic Haunch of Venison pub.

Other good drinking options include the **Ox Row Inn** (11 Ox Row) for local ales, and the 14th-century **New Inn** (41 New St) with beer garden and cathedral views.

Getting There & Away

National Express coaches run to/from London via Heathrow three times per day (£14, 3½ hours). There's a daily coach to Bath (£9, 1½ hours) and Bristol (£9, two hours).

Trains run half-hourly to/from London Waterloo (£27, 1½ hours) and hourly to Exeter (£26, two hours). You can also reach Portsmouth (£14, 1½ hours, hourly), Bath (£8, one hour, hourly) and Bristol (£10, 1¼ hours, hourly).

STONEHENGE

Britain's best-known and most iconic archaeological site, **Stonehenge** (☎ 01980-624715; adult £6.50; ⏲ 9am-7pm Jul-Aug, 9.30am-6pm mid-Mar–May & Sep–mid-Oct, 9.30am-4pm Oct–mid-Mar) has attracted pilgrims, poets and philosophers for millennia. Most visitors today seek spooky mysticism or just want to marvel at the prehistoric engineering project that brought these huge rocks from Wales about 5000 years ago. The reality is a ring of stones surrounded by barbed wire in a field next to a noisy main road, so the best time to arrive is in the morning when the crowds are small, and with luck some mist to disguise modern trappings. Even better, **Stone Circle Access Visits** (☎ 343834; adult £13) are available in the evening and early morning; with only 26 places, you'll need to book, but the VIP viewing is worth the expense.

Stonehenge is around 9 miles north of Salisbury. The **Stonehenge Tour** (☎ 336855; £11) leaves Salisbury's railway and bus stations hourly (half-hourly June to August); and you can hop off at Old Sarum (p185) on the way back.

AVEBURY

Older and more tranquil than Stonehenge, and one of the largest megalithic monuments in Britain, **Avebury Stone Circle** (☎ 01672-539250; admission free) surrounds the pretty village of the same name. The stones themselves are smaller than Stonehenge's, but it's great to stroll around without restriction.

The fascinating **Alexander Keiller Museum** (☎ 01672-539250; admission £4.20; ⏲ 10am-6pm Apr-Oct, 10am-4pm Nov-Mar) provides interesting context on the region's mysterious past and other nearby features, including pyramid-shaped **Silbury Hill**, Europe's largest prehistoric construction, a couple of (walkable) miles away.

To reach Avebury, buses run hourly from Salisbury (£6.50 return).

BATH

☎ 01225 / pop 90,100

Getting lost is the first thing any visitor to Bath should do. Its grand streets and teeming alleys, lined with honey-coloured stone buildings, are a stroller's delight and perfect for unplanned exploration. But while it's tempting to just keep walking, there are some sights in this Unesco World Heritage city that are well worth stopping for.

History

Bath's enduring popularity for visitors is based on a stroke of geological luck. Hot springs bubble to the surface here, and legend has it King Bladud, father of King Lear, founded the city some 2800 years ago after he was cured of leprosy by a dip in the waters. A few centuries later, the Romans created Aquae Sulis, an enormous complex of public baths and temples, and the medieval era was one of monastic devotion with the town becoming a religious centre and the site of an important abbey. In the early 18th century, Bath's hot waters attracted the fashionable glitterati for restorative sojourns, and the present-day city owes much of its appearance to this golden age.

Orientation & Information

Bath's train station (called Bath Spa) is on the southern edge of the centre. When we were researching here, the bus station was temporarily on Avon St, about 500m away; by mid-2009 it's due back near the train station. The main historic attractions occupy an area north of the train station.

The **TIC** (☎ 0906-711 2000; www.visitbath.co.uk; Abbey Churchyard; per min £0.50; ⏰ 9.30am-5pm Mon-Sat, 10am-4pm Sun) is on the southern side of the abbey. Internet access is available at **Retailer Internet** (☎ 443181; 13 Manvers St; per 20 min £1; ⏰ 9am-9pm Mon-Sat, 3-9pm Sun) near the train station.

Sights

ROMAN BATHS

The unmissable heart of any visit, the **Roman Baths Museum** (☎ 477785; www.romanbaths.co.uk; Abbey Churchyard; adult £11; ⏰ 9am-6pm Mar-Jun & Sep-Oct, 9am-10pm Jul & Aug, 9.30am-5.30pm Nov-Feb) offers a tangible link with Britain's historic past. While you may not want to dive into the steaming green pools, the largely intact Roman engineering is fascinating. It gets very busy in summer; you can usually dodge the worst crowds by visiting early on a midweek morning.

BATH ABBEY

Edgar, the first king of united England, was crowned in a church here in 973, and the present **Bath Abbey** (☎ 422462; www.bathabbey.org; admission £2.50; ⏰ 9am-6pm Mon-Sat Easter-Oct, 9am-4.30pm Nov-Easter, afternoons only Sun) dates from 1499 to 1616, making it the last great medieval church built in England. Before you go in, take a moment to marvel at the extraordinary exterior of heavenly ladders with angels ascending and descending (head first). Highlights of the well-scrubbed interior include a spider-web vaulted ceiling and intricate stained-glass windows.

ROYAL CRESCENT & THE CIRCUS

The crowning glory of Georgian Bath is the **Royal Crescent**, a semicircular terrace of majestic houses overlooking a private lawn and the green sweep of Royal Victoria Park. Built between 1767 and 1775, the houses were originally rented for the season by wealthy socialites. These days, flats are keenly sought after, and entire houses almost never come up for sale.

For a glimpse into the splendour of Georgian life, head for **No 1 Royal Crescent** (☎ 428126; www.bath-preservation-trust.org.uk; adult £5; ⏰ 10.30am-4pm Tue-Sun Feb-Oct), which contains an astonishing amount of period furniture.

Nearby is **The Circus**, a magnificent circle of 30 Georgian townhouses, where plaques commemorate famous residents such as Thomas Gainsborough, Clive of India and David Livingstone.

ASSEMBLY ROOMS

Opened in 1771, the city's glorious **Assembly Rooms** (☎ 477789; Bennett St; admission free; ⏰ 11am-6pm Mar-Oct, 11am-5pm Nov-Feb) were where fashionable Bath socialites once gathered to waltz, play cards and listen to the latest chamber music. Most days, you're free to wander; highlights include the card-room, tearoom and the truly splendid ballroom – all lit by their original 18th-century chandeliers.

Sleeping

Bath gets busy in summer, so book ahead if you can. B&Bs generally give better value for money the further you head from the city centre.

Bath Backpackers' Hostel (☎ 446787; bath@hostels.co.uk; 13 Pierrepont St; dm £12-13; 💻) It may be grungy (worn carpets, saggy beds), but this

BRITAIN

hostel is central and friendly, with a party 'dungeon', no curfew and (therefore) a fair bit of noise at night.

Bath YHA Hostel (☎ 0870 770 5688; bath@yha.org.uk; dm £14, d from £35; ⊠ 💻) With refurbished rooms, hostels don't come much grander than this Italianate mansion, a mile and a steep climb (or a short hop on bus 18) from the centre.

YMCA (☎ 325900; www.bathymca.co.uk; Broad St Pl; dm £14-16, s/d £30/40; ⊠ 💻) Bright fabrics in the dorms, excellent facilities, onsite cafe, super-central location and knock-down prices – what's not to like?

Henry Guest House (☎ 424052; 6 Henry St; www.thehenry.com; s £35-65, d £70-130; ⊠) Some of the best-value rooms in town, just five minutes'

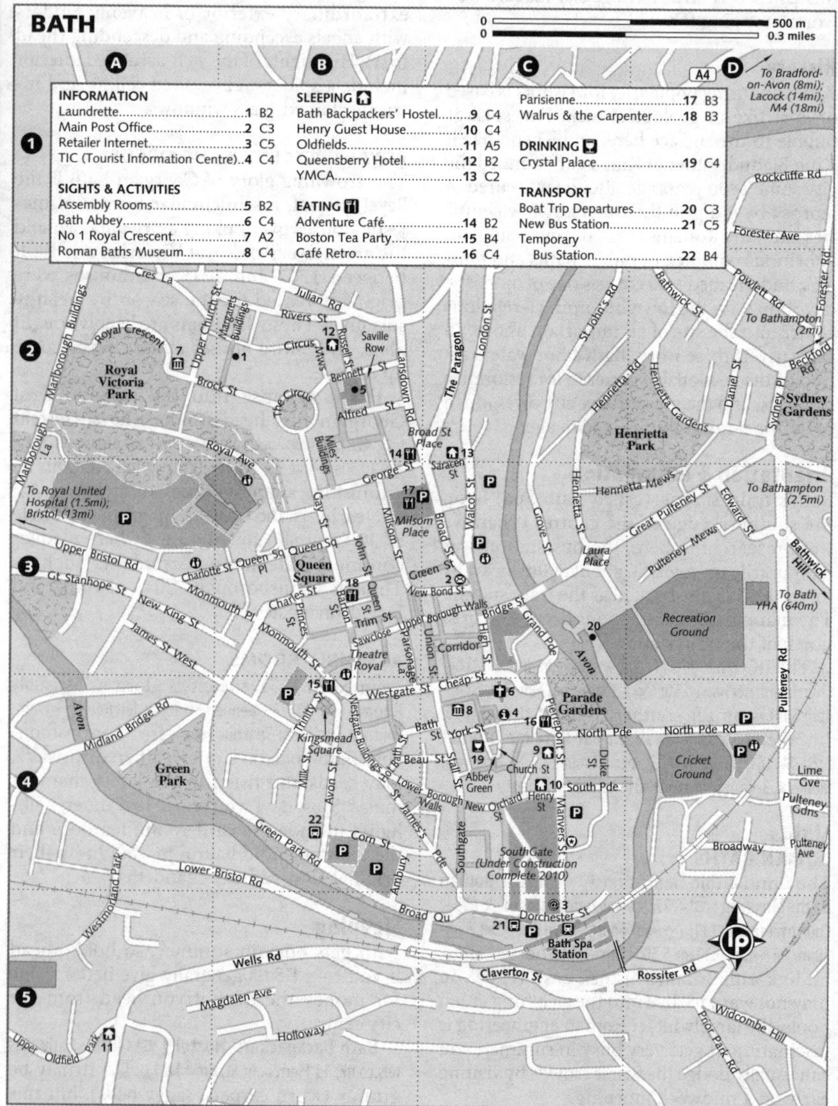

SPLURGE

OUR PICK **Queensberry Hotel** (☎ 447928; www.thequeensberry.co.uk; 4 Russell St; s/d from £95/105; ☒) One to save your pennies for. This boutique barnstormer is sexy, swanky and super, a place where modern fabrics, muted colour schemes and funky throws meet polished wardrobes, feature fireplaces and Zen-tinged furniture. Not to mention gleaming bathrooms, designer-print cushions and oversized beds. Prepare to be pampered.

walk from the centre. Crisp linens, ornate fireplaces and mock-Georgian chairs.

Oldfields (☎ 317984; www.oldfields.co.uk; 102 Wells Rd; s £49-99, d £65-135; ☒) One of the best deals in Bath: spacious rooms and soft beds for comfort, brass bedsteads and antiques for character.

Eating & Drinking

Plenty of eating options line the main streets of Bath, but it's worth exploring the back alleys for something unexpected.

Boston Tea Party (19 Kingsmead Sq; mains from £4; ⌚ Mon-Sat) Popular cafe with outside tables, and more chance of finding a seat than the places near the Abbey.

Adventure Café (5 Princes Bldgs; mains £4-8) Californian bohemia meets urban chic – cappuccinos by morning, ciabattas at noon, cocktails after dark.

Café Retro (☎ 339347; 18 York St; mains £5-11; ⌚ breakfast, lunch & dinner, closed Sun & Mon eve) A quirky gem and ideal spot to munch a burger, linger over lunch or sink a salad.

Parisienne (Milsom Pl; mains £7-13; ⌚ breakfast & lunch) This delightful cafe has a Left Bank air thanks to a courtyard terrace and menu of baguettes, croissants and more.

Walrus & the Carpenter (☎ 314864; 28 Barton St; mains £7-15; ⌚ lunch & dinner) A classic Bath bistro with mismatched furniture, chummy service and down-home food.

Crystal Palace (Abbey Green) This popular pub is tucked away in the shadow of the abbey on a tree-shaded green.

Getting There & Away

National Express coaches run to/from London (£21, 3½ hours, 10 daily) via Heathrow (£17.50, three hours). Trains run to/from London Paddington (advance/peak £20/60, 1½ hours, half hourly) and Cardiff (£15, 1¼ hours, four hourly), plus several each hour to/from Bristol (£5, 11 minutes). Trains also go to/from Oxford approximately hourly (£17, 1½ hours, change at Didcot Parkway), and Portsmouth (£29, 2½ hours) hourly via Salisbury (£13, one hour).

BRISTOL

☎ 0117 / pop 393,300

The most exciting city in the southwest, this once-decrepit port now boasts a hip cultural scene, trend-setting populace and a wealth of historic and modern attractions. Under the new-found swagger, Bristol's past includes the legacies of engineering genius Isambard Kingdom Brunel as well as the transatlantic slave trade. Mix in the work of guerrilla graffiti artist Banksy and a cutting-edge club-scene and you get something real and raw – and just a little rough around the edges.

Orientation & Information

The heart of the city centre is around the markets and redeveloped docklands. Park St is lined with trendy shops and cafes, while a strip of Whiteladies Rd is the hub of bar and restaurant life. West of the centre is the genteel suburb of Clifton and iconic Bristol landmark Clifton Suspension Bridge. The main train station is Bristol Temple Meads, about a mile southeast of the centre. The coach station is northeast of the city centre.

As in any city, keep your wits about you after dark, especially around St Paul's, a run-down area with a heavy drug scene, just north-east of the centre.

The **TIC** (☎ enquiries 0906 711 2191 per min 50p, accommodation 0845 408 0474; www.visitbristol.co.uk; Harbourside; ⌚ 10am-6pm Mar-Oct, 10am-5pm Mon-Sat, 11am-4pm Sun Nov-Feb) is well stocked with local info. For internet, try **Bristol Central Library** (☎ 903 7200; College Green; internet access free; ⌚ 9.30am-7.30pm Mon, Tue & Thu, 10am-5pm Wed, 9am-5pm Fri & Sat, 1-5pm Sun).

Sights

Explore@Bristol (☎ 915 5000; www.at-bristol.org.uk; Anchor Rd; adult £9; ⌚ 10am-5pm) is Bristol's impressive science museum, with zones spanning space, technology and the human brain. It's fun, imaginative and highly interactive. A

Book your stay at lonelyplanet.com/hotels

GO BY BOAT

As befitting a city with nautical heritage, a great way to get around is on the **Bristol Ferry Boat** (☎ 927 3416; www.bristolferry.com), cruising between the city centre and Hotwells (40 minutes, 12 to 16 daily year-round), via *SS Great Britain* and Mardyke. There's also a service from the city centre to Temple Meads (40 minutes, six to 10 daily April to September, weekends only October to March), via Welsh Back, Bristol Bridge and Castle Park. An adult single fare is £1.60, or £7 for a day's unlimited travel.

£4 million aquarium at the same site should be open by the time you read this.

Victorian engineer Isambard Kingdom Brunel designed the mighty transatlantic steamship **SS Great Britain** (☎ 926 0680; www.ssgreatbritain.org; adult £10.95; ⏲ 10am-4.30pm) in 1843. Abandoned in the South Atlantic, and finally towed back to Bristol in 1970, a renovation program has restored the ship's former splendour.

The avant-garde **Arnolfini Arts Centre** (☎ 917 2300; www.arnolfini.org.uk; 16 Narrow Quay; admission free; ⏲ 10am-6pm Tue-Sun) remains the top venue in town for dance, photography and art exhibitions.

A £25 million scheme to turn the city's old Industrial Museum into a flagship **Museum of Bristol** is due to be completed by 2011.

Sleeping

Bristol Backpackers (☎ 925 7900; www.bristolbackpackers.co.uk; 17 St Stephen's St; dm/tw £15/36; ⊠ 🖳) This longstanding traveller's friend is a decent budget option, although the dorms and doubles are cramped and crowded in summer.

Bristol YHA Hostel (☎ 0870 770 5726; bristol@yha.org.uk; 14 Narrow Quay; dm £18-20, s/d £25/40; ⊠ 🖳) A great option with fantastic location, superb facilities, en-suite four-bed dorms and doubles, and excellent coffee lounge.

Arches House (☎ 924 7398; www.arches-hotel.co.uk; 132 Cotham Brow; s £30-45, d £52-63; ⊠) Vegetarian organic breakfasts and renewable energy – an eco-friendly gem.

Downs Edge (☎ 968 3264; www.downsedge.com; Saville Rd; s/d from £55/75; ⊠ 🖳) A few miles from the centre and surrounded by botanical gardens, the antique-filled rooms create a country house atmosphere. Wi-fi available.

Eating & Drinking

Good options line the Harbourside – the alfresco dining areas here are especially popular in summer – and you'll find plenty more options around the city centre. Our favourites:

Pieminister (24 Stokes Croft; pies £3; ⏲ 10am-7pm Sat, 11am-4pm Sun) Dragging the good old British pie into the 21st-century.

Rocotillo's (☎ 929 7207; 1 Queens Row; mains from £4; ⏲ breakfast & lunch) Bristol's version of a traditional American diner, complete with leather booths.

Planet Pizza (☎ 907 7112; 83 Whiteladies Rd; pizzas from £10; ⏲ 11am-11pm; 🖳) Technicolour eatery with 12-inch specials big enough to share. Wi-fi, too.

Clifton Sausage (☎ 973 11192; 7-9 Portland St; mains £10-18; ⏲ lunch & dinner) Groovy gastro-pub serving up eight types of bangers 'n' mash.

Elbow Room (64 Park St) Part dimly lit bar, part hustler's pool hall, favourite hang-out for a style-conscious crowd.

Avon Gorge Hotel (Sion Hill; www.avongorge-hotel-bristol.com) This hotel's heyday has passed, but its panoramic drinks terrace is the place to watch the sun set.

Pipe & Slippers (118 Cheltenham Rd) Unpretentious pub with real ale on tap.

Clubbing

The Bristol club scene moves fast; a copy of listings mag **Venue** (www.venue.co.uk; £1.50) is a sound investment.

Timbuk2 (☎ 945 8459; 22 Small St; admission £5-10; ⏲ 9am-2pm) Scruffy-chic club-venue, with a mixed bag of breaks, house and jungle.

Native (☎ 930 4217; www.nativebristol.co.uk; 15 Small St; admission £5-8) Bristol's top ticket, a tiny 200-cover club always on the cutting edge.

Getting There & Away

National Express coaches go to/from London (from £10, 2½ hours, at least hourly), Cardiff (£7, 1¼ hours, nine daily) and Exeter (£12, two hours, four daily). Bus 375/376 goes to Glastonbury (1¼ hours) every half-hour (hourly on Sunday).

Bristol has two main train stations: Bristol Temple Meads is near the city centre; Bristol Parkway is several miles north. From Temple Meads, there are services to Bath (single £5.50, 11 minutes, four per hour) and London (from £20, 1¾ hours, at least hourly) and numerous southwest destinations.

GLASTONBURY

☎ 01458 / pop 8430

Druids, mystics and straggle-haired hippies converge like ley lines on this pretty Somerset town that has reinvented itself as a New Age capital of England.

The **TIC** (☎ 832954; www.glastonburytic.co.uk; The Tribunal, 9 High St; 10am-5pm Apr-Sep, 10am-4pm Oct-Mar) is used to fielding questions about vegie restaurants and the likely remains of King Arthur.

The town's youthful summer vibe is exemplified by **Glastonbury Festival** (☎ tickets 0870 120 0332; www.glastonburyfestivals.co.uk), a long weekend of music, theatre and New Age shenanigans – and one of England's favourite outdoor events. More than 100,000 turn up to writhe around in the grassy fields (or deep mud) at Pilton Farm, 8 miles east of Glastonbury.

Sights

Beyond the joss-sticks, Glastonbury is reputed to be the birthplace of English Christianity, and the main attraction is romantically ruined **Glastonbury Abbey** (☎ 832267; www.glastonburyabbey.com; Magdalene St; adult £5; 9.30am-6pm), where intricately carved arch and pillar remnants indicate a once-stunning structure. Most visitors spend a couple of minutes reflecting in front of an area marked as King Arthur's grave. As with many of Glastonbury's attractions, faith is the key.

On the edge of town, **Glastonbury Tor** is a derelict hilltop church tower. Even if you don't believe it's the mythic Isle of Avalon, or a gateway to the underworld, it's a lovely spot to bring a picnic and enjoy the panoramic views.

Sleeping

If you're a fan of wind chimes and homemade muesli, then Glastonbury's accommodation won't disappoint.

Glastonbury Backpackers (☎ 833353; www.glastonburybackpackers.com; 4 Market Pl; dm/tw/d £14/35/40;) A happy, hippy hang-out, with doubles and dorms in jazzy colours, TV lounge, kitchen and cafe-bar.

Parsnips (☎ 835599; www.parsnips-glastonbury.co.uk; 99 Bere Lane; s/d £50/65;) Swimming against the tie-die and crystal tide, this stylish B&B opts instead for a fresh design with gingham flourishes and plumped up quilts.

Eating & Drinking

Rainbow's End (17A High St; mains £4-7; 10am-4pm) The classic wholefood cafe, with potted plants, wooden tables and a rotating menu of organic offerings.

Mocha Berry (14 Market Pl; mains £5-8; Sun-Wed) This ever-popular cafe is the top spot for a frothy latte or a stack of breakfast pancakes.

George & Pilgrim (☎ 831146; 1 High St; mains £7-10; lunch daily, dinner Mon-Sat) The creaking timbers and stone arches in this 15th-century inn show that Glastonbury's New Age incarnation is a mere blip on a very ancient time line.

Getting There & Away

There's one early-morning National Express coach to Bath (£6, 1¼ hours) and on to London (£19, 4¼ hours). Bus 376 serves Wells (30 minutes, hourly) and Bristol (1¼ hours).

EXMOOR NATIONAL PARK

Straddling the counties of Somerset and Devon, and perched on the coast, exquisite Exmoor offers lovely beaches, dramatic seacliffs, verdant valleys, tumbling streams, peaceful farmland and expansive moors perfect for strolls and hikes.

The park is about 21 miles wide and just 12 miles from north to south. Main towns with TICs include Lynton and Porlock, and two good websites are www.exmoor-nationalpark.gov.uk and www.visit-exmoor.info.

There are plenty of places to sleep and eat in Exmoor, catering for all budgets. **Exford YHA Hostel** (☎ 0870 770 5828; exford@yha.org.uk; Exe Mead; dm £13.95;) makes an excellent budget base, a short walk from the village centre – and pub. In Porlock are two favourites:

Reines House (☎ 01643-862913; www.reineshouse.co.uk; Parson St; s £25, d £50-54;) Simplicity and bargain prices define this snug B&B.

Ship Inn (☎ 01643-862507; www.shipinnporlock.co.uk; High St; mains £7-14; s/d £40/60; lunch & dinner) Favoured haunt of smugglers; great beer and pub grub.

For getting around, bus 400, the Exmoor Explorer (round trip £6) runs a circular route via Minehead, Dunster, Exford and Porlock, twice daily Saturdays and Sundays June to September, plus Tuesday and Thursday late July to the end of August.

DARTMOOR NATIONAL PARK

Dartmoor is an ancient and compelling landscape, very different from the rest of Devon. Exposed granite hills (called tors) dot the horizon, each linked by swathes of honey-tinged moorland – wild and treeless on the high ground. You'll find its desolate beauty exhilarating or chilling – or quite possibly a bit of both.

Orientation & Information

This 368-sq-mile park is popular with hikers and mountain-bikers, but with notoriously changeable weather and visibility-crushing fog it's not a place for the unprepared. Most visitors stick to the eastern side, near the main settlements, while serious walkers get away from it all on the western edge.

For local information, the **High Moorland Visitor Centre** (☎ 01822-890414; www.dartmoor-npa.gov.uk; 10am-4pm) is in Princetown, a large village at the heart of the moor. Smaller centres include **Postbridge** (☎ 01822-880272) and **Haytor** (☎ 01364-661520).

Note that the military uses part of Dartmoor for training – with live ammunition. Details are available at TICs or the **Firing Information Service** (☎ 08004 584858; www.dartmoor-ranges.co.uk).

Sleeping

B&Bs are plentiful in the larger settlements on the edge of the park (like Buckfastleigh, Okehampton and Tavistock) plus in the villages on the moor itself. The following are some ideas to get you started:

Plume of Feathers (☎ 01822-890240; www.theplumeoffeathers.co.uk; Plymouth Hill, Princetown; dm/s/d £13/35/70; 11.30am-8.30pm) This place offers no-nonsense B&B, bunk-bed dorms and bar food.

Bellever YHA Hostel (☎ 0870 770 5692; bellever@yha.org.uk; Postbridge; dm £14; Mar-Oct) This former farm, 1 mile south of Postbridge, has bags of character, a huge kitchen, lots of rustic stone walls and cosy dorms.

Sparrowhawk Backpackers (☎ 01647-440318; www.sparrowhawkbackpackers.co.uk; 45 Ford St, Moretonhampstead; dm/d £15/35) Eco-friendly hostel with bright dorms in converted stables.

Railway Inn (☎ 01822-890240; Plymouth Hill, Princetown; s/d £35/70) Similar to the Plume of Feathers, and right next door.

Getting Around

Late July to late August, bus 82, the Transmoor Link, runs twice each weekday between Exeter and Plymouth, across the moor via Postbridge, Princetown and Moretonhampstead. It also runs twice on Saturdays from May to September. On Sundays year round there are two to five services.

NEWQUAY

☎ 01637 / pop 19,570

The surf capital of Cornwall (and the whole of Britain), noisy Newquay seems like a great summer-long party. If you're here for the waves, you'll meet plenty of like-minded souls on the 11 sandy stretches around town, especially the ever-popular **Fistral Beach** and the learner-friendly **Watergate Bay**. There's a **TIC** (☎ 854020; www.newquay.co.uk; Marcus Hill; 9.30am-5.30pm Mon-Sat, 9.30am-12.30pm Sun), and for board rental or lessons surf shops are dotted around the town.

Sleeping

Newquay has stacks of surf-happy lodges and hostels:

Reef Surf Lodge (☎ 879058; www.reefsurflodge.info; 10-12 Berry Rd; dm £15-30, d £35-70;) Clean, smart and well organised – but it is still a surf lodge, so expect dorms, shared facilities and chronic overcrowding in summer.

Base Surf Lodge (☎ 874852; www.basesurflodge.com; 20 Tower Rd; dm £15-20) Superior surf lodge with slatted blinds, tiled floors, sunset murals and pine bunks.

Goofys (☎ 872684; www.goofys.co.uk; 5 Headland Rd; dm £15-25, d £30-60;) Friendly, funky place bridging the gap between surf lodge and B&B.

Carlton Hotel (☎ 872658; www.carltonhotelnewquay.co.uk; 6 Dane Rd; s £45, d £68-94;) B&B with frilly beds, DVD players and country-cream furnishings.

ST IVES

☎ 01736 / pop 9870

Once a busy fishing port, St Ives is now best known for its wonderful beaches and as a centre for the arts, with cobbled alleyways lined with galleries, shops and cafes – an intriguing mix of boutique chic and traditional seaside.

For all the usual info there's a **TIC** (☎ 796297; ivtic@penwith.gov.uk; Street-an-Pol; 9am-5pm Mon-Sat, 10am-4pm Sun) while the top sight is **Tate St Ives** (☎ 796226; www.tate.org.uk/stives; adult £5.75; 10am-5pm Mar-Oct, 10am-4pm Tue-Sun Nov-Feb), the southwest satellite of the popular London gallery, showcasing local legends like Barbara Hepworth and John Wells. There's a panoramic top-floor cafe, plus free talks and tours, keeping the place livelier than a hungry seagull.

Sleeping options include **St Ives International Backpackers** (☎ 799444; www.backpackers.co.uk/st-ives; The Stennack; dm £12-18;), a longstanding shabby hostel; and **Treliska** (☎ 797678; www.treliska.com; 3 Bedford Rd; s/d from £40/64;), a beautifully finished B&B far beyond lace doilies.

> **DETOUR: EDEN PROJECT**
>
> If anything is emblematic of Cornwall's regeneration, it's the **Eden Project** (☎ 01726-811911; www.edenproject.com; adult £15; ⏲ 10am-6pm Apr-Oct, 10am-4.30pm Nov-Mar). Just a few years ago it was an abandoned clay pit, a symbol of the county's industrial decline. Now it's home to the largest plant-filled greenhouses in the world and a monumental education project about the natural world. Tropical, temperate and desert environments have been recreated, so a single visit carries you from the steaming rainforests of South America to the dry deserts of Northern Africa.

PENZANCE

☎ 01736 / pop 21,168

The westernmost town in Britain, Penzance is larger and a bit scruffier than other Cornish neighbours, but some say it's better for it, and it makes an excellent base for exploring the rest of west Cornwall and around Land's End.

The **TIC** (☎ 362207; www.visit-westcornwall.com; ⏲ 9am-5pm Mon-Fri, plus 10am-4pm Sat Easter-Sep, plus 10am-2pm Sun Jul & Aug) is next to the bus station.

The top sight is the island abbey of **St Michael's Mount** (☎ 710507; adult £6.60; ⏲ 10.30am-5pm Sun-Fri Mar-Oct) – one of Cornwall's iconic landmarks. Set on craggy cliffs and connected to the mainland by a cobbled causeway, there's been a monastery here since at least the 5th century. You can walk across at low tide and there are ferries at high tide in summer.

Places to stay:

Penzance Backpackers (☎ 363836; www.pzbackpack.com; Alexandra Rd; dm/d £15/32; 💻) Laid-back indie hostel; a touch worn, but clean, fun and friendly.

Penzance YHA Hostel (☎ 0870 770 5992; penzance@yha.org.uk; Castle Horneck, Alverton; dm £15.50; 💻) A Georgian manor on the outskirts of town.

Glencree House (☎ 362026; www.glencreehouse.co.uk; 2 Mennaye Rd; d £40-62, ⊠) Sea-views and great breakfasts make this a great budget B&B.

LAND'S END

At the extreme southwesterly point of mainland Britain, the coal-black cliffs, heather-covered headlands and booming Atlantic surf should steal the show. Unfortunately the view is rather spoilt by a tawdry theme park called **Legendary Land's End** (☎ 0870 458 0099; www.landsend-landmark.co.uk; adult £11; ⏲ 10am-5pm summer, 10am-3pm winter). But you can bypass the kitsch and tat, and opt for an exhilarating clifftop stroll instead.

Land's End is 9 miles from Penzance (and 874 miles from John O'Groats – see p225). Bus 1/1A travels to/from Penzance (around seven daily Monday to Saturday), while bus 300 serves St Ives (four daily May to October).

CENTRAL ENGLAND

The geographic heartland of England is a mix of wildly differing scenes, with historic towns like Oxford and Stratford-upon-Avon and the flower-decked villages in the Cotswolds. In this section we also cover the lush dales and peaty moors of the Peak District, although some locals would say they're in northern, not central, England. Either way, this region which should definitely feature on your itinerary.

Destinations are listed roughly south to north. For local information, see www.visitheartofengland.com, www.oxfordshirecotswolds.org and www.visitpeakdistrict.com.

OXFORD

☎ 01865 / pop 134,200

Renowned as one of the world's most famous university towns, Oxford lives up to its advance billing as a fascinating, colourful, history-flavoured place. It's also a crowded hotspot in summer – so bypass jostling tour groups by coming early or late in the season if you can.

For visitors short on time, 'Oxford or Cambridge?' is a common conundrum. Though Oxford is not quite as quaint or pretty as Cambridge, it makes up for this with its more vibrant atmosphere and wider array of attractions.

History

Oxford University is the oldest in Britain, with the first of its 39 colleges dating from the 13th century. This august institution's history includes a 14th-century riot over the quality of a local innkeeper's wine (it seems students have changed little since), and its plethora of notable graduates includes William Morris, Oscar Wilde, Lewis Carroll and, the evidence suggests, Sherlock Holmes. All men, you note. Women were not admitted to Oxford's

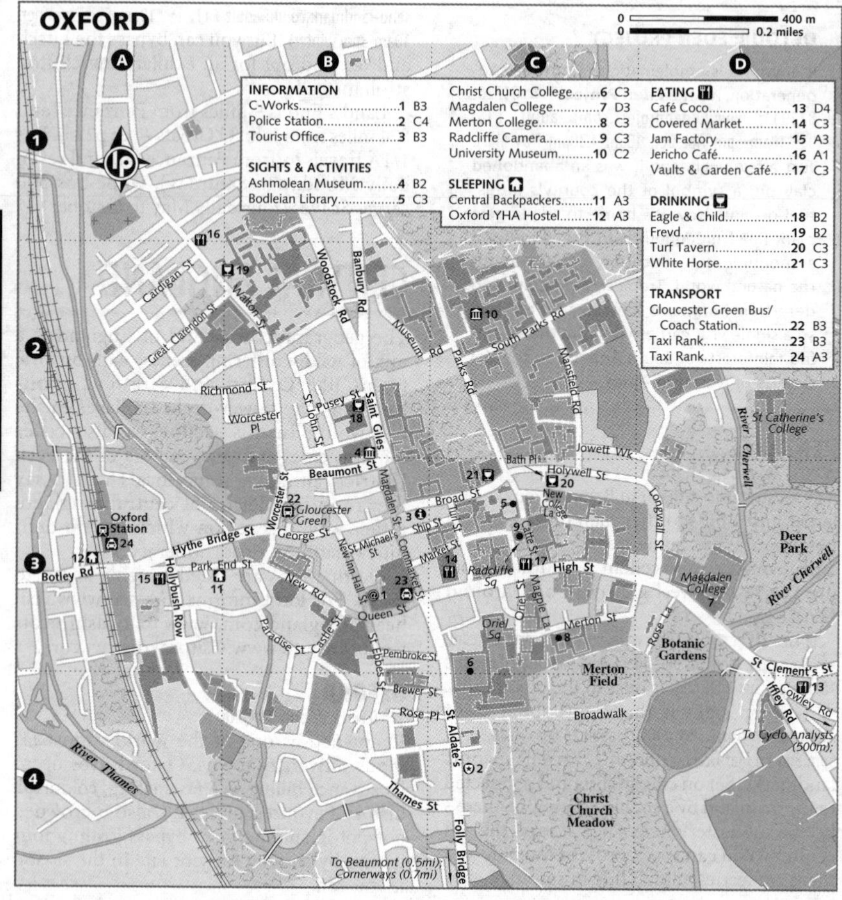

closeted halls until 1878 and even then were not allowed to receive degrees until the 1920s.

Orientation & Information

Surrounded by rivers on its eastern, southern and western edges, pedestrian-friendly Oxford is best explored on foot (or by bike, as per the locals – keep an eye out for zooming cyclists). The train station is a 10-minute stroll west of the centre. The bus station on Gloucester Green (there's no green) is even nearer.

The **TIC** (☎ 252200; www.visitoxford.org; 15-16 Broad St; 🕑 9.30am-5pm Mon-Sat, to 6pm Thu-Sat Jul & Aug, 10am-4pm Sun) is packed with maps and brochures. Web access is available at **C-Works** (☎ 722044; 1st fl, New Bailey House, New Inn Hall St; per 50min £1; 🕑 9am-9pm Mon-Sat, 9am-7pm Sun).

Sights

It is absolutely impossible to miss Oxford's crenulated college buildings, some surrounded by fortress-like walls to keep out intellectual inferiors. Fool the dons by assuming a foppish haircut and clutching weighty tomes as you stroll around town. The following colleges are highlights (though note that colleges may sometimes unexpectedly close to visitors).

The largest and grandest of all of Oxford's colleges, **Christ Church** (☎ 276492; www.chch.ox.ac.uk; St Aldate's; adult £4.90; 🕑 9am-5pm Mon-Sat, 1-5pm Sun) is also its most popular. The magnificent buildings, illustrious history and latter-day fame as a Harry Potter location has tourists coming in droves.

Arguably Oxford's prettiest college, **Magdalen** (☎ 276000; www.magd.ox.ac.uk; High St; adult £4; ⌚ noon-6pm Jul-Sep, 1-6pm/dusk Oct-Jun) combines stately buildings with a verdant tapestry of landscaped grounds. Enhance your credentials by pronouncing it properly: mawd-len. The architectural highlight is the **cloister**, featuring fantastical carvings said to have inspired the stone statues in CS Lewis' *Chronicles of Narnia*.

From the High St follow wonderfully named Logic Lane to **Merton College** (☎ 276310; www.merton.ox.ac.uk; Merton St; admission free; ⌚ 2-4pm Mon-Fri, 10am-4pm Sat & Sun), one of Oxford's original three colleges.

Oxford's **Bodleian Library** (☎ 277224; www.bodley.ox.ac.uk; Broad St) is one of the oldest public libraries in the world, with more than seven million items on 118 miles of shelving, and seating for 2500 readers.

Nearby is the **Radcliffe Camera** (Radcliffe Sq; ⌚ no public access), a quintessential Oxford landmark and one of the city's most photographed buildings, boasting Britain's third-largest dome.

A vast collection is on display at the **Ashmolean Museum** (☎ 278000; www.ashmolean.org; Beaumont St; admission free; ⌚ 10am-5pm Tue-Sat, noon-5pm Sun), Britain's oldest public museum, including European, Egyptian, Islamic and Chinese art, rare porcelain, tapestries, silverware, and priceless musical instruments.

In a glorious Victorian Gothic building with cast-iron columns, ornate capitals and a soaring glass roof, the **University Museum** (☎ 272950; www.oum.ox.ac.uk; Parks Rd; admission free; ⌚ 10am-5pm) is worth a visit for its architecture alone. But the real draw is the mammoth natural history collection ranging from exotic insects to a towering T-Rex skeleton.

Sleeping

You'll find endless B&Bs along the Iffley, Abingdon, Banbury and Headington roads, and the TIC's *Staying in Oxford* guide (£1) details a wide range of additional options.

Central Backpackers (☎ 242288; www.centralbackpackers.co.uk; 13 Park End St; dm £16-19; 💻) Central, with basic but bright dorms, a decent lounge, satellite TV, rooftop terrace, free internet and luggage storage.

Oxford YHA Hostel (☎ 727275; oxford@yha.org.uk; 2A Botley Rd; dm/d £22/56; 💻) Well-kept and tidy, this is Oxford's best budget option with comfortable dorms and en-suite rooms plus restaurant, library, garden, laundry and lounges.

Budget B&B options:

Beaumont (☎ 241767; www.oxfordcity.co.uk/accom/beaumont; 234 Abingdon Rd; s £45-55, d £ 60-78) A class above most B&Bs at this price; all crisp white linen, mosaic bathrooms and beautiful furniture.

Cornerways (☎ 240135; jeakings@btopenworld.com; 282 Abingdon Rd; s £48, d £76-98) Genial hosts, bright rooms and contemporary decor make this a good bet within walking distance of town.

Eating & Drinking

There's an array of eateries to suit all budgets in Oxford. Bland chain restaurants dominate the scene, especially along George St; head to Walton St or up Cowley Rd for a more interesting selection.

Covered Market (Market St; ⌚ 8am-5.30pm Mon-Sat) Not everything's for eating on the spot, but it's hard to shake the idea that you're wandering around a smorgasbord. A couple of small cafes are ideal for a coffee in a buzzy atmosphere.

Vaults (St Mary's Church; mains £3.25-4.95; ⌚ 10am-5pm) Great selection of wholesome soups, salads and pastas, plus fine views and historic setting – one of the best lunch venues in Oxford.

Jericho Café (112 Walton St; mains £7-9) Everything from coffee and cake to sausages and mash to Lebanese lamb kibbeh.

Café Coco (☎ 200232; 23 Cowley Rd; mains £7-14) Hip hang-out, with classic posters on the walls, vaguely Mediterranean menu and lively atmosphere.

Jam Factory (☎ 244613; www.thejamfactoryoxford.com; 27 Park End St; mains £8-12) Arts centre, bar and restaurant with exhibitions, hearty breakfasts and excellent-value modern British dishes.

Our favourite Oxford drinkeries:

Eagle & Child (49 St Giles) Atmospheric and historic pub with a hotchpotch of nooks and crannies.

Frevd (119 Walton St) Once a neoclassical church, now a happening bar.

Turf Tavern (4 Bath Pl) Much loved and often crowded medieval pub.

White Horse (52 Broad St) Delightful olde-worlde pub; quiet in the afternoon, lively in the evening.

Getting There & Around

Competition on the Oxford–London route is fierce, with **Oxford Espress** (☎ 785400; www.oxfordbus.co.uk) and **Oxford Tube** (☎ 772250; www.oxfordtube.com) running buses (£15 return, 90 minutes) up to every 10 to 15 minutes at peak times.

WORTH THE TRIP: BLENHEIM PALACE

About 8 miles from Oxford is the monumental Baroque fantasy of **Blenheim Palace** (☎ 08700 602080; www.blenheimpalace.com; adult £16.50; ⏲ 10.30am-5.30pm mid-Feb–Oct, Wed-Sun Nov–mid-Dec, park open year-round). The funds to build the house were awarded by a grateful Queen Anne to John Churchill, Duke of Marlborough, after his decisive victory over France at the Battle of Blenheim in 1704, and it was completed in 1722. Now a Unesco World Heritage site, Blenheim (pronounced blen-um) is home to the 11th Duke of Marlborough, and is the historic birthplace of Winston Churchill. The **Churchill Exhibition** explores the life of this still-revered wartime leader. The beautifully landscaped **gardens** are another attraction, making a day trip well worthwhile. To get here from Oxford, bus 20 (£4.20 return, 30 minutes, twice hourly) runs from the train and bus stations to Woodstock village, in the shadow of the palace.

There are half-hourly trains to/from London Paddington (£22.50, one hour). Hourly services also run to/from Bath (£20, 1¼ hours) and Bristol (£21, 1½ hours), changing at Didcot Parkway.

Oxford is best explored on foot – almost everything is within easy reach if you hoof it – or grab the *Cycle into Oxford* map at the TIC and hire some wheels from **Cyclo Analysts** (☎ 424444; 150 Cowley Rd; per day/week £14/40).

THE COTSWOLDS

Dripping with beautiful scenery, glorious villages, atmospheric churches and olde-worlde charm – not to mention celeb hideouts and fine pubs – the Cotswold Hills are as close to chocolate-box England as you'll get, but despite its popularity you can still get off the beaten track.

Orientation

The western side of the Cotswolds is an escarpment running for around 100 miles from Bath towards Stratford-upon-Avon, while the area around Oxford marks the eastern extremity. The northern part of the Cotswolds attracts most visitors – mainly because the local stone (and therefore the buildings) is honey-coloured, whereas further south it tends towards grey. The northern Cotswolds is also where you find three of the most famous towns: Moreton-in-Marsh, Stow-on-the-Wold and Chipping Campden.

Getting There & Away

Coming from London, your best bet for reaching the Cotswolds is the train to Moreton-in-Marsh from London Paddington (£29, 1½ hours, every 1½ hours) via Oxford (£9.70, 35 minutes).

Moreton-in-Marsh

Home to some beautiful buildings (and a main street busy with through traffic), Moreton-in-Marsh is an excellent gateway to the Cotswolds, with several B&Bs, pubs and places to eat. On Tuesday the town bursts into life for its weekly market. For onward travel, **Pulhams Coaches** (☎ 01451-820369; www.pulhamscoaches.com) runs seven services daily between Moreton and Cheltenham (one hour, Monday to Saturday) via Stow-on-the-Wold (15 minutes). Two Sunday services run from May to September only.

Stow-on-the-Wold

With a large market square surrounded by handsome buildings, Stow-on-the-Wold was a wealthy trade town in medieval times. Today it's littered with antique shops, boutiques, tearooms and delis thronged with passengers from passing coach tours. On a quiet day it's a wonderful place but all a little artificial if you're looking for true Cotswold charm. The **TIC** (☎ 01451-831082; Hollis House; ⏲ 9.30-5.30pm Mon-Sat) is on Market Sq. **Stow-on-the-Wold YHA Hostel** (☎ 0870 770 6050; www.yha.org.uk; The Square; dm £15.95; 💻) is a great budget option, with small dorms and a warm welcome.

Chipping Campden

A gem in an area full of achingly pretty villages, Chipping's graceful main street is flanked by a wonderful array of wayward stone cottages, fine terraced houses, ancient inns and historic homes, liberally sprinkled with chichi boutiques and upmarket shops. The helpful **TIC** (☎ 01386-841206; www.visitchippingcampden.com; High St; ⏲ 10am-5pm Mon-Fri) has a town trail guide about the historic buildings. B&B options include **Manor Farm** (☎ 01386-840390; www.manorfarmbnb.demon.co.uk; s/d £55/65), a perfect mix of period charm and contemporary style. Buses 21 and 22 run around hourly to/from Stratford-upon-Avon or Moreton-in-Marsh (no Sunday services). To really get into the countryside, hire a bike from **Cotswold Country Cycles** (☎ 01386-438706; www.cotswoldcountrycycles.com; per day £15).

STRATFORD-UPON-AVON

☎ 01789 / pop 22,200

Few towns are so dominated by one man's legacy as Stratford is by William Shakespeare – England's most famous wordsmith. It's a very popular spot, so be prepared to fight for breathing space in the historic buildings, but if you choose your time, this pretty market town should definitely be on your hit list. Whatever you do, remember that the play's the thing and make sure you catch a performance by the resident Royal Shakespeare Company. It will remind you what all the fuss is about, 450 years after the Bard shuffled off this mortal coil.

Orientation & Information

Stratford's compact old centre is easily explored on foot. The train station is a 15-minute walk west. You can book accommodation, buy theatre tickets and exchange currency at the **TIC** (☎ 0870 160 7930; www.shakespeare-country.co.uk; Bridgefoot; 9am-5pm Mon-Sat, 10am-3pm Sun). For internet access, head to **Cyber Junction** (☎ 263400; www.cyberjunction.co.uk; 28 Greenhill St; per hr £4; 10.30am-5.30pm Mon-Sat).

Sights

Like artefacts in glass cases, there's an unreal quality to the five timber-framed Shakespeare-related houses on Stratford's mostly modern streets. Three are central, one is an easy walk away, and the fifth a drive or bike ride out; all are managed by the **Shakespeare Birthplace Trust** (☎ 204016; www.shakespeare.org.uk; all 5 properties £15, three in-town houses £9; 9am-5pm Mon-Sat, 10am-5pm Sun Jun-Aug, variable at other times).

Shakespeare's Birthplace is a scrubbed-clean Tudor building reputed to be where the Bard entered the world mewling and puking; today, chatty interpreters explain the history.

Shakespeare's daughter Susanna married doctor John Hall, and their fine Elizabethan town house, **Hall's Croft**, stands near **Holy Trinity Church** – where Will is now buried. **Nash's House**, where Shakespeare's granddaughter lived, describes the town's history and contains a collection of 17th-century furniture and tapestries.

Located a mile from the centre, **Anne Hathaway's Cottage** is an idyllic thatch-roofed farmhouse where Shakespeare's wife was raised. **Mary Arden's House**, the childhood home of Shakespeare's mother, is at Wilmcote, 3 miles west. It's now the **Shakespeare Countryside Museum**, with exhibits tracing local rural life over the past four centuries.

Seeing the **Royal Shakespeare Company** (☎ 0844 800 1110; www.rsc.org.uk; tickets £8-38; 9.30am-8pm Mon-Sat) is a must. Several major stars have trod the boards here and production standards are very high. The main Royal Shakespeare Theatre is closed for renovations and due to reopen in 2010. In the meantime, the Company's performances are in the striking temporary Courtyard Theatre by the Other Place. The box office is in the foyer of the Courtyard Theatre until the main theatre reopens.

Sleeping

Stratford's big hotels tend to be geared towards group travel, but B&Bs are plentiful – especially along Grove Rd and Evesham Pl, between the train station and town centre.

Stratford-upon-Avon YHA Hostel (☎ 0870 160 7930; stratford@yha.org.uk; Alveston; dm incl breakfast £19.95;) This four-star youth hostel is in a large, 200-year-old mansion 1.5 miles east of the town centre.

Stratford's cheaper B&B options:

Arrandale (☎ 267112; www.arrandale.netfirms.com; 208 Evesham Rd; s/d incl breakfast £23-46) Neatly kept lodgings, 10 minutes' walk from the centre.

Ambleside Guest House (☎ 297239; www.amblesideguesthouse.co.uk; 41 Grove Rd; s/d from £30/50;) Great non-frilly B&B, with spotless rooms and amiable hosts.

Moonraker House (☎ 268774; www.moonrakerhouse.com; 40 Alcester Rd; s/d incl breakfast from £47/70;) The pristine rooms behind the whitewashed facade of this memorable B&B have a Shakespeare theme.

Eating & Drinking

Shakespeare pilgrimages clearly work up an appetite: there's no shortage of good restaurants. Sheep St is clustered with refined but relaxed eating options, mostly aimed at theatregoers.

Book your stay at lonelyplanet.com/hotels

Vintner Wine Bar (5 Sheep St; mains £6-13; ⌚ 9.30am-10pm Mon-Fri, to 9.30pm Sun) This quirky space has low ceilings, a relaxed atmosphere and a tasty menu of burgers, pastas and good vegetarian options.

Dirty Duck (Waterside) This enchantingly old riverside alehouse is a favourite post-performance thespian watering hole, and the adjoining restaurant (open 11am to 10pm) is good value.

Cox's Yard (Bridgefoot) This large riverside complex, with a pub, cafe and music venue, is a lovely place to enjoy a drink or meal.

Getting There & Around

National Express destinations include Oxford (£9, one hour, daily) and London Victoria (£16.00, 3½ hours, five daily). Trains run to/from London Marylebone (£16, 2¼ hours).

Stratford is small enough to explore on foot, but a bike is good for getting out to the surrounding countryside or rural Shakespeare properties. For rental, contact **Clarkes Cycles** (☎ 205057; Guild St; per half/full day from £6/10; ⌚ 9.15am-5pm Tue-Sat).

PEAK DISTRICT NATIONAL PARK

Squeezed between the industrial Midlands to the south, and the cities of Manchester and Sheffield to the west and east, the 555-sq-mile Peak District is a surprisingly rural area – and one of the finest parts of England for walking, cycling and other outdoor activities. Don't be misled by the name; there are few 'peaks', but plenty of wild moors, rolling farmland and deep valleys – plus prehistoric sites, limestone caves and stately Chatsworth House.

The region is divided into the wilder scenery of the Dark Peak in the north, and the gentler dales of the White Peak in the south. The towns of Buxton to the west or Matlock to the east are good gateways and bases, or you can stay right in the centre at Edale, Bakewell or Castleton.

In and around the park, there are several **TICs** Bakewell (☎ 01629-813227; Bridge St); Buxton (☎ 01298-25106; Pavilion Gardens); Edale (☎ 01433-670207; Grindsbrook); Castleton (☎ 01433-620679; Buxton Rd).

Sleeping

The Peak District has a great selection of B&Bs, hotels and pubs with accommodation. Recommendations include:

Mam Tor House (☎ 01433-670253; www.mamtorhouse.co.uk; Grindsbrook, Edale; r £25) Lovely stained-glass windows distinguish this charming B&B next to the church.

Rambler's Rest (☎ 01433-620125; www.ramblersrest-castleton.co.uk; Mill Bridge, Castleton; s/d from £25/40) This well-appointed 17th-century cottage has comfortable rooms, and is near several great pubs.

our pick **Roseleigh Hotel** (☎ 01298-24904; www.roseleighhotel.co.uk; 19 Broad Walk, Buxton; s/d from £33/70; ⊠ 💻) Travellers get a great welcome in this gorgeous B&B with fine views over picturesque Pavilion Gardens. Also has wi-fi.

Melbourne House (☎ 01629-815357; Buxton Rd, Bakewell; s/d £35/50; ⊠) An inviting B&B in the very best Peak District tradition.

In the heart of the national park are **Castleton YHA Hostel** (☎ 0870 770 5758; castleton@yha.org.uk; Castle St; dm £14; 💻) and **Edale YHA Hostel** (☎ 0870 770 5808; edale@yha.org.uk; dm from £11.95; 💻), the latter also an activity centre to try your hand at caving, kayaking or climbing.

Getting There & Around

National Express coaches run from London Victoria to Manchester and Buxton, from where you can switch to local bus. Derby, south of the park, is another good gateway, from where trains run to Matlock. Trains also run between Sheffield and Manchester via Edale and several other Peak villages. The handiest local bus is the hourly Transpeak service that cuts across the Peak District from Nottingham and Derby to Manchester, via Matlock, Bakewell and Buxton.

EASTERN ENGLAND

Apart from the bustling magnet of Cambridge, few parts of eastern England see many visitors. But Norfolk, Suffolk and Lincolnshire are picturesque counties, and the absence of tourists belies a region well worth exploring, with pretty market towns, gently undulating farm-strewn landscapes, winding rivers and lakes, swathes of beautifully desolate coastline, and gallons of colourful history.

Places in this section are listed roughly north to south. For information see www.visiteastofengland.com.

CAMBRIDGE

☎ 01223 / pop 108,900

Hallowed home of one of the world's most prestigious centres of learning, Cambridge has exquisite architecture and is steeped in scholarly ambience. The university was founded in the 13th century by a splinter group from Oxford – still known locally as the 'other place'. The rivalry has been barely concealed ever since. Famous former students include William Wordsworth, Isaac Newton, Charles Darwin, Stephen Hawking and John Cleese. Yet Cambridge does not rest only on its swotty laurels; it's a lively city with enough designer boutiques and trendy cafes to keep its compact centre teeming with locals and visitors.

Orientation & Information

Cambridge is easily explored on foot or by bike. The main university buildings occupy the city centre. The bus station is also central, while the train station is a 20-minute walk south. The **TIC** (☎ 0871 266 8006; www.visitcambridge.org; Wheeler St; 🕑 10am-5.30pm Mon-Fri, 10am-5pm Sat year-round, 11am-3pm Sun Apr-Sep) is crowded in summer. For internet access, go to **Budget Internet Café** (☎ 313875; 30 Hills Rd; 🕑 9am-11pm) or **CB2** (☎ 508503; 5-7 Norfolk St; 🕑 noon-midnight).

Sights

Cambridge University comprises 31 colleges, and five of these – King's, Queen's, Clare, Trinity and St John's – charge tourists admission. Some other colleges deem visitors too disruptive and simply deny entry. Most colleges close to visitors for the Easter term and all are closed for exams from mid-May to mid-June.

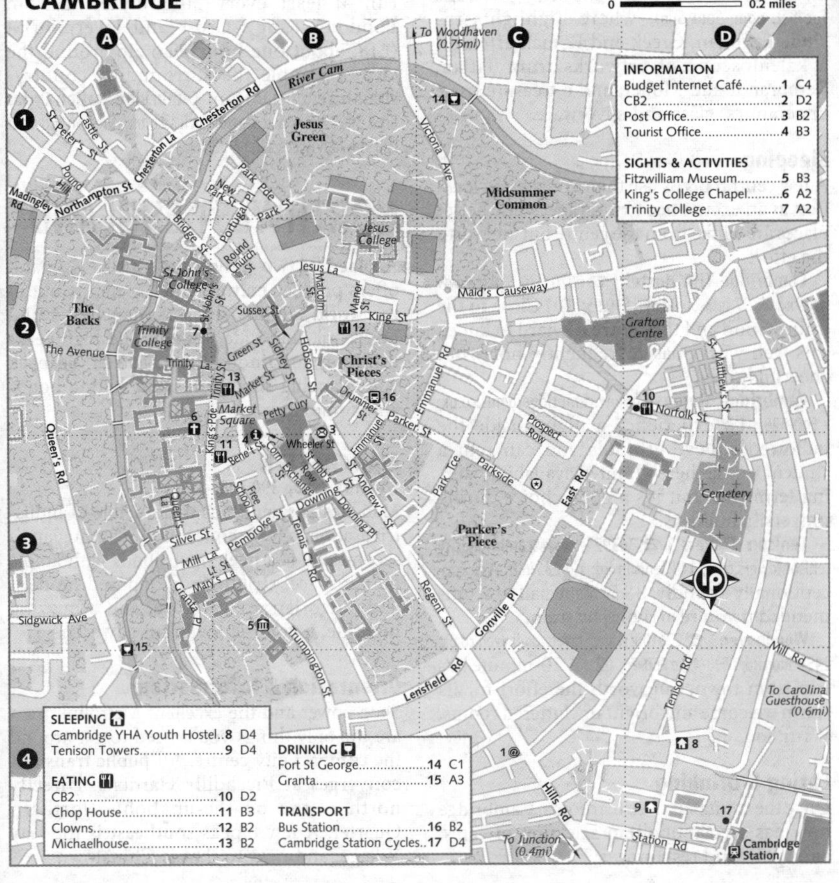

Book your stay at lonelyplanet.com/hotels

Among the unmissable highlights is **King's College Chapel** (☎ 331212; www.kings.cam.ac.uk/chapel; King's Pde; adult £5; ⌚ during term 9.30am-3.30pm Mon-Fri, 9.30am-3.15pm Sat, 1.15pm-2.30pm Sun, outside term 9.30am-4.30pm Mon-Sat, 10am-5pm Sun), a dazzling Tudor testament to Christian devotion with the power to impress even ardent atheists.

Nearby **Trinity College** (☎ 338400; www.trin.cam.ac.uk; Trinity St; admission Mar-Oct £2.50, Nov-Feb free; ⌚ library noon-2pm Mon-Fri, hall 3-5pm, chapel 10am-5pm) is one of the university's grandest and most attractive academic piles. Don't miss the **Wren Library**; its collection includes AA Milne's original *Winnie the Pooh*.

Echoing its history as a centre of discovery, many Cambridge colleges have their own museums, our favourite being the **Fitzwilliam Museum** (☎ 332900; www.fitzmuseum.cam.ac.uk; Trumpington St; admission free; ⌚ 10am-5pm Tue-Sat, noon-5pm Sun), where highlights include Egyptian, Greek and Roman artefacts, a kaleidoscope of artworks from Titian, Rembrandt and Monet, and a treasure trove of ceramics, glass and silverware.

Sleeping

A few central B&Bs use their convenient location as an excuse not to upgrade; some better places are a hike from the centre but are worth the effort.

Cambridge YHA Hostel (☎ 0870 770 5742; www.yha.org.uk; 97 Tenison Rd; dm £19.95; 💻) Close to the train station and the centre it's hard to knock this well-worn, basic, frequently noisy but cheerful hostel.

Cambridge Rooms (www.cambridgerooms.co.uk; r £40-120) To experience a night inside the hallowed college grounds you can rent a student room; there's limited availability during term time but it's a good choice during university holidays.

Tenison Towers (☎ 363924; www.cambridgecitytenisontowers.com; 148 Tenison Rd; s/d £35/60) An exceptionally friendly B&B, especially recommended if you're arriving by train.

Woodhaven (☎ 226108; www.stayatwoodhaven.co.uk; 245 Milton Rd; s £30-45, d £60-75; 💻) A 10-minute bus trip from town, but worth the effort for its warm welcome and bright uncluttered rooms. Wi-fi, too.

Eating & Drinking

Once the capital of twee tearooms, Cambridge now has a cosmopolitan selection of cafes, bars, pubs and restaurants:

our pick **Michaelhouse** (☎ 309167; Trinity St; mains £3.55-6.35; ⌚ 9.30am-5pm Mon-Sat) Sup fairtrade coffee and nibble focaccia in this stylishly converted church.

CB2 (5-7 Norfolk St; mains £4-13) Internet cafe, bistro and music venue, dishing up global cuisine in a relaxed atmosphere.

Clowns (☎ 355711; 54 King St; mains £5-9; ⌚ 8am-midnight) Cheap and cheerful Cambridge institution, with great Italian food.

Chop House (☎ 359506; 1 Kings Pde; mains £9-15) A great place to enjoy classic British cuisine.

Fort St George (Midsummer Common) Ideal summertime pub with river views.

Granta (Newnham Rd) Picturesque waterside pub.

Getting There & Around

Buses to/from Oxford (£9, 3¼ hours) are regular but take a convoluted route. Trains run at least every 30 minutes to/from London's King's Cross and Liverpool St (£18, about one hour). To zip around the city or sample the surrounding countryside, hire a bike from **Cambridge Station Cycles** (☎ 307125; www.stationcycles.co.uk; Station Rd; per half-day/day/week £8/10/20).

NORTHWEST ENGLAND

A place of two halves, northwest England offers popular culture and big nights out in the world-famous cities of Manchester and Liverpool, alongside fresh air and high peaks in the mountainous Lake District. So pack your dancing shoes and your hiking boots, and come on over.

MANCHESTER

☎ 0161 / pop 390,000

Manchester's zenith as the crucible of industrialisation is long gone, and today England's second city is a lively metropolis with ample public space, strikingly juxtaposed modern and Victorian architecture, and a buzzing nightlife, including a vibrant gay scene.

Orientation & Information

Shoe power and the excellent Metrolink tram are the only things you'll need to get around the compact city centre. All public transport converges at Piccadilly Gardens. Directly north is the on-the-up boho Northern Quarter. A few blocks southeast is the Gay Village, and next to that is Chinatown.

The **TIC** (☎ 0871 222 8223; www.visitmanchester.com; Town Hall Extension, St Peter's Sq; ⌚ 10am-5.15pm Mon-Sat, 10am-4.30pm Sun) sells tickets for all sorts of guided walks (£5). Internet access is available at **Central Library** (St Peter's Sq; per 30min £1; ⌚ internet access 1-6pm Mon-Sat) and **L2K Internet Gaming Cafe** (32 Princess St; per 30min £2; ⌚ 9am-9pm).

Sights

Explore the city centre on foot and you'll find some grand Victorian architecture, most notably in Albert Sq, home of the enormous Victorian Gothic **Town Hall**.

Further south, the **Castlefield** district (now dubbed 'urban heritage park') offers a fascinating mosaic of solid old civic structures, warehouses, Roman ruins, serene canalside paths and old pubs – with modern skyscrapers jostling for space in between. The area also contains the excellent **Museum of Science & Industry** (☎ 832 1830; www.msim.org.uk; Liverpool Rd; admission free; ⌚ 10am-5pm) with interactive displays on the city's textile and engineering industries.

The stunning glass triangle that is **Urbis** (☎ 907 9099; www.urbis.org.uk; City Park, Corporation St; admission free; ⌚ 10am-6pm Sun-Wed, 10am-8pm Thu-Sat) is a museum about how a city works and – often – doesn't work, with three floors covered in compelling photographs and interactive videos.

Out in Manchester's rapidly regenerating **Salford Quays** area (take the Metrolink to Broadway or Harbour City), the visually stunning and truly thought-provoking **Imperial War Museum North** (☎ 836 4000; www.iwm.org.uk/north; Trafford Wharf Rd; admission free; ⌚ 10am-5pm) is a cut above the usual dusty repository of guns and badges.

You may begin to understand the passion surrounding the city's most famous football club if you head to **Old Trafford stadium**, the home of **Manchester United** (www.manutd.com). There's a great **museum** (admission £8.50), but for true fans the **stadium tours** (☎ 0870 442 1994; tour & museum entry £12; ⌚ every 10min, 9.40am-4.30pm except match days) are most rewarding.

Sleeping

Manchester YHA Hostel (☎ 839 9960; www.yha.org.uk; Potato Wharf; dm incl breakfast from £13.50; 💻) This purpose-built canalside hostel in the Castlefield area is one of the best in the country.

Manchester Backpackers' Hostel (☎ 865 9296; 64 Cromwell Rd; dm £15) A great indie hostel, 2 miles south of the city centre (take Metrolink to the Stretford stop), with cooking facilities, a TV lounge and some doubles.

Hatters (☎ 236 9500; www.hattersgroup.com; 50 Newton St; dm/s/d from £17/28/50; 💻) One of the best hostels in town, in a great location for enjoying alternative Manchester.

New Union Hotel (☎ 228 1492; www.newunionhotel.com; 111 Princess St; s/d from £40/50) In the heart of the Gay Village but not exclusively pink, this terrific little hotel is all about affordable fun.

Eating

Only London can outdo Manchester for the choice of cafes and restaurants. There's something for every palate: ubiquitous-but-excellent selections in Chinatown; south Asian specials on Wilmslow Rd, aka the Curry Mile; organic and vegie in the Northern Quarter. Following is but a small starter course.

Eighth Day (☎ 273 4878; 111 Oxford Rd; mains £5; ⌚ 9.30am-5pm Mon-Sat) Eco-friendly hang-out, a favourite with students.

Trof (☎ 832 1870; 5-8 Thomas St; sandwiches £4, mains £8; ⌚ 9.30am-midnight) Great music, top staff and a fab selection of beer and food.

Love Saves the Day (☎ 832 0777; Tib St) The Northern Quarter's most popular cafe is a New York–style deli and eatery.

Al Bilal (☎ 257 0006; 87-81 Wilmslow Rd; mains £7-14; ⌚ lunch & dinner Sun-Fri) You're spoilt for choice on the Curry Mile but this is always a good bet.

Drinking

Every neighbourhood has its favourites. Here's a few to get you going:

A Place Called Common (39-41 Edge St) Art on the walls and DJs on the decks, favoured by an unpretentious crowd.

Dry Bar (28-30 Oldham Rd) The former HQ of Madchester's maddest protagonists is still one of the best bars in the Northern Quarter.

Dukes 92 (2 Castle St) Castlefield's best canalside pub – if it's sunny.

Lass O'Gowrie (36 Charles St) Victorian classic pub; good-value beer and food (mains around £6) attract students, old-timers and BBC employees.

Old Wellington Inn (4 Cathedral Gates) One of the oldest buildings in the city and a lovely pub for a pint of genuine ale.

Peveril of the Peak (127 Great Bridgewater St) An unpretentious pub with wonderful Victorian glazed tilework outside.

Clubbing

Madchester is so yesterday, but Manchester remains at the vanguard of dance-floor culture. The following are our favourites:

Attic (☎ 236 6071; www.theatticmcr.co.uk; New Wakefield St; admission free; daily) Northern soul shares with techno, alt grunge and live music.

Music Box (☎ 236 9971; www.musicboxmanchester.com; 65 Oxford St; admission £6-12; Wed-Sat) Our favourite club in town and – judging by the queues – almost everyone else's too. But worth it.

Sankey's (☎ 950 4201; www.sankeys.info; Radium St, Ancoats; admission free-£12; Fri & Sat) The place for hard-core clubbers.

Getting There & Away

National Express coaches serve most major cities from Chorlton St coach station in the city centre, including Liverpool (£5, 1¼ hours, hourly) and London (£23, 3¾ hours, hourly).

Manchester Piccadilly is the main station for trains to/from the rest of the country, including London (£115 on the spot, from £20 with advance booking, three hours, seven daily). Local services run to/from Liverpool (£8.80, 45 minutes, half-hourly).

LIVERPOOL

☎ 0151 / pop 510,000

Visually more striking than Manchester, with some fantastic architecture, a grand waterfront facing the River Mersey and towering cathedrals, infectiously friendly Liverpool, with its busy nightlife, is on the up – finally emerging from decades of economic depression and industrial decline.

Orientation & Information

Liverpool is simple to get around. The main attractions are Albert Dock, west of the city centre, and the trendy Ropewalks area, south of Hanover St. Lime St station, the bus station, the tourist office and the Cavern Quarter – a mecca for Beatles fans – lie just to the north.

There's a central **TIC** (☎ 233 2008; 08 Place, Whitechapel; 9am-8pm Mon-Sat & 11am-4pm Sun Apr-Sep, 9am-6pm Mon-Sat & 11am-4pm Sun Oct-Mar) and another branch at Albert Dock. For internet, try **CaféLatte.net** (☎ 709 9683; 4 S Hunter St; per 30min £1.50; 9am-6pm) or **Planet Electra** (☎ 708 0303; 36 London Rd; per 30min £1.50; 9am-5pm).

Sights

In the city centre, **St George's Hall** (☎ 707 2391; admission free; 10am-5pm Tue-Sat, 1-5pm Sun) is arguably Liverpool's most impressive building, built in 1854 and recently restored to former glory.

At the vastly entertaining **World Museum** (☎ 478 4399; www.liverpoolmuseums.org.uk/wml; William Brown St; admission free; 10am-5pm), exhibits range from live insect colonies to space exploration.

A £100 million renovation helped make **Albert Dock** (www.albertdock.com) Liverpool's number one tourist attraction, with a number of worthwhile sights:

Beatles Story (☎ 709 1963; www.beatlesstory.com; Albert Dock; admission £12.50; 9am-7pm) Sanitised coverage of Liverpool's famous sons, with plenty of genuine memorabilia.

International Slavery Museum (☎ 478 4499; www.liverpoolmuseums.org.uk/ism; admission free; 10am-5pm) Revealing slavery's unimaginable horrors – including Liverpool's own role in the trade.

Merseyside Maritime Museum (☎ 478 4499; www.liverpoolmuseums.org.uk/maritime; admission free; 10am-5pm) Celebrating this city's place as a world port, with several absorbing exhibition spaces.

Tate Liverpool (☎ 702 7400; www.tate.org.uk/liverpool; admission free, 10am-6pm Tue-Sun & bank holiday Mon) Displaying a roll-call of 20th-century artistic talent.

North of Albert Dock is **Pier Head**, still the departure point for ferries across the Mersey and in previous centuries the final contact with European soil for millions of migrants. Their story – and that of the city – will be told in the **Museum of Liverpool**, due to open 2010–11. Also here is a trio of buildings known as the 'Three Graces', a reminder of Liverpool's Edwardian hey-day: the **Port of Liverpool Building**, with its giant dome; the **Cunard Building**, once HQ to the Cunard Steamship Line; and the **Royal Liver Building**, crowned by the iconic Liver Bird.

Sleeping

International Inn (☎ 709 8135; www.internationalinn.co.uk; 4 S Hunter St; dm/d from £15/36) A converted warehouse in uni-land, with tidy dorms, en-suite rooms, lounge, baggage storage, laundry and friendly staff on the 24-hour front desk.

University of Liverpool (☎ 794 6440; www.liv.ac.uk; Greenbank La; r from £17.50) Accommodation in modern rooms is provided out of term in a beautiful part of the city near Penny Lane.

Liverpool International YHA Hostel (☎ 0870 770 5924; www.yha.org.uk; 25 Tabley St; dm £15.95) This award-winning hostel on Albert Dock, adorned – inevitably – with Beatles memorabilia, is one of the best in the country.

Aachen Hotel (☎ 709 3477; www.aachenhotel.co.uk; 89-91 Mt Pleasant; s/d from £50/70) A perennial favourite with a mix of rooms, retro decor and a welcoming, offbeat atmosphere.

Eating

Liverpool's dining scene is getting better all the time. There are plenty of choices in Ropewalks, along Hardman St and Hope St, and along Nelson St in the heart of Chinatown.

Lucy in the Sky with Diamonds (8 Cavern Walks; mains £4; 8am-5pm Mon-Sat) It's hard to imagine that a cafe with this name in this touristy part of town could be authentic in any way, but Lucy is. And we love her.

Everyman Bistro (13 Hope St; mains £5-8; noon-2am Mon-Fri, 11am-2am Sat, 7-10.30pm Sun) Out-of-work actors and other creative types favour this great cafe-restaurant beneath the Everyman Theatre.

Keith's Wine Bar (☎ 728 7688; 107 Lark Lane; mains £5; 11am-11pm) This friendly, bohemian and mostly vegetarian hang-out is the favourite resting place of the city's alternative-lifestyle crowd.

Tea Factory (☎ 708 7008; 79 Wood St; mains £7-12; 11am-late) The wide-ranging menu covers all bases from typical Brit fare to international tapas, but it's the room, darling, that makes this place so popular. Rock stars' favourite.

Drinking & Clubbing

Health officials may despair, but Liverpool's wealth of pubs, clubs and bars satisfy the locals' seemingly inexhaustible desire to get loaded, especially in the party zone that is Ropewalks. Here's a few favourites:

Bar Ça Va (4A Wood St) Indie vibe and discerning crowd.

Hannah's (2 Leece St) One of the top student bars in town.

Magnet (39 Hardman St) With a New York–dive atmosphere, the upstairs bar is cool, while the downstairs dance-floor shakes.

Barfly (90 Seel St; admission £4-11; Mon-Sat) The fortnightly Chibuku Shake-Shake (www.chibuku.com) is one of the best club nights in England.

Nation (40 Slater St/Wolstenholme Sq; admission £4-13) The city's premier dance club with big-name DJs plus live bands and pumping techno nights.

Getting There & Away

National Express coaches run to/from Manchester (£5, 1¼ hours, hourly), London (£24, five to six hours, seven daily) and Newcastle (£20.50, 6½ hours, three daily).

Trains run hourly to/from London (£25 to £60 depending on time of travel, 3¼ hours) and there are regular local services to/from Manchester.

LAKE DISTRICT NATIONAL PARK

A dramatic landscape of high peaks, dizzying ridges and huge lakes gouged by the march of Ice Age glaciers, the Lake District is simply beautiful, and for England, as extreme as it gets. Not surprisingly, the awe-inspiring geography here shaped the literary persona of one of Britain's best-known poets, William Wordsworth.

Often called simply The Lakes (but never – note, Australians – the 'Lakes District'), the national park and surrounding area attract around 15 million visitors yearly who come for serious hiking or to potter gently around the souvenir shops of the countless pretty villages. If you avoid summer weekends, it's easy enough to miss the crush.

Orientation & Information

The key valleys of the Lake District radiate from a central high point like the spokes of a wheel, with most of the larger gateway towns on the outer rim, including Windermere and Bowness in the south, Ambleside slightly nearer the centre, and Keswick in the north. Other focal points include the village of Grasmere. All have hostels, B&Bs, places to eat and shops selling maps and outdoor equipment.

The shelves of the local TICs groan with guidebooks and brochures, and both Windermere and Keswick have decent information centres with free accommodation booking services. Portal websites include www.lake-district.gov.uk and www.golakes.co.uk.

The Lake District is home to England's highest peak (Scafell; 978m), the wettest inhabited place (Seathwaite; over 3m of rain a year), and notoriously changeable weather conditions – which prove fatal to a few unlucky/unready souls each year – so make sure you're prepared if you venture into the hills.

Sleeping

There's a host of B&Bs and country-house hotels in the Lakes, plus over 20 YHA hostels, many of which can be linked by foot. The YHA also runs a shuttle-bus between the busiest hostels during summer.

WINDERMERE & BOWNESS

☎ 015394

Thanks to the railway, Windermere is an excellent gateway and the largest tourist town in the area. Bowness, on the lake shore, is a 30-minute downhill walk. Windermere's busy **TIC** (☎ 46499; windermeretic@southlakeland.gov.uk; Victoria St; 9.30am-5.30pm) is near the train station, and there's a branch in Bowness. Places to stay:

Lake District Backpackers Lodge (☎ 46374; www.lakedistrictbackpackers.co.uk; High St; dm £10-12;) Cramped but cheap, with a cosy lounge and biking and hiking trips available.

Windermere YHA Hostel (☎ 0870 770 6094; windermere@yha.org.uk; Bridge Lane, Troutbeck; dm from £12; mid-Feb–Nov;) Top-notch facilities, panoramic lake views, shop, canteen and gear-drying room. A couple of miles outside town; buses run to Troutbeck Bridge, then it's a mile uphill walk.

Fair Rigg (☎ 43941; www.fairrigg.co.uk; Ferry View; d £66-84) A decent B&B option with simple, spick-and-span rooms.

AMBLESIDE

☎ 015394

Towards the northern end of Windermere (the lake), Ambleside is a good base for hardy hikers and village amblers. Sleeping options:

Ambleside Backpackers (☎ 32340; www.englishlakesbackpackers.co.uk; Old Lake Rd; dm £16;) Popular indie hostel, with close-packed dorms and huge kitchen.

Ambleside YHA Hostel (☎ 0870-770 5672; ambleside@yha.org.uk; Windermere Rd; dm from £17.95;) Supremely well-organised YHA hostel, popular for activity breaks; due to reopen after refurbishment in 2009.

Easedale Lodge (☎ 32112; www.easedaleambleside.co.uk; Compston Rd; d £70-96) Immaculate B&B in handy location.

GRASMERE

☎ 015394

Occupying a graceful spot amid meadows, with Wordsworth connections, Grasmere is a delight – and busy in summer. Options for a bed:

Butharlyp How YHA Hostel (☎ 0870 770 5836; grasmere@yha.org.uk; dm £15.50; daily Feb-Nov, Sat & Sun Dec-Jan;) Outside the village, with modernish dorms, lovely grounds and decent bar-restaurant.

Grasmere Hostel (☎ 35055; www.grasmerehostel.co.uk; Broadrayne Farm; dm £17.50) Quaint farmhouse turned excellent indie hostel, outside the village near the Traveller's Rest pub.

How Foot Lodge (☎ 35366; www.howfoot.co.uk; Town End; d £66-76) Stone cottage B&B with contemporary rooms – one with private sun-lounge.

KESWICK

☎ 017687

Sturdy slate-town Keswick lacks the green charm of Windermere, but is an excellent walking base. The **TIC** (☎ 72645; keswicktic@lake-district.gov.uk; Market Pl; 9.30am-5pm) is helpful, and there's an internet cafe above the post office. Places to stay and eat:

Keswick YHA Hostel (☎ 0870-770 5894; keswick@yha.org.uk; Station Rd; dm £22.95;) Fresh from a refit, this former woollen mill is now a Lakeland top spot.

Hetherlea (☎ 72430; www.heatherlea-keswick.co.uk; 26 Blencathra St; d £54) One of the best choices in the B&B-heavy area around Blencathra St.

Lakeland Pedlar (www.lakelandpedlar.co.uk; Hendersons Yard; mains £3-10; 9am-5pm) Our favourite Lakes cafe, with mainly wholefood choices plus bike hire.

Getting There & Around

National Express coaches have direct connections between Windermere and London (£32, 8½ hours, daily); other services require a change at Preston.

Via train, Windermere is at the end of a branch off the main line between London Euston and Glasgow. Destinations include Manchester (£25, hourly, two hours).

For getting around, the handiest bus service is bus 555, cruising regularly through the park via Kendal, Windermere, Ambleside, Grasmere and Keswick, with occasional 554 and 559 variants and extensions north to Carlisle and south to Lancaster. Timetables are available at TICs.

NORTHEAST ENGLAND

By turns wild and pretty, rural and urban, modern and historic, this part of England contains the large and varied counties of Yorkshire and Northumberland, and three of Britain's great cities: historic York and Durham, and resurgent Newcastle. This region also offers national parks with excellent walking and other outdoor activities, great expanses of empty beach, plus a hoard of world-class relics and ruins. For general information, see www.yorkshirevisitor.com and www.visitnortheastengland.com.

YORK

☎ 01904 / pop 180,000

York has been a military, political, religious and commercial settlement dating back to the Roman era, and time-travellers from the city's medieval past would still recognise many of its wonderfully preserved buildings, such as the spectacular Minster and the stout wall girdling the centre's ancient alleyways – although they might be surprised at the modern profusion of giftshops and tearooms, not to mention the mass of sightseeing visitors. But York wears its popularity well and retains an undiluted appeal, making it one of Britain's finest attractions.

Orientation & Information

The city centre is relatively small, though a tangle of medieval alleys is further confused by the fact that 'gate' means street, and 'bar' means gate. The **TIC** (☎ 550099; www.visityork.org; Exhibition Sq; 🕑 9am-6pm Mon-Sat, 10am-5pm Sun) can help with accommodation (£3 booking fee). For internet, try the **City Library** (☎ 552815; Museum St; per 30min £1; 🕑 9am-8pm Mon-Wed & Fri, to 5pm Thu & Sat).

Sights

Northern Europe's largest Gothic cathedral, **York Minster** (☎ 557200; www.yorkminster.org; adult £5.50; 🕑 9am-5pm Mon-Sat, noon-3.45pm Sun) is a 1000-year-old treasure house of architecture and richly coloured stained-glass windows. Take an audio tour of the **Undercroft** (admission £3) for subterranean Roman, Norman and Viking remains, or climb the Minster's 275-step **Tower** for a spectacular view past gargoyles and over the city.

If the weather's good, a walk round the **City Walls** (admission free; 🕑 8am-dusk) gives a whole new perspective on the city. The full circuit is 4.5 miles (allow two hours); if you're pushed for time, the stretch from Bootham Bar to Monk Bar is best.

The cobbled lane called the **Shambles** (www.yorkshambles.com), lined with 15th-century Tudor buildings that overhang so much they almost meet above your head, is the most visited street in Europe. Quaint and picturesque, it hints at what a medieval street may have looked like – if you forget the boutiques and gift shops.

Interactive multimedia exhibits aimed at 'bringing history to life' often achieve just the opposite, but the much-hyped **Jorvik** (☎ 543403; www.vikingjorvik.com; Coppergate; admission £8.50; 🕑 10am-5pm), a smells-and-all reconstruction of the original Viking settlement that gave York its name, manages to pull it off.

The **National Railway Museum** (☎ 621261; Leeman Rd; admission free; 🕑 10am-6pm) is a homage to train travel, especially the age of steam – but there's also a Japanese bullet train, and a nod to the Channel Tunnel. Nearby is the **Yorkshire Wheel** (a smaller version of the London Eye), with great views over the city.

York Castle Museum (☎ 653611; www.yorkcastlemuseum.org.uk; adult £7.50; 🕑 9.30am-5pm) contains a labyrinth of rooms exploring 600 years of British life from medieval prisons to Victorian parlours, plus a less-than-homely prison cell of notorious highwayman Dick Turpin.

The Association of Voluntary Guides offers free two-hour **walking tours** (🕑 10.15am & 2.15pm Apr-Oct, plus 6.45pm Jun-Aug), departing across the street from the TIC. There's a bewildering range of **ghost tours** – York is reputed to be England's most haunted city. For your own wanderings, check the tourist office's own suggestions for walking itineraries at www.visityork.org/explore.

Sleeping

York YHA Hostel (☎ 0870 770 6102; www.yha.org.uk; 42 Water End, Clifton; dm £18.50; 💻) Historic mansion about a mile northwest of the centre with spacious four-bed dorms and good facilities.

Dairy Guesthouse (☎ 639367; www.dairyguesthouse.co.uk; 3 Scarcroft Rd; s/d from £55/75) This lovely Victorian home has many original features, but the real treat is the flower-filled courtyard.

Also recommended:

Briar Lea Guest House (☎ 635061; www.briarlea.co.uk; 8 Longfield Tce; s/d from £35/60) Clean, simple rooms and a friendly welcome in a central location.

Alcuin Lodge (☎ 632222; www.alcuinlodge.com; 15 Sycamore Pl; s/d from £35/60; 💻) Elegant rooms in a beautiful house.

Eating & Drinking

Eating well in York is not a problem – there are plenty of fine options throughout the city centre. Most pubs also serve food.

Café Concerto (21 High Petergate; snacks £2-6, mains £9-14; 🕑 10am-10pm) Breakfasts and bagels during the day; sophisticated bistro menu in the evening.

Blake Head Vegetarian Café (104 Micklegate; mains £4-6; 🕑 9.30am-5pm Mon-Sat, 10am-5pm Sun) A bright and airy space at the back of a bookshop.

King's Arms (King's Staith; lunch £6) Creaky old place with a fabulous riverside location – a perfect spot for a summer's evening.

Black Swan (Peasholme Green) Classic black-and-white building with decent beer, friendly people and live jazz on Sundays.

our pick Blue Bell (53 Fossgate) Typical English pub with fireplace, beer-stained decor, real ale and friendly staff.

Little John (5 Castlegate) Historic pub and top gay venue, haunted by the ghost of Dick Turpin. Thursday night karaoke is even scarier…

Getting There & Away

National Express coaches run to/from London (£24, 5¼ hours, four daily) and many other destinations including Newcastle (£14, 2¾ hours, four daily).

On the train, York is a major railway hub with frequent direct services to London's King's Cross (£20 to £100 depending when

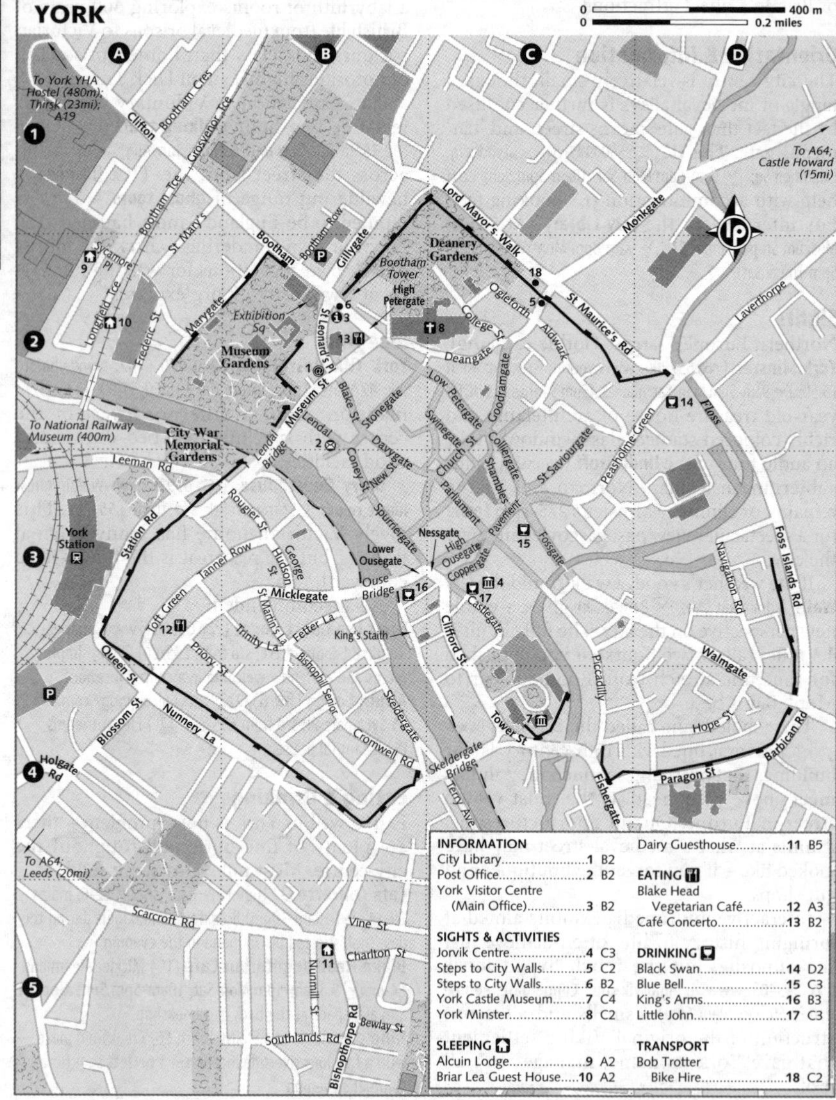

WORTH THE TRIP: CASTLE HOWARD

There are big posh houses, there are stately homes – and then there's **Castle Howard** (☎ 01653-648333; www.castlehoward.co.uk; house & grounds £10.50, grounds only £8; 🕑 house 11am-4.30pm, grounds 10am-4.30pm Mar-Oct & 1st three weeks of Dec), a work of theatrical grandeur, instantly recognisable from its starring role in the *Brideshead Revisited* TV series, first aired in the early 1980s. The ostentatious Renaissance exteriors are complemented by sumptuous interiors of priceless art and artefacts, while the surrounding landscaped parkland boasts temples, fountains and strutting peacocks. About 15 miles from York, it's a popular tour excursion. Or you can get there on Yorkshire Coastliner bus 840 (40 minutes, one daily).

you book and travel, two hours), Newcastle (£25, one hour) and Manchester (£20, 1½ hours).

Getting Around

York is easy to get around on foot – you're never more than 20 minutes from the next major sight. For further exploration, the energetic could pedal out to Castle Howard (15 miles) on bikes rented from **Bob Trotter** (☎ 622868; 13 Lord Mayor's Walk; per day £10; 🕑 9am-5.30pm Mon-Sat, 10am-4pm Sun).

DURHAM

☎ 0191 / pop 100,000

The grand city of Durham is crowned by a magnificent castle and Britain's finest Norman cathedral. Surrounding them both is a maze of cobbled streets, usually full of upper-crust students attending Durham's prestigious university. It's a place rich in history and (thanks to those students) also packed with busy pubs and bars. But apart from that, there isn't much, so we recommend you visit as a day trip from Newcastle (right).

Orientation & Information

Market Place, the tourist office, castle and cathedral are all on a steep-sided peninsula surrounded by the River Wear. The train and bus stations are to the west, on the other side of the river. Using the cathedral as your landmark, you can't really go wrong.

The **TIC** (☎ 384 3720; www.durhamtourism.co.uk; 2 Millennium Pl; 🕑 9.30am-5.30pm Mon-Sat, 10am-4pm Sun) books accommodation for free.

Sights

If you need one good reason to visit the city, it's **Durham Cathedral** (☎ 386 4266; www.durhamcathedral.co.uk; 🕑 9.30am-8pm mid-Jun–Aug, 9.30am-6.15pm Mon-Sat & 12.30-5pm Sun Sep–mid-Jun). A magnificent Unesco-listed landmark, its rib-vaulted architecture was an engineering breakthrough and remains an architectural marvel today. For the inside story, take an illuminating **guided tour** (£3.50) or climb the 66m **tower** (£3) for spectacular views.

The city's other great sight is stout and sturdy **Durham Castle** (☎ 374 3800; www.durhamcastle.com; adult £5; 🕑 tours only, on the hr 10am-12.30pm & 2-4pm Jun-Oct, 2-4pm Mon, Wed, Sat & Sun Nov-May), dating from 1072 and now part of the university. Highlights of the 45-minute tour include the groaning 17th-century Black Staircase and the beautifully preserved Norman chapel.

Getting There & Away

National Express coaches run to/from London (£27, seven hours, four daily) and Edinburgh (£23, four hours, one daily). By train, destinations include Newcastle (£6.80, 20 minutes) and York (£24, one hour).

NEWCASTLE-UPON-TYNE

☎ 0191 / pop 470,000 (including Gateshead)

Once synonymous with post-industrial decline and decay, today's Newcastle is reborn and brimming with confidence. With its distinctive Geordie accent thicker than molasses, this unfailingly friendly city has kick-started a brand new arts and entertainment scene – while riotous nightlife remains an established tradition.

Orientation & Information

Newcastle's compact city centre is easy to navigate on foot and it has excellent public transport, including a metro system circling the centre. The main train and bus station is just south of the city centre.

The River Tyne is a focal point, and also the boundary between Newcastle to the north and the separate entity of Gateshead to the south, although the local tourism authorities bill the area as a combined Newcastle-Gateshead.

DETOUR: ANGEL OF THE NORTH

South of Newcastle, on the outer edge of Gateshead, is a potent symbol of restored northeast pride, and (thanks to its position next to a busy highway) the world's most viewed work of art – the towering, rusting, forbidding, welcoming, redemptive, apocalyptic **Angel of the North** (admission free). This is artist Antony Gormley's (1950–) best-known and most successful work, and Britain's largest sculpture – 20m high with a wingspan (54m) wider than a Boeing 767. For more information, see www.gateshead.gov.uk and follow links to Angel of the North. To get there from central Newcastle, take bus 723/724 from Eldon Sq, or bus 21/21A/21B from Pilgrim St.

Newcastle has two main **TICs** Grainger St (☎ 277 8000; 132 Grainger St; ⌚ 9.30am-5.30pm Mon-Wed, Fri & Sat, to 7.30pm Thu year-round, plus 10am-4pm Sun Jun-Sep); Guildhall (☎ 277 8000; ⌚ 11am-6pm Mon-Fri, 9am-6pm Sat, 9am-4pm Sun).

Sights

Make sure you take a stroll along the quays beside the River Tyne, under the famous **Tyne Bridges**, where many of Newcastle's and Gateshead's great buildings jostle for your attention. On the Gateshead side, you can't miss **Baltic** (☎ 478 1810; www.balticmill.com; admission free; ⌚ 10am-6pm), a former flourmill, now a contemporary art centre. It's reached from the Newcastle side via the **Millennium Bridge**, a pedestrian walkway that opens like an eye for passing ships. Nearby, in sharp architectural contrast, is **The Sage** (☎ 443 4666; www.thesagegateshead.org), a magnificent chrome-and-glass concert hall.

Sleeping & Eating

Newcastle YHA Hostel (☎ 0870 770 5972; www.yha.org.uk; 107 Jesmond Rd; dm/d £16.50/40; ⌚ end Jan-end Dec) In the suburb of Jesmond, this nice, rambling place has small dorms that are generally full, so book in advance.

Albatross Inl (☎ 233 1330; www.albatrossnewcastle.com; 51 Grainger St; dm/d from £17.50/45; 💻) Fully equipped hostel with decent-sized dorms, a self-catering kitchen, top-notch bathroom facilities and an internet station.

Euro-Hostel Newcastle (☎ 0845 490 0371; www.euro-hostel.co.uk; Garth Heads St; dm/d £17/60; 💻) With a broader range of options than most hotels, from a bed in a dorm to a private room or self-catering apartment, this is a good spot.

Blake's Coffee House (53 Grey St; sandwiches £3-4; ⌚ 9am-6pm) This friendly, relaxed cafe serves up the biggest selection of coffees in town. We love it.

Big Mussel (☎ 232 1057; 15 The Side; mains £6-12; ⌚ lunch & dinner) Shellfish – with chips – are a popular choice at this informal diner. There are pasta and vegetarian options as well.

Drinking

Geordies are famous (or infamous) for a good night out. You can join the masses staggering from booze-shed to booze-shed in the Bigg Market and Quayside areas – or you can seek out pubs, bars and nightlife that are infinitely more satisfying. Ouseburn Valley is our area of choice, but it's also worth checking the western end of Neville St – with a decent mix of great bars and the best of the gay scene. Here's a small selection in the city centre to get you started:

Crown Posada (31 The Side) Unspoilt real-ale pub, loved by seasoned drinkers.

Forth (Pink Lane) In the heart of the gay district, this great old pub draws all kinds.

Tokyo (17 Westgate Rd) The best cocktails in town, with upstairs garden bar.

our pick **Trent House Soul Bar** (1-2 Leazes Lane) Totally relaxed and utterly devoid of pretentiousness, this old-school boozer out-cools every other bar.

Clubbing

Once again, a massive choice, so just a few of our favourites follow. For the full listings, see www.thecrackmagazine.com.

Digital (☎ 261 9755; www.yourfutureisdigital.com; Times Sq) Two-floored cathedral to dance music.

Foundation (☎ 261 8985; www.foundation-club.com; 57-59 Melbourne St) Serves up all you need for a night of hard-core clubbing.

Head of Steam @The Cluny (☎ 230 4474; www.headofsteam.co.uk; 36 Lime St, Ouseburn Valley) Top spot for live music, touring acts and local talent.

Getting There & Away

National Express coaches go to/from London (£27, seven hours, six daily) and Manchester

(£17.50, five hours, six daily) and many other cities in England and Scotland. Newcastle is on the main rail line between London and Edinburgh, via York (£20, 45 minutes, every 20 minutes).

HADRIAN'S WALL

Built in AD 122 to mark the edge of the Roman empire, this 73-mile coast-to-coast barrier across England is mightily impressive to this day. Very little remains in some parts, while other stretches are remarkably well preserved and simply spectacular, notably the section between Hexham and Brampton.

Good gateways include the tiny settlements of Once Brewed and Twice Brewed, and the small towns of Haltwhistle and Greenhead, all with accommodation (ranging from YHA hostels to pubs and B&Bs), and TICs packed with maps and information about the wall and surrounding area. The best portal site for information is www.hadrians-wall.org.

Walkers and cyclists can follow the **Hadrian's Wall Path** (www.nationaltrail.co.uk/hadrianswall) or **Hadrian's Wall Cycleway** (www.cycle-routes.org/hadrianscycleway). Or, if you want to learn more about local history, **Hadrian's Wall Adventure** (☎ 01343-344650; www.hadrianswalladventure.com) offers tours by bike or foot, as well as sightseeing trips by 4WD. You can also hire bikes from their base (a cosy cafe and outdoor shop) at Haltwhistle train station, so you can arrive by rail and hop straight on a bike.

As well as the wall itself, you can also marvel at the Roman forts and castles along its length.

Chesters (☎ 01434-681379; admission £4.50; 🕑 9.30am-6pm Apr-Sep, 10am-4pm Oct-Mar) is a well-preserved fortification with an impressive bathhouse, and museum with a fascinating array of Roman sculptures and drawings found in the area.

Vindolanda (☎ 01434-344277; www.vindolanda.com; admission £5.20; 🕑 10am-6pm Apr-Sep, to 5pm Feb-Mar & Oct-Nov), about 1 mile from Once Brewed, offers a fascinating glimpse into the daily life of a Roman garrison town.

Housesteads (☎ 01434-344363; adult/concession £3.80/2.90; 🕑 10am-6pm Apr-Sep, 10am-4pm Oct-Mar), the wall's most dramatic and popular ruin, has a famous public latrine and iconic gateway overlooking wild Northumbrian countryside. It's a spectacular walk (3 miles) along the wall from Once Brewed.

Reaching Hadrian's Wall is straightforward. The Newcastle–Carlisle train line runs parallel to the wall a mile or two to the south, with stations at Hexham, Haydon Bridge, Bardon Mill, Haltwhistle and Brampton. There are also hourly buses between Carlisle and Newcastle via most of the same towns. From June to September the hail-and-ride Hadrian's Wall Bus (number AD 122 – gedit?) shuttles between all the major sites, towns and villages along the way. For timetables and other information, see www.hadrians-wall.org.

CARDIFF

☎ 029 / pop 285,000

Cool Cardiff. Contemporary Cardiff. Changing Cardiff. The Welsh capital labours under many sobriquets these days, but one thing is certain: Cardiff feels very much alive, and is currently emerging as one of Britain's leading urban centres of the 21st century, with a redefined cityscape, creative buzz and a vibrant nightlife.

ORIENTATION & INFORMATION

The central area of Cardiff (Caerdydd in Welsh) is small enough to explore on foot, with two unmistakable landmarks – the castle on the northern side, and the enormous Millennium Stadium to the southwest. The compact shopping and restaurant zone, including the tourist office, is east of the stadium. The central bus and train stations mark the southern extent of downtown. Cardiff Bay waterfront lies about 2 miles southeast of the centre.

The **TIC** (☎ 0870 121 1258; www.visitcardiff.com; Old Library, The Hayes; 🕑 9.30am-6pm Mon-Sat, 10am-4pm Sun; 💻) has piles of information covering all Wales. Internet access is £2 per hour; left luggage £3 per locker. You can also surf at **Cardiff Central Library** (☎ 2038 2116; internet access free; 🕑 9am-6pm Mon-Wed & Fri, 9am-7pm Thu, 9am-5.30pm Sat), which is temporarily on Bute St, but moving to Mill Lane.

SIGHTS

Dazzling Victorian style and mock-Gothic folly make **Cardiff Castle** (☎ 2087 8100; www.cardiffcastle.com; Castle St; grounds only £3.50, with castle tour £8.95; 🕑 9am-6pm Mar-Oct, 9.30am-5pm Nov-Feb) an entertaining visit. Nearby, the **National Museum Cardiff** (☎ 2039 7951; www.museumwales.ac.uk; Cathays Park; admission free; 🕑 10am-5pm Tue-Sun) has international-quality galleries and enthralling natural history exhibits, as well as a handy crash course in Welsh culture.

Cardiff's **arcades**, enclosed shopping streets with ornate roofs, are the city's best-kept secret, offering a vibrant mix of independent retailers and eateries, and a welcome counterpoint to the chain-dominated behemoth that will be **St Davids 2** (www.stdavids2.com), due for completion in 2010.

Most cities have their stadium on the outskirts. Cardiff's spectacular **Millennium Stadium** (☎ tours 2082 2228, box office 0870 558 2582; www.millenniumstadium.co.uk; tours £6.50; ⏲ 10am-5pm Mon-Sat, 10am-4pm Sun & bank holidays), on the site of the famous Arms Park, sits smack bang in the middle of town like an invading spaceship.

Of the many stunning new buildings at Cardiff Bay, the **Wales Millennium Centre** (☎ box office 0870 040 2000; www.wmc.org.uk; Bute Pl) stands out the most, with its golden roof and mauve slate panelling. Not to be confused with Millennium Stadium, this is Wales' premier arts complex and home to the Welsh National Opera. Next door, **Y Senedd** (www.assemblywales.org), the National Assembly for Wales, is another distinctive structure of glass, steel and slate. And the past is not forgotten, thanks to the red-brick **Pierhead Building** and **Norwegian Church** overlooking the bay.

SLEEPING

River House Backpackers (☎ 2039 9810; www.riverhousebackpackers.com; 59 Fitzhamon Embankment; dm/r

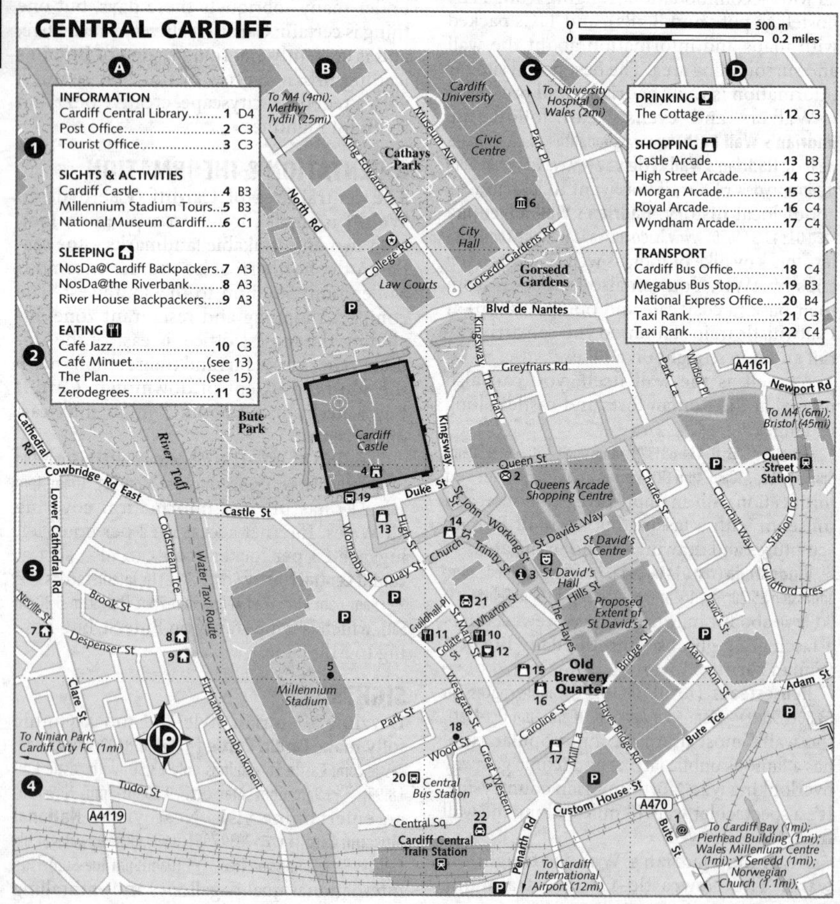

with breakfast £17.50/25; 💻) This smart new place is modern and clean, with a garden, well-equipped kitchen and TV lounge.

NosDa@Cardiff Backpackers (☎ 2034 5577; www.nosda.co.uk; 96-98 Neville St; dm with breakfast from £18; 💻) A stalwart of the Cardiff budget scene, this independent hostel has well-maintained facilities and a central location.

NosDa@the Riverbank (☎ 2034 8866; www.nosda.co.uk; 53-59 Despenser St; s/d from £35/55; 💻) An upscale hostel experience with more privacy, home-cooked meals and a cool bar area.

EATING & DRINKING

The following places are our city centre favourites. More upmarket options await your exploration in Cardiff Bay.

our pick **Café Minuet** (☎ 2034 1794; 42 Castle Arcade; 🕒 10am-5pm Mon-Sat) A classical music-themed cafe with Italian-influenced dishes.

The Plan (☎ 2039 8464; 28-29 Morgan Arcade; 🕒 8.30am-5pm Mon-Sat, 10.30am-4pm Sun) This small but satisfying place is a haven for healthy options.

The Cottage (☎ 2033 7195; 25 St Mary St) This friendly old pub is great for a pint and no-nonsense bar meals.

Café Jazz (☎ 2023 2161; www.cafejazzcardiff.com; St Mary St; 2-/3-course set menu from £7.95/10.95; 🕒 lunch & dinner Mon-Sat, noon-5pm Sun) Cool venue by night, relaxed cafe by day.

Zerodegrees (☎ 2022 9494; www.zerodegrees.co.uk; 27 Watergate St) A bright and buzzy bar-restaurant (and microbrewery) with all-day food.

GETTING THERE & AWAY

Coaches run to/from Bristol (£7.20, one hour, seven daily) and London (£21, 3½ hours, hourly), competing with low-cost Megabus (from £2, 3½ hours, seven daily) on the London route. Regular train services include to/from London Paddington (£24, two hours, at least half-hourly).

SOUTHERN & WESTERN WALES

South Wales extends north, west and east from Cardiff, and includes the former industrial heartland of The Valleys with the hills of the Brecon Beacons beyond, and the ports of Swansea and Newport along the coast. Beyond Swansea is the delightful Gower Peninsula – with quiet villages and sandy beaches – and then you get into West Wales, a rural area with a stunning coastline. For the sake of convenience, we've combined them all in this section, describing places roughly east to west.

BRECON BEACONS NATIONAL PARK

The Brecon Beacons National Park covers 519 sq miles of grassy whale-back mountains, marking the border between south and mid Wales. The park's northern flank is lined with several attractive market towns – Llandovery, Brecon, Crickhowell, Talgarth and Hay-on-Wye – all making good bases, and easily reached by bus from Cardiff. Abergavenny is another gateway, accessible by train from Cardiff. All these towns have TICs, providing information on accommodation and activities.

For information on the park, the main **National Park Visitor Centre** (☎ 01874-623366) is at the village of Libanus, about 4 miles from Brecon. Or see www.visitbreconbeacons.com.

If you want to combine reaching the park with seeing the park, a 55-mile cycleway/footpath, the **Taff Trail** (www.tafftrail.org.uk), connects Cardiff with Brecon.

From late May to the end of September, on Sunday and bank holidays, the **Beacons Bus** (☎ 01873-853254; www.breconbeacons.org) operates several routes in and around the park, with a central hub in Brecon, and links to Cardiff, Merthyr Tydfil, Swansea and Carmarthen.

BRECON

☎ 01874 / pop 7800

Brecon (Aberhonddu in Welsh) is an attractive, historic market town and an excellent base for walking in the magnificent surrounding countryside. There's also a **cathedral** dating from the 13th century, and a helpful **TIC** (☎ 622485; brectic@powys.gov.uk; 🕒 9.30am-5pm Mon-Sat, to 4pm Sun Apr-Sep, 9.30am-5pm Mon-Fri, to 4pm Sat & Sun Oct-Mar).

Brecon is stuffed with B&Bs, with more options (including hostels) in the surrounding area. The town also has cafes and pubs.

Two miles east of Brecon, the **Brecon YHA Hostel** (☎ 0870 770 5718; brecon@yha.org.uk; Groesffordd; dm £15.95; 🕒 reception 7.30-11.30am & 5-10.30pm) has good facilities, simple but comfortable rooms and a lovely farmhouse location. **Beacons Guesthouse** (☎ 623339; 16 Bridge St; s/d £50/56) is a straightforward place with a warm welcome.

BRITAIN

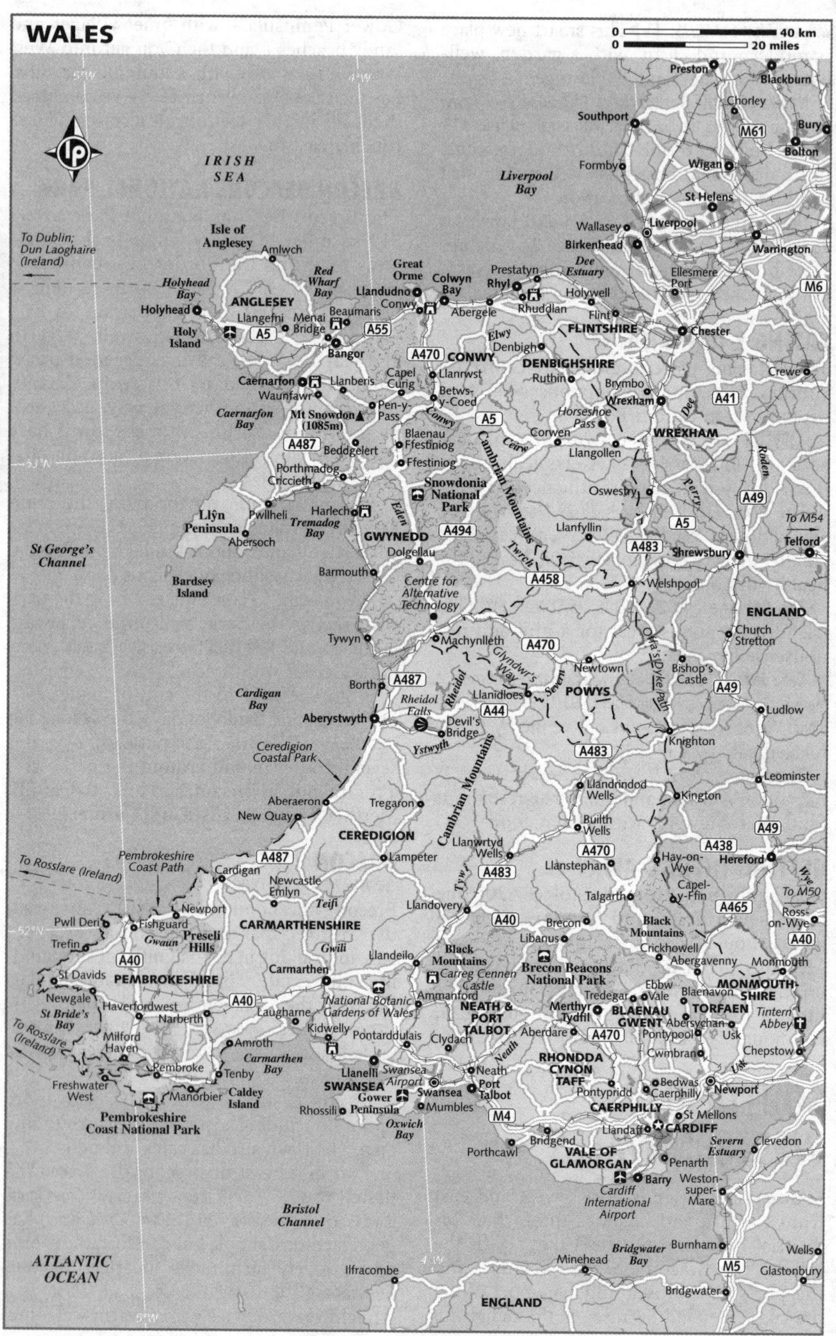
WALES
0 40 km
0 20 miles
IRISH SEA
Liverpool Bay
St George's Channel
Cardigan Bay
Bristol Channel
ATLANTIC OCEAN
To Dublin; Dun Laoghaire (Ireland)
To Rosslare (Ireland)
Isle of Anglesey
ANGLESEY
Holyhead
Holyhead Bay
Holy Island
Amlwch
Red Wharf Bay
Llangefni
Menai Bridge
Beaumaris
Bangor
Great Orme
Llandudno
Conwy
Colwyn Bay
Abergele
Rhyl
Prestatyn
Rhuddlan
Dee Estuary
Holywell
Flint
FLINTSHIRE
Chester
CONWY
DENBIGHSHIRE
Denbigh
Ruthin
Llanrwst
Betws-y-Coed
Capel Curig
Caernarfon
Llanberis
Waunfawr
Pen-y-Pass
Mt Snowdon (1085m)
Caernarfon Bay
Beddgelert
Blaenau Ffestiniog
Ffestiniog
Porthmadog
Criccieth
Llŷn Peninsula
Pwllheli
Abersoch
Harlech
Tremadog Bay
Bardsey Island
Snowdonia National Park
GWYNEDD
Dolgellau
Barmouth
Cambrian Mountains
Centre for Alternative Technology
Tywyn
Machynlleth
Glyndwr's Way
Borth
Aberystwyth
Rheidol Falls
Devil's Bridge
Ystwyth
Ceredigion Coastal Park
Aberaeron
New Quay
Tregaron
CEREDIGION
Lampeter
Llanwrtyd Wells
Cardigan
Pembrokeshire Coast Path
Newport
Fishguard
Pwll Deri
Trefin
Preseli Hills
Gwaun
Newcastle Emlyn
Teifi
CARMARTHENSHIRE
St Davids
PEMBROKESHIRE
Newgale
St Bride's Bay
Haverfordwest
Narberth
Milford Haven
Pembroke
Tenby
Amroth
Freshwater West
Manorbier
Caldey Island
Pembrokeshire Coast National Park
Carmarthen
Laugharne
Kidwelly
Llanelli
Carmarthen Bay
Gwili
Llandeilo
Llandovery
National Botanic Gardens of Wales
Black Mountains
Carreg Cennen Castle
Ammanford
Pontarddulais
Clydach
SWANSEA
Swansea Airport
Swansea
Gower Peninsula
Rhossili
Mumbles
Oxwich Bay
NEATH & PORT TALBOT
Neath
Port Talbot
Porthcawl
Bridgend
Brecon Beacons National Park
Brecon
Libanus
Merthyr Tydfil
Aberdare
RHONDDA CYNON TAFF
Pontypridd
Tredegar
Ebbw Vale
BLAENAU GWENT
Blaenavon
TORFAEN
Abersychan
Pontypool
Cwmbran
CAERPHILLY
Caerphilly
Bedwas
Newport
CARDIFF
Llandaff
St Mellons
VALE OF GLAMORGAN
Penarth
Barry
Cardiff International Airport
Severn Estuary
Clevedon
Weston-super-Mare
Burnham
Bridgwater Bay
Minehead
Ilfracombe
Bridgwater
Wells
Glastonbury
ENGLAND
Preston
Blackburn
Chorley
Southport
Bury
Bolton
Formby
Wigan
St Helens
Wallasey
Liverpool
Birkenhead
Warrington
Ellesmere Port
Crewe
Brymbo
Wrexham
WREXHAM
Horseshoe Pass
Corwen
Llangollen
Ceirw
Dee
Roden
Perry
Oswestry
Llanfyllin
Shrewsbury
Telford
To M54
Welshpool
Twrch
ENGLAND
Church Stretton
Newtown
Bishop's Castle
Offa's Dyke Path
Llanidloes
Severn
POWYS
Rheidol
Ludlow
Knighton
Leominster
Llandrindod Wells
Kington
Builth Wells
Llanstephan
Hay-on-Wye
Hereford
Wye
To M50
Capel-y-Ffin
Talgarth
Black Mountains
Crickhowell
Abergavenny
Ross-on-Wye
Monmouth
MONMOUTHSHIRE
Tintern Abbey
Usk
Chepstow
Tywi
Elwy
Neath
A5
A55
A470
A487
A494
A458
A483
A44
A40
A41
A49
A438
A465
M4
M5
M6
M61

The **Bridge Café** (☎ 622024; www.bridgecafe.co.uk; 7 Bridge St; 🕑 10am-5pm Wed-Fri, 10am-6pm Sat & during bank holiday weekends & school holidays) is the best place in town, with beautiful home-cooked food and spacious bedrooms.

National Express coaches run to Cardiff (1¼ hours) en route to London (£23.50, five hours and 20 minutes).

PEMBROKESHIRE COAST NATIONAL PARK

Sparkling and remote, the wonders of the Pembrokeshire Coast National Park are unmissable, with a stunning coastline of soaring cliffs and golden beaches, set against a backdrop of boiling surf or sheltered crystal coves.

To explore the park on foot, you can follow all or some of the **Pembrokeshire Coast Path** (www.nationaltrail.co.uk). For another view, try sea-kayaking or the whacky sport of **coasteering** (www.coasteering.org) – reputedly invented here.

For information, see www.pcnpa.org.uk and www.visitpembrokeshirecoast.org.uk, or visit the TICs in places such as Fishguard and St Davids.

Activities

Several tour and activity operators are based in the park:

Preseli Venture (☎ 01348-837709; www.preseliventure.com) Coasteering, kayaking and mountain-biking weekends in stunning eco-friendly accommodation.

Thousand Islands Expeditions (☎ 01437-721721; www.thousandislands.co.uk) Bird-spotting, whale watching, fishing trips, island cruises and landings.

TYF Adventure (☎ 01437-721611; www.tyf.com) Coasteering, kayaking, surfing and rock climbing, also with an eco-friendly base.

Getting There & Around

Frequent train services run from Cardiff and London Paddington to Pembrokeshire's major transport hubs: Haverfordwest, and the ports of Pembroke Dock and Fishguard. For getting around between May and September, local buses such as the Poppit Rocket, Celtic Coaster and Puffin Shuttle are operated under the auspices of **Pembrokeshire Greenways** (www.pembrokeshiregreenways.co.uk).

ST DAVIDS

☎ 01437 / pop 1450

Beautiful little St Davids (Tyddewi) ranks as Britain's smallest city, its status ensured by magnificent 12th-century **St David's cathedral** (www.stdavidscathedral.org.uk; 🕑 8.30am-5.30pm Mon-Sat, 12.45-5.30pm Sun) – the home of Welsh Christianity. Today, the tiny streets boast several cafes, a good old-fashioned pub, outdoor gear shops, some smart galleries and several excellent restaurants.

The **TIC** (☎ 720392; enquiries@stdavids.pembrokeshirecoast.org.uk; 🕑 9.30am-5.30pm daily summer, 10am-4pm Mon-Sat winter) is on the eastern side of town.

Sleeping options include: **St Davids YHA Hostel** (☎ 0870 770 6042; stdavids@yha.org; Llaethdy; dm £11.95), a basic but functional farmhouse hostel, 2 miles northwest of town; and **Alandale** (☎ 720404; www.stdavids.co.uk/guesthouse/alandale.htm; 43 Nun St; s/d £36/72), a homely B&B with panoramic views from some rooms.

FISHGUARD

☎ 01348 / pop 3190

Most people come to Fishguard (Abergwaun) to catch a ferry to Ireland, while movie fans like the old part of town, Lower Fishguard, the location for the 1971 film of Dylan Thomas' *Under Milk Wood.*

In the town centre is the **TIC** (☎ 776636; fishguard.tic@pembrokeshire.gov.uk; Market Sq; 🕑 9.30am-5pm Mon-Sat, 10am-4pm Sun Jul & Aug). The train station (Fishguard Harbour) and ferry terminal are a mile northwest of town at Goodwick. There's another TIC here, too.

For a bed, **Hamilton Backpackers** (☎ 874797; 21 Hamilton St; dm/d £16/19; 💻) is a deserved long-standing favourite. The best midrange option is **Manor Town House** (☎ 873260; www.manortownhouse.com; Main St; s/d from £45/75).

NORTHERN WALES

North Wales is dominated by the mountains of Snowdonia, and is surrounded by beautiful coastline with pretty harbour towns and popular holiday beaches. There are sturdy castles at Harlech, Beaumaris and Conwy, and the island of Anglesey is always a good bet for fine weather when thick cloud covers the mountains inland.

SNOWDONIA NATIONAL PARK

The jagged peaks of Snowdonia offer the most spectacular scenery in Wales. The most popular region is in the north around Snowdon (at 1085m the highest peak in Britain south of the Scottish Highlands), although the park extends all the way south to Machynlleth. For outdoor types, walking on the mountains is the main activity. For mountain-bikers there are excellent trails in the surrounding forests. For more information, see www.visitsnowdonia.info and www.snowdonia-npa.gov.uk.

A good base and gateway is the busy village of **Betws-y-Coed** on the eastern side of the park. Pretty **Beddgelert** and former slate-mining town **Blaenau Ffestiniog** are handy for the south.

Most convenient for Snowdon itself is the town of **Llanberis** – a former slate-mining village attracting walkers, climbers and mountain-bikers year round – with a great range of cafes, shops, pubs and B&Bs. The helpful **TIC** (☎ 01286 870765; llanberis.tic@gwynedd.gov.uk; 41 High St; ⏰ 9.30am-4.30pm Easter-Oct, 10.30am-4.30pm Fri-Mon Nov-Easter) stocks a good range of maps, and can advise on the local accommodation.

If walking up mountains isn't for you, from Llanberis you can take the **Snowdon Mountain Railway** (☎ 0870-4580033; www.snowdonrailway.co.uk; ⏰ 9am-5pm Mar-Oct) to the top of Wales' highest peak.

To reach Snowdonia, the handiest train line runs along the North Wales coast between Chester and Holyhead, via Llandudno Junction and Bangor (from where you can get buses into the park itself), with a branch line down to Betws-y-Coed and Blaenau Ffestiniog. An excellent local bus network called the **Snowdon Sherpa** serves the park, with connections between Bangor, Llandudno, Betws-y-Coed and Llanberis.

EDINBURGH & GLASGOW

The Scottish capital, Edinburgh, and neighbouring Glasgow, with several other nearby towns, together make up the 'Central Belt' – by far the most urban area of Scotland. For many years, visitors tended to overlook Glasgow and head instead for Edinburgh, but recently Scotland's second city has enjoyed a cultural and architectural renaissance. Rather than weighing up which of the two cities to see, it's well worth making the effort to fit them both on your itinerary.

EDINBURGH

☎ 0131 / pop 440,000

Scotland's proud and historic capital city is a visual delight, built on a grand scale around two hills – one topped by its impressive castle, the other a big chunk of undeveloped mountain seemingly helicoptered in for effect. Among the well-proportioned buildings and the tangle of historic walkways you'll find a rich haul of excellent museums, galleries, pubs and entertainment options, while every house seems to have its own ghost story. And with the UK's most popular and comprehensive summer festival scene (see www.edinburghfestivals.co.uk), visitors who plan a brief stopover often end up staying longer.

Orientation

The city's most prominent landmarks are Edinburgh Castle at the western end of the Old Town, and the rocky peak of Arthur's Seat southeast of the centre. The Old and New Towns are separated by Princes Street Gardens, with Waverley train station (the main train station in Edinburgh) at their eastern end. Trains to/from the west also stop at Haymarket station. Edinburgh bus station is at the northeast corner of St Andrew Sq.

Information

The **Edinburgh & Scotland Information Centre** (☎ 0845 225 5121; info@visitscotland.com; 3 Princes St; ⏰ 9am-9pm Mon-Sat, 10am-8pm Sun Jul & Aug, 9am-7pm Mon-Sat, 10am-7pm Sun May, Jun & Sep, 9am-5pm Mon-Wed, 9am-6pm Thu-Sun Oct-Apr) offers an accommodation booking service, currency exchange, gift and bookshop, internet access, and tickets for Edinburgh city tours and Scottish Citylink bus services.

Other options for internet include **easyInternetcafé** (☎ 220 3580; www.easy-everything.com; 58 Rose St; ⏰ 7.30am-10.30pm) and **Internet Café** (☎ 226 5400; www.edininternetcafe.com; 98 West Bow, Victoria St; ⏰ 10am-11pm).

Sights

Dominating the skyline like a city in the clouds, the hilltop complex of **Edinburgh Castle** (☎ 225 9846; www.edinburghcastle.gov.uk; Castlehill; adult £12; ⏰ 9.30am-6pm Apr-Oct, 9.30am-5pm Nov-Mar) should be the first stop for any visitor. It's a mix of architectural styles, representing centuries of myriad historic uses. Highlights include **St Margaret's Chapel** (the oldest building in Edinburgh) and the **Royal Palace** (including the Stone of Destiny and the Scottish Crown Jewels).

Sealed off for 250 years beneath the City Chambers, **Real Mary King's Close** (☎ 0870 243 0160; 2 Warriston's Close; adult £10; ⏰ 9am-9pm Aug, 10am-9pm

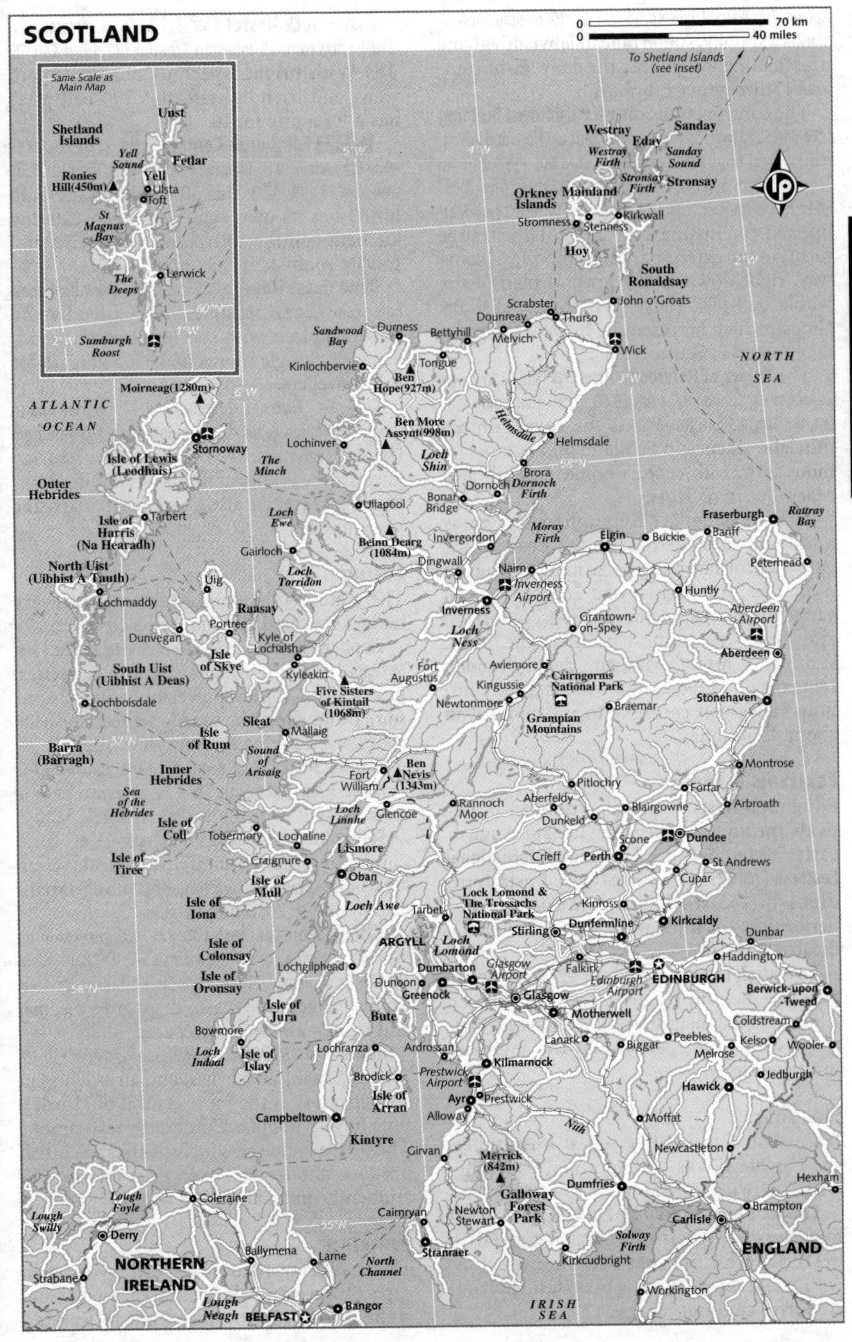
SCOTLAND
0 70 km
0 40 miles
To Shetland Islands (see inset)
Same Scale as Main Map
Shetland Islands
Unst
Yell Sound
Fetlar
Yell
Ronies Hill(450m)
Ulsta
Toft
St Magnus Bay
Lerwick
The Deeps
Sumburgh Roost
Westray
Sanday
Eday
Westray Firth
Sanday Sound
Stronsay Firth
Stronsay
Orkney Islands
Mainland
Kirkwall
Stromness
Stenness
Hoy
South Ronaldsay
John o'Groats
Scrabster
Thurso
Dounreay
Melvich
Bettyhill
Durness
Sandwood Bay
Tongue
Wick
Kinlochbervie
Ben Hope(927m)
NORTH SEA
Moirneag(1280m)
ATLANTIC OCEAN
Stornoway
Ben More Assynt(998m)
Helmsdale
Lochinver
Isle of Lewis (Leodhais)
The Minch
Loch Shin
Brora
Outer Hebrides
Dornoch
Dornoch Firth
Bonar Bridge
Ullapool
Isle of Harris (Na Hearadh)
Tarbert
Loch Ewe
Fraserburgh
Rattray Bay
Banff
Buckie
Elgin
Moray Firth
Invergordon
Beinn Dearg (1084m)
Gairloch
Peterhead
North Uist (Uibhist A Tauth)
Loch Torridon
Dingwall
Nairn
Inverness Airport
Huntly
Uig
Lochmaddy
Raasay
Inverness
Aberdeen Airport
Portree
Grantown-on-Spey
Dunvegan
Kyle of Lochalsh
Loch Ness
Aberdeen
Isle of Skye
South Uist (Uibhist A Deas)
Kyleakin
Fort Augustus
Aviemore
Cairngorms National Park
Five Sisters of Kintail (1068m)
Kingussie
Lochboisdale
Newtonmore
Stonehaven
Braemar
Sleat
Grampian Mountains
Isle of Rum
Mallaig
Barra (Barragh)
Sound of Arisaig
Ben Nevis (1343m)
Montrose
Inner Hebrides
Fort William
Pitlochry
Forfar
Sea of the Hebrides
Glencoe
Rannoch Moor
Aberfeldy
Arbroath
Loch Linnhe
Blairgowrie
Isle of Coll
Dunkeld
Tobermory
Lochaline
Scone
Dundee
Lismore
Crieff
Perth
Isle of Tiree
Craignure
St Andrews
Oban
Cupar
Isle of Mull
Loch Awe
Lock Lomond & The Trossachs National Park
Kinross
Isle of Iona
Tarbet
Kirkcaldy
Dunfermline
Stirling
Dunbar
ARGYLL
Loch Lomond
Isle of Colonsay
Haddington
Glasgow Airport
Falkirk
Lochgilphead
Dumbarton
EDINBURGH
Isle of Oronsay
Edinburgh Airport
Berwick-upon-Tweed
Dunoon
Greenock
Glasgow
Isle of Jura
Motherwell
Bute
Coldstream
Bowmore
Lanark
Peebles
Kelso
Loch Indaal
Isle of Islay
Lochranza
Ardrossan
Biggar
Melrose
Wooler
Kilmarnock
Prestwick Airport
Jedburgh
Brodick
Isle of Arran
Hawick
Ayr
Prestwick
Alloway
Campbeltown
Moffat
Nith
Kintyre
Newcastleton
Girvan
Merrick (842m)
Hexham
Lough Foyle
Coleraine
Galloway Forest Park
Dumfries
Brampton
Lough Swilly
Cairnryan
Newton Stewart
Carlisle
Derry
Solway Firth
Ballymena
Larne
North Channel
Stranraer
Kirkcudbright
ENGLAND
NORTHERN IRELAND
Strabane
Workington
Lough Neagh
BELFAST
Bangor
IRISH SEA
Helmsdale
BRITAIN

Apr-Jul, Sep & Oct, 10am-4pm Sun-Fri & 10am-9pm Sat Nov-Mar) is a spooky, subterranean labyrinth giving a fascinating insight into the daily life of 16th- and 17th-century Edinburgh.

The controversial **Scottish Parliament Building** (☎ 348 5200; www.scottish.parliament.uk; Holyrood Rd; admission free, tours adult/concession £6/3.60; 9am-6pm Tue-Thu, 10am-5pm Mon & Fri in session, 10am-5pm Mon-Fri in recess Apr-Oct, 10am-4pm Mon-Fri in recess Nov-Mar) opened for business in 2005. The strange forms of the exterior are all symbolic in some way, right down to the ground plan of the whole complex (best seen from Salisbury Crags), which represents a 'flower of democracy rooted in Scottish soil'.

The **Palace of Holyroodhouse** (☎ 556 5100; www.royal.gov.uk; Canongate; adult £9.80; 9.30am-6pm Apr-Oct, 9.30am-4.30pm Nov-Mar) is the royal family's official residence in Scotland, but is most famous as the 16th-century home of the ill-fated Mary Queen of Scots.

In **Holyrood Park**, Edinburghers can enjoy a little bit of wilderness in the heart of the city. The former hunting ground of Scottish monarchs, the park covers 263 hectares of varied landscape, including crags, moorland and loch. The highest point is the 251m summit of **Arthur's Seat**, the deeply eroded remnant of a long-extinct volcano; for stunning views you can hike to the summit in about 45 minutes.

Festivals & Events

Edinburgh hosts an amazing number of festivals throughout the year. In late August/early September, the **Edinburgh International Festival** (☎ 473 2099; www.eif.co.uk) hosts hundreds of the world's top musicians and performers for three weeks of music, opera, theatre and dance.

Edinburgh Festival Fringe (☎ 226 0026; www.edfringe.com), held in August, was originally an adjunct to the main festival; it's now *the* biggest festival of the performing arts anywhere in the world.

Sleeping

It's essential to book a bed at busy times, such as New Year and summer, especially when there's a festival on.

Budget Backpackers (☎ 226 6351; www.budgetbackpackers.com; 39 Cowgate, The Grassmarket; dm £11-14, tw £44;) This fun spot piles on the extras, with pool tables, laundry, breakfast (£2) and colourful chill-out lounge.

Castle Rock Hostel (☎ 225 9666; www.scotlands-top-hostels.com; 15 Johnston Tce; dm £13-15, d £40-55;) With bright, spacious dorms, superb views and friendly staff, this 200-bed place has a lot going for it.

our pick **Edinburgh Central SYHA** (☎ 524 2090; www.syha.org.uk; 9 Haddington Pl, Leith Walk; dm £10-25.50, s/tw from £33/49;) This 300-bed purpose-built hostel has its own cafe-bistro, self-catering kitchen, comfortable eight-bed dorms and private rooms.

Dene Guest House (☎ 556 2700; www.deneguesthouse.com; 7 Eyre Pl; s/d from £30/60) A friendly and informal place, with spacious bedrooms; inexpensive single rooms make it a bargain for solo travellers.

Cluaran House (☎ 221 0047; www.cluaran-house-edinburgh.co.uk; 47 Leamington Tce; s/d & tw from £50/80) Bright and arty, this stylish Victorian guest house is known for its welcoming owners. Breakfasts are also good, particularly the vegie option.

Eating

There are good-value restaurants for every budget scattered all around the city.

Elephant House (21 George IV Bridge; snacks £3-6; 8am-11pm;) Brilliant cafe with baguettes, pastries and coffees powerful enough to inspire JK Rowling (she used to write in the back room, overlooking Edinburgh Castle).

Engine Shed (19 St Leonard's Lane; lunches £3-6; 10am-3.30pm Mon-Sat) This vegetarian cafe is an ideal spot after hiking on Arthur's Seat.

Forest (2 Bristo Pl; mains £3-5; noon-11pm;) A comfortably scuffed antidote to squeaky-clean style bars, serving huge helpings of vegetarian/vegan fodder. Also has wi-fi.

our pick **Monster Mash** (☎ 225 7069; www.monstermashcafe.co.uk; 4a Forrest Rd; mains £5-7; 8am-10pm Mon-Fri, 9am-10pm Sat, 10am-10pm Sun) Classic British grub – bangers and mash, shepherd's pie, fish and chips – all freshly prepared.

Howie's (☎ 556 5766; 29 Waterloo Pl; mains £10-15; lunch & dinner) This bright and airy Georgian corner-house is the most central of Howie's four hugely popular Edinburgh restaurants. The recipe for success includes fresh Scottish produce, good-value, fixed-price menus, and eminently quaffable house wines.

Drinking

The array of pubs and bars is vast, as you might expect from a capital city, tourist hotspot and student town. If you just want to wander,

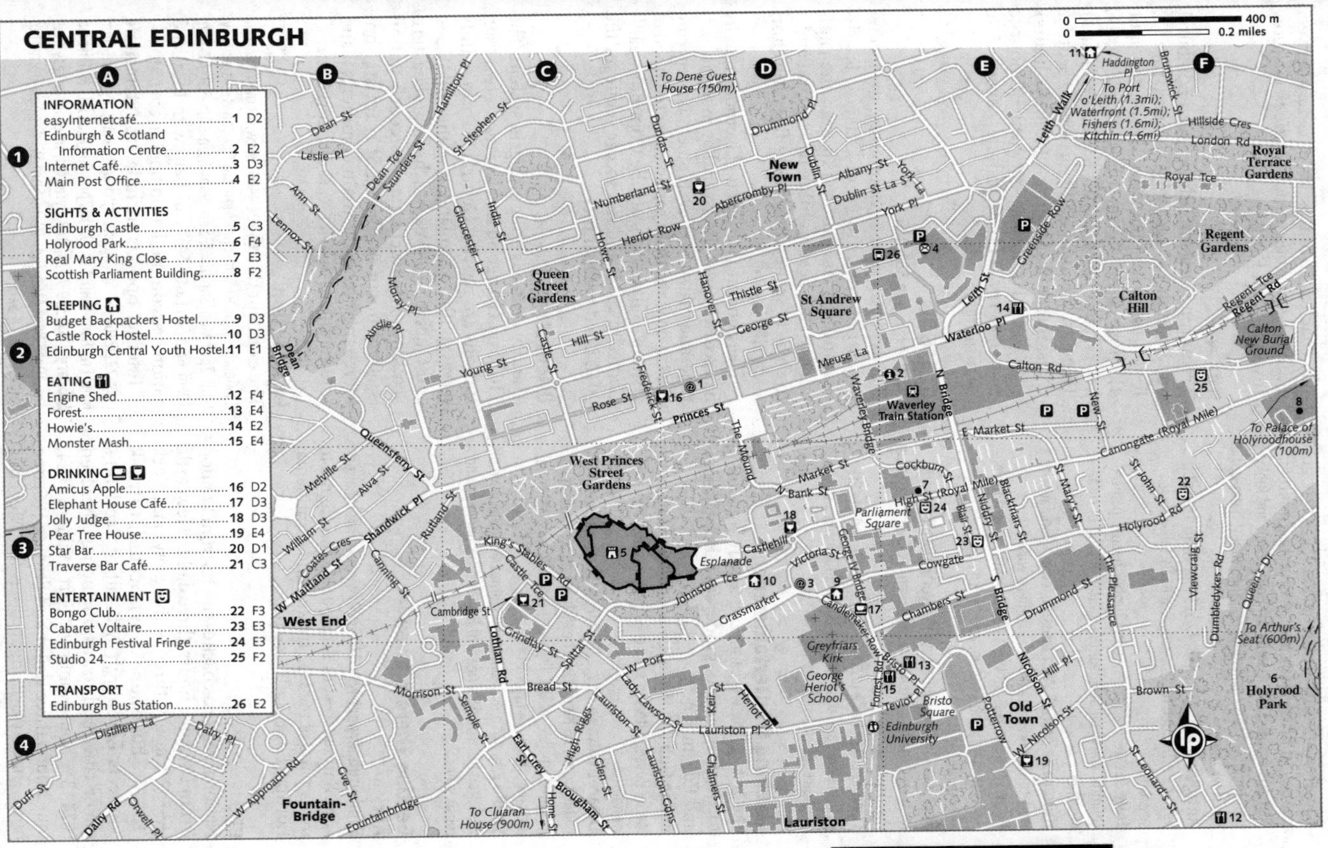
CENTRAL EDINBURGH
INFORMATION
easyInternetcafé 1 D2
Edinburgh & Scotland Information Centre 2 E2
Internet Café 3 D3
Main Post Office 4 E2
SIGHTS & ACTIVITIES
Edinburgh Castle 5 C3
Holyrood Park 6 F4
Real Mary King Close 7 E3
Scottish Parliament Building 8 F2
SLEEPING
Budget Backpackers Hostel 9 D3
Castle Rock Hostel 10 D3
Edinburgh Central Youth Hostel 11 E1
EATING
Engine Shed 12 F4
Forest 13 E4
Howie's 14 E2
Monster Mash 15 E4
DRINKING
Amicus Apple 16 D2
Elephant House Café 17 D3
Jolly Judge 18 D3
Pear Tree House 19 E4
Star Bar 20 D1
Traverse Bar Café 21 C3
ENTERTAINMENT
Bongo Club 22 F3
Cabaret Voltaire 23 E3
Edinburgh Festival Fringe 24 E3
Studio 24 25 F2
TRANSPORT
Edinburgh Bus Station 26 E2
400 m
0.2 miles
To Dene Guest House (150m)
To Port o'Leith (1.3mi); Waterfront (1.5mi); Fishers (1.6mi); Kitchin (1.6mi)
To Palace of Holyroodhouse (100m)
To Arthur's Seat (600m)
To Cluaran House (900m)
New Town
Old Town
West End
Fountain-Bridge
Lauriston
Queen Street Gardens
St Andrew Square
Regent Gardens
Royal Terrace Gardens
Calton Hill
Calton New Burial Ground
West Princes Street Gardens
Waverley Train Station
Parliament Square
Esplanade
Greyfriars Kirk
George Heriot's School
Bristo Square
Edinburgh University
Holyrood Park
Princes St
BRITAIN

the area around Grassmarket has a few good places in close proximity. Our favourites:

Amicus Apple (15 Frederick St) Bold design and funky lighting make this cocktail lounge the hippest hang-out in the New Town.

Antiquary (☎ 225 2858; 72 St Stephen St) Trad pub with bare wooden floorboards and lively folk-music sessions.

Jolly Judge (7a James Court) Timber beams, painted ceilings, convivial atmosphere, plus a log fire in cold weather.

Human Be-in (2-8 West Crosscauseway) Popular with a well-to-do university crowd; excellent wine list.

Pear Tree House (38 West Nicolson St) Student favourite, with comfy sofas inside, and the city centre's biggest beer garden.

Star Bar (1 Northumberland Pl) Worth the pilgrimage for one of the New Town's best jukeboxes. Don't ask about the skull.

Traverse Bar Café (☎ 228 5383; 10 Cambridge St) Bustling pre- and post-theatre bar in Edinburgh's top drama venue.

Clubbing & Entertainment

The List (£2.20; www.list.co.uk) is an invaluable fortnightly events guide covering Glasgow and Edinburgh.

Bongo Club (☎ 558 7604; www.thebongoclub.co.uk; Moray House, Paterson's Land, 37 Holyrood Rd) Weird and wonderful.

Cabaret Voltaire (☎ 220 6176; www.thecabaretvoltaire.com; 36 Blair St) Eschews huge dance floors for a 'creative crucible' of DJs, live acts, comedy, theatre, visual arts and the spoken word.

Studio 24 (☎ 558 3758; www.studio24edinburgh.co.uk; 24 Calton Rd) The dark heart of Edinburgh's underground music scene.

Getting There & Away

AIR

Edinburgh airport (☎ 333 1000; www.edinburghairport.com), 8 miles west of Edinburgh, has flights to many parts of the UK, Ireland and Continental Europe. For details, see p155.

BUS

National Express coaches run to/from London (from £34, nine hours, three daily), Newcastle (£17, 2¾ hours, three to five daily) and York (£34, 5¾ hours, one daily). Scottish Citylink connects Edinburgh with all of Scotland's major cities and towns, including Aberdeen (£24, 3¼ hours, hourly), Fort William (£24, four hours, three daily) and Stirling (£6, one hour, hourly). Budget operator Megabus has coaches (from as little as £2) between Edinburgh, Aberdeen, Dundee, Glasgow, Inverness and Perth.

TRAIN

Trains run at least hourly between Edinburgh and London's Kings Cross station (from £25 if you book in advance, £126 on the spot, 4½ hours) via Newcastle (£20 to £40, 1½ hours) and York (£30 to £70, 2½ hours). There are frequent daily services to Scottish cities, including Inverness (£38, 3¼ hours), and a regular shuttle between Edinburgh and Glasgow (£11, 50 minutes, every 15 to 30 minutes).

GLASGOW

☎ 0141 / pop 581,000

Not as picturesque as Edinburgh, the former industrial powerhouse of Glasgow is grittier and arguably more fun than the capital, with the best nightlife in Scotland and a lively arts scene, plus many fine museums and galleries.

Like London, Cardiff and Liverpool, the city has rediscovered the river that made its fortune, and massive redevelopment is preparing the Clyde waterfront for an expected flood of visitors – Glasgow hosts the Commonwealth Games in 2014, and is a soccer venue for the 2012 London Olympics.

Orientation

The city centre is built on a grid system. The TIC is on George Sq and Glasgow's two train stations are nearby; Central Station mainly serves southern Scotland, England and Wales, and Queen St serves northern and eastern Scotland. The Buchanan bus/coach station is 300m north of Queen St train station. Merchant City is the main commercial and entertainment district, east of George Sq.

Information

The excellent **TIC** (☎ 204 4400; www.seeglasgow.com; 11 George Sq; 🕒 9am-6pm Mon-Sat Oct-Jan & Easter-May, 9am-7pm Mon-Sat Jun & Sep, 9am-8pm Mon-Sat Jul-Aug, 10am-6pm Sun Easter-Sep) can help with local and national accommodation bookings (£3).

Internet options include **easyInternetcafé** (☎ 222 2364; 57 St Vincent St; charges vary; 🕒 7am-9pm Mon-Fri, 8am-9pm Sat, 9am-7pm Sun) and **Hillhead Library** (☎ 339 7223; 348 Byres Rd; internet access free; 🕒 10am-8pm Mon-Tue, 10am-5pm Wed, noon-8pm Thu, 9am-5pm Fri & Sat).

Sights

Glasgow's main square is **George Square**, a grand public space built in the Victorian era to show off the city's wealth and dignified by statues of notable Glaswegians and Scots, including Robert Burns, James Watt, John Moore and Sir Walter Scott.

The prosperity of Glasgow's 18th-century 'tobacco lords', who made vast profits importing tobacco and sugar via lucrative transatlantic trade routes, is reflected in the grand buildings they erected in the area east of George Square, now known as the **Merchant City**; many have been renewed as stylish apartments, bars and restaurants.

Recently reopened, Glasgow's much-loved cultural icon, the **Kelvingrove Art Gallery & Museum** (☎ 276 9599; Argyle St; admission free; 10am-5pm Mon-Thu & Sat, 11am-5pm Fri & Sun), is the most visited museum in Britain outside London, with a superb collection of Scottish and European art, a fascinating series of natural-history exhibits, and plenty on Scottish history including the Viking influence. If you only visit one museum in Glasgow, make it this one.

Strolling along the **River Clyde** gives two very different insights into the city. First there's **Glasgow Science Centre** (☎ 420 5000; www.glasgowsciencecentre.org; 50 Pacific Quay; adult £7.95; 10am-6pm), which brings science and technology alive through hundreds of interactive exhibits. Then, 3 miles downstream, **Clydebuilt** (☎ 886 1013; www.scottishmaritimemuseum.org; Braehead Shopping Centre, Kings Inch Rd; adult £4.25; 10am-5.30pm Mon-Sat, 11am-5.30pm Sun) has a superb collection of model ships, industrial displays and narrative that vividly depicts the history of the Clyde, which has been inextricably linked with Glasgow and its people.

Sleeping

Bunkum Backpackers (☎ 581 4481; www.bunkumglasgow.co.uk; 26 Hillhead St; dm/tw £12/32) A quieter place with a homely feel with spacious dorms (which include lockers), and a comfy lounge room.

Blue Sky Backpackers (☎ 221 1710; www.blueskyhostel.com; 65 Berkeley St; dm £13-15, d £38;) Another party joint, fairly basic, but a good spot to dump your bag and head out for the night. Don't confuse this place with other hostels in the street, which aren't as nice.

our pick **Glasgow SYHA Hostel** (☎ 332 3004; www.syha.org.uk; 8 Park Tce; dm £15.50-20;) In a charming town house overlooking Kelvingrove Park, this place is simply fabulous and one of Scotland's best official hostels.

Euro Hostel (☎ 222 2828; www.euro-hostels.co.uk; 318 Clyde St; dm £16-18, s/tw from £30/40;) This institutional slab wouldn't look out of place in Soviet-era Poland, and dorms can be crowded, but with the city so handy you'll be out partying most of the night, so who cares?

Eating

Café Lava (☎ 553 1123; 24 St Andrew's St; mains £2-6; 8am-6pm Mon-Fri, 10am-5pm Sat & Sun;) Everyone wants to live next door to a cafe like this: delicious home cooking, the best coffee in town, and the best carrot cake in Scotland. Wi-fi, too.

University Café (☎ 339 5217; 87 Byres Rd; mains £3-6; 9am-10pm Mon-Sat, 10am-10pm Sun) This classic cafe has been serving fried breakfasts to hungover students for almost a century.

Mono (☎ 553 2400; 12 Kings Ct; mains £3-7; noon-10pm) Not content to be one of Glasgow's best vegetarian cafes, this place also crams in an indie record store, organic grocery shop and occasional live-music venue.

Wee Curry Shop (☎ 353 0777; 7 Buccleuch St; 2-course lunch £6, dinner mains £11; lunch Mon-Sat, dinner daily) An Indian restaurant decked out in tartan? The food is authentic though, so there's no fear of a faulty balti.

Drinking

Some of Scotland's best nightlife is to be found in the din and roar of Glasgow's crowded pubs and bars. Merchant City and the West End are the twin epicentres of fashionable drinking with any number of different concept bars, while Sauchiehall St has mainstream boozers that attract their fair share of stag and hen nights. For starters:

Arches (253 Argyle St) Bar-club-theatre where bearded guys in hiking boots rub shoulders with suited city boys.

Bloc (117 Bath St) Buzzing basement bar with young party crowd.

Centre for Contemporary Arts (350 Sauchiehall St) Refined boho spot, ideal for a relaxed drink.

Horse Shoe Bar (17 Drury St) Legendary city-centre pub; tops for real ale and the best-value three-course lunches (£3.50) in town.

Liquid Ship (171-175 Great Western Rd) The best of Glasgow's style bars distilled into a single venue.

Uisge Beatha (☎ 232-246 Woodlands Rd) Traditional boozer with more than 100 single malts on offer.

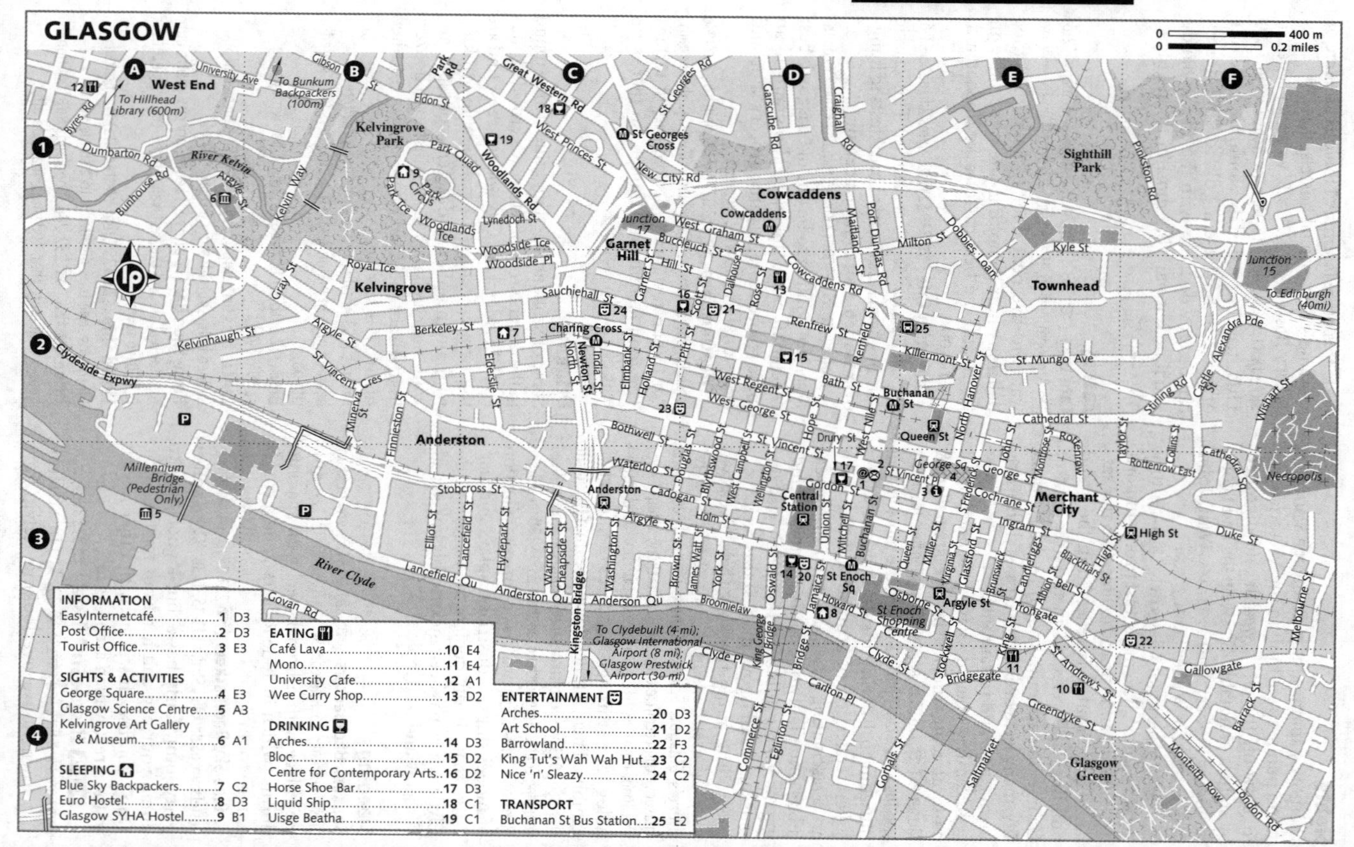
GLASGOW
0 400 m
0 0.2 miles
INFORMATION
EasyInternetcafé 1 D3
Post Office 2 D3
Tourist Office 3 E3
SIGHTS & ACTIVITIES
George Square 4 E3
Glasgow Science Centre 5 A3
Kelvingrove Art Gallery & Museum 6 A1
SLEEPING
Blue Sky Backpackers 7 C2
Euro Hostel 8 D3
Glasgow SYHA Hostel 9 B1
EATING
Café Lava 10 E4
Mono 11 E4
University Cafe 12 A1
Wee Curry Shop 13 D2
DRINKING
Arches 14 D3
Bloc 15 D2
Centre for Contemporary Arts 16 D2
Horse Shoe Bar 17 D3
Liquid Ship 18 C1
Uisge Beatha 19 B1
ENTERTAINMENT
Arches 20 D3
Art School 21 D2
Barrowland 22 F3
King Tut's Wah Wah Hut 23 C2
Nice 'n' Sleazy 24 C2
TRANSPORT
Buchanan St Bus Station 25 E2

Clubbing

Glasgow has long been regarded as the centre of Scotland's live-music scene and has one of Britain's biggest club scenes. Don't believe us? Try the following:

Arches (☎ 565 1000; www.thearches.co.uk; 253 Argyle St; ⏲ club nights Wed, Fri & Sat) The Godfather of Glaswegian clubs.

Art School (☎ 353 4530; www.theartschool.co.uk; 168 Renfrew St; ⏲ Tue-Sun during term time) For innovative DJs and legendary dance nights.

Barrowland (☎ 552 4601; www.glasgow-barrowland.com; 244 Gallowgate) Stalwart live music venue.

King Tut's Wah Wah Hut (☎ 221 5279; www.kingtuts.co.uk; 272a St Vincent St) One of the city's premier live-music pub venues.

Nice 'n' Sleazy (☎ 333 0900; www.nicensleazy.com; 421 Sauchiehall St) The place to catch emerging indie bands.

Getting There & Away

AIR

Ten miles west of the city, **Glasgow International airport** (☎ 887 1111; www.baa.co.uk/glasgow) handles international routes, domestic UK traffic and most flights to/from the Scottish islands. Do not confuse it with **Glasgow Prestwick airport** (☎ 0871 223 0700; www.gpia.co.uk), 30 miles southwest of Glasgow.

BUS

National Express coaches run to/from London (£34, nine hours, at least four daily), Manchester (£28, five hours, four daily), Newcastle (£30, four hours, one daily) and York (£34, seven hours, one daily). Also to/from London, Megabus has one-way fares from around £10.

Scottish Citylink has coaches to/from most major towns in Scotland, including Stirling (£6, 45 minutes, hourly) and Aberdeen (£24, three hours, hourly).

TRAIN

There are direct trains to/from London's King's Cross and Euston stations (from £25 for advance bookings, up to £125 on the spot, 5½ hours, 12 daily). Within Scotland, trains run to/from Aberdeen (£38, hourly, 1¾ hours) and Inverness (£38, three hours, one direct service daily), and along the scenic West Highland line to Oban and Fort William. There are shuttle trains every 15 to 30 minutes to/from Edinburgh (£11, 50 minutes).

CENTRAL & EASTERN SCOTLAND

This vast region includes everything north of the big cities of Glasgow and Edinburgh, and everything east of a line between the Trossach hills and Inverness. Highlights include the historic towns of Stirling and St Andrews – also the spiritual home of the game of golf.

STIRLING

☎ 01786 / pop 41,200

With an impregnable position atop a mighty rocky crag, Stirling's beautifully preserved old town is a treasure of noble buildings and cobbled streets winding up to the ramparts of its dominant castle, offering views for miles around. Clearly visible is the brooding Wallace monument, honouring the freedom fighter of *Braveheart* fame.

The **TIC** (☎ 475019; stirling@visitscotland.com; 41 Dumbarton Rd; ⏲ Mon-Sat Oct-May, daily Jun-Sep) has info and coin-operated internet.

Stirling Castle (☎ 450000; admission £8.50; ⏲ 9.30am-6pm Apr-Sep, 9.30am-5pm Oct-Mar) has existed since prehistoric times, and the location, architecture and historical significance combine to make it a memorable visit today. Many visitors come on daytrips from Edinburgh, so you may have the castle to yourself by about 4pm.

Sleeping options:

Stirling SYHA Hostel (☎ 473442; www.syha.org.uk; St John St; dm £16.25; 💻) Unbeatable location and great facilities.

Willy Wallace Backpackers Hostel (☎ 446773; www.willywallacehostel.com; 77 Murray Pl; dm £14-16, tw £34-37; 💻) Convenient, central, friendly, spacious.

Forth Guest House (☎ 471020; www.forthguesthouse.co.uk; 23 Forth Pl; d £50) Attractive and stylish accommodation at a fair price.

Munro Guest House (☎ 472685; www.munroguesthouse.co.uk; 14 Princes St; s/d £42/58) Cosy and cheery, in the centre of town.

Trains run half-hourly to Edinburgh (£6.50, 55 minutes) and Glasgow (£6.70, 40 minutes), and hourly to Aberdeen (£36.60, 2¼ hours).

ST ANDREWS

☎ 01334 / pop 14,200

For a small place, St Andrews made a big name for itself, firstly as religious centre, then as Scotland's oldest university town, and

BRITAIN

finally as the home of golf. It's a lovely place to visit, even if you've no interest in little white balls, with medieval ruins, stately buildings, idyllic white sands, and many good sleeping and eating options.

The **TIC** (☎ 472021; standrews@visitscotland.com; 70 Market St; Mon-Sat Nov-Easter, daily Easter-Oct) also offers internet access.

Ruined **St Andrews cathedral** (☎ 472563; cathedral & castle £7.20, cathedral £4.20; 9.30am-5.30pm Apr-Sep, 9.30am-4.30pm Oct-Mar) was one of Britain's most magnificent medieval buildings. You can appreciate the scale and majesty of the edifice from the small sections that remain standing. Nearby, with dramatic coastline views, **St Andrews castle** is also mainly ruinous, but the site is evocative.

The **British Golf Museum** (☎ 460046; www.britishgolfmuseum.co.uk; Bruce Embankment; admission £5.50; 9.30am-5.30pm Mon-Sat & 10am-5pm Sun Apr-Oct, 10am-4pm Nov-Mar) has an extraordinarily comprehensive overview of the history and development of the game. Nearby is the **Royal & Ancient Golf Club**, at the head of the **Old Course**, which you can stroll on once play is finished for the day.

Places to stay:

St Andrews Tourist Hostel (☎ 479911; www.standrewshostel.com; St Marys Pl; dm £13-15;) Central, with high corniced ceilings and a laissez-faire approach.

Meade B&B (☎ 477350; annmeade10@hotmail.com; 5 Albany Pl; s/d with shared bathroom £25/50, s/d with private bathroom £37/57) Economical gem run by a friendly family and their pets.

our pick **Abbey Cottage** (☎ 473727; www.abbeycottage.co.uk; Abbey Walk; s £40, d £54-58) Engaging spot below the town, with stone walls and rambling garden.

You can get here on the bus from Edinburgh (£9, two hours, hourly), Glasgow (£9, 2½ hours, hourly) and Stirling (£7, two hours, six to seven Monday to Saturday). The nearest train station is Leuchars (5 miles away but connected by frequent buses), with trains to Edinburgh (£10.60, one hour, hourly).

WESTERN & NORTHERN SCOTLAND

It's a long way north, and takes effort to reach, but this is by far the best bit of Scotland, and one of the best bits of Britain too. Some folks (well, those that love mountains and wild places) might even say that it's one of the finest parts of the whole of Europe.

The western area includes deep lochs, misty glens and towering snow-covered mountains. Famous name-checks include Loch Lomond, the Isle of Skye and Ben Nevis. The northern area, often called the Northwest Highlands, is the land beyond the Great Glen, the fault-line that separates this remote and ruggedly beautiful part of Scotland from the rest of the country.

Places are listed roughly southwest to northeast. It's easy to underestimate the size of the region, so give yourself extra time to explore. See www.visithighlands.com for transport and accommodation advice throughout the region, or drop by one of the local TICs that dot the area.

LOCH LOMOND

You take the high road, and I'll take the low road. Legendary Loch Lomond, not 20 miles from central Glasgow, gives you the first taste of the epic scenery awaiting you in Britain's northern reaches. This makes the lake incredibly popular, and you might be disappointed at first glimpse. But get onto a boat, or explore the forest paths on its eastern side, and you'll soon be beguiled by its charms.

Loch Lomond forms the western half of the **Loch Lomond & The Trossachs National Park** (www.lochlomond-trossachs.org). The eastern half of the park, the Trossach hills, is best reached from Stirling, as there's virtually no road link between the west and east sides.

Along Loch Lomond's western shore, the busy A82 hums with traffic. At Balloch you'll find the main 'gateway' centre for the park, **Loch Lomond Shores** (☎ 01389-721500; www.lochlomondshores.com; 9.30am-5.30pm Apr-Sep, 10am-5.30pm Oct-Mar;), with information, audiovisual entertainment, wi-fi, and a giant parking area and retail complex hinting at motives beyond conservation.

The eastern shore is better territory for exploration. The road runs as far as Rowardennan; beyond there, walkers can follow the West Highland Way along the shore through beautiful woodland for a few miles. Or all the way to Fort William…

OBAN

☎ 01631 / pop 8120

A major launchpad for the islands off Scotland's west coast, especially Mull, the harbour town of Oban enjoys a splendid bayside location. The **TIC** (☎ 563122; info@oban.visitscotland.com; Argyll Sq; ⏲ 9am-5.30pm Mon-Sat, 10am-4pm Sun Apr-Oct, 10am-5pm Mon-Sat, noon-4pm Sun Nov-Mar) also has internet access.

As befitting a ferry town, there are a lot of fairly mediocre B&Bs here, and a racket at the northern end of George St involving outrageous prices for substandard rooms across various premises. Instead, try the following places:

Jeremy Inglis Hostel (☎ 565065; 21 Airds Cres; dm £12, s £17-20) Curious part-B&B-part-hostel, exuding offbeat character but fairly priced.

our pick **Oban Backpackers** (☎ 562107; www.scotlandstophostels.com; Breadalbane St; dm £13.50; 💻) Space isn't a worry at this sociable hostel; you could dock the Mull ferry in the enormous lounge. Also has wi-fi.

Maridon House (☎ 562670; Dunuaran Rd; s/d £28/50) The personable owner charges a very fair price for appealing rooms, some with sea/harbour views.

Citylink buses run to/from Glasgow (£13.20, three hours, eight daily) and Fort William (£10.40, 1½ hours, two to four daily Monday to Saturday). Trains run to/from Glasgow (£18.30, three hours, three daily).

ISLE OF MULL

☎ 01688

Just a short ferry hop from the coast, Mull attracts wildlife enthusiasts with eagles and dolphins, while hillwalkers tackle Ben More for magnificent views from its summit.

The Oban ferry arrives at Craignure, on the eastern coast, but most Mull residents live in Tobermory, in the north, an achingly pretty ensemble of colourful shorefront houses straight out of a picturebook (and featuring in a popular children's TV series), with many sleeping and eating options:

Tobermory SYHA Hostel (☎ 01688-302481; www.syha.org.uk; Main St; dm £14; ⏲ mid-Mar–Oct; 💻) Simple and friendly, in a creaky waterfront building.

Fàilte Guest House (☎ 01688-302495; www.failteguesthouse.com; 27 Main St; s/d from £32/64; ⏲ Apr-Oct) Cosy B&B on the colourful waterfront.

our pick **Mishnish Hotel** (☎ 01688-302009; Main St; bar meals £5-9; ⏲ lunch & dinner, bar open till 1am, 2am at weekends) Spend your life-savings on ferry tickets, but you won't find a better island pub than this. Good beer, good crowd, good food.

From Oban you reach Mull on a CalMac ferry (foot passenger £4.25, 45 minutes, five to seven daily). For getting around the island, **Bowman's Coaches** (☎ 812313; www.bowmanstours.co.uk) connects Craignure with Tobermory (£7 return, 50 minutes, four to seven daily summer, three to five Monday to Saturday winter). Or hire a bike at the legendary **Archibald Brown & Son** (☎ 01688-302020; www.browns-tobermory.co.uk; 21 Main St; per day £13; ⏲ Mon-Sat).

FORT WILLIAM

☎ 01397 / pop 9910

On the banks of Loch Linnhe and towered over by majestic mountains, Fort William should be magnificent but it's spoilt by an ugly bypass and a row of depressing shops along the pedestrianised main street. But you're not here to hang around town. Fort William is a jumping-off point dubbed 'Outdoor Capital of the UK', and there's much to do in the surrounding area. Trot up **Ben Nevis** to reach the highest point in Britain. Or, if downhill's more your thing, go to the nearby **Nevis Range** for mountain-biking or skiing.

The **TIC** (☎ 0845 225 5121; fortwilliam@visitscotland.com; 15 High St; ⏲ 9am-6pm Mon-Sat, 10am-5pm Sun Jun-Sep, 9am-5pm Mon-Sat Oct-May) is helpful and has internet access (£1 per 20 minutes).

Sleeping options:

Fort William Backpackers (☎ 700711; www.scotlands-top-hostels.com; Alma Rd; dm £13; 💻) Welcoming place near train and bus stations.

Ben Nevis Inn (☎ 701227; www.ben-nevis-inn.co.uk; dm £14) Under a cracking pub at the Ben Nevis trailhead, with no-nonsense bunks in little alcoves.

Bank Street Lodge (☎ 700070; www.bankstreetlodge.co.uk; Bank St; dm/s/d £14/25/45) No-nonsense guest house and hostel with spick-and-span rooms.

Glen Nevis SYHA Hostel (☎ 702336; www.syha.org.uk; Glen Nevis; dm/tw £17.50/46; 💻) Well-equipped hostel at the foot of The Ben, 2½ miles from town.

Citylink coaches run to/from Edinburgh (£25.20, four hours, one direct daily) and Glasgow (£17.80, three hours, eight daily), Inverness (£11.30, two hours, five to seven daily) and Oban (£10.40, 1½ hours, two to four daily Monday to Saturday). Trains run to/from Glasgow (£22.20, 3¾ hours, three to four daily).

For getting around locally, buses trundle between the bus station, Glen Nevis SYHA and the Nevis Range. Or rent wheels from **Off-Beat Bikes** (☎ 704008; www.offbeatbikes.co.uk; 117 High St; half-/full-day hire £10/15; ⏲ daily). For walking info, especially if you're considering Ben Nevis, visit the **Glen Nevis Visitor Centre** (☎ 705922; www.bennevisweather.co.uk; ⌚ 9am-5pm Easter-Oct, 9am-4pm Nov-Easter) about 2 miles from town.

ISLE OF SKYE

☎ 01478

The Isle of Skye's romantic and lofty reputation is well deserved, and the scenic splendour of Scotland's largest island rarely disappoints. Even if your stay is marked by the typical mist and drizzle (Skye owes its name to a Norse word for 'cloud'), you'll likely feel the magic, especially around the striking Cuillin Hills at the island's southern end.

BRITAIN

The helpful **TIC** (☎ 01478-612137; portree@visitscotland.com; Bayfield Rd; ⌚ Mon-Sat Oct-Easter, daily Easter-Sep) offers accommodation booking, internet (£1 per 20 minutes) and foreign exchange.

Portree, the island's capital, has the largest range of sleeping and eating places. A small selection of favourites is listed here, but there are many more hostels and B&Bs dotted around the island.

Bayfield Backpackers (☎ 612231; Bayfield; dm £14) Smart and functional with great views, few frills but lots of sensible details (including wi-fi).

Bayview House (☎ 613340; www.bayviewhouse.co.uk; Bayfield; d £45-50) Solid comfort is the keyword at this great-value stalwart. Wi-fi available.

Braeside B&B (☎ 612613; www.braesideportree.co.uk; Stormy Hill; d £54-60; ⌚ Jan-Oct) Bright and friendly with good breakfasts.

Ben Tianavaig (☎ 612152; www.ben-tianavaig.co.uk; 5 Bosville Tce; d £60) Memorable views, friendly hosts and antipodean flavour.

Most visitors arrive across the bridge from Kyle of Lochalsh on the mainland. Citylink runs buses to Portree from Glasgow (£31, 6½ hours, three daily) and Inverness (£18, 3¼ hours, three daily). A slower but infinitely more rewarding route involves the train on the famously scenic West Highland Line from Fort William, or all the way from Glasgow to Mallaig on the mainland, from where a ferry runs across to Skye.

On the island, the Skye Roverbus ticket gives unlimited travel for one/three days for £6/15, although Sunday services are scant. Bike hire is available from **Fairwinds** (☎ 822270; standonaldson@aol.com; Elgol Rd, Broadford) and **Island Cycles** (☎ 613121; The Green, Portree).

INVERNESS

☎ 01463 / pop 44,500

By far the region's largest settlement, friendly Inverness is an important service centre for Highlanders and visitors, as well as a transport hub, so you're bound to pass through at some point in your wanderings. The River Ness is the city's chief delight, and a summer evening stroll along its banks is soothingly romantic. On a riverside hillock, **Inverness Castle** is a lightweight compared with most Scottish fortifications, but its rosy walls are beautiful at sunset. Inverness is also a fine gateway: monster-famous **Loch Ness** is on the doorstep, while tours and buses serve the Highlands.

The friendly **TIC** (☎ 234353; invernesstic@visitscotland.com; Castle Wynd; ⌚ 9am-5pm Mon-Sat, 10am-4pm Sun Sep-May, 9am-6pm Mon-Sat, 9.30am-5pm Sun Jun-Aug) offers currency exchange, internet access (£3 per hour), tour, ferry and accommodation bookings.

Sleeping

Inverness has a good range of sleeping options. B&Bs along the river tend to be more pricey, while Old Edinburgh Rd, Kenneth St and Ardconnel St are cheaper.

our pick **Bazpackers Backpackers** (☎ 717663; bazmail@btopenworld.com; 4 Culduthel Rd; dm/d £13/32; 💻) This cosy hostel is hard to beat with its relaxed vibe, log fire, Ness-view dorms, wi-fi and great location.

Inverness SYHA Hostel (☎ 231771; www.syha.org.uk; Victoria Dr; dm/d £17/34; 💻) Offering excellent facilities, spacious dorms and rooms, a pine feel, space-age kitchen and two lounges, this is one of the SYHA's best.

Hornbeam (☎ 225655; ian.barron@btinternet.com; 12A Lovat Rd; d with shared/private bathroom £44/52) A gentle welcome and a genuine wish to make guests feel at home awaits at this understated B&B, one of several in the surrounding streets.

Ivybank Guest House (☎ 232796; www.ivybankguesthouse.com; 28 Old Edinburgh Rd; s £40, d with shared/private bathroom £60/80) This noble heritage-listed Georgian building brims with welcome and character.

Eating & Drinking

Mustard Seed (☎ 220220; 16 Fraser St; 2-course lunch £5.95, mains £11-19; ⌚ lunch & dinner) Visionary conversion of a riverside church with open-plan dining, cordial service, and smart Med-Scottish cuisine.

our pick **Hootananny** (☎ 233651; www.hootananny.co.uk; 67 Church St; ⏰ 11am-late) Something for everyone: a mixed crowd dance to ceilidh bands downstairs, cooler cats prowl the rock bar and top-floor chill-out zone.

Johnny Foxes (☎ 236577; cnr Bridge & Bank Sts) A cheery riverside watering hole where sauced-up locals take the odd swim.

Ironworks (☎ 0871-789 4173; www.ironworksvenue.com; 122b Academy St) The main place when someone big is in town, with regular live bands.

Getting There & Away

National Express coaches run to/from London (£40, 13 hours, one daily). Citylink coaches serve Edinburgh and Glasgow (both £21.20, four hours, hourly) and go to/from Fort William (£11.30, two hours, five to seven daily). On the train, destinations include Edinburgh and Glasgow (£38, 3½ hours, six and three daily services respectively), while the service round to Kyle of Lochalsh (£17.30, 2½ hours, three daily), for Skye, is another great scenic rail journey.

JOHN O'GROATS

☎ 01955 / pop 510

Mainland Britain's northeasterly extreme, John O'Groats should be an epic location. Instead it's a car park surrounded by tourist shops, offering little of interest apart from ferries to Orkney, and a signpost indicating the endpoint of the 874-mile trek from Land's End (p193) – a popular if arduous route for cyclists and walkers, many raising money for charity. If you see someone stagger in, give them a round of applause.

BRITAIN DIRECTORY

ACCOMMODATION

Reflecting the wide array of sleepover options available in Britain, accommodation in this chapter has been listed with the lowest-priced first. We've focused on budget places (hostels and backpacker joints) with some midrange options, and a few top-end temptations if you fancy a splurge. The rates we quote are usually high-season prices; they tend to drop in low season. Local TICs can help you find accommodation, or book for you ahead of your arrival; a fee around £3 is charged, but it saves you hiking or phoning round loads of places.

Free camping is rare in Britain, but there are many camping grounds on the edge of towns and in the countryside. Rates range from £5 to £10 per person, depending on location, season and facilities. We don't list specific camping grounds in this Britain chapter, as budget travellers tend to prefer hostels (as the costs are only slightly more, and they offer more facilities – not to mention shelter from the sometimes inclement British weather).

Britain has two national hostelling organisations: **Youth Hostels Association** (YHA; ☎ 01629-592700; www.yha.org.uk), covering England and Wales; and **Scottish Youth Hostels Association** (SYHA; ☎ 0870 155 3255; www.syha.org.uk). Dorm beds range from £9 to £20 per night, and many hostels also have double and four-bed rooms. You don't have to be a member of YHA or SHYA – or another Hostelling International (HI) organisation – to stay, but nonmembers pay extra: it's £3 per person per night in England and Wales, and £1 in Scotland. Annual YHA membership costs £16; SYHA is £9. Under-26s get discounts.

Most hostel prices vary according to demand and season. So book early for a Tuesday night in May and you'll get a cheap rate. Book late for a weekend in August and you'll pay top whack – if there's space at all. Throughout this Britain chapter, we've generally quoted the cheaper rates for YHA and SYHA hostels (in line with those on YHA's and SYHA's websites), even though we generally quote high-season prices for hotels and B&Bs. Some hostels also have varying opening times/days, especially in remote locations or out of tourist season, so check before turning up.

There's a growing array of independent hostels and backpackers across Britain, varying widely in quality, facilities and price (typically from £10 to £25). Some are quiet and cosy, while others are for serious party travellers. The print and online **Independent Hostel Guide** (www.independenthostelguide.co.uk) is the best listing. North of the border, an excellent site is www.hostel-scotland.co.uk.

Many universities offer student accommodation to visitors during Christmas, Easter and summer holidays. Usually in basic single study rooms, rates typically range from £15 to £30 per person. The useful website www.budgetstayuk.com represents many unis and colleges, and offers online bookings.

The B&B (bed and breakfast) is a great British institution. Basically, you get a room in somebody's house, and at smaller places you'll really feel part of the family. Larger B&Bs may have around 10 rooms and more facilities. 'Guest house' is sometimes just another name for a B&B, although they can be more like a hotel, with higher rates. Room rates are nearly always quoted per person, but based on two people sharing. Single rooms cost more. Bottom-end you'll pay around £20 per person; in the midrange you're looking at around £35 or £40. Most B&Bs serve enormous breakfasts; some also offer packed lunches (around £5) and evening meals (around £10 to £15).

ACTIVITIES

Britain is a great destination for outdoor enthusiasts. Walking (hiking) and cycling are the most popular and accessible activities – and the perfect way to open up some beautiful corners of the country – while the coast has excellent spots for surfing and the whacky sport of coasteering. TICs stock local route maps and guidebooks, and a good website for ideas and inspiration is www.visitbritain.com – follow links to Holiday Ideas and Outdoor Activities.

Cycling

Compact Britain is an excellent destination to explore by bike, whether it's pottering around a cycle-friendly city like Oxford or Bristol, heading into surrounding countryside, or making a grand tour of the whole country. The 10,000-mile **National Cycle Network** (www.nationalcyclenetwork.org.uk) is a web of quiet roads and traffic-free tracks through busy cities and remote rural areas, with some sections designed as tours of a few days or longer. The **Cyclists' Touring Club** (☎ 0870 873 0060; www.ctc.org.uk) is the leading organisation; the website includes a bike-hire directory and mail-order service for maps and books. There are bike-hire outlets in most tourist centres; rates range from £6 for a half-day to £60 for a week.

Walking

Britain's picturesque terrains are great for walking – from short strolls to hardy hikes. Every town is surrounded by a web of footpaths, with more choice in national parks and mountain areas such as the Lake District, North Wales and Highlands of Scotland. **The Ramblers** (☎ 020-7339 8500; www.ramblers.org.uk) is the leading organisation, and their website is a mine of information.

For keen walkers, Britain boasts many multi-day routes:

Coast to Coast Popular trek across three northern England national parks.

Cotswold Way Delightful ramble through southern hills and countryside.

Pembrokeshire Coast Path Rollercoaster romp round the West Wales peninsula.

West Highland Way Classic route through southern Scotland.

Some long routes are designated **National Trails** (www.nationaltrails.co.uk) but you don't have to do the whole thing; many people follow sections for a day or two, or just a few hours. It still makes for a great day out.

Other Activities

As long as you've got a wetsuit, Britain offers many excellent **surfing** opportunities, including Southwest Wales, Cornwall and Devon. For more info, see www.britsurf.co.uk. The fast-growing watersport of **kitesurfing** is also popular in these areas. See www.kitesurfing.org. Or try your hand at **coasteering** (see www.coasteering.org). It's like mountaineering, although instead of going up a mountain, you go along the coast – a steep rocky coast, often with waves breaking around your feet. And if the rock gets too steep, you jump in and start swimming. Outdoor centres – notably in Cornwall and Pembrokeshire – provide guides and all the gear. You provide the sense of adventure.

BUSINESS HOURS

Banks (🕑 9.30am-5pm Mon-Fri) Larger branches also open Sat morning.

Post Offices (🕑 9.30am-5pm Mon-Sat)

Pubs (🕑 11am-11pm Mon-Sat, to 10.30pm Sun) Some pubs – and many bars, particularly in the cities – stay open later, especially on weekends.

Restaurants (🕑 lunch 11am-3pm, dinner 6pm-10pm) Specific hours vary widely.

Shops (🕑 9am-5pm Mon-Sat, 10am-4pm Sun)

DANGERS & ANNOYANCES

It's worth noting that some city centres can get rowdy late on Friday and Saturday night, and rowdy sometimes turns nasty. Beware of drunken fights, random vandalism – and piles of vomit.

EMBASSIES & CONSULATES

The following is a selection in London. For a complete list in the UK, see the website of the **Foreign & Commonwealth Office** (www.fco.gov.uk), which also lists Britain's embassies overseas.

Australia (Map pp162-3; ☎ 020-73794334; www.australia.org.uk; Strand, WC2B 4LA)

Canada (Map pp162-3; ☎ 020-7258 6600; www.canada.org.uk; 1 Grosvenor Sq, W1X 0AB)

France (Map pp172-3; ☎ 020-7073 1000; www.ambafrance-uk.org; 58 Knightsbridge, SW1 7JT)

Germany (Map pp162-3; ☎ 020-7824 1300; www.london.diplo.de; 23 Belgrave Sq, SW1X 8PX)

Ireland (Map pp162-3; ☎ 020-7235 2171; www.embassyofireland.co.uk; 17 Grosvenor Pl, SW1X 7HR)

Japan (Map pp162-3; ☎ 020-7465 6500; www.uk.emb-japan.go.jp; 101 Piccadilly, W1J 7JT)

Netherlands (Map pp172-3; ☎ 020-7590 3200; www.netherlands-embassy.org.uk; 38 Hyde Park Gate, SW7 5DP)

New Zealand (Map pp162-3; ☎ 020-7930 8422; www.nzembassy.com/uk; 80 Haymarket, SW1Y 4TQ)

USA (Map pp162-3; ☎ 020-7499 9000; www.usembassy.org.uk; 24 Grosvenor Sq, W1A 1AE)

FESTIVALS & EVENTS

There are countless traditional fetes and local events around Britain throughout the year, many based on centuries-old customs.

April

Grand National (www.aintree.co.uk) Britain's top annual horse race, when the whole nation stops to watch the gee-gees. Aintree, Liverpool, early April.

May

FA Cup Final (www.thefa.com) Nail-biting conclusion to England's annual knock-out football club competition. Wembley Stadium, London, mid-May.

June

Trooping the Colour (www.royal.gov.uk) The Queen's official birthday is celebrated with pomp and pageantry. Horse Guards Pde, London, mid-June.

Glastonbury Festival (www.glastonburyfestivals.co.uk) Giant open-air extravaganza of music and sunshine (or mud). Glastonbury, Somerset, late June.

July

Llangollen International Musical Eisteddfod (www.international-eisteddfod.co.uk) Celebration of international folk music and dance. Llangollen, Wales, early July.

T in the Park (www.tinthepark.com) Scotland's leading open-air rock and pop festival. Glasgow, mid-July.

August

Edinburgh Fringe Festival (www.edfringe.com) Sprawling three-week comedy and avant-garde performance fest. Edinburgh, from early August.

Brecon Jazz Festival (www.breconjazz.co.uk) Indoor and outdoor jazz concerts. Brecon, Wales, mid-August.

September

Braemar Gathering (www.braemargathering.org) Caber tossing and other Highland sports, attended by kilted Royal Family. Braemar, Scotland, early September.

November

Guy Fawkes Night Bonfires and fireworks nationwide, recalling a failed antigovernment plot from the 1600s. Held 5 November.

December

Edinburgh Hogmanay (www.edinburghshogmanay.org) Huge street party to see in New Year. Princes St, Edinburgh, from late 31 December to early 1 January. Echoed by other versions in London and other cities and towns around Britain.

HOLIDAYS

Public Holidays

Called 'bank holidays' in Britain, these affect most businesses, although larger shops increasingly remain open.

New Year's Day 1 January
New Year's Holiday 2 January (Scotland only)
Good Friday March/April, Friday before Easter
Easter Monday March/April (except Scotland)
May Day First Monday in May
Spring Bank Holiday Last Monday in May
Summer Bank Holiday First Monday in August (Scotland only)
Summer Bank Holiday Last Monday in August (England and Wales only)
Christmas Day 25 December
Boxing Day 26 December

If a public holiday falls on a weekend, the nearest Monday is usually taken instead.

MONEY

Britain's currency is the pound sterling (£), split into 100 pennies (p), using a variety of coins and banknotes issued by the Bank of England. Banks in Scotland issue their own banknotes, which are legal tender across Britain: if you have trouble using them in England, exchange them at any bank for free.

ATMs

ATMs – usually called 'cashpoints' – in Britain are located outside banks and large supermarkets, and at train stations. Some in locations like pubs and motorway service stations charge extra withdrawal fees.

Credit Cards & Debit Cards

MasterCard and Visa are the most acceptable cards in Britain, with Amex not far behind. Britain uses a 'Chip & Pin' debit/credit card payment system that requires a security number to be entered (instead of a handwritten signature). This usually does not apply to cards issued overseas: you should be able to use your card as usual.

Moneychangers

Many *bureaux de change* advertise good rates but some levy outrageous fees and commissions; always ask about 'extras' before making a transaction. High street banks are a safe money-changing option, offering fair rates, as are larger post offices – particularly useful in country areas.

POST

There are two classes of post within Britain: a standard letter (under 100g and smaller than 240 x 165 x 5mm) costs 36p first-class (normally delivered next day) and 27p second-class (up to three days). Stamps for straightforward 1st- and 2nd-class mail can also be bought at shops and newsagents. Letters by airmail cost 50p to EU countries and 56p to the rest of the world (up to 10g). For details on all prices, see www.postoffice.co.uk.

TELEPHONE

Phone boxes are still common on city streets and most take coins, credit cards, phonecards or all three. Coin phones charge a minimum of 20p or 40p. Local calls are charged by time, while national calls are by time and distance: it's cheaper to call before 8am or after 6pm Monday to Friday or any time on weekends. Many hotels charge high fees for in-room phone usage – you may need to sell your body if you want to make an international call.

For the operator, call ☎ 100. For directory inquiries, a host of agencies compete for your business and charge from 10p to 40p; numbers include ☎ 118 192, ☎ 118 118, ☎ 118 500 and ☎ 118 811.

Phone Codes

To call outside the UK dial ☎ 00, then the country code (☎ 1 for USA, ☎ 61 for Australia, etc), the area code (you usually drop the initial zero) and the number.

In Britain, area codes do not have a standard format and vary in length, which can be confusing for foreigners (and locals); for example ☎ 020 for London, ☎ 0131 for Edinburgh, ☎ 01225 for Bath, and ☎ 015394 for Ambleside.

As well as geographical area codes, other 'codes' include: ☎ 0500 or ☎ 0800 for free calls, and ☎ 0845 for national calls at a local rate. Numbers starting ☎ 087 are charged at national-call rate, while numbers starting ☎ 089 or ☎ 09 are premium rate, and often very expensive.

Codes for mobile phones usually start with ☎ 07 – and are more expensive than calling a land line.

TOURIST INFORMATION

The website of **Visit Britain** (www.visitbritain.com) is stuffed with resources. **England** (www.enjoyengland.com), **Scotland** (www.visitscotland.com) and **Wales** (www.visitwales.com) also have dedicated tourism agencies. Most regions and cities have their own visitor websites – they are listed throughout this chapter.

All British cities and towns have a tourist information centre (TIC), with helpful staff, books and maps for sale, leaflets to give away and loads of advice on things to see or do. For a list, see www.visitmap.info/tic.

VISAS

If you're a European Economic Area (EEA) national, you don't need a visa to visit (or work in) Britain. Citizens of Australia, Canada, New Zealand, South Africa and the USA are given leave to enter at their point of arrival for up to six months (three months for some nationalities), but are prohibited from working.

Visa and entry regulations are always subject to change, so it's vital to check before leaving home. Your first stop should be www.ukvisas.gov.uk or www.ukba.homeoffice.gov.uk.

Bulgaria България

HIGHLIGHTS

- **Veliko Târnovo** Chilled-out student town boasting hiking, cycling, rock-climbing and a sprawling citadel along a gorge that hosts a night light show (p240)
- **Varna** It'd be cool even if it weren't on the Black Sea, with good beaches, open-air clubs at night, and day trips to resorts and rock-climbing spots hanging over the water (p243)
- **Sinemorets** The remote beach village, near Turkey, isn't much to look at until you reach the southernmost beach via a cliff-top hike (p247)
- **Plovdiv** Roman ruins litter the laid-back central streets, including the cobbled hilltop Old Town with a couple of hostels and open-air bars (p238)

FAST FACTS

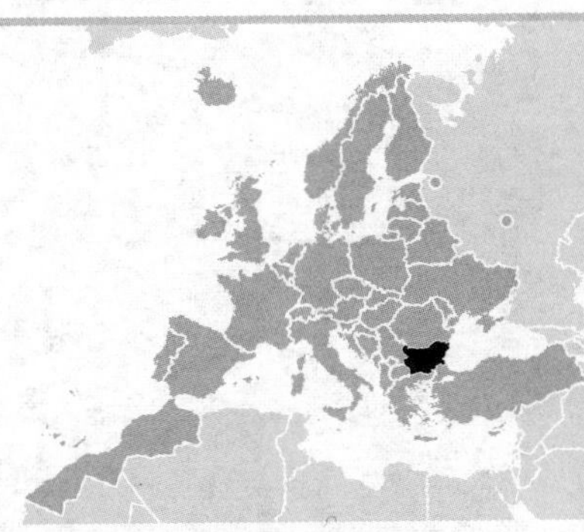

- **Area** 110,910 sq km (about one-third of Finland)
- **Budget** 45lv to 75lv per day
- **Capital** Sofia
- **Country code** ☎ 359
- **Famous for** Black Sea beaches, 'cheap' ski runs, yoghurt
- **Language** Bulgarian
- **Money** leva (lv); A$1 = 1.08lv; C$1 = 1.23lv; €1 = 1.95lv; ¥100 = 1.53; NZ$1 = 0.85; UK£1 = 2.20lv; US$1 = 1.45lv
- **Phrases** *zdrasti* (hello), *blagodarya* (thank you), *imati li?* (do you have?), *kolko strubo?* (how much?), *oshte bira molya* (another beer please)
- **Population** 7.3 million
- **Visas** not required for citizens of Australia, Canada, EU, New Zealand, USA and several others for stays of up to 90 days (p248)

TRAVEL HINTS

Buddy up with travellers and rent a car for DIY day-trip experiments from only 25lv per day – the steal of the country.

ROAMING BULGARIA

Start in Sofia, bus to Veliko Târnovo, then on to Varna, where – with time – you can bus via Burgas to Sinemorets.

The last postcommunist stop heading south, newly EU-christened Bulgaria is having its coming-of-age party at last. For good and bad. Brits are buying up beach property, so free spots of Black Sea sand are running out, but there are still a couple of stray golden beaches. Inland offers many pockets of Alplike mountain villages with hut-to-hut walks in summer and good skiing in winter.

This chapter focuses on the 'big four': Sofia, the busy capital; Veliko Târnovo, the chilled student town; Varna, the bustling sea hub; and Plovdiv, the Roman survivor in the Thracian plain. All have hostels and day trips that could detain you several days. The best is in-between them, where you're still likely to spot shepherds taking their four-legged pals by whitewashed revival-era homes from the 19th century. Go and explore now; things may look different in a few years.

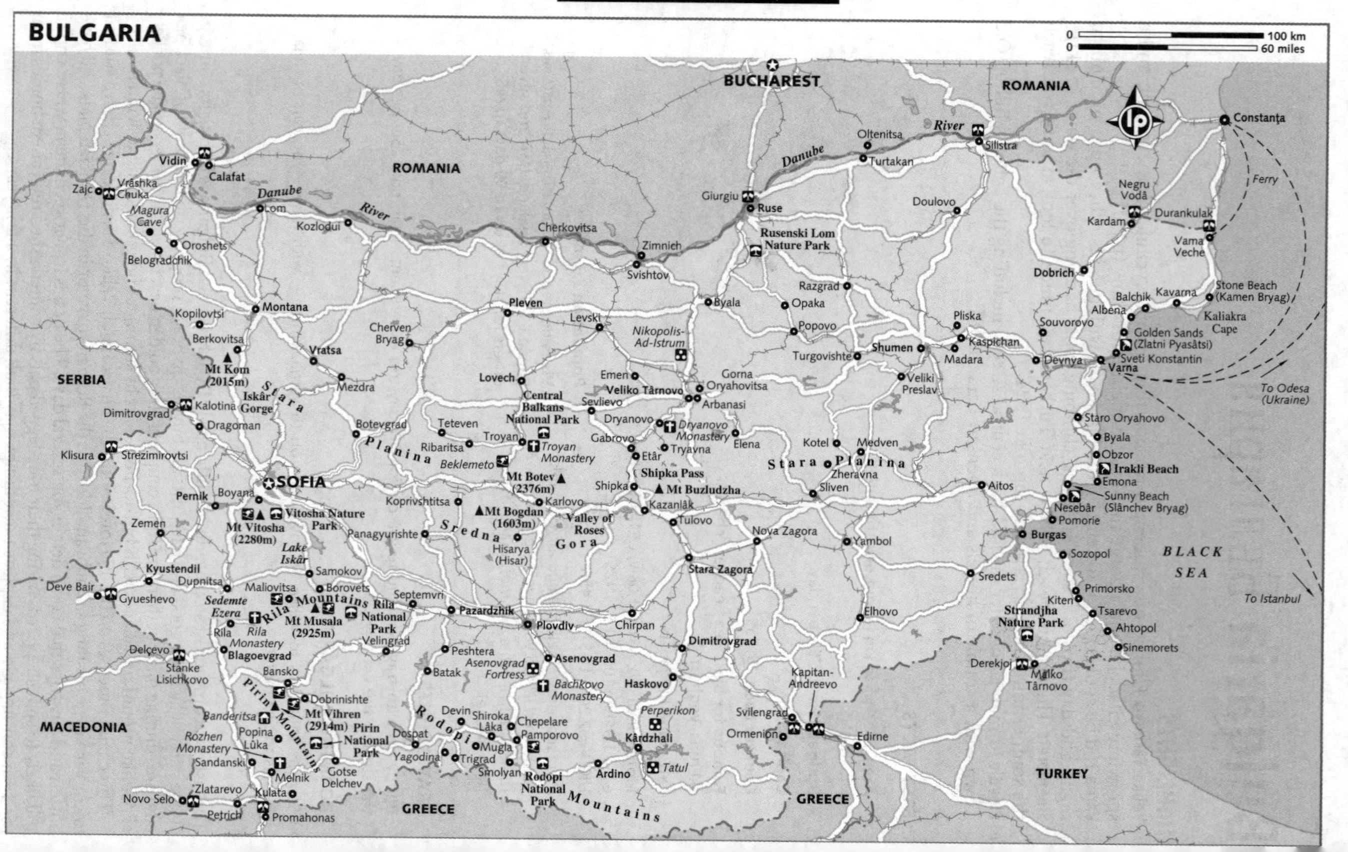
BULGARIA
0 100 km
0 60 miles
ROMANIA
BUCHAREST
SERBIA
MACEDONIA
GREECE
TURKEY
BLACK SEA
Danube River
Ferry
To Odesa (Ukraine)
To Istanbul
SOFIA
Plovdiv
Varna
Burgas
Ruse
Giurgiu
Pleven
Vidin
Calafat
Zajc
Vrâshka Chuka
Magura Cave
Oroshets
Belogradchik
Lom
Kozlodui
Montana
Kopilovtsi
Berkovitsa
Mt Kom (2015m)
Vratsa
Mezdra
Botevgrad
Cherven Bryag
Iskâr Gorge
Kalotina
Dimitrovgrad
Dragoman
Klisura
Strezimirovtsi
Pernik
Boyana
Zemen
Kyustendil
Dupnitsa
Deve Bair
Gyueshevo
Delčevo
Stanke Lisichkovo
Blagoevgrad
Rila
Rila Monastery
Sedemte Ezera
Maliovitsa
Rila Mountains
Rila National Park
Mt Musala (2925m)
Samokov
Borovets
Lake Iskâr
Mt Vitosha (2280m)
Vitosha Nature Park
Bansko
Dobrinishte
Pirin Mountains
Mt Vihren (2914m)
Pirin National Park
Banderitsa
Popina Lûka
Rozhen Monastery
Sandanski
Melnik
Gotse Delchev
Zlatarevo
Kulata
Novo Selo
Petrich
Promahonas
Stara Planina
Sredna Gora
Koprivshtitsa
Panagyurishte
Mt Bogdan (1603m)
Hisarya (Hisar)
Karlovo
Valley of Roses
Mt Botev (2376m)
Beklemeto
Teteven
Ribaritsa
Troyan
Troyan Monastery
Central Balkans National Park
Lovech
Levski
Nikopolis-Ad-Istrum
Emen
Veliko Târnovo
Gorna Oryahovitsa
Arbanasi
Sevlievo
Dryanovo
Dryanovo Monastery
Elena
Gabrovo
Etâr
Tryavna
Shipka Pass
Shipka
Mt Buzludzha
Kazanlâk
Tulovo
Septemvri
Pazardzhik
Velingrad
Peshtera
Batak
Asenovgrad
Asenovgrad Fortress
Bachkovo Monastery
Chirpan
Stara Zagora
Nova Zagora
Dimitrovgrad
Haskovo
Perperikon
Kârdzhali
Tatul
Ardino
Devin
Shiroka Lâka
Chepelare
Pamporovo
Mugla
Dospat
Yagodina
Trigrad
Smolyan
Rodopi National Park
Rodopi Mountains
Cherkovitsa
Zimnich
Svishtov
Byala
Rusenski Lom Nature Park
Razgrad
Opaka
Popovo
Turgovishte
Shumen
Veliki Preslav
Pliska
Kaspichan
Madara
Kotel
Medven
Zheravna
Sliven
Yambol
Elhovo
Aitos
Sredets
Svilengrad
Kapitan-Andreevo
Ormenion
Edirne
Oltenitsa
Turtakan
Silistra
Doulovo
Negru Vodă
Kardam
Durankulak
Vama Veche
Constanța
Dobrich
Balchik
Kavarna
Stone Beach (Kamen Bryag)
Kaliakra Cape
Albena
Golden Sands (Zlatni Pyasâtsi)
Sveti Konstantin
Souvorovo
Devnya
Staro Oryahovo
Byala
Obzor
Irakli Beach
Emona
Sunny Beach (Slânchev Bryag)
Nesebâr
Pomorie
Sozopol
Primorsko
Kiten
Tsarevo
Ahtopol
Sinemorets
Strandjha Nature Park
Derekjoj
Malko Târnovo

HISTORY

The first Slavs migrated to this Thracian (then Roman) ground in the 5th century AD, and the first Bulgarian state was formed in 681. The Byzantines conquered Bulgaria in 1014, but not until the state had created a language, the Cyrillic alphabet, a church and a people (a mix of Slavs, Proto-Bulgarians and Thracians).

Bulgaria's second kingdom, based in Veliko Târnovo, lasted until the Ottoman army took over in 1396. The next 500 years were spent living 'under the yoke' of Ottoman rule.

During the 18th and 19th centuries, many 'awakeners' are credited with reviving Bulgarian culture, including Bulgaria's own 'Che Guevara', Vasil Levski. With Russia stepping in, the Ottoman army was defeated in 1878.

Hoping to annex Macedonia, Bulgaria aligned with Germany in WWII, but famously said 'no' to Hitler by refusing to send its Jewish population to concentration camps, sparing up to 50,000 lives. After the war, Bulgaria embraced communism wholeheartedly (even proposing in 1973 to join the USSR).

Since 1989, Bulgaria has stumbled slightly as a new democracy. NATO said 'yes' to Bulgaria in 2004, then the EU welcomed Bulgaria (and Romania) in 2007 (though noted that Bulgaria's record of corruption and organised crime continue to get rebukes from Brussels).

THE CULTURE

Of Bulgaria's 7.3 million people, Bulgarians and Slavs constitute 84%. The largest minorities are Turks (9.4%) and Roma (4.7%), with smaller populations of Russians, Jews and Greeks.

Bulgarians can be quite friendly, but help (with directions etc) isn't always volunteered. Ask, and locals often go out of their way to help.

RELIGION

During the communist era Bulgaria was officially atheist. These days about 83% of the population is Orthodox Christian and 12% is Muslim (almost all Sunni).

ARTS

Bulgaria's proud 19th-century revival saw many town makeovers, with traditionally styled *kâshta* buildings (whitewashed walls, wood-carved ceilings, hand-woven rugs).

Bulgaria's most treasured art is on the walls of medieval monasteries and churches, such as the 19th-century paintings at Rila Monastery (p238).

> **READING UP**
>
> Lonely Planet's *Bulgaria* offers comprehensive coverage of the country. Ivan Ilchev's *The Rose of the Balkans* is a recent historical overview of Bulgaria translated into English, available in Sofia.

The currently popular 'wedding music', aka *chalga,* is Turkish-sounding synth-pop with dumb lyrics. Essentially no one in the country admits to liking Azis, a seriously flamboyant, sexually ambiguous *chalga* performer who sells many, many CDs.

For more traditional music, click on the TV – there are shows nightly.

ENVIRONMENT

Bulgaria lies in the heart of the Balkan Peninsula, stretching 502km from the Serbian border to the 378km-long Black Sea coast.

The Stara Planina (Balkan Mountain) range stretches across central Bulgaria. In the southwest are three higher ranges – the Rila Mountains (home to Mt Musala, Bulgaria's highest point at 2925m), Pirin Mountains and Rodopi Mountains.

Bulgaria has some 56,000 kinds of living creatures, including bears, wild goats and deer. It maintains three national parks (Rila, Pirin and Central Balkans) and 10 nature parks.

Recent controversial development of the Rila Mountains, southwest of Borovets, has involved tree-clearing roads towards the supposedly protected hiking area of the 'Seven Lakes' hike.

TRANSPORT

GETTING THERE & AWAY

Air

Bulgaria's most active airports are Sofia and (in summer) Varna and Burgas. There is no additional departure tax levied at the airport.

Airlines flying to/from Bulgaria have offices in Sofia:

Aeroflot (SU; www.aeroflot.ru; ☎ 02-943 4489; ul Oborishte 23)

Air France (AF; www.airfrance.com; ☎ 02-939 7010; ul Sâborna 5)

Alitalia (AZ; www.alitalia.com; ☎ 02-981 6702; ul Kânchev 5)

> **'YES OR NO?'**
>
> Bulgarians shake their head 'yes' and nod their head 'no'. Confusing at first, then fun. Just try to think that a shake is sweeping the floor clean ('yes, come in') and a nod is slamming shut a garage door ('no, go away'). If in doubt, ask '*Da ili ne?*' (Yes or no?).

Austrian Airlines (OS; www.aua.com; ☎ 02-806 000; bul Zlaten rog 12)
British Airways (AS; www.britishairways.com; ☎ 02-945 7000; bul Patraiarh Evtimii 49)
Bulgaria Air (FB; www.air.bg; ☎ 02-402 0406; NDK underpass)
ČSA (OK; Czech Airlines; www.czechairlines.com; ☎ 02-981 5408; ul Sâborna 9)
easyJet (EZY; www.easyjet.com) Flies daily to London's Gatwick.
LOT Polish Airlines (LO; www.lot.com; ☎ 02-987 4562; bul Aleksandâr Stamboliski 27A)
Lufthansa (LH; www.lufthansa.com; ☎ 02-930 4242; ul Bacho Kiro 26-30)
Malév (MA; www.malev.com; ☎ 02-981 5091; bul Patriarh Evtimii 19)
Sky Europe (NE; www.skyeurope.com) Flies to Prague.
Turkish Airlines (TK; www.turkishairlines.com; ☎ 02-988 3596; ul Sâborna 11A)
Wizz Air (8Z; www.wizzair.com; ☎ 960 3888) Flies daily to London's Luton airport and a couple of times weekly to Brussels, Rome and Barcelona.

BULGARIA

Boat

You can take a ferry across the Danube River from Vidin or Ruse. From Varna, the ferry service is to Odesa, Ukraine, or Constanţa, Romania.

Bus

International tickets to the region are available at practically any bus station in the country. Often, there's not one set price, so it's worth checking a couple of companies to find the cheapest fare.

Car & Motorcycle

Drivers pay a weekly €5 road tax.

Train

Tickets for international trains can be bought at any government-run **Rila Bureau** (www.bdz-rila.com; 🕑 most closed Sun) or at some stations' dedicated ticket offices (most open daily) at larger stations with international connections.

The daily *Trans-Balkan Express* (between Budapest and Thessaloniki, Greece) stops at Ruse, Gorna Oryahovitsa (near Veliko Târnovo) and Sofia.

The *Balkan Express* normally goes daily between Belgrade and Istanbul, with stops in Sofia and Plovdiv, though at research time only Sofia–Belgrade train No 292 linked Sofia and Belgrade; the *Balkan Express* may resume full service by the time you arrive.

The *Bulgaria Express* (aka 'the Russian train', between Sofia and Moscow) is useful as an overnighter between Sofia and Bucharest.

GETTING AROUND

Air

Bulgaria Air (www.air.bg), which merged with Hemus Air in 2007, flies between Sofia and Varna daily (about 210lv/350lv one-way/return); it also flies to Burgas.

Bicycle

Traffic is relatively light outside the cities on many highways, but winding curves in the mountains and/or potholes anywhere can be obstacles.

Bulgaria has few bike-rental options (try Sofia and Veliko Târnovo), but most towns have bike shops that can make repairs or sell parts.

Bus

This chapter lists the price and duration of trips and number of buses daily – *use these as a gauge only*. The best web source is www.avtogari.info (in Bulgarian only); also try www.centralnaavtogara.bg for international routes.

Bigger bus stations generally have a confusing array of private bus booths advertising the same destinations. The public bus stops generally have a few windows and a list of timetables outside. In most cases, buses leave between around 7am and 7pm.

> **KEY BORDER CROSSINGS**
>
> The most popular entry/exit point from the north is by train between Belgrade and Sofia; another is the Ruse–Giurgiu border, used for journeys between Bucharest and Sofia or Veliko Târnovo; the trickiest tends to be rail links with Istanbul, which often include a bus-clearing customs check, and wee-hour train check too. There's less hassle entering Greece, south of Sofia at Kulata–Promahonas.

CONNECTIONS

It's not necessary to backtrack to Sofia if you're heading to Bucharest or Istanbul. From central Veliko Târnovo (p243), for example, there are daily trains both ways – and you can catch overnight buses to Istanbul from many places in the country. Heading to Greece or Belgrade by train means going through Sofia (p237), and for Skopje, you'll need to catch a bus there too.

Most bus stations have a left-luggage service.

Car & Motorcycle

If you're with a gang of four, are 21 and have a driver's licence from your country, renting a car from a local agent can be a good way to beach hop or drive on mountain back roads. The cheapest place to rent, by far, is Veliko Târnovo, where hostels find cars from 25lv per day.

Train

Trains, all run by the Bulgarian State Railways (BDZh), are a bit cheaper than buses, but take longer. *Ekspresen* (express) and *bârz* (fast) trains zip along at a speed akin to a bus, while the slow *pâtnicheski* (passenger) trains tinker along.

Listings in this chapter are for 2nd-class seats and peak-season schedules. First-class seats – usually costing an extra leva or three – are in six-seat carriages, 2nd-class in eight-seat carriages. You can buy tickets on board but it's up to 50% more expensive. Check updated schedules at www.bdz.bg.

Europe-wide rail passes are not good value in Bulgaria.

Bring food and water on board with you. Most train stations are signposted in Cyrillic. Nearly all train stations have left-luggage offices.

SOFIA СОФИЯ

☎ 02 / pop 1.4 million

Don't expect to uncover the 'new Prague' here in this mostly modern city at the base of towering Mt Vitosha. Filling fast with more and more cars, Sofia's an energetic little place – far more 20th century than most Eastern European capitals. But you'll find its charm in random encounters in arty nooks of south-central neighbourhoods, the golden-brick roads around the centre, or the delirious nightlife scene.

EMERGENCY NUMBERS

- Ambulance ☎ 150
- Fire ☎ 160
- Police ☎ 166

Lived in by Thracians, Romans and now Bulgarians for up to 7000 years, Sofia was an outpost of 1200 residents when it became the nation's unlikely fourth capital in 1879.

ORIENTATION

Sofia's main bus and train station are across bul Maria Luisa from each other, about 500m north of the centre. Thoroughfares bul Maria Luisa and Vitosha meet at central pl Sveta Nedelya.

INFORMATION

Bookshops

Booktrading (ul Graf Ignatiev 50; ⏲ 8.30am-8.30pm Mon-Sat, 10am-8pm Sun) Super selection of English-language books.

Internet Access

Site (bul Vitosha 45; per hr 4.20lv; ⏲ 24hr) Make international calls for 0.20lv per minute to the USA and Australia, from 0.60lv to the UK.

Medical Services

Poliklinika Torax (☎ 91285; www.thorax.bg; bul Stamboliyski 57; ⏲ 24hr) Good private clinic west of the centre.

Money

Unicredit Bulbank (ul Lavele & ul Todor Aleksandrov; ⏲ 8.30am-6pm Mon-Fri) Changes travellers cheques for 4% commission.

Telephone

BTC (ul General Gurko; ⏲ 8am-8pm Mon-Fri, 10am-4pm Sat) It's 0.32lv per minute for international calls.

Travel Agencies

Eurotours (Evroturs; ☎ 0878 258 468; Traffic Market, office 61; ⏲ 6.30am-7pm Mon-Fri, 6.30am-5pm Sat & Sun) Bus station agent helps with accommodation.

Usit Colours (☎ 981 1900; www.usitcolours.bg; ul Vasil Levski 35; ⏲ 9.30am-6.30pm Mon-Fri) Sells ISIC cards (10lv) and offers discounted air fares for students.

Zig Zag/Odysseia-In (☎ 980 5102; www.zigzagbg.com; bul Stamboliyski 20V; ⏲ 8.30am-7.30pm Mon-Fri,

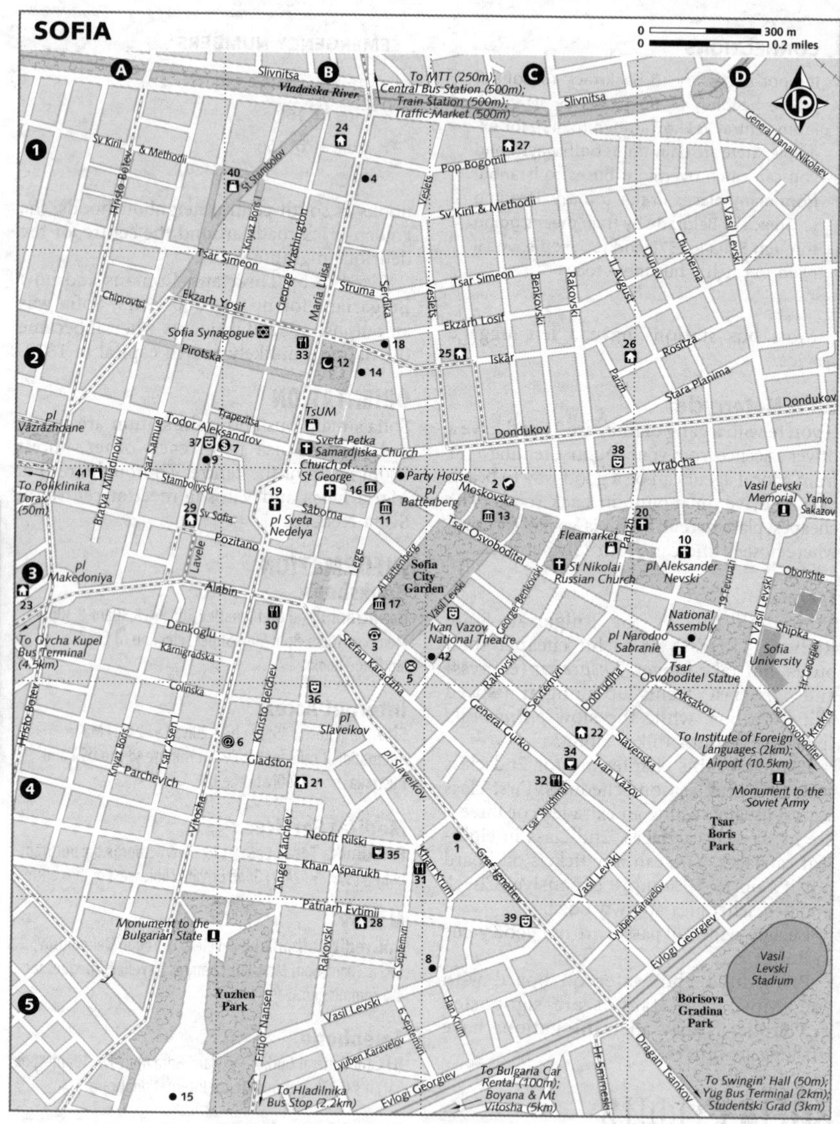

Sat in summer) Super-helpful English-language staff charge 5lv for a 30-minute consultation on priceless hiking tips. Can also book rooms, sells trail maps (6lv) and offers a host of day trips. Enter from ul Lavele.

Visas

Immigration Office (☎ 982 3316; bul Maria Luisa 48; foreigner services 12.15-1.30pm Mon-Fri) This hectic office (in the MVR building) can extend visas and entry stamps beyond 90 days.

SIGHTS & ACTIVITIES

Ploshad Aleksander Nevski

Gold domed and massive, **Aleksander Nevski Church** (pl Aleksander Nevski; admission free; 7am-7pm) is the city's focal point. Built between

INFORMATION		
Booktrading	1	C4
British Embassy	2	C3
BTC	3	B3
Canadian Embassy	(see 2)	
Immigration Office	4	B1
Post Office	5	B3
Site	6	B4
Unicredit Bulbank	7	B2
Usit Colours	8	C5
Zig Zag/Odysseia-In	9	A2
SIGHTS & ACTIVITIES		
Aleksander Nevski Church	10	D3
Aleksander Nevski Crypt	(see 10)	
Archaeological Museum	11	B3
Banya Bashi Mosque	12	B2
Ethnographical Museum	13	C3
Mineral Baths	14	B2
National Art Gallery	(see 13)	
NDK	15	A5
President's Building	16	B3
Sofia City Art Gallery	17	B3
Spring Wells	18	B2
Sveta Nedelya Cathedral	19	B3
Sveta Sofia Church	20	D3
SLEEPING		
Art Hostel	21	B4
Be My Guest Hostel	22	C4
Hostel Mostel	23	A3
Hotel Enny	24	B1
Hotel Iskâr	25	C2
Kervan Hostel	26	C2
Rooms	27	C1
Sofia Guesthouse	28	B5
Sofia Hostel	29	A3
EATING		
Dream House	30	B3
Krâchme Divaka	31	B4
Trops Kâshta	32	C4
Tsentralni Hali	33	B2
DRINKING		
Bilkovata	34	C4
The Apartment	35	B4
ENTERTAINMENT		
Escape	36	B4
Exit Club	37	A2
National Opera House	38	C2
Odeon	39	C5
SHOPPING		
Ladies Market	40	B1
Stenata	41	A3
TRANSPORT		
Rila Bureau Centre Office	42	C3

1892 and 1912, it's named after a Russian warrior. In its basement, the **Aleksander Nevski Crypt** (☎ 981 5775; adult/student 6/3lv; 10.30am-5.30pm Wed & Fri-Sun, 10am-6.30pm Tue & Thu) features many national icons dating to the 5th century AD.

On the sidewalks leading to the church from ul Rakovski are stalls selling communist-era tidbits.

Earthquake-battered **Sveta Sofia Church** (admission free; 7am-6pm or 7pm) inspired the name of the city.

Around Sofia City Garden

Surrounded by an Oz-like yellow-brick road, this fountain-filled park is near several attractions, including the super **Archaeological Museum** (adult/student 10/2lv; 10am-6pm May-Oct, 10am-5pm Tue-Sun Nov-Apr). Housed in a former mosque, it gives a good overview of Bulgaria's Thracian and Roman past; particularly worthwhile is staring into the (ivory) eyeballs of a 4th-century Thracian king bust found in 2004.

Across the street is the **President's Building** (closed to the public), the site of the boot sole–slapping **changing of the guards**, staged on the hour during daylight hours.

Facing the park nearby is the former Royal Palace, housing two museums: the squeaky-floored **National Art Gallery** (☎ 980 0093; ul Tsar Osvoboditel; adult/student 6/3lv; 10am-5.30pm Wed & Fri-Sun, 10am-6.30pm Tue & Thu) and the **Ethnographical Museum**, which should reopen after a renovation in mid-2009.

The **Sofia City Art Gallery** (ul General Gurko 1; admission free; 10am-7pm Tue-Sat, 11am-6pm Sun) is well worth ducking into for a mix of local art.

Around Ploshad Sveta Nedelya

In the heart of pl Sveta Nedelya is well-lit, ornate **Sveta Nedelya Cathedral** (admission free; 7am-7pm).

North on bul Maria Luisa, behind unmistakable **Banya Bashi Mosque** (admission free; dawn-dusk) is the red-and-gold **mineral baths** (aka Turkish Baths), undergoing a loooong renovation. Across the street, locals fill – with fervour – bottles at the modern **spring wells**.

South 1km from pl Sveta Nedelya, via ritzy bul Vitosha, is the huge **NDK** (National Palace of Culture) complex, with a viewing deck.

Mt Vitosha & Boyana

The feather in Sofia's cap, **Mt Vitosha** (at the southern end of town) is popular for summer hikes and winter skiing that's cheaper than ski resorts (about 30lv for a lift ticket). Get the trail map *Vitosha Turisticheska Karta* (1:50,000) in Sofia.

GETTING INTO TOWN

Sofia's main bus and train stations are next to each other, about 500m north of the start of the centre. Take tram 1 or 7 from outside the train station to central pl Sveta Nedelya. Buy *two* tickets from the ticket booth on the platform – one for you, and one for your bag (if you have a big backpack or suitcase); you may be fined if you don't have both. If you're travelling with a couple of people, it's often quicker and just as cheap to go by taxi. The **OK Taxi** (☎ 973 2121) stands in front of the central bus station or airport terminal (about 10lv) are dependable.

BULGARIA

SCAMS

Mean taxi drivers – including 'fake' OK Taxi taxis – often overcharge the innocent. Have your hostel or a restaurant call a dependable one for you, and see that the meter's on and that the taxi's posted rates aren't exorbitant.

Chairlifts run all year. **Dragalevtsi**, 2km up from the village, has two lifts that lead up to Goli Vrâh (1837m). Another option is the six-person gondolas at **Simeonovo**, which runs Friday through Sunday only.

A visit theoretically could be combined with the outskirts village Boyana, home to the **National Historical Museum** (☎ 955 4280; www.historymuseum.org; bul Vitoshko Lale 16; adult/student 10/1lv, combo ticket with Boyana Church 12lv, guide 20lv; 9.30am-6pm Apr-Oct, 9am-5.30pm Nov-Mar), which outlines Bulgaria's past from Thracian towns to EU signatures (though many pieces are fakes).

More rewarding is the **Boyana Church** (☎ 959 0939; adult/student 10/1lv, combo ticket with National Historical Museum 12lv, guide 10lv; 9.30am-5.30pm Apr-Dec, 9am-5pm Jan-Mar), 1.5km south of the museum. Built between the 11th and 19th centuries, the three-part, mural-filled medieval church allows 10-minute visits only.

From Sofia's **Hladilnika bus stop** (ul Srebârna), near bul Cherni Vrâh 2km south of the NDK, take bus 122 to Simeonovo and bus 64 to Dragalevtsi or Boyana.

BULGARIA

COURSES

Sofia University's **Institute of Foreign Languages** (☎ 871 0069; www.deo.uni-sofia.bg; ul Lulchev 27) offers Bulgarian-language courses (eg private tutors for 17lv per hour, three-week courses for 510lv).

SLEEPING

Some travel agents book private rooms.

Prices here include breakfast and free internet (many with wi-fi access), and are for summer; most drop by €1 or €2 in winter. Many hostels also keep a private room or two available.

Sofia Guesthouse (☎ 403 0100; www.sofiaguest.com; ul Patriarkh Evtimii 27; dm/r incl breakfast €9/30;) Filling a little house off the busy street, this friendly hostel has a travel agent on hand, but a rather clinical feel inside.

Kervan Hostel (☎ 983 9428; www.kervanhostel.com; ul Rositza 3; dm incl breakfast €10) Cute and grandma-clean, the Kervan has an entry lined with antique radios, a 'Spanish' tiled kitchen and three dorms and a single bathroom.

Be My Guest Hostel (☎ 989 5092; http://hostel-sofia.com; ul Ivan Vazov 13; dm €10-12, s/d €15/30, incl breakfast;) Oodles of homey style in this house-turned-hostel on a graffitied sidestreet near many student hang-outs.

Hostel Mostel (☎ 0889-223 296; www.hostelmostel.com; ul Makedoniya 2; dm incl breakfast €10-13, s €25, d €30-39;) The lovingly run Mostel fills the sweeping 1st floor of an old roadside tavern with sofas, a pool table and a shoes-off TV pit. It's not a party pad though – drinking's forbidden after 9pm. It's just west of pl Makedoniya.

Sofia Hostel (☎ 989 8582; hostel-sofia@yahoo.com; ul Pozitano 16; dm incl breakfast €10) Bulgaria's first hostel has family decorations giving the small place a kindergarten feel, but it's starting to wear a little and the lone bathroom gets busy.

Art Hostel (☎ 987 0545; www.art-hostel.com; ul Angel Kânchev 21a; dm incl breakfast €11, s/d €14/28;) 'Let it be' with a roar, this popular Boho hang-out has a back garden, dark TV area and less attention paid to rooms than the cool basement bar.

Rooms (☎ 983 3508; the roomshostel@yahoo.com; ul Pop Bogomil 10; dm/s/d incl breakfast 20/34/46lv;) A purple-and-gold house on a grey street, the seven-room guesthouse offers tidy but tiny themed rooms (and one dorm).

Hotel Enny (☎ 983 4395; www.enyhotel.com; ul Pop Bogomil 46; s/d 30/40lv) This central back-up has simple rooms (no air-con or fan) that can get you to the next day OK.

Hotel Iskâr (☎ 986 6750; ul Iskâr 11; r 50-59lv) The 11 rooms are nice if a bit small. Private bathrooms are across the hall.

EATING

Cheap pizza slices and kebabs (from 2lv) are available everywhere.

Tsentralni Hali (cnr bul Maria Luisa & ul Ekzarh Iosif; 7am-midnight) This refurbished covered market has fresh produce, baked goods, produce, ice cream, wine and cheap meals (kebabs are 2.20lv).

Trops Kâshta (ul General Gurko 38; mains from 2.50lv; 8am-8.30pm) For cheap, fast, fresh, point-and-eat cafeteria-style food, Trops is your new comrade. It's 30% off after 8pm.

OUR PICK Dream House (ul Alabin 50A; mains 3.90-7.80lv; 11am-10pm) Offering Sofia's best meatless dining, this place changes its menu seasonally, with tons of inspired veggie and vegan choices, plus a Sunday buffet from 11am to 4pm (7lv).

Krâchme Divaka (986 6971; ul 6 Septemvri 41a; mains 4.30lv; 24hr) A quick-filling four-room restaurant made from an old back-street home is an appealing place for a nicely prepared Bulgarian meal.

DRINKING

Several English-language publications list bars; the best is the excellent free quarterly *Sofia: In Your Pocket*.

Bilkovata (ul Tsar Shushman 22; 10am-2am) See if you can't squeeze into this unpretentious, unsigned (other than 'Heineken') basement bar with couples and a welcoming vibe.

The Apartment (ul Neofit Rilski 68; 10am-2am) A full century-old apartment as a bar; it's a tad Boho, with soft lighting, sofas under chandeliers and the occasional making-out couple.

OUR PICK Studentski Grad (Student Town) is literally that: an enclave of college students living in drab communist-era apartment blocks with nightly action found on ground-floor bars. **Strozha** (Block 23B) is an indie-rock dive designed to look like a construction site, **Avenue** (ul Manchev 1A) goes for on-top, hip-shake dancing *chalga*, and **Maskata** (Block 19) has a legendary Monday night karaoke. Get there by minibus 7 from bul Maria Luisa or 8 along ul Rakovski (one-way 1.50lv).

ENTERTAINMENT

One of Sofia's favourite central discos is **Escape** (0887-990 000; www.clubescape,bg; ul Angel Kânchev 1; cover 10lv; 10pm-late Thu-Sun). **Exit Club** (0888-140 133; ul Lavele 16; 6pm-late) is a gay-friendly club.

The coolest cellar-fashioned live-music venue (rock, blues, jazz) is **Swingin' Hall** (963 0696; bul Dragan Tsankov 8; Tue-Sun).

If you're feeling polite, go for opera at the **National Opera House** (987 1366; www.operasofia.com; ul Vrabcha 1; ticket office 9.30am-6.30pm Mon-Fri, 10.30am-6pm Sat & Sun) or indie films at **Odeon** (989 2469; bul Patriarkh Evtimii 1; tickets 4lv).

SHOPPING

Stenata (980 5491; www.stenata.com; ul Bratya Miladinovi 5; 10am-7pm Mon-Fri, 10am-6pm Sat) Bulgaria's best outfitter for the outdoors-bound and active.

Ladies Market (ul St Stambolov; dawn-dusk) A lively, messy market (mostly food).

GETTING THERE & AWAY

Air

Sofia's airport has two terminals; most flights land in the new terminal two, where there's a taxi stand, ATM and **information booth** (937 2211; www.sofia-airport.bg).

Bus

DOMESTIC BUSES

Sofia's **Central Bus Station** (0900 21000; www.centralnaavtogara.bg; bul Maria Luisa; 24hr) is 100m south of the train station, with assorted stands (serving some international destinations) in the nuttier **Traffic Market** in between. The following bus routes are frequent unless otherwise noted.

Belogradchik 15lv, four hours, one or two daily
Burgas 30lv, six hours
Plovdiv 13lv, two hours
Ruse 15lv, 4½ hours
Varna 29lv, six hours
Veliko Târnovo 17lv, 3½ hours

At research time, two buses connected Sofia with the Rila monastery (10lv, 2½ hours), leaving at 10.20am and 6.20pm from the **Ovcha Kupel Bus Terminal** (aka Zapad; 955 5362; bul Tsar Boris III). Reach the station by tram 5 from pl Makedoniya, west of the centre on ul Alabin (it's a 20-minute ride).

INTERNATIONAL BUSES

Most international buses go from the Traffic Market. **Matpu** (981 5653; www.matpu.com; office 58, Traffic Market) sells tickets for Skopje (24lv, six hours, three daily) and Belgrade (54lv, eight hours, two daily) with a change in Nish. Other stands sell tickets for Budapest, Bratislava and Prague.

South a couple of hundred metres, **MTT** (bul Maria Luisa; 8.30am-5.30pm Mon-Fri, 8.30am-4.30pm Sat) sends buses to Thessaloniki, Greece (48lv, 6½ hours) and Athens (108lv, 12 to 13 hours).

Several companies go daily to Istanbul (40lv to 50lv, eight to 10 hours) from the central station.

Train

At Sofia's **Central Train Station** (931 1111; www.bdz.bg; bul Maria Luisa) buy same-day tickets for

Vidin, Ruse and Varna on the main floor; all other domestic destinations are downstairs.

International tickets can be purchased at the **Rila Bureau** (☎ 932 3346; 24hr) in the northern part of the main floor, or at its **centre office** (☎ 987 0777; ul General Gurko 5; 7am-7.30pm Mon-Fri, 7am-6.30pm Sat).

Sample train routes (sleeper rates for international trains):

Athens 95lv, 15 hours, one daily
Belgrade 58lv, 7½ hours, two daily
Bucharest 57lv sleeper, 10½ hours, two daily
Burgas 17.20lv, 6½ to 7½ hours, six daily (others change in Karnobat)
Gorna Oryahovitsa (near Veliko Târnovo) 13.40lv, 4½ hours, 10 daily
Istanbul 82lv, 12 to 14 hours, one daily
Plovdiv 8.10lv, 2½ hours, 12 daily
Ruse 17.20lv, 6½ hours, four daily
Varna 21.90lv, eight to nine hours, six daily

GETTING AROUND

Car & Motorcycle

The literally named **Bulgaria Car Rental** (☎ 400 1060; www.bulgariacarrent.com; ul Orfei 9) rents cars from 30lv per day outside the July and August period (when they rise to 50lv).

Public Transport

Sofia's trams, buses and metro line run 5.30am to 11pm and share a ticket system. A single ride is 1lv, a day pass is 4lv. There are no transfers. Blue ticket booths are near most stops and many newsstands sell tickets too. Single-ride tickets must be validated once you board.

Minibuses ply many useful city routes at 1.50lv per ride.

The dependable **OK Taxi** (☎ 973 2121) uses the meter.

SOUTHERN BULGARIA

Most of Bulgaria's most popular hikes or ski runs are in the mountainous southwest, filled by three chains: the Rila Mountains (www.rilanationalpark.org) are south of Sofia, the Pirins (www.pirin-np.com) are further south towards the Greek border, and the Rodopis are just east and south of the popular hub Plovdiv.

Check www.bulgariaski.com for loads of ski info on the three main resorts: Borovets, Bansko and Pamporovo.

Drop by Zig Zag (p233) in Sofia for tips on activities.

RILA MONASTERY РИЛСКИ МАНАСТИР

☎ 07054

Many Bulgarians say you haven't been to Bulgaria without paying your respects to this **monastery** (admission free; 6am-9pm or 10pm) 120km south of Sofia. Set in a forested valley, it's near excellent hikes (multiday ones lead to *hizhas;* mountain huts) and is famed for its mural-filled **Nativity Church**, built in the 1830s.

Built in 927, and heavily restored in 1469, the monastery helped keep Bulgarian culture and language alive during the Ottoman rule.

If you have time, you can hike up the **Tomb of St Ivan** (grobyat na Sv Ivan Rilski). The 15-minute hike begins along the road 3.7km east behind the monastery.

There are hotels and camping grounds nearby; or you could sleep in the monastery's **rooms** (☎ 2208; r about €15).

At research time, two daily direct buses connected the monastery with Sofia's Ovcha Kupel bus terminal (10lv, 2½ hours), with one returning at 3pm. Five daily buses reach nearby Rila village (2lv, 30 minutes), where hourly buses go south to Blagoevgrad (1.70lv, 25 minutes) for more connections.

PLOVDIV ПЛОВДИВ

☎ 032 / pop 375,000

Despite its sprawl, Bulgaria's second city lives more like a town, particularly around its legendary cafe-lined pedestrian malls and laid-back, cobbled, hilltop 'Old Town'. It's got a lot to take in – student life, Roman theatres still in use, cobbled 19th-century revival-era taverns, and local wines galore.

Plovdiv was known as Philippopolis to the Romans in the 3rd century AD, but it was settled thousands of years earlier by Thracians.

Orientation

Plovdiv's train station and (main) Yug Bus Terminal are about 600m southwest of the central pl Tsentralen. From the square, the main pedestrian mall, ul Knyaz Aleksandâr, stretches 500m north to pl Dzhumaya, near Old Town just east.

On arrival, take bus 7, 20 or 26 in front of the train station (1lv, buy on board) and exit on ul Tsar Boris III Obedinitel past the tunnel to reach Old Town.

Information

Left Luggage The train station has 24-hour luggage storage (3lv per piece per day); the Yug and Rodopi bus stations both hold bags for 1lv per day.

Tourist Information Centre (☎ 656 794; www.plovdiv-tour.info; pl Tsentralen; 9am-6pm Mon-Fri, 10am-2pm Sat & Sun) Staff have free local maps and can find private accommodation.

Unicredit Bulbank (ul Ivan Vazov 4; 8am-6pm Mon-Fri)

Sights

Plovdiv likes calling itself the 'city of seven hills' (like Rome). Too bad it isn't true – the smallest was knocked down half a century ago to recobble Old Town. Of the remaining six, the best vantage point is up the **Hill of the Liberators** (Bunardjika Park), where 'Alyosha' (a statue of a Russian soldier) will greet you.

OLD TOWN

Old Town – with lanes of antiques shops and outdoor cafes – is a living museum. Seeing the 22 rooms inside the area's most striking building (built in 1847) is an added bonus to the country's finest **Ethnographical Museum** (☎ 625 654; ul Dr Chomakov 2; admission 4lv; 9am-noon & 2-5pm or 5.30pm) – with *Star Wars*-like masked *kukeri* costumes.

There are more nice views nearby at the **Ruins of Eumolpias** (ul Dr Chomakov; admission free; 24hr), scattered upon Nebet Tepe hilltop.

The amazing **Roman Amphitheatre** (admission 3lv; 10am-5pm) is easily seen from the cafe set up outside the gates, but entry lets you tread on worn steps approaching their 2000th birthday. The theatre holds various events from June to August.

OTHER SIGHTS

Dzhumaya Mosque (pl Dzhumaya; admission free; dawn-dusk) – the first in Balkan Europe – is not your usual Bulgarian centrepiece. It initially dates from 1368, but has been renovated a couple of times since a 1928 earthquake. Outside a shiny **statue of Philip II** (Alexander the Great's dad) looks over the **Roman stadium ruins**, providing a bizarre peek into the past from below the pedestrian walkway.

Sleeping

For private rooms, drop by **Esperansa** (☎ office 260 653, 24hr cell phone 0897-944 951; travel_plovdiv@abv.bg; ul Ivan Vazov 14; s/d 25/50lv, apt from 80lv; approx 10am-8pm), a nine-minute walk from the main stations.

Gusto Hostel (☎ 625 258; www.gustohostel.com; ul Petko Karavelov 2; dm/d incl breakfast €10/25;) Staff keep things neat at this simple new hostel with six- and eight-bunk dorms and a private double.

Plovdiv Guesthouse (☎ 622 432; www.plovdivguest.com; ul Sâborna 20; dm/s/d incl breakfast €10/28/36;) Home to a travel agency, this clean all-pink house in Old Town is half hostel, half guesthouse.

our pick **Hiker's Hostel** (☎ 0885-194 553, www.hikers-hostel.org; ul Sâborna 53; tent/dm incl breakfast 14/22lv, d incl breakfast 52-60lv;) Plovdiv's top backpacker stop occupies a cosy little house in Old Town. The laid-back staff keep a couple of tents to use in the courtyard, plus a claustrophobic private room.

Hotel Elite (☎ 624 537; www.hotel-elite.eu; ul Raiko Daskalov 53; r from 39lv) Rooms vary, but are clean with views of Imaret Mosque. TV, no breakfast or internet.

Dafi Hotel (☎ 620 041; www.hoteldafi.com; ul Benkovski 23; s/d incl breakfast from 85/105lv;) The modern Dafi's 20 rooms offer nice, midrange, carpeted comfort near several bars.

Eating

North of pl Dzhumaya, you'll find a popular **banitsa stand** (ul Daskalov; banitsas 0.80lv), selling cheese-filled pastries. The best spot for kebabs or falafel is the alley-hub **Alaeddin** (ul Kynaz Aleksandâr; kebab 1.60lv, falafel 2lv; 24hr).

Dayana (ul Dondukov; dishes from 2.80lv, grills from 8lv; 24hr) Aside the rocky walls of Sahat Tepe hill, this sprawling spot goes with the usual Bulgarian grill items plus skewers of vegetables (4.90lv).

Gradzhanski Klub (ul Chalkov; dishes 5-12lv; 8.30am-midnight) A local hang-out in Old Town: a three-room smoky spot with students yapping over coffee, Kamenitza beers or *shopska* salads (tomatoes, cucumber, onions and cheese).

Drinking

King's Stable (ul Sâborna; cocktails 3.40lv; 8.30am-2am Apr-Sep) This great open-air bar/cafe is in the Old Town.

Marmalad (ul Bratya Pulievi 3; cocktails 3lv; 9am-2am) The ultramod Marmalad has cream leather booths and local dress-uppers who sip to house music.

our pick **Nylon** (ul Benkovski 8; noon-4am) This classic local dive – across the street from Marmalad – has a leaky ceiling and ancient trumpets hanging over the long wood bar.

Entertainment

Petnoto (ul Yoakim Gruev 36) Local bands and DJs mixing things up in a mod setting geared to fulfil local indie-rock hearts.

Caligula (ul Knyaz Aleksandâr 30) Plovdiv's only gay club appeals to folks of all stripes.

Getting There & Away

BUS

Yug Bus Terminal (☎ 626 916; bul Hristo Botev), 100m northeast of the train station, sends frequent buses to Sofia (13lv, two hours) every half-hour or hour, plus a few daily buses to Varna (26lv, seven hours), Burgas (20lv, four hours) and half a dozen to İstanbul (35lv, six hours).

More than 1km north of the river, **Sever Bus Terminal** (☎ 935 705) has four daily buses to Veliko Târnovo (14lv, 4½ hours). Get there by minibus 4 from ul Tsar Boris III Obedinitel.

About 100m south of the Yug bus station, **Rodopi Bus Terminal** (☎ 765 160), accessible by underpass from the train station, sends buses into the Rodopi Mountains, stopping in Asenovgrad.

TRAIN

Daily direct trains from the **train station** (☎ 622 729; bul Hristo Botev) include: Burgas (13.40lv, five hours, five daily), Istanbul (49lv, 11 hours, one daily), Sofia (8.10lv, 2½ hours, frequent), Varna (16.70lv, six hours, four daily) and Veliko Târnovo (11lv, five hours, one daily).

For international tickets, go to **Rila Bureau** (☎ 643 120; bul Hristo Botev 31a; summer 7.30am-7.30pm Mon-Fri, 8am-6pm Sat, winter 7.30am-5.30pm Mon-Fri, 8am-5pm Sat).

CENTRAL BULGARIA

Bulgaria's crossed by the long Stara Planina range (www.staraplanina.org), the local name for the Balkans. Some appealing highway towns line the south side of the towering range – like **Kazanlâk** in the Valley of the Roses, near Thracian tombs and gorgeous **Shipka Pass** – and see a few tourists. Most visitors go to Central Bulgaria's main hub, the former capital of Veliko Târnovo.

VELIKO TÂRNOVO ВЕЛИКО ТЪРНОВО

☎ 062 / pop 72,000

Clinging to a sharp S-shaped gorge split by a snaking river between Sofia and Varna, Bucharest and Istanbul, Veliko Târnovo is too convenient and lovely to miss. The former capital (1185–393) and busy student hub is easy-going and filled with days of potential.

Orientation

From the train platform, a walkway heads northwest towards an underpass that leads to ul Hristo Botev, near the Yug Bus Terminal. Alternatively, there are several buses to the centre from in front of the train station; and taxis cost 3lv or 4lv to the centre. From the bus station, it's an inclined walk up to pl Maika Bulgaria, where ul Vasil Levski heads west and the main crawl, ul Nezavisimost (then ul Stefan Stambolov), heads east.

Information

Navigator (ul Nezavisimost 3; per hr 0.90-1.20lv; 24hr) Internet cafe in basement of corner mall.

Tourist Information Centre (☎ 622 148; www.velikotarnovo.info; ul Hristo Botev 5; 9am-6pm Mon-Fri, Mon-Sat in summer) Staff will call for accommodation reservations, rent cars (30lv to 40lv per day) and sell regional maps (from 3lv).

United Bulgarian Bank (ul Hristo Botev; 8.30am-4.30pm) Cashes travellers cheques.

USIT Colours (☎ 601 751; pl Slaveikov 7; 9.30am-6pm Mon-Fri) Sells ISIC cards for 10lv.

Wash & Dry (ul Nezavisimost 3; per load 6.50lv; 8.30am-7pm) Laundry drop-off service next to Navigator.

Sights

At research time, Veliko was considering upping the costs of its museums and many churches to a hefty 6lv each.

TSAREVETS FORTRESS

About 1km from the centre, this mammoth **citadel** (admission 4lv; 8am-7pm Apr-Sep, 9am-5pm Oct-Mar) sits stoic and sprawling on a site shared over the centuries by Thracians, Romans and Byzantines. What's seen now – a triangular, high-walled fortress – was largely built between the 5th and 12th centuries.

Some tour groups shell out about €300 (per group) for the after-dusk, rather cheesy 40-

minute **sound and light show**, which lights up the fortress with laser beams and coloured bulbs. It's easy to watch for free outside the gates.

HIKES

Veliko's valley setting begs for some footfall. From town, you can walk 6km to a ridgetop **Preobrazhenski Monastery**, with boulders fallen after a 1991 earthquake strewn about a (narrowly missed) mural-filled **church** (admission 2lv). The path there begins near Hikers Hostel – up from the centre.

Another great hike is to the hilltop **Arbanasi** (4km northeast), a village of walled villas that once housed the king's royal entourage. It's worth seeking out the 16th-century **Nativity**

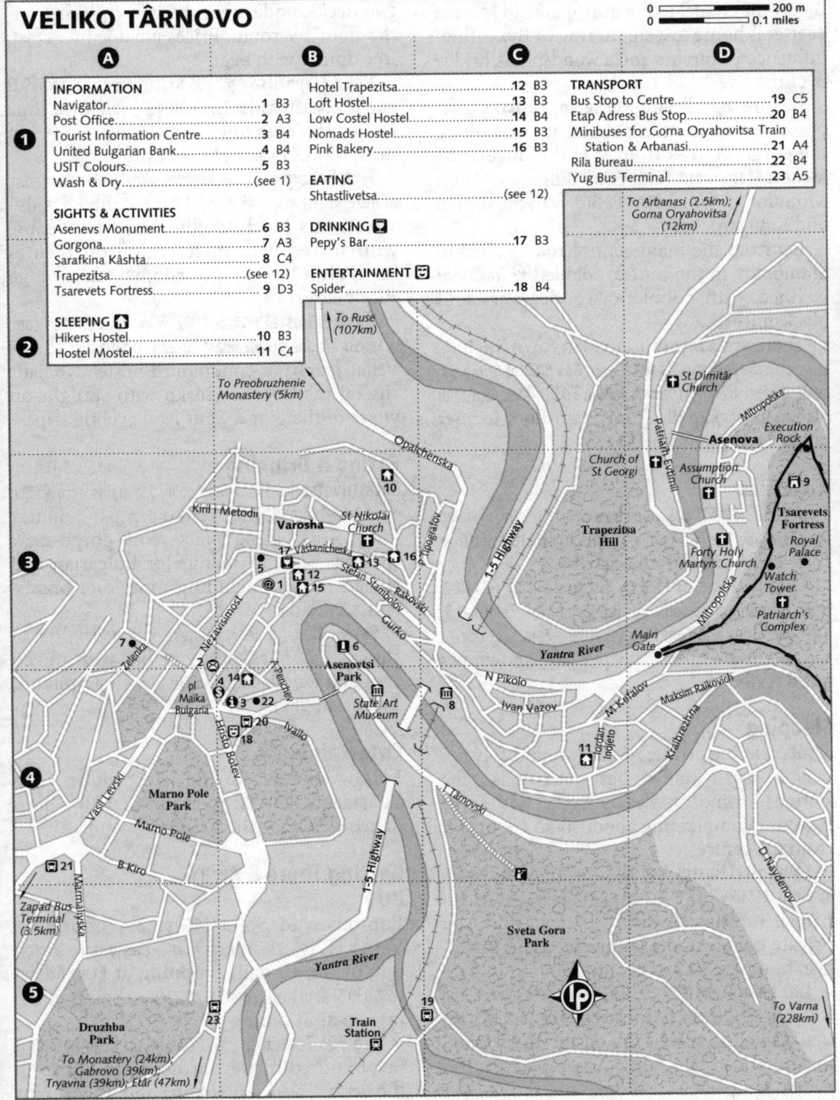

Book your stay at lonelyplanet.com/hotels

Church (adult/student 4/2lv; 9am-5pm or 6pm), 200m west of the bus stop/centre. It's humble outside (intentionally to obscure religious purposes of buildings to Ottomans) but packed with evocative murals inside. The hike begins across a small bridge behind Tsaravets (go around to the left side); or you can bus up.

OTHER SIGHTS

Below the citadel to the north, the old **Asenova quarter** is home to a smattering of Byzantine-influenced churches and a wood-plank bridge over the river.

Be sure to walk along **ul Gurko**, Veliko's best-preserved street that cobbles its way along the gorge. Across from it is the huge 1985 **Asenevs Monument** (aka Four Bulgarian Kings Monument, for Assen, Petâr, Ivan Shishman and Kaloyan).

Up from the main central road, called ul Stambolov in the centre, cobbled **ul Rakovski** is lined with cobblers, woodcarvers and blacksmiths.

There are a few museums in town, including the **Sarafkina Kâshta** (635 802; ul Gurko 88; adult/student 4/2lv; 9am-5pm Mon-Fri Dec-Mar, 9am-6pm Tue-Sun Apr-Nov), made from a two-floor former banker's home from 1861.

Activities

Trapezitsa (635 823; www.trapezitca1902.com; ul Stefan Stambolov 79; 9am-6pm Mon-Fri) can help arrange rock-climbing and hiking trips.

For cycling options, **Gorgona** (601 400; www.gorgona-shop.com, in Bulgarian; ul Zelenka 2; 10am-1pm & 2-7pm Mon-Fri, 10am-2pm Sat) rents out mountain bikes (10lv per day) and knows good trails.

Sleeping

Touts offering private rooms (around 15lv per person) usually wait for buses and trains at the stations – some travellers end up at hostels the next day complaining about so-so rooms far from the centre.

Low Costel Hostel (0885-726 733; ul Assen Ruskov 6; dm/d 16/40lv;) Compact and colourful British-run hostel, with two clean dorms, a private double and a lounge area. No breakfast, but there's a kitchen to use.

Loft Hostel (0877-323 255; www.thelofthostel.com; ul Kapitan Diado Nikola 2a; dm incl breakfast 18-20lv, d incl breakfast 44lv;) Overlooking the main drag, the American-run Loft is a compact, stylish hostel. Only one bathroom.

Hikers Hostel (0889-691 661; www.hikers-hostel.org; ul Rezevoarska 91; camp sites/dm/r incl breakfast €7/10/26;) Way up a cobbled path, this super, intimate hostel is a hike to reach but has superb views.

Hostel Mostel (0897-859 359; www.hostelmostel.com; ul Iordan Indjeto 10; camp sites €9, dm €10-13, s/d €23/30;) This stunner resides in a transformation of an old Turkish home, with sitting areas on two decks, under vines or in a cushions-on-the-floor TV room. Prices include breakfast; free dinner with beer.

Hotel Trapezitsa (635 823; wwww.trapezitca1902.com; ul Stefan Stambolov 79; s/d 30/40lv) Once the lone budget choice in town, it's a bit worn out, but most rooms look right over the gorge.

Pink Bakery (633 339; www.the-pink-bakery.com; ul Rezervoarska 5; r 45-55lv) On a cobbled side-street, this lovely dollhouse-style cheapie with shared bath mixes colourful themes in a grab-bag of six rooms (eg orange slice bedspreads).

Nomads Hostel (603 092; www.nomadshostel.com; ul Gurko 27; dm incl breakfast 20-22lv, d 50-54lv;) Veliko's only air-conditioned hostel, Nomads sits on the historic Gurko with straight-on views of the gorge. Staff lead cycling trips.

Eating & Drinking

Shtastlivetsa (ul Stefan Stambolov 79; mains from 4.50lv; 10am-11pm) Long Veliko's most popular (and best) eating place, this gorge-view spot has separate menus for Bulgarian and Italian dishes, including nine 'diet pizzas' and 82 salads!

Pepy's Bar (ul Veneta Boteva 5; beer 2lv; 8am-11pm) A laid-back, softly lit bar with mixed ages and a grab-bag decor (Jackie O photos, Bulgarian 78s).

Entertainment

Follow students to the latest clubs, such as **Spider** (ul Hristo Botev; entry 2-3lv), a two-floor dance club near the Etap bus stand.

Getting There & Away

BUS

For buses to Sofia (17lv, 3½ hours) or Varna (17lv, 3½ hours), it's easiest to catch one of the 10 daily stopping at **Etap Adress** (630 564; ul Ivaylo, Hotel Etâr), 100m south of the information centre.

Yug Bus Terminal (620 014; ul Hristo Botev), a few hundred metres farther downhill from the centre, also serves Sofia and Varna, plus

Plovdiv (14lv, four hours, one daily), Burgas (18lv to 23lv, four hours) four times daily, a midday bus with quick transfer in Ruse to Bucharest (28lv) and a night bus to Istanbul (40lv, seven hours).

Regional buses, plus more to Plovdiv, leave from the **Zapad Bus Terminal** (☎ 640 908), 4km west of the centre.

TRAIN

Veliko's small **train station** (☎ 622 130, 620 065) sends about one direct train a day to Plovdiv (11lv, five hours). Five daily trains to Sofia (15.40lv, five to six hours) and four to Varna (12.50lv, four or five hours) require a change at the busier **Gorna Oryahovitsa train station** (☎ 0618-26 118), 13km north of town. Minibuses along ul Vasil Levski, or bus 10 east from the centre, head there every 10 or 15 minutes.

An overnight train to Istanbul (couchette/sleeper 58/72lv, 13¾ hours) and midmorning train to Bucharest (29lv, six hours) stop in Veliko. Buy international tickets at **Rila Bureau** (☎ 622 2042; ul Tsar Kolyan; 🕑 7.30am-6pm Mon-Sat Jul & Aug, 8am-4pm Mon-Sat Sep-Jun), behind the information centre.

BLACK SEA COAST

Every summer hordes of package trippers flood the crowded, overdeveloped resorts like Sunny Beach and Golden Sands. You can skip those places entirely and enjoy the turquoise (not black) waters of this interesting sea more. Varna is a real-deal town with lively beaches (and the coast's only hostels), but the best stretches of sand are found to the south (where bus services are less frequent).

Hotel rates are most expensive in July and August, a bit less in June and September.

VARNA ВАРНА

☎ 052 / pop 357,000

Varna – with Roman ruins and shady cosmopolitan streets – would be a highlight even without the Black Sea at its lip – but it's sure nice having its long beach as a bonus. Briefly called 'Stalin' after WWII, its roots date to the Thracians from 4000 BC until it got refashioned as Odessos by Greek sailors in the 6th century BC.

The renowned **Varna Summer International Festival** is held between May and October.

Orientation

The train station is 650m south of central pl Nezavisimost, where pedestrian mall ul Knyaz Boris I heads west to ul Slivnitsa, which goes southeast to seaside Primorski Park. The bus station is 2km north of the centre; take bus 409 or 148.

Information

Find entertainment listings in the free seasonal guide *Varna In Your Pocket* (www.inyourpocket.com).

Bulbank (ul Slivnitsa; 🕑 8am-6pm Mon-Fri)

Frag (pl Nezavisimost; per hr 1lv; 🕑 24hr) Internet access in the opera building's basement.

Global Tours (☎ 601 085; www.globaltours-bg.com; ul Kynaz Boris I 67; 🕑 8am-8pm Mon-Fri, 10am-6pm Sat Jun-Sep, 9am-6pm Mon-Fri Oct-May) This travel agent books private apartments (from €25 in summer), rents cars and offers group bus tours to Balchik and Kaliakra Cape (82lv) or yacht trips (72lv).

Left Luggage (main bus terminal; bul Vladislav Varenchik; per day 5lv; 🕑 7am-7pm)

Municipal Tourist Information Centre (☎ 602 907; office@vct-bg.org; ul Batenberg; 🕑 approx 9am-7pm Mon-Sat May-Sep, 9am-6pm Mon-Sat Oct-Apr) Drop by for area tips, plus homestay hook-ups (s/d 30/40lv).

Peralnya (ul Voden; per load 6lv; 🕑 9am-7pm Mon-Sat) Laundry service.

Sights

The beach is a big part of why people come, but there's a lot more to Varna.

BEACH

Starting just steps from the train station, **Varna city beach** is 8km long and has three essential parts: the south beach (with water slides and pirate ship restaurant) has a nice but busy stretch; the thinner central beach is dominated by clubs; another 1.5km up is the north beach, with nicer sandy stretches and a great old-school **thermal pool** with year-round hot water.

Just in from the beach is the 8km-long, Vienna-inspired **Primorski Park**, a lovely strolling ground freckled with open-air cafes and a monument or two.

RESORTS

Another beach option is bussing north to mingle with the resort crowd. Just 9km north of Varna, **Sveti Konstantin** is a leafy area, with a pleasant monastery and a beach crammed with nicer-than-usual midrange resorts. Take bus 8 from ul Maria Luisa.

Another 9km north you'll find **Golden Sands** (Zlatni Pyasâtsi), a tackier resort-burg with a busy 4km-long beach lined with kebab stands and a fake Eiffel Tower. In the nearby hills, the interesting **Aladzha Monastery** (☎ 052-355-460; adult/student 5/2lv; ⌚ 9am-6pm May-Oct, 9am-4pm Tue-Sat Nov-Apr) is a 13th-century rock monastery.

Buses 109, 209, 309 and 409 pass near Golden Sands. The monastery is an hour's hike up by road or trails marked with blue or gold signs).

OTHER SIGHTS

The large **Archeological Museum** (☎ 681 030; ul Maria Luisa 41; adult/student 10/2lv; ⌚ 10am-5pm Tue-Sun Apr-

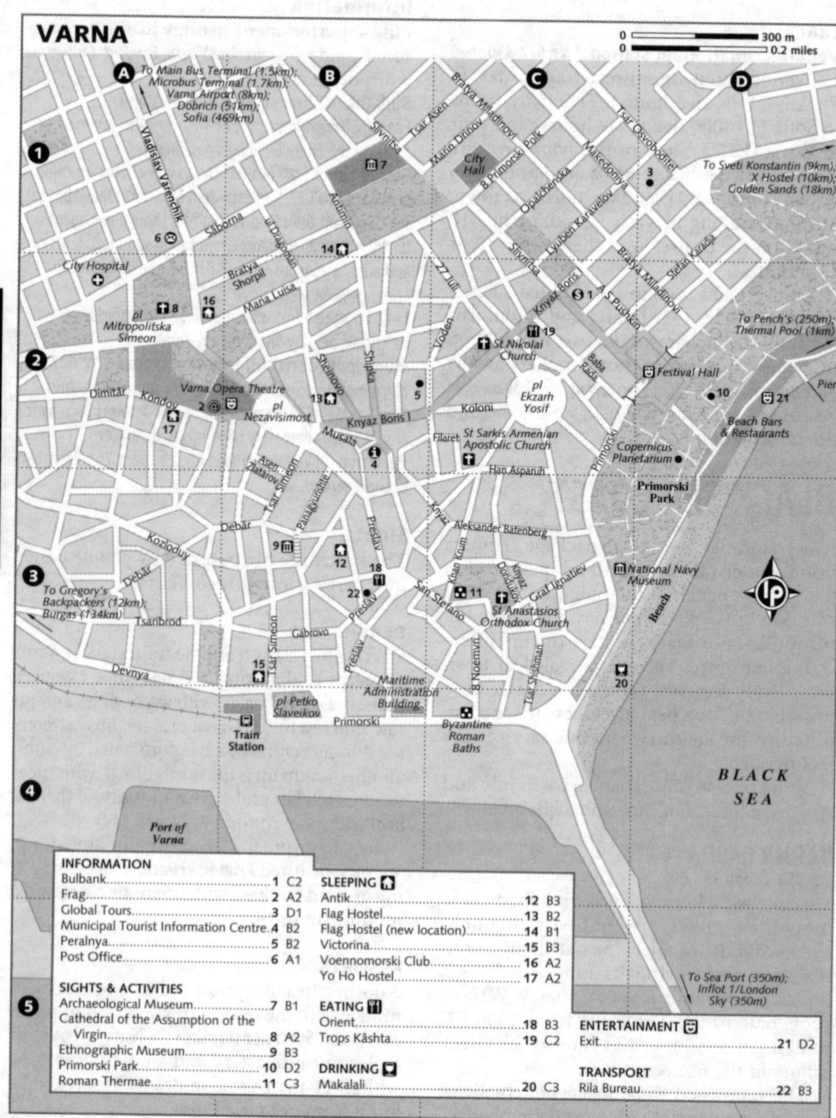

SCAMS

Every year beach bums lose bags and cameras on the Varna beach. Always have someone in your group sitting with your things.

Sep, 10am-5pm Tue-Sat Oct-Mar) is one of Bulgaria's best. Housed in a former girls' school – a grand old two storey – it is filled with more than 100,000 pieces from some 6000 years of the area's history, all well explained in English. Look out for the sculpted Thracian goatee.

Built in the 1880s, the towering, gold onion-domed **Cathedral of the Assumption of the Virgin** (pl Mitropolitska Simeon), a 10-min walk west of the museum, is one of the city symbols.

South of the central pedestrian crawl, Varna's second-best museum, housed in an 1860 revival building, is the **Ethnographic Museum** (☎ 630 588; ul Panagyurishte 22; adult/student 4/2lv; 🕑 10am-5pm Tue-Sun Apr-Sep, 10am-5pm Tue-Fri Oct-Mar).

Wedged impossibly between a church and modern housing, the leftovers of the 2nd-century AD **Roman Thermae** (ul Khan Krum & ul San Stefano; adult/student 4/2lv; 🕑 10am-5pm May-Oct, 10am-5pm Tue-Sat Nov-Apr) are easily seen from outside for free.

Sleeping

HOSTELS

Across from the train station, **Victorina** (☎ 603 541; http://victorina.borsabg.com; Tsar Simeon 36; r with family/private apt from 30/40lv; 🕑 7am-9pm Jun-Sep, 10am-6pm Mon-Fri Oct-May) arranges rooms all year. The Varna area has the only hostels on the Black Sea.

Gregory's Backpackers (☎ 379 909; www.hostelvarna.com; 82 Fenix St, Zvezditsa village; camp sites/dm/d incl breakfast €6.50/11/28; 💻 🚭) Run by Brits, Gregory's is a great kick-back hostel base, but it's a 15-minute ride outside Varna. Staff offer rides daily, while bus 36 makes its way hourly. Open April to October only.

Flag Hostel (☎ 089 740 8115; www.varnahostel.com; 2nd fl, ul Sheinovo 2; dm incl breakfast €10; 💻) Also run by a Brit, the all-year Flag is a toaster's paradise – free beer in the evening, free toast-and-vodka breakfasts. Note: it may be moving to a new location (ul Maria Luisa 35).

Yo Ho Hostel (☎ 088 760 1691; 088 793 3340; www.yohohostel.com; ul Ruse 23; dm/r 22/28lv; 💻) Nothing pirate about the place; the laid-back Bulgarian guys running this urban-style hostel are more into surfing and anime-style art.

X Hostel (☎ 054-361 881; www.xhostel.eu; Evksinograd 19, 16th Rd, Sveti Konstantin; dm/d €11/32; 💻) About 10km north of Varna, the X is in a '70s-style party-pad hostel on a hill (15 minutes' walk from the beach). Exit the bus 1km south of the main Sveti Konstanti stop, then follow the 'Villa Waikiki' signs.

Voennomorski Club (☎ 617 965; ul Vladislav Varenchik 2; s 21-31lv, d 42-46lv; ❄) Filling the top two floors of the sky-blue building, rooms are a little musty and the staff grumpy, but it'll work if the hostels are full.

Antik (☎ 632 167; www.galia-online.com/antik; ul Ohrid 10; r from 50lv; ❄ 💻) On a cobbled shady lane, the friendly Antik has a mix of rooms between the train station and central pedestrian zone.

Eating

Trops Kâshta (bul Knyaz Boris I 48; dishes 2-5lv; 🕑 8.30am-11pm) This bright pick-and-point chain offers fresh, cheap and fast Bulgarian staples.

Orient (☎ 602 380; ul Tsaribrod 1; dishes from 4lv; 🕑 8am-11pm or midnight) This atmospheric Turkish eatery, located between the train station and pedestrian crawl, fills with locals coming for fresh hummus (3.80lv) or lamb kebabs (7lv).

Drinking

In summer, the bars of the beach nightlife zone – mostly grouped about 400m north along the beach – open their doors on the beach. At last pass, a few good 'chill-out' bars clustered near the south end, including the glassed-in **Makalali**.

Just north, in a long old seaside complex, you'll find clubs like **Exit** (🕑 10pm-4am) and the classic frat-friendly **Pench's**.

Getting There & Away

AIR

Varna airport (VAR; ☎ 573 323; www.varna-airport.bg) is 8km northwest of town. Bus 409 goes there.

BUS

The confusing **main bus terminal** (☎ 748 349; www.autogaravn.com; bul Vladislav Varenchik 158), 2km north of the city centre, is three stops north of the main cathedral on bus 409 or 148. Bus service includes: Athens (141lv, 26 hours), Bucharest (70lv, seven hours, daily in summer), Burgas (12lv, 2½ hours, frequent), Istanbul (50lv, 10 hours, twice daily), Plovdiv

Book your stay at lonelyplanet.com/hotels

(26lv, six hours, two daily), Ruse (16lv, four hours, two daily), Sofia (30lv, seven to eight hours, half hourly) and Veliko Târnovo (17lv, four hours, half hourly).

FERRY

From June through early September, **Inflot 1/London Sky** (☎ 692 099, 617 577; inflot@varna.tea.bg, www.londonsky-bg.com; ul Shishman 20) sends ferries to Odessa (from €95, nine hours) twice weekly, stopping in Constanţa, Romania (from €30, four hours).

MICROBUS

The **microbus terminal** (Avtogara Mladost; ☎ 500 039; ul Knyaz Cherkazki), 200m west of the bus station (cross the street via an underpass and go left 50m, then right past the next block), sends microbuses hourly to Burgas (12lv) from 7am to 7pm, Less frequent services go to Nesebâr (via Sunny Beach, 10v).

TRAIN

Direct train services from the **main train station** (☎ 630 444; bul Primorski) link Varna to Sofia (25.20lv, eight to nine hours, six daily), Plovdiv (16.70lv, 6½ to 7½ hours, four daily), Ruse (11lv, 3¾ hours, two daily), and Gorna Oryahovitsa (for Veliko Târnovo; 14.10lv, 3½ hours, five daily).

Direct trains to Bucharest (41lv, 13 hours) are available on an overnight Russia-bound Russian train from mid-June to early September only. The rest of the year you have to change in Ruse. International tickets must be purchased at **Rila Bureau** (☎ 632 348; ul Preslav 13; 8am-7.30pm Mon-Fri, 8am-3.30pm Sat), a few minutes' walk from the station.

NORTH COAST

As well as the resorts north of town (p243), it's possible to daytrip or overnight in historic **Balchik.** The beach is nothing much here – most of the north coast is rocky – but there's the posh **Summer Palace Queen Marie & Botanical Gardens** (Dvoretsa; ☎ 76854; mandatory separate admission 5lv each; 8am-8pm May–mid-October, 8.30am-6.30pm mid-October–Apr), designed as something 'small and romantic' by the Romanian queen in the 1920s. **JJ's** (☎ 0887-844 953; jayjaysbalchik@yahoo.co.uk; ul Primorska 33; s/d 35/40lv) is an English-run pub/guesthouse near the small beach.

From Balchik you can bus 30km northeast once daily to lovely Kaliakra Cape (5lv, 45 minutes), where the 2km-long **Kaliakra Nature Reserve** (admission 3lv; 24hr) pokes out into the Black Sea and features Thracian ruins, dating from the 4th century BC.

NESEBÂR НЕСЕБЪР

☎ 0554 / pop 10,000

About 95km south of Burgas on the central coast, historic (Thracians settled Mesembria here in 3000 BC) but touristy Nesebâr sits on a small rocky isthmus on the south end of the wide, practically perfect bay that's home to built-for-tourism **Sunny Beach** (Slânchev Bryag), a jam-packed 8km beach a couple of kilometres north.

Even the churched-out should stroll past Nesebâr's Byzantine-inspired, ceramic disc-adorned **churches**, including the ruined 6th-century **basilica** (ul Mitropolitska).

'New Nesebâr', a kilometre inland, has many hotels and possible homestays. At the north end of town, **Hotel Toni** (☎ 42 403, 0889-268 004; ul Kraybrezhna 20; r 50lv; ❄) is a cosy hotel with some balconies facing Sunny Beach.

Most Varna–Burgas buses stop on the main highway, 2km west of town. Nesebâr's bus stand is at the old town gate, where you can catch buses to Burgas (5lv, 40 minutes) every 40 minutes, or six daily to Varna (10lv, two hours).

BURGAS БУРГАС

☎ 056 / pop 189,500

A major gateway to the Black Sea, Burgas is an unappealing port town you'll probably be happy to skip. If you do stay, the 2km **beach** isn't bad (MTV chose it for a 2008 festival). Meanwhile, you'll find plenty of action on the lively pedestrianised ul Aleksandrovska, which runs north (across ul Bulair) from the train station and Yug Bus Terminal. At pl Svoboda it meets another mall, ul Bogoridi – the busier of the two – which extends east towards the beach.

Sleeping

Dim-ant (☎ 840 779; dimant91@abv.bg; ul Tsar Simeon 15; 8am-9pm or 10pm summer, 8am-5.30pm Mon-Fri winter) Helps find homestay rooms.

Hotel Elite (☎ 845 780; ul Morska 35; s/d incl breakfast 45/50lv) Off ul Bogodini, the Elite has comfortable rooms – some with a balcony.

Getting There & Away

AIR

Wizz Air (p232) connects London's Luton with Burgas' airport (8km north); take bus 15 (11lv) to the centre.

BUS

From **Yug Bus Terminal** (☎ 842 692; near cnr ul Aleksandrovska & ul Bulair), buses go to Varna (12lv, 2½ hours, half hourly), Nesebâr (5lv, 45 minutes, frequent), Sozopol (4lv, 40 minutes, frequent), Sofia (25lv to 30lv, 6¼ hours, eight daily), Plovdiv (20lv to 26lv, four hours, several daily), and Veliko Târnovo (26lv, 4½ hours, two daily).

Enturtrans/Istanbul Seyahat (☎ 844 708; www.istanbulseyahat.com.tr; ul Bulair 22; 6.30-1am), 200m north, sells tickets for Istanbul (adult/student 50/40lv, seven hours).

TRAIN

The **train station** (☎ 845 022) has direct trains to Sofia (18.80lv, 7½ hours, seven daily) and Plovdiv (13.40lv, four to five hours, three daily). Trains to Bucharest (53lv, 11 hours, twice weekly) leave June through August only and require a transfer in Ruse. Buy international tickets at **Rila Bureau** (☎ 845 242; 8am-4pm Mon-Fri, 8am-2.30pm Sat) in the station.

SOUTH COAST

Fine sandy beaches dot the coast south from Sozopol to Turkey, though some come with the less appealing modern beach resorts of **Primorsko** and **Kiten** that cater mostly to Bulgarians.

Sozopol Созопол

☎ 0550 / pop 4650

A jutting peninsula of cobbled streets, beaches and Greek roots, touristy Sozopol is a favourite Bulgarian summer destination.

The bus stop, 31km south of Burgas, is roughly between the old town and inland new town (Harmanite). There are two small beaches in town, and a longer, less-developed one just north, **Gradina Beach**.

Gradina Camping has bungalows and tent space near the beach, 2km north of town. **Sasha Khristov's Private Rooms** (☎ 23 434; ul Venets 17; r with shared bathroom 25lv) offers four rooms in old town. Agents like **Enigma Tours** (☎ 22 693; ul Kulata 5) find private accommodation from 35lv. The 'new town' is full of four-floor guesthouses with doubles for 40lv or 50lv.

Buses and minibuses leave the **bus terminal** (☎ 22 239; ul Han Krum) for Burgas (5lv, 40 minutes, half-hourly 6am to 9pm) all year.

Sinemorets Синеморец

☎ 0590

Nearly to the Turkish border, this remote bluff-top village of new villas, a few hotels and ongoing construction is nevertheless a lovely place to visit for its three beaches – particularly the one farthest south, reached via a short walk over rocky cliffs.

Near the town entrance, you can take 90-minute boat trips into the marshy riverway of the **Strandjha Nature Park** for 15lv per person.

Casa Domingo (☎ 0888-744 019; 66 093; www.casadomingo.info; r 22-35lv) is a simple hotel with pool.

One daily bus connects Sinemorets with Burgas.

BULGARIA DIRECTORY

ACCOMMODATION

Bulgaria's hostel count has grown in recent years, with Sofia, Plovdiv, Veliko Târnovo and Varna represented with rooms from 18lv.

The next cheapest option is safe, clean homestays, found in summer from the bus- and train-station touts, accommodation agencies or by posted *'stai pod naem'* (rooms for rent) signs. Rates are 10lv to 25lv per person.

Average rates for hotels (which usually have private bathroom, TV and air-con) are around 35lv for a single, 45lv for a double.

'Camping' for most Bulgarians means an area with side-by-side basic bungalows and a couple of spots to pitch a tent.

Up in the mountains there are many *hizhas* (mountain huts) of varying condition. Check Bulgaria maps for locations.

ACTIVITIES

The hiking options in Bulgaria's mountains abound (with more than 37,000km of hiking trails in all). Visit Zig Zag (p233) in Sofia for trip info, tips and trail maps.

In winter, Bulgaria's excellent slopes at southwestern resorts such as Borovets, Bansko and Pamporovo bring in skiers, many on package trips. Lift tickets at these places run at about 50lv per day, while Sofia's Mt Vitosha is about 20lv cheaper.

There's good rock climbing and cycling outside Veliko Târnovo.

DANGERS & ANNOYANCES

Bulgaria feels a lot safer than some of its neighbours. Grab-and-run incidents can happen in Sofia or Varna, particularly in summer. Cigarette smoke is another matter – there's no escaping it, despite the recent regulation to set aside at least a *table* for nonsmoking customers.

DISCOUNT CARDS

Students can save up to 75% on admission to most museums, and on air fares at some travel agents.

EMBASSIES & CONSULATES

New Zealanders can turn to the UK Embassy for assistance, or contact their **consulate general** (☎ 210-6924 136; 76 Kifissias Ave, Ambelokipi) in Athens.

All of the below are in Sofia unless stated:

Australia (☎ 02-946 1334; ul Trakia 37) Main office in Athens.
Canada (☎ 02-969 9710; ul Moskovska 9)
France (☎ 02-965 1100; www.ambafrance-bg.org; ul Oborishte 27-29)
Germany (☎ 02-918 380; www.sofia.diplo.de; ul Frederic Joliot-Curie 25)
Turkey (☎ 02-935 5500; bul Vasil Levski 80); Plovdiv (☎ 032-632 309; ul Filip Makedonski 10)
UK (☎ 02-933 9222; www.british-embassy.bg; ul Moskovksa 9)
USA (☎ 02-937 5100; www.usembassy.bg; ul Kozyak 16)

FESTIVALS & EVENTS

Bulgaria hosts many fascinating shindigs. City-run music and cultural events go all through summer, particularly Varna's music festival.

During the whole of March you can take part in the national custom of Martenitsa, when Bulgarians exchange red-and-white figures and wear them until they see a stork.

In Kavarna, north of Varna, the Kaliakra Rock Fest is a three-day head-banging heavy-metal festival held every June.

GAY & LESBIAN TRAVELLERS

Consensual homosexual sex is legal in Bulgaria, and the age of consent is 16, but Bulgaria is far from openly tolerant (a 2008 poll found 80% of the nation had 'negative attitudes' towards homosexuality). Some gay clubs are listed in this chapter; also check www.gayguidebg.com.

HOLIDAYS

New Year's Day 1 January
Liberation Day (National Day) 3 March
Orthodox Easter Sunday & Monday March/April; one week after Catholic/Protestant Easter
St George's Day 6 May
Cyrillic Alphabet Day 24 May
Unification Day (National Day) 6 September
Bulgarian Independence Day 22 September
National Revival Day 1 November
Christmas 25 and 26 December

INTERNET RESOURCES

A few helpful sites:

www.bdz.bg Train schedule and fares.
www.bulgariatravel.org Official tourist site, with detailed background and photos.
www.inyourpocket.com Online guides to Sofia, Burgas and Varna
www.sofiaecho.com English-language paper that has national coverage, travel tips and extensive archives.

LANGUAGE

Almost everything is written in Cyrillic, a Bulgarian (not Russian) creation. Many Bulgarians know some Russian, German or English. See p1252 for a few useful words.

MONEY

The leva (lv) comprises 100 stotinki. It's pegged to the euro (roughly 2lv to €1). Prices in this chapter conform to local prices (alternating between euro and leva). Banknotes come in denominations of one, two, five, 10, 20 and 50 leva and coins in one, two, five, 10, 20 and 50 stotinki. Bulgaria won't adopt the euro during the life of this book.

ATMs (cash points) and foreign-exchange offices are found in all towns listed here except Rila and Sinemorets.

American Express and Thomas Cook cheques can be cashed at most banks (for approximately 4% commission).

POST

Sending a postcard to Europe costs 1lv, elsewhere 1.40lv. Many post offices in bigger cities are open daily and have internet to use.

TELEPHONE

At Bulgarian Telecommunications Centre (BTC), often found at main post offices, you can make international calls for about 0.32lv per minute. It's cheaper to call from internet cafes (as little as 0.20lv per minute). Mobika and BulFon telephone booths use *fonkarta* (phonecards).

VISAS

Citizens of other EU member states and Australia, Canada, Israel, Japan, New Zealand and the USA can stay in Bulgaria visa-free for up to 90 days. If you need to extend, it may be easier to hop across the border than deal with the headaches of Sofia's Immigration Office (p234). EU citizens can stay up to five years by registering for a permit.

Croatia

HIGHLIGHTS

- **Dubrovnik** The walled Old Town that surrounds luminous marble streets and finely ornamented buildings surrounded by the glistening Adriatic (p266)
- **Hvar Town** The Venetian architecture and vibrant nightlife are what keeps travellers returning to one of Croatia's most stunning islands (p263)
- **Split** The incredible, lively and historic delights of Diocletian's Palace are combined with good food, beaches and perfect location for island hopping (p262)

FAST FACTS

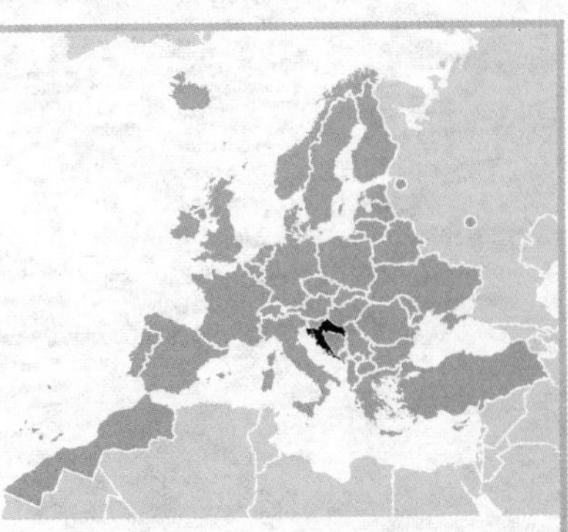

- **Area** 56,538 sq km
- **Budget** around 300KN per day
- **Capital** Zagreb
- **Country code** ☎ 385
- **Famous for** neckties, Slaven Bilić, Tito
- **Language** Croatian
- **Money** kuna (KN); A$1 = 4.10KN; C$1 = 4.65KN; €1 = 7.36KN; ¥100 = 5.79KN; NZ$1 = 3.20KN; UK£1 = 8.30KN; US$1 = 5.49KN
- **Phrases** *bog* (hello), *doviđenja* (goodbye), *hvala* (thanks), *pardon* (sorry)
- **Population** 4.5 million
- **Visas** not required for citizens of the EU, USA, Australia and Canada (see p271)

TRAVEL HINT

Check out Croatia's lovely fresh food markets.

ROAMING CROATIA

Start in Zagreb, head down to Pula, then follow the coast south hitting Split, Hvar, Korčula and Dubrovnik.

Touted as the 'new this' and the 'new that' for years upon its re-emergence on the world tourism scene, it is now blatant that Croatia is a unique destination that can hold its own, and then some. The Adriatic coast is a knockout: its limpid sapphirine waters pull visitors to remote islands, hidden coves and traditional fishing villages, while touting the glitzy beach and yacht scene. Istria is captivating with its gastronomic and wine offerings, and the bars, clubs and festivals of Zagreb and Split remain little-explored delights. Punctuate all this by Dubrovnik in the south and a country couldn't wish for a better finale.

Sitting on a see-saw between the Balkans and central Europe, Croatia has suffered from something of a love-hate-love affair with the EU as the elusive joining date snags on a number of hurdles. The country has managed to keep the lack of (massive) development at bay and maintain the extraordinary beauty of the coast – and the coast's beauty, combined with stunning historic towns and cities that straddle it, is the very thing that brings back travellers year after year.

CROATIA

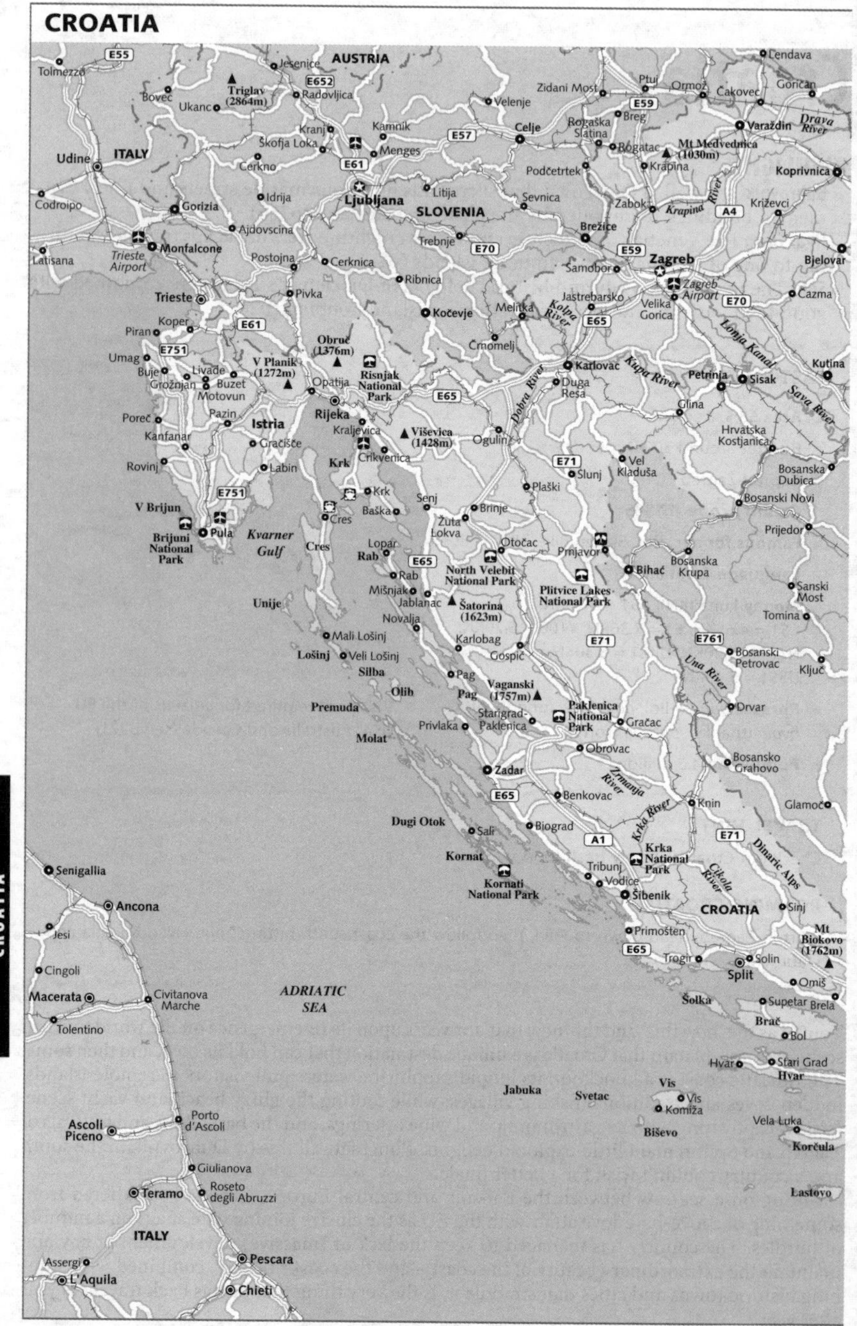
AUSTRIA
ITALY
SLOVENIA
CROATIA
ITALY
ADRIATIC SEA
Kvarner Gulf
Istria
Tolmezzo
Jesenice
Lendava
Triglav (2864m)
Radovljica
Bovec
Ukanc
Zidani Most
Ptuj
Ormož
Čakovec
Goričan
Velenje
Breg
Kranj
Kamnik
Celje
Rogaška Slatina
Varaždin
Drava River
Škofja Loka
Menges
Bogatac
Mt Medvednica (1030m)
Udine
Cerkno
Podčetrtek
Krapina
Koprivnica
Litija
Idrija
Ljubljana
Sevnica
Zabok
Krapina River
Križevci
Codroipo
Gorizia
Ajdovscina
Trebnje
Brežice
Monfalcone
Trieste Airport
Latisana
Postojna
Cerknica
Samobor
Zagreb
Zagreb Airport
Bjelovar
Ribnica
Trieste
Pivka
Jastrebarsko
Velika Gorica
Čazma
Kočevje
Metlika
Kolpa River
Lonja Kanal
Koper
Piran
Obruč (1376m)
Črnomelj
Umag
V Planik (1272m)
Risnjak National Park
Karlovac
Kupa River
Kutina
Buje
Livade
Buzet
Opatija
Duga Resa
Petrinja
Sisak
Grožnjan
Motovun
Dobra River
Sava River
Poreč
Pazin
Rijeka
Glina
Kraljevica
Višević (1428m)
Ogulin
Hrvatska Kostjanica
Kanfanar
Gračišće
Rovinj
Labin
Crikvenica
Krk
Vel Kladuša
Slunj
Bosanska Dubica
Plaški
Bosanski Novi
V Brijun
Senj
Baška
Brinje
Cres
Žuta Lokva
Prijedor
Pula
Brijuni National Park
Lopar
Otočac
Prnjavor
Rab
Bosanska Krupa
North Velebit National Park
Bihać
Rab
Mišnjak
Jablanac
Šatorina (1623m)
Plitvice Lakes National Park
Sanski Most
Unije
Novalja
Tomina
Mali Lošinj
Karlobag
Lošinj
Veli Lošinj
Gospić
Bosanski Petrovac
Silba
Una River
Ključ
Pag
Vaganski (1757m)
Olib
Pag
Premuda
Starigrad-Paklenica
Paklenica National Park
Drvar
Privlaka
Gračac
Molat
Obrovac
Zadar
Bosansko Grahovo
Zrmanja River
Benkovac
Knin
Glamoč
Krka River
Dugi Otok
Sali
Biograd
Dinaric Alps
Kornat
Krka National Park
Kornati National Park
Tribunj
Vodice
Cikola River
Šibenik
Sinj
Senigallia
Ancona
Primošten
Mt Biokovo (1762m)
Jesi
Trogir
Solin
Split
Cingoli
Omiš
Macerata
Civitanova Marche
Šolka
Supetar
Brela
Brač
Tolentino
Bol
Hvar
Stari Grad
Hvar
Vis
Jabuka
Svetac
Vis
Komiža
Porto d'Ascoli
Ascoli Piceno
Biševo
Vela Luka
Korčula
Giulianova
Roseto degli Abruzzi
Teramo
Lastovo
Assergi
Pescara
L'Aquila
Chieti
E55
E652
E59
E57
E61
A4
E70
E59
E70
E65
E61
E751
E65
E751
E71
E65
E71
E761
E65
E71
A1
E65

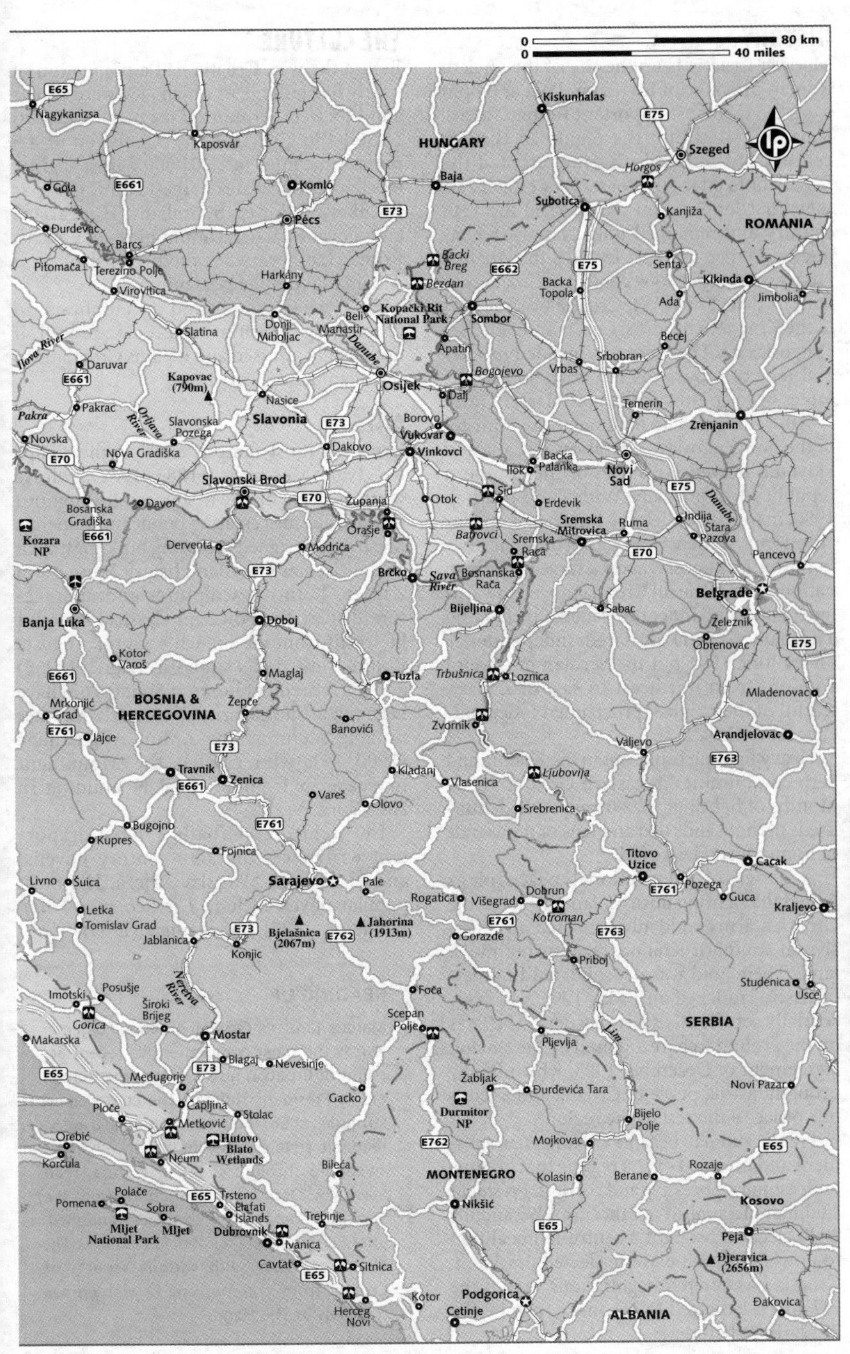
0 80 km
0 40 miles
E65
Nagykanizsa
Kiskunhalas
E75
Kaposvár
HUNGARY
Szeged
Horgos
Gola
E661
Komló
Baja
Subotica
Kanjiža
Đurđevac
Pécs
E73
ROMANIA
Barcs
Backi Breg
Senta
Pitomača
Terezino Polje
Harkány
Bezdan
E662
E75
Kikinda
Virovitica
Backa Topola
Ada
Jimbolia
Beli Manastir
Kopački Rit National Park
Sombor
Slatina
Donji Miholjac
Danube
Apatin
Becej
Ilova River
Srbobran
Daruvar
Vrbas
E661
Kapovac (790m)
Osijek
Bogojevo
Nasice
Dalj
Temerin
Pakra
Pakrac
Orljava River
Slavonska Pozega
Slavonia
E73
Borovo
Zrenjanin
Novska
Vukovar
Nova Gradiška
Dakovo
Vinkovci
E70
Backa Palanka
Ilok
Novi Sad
Slavonski Brod
Sid
E75
Davor
E70
Županja
Otok
Erdevik
Danube
Bosanska Gradiška
Orašje
Sremska Mitrovica
Ruma
Indija
Kozara NP
E661
Batrovci
Sremska Raca
Stara Pazova
Derventa
Modriča
E70
Pancevo
E73
Brčko
Sava River
Bosnanska Rača
Belgrade
Bijeljina
Sabac
Banja Luka
Doboj
Železnik
Obrenovac
E75
Kotor Varoš
Maglaj
Tuzla
Trbušnica
Loznica
E661
BOSNIA & HERCEGOVINA
Mladenovac
Mrkonjić Grad
Žepče
Banovići
Zvornik
E761
Jajce
Valjevo
Arandjelovac
E73
E763
Travnik
Kladanj
Ljubovija
Zenica
E661
Vlasenica
Vareš
Olovo
Srebrenica
E761
Bugojno
Kupres
Fojnica
Titovo Uzice
Cacak
Livno
Šuica
Sarajevo
Pale
E761
Pozega
Dobrun
Guca
Rogatica
Višegrad
Letka
Kraljevo
E761
Kotroman
Tomislav Grad
Bjelašnica (2067m)
Jahorina (1913m)
E73
E762
Gorazde
E763
Jablanica
Konjic
Priboj
Neretva River
Imotski
Posušje
Studenica
Usce
Foča
Široki Brijeg
Gorica
Scepan Polje
SERBIA
Makarska
Mostar
Lim
Pljevlja
Blagaj
Nevesinje
E65
E73
Međugorje
Žabljak
Đurđevića Tara
Novi Pazar
Gacko
Ploče
Čapljina
Durmitor NP
Stolac
Metković
Bijelo Polje
Orebić
Hutovo Blato Wetlands
Mojkovac
E762
Korčula
Neum
E65
Bileća
MONTENEGRO
Kolasin
Berane
Rozaje
Polače
Trsteno
E65
Pomena
Sobra
Elafati Islands
Nikšić
Kosovo
Trebinje
Mljet National Park
Mljet
Dubrovnik
E65
Peja
Ivanica
Đjeravica (2656m)
Cavtat
Sitnica
E65
Kotor
Podgorica
Herceg Novi
Cetinje
ALBANIA
Đakovica
CROATIA

HISTORY

Modern Croatia is on the site of the ancient Roman province of Illyricum. Pula and Split were the two most important Roman towns. Slavs migrated into the region in the 7th century but political disarray tempted the Venetians to attack the coast. They established their first foothold on the coast in the 11th century and remained until Napoleon conquered Venice in 1797. In 1815 the Austro-Hungarian empire took control of Croatia, but with its defeat in WWI, Croatia became part of the Kingdom of Serbs, Croats and Slovenes (Yugoslavia). The Germans invaded in 1941 and tens of thousands of Croats joined the forces of Josip Broz, known as Maršal Tito.

After the war, Tito became prime minister of the new Yugoslav Federation. Croatia and Slovenia moved far ahead of the southern republics economically. With Tito's death in 1980, many Croats felt the time had come for autonomy. When Slobodan Milošević rose to power in Yugoslavia on a wave of Serbian nationalism, a fearful Croatia moved towards independence. Under the leadership of Franjo Tuđman, Croatia declared independence on 25 June 1991 but the Serbian enclave of Krajina (from northeast to east of Zadar), fearful of their rights, proclaimed independence from Croatia.

Heavy fighting broke out in the Krajina and Serb communities in eastern Croatia. In six months of fighting, 10,000 people died, hundreds of thousands fled and tens of thousands of homes were destroyed.

A series of international peace plans halted the fighting until, in January 1993, the Croatian army suddenly launched an offensive in southern Krajina, recapturing much land. Their hold was consolidated in a new offensive launched on 1 May 1995, which essentially set Croatia's new borders. The facts on the ground were recognised by the Dayton Agreement of December 1995, which finally brought lasting peace to Croatia and a tenuous peace to the rest of the region.

Franjo Tuđman became Croatia's first president and presided over a regime that became increasingly oppressive and corrupt. President Tuđman succumbed to cancer in 1999 and the 2000 election brought a centre-left coalition to power with Stipe Mesić elected president. Croatia has entered negotiations to join the EU and is expected to become a member by 2012, if not before.

THE CULTURE

Before the war, Croatia had a population of nearly five million, of which 78% were Croats and 12% were Serbs. After the massive exodus of Serbs in 1995, today's population of 4.5 million includes just 201,000 Serbs, slightly less than 5%. The next largest ethnic group is Bosnians, followed by Italians, Hungarians and Slovenes. Small communities of Czechs, Roma (sometimes called Gypsies) and Albanians complete the mosaic.

Everywhere you'll find an emphasis on keeping up appearances. People are well, if not flashily, dressed and it pains Croatians to see dilapidation anywhere.

ARTS

Croatia's most famous artist is the sculptor Ivan Meštrović (1883–1962), whose work is seen in town squares throughout Croatia. Besides creating public monuments, Meštrović designed imposing buildings, such as the circular Croatian History Museum in Zagreb. Both his sculptures and architecture display the powerful classical restraint he learnt from the French sculptor Auguste Rodin. Meštrović's studio in Zagreb (p255) and his retirement home at Split (p262) have been made into galleries of his work. Another notable sculptor was Antun Augustinčić (1900–79), who created the Monument to Peace in front of the UN building in New York.

In literature, Croatia's most important writer was the 20th-century novelist and playwright Miroslav Krleža. His most popular novels include *The Return of Philip Latinović* (1932) and *Banners* (1963).

READING UP

Marcus Tanner's *Croatia: A Nation Forged in War* is the most comprehensive recent account of Croatian history. From the Roman era to President Tuđman, the complicated struggles of Croatia are presented in a lively, readable style. For insight into the changes sweeping through Croatian culture, read Slavenka Drakulić's nonfiction: *How We Survived Communism and Even Laughed, Café Europa* and *They Wouldn't Hurt a Fly*. The books deal with various aspects of Croatia from communism to war crimes tribunals in The Hague.

ENVIRONMENT

Croatia has a diverse topography, from the Pannonian plains of Slavonia between the Sava, Drava and Danube Rivers, across hilly central Croatia to the Istrian Peninsula, then south through Dalmatia along the rugged Adriatic coast. Of Croatia's 1185 islands and islets, only 66 are inhabited. There are eight national parks and a generally high level of environmental consciousness among Croatians. The lack of heavy industry has left Croatia largely free of industrial pollution.

TRANSPORT

GETTING THERE & AWAY

Air

There are flights to Rome and Prague from both Split and Zagreb, plus flights go between Split and Zagreb.

Adria Airways (JD; www.adria-airways.com; ☎ 01-48 10 011)
Aeroflot (SU; www.aeroflot.ru; ☎ 01-48 72 055)
Air Canada (AC; www.aircanada.ca; ☎ 01-48 22 033)
Air France (AF; www.airfrance.com; ☎ 01-48 37 100)
Alitalia (AZ; www.alitalia.it; ☎ 01-48 10 413)
Austrian Airlines (OS; www.aua.com; ☎ 062 65 900)
British Airways (BA; www.british-airways.com)
Croatia Airlines (OU; ☎ 01-48 19 633; www.croatiaairlines.hr; Zrinjevac 17, Zagreb) Croatia's national carrier.
ČSA (OK; www.csa.cz; ☎ 01-48 73 301)
Delta Airlines (DL; www.delta.com; ☎ 01-48 78 760)
Easyjet (EZY; www.easyjet.com)
Germanwings (GWI; www.germanwings.com)
Hapag Lloyd Express (HLX; www.hlx.com)
KLM-Northwest (KL; www.klm.com; ☎ 01-48 78 601)
LOT Polish Airlines (LO; www.lot.com; ☎ 01-48 37 500)
Lufthansa (LH; www.lufthansa.com; ☎ 01-48 73 121)
Malév Hungarian Airlines (MA; www.malev.hu; ☎ 01-48 36 935)
SNBrussels (SN; www.flysn.com)
Turkish Airlines (TK; www.turkishairlines.com; ☎ 01-49 21 854)
Wizzair (W6; www.wizzair.com)

There are international airports in **Dubrovnik** (☎ 020-773 377; www.airport-dubrovnik.hr), **Zagreb** (☎ 01-62 65 222; www.zagreb-airport.hr), **Split** (☎ 021-203 506; www.split-airport.hr) and **Rijeka** (☎ 051-842 132; www.rijeka-airport.hr).

Boat

Regular boats from several companies connect Croatia with Italy and Slovenia. Prices quoted refer to deck passage in the summer season.

Jadrolinija (www.jadrolinija.hr; Ancona ☎ 071-20 71 465; Bari ☎ 080-52 75 439; Rijeka ☎ 051-211 444), Croatia's national boat line, runs car ferries from Ancona to Split (346KN to 477KN, 10 hours, three to seven weekly), a line from Bari to Dubrovnik (346KN to 477KN, eight hours, one to four weekly), a year-round ferry from Pescara to Split (346KN to 477KN, 10 hours, twice weekly) and a summer ferry from Pescara to Hvar (346KN to 477KN, nine hours, once weekly).

Split Tours (www.splittours.hr; Ancona ☎ 071-20 40 90; Split ☎ 021-352 553) runs the Blue Line car ferries connecting Ancona with Split, and continuing on to Stari Grad (Hvar) for the same prices as Jadrolinija.

SNAV (www.snav.com; Ancona ☎ 071-20 76 116; Naples ☎ 081-76 12 348; Split ☎ 021-322 252) has a fast car ferry that links Split with Pescara (€36 to €90, 4¾ hours, daily) and Ancona (€36 to €90, 4½ hours, three to seven weekly), and Pescara with Hvar (€36 to €90, 3¼ hours, daily).

Venezia Lines (☎ 041-52 22 568; www.venezialines.com; Santa Croce 518/a, Venice 30135) runs passenger boats from Venice to Pula (€55, three hours).

Emilia Romagna Lines (www.emiliaromagnalines.it) runs summer passenger boats (14 April to 30 September) from Italy to Croatia. Routes run from Cesenatico, stopping at Rimini and Pesaro, to Hvar (€82, five hours 30 minutes).

In Croatia, contact **Jadroagent** (☎ 052-210 431; jadroagent-pula@pu.t-com.hr; Riva 14) in Pula for information and tickets on boats between Italy and Croatia.

Bus

The border between Montenegro and Croatia is open to visitors, allowing Americans, Australians, Canadians and Brits to enter visa-free.

For specific details on international bus trips, see the relevant towns.

Train

For specific details on international train trips, see the relevant towns.

GETTING AROUND

Boat

Year-round Jadrolinija car ferries operate along the Bari–Rijeka–Dubrovnik coastal route, stopping at Split and Hvar and Korčula Islands. Services are less frequent in winter. The most scenic section is Split to Dubrovnik, which all Jadrolinija ferries cover during the day. You must buy tickets in advance at an agency or Jadrolinija office, since they are not sold on board.

Bus

At large stations bus tickets must be purchased at the office; book ahead to be sure of a seat. Tickets for buses that arrive from somewhere else are usually purchased from the conductor. Buy a one-way ticket only or you'll be locked into one company's schedule for the return

On schedules, *vozi svaki dan* means 'every day' and *ne vozi nedjeljom ni praznikom* means 'not Sunday and public holidays'. Check www.akz.hr (in Croatian) for information on schedules and fares to and from Zagreb.

Car & Motorcycle

Motorists require vehicle registration papers and Green Card insurance (which proves drivers travelling through Europe have insurance that complies with the minimum insurance requirements of the places that they drive through) to enter Croatia. Hrvatski Autoklub (HAK; Croatian Auto Club) offers help and advice; contact the nationwide **HAK road assistance** (vučna služba; ☎ 987).

The large car-rental chains represented are Avis, Budget, Europcar and Hertz.

Hitching

Hitching is never entirely safe, and we don't recommend it. Hitchhiking in Croatia is unreliable. You'll have better luck on the islands, but in the interior cars are small and usually full.

CONNECTIONS

Croatia is a handy transport hub for south-eastern Europe and the Adriatic. Zagreb is connected by train (p253) and/or bus (p253) to Venice, Budapest, Belgrade and Ljubljana, and Sarajevo. Down south there are easy bus connections from Dubrovnik (p269) to Mostar and Sarajevo, and to Kotor. There are a number of ferries linking Croatia with Italy (p253), including from Dubrovnik to Bari, and Split to Ancona.

BORDER CROSSINGS

There ar`e dozens of crossings points to/from Slovenia, too many to list here. There are 23 border crossings into Bosnia and Hercegovina, and 10 into Serbia and Montenegro respectively.

Local Transport

Zagreb has a well-developed tram system as well as local buses, but in the rest of the country you'll only find buses. In major cities such as Split and Dubrovnik, buses run about every 20 minutes, and less often on Sunday.

Taxis are available in all cities and towns, but they must be called or boarded at a taxi stand. Prices are rather high (meters start at 25KN).

Train

Train travel is about 15% cheaper than bus travel and often more comfortable, although slower. The main lines run from Zagreb to Rijeka, Zadar and Split and east to Osijek. There are no trains along the coast.

On posted timetables in Croatia, the word for arrivals is *dolazak* and for departures it's *odlazak* or *polazak*. For train information check out **Croatian Railway** (www.hznet.hr).

ZAGREB

☎ 01 / pop 780,000

Everyone knows about Croatia, its coast, beaches and islands, but a mention of the country's capital still draws confused questions of whether 'it's nice' or 'worth going to for a weekend'. Well, here it is, once and for all: yes, Zagreb is a great destination, weekend or weeklong. There's lots of culture, arts, music, architecture, gastronomy and all the other things that make a quality capital. Admittedly, it doesn't register highly on a nightlife Richter scale, but it does have an ever-developing art and music scene and a growing influx of fun-seeking travellers.

Zagreb is made for strolling, drinking coffee in the almost permanently full cafes, popping into museums and galleries and enjoying the theatres, concerts, cinema and music.

ORIENTATION

The city is divided into Lower Zagreb, where you'll find most shops, restaurants and businesses, and Upper Zagreb, defined by the two hills of Kaptol and Gradec. As you come out of the train station, you'll see a series of parks and pavilions directly in front of you and the twin neo-Gothic towers of the cathedral in the distance. Trg Jelačića, beyond the northern end of the parks, is the main city square.

INFORMATION

Discount Cards

If you're in Zagreb for a day or three, getting the Zagreb Card is a pretty good way to save money. You can choose either 24 or 72 hours (60/90KN) and you get free travel on all public transport, and a 50% discount on museum and gallery entries. The card is sold at the main tourist office and many hostels, hotels, bars and shops.

Internet Access

Sublink (☎ 48 11 329; Teslina 12; per hr 15KN; 9am-10pm Mon-Sat, 3-10pm Sun) It was the city's first cybercafe and it remains its best.

Medical Services

KBC Rebro (☎ 23 88 888; Kišpatićeva 12; 24hr) East of the city, it provides emergency aid.

Money

There are ATMs at the bus and train stations and the airport, as well as numerous locations around town.

Atlas (☎ 48 13 933; www.atlas-croatia.com; Zrinjevac 17) The American Express representative in Zagreb.

Tourist Information

Main tourist office (☎ 48 14 051; www.zagreb-touristinfo.hr; Trg Jelaèiæa 11; 8.30am-8pm Mon-Fri, 9am-5pm Sat, 10am-2pm Sun) Distributes city maps and free leaflets. It also sells the Zagreb Card.

Marko Polo (☎ 48 15 216; Masarykova 24) Handles information and ticketing for Jadrolinija's coastal ferries.

Tourist office annexe (☎ 49 21 645; Zrinjevac 14; 9am-6pm Mon-Fri) Same services but fewer brochures.

Travel Agencies

Dali Travel (☎ 48 47 472; travelsection@hfhs.hr; Dežmanova 9; 9am-5pm Mon-Fri) The travel branch of the Croatian Youth Hostel Association (YHA), it can provide information on Hostelling International (HI) hostels throughout Croatia and make advance bookings. It also sells ISIC (International Student Identity Card) identification for 50KN.

EMERGENCY NUMBERS

- Ambulance ☎ 94
- Fire Service ☎ 93
- Police ☎ 92
- Roadside Assistance ☎ 987

SIGHTS

Kaptol

The twin neo-Gothic spires of the **Cathedral of the Assumption of the Blessed Virgin Mary** (☎ 48 14 727; 7am-7pm), built in 1899, contains elements from the medieval cathedral on its site, destroyed by an earthquake in 1880. Remnants include 13th-century frescoes, Renaissance pews, marble altars and a baroque pulpit. The baroque **Archiepiscopal Palace** surrounds the cathedral, as do 16th-century **fortifications** constructed when Zagreb was threatened by the Turks.

Gradec

From Radićeva 5, off Trg Jelačića, a pedestrian walkway called stube Ivana Zakmardija leads you to the **Lotrščak Tower** (11am-8pm Mon-Sat) and a **funicular railway** (3KN), which was constructed in 1888, and connects the lower and upper towns. To the right is the baroque **St Catherine's Church**, with Jezuitski trg beyond. The **Gallery Klovićevi Dvori** (☎ 48 51 926; Jezuitski trg 4; adult/student 40/20KN; 11am-7pm Tue-Sun) is Zagreb's premier exhibition hall. Further north and to the right is the 13th-century **Stone Gate**, with a painting of the Virgin.

The colourful painted-tile roof of the Gothic **St Mark's Church** (☎ 48 51 611; Markov trg; 11am-4pm & 5.30-7pm) marks the centre of Gradec. Inside are works by Ivan Meštrović, Croatia's most famous modern sculptor. On the eastern side of St Mark's is the **Sabor** (1908), Croatia's National Assembly. To the west of St Mark's is the 18th-century **Banski Dvori**, the presidential palace.

Nearby is the former **Meštrović Studio** (☎ 48 51 123; Mletačka 8; adult/concession 30/15KN; 10am-6pm Tue-Fri, to 2pm Sat & Sun), which now presents an excellent collection of some 100 sculptures, drawings, lithographs and furniture created by the artist.

Lower Town

Zagreb really is a city of museums. There are four just in the parks between the train station

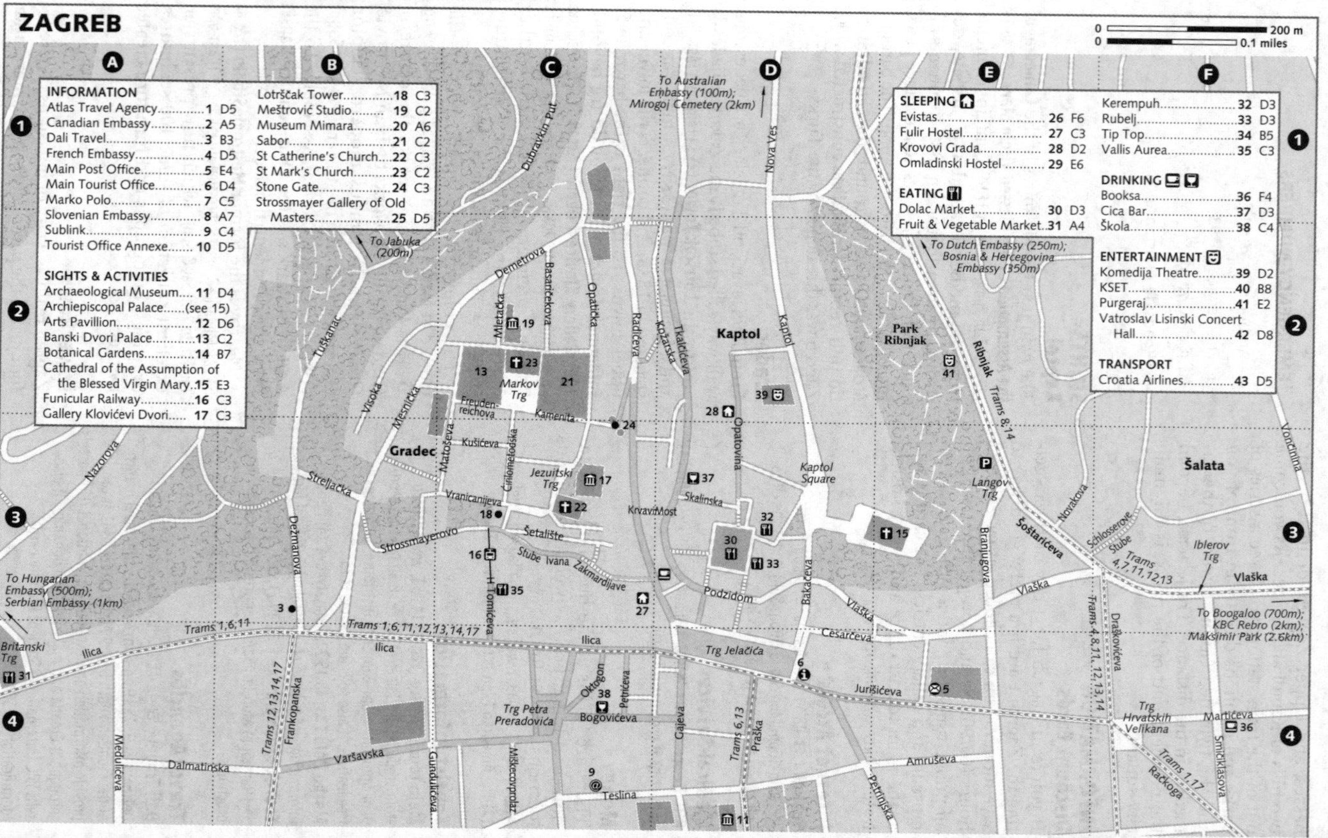
ZAGREB
0 200 m
0 0.1 miles
INFORMATION
Atlas Travel Agency 1 D5
Canadian Embassy 2 A5
Dali Travel 3 B3
French Embassy 4 D5
Main Post Office 5 E4
Main Tourist Office 6 D4
Marko Polo 7 C5
Slovenian Embassy 8 A7
Sublink 9 C4
Tourist Office Annexe 10 D5
SIGHTS & ACTIVITIES
Archaeological Museum 11 D4
Archiepiscopal Palace (see 15)
Arts Pavillion 12 D6
Banski Dvori Palace 13 C2
Botanical Gardens 14 B7
Cathedral of the Assumption of the Blessed Virgin Mary 15 E3
Funicular Railway 16 C3
Gallery Klovićevi Dvori 17 C3
Lotrščak Tower 18 C3
Meštrović Studio 19 C2
Museum Mimara 20 A6
Sabor 21 C2
St Catherine's Church 22 C3
St Mark's Church 23 C2
Stone Gate 24 C3
Strossmayer Gallery of Old Masters 25 D5
SLEEPING
Evistas 26 F6
Fulir Hostel 27 C3
Krovovi Grada 28 D2
Omladinski Hostel 29 E6
EATING
Dolac Market 30 D3
Fruit & Vegetable Market 31 A4
Kerempuh 32 D3
Rubelj 33 D3
Tip Top 34 B5
Vallis Aurea 35 C3
DRINKING
Booksa 36 F4
Cica Bar 37 D3
Škola 38 C4
ENTERTAINMENT
Komedija Theatre 39 D2
KSET 40 B8
Purgeraj 41 E2
Vatroslav Lisinski Concert Hall 42 D8
TRANSPORT
Croatia Airlines 43 D5
To Australian Embassy (100m); Mirogoj Cemetery (2km)
To Jabuka (200m)
To Dutch Embassy (250m); Bosnia & Hercegovina Embassy (350m)
To Hungarian Embassy (500m); Serbian Embassy (1km)
To Boogaloo (700m); KBC Rebro (2km); Maksimir Park (2.6km)
Kaptol
Gradec
Park Ribnjak
Šalata
Markov Trg
Jezuitski Trg
Kaptol Square
Langov Trg
Iblerov Trg
Britanski Trg
Trg Jelačića
Trg Petra Preradovića
Trg Hrvatskih Velikana
Dubravkin Put
Tuškanac
Demetrova
Basaričekova
Opatička
Radićeva
Kožarska
Tkalčićeva
Nova Ves
Kaptol
Opatovina
Ribnjak
Vončinina
Novakova
Schlosserove Stube
Šoštarićeva
Branjugova
Vlaška
Bakačeva
Cesarčeva
Juršićeva
Draškovićeva
Smičiklasova
Martićeva
Račkoga
Amruševa
Petrinjska
Praška
Gajeva
Petrićeva
Oktogon
Bogovićeva
Teslina
Miškecovprolaz
Gundulićeva
Varšavska
Dalmatinska
Medulićeva
Frankopanska
Dežmanova
Ilica
Nazorova
Visoka
Mesnička
Matoševa
Mletačka
Freudenreichova
Kamenita
Kušićeva
Ćirilometodska
Streljačka
Vranicanijeva
Šetalište
Strossmayerovo
Stube Ivana Zakmardijave
Tomićeva
Skalinska
Krvavi Most
Podzidom
Trams 1,6,11
Trams 1,6,11,12,13,14,17
Trams 12,13,14,17
Trams 6,13
Trams 8,14
Trams 4,7,11,12,13
Trams 4,8,11,12,13,14
Trams 1,17

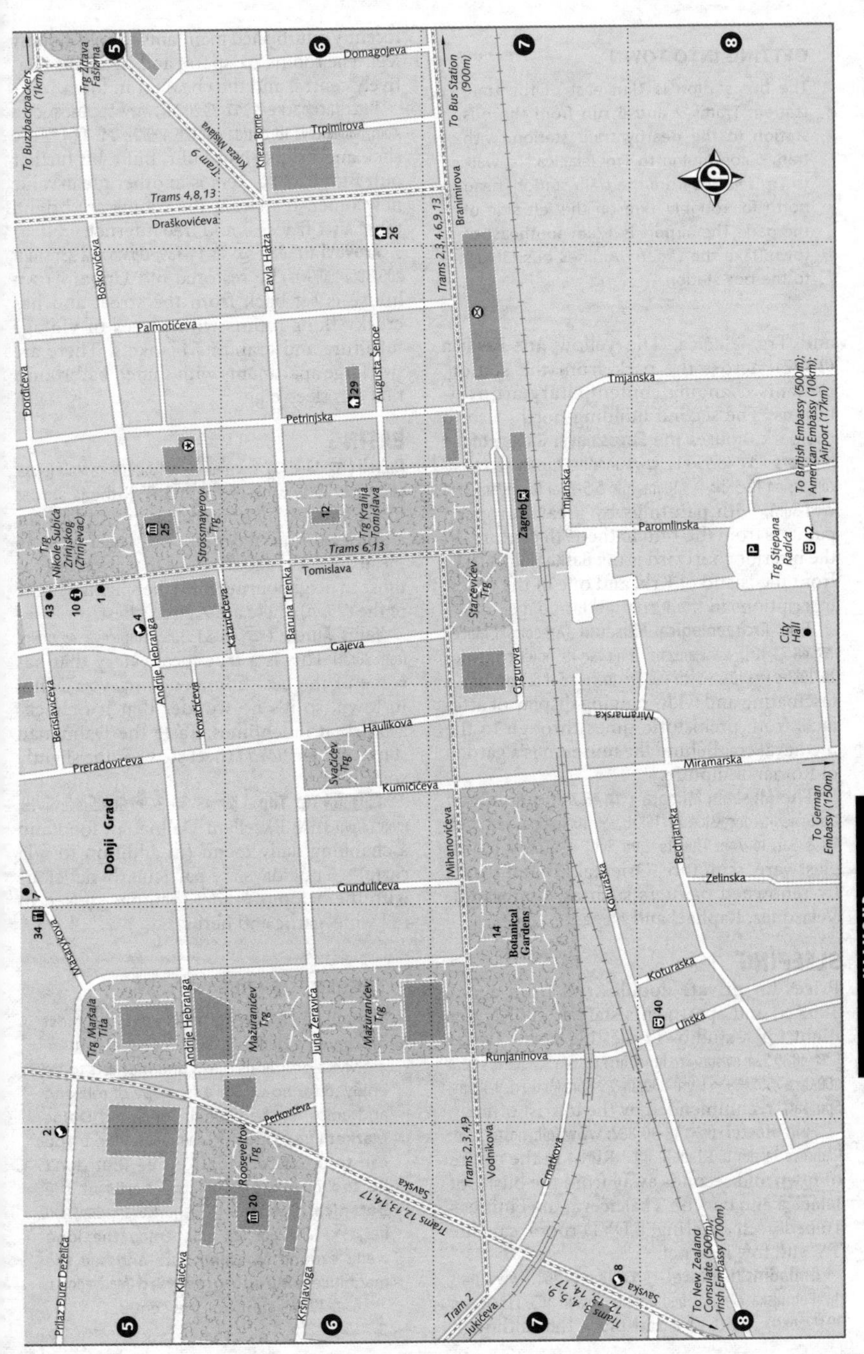
To Buzzbackpackers (1km)
Trg Žrtava Fašizma
Domagojeva
To Bus Station (900m)
Trpimirova
Tram 9
Kneza Mislava
Kneza Borne
Trams 4,8,13
Draškovićeva
Trams 2,3,4,6,9,13
Branimirova
Boškovićeva
Pavla Hatza
26
Palmotićeva
Augusta Šenoe
Đorđićeva
29
Petrinjska
Tmjanska
To British Embassy (500m); American Embassy (10km); Airport (17km)
Trg Nikole Subića Zrinjskog (Zrinjevac)
25
Strossmayerov Trg
12
Trg Kralja Tomislava
Trams 6,13
Zagreb
Paromlinska
Trg Stjepana Radića
42
Tomislava
43
10
1
4
Starčevićev Trg
Andrije Hebranga
Katančićeva
Baruna Trenka
Gajeva
City Hall
Grgurova
Berislavićeva
Kovačićeva
Miramarska
Haulikova
Preradovićeva
Svačićev Trg
Kumičićeva
To German Embassy (150m)
Donji Grad
Mihanovićeva
Bednjanska
Gundulićeva
Zelinska
7
34
Masarykova
Koturaška
14
Botanical Gardens
Trg Maršala Tita
Mažuranićev Trg
Jurja Žerjavića
40
Unska
Runjaninova
Perkovčeva
2
Rooseveltov Trg
20
Trams 2,3,4,9
Vodnikova
Savska
Trams 12,13,14,17
Crnatkova
To New Zealand Consulate (500m); Irish Embassy (700m)
8
Prilaz Đure Deželića
Klaićeva
Kršnjavoga
Tram 2
Jukićeva
Trams 3, 4, 5, 9, 12, 13, 14, 17
5
6
7
8
CROATIA

Book your stay at lonelyplanet.com/hotels

GETTING INTO TOWN

The bus station is 1km east of the train station. Trams 2 and 6 run from the bus station to the nearby train station, with tram 6 continuing to Trg Jelačića. To walk to Trg Jelačića from the train station, head north for roughly 1km on the left side of the park. The airport is 17km southeast of town; take the Croatia Airlines bus (30KN) to the bus station.

and Trg Jelačića. The yellow **Arts Pavilion** (1897), across the park from the station, presents changing contemporary art exhibitions. The second building north, also in the park, houses the **Strossmayer Gallery of Old Masters** (☎ 48 95 115; www.mdc.hr/strossmayer; adult/concession 10/5KN; 🕑 10am-1pm & 5-7pm Tue, 10am-1pm Wed-Sun), with paintings by great European painters from the 14th to the 17th century. In the interior courtyard is the **Baška Slab** (1102), from the island of Krk, and one of the oldest inscriptions in the Croatian language.

The **Archaeological Museum** (Arheološki Muzej; ☎ 48 73 101; www.amz.hr; Zrinjevac 19; adult/concession 20/10KN; 🕑 10am-5pm Tue-Fri, to 1pm Sat & Sun) has a fascinating and wide-ranging display of artefacts from prehistoric times through to the medieval era. Behind the museum is a garden of Roman sculpture.

The **Museum Mimara** (☎ 48 28 100; Rooseveltov trg 5; adult/concession 20/15KN; 🕑 10am-5pm Tue, Wed, Fri & Sat, to 7pm Thu, to 2pm Sun) houses icons, glassware, sculpture, Oriental art and works by renowned painters such as Rembrandt, Velasquez, Raphael and Degas.

CROATIA

SLEEPING

Prices for private doubles run from about 300KN, and apartments start at 400KN per night for a studio. Try letting agent **Evistas** (☎ 48 39 554; evistas@zg.htnet.hr; Augusta Šenoe 28; s from 200KN, d 250KN, 🕑 9am-1.30pm & 3-8pm Mon-Fri, 9.30am-5pm Sat), recommended by the tourist office.

Fulir Hostel (☎ 48 30 882; www.fulir-hostel.com; Radićeva 3a; dm 100-140KN; 💻) Right in the centre of town and seconds away from the bustle of Jelačića and bars on Tkalčićeva, the Fulir has 16 beds, self-catering, a DVD room, satellite TV and free internet.

Omladinski Hostel (☎ 48 41 261; www.hfhs.hr; Petrinjska 77; 6-/3-bed dm per person 103/113KN, s/d 193/256KN) A bit of a sad place that although recently refurbished maintains the old gloomy feel. The rooms are sparse and clean, it's relatively central and the cheapest in town.

Buzzbackpackers (☎ 23 20 267; www.buzzbackpackers.com; Babukićeva 1b; dm/d from 120/400KN; 🖧 💻) More slick and bright than Fulir, but a bit further out, Buzzbackpackers is another great-value newcomer. It's clean, the rooms are bright, there's wi-fi access and free internet.

Krovovi Grada (☎ 48 14 189; Opatovina 33; s/d/tr 200/300/400KN) The restored old Upper Town house is set back from the street and has creaky-floor rooms with pieces of vintage furniture and grandma blankets. There are two large apartments with shared bathrooms that can sleep eight.

EATING

Rubelj (☎ 48 18 777; www.rubelj-grill.hr; Tržnica Mala Terasa; mains from 25KN) One of the many Rubeljs across town, this Dolac branch is a great place for a quick portion of *ćevapi* (spicy beef or lamb meatballs). And though none that are as tasty as those in neighbouring BiH (the spiritual home of the *ćevap*), these are Zagreb's best.

Vallis Aurea (☎ 48 31 305; Tomićeva 4; mains from 30KN) This is a true local eatery that has some of the best home cooking you'll find in town, so it's no wonder that it's chock-a-block at lunchtimes. Taste the Dalmatian staple, the *pašticada* (beef stew) or the slightly spicy beans.

our pick **Tip Top** (☎ 48 30 349; Gundulićeva 18; mains from 35KN) Excellent Dalmatian food and a changing daily menu (in addition to á la carte) – Thursdays are particularly delicious with the octopus *brodet* (octopus stewed in red wine, garlic and herbs).

ZAGREB FOR FREE

Though you'll have to pay to get into most of Zagreb's galleries and museums, there are some gorgeous parks and markets to be enjoyed for nowt. For a free day of relaxing and enjoying the capital, check out **Dolac Market** (Trg Jelačića; 🕑 7am-3pm) where you can taste bits of food for free (but don't be too cheeky!), smell the herbs at the **Botanical Gardens** (Mihanovićeva; admission free; 🕑 9am-7pm Tue-Sun), enjoy the long walks around Maksimir Park and see the magnificent **Mirogoj graveyard** (Medvednica; 🕑 6am-10pm), north of the centre.

Kerempuh (☎ 48 19 000; Kaptol 3; mains 50-70) Overlooking Dolac market, this is a fabulous place to taste: a) Croatian cuisine cooked well and simply, and b) the market's ingredients on your plate. The daily dishes are decided on in the morning, when the chef gets that day's freshest ingredients from Dolac.

There's also a **fruit and vegetable market** (Britanski trg; 7am-3pm).

DRINKING

In the Upper Town, the chic Tkalčićeva is throbbing with bars. In the Lower Town, Trg Petra Preradovića is the most popular spot for street performers and occasional bands in mild weather.

our pick **Booksa** (☎ 46 16 124; www.booksa.hr; Martićeva 14d; 9am-11pm Tue-Sun) Anyone on the creative side of things in Zagreb comes to chat and drink coffee, buy books and hear readings at this lovely bookshop. There are English-language readings here too, so check the website.

Škola (☎ 48 28 197; www.skolaloungebar.com; Bogovićeva 7) This has to be the best designed bar in the whole of Zagreb with its huge, differently themed rooms, lounge sofas and an olive tree in the middle of the main room. There are weekly DJ nights.

Cica Bar (Tkalčićeva 18) It's the size of an east London bedsit, with a great, punk vibe: an underground place with a massive choice of *rakija* (grape brandy) in all flavours – herbal, nutty, fruity – you think it, it has it.

CLUBBING

The dress code is relaxed in most Zagreb clubs. It doesn't get lively until near midnight.

KSET (☎ 61 29 999; www.kset.org; Unska 3; 8pm-midnight Mon-Fri, to 3am Sat) Zagreb's best music venue, with anyone who's anyone performing here.

Boogaloo (☎ 63 13 021; www.boogaloo.hr; OTV Dom, Vukovarska 68) A great venue that hosts DJ nights and live music. It's just east of the centre.

Purgeraj (☎ 48 14 734; Park Ribnjak) Live rock, blues, rock-blues, blues-rock, country rock and avant-garde jazz.

ENTERTAINMENT

Komedija Theatre (☎ 48 14 566; Kaptol 9) Near the cathedral, the Komedija Theatre stages operettas and musicals.

Vatroslav Lisinski Concert Hall (☎ ticket office 61 21 166; Trg Stjepana Radica 4; 9am-8pm Mon-Fri, to 2pm Sat) Just south of the train station, this concert hall is a prestigious venue where symphony concerts are held regularly.

GETTING THERE & AWAY

Croatia Airlines (☎ 48 19 633; www.croatiaairlines.hr; Zrinjevac 17) operates flights between Zagreb and Split (from 500KN, one hour, up to four daily).

Domestic buses depart from Zagreb **bus station** (☎ 61 57 983; www.akz.hr, in Croatian), to most major destinations in Croatia, including Dubrovnik (250KN, 11 hours, seven daily), Korčula (224KN, 12 hours, daily), Pula (175KN to 230KN, four to six hours, 13 daily) and Split (195KN, five to nine hours, 27 daily).

There are three daily buses from Sarajevo to Zagreb (€18, eight hours, three daily), and six daily buses from Zagreb to Belgrade (€20, six hours). At Bajakovo on the border, a Serbian bus takes you on to Belgrade. There two daily buses from Ljubljana to Zagreb (110KN, three hours).

Domestic trains depart from **Zagreb train station** (☎ 060 33 34 44; www.hznet.hr) to Pula (131KN, 5½ hours, two daily) and Split (160KN, six to nine hours, 27 daily). Reservations are required on fast InterCity (IC) trains and there's a supplement that costs 5KN to 15KN for fast or express trains. There's a daily train service to Zagreb from Sarajevo each morning (260KN, eight hours); five daily trains connect Zagreb with Belgrade (€25, seven hours); and there are up to 11 trains daily between Zagreb and Ljubljana (€16, 2¼ hours).

GETTING AROUND

Public transport is based on an efficient network of trams, though the city centre is compact enough to make them unnecessary. Buy tickets at newspaper kiosks for 8KN. Each ticket must be stamped when you board. You can use your ticket for transfers within 90 minutes but only in one direction.

A *dnevna karta* (day ticket), valid on all public transport until 4am the next morning, is 25KN at most Vjesnik or Tisak news outlets. Controls are frequent on the tram system with substantial fines for not having the proper ticket.

Zagreb's taxis ring up 8KN per kilometre after a flag fall of 25KN. On Sunday and from 10pm to 5am any day there's a 20% surcharge.

ISTRIA (ISTRA)

☎ 052

Continental Croatia meets the Adriatic coast in Istria (Istra to Croatians), the heart-shaped 3600-sq-km peninsula just south of Trieste in Italy. While the bucolic interior of rolling hills and fertile plains has been attracting artists and visitors to its hilltop villages, rural hotels and farmhouse restaurants, the verdant indented coastline is enormously popular with the sun 'n' sea set. Vast hotel complexes now line much of the coast and although its rocky beaches are not Croatia's best, the facilities are wide ranging, the sea is clean and secluded spots are still aplenty.

PULA

pop 65,000

The wealth of Roman architecture makes the otherwise workaday Pula (ancient Polensium) a standout among Croatia's larger cities. The star of the Roman show is the remarkably well-preserved Roman amphitheatre, which dominates the streetscape and doubles as a venue for summer concerts and performances. Historical attractions aside, Pula is a busy commercial city on the sea that has managed to retain a friendly small-town appeal.

Orientation

The oldest part of the city follows the ancient Roman plan of streets circling the central citadel. Most shops, agencies and businesses are clustered in and around the old town as well as on Giardini, Carrarina, Istarska and Riva, which runs along the harbour. The bus station is 500m northeast of the town centre. The harbour is west of the bus station. The train station is near the sea less than a kilometre north of town.

CROATIA

Information

You can exchange money in travel agencies, banks or at the post offices. There are numerous ATMs around town.

Tourist information centre (☎ 212 987; www.pula info.hr; Forum 3; ⏲ 8am-9pm Mon-Fri, 9am-9pm Sat & Sun summer, 8am-7pm Mon-Fri, 9am-7pm Sat, 10am-4pm Sun winter) Knowledgeable and friendly, it provides heaps of maps and brochures. Pick up the useful *Domus Bonus* booklet, which lists the best-quality private accommodation in Istria.

Sights

Pula's most imposing sight is the 1st-century **Roman amphitheatre** (☎ 219 028; Flavijevska bb; adult/concession 40/20KN; ⏲ 8am-9pm summer, 9am-8pm spring & autumn, 9am-5pm winter) overlooking the harbour northeast of the old town. Built entirely from local limestone, the amphitheatre with seating for up to 20,000 spectators was designed to host gladiatorial contests.

The **Archaeological Museum** (Arheološki Muzej; ☎ 218 603; Carrarina 3; adult/concession 20/10KN; ⏲ 9am-8pm Mon-Sat, 10am-3pm Sun May-Sep, 9am-2pm Mon-Fri Oct-Apr) presents archaeological finds from all over Istria. Even if you don't enter the museum, be sure to visit the large sculpture garden around it, and the **Roman theatre** behind.

Along Carrarina are **Roman walls**, which mark the eastern boundary of old Pula. Follow these walls south and continue down Giardini to the **Triumphal Arch of Sergius** (27 BC). The street beyond the arch winds right around old Pula, changing names several times. Follow it to the ancient **Temple of Augustus** (☎ 218 603; Forum; adult/concession 10/5KN; ⏲ 9am-8pm Mon-Fri, 10am-3pm Sat & Sun summer, by appointment otherwise), erected from 2 BC to AD 14 and now housing a small historical museum with captions in English.

The 17th-century **Venetian citadel**, on a high hill in the centre of the old town, is worth the climb for the view if not for the meagre maritime-related exhibits in the tiny **Museum of History** (Povijesni Muzej Istre; ☎ 211 566; Gradinski Uspon 6; adult/concession 15/7KN; ⏲ 8am-9pm Jun-Sep, 9am-5pm Oct-May) inside.

BEACHES

The most tourist-packed beaches are undoubtedly those surrounding the hotel complex on the **Verudela Peninsula**, although some locals will dare to be seen at the small turquoise-coloured **Hawaii Beach** near the Hotel Park.

For more seclusion, head out to the wild **Rt Kamenjak** (www.kamenjak.hr, in Croatian; pedestrians & cyclists free, cars 20KN, scooters 10KN; ⏲ 7am-10pm) on the Premantura Peninsula 10km south of town.

Festivals & Events

Every summer, **Pula Film Festival** is held in the Roman amphitheatre. International pop and classical stars give concerts in the Roman Amphitheatre during the **Pula Summer Festival** (July to August).

Sleeping & Eating

Any travel agency can give you information and book you into one of the hotels, or you can contact **Arenaturist** (☎ 529 400; www.arenaturist.hr; Splitska 1a; 🕑 8am-8pm Mon-Fri, to 6pm Sat). Travel agencies can find private accommodation but there is little available in the town centre. Count on paying from 250KN to 490KN for a double room (up to 535KN for a two-person apartment).

Camping Stoja (☎ 387 144; www.arenaturist.hr; Stoja 37; per person/tent 52/30KN; 🕑 Apr-Oct) The closest camping ground to Pula, 3km southwest of the centre, has lots of space on the shady promontory, with a restaurant, diving centre and swimming possible off the rocks. Take bus 1 to Stoja.

Youth Hostel (☎ 391 133; www.hfhs.hr; Valsaline 4; camp sites per person/tent 70/15KN, dm 114KN, mobile homes 134KN; 💻) This hostel overlooks a beach in Valsaline bay, 3km south of central Pula. There are dorms and mobile homes split into two tiny four-bed units, each with bathroom, and air-con on request (15KN per day). There's bike rental (80KN per day). Take the bus 2 or 3 to the 'Piramida' stop, walk back to the first street, then turn left and look for the sign.

our pick **Hotel Scaletta** (☎ 541 599; www.hotel-scaletta.com; Flavijevska 26; s 498KN, d 718KN; P) There's a friendly family vibe, the rooms have tasteful decor and a bagful of trimmings, like minibars, and the restaurant serves good food. Plus it's just a hop from town.

Vodnjanka (☎ 210 655; Vitezića 4; mains from 30KN; 🕑 closed Sat dinner & Sun) Locals swear by the home cooking here. It's cheap, casual, cash-only and has a small menu that concentrates on simple Istrian dishes. To get here, walk south on Radićeva to Vitezića.

our pick **Gina** (☎ 387 943; Stoja 23; mains from 60KN) Istrian mainstays like *maneštra* (vegetable-and-bean soup similar to minestrone) and *fritaja* (omelette) are prepared with care, pastas are handmade, and veggies picked from the garden.

Drinking & Entertainment

You should definitely try to catch a concert in the spectacular amphitheatre; the tourist office has schedules.

Cabahia (Širolina 4) An artsy hideaway in Veruda, with cosy wood-beamed interior, eclectic decor of old objects, dim lighting and South American flair.

Getting There & Away

From the Pula **bus station** (☎ 500 012; Trg 1 Istarske Brigade bb) there are buses heading to Zagreb (210KN, four to five hours, 18 daily), Split (360KN to 396KN, 10 hours, three daily) and Dubrovnik (568KN, 10½ hours, one daily).

There are four daily trains to Zagreb (125KN to 148KN, 6½ hours), but you must board a bus for part of the trip, from Lupoglav to Rijeka.

Getting Around

The city buses of use to visitors are bus 1, which runs to the Autocamp Stoja, and buses 2 and 3 to Verudela. Tickets are sold at *tisak* (news-stands) for 6KN, or 10KN from the driver.

DALMATIA (DALMACIJA)

Roman ruins, spectacular beaches, old fishing ports, medieval architecture and unspoilt offshore islands make a trip to Dalmatia (Dalmacija) unforgettable. Occupying the central 375km of Croatia's Adriatic coast, Dalmatia offers a matchless combination of hedonism and historical discovery. The jagged coast is speckled with lush offshore islands and dotted with historic cities.

SPLIT (SPALATO)

☎ 021 / pop 188,700

The second largest city in Croatia, Split (Spalato in Italian), is a great place to see Dalmatian life as it's really lived. Free of mass tourism and always buzzing, this is a city with just the right balance of tradition and modernity. Just step inside Diocletian's Palace – a Unesco World Heritage site and one of the world's most impressive Roman monuments – and you'll see dozens of bars, restaurants and shops thriving amid the atmospheric old walls. Split's unique setting and exuberant nature make it one of the most delectable cities in Europe.

Orientation

The bus, train and ferry terminals are adjacent on the eastern side of the harbour, a short walk from the Old Town. The seafront promenade, Obala hrvatskog narodnog preporoda, better known as Riva, is the best central reference point.

Information

DISCOUNT CARD

Get the Split Card for 36KN for one day and you can use it for three days without paying anything extra. You get free access to most of the city museums and half-price discounts to many galleries.

INTERNET ACCESS

Mriža (☎ 321 320; Kružićeva 3; per hr 20KN)

MONEY

Change money at travel agencies or the post office. You'll find ATMs around the bus and train stations.

TOURIST INFORMATION

Hostelling International (HI; ☎ 321 614; Domilijina 8) Sells HI cards and is a good source of information about Croatian hostels.

Turist Biro (☎ /fax 342 142; www.turistbiro-split.hr; Obala hrvatskog narodnog preporoda 12; 🕑 9am-7pm Mon-Fri, to 4pm Sat) This office arranges private accommodation and sells guidebooks and the Split Card.

Turistička Zajednica (☎ /fax 342 606; www.visitsplit.com; Peristile; 🕑 9am-8.30pm Mon-Sat, 8am-1pm Sun) Has information on Split; sells the Split Card.

TRAVEL AGENCIES

Daluma Travel (☎ /fax 338 484; www.daluma.hr; Obala Kneza Domagoja 1) Finds private accommodation and has information on boat schedules.

Sights

DIOCLETIAN'S PALACE

The Old Town is a vast open-air museum and the new information signs at the important sights explain a great deal of Split's history. **Diocletian's Palace** (entrance: Obala hrvatskog narodnog preporoda 22), facing the harbour, is one of the most imposing Roman ruins in existence. It was built as a strong rectangular fortress, with walls measuring 215m from east to west, 181m wide at the southernmost point and reinforced by square corner towers. The imperial residence, mausoleum and temples were south of the main street, now called Krešimirova, connecting the east and west palace gates. Its main features include the **Peristyle**, a picturesque colonnaded square; the open-area **Temple of Jupiter**, now a baptistry; and the **Cathedral** (🕑 7am-noon & 4-7pm), originally Diocletian's mausoleum.

In the Middle Ages the nobility and rich merchants built their residences within the old palace walls; the Papalić Palace is now the **Town Museum** (Gradski Muzej; ☎ 341 240; Papalićeva ul 5; adult/concession 10/5KN; 🕑 9am-noon & 5-8pm Tue-Fri, 10am-noon Sat & Sun Jun-Sep, 10am-5pm Tue-Fri, 10am-noon Sat & Sun Oct-May). It has a tidy collection of artefacts, paintings, furniture and clothes from Split; captions are in Croatian.

Go through the **North Palace Gate** to see Ivan Meštrović's powerful 1929 **statue of Gregorius of Nin**.

OUTSIDE CENTRAL SPLIT

The **Archaeological Museum** (Arheološki Muzej; ☎ 318 720; Zrinjsko-Frankopanska 25; adult/student 20/10KN; 🕑 9am-2pm Tue-Fri, to 1pm Sat & Sun), north of town, is a fascinating supplement to your walk around Diocletian's Palace, and to the site of ancient Salona. The history of Split is traced from Illyrian times to the Middle Ages.

The finest art museum in Split is **Meštrović Gallery** (Galerija Meštrović; ☎ 358 450; Šetalište Ivana Meštrovića 46; adult/student 30/15KN; 🕑 9am-9pm Tue-Sun Jun-Sep, 9am-4pm Tue-Sat, 10am-3pm Sun Oct-May). You'll see a comprehensive, well-arranged collection of works by Ivan Meštrović, Croatia's premier modern sculptor.

Sleeping & Eating

Book private accommodation through the **Turist Biro** (☎ /fax 342 142; www.turistbiro-split.hr; Obala hrvatskog narodnog preporoda 12; 🕑 9am-7pm Mon-Fri, to 4pm Sat). Expect to pay between 145KN and 220KN for a double room where you will probably share the bathroom with the proprietor.

Hostel Split Mediterranean House (☎ 098 987 1312; www.hostel-split.com; Vukasovićeva 21; dm from 100KN; ⊠) It's a 10-minute walk from the Northern Gate to this friendly, family-run hostel set in a lovely old stone building. There are two six-bed dorms and some newer en suite three-bed dorms.

Split Hostel booze & snooze (☎ 342 787; www.splithostel.com; Narodni Trg 8; dm 180KN; ⊠) A great new addition to Split's backpacker scene, this hostel is run by Aussie Croats and does exactly what it says on the tin – it's a party place, with 23 beds to snooze in, a nice terrace and it's right in the centre of town.

Makrovega (☎ 394 440; www.makrovega.hr; Leština 2; mains from 40KN; 🕑 9am-7pm Mon-Fri, to 4pm Sat) A meat-free haven with a clean, spacious (non-smoking!) interior and delicious buffet and à la carte food that alternates between macrobiotic and vegetarian.

Buffet Fife (☎ 345 223; Trumbićeva Obala 11; mains around 40KN) Dragomir presides over a motley crew of sailors and misfits who drop in for the simple home cooking (especially the *pašticada;* beef stew with wine and spices) and his own brand of grumpy but loving hospitality.

Supermarket/delicatessen (Svačićeva 1) This vast place has a wide selection of meat and cheese for sandwiches.

The **vegetable market** (🕒 6am-2pm), outside the east palace gate, has a wide array of fresh local produce.

Drinking & Entertainment

Split is great for nightlife, especially (or more so) in the spring and summer months. The palace walls are generally throbbing with loud music on Friday and Saturday nights.

Le Porta (Majstora Jurja) Next door to Teak Caffe, Le Porta is renowned for its cocktails. On the same square – Majstora Jurja – are Kala, Dante, Whisky Bar and Na Kantunu, all of which end up merging into one when the night gets busy.

Café Puls (Mihovilova Širina) and **Café Shook** (Mihovilova Širina) are pretty much indistinguishable late on Friday or Saturday night, when the dozen steps that link these two bars are chock-a-block with youngsters.

Croatian National Theatre (Trg Gaje Bulata; best seats about 60KN) During winter, opera and ballet are presented here. Erected in 1891, the theatre was fully restored in 1979 in its original style; it's worth attending a performance for the architecture alone.

Getting There & Away

AIR

The country's national air carrier, **Croatia Airlines** (☎ 062-777 777; Obala Hrvatskog Narodnog Preporoda 8), operates flights between Zagreb and Split (170KN to 350KN, 45 minutes) up to four times every day. Rates are lower if you book in advance. There's also **Easyjet** (www.easyjet.com).

BOAT

All of the boat-company offices in Split are located inside the ferry terminal.

You can buy tickets for passenger ferries at the **Jadrolinija stall** (Obala Kneza Domagoja). There are also several agents in the large ferry terminal opposite the bus station that can assist with boat trips from Split: **Jadroagent** (☎ 338 335) represents Adriatica Navigazione for its connections between Split and Ancona; **Jadrolinija** (☎ 338 333) handles all car-ferry services that depart from the docks around the ferry terminal; **SEM agency** (☎ 060 325 523) handles tickets between Ancona, Split and Hvar. **SNAV** (☎ 322 252) has a four-hour connection to Ancona and Pescara.

For more details on connections to/from Italy see p253.

BUS

Advance bus tickets with seat reservations are recommended. There are buses from the main **bus station** (☎ 060 327 327; www.ak-split.hr, in Croatian) beside the harbour to Dubrovnik (105KN to 166KN, 4½ hours, 12 daily), and Zagreb (195KN, five to nine hours, 27 daily). There are four daily buses to Mostar (120KN, three hours, four daily), and buses to Split from Sarajevo (€19, seven hours, five daily) and Ljubljana (310KN, 10½ hours, one daily).

There are three fast trains (138KN, six hours) and three overnight trains (138KN, 8½ hours) between Split and Zagreb, via Šibenik.

HVAR ISLAND

☎ 021 / pop 12,600

Hvar is the number one-carrier of Croatia's superlatives: it's the most luxurious island, the sunniest place in the country (2724 sunny hours each year), and, along with Dubrovnik, the most popular tourist destination. Hvar is also famed for its verdancy and its lilac lavender fields, as well as other aromatic herbs such as rosemary and heather.

Hvar Town

The island's hub and busiest destination, Hvar Town is estimated to draw around 30,000 people a day in the high season. It's odd that they can all fit in the small bay town, but fit they do. Visitors wander along the main square, explore the sights on the winding stone streets, swim on the numerous beaches or pop off to nudist Pakleni Islands. There are several good restaurants and a number of great hotels, as well as a couple of hostels.

ORIENTATION & INFORMATION

Car ferries from Split deposit you in Stari Grad but local buses meet most ferries in summer for the trip to Hvar Town. The town

Book your stay at lonelyplanet.com/hotels

centre is Trg Sv Stjepana, 100m west of the bus station. Passenger ferries tie up on Riva, the eastern quay, across from Hotel Slavija.

Pelegrini Travel (☎ /fax 742 250; pelegrini@inet.hr) Also finds private accommodation.

Tourist office (☎ /fax 742 977; www.tzhvar.hr; 🕑 8am-1pm & 5-9pm Mon-Sat, 9am-noon Sun Jun-Sep, 8am-2pm Mon-Sat Oct-May) In the arsenal building on the corner of Trg Sv Stjepana.

SIGHTS & ACTIVITIES

The full flavour of medieval Hvar is best savoured on the backstreets of the Old Town. At each end of Hvar is a monastery with a prominent tower. The Dominican **Church of St Marko** at the head of the bay was largely destroyed by Turks in the 16th century but you can visit the local **Archaeological Museum** (admission 10KN; 🕑 10am-noon Jun-Sep) in the ruins.

At the southeastern end of Hvar you'll find the 15th-century Renaissance **Franciscan Monastery** (🕑 10am-noon & 5-7pm Jun-Sep, plus Christmas week & Holy Week), with a wonderful collection of Venetian paintings in the church and adjacent **museum** (admission 15KN; 🕑 10am-noon & 5-7pm Mon-Sat Jun-Sep).

Smack in the middle of Hvar is the imposing Gothic **arsenal**, and upstairs is Hvar's prize, the first **municipal theatre** in Europe (1612) – both under extensive renovations at the time of research. On the hill high above Hvar Town is a **Venetian fortress** (1551), and it's worth the climb up to appreciate the lovely, sweeping panoramic views.

For more activity, hop on a launch to the **Pakleni Islands**, famous for nude sunbathing.

SLEEPING & EATING

Accommodation in Hvar is extremely tight in July and August: a reservation is highly recommended. For private accommodation, try **Pelegrini Travel** (☎ /fax 742 250; pelegrini@inet.hr). Expect to pay from 160/280KN per single/double with bathroom in the town centre.

Jagoda & Ante Bracanović Guesthouse (☎ 741 416, 091 520 3796; www.geocities.com/virgilye/hvar-jagoda.html; Poviše Škole; s/d 120/220KN) The Bracanović family has turned a traditional stone building into a small pension. Rooms come with balconies, private bathrooms and access to a kitchen, and the family goes out of their way for guests.

Green Lizard Hostel (☎ 742 560; www.greenlizard.hr; Lučića bb; dm 110KN, d per person 135KN; 🕑 Apr-Nov) This privately run hostel is a welcome and most necessary budget option on Hvar. Rooms are simple and immaculately clean, there's a communal kitchen and a few doubles with private and shared facilities.

Konoba Menego (☎ 742 036; mains from 70KN) This is a rustic old house where everything is decked out in Hvar antiques, and the staff wear traditional outfits. Try the cheeses and vegetables, prepared the old-fashioned Dalmatian way.

The pizzerias along the harbour offer predictable but inexpensive eating. The **grocery store** (Trg Sv Stjepana) is a viable restaurant alternative, and there's a morning market next to the bus station.

GETTING THERE & AWAY

The Jadrolinija ferries between Rijeka and Dubrovnik stop in Stari Grad before continuing to Korčula. The **Jadrolinija agency** (☎ 741 132; Riva) sells boat tickets. Car ferries from Split call at Stari Grad (42KN, one hour) three times daily (five daily in July and August). The speedy catamaran goes five times a day between Split and Hvar Town in the summer months (22KN, one hour). The **Jadrolinija agency** (☎ 741 132; www.jadrolinija.hr) is beside the landing in Stari Grad. There are at least 10 shuttle ferries (less off season) running from Drvenik, on the mainland, to Sućuraj on the tip of Hvar island (13KN, 25 minutes).

Buses meet most ferries that dock at Stari Grad in July and August, but if you come in the off season it's best to check at the tourist office or at Pelegrini Travel to make sure the bus is running. A taxi costs from 150KN to 200KN. **Radio Taxi Tihi** (☎ 098 338 824) is cheaper if there are a number of passengers to fill up the minivan. It's easy to recognise with the photo of Hvar painted on the side.

KORČULA ISLAND

☎ 020 / pop 16,200

Rich in vineyards and olive trees, the island of Korčula was named Korkyra Melaina (Black Korčula) by the original Greek settlers because of its dense woods and plant life. As the largest island in an archipelago of 48, it provides plenty of opportunities for scenic drives, particularly along the southern coast.

Swimming opportunities abound in the many quiet coves and secluded beaches, while the interior produces some of Croatia's finest wine, especially dessert wines made from *grk* grapes grown around Lumbarda. Local olive oil is another product worth seeking out.

On a hilly peninsula jutting into the Adriatic sits Korčula Town, a striking walled town of round defensive towers and red-roofed houses. Resembling a miniature Dubrovnik, the gated, walled Old Town is criss-crossed by narrow stone streets designed to protect its inhabitants from the winds swirling around the peninsula.

Orientation & Information

The big Jadrolinija car ferry drops you off either in the west harbour next to the Hotel Korčula or the east harbour next to Marko Polo Tours. The Old Town lies between the two harbours. The large hotels and main beach lie south of the east harbour, and the residential neighbourhood Sveti Nikola (with a smaller beach) is southwest of the west harbour. The town bus station is 100m south of the Old Town centre.

There are ATMs in the town centre at HVB Splitska Banka and Dubrovačka Banka. The post office is hidden next to the stairway up to the Old Town. The post office also has telephones.

Atlas travel agency (☎ 711 231; Trg Kralja Tomislava) Represents Amex, runs excursions and finds private accommodation. There's another office nearby.

Marko Polo Tours (☎ 715 400; marko-polo-tours@du.t-com.hr; Biline 5) Finds private accommodation and organises excursions.

Tino's Internet (☎ 091 50 91 182; ul Tri Sulara; per hr 30KN) Tino's other outlet is at the ACI Marina; both are open long hours.

Tourist office (☎ 715 701; tzg-korcule@du.t-com.hr; Obala Franje Tudjmana bb; 🕑 8am-3pm & 5-9pm Mon-Sat, 8am-3pm Sun Jun-Sep, 8am-1pm & 5-9pm Mon-Sat Oct-May) An excellent source of information, located on the west harbour.

Sights

Other than following the circuit of the former city walls or walking along the shore, sightseeing in Korčula centres on Cathedral Sq. The Gothic **Cathedral of St Mark** features two paintings by the Italian Renaissance master Jacopo Tintoretto (*Three Saints* on the altar and *Annunciation* to one side). The **treasury** (☎ 711 049; Trg Sv Marka; admission 15KN; 🕑 9am-7pm Jun-Aug), in the 14th-century Abbey Palace next to the cathedral, is worth a look. Even better is the **town museum** (☎ 711 420; Trg Sv Marka; admission 10KN; 🕑 10am-1pm Nov-Mar, 10am-2pm Apr-May, 10am-2pm & 7-9pm Jun, Sep & Oct, 10am-9pm Jul & Aug), in the 15th-century Gabriellis Palace opposite. It's said that Marco Polo was born in Korčula in 1254; for 10KN you can climb the tower of what is believed to have been his house.

Sleeping & Eating

The big hotels in Korčula are overpriced, but there are a wealth of guest houses that offer clean, attractive rooms and friendly service. Atlas and Marko Polo Tours arrange private rooms, charging from 200KN to 220KN for a room with a bathroom, and starting at about 400KN for an apartment. Or you could try one of the following options.

Autocamp Kalac (☎ 711 182; fax 711 146; per person/camp site €5.40/8.20) This attractive camping ground is behind Hotel Bon Repos, about 4km from the west harbour, in a dense pine grove near the beach.

Onelove Hostel (☎ 716 755; www.korculabackpacker.com; Hrvatske Bratske Zajednice 6; dm 100KN) Prepare for hedonism at this South African/Croatian-run hostel, where, according to travellers' feedback, good-looking girls and heavy boozers get priority booking. It's booze, dance and stay-up-all-night.

Pansion Marinka (☎ 712 007, 098 344 712; marinka.milina-bire@du.t-com.hr; d 230KN) This is a working farm and winery situated in Lumbarda, in a beautiful setting within walking distance of the beach.

Fresh (☎ 091 799 2086; www.igotfresh.com; 1 Kod Kina Liburne; snacks from 20KN) Right across from the bus station, Fresh is fab for breakfast smoothies, lunch wraps or beers and cocktails in the evening.

Planjak (☎ 711 015; Plokata 19 Travnja; mains from 50KN) Meat lovers should head here for the mixed grill and proper Balkan dishes, served on a covered terrace.

Entertainment

Between June and October there's **moreška sword dancing** (tickets 100KN; 🕑 show 9pm Thu) by the Old Town gate; performances are more frequent during July and August. The clash of swords and the graceful movements of the dancers/fighters make an exciting show. Atlas, the tourist office and Marko Polo Tours sell tickets.

Getting There & Away

There's a **Jadrolinija office** (☎ 715 410) about 25m up from the west harbour. A bus goes every day from Dubrovnik (87KN, three hours), one daily from Zagreb (195KN, 12 hours), and one a week from Sarajevo (165KN, eight hours).

DUBROVNIK

☎ 020 / pop 43,800

No matter whether you are visiting Dubrovnik for the first time or if you're returning again and again to this marvellous city, the sense of awe and beauty when you set eyes on the Stradun never fades. It's hard to imagine anyone, even the city's inhabitants, becoming jaded by its marble streets and baroque buildings, or failing to be inspired by a walk along the ancient city walls that protected a civilised, sophisticated republic for five centuries and that now look out onto the endless shimmer of the peaceful Adriatic.

Orientation

The Jadrolinija ferry terminal and the bus station are next to each other at Gruž, several kilometres northwest of the Old Town, which is closed to cars. The main street in the Old Town is Placa (better known as Stradun). Most accommodation is on the leafy Lapad Peninsula, west of the bus station.

Information

Atlas travel agency Obala Papa Ivana Pavla II (Map p267; ☎ 418 001; Obala Papa Ivana Pavla II 1); Sv Đurđa (off Map p268; ☎ 442 574; Sv Đurđa 1) In convenient locations, this agency is extremely helpful for general information as well as finding private accommodation. All excursions are run by Atlas.

Netcafé (Map p268; ☎ 321 125; www.netcafe.hr; Prijeko 21; per hr 30KN; 9am-11pm) A wonderfully friendly cafe with a fast connection and good services.

Tourist office (www.tzdubrovnik.hr) Bus Station (Map p267; ☎ 417 581; Obala Pape Ivana Pavla II 24; 8am-8pm daily Jun-Sep, 8am-3pm Mon-Fri, 9am-2pm Sat Oct-May); Gruž Harbour (Map p267; ☎ 417 983; Obala Stjepana Radića 27; 8am-8pm daily Jun-Sep, 8am-3pm Mon-Fri, 9am-2pm Sat Oct-May); Old Town (Map p268; ☎ 323 587; Široka 1; 8am-8pm daily Jun-Sep, 8am-3pm Mon-Fri, 9am-2pm Sat Oct-May); Lapad (Map p267; ☎ 437 460; Šetalište Kralja Zvonimira 25; 8am-8pm daily Jun-Sep, 8am-3pm Mon-Fri, 9am-2pm Sat, closed Sun Oct-May); Pile Gate (Map p268; ☎ 427 591; Branitelja Dubrovnika 7; 8am-8pm daily Jun-Sep, 8am-3pm Mon-Fri, 9am-2pm Sat Oct-May) Maps, information and the indispensable *Dubrovnik Riviera* guide.

CROATIA

Sights

You'll probably begin your visit at the bus stop outside **Pile Gate** (Map p268). As you enter the city, Dubrovnik's wonderful pedestrian promenade, the Placa, extends all the way to the clock tower at the other end of town. Just inside Pile Gate is the huge **Onofrio Fountain** (Map p268), completed in 1438, and the **Franciscan monastery** (Map p268), with a splendid cloister and the third-oldest functioning pharmacy, dating from 1391, in Europe. The **monastery museum** (Map p268; ☎ 321 410; Placa 2; adult/concession 20/10KN; 9am-6pm) presents a collection of liturgical objects, paintings and pharmacy equipment.

In front of the clock tower, at the eastern end of Placa, you'll find the **Orlando Column** (Map p268), which dates from 1419. On opposite sides of the Orlando Column are the 16th-century **Sponza Palace** (Map p268; admission free; 8am-3pm Mon-Fri, to 1pm Sat) and **St Blaise's Church** (Map p268; for morning & late-afternoon Mass Mon-Sat), a lovely Italian baroque building.

At the end of the broad street called Pred Dvorom, beside St Blaise, is the baroque **Cathedral of the Assumption of the Virgin** (Map p268; Poljana M Držića; for morning & late-afternoon Mass) and, between the two churches, the Gothic **Rector's Palace** (Map p268; ☎ 426 469; Pred Dvorom 3; adult/student 35/15KN, audio guide 30KN; 9am-6pm), built in 1441.

As you proceed up Placa, make a detour to the **Museum of the Orthodox Church** (Map p268; ☎ 323 283; Od Puča 8; adult/concession 10/5KN; 9am-1pm Mon-Fri) for a look at a fascinating collection of 15th- to 19th-century icons.

By this time you'll be ready for a walk around the **city walls** (Map p268; adult/concession 50/20KN; 9am-7pm), which have entrances just inside Pile Gate, across from the Dominican monastery and near Fort St John. These powerful walls are the finest in the world and Dubrovnik's main claim to fame. The views are great – this walk could be the high point of your visit.

Whichever way you go, you will notice the 14th-century **Dominican monastery** (Map p268; ☎ 321 421; Svetog Dominika 4; admission 20KN; 9am-5pm) in the northeastern corner of the city, the forbidding fortresslike exterior of which shelters a rich trove of paintings from Dubrovnik's finest 15th- and 16th-century artists.

The closest beach to the Old Town, **Banje Beach**, is outside Ploče Gate. There are also hotel beaches on the **Lapad Peninsula** (Map p267).

An even better option is to take the ferry (services operate from 9am to 6pm) from the old port (Map p268) that shuttles half-hourly

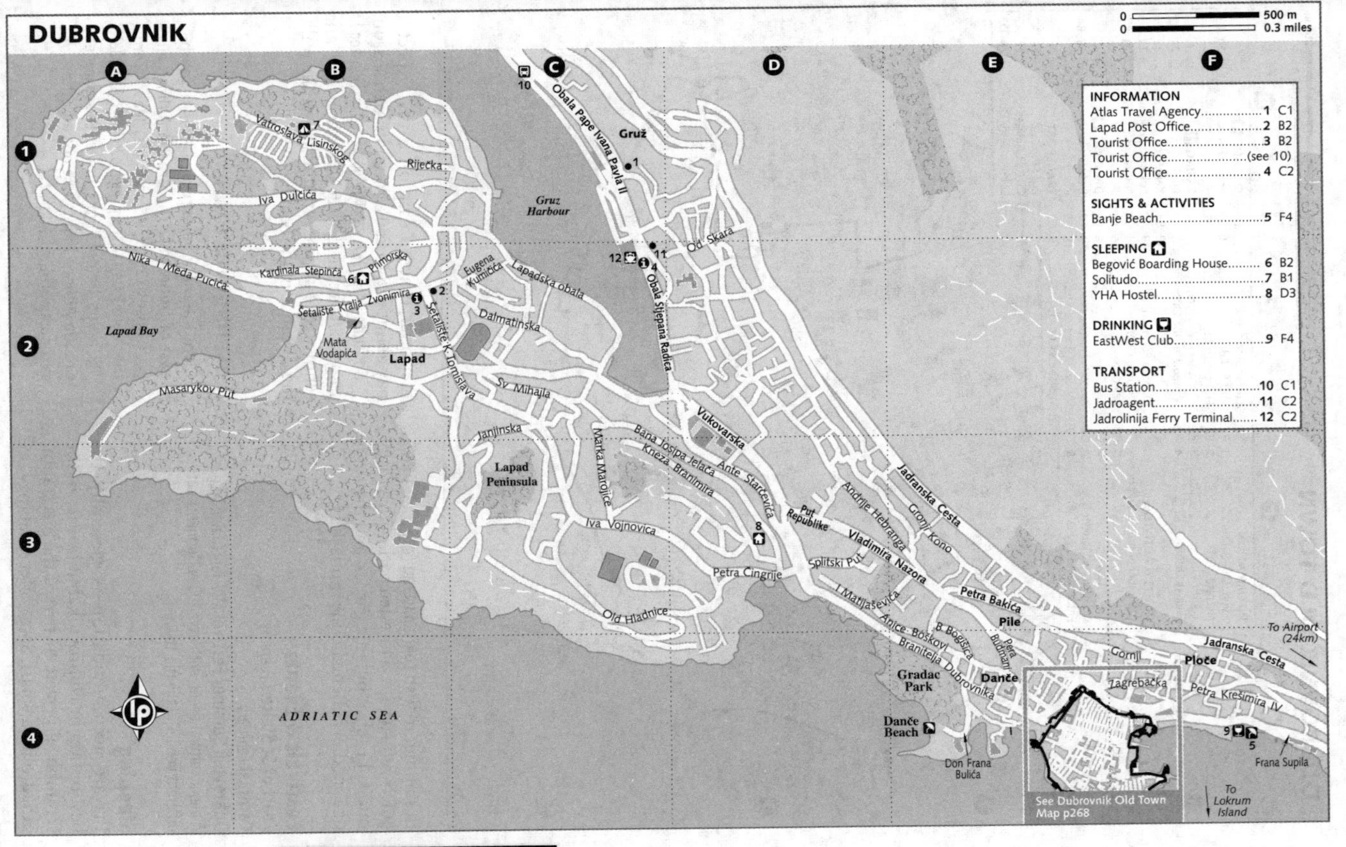
DUBROVNIK
0 500 m
0 0.3 miles
INFORMATION
Atlas Travel Agency 1 C1
Lapad Post Office 2 B2
Tourist Office 3 B2
Tourist Office (see 10)
Tourist Office 4 C2
SIGHTS & ACTIVITIES
Banje Beach 5 F4
SLEEPING
Begović Boarding House 6 B2
Solitudo 7 B1
YHA Hostel 8 D3
DRINKING
EastWest Club 9 F4
TRANSPORT
Bus Station 10 C1
Jadroagent 11 C2
Jadrolinija Ferry Terminal 12 C2
Gruž
Gruz Harbour
Obala Pape Ivana Pavla II
Obala Stjepana Radića
Od Skara
Vatroslava Lisinskog
Riječka
Iva Dulčića
Nika i Meda Pucića
Kardinala Stepinča
Primorska
Eugena Kumičića
Lapadska obala
Šetalište Kralja Zvonimira
Šetalište K. Tomislava
Dalmatinska
Lapad Bay
Mata Vodapića
Lapad
Masarykov Put
Sv Mihajla
Janjinska
Lapad Peninsula
Marka Marojice
Bana Josipa Jelača
Kneza Branimira
Vukovarska
Ante Starčevića
Iva Vojnovica
Petra Čingrije
Old Hladnice
Put Republike
Andrije Hebranga
Gronji Kono
Jadranska Cesta
Vladimira Nazora
Splitski Put
I Matijaševića
Anice Boškovi
B Bogišića
Pera Budmani
Branitelja Dubrovnika
Petra Bakića
Pile
Gradac Park
Danče
Danče Beach
Don Frana Bulića
Gornji
Zagrebačka
Ploče
Petra Krešimira IV
Frana Supila
To Airport (24km)
To Lokrum Island
See Dubrovnik Old Town Map p268
ADRIATIC SEA

Book your stay at lonelyplanet.com/hotels

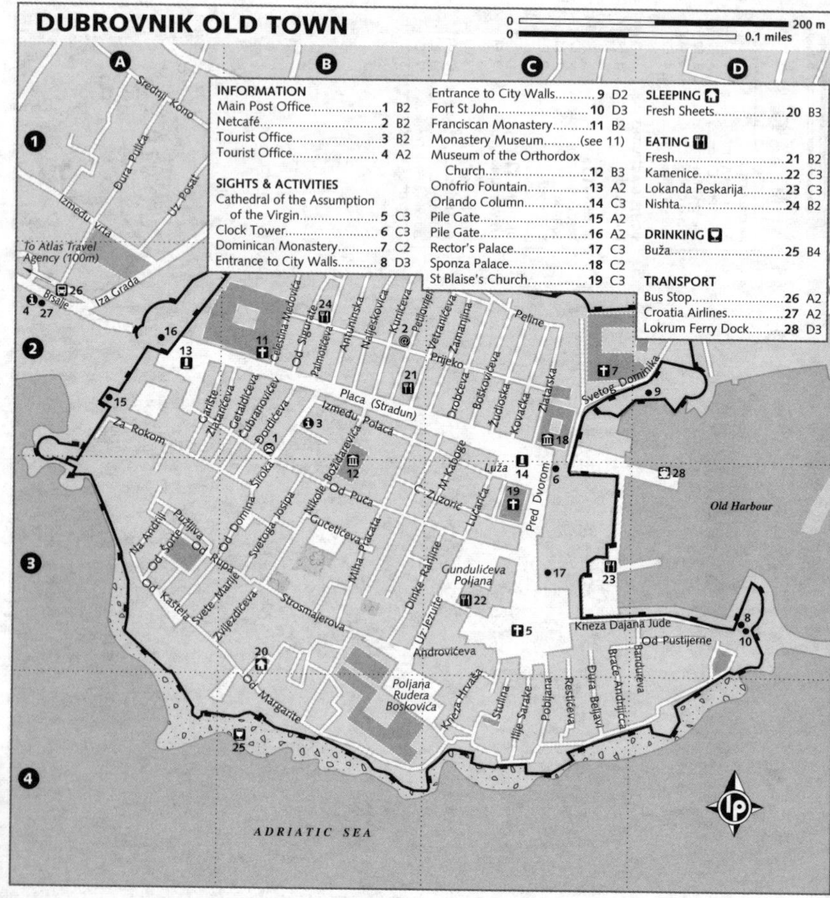

in summer to lush **Lokrum Island** (off Map p267; 40KN return trip), a forested park with a rocky nudist beach, a botanic garden and the ruins of a medieval Benedictine monastery.

Festivals & Events

Feast of St Blaise 3 February
Carnival February
Dubrovnik Summer Festival Mid-July to mid-August. A major cultural event, with over 100 performances at different venues in the Old Town.

Sleeping

Private accommodation is generally the best option in Dubrovnik, but beware of the scramble of private owners at the bus station or Jadrolinija wharf. Some offer what they say they offer, others are rip-off artists. Expect to pay about €28 to €50 a room in high season.

Solitudo (Map p267; ☎ 448 200; Vatroslava Lisinskog 17; per person/camp site €5.40/10.20) This pretty and renovated camping ground is within walking distance of the beach.

GETTING INTO TOWN

Čilipi international airport is 24km south-east of Dubrovnik. The Croatia Airlines airport buses (25KN, 45 minutes) leave from the main **bus station** (Map p267; ☎ 357 088) 1½ hours before flight times. Buses meet Croatia Airlines flights but not all others. A taxi costs around 200KN.

our pick **Fresh Sheets** (Map p268; ☎ 091 799 2086; beds@igotfresh.com; Sv Šimuna 15; per person €25; 💻) A brand-new place, this is a collection of four individually decorated apartments, each sleeping two to four people (plus a sofa), and one double room. The location is excellent – in the heart of Old Town – you get free internet and wi-fi and, when the Fresh bar's kitchen is open, a free smoothie.

Begović Boarding House (Map p267; ☎ 435 191; http://begovic-boarding-house.com; Primorska 17; dm/s/d €19/32/40) A long-time favourite with our readers, this friendly place in Lapad has three rooms with shared bathroom and three apartments. There's a terrace out the back with a good view. Breakfast is an additional 30KN.

YHA Hostel (Map p267; ☎ 423 241; dubrovnik@hfhs.hr; Vinka Sagrestana 3; B&B per person 120KN) Basic in decor, the YHA Hostel is clean and, as travellers report, a lot of fun. The best dorms are room Nos 31 and 32, for their 'secret' roof terrace.

Eating

Fresh (Map p268; ☎ 091 896 7509; www.igotfresh.com; Vetranićeva 4; wraps from 20KN) A mecca for young travellers who gather here for the smoothies, wraps and other healthy snacks, as well as drinks and music in the evening.

Nishta (Map p268; ☎ 091 896 7509; Prijeko 30; mains from 30KN) Head here for a refreshing gazpacho, a heart-warming miso soup, Thai curries, veggies and noodles, and many more veggie delights.

Kamenice (Map p268; ☎ 421 499; Gundulićeva Poljana 8; mains from 40KN) It's been here since the 1970s and not much has changed: the socialist-style waiting uniforms, the simple interior, the massive portions of mussels, grilled or fried squid and griddled anchovies, and *kamenice* (oysters) too.

our pick **Lokanda Peskarija** (Map p268; ☎ 324 750; Ribarnica bb; mains from 40KN) Located on the Old Harbour right next to the fish market, this is undoubtedly one of Dubrovnik's best eateries. The quality of the seafood dishes is unfaltering, the prices are good, and the location is gorgeous.

Drinking

EastWest Club (Map p267; ☎ 412 220; Frana Supila bb) By day this outfit on Banje Beach rents out beach chairs and umbrellas and serves drinks to the bathers. When the rays lengthen, the cocktail bar opens.

our pick **Buža** (Map p268; Ilije Sarake) The Buža is just a simple place on the outside of the city walls, facing out onto the open sea, with simple drinks and blissful punters.

Getting There & Away

Daily flights to/from Zagreb are operated by **Croatia Airlines** (Map p268; ☎ 413 777; Brsalje 9). The fare costs from about 400KN one way (one hour), up to 800KN in high season. The Jadrolinija coastal ferry travels north to Hvar and Split. **Jadrolinija** (Map p267; ☎ 418 000; Gruž) sells tickets and can provide information on coastal, international and local ferries. **Jadroagent** (Map p267; ☎ 419 009; fax 419 029; Stjepana Radića 32) handles ticketing for most international boats to/from Croatia.

There are daily bus connections to Dubrovnik from Kotor (120KN, 2½ hours), Međugorje (€18, three hours, two daily), Mostar (€15, three hours, two daily), Sarajevo (€18, five hours, daily).

Buses go daily from Dubrovnik to Korčula (95KN, three hours, one daily), Split (120KN to 111KN, 4½ hours, 14 daily) and Zagreb (250KN, 11 hours, seven daily).

Getting Around

Dubrovnik's buses run frequently and generally on time. The fare is 10KN if you buy from the driver but only 8KN if you buy a ticket at a kiosk.

CROATIA DIRECTORY

ACCOMMODATION

Accommodation listings in this guide have been arranged in order of price. Many hotels, rooms and camping grounds issue their prices in euros but some places to stay have stuck with the kuna. Although you can usually pay with either currency, we have listed the primary currency the establishment uses in setting its prices.

Along the Croatian coast, accommodation is priced according to three seasons, which tend to vary from place to place. Generally October to May are the cheapest months, June and September are midpriced, but count on paying top price for the peak season, which runs for a six-week period in July and August. High-season prices have been given in this chapter. Note that prices for rooms in Zagreb are pretty much constant all year and that many hotels on the coast close in winter.

Camping
Nearly 100 camping grounds are scattered along the Croatian coast. Opening times of camping grounds generally run from mid-April to September, give or take a few weeks. The exact times change from year to year, so it's wise to call in advance if you're arriving at either end of the season.

A good site for camping information is www.camping.hr.

Hostels
The **Croatian YHA** (☎ 01-48 47 472; www.hfhs.hr; Dežmanova 9, Zagreb) operates youth hostels in Dubrovnik, Zadar, Zagreb and Pula. Nonmembers pay an additional 10KN per person daily for a stamp on a welcome card; six stamps entitles you to a membership.

Hotels
Hotels are ranked from one to five stars with the most in the two- and three-star range. In August some hotels may demand a surcharge for stays of less than four nights but this surcharge is usually waived during the rest of the year, when prices drop steeply. Breakfast is included in hotel prices.

Private Rooms
Private rooms or apartments are the best accommodation in Croatia. Service is excellent and the rooms are usually extremely well kept. You may very well be greeted by offers of *sobe* as you step off your bus and boat, but rooms are most often arranged by travel agencies or the local tourist office. Booking through an agency will ensure that the place you're staying in is officially registered and has insurance.

It makes little sense to price-shop from agency to agency since prices are fixed by the local tourist association. Whether you deal with the owner directly or book through an agency, you'll pay a 30% surcharge for stays of less than four nights and sometimes 50% or even 100% more for a one-night stay, although you may be able to get them to waive the surcharge if you arrive in the low season. Prices for private rooms in this chapter are for a four-night stay in peak season.

ACTIVITIES
The clear waters and varied underwater life of the Adriatic have led to a flourishing dive industry along the coast. The real speciality in Croatia is cave diving; night diving and wreck diving are also offered, and there are coral reefs in some places but in rather deep water. You must get a permit for a boat dive: go to the harbour captain in any port with your passport, diving certification card and 100KN. Permission is valid for a year. If you dive with a dive centre, it will take care of the paperwork. Most of the coastal resorts mentioned in this chapter have dive shops. See **Diving Croatia** (www.diving-hrs.hr) for contact information.

BUSINESS HOURS
Banking and post office hours are 7.30am to 7pm on weekdays and 8am to noon on Saturday. Many shops are open 8am to 7pm on weekdays and until 2pm on Saturday. Along the coast life is more relaxed; shops and offices frequently close around noon for an afternoon break and reopen around 4pm. Restaurants are open long hours, often noon to midnight, with Sunday closings outside of peak season.

EMBASSIES & CONSULATES
The following addresses are in Zagreb:

Australia (off Map pp256-7; ☎ 01-48 91 200; www.auembassy.hr; Kaptol Centar, Nova Ves 11) North of the centre.

Bosnia & Hercegovina (off Map pp256-7; ☎ 01-46 83 761; Torbarova 9) Northwest of the centre.

Canada (Map pp256-7; ☎ 01-48 81 200; zagreb@dfait-maeci.gc.ca; Prilaz Gjure Deželića 4)

France (Map pp256-7; ☎ 01-48 93 680; consulat@ambafrance.hr; Hebrangova 2)

Germany (off Map pp256-7; ☎ 01-61 58 105; www.deutschebotschaft-zagreb.hr, in German; ul grada Vukovara 64) South of the centre.

Hungary (off Map pp256-7; ☎ 01-48 22 051; Pantovčak 128/I) Northwest of the centre.

Ireland (Map pp256-7 ☎ 01-66 74 455; Turinina 3)

Netherlands (off Map pp256-7; ☎ 01-46 84 880; nlgovzag@zg.t-com.hr; Medveščak 56)

New Zealand (off Map pp256-7; ☎ 01-61 51 382; Trg Stjepana Radića 3) Southwest of the centre.

Serbia (off Map pp256-7; ☎ 01-45 79 067; Pantovčak 245) Northwest of the centre.

Slovenia (Map pp256-7; ☎ 01-63 11 000; Savska 41)

UK (off Map pp256-7; ☎ 01-60 09 100; I Lučića 4) East of the centre.

USA (off Map pp256-7; ☎ 01-66 12 200; www.usembassy.hr; ul Thomasa Jeffersona 2) South of the centre.

FESTIVALS & EVENTS
Revived shortly after Croatian independence, the pre-Lent festival of **Mardi Gras** has gathered force in Croatia. Held in February,

HOLIDAYS

New Year's Day 1 January
Epiphany 6 January
Easter Monday March/April
Labour Day 1 May
Corpus Christi 10 June
Day of Antifascist Resistance 22 June; marks the outbreak of resistance in 1941
Statehood Day 25 June
Victory Day and National Thanksgiving Day 5 August
Feast of the Assumption 15 August
Independence Day 8 October
All Saints' Day 1 November
Christmas 25 & 26 December

INTERNET RESOURCES

Croatia Homepage (www.hr.hr) Hundreds of links to everything you want to know about Croatia.

MONEY

The currency is the kuna (KN). Banknotes are in denominations of 500, 200, 100, 50, 20, 10 and five. Each kuna is divided into 100 lipa in coins of 50, 20 and 10. Many places exchange money, all with similar rates. Exchange offices may deduct a commission of 1% to change cash or travellers cheques, but some banks do not.

Although they are widely accepted in upmarket places, don't count on credit cards to pay for private accommodation or meals in small restaurants. ATMs are available in most bus and train stations, airports, all major cities and most small towns. Many branches of Privredna Banka have ATMs that allow cash withdrawals on an American Express card.

POST

Mail sent to Poste Restante, 10000 Zagreb, Croatia, is held at the **main post office** (Branimirova 4; 24hr Mon-Sat, 1pm-midnight Sun) next to the Zagreb train station. A good coastal address to use is c/o Poste Restante, Main Post Office, 21000 Split, Croatia. If you have an Amex card, most Atlas travel agencies will hold your mail.

TELEPHONE

To call Croatia from abroad, dial your international access code, ☎ 385 (Croatia's country code), the area code (without the initial zero) and the local number. When calling from one region to another within Croatia, use the initial zero. When in Croatia, dial ☎ 00 to speak to the international operator. To make a phone call from Croatia, go to the town's main post office. Phonecards are sold according to *impulsi* (units), and you can buy cards of 25 (15KN), 50 (30KN), 100 (50KN) and 200 (100KN) units. These can be purchased at any post office and most tobacco shops and newspaper kiosks. Mobile phone numbers start with 091.

VISAS

Visitors from Australia, Canada, New Zealand, the EU and the USA do not require a visa for stays of less than 90 days. For other nationalities, visas are issued free of charge at Croatian consulates.

Cyprus Κύπρος

HIGHLIGHTS

- **Kourion** Near Lemesos, this is a top spot for history buffs keen on Cyprus' ruins (p277)
- **Salamis** One of Cyprus' most fascinating archaeological sites (p281)
- **Troodos Massif** The Byzantine churches and monasteries of the Troodos are illuminated by glorious frescoes (p278)
- **Best journey** Driving past ruined basilicas and untouched beaches to the tip of the Karpas Peninsula (p281)
- **Off-the-beaten track** Share gorgeous Altinkum Beach with nobody but the turtles (p281)

FAST FACTS

- **Area** 9250 sq km (about 30 Maltas).
- **Budget** €22 to €40/TL50 to TL90 per day
- **Capital** Republic of Cyprus: Lefkosia; North Cyprus: Lefkoşa
- **Country codes** Republic of Cyprus: ☎ 357; North Cyprus: ☎ 90 392
- **Famous for** beaches, mezes, mosaics and monasteries
- **Languages** Greek; Turkish
- **Money** Republic of Cyprus: Euro (€); North Cyprus: Turkish Lira (TL); A$1 = €0.55/TL1.16; C$1 = €0.60/TL1.32; €1 = TL2.10; ¥100 = €0.78/TL1.65; NZ$1 = €0.43/TL0.92; UK£1 = €1.12/TL2.38; US$1 = €0.74/TL1.57
- **Phrases** Republic: *yasas* (hello), *signomi* (excuse me), *poso kani?* (how much?); North Cyprus: *merhaba* (hello), *affedersiniz* (excuse me), *ne kadar?* (how much?)
- **Population** 780,130 (plus around 120,000 Turkish settlers in North Cyprus)
- **Visas** none required for most nationalities (p282)

TRAVEL HINTS

Eat where the locals eat – the best *tavernas* are simple, rustic and crowded with Cypriots.

ROAMING CYPRUS

In the south, walk on the Akamas, and explore old Lefkosia and monasteries in the Troodos. In the north, discover the Karpas Peninsula.

Cyprus (Kibris in Turkish) is a kaleidoscopic blend: divided for 30-odd years between the Greek South and the Turkish North, and close to Europe economically and politically, the island's character is stirred by its physical proximity to Asia and the Middle East. It is a place that can be both rewarding and repelling, and a visitor needs to exercise discernment in order to get the best out of the island. Avoid overdeveloped, tourist-swamped places and concentrate on exploring eco options, medieval churches, castles and the abundance of activities on offer along the island's many beaches and gorgeous mountain ranges. Alternatively, dive into the urbanity of Lefkosia/North Nicosia where you can see the merging of modern and traditional Cyprus. If time allows, visit both sides of the island – you'll get a fuller picture of the complex and fractured Cypriot identity.

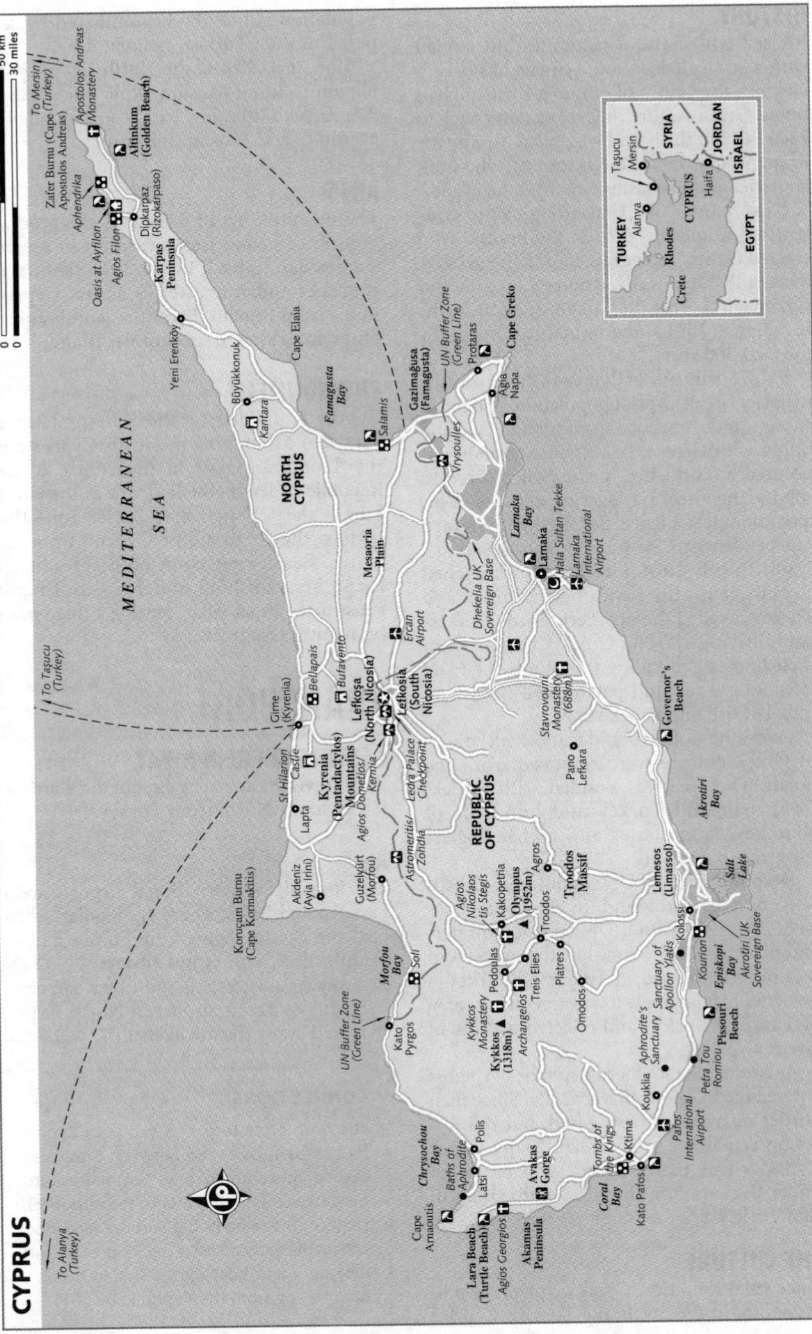

CYPRUS

MEDITERRANEAN SEA

To Alanya (Turkey)
To Taşucu (Turkey)
To Mersin (Turkey)

0 50 km
0 30 miles

NORTH CYPRUS
REPUBLIC OF CYPRUS

Zafer Burnu (Cape Apostolos Andreas)
Apostolos Andreas Monastery
Aphendrika
Oasis at Ayfilon
Agios Filon
Dipkarpaz (Rizokarpaso)
Altinkum (Golden Beach)
Karpas Peninsula
Yeni Erenköy
Cape Elaia
Büyükkonuk
Kantara
Famagusta Bay
Salamis
Gazimağusa (Famagusta)
UN Buffer Zone (Green Line)
Protaras
Cape Greko
Agia Napa
Vrysoulles
Larnaka Bay
Hala Sultan Tekke
Larnaka
Larnaka International Airport
Dhekelia UK Sovereign Base
Mesaoria Plain
Ercan Airport
Bufavento
Bellapais
Girne (Kyrenia)
St Hilarion Castle
Kyrenia (Pentadactylos) Mountains
Lefkoşa (North Nicosia)
Lefkosia (South Nicosia)
Agios Dometios/Kermia
Ledra Palace Checkpoint
Lapta
Stavrovouni Monastery (688m)
Pano Lefkara
Governor's Beach
Akrotiri Bay
Koruçam Burnu (Cape Kormakitis)
Akdeniz (Ayia Irini)
Guzelyurt (Morfou)
Astromeritis/Zohdia
Agios Nikolaos tis Stegis
Kakopetria
Olympus (1952m)
Agros
Troodos Massif
Troodos
Lemesos (Limassol)
Salt Lake
Akrotiri UK Sovereign Base
Morfou Bay
Soli
Pedoulas
Treis Elies
Platres
Omodos
Kolossi
Kourion
Episkopi Bay
Sanctuary of Apollon Ylatis
Kykkos Monastery
Kykkos (1318m)
Archangelos
Kato Pyrgos
UN Buffer Zone (Green Line)
Aphrodite's Sanctuary
Pissouri Beach
Petra Tou Romiou
Kouklia
Pafos International Airport
Tombs of the Kings
Ktima
Kato Pafos
Coral Bay
Chrysochou Bay
Polis
Baths of Aphrodite
Latsi
Avakas Gorge
Cape Arnaoutis
Lara Beach (Turtle Beach)
Agios Georgios
Akamas Peninsula

TURKEY
Alanya
Taşucu
Mersin
SYRIA
CYPRUS
Rhodes
Crete
Haifa
JORDAN
ISRAEL
EGYPT

HISTORY

Blessed with natural resources but cursed with a strategic location, Cyprus has been a pawn in the games of empires since ancient times. Greek culture in Cyprus dates back to 2500 BC, but the island was taken over by the Romans and then the Byzantines, who built churches and monasteries across the island.

Next came the Crusaders, who constructed numerous castles; the Franks, who erected Gothic cathedrals; and the Venetians, who built huge walls around Lefkosia and Gazimağusa. This didn't stop the Ottomans invading in 1571 and dominating Cyprus for the next 300 years.

In 1878 Turkey sold Cyprus to Britain but the majority Greek Cypriot population demanded *enosis* – independence from foreign rule and union with Greece. In response, Britain appointed a Turkish Cypriot police force to subdue the Greeks, triggering decades of intercommunal violence. Britain finally granted independence to Cyprus in August 1960.

On 15 July 1974, Greek forces launched a coup against the Cypriot government and Turkey invaded the northern third of the island, driving 180,000 Greek Cypriots from their homes and killing thousands. The UN later interceded and partitioned the island into Turkish and Greek states.

Over the following decades, all traces of Greek culture were removed from the north. The area was flooded with settlers from mainland Turkey and hundreds of churches, monasteries and archaeological sites were plundered.

Despite a series of UN resolutions, Cyprus remains a divided island. In 2004 both sides were presented with a UN-sponsored referendum on reunification, but the agreement was heavily skewed in favour of Turkey – perhaps unsuprisingly it was accepted by 65% of Turkish Cypriots and rejected by 75% of Greek Cypriots.

As a result, the southern Republic of Cyprus entered the EU alone in May 2004. Since then border restrictions have eased, but reunification remains controversial. Many Greek Cypriots fear their struggle will be swept under the carpet in the EU's enthusiasm to sign Turkey as a new member state.

THE CULTURE

Since partition, most Greek Cypriots live in the south. In the north, the Turkish Cypriot population is heavily outnumbered by settlers from the Turkish mainland.

More than 99% of the North Cyprus population is Sunni Muslim, while the south is 94% Greek Orthodox, with Roman Catholic, Maronite and Muslim minorities.

ARTS

The definitive art of Cyprus is the production of icons and frescoes; you can see examples dating back to the 12th century in churches and monasteries across Cyprus. Ruins from Roman, Byzantine and Frankish times are scattered around the island.

ENVIRONMENT

Cyprus is divided by the Kyrenia (Pentadactylos) Mountains in North Cyprus and the Troodos Massif in the centre of the Republic. A less tangible divide is the Green Line – the UN-patrolled buffer zone that divides the Republic of Cyprus from the North. Beach resorts on both sides of the island are vanishing under a sea of newly constructed expat villas, putting a huge strain on natural resources.

TRANSPORT

GETTING THERE & AWAY

Most travellers arrive by air, but there are also ferries to the North from Turkey.

Air

The Republic's international airports are at Larnaka and Pafos. There are regular scheduled and charter flights from Europe and the Middle East with **Cyprus Airways** (CY; ☎ 2266 3054; www.cyprusairways.com) and other carriers.

Flights to Ercan airport in North Cyprus start in Turkey. **Turkish Airlines** (TK; ☎ 227 1061;

CONNECTIONS

The main place to get to and from Cyprus by boat is Turkey – go between Girne and Taşucu in summer, and Gazimağusa to Mersin overnight (for details, see opposite). Lemesos is having its old harbour facelifted with some hefty millions (see opposite), and new ferry and boat routes should be running to and from the Republic by 2011.

www.turkishairlines.com) and **Cyprus Turkish Airlines** (YK; ☎ 227 3820; www.kthy.net) are the main carriers.

Discount airlines flying to Cyprus:

Aegean Airlines (www.aegeanair.com)
Atlasjet (www.atlasjet.com)
Eurocypria (www.eurocypria.com)

One cheap option is to join a discount package tour – in the peak season, this is often cheaper than buying a scheduled flight.

Boat

Passenger services to the Republic's main port at Lemesos are currently suspended – contact **Salamis Shipping** (☎ 2589 9999) and **Louis Cruise Lines** (☎ 7777 8555) for the latest information.

Ferries connect North Cyprus to mainland Turkey. **KT Denizcilik** (Cyprus Turkish Shipping; ☎ 366 5786) sails three times a week between Gazimağusa and Mersin (TL65 one way, 12 hours). **Fergün** (☎ 815 4993) and **Akgünler** (☎ 815 6002) have daily passenger ferries between Girne and Taşucu (TL60 to TL71 per person, two to five hours). In summer there's also a twice-weekly ferry from Girne to Alanya (TL75, five hours).

GETTING AROUND

Inexpensive buses link the major cities, except on Sunday. Shared service-taxis cover similar routes for similar prices.

Cheap car and motorbike rental is available in most towns. Most national driving licences are valid in the Republic, but only British and international licences are accepted in North Cyprus. The boxed text (p280) has information on crossing the border.

REPUBLIC OF CYPRUS

Covering the southern 63% of the island, the Greek-speaking Republic of Cyprus has the lion's share of the beaches and historical treasures. Development is rampant at the main beach resorts, but inland are quiet stone villages that have hardly changed in centuries.

> **READING UP**
>
> To understand the glory of undivided Cyprus, read Colin Thubron's *Journey into Cyprus* (1975) or Lawrence Durrell's *Bitter Lemons* (1957), set around Bellapais.

> **EMERGENCY NUMBERS**
>
> - Ambulance, fire or police (Republic of Cyprus) ☎ 112 or ☎ 199
> - Ambulance (North Cyprus) ☎ 112
> - Police (North Cyprus) ☎ 155

LEFKOSIA (SOUTH NICOSIA) ΛΕΦΚΩΣΙΑ

pop 213,500

Lefkosia is an attractive, enticing city and Cyprus' cultural heart; it's ideal for experiencing what modern Cyprus is about. The Old City's curious shape has been likened to a snowflake or a hand grenade – depending on how romantic your vision is. Its narrow streets are a labyrinth, teeming during the day and ghostly at night, hiding churches, mosques, and unique bars and restaurants that sit inside beautiful old colonial houses.

The city is split almost evenly between the Turkish-occupied North and the Republican South. Lefkosia/Lefkoşa (p279) as a whole reflects the story of Cyprus: its two people, divided, are glancing at a future that might bring a better solution. With crossing to and fro made easier, it's possible to see and feel Lefkosia as one city, though it may be years still until it's truly that way.

Orientation

The city centre is Plateia Eleftherias, located by the city walls; Lidras St is the main shopping street, at the end of which now sits the pedestrian crossing into the North (24 hours, passport necessary). Most tourist attractions are tucked away on the alleys leading down to the Green Line.

Information

Plateia Eleftherias has banks, the main post office and numerous payphones.

Cyprus Tourist Organisation (CTO; ☎ 2267 4264; cytour@cto.org.cy; Aristokyprou; 🕑 8.30am-4pm Mon-Fri, to 2pm Sat) In the alleys of Laiki Yeitonia.

Lefkosia General Hospital (☎ 2280 1400; Nechrou) In Engkomi.

PS Printways (☎ 2266 1628; Rigainis 63B; per hr €2; 🕑 8am-midnight) Internet access near Plateia Solomou.

Sights

Near the old Pafos Gate, the **Cyprus Museum** (☎ 2286 5864; Mouseiou 1; admission €4; 9am-5pm Mon-Sat, 10am-1pm Sun) houses an incredible collection of pots, statues and tomb offerings, but come early to beat the guided tours.

The outline of the **Venetian Walls** makes Lefkosia's logo. The Venetian rulers erected the walls between 1567 and 1570 with the express aim of keeping the feared Ottoman invaders out of Lefkosia. Five of the bastions, **Tripoli**, **D'Avila**, **Constanza**, **Podocataro** and **Caraffa**, are in the southern sector of Lefkosia. The easternmost **Famagusta Gate** (Pyli Ammohostou; 9am-1pm & 4-7pm Mon-Fri) is the most photographed and best preserved of the three original gates that led into the Old City of Lefkosia.

Just off Lidras St, the intriguing **Leventis Municipal Museum** (☎ 2266 1475; Ippokratous 17; admission free; 10am-4.30pm Tue-Sun) traces the history of Lefkosia, while the **Shacolas Tower Museum & Observatory** (☎ 2267 9396; 11th fl, Shakolas Tower, cnr Ledra & Arsinois; admission €0.85; 10am-6.30pm daily) offers stupendous views across the city.

On Plateia Tillirias are the recently restored **Omeriye Mosque** and the swish and indulgent **Hamam Omerye** (Turkish Baths; ☎ 2275 0550; www.hamambaths.com; Plateia Tyllirias 8; admission & Turkish bath 2hrs €20; men 9am-9pm Tue, Thu & Sat, women 9am-9pm Wed, Fri & Sun, couples 11am-7pm Mon).

Lefkosia has many **art galleries, churches** and **museums** – contact the tourist office or follow the brown signs.

Sleeping & Eating

HI Hostel (☎ 9943 8360; Tefkrou 5; dm €10-15) About 1.5km from the city walls, this brightly painted hostel has a guest kitchen, fan-cooled dorms and resident cats. Bus 12 passes nearby.

our pick **Sky Hotel** (☎ 2266 6880; www.skyhotel.ws; Solonos 7C; s/d €43/60;) The best budget place in Lefkosia, Sky is bang in the centre of the Old Town, with good, spacious rooms overlooking the surrounding rooftops.

our pick **Shiantris** (☎ 2267 1549; Pericleous 21; mains from €6; lunch) Head here for a really good, simple, homemade Cypriot lunch.

Inga's Veggie Heaven (☎ 2234 4674; 2 Dimonaktos, Chrisaliniotissa Crafts Centre; mains €8-10; 9am-5pm) Vegies will delight in offerings at Inga's.

Double Six Coffee Bar (☎ 2266 8998; Faneromenis; snacks €3.50, juice from €3; 8.30am-7pm Mon-Sat) A fabulous breakfast spot that turns into a fun bar at night.

Drinking & Entertainment

Explore the bar scene in the Old Town for the most gorgeous spots:

Hammam (☎ 2276 6202; Soutsou 9) Right behind Hamam Omerye, this heavenly old colonial house, with a grand arched door and beautifully tiled floors, is perfect for sitting under the stars and sipping a cocktail beneath the aromatic fig tree. The music is good and the atmosphere relaxed. It's superpopular and always packed.

our pick **Oktana** (☎ 2276 0099; Aristidou 6) One of Lefkosia's most popular bars, this place will serve just as well as a cafe, though it's at its most packed in the evening. There is a fantastic garden at the back, a bookshop and interior seating area in the old house, where Oktana is set, and a wide range of board games that are happily perused by the Lefkosians. Try their crêpes.

Uqbar (☎ 2276 0099; Aristidou 6) Owned by the same people as Oktana, this is an interior basement space that's favoured by the nargile smokers, who lounge around on the large cushions, chat each other up and sip cocktails.

Brew (☎ 2210 0133; Ippocratous 30) A gorgeous space that stretches through the ground floor of an old mansion, Brew is airy, spacious, with good music, painted white wood furniture and lots of tea, cocktails and food.

Inofroudistiriou (☎ 99 788 486; Areos 42) A bit of a mouthful, we agree, but this place has one of the loveliest gardens in town. It's popular with the hippies too, so you might get a juggling act while you drink.

Getting There & Away

Buses leave from several stands around the old city wall, except on Sunday.

From Plateia Solomou, **Intercity** (Green Bus; ☎ 2464 3492) runs regularly to Larnaka (€10, 45 minutes); **Alepa** (☎ 2266 4636) and **LLL Bus** (☎ 2266 5814) operate services to Lemesos (€10, one hour). Alepa also has a daily bus from Tripolis Bastion to Pafos (€10, 2½ hours). **Eman** (☎ 2372 1321) goes from Constanza Bastion to Agia Napa (€10, one hour).

For the Troodos, **Clarios** (☎ 2275 3234; Constanza Bastion) has a morning bus to Kakopetria (€12, one hour) and Troodos town (€10, 1½ hours). **Pedoulas-Platres Bus** (☎ 9961 8865, 2295 2437; Leonidou 34) runs a daily bus at 12.15pm Monday to Saturday to Pedoulas and Platres (€10, 2 hours 30 minutes). The Saturday bus doesn't continue to Platres. **Kambos** (☎ 9962 3604) runs from Tripolis Bastion to Kykkos Monastery (€12, 2½ hours).

Behind Podocataro Bastion, **Travel & Express** (☎ 7777 7474; www.travelexpress.com.cy; Salaminos) has frequent service-taxis to Larnaka (€9, one hour), Lemesos (€12, 1½ hours) and Pafos (€22, 2½ hours).

For car hire, try **Petsas** (☎ 7777 1515; Kostaki Pantelidi 24; per day from €20).

LARNAKA ΛΑΡΝΑΚΑ

pop 71,740

Calmer and friendlier than the other coastal towns, Larnaka has the beautiful Old Turkish quarter, a maze of whitewashed, sleepy streets that hide numerous ceramics studios. Ancient Cypriot crafts thrive among the shabby streets that surround the beautiful Agios Lazaros church.

Back from the seafront are the **CTO** (☎ 2465 4322; Plateia Vasileos Pavlou; 8.15am-2.30pm & 3-6.15pm Mon-Fri, to 1pm Sat, closed Wed afternoon), the post office and several banks. For internet access, try **Livadhiotis Hotel** (☎ 2462 6222; Nikolaou Rossou 50; per hr €2) opposite the HI Hostel.

Sights

In the old town, **Agios Lazaros church** (Agiou Lazarou; 8am-12.30pm & 3.30-6.30pm) contains fabulous icons and the tomb of Lazarus. Near the tourist office, **Pierides Museum** (☎ 2481 4555; Zinonos Kitieos 4; admission €2; 9am-4pm Mon-Thu, to 1pm Fri & Sat) displays an amazing collection of folk art amassed by the kleptomaniac Pierides family. Larnaka also has a **castle**, a **museum** and several **mosques**; the tourist office has details.

Sleeping & Eating

HI Hostel (☎ 2462 8811; Nikolaou Rossou 27; dm €10) Upstairs by the Bekir Pasa mosque, the hostel is old and creaky but OK for the money. Family rooms sleep four.

Prasino Amaxoudi (☎ 2462 2939; Agias Faneromenis; mains €5; noon-10pm) For a fantastic yet cheap kebab, right next to the mosque.

Art Café 1900 (☎ 2465 3027; Stasinou 6; mains from €8; from 6pm, closed Tue) This classy place serves fine wines and even finer Cypriot food in a dining room full of old movie posters.

> **SPLURGE**
>
> **Les Palmiers Beach Hotel** (☎ 2462 7200; www.lespalmierscityhotel.com; Leoforos Athinon 12; s €42-60, d €60-78;) What was once the grimmest hotel in town has been turned into a knockout boutique hotel that has great prices and friendly service to boot. Decorated simply and tastefully, with elegant camel-coloured rooms, Les Palmiers is the town's best sleeping option.

Getting There & Away

Buses stop on the waterfront, opposite the old Four Lanterns Hotel. **Eman** (☎ 2372 1321) and **Intercity** (☎ 2462 3492) run daily to Agia Napa (€4, 45 minutes), except on Sunday. **Travel & Express** (☎ 7777 7474; www.travelexpress.com.cy; Papakyriakou) operates frequent service-taxis to Lemesos (€11, one hour) and Lefkosia (€9, one hour).

For the airport, take a taxi (€10, 20 minutes) or local bus 22 or 24 (€1, 30 minutes, not Sunday) from Ermou. Car hire companies have desks at the terminal.

LEMESOS (LIMASOL) ΛΕΜΕΣΟΣ

pop 160,730

Part beach resort, part economic hub, Lemesos is the second-largest town in Cyprus. Its Old City is a much-renovated, historic part of town with stylish cafes, restaurants, shops and bars around the Old Fishing Harbour. The tourist area is a rather abysmal stretch of town around 3km to the east of the Old City.

The **CTO** (☎ 2536 2756; cnr Spyros Araouzou & Dimitriou Nikolaidi; 8.15am-2.30pm & 3-6.15pm Mon-Fri, to 1.30pm Sat, closed Wed afternoon) is on the waterfront. There are banks all over town. **CyberNet** (Eleftherias 79; per hr €2.50; 1-11pm Mon-Fri, 10am-11pm Sat & Sun) offers internet access in the old town.

Sights

The main attraction in Lemesos is the solid-looking **Lemesos Castle Medieval Museum** (☎ 2533 0419; admission €3.40; 9am-5pm Mon-Sat, 10am-1pm Sun), with Crusader gravestones and Byzantine sgraffito pottery. Lemesos also has a **mosque**, **hamam** and **museum** – the tourist office has details.

About 19km towards Pafos, **Kourion** (Curium; ☎ 2599 5048; admission €1.70; 8am-7.30pm Jul & Aug, 7.30am-5pm Sep-Jun) has the finest Graeco-Roman ruins in the south, overlooking a rugged strip of coast. The nearby **Sanctuary of Apollon Ylatis** (☎ 2599 5049; admission €1.70; 9am-7.30pm May-Sep,

Book your stay at lonelyplanet.com/hotels

9am-5.30pm Oct-Apr) and **Kolossi Castle** (☎ 2593 4907; admission €1.70; 9am-7.30pm Jul-Aug, 9am-5pm Sep-Jun) are open similar hours.

Sleeping & Eating

Luxor Guest House (☎ 2536 2265; Agiou Andreou 101; dm €11, r per person €13;) Rooms at this old-fashioned guest house have lumpy beds and shared bathrooms, but the welcome is friendly.

our pick **127** (☎ 2534 3990; Eleni Paleologinas 5; salads & sandwiches from €5) This is a lovely boho salad bar, with meat options too.

There's a cluster of excellent open-air **kebab restaurants** near the municipal market on Saripolou.

Getting There & Away

Long-distance buses run from the market on Andrea Themistokleous, except on Sunday. **Alepa** (☎ 9962 5027) has several daily buses to Lefkosia (€10, one hour). On weekdays, **Troodos Mountain Bus** (☎ 2555 2220) has a morning bus to Platres (€5, two hours). **Intercity** (☎ 2264 3492) runs from the old port roundabout to Larnaka (€10, one hour), while **Alepa** (☎ 9962 5027) runs to Pafos (€10, 1½ hours) from the seafront.

Travel & Express (☎ 7777 7474; www.travelexpress.com.cy; Thessalonikis) has service-taxis to Pafos (€10, 40 minutes), Lefkosia (€12, 1½ hours) and Larnaka (€11, one hour).

There are numerous car-rental offices on the tourist strip.

TROODOS MASSIF ΤΡΟΟΔΟΣ

Wild and rugged, the Troodos Massif is a haven for walkers and nature buffs. Dotted amongst the black pines are waterfalls, wine-making villages and World Heritage-listed Byzantine churches and monasteries.

The village of Platres has banks, a post office and a **CTO** (☎ 2542 1316; 8.30am-4pm Mon-Fri). Just south of Troodos town is the **Troodos Visitor Centre** (☎ 2542 0144; admission €0.85; 10am-4pm) with a museum, video show and nature leaflets.

Sights & Activities

Nearby Pedoulas has the teeny stone **Church of Archangelos** (admission by donation, key in museum opposite) with hellfire-and-brimstone frescoes from 1474. Near Kakopetria, **Agios Nikolaos tis Stegis** (admission by donation; 9am-4pm Tue-Sat, 11am-4pm Sun) has 12th-century paintings of stern-looking saints.

Other interesting detours include the wine-making village of **Omodos** and the historic monastery of **Kykkos**, with its intriguing religious **museum** (☎ 2294 2736; www.kykkos-museum.cy.net; admission €3.40; 10am-6pm Jun-Sep, 10am-4pm Oct-May). The mountains are crisscrossed by **walking trails** – walkers can pick up trail brochures from the Troodos Visitor Centre.

Sleeping & Eating

There are some choice places to stay and eat in the mountains.

our pick **To Spitiko tou Arhonta** (☎ 9952 7117, 2546 2120; 2-/4-person apt €75/85) This is a traditional house converted for ecotourism in the village of Treis Elies. It has two one-bedroom apartments and one two-bedroom apartment, plus space for a party of six, all self-catering.

our pick **Two Flowers** (☎ 2295 2372; r per person €25 Sep-Jul, full board per person €50 Aug) A lovely little B&B in Pedoulas with 19 simple, clean and bright rooms, five of which sit in an old house that overlooks the valley.

Getting There & Away

A rental car is the best way to get around. On weekdays, **Troodos Mountain Bus** (☎ 2555 2220) has a daily bus from Troodos to Lemesos (€10, 1¾ hours), via Platres (€3, 20 minutes). See p276 for buses from Lefkosia.

PAFOS ΠΑΦΟΣ

pop 47,200

The former capital of Cyprus, Pafos is packed with historical relics…and tourists. Pafos consists of Kato Pafos (Lower Pafos) and Ktima (Upper Pafos). They are connected by a traffic artery. If you find the beach strip at Kato Pafos too developed, head up to quieter Ktima on the hillside.

A private taxi to/from the airport, 8km southeast of town, costs from €30 – you're better off getting a service-taxi.

The main **CTO** (☎ 2693 2841; Gladstonos 3; 8.15am-2.30pm & 3-6.15pm Mon-Fri, to 1.30pm Sat, closed Wed afternoon) is just down from Ktima's main square. There are banks and post offices in both Ktima and Kato Pafos. **Maroushia Internet** (☎ 2694 7240; Plateia Kennedy 6, Ktima; per hr €3; 10am-11pm Mon-Sat, 3-10pm Sun) is the best internet cafe.

Sights

Pafos Archaeological Site (☎ 2694 0217; admission €3.40; 🕑 8am-7.30pm) has astounding Roman mosaics, many featuring the inebriated exploits of Dionysus.

The Unesco World Heritage site, **Tombs of the Kings** (☎ 2694 0295; admission €1.70; 🕑 8.30am-7.30pm May-Sep, 8.30am-5pm Oct-Apr), was hewn by hand in the 3rd century BC. Pafos also has a **castle**, a **Roman basilica** and several **museums**.

Sleeping & Eating

our pick Pyramos Hotel (☎ 2693 0222; www.pyramos-hotel.com; Agias Anastasias 4, Kato Pafos; s/d €45/55) A marvellous change from the old Pyramos, the newly refurbished hotel is gleaming, tasteful and well-equipped. The 21 rooms are simple but just right, with orange bed throws and stylishly tiled modern showers. There is free wi-fi in the lobby and cafe (nonguests can use the wi-fi in the cafe if they are drinking). The service is friendly. One of the best small hotels in Kato Pafos.

Kiniras Hotel (☎ 2694 1604; www.kiniras.cy.net; Arhiepiskopou Makariou III 91, Ktima; s €45-60, d €60-85; ❄) A sweet hotel, with an elegant courtyard full of statuary and potted plants and a good restaurant.

Nikos Tyrimos Fish Tavern (☎ 2694 2846; Agapinoros 71, Kato Pafos; fish dishes from €8) Inland from the tourist strip, Tyrimos serves fabulous fish, cooked the way locals like it.

Getting There & Away

Buses leave from the Karavella bus stand near the market in Ktima, except Sunday. **Alepa** (☎ 2693 1755) has a morning bus to Lefkosia (€10, 2½ hours) via Lemesos (€10, 1½ hours) and frequent local buses from Ktima to Kato Pafos (€1, 15 minutes). **Nea Amoroza Co** (☎ 2693 6822) runs hourly buses to Polis (€5, 45 minutes).

Alternatively, **Travel & Express** (☎ 7777 7474; www.travelexpress.com.cy; Evagora Pallikaridi, Ktima) has frequent service-taxis to Lemesos (€10, 40 minutes) and other main cities on the island.

Dozens of hire places in Kato Pafos rent bikes, mopeds and cars.

POLIS ΠΟΛΙΣ

Built over the ruins of ancient Marion, Polis is the Mediterranean the way it used to be – orange groves above a pretty beach and small *tavernas* around the village square. There's a **CTO** (☎ 2632 2468; Vasileos Stasioikou 2; 🕑 9am-1.30pm Mon-Fri, 9am-2pm Sat).

You can hike to remote, empty beaches in the nearby **Akamas Peninsula**. Turtles nest on remote **Lara Beach** from June to August. Top walks include the **Avakas Gorge** on the south coast and the nature trails around the **Baths of Aphrodite**, a natural pool inside a grotto, on the north coast.

Polis square is packed with pavement cafes, and **Bougainvillea Hotel Apartments** (☎ 2632 2201; fax 2632 2203; Verginas 13; studio/apt €50/65; ❄ 🏊) has appealing self-catering apartments set around a pool. The Polis **camping ground** (☎ 2681 5080; camp sites per tent/person €3.50/3) is behind the beach.

Nea Amoroza Co (☎ 2632 1114; Kyproleontos) has hourly buses to Pafos (€5, 45 minutes) and weekday buses to the Baths of Aphrodite (€1, 20 minutes).

NORTH CYPRUS

Growing numbers of tourists are exploring the Turkish Republic of Northern Cyprus (TRNC). Historic ruins abound and beaches are breathtaking, but the legacy of 1974 casts a long shadow in the form of looted churches and neglected national treasures.

LEFKOŞA (NORTH NICOSIA)

pop 39,180

Life moves at a snail's pace in the northern half of the capital and the dusty streets are lined with ancient mosques and Frankish ruins. With the relaxing of border restrictions, many people day-trip across from the Republic.

Sights

The well-preserved Kyrenia Gate contains the main **tourist office** (☎ 227 2994; 🕑 9am-4pm Mon-Fri, 9am-1pm Sat & Sun) and there are several banks on Girne Caddesi, the main street. **Orbit Internet Café** (Girne Caddesi 180; per hr 2TL; 🕑 24hr) has fast connections.

Just inside the walls, the **Mevlevi Shrine Museum** (☎ 227 1283; Girne Caddesi; admission TL5; 🕑 9am-1pm & 2-4.45pm Mon-Fri) tells the story of a local sect of whirling Sufi dervishes (Muslim mystics).

The historic Selimiye quarter is dominated by the grand **Selimiye Mosque** (San Sophia Mosque, Agios Nikolaos Cathedral; Selimiye Sokak), built as a cathedral between 1209 and 1326.

Book your stay at lonelyplanet.com/hotels

CROSSING THE LINE

Border restrictions were further relaxed in 2005, allowing tourists to cross from south to north (or vice versa) and stay for up to three months.

However, you must leave Cyprus from the same side you arrived on. To avoid ruffling Greek feathers, entry stamps for Turkey go on a separate piece of paper, not your passport. The main crossing points are the Ledra St crossing in Lefkosia, Ledra Palace Hotel in Lefkosia, Agios Dometios/Kermia (west of Lefkosia), Vrysoulles (near Agia Napa) and Astrometiris/Zohdia (near Güzelyurt). Temporary car insurance is available at the border but it's not advisable to take hire cars across (though you can only take cars from south to north, not the other way round) as the insurance on offer can be elusive.

Sleeping & Eating

Seslikaya Otel (☎ 227 4193; Cumhuriyet Sokak; s/d TL30/35) Dust hardly dares to settle at this bright and clean *pansiyon* (guest house) near the main square. Rooms have fans, cartoon bedspreads and tiny TVs.

Saray Hotel (☎ 228 3115; fax 228 4808; Atatürk Meydanı; s/d with air-con TL90/150; P) It's worth upgrading to this tasteful hotel right in the centre for city views, tiny balconies and luscious deep-pile carpets.

our pick Bereket (☎ 227 1166; Irfan Bey Sokak; pide & lahmacun 7-10TL; lunch) Ahmet makes the best pide and *lahmacun* (Turkish-style pizza with minced lamb) in town, in his stone oven.

Getting There & Around

A private taxi to/from Ercan airport costs TL30 (40 minutes).

The bus station is north of the centre on Gazeteci Kemal Aşik Caddesi. Buses leave regularly for Girne (TL3, 30 minutes). **İtimat** (☎ 227 1617) minibuses to Gazimağusa (TL5, one hour) leave half-hourly from Kaymakli Yolu Sokak.

Kombos (☎ 227 2929) service-taxis to Girne (TL3, 30 minutes) run from Mevlevi Tekke Sokak inside the walls.

For car hire, try **Sun Rent-a-Car** (☎ 227 2303; www.sunrentacar.com; Abdi Ipekci Ave 10; per day from 47TL).

GIRNE (KYRENIA)

pop 14,200

Girne's picturesque stone harbour ends abruptly at a looming Byzantine castle. The old part of Girne is delightful, but the surrounding countryside is vanishing under a sea of holiday homes. The **tourist office** (☎ 815 2145; 9am-5pm) is at the west end of the harbour.

Dominating the seafront, **Kyrenia Castle & Shipwreck Museum** (Girne Kalesi; ☎ 815 2142; admission TL12; 9am-4pm) has spooky dungeons and a 5000-year-old shipwreck. The tourist office has details of other **museums** in town.

Draped along the highest, rockiest ridge above Girne, **St Hilarion Castle** (admission TL7; 9am-6pm) offers stupendous views over the coast. Nearby are Byzantine cathedral ruins at **Bellapais** (admission TL9; 9am-6pm).

Sleeping & Eating

Bingöl Guest House (☎ 815 2749; Efeler Sokak; r from TL30) Below the main roundabout, this workers' hostel is grungy but cheap – the tiny rooms have fans and bathrooms. Few women stay here.

White Pearl Hotel (☎ 815 4677; fax 815 6010; Girne Harbour; s/d TL100/140) The best value of the harbour-front hotels, with cracking seas views and a rooftop terrace.

The waterfront has dozens of expensive **tourist restaurants** serving kebabs and seafood, or there are cheaper **kebab houses** just west of Ramadan Cemil Meydanı.

Getting There & Around

Buses and service-taxis leave regularly from Ramadan Cemil Meydanı to Gazimağusa (TL5, one hour) and Lefkoşa (TL3, 30 minutes). See p275 for ferry services to Turkey. Private taxis charge TL8 to the ferry terminal and TL60 to Ercan airport.

Dozens of rental firms on Ziya Rifki Caddesi rent out mopeds and cars.

AROUND NORTH CYPRUS

In the island's northwest, the ancient walled city of **Gazimağusa** (Famagusta) is dotted with ruined Frankish churches. There's a **tourist office** (☎ 366 2864; Akkule Bastion, İstiklal Caddesi; 7.30am-4pm Mon-Fri, 9am-6pm Sat & Sun) and several cheap hotels.

Buses and service-taxis run here from Girne and Lefkoşa. See p275 for ferries to Turkey.

About 9km north of Gazimağusa are the impressive but overgrown Graeco-Roman ruins of **Salamis** (admission TL12; 8am-6pm), overlooking a sandy beach with interesting snorkelling – a return taxi from Gazimağusa costs TL35.

A reminder of what Cyprus was like before partition, the remote **Karpas Peninsula** has incredible **beaches**, Byzantine **basilicas**, a handful of unmolested Greek Orthodox **monasteries** and the romantic Crusader castle of **Kantara** (admission TL6; 9am-5pm). **Altinkum** (Golden Beach) has nesting turtles from June to August.

our pick **Oasis at Ayfilon** (0533 840 5082; www.oasishotelkarpas.com; s/d with shared bathroom UK£24/32, with private bathroom UK£32/38) is a lovely place to stay at.

CYPRUS DIRECTORY

ACCOMMODATION

There are cheap hotels or guest houses in most towns, plus a few camping grounds and two youth hostels (in Lefkosia and Larnaka). Rooms in hotels or guest houses start at €10 in the Republic and TL30 (single room) or TL50 (double) in the North. Prices increase by 20% to 30% from June to August.

ACTIVITIES

All the seaside resorts offer banana-boat rides, scuba dives, boat trips and paragliding. The Akamas and Karpas Peninsulas and the Troodos Massif and Pentadaktylos Mountains are fantastic for hiking and mountain biking.

BUSINESS HOURS

Usual opening times in Cyprus:

Banks Open from 8.30am to 12.30pm Monday to Friday, plus Mon afternoon in the Republic.

Government offices Open 7.30am to 2.30pm Monday to Friday and from 3pm to 6pm Thursday (in the Republic) or Monday (in the North).

Restaurants Open 11am to 2pm and 7pm to 11pm.

Shops (8.30am-7.30pm Mon-Sat Jun–mid-Sep, to 7pm Apr, May & mid-Sep–Oct, to 6pm Nov-Mar) In the major cities there is an afternoon break from 1pm to 4pm. On Wednesday and Saturday early closing is at 2pm, and shops do not open on Sunday.

EMBASSIES & CONSULATES

Countries with diplomatic representation in the Republic of Cyprus include the following, all in Lefkosia:

Australia (2275 3001; fax 2276 6486; cnr Leoforos Stasinou & Annis Komninis 4)

Canada (2277 5508; fax 2277 9905; Lambousa 1)

France (2277 9910; fax 2278 1052; Ploutarhou 12, Engomi)

Germany (2245 1145; fax 2266 5694; Nikitara 10)

Greece (2268 0645; fax 2268 0649; Leoforos Lordou Vyronos 8-10)

Ireland (2281 8183; fax 2266 0050; 7 Aiantas)

Netherlands (2265 3451; fax 2237 7956; Hilton Hotel, Leoforos Arhiepiskopou Makariou III)

UK (British High Commission; 2286 1100; fax 2286 1125; Alexandrou Palli)

USA (2277 6400; fax 2278 0944; cnr Metohiou & Agiou Ploutarhou, Engomi)

Countries with diplomatic representation in North Cyprus include the following, all in Lefkoşa:

Australia (227 7332; Güner Türkmen Sokak 20, Köşklüçiftlik)

Germany (227 5161; Kasım 15)

Turkey (227 2314; fax 228 2209; Bedrettin Demirel Caddesi)

UK (228 3861; Mehmet Akif Caddesi 29, Köşklüçiftlik)

USA (227 8295; Güner Türkmen Sokak 20, Köşklüçiftlik)

See p282 for visa information.

FESTIVALS & EVENTS

As well as national holidays, both sides of Cyprus celebrate numerous festivals, some religious and some laid on specifically for tourists. The tourism websites have dates (see below).

HOLIDAYS

Holidays in the Republic are the same as those in Greece, with the addition of Greek Cypriot Day (1 April) and Cyprus Independence Day (1 October). North Cyprus observes Muslim holidays and a host of national holidays – www.holidayinnorthcyprus.com has dates.

INTERNET RESOURCES

Useful web resources on Cyprus:

Cyprus Tourism Organisation (www.cyprustourism.org) Covers the Republic.

North Cyprus Home Page (www.cypnet.co.uk/cyradise/index.html) Comprehensive coverage.
North Cyprus Tourism (www.holidayinnorthcyprus.com) Covers North Cyprus.
World of Cyprus (www.kypros.org) News, tourist information, weather and more.

LANGUAGE

Cypriots on both sides of the divide usually speak some English, but settlers in the north tend to speak only Turkish.

MONEY

Banks and private exchange offices will change cash and cheques. Prices at most hotels and restaurants include a 10% service charge.

POST

For poste restante, stick to the main post offices in Lefkosia and Lefkoşa. Mail to North Cyprus must be addressed to Mersin 10, Turkey, *not* North Cyprus.

TELEPHONE

Roaming-enabled GSM mobile phones can be used all over Cyprus. Payphones take phonecards, available from shops and kiosks. There are no area codes in Cyprus.

Useful numbers:

International access code ☎ 00 Republic & North Cyprus
International operator ☎ 80000198 Republic; ☎ 115 North Cyprus

VISAS

In both the Republic and North Cyprus, nationals of Australia, New Zealand, USA, Canada and EU countries can stay for up to three months without a visa. When entering the north, you'll have to fill out a small visa application, granted on the spot (free).

Czech Republic

HIGHLIGHTS

- **Prague** Experience Europe's past, present and future in the capital's vibrant mix of history, art and architecture, and nightlife (p287)
- **Český Krumlov** Enjoy lazy days on the Vltava River and energetic nights in riverside cafes (p300)
- **Loket** Discover this sleepy gem, which winds around a serpentine river (p298)
- **Olomouc** Unearth the easygoing appeal of this Moravian student town (p303)
- **Plzeň and České Budějovice** Create your own beer taste test in the 'Big Two' of Bohemian brewing (p298 and p299)

FAST FACTS

- **Area** 78,864 sq km
- **Budget** 700-1000Kč per day
- **Capital** Prague
- **Country code** ☎ 420
- **Famous for** beer, ice hockey, Franz Kafka, supermodels
- **Language** Czech
- **Money** Czech crown (Kč); A$1 = 14.94Kč; C$1 = 16.96Kč; €1 = 26.87Kč; ¥100 = 21.13Kč; NZ$1 = 11.70Kč; UK£1 = 30.32Kč; US$1 = 20.00Kč
- **Phrases** *dobrý den/ahoj* (hello/informal); *na shledanou* (goodbye); *dìkuji* (thank you); *prominňtě* (excuse me)

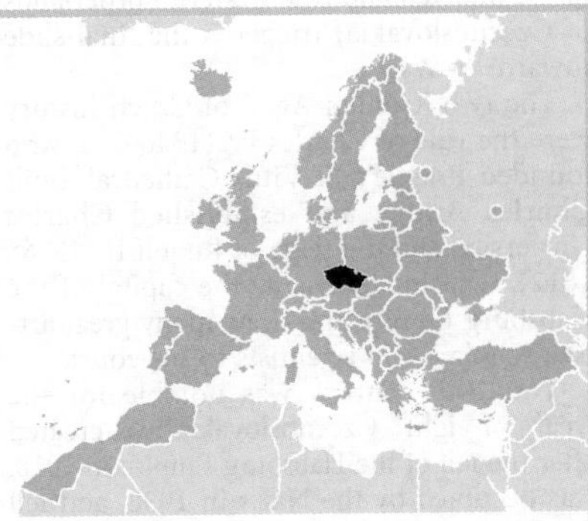

- **Population** 10.2 million
- **Visas** none required for most travellers (see p305)

TRAVEL HINT

Base yourself in Prague's up-and-coming Vinohrady and Žižkov neighbourhoods to enjoy Prague without the tourist commotion.

ROAMING THE CZECH REPUBLIC

Experience Prague's buzz before getting active on Český Krumlov's meandering river. After reflective times in Loket, head to underrated Olomouc.

Located in the absolute centre of Europe, the Czech Republic is likely to pop up as at least a through-road in your travels. Try not to rush your visit though, and be sure to venture beyond the obvious attractions. Definitely spend time exploring the beauty, culture and energy of Prague, and a lazy sojourn on the Vltava River around Český Krumlov is also mandatory. But once you've ticked off those 'Must Do' destinations, venture off the beaten path to fully understand the Czech Republic's thrilling history. Castles and chateaux abound, bringing the past to life, and illuminating the stories of families and individuals whose influence was felt well beyond the nation's current borders. The pristine old towns of Loket, Telč and Olomouc provide your best chance to ease off the travel accelerator, and in quickly changing cities like Plzeň, Brno and České Budějovice, you'll soon discover 21st-century Czech life beyond Prague's tourist bustle.

HISTORY

The Good King Wenceslas of the Christmas carol fame was actually a prince, and the land he looked out over was the ancient territory of Bohemia. Beatified as St Wenceslas (svatý Václav in Czech), he remains the country's patron saint.

The tides of war and imperial domination have washed through Bohemia and Moravia for centuries. Events in Czech history have impacted throughout Europe. Two Habsburg councillors were thrown from a Prague Castle window in 1618 (the famous Defenestration of Prague), igniting the Thirty Years War. Hitler's 1938 annexation of the Sudetenland (the western borderlands of Czechoslovakia) triggered the final slide towards WWII.

The two 'Golden Ages' of Czech history were the rule of Charles IV (1346–78), who founded Prague's St Vitus Cathedral, built Charles Bridge and established Charles University; and the reign of Rudolf II (1576–1612), who made Prague the capital of the Habsburg Empire and drew many great artists, scholars and scientists to his court.

The 20th century was notable for the 'years of eight'. Czechoslovakia was created after the fall of the Habsburg Empire in 1918, was occupied by the Nazis in 1938, and fell to a communist coup in 1948. The hopeful 'Prague Spring', when censorship was relaxed and political prisoners were released, was crushed by the Soviet invasion of 1968.

The Velvet Revolution – the bloodless overthrow of the communist regime – didn't happen until 1989. It was soon followed by the Velvet Divorce of 1993, when Czechoslovakia split into separate Czech and Slovak republics, the former led by famous playwright and former political prisoner Václav Havel.

The Czech Republic joined the EU on 1 May 2004. The Czech Republic is currently scheduled to adopt the euro in 2012.

THE CULTURE

The population of the Czech Republic is 10.2 million; 95% of the population are Czech and 3% are Slovak. A significant Roma population (0.3%) is subject to hostility and racism, and suffers from poverty and unemployment.

ARTS

Famous Czech writers include Franz Kafka (1883–1924; *The Trial, Metamorphosis*), Milan Kundera (b 1929; *The Book of Laughter and Forgetting, The Unbearable Lightness of Being*) and Bohumil Hrabal (1914–97; *I Served The King of England*).

Antonín Dvořák (1841–1904; *New World Symphony*) is the country's best-known composer, and painter Alfons Mucha (1860–1939) is famous for his art nouveau posters.

The films of Jan Hrebejk, *Musíme si pomáhat* (Divided We Fall; 2000), *Pupendo* (2003), and *Horem pádem* (Up and Down; 2004) all cover different times in the country's tumultuous 20th-century history. Buy subtitled Czech films on DVD at Kino Světozor (p296).

ENVIRONMENT

The Czech Republic consists of two low-lying river basins ringed by rounded, forest-clad hills. Acid rain caused by air pollution from intensive industry has damaged the forests in northern Bohemia and Moravia, but the situation has improved since the fall of communism.

Following the Czech Republic entry to the EU, local industries are now forced to adopt stronger environmental codes.

In 2008, the Czech environmental group Friends of the Earth made a formal complaint to the EU that German and Austrian clear-felling of forest just across the border was threatening Czech forests.

TRANSPORT

GETTING THERE & AWAY

Air

Low-cost airlines flying to Prague from other European cities include **bmibaby** (www.bmibaby.com), **clickair** (www.clickair.com), **easyJet** (www.easyjet.com), **germanwings** (www.germanwings.com), **Jet2.com** (www.jet2.com), **Ryanair** (www.ryanair.com), **SkyEurope** (www.skyeurope.com) and **Smart Wings** (www.smartwings.com). Ryanair also connects London with Brno.

Bus

Prague's main international bus terminal is Florenc Bus Station, 600m north of the main train station. The peak season for bus travel is mid-June to the end of September, with daily buses to major European cities. Outside this season, frequency falls to two or three a week.

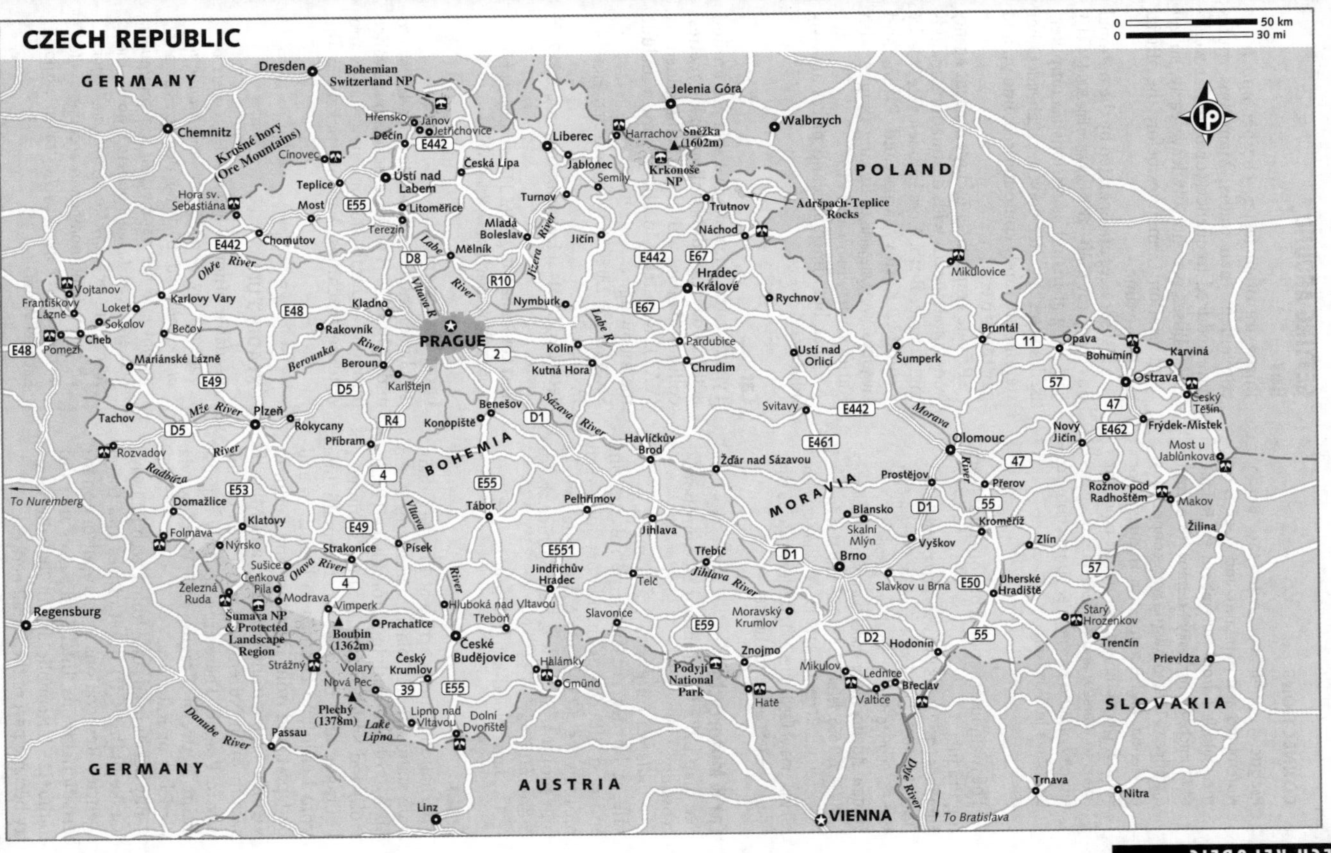
CZECH REPUBLIC
0 50 km
0 30 mi
GERMANY
POLAND
SLOVAKIA
AUSTRIA
GERMANY
VIENNA
BOHEMIA
MORAVIA
PRAGUE
Dresden
Chemnitz
Bohemian Switzerland NP
Krušné hory (Ore Mountains)
Hřensko
Janov
Jetřichovice
Děčín
Ústí nad Labem
Česká Lípa
Liberec
Jablonec
Harrachov
Krkonoše NP
Sněžka (1602m)
Jelenia Góra
Walbrzych
Semily
Trutnov
Adršpach-Teplice Rocks
Náchod
Mikulovice
Hradec Králové
Rychnov
Ústí nad Orlicí
Šumperk
Bruntál
Opava
Bohumín
Ostrava
Karviná
Český Těšín
Frýdek-Mistek
Most u Jablůnkova
Makov
Žilina
Rožnov pod Radhoštěm
Nový Jičín
Olomouc
Přerov
Kroměříž
Zlín
Uherské Hradiště
Starý Hrozenkov
Trenčín
Prievidza
Nitra
Trnava
To Bratislava
Hodonín
Břeclav
Lednice
Valtice
Mikulov
Dyje River
Morava River
Prostějov
Vyškov
Slavkov u Brna
Blansko
Skalní Mlýn
Brno
Svitavy
Žďár nad Sázavou
Moravský Krumlov
Znojmo
Hatě
Podyjí National Park
Třebíč
Jihlava River
Jihlava
Telč
Slavonice
Havlíčkův Brod
Pardubice
Chrudim
Kolín
Kutná Hora
Labe R
Sázava River
Pelhřimov
Jindřichův Hradec
Gmünd
Halámky
Nymburk
Jičín
Turnov
Jizera River
Mladá Boleslav
Mělník
Litoměřice
Terezín
Labe River
Vltava R
Teplice
Cínovec
Most
Hora sv. Sebastiána
Chomutov
Kladno
Rakovník
Beroun
Karlštejn
Konopiště
Benešov
Tábor
Třeboň
Hluboká nad Vltavou
České Budějovice
Dolní Dvořiště
Lipno nad Vltavou
Linz
Český Krumlov
Prachatice
Vltava River
Písek
Příbram
Rokycany
Berounka River
Strakonice
Otava River
Vimperk
Boubín (1362m)
Volary
Nová Pec
Plechý (1378m)
Lake Lipno
Strážný
Passau
Danube River
Šumava NP & Protected Landscape Region
Modrava
Čeňkova Pila
Sušice
Klatovy
Nýrsko
Železná Ruda
Domažlice
Folmava
Plzeň
Mže River
Radbuza River
Rozvadov
Tachov
Mariánské Lázně
Bečov
Karlovy Vary
Ohře River
Loket
Sokolov
Vojtanov
Cheb
Františkovy Lázně
Pomezí
Regensburg
To Nuremberg
E48
E49
E53
D5
E442
E55
D8
R10
R4
2
4
D1
E67
E551
E50
E59
E461
E462
47
57
11
55
D2
39

CONNECTIONS

Prague is well connected to Berlin, Nuremberg and Hamburg, and Plzeň is on the main line from Nuremberg via Prague to Munich. From Český Krumlov it's a short distance to Linz in Austria with connections to Vienna, and Budapest in Hungary. For Poland, Olomouc is a key transit point for trains to Warsaw and Krakow, and the eastern city of Brno has regular connections to Bratislava in Slovakia.

The main international bus operators serving Prague:

Eurolines (☎ 224 218 680; www.bei.cz; ÚAN Praha Florenc Bus Station, Křižíkova 4-6, Karlín; 🕑 8am-6pm Mon-Fri) Buses to destinations all over Europe.

Student Agency (www.studentagency.cz) Central Prague (☎ 224 999 666; Ječná 37; 🕑 9am-6pm Mon-Fri); Florenc bus station (☎ 224 894 430; 🕑 9am-6pm Mon-Fri) Links major Czech cities and provides services to other cities in Western and Central Europe.

Car & Motorcycle

See map p285 for all major 24-hour border crossings.

A *nálepka* (motorway tax coupon) – on sale at border crossings, petrol stations and post offices – is mandatory for Czech motorways (220/330Kč for one week/one month). See www.ceskedalnice.cz for more information.

The legal blood-alcohol limit is zero.

Train

International trains arrive at Prague's main train station (Praha-hlavní nádraží, or Praha hl. n.), or the outlying Holešovice (Praha Hol.) and Smíchov (Praha Smv.) stations.

Prague and Brno lie on the main line from Berlin and Dresden to Bratislava and Budapest, and from Hamburg and Berlin to Vienna. Trains from Frankfurt and Munich pass through Nuremberg and Plzeň on the way to Prague. There are also daily express trains between Prague and Warsaw via Wrocław or Katowice.

Buy tickets in advance from Czech Railways (České dráhy; ČD) ticket offices and travel agencies. Reservations are compulsory on international trains. Inter-Rail passes are valid in the Czech Republic, and in 2009 the country became part of the Eurail network.

GETTING AROUND

Bus

Buses are often faster, cheaper and more convenient than trains. Many bus routes have reduced frequency (or none) at weekends. Buses occasionally leave early, so get to the station 15 minutes before the official departure time.

Most services are operated by the national bus company **ČSAD** (☎ information line 900 144 444). Ticketing at main bus stations is computerised, so you can often book a seat ahead. Other stations are rarely computerised; line up and pay the driver.

Private companies include **Student Agency** (www.studentagency.cz) with destinations including Prague, Brno, České Budějovice, Český Krumlov, Karlovy Vary and Plzeň, and **Megabus** (www.megabus.cz) linking Prague with Karlovy Vary, Brno and Plzeň.

Check bus timetables and prices at www.idos.cz.

Car

Typical rates for a Škoda Fabia are around 800Kč a day including unlimited kilometres, collision-damage waiver and value-added tax (VAT). Reputable local companies include the following:

Secco Car (☎ 220 802 361; www.seccocar.cz; Přístavní 39, Holešovice)

Vecar (☎ 224 314 361; www.vecar.org; Svatovítská 7, Dejvice)

West Car Praha (☎ 235 365 307; www.westcarpraha.cz, in Czech; Veleslavínská 17, Veleslavín)

Local Transport

City buses and trams operate from 4.30am to midnight daily. Purchase tickets in advance from bus and train stations, newsstands and vending machines. Validate tickets in the

READING UP

Readable histories include *The Coasts of Bohemia*, by Derek Sayer, and *Prague in Black and Gold*, by Peter Demetz. For an insight into the paranoia of the communist era, read Milan Kundera's novel *The Joke*. More recent is *Me, Myself and Prague*, an entertaining non-fiction account of life in the Czech capital by Australian author Rachael Weiss.

EMERGENCY NUMBERS

- Ambulance ☎ 155
- EU-wide Emergency Hotline ☎ 112
- Fire ☎ 150
- Motoring Assistance (ÚAMK) ☎ 1230
- Municipal Police ☎ 156
- State Police ☎ 158

time-stamping machines on buses and trams, and at the entrance to metro stations. Tickets are hard to find at night, at weekends and out in residential areas, so carry a good supply.

Make sure taxi meters are switched on.

Train

Czech Railways provides efficient train services throughout the country. For travel within the Czech Republic only, the Czech Flexipass is available (from US$112 to US$268 for three to eight days travel in a 15-day period). The sales clerks at ticket counters outside Prague may not speak English, so write down your destination with the date and time you wish to travel. If you're paying by credit card, let them know *before* they issue the ticket.

If you need to purchase a ticket or pay a supplement on the train, advise the conductor *before* they ask for your ticket or you'll have to pay a fine. Don't pay any 'fine', 'supplement' or 'reservation fee' unless you first get a *doklad* (written receipt).

Check www.idos.cz for train timetables.

PRAGUE

pop 1.22 million

It's Prague's perfect irony. You are lured by the past, but compelled to linger by the present and the future. Fill your days with Prague's artistic and architectural heritage, but after dark move your focus to the here and now in the lively restaurants, bars and clubs in emerging neighbourhoods like Vinohrady and Žižkov.

If Prague's seasonal legions of tourists sometimes wear you down, just drink a glass of Bohemian lager, relax, and be reassured that quiet moments still exist: enjoying a private dawn on Charles Bridge; sipping a chilled beer in Letná above the improbable cityscape of Staré Město; or getting reassuringly lost in the intimate lanes of Malá Strana or Josefov.

Everyday you'll uncover more reasons to support Prague's enduring reputation as one of Europe's most exciting cities.

ORIENTATION

Central Prague nestles on the Vltava River, which separates Hradčany, the medieval castle district, and Malá Strana (Little Quarter) on the west bank from Staré Město (Old Town) and Nové Město (New Town) on the east.

Prague Castle overlooks Malá Strana, while the twin Gothic spires of Týn Church dominate the open space of Staroměstské nám, the Old Town Square. The broad avenue of Václavské nám (Wenceslas Sq) stretches southeast from Staré Město towards the National Museum and the main train station.

All places mentioned in the Prague section of this chapter appear on the Central Prague map (pp290–1) unless otherwise stated.

INFORMATION

Internet Access

Many hotels, bars, fast-food restaurants and internet cafes provide wi-fi hotspots.

Globe Café & Bookstore (☎ 224 934 203; www.globebookstore.cz; Pštrossova 6, Nové Město; per min 1.50Kč; 🕑 9.30am-midnight) Weekly (800Kč) and monthly (2250Kč) rates with your own laptop.

Mobilarium (☎ 221 967 327; Rathova Pasaž, Na příkopě 23, Staré Město; per min 1.50Kč; 🕑 10am-7pm Mon-Fri, 11am-6pm Sat) Also cheap international phone calls.

Laundry

Laundryland (☎ 221 014 632; Na příkopě 12, Staré Město; 🕑 9am-8pm Mon-Fri, 9am-7pm Sat, 11am-7pm Sun) On the 1st floor of Černá Růže shopping centre, above the Panská entrance.

GETTING INTO TOWN

You can walk from the main train station, Praha-hlávní nádraží, to Staroměstské nám (Old Town Square) in around 10 minutes. From Praha-Holešovice, take the metro (10 minutes to Staroměstské nám).

There's a metro station at ÚAN Praha Florenc bus station too – take Line B (yellow) two stops west to Můstek for the city centre.

Medical Services

Praha lékárna (☎ 224 946 982; Palackého 5, Nové Město) 24-hour pharmacy; for emergency service after business hours, ring the bell.

Canadian Medical Care (☎ 235 360 133, after hr 724 300 301; www.cmcpraha.cz; Veleslavínská 1, Veleslavín; 8am-6pm Mon, Wed & Fri, 8am-8pm Tue & Thu) Expat centre with English-speaking doctors, 24-hour medical aid and pharmacy.

Na Homolce Hospital (☎ 257 271 111, after hr 257 272 527; www.homolka.cz; 5th fl, Foreign Pavilion, Roentgenova 2, Motol) Prague's main casualty department.

Polyclinic at Národní (☎ 222 075 120, 24hr emergencies 720 427 634; www.poliklinika.narodni.cz; Národní třída 9, Nové Město; 8.30am-5pm Mon-Fri) English-, French- and German-speaking staff.

Money

Avoid *směnárna* (private exchange booths), which advertise misleading rates and have exorbitant charges. Banks with ATM and exchange facilities are widespread throughout central Prague.

Telephone

There's a 24-hour telephone centre to the left of the right-hand entrance to the central post office at Jindřišská 14 in Nové Mesto.

Tourist Information

Czech Tourism (www.czechtourism.com; Staroměstské nám, Staré Město; 9am-5pm Mon-Fri) has an office in Prague's Old Town Square.

Prague Information Service (Pražská infor mační služba, PIS; ☎ 12 444, in English & German 221 714 444; www.pis.cz) has three main offices:

Old Town Hall (Staroměstské nám 5, Staré Město; 9am-7pm Mon-Fri, to 6pm Sat & Sun Apr-Oct, 9am-6pm Mon-Fri, to 5pm Sat & Sun Nov-Mar)

Main train station (Praha hlavní nádraží; Wilsonova 2, Nové Město; 9am-7pm Mon-Fri, 9am-6pm Sat & Sun)

Malá Strana Bridge Tower (Charles Bridge; 10am-6pm Apr-Oct)

Travel Agencies

CKM Travel Centre (☎ 222 721 595; www.ckm.cz; Mánesova 77, Vinohrady; 10am-6pm Mon-Thu, 10am-4pm Fri) Books air and bus tickets and sells youth cards.

GTS International (☎ 222 119 700; www.gtstravel.cz; Ve Smečkách 33, Nové Město; 9am-6pm Mon-Fri, 10am-3pm Sat) Youth cards and air, bus and train tickets.

Student Agency (☎ 0800 100 1300; www.studentagency.cz; Ječná 37, Vinohrady; 9am-6pm Mon-Fri, 9am-1pm Sat) Air and domestic and international bus tickets. Also has an office in the Florenc bus station.

SIGHTS

Prague Castle & Hradčany

The city's number-one attraction is **Prague Castle** (Pražský hrad; ☎ 224 373 368; www.hrad.cz, in Czech; 9am-5pm Apr-Oct, 9am-4pm Nov-Mar, grounds 5am-midnight Apr-Oct, 9am-11pm Nov-Mar). Castle highlights include jewel-studded **St Wenceslas Chapel** in **St Vitus Cathedral**; the view from the **cathedral tower**; the spectacular **Vladislav Hall** in the Old Royal Palace; and the **Basilica of St George**, Prague's finest Romanesque church. The Long Tour (adult/concession 350/175Kč) gives access to the Basilica of St George, the Convent of St George, the Old Royal Palace, Golden Lane and the Story of Prague Castle Exhibit (essential for taking in the castle's history and scope). The truncated Short Tour (250/125Kč) omits a visit to the Old Royal Palace.

There's no charge to wander around the castle courtyards and gardens, and you can also watch the changing of the guard at noon for free. Tickets are valid for two days, but you can only visit each attraction once. Get to the castle on tram 22 or 23 (from Národní třída on the

GETTING INTO TOWN FROM THE AIRPORT

Prague's Ruzyně airport is 17km west of the city centre. Buy a ticket from the public transport (DPP) desk in arrivals and take bus 119 (26Kč, 20 minutes, every 15 minutes) to the end of the line (Dejvická), then continue by metro into the city centre (another 10 minutes; no new ticket needed). You'll also need a half-fare ticket (13Kč) for your backpack or suitcase.

Alternatively, the **Airport Express** (45Kč; 5am-9pm) goes direct to the Holešovice metro station. Luggage is free; buy your ticket from the driver.

A third option from the airport is the **Cedaz minibus** (☎ 220 114 296) to the city centre at nám Republiky (120Kč, 20 minutes, every 30 minutes 6am to 9pm); buy your ticket from the driver.

Arriving at Florenc bus station or at one of Prague's three main train stations, you can link with the city's excellent metro system to the centre.

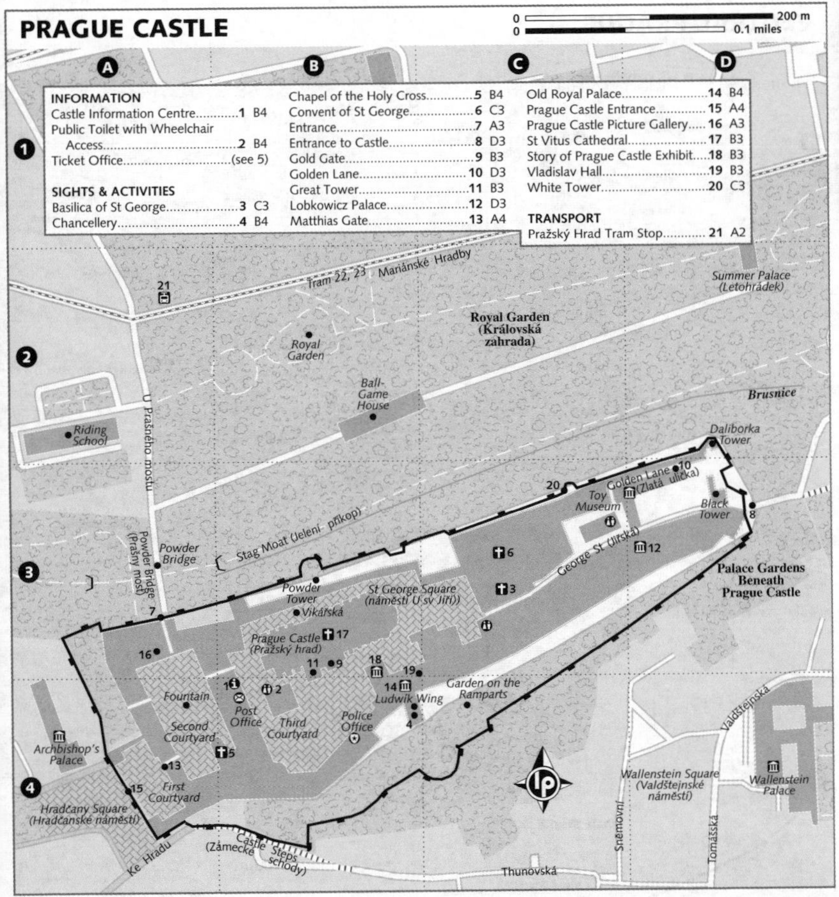

southern edge of Staré Město, Malostranská nám in Malá Strana, or Malostranská metro station) to the Prazský Hrad tram stop.

The **Convent of St George** (www.ngprague.cz; adult/concession 100/50Kč; 10am-6pm Tue-Sun) houses the National Gallery's collection of Czech art from the 16th to 18th centuries. Outside the castle entrance is the 18th-century Šternberg Palace housing the **National Gallery** (☎ 220 514 599; www.ngprague.cz; adult/concession 150/80Kč; 10am-6pm Tue-Sun), the country's principal collection of 14th- to 18th-century European art.

Malá Strana

Head downhill from the castle to the baroque backstreets of Malá Strana (Little Quarter). Close to the cafe-crowded main square, Malostranské nám, is **St Nicholas Church** (www.psalterium.cz; adult/concession 70/35Kč; 9am-5pm Mar-Oct, 9am-4pm Nov-Feb), one of the city's greatest baroque buildings.

To escape Malá Strana's tourist throng, head for **Kampa**, a broad park beside the river. The innovative **Franz Kafka Museum** (☎ 257 535 507; www.kafkamuseum.cz; Cihelná 2b; adult/concession 120/60Kč; 10am-6pm) proves the writer was much more than the T-shirt logo he's become.

Adjacent is the **'Piss' sculpture** by Czech artist David Černý with two stylised figures piddling in a puddle shaped like the Czech Republic. Interrupt the flow of famous Prague literary quotations by sending your own message via SMS to ☎ 420 724 370 770.

CENTRAL PRAGUE

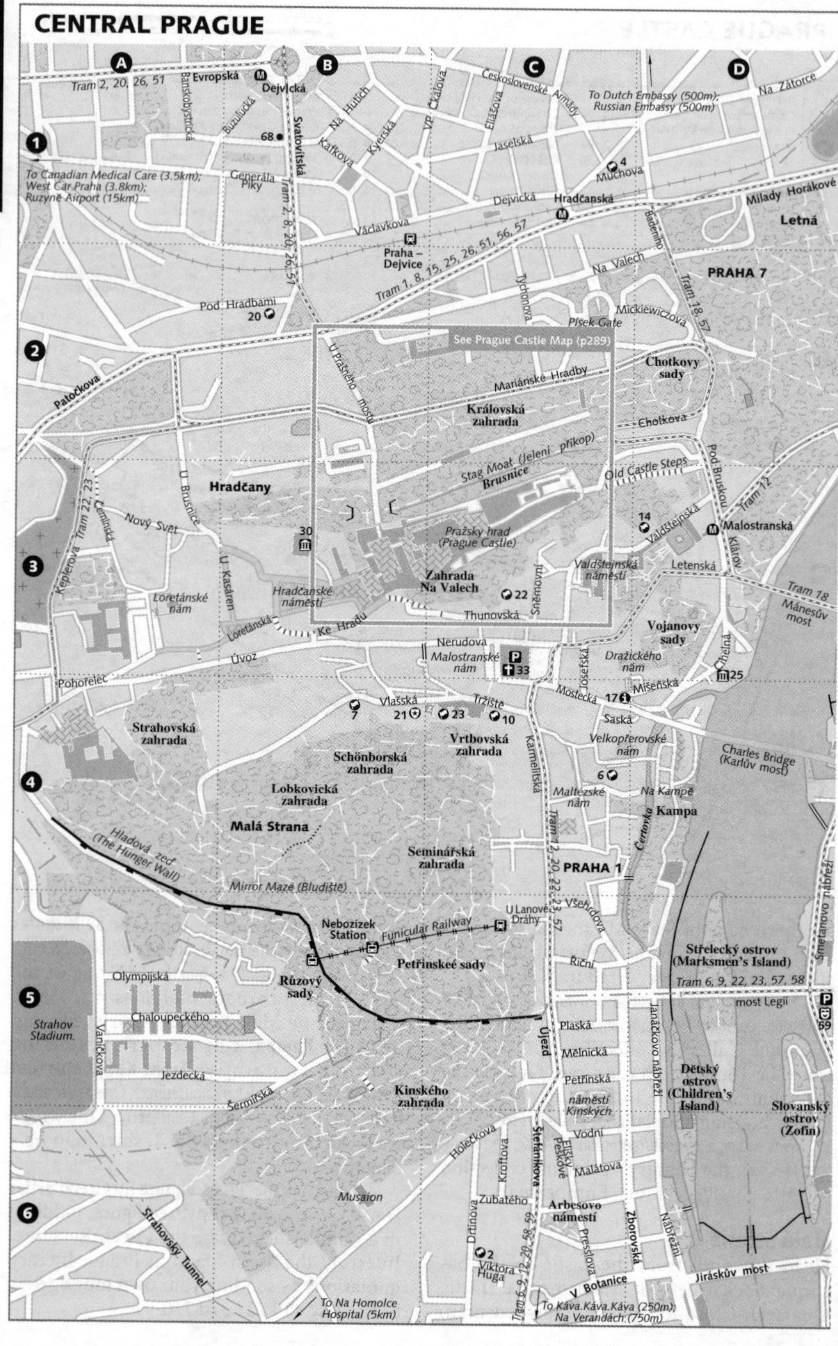

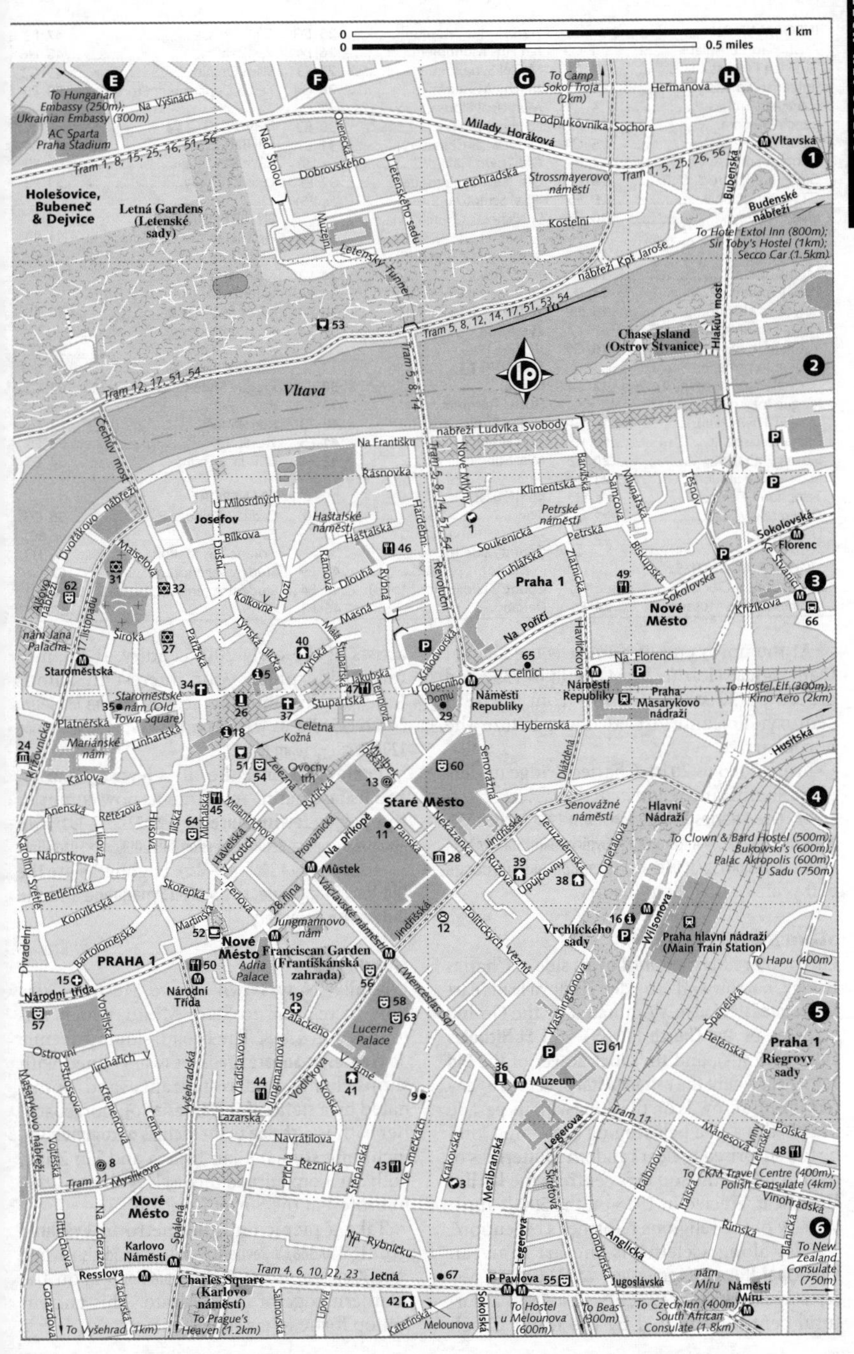
0 1 km
0 0.5 miles
To Hungarian Embassy (250m); Ukrainian Embassy (300m)
AC Sparta Praha Stadium
Holešovice, Bubeneč & Dejvice
Letná Gardens (Letenské sady)
To Camp Sokol Troja (2km)
Vltavská
To Hotel Extol Inn (800m); Sir Toby's Hostel (1km); Secco Car (1.5km)
Chase Island (Ostrov Štvanice)
Vltava
Josefov
Praha 1
Nové Město
Florenc
Staroměstská
Staroměstské nám (Old Town Square)
Náměstí Republiky
Praha-Masarykovo nádraží
To Hostel Elf (300m); Kino Aero (2km)
Staré Město
Hlavní Nádraží
To Clown & Bard Hostel (500m); Bukowski's (600m); Palác Akropolis (600m); U Sadu (750m)
Můstek
Vrchlického sady
Praha hlavní nádraží (Main Train Station)
To Hapu (400m)
Nové Město
Franciscan Garden (Františkánská zahrada)
Adria Palace
PRAHA 1
Národní Třída
Lucerne Palace
Muzeum
Praha 1
Riegrovy sady
To CKM Travel Centre (400m); Polish Consulate (4km)
To New Zealand Consulate (750m)
Nové Město
Karlovo Náměstí
Charles Square (Karlovo náměstí)
To Prague's Heaven (1.2km)
To Vyšehrad (1km)
IP Pavlova
To Hostel u Melounova (600m)
To Beas (300m)
To Czech Inn (400m); South African Consulate (1.8km)
Náměstí Míru
nám Míru
Wenceslas Sq

INFORMATION

Australian Consulate	1	G3
Austrian Embassy	2	C6
Bulgarian Embassy	3	G6
Canadian Embassy	4	C1
Czech Tourism	5	F3
French Embassy	6	C4
German Embassy	7	B4
Globe Bookstore & Café	8	E6
GTS International	9	F5
Irish Embassy	10	C4
Laundryland	11	F4
Main Post Office	12	G5
Mobilarium	13	F4
Polish Embassy	14	D3
Polyclinic at Národní	15	E5
Prague Information Service (main train station)	16	G5
Prague Information Service (Malá Strana Bridge Tower)	17	C4
Prague Information Service (Old Town Hall)	18	F4
Praha Lékárna	19	F5
Slovak Embassy	20	B2
State Police Station	21	B4
Telephone Centre	(see 12)	
UK Embassy	22	C3
US Embassy	23	C4

SIGHTS & ACTIVITIES

Astronomical Clock	(see 18)	
Charles Bridge Museum	24	E4
Franz Kafka Museum	25	D3
Jan Hus Monument	26	F4
Maisel Synagogue	27	E3
Mucha Museum	28	G4
Municipal House	29	G4
National Gallery	30	B3
Old Jewish Cemetery	31	E3
Old Town Hall	(see 18)	
Old-New Synagogue	32	E3
'Piss' Sculpture	(see 25)	
St Nicholas Church (Malá Strana)	33	C3
St Nicholas Church (Staré Město)	34	E3
Staroměstské nám	35	E4
Statue of St Wenceslas	36	G5
Týn Church	37	F4

SLEEPING

Dasha	38	G4
Hostel Rosemary	39	G4
Hostel Týn	40	F3
Icon Hotel	41	F5
Miss Sophies	42	F6

EATING

Beas	(see 40)	
Café Vesmírna	43	F6
Country Life (Nové Město)	44	F5
Country Life (Staré Město)	45	E4
Dahab	46	F3
Giallo Rossa	47	F3
Pastička	48	H6
Siam Orchid	49	G3
Tesco Department Store	50	E5

DRINKING

Čili Bar	51	F4
Káva.Káva.Káva	52	E5
Letenské sady	53	F2

ENTERTAINMENT

AghaRTA Jazz Centrum	54	F4
Club Radost FX	55	G6
Kino Světozor	56	F5
Laterna Magika	57	E5
Lucerna Music Bar	58	F5
Municipal House	(see 29)	
National Theatre	59	D5
Palace Cinemas	60	G4
Prague State Opera	61	G5
Roxy	(see 46)	
Rudolfinum	62	E3
Ticketpro	63	F5
USP Jazz Lounge	64	E4

TRANSPORT

Cedaz Minibus Stop	65	G3
Eurolines	(see 66)	
Florenc Bus Station	66	H3
Student Agency	67	G6
Student Agency	(see 66)	
Vecar	68	B1

At the north end of Kampa is the elegant **Charles Bridge** (Karlův Most), built in 1357 and graced by 30 statues dating from the 18th century. Try and visit at dawn before the hordes arrive.

From 2006 to 2010, Charles Bridge underwent significant reconstruction. Across the river, the **Charles Bridge Museum** (☎ 739 309 551; www.muzeumkarlovamostu.cz; Křížovnické nám, Staré Město; adult/concession150/100Kč; 10am-8pm) showcases 650 years of turbulent history.

Staré Město

On the Staré Město (Old Town) side of Charles Bridge, narrow and crowded Karlova leads east to **Staroměstské nám**, dominated by the Gothic steeples of **Týn Church** (1365) and **St Nicholas Church** (1730s), and the clock tower of the **Old Town Hall**, where the **astronomical clock** (1410) entertains the crowds on the hour with its parade of apostles and a bell-ringing skeleton. Don't be too surprised to hear random mutterings of 'Is that it?' At the square's centre is the **Jan Hus Monument**, erected in 1915 on the 500th anniversary of the religious reformer's execution.

East along Celetná is the art nouveau **Municipal House** (Obecní dům; ☎ 222 002 100; nám Republiky 5; guided tours 150Kč; 10am-1pm), a cultural centre decorated by the finest Czech artists of the early 20th century. If the murals inside pique your interest in Alfons Mucha, delve into the nearby **Mucha Museum** (☎ 221 451 333; www.mucha.cz; Panská 7; adult/concession 120/60Kč; 10am-6pm).

Josefov was once the city's Jewish Quarter, and its fascinating monuments now comprise the **Prague Jewish Museum** (☎ 222 317 191; www.jewishmuseum.cz; adult/concession 300/200Kč; 9am-6pm Sun-Fri Apr-Oct, to 4.30pm Nov-Mar). Highlights are the **Old-New Synagogue**, the **Maisel Synagogue** and the **Old Jewish Cemetery**.

Nové Město

Literally 'New Town', Nové Město is new only in relation to Staré Město, which was founded in 1348. The broad, sloping avenue of **Wenceslas Square** (Václavské nám) is lined with shops, banks and restaurants, and dominated by a **statue of St Wenceslas** on horseback. Beneath is a **shrine to the victims of communism**, including students Jan Palach and Jan Zajíc, both of whom burned themselves alive in 1969 in protest at the Soviet invasion.

Take a picnic and the metro to **Vyšehrad** (☎ 241 410 348; V Pevnosti 5, Vyšehrad; admission free; 9.30am-6pm Apr-Oct, 9.30am-5pm Nov-Mar) on the southern edge of Nové Město. This ancient hilltop fortress has superb views.

FESTIVALS & EVENTS

Prague Spring (www.festival.cz) From 12 May to 3 June, classical music kicks off summer.

Prague Fringe Festival (www.praguefringe.com) Eclectic action in late May.

Khamoro (www.khamoro.cz) Late May's annual celebration of Roma culture.

United Islands (www.unitedislands.cz) World music in mid-June.

Prague Autumn (www.pragueautumn.cz) Celebrates summer's end from 12 September to 1 October.

Prague International Jazz Festival (www.jazzfestivalpraha.cz) Late November.

SLEEPING

For Christmas and Easter, or from May to September, book ahead. High-season prices, charged from April to October, are quoted in the following reviews. These rates can increase a further 15% at Christmas, New Year, Easter and in May during the Prague Spring festival. Some hotels have slightly lower rates in July and August, and from November to March rates drop further.

Hostel.cz (☎ 415 658 580; www.hostel.cz) offers around 60 hostels with online booking. **Prague Apartments** (☎ 224 990 900; www.prague-apartments.com) has a web-based offering of furnished apartments.

Camp Sokol Troja (☎ 233 542 908; www.camp-sokol-troja.cz; Trojská 171a, Troja 102; camp site per person/car 130/90Kč; P 💻) A riverside campground with kitchen and laundry in Troja, 15 minutes north of the centre on tram 5, 14 or 17.

Clown & Bard Hostel (☎ 222 716 453; www.clownandbard.com; Bořivojova 102, Žižkov; dm 300-380Kč, d 1000-1160Kč; P 💻) Party hard in the basement bar, and recharge at the all-you-can-eat breakfast any time until 2pm. Double rooms offer (slightly) more seclusion.

PRAGUE FOR FREE

Prague's great for walking, and some of the city's best sights are free of charge.

- Stroll through the gardens and courtyards at **Prague Castle** (p288)
- Visit **Charles Bridge** (opposite) at dawn
- Explore **Vyšehrad** (opposite)
- Visit the varied locations of the **National Gallery** (www.ngprague.cz) for free from 3pm to 8pm on the first Wednesday of every month

SPLURGE

Icon Hotel (☎ 221 634 100; www.iconhotel.eu; V jámě 6, Nové Město; d €165-210; ⊠ 💻) Here's design-savvy cool concealed down a quiet laneway. The handmade beds are extra-wide, and the crew at reception are unpretentious and hip. Linger in the downstairs bar before exploring Prague's nightlife.

our pick **Prague's Heaven** (☎ 603 153 617; www.hostelpraha.eu; Jaromírova 20, Vyšehrad; dm 320-350Kč, s/d/tr/q from 850/1300/1500/1980; 💻) This quieter spot in Vyšehrad is ideal for travellers not interested in Prague's reputation as a party town. Apartment-style rooms and shiny new bathrooms huddle around a central lounge and shared kitchen. It's a 15-minute journey to central Prague on tram 7, 18 or 24 (Svatoplukova stop). Credit cards are not accepted and there's free wi-fi.

Hostel Elf (☎ 222 540 963; www.hostelelf.com; Husitská 11, Žižkov; dm 320-390Kč, s/d/tr 750/950/1450Kč; 💻) This hip hostel is near Žižkov's bars. Swap tales in the beer garden or grab quiet time in the hidden nooks and crannies. More expensive rooms have ensuite bathrooms.

Czech Inn (☎ 267 267 600; www.czech-inn.com; Francouzská 76, Vinohrady; dm 295-545Kč, s/d/tw from 990/1320/1320Kč, apt from 1650Kč; P ⊠ 💻) From dorms to private apartments, everything's covered at this designer hostel with good transport links. There are no kitchen facilities, but Vinohrady's restaurants and cheap eats are minutes away. Breakfast costs an additional 140Kč.

Sir Toby's Hostel (☎ 283 870 635; www.sirtobys.com; Dělnická 24, Holešovice; dm 330-470Kč, s/d/tw/tr 1150/1400/1600/1800Kč; P ⊠ 💻) Just a 10-minute tram ride from the city centre, Sir Toby's is in a refurbished apartment building on a quiet street. The staff are friendly and knowledgeable, and there is a shared kitchen and lounge.

Hostel U Melounu (☎ 224 918 322; www.hostelumelounu.cz; Ke Karlovu 7, Vinohrady; dm/s/d 400/750/1200Kč; P 💻) An attractive hostel in an historic building on a quiet street, U Melounu features a sunny barbecue area, and shared kitchen and laundry facilities. A few pricier rooms have private bathrooms.

Hostel Týn (☎ 224 808 333; www.tyn.prague-hostels.cz; Týnská 19, Staré Město; dm/s/d/tr 420/1240/1240/1410Kč; ⊠ 💻) In a quiet lane metres from Old Town Square, you'll struggle to find better-value central accommodation. Look forward to occasional church bells.

Dasha (☎ 602 210 716; www.accommodation-dasha.cz; Jeruzalémská 10, Nové Město; s/d from €30/40, apt €70-90) A restored apartment building 200m from the main train station has private rooms and apartments for up to 10 people – a good choice for larger groups. Forward bookings are essential.

Hotel Extol Inn (☎ 220 876 541; www.extolinn.cz; Přístavní 2, Holešovice; s/d from 820/1400Kč;) The reader-recommended rooms here are all excellent value. The cheapest rooms with shared bathrooms are no-frills but spick and span, while the three-star rooms with private bathroom include use of the sauna and spa. Breakfast is included, and the city is 10 minutes by tram.

Hostel Rosemary (☎ 222 211 124; www.praguecityhostel.cz; Růžová 5, Nové Město; dm 450-500Kč, s/tw/tr from 900/1400/1650Kč;) Hostel Rosemary enjoys a quiet location near Wenceslas Sq. Rooms are light and airy with high ceilings; some include a private bathroom and kitchen.

Miss Sophies (☎ 296 303 530; www.miss-sophies.com; Melounova 3, Nové Město; dm 560Kč, s/d from 1790/2050Kč, apt from 2290Kč;) 'Boutique hostel' sums up this converted apartment building. Polished concrete blends with oak flooring, and the basement lounge is all bricks and black leather. Good restaurants await outside.

EATING

Traditional Czech cuisine is strong on meat, dumplings and gravy. Try *knedlo-zelo-vepřo* (bread dumplings, sauerkraut and roast pork), *cesneková* (garlic soup) or *kapr na kmíní* (carp with caraway seed). Prague's also got an eclectic range of international eateries.

Café Vesmírna (☎ 222 212 363; Ve Smečkách 5, Nové Město; snacks 30-70Kč; 9am-10pm Mon-Fri, noon-8pm Sat, closed Sun;) Vesmírna provides training and opportunities for people with special needs. There are healthy snacks like savoury crepes and a 'how do I choose?' selection of teas and coffees.

Country Life Nové Město (☎ 224 247 280; Jungmannova 1; 9.30am-6.30pm Mon-Thu, 9am-6pm Fri); Staré Město (☎ 224 213 366; Melantrichova 15; mains 75-150Kč; 9am-8.30pm Mon-Thu, 9am-6pm Fri, 11am-8.30pm Sat & Sun) These all-vegan cafeterias feature inexpensive salads, sandwiches, soy drinks and sunflower-seed burgers.

Beas (☎ 608 035 727; Týnská 19, Staré Město; mains 90-120Kč) Tucked away in an Old Town courtyard, Beas dishes up good-value Indian vegetarian food. There's another branch (at Bělehradská 90, Vinohrady; ☎ 608 035 727) near the IP Pavlova metro station.

Giallo Rossa (☎ 604 898 989; Jakubská 2; mains 100-180Kč;) Dine in on rustic pizza'n'pasta, or duck next door to the takeaway window and grab a few late night/early morning slices (from 30Kč). Another deal you can't refuse is free internet.

Siam Orchid (☎ 222 319 410; Na poříčí 21, Nové Město; mains 160-280Kč) The waiter's Cambodian, but that doesn't stop this Thai restaurant from being Prague's most authentic Asian eatery.

Na Verandách (☎ 257 191 200; Nádražní 84, Smíchov; meals 150-300Kč) Across the river in Smíchov, the Staropramen brewery's restaurant is a modern spot crowded with locals enjoying superior versions of favourite Czech dishes, and lots of different brews. Na Verandách is a short walk from Anděl metro station.

OUR PICK **Pastička** (☎ 222 253 228; Blanikcá 24, Vinohrady; mains 150-350Kč; from 5pm Sat & Sun) Vinohrady's emerging dining scene around Mánesova now features the unpretentious 'Mousetrap'. Locals come for excellent Bernard beer, huge meaty meals, and to feel good about living in the funky part of town.

Dahab (☎ 224 837 375; Dlouhá 33, Staré Město; mains 200-400Kč; noon-1am) Morocco meets the Middle East amid Dahab's softly lit *souk*-like ambience. Relax with a mint tea and a hookah (hubble-bubble pipe) before diving into tagines and couscous. There's also takeaway falafel and shawarma wraps.

Tesco (☎ 222 003 111; Národní třída 26, Nové Město; 7am-10pm Mon-Fri, 8am-8pm Sat, 9am-8pm Sun) Prague's best-stocked supermarket.

DRINKING

Bohemian beer is one of the world's best. The most famous brands are Budvar, Plzeňský Prazdroj (Pilsner Urquell) and Prague's own Staropramen. Avoid the tourist areas and you'll discover local bars selling half-litres for 35Kč or less.

Cafes

Káva.Káva.Káva Nové Město (☎ 224 228 862; Národní třída 37; 7am-10pm Mon-Fri, 9am-10pm Sat & Sun;); Smíchov (☎ 257 314 277; Lidicka 42; 7am-10pm Mon-Thu, 7am-midnight Fri, 9am-midnight Sat, 9am-10pm Sun;) This courtyard cafe offers smoothies and tasty nibbles. Access the internet (2Kč per minute or 15 minutes free with a purchase) or use the inhouse wi-fi.

Pubs & Bars

our pick **Čili Bar** (Kožná 10, Staré Město; from 5pm) This raffish bar is more Žižkov than Staré Město, with cool cocktails and a grungy style in welcome contrast to the crystal shops and Russian dolls just around the corner.

Bukowski's (Bořivojova 86, Žižkov; from 6pm) This late-night cocktail bar is driving grungy Žižkov's inevitable transformation into Prague's hottest after-dark neighbourhood. Leave the Old Town pubs to the easyJet masses, and sip on cool concoctions here instead.

U Sadu (☎ 222 727 072; Škroupovo nám, Žižkov) Escape the overpriced tyranny of central Prague at this neighbourhood pub in Žižkov. With its ragtag collection of memorabilia including Communist-era posters of forgotten politicians, nothing's really changed here in a few decades. An essential stop before or after gigs at the Palác Akropolis (below).

Hapu (☎ 222 720 158; Orlická 8, Vinohrady; from 6pm) 'Pop round for a drink after work.' Well, that's what it feels like anyway at this shabby but chic basement bar that's a deadringer for a friend's front room. That's if you had mates with superb cocktail-making skills anyway.

Letenské sady (Letna Gardens, Bubeneč) This garden bar has views across the river of the Old Town and southwest to the castle. In summer it's packed with a young crowd enjoying cheap beer and grilled sausages. Sometimes the simple things in life are the best.

CLUBBING

Lucerna Music Bar (☎ 224 217 108; www.musicbar.cz; Lucerna pasaž, Vodičkova 36, Nové Město; 8pm-3am) Lucerna features local bands and almost-famous international acts. Jettison your musical snobbery at the wildly popular '80s and '90s nights (admission 100Kč, open 8pm to 1am Friday and Saturday).

Palác Akropolis (☎ 296 330 911; www.palacakropolis.cz; Kubelikova 27, Žižkov; club 7pm-5am) Get lost in the labyrinth of theatre, live music, clubbing, drinking and eating that makes up Prague's coolest venue. Hip-hop, house, reggae or rocking Gypsy bands from Romania – anything goes. Kick off at the nearby U Sadu (above).

Club Radost FX (☎ 224 254 776; www.radostfx.cz; Bělehradská 120, Vinohrady; admission 120-280Kč; 10pm-6am) Prague's most stylish club remains hip for its bohemian-boudoir decor and its popular Thursday hip-hop night FXBounce (www.fxbounce.com).

Roxy (☎ 224 826 296; www.roxy.cz; Dlouhá 33, Staré Město; admission 120-250Kč; 10pm-4am) In a resurrected old cinema, the Roxy presents innovative DJs and the occasional global act. 'Free Mondays' will give you more money for beer.

ENTERTAINMENT

For current listings, see *Culture in Prague* (available from PIS offices; see p288), www.prague.tv, or the monthly free *Provokátor* magazine (www.provokator.org), from clubs, cafes and art-house cinemas.

For classical music, opera, ballet, theatre and some rock concerts – even the most *vyprodáno* (sold-out) events – a few tickets are usually on sale at the box office 30 minutes before concert time. Tickets can cost as little as 100Kč for standing-room only to over 1000Kč for the best seats; the average price is about 600Kč.

Be wary of touts selling concert tickets in the street. You may end up sitting on stacking chairs in a cramped hall listening to amateur musicians, rather than in the grand concert hall that was implied.

Ticket agencies include the following:

Ticketpro (☎ 296 333 333; www.ticket pro.cz; pasáž Lucerna, Štěpánská 61, Nové Město; 9am-12.30pm & 1-5pm Mon-Fri) Also has branches in PIS offices (p288).

Ticketstream (www.ticketstream.cz) Online bookings.

Live Music

USP Jazz Lounge (☎ 603 551 680; www.jazzlounge.cz; Michalská 9, Staré Město; 8pm-3am) Modern jazz from 10pm with DJs after midnight.

AghaRTA Jazz Centrum (☎ 222 221 275; www.agharta.cz; Železná 16, Staré Město; admission 200Kč; 6pm-1am) Rock up early for a table or book online the day before.

Cinemas

Most films are screened in their original language with Czech subtitles *(české titulky)*, but Hollywood blockbusters are sometimes dubbed into Czech *(dabing)*; look for the labels 'tit.' or 'dab.' on listings. Tickets are around 180Kč.

Kino Aero (☎ 271 771 349; www.kinoaero.cz; Biskupcova 31, Žižkov) This art-house cinema offers themed weeks and retrospectives; it often uses English subtitles.

Kino Světozor (☎ 224 946 824; www.kinosvetozor.cz; Vodičkova 41, Nové Město) The same management as Kino Aero but more central, and with a good Czech DVD shop.

Palace Cinemas (☎ 257 181 212; www.palacecinemas.cz; Slovanský dům, Na příkopě 22, Nové Město) For Hollywood blockbusters.

Classical Music & Performance Arts

Prague's main venues are the **Rudolfinum** (nám Jana Palacha, Staré Město) and the art nouveau **Municipal House** (Obecní dům; nám Republiky 5, Staré Město). See www.obecnidum.cz.

Opera and ballet is performed at the **Prague State Opera** (☎ 224 227 266; Wilsonova, Nové Město) and **National Theatre** (☎ 224 901 377; Národní třída 2, Nové Město). Adjacent is **Laterna Magika** (☎ 224 931 482; Národní třída 4, Nové Město), combining theatre, dance and film.

GETTING THERE & AWAY

See p284 for details of main overland and air routes to Prague and the Czech Republic.

GETTING AROUND

Public Transport

Buy a ticket before you enter a tram, bus or metro – available from metro stations, vending machines, newsstands, tobacco kiosks, hotels and tourist information offices.

Validate your ticket in the yellow machine in the metro station or on the bus or tram. Once validated, a 26Kč *jízdenka* (ticket) remains valid for 75 minutes from the time of stamping (90 minutes if stamped between 8pm and 5am weekdays, or at any time on weekends). Within this period, unlimited transfers between tram, metro and bus are allowed. You also need a half-fare ticket (13Kč) for large backpacks.

There's also an 18Kč ticket, valid for 20 minutes on buses and trams, or for up to five metro stations. No transfers are allowed, and they're not valid on night trams or night buses.

The metro operates from 5am to midnight daily. Night trams and buses traverse the city every 40 minutes.

Taxi

Avoid getting a taxi in tourist areas. To avoid being ripped off, phone a reliable company such as **AAA** (☎ 14 014; www.aaa.radiotaxi.cz) or **City Taxi** (☎ 257 257 257; www.citytaxi.cz). Both companies offer online bookings.

Prague has the 'Taxi Fair Place' scheme with authorised taxis. Drivers can charge a maximum of 28Kč per kilometre and must announce the estimated price in advance. Look for the yellow and red signs.

AROUND PRAGUE

The following are easy day trips.

KARLŠTEJN

Erected by the Emperor Charles IV in the mid-14th century, **Karlštejn Castle** (☎ 274 008 154; www.hradkarlstejn.cz; Karlštejn; 9am-6pm Tue-Sun Jul & Aug, 9am-5pm May, Jun & Sep, 9am-4pm Apr & Oct, 9am-3pm Mar & Nov, closed Jan, Feb & Dec) crowns a ridge above Karlštejn village. It's a 20-minute walk from the train station.

The **Chapel of the Holy Rood** is where the Bohemian crown jewels were kept until 1420. Guided tours on Route I cost 200/120Kč for adult/concession tickets. Route II, which includes the chapel (June to October only), is 300/150Kč adult/concession per person and must be pre-booked.

Trains from Praha-hlavní nádraží station to Beroun stop at Karlštejn (46Kč, 45 minutes, hourly).

KUTNÁ HORA

pop 22,000

In the 14th century, Kutná Hora rivalled Prague as the most important town in Bohemia, growing rich on the silver ore lacing the rocks beneath it. Today it's an attractive medieval town with historical attractions.

The **information centre** (☎ 327 512 378; www.kutnahora.cz; Palackého nám 377; 9am-6pm Apr-Sep, 9am-5pm Mon-Fri, 10am-4pm Sat & Sun Oct-Mar) books accommodation, has internet access and rents out bicycles.

Walk 10 minutes south from Kutná Hora hlavní nádraží to the remarkable **Sedlec Ossuary** (Kostnice; ☎ 327 561 143; www.kostnice.cz; adult/concession 50/30Kč; 8am-6pm Apr-Sep, 9am-noon & 1-5pm Oct & Mar, 9am-noon & 1-4pm Nov-Mar). When the Schwarzenberg family purchased Sedlec monastery in 1870, a local woodcarver got creative with the bones of 40,000 people from the centuries-old crypt. From the Kutná Hora bus station, catch bus 1B and get off at the 'Tabak' stop.

In the town centre is the **Hrádek** (Little Castle), a 15th-century palace housing the **Czech Silver Museum** (České Muzeum Stříbra; ☎ 327

512 159; www.cms-kh.cz; adult/concession 60/30Kč; ⌚ 10am-6pm Jul & Aug, 9am-6pm May, Jun & Sep, 9am-5pm Apr & Oct, 10am-4pm Sat & Sun Nov, closed Mon year-round). Don a miner's helmet to join the 1½ hour **'Way of Silver' tour** (adult/concession 110/70Kč) through 500m of medieval mine shaft. A combination ticket for the museum and the mine tour is 130Kč.

The Gothic **Cathedral of St Barbara** (☎ 327 512 115; adult/concession 50/30Kč; ⌚ 9am-5.30pm Tue-Sun, 10am-4pm Mon May-Sep, 10am-4pm Oct-Apr) rivals Prague's St Vitus in magnificence; its soaring nave culminates in elegant, ribbed vaulting.

There are direct trains from Prague's hlavní nádraží to Kutná Hora hlavní nádraží (98Kč, 55 minutes, seven daily).

Buses to Kutná Hora from Prague (62Kč, 1¼ hours, hourly) depart from Florenc bus station; services are less frequent at weekends. A bus leaves Prague Florenc at 8.10am for an early start.

BOHEMIA

KARLOVY VARY

pop 60,000

According to legend, Emperor Charles IV discovered Karlovy Vary's hot springs accidentally in 1350 when one of his hunting dogs fell into the waters. Now well-heeled hypochondriacs from Germany, Austria and (especially) Russia make the pilgrimage for courses of lymphatic drainage, hydrocolonotherapy and other scary-sounding treatments. The preferred form is to sip the mineral-laden waters from a dainty porcelain cup, but the caffeine-enriched offerings from the town's cafes are actually much tastier.

The Karlovy Vary International Film Festival in early July is well worth attending. More than 200 films are shown, tickets are easy to get, and concurrent events including buskers and world-music concerts give the genteel town a much-needed annual energy transfusion.

Orientation

Karlovy Vary has two train stations: Dolní nádraží (Lower Station), beside the main bus station, and Horní nádraží (Upper Station), across the Ohře River to the north.

Prague trains arrive at Horní nádraží. Take bus 11, 12 or 13 (12Kč) from across the road to the Tržnice station; 11 continues to Divadelni nám in the spa district.

Alternatively, it's 10 minutes on foot: cross the road outside the station and go right, then first left on a footpath that leads downhill under the highway. At its foot, turn right on U Spořitelny, then left at the far end of the big building and head for the bridge over the river.

The Tržnice bus stop is three blocks east of Dolní nádraží, in the middle of the town's modern commercial district. Pedestrianised TG Masaryka leads east to the Teplá River; from here the old spa district stretches upstream for 2km along a steep-sided valley.

Information

Infocentrum Dolni nádraží (☎ 353 232 838; www.karlovyvary.cz; Západni; ⌚ 9am-5pm Mon-Fri, 10am-4pm Sat & Sun); Lázeňska (☎ 353 224 097; Lázeňska 1; ⌚ 10am-6pm Mon-Fri, 10am-5pm Sat & Sun) Maps, accommodation and internet (per min 2Kč).

Moonstorm Internet (TG Masaryka 31; per min 1Kč; ⌚ 9am-9pm)

Sights & Activities

At the heart of the old spa district, on the west bank of the river, is the neoclassical **Mlýnská Kolonáda** (Mill Colonnade; Lazeňská), where bands play in summer. Other elegant colonnades and imposing 19th-century spa centres punctuate the Teplá River, though the ugly 1970s **Hotel Thermal** and the **Vřídelní Kolonáda** (Geyser Colonnade) spoil the effect slightly.

Pretend to be a spa patient by purchasing a *lázenské pohár* (spa cup) and a box of *oplátky* (spa wafers), and sampling the various hot springs (free). There are 12 springs in the 'drinking cure', ranging from the **Skalní Pramen** (Rock Spring), which dribbles a measly 1.3L per minute, to the **Vřídlo** (Geyser), which spurts 2000L per minute in a steaming, 14m-high jet.

You can swim in the **open-air thermal pool** (admission per hr 80Kč; ⌚ 8am-8pm Mon-Sat, to 9pm Sun). Follow the 'Bazén' signs up the hill behind Hotel Thermal.

Sleeping

Accommodation is pricey, especially during weekends and festivals; book ahead. Infocentrum can find hostel, *pension* and hotel rooms. Consider staying in Loket (p298) and visiting Karlovy Vary as a day trip.

Quest Hostel & Apartments (☎ 353 820 030; www.hostel-karlovy-vary.cz; Moravská 44; dm from 410Kč, s/tw from 845/1090Kč; P 💻) The well-run Quest has

LOKET – A QUIET & AFFORDABLE GEM

Avoid Karlovy Vary's high prices by staying in the nearby riverside village of Loket. Loket Castle is one of the Czech Republic's most dramatic structures, and the sleepy village also makes a good alternative to Český Krumlov for river rafting.

The **Lazy River Hostel** (☎ 352 684 587; www.lazyriverhostel.com; Kostelní 61; dm/d/tr 300/750/1125Kč) is an easygoing place crammed with ideas for day trips.

A few enthusiastic locals brew what could be Bohemia's best beer at **Pivovar Sv. Florian** (☎ 352 225 959; TG Masaryka 81).

Buses to Karlovy Vary run throughout the day, or you can walk via a pretty 17km (four hours) track.

spacious budget dorms and apartments with two, four or six beds. Catch bus 8 (12Kč) from Tržnice to the Černý Kůn stop (five stops). Cross the road behind you and walk down the steps 100m to your right.

Hotel Kavalerie (☎ 353 229 613; www.kavalerie.cz; TG Masaryka 43; s/d incl breakfast from 950/1225Kč) Friendly staff abound in this cosy spot above a cafe. It's near the bus and train stations, and adjacent eateries let you avoid the spa district's high restaurant prices.

Eating

Steakhouse Sklipek (☎ 353 229 197; Zeyerova 1; meals 140-180Kč) Red-checked tablecloths and an emphasis on good steaks, fish and pasta give this place an honest, rustic ambience missing from the more expensive chichi spots down the hill in the spa district.

An **Albert supermarket** is near the Tržnice bus station.

Also recommended:

Café Elefant (☎ 353 223 406; Stará Louka 30; coffee 50Kč) A tad touristy, but an elegant spot for coffee and cake.

Kafé Brejk (Stará Louka 62; coffee 45Kč, baguettes 60Kč) Takeaway coffees and baguettes.

Getting There & Away

Student Agency and Megabus run buses to/from Prague Florenc (130Kč, 2¼ hours, eight daily), departing from the main bus station beside Dolní nádraží train station. There are direct buses to Plzeň (84Kč, 1½ hours, hourly).

There are direct (but slow) trains from Karlovy Vary to Prague Holešovice (288Kč, three hours). Heading west from Karlovy Vary to Nuremberg, Germany (4½ hours, two daily), and beyond, you'll have to change at Cheb (Eger in German). Check online at www.idos.cz and www.bahn.de.

Buses to/from Loket run throughout the day (26Kč, 20 minutes).

PLZEŇ

pop 175,000

Brew aficionados flock to this city where lager was invented in 1842. Plzeň (Pilsen in German) is the hometown of Pilsner Urquell (Plzeňský prazdroj), the world's first lager beer, and now imitated around the world. Pilsner Urquell is now owned by international conglomerate SAB-Miller, and some beer buffs claim the brew's not as good as before. One taste of the town's tasty *nefiltrované pivo* (unfiltered beer) will have you disputing that claim, and the original brewery is still an essential stop for beer fans.

Plzeň is an easy day trip from Prague, but the pubs of this university town also reward an overnight stay.

The central bus station is west of the centre on Husova. The main train station is on the eastern side of town, 10 minutes' walk from the old town square. Tram 2 (12Kč) goes from the train station through the centre of town and on to the bus station.

Information

City Information Centre (www.plzen.eu) nám Republiky (městské informační středisko; ☎ 378 035 330; nám Republiky 41; ⏲ 9am-6pm); train station (☎ 972 524 313; ⏲ 9am-7pm Apr-Sep, to 6pm Oct-Mar) Arranges accommodation.

Matrix Internet (Sedláčkova; per hr 40Kč; ⏲ 8.30am-8pm Mon-Fri, 10am-8pm Fri, noon-10pm Sat & Sun) Down arcade beside Oberbank.

Sights

In summer people congregate at the outdoor beer bar in nám Republiky beneath the towering, Gothic **Church of St Bartholomew**. Climb the 102m **church tower** (adult/concession 20/10Kč; ⏲ 10am-6pm Wed-Sat Apr-Sep, Wed-Fri Oct-Dec), the highest in Bohemia.

The **Brewery Museum** (☎ 377 235 574; www.prazdroj.cz; Veleslavínova 6; guided tour adult/concession 120/100Kč; ⏲ 10am-6pm Apr-Dec, 10am-5pm Jan-Mar) is in a medieval malt house. Combined entry (250Kč), including the Pilsner Urquell Brewery, is available.

In previous centuries beer was brewed, stored and served beneath Plzeň. The earliest tunnels were dug in the 14th century and the latest date from the 19th century. Take a 30-minute subterranean guided tour at the **Plzeň Historical Underground** (☎ 377 225 214; Perlová 4; adult/concession 55/35Kč; 🕑 9am-5pm Tue-Sun Jul-Sep, Wed-Sun Apr-Jun, Oct & Nov). The temperature is only 10°C; remember to bring a torch (flashlight).

Across the river is the essential **Pilsner Urquell Brewery** (☎ 377 062 888; www.prazdroj.cz; guided tour adult/concession 150/80Kč; 🕑 10am-6pm).

Sleeping

Autocamp Ostende (☎ 377 520 194; www.ostende.webnode.cz; tent/bungalow per person 100/300Kč; 🕑 May-Sep; Ⓟ) The camping ground is on Velký Bolevecký rybník, a lake about 6km north of the city centre, and accessible by bus 20 from near the train station.

Euro Hostel (☎ 377 373 729; www.eurohostel.cz; Na Roudne 1; dm €14, s/d/tr €39/39/57) Housed in a grand building 400m from Plzeň's old town. It lacks atmosphere, but the location is good. Walk north on Rooseveltova across the river and veer right on Luční.

Pension City (☎ 377 326 069; www.pensioncityplzen.cz; Sady 5 kvetna 52; s/d incl breakfast 1050/1450Kč; Ⓟ) On a quiet street near the river, the City is popular with both local and international guests. The welcoming English-speaking staff are a good source of local information.

Eating & Drinking

Na Parkanu (Veleslavínova 4; mains 100-150Kč) Attached to the Brewery Museum, Na Parkanu lures tourists and locals with good-value meals and a garden bar. Don't leave without trying the *nefiltrované pivo* (unfiltered beer). It's not our fault if you stay for another.

Dominik Jazz Rock Café (☎ 377 323 226; Dominikánská 3; mains 120Kč) Get lost in the nooks and crannies of this vast student hang-out with cool beats and good-value salads, pizza and sandwiches. Downstairs they've just added a nicely grungy beer garden.

Also recommended:

Albert supermarket (Plzeň Plaza Shopping Centre) Catch tram 2 en route to the bus station.

Slunečnice (Jungmanova 10; baguettes 60Kč; 🕑 7.30am-6pm) For sandwiches, salads and vegetarian eats.

Getting There & Away

All trains travelling from Munich and Nuremberg to Prague stop at Plzeň. Fast trains run to/from Plzeň and Prague Smíchov (140Kč, 1½ hours, eight daily) and České Budějovice (172Kč, two hours, five daily).

For Karlovy Vary, take a bus (80Kč, 1¾ hours, five daily). To Prague there are express buses (90Kč, 1½ hours, hourly), and trains (98Kč, 1½ hours, eight daily).

ČESKÉ BUDĚJOVICE

pop 100,000

Post Plzeň, you can conduct the ultimate Bohemian beer taste test at České Budějovice (Budweis in German), the home of Budvar lager. The regional capital of south Bohemia is a picturesque medieval city with one of Europe's largest old town squares.

The **City Information Centre** (Městské Informarční Centrum; ☎ 386 801 413; www.c-budejovice.cz; nám Přemysla Otakara II 2; 🕑 8.30am-6pm Mon-Fri, 8.30am-5pm Sat, 10am-4pm Sun May-Sep, 9am-5pm Mon-Fri, 9am-1pm Sat, closed Sun Oct-Apr) books tickets, tours and accommodation, and has free internet.

From the train station it's a 10-minute walk west down Lannova třída, then Kanovnická, to nám Přemysla Otakara II, the main square. České Budějovice's flash new bus station is 300m southeast of the train station above the Mercury Central shopping centre on Dvořákova.

The **Budweiser Budvar Brewery** (☎ 387 705 341; www.budvar.cz; cnr Pražská & K Světlé; admission 100Kč; 🕑 9am-4pm) is 3km north of the main square. The 2pm tour (Monday to Friday only) is open to individual travellers. Catch bus 2 to the Budvar stop (12Kč).

In 1876 the founders of US brewer Anheuser-Busch chose the brand name Budweiser because it was synonymous with good beer. Since the late 19th century, both breweries have used the name, and a legal arm wrestle over the brand continues.

Sleeping

Motel Dlouhá Louka Autocamp (☎ 387 203 601; www.dlouhalouka.cz; Stromovka 8; tent/s/d 75/750/1000Kč) Take bus 6 to 'Autocamping' from the main square for functional camp sites (May to September), or uninspiring motel rooms year round.

Pension U výstaviště (☎ 387 240 148; U výzstaviště 17; per person 270Kč; Ⓟ) The city's closest thing to a travellers hostel is 20 minutes from the city centre on bus 1 from the bus station to the fifth stop (U parku). From the bus stop, veer right on U výstaviště for 250m. On your left after crossing Čajkovského is the pension. New arrivals after 9pm won't be accepted.

AT Pension (☎ 603 441 069; www.atpension.cz; Dukelská 15; s/d 490/750Kč; P) In a quiet riverside neighbourhood, this great-value spot still has the Czech Republic's biggest breakfasts (50Kč). Don't go making plans for a big lunch.

Eating & Drinking

Fresh Salad & Pizza (☎ 387 200 991; Hroznová 21; salads 70-90Kč, pizza 100-130Kč) This lunch spot with outdoor tables does exactly what it says on the tin: healthy salads and (slightly) less healthy pizza dished up by a fresh and funky youthful crew.

Indická (Gateway of India; ☎ 386 359 355; 1st fl, Chelčického 11; mains 100-150Kč; closed Sun) From Chennai to České comes respite for travellers wanting something different. Request 'spicy' because the kitchen is used to dealing with more timid Czech palates.

Pekarna Rolo (Dr Stejskala 7; 7.30am-6pm Mon-Fri, 7am-noon Sat) Baked goodies, open sandwiches and fresh fruit cover all the bases for eating and strolling.

Albert supermarket (Lannova 22) To the east of the square.

Singer Pub (Česká 55) With Czech and Irish beers, and good cocktails, don't be surprised if you get the urge to rustle up something on the Singer sewing machines on every table. If not, challenge the regulars to a game of *foosball* with a soundtrack of noisy rock.

Getting There & Away

Trains run to Prague (211Kč, 2½ hours, hourly), Plzeň (172Kč, two hours, five daily) and Český Krumlov (44Kč, 45 minutes, frequent).

Heading for Vienna (620Kč, four hours, two daily), change at Gmünd, or take a direct train to Linz (420Kč, 2¼ hours, one daily) and change there. The bus to Brno (194Kč, 3½ to 4½ hours, four daily) travels via Telč (92Kč, two hours). Buses regularly shuttle south to Český Krumlov (32Kč, 45 minutes). Frequent minibuses shuttle from Český Krumlov to Linz in Austria.

ČESKÝ KRUMLOV

pop 14,600

Crowned by a stunning castle, and centred on an elegant old-town square, Český Krumlov's Renaissance and baroque buildings enclose the meandering arc of the Vltava River.

During summer, pigeons dart through busloads of day-trippers exploring the town's narrow lanes and footbridges. Either side of July and August, the town is (slightly) more subdued and secluded. Come in winter to experience the castle blanketed in snow.

For too many travellers, Český Krumlov is just a hurried day trip, but its combination of glorious architecture and waterborne fun deserves more attention. Add in the rugged attractions of the nearby Šumava region, and you can easily fill three days.

If arriving by bus from České Budějovice, get off at the Špičák bus stop, the first in town. The train station is located about 1.5km north of the old town centre; buses 1, 2 and 3 make the run from the station to the Špičák bus stop.

Information

Deli 99 (Latrán 106; 7am-7pm Mon-Sat, 8am-5pm Sun) Offers wi-fi internet access.

Infocentrum (☎ 380 704 622; www.ckrumlov.cz; nám Svornosti 1; 9am-6pm) Transport and accommodation information, maps, plus internet access and audio guides (100Kč per hour). Also a good source of information on the Šumava region.

Laundromat (☎ 380 713 153; Pension Lobo, Latrán 73; washing per load 140Kč; 9am-noon & 1-4pm Mon-Fri, 9-11am Sat, closed Sun)

Shakespeare & Sons (☎ 380 711 203; Soukenická 44; 11am-7pm) English-language paperbacks.

Unios Tourist Service (☎ 380 725 110; www.visitceskykrumlov.cz; Zámek 57; 9am-6pm) Accommodation booking and an internet cafe with international calling.

Sights & Activities

Wander for free through the courtyards and gardens of **Český Krumlov Castle** (☎ 380 704 721; 9am-6pm Tue-Sun Jun-Aug, 9am-5pm Apr, May, Sep & Oct); guided tour 1 (adult/concession 230/130Kč) takes in the Renaissance and baroque apartments. The **Castle Tower** (adult/concession 45/30Kč) provides superb views. The **Theatre Tour** (adult/concession 350/200Kč; 10am-4pm Tue-Sun May-Oct) explores the chateau's remarkable rococo theatre.

Rent canoes, rafts and rubber rings from **Maleček** (☎ 380 712 508; http://en.malecek.cz; Rooseveltova 28; 9am-5pm). A half-hour splash in a two-person canoe costs 350Kč. A canoe for a full day trip down the river from Rožmberk is 850Kč (six to eight hours).

Expedicion (☎ 607 963 868; www.expedicion.cz; Soukenická 33; 9am-7pm) rents out bicycles (280Kč for a day), arranges horse riding (250Kč per hour), and operates action-packed day trips (1680Kč including lunch) incorporating horse riding, fishing, mountain biking and rafting in the nearby Šumava region.

Krumlov Tours (☎ 723 069 561; www.krumlovtours.com; nám Svornosti; per person 200-250Kč) organises walking tours with regular departure times. It's good for solo travellers.

For details on the Five-Petalled Rose Festival and the Český Krumlov International Music Festival, see p304.

Sleeping

Kemp Nové Spolí (☎ 380 728 305; www.kempkrumlov.cz; camp site per person 70Kč; Jun-Aug; P) Located on the Vltava River about 2km south of town. Take bus 3 from the train or bus station to the Spolí mat. šk. stop; otherwise it's a half-hour walk from the old town.

hostel postel (☎ 380 715 631; www.hostelpostel.cz; Rybářská 35; dm/d 300/650Kč) Conveniently situated near good bars in Rybářská, hostel postel has a sunny courtyard with shady umbrellas to wake you up slowly after a big night.

Krumlov House (☎ 380 711 935; www.krumlovhostel.com; Rooseveltova 68; dm/d 300/650Kč; ☒) Perched above the river, Krumlov House is friendly and comfortable, and has plenty of local information to feed your inner backpacker. Lots of day trips are available.

Pension Sebastian (☎ 608 357 581; www.sebastianck.com; 5 Května Ul, Plešivec; s/d/tr incl breakfast 790/990/1490Kč; Apr-Oct) Just 10 minutes' walk from the old town, and therefore slightly cheaper. Larger four-bed rooms (1780Kč) are good for families, and there's a pretty garden for end-of-day drinks and diary writing.

Pension Lobo (☎ 380 713 153; www.pensionlobo.cz; Latrán 73; d incl breakfast 1200Kč) Pension Lobo offers spotless, central rooms and a handy laundromat.

Eating & Drinking

our pick Laibon (☎ 728 676 654; Parkán 105; mains 90-180Kč) Candles and vaulted ceilings create a great boho ambience in the best little vegetarian teahouse in Bohemia. The riverside setting's pretty fine as well. Order the blueberry dumplings for dessert, and don't miss the special 'yeast beer' from the Bernard brewery.

SPLURGE

Castle View Apartments (☎ 731 108 677; http://accommodation-cesky-krumlov.castleview.cz; Satlavska; d incl breakfast 2900-3500Kč; ☒) Furnished apartments are better value than top-end hotels in Český Krumlov. Castle View has seven apartments with spacious bathrooms and decor combining sophistication and romance in equal measure. Infocentrum (opposite) can also recommend other furnished apartments, easily Krumlov's best option for romantic couples.

Nonna Gina (☎ 380 717 187; Klášterіní ul 52; pizza 90-155Kč) Authentic Italian flavours from the authentic Italian Massaro family feature in this pizzeria down a quiet lane. Grab an outdoor table and pretend you're in Naples.

Divadelní Klub Ántré (☎ 602 336 320; Horní Braná 2; www.klubantre.cz; ☒) This arty cafe/bar in the town theatre has a sprawling terrace overlooking the river. There's free wi-fi, and it's always worth dropping by to see if any music gigs are scheduled.

Also recommended:

Deli 99 (Latrán 106; snacks 50-80Kč; 7am-7pm Mon-Sat, 8am-5pm Sun) Bagels, sandwiches, organic juices and wi-fi all tick the box 'Slightly Homesick Traveller'.

Potraviny (supermarket; Latrán 55) Self-catering central.

Getting There & Away

Buses depart from Prague Florenc to Český Krumlov (160Kč, three hours, daily) via České Budějovice. Student Agency leaves from Prague Ná Knížecí (140Kč). In July and August this route is popular and booking several days ahead is recommended.

Local buses (32Kč, 50 minutes, seven daily) and trains (46Kč, one hour, eight daily) run to České Budějovice, for onward travel to Brno or Plzeň.

The most straightforward way to get to Austria is on one of the direct shuttle buses offered by several Český Krumlov companies, which travel to Vienna (1100Kč), Salzburg (1100Kč) and Linz (350Kč). From Linz there are regular trains to Vienna, Salzburg and Munich (Germany).

Public transport to Austria involves heading north to České Budějovice and catching an infrequent train to Linz (2¼ hours).

MORAVIA

BRNO

pop 387,200

Brno's attractions aren't obvious after Prague's showy buzz, but you'll soon see the traditional Moravian reserve melting away in the old town's bars and restaurants. Leave the touristy commotion in the capital, and have a stellar array of museums and galleries almost to yourself.

The train station (Brno-hlavní nádraží) is at the southern edge of the old town, just a short stroll on foot. The main bus station (Brno ÚAN Zvonařka) is 800m south of the train station (Zvonařka) through the Galerie Vaňkovka shopping centre. Brno's Tuřany airport is 7.5km southeast of the train station.

Information

Cyber Café (Velký Spalicek shopping centre, Mečova 2; per hr 60Kč; 9am-11pm) Also provides wi-fi access.

Tourist information office (Kulturní a Informační Centrum; KIC; 542 211 090; www.ticbrno.cz; Radnická 8; 8am-6pm Mon-Fri, 9am-5.30pm Sat & Sun Apr-Sep, 9am-5pm Sat, 9am-3pm Sun Oct-Mar) Sells maps and books accommodation.

Sights & Activities

Above the old town looms **Špilberk Castle** (542 215 012; www.spilberk.cz; 9am-6pm May-Sep, to 5pm Oct-Apr, closed Mon Sep-Jun). Founded in the 13th century and converted into a citadel during the 17th century, it imprisoned opponents of the Habsburgs until 1855. The underground **Casemates** (adult/concession 70/35Kč) house a creepy prison museum, and the main building houses the **Brno City Museum** (adult/concession 120/60Kč).

The gruesome **Capuchin Monastery** (542 213 232; Kapucínské nám 5; adult/concession 60/30Kč; 9am-noon & 2-4.30pm Mon-Sat, 11-11.45am & 2-4.30pm Sun May-Sep, closed Mon Oct-Apr, closed daily Dec 15-Jan 31) displays the desiccated corpses of 18th-century monks and local aristocrats.

Architecture buffs shouldn't miss the 1930 **Vila Tugendhat** 545 212 118; www.tugendhat-villa.cz; Černopolni 45; admission 120Kč; 10am-6pm Wed-Sun), northeast of town, designed by Mies van der Rohe. Catch tram 3, 5 or 11 to the Dětská nemocnice stop. Advance booking essential.

Ask at the tourist information office about Brno's many other galleries and museums.

Sleeping

Obora Camping (546 223 334; www.autocampobora.cz; tent per person 80Kč, bungalow per person 230Kč; May-Sep; P) At the Brněnská přehrada (Brno dam), northwest of the city centre. Take tram 1 from the train station to the zoo and change to bus 103, alighting at the seventh stop.

Travellers' Hostel (542 213 573; www.travellers.cz; Jánská 22; dm incl breakfast 290Kč; Jul-Aug) This place provides the most central cheap beds in the city – for July and August anyway.

Hotel Omega (543 213 876; www.hotelomega.cz; Křídloviská 19b; s/d incl breakfast 950/1450Kč; P) In a quiet neighbourhood, 1km from the centre, this tourist information favourite has spacious rooms with modern pine furniture. A couple of three- and four-bed rooms cater to travelling families. Catch tram 1 from the railway station to the Václavská stop.

Eating & Drinking

Minach (Poštovská 6; per chocolate 13Kč; 10am-7pm Mon-Sat, from 2pm Sun) More than 50 kinds of handmade chocolates and bracing coffee make this an essential detour.

Rebio (542 211 110; Orli 16; mains 70-100Kč; 8am-8pm Mon-Fri, 10am-3pm Sat) Healthy risottos and vegie pies stand out in this self-service spot.

Spolek (542 213 002; Orli 22; mains 70-100Kč; closed Sun) The service is unpretentious at this cool students' haven with interesting salads, soups, pasta and wine.

Pivnice Pegas (Jakubská 4) *Pivo* melts that old Moravian reserve as the locals become pleasantly noisy. Don't miss the wheat beer with a slice of lemon.

Café Alfa (Poštovská 6; 8am-midnight Mon-Sat, 3-11pm Sun) Start the day with coffee and return for Alfa's nocturnal transformation from groovy cafe to funky bar.

A **Tesco supermarket** is 300m south of the train station through a pedestrian tunnel.

Getting There & Away

There are frequent buses from Brno to Prague (130Kč, 2½ hours, hourly), Bratislava (110Kč, 2¼ hours, hourly) and Vienna (200Kč, 2½ hours, two daily). The departure point is either the bus station or near the railway station opposite the Grand Hotel. Check your ticket. Private companies Student Agency and Megabus both leave opposite the Grand Hotel.

Trains run to Prague (160Kč, three hours, every two hours). Direct Eurocity trains from Brno to Vienna (5725Kč, 1¾ hours, five daily) arrive at Vienna's Südbahnhof. There are frequent trains to Bratislava in

BREAK YOUR JOURNEY TO POLAND IN OLOMOUC

Olomouc (pronounced 'Olla-moats') is one of the Czech Republic's most underrated destinations.

The superb **Archdiocesan Museum** (☎ 585 514 111; www.olumart.cz; Václavské nám 3; adult/concession 50/25Kč; ⏰ 10am-6pm Tue-Sun) is world class, and there's good nightlife fuelled by a cosmopolitan student population.

Stay at **Poet's Corner** (☎ 777 570 730; www.hostelolomouc.com; 3rd fl, Sokolská 1; dm/tw/tr/q 350/900/1200/1600Kč), a friendly and well-run hostel. In summer, there's a two-night minimum stay, but Olomouc is definitely worth it.

From Olomouc to Poland there is one direct train to Warsaw at 12.57pm daily (750Kč, six hours), and one to Krakow at 4.57pm (430Kč, 4½ hours).

Slovakia (188Kč, two hours). See www.idos.cz for bus and train information.

ČSA (www.csa.cz) flies from Prague and **Ryan Air** (www.ryanair.com) flies daily from London.

TELČ

pop 6000

Telč's gorgeous old centre is ringed by medieval fishponds and unspoilt by modern buildings. Unwind with a glass of Moravian wine at one of the local cafes. The bus and train stations are a few hundred metres apart on the eastern side of town. A 10-minute walk along Masarykova leads to nám Zachariáše z Hradce, the old town square.

The **information office** (☎ 567 243 145; www.telc-etc.cz; nám Zachariáše z Hradce 10; ⏰ 8am-5pm Mon-Fri, 10am-5pm Sat & Sun) books accommodation in private homes (around 350Kč to 400Kč per person). Internet access is 1Kč per minute.

Telč's pristine old town square, ringed with Gothic arcades and elegant Renaissance facades, is a Unesco World Heritage site. At the square's northwestern end is the **Water Chateau** (☎ 567 243 943; www.zamek-telc.cz). **Tour A** (adult/concession 90/45Kč, in English 180Kč, 1hr; ⏰ 9am-5pm Tue-Sun May-Sep, to 4pm Apr & Oct) visits the Renaissance halls, while **Tour B** (adult 80Kč, 45min; ⏰ 9am-5pm Tue-Sun May-Sep) visits the private apartments, inhabited by the aristocratic owners until 1945.

Penzión u Rudolfa (☎ 567 243 094; nám Zachariáše z Hradce 58; s/d 300/600Kč; ⏰ Jul-Aug), a pretty merchant's house on the main square, conceals a friendly *pension* with shared kitchen facilities.

Telč's hipper younger citizens crowd the buzzy **U Marušky** (☎ 605 870 854; Palackého) for cool jazz and tasty eats.

Five buses travel daily from Prague Roztyly to Telč (124Kč, 2½ hours). Buses between České Budějovice and Brno also stop at Telč (92Kč, two hours, two daily).

CZECH REPUBLIC DIRECTORY

ACCOMMODATION

There are several hundred camping grounds spread around the Czech Republic; most are open from May to September only and charge around 70Kč to 100Kč per person. Camping on public land is prohibited.

In July and August many student dormitories become temporary hostels, and some in Prague are also year-round backpacker hostels. Prague and Český Krumlov are the only places with a range of backpacker-oriented hostels. Dorm beds cost around 400Kč in Prague and 300Kč to 350Kč elsewhere. Book ahead in summer. An HI-membership card is not usually needed, although it will often get you a reduced rate. An ISIC, ITIC, IYTC or Euro26 card may also get you a discount.

Another category of hostel accommodation is *turistické ubytovny* (tourist hostels), with basic dormitory accommodation (200Kč to 300Kč). Rooms can be booked through the local tourist information office. Look for signs advertising private rooms (*privát* or *Zimmer frei* – like B&Bs without the breakfast). Expect to pay from 400Kč to 550Kč per person outside Prague.

Pensions (penzióny) are homely and family-run, offering rooms with private bathroom, often including breakfast. Rates range from 900Kč to 1500Kč for a double room (1800Kč to 2500Kč in Prague).

Hotels in central Prague, Český Krumlov and Brno can be expensive, but smaller towns are usually significantly cheaper. Two-star hotels offer reasonable comfort for 900Kč to 1000Kč for a double, or 1100Kč to 1500Kč with private bathroom (50% higher in Prague).

ACTIVITIES

There is good hiking in the Šumava hills south of Český Krumlov, in the forests around Karlovy Vary and in the Moravian Karst area north of Brno. Canoeing and rafting are popular on the Vltava River around Český Krumlov and the whole country is ideal for cycling and cycle touring.

BUSINESS HOURS

Most restaurants are open every day; most museums, castles and chateaux are closed on Mondays year-round.

Banks 8am to 4.30pm Monday to Friday.

Bars 11am to midnight daily.

Post offices 8am to 6pm Monday to Friday, 8am to noon Sat.

Restaurants 11am to 11pm daily.

Shops 8.30am to 5pm or 6pm Monday to Friday, 8.30am to noon or 1pm Saturday.

DANGERS & ANNOYANCES

Pickpocketing can be a problem in Prague's tourist zone, and there are occasional reports of robberies on overnight international trains. There is racism towards the local Roma population, but Prague's increasingly cosmopolitan society means that abuse directed at darker-skinned travellers is becoming less prevalent.

EMBASSIES & CONSULATES

Most are open 9am to noon Monday to Friday.

Australia (☎ 296 578 350; www.embassy.gov.au/cz.html; 6th fl, Klimentská 10, Nové Město) Honorary consulate for emergency assistance only; the nearest Australian embassy is in Vienna.

Austria (☎ 257 090 511; www.austria.cz, in German & Czech; Viktora Huga 10, Smíchov)

Bulgaria (☎ 222 211 258; bulvelv@mbox.vol.cz; Krakovská 6, Nové Město)

Canada (☎ 272 101 800; www.canada.cz; Muchova 6, Bubeneč)

France (☎ 251 171 711; www.france.cz, in French & Czech; Velkopřerovské nám 2, Malá Strana)

Germany (☎ 257 113 111; www.deutschland.cz, in German & Czech; Vlašská 19, Malá Strana)

Hungary (☎ 233 324 454; huembprg@vol.cz; Českomalínská 20, Bubeneč)

Ireland (☎ 257 530 061; www.embassyofireland.cz; Tržiště 13, Malá Strana)

Netherlands (☎ 233 015 200; www.netherlandsembassy.cz; Gotthardská 6/27, Bubeneč)

New Zealand (☎ 222 514 672; egermayer@nzconsul.cz; Dykova 19, Vinohrady) Honorary consulate providing emergency assistance only (eg stolen passport); the nearest NZ embassy is in Berlin. Visits only by appointment.

Poland Consulate (☎ 224 228 722; konspol@mbox.vol.cz; Vúžlabině 14, Strašnice); Embassy (☎ 257 099 500; www.ambpol.cz; Valdštejnská 8, Malá Strana) Go to the consular department for visas.

Russia (☎ 233 374 100; rusembas@bohem-net.cz; Pod Kaštany 1, Bubeneč)

Slovakia (☎ 233 113 051; www.slovakemb.cz, in Slovak; Pod Hradbami 1, Dejvice)

South Africa (☎ 267 311 114; www.saprague.cz; Ruská 65, Vršovice)

Ukraine (☎ 233 342 000; emb_cz@mfa.gov.ua; Charlese de Gaulla 29, Bubeneč)

UK (☎ 257 402 111; www.britain.cz; Thunovská 14, Malá Strana)

USA (☎ 257 022 000; www.usembassy.cz; Tržiště 15, Malá Strana)

FESTIVALS & EVENTS

Festival of Sacred Music (www.mhf-brno.cz) Easter in Brno.

Prague Spring (www.festival.cz) May; international music festival.

Prague Fringe Festival (www.praguefringe.com) Eclectic action in late May.

Khamoro (www.khamoro.cz) Late May's annual celebration of Roma culture.

United Islands (www.unitedislands.cz) June; World music festival, Prague.

Five-Petalled Rose Festival June; medieval festival, Český Krumlov.

Karlovy Vary International Film Festival (www.kviff.com) July.

Český Krumlov International Music Festival (www.festivalkrumlov.cz) July to August.

Dvořák Autumn September; classical-music festival, Karlovy Vary.

Prague Autumn (www.pragueautumn.cz) September; international music festival.

GAY & LESBIAN TRAVELLERS

Homosexuality is legal in the Czech Republic and the age of consent is 15 years old. **Prague Saints** (www.praguesaints.cz) is a comprehensive online source for English-language information and has links to gay-friendly accommodation and bars. Also worth checking out is www.prague.gayguide.net.

HOLIDAYS

New Year's Day 1 January; also anniversary of the founding of the Czech Republic
Easter Monday March/April
Labour Day 1 May
Liberation Day 8 May
SS Cyril and Methodius Day 5 July
Jan Hus Day 6 July
Czech Statehood Day 28 September
Republic Day 28 October
Struggle for Freedom and Democracy Day 17 November
Christmas 24 to 26 December

INTERNET RESOURCES

ABC Prague (www.abcprague.com) English-language news.
Czech Tourism (www.czechtourism.com) Official tourist information.
Czech.cz (www.czech.cz) Informative government site on travel and tourism, including visa requirements.
IDOS (www.idos.cz) Train and bus timetables.
Mapy (www.mapy.cz) Online maps.
Prague Information Service (www.prague-info.cz) Official tourist site for Prague.
PragueTV (www.praguetv.cz) Prague events and entertainment listings.
Radio Prague (www.radio.cz) Dedicated to Czech news, language and culture.

MONEY

Czech crown (Koruna česká, or Kč) banknotes come in denominations of 20, 50, 100, 200, 500, 1000, 2000 and 5000Kč, and coins in one, two, five, 10, 20 and 50Kč.

Keep small change for use in public toilets, telephones and tram-ticket machines, and keep small denomination notes for shops, cafes and restaurants. Changing larger notes from ATMs can be difficult.

Exchanging Money

There's a nationwide network of ATMs *(bankomaty)*. The main banks are the best places to change cash and travellers cheques or get a cash advance on Visa or MasterCard.

Beware of the private exchange offices *(směnárna)*, especially in Prague – they advertise misleading rates and often charge exorbitant commissions or 'handling fees'.

Credit cards are widely accepted in petrol stations, midrange and top-end hotels, restaurants and shops.

Tipping

Tipping in restaurants is optional, but increasingly expected in Prague. If there is no service charge you should certainly round up the bill to the next 10Kč or 20Kč (5% to 10% is normal in Prague). The same applies to tipping taxi drivers.

POST

General delivery mail can be addressed to Poste Restante, Pošta 1, in most major cities. For Prague, the address is Poste Restante, Jindřišská 14, 11000 Praha 1, Czech Republic. International postcards cost 15Kč.

TELEPHONE

All Czech phone numbers have nine digits – you have to dial all nine for any call, local or long distance. Make international calls at main post offices, via Skype, or from phonecard booths. The international access code is ☎ 00. The Czech Republic's country code is ☎ 420.

Payphones are widespread, some taking coins and some phonecards. Buy phonecards from post offices, hotels, newsstands and department stores for 150Kč or 1000Kč.

Mobile-phone coverage (GSM 900) is excellent. If you're from Europe, Australia or New Zealand, your own mobile phone should be compatible. Get a Czech SIM card for around 500Kč (including 300Kč of calling credit).

Local mobile-phone numbers start with the numbers ☎ 601-608 and 720-779.

VISAS

Everyone requires a valid passport (or identity card for EU citizens) to enter the Czech Republic.

Since March 2008, the Czech Republic has been part of the Schengen Agreement, and citizens of EU and EEA countries do not need a visa. Citizens of Australia, Canada, Israel, Japan, Malaysia, New Zealand, Singapore, the US and 22 other countries can stay for up to 90 days in a six-month period without a visa. If you are also travelling in other Schengen Agreement countries, note you can still only stay for a maximum of 90 days in any six-month period.

For travellers from other countries, obtaining a Schengen Visa is required. You can only do this from your country of residence. Most – but not all – Schengen Agreement countries will honour Schengen Visas issued by other member countries. Visa regulations often change. See www.czech.cz.

Denmark

HIGHLIGHTS

- **Copenhagen** Historical interest aplenty, cool cafes, cutting-edge design, cosy bars and lively clubs (p311)
- **Helsingør** Soak up the history in Hamlet's castle, one of the country's outstanding Renaissance castles (p318)
- **Bornholm** Escape to empty beaches and extensive forests, and relax beside picture-postcard harbours on this idyllic island (p319)
- **Skagen** Watch angry seas collide above luminous Skagen on Denmark's slender northern tip (p325)

FAST FACTS

- **Area** 43,075 sq km (the same as Switzerland)
- **Budget** Dkr400 to Dkr550 per day
- **Capital** Copenhagen
- **Country code** ☎ 45
- **Famous for** Hans Christian Andersen, the Little Mermaid, marauding Vikings
- **Language** Danish
- **Money** Danish krona (Dkr); A$1 = Dkr4.13; CA$1 = Dkr4.69; €1 = Dkr7.45; ¥100 = Dkr5.85; NZ$1 = Dkr3.23; UK£1 = Dkr8.38; US$1 = Dkr5.53
- **Phrases** *ja/nej* (yes/no), *tak* (thanks), *farvel* (goodbye), *skal* (cheers)

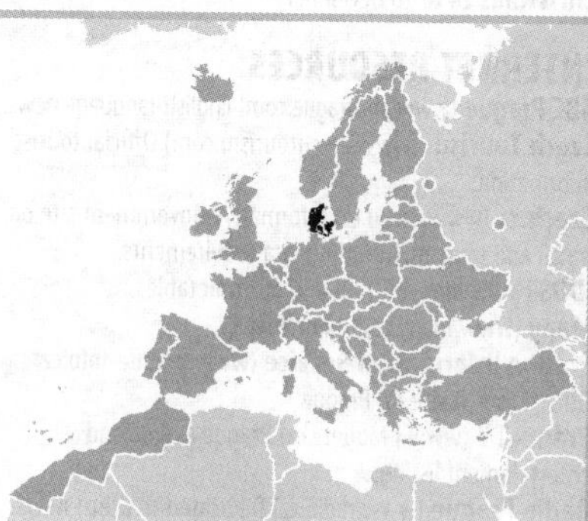

- **Population** 5.5 million
- **Visas** not needed for citizens of EU, USA, Canada, Australia and New Zealand (p328)

TRAVEL HINTS

Rail travel is the best way to go. Takeaway beer and wine are cheap, and there's good value in the bars during happy hour. Cheap and tasty food includes pastries and smørrebrød (open sandwiches).

ROAMING DENMARK

Three days is enough for a taste of Copenhagen, then head to Jutland for a night in happening Århus, on to party town Aalborg and then further north still for a taste of Jutland's wilder, open spaces.

Denmark is the bridge between Scandinavia and northern Europe. To the rest of Scandinavia, the Danes are fun-loving, frivolous party animals, with relatively liberal, progressive attitudes to most things. Their culture, food, architecture and appetite for conspicuous consumption owes as much, if not more, to their German neighbours to the south, than their former colonies – Sweden, Norway and Iceland to the north.

The capital, Copenhagen, is one of the most charming and accessible cities in northern Europe, with excellent museums, shops, bars, nightlife and, in particular, restaurants. Other cities of interest include Odense and Århus, but Denmark's chief appeal lies in its gently idyllic countryside, coastline and history. Make sure to see the Neolithic burial chambers; well-preserved Iron Age people exhumed from their slumber in peat bogs; and atmospheric Viking ruins and treasures.

HISTORY

The Danes themselves are thought to have migrated south from Sweden around AD 500. What we think of as modern Denmark was an important trading centre within the Viking empire and, again, the physical evidence of this part of the country's history is to be found throughout the country today. In the late 9th century, warriors led by the Viking chieftain, Hardegon, conquered the Jutland Peninsula. The Danish monarchy, Europe's oldest, dates back to Hardegon's son, Gorm the Old, who reigned in the early 10th century. Gorm's son, Harald Bluetooth, completed the conquest of Denmark and spearheaded the conversion of the Danes to Christianity. Successive Danish kings sent their subjects to row their longboats to England and to conquer most of the Baltic region.

In 1397 Margrethe I of Denmark established a union between Denmark, Norway and Sweden to counter the influence of the powerful Hanseatic League that had come to dominate the region's trade. Sweden withdrew from the union in 1523 and over the next few hundred years Denmark and Sweden fought numerous border skirmishes and a few fully fledged wars, largely over control of the Baltic Sea. Norway remained under Danish rule until 1814.

In the 16th century the Reformation swept through the country, accompanied by church burnings and civil warfare. The fighting ended in 1536, the Catholic Church was ousted and the Danish Lutheran Church headed by the monarchy established.

Denmark's 'Golden Age' was under Christian IV (1588–1648), with Renaissance cities, castles and fortresses flourishing throughout his kingdom. In 1625 Christian IV, hoping to neutralise Swedish expansion, entered an ill-advised and protracted struggle known as the Thirty Years War. The Swedes triumphed and won large chunks of Danish territory.

Denmark remained neutral throughout WWI and also declared its neutrality at the outbreak of WWII. Nevertheless, on 9 April 1940, the Germans invaded, albeit allowing the Danes a degree of autonomy. For three years the Danes managed to walk a thin line, running their own internal affairs under Nazi supervision, until in August 1943 the Germans took outright control. The Danish Resistance movement mushroomed and 7000 Jewish Danes were smuggled into neutral Sweden.

Denmark joined NATO in 1949, and the European Community, now the EU, in 1973. The Danes offer tepid support for an expanding EU. In 1993 they narrowly voted to accept the Maastricht Treaty, which established the terms of a European economic and political union, but only after being granted exemptions from common-defence and single-currency provisions. They also voted not to adopt the euro in 2000.

In 2004 the country's most eligible bachelor Crown Prince Frederik married Australian Mary Donaldson in a hugely popular and exhaustively covered fairy-tale wedding. They now have two children.

It has not all been fairytales though. Accustomed to being a blameless paragon of international virtue, Denmark has experienced harsh criticism from some unusual quarters. Critics say its increasingly tough immigration laws are proof of creeping xenophobia and racism, earning it a rebuke from the European Council.

Meanwhile, in 2006 the Danes were deeply traumatised by the now notorious Islamic cartoons scandal, in which the national newspaper *Jyllands Posten* printed some controversial depictions of the prophet Mohammed, leading to outrage and violence against Danish embassies in the Middle East. This seemed to have little impact on the popularity of their long-serving Prime Minister Anders Fogh Rasmussen, who was returned to power in 2007 after which he handed over to his cabinet colleague Lars Løkke Rasmussen to take up a new job as NATO Secretary General.

THE CULTURE

The Danes are tolerant and modest yet confident in their country and its achievements. They are an outwardly serious people, yet with an ironic sense of humour closely akin to the English. They have a strong sense of family and an admirable environmental sensitivity. Above all, they are the most egalitarian of people – they officially have the smallest gap between rich and poor in the world – proud of their social equality in which none have too much or too little, although this can lead to a sense that they are somewhat homogenous.

Denmark's population is about 5.5 million, with 70% living in urban areas, 1.5 million of them in Copenhagen. Foreign nationals account for 7.8% of Denmark's population.

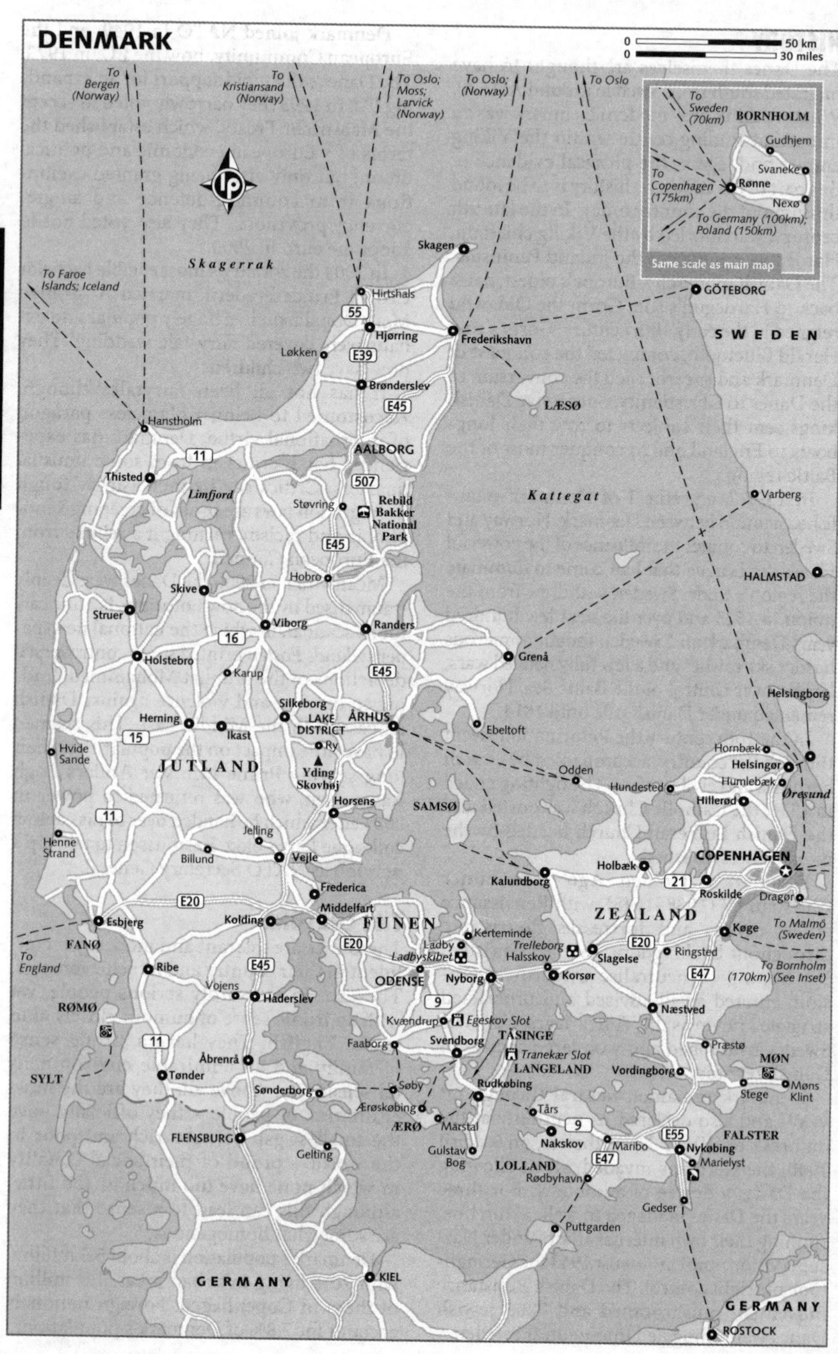
DENMARK
0 50 km
0 30 miles
To Bergen (Norway)
To Kristiansand (Norway)
To Oslo; Moss; Larvick (Norway)
To Oslo; (Norway)
To Oslo
To Sweden (70km)
BORNHOLM
Gudhjem
Svaneke
To Copenhagen (175km)
Rønne
Nexø
To Germany (100km); Poland (150km)
Same scale as main map
Skagerrak
To Faroe Islands; Iceland
Skagen
Hirtshals
GÖTEBORG
SWEDEN
Hjørring
Frederikshavn
Løkken
Brønderslev
LÆSØ
Hanstholm
AALBORG
Thisted
Limfjord
Støvring
Rebild Bakker National Park
Kattegat
Varberg
Hobro
HALMSTAD
Skive
Struer
Viborg
Randers
Holstebro
Grenå
Karup
Helsingborg
Silkeborg
ÅRHUS
Herning
Ikast
LAKE DISTRICT
Ebeltoft
Hvide Sande
Ry
Hornbæk
JUTLAND
Yding Skovhøj
Odden
Helsingør
Humlebæk
Hundested
Øresund
Horsens
SAMSØ
Hillerød
Jelling
Henne Strand
Billund
Vejle
COPENHAGEN
Holbæk
Kalundborg
Frederica
Roskilde
Dragør
Esbjerg
Middelfart
Kolding
FUNEN
ZEALAND
Kerteminde
Køge
To Malmö (Sweden)
FANØ
Ladby
Trelleborg
Halsskov
Slagelse
Ladbyskibet
Ringsted
To England
Ribe
ODENSE
Nyborg
Korsør
To Bornholm (170km) (See Inset)
Vojens
Haderslev
RØMØ
Næstved
Kværndrup
Egeskov Slot
Faaborg
Svendborg
TÅSINGE
Præstø
Tranekær Slot
MØN
Åbrenrå
LANGELAND
Vordingborg
SYLT
Tønder
Søby
Rudkøbing
Møns Klint
Stege
Sønderborg
Tårs
Ærøskøbing
ÆRØ
Marstal
FALSTER
FLENSBURG
Nakskov
Maribo
Nykøbing
Gelting
Gulstav Bog
LOLLAND
Marielyst
Rødbyhavn
Gedser
Puttgarden
GERMANY
KIEL
ROSTOCK
55
E39
E45
11
507
16
15
E20
9
21
E47
E55

ARTS

By far the most famous Danish author is Hans Christian Andersen, but following the 2004 bicentennial celebrations, if they were honest, most Danes would say they had probably had enough of him for a while. This probably goes double for the residents of Odense, whose city has been turned into a permanent shrine to the lanky fairy-tale writer.

For a small country Denmark has had a massive global impact in the fields of architecture and design. Arne Jacobsen, Verner Panton, the recently deceased Jørn Utzon and Hans J Wegner are now considered among the foremost designers of the 20th century.

The last decade or so has seen director Lars von Trier stir up repeated controversy – and win numerous international film prizes – with his challenging films such as *Breaking the Waves*, *Dancer in the Dark*, and *Dogville*, starring Nicole Kidman.

Before the 19th century, Danish art had consisted mainly of formal portraiture. Later in the century, though, the 'Skagen School' evolved towards outdoor painting of scenes from working life, especially of fishing communities on the northern coasts of Jutland and Zealand.

ENVIRONMENT

If you arrive in Denmark by plane at Copenhagen Airport you will see the country's major contribution to improving the global environment: a row of wind turbines. Turbines such as these provide the country with almost 20% of its energy requirements and the company that makes them, Vestas, is the world leader in wind turbine technology. Danes also lead the way in the consumption of organic produce, recycling and environmentally friendly transport: more Danes commute by bicycle than any other European nationality.

Still commonly seen in Denmark are wild hare, deer and many species of birds, including magpies, coots, swans and ducks. Restoration programs have brought some wetland habitats back from the brink, helping endangered species such as the freshwater otter as well as beavers, which have been re-introduced to Denmark. The Danes are particularly proud of their eagles – they have two pairs of golden eagles who live in Lille Vildemose, close to Aalborg on Jutland, and are national celebrities.

TRANSPORT

GETTING THERE & AWAY

Air

The profusion of budget carriers and flights into Denmark from elsewhere on the Continent, Ireland and the UK makes flying here very affordable indeed. If you're coming from European destinations, consider flying into an airport other than Copenhagen, such as Århus or Billund; air fares can be competitive, and the airports are well connected by bus with neighbouring towns and afford fast access to some great parts of northern and central Jutland.

The budget carrier Ryanair, for instance, has regular, cheap flights from Stansted Airport in England to Århus airport and to Malmö, in Sweden (a short hop by rail from Copenhagen). See the following airport websites for full details.

AIRLINES

SAS (SK; ☎ 70 10 30 00; www.flysas.com) is the largest carrier serving Denmark, connecting it with much of Europe and the rest of the world.

Many other airlines fly into Denmark including the following ones.

Aer Lingus (EI; ☎ +353 818 365 000; www.aerlingus.com)
Air France (AF; ☎ 82 33 27 01; www.airfrance.com)
Alitalia (AZ; ☎ 70 27 02 90; www.alitalia.com)
BMI British Midland (BD; ☎ 70 10 20 00; www.flybmi.com)
British Airways (BA; ☎ 70 12 80 22; www.britishairways.com)
easyJet (U2; ☎ 70 12 43 21; www.easyjet.com)
Finnair (AY; ☎ 33 36 45 45; www.finnair.com)
Icelandair (FI; ☎ 33 70 22 00; www.icelandexpress.com)
KLM Royal Dutch Airlines (KL; ☎ 70 10 07 47; www.klm.com)
Lufthansa (LH; ☎ 70 10 20 00; www.lufthansa.com)
Ryanair (FR; ☎ +353 818 303 030; www.ryanair.com)
Sterling (NB; ☎ 70 10 84 84; www.sterling.dk)

MAIN DANISH AIRPORTS

Århus (☎ 87 75 70 00; www.aar.dk)
Billund (☎ 76 50 50 50; www.bll.dk)
Copenhagen (☎ 32 31 32 31; www.cph.dk)

Boat

TO/FROM GERMANY

The frequent Rødbyhavn–Puttgarden ferry takes 45 minutes and is included in train

DENMARK

DENMARK

CONNECTIONS

Denmark's modern and brilliantly efficient transport network is about as well connected to the region and the rest of the world as it could be. Its main airport Kastrup (Copenhagen) offers excellent and numerous long- and short-haul connections while its regional airports Billund on Funen, and Århus in Jutland offer plenty of European short-haul options. Good road and rail connections link Sweden and Germany to Denmark. Ferry links, meanwhile, are plentiful, linking Denmark with all major Baltic destinations and also with Atlantic coast destinations in Norway, Faroe Islands, Iceland and the UK.

tickets for those travelling by rail; otherwise, the cost per adult is Dkr40 and for a car with up to nine passengers it's Dkr480.

Bornholmstrafikken (☎ 56 95 18 66; www.bornholmstrafikken.dk) operates a ferry service at least once a day between Rønne and Sassnitz, Germany (Dkr102 to Dkr203 one way, 3½ hours).

TO/FROM NORWAY

DFDS (☎ 33 42 30 00; www.dfds.dk) operates a daily overnight ferry between Copenhagen and Oslo.
Colorline (☎ 99 56 19 77; www.colorline.dk) sails from Hirtshals to Larvik, Kristiansand, Stavanger and Bergen; and from Frederikshavn to Oslo. See the relevant Getting There & Away sections of the cities for details.

TO/FROM POLAND

Polferries (☎ 33 11 46 45; www.polferries.pl) operates ferries to Świnoujście from both Copenhagen (from Dkr420, 10 hours, four times weekly) and Rønne (from Dkr260, five hours, on Saturday).

TO/FROM SWEDEN

Scandlines (☎ 33 15 15 15; www.scandlines.dk) and **HH Ferries** (☎ 46 42 19 80 00; http://hh.net.dynamicweb.se) sail every half hour from Helsingør to Helsingborg, in Sweden. Prices vary, but are roughly Dkr48 return per adult or from Dkr600 return if you are taking a car with two passengers.

Other ferries go from Frederikshavn to Göteborg and Oslo, and Rønne to Ystad. See the relevant Getting There & Away sections in this chapter.

TO/FROM UK

DFDS Seaways (☎ in UK 08705 333 000, in Denmark 33 42 30 00; www.dfdsseaways.co.uk) sails from Esbjerg to Harwich at least three times a week at 6pm year-round. It takes 19 hours. The cost for passage in a chair starts from £38 per person, one way.

Bus

Eurolines operates buses from Copenhagen to Berlin (Dkr274, seven hours) and Frankfurt via Hamburg (Dkr734, 13 hours), and 17 other German cities (as well as most European countries) several times a week. They also offer a daily bus service between Oslo and Copenhagen (Dkr385, nine hours) via Göteborg. There are numerous and frequent bus services between Copenhagen and Sweden, including Eurolines buses to Göteborg (Dkr275, 4½ hours) and Stockholm (Dkr385, 9½ hours).

Car & Motorcycle

For those travelling by car, there's a Dkr260 toll per vehicle for the bridge crossing to Sweden.

Train

Three railway lines link Denmark with Germany. Second-class fares from Copenhagen to Frankfurt are Dkr1307, and to Berlin Dkr1010, although be advised fares booked in advance can be substantially cheaper than the prices listed here (see www.dsb.dk for more information). Trains operate between Copenhagen and Oslo; the 2nd-class fare (via Sweden; 7½ hours, one or two daily) is Dkr1050. Trains run many times a day between Denmark and Sweden via a bridge linking Copenhagen with Malmö (Dkr90, 40 minutes), Göteborg (Dkr385; four hours) and Stockholm (Dkr965, five hours). If you're travelling by train, the bridge crossing is included in the fare.

GETTING AROUND

Air

Most internal flights cost around Dkr500 for a standard ticket and can be much cheaper if you book in advance.

Denmark's domestic air routes are operated by the airlines listed here.

Cimber Air (☎ 70 10 12 18; www.cimber.dk) Services include Copenhagen to Aalborg (50 minutes, three times daily), Rønne (Bornholm, 40 minutes, at least four times daily) and Karup (central Jutland, 50 minutes, 12 times daily weekdays, at least twice on weekends).

SAS (☎ 70 10 30 00; www.scandinavian.net) Links Copenhagen with Aalborg, Århus and Billund about a dozen times a day.

Bicycle

Cycling is a practical way to get around Denmark. There are extensive bike paths linking towns throughout the country and bike lanes through most city centres. You can rent bikes in most towns for around Dkr70 a day, plus a deposit of about Dkr250. Bikes can be taken on ferries and most trains for a modest cost; make sure you pick up the DSB pamphlet *Cykler i tog*.

Boat

A network of ferries links virtually all of Denmark's populated islands. Where there's not a bridge, there's usually a ferry, most of which take cars.

Bus

All large cities and towns have a local bus system and most places are also served by regional buses, many of which connect with trains. There are also a few long-distance bus routes, including from Copenhagen to Aalborg or Århus. Travelling by bus on long-distance routes costs about 20% less than travel by train, although it's usually a bit slower than the train.

Car & Motorcycle

Denmark is perfect for touring by car. Roads are in good condition and well signposted. Traffic is manageable, even in major cities such as Copenhagen (rush hours excepted).

Access to and from motorways is made easy since roads leading out of city and town centres are sensibly named after the main city to which they're routed. For instance, the road leading out of Odense to Faaborg is Faaborgvej, the road leading to Nyborg is Nyborgvej, and so on.

Denmark's extensive network of ferries carries motor vehicles for reasonable rates. It's always a good idea for drivers to call ahead and make reservations.

Train

With the exception of a few short private lines, the **Danish State Railways** (DSB; www.dsb.dk) runs all Danish train services. There are two types of long-distance trains: sleek intercity (IC) trains that generally require reservations (Dkr35) and older, slower inter-regional (IR) trains that make more stops and don't require reservations. Both cost the same, apart from the InterCity-Lyn, a cushy, pricier express train aimed at business-people. Rail passes don't cover reservation fees or surcharges.

Overall, train travel in Denmark is not expensive, in large part because the distances are short. Scanrail, Eurail and other rail passes are valid on DSB ferries and trains, but not on the private lines.

> **EMERGENCY NUMBER**
>
> Police, fire and ambulance ☎ 112

COPENHAGEN

pop 1.5 million

Stockholm might be more grandiose and Oslo more spectacularly located, but there is no more charming, exciting and stimulating city in Scandinavia than Copenhagen.

This 1000-year-old harbour town has managed to retain much of its historic charm – with its copper spires, cobbled squares and pastel-coloured gabled town houses – while at the same time being everything a modern metropolis should be, home to cutting edge designers, a super efficient transport system and an impressive environmental conscience. It has intriguing, independent shops galore; excellent restaurants and bars; world-class museums and art collections; and brave new architecture. This is also a royal city, home to the beloved Queen Margrethe II and her family. Copenhagen is proud of its regal past and the architectural legacy of one king in particular, Christian IV, to whose reign in the 17th century we can credit some of the city's most picturesque buildings.

ORIENTATION

Whether travellers land at Copenhagen airport, just 12 minutes away from the city centre by train, or arrive from elsewhere in Europe, most people's first view of Copenhagen is of its Central Station (Hovedbanegården). Just across the street, to the east of the station's main entrance, is Denmark's number one tourist attraction, Tivoli Gardens. Beyond that is the town

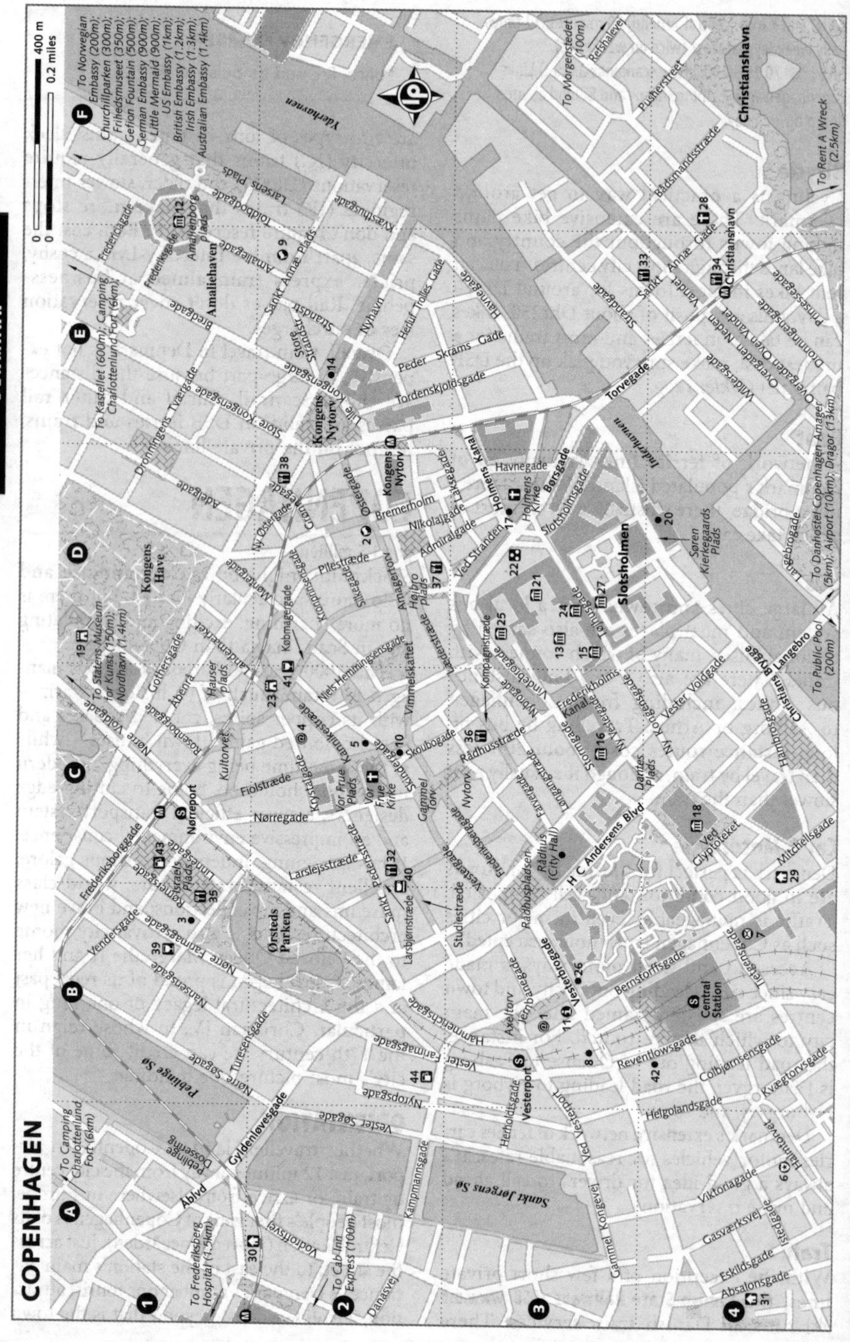
COPENHAGEN
A
B
C
D
E
F
1
2
3
4
0
400 m
0.2 miles
To Norwegian Embassy (200m); Churchillparken (300m); Frihedsmuseet (350m); Gefion Fountain (500m); German Embassy (900m); Little Mermaid (900m); US Embassy (1km); British Embassy (1.2km); Irish Embassy (1.3km); Australian Embassy (1.4km)
To Kastellet (600m); Camping Charlottenlund Fort (6km)
To Statens Museum for Kunst (150m); Nordhavn (1.4km)
To Camping Charlottenlund Fort (6km)
To Frederiksberg Hospital (1.5km)
To Cab Inn Express (100m)
To Morgenstedet (100m)
To Rent A Wreck (2.5km)
To Danhostel Copenhagen Amager (5km); Airport (10km); Dragør (13km)
To Public Pool (200m)
Yderhavnen
Inderhavnen
Christianshavn
Slotsholmen
Amalienhaven
Amalienborg Plads
Kongens Have
Kongens Nytorv
Ørsteds Parken
Peblinge Sø
Sankt Jørgens Sø
Nørreport
Vesterport
Central Station
Rådhus (City Hall)
Rådhuspladsen
Israels Plads
Kultorvet
Hauser Plads
Vor Frue Plads
Vor Frue Kirke
Gammel Torv
Nytorv
Højbro Plads
Holmens Kirke
Holmens Kanal
Frederiksholms Kanal
Søren Kierkegaards Plads
Dantes Plads
Ved Glyptoteket
Larsens Plads
Toldbodgade
Kvæsthusgade
Sankt Annæ Plads
Amaliegade
Frederiksgade
Fredericiagade
Bredgade
Store Kongensgade
Dronningens Tværgade
Adelgade
Gothersgade
Nyhavn
Store Strandstræde
Lille Strandstræde
Lille Kongensgade
Heluf Trolles Gade
Havnegade
Peder Skrams Gade
Tordenskjoldsgade
Holbergsgade
Bremerholm
Østergade
Ny Østergade
Grønnegade
Møntergade
Kronprinsensgade
Pilestræde
Silkegade
Købmagergade
Amagertorv
Nikolajgade
Laksegade
Admiralgade
Ved Stranden
Børsgade
Slotsholmsgade
Havnegade
Torvegade
Strandgade
Sankt Annæ Gade
Vandet
Bådsmandsstræde
Pusherstreet
Refshalevej
Overgaden Oven Vandet
Overgaden Neden Vandet
Wildersgade
Dronningensgade
Prinsessegade
Langebrogade
Langebro
Christians Brygge
Hambrosgade
Mitchellsgade
Tietgensgade
Bernstorffsgade
Reventlowsgade
Colbjørnsensgade
Kvægtorvsgade
Helgolandsgade
Halmtorvet
Viktoriagade
Gasværksvej
Istedgade
Eskildsgade
Absalonsgade
Ved Vesterport
Gammel Kongevej
Vesterbrogade
Axeltorv
Jernbanegade
Herholdtsgade
Vester Farimagsgade
Hammerichsgade
Nyropsgade
Vester Søgade
Kampmannsgade
Danasvej
Vodroffsvej
Åboulevard
Gyldenløvesgade
Peblinge Dossering
Nørre Søgade
Turesensgade
Nansensgade
Nørre Farimagsgade
Vendersgade
Rømersgade
Linnésgade
Frederiksborggade
Nørre Voldgade
Rosenborggade
Åbenrå
Landemærket
Fiolstræde
Nørregade
Krystalgade
Kannikestræde
Store Kannikestræde
Niels Hemmingsensgade
Vimmelskaftet
Skindergade
Skoubogade
Larslejsstræde
Sankt Peders Stræde
Larsbjørnsstræde
Studiestræde
Vestergade
Frederiksberggade
Lavendelstræde
Rådhusstræde
Kompagnistræde
Magstræde
Vindebrogade
Nybrogade
Stormgade
Ny Vestergade
Ny Kongensgade
Vester Voldgade
Longangstræde
Farvergade
H C Andersens Blvd
Tøjhusgade
Vester Voldgade
Rådhuspladsen

INFORMATION	
Boomtown	1 B3
Canadian Embassy	2 D2
Dansk Cyklist Forbund	3 B1
Hovedbiblioteket	4 C2
Kilroy Travels	5 C2
Police Station	6 A4
Post Office	7 B4
Steno Apotek	8 B3
Swedish Embassy	9 E2
Wasteels	10 C2
Wonderful Copenhagen	11 B3
SIGHTS & ACTIVITIES	
Amalienborg Palace	12 F1
Christiansborg Palace	13 D3
DFDS Canal Tours	14 E2
Museum of Royal Coaches	15 D3
Nationalmuseet	16 C3
Netto-Boats	17 D3
Ny Carlsberg Glyptotek	18 C4
Rosenborg Slot	19 D1
Royal Library	20 D4
Royal Reception Chambers	21 D3
Ruins of Absalon's Fortress	22 D3
Rundetårn	23 C2
Slots-og Ejendomysstyrelsen	(see 21)
Teatermuseet	24 D3
Thorvaldsens Museum	25 D3
Tivoli	26 B3
Tøjhusmuseet (Armoury Museum)	27 D3
Vor Frelsers Kirke	28 F4
SLEEPING	
Cab Inn City	29 C4
Cab Inn Scandinavia	30 A2
City Public Hostel	31 A4
EATING	
Atlas Bar	32 C2
Café Wilder	33 E3
Lagkagehuset	34 E4
Produce Market	35 B1
Riz Raz	36 C3
Slotskælderen Hos Gitte Kik	37 D2
Wokshop Cantina	38 D2
DRINKING	
Barbarellah Bar	39 B1
Roberts Coffee	40 C2
Studenterhuset	41 C2
TRANSPORT	
Eurolines Office	42 B4
Petrol Station	43 C1
Petrol Station	44 B2

hall square (Rådhuspladsen), from where the main shopping street, Strøget (several connecting streets and squares), leads to the other main square, Kongens Nytorv. From here the bustling quayside of Nyhavn, with its countless cafes, bars and restaurants, leads to the harbour.

INFORMATION

Internet Access

Boomtown (☎ 33 32 10 32; www.boomtown.net; Axeltorv 1-3; per hr Dkr35; 24hr) There's wi-fi access, too.

Hovedbiblioteket (☎ 33 73 60 60; 15 Krystalgade; 10am-7pm Mon-Fri, 10am-2pm Sat) A public library offering free internet access on one of four computers.

Left Luggage

Central Station (per 24hr small/large locker Dkr25/35, maximum 72hr; 5.30am-1.00am Mon-Sat, 6am-1am Sun) Lockers are in the lower level near the Reventlowsgade exit.

Medical Services

Frederiksberg Hospital (☎ 38 16 38 16; Nordre Fasanvej 57) West of the city centre, has a 24-hour emergency ward.

Steno Apotek (Vesterbrogade 6c; 24hr) Pharmacy opposite Central Station.

Money

Banks, all of which charge transaction fees, are found throughout the city centre. Banks in the airport arrival and transit halls are open 6am to 10pm daily. The **Forex exchange booth** (Central Station; 7am-9pm) has the lowest fees but you will find other exchange shops all along Strøget.

Tourist Information

Wonderful Copenhagen (☎ 70 22 24 42; www.visitcopenhagen.dk; Vesterbrogade 4a; 9am-4pm Mon-Fri, to 2pm Sat Jan-Apr & Sep-Dec, 9am-6pm Mon- Sat May-Jun, to 8pm Mon-Sat, 10am-6pm Sun Jul-Aug) is a tourist information centre that distributes the informative *Tourist in Copenhagen* as well as *Copenhagen This Week*, a free city map, and brochures covering all the regions of Denmark.

Travel Agencies

Kilroy Travels (☎ 33 11 00 44; www.kilroytravels.com; Skindergade 28; 10am-5.30pm Mon-Fri, to 2pm Sat)

Wasteels (☎ 33 14 46 33; Skoubogade 6; 9am-5pm Mon-Fri, 10am-noon Sat)

SIGHTS

Tivoli

Copenhagen's historic **amusement park** (☎ 33 15 10 01; www.tivoli.dk, in Danish; adult Dkr85; 11am-11pm Sat-Thu, 11am-1am Fri mid-Apr–mid-Jun & mid-Aug–mid-Sep, 11am-midnight Sun-Thu, 11am-1am Fri & Sat mid-Jun–mid-Aug) has been Denmark's number one tourist attraction pretty much since the day it opened over 160 years ago. At first glance, visitors more used to the scale and glitz of Disneyland might wonder what the fuss is about, but Tivoli Gardens has a unique atmosphere and no one can deny its appeal, particularly after dark when its wonderful illuminations work their magic. The gardens have an innocent, old-fashioned charm. There are flower beds, food pavilions, amusement rides, carnival games and various stage shows.

Nationalmuseet

For a whistle-stop tour through the history of Denmark, nothing can beat the **Nationalmuseet** (National Museum; ☎ 33 13 44 11; www.natmus.dk; Ny Vestergade 10; admission free; 10am-5pm Tue-Sun). Here you will find the world's most extensive collection of Danish artefacts from the Palaeolithic period to the 19th century. Naturally, the stars of the show are the Vikings, those much maligned, but actually very sophisticated Scandinavian marauders. Highlights include Bronze Age burial remains in oak coffins and various examples of *lur* (musical horns) that were used for ceremony and communication, ancient rune stones, a golden sun chariot, the silver Gundestrip cauldron and Viking weaponry. But the displays don't stop with the Vikings; there are excellent collections covering the Middle Ages and the Renaissance period, plus delightful Egyptian and classical antiquities, as well as frequently changing special exhibitions.

Rosenborg Slot

This early 17th-century **castle** (☎ 33 15 32 86; www.rosenborgslot.dk; admission Dkr70; 10am-4pm May & Sep, to 5pm Jun-Aug, 11am-3pm Oct, to 2pm Tue-Sun Nov-Apr), built by Christian IV in the Dutch Renaissance style, stands at the edge of **Kongens Have** (King's Gardens; admission free). It is a fairy-tale castle and one of Copenhagen's great landmarks. Inside you'll find glorious marbled and painted ceilings, gilded mirrors, priceless Dutch tapestries, solid silver lions, and gold- and enamel-ware. The Royal Treasury, in the castle basement, is home to the Danish crown jewels.

Statens Museum for Kunst

Denmark's national **gallery** (☎ 33 74 84 94; www.smk.dk; Sølvgade 48-50; admission free; 10am-5pm Tue & Thu-Sun, to 8pm Wed) houses an impressive collection of works from Danish artists in the original building, particularly those of the 19th-century 'Golden Age' such as Hammershøj and Eckersberg. The dramatic glass extension contains more modern works from international names like Picasso and Munch as well as more contemporary Danish artists such as Per Kirkeby, Søren Jensen, Michael Ancher and Richard Mortensen.

Ny Carlsberg Glyptotek

This splendid **museum** (☎ 33 41 81 41; www.glyptoteket.dk; Dantes Plads 7, HC Andersens Blvd; admission Dkr50, Wed & Sun free; 10am-4pm Tue-Sun), occupying a grand period building near Tivoli Gardens, has now received a thorough restoration program. The museum's impressive collection features Etruscan art, 18th- and 19th-century paintings from France and Denmark (the Gauguins are particularly notable) and sculpture spanning five millennia (including over 30 works by Rodin). At its heart is a beautiful tropical winter garden with a cafe.

Slotsholmen

An island separated from the city centre by a moat-like canal on three sides and the harbour on the other side, Slotsholmen is the site of **Christiansborg Palace** (☎ 33 92 64 92) home to Denmark's parliament. There are many sites on the island, including a **Teatermuseet** (theatre museum), a museum housing the **royal coaches**, and a magnificent **Tøjhusmuseet** (armoury museum), but the grandest is the **Slots-og Ejendomysstyrelsen** (Royal Reception Chambers; ☎ 33 92 64 92; www.ses.dk; admission Dkr65; guided tours in English 11am, 1pm & 3pm May-Sep, 3pm Tue-Sun Oct-Apr), the ornate Renaissance hall where the queen entertains heads of state.

The **Ruins of Absalon's Fortress** (admission Dkr40; 10am-4pm, closed Mon during winter) are the excavated foundations of Bishop Absalon's original castle of 1167 and of its successor, Copenhagen Slot. They can be visited in the basement of the present palace.

Thorvaldsens Museum (☎ 33 32 15 32; Bertel Thorvaldsens Plads; admission Dkr20, Wed free; 10am-5pm Tue-Sun) features imposing statues by the famed Danish sculptor Bertel Thorvaldsen, who was heavily influenced by Greek and Roman mythology. Enter from the direction of Vindebrogade.

The **Royal Library** (☎ 33 47 47 47; Søren Kierkegaards Plads; 10am-7pm Mon-Sat) dates from the 17th century, but the focal point these days is its ultramodern walkway-connected extension dubbed the 'Black Diamond' for its shiny black granite facade. The sleek, seven-storey building houses 21 million books and other literary items such as Hans Christian Andersen's

GETTING INTO TOWN

A train links the airport with Central Station (Dkr30, 17 minutes, three times hourly). The airport is 15 minutes and about Dkr250 from the city centre by taxi. The **Metro** (www.m.dk) links the airport to the eastern side of the city, stopping at Christianshavn Torv, Kongens Nytorv and Nørreport stations (Dkr30, 12 minutes, every five minutes).

original manuscripts. The building itself is open for **visits and guided tours** (Dkr25; 10am-6pm) and has a cafe and restaurant.

Rundetårn

The **Round Tower** (☎ 33 73 03 73; Købmagergade 52; www.rundetaarn.dk; admission Dkr25; 10am-8pm Mon-Sat, noon-8pm Sun Jun-Aug, 10am-5pm Mon-Sat, noon-5pm Sun Sep-May) provides a fine vantage point for viewing the old city. It was built by Christian IV in 1642 as an astronomical observatory for the famous silver-nosed astronomer Tycho Brahe. Halfway up the 209m-high spiral walkway is a hall with changing exhibits. The tower houses the oldest functioning observatory.

Christianshavn

Copenhagen's picturesque canal quarter was built on reclaimed land in the 17th century by Christian IV. Most visitors come to visit the alternative commune at Freetown of Christiania but it's equally pleasurable to wander beside the canals and visit the quarter's pleasant cafes.

To get there, walk over the bridge from the northeastern side of Slotsholmen or you can take the Metro from Kongens Nytorv or Nørreport direct to Christianshavnstorv.

Close to Freetown of Christiania is the 17th-century **Vor Frelsers Kirke** (☎ 31 57 27 98; www.vorfrelserskirke.dk; Sankt Annæ Gade 29; admission free, tower admission Dkr20; 11am-4.30pm Apr-Aug, to 3.30pm Sep-Mar, closed during services, tower closed Nov-Mar). For a panoramic view of the city and across to Sweden, climb the 400 steps of the church's 95m-high spiral tower. The last 160 steps run spectacularly and dizzyingly along the outside rim.

Waterfront

The home of the royal family since 1794, **Amalienborg Palace** (admission Dkr55; 10am-4pm) comprises four austere mansions surrounding the central square and guarded by sentries, who are relieved at noon by a ceremonial changing of the guard. You can view the interior of the northwestern mansion, with its royal memorabilia and the study rooms of three kings.

Back on Amalienborg Plads, and 500m north along Amaliegade, is Churchillparken, where you'll find **Frihedsmuseet** (admission free; 10am-4pm Tue-Sat, to 5pm Sun), with moving relics from the time of the Danish Resistance against Nazi occupation.

About 150m north of the Frihedsmuseet you pass the spectacular **Gefion Fountain** that features the goddess Gefion, ploughing the island of Zealand with her four sons yoked as oxen. Another 400m north along the waterfront is the statue of the unjustly famed **Little Mermaid** (Den Lille Havfrue) – a rather forlorn statue that is actually one of the least interesting of all Copenhagen's many sights.

TOURS

The best way to see Copenhagen is from the water. There are several ways to take a boat tour around the city's canals and harbour from April to mid-October. Multilingual guides give a lively commentary in English. **DFDS Canal Tours** (www.canaltours.dk; adult Dkr60) leave from the head of Nyhavn or the Marriott Hotel. Tours take 50 minutes, passing by the Little Mermaid, Christianshavn and Christiansborg Palace, and leave every half hour between 10am and 5pm. **Netto-Boats** (☎ 32 54 41 02; www.netto-baadene.dk; adult Dkr30) are cheaper, run the same times and depart from Holmens Kirke and from Nyhavn.

FESTIVALS

The **Copenhagen Jazz Festival** (☎ 33 93 20 13; www.jazzfestival.dk) is the city's largest music event, invigorating the whole city with 10 days of music in early July. The festival presents a wide range of Danish and international jazz, blues and fusion music in over 500 indoor and outdoor venues, with music wafting out of practically every public square, park, pub and cafe from Strøget to Tivoli Gardens.

SLEEPING

Camping Charlottenlund Fort (☎ 39 62 36 88; www.campingcopenhagen.dk; Strandvejen 144, Charlottenlund; camp site per adult/tent Dkr80/25) This is 6km north of the city centre beside a delightful sandy beach

Book your stay at lonelyplanet.com/hotels

overlooking the Øresund sea. Take bus 14 for a half-hour trip.

City Public Hostel (☎ 33 31 20 70; www.citypublichostel.dk; Absalonsgade 8; dm Dkr110-150; ⌚ early May–mid-Aug, 24hr reception; 💻) A central, well-run hostel with dorms sleeping six to 23; they are both mixed gender and separate gender. Breakfast costs Dkr25, or Dkr20 if it's included with the bed price. There is wi-fi access and an outdoor barbecue area.

Danhostel Copenhagen Amager (☎ 32 52 29 08; www.danhostel.dk/copenhagen; Vejlands Allé 200, Amager; dm/d Dkr110/340; ⌚ early Jan–mid-Dec; P 💻) Located in an isolated part of Amager just off the E20, this is one of the largest hostels in Europe, with 528 beds in two-, three-, four- and five-bed rooms. Take bus 5A from Rådhuspladsen to Sundbyvesterplads and change to bus 77. Until 5pm Monday to Friday, bus 46 runs from Central Station directly to the hostel.

Danhostel Copenhagen Downtown (☎ 70 23 21 10; www.copenhagendowntown.com; Vandkunsten 5; dm/d Dkr130/549; ⌚ year-round) This characterful, buzzing new hostel could not be more centrally located, right beside the main pedestrian shopping street, Strøget, and prides itself on its cultural dynamism, with several artists in residence.

Danhostel Copenhagen City (☎ 33 11 85 85; www.danhostel.dk; HC Andersens Blvd 50; dm Dkr150; ⌚ year-round) The best of Copenhagen's hostels occupies a modern high-rise overlooking the harbour a short walk from the Central Station. With a reception that resembles a boutique hotel, a great cafe and a 25% discount on the facilities at the DGI-Byen swimming pool and sports centre included in the price, it is wise to book ahead.

Cab Inn City (☎ 33 46 16 16; www.cabinn.com; Mitchellsgade 14; s/d/tr Dkr545/675/805; 💻 P ⊠) Cab Inns are modern, and rather clinical but boast good facilities (including kettle and TV) and reliable levels of comfort, although the ship's cabin (cab-in, geddit?) style means small rooms and rather narrow bunk-style beds. This is the best located of all Copenhagen's Cab Inns, considering it's a short walk south of Tivoli Gardens. Book ahead.

Its sister hotels are **Cab Inn Scandinavia** (☎ 35 36 11 11; www.cabinn.com; Vodroffsvej 57; s/d/tr/q Dkr545/665/785/905; P) and **Cab Inn Express** (☎ 33 21 04 00; www.cabinn.com; Danasvej 32-34; s/d/tr/q Dkr545/665/785/905; P).

EATING

Produce market (Israels Plads; ⌚ 9am-5pm Mon-Fri, to 2pm Sat) This is the main city produce market, just a few minutes' walk north of Nørreport Station.

Lagkagehuset (☎ 32 57 36 07; Torvegade 45; www.lagkagehuset.dk; ⌚ 6am-7pm) One of the best bakeries in town lies right in the heart of Christianshavn and is highly recommended for sandwiches (Dkr45) and salads (Dkr45).

Wokshop Cantina (☎ 33 91 61 21; Ny Adelgade 6; www.wokshop.dk; soups Dkr60-99, curry Dkr109; ⌚ noon-2pm & 5.30pm-10pm Mon-Fri, 6-10pm Sat) This basement canteen in a street just off Kongens Nytorv serves excellent, cheap Thai and Vietnamese staples.

Morgenstedet (www.morgenstedet.dk; Langgaden; mains Dkr70; ⌚ noon-9pm Tue-Sun) This long-established vegetarian and vegan place has a pretty garden in the heart of Christiania. Its dish of the day – usually a curry – is Dkr70.

Café Wilder (☎ 32 54 71 83; Wildersgade 56; www.cafewilder.dk; mains Dkr85-145; ⌚ 9am-midnight) The archetypal Christianshavn cafe serves good salads and pastas by day and French brasserie food by night to a groovy local crowd.

Slotskælderen Hos Gitte Kik (☎ 33 11 15 37; Fortunstræde 4; mains Dkr89; ⌚ 11.30am-3.30pm Mon-Fri) Hidden away in a quiet sidestreet off Amagertorv, this traditional Danish lunch restaurant is a great place to try classic Danish staples like *frikadeller* (meatballs), *sild* (herring) and, of course, a wide range of smørrebrød (all for under Dkr100).

Atlas Bar (☎ 33 15 03 52; Larsbjørnstræde 18; ⌚ noon-midnight Mon-Sat) Atlas Bar is an enduringly popular semi-subterranean corner restaurant in the heart of the Latin Quarter. Its globally inspired blackboard menu changes regularly but there is always a good vegetarian option and the portions are generous. You can eat very well here for under Dkr100.

Riz Raz (☎ 33 15 05 75; Kompagnistræde 20; buffet lunch/dinner Dkr79/89, mains Dkr139; ⌚ 11.30am-11pm) Regularly voted by the media as one of the city's best cheap eats, Riz Raz offers a great-value southern Mediterranean buffet, and plenty of outside seating. There are good meat mains, too.

DRINKING

Drinking is one of the Danes' chief pastimes and Copenhagen is packed with a huge range of places, from cosy, old-school cellar bars or 'bodegas', to the cavernous fleshpots close to Rådhuspladsen, and the many more quirky, characterful, loungey, grungy, design-ey, boozy, artsy places elsewhere. The line is often blurred between cafe, bar and restaurant, with many places changing roles as the day progresses.

Barbarellah Bar (☎ 33 32 00 61; Nørre Farimagsagde 41; 4pm-2am Mon-Thu, 4pm-4am Fri & Sat) Close to groovy Nansensgade, where you'll find several more bars, restaurants and boutiques worth visiting, this spacey cafe-cum-cocktail bar is named after owner Barbara (and the Roger Vadim film, of course), who also does a nice line in trendy clothes and furniture. A honey pot for the city's best DJs.

Roberts Coffee (☎ 33 32 66 10; www.robertscoffee.dk; Larsbjørnstræde 17; 10am-11pm Mon-Thu, 10am-1am Fri, 11am-midnight Sat, noon-7pm Sun) Organic, fresh, expertly roasted and brewed coffee with a great view over the busy crossroads in the heart of Pisserendern.

Studenterhuset (☎ 35 32 38 61; Købmagergade 52; www.studenterhuset.com; sandwiches Dkr40; noon-midnight or later Tue-Sun) There is something happening – live music, DJs, quizzes, table football competitions – most nights at Copenhagen's perennially popular student bar (open to all). This is a relaxed student hang-out with drinks and light eats, including vegetarian or meat sandwiches during the day.

ENTERTAINMENT

Copenhagen really revs into gear from Thursday to Saturday when it turns into a genuine 24-hour party city. Club admission is usually around Dkr60, but you can often get in for free before a certain time in the evening. Major international rock acts often play the national stadium. Visit www.aok.dk for full listings. The monthly, free magazine *Copenhagen This Week* also lists concerts and entertainment schedules in detail.

GETTING THERE & AWAY

Air

Copenhagen's modern international airport is in Kastrup, 10km southeast of the city centre. Flights connect frequently with most major Danish and Scandinavian destinations. Many airline offices are north of Central Station near the intersection of Vester Farimagsgade and Vesterbrogade.

Boat

The ferry to Oslo, operated by **DFDS Seaways** (☎ 33 42 30 00/+44 871 522 9955; www.dfdsseaways.co.uk; Dampfærgevej 30), departs from the Nordhavn area north of the city (past Kastellet).

Bus

International buses leave from Central Station; advance reservations on most routes can be made at **Eurolines** (☎ 33 88 70 00; www.eurolines.dk; Reventlowsgade 8).

Car

Close to Copenhagen airport, **Rent A Wreck** (☎ 32 54 00 33; Amagerstrandvej 418; www.rent-a-wreck) hires out cars from as little as Dkr363 per day (actually not that old, but usually quite used). Rates are even more competitive on longer hires. The downside is having to drive around with the company name emblazoned on the doors.

Train

Long-distance trains arrive and depart from Central Station (Hovedbanegården), a huge complex with numerous eateries and all sorts of services. There are even public showers (Dkr15, towel hire Dkr6) located at the underground toilets opposite the police office.

There are three ways of buying a ticket, and the choice can be important, depending on how much time you have before your train leaves. *Billetautomats* are coin-operated machines and are the quickest, but only if you've mastered the zone-system prices. They are best for S-train tickets. If you're not rushed, then **DSB Billetsalg** (8am-7pm Mon-Fri, 9.30am-4pm Sat) is best for reservations. There's a numbered-ticket queuing system. **DSB Kviksalg** (5.45am-11.30pm) is for quick ticket buying, although queues can build up quite a bit at busy times (ie rush hour). Alternatively you can make reservations at www.dsb.dk, which has an English-language option.

GETTING AROUND

Copenhagen has a large public-transport system consisting of a small but excellent new underground and overground driverless **Metro system** (www.m.dk), in which trains run a minimum of every three minutes; an extensive metropolitan rail network called **S-Tog** (S-Train; www.dsb.dk), whose 10 lines pass through Central Station (København H); and a vast bus system, whose main terminus is nearby at Rådhuspladsen.

Buses, Metro and trains use a common fare system based on the number of zones you pass through. The basic fare of Dkr20 for up to two zones covers most city runs and allows transfers between buses and trains on a single ticket as long as they're made within an hour. A 24-hour pass permits unlimited travel in all zones for Dk115.

At Central Station beneath platform 12, **Københavns Cykler** (per day Dkr75) rents out bikes.

Taxi

Taxis with signs saying '*fri*' (meaning 'free') can be flagged down or you can phone ☎ 35 35 35 35.

ZEALAND

Though Copenhagen is the centre of gravity for most visitors to Denmark's eastern island, there is plenty to make it worth your while to explore beyond the city limits. This is an island with a rich history, a beautiful coastline and plenty of gentle rolling countryside – it's hardly surprising that many Copenhageners choose to holiday on their home island in summer houses rather than head abroad.

HELSINGØR (ELSINORE)

pop 34,000

Helsingør's top sight is **Kronborg Slot** (☎ 49 21 30 78; www.kronborg.dk; admission Dkr85; 11am-3pm Tue-Sun Jan-Mar, to 4pm Tue-Sun Apr, 10.30am-5pm May-Sep, 11am-4pm Tue-Sun Oct, 11am-3pm Tue-Sun Nov & Dec), made famous as the Elsinore Castle of Shakespeare's *Hamlet*. Kronborg's primary function was not as a royal residence, but rather as a grandiose tollhouse, wresting taxes (the infamous and lucrative 'Sound Dues') for more than 400 years from ships passing through the narrow Øresund. The castle is on the northern side of the harbour within easy walking distance of the station.

The **tourist office** (☎ 49 21 13 33; www.visithelsingor.dk; Havnepladsen 3; 10am-4pm Mon-Fri, closed Sat & Sun) is opposite the train station.

Sleeping & Eating

Helsingør Camping Grønnehave (☎ 49 28 49 50; www.helsingor.dk/campingpladsen; Strandalleen 2; camp site per adult/cabin Dkr60/350) A well-spaced beachside camping ground, east of the hostel and close to one of the area's best beaches.

Danhostel Helsingør (☎ 49 21 16 40; www.helsingorhostel.dk; Nordre Strandvej 24; dm Dkr175, r Dkr475-850; Feb-Nov; P) The hostel, housed in the imposing red-brick Villa Moltke, is 2km northwest of the centre, and is right by the water with its own beach. Rooms are simple but clean.

Brasserie Kosten (☎ 49 20 0014; www.kosten.dk; Stengade 81B; mains Dkr99-180; noon-10pm Mon-Fri, 11am-10pm Sat & Sun) Sturdy traditional Danish food, such as *frikadeller* and steaks, are the menu staples at this simple but light-filled, unpretentious restaurant – part of a small restaurant complex that also includes Chinese and Mexican places, in a converted harbour building.

Getting There & Away

Trains departing from Hillerød (Dkr60, 30 minutes) run at least once hourly. Trains from Copenhagen run a few times hourly (Dkr90, 50 minutes). **Scandlines** (☎ 33 15 15 15; www.scandlines.dk) and **HH Ferries** (☎ +46 42 19 80 00; http://hh.net.dynamicweb.se) sail every half hour from Helsingør to Helsingborg, in Sweden. Prices vary, but are roughly Dkr48 return per adult or from Dkr600 return if you are taking a car with two passengers.

ROSKILDE

pop 45,000

Home to one of Northern Europe's best outdoor music festivals, resting place of a millennia of Danish royalty and the site of several remarkable Viking ship finds, Roskilde is worth the day trip. For information, see the **tourist office** (☎ 46 31 65 65; www.visitroskilde.com; Gullandsstræde 15; 9am-5pm Mon-Fri, 10am-1pm Sat, to 2pm Sat in summer).

Though most of Roskilde's medieval buildings have vanished in fires over the centuries, the imposing twin-spired **Roskilde Domkirke** (☎ 46 35 16 24; www.roskildedomkirke.dk; Domkirkepladsen; admission Dkr25, tours Dkr20; 9am-5pm Mon-Sat & 12.30-5pm Sun Apr-Sep, 10am-4pm Tue-Sat & 12.30-4pm Sun Oct-Mar) still dominates the city centre. Started by Bishop Absalon in 1170, its **crypts** contain the sarcophagi of 39 Danish kings and queens. Some are lavishly embellished and guarded by marble statues of knights and women in mourning. Others are simple and unadorned. Guided tours run 11am and 2pm weekdays, 11am Saturday and 2pm Sunday.

Don't miss the excellent purpose-built **Viking Ship Museum** (☎ 46 30 02 53; Vindeboder 12;

www.viksingskibesmuseet.dk; admission May-Sep Dkr95, Oct-Apr Dkr60; 10am-5pm), which contains five reconstructed Viking longboats.

Trains from Copenhagen to Roskilde are frequent (Dkr70, 25 minutes). From Copenhagen by car, Rte 21 leads to Roskilde; upon approaching the city, exit onto Rte 156, which leads into the centre.

BORNHOLM

pop 44,000

Bornholm is a little Baltic pearl. Though a Danish island, it lies some 200km east of the mainland, north of Poland, and boasts more hours of sunshine than any other part of the country. It also has gorgeous sandy beaches, idyllic fishing villages, numerous historic sights, endless cycle paths and a burgeoning reputation for culinary curiosities, ceramic artists and glass makers. The island's tourist website, with information on accommodation, activities, events and transport, is at www.bornholm.info.

The **tourist office** (Bornholms Velkomstcenter; 56 95 95 00; www.bornholm.info; Nordre Kystvej 3, Rønne; 9am-5pm Mon-Sat, 10am-3pm Sun mid-Jun–Aug, 9am-4pm Mon-Fri, to noon Sat Feb-May, Sep & Oct, to 4pm Mon-Fri Nov-Jan) is a few minutes' walk from the harbour and has masses of information on all of Bornholm. There's free internet access at the **public library** (Pingels Allé; 10am-7pm Mon-Tue & Thu, to 3pm Fri, 1-8pm Wed, 10am-2pm Sat) for which you must book a slot first.

SIGHTS & ACTIVITIES

The harbour town of **Svaneke** has award-winning historic buildings, especially those near the village church, a few minutes' walk south of the centre. The **tourist office** (56 49 70 79; Storegade 24; noon-4.30pm Mon-Fri) is in the post office building, two blocks north of the central square.

Gudhjem is the perfect Danish seaside holiday village, with plenty of places to eat and stay, and excellent beaches within a kilometre or so. Its charming half-timbered houses and sloping streets rolling down to the pleasant harbour front make it one of the island's most attractive towns. The **tourist office** (56 48 52 10; Åbogade 7; 10am-4pm Jul-Aug, 1-4pm Mon-Sat Sep & Mar-Jun) is a block inland from the harbour alongside the library. Gudhjem has narrow streets and parking can be difficult. There's a public car park northwest of the harbour.

SLEEPING & EATING

Fifty metres from the harbourside bus stop, **Danhostel Gudhjem** (56 48 50 35; www.danhostel-gudhjem.dk; dm/s/d Dkr165/320/410) is in an attractive spot right by the harbour with small cosy, bright white six-bed dorms. The management also handles the pleasant **Therns Hotel** (56 48 50 35; www.therns-hotel.dk; Brøddegade 31; s Dkr500, d Dkr650-850).

Further along is the waterfront smokehouse **Gudhjem Rogeri** (56 48 57 08; buffet Dkr95), the oldest on the island (dating from 1910), with an all-you-can-eat buffet and some challenging seating, including on the upper floor, which is reached by rope ladder. It has live folk, country and rock music most nights in summer.

GETTING THERE & AROUND

The most cost- and time-efficient way to get to Bornholm is to take the train from Copenhagen to Ystad in Sweden, from where you can take the high-speed catamaran for one hour across the Baltic Sea to the town of Rønne. The service is operated on a single ticket from **DSB** (70 13 14 15; www.dsb.dk). This trip goes several times a day, takes just over three hours in total and costs Dkr265 one way with a seat reservation (or Dkr530 return).

Bornholmstrafikken (56 95 18 66; www.bornholmstrafikken.dk; adult Dkr250, car Dkr1350-1435) operates a ferry service from Køge, around 30 minutes south of Copenhagen by train, to Bornholm. The overnight ferry departs daily at 11.30pm and arrives at 6am.

Cycling is a great way to get around. Bornholm is crisscrossed by more than 200km of bike trails, many built over former rail routes. You can download bicycle routes across the island for free at www.cykel.bornholm.info.

In Rønne, **Bornholms Cykeludlejning** (56 95 13 59; www.bornholms-cykeludlejning.dk, in Danish; Nordre Kystvej 5; per day/week Dkr60/250), next to the tourist office, has a large fleet of bikes for hire. Bicycles can usually be rented from hostels and camping grounds around the island for about Dkr60 a day.

A good, inexpensive bus service around the island is operated by **Bornholms Amts Trafikselskab** (BAT; www.bat.dk; day/weekly passes Dkr140/450). Fares are based on a zone system and cost Dkr10 per zone; the maximum fare is for 10 zones.

Book your stay at lonelyplanet.com/hotels

FUNEN

pop 476,000

As a stepping stone from Zealand to the Jutland Peninsula, the rural island of Funen is often overlooked by visitors who, at most, make a whistle-stop visit to Hans Christian Andersen's birthplace and museum in the island's capital, Odense. But there is more to Funen ('Fyn' in Danish) than this: the towns of Svendborg and Faaborg have a gentle charm, particularly in summer, and there are excellent, clean beaches all around the island.

ODENSE

pop 158,000

There's plenty more to Odense than the legacy of Denmark's most famous son, the writer and traveller Hans Christian Andersen. Nevertheless, HCA's birthplace and adjoining museum are the number one draw, even if there is no concrete evidence to show he ever lived in the house in question. For more information on the city, go to www.visitodense.com.

The **tourist office** (☎ 66 12 75 20; www.visitodense.com; 9.30am-4.30pm Mon-Fri, 10am-3pm Sat & Sun mid-Jun–Aug, 9.30am-4.30pm Mon-Fri, 10am-3pm Sat & Sun Sep–mid-Jun) is at Rådhus, a 15-minute walk from the train station.

Sights

The **HC Andersens Museum** (☎ 65 51 46 01; Bangs Boder 29; admission Dkr60; 10am-4pm Tue-Sun Jan-May & Sep-Dec, 9am-6pm Jun-Aug) lies amid the picturesque houses of the old, working-class part of Odense, now often referred to as the 'HCA Quarter'. The museum puts Andersen's life into an interesting historical context and is leavened by some good audiovisual material.

Odense's 13th-century Gothic cathedral **Sankt Knuds Kirke** (☎ 66 12 03 92; Flakhaven; admission free; 9am-5pm Mon-Sat, noon-5pm Sun) reflects Odense's medieval wealth and stature. The stark white interior has a handsome rococo pulpit, a dazzling 16th-century altarpiece and a gilded wooden triptych crowded with over 300 carved figures, and is said to be one of the finest pieces of religious art in northern Europe.

Sleeping

DCU Camping (☎ 66 11 47 02; Odensevej 102; www.camping-odense.dk; adult/tent Dkr73/45) Just under 4km from the city centre, this camping ground is top notch, with an open-air pool, various sports facilities and 12 cabins for rent. Prices drop in low season.

Danhostel Odense City (☎ 63 11 04 25; www.cityhostel.dk; dm/s/d/tr/q incl breakfast Dkr160/465/630/695/760;) An excellent, modern 140-bed place with four- and six-bed dorms, a kitchen and laundry facilities located alongside the train and bus stations.

Cab Inn (☎ 63 14 57 00; Østre Stationsvej 7; www.cabinn.dk; s Dkr485, d Dkr675-805) The reliably cheap and modern bargain hotel chain has arrived in Odense with a 200-plus room place right beside the station.

Eating & Drinking

There are numerous fast-food places along Kongensgade and an excellent bakery at Vestergade 26, the main shopping street.

Cuckoos Nest (☎ 65 91 57 87; Vestergade 73; www.cuckoos.dk; mains Dkr139-159; 9am-midnight Mon-Wed, 9am-1am Thu, 9am-2am Fri & Sat, 10am-11pm Sun) A great stalwart of Odense's nightlife scene is this cavernous bar and restaurant on the corner of the main shopping street and Brandts Passage. A lengthy, wide-ranging menu includes everything from nachos and burgers to *confit de canard* (duck confit).

Bryggeriet Flakhaven (☎ 566 12 02 99; Flakhaven 2; www.bryggeriet.dk/flakhaven; mains Dkr170-220; 11.30am-10pm Mon-Sat, 3-10pm Sun) This colourful microbrewery close to the town hall brews a variety of beers and bitters on site and serves a decent global menu of Mexican, Spanish, Texan and Danish classics, such as beer-marinated chicken breast.

Odense Banegård Center, which incorporates the train and bus stations, has low-priced options including a **DSB Café** (5am-10pm Mon-Fri, 8am-10pm Sat & Sun), a supermarket and a pub.

Getting There & Around

Odense is on the main railway line between Copenhagen (Dkr224, 1½ hours, every 15 minutes), Århus (Dkr195, 1¾ hours, hourly), Aalborg (Dkr300, three hours, hourly) and Esbjerg (Dkr177, 1½ to two hours, every 30 minutes). The ticket office is open from about 6am to 8.15pm most days, but closes at 5pm on Saturday. Buses leave from the rear of the train station.

You can rent bikes at **City Cykler** (☎ 66 13 97 83; www.citycykler.dk; Vesterbro 27; per day Dk155; 10am-5.30pm Mon-Fri, to 1pm Sat), west of the city centre.

JUTLAND

Jutland (Jylland) is Denmark's largest land mass by far. The area where the borders meet is a rather monotonous procession of moor and marsh but further north things improve as you hit the pretty, forested lake district. Cosmopolitan Århus, Denmark's second city, hugs the eastern coast of this landmass. Further north still there's the windswept western and northern coasts (a windsurfer's dream) lined with vast sandy beaches and an incredible, constantly shifting landscape of mammoth, grassy dunes. Then there's Grenen, a bracing, epic sandy spit where the currents collide in a maelstrom of white water.

ÅRHUS

pop 238,000

Århus (the second-largest city in Denmark) has tended to labour in the shadows of Copenhagen in terms of its cultural attractions for visitors, but all the same this is a terrific city in which to spend a day or two. It is the cultural and commercial heart of Jutland and has one of Denmark's best music and entertainment scenes (there is a very large student population on account of the city's university), a well-preserved historic quarter, and plenty to see and do.

Orientation

Århus is fairly compact and easy to get around. The train station is on the southern side of the city centre. The pedestrian shopping streets of Ryesgade, Søndergade and Sankt Clements Torv extend around 1km from the station to the cathedral at the heart of the old city.

Information

Lockers are available at the bus and train stations. Both charge Dkr12 for 24 hours.

Boomtown (Åboulevarden 21; internet access per 30min Dkr25; ⌚ 10am-2am Mon-Thu, to 8am Fri & Sat, 11am-midnight Sun)

Kilroy Travels (☎ 86 20 11 44; Fredensgade 40) Specialises in discount and student travel and has friendly, helpful staff.

Tourist Office (☎ 87 31 50 10; www.visitaarhus.com; Banegårdspladsen; ⌚ 9.30am-6pm Mon-Fri, to 5pm Sat, to 1pm Sun mid-Jun–mid-Sep, 9.30am-5pm Mon-Fri, 10am-1pm Sat May–mid-Jun, 9am-4pm Mon-Fri, to 1pm Sat mid-Sep–Apr) Well stocked with brochures and leaflets on the city and its surroundings, and on the rest of Jutland and Denmark.

Sights & Activities

The towering brick walls of **ARoS** (☎ 87 30 66 00; www.aros.dk; Aros Allé 2; admission Dkr90; ⌚ 10am-5pm Thu-Sun & Tue, to 10pm Wed), Århus' showpiece art museum, look rather mundane from the outside but inside it's all sweeping curves, soaring spaces and white walls. One of the top three art galleries in Denmark, it is home to a comprehensive collection of 19th- and 20th-century Danish art and a wide range of arresting and vivid contemporary art.

The Danes' seemingly limitless enthusiasm for dressing up and recreating history reaches its zenith at **Den Gamle By** (The Old Town; ☎ 86 12 31 88; www.dengamleby.dk; Viborgvej 2; admission Dkr100; ⌚ 9am-6pm Jul-Aug, 10am-5pm Apr-Jun & Sep-Nov, to 4pm Feb & Mar, 10am-5pm Dec, 11am-3pm Jan). It's an engaging open-air museum of 75 half-timbered houses brought here from around Denmark and reconstructed as a provincial town, complete with a functioning bakery, silversmith and bookbinder. It's on Viborgvej, a 20-minute walk from the city centre. Buses 3, 14, 25 and 55 will take you there.

The impressive **Århus Domkirke** (☎ 86 20 54 00; Bispetorv; admission free; ⌚ 9.30am-4pm Mon-Sat May-Sep, 10am-3pm Mon-Sat Oct-Apr) is Denmark's longest, with a lofty nave that spans nearly 100m. The original Romanesque chapel at the eastern end dates from the 12th century, while most of the rest of the church is 15th-century Gothic.

Visit **Moesgård**, 5km south of the city centre, for its glorious beech woods and the trails threading through them towards sandy beaches. Visit for the well-presented history exhibits from the Stone Age to the Viking Age at **Moesgård Museum of Prehistory** (admission Dkr60; ⌚ 10am-5pm Apr-Sep, to 4pm Tue-Sun Oct-May). But above all else, visit Moesgård for the museum's most dramatic exhibit: the 2000-year-old **Grauballe Man**, or Grauballemanden, whose astonishingly well-preserved body was found in 1952 at the village of Grauballe, 35km west of Århus.

The superb new display on the Grauballe Man is part history lesson, part forensics lesson. Was he a sacrifice to Iron Age fertility gods, an executed prisoner perhaps, or simply a victim of murder?

Bus 6 from Århus train station terminates at the museum year-round and runs twice an hour.

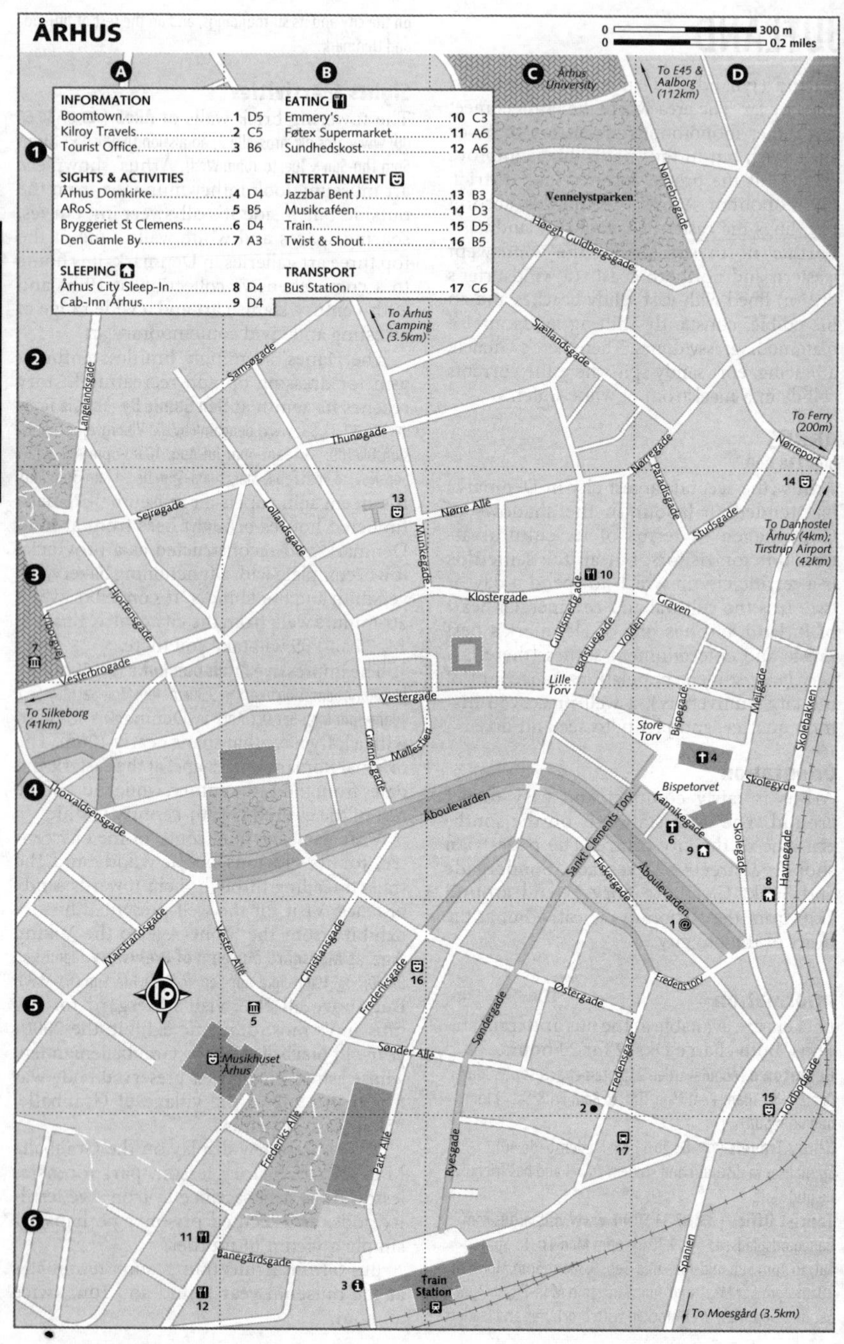
ÅRHUS
0 300 m
0 0.2 miles
INFORMATION
Boomtown 1 D5
Kilroy Travels 2 C5
Tourist Office 3 B6
SIGHTS & ACTIVITIES
Århus Domkirke 4 D4
ARoS 5 B5
Bryggeriet St Clemens 6 D4
Den Gamle By 7 A3
SLEEPING
Århus City Sleep-In 8 D4
Cab-Inn Århus 9 D4
EATING
Emmery's 10 C3
Føtex Supermarket 11 A6
Sundhedskost 12 A6
ENTERTAINMENT
Jazzbar Bent J 13 B3
Musikcaféen 14 D3
Train 15 D5
Twist & Shout 16 B5
TRANSPORT
Bus Station 17 C6
Århus University
To E45 & Aalborg (112km)
Vennelystparken
Nørrebrogade
Høegh Guldbergsgade
To Århus Camping (3.5km)
Sjællandsgade
Samsøgade
Langelandsgade
Thunøgade
To Ferry (200m)
Nørreport
Nørregade
Paradisgade
Studsgade
To Danhostel Århus (4km); Tirstrup Airport (42km)
Sejrøgade
Lollandsgade
Nørre Allé
Munkegade
Klostergade
Guldsmedgade
Graven
Hjortensgade
Viborgvej
Badstuegade
Volden
Vesterbrogade
Lille Torv
Vestergade
To Silkeborg (41km)
Bispegade
Store Torv
Mejlgade
Skolebakken
Grønnegade
Møllestien
Bispetorvet
Skolegyde
Thorvaldsensgade
Åboulevarden
Sankt Clements Torv
Kannikegade
Skolegade
Havnegade
Fiskergade
Marstrandsgade
Vester Allé
Christiansgade
Fredensgade
Fredens Torv
Frederiksgade
Østergade
Søndergade
Musikhuset Århus
Sønder Allé
Toldbodgade
Frederiks Allé
Park Allé
Ryesgade
Banegårdsgade
Spanien
Train Station
To Moesgård (3.5km)

DENMARK

Festival & Events

The 10-day **Århus Festival** (www.aarhusfestuge.dk) in early September turns the city into a stage for nonstop revelry with jazz, rock, classical music, theatre and dance.

Sleeping

The tourist office books rooms in private homes for around Dkr200/300 per single/double, plus a Dkr25 booking fee.

Århus Camping (☎ 86 23 11 33; www.aarhusnord.dk; Randersvej 400, Lisbjerg; adult/tent Dkr77/20; year-round) This large, decent, three-star camping ground is about 3.5km north of Århus.

Århus City Sleep-In (☎ 86 19 20 55; www.citysleep-in.dk; Havnegade 20; dm Dkr130, d with shared/private bathroom Dkr400/460; 24hr reception) Run by a youth organisation, the Århus City Sleep-In is in a central former mariners' hotel. It's casual, the rooms are a bit rundown but it's a cheerful place and by far the best budget option in the centre. Sheet hire costs Dkr45 and safety boxes are Dkr20, with Dkr100 deposit. Key deposit is Dkr50. There's a TV and pool table, guest kitchen and laundry facilities. Bike hire costs Dkr60 a day.

Danhostel Århus (☎ 86 16 72 98; www.hostel-aarhus.dk; Marienlundsvej 10; dm Dkr160, r Dkr506-620; late Jan–mid-Dec) It's 4km north of the city centre but well worth considering for the lovely parkland setting in a renovated 1850s dance hall. It's at the edge of the Risskov Woods and not far from the beach. Buses 6 or 9 pass nearby.

Cab Inn Århus (☎ 86 75 70 00; www.cabinn.com; Kannikegade 14; s from Dkr485-545, d Dkr615-675; P) In an ideal central location opposite the Domkirke. The style is standard Cab Inn with small, rather bare but usually clean rooms. Parking costs Dkr60. There's free internet and wi-fi access.

Eating

The Åboulevarden canal area is the place to head for the most high-profile restaurants and cafes. Nearby Skolegade is packed with popular, studenty pubs and clubs. The narrow streets of the old quarter north of the cathedral are also thick with cafes serving Danish and ethnic foods.

Emmery's (☎ 86 13 04 00; Guldsmedgade 24-26; brunch Dkr95, breakfast Dkr23; 7.30am-6pm Mon-Fri, 8am-4pm Sat & Sun) A stylish and friendly cafe-cum-delicatessen that serves its own delicious bread, tapas (Dkr95) and sandwiches (Dkr60 to Dkr78), some with vegetarian fillings.

Bryggeriet St Clemens (☎ 86 13 80 00; www.bryggeriet.dk, in Danish; Kannikegade 10 & 12; mains Dkr170-220; 11.30am-midnight Mon-Wed, to 2am Thu-Sat) This cosy microbrewery is a short walk from Åboulevarden and serves a range of home-brewed beers, as well as a decent range of cheap-ish fast food. This is part of the Hereford Beefstouw chain, so the menu is predictably steak-centric (although, less predictably this includes Wagyu beef).

The train station has a DSB cafe, a snack bar and a small **supermarket** (to midnight). Two blocks west is **Føtex supermarket** (Frederiks Allé), with a cheap bakery and deli, and **Sundhedskost** (Frederiks Allé), the city's largest health-food store.

DENMARK

Drinking & Clubbing

The monthly free publication *What's On in Århus* lists current happenings in detail and is available at the tourist office and venues around town. Århus has a vibrant music scene with something for all ages and tastes.

Train (☎ 86 13 47 22; Toldbodgade 6; until 5am Thu-Sat) One of the biggest venues in Denmark stages concerts by international rock, pop and country stars and there's a late-night disco.

Musikcaféen (☎ 86 76 03 44; Mejlgade 53; 8.30pm-2am Mon-Sat) Along with the adjacent Gyngen, this place is an alternative and often vibrant venue with rock, jazz and world music. Both are a showcase for hopefuls and up-and-coming acts.

Jazzbar Bent J (☎ 86 12 04 92; Nørre Allé 66; from 3.30pm Mon-Fri) This is a jazz only, very long-established bar with an impressive guest list. Entry is Dkr80 on guest nights.

Twist & Shout (☎ 86 18 08 55; Frederiksgade 29; 10am-5am Mon-Thu, from 5pm Fri & 10pm Sat) Lively, small, often packed and friendly, this three-floor club is the place to head to later in the evening. It's not too precious, there's a mix of music from '60s to house (depending on the floor) and everyone has fun.

Getting There & Away

AIR

SAS (www.flysas.com) flies one way for around Dkr300 from Copenhagen. The airport, in Tirstrup, 44km northeast of Århus, also has direct flights from London. Budget carrier Ryanair flies twice daily between London Stansted and Århus on weekdays and once on Saturday and Sunday.

Book your stay at lonelyplanet.com/hotels

BOAT
The ferry operator is **Mols-Linien** (☎ 70 10 14 18). It runs car ferries from Århus to Odden in northwest Zealand (adult Dkr315, car and five passengers Dkr695, 65 minutes).

BUS
The bus station (Fredensgade) has a DSB cafe and small supermarket. **Abildskou buses** (☎ 70 21 08 88; www.abildskou.dk) run a few times daily between Århus and Copenhagen's Valby Station and the airport, also stopping in Odense (Dkr270, three hours). For info on travel to other destinations in Jutland, see www.dsb.dk.

TRAIN
Trains to Århus, via Odense, leave Copenhagen hourly from early morning to 10pm (Dkr311, three hours) and there's a night train at 2am. There are regular trains to Aalborg (Dkr157, 1½ hours) and Esbjerg (Dkr216, 2½ hours). There's a ticket-queuing system at the station.

Getting Around
The airport bus to Århus train station costs Dkr90 and takes approximately 45 minutes. Check times to the airport at the stands outside the train station; some services start only in August. The taxi fare to the airport is about Dkr750.

Most in-town buses stop in front of the train station or around the corner on Park Allé.

AALBORG
pop 121,000

Aalborg has a vibrant nightlife, thanks to a large student population, and several worthwhile sights, not least the remarkable Lindholm Høje, Denmark's largest Viking burial ground.

The town centre is a 10-minute walk north on Boulevarden from the train and bus stations. The **tourist office** (☎ 99 31 75 00; www.visitaalborg.com; Østerågade 8; 9am-5.30pm Mon-Fri, 10am-1pm Sat mid-Jun–Aug, to 4.30pm Mon-Fri, 10am-1pm Sat Sep–mid-Jun) has friendly and helpful staff, with masses of information, including a diary of events, *What's on in Aalborg*. **Hovedbiblioteket** (City library; Rendsburggade 2; 10am-8pm Mon-Fri, 10am-3pm Sat) offers free internet access.

Sights
The whitewashed **Buldolfi Domkirke** marks the centre of the old town, and has colourful frescoes in the foyer. About 75m east of the cathedral is the **Aalborg Historiske Museum** (Algade 48; admission Dkr20; 9am-4pm Mon-Fri, to 2pm Sat), with artefacts from prehistory to the present, and furnishings and interiors that hint at the wealth Aalborg's merchants enjoyed during the Renaissance.

The Limfjorden (chalk fjord) was a kind of Viking motorway providing easy and speedy access to the Atlantic for longboat raiding parties. It's perhaps not surprising then that by far the most important piece of Aalborg's historical heritage is the Viking one. The hugely atmospheric **Lindholm Høje** (admission free; dawn-dusk) is a Viking burial ground where nearly 700 graves from the Iron Age and Viking Age are strewn around a hilltop pasture ringed by a wall of tall beech trees. The **museum** (☎ 96 31 04 28; admission free; 10am-5pm Apr-Oct), adjacent to the field, depicts the site's history while huge murals behind the exhibits speculate on what the people of Lindholm looked like and how they lived. Lindholm Høje is 15 minutes from Aalborg centre on bus 2.

Sleeping
Accommodation options are pretty good in town, inexpensive compared to other Danish destinations and not generally in massive demand.

Aalborg Camping & Hytteø (☎ 98 11 60 44; www.aalborgcamping.dk; Skydebanevej 50; adult/tent Dkr50/22; year-round) In the process of being modernised, this pleasant two-star camping ground is popular with naturists.

Danhostel Aalborg (☎ 98 11 60 44; www.danhostel.dk/aalborg; Skydebanevej 50; Jan-Jun & mid-Sep–Dec dm/s/d Dkr190/378/428, Jul–mid-Sep dm/s/d Dkr285/478/528; P) Handy for boating activities on the fjord but hardly central, the hostel is at the marina 4km west of the centre. It also runs an adjacent camping ground with cabins. Otherwise, the facilities are rather basic.

Zleep Hotel Aalborg (☎ 98 10 97 00; www.zleep.dk; Hadsundvej 182; s/d Dkr449/550) Part of a small chain of no-frills hotels, usually located a little out of town centres. This one is a 15-minute ride on bus 182 from Aalborg centre. The rooms are sparse but tidy and have cable TV.

Eating & Drinking
Eating out in Aalborg is very much about quantity rather than quality. If it's just ballast you want with your alcohol, then Jomfru Ane Gade, a lively, pedestrian street jammed solid

with fast-food style restaurants and bars, is the place to go.

Penny Lane (Boulevarden 10; ⏰ 10am-6pm Mon-Fri, 10am-2pm Sat) This is one of the most charming cafes in Jutland, featuring a well-stocked delicatessen and terrific cakes and pastries.

Studenterhuset (Student Union; ☎ 98 11 05 22; Gammeltorv 10) A convivial budget drinking and entertainment option. Lined with bookshelves, it's surprisingly upmarket and, well, studious for a student union. There's inexpensive beer, regular live bands and DJ nights.

Getting There & Around

Trains run to Århus (Dkr157, 1½ hours, at least hourly) and Frederikshavn (Dkr88, one hour, every two hours). **Abildskov buses** (☎ 70 21 08 88) run to Copenhagen (bus 888; Monday to Thursday Dkr170, Friday to Saturday Dkr310; five hours).

City buses leave from the intersection of Østerågade and Nytorv. The bus fare is Dkr16 to any place in greater Aalborg.

FREDERIKSHAVN

pop 23,500

A transport hub rather than a compelling destination, this bustling port town is pleasant enough but not one to linger in.

An overhead walkway leads from the ferry terminal to the **tourist office** (☎ 98 42 32 66; www.visitfrederikshavn.dk; Skandiatorv 1; ⏰ 9am-6pm Mon-Sat, to 2pm Sun end-Jun–mid-Aug, 9am-6pm last 2 weeks Jun & Aug, to 4pm Mon-Fri, 11am-2pm Sat Sep–mid-Jun). The train station and adjacent bus terminal are a 10-minute walk to the north.

Danhostel Frederikshavn (☎ 98 42 14 75; www.danhostel.dk/frederikshavn; Buhlsvej 6; dm/s/d Dkr100/250/300; ⏰ Feb–mid-Dec; P ☒) is a pleasant place, 2km north of the ferry terminal, with chalet-style, six-bed dorms.

If you're catching a ferry, **Havne Super** (Sydhavnesvej 8) is a supermarket at the harbour with a cafeteria and long hours. Consider picking up provisions if you're going on to expensive Norway.

From Frederikshavn, **Stena Line** (☎ 96 20 02 00) runs ferries six to 10 times daily (Dkr95 to Dkr215, two to 3¼ hours) to Göteborg, Sweden. **Color Line** (☎ 99 56 19 77; www.colorline.com) runs to Oslo once daily (8½ hours). Prices vary by season.

Frederikshavn is the northern terminus of the DSB train line. Trains run about hourly south to Aalborg (Dkr88) and then onto Copenhagen (Dkr343). **Nordjyske Jernbaner** (☎ 98 45 45 10; www.njba.dk) runs smart new trains every two hours to Skagen (Dkr48) and to Hirtshals at least once a day.

SKAGEN

Skagen is a magical place, both bracing and beautiful. Artists discovered its luminous light and its colourful, wind-blasted, heath-and-dune landscape in the mid-19th century.

Today, Skagen is a very popular tourist resort, packed in high summer. But the sense of a more picturesque Skagen survives and the town's older neighbourhood, Gammel Skagen, 5km west, is filled with distinctive, single-storey, yellow-walled, red-roofed houses. The peninsula is lined with fine beaches, including a sandy stretch on the eastern end of Østre Strandvej, a 15-minute walk from the town centre.

Sankt Laurentii Vej, Skagen's main street, runs almost the entire length of this long thin town, and is never more than five minutes from the waterfront. The **tourist office** (☎ 98 44 13 77; www.skagen-tourist.dk; Sankt Laurentii Vej 22; ⏰ 10am-4pm Mon-Fri, 10am-1pm Sat Jan-Mar, 9am-4pm Mon-Fri, 10am-2pm Sat Apr-Jun & late Aug-Oct, 9am-6pm Mon-Sat, 10am-4pm Sun Jul-early Aug) is in the train/bus station.

Sleeping & Eating

Grenen Camping (☎ 98 44 25 46; adult Dkr81) A fine seaside location, semi-private tent sites and pleasant four-bunk huts, 1.5km northeast of Skagen centre. The only downside is the rather tightly bunched sites.

Danhostel Skagen (☎ 98 44 22 00; www.danhostel.dk/skagen; Rolighedsvej 2; dm Dkr150, s/d from Dkr500/600; ⏰ mid-Feb–late Nov; P) Danhostel is well-kept, very popular and 1km from the centre, so book ahead in summer. Rates drop sharply in low season.

You'll find a couple of pizzerias, a kebab shop, a burger joint and an ice-cream shop clustered near each other on Havnevej. **Super Brugsen** (Sankt Laurentii Vej 28), a grocery store just west of the tourist office, has a bakery.

Getting There & Around

Nordjyske Jernbaner (☎ 98 45 45 10; www.njba.dk, in Danish) runs smart new trains every two hours (Dkr48) to Frederikshavn. The seasonal Skagerakkeren bus 99 runs between Hirtshals and Skagen (Dkr37, 1½ hours, six daily mid-June to mid-August). The same bus continues to Hjørring and Løkken.

Cycling is an excellent way of exploring Skagen and the surrounding area. **Skagen Cykeludlejning** (☎ 98 44 10 70; Banegårdspladsen; per day Dkr75, deposit Dkr200) rents out bicycles and has a stand on the western side of the train station and at the harbour.

Skagen is very busy with traffic in high season. There is free parking for short periods and convenient metered parking (Dkr10 per hour) just by the train station.

HIRTSHALS

A busy, modern little town thanks to a large commercial fishing harbour and ferry terminal, Hirtshals has an easy, friendly character, an excellent aquarium and some fine stretches of beach. For information, pop in to the **tourist office** (☎ 98 94 22 20; www.visithirtshals.com; Nørregade 40; 9am-4pm Mon-Fri & 9am-noon Sat Apr-Jun, 9am-4pm Mon-Sat Jul–mid-Aug).

Hirtshals' big draw is the **Nordsømuseet** (☎ 98 94 41 88; Willemoesvej 2; admission Dkr110; 10am-6pm mid-Jun–mid-Aug, to 5pm mid-Aug–mid-Jun), an impressive aquarium that recreates a slice of the North Sea in a massive four-storey tank, containing elegantly balletic schools of thousands of fish. Divers feed the fish at 1pm and the seals at 11am and 3pm.

Hirtshals Hostel (☎ 98 94 12 48; www.danhostelnord.dk/hirtshals; Kystvejen 53; dm/s/d Dkr150/370/420; Mar-Nov) occupies a bland building and offers basic facilities about 1km from the centre. The saving grace of this hostel is its location a bucket and spade's throw from the beach.

The ferry company **Color Line** (☎ 99 56 20 00; www.colorline.com) runs year-round ferries to the Norwegian ports of Larvik (6½ hours, twice daily from May to September) and Kristiansand (2½, twice daily). Fares on both routes range from Dkr180 per adult midweek in the low season to Dkr460 on summer weekends for passengers, and Dkr720 to Dkr1760 for cars. A new service from **Fjord Line** (☎ 97 96 30 00; www.fjordline.dk) goes to Stavanger and Bergen in Norway (car to Stavanger from Dkr654; to Bergen from Dkr744).

Hirtshals' main train station, 500m south of the ferry harbour, connects Hirtshals with Hjørring (Dkr24), 20 minutes to the south. Trains run at least hourly. From Hjørring you can take a DSB train to Aalborg (Dkr72) or Frederikshavn (Dkr48).

RIBE

The charming, crooked cobblestone streets of Ribe date from 869, making it one of Scandinavia's oldest and Denmark's most attractive towns. It is a delightful chocolate-box confection of half-timbered, 16th-century houses, clear-flowing streams and water meadows.

There's a **tourist office** (☎ 75 42 15 00; www.visitribe.dk; Torvet 3; 9am-6pm Mon-Fri, 10am-5pm Sat, to 2pm Sun Jul & Aug, 9am-5pm Mon-Fri Apr-Jun & Sep-Oct, 10am-1pm Sat Apr-Jun & Sep-Dec) and the **Danske Bank** (☎ 76 88 68 20; Overdammen 4).

Dominating the heart of the town, **Ribe Domkirke** (☎ 75 42 06 19; Torvet; admission Dkr10) boasts a variety of styles from Romanesque to Gothic. The highlight is the climb up the steeple for breathtaking views.

Ribes Vikinger (☎ 76 88 11 22; Odins Plads 1; admission Dkr60; 10am-6pm Jul & Aug, to 4pm Apr-Jun, Sep & Oct, to 4pm Tue-Sun Nov-Mar) is a substantial museum opposite the train station; it has archaeological displays of Ribe's Viking past, including a reconstructed marketplace and Viking ship, with lots of hands-on features.

The tourist office maintains a list of singles/doubles in private homes from around Dkr250/350.

Danhostel Ribe (☎ 75 42 06 20; www.danhostel.dk/ribe; Sankt Pedersgade 16; dm/s Dkr160/325, d Dkr360-560; Feb–late-Nov; P) is a modern, 140-bed hostel with friendly staff and a good, uncrowded location. The new rooms at the top are especially appealing and worth the extra cost.

Trains run hourly between Esbjerg and Ribe (Dkr65, 40 minutes).

DENMARK DIRECTORY

ACCOMMODATION

Camping & Cabins

Denmark's 516 camping grounds typically charge from Dkr50 to Dkr65 per person to pitch a tent. Many places add about Dkr20 for the tent. A camping pass (available at any camping ground) is required (Dkr90). If you do not have a seasonal pass you pay an extra Dkr20 a night for a temporary pass.

The **Danish Camping Association** (☎ 39 27 88 44; www.campingraadet.dk; Campingrådet, Mosedalvej 15, Valby) inspects and grades Danish camping grounds using a star system and carries a full list on its website.

Hostels

The national Hostelling International office is **Danhostel** (☎ 33 31 36 12; www.danhostel.dk; Vesterbrogade 39, 1620 Copenhagen V).

Most of Denmark's 100 *vandrerhjem* (hostels) in its Danhostel association have private rooms in addition to dormitories, making hostels an affordable and popular alternative to hotels (so book ahead from June to August). Dorm beds cost from about Dkr150, while private rooms range from Dkr280 to Dkr400 for singles, and Dkr400 to Dkr500 for doubles.

Hotels

Budget hotels start at around Dkr500/650 for singles/doubles. Kro, a name that implies country inn but is more often the Danish version of a motel, are generally cheaper, often occupy pleasing period houses and more often than not offer a sense of homeliness and hospitality that chain hotels cannot hope to compete with. Both hotels and kros usually include an all-you-can-eat breakfast. You can find out more about some of Denmark's inns and make online bookings at www.krohotel.dk (though not all are listed online – those listed pay to be included).

ACTIVITIES

Cycling is a popular holiday activity and there are thousands of kilometres of established cycling routes. Those around Bornholm, Funen and Møn, as well as the 440km Old Military Rd (Hærvejen) through central Jutland, are among the most popular.

Dansk Cyklist Forbund (DCF; ☎ 33 32 31 21; www.dcf.dk; Rømersgade 7, 1362 Copenhagen K) publishes *Cykelferiekort*, a cycling map of the entire country (Dkr60), as well as more detailed regional cycling maps.

DCF also publishes *Overnatning i det fri*, which lists hundreds of farmers who provide cyclists with a place to pitch a tent for Dkr15 a night.

Canoeing possibilities on Denmark's inland lakes, such as canoe touring between lakeside camping grounds in Jutland's Lake District, are superb. You can hire canoes and equipment at many camping grounds or in main centres.

Denmark's remarkable coastline offers terrific wind- and kite-surfing. Good areas are along the northern coast of Zealand at places such as Smidstrup Strand, and in northwest Jutland. The Limfjord area of northwest Jutland is particularly suitable.

BUSINESS HOURS

Office hours are generally 9am to 5pm Monday to Friday. Most banks are open from 9.30am to 4pm Monday to Friday (to 6pm Thursday), but some still close earlier. Shops are usually open 9.30am to 5.30pm Monday to Thursday, to 7pm on Friday, and to 2pm on Saturday.

EMBASSIES & CONSULATES

The following embassies and consulates are in Copenhagen, unless mentioned otherwise.

Australia (☎ 70 26 36 76; www.denmark.embassy.gov.au; Dampfærgevej 26, Copenhagen)
Canada (☎ 33 48 32 00; www.canada.dk; Kristen Bernikows Gade1, Copenhagen)
Germany (☎ 35 45 99 00; www.kopenhagen.diplo.de; Stockholmsgade 57, Copenhagen)
Ireland (☎ 35 42 32 33; Østbanegade 21, Copenhagen)
Norway (☎ 33 14 01 24; www.norsk.dk; Amaliegade 39, Copenhagen)
Poland (☎ 39 46 77 00; www.ambpol.dk; Richelius Allé 12, Hellerup)
Sweden (☎ 33 36 03 70; www.sverigesambassad.dk; Sankt Annæ Plads 15A, Copenhagen)
UK (☎ 35 44 52 00; www.britishembassy.dk; Kastelsvej 36-40, Copenhagen)
USA (☎ 33 41 71 00; www.usembassy.dk; Dag Hammarskjölds Allé 24, Copenhagen)

FESTIVALS & EVENTS

Midsummer's Eve Starting with bonfires in late June, Denmark buzzes with outdoor activity throughout the summer. Main attractions are the 180 music festivals that run throughout the country, covering a broad spectrum of music that includes not only jazz, rock and blues but also gospel, folk, classical, country, Cajun and much more.
Roskilde Rock festival (www.roskilde-festival.dk) Last weekend of June; a single admission fee includes camping space and entry to all concerts.
Copenhagen Jazz Festival (http://festival.jazz.dk, in Danish) A 10-day festival held in early July, with outdoor concerts and numerous performances in clubs around the city.
Århus Festival Early September, features music and multicultural events.
Skanderborg Festival (www.smukfest.dk) An August rock and pop festival said to be Denmark's most beautiful.

GAY & LESBIAN TRAVELLERS

Denmark is a popular destination for gay and lesbian travellers. Copenhagen, in particular, has an active, open gay community and lots of nightlife options. A good English-language website with links to LBL and other gay organisations is www.copenhagen-gay-life.dk.

HOLIDAYS

Summer holidays for schoolchildren begin around 20 June and end around 10 August. Many Danes go on holiday during the first three weeks of July. The following public holidays are observed in Denmark:

New Year's Day (1 January)
Maundy Thursday (Thursday before Easter)
Good Friday to Easter Monday (March/April)
Common Prayer Day (Fourth Friday after Easter)
Ascension Day (Fifth Thursday after Easter)
Whit Sunday (Fifth Sunday after Easter)
Whit Monday (Fifth Monday after Easter)
Constitution Day (5 Jun)
Christmas Eve (24 December from noon)
Christmas Day (25 December)

LEGAL MATTERS

Denmark is taking a much harder line on even the 'softest' drugs these days. All forms of cannabis and harder drugs are illegal.

MONEY

ATMs

Major banks have ATMs, which accept Visa, MasterCard and the Cirrus and Plus bank cards. All major credit and debit cards are widely accepted throughout Denmark, although some shops impose a surcharge of up to 5% if you use them, even in the case of debit cards.

The Euro

Although Denmark remains outside the Euro zone, acceptance of euros is commonplace. Most hotels and restaurants will take euros, as do many bars, cafes and shops, although you may find reluctance to do so in more remote areas or from very small businesses. Government institutions do not accept euros.

Tipping

Restaurant bills and taxi fares include service charges in the quoted prices, and further tipping is unnecessary.

POST

Denmark has an efficient postal system. Most post offices are open 9am or 10am to 5pm or 5.30pm Monday to Friday and 9am to noon on Saturday. You can receive mail poste restante at any post office in Denmark.

TELEPHONE

It costs Dkr5 to make a local call at coin phones. You get about twice as much calling time for your money on domestic calls made between 7.30pm and 8am daily and all day on Sunday. Phonecards (Dkr50 to Dkr100) can be bought at post offices and newspaper kiosks throughout the country.

VISAS

Citizens of the EU, USA, Canada, Australia and New Zealand need a valid passport to enter Denmark, but don't need a visa for stays of less than three months. If you wish to apply for a visa, do so at least three months in advance of your planned arrival.

Estonia

HIGHLIGHTS

- **Tallinn** Find medieval bliss exploring the Old Town, then unwind at Kadriorg Park (p333)
- **Pärnu** Get sand in your shorts at Estonia's beachy-keen summertime mecca (p342)
- **Tartu** Further your local education among the bars and cafes of Estonia's second city (p339)
- **Lahemaa National Park** Look for shy beavers, go cycling and discover your own slice of deserted coast (p339)

FAST FACTS

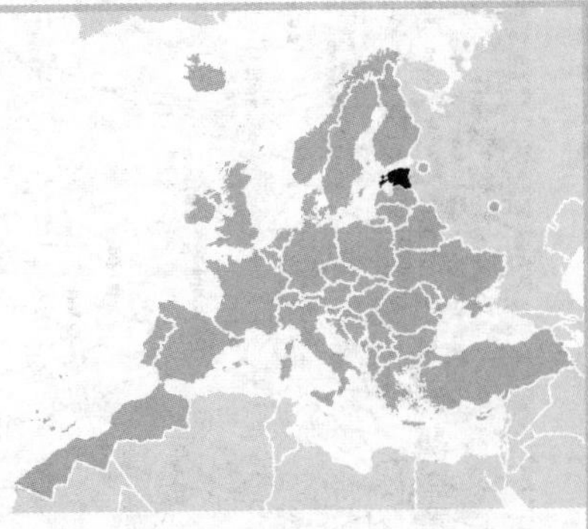

- **Area** 45,226 sq km (slightly larger than Denmark)
- **Budget** 500-600EEK per day
- **Capital** Tallinn
- **Country code** ☎ 372
- **Famous for** song festivals, Skype & Kazaa, saunas, forest, supermodel Carmen Kass
- **Language** Estonian (a Finno-Ugric language)
- **Money** kroon (EEK); A$1 = 8.69EEK; C$1 = 9.88EEK; €1 = 15.65EEK; ¥100 = 12.30EEK; NZ$1 = 6.80EEK; UK£1 = 17.63EEK; US$1 = 11.64EEK
- **Phrases** *aitäh* (thanks), *tere!* (hi!), *mis te nimi on?* (what's your name?), *kui palju see maksab?* (how much does this cost?)
- **Population** 1.3 million
- **Visas** none required for travellers from the EU, the USA, Canada and Australia (p344)

TRAVEL HINTS

Buses are the way to get around (trains are minimal). Internet access is usually free at libraries.

ROAMING ESTONIA

Tallinn's Old Town is *the* must-see, but also check out student-savvy Tartu and/or the beaches of Pärnu.

The 20th century was full of twists and turns for Estonia, but it's now primped and primed and waiting to shine in the spotlight.

This diminutive country has shaken off the dead weight of the Soviet era and turned its focus to the West, and to promises of a richer, shinier future. In recent years it's claimed EU membership and one of Europe's fastest-growing economies, and the country is now patting itself on the back and celebrating its return to the world stage – independent, economically robust and tech-savvy.

And the world is tuning in to the low-key, lovely Estonian charms, an irresistible blend of Eastern European and Nordic. Soaking up Tallinn's long white nights and medieval history, or exploring the country's coastline, studded with islands, are joys to be savoured. National parks provide plenty of elbow room, quaint villages evoke a timeless sense of history, and uplifting song festivals celebrate age-old traditions.

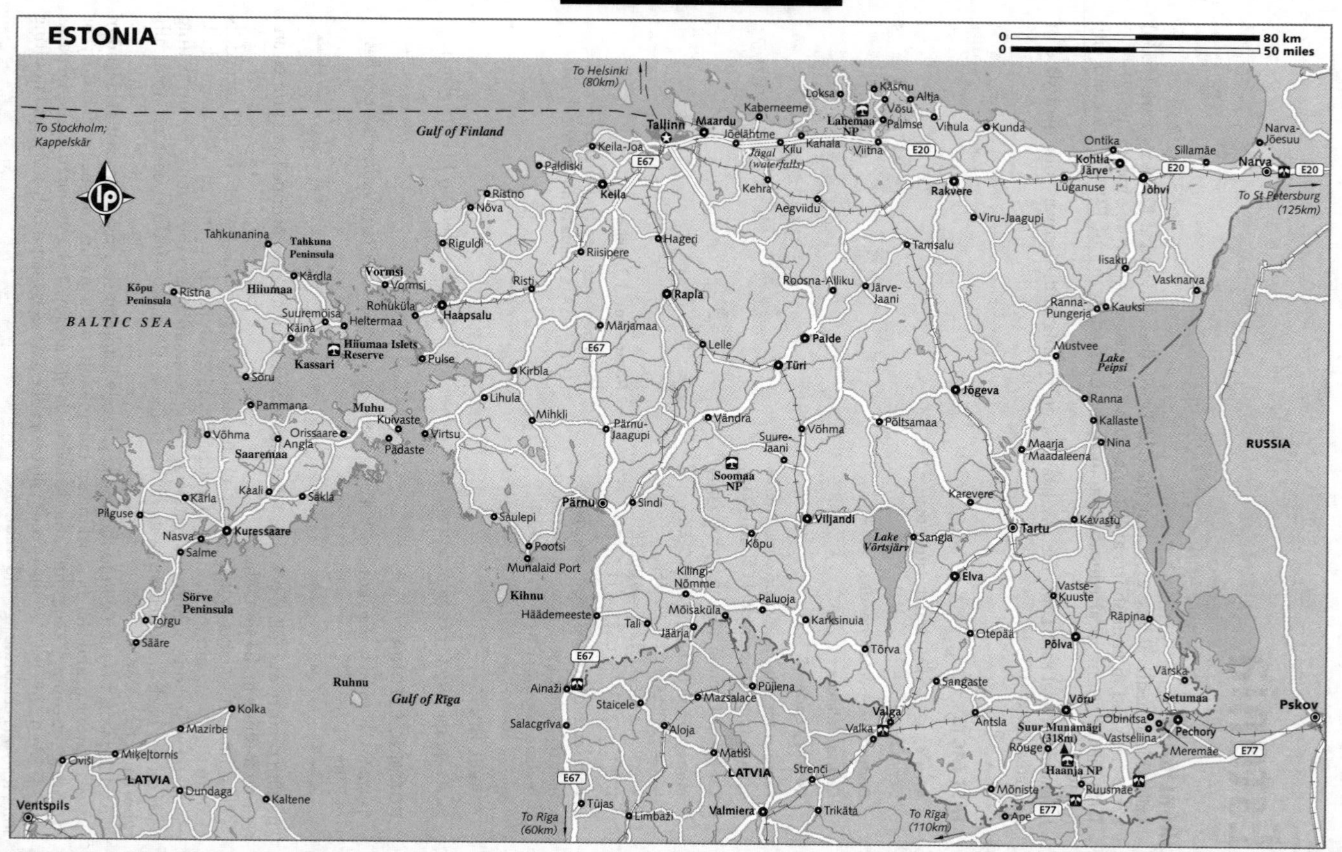
ESTONIA
0 80 km
0 50 miles
To Helsinki (80km)
To Stockholm; Kappelskär
Gulf of Finland
To St Petersburg (125km)
To Rīga (60km)
To Rīga (110km)
RUSSIA
LATVIA
BALTIC SEA
Gulf of Rīga
Lake Peipsi
Lake Võrtsjärv
Tallinn
Maardu
Jõelähtme
Kaberneeme
Jägala (waterfalls)
Kiiu
Kahala
Kehra
Aegviidu
Loksa
Lahemaa NP
Käsmu
Võsu
Altja
Palmse
Vihula
Viitna
Kunda
Rakvere
Viru-Jaagupi
Tamsalu
Ontika
Kohtla-Järve
Lüganuse
Jõhvi
Sillamäe
Narva
Narva-Jõesuu
Iisaku
Vasknarva
Ranna-Pungerja
Kauksi
Mustvee
Ranna
Kallaste
Nina
Maarja Maadaleena
Kavastu
Tartu
Karevere
Jõgeva
Põltsamaa
Järve-Jaani
Roosna-Alliku
Paide
Türi
Võhma
Suure-Jaani
Vändra
Soomaa NP
Viljandi
Kõpu
Sangla
Elva
Lelle
Rapla
Hageri
Keila
Keila-Joa
Paldiski
Riisipere
Märjamaa
Pärnu-Jaagupi
Sindi
Pärnu
Saulepi
Pootsi
Munalaid Port
Kihnu
Häädemeeste
Tali
Jäärja
Mõisaküla
Kilingi-Nõmme
Paluoja
Karksinuia
Tõrva
Otepää
Sangaste
Valga
Valka
Antsla
Võru
Põlva
Vastse-Kuuste
Räpina
Värska
Setumaa
Obinitsa
Vastseliina
Pechory
Meremäe
Suur Munamägi (318m)
Rõuge
Haanja NP
Ruusmäe
Mõniste
Ape
Pskov
E20
E67
E77
Ristno
Nõva
Riguldi
Risti
Haapsalu
Rohuküla
Vormsi
Heltermaa
Hiiumaa Islets Reserve
Kassari
Käina
Suuremõisa
Kärdla
Tahkuna Peninsula
Tahkunanina
Hiiumaa
Ristna
Kõpu Peninsula
Sõru
Pulse
Kirbla
Lihula
Mihkli
Virtsu
Muhu
Kuivaste
Pädaste
Pammana
Orissaare
Angla
Võhma
Saaremaa
Kaali
Sakla
Kärla
Pilguse
Kuressaare
Nasva
Salme
Sõrve Peninsula
Torgu
Sääre
Ruhnu
Ainaži
Salacgrīva
Staicele
Aloja
Mazsalace
Pūjiena
Matīši
Strenči
Valmiera
Trikāta
Limbaži
Tūjas
Kolka
Mazirbe
Mikeļtornis
Ovīši
Dundaga
Kaltene
Ventspils

HISTORY

Most of Estonia's history has been one of occupation and domination. Bandied about between European major powers, it has enjoyed only sparse periods of independence, notably in the 20th century between the world wars, and since 1991.

In the 3rd millennium BC Finno-Ugric tribes from the east mixed with the Baltic tribes already there. The Germanic Teutonic Order took control in 1346, placing Estonians under servitude to a German nobility that would last until the early 20th century despite Danish, Swedish and Russian rulers.

After the Great Northern War (1700–21), Estonia became part of the Russian empire. During WWI, the Soviet government relinquished Estonia. Until 1940 Estonia was ruled by benevolent dictator Konstantin Päts, who was forced to accept Soviet occupation. Estonia was 'accepted' into the USSR after fabricated elections and, within a year, over 10,000 people in Estonia were killed or deported before the German occupation. Between 1945 and 1949 a further 60,000 Estonians were killed or deported.

Estonia declared independence from the USSR on 20 August 1991. The following decade saw frequent changes of government and no shortage of scandal as it tried to find its footing. Estonia is an independent parliamentary republic led by Prime Minister Ansip; the head of state is President Ilves. It's now a member of NATO and the EU, business is booming, and Estonia intends to continue the Euro party until well into the wee hours.

THE CULTURE

Estonia's population of 1.3 million is 69% Estonian, 26% Russian, and 3% Ukrainian and Belarusian. The Russian speakers are concentrated in Tallinn and in the industrial northeast, forming around 37% and up to 95% of the respective populations.

The Estonians are historically a rural people cautious of outsiders and stereotypically shy and reticent. They are nature lovers who enjoy a sauna with friends by a lake, and are emotionally connected to their history, folklore and national song tradition.

ARTS

Estonia has a strong and internationally well-respected classical music tradition, most notably its choirs. Composer Arvo Pärt is among the world's most renowned living composers.

Hard rock thrives in Estonia – Ultima Thule, Genialistid and Smilers are among the country's longest-running and most beloved bands. The pop- and dance-music scenes are also strong here (Eurovision is serious business). See www.estmusic.com for detailed listings and streaming samples of Estonian musicians of all genres.

> **READING UP**
>
> Former president Lennart Meri's *Hõbevalge* (Silver White) masterfully incorporates history and folklore to weave a unique recounting of Estonia's history and destiny. Douglas Wells spent years in Estonia in the US Peace Corps and wrote the entertaining *In Search of the Elusive Peace Corps Moment: Destination: Estonia* as a result. Also worth reading is Jaan Kross' *The Czar's Madman.*

ENVIRONMENT

Estonia is a low-lying land whose highest peak (Suur Munamägi) stands at just 318m. Despite its tiny size, it boasts some 1500 islands and 3794km of coastline.

Since independence there have been major 'clean-up' attempts to counter the effects of Soviet-era industrialisation. Toxic emissions in the industrialised northeast of Estonia have been reduced sharply and new environmental-impact legislation aims to minimise the environmental effects of future development.

TRANSPORT

GETTING THERE & AWAY

Air

The national carrier **Estonian Air** (OV; ☎ 640 1163; www.estonian-air.ee; Vabaduse väljak 10, Tallinn) links Tallinn with some 20 cities in Europe and Russia. Other airlines serving **Tallinn airport** (www.tallinn-airport.ee) include **Air Baltic** (BT; ☎ 640 7750; www.airbaltic.com), with flights to Vilnius and Rīga, and **Finnair** (AY; ☎ 626 6309; www.finnair.com), with flights to Helsinki. **easyJet** (www.easyjet.com) links Tallinn with both London and Berlin.

Boat

TO/FROM FINLAND

Oodles of daily ferries ply the 85km separating Helsinki and Tallinn (ships take two to 3½ hours, hydrofoils approximately 1½ hours). In high winds or bad weather, hydrofoils are often cancelled; they operate only when the sea is free from ice (generally around late March/April to late December). Larger ferries sail year-round.

All companies provide concessions. Prices are cheaper on weekdays, and outside summer. There's lots of competition, so shop around.

Eckerö Line (☎ 664 6000; www.eckeroline.ee; Terminal A, Tallinn) Sails once daily back and forth year-round (300EEK to 390EEK, three to 3½ hours).

Linda Line (☎ 699 9333; www.lindaliini.ee; Linnahall Terminal, Tallinn) Small, passenger-only hydrofoils up to seven times daily late March to late December (295EEK to 455EEK, 1½ hours).

Nordic Jet (☎ 613 7000; www.njl.info; Terminal C, Tallinn) Seven daily crossings with jet catamarans, generally from May to September (from 440EEK, 1¾ hours).

Tallink (☎ 640 9808; www.tallinksilja.com; Terminal D, Tallinn) At least five services daily in each direction; the huge *Baltic Princess* takes 3½ hours, brand-new high-speed ferries take two hours and operate year-round. Prices start at 360EEK.

Viking Line (☎ 666 3966; www.vikingline.ee; Terminal A, Tallinn) Operates a giant car ferry, with two departures daily (from 300EEK, 2½ hours).

TO/FROM SWEDEN

Tallink (☎ 640 9808; www.tallinksilja.com) sails every night year-round between Tallinn's Terminal D and Stockholm (cabin berth from 2250EEK, 16 hours). Book ahead.

Bus

Eurolines (☎ 680 0909; www.eurolines.ee; Bus Station, Lastekodu 46, Tallinn) connects Tallinn with several cities in Germany and Poland, and from there to cities throughout Europe.

> **CONNECTIONS**
>
> Estonia's an easy northern addition to Eastern European roaming: plenty of daily buses connect with Latvia and Lithuania (Tallinn–Rīga buses are particularly plentiful). You could follow the white nights to Scandinavia – Tallinn has daily ferry connections to/from Stockholm and Helsinki. Or if you're hearing the siren call of Russia, nightly trains connect Tallinn with Moscow, and half-a-dozen daily buses run between Tallinn and St Petersburg (you can also reach St Pete by daily bus from Tartu).

Direct services connect Tallinn to Rīga (190EEK to 295EEK, 4½ hours, seven daily) and Vilnius (465EEK to 570EEK, 9½ to 12 hours, six daily via Rīga). Buses leave Tallinn for St Petersburg seven or eight times daily (495EEK, eight hours). One daily bus connects Tartu with St Pete (370EEK, eight hours).

Car & Motorcycle

From Finland, put your vehicle on a Helsinki–Tallinn ferry (p331).

Train

The on-again, off-again Tallinn–St Petersburg service was off at the time of research. An overnight train runs every evening between Moscow and Tallinn (1500EEK in a four-berth compartment, 14 hours) operated by **GO Rail** (☎ 631 0044; www.gorail.ee).

GETTING AROUND

Bicycle

The flatness and small scale of Estonia, and the light traffic on most roads, make it excellent cycling territory. Plenty of places rent bikes out; see City Bike, p339.

Bus

Buses are the best option, as they're more frequent and faster than trains, and cover destinations not serviced by the limited rail network. For bus information and advance tickets, contact Tallinn's central bus station, **Autobussijaam** (☎ 680 0900; Lastekodu 46). The excellent website www.bussireisid.ee has schedules and prices for all national bus services.

Train

Trains are slower and rarer than buses. Regional train schedules are listed at www.edel.ee, in Estonian (click on Sõiduplannid ja-hinnad to access timetables and prices).

TALLINN

pop 400,000

Today's Tallinn fuses medieval and cutting-edge to come up with an energetic new mood all its own – an intoxicating traveller mix of ancient church spires, glass-and-chrome skyscrapers, cosy wine cellars inside 15th-century basements, lazy afternoons soaking up sun and beer suds on Raekoja plats, and bike paths to beaches and forests – with a few Soviet throwbacks in the mix, for added spice. Despite its fiercely forward focus and the boom of 21st-century development, Tallinn remains loyal to the fairy-tale charms of the Old Town, and compact enough to explore on foot (or there's the option of an easy tram or bus ride should you seek leafy parks or beachside downtime).

The jewel in Tallinn's crown remains the two-tiered Old Town, a 14th- and 15th-century jumble of turrets, spires and winding streets. Most tourists see nothing other than this cobblestoned labyrinth of intertwining alleys and picturesque courtyards. Tallinn's modern dimension – its growing skyline, shiny shopping malls, cutting-edge new art museum, the wi-fi that bathes much of the city – is a cool surprise.

ORIENTATION

The medieval Old Town, just to the south of Tallinn Bay, comprises Toompea (the upper town) and the lower town, which is still surrounded by much of its 2.5km defensive wall. Its centre is Raekoja plats (Town Hall Sq). Immediately east of the Old Town is the modern city centre.

INFORMATION

Discount Cards

Tallinn Card (www.tallinncard.ee; per person 185-495EEK) Offers free rides on public transport, admission to museums, free excursions and discounts at restaurants; valid for six to 72 hours.

Internet Access

Metro (Viru Keskus; per hr 40EEK; 9am-11pm) By the bus terminal, on the basement level of Viru Keskus shopping centre.

Medical Services

Apteek 1 (☎ 627 3607; Aia 7) One of many well-stocked pharmacies in town; open daily.

Tallinn Central Hospital (☎ 620 7070, emergency department 620 7040; Ravi 18) Has a full range of services and a 24-hour emergency room.

Money

Tavid Exchange Bureau (☎ 627 9900; Aia 5; 24hr) Currency exchange; reliably good rates.

Telephone

You can buy 50EEK and 100EEK chip cards from newsstands to use for local and international calls at any one of the blue phone boxes scattered around town.

EMERGENCY NUMBERS

- 24-hour roadside assistance for drivers ☎ 1888
- Fire, ambulance and urgent medical advice ☎ 112
- Police ☎ 110
- Tallinn's First Aid hotline (☎ 697 1145) can advise in English about the nearest treatment centres.

Post offices, supermarkets and kiosks sell mobile-phone starter kits with prepaid SIM cards (from 50EEK).

Tourist Information

Tallinn In Your Pocket (www.inyourpocket.com) The king of the region's listings. Its booklets are on sale at bookshops, or can be downloaded free from its website.

Tourist Information Centre (☎ 645 7777; www.tourism.tallinn.ee; cnr Kullassepa & Niguliste; 9am-5pm Mon-Fri, 10am-3pm Sat Oct-Apr, 9am-7pm Mon-Fri, 10am-5pm Sat & Sun May-Jun, 9am-8pm Mon-Fri, 10am-6pm Sat & Sun Jul-Aug, 9am-6pm Mon-Fri, 10am-5pm Sat & Sun Sep) A block south of Raekoja plats. There are also small information desks at the port (Terminal A), and inside Viru Keskus shopping centre.

Traveller Info Tent (☎ 5814 0442; www.traveller-info.com; Niguliste; 9am-9pm or 10pm Jun–mid-Sep) Fabulous source of information, set up by locals in a tent opposite the official tourist info centre. They produce a map of Tallinn with loads of recommended places (and similar maps to Tartu and Pärnu), dispense lots of local tips, keep a 'what's on' board, and operate entertaining, well-priced walking and cycling tours.

Travel Agencies

Bookingestonia.com (☎ 712 2102; Voorimehe 1, 2nd fl; www.bookingestonia.com) Books bus, train and ferry tickets (no commission), and helps arrange accommodation and car rental.

Union Travel (☎ 627 0627; Lembitu 14) Can help arrange visas to Russia.

SIGHTS

Raekoja Plats & Lower Town

Raekoja plats has been the centre of Tallinn life since the 11th century; bathed in sunlight or sprinkled with snow, it's always a photogenic spot. It's dominated by northern Europe's only surviving Gothic **town hall** (☎ 645 7900; adult/student 40/25EEK; 10am-4pm

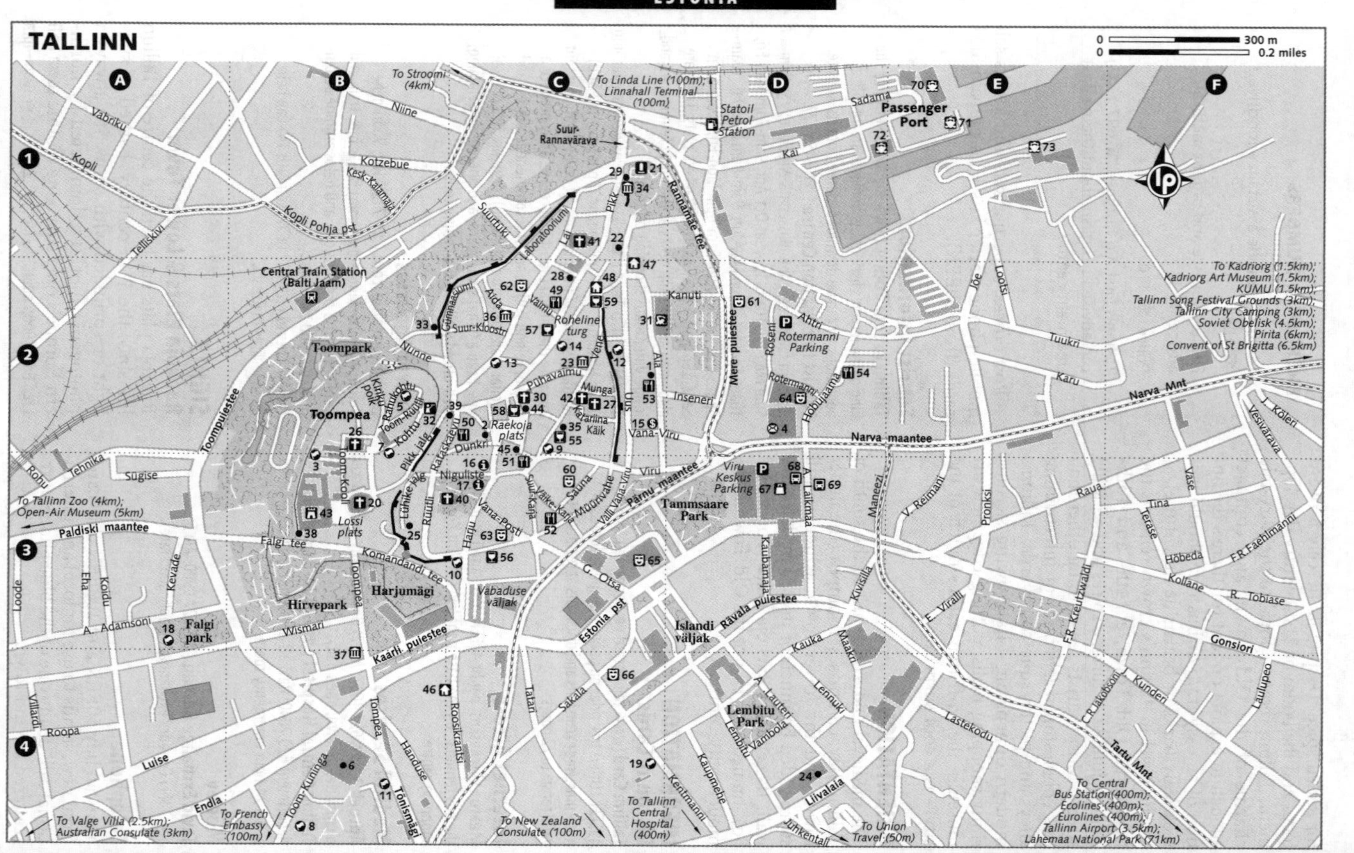
TALLINN
300 m
0.2 miles
To Stroomi (4km)
To Linda Line (100m); Linnahall Terminal (100m)
Statoil Petrol Station
Passenger Port
Sadama
Kai
Suur-Rannavärava
Central Train Station (Balti Jaam)
Toompark
Toompea
Kiriku poik
Rahukohtu
Toom-Rüütli
Kohtu
Toom-Kooli
Pikk jalg
Lühike jalg
Lossi plats
Raekoja plats
Rataskaevu
Dunkri
Niguliste
Pühavaimu
Roheline turg
Vaimu
Aida
Suur-Kloostri
Gümnaasiumi
Laboratooriumi
Suurtüki
Nunne
Lai
Pikk
Vene
Munga
Katariina Käik
Uus
Ala
Inseneri
Kanuti
Vana-Viru
Viru
Välli Vana-Viru
Müürivahe
Sauna
Väike-Karja
Suur-Karja
Vana-Posti
Harju
Rüütli
Komandandi tee
Falgi tee
Vabaduse väljak
Harjumägi
Hirvepark
Falgi park
Tõnismägi
Tammsaare Park
Viru Keskus Parking
Kaubamaja
Islandi väljak
Lembitu Park
Rotermanni Parking
Rotermanni
Roseni
Ahtri
Hobujaama
Mere puiestee
Rannamäe tee
Narva maantee
Narva Mnt
Pärnu maantee
Estonia pst
G. Otsa
Rävala puiestee
Kaarli puiestee
Toompuiestee
Paldiski maantee
Tartu Mnt
Gonsiori
Kopli
Kopli Pohja pst
Vabriku
Niine
Kotzebue
Kesk-Kalamaja
Telliskivi
Rohu
Tehnika
Sügise
Loode
Eha
Koidu
Kevade
A. Adamsoni
Wismari
Villardi
Roopa
Luise
Endla
Toom-Kuninga
Tompea
Toompea
Handuse
Roosikrantsi
Tatari
Sakala
Kentmanni
Kaupmehe
Lembitu
Vambola
A. Lauteri
Liivalaia
Juhkentali
Kauka
Maakri
Lennuki
Kivisilla
Maneezi
V. Reimani
E. Vilde
Pronksi
F.R. Kreutzwaldi
Lastekodu
C.R. Jakobsoni
J. Kunderi
Laulupeo
Raua
Tina
Terase
Hõbeda
Kollane
R. Tobiase
F.R. Faehlmanni
Vase
Vesivärava
J. Köleri
Joe
Lootsi
Tuukri
Karu
A. Laikmaa
To Kadriorg (1.5km); Kadriorg Art Museum (1.5km); KUMU (1.5km); Tallinn Song Festival Grounds (3km); Tallinn City Camping (3km); Soviet Obelisk (4.5km); Pirita (6km); Convent of St Brigitta (6.5km)
To Tallinn Zoo (4km); Open-Air Museum (5km)
To Valge Villa (2.5km); Australian Consulate (3km)
To French Embassy (100m)
To New Zealand Consulate (100m)
To Tallinn Central Hospital (400m)
To Union Travel (50m)
To Central Bus Station (400m); Ecolines (400m); Eurolines (400m); Tallinn Airport (3.5km); Lahemaa National Park (71km)

INFORMATION

- Apteek 1 ... 1 C2
- Bookingestonia ... 2 C2
- Canadian Embassy ... 3 B3
- Central Post Office ... 4 D2
- Dutch Embassy ... 5 B2
- Estonian National Library ... 6 B4
- Finnish Embassy ... 7 B2
- German Embassy ... 8 B4
- Irish Embassy ... 9 C2
- Japanese Embassy ... 10 C3
- Latvian Embassy ... 11 B4
- Lithuanian Embassy ... 12 C2
- Russian Embassy ... 13 C2
- Swedish Embassy ... 14 C2
- Tavid Exchange Bureau ... 15 C2
- Tourist Information Centre ... 16 C3
- Tourist Information Centre (Port) ... (see 70)
- Tourist Information Centre (Viru Keskus) ... (see 67)
- Traveller Info Tent ... 17 C3
- UK Embassy ... 18 A3
- US Embassy ... 19 C4

SIGHTS & ACTIVITIES

- Alexander Nevsky Cathedral ... 20 B3
- Broken Line Monument ... 21 C1
- City Bike ... 22 C1
- City Museum ... 23 C2
- Club 26 ... 24 D4
- Danish King's Courtyard ... 25 B3
- Dome Church ... 26 B2
- Dominican Monastery ... 27 C2
- Former KGB Headquarters ... 28 C2
- Great Coast Gate ... 29 C1
- Holy Spirit Church ... 30 C2
- Kalev Spa Waterpark ... 31 C2
- Lookout ... 32 B2
- Lower Town Wall ... 33 B2
- Maritime Museum ... 34 C1
- Masters' Courtyard ... 35 C2
- Museum of Applied Art & Design ... 36 C2
- Museum of Occupation & Fight for Freedom ... 37 B4
- Niguliste Museum & Concert Hall ... (see 40)
- Observation Tower ... (see 41)
- Pikk Hermann Bastion ... 38 B3
- Pikk jalg Gate Tower ... 39 C2
- St Nicholas' Church ... 40 C3
- St Olaf's Church ... 41 C1
- Sts Peter & Paul's Catholic Church ... 42 C2
- Toompea Castle ... 43 B3
- Town Council Pharmacy ... 44 C2
- Town Hall ... 45 C2
- Traveller Info Tent ... (see 17)

SLEEPING

- Euphoria ... 46 B4
- Old House Hostel ... 47 C2
- Tallinn Backpackers ... 48 C2

EATING

- Bonaparte Café ... 49 C2
- Kompressor ... 50 C2
- Olde Hansa ... 51 C3
- Pizza Grande ... 52 C3
- Rimi ... 53 C2
- Vapiano ... 54 D2

DRINKING

- Café-Chocolaterie de Pierre ... 55 C2
- Gloria Wine Cellar ... 56 C3
- Hell Hunt ... 57 C2
- Kehrwieder ... 58 C2
- Levist Väljas ... 59 C2

ENTERTAINMENT

- Angel ... 60 C3
- Bon Bon ... 61 D2
- City Theatre ... 62 C2
- Club Hollywood ... 63 C3
- Coca-Cola Plaza ... 64 D2
- Estonia Concert Hall & National Opera ... 65 C3
- Kino Sõprus ... (see 63)
- Piletilevi ... (see 67)
- Teater No99 ... 66 C4

SHOPPING

- Masters' Courtyard ... (see 35)
- Viru Keskus ... 67 D3

TRANSPORT

- Bookingestonia.com ... (see 2)
- Bus to Airport ... 68 D3
- Bus to Port ... 69 D3
- Eckerö Lines ... (see 70)
- Local Bus Terminus ... (see 67)
- Nordic Jet ... (see 72)
- Sea-Passenger Terminal A ... 70 E1
- Sea-Passenger Terminal B ... 71 E1
- Sea-Passenger Terminal C ... 72 D1
- Sea-Passenger Terminal D ... 73 E1
- Tallink ... (see 73)
- Viking Line ... (see 70)

Mon-Sat Jul-Aug, by appointment Sep-Jun), built from 1371 to 1404. Climb the **tower** (adult/student 30/15EEK; 11am-6pm Jun-Aug) for fine Old Town views.

The nearby **Town Council Pharmacy** (Raeapteek; Raekoja plats 11) is another ancient Tallinn institution; there's been a pharmacy or apothecary here since 1422. An arch beside it leads into narrow Saiakang (White Bread Passage), at the far end of which is the lovely 14th-century Gothic **Holy Spirit Church** (644 1487; adult/student 15/7.50EEK; 9am-5pm Mon-Sat May-Sep, 10am-2pm Mon-Fri Oct-Apr), with carvings from 1684 and a tower bell cast in 1433.

From the church, stroll along Pikk (Long St), which runs north to the **Great Coast Gate** – the medieval exit to Tallinn's port. Pikk is lined with the 15th-century houses of merchants and gentry (check out the fabulous sculpted facade of the art gallery at number 18).

At the northern end of Pikk stands a chief Tallinn landmark, the gargantuan **St Olaf's Church** (Oleviste Kirik; Pikk 48; admission free). View-seekers unafraid of a bit of sweat should head up to the **observation tower** (621 2241; adult/student 30/15EEK; 10am-6pm Apr-Oct).

Just south of the church is the **former KGB headquarters** (Pikk 59), whose basement windows were sealed to conceal the sounds of cruel interrogations.

A medieval merchant's home houses the **City Museum** (644 6553; www.linnamuuseum.ee; Vene 17; adult/student 35/10EEK; 10.30am-6pm Wed-Mon Mar-Oct, to 5pm Wed-Mon Nov-Feb), which traces Tallinn's development from its

GETTING INTO TOWN

From the airport, just 4km from the centre, take bus 2 for five stops to the city centre; taxis shouldn't charge more than 100EEK to 120EEK for the same journey. From the Autobussijaam (bus station), walk one block east to Tartu maantee, cross the street and hop on any tram into town; the Old Town's but four stops away. The train station is directly across the street, to the northwest, from the Old Town and is served by trams 1 and 2, which whisk you downtown in three or four stops. The main ferry terminals are just 350m from the northeastern edge of Old Town – from these it's best to walk.

TALLINN FOR FREE

- Absorb the medieval magic wandering **Old Town** (p333)
- Get a breath of fresh air at **Kadriorg Park** (right)
- Hit the beach at **Pirita** or retro-Soviet **Stroomi** (right)
- Browse the artisans' studios of **Katariina käik** and **Masters' Courtyard** (below)

beginnings through to 1940 with some quirky displays and curious artefacts. The 20th-century section will satisfy any thirst for Soviet propaganda material.

Vene is home to some lovely passageways and courtyards – check out **Katariina käik** (Vene 12), home to artisans' studios, and **Masters' Courtyard** (Vene 6), a cobblestoned charmer, some of it dating from the 13th century. It's home to craft stores and a sweet chocolaterie.

Also on Vene is the whitewashed, 1844 **Sts Peter & Paul's Catholic Church** (Vene 16), looking like it belongs in Spain. A door in the courtyard leads into the **Dominican Monastery** (☎ 515 5489; www.kloostri.ee; Vene 16; adult/student 90/45EEK; 🕑 10am-6pm mid-May–Aug, visits other times by appt), founded in 1246 as a base for Scandinavian monks.

The majestic St Nicholas' Church (Niguliste Kirik), now known as the **Niguliste Museum & Concert Hall** (☎ 631 4330; Niguliste 3; adult/student 35/20EEK; 🕑 10am-5pm Wed-Sun), stages concerts and serves as a museum of medieval church art.

Toompea

A regal approach to Toompea is through the red-roofed 1380 **gate tower** at the western end of Pikk in the lower town, and then uphill along Pikk jalg (Long Leg). The 19th-century Russian Orthodox **Alexander Nevsky Cathedral** (Lossi plats; 🕑 8am-8pm) greets you at the top, planted strategically across from **Toompea Castle**, traditionally Estonia's seat of power. Only a section of the Old Town wall and the **Pikk Hermann Bastion**, from which the state flag flies, are left from medieval times. The *riigikogu* (parliament) meets in the pink, baroque-style building in front, which is an 18th-century addition. A path leads down from Lossi plats through an opening in the wall to the **Danish King's Courtyard**, where, in summer, artists set up their easels.

The Lutheran **Dome Church** (Toomkirik; ☎ 644 4140; Toom-Kooli 6; 🕑 9am-4pm Tue-Sun), sombre and austere, was founded in 1233, though this edifice dates from the 14th century. From the Dome Church, follow Kohtu to the city's favourite **lookout** over the lower town, cameras at the ready.

The absorbing **Museum of Occupation & Fight for Freedom** (☎ 668 0250; www.okupatsioon.ee; Toompea 8; adult/student 20/10EEK; 🕑 11am-6pm Tue-Sun), just downhill from Toompea, focuses on Estonia's 20th-century occupations (Nazi and Soviet) – and the joy of a happy ending.

Kadriorg

To reach **Kadriorg Park**, 2km east of Old Town along Narva maantee, take tram 1 or 3 to the last stop.

The lovely, wooded park and its palace were designed for Peter the Great for his wife Catherine I. The park's original centrepiece is Kadriorg Palace (1718–36), now home to the **Kadriorg Art Museum** (☎ 606 6403; www.ekm.ee; Weizenbergi 37; adult/student 55/30EEK; 🕑 10am-5pm Tue-Sun May-Sep, 10am-5pm Wed-Sun Oct-Apr). The 17th- and 18th-century foreign art is mainly unabashedly romantic, and the palace unashamedly splendid.

The grand new showpiece of Kadriorg (and Tallinn) is **KUMU** (Kunstimuuseum; ☎ 602 6000; www.ekm.ee; Weizenbergi 34; adult/student 80/45EEK; 🕑 11am-6pm Tue-Sun May-Sep, 11am-6pm Wed-Sun Oct-Apr), also known as the Art Museum of Estonia. It's a spectacular structure of limestone, glass and copper, and contains the largest repository of Estonian art as well as constantly changing contemporary exhibits.

ACTIVITIES

Waterparks are all the rage in Estonia; the biggest in Tallinn is the **Kalev Spa Waterpark** (☎ 649 3370; www.kalevspa.ee; Aia 18), offering plenty of ways to wrinkle your skin.

In Estonia, saunas come close to being a religious experience. If you're looking to convert, splurge at **Club 26** (☎ 631 5585; 26th fl, Liivalaia 33; per hr before/after 3pm 300/600EEK; 🕑 8am-11pm), on the top floor of the Reval Hotel Olümpia and with outstanding views.

The most popular **beaches** are at Pirita (northeast of the centre; bus 1A, 8, 34A and 38) and Stroomi (4km due west of the centre; bus 40 or 48).

City Bike (☎ 683 6383; www.citybike.ee; Uus 33) rents bikes for city- or country-wide exploring, and has a range of Tallinn tours, as well as tours (cycling or bus) to Lahemaa National Park (p339). The guys behind the Traveller Info Tent (p333) also run recommended walking or cycling city tours.

FESTIVALS & EVENTS

Expect an extra-full calendar of events in 2011 as Tallinn celebrates its status as a European City of Culture; check www.tallinn2011.ee. For a complete list of Tallinn festivals, visit the events pages of www.tourism.tallinn.ee.

Jazzkaar (www.jazzkaar.ee) Jazz greats from around the world converge in mid-April.

Old Town Days (www.vanalinnapaevad.ee) Week-long fest in early June featuring dancing, concerts, costumed performers and plenty of medieval merrymaking.

Õllesummer (Beer Summer; www.ollesummer.ee) Popular ale-guzzling, rock-music extravaganza over five days in early July.

Black Nights Film Festival (www.poff.ee) Films and animations from all over the world, bringing life to cold nights from mid-November to mid-December.

SLEEPING

Tallinn City Camping (☎ 613 7322; www.tallinn-city-camping.ee; Pirita tee 28; tent & caravan site 200Kr, plus per car/adult/child 100/50/25Kr; mid-May–mid-Sep;) Right by the Tallin Song Festival Grounds, this well-equipped site is an amble away from Pirita beach and Kadriorg Park, and just a short bus ride into town (bus 1A, 8, 34A and 38 to Lauluväljak stop), or you can rent bikes here.

Euphoria (☎ 5837 3602; www.euphoria.ee; Roosikrantsi 4; dm/d 200/600EEK;) So laid-back it's almost horizontal, this new backpackers hostel, just south of Old Town, has adopted some very '60s hippie vibes and given them a modern twist, creating a fun place to stay with a sense of traveller community – especially if you like hookah pipes, bongo drums, jugglers, musos, artists and impromptu late-night jam sessions (pack earplugs if you don't).

Tallinn Backpackers (☎ 644 0298; www.tallinnbackpackers.com; Olevimägi 11; dm 200-225EEK;) Staffed by backpackers who are more than happy to go drinking with guests, and in a perfect Old Town location, this place has a global feel and a roll-call of traveller-happy features: free wi-fi and internet, lockers, free sauna, snazzy bathrooms, big-screen movies in the common room, a foosball table and day-trips to nearby attractions.

Old House Hostel (☎ 641 1464; www.oldhouse.ee; Uus 26; dm/s/tw 290/550/690EEK;) Has a more refined, mature atmosphere than the party-oriented places listed above: wooden floors and old-world decor, plus no bunks, and a choice of private rooms. In summer it expands into a nearby local school. Kitchen, living room, wi-fi and parking are good extras. Management also has a guest house nearby, and rents fantastic Old Town apartments at reasonable prices.

EATING

Bonaparte Café (☎ 646 4444; Pikk 45; pastries 14-20EEK, meals 55-130EEK) Flaky croissants and raspberry-mousse cake are a few reasons why Bonaparte ranks as Tallinn's best patisserie. It's also a supremely civilised lunch stop, with the likes of French onion soup and salad Niçoise on the menu. And the quiches – *très magnifiques*!

Pizza Grande (☎ 641 8718; Väike-Karja 6; small pizzas 39-69EEK) Local students vote this their favourite pizza spot. Enter from the courtyard and check the menu, where some left-of-centre topping combos (chicken, shrimps, blue cheese and peach?) stand alongside the tried-and-true. Salads and pasta dishes all come in under 70EEK.

Kompressor (☎ 646 4210; Rataskaevu 3; pancakes 50-55EEK) Under an industrial ceiling you can plug any holes in your stomach with cheap pancakes of the sweet or savoury persuasion. The smoked cheese and bacon is a treat, but don't go thinking you'll have room for dessert. By night, this is a decent detour for a drink.

our pick **Vapiano** (☎ 682 9010; Hobujaama 10; pizzas & pasta 50-125EEK) Choose your pasta or salad from the appropriate counter and watch as it's prepared in front of you. If it's pizza you're after, you'll receive a pager to notify you when it's ready. This is 'fast' food done healthy, fresh and cheap (without sacrificing quality), and the restaurant is big, bright and buzzing.

For groceries, hit **Rimi supermarket** (Aia 7; 9am-10pm).

DRINKING

Tallinn without its cafe and bar culture is simply inconceivable. Due to the charm of its surroundings, the Old Town is the obvious place to head to for cellar bars and absurdly cosy cafes.

Kehrwieder (☎ 505 258; Saiakang 1) Sure, there's seating on Raekoja plats, but inside the city's cosiest cafe is where the real ambience is

ESTONIA

SPLURGE

Olde Hansa (☎ 627 9020; www.oldehansa.ee; Vana Turg 1; mains 155-365EEK) One of the few touristy places that's truly worth a visit, this candlelit, medieval-themed restaurant boasts the friendliest service in the country, delicacies like juniper cheese and forest-mushroom soup, and exotic meats such as boar and bear, all impeccably presented.

found in spades – stretch out on a couch, read by lamplight and bump your head on the arched ceilings.

Gloria Wine Cellar (☎ 640 6804; Müürivahe 2) This maze-like cellar has a number of nooks and crannies where you can secrete yourself with a date and/or a good bottle of shiraz. Antique furnishings and flickering candles add to the allure.

our pick **Hell Hunt** (☎ 681 8333; Pikk 39) Try to score a few of the comfy armchairs out the back of this trouper on the pub circuit, beloved of discerning locals of all ages. It boasts an amiable air and reasonable prices for locally brewed beer and cider, plus decent pub grub. Don't let the menacing-sounding name put you off – it actually means 'gentle wolf'.

Levist Väljas (☎ 507 7372; Olevimägi 12) Inside this cellar bar (usually the last pitstop of the night) you'll find broken furniture, cheap booze and a refreshingly motley crew of friendly punks, grunge kings, has-beens and anyone else who strays from the tourist path.

CLUBBING

Club Hollywood (☎ 627 4770; www.club-hollywood.ee; Vana-Posti 8; ⏲ from 11pm Wed-Sat) A multilevel emporium of mayhem, this is the one to draw the largest crowds, especially of foreigners. Plenty of tourists and Tallin's young party crowd mix it up to international and local DJs.

Bon Bon (☎ 661 6080; www.bonbon.ee; Mere pst 6e; ⏲ 11pm-5am Fri & Sat) With enormous chandeliers and a portrait of Bacchus, the god of decadence, overlooking the dance floor, Bon Bon is renowned for its chichi attitude. It attracts a 25- to 30-something A-list clientele who still want to party, in style. Frock up to fit in.

Angel (☎ 641 6880; www.clubangel.ee; Sauna 1; ⏲ 10pm-5am Wed, Fri, Sat) Open to both sexes and all orientations (but with strict door control, particularly on Friday and Saturday when ladies may struggle to get in), this mainly gay club has become one of the liveliest spots in town. See www.gay.ee for more on the (small) gay scene in Tallinn.

ENTERTAINMENT

Buy tickets for concerts and main events at any central branch of **Piletilevi** (www.piletilevi.ee), such as the one inside Viru Keskus.

Theatre

Estonia Concert Hall & National Opera (concert hall ☎ 614 7760, opera 683 1201; www.concert.ee & www.opera.ee; Estonia pst 4) The city's biggest concerts are held here, in this double-barrelled venue. It's Tallinn's main theatre, and also houses the Estonian national opera and ballet.

City Theatre (Linnateater; ☎ 665 0800; www.linnateater.ee; Lai 23) The most beloved theatre in town always stages something memorable. Watch for its summer plays on an outdoor stage.

Teater No99 (☎ 660 5051; www.no99.ee; Sakala 3) More-experimental productions happen here, but come by for the jazz bar downstairs on Friday and Saturday evenings.

Cinemas

Kino Sõprus (☎ 644 1919; Vana-Posti 8) An art-house cinema set in a magnificent Stalin-era theatre.

Coca-Cola Plaza (☎ 1182; www.superkinod.ee; Hobujaama 5) Modern 11-screen cinema playing the latest Hollywood releases.

SHOPPING

You'll be tripping over handicraft stores – look for signs for *käsitöö*. Dozens of small shops sell Estonian-made handicrafts, linen, leather-bound books, ceramics, jewellery, silverware, stained glass and objects carved from juniper wood. These are all traditional Estonian souvenirs – and a bottle of Vana Tallinn liqueur, of course!

Tallinn's showpiece shopping mall **Viru Keskus** (www.virukeskus.com; Viru väljak 4; ⏲ 9am-9pm), aka Viru Centre, lies just outside Old Town.

GETTING THERE & AWAY

See p331 for details on getting to Tallinn.

GETTING AROUND

Tallinn has an excellent network of buses, trolleybuses and trams that run from 6am to midnight; all three modes of local transport

ESTONIA

use the same ticket system. Buy *piletid* (tickets) from street kiosks (13EEK, or a book of 10 single tickets for 90EEK) or from the driver (20EEK). Validate your ticket using the hole puncher inside the vehicle – watch a local to see how it's done.

The major bus terminal for local buses is at the basement level of Viru Keskus shopping centre or the surrounding streets (just east of Old Town). Public transport timetables are at www.tallinn.ee.

City Bike (☎ 683 6383; www.citybike.ee; Uus 33; rental per hr/day/week 35/200/765EEK) can help you get around by bike, within Tallinn and around Estonia.

Taxis are plentiful, but it's best to order one by phone: **Krooni Takso** (☎ 1212, 638 1111) and **Tulika Takso** (☎ 1200, 612 0000).

AROUND TALLINN

LAHEMAA NATIONAL PARK

The perfect retreat from the capital, Lahemaa takes in a stretch of deeply indented coast with several peninsulas and bays, plus 475 sq km of pine-fresh forested hinterland. Visitors are well looked after: there are cosy guest houses, restored manor houses, remote camp sites along the sea and an extensive network of nature trails and cycling paths.

A good first stop is the **visitor centre** (☎ 329 5555; www.lahemaa.ee; 🕑 9am-7pm May-Aug, 9am-5pm Sep, 9am-5pm Mon-Fri Oct-Apr) in Palmse, 8km north of Viitna (71km east of Tallinn) in the park's southeast. Nearby is **Palmse Manor** (☎ 324 0070; www.svm.ee; adult/student 60/30EEK; 🕑 10am-7pm May-Sep, 10am-6pm Wed-Sun Oct-Apr), once a wholly self-contained Baltic-German estate.

The small coastal towns of **Võsu**, **Käsmu** and (to a lesser extent) **Loksa** are popular seaside spots in summer. Käsmu is a particularly enchanting village.

Toomarahva Turismitalu (☎ 325 2511; www.zone.ee/toomarahva; Altja; camping per person 25EEK, d incl breakfast 500EEK) is a gem, offering a gorgeous taste of rural Estonia – a farmstead with thatch-roofed wooden outhouses and a garden full of flowers and sculptures. Signage is minimal – look for it opposite the yard of the farmhouse tavern, **Altja Kõrts** (☎ 326 8681; mains 65-190Kr), itself worth a visit for its rustic interior and traditional dishes.

Hiring a car is a good way to reach and explore the park, or take a tour from Tallinn – **City Bike** (☎ 683 6383; www.citybike.ee; Uus 33, Tallinn) offers excellent park tours by bus or bike. From Tallinn a bus runs daily to Käsmu, Võsu and Altja.

SOUTHEASTERN ESTONIA

TARTU

pop 102,000

If Tallinn is Estonia's head, Tartu may well be its heart (and in some ways its university-educated brains trust, too). Tartu lays claim to being Estonia's spiritual capital – locals talk about a special Tartu *vaim* (spirit), encompassed by the time-stands-still, 19th-century feel of many of its streets. Small and provincial, Tartu is Estonia's premier university town, with students making up nearly one-fifth of the population. This injects a boisterous vitality into the leafy, historic setting and grants it a surprising sophistication for a city of its size. During the Student Days festival at the end of April, carnival-like mayhem erupts throughout the city.

The Estonian nationalist revival in the 19th century had its origins here and Tartu was the location for the first Estonian Song Festival in 1869. Tartu provides visitors with a true glimpse of the Estonian rhythm of life.

Orientation & Information

Toomemägi hill and the area of older buildings between it and the Emajõgi River are the focus of 'old' Tartu. Its heart is Raekoja plats (Town Hall Square).

City Library (☎ 736 1379; Kompanii 3) Free internet upstairs.

Tartu In Your Pocket (www.inyourpocket.com) Listings guide, available in bookshops or online.

Tourist information centre (☎ 744 2111; www.visittartu.com; Raekoja plats; 🕑 9am-6pm Mon-Fri, 10am-5pm Sat, 10am-3pm Sun mid-May–mid-Sep, 9am-5pm Mon-Fri, 10am-3pm Sat mid-Sep–mid-May) Friendly office inside the Town Hall; can book accommodation and tour guides. Free internet access available.

Sights & Activities

At the town centre on Raekoja plats is the **town hall** (1782–89), fronted by a statue of lovers

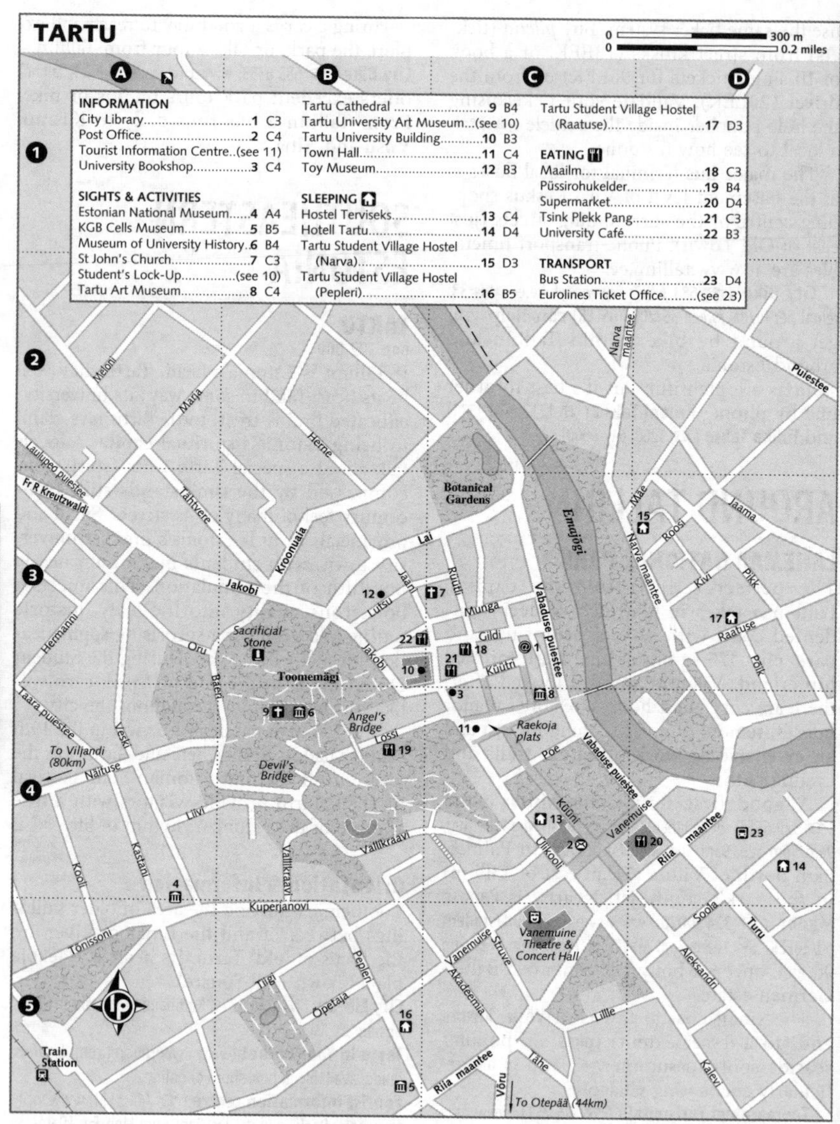

kissing under an umbrella. At the other end of the square is a wonderfully wonky building housing the **Tartu Art Museum** (☎ 744 1080; Raekoja plats 18; adult/student 30/20EEK; 🕑 11am-6pm Wed-Sun).

The university was founded in 1632; the main **university building** (☎ 737 5100; www.ut.ee; Ülikooli 18) dates from 1804. It houses the **Tartu University Art Museum** (adult/child 10/5EEK; 🕑 11am-5pm Mon-Fri) and **Student's Lock-Up** (admission 5EEK; 🕑 11am-5pm Mon-Fri), where 19th-century students were held for their misdeeds.

North of the university stands the magnificent Gothic **St John's Church** (☎ 744 2229; Jaani 5; 🕑 10am-7pm Tue-Sat), dating back to at least 1323. Climb the 135 steps of the 30m **observation tower** (adult/child 25/15EEK) for a bird's-eye view of Tartu.

Rising to the west of Raekoja plats is the splendid Toomemägi (Cathedral Hill), landscaped in the manner of a 19th-century English park and perfect for a stroll. The 13th-century Gothic **Tartu Cathedral** (Toomkirik), at the top, was rebuilt in the 15th century, despoiled during the Reformation in 1525, and partly rebuilt in 1804–07 to accommodate the university library, which is now the **Museum of University History** (☎ 737 5674; adult/student 25/15EEK; 🕑 11am-5pm Wed-Sun).

Tartu, as the major repository of Estonia's cultural heritage, has an abundance of first-rate museums. Among them is the absorbing **Estonian National Museum** (☎ 742 1311; www.erm.ee; Kuperjanovi 9; adult/student 20/15EEK, Fri free; 🕑 11am-6pm Wed-Sun), which traces the history, life and traditions of the Estonian people.

The former KGB headquarters now houses the sombre and highly worthwhile **KGB Cells Museum** (☎ 746 1717; Riia mnt 15b, entrance on Pepleri; adult/student 12/8EEK; 🕑 11am-4pm Tue-Sat).

The best place to pass a few rainy hours is the **Toy Museum** (☎ 736 1550; www.mm.ee; Lutsu 8; adult/student 25/20EEK; 🕑 11am-6pm Wed-Sun). It showcases dolls, model trains, rocking horses, toy soldiers and lots of other desirables dating back a century or so. Be sure to wander through the adjacent TEFI House, home to an outstanding collection of theatre and animation puppets.

Sleeping

Hostel Terviseks (☎ 5353 1153; www.hostelterviseks.blogspot.com; Ülikooli 1, apt 6, 4th fl; dm 200-250EEK; 💻) A real travellers hostel (run by an Australian and a Canadian) that's best described as staying at your mate's place (albeit a mate with quite a few bunks in their apartment). There are 14 beds spread over two dorm rooms, plus a decent kitchen and cosy, orange-coloured lounge, but only one bathroom. It can be a little tricky to find – check directions on the website, or call if you're lost.

Tartu Student Village Hostels (☎ 740 9955; www.tartuhostel.eu; s/d from 350/600EEK; Pepleri dorm **Pepleri 14**; Raatuse dorm **Raatuse 22**; Narva dorm **Narva mnt 27**) These student dorms offer cheap, clean, central accommodation (only Pepleri is south of the river). The Raatuse dorm is newest but somewhat institutional; it's the cheapest, as every three rooms share a kitchen and bathroom. The Narva option has two rooms sharing kitchen and bathroom. The Pepleri dorm is the best pick – it's older but a bit cosier, and there's a private kitchenette and bathroom in each room (there are also larger suites here that are excellent value). Advance reservations are a must.

Hotell Tartu (☎ 731 4300; www.tartuhotell.ee; Soola 3; hostel dm/tw/tr 325/800/900EEK, hotel s/d/f 750/1150/1650EEK) Being across from the bus station doesn't make for the most charming of locations, but this hotel's modernised rooms are sleek, bright and comfy. The 'hostel' is actually six spotless, older-style hotel rooms (shared bathrooms in the corridor) sleeping only three.

Eating & Drinking

University Café (☎ 737 5405; Ülikooli 20; buffet per 100g 13EEK, snacks & meals from 50EEK) Some of the most economical meals in town await at the ground-floor cafeteria, which serves up decent breakfasts and a simple daytime buffet. Upstairs is a labyrinth of elegantly decorated rooms that create worlds unto themselves, both old-world grand and embracingly cosy.

our pick Tsink Plekk Pang (☎ 730 3415; Küütri 6; dishes 50-150EEK) Behind Tartu's funkiest facade (look for the stripey paintwork) and over three floors is this cool Chinese-flavoured restaurant-lounge, named after the zinc buckets that are suspended from the ceiling as lampshades. You'll need time to peruse the huge, veg-friendly menu – well-priced noodles and soups, plus a decent Indian selection and even a handful of Japanese dishes. Or simply stop by to enjoy drinks with a DJ-spun soundtrack on weekends.

Maailm (☎ 742 9099; Rüütli 12; mains 70-115Kr) Artlessly hip Maailm (meaning 'world') is a chilled-out place for a bite and/or a beer, with a cheap-and-cheerful menu of eclectic options, from Irish stew to chili con carne.

Püssirohukelder (☎ 730 3555; Lossi 28; mains 70-260EEK) Set in a cavernous old gunpowder cellar under a soaring, 10m-high vaulted ceiling, this is both a boisterous pub and a good choice for tasty meat and fish dishes. When the regular live music kicks in later in the night (sometimes with a cover charge), you'll find the older crowd withdrawing to the more secluded wine cellar.

The most central **supermarket** (Riia 1) is in the basement of the Tartu Kaubamaja shopping centre.

Getting There & Away

From the **Tartu bus station** (Autobussijaam; ☎ 733 1277; Turu 2), daily buses run to/from Tallinn

(125EEK to 160EEK, 2½ to 3½ hours) about every 15 to 30 minutes. Three daily trains make the same journey (95EEK to 140EEK, 2¼ hours). Ten buses a day serve Pärnu (135EEK to 150EEK, 2¾ hours).

SOUTHWESTERN ESTONIA

PÄRNU

pop 44,000

Local families, young party-goers and German and Finnish holidaymakers join together in a collective prayer for sunny weather while strolling the golden-sand beaches, sprawling parks and historic, picturesque centre of Pärnu (*pair*-nu), Estonia's premier seaside resort, 130km south of Tallinn on the main road to Rīga.

Orientation & Information

Pärnu lies on either side of the Pärnu River estuary, which empties into Pärnu Bay. The tourist office is on the main commercial street in the heart of the Old Town, around 150m southwest of the bus station.

Central Library (☎ 445 5706; Akadeemia 3) Free internet.

Pärnu In Your Pocket (www.inyourpocket.com) More great info from this listings guide, available in bookshops or online.

Tourist information centre (☎ 447 3000; www.visitparnu.com; Rüütli 16; 🕑 9am-6pm Mon-Fri, 10am-4pm Sat, 10am-3pm Sun Jun-Aug, 9am-5pm Mon-Fri Sep-May) Helpful staff will book accommodation for a 25EEK fee.

Sights & Activities

The wide, golden-sand **beach** and **Ranna puiestee**, whose buildings date from the early 20th century, are Pärnu's prime attractions. The handsome 1927 neoclassical **Mudaravila** is a symbol of the town's history. The legendary mud baths that once operated here have closed; new owners are planning to restore the building and add an adjacent spa hotel. Stay tuned.

A fine new beach promenade curves along the sand, lined with fountains and park benches. At the far end, Estonia's largest waterpark, **Veekeskus** (☎ 445 1166; www.tervisedparadiis.ee; Side 14; adult 115-290EEK, student 75-205EEK; 🕑 10am-10pm), beckons with pools, slides, tubes etc – it holds special appeal when bad weather ruins beach plans. It's part of the huge Tervise Paradiis hotel complex.

Sleeping & Eating

Camping Konse (☎ 5343 5092; www.konse.ee; Suur-Jõe 44a; tent sites 60EEK plus 60EEK per person, r with shared/private bathroom 550/700EEK) Perched on a spot by the river 1km from the Old Town, Konse offers tent and campervan sites and a variety of rooms (half with private bathroom, half with shared facilities, all with kitchen access). There's sauna, rowboat and bike rental. It can get crowded, but that just makes it easier to meet people. Open year-round.

Hommiku Hostel (☎ 445 1122; www.hommikuhostel.ee; Hommiku 17; dm/s/d/tr/q 300/600/900/1200/1400EEK) Hommiku is far more like a hotel than a hostel, except for its prices. This modern place has handsome rooms with private bathrooms, TV and kitchenettes, and some with old-beamed ceilings. It's in a prime in-town position with good eateries as its neighbours.

Mõnus Margarita (☎ 443 0929; Akadeemia 5; mains 69-310EEK) Huge, colourful and decidedly upbeat, as all good Tex-Mex places should be – but if you're looking for heavy-duty spice, you won't find it here. Fajitas, burritos and quesadillas all score goals, as do margaritas and tequilas.

Steffani Pizzeria (☎ 443 1170; Nikolai 24; pizzas 75-105EEK) The queue out front should alert you – this is a top choice for pizza, particularly in summer when you can dine al fresco on the big, flower-filled terrace. In a smart business move, a second summertime branch opens near the beach at Ranna puiestee 1.

Getting There & Away

About 30 daily buses connect Pärnu with Tallinn (115EEK to 125EEK, two hours), and 10 services connect Pärnu with Tartu (135EEK to 150EEK, 2½ to three hours). Tickets for other destinations, including Rīga (Latvia) and beyond, are available at the Pärnu bus station **ticket office** (☎ 447 1002; Ringi; 🕑 6.15am-7.30pm).

There are two daily Tallinn–Pärnu trains (75EEK, 2¾ hours), though the train station is an inconvenient 5km east of the town centre.

ESTONIA DIRECTORY

ACCOMMODATION

Finding a decent place to lay your head in Estonia is not a problem. Peak tourist season is June through August – if you visit then, book your accommodation in advance.

There are a few *kämpingud* (camping grounds), which are open from mid-May to September and allow you to pitch a tent, though most consist mainly of permanent wooden cabins, with communal showers and toilets.

Farms and homestays offer more than a choice of rooms and in many cases meals, sauna and a range of activities are on offer.

The following websites are useful:

Estonian Rural Tourism (www.maaturism.ee)

Visit Estonia (www.visitestonia.com) Has a search engine for all types of accommodation throughout the country.

ACTIVITIES

A list of companies keeping tourists active can be found at www.turismiweb.ee.

For a range of eco-friendly activities, from kayaking to kicksledding, contact **Reimann Retked** (☎ 511 4099; www.retked.ee). This company offers sea-kayaking excursions, including guided overnight trips or a four-hour paddle out to Aegna island, 14km offshore from Tallinn (450EEK). Other possibilities include diving, rafting, bogwalking and snowshoeing, and kicksledding on sea ice, frozen lakes or in snowy forests. Most arrangements need a minimum of eight to 10 people, although smaller groups should still enquire (as you may be able to tag along with another group).

As well as offering Tallinn hostels and tours, **City Bike** (☎ 683 6383; www.citybike.ee; Uus 33, Tallinn) can take care of all your needs to get around by bike, within Tallinn, around Estonia or throughout the Baltic region.

EMBASSIES & CONSULATES

For up-to-date details of Estonian diplomatic organisations as well as foreign embassies and consulates in Estonia, check the website of the **Estonian Foreign Ministry** (☎ 637 7000; www.vm.ee; Islandi väljak 1, Tallinn).

The following embassies and consulates are in Tallinn unless otherwise indicated:

Australia (☎ 650 9308; mati@standard.ee; Marja 9)

Canada (☎ 627 3311; tallinn@canada.ee; Toom-Kooli 13, 2nd fl)

Finland (☎ 610 3200; www.finland.ee; Kohtu 4)

Germany (☎ 627 5300, www.tallinn.diplo.ee; Toom-Kuninga 11)

Ireland (☎ 681 1888; tallinnembassy@dfa.ie; Vene 2, 2nd fl)

Latvia (☎ 627 7860; embassy.estonia@mfa.gov.lv; Tõnismägi 10)

Lithuania (☎ 616 4991; http://ee.mfa.lt; Uus 15)

Russia Narva (☎ 356 0652; narvacon@narvacon.neti.ee; Kiriku 8, Narva) Tallinn (☎ 646 4166; www.rusemb.ee; Lai 18)

Sweden (☎ 640 5600; www.sweden.ee; Pikk 28)

UK (☎ 667 4700; www.britishembassy.ee; Wismari 6)

USA (☎ 668 8100; www.usemb.ee; Kentmanni 20)

FESTIVALS & EVENTS

Estonia has a busy festival calendar hitting its peak in summer. A good list of upcoming major events can be found at www.culture.ee.

Estonian Song & Dance Celebration (www.laulupidu.ee) Convenes every five years and culminates in a 30,000-strong traditional choir, due in Tallinn in 2009.

Baltica International Folk Festival A week of music, dance and displays focusing on Baltic and other folk traditions, this festival is shared between Rīga, Vilnius and Tallinn; it's Tallinn's turn to play host in 2010.

Jaanipäev (St John's Eve; 24 June) A celebration of the pagan Midsummer or summer solstice, this is the biggest occasion in Estonia. Celebrations peak on the evening of 23 June, and are best experienced far from the city along a stretch of beach, where huge bonfires are lit for all-night parties.

HOLIDAYS

New Year's Day 1 January

Independence Day 24 February

Good Friday & Easter March/April

Spring Day 1 May

Whitsunday Seventh Sunday after Easter; May/June

Victory Day (1919; Battle of Võnnu) 23 June

Jaanipäev (St John's Day or Midsummer Day) 24 June

Day of Restoration of Independence (1991) 20 August

Christmas Eve 24 December

Christmas Day 25 December

Boxing Day 26 December

MONEY

Estonia's currency is the kroon (EEK; pronounced krohn), which is pegged to the euro (€1 = 15.65EEK). The kroon comes in notes of two, five, 10, 25, 50, 100 and 500EEK. One kroon is divided into 100 senti (cents), and there are coins of five, 10, 20 and 50 senti, as well as one- and five-kroon coins. The euro is expected to be introduced in Estonia as common currency sometime between 2010 and 2013.

The best foreign currencies to bring into Estonia are euros and US dollars, although all Western currencies are readily exchangeable.

All major credit cards are widely accepted. Most banks (but not stores and restaurants) accept travellers cheques, but their commissions can be high. There are frequent student, pensioner and group discounts on transport, in museums and in some shops upon presentation of accredited ID.

Tipping in service industries has become the norm, but generally no more than 10% is expected.

POST

Mail service in/out of Estonia is highly efficient. To post a letter up to 50g anywhere in the world costs 9EEK.

TELEPHONE

There are no area codes in Estonia. All landline phone numbers have seven digits; mobile (cell) numbers have seven or eight digits, and begin with ☎ 5.

To call Estonia from abroad, dial the country code ☎ 372.

VISAS

Ensure your passport is valid for three months more than your travels. Citizens of EU countries, plus Australia, Canada, the USA and many other countries can enter Estonia visa-free for a maximum 90-day stay over a six-month period. For more info, see the website of the **Estonian Foreign Ministry** (www.vm.ee).

Finland

HIGHLIGHTS

- **Helsinki** National capital, serene harbour city, buzzing nightlife and creative melting pot for the latest in Finnish design (p350).
- **Kuopio** Cruise Lakeland waterways, gorge on tiny fish, or sweat it in the world's largest smoke sauna (p363).
- **Inari** Finland's Sámi capital has a spectacular lake and marvellous resources for learning about Lapland (p367).
- **Savonlinna** Shimmering lakescapes, handsome town and fabulous opera in Finland's most spectacular castle make this a don't miss (p362).

FAST FACTS

- **Area** 338,145 sq km
- **Budget** €70-130 per day
- **Capital** Helsinki
- **Country code** ☎ 358
- **Famous for** saunas, reindeer, racing drivers, heavy metal, Nokia
- **Languages** Finnish, Swedish, Sámi languages
- **Money** euro (€); A$1 = €0.55; C$1 = €0.60; ¥100 = €0.78; NZ$1 = €0.43; UK£1 = €1.12; US$1 = €0.74
- **Phrases** *kiitos* (thank you), *moi/hei* (hello), *anteeksi* (excuse me), *kippis* (cheers)

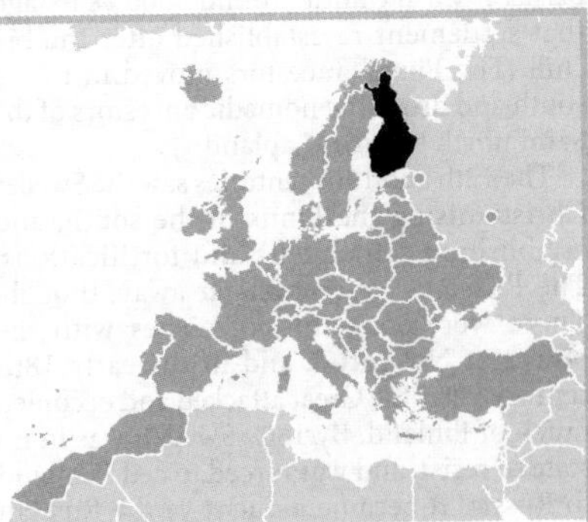

- **Population** 5.31 million
- **Visas** not required for most visitors for stays of up to 90 days (see p369)

TRAVEL HINTS

Fill up on inexpensive breakfast and lunchtime buffets. Check the *kauppahalli* (market hall) in every town to see what local foods are on offer. Buy alcohol cheaply at Alko shops, supermarkets or R-kioskis (convenience stores). Internet access is free at libraries.

ROAMING FINLAND

For a quick tour of Finland, spend a day in Helsinki, take a train to Turku or Tampere, track up to Rovaniemi to sample Lapland, then head south to Kuopio's smoke sauna and back to Helsinki.

Remote, forested, cold, sparsely populated Finland has had a hell of a last hundred years. It's propelled itself from agricultural backwater of the Russian Empire to one of the world's most prosperous and forward-looking nations, with a great standard of living and education, and a booming technology industry. Although socially and economically in the vanguard of nations, parts of Finland remain gloriously remote; trendsetting Helsinki is counterbalanced by vast forested wildernesses.

There's something pure in the Finnish air and spirit that's incredibly vital and exciting. It's an invitation to get out and active year-round. A postsauna dip in an ice hole under the majestic aurora borealis, after whooshing across the snow behind a team of huskies, isn't a typical winter's day just anywhere. And hiking or canoeing under midnight sun through pine forests populated by wolves and bears isn't your typical tanning-oil summer either.

Nordic peace in a lakeside cottage, summer sunshine on convivial beer terraces, avant-garde Helsinki design, dark melodic music, and cafes warm with cinnamon aromas are just the beginning of Suomi seduction. The real bonus? The Finns, who do their own thing and are much the better for it. Independent, loyal, warm and welcoming – a memorable people in an inspirational country.

HISTORY

Finland's story is that of a wrestling mat under two heavyweights, Sweden and Russia, and the nation's eventful emergence from between their grip to become one of the world's most progressive and prosperous nations.

Though evidence of pre–Ice Age habitation exists, it wasn't until around 9000 years ago that settlement re-established after the big chill. The Finns' ancestors moved in to the south and drove the nomadic ancestors of the Sámi north towards Lapland.

The 12th and 13th centuries saw the Swedes Christianising the Finns in the south, and establishing settlements and fortifications. The Russians were never far away, though. There were constant skirmishes with the power of Novgorod, and in the early 18th century Peter the Great attacked and occupied much of Finland. By 1809 Sweden was in no state to resist, and was forced to cede Finland to Russia. It became a duchy of the Russian Empire and the capital was moved to Helsinki, but the Revolution of October 1917 enabled the Finnish senate to declare independence.

Stalin's aggressive territorial demands in 1939 led to the Winter War between Finland and the Soviet Union, conducted in horribly low temperatures. Little Finland resisted heroically, but was defeated and forced to cede a tenth of its territory. When pressured for more, Finland accepted assistance from Germany. This 'Continuation War' against the Russians cost Finland almost 100,000 lives. Eventually general-turned-president Mannerheim negotiated an armistice with the Russians, ceding more land, and then waged a bitter war in Lapland to oust the Germans. Against the odds, Finland remained independent, but at a heavy price.

Finland managed to take a neutral stance during the Cold War, and once the USSR collapsed, it joined the EU in 1995, and adopted the euro in 2002.

In the new millennium, Finland has boomed, on the back of a strong technology sector, the important forestry industry, design and manufacturing, and, increasingly, tourism. It's a major success story of the new Europe with strong economy, robust social values, and superlow crime and corruption.

Some of this gloss was tarnished in 2008 however, when, in the second such incident in less than a year, 22-year-old Matti Saari went on a shooting spree in a vocational college, killing 10 before turning the gun on himself. It sent the country into shock and a re-examination of its liberal gun laws.

THE CULTURE

Finland has only 17 people per square kilometre, falling to under one person in parts of Lapland. There are around 300,000 Swedish-speaking Finns on the west and south coasts and the Åland Islands. Finland's immigrant population of some 150,000 is the EU's lowest; Russians are the biggest group.

The indigenous Sámi (Lapp) population of around 7000 in the north consists of three distinct groups, with the majority involved in reindeer husbandry.

A capacity for silence and reflection is the trait that best sums up the Finnish character. The image of a log cabin with a sauna by a lake tells much about Finnish culture: independence, endurance (*sisu*, or 'guts') and a love of space and nature.

ARTS

Jean Sibelius (1865–1957) was at the forefront of the Finnish nationalist movement. His stirring *Finlandia* has been raised to the status of national hymn. Sibelius and nationalistic painter Akseli Gallen-Kallela fell under the spell of Karelianism, a movement that drew its inspiration from the folk songs collected in the 1830s by Elias Lönnrot to form the national epic *Kalevala*.

Other famed Finnish writers include Tove Jansson, creator of the Moomintrolls, and novelist Arto Paasilinna. Finland's preeminence in architecture and design owes much to Alvar Aalto, who designed everything from public buildings to furniture and vases.

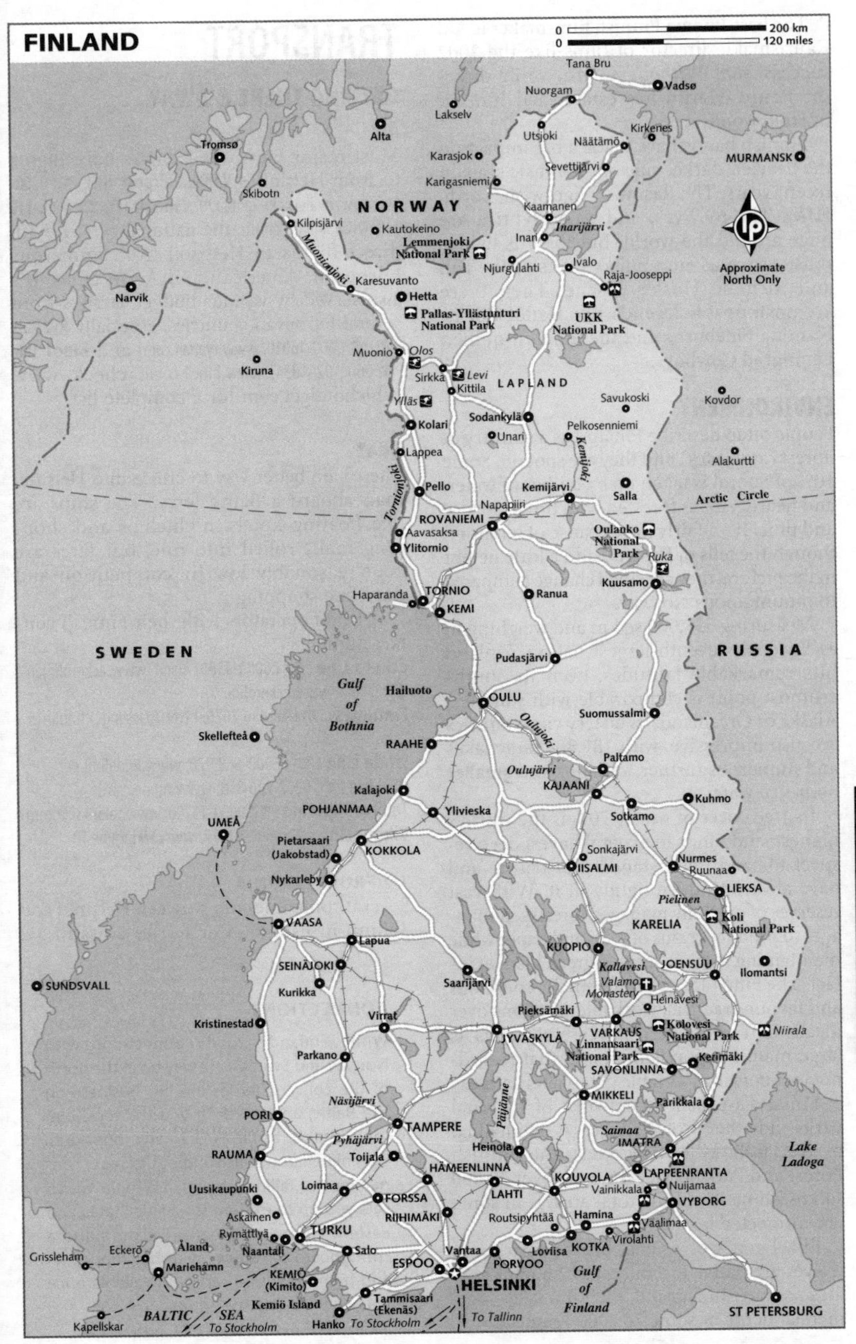
FINLAND
0 200 km
0 120 miles
Approximate North Only
NORWAY
SWEDEN
RUSSIA
LAPLAND
KARELIA
POHJANMAA
Arctic Circle
Gulf of Bothnia
Gulf of Finland
BALTIC SEA
Lake Ladoga
Tana Bru
Vadsø
Nuorgam
Lakselv
Alta
Kirkenes
Utsjoki
Näätämö
Tromsø
Karasjok
MURMANSK
Sevettijärvi
Karigasniemi
Skibotn
Kaamanen
Inarijärvi
Kilpisjärvi
Kautokeino
Inari
Lemmenjoki National Park
Ivalo
Njurgulahti
Raja-Jooseppi
Muonionjoki
Karesuvanto
Narvik
Hetta
UKK National Park
Pallas-Yllästunturi National Park
Muonio
Olos
Kiruna
Sirkka
Levi
Kittila
Savukoski
Kovdor
Ylläs
Sodankylä
Kolari
Pelkosenniemi
Unari
Kemijoki
Alakurtti
Lappea
Tornionjoki
Pello
Kemijärvi
Salla
Napapiiri
ROVANIEMI
Oulanko National Park
Aavasaksa
Ylitornio
Ruka
Kuusamo
Haparanda
TORNIO
Ranua
KEMI
Pudasjärvi
Gulf of Bothnia
Hailuoto
OULU
Oulujoki
Suomussalmi
Skellefteå
RAAHE
Paltamo
Oulujärvi
KAJAANI
Kalajoki
Kuhmo
Ylivieska
Sotkamo
UMEÅ
Pietarsaari (Jakobstad)
KOKKOLA
Sonkajärvi
Nurmes
IISALMI
Ruunaa
Nykarleby
LIEKSA
Pielinen
Koli National Park
VAASA
Lapua
KUOPIO
SEINÄJOKI
Kallavesi
JOENSUU
Ilomantsi
Valamo Monastery
Saarijärvi
Kurikka
SUNDSVALL
Heinävesi
Virrat
Pieksämäki
Kolovesi National Park
Kristinestad
JYVÄSKYLÄ
VARKAUS
Niirala
Linnansaari National Park
Parkano
Kerimäki
SAVONLINNA
Päijänne
Näsijärvi
MIKKELI
Parikkala
PORI
TAMPERE
Saimaa
Pyhäjärvi
IMATRA
Heinola
RAUMA
Toijala
HÄMEENLINNA
LAPPEENRANTA
KOUVOLA
Nuijamaa
Uusikaupunki
Loimaa
Vainikkala
FORSSA
LAHTI
VYBORG
Askainen
RIIHIMÄKI
Hamina
Rymättylä
Routsipyhtää
Vaalimaa
TURKU
KOTKA
Åland
Loviisa
Virolahti
Eckerö
Naantali
Salo
Grissleham
Vantaa
Mariehamn
ESPOO
PORVOO
KEMIÖ (Kimito)
HELSINKI
Kemiö Island
Tammisaari (Ekenäs)
Kapellskar
To Stockholm
Hanko
To Tallinn
ST PETERSBURG

The best-known Finnish film-maker is Aki Kaurismäki, director of films like the 2002 success *Man Without A Past*, while director Renny Harlin has established himself in Hollywood.

Finnish bands have made a big impact on the heavier, darker side of the music scale in recent years. The Rasmus, Nightwish, Lordi, HIM, The 69 Eyes, and Apocalyptica are huge around the world. But there is lighter music, such as emo-punks Poets of the Fall and melodic Husky Rescue. Then there are unstoppable legends like Hanoi Rocks, Flaming Sideburns and the unicorn-quiffed Leningrad Cowboys.

ENVIRONMENT

People often describe Finland as a country of 'forests and lakes', and they are spot on. Some 10% of Suomi is taken up by bodies of water, and nearly 70% is forested with birch, spruce and pine. It's a fairly flat expanse of territory: though the fells of Lapland add a little height to the picture, they are small change compared to mountainous Norway.

Measuring 338,000 sq km and weighing in as Europe's seventh-largest nation, Finland hits remarkable latitudes: even its southernmost point is comparable with southern Alaska or Greenland. Its watery vital statistics are also impressive, with 187,888 large lakes and numerous further wetlands and smaller bodies of water.

Its tree cover of nearly 70% is the world's highest, and Finns in general have a deep respect for and understanding of nature and have always trodden lightly in it. With vast reserves of carefully managed forestry, it manages to produce reams of pulp and paper while maintaining its pine-scented green blanket intact. The Finns are environmentally conscious and favour practical, workable solutions over idealism. It's a country that carefully culls its large mammal population, and that regards nuclear power as a viable green alternative.

Finland's excellent network of national parks and other protected areas is maintained by **Metsähallitus** (www.outdoors.fi), the Finnish Forest and Park Service. In total, over 30,000 sq km, some 9% of the total area, is in some way protected land.

Elk, lynx, wolverines, brown bears and wolves are native to Finland, although sightings are rare. In Lapland, the Sámi keep commercial herds of some 200,000 reindeer.

TRANSPORT

GETTING THERE & AWAY

Air

Most major European carriers have flights to/from Helsinki's **Vantaa airport** (HEL; ☎ 0200-14636; www.helsinki-vantaa.fi). **Finnair** (AY; ☎ 0600-140 140; www.finnair.com) is the national carrier, with direct flights to Helsinki from numerous European, American and Asian cities. It's also served by various budget carriers from several European countries, especially **Ryanair** (FR; ☎ 0600-16010; www.ryanair.com) and **Blue1** (KF; ☎ 0600-025 831; www.blue1.com); check www.whichbudget.com for a complete list.

Boat

There's no better way to cruise into Helsinki than aboard a Baltic ferry. The ships are like floating hotels, nightclubs and shopping malls rolled into one, but fares are kept reasonably low by competition and duty-free shopping.

A list of operators with their Finnish contact numbers:

Eckerö Line (☎ 06000-4300) Åland (www.eckerolinjen.fi); Tallinn (www.eckeroline.fi)
Finnlines (☎ 010-436 7676; http://passenger.finnlines.com)
Linda Line (☎ 06000-668 970; www.lindaliini.ee)
RG Line (☎ 0207-716 810; www.rgline.com)
Tallink/Silja Line (☎ 0600-15700; www.tallinksilja.com)
Viking Line (☎ 0600-41577; www.vikingline.fi)

TO/FROM ESTONIA

Several companies nip between Helsinki and Tallinn in Estonia. Car ferries cross in 3½

CONNECTIONS

While Finland's road connections with Norway and Sweden are way up in the north of the country, ferries are big business on the Baltic, and can take you to Stockholm (opposite) or as far as Germany (opposite). Helsinki's harbour also offers quick, easy connections to Tallinn (above) in Estonia, which sets you up to explore the Baltic States and Eastern Europe in general. Finland's also a springboard for Russia, with bus (opposite) and train (opposite) services available once you've got a visa sorted out.

hours, catamarans and hydrofoils in about 1½ hours, although in winter there are fewer departures and the crossing is slower due to the ice.

Ferries are cheapest: Eckerö Line has only one departure daily but is the cheapest with a return fare from €30 to €39 in high season.

TO/FROM GERMANY

Finnlines has a year-round service from Helsinki to Travemünde (from €196 September to May, from €244 June to August one way, plus €100 per vehicle) with a connecting bus service to Hamburg. The faster Star boats (27 hours) are cheaper than the Hansa Class boats (35 hours), which you stay on for two nights. Tallink/Silja also runs a fast ferry from Helsinki to Rostock (27 hours), with seats costing €72 to €97, and berths starting at €127. Vehicle places are available from €115.

TO/FROM SWEDEN

The Stockholm–Helsinki, Stockholm–Turku and Kapellskär–Mariehamn (Åland) runs are dominated by Tallink/Silja and Viking Lines, with daily departures. Viking is cheaper, with a passenger ticket between Stockholm and Helsinki costing from €34 to €51 (up to €62 on Fridays). In summer you can doss down in chairs or on the floor, but an extra cabin ticket is obligatory from September to May: the cheapest berths start at €24.

Tallink/Silja don't offer deck tickets on the Helsinki run: the cheapest cabins start at €122 for the crossing.

It's usually much cheaper to cross to Turku (11 to 12 hours), with tickets starting at €10 on the day ferries. Note that Åbo is Swedish for Turku.

Eckerö Line sails from Grisslehamn, located north of Stockholm, to Eckerö in Åland. It's the quickest, at just two hours, and, with prices starting from €8.90 return, it's a bargain. There's a connecting bus from Stockholm.

Bus

Five daily routes link Finnish Lapland with northern Norway, some running only in summer.

Buses link Tornio in Finland with adjoining Haparanda in Sweden; you can get onward transport from either.

Daily buses run from Helsinki to St Petersburg (€63.70, 8½ to nine hours) in Russia. You'll need a visa.

Timetables for all these buses appear on the Finnish bus website (www.matkahuolto.fi).

Train

The only international train links to Finland are with Russia. There are three trains daily from Helsinki. You must have a Russian visa, which gets processed aboard. The *Sibelius* and *Repin* run daily from Helsinki to St Petersburg (€54.80, six hours). In 2010 new high-speed trains are scheduled to cut this journey to 3½ hours. The *Tolstoi* sleeper runs from Helsinki via St Petersburg to Moscow (1st/2nd class €139/93, 13 hours). The fare includes a sleeper berth. See www.vr.fi for details.

GETTING AROUND

Air

Finnair and its budget affiliate **Finncomm** (www.fc.fi) run a comprehensive domestic service mainly out of Helsinki. Budget carrier **Blue1** (☎ 0600-025 831; www.blue1.com) also offers cheap fares on certain routes.

Bicycle

Finland is flat, with miles of bike paths – also used by in-line skaters in summer and cross-country skiers in winter. The only drawback to an extensive tour is distance, but bikes can be carried on most public transport. Daily/weekly hire from €15/70 is possible in most cities; check with the local tourist office. Hostels and camping grounds have cheaper or free bikes best for local exploration rather than long routes. The Åland Islands are great for cycle touring.

Boat

Lake and river ferries operate in summer (June to August). More than mere transport, a cruise is a bona-fide Finnish experience. Some of the best routes are Savonlinna–Kuopio, Tampere–Hämeenlinna, Lake Pielinen and the coastal ferries from Turku. Many ferries that run between the islands along the coast are free, especially in Åland.

Bus

All long-distance bus ticketing is handled by **Matkahuolto** (☎ 0200-4000; www.matkahuolto.fi); its excellent website has all timetables. Each town and municipal centre has a *linja-autoasema* (bus terminal), with local timetables displayed (*lähtevät* is departures, *saapuvat* arrivals). Ticket offices tend to work normal business hours, but you can always buy the ticket from the driver.

Buses are express *(pikavuoro)* or regular *(vakiovuoro)*. Fares are based on distance travelled. The one-way fare for a 100km trip is normal/express €16.30/19.20. For student discounts, you need to be studying full time in Finland and buy a student coach discount card (€6). If booking three or more adult tickets together, a 25% discount applies, meaning good news for groups.

Car & Motorcycle

Car rental in Finland is much more expensive than elsewhere in Europe. A small car costs from €77/320 per day/week with 300km free per day. As ever, there are much cheaper deals online. Look out for weekend rates, which can cost little more than the rate for a single day. One of the cheapest operators is **Sixt** (☎ 09-350 5590; www.sixt.fi).

Hitching

Hitching in Finland is possible but expect long waits and pack waterproofs. Your greatest friend will be your insect repellent. Mosquitoes can't believe their luck that a large juicy mammal will stand in one place for such a very long time.

Train

Finnish trains are run by the state-owned **Valtion Rautatiet** (VR; ☎ 0600-41900; www.vr.fi) and are an excellent service: fast, efficient and cheaper than the bus. They are the best form of transport between major cities.

VR's website is excellent, with comprehensive timetable information, and some ticket sales. Major stations have a VR office: this is where to buy your ticket, as the automated machines only accept Finnish bankcards. You can also just hop aboard, find a seat and pay the conductor, but if the ticket office was open where you boarded, you'll be charged a small penalty fee (€3 to €6).

The Finland Eurail Pass costs €128/169/230 for three/five/10 days' second-class travel in a one-month period within Finland. The InterRail Finland pass offers travel only in Finland for three/four/six/eight days in a one-month period, costing €109/139/189/229 in second class. The **Finnrail Pass** (www.vr.fi) offers a similar deal to the InterRail and Eurail passes though it's slightly more expensive.

HELSINKI

☎ 09 / pop 568,600

It's fitting that harbourside Helsinki, capital of a country with such a watery geography, melds so graciously with the Baltic Sea. Half the city seems to be liquid, and the tortured writhings of the complex coastline includes any number of bays and inlets, and a speckling of islands.

Though Helsinki can seem like a younger sibling to other Scandinavian capitals, it's the one that went to art school, scorns pop music, is working in a cutting-edge design studio and hangs out with friends who like black and plenty of piercings. The city's design shops are legendary, and its music and nightlife scene kicking.

HISTORY

Helsinki was founded in 1550 by the Swedish king Gustav Vasa. In the 18th century the Swedes built a mammoth fortress on the nearby island of Suomenlinna, but it wasn't enough to keep the Russians out. Once the Russians were in control of Finland, they needed a capital a bit closer to home than the Swedish-influenced west coast. Helsinki was it and it grew rapidly, with German architect CL Engel responsible for many noble central buildings. In the bitter postwar years, the 1952 Olympic Games symbolised the city's gradual revival.

ORIENTATION

Helsinki occupies a peninsula, surrounded by an archipelago of islands. The compact city centre stretches from the harbourside *kauppatori* (market square), between the international ferry terminals, to Kamppi, the bus station. The train station is nearby.

INFORMATION

Bookshops

Akateeminen Kirjakauppa (☎ 12141; Pohjoisesplanadi 39; 🕒 9am-9pm Mon-Fri, 9am-6pm Sat, noon-6pm Sun) Huge travel section, maps, Finnish literature and impressive English section.

EMERGENCY NUMBERS

- Police, fire & ambulance ☎ 112

Discount Cards

Helsinki Card (☎ 2288 1200; www.helsinkicard.fi; 24/48/72hr €33/43/53) If you plan to see a lot of sights, the Helsinki Card gives you free travel, and entry to more than 50 attractions in and around Helsinki. Buy it at the tourist office, hotels, R-kioskis and transport terminals.

Emergencies

Dial ☎ 112 for all emergencies and ☎ 10023 for 24-hour medical advice.

Internet Access

Internet access at Helsinki's public libraries is free. Large parts of the city centre have free wi-fi, as do many bars and cafes.

Library 10 (☎ 3108 5000; Elielinkatu 2; 10am-10pm Mon-Thu, 10am-6pm Fri, noon-6pm Sat & Sun, shorter hours summer) On the 1st floor of the main post office, by the railway station. Several half-hour terminals and others bookable by phone.

mbar (☎ 6124 5420; Mannerheimintie 22; per hr €5; 9am-midnight, later at weekends) In the Lasipalatsi building. Heaps of terminals.

TeleCenter (☎ 670 612; Vuorikatu 8; per hr €2; 10am-9pm Mon-Fri, 11am-7pm Sat, noon-7pm Sun) Slowish but cheap.

Left Luggage

At the bus and train station it costs €3/4 for small/large lockers. There are similar lockers and left-luggage counters at the ferry terminals.

Medical Services

Maria Hospital (☎ 3106 3231; Lapinlahdenkatu 16; 24hr) For emergency medical assistance.

GETTING INTO TOWN

Bus 615 (€3.40, 50 minutes) shuttles between Vantaa airport and Rautatientori next to the main train station. Bus stops are marked with a blue sign featuring a plane. Faster Finnair buses (€5.90, 30 minutes, every 20 minutes) also depart from the railway station, stopping a couple of times en route. Both run from 5am to midnight.

If you arrive by ferry from Sweden or Estonia, or by bus or train, you'll be deposited right in the middle of town.

Töölö Health Station (☎ 310 5015; Sibeliuksenkatu 14; 8am-6pm Mon, to 4pm Tue-Fri) A day-only medical centre.

Money

There are currency exchange counters at the airport and ferry terminals. ATMs (Otto) are plentiful.

Forex (8am-9pm summer, to 7pm Mon-Sat autumn-spring) At Pohjoisesplanadi 27, Mannerheimintie 10 and at the train station, Forex offers good rates and is the best place to change cash or travellers cheques (flat fee €2).

Tourist Information

Helsinki City Tourist Office (☎ 169 3757; www.hel.fi/tourism; Pohjoisesplanadi 19; 9am-8pm Mon-Fri, to 6pm Sat & Sun May-Sep, 9am-6pm Mon-Fri, 10am-4pm Sat & Sun Oct-Apr) Busy multilingual office with booking desk. In summer, it sends out uniformed 'Helsinki Helpers'; grab one on the street and ask away. A cut-down version of the city tourism website can be delivered to your mobile at www.helsinki.mobi.

SIGHTS

Historic Helsinki

Helsinki's **kauppatori** sits right by the passenger harbour in the old part of town. It's a forum for selling fish off the boats, as well as other fresh garden produce and seasonal berries. Just north of it, chalk-white **Tuomiokirkko** (Lutheran Cathedral; ☎ 709 2455; Unioninkatu 29; 9am-6pm Mon-Sat, noon-6pm Sun Sep-May, 9am-midnight Jun-Aug) presides over Senate Sq. Its interior is fairly unadorned, unlike that of red-brick **Uspenski Cathedral** (☎ 634 267; Kanavakatu 1; 9.30am-4pm Mon-Fri, 9.30am-2pm Sat, noon-3pm Sun, closed Mon Oct-Apr), the lavishly decorated Orthodox cathedral topped with onion domes on nearby Katajanokka island.

From the *kauppatori* it's an entertaining day or half-day boat trip to the islands of **Suomenlinna** (Sveaborg), the 'fortress of Finland', founded by the Swedes in 1748 to protect the eastern part of the empire against the Russians. At the bridge connecting the two main islands is the **Inventory Chamber Visitor Centre** (☎ 668 800; www.suomenlinna.fi; walking tours €6.50 or free with Helsinki Card; 10am-6pm May-Sep), which has tourist information, maps and guided walking tours in summer. Here too is **Suomenlinna Museum** (☎ 684 1880; admission €5; 10am-6pm May-Sep, to 4pm Oct-Apr), featuring a scale model of Suomenlinna as it looked in 1808 and a 30-minute audiovisual display. The most interesting of the other island attractions

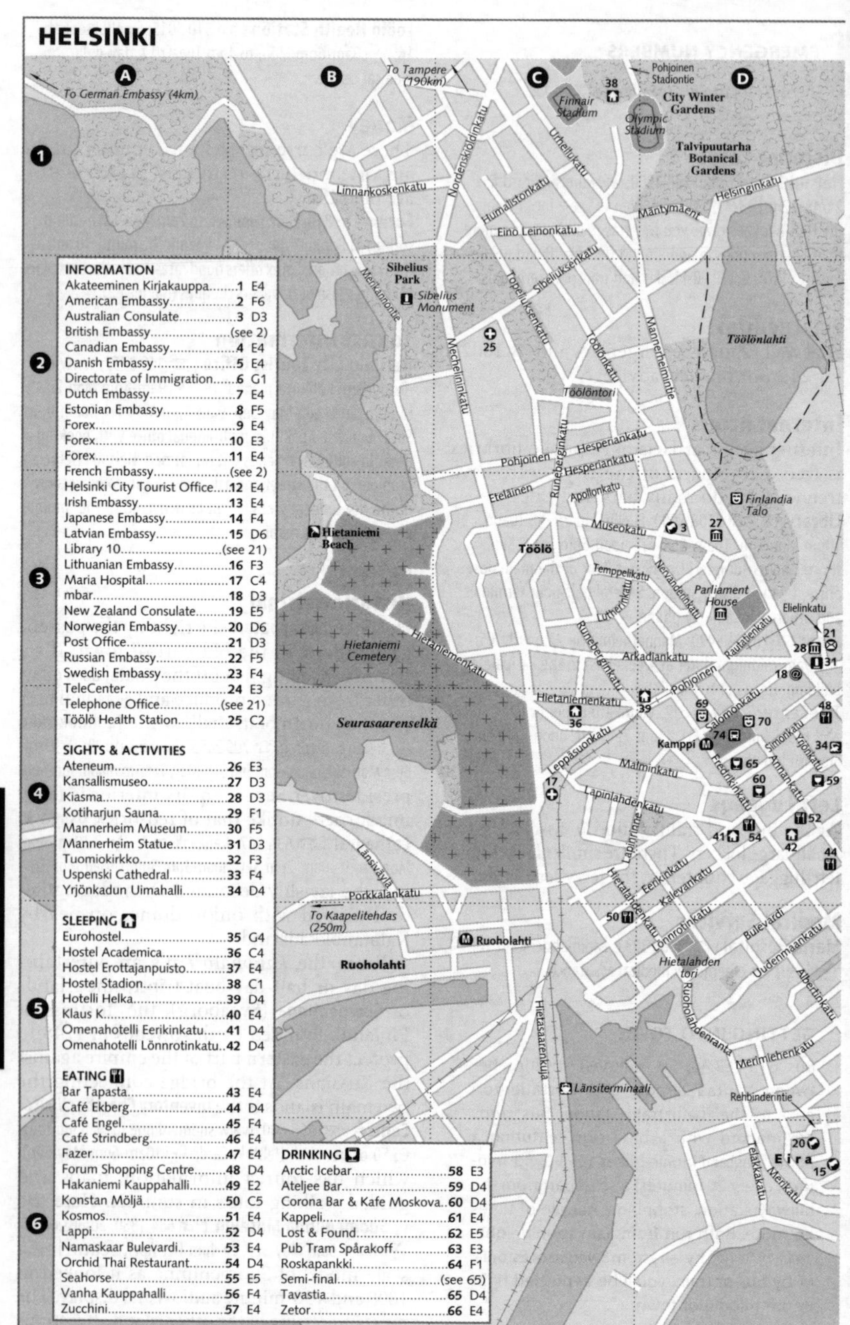
HELSINKI
A
B
C
D
1
2
3
4
5
6
To German Embassy (4km)
To Tampere (190km)
Pohjoinen Stadiontie
38
Finnair Stadium
Olympic Stadium
City Winter Gardens
Talvipuutarha Botanical Gardens
Urheilukatu
Nordenskiöldinkatu
Linnankoskenkatu
Humalistonkatu
Helsinginkatu
Mäntymäent
Eino Leinonkatu
Sibeliuksenkatu
Topeliuksenkatu
Sibelius Park
Sibelius Monument
Merikannontie
Mechelininkatu
25
Töölönkatu
Mannerheimintie
Töölönlahti
Töölöntori
Runeberginkatu
Pohjoinen Hesperiankatu
Eteläinen Hesperiankatu
Apollonkatu
Finlandia Talo
Hietaniemi Beach
Museokatu
3
27
Töölö
Temppelikatu
Nervanderinkatu
Parliament House
Lutherinkatu
Elielinkatu
Hietaniemi Cemetery
Hietaniemenkatu
Rautatienkatu
21
28
31
Arkadiankatu
18
Pohjoinen
Hietaniemenkatu
36
39
69
Salomonkatu
70
48
Seurasaarenselkä
Leppäsuonkatu
Kamppi
74
Simonkatu
34
Yrjönkatu
Malminkatu
65
Annankatu
Fredrikinkatu
60
59
17
Lapinlahdenkatu
52
41
54
42
44
Länsiväylä
Lapinrinne
Eerikinkatu
Kalevankatu
Porkkalankatu
Hietalahdenkatu
To Kaapelitehdas (250m)
50
Lönnrotinkatu
Bulevardi
Ruoholahti
Ruoholahti
Uudenmaankatu
Hietalahden tori
Albertinkatu
Hietasaarenkuja
Ruoholahdenranta
Merimiehenkatu
Länsiterminaali
Rehbinderintie
20
Eira
15
Telakkakatu
Merikatu
INFORMATION
Akateeminen Kirjakauppa.......1 E4
American Embassy.......2 F6
Australian Consulate.......3 D3
British Embassy.......(see 2)
Canadian Embassy.......4 E4
Danish Embassy.......5 E4
Directorate of Immigration.......6 G1
Dutch Embassy.......7 E4
Estonian Embassy.......8 F5
Forex.......9 E4
Forex.......10 E3
Forex.......11 E4
French Embassy.......(see 2)
Helsinki City Tourist Office.......12 E4
Irish Embassy.......13 E4
Japanese Embassy.......14 F4
Latvian Embassy.......15 D6
Library 10.......(see 21)
Lithuanian Embassy.......16 F3
Maria Hospital.......17 C4
mbar.......18 D3
New Zealand Consulate.......19 E5
Norwegian Embassy.......20 D6
Post Office.......21 D3
Russian Embassy.......22 F5
Swedish Embassy.......23 F4
TeleCenter.......24 E3
Telephone Office.......(see 21)
Töölö Health Station.......25 C2
SIGHTS & ACTIVITIES
Ateneum.......26 E3
Kansallismuseo.......27 D3
Kiasma.......28 D3
Kotiharjun Sauna.......29 F1
Mannerheim Museum.......30 F5
Mannerheim Statue.......31 D3
Tuomiokirkko.......32 F3
Uspenski Cathedral.......33 F4
Yrjönkadun Uimahalli.......34 D4
SLEEPING
Eurohostel.......35 G4
Hostel Academica.......36 C4
Hostel Erottajanpuisto.......37 E4
Hostel Stadion.......38 C1
Hotelli Helka.......39 D4
Klaus K.......40 E4
Omenahotelli Eerikinkatu.......41 D4
Omenahotelli Lönnrotinkatu.......42 D4
EATING
Bar Tapasta.......43 E4
Café Ekberg.......44 D4
Café Engel.......45 F4
Café Strindberg.......46 E4
Fazer.......47 E4
Forum Shopping Centre.......48 D4
Hakaniemi Kauppahalli.......49 E2
Konstan Möljä.......50 C5
Kosmos.......51 E4
Lappi.......52 D4
Namaskaar Bulevardi.......53 E4
Orchid Thai Restaurant.......54 D4
Seahorse.......55 E5
Vanha Kauppahalli.......56 F4
Zucchini.......57 E4
DRINKING
Arctic Icebar.......58 E3
Ateljee Bar.......59 D4
Corona Bar & Kafe Moskova.......60 D4
Kappeli.......61 E4
Lost & Found.......62 E5
Pub Tram Spårakoff.......63 E3
Roskapankki.......64 F1
Semi-final.......(see 65)
Tavastia.......65 D4
Zetor.......66 E4

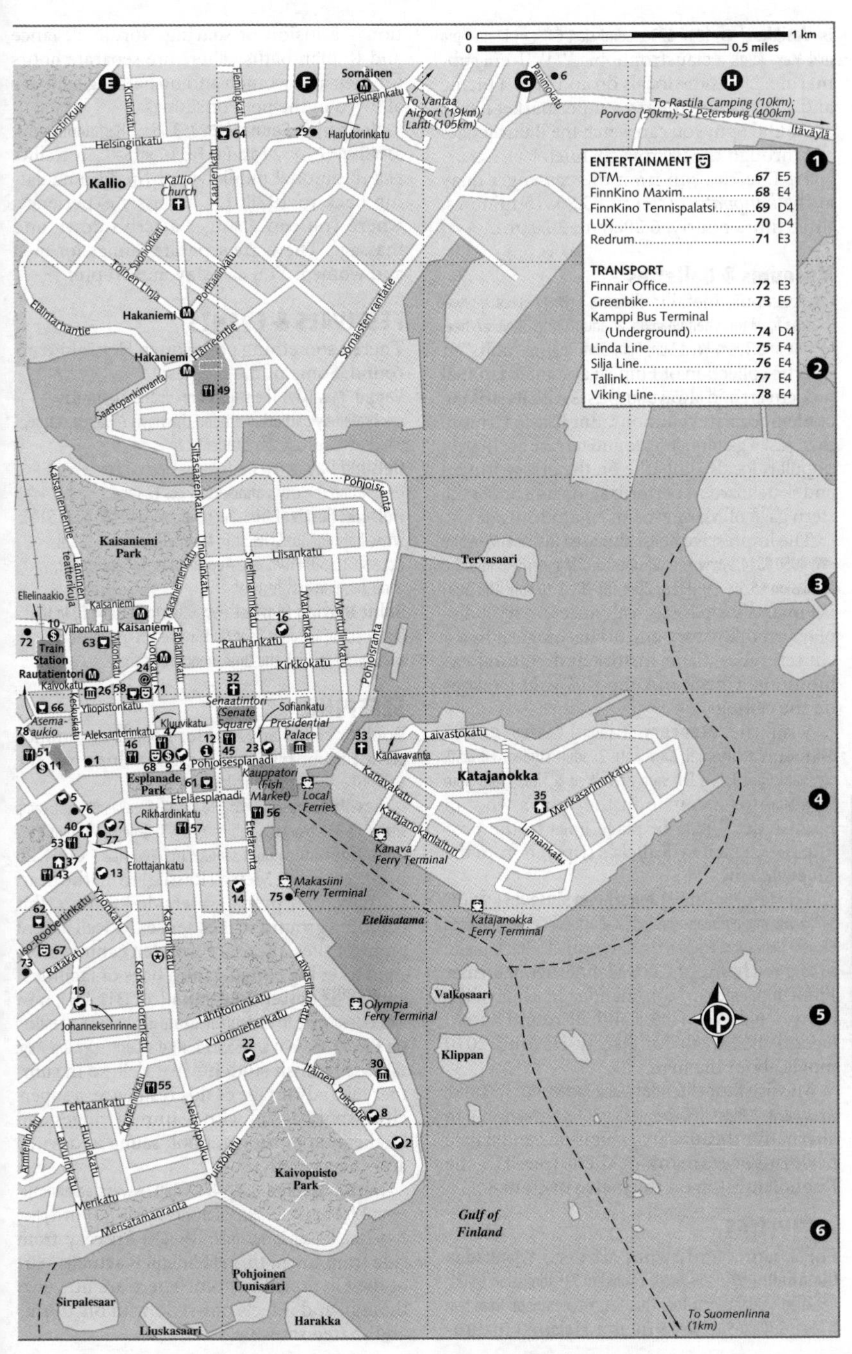
0 1 km
0 0.5 miles
E
F
G
H
1
2
3
4
5
6
ENTERTAINMENT
DTM 67 E5
FinnKino Maxim 68 E4
FinnKino Tennispalatsi 69 D4
LUX 70 D4
Redrum 71 E3
TRANSPORT
Finnair Office 72 E3
Greenbike 73 E5
Kamppi Bus Terminal (Underground) 74 D4
Linda Line 75 F4
Silja Line 76 E4
Tallink 77 E4
Viking Line 78 E4
Sornäinen
To Vantaa Airport (19km); Lahti (105km)
To Rastila Camping (10km); Porvoo (50km); St Petersburg (400km)
Itäväylä
Panimokatu
Helsinginkatu
Harjutorinkatu
Kirstinkuja
Kirstinkatu
Flemingkatu
Kaarlenkatu
Kallio
Kallio Church
Suonionkatu
Toinen Linja
Porthaninkatu
Eläintarhantie
Hakaniemi
Hämeentie
Saastopankinranta
Sörnäisten rantatie
Siltasaarenkatu
Pohjoisranta
Kaisaniemi Park
Kaisaniementie
Läntinen teatterikuja
Elielinaakio
Unioninkatu
Kaisaniemenkatu
Snellmaninkatu
Liisankatu
Tervasaari
Mariankatu
Meritullinkatu
Kaisaniemi
Vilhonkatu
Train Station
Rautatientori
Kaivokatu
Mikonkatu
Vuorikatu
Fabianinkatu
Rauhankatu
Kirkkokatu
Yliopistonkatu
Keskuskatu
Asema-aukio
Kluuvikatu
Aleksanterinkatu
Senaatintori (Senate Square)
Sofiankatu
Presidential Palace
Laivastokatu
Kanavaranta
Katajanokka
Pohjoisesplanadi
Esplanade Park
Eteläesplanadi
Kauppatori (Fish Market)
Local Ferries
Kanavakatu
Katajanokanlaituri
Merikasarminkatu
Linnankatu
Rikhardinkatu
Eteläranta
Kanava Ferry Terminal
Erottajankatu
Makasiini Ferry Terminal
Yrjönkatu
Iso-Roobertinkatu
Kasarmikatu
Eteläsatama
Katajanokka Ferry Terminal
Ratakatu
Korkeavuorenkatu
Laivasillankatu
Valkosaari
Johanneksenrinne
Tähtitorninkatu
Vuorimiehenkatu
Olympia Ferry Terminal
Klippan
Itäinen Puistotie
Tehtaankatu
Kapteeninkatu
Neitsytpolku
Armfeltintie
Laivurinkatu
Huvilakatu
Puistokatu
Kaivopuisto Park
Merikatu
Merisatamanranta
Gulf of Finland
Pohjoinen Uunisaari
Sirpalesaar
Liuskasaari
Harakka
To Suomenlinna (1km)
FINLAND

Book your stay at lonelyplanet.com/hotels

is **Vesikko** (☎ 1814 6238; admission €4, ⏰ 11am-6pm mid-May–Aug), a claustrophobic WWII-era submarine. Do as the locals do and grab a picnic and a few beers (there's a supermarket here); at around 5pm you can watch the Baltic ferries sail through the narrow channel.

HKL ferries run from the passenger quay at the *kauppatori* (return €3.80, 15 minutes, three times hourly, 6.20am to 2.20am).

Museums & Galleries

Curvaceous, metallic **Kiasma** (☎ 1733 6501; www.kiasma.fi; Mannerheiminaukio 2; adult/under 18yr €7/free; ⏰ 10am-8.30pm Wed-Sun, 9am-5pm Tue) exhibits an eclectic collection of Finnish and international modern art and always surprises with its striking contemporary exhibitions. But Kiasma's more than just a gallery; its cafe and terrace are hugely popular, locals sunbathe on the grassy fringes and skateboarders perform aerobatics under the stern gaze of Mannerheim's statue outside.

The impressive **Kansallismuseo** (National Museum; ☎ 4050 9544; www.kansallismuseo.fi; Mannerheimintie 34; admission €5.50; ⏰ 11am-8pm Tue-Wed, to 6pm Thu-Sun) is Finland's top historical museum, with displays on prehistory and archaeological finds, church relics, Sámi history and cultural exhibitions. Check out the *Kalevala* frescoes on the ceiling.

Visit the **Ateneum** (National Gallery; ☎ 1733 6401; www.ateneum.fi; Kaivokatu 2; adult/student €8/6.50; ⏰ 9am-6pm Tue & Fri, 9am-8pm Wed & Thu, 11am-5pm Sat & Sun) for a course in the 'who's who' of Finnish art. Pride of place goes to the prolific Akseli Gallen-Kallela's triptych from the *Kalevala* epic.

The fascinating **Mannerheim Museum** (☎ 635 443; www.mannerheim-museo.fi; Kalliolinnantie 14; admission €8; ⏰ 11am-4pm Fri-Sun) in Kaivopuisto Park is the preserved home of CGE Mannerheim, former Finnish president, commander-in-chief of the army, Civil War victor and all-round Suomi legend. Look out for Renny Harlin's 2010 movie about the man.

Massive **Kaapelitehdas** (Cable Factory; ☎ 4763 8300; www.kaapelitehdas.fi; Tallberginkatu 1C) is now home to alternative theatre, art exhibitions and dance performances, many of them free. Hit the Ruoholahti stop on the metro or tram 8.

ACTIVITIES

For a sauna and swim, art deco **Yrjönkadun Uimahalli** (☎ 3108 7400; Yrjönkatu 21; admission €4-11; ⏰ men 6.30am-9pm Tue, Thu, Sat, women noon-9pm Sun & Mon, 6.30am-9pm Wed & Fri) is a Helsinki institution – a fusion of soaring Nordic elegance and Roman baths. There are separate hours for men and women and no bathing suits are allowed in the pool or saunas.

Kotiharjun Sauna (☎ 753 1535; Harjutorinkatu 1; admission €7; ⏰ 2-8pm Tue-Fri, 1-7pm Sat), in Kallio, is a traditional public wood-fired sauna dating back to 1928. It's a classic experience, where you can also get a scrub-down and massage. There are separate saunas for men and women. You can stay until 10pm.

FESTIVALS & EVENTS

There's something going on in Helsinki year-round. Some of the biggies:

Vappu (May Day) The student graduation festival is celebrated by gathering around the Havis Amanda statue, which receives a white 'student cap'.

Helsinki Day (www.hel.fi/helsinkipaiva) Free events celebrating the city's anniversary on 12 June.

Helsinki Festival (Helsingin Juhlaviikot; ☎ 6126 5100; www.helsinginjuhlaviikot.fi; Mannerheimintie 22-24; tickets €10-50) From late August to early September; wide-ranging arts festival.

Baltic Herring Market (www.portofhelsinki.fi) In the first week of October fisherfolk and chefs gather at the *kauppatori* to cook the time-honoured fish.

SLEEPING

Book or call in advance for hostels in summer. At a pinch, try booking something via the website www.helsinkiexpert.fi.

Rastila Camping (☎ 3107 8517; Karavaanikatu 4; camp sites €13-15, 2-person cabins €38-45, 4-person cabins €53-64, cottage with/without sauna €165/100; 💻) Only 20 minutes on the Metro (Rastila) from the heart of town, in a pretty waterside location, this camping ground makes sense. As well as tent and van sites, there are wooden cabins, more upmarket log cottages, and bags of facilities.

our pick **Hostel Academica** (☎ 1311 4334; www.hostelacademica.fi; Hietaniemenkatu 14; dm €18, standard s/d €40/60, modern s/d €55/75, HI discount; ⏰ Jun-Aug; 💻 ♿) Finnish students live well, so in summer take advantage of this residence, a super-clean spot packed with features (fridges and kitchenette in rooms, pool, sauna and wi-fi) and cheery staff.

Hostel Stadion (☎ 477 8480; www.stadionhostel.com; Pohjoinen Stadiontie 3; dm/s/d €19/38/47; ⏰ reception 7am-2am, to 3am in summer; 🅿 💻) An easy tram ride from town, this HI hostel is actually part of the Olympic Stadium. There are no views though, and it feels old-style with big dorms and shared showers.

SPLURGE

Klaus K (☎ 020-770 4700; www.klauskhotel.com; Bulevardi 2, Helsinki; s/d from €140/180; 💻) Confidently Finnish, with an elegant *Kalevala*-epic theme, luxurious birch toiletries, space-conscious architecture and sauna-style bathroom ceilings, this design hotel is hard to beat for sleeping in style. It backs it up with comforts like high-speed wi-fi and DVDs in all rooms, plus two good restaurants and a frostily cool bar.

Eurohostel (☎ 622 0470; www.eurohostel.fi; Linnankatu 9; dm €22-24, s €38-44, d €43-55; 💻) On Katajanokka island less than 500m from the Viking Line terminal, this HI-affiliate is busy but a bit soulless and offers both backpacker and 'hotel' rooms. Both share common bathrooms. The small cafe serves a breakfast buffet (€7) and other meals and there's a morning sauna included.

Hostel Erottajanpuisto (☎ 642 169; www.erottajanpuisto.com; Uudenmaankatu 9; dm/s/d/tr €23.50/49/68/81; 💻) Helsinki's smallest and most laid-back hostel occupies the top floor of a building in a lively street of bars and restaurants close to the heart of the city.

Hotelli Finn (☎ 684 4360; www.hotellifinn.fi; Kalevankatu 3b; s/d with toilet €65/75, with toilet & shower €65/80) Although not flash, this small, friendly hotel on the top floor of a central-city building offers very reasonable rates for the location. Rooms are compact but tidy, with TV.

Omenahotelli (☎ 0600-18018; www.omena.com; Eerikinkatu 24 & Lönnrotinkatu 13; r €90) This good-value staffless hotel chain has two handy Helsinki locations. As well as a double bed, rooms have a fold-out sofa that can sleep two more, plus there's a microwave and minifridge. Book online or via a terminal in the lobby.

Hotelli Helka (☎ 613 580; www.helka.fi; Pohjoinen Rautatiekatu 23a; s/d €136/171, weekends & summer €90/112; Ⓟ 💻) A substantial renovation has made this a hip hotel with rooms decked out in chocolate browns and wheaty shades. You can often bag cheap deals here on discount hotel websites. Bikes are for hire at €15 per day.

EATING

Helsinki has by far Finland's best range of cafes and restaurants, from Finnish and Russian to Asian and Italian, sushi joints to kebab stands and terrace cafes to fine French dining. Seek out the lunchtime specials – many restaurants (even the fancy ones) have buffet lunch deals for under €10.

Quick Eats

In summer there are food stalls, fresh produce and expensive berries at the *kauppatori*, but the real picnic treats are in the fabulous **Vanha Kauppahalli** (Old Market Hall; Eteläranta 1; 🕒 6.30am-6pm Mon-Fri, 6.30am-4pm Sat, 10am-4pm Sun summer only) nearby, where you can get filled rolls, cheese, breads, fish and an array of Finnish snacks and delicacies. A less touristed traditional market hall is **Hakaniemi Kauppahalli** (🕒 8am-6pm Mon-Fri, to 4pm Sat), by Hakaniemi metro.

For everything from Asian noodles to burgers and kebabs, head to the food court in the basement of the **Forum shopping centre** (Mannerheimintie 20), where you'll also find a supermarket and Alko store.

Cafes

Café Strindberg (☎ 681 2030; Pohjoisesplanadi 33; pastries €4-8; 🕒 9am-10pm Mon-Sat, 10am-10pm Sun) This upmarket cafe is a classic place to see and be seen on the esplanade, with a terrace whose waiter-served seats are much in demand. There's a sumptuous lounge and classy bistro upstairs too.

Fazer (☎ 6159 2959; Kluuvikatu 3; sandwiches & pies €7-10; 🕒 7.30am-10pm Mon-Fri, 9am-10pm Sat) Founded in 1891 by the Finnish confectionary-making family (you'll see Fazer sweets and chocolate everywhere), this place does amazing ice-cream sundaes and also sells cakes and tea to take away.

Café Engel (☎ 652 776; Senaatintori; meals €10-18; 🕒 8am-10pm Mon-Fri, 9am-10pm Sat, 10am-10pm Sun) There's always a good selection of cakes and enticing meals, often of a vegetarian bent, at this popular cultural hub. Films show in the courtyard in summer.

Restaurants

Bar Tapasta (☎ 640 724; Uudenmaankatu 13; tapas €3-5; 🕒 11am-midnight Mon-Thu, 11am-2am Fri, 2pm-2am Sat) This is an intimate and welcoming bar with quirky Mediterranean decor and friendly staff. The tapas are cheap and generous; there is also (how did you guess?) pasta, wines by the glass and popular sangria.

Zucchini (☎ 622 2907; Fabianinkatu 4; lunch €6-9; 🕒 11am-4pm Mon-Fri) One of the city's few vegetarian eateries, this covers a lot of bases with friendliness, fresh baked quiches and piping soups. The sunny terrace out the back is stunning in summer.

our pick **Konstan Möljä** (☎ 694 7504; Hietalahdenkatu 14; lunch/dinner buffet €7.50/14; ⌚ 11am-10pm Mon-Fri, 2-10pm Sat, dinner buffet starts 4pm) You can almost smell the sea in the maritime interior of this old sailors' eatery. It's real working-man's food with a huge buffet that includes soup, salad, bread, meat (always reindeer) and vegetable dishes.

Namaskaar Bulevardi (☎ 6220 1155; Bulevardi 6; lunch €7.50-12, mains €12-18; ⌚ lunch & dinner) There are several branches of this Indian buffet throughout the city, but this is the best, with interesting, stylish decor and an excellent terrace.

Café Ekberg (☎ 6811 8660; Bulevardi 9; buffet breakfast & lunch €9; ⌚ 7.30am-7pm Mon-Fri, 8.30am-5pm Sat, 10am-5pm Sun) There's been a cafe of this name in Helsinki since 1861 and today it continues to be a family-run place renowned for its pastries, like the Napoleon cake. Its buffet breakfasts and lunches are also popular, plus there's fresh bread to take away.

Orchid Thai Restaurant (☎ 694 5491; Eerikinkatu 20; mains €9-15; ⌚ 10.30am-10pm Mon-Fri, noon-10pm Sat, 2-10pm Sun) This cheap and cheerful little spot does tasty Thai, with scrumptious stir-fried duck alongside classics such as green curry and cashew-nut chicken.

Seahorse (☎ 628 169; www.seahorse.fi; Kapteeninkatu 11; mains €12-21; ⌚ 10.30am-midnight) Seahorse dates back to the '30s and is as traditional a Finnish restaurant as you'll find anywhere. Locals gather in the gloriously unchanged interior to meet and drink over hefty dishes of Baltic herring, Finnish meatballs and cabbage rolls.

Lappi (☎ 645 550; Annankatu 22; mains €15-30; ⌚ noon-10.30pm Mon-Fri, 1-10.30pm Sat & Sun) This Lapland-themed restaurant is enjoyably kitschy, with the rustic decor and Sámi culture laid on thick. The food's pretty good, with plenty of berries, and the chance to add Rudolf or Bullwinkle to your list of carnivorous conquests.

Kosmos (☎ 647 255; Kalevankatu 3; mains €15-25, menu €40; ⌚ 11.30am-1am Mon-Fri, 4pm-1am Sat, closed Jul) Designed by Alvar Aalto, this classical place could qualify as an institution on that fact alone, but the great formal service and reliably excellent food make it a real Helsinki redoubt. A Finnish antipasto plate (including smoked reindeer and Baltic herring) is the ideal start before moving on to meaty mains such as Russian chicken breast served with roe and sauerkraut or lamb kidneys with pilaf.

FINLAND

DRINKING

Helsinki has some of Scandinavia's most diverse nightlife. In winter locals gather in cosy bars, while in summer beer terraces sprout all over town.

The centre's full of bars and clubs, with the Punavuori area around Iso-Roobertinkatu one of the most worthwhile for trendy alternative choices. For the cheapest beer, try the working-class suburb of Kallio (metro: Sörnäinen), north of the centre.

Ateljee Bar (Sokos Hotel Torni, Yrjönkatu 26; ⌚ 2pm-2am Mon-Thu, noon-2am Fri & Sat, 2pm-1am Sun) It's worth the climb up to this tiny perch on the roof of the Sokos Hotel Torni for the city panorama. Taking the lift to the 12th floor is the best option, then there's a narrow winding staircase to the top. Downstairs, the courtyard Tornin Piha is a cute little terrace with good wines by the glass. The rooftop bars of the Palace and the Sokos Vaakuna hotels are also notable for their great views.

Arctic Icebar (☎ 278 1855; Yliopistonkatu 5; admission €10; ⌚ 10pm-4am Wed-Sat) Not cold enough outside? Then try this bar that's literally carved out of ice, including tables and bar. It's minus 5°C so you'll need the furry cape they loan you on entry and the complimentary warming drink included in the price. There's an age minimum of 24. It's above La Bodega.

Corona Bar & Kafe Moskova (☎ 611 200; Eerikinkatu 11-15; ⌚ bar 11am-2am, cafe 6pm-2am) Those offbeat film-making Kaurismäki brothers are up to their old tricks with this pair of conjoined drinking dens. Corona plays the straight man with 20 pool tables and cheap beer, while Moskova is back in the USSR with a bubbling samovar, Soviet vinyl and lugubrious Brezhnev speeches. Dubrovnik in the same complex does regular live jazz.

Pub Tram Spårakoff (☎ 123 4800; departs Mikonkatu, east of train station; tickets €8.50, beers €5; ⌚ Departs hourly 2pm-3pm & 5pm-8pm, Tue-Sat mid-May–mid-Aug) Not sure whether to go sightseeing or booze the day away? Do both in this bright red pub tram, the tipsy alternative to traditional tours around town.

Zetor (☎ 010 766 4450; www.ravintolazetor.fi; Mannerheimintie 3-5; mains €10-22; ⌚ 11am-4am Sat, 3pm-1am Sun & Mon, 3pm-3am Tue, 3pm-4am Wed & Thu) A fun Finnish restaurant and pub with deeply ironic tractor decor. It's owned by film-maker Aki Kaurismäki and designed by the Leningrad Cowboys. It's worth going in just for a drink and a ride on a tractor, but the food is decent value too.

Kappeli (☎ 681 244; Eteläesplanadi 1; ⏰ 10am-midnight Mon-Sat, to 11pm Sun) In the middle of the park near the *kauppatori*, this has one of the most popular summer terraces, facing a stage where various bands and musicians regularly play in summer. Inside, there's a vaulted cellar bar, which is fantastic later in the evening or when the sun's not shining. There are also restaurant and cafe sections.

Lost & Found (☎ 680 1010; www.lostandfound.fi; Annankatu 6; ⏰ to 4am) This sophisticated gay-hetero bar is still a hugely popular late-night hang-out with people of all persuasions. Head downstairs to the grottolike dance floor and wait for your favourite chart hits to spin.

Tavastia & Semi-final (☎ 694 8511; www.tavastiaklubi.fi; Urho Kekkosenkatu 4; tickets from €10; ⏰ 9pm-late) There's always something happening at Finland's biggest rock music club. Live bands, including international acts, hit the stage in this hangar-sized venue. Also check out what's on at Semi-final (same contact and opening times), the smaller sister venue.

There's a string of local pubs along Helsinginkatu, such as the grungy local favourite **Roskapankki** (☎ 735 488; Helsingkatu 20) – the name means 'trash bank' – and a growing number of trendy bars and cafes.

CLUBBING

Helsinki has a dynamic club scene; some nights have age limits (often over 20).

LUX (☎ 020-775 9350; www.luxnightclub.fi; Urho Kekkosen katu 1A, entrance via Kamppi Sq; door charge €5-10; ⏰ 10pm-4am Wed-Sat) Ascend into clubbing heaven at this superslick club with stellar lighting, Kamppi-top views and high-altitude cocktails. Music runs from sexy lounge to sweaty funk with local DJs and international visitors.

Redrum (☎ 045 6355 450; www.redrum.fi; Vuorikatu 2; DJs €3-10; ⏰ from 8pm) The wood-panelled interior is drenched in red lighting and a murderous sound system that pushes out house, hip hop and even spacey disco. Sunday is a chill-down with reggae but most nights have good dancing.

DTM (☎ 676 315; www.dtm.fi; Iso Roobertinkatu 28; admission €2-10, cafe free; ⏰ 9am-4am Mon-Sat, noon-4am Sun; 💻) Scandinavia's biggest gay club (Don't Tell Mum) is a multilevel complex with an early-opening cafe/bar. There are a couple of dance floors with regular club nights as well as drag shows or women-only sessions.

ENTERTAINMENT

For concerts and performances, see *Helsinki This Week*, inquire at the tourist office or check the website of ticket outlet **Lippupiste** (☎ 0600-900 900; www.lippu.fi). **FinnKino** (☎ 0600-007 007; www.finnkino.fi; adults €9) operates several Helsinki cinemas that screen big-name films in English or with subtitles, including **Tennispalatsi** (Salomonkatu 15) and **Maxim** (Kluuvikatu 1).

SHOPPING

Helsinki is an epicentre of Nordic art and design, from fashion to the latest furniture and homewares. The hippest area is definitely Punavuori, which has several good boutiques and art galleries to explore. Look out for the sticker of **Design District Helsinki** (www.designdistrict.fi).

GETTING THERE & AWAY

Air

Finnair (☎ 0600-140140; www.finnair.fi; Asema-aukio 3; ⏰ 8am-8pm Mon-Fri, 10am-5pm Sat) and its cheaper partner **Finncomm** (www.fc.fi) fly to 20 Finnish cities, generally at least once a day. **Blue1** (☎ 0600-25831; www.blue1.com) has budget flights to a handful of major Finnish destinations.

Bus

Regional and long-distance buses arrive and depart from underground **Kamppi Bus Terminal** (www.matkahuolto.fi; ⏰ 24hr, tickets 7am-7pm Mon-Fri, to 5pm Sat, 9am-6pm Sun), below the Kamppi Centre off Salomonkatu or Frederikinkatu. You can always buy your ticket on the bus.

Train

Helsinki's **train station** (rautatieasema; ☎ 0600-41902; ⏰ 24hr, tickets 6.30am-9.30pm) is central and easy to find your way around. It's linked by subway to the Metro (Rautatientori stop), and is a short walk from the bus station.

GETTING AROUND

Central Helsinki is easy enough to get around on foot or by bicycle, but there's also a reasonably comprehensive metro, tram, bus and train network. A one-hour flat-fare ticket within Helsinki's **HKL network** (☎ 310 1071; www.hkl.fi) costs €2 from a ticket machine (€2.20 from a driver). Tourist tickets cost €6/12/18 for 1/3/5 days. Tram 3T from the *kauppatori* makes a good sightseeing trip.

There are well-marked bicycle paths. In summer, the city provides distinctive green 'City Bikes' at some 26 stands (€2 refundable deposit). **Greenbike** (☎ 8502 2850; www.greenbike.fi; Fredrikinkatu 31; bikes from €15/20/60 per day/24hr/week) rents out quality bikes.

AROUND HELSINKI

PORVOO

☎ 019 / pop 47,900

With its picture-postcard medieval Old Town, rust-coloured timber houses lining the river, and quaint cafes, Porvoo (Borgå) makes a perfect day or overnight trip from Helsinki, 50km away.

The **tourist office** (☎ 520 2316; www.porvoo.fi; Rihkamakatu 4; 9am-6pm Mon-Fri, 10am-4pm Sat & Sun early Jun-Aug, 9.30am-4.30pm Mon-Fri, 10am-2pm Sat Sep-early Jun), on the southern edge the Old Town, has plenty of information and a free internet terminal.

Porvoon Retkeilymaja (☎ 523 0012; http://personal.inet.fi/yritys/porvoohostel/; Linnankoskenkatu 1-3; dm/s/d €16/29/38; check-in 4-7pm; P) is a well-kept hostel in a grassy garden 10 minutes' walk southeast of the Old Town. It's a bit old school but it's the cheapest bed in town. **Gasthaus Werneri** (☎ 0400-494 876; www.werneri.net, in Finnish; Adlercreutzinkatu 29; s/d/tr €35/50/75) is a cosy family-run guest house, located about 1km east of the Old Town.

Porvoo's most atmospheric cafes, restaurants and bars are in the Old Town and along the riverfront. **Porvoon Paahtimo** (☎ 617 040; Mannerheiminkatu 2; noon-10pm Mon-Thu, noon-2am Fri, 11-2am Sat, noon-10pm Sun) is at the main bridge, with a great little terrace hanging over the water. The atmospheric red-brick former storehouse is part cosy bar, part cafe – fresh coffee is roasted here.

The bus station is on the *kauppatori*; buses run every half-hour between Porvoo and Helsinki (€10.30, one hour). In summer (exact dates vary) the historic steamship **JL Runeberg** (☎ 524 3331; www.msjlruneberg.fi; one way/return €22/33) sails from Helsinki, as do faster **Royal Line** (☎ 020-711 8333; www.royalline.fi) boats.

FINLAND

SOUTHWESTERN FINLAND

Finland's southwestern corner is an archipelago of numerous islands clustered around the harbour town of Turku and stretching right out to the semi-independent Åland Islands. Turku is the natural base, but if you have time you could explore this coastline by local ferry or even canoe.

TURKU

☎ 02 / pop 175,300

Turku is Finland's oldest town, but today it's a modern maritime city, brimming with museums and boasting a robust harbourside castle and magnificent cathedral. Its heart and soul is the lovely Aurajoki (Aura River), a broad ribbon spilling into the Baltic Sea harbour and lined with riverboat bars and restaurants.

For travellers, Turku is one of Finland's most visited cities after Helsinki, thanks to the direct ferries from Stockholm, and this is the place to catch a ferry to the Åland Islands. In 2011 it'll be Finland's party town as it's been chosen as one of the EU's Capitals of Culture (see www.turku2011.fi).

Information

Forex (☎ 751 2650; www.forex.fi; Eerikinkatu 23 & 12; 8am-7pm Mon-Fri, 9am-3pm Sat) Best places to change cash and travellers cheques.

Public Library (☎ 262 3611; Linnankatu 2; 11am-8pm Mon-Thu, to 6pm Fri, to 4pm Sat) Free internet terminals (15-minute maximum).

Tourist office (☎ 262 7444; www.turkutouring.fi; Aurakatu 4; bike hire per day €15, internet per hr €5; 8.30am-6pm Mon-Fri, 9am-4pm Sat & Sun, 10am-3pm winter weekends) Busy, very helpful, information on entire region. Rents bikes; free internet access for short periods. Ask about the Turku Card discount card.

Sights & Activities

A great way to soak up Turku's summertime vibe is simply to walk or cycle along the river bank between the cathedral and the castle, crossing the bridges or taking the free pedestrian ferry *Föri*.

At the western (harbour) end, **Turku Castle** (Turun Linna; ☎ 262 0300; admission €7, guided tours €2; 10am-6pm daily mid-Apr–mid-Sep, 10am-3pm Tue-Sun mid-Sep–mid-Apr) is a historical highlight, dating from 1280 and boasting dungeons, banquet halls and a medieval museum.

Forum Marinum (☎ 282 9511; www.forum-marinum.fi; Linnankatu 72; admission €7, with museum ships €12; 11am-7pm daily May-Sep, 10am-6pm Tue-Sun Oct-Apr) is an impressive maritime museum near Turku Castle. As well as a nautically crammed exhibition space devoted to Turku's shipping background, it incorporates a moored fleet of **museum ships** including the beautiful 1902 sailing ship *Suomen Joutsen* (Swan of Finland).

Aboa Vetus & Ars Nova (☎ 250 0552; www.aboavetusarsnova.fi; Itäinen Rantakatu 4-6; admission €8; 11am-7pm, closed Mon mid-Sep–Mar, English-language tour 11.30am Jul-Aug) are two museums under one roof: a fascinating display of live archaeology and a contemporary art gallery.

The open-air **Luostarinmäki Handicrafts Museum** (☎ 262 0350; admission €5; 10am-6pm daily mid-Apr–mid-Sep, 10am-3pm Tue-Sun mid-Sep–mid-Apr) is worth a look in summer – it's the only surviving 18th-century area of this medieval town, and includes around 40 restored wooden houses and working craftspeople.

Archipelago cruises are popular in summer, with daily departures from Martinsilta bridge.

Sleeping

Ruissalo Camping (☎ 262 5100; camp sites €10, plus per person €4, d/q €35/60; Jun-Aug) A popular camping area on Ruissalo island, 10km west of the city centre. Take bus 8 from the market square.

Hostel Turku (☎ 262 7680; www.turku.fi/hostelturku; Linnankatu 39; dm/s/tw €16/36/42; reception 6-10am & 3pm-midnight;) Well located on the river close to the town centre, this is a neat place with good lockers, spacious dorms, internet and bike hire.

our pick **Bed & Breakfast Tuure** (☎ 233 0230; www.netti.fi/~tuure2; Tuureporinkatu 17c; s/d €37/50;) Very handy for the bus station, and close to the market square, this tidy and friendly guest house has bright and thoughtfully decorated rooms. Guests get a key, as well as use of microwave, fridge and internet.

Eating

There are plenty of cheap eateries on and around Turku's bustling central *kauppatori*. The **kauppahalli** (Eerikinkatu 16; 7am-5.30pm Mon-Fri, to 3pm Sat) is packed with produce, meat, a sushi bar, and a cool cafe in a converted train carriage.

Baan Thai (☎ 233 8290; Kauppiaskatu 15; lunch from €6, mains €7-13; 11am-9pm Mon-Thu, 11am-10pm Fri & Sat, noon-9pm Sun) Authentic spicy Thai food with great-value lunch specials.

Pizzeria Dennis (☎ 469 1191; Linnankatu 17; dishes €8-15; 11am-11.30pm Mon-Thu, 11am-midnight Fri & Sat, 12.30-11pm Sun) A genuine Italian flavour and cosy dining rooms put this above most Finnish pizza-and-pasta places.

Vaakahuoneen Paviljonki (☎ 515 3324; Linnankatu 38; fish buffet €9, mains €8-18; food served 11am-10pm May-Aug) This riverfront jazz restaurant is the place to go for great-value food and entertainment in summer. There's a daily 'archipelago fish buffet' (June to August), plus a changing ethnic buffet.

Viikinkiravintola Harald (☎ 276 5050; www.ravintolaharald.fi; Aurakatu 3; mains €10-22, menus €27-45; 11am-midnight) Dust off your horned helmet for this Viking restaurant where subtlety is run through with a berserker's broadsword. It's not exactly gourmet, but great fun.

Drinking

In summer the decks of Turku's boat bars, which line the river bank on the southeast side of Auransilta bridge, are crammed with drinkers, but the town also has some charmingly eccentric bars: **Puutorin Vessa** (☎ 233 8123; Puutori; noon-midnight Mon-Sat, 3pm-midnight Sun) was a public toilet in a former life; **Uusi Apteeki** (☎ 250 2595; Kaskenkatu 1; 10am-3am) is a converted pharmacy; and **Panimoravintola Koulu** (☎ 274 5757; Eerikinkatu 18; 11am-midnight Mon-Fri, noon-midnight Sat) is an enormous brewery-restaurant in an old school.

Getting There & Away

From the main **bus terminal** (☎ 0200-4000; Aninkaistenkatu 20) there are hourly express buses to Helsinki (€27.50, 2½ hours), and frequent services to Tampere (€22.40, three hours) and other points in southern Finland.

The train station is a short walk northwest of the centre; trains also stop at the ferry harbour and at Kupittaa train station east of the centre. Bus 32 shuttles between the centre and the main train station. Express trains run frequently to and from Helsinki (€32, two hours), Tampere (€22, 1¾ hours) and beyond.

Tallink/Silja Line (☎ 0600-15700; www.tallinksilja.com) and **Viking Line** (☎ 333 1331; www.vikingline.fi) both sail to Stockholm (11 hours) and Mariehamn (six hours). Prices vary widely according to season and class, with deck class

Book your stay at lonelyplanet.com/hotels

one-way tickets ranging from €14 to €35. Both have offices at the harbour, southwest of the centre, and in town.

TAMPERE

☎ 03 / pop 207,900

For many travellers, Tampere is the number-one Finnish city. It combines Nordic sophistication with urban vitality and a most scenic location between two vast lakes. Through its centre churn the Tammerkoski rapids, whose grassy banks contrast with the red brick of the imposing chimneys of the fabric mills that once drove the economy. Tampere's students ensure plenty of evening action, and its regenerated industrial buildings house quirky museums, enticing shops, pubs, cinemas and cafes.

Information

GoTampere Oy (tourist office; ☎ 5656 6800; www.gotampere.fi; Rautatienkatu 25; 9am-5pm Mon-Fri Jan-May, 9am-8pm Mon-Fri, 9.30am-5pm Sat & Sun Jun-Aug, 9am-5pm Mon-Fri, 9.30am-5pm Sat & Sun Sep, 9am-5pm Mon-Fri, 11am-3pm Sat & Sun Oct-Dec) In the railway station. Has free internet terminals and booking desk.

Internet Café Madi (☎ 050-922 2346; Tuomiokirkonkatu 36; per hr €3; 10am-10pm Mon-Fri, 11am-10pm Sat & Sun) Free tea and coffee.

Tampere City Library (Metso; ☎ 565 614; Pirkankatu 2; 10am-8pm Mon-Fri, 10am-4pm Sat, 11am-5pm Sun Sep-May, 10am-7pm Mon-Fri Jun-Aug) Has several internet terminals, some first-come, first-served (15 minute time limit).

Sights & Activities

A walk along the banks of the Tammerkoski rapids will give you a good feel for Tampere's industrial past; check out the renovated **Finlayson Centre**, which houses restaurants, a cinema and the offbeat **Vakoilumuseo** (Spy Museum; ☎ 212 3007; www.vakoilumuseo.fi; Satakunnankatu 18; admission €7; noon-6pm Mon-Sat, 11am-5pm Sun May-Aug, 11am-5pm daily Sep-Apr), which plays to the budding secret agent in all of us.

Admirers of bearded revolutionaries won't want to miss the small **Lenin Museum** (☎ 276 8100; www.lenin.fi; Hämeenpuisto 28; admission €5; 9am-6pm Mon-Fri, 11am-4pm Sat & Sun), which has a crazy gift shop with Soviet souvenirs.

In the basement of the public library, **Moominvalley** (Muumilaakso; ☎ 5656 6578; Hämeenpuisto 20; admission €4; 9am-5pm Mon-Fri, 10am-6pm Sat & Sun, closed Mon Sep-May) is a whimsical exhibition based on the children's books of Tove Jansson.

Intriguing **Tampere Cathedral** (Tuomiokirkonkatu 3; 9am-6pm May-Aug, 11am-3pm Sep-Apr) features Hugo Simberg's haunting frescoes of a procession of ghostly childlike apostles holding the 'garland of life'.

Trips on Tampere's two magnificent lakes are extremely popular in summer and there are plenty of options. All cruises can be booked at the tourist office.

Traditional **Rajaportin Sauna** (☎ 222 3823; Pispalan Valtatie 9; admission €5; 6-10pm Wed, 3-9pm Fri, 2-10pm Sat) is Finland's oldest operating public sauna.

Sleeping

our pick **Hostel Sofia** (☎ 254 4020; www.hostelsofia.fi; Tuomiokirkonkatu 12a; dm/s/d €25/45/65;) Tampere's only hostel is right opposite the cathedral and fills up fast. A recent refit has left it looking very spruce, offering rooms with comfortable beds (no bunks), as well as good showers and a kitchenette on every colour-coded floor. If you're going to arrive late, they'll text you a door code.

Omenahotelli (☎ 020-771 6555; www.omenahotelli.fi; Hämeenkatu 28; r to €65;) At the western end of the main drag, this receptionless hotel offers comfortable rooms with twin beds, microwave, kettle, and a fold-out couch. Great value for two couples. Book online or via the terminal at the entrance.

Hotelli Victoria (☎ 242 5111; www.hotellivictoria.fi; Itsenäisyydenkatu 1; s/d €109/142, Fri-Sun & summer €79/89; P) Just on the other side of the railway station from the city centre, this friendly hotel offers sound summer value with its spruce rooms, free internet and commendable breakfast spread including waffles, sausage omelette and berry pudding options.

Eating

Kauppahalli (Hämeenkatu 19; 8am-6pm Mon-Fri, to 3pm Sat) This intriguing indoor market is one of Finland's best, with picturesque wooden stalls serving a dazzling array of wonderful meat, fruit, baked goodies and fish. There's also Neljä Vuodenaikaa, a great French cafe-bistro, and places to try Tampere's speciality, *mustamakkara*, a tasty black sausage made with cow's blood.

Vohvelikahvila (☎ 214 4225; Ojakatu 2; waffles €3-6; 9am-8pm Mon-Sat, 10am-8pm Sun) This homey cafe in a quaint stone house specialises in Tampere's best waffles.

Veganissimo (☎ 213 0323; Otavalankatu 10; ⌚ 11am-8pm Mon & Tue, 11am-10pm Wed & Thu, 11am-midnight Fri, 1pm-midnight Sat, 1-7pm Sun) A short stroll from the station brings you to this pleasing new vegan restaurant with smart contemporary decor and a good feeling about the place. Lunch (€7 to €9) is a bargain, with delicious salads.

Panimoravintola Plevna (☎ 260 1200, Itäinenkatu 8; mains €9-24; ⌚ food served 11am-10pm) Inside the old Finlayson textile mill, this big barn of a place offers a wide range of delicious beer, cider and perry (pear cider) brewed on the premises, including an excellent strong stout. Meals are large and designed for soaking it all up: massive sausage platters and enormous slabs of pork.

Drinking & Entertainment

Café Europa (☎ 223 5526; Aleksanterinkatu 29; ⌚ noon-1am Sun-Tue, to 2am Wed-Thu, to 3am Fri & Sat) Tampere's coolest bar for the decor alone, with old-world couches, candlelight and a good summer terrace. Upstairs is a small but stylish dance club.

O'Connell's (☎ 222 7032; Rautatienkatu 24; ⌚ 4pm-2am) Popular with both Finns and expats, this rambling Irish pub is handy for the train station and has plenty of time-worn, comfortable seating and an air of bonhomie.

Fall's Café (☎ 223 0061; Kehräsaari; ⌚ noon-midnight Sun-Tue, to 3am Wed-Sat) Set among craft shops in a converted brick factory, this bar has Tampere's cutest terrace, a wedge-shaped balcony right by the water.

Suvi (☎ 211 0150; Laukontori; ⌚ 10am-late) Moored alongside the Laukontori quay, this is a typical Finnish boat bar offering no-nonsense deck-top drinking. Prepare a boarding party and lap up the afternoon sun.

Tullikamari klubi (☎ 343 9933; www.tullikamari.net; Tullikamarinaukio 2; ⌚ 11am-10pm Mon-Tue, 11am-4am Wed-Fri, 3pm-4am Sat) This cavernous place near the train station is Tampere's main indoor live-music venue.

Getting There & Away

Ryanair (☎ 0200-39000; www.ryanair.com) flies from London Stansted and other European cities. **Blue 1** (☎ 06000-25831; www.blue1.com) hits Stockholm and **Air Baltic** (www.airbaltic.com) flys to Riga. The airport is 15km southwest of the centre, but all flights are met by a bus.

The **bus station** (Hatanpäänvaltatie 7) is in the south of town. Regular express buses run from Helsinki (€31.70, 2½ hours) and Turku (€28.70, three hours), and most other major towns in Finland are served from here.

Express trains run hourly to/from Helsinki (€24.60, two hours). There are direct trains to Turku (€22, 1¾ hours), Oulu (€53.10, five hours) and other cities.

ÅLAND

☎ **018 / pop 27,200**

This sweeping archipelago spattered between Finland and Sweden is a curious geopolitical entity that belongs to Finland, speaks Swedish, but has its own parliament, flies its own flag proudly from every pole, and issues its own national stamps.

There are over 6500 islands, although many of these are merely little mounds of granite rising centimetres above the sea. Indeed, the islands are all remarkably flat: Ålanders are even less thrilled by global warming than most. This flatness, however, makes the islands ideal for exploration by bike.

Getting There & Around

Viking Line (☎ 26211; www.vikingline.fi; Storagatan 2) and **Tallink/Silja Line** (☎ 0600-15700; www.tallinksilja.com; Torggatan 14) have daily ferries between Helsinki/Turku and Mariehamn, continuing on to Stockholm – the cruise through the archipelago is awesome.

Eckerö Linjen (☎ 28000; www.eckerolinjen.fi; Torggatan 2, Mariehamn) sails to Grisslehamn in Sweden (€8.90, three hours) from Eckerö.

There's an island bus service, but a bike is the way to go. **Ro-No Rent** (☎ 12820; www.visitaland.com/rono; bicycles per day/week from €8/40, mopeds per day/week €65/210; ⌚ May-Aug) has offices at Mariehamn and Eckerö harbours.

MARIEHAMN

☎ **018 / pop 11,000**

Villagey Mariehamn is Åland's main port and capital, a pretty place lined with linden trees and timber houses set between two large harbours. Compared to the rest of the archipelago, it's a metropolis, and gets busy in summer with tourists off the ferries and yachts stocking the marinas.

The **tourist office** (☎ 24000; www.visitaland.com; Storagatan 8; ⌚ 9am-4pm Mon-Fri Sep-May, 10am-3pm Sat Apr-May & Sep, 9am-5pm Mon-Fri, 9am-4pm Sat & Sun Jun-Aug; 💻) has plenty of island info, books tours and has internet access (€1 for 15 minutes).

FINLAND

Book your stay at lonelyplanet.com/hotels

Sights

Sjöfartsmuseum (Maritime Museum; ☎ 19930; Hamngatan 2; admission €5, joint ticket with Pommern €8; 🕓 9am-5pm May, Jun & Aug, to 7pm Jul, 10am-4pm Sep-Apr) is a wonderfully kitsch museum of fishing and maritime commerce. Outside is the museum ship **Pommern** (admission €5), a beautifully preserved four-masted barque built in Glasgow in 1903.

Ålands Museum & Ålands Konstmuseum (☎ 25426; Stadhusparken; admission €3; 🕓 10am-4pm Wed-Mon, 10am-7pm Tue Jun & Aug, 10am-7pm daily Jul, 10am-4pm Wed-Sun, 10am-8pm Tue Sep-May) gives an absorbing account of Åland's history and culture from prehistory to the present and displays a collection of work by islander artists.

Sleeping & Eating

Gröna Uddens Camping (☎ 21151; www.gronaudden.com; camp sites €6 plus per adult €6, 2-/4-person cabins €60/85, r €60; 🕓 mid-May–Aug) In a beachside park 1km south of town, Mariehamn's camping ground has tent and van sites, cabins, bike and canoe rental, and saunas on the water's edge.

Gästhem Kronan (☎ 12617; Neptunigatan 52; s/d with shared bathroom €48/69) A good-value guest house with basic but spotless renovated rooms. It's in a quiet street five minutes' walk east of the ferry terminal. It's much cheaper in the off season.

Café Bönan (☎ 21735; Sjökvarteret; lunch buffet €8; 🕓 10:30am-2pm) This vegetarian place does healthy salad buffets sourced from ethical producers so it's total guilt-free lunching.

Dino's Bar & Grill (☎ 13939; www.dinosbar.net; Strandgatan 12; mains €13-25; 🕓 lunch & dinner Mon-Sat, dinner Sun) Popular as a meeting spot, this bar does thick burgers and creative pastas and steaks, best eaten on its great outdoor deck.

Mariehamn's many cafes serve the local speciality, *Ålandspannkaka* (Åland pancakes), a fluffy square pudding made with semolina and served with stewed prunes.

THE ISLANDS

You can explore most of the main islands in a few days' biking. The central group comprises **Jomala** and **Sund**, north of Mariehamn, and **Eckerö** to the west. Pick up a copy of the *Visit Åland* brochure and the camping guide from the Mariehamn tourist office for details of places to stay.

Åland's most striking attraction is the medieval castle **Kastelholm** (☎ 432 156; admission €5; 🕓 10am-5pm Mon-Fri May, 10am-5pm daily Jun & Aug, 10am-6pm daily Jul, 10am-4pm Mon-Fri early–mid-Sep) in Sund, about 25km northeast of Mariehamn. Catch bus 4 from Mariehamn or go by bike.

SOUTHEASTERN FINLAND

Most of southern Finland could be dubbed Lakeland, but this spectacular area takes it to extremes. It often seems there's more water than land here, and what water it is – sublime, sparkling and clean, reflecting sky and forests as clearly as a mirror. It's a land that leaves an indelible impression on every visitor. If you've only got the time or money to visit one part of Finland outside Helsinki in summer, make this the place.

SAVONLINNA

☎ 015 / pop 26,800

Gorgeous Savonlinna shimmers on a sunny day as the water ripples around its centre. Set on two islands between lakes, it's a classic Lakeland settlement with a major attraction: perched on a rocky islet, one of Europe's most visually dramatic castles lords it over the picturesque centre and in July hosts world-famous opera festival in a spectacular setting.

Hit **Savonlinna Travel** (☎ 517 510; www.savonlinna.travel; Puistokatu 1; 🕓 9am-5pm Mon-Fri Aug-Jun, 9am-7pm daily Jul) for tourist information including accommodation reservation, farmstays, festival tickets, free internet and tours.

Sights & Activities

Standing immense and haughty on a rock in the lake, 15th-century **Olavinlinna** (☎ 531 164; www.olavinlinna.fi; admission €5; 🕓 10am-6pm Jun–mid-Aug, 10am-4pm Mon-Fri, 11am-4pm Sat & Sun mid-Aug–May, last tour leaves 1 hour before close) is one of the most spectacular castles in northern Europe. You visit with a multilingual guided tour (around 45 minutes); guides are good at bringing the castle to life.

Walk to the castle from the market square along the lakefront and back along **Linnankatu**, a charming street lined with old wooden houses, craft shops, studios and cafes.

Dozens of 1½-hour **scenic cruises** (€8 to €12) leave from the harbour near the *kauppatori* daily in summer, including cruises to Linnansaari National Park and Punkaharju.

Festivals & Events

Savonlinna Opera Festival (☎ 476 750; www.operafestival.fi; Olavinkatu 27) Held throughout July. Tickets cost €80 to €108; the few cheap seats (€38 to €43) have a severely restricted view. Buy tickets up to a year in advance online or from Savonlinna Travel. Worth the splurge.

Mobile Phone Throwing World Championships (www.savonlinnafestivals.com) Enthusiastically contested in late August most years.

Sleeping & Eating

Book accommodation well in advance during the opera festival. The lively market at the *kauppatori* is where to find local pastries such as *omena-lörtsy* (a tasty apple turnover) and fried *muikku* (vendace, a small lake fish).

Vuohimäki Camping (☎ 537 353; www.fontana.fi; camp sites €12 plus per person €4, q €58-68, 4-/6-person cabins €76/84; Jun-Aug) Located 7km southwest of town, this has good facilities but fills quickly in July.

SS Heinävesi (☎ 533 120; www.savonlinnanlaivat.com; cabins lower/upper deck per person €25/28) During summer this steamer offers cramped but cute two-bunk cabins after the last cruise every afternoon/evening. Other boats nearby also offer cabins (☎ 0400-200 117; www.lakestar.info; double €40).

our pick **Vuorilinna** (☎ 73950; www.spahotelcasino.fi; Kylpylaitoksentie; dm/s/d €28/60/74; P) Set in several buildings mostly used by students, this friendly complex has an appealing location across a footbridge from the centre. Rooms share bathroom and kitchen between two. HI discount.

our pick **Majakka** (☎ 206 2825; Satamakatu 11; mains €13-24; 11am-11.30pm Mon-Sat, noon-11.30pm Sun) This restaurant has a decklike terrace fitting the nautical theme (the name means 'lighthouse'). Local meat and fish specialities are tasty, generously sized and fairly priced.

SPLURGE

Lossiranta Lodge (☎ 511 2323; www.lossiranta.net; Aino Acktén puistotie; r €100-140, during Opera €160-210) This beautifully designed boutique villa boasts a stunning lakeside location and the closest possible view of Olavinlinna. The five unique rooms are impossibly cute, lovingly designed and surprisingly functional.

Getting There & Away

From the bus station on the western side of town there are several daily express buses to Helsinki (€52.60, 4½ to 5½ hours), Kuopio (€28.70, three hours) and other towns in the area.

Trains from Helsinki (€49, five hours) require a change in Parikkala. For Kuopio and Tampere, railbuses run the two hours to Pieksämäki to connect with trains. The main train station is a walk from the centre of Savonlinna; board and alight at the Kauppatori station instead.

Check out www.mspuijo.fi and www.kristinacruises.com for some great lake-cruising options from Savonlinna to other towns and attractions in the region.

KUOPIO

☎ 017 / pop 91,400

Most things a reasonable person could desire are in Kuopio, with pleasure cruises on the azure water, spruce forests to stroll in, wooden waterside pubs, and local fish specialities to taste. And the world's biggest smoke sauna; visit on Tuesday (also Thursday in summer) when it's open.

The **Kuopio Tourist Service** (☎ 182 585; www.kuopioinfo.fi; Haapaniemenkatu 17; 9.30am-4.30pm Mon-Fri Sep-May, to 5pm Jun-Aug, also 9.30am-3pm Sat in Jul) is by the *kauppatori*.

In a country as flat as Finland, **Puijo Hill** is highly regarded. Take the lift to the top of the 75m-high **Puijon Torni** (☎ 255 255; adult €4, free in winter; 9am-10pm) for vast perspectives of (yes, you guessed correctly) lakes and forests. There's a giant all-season ski jump here where you can often see jumpers in training.

South of the centre, **Jätkänkämppä sauna** (☎ 030-60830; www.rauhalahti.com; admission €11; 4-10pm Tue, also Thu Jun-Aug) is a memorable and sociable experience. The world's largest *savusauna* (smoke sauna) seats 60; it's mixed, and guests are given towels to wear. Bring a swimsuit for a dip in the lake between sweats.

You can get to the sauna by boat from the harbour, from where there are also regular summer lake and canal cruises. Ninety-minute jaunts cost €11 and depart hourly from 11am to 6pm.

FINLAND

Sleeping

Hostelli Hermanni (☎ 040-910 9083; www.hostellihermanni.net; Hermanninaukio 3e; dm/s/d €20/40/50) Tucked away in a quiet area 1.5km south of the *kauppatori*, this is a well-run little hostel with comfy wooden bunks and beds, high ceilings and decent shared bathrooms and kitchen.

Matkustajakoti Rautatie (☎ 580 0569; www.kuopionasemagrilli.com; Asemakatu 1 & Vuorikatu 35; s/d with shared bathroom €40/60, with private bathroom €50/79) This friendly place, run out of the *grilli* (fast food take away) in the railway station, actually offers en suite rooms in the building itself as well as cheaper, but most acceptable rooms with shared bathroom across the road.

our pick **Kesähotelli Lokki** (☎ 261 4101; www.kesahotellilokki.fi; Satamakatu 26; s/studio/apt Sun-Wed €48/55/75, Thu-Sat €58/75/95; early Jun-early Aug; P) In a perfect harbourside location, this summer hotel offers spotless industrial studios with heavy doors, bags of space, comfortable new beds and a kitchenette.

Eating & Drinking

Kaneli (☎ 040-835 8187; Kauppakatu 22; 10am-7pm Mon-Fri, 10am-5pm Sat, 11am-4pm Sun) This cracking cafe just off the *kauppatori* evokes a bygone age with much of its decor but offers modern comfort with its shiny espresso machine.

Vapaasatama Sampo (☎ 581 0458; Kauppakatu 13; muikku dishes €10-14; 11am-midnight Mon-Sat, noon-midnight Sun) Stewed, fried, smoked or in a soup, it's all about *muikku* here. This is one of Finland's most famous spots to try the small lake fish.

> **DETOUR: THE SEAL LAKES**
>
> Linnansaari and Kolovesi, two watery national parks in the Savonlinna area, offer fabulous lakescapes dotted with islands; all best explored by hiring a canoe or rowing boat. Several outfitters offer these services, and free camping spots dot the lakes' shores.
>
> This is the habitat of the Saimaa ringed seal, an endangered freshwater species. The parks both have information points, but a good place to start is Nestori centre in the Savonlinna local museum. **Saimaaholiday** (www.saimaaholiday.net) and **Kolovesi Retkeily** (☎ 040-558 9163; www.sealtrail.com) are experienced operators for Linnansaari and Kolovesi respectively.

The **kauppahalli** (8am-5pm Mon-Fri, to 3pm Sat) on the *kauppatori* is a classic Finnish indoor market hall. Stalls sell *kalakukko*, a large rye loaf stuffed with whitefish.

Kuopio's nightlife area is around Kauppakatu, east of the *kauppatori*. Nearby, **Henry's Pub** (☎ 262 2002; www.henryspub.net; Käsityökatu 17; 9pm-4am) is an atmospheric underworld with bands playing several times a week.

Down by the harbour in massive wooden warehouses, **Wanha Satama** (☎ 197 304; mains €14-18; 11am-11pm Sun-Tue, to 4am Wed-Sat summer) and **Albatrossi** (☎ 368 8000; 11am-midnight or later May-Sep) have big summer terraces

Getting There & Away

Finncomm (☎ 580 7400; www.fc.fi) and **Blue1** (☎ 06000-25831; www.blue1.com) fly cheaply to Helsinki. The adjacent train and bus stations are 400m north of the centre on Asemakatu. Express bus services to/from Kuopio include Helsinki (€58.10, 6½ hours) and Savonlinna (€28.70, three hours). There are direct trains to Helsinki (€50.40, 4½ to five hours).

Kuopio is a good base to experience lake travel: from mid-June to mid-August, lake ferry **MS Puijo** (www.mspuijo.fi) travels to Savonlinna.

NORTHERN FINLAND

Northern Finland is a true wilderness and place of extremes: continuous daylight in summer and continuous night in winter. October, February and March are ideal times to see the stunning aurora borealis. September brings exceptional autumn colours, and in the far north *kaamos*, the season of eerie bluish light, begins in late October. The region includes pristine national parks, ski resorts, husky-sledding opportunities, reindeer, Santa Claus and an Arctic ice-breaker ship and winter ice castle at Kemi.

The northernmost part, Finnish Lapland is a mysterious land of clear Arctic air and unpopulated vastnesses. It's home to the Sámi, who have traditionally made their living from their domesticated reindeer herds, which number some 200,000 antlered beasts.

OULU

☎ 08 / pop 131,600

Prosperous Oulu, one of Europe's foremost IT centres, is spread across several islands, elegantly connected by pedestrian bridges, and water never seems far away. In summer,

SHE AIN'T HEAVY, SHE'S MY WIFE

What may have begun as a debauched habit of stealing maidens from neighbouring villages has morphed into one of Finland's maddest but most entertaining events. The **Wife-Carrying World Championships** (www.sonkajarvi.fi), held on the first weekend of July, has put the tiny village of Sonkajärvi, about 80km north of Kuopio, on the map.

The championship is a race over a 253.5m obstacle course, where competitors must carry their 'wives' through water traps and over hurdles to achieve the fastest time. The winners get the wife's weight in beer. Along with the heats, finals and novelty races, this is a big weekend of drinking, dancing and mayhem. Don't miss it!

Buses and trains connect Kuopio with Iisalmi, from where buses run to Sonkajärvi, 18km northeast.

the angled sun bathes the *kauppatori* in light and all seems well with the world. Locals, who appreciate daylight when they get it, crowd the terraces, and stalls groan under the weight of Arctic berries.

For travellers, Oulu's summertime energy, superb cycling paths, friendly locals and frenetic nightlife make it worth a stop on your way north.

The **tourist office** (☎ 5584 1330; www.visitoulu.fi; Torikatu 10; 🕑 9am-4pm Mon-Fri) is about 200m southeast of the *kauppatori*.

In a country that wrote the book on oddball festivals, Oulu hosts more than its fair share. Take the **World Air Guitar Championships** (www.airguitarworldchampionships.com), which is part of the **Oulu Music Video Festival** (www.omvf.net) in late August. Contestants from all over the world take the stage to show what they can do with their imaginary instruments.

Sleeping

There's precious little budget accommodation in Oulu.

Nallikari Camping (☎ 5586 1350; www.nallikari.fi; Hietasaari; camp sites €10-17 plus per adult €4, cabins €35-40, cottages €80-135; P 💻) Resembling a small town, this excellent camping ground offers all sorts of options in a location close to the beach on Hietasaari, a 40-minute walk to town via pedestrian bridges. Bus 17 gets you there from the *kauppatori* (€2.80).

Hotelli Turisti (☎ 563 6100; www.hotellituristi.fi; Rautatienkatu 9; s/d Fri-Sun & summer €55/65, Mon-Thu €80/95; P) You can't beat this spot for convenience: it's bang opposite the train station. It's a no-nonsense affair with reception doubling as a convenience kiosk, but offers value, with bright, modern rooms that have plenty of space. There are rooms sleeping up to five; rates include sauna and breakfast.

Eating & Drinking

Local specialities can be found in and around the lively *kauppatori*.

ourpick **Café Bisketti** (☎ 375 768; Kirkkokatu 8; 🕑 8am-10pm Mon-Thu, 8am-1am Fri & Sat, noon-10pm Sun) This top double-sided spot transforms itself throughout the day. Think twice before getting that pastry with your morning coffee; they're enormous and might not leave room for lunch, when soup, salad, coffee and a pastry are €6.30, and only €7.80 with a tasty hot dish. In the evenings, the terrace is a decent spot for a people-watching beer.

Grilleriina (☎ 370 927; Asemakatu 29; snacks €2-6; 🕑 6pm-5am) There are *grillis*, and then there's this, a class above and a step beyond the standard. The usual all-possible-permutations menu is tastier than most, and there's a dining room to enjoy the abundant portions at any hour of the night.

On the square is the **kauppahalli** (🕑 8am-6pm Mon-Fri, to 3pm Sat), with freshly filleted salmon glistening in the market stalls and plenty of spots to snack on anything from cloudberries to sushi.

Never Grow Old (☎ 311 3936; Hallituskatu 17; 🕑 2pm-2am, to 3am weekends) This enduringly popular bar hits its stride after 10pm, with plenty of dancing, DJs and revelry. The goofy decor includes some seriously comfortable and extremely uncomfortable places to sit, and a log-palisade bar that seems designed to get you to wear your drink.

On the same block is convivial St Michaels, an Irish bar, and Sarkka, an old-time Finnish bar that charges a €1.50 entrance fee at night but is worth it for the downbeat traditional atmosphere and heroic 9am to 3am opening hours.

Book your stay at lonelyplanet.com/hotels

Getting There & Away

Finncomm and Blue1 have affordable flights from Helsinki. Trains and buses connect Oulu with all main centres; six to 10 trains a day (€63.50, seven to nine hours) run from Helsinki to Oulu; the Pendolino service takes only 6¼ hours (€72).

ROVANIEMI

☎ 016 / pop 58,900

Expanding rapidly on the back of a tourism boom, the 'official' terrestrial residence of Santa Claus is the capital of Finnish Lapland and a more-or-less obligatory northern stop. Its wonderful Arktikum museum is the perfect introduction to the mysteries of these latitudes, and Rovaniemi is a good place to organise activities from.

Thoroughly destroyed by the retreating Wehrmacht in 1944, the town was rebuilt to an Alvar Aalto plan, with major streets in the shape of reindeer antlers (no, us neither). Best is its marvellous location on the fast-flowing Kemijoki.

The **tourist office** (☎ 346 270; www.visitrovaniemi.fi; Maakuntakatu 29; 8am-5pm Mon-Fri Sep-May, 8am-6pm Mon-Fri, 10am-4pm Sat & Sun Jun-Aug, also opens some weekends in Sep & Dec) is on the square in the middle of town and has a free internet terminal. The Alvar Aalto–designed **regional library** (☎ 322 2463; Hallituskatu 9; 11am-7pm Mon-Fri, to 5pm Sat) also has free internet access.

Sights & Activities

With its beautifully designed glass tunnel stretching out to the Ounasjoki, **Arktikum** (☎ 322 3260; www.arktikum.fi; Pohjoisranta 4; adult/student €12/8; 9am-7pm mid-Jun–mid-Aug, 10am-6pm early Jun, late Aug & Dec, 10am-5pm Tue-Sun Sep-Nov, 10am-6pm Tue-Sun Jan-May) is one of Finland's best museums and well worth the admission fee if you are interested in the north. One side deals with Lapland, with some information on Sámi culture. The highlight, though, is the other side, with a wide-ranging display on the Arctic itself.

The **Arctic Circle marker** (Napapiiri) is 8km north of Rovaniemi. Here is the 'official' **Santa Claus Village** (www.santaclausvillage.info; admission free; 10am-5pm Sep-May, 9am-6pm early Jun & late Aug, 9am-7pm mid-Jun–mid-Aug). The post office receives three quarters of a million letters each year. You can send a postcard home with an official Santa stamp (to be delivered at Christmas) and meet the man himself, who likes a chat in many languages, in his impressive new **grotto** (☎ 020-799 999; www.santaclauslive.com; admission free; 9am-6pm Jun-Aug, 10am-5pm Sep-May). It's free to yarn with old beardie, but a souvenir photo sets you back €25 (no misprint). Bus 8 heads there from the train station, passing through the centre (€6.40 return).

Sleeping

Ounaskoski Camping (☎ 345 304; Jäämerentie 1; camp sites €14 plus per adult €4.50; late May–mid-Sep) Just across the elegant bridge from the town centre, this camping ground is perfectly situated on the riverbank.

Hostel Rudolf (☎ 321 321; www.rudolf.fi; Koskikatu 41; dm/s/d summer €30/41/52, winter €44/60/88) Run by Hotel Santa Claus (in the centre of town near the tourist office), where you inconveniently have to go to check in, this staffless hostel is Rovaniemi's only one and can fill up fast. It's excellent for the price, with spotless bathrooms and a kitchen available. HI discount.

Also recommended:

Guesthouse Borealis (☎ 342 0130; www.guesthouseborealis.com; Asemieskatu 1; s/d/tr €45/56/77;) The cordial hospitality and proximity to the train station make this family-run spot a winner.

Hotelli Aakenus (☎ 342 2051; www.hotelliaakenus.net; Koskikatu 47; s/d in summer €55/59, rest of year €70/80; P) Offers excellent summer value right from mid-May to the end of August. A block beyond Hostel Rudolf.

Eating & Drinking

Koskikatu has many inexpensive and midrange restaurants. You'll also find the world's northernmost McDonald's here. Rovaniemi has loads of bars and nightclubs in the town centre, including a winter ice bar.

our pick **Kauppayhtiö** (☎ 342 2422; Valtakatu 24; 10.30am-8pm Mon-Thu, to 2am Fri & Sat) Rovaniemi's best cafe, this is an oddball collection of retro curios with a coffee-bean and gasoline theme and colourful plastic tables.

Mariza (☎ 319 616; Ruokasenkatu 2; lunch €6.20-7.20; 9.30am-3pm Mon-Fri) A couple of blocks from the centre in untouristed territory, this simple lunch place is a real find, and offers a great buffet of home-cooked Finnish food, including changing daily hot dishes, soup and salad.

Xiang Long (☎ 319 331; Koskikatu 21; mains €11-17; 11am-10pm Mon-Fri, noon-10pm Sat & Sun) This main-street Chinese has friendly service, tasty steamed prawn dim sum, a salad bar and several reindeer dishes, including one served on a sizzling platter. The lunch buffet (€8.40 Monday to Friday) is great value.

ZoomIt (☎ 321 321; Koskikatu; 🕑 11am-11pm, later at weekends) Large, light, modern ZoomIt is a popular, buzzy central bar and cafe, a good place for a drink or coffee while you scope out Rovaniemi.

Roy Club (☎ 313 705; Maakuntakatu 24; 🕑 9pm-4am) This friendly bar has a sedate, comfortable top half with cosy seating, a very cheap happy hour until 1am nightly, and well-attended Monday karaoke. There's also a downstairs nightclub.

Getting There & Away

Finnair flies daily from Helsinki and Oulu. The budget carrier Blue1 also flies to Helsinki. Buses meet each arriving flight (€5, 15 minutes).

Rovaniemi is Lapland's transport hub. Frequent express buses go south to Oulu (€38.40, 3½ hours); two daily buses go to Inari (€52.60, 5¼ hours), continuing to Norway; one goes to Karasjok, and on to Nordkapp in summer; and another to Tana Bru. In summer there's also a bus to Kirkenes.

The train between Helsinki and Rovaniemi (€70 to €75, 10 to 12 hours) is quicker, cheaper and comfier than the bus. It goes via Oulu; there are various sleeping options.

INARI

☎ 016 / pop 550

Finland's most significant Sámi centre, this tiny village on the shores of spectacular Inarijärvi, Lapland's largest lake, is the place to learn something of their culture, with authentic handcraft shops and a brilliant museum. Hit **Inari Info** (☎ 661 666; www.inarilapland.org; 🕑 9am-6pm Jun-Aug, 10am-5pm early Sep, 10am-5pm Mon-Fri mid-Sep–May), in the centre of the village, for excellent information, bike and canoe rental, tours and internet access (€2 per 15 minutes).

Siida (☎ 665 212, www.siida.fi; adult/student €8/6.50; 🕑 9am-8pm Jun-Sep, 10am-5pm Tue-Sun Oct-May) should not be missed. It's a comprehensive overview of the Sámi and their environment that's actually two museums skilfully interwoven. Outside is the original museum, a complex of **open-air buildings** that reflect post-nomadic Sámi life. There's also a fine craft shop and top-value cafe, where the €9.50 lunch gets you a hot dish and free use of the salad bar.

Siida's website is itself worth a mention: via the 'services' and 'links' menus of Siida's website you can access a series of excellent pages on Sámi culture.

The closest cabin accommodation to town, **Lomakylä Inari** (☎ 671 108; www.lomakyla-inari.fi; 2-/4-person cabins with shared bathroom €35/45, with private bathroom €50/65, cottages with sauna €75-150, camp sites for 1-2 people €22; 🕑 Jun-late Sep; Ⓟ 💻) is 500m south of the centre and a good option.

Opposite the tourist office, **Villa Lanca** (☎ 040-748 0984; www.villalanca.com; s/d €43/68, with kitchen €53/78; Ⓟ) is Inari's most characterful lodging, with superb boutique rooms decorated with Asian fabrics, feather charms and real artistic flair.

The restaurant-bar of **Hotelli Inari** (☎ 671 026; www.hotelliinari.fi; s/d €65/82) is the heart of the village and serves burgers and offbeat pizzas (€5 to €9) as well as uncomplicated Lappish dishes (€11 to €19), with little sophistication but plenty of quantity.

Buses from Rovaniemi ply the route right through to Nordkapp (Norway) in summer.

FINLAND DIRECTORY

ACCOMMODATION

Most camping grounds are open only from June to August. Sites usually cost around €10 plus €4 per person. Almost all camping grounds have cabins or cottages for rent, which are usually excellent value from €35 for a basic double cabin. Contact the **Finnish Camping Association** (☎ 09-4774 0740; www.camping.fi) for more information.

Finnish hostels are invariably clean, comfortable and very well equipped, if sometimes short on atmosphere. It's worth being a member of **HI** (www.hihostels.com), as members save €2.50 per night at affiliated places. You'll save money with a sleep sheet or your own linen, as hostels tend to charge €4 to €8 for this.

From June to August, many student residences function as hostels and hotels. These can be great value, as you often get your own room, with kitchen (not always equipped) and bathroom either to yourself or shared between two. Double rooms in these places cost around €50 to €60. In summer and at weekends, the big hotels lower their prices, so that a double that would normally cost €110 might be €70.

All hotels and hostels in Finland are partially or wholly nonsmoking.

ACTIVITIES

Finland is all about nature and the great outdoors. Hiking or trekking is best from June to September, although in July mosquitoes and other insects are a problem in Lapland. Wilderness huts line the northern trails (free and shared), and you're generally allowed to hike in any forested or wilderness area and camp for a night anywhere outside inhabited, privately owned areas.

Canoes and kayaks can be hired in most towns near a lake, often from camp sites.

Nordic and downhill skiing are popular and the season runs from October to April. Other winter activities include reindeer-sledding, dogsledding and snowmobiling, best organised through tour companies, such as those in Rovaniemi, which include the following:

Eräsetti Safaris (☎ 016-362 811; www.erasetti.fi; Valtakatu 31)
Lapland Safaris/Arctic Safaris (☎ 016-340 0400, 0207-868 700; www.arcticsafaris.fi, www.laplandsafaris.fi; Koskikatu 6)
Lapland VIP Tour (☎ 0400-542 868; www.laplandviptour.fi; Valtakatu 33)
Safartica (☎ 016-311 484; www.safartica.com; Valtakatu 20)

Many hostels, camping grounds and hotels have a sauna. Towns usually have an indoor swimming pool *(uimahalli)* with saunas and spas.

BUSINESS HOURS

Usual business hours in Finland:

Alko (state alcohol store; 9am-8pm Mon-Fri, to 6pm Sat)
Banks (9.15am-4.15pm Mon-Fri)
Nightclubs (until as late as 4am)
Pubs (11am-1am, often later on Fri & Sat)
Restaurants (11am-10pm, lunch 11am-3pm)
Shops (9am-5pm Mon-Fri, to 1pm Sat)

EMBASSIES & CONSULATES

The following is a list of foreign government representatives in Helsinki. Use the Helsinki area telephone code (☎ 09) if calling from elsewhere.

Australia (☎ 4777 6640; australian.consulate@tradimex.fi; Museokatu 25B) Consulate; the nearest embassy is in Stockholm (p1146).
Canada (☎ 228 530; www.canada.fi; Pohjoisesplanadi 25b)
Denmark (☎ 684 1050; www.denmark.fi; Mannerheimintie 8)
Estonia (☎ 622 0260; www.estemb.fi; Itäinen Puistotie 10)
France (☎ 618 780; www.france.fi; Itäinen Puistotie 13)
Germany (☎ 458 580; www.helsinki.diplo.de; Krogiuksentie 4)
Ireland (☎ 646 006; embassy.ireland@welho.com; Erottajankatu 7a)
Japan (☎ 686 0200; www.fi.emb-japan.go.jp; Unioninkatu 20)
Latvia (☎ 4764 720; www.mfa.gov.lv/en/helsinki/; Armfeltintie 10)
Lithuania (☎ 684 4880; www.lithuania.fi; Rauhankatu 13a)
Netherlands (☎ 228 920; www.netherlands.fi; Erottajankatu 19B)
New Zealand (☎ 470 1818; paddais@paddais.net; Johanneksenrinne 2) Consulate general; otherwise contact the embassy in the Netherlands (p858).
Norway (☎ 686 0180; www.norge.fi; Rehbinderintie 17)
Russia (☎ 661 877; http://helsinki.rusembassy.org/; Tehtaankatu 1b)
Sweden (☎ 687 7660; www.sverige.fi; Pohjoisesplanadi 7b)
UK (☎ 2286 5100; http://ukinfinland.fco.gov.uk; Itäinen Puistotie 17)
USA (☎ 616 250; www.usembassy.fi; Itäinen Puistotie 14B)

FESTIVALS & EVENTS

Finland puts on a barrage of music, arts, cultural, sporting and just plain nutty festivals year-round, but especially between June and mid-August. Midsummer is a big deal in any part of Finland, though for most Finns it's a family time when they disappear to their summer cottages. Pick up the *Finland Festivals* booklet in any tourist office or check out www.festivals.fi.

World Wife-Carrying Championships (p365, Sonkajärvi, early July)
Pori Jazz Festival (Pori, July)
Ruisrock (Turku, early July)
Vappu (May Day) A big day for Finns, especially students, this holiday is celebrated nationally.
Savonlinna Opera Festival (Savonlinna, throughout July)
Air Guitar World Championships (p365; Oulu, late August)

FOOD & DRINK

Typical Finnish food is heavy on fish, potatoes, dark rye bread, hearty soups and stews. In Lapland or Lappish restaurants reindeer is commonly served. Most restaurants offer special lunch menus for under €10, which include a buffet of salad, bread, juice, coffee and dessert, plus big helpings of fish, meat or pasta. Fill up between 11am and 2pm.

Most towns have an outdoor marketplace *(kauppatori)* and a covered market hall *(kauppahalli)* where you can buy fresh produce and cheap sandwiches and snacks. Inexpensive kebab and pizza joints are everywhere – Golden Rax has all-you-can-eat pizza, pasta and more for €9.

Finns are the world's biggest coffee drinkers, and cafes abound. Percolated coffee sits on a warmer; grab one with a *pulla* (cardamom bun) or other sticky pastry for €2 to €4 total. A large beer in a bar costs around €4.50, but scout around for cheap pubs and happy hours. To drink cheaply, visit the state-run Alko shops, which sell all kinds of beer, wine and spirits; for beer and cider under 5%, go to any supermarket, R-kioski or petrol station.

Restaurants and bars are non-smoking, although there may be a small ventilated smoking area.

HOLIDAYS

Finland grinds to a halt around Christmas and during the Midsummer weekend. National public holidays:

New Year's Day 1 January
Epiphany 6 January
Easter March/April
May Day 1 May
Ascension Day May
Whitsunday Late May or early June
Midsummer's Eve & Day Weekend in June closest to the 24th
All Saints Day 1st Saturday in November
Independence Day 6 December
Christmas Eve 24 December
Christmas Day 25 December
Boxing Day 26 December

INTERNET RESOURCES

Almost every town in Finland has a website chock-full of information, nearly always: www.[townname].fi.

Finnish Tourist Board (www.visitfinland.com) Official site full of excellent information from the practical to the whimsical.

Forest and Park Service (www.outdoors.fi) Truly excellent resource, with detailed information on all Finland's national parks and protected areas, as well as activities listings.

Helsingin Sanomat (www.hs.fi/english/) International edition of Finland's best daily newspaper.

Virtual Finland (www.virtual.finland.fi) Maintained by the Ministry of Foreign Affairs, this is an excellent, informative and entertaining website.

MONEY

Finland uses the euro. In cities, independent exchangers such as **Forex** (www.forex.fi) are a better alternative to banks for exchanging cash and travellers cheques.

Undoubtedly the best way to get by in Finland is with plastic – a debit or credit card. Finnish ATMs, called 'Otto', are everywhere, and all are linked to international networks. Credit cards are accepted throughout.

POST

Stamps can be bought at bus or train stations and R-kioski newsstands as well as at the **posti** (post office; www.posti.fi). Airmail postcards and letters weighing up to 20g cost €0.80 to anywhere in the world or €0.70 by slower economy rate.

There are also two main rates for international parcels: a 5kg package to Europe will cost €46 to €49 sent priority, and €31 to €35 sent economy, for example.

TELEPHONE

Public telephones basically no longer exist on the street, so if you don't have a mobile you're reduced to finding a cybercafe and talking over the internet, or tracking down a telecentre, which only really exist in the big cities.

The cheapest and most practical solution is to purchase a Finnish SIM card and pop it in your own phone. Make sure your phone isn't blocked from doing this. You can buy a prepaid SIM card at any R-Kioski shop. There are always several deals on offer, and you might be able to pick up a card for as little as €10, including some call credit.

The country code for Finland is ☎ 358. To dial abroad it's ☎ 00. The number for the international operator is ☎ 020208.

VISAS

A valid passport or EU identity card is required to enter Finland. Most Western nationals don't need a tourist visa for stays of less than three months; South Africans, Indians and Chinese, however, are among those who need a Schengen visa (see p1230). For more information contact the nearest Finnish embassy or consulate, or the **Directorate of Immigration** (☎ 071-873 0431; www.uvi.fi; Panimokatu 2a, Helsinki).

Australian and New Zealand citizens aged between 18 and 30 can apply for a 12-month working holiday visa; contact the Finnish embassy in your home country.

France

HIGHLIGHTS

- **Paris** Every French adventure begins in the capital. With its chic boulevards, fabulous museums and historic brasseries, Paris is a complete *coup de coeur* (p376)
- **Loire Valley** Marvel at the ostentatious architecture of the Loire's stellar chateaux (p408)
- **Lyon** If it's classic French cooking you're after, Lyon's the only place to be. Tiny *bouchons* and brasseries line practically every street and square (p415)
- **Provence** Lavender fields and olive groves, artistic cachet and buzzy multicultural cities – picture-perfect Provence has it all (p428)
- **Nice** Slap bang in the heart of the Côte d'Azur, Nice has been *the* French beach destination for well over a century (p434)

FAST FACTS

- **Area** 551,000 sq km
- **Budget** €40to €50 per day
- **Capital** Paris
- **Country code** ☎ 33
- **Famous for** croissants, cheese, food, wine, the Eiffel Tower, the Alps, bad driving, the Gallic shrug
- **Language** French
- **Money** euro (€); A$1 = €0.55; C$1 = 0.60; ¥100 = €0.78; NZ$1 = €0.43; UK£1 = €1.12; US$1 = €0.74
- **Phrases** *s'il vous plaît* (please); *merci* (thank you); *parlez-vous Anglais?* (do you speak English?); *excusez-moi* (excuse me); *où est* (where is)

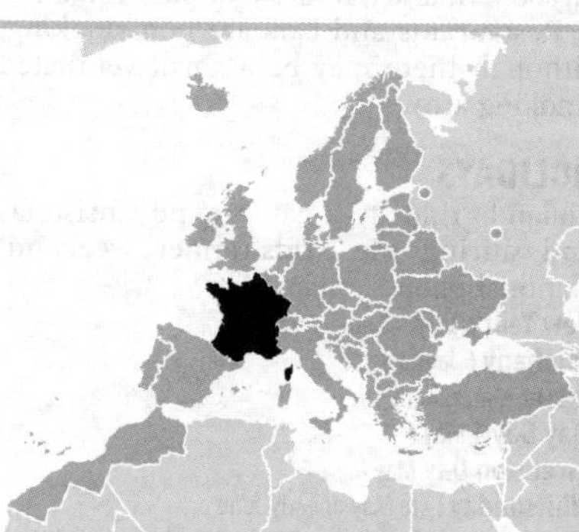

- **Population** 63.4 million
- **Visas** not required for citizens of the EU, US, Australia, Japan and most other western nations (see p446)

TRAVEL HINTS

Always say *bonjour* and *au revoir* when entering a shop, remember to stamp your transport ticket in a *composteur* and never call a waiter *garçon*.

ROAMING FRANCE

Paris has high-speed rail-links to practically everywhere in France. Lyon and Dijon are ideal for exploring the Rhone and Burgundy, while Nice is a convenient launchpad for exploring the Côte d'Azur.

Love it or loathe it, everyone has their own opinion about this Gallic giant. Snooty, sexy, superior, chic, infuriating, arrogant, officious and inspired, the French have long lived according to their own idiosyncratic rules, and if the rest of the world doesn't always see eye-to-eye with them – well, *tant pis* (too bad). That's just the price you pay for being a culinary trendsetter, artistic pioneer and all-round cultural icon.

In many ways France is a deeply traditional place: castles, chateaux and ancient churches litter the landscape, centuries-old principles of food, fine wine and *joie de vivre* underpin everyday life, and any decision to meddle with the status quo brings out half the nation in protest.

But France also boasts one of one of the most multicultural make-ups of any European country, as well as a well-deserved reputation for artistic experimentation and architectural invention. And with their vertically challenged, personality-driven, supermodel-marrying president Nicolas Sarkozy advocating the need for profound change in years to come, there are bound to be a few fireworks on the horizon. Time to join the party.

HISTORY

France's early history is encapsulated in the *Astérix* comic books: the Celtic Gauls arrived between 1500 and 500 BC, and were under Roman rule from 52 BC until the 5th century. After the Roman Empire's decline, France was governed by monarchs including Charlemagne (from 800). William the Conqueror extended French rule to England in 1066.

During the Reformation, fighting between Catholics and Protestants brought France close to disintegration. However, that paled beside the seismic events of the 1780s, when the population rose up against Louis XVI and his queen, Marie Antoinette. On 14 July 1789, a Parisian mob stormed the Bastille, unleashing the French Revolution. The vicious Reign of Terror followed; thousands of aristocrats were guillotined, including Louis XVI and his queen in 1793.

A young Corsican general by the name of Napoleon Bonaparte assumed power in 1799 and embarked on European conquest. Initially defeated and exiled to the island of Elba, he

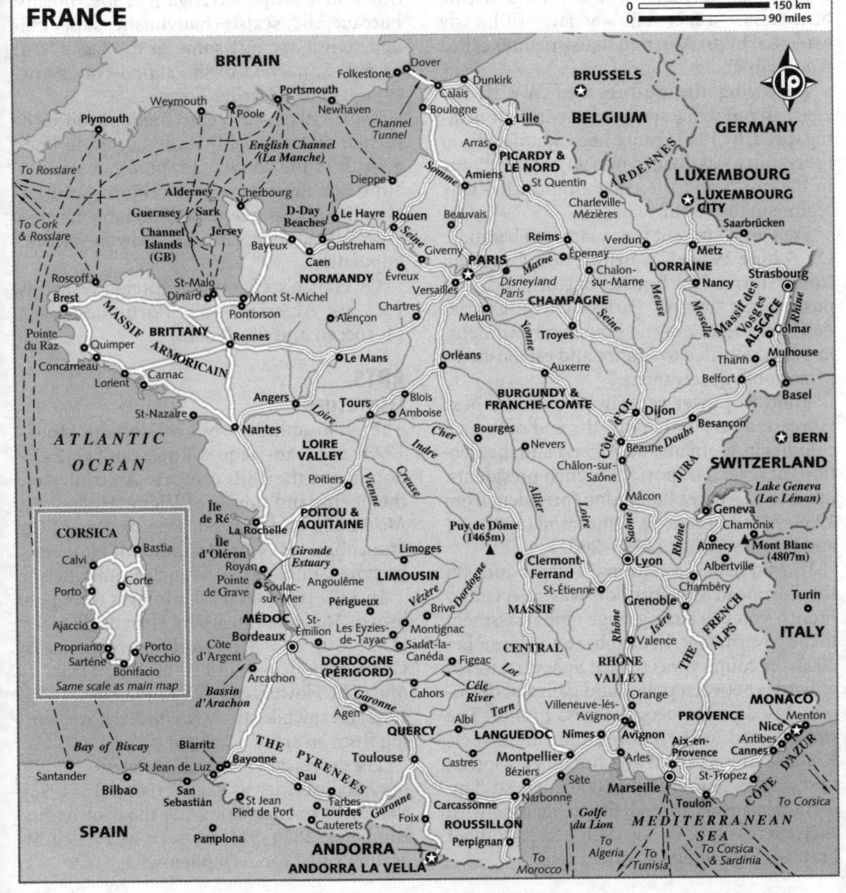

staged a short comeback before meeting his final defeat at Waterloo in 1815.

The subsequent years were marked by civil strife, with monarchists and revolutionaries vying for power. Napoleon's nephew Louis-Napoleon Bonaparte seized power in 1851, declaring himself Emperor Napoleon III, but proved no match for his uncle in terms of military prowess: he embroiled France in various catastrophic conflicts, including the Crimean War (1853–56) and the Franco-Prussian War (1870–71).

Central to France's entry into WWI was the desire to regain Alsace and Lorraine, lost to Germany in 1871. This was achieved but at immense cost: 1.3 million killed and almost one million crippled. The Treaty of Versailles, signed in 1919, demanded punitive reparations from Germany, causing long-lasting bitterness – a fact that was later ruthlessly exploited by an Austrian house painter called Adolf Hitler.

Following the outbreak of WWII, the German *blitzkrieg* swept west with astonishing speed; by 1940 France had capitulated and the country was divided into an occupied zone in the north and the collaborationist Vichy regime in the south.

France had to wait four years for liberation. On 6 June 1944, US, British and Canadian troops stormed the beaches of Normandy and pushed east towards Paris. General Charles de Gaulle, leader of the French government-in-exile, returned to France and established a provisional government.

Political power see-sawed over the next 50 years, a period that saw the end of French colonies in Vietnam and Algeria and the elections of several important French presidents, including Georges Pompidou (president from 1969–74) and François Mitterrand (1981–95) and Jacques Chirac (1995–2007).

In May 2005, a national referendum on the European Constitution was rejected by French voters, causing huge embarrassment to the government. In October and November 2005, the country was rocked by several weeks of battles between police and gangs of disenfranchised young people across France. The riots started in the poor, ethnically diverse *banlieue* (suburbs) of Paris, but quickly spread to several major cities. In 2006, huge student demonstrations forced the government to shelve a new labour law designed to combat France's high unemployment rate.

The presidential race in 2007 was contested by socialist Ségolène Royal (the first female presidential candidate) and the dynamic Nicolas Sarkozy of Chirac's centre-right UMP party. Sarkozy eventually won with 53% of votes compared to Royal's 47%. Sarkozy's first period in office has been dogged by controversy, not least thanks to his infamous split with his second wife in order to marry the sexy *chanteuse* and supermodel Carla Bruni.

But beyond Sarkozy's high-profile private life, there have been some major political developments too, including the banning of smoking in public places in 2007 and the ratification of a new EU treaty in 2008.

THE CULTURE

France attracts more stereotypes than any other in Europe. Arrogant, rude, bolshy, bureaucratic, sexist, chauvinistic, super chic and stylish are just some of the tags – true or not – attached to the supposedly garlic-eating, beret-wearing French.

Most citizens are extremely proud to be French and staunchly nationalistic to boot, a result of the country's republican stance – although the conflict of religion and nationality is a source of considerable tension, especially among France's growing Muslim population.

Of France's 4.3 million foreign residents, 13% are Algerian, 13% Portuguese, 12% Moroccan and 9% Italian.

ARTS

Literature

The philosophical work of Voltaire (1694–1778) and Jean-Jacques Rousseau (1712–78) dominated the 18th century. A century on, the poems and novels of Victor Hugo – *Les Misérables* and *Notre Dame de Paris* (The Hunchback of Notre Dame) among them – became landmarks of French Romanticism.

In 1857 two literary landmarks were published: *Madame Bovary* by Gustave Flaubert (1821–80) and a collection of poems by Charles Baudelaire (1821–67), *Les Fleurs du Mal* (The Flowers of Evil). Émile Zola (1840–1902) meanwhile strove to convert novel writing from an art to a science.

The expression of mental states was the aim of symbolists such as Paul Verlaine (1844–96). Verlaine's poems, alongside those of Arthur Rimbaud (1854–91), are seen as French literature's first modern poems.

After WWII, existentialism developed around the lively debates of Jean-Paul Sartre (1905–80), Simone de Beauvoir (1908–86) and Albert Camus (1913–60) in Paris' Left Bank cafes.

Contemporary authors include Françoise Sagan, Pascal Quignard, Anna Gavalda, Emmanuel Carrère, Stéphane Bourguignon and Martin Page, whose novel *Comment Je Suis Devenu Stupide* (How I Became Stupid) explores a 25-year-old Sorbonne student's methodical attempt to become stupid.

Cinema

Cinema is known as the *septième art* (seventh art) in France, and the French have taken their cinema very seriously ever since the Lumière brothers shot the world's first-ever motion picture in March 1895.

France's best-known cinematic movement was the *nouvelle vague* (new wave), which emerged in the late 1950s and the 1960s. With small budgets and no big-name stars, film-makers produced uniquely personal films using real-life subject matter: Claude Chabrol, Alain Resnais, François Truffaut and Jean-Luc Godard (who directed the classic *À Bout de Souffle*) were pioneers of the movement.

Big-name stars and nostalgic narratives dominated some of the most notable French films of subsequent years. Claude Berri's presentation of prewar Provence in *Jean de Florette* (1986), Jean-Paul Rappeneau's *Cyrano de Bergerac* (1990) and *Bon Voyage* (2003), set in 1940s Paris, found huge audiences in France and abroad.

La Haine (1995), directed by Mathieu Kassovitz, documented the bleak reality of life in the Parisian suburbs, while at the other end of the spectrum, *Le Fabuleux Destin de Amélie Poulain* (Amélie; 2001) is a feel-good story about a Parisian do-gooder, directed by Jean-Pierre Jeunet. In 2008, *Bienvenue chez les Ch'tis*, a broad comic caper debunking grim stereotypes about the industrialised regions of northern France, became the highest-grossing film in French box office history. *The Class* (2008) gained international attention when it became the first French film to scoop the Palme d'Or in over twenty years.

Music

France produced a string of great 19th-century composers, including *Carmen*-creator Georges Bizet (1838–75) and Claude Debussy (1862–1918). Jazz hit 1920s Paris, while the *chanson française* (French song) was revived in the 1930s by Édith Piaf and Charles Trenet. In the 1950s the Left Bank cabarets nurtured *chansonniers* (cabaret singers) such as Léo Ferré, Georges Brassens, Claude Nougaro, Jacques Brel and Serge Gainsbourg.

French pop music has evolved massively since the 1960s *yéyé* (imitative rock) days of Johnny Halliday. There's a strong tradition of world music, ranging from Senegalese *mbalax* (Youssou N'Dour) to West Indian *zouk* (Zouk Machine); one of the most popular figures is Paris-born Manu Chao. Electronic music (Daft Punk, Air) has found a global following, while French rap continues to break new ground: pioneered in the 1990s by MC Solaar and continued by young French rappers such as Disiz La Peste, Monsieur R, Rohff and Marseille's IAM (www.iam.tm.fr).

Architecture

Southern France is the place to find France's Gallo-Roman legacy, especially at the Pont du Gard (p426) and the amphitheatres in Nîmes (p425).

Several centuries later, architects adopted Gallo-Roman motifs in (Romanesque) masterpieces such as the original portions of the cathedral in Chartres (p396), as well as Toulouse's huge Basilique St-Sernin (p427) and the lovely Église St-Germain des Prés in Paris (p384).

Impressive 12th-century Gothic structures include Avignon's pontifical palace (p432), Chartres Cathedral (p396) and, of course, Notre Dame (p384) in Paris.

Art nouveau (1850–1910) combined iron, brick, glass and ceramics in new ways. See it for yourself at Paris' metro entrances and in the Musée d'Orsay (p381).

Contemporary buildings to look out for include the once-reviled (now much-revered) Centre Pompidou (p385) and IM Pei's glass pyramid (p385) at the Louvre. In the provinces, notable buildings include Strasbourg's European Parliament, the stunning new Musée des Confluences in Lyon and a 1920s art-deco swimming pool–turned–art museum in Lille (p397).

Painting

An extraordinary flowering of artistic talent occurred in 19th- and 20th-century France. The impressionists, who endeavoured to capture the ever-changing aspects of reflected light, included Edouard Manet, Claude Monet (p400), Edgar Degas, Camille Pisarro and Pierre-Auguste Renoir. They were followed by the likes of Paul Cézanne (who lived in Aix-en-Provence; see p431) and Paul Gauguin, as well as the 'fauvist' Henry Matisse (a Niçois resident, p435) and 'cubists' including Spanish-born Pablo Picasso and Georges Braque (1882–1963).

ENVIRONMENT

Hexagon-shaped France is the largest country in Europe after Russia and Ukraine. Europe's highest peak, Mont Blanc (4807m), crowns the French Alps along France's eastern border, while the rugged Pyrenees define France's 450km-long border with Spain, peaking at 3404m. The country's major river systems include the Garonne, Rhône, Seine, and France's longest river, the Loire.

France has more mammals (around 110) than any other country in Europe, as well as 363 bird species, 30 types of amphibian, 36 varieties of reptile and 72 kinds of fish. Around 80% of its electricity comes from nuclear power stations – the highest ratio in the world – with the rest from carbon-fuelled power stations, wind farms and hydro-electric dams.

France is lagging behind many other European countries on the sustainable travel front, although on the plus side, it boasts one of the finest and most efficient train systems in Europe – so there's no excuse not to use public transport. Shopping at local markets rather than supermarkets is an excellent way of cutting down on food miles, and *restaurants bios* (organic restaurants) are steadily gaining ground in many areas.

TRANSPORT

GETTING THERE & AWAY

Air

Air France (AF; ☎ 08 20 820 820; www.airfrance.com) and many other airlines travel regularly to Paris and other French cities, including Bordeaux, Lyon, Marseille, Nice, Strasbourg and Toulouse.

Cheap flights can be found online, or try agencies such as the French student travel company **OTU** (☎ 08 20 81 78 17; www.otu.fr) and **Nouvelles Frontières** (☎ 08 25 00 08 25; www.nouvelles-frontieres.fr).

CONNECTIONS

France is well connected to practically everywhere in Western Europe. High-speed trains travel from Paris to many major European cities, including Milan, Brussels, Cologne, Amsterdam, Frankfurt and Zurich, as well as London via the Channel Tunnel/Eurostar service. Ferry links from Cherbourg, St-Malo, Calais and other north coast ports travel to England and Ireland, while ferries from Marseille, Nice and Toulon provide regular ferry links with Corsica, Italy and North Africa. Regular bus and rail links cross the French-Spanish border via the Pyrenees, and the French-Italian border via the Alps and the southern Mediterranean coast.

Budget carriers include the following:

Air Berlin (www.airberlin.com) Links EuroAirport (Mulhouse) and Nice with destinations around Western Europe.
Air Transat (www.airtransat.com) Flights from Canada.
bmibaby (www.bmibaby.com)
easyJet (www.easyjet.com) UK budget carrier.
Flybe (www.flybe.com) Links a dozen French cities with the UK.
Flyglobespan (www.flyglobespan.com) Scottish budget carrier.
Jet2.com (www.jet2.com) Links French cities with the UK.
Myair (www.myair.com) Flights to Italy.
Ryanair (www.ryanair.com) Services from Ireland and the UK.
Transavia.com (www.transavia.com) Budget subsidiary of Air France–KLM.
TUIfly (www.tuifly.com) German budget carrier.

Boat

Regular ferries travel to France from Italy, the UK, Channel Islands and Ireland.

TO/FROM IRELAND

Irish Ferries (☎ in UK 08705 17 17 17; in Ireland 0818 300 400; www.irishferries.ie) has overnight services from Rosslare to either Cherbourg (17½ hours) or Roscoff (17½ hours; mid-May to mid-September only) every other day (three times a week from October to May, except late December and January).

From about March to early November, **Brittany Ferries** (☎ in UK 0871 244 0744; www.brittanyferries.co.uk) runs a car ferry from Cork (Ringaskiddy) to Roscoff (14 hours).

TO/FROM ITALY

Every two or three days during the warm half of the year, **SNCM** (☎ in France 00 33 825 88 80 88; www.sncm.fr) runs an overnight car ferry from Marseille to Porto Torres on the Italian island of Sardinia. The crossing takes 14½ to 17½ hours. Several companies ply the waters between Corsica and Italy.

TO/FROM UK

As with budget airlines, ferry travel costs to the UK vary hugely depending on when you travel: booking early, avoiding peak times and avoiding July and August will cut costs. To get the best fare, check out the comparison service offered by **Ferry Savers** (☎ in UK 0844-576 8835; www.ferrysavers.com). Booking by phone incurs a UK£25 fee.

To/From Brittany

Condor Ferries (☎ for bookings in UK 0845 609 1024; www.condorferries.co.uk) runs car ferries from Poole to St-Malo (from 4½ hours) from late May to September; and from Weymouth to St-Malo (5¼ hours) daily from late March to October and at least once a week in winter.

Brittany Ferries links Plymouth with Roscoff (6½ hours by day, nine hours overnight, one to three daily from mid-March to early November, almost daily in winter); and Portsmouth with St-Malo (8¾ hours by day, 10¾ hours overnight, one daily from March to October, almost daily in winter).

To/From Normandy

Transmanche Ferries (☎ in UK 0800 917 1201, in France 0800 650 100; www.transmancheferries.com) operates car ferries from Newhaven to Dieppe (up to three daily, four hours).

Condor Ferries links Portsmouth with Cherbourg (5½ hours) each Sunday from late May to early September.

Brittany Ferries links Cherbourg with both Poole (high-speed ferry 2¼ hours, regular ferry 4½ to 6½ hours, two or three daily) and Portsmouth (three hours, one or two sailings daily). The company also has car-ferry services from Portsmouth to Ouistreham (5¾ to seven hours, two to four daily), 14km northeast of Caen; high-speed ferries (3¾ hours) ply this route from mid-March to late October.

To/From Northern France

The extremely popular Dover–Calais crossing is handled by **SeaFrance** (☎ in UK 0871 22 22 500; www.seafrance.com; 80-90 min, 15 daily) and **P&O Ferries** (☎ in UK 08716 645 645; www.poferries.com; 75-90 min, 35 daily). Foot passengers are not allowed on night sailings (ie sailings departing sometime between 7pm and 9.30pm and before 7am or 8am).

Car ferries run by **Norfolk Line** (☎ in UK 0844 847 5042; www.norfolkline.com) link Loon Plage, about 25km west of Dunkirk (Dunkerque), with Dover (1¾ hours).

Bus

Europe's international buses are slower than trains but considerably cheaper, especially if you are under 26 or over 60.

Eurolines (☎ 08 92 89 90 91; www.eurolines.eu) provides bus services to various destinations throughout France (see p1238). Return fares are about 20% cheaper than two one-way fares. In summer, reservations are recommended at least two days in advance.

Buses run by London-based **Busabout** (☎ in UK 0207 950 1661; www.busabout.com; 1/2/3 loops US$829/1399/1699) link 29 continental European cities from early May to October. In France, stops are in Bordeaux, Tours, Paris, Avignon and Nice.

Train

Rail services link France with just about every country in Europe. Tickets and information are available from **Rail Europe** (www.raileurope.com). In France ticketing is handled by **SNCF** (☎ in France 36 35, from abroad 08 92 35 35 35; www.sncf.com).

The **Eurostar** (☎ in UK 08705 186 186, in France 08 92 35 35 39; www.eurostar.com) travels between London St Pancras and Paris Gare du Nord in just 2¼ hours. As always, booking early secures the best fares: a standard 2nd-class one-way/return ticket from London to Paris costs a whopping UK£154.50/309 (€232.50/435), but superdiscount returns can be just UK£59.

For details on Europe-wide rail passes, see p1243.

GETTING AROUND

Air

Air France (☎ 36 54; www.airfrance.com) and its subsidiaries **Brit Air** (www.britair.fr) and **Régional** (☎ 36 54; www.regional.com) control the lion's share of France's domestic airline industry, although budget airlines including **easyJet** (www.easyjet.com), **Airlinair** (www.airlinair.com) and **Twin Jet** (www.twinjet.fr) are steadily making inroads.

Students and people aged 12 to 24 receive hefty discounts. Special last-minute offers appear on the Air France website every Wednesday.

Bus

You're nearly always better off travelling by train in France. Nevertheless, buses are widely used for short-distance travel within *départements,* especially in rural areas with relatively few train lines (eg Brittany and Normandy).

Car & Motorcycle

Having your own wheels gives you exceptional freedom but can be expensive once you factor in petrol costs and *autoroute* (motorway) tolls. The websites www.viamichelin.com, www.autoroutes.fr and www.mappy.fr can help you work out likely costs for specified routes.

To hire a car you'll need to be over 21 and in possession of a valid *permis de conduire* (driving licence) and a credit card. Third party liability insurance is provided, but collision-damage waivers (CDW) vary; make sure you check the *franchise* (excess) when comparing rates. Automatic transmissions are *very* rare in France.

Cheap deals can be found with **Auto Europe** (☎ in USA 1 888 223 5555; www.autoeurope.com) in the US and **Holiday Autos** (☎ in UK 0871 472 5229; www.holidayautos.co.uk) in the UK. Otherwise, try the majors:

ADA (☎ 08 25 16 91 69; www.ada.fr, in French)
Avis (☎ 08 20 05 05 05; www.avis.com)
Budget (☎ 08 25 00 35 64; www.budget.com or www.budget.fr, in French)
Easycar (☎ in UK 08710 500 444; www.easycar.com)
Europcar (☎ 08 25 35 83 58; www.europcar.com)
Hertz (☎ 01 39 38 38 38; www.hertz.com)
National-Citer (www.nationalcar.com or www.citer.fr)
Renault Rent (☎ 08 10 40 50 60; www.renault-rent.com, in French) Renault's new car-rental arm.
Sixt (☎ 08 20 00 74 98; www.sixt.fr, in French)

Hitching

Hitching is rare in France and is not recommended for women, even in pairs. Remote rural areas are a better bet, but once you get off the *routes nationales*, traffic can be light and local; it's also illegal to hitch on autoroutes. Remember, hitching is never entirely safe wherever you are in the world, so be aware of the risks and if in doubt, just take the bus or train instead.

Train

France's rail network is operated by the state-owned **SNCF** (www.sncf.com). Many towns not on the SNCF train network are served by SNCF buses. The flagship trains are the superfast TGVs:

TGV Atlantique Sud-Ouest & TGV Atlantique Ouest Paris' Gare Montparnasse to western and southwestern France, including Brittany (Rennes, Brest, Quimper), Nantes, Tours, Poitiers, La Rochelle, Bordeaux, Biarritz and Toulouse.
TGV Est Européen New line connecting Paris' Gare de l'Est with Reims, Nancy, Metz, Strasbourg, Zürich and Germany, including Frankfurt, Stuttgart and Luxembourg. At the time of writing, the high-speed section of the line only stretched as far east as Lorraine; plans to extend the superfast line all the way to Strasbourg are scheduled for completion in 2012.
TGV Nord, Thalys & Eurostar Paris' Gare du Nord to Arras, Lille, Calais, Brussels, Amsterdam, Cologne and London St Pancras.
TGV Sud-Est & TGV Midi-Méditerranée Paris' Gare de Lyon with the southeast, including Dijon, Lyon, Geneva, the Alps, Avignon, Marseille, Nice and Montpellier.

A non-TGV train is referred to as a *corail* or TER *(train express régional).*

Full-fare tickets can be expensive, and are always pricier during peak periods (eg workday rush hours, on Friday evening and holiday periods). Special deals are published online every Tuesday at www.sncf.com, and www.idtgv.com sells tickets for as little as €19 for TGV travel on 20 routes to/from Paris.

Discount cards include the following:

Carte 12-25 (www.12-25-sncf.com; €49) For travellers aged 12 to 25.
Carte Escapades (www.escapades-sncf.com, in French; €85) For people aged 26 to 59. Discounts on return journeys of at least 200km including a Saturday night away or weekend-only travel.

The **InterRail One Country Pass** (www.interrailnet.com), valid in France, entitles nonresidents to unlimited travel on SNCF trains for three to eight days over a month. For three/four/six/eight days, the cost is €189/209/269/299 for adults and €125/139/175/194 for people aged 12 to 25.

PARIS

pop 2.15 million

What can be said about the sexy, sophisticated City of Lights that hasn't already been said a thousand times before? Quite simply, this is one of the world's great metropolises, a trend-setter, market-leader and cultural capital for

EMERGENCY NUMBERS

- Ambulance (SAMU) ☎ 15
- Police ☎ 17
- Fire ☎ 18

over a thousand years and still going strong. This is the place that gave the world the cancan and the cinematograph, a city that reinvented itself during the Renaissance, bopped to the beat of the Jazz Age and positively glittered during the *belle époque* (beautiful era). As you might expect, Paris is strewn with historic architecture, glorious galleries and cultural treasures galore, but the modern-day city is much more than just a museum piece. It's a heady hotchpotch of cultures and ideas – a place to stroll the boulevards, shop till you drop or just do as the Parisians do and watch the world buzz by from a streetside cafe. Savour every moment.

ORIENTATION

Central Paris is small: 9.5km (north to south) by 11km (east to west). Excluding the Bois de Boulogne and the Bois de Vincennes, its total area is 105 sq km. The Seine River flows east–west through the city; the Rive Droite (Right Bank) is north of the river, while the Rive Gauche (Left Bank) is to the south. Paris is divided into 20 *arrondissements* (districts).

INFORMATION

Internet Access

Wi-fi is widespread. For a list of free-access wi-fi cafes, visit www.cafes-wifi.com. If you're laptop-less, Paris is awash in internet cafes:

Cyber Cube (Map pp378-9; ☎ 01 56 80 08 08; www.cybercube.fr; 9 rue d'Odessa, 14e; per 15/30min €1/2, per 5/10hr €30/40; 🕑 10am-10pm; Ⓜ Montparnasse Bienvenüe) Expensive but handy for Gare Montparnasse.

Milk (☎ 08 20 00 10 00; www.milklub.com; per 1/2/3/5hr €4/7/9/12, night-time per 3/10hr €6/13; 🕑 24hr) Panthéon (Map pp382-3; 17 rue Soufflot, 5e; Ⓜ Luxembourg); Les Halles (Map pp382-3; 31 bd de Sébastopol, 1er; Ⓜ Les Halles) This chain of seven internet cafes is bright, buzzy and open round the clock.

Phon'net (Map pp378-9; ☎ 01 42 05 10 73; 74 rue de Charonne, 11e; per 1/5/15/30hr €5/16/30/45; 🕑 10am-midnight; Ⓜ Charonne or Ledru Rollin)

Web 46 (Map pp382-3; ☎ 01 40 27 02 89; 46 rue du Roi de Sicile, 4e; per 15/30min €2.50/4, per 1/5hr €7/29; 🕑 10am-11pm Mon-Fri, 10am-9pm Sat, noon-11pm Sun; Ⓜ St-Paul) Cybercafe in the heart of the Marais.

Internet Resources

Go Go Paris! Culture! (www.gogoparis.com) All things cultural: clubs, art, gigs, food and drink.

Mairie de Paris (www.paris.fr) Comprehensive Paris info from opening times to city stats.

Paris Convention & Visitors Bureau (www.parisinfo.com) Official tourist office site.

Paris Pages (www.paris.org) Museums and cultural events.

Laundry

There's a *laverie* (laundrette) on practically every Parisian street-corner; your hotel or hostel can point you to one.

Medical Services

These are major 24-hour accident-and-emergency hospitals:

American Hospital of Paris (Map pp378-9; ☎ 01 46 41 25 25; www.american-hospital.org; 63 bd Victor Hugo, 92200 Neuilly-sur-Seine; Ⓜ Pont de Levallois Bécon)

Hertford British Hospital (Map pp378-9; ☎ 01 46 39 22 22; www.british-hospital.org; 3 rue Barbès, 92300 Levallois-Perret; Ⓜ Anatole France)

Hôpital Hôtel Dieu (Map pp382-3; ☎ 01 42 34 82 34; www.aphp.fr; 1 place du Parvis Notre Dame, 4e; Ⓜ Cité) One of the city's main government-run public hospitals; after 8pm use the emergency entrance on rue de la Cité, 4e.

Money

Post offices with a Banque Postale offer the best exchange rates, and accept banknotes (commission €4.50) and travellers cheques. *Bureaux de change* are faster and easier, open longer hours and give better rates than commercial banks.

Toilets

The public toilets in Paris are signposted *toilettes* or *WC*. The tan-coloured, self-cleaning toilets you see on Parisian pavements are open 24 hours and are free of charge. *Libre* means 'free'; *occupé* means 'occupied'.

Tourist Information

The main branch of the **Paris Convention & Visitors Bureau** (Office de Tourisme et de Congrès de Paris; Map pp378-9; ☎ 08 92 68 30 00; www.parisinfo.com; 25-27 rue des Pyramides, 1er; 🕑 9am-7pm Jun-Oct, 10am-7pm Mon-Sat & 11am-7pm Sun Nov-May, closed 1 May; Ⓜ Pyramides) is 500m northwest of the Louvre.

PARIS

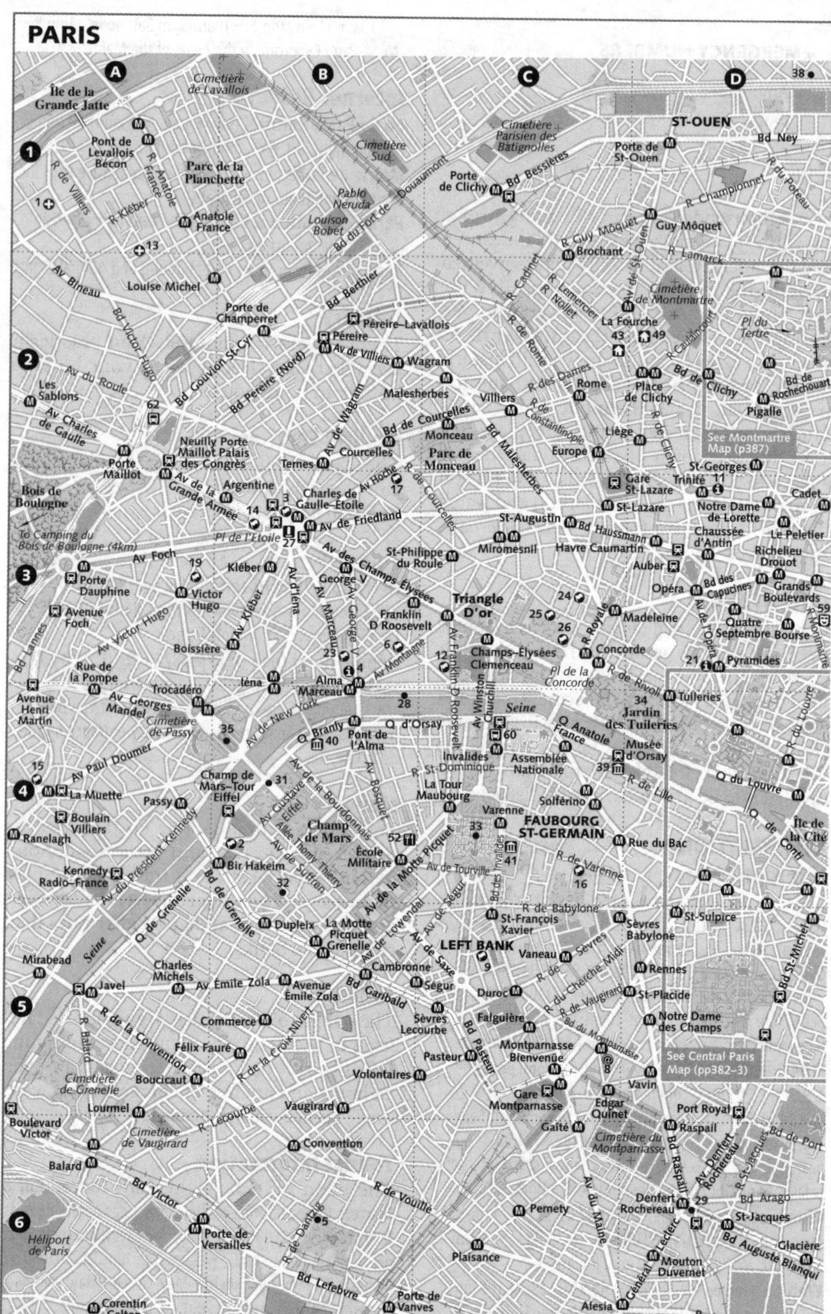
Île de la Grande Jatte
Cimetière de Lavallois
Cimetière Parisien des Batignolles
ST-OUEN
Bd Ney
Porte de St-Ouen
Pont de Levallois Bécon
Parc de la Planchette
Cimetière Sud
Porte de Clichy
Bd Bessières
R Championnet
R du Poteau
Anatole France
Guy Môquet
Brochant
R Lamarck
Cimetière de Montmartre
Louise Michel
Av Bineau
Porte de Champerret
Bd Berthier
Péreire-Lavallois
Péreire
Wagram
La Fourche
Pl du Tertre
Les Sablons
Av du Roule
Malesherbes
Villiers
Rome
Place de Clichy
Bd de Clichy
Pigalle
Neuilly Porte Maillot Palais des Congrès
Porte Maillot
Bd de Courcelles
Monceau
Parc de Monceau
Courcelles
Ternes
Liège
Europe
See Montmartre Map (p387)
Bois de Boulogne
Argentine
Charles de Gaulle-Étoile
Gare St-Lazare
St-Lazare
Trinité
St-Georges
Cadet
Notre Dame de Lorette
To Camping du Bois de Boulogne (4km)
Pl de l'Étoile
Av de Friedland
St-Augustin
Bd Haussmann
Chaussée d'Antin
Le Peletier
Av Foch
St-Philippe du Roule
Miromesnil
Havre Caumartin
Richelieu Drouot
Porte Dauphine
Kléber
Victor Hugo
Av des Champs Élysées
George V
Auber
Opéra
Grands Boulevards
Triangle D'or
Franklin D Roosevelt
Madeleine
Quatre Septembre
Bourse
Avenue Foch
Boissière
Champs-Élysées Clemenceau
Concorde
Pyramides
Rue de la Pompe
Trocadéro
Iéna
Alma Marceau
Pl de la Concorde
R de Rivoli
Tuileries
Avenue Henri Martin
Av Georges Mandel
Cimetière de Passy
Seine
Jardin des Tuileries
Q d'Orsay
Pont de l'Alma
Invalides
Assemblée Nationale
Musée d'Orsay
Q Anatole France
Av Paul Doumer
Champ de Mars-Tour Eiffel
La Tour Maubourg
R St-Dominique
Solférino
Q du Louvre
La Muette
Passy
Varenne
FAUBOURG ST-GERMAIN
Île de la Cité
Boulain Villiers
Ranelagh
Champ de Mars
École Militaire
Rue du Bac
Kennedy Radio-France
Bir Hakeim
Av de Tourville
R de Varenne
R de Babylone
St-François Xavier
St-Sulpice
Dupleix
La Motte Picquet Grenelle
Sèvres Babylone
LEFT BANK
Vaneau
Mirabead
Charles Michels
Cambronne
Rennes
Javel
Av Émile Zola
Avenue Émile Zola
Ségur
Duroc
St-Placide
Commerce
Sèvres Lecourbe
Falguière
Notre Dame des Champs
Félix Faure
Pasteur
Montparnasse Bienvenüe
R de la Convention
See Central Paris Map (pp382-3)
Boucicaut
Volontaires
Vavin
Cimetière de Grenelle
Gare Montparnasse
Edgar Quinet
Port Royal
Lourmel
Vaugirard
Gaîté
Raspail
Boulevard Victor
Cimetière de Vaugirard
Convention
Cimetière du Montparnasse
Balard
R de Vouillé
Bd Victor
Pernety
Denfert Rochereau
Bd Arago
St-Jacques
Porte de Versailles
Héliport de Paris
Plaisance
Glacière
Bd Auguste Blanqui
Mouton Duvernet
Bd Lefebvre
Porte de Vanves
Corentin Celton
Alésia
R d'Alésia

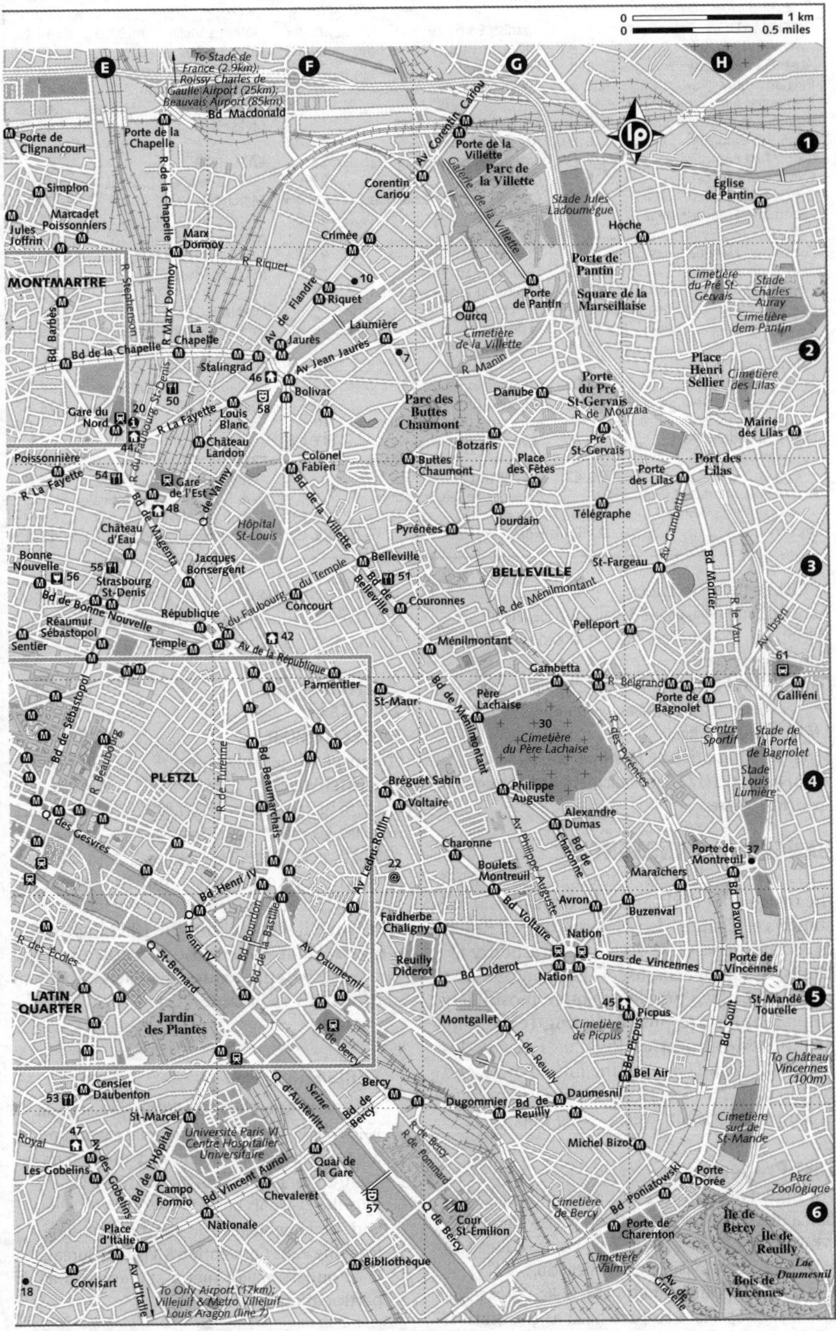
0 1 km
0 0.5 miles
E
F
G
H
1
2
3
4
5
6
To Stade de France (2.9km); Roissy Charles de Gaulle Airport (25km); Beauvais Airport (85km)
Bd Macdonald
Porte de Clignancourt
Porte de la Chapelle
R de la Chapelle
Simplon
Marcadet Poissonniers
Jules Joffrin
Marx Dormoy
R Riquet
MONTMARTRE
R Stephenson
R Marx Dormoy
Barbès
Bd Barbès
Bd de la Chapelle
La Chapelle
Stalingrad
Gare du Nord
R du Faubourg St-Denis
R La Fayette
Louis Blanc
Château Landon
Poissonnière
Gare de l'Est
Q de Valmy
Bd de Magenta
Château d'Eau
Bonne Nouvelle
Strasbourg St-Denis
Bd de Bonne Nouvelle
Réaumur Sébastopol
Sentier
République
Temple
Av Corentin Cariou
Porte de la Villette
Corentin Cariou
Parc de la Villette
Galerie de la Villette
Crimée
Av de Flandre
Riquet
Laumière
Jaurès
Av Jean Jaurès
Bolivar
Colonel Fabien
Bd de la Villette
Hôpital St-Louis
Jacques Bonsergent
Belleville
Bd de Belleville
R du Faubourg du Temple
Goncourt
Couronnes
Av de la République
Parmentier
Stade Jules Ladoumègue
Porte de Pantin
Ourcq
Cimetière de la Villette
R Manin
Porte de Pantin
Square de la Marseillaise
Parc des Buttes Chaumont
Danube
Porte du Pré St-Gervais
R de Mouzaia
Pré St-Gervais
Botzaris
Buttes Chaumont
Place des Fêtes
Jourdain
Pyrénées
Télégraphe
BELLEVILLE
R de Ménilmontant
Ménilmontant
Église de Pantin
Hoche
Cimetière du Pré St-Gervais
Stade Charles Auray
Cimetière dem Pantin
Place Henri Sellier
Cimetière des Lilas
Mairie des Lilas
Porte des Lilas
Port des Lilas
St-Fargeau
Av Gambetta
Bd Mortier
R le Vau
Av Ibsen
Pelleport
Gambetta
R Belgrand
Porte de Bagnolet
Gallieni
Centre Sportif
Stade de la Porte de Bagnolet
Stade Louis Lumière
St-Maur
Bd de Ménilmontant
Père Lachaise
Cimetière du Père Lachaise
R des Pyrénées
Bd de Sébastopol
R Beaubourg
PLETZL
R de Turenne
Bd Beaumarchais
Q des Gesvres
Bd Henri IV
Bd Bourdon
Bd de la Bastille
Q Henri IV
Q St-Bernard
R des Écoles
LATIN QUARTER
Jardin des Plantes
Av Daumesnil
R de Bercy
Av Ledru-Rollin
Bréguet Sabin
Voltaire
Philippe Auguste
Av Philippe Auguste
Alexandre Dumas
Bd de Charonne
Charonne
Boulets Montreuil
Bd Voltaire
Avron
Buzenval
Maraîchers
Porte de Montreuil
Bd Davout
Faidherbe Chaligny
Reuilly Diderot
Bd Diderot
Nation
Cours de Vincennes
Porte de Vincennes
St-Mandé Tourelle
Montgallet
R de Reuilly
Picpus
Cimetière de Picpus
Bd de Picpus
Bel Air
Bd Soult
To Château Vincennes (100m)
Censier Daubenton
St-Marcel
Université Paris VI Centre Hospitalier Universitaire
Royal
Av des Gobelins
Les Gobelins
Bd de l'Hôpital
Campo Formio
Bd Vincent Auriol
Chevaleret
Nationale
Place d'Italie
Av d'Italie
Corvisart
Q d'Austerlitz
Seine
Bd de Bercy
Bercy
Quai de la Gare
R de Bercy
R de Pommard
Q de Bercy
Cour St-Émilion
Bibliothèque
Dugommier
Bd de Reuilly
Daumesnil
Michel Bizot
Cimetière sud de St-Mandé
Bd Poniatowski
Porte Dorée
Parc Zoologique
Cimetière de Bercy
Porte de Charenton
Cimetière Valmy
Av de Gravelle
Île de Bercy
Île de Reuilly
Lac Daumesnil
Bois de Vincennes
To Orly Airport (17km); Villejuif & Metro Villejuif Louis Aragon (line 7)
7
10
18
20
22
30
37
42
44
45
46
47
48
50
51
53
54
55
56
57
58
61

FRANCE

INFORMATION
American Hospital of Paris........ **1** A1
Australian Embassy........ **2** B4
Belgian Embassy........ **3** B3
Bienvenue à la Ferme........ **4** B3
Bureau des Objets Trouvés........ **5** B6
Canadian Embassy........ **6** B3
Club Alpin Français........ **7** F2
Cyber Cube........ **8** C5
Dutch Embassy........ **9** C5
Fédération Française de la Randonnée Pédestre........ **10** F2
Fédération Nationale des Gîtes de France........ **11** D3
German Embassy........ **12** C3
Hertford British Hospital........ **13** A1
Irish Embassy........ **14** B3
Italian Consulate........ **15** A4
Italian Embassy........ **16** C4
Japanese Embassy........ **17** B3
Ligue Française pour les Auberges de la Jeunesse........ **18** E6
New Zealand Embassy........ **19** A3
Paris Convention & Visitors Bureau........ **20** E2
Paris Convention & Visitors Bureau (Main Branch)........ **21** D3
Phon'net........ **22** F4
Spanish Embassy........ **23** B3
UK Consulate (Visa Section)........ **24** C3
UK Embassy........ **25** C3
US Embassy........ **26** C3

SIGHTS & ACTIVITIES
Arc de Triomphe........ **27** B3
Bateaux Mouches........ **28** B4
Catacombes........ **29** D6
Cimetière du Père Lachaise........ **30** G4
Eiffel Tower........ **31** B4
Fat Tire Bike Tours........ **32** B4
Hôtel des Invalides........ **33** C4
Jardin des Tuileries........ **34** D4
Jardins du Trocadéro........ **35** B4
Marché aux Puces de la Porte de Vanves........ **36** B6
Marché aux Puces de Montreuil........ **37** H4
Marché aux Puces de St-Ouen........ **38** D1
Musée d'Orsay........ **39** C4
Musée du Quai Branly........ **40** B4
Musée Rodin........ **41** C4

SLEEPING
Auberge de Jeunesse Jules Ferry........ **42** F3
Hôtel Eldorado........ **43** C2
Hôtel La Vieille France........ **44** E2
Hôtel Le Cosy........ **45** G5
Peace & Love Hostel........ **46** F2
Port Royal Hôtel........ **47** E6
Sibour Hôtel........ **48** E3
Style Hôtel........ **49** D2

EATING
Krishna Bhavan........ **50** E2
Marché Belleville........ **51** F3
Marché Rue Cler........ **52** B4
Marché Rue Mouffetard........ **53** E5
Marché St-Quentin........ **54** E3
Passage Brady........ **55** E3

DRINKING
De La Ville Café........ **56** E3

ENTERTAINMENT
La Dame de Canton........ **57** F6
Point Éphémère........ **58** F2
Social Club........ **59** D3

TRANSPORT
Aérogare des Invalides........ **60** C4
Gare Routière Internationale de Paris-Galliéni........ **61** H3
Parking Pershing Express Bus........ **62** A2

Other tourist offices:

Gare de Lyon (Map pp382-3; Hall d'Arrivée, 20 bd Diderot, 12e; 8am-6pm Mon-Sat, closed Sun & 1 May; M Gare de Lyon)

Gare du Nord (Map pp378-9; 18 rue de Dunkerque, 10e; 8am-6pm, closed Christmas Day, New Year's Day & 1 May; M Gare du Nord)

Syndicat d'Initiative de Montmartre (Map p387; ☎ 01 42 62 21 21; 21 place du Tertre, 18e; 10am-7pm; M Abbesses)

DANGERS & ANNOYANCES

Paris is generally safe, but take extra care on the metro after dark, and take extra care at the stations at Châtelet-Les Halles, Château Rouge in Montmartre, Gare du Nord, Strasbourg St-Denis, Réaumur Sébastopol and Montparnasse Bienvenüe. Two problems you're most likely to encounter are pickpocketing (especially around Montmartre, Pigalle, Forum des Halles, the Latin Quarter, the Eiffel Tower, and on the rush-hour metro) and the ever-present scourge of Parisian streets – dog poo.

Lost Property

All objects found in Paris are brought to the **Bureau des Objets Trouvés** (Lost Property Office; Map pp378-9; ☎ 08 21 00 25 25; 36 rue des Morillons, 15e; 8.30am-5pm Mon-Thu, 8.30am-4.30pm Fri; M Convention).

Items lost on the **metro** (☎ 32 46; 7am-9pm Mon-Fri, 9am-5pm Sat & Sun) are held at the station before being sent to the Bureau des Objets Trouvés, while lost property on trains is taken to the station's lost-property office.

SIGHTS

Left Bank

EIFFEL TOWER

It's impossible to imagine Paris without the **Tour Eiffel** (Map pp378-9; ☎ 01 44 11 23 23; www.tour-eiffel.fr; lifts to 1st/2nd/top level €4.80/7.80/12; lifts 9am-midnight mid-Jun–Aug, 9.30am-11pm Sep–mid-Jun, stairs 9am-midnight mid-Jun–Aug, 9.30am-6pm Sep–mid-Jun; M Champ de Mars-Tour Eiffel or Bir Hakeim), but the 'metal asparagus' faced opposition from Paris' artistic elite when it was built for the 1889 Exposition Universelle. It was almost torn down in 1909 but was spared because it proved an ideal platform for radio antennas.

PARIS PASS

The **Paris Museum Pass** (www.parismuseumpass.fr; 2/4/6 days €30/45/60) is valid for around 38 Parisian sights – including the Louvre, Centre Pompidou and the Musée d'Orsay, plus the St-Denis basilica, parts of Versailles and Fontainebleau. You can buy it online, from the Paris Convention & Visitors Bureau, Fnac outlets, major metro stations and all participating venues.

GETTING INTO TOWN

From both of Paris' main airports – Roissy Charles de Gaulle in the north and Orly in the south – RER trains travel to the city centre and several mainline train stations. There are also public buses from both airports to various areas of Paris. A taxi will cost around €40 to €50 from Orly, €40 to €60 from Roissy Charles de Gaulle.

Private shuttle buses are around €25 from Orly or Roissy Charles de Gaulle; departures between 8pm and 6am cost around €40. Book ahead and allow time for pick-ups and drop-offs.

Allô Shuttle (☎ 01 34 29 00 80; www.alloshuttle.com)
Paris Airports Service (☎ 01 55 98 10 80; www.parisairportservice.com)
PariShuttle (☎ 01 53 39 18 18; www.parishuttle.com)

These days some 6.9 million people make the 324m trek to the top each year. If you're feeling steely-legged, you can dodge the lift fees by taking the stairs (€4/3.10 over/under 25 years old) to the 1st and 2nd platforms, but be warned: it's steep. Really, really steep.

Spreading out around the Eiffel Tower are the **Jardins du Trocadéro** (Trocadero Gardens; Map pp378-9; Ⓜ Trocadéro), whose fountains and statue garden are grandly illuminated at night.

MUSÉE D'ORSAY

The **Musée d'Orsay** (Orsay Museum; Map pp378-9; ☎ 01 40 49 48 14; www.musee-orsay.fr; 62 rue de Lille, 7e; adult/18-30yr €8/5.50, 1st Sun of month free; 🕑 9.30am-6pm Tue, Wed & Fri-Sun, 9.30am-9.45pm Thu; Ⓜ Musée d'Orsay or Solférino), housed in a turn-of-the-20th-century train station, displays France's national collection of paintings, sculptures and artwork produced between the 1840s and 1914, including the fruits of the impressionist, postimpressionist and art nouveau movements. Among its exhibits are works by Monet, Renoir, Pissarro, Sisley, Degas, Manet, Gauguin, Cézanne, Van Gogh, Seurat and Matisse.

Tickets are valid all day so you can come and go as you please. The reduced entrance fee of €5.50 applies to everyone after 4.15pm (6pm on Thursday). A combined ticket with the Musée Rodin costs €12.

PANTHÉON

The domed landmark known as the **Panthéon** (Map pp382-3; ☎ 01 44 32 18 00; www.monuments-nationaux.fr; place du Panthéon, 5e; adult/18-25yr €7.50/4.80, 1st Sun of month Oct-Mar free; 🕑 10am-6.30pm Apr-Sep, to 6.15pm Oct-Mar; Ⓜ Luxembourg) was completed in 1789. The crypt houses the tombs of French luminaries such as Voltaire, Jean-Jacques Rousseau, Victor Hugo, Émile Zola, Jean Moulin and Marie Curie. A working model of Foucault's Pendulum demonstrates the rotation of the earth.

MUSÉE RODIN

The **Musée Rodin** (Rodin Museum; Map pp378-9; ☎ 01 44 18 61 10; www.musee-rodin.fr; 79 rue de Varenne, 7e; adult/18-25yr permanent or temporary exhibition plus garden €6/4, both exhibitions plus garden €9/7, garden only €1, 1st Sun of month free; 🕑 9.30am-5.45pm Tue-Sun Apr-Sep, 9.30am-4.45pm Tue-Sun Oct-Mar; Ⓜ Varenne) displays some of Rodin's most famous works, including *The Burghers of Calais (Les Bourgeois de Calais), Cathedral, The Thinker (Le Penseur)* and *The Kiss (Le Baiser)*.

HÔTEL DES INVALIDES

The **Hôtel des Invalides** (Map pp378-9; Ⓜ Varenne or La Tour Maubourg) was built in the 1670s as housing for 4000 *invalides* (disabled war veterans). On 14 July 1789, a mob forced its way into the building and seized 28,000 rifles before heading to the prison at Bastille, starting the revolution.

MUSÉE DU QUAI BRANLY

The new **Musée du Quai Branly** (Quai Branly Museum; Map pp378-9; ☎ 01 56 61 70 00; www.quaibranly.fr; 37 quai Branly, 7e; adult/student & 18-25yr €8.50/6, free after 6pm Sat for 18-25yr, 1st Sun of month for all; 🕑 11am-7pm Tue, Wed & Sun, to 9pm Thu-Sat; Ⓜ Pont de l'Alma or Alma-Marceau), in a fabulous building designed by architect Jean Nouvel, explores the cultures of Africa, Oceania, Asia and the Americas through a range of multimedia exhibits.

JARDIN DU LUXEMBOURG

When the weather is fine Parisians flock to the 23-hectare **Jardin du Luxembourg** (Luxembourg Garden; Map pp378-9; 🕑 7am-9.30pm Apr-Oct, 8am-sunset Nov-Mar; Ⓜ Luxembourg) to relax and sunbathe.

CATACOMBES

There are few spookier sights in Paris than the **Catacombes** (Map pp378-9; ☎ 01 43 22 47 63; www.catacombes.paris.fr, in French; 1 av Colonel Henri

CENTRAL PARIS

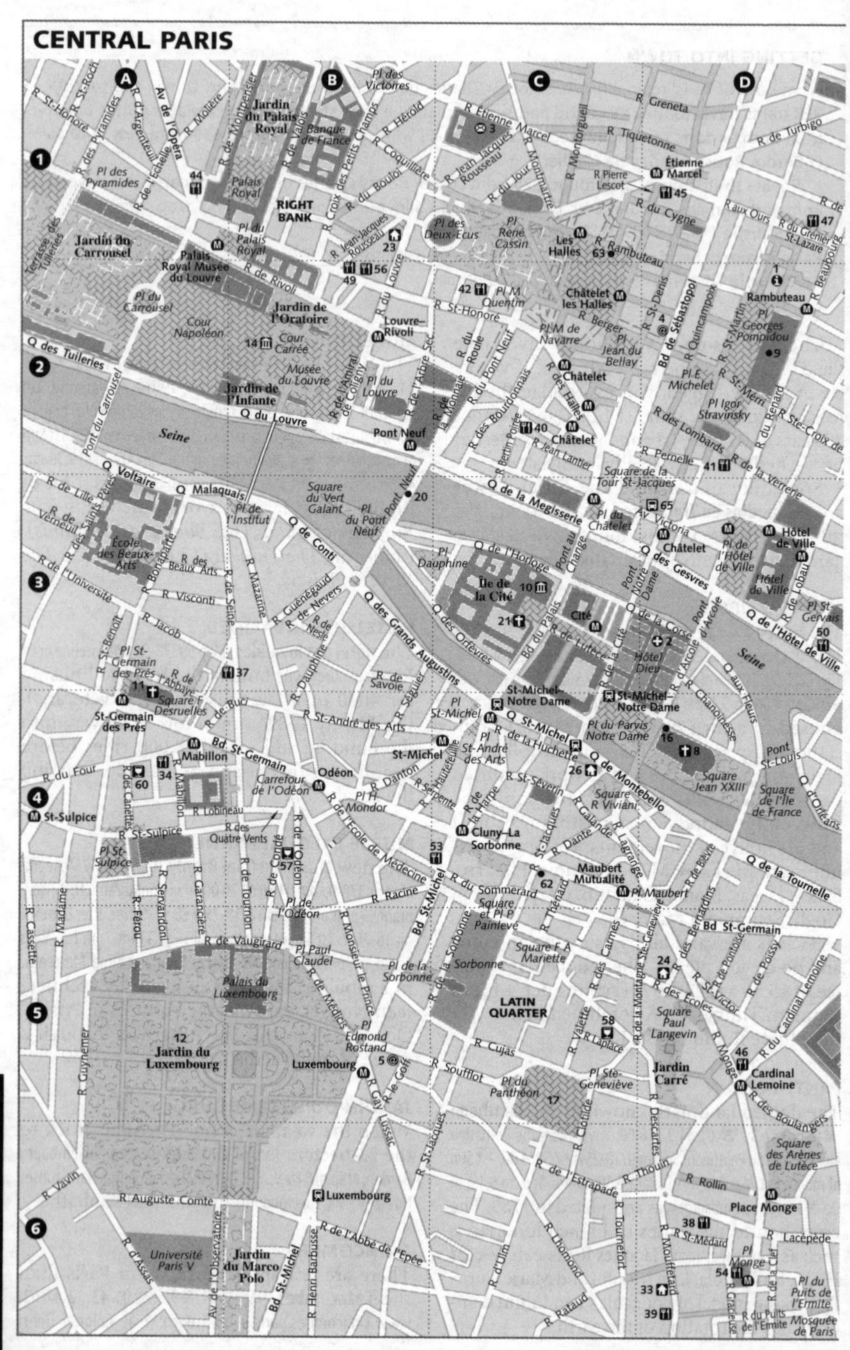

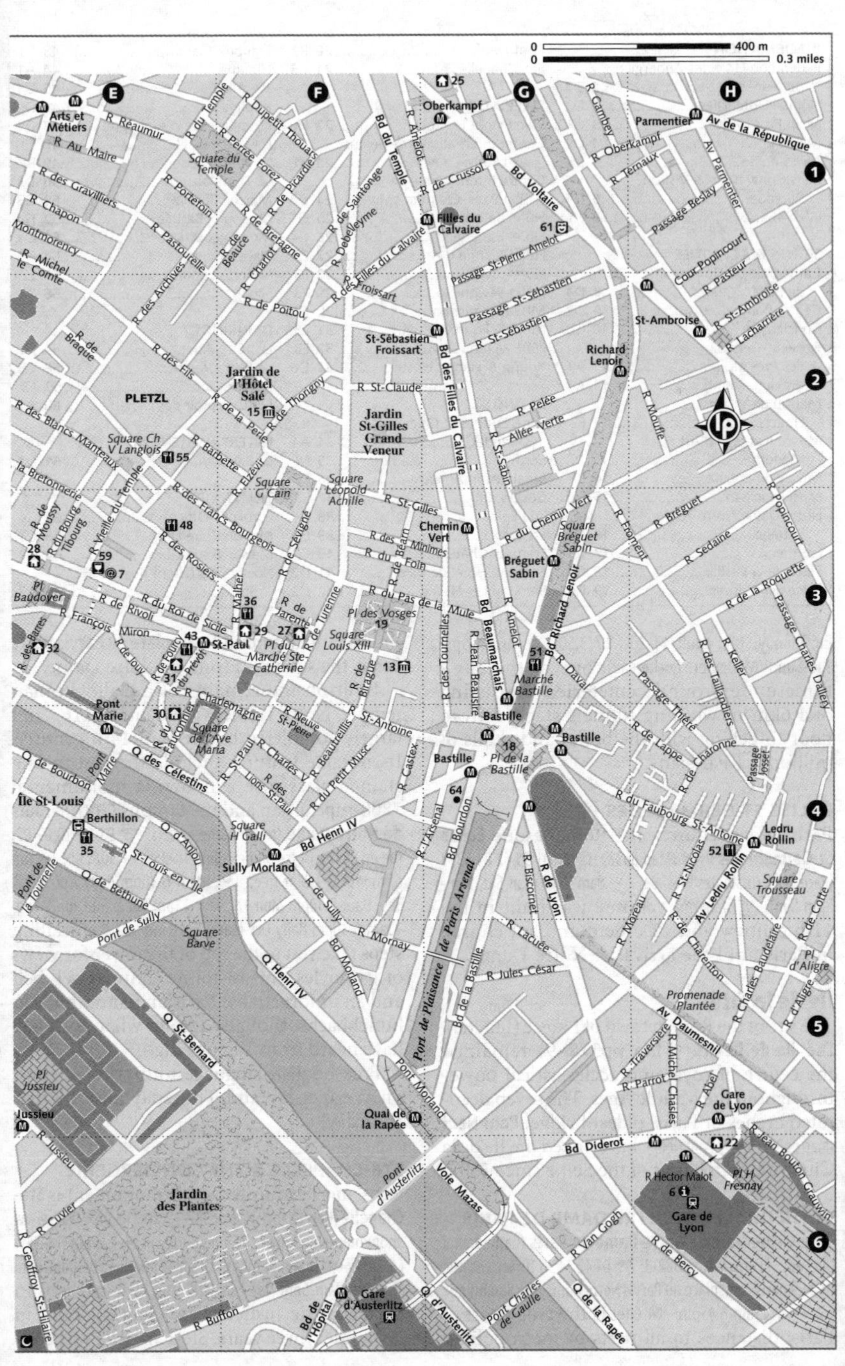
400 m
0.3 miles
Arts et Métiers
Oberkampf
Parmentier
Av de la République
Square du Temple
Filles du Calvaire
St-Sébastien Froissart
St-Ambroise
Richard Lenoir
Jardin de l'Hôtel Salé
PLETZL
Jardin St-Gilles Grand Veneur
Chemin Vert
Bréguet Sabin
Pl des Vosges
Square Louis XIII
St-Paul
Pont Marie
Bastille
Pl de la Bastille
Marché Bastille
Île St-Louis
Berthillon
Sully Morland
Bd Henri IV
Port de Plaisance de Paris Arsenal
Ledru Rollin
Square Trousseau
Pl d'Aligre
Promenade Plantée
Av Daumesnil
Gare de Lyon
Bd Diderot
Quai de la Rapée
Pont d'Austerlitz
Jardin des Plantes
Pl Jussieu
Jussieu
Gare d'Austerlitz
Q d'Austerlitz
Q de la Rapée
Pont Charles de Gaulle
Pl H Fresnay
R de Bercy
Bd Beaumarchais
Bd des Filles du Calvaire
Bd du Temple
Bd Voltaire
Bd Richard Lenoir
R de Rivoli
R St-Antoine
R du Faubourg St-Antoine
R de la Roquette
R de Charonne
R de Lyon
Q des Célestins
Q Henri IV
Q St-Bernard
FRANCE

INFORMATION
- Fédération Unie des Auberges de Jeunesse 1 D2
- Hôpital Hôtel Dieu 2 D3
- Main Post Office 3 C1
- Milk 4 D2
- Milk 5 B5
- Paris Convention & Visitors Bureau 6 H6
- Web 46 ..... 7 E3

SIGHTS & ACTIVITIES
- Cathédrale de Notre Dame de Paris 8 D4
- Centre Pompidou 9 D2
- Conciergerie 10 C3
- Église St-Germain des Prés 11 A3
- Jardin du Luxembourg 12 A5
- Maison de Victor Hugo 13 F3
- Musée National d'Art Moderne ..... (see 9)
- Musée du Louvre 14 B2
- Musée Picasso 15 F2
- Notre Dame North Tower Entrance 16 D4
- Panthéon 17 C5
- Place de la Bastille 18 G4
- Place des Vosges 19 F3
- Pont Neuf 20 B3
- Ste-Chapelle 21 C3

SLEEPING
- Blue Planet Hostel 22 H6
- Centre International de Séjour BVJ Paris–Louvre 23 B1
- Centre International de Séjour BVJ Paris–Quartier Latin 24 D5
- Hôtel de Nevers 25 G1
- Hôtel Esmeralda 26 C4
- Hôtel Jeanne d'Arc 27 F3
- Hôtel Rivoli 28 E3
- Hôtel Sévigné 29 F3
- MIJE Le Fauconnier 30 E4
- MIJE Le Fourcy 31 E3
- MIJE Maubuisson 32 E3
- Young & Happy Hostel 33 D6

EATING
- Bar à Soupes et Quenelles Giraudet 34 A4
- Berthillon 35 E4
- Breakfast in America 36 F3
- Cosi 37 B3
- Ed l'Épicier 38 D6
- Franprix 39 D6
- Franprix Châtelet 40 C2
- Franprix Hôtel de Ville 41 D2
- Franprix Les Halles 42 C2
- Franprix Marais 43 E3
- Higuma 44 A1
- Joe Allen 45 D1
- Kootchi 46 D5
- L'Ambassade d'Auvergne 47 D1
- L'As de Felafel 48 E3
- Le Petit Mâchon 49 B2
- Le Trumilou 50 D3
- Marché Bastille 51 G3
- Monoprix Bastille 52 H4
- Monoprix St-Michel 53 C4
- Place Monge 54 D6
- Robert et Louise 55 E2
- Scoop 56 B2

DRINKING
- Le 10 ..... 57 B4
- Le Piano Vache 58 C5
- Le Pick Clops 59 E3
- Les Comptoir des Canettes 60 A4

ENTERTAINMENT
- Le Bataclan 61 G1

TRANSPORT
- Eurolines Office 62 C4
- Maison Roue Libre 63 C1
- Maison Roue Libre 64 G4
- Noctambus (Night Bus) Stops 65 D3

Roi-Tanguy, 14e; adult/14-26yr €7/3.50; 10am-5pm Tue-Sun; M Denfert Rochereau), one of the city's three underground cemeteries, consisting of 1.6km of winding tunnels stacked from floor-to-ceiling with the bones and skulls of millions of Parisians.

ÉGLISE ST-GERMAIN DES PRÉS

Paris' oldest church, the Romanesque **Église St-Germain des Prés** (Map pp382-3; ☎ 01 55 42 81 33; 3 place St-Germain des Prés, 6e; 8am-7pm Mon-Sat, 9am-8pm Sun; M St-Germain des Prés) was built in the 11th century and was the dominant church in Paris until the arrival of Notre Dame.

Île de la Cité

The site of the Roman town of Lutèce (Lutetia), the **Île de la Cité** (Map pp378–9) remained the centre of royal and ecclesiastical power throughout the Middle Ages. The seven decorated arches of Paris' oldest bridge, **Pont Neuf** (Map pp382-3; M Pont Neuf), have linked the Île de la Cité with both banks of the Seine since 1607.

CATHÉDRALE DE NOTRE DAME DE PARIS

The **Cathédrale de Notre Dame de Paris** (Cathedral of Our Lady of Paris; Map pp382-3; ☎ 01 42 34 56 10; www.cathedraledeparis.com; place du Parvis Notre Dame, 4e; audioguide €5; 7.45am-6.45pm; M Cité) is the true heart of Paris; distances to all parts of metropolitan France are measured from **place du Parvis Notre Dame**, the square in front of Notre Dame.

Built on the remains of a Gallo-Roman temple, Notre Dame was begun in 1163 and largely completed by the mid-14th century. Its notable features include three stunning stained-glass rose windows, a monumental 7800-pipe organ and the famous Gothic **tours de Notre Dame** (Notre Dame towers; ☎ 01 53 10 07 02; rue du Cloître Notre Dame; adult/18-25yr €7.50/4.80, 1st Sun of month Oct-Mar free; 10am-6.30pm daily Apr-Jun & Sep, 9am-7.30pm Mon-Fri, 9am-11pm Sat & Sun Jul & Aug, 10am-5.30pm daily Oct-Mar), whose 422 spiralling steps take you to the top of the tower for views of gargoyles, the 13-tonne 'Emmanuel' bell and an unforgettable Parisian panorama. No hunchbacks, though, despite what you may have heard from Victor Hugo.

Free English-language tours run at noon on Wednesday and Thursday and 2.30pm Saturday.

STE-CHAPELLE & THE CONCIERGERIE

Paris' most exquisite Gothic monument is **Ste-Chapelle** (Holy Chapel; Map pp382-3; ☎ 01 53 40 60 97; www.monuments-nationaux.fr; 4 bd du Palais, 1er; adult/18-25yr €6.50/4.50, 1st Sun of month Oct-Mar free; 9.30am-6pm Mar-Oct, 9am-5pm Nov-Feb; M Cité), tucked within the Palais de Justice (Law Courts). Built in just under three years, Ste-Chapelle was consecrated in 1248. The chapel was conceived by Louis IX to house his sacred relics, now kept in the treasury of Notre Dame.

Nearby, the 14th-century palace known as the **Conciergerie** (Map pp382-3; ☎ 01 53 40 60 97; www.monuments-nationaux.fr; 2 bd du Palais, 1er; adult/18-25yr €8/6, 1st Sun of month Oct-Mar free; 9.30am-6pm Mar-Oct, 9am-5pm Nov-Feb; M Cité) became the city's main prison during the Reign of Terror (1793–94). Many famous inmates, including Marie-Antoinette and the radicals Danton and Robespierre, were incarcerated here before meeting their eventual fate beneath the guillotine. You can also visit Europe's largest surviving medieval hall, the **Salle des Gens d'Armes** (Cavalrymen's Hall). A joint ticket with Ste-Chapelle (opposite) costs €11.50 (€9 for those 18 to 25 years old).

Right Bank

MUSÉE DU LOUVRE

The vast Palais du Louvre was constructed as a fortress by Philippe-Auguste in the 13th century and rebuilt in the mid-16th century. In 1793 the Revolutionary Convention transformed it into the **Musée du Louvre** (Louvre Museum; Map pp382-3; ☎ 01 40 20 53 17; www.louvre.fr; admission to permanent collections/permanent collections & temporary exhibits €9/13, after 6pm Wed & Fri €6/11; 9am-6pm Mon, Thu, Sat & Sun, 9am-10pm Wed & Fri; M Palais Royal-Musée du Louvre), the nation's first (and foremost) national museum.

The Louvre's top attractions are da Vinci's mischievous *Mona Lisa* and the *Venus de Milo*, but there's much, much more to see. Other highlights include key works by Raphael, Botticelli, Delacroix and Titian, the lavish apartments of Napoleon III's Minister of State, and a glorious collection of Greek and Roman sculpture. Tickets remain valid for the whole day, so take your time – you'll enjoy it more if you don't try and pack too much into one day.

The main entrance in the Cour Napoléon is covered by the 21m-high glass **Pyramide du Louvre**. You can dodge queues by buying advance tickets from machines in the Carrousel du Louvre, by ringing ☎ 08 92 68 36 22 or ☎ 08 25 34 63 46, or booking online at www.louvre.fr. Note that entry to the permanent collections is free after 6pm on Friday for those under 26; entry is free for all on the first Sunday of the month.

JARDIN DES TUILERIES

Joggers and picnickers congregate in the 28-hectare **Jardin des Tuileries** (Tuileries Garden; Map pp378-9; ☎ 01 40 20 90 43; 7am-9pm Apr, May & Sep, 7am-11pm Jun-Aug, 7.30am-7.30pm Oct-Mar; M Tuileries or Concorde), laid out in the mid-17th century by André Le Nôtre, designer of the Versailles gardens (p396).

> **PARIS FOR FREE**
>
> Paris sure ain't cheap, but a visit to the City of Lights doesn't have to blow your budget. Here are a few of our favourite free treats:
>
> - Turn up some treasures at the **Marché aux Puces de St-Ouen** (p387)
> - Pack a picnic for the **Jardin du Luxembourg** (p381)
> - Wander the celebrity gravestones at the **Cimetière du Père Lachaise** (p386)
> - Marvel at the architectural ambition of **Cathédrale de Notre Dame** (opposite)
> - Watch the painters and portraitists at work on **place du Tertre** (p386) in Montmartre

ARC DE TRIOMPHE

The **Arc de Triomphe** (Map pp378-9; ☎ 01 55 37 73 77; www.monuments-nationaux.fr; viewing platform adult/18-25yr €9/6.50, 1st Sun of month Nov-Mar free; 10am-11pm Apr-Sep, to 10.30pm Oct-Mar; M Charles de Gaulle-Étoile) stands in the middle of the world's largest traffic roundabout, **place de l'Étoile** (Map pp378-9; M Charles de Gaulle Étoile), officially known as place Charles de Gaulle. The 'triumphal arch' was commissioned in 1806 by Napoleon to commemorate his victories, but remained unfinished when he started losing battles, and wasn't completed until 1836. Since 1920, the body of an **unknown soldier** from WWI has lain beneath the arch; a memorial flame is rekindled each evening around 6.30pm.

The **viewing platform** affords wonderful views of the dozen avenues that radiate out from the arch, many of which are named after Napoleonic generals. **Av Foch** is Paris' widest boulevard, while **av des Champs-Elysées** leads south to place de la Concorde and its famous 3300-year-old pink granite obelisk, which once stood in the Temple of Ramses at Thebes (present-day Luxor).

CENTRE POMPIDOU

Opened in 1977, the inside-out **Centre National d'Art et de Culture Georges Pompidou** (Georges Pompidou National Centre of Art & Culture; Map pp382-3;

(☎ 01 44 78 12 33; www.centrepompidou.fr; place Georges Pompidou, 4e; Ⓜ Rambuteau) is a huge cultural and artistic centre, housing the **Musée National d'Art Moderne** (MNAM, National Museum of Modern Art; Map pp382-3; adult €10-12, 18-25yr €8-10, 6-9pm Wed free for 18-25yr, 1st Sun of month free for all; 🕒 11am-9pm Wed-Mon). Nearby place Igor Stravinsky is famous for its fanciful mechanical fountains.

PLACE DES VOSGES

The Marais, the area of the Right Bank north of Île St-Louis in the 3e and 4e, was transformed into one of the city's most fashionable districts by Henri IV, who constructed the elegant *hôtels particuliers* around place Royale – today known as the **Place des Vosges** (Map pp382-3; Ⓜ St-Paul or Bastille).

The novelist Victor Hugo lived here from 1832 to 1848, and the **Maison de Victor Hugo** (Victor Hugo House; Map pp382-3; ☎ 01 42 72 10 16; www.musee-hugo.paris.fr, in French; permanent collections admission free, temporary exhibitions adult/14-26yr/student €7.50/5.50/3.50; 🕒 10am-6pm Tue-Sun) contains drawings, paintings and memorabilia relating to the author.

MUSÉE PICASSO

The **Picasso Museum** (Map pp382-3; ☎ 01 42 71 25 21; www.musee-picasso.fr, in French; 5 rue de Thorigny, 3e; adult/18-25yr €7.70/5.70, 1st Sun of month free; 🕒 9.30am-6pm Wed-Mon Apr-Sep, 9.30am-5.30pm Wed-Mon Oct-Mar; Ⓜ St-Paul or Chemin Vert) contains more than 3500 of the *grand maître*'s engravings, paintings, ceramics and sculptures.

PLACE DE LA BASTILLE

The Bastille is the most famous monument in Paris that no longer exists; the notorious prison was demolished by a revolutionary mob on 14 July 1789, and the **place de la Bastille** (Map pp382-3; Ⓜ Bastille), where the prison once stood, is now a busy traffic roundabout. The 52m-high **Colonne de Juillet** (July Column) was erected in memory of Parisians killed during the July Revolution of 1830.

Other Districts

MONTMARTRE & PIGALLE

During the late 19th and early 20th centuries, bohemian **Montmartre** attracted a number of important writers and artists, including Picasso, who lived at the studio called **Bateau Lavoir** (Map p387; 11bis Émile Goudeau; Ⓜ Abbesses) from 1908 to 1912.

Montmartre's most famous landmark is the **Basilique du Sacré Cœur** (Basilica of the Sacred Heart; Map p387; ☎ 01 53 41 89 00; www.sacre-coeur-montmartre.com; place du Parvis du Sacré Cœur, 18e; 🕒 6am-10.30pm; Ⓜ Anvers), whose gleaming white **dome** (admission €5; 🕒 9am-7pm Apr-Sep, 9am-6pm Oct-Mar) has one of the most spectacular city panoramas anywhere in Paris.

Nearby **place du Tertre** (Map pp378-9; Ⓜ Abbesses) was once the main square of the village of Montmartre; these days it's filled with cafes, restaurants, endless tourists and a concentrated cluster of caricaturists and painters – if you want to get your portrait painted in Paris, this is definitely the place.

Only a few blocks southwest of the tranquil residential streets of Montmartre is lively, neon-lit **Pigalle** (9e and 18e), one of Paris' two main sex districts. It's connected to the top of Butte de Montmartre (Montmartre Hill) by a funicular.

DALÍ ESPACE MONTMARTRE

More than 300 works by Salvador Dalí (1904–89), the flamboyant Catalan surrealist printmaker, painter, sculptor and self-promoter, are on display at the **Dalí Espace Montmartre** (Dalí Exhibition Space Montmartre; Map p387; ☎ 01 42 64 40 10; www.daliparis.com; 11 rue Poulbot, 18e; adult/student & 8-26yr €10/6; 🕒 10am-6.30pm; Ⓜ Abbesses).

CIMETIÈRE DU PÈRE LACHAISE

The world's most-visited graveyard, **Cimetière du Père Lachaise** (Père Lachaise Cemetery; Map pp378-9; ☎ 01 55 25 82 10; admission free; 🕒 8am-6pm Mon-Fri, 8.30am-6pm Sat, 9am-6pm Sun mid-Mar–early Nov, 8am-5.30pm Mon-Fri, 8.30am-5.30pm Sat, 9am-5.30pm Sun early Nov–mid-Mar; Ⓜ Philippe Auguste, Gambetta or Père Lachaise) contains the tombs of over 800,000 people, including Chopin, Molière, Balzac, Proust, Gertrude Stein, Pissarro, Seurat, Modigliani, Édith Piaf, Oscar Wilde and the lizard king himself, Jim Morrison. Free maps are available from the **conservation office** (Map pp378-9; 16 rue du Repos, 20e).

TOURS

Fat Tire Bike Tours (Map pp378-9; ☎ 01 56 58 10 54; www.fattirebiketoursparis.com; 24 rue Edgar Faure, 15e; 🕒 office 9am-6pm; Ⓜ La Motte Picquet Grenelle) runs a daily cycling tour (adult/student €24/22) at 11am, plus 3pm from April to October. Night tours (adult/student €28/26) depart at 7pm daily from mid-March to October, and on Tuesday, Thursday, Saturday and Sunday in winter. Tours start near the Eiffel Tower's South Pillar.

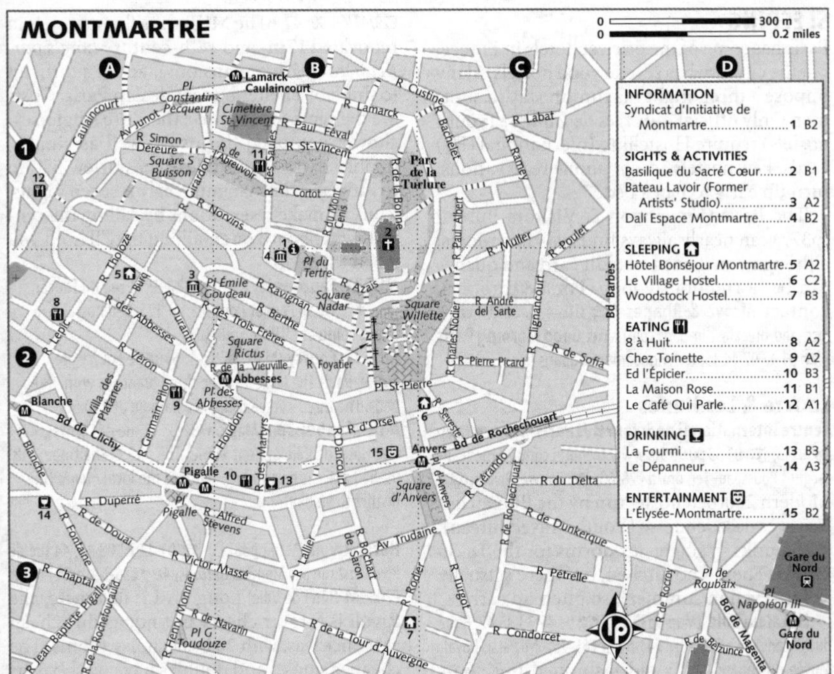

Bateaux Mouches (Map pp378-9; ☎ 01 42 25 96 10; www.bateauxmouches.com, in French; Port de la Conférence, 8e; adult €9; 🕒 mid-Mar–mid-Nov; Ⓜ Alma Marceau) is based just east of the Pont de l'Alma. From April to September, 1000-seater cruises (70 minutes) depart eight times daily between 10.15am and 3.15pm and then every 20 minutes till 11pm. They depart 10 times a day between 10.15am and 9pm the rest of the year. Commentary is in French and English.

Paris Walks (☎ 01 48 09 21 40; www.paris-walks.com; adult/student under 21yr from €10/8) has English-language tours of Montmartre at 10.30am on Sunday and Wednesday (leaving from Abbesses metro station; Map pp378–9) and the Marais at 10.30am on Tuesday and at 2.30pm on Sunday (departing from St-Paul metro station; Map pp378–9). There are other tours focusing on Hemingway, medieval Paris, the Latin Quarter, fashion, the Revolution and even chocolate.

FLEA MARKETS

Even the most chi-chi Parisians aren't above rummaging around the city's wonderful *marchés aux puces* (flea markets).

Marché aux Puces de St-Ouen (Map pp378-9; rue des Rosiers, av Michelet, rue Voltaire, rue Paul Bert & rue Jean-Henri Fabre, 18e; 🕒 11am-5pm Mon, 9am-6pm Sat, 10am-6pm Sun; Ⓜ Porte de Clignancourt) This is the largest, with 2500 stalls grouped into 10 *marchés* (market areas).

Marché aux Puces de la Porte de Vanves (Map pp378-9; av Georges Lafenestre & av Marc Sangnier, 14e; 🕒 7am-6pm or later Sat & Sun; Ⓜ Porte de Vanves) The Porte de Vanves flea market is the smallest and friendliest of the big three, with everything from designer curios to handbags and household goods.

Marché aux Puces de Montreuil (Map pp378-9; av du Professeur André Lemière, 20e; 🕒 8am-7.30pm Sat-Mon; Ⓜ Porte de Montreuil) Established in the 19th century, this flea market is renowned for its second-hand clothing, jewellery and designer seconds.

Book your stay at lonelyplanet.com/hotels

SLEEPING

Paris has some of the priciest hotels in France, but the city also has several good hostels. Many impose a three-night maximum stay in summer. Only official *auberges de jeunesse* (youth hostels) require Hostelling International (HI) cards. Few hostels accept phone reservations; turn up early to bag a bed.

The Paris Convention & Visitors Bureau (p377) can nearly always find available rooms, although you'll need a credit card and queues can be horrendously long. For B&B rooms, contact **Alcôve & Agapes** (☎ 01 44 85 06 05; www.bed-and-breakfast-in-paris.com) and **Good Morning Paris** (☎ 01 47 07 44 45; www.goodmorningparis.fr).

Louvre & Les Halles

Centre International de Séjour BVJ Paris–Louvre (Map pp382-3; ☎ 01 53 00 90 90; www.bvjhotel.com; 20 rue Jean-Jacques Rousseau, 1er; dm/d €28/60; Ⓜ Louvre-Rivoli; 💻) Modern 200-bed hostel run by the Bureau des Voyages de la Jeunesse (Youth Travel Bureau), with bunks in single-sex dorms for the 18-35 crowd. There's no kitchen, but there's usually space (even in summer), so pitch up early.

Hôtel de Lille (Map pp378-9; ☎ 01 42 33 33 42; 8 rue du Pélican, 1er; s €35-38, d €43-50, tr €65-75; Ⓜ Palais Royal-Musée du Louvre) This old-fashioned but spotlessly clean 13-room hotel is down a quiet side street. Some rooms have just washbasin and bidet (communal showers cost €3), while the rest have showers too.

Marais & Bastille

Auberge de Jeunesse Jules Ferry (Map pp378-9; ☎ 01 43 57 55 60; www.fuaj.fr; 8 bd Jules Ferry, 11e; dm/d €21/42; Ⓜ République or Goncourt; ⌘ 💻) This 'official' hostel offers 99 beds in two- to six-person rooms, all locked between 10.30am and 2pm for housekeeping (but there's no curfew). HI cards buy a discount of €2.90 per night.

our pick **Maison Internationale de la Jeunesse et des Étudiants** (☎ 01 42 74 23 45; www.mije.com; dm/s/d/tr €29/47/68/90; 💻) The MIJE runs three hostels in renovated 17th- and 18th-century *hôtels particuliers* (private mansions), and it's difficult to think of a better budget deal in Paris. Costs are the same for all three; there are single-sex, shower-equipped dorms, as well as singles, doubles/twins and triples. The curfew is 1am to 7am, and the maximum stay is seven nights. You can make reservations by calling the central switchboard or emailing; they'll hold you a bed till noon.

MIJE Le Fauconnier (Map pp382-3; 11 rue du Fauconnier, 4e; Ⓜ St-Paul or Pont Marie) 125-bed hostel two blocks south of MIJE Le Fourcy.

MIJE Le Fourcy (Map pp382-3; 6 rue de Fourcy, 4e; Ⓜ St-Paul) The largest of the three branches with 180 beds. The three-course *menu* is a bargain at €10.50.

MIJE Maubuisson (Map pp382-3; 12 rue des Barres, 4e; Ⓜ Hôtel de Ville or Pont Marie) The pick of the three, this 99-bed place is half a block south of the local *mairie* (the district town hall).

Hôtel Rivoli (Map pp382-3; ☎ 01 42 72 08 41; 44 rue de Rivoli or 2 rue des Mauvais Garçons, 4e; s €35-55, d €44-55, tr €70; Ⓜ Hôtel de Ville) Long an LP favourite, the Rivoli is forever cheery but not as dirt cheap as it once was, with 20 basic, noisy rooms. The cheaper singles and doubles have washbasins only but showers are free. The front door is locked from 2am to 7am.

Hôtel de Nevers (Map pp382-3; ☎ 01 47 00 56 18; www.hoteldenevers.com; 53 rue de Malte, 11e; s €39, d €45-55, tr €75-87; Ⓜ Oberkampf; 💻) This 32-room budget hotel is handy for the Marais nightlife. Cheaper rooms share bathing facilities, and if you like cats you'll be happy here – there are three in-house moggies to greet prospective guests.

Hôtel Jeanne d'Arc (Map pp382-3; ☎ 01 48 87 62 11; www.hoteljeannedarc.com; 3 rue de Jarente, 4e; s €60-97, d €84-97, tr/q €116/146; Ⓜ St-Paul; 💻) Near place du Marché Ste-Catherine, this cosy, 36-room hotel almost has a country feel and is a great little base for exploring the Marais.

CAMPING IN PARIS

Camping du Bois de Boulogne (☎ 01 45 24 30 00; www.campingparis.fr; 2 allée du Bord de l'Eau, 16e; camp sites low/mid/peak season €11/15.20/16.80, with vehicle, tent & 2 people €24/28.60/31.90, 1st-time booking fee €14) The only camping ground within the city limits covers 7 hectares along the Seine at the far-western edge of the Bois de Boulogne. Be warned – it gets *very* crowded in summer.

Porte Maillot metro station, 4.5km northeast, is linked to the camping ground by RATP bus No 244; alight at Les Moulins-Camping stop. From April to October the camping ground runs a shuttle bus (€1.80; from 8.45am to 12.15pm and 6.30pm to midnight) from the metro.

SPLURGE

our pick Hôtel Caron de Beaumarchais (Map pp378-9; ☎ 01 42 72 34 12; www.carondebeaumarchais.com; 12 rue Vieille du Temple, 4e; r €125-162; Ⓜ St-Paul; ✇ 💻) Decorated as an 18th-century private house, this is an ostentatious little gem. An 18th-century *pianoforte,* gaming tables, gilded mirrors and candelabras set the tone in the palatial lobby, but the 19 rooms are smallish and the welcome's rather frosty.

Hôtel Sévigné (Map pp382-3; ☎ 01 42 72 76 17; www.le-sevigne.com; 2 rue Malher, 4e; s €67, d & tw €80-91, tr €107; Ⓜ St-Paul; ✇) Named after the celebrated 17th-century writer the Marquise de Sévigné, and offering an excellent price:location ratio. The hotel's 29 rooms, spread over six lift-accessible floors, are basic but comfortably furnished.

Latin Quarter

Young & Happy Hostel (Map pp382-3; ☎ 01 47 07 47 07; www.youngandhappy.fr; 80 rue Mouffetard, 5e; dm/d €23/52; Ⓜ Place Monge; 💻) Frayed but friendly spot, popular with a slightly older crowd. Beds are in cramped rooms for two to eight people with washbasins. Turn up pre-8am if you want to bag a bed in summer.

Centre International de Séjour BVJ Paris–Quartier Latin (Map pp382-3; ☎ 01 43 29 34 80; www.bvjhotel.com; 44 rue des Bernardins, 5e; dm/s/d €28/42/64; Ⓜ Maubert Mutualité; 💻) This Left Bank hostel is a sister branch of the Centre International BVJ Paris–Louvre. It offers 100 beds in singles, doubles and single-sex dorms for four to 10 people, all with showers and telephones.

Port Royal Hôtel (Map pp378-9; ☎ 01 43 31 70 06; www.hotelportroyal.fr; 8 bd de Port Royal, 5e; s €41-89, d €52.50-89; Ⓜ Les Gobelins) It's hard to believe that this 46-room hotel, owned and managed by the same family for three generations, still only bears one star. The spotless, quiet rooms overlook a glassed-in courtyard (eg No 15) or the street (No 14), but we especially like room No 11, with its colourful bed frame and pretty bathroom.

Hôtel Esmeralda (Map pp382-3; ☎ 01 43 54 19 20; fax 01 40 51 00 68; 4 rue St-Julien le Pauvre, 5e; s €35-95, d €85-95, tr/q €110/120; Ⓜ St-Michel) Tucked away in a quiet street with full views of Notre Dame (choose room No 12!), the Esmeralda has been everyone's secret 'find' for years now, so book well in advance. The three cheapest singles have washbasin only, there's no lift and some rooms share a toilet.

Clichy & Gare St-Lazare

Style Hôtel (Map pp378-9; ☎ 01 45 22 37 59; fax 01 45 22 81 03; 8 rue Ganneron, 18e; s & d €35-50, tr/q €57/67; Ⓜ La Fourche) This 36-room hotel is a bit rough around the edges (rough wooden floors, old runner carpets in the hallways) but is loaded with character and the welcome is always charming.

Hôtel Eldorado (Map pp378-9; ☎ 01 45 22 35 21; www.eldoradohotel.fr; 18 rue des Dames, 17e; s €35-57, d & tw €68-80, tr €80-90; Ⓜ Place de Clichy) The bohemian Eldorado is one of Paris' great finds: a welcoming, well-run place with 23 colourfully decorated rooms divided between a quiet main building and a garden-backed annexe.

Gare du Nord, Gare de l'Est & République

Peace & Love Hostel (Map pp378-9; ☎ 01 46 07 65 11; www.paris-hostels.com; 245 rue La Fayette, 10e; dm/d €25/60; Ⓜ Jaurès or Louis Blanc; 💻) This modern-day hippy hang-out is a groovy though chronically crowded hostel with beds in 21 smallish, shower-equipped rooms for two to four people. There's a great kitchen and eating area, and the bar stays open till 2am.

Sibour Hôtel (Map pp378-9; ☎ 01 46 07 20 74; www.hotel-sibour.com; 4 rue Sibour, 10e; s €40-55, d €45-65, tr/q €80/110; Ⓜ Gare de l'Est) This friendly place has 45 well-kept rooms, including some old-fashioned ones – the cheapest singles and doubles – with washbasins only. Hall showers cost €3. Some of the rooms overlook pretty Église de St-Laurent.

Hôtel La Vieille France (Map pp378-9; ☎ 01 45 26 42 37; la.vieille.france@wanadoo.fr; 151 rue La Fayette, 10e; s €48, d €75-85, tr €120; Ⓜ Gare du Nord; 💻) The 'Old France' is an upbeat, 34-room place with relatively spacious and pleasant rooms, though with the Gare du Nord so close it's bound to be somewhat noisy.

Gare de Lyon, Nation & Bercy

Blue Planet Hostel (Map pp382-3; ☎ 01 43 42 06 18; www.hostelblueplanet.com; 5 rue Hector Malot, 12e; dm €21; Ⓜ Gare de Lyon; 💻) This 43-room hostel is very close to Gare de Lyon – convenient if you're heading south or west at the crack of dawn. Dorm beds are in rooms for two to four people. The hostel closes between 11am and 3pm, but there's no curfew.

Hôtel Le Cosy (Map pp378-9; ☎ 01 43 43 10 02; www.hotel-cosy.com; 50 av de St-Mandé, 12e; s €40-65, d €50-99;

M Picpus;) This family-run budget hotel oozes charm. The 28 rooms, though basic, are decorated in original artwork and hardwood floors; for extra luxury there are four 'VIP' rooms.

Montmartre & Pigalle

Woodstock Hostel (Map p387; ☎ 01 48 78 87 76; www.woodstock.fr; 48 rue Rodier, 9e; dm €18-21, d €42-48; M Anvers;) Woodstock is just downhill from raucous Pigalle in a quiet, residential quarter. Dorm beds are in rooms for four to six people; showers and toilets are off the corridor. Rooms are shut from 11am to 3pm, and the curfew is at 2am. Recent additions include a spanking new eat-in kitchen.

Le Village Hostel (Map p387; ☎ 01 42 64 22 02; www.villagehostel.fr; 20 rue d'Orsel, 18e; dm/d/tr €24/60/81; M Anvers;) A fine 25-room hostel with beamed ceilings and views of Sacré Cœur. Dorms all have showers and toilets. Kitchen facilities are available, and there's a bar too (no curfew).

Hôtel Bonséjour Montmartre (Map p387; ☎ 01 42 54 22 53; www.hotel-bonsejour-montmartre.fr; 11 rue Burq, 18e; s €33-40, d €44-55, tr €58-65; M Abbesses;) The 'Good Stay' is a perennial budget favourite. It's a simple place – hall showers, no lift – but welcoming and comfortable. Some rooms (14, 23, 33, 43 and 53) have little balconies.

EATING

When it comes to food, Paris has everything. As the culinary centre of the most aggressively gastronomic country in the world, the city has more 'generic French', regional and ethnic restaurants than any other place in France.

Louvre & Les Halles

Higuma (Map pp382-3; ☎ 01 58 62 49 22; 163 rue St-Honoré, 1er; dishes €7-12.50, menus €10-€11.50; lunch & dinner; M Palais Royal-Musée du Louvre) This no-nonsense Japanese noodle shop offers incredible value. Try the *gyoza* (dumplings) and the fried noodles with pork.

Le Petit Mâchon (Map pp382-3; ☎ 01 42 60 08 06; 158 rue St-Honoré, 1er; starters €7-12.50, mains €14-22; lunch & dinner Tue-Sun; M Palais Royal-Musée du Louvre) An upbeat bistro with Lyon-inspired specialities. Try the *saucisson de Lyon* (Lyon sausage) studded with pistachios.

Scoop (Map pp382-3; ☎ 01 42 60 31 84; 154 rue St-Honoré, 1er; dishes €10.90-16.90; 11am-7pm; M Palais Royal-Musée du Louvre) This American-style ice-cream parlour has been making quite a splash for its wraps, burgers, tarts and soups and central, trendy location. Sunday brunch (11.30am to 4pm) includes pancakes with maple syrup.

Joe Allen (Map pp382-3; ☎ 01 42 36 70 13; 30 rue Pierre Lescot, 1er; starters €7.50-10.30, mains €15.50-26, lunch menus €13.90-22.50, dinner menus €18-22.50; noon-1am; M Étienne Marcel) An institution in Paris since 1972, Joe Allen is a little bit of New York in Paris. There's an excellent brunch (€19.50 to €23.50) from noon to 4pm at the weekend.

Supermarkets around Forum des Halles include **Franprix Les Halles** (Map pp378-9; 35 rue Berger, 1er; 8.30am-9.50pm Mon-Sat; M Châtelet) and the **Franprix Châtelet** (Map pp382-3; 16 rue Bertin Poirée, 1er; 8.30am-8pm Mon-Sat; M Châtelet).

Marais & Bastille

L'As de Felafel (Map pp382-3; ☎ 01 48 87 63 60; 34 rue des Rosiers, 4e; dishes €5-7; noon-midnight Sun-Thu,

TO MARKET, TO MARKET

Paris has about 70 *marchés découverts* (open-air markets) and another dozen *marchés couverts* (covered markets, open generally from 8am to 1pm and 3.30pm to 7pm Tuesday to Saturday, to lunchtime on Sunday).

Marché Bastille (Map pp382-3; bd Richard Lenoir, 11e; 7am-2.30pm Tue & Sun; M Bastille or Richard Lenoir) Arguably the best open-air market in Paris.

Marché Belleville (Map pp378-9; bd de Belleville btwn rue Jean-Pierre Timbaud & rue du Faubourg du Temple, 11e & 20e; 7am-2.30pm Tue & Fri; M Belleville or Couronne) Large ethnic market popular with the African, Asian and Middle Eastern immigrants of the *quartiers de l'est* (eastern neighbourhoods).

Marché Rue Cler (Map pp378-9; rue Cler, 7e; 8am-7pm Tue-Sat, 8am-noon Sun; M École Militaire) Commercial street market in the sometimes-stuffy 7e, with an almost party-like atmosphere on weekends.

Marché Rue Mouffetard (Map pp378-9; rue Mouffetard around rue de l'Arbalète; 8am-7.30pm Tue-Sat, 8am-noon Sun; M Censier Daubenton) Rue Mouffetard is the city's most photogenic market street – the place where Parisians send tourists (travellers go to Marché Bastille.

Marché St-Quentin (Map pp378-9; 85 bd de Magenta, 10e; 8am-1pm & 3.30-7.30pm Tue-Sat, 8.30am-1pm Sun; M Gare de l'Est) Iron-and-glass covered market built in 1866 lined with gourmet food stalls.

SPLURGE

our pick L'Ambassade d'Auvergne (Map pp382-3; ☎ 01 42 72 31 22; 22 rue du Grenier St-Lazare, 3e; starters €8-16, mains €14-22, lunch menus €20-28, dinner menus €28; lunch & dinner; M Rambuteau) The 100-year-old 'Auvergne Embassy' is the place to go if you're hungry; the sausages and hams of this region are among the best in France. The house special is *clafoutis,* a custard and cherry tart baked upside down like a *tarte tatin* (caramelised apple pie).

noon-5pm Fri; M St-Paul) Our favourite place for deep-fried falafels (€6.50). It's always packed at lunchtime.

Breakfast in America (Map pp382-3; ☎ 01 42 72 40 21; 4 rue Malher, 4e; meals €6.50-12; 8.30am-11.30pm; M St-Paul) American-style diner, complete with red banquettes and Formica surfaces. Breakfast, served all day and with free coffee refills, starts at €6.50, and there are generous burgers, chicken wings and fish and chips.

Le Trumilou (Map pp382-3; ☎ 01 42 77 63 98; 84 quai de l'Hôtel de Ville, 4e; starters €4.50-13, mains €15-22, menus €16.50 & €19.50; lunch & dinner; M Hôtel de Ville) This no-frills bistro is a Parisian institution for classic French cooking: try *confit aux pruneaux* (duck with prunes) and the *ris de veau grand-mère* (veal sweetbreads).

Robert et Louise (Map pp382-3; ☎ 01 42 78 55 89; 64 rue Vieille du Temple, 3e; starters €6-13, mains €12-18, lunch menus €12; lunch & dinner Tue-Sat; M St-Sébastien Froissart) This 'country inn', complete with its red gingham curtains, offers delightful, simple and inexpensive French food, including *côte de bœuf* (side of beef, €40 for two).

For all-round atmosphere, check out the Marché Bastille (opposite), and for general supplies try **Franprix** Marais (Map pp382-3; 135 rue St-Antoine, 4e; 9am-9pm Mon-Sat; M St-Paul); Hôtel de Ville (Map pp382-3; 87 rue de la Verrerie, 4e; 9.30am-9pm Mon-Sat; M Hôtel de Ville) or **Monoprix** Marais (Map pp378-9; 71 rue St- Antoine, 4e; 9am-9pm Mon-Sat; M St-Paul); Bastille (Map pp382-3; 97 rue du Faubourg St-Antoine, 11e; 9am-9.45pm Mon-Sat; M Ledru Rollin).

Latin Quarter & Jardin des Plantes

Kootchi (Map pp382-3; ☎ 01 44 07 20 56; 40 rue du Cardinal Lemoine, 5e; mains €12, lunch menus €9.50-15.50, dinner menus €12.50-15.50; lunch & dinner Mon-Sat; M Cardinal Lemoine) Afghan grub such as *qhaboli palawo* (veal 'stew' with nuts and spices) and traditional halva perfumed with rose and cardamom.

Le Baba Bourgeois (Map pp378-9; ☎ 01 44 07 46 75; 5 quai de la Tournelle, 5e; mains €15-20; lunch & dinner Wed-Sat, 11.30am-5pm Sun; M Cardinal Lemoine or Pont Marie) Contemporary dining in a former architect's studio. Its *tartines* (open-face sandwiches), terrines, *tartes salées* (savoury tarts) and salads are delicious, and there's an all-you-can-eat Sunday buffet.

Place Maubert becomes the lively food market Marché Maubert on Tuesday, Thursday and Saturday mornings, while rue Mouffetard (opposite) and **place Monge** (Map pp378-9; place Monge, 5e; 7am-2pm Wed, Fri & Sun; M Place Monge) both have their own street markets.

Supermarkets:

Ed l'Épicier (Map pp382-3; 37 rue Lacépède, 5e; 9am-1pm & 3-7.30pm Mon-Fri, 9am-7.30pm Sat; M Place Monge)

Franprix (Map pp382-3; 82 rue Mouffetard, 5e; 8.30am-8.50pm Mon-Sat; M Censier Daubenton or Place Monge)

Monoprix (Map pp382-3; 24 bd St-Michel, 5e; 9am-midnight Mon-Sat; M St-Michel)

St-Germain, Odéon & Luxembourg

Bar à Soupes et Quenelles Giraudet (Map pp382-3; ☎ 01 43 25 44 44; 5 rue Princesse, 6e; meals from €7.50; 10am-5pm Mon, 10am-5pm & 7-11.30pm Tue-Fri, 10am-11.30pm Sat; M Mabillon) This soup and dumpling bar serves unusual soups – pear and litchi (lychee), chestnut or cardoon – plus Lyonnais-style *quenelles* (pike-perch dumplings).

Cosi (Map pp382-3; ☎ 01 46 33 35 36; 54 rue de Seine, 6e; sandwich menus €9-11; noon-11pm; M Odéon) With sandwich names like Stonker, Tom Dooley and Naked Willi, Kiwi-owned Cosi could easily run for Paris' most imaginative sandwich maker.

THE GOURMET GLACIER

our pick Berthillon (Map pp382-3; ☎ 01 43 54 31 61; 31 rue St-Louis en l'Île, 4e; ice cream €2-5.40; 10am-8pm Wed-Sun; M Pont Marie) For Paris' finest ice-cream, head for Berthillon on Île St-Louis. There are some 70 flavours to choose from, ranging from fruity cassis to chocolate, coffee, *marrons glacés* (candied chestnuts), *Agenaise* (Armagnac and prunes), *noisette* (hazelnut) and *nougat au miel* (honey nougat). One just won't be enough…

Gare du Nord, Gare de l'Est & République

Krishna Bhavan (Map pp378-9; ☎ 01 42 05 78 43; 2 rue Cail, 10e; dishes €1.50-7.50, menus €10.50; lunch & dinner Tue-Sun; Ⓜ La Chapelle) This is about as authentic an Indian vegetarian canteen as you'll find in Paris. If in doubt, ask for a *thali* (€7.50) of samosas, dosas and other wrapped goodies.

Passage Brady (Map pp378-9; 46 rue du Faubourg St-Denis & 33 bd de Strasbourg, 10e; lunch & dinner; Ⓜ Château d'Eau) This covered arcade has dozens of cheap Indian, Pakistani and Bangladeshi cafes offering excellent-value lunches – meat curry, rice and a tiny salad (€5 to €9.50), chicken or lamb biriani (€10.50 to €14.50) and *thalis* (€7 to €9.50). Dinner menus are from €12.50 to €24.

Montmartre & Pigalle

Chez Toinette (Map p387; ☎ 01 42 54 44 36; 20 rue Germain Pilon, 18e; starters €6-9, mains €15-20; dinner Tue-Sat; Ⓜ Abbesses) This convivial authentic French restaurant has somehow managed to keep alive the tradition of old Montmartre in one of the capital's most touristy neighbourhoods.

Le Café Qui Parle (Map p387; ☎ 01 46 06 06 88; 24 rue Caulaincourt, 18e; starters €7-14, mains €13.50-20, menus €12.50-17; lunch & dinner Thu-Tue; Ⓜ Lamarck Caulaincourt or Blanche) 'The Talking Cafe' offers inventive, reasonably priced dishes. We love the art on the walls. Brunch (€15) is served from 10am on Saturday and Sunday.

La Maison Rose (Map p387; ☎ 01 42 57 66 75; 2 rue de l'Abreuvoir, 18e; starters €7.20-13, mains €14.50-16.50, menus €16.50; lunch & dinner daily Mar-Oct, lunch & dinner to 9pm Thu-Mon Nov-Feb; Ⓜ Lamarck Caulaincourt) Looking for the quintessential Montmartre bistro? Head for the tiny 'Pink House' just north of place du Tertre. It's not so much about food but rather location, location, location.

Self-catering options:

8 à Huit (Map p387; 24 rue Lepic, 18e; 8.30am-10.30pm Mon-Sat; Ⓜ Abbesses)

Ed l'Épicier (Map p387; 6 bd de Clichy, 18e; 9am-9pm Mon-Sat; Ⓜ Pigalle)

DRINKING

Drinking in Paris means paying the rent for the space you are occupying – it costs more sitting at tables than standing, more on a fancy square than a backstreet, more in the 8e than the 18e.

Louvre & Les Halles

Le Fumoir (Map pp378-9; ☎ 01 42 92 00 24; 6 rue de l'Amiral Coligny, 1er; 11am-2am; Ⓜ Louvre-Rivoli) The 'Smoking Room' is a huge, stylish colonial-style bar-cafe opposite the Louvre. It's a fine place to sip top-notch gin while nibbling on olives; during happy hour (6pm to 8pm), cocktails, usually €8.50 to €11, drop to €6.

Marais & Bastille

La Perle (Map pp378-9; ☎ 01 42 72 69 93; 78 rue Vieille du Temple, 3e; 6am-2am Mon-Fri, 8am-2am Sat & Sun; Ⓜ St-Paul or Chemin Vert) This is where *bobos* (bohemian bourgeois types) come to slum it over *un rouge* (glass of red wine) until the DJ arrives and things liven up.

our pick **Le Loir dans la Théière** (Map pp378-9; ☎ 01 42 72 90 61; 3 rue des Rosiers, 4e; 9.30am-7pm; Ⓜ St-Paul) The 'Dormouse in the Teapot' is filled with retro toys and comfy couches, while scenes of *Through the Looking Glass* decorate the walls. It serves sandwiches, sticky puddings and a dozen teas, plus stronger stuff after dark.

Le Pick Clops (Map pp378-9; ☎ 01 40 29 02 18; 16 rue Vieille du Temple, 4e; 7am-2am Mon-Sat, 8am-2am Sun; Ⓜ Hôtel de Ville or St-Paul) Retro neon-lit cafe-bar with formica tables, ancient bar stools and mirrors. Try the rum punch.

Latin Quarter & Jardin des Plantes

Le Piano Vache (Map pp382-3; ☎ 01 46 33 75 03; 8 rue Laplace, 5e; noon-2am Mon-Fri, 9pm-2am Sat & Sun; Ⓜ Maubert Mutualité) Just downhill from the Panthéon, the 'Mean Piano' is effortlessly underground, and a huge favourite with students. Bands and DJs play mainly rock, plus some Goth, reggae and pop.

Le Pub St-Hilaire (Map pp378-9; www.pubsthilaire.com; 2 rue Valette, 5e; 11am-2am Mon-Thu, 11am-4am Fri, 4pm-4am Sat, 3pm-midnight Sun; Ⓜ Maubert Mutualité) 'Buzzing' fails to do justice to this student-loved pub. Happy hours last forever, while pool tables, boardgames, and music on two floors keep the punters happy.

St-Germain, Odéon & Luxembourg

Le 10 (Map pp378-9; ☎ 01 43 26 66 83; 10 rue de l'Odéon, 6e; 5.30pm-2am; Ⓜ Odéon) A local institution, this cellar pub groans with students, smoky ambience and cheap sangria. Posters adorn the walls, and an eclectic jukebox jumps from jazz and the Doors to *chansons françaises*.

Le Comptoir des Canettes (Map pp382-3; ☎ 01 43 26 79 15; 11 rue des Canettes, 6e; noon-2am Tue-Sat; Ⓜ Mabillon) A faithful local following pours into this basement bar, draped with red tablecloths, melting candles and nostalgic photos of musicians.

Opéra & Grands Boulevards

De la Ville Café (Map pp378-9; ☎ 01 48 24 48 09; 34 bd de Bonne Nouvelle, 10e; 🕑 11am-2.30am; Ⓜ Bonne Nouvelle) This one-time brothel has an alluring mix of restored history and modern design. DJs play most nights, so it's popular with the preclub crowd.

Montmartre & Pigalle

La Fourmi (Map p387; ☎ 01 42 64 70 35; 74 rue des Martyrs, 18e; 🕑 8am-2am Mon-Thu, 8am-4am Fri & Sat, 10am-2am Sun; Ⓜ Pigalle) A Pigalle stayer, 'The Ant' always hits the mark: hip but not snobby, with a laid-back crowd and a rock-oriented playlist.

Le Dépanneur (Map p387; ☎ 01 44 53 03 78; 27 rue Pierre Fontaine, 9e; 🕑 10am-2am Mon-Thu, 24hr Fri-Sun; Ⓜ Blanche) An American-style diner-cum-bar open (almost) round-the-clock, 'The Repairman' specialises in fancy cocktails (€7.50) and DJs after 11pm from Thursday to Saturday.

CLUBBING

Paris' clubbing scene changes fast – the internet's usually the best place to find out where the action's at. Admission costs anything from €5 to €20 and is usually cheaper before 1am.

La Dame de Canton (Map pp378-9; ☎ 01 53 61 08 49, 06 10 41 02 29; www.damedecanton.com, in French; opp 11 quai François Mauriac, 13e; admission €10; 🕑 7pm-2am Tue-Thu, 7pm-dawn Fri & Sat; Ⓜ Quai de la Gare or Bibliothèque) This floating *boîte* (club) aboard a three-masted Chinese junk hosts DJs and concerts (8.30pm) ranging from pop and indie to electro, hip-hop and rock.

Point Éphémère (Map pp378-9; ☎ 01 40 34 02 48; www.pointephemere.org; 200 quai de Valmy, 10e; admission free-€14; 🕑 10am-2am; Ⓜ Louis Blanc) A new arrival by the Canal St-Martin with some of the best electronic music nights in town. Once this self-proclaimed 'centre for dynamic artists' gets in gear, '*on y danse, on danse*' (you'll dance your arse off).

Social Club (Map pp378-9; ☎ 01 40 28 05 55; www.myspace.com/parissocialclub; 142 rue Montmartre, 2e; admission free-€20; 🕑 11pm-3am Wed & Sun, to 6am Thu-Sat; Ⓜ Grands Boulevards) Once known as Triptyque, this vast club occupies three underground rooms pumping out electro, hip-hop and funk, as well as jazz and live acts.

DIGITAL CLUBBING

Track tomorrow's hot 'n' happening *soirée au feeling* with these Parisian nightlife links.

- www.gogoparis.com
- www.lemonsound.com, in French
- www.novaplanet.com, in French
- www.parisbouge.com, in French
- www.parissi.com, in French
- www.radiofg.com, in French
- www.tribudenuit.com, in French

ENTERTAINMENT

All the latest listings are covered in *Pariscope* (€0.40) or *Officiel des Spectacles* (€0.35), published every Wednesday. For more general info, try the freebies such as **À Nous Paris** (www.anous.fr/paris, in French) and **LYLO** (www.lylo.fr, in French), both available at bars and cafes.

Tickets are sold at *billeteries* (ticket offices) in **Fnac** (☎ 08 92 68 36 22; www.fnacspectacles.com, in French) or **Virgin Megastores** (☎ 08 25 12 91 39; www.virginmega.fr, in French).

Live Music

La Cigale (Map pp378-9; ☎ 01 49 25 89 99; www.lacigale.fr; 120 bd de Rochechouart, 18e; admission €25-60; Ⓜ Anvers or Pigalle) A music hall dating from 1887, which prides itself on its avant-garde musical program.

L'Élysée-Montmartre (Map p387; ☎ 01 44 92 45 47; www.elyseemontmartre.com; 72 bd de Rochechouart, 18e; admission €15-45; Ⓜ Anvers) Another old music hall specialising in one-off rock and indie concerts.

Le Bataclan (Map pp382-3; ☎ 01 43 14 00 30; www.bataclan.fr, in French; 50 bd Voltaire, 11e; admission €20-45; Ⓜ Oberkampf or St-Ambroise) Actor and singer Maurice Chevalier's debut venue still draws French and international acts.

GETTING THERE & AWAY

Air

AÉROPORT D'ORLY

Orly (ORY; off Map pp378-9; ☎ 39 50, 01 70 36 39 50; www.aeroportsdeparis.fr), the older and smaller of Paris' two major airports, is 18km south of the city.

AÉROPORT ROISSY CHARLES DE GAULLE

Roissy Charles de Gaulle (CDG; off Map pp378-9; ☎ 39 50, 01 70 36 39 50; www.aeroportsdeparis.fr), 30km northeast of central Paris, consists of three terminal complexes and two train stations, linked to the TGV network.

AÉROPORT PARIS-BEAUVAIS

Charter companies as well as Ryanair, Central Wings and other budget airlines use the international airport at **Beauvais** (BVA; off Map pp378-9; ☎ 08 92 68 20 66, 03 44 11 46 86; www.aeroportbeauvais.com), 85km north of Paris.

Bus

DOMESTIC

France's intercity bus system is practically nonexistent – for domestic destinations, you're much better off travelling by train.

INTERNATIONAL

Eurolines links Paris with most parts of Western and Central Europe, Scandinavia and Morocco. The central **Eurolines office** (Map pp382-3; ☎ 01 43 54 11 99; www.eurolines.fr; 55 rue St-Jacques, 5e; 9.30am-6.30pm Mon-Fri, 10am-1pm & 2-5pm Sat; M Cluny-La Sorbonne) takes reservations and sells tickets. The **Gare Routière Internationale de Paris-Galliéni** (Map pp378-9; ☎ 08 92 89 90 91; 28 av du Général de Gaulle; M Galliéni), the city's international bus terminal, is in the eastern suburb of Bagnolet.

Train

Paris has six major train stations, each serving different parts of France:

Gare d'Austerlitz (Map pp382-3; bd de l'Hôpital, 13e; M Gare d'Austerlitz) Spain and Portugal; Loire Valley and non-TGV trains to southwestern France.

Gare de l'Est (Map pp378-9; bd de Strasbourg, 10e; M Gare de l'Est) Luxembourg, parts of Switzerland (Basel, Lucerne, Zurich), southern Germany (Frankfurt, Munich) and points further east; regular and TGV Est trains to Champagne, Alsace and Lorraine.

Gare de Lyon (Map pp382-3; bd Diderot, 12e; M Gare de Lyon) Parts of Switzerland (Bern, Geneva, Lausanne), Italy and points beyond; regular and TGV Sud–Est and TGV Midi-Méditerranée trains to areas southeast of Paris, including Dijon, Lyon, Provence, the Côte d'Azur and the Alps.

Gare du Nord (Map pp378-9; rue de Dunkerque, 10e; M Gare du Nord) UK, Belgium, northern Germany, Scandinavia, Moscow etc (terminus of the high-speed Thalys trains to/from Amsterdam, Brussels, Cologne and Geneva and Eurostar to London); trains to northern France, including TGV Nord trains to Lille and Calais.

Gare Montparnasse (Map pp378-9; av du Maine & bd de Vaugirard, 15e; M Montparnasse Bienvenüe) Brittany and places en route from Paris (Chartres, Angers, Nantes); TGV Atlantique Ouest and TGV Atlantique Sud–Ouest trains to Tours, Nantes, Bordeaux and other destinations in southwestern France.

Gare St-Lazare (Map pp378-9; rue St-Lazare & rue d'Amsterdam, 8e; M St-Lazare) Normandy (Dieppe, Le Havre, Cherbourg).

GETTING AROUND

To/From the Airports

AÉROPORT D'ORLY

There are loads of public-transport options to and from Orly airport. Apart from RATP bus 183, all services call at both terminals. Tickets are sold on board.

Air France Bus No 1 (☎ 08 92 35 08 20; www.cars-airfrance.com; one way/return €9/14; 30-45min; every 15min 6am-11.30pm from Orly, 5.45am-11pm from Invalides) This shuttle bus runs to/from the eastern side of Gare Montparnasse (Map pp378-9; rue du Commandant René Mouchotte, 15e; M Montparnasse Bienvenüe) as well as Aérogare des Invalides (Map pp378-9; M Invalides) in the 7e. Request stops include metro stations Porte d'Orléans or Duroc.

Jetbus (☎ 01 69 01 00 09; adult €5.70; 55min; every 15-25min 6.20am-11.10pm from Orly, 6.15am-10.30pm from Paris) Jetbus runs to/from metro Villejuif Louis Aragon (off Map pp378-9) on the city's southern fringe. From there a regular metro/bus ticket will get you into the centre of Paris.

Noctilien Bus No 31 (☎ 08 92 68 77 14, in English 08 92 68 41 14; adult €6; 45min; every 60min 12.30am-5.30pm) Part of the RATP night service, Noctilien bus 31 links Gare de Lyon, Place d'Italie and Gare d'Austerlitz with Orly-Sud.

Orlybus (☎ 08 92 68 77 14; adult €6.10; 30min; every 15-20min 6am-11.50pm from Orly, 5.35am-11.25pm from Paris) This RATP bus runs to/from metro Denfert Rochereau (Map pp378-9) and stops in the eastern 14e.

Orlyval ☎ 08 92 68 77 14; adult €9.30; 35-40min; every 4-12min 6am-11pm) This RATP service links Orly with the city centre via a shuttle train and the RER (see opposite). An automated shuttle train runs between the airport and Antony RER station (eight minutes) on RER line B, from where it's an easy journey into the city; to get to Antony from the city (26 minutes), take line B4 towards St-Rémy-lès-Chevreuse. Orlyval tickets are valid for travel on the RER and metro.

RATP Bus 183 (☎ 08 92 68 77 14; adult €1.50 or 1 metro/bus ticket; 1hr; every 35min 5.35am-8.35pm) Cheap but very slow public bus that links Orly-Sud (only) with Porte de Choisy metro station (Map pp378-9).

RER C (☎ 08 90 36 10 10; adult €6; 50min; every 15-30min 5.30am-11.50pm) An Aéroports de Paris (ADP) shuttle bus links the airport with RER line C at Pont de Rungis-Aéroport d'Orly RER station. From the city, take a C2 train towards Pont de Rungis or Massy-Palaiseau. Tickets remain valid on the metro.

AÉROPORT ROISSY CHARLES DE GAULLE

Roissy Charles de Gaulle has two train stations: Aéroport Charles de Gaulle 1 (CDG1) and the sleek Aéroport Charles de Gaulle 2 (CDG2). Both are served by RER line B3. A free shuttle bus links the terminals with the train stations.

Air France bus 2 (☎ 08 92 35 08 20; www.cars-airfrance.com; one way/return €13/18; 35-50min; every 15min 5.45am-11pm) Air France bus No 2 links the airport with two locations on the Right Bank: near the Arc de Triomphe just outside 2 av Carnot, 17e (Map pp378-9; Ⓜ Charles de Gaulle-Étoile) and the Palais des Congrès de Paris (Map pp378-9; bd Gouvion St-Cyr, 17e; Ⓜ Porte Maillot).
Air France bus 4 (☎ 08 92 35 08 20; www.cars-airfrance.com; one way/return €14/22; 45-55min; every 30min 7am-9pm from Roissy Charles de Gaulle, 6.30am-9.30pm from Paris) Air France bus 4 links the airport with Gare de Lyon (Map pp382-3; 20bis bd Diderot, 12e; Ⓜ Gare de Lyon) and Gare Montparnasse (Map pp378-9; rue du Commandant René Mouchotte, 15e; Ⓜ Montparnasse Bienvenüe).
Noctilien Bus 120, 121 & 140 (☎ 08 92 68 77 14, in English 08 92 68 41 14; adult €7.50; every 60min 12.30am-5.30pm) Part of RATP's night service, Noctilien bus 120 and 121 link Montparnasse, Châtelet and Gare du Nord with Roissy Charles de Gaulle, and bus 140 links Gare du Nord and Gare de l'Est with the airport.
RATP Bus 350 (☎ 08 92 68 77 14; adult €4.50 or 3 metro/bus tickets; 1hr; every 30min 5.45am-7pm) This public bus links Aérogares 1 & 2 with Gare de l'Est (Map pp378-9; rue du 8 Mai 1945, 10e; Ⓜ Gare de l'Est) and with Gare du Nord (Map pp378-9; 184 rue du Faubourg St-Denis, 10e; Ⓜ Gare du Nord).
RATP Bus 351 (☎ 08 92 68 77 14; adult €4.50 or 3 metro/bus tickets; 1hr; every 30min 7am-9.30pm from Roissy Charles de Gaulle, 8.30am-8.20pm from Paris) This public bus links the eastern side of place de la Nation (Map pp378-9; av du Trône, 11e; Ⓜ Nation) with the airport.
RER B (☎ 08 90 36 10 10; adult €8.20; 30min; every 10-15min 5am-midnight) RER line B3 links CDG1 and CDG2 with the city. To get to the airport, take any RER line B train whose four-letter destination code begins with E (eg EIRE), and a shuttle bus (every five to eight minutes) will ferry you to the appropriate terminal. Regular ticket windows don't always sell RER tickets as far as the airport so you may have to buy one at the RER station where you board.
Roissybus (☎ 08 92 68 77 14; €8.60; 45-60min; every 15min 5.45am-11pm) This direct public bus links both terminals with rue Scribe (Map pp378-9; Ⓜ Opéra) behind the Palais Garnier in the 9e.

AÉROPORT PARIS-BEAUVAIS

The special **Express Bus** (☎ 08 92 68 20 64; €13; 1-1¼hr; 8.05am-10.40pm from Beauvais, 5.45am-8.05pm from Paris) leaves **Parking Pershing** (Map pp378-9; 1 bd Pershing, 17e; Ⓜ Porte Maillot), just west of Palais des Congrès de Paris, three hours before Ryanair departures (you can board up to 15 minutes before) and leaves the airport 20 to 30 minutes after each arrival, dropping off just south of Palais des Congrès on Place de la Porte Maillot. Tickets can be purchased up to 24 hours in advance online (http://ticket.aeroportbeauvais.com), at the airport from **Ryanair** (☎ 03 44 11 41 41) or at a car-park kiosk.

Bicycle

For bike hire, try **Maison Roue Libre** (☎ 08 10 44 15 34; www.rouelibre.fr; 🕑 9am-7pm daily Feb-Oct, 10am-6pm Wed-Sun Nov & Jan) Forum des Halles (Map pp382-3; Forum des Halles, 1 passage Mondétour, 1er; Ⓜ Les Halles); Bastille (Map pp382-3; 37 bd Bourdon, 4e; Ⓜ Bastille). Bicycles cost €4/10/15/28 per hour/half-day/day/weekend (plus €150 deposit).

Public Transport

Paris' public transit system is operated by **RATP** (Régie Autonome des Transports Parisians; ☎ 32 46, 08 92 69 32 46; www.ratp.fr; 🕑 7am-9pm Mon-Fri, 9am-5pm Sat & Sun). The same RATP tickets are valid on the metro, the RER, buses, the Montmartre funicular and Paris' three tramlines. A single ticket costs €1.50; a *carnet* (book) of 10 is €11.10. Tickets and maps are available from all metro stations.

The Mobilis card allows unlimited travel for one day in two to six zones (€5.60 to €15.90), while the Paris Visite pass allows unlimited travel (including to/from airports) plus discounted entry to museums and activities. The version covering one to three zones costs €8.50/14/19/27.50 for one/two/three/five days. Both passes are valid on the metro, the RER, buses, trams and the Montmartre funicular.

BUS

Paris' bus system runs between 5.45am and 12.30am Monday to Saturday. Services are reduced on Sunday and public holidays (when buses run from 7am to 8.30pm).

Noctilien (www.noctilien.fr) night buses depart every hour between 12.30am and 5.30am. There are two circular lines (the N01 and N02) linking the four main stations, St-Lazare, Gare de l'Est, Gare de Lyon and Montparnasse, plus popular nightspots such as Bastille, the Champs-Élysées, Pigalle and St-Germain. Look for blue 'N' or 'Noctilien' signs.

Remember to *oblitérer* (cancel) tickets in the cancelling machine *(composteur)* next to the driver.

METRO & RER NETWORK

Paris' underground network consists of two interlinked systems: the **Métropolitain** (metro) with 14 lines and 372 stations; and the **RER**

(Réseau Express Régional), a network of suburban train lines.

Each metro train is known by the name of its terminus. On lines that split into several branches (such as lines 3, 7 and 13), the terminus is indicated on the cars with backlit panels, and often on electronic signs on the station platforms. The last metro train on each line begins sometime between 12.35am and 1.04am, and trains start up again around 5.30am.

The RER is faster than the metro, but the stops are further apart. RER lines are known by an alphanumeric combination – the letter (A to E) refers to the line, the number to the spur it follows to the suburbs.

Taxi

The *prise en charge* (flag fall) in a Parisian taxi is €2.10. Within the city limits, it costs €0.82 per kilometre between 10am and 5pm Monday to Saturday (*Tarif A;* white light on meter), and €1.10 per kilometre from 5pm to 10am, all day Sunday, and public holidays (*Tarif B;* orange light on meter).

The first piece of baggage is free; additional pieces over 5kg cost €1 extra, as do pick-ups from SNCF mainline stations. Most drivers won't carry more than three people for insurance reasons.

To order a taxi, call Paris' **central taxi switchboard** (☎ 01 45 30 30 30; passengers with reduced mobility ☎ 01 47 39 00 91; 24hr).

Local taxi companies:

Alpha Taxis (☎ 01 45 85 85 85; www.alphataxis.com)
Taxis Bleus (☎ 01 49 36 29 48, 08 91 70 10 10; www.taxis-bleus.com)
Taxis G7 (☎ 01 47 39 47 39; www.taxisg7.fr, in French)

AROUND PARIS

VERSAILLES

pop 85,300

The leafy, bourgeois suburb of Versailles, 21km southwest of Paris, is the site of France's grandest and most famous royal residence, the **Château de Versailles** (Versailles Palace; ☎ 08 10 81 16 14; www.chateauversailles.fr; admission €13.50; 9am-6.30pm Tue-Sun Apr-Oct, to 5.30pm Tue-Sun Nov-Mar), built in the mid-17th century by Louis XIV – the Roi Soleil (Sun King) – to project the power of the French monarchy. The 580m-long palace itself is split into several wings, each with its own astonishing array of grand halls, wood-panelled corridors and sumptuous bedchambers, including the **Grand Appartement du Roi** (King's Suite) and the **Galerie des Glaces** (Hall of Mirrors), a fabulous 75m-long mirrored ballroom. Outside, the **landscaped gardens** are filled with canals, pools, fountains and neatly trimmed hedges, and two outbuildings, the **Grand Trianon** and the **Petit Trianon**. Versailles is currently undergoing a €370 million restoration program, so you'll see some scaffolding until at least 2020.

Getting There & Away

RER line C5 (€2.80, every 15 minutes) goes from Paris' Left Bank RER stations to Versailles-Rive Gauche, 700m southeast of the chateau.

SNCF operates up to 70 trains daily from Paris' Gare St-Lazare (€2.80) to Versailles-Rive Droite, 1.2km from the chateau. Versailles-Chantiers is served by half-hourly SNCF trains daily from Gare Montparnasse (€2.80); trains continue to Chartres (€10.90, 45 to 60 minutes). An SNCF package (*forfait loisir*) covering the metro, return train journey to/from Versailles and chateau admission costs €19.20.

CHARTRES

pop 40,250

The medieval town of Chartres is famous for its stunning cathedral, the 130m-long **Cathédrale Notre Dame de Chartres** (Cathedral of Our Lady of Chartres; ☎ 02 37 21 22 07; www.diocese-chartres.com, in French; place de la Cathédrale; 8.30am-7.30pm). The original Romanesque cathedral was devastated in a fire in 1194, but remnants of it remain in the **Portail Royal** (Royal Portal) and the 103m-high **Clocher Vieux** (Old Bell Tower, also known as the South Tower). The rest of the cathedral dates mainly from the 13th century, including many of the 172 glorious stained-glass windows, which are renowned for their intense 'Chartre blue' tones.

A platform emerges some 70m up the 112m-high **Clocher Neuf** (New Bell Tower; adult/18-25yr €6.50/4.50, admission free on 1st Sun of certain months; 9.30am-noon & 2-5.30pm Mon-Sat, 2-5.30pm Sun May-Aug, 9.30am-noon & 2-4.30pm Mon-Sat, 2-4.30pm Sun Sep-Apr), with superb views of the cathedral's three-tiered flying buttresses and 19th-century copper roof.

Getting There & Away

More than 30 SNCF trains a day (20 on Sunday) link Paris' Gare Montparnasse

(€12.90, 70 minutes) with Chartres via Versailles–Chantiers (€10.90, 45 minutes to one hour).

FAR NORTHERN FRANCE

It's grim up north – or so the stereotype goes. But while France's northernmost corner is one of the most densely populated and heavily industrialised areas of the country, there's still plenty to see – including the Flemish-style city of Lille, the cross-channel shopping centre of Calais and the moving battlefields of WWI.

LILLE

pop 1.22 million

Lille (Rijsel in Flemish) may be France's most underrated major city. In recent decades this once-grimy industrial metropolis has transformed itself – with generous government help – into a glittering and self-confident cultural and commercial hub. Highlights include an attractive old town with a strong Flemish accent, three renowned art museums, and a cutting-edge, student-driven nightlife.

Information

4 Players (☎ 03 20 07 43 18; 9 rue Maertens; per 10min/hr prepaid €0.50/3; 🕑 11am-10.30pm Mon-Fri, 10am-11.30pm Sat, 2-10pm Sun; Ⓜ République Beaux Arts) Cybercafe. Yes, it's pronounced 'foreplayers'.

Laundrette (4 rue Ovigneur; 🕑 7am-8pm; Ⓜ République Beaux Arts)

Net Arena (☎ 03 28 38 09 20; 10 rue des Bouchers; per hr €3; 🕑 10am-10pm Mon-Sat, 2-8pm Sun) Thirty internet-access computers.

Tourist Office (☎ from abroad 03 59 57 94 00, in France 08 91 56 20 04; www.lilletourism.com; place Rihour; 🕑 9.30am-6.30pm Mon-Sat, 10am-noon & 2-5pm Sun & holidays; Ⓜ Rihour) Sells the Lille City Pass (one-/two-/three-day €18/30/45) covering Lille's museums and public transport.

Sights

Vieux Lille (Old Lille), which begins just north of place du Général de Gaulle, is justly proud of its restored 17th- and 18th-century houses. The old brick residences along **rue de la Monnaie** were all but abandoned by the 1970s, but now house the city's chicest boutiques, as well as the **Hospice Comtesse Museum** (☎ 03 28 36 84 00; 32 rue de la Monnaie; adult/student €3/2; 🕑 10am-12.30pm & 2-6pm, closed Mon morning & Tue), featuring mainly religious art.

Lille's world-renowned **Fine Arts Museum** (☎ 03 20 06 78 00; www.pba-lille.fr; place de la République; adult/12-25yr €5/3.50; 🕑 2-6pm Mon, 10am-6pm Wed-Sun; Ⓜ République Beaux Arts) has a truly first-rate collection of 15th- to 20th-century paintings, including works by Rubens, Van Dyck and Manet.

Housed in an art-deco swimming pool (built 1927–32), **La Piscine Musée d'Art et d'Industrie** (☎ 03 20 69 23 60; www.roubaix-lapiscine.com; 23 rue de l'Espérance, Roubaix; admission €3.50; 🕑 11am-6pm Tue-Thu, 11am-8pm Fri, 1-6pm Sat & Sun; Ⓜ République Beaux Arts), 12km northeast of Gare Lille-Europe, showcases fine arts and sculpture.

Sleeping

Auberge de Jeunesse (☎ 03 20 57 08 94; www.hihostels.com; lille@fuaj.org; 12 rue Malpart; dm with breakfast €16.85, d €33.70; 🕑 closed 23 Dec–mid-Jan; Ⓜ Mairie de Lille; 💻) This former maternity hospital has 165 beds (two to eight beds per room), hall showers, kitchen facilities and a rather spartan atmosphere.

Hôtel Faidherbe (☎ 03 20 06 27 93; hotelfaidherbe@wanadoo.fr; 42 place de la Gare; d with washbasin €33, d with private bathroom from €47; Ⓜ Gare Lille-Flandres) The 40 one-star rooms are compact, cheerful, pastel and very simply furnished. The perfect choice for linoleum fans.

Hôtel Kanaï (☎ 03 20 57 14 78; www.hotelkanai.com; 10 rue de Béthune; d Mon-Thu €75-95, Fri-Sun €60-65, festival period €105; Ⓜ Rihour; ❄) Completely renovated in 2007, the 31 rooms at this super-central hotel have clean, minimalist lines; top-floor rooms have views.

Eating

The *estaminets* (traditional eateries) of Lille, especially Vieux Lille, specialise in Flemish dishes such as as *carbonnade* (beef stewed with beer and brown sugar).

Estaminet 'T Rijsel (☎ 03 20 15 01 59; 25 rue de Gand; mains €9.90-19.90; 🕑 noon-1.30pm & 7.30-9.30pm, to 10pm or 10.30pm Fri & Sat, closed Mon lunch & Sun) This homey, unpretentious eatery serves up local specialities such as *carbonnade* (€9.90), *pot'je vleesch* (a cold meat terrine; €11.90) and *poulet au Maroilles* (chicken with Maroilles cheese).

Tous Les Jours Dimanche (☎ 03 28 36 05 92; 13 rue Masurel; menus €15.50-16.50; 🕑 restaurant noon-2.30pm, salon de thé noon-6.30pm, closed Mon, also closed Sun May-Sep) Surrounded by antique furniture and *objets d'art*, lunch here feels like hanging out in an arty friend's living room. Specialities include salads, sandwiches (€11) and quiche-like *tartes*.

Book your stay at lonelyplanet.com/hotels

SPLURGE

our pick **À l'Huîtrière** (☎ 03 20 55 43 41; www.huitriere.fr, in French; 3 rue des Chats Bossus; lunch menu €45, other menus €100-140; ⏰ noon-2pm & 7-9.30pm, closed dinner Sun & late Jul-late Aug) On the 'Street of the Hunchback Cats', this sophisticated restaurant is almost as well-known for its art deco trappings as for its fabulous seafood – weekend bookings are essential.

Lille's beloved **Wazemmes food market** (place de la Nouvelle Aventure; ⏰ 8am-2pm Tue-Thu, 8am-8pm Fri & Sat, 8am-3pm Sun & holidays; Ⓜ Gambetta) is in the ethnically mixed Wazemmes district, 1.5km southwest of the tourist office. The city's largest **outdoor market** (⏰ 7am-1.30pm or 2pm Tue, Thu & Sun) takes place outside on Sunday morning.

The largest supermarket is **Carrefour** (Euralille shopping mall; ⏰ 9am-9.30pm Mon-Sat; Ⓜ Gare Lille-Europe).

Drinking

Meert (☎ 03 20 57 07 44; www.meert.fr; 27 rue Esquermoise; ⏰ 9.30am-7.30pm Tue-Fri, 9am-7.30pm Sat, 9am-1pm & 3-7pm Sun; Ⓜ Rihour) Vanilla-flavoured *gaufres* (waffles; €2.30 each) are the speciality of Meert, a luxury tearoom-cum-pastry-and-sweets-shop, in business since 1761.

L'Illustration Café (☎ 03 20 12 00 90; www.bar-lillustration.com, in French; 18 rue Royale; ⏰ 12.30pm-3am Mon-Sat, 2pm-3am Sun) A quintessentially French cafe, adorned with art-nouveau woodwork and frequented by an intellectual crowd.

Le Balatum (☎ 03 20 57 41 81; www.myspace.com/balatum; 13 rue de la Barre; ⏰ 4pm-3am Sun-Fri, 2pm-3am Sat) Funky, dimly-lit place favoured by a *branché* (in-the-know) crowd, with weekend gigs and DJs.

Getting There & Away

Eurolines (☎ 03 20 78 18 88; 23 parvis St-Maurice; ⏰ 9.30am-6pm Mon-Fri, 10am-noon & 1-6pm Sat; Ⓜ Gare Lille-Flandres) serves cities such as Brussels (€15, 1½ to two hours), Amsterdam (€30, five hours) and London (€34, 5½ hours). Buses depart from bd de Leeds, near Gare Lille-Europe.

The city has two train stations. Gare Lille-Flandres is used by regional services and TGVs to Paris' Gare du Nord (€37.60 to €52.20, one hour, 14 to 18 daily), while ultra-modern Gare Lille-Europe handles everything else, including Eurostar trains to London, TGVs/Eurostars to Brussels-Nord (Monday to Friday/weekend €25.20/16.30, 35 minutes, 12 daily); and TGVs to Nice (€110 to €132.70, 7½ hours, two direct daily).

CALAIS

pop 74,200

Over 15 million people pass through Calais en route to the cross-channel ferries, but precious few take the time to explore the town itself – and while it's far from the most fascinating town in France, it's worth a stop for Rodin's famous sculpture, *The Burghers of Calais*, housed at the town hall.

Orientation & Information

Gare Calais-Ville (the train station) is 650m south of the main square, place d'Armes. The car-ferry terminal is 1.5km northeast of place d'Armes (by car the distance is double that). The Channel Tunnel's vehicle-loading area is 6km southwest of the town centre. The **tourist office** (☎ 03 21 96 62 40; www.calais-cotedopale.com; 12 bd Georges Clemenceau; ⏰ 10am-1pm & 2-6.30pm Mon-Sat year-round, 10am-1pm Sun Jul & Aug) is a short walk north across the river from the station along blvd Georges Clemenceau.

Sleeping & Eating

Auberge de Jeunesse (☎ 03 21 34 70 20; www.auberge-jeunesse-calais.com; av Maréchal de Lattre de Tassigny; dm in a double r €18, s €24, incl breakfast; ⏰ 24hr) Modern, well equipped and just 200m from the beach, this 162-bed hostel is served by buses 3 and 9.

Hôtel Victoria (☎ 03 21 34 38 32; hotelvictoriacalais@wanadoo.fr; 8 rue du Commandant Bonningue; d with washbasin €30, with private bathroom €42) A hotel so ordinary that it could be described as 'extraordinarily ordinary'. The 14 two-star rooms are clean, comfortable and in good repair.

Tonnerre de Brest (☎ 03 21 96 95 35; 16 place d'Armes; weekday lunch menus €10.50-18.50; ⏰ closed Mon except Jul & Aug) At this rustic eatery run by two sisters, you can tuck into 28 savoury galettes or 31 sweet crêpes washed down with local cider.

Getting There & Around

BOAT

For details on ferry travel, see p374.

BUS

Ligne BCD (☎ 08 00 62 00 59) is an express service linking Calais' train station with Dunkirk

(€7.70, 45 minutes, 11 daily Monday to Friday, three on Saturday) and Boulogne (€7.20, 40 minutes, five daily Monday to Friday, two on Saturday).

CAR & MOTORCYCLE

To reach the Channel Tunnel's vehicle-loading area at Coquelles, follow the road signs on the A16 to 'Tunnel Sous La Manche' and get off at exit 42.

TRAIN

Calais has two train stations: central Gare Calais-Ville and Gare Calais-Fréthun, a TGV station 10km southwest of town near the Channel Tunnel entrance. They are linked by trains and shuttle buses.

Gare Calais-Ville serves Amiens (€22.10, 2½ to 3½ hours, six to eight daily), Boulogne (€7.20, 30 minutes, 15 to 18 daily Monday to Saturday, eight on Sunday), Dunkirk (€7.70, 50 minutes, two to five Monday to Saturday) and Lille-Flandres (€15.30, 1¼ hours, seven to 11 daily).

Gare Calais-Fréthun is served by TGVs to Paris' Gare du Nord (€39.60 to €54.60, 1½ hours, six daily Monday to Saturday, three on Sunday) as well as Eurostars to London (one hour, three daily).

NORMANDY

Famous for cows, cider and Camembert, the largely rural region of Normandy (www.normandie-tourisme.fr) is one of the most traditional areas of France, home to the historic D-Day beaches, the otherworldy spires of Mont St-Michel and the half-timbered houses of Rouen, as well as the world's largest comic-strip – the Bayeux tapestry.

ROUEN

pop 108,750

With its elegant church spires, beautifully restored medieval quarter and soaring Gothic cathedral, the ancient city of Rouen is definitely one of Normandy's highlights. Devastated several times during the Middle Ages by fire and plague, the city was later badly damaged by WWII bombing raids, but has been meticulously rebuilt over the last six decades or so, and the city makes an ideal base for exploring the northern Normandy coast.

Orientation

The main train station (Gare Rouen-Rive Droite) is at the northern end of rue Jeanne d'Arc, the main thoroughfare running south to the Seine. The old city is centred around rue du Gros Horloge between the place du Vieux Marché and the cathedral.

Information

Cybernet (☎ 02 35 07 73 02; 47 place du Vieux Marché; internet per hr €4; ⏰ 10am-8pm Mon-Sat, 2-7pm Sun)

Laundrettes 56 rue Cauchoise (⏰ 7am-9pm); 55 rue d'Amiens (⏰ 7am-9pm)

PlaceNet (☎ 02 77 76 90 21; 37 rue de la République; internet per 15min/hr €1/3; ⏰ 2.30pm-12.30am Sun & Mon, 10.30am-12.30am Tue-Thu, 10.30am-3am Fri & Sat)

Tourist Office (☎ 02 32 08 32 40; www.rouentourisme.com; 25 place de la Cathédrale; ⏰ 9am-7pm Mon-Sat, 9.30am-12.30pm & 2-6pm Sun & holidays May-Sep; 9.30am-12.30pm & 1.30-6pm Mon-Sat, 2-6pm Sun & holidays Oct-Apr) Opposite the cathedral.

Sights

The old city's main thoroughfare, rue du Gros Horloge, runs from the cathedral west to **place du Vieux Marché**, where 19-year-old Joan of Arc was executed for heresy in 1431. Dedicated in 1979, the modernist **Église Jeanne d'Arc** (⏰ 10am-noon & 2-6pm Apr-Oct, to 5.30pm Nov-Mar) marks the spot where Joan was burned at the stake.

Rouen's stunning Gothic **Cathédrale Notre Dame** (⏰ 2-6pm Mon, 8am-6pm Tue-Sun) is the famous subject of a series of paintings by Monet, although the great man would hardly recognise the place these days – an ongoing restoration project has polished up the soot-blackened stone to its original brilliant white colour.

Inside a desanctified 16th-century church, the riveting **Musée Le Secq des Tournelles** (☎ 02 35 88 42 92; 2 rue Jacques Villon; adult/student €2.30/1.55; ⏰ 10am-1pm & 2-6pm Wed-Mon) is devoted to the blacksmith's craft, with some 5000 wrought-iron items ranging from shop signs to an elaborate choir grille from 1202.

The **Musée des Beaux-Arts** (Fine Arts Museum; ☎ 02 35 71 28 40; esplanade Marcel Duchamp; adult/student €3/2; ⏰ 10am-6pm Wed-Mon), housed in a grand structure erected in 1870, features canvases by Caravaggio, Rubens, Modigliani, Pissarro, Renoir, Sisley (lots) and (of course) several works by Monet, including a study of Rouen's cathedral (in Room 2.33).

DETOUR: MAISON DE CLAUDE MONET

Monet's home for the last 43 years of his life is now the delightful **Maison et Jardins de Claude Monet** (☎ 02 32 51 28 21; www.fondation-monet.com; adult/student €5.50/4, gardens only €4; 9.30am-6pm Tue-Sun Apr-Oct), where you can view the famous gardens and lily ponds that often featured in his canvases, and take in other impressionist masterpieces at the nearby **Musée d'Art Américain** (☎ 02 32 51 94 65; www.maag.org; 99 rue Claude Monet; adult/student €5.50/4; 10am-6pm Tue-Sun Apr-Oct).

The gardens are in Giverny, 66km southeast of Rouen. Several trains (€9.60, 40 minutes) leave Rouen before noon; to get back, there are hourly return trains between 5pm and 10pm (to 9pm on Saturday). From Paris' Gare St-Lazare, two early morning trains run to Vernon (€11.90, 50 minutes), 7km to the west of Giverny.

Sleeping

Hôtel Le Palais (☎ 02 35 71 41 40; 12 rue du Tambour; s/d with hall shower €24/30, with private bathroom €36/42) The rooms are basic and not all have private bathrooms but this old-school cheapie is bang in the middle of the old city.

Hôtel Andersen (☎ 02 35 71 88 51; www.hotelandersen.com; 4 rue Pouchet; s/d with hall shower €40/45, d with private bathroom €53-63) This is the best of the station hotels, ensconced in an early 19th-century mansion. Classical music wafts through the lobby and the 15 spare but imaginative rooms feature Laura Ashley wallpaper.

Hôtel des Carmes (☎ 02 35 71 92 31; www.hoteldescarmes.com, in French; 33 place des Carmes; d €49-65, tr €67-77; 💻) This sweet little hotel offers 12 rooms decked out with patchwork quilts and vibrant colours; some have cerulean-blue cloudscapes painted on the ceilings.

Eating

Thé Majuscule (☎ 02 35 71 15 66; 8 place de la Calende; plat du jour €10.50; restaurant noon-2pm Mon-Sat, salon de thé 2.30-6.30pm Mon-Sat) Downstairs it's a typically chaotic French second-hand bookshop, upstairs a homey tearoom with homemade *tartes*, salads, cakes and exotic teas (€3.30).

Pascaline (☎ 02 35 89 67 44; 5 rue de la Poterne; menus €14.90-26.90; lunch & dinner) A top spot for a great-value *formule midi* (lunchtime menu), this bustling bistro serves up French cuisine in typically Parisian surroundings – think net curtains, white tablecloths and chuffing coffee machines.

A few self-catering options:

Halles du Vieux Marché (place du Vieux Marché; 7am-7pm Tue-Sat, 7am-1pm Sun) A small covered market with an excellent *fromagerie* (cheese shop).

Monoprix (65 rue du Gros Horloge; 8.30am-9pm Mon-Sat)

Getting There & Away

From **Gare Rouen-Rive Droite** (rue Jeanne d'Arc), trains go direct to Paris' Gare St-Lazare (€19.30, 1¼ hours, 25 daily Monday to Friday, 14 to 19 daily weekends), Caen (€21.80, 1½ hours, eight daily), Dieppe (€9.90, 45 minutes, 10 to 15 daily Monday to Saturday, five Sunday) and Le Havre (€12.90, 50 minutes, 18 daily Monday to Saturday, 10 Sunday). Tickets are sold at the **Boutique SNCF** (20 rue aux Juifs; 10am-7pm Mon-Sat).

BAYEUX

pop 14,600

Bayeux is world-famous for a 68m-long piece of painstakingly embroidered cloth: the 11th-century Bayeux Tapestry, which relates the story of the Norman invasion of England in 1066. The town is one of the few in Normandy to have survived WWII practically unscathed, with a centre crammed with 13th- to 18th-century buildings, wooden-framed Norman-style houses, and a fine Gothic cathedral.

Information

La Paillote (☎ 02 31 10 08 73; 25 rue Montfiquet; 5pm-2am Sun-Thu, to 3am Fri & Sat, closed Sun & Mon in winter) A laid-back pub with internet access.

Laundrettes 67 rue des Bouchers (7am-9pm); 13 rue Maréchal Foch (7am-9pm)

Tourist Office (☎ 02 31 51 28 28; www.bayeux-bessin-tourism.com; pont St-Jean; 9am-7pm Mon-Sat, 9am-1pm & 2-6pm Sun & holidays Jul & Aug, 9.30am-12.30pm & 2-6pm Apr-Jun, Sep & Oct, 9.30am-12.30pm & 2-5.30pm Nov-Mar)

Sights

The world's most celebrated embroidery, the **Bayeux Tapestry** (☎ 02 31 51 25 50; www.tapisserie-bayeux.fr; rue de Nesmond; adult/student incl audioguide €7.80/3.80; 9am-6.30pm mid-Mar–Apr & Sep–mid-Nov,

9am-7pm May-Aug, 9.30am-12.30pm & 2-6pm mid-Nov–mid-Mar) recounts William the Conqueror's conquest of England over 58 remarkable (and sometimes graphic) scenes (plenty of lopped-off heads and severed limbs).

Bayeux was the first Normandy town liberated after D-Day, and the **Memorial Museum** (Musée Mémorial de la Bataille Normandie; ☎ 02 31 51 46 90; bd Fabien Ware; adult/student €6.50/3.80; ⏲ 9.30am-6.30pm May-Sep, 10am-12.30pm & 2-6pm Oct-Apr) explores the events using photos, personal accounts, dioramas and wartime objects. Nearby, the **Bayeux war cemetery** (☎ 02 21 21 77 00; blvd Fabien Ware) contains the graves of 4848 soldiers from the UK and 10 other countries (including Germany). Some 1807 other Commonweath soldiers, whose bodies were sadly never found, are commemorated on the memorial across the road.

Most of Bayeux's spectacular Norman-Gothic **Cathédrale Notre Dame** (rue du Bienvenu; ⏲ 8.30am-7pm Jul-Sep, 8.30am-6pm Apr-Jun & Oct, 9am-5pm Nov-Mar) dates from the 13th century.

Sleeping

our pick **Family Home** (☎ 02 31 92 15 22; www.fuaj.org; 39 rue Général de Dais; dm €19, s €30) One of France's most charming youth hostels, this place sports a 17th-century dining room, a delightful 16th-century courtyard and 80 beds in rooms for one to four people. If reception isn't staffed, phone and someone will pop by.

Hôtel de la Gare (☎ 02 31 92 10 70; www.normandy-tours-hotel.com; 26 place de la Gare; d with hall bathroom €28, d/q with private shower €38/55) Across the parking lot from the train station, this place has 15 tired but serviceable rooms.

Hôtel Mogador (☎ 02 31 92 24 58; hotel.mogador@wanadoo.fr; 20 rue Alain Chartier; d €44-54) On the market square, this friendly, family-run, two-star hotel has 14 rooms with pastel curtains and lots of old wood beams. The small patio is a lovely spot for a morning croissant.

Eating

La Reine Mathilde (☎ 02 31 92 00 59; 47 rue St-Martin; cakes €2.30; ⏲ 8.30am-7.30pm Tue-Sun) A sumptuous, c 1900-style *pâtisserie* and *salon de thé* that's ideal if you've got a hankering for something sweet.

La Table du Terroir (☎ 02 31 92 05 53; 42 rue St-Jean; lunch menus €12.50-14, dinner menus €21-28; ⏲ closed dinner Sun) At this country-style restaurant, crimson chairs and white tablecloths provide an enjoyable backdrop for specialities such as grilled salmon, pork fillet and *tripes à la Caen* (tripe stew).

Self-catering options:

Food markets rue St-Jean (⏲ Wed morning); place St-Patrice (⏲ Sat morning)

Marché Plus (16 rue St-Jean; 7am-9pm Mon-Sat, 8.30am-12.30pm Sun)

Getting There & Away

Bus Verts (☎ 08 10 21 42 14; www.busverts.fr) runs to Caen (Bus 30; €4, one hour, three or four daily Monday to Friday except holidays) and provides regular buses to the D-Day beaches (p402).

The most useful train link from Bayeux is Caen (€5.50, 20 minutes, 13 to 19 daily Monday to Saturday, eight Sunday), from where there are regular connections to Paris' Gare St-Lazare (€32) and Rouen (€24.60).

MONT ST-MICHEL

Standing on a rocky island opposite the town of Pontorson, connected to the mainland by a narrow causeway, the sky-scraping turrets of the abbey of **Mont St-Michel** (☎ 02 33 89 80 00; www.monuments-nationaux.fr; adult/18-25yr incl guided tour €8.50/5; ⏲ 9am-7pm May-Aug, 9.30am-6pm Sep-Apr, last entry 1hr before closing) provide one of France's most iconic sights. The surrounding bay is notorious for its fast-rising tides: at low tide the Mont is surrounded by bare sand for miles around, but at high tide, barely six hours later, the bay, causeway and nearby car parks can be submerged under several feet of water.

At the base of the mount, just inside Porte de l'Avancée as you enter the abbey, the **Mont St-Michel tourist office** (☎ 02 33 60 14 30; www.ot-montsaintmichel.com; ⏲ 9am-7pm Jul & Aug, 9am-12.30pm & 2-6.30pm Mon-Sat, 9am-noon & 2-6pm Sun Apr-Jun & Sep, 9am-noon & 2-6pm Mon-Sat, 10am-noon & 2-5pm Sun Oct-Mar) sells detailed visitor maps (€3). From here, a winding cobbled street leads up to the **Église Abbatiale** (Abbey Church), incorporating elements of both Norman and Gothic architecture. Other notable sights include the arched **cloître** (cloister), the barrel-roofed **réfectoire** (dining hall), and the Gothic **Salle des Hôtes** (Guest Hall), dating from 1213. A one-hour tour is included in the ticket price: English tours are run twice a day (11am and 3pm) in winter, hourly in summer. From Monday to Saturday in July and August, there are illuminated *nocturnes* (night-time visits) with music from 7pm to 10pm.

DETOUR: D-DAY BEACHES

On 6 June 1944, Allied troops stormed 80km of beaches north of Bayeux, code-named (from west to east) Utah, Omaha, Gold, Juno and Sword. The audacious invasion of D-Day – known as Jour J in French – ultimately liberated the European mainland from Nazi occupation. For context, see www.normandiememoire.com and www.6juin1944.com.

The most brutal fighting took place 15km northwest of Bayeux at **Omaha Beach**, now home to the huge **American Military Cemetery** (☎ 02 31 51 62 00; www.abmc.gov; Colleville-sur-Mer; 9am-6pm mid-Apr–mid-Sep, 9am-5pm mid-Sep–mid-Apr). Nearby **Juno Beach**, 12km east of Arromanches, was stormed by Canadian troops, while bomb craters and German gun emplacements dot the **Pointe du Hoc Ranger Memorial** (☎ 02 31 51 90 70; admission free; 24hr). One of the Allies' prefabricated 'Mulberry Harbours' can be seen at low-tide at **Arromanches**, 10km northeast of Bayeux.

Caen's hi-tech museum, **Mémorial – Un Musée pour la Paix** (Memorial – A Museum for Peace; ☎ 02 31 06 06 45; www.memorial-caen.fr; esplanade Général Eisenhower; adult/student/war veteran €16/15/free; 9am-7pm Mar-Oct, 9.30am-6pm Nov-Feb, closed last 3 weeks Jan), uses sound, film and animation to explore the events of WWII, D-Day and the Cold War.

Several companies offer guided tours:

- **Caen Mémorial** (☎ 02 31 06 06 45; www.memorial-caen.fr; adult €69; 1pm Oct-Mar, 9am & 2pm Apr-Sep) Four- to five-hour minibus tours around the landing beaches, including entry to the museum.
- **Normandy Sightseeing Tours** (☎ 02 31 51 70 52; www.normandywebguide.com; May-Oct) Offers morning (adult/student €40/35) and afternoon tours (€45/40), which can be combined into an all-day excursion (€75/65).
- **Normandy Tours** (☎ 02 31 92 10 70; www.normandy-tours-hotel.com; 26 place de la Gare; adult/student €41/36; year-round) Bayeux-based operator offering four- or five-hour tours at 8.15am and 1.15pm.

Getting There & Away

Les Couriers Bretons (☎ 02 99 19 70 80) links Pontorson with St-Malo (1¼ hours, one round-trip daily). Trains from Pontorson include Bayeux (€19.60, 1¾ hours, two or three direct daily), Cherbourg (€24.50, 2¼ hours, two daily) and Rennes (€11.90, 1¾ hours, two or three daily).

BRITTANY

Thrust out into the Atlantic, France's westernmost promontory might be called Finistère, meaning 'land's end', but its Breton name, *Penn ar Bed*, translates as the 'head of the world'. It's long considered itself a separate nation from the rest of France, with its own history, customs and Breton language; chuck in some scenic coastline, windswept islands and the eeriest stone circles this side of Stonehenge, and you'll discover one of France's most fascinating corners.

QUIMPER

pop 64,900

Small enough to feel like a village – with its slanted half-timbered houses and narrow cobbled streets – and large enough to champion itself as the troubadour of Breton culture, Quimper (pronounced *kam-pair*) is Finistère's thriving capital.

Information

Eixxos (☎ 02 98 64 40 56; 12 bd Dupleix; per hr €3.50; 11am-10pm Mon-Thu, 11am-1am Fri & Sat, 2-10pm Sun) Internet access.

Laverie de la Gare (4 av de la Gare; 8am-8pm) Laundry.

Tourist Office (☎ 02 98 53 04 05; www.quimper-tourisme.com, in French; place de la Résistance; 9am-7pm Mon-Sat, 10am-12.45pm & 3-5.45pm Sun Jul & Aug, 9.30am-12.30pm & 1.30-6pm or 6.30pm Mon-Sat Sep-Jun, 10am-12.45pm Sun Jun & 1-15 Sep) Runs weekly 1½-hour guided city tours in English (€5.20) in July and August, and sells the *Pass' Quimper* (€13) to four attractions/tours.

Sights

Quimper's **cathedral** (9.30am-noon & 1.30-6.30pm Mon-Sat May-Oct, 9am-noon & 1.30-6.30pm Mon-Sat Nov-Apr, 1.30-6.30pm Sun year-round) was begun in 1239, but the cathedral's dramatic twin spires were added in the 19th century – high on the west facade, look out for an equestrian statue of King Gradlon, the city's mythical 5th-century founder.

The **Musée des Beaux-Arts** (☎ 02 98 95 45 20; 40 place St-Corentin; admission €4.50; ⏲ 10am-7pm daily Jul & Aug, 10am-noon & 2-6pm Wed-Mon Apr-Jun & Sep-Oct, 10am-noon & 2-6pm Wed-Sat & Mon, 2-6pm Sun Nov-Mar) is a mite gloomy, although the upper levels are brightened up by Picasso sketches and a room dedicated to Quimper-born poet Max Jacob.

Recessed behind a magnificent stone courtyard beside the cathedral, the **Musée Départemental Breton** (☎ 02 98 95 21 60; 1 rue du Roi Gradlon; admission €4; ⏲ 9am-6pm daily Jun-Sep, 9am-noon & 2-5pm Tue-Sat, 2-5pm Sun Oct-May) showcases Breton history, furniture, costumes, crafts and archaeology. Adjoining the museum is the **Jardin de l'Évêché** (Bishop's Palace Garden; admission free; ⏲ 9am-5pm or 6pm).

Sleeping

Auberge de Jeunesse (☎ 02 98 64 97 97; quimper@fuaj.org; 6 av des Oiseaux; camp sites €6, dm incl breakfast €15.20, sheets €2.80; ⏲ Apr-Sep) Quimper's seasonal youth hostel has self-catering facilities.

Camping Municipal (☎/fax 02 98 55 61 09; av des Oiseaux; camp sites from €9; ⏲ tents Apr-Sep, campervans year-round) This wooded park is 1km west of the old city (3km from the train station). Take bus 1 from the train station to the Chaptal stop.

Hôtel TGV (☎ 02 98 90 54 00; www.hoteltgv.com; 4 rue de Concarneau; s/d €36/38) The cheapest of several hotels around the train station, 800m from the old city, the TGV has 22 small but bright en-suite rooms. Light sleepers will find the top-floor rooms quieter. Wi-fi's free.

Eating

Crêpes are king in Quimper, but fine-diners won't be disappointed either.

our pick **Crêperie la Krampouzerie** (☎ 02 98 95 13 08; 9 rue du Sallé; galettes €3.50-7.70; ⏲ lunch & dinner Tue-Sat) The best crêpes in town, made from organic flours and regional ingredients like *algues d'Ouessant* (seaweed), Roscoff onions and homemade ginger caramel.

Le Bistro á Lire (☎ 02 98 95 30 86; 18 rue des Boucheries; snacks around €4.50, mains €7.80; ⏲ lunch Tue-Sat, salon de thé 9am-7pm Tue-Sat, plus Mon afternoon Jul & Aug) Amid the shelves at this bookshop–*salon de thé*, you can tuck into lasagne and the *gâteau du jour* (cake of the day) for €5.50.

Getting There & Away

CAT/Connex Tourisme (☎ 02 98 90 68 40) bus destinations include Brest (€6, 1¼ hours), while **Le Coeur** (☎ 02 98 54 40 15) runs to Concarneau (€2, 45 minutes, seven to 10 daily).

There are frequent trains to Brest (€14, 1¼ hours, up to 10 daily), Rennes (€30.10, 2½ hours, five daily) and Paris (Gare Montparnasse; €68.20, 4¾ hours, eight daily).

ST-MALO

pop 49,600

The pretty port of St-Malo is inextricably tied up with the briny blue: the town became a key harbour during the 17th and 18th centuries as a base for merchant ships and government-sanctioned privateers, and these days it's a busy cross-channel ferry-port and summertime getaway.

Orientation

The old walled city of St-Malo is known as Intra-Muros (within the walls) or Ville Close. From the train station, it's a 15-minute walk westwards along av Louis Martin.

Information

Cyberm@lo (☎ 02 99 56 07 78; 68 chaussée du Sillon; per 15 min/hr €1.50/4; ⏲ 10am-1am Mon-Sat, 11am-11pm Sun mid-Jun–mid-Sep, 11am-9pm Tue-Thu, 11am-11pm Fri & Sat, 3-8pm Sun mid-Sep–mid-Jun) Internet access along the seafront.

Tourist Office (☎ 08 25 13 52 00, 02 99 56 64 43; www.saint-malo-tourisme.com; esplanade St-Vincent; ⏲ 9am-7.30pm Mon-Sat, 10am-6pm Sun Jul & Aug, 9am-12.30pm & 1.30-6pm or 6.30pm Mon-Sat Sep-Jun, 10am-12.30pm & 2.30-6pm Sun Easter-Jun & Sep)

Sights

The city's sturdy ramparts were constructed at the end of the 17th century by the military architect Vauban, and afford fine views of the old walled city – you can access them from all of the main city *portes* (gates). From their northern stretch, you'll see the remains of the former prison, the **Fort National** (admission €4; ⏲ Jun-Sep), and the rocky islet of **Île du Grand Bé**, where the great St-Malo–born 18th-century writer Chateaubriand is buried. You can walk across at low tide, but check the tide times with the tourist office.

The battle to liberate St-Malo destroyed around 80% of the old city during August 1944; damage to the **Cathédrale St-Vincent** (place Jean de Châtillon; ⏲ 9.30am-6pm except during Mass) was particularly severe.

Within **Château de St-Malo**, built by the dukes of Brittany in the 15th and 16th centuries, is the **Musée du Château** (☎ 02 99 40 71 57; admission €5.20; ⏲ 10am-noon & 2-6pm daily Apr-Sep, Tue-Sun Oct-Mar). The museum's most interesting exhibits – the history of cod fishing and photos of St-Malo after WWII – are in the Tour Générale.

The attractions at the **Grand Aquarium** (☎ 02 99 21 19 00; av Général Patton; admission €14; ⌚ at least 10am-6pm Feb-Dec, to 8pm Jul & Aug) include a minisubmarine descent and a *bassin tactile* (touch pool). The aquarium is 4km south of the city; Bus C1 travels from the train station every half-hour.

If you're hardy enough to brave the Atlantic swells, there are several pleasant **beaches** around St-Malo.

Sleeping

Camping Aleth (☎ 02 99 81 60 91; camping@ville-saint-malo.fr; allée Gaston Buy, St-Servan; camp sites €12; ⌚ May-Sep) Perched on a peninsula, Camping Aleth (also spelt Alet) has panoramic 360° views and is close to beaches and some lively bars.

Auberge de Jeunesse Éthic Étapes (☎ 02 99 40 29 80; www.centrevarangot.com; 37 av du Père Umbricht; dm incl breakfast €15.50-18.70; 💻) This efficient place has a self-catering kitchen as well as free sports facilities. Take bus C1 from the train station.

Hôtel San Pedro (☎ 02 99 40 88 57; www.sanpedro-hotel.com; 1 rue Ste-Anne; s €46-48, d €53-70; ⌚ Feb-Nov; 💻) Tucked at the back of the old city, the San Pedro has cool, crisp, neutral-toned decor with subtle splashes of colour, friendly service and superb sea views.

Eating

Le Biniou (☎ 02 99 56 47 57; 3 place de la Croix du Fief; crêpes €2-8, menus around €10; ⌚ 10am-1am summer, closed Thu winter) St-Malo has no shortage of crêperies but this one – with cute illustrations of Breton *biniou* (bagpipes) – is a fave. Savour 100 *galettes* and *crêpes,* including the house speciality: apples flambéed in Calvados.

Crêperie Margaux (☎ 02 99 20 26 02; 3 place du Marché aux Légumes; crêpes €7.50-13; ⌚ closed Tue & Wed, daily during school holidays) The owner of this wonderful crêperie makes traditional crêpes by hand (her motto: 'if you're in a hurry, don't come here'). They're worth the wait.

Jean-Yves Bordier (9 rue de l'Orme; ⌚ Tue-Sat) is the place for cheeses and butters, while the **Halle au Blé** (rue de la Herse; ⌚ 8am-noon Tue & Fri) covered market and the **Marché Plus** (cnr rue St-Vincent & rue St-Barbe; ⌚ 7am-9pm Mon-Sat, to noon Sun) sell general supplies.

Getting There & Away

Brittany Ferries (☎ reservations in France 08 25 82 88 28, in UK 0870 556 1600; www.brittany-ferries.com) sails between St-Malo and Portsmouth, and **Condor Ferries** (☎ France 08 25 13 51 35, UK 0870 243 5140; www.condorferries.co.uk) runs to/from Poole and Weymouth via Jersey or Guernsey.

From April to September, **Compagnie Corsaire** (☎ 08 25 13 80 35) and **Vedettes de St-Malo** (☎ 02 23 18 41 08; www.vedettes-saint-malo.com) run a **Bus de Mer** (Sea Bus; return €6; ⌚ hourly) shuttle service (10 minutes) between St-Malo and Dinard.

Courriers Bretons (☎ 02 99 19 70 80) runs buses to Pontorson (€2.50, one hour) and Mont St-Michel (€4.30, 1½ hours, three to four daily). **TIV** (☎ 02 99 82 26 26) has buses to Dinard (€1.50, 30 minutes, hourly) and Rennes (€3, one to 1½ hours, three to six daily).

TGV train services run between St-Malo and Rennes (€11.60, one hour), and there are direct trains to Paris' Gare Montparnasse (€58, three hours).

ALSACE & LORRAINE

Teetering on the tempestuous frontier between France and Germany, the neighbouring regions of Alsace and Lorraine are where the worlds of Gallic and Germanic culture collide. Half-timbered houses, lush vineyards and forest-clad mountains hint at Alsace's Teutonic leanings, while nearby Lorraine is indisputably Francophile.

STRASBOURG

pop 427,000

Prosperous, cosmopolitan Strasbourg (City of the Roads) is the intellectual and cultural capital of Alsace, as well as the unofficial seat of European power – the European Parliament, the Council of Europe and the European Court of Human Rights are all based here. The city's most famous landmark is its pink sandstone cathedral, towering above the restaurants, *winstubs* (traditional Alsatian eateries) and pubs of the lively old city.

Orientation

The train station is 400m west of the Grande Île (Big Island), the core of ancient and modern Strasbourg, whose main squares are place Kléber, place Broglie (*broag*-lee), place Gutenberg and place du Château. The quaint Petite France area, on the Grande Île's south-western corner, is subdivided by canals.

Information

Laundrettes 29 Grand' Rue (7.30am-8pm; Alt Winmärik); 8 rue de la Nuée Bleue (7am-9pm; Broglie); 15 rue des Veaux (7am-9pm)

L'Utopie (03 88 23 89 21; 21-23 rue du Fossé des Tanneurs; per 1/20hr €3/20; 7am-11.30pm; Homme de Fer) Cybercafe with free wi-fi.

Milk (03 88 32 06 02; 32-34 rue du Vieux Marché aux Vins; per hr €4, discounts available; 24hr; Homme de Fer) One hundred internet-access computers.

Tourist Office (03 88 52 28 28; www.otstrasbourg.fr; 17 place de la Cathédrale; 9am-7pm; Langstross Grand' Rue) A city-centre walking map costs €1, and the Strasbourg Pass (adult €11.40) will save you some sightseeing cash.

Tourist Office Annexe (03 88 32 51 49; 9am-7pm; Gare Centrale) In the train station's southern wing.

Sights & Activities

With its bustling squares and upmarket shopping streets, the Grande Île was Unesco-listed in 1988. The narrow streets of the **old city** are especially enchanting at night, while the half-timbered buildings and flowery canals around **Petite France** are fairy-tale pretty. The romantic **Terrasse Panoramique** (admission free; 9am-7.30pm) on top of **Barrage Vauban** (7.30am-7.30pm) affords the best views.

Strasbourg's lacy, candy-coloured Gothic **Cathédrale Notre Dame** (admission free; 7am-7pm) is one of the marvels of European architecture. The west facade was completed in 1284, but the 142m spire wasn't finished till 1439. Inside, a stunning 16th-century *horloge astronomique* (astronomical clock) strikes solar noon at 12.30pm. The 66m-high **platform** (03 88 43 60 40; adult/student €3/1.50; 9am-5pm Mon-Fri, 10am-5pm Sat & Sun Apr-Oct, to 4.30pm Nov-Mar) provides a stork's-eye view of Strasbourg.

The world-renowned **Musée de l'Œuvre Notre-Dame** (03 88 32 88 17; 3 place du Château; adult/student under 25yr incl audioguide €4/2; noon-6pm Tue-Sun; Langstross Grand' Rue) has one of Europe's premier collections of Romanesque, Gothic and Renaissance sculptures, 15th-century paintings and stained glass.

The **Musée d'Art Moderne et Contemporain** (MAMC, Museum of Modern & Contemporary Art; 03 88 23 31 31; place Hans Jean Arp; adult/student under 25yr €5/2.50; noon-7pm Tue, Wed & Fri, noon-9pm Thu, 10am-6pm Sat & Sun; Musée d'Art Moderne) covers every major art movement from impressionism to cubism and surrealism.

The **Palais Rohan** (03 88 52 50 00; 2 place du Château; for whole complex adult/student under 25yr €6/3, for each museum €4/2; noon-6pm Mon & Wed-Fri, 10am-6pm Sat & Sun) was built between 1732 and 1742 as a bishops' residence. It houses several museums including the **Musée Archéologique**.

Tours

Batorama (03 88 84 13 13; www.batorama.fr, in French; 9 rue de Nantes; adult/student 25yr & under €7.60/3.80; excursions begin at 10.30am, 1pm, 2.30pm & 4pm Nov & Jan-Mar, till 9pm or 10pm Apr-Oct; Porte de l'Hôpital) runs boat trips in nine languages, taking in Petite France and the European institutions.

Sleeping

Ciarus (03 88 15 27 88; www.ciarus.com; 7 rue Finkmatt; dm in 8-/4-/2-bed room incl breakfast €21.50/25.50/28, s €44.50;) Hostels don't get more stylish than this 295-bed place; the dorms have industrial-strength furniture, toilets and showers. There's also a self-service restaurant. By bus, take 2, 4 or 10 to the place de Pierre stop.

Hôtel Le Colmar (03 88 32 16 89; hotel.le.colmar@wanadoo.fr; 1 rue du Maire Kuss; s/d with washbasin €27/34, with private bathroom €42/45, hall shower €1.50; Alt Winmärik) This cash-only cheapie mixes light and linoleum – stylish it ain't but it's convenient and good value. Some rooms have great river views.

Hôtel Patricia (03 88 32 14 60; www.hotelpatricia.fr; 1a rue du Puits; s with washbasin €28, d with private bathroom €43-45; reception 8-11am & 2-8pm Mon-Sat, 8-11am Sun; Langstross Grand' Rue) The dark, rustic interior and Vosges sandstone floors of this former convent fit in well with the local ambience. The 22 rooms are simply furnished but immaculate and spacious; some (eg rooms 3 and 6) have great views. The best budget bet on the island.

Eating & Drinking

Moozé (03 88 22 68 46; 1 rue de la Demi-Lune, cnr rue Ste-Barbe; dishes €2.50-6; lunch & dinner Mon-Sat; Langstross Grand' Rue) A hip Japanese fusion place where colour-coded plates go round on a dual-carriageway conveyor belt.

Restaurant La Victoire (03 88 35 39 35; 24 quai des Pêcheurs; menu €8.70; 11.30am-2pm & 6.30pm-1am, closed Sat & Sun; Gallia) A great place for a hearty French or Alsatian meal, especially late at night. Vegetarians can order *bibeleskaes* (Alsace cheese, €8.50).

Le Michel (03 88 35 45 40; 20 av de la Marseillaise; menus €9.50-15; 6am-9pm Mon-Fri, 6am-7pm Sat; Gallia) Hugely popular with locals, this Paris-style cafe-brasserie – locally known as

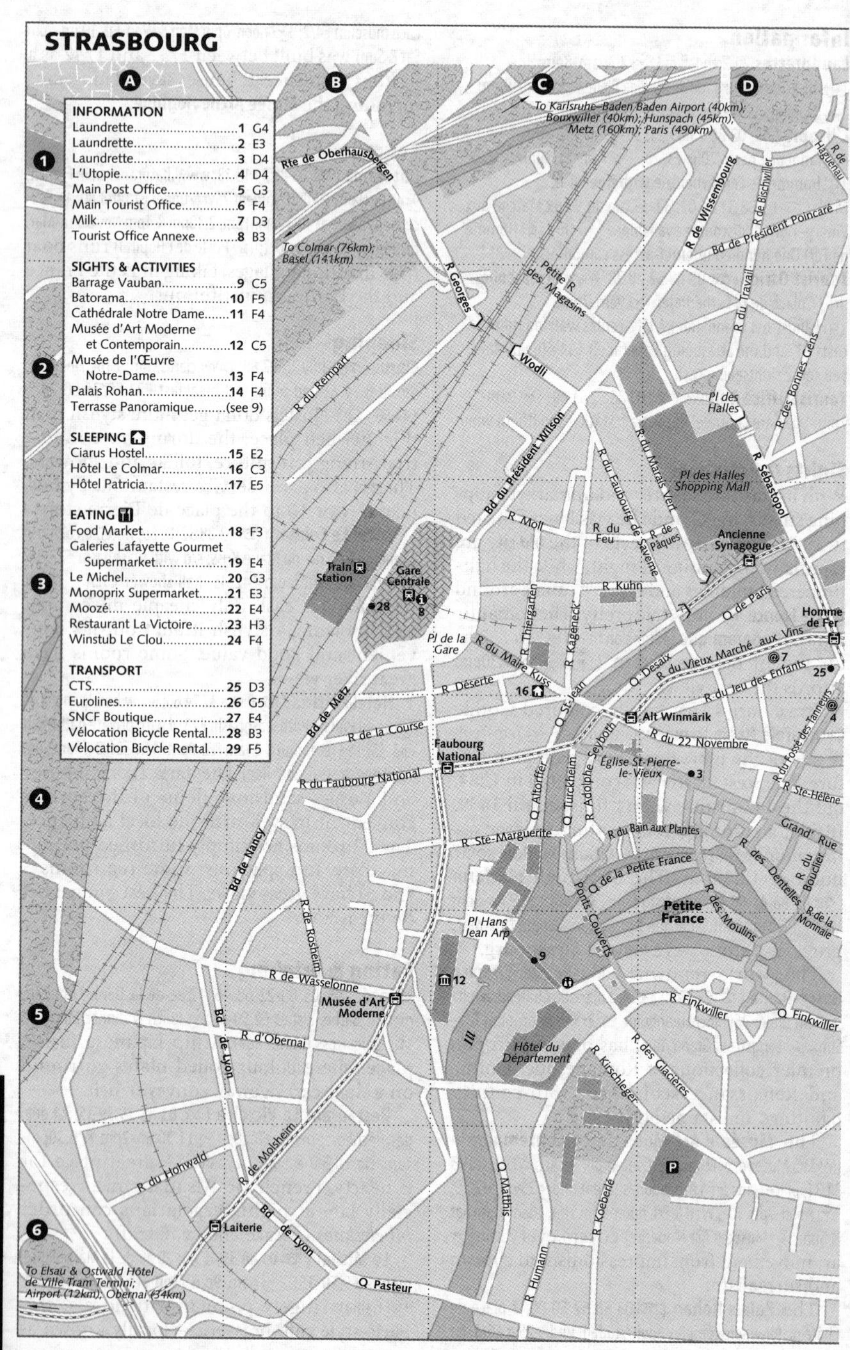
STRASBOURG
INFORMATION
Laundrette 1 G4
Laundrette 2 E3
Laundrette 3 D4
L'Utopie 4 D4
Main Post Office 5 G3
Main Tourist Office 6 F4
Milk 7 D3
Tourist Office Annexe 8 B3
SIGHTS & ACTIVITIES
Barrage Vauban 9 C5
Batorama 10 F5
Cathédrale Notre Dame 11 F4
Musée d'Art Moderne et Contemporain 12 C5
Musée de l'Œuvre Notre-Dame 13 F4
Palais Rohan 14 F4
Terrasse Panoramique (see 9)
SLEEPING
Ciarus Hostel 15 E2
Hôtel Le Colmar 16 C3
Hôtel Patricia 17 E5
EATING
Food Market 18 F3
Galeries Lafayette Gourmet Supermarket 19 E4
Le Michel 20 G3
Monoprix Supermarket 21 E3
Moozé 22 E4
Restaurant La Victoire 23 H3
Winstub Le Clou 24 F4
TRANSPORT
CTS 25 D3
Eurolines 26 G5
SNCF Boutique 27 E4
Vélocation Bicycle Rental 28 B3
Vélocation Bicycle Rental 29 F5
To Karlsruhe–Baden Baden Airport (40km); Bouxwiller (40km); Hunspach (45km); Metz (160km); Paris (490km)
To Colmar (76km); Basel (141km)
To Elsau & Ostwald Hôtel de Ville Tram Termini; Airport (12km); Obernai (34km)
Rte de Oberhausbergen
R Georges
Wodli
R du Rempart
Petite R des Magasins
R de Wissembourg
R de Bischwiller
Bd de Président Poincaré
R du Travail
R de Haguenau
R des Bonnes Gens
Pl des Halles
Pl des Halles Shopping Mall
R Sébastopol
R du Marais Vert
R du Faubourg de Saverne
Bd du Président Wilson
R Moll
R du Feu
R de Pâques
Ancienne Synagogue
R Kuhn
Train Station
Gare Centrale
Pl de la Gare
R du Maire Kuss
R Thiergarten
R Kageneck
Q de Paris
Homme de Fer
Q Desaix
R du Vieux Marché aux Vins
R du Jeu des Enfants
R Déserte
Q St-Jean
Alt Winmärik
R du Fossé des Tanneurs
Bd de Metz
R de la Course
R du 22 Novembre
Faubourg National
R du Faubourg National
Q Altorffer
Q Turckheim
R Adolphe Seyboth
Église St-Pierre-le-Vieux
R Ste-Hélène
Grand' Rue
R du Bain aux Plantes
R Ste-Marguerite
Q de la Petite France
R des Dentelles
R du Bouclier
Ponts Couverts
Petite France
R des Moulins
R de la Monnaie
Bd de Nancy
R de Rosheim
Pl Hans Jean Arp
R de Wasselonne
Musée d'Art Moderne
R Finkwiller
Q Finkwiller
Ill
Hôtel du Département
R des Glacières
R Kirschleger
R d'Obernai
Bd de Lyon
R du Hohwald
R de Molsheim
Laiterie
Q Matthis
R Koeberlé
R Humann
Q Pasteur
FRANCE

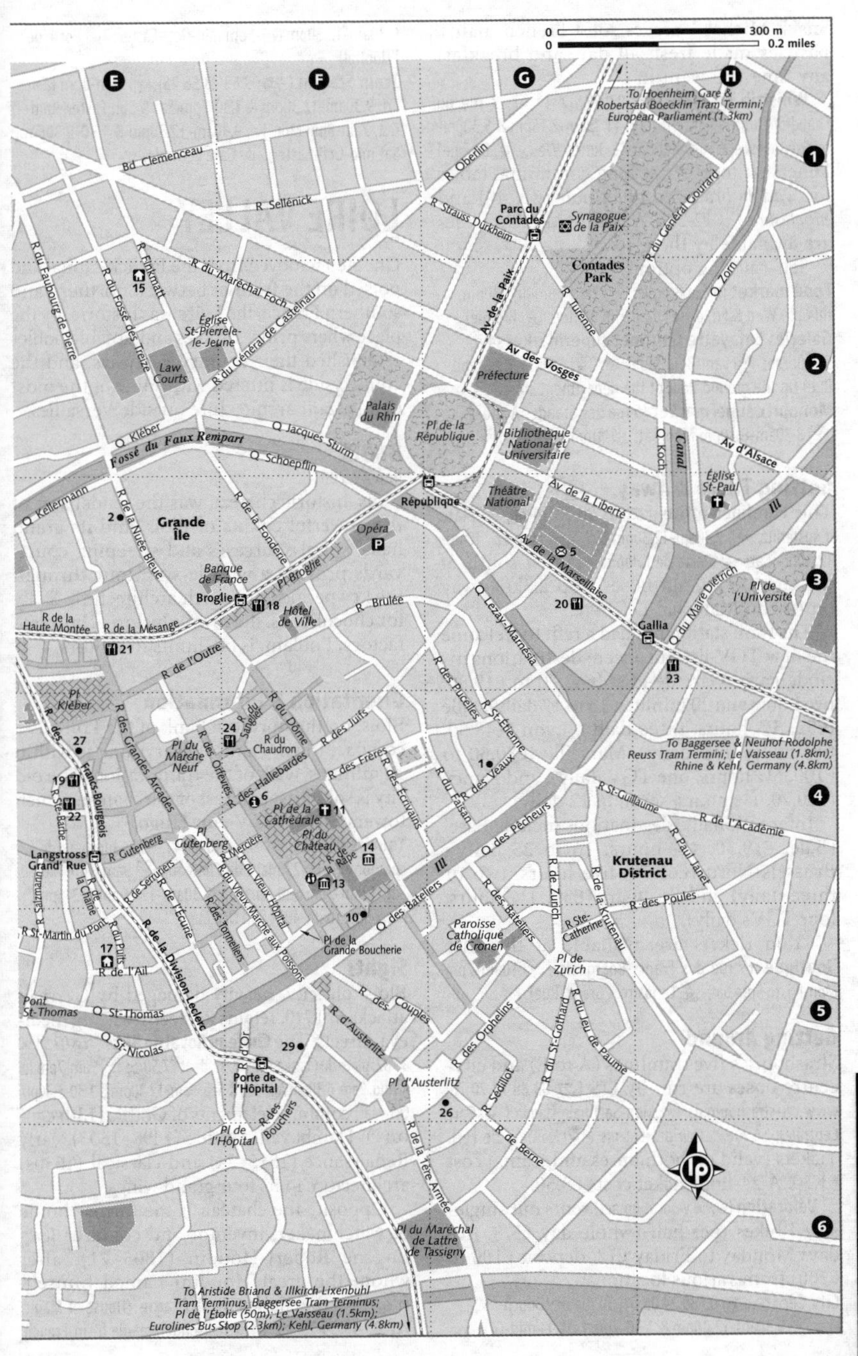
To Hoenheim Gare & Robertsau Boecklin Tram Termini; European Parliament (1.3km)
Bd Clemenceau
R Oberlin
R Sellénick
R Strauss Dürkheim
Parc du Contades
Synagogue de la Paix
Contades Park
R du Général Gourard
R du Faubourg de Pierre
R Finkmatt
R du Fossé des Treize
R du Maréchal Foch
R du Général de Castelnau
Av de la Paix
R Turenne
Q Zorn
Église St-Pierre-le-Jeune
Law Courts
Av des Vosges
Préfecture
Palais du Rhin
Pl de la République
Bibliothèque National et Universitaire
Q Kléber
Fossé du Faux Rempart
Q Jacques Sturm
Q Schoepflin
Q Koch
Canal
Av d'Alsace
Église St-Paul
Q Kellermann
Grande Île
R de la Nuée Bleue
R de la Fonderie
République
Théâtre National
Av de la Liberté
Ill
Opéra
Av de la Marseillaise
Banque de France
Pl Broglie
Broglie
Hôtel de Ville
R Brulée
Q Lezay-Marnésia
Q du Maire Dietrich
Pl de l'Université
Gallia
R de la Haute Montée
R de la Mésange
R de l'Outre
R des Pucelles
Pl Kléber
R des Francs-Bourgeois
R des Grandes Arcades
R du Sanglier
R du Dôme
R des Juifs
R St-Etienne
R du Chaudron
Pl du Marché Neuf
R des Orfèvres
R des Hallebardes
R des Frères
R des Écrivains
R du Faisan
R des Veaux
To Baggersee & Neuhof Rodolphe Reuss Tram Termini; Le Vaisseau (1.8km); Rhine & Kehl, Germany (4.8km)
R St-Guillaume
R de l'Académie
R Ste-Barbe
Pl de la Cathédrale
Pl du Château
R de la Râpe
Q des Pêcheurs
R Paul Janet
Krutenau District
Langstross Grand' Rue
R Gutenberg
Pl Gutenberg
R Mercière
R du Vieux Hôpital
R de Zurich
R de la Krutenau
R Salzmann
R de la Chaîne
R des Serruriers
R de l'Écurie
R des Tonneliers
R du Vieux Marché aux Poissons
Q des Bateliers
R des Bateliers
R des Poules
R Ste-Catherine
R St-Martin du Pont
R du Puits
Pl de la Grande Boucherie
Paroisse Catholique de Cronen
R de l'Ail
R de la Division Leclerc
Pl de Zurich
Pont St-Thomas
Q St-Thomas
R des Couples
R d'Austerlitz
R du St-Gothard
R du Jeu de Paume
Q St-Nicolas
R d'Or
R des Orphelins
Porte de l'Hôpital
Pl d'Austerlitz
R Sédillot
R des Bouchers
Pl de l'Hôpital
R de la 1ère Armée
R de Berne
Pl du Maréchal de Lattre de Tassigny
To Aristide Briand & Illkirch Lixenbuhl Tram Terminus, Baggersee Tram Terminus; Pl de l'Étoile (50m), Le Vaisseau (1.5km); Eurolines Bus Stop (2.3km); Kehl, Germany (4.8km)
0 300 m
0 0.2 miles

FRANCE

Snack Michel – serves solid French mains, pastries made fresh all day, and breakfast any time you want it.

Winstub Le Clou (☎ 03 88 32 11 67; 3 rue du Chaudron; lunch menu €15; 11.45am-2.15pm & 5.30pm-midnight except Sun, holidays & lunch Wed; Broglie) Diners sit together at long communal tables for *wädele braisé au pinot noir* (€16.40) and *bibeleskaes* (€12.20). A dozen Alsatian wines are available by the glass.

Self-catering options:

Food market (place Broglie; 7am-5pm or 5.30pm, till 6pm Wed & Fri, closes earlier in winter; Broglie)

Galeries Lafayette Gourmet supermarket (4 rue Ste-Barbe; 9am-8pm Mon-Sat; Langstross Grand' Rue) On the ground floor of the department store.

Monoprix supermarket (5 rue des Grandes Arcades; 8.30am-8.30pm Mon-Sat; Homme de Fer)

Getting There & Away

The **Eurolines office** (☎ 03 90 22 14 60; 6D place d'Austerlitz; 9.30am-12.30pm & 2-6pm Mon-Fri, 10am-12.30pm Sat; Porte de l'Hôpital) is just south of the Grande Île, but buses stop 2.5km away on rue du Maréchal Lefèbvre.

The train station has had a refit to welcome the new TGV Est Européen; destinations include Paris' Gare de l'Est (€63.70 to €19.80, two hours and 20 minutes, 13 to 17 daily), Lille (€52, 3½ hours, three daily), Lyon (€48.30, five hours, five daily), Marseille (€80.50 to €100, 6½ hours, one TGV daily), and Nancy (€20.70, 1½ hours, seven to 12 daily).

Internationally, destinations include Basel (Bâle; €19.30, 1¼ hours, 16 to 25 daily), Brussels-Nord (€61.70, five hours, two or three daily) and Stuttgart (€39, 1¼ hours, four TGVs daily).

Train tickets are available at the **SNCF Boutique** (5 rue des Francs-Bourgeois; 10am-7pm Mon-Fri, to 5pm Sat; Langstross Grand' Rue).

Getting Around

Strasbourg's five tramlines (A to E) and city-centre buses are run by **CTS** (☎ 03 88 77 70 70; www.cts-strasbourg.fr; Mon-Sat) train station (Gare Centrale); 56 rue du Jeu des Enfants (Homme de Fer). Tickets (valid on both buses and trams) cost €1.30. A 24-hour ticket costs €3.50.

Vélocation (www.velocation.net) rents out single-speed bikes (per half-/whole day €5/8, five days Monday to Friday €12, deposit €100 to €200) from various locations:

City Centre (☎ 03 88 24 05 61; 10 rue des Bouchers; 9.30am-12.30pm & 1.30-7pm Easter–mid-Oct, 9.30am-12.30pm & 1-5pm mid-Oct–Easter; Porte de l'Hôpital)

Train Station (☎ 03 88 23 56 75; 7am-8pm Mon-Fri, 9.30am-12.30pm & 1.30-7pm Sat & Sun Easter–mid-Oct, 7am-8pm Mon-Fri, 9.30am-12.30pm & 1.30-5.30pm Sat mid-Oct–Easter; Gare Centrale)

LOIRE VALLEY

One step removed from the French capital and poised on the frontier between northern and southern France, the Loire was historically the place where princes, dukes and notable nobles established their country getaways, and the countryside is littered with some of the most extravagant architecture outside Versailles.

BLOIS

pop 49,200

Blois' historic chateau was the feudal seat of the powerful counts of Blois, and its grand halls, spiral staircases and sweeping courtyards provide a whistle-stop tour through the key periods of French architecture. Sadly for chocoholics, the town's historic chocolate factory, Poulain, is off-limits to visitors.

Orientation & Information

Blois, on the northern bank of the Loire, is a compact town – almost everything is within 10 minutes' walk of the train station. The old city is southeast and east of the chateau, which towers over place Victor Hugo.

Tourist Office (☎ 02 54 90 41 41; www.bloispaysdechambord.com; 23 place du Château; 9am-7pm Mon-Sat, 10am-7pm Sun Apr-Sep, 9.30am-12.30pm & 2-6pm Mon-Sat, 10am-4pm Sun Oct-Mar)

Sights

Blois' old city, heavily damaged by German attacks in 1940, retains its steep, twisting medieval streets. The **Château Royal de Blois** (☎ 02 54 90 33 32; place du Château; adult/student €7.50/5; 9am-7pm Jul & Aug, 9am-6.30pm Apr-Jun & Sep, 9am-12.30pm & 1.30-5.30pm Oct-Mar) combines elements of Gothic (13th century); Flamboyant Gothic (1498–1503), early Renaissance (1515–24) and classical (1630s) architecture in its four grand wings.

Opposite the chateau is the former home of watchmaker, inventor and conjurer Jean Eugène Robert-Houdin (1805–71), after whom the great Houdini named himself. It's now the **Maison de la Magie** (House of Magic; ☎ 02 54 55 26 26; www.maisondelamagie.fr, in French;

1 place du Château; adult/student €7.50/6.50, incl chateau €12.50/8.50; 10am-12.30pm & 2-6.30pm Mar-late Sep & late Oct-early Nov).

The brilliant (and very French) **Musée de l'Objet** (02 54 55 37 45; www.museedelobjet.org; 6 rue Franciade; adult/student €4/2; 1.30-6.30pm Wed-Sun late Jun-Aug, 1.30-6.30pm Fri-Sun late Feb-late Jun & Sep-Dec) is a treasure trove of modern art based around everyday materials – look out for works by Dali and Man Ray.

Sleeping & Eating

Hôtel Le Savoie (02 54 74 32 21; hotel.le.savoie@wanadoo.fr; 6 rue Ducoux; s €41-45, d €48-54) Straightforward station hotel. The modern chain-style rooms are hardly award-winning: expect prefab furniture and easy-clean fabrics.

Hôtel de France (02 54 78 00 53; www.franceetguise.com; 3 rue Gallois; s €45, d 49-53) Chandeliers, glass and brass left from this hotel's *belle époque* heyday decorate the lobby, but the musty rooms are looking tired: ask for a balcony overlooking the Église St-Vincent.

Côté Loire (02 54 78 07 86; www.coteloire.com; 2 place de la Grève; d early Nov-Mar €48-67, Apr-early Nov €53-72) If it's charm and colours you want, the homely Loire Coast has haphazard rooms decked out in checks, pastels and the odd exposed brick.

Au Bouchon Lyonnais (02 54 74 12 87; 25 rue des Violettes; mains €12-14) Classic neighbourhood bistro with a flavour of bygone days, where the food is straight out of the Lyonnaise cookbook: snails, duck steaks and *la veritable andouillette* (true tripe sausage).

Self-catering options:

Food market (rue Anne de Bretagne; 7.30am or 8am-1pm Tue, Thu & Sat)

Intermarché supermarket (16 av Gambetta)

Getting There & Around

TLC (02 54 58 55 44; www.tlcinfo.net) buses run to Chambord (€3.99, Line 2, 40 minutes, four Monday to Saturday, one on Sunday) and Cheverny (€1.10, Line 4, 45 minutes, six to eight Monday to Friday, three on Saturday, two on Sunday).

There are regular trains to Amboise (€6, 20 minutes, at least 10 daily), Orléans (€9.30, 45 minutes, at least hourly) and Tours (€9.10, 40 minutes, hourly), plus Paris' Gare d'Austerlitz (€23.30, two hours, eight to 13 daily).

The **Châteaux à Vélo** (www.chateauxavelo.com) network offers 11 waymarked cycling routes in the Blois area. For bike hire:

Cycles Leblond (02 54 74 30 13; 44 Levée des Tuileries; per half-/full day €9/12; 9am-9pm)

Randovélo (02 54 78 62 52; www.randovelo.fr; 29 rue du Puits Neuf; per day €14; 9am-6pm Mon-Fri Apr-Oct)

AROUND BLOIS

Château de Chambord

For full-blown chateau splendour, you can't top **Chambord** (02 54 50 50 20; www.chambord.org; adult/18-25yr €9.50/7.50, €1 reduction Jan-Mar & Oct-Dec; 9am-7.30pm mid-Jul–mid-Aug, 9am-6.15pm mid-Mar–mid-Jul & mid-Aug–Sep, 9am-5.15pm Jan–mid-Mar & Oct-Dec).

The chateau's most famous feature is the double-helix staircase, attributed by some to Leonardo da Vinci, who lived in Amboise (34km southwest) from 1516 until his death three years later. The Italianate rooftop terrace, surrounded by cupolas, domes, chimneys and slate roofs, was where the royal court assembled to watch military exercises and hunting parties returning at the end of the day.

Several times daily there are 1½-hour **guided tours** (€4) in English. Free *son et lumière* shows, known as **Les Clairs de Lune**, are projected onto the chateau's facade nightly from July to mid-September.

Chambord is 16km east of Blois, 45km southwest of Orléans and 17km northeast of Cheverny. For details on public transport options, see left.

Château de Cheverny

Thought by many to be the most perfectly proportioned chateau, **Cheverny** (02 54 79 96 29; www.chateau-cheverny.fr; admission €7; 9.15am-6.45pm Jul & Aug, 9.15am-6.15pm Apr-Jun & Sep, 9.45am-5.30pm Oct, 9.45am-5pm Nov-Mar) has hardly been altered since its construction between 1625 and 1634. Inside you'll find a formal dining room, bridal chamber and children's playroom (complete with Napoléon III–era toys), as well as a guards' room full of pikestaffs, claymores and suits of armour. Many priceless artworks (including the *Mona Lisa)* were stashed in the 18th-century **Orangerie** during WWII.

Cheverny is 16km southeast of Blois and 17km southwest of Chambord. For information on the bus from Blois, see left.

Château de Chaumont

It's a brisk climb up to **Château de Chaumont-sur-Loire** (02 54 51 26 26; admission €7.50; 10am-6pm mid-May–mid-Sep, 10.30am-5.30pm Apr–mid-May & mid-Sep–end Sep, 10am-5pm Oct-Mar), which is set on a

CHÂTEAUX TOURS

The **Pass'-Châteaux**, available from local tourist offices, covers several chateaux, including **Chambord–Cheverny–Blois** (€19) and **Blois–Cheverny–Chaumont–Chambord** (€25.20).

Several operators offer minibus trips if you're short on time: half-day trips cost between €18 and €33; full-day trips range from €40 to €50 (chateau admission is extra).

- **Acco-Dispo** (☎ 06 82 00 64 51; www.accodispo-tours.com)
- **Alienor** (☎ 02 47 61 22 23, 06 10 85 35 39; www.locationdevelos.com)
- **Quart de Tours** (☎ 06 85 72 16 22; www.quartdetours.com)
- **St-Eloi Excursions** (☎ 02 47 37 08 04; www.saint-eloi.com)

bluff overlooking the Loire. The entrance, across a wooden drawbridge between two wide towers, opens onto an inner courtyard from where there are stunning views. Opposite the main entrance are the luxurious stables, built in 1877.

Chaumont-sur-Loire is 17km southwest of Blois and 20km northeast of Amboise. Onzain, an easyish walk from Chaumont across the Loire, has trains to Blois (€3, 10 minutes, 10 to 14 daily) and Tours (€7.20, 35 minutes).

TOURS

pop 298,000

Hovering somewhere between the style of Paris and the conservative sturdiness of central France, Tours is one of the principal cities of the Loire Valley. It's a smart, solidly bourgeois kind of place, filled with wide 18th-century boulevards, parks and imposing public buildings, as well as a busy university of some 25,000 students.

Orientation & Information

The central hub of place Jean-Jaurès connects the main thoroughfares – west–east bd Béranger and bd Heurteloup, and north–south rue Nationale and av de Grammont. The old city encircles place Plumereau, 400m west of rue Nationale.

Emega Cyberstation (43 rue du Grand Marché; per hr €2; ⌚ noon-midnight Mon-Sat, 2-11pm Sun) Internet access.

Tourist Office (☎ 02 47 70 37 37; www.ligeris.com; 78-82 rue Bernard Palissy; ⌚ 8.30am-7pm Mon-Sat, 10am-12.30pm & 2.30-5pm Sun mid-Apr–mid-Oct, 9am-12.30pm & 1.30-6pm Mon-Sat, 10am-1pm Sun mid-Oct–mid-Apr)

Sights

Arranged around the courtyard of the former archbishop's palace, the **Musée des Beaux-Arts** (☎ 02 47 05 68 73; 18 place François Sicard; adult/student €4/2; ⌚ 9am-12.45pm & 2-6pm Wed-Mon) is a fine example of a French provincial arts museum – look out for works by Delacroix, Degas, Monet, Rembrandt and Rubens.

With its twin west towers and Gothic arches and gargoyles, the **Cathédrale St-Gatien** (place de la Cathédrale; ⌚ 9am-7pm) is a show-stopper. It's particularly known for its stained glass; the interior dates from the 13th to 16th centuries, and the domed tops of the 70m-high towers date from the Renaissance.

France's skilled labourers, including pastry chefs, coopers and locksmiths, are celebrated at the **Musée du Compagnonnage** (☎ 02 47 61 07 93; 8 rue Nationale; adult/student €5/3; ⌚ 9am-12.30pm & 2-6pm mid-Jun–mid-Sep, 9am-noon & 2-6pm Wed-Mon mid-Sep–mid-Jun).

Tours has several public parks, including the 19th-century **botanic garden** (bd Tonnelle; admission free; ⌚ 7.45am-sunset) a five-hectare landscaped park with a tropical greenhouse, medicinal herb garden and petting zoo. The park is 1.6km west of place Jean Jaurès; bus 4 along bd Béranger stops nearby.

Sleeping

Auberge de Jeunesse du Vieux Tours (☎ 02 47 37 81 58; www.ajtours.org; 5 rue Bretonneau; dm €17.40; ⌚ reception 8am-noon & 6-11pm; 💻) Friendly, bustling hostel with a large foreign-student and young-worker contingent; there are several kitchens and lounges, but no en suites.

Hôtel Régina (☎ 02 47 05 25 36; fax 02 47 66 08 72; 2 rue Pimbert; d with shower €26.60-44, d with shower & toilet €31.60-50) Budget cheapie with a bedsit vibe, offering simple rooms with mix-and-match furniture and a choice of pinks, blues and pale whites. Curfew is 1am.

Hôtel Val de Loire (☎ 02 47 05 37 86; hotel.val.de.loire@club-Internet.fr; 33 bd Heurteloup; s €30-40, d €40-50) Higgledy-piggledy rooms spread around an 1870 townhouse, with period features in-

SPLURGE

our pick **L'Adresse** (☎ 02 47 20 85 76; www.hotel-ladresse.com; 12 rue de la Rôtisserie; s €50, d €70-90) Looking for Parisian style in provincial Tours? Then you're in luck – 'The Address' is a boutique bonanza, with rooms finished in sleek slates and ochres, topped off with wi-fi, flat-screen TVs and designer sinks.

cluding parquet floors, faded rugs and scruffy furniture, as well as double glazing to shut out the road noise.

Eating

In the old city, place Plumereau, rue du Grand Marché and rue de la Rôtisserie are loaded with restaurants and cafes.

Tartines & Co (☎ 02 47 20 50 60; 6 rue des Fusillés; mains from €8.50, lunch menu €13.20; 10am-5pm) Snazzy little bistro that reinvents the traditional *croque* (toasted sandwich). Choose your topping – chicken, roasted veg, carpaccio beef – and it's served on toasted artisan bread.

Comme Autre Fouée (☎ 02 47 05 94 78; 11 rue de la Monnaie; lunch menu €10, other menus €16-19.50; lunch Sat & Sun, dinner Tue-Sat, lunch Tue-Thu mid-May–mid-Sep) For local flavour, you can't top this place, which churns out the house speciality of *fouées*, a pitta-like disc of dough stuffed with pork rillettes, *haricots blancs* (white beans) or goat's cheese.

For all your picnicking needs:

Atac supermarket 5 place du Général Leclerc (7.30am-8pm Mon-Sat); 19 place Jean Jaurès (9am-7.30pm Mon-Sat) The place Jean Jaurès branch is inside the shopping centre.

Les Halles (covered market; place Gaston Pailhou; 7am-7pm)

Drinking

Place Plum and the surrounding streets are plastered in grungy drinking dens.

Bistro 64 (64 rue du Grand Marché; 11am-2am Mon-Sat) Cosy neighbourhood bar that's one step removed from the place Plum hustle. Scuffed-up decor, jazz combos and plenty of house beers keep the local crowd happy.

L'Alexandra (☎ 02 47 61 48 30; 106 rue du Commerce; noon-2am Mon-Fri, 3pm-2am Sat & Sun) Popular Anglo-Saxon bar crammed with students and late-night boozers. Wi-fi's €2.

Getting There & Away

Tours–Val de Loire Airport (☎ 02 47 49 37 00; www.tours-aeroport.com), about 5km northeast of central Tours, is linked to London's Stansted airport and Dublin by Ryanair. A shuttle bus (€5) leaves the bus station two hours before and half an hour after each Ryanair flight.

Touraine Fil Vert (☎ 02 47 47 17 18; www.touraine-filvert.com, in French) runs buses to Amboise (35 minutes, 12 daily Monday to Saturday) and Chenonceaux (1¼ hours, two daily).

Tours is the Loire's main rail hub. The train station is linked to St-Pierre-des-Corps, Tours' TGV train station, by frequent shuttle trains. Trains run at least hourly between Tours and Orléans (€16.60, one to 1½ hours), stopping at Amboise (€4.60, 20 minutes) and Blois (€9.10, 40 minutes). High-speed TGVs rocket to Paris-Gare Montparnasse (€39.10 to €55.10, 1¼ hours, around 15 daily), Bordeaux (€45, 2¾ hours), Poitiers (€18.50 to €20.40, one hour) and Nantes (€25 to €26.90, 1½ hours).

AROUND TOURS

Tours is an excellent base for exploring nearby chateaux.

The 16th-century **Château de Chenonceau** (☎ 02 47 23 90 07; www.chenonceau.com; adult/student €10/7.50, with audioguide €14/11.50; 9am-8pm Jul-Aug, 9am-7.30pm Jun & Sep, 9am-7pm Apr & May, 9.30am-5pm or 6pm rest of year) is one of the most architecturally attractive (and busiest) of the Loire chateaux, surrounded by a glassy moat and sweeping gardens, and topped by turrets and towers. The highlight is the stunning 60m-long Grande Gallerie spanning the Cher River.

Built in the 1500s on an island in the River Indre, **Azay-le-Rideau** (☎ 02 47 45 42 04; adult/18-25yr €7.50/4.80; 9.30am-7pm Jul & Aug, 9.30am-6pm Apr-Jun & Sep, 10am-12.30pm & 2-5.30pm Oct-Mar) is another moat-ringed wonder, decorated with geometric windows, ordered turrets and decorative stonework, as well as a famous loggia staircase.

For medieval atmosphere, head for **Château de Langeais** (☎ 02 47 96 72 60; admission €7.50; 9.30am-7pm Jul & Aug, to 6.30pm Feb-Jun & Sep–mid-Nov, 10am-5pm mid-Nov-Jan), complete with its own working drawbridge, crenellated battlements and ruined 10th-century *donjon* (keep), thought to be the oldest in France.

AMBOISE

pop 11,500

The childhood home of Charles VIII and the final resting place of Leonardo da Vinci, upmarket Amboise is an elegant provincial town, perched along the Loire and overlooked by its fortified 15th-century chateau. Da Vinci whiled away his last three years here under the patronage of François I; you can view many of his wackiest contraptions at the mansion of Clos Lucé (below).

Information

Laundrette (7 allée du Sergent Turpin; ⌚ 7am-8pm)
Playconnect (119 rue Nationale; per hr €3; ⌚ 3-10pm Sun & Mon, 10am-10pm Tue-Sat) Internet access.
Tourist Office (☎ 02 47 57 09 28; www.amboise-valdeloire.com; ⌚ 9am-8pm Mon-Sat & 10am-6pm Sun Jul & Aug, 10am-1pm & 2-6pm Mon-Sat, 10am-1pm Sun Apr-Jun & Sep, 10am-1pm & 2-6pm Mon-Sat Oct-Mar) Sells walking and cycling maps and a discount ticket for the chateau and Clos Lucé.

Sights

The **Château Royal d'Amboise** (☎ 02 47 57 00 98; place Michel Debré; adult/15-25yr €9/7.50; ⌚ 9am-7pm Jul-Aug, 9am-6.30pm Apr-Jun, 9am-6pm Sep-Oct, 9am-5.30pm Mar & early Nov, 9am-12.30pm mid-Nov–Feb) sprawls on a rocky bluff above town. Charles VIII (r 1483–98) was responsible for the chateau's Italianate remodelling in 1492. Today, just a few of the original 15th- and 16th-century structures survive, notably the **Flamboyant Gothic wing** and the **Chapelle St-Hubert**, believed to be the final resting place of da Vinci.

Leonardo da Vinci moved into nearby **Clos Lucé** (☎ 02 47 57 00 73; www.vinci-closluce.com; 2 rue du Clos Lucé; adult/student Mar–mid-Nov €12.50/9.50, mid-Nov–Mar €9.50/7; ⌚ 9am-8pm Jul-Aug, 9am-7pm Feb-Jun & Sep-Oct, 9am-6pm Nov-Jan) in 1516, and the house and grounds feature scale models of his inventions, including a protoautomobile, tank, parachute, hydraulic turbine and even a primitive helicopter.

Sleeping

Camping Municipal de l'Île d'Or (☎ 02 47 57 23 37; Île d'Or; adult €2.45-2.50, tent €3.25-3.30; ⌚ mid-Mar-early Oct; ♿) Pleasant camping ground on a peaceful river island, with tennis courts, ping pong and canoe hire.

Centre Charles Péguy-Auberge de Jeunesse (☎ 02 47 30 60 90; www.mjcamboise.fr; Île d'Or; dm €12; ⌚ reception 2-8pm Mon-Fri, 5-8pm Sat & Sun; 💻) Efficient boarding school–style hostel on the Île d'Or, with 72 beds mostly in three- or four-bed dorms, and treats including table football and bike hire.

Hotel Blason (☎ 02 47 23 22 41; www.leblason.fr; 11 place Richelieu; d €44-58, tr €66-68; 💻 P) Quirky, creaky budget hotel, on a quiet square in a wood-fronted building that previously served as a convent school, laundry and blacksmith's. The 25 higgledy-piggledy rooms are titchy, flowery and timber-beamed.

Eating

Café des Arts (☎/fax 02 47 57 25 04; 32 rue Victor Hugo; meals €4-12) Spit-and-sawdust local's bar, dishing up beer and bar snacks near the chateau's old gate.

Bigot (☎ 02 47 57 59 32; 2 rue Nationale; ⌚ 9am-7.30pm Tue-Fri, 8.30am-7.30pm Sat & Sun) Since 1913 this award-winning chocolatier and pâtisserie has been whipping up some of the Loire's creamiest cakes and gooiest treats: multicoloured *macarrons*, buttery biscuits and handmade *petits fours*.

Chez Bruno (☎ 02 47 57 73 49; place Michel Debré; 2-/3-course menu €11/15; ⌚ lunch Wed-Sun, dinner Fri & Sat) Amboise's new boy uncorks a host of local vintages in a coolly contemporary setting (white tablecloths, big gleaming glasses, snazzy artwork), accompanied by honest regional cooking.

Amboise's outdoor **food market** (⌚ 8am-1pm Fri & Sun) fills the river-bank car parks west of the tourist office. There's also a **Marché Plus** (5 quai du Général de Gaulle; ⌚ 7am-9pm Mon-Sat, 10am-2pm Sun).

Getting There & Around

Touraine Fil Vert's line C1 links Amboise with Tours (€1.50, 45 minutes, nine daily Monday to Saturday). One bus continues on to Chenonceaux (15 minutes) from Monday to Saturday, with an extra afternoon bus in summer.

The **train station** (bd Gambetta) is served by trains from Paris' Gare d'Austerlitz (€24.20, 2¼ to three hours, 11 daily), Blois (€5.60, 20 minutes, 10 to 20 daily) and Tours (€4.50, 15 minutes, 10 to 20 daily).

Hire mountain bikes at **Cycles Richard** (☎ 02 47 57 01 79; 2 rue de Nazelles; per day €15; 🕒 9am-noon & 2.30-7pm Tue-Sat).

BURGUNDY & THE RHÔNE VALLEY

If there's one place in France where you're really going to find out what makes the nation tick, it's Burgundy. Two of the country's enduring passions – food and wine – come together in this gorgeously rural region, and if you're a sucker for hearty food and the fruits of the vine, you'll be in seventh heaven.

DIJON

pop 230,000

Filled with elegant medieval and Renaissance buildings, dashing Dijon is the region's lively capital, as well as the spiritual home of French mustard. The city makes an excellent launchpad for exploring wider Burgundy, and a population of some 25,000 students keeps the nightlife snappy.

Orientation

Dijon's main thoroughfare stretches from the train station eastwards to the Palais des Ducs to Église St-Michel. The main shopping precinct is around rue de la Liberté and rue du Bourg. The old town centres on place François Rude.

Information

Cyberbisey (☎ 03 80 30 95 41; 53 rue Berbisey; per hr €3; 🕒 10am-8pm Mon-Fri, noon-8pm Sat) Internet access.

Cyberspace 21 (☎ 03 80 30 57 43; 46 rue Monge; per hr €4; 🕒 11am-midnight Mon-Sat, 2pm-midnight Sun & holidays) Internet access.

Laundrettes 41 rue Auguste Comte (🕒 6am-9pm); 28 rue Berbisey (🕒 6am-9pm); 55 rue Berbisey (🕒 7am-8.30pm); 8 place de la Banque (🕒 7am-8.30pm)

Tourist Office (☎ 08 92 70 05 58; www.dijon-tourism.com; 11 rue des Forges; 🕒 9am-7pm Mon-Sat, 9am-12.30pm & 2.30-5pm Sun & holidays May-Oct, 10am-noon & 2-6pm Mon-Sat, 2.30-5.30pm Sun & holidays Nov-Apr) *The Owl's Trail* (€2.50), available in 11 languages, details a city-centre walking tour (follow bronze triangles).

Tourist Office Annexe (place Darcy; 🕒 9am-12.30pm & 2.30-6pm Mon-Sat, 2-6pm Sun & holidays May-Oct, 10am-12.30pm & 2.30-6pm Mon-Sat Nov-Apr)

Sights & Activities

Once home to the region's rulers, the elaborate **Palais des Ducs et des États de Bourgogne** complex lies at the heart of old Dijon. The 15th-century **Tour Philippe le Bon** (Tower of Philip the Good; ☎ 03 80 74 52 71; adult/student €2.30/1.20; 🕒 accompanied climbs every 45min 9am-noon & 1.45-5.30pm Easter-late Nov, 9-11am & 1.30-3.30pm Wed afternoon, Sat & Sun late Nov-Easter) affords fantastic views over the city.

Housed in the palace's east wing, the **Musée des Beaux-Arts** (☎ 03 80 74 52 09; admission free, audioguide €3.90; 🕒 9.30am-6pm Wed-Mon May-Oct, 10am-5pm Wed-Mon Nov-Apr) has an enormous collection ranging from medieval paintings to sculptures by Dijon-born François Rude (1784–1855). You can also visit the **ducal kitchens** and the wood-panelled **Salle des Gardes** (Guards' Room).

The **Musée Archéologique** (☎ 03 80 30 88 54; 5 rue du Docteur Maret; 🕒 9am-12.30pm & 1.30-6pm Wed-Sun, also open Mon mid-May–Sep) displays Celtic, Roman and Merovingian artefacts, including a 1st-century bronze of the goddess Sequana standing on a boat.

The **Musée de la Vie Bourguignonne** (☎ 03 80 44 12 69; 17 rue Ste Anne; 🕒 9am-noon & 2-6pm Wed-Mon) explores rural Burgundian life and the **Musée d'Art Sacré** (☎ 03 80 44 12 69; 15 rue Ste Anne; 🕒 9am-noon & 2-6pm Wed-Mon) displays ritual objects from the 12th to 19th centuries.

Sleeping

Ethic Étapes Dijon (CRISD; ☎ 03 80 72 95 20; www.auberge-cri-dijon.com; 1 bd Champollion; dm/s/d incl breakfast €19.50/36.50/49, €1.50 less per person after 1st night; 💻) This institutional (though friendly) 216-bed hostel, 2.5km northeast of the centre, was completely renovated in 2006. Most beds are in modern, airy rooms for two. By bus, take Liane 4 to the Epirey CRI stop.

Hôtel Chambellan (☎ 03 80 67 12 67; www.hotel-chambellan.com; 92 rue Vannerie; s/d with washbasin €29/32, with private bathroom from €43/48) Built in 1730, this two-star place has a vaguely medieval feel. Most of the rooms, decorated in cheerful tones of red, orange, pink and white, have courtyard views.

Hôtel Chateaubriand (☎ 03 80 41 42 18; www.hotelchateaubriand.fr, in French; 3 av Maréchal Foch; d with washbasin €35.60, with private bathroom €40.60-45.60) An old-fashioned cheapie, this 23-room place has the air of a well-worn dive but has far more character than the sterile chain hotels down the block.

Hôtel du Palais (☎ 03 80 67 16 26; www.hoteldupalais-dijon.com; 23 rue du Palais; d €44-68, q €83) A two-starrer in a 17th-century *hôtel particulier* (private mansion). The 13 rooms are spacious and welcoming and the public spaces exude old-fashioned charm.

Eating

Café Chez Nous (☎ 03 80 50 12 98; impasse Quentin; ⏰ lunch noon-2pm, bar 10am-2am, closed Mon to 2pm & Sun) Quintessentially French *bar du coin* (neighbourhood bar) down an alleyway from the market. The decor's scruffy, the grub's solid, and fine wines are served by the glass.

our pick **Le Petit Roi de la Lune** (☎ 03 80 49 89 93; 28 rue Amiral Roussin; lunch menu €13.80; ⏰ closed Sun & lunch Mon) 'The Little King of the Moon' specialises in reinvented French cuisine – *Camembert frit avec gelée de mûre* (breadcrumbed Camembert served with blackberry jelly; €9.80), or the bizarrely brilliant *aiguillettes de canard au Coca Cola* (duck strips in Coca-Cola sauce; €14.90).

La Petite Marche (☎ 03 80 30 15 10; 27-29 rue Musette; menus €10.50-14; ⏰ lunch Mon-Sat) An organic restaurant with loads of salads and veggie options – a welcome change from stodgy Burgundian classics.

Self-catering options:

Covered Market (Halles du Marché; rue Quentin; ⏰ 7am-1pm Tue & Thu-Sat) A huge market on Fridays and Saturdays, with a smaller version on Tuesdays & Thursdays.

Fromagerie (28 rue Musette; ⏰ 6am or 7am-12.30pm or 1pm & 2.30-7pm, no midday closure Fri & Sat, closed Mon morning & Sun) A friendly, top-quality cheese shop.

Monoprix supermarket (11-13 rue Piron; ⏰ 9am-8.45pm Mon-Sat)

Drinking & Entertainment

For the latest on Dijon's cultural scene, pick up the free zine *Spectacles*.

Le Cappuccino (☎ 03 80 41 06 35; 132 rue Berbisey; ⏰ 5pm-2am Mon-Sat) Previously a coffee bar, this nightspot now focuses on wine by the glass and a varied selection of 80 beers, including Mandubienne, Dijon's local brew.

Café de l'Univers (☎ 03 80 30 98 29; 47 rue Berbisey; ⏰ 5pm-2am) Mirrors and beer ads cover the walls of this ground-floor bar. There's live music from 9pm to 1am on Friday and Saturday.

Getting There & Away

Trains run to Paris' Gare de Lyon (€43.40 to €54.10 by TGV, 1¾ hours, 10 to 14 daily, most frequent in the early morning and evening), Lyon-Part Dieu (€25.10, two hours, 11 to 19 daily), Nice (€79.10 to €91.30 by TGV, 6¼ hours, two direct daily) and Strasbourg (€38.90, 3½ hours, three or four nondirect daily). There's a city-centre **SNCF Boutique** (55 rue du Bourg; ⏰ 12.30-7pm Mon, 10am-7pm Tue-Sat).

Buses run from the train station. An **information and ticket counter** (⏰ 5.45am-9pm Sun-Thu, to 9.30pm Fri, to 8pm Sat) deals with TER trains and regional Transco buses: bus 60 (18 to 21 daily Monday to Friday, 10 on Saturday, two on Sunday) links Dijon with the northern Côte de Nuits wine villages. Other Transco buses travel to various destinations around Burgundy.

International bus travel is handled by **Eurolines** (☎ 03 80 68 20 44; 53 rue Guillaume Tell; ⏰ Mon-Fri & Sat morning).

Getting Around

Details on Dijon's bus network, operated by Divia, are available at **L'Espace Bus** (☎ 08 00 10 20 04; www.divia.fr, in French; place Grangier; ⏰ 7.30am-6.45pm Mon-Fri, 8.30am-6.30pm Sat). Single tickets cost €0.95; a Forfait Journée ticket (€3.20) is available from the tourist office or L'Espace Bus.

BEAUNE

pop 21,300

Beaune (pronounced 'bone'), 44km south of Dijon, is the unofficial capital of the Côte d'Or. This thriving town's *raison d'être* is wine – making it, tasting it, selling it, but most of all, drinking it.

Information

Laundrettes 19 rue du Faubourg St-Jean (⏰ 6am-9pm); 63 rue de Lorraine (⏰ 7am-9pm)

Le Clos Carnot (☎ 03 80 22 73 43; 34 place Carnot; per hr €3; ⏰ 8am-midnight) A cafe-brasserie with two internet computers.

Tourist Office (☎ 03 80 26 21 30; www.beaune-burgundy.com; 6 bd Perpreuil; ⏰ 9am-7pm Mon-Sat, 9am-6pm Sun Easter–mid-Nov, 9am-12.30pm & 1.30-6pm Mon-Sat, 10am-12.30pm & 1.30-5pm Sun mid-Nov–Easter) Has an internet computer (per 15min €1.50) and sells the Pass Beaune, offering 5% to 15% discounts on local attractions.

Sights & Activities

Founded in 1443, the celebrated Gothic **Hôtel-Dieu des Hospices de Beaune** (☎ 03 80 24 45 00; rue de l'Hôtel-Dieu; adult/student €6/4.80; ⏰ tickets sold 9am-6.30pm Easter–mid-Nov, 9am-11.30am & 2-5.30pm mid-Nov–Easter, interior closes 1hr later) was originally built as a charity hospital; its highlights include the barrel-vaulted Grande Salle, an 18th-century pharmacy and **Polyptych of the Last Judgement** by the Flemish painter Roger van der Weyden, depicting Judgment Day in glorious technicolour.

Underneath Beaune's streets, millions of dusty bottles of wine are being aged to perfection in cool, dark, cobweb-lined cellars. Several local cellars offer wine-tasting tours, including **Marché aux Vins** (☎ 03 80 25 08 20; www.marcheauxvins.com, in French; 2 rue Nicolas Rolin; admission €10; 🕑 9.30-11.30am & 2-5.30pm, no midday closure mid-Jun–Aug), where you'll taste 15 wines from a special *tastevin* cup; and **Patriarche Père et Fils** (☎ 03 80 24 53 78; www.patriarche.com; 5 rue du Collège; audioguide tour €10; 🕑 9.30-11.30am & 2-5.30pm), the largest cellars in Burgundy.

Sleeping & Eating

Campground (☎ 03 80 22 03 91; campinglescentvignes@mairie-beaune.fr; 10 rue Auguste Dubois; per adult/tent €3.60/4.35; 🕑 mid-Mar–Oct) A flowery, four-star camping ground 700m north of the centre.

Hôtel Rousseau (☎ 03 80 22 13 59; 11 place Madeleine;, s/d with washbasin from €30/38, d with private bathroom €55, hall shower €3) An endearingly old-fashioned, 12-room hotel run since 1959 by a friendly lady *d'un certain âge*. Reception occasionally shuts without warning so she can go shopping.

Caves Madeleine (☎ 03 80 22 93 30; 8 rue du Faubourg Madeleine; menus €12-22; 🕑 closed Thu, Sun & lunch Fri) A convivial Burgundian restaurant, where locals share tables for regional classics such as *boeuf bourguignon*, *cassolette d'escargots* and *jambon persillé* (jellied ham).

Le Bistrot Bourguignon (☎ 03 80 22 23 24; www.restaurant-lebistrotbourguignon.com; 8 rue Monge; lunch menu €12.90; 🕑 closed Sun & Mon) A cosy bistro-style restaurant that serves regional cuisine and 17 Burgundies by the glass (€2.60 to €7).

The covered market hall at place de la Halle hosts a **food market** (🕑 until 12.30pm Sat) and a smaller **marché gourmand** (gourmet market; 🕑 Wed morning). **Casino supermarket** (28 rue du Faubourg Madeleine; 🕑 8.30am-7.30pm Mon-Sat, 9am-noon Sun) is through an archway on rue du Faubourg Madeleine.

Getting There & Away

Bus 44, run by **Transco** (☎ 08 00 10 20 04), travels to Dijon (€6.30, one hour, seven daily Monday to Friday, six Saturday, two Sunday and holidays), stopping at Côte d'Or wine-growing villages such as Vougeot, Nuits-St-Georges and Aloxe-Corton. Some line 44 buses also serve villages south of Beaune, including Pommard, Volnay, Meursault and La Rochepot.

Beaune has frequent trains to Dijon (€6.50, 25 minutes, 25 to 40 daily) via Nuits-St-Georges (€3, 10 minutes), Paris' Gare de Lyon (€50.50 to €62.40, two direct TGVs daily) and Lyon–Part Dieu (€21.60, 1¾ hours, 11 to 17 daily).

LYON

pop 467,400

Gourmets, eat your heart out: Lyon is *the* gastronomic capital of France, with a lavish table of piggy-driven dishes and delicacies to savour. The city has been a commercial, industrial and banking powerhouse for the past 500 years, and is still France's second-largest conurbation, with outstanding art museums, a dynamic nightlife, green parks and a Unesco-listed old town.

Information

AOC Exchange (20 rue Gasparin, 2e; 🕑 9.30am-6.30pm Mon-Sat; Ⓜ Bellecour) Currency exchange.

Laverie de la Fresque (1 rue de la Martinière, 1er; 🕑 6am-10pm; Ⓜ Hôtel de Ville) Laundry.

Raconte-Moi La Terre (☎ 04 78 92 60 22; www.raconte-moi.com; 38 rue Thomassin, 2e; per hr €4; 🕑 10am-7.30pm Mon-Sat; Ⓜ Cordeliers) Stylish surfing in the 1st-floor cafe of a travel bookshop.

Tourist Office (☎ 04 72 77 69 69; www.lyon-france.com; place Bellecour, 2e; 🕑 9am-6pm; Ⓜ Bellecour)

Sights

VIEUX LYON

Old Lyon is divided into three quarters: St-Paul at the northern end, St-Jean in the middle and St-Georges in the south. Lovely old buildings languish on **rue du Bœuf**, **rue St-Jean** and **rue des Trois Maries**. The part-Romanesque **Cathédrale St-Jean** (place St-Jean, 5e; 🕑 8am-noon & 2-7.30pm Mon-Fri, 8am-noon & 2-7pm Sat & Sun; Ⓜ Vieux Lyon) was built from the late 11th to the early 16th centuries. The **astronomical clock** chimes at noon, 2pm, 3pm and 4pm.

FOURVIÈRE

Over two millennia ago, the Romans built the city of Lugdunum on the slopes of Fourvière. Today, Lyon's 'hill of prayer' is topped by the 27m-high **Basilique Notre Dame de Fourvière**

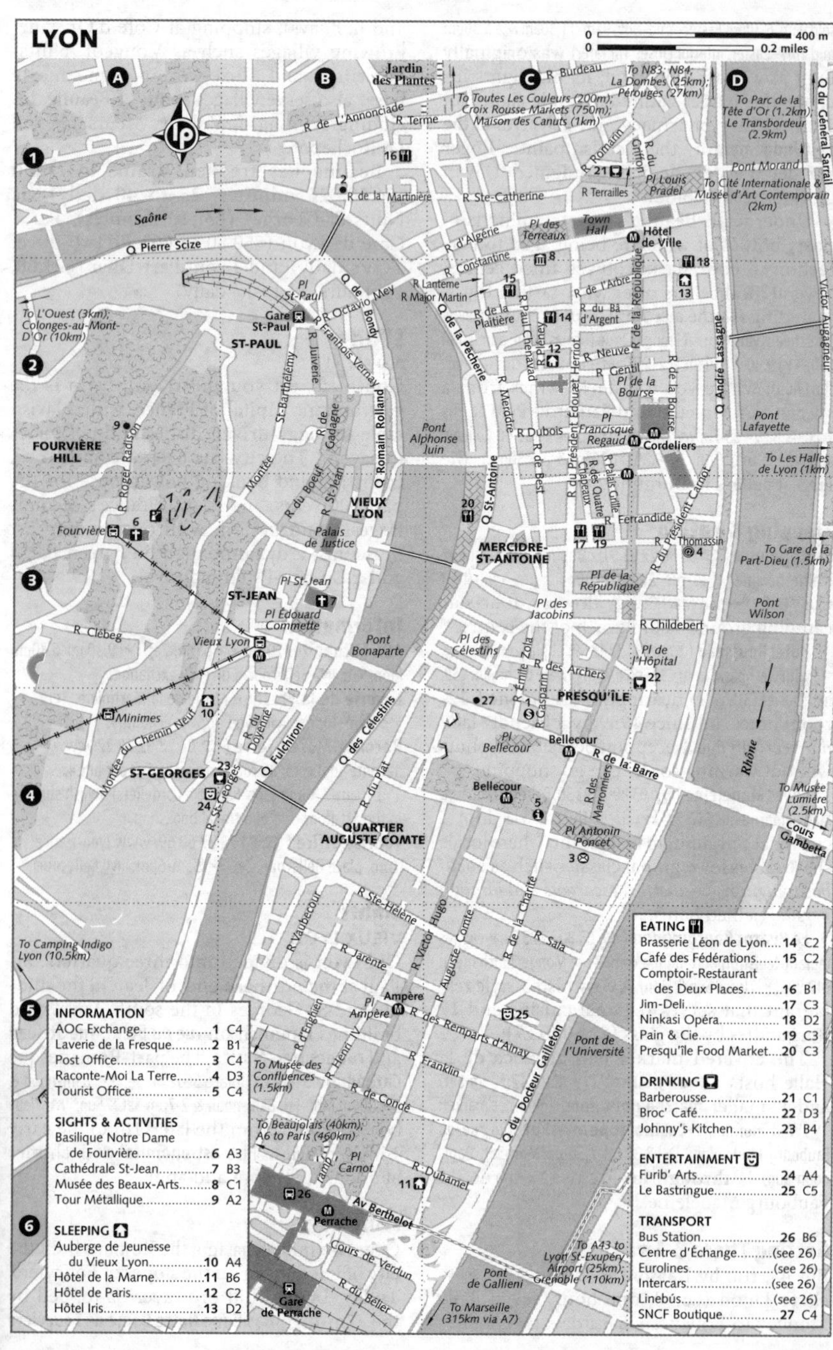
LYON
0 400 m
0 0.2 miles
A
B
C
D
1
2
3
4
5
6
Jardin des Plantes
R Burdeau
To N83; N84; La Dombes (25km); Pérouges (27km)
To Toutes Les Couleurs (200m); Croix Rousse Markets (750m); Maison des Canuts (1km)
To Parc de la Tête d'Or (1.2km); Le Transbordeur (2.9km)
Q du Général Sarrail
R de L'Annonciade
R Terme
R Romarin
R du Griffon
Pont Morand
R Terraille
Pl Louis Pradel
To Cité Internationale & Musée d'Art Contemporain (2km)
R de la Martinière
R Ste-Catherine
Saône
Pl des Terreaux
Town Hall
Hôtel de Ville
R d'Algérie
Q Pierre Scize
R Constantine
R de la République
Pl St-Paul
Q de Bondy
R Lanterne
R Major Martin
R de l'Arbre Sec
R Octavio Mey
To L'Ouest (3km); Colonges-au-Mont-D'Or (10km)
Gare St-Paul
R François Vernay
R de la Plaitière
R Paul Chenavard
R du Bât d'Argent
ST-PAUL
R Juiverie
Q de la Pêcherie
R Pléney
R Neuve
Q André Lassagne
Victor Augagneur
R St-Barthélemy
R Gentil
R de la Bourse
Pl de la Bourse
R Mercière
R Président Édouard Herriot
Pont Lafayette
R de Gadagne
Q Romain Rolland
Pont Alphonse Juin
R Dubois
Pl Francisque Regaud
Cordeliers
FOURVIÈRE HILL
R Roger Radisson
Montée St-Barthélemy
R de Brest
R des Quatre Chapeaux
R Palais Grillet
To Les Halles de Lyon (1km)
R du Boeuf
R St-Jean
VIEUX LYON
Q St-Antoine
R Ferrandière
R du Président Carnot
Fourvière
Palais de Justice
MERCIÈRE-ST-ANTOINE
R Thomassin
To Gare de la Part-Dieu (1.5km)
Pl de la République
Pl St-Jean
ST-JEAN
Pl Édouard Commette
Pl des Jacobins
Pont Wilson
R Childebert
R Clébeg
Vieux Lyon
Pont Bonaparte
Pl des Célestins
Pl de l'Hôpital
R des Archers
R Émile Zola
R Gasparin
PRESQU'ÎLE
Minimes
Montée du Chemin Neuf
R du Doyenné
Q Fulchiron
Q des Célestins
Pl Bellecour
Bellecour
R de la Barre
Rhône
ST-GEORGES
R St-Georges
R du Plat
R des Marronniers
To Musée Lumière (2.5km)
Cours Gambetta
QUARTIER AUGUSTE COMTE
Pl Antonin Poncet
R Ste-Hélène
R Vaubecour
R Victor Hugo
R Auguste Comte
R de la Charité
R Sala
To Camping Indigo Lyon (10.5km)
R Jarente
Ampère
Pl Ampère
R des Remparts d'Ainay
Pont de l'Université
R d'Enghien
R Henri IV
R Franklin
Q du Docteur Gailleton
To Musée des Confluences (1.5km)
R de Condé
To Beaujolais (40km); A6 to Paris (460km)
Pl Carnot
R Duhamel
Perrache
Av Berthelot
To A43 to Lyon St-Exupéry Airport (25km); Grenoble (110km)
Cours de Verdun
Pont de Gallieni
R du Bélier
Gare de Perrache
To Marseille (315km via A7)
INFORMATION
AOC Exchange....1 C4
Laverie de la Fresque....2 B1
Post Office....3 C4
Raconte-Moi La Terre....4 D3
Tourist Office....5 C4
SIGHTS & ACTIVITIES
Basilique Notre Dame de Fourvière....6 A3
Cathédrale St-Jean....7 B3
Musée des Beaux-Arts....8 C1
Tour Métallique....9 A2
SLEEPING
Auberge de Jeunesse du Vieux Lyon....10 A4
Hôtel de la Marne....11 B6
Hôtel de Paris....12 C2
Hôtel Iris....13 D2
EATING
Brasserie Léon de Lyon....14 C2
Café des Fédérations....15 C2
Comptoir-Restaurant des Deux Places....16 B1
Jim-Deli....17 C3
Ninkasi Opéra....18 D2
Pain & Cie....19 C3
Presqu'île Food Market....20 C3
DRINKING
Barberousse....21 C1
Broc' Café....22 D3
Johnny's Kitchen....23 B4
ENTERTAINMENT
Furib' Arts....24 A4
Le Bastringue....25 C5
TRANSPORT
Bus Station....26 B6
Centre d'Échange....(see 26)
Eurolines....(see 26)
Intercars....(see 26)
Linebús....(see 26)
SNCF Boutique....27 C4

GETTING INTO TOWN

From Lyon-St-Exupéry airport, **Satobus** (☎ 04 72 68 72 17; www.satobus.com) runs shuttle buses to the city centre (single/return €8.60/15.20) every 20 minutes from early in the morning until midnight.

(☎ 04 78 25 86 19; www.fourviere.org; 🕑 7am-7pm) and the **Tour Métallique**, an Eiffel Tower–like structure built in 1893 and used as a TV transmitter. The hill affords spectacular views of the city; the easiest way up is via the funicular from place Édouard Commette. A return ticket costs €2.20.

PRESQU'ÎLE

The centrepiece of **place des Terreaux** (Ⓜ Hôtel de Ville) is the 19th-century fountain sculpted by Frédéric-Auguste Bartholdi, creator of the Statue of Liberty.

Nearby, the **Musée des Beaux-Arts** (Museum of Fine Arts; ☎ 04 72 10 17 40; www.mba-lyon.fr; 20 place des Terreaux, 1er; admission €6; 🕑 10am-6pm Wed, Thu & Sat-Mon, 10.30am-6pm Fri; Ⓜ Hôtel de Ville) showcases France's finest collection of sculptures and paintings outside Paris.

Laid out in the 17th century, **place Bellecour** (Ⓜ Bellecour) – one of Europe's largest public squares – is pierced by an equestrian **statue of Louis XIV**.

OTHER ATTRACTIONS

The hilltop quarter of **Croix Rousse** (Ⓜ Croix Rousse) is famed for its bohemian inhabitants, outdoor food market and silk-weaving tradition, illustrated by the **Maison des Canuts** (☎ 04 78 28 62 04; www.maisondescanuts.com; 10-12 rue d'Ivry, 4e; adult/student €6/3; 🕑 10am-6.30pm Tue-Sat, guided tours 11am & 3.30pm; Ⓜ Croix Rousse).

Lyon's graceful 117-hectare **Parc de la Tête d'Or** (☎ 04 72 69 47 60; bd des Belges, 6e; 🕑 6am-11pm mid-Apr–mid-Oct, to 9pm mid-Oct–mid-Apr; Ⓜ Masséna), landscaped in the 1860s, is graced by a lake, botanic garden with greenhouses, rose garden and zoo. Bus 41 or 47 links it with metro Part-Dieu. Nearby, post-1960 art is the focus of the **Musée d'Art Contemporain** (Museum of Contemporary Art; ☎ 04 72 69 17 17; www.moca-lyon.org; 81 quai Charles de Gaulle, 6e; adult/18-25yr €8/6; 🕑 noon-7pm Wed-Fri, 10am-7pm Sat & Sun).

Cinema's glorious beginnings are showcased at the **Musée Lumière** (☎ 04 78 78 18 95; www.institut-lumiere.org; 25 rue du Premier Film, 8e; admission €6, audioguide €3; 🕑 11am-6.30pm Tue-Sun; Ⓜ Monplaisir-Lumière), 3km southeast along cours Gambetta. The museum is housed inside the art nouveau home of Antoine Lumière, whose sons Auguste and Louis shot the world's first motion picture, *La Sortie des Usines Lumières* (Exit of the Lumières Factories) in 19 March 1895.

Sleeping

Camping Indigo Lyon (☎ 04 78 35 64 55; www.camping-indigo.com; Porte de Lyon, Dardilly; tent/adult €9.90/4.40, 5-person chalet per night/week from €50/210;) Fancy a bijou wooden chalet between trees or a green plot of shade to pitch up on? Then head out of town to this eco-friendly camping ground.

Auberge de Jeunesse du Vieux Lyon (☎ 04 78 15 05 50; lyon@fuaj.org; 41-45 montée du Chemin Neuf, 5e; dm incl breakfast €16.60; 🕑 reception 7am-1pm, 2-8pm & 9pm-1am; Ⓜ Vieux Lyon) The main draw of this superbly located hostel above Vieux Lyon is the sweeping city views from its garden and terrace.

Hôtel de Paris (☎ 04 78 28 00 95; www.hoteldeparis-lyon.com; 16 rue de la Platière, 1er; s/d from €48/62; Ⓜ Hôtel de Ville;) This fantastic-value hotel resides in a 19th-century bourgeois building. The funkiest rooms sport retro 1970s decor with a chocolate-and-turquoise or candyfloss-pink colour scheme.

Hôtel Iris (☎ 04 78 39 93 80; hoteliris@freesurf.fr; 36 rue de l'Arbre Sec, 1er; s/d with shared bathroom €40/42, s/d/tr with private bathroom €50/60/72; Ⓜ Hôtel de Ville) The location of this colourful dame in a centuries-old convent couldn't be better: its street brims with hip places to eat and drink.

our pick **Hôtel de la Marne** (☎ 04 78 37 07 46; www.hoteldelamarne.fr; 78 rue de la Charité, 2e; s/d/tr/q €51/57/73/81; Ⓜ Gare de Perrache) A real charmer, this Perrache hotel has 23 rooms, some of which open onto a sky-topped courtyard. Blue carpets and slate-grey paintwork mix with knick-knacks and a reception desk made of a vintage hot-air balloon basket.

Eating

Ninkasi Opéra (☎ 04 78 28 37 74; www.ninkasi.fr, in French; 27 rue de l'Arbre Sec, 1er; salads €6-9, burgers €5.20; 🕑 10am-1am Mon-Thu, 10am-3am Fri & Sat, 6pm-midnight Sun; Ⓜ Hôtel de Ville) If meaty burgers or fish and chips are your cup of tea, this microbrewery grub stop is for you. DJs spin tunes on Saturdays, followed by films and bands on Sunday.

Pain & Cie (☎ 04 78 38 29 84; 13-15 rue des Quatre Chapeaux, 2e; salads €3.50-14.50; 🕑 7am-10.30pm Mon-Sat, 7am-7pm Sun; Ⓜ Bellecour) Join the crowds for a well-topped *tartine* (thick toast with topping) or weekend brunch (€9 to €21).

Jim-Deli (☎ 04 78 38 31 67; 14 rue des Quatre Chapeaux, 2e; starters/pasta €8/15; 🕑 lunch & dinner Mon-Sat; Ⓜ Bellecour) Half of this Italian duo serves panini to take away; the other half carpaccio, pasta and salads.

Toutes les Couleurs (☎ 04 72 00 03 95; 26 rue Imbert Colomès, 1er; plat du jour €9.50, 2-course menus €13 & €16.50, 3-course menus €18, €21 & €25; 🕑 lunch Tue-Fri, lunch & dinner Fri & Sat; Ⓜ Croix-Paquet) Vegetarians will love this *restaurant bio* (organic restaurant). Its veggie menu includes vegan and gluten-free dishes.

Comptoir-Restaurant des Deux Places (☎ 04 78 28 95 10; 5 place Fernand Rey, 1er; lunch/dinner menu €15/28; 🕑 lunch & dinner Tue-Sat; Ⓜ Hôtel de Ville) Red-and-white checked curtains, an old-world interior and a menu scribed in black ink contribute to the overwhelmingly traditional feel here.

our pick **Café des Fédérations** (☎ 04 78 28 26 00; www.lesfedeslyon.com, in French; 8 rue Major Martin, 1er; lunch/dinner menu €19.50/24; 🕑 lunch & dinner Mon-Fri; Ⓜ Hôtel de Ville) B&W photos of old Lyon speckle the wood-panelled walls of the city's best-known *bouchon*. Feast on *caviar de la Croix Rousse* (lentils in creamy sauce), followed by *andouillette* (tripe sausage).

Lyon has two superb **outdoor food markets**: Presqu'île (quai St-Antoine, 2e; 🕑 Tue-Sun morning; Ⓜ Bellecour or Cordeliers); Croix Rousse (bd de la Croix Rousse, 4e; 🕑 Tue-Sun morning; Ⓜ Croix Rousse), as well as a legendary indoor market, **Les Halles de Lyon** (102 cours Lafayette, 3e; 🕑 8am-7pm Tue-Sat, 8am-2pm Sun; Ⓜ Part-Dieu).

Drinking

The bounty of cafe terraces on place des Terreaux buzz with all-hours drinkers.

Barberousse (☎ 04 72 00 80 53; 18 rue Terrailles, 1er; 🕑 7pm-3am Tue-Sat; Ⓜ Hôtel de Ville) Student-loved shooter bar on the buzzy back-alley of rue Terrailles, famous for flavoured rums.

Broc' Café (☎ 04 72 40 46 01; 2 place de l'Hôpital, 2e; 🕑 8am-1am Mon-Sat; Ⓜ Bellecour) This laid-back cafe-bar is stocked with jumble-sale furniture and its student crowd oozes street cred.

Johnny's Kitchen (☎ 04 78 37 94 13; www.myspace.com/johnnyskitchen; 48 rue St-Georges, 5e; 🕑 noon-1am; Ⓜ Vieux Lyon) Busy pub in St-Georges, where Johnny dishes up burger-shaped world cuisine and bands jam in the cellar.

SPLURGE

Brasserie Léon de Lyon (☎ 04 72 10 11 12; www.leondelyon.com; 1 rue Pléney, 1er; 2-/3-course menu du jour €22.80/26, entrée/plat/dessert du jour €7/14.80/5.80; 🕑 lunch & dinner Mon-Sun; Ⓜ Hôtel de Ville) In keeping with dining trends, legendary Lyonnais chef Jean-Paul Lacombe has turned his Michelin-starred gastronomic restaurant into a soulful brasserie – same 1904 decor, similar culinary products, more affordable prices.

Entertainment

The cultural scene is dynamic. Listings guides include weekly **Lyon Poche** (www.lyonpoche.com, in French; €1 at newsagents) and the free **Le Petit Bulletin** (www.petit-bulletin.fr, in French), available on street corners.

Lyon's top gig venues include grungy **Furib' Arts** (☎ 04 72 00 26 41; www.myspace.com/lefuribart; 60 rue St-Georges, 5e; admission free-€4; 🕑 3pm-1am Tue-Sat; Ⓜ Vieux Lyon) and **Le Bastringue** (☎ 06 70 15 81 39; http://lebastringue.free.fr, in French; 14 rue Laurencin, 2e; 🕑 8pm-1am Tue-Sat; Ⓜ Ampère), while touring bands head for **Le Transbordeur** (☎ 04 78 93 08 33; www.transbordeur.fr, in French; 3 bd de Stalingrad, Villeurbanne). Take bus 59 from metro Part-Dieu to Cité Inter Transbordeur stop.

For the hottest clubbing venues, check out www.lyonclubbing.com, www.lyon2night.com and www.night4lyon.com (all in French).

Getting There & Away

Flights to/from European cities land at **Lyon-St-Exupéry Airport** (☎ 08 26 80 08 26; www.lyon.aeroport.fr), 25km east of the city. **Satobus** (☎ 04 72 68 72 17; www.satobus.com) runs city-centre shuttles (single/return €8.60/15.20) every 20 minutes between 5am or 6am and midnight.

In the Perrache complex, **Eurolines** (☎ 04 72 56 95 30), **Intercars** (☎ 04 78 37 20 80) and Spain-oriented **Linebús** (☎ 04 72 41 72 27) have offices on the bus-station level of the Centre d'Échange.

Lyon has two train stations: **Gare de Perrache** (Ⓜ Perrache) and **Gare de la Part-Dieu** (Ⓜ Part-Dieu), which mainly handles long-haul trains. Tickets are sold at the **SNCF Boutique** (2 place Bellecour, 2e; Ⓜ Bellecour; 🕑 9am-6.45pm Mon-Fri, 10am-6.30pm Sat).

TGV destinations include Paris' Gare de Lyon (€61, two hours, every 30 to 60 minutes), Lille–Europe (€80.20, 3¼ hours, nine daily), Nantes (€89.20, 4½ hours, five daily), Dijon (€28.50, 2¾ hours, at least 12 daily) and Strasbourg (€52.80, 5¼ hours, five daily).

Getting Around

Buses, trams, a four-line metro and two funiculars linking Vieux Lyon to Fourvière are run by **TCL** (☎ 08 20 42 70 00; www.tcl.fr, in French; 5 rue de la République, 1er; 🕑 7.30am-6.30pm Mon-Fri, 9am-noon & 1.30-5pm Sat; Ⓜ Bellecour). Public transport runs from around 5am to midnight. Tickets cost €1.50/12.50 for one/*carnet* (booklet) of 10.

Bicycles are available from 200-odd drop-off points run by **vélo'v** (☎ 08 00 08 35 68; www.velov.grandlyon.com; first 30min free, 1st/subsequent hr €1/2).

FRENCH ALPS

The French Alps is the undisputed centre of adventure sports in France, whether it's paragliding among the peaks, hiking the trails or hurtling down a mountainside strapped to a pair of glorified toothpicks. It's also home to Europe's highest peak, Mont Blanc (4810m).

CHAMONIX

pop 9086 / elevation 1037m

Supercharged Chamonix is the mecca of French mountaineering, and its knife-edge peaks, plunging slopes and massive glaciers have enthralled generations of adventurers and thrill-seekers (not to mention thousands of holidaying French and Brits). It's renowned for its pumping après-ski scene, and adventurous souls can brave the world's highest (and most terrifying) cable car.

Information

Laverie Automatique (174 av de l'Aiguille du Midi; 7/16kg wash €5.50/10; 🕑 8am-10pm)

Mojo (21 place Balmat; sandwich €5-6; 🕑 9am-8pm) Cafe with internet-connected computers.

PGHM (Peloton de Gendarmerie de Haute-Montagne; ☎ 04 50 53 16 89; 69 rue de la Mollard) Mountain rescue service.

Shop 74 (☎ 04 50 90 73 17; impasse du Bartavel; per hr €6; 🕑 10am-8pm) Internet access.

Tourist Office (☎ 04 50 53 00 24; www.chamonix.com; 85 place du Triangle de l'Amitié; 🕑 8.30am-7.30pm Dec-Apr, 9am-12.30pm & 2-6.30pm Mon-Sat, 9am-12.30pm Sun May-Nov) Accommodation & activity information, plus ski passes & free wi-fi.

Sights

AIGUILLE DU MIDI

A jagged pinnacle of rock 8km from the domed summit of Mont Blanc, the **Aiguille du Midi** (3842m) is one of Chamonix' iconic landmarks. If you can handle the height, the panoramic views from the summit are unforgettable.

The **Téléphérique du l'Aiguille du Midi** (Aiguille du Midi Cable Car; ☎ 04 50 53 30 80, advance reservations 24hr ☎ 04 50 53 22 75; 100 place de l'Aiguille du Midi; adult return €38, adult return to midstation Plan de l'Aiguille €21; 🕑 6.30am-6pm Jul & Aug, 8.30am-4.30pm late-Dec–Mar, hr vary rest of year) links Chamonix with the Aiguille du Midi. Be prepared for long queues, and bring warm clothes – the temperature at the top rarely rises above -10°C.

Between mid-May and mid-September the **Télécabine Panoramic Mont Blanc** (Panoramic Mont Blanc Cable Car; ☎ 04 50 53 30 80; adult return from Chamonix €54; 🕑 8.50am-4pm mid-May–Jun & Sep, 8.15am-4.30pm Jul & Aug) to **Pointe Helbronner** (3466m) continues for another 30 minutes over the French–Italian border, affording views of glaciers, snowfields and seracs.

MER DE GLACE

The **Mer de Glace** (Sea of Ice) is the second-largest glacier in the Alps, 14km long, 1800m wide and up to 400m deep. A quaint red mountain train links **Gare du Montenvers** (☎ 04 50 53 12 54; 35 place de la Mer de Glace; adult €21; 🕑 9am-4.30pm mid-Dec–Apr, 8am-6.30pm Jul & Aug, hr vary rest of year) in Chamonix with Montenvers (1913m), from where a cable car transports tourists in summer down to the glacier and the **Grotte de la Mer de Glace** (🕑 late Dec-Apr & mid-Jun–Sep), an ice cave that has been carved every spring since 1946.

Activities

For activities out and about on the mountain – whether that means summer hiking or winter skiing – the **Maison de la Montagne** (190 place de l'Église; 🕑 8.30am-noon & 3-7pm), across the square from the tourist office, supplies comprehensive details on practically every imaginable pastime in the Mont Blanc area.

Sleeping

Les Deux Glaciers (☎ 04 50 53 15 84; http://les2glaciers.com; 80 rte des Tissières; 2-adult tent pitch €14.30; 🕑 mid-Dec–mid-Nov) The only year-round camping ground, the Two Glaciers is in Les Bossons, 3km south of Chamonix.

Gîte Le Vagabond (☎ 04 50 53 15 43; www.gitevagabond.com; 365 av Ravanel-le-Rouge; dm €16.80, with breakfast/half-board €19.40/38.60; reception 8-10am & 4.30-10pm;) This legendary bunkhouse, where cool dudes free-ride by day, and eat, drink and party by night, is run and populated almost exclusively by Brits.

Auberge de Jeunesse Chamonix (☎ 04 50 53 14 52; www.fuaj.org; 127 montée Jacques Balmat; dm incl sheets & breakfast €18, half-board €27.80; reception 8am-noon, 5-7.30pm & 8.30-10pm Dec-May & Jun-Sep) A bright, well-run hostel with impeccable two- to six-bed dorms (but no kitchen). It's 2km south of Chamonix in Les Pélerins. Take the Chamonix–Les Houches bus line and get off in Les Pélerins d'en Haut.

Le Vert Hôtel (☎ 04 50 53 13 58; www.verthotel.com; 964 route des Gaillands; low season s/d/tr/q from €25/40/60/75, high season from €62/78/108/122) Chamonix's self-proclaimed house of fun, sports and creativity, 2km out of town. Rooms are unremarkable (some with bathroom cabins the size of an aeroplane toilet), but it's the happening bar most guests come for.

Eating

Mojo (21 place Balmat; sandwiches €5-6; 9am-8pm) The latest arrival on the sandwich scene, Mojo is smack bang on the main square, with views of Le Brévent, Mont Blanc and l'Aiguille du Midi to boot. *Bon appétit.*

Annapurna (☎ 04 50 55 81 39; 62 av Ravanel-le-Rouge; mains €10-15; lunch & dinner Wed-Sun, dinner Tue) Named after the 8000m-plus Himalayan mountain, this place serves spicy tandooris, birianis and kormas either inhouse or to take away.

Casa Valério (☎ 04 50 55 93 40; 88 rue du Lyret; mains €10-20; lunch & dinner, closes at 2am) One of Chamonix's most popular eateries, this restaurant doubles up as a happening hangout when young 'seasonaires' devour pasta or pizza by the bar counter.

A food market fills place du Mont Blanc on Saturday morning.

Other self-catering options:

Camp de Base (☎ 04 50 18 47 76; 107 rue des Moulins; 3-8pm) English grocery shop, combined with internet cafe (per hour €5).

Le Refuge Payot (☎ 04 50 53 18 71; www.refugepayot.com; 166 rue Joseph Vallot) Local produce: cheese, smoked meats, sausages.

Super U (117 rue Joseph Vallot) Supermarket.

Getting There & Away

Next to the train station, **Chamonix bus station** (☎ 04 50 53 01 15; www.altibus.com; 6.45-10.30am & 1.25-4.45pm Mon-Fri, 6.45-11am Sat & Sun) runs buses to/from Geneva airport and bus station (one way/return €35/55, 1½ to 2 hours, three daily) and Courmayeur (one way/return €11/18, 45 minutes, two to three daily). Advance booking only.

From **Chamonix–Mont Blanc train station** (☎ 04 50 53 12 98; place de la Gare), trains trundle to St-Gervais–Le Fayet station, 23km west of Chamonix, from where there are trains to most major French cities.

Getting Around

Local buses are provided by **Chamonix Bus** (☎ 04 50 53 05 55; www.chamonix-bus.com; 591 promenade Marie-Paradis; 7am-7pm winter, 8am-noon & 2-7pm Jun-Aug).

Le Grand Bi Cycles (☎ 04 50 53 14 16; 240 rte du Bouchet; 9am-7pm Jul & Aug, 9am-7pm Tue-Sun Sep-Oct & Dec-Jun, closed Nov) rents out bikes for €25 a day.

DORDOGNE & QUERCY

If it's the heart and soul of France you're searching for, then look no longer. Tucked away in the country's southwestern corner, the neighbouring regions of the Dordogne and Quercy combine history, culture and culinary sophistication in one unforgettably scenic package. The Dordogne is best-known for its sturdy *bastides* (fortified towns), clifftop chateaux and spectacular prehistoric cave paintings, while the Mediterranean-tinged region of Quercy is home to endless vintage vineyards and the historic city of Cahors.

SARLAT-LA-CANÉDA

pop 10,000

A pretty tangle of honey-coloured buildings, alleyways and secret squares make up Sarlat-la-Canéda, one of the unmissable villages of the Dordogne, and an ideal (if highly touristy) launchpad for exploring the Vézère Valley.

Sarlat's **tourist office** (☎ 05 53 31 45 45; www.ot-sarlat-perigord.fr; rue Tourny; 9am-7pm Mon-Sat, 10am-noon Sun Apr-Oct, 9am-noon & 2-7pm Mon-Sat Nov-Mar) is attached to a building next to the cathedral.

Part of the fun in Sarlat is getting well and truly lost in the twisting alleyways and back streets. **Rue Jean-Jacques Rousseau** or the area around **Le Présidial** both make good starting points, but the grandest buildings and *hôtels particuliers* are along **rue des Consuls**.

The **Cathédrale St-Sacerdos** was once part of Sarlat's Cluniac abbey, and is a real mix of architectural styles and periods; the belfry and western facade are the oldest parts while the nave, organ and chapels are later additions.

Two medieval courtyards, the **Cour des Fontaines** and the **Cour des Chanoines**, can be reached off rue Tourny. Nearby is the **Jardin des Enfeus**, Sarlat's first cemetery, and the rocket-shaped **Lanterne des Morts** (Lantern of the Dead), built to honour a visit by St Bernard, one of the founders of the Cistercian order, in 1147.

Sleeping & Eating

Hôtel Les Récollets (☎ 05 53 31 36 00; www.hotel-recollets-sarlat.com; 4 rue Jean-Jacques Rousseau; d €43-69) Lost in the medieval maze of the old town, the Récollets is a budget beauty. Nineteen topsy-turvy rooms and a charming vaulted breakfast room are rammed in around the medieval *maison* (home).

Hôtel Montaigne (☎ 05 53 31 93 88; www.hotelmontaigne.fr; 2 place Pasteur; d €54-64; P) Popular with the coach-tour crowd, this imposing stone-front hotel offers modern rooms, all with private bathrooms and cosy decor. They're hardly exciting, but the buffet brekkie is great.

Chez Le Gaulois (☎ 05 53 59 50 64; 3 rue Tourny; mains €9-13; lunch & dinner Tue-Sat) Fondues and stonking plates of smoked sausage, cold meats and cheese are served up Savoyard-style on wooden platters.

Le Bistrot (☎ 05 53 28 28 40; place du Peyrou; menus €15-24; lunch & dinner Mon-Sat) Best of the bunch on place du Peyrou. Red-check tablecloths create an intimate atmosphere, and the menu's heavy on Sarlat classics: *magret de canard* (duck breast) and *pommes sarlardaises* (potatoes cooked in duck fat).

Sarlat's chaotic **Saturday market** (place de la Liberté & rue de la République) takes over the streets around the cathedral from 8am. A smaller **fruit and vegetable market** (8.30am-1pm) is held on Wednesday mornings on place de la Liberté.

Getting There & Away

Bus services from Sarlat are practically non-existent. The **train station** (☎ 05 53 59 00 21) is 1.3km south of the old city. Destinations include Périgueux (via Le Buisson; €13.20, 1¾ hours, three daily) and Les Eyzies (change at Le Buisson; €8.20, 50 minutes to 2½ hours depending on connections, three daily).

ATLANTIC COAST & FRENCH BASQUE COUNTRY

Though the Côte d'Azur is the most popular beach spot in France, the many seaside resorts along the Atlantic Coast are fast catching up. If you're a surf-nut or a beach bum, the sandy bays around Biarritz will be right up your alley, while oenophiles can sample the fruits of the vine in the capital of French winemaking, Bordeaux. Towards the Pyrenees you'll find the Basque Country, which feels closer to northern Spain than to the rest of France.

BORDEAUX

pop 229,500

The new millennium was a major turning point for the city long known as *La Belle Au Bois Dormant* (Sleeping Beauty), when the mayor, ex-Prime Minister Alain Juppé, roused Bordeaux, pedestrianising its boulevards, restoring its neoclassical architecture, and implementing a high-tech public-transport system. His efforts paid off: in mid-2007 half of the entire city was Unesco-listed, making it the largest urban World Heritage Site. Bolstered by its students and some 2.5 million tourists annually, La Belle Bordeaux now scarcely seems to sleep at all.

Orientation

The city centre lies between the flower-filled place Gambetta and the Garonne River. From place Gambetta, place de Tourny is 500m northeast, from where the tourist office is 400m to the east. Bordeaux's train station, Gare St-Jean, is about 3km southeast of the city centre.

Information

Bordeaux Monumental (☎ 05 56 48 04 24; 28 rue des Argentiers; 9.30am-1pm & 2-7pm Mon-Sat, 10am-1pm & 2-6pm Sun Jul & Aug, 9.30am-1pm & 2-6pm Mon-Sat, 10am-1pm & 2-6pm Sun May, Jun, Sep & Oct, 10am-1pm & 2-6pm Mon-Sat, 2-6pm Sun Nov-Apr)

DETOUR: PREHISTORIC PAINTINGS

The Vézère Valley is renowned for its prehistoric **cave art.** The most famous site is the **Lascaux Caves** (☎ 05 53 51 95 03; www.semitour.com; adult €8.30; 9am-8pm Jul-Aug, 9.30am-6.30pm Sep & Apr-Jun, 10am-12.30pm & 2-6pm Oct–mid-Nov, 10am-12.30pm & 2-5.30pm mid-Nov–Mar), 2km southeast of Montignac, featuring oxen, deer, horses, reindeer and mammoths, as well as a 5.5m bull, the largest cave drawing ever found. The original cave was closed in 1963 to prevent damage to the paintings, but the most famous sections have been recreated in a second cave nearby.

Other sites include the **Grotte de Font de Gaume** (☎ 05 53 06 86 00; www.leseyzies.com/grottes-ornees; adult/18-25yr €6.50/4.50; 9.30am-5.30pm mid-May–mid-Sep, 9.30am-12.30pm & 2-5.30pm mid-Sep–mid-May), 1km northeast of Les Eyzies, where you can see around two dozen paintings of bison, reindeer, horses, mammoths, bears and wolves.

The **Abri du Cap Blanc** (☎ 05 53 06 86 00; adult €6.50; 9.30am-5.30pm mid-May–mid-Sep, 9.30am-12.30pm & 2-5.30pm mid-Sep–mid-May, closed Sat year-round) contains a sculpture gallery of horses, bison and deer about 7km east of Les Eyzies.

Fifteen kilometres north of Les Eyzies, **Grotte de Rouffignac** (☎ 05 53 05 41 71; www.grottederouffignac.fr; admission €6.20; tours in French 9-11.30am & 2-6pm Jul-Aug, 10-11.30am & 2-5pm Mar-Jun & Sep-Oct) is sometimes known as the 'Cave of 100 Mammoths', thanks to the large number of mammoths painted onto the ceiling and walls. Access is provided by an underground electric train.

Most of the caves are closed in winter, and summer visitor numbers are limited, so you'll need to reserve ahead. There's no public transport to the caves, but trains run from Sarlat, and several campsites and the Les Eyzies tourist office provide bike rental.

Specialist tourist office dedicated to the city's history.

Cyberstation (☎ 05 56 01 15 15; 23 cours Pasteur; per hr €2; 9.30am-2am Mon-Sat, 2pm-2am Sun)

Laundrette (32 rue des Augustins; 7.30am-9pm)

Main Tourist Office (☎ 05 56 00 66 00; www.bordeaux-tourisme.com; 12 cours du 30 Juillet; 9am-7.30pm Mon-Sat, 9.30am-6.30pm Sun Jul & Aug, 9am-6.30pm Mon-Sat, 9.30am-6.30pm Sun May, Jun, Sep & Oct, 9am-6.30pm Mon-Sat, 9.45am-4.30pm Sun Nov-Apr) Runs an excellent range of city and regional tours.

Police Station (☎ 05 57 85 77 77; 23 rue François de Sourdis; 24hr)

Train Station Tourist Office (9am-noon & 1-6pm Mon-Sat, 10am-noon & 1-3pm Sun May-Oct, 9.30am-12.30pm & 2-6pm Mon-Fri Nov-Apr) Small but helpful office outside the train-station building.

Sights

The Unesco-listed **Cathédrale St-André** is almost overshadowed by the gargoyled, 50m-high Gothic belfry, **Tour Pey-Berland** (adult/student €5/3.50; 10am-1.15pm & 2-6pm Jun-Sep, 10am-12.30pm & 2-5.30pm Tue-Sun Oct-May). Erected between 1440 and 1466, its spire was later topped off with the statue of Notre Dame de l'Aquitaine. Scaling the tower's 232 narrow steps rewards you with a spectacular panorama of the city.

Bordeaux's museums offer free entry for permanent collections. Gallo-Roman relics are the highlights at the **Musée d'Aquitaine** (Museum of Aquitaine; ☎ 05 56 01 51 00; 20 cours Pasteur; 11am-6pm Tue-Sun), while more than 700 post-1960s works are featured at the **CAPC Musée d'Art Contemporain** (Museum of Contemporary Art; ☎ 05 56 00 81 50; Entrepôt 7, rue Ferrére; 11am-6pm Tue & Thu-Sun, to 8pm Wed, closed Mon).

The evolution of Occidental art from the Renaissance to the mid-20th century is explored at Bordeaux's **Musée des Beaux-Arts** (Museum of Fine Arts; ☎ 05 56 10 20 56; 20 cours d'Albret; 11am-6pm Wed-Mon), while *faïence* pottery, porcelain, gold, iron, glasswork and furniture are displayed at the **Musée des Arts Décoratifs** (Museum of Decorative Arts; ☎ 05 56 00 72 50; 39 rue Bouffard; museum 2-6pm Wed-Mon, temporary exhibits from 11am Mon-Fri).

The only remains of the Roman city of Burdigala are the crumbling ruins of the 3rd-century amphitheatre, **Palais Gallien** (rue du Docteur Albert Barraud; admission €3; 2-7pm Jun-Sep).

The **Jardin Public** (cours de Verdun) was established in 1755 and reworked in the English style a century later. There's been a **Jardin Botanique** (☎ 05 56 52 18 77; admission free; 8.30am-6pm) on this site since 1855.

Sleeping

Auberge de Jeunesse (☎ 05 56 33 00 70; www.auberge-jeunesse-bordeaux.com; 22 cours Barbey; dm incl sheets & breakfast €21; reception 7.30am-1.30pm & 3.30-9.30pm;) Bordeaux's only hostel is housed in an ultramodern building with a self-catering kitchen, good wheelchair access and fussball, to boot. From the train station, follow cours de la Marne for 300m; the hostel's about 250m ahead on your left.

Hôtel Studio (☎ 05 56 48 00 14; www.hotel-bordeaux.com; 26 rue Huguerie; s/d €29/35; 💻) Hôtel Studio's private rooms work out cheaper for two people than two dorm beds at Bordeaux's hostel. Sure, there are no lifts, and the blue-and-white rooms are plain (with paper-thin walls – bring ear plugs), but they're comfortable, and some have balconies and/or TVs.

Hôtel Touring (☎ 05 56 81 56 73; www.hoteltouring.fr; 16 rue Huguerie; s/d with shared bathroom €35/40, s with private bathroom €42-45, d with private bathroom €49-53) Run with pride by a warm-hearted local family, the Touring's rooms are furnished with original 1940s and '50s furniture, like flip-up school-style desks and club chairs, and most have fridges, TVs and telephones.

Eating

Cassolette Café (☎ 05 56 92 94 96; 20 place de la Victoire; menu €11.90, individual dishes €2.60-7.60; 🕑 noon-midnight) Fun, friendly and fantastic value, this lively place serves up *cassoulets* (casserole dishes) cooked on terracotta plates, created from ingredients you tick off on a checklist.

L'Entrecôte (☎ 05 56 81 76 10; 4 cours du 30 Juillet; menu €16.50; 🕑 lunch & dinner) Opened in 1966, this unpretentious place doesn't take reservations, and it only has one menu option: succulent thin-sliced meat, heated by tea-lights, cooked in a special shallot sauce and accompanied by homemade *frites*.

On Sunday mornings head to quai des Chartrons' **bio (organic) market**; otherwise, stock up at **Marché des Capucins** (place des Capuchins; 🕑 6am-1pm Tue-Sun).

Getting There & Away

Citram Aquitaine (☎ 05 56 43 68 43; www.citram.fr, in French) runs most buses to destinations in the Gironde. **Eurolines** (☎ 05 56 92 50 42; 32 rue Charles Domercq; 🕑 9am-12.30pm & 1.30-7pm Mon-Fri, 9am-noon & 2-6pm Sat) faces the train station.

Bordeaux's Gare St-Jean is about 3km from the city centre. Destinations include Paris' Gare Montparnasse (€66.20, three hours, at least 16 daily), Bayonne (€28.80, 1¾ hours), Nantes (€41.60, four hours), Poitiers (€33.90, 1¾ hours) and Toulouse (€33.30, 2¼ hours).

BIARRITZ

pop 30,700

As ritzy as its name suggests, this stylish coastal town took off in the mid-19th century when Napoléon III visited. It glimmers with architectural treasures from the *belle époque* and art deco eras, but these days its big waves and beachy lifestyle are more popular with European surfers.

Orientation

Place Clemenceau, the heart of town, is just south of the main beach (La Grande Plage). Pointe St-Martin rounds off Plage Miramar, the northern continuation of La Grande Plage, bounded on its southern side by Pointe Atalaye. The train station and airport are about 3km southeast of the centre.

Information

Form@tic (☎ 05 59 22 12 79; 15 av de la Marne; per hr €4; 🕑 9am-8pm Mon-Sat) Bright, stylish internet cafe.

Laundrettes (🕑 7am-9pm) Wash your togs at 11 av de la Marne and 4 av Jaulerry.

Tourist Office (☎ 05 59 22 37 00; www.biarritz.fr; square d'Ixelles; 🕑 9am-7pm daily Jul & Aug, 9am-6pm Mon-Sat, 10am-5pm Sun Sep-Jun) Has internet access (€3 for every 15 minutes) and publishes *Biarritz Scope et Shops*, a free what's-on guide.

Sights & Activities

Biarritz' fashionable beaches, particularly the **Grande Plage** and **Plage Miramar**, are end-to-end bodies on hot summer days. North of Pointe St-Martin, the adrenaline-pumping surfing beaches of **Anglet** (the *t* is pronounced) continue northwards for more than 4km, and provide some of Europe's finest surfing. Take eastbound bus 9 (Line C on Sunday and public holidays) from the bottom of av Verdun (just near av Édouard VII). For gear, try **Rip Curl Surf Shop** (☎ 05 59 24 38 40; 2 av de la Reine Victoria) or the **Quiksilver Surf School** (☎ 05 59 22 03 12; www.biarritz-boardriders.com, in French).

Beyond **Plage de la Côte des Basques**, some 500m south of Port Vieux, are **Plage de Marbella** and **Plage de la Milady**. Take westbound bus 9 (Line C on Sunday and public holidays) from rue Gambetta.

Biarritz' history as a fishing and whaling centre is explored at the **Musée de la Mer** (☎ 05 59 22 33 34; www.museedelamer.com; Esplanade du Rocher de la Vierge; admission €7.80; 🕑 9.30am-12.30pm & 2-6pm, closed Mon Nov-Mar) alongside underwater life collected from the Bay of Biscay (Golfe de Gascogne).

Sleeping

Biarritz Camping (☎ 05 59 23 00 12; www.biarritz-camping.fr; 28 rue d'Harcet; camp sites €15-23; mid-May–mid-Oct;) This camping ground, 2km southwest of the centre, has spacious, shady pitches. Take westbound bus 9 to the Biarritz Camping stop.

Auberge de Jeunesse de Biarritz (☎ 05 59 41 76 00; www.hibiarritz.org; 8 rue Chiquito de Cambo; dm incl sheets & breakfast €17.10-18.10; reception 8.30-11.30am & 6-9pm Oct–mid-Dec & Jan-Mar, 8.30am-noon & 6-10pm Apr-Sep, closed mid-Dec–early Jan;) This popular place offers outdoor activities including surfing. Rooms for two to four hostellers have an ensuite bathroom. From the train station, follow the railway westwards for 800m.

Hôtel Maïtagaria (☎ 05 59 24 26 65; www.hotel-maitagaria.com; 34 av Carnot; s €49-54, d €57-69, tr €76-90) Spotless modern rooms with art-deco furniture and immaculate bathrooms, as well as a lovely summer terrace tailor-made for lounging.

Eating

Bleu Café (☎ 05 59 22 34 53; Grand Plage; breakfast €9, dishes €7-9; 9am-midnight Jul & Aug, 9am-5pm Sep-Jun) Sip Lavazza coffee or dine on Poilâne bread with fresh veggies while watching surfers battle the rollers.

Bistrot des Halles (☎ 05 59 24 21 22; 1 rue du Centre; mains €14.50-17; lunch & dinner) One of a cluster of decent restaurants along rue du Centre that get their produce directly from the nearby covered market, this bustling place serves excellent fish and other fresh fare from the blackboard menu.

Le Corsaire (☎ 05 59 24 63 72; Port des Pêcheurs; mains €11-23.50; lunch & dinner Tue-Sat) Down by the water's edge, sit out on the terrace to savour dishes like grilled cod with chorizo. The neighbouring seafood restaurants in this little harbourside setting offer similar quality and prices.

Just downhill from Biarritz' **covered market**, **La Table de Don Quichotte** (12 av Victor Hugo) sells Spanish hams, sausages, pickles and wines. You'll find a tempting array of cheeses, wines and pâtés at nearby **Mille et Un Fromages** (8 av Victor Hugo). At sea level, **Épicerie Fine du Port Vieux** (41bis rue Mazagran) is another excellent delicatessen.

Drinking

There are great bars around rue du Port Vieux and place Clemenceau.

Bar Basque (☎ 05 59 24 60 92; 1 rue du Port Vieux) This rustic-chic newcomer serves bite-size Basque tapas (€1.20 to €7) washed down with a selection of wines.

Le Surfing (☎ 05 59 24 78 72; 9 bd Prince des Galles) After a hard day's surfing, drop in to this memorabilia-filled surf bar to compare waves and wipe-outs.

Arena Café Bar (☎ 05 59 24 88 98; Plage du Port Vieux; 9am-2am daily Apr-Sep, 10am-2am Wed-Sun Oct-Mar) Tucked into a tiny cove, this beachfront hangout combines a style-conscious restaurant (mains €15 to €22) with a fuchsia-tinged bar with DJs on the turntables.

Getting There & Away

Biarritz–La Négresse train station is about 3km south of the town centre, and is served by buses 2 and 9 (B and C on Sundays).

From place des Basques, **ATCRB buses** (☎ 05 59 26 06 99) follow the coast to the Spanish border. There are nine services daily to St-Jean de Luz (€3, 40 minutes) with connections for Hendaye (€3, one hour). Summer beach traffic can double journey times.

Transportes Pesa (☎ in Spain 902 10 12 10; www.pesa.net) buses leave twice a day Monday to Saturday for Bilbao in Spain, calling by Biarritz, St-Jean de Luz and San Sebastián.

From the train station, **RDTL** (☎ 05 59 55 17 59; www.rdtl.fr, in French) runs services northwards into Les Landes. For beaches north of Bayonne, such as Mimizan Plage and Moliets Plage, get off at Vieux Boucau (1¼ hours, six or seven daily).

Eurolines is represented by **Voyages Domejean** (☎ 05 59 59 19 33; 3 place Charles de Gaulle). Buses stop in the square, opposite this travel agent's office.

LOURDES

pop 15,700 / elevation 400m

Lourdes has been one of the world's most important pilgrimage sites since 1858, when 14-year-old Bernadette Soubirous (1844–79) saw the Virgin Mary in a series of 18 visions. Over six million miracle-seeking visitors now descend on the town every year, and despite the endless tacky souvenir shops, it's still a fascinating place to visit.

The most revered site is the candle-lit **Grotte de Massabielle** (Massabielle Cave). The 19 holy **baths** (generally 9am-11am & 2.30-4pm Mon-Sat, 2-4pm Sun & holy days) are said to cure all kinds of diseases and ailments – the most recent confirmed case was that of an Italian, Anna Santaniello, who was apparently cured of chronic rheumatism in 2005. The main 19th-century section of the **sanctuaries** is divided between the neo-Byzantine Basilique du Rosaire, the crypt and the spire-topped Basilique Supérieure (Upper Basilica).

Lourdes is well connected by train; destinations include Bayonne (€18.90, 1¾ hours, up to four daily) and Toulouse (€22.20, 1¾ hours, six daily). There are four daily TGVs to Paris' Gare Montparnasse (€91.80, six hours).

LANGUEDOC-ROUSSILLON

Languedoc-Roussillon is three separate regions rolled into one. Bas Languedoc (Lower Languedoc) is known for bullfighting, rugby and robust red wines, while Roussillon straddles the rugged Pyrenees and has an unmistakeably Spanish atmosphere. Inland is mountainous Haut Languedoc (Upper Languedoc), whose traditional centre, Toulouse, was hived off when regional boundaries were redrawn almost half a century ago; we've chosen to include it in this section.

CARCASSONNE

pop 45,500

With its witch's hat turrets and walled city, Carcassonne looks like some fairy-tale fortress from afar – but the medieval magic's more than a little tarnished by an annual influx of over four million visitors. It can be a tourist hell in high summer, so pitch up out of season to see the town at its best (and quietest).

You can borrow an audioguide to **La Cité** (The Old City; per 2hr €3) at the **tourist office** (☎ 04 68 10 24 30; www.carcassonne-tourisme.com; 28 rue de Verdun; ⏲ 9am-7pm Jul & Aug, 9am-6pm Mon-Sat, 9am-1pm Sun Sep-Jun) or one of the summer **annexes** La Cité (Porte Narbonnaise; ⏲ year-round); Ville Basse (av Joffre; ⏲ mid-Apr–Oct).

The old city is dramatically illuminated at night and enclosed by two **rampart walls** punctuated by 52 stone towers, Europe's largest city fortifications. Successive generations of Gauls, Romans, Visigoths, Moors, Franks and Cathars reinforced the walls, but only the lower sections are original; the rest, including the turrets, were stuck on by the 19th-century architect Viollet-le-Duc.

A drawbridge leads to the the old gate of **Porte Narbonnaise** and rue Cros Mayrevieille en route to place du Château and the 12th-century **Château Comtal** (adult/18-25yr €7.50/4.80; ⏲ 10am-6.30pm Apr-Sep, 9.30am-5pm Oct-Mar). South of place du Château is **Basilique St-Nazaire** (⏲ 9am-11.45am & 1.45-5.30pm Mon-Sat, 9-10.45am & 2-6pm Sun), illuminated by delicate medieval rose windows.

Carcassonne's hotels can be chronically overpriced in season, so you'll be better off visiting as a day-trip from Toulouse.

Bus services are extremely patchy, but Carcassonne is on the main line to Toulouse (€13.30, 50 minutes, frequent).

NÎMES

pop 145,000

Though the buzzy city of Nîmes boasts some of France's best-preserved classical buildings, including a famous Roman amphitheatre, the city is most famous for its sartorial export, *serge de Nîmes* – better-known to cowboys, clubbers and couturiers as denim.

Information

Avenue PC Gamer (2 rue Nationale; per hr €2; ⏲ 10.30am-11.30pm) Internet access.

Laundrette (14 rue Nationale; ⏲ 7am-9pm)

Net@Games (place de la Maison Carrée; per hr €2.50, wi-fi per hr €2; ⏲ 9am-1am Mon-Sat, noon-1am Sun) Internet access.

Tourist Office (☎ 04 66 58 38 00; www.ot-nimes.fr; 6 rue Auguste; ⏲ 8.30am-8pm Mon-Fri, 9am-7pm Sat, 10am-6pm Sun Jul & Aug, 8.30am-6.30pm Mon-Fri, 9am-6.30pm Sat, 10am-5pm Sun Sep-Jun) Rents out audioguides (one/two terminals €8/10).

Sights

A combination ticket (€9.80) covers all three of Nîmes' major sights.

The magnificent **Roman Amphitheatre** (adult incl audioguide €7.70; ⏲ 9am-7pm Jun-Aug, 9am-6pm or 6.30pm Mar-May, Sep & Oct, 9.30am-5pm Nov-Feb), the best preserved in the Roman empire, was built around AD 100 to seat 24,000 spectators.

The **Maison Carrée** (Square House; place de la Maison Carrée; adult €4.50; ⏲ 10am-7pm or 7.30pm Apr-Sep, 10am-6.30pm Mar & Oct, 10am-1pm & 2-5pm Nov-Feb) is a rectangular Roman temple, constructed around AD 5 to honour Emperor Augustus' two adopted sons.

A 10- to 15-minute uphill walk brings you to the crumbling shell of the **Tour Magne** (admission €2.70; ⏲ 9.30am-6.30pm or 7pm Jun-Sep,

9.30am-1pm & 2-4.30pm or 6pm Oct-May), raised around 15 BC and the largest of a chain of towers that once punctuated the city's 7km-long Roman ramparts.

Nîmes also has a **Musée des Beaux-Arts** (Fine Arts Museum; rue de la Cité Foulc; admission €5.10) and the **Musée d'Art Contemporain** (Contemporary Art Museum; place de la Maison Carrée; admission €5.10).

Festivals & Events

Nîmes becomes more Spanish than French during its two *férias* (bullfighting festivals): the five-day **Féria de Pentecôte** (Whitsuntide Festival) in June, and the three-day **Féria des Vendanges**, celebrating the grape harvest on the third weekend in September.

Sleeping

Auberge de Jeunesse (☎ 04 66 68 03 20; www.hinimes.com; 257 chemin de l'Auberge de Jeunesse, la Cigale; dm/d/q €12.75/32/51; ⏰ Feb-Dec) This sterling, well-equipped youth hostel with self-catering facilities has everything from dorms to cute houses for two to six in its extensive grounds, 3.5km northwest of the train station. Take bus I, direction Alès or Villeverte, and get off at the Stade stop.

Hôtel Central (☎ 04 66 67 27 75; www.hotel-central.org; 2 place du Château; s/d with shared bathroom €35/40, s/d/tr/q with private bathroom €43/48/58/68) With its creaky floorboards and bunches of wild flowers painted on each bedroom door, this friendly hotel is full of character.

our pick **Hôtel Amphithéâtre** (☎ 04 66 67 28 51; http://pagesperso-orange.fr/hotel-amphitheatre; rue des Arènes; s €41-45, d €53-70; ⏰ Feb-Dec; ☒) The welcoming, family-run Amphithéâtre is just up the road from its namesake. Once a pair of 18th-century mansions, it has 15 rooms decorated in warm, woody colours, each named after a writer or painter.

Eating

Haddock Café (☎ 04 66 67 86 57; www.haddock-cafe.fr, in French; 13 rue de l'Agau; daily special €8, menus €15-20, mains €10-14.50; ⏰ lunch & dinner Mon-Fri, 7pm-2am Sat) This cheerful cafe began life as a convent. Traditional food, local wines and live music at least twice a week.

Le Marché sur la Table (☎ 04 66 67 22 50; 10 rue Littré; mains €15-18; ⏰ Tue-Sun) You *could* just pop in for a glass of wine at this up-and-coming bistro, but you'd be missing out on Éric Vidal's market-fresh food. Eat in the attractively furnished interior or quiet rear courtyard.

Le 9 (☎ 04 66 21 80 77; 9 rue de l'Étoile; lunch menu €15, mains €15-18; ⏰ Mon-Sat & lunch Sun May-Sep, dinner Fri & Sat only Oct-Apr) Tucked away behind high green doors, you'll find a converted stables and a vine-clad courtyard. Everything except the lunch menu is à la carte.

For a quick snack or a picnic, try the following:

La Ferme (☎ 04 68 25 02 15; 26 rue Chartran) Well-stocked deli.
L'Art Gourmand (13 rue St-Louis) Divine chocolates and 33 ice-cream flavours.
Covered market (rue Aimé Ramond; ⏰ Mon-Sat)
Open-air market (place Carnot; ⏰ Tue, Thu & Sat)

Getting There & Away

Nîmes' **airport** (☎ 04 66 70 49 49), 10km southeast of the city on the A54, is served by Ryanair to/from London (Luton), Liverpool and Nottingham East Midlands.

The **bus station** (☎ 04 66 38 59 43; rue Ste-Félicité) is connected to the train station. International operators **Eurolines** (☎ 04 66 29 49 02) and **Line Bus** (☎ 04 66 29 50 62) both have kiosks. Regional destinations include Pont du Gard (€6.50, 30 minutes, five daily) and Alès (€8, 1¼ hours, five daily).

More than 12 TGVs daily run to/from Paris' Gare de Lyon (€68.50 to €96, three hours), while regional trains run to Avignon (€8.10, 30 minutes), Marseille (€17.90, 1¼ hours) and Montpellier (€8.20, 30 minutes).

PONT DU GARD

This Unesco World Heritage Site, is an exceptionally well-preserved, three-tiered Roman aqueduct. It's part of a 50km-long system of canals built about 19 BC by the Romans to bring water from near Uzès to Nîmes. The scale is huge: the 35 arches of the 275m-long upper tier, running 50m above the Gard River, contain a watercourse designed to carry 20,000 cubic metres of water per day, and the largest construction blocks weigh over five tonnes.

From car parks (€5) either side of the Gard River, you can walk along the road bridge, built in 1743. The best view of the Pont du Gard is from upstream, beside the river, where you can swim on hot days. For information on buses from Nîmes, see above.

TOULOUSE

pop 437,100

Often known as *la ville rose* (the pink city), funky Toulouse is one of the nation's liveliest and fastest-growing metropolises. Sliced through by the twin rivers of Canal du Midi and River Garonne, it's a city with both a long history and a forward-looking attitude: medieval streets and old churches fill the old town, while buzzy bars, grungy gig venues and over 100,000 students give the place a youthful kick.

Orientation

The heart of Toulouse is bounded by the River Garonne (west), bd de Strasbourg and bd Lazare Carnot (east). From place Wilson, allée Jean Jaurès leads to the bus station and Gare Matabiau, the train station.

Information

Laverie des Lois (☎ 05 61 23 71 45; 19 rue des Lois; http://laveriedeslois.spaces.live.com; per hr €4; ⏰ cybercafe 11am-9pm Tue-Sat, laundrette 8am-9pm daily) Surf the internet while your smocks wash.

Tourist Office (☎ 05 61 11 02 22; www.toulouse-tourisme.com; square Charles de Gaulle; ⏰ 9am-7pm Mon-Sat, 10am-1pm & 2-6.15pm Sun Jun-Sep, 9am-6pm Mon-Fri, 9am-12.30pm & 2-6pm Sat, 10am-12.30pm & 2-5pm Sun Oct-May) Inside a 16th-century tower. Runs walking tours (2hr tours €9) of historic Toulouse, metro art and night-time Toulouse (tours €10).

Sights

Bustling **place du Capitole** is the city's main square.

The predominantly 18th-century **Vieux Quartier** is a tiny web of narrow lanes and squares. The vast **Basilique St-Sernin** (☎ 05 61 21 80 45; place St-Sernin; ⏰ 8.30am-6.15pm Mon-Sat, 8.30am-7.30pm Sun Jul-Sep, 8.30-11.45am & 2-5.45pm Mon-Sat, 8.30am-12.30pm & 2-7.30pm Sun Oct-Jun) is France's largest Romanesque structure, topped by an octagonal 13th-century tower and 15th-century spire.

Inside an old Augustinian monastery, the **Musée des Augustins** (☎ 05 61 22 21 82; 21 rue de Metz; admission €3, temporary exhibitions €6, 1st Sun of month free; ⏰ 10am-6pm Thu-Tue, 10am-9pm Wed) houses everything from Roman artefacts to paintings by Rubens, Delacroix and Toulouse-Lautrec.

The **Cathédrale St-Étienne** (Cathedral of St Stephen; place St-Étienne; ⏰ 8am-7pm Mon-Sat, 9am-7pm Sun) is a hotchpotch of styles: highlights include a glorious 13th-century rose window and the choir.

The city's old red-brick abattoir is now the cutting-edge **Musée d'Art Moderne et Contemporain** (☎ 05 62 48 58 00; www.lesabattoirs.org, in French; 76 allées Charles de Fitte; admission €5-10 depending on exhibition, 1st Sun of month free; ⏰ 11am-7pm Tue-Sun).

Boat trips (from €5) along the Canal du Midi and River Garonne, run by **Toulouse Croisières** (☎ 05 61 25 72 57; www.toulouse-croisieres.com, in French) and **Les Bateaux Toulousains** (☎ 05 61 80 22 26; www.bateaux-toulousains.com), leave from quai de la Daurade.

Sleeping

Camping de Rupé (☎ 05 61 70 07 35; 21 chemin du Pont de Rupé; 2 adults, tent & car €14.50; ⏰ reception 9am-12.30pm & 5-8pm) Find this jam-packed camping ground 6km northwest of the train station; take bus 59 from place Jeanne d'Arc. Pitch tents in summer, and caravans year-round.

Hôtel La Chartreuse (☎ 05 61 62 93 39; www.chartreusehotel.com; 4bis bd de Bonrepos; d/tr €37/48) *Bon repos* (good rest) is the order of the day at this good-value hotel across from the train station.

Hôtel des Arts (☎ 05 61 23 36 21; couleurs.suds@club-internet.fr; 1bis rue Cantegril; d with shared/private shower €42/54) Price is the trump card for this modest place: all rooms feature shared toilets and in-room shower cubicles.

our pick **Hôtel St-Sernin** (☎ 05 61 21 73 08; www.hotelstsernin.com; 2 rue St-Bernard; s/d/tr from €58/68/83) Exciting change is afoot at this boutique hotel: Parisian couple Julien and Aurore bought it in 2008 and are renovating floor by floor. Many rooms have prime views of Basilique St-Sernin, and rooms four, nine, 15 and 20 are to die for.

Eating

our pick **Les Halles Victor Hugo** (place Victor Hugo; menus €10-20; ⏰ lunch Tue-Sun) Many of Toulouse's best-value places are the small, spartan, lunchtime-only restaurants above Toulouse's busy covered market. Fast, packed and no-nonsense, catering for market vendors and shoppers alike, they serve up generous, delicious menus of hearty fare.

Michel, Marcel, Pierre et les Autres (☎ 05 61 22 47 05; www.michelmarcelpierre.com; 35 rue de Rémusat; starter/main/dessert €7/13/7, 2-/3-course menu €17/23; ⏰ lunch & dinner Tue-Sat) This classic bistro with a twist is *the* place for bistro fare (mackerel fillets, pastry-baked cheese, *rillettes de canard* etc).

Chez Navarre (☎ 05 62 26 43 06; 49 Grande Rue Nazareth; lunch/dinner menu €12.50/20; ⏰ lunch & dinner Tue-Fri, dinner Sat) Fed up with restaurant dining? This fabulous 16th-century *table d'hôtes*, with red-brick walls, beamed ceiling and shared candlelit tables, is perfect. The rustic French cuisine of terrines, soups and one fixed meal emphasise the down-home feel.

Buy fresh produce (and/or wine for €1.20 a litre!) at **Les Halles Victor Hugo** (place Victor Hugo; 7am-1pm Tue-Sun) or **Marché des Carmes** (place des Carmes; 7am-1pm Tue-Sun).

Drinking

Almost every square in the Vieux Quartier has at least one bustling cafe.

Au Père Louis (05 61 21 33 45; 45 rue des Tourneurs; 8.30am-3pm & 5-10.30pm Mon-Sat) Top of our list for irresistible old-fashioned charm, Father Louis' is Toulouse's oldest bar (founded 1889).

La Maison (05 61 62 87 22; 9 rue Gabriel Péri; 5pm-2am Sun-Fri, 5pm-5am Sat) This crumbling old house is all about old-fashioned atmosphere – there's a vintage fireplace, retro chairs and sofas to lounge on.

La Tireuse (05 61 12 28 29; 24 rue Pargaminières; 5pm-2am Mon-Sat, 6pm-2am Sun) Friendly beer bar with 20 beers *en pression* (on tap), surrounded by kebab and burger joints.

Havana Café (05 62 88 34 94; www.havana-cafe.fr; 2 av des Crêtes, Ramonville St-Agne; admission free-€20) Reggae, rock, blues, heavy metal and gospel make this Toulouse's best live-music venue; it's at the end of metro line B, 8km south of the city (Ramonville stop).

Le Bikini (05 62 24 09 50; www.lebikini.com; rue Hermès, Ramonville St-Agne; admission €5-20) The stuff of Toulousien legend, around for 25 years or so, is also at the end of metro line B (Ramonville metro stop).

Getting There & Away

From **Toulouse-Blagnac Airport** (08 25 38 00 00; www.toulouse.aeroport.fr), 8km northwest of the centre, there are daily flights to/from Paris (Air France and easyJet) and other European cities. The **Navette Aéroport** (airport shuttle; 05 34 60 64 00; www.navette-tisseo-aeroport.com) links the airport (one-way/return €4/6.30, 20 minutes, every 20 minutes from 5am/7.25am to 8.20pm/midnight from town/airport) with the bus station, Jean Jaurès metro station or place Jeanne d'Arc.

Useful trains travel to Bordeaux (€34.80, two to three hours), Carcassonne (€13.30, one hour) and Lourdes (€23.40, 1¾ hours). Buy tickets at the **SNCF boutique** (5 rue Peyras) or **Gare Matabiau** (bd Pierre Sémard), 1km northeast of the centre.

Local buses and the two-line metro are run by **Tisséo** (05 61 41 70 70; www.tisseo.fr, in French), which has ticket kiosks on place Jeanne d'Arc and cours Dillon. A one-way/return ticket for either costs €1.40/2.50, a 10-ticket *carnet* is €11.70 and a one-/two-day pass is €4.20/7.

PROVENCE

Provence conjures up images of rolling lavender fields, blue skies, gorgeous villages, wonderful food and superb wine. It certainly delivers on all those fronts, but it's not just worth visiting for its good looks – dig a little deeper and you'll also discover the multicultural metropolis of Marseille, the artistic haven of Aix-en-Provence and the old Roman city of Arles.

MARSEILLE

pop 826,700

There was a time when Marseille was on the receiving end of some pretty bad press. No longer. The *cité phocéenne* has made an unprecedented comeback, undergoing a vast makeover. Marseillais will tell you that the city's rough-and-tumble edginess is part of its charm and that, for all its flaws, it is a very endearing place. They're right: Marseille grows on you, with its unique history, souk-like markets, millennia-old port and spectacular *corniches* (coastal roads).

Orientation

The city's main thoroughfare, blvd La Canebière, stretches eastwards from the Vieux Port (Old Port). The train station is north of La Canebière at the northern end of blvd d'Athènes. A few blocks south of La Canebière is the cours Julien, a large pedestrianised square. The ferry terminal is west of place de la Joliette, a few minutes' walk north of the Nouvelle Cathédrale. Addresses below include arrondissements (1er being the most central).

Information

There are banks and exchange bureaux on La Canebière near the Vieux Port.

Canebière Change (39 La Canebière, 1er; 8am-6pm Mon-Fri, 8.30am-noon & 2-4.30pm Sat; M Vieux Port)

Info Café (04 91 33 74 98; 1 quai de Rive Neuve, 1er; per hr adult/student €3.80/3; 9am-9pm Mon-Sat, 2.30-7.30pm Sun; M Vieux Port) Internet access.

Laverie des Allées (15 allées Léon Gambetta, 1er; 8am-8pm; M Réformés Canebière) Laundry.

FRANCE

GETTING INTO TOWN

Navette shuttle buses (☎ in Marseille 04 91 50 59 34, in airport 04 42 14 31 27) travel between Marseille's airport and train station every 20 minutes between 5.30am and 10.50pm (€8, 25 minutes).

Tourist Office (☎ 04 91 13 89 00; www.marseille-tourisme.com; 4 La Canebière, 1er; 9am-7pm Mon-Sat, 10am-5pm Sun; M Vieux Port)

Dangers & Annoyances

Marseille has a reputation for street crime; there's no need for paranoia but you should avoid the Belsunce area. Women *will* get unsolicited attention, ranging from wolf-whistling to occasionally aggressive chat-up routines.

Sights

The courtyard of the **Centre de la Vieille Charité** (Old Charity Cultural Centre; ☎ 04 91 14 58 80; 2 rue de la Charité, 2e; M Joliette) contains Marseille's **Musée d'Archéologie Méditerranéenne** (Museum of Mediterranean Archeology; ☎ 04 91 14 58 59) and **Musée d'Arts Africains, Océaniens & Amérindiens** (Museum of African, Oceanic & American Indian Art; ☎ 04 91 14 58 38). An all-inclusive ticket costs €5/2.50 per adult/student.

The hilltop **Basilique Notre Dame de la Garde** (☎ 04 91 13 40 80; montée de la Bonne Mère; admission free; basilica & crypt 7am-7pm, longer hr in summer), 1km south of the Vieux Port, dominates Marseille's skyline. The domed basilica was built between 1853 and 1864 and is ornamented with coloured marble, murals and mosaics. Bus 60 runs from the Vieux Port.

Immortalised in Alexandre Dumas' 1840s novel *Le Comte de Monte Cristo* (The Count of Monte Cristo), the 16th-century island prison of **Château d'If** (☎ 04 91 59 02 30; adult/student €5/3.50; 9.30am-6.30pm daily May-Aug, 9.30am-5.30pm Tue-Sun Sep-Mar, 9.30am-5.30pm daily Apr) sits 3.5km west of the Vieux Port. Political prisoners of all persuasions were incarcerated here, along with Protestants, the Revolutionary hero Mirabeau and the Communards of 1871.

Boats run by **Frioul If Express** (☎ 04 91 46 54 65; www.frioul-if-express.com; 1 quai des Belges, 1er) leave from the Vieux Port (€10 return, 20 minutes, 15 boats daily in summer, fewer in winter).

Sleeping

Auberge de Jeunesse de Bonneveine (☎ 04 91 17 63 30; www.fuaj.org; impasse du Docteur Bonfils, 8e; dm €17.10, d incl sheets & breakfast €40.60; Feb-Dec;) The building looks like a primary school, the rooms are spartan and it's miles from town, but beach activities including kayaking, hiking and kitesurfing make up for that. Bus 44 (stop Bonnefon) is 200m away.

our pick **Vertigo** (☎ 04 91 91 07 11; www.hotelvertigo.fr; 42 rue des Petites Maries, 1er; dm €23.90, d €55-65; M Gare St-Charles SNCF;) This new boutique hostel swaps dodgy bunk beds and hospital-like decor for vintage posters, a chrome kitchen and groovy communal spaces. Obviously, there's no curfew. Check out the *cabanons* (fishing cabins) doubles.

Hôtel Le Richelieu (☎ 04 91 31 01 92; www.leriche lieu-marseille.com; 52 corniche Président John F Kennedy, 7e; d €46-110) This beach house–style hotel has gone a little over-the-top on the colours, but the balconies, sea views and breakfast terrace are fab.

Etap Hotel (☎ 08 92 68 05 82; fax 04 91 54 95 67; 46 rue Sainte, 1er; s/d/tr €49/58/67; M Vieux Port;) Try for one of the large, wood-beamed rooms in the old building (a former sea-captain's house), which add a smidgen of charm to this somewhat soulless chain establishment.

Hôtel Relax (☎ 04 91 33 15 87; http://relaxhotel.free.fr, in French; 4 rue Corneille, 1er; s €40, d €55-60; M Vieux Port;) In a dress-circle location overlooking Marseille's art deco Opera House, this 20-room hotel is run by a lovely family. Noise insulation isn't great, but it's a bargain for the location.

Eating

The Vieux Port overflows with restaurants. Cours Julien and its surrounding streets are jammed with ethnic restaurants.

Le Femina (☎ 04 91 54 03 56; 1 rue de Musée, 1er; menus €15; closed Sun & Mon; Canebière Garibaldi, M Noailles) Heading east from the Vieux Port towards cours Julien, Le Femina is a great Algerian place for succulent couscous.

Pain & Cie (☎ 04 91 33 55 00; 18 place aux Huiles, 1er; brunch €19; 8am-10.30pm Tue-Sat, 8am-6pm Sun & Mon; M Vieux Port) Trendy locals brunch here at the weekend or come for a quick lunchtime *tartine* (open sandwich).

Chez Jeannot (☎ 04 91 52 11 28; 129 rue du Vallon des Auffes; mains €15-22; lunch & dinner Tue-Sat, lunch Sun, closed Mon) An institution among

SPLURGE

ourpick **Chez Madie Les Galinettes** (☎ 04 91 90 40 87; 138 quai du Port, 2e; mains €25-50, menus €15-27; ⏲ lunch & dinner Mon-Sat, closed Sat lunch in summer) They're so friendly at Madie's that you'll leave feeling as though you've just had dinner with friends. The portside terrace is perfect for those long summer evenings, and the menu's stocked with fish and a fantastic *bouillabaisse* that you'll need to order in advance.

Marseillais for thin-crust pizzas, *grillades* (grilled meats) and seafood, the rooftop terrace overlooking the stunning Vallon des Auffes is booked out days in advance.

The fascinating **fish market** (quai des Belges; ⏲ 8am-1pm; Ⓜ Vieux Port) is a daily fixture at the Vieux Port. Cours Julien hosts a Wednesday-morning **organic fruit and vegetable market**.

Stock up on fruit and vegetables at **Marché des Capucins** (place des Capucins, 1er; ⏲ 8am-7pm Mon-Sat; 🚊 Canebière Garibaldi, Ⓜ Noailles) and the **fruit and vegetable market** (cours Pierre Puget, 6e; ⏲ 8am-1pm Mon-Fri; Ⓜ Estrangin Préfecture).

There are supermarkets in the Centre Bourse shopping centre.

Drinking & Entertainment

Options for a coffee or something stronger abound on and around the Vieux Port.

Au Petit Nice (☎ 04 91 48 43 04; 28 place Jean Jaurès, 6e; ⏲ 6.30am-2am; Ⓜ Notre Dame du Mont-Cours Julien) A perfect illustration of what cheap and cheerful means: €2 a drink, whatever it is – how could you not be happy?

Le Bar de la Marine (☎ 04 91 54 95 42; 15 quai de Rive Neuve, 7e; ⏲ 7am-1am; Ⓜ Vieux Port) Marcel Pagnol filmed the card party scenes in his 1931 film *Marius* at this Marseille institution.

L'Intermédiaire (☎ 04 91 47 01 25; 63 place Jean Jaurès, 6e; ⏲ 7pm-2am Mon-Sat; Ⓜ Notre Dame du Mont-Cours Julien) This graffitied, grungy venue is one of the best bets in town for live music, bands or DJs.

Getting There & Away

AIR

Aéroport Marseille-Provence (☎ 04 42 14 14 14; www.marseille.aeroport.fr), also known as Aéroport Marseille–Marignane, is 25km northwest of town. It has numerous budget flights to various European destinations. **Navette shuttle buses** (☎ in Marseilles 04 91 50 59 34, in airport 04 42 14 31 27) run to Marseille's train station every 20 minutes between 5.30am and 10.50pm (€8, 25 minutes).

BOAT

Marseille's **passenger ferry terminal** (☎ 04 91 39 40 00; www.marseille-port.fr; 🚊 Ⓜ Joliette) is 250m south of place de la Joliette (1er). The **Société Nationale Maritime Corse-Méditerranée** (SNCM; ☎ 08 25 88 80 88; www.sncm.fr; 61 bd des Dames, 2e; ⏲ 8am-6pm Mon-Fri, 8.30am-noon & 2-5.30pm Sat; 🚊 Ⓜ Joliette) links Marseille with Corsica, Sardinia and Tunisia.

BUS

The **bus station** (☎ 08 91 02 40 25; 3 rue Honnorat, 3e; Ⓜ Gare St-Charles SNCF) is at the back of the train station. Tickets can be purchased from the information desk inside the train station or from the driver. Buses travel to Aix-en-Provence (€4.60, 35 minutes, every five to 10 minutes), Avignon (€18.50, two hours, one daily), Cannes (€25, two hours, up to three daily), Nice (€26.50, three hours, up to three daily) and other destinations.

Eurolines (☎ 08 92 89 90 91; www.eurolines.com; 3 allées Léon Gambetta; ⏲ 10am-6pm Mon-Fri, 10am-2pm Sat) has international coach services.

TRAIN

Marseille's passenger train station, Gare St-Charles, is served by both metro lines. There's an **information and ticket reservation office** (⏲ 9am-8pm Mon-Sat, 5.15am-10pm for ticket purchases), plus a **left-luggage office** (from €3.50; ⏲ 7.30am-10pm) next to platform A. In town, tickets can be bought at the SNCF Boutique inside the Centre Bourse shopping centre.

Useful destinations include Paris' Gare de Lyon (€80.20, three hours, 21 daily), Nice (€27.80, 2½ hours, 21 daily), Avignon (€23.10, 35 minutes, 27 daily) and Lyon (€57.60, 1¾ hours, 16 daily).

Getting Around

Marseille has two metro lines (Métro 1 and Métro 2), two tram lines (yellow and green) and an extensive bus network. The metro runs between 5am and 10.30pm Monday to Thursday and until 12.30am Friday to Sunday; the tram runs between 5am and 1am. Bus services stop around 9.30pm, when night buses take over until 12.30am. Bus, metro or tram tickets (€1.70) are valid for one hour after being time-stamped. A one-/three-day pass costs €4.50/10.

AIX-EN-PROVENCE

pop 141,200

Aix-en-Provence is to Provence what the Left Bank is to Paris: a pocket of bohemian chic with an edgy student crowd. It's hard to believe Aix (pronounced ex) is just 25km from chaotic, exotic Marseille. The city has been a cultural centre since the Middle Ages (two of the town's most famous sons are painter Paul Cézanne and novelist Émile Zola) but for all its polish, it's a laid-back Provençal town at heart.

Information

Netgames (☎ 04 42 26 60 41; 52 rue Aumône Vieille; per hr €3; ⏰ 10am-midnight) Central and state of the art.

Tourist Office (☎ 04 42 16 11 61; www.aixenprovencetourism.com; 2 place du Général de Gaulle; ⏰ 8.30am-7pm Mon-Sat, 10am-1pm & 2-6pm Sun) Longer hours in summer; very proactive and helpful.

Sights

Art, culture, and architecture abound in Aix, thanks to local lad Paul Cézanne (1839–1906). To see where he ate, drank, studied and painted, you can follow the **Circuit de Cézanne** (Cézanne Trail), marked by footpath-embedded bronze plaques inscribed with the letter C. An English-language guide, *Cézanne's Footsteps*, is available free from the tourist office.

The trail takes in Cézanne's last studio, **Atelier Paul Cézanne** (☎ 04 42 21 06 53; www.atelier-cezanne.com; 9 av Paul Cézanne; adult/student €5.50/2; ⏰ 10am-noon & 2-5pm Oct-Mar, to 6pm Apr-Jun & Sep, 10am-6pm Jul & Aug), 1.5km north of the tourist office.

Cézanne also features at the **Musée Granet** (☎ 04 42 52 88 32; place St-Jean de Malte; ⏰ 11am-7pm Wed-Mon Jun-Sep, noon-6pm Wed-Mon Oct-May), which houses nine of the artists' canvases alongside works by Picasso, Léger, Matisse, Tal Coat and Giacometti.

Sleeping

Camping Arc-en-Ciel (☎ 04 42 26 14 28; rte de Nice; camp site for 2 people plus car €18.50; ⏰ Apr-Sep; 🏊) Tranquil wooded hills and a busy motorway frame this four-star camping ground. It's 2km southeast of town; take bus 3 to Les Trois Sautets stop.

Auberge de Jeunesse du Jas de Bouffan (☎ 04 42 20 15 99; www.fuaj.org; 3 av Marcel Pagnol; dm incl breakfast & sheets €17.50-29.50; ⏰ reception 7am-1pm & 5pm-midnight, closed mid-Dec–Jan) Shiny new, with a bar, tennis courts, bike shed and massive summer BBQs, this HI hostel is 2km west of the centre; shame about the motorway. Take bus 4 from La Rotonde to the Vasarely stop.

Hôtel La Caravelle (☎ 04 42 21 53 05; www.lacaravelle-hotel.com; 29 bd du Roi René; s €45, d €65-70) Central and friendly, La Caravelle has 30 rooms ranging from air-conditioned doubles to singles with adjoining toilets. Wi-fi's free and wheelchair access is good.

Eating & Drinking

Charlotte (☎ 04 42 26 77 56; 32 rue des Bernardines; 2-/3-course menu €14/17.50; ⏰ lunch & dinner Tue-Sat) Townspeople congregate like a big extended family for home-cooked terrines, soups and savoury tarts. In summer, feasting takes place outdoors in the garden.

Le Zinc d'Hugo (☎ 04 42 27 69 69; 22 rue Lieutaud; mains €14-18; ⏰ lunch & dinner Tue-Sat) Stone walls, wooden tables and a blackboard menu make for a lovely rustic bistro, so it unsurprisingly gets rammed on market days.

The daily **produce market** (place Richelme) sells olives, goats' cheese, garlic, lavender, honey, peaches, melons and other sun-kissed products. Another **food market** (place des Prêcheurs) takes place on Tuesday, Thursday and Saturday mornings. Groceries are available at **Monoprix** (cours Mirabeau; ⏰ 8.30am-9pm Mon-Sat) and **Petit Casino** (rue d'Italie; ⏰ 9am-7pm Mon-Sat).

Getting There & Away

Aix' **bus station** (☎ 08 91 02 40 25; av de l'Europe) is 10 minutes southwest from La Rotonde. Routes include Marseille (€4.60, 30 to 50 minutes, every 10 minutes, every 20 minutes on Sunday), Arles (€10.40, 1½ hours, six daily Monday to Saturday) and Avignon (€14, 1¼ hours, six daily Monday to Saturday).

The only useful train from Aix' city-centre **train station** (⏰ 7am-7pm) goes to Marseille (€6.50, 50 minutes). For other routes, you'll have to travel to the **TGV station**, 8km from the city centre.

Half-hourly shuttle buses run from the bus station to the TGV station (€3.70) and Aéroport Marseille-Provence (€7.90) from 4.40am to 10.30pm.

AVIGNON

pop 90,800

Hooped by 4.3km of superbly preserved stone ramparts, this graceful city is the belle of Provence's ball. Famed for its annual

Book your stay at lonelyplanet.com/hotels

performing-arts festival and its fabled bridge, the Pont St-Bénezet (aka the Pont d'Avignon), Avignon is an ideal spot from which to step out into the surrounding region.

Information

Chez W@m (☎ 04 90 86 19 03; 34 rue Bonneterie; per hr €3; 10am-8pm Mon-Thu & 10am-10pm Fri & Sat) Cybercafe.

Lavmatic (9 rue du Chapeau Rouge; 7am-8.30pm) 21st-century laundrette with wi-fi.

Tourist Office (☎ 04 32 74 32 74; www.avignon-tourisme.com; 41 cours Jean Jaurès; 9am-5pm Mon-Sat, 9.45am-5pm Sun Apr-Jun & Aug-Oct, 9am-7pm Mon-Sat, 9.45am-5pm Sun Jul, 9am-6pm Mon-Fri, 9am-5pm Sat & 10am-noon Sun Nov-Mar) Around 300m north of the train station. The *Avignon Passion* pass entitles you to discounted museum entry.

Sights

The fabled **Pont St-Bénezet** (St Bénezet's Bridge; ☎ 04 90 27 51 16; full price/pass & student €4.50/3.50; 9am-9pm Aug, 9am-8pm Jul & early–mid-Sep, 9am-7pm Apr-Jun & mid-Sep–Oct, 9.30am-5.45pm Nov-Mar), immortalised in the French nursery rhyme *Sur le Pont d'Avignon*, was completed in 1185. The 900m-long wooden structure was repaired and rebuilt several times before all but four of its 22 spans were washed away in the mid-1600s. You can see it for free from the Rocher des Doms park, Pont Édouard Daladier or from across the river on the Île de la Barthelasse's chemin des Berges.

Wrapping around the city, Avignon's ramparts were built between 1359 and 1370. They were restored during the 19th century, minus their original moats. Within the walls is a wealth of fine museums, including the **Palais des Papes** (Palace of the Popes; ☎ 04 90 27 50 00; place du Palais; full price/pass & student €6/3; 9am-9pm Aug, 9am-8pm Jul & early–mid-Sep, 9am-7pm Apr-Jun & mid-Sep–Oct, 9.30am-5.45pm Nov-Mar). Built during the 14th century and intended as a fortified palace for the papal court, it's the largest Gothic palace in Europe, but its rooms are rather bare.

The **Musée Lapidaire** (☎ 04 90 86 33 84; 27 rue de la République; full price/pass €2/1; 10am-6pm Wed-Mon Jun-Sep, 10am-1pm & 2-6pm Wed-Mon Oct-May) houses a collection of Egyptian, Roman, Etruscan and early Christian pieces, while works by Cézanne, Manet, Degas, Modigliani and the only Van Gogh painting in Provence can be seen at the charming **Musée Angladon** (☎ 04 90 82 29 03; www.angladon.com; 5 rue Laboureur; full price/pass & student €6/4; 1-6pm Tue-Sun mid-Mar–mid-Nov, 1-6pm Wed-Sun mid-Nov–mid-Mar).

Fine views of the old city are afforded by the **Tour Philippe-le-Bel** (☎ 04 32 70 08 57; full price/pass €2/1.50; 10am-12.30pm & 2-6.30pm Tue-Sun Apr-Sep, 10am-noon & 2-5pm Tue-Sun Oct, Nov & Mar), 3km across the Rhône in neighbouring Villeneuve-lès-Avignon.

Festivals & Events

Hundreds of artists take to the stage and streets during the world-famous **Festival d'Avignon** (www.festival-avignon.com), held every year from early July to early August. The more experimental (and cheaper) fringe event, **Festival Off** (☎ 04 90 85 13 08; www.avignonleoff.com, in French), runs alongside the main festival.

Sleeping

Camping Bagatelle (☎ 04 90 86 30 39; camping.bagatelle@wanadoo.fr; Île de la Barthelasse; tent only per person €4.66-6.16, 2 people with car €11.32-19.32; reception 8am-9pm) Multilingual, shaded and only 20 minutes' walk from the centre on Île de la Barthelasse, this camping ground offers discounts for carless campers.

YMCA-UCJG (☎ 04 90 25 46 20; www.ymca-avignon.com; 7bis chemin de la Justice; d/tr/q with shared bathroom €30/36/48, with private bathroom €45/54/54; reception 8.30am-6pm, closed Dec-early Jan;) If you're after your own space on a shoestring, head to this spotless hostel outside Villeneuve-lès-Avignon. There's a massive swimming pool and terrace with panoramic views of the city. Take bus 10 to the Monteau stop or take the 30-minute stroll across the bridge.

Hôtel Splendid (☎ 04 90 86 14 46; www.avignon-splendid-hotel.com; 17 rue Agricol Perdiguier; s €32-46, d €48-70, apt €70-90) This eco-conscious, cyclist-friendly place has charming rooms and self-contained studios, half overlooking the pretty neighbouring park.

Hôtel Boquier (☎ 04 90 82 34 43; www.hotel-boquier.com, in French; 6 rue du Portail Boquier; d €45-66;) Run by new owners, this great little hotel is bright, airy, spacious and central, and the themed rooms are particularly attractive (try for Morocco or Lavender).

Eating

Numéro 75 (☎ 04 90 27 16 00; 75 rue Guillaume Puy; mains from €10; lunch & dinner Mon-Sat) Lodged inside the house of absinthe inventor Jules

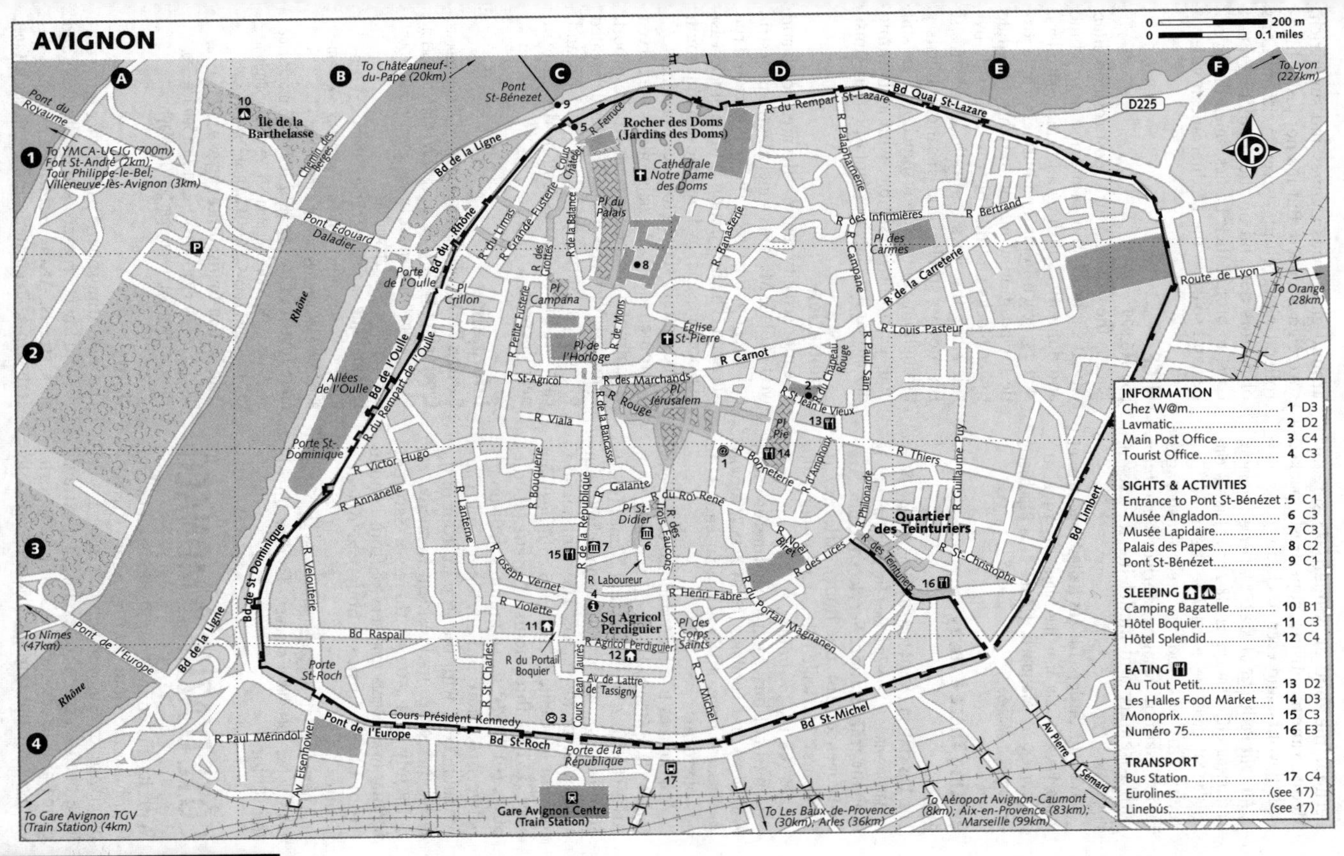
AVIGNON
0 200 m
0 0.1 miles
A
B
C
D
E
F
1
2
3
4
To Châteauneuf-du-Pape (20km)
To Lyon (227km)
To Orange (28km)
To YMCA-UCJG (700m); Fort St-André (2km); Tour Philippe-le-Bel; Villeneuve-lès-Avignon (3km)
To Nîmes (47km)
To Gare Avignon TGV (Train Station) (4km)
To Les Baux-de-Provence (30km); Arles (36km)
To Aéroport Avignon-Caumont (8km); Aix-en-Provence (83km); Marseille (99km)
Pont du Royaume
Île de la Barthelasse
Chemin des Berges
Pont St-Bénezet
Pont Édouard Daladier
Rhône
D225
Rocher des Doms (Jardins des Doms)
Cathédrale Notre Dame des Doms
Pl du Palais
Pl Campana
Pl de l'Horloge
Église St-Pierre
Pl Jérusalem
Pl Pie
Pl St-Didier
Pl des Carmes
Pl Crillon
Pl des Corps Saints
Sq Agricol Perdiguier
Quartier des Teinturiers
Allées de l'Oulle
Porte de l'Oulle
Porte St-Dominique
Porte St-Roch
Porte de la République
Gare Avignon Centre (Train Station)
Bd Quai St-Lazare
R du Rempart St-Lazare
Bd de la Ligne
Bd du Rhône
Bd de l'Oulle
R du Rempart de l'Oulle
Bd de St Dominique
Pont de l'Europe
Bd St-Roch
Bd St-Michel
Bd Limbert
Route de Lyon
R de la Carreterie
R Carnot
R des Marchands
R Rouge
R de la République
Cours Jean Jaurès
Cours Président Kennedy
Bd Raspail
R Joseph Vernet
R Victor Hugo
R Annanelle
R Velouterie
R Lanterne
R St Charles
R Paul Mérindol
Av Eisenhower
Av Pierre Sémard
Av de Lattre de Tassigny
R du Portail Boquier
R Agricol Perdiguier
R Violette
R Labroueur
R Henri Fabre
R du Portail Magnanen
R St Michel
R des Lices
R des Teinturiers
R Noël Biret
R St-Christophe
R Guillaume Puy
R Thiers
R Philonarde
R Paul Saïn
R Bonneterie
R d'Amphoux
R St Jean le Vieux
R du Chapeau Rouge
R Louis Pasteur
R Campane
R des Infirmières
R Bertrand
R Palapharnerie
R Banasterie
R Ferruce
Cours Châtelet
R de la Balance
R des Grottes
R Grande Fusterie
R du Limas
R Petite Fusterie
R St-Agricol
R Viala
R de la Bancasse
R de Mons
R Bouquerie
R Galante
R du Roi René
R des Trois Faucons
INFORMATION
Chez W@m 1 D3
Lavmatic 2 D2
Main Post Office 3 C4
Tourist Office 4 C3
SIGHTS & ACTIVITIES
Entrance to Pont St-Bénézet 5 C1
Musée Angladon 6 C3
Musée Lapidaire 7 C3
Palais des Papes 8 C2
Pont St-Bénézet 9 C1
SLEEPING
Camping Bagatelle 10 B1
Hôtel Boquier 11 C3
Hôtel Splendid 12 C4
EATING
Au Tout Petit 13 D2
Les Halles Food Market 14 D3
Monoprix 15 C3
Numéro 75 16 E3
TRANSPORT
Bus Station 17 C4
Eurolines (see 17)
Linebús (see 17)

FRANCE

Pernod, the food at Numéro 75 screams Mediterranean cuisine: superfresh, packed with flavours, and ever so cheap.

Au Tout Petit (☎ 04 90 82 38 86; 4 rue d'Amphoux; lunch menu €10, dinner menu €18-24; ⏰ lunch & dinner Mon-Sat, closed Wed night) The menu of 'The Teeny Tiny' is a foodies' treat – asparagus ravioli, salmon lasagne, apricot *tarte tatin* with rosemary-and-madeleine ice cream. Food poetry.

Over 40 outlets fill **Les Halles' food market** (place Pie; ⏰ 7am-1pm Tue-Sun), or pick up groceries at **Monoprix** (24 rue de la République; ⏰ 8am-9pm Mon-Sat).

Getting There & Away

BUS

The **bus station** (☎ 04 90 82 07 35; bd St-Roch; ⏰ information window 8am-7pm Mon-Fri, 8am-1pm Sat) is near the train station. Services include Aix-en-Provence (€14, one hour), Arles (€7.10, 1½ hours), Marseille (€18.50, two hours) and Nîmes (€8.10, 1¼ hours).

Long-haul bus companies **Linebús** (☎ 04 90 85 30 48) and **Eurolines** (☎ 04 90 85 27 60; www.eurolines.com) have offices at the far end of the bus platforms.

Avignon has two train stations: **Gare Avignon Centre** (42 bd St-Roch) has local trains to/from Arles (€6.30, 20 minutes) and Nîmes (€8.10, 30 minutes), while **Gare Avignon TGV**, 4km southwest of town, has TGV connections to/from Marseille (€23.10, 35 minutes) and Nice (€51.80, three hours). *Navette* (shuttle) buses (€1.10, 10 to 13 minutes, half-hourly between 6.15am and 11.30pm) link Gare Avignon TGV with the stop in front of the post office on cours Président Kennedy.

In July and August there's a Saturday **Eurostar** (www.eurostar.com) service from London (from €125 return, six hours) to Avignon Centre.

There is a **left luggage** (per bag from €4; ⏰ 7am-7pm winter, 7am-10pm summer) facility inside the station.

CÔTE D'AZUR & MONACO

With its glistening seas, idyllic beaches and lush hills, the Côte d'Azur (Azure Coast) – otherwise known as the French Riviera – has long been a symbol of exclusivity, extravagance and excess, and it's still a favourite getaway for the European jetset, especially around glamorous Cannes and super-rich, sovereign Monaco. But it's not just a high-roller's playground – every year millions of visitors descend on the southern French coast to bronze their bodies, smell the lavender and soak up the Mediterranean vibe.

NICE

pop 346,900

Nice is the Côte d'Azur's most cosmopolitan city. It's a heady mix of old and new, ethnic and domestic, sunshine and smog: strollers, skaters, beach-bums, and businesspeople jostle for position along the beachfront, while tower blocks and tiny bistros stand side-by-side along the city's traffic-thronged streets. It's noisy, smelly and insanely touristy throughout summer, but somehow Nice still manages to be irresistible, with a charming old city and a clutch of fantastic museums.

Orientation

The modern city centre – the area north and west of place Masséna – includes the pedestrianised shopping streets rue de France and rue Masséna. The bus station is three blocks east of place Masséna. Av Jean Médecin runs south from the train station to place Masséna.

Promenade des Anglais follows the curved beachfront from the city centre to the airport, 6km west. Vieux Nice (Old Nice) is delineated by bd Jean Jaurès, quai des États-Unis and, east, the hill known as Colline du Château, near the port.

Information

Barclays Bank (2 rue Alphonse Karr) Has a change counter.
Cyberpoint (☎ 04 93 92 70 63; 10 av Félix Faure; per hr €4; ⏰ 10am-9pm Mon-Sat, later in summer, 3-9pm Sun) One of endless cybercafes in Nice.
Lavomatique rue Pertinax (22 rue Pertinax; ⏰ 7am-8pm); rue du Pont Vieux (11 rue du Pont Vieux; ⏰ 7am-8pm) More laundrettes surround the station.
Main Tourist Office (☎ 08 92 70 74 07; 5 promenade des Anglais; ⏰ 8am-8pm Mon-Sat, 9am-7pm Sun Jun-Sep, 9am-6pm Mon-Sat Oct-May) Right by the beach.
Train Station Tourist Office (☎ 08 92 35 35 35; av Thiers; ⏰ 8am-8pm Mon-Sat, 9am-7pm Sun Jun-Sep, 8am-7pm Mon-Sat, 10am-5pm Sun Oct-May)

Sights

The most atmospheric part of Nice is the tangled old town, criss-crossed by alleyways and back-streets. At the eastern end of quai des États-Unis, steep steps and a **cliffside lift** (per person €1; 9am-8pm Jun-Aug, 9am-7pm Apr, May & Sep, 10am-6pm Oct-Mar) climb to the **Parc du Château**, a beautiful hilltop park with great views over the old city and the beachfront.

The excellent **Mamac** (Museum of Modern & Contemporary Art; ☎ 04 97 13 42 01; www.mamac-nice.org; Promenade des Arts; admission free; 10am-6pm Tue-Sun) houses some fantastic avant-garde art from the 1960s to the present, including pop art from Roy Lichtenstein and Andy Warhol's 1965 *Campbell's Soup Can*.

The small **Musée National Message Biblique Marc Chagall** (Marc Chagall Biblical Message Museum; ☎ 04 93 53 87 20; www.musee-chagall.fr, in French; 4 av Dr Ménard; permanent collection adult/student €6.50/4.50, temporary exhibitions additional €1.20; 10am-5pm Wed-Mon Oct-Jun, to 6pm Jul-Sep) houses the largest public collection of the Russian-born artist's seminal *Old Testament* paintings.

Heading northeast from the Chagall museum (about 2.5km from the city centre) brings you to the **Musée Matisse** (☎ 04 93 81 08 08; www.musee-matisse-nice.org; 164 av des Arènes de Cimiez; admission free; 10am-6pm Wed-Mon), which contains a fantastic collection of exhibits and paintings spanning Matisse's entire career, including his famous paper cut-outs *Blue Nude IV* and mixed-media *Woman with Amphora*.

Free sections of beach alternate with 15 sun lounge–lined **plages concédées** (private beaches; late Apr or early May-15 Sep), for which you have to pay by renting a chair (around €15 a day) or mattress (around €10).There are outdoor showers on every beach, and indoor toilets and showers opposite 50 promenade des Anglais.

Sleeping

our pick **Villa Saint-Exupéry** (☎ 04 93 84 42 83; www.vsaint.com; 22 av Gravier; dm €18-25, s €35, d €55-80, all incl breakfast;) Why can't all hostels be like this? Set in a converted monastery in the north of the city, this backpacker's palace features a 24-hour common room, state-of-the-art-kitchens, BBQ terraces and lovely dorms; staff will even pick you up from the nearby Comte de Falicon tram stop or St Maurice stop for bus 23 (from the airport).

Auberge de Jeunesse – Les Camélias (☎ 04 93 62 15 54; www.fuaj.org, in French; 3 rue Spitalieri; dm incl breakfast & sheets €20.70;) This squeaky-clean 136-bed hostel is a signature Fédération Unie des Auberges de Jeunesse (FUAJ) establishment: bright and spacious, with bar, self-catering kitchen and laundry. No curfew, but it's closed from 11am to 3pm.

SPLURGE

Hôtel Windsor (☎ 04 93 88 59 35; www.hotelwindsornice.com; 11 rue Dalpozzo; d €90-175;) This original boutique hotel has given free reign to artists' imaginations – with the graffiti mural by the pool; the weird and wonderful artists' rooms customised from bathroom to bedspread; the more 'traditional' rooms (although there's no such thing as traditional at the Windsor) with their large frescoes; and the luxurious garden with its unconventional exotic plants.

Backpackers Chez Patrick (☎ 04 93 80 30 72; www.chezpatrick.com; 32 rue Pertinax; dm/d €22/50;) Ultrahandy for the station, you'll find this 24-bed independent hostel inconspicuously situated on the 1st floor, above a restaurant (look for Chez Patrick's doorbell). Chill out in the air-conditioned, tiled common room, or in the high-ceilinged rooms.

our pick **Hôtel Wilson** (☎ 04 93 85 47 79; www.hotel-wilson-nice.com; 39 rue de l'Hôtel des Postes; s €29-50, d €34-65) Jean-Marie's many years of travelling and an experimental nature have turned his rambling flat into a compelling place to stay. The 16 rooms have carefully crafted decor, and there's a dining room filled with photos, African statues and a pair of resident tortoises.

Hôtel Paradis (☎ 04 93 87 71 23; www.paradishotel.com; 1 rue Paradis; d €55-110) This sun-filled, spotless hotel is a stone's throw from the promenade. Top-floor and courtyard rooms have air-con and all rooms are equipped with fridges; three have balconies.

Eating

Niçois nibbles include *socca* (a thin layer of chickpea flour and olive oil batter), *salade niçoise*, and *farcis* (stuffed vegetables). Restaurants in Vieux Nice are a mixed bag, so choose carefully.

Chez René Socca (☎ 04 93 92 05 73; 2 rue Miralhéti; dishes from €2; 9am-9pm Tue-Sun, to 10.30pm Jul & Aug, closed Nov) Forget about presentation; here, it's all about taste. Grab a portion of *socca* or a plate of *petits farçis* and head across the street for a *grand pointu* (glass) of red, white or rosé.

our pick **Lou Pilha Leva** (10-13 rue Collet; dishes from €3; 10am-10pm) With its outdoor wooden tables crammed under a tight awning, this is Nice's version of a fast-food joint. Courgette

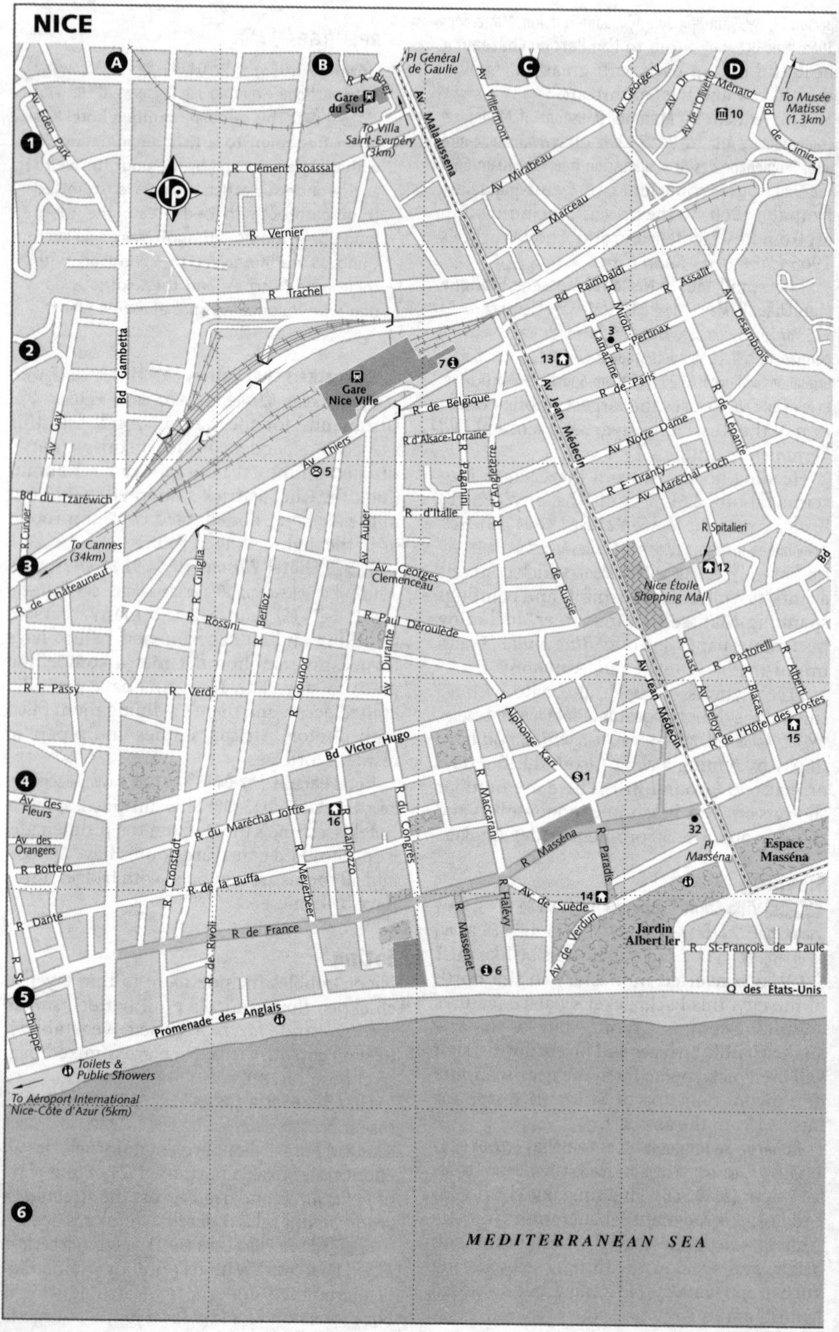

NICE

A
B
C
D
1
2
3
4
5
6

Gare du Sud
To Villa Saint-Exupéry (3km)
Pl Général de Gaulle
To Musée Matisse (1.3km)
10
Av Eden Park
R A Binet
Av Malausséna
Av Villermont
Av George V
Av Dr Ménard
Av de l'Olivetto
Bd de Cimiez
R Clément Roassal
Av Mirabeau
R Marceau
R Vernier
R Trachel
Bd Raimbaldi
R Miroir
R Assalit
Av Desambrois
R Lamartine
R Pertinax
3
13
7
Gare Nice Ville
Bd Gambetta
Av Gay
Av Jean Médecin
R de Paris
R de Belgique
R de Lépante
R d'Alsace-Lorraine
Av Notre Dame
Av Thiers
5
R Paganini
R d'Angleterre
R E Tiranty
Av Maréchal Foch
Bd du Tzaréwich
R Curvier
R d'Italie
R Spitalieri
12
To Cannes (34km)
R de Châteauneuf
R Guiglia
Av Auber
Av Georges Clemenceau
R de Russie
Nice Étoile Shopping Mall
Bd
R Rossini
R Berlioz
R Paul Déroulède
R Gounod
Av Durante
R Cast
R Pastorelli
R Alberti
R F Passy
R Verdi
Av Jean Médecin
Av Deloye
R Blacas
R de l'Hôtel des Postes
15
R Alphonse Karr
Bd Victor Hugo
Av des Fleurs
R Maccarani
1
R du Maréchal Joffre
16
R Dalpozzo
R du Congrès
Av des Orangers
R Bottero
R Meyerbeer
R Cronstadt
R Masséna
R Paradis
32
Pl Masséna
Espace Masséna
R de la Buffa
R Halévy
Av de Suède
14
R Dante
R de France
R Massenet
Av de Verdun
Jardin Albert Ier
R St-François de Paule
R St Philippe
R de Rivoli
6
Q des États-Unis
Promenade des Anglais
Toilets & Public Showers
To Aéroport International Nice-Côte d'Azur (5km)

MEDITERRANEAN SEA

FRANCE

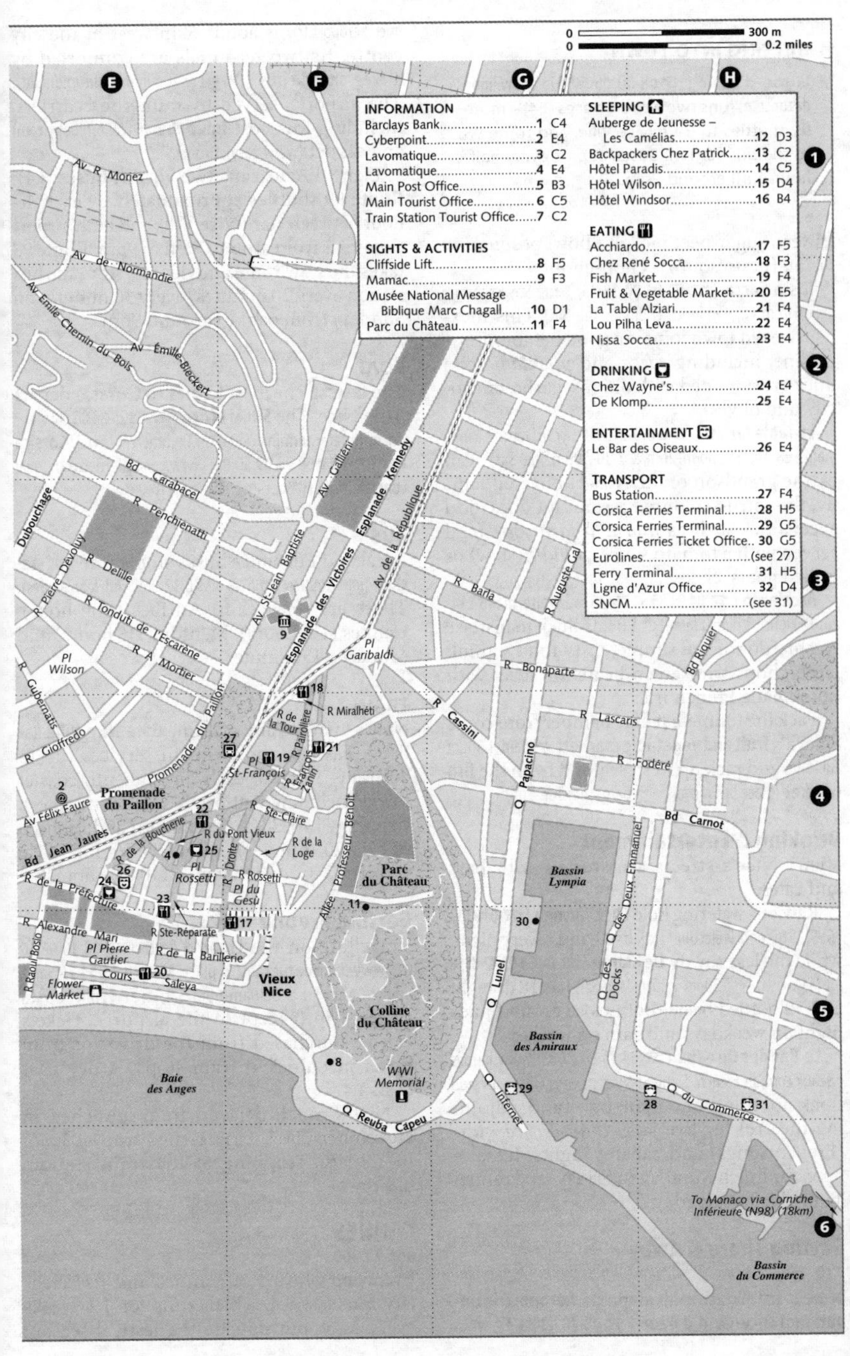
0 300 m
0 0.2 miles
E
F
G
H
1
2
3
4
5
6
INFORMATION
Barclays Bank....1 C4
Cyberpoint....2 E4
Lavomatique....3 C2
Lavomatique....4 E4
Main Post Office....5 B3
Main Tourist Office....6 C5
Train Station Tourist Office....7 C2
SIGHTS & ACTIVITIES
Cliffside Lift....8 F5
Mamac....9 F3
Musée National Message Biblique Marc Chagall....10 D1
Parc du Château....11 F4
SLEEPING
Auberge de Jeunesse – Les Camélias....12 D3
Backpackers Chez Patrick....13 C2
Hôtel Paradis....14 C5
Hôtel Wilson....15 D4
Hôtel Windsor....16 B4
EATING
Acchiardo....17 F5
Chez René Socca....18 F3
Fish Market....19 F4
Fruit & Vegetable Market....20 E5
La Table Alziari....21 F4
Lou Pilha Leva....22 E4
Nissa Socca....23 E4
DRINKING
Chez Wayne's....24 E4
De Klomp....25 E4
ENTERTAINMENT
Le Bar des Oiseaux....26 E4
TRANSPORT
Bus Station....27 F4
Corsica Ferries Terminal....28 H5
Corsica Ferries Terminal....29 G5
Corsica Ferries Ticket Office....30 G5
Eurolines....(see 27)
Ferry Terminal....31 H5
Ligne d'Azur Office....32 D4
SNCM....(see 31)
Av R Moniez
Av de Normandie
Av Emile Chemin du Bois
Av Émille Bieckert
Bd Carabacel
R Penchienatti
Dubouchage
R Pierre Dévoluy
R Delille
R Tonduti de l'Escarène
R A Mortier
Pl Wilson
R Gubernatis
R Gioffredo
Av Gallieni
Esplanade Kennedy
Av St-Jean Baptiste
Esplanade des Victoires
Av de la République
R Barla
R Auguste Gal
Pl Garibaldi
R Bonaparte
Bd Riquier
R Cassini
R Lascaris
R Fodéré
Q Papacino
Bd Carnot
R de la Tour
R Pairolière
R Miralhéti
Pl St-François
R François Zanin
Promenade du Paillon
Av Félix Faure
Bd Jean Jaurès
R Ste-Claire
R du Pont Vieux
R de la Boucherie
R de la Loge
Pl Rossetti
R Rossetti
Droite
Pl du Gesù
R de la Préfecture
R Alexandre Mari
R Ste-Réparate
Pl Pierre Gautier
R de la Barillerie
Cours Saleya
R Raoul Bosio
Flower Market
Vieux Nice
Allée Professeur Benoît
Parc du Château
Colline du Château
WWI Memorial
Q Reuba Capeu
Baie des Anges
Q Lunel
Bassin Lympia
Q des Deux Emmanuel
Q des Docks
Bassin des Amiraux
Q Infernet
Q du Commerce
To Monaco via Corniche Inférieure (N98) (18km)
Bassin du Commerce

FRANCE

GETTING INTO TOWN

Ligne d'Azur (☎ 08 10 06 10 07; www.lignedazur.com) runs two airport buses (€4) – route 99 shuttles to Gare Nice Ville, and route 98 to the bus station. Buses depart every half-hour until around 9pm.

fritters, sugar-beet pie, or a bowl of *soupe au pistou* (pesto soup) – chop-chop!

Nissa Socca (☎ 04 93 80 18 35; 7 rue Ste-Réparate; mains from €8; lunch & dinner Tue-Sat) This inexpensive old town joint is a good bet for *niçoise* cuisine, including *socca* and *pissaladière* (a thick crust topped with onions, garlic, anchovies and olives).

La Table Alziari (☎ 04 93 80 34 03; 4 rue François Zanin; mains €8-14, noon-2pm & 7.30-10pm Tue-Sat) Run by the grandson of the Alziari olive oil family, this citrus-coloured restaurant does local specialities such as *morue à la niçoise* (cod served with a tomato sauce), *daube* (stew) or grilled goats' cheese.

Acchiardo (☎ 04 93 85 51 16; 38 rue Droite; mains €14-20; lunch & dinner Mon-Fri) Locals flock to historic Acchiardo for the simple, tasty food – think lamb chops with green beans or steak with homemade French fries.

Pack the ultimate picnic hamper from cours Saleya's **fruit and vegetable market**(6am-1.30pm Tue-Sun) and pick up fresh seafood from the **fish market** (place St-François; 6am-1pm Tue-Sun).

Drinking & Entertainment

Vieux Nice's streets are stuffed with bars and cafes.

Raucous watering hole **Chez Wayne's** (☎ 04 93 13 46 99; 15 rue de la Préfecture) has live bands every night, while the less rowdy **De Klomp** (☎ 04 93 92 42 85; 8 rue Mascoïnat; 5.30pm-2.30am Mon-Sat) has 18 draught and 50 bottled beers. Both close around midnight on weekdays and 3am on weekends.

Le Bar des Oiseaux (☎ 04 93 80 27 33; www.bardesoiseaux.com, in French; 5 rue St-Vincent) Artistic types flock to this bohemian bar (and adjoining theatre) for live jazz, *chanson française* (French songs) and cabaret nights. It's also open for lunch Monday to Friday, and dinner Thursday to Saturday.

Getting There & Away

AIR

Nice's international airport, **Aéroport International Nice-Côte d'Azur** (☎ 08 20 42 33 33; www.nice.aeroport.fr), is about 6km west of the city centre. Its two terminals are connected by a free **shuttle bus** (every 10min 4.30am-midnight). The airport's served by numerous carriers, including low-cost **bmibaby** (www.bmibaby.com) and **easyJet** (www.easyjet.com).

Ligne d'Azur runs two airport buses (€4). Route 99 shuttles approximately every half-hour between Gare Nice Ville and both airport terminals from around 8am to 9pm. Route 98 takes the slow route and departs from the bus station every 20 minutes (every 30 minutes on Sunday) from 6am to around 9pm.

BOAT

The fastest, cheapest ferries to Corsica depart from Nice. The **SNCM office** (☎ 08 25 88 80 88; www.sncm.fr; ferry terminal, quai du Commerce) and **Corsica Ferries** (☎ 08 25 09 50 95; www.corsicaferries.com; quai Lunel) issue tickets at the port.

BUS

Local and Eurolines buses stop at the **bus station** (gare routière; ☎ 08 92 70 12 06; 5 bd Jean Jaurès). There are services to Antibes (one hour), Cannes (1½ hours), Menton (1½ hours) and Monaco (45 minutes).

TRAIN

Nice's main train station, **Gare Nice Ville** (av Thiers), has fast and frequent services (up to 40 trains a day in each direction) to coastal towns including Antibes (€3.80, 30 minutes), Cannes (€5.70, 30 to 40 minutes) and Monaco (€3.20, 20 minutes). Direct TGVs link Nice with Paris' Gare de Lyon (€110, 5½ hours).

Getting Around

Travelling on the **Ligne d'Azur** (☎ 08 10 06 10 07; www.lignedazur.com; 3 place Masséna; 7.45am-6.30pm Mon-Fri & 8.30am-6pm Sat) network costs €1 per trip (except to the airport). Tickets can be purchased from the driver or from ticket machines at tram stops. A day pass costs €4.

Nice's much-delayed tram launched in November 2007. Line 1 runs from 4.30am to 1.30am, stopping at the train station, old town.

CANNES

pop 70,400

Everyone's heard of Cannes and its celebrity film festival, which runs for 1½ weeks every May, but outside the festival season,

Cannes retains a genuine small-town feel, with pleasant shops, sparkling beaches, buzzy markets and the idyllic Îles de Lérins just offshore.

The **tourist office** (☎ 04 92 99 84 22; www.cannes.travel; bd de la Croisette; ⌚ 9am-8pm Jul & Aug, 9am-7pm Mon-Sat Sep-Jun) is on the ground floor of the Palais des Festivals.

Sights & Activities

The best public beaches are **Plages du Midi** and **Plages de la Bocca**, west from the Vieux Port along bd Jean Hibert and bd du Midi.

The **Musée de la Castre** (☎ 04 93 38 55 26; place de la Castre, Le Suquet; adult/student €3.20/free; ⌚ 10am-7pm Jul & Aug, 10am-1pm & 2-6pm Tue-Sun Apr-Jun & Sep, 10am-1pm & 2-5pm Tue-Sun Oct-Mar) houses ethnographic exhibits in a castle at the top of Cannes' old town.

Twenty minutes away by boat are the **Îles de Lérins**. The closest is **Île Ste-Marguerite**, where the mysterious Man in the Iron Mask was incarcerated during the late 17th century; it's now better known for its bone-white beaches, eucalyptus groves and small marine museum. Smaller still is **Île St-Honorat**, which has been a monastery since the 5th century.

Boats for the islands travel from quai des Îles on the western side of the harbour. **Riviera Lines** (☎ 04 92 98 71 31; ww.riviera-lines.com) runs ferries to Île Ste-Marguerite (return €11), while **Compagnie Planaria** (☎ 04 92 98 71 38; www.cannes-ilesdelerins.com) operates boats to Île St-Honorat (return €11).

Sleeping

Parc Bellevue (☎ 04 93 47 28 97; www.parcbellevue.com; 67 av Maurice Chevalier, Cannes-la-Bocca; powered site per 2 adults, tent & car €26; ⌚ Apr-Sep; 🏊) About 5.5km west of the city, this is the closest camping ground to Cannes, with a huge pool and facilities galore. The 9 bus from the bus station stops 400m away.

Hôtel Albe (☎ 04 97 06 21 21; www.albe-hotel.fr; 31 rue Bivouac Napoléon; s/d from €35/45; ❄) The rooms are nothing to write home about, but this hotel is right in the heart of the action: the street is about to become pedestrianised, which should guarantee a good night's sleep.

Le Chanteclair (☎/fax 04 93 39 68 88; 12 rue Forville; d from €48; ⌚ closed mid-Nov–mid-Jan) Right in the heart of Le Suquet and moments from the Forville Provençal market, this sweet 15-room place has an enchanting courtyard garden.

Eating

La Tarterie (☎ 04 93 39 67 43; 33 rue Bivouac Napoléon; dishes €6-13; ⌚ 8.30am-6pm Mon-Sat) A bakery with a difference, offering mega salads and fancy tarts at a fast-food price. We like it.

Volupté (☎ 04 93 39 60 32; 32 rue Hoche; snacks €4.50, mains €13-15; ⌚ 9am-8pm Mon-Sat) With its 140 types of tea, all neatly stocked in red and white tins, this elegant tearoom draws a happening crowd of young and beautiful things.

Barbarella (☎ 04 92 99 17 33; 16 rue St-Dizier; mains €25-35; ⌚ 7-11.30pm Tue-Sun) You've seen the film, now go to the err…restaurant. It's as kitsch as the movie (trompe l'œil–painted building, see-through chairs, psychedelic lighting, groovy atmosphere) and its fusion food is fine.

The **Marché Forville** (rue du Marché Forville; ⌚ mornings Tue-Sun) and the **food market** (place Gambetta; ⌚ morning) are where many of the city's chefs shop for ingredients.

Large supermarkets:

Champion (6 rue Meynadier; ⌚ 8.30am-7.30pm Mon-Sat)
Monoprix (9 rue Maréchal Foch; ⌚ 8.30am-8pm Mon-Sat)

Getting There & Away

Regular buses go to Nice (bus 200, €1, 1½ hours) and Nice airport (bus 210, €14.20, 50 minutes, half-hourly from 8am to 6pm). Trains serve Nice (€5.70, 30 to 40 minutes), Grasse (€3.60, 25 minutes) and Marseille (€24.80, two hours).

MONACO

☎ 377 / pop 32,000

This pocket-sized principality has long been a favourite haunt of super-rich celebs, high-rolling gamblers and tax exiles, and even the prices for a humble morning *café* will probably make your heart sink. But it's worth a visit for its sparkling harbour, lined with luxury yachts and cruisers, and a fantastic aquarium in the hilltop quarter of Monaco Ville.

Since 1297, Monaco has been ruled by the Grimaldi family and has its own flag, national holiday (19 November), postal system and telephone code. Monaco's long-term monarch, Prince Rainier, was famous for marrying Hollywood starlet Grace Kelly; since his death in 2005, his son Prince Albert (b 1958) has been the man in charge of the principality.

Information

Tourist Office (☎ 92 16 61 16; www.visitmonaco.com; 2a bd des Moulins; ⌚ 9am-7pm Mon-Sat, 10am-1pm Sun) Across the public gardens from the casino. From mid-June to late-September additional tourist information kiosks open around the harbour and the train station.

Sights & Activities

At 11.55am every day, guards are changed at Monaco's **Palais du Prince** (Prince's Palace; ☎ 93 25 18 31) in Monaco Ville. For a glimpse into royal life, you can tour the **state apartments** (admission €7; 🕑 9.30am-6.30pm May-Sep, 10.30am-6pm Apr, 10am-5.30pm Oct). A combined ticket (€9) also covers the **Musée des Souvenirs Napoléoniens** (🕑 10.30am-5pm Dec-Mar, to 5.30pm Oct & Apr, 9.30am-6.30pm May-Sep), which displays some of Napoléon's personal effects.

The graceful 1910 **Musée Océanographique de Monaco** (Monaco Oceanographic Museum; ☎ 93 15 36 00; av St-Martin; adult/student €12.50/6; 🕑 9.30am-7pm Jul & Aug, to 6.30pm Apr-Jun & Sep, to 6pm Oct-Mar) houses an aquarium stocked with sharks, tropical fish and other local sea creatures.

The famous **Formula 1 Grand Prix** hits Monaco's streets in late May, and there's also an **International Circus Festival of Monaco** (www.montecarlofestivals.com) held in late January.

Getting There & Away

Monaco's **train station** (av Prince Pierre) has frequent trains to Nice (€3.20, 20 minutes), and east to Menton (€1.80, 10 minutes), and the Italian town of Ventimiglia (€3.20, 20 minutes).

CORSICA

The rugged island of Corsica (*Corse* in French) is officially a part of France, but remains fiercely proud of its own culture, history and language. It's one of the Med's most dramatic islands, with a bevy of beautiful beaches, glitzy ports, and a mountainous, maquis-covered interior to explore, as well as a wild, independent spirit all of its own.

AJACCIO

pop 52,880

The spectre of Corsica's great (little) general looms over the elegant port city of Ajaccio (pronounced a·zhaks·jo). Napoléon Bonaparte was born here in 1769, and the city is dotted with relics relating to the diminutive dictator. Often dubbed *La Cité Imperiale* in recognition of its historic importance, Ajaccio is the capital of the Corse-du-Sud *département* and is the island's main metropolis.

Information

Cyber Espace (rue Docteur Versini; per 30min/hr €2/3; 🕑 10am-12.30am Mon-Sat)

Tourist Office (☎ 04 95 51 53 03; www.ajaccio-tourisme.com; 3 bd du Roi Jérôme; 🕑 9am-6pm Mon-Sat, 9am-1pm Sun Jun-Sep, 8.30am-11.30am & 1.30-4pm Mon-Fri Oct-May) Free internet kiosk.

Sights

The Napoleonic saga begins at the **Musée National de la Maison Bonaparte** (☎ 04 95 21 43 89; rue St-Charles; adult/concession €5/3.50; 🕑 9-11.30am & 2-5.30pm Tue-Sun, 2-5.50pm Mon Apr-Sep, 10-11.30am & 2-4.15pm Tue-Sun, 2-4.15pm Mon Oct-Mar), where Napoleon was born and spent the first nine years of his childhood.

Established by Napoléon's uncle, the **Musée Fesch** (rue du Cardinal Fesch), one of the island's flagship museums, is closed for major renovations until late 2009.

Two companies run boat trips around the Golfe d'Ajaccio and the Îles Sanguinaires (€25), and excursions to the Scandola Nature Reserve (€50). **Découvertes Naturelles** (☎ 06 24 69 48 80; www.promenades-en-mer.org; 🕑 May-Sep) also offers a sunset cruise to the Îles Sanguinaires (€25), returning around 10pm, while **Nave Va** (☎ 04 95 51 31 31; www.naveva.com; 🕑 May-Sep) offers a cultural tour (€28) and a voyage down to Bonifacio (€57).

Sleeping

Ajaccio's hotels are pricey, especially in the high season.

Hôtel Le Dauphin (☎ 04 95 21 12 94; www.ledauphinhotel.com; 11 bd Sampiero; s €52-59, d €60-79, tr €79-96; ❄) Ajaccio's idea of a budget hotel, with cheap(ish), functional rooms, some with port-view balconies overlooking the hectic road and ground-floor cafe-bar.

our pick **Hôtel Kallisté** (☎ 04 95 51 34 45; www.hotel-kalliste-ajaccio.com, in French; 51 cours Napoléon; s €56-69, d €64-79, tr €79-99; ❄ 💻) Exposed brick, neutral tones, terracotta tiles and a glass lift conjure a neo-boutique feel, and the facilities are fab – wi-fi, satellite TV, and a stonking buffet brekkie.

Hôtel Marengo (☎ 04 95 21 43 66; www.hotel-marengo.com; 2 rue Marengo; d €61-79, tr €75-95; ❄) For something more personal, try this jolly, hospitably run little bolthole. Expect pastel rooms (all with balconies) and a quiet courtyard, all a stroll from the beach.

Eating

Il Passaggero (☎ 04 95 21 30 52; 3 bd du Roi Jérôme; mains €12-18; 🕑 daily) Hip new Italian-slash-

Mediterranean restaurant by the harbour, specialising in authentic pastas, fresh fish and inventive risottos.

Le Spago (☎ 04 95 21 15 71; rue Emmanuel Arène; mains €14-22; ⏰ lunch & dinner Mon-Fri, dinner Sat) Sleekly styled fusion restaurant – think chicken kebabs, pesto gnocchi, Moroccan *tajines* (slow-cooked stews).

U Pampasgiolu (☎ 06 09 39 26 92; 15 rue de la Porta; mains €14-24, platters €26-27; ⏰ dinner) The arch-vaulted dining room of this Ajaccio institution is always packed thanks to the first-rate Corsican food. If you're a novice, the *planches* (platters) offer bite-sized dishes of local staples.

L'Altru Versu (☎ 04 95 50 05 22; 16 rue J Baptiste Marcaggi; mains €22-28; ⏰ lunch Tue-Sat, dinner Tue-Sun) One of the top tables for Corsican cuisine: dishes at 'The Other Side' include prawn and *brocciu* tart, pork with almonds, and sorbet tinged with Pietra beer.

The open-air **food market** (⏰ to noon, closed Mon) is on Sq Campinchi, while Corsican produce is sold at **U Stazzu** (☎ 04 95 51 10 80; 1 rue Bonaparte; ⏰ 9am-12.30pm & 2.30-7pm). Supermarkets include **Spar** (cours Grandval; ⏰ 8.30am-12.30pm & 3-7.30pm Mon-Sat) and **Monoprix** (cours Napoléon; ⏰ 8.30am-7.15pm Mon-Sat).

Getting There & Away

AIR

Aéroport d'Ajaccio-Campo dell'Oro (☎ 04 95 23 56 56) is 8km east of the city centre. Transports Corse d'Ajaccio (TCA) bus 8 links the airport with Ajaccio's train and bus stations (€4.50).

BOAT

Boats depart from **Terminal Maritime et Routier** (quai l'Herminier), the combined bus/ferry terminal.

CMN (☎ 08 10 20 13 20; www.cmn.fr; bd Sampiero; ⏰ 8.15am-6pm Mon-Fri, 8.15am-noon Sat, departure days open to 7pm Mon-Fri & from 4.30-7pm Sat) Located inside the terminal.

Corsica Ferries (☎ 08 25 09 50 95; www.corsicaferries.fr) Inside the terminal.

SNCM (☎ 04 95 29 66 99; www.sncm.fr; ⏰ 8am-8pm Tue-Fri, 8am-1pm Sat) The main office is on quai L'Herminier, and there's a ticket and information kiosk inside the terminal.

BUS

Lots of local bus companies have kiosks inside the terminal building. **Eurocorse** (☎ 04 95 21 06 30) travels to Bastia (€22, three hours, two daily), Corte (1¾ hours) and Ponte Lecchia (two hours). There's also a route to Bonifacio (€22, four hours, two daily).

TRAIN

The **train station** (☎ 04 95 23 11 03; place de la Gare) has trains to Bastia (€23.90, four hours, three to four daily), Corte (€12.70, two hours, three to four daily) and Calvi (€27.80, five hours, two daily).

BONIFACIO

pop 2700

With its glittering harbour, creamy cliffs and stout citadel, this dazzling port has a distinctly Italianate feel: sun-bleached townhouses, washing lines and murky chapels cram the old citadel, while on the harbourside, brasseries and boat-kiosks tout their wares.

A steep staircase links the harbour with the citadel's old gateway, the **Porte de Gênes**, complete with its original 16th-century drawbridge. Inside the gateway is the 13th-century **Bastion l'Étendard**, which houses a small historical museum exploring Bonifacio's past. Nearby is the **tourist office** (☎ 04 95 73 11 88; www.bonifacio.fr; 2 rue Fred Scamaroni; ⏰ 9am-8pm Jul & Aug, 9am-7pm May, Jun & Sep, 9am-noon & 2-6pm Mon-Fri Oct-Apr). Along the ramparts, fabulous panoramic views unfold from **place du Marché** and **place Manichella**.

From the citadel, the **Escalier du Roi d'Aragon** (Staircase of the King of Aragon; admission €2; ⏰ 9am-6pm Mon-Sat Apr-May & Sep-Oct, daily Jul & Aug) leads down the cliff.

Boat trips (€25) to the offshore **Îles Lavezzi** (Lavezzi Islands) run from the quayside.

Sleeping

Camping L'Araguina (☎ 04 95 73 02 96; av Sylvère Bohn; per person/tent/car €5.85/2.40/2.40; ⏰ Mar-Oct) Bonifacio's main camping ground has plenty of tent sites, but the roadside location is less than soothing.

Hôtel des Étrangers (☎ 04 95 73 01 09; http://hoteldesetrangers.ifrance.com, in French; av Sylvère Bohn; d €35-70; ⏰ Apr-Oct; ❄ P) Bonifacio's only budget option is the Foreigners' Hotel. Spick-and-span rooms, all with tiled floors, clean bathrooms and simple colour schemes almost make up for the road racket.

Eating

Kissing Pigs (☎ 04 95 73 56 09; quai Banda del Ferro; mains €8-15; ⏰ lunch & dinner daily) Diners pack into this cosy wine bar among swinging sausages for platters of Corsican meats and cheeses.

our pick Cantina Doria (☎ 04 95 73 50 49; 27 rue Doria; mains €10-14; ⏰ Apr-Oct) *The* place in Bonifacio for Corsican country food, served at wooden benches amid copper pots, rustic tools and dented signs. There's a sister place on the quay, Cantina Grill (☎ 04 95 70 49 86).

Getting There & Away

AIR

Bonifacio's airport, **Aéroport de Figari** (☎ 04 95 71 10 10), is 21km north of town. A shuttle bus runs from the town centre in July and August (€9, 30 to 40 minutes) five times daily.

BOAT

Saremar (☎ 04 95 73 00 96; www.saremar.it, in Italian) and **Moby Lines** (☎ 04 95 73 00 29; www.mobylines.it) offer services between Bonifacio and Santa Teresa (on the neighbouring island of Sardinia) in summer.

BUS

From Monday to Saturday, **Eurocorse** (☎ 04 95 21 06 30) has a twice-daily service to Porto-Vecchio (€7.50, 30 minutes), with onward connections to Ajaccio (€22, four hours).

BASTIA

pop 37,800

Ramshackle Bastia might not measure up to the sexy style of Ajaccio or the architectural appeal of Bonifacio, but in many ways it's a more authentic snapshot of modern-day Corsica, a lived-in, well-loved city that's resisted the urge to polish up its image just to please the tourists.

Information

Oxy Cyber Café (☎ 06 84 76 11 65; 1 rue Salvatore Viale; per hr €3.10; ⏰ 10am-2am Mon-Sat, 1pm-2am Sun)

Tourist Office (☎ 04 95 54 20 40; www.bastia-tourisme.com; place St-Nicolas; ⏰ 8am-8pm Mon-Sat, 9am-noon & 4-7pm Sun Jul & Aug, 8.30am-noon & 2-6pm Mon-Sat, 9.30am-1pm Sun Apr-Jun, Sep & Oct, 8.30am-noon & 2-6pm Mon-Fri, 8.30am-noon Sun Nov-Mar) Multilingual tourist office on place St-Nicholas.

Sights & Activities

Even by Corsican standards, Bastia is a pocket-sized city. The 19th-century square of **place St-Nicholas** sprawls along the seafront between the ferry port and the harbour. The square is lined with plane trees and busy cafes, as well as a **statue of Napoléon Bonaparte**, Corsica's most famous son.

A network of lanes leads south towards the old port and the attractive neighbourhood of **Terra Vecchia**. Further south is the Vieux Port (Old Port), ringed by pastel-coloured tenements and buzzy brasseries, as well as the twin-towered **Église St-Jean Baptiste**. Behind the port looms Bastia's sunbaked **citadel**, built from the 15th to 17th centuries by the city's Genoese masters.

Sleeping

Camping San Damiano (☎ 04 95 33 68 02; www.campingsandamiano.com; camp site tent & vehicle €5-7 plus per person €5-7.50, chalets per week €441-798 Jul & Aug, per night €45-72, per week €315-504 Apr-Jun, Sep & Oct; ⏰ Apr-Oct) An idyllic beachfront camping ground, shaded under pines about 6km south of Bastia.

Hôtel Athéna (☎ 04 95 34 88 40; 2 rue Miot; d €40-60) This cut-price hotel is about the cheapest sleep in town, so you can forgive it a few bits of battered furniture and flaking paint. Rooms are clean, spartan and simple.

Hôtel Univers (☎ 04 95 31 03 38; www.hoteluniv ers.org, in French; 3 av Maréchal Sébastiani; s €45-60, d €50-70; ❄) Near place St-Nicholas, the Univers makes a decent base, but don't expect frills. A scruffy staircase leads to whitewashed rooms with blue-and-yellow bedspreads and laminate floors.

Hôtel Posta Vecchia (☎ 04 95 32 32 38; www.hotel-postavecchia.com; quai des Martyrs de la Libération; d €55-92, f €65-100; ❄) If it's sea views you're after, make a beeline for the Posta Vecchia – the only place in town where you can watch bobbing boats and Mediterranean waves from your bed.

Eating

Cafes and restaurants line place St-Nicolas and the old port.

our pick A Casarella (☎ 04 95 32 02 32; rue du Dragon; mains €9-28; ⏰ lunch Mon-Fri, dinner Mon-Sat) In the citadel, this well-hidden restaurant boasts the loveliest port-view patio in Bastia. Tuck into traditional Corsican cuisine – tuna with caramelised figs, or sardines stuffed with *brocciu* (ewe or goat's milk cheese).

Chez Vincent (☎ 04 95 31 62 50; 12 rue St-Michel; mains €8-18; ⏰ lunch & dinner Mon-Fri, dinner Sat) Next door to A Casarella, this place offers Corsican staples and wood-fired pizzas. The *Assiette du Bandit Corse* (€18) features Corsican meats, chestnuts, cheese and boar.

U Tianu (☎ 04 95 31 36 67; 4 rue Rigo; menus €19; ⏰ dinner Mon-Sat, closed Aug) A tiny backstreet restaurant with the air of a traditional Corsican kitchen. Hunting rifles and country knick-knacks cover the walls, and you'll tuck into five-course platters of Corsican food including cheese, aperitif and coffee.

Cheese, fish, fruit, veg and Corsican charcuterie fills the morning **food market** (place de l'Hôtel de Ville; ⏰ Tue-Sun), or you can pick up supplies at Spar supermarkets on rue César Campinchi and bd Paoli.

Getting There & Away

AIR

Aéroport Bastia-Poretta (☎ 04 95 54 54 54; www.bastia.aeroport.fr) is 24km south of the city. Buses (€8.50, eight daily) depart from outside the Préfecture building. The first bus from town is around 6am and the last bus from the airport is around 9pm; schedules are posted at the bus stop.

BOAT

Bastia's two ferry terminals are connected by a free shuttle bus. All the ferry companies have information offices in the southern terminal, which usually open for same-day ticket sales a couple of hours before each sailing.

Corsica Ferries (☎ 04 95 32 95 95; www.corsicaferries.com; 15bis rue Chanoine Leschi; ⏰ 8.30am-noon & 2-6pm Mon-Fri, 9am-noon Sat) Opposite the northern terminal.

Moby Lines (☎ 04 95 34 84 94; www.mobylines.it; 4 rue du Commandant Luce de Casabianca; ⏰ 8am-noon & 2-6pm Mon-Fri, 8am-noon Sat)

SNCM (☎ 04 95 54 66 81; www.sncm.com; inside Southern Terminal; ⏰ 8-11.45am & 2-5.45pm Mon-Fri, 8am-noon Sat)

BUS

There are three bus stops in Bastia: outside the tourist office, at the train station, and at the 'bus station' north of Square St-Victor.

Beaux Voyages (☎ 04 95 65 11 35) Travels to Île Rousse (€10, 90 minutes) and Calvi (€16, two hours) daily except Sunday. Buses leave from the train station.

Eurocorse (☎ 04 95 31 73 76) Travels to Ajaccio (€22, three hours) via Corte (€11, two hours) twice daily except on Sundays from Bastia's 'bus station'.

TRAIN

The **train station** (☎ 04 95 32 80 61; av Maréchal Sébastiani; ⏰ 6am-8.30pm Mon-Sat, 8.30am-8.30pm Sun) is on Square Maréchal Leclerc. Main destinations include Ajaccio (€23.90, four daily) via Corte (€11.20), and Calvi (€18.10, three hours, three or four daily) via Île Rousse (€15).

FRANCE DIRECTORY

ACCOMMODATION

Accommodation and space are both at a premium in France during the high season in July and August (when many French people take their annual holiday), as well as Christmas and Easter.

B&Bs

Some of France's most charming (and best value) accommodation can be found in *chambres d'hôtes* (bed and breakfasts). Local tourist offices always have a list of local establishments, or you can contact the **Fédération Nationale des Gîtes de France** (Map pp378-9; ☎ 01 49 70 75 75; www.gites-de-france.fr; 59 rue St-Lazare, 9e, Paris; Ⓜ Trinité). Other useful websites:

Bienvenue à la Ferme (Map pp378-9; ☎ 01 53 57 11 44; www.bienvenue-a-la-ferme.com; 9 av George V, 8e, Paris; Ⓜ Alma-Marceau, George V) Specialist for farm-stays.

Fleurs de Soleil (http://fleursdesoleil.fr, in French)

Samedi Midi Éditions (www.samedimidi.com)

Camping & Caravan Parks

Camping is popular in France, although many camping grounds close from October to April. Hostels sometimes let travellers pitch tents in their grounds. Gîtes de France and Bienvenue à la Ferme coordinate camping on farms. Camping in nondesignated spots, or *camping sauvage*, is usually illegal.

Hostels

Official hostels are known as *auberges de jeunesse*. Dorm beds cost about €25 in Paris, and anything from €10.30 to €28 in the provinces; breakfast is often included. Sheets are usually provided.

You'll need an annual Hostelling International card (€11/16 for under/over 26s) or a nightly Welcome Stamp (€1.80-2.90) to stay at the official hostels run by **Fédération Unie des Auberges de Jeunesse** (FUAJ; Map pp382-3; ☎ 01 44 89 87 27; www.fuaj.org; 27 rue Pajol, 18e, Paris; Ⓜ Marx Dormoy) and **Ligue Française pour les Auberges de la Jeunesse** (LFAJ; Map pp378-9; ☎ 01 44 16 78 78; www.auberges-de-jeunesse.com; 7 rue Vergniaud, 13e, Paris; Ⓜ Glacière).

TOP TIP

In France, computer keyboards are laid-out differently, which can make typing difficult. To change the keyboard language, hold down Alt and the Maj *(majiscule)* keys – and hey presto, you can type away to your heart's content.

Hotels

A double has one double bed, so specify if you prefer *deux lits séparés* (two twin beds). French hotels almost never include breakfast in their nightly rates.

ACTIVITIES

From the peaks, rivers and canyons of the Alps to the shining coastline, France offers a cornucopia of outdoor adventures.

Adventure Sports

Whether it's canyoning, diving, ice-driving or kite-surfing, France really sets the pulse racing. Adventures in *alpinisme* (mountaineering), *escalade* (rock climbing) and *escalade de glace* (ice climbing) can all be arranged through the **Club Alpin Français** (www.ffcam.fr, in French).

Cycling

The French take cycling very seriously – the country practically grinds to a halt during the annual Tour de France. Mountain-biking (known in France as VTT, or *vélo tout-terrain*) is gaining popularity around the Alps and Pyrenees, but road-cycling still rules the roost. A *piste cyclable* is a cycling path – you'll find plenty of routes in the Dordogne and the Loire Valley.

Skiing & Snowboarding

France has over 400 ski resorts in the Alps, the Jura, the Pyrenees, the Vosges and Massif Central – and even the mountains of Corsica. The season generally lasts from mid-December to late March or April, but the slopes get very crowded during the February–March school holidays. Package deals, including lift passes and accommodation, are available for all main resorts.

Paris-based **Ski France** (www.skifrance.fr) has information and an annual brochure covering more than 90 ski resorts.

Walking

The French countryside is criss-crossed by a staggering 120,000km of *sentiers balisés* (marked walking paths), including the long-distance *sentiers de grande randonnée* (GR) trails.

The **Fédération Française de la Randonnée Pédestre** (FFRP; French Ramblers' Association; www.ffrp.asso.fr, in French) has an **information centre** (Map pp378-9; ☎ 01 44 89 93 93; 64 rue du Dessous des Berges, 13e, Paris; Ⓜ Bibliothèque François Mitterrand) in Paris.

Water Sports

France has fine beaches along all its coasts – the English Channel, the Atlantic and the Mediterranean. The beautifully sandy beaches along the Atlantic Coast are less crowded than their counterparts on the Côte d'Azur and Corsica, while Brittany, Normandy and the Channel coast are also popular, albeit cooler, beach destinations.

The best surfing in France is on the Atlantic Coast around Biarritz (p423). White-water rafting, canoeing and kayaking are practised on many French rivers, especially in the Massif Central and the Alps.

BUSINESS HOURS

French business hours are usually 9am or 9.30am to 7pm or 8pm, often with a midday break from noon or 1pm to 2pm or 3pm. Most businesses close on Sunday (and sometimes Monday); exceptions include grocery stores, *boulangeries* and cake shops.

Cafes 🕒 early morning until midnight.
Banks 🕒 8am or 9am to 11.30am or 1pm and then 1.30pm or 2pm to 4.30pm or 5pm, Monday to Friday or Tuesday to Saturday.
Bars 🕒 early evening until 1am or 2am.
Post offices 🕒 8.30am or 9am to 5pm or 6pm Monday to Friday (often with a midday break), Saturday morning from 8am to noon.
Restaurants 🕒 lunch between noon and 2pm and for dinner from 7.30pm.
Supermarkets 🕒 9am or 9.30am to 7pm or 8pm Monday to Saturday; some open on Sunday morning.

EMBASSIES & CONSULATES

All foreign embassies are in Paris. Many countries – including the United States, Canada and a number of European countries – also have consulates in other major cities.

Australia (Map pp378-9; ☎ 01 40 59 33 00; www.france.embassy.gov.au; 4 rue Jean Rey, 15e, Paris; Ⓜ Bir Hakeim)

FRANCE

Belgium (Map pp378-9; ☎ 01 44 09 39 39; www.diplomatie.be/paris; 9 rue de Tilsitt, 17e, Paris; Ⓜ Charles de Gaulle-Étoile)
Canada Paris (Map pp378-9; ☎ 01 44 43 29 00; www.amb-canada.fr; 35 av Montaigne, 8e; Ⓜ Franklin D Roosevelt); Nice consulate (☎ 04 93 92 93 22; 10 rue Lamartine)
Germany (Map pp378-9; ☎ 01 53 83 45 00; www.paris.diplo.de, in French & German; 13 av Franklin D Roosevelt, 8e, Paris; Ⓜ Franklin D Roosevelt)
Ireland (Map pp378-9; ☎ 01 44 17 67 00; www.embassyofirelandparis.com; 12 av Foch, 16e, Paris; Ⓜ Argentine)
Italy Paris Embassy (Map pp378-9; ☎ 01 49 54 03 00; www.amb-italie.fr; 51 rue de Varenne, 7e; Ⓜ Rue du Bac); Paris Consulate (Map pp378-9; ☎ 01 44 30 47 00; 5 bd Émile Augier, 16e; Ⓜ La Muette)
Japan (Map pp378-9; ☎ 01 48 88 62 00; www.amb-japon.fr; 7 av Hoche, 8e, Paris; Ⓜ Courcelles)
Netherlands (Map pp378-9; ☎ 01 40 62 33 00; www.amb-pays-bas.fr; 7 rue Eblé, 7e, Paris; Ⓜ St-François Xavier)
New Zealand (Map pp378-9; ☎ 01 45 01 43 43; www.nzembassy.com; 7ter rue Léonard de Vinci, 16e, Paris; Ⓜ Victor Hugo)
Spain (Map pp378-9; ☎ 01 44 43 18 00; www.amb-espagne.fr; 22 av Marceau, 8e, Paris; Ⓜ Alma-Marceau)
UK Paris Embassy (Map pp378-9; ☎ 01 44 51 31 00; www.amb-grandebretagne.fr; 35 rue du Faubourg St-Honoré, 8e; Ⓜ Concorde); Paris Consulate (Map pp378-9; ☎ 01 44 51 31 00; 18bis rue d'Anjou, 8e; Ⓜ Madeleine); Marseille Consulate (☎ 04 91 54 92 00; place Varian Fry, 6e)
USA Paris Embassy (Map pp378-9; ☎ 01 43 12 22 22; http://france.usembassy.gov; 2 av Gabriel, 8e; Ⓜ Concorde); US citizen services (Map pp378-9; ☎ 01 43 12 26 71; 4 av Gabriel, 8e; Ⓜ Concorde; 🕑 9am-noon Mon-Fri except US & French holidays); Nice Consular Agency (Map pp378-9; ☎ 04 93 88 89 55; 3rd fl, 7 av Gustave V); Marseille Consulate (☎ 04 91 54 92 00; place Varian Fry, 6e)

FESTIVALS & EVENTS

Most French cities, towns and villages have at least one major arts festival each year.

February

Carnaval de Nice (p434; www.nicecarnaval.com) Merrymaking in Nice during France's largest street carnival (last half of February)

May & June

May Day Across France, workers' day is celebrated with parades and protests. People give each other *muguets* (lilies of the valley) for good luck. No-one works – except waiters and *muguet* sellers (1 May).
Fête de la Musique (www.fetedelamusique.culture.fr, in French) Bands and buskers take to the streets for this nationwide celebration of music (21 June).

July

Festival d'Aix-en-Provence (p431; www.festival-aix.com) Attracts some of the world's best classical music, opera, ballet and buskers (late June to mid-July).
Bastille Day Fireworks, balls, processions – including a military parade down Paris' Champs-Élysées for France's National Day (14 July).
Festival d'Avignon (p431; www.festival-avignon.com) Avignon has an official and fringe festival (mid-July).
Nice Jazz Festival (p431; www.nicejazzfest.fr) Jazz cats among the Roman ruins of Nice (mid-July).

August & September

Braderie de Lille (p397) Three days of mussel-munching as this colossal flea market engulfs the city with antiques, handicrafts and bric-a-brac (first weekend in September).

December

Christmas Markets in Alsace (p404) Last weekend in November through to Christmas or New Year.
Fête des Lumières (p415; www.lumieres.lyon.fr) France's biggest and best light show transforms Lyon (8 December).

HOLIDAYS

The following *jours fériés* (public holidays) are observed in France:

New Year's Day (Jour de l'An) 1 January.
Easter Sunday & Monday (Pâques & lundi de Pâques) Late March/April.
May Day (Fête du Travail) 1 May – traditional parades.
Victoire 1945 8 May – commemorates the Allied victory in Europe that ended WWII.
Ascension Thursday (Ascension) May – celebrated on the 40th day after Easter.
Pentecost/Whit Sunday & Whit Monday (Pentecôte & lundi de Pentecôte) Mid-May to mid-June – celebrated on the seventh Sunday after Easter.
Bastille Day/National Day (Fête Nationale) 14 July – *the* national holiday.
Assumption Day (Assomption) 15 August.
All Saints' Day (Toussaint) 1 November.
Remembrance Day (L'onze novembre) 11 November – marks the WWI armistice.
Christmas (Noël) 25 December.

LEGAL MATTERS

French police have wide powers of stop-and-search and can demand proof of identity at any time. Foreigners must be able to prove their legal status in France (eg passport, visa, residency permit). If the police stop you, be polite and don't argue.

MONEY

The official currency of France is the euro.

Bureaux de change are available in most major cities, and most large post offices offer currency exchange and cash travellers cheques. Commercial banks charge a stiff fee for changing money – generally it's cheaper to use the *distributeurs automatiques de billets* (DAB, otherwise known as ATMs). Most ATMs are linked to the Cirrus, Plus and Maestro networks – check with your bank back home for overseas fees.

Visa and MasterCard (Access or Eurocard) are widely accepted at shops, restaurants and hotels; you'll need to know your *code* (PIN number).

For lost cards:

Amex (☎ 01 47 77 72 00)
Diners Club (☎ 08 10 31 41 59)
MasterCard, Eurocard & Access (Eurocard France; ☎ 08 00 90 13 87, 01 45 67 84 84)
Visa (Carte Bleue; ☎ 08 00 90 20 33)

POST

French post offices are flagged with a yellow or brown sign reading 'La Poste'.

Postal Rates

Domestic letters weighing up to 20g currently cost €0.55. For international post, a letter/package under 20g/2kg costs €0.65/12.30 to Zone 1 (EU and Switzerland) and €0.85/14 to Zone 2 (the rest of the world). All mail to France *must* include the five-digit *code postal* (postcode/ZIP code), which begins with the two-digit number of the *département*.

TELEPHONE

International Dialling

To call someone outside France, dial the international access code (☎ 00), the country code, the area code (without the initial zero if there is one) and the local number. Numbers beginning ☎ 08 00 or ☎ 08 05 are free, but other ☎ 08 numbers are not.

For France Telecom's *service des renseignements* (directory inquiries) dial ☎ 11 87 12 (€1.18 per call from a fixed-line phone). Not all operators speak English. For help in English with France Telecom's services, see www.francetelecom.com or call ☎ 08 00 36 47 75.

Mobile Phones

French mobiles use the GSM 900/1800 system and phone numbers begin ☎ 06. Buying your own French SIM card (€20 to €30) is a good idea if you're staying in the country for long; they're available from *tabacs* and newsagents for all three of France's mobile companies: **Bouygues** (☎ 08 10 63 01 00; www.bouyguestelecom.fr), France Telecom's **Orange** (www.orange.fr, in French) and **SFR** (☎ 08 11 70 70 73; www.sfr.com).

Public Phones & Telephone Cards

Most public phones operate using a credit card or two kinds of *télécartes* (phonecards): *cartes à puce* (cards with a magnetic chip) and *cartes à code* (which use a free access number and a scratch-off code). Both types are sold at *tabacs*, newsagents and post offices in various denominations; phonecards with codes offer *much* better international rates than their chip equivalents.

VISAS

For visa requirements, see the **French Foreign Affairs Ministry site** (www.diplomatie.gouv.fr) and click 'Going to France'. EU nationals and citizens of Iceland, Norway and Switzerland need only a passport or a national identity card in order to enter France. Citizens of Australia, Canada, Israel, Hong Kong, Japan, Malaysia, New Zealand, Singapore, the USA and many Latin American countries do not need visas to visit France as tourists for up to 90 days. Citizens of other countries will require a visa.

Germany

HIGHLIGHTS

- **Berlin** The reborn capital is a shape-shifting creature that never sleeps (p452)
- **Dresden** Rebuilt grandeur by day, endless partying by night (p465)
- **Munich** Beer gardens and naked sunbathing; big sausages too (p472)
- **Hamburg** Its huge harbour has made it rich, but you needn't be to enjoy this forward-looking hotspot (p506)
- **Best journey** Cruise up the Rhine from Koblenz, stopping at whatever fun town grabs your fancy (p491)
- **Off-the-beaten track** Head for trails lacing the green hills of the Harz Mountains (p504)

FAST FACTS

- **Area** 356,866 sq km (about two-thirds the size of France)
- **Budget** €35-75 per day
- **Capital** Berlin
- **Country code** ☎ 49
- **Famous for** beer, BMWs, kicking ass in football/soccer
- **Language** German
- **Money** euro (€); A$1 = €0.55; C$1 = €0.60; ¥100 = €0.78; NZ$1 = €0.43; UK£1 = €1.12; US$1 = €0.74
- **Phrases** *Hallo* (hello), *tschüss* (goodbye), *danke* (thank you), *Entschuldigung* (sorry), *Igitt!* (yuck)

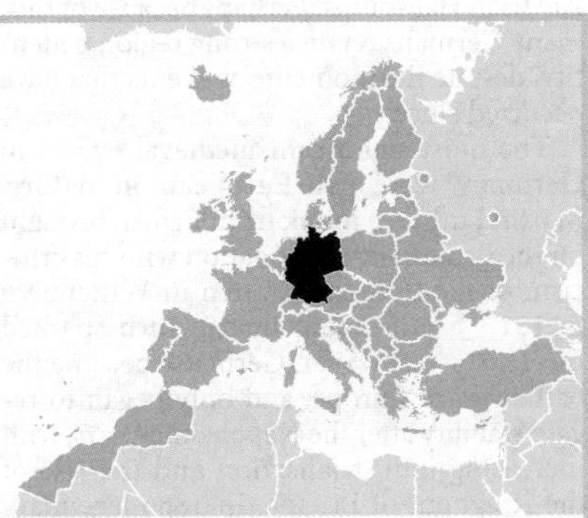

- **Population** 82 million
- **Visas** none required for passport holders of the EU, the USA, Canada, Australia and New Zealand (see p516)

TRAVEL HINTS

Try the end coaches on busy trains – most people head for the middle. Bring your own picnic to beer gardens.

ROAMING GERMANY

Try combining major cities (Berlin, Dresden, Munich, Hamburg) with the scenic heartlands (Thuringia, the Rhine Valley, Bavaria).

Germany has been the major force in Europe for over a century. Often its influence has been bad (world wars and the Holocaust), but often it has been good (driving force of the unifying EU and open confrontation of past crimes). Perhaps it is the latter that propelled Germany to become the moneybags of the continent for the past few decades. Money has flowed out to other European countries, including basket cases such as Ireland in the 1980s and Eastern Europe today. The same generous German taxpayers have spent a remarkable fortune building up and integrating the old East Germany since 1989.

Today the country is a place more concerned with its future than its past. Although the economy seems to be permanently stuck in neutral (and this in the country of Porsche, BMW,

Audi, Mercedes etc), Germans have done an amazing job of transforming themselves into forward-thinking people.

But it's the past that will draw many to Germany, whether it's the beer-drinking traditions of Bavaria, the scores and scores of historic sights such as castles and cathedrals, or the darker corners as found at places like Dachau. Modernity, from the great transport system to cutting-edge music and raucous nightlife, is a bonus every traveller will enjoy.

HISTORY

Events in Germany have often dominated the European stage, but the country itself is a relatively recent invention: for most of its history Germany has been a patchwork of semi-independent principalities and city-states, occupied first by the Roman Empire, then the Holy Roman Empire and finally the Austrian Habsburgs. Perhaps because of this, many Germans retain a strong regional identity, despite the momentous events that have occurred since.

The most significant medieval events in Germany were pan-European in nature. Martin Luther, a monk from Erfurt, brought on the Protestant Reformation with his criticism of the Catholic Church in Wittenberg in 1517, a movement that in turn sparked the Thirty Years' War. Germany became the battlefield of Europe, and only began to regain stability after the Napoleonic Wars, with increasing industrialisation and the rise of the Kingdom of Prussia. In 1866 legendary Prussian 'Iron Chancellor' Otto von Bismarck succeeded in bringing the German states together, largely by force, and a united Germany emerged for the first time in 1871, under Kaiser Wilhelm I.

Germany's rapid growth led to mounting tensions with England, Russia and France, sparking WWI. After Germany's defeat the Weimar Republic was proclaimed, but the new government was hampered by impossible reparation payments. Hyperinflation and economic depression bolstered support for extremist groups, including Adolf Hitler's National Socialists (Nazis).

By 1933, the Nazis had manoeuvred themselves into a position of political dominance: Hitler was appointed chancellor, dissolved parliament and assumed control. In September 1939 he attacked Poland, provoking war with Britain and France. Behind the scenes, concentration camps exterminated an estimated six million Jews and another one million 'enemies of state'. Germany surrendered in May 1945, soon after Hitler's suicide.

After the war, the USA, Britain, France and the Soviet Union divided the country into four occupation zones. In September 1949 the Federal Republic of Germany (FRG) was formed from the three western zones. In response, the communist German Democratic Republic (GDR) was founded in the Soviet zone, with (East) Berlin as its capital. To prevent skilled workers emigrating, the GDR built a wall around West Berlin in 1961, closing its border with the FRG.

For almost 40 years capitalist and socialist Germany coexisted uneasily. In 1989, however, the Peaceful Revolution overtook the reform-shy GDR regime. On 9 November 1989 the Berlin Wall opened, and in 1990 East Germans voted clearly for reunification, which occurred on 3 October 1990.

In recent years the dodgy economy (9% unemployment) has been the major domestic issue, a situation made worse by global recession. In 2005 Angela Merkel was elected as the first female German chancellor and since then has tried to govern through a broad coalition of parties.

THE CULTURE

With 82 million people, Germany is the most populous country in Europe after Russia. Immigration compensates for declining birth rates among the established German population. More than seven million foreigners now live in Germany, mostly in the west. The biggest minority by far is the Turkish population (Berlin is reputedly the biggest Turkish community outside Istanbul), followed by immigrants from Eastern Europe, Russia and the former Soviet states.

Racial problems are relatively rare in Germany, but the international climate since the USA's 'war on terror' has increased tension between local and Muslim communities, often hindering the integration process. Also troubling is the ongoing problem in the east with violent neo-Nazis and skinheads.

On a personal level Germans are generally open, personable and interested in enjoying life, a far cry from their strict and

GERMANY
0 100 km
0 60 miles
DENMARK
SWEDEN
COPENHAGEN
Bornholm
BALTIC SEA
NORTH SEA
Sylt Island
Amrum Island
North Frisian Islands
Rügen Island
Sassnitz
Binz
Schleswig
Heide
Kiel
Stralsund
Warnemünde
Rostock
SCHLESWIG-HOLSTEIN
East Frisian Islands
Cuxhaven
Lübeck
Wismar
MECKLENBURG-WESTERN POMERANIA
Wilhelmshaven
HAMBURG
Hamburg
Schwerin
A24
A241
A19
A1
BREMEN
Bremen
A7
Elbe River
A11
NETHERLANDS
POLAND
BRANDENBURG
Oder
A31
LOWER SAXONY
A1
A19
BERLIN
SAXONY-ANHALT
Potsdam
Frankfurt/Oder
Hanover
A12
A2
A2
River
A30
Hamelin
Magdeburg
A13
Badenwerder
Goslar
Wernigerode
Lutherstadt Wittenberg
NORTH RHINE-WESTPHALIA
Clausthal-Zellerfeld
Quedlinburg
Dessau
Rhine
A9
A15
A44
Dortmund
Göttingen
A13
A7
Halle
Nordhausen
Düsseldorf
Kassel
Leipzig
Meissen
Görlitz
A4
THURINGIA
Naumburg
Cologne
Eisenach
Erfurt
Weimar
Dresden
Aachen
A45
Marburg
A4
Bonn
A4
SAXONY
A5
A9
A72
BELGIUM
61
HESSE
River
Cochem
Koblenz
Frankfurt-am-Main
A48
A3
A7
RHINELAND-PALATINATE
River
Wiesbaden
Hanau
PRAGUE
Rüdesheim
Mainz
Marktredwitz
LUXEMBOURG
Trier
Würzburg
Bamberg
A3
CZECH REPUBLIC
SAARLAND
Mannheim
Moselle
Heidelberg
Nuremberg
Saarbrücken
Rothenburg ob der Tauber
BAVARIA
A6
Dinkelsbühl
A19
Regensburg
Karlsruhe
Danube
A3
River
Nördlingen
Baden-Baden
Stuttgart
River
Passau
A8
A92
A5
BADEN-WÜRTTEMBERG
Ulm
Augsburg
Rhine
A81
FRANCE
A7
Munich
Freiburg
Donaueschingen
A95
A8
Constance
Berchtesgaden
Füssen
Lake Constance
Lindau
Garmisch-Partenkirchen
Oberstdorf
AUSTRIA
LIECHTENSTEIN
SWITZERLAND

humourless reputation. However, in public they have quite a formal culture, and manners remain very important. A little politeness goes a long way with officialdom in particular, and remember to always introduce yourself by name when making a phone call.

ARTS

Historically Germany has always been strong in the arts, with the legacies of such literary, musical, artistic and architectural greats as Goethe, JS Bach, Karl Friedrich Schinkel and Caspar David Friedrich providing a rich vein of inspiration for modern successors like Günter Grass, Arnold Schönberg, Walter Gropius and Paul Klee.

Today the arts still occupy a key place at the heart of German culture. Tradition is scrupulously preserved around the country, but for the new generation of artists experimentation is the way forward. Germany is a hotbed of exciting new architecture, avant-garde art and left-field literature. Above all, the popular music scene is much more wide-ranging than radio playlists suggest, particularly where electronic dance music is concerned. Berlin and Frankfurt are centres of techno.

ENVIRONMENT

Germany can be divided from north to south into several geographical regions, including the Northern Lowlands, the Central Uplands (Germany's heartland), the Alpine Foothills and the Alps.

German weather can be variable. The most reliable weather is from May to October. However, shoulder periods (late March to May and September to October) can bring fewer tourists and surprisingly pleasant weather. Camping season is May to September.

Environmental issues are taken seriously in Germany, and almost every household will have several separate bins for recycling glass, packaging, paper and organic waste. On a national level, Germany regularly introduces environmental initiatives to combat problems such as industrial emissions and energy wastage, actively supports international agreements such as the Kyoto Protocol and is a huge proponent of solar power despite the often dodgy weather.

READING UP

Still the most important German novel post-WWI, Günter Grass's *The Tin Drum* (1959) takes a magical realist tour through 19th- and 20th-century German history. Australian journalist Anna Funder's award-winning *Stasiland* (2002) probes how the East German intelligence service destroyed ordinary lives, interviewing former Stasi men and their victims. The explicit tales of an 18-year-old girl, *Wetlands* (2008) by Charlotte Roche, have set tongues wagging even in nonprudish Germany.

TRANSPORT

GETTING THERE & AWAY

Air

The main arrival and departure points in Germany are proliferating as budget airlines expand. **Frankfurt airport** (FRA; www.airportcity-frankfurt.com) and **Munich airport** (MUC; www.munich-airport.de) are still the main destinations for long-haul flights, but are joined for intra-Europe flights by **Berlin Schönefeld** (SXI; www.berlin-airport.de), which is soon to be renamed Berlin Brandenburg International (BER or BBI); **Nuremberg** (NUE; www.airport-nuernberg.de); and the misleadingly named and inconvenient **Frankfurt-Hahn airport** (HHN; www.hahn-airport.de) among many others.

From North America, Lufthansa and its partners United Airlines and Air Canada have the most nonstop flights to Germany. Asian carriers offer the main connections from Australia and New Zealand.

European budget airlines serving Germany include Ryanair, easyJet, Air Berlin and Germanwings. And don't count out huge

CONNECTIONS

At the heart of Europe, Germany's superb railway (opposite) is well linked to surrounding countries. Freiburg and Stuttgart have services south to Switzerland and Italy, Munich is close to Austria and the Czech Republic, Berlin is close to Poland, Hamburg has frequent services to Denmark, Cologne is good for both the Netherlands and Belgium and Frankfurt is the base for fast trains to France, including Paris (four hours).

Lufthansa, which often competes with the cheapies on price.

Boat

If you're heading to Scandinavia or the UK, the German port options are Lübeck, Kiel, Rostock and Sassnitz. The most common destinations are Trelleborg, Gothenburg and Oslo.

Bus

With bargain-priced fares from the UK to Germany, budget airlines have largely eclipsed bus operators. Still, **Eurolines** (www.eurolines.com), a consortium of national bus companies, may prove useful. See the website for the latest fares and increasing number of specials. **Deutsche-Touring** (☎ 069-790 350; www.deutsche-touring.com) is the local Eurolines affiliate.

Car & Motorcycle

Germany is served by an excellent *autobahn* (motorway) system. If you're coming from the UK, the quickest option is via the Channel Tunnel; ferries take longer but are cheaper. Either way, you can be in Germany four hours after arriving in France.

You must have third-party insurance to enter Germany with a car or motorcycle.

Hitching & Ride Services

Lonely Planet does not recommend hitching, but should you decide to try it you may encounter long delays. The best way to pick up lifts is to head for a service area on the main route you wish to use.

Aside from hitching, the cheapest way to get to Germany is as a paying passenger in a private car. Rides are arranged through *Mitfahrzentrale* (ride-sharing agencies) in many German cities; you pay a reservation fee to the agency and a share of petrol and costs to the driver. Tourist offices can direct you to local agencies, or call ☎ 194 40 in large German cities.

Train

Trains are a lot more comfortable (and expensive) than buses. Some long-distance trains between major German cities and other countries are called EuroCity (EC) or InterCityExpress (ICE) trains. The main German hubs with the best connections to/from major European cities are Hamburg (for Scandinavia), Cologne (for France, Belgium and the Netherlands, plus London via Eurostar), Frankfurt (for Paris), Munich (for southern and southeastern Europe) and Berlin (for Eastern Europe).

Generally the longer international routes are served by at least one day-time train and often a night train as well. Many night trains only carry sleeping cars, which cost more but are considerably more comfortable.

GETTING AROUND

Bicycle

Radwandern (bicycle touring) is very popular in Germany. Favoured routes include along the Rhine, Moselle, Elbe and Danube Rivers and around the Lake Constance area. Cycling is strictly *verboten* (forbidden) on *autobahns*. There are well-equipped cycling shops in almost every town, and a fairly active market for used touring bikes. Simple three-gear bicycles can be hired from around €15/40 per day/week, and more robust mountain bikes from €20/50.

Deutsche Bahn (DB, www.bahn.de) publishes *Bahn&Bike,* an excellent handbook covering shops, routes, maps and other resources, and has a good website (www.bahn.de/bahnundbike).

Bicycles may be taken on most trains but you must purchase a separate *Fahrradkarte* (bicycle ticket). These cost €9 on long-distance trains and €4.50 on regional trains (RB, RE and S-Bahn). Bicycles are not allowed on high-speed ICE trains. There is no charge at all on some trains; for specifics enquire at a local station or call DB on the **DB Radfahrer-Hotline** (bicycle hotline; ☎ 01805-151 415). Free lines are also listed in DB's complimentary *Bahn&Bike* brochure (in German), as are the almost 250 stations throughout the country where you can hire bikes for between €3 and €13.

Boat

Boats are most likely to be used for transport when travelling along the delightful Rhine, Elbe and Moselle Rivers.

Bus

The bus network functions primarily in support of the rail network, cutting corners and going where trains don't. Bus stations or stops are usually near the train station in any town.

DB agents have information on certain regional services; otherwise, check with tourist offices. Deutsche-Touring services include the Romantic Rd buses in southern Germany; see p478 for details.

Car & Motorcycle

Although hiring a vehicle can be a great way to tour the country, it's expensive. For information, contact the Munich-based **Allgemeiner Deutscher Automobil Club** (ADAC; ☎ 089-767 60; www.adac.de); it has offices in all major cities and a national breakdown service.

Local Transport

Local transport is excellent within big cities and small towns, and is generally based on buses, *Strassenbahn* (trams), S-Bahn and/or U-Bahn (underground trains). Fares cover all these and are generally determined by zones or the time travelled. Multiticket strips or day passes are generally better value than single-ride tickets.

Train

Operated mostly by **Deutsche Bahn** (DB; www.bahn.de), the German train system is one of the best in Europe. Schedules are integrated throughout the country so that connections between trains are tight, often only five minutes. Of course, this means that when a train is late, connections are missed. Put some slack in your itinerary so you won't miss a connection and be stranded.

German trains fall into specific classifications. From fastest to slowest, these include InterCityExpress (ICE), InterCity (IC) or EuroCity (EC), RegionalExpress (RE), RegionalBahn (RB) and S-Bahn (not to be confused with U-Bahn, which are run by local authorities that don't honour rail passes). EN and CNL trains are generally night services. *Zuschläge* (supplements) for faster trains are built into fares.

Buy your ticket before boarding, as buying from a conductor carries a surcharge (€3 to €8). Ticket agents cheerfully accept credit cards, as do most machines. During peak travel periods, a reservation (€3.50) on a long-distance train can mean the difference between squatting by the toilets and relaxing in your own seat.

A host of special train fares offered by DB allow you to cut costs for journeys. Most ticket agents are quite willing to help you find the cheapest options for your intended trip. Or go online (www.bahn.de) and look for Savings Fares 25 and 50, which carry restrictions similar to discount airline tickets.

For train schedule and fare information (also available in English), you can call ☎ 01805-996 633 from anywhere in Germany (€0.13 per minute) or – better – use the very helpful International Guests pages of the DB website.

Travel agents outside Germany sell German Rail Passes valid for unlimited travel on all DB trains for a given number of days within a 30-day period; prices start at €160 for four days. They're worth it if you're going to do a few long intercity journeys with stops in between. These are only available to visitors from outside Germany.

Eurail and Inter-Rail passes are valid in Germany.

BERLIN

☎ 030 / pop 3.41 million

Something old, something new. Reminders of Berlin's once-divided past sit side-by-side with its united present – Norman Foster's Reichstag dome, Peter Eisenman's Holocaust Memorial and the iconic Brandenburg Gate are all contained within a few blocks of each other. Strolling along Bernauerstrasse near trendy Prenzlauer Berg, you suddenly place your foot on a brick-marked line in the pavement showing where the wall once stood, a past that is rapidly receding.

Renowned for its diversity and tolerance, its alternative culture and night-owl stamina, the best thing about the German capital is the way it reinvents itself and isn't shackled by its mind-numbing history. And the world is catching on – as evidenced by the surge of expatriates and steady increase in out-of-towners coming to see what all the fuss is about.

In the midst of it all, students rub shoulders with Russian émigrés, fashion boutiques inhabit monumental GDR buildings, Turkish residents live next door to famous DJs and the nightlife has long left the American sector as edgy clubbers watch the sun rise over the neon-lit Universal Music headquarters in the city's east.

In short, all human life is here, and don't expect to get much sleep.

EMERGENCY NUMBERS

- Ambulance (☎ 112)
- Fire brigade (☎ 112)
- Police (☎ 110)

ORIENTATION

The major sights are laid out roughly along an east–west axis going through the Brandenburger Tor (Brandenburg Gate). East of the gate lies Unter den Linden, the Museumsinsel (Museum Island) and the needle-shaped Fernsehturm (TV tower) at Alexanderplatz. Heading west you encounter the Reichstag, Holocaust Memorial, Tiergarten and Siegessäule (Victory Column), plus Potsdamer Platz to the south.

Most of the action now happens in the east – which includes the 'centra' area of Mitte and the districts of Prenzlauer Berg and Friedrichshain. Meanwhile, on the far western side of the Tiergarten, near the Zoo station, lies the Kurfürstendamm, the one-time centre of West Berlin.

INFORMATION

Internet access is a breeze to find in Berlin – and the entire Sony Center at Potsdamerplatz (p457) is a free public hot spot.

Al Hamra (Map pp454-5; ☎ 4285 0095; Raumerstrasse 16; per hr €1; 9-4am; M Eberswalder Strasse) Internet access.

Berlin Tourismus (☎ 250 025; www.berlin-tourist-information.de) Alexanderplatz (Map pp454-5; Alexa Shopping Centre; 10am-6pm); Brandenburger Tor (Map pp454-5; 10am-6pm); Hauptbahnhof/Main Train Station (Map pp454-5; Ground fl/Europa Platz Entrance; 8am-10pm); Reichstag (Map pp454-5; 10am-6pm); Zoologisher Garten Station (Map p458; Kurfürstendamm 21; 10am-8pm Mon-Sat, to 6pm Sun) Tourist information.

Berlin Welcome Card (www.berlin-welcomecard.de; 48/72hr card €16.50/21.50, incl Potsdam & up to 3 children €18/24.50) A discount card giving free public transport, plus museum and entertainment discounts.

Kassenärztliche Bereitschaftsdienst (Public Physicians' Emergency Service; ☎ 310 031; www.kvberlin.de, in German) Phone referral for medical services.

Surf & Sushi (Map pp454-5; ☎ 2838 4898; www.surfandsushi.de; Oranienburger Strasse 17; per hr €2, free if you eat a bite of sushi; from noon Mon-Sat, from 1pm Sun; M Oranienburger Strasse/Hackescher Markt) Internet access.

SIGHTS

Brandenburg Gate Area

Finished in 1791 as one of 18 city gates, the neoclassical **Brandenburger Tor** (Map pp454-5; Pariser Platz; M S-Bahn Unter den Linden) became an east–west crossing point after the Wall was built in 1961. The crowning Quadriga statue, a winged goddess in a horse-drawn chariot, was once kidnapped by Napoleon and briefly taken to Paris. It's back in place now. Before reunification it faced east, but has since been reversed.

Just to the west of the gate stands the glass-domed **Reichstaggebäude** (Parliament Bldg; Map pp454-5; ☎ 2273 2152; www.bundestag.de; Platz der Republik 1; admission free; 8am-midnight, last admission 10pm). A fire here in 1933 allowed Hitler to blame the communists and grab power, while the Soviets raised their flag here in 1945 to signal Nazi Germany's defeat. Today, the glass cupola added in 1999 by architect Lord Norman Foster is the highlight. Queues to visit the internal spiral walkway are long, so arrive early.

The Reichstag overlooks the **Tiergarten** (see p457) and further south again is the **Holocaust Memorial** (Denkmal für die ermordeten Juden Europas; Map pp454-5; ☎ 2639 4336; www.stiftung-denkmal.de; Cora-Berliner-Strasse 1; admission free; field 24hr, information centre 10am-8pm Tue-Sun, last entry 7.15pm Apr-Sep, to 7pm, last entry 6.15pm Oct-Mar; M Potsdamer Platz/S-Bahn Unter den Linden), a grid of 2711 'stelae' or differently shaped concrete columns set over 19,000 sq metres of gently undulating ground. This slate-grey expanse of walkways and pillars can be entered from any side, but presents varied sombre perspectives as you move through it. For historical background, designer Peter Eisenman has created an underground information centre in the southeast corner of the site. Highly recommended are the weekly **English tours** (tours €3; 4pm Sun).

Unter den Linden

Lined with lime (or linden) trees, the street **Unter den Linden** (M S-Bahn Unter den Linden) was the fashionable avenue of old Berlin. Today, after decades of communist neglect, it's been rejuvenated. The thoroughfare stretches east from Brandenburger Tor to the Museumsinsel, passing shops, embassies, operas and a university.

Don't forget to stop awhile at **Bebelplatz** (Map pp454-5; M Französische Strasse). There's a book-burning memorial – a chastening reminder

MITTE & PRENZLAUER BERG

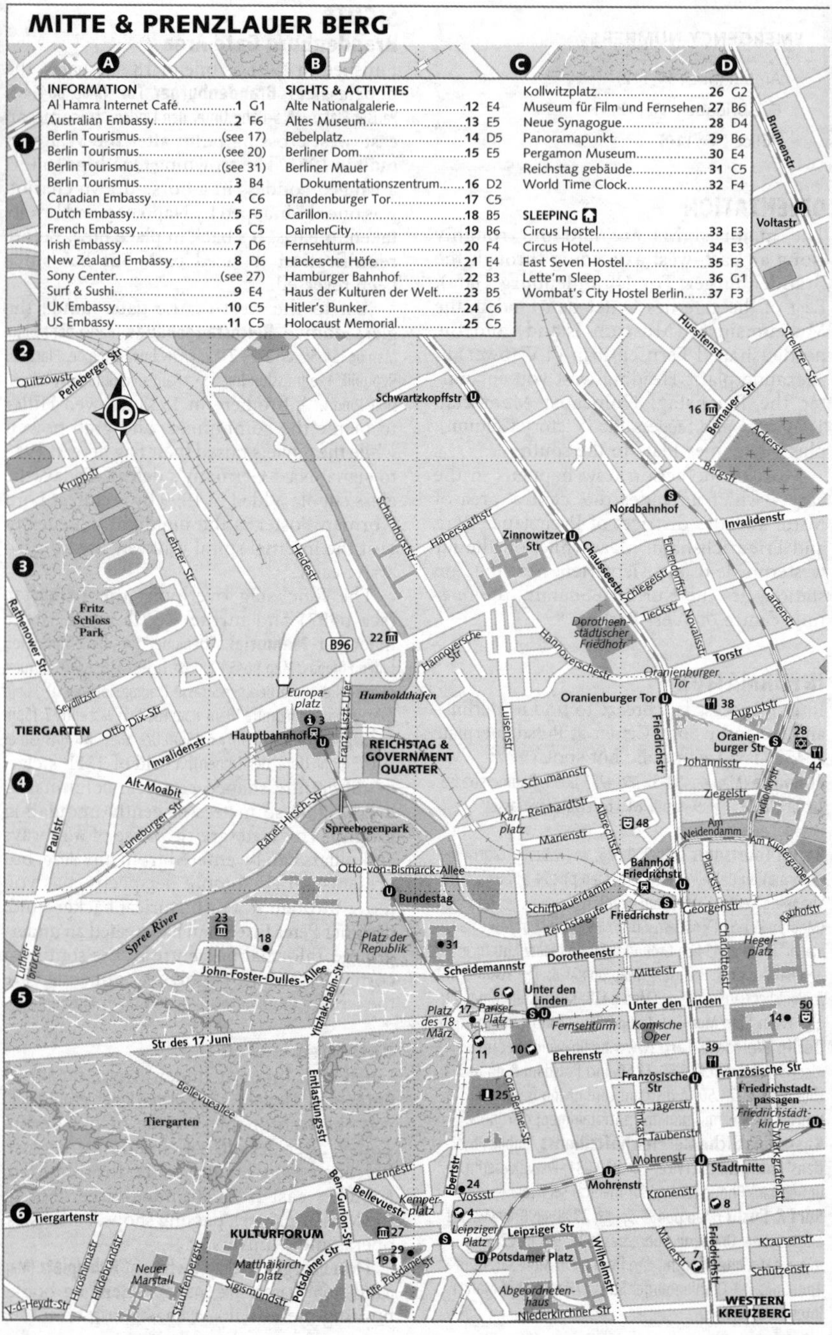

INFORMATION

Al Hamra Internet Café	1	G1
Australian Embassy	2	F6
Berlin Tourismus	(see 17)	
Berlin Tourismus	(see 20)	
Berlin Tourismus	(see 31)	
Berlin Tourismus	3	B4
Canadian Embassy	4	C6
Dutch Embassy	5	F5
French Embassy	6	C5
Irish Embassy	7	D6
New Zealand Embassy	8	D6
Sony Center	(see 27)	
Surf & Sushi	9	E4
UK Embassy	10	C5
US Embassy	11	C5

SIGHTS & ACTIVITIES

Alte Nationalgalerie	12	E4
Altes Museum	13	E5
Bebelplatz	14	D5
Berliner Dom	15	E5
Berliner Mauer Dokumentationszentrum	16	D2
Brandenburger Tor	17	C5
Carillon	18	B5
DaimlerCity	19	B6
Fernsehturm	20	F4
Hackesche Höfe	21	E4
Hamburger Bahnhof	22	B3
Haus der Kulturen der Welt	23	B5
Hitler's Bunker	24	C6
Holocaust Memorial	25	C5
Kollwitzplatz	26	G2
Museum für Film und Fernsehen	27	B6
Neue Synagogue	28	D4
Panoramapunkt	29	B6
Pergamon Museum	30	E4
Reichstag gebäude	31	C5
World Time Clock	32	F4

SLEEPING

Circus Hostel	33	E3
Circus Hotel	34	E3
East Seven Hostel	35	F3
Lette'm Sleep	36	G1
Wombat's City Hostel Berlin	37	F3

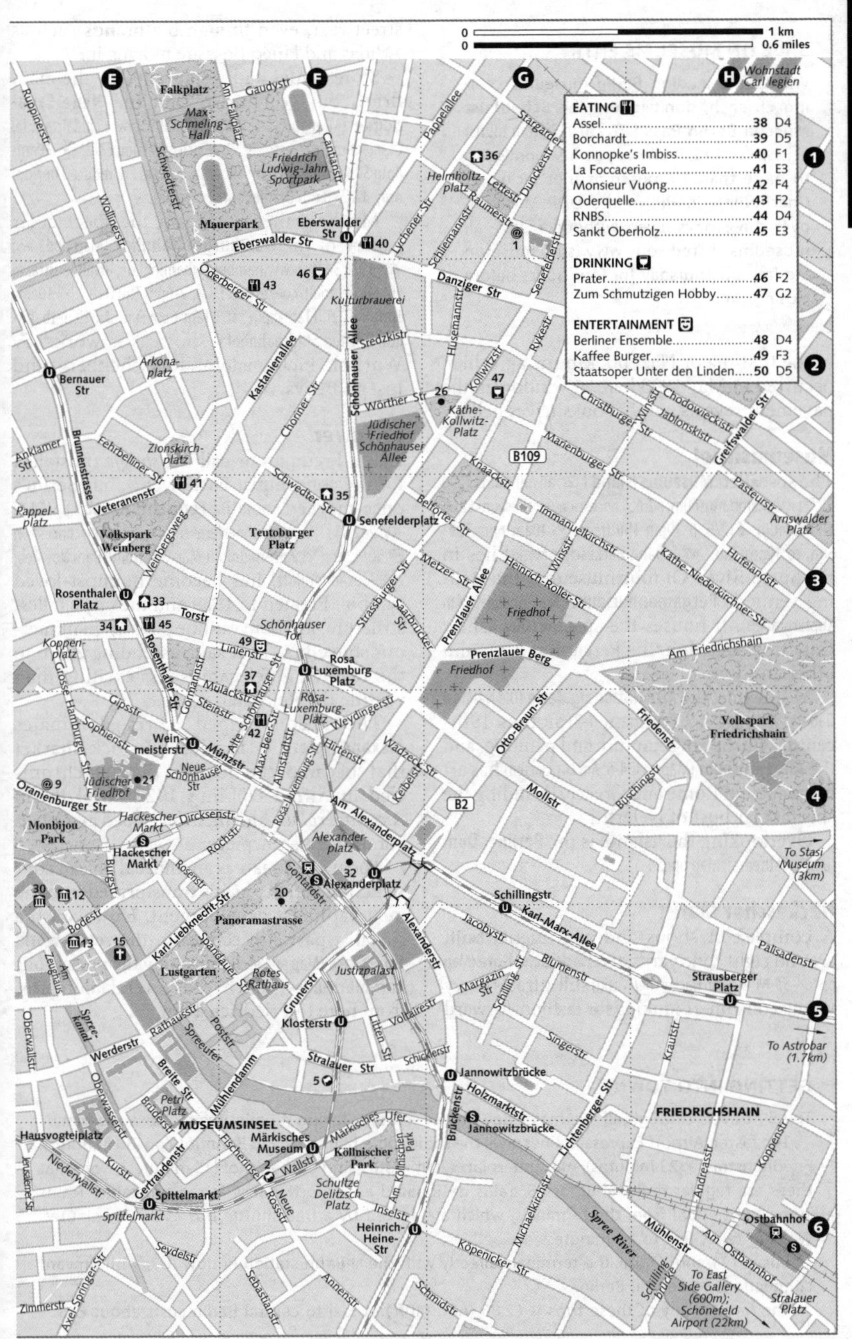
EATING
Assel 38 D4
Borchardt 39 D5
Konnopke's Imbiss 40 F1
La Foccaceria 41 E3
Monsieur Vuong 42 F4
Oderquelle 43 F2
RNBS 44 D4
Sankt Oberholz 45 E3
DRINKING
Prater 46 F2
Zum Schmutzigen Hobby 47 G2
ENTERTAINMENT
Berliner Ensemble 48 D4
Kaffee Burger 49 F3
Staatsoper Unter den Linden 50 D5
0 1 km
0 0.6 miles
Mauerpark
Falkplatz
Max-Schmeling-Hall
Friedrich Ludwig-Jahn Sportpark
Eberswalder Str
Kulturbrauerei
Volkspark Weinberg
Teutoburger Platz
Rosenthaler Platz
Rosa Luxemburg Platz
Friedhof
Volkspark Friedrichshain
Alexanderplatz
Monbijou Park
Hackescher Markt
Lustgarten
Rotes Rathaus
MUSEUMSINSEL
Märkisches Museum
Köllnischer Park
FRIEDRICHSHAIN
Ostbahnhof
Jannowitzbrücke
Spree River
To Stasi Museum (3km)
To Astrobar (1.7km)
To East Side Gallery (600m); Schönefeld Airport (22km)

SAVE ON MUSEUMS ENTRY

With some leading Berlin museums costing €8 each, don't ignore the **SchauLust Museen Berlin Pass** (☎ 250 025; from tourist offices). For €15, it allows you free admission to more than 70 museums (not including Checkpoint Charlie or the DDR Museum) over three days. Even without a pass, all museums listed on www.smb.museum are free on Thursday for four hours before closing time.

of the first major Nazi book-burning, which occurred in May 1933 here. A window in the pavement reveals empty bookshelves below.

Museumsinsel

The so-called **Museums Island** (☎ all museums 2090 5577; www.smb.museum; adult/concession per museum €8/4, all museums €12/6, 6-10pm Thu free; 10am-6pm Tue-Sun, to 10pm Thu; M S-Bahn Hackescher Markt) lies in the Spree River. Of four museums, the leading venue is **Pergamonmuseum** (Map pp454-5; Am Kupfergraben). It houses the spectacular Ishtar Gate from Babylon, the Pergamon Altar and other antiquities.

Meanwhile, the **Alte Nationalgalerie** (Old National Gallery; Map pp454-5; Bodestrasse 1-3) houses 19th-century European sculpture and painting, and the **Altes Museum** (Map pp454-5; Am Lustgarten) has art from ancient Rome and Greece, including the spectacular bust of Nefertiti.

Overlooking the 'island' is the **Berliner Dom** (Berlin Cathedral; Map pp454-5).

Hackescher Markt

A complex of shops and apartments built around eight courtyards, the **Hackesche Höfe** (Map pp454-5; M S-Bahn Hackescher Markt) still attracts savvy young consumers looking for fashion-forward streetwear, even though big brands such as Adidas and Hugo Boss are moving in.

Stores, cafes and restaurants are the main draw, but you'll also find the **Neue Synagogue** (Map pp454-5; ☎ 8802 8300; www.cjudaicum.de; Oranienburger Strasse 28-30; adult/concession €3/2; 10am-8pm Sun & Mon, to 6pm Tue-Thu, to 5pm Fri, reduced hr Nov-Apr; M S-Bahn Oranienburgerstrasse).

Much further northeast, the spectacular gallery of the **Hamburger Bahnhof** (Map pp454-5; ☎ 3978 3439; www.hamburgerbahnhof.de; Invalidenstrasse 50, Mitte; adult/concession €8/4, 2-6pm Thu free; 10am-6pm Tue-Fri, 11am-8pm Sat, 11am-6pm Sun; M Hauptbahnhof/Lehrter Stadtbahnhof) showcases works by Warhol, Lichtenstein, Rauschenberg and Joseph Beuys.

TV Tower

Call it Freudian or call it *Ostalgie* (nostalgia for the communist East or *Ost*), but Berlin's once-mocked socialist **Fernsehturm** (Map pp454-5; ☎ 242 3333; www.berlinerfernsehturm.de; adult/concession €9.50/4.50; 9am-midnight Mar-Oct, from 10am Nov-Feb; M Alexanderplatz) has become its most-loved symbol. Erected in 1969 and the city's tallest structure, its 368m outline pops up in numerous souvenirs. That said, ascending 207m to the revolving Telecafé is less exciting than visiting the Reichstag dome.

The needle-shaped Turm dominates **Alexanderplatz**, a former livestock market that became the lowlife district chronicled in Alfred Döblin's 1929 novel *Berlin Alexanderplatz*, and then developed as a 1960s communist showpiece.

Today the square is an unusual hive of construction activity as it's transformed into the next capitalist development. However, the socialist past still echoes in the retro **World Time Clock** (Map pp454-5) and along the portentous **Karl-Marx-Allee**, which leads several kilometres from here to Friedrichshain.

GETTING INTO TOWN

The S9 travels through all the major downtown stations, taking 40 minutes to Alexanderplatz.

The faster 'Airport Express' trains travel the same route half-hourly to Bahnhof Zoo (30 minutes), Friedrichstrasse (23 minutes), Alexanderplatz (20 minutes) and Ostbahnhof (15 minutes). Note that these are regular regional RE or RB trains designated as AirportExpress in the timetable. Trains stop about 400m from the terminals, which are served by a free shuttle bus every 10 minutes. Walking takes five to 10 minutes.

Buses 171 and X7 link the terminals directly with the U-Bahn station Rudow (U7) with onward connections to central Berlin.

The fare for any of these trips is €2.80 (ABC tariff). A taxi to central Berlin costs about €35.

Berlin Wall

The infamous Wall snaked through Berlin, so today's remnants are scattered across the city. The longest surviving stretch is the so-called **East Side Gallery** (off Map pp454-5; www.eastsidegallery.com; Mühlenstrasse; Ⓜ S-Bahn Warschauer Strasse) in Friedrichshain. Panels along this 1.3km of graffiti and art include the famous portrait of Soviet leader Brezhnev kissing GDR leader Erich Hönecker and a Trabant car seemingly bursting through the (now crumbling) concrete.

Climbing the tower at the **Berliner Mauer Dokumentationszentrum** (Berlin Wall Documentation Centre; Map pp454-5; ☎ 464 1030; Bernauer Strasse 111; admission free; 🕑 10am-5pm; Ⓜ S-Bahn Nordbahnhof) you overlook a memorial across the street – an artist's impression of the death strip behind an original stretch of wall.

In Kreuzberg, the renowned sign saying 'You are now leaving the American sector' still stands, marking the position of **Checkpoint Charlie** (Map p460; cnr Friedrichstrasse & Zimmerstrasse). Nearby, the touristy **Haus am Checkpoint Charlie** (Map p460; ☎ 253 7250; www.mauer-museum.com; Friedrichstrasse 43-45; adult/concession €12.50/9.50; 🕑 9am-10pm; Ⓜ Kochstrasse/Stadtmitte) chronicles tales of spectacular escape attempts, including through tunnels, in hot-air balloons and even with a one-man submarine.

Tiergarten

From the Reichstag, you can see the Tiergarten's **carillon** (Map pp454-5; John-Foster-Dulles-Allee; bus 100 or 200) and the **Haus der Kulturen der Welt** (House of World Cultures; Map pp454-5; John-Foster-Dulles-Allee). The latter was erected during a 1950s building expo and is nicknamed the 'pregnant oyster'.

Further west is the **Siegessäule** (Victory Column; Map p458; bus 100 or 200), a golden angel built to commemorate 19th-century Prussian military victories. Be aware that there are better views than those from the column's peak.

A short walk south is a cluster of embassy buildings and museums, including the **Bauhaus Archiv** (Map p458; ☎ 254 0020; www.bauhaus.de; Klingelhöferstrasse 14; adult/concession €7/4 Sat-Mon, €6/3 Wed-Fri; 🕑 10am-5pm Wed-Mon; Ⓜ Nollendorfplatz), with Modernist objects from the influential Bauhaus design school. The school itself survives in Dessau (see www.bauhaus-dessau.de), not far from Berlin.

The **Berliner Philharmonie** (1961; www.berliner-philharmoniker.de) and yet more stunning art museums lie a little to the east in the **Kulturforum** (Map pp454-5; www.kulturforum-berlin.de), south of Tiergartenstrasse. Check the website to see if anything appeals.

Potsdamer Platz

This postmodern temple to Mammon was erected in 2000 in the former death strip. Under the big-top, glass-tent roof of the **Sony Center** (Map pp454-5; Ⓜ or S-Bahn Potsdamer Platz) and along the malls of the Lego-like **DaimlerCity** (Map pp454-5), people swarm in and around shops, restaurants, offices, loft apartments, clubs, a cinema, a luxury hotel and a casino – all revitalising what was the busiest square in prewar Europe.

There's a **Filmmuseum** (Map pp454-5; ☎ 300 9030; www.filmmuseum-berlin.de; Potsdamer Strasse 2, Tiergarten; adult/concession €6/4.50; 🕑 10am-6pm Tue-Sun, to 8pm Thu) and 'Europe's fastest' lift to the **Panorama Observation Deck** (Map pp454-5; www.panoramapunkt.de; adult/concession €3.50/2.50; 🕑 11am-8pm).

But, as ever in Berlin, the past refuses to go quietly. Just north of Potsdamer Platz lies the former site of **Hitler's Bunker** (Map pp454-5). To the southeast lies the **Topographie des Terrors** (Map p460; ☎ 2548 6703; www.topographie.de; Niederkirchner Strasse; admission free; 🕑 10am-8pm May-Sep, to dusk Oct-Apr), a sometimes shockingly graphic record of the Gestapo and SS headquarters that once stood here.

Jewish Museum

The **Jüdisches Museum** (Map p460; ☎ 2599 3300; www.juedisches-museum-berlin.de; Lindenstrasse 9-14; adult/concession €5/2.50; 🕑 10am-10pm Mon, to 8pm Tue-Sun, last entry 1hr before closing; Ⓜ Hallesches Tor) is as much about the Daniel Libeskind building as the collection of Jewish-German history within. Designed to disorient with its 'voids', culs-de-sac, barbed metal fittings, slit windows and uneven floors, this still-somehow-beautiful structure swiftly conveys the uncertainty and sometime terror of past Jewish life in Germany.

Kurfürstendamm

West Berlin's legendary shopping thoroughfare, the Ku'damm has lost some of its cachet since the Wall fell, but is worth visiting for old times' sake. Here you'll find the **Kaiser-Wilhelm-Gedächtniskirche** (Map p458; ☎ 218 5023; Breitscheidplatz; 🕑 Memorial Hall 10am-4pm Mon-Sat, Hall of Worship 9am-7pm), which remains in ruins – just as British bombers on 22 November 1943

left it – as an antiwar memorial. Only the broken west tower still stands.

Stasi Museum

The one-time secret police headquarters now houses the **Stasi Museum** (off Map p458; ☎ 553 6854; House 1, Ruschestrasse 103; adult/concession €4/3; 🕒 11am-6pm Tue-Fri, 2-6pm Sat & Sun; Ⓜ Magdalenenstrasse). It's largely in German, but worth a visit to see the cunning surveillance devices and communist paraphernalia.

FESTIVALS & EVENTS

International Film Festival Berlin (☎ 259 200; www.berlinale.de) The Berlinale, held in February, is Germany's answer to the Cannes and Venice film festivals.

Christopher Street Day (☎ 2362 8632; www.csd-berlin.de) Held on the last weekend in June, Germany's largest gay event celebrated its 30th anniversary in 2008.

B-Parade (www.b-parade.eu) Held each July, Berlin's huge techno street parade is the Loveparade's successor.

Fuckparade (www.fuckparade.org) Each August, this anti-establishment, anti-gentrification demonstration dances to its own noncommercial techno beat.

SLEEPING

Berlin's independent hostels outdo the **DJH/HI** (www.jugendherberge.de) offerings in the city.

Ostel (Map p460; ☎ 2576 8660; www.ostel.eu; Wriezener Karree 5; dm/d/apt €9/61/120; 💻 Ⓟ ⊠; Ⓜ Ostbahnhof) *Ostalgie* – nostalgia for the communist East – is taken to a whole new level at this hostel/hotel with original socialist GDR furnishings and portraits of Honecker and other former socialist leaders. You can even stay in a 'bugged' Stasi Suite. You might think you've entered a surreal time machine – until you access the free wi-fi in the lobby, that is.

Lette 'M Sleep (Map pp454-5; ☎ 4473 3623; www.backpackers.de; Lettestrasse 7; dm from €11, tw with shared bathroom from €40, apt from €69; 🖳 ⊠; Ⓜ Eberswalder Strasse) Located within stumbling distance of the Prenzlauer Berg nightlife action, this colourful and convenient party hostel is simply groovy, baby, groovy.

EastSeven (Map pp454-5; ☎ 9362 2240; www.eastseven.de; Schwedter Strasse 7; dm from €13, s/d/tr/q per person from €30/21/17/16.50, bedding €3; 🖳; Ⓜ Senefelder Platz) Retro and homey with spotless rooms and sturdy pine furniture, there is a youthful elegance here rarely present in hostels. The lovely garden is perfect for summer barbecues.

our pick Die Fabrik (Map p460; ☎ 611 7716; www.diefabrik.com; Schlesischestrasse 18; dm €18, s/d/tr from €52/69/84; 🖳 ⊠; Ⓜ Schlesisches Tor) A cross between a hostel and a hotel (feels more like the latter), these tidy and simple rooms are a steal. Plenty of spotless shower and toilet facilities are located on each floor and larger doubles come with washbasins and tiny sitting areas – oh, and solar power heats 100% of your hot water in the sunny months (and a smaller percentage in other seasons).

Circus Hostel (Map pp454-5; ☎ 2839 1433; www.circus-hostel.de; Weinbergsweg 1a; dm €19-25, s/d €50/70, s/d without bathroom €40/56, 2-/4-person apt €85/140; 🖳; Ⓜ U-Bahn Rosenthaler Platz) This stalwart is one of the most popular hostels in town, with a great central location, friendly staff and tastefully decorated rooms in cheerful colours. A two-night minimum stay applies to the apartments.

Wombat City Hostel Map pp454-5; ☎ 8471 0820; www.wombats-hostels.com; Alte Schönhauser Strasse 2; dm/d €21/58, apt with kitchen €100, discounts Nov-Feb; 🖳; Ⓜ Rosa-Luxemburg-Platz) A newcomer to the Mitte hostel scene, rooms and dorms (all en suite) are decorated Ikea-style and doubles have long balconies. A hopping lounge and all-you-can-eat breakfast buffet (€3.50) round out the package.

Berliner Bed & Breakfast (off Map p458; ☎ 2437 3962; www.berliner-bed-and-breakfast.de; Langenscheidtstrasse 5; s/d/tr/q shared bathroom €30/50/65/75; Ⓜ Kleistpark). Lofty ceilings and gorgeous wood floors dominate in this small, unique space with themed rooms (Asia, retro, fashionable). Excellent breakfast food is left for guests each day, which you prepare yourself in the communal kitchen.

TOUR BERLIN FOR FREE (OR A FEW EUROS)

Guided tours are phenomenally popular in Berlin, covering many themes, but the best introduction to the city is a free 3½-hour introductory walking tour offered by **New Berlin**. They leave at 10:30am and 12:30pm from the Dunkin' Donuts opposite the Zoologisher Gartern train station and 11am and 1pm outside the Starbucks at Pariser Platz near the Brandenburg Gate. Guides accept tips.

Alternatively, bus 100, the Museenlinie, runs a route past scores of museums, including all the Pinokotheks, between the Hauptbahnhof (north side) and the Ostbahnhof. Ask the tourists offices for details.

Circus Hotel (Map pp454-5; ☎ 2000 3939; www.circus-berlin.de; Rosenthalerstrasse 1; s €68, d from €78, ste €98, 2-/3-room apt €110/160; 🖳 ⊠; Ⓜ U-Bahn Rosenthaler Platz) The fancier younger sister to the Circus Hostel (left) across the intersection, every detail in this brand-spanking new hotel has been given careful attention – the result is a retro twist on minimalism, airy rooms, bold-coloured walls and supershiny wood flooring.

EATING

Berliners love eating out and you needn't walk far for a feed. Restaurants usually open from 11am to midnight, with varying *Ruhetage* or rest days, and many close during the day from 3pm to 6pm. Cafes often close around 8pm, though equal numbers stay open until 2am or later.

There's the excellent organic **Kollwitzplatz market** (Map pp454-5; 🕑 9am-4pm Sat & Sun), the relaxed **Winterfeldtplatz farmers market** (Map p458; 🕑 Wed & Sat) and the bustling, ultracheap **Türkenmarkt** (Map p460; Turkish market, 🕑 noon-6:30pm Tue & Fri).

Mitte & Prenzlauer Berg

La Focacceria (Map pp454-5; ☎ 4403 2771; Fehrbelliner Strasse 24; slices €1.50; 🕑 11am-11pm; Ⓜ Rosethaler Platz) A character-filled foccacia and pizza joint with an intense local following – perfect for an afternoon snack after a hard day's shopping or sightseeing.

Konnopke's Imbiss (Map pp454-5; Schönhauser Allee 44a; snacks €1.50-5; 🕑 6am-8pm Mon-Fri, 12-7pm Sat; Ⓜ Eberswalder Strasse) The quintessential Wurst

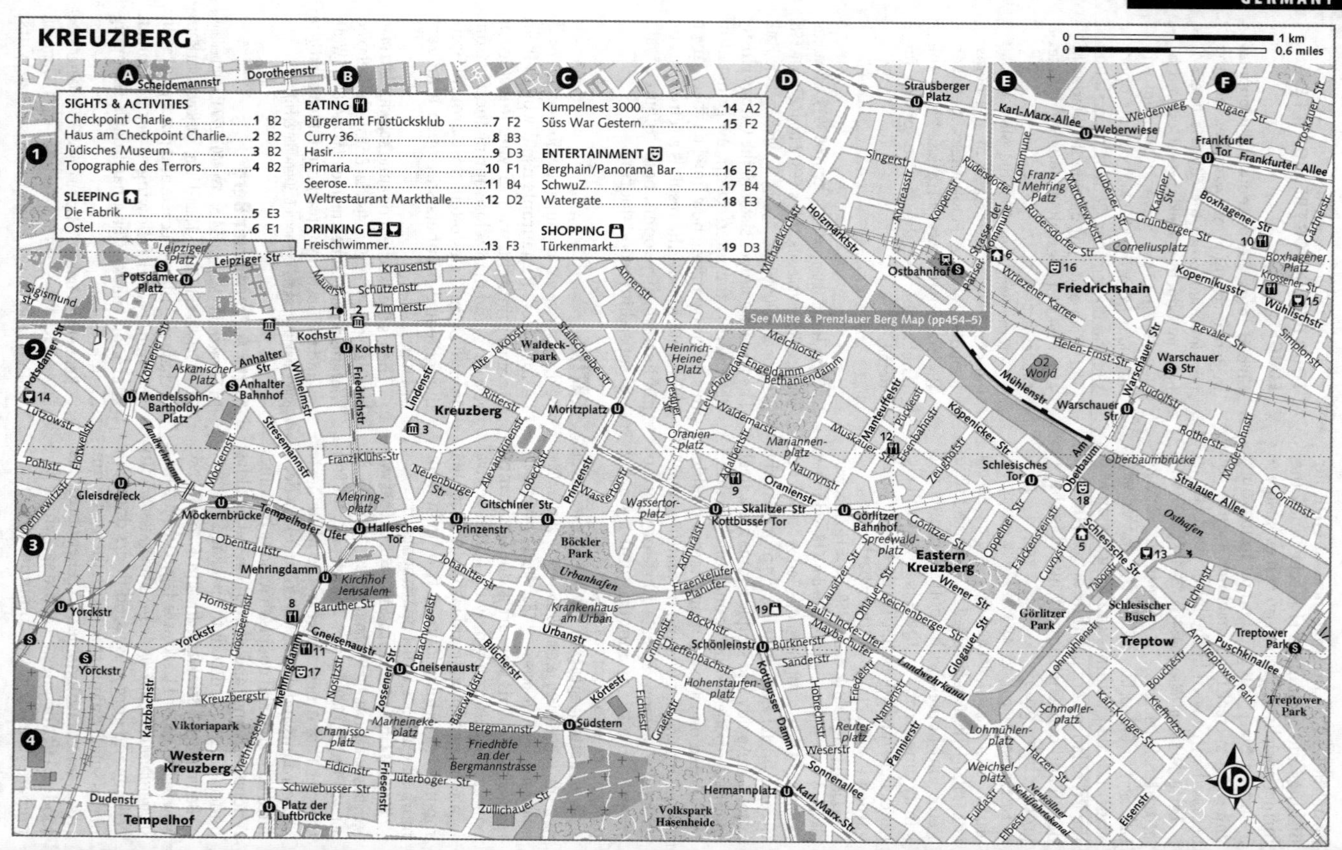
KREUZBERG
SIGHTS & ACTIVITIES
Checkpoint Charlie 1 B2
Haus am Checkpoint Charlie 2 B2
Jüdisches Museum 3 B2
Topographie des Terrors 4 B2
SLEEPING
Die Fabrik 5 E3
Ostel 6 E1
EATING
Bürgeramt Frühstücksklub 7 F2
Curry 36 8 B3
Hasir 9 D3
Primaria 10 F1
Seerose 11 B4
Weltrestaurant Markthalle 12 D2
DRINKING
Freischwimmer 13 F3
Kumpelnest 3000 14 A2
Süss War Gestern 15 F2
ENTERTAINMENT
Berghain/Panorama Bar 16 E2
SchwuZ 17 B4
Watergate 18 E3
SHOPPING
Türkenmarkt 19 D3
See Mitte & Prenzlauer Berg Map (pp454–5)
Friedrichshain
Kreuzberg
Eastern Kreuzberg
Western Kreuzberg
Treptow
Tempelhof

stand under the elevated U-Bahn tracks. We think Konnopke's serves the best *Currywurst* in town.

RNBS (Map pp454-5; ☎ 540 2505; Oranienburger Strasse 50; mains €3.50-6; M Oranienburger Strasse/Hackescher Markt) The Asian soups and noodle dishes served up by this tiny orange-and-white outlet are as delicious as they are healthy: no preservatives, no MSG, no artificial flavourings.

Sankt Oberholz (Map pp454-5; ☎ 2408 5586; Rosenthaler Strasse 72a; dishes €4-7; M Rosenthaler Platz) Berlin's '*Urbanen Pennern*' (officeless, self-employed creatives-types) have been flocking here for years with their laptops for the free wi-fi access, but we like it for the people-watching – especially from the lofty lifeguard chairs out front. Soups, sandwiches and salads are always satisfying.

our pick Assel (Map pp454-5; ☎ 281 2056; Oranienburgerstrasse 61; mains €5-15; M Oranienburger Strasse or Hackescher Markt) One of the few exceptional picks on a particularly touristy and busy stretch of Mitte, come for coffee, a bite or a full meal and stretch out in the wooden booths made from old S-Bahn seats. Plus, the toilets are entertaining (you'll see).

Monsieur Vuong (Map pp454-5; ☎ 3087 2643; Alte Schönhauser Strasse 46; mains €6.90; M Weinmeisterstrasse, Rosa-Luxemburg-Platz or Alexanderplatz) Berlin's original designer Asian soup den is trendy, packed and consistently serves amazing Vietnamese fare. Arrive early to avoid queuing.

Oderquelle (Map pp454-5; ☎ 4400 8080; Oderberger Strasse 27; mains €8-16; ⏲ dinner; M Eberswalder Strasse) Modern German food in such mellow, convivial digs is rare, almost as rare as snagging a table here after 7pm, so be sure to make reservations.

Borchardt (Map pp454-5; ☎ 8188 6250; Französische Strasse 47; mains €18-40; M Französische Strasse) On every Berlin *promi*'s (celeb's) speed-dial list, this refined French-German bistro also tolerates ordinary civilians.

Friedrichshain, Kreuzberg & Kreuzköln

Bürgeramt Früstücksklub (Map p460; Krossenerstrasse 22; burgers €2-4; ⏲ from 10am Sat & Sun, from 11am Mon-Fri; M Samariterstrasse) A mere 13 types of burgers, including chicken and veggie versions, are cooked up with love and a smile in this wee space – if you can't snag a seat head to the tree-filled square opposite. Hearty breakfast fare is also available.

Curry 36 (Map p460; ☎ 881 4710; Mehringdamm 36; snacks €2-6; ⏲ 9am-4pm Mon-Sat, to 3pm Sun; M Mehringdamm) This is Kreuzberg's most popular sausage stand, as evidenced by the daily queues (yes, it really is worth the wait).

Primaria (Map p460; ☎ 2904 4976; Boxhagener Strasse 26; mains €2-6; M Frankfurter Tor) Mostly meatless Bulgarian fare (salads, casseroles, lots of feta) in cosy digs and a friendly, helpful staff.

Hasir (Map p460; Adalbertstrasse 10; mains €5-10; ⏲ 24hr; M Kottbusser Tor) Local lore says this is the birthplace of the doner kebab – we haven't seen proof but we do know it tastes fantastic and we can indulge on proper chairs.

Seerose (Map p460; ☎ 6981 5927; Mehringdamm 47; dishes €7.50-8; M Mehringdamm) One of the most popular veggie restaurants in town serves imaginative organic fare – of pastas, soups and salads.

Weltrestaurant Markthalle (Map p460; ☎ 617 5502; Pücklerstrasse 34; mains €11.50-17; M Görlitzer Bahnhof) This wood-lined, century-old pub draws a mixed clientele of ageing hipsters and neighbourhood folk with its relaxed vibe and interesting German fare.

Charlottenburg & Schöneberg

Schwarzes Café (Map p458; ☎ 313 8038; Kantstrasse 148; dishes €4.50-10; M S-Bahn Zoo/Savignyplatz) Founded in 1978, this 24-hour food'n'booze institution must have seen half of Berlin pass through it (or out in it) at some point. Don't leave without checking out the toilets.

Petite Europe (off Map p458; ☎ 781 2964; Langenscheidtstrasse 1; mains €5-12; ⏲ dinner; M Kleistpark) Pizzas, pastas and other straightforward Italian fare are still going strong at this 40-year-old institution.

Engelbecken (off Map p458; ☎ 615 2810; Witzlebenstrasse 31; mains €8-18; ⏲ dinner only Mon-Sat, lunch & dinner Sun; M Sophie Charlotte Platz) Come here for what many rate as Berlin's best Bavarian food, with *Schweinsbraten*, schnitzels, dumplings and sauerkraut. All the meat is organic.

Café Einstein Stammhaus (Map p458; ☎ 261 5096; www.cafeeinstein.com, in German; Kurfürstenstrasse 58; breakfast €6-15, mains €15-23; ⏲ 9-1am; M Nollendorfplatz) You'll think you've hopped to another capital at this Viennese coffee house. Choose from schnitzel, strudel and other Austrian fare in the polished, palatial digs.

DRINKING

Gemütlichkeit, which roughly translates as cosy, warm and friendly, with a decided lack of anything hectic, dominates the upmarket

GAY & LESBIAN BERLIN

Still going strong since the 1920s, Schöneberg is the original gay area, but these days Prenzlauer Berg is the trendiest. Skim through **Berlin Gay Web** (http://berlin.gay-web.de, in German) for all things gay in Berlin.

SchwuZ (Map p460; ☎ 693 7025; www.schwuz.de; Mehringdamm 61; ⏲ from 11pm Fri & Sat; Ⓜ Mehringdamm) is one of the longest-running mixed institutions; there's a cafe here all week too.

A popular bar attracting a mixed crowd is **Zum Schmutzigen Hobby** (Map pp454-5; Rykestrasse 45; ⏲ from 5pm; Ⓜ Eberswalder Strasse) run by well-known drag queen Nina Queer.

bars of the west as well as the hipper, more underground venues in the east. Prenzlauer Berg, the first GDR sector to develop a happening nightlife, still attracts visitors, creative types and gay customers, but as its residents have aged (and produced many, many babies) its nightlife has become more subdued. Clubs and bars in Mitte around Hackescher Markt cater to a cool, slightly older and wealthier crowd. Friedrichshain boasts a young hipster feel and Kreuzberg remains the alternative hub, becoming grungier as you move east. Charlottenburg and Winterfeldtplatz are fairly upmarket and mature, but liberal.

Bars without food open between 5pm and 8pm and may close as late as 5am (if at all).

Astrobar (off Map pp454-5; ☎ 2966 1615; Simon-Dach-Strasse 40; Ⓜ S-Bahn Warschauer Strasse) The Astro offers the future as it looked in the 1960s, with spaceships, robots and classic computer games in the back room. DJs start spinning after 10pm.

Kumpelnest 3000 (Map p460; ☎ 8891 7960; Lützowstrasse 23; Ⓜ Kurfürstenstrasse) Once a brothel, always an experience – the Kumpelnest has been famed since the '80s for its wild, inhibition-free nights. Much of the original whorehouse decor remains intact. We've had reports that pickpockets operate here – be aware.

Prater (Map pp454-5; Kastanienallee 7-9; Ⓜ Eberswalder Strasse) A summer institution, come to Berlin's oldest beer garden (since 1837) for a tall chilled draught under the canopy of chestnut trees.

our pick **Freischwimmer** (Map p460; ☎ 6107 4309; Vor dem Schlesischen Tor 2a; ⏲ from 2pm Mon-Fri, from 11am Sat & Sun, reduced hours in winter; Ⓜ Schlesisches Tor) It was a boathouse, now it's a bar that entices with its chill vibe and a view of the tranquil canal.

Süss War Gestern (Map p460; Wülischstrasse 43; Ⓜ S-Bahn Ostkreuz) Street art–covered walls, 1970s decorations and comfortable sofas make this outpost worth the trek. Most nights feature a DJ spinning anything from funk to soul to electric music.

CLUBBING

Few club opens before 11pm (and if you arrive before midnight you may be dancing solo) but they stay open well into the early hours – usually sunrise at least. As the scene changes so rapidly, it's always wise to double-check listings magazines or ask locals. Admission charges, when they apply, range from €5 to €15.

Berghain/Panorama Bar (Map p460; www.berghain.de; Am Wriezener Bahnhof; ⏲ from midnight Thu-Sat; Ⓜ Ostbahnhof) If you only make it to one club in Berlin, this is where you need to go. The upper floor (Panoramabar, aka 'Pannebar') is all about house; the big factory hall below (Berghain) goes hardcore techno. Expect cutting-edge sounds in industrial surrounds.

Kaffee Burger (Map pp454-5; ☎ 2804 6495; www.kaffeeburger.de; Torstrasse 60; Ⓜ Rosa-Luxemburg-Platz) The original GDR '60s wallpaper is part of the decor at this arty bar, club and music venue in Mitte. Burger hosts popular monthly readings by local (mainly expat) writers in English, but many come here for indie, rock, punk and cult author Wladimir Kaminer's fortnightly *Russendisko* (Russian disco; www.russendisko.de).

Watergate (Map p460; ☎ 6128 0394; www.water-gate.de; Falckensteinstrasse 49a; ⏲ from 11pm Fri & Sat; Ⓜ Schlesisches Tor) Watch the sun rise over the Spree River through the floor-to-ceiling windows of this fantastic lounge. The music is mainly electro, drum'n'bass and hip-hop.

ENTERTAINMENT

Berlin is not only famous for its clubs – its cultural offerings are also renowned. So if you fancy splashing out on a quieter, more refined evening, try one of the following.

Staatsoper Unter den Linden (Map pp454-5; ☎ information 203 540, tickets 2035 4555; www.staatsoper-berlin.de; Unter den Linden 5-7; Ⓜ S-Bahn Unter den Linden) This is the handiest and most prestigious of Berlin's three opera houses, where unsold seats go on sale cheap an hour before curtains-up.

Berliner Ensemble (Map pp454-5; ☎ information 284 080, tickets 2840 8155; www.berliner-ensemble.de; Bertolt-Brecht-Platz 1; Ⓜ Friedrichstrasse) 'Mack the Knife' had its first public airing here, during the *Threepenny Opera's* premiere in 1928. Bertolt Brecht's former theatrical home continues to present his plays.

GETTING THERE & AWAY

Air

Berlin has two international airports, reflecting the legacy of the divided city. The larger one is in the northwestern suburb of Tegel (TXL), about 8km from the city centre; the other is in Schönefeld (SXF), about 22km southeast of town. For information about either, go to www.berlin-airport.de or call ☎ 0180-500 0186.

Berlin will eventually get its own major international airport, as Schönefeld is being expanded into Berlin Brandenburg International (BBI or BER); estimated completion date is 2011.

Bus

Most buses arrive at and depart from the **Zentraler Omnibusbahnhof** (ZOB; off Map p458; ☎ 302 5361; Masurenallee 4-6; Ⓜ Kaiserdamm/Witzleben), opposite the Funkturm radio tower. Tickets are available from travel agencies or at the bus station.

Car

Lifts can be organised by **ADM Mitfahrzentrale** (www.mitfahrzentralen.org, in German; ride-share agencies); two branches are located in Berlin, one in **Zoo station** (Map p458; ☎ 194 40; 🕓 9am-8pm Mon-Fri, 10am-6pm Sat & Sun), the other nearby in **Hardenbergplatz** (Map p458; ☎ 194 240; Hardenbergplatz 14; 🕓 9am-8pm Mon-Fri, 10am-2pm Sat, 10am-4pm Sun).

Train

Long-distance services arrive at the architecturally spectacular Hauptbahnhof (also called Lehrter Bahnhof), with many continuing east to Ostbahnhof and Lichtenberg. ICE and IC trains leave hourly to every major city in Germany and there are connections to central Europe. Sample fares include Leipzig (€34, 1¼ hours), Hamburg (€65, 1½ to two hours) and Prague (€56.80, 4½ to five hours).

GETTING AROUND

Berlin's public transport system is excellent and a much better choice than driving around the city. One type of ticket is valid on all transport and three tariff zones exist – A, B and C. Unless venturing to Potsdam or the outer suburbs, you'll only need an AB ticket, costing €2.10 for a single, €6.10 for a day pass and €15.40 for a group day pass for up to five people.

Most tickets are available from vending machines in stations, but must be validated before hopping on the train or bus, or as you enter them.

Services operate from 4am until just after midnight on weekdays, with many *Nachtbus* (night bus) services in between. At weekends, they run all night long (except the U4).

AROUND BERLIN

Despite its proximity to Berlin, Brandenburg has suffered from a poor reputation since reunification. Many western Germans still think of Brandenburgers as archetypal Ossis, ambivalent about the demise of the GDR and perhaps even a touch xenophobic. However, even the most sneering Wessi will happily go to Potsdam on a day trip.

POTSDAM

☎ 0331 / pop 150,000

With ornate palaces and manicured gardens dotted around a huge riverside park, the Prussian royal seat of Potsdam makes a relaxing break from wired Berlin. Elector Friedrich Wilhelm of Brandenburg made the town his second home in the 17th century, but it was Friedrich II (Frederick the Great) who sealed its fame by commissioning the palaces in the mid-18th century.

In August 1945, the victorious WWII Allies chose nearby Schloss Cecilienhof for the Potsdam Conference, which set the stage for the division of Berlin and Germany into occupation zones.

Orientation

Potsdam Hauptbahnhof is just southeast of the city centre, across the Havel River. As this is still quite a way (2km) from Sansoucci Park, you might like to change trains here; see Getting There & Around for more details.

Information

Potsdam Information (☎ 275 580; www.potsdamtourismus.de; Brandenburger Strasse 3; 🕓 9.30am-6pm

Mon-Fri, 9.30am-4pm Sat & Sun Apr-Oct, 10am-6pm Mon-Fri, 9.30am-2pm Sat & Sun Nov-Mar) Near the Hauptbahnhof.

Sanssouci Besucherzentrum (☎ 969 4202; www.spsg.de; An der Orangerie 1; ⏰ 8.30am-5pm Mar-Oct, 9am-4pm Nov-Feb) Near the windmill and Schloss Sanssouci.

Sights

SANSSOUCI PARK

At the heart of **Sanssouci Park** (admission free; ⏰ dawn to dusk) lies a celebrated rococo palace, **Schloss Sanssouci** (☎ 969 4190; adult/concession €12/8 Apr-Oct, €8/5 Nov-Mar; ⏰ 10am-6pm Tue-Sun Apr-Oct, to 5pm Nov-Mar). Built in 1747, it has some glorious interiors. Only 2000 visitors are allowed entry each day (a Unesco rule), so tickets are usually sold by 2.30pm, even in quiet seasons. Tours run by the tourist office guarantee entry.

The late-baroque **Neues Palais** (New Palace; ☎ 969 4255; adult/concession €6/5; ⏰ 10am-6pm, closed Tue, to 5pm Nov-Mar) was built in 1769 as the royal family's summer residence. It's one of the most imposing buildings in the park and the one to see if your time is limited.

The **Bildergalerie** (Picture Gallery; ☎ 969 4181; adult/concession €3/2.50; ⏰ 10am-6pm Tue-Sun 15 May-Oct) contains a rich collection of 17th-century paintings by Rubens, Caravaggio and other big names.

Many consider the **Chinesisches Haus** (Chinese Teahouse; ☎ 969 4222; admission €2; ⏰ 10am-6pm Tue-Sun 15 May-Oct) to be the pearl of the park. It's a circular pavilion of gilded columns, palm trees and figures of Chinese musicians and animals, built in 1757.

NEUER GARTEN

Located in the separate New Garden, northeast of the centre on the bank of Heiliger See, **Schloss Cecilienhof** (☎ 969 4244; tours adult/concession €4/3; ⏰ 9am-5pm Tue-Sun) is an incongruously English-style country manor in rococo-heavy Potsdam.

British PM Winston Churchill, US President Harry Truman and Soviet leader Josef Stalin met here in 1945 for the Potsdam Conference on administering postwar Germany. Large photos of the participants are displayed inside.

OTHER ATTRACTIONS

In April 1945, Royal Air Force bombers devastated the historic centre of Potsdam, but fortunately some pivotal features survived undamaged.

The **Brandenburger Tor** (Brandenburg Gate) at the western end of the old town on Luisenplatz isn't a patch on the one in Berlin, but it is older, dating from 1770. From here, pedestrianised Brandenburger Strasse runs due east, providing the town's main eating strip.

Standing out from its surrounds is the pretty **Holländisches Viertel** (Dutch Quarter). Towards the northern end of Friedrich-Ebert-Strasse, it has 134 gabled red-brick houses, built for Dutch workers who came to Potsdam in the 1730s at the invitation of Friedrich Wilhelm I.

Germany's **UFA Film Studios** (☎ 721 2755; www.filmpark.de; Grossbeerenstrasse; adult/concession €19/16; ⏰ 10am-6pm 7 Apr-31 Oct) was where Fritz Lang's *Metropolis* was shot and FW Murnau filmed the first Dracula movie, *Nosferatu*. Since a relaunch in 1999, it's helped Berlin regain its film-making crown. At research time, Quentin Tarantino's *Inglorious Bastards* starring Brad Pitt was making local headlines. The studios are east of the city centre.

Tours

Boats belonging to **Weisse Flotte** (☎ 275 9210; www.schiffahrt-in-potsdam.de; Lange Brücke 6; ⏰ 9.45am-7pm Apr-Oct) cruise the Havel and the lakes around Potsdam, departing regularly from the dock near Lange Brücke, with frequent trips to Wannsee (€8/11 one way/return) and around the castles (€10).

Getting There & Around

S-Bahn line S7 links central Berlin with Potsdam Hauptbahnhof about every 10 minutes. Some regional (RB/RE) trains from Berlin stop at all three stations in Potsdam. Your ticket must cover Berlin Zones A, B and C (€2.80) to come here.

SACHSENHAUSEN CONCENTRATION CAMP

In 1936 the Nazis opened a 'model' **concentration camp** (☎ 03301-200 200; www.gedenkstaette-sachsenhausen.de; admission free; ⏰ 8.30am-6pm Tue-Sun Apr-Sep, to 4.30pm Oct-Mar) near Oranienburg some 35km north of Berlin. By 1945 about 220,000 prisoners had passed through the gates of Sachsenhausen. About 100,000 people died here. After the war, the Soviets and the communist leaders of the new GDR used the camp for *their* undesirables.

Plan on spending at least two hours. Among the many monuments and museums are **Barracks 38 & 39**, with excellent displays on the camp's history. Maps, brochures, booklets and audio guides (also in English) are available.

The easiest way to get to Sachsenhausen from Berlin is to take the frequent S1 to Oranienburg (€2.80, 50 minutes). The walled camp is a signposted 20-minute walk from Oranienburg station.

EASTERN GERMANY

Germany's eastern heartland is for many people (Germans included) the most historically German. Its three states all have their own distinct character. Saxony lives off its reputation based on the momentous history of cities such as Leipzig and Dresden. Thuringia, the self-touted 'green heart' of Germany, entices hordes of visitors to the humanist bastion of Weimar and the state capital Erfurt. Saxony-Anhalt boasts a good swathe of the lovely Harz Mountains (sharing them with Lower Saxony).

Together with Brandenburg, East Berlin and Mecklenburg-Western Pomerania, these states made up the GDR. In the popular towns such as Dresden you'll still easily see vestiges of things past in the monumental – and monumentally ugly – 1960s blocks of buildings around (and sometimes in) the centre.

Any trips south of Berlin should really include stops in this fun and fascinating region.

DRESDEN

☎ 0351 / pop 484,000

In life, Dresden was famous throughout Europe as 'Florence on the Elbe', owing to the efforts of Italian artists, musicians, actors and master craftsmen who flocked to the court of Augustus the Strong, bestowing countless masterpieces upon the city. In death, Dresden became even more famous. Shortly before the end of WWII, Allied bombers blasted and incinerated much of the historic centre, a beautiful jewel-like area dating from the 18th century. More than 35,000 people died, and in bookshops throughout town you can find books showing the destruction (or read about it in Kurt Vonnegut's classic *Slaughterhouse Five*).

Rebuilding began under the communist regime in the 1950s and accelerated greatly after reunification. The city celebrated its 800th anniversary in 2006 and while much focus is on the restored centre, you should cross the Elbe River to the Neustadt, where edgy new clubs and cafes open every week, joining the 150 already there.

Information

Dresden Information Prager Strasse 2 (☎ 4919 2100; www.dresden.de; 🕒 10am-7pm Mon-Sat); Theaterplatz 2 (🕒 10am-6pm Mon-Fri, to 4pm Sat & Sun) Discount cards from €21.

Haus Des Buches (☎ 497 369; Dr-Külz-Ring 12) Bookshop with huge selection on local history and culture.

K&E Callshop (Wiener Passage; per hr €2; 🕒 10am-10pm) In the subterranean passageway outside the Hauptbahnhof.

Sights

Dresden straddles the Elbe River, with the attraction-studded Altstadt (old town) in the south and the livelier Neustadt to the north. One of Dresden's most beloved icons, the **Frauenkirche** (Church of Our Lady; ☎ 439 3934; www.frauenkirche-dresden.org; Neumarkt; 🕒 10am-6pm) on **Neumarkt**, was rebuilt in time for the city's 800th anniversary celebrations. Built between 1726 and 1743 under the direction of baroque architect George Bähr, it was Germany's greatest Protestant church until February 1945, when bombing raids flattened it.

Leading northwest from Neumarkt is Augustusstrasse, with the stunning 102m-long **Procession of Princes** porcelain mural covering the outer wall of the old royal stables. Augustusstrasse leads directly to Schlossplatz and the baroque Catholic **Hofkirche** (1755). Just south of the church is the Renaissance **Schloss**, which is being reconstructed. Outside, don't miss the amazing 102m-long tiled mural, the **Fürstenzug** (Procession of Princes; Augustusstrasse), on the wall of the former Stendehaus (Royal Stables). The scene, a long row of royalty on horses, was painted in 1876 and then transferred to some 24,000 Meissen porcelain tiles in 1906.

THEATERPLATZ

On the western side of the Hofkirche is Theaterplatz, with Dresden's glorious opera house, the neo-Renaissance **Semperoper** (☎ 491 1496; www.semperoper.de; Theaterplatz; tours €7) – if you've watched any German TV you'll probably recognise it from a certain beer commercial. The opera tradition goes back 350 years, and many works by Richard Strauss, Carl Maria von Weber and Richard Wagner premiered here.

Next door, the baroque **Zwinger fortress** (☎ 491 4622; Theaterplatz 1; ⏰ 10am-6pm Tue-Sun) is another great Dresden heavyweight, with no fewer than six museums within its ornate walls. The most important are the **Rüstkammer**, with its superb collection of ceremonial weapons, and the **Galerie Alte Meister** (admission €7, incl entry to Rüstkammer), which features masterpieces including Raphael's *Sistine Madonna*. The dazzling **Porcelain Collection** (☎ 491 4622; adult/concession €6/3.50) includes plenty of local Meissen classics.

BRÜHLSCHE TERRASSE

The imposing block **Albertinum** (☎ 491 4619; Brühlsche Terrasse) houses many of Dresden's art treasures, including the **Galerie Neue Meister**, renowned for its 19th- and 20th-century paintings from leading French and German impressionists. The complex is meant to reopen in 2010 after a massive reconstruction. **Sächsische Dampfschiffahrt** (☎ 866 090; tours from €16) runs river tours on rebuilt steam ships from the docks below the terrace.

Sleeping

Accommodation in Dresden can be very expensive in the high season. Luckily, several good-value budget places can be found in the lively Neustadt.

Hostel & Backpacker kangaroo-stop (☎ 314 3455; www.kangaroo-stop.de; Erna-Berger-Strasse 8-10; dm/s/d from €13/29/38; P ⊠ 💻) Welcoming and low-key, with rooms spread over two buildings; one for backpackers and the other for families. So which will see more immature behaviour? The internet is free and the big breakfast buffet costs €5. Dresden-Neustadt station is nearby.

Hostel Louise 20 (☎ 889 4894; www.louise20.de; Louisenstrasse 20; dm/s/d from €14/30/40; 💻) Rooms are divided between two buildings here. Basic ones are off a courtyard at the back while more expensive – and Ikea-styled – units are up front. Families can rent entire suites of rooms. The Dresden-Neustadt station is a 10-minute walk away.

Jugendgästehaus Dresden (☎ 492 620; www.jugendherberge.de; Maternistrasse 22; dm €19; 💻 ⊠) This tower block was once a Communist Party training centre; now it's a huge hostel (HI), with 480 beds in small dorms and a bistro (breakfast included). Take tram 7 or 10 to the corner of Ammonstrasse and Freiberger Strasse.

Hotel Martha Hospiz (☎ 817 60; www.hotel-martha-hospiz.de; Nieritzstrasse 11; s/d €55/120; P 💻) Hospitality is taken very seriously at this lovely quiet inn, which is close to the lively Königstrasse. Newer rooms are decked out in Biedermeier-style. There's wi-fi, and breakfast is €10.

EV-Ref Gemeinde zu Dresden (☎ 438 230; www.ev-ref-gem-dresden.de; Brühlscher Garten 4; s/d €60/75) The name is not a marketer's dream, but this pension is amazing value in a great location – right across from the Albertinum and on the river. This historic retirement home makes rooms available for travellers whenever a resident has permanently 'checked out'. Rooms have showers and TV and often great views; breakfast is included.

Eating

It's no problem finding somewhere to eat in the Neustadt, with oodles of cafes and restaurants found along Königstrasse and the streets north of Albertplatz. This is the centre of nightlife. You'll be going until dawn, with dozens of choices.

Raskolnikoff (☎ 804 5706; www.raskolnikoff.de; Böhmische Strasse 34; mains €4-12) This bohemian cafe in a former artists' squat was one of the Neustadt's first post-Wende pubs. The menu is sorted by compass direction (borscht to quiche Lorraine to smoked fish), there's a sweet, ivy-lined little beer garden out back, and a gallery and pension (rooms €40 to €55) upstairs.

Cafe Kontinental (☎ 801 3531; Görlitzer Strasse 1; mains €5-15; ⏰ 24hr; 💻) A bustling place open around the clock, this trendy cafe caters to a broad swath of Neustadt characters.

Lloyd's Café & Bar (☎ 5018774; Martin-Luther-Strasse 17; mains €6-10) Across a square from the Martin Luther Kirche, this swank place is a bargain given the creamy leather seating, high style and year-round gelato sales. Breakfast is served all day. Also salads, paninis and pasta.

Drinking

The places listed under Eating above are also good just for a drink.

Blue Note (☎ 801 4275; www.jazzdepartment.com; Görlitzer Strasse 2b; ⏰ until 5am or later) Small, smoky and smooth, this converted smithy has live jazz almost nightly until 11pm, then turns into a night owl magnet until the wee hours. The talent is mostly regional.

Café 100 (☎ 801 7729; Alaunstrasse 100) Off a courtyard, you'll pass hundreds of empty bottles on the way in, a foreshadowing of the lengthy wine list and delights that follow. Candles give the underground space a romantic yet edgy glow.

Katy's Garage (☎ 656 7701; Alaunstrasse 48) This place, a key venue for indie gigs and club nights throughout the week, is in a former tyre shop.

Queens (☎ 810 8108; Görlitzerstrasse 3) This hopping gay bar/lounge/disco is a good first stop to find out what's happening locally.

Scheunecafé (☎ 802 6619; Alaunstrasse 36-40; mains €7-12) Set back from the street, Indian food, a vast beer garden, live music and DJs all combine here for a fun and funky stew.

Entertainment

Dresden is synonymous with opera, and performances at the spectacular **Semperoper** (☎ 491 1496; www.semperoper.de; Theaterplatz), opposite the Zwinger, are brilliant. Tickets cost from €10, but they're usually booked out well in advance. Some performances by the renowned Philharmonic are also held here.

Getting There & Around

Dresden Airport (DRS; www.dresden-airport.de), served by Lufthansa and Air Berlin among others, is 9km north of the city centre.

Dresden is well linked by regular services throughout the day to Leipzig (€26, 70 minutes), Berlin-Hauptbahnhof by IC/EC train (€36, 2¼ hours) and Frankfurt-am-Main by ICE (€85, 4½ hours).

Trams 3, 7, 8 and 9 (€1.80) provide good links between the Hauptbahnhof and Neustadt.

AROUND DRESDEN

Meissen

☎ 03521 / pop 29,000

Some 27km northwest of Dresden, Meissen is a compact, perfectly preserved old town and the centre of a rich wine-growing region. It makes for a good day trip out of Dresden by train or boat and beguiles with its red-tiled roofs and old Saxon charm.

The tourist office is at **Meissen-Information** (☎ 419 40; www.touristinfo-meissen.de; Markt 3; ⌚ 10am-6pm Mon-Fri, to 4pm Sat & Sun Apr-Oct, to 4pm Mon-Fri, to 3pm Sat Nov-Mar). Staff can help find accommodation. The Markt is framed by the **Rathaus** (town hall; 1472) and the Gothic **Frauenkirch**, which – fittingly – has a porcelain carillon.

Meissen's medieval fortress, the 15th-century **Albrechtsburg** (☎ 470 70; Domplatz 1; admission €4; ⌚ 10am-6pm Mar-Oct, to 5pm Nov-Feb), crowns a ridge high above the Elbe River reached by steep lanes. It contains the former ducal palace and Meissen Cathedral, a magnificent Gothic structure.

Next door, the towering 13th-century **Albrechtsburg Cathedral** (☎ 452 490; Domplatz 7; admission €3.50; ⌚ 10am-6pm Mar-Oct, to 4pm Nov-Feb) contains an altarpiece by Lucas Cranach the Elder.

Meissen has long been renowned for its chinaware, with its trademark insignia of blue crossed swords. Meissen's porcelain factory is now 1km southwest of the Altstadt in an appropriately beautiful building, the **Porzellan-Museum** (☎ 468 700; Talstrasse 9; admission €8; ⌚ 9am-6pm May-Oct, to 5pm Nov-Apr), which dates to 1916.

Half-hourly S-Bahn trains run from Dresden's Hauptbahnhof and Neustadt train stations (€5.50, 40 minutes). To visit the porcelain factory, get off at Meissen-Triebischtal (one stop after Meissen).

LEIPZIG

☎ 0341 / pop 498,000

Leipzig is the busiest city in Saxony, a bustling, more commercial alternative to Dresden. Although it lacks the capital's busload of museums, Leipzig is not weighed down by the past and like its shopping passages, invites exploration.

Leipzig also has some of the finest classical music and opera in the country, and its art and literary scenes are flourishing. It was once home to Bach, Wagner and Mendelssohn, as well as Goethe, who set a key scene of *Faust* in the cellar of his favourite watering hole. More recently, it earned the sobriquet *Stadt der Helden* (City of Heroes) for its leading role in the 1989 democratic revolution.

Information

The Hauptbahnhof contains a modern mall with more than 140 shops and, radically for Germany, it is open 6am to 10pm seven days a week. You'll find good bookshops, a post office, banks and much more.

Internetcafé (☎ 993 9530; Reichsstrasse 18; per 30min €1; ⏰ 10am-10pm) A full-service internet shop for CD burning plus cheap calls and copies.

Leipzig Tourist Service (☎ 710 4260; www.leipzig.de; Richard-Wagner-Strasse 1; ⏰ 9.30am-6pm Mon-Fri, to 4pm Sat, to 3pm Sun) One of the most helpful in Germany, with discount cards from €9.

Sights

Don't rush from sight to sight – wandering around Leipzig is a pleasure in itself, with many of the blocks around the central Markt crisscrossed by old internal shopping passages, including the classic **Mädlerpassage**.

MONUMENTS & LANDMARKS

Off the southern ring road is the impressive 108m-high tower of the baroque **Neues Rathaus** (New Town Hall; ☎ 1230; Martin-Luther-Ring; ⏰ 7am-4.30pm Mon-Fri). Although the building's origins date back to the 16th century, its current manifestation was completed in 1905.

Located 4km southeast of the centre, the **Völkerschlachtdenkmal** (Battle of Nations Monument; ☎ 878 0471; Prager Strasse; admission €5; ⏰ 10am-6pm Apr-Oct, to 4pm Nov-Mar) is a massive 91m-high monument commemorating the decisive victory here by the combined Prussian, Austrian and Russian forces over Napoleon's army in 1813. Climb the 500 steps for a view of the region. Take tram 15 from the station (direction Meusdorf).

MUSEUMS

Leipzig's finest museum, the **Museum der Bildenden Künste** (Museum of Fine Arts; ☎ 216 990; Grimmaische Strasse 1-7; admission €5; ⏰ 10am-6pm Tue & Thu-Sun, noon-8pm Wed) is housed in a stunning building that provides a dramatic backdrop to its collection, which spans old masters and the latest efforts of the many noted local artists.

Haunting and uplifting by turns, the **Zeitgeschichtliches Forum** (Forum of Contemporary History; ☎ 222 20; Grimmaische Strasse 6; admission free; ⏰ 9am-6pm Tue-Fri, 10am-6pm Sat & Sun) tells the story of the GDR from division and dictatorship to resistance and reform.

Former headquarters of the East German secret police, the **Stasi Museum** (☎ 961 2443; Dittrichring 24; admission free; ⏰ 10am-6pm) has exhibits on propaganda, amazingly hokey disguises, surveillance photos and other forms of 'intelligence'.

Opposite the Thomaskirche is the **Bach Museum** (☎ 964 110; Thomaskirchhof 16; admission free; ⏰ 11am-6pm), where JS Bach worked from 1723 until his death in 1750. This collection focuses on the composer's busy life in Leipzig. Displays are temporary while restorations continue.

Sleeping

Leipzig Tourist Service offers free booking in private homes near the centre. Average cost is €30 to €50.

Camping Am Auensee (☎ 465 1600; www.motel-auensee.de; Gustav-Esche-Strasse 5; camp sites per person from €5, cabins €35-60) This camping ground is in a pleasant wooded spot on the city's northwestern outskirts (take tram 10 or 11 to Wahren). The cabins are A-frame bungalows.

Central Globetrotter Hostel (☎ 149 8960; www.globetrotter-leipzig.de; Kurt-Schumacher-Strasse 41; dm €13-15, s/d €24/36, linen €2, breakfast €4; ⊠ 💻) In a busy location just north of the train station, this 80-room hostel offers bare-bones accommodation, although some rooms boast murals, albeit ones that won't win any scholarships to the Art Academy of Leipzig.

Hostel Sleepy Lion (☎ 993 9480; www.hostel-leipzig.de; Käthe-Kollwitz-Strasse 3; dm from €14, s/d €30/45; ⊠ 💻) Budget-minded nomads will feel welcome at this low-key hostel, with 60 clean and comfy beds in cheerfully painted rooms with private facilities. Major sights are just steps away; breakfast is €4.

Hotel Kosmos (☎ 233 44 22; www.hotel-kosmos.de; Gottschedstrasse 1; s/d from €50/80) Right on a street with burgeoning nightlife, this low-key place in a grand building combines GDR-era furniture with murals in themed rooms. The murals next to the bed in the Marilyn Monroe room may fool the foolhardy.

Eating

Zum Arabischen Coffe Baum (☎ 965 1321; Kleine Fleischergasse 4; mains €6-15) Leipzig's oldest coffee bar has a restaurant and cafe offering excellent meals over three floors, plus a free coffee museum at the top. Composer Robert Schumann met friends here, and if you ask nicely you can sit at his regular table.

Barthel's Hof (☎ 141 310; Hainstrasse 1; mains €7-22) This is a sprawling place with outdoor seating in a courtyard, lots of roasts with thick, oniony sauces and quirky Saxon dishes such as *Heubraten* (marinated lamb roasted on hay).

Koslik (☎ 998 5993; Zentralstrasse 1; mains €8-14; 🕑 9-1am) A stylish wood interior complements the tasty world cuisine offered here, with great breakfasts and meals from pizza to Thai soup to Swiss potato *rösti*.

Auerbachs Keller (☎ 216 100; www.auerbachs-keller-leipzig.de; Mädlerpassage; mains €14-22) Founded in 1525, Auerbachs Keller is one of Germany's classic restaurants, serving typically hearty fare. Goethe's *Faust – Part I* includes a scene here, in which Mephistopheles and Faust carouse with some students before they ride off on a barrel.

Drinking

Barfussgässchen and Kleine Fleischergasse, west of the Markt, form one of Leipzig's two 'pub miles', packed with outdoor tables that fill up the second the weather turns warm. The other is on Gottschedstrasse, a wider cafe strip just west of the Altstadt.

Moritz-Bastei (☎ 702 590; www.moritzbastei.de; Universitätsstrasse 9) One of the best student clubs in Germany, in a spacious cellar below the old city walls. It has live music or DJs most nights and runs films outside in summer.

Sixtina (☎ 0177-476 4855; Katharinenstrasse 11) At some point in the last few years the word 'absinthe' has ceased to mean 'bad idea', and the result is places like Sixtina, wholly dedicated to the deadly green fairy. Part the foliage on the way in.

our pick **Spizz** (☎ 960 8043; Markt 9) Classic brass instruments dangle above the stage at this city slicker, where you might catch some cool jazz. It has three levels, a good range of wines and beers and a fine sidewalk cafe that's good day or night.

Getting There & Around

Leipzig-Halle airport (LEJ; www.leipzig-halle-airport.de) has only a few flights. Ryanair serves tiny **Altenburg airport** (ADC; www.flughafen-altenburg.de), some 53km from Leipzig. There's a shuttle bus (€12, 1¾ hours) timed to coincide with the flights to/from London.

Regular service through the day includes Dresden (€26, 70 minutes), Munich by ICE (€84, five hours), Berlin-Hauptbahnhof by ICE (€40, 70 minutes) and Frankfurt-am-Main (€63, 3½ hours).

Trams are the main public transport option, with most lines running via the Hauptbahnhof. A single ticket costs €2 and a day card is €5.20.

ERFURT

☎ 0361 / pop 203,000

Thuringia's capital was founded by St Boniface as a bishopric in 742. In the Middle Ages the city shot to prominence and prosperity as an important trading post. The Altstadt's many well-preserved 16th-century and later buildings attest to its wealth.

Damage during WWII was extensive, and the GDR regime did little to restore the city's former glories. Over the past decade, however, Erfurt has spiffed up what it has and a stroll through the old streets and across the rivers is a delight.

Information

Erfurt Tourismus (☎ 664 00; www.erfurt-tourist-info.de; Benediktsplatz 1; 🕑 10am-7pm Mon-Fri, to 4pm Sat & Sun) Has a discount card from €9.90.

Tourist Thüringen (☎ 374 2388; Willy-Brandt-Platz 1; 🕑 9am-7pm Mon-Fri, 10am-4pm Sat & Sun) Regional tourism office is directly in front of the station.

Sights

The numerous interesting lanes and alleys in Erfurt's surprisingly large Altstadt make this a fascinating place to explore. Whatever you do, though, you shouldn't miss the massive 13th-century Gothic **Dom St Marien** (☎ 646 1265; Domplatz; tours €2.50; 🕑 9am-5pm Mon-Fri, to 4.30pm Sat, 1-5pm Sun, less in winter) and **Severikirche**, which dominate the central Domplatz square. The stained glass and elaborate portals make the cathedral one of the most richly ornamented medieval churches in Germany. The Severikirche, meanwhile, boasts the sarcophagus of St Severus.

The eastbound street beside the Rathaus leads to the restored **Krämerbrücke** (1325), a narrow medieval bridge lined with timber-framed shops – it's the only such structure north of the Alps. Further north, on the same side of the river, is the **Augustinerkloster** (☎ 576 600; Augustinerstrasse; admission €8; 🕑 tours 10am-noon & 2-5pm Tue-Sat, 11am-2pm Sun), a late-medieval monastery that was home to Martin Luther in the 16th century and now puts up tourists and conference guests.

Sleeping & Eating

Re_4Hostel (☎ 6000 110; www.re4hostel.de; Pushkinstrasse 21; dm €13-16, s/d €26/52; P ⊠ 💻) Rooms in this former police station range from hotel-like twins to hostel-like dorms. Bedding and towels cost extra. Breakfast and bike rental both cost €5 (the latter per day).

Hotel & Gasthof Nikolai (☎ 5981 7119; www.hotel-nikolai-erfurt.com; Augustinerstrasse 30; r €80-100; P ☒) The location alongside the river, the overall high standard of the 17 rooms, and the friendly owners make this a prime choice. The restaurant is good and there's a fine garden plus a beautiful curved wooden staircase.

Anger Maier (☎ 566 1058; Schlösserstrasse 8; meals €6-12) This tunnel-like restaurant is an Erfurt student institution, with cheap, quality eats in a busy, smoky old warren. Set your lungs free in the leafy beer garden.

Zum Goldenen Schwann (☎ 2623 742; Michaelisstrasse 9; mains €5-12.50) It's not so much the unpretentious traditional food that makes this place popular locally, rather the highly rated unfiltered boutique beer.

Look for interesting and trendy restaurants and cafes along Michaelisstrasse and Marbacher Gasse. For a quick treat, have a *thuringer Bratwurst* hot off the grill from a **stand** (☎ 793 5250; Schlösserstrasse; meals €2) near a small waterfall.

Getting There & Away

Erfurt's flashy Hauptbahnhof is on a line with frequent services linking Leipzig (€25, one hour) and Weimar (€7.50, 15 minutes). Hourly ICE/IC service goes to Frankfurt (€48, 2¼ hours) and Berlin-Hauptbahnhof (€54, 2½ hours).

AROUND ERFURT

Eisenach is home to the Wartburg, the only German castle to be named a Unesco World Heritage site. Composer Johann Sebastian Bach was born here but he plays second fiddle to the awe-inspiring edifice in stone and half-timber high on the hill.

The small town has a good **tourist office** (☎ 792 30; www.eisenach.de; Markt 9; ⌚ 10am-6pm Mon-Fri, 10am-4pm Sat year-round, 11am-1pm Sun Apr-Oct), which can help you find accommodation if your day trip gets extended.

The **Wartburg** (☎ 2500; www.wartburg-eisenach.de; tours €7; ⌚ tours 8.30am-5pm Mar-Oct, 9am-3.30pm Nov-Feb), parts of which date to the 11th century, is perched high above the town on a wooded hill and is said to go back to Count Ludwig der Springer (the Jumper); you'll hear the story of how the castle got its name many times, but listen out for how Ludwig got his peculiar moniker as well.

The castle owes its huge popularity to Martin Luther, who went into hiding here from 1521 to 1522 after being excommunicated; during this time he translated the entire New Testament from Greek into German, contributing enormously to the development of the written German language. His modest, wood-panelled **study** is part of the guided tour (available in English), which is the only way to view the interior. The **museum** houses the famous Cranach paintings of Luther and important Christian artefacts from all over Germany. Most of the rooms you'll see here are extravagant 19th-century impressions of medieval life rather than original fittings; the re-imagined Great Hall inspired Richard Wagner's opera *Tannhäuser*. Between Easter and October, crowds can be horrendous; arrive before 11am.

Frequent direct trains run to Erfurt (€11 to €14, 30 to 45 minutes) and most continue on the short distance to Weimar.

WEIMAR & AROUND

☎ 03643 / pop 65,200

The city that was once home to Goethe is not impressive at first glance. There are no vast cathedrals or palaces, nor are there any world-renowned museums. But spend a little time wandering its enchanting old streets and visiting its fascinating little museums and historic houses and soon you will understand the allure. You'll feel the presence of notables like Luther, Schiller and Liszt, and you'll begin to understand the remarkable cultural accomplishments achieved in Weimar over the centuries. While the city can sometimes feel like a giant museum teeming with tourists, it is one of Germany's most fascinating places and should not be missed.

Information

There are scores of little book and music shops in town.

Die Eule (☎ 850 388; Frauentorstrasse 9-11; per 30min €1; ⌚ 10am-6pm Mon-Fri, to 1pm Sat) Internet and books.

Tourist Information (☎ 240 00; www.weimar.de; Markt 10; ⌚ 9.30am-6pm Mon-Fri, to 4pm Sat & Sun) Discount cards start at €10.

Sights

A good place to begin a tour is in front of the neo-Gothic 1841 **Rathaus** on the Markt. For in-depth museum information and high-end souvenirs try the **Stiftung Weimarer Klassik** (Weimar Classics Foundation; ☎ 545 401; www.swkk.de; Frauentorstrasse 4; ⌚ 10am-6pm Mon-Sat, 11am-4pm Sun).

Those who visit the **Goethe Nationalmuseum** (☎ 545 347; Frauenplan 1; admission €8.50; ⌚ 9am-6pm Tue-Sun) expecting to learn all about the great man of letters will probably be disappointed. Rather than focusing on Goethe himself, the museum offers a broad overview of German Classicism, from its proponents to its patrons. The adjoining **Goethe Haus**, where such works as *Faust* were written, focuses much more on the man. He lived here from 1775 until his death in 1832. Goethe's original 1st-floor living quarters are reached via an expansive Italian Renaissance staircase decorated with sculpture and paintings brought back from his travels to Italy.

The Bauhaus School and movement was founded in Weimar in 1919 by Walter Gropius, who managed to draw top artists including Kandinsky, Klee, Feininger and Schlemmer as teachers. The exhibition at the **Bauhaus Museum** (☎ 545 961; Theaterplatz; admission €5; ⌚ 10am-6pm) chronicles the evolution of the group, explains their innovations and spotlights the main players.

Housed in the **Stadtschloss**, the former residence of the ducal family of Saxe-Weimar, the **Schlossmuseum** (☎ 545 960; Burgplatz 4; admission €5; ⌚ 10am-6pm Tue-Sun Apr-Oct, to 4pm Nov-Mar) boasts the Cranach Gallery, several portraits by Albrecht Dürer and collections of Dutch masters and German romanticists. A €90 million project for a full restoration is now in the works.

Goethe's fellow dramatist Friedrich von Schiller lived in Weimar from 1799 until his early death in 1805. Unlike his mentor, he had to buy his own house, now known as **Schiller Museum** (☎ 545 350; Schillerstrasse 12; admission €4; ⌚ 9am-6pm Wed-Mon). The study at the end of the 2nd floor contains the desk where he penned *Wilhelm Tell* and other works, and also holds his deathbed.

BUCHENWALD

The **Buchenwald** (☎ 03643-4300; www.buchenwald.de; ⌚ 9am-6pm Apr-Oct, to 4pm Nov-Mar) concentration-camp museum and memorial are 10km north of Weimar. The contrast between the brutality of the former and the liberal humanism of the latter is hard to comprehend.

Between 1937 and 1945, more than one-fifth of the 250,000 people incarcerated here (Jews, Roma, children, political opponents etc) died. The location on the side of a hill only added to the torture of the inmates as there are sweeping views of the region – a place where people were free while those here died. Various parts of the camp have been restored and there is an essential **museum** with excellent exhibits.

The Weimar tourist office has a useful desk with Buchenwald information. To reach the camp, take bus 6 (€1.70, 15 minutes), which runs regularly.

Sleeping & Eating

The tourist office can help find accommodation, especially at busy times. There are many small pensions scattered about the centre, which is where you should try to stay.

Hababusch (☎ 850737; www.hababusch.de; Geleitstrasse 4; dm/s/d from €10/15/26) Get in touch with the town's past at this unrestored 19th-century house run – and furnished – by students. Perfectly located with no shortage of funky charm. Cook your own brekkie in the kitchen.

Am Poseckschen Garten (☎ 850 792; www.weimar-posgarten.jugendherberge.de; Humboldtstrasse 17; dm from €24; ⊠ 💻) An official DJH/HI hostel in a vintage building near the Historischer Friedhof. Dorms have eight to 10 beds.

Hotel Am Frauenplan (☎ 494 40; www.hotel-am-frauenplan.de; Brauhausgasse 10; r €45-80; 💻 P ⊠) A classic vintage German building that's no nonsense inside and out. The 46 rooms are clean; interior details are kept to a minimum although breakfast is included.

Residenz-Café (☎ 594 08; www.residenz-cafe.de; Grüner Markt 4; mains €5-15) For more than 160 years, the 'Resi' has been an enduring favourite, and for good reason: everyone finds something to their taste here. Meaty platters let you sample local specialities – all best accented with local mustard.

Johanns Hof (☎ 493 617; Scherfgasse 1; mains €6-16) Large windows punctuate the maroon walls in this historic and stylish cafe. The long wine list specialises in German white wines. Creative dishes include many changing specials.

Drinking

Studentenclub Kasseturm (☎ 851 670; www.kasseturm.de; Goetheplatz 10; ⌚ 6pm-late) A classic, the Kasseturm is a historic round tower with three floors of live music, DJs, cabaret and €2 beer.

Getting There & Away

Weimar's Hauptbahnhof is on a line with frequent service linking Leipzig (€22, one hour) and Erfurt (€7.50, 15 minutes). Two-hourly ICE/IC services go to Berlin-Hauptbahnhof (€51, 2¼ hours).

Most buses serve Goetheplatz, on the northwestern edge of the Altstadt. Don't have time for the 20-minute walk before the next train? A cab costs €6.

BAVARIA

Bavaria (Bayern) can seem like every German stereotype rolled into one. Lederhosen, beer halls, oompah bands and romantic castles are just some Bavarian clichés associated with Germany as a whole. But as any Bavarian will tell you, the state thinks of itself as Bavarian first and German second. And as any German outside of Bavaria will tell you, the Bavarian stereotypes aren't representative of the rest of Germany.

Bavaria draws visitors year-round. If you only have time for one part of Germany after Berlin, this is it. Munich, the capital, is the heart and soul. The Bavarian Alps, Nuremberg and the medieval towns on the Romantic Rd are other important attractions.

MUNICH

☎ 089 / pop 1.25 million

Munich (München) is truly the capital of all things Bavarian. It's a heady mix of world-class museums, historic sites, cosmopolitan shopping, exhausting nightlife, trendy restaurants, roaring beer halls, vast parks and, of course, Oktoberfest.

Navigating and enjoying all of this blue-and-white-checked fun (the colours of Bavaria) will take a few days. The efficient public transport system can whisk you around town – although if you stay above ground you might be surprised at how walkable the centre really is. Against all this urban life is the backdrop of the Alps, peaks that exude an allure that many locals – and visitors – find inescapable. No visit to Germany is complete without at least some time spent in this storied city.

Munich didn't really achieve prominence until the 19th century, under the guiding hand of King Ludwig I. In the aftermath of WWI, the city became a hotbed of right-wing political ferment. Hitler staged a failed coup attempt here in 1923. WWII brought bombing and more than 6000 civilian deaths. Today it is a growing city with a diversified economy.

Orientation

The main train station is just west of the centre. From the station, head east along Bayerstrasse, through Karlsplatz, and then along Neuhauser Strasse and Kaufingerstrasse to Marienplatz, the hub of Munich.

North of Marienplatz are the Residenz (the former royal palace), Schwabing (the famous student section) and the parklands of the Englischer Garten through which the Isar River runs.

Information

For late-night shopping and services such as pharmacies and currency exchange, the Hauptbahnhof's multilevel shopping arcades cannot be beaten.

BOOKSHOPS

Hugendubel Marienplatz (☎ 484 484; Marienplatz 22); Salvatorplatz (☎ 484 484; Salvatorplatz 2) Marienplatz has a good selection of guides and maps (and good Glockenspiel views from the top floor); the Salvatorplatz outlet has all English titles.

Max&Milian (☎ 260 3320; Ickstattstrasse 2) Gay bookshop and unofficial community centre.

DISCOUNT CARDS

City Tour Card (www.citytourcard.com; 1/3 days €9.80/18.80) Includes transportation and discounts of between 10% and 50% for about 30 attractions. Available at some hotels, MVV (Munich public transport authority) offices and U-Bahn and S-Bahn vending machines.

INTERNET ACCESS

Internet + Callshop (☎ 2423 1767; Thomas-Wimmer-Ring 1; per 30min €1; 🕒 9am-11pm) Full-service shop and office for Munich Walk Tours (p475).

INTERNET RESOURCES

www.muenchen-tourist.de Munich's official website.

www.munichfound.de Munich's expat magazine.

www.mvv-muenchen.de Everything about Munich's transport system.

www.toytowngermany.com English-language community website with specialised Munich pages.

LAUNDRY

City SB-Waschcenter (Paul-Heysestrasse 21; loads €6; 🕒 7am-11pm) Close to the Hauptbahnhof.

MEDICAL SERVICES

Bahnhof-Apotheke (☎ 598 119; Bahnhofplatz 2, Ludwigsvorstadt)

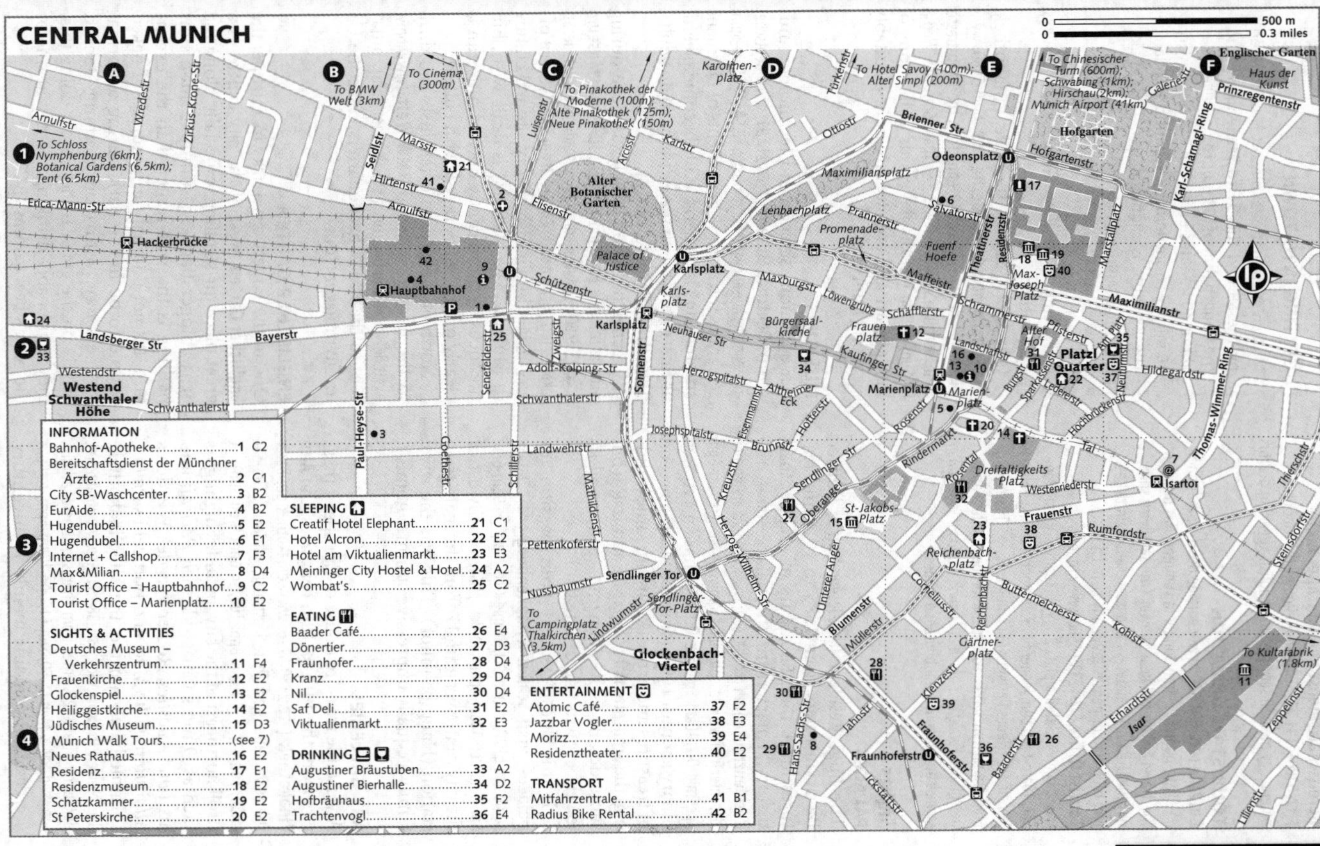
CENTRAL MUNICH
0 500 m
0 0.3 miles
To Schloss Nymphenburg (6km); Botanical Gardens (6.5km); Tent (6.5km)
To BMW Welt (3km)
To Cinema (300m)
To Pinakothek der Moderne (100m); Alte Pinakothek (125m); Neue Pinakothek (150m)
To Hotel Savoy (100m); Alter Simpl (200m)
To Chinesischer Turm (600m); Schwabing (1km); Hirschau (2km); Munich Airport (41km)
To Campingplatz Thalkirchen (3.5km)
To Kultfabrik (1.8km)
Englischer Garten
Haus der Kunst
Hofgarten
Alter Botanischer Garten
Palace of Justice
Hauptbahnhof
Hackerbrücke
Karlsplatz
Odeonsplatz
Marienplatz
Sendlinger Tor
Isartor
Fraunhoferstr
Platzl Quarter
Glockenbach-Viertel
Westend Schwanthaler Höhe
Isar
INFORMATION
Bahnhof-Apotheke 1 C2
Bereitschaftsdienst der Münchner Ärzte 2 C1
City SB-Waschcenter 3 B2
EurAide 4 B2
Hugendubel 5 E2
Hugendubel 6 E1
Internet + Callshop 7 F3
Max&Milian 8 D4
Tourist Office – Hauptbahnhof 9 C2
Tourist Office – Marienplatz 10 E2
SIGHTS & ACTIVITIES
Deutsches Museum – Verkehrszentrum 11 F4
Frauenkirche 12 E2
Glockenspiel 13 E2
Heiliggeistkirche 14 E2
Jüdisches Museum 15 D3
Munich Walk Tours (see 7)
Neues Rathaus 16 E2
Residenz 17 E1
Residenzmuseum 18 E2
Schatzkammer 19 E2
St Peterskirche 20 E2
SLEEPING
Creatif Hotel Elephant 21 C1
Hotel Alcron 22 E2
Hotel am Viktualienmarkt 23 E3
Meininger City Hostel & Hotel 24 A2
Wombat's 25 C2
EATING
Baader Café 26 E4
Dönertier 27 D3
Fraunhofer 28 D4
Kranz 29 D4
Nil 30 D4
Saf Deli 31 E2
Viktualienmarkt 32 E3
DRINKING
Augustiner Bräustuben 33 A2
Augustiner Bierhalle 34 D2
Hofbräuhaus 35 F2
Trachtenvogl 36 E4
ENTERTAINMENT
Atomic Café 37 F2
Jazzbar Vogler 38 E3
Morizz 39 E4
Residenztheater 40 E2
TRANSPORT
Mitfahrzentrale 41 B1
Radius Bike Rental 42 B2

Bereitschaftsdienst der Münchner Ärzte (☎ 01805-191 212; Elisenhof) Round-the-clock non-emergency medical services with English-speaking doctors.

TOURIST INFORMATION

EurAide (☎ 593 889; www.euraide.de; Hauptbahnhof; 8am-noon & 1-4pm, longer in summer) Has desks in the Travel Centre and near Subway (the sandwich shop, not the U-Bahn). Validates rail passes, sells train tickets and tours and dispenses savvy advice in English.

Tourist Office (☎ 2339 6500; www.muenchen.de) Hauptbahnhof (Bahnhofplatz 2; 9.30am-6.30pm Mon-Sat, 10am-6pm Sun, longer hr in summer & during holidays); Marienplatz (Neues Rathaus, Marienplatz 8; 10am-8pm Mon-Fri, to 4pm Sat) Be sure to ask for the excellent and free guides *Young and About in Munich, National Socialism in Munich* and various neighbourhood guides.

Sights

PALACES

The huge **Residenz** (Max-Joseph-Platz 3) housed Bavarian rulers from 1385 to 1918 and features more than 500 years of architectural history. Apart from the palace itself, the **Residenzmuseum** (☎ 290 671; www.residenz-muenchen.de; enter from Max-Joseph-Platz; admission €6; 9am-6pm Apr–mid-Oct, 10am-5pm mid-Oct–Mar) has an extraordinary array of 100 rooms containing no end of treasures and artworks. In the same building, the **Schatzkammer** (separate admission but same details as Residenzmuseum) exhibits jewels, crowns and ornate gold.

If this doesn't satisfy your passion for palaces, visit **Schloss Nymphenburg** (☎ 179 080; admission €10 Apr–mid-Oct, €8 mid-Oct–Mar; 9am-6pm Apr–mid-Oct, 10am-4pm mid-Oct–Mar), northwest of the city centre via tram 17 from the main train station (Hauptbahnhof). This was the royal family's equally impressive summer home.

ART GALLERIES

A veritable treasure house of European masters from the 14th to 18th centuries, the **Alte Pinakothek** (☎ 2380 5216; www.pinakothek.de; Barer Strasse 27, enter from Theresienstrasse; admission Tue-Sat €5.50, Sun €1; 10am-8pm Tue, to 6pm Wed-Sun), a stroll northeast of the city, includes highlights such as Dürer's Christ-like *Self Portrait* and his *Four Apostles*, Rogier van der Weyden's *Adoration of the Magi* and Botticelli's *Pietà*.

Immediately north of the Alte Pinakothek, the **Neue Pinakothek** (☎ 2380 5195; www.pinakothek.de/; Barer Strasse 29, enter from Theresienstrasse; admission Wed-Sat & Mon €5.50, Sun €1; 10am-5pm, to 8pm Wed, closed Tue) contains mainly 19th-century works, including Van Gogh's *Sunflowers*, and sculpture.

One block east of the Alte Pinakothek, the **Pinakothek der Moderne** (☎ 2380 5360; www.pinakothek.de; Barer Strasse 40, enter from Theresienstrasse; admission Tue-Sat €8, Sun €1; 10am-6pm Tue, Wed & Fri-Sun, to 8pm Thu) displays four collections of modern art and architecture in one suitably arresting building.

GETTING INTO TOWN

Munich's international airport is connected by the S8 and the S1 to Marienplatz and the Hauptbahnhof (€8.80). The service takes about 40 minutes and there is a train every 10 minutes from 4am until around 12.30am. The S8 route is slightly faster. Taxis make the long haul for at least €60.

MUSEUMS

An enormous science and technology museum, **Deutches Museum** (☎ 217 91; www.deutsches-museum.de; Museumsinsel 1; admission €8.50; 9am-5pm) celebrates the many achievements of Germans and humans in general. Kids become gleeful as they interact with the exhibits; so do adults. Take the S-Bahn to Isartor.

Tracing the lives of local Jews before, during and after the Holocaust, the **Jüdisches Museum** (☎ 2339 6096; www.juedisches-museum.muenchen.de; St-Jakobs-Platz 16; admission €6; 10am-6pm Tue-Sun) offers insight into Jewish history, life and culture in Munich. The Nazi era is dealt with, but the focus of this recently opened museum is clearly on contemporary Jewish culture.

North of the city, auto-fetishists can thrill to the newly expanded **BMW Welt** (www.bmw-welt.de; admission free, tours €6; 9am-8pm), adjacent to the BMW headquarters. Take the U3 to Olympiazentrum.

ENGLISCHER GARTEN

One of the largest city parks in Europe, the **Englischer Garten**, west of the city centre, is a great place for strolling, especially along the Schwabinger Bach. In summer, nude sunbathing is the rule rather than the exception. It's not unusual for hundreds of naked people to be in the park during a normal business day, with their clothing stacked primly on the grass. If they're not doing this, they're probably drinking merrily at one of the park's **beer gardens** (p477).

HISTORIC BUILDINGS

The **Marienplatz** is a good starting point for historic buildings. Dominating the square is the towering neo-Gothic **Neues Rathaus**, with its ever-dancing **Glockenspiel** (carillon), which performs at 11am and noon daily (also at 5pm from March to October), bringing the square to an expectant standstill (note the fate of the Austrian knight…). Two important churches are on this square: the baroque star **St Peterskirche** (☎ 260 4828; Rindermarkt 1; tower adult/child €1.50/0.30; 9am-7pm Apr-Oct, to 6pm Nov-Mar) and, behind the Altes Rathaus, the often forgotten but equally important **Heiliggeistkirche** (Tal 77; 7am-6pm).

Head west along shopping street Kaufingerstrasse to landmark of Munich, the late-Gothic **Frauenkirche** (Church of Our Lady; ☎ 290 0820; Frauenplatz 1; admission free; 7am-7pm Sat-Wed, to 8.30pm Thu, to 6pm Fri) with its then-trendy 16th-century twin onion domes. Go inside and join the hordes gazing at the grandeur of the place, or climb the tower for majestic views of Munich.

DACHAU

The first Nazi concentration camp was **Dachau** (☎ 08131-669 970; www.kz-gedenkstaette-dachau.de; Alte-Roemerstrasse 75; admission free; 9am-5pm Tue-Sun), built in March 1933. Jews, political prisoners, homosexuals and others deemed 'undesirable' by the Third Reich were imprisoned in the camp. More than 200,000 people were sent here; more than 30,000 died at Dachau and countless others died after being transferred to other death camps. An English-language documentary is shown at 11.30am and 3.30pm. Take the S2 (direction Petershausen) to Dachau and then bus 726 to the camp. A Munich XXL day ticket (€6.70) will cover the trip.

Tours

The hordes of visitors and plethora of sights mean there's lots of people willing to show you around – an excellent way to gain background and context on what you see.

Mike's Bike Tours (☎ 2554 3987; www.mikesbiketours.com; tours from €24) Enjoyable (and leisurely) city cycling tours in English. Tours depart from the archway at the Altes Rathaus on Marienplatz.

Munich Walk Tours (☎ 2423 1767; www.munichwalktours; Thomas-Wimmer-Ring 1; tours from €10) Walking tours of the city and a tour focused on 'beer, brewing and boozing'.

OKTOBERFEST

Hordes come to Munich for **Oktoberfest** (www.oktoberfest.de), running the 15 days before the first Sunday in October. Although its origins are in the marriage celebrations of Crown Prince Ludwig in 1810, there's nothing regal about this beery bacchanalia now: expect mobs, expect to meet new and drunken friends, expect decorum to vanish as night sets in, and you'll have a blast.

Reserve accommodation well ahead and go early so you can grab a seat in one of the hangar-sized beer 'tents'. The action takes place at the Theresienwiese grounds, about a 10-minute walk southwest of the Hauptbahnhof. While there is no entrance fee, those €7 steins of beer add up fast.

New Munich Free Tour (www.newmunich.com; tours free; 10.45am & 1pm) English-language walking tours tick off all of Munich's central landmarks and historical milestones in three hours. Guides are well-informed and work only for tips. Tours depart from Marienplatz by Mary's Column.

Sleeping

Munich has no shortage of places to stay – except during Oktoberfest or some busy summer periods, when the wise (meaning those with a room) will have booked.

Campingplatz Thalkirchen (☎ 7243 0808; www.camping-muenchen.de; Zentralländstrasse 49; camp sites per person/tent €5/4, heated cabin per person €13; mid-Mar–end Oct) To get to this camping ground, southwest of the city centre, take the U3 to Thalkirchen and then catch bus 57 (about 20 minutes).

The Tent (☎ 141 4300; www.the-tent.com; In den Kirschen 30; camp sites per tent/person €5.50/5.50, bed in main tent €11; Jun-Sep) Pads and blankets provided for the bagless, bring your own lock for the lockers. Take tram 17 to the Botanic Gardens then follow the signs to a legendary international party.

Wombat's (☎ 5998 9180; www.wombats-hostels.com; Senefelderstrasse 1; dm €12-24, r from €68; P) This hostel-hotel combo gets top marks for style, comfort and location. You'll sleep well in pine beds with real mattresses (free linen) and reading lamps in doubles and dorms with en suite bathrooms. Breakfast is an extra €4.

Meininger City Hostel & Hotel (☎ 420 956 053; www.meininger-hostels.de; Landsbergerstrasse 20; dm/s/d from

€17/43/62; 💻 P ⊠) This hotel-hostel combo scores big points for three reasons: location, amenities and service. Just west of the Hauptbahnhof, it has 380 beds in 95 cheerful rooms ranging in size from singles to 12-bed dorms. Rates include a generous buffet breakfast and wi-fi throughout.

our pick **Hotel am Viktualienmarkt** (☎ 231 1090; www.hotel-am-viktualienmarkt.de; Utzschneiderstrasse 14; s/d from €48/98; ⊠) Owners Elke and her daughter Stephanie run this good-value property with panache and a sunny attitude. A steep staircase (no lift) leads to rooms, the nicest of which have wooden floors and framed poster art. Book far ahead.

Creatif Hotel Elephant (☎ 555 785; www.creatif-hotel-elephant.com; Lämmerstrasse 6; r €50-150; 💻 ⊠) The Creatif is a polychromatic and friendly place bursting with flowers. Its 44 rooms are stylish and comfortable in an Ikea sort of way, and there's free wi-fi.

Hotel Alcron (☎ 228 3511; www.hotel-alcron.de, in German; Ledererstrasse 13; s €60-70, d €80-95, tr €90-105; ⊠ 💻) Within stumbling distance of the Hofbräuhaus, this quaint hotel has a dizzying spiral staircase leading up to traditionally furnished rooms that don't spoil you with space. Beds, though, are comfortable enough to sleep off any excesses.

Hotel Savoy (☎ 287 870; www.pension-haydn.de; Amalienstrasse 25; r €60-150; P 💻) In a Maxvorstadt area thick with modest hotels and cafes, the Savoy stands out for good service, a lift and 74 large rooms with wi-fi. Big windows look across to other inns so you can compare rooms. Breakfast is extra.

Eating

Clusters of restaurants can be found anywhere there's pedestrian life. The streets in and around Gärtnerplatz and Glockenbach-Viertel are the flavour-of-the-moment. You can always do well in and around Marienplatz and the wonderful Viktualienmarkt.

Viktualienmarkt, just south of Marienplatz, is a large open-air market open daily except Saturday afternoon and Sunday. You can put together a picnic feast to take to the Englischer Garten. The fresh produce, cheese and baked goods are hard to resist. Or relax here under the trees, at tables provided by one of the many beer and sausage vendors. This is the place to see the German's love of all things organic.

Dönertier (Sendlinger Strasse 31; döners €3.60-4.20; 🕑 10.30am-8.30pm Mon-Fri, 11am-8pm Sat) This spacey döner bar takes the humble snack to new heights. Go classic or try the 'deluxe' version with *rucola* and mozzarella, and definitely top it off with the refreshing mango yoghurt.

Saf Deli (☎ 1892 2813; Ledererstrasse 3; mains from €6; 🕑 11am-7pm Mon-Sat) Vegan fair for the faint of heart is served in this stylish cafe right in the heart of roasted-meat land. The curried pea soup's a winner, as is the huge range of salads and sandwiches. It's the perfect start after a long night.

Fraunhofer (☎ 266 460; Fraunhoferstrasse 9; mains €5-14; 🕑 4.30pm-1am) This classic brewpub brings tradition into the 21st century. The olde-worlde atmosphere (mounted animal heads and a portrait of Ludwig II) contrasts with the clued-in, intergenerational crowd and a menu that offers progressive takes on classical fare.

CAFES

Nil (☎ 265 545; Hans-Sachs-Strasse 2; meals €7-12; 🕑 8am-4am) Right in trendy Glockenbach-Viertel, this hip place draws a straight and gay crowd in the know. Tables outside are packed when the sun shines, inside it's packed all night long.

Kranz (☎ 2166 8250; Hans-Sache-Strasse 12; mains €8-16) A luxe cafe in the heart of the edgy and trendy streets of the Glockenbach-Viertel. Posh desserts beg you to go easy on the organic burgers etc. Excellent sidewalk tables.

Baader Café (☎ 201 0638; Baaderstrasse 47; 🕑 9.30am-1am) This literary think-and-drink place gets everyone from short skirts to tweed jackets to mingle beneath the conversation-fuelling map of the world. Lines form early for Sunday brunch.

Drinking

Outside of the beer halls and gardens, Munich has no shortage of lively pubs. Schwabing and Glockenbach-Viertel are good places to follow your ears. Many serve food.

BARS

Alter Simpl (☎ 272 3083; Türkenstrasse 57, Maxvorstadt) Thomas Mann and Hermann Hesse used to knock 'em back at this legendary thirst parlour, which is also a good place to satisfy midnight munchies as bar bites are available until one hour before closing time.

Trachtenvogl (☎ 201 5160; Reichenbachstrasse 47, Gärtnerplatzviertel; 🕑 10am-1am) At night you'll have to shoehorn your way into this buzzy lair fa-

BEER HALLS & BEER GARDENS

Beer drinking is not just an integral part of Munich's entertainment scene, it's a reason to visit. Germans drink an average of 130L of the amber liquid each per year, while Munich residents manage to drink much more.

Beer halls can be vast boozy affairs seating thousands, or much more modest neighbourhood hang-outs. The same goes for beer gardens. Both come in all shapes and sizes. Note that beer garden tradition allows you to bring your own food, a boon if you want a cheap option.

On a warm day there's nothing better than sitting and sipping among the greenery at one of the Englischer Garten's classic beer gardens. **Chinesischer Turm** (☎ 383 8730) is justifiably popular while the nearby **Hirschau** (☎ 369 942) on the banks of Kleinhesseloher See is less crowded.

our pick **Augustiner Bräustuben** (☎ 507 047; Landsberger Strasse 19) Depending on the wind, an aroma of hops envelops you as you approach this ultra-authentic beer hall inside the actual Augustiner brewery. The Bavarian grub here is superb, especially the *Schweinshaxe* (big hunk of roasted pork). Giant black draft horses are stabled behind glass on your way to the loo.

Augustiner Bierhalle (☎ 5519 9257; Neuhauser Strasse 27) What you probably imagine an old-style Munich beer hall looks like, filled with laughter, smoke and clinking glasses.

Hofbräuhaus (☎ 2901 3610; Am Platzl 9) The ultimate cliché of Munich beer halls. Tourists arrive by the busload but no one seems to mind that this could be Disneyland (although the theme park wasn't once home to Hitler's early speeches, like this place was).

voured by a chatty, boozy crowd of scenesters, artists and students. Daytimes are mellower at this former folkloric garment shop.

CLUBS

Jazzbar Vogler (☎ 294 662; Rumfordstrasse 17, Gärtnerplatzviertel) This intimate watering hole brings some of Munich's baddest cats to the stage. You never know who'll show up for Monday's blues-jazz-Latin jam session.

Kultafabrik (www.kultafabrik.de; Grafingerstrasse 6; 🕑 8pm-6am or later) There are more than 25 clubs in this old potato factory that you can sample before you end up mashed or fried. Electro and house beats charge up the crowd at the loungy apartment 11, the Asian-themed Koi and at the small red cocktail cantina called Die Bar. It's close to the Ostbahnhof station.

Atomic Café (☎ 228 3054; www.atomic.de; Neuturmstrasse 5; 🕑 10pm-4am Tue-Sun, opens 9pm on concert nights) This bastion of indie sounds with funky '60s decor is known for bookers with a knack for catching upwardly hopeful bands before their big break.

GAY & LESBIAN VENUES

Much of Munich's gay and lesbian nightlife is around Gärtnerplatz and the Glockenbach-Viertel. *Our Munich* and *Sergej* are monthly guides easily found in this neighbourhood. Another good resource is Max&Milian (p472).

Morizz (☎ 201 6776; Klenzestrasse 43) This mod art deco–style lounge with red leather armchairs and mirrors for posing and preening goes for a moneyed clientele and even gets the occasional local celebrity drop-in. Packed on weekends.

Entertainment

Munich is one of the cultural capitals of Germany; the publications and websites listed on p472 can guide you to the best events. For tickets, try **Munchën Ticket** (☎ 5481 8154; www.muenchenticket.de).

Residenztheater (☎ 2185 1920; Max-Joseph-Platz 2) Home of the Bavarian State Opera (www.staatsoper.de) and the site of many cultural events (particularly during the opera festival in July).

Getting There & Away

AIR

Munich's **airport** (MUC; www.munich-airport.de) is second in importance only to Frankfurt-am-Main for international and national connections. EasyJet is a major budget carrier here.

BUS

Munich is linked to the Romantic Rd by the popular **Deutsche-Touring** (☎ 8898 9513; www.touring.com; Hirtenallee 14) Munich–Frankfurt service. Buses stop along the northern side of the train station on Arnulfstrasse.

RIDE SERVICES

For arranged rides, the **Mitfahrzentrale** (☎ 194 40; www.mitfahrzentrale.de; Lämmerstrasse 6; 🕒 8am-8pm) is near the Hauptbahnhof. The cost is split with the driver and you can reach most parts of Germany for well under €40.

TRAIN

Train services to/from Munich are excellent. There are rapid connections at least every two hours to all major cities in Germany, as well as daily trains to other European cities such as Paris (€135, 6¼ hours), Vienna (€76, four hours) and Zurich (€64, 4¼ hours).

High-speed ICE services from Munich include Frankfurt (€89, three hours, hourly), Hamburg (€115, 5½ hours, hourly) and Berlin (€113, 5¾ hours, every two hours).

Getting Around

BICYCLE

Pedal power is popular in relatively flat Munich. **Radius Bike Rental** (☎ 596 113; www.radiustours.com; Hauptbahnhof near track 32; 🕒 10am-6pm May-Sep) rents out two-wheelers from €15 per day.

PUBLIC TRANSPORT

Munich's excellent **public transport network** (MVV; www.mvv-muenchen.de) is zone-based, and most places of interest to tourists (except Dachau and the airport) are within the 'blue' inner zone (Innenraum; single ride/day pass €2.30/5). MVV tickets are valid for the S-Bahn, U-Bahn, trams and buses, but must be validated before use. The U-Bahn stops operating around 12.30am Monday to Friday and 1.30am Saturday and Sunday, but there are some later buses and S-Bahns. Rail passes are valid only on the S-Bahn.

ROMANTIC ROAD

The popular and schmaltzily named Romantic Rd (Romantische Strasse) links a series of picturesque Bavarian towns and cities. It's not actually one road per se, but rather a 353km route chosen to highlight as many quaint towns and cities as possible in western Bavaria. From north to south the Romantic Rd includes the following major stops:

Würzburg (right) Starting point and featuring 18th-century artistic splendour among the vineyards.

Rothenburg ob der Tauber (p480) The medieval walled hub of cutesy picturesque Bavarian touring.

Dinkelsbühl Another medieval walled town replete with moat and watchtowers, a smaller Rothenberg. The town is best reached by the Romantic Rd by bus or car.

Augsburg A medieval and Renaissance city with many good places for a beer.

Füssen (p482) The southern end of the route and the cute and overrun home of mad King Ludwig's castles.

Getting There & Around

The principal cities and towns we've listed are all easily reached by train; see individual listings for details. But to really explore the route you are best off with your own transport. With a car, you can blow through places of little interest and linger at those which attract.

A popular way to tour the Romantic Rd is the Deutsche-Touring **Romantic Road bus** (www.deutsche-touring.com). Starting in Frankfurt in the north and Füssen in the south, a bus runs in each direction each day covering the entire route between Würzburg and Füssen. However, seeing the whole thing in one day is only for those with unusual fortitude and a love of buses. Stops are brief (17 minutes for Wieskirche, *Schnell!* 35 minutes for Rothenburg, *Schnell!* etc) so you'll want to choose places where you can break the trip for a day (stopovers are allowed). But of course this leads you to decide between a 30-minute visit and a 24-hour one.

The buses depart April to October south from Frankfurt Hauptbahnhof at 8am and north from Füssen at 8am and Munich Hauptbahnhof (north side) at 11am and take about 11 hours. The total fare (tickets are bought on board) is a pricey €150. Railpass holders get a paltry 20% discount. You can also just ride for individual segments (eg Rothenberg to Augsburg costs €31), which may be the best use.

WÜRZBURG

☎ 0931 / pop 131,000

Nestled among river valleys lined with vineyards, Würzburg beguiles even before you reach the city centre. Three of the four largest wine-growing estates in all of Germany are here and most of the delicate whites produced locally never leave the region. The locals will always reach for a wine glass first – so should you.

The **tourist office** (☎ 372 398; www.wuerzburg.de; Marktplatz; 🕒 10am-6pm Mon-Fri, to 2pm Sat & Sun May-Oct, reduced hr & closed Sun other times) is in the rococo masterpiece Haus zum Falken.

The magnificent, sprawling **Residenz** (☎ 355 170; Balthasar-Neumann-Promenade; admission €5; ⌚ 9am-6pm Apr-Oct, 10am-4pm Oct-Mar), a baroque tour de force by Neumann, took a generation to build and boasts the world's largest ceiling fresco painting. The interior of the **Dom St Kilian** (☎ 3866 5600; museum admission €5; ⌚ 10am-7pm Tue-Sun Apr-Oct, to 5pm Tue-Sun Nov-Mar) and the adjacent **Neumünster**, an 11th-century church in the old town housing the bones of St Kilian (the patron Saint of Würzburg), continue the baroque themes of the Residenz.

Neumann's fortified **Alter Kranen** (old crane), which serviced a dock on the river-bank south of Friedensbrücke, is now the **Haus des Frankenweins** (☎ 390 1111; Kranenkai 1), where you can taste Franconian wines (around €3 per glass).

The medieval fortress **Marienberg**, across the river on the hill, is reached by crossing the 15th-century stone **Alte Mainbrücke** (bridge) from the city and walking up Tellstiege, a small alley. It encloses the **Fürstenbau Museum** (☎ 355 1753; admission €4; ⌚ 9am-6pm Tue-Sun Apr-Oct) featuring some killer decor. For a simple thrill, wander the walls enjoying the panoramic views.

Sleeping & Eating

Würzburg's many *weinstuben* are excellent places to sample the local vintages. Look for crests of gilded grapes over entrances. Sanderstrasse has a good strip of lively bars.

Kanu-Club (☎ 725 36; Mergentheimer Strasse 13b; camp sites per person/tent €6/6; ⌚ Apr-Sep) A camping ground on the west bank of the Main; take tram 3 or 5 to Jugendbühlweg.

Babelfish Hostel (☎ 304 0430; www.babelfish-hostel.de; Prymstrasse 3; dm €16-18; P ⊠ 💻) This green-powered, independent hostel is operated by two fun-loving locals. Facilities include spotless dorms and a chilled common room/kitchen.

Pension Spehnkuch (☎ 547 52; www.pension-spehnkuch.de; Röntgenring 7; r €32-65; 💻) This little pension 100m from the train station has few frills (other than wi-fi), but the seven rooms are clean. Breakfast is served in a sunny room with a balcony.

Kult (☎ 531 43; Landwehrstrasse 10; mains €5.50-8.50) Old washing machine and dryer drums have been turned into light fittings at this cafe that draws an alternative crowd for its organic food, steaming mugs of Ovaltine and good beer.

Weinstuben Juliusspital (☎ 540 80; Juliuspromenade 19; meals €8-20) This rambling place serves from a long list of wines (especially local whites). You can have a meal or just a drink at one of the many old wooden tables.

Getting There & Away

Würzburg is served by frequent ICE trains from Frankfurt (€32, 70 minutes) and Nuremberg (€32, 69 minutes). It's a major stop for the ICE trains on the Hamburg–Munich line. It is also on the Deutsche-Touring Romantic Rd bus route (€14, 1½ hours to/from Rothenburg). The stop is in front of the train station.

BAMBERG

☎ 0951 / pop 71,000

Off the major tourist routes, Bamberg is celebrated by those in the know. It boasts an amazing and well-preserved collection of 17th- and 18th-century buildings, palaces and churches and its own local style of beer. No wonder it has been recognised by Unesco as a World Heritage Site. This is one of the most alluring small towns in Germany.

The **tourist office** (☎ 297 6200; www.bamberg.info; Geyerswörthstrasse 3; ⌚ 9.30am-6pm Mon-Fri, to 2.30pm Sat year-round, plus 9.30am-2.30pm Sun Apr-Dec) is situated on an island in the Regnitz River.

Bamberg's main appeal is its fine buildings: their sheer number, their jumble of styles and the ambience this creates. Most attractions are spread either side of the Regnitz River, but the colourful **Altes Rathaus** (Obere Brücke) is solidly perched on its own islet. Its lavish murals are among many around town.

The princely and ecclesiastical district is centred on Domplatz, where the Romanesque and Gothic **cathedral** (Domplatz; ⌚ 8am-6pm Apr-Sep, to 5pm Oct-Mar) is the biggest attraction. Across the square, the imposing 17th-century **Neue Residenz** (☎ 519 390; Domplatz 8; admission €4; ⌚ 9am-6pm Apr-Sep, 10am-4pm Oct-Mar) is filled with treasures and opulent decor.

Above Domplatz is the former Benedictine monastery of St Michael, at the top of Michaelsberg. The **Kirche St Michael** (Franziskanergasse 2; ⌚ 9am-6pm) is a must-see for its baroque art.

Sleeping & Eating

Bamberg's unique style of beer is called *Rauchbier*, which literally means smoked beer. Sort of bacony at first, it is a smooth brew that goes down easily. Happily, many of the local breweries also rent rooms.

Campingplatz Insel (☎ 563 20; www.campinginsel.de; Am Campingplatz 1; camp sites per adult €3, per tent €3.50-7; P) A well-equipped place in a tranquil spot right on the river. Take bus 18 to Campingplatz.

Backpackers Bamberg (☎ 2221 718; www.backpackerrsbamberg.de; Memmelsdorfer Strasse 21; dm €16-19; ☒) This little eight-bed hostel is set within an old half-timbered house. You can cook in the kitchen and dine on the rooftop terrace, before bedding down in spotless dorms. It's a five-minute walk to the Hauptbahnhof.

Brauerei Spezial (☎ 243 04; www.brauerei-spezial.de; Obere Königstrasse 10; r €25-60, meals €8-15) This half-timbered brewery has cosy drinking and dining areas featuring old tile stoves. The seven rooms are simple but comfortable.

Klosterbräu (☎ 522 65; Obere Mühlbrücke 3; meals €8-15; Thu-Tue) This beautiful half-timbered brewery is Bamberg's oldest, with a young, fun crowd and friendly staff.

our pick **Schlenkerla** (☎ 560 60; Dominikanerstrasse 6; meals €8-15; Wed-Mon) Decked out with lamps fashioned from antlers, this 16th-century restaurant is famous for its tasty Franconian specialities (many seasonal) and its *Rauchbier*, served directly from oak barrels.

Getting There & Away

There are two trains per hour to/from both Würzburg (€15.50, one hour) and Nuremberg (€18, one hour). Bamberg is also served by ICE trains running between Munich (€56, two hours) and Berlin (€72, 3¾ hours) every two hours.

ROTHENBURG OB DER TAUBER

☎ 09861 / pop 12,000

In the Middle Ages, the town fathers of Rothenburg built strong walls to protect the town from siege. Today those same walls are the reason the town is under siege from tourists. Possibly the most stereotypical of all German walled towns, Rothenburg can't help being so cute.

The **tourist office** (☎ 194 12; www.rothenburg.de; Marktplatz 2; 9am-6pm Mon-Fri, 10am-3pm Sat & Sun Apr-Oct, 9am-5pm Mon-Fri, 10am-1pm Sat Nov-Mar) can help you find a room, which is a good idea because after dark the streets are quiet and the underlying charm comes out.

The **Rathaus on Markt** was begun in Gothic style in the 14th century, but completed in Renaissance style. The **tower** (admission €1) gives a majestic view over the town and the Tauber Valley. The **Meistertrunk** scene is reenacted by the clock figures on the tourist-office building (eight times daily in summer).

The totally uncommercial **Jakobskirche** (☎ 700 60; Klingengasse 1; admission €2; 9am-4pm) is sober and Gothic. Marvel at the carved *Heilige Blut alter* (Holy Blood altar). Elsewhere, you won't be able to avoid the legion of Christmas shops and other places aimed right at your dowager aunt.

Pension Raidel (☎ 3115; www.romanticroad.com/raidel; Wenggasse 3; r €25-60; P) is a half-timbered inn with 500-year-old exposed beams studded with wooden nails, and musical instruments for guests to play. Some rooms share baths.

Restaurant Bürgerkeller (☎ 2126; Herrngasse 24; mains €8-16; Thu-Tue) is down a short flight of stairs in a frescoed 16th-century cellar. This hidden spot serves local, seasonal fare.

There are hourly trains to/from Steinach, a transfer point for service to Würzburg (total journey €12, 70 minutes). Rothenburg is a cross-road for tourist buses. Deutsche-Touring Romantic Rd buses pause here for 35 minutes.

NUREMBERG

☎ 0911 / pop 498,000

Nuremberg (Nürnberg) woos visitors with its wonderfully restored medieval Altstadt, its grand castle and its magical Christkindlesmarkt (Christmas market). Thriving traditions also include sizzling *Nürnberger Bratwürste* (finger-sized sausages) and *Lebkuchen* – large, soft gingerbread cookies, traditionally eaten at Christmastime but available here year-round.

Nuremberg played a major role during the Nazi years, as documented in Leni Riefenstahl's film *Triumph of Will* and during the war crimes trials afterwards. It has done an admirable job of confronting this ugly past with museums and exhibits.

The main artery, the mostly pedestrian Königstrasse, takes you through the old town and its major squares.

Information

The Hauptbahnhof has several internet cafes, most serving beer so you can email things you later regret.

Tourist office (www.tourismus.nuernberg.de) Hauptmarkt (☎ 2336 135; Hauptmarkt 18; 9am-6pm Mon-Sat,

10am-4pm Sun May-Oct, 9am-6pm Mon-Sat Nov & Jan-Apr, 10am-7pm daily during Christkindlesmarkt); Künstlerhaus (☎ 233 6131; Königstrasse 93; 🕑 9am-7pm Mon-Sat year-round, plus 10am-4pm Sun during Christkindlesmarkt) Staff sell the Nürnberg + Fürth Card (€19), good for two days of unlimited public transport and admissions.

Sights

The stunning **Germanisches Nationalmuseum** (☎ 133 10; Kartäusergasse 1; admission €6; 🕑 10am-6pm Tue & Thu-Sun, to 9pm Wed) is the most important general museum of German culture. It displays works by German painters and sculptors, an archaeological collection, arms and armour, musical and scientific instruments, and toys.

The scenic **Altstadt** is easily covered on foot. On Lorenzer Platz there's **St Lorenzkirche**, noted for the 15th-century tabernacle that climbs like a vine up a pillar to the vaulted ceiling.

To the north is the bustling **Hauptmarkt**, where the most famous Christkindlesmarkt in Germany is held from the Friday before Advent to Christmas Eve. The church here is the ornate **Pfarrkirche Unsere Liebe Frau**; the clock's figures go strolling at noon. Near the Rathaus is **St Sebalduskirche**, Nuremberg's oldest church (dating from the 13th century).

Climb up Burgstrasse to the enormous 15th-century **Kaiserburg complex** (☎ 200 9540; admission incl museum €6; 🕑 9am-6pm Apr-Sep, 10am-4pm Oct-Mar) for good views of the city. The walls spread west to the tunnel-gate of **Tiergärtnertor**, where you can stroll behind the castle to the gardens. Nearby is the renovated **Albrecht-Dürer-Haus** (☎ 231 2568; Albrecht-Dürer-Strasse 39; admission €5; 🕑 10am-5pm Fri-Wed, to 8pm Thu), where Dürer, Germany's renowned Renaissance draughtsperson and artist, lived from 1509 to 1528.

The Nazis chose Nuremberg as their propaganda centre and for mass rallies, which were held at **Luitpoldhain**, a (never-completed) sports complex of megalomaniacal proportions. After the war, the Allies deliberately chose Nuremberg as the site for the trials of Nazi war criminals. Not to be missed is the **Dokumentationzentrum** (☎ 231 5666; www.museen.nuernberg.de; Bayernstrasse 110; admission €5; 🕑 9am-6pm Mon-Fri, 10am-6pm Sat & Sun) in the north wing of the massive unfinished Congress Hall, which would have held 50,000 people for Hitler's spectacles. The museum's absorbing exhibits trace the rise of Hitler and the Nazis and the important role Nuremberg played in the mythology. Take tram 9 or 6 to Doku-Zentrum.

Sleeping & Eating

Don't leave Nuremberg without trying its famous finger-sized grilled sausages. Order 'em by the dozen with *meerrettich* (horseradish) on the side.

Lette 'm Sleep (☎ 992 8128; www.backpackers.de; Frauentormauer 42; dm €16-25, sheets €3, s/d from €30/50; ⊠ 💻) A backpacker favourite, this independent hostel is just five minutes' walk from the Hauptbahnhof, with a laundry, colourfully painted dorms and wi-fi.

Probst-Garni Hotel (☎ 203 433; www.hotel-garni-probst.de; Luitpoldstrasse 9; r €35-110) Nuremberg's most reasonably priced pension is squeezed on the 3rd floor of a vintage building. Some singles are tiny and some share bathrooms.

Café am Trödelmarkt (☎ 208 877; Trödelmarkt 42; dishes €3-5; 🕑 9am-6pm) A gorgeous place on a sunny day, this multilevel waterfront cafe overlooks the covered Henkersteg bridge.

our pick Bratwursthäusle (☎ 227 695; Rathausplatz 2; meals €6-12) A local legend and *the* place for local sausages, flame-grilled and scrumptious. Get them with *Kartoffelsalat* (potato salad). There are also nice tree-shaded tables outside.

Kettensteg (☎ 221 081; Maxplatz 35; mains €7-15) Right by the river and with its own suspension bridge to the other side, this beer garden and restaurant is fine on a summer day and cosy in winter. The basic fare is tasty and absorbs lots of beer.

Getting There & Around

Nuremberg's **airport** (NUE; www.airport-nuernberg.de) is a hub for budget carrier Air Berlin, which has service throughout Germany, as well as flights to London. There's frequent service to the airport on the S-2 line (€2, 12 minutes).

The city is also a hub for train service. ICE trains run to/from Berlin-Hauptbahnhof (€89, 4½ hours, every two hours), Frankfurt-am-Main (€48, two hours, hourly) and on the new fast line to Munich (€49, one hour, hourly). Trains run hourly to Stuttgart (€38, 2¼ hours).

Tickets on the bus, tram and U-Bahn system cost €1.80 each. Day passes are €4.

REGENSBURG

☎ 0941 / pop 129,000

On the wide Danube River, student-filled Regensburg has relics of all historic periods as far back as the Romans, yet doesn't have the tourist mobs you'll find in other equally attractive German cities. The centre escaped WWII's carpet bombing and boasts Renaissance towers that could be in Florence mixed with half-timbered charm. Throngs of students keep things from getting too mouldy.

From the main train station, you walk up Maximillianstrasse for 10 minutes to reach the centre. There's internet access at coin-op terminals (€1 per 15 minutes) on the top level of the train station. The **tourist office** (☎ 507 4410; www.regensburg.de; Altes Rathaus; ⏰ 9am-6pm Mon-Fri, to 4pm Sat & Sun) is in the centre.

Dominating the skyline are the twin spires of the Gothic **Dom St Peter** (☎ 597 1002; Domplatz; admission free; ⏰ 6.30am-6pm Apr-Oct, to 5pm Nov-Mar), built during the 14th and 15th centuries from unusual green limestone.

The **Altes Rathaus** (507 4411; admission incl museum €6; ⏰ tours in English 3pm Apr-Oct, 2pm Nov, Dec & Mar) was progressively extended from medieval to baroque times.

Bus 6 from the train station goes to the entrance of **Azur-Camping** (☎ 270 025; www.azur-camping.de; Weinweg 40; per person €5.50-7, camp sites €6-8). The **DJH Hostel** (☎ 574 02; www.djh.de; Wöhrdstrasse 60; dm €17; 💻) is in a beautiful old building on Unterer Wöhrd island about a 10-minute walk north of the Altstadt. Take bus 3 from Albertstrasse to Eisstadion.

An ever-expanding indie hostel, **Brook Lane Hostel** (☎ 690 0966; www.hostel-regensburg.de, in German; Obere Bachgasse 21; dm €15, d with shared bathroom €35) is in the heart of town. It has a full kitchen, colourful dorms with timber bunks, and a small supermarket downstairs.

Don't miss the **Historische Wurstküche** (☎ 466 210; Thundorferstrasse 3; meals €7). The Danube rushes past this little house that's been cooking up the addictive local version of Nuremberg sausages (slightly spicy) for centuries.

Regensburg is on the train line between Nuremberg (€18 to €24, one hour, hourly) and Austria (Vienna: €70, four hours). There are hourly trains to Munich (€24, 1½ hours).

FÜSSEN

☎ 08362 / pop 14,000

Close to the Austrian border and the foothills of the Alps, Füssen is primarily visited for the two castles in nearby Schwangau associated with King Ludwig II. The **tourist office** (☎ 938 50; www.fuessen.de; Kaiser-Maximillian-Platz 1; ⏰ 9am-5pm Mon-Fri, 10am-2pm Sat, 10am-noon Sun) is often overrun. This place is really best seen as a day trip from Munich.

Neuschwanstein & Hohenschwangau Castles

The castles provide a fascinating glimpse into the romantic king's state of mind (or lack thereof) and well-developed ego. **Hohenschwangau** is where Ludwig lived as a child, but more interesting is the adjacent **Neuschwanstein**, his own creation (albeit with the help of a theatrical designer). Although it was unfinished when he died in 1886, there is plenty of evidence of Ludwig's twin obsessions: swans and Wagnerian opera. The sugary pastiche of architectural styles, alternatively overwhelmingly beautiful and just a little too much, reputedly inspired Disney's Fantasyland castle.

Tickets must be bought from the **Ticket Centre** (☎ 930 830; www.ticket-center-hohenschwangau.de; Alpenseestrasse 12, Hohenschwangau; admission €9, incl Schloss Hohenschwangau €17; ⏰ tickets on sale 8am-5pm Apr-Sep, 9am-3pm Oct-Mar). In summer it's worth the €1.80 surcharge each to reserve ahead. To walk to Hohenschwangau takes 20 minutes while Neuschwanstein is a 45-minute steep hike. The walk between the castles is a piney 45-minute stroll.

Take the bus from Füssen train station (€2, 15 minutes, hourly) or share a taxi (☎ 7700; €10 for up to four people). Go early to avoid the worst of the rush.

Getting There & Away

Train connections to Munich (€24, two hours) run every two hours. Füssen is the start of the Romantic Rd. Deutsche-Touring buses (p478) start here.

BAVARIAN ALPS

While not quite as high as their sister summits further south in Austria and Switzerland, the Bavarian Alps (Bayerische Alpen) are still standouts, owing to their abrupt rise from the rolling Bavarian foothills. Stretching westward from Germany's southeastern corner to the Allgäu region near Lake Constance, the Alps take in most of the mountainous country fringing the southern border with Austria.

BERCHTESGADEN

☎ 08652 / pop 7900

Berchtesgaden is easily the most dramatically scenic corner of the Bavarian Alps, which hang down into Austria like an appendix here. The views over the steep valleys and craggy peaks go on forever. To reach the centre from the train station, cross the footbridge and walk up Bahnhofstrasse. The **tourist office** (☎ 9670; www.berchtesgaden.de; Königsseer Strasse 2; 8.30am-6pm Mon-Fri, 8.30am-5pm Sat, 9am-3pm Sun mid-Jun–Sep, less other times) is just across the river from the train station and has internet access.

In 1933, the quiet mountain retreat of Obersalzberg (some 3km from Berchtesgaden) became the southern headquarters of Hitler's government, a dark period that's given the full historical treatment at the **Dokumentation Obersalzberg** (☎ 947 960; www.obersalzberg.de; Salzbergstrasse 41, Obersalzberg; adult/student €3/free; 9am-5pm Apr-Oct, 10am-3pm Tue-Sun Nov-Apr). To get there take bus 838 from the Hauptbahnhof in Berchtesgaden.

Berchtesgaden's creepiest – yet impressive – draw is the **Eagle's Nest** atop Mt Kehlstein, a sheer-sided peak at Obersalzberg. Perched at 1834m, the innocent-looking lodge (called Kehlsteinhaus in German) has sweeping views across the mountains and down into the valley where the Königssee shimmers. Ironically, Hitler is said to have suffered from vertigo and rarely enjoyed the spectacular views himself.

Drive or take bus 849 from the Berchtesgaden Hauptbahnhof to the Kehlstein stop, where you board a special **bus** (www.kehlsteinhaus.de; tickets €13) that drives you up the mountain. It runs between 7.20am and 4pm, and takes 35 minutes.

Eagle's Nest Tours (☎ 649 71; www.eagles-nest-tours.com; tours €45; 1.30pm mid-May–Oct) has four-hour tours in English that cover the war years.

You can forget the horrors of war at **Königssee**, a beautiful alpine lake situated 5km south of Berchtesgaden (linked by buses in summer). There are frequent boat tours across the lake to the chapel at St Bartholomä (€12).

The nicest camping grounds are at Königssee. **Grafenlehen** (☎ 4140; www.camping-grafenlehen.de; Königsseerfussweg 71, Schönau; per camp site/person €6.50/5.50) has a playground and mountain views.

Take bus 9539 to the busy **Jugendherberge** (☎ 943 70; www.berchtesgaden.jugendherberge.de; Struberweg 6, Bischofswiesen; dm €16-20, s/d from €24/40; closed Nov–late-Dec; ⊠).

There is hourly service to Berchtesgaden from Munich (€34, 2½ hours), which usually requires a change in Frilassing. There's hourly service to nearby Salzburg in Austria (€9, one hour).

BADEN-WÜRTTEMBERG

Most people don't realise it (even as they're enjoying it), but Baden-Württemberg is one of Germany's best tourist regions. For starters, there's the Black Forest – a place on almost every itinerary. Ditto for Heidelberg and its half-timbered charms. Slightly less known but possibly even more worth exploring are the rollicking student town of Freiburg and misty waters of Lake Constance.

STUTTGART

☎ 0711 / pop 590,000

Hemmed in by vine-covered hills and full of greenery, Stuttgart is a haven for its residents, who enjoy a high quality of life. For tourists, it's another matter: come for the car museums and leave (especially to Tübingen). It's not a major stop for budget travellers.

Information

Königstrasse is the spine of central Stuttgart, with most of the major stores and malls.

Coffee Fellows (Hauptbahnhoff; per hr €2; 8am-11pm) Has computers and free wi-fi across from track 4.

Tourist office (☎ 222 80; www.stuttgart-tourist.de; Königstrasse 1a; 9am-8pm Mon-Fri, 9am-6pm Sat, 11am-6pm Sun) Sells the three-day Stuttcard discount card for €18.

Sights

An arms race has broken out among the two local car companies, with both building new and costly monuments to themselves.

The motor car was first developed by Gottlieb Daimler and Carl Benz at the end of the 19th century. The impressive new-for-2006 **Mercedes-Benz Museum** (☎ 172 2578; Mercedesstrasse 137; admission €8; 9am-6pm Tue-Sun) is in the suburb of Bad-Cannstatt; take S-Bahn 1 to Neckarstadion. For even faster cars, cruise over to the striking new-for-2009 **Porsche Museum** (☎ 911 5685; Porscheplatz 1; admission €8; 9am-6pm Tue-Sun); take S-Bahn 6 to Neuwirtshaus, north of the city.

In town and stretching southwest from the Neckar River to the city centre is the **Schlossgarten**, complete with ponds, swans, street entertainers and modern sculptures. At the southern end, the gardens encompass the sprawling baroque **Neues Schloss** and the Renaissance **Altes Schloss**.

Possibly more beautiful than the works within, the **Kunstmuseum Stuttgart** (☎ 216 2188; www.kunstmuseum-stuttgart.de; Kleiner Schlossplatz 1;

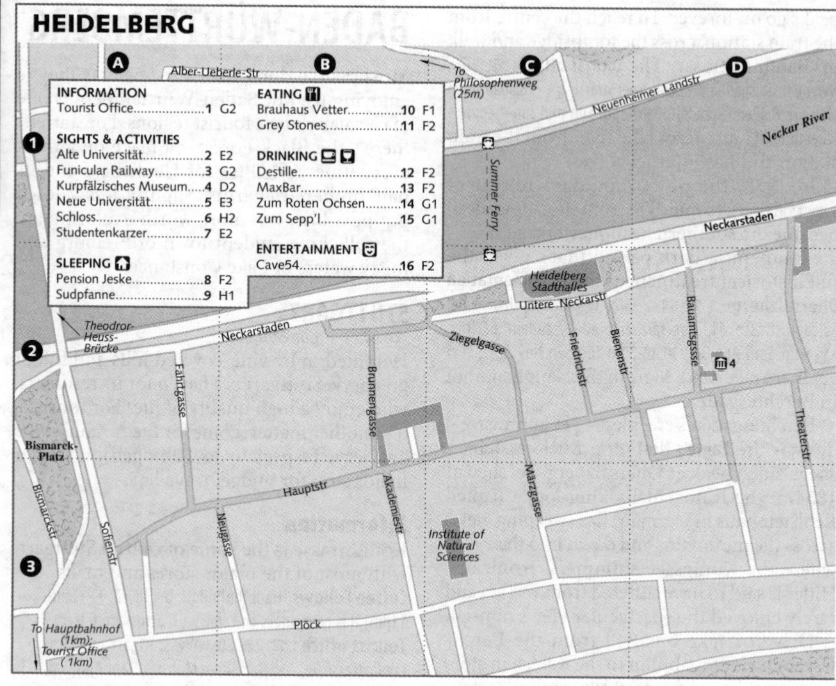

admission €5; ⌚ 10am-6pm Tue-Sun, to 9pm Wed & Fri) glows like a radioactive sugarcube at night. Highlights include works by Otto Dix, Dieter Roth and Willi Baumeister.

Sleeping & Eating

Stuttgart is a great place to sample Swabian specialities such as *Spätzle* (homemade noodles) and *Maultaschen* (a hearty ravioli in broth).

Alex 30 Hostel (838 8950; www.alex30-hostel.de; Alexanderstrasse 30; dm €22, r €35-100; 💻 P ⊠) Tidy and orderly in an interesting neighbourhood. Take U-Bahn lines 5, 6 or 7 to Olgaeck.

Museumstube (☎ 296 810; www.museumstube.de; Hospitalstrasse 9; s/d from €32/47) A modest, family-run place with 14 rooms that are clean and functional, like that generic Ford you rented many years back. Confirm that reception will be open when you arrive.

Markthalle (market hall; Dorotheenstrasse 4; ⌚ 7am-6.30pm Mon-Fri, to 4pm Sat) Sells picnic fixin's and has Italian and Swabian restaurants.

Café Künstlerbund (☎ 227 0036; Schlossplatz 2; mains €7-10) Shelter under the arches facing the park or out in the sunshine at this funky cafe that's part of a large gallery. The drinks menu is huge, as are the choices for breakfast. When the weather gets nasty, duck into the groovy upstairs room.

Drinking

Palast der Republik (☎ 226 4887; Friedrichstrasse 27) A legendary and tiny pillbox of a bar that pulls a huge crowd of laid-back, genial drinkers. Statuary and stickers abound.

There's a **beer garden** (☎ 226 1274; Canstatterstr 18) in the Mittlerer Schlossgarten northeast of the main train station, with beautiful views over the city.

Getting There & Around

Stuttgart's international **airport** (SGT; www.stuttgart-airport.com) is south of the city and includes service from Air Berlin (Germany), Germanwings (Germany, London, Eastern Europe and the Mediterranean) and Lufthansa. It's served by S2 and S3 trains (€3.10, 30 minutes from the Hauptbahnhof).

There are frequent train departures for all major German, and many international, cities. ICE trains run to Frankfurt (€56, 1¼ hours, hourly) and Munich (€39 to €52, 2¼ hours,

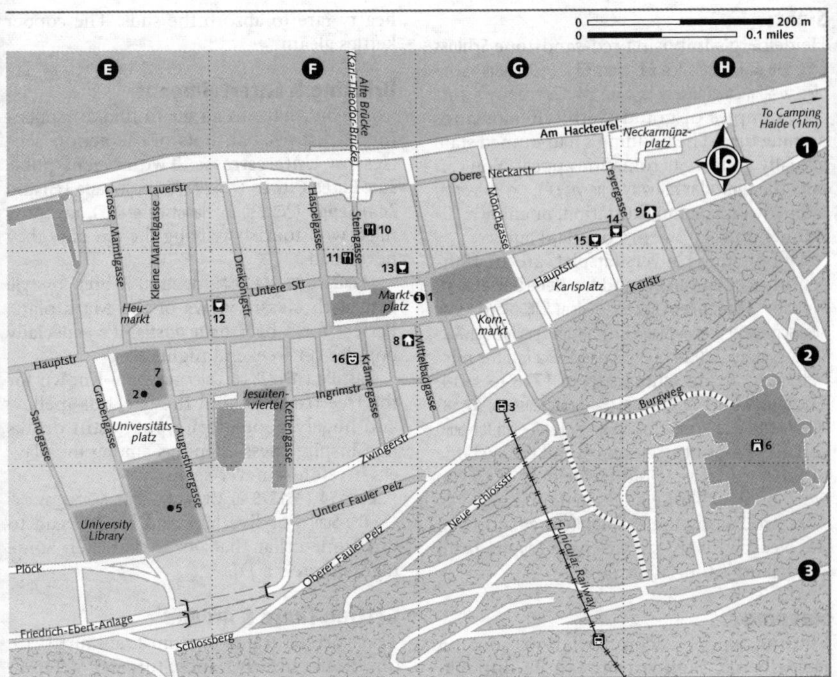

two hourly). Trains run hourly to Nuremberg (€38, 2¼ hours).

One-way fares on Stuttgart's public transport network (www.vvs.de) are €2 in the central zone; a central zone day pass is €5.80.

AROUND STUTTGART

Tübingen

☎ 07071 / pop 83,200

Swans set the mood for this hilly, picturesque town. And as the university (founded 1477) has 22,000 students, there's an appealing edge to it all. On **Marktplatz** is the 1435 **Rathaus** with its ornate baroque facade and astronomical clock. From the Renaissance **Schloss Hohentübingen** (Burgsteig 11) there are fine views over the steep rooftops of the old town. The **tourist office** (☎ 913 60; www.tuebingen-info.de; An der Neckarbrücke 1; 9am-7pm Mon-Fri, 9am-5pm Sat, 11am-4pm Sun May-Oct) is by the bridge.

The **Jugendherberge Tübingen** (☎ 230 02; www.djh.de; Gartenstrasse 22/2; dm €22-25;) has a delightful location by the river.

No one has said this before: get shlossed at the **Schloss Café** (☎ 965 153), a fine student hang with live music and poetry.

There are half-hourly RE trains between Tübingen and Stuttgart (€11.30, one hour).

HEIDELBERG

☎ 06221 / 143,000

Heidelberg's baroque old town, lively university atmosphere, excellent pubs and evocative half-ruined castle make it popular with visitors: 3.5 million flock here each year. They are following in the footsteps of the 19th-century romantics, most notably the poet Goethe. Britain's William Turner also loved the city, which inspired him to paint some of his greatest landscapes.

Heidelberg's captivating old town starts to reveal itself after a 15-minute walk that holds very little of interest west of the main train station, along the Kurfürsten-Anlage.

Information

There are internet places in the train station.

Tourist office (☎ 194 33; www.heidelberg-marketing.de) Hauptbahnhof (Willy-Brandt-Platz 1; 9am-7pm Mon-Sat year-round, 10am-6pm Sun Apr-Nov); Marktplatz (8am-5pm Mon-Fri, 10am-5pm Sat) The Hauptbahnhof branch is outside the train station. The €10 Heidelberg Card offers discounts and free admission to many sights.

Sights

Heidelberg's imposing red-sandstone **Schloss** (☎ 538 421; admission €4, tours €4; ⏰ 9am-8pm summer, to 5pm other times) is one of Germany's finest examples of grand Gothic-Renaissance architecture. The building's half-ruined state actually adds to its romantic appeal. You can take the **funicular railway** (one-way €3; ⏰ 9am-5pm) from lower Kornmarkt station, or enjoy a 10-minute walk up steep, stone-laid lanes.

Dominating Universitätsplatz are the 18th-century **Alte Universität** and the **Neue Universität**. Nearby **Studentenkarzer** (student jail; ☎ 543 554; Augustinergasse 2; admission €3; ⏰ 10am-6pm Tue-Sun Apr-Sep, to 4pm Tue-Sat Oct-Mar) was used as a jail for misbehaving young scholars from 1778 to 1914. The **Kurpfälzisches Museum** (Palatinate Museum; ☎ 583 402; Hauptstrasse 97; admission €3; ⏰ 10am-6pm Tue-Sun) contains paintings, sculptures and the jawbone of the 600,000-year-old Heidelberg Man (no word on whether he graduated on time).

A stroll along the **Philosophenweg**, north of the Neckar River, is a welcome respite from Heidelberg's tourist hordes.

Sleeping

Finding any accommodation during Heidelberg's high season can be difficult. Arrive early in the day or book ahead.

Camping Haide (☎ 802 506; www.camping-heidelberg.de; Schlierbacher Landstrasse 151; camp sites per person €6, per tent €3.50-6) These grounds are in a pretty spot on the river. Take bus 35 to Orthopädie.

Sudpfanne (☎ 163 636; www.heidelberger-sudpfanne.de; Hauptstrasse 223; dm/s/d €20/30/60; 💻 P ⊠) Right in the centre of things, the mood is set by the wine-barrel entrance (it's also a cafe). Bathrooms are shared and it's all rather bare-bones (although there is wi-fi) but you can't beat the price.

Pension Jeske (☎ 237 33; www.pension-jeske-heidelberg.de; Mittelbadgasse 2; r €25-65; ⊠) Large, colourful and decorated with flair, the rooms in this 250-year-old house are the antithesis of cookie-cutter, chain-hotel blandness. The cheapest singles share bathrooms.

Eating

Find cheap, fresh food and spicy wursts at the centuries-old market on Marktplatz.

Grey Stones (☎ 588 0280; Steingasse 16A; meals €4-10) A new-age cafe with comfy tables out front for hanging out over long, shared breakfasts. Inside is a techno beat that lasts well into the night.

Brauhaus Vetter (☎ 165 850; Steingasse 9; mains €5-12) A popular brewery that serves up lots of hearty fare to absorb the suds. The copper kettles gleam.

Drinking & Entertainment

You won't have to go far to find a happening backstreet bar. Lots of the action centres on Unterestrasse. Two ancient pubs, **Zum Roten Oschen** (☎ 209 77; Hauptstrasse 213) and **Zum Sepp'l** (☎ 230 85; Hauptstrasse 217), are now filled with tourists reliving the uni days they never had.

MaxBar (☎ 244 19; Marktplatz 5t) A French-style cafe with classic views of the Marktplatz. Perfect for a beer or a *pastis*, it's especially popular on weekend nights.

Destille (☎ 228 08; Unterestrasse 16) Known for the tree trunk behind the bar, this mellow and hugely popular pub pours stiff drinks that inspire chess openings among the players heretofore never seen.

Cave54 (☎ 278 40; www.cave54.de; Krämergasse 2; ⏰ Thu-Sun) For live jazz and blues, head to this stone cellar that oozes character. Some nights there's a DJ.

Getting There & Around

There are IC trains to/from Frankfurt (€19, one hour, hourly) and Stuttgart (€24, 40 minutes, hourly). The frequent service to Mannheim (€5, 15 minutes) has connections to cities throughout Germany.

Bismarckplatz is the main public transport hub. One-way tickets for the excellent bus and tram system are €2.10. Greatly shorten the trek from the train station to the Altstadt with bus 32 or 33 to the Bergbahn stop.

BLACK FOREST

The Black Forest (Schwarzwald) gets its name from the dark canopy of evergreens, though it's also dotted with open slopes and farmland. And while some parts heave with visitors, a 20-minute walk from even the most crowded spot will put you in quiet countryside dotted with enormous traditional farmhouses and patrolled by amiable dairy cows. It's not nature wild and remote, but bucolic and picturesque.

The Black Forest is east of the Rhine between Karlsruhe and Basel. It's shaped like a bean, about 160km long and 50km wide. From north to south there are three good bases for your visit: Schiltach, Triberg and Titisee. Each has good train links.

If you have a car, you'll find your visit especially rewarding as you can wander the rolling hills and deep valleys at will. One of the main tourist roads is the Schwarzwald-Hochstrasse (B500), which runs from Baden-Baden to Freudenstadt and from Triberg to Waldshut. And, yes, there are many, many places to buy cuckoo clocks (at €150 or more for a good one, buyers are, well, cuckoo).

Activities

With more than 7000km of marked trails, hiking possibilities during summer are, almost literally, endless. A simple inquiry at any tourist office will yield lots of local options for exploration.

Cross-country skiing is big on all these trails through the winter. For downhill fun, there are runs galore around Feldberg.

Freudenstadt

☎ 07441 / pop 23,000

Freudenstadt is a good base for exploring the northern part of the Black Forest and for hikes into the surrounding countryside. It's most notable feature is a vast **marketplace** that is the largest in the country. The **tourist office** (☎ 8640; www.freudenstadt.de; Marktplatz 64; ⌚ 9am-6pm Mon-Fri, 10am-2pm Sat & Sun May-Oct, 10am-5pm Mon-Fri, 10am-1pm Sat, 11am-1pm Sun Nov-Apr) has internet access and is good for local hiking ideas.

The **DJH Hostel** (☎ 7720; www.jugendherberge.de; Eugen-Nägele-Strasse 69; dm €19; ⊠) has 138 beds in a central and classic 1960s building. **Hotel Schwanen** (☎ 915 50; www.schwanen-freudenstadt.de, in German; Forststrasse 6; r €40-90; 🖳 P ⊠) has spruced-up rooms with wi-fi.

From Freudenstadt, hourly trains run south to Schiltach (€7, 30 minutes) and north to the important transfer point of Karlsruhe (€16,1½ hours). Stuttgart has hourly trains (€16, 1½ hours).

Schiltach

☎ 07836

Schiltach is easily the prettiest town in the Black Forest – there is the always underlying roar of the Kinzig and Schiltach Rivers, which meet here. Half-timbered buildings lean at varying angles along the crisscrossing hillside lanes. The **Markt**, the town square, has several tiny museums that cover local history and culture.

The **tourist office** (☎ 58 50; www.schiltach.de; Hauptstrasse 5; ⌚ 10am-5pm Mon-Fri, to 2pm Sat) can help with accommodation and has a lot of English-language information.

Schiltach is on a small train line linking Offenburg (€8, 45 minutes) via Hausach to Freudenstadt (€5, 30 minutes) with hourly services.

Triberg

☎ 07722

Framed by three mountains (hence the name), Triberg has two duelling cuckoo clocks that claim to be the world's largest – it's a close call on these house-sized oddities.

It also has an appealing old centre and plenty of chances to go for a stroll. There's a one-hour walk to a roaring waterfall (and even better hiking beyond) that starts near the **tourist office** (☎ 866 490; www.triberg.de; Wallfahrtstrasse 4; ⌚ 10am-5pm).

Kukucksnest (☎ 869 487; Wallfahrtstrasse 15; r €50; ⊠) has the shop of master woodcarver Gerald Burger. Above is the beautiful nest he has carved for his guests.

The Black Forest cake at **Café Schäfer** (☎ 44 65; www.cafe-schaefer-triberg.de; Hauptstrasse 33; coffee & cake €4-6; ⌚ 9am-6pm Mon-Fri, 8am-6pm Sat, 11am-6pm Sun, closed Wed) is the real deal; they have the original recipe to prove it.

Triberg is midway on the spectacular Karlsruhe (€22, 1½ hours) to Constance (€22, 1½ hours) train line. There's hourly service and good connections. Change at Hausach for Schiltach and Freudenstadt. The station is 1.7km from the centre; take any bus to Markt.

Titisee

☎ 07651

The iconic glacial **lake** draws no shortage of visitors to the busy village of Titisee. Walking around Titisee or paddle-boating across it are major activities. But if you can, drive into the surrounding rolling meadows to see some of the truly enormous traditional house-barn combos ('Is that the cow or is it your feet?').

The **tourist office** (☎ 980 40; www.titisee-neustadt.de; Strandbadstrasse 4; ⌚ 9am-6pm Mon-Fri, 10am-1pm Sat & Sun May-Oct, 9am-noon & 1.30-5pm Mon-Fri Nov-Apr) can help you arrange a farm stay.

There are four campgrounds around the lake. **Jugendherberge Veltishof am Titisee** (☎ 07652-238; www.jugendherberge-titisee-veltishof.de; Bruderhalde 27; dm from €20; ⊠) is in a huge farmhouse and

Book your stay at lonelyplanet.com/hotels

is reached by bus 7300 from Titisee or by foot (30 minutes).

Bergseeblick (☎ 8257; www.bergseeblick-titisee.de; Erlenweg 3; s €24-30, d €48-58; Ⓟ) is a family-run chalet near the church that offers quiet rooms and gnomes themed for Snow White and her Seven Dwarfs.

Titisee is linked to Freiburg by frequent train service (€10, 40 minutes). To reach Triberg to the north, there are scenic hourly connections via Neustadt and Donaueschigen (€16, two hours).

Around Titisee

The Black Forest **ski season** runs from late December to March. While there is good downhill skiing, the area is more suited to cross-country. The centre for winter sports is around Titisee, with uncrowded downhill ski runs at **Feldberg** (www.liftverbund-feldberg.de; lift tickets €25, rental equipment available) and numerous graded cross-country trails.

In summer you can use the lifts to reach the summit of the sallow-sloped Feldberg (1493m) for a wondrous panorama that stretches to the Alps.

Feldberg is 15km south of Titisee. It can be reached by bus 7300 from Titisee (€4, 12 minutes, hourly) or in season by free ski shuttles.

FREIBURG

☎ 0761 / pop 213,500

Nestled between hills and vineyards, Freiburg im Breisgau is a fun place, thanks to the city's large and thriving university community. There's a sense of fun here best exemplified by the tiny medieval canals *(bächle)* running right down the middle of streets. The monumental 13th-century cathedral is the city's key landmark, but the real attractions are the vibrant cafes, bars and street life, plus the local wines.

Information

Tourist office (☎ 388 1880; www.freiburg.de; Rathausplatz 2-4; 🕑 8am-8pm Mon-Fri, 9.30am-5pm Sat, 10am-noon Sun Jun-Sep, 8am-6pm Mon-Fri, 9.30am-2.30pm Sat, 10am-noon Sun Oct-May) Well stocked with hiking and cycling maps of the region.

Wash & Tours (☎ 288 866; Salzstrasse 22; wash €5, internet per hr €2.50; 🕑 9am-7pm) There's a drop-off laundry downstairs and an internet cafe upstairs.

Sights

The major sight in Freiburg is the 700-year-old **Münster** (Cathedral; Münsterplatz; tower €1.50; 🕑 9.30am-5pm Mon-Sat, 1-5pm Sun), a classic example of both high- and late-Gothic architecture that looms over Münsterplatz, Freiburg's market square. The bustling **university quarter** is northwest of the Martinstor (one of the old city gates).

The trip by cable car to the 1286m **Schauinsland peak** (one way/return €8/12; 🕑 9am-5pm Jan-Jun, to 6pm Jul-Sep, 9.30am-5pm Oct-Dec) is a quick way to reach the Black Forest highlands. Numerous easy and well-marked trails make the Schauinsland area ideal for day walks. From Freiburg take tram 4 south to Günterstal and then bus 21 to Talstation.

Sleeping

Hirzberg Camping (☎ 350 54; www.freiburg-camping.de; Kartäuserstrasse 99; camp sites per adult/tent €6/3.50; 💻 Ⓟ) Pitch a tent at this serene woodland camping ground 1.5km east of Schwabentor.

Black Forest Hostel (☎ 881 7870; www.blackforest-hostel.de; Kartäuserstrasse 33; dm €13-21, s/d €30/50; 💻 ⊠) Freiburg's funkiest budget digs are five minutes' stroll from the centre. Overlooking vineyards, this former factory has been lovingly revamped as an industrial-themed hostel. Bike hire costs €5 per day.

Pension Paradies (☎ 273 700; www.paradies-freiburg.de; Friedrich-Ebert-Platz; r €36-75; 💻 Ⓟ) This treasure over the train tracks (take tram 4) has simple but stylish rooms. There is a vast cafe with vegetarian specials and a large terrace.

Hotel Schwarzwälder Hof (☎ 380 30; www.schwarzwaelder-hof.eu; Herrenstrasse 43; r €45-120; ⊠ 💻) This bijou hotel has an unrivalled style-for-euro ratio. A wrought-iron staircase sweeps up to snazzy rooms, some with postcard views of the Altstadt. Bargain singles share bathrooms.

Eating & Drinking

There's a good selection of *Wurst* and other quick eats from stalls set up in the market square during lunch.

UC Uni-Café (☎ 383 355; Niemensstrasse 7; meals €3-7) A popular hang-out that serves snacks on its see-and-be-seen outdoor terrace.

Markthalle (Grünwälderstrasse 2; meals €3-8; 🕑 7am-7pm) A dozen stands selling ethnic food cluster around a bar selling local wine. A fun and fine deal.

Beirgarten Greiffenegg-Schlössle (☎ 327 28; Schlossbergring 3; mains €5) Perched above Freiburg, this terrace beer garden is great for watching the sun set over the city's red rooftops. The restaurant inside the villa is posh.

our pick **Schlappen** (☎ 334 94; Löwenstrasse 2; ⏲ 11am-1am Mon-Thu, 11am-3am Fri & Sat, 3pm-1am Sun) With its jazz-themed back room and poster-plastered walls, this student watering hole is a perennial fave. Try a Flammkuche, then forget about it with absinthe.

Jazzhaus (☎ 349 73; www.jazzhaus.de; Schnewlinstrasse 1) Under the brick arches of a wine cellar, this venue hosts first-rate jazz, rock and hip-hop concerts (€10 to €30) at 8pm at least three nights a week. It morphs into a club at weekends.

Jos Fritz Cafe (☎ 300 19; www.josfritzcafe.de; Wilhelmstrasse 15) Down a little alley past the recycling bins, this cafe hosts concerts of alternative bands and events such as political discussions (stir things up with 'Is Merkel too liberal?').

Getting There & Around

Freiburg is on the busy Mannheim to Basel, Switzerland (€22, 45 minutes, hourly) train line. ICE service includes Frankfurt (€61, two hours, hourly). Freiburg is linked to Titisee by frequent trains (€10, 40 minutes).

Single rides on the efficient local bus and tram system cost €2. A 24-hour pass costs €5. Trams depart from the bridge over the train tracks.

LAKE CONSTANCE

☎ **07531 / pop 81,000**

Lake Constance (Bodensee) is an oasis in landlocked southern Germany. Even if you never make contact with the water, this giant bulge in the sinewy course of the Rhine can offer a splash of refreshment. There are many historic towns around its periphery, which can be explored by boat or bicycle and on foot. Two good places to start are the namesake Constance, a tidy lake town, and Lindau, a misplaced corner of Bavaria.

Information

Constance Tourist Office (☎ 133 030; www.konstanz.de/tourismus; Bahnhofplatz 13; ⏲ 9am-6.30pm Mon-Fri, to 4pm Sat, 10am-1pm Sun Apr-Oct, 9.30am-12.30pm, 2-6pm Mon-Fri Nov-Mar) About 150m to the right from the train station exit.

Lindau Tourist Office (☎ 260 030; www.lindau.de; Ludwigstrasse 68; ⏲ 9am-1pm & 2-7pm Mon-Fri, 2-7pm Sat & Sun May-Sep, 9am-1pm & 2-5pm Mon-Fri Oct-Apr) Directly opposite the train station.

Sights & Activities

From Constance, head across to **Mainau Island** (☎ 3030; www.mainau.de; admission €14; ⏲ 7am-8pm mid-Mar–Nov, 9am-6pm Nov–mid-Mar), with its baroque castle set among vast and gorgeous gardens that include a butterfly house and beaches. Take bus 4 (€2, 25 minutes) or a BSB ferry from the harbour behind the station.

Connected to the nearby lakeshore by bridges, the key sights of the oh-so-charming island town of Lindau all have murals: **Altes Rathaus** (Reichsplatz), the **city theatre** (Barfüsserplatz) and the harbour's **Seepromenade**, with its Bavarian Lion monument and lighthouse.

Other lakeside towns worth a visit include **Meersburg** and **Friedrichshafen**.

A 270km international **bike route** circumnavigates Lake Constance through Germany, Austria and Switzerland, tracing the often-steep shoreline beside vineyards and pebble beaches. You can rent bikes in any town. Popular watery pursuits include sailing and wind-boarding.

A fun way to explore is by **Bodensee-Schiffsbetriebe boats** (BSB; www.bsb-online.com), which, from Easter to late October, call several times a day at the larger towns along the lake; there are discounts for rail-pass holders.

Sleeping & Eating

Lakeside beer gardens and cafes can be found in every town.

Campingplatz Bruderhofer (☎ 31 388; www.campingplatz-konstanz.de; Fohrenbühlweg 45, Constance; camp sites per adult/car/tent €4/3/4; Ⓟ) This modern camping ground, in Constance's northeastern suburb of Staad, is 3km northeast of the Altstadt and 800m south of the Meersburg car-ferry dock.

Park Camping Lindau am See (☎ 722 36; www.park-camping.de; Fraunhoferstrasse 20, Lindau; camp sites for 2 people €20) Is on a beach 3km southeast of Lindau. Take bus 1 or 2 to the bus station, then bus 3.

Jugendherberge Konstanz (☎ 322 60; www.jugendherberge-konstanz.de; Zur Allmannshöhe 18, Constance; dm €25; ⊠) This 178-bed hostel is in a white cylindrical one-time water tower. Take bus 4 (to Jugendherberge).

Hotel Gasthof Goldenes Lamm (☎ 5732; www.goldenes-lamm-lindau.de; Schafgasse 3, Lindau; r €60-120) The attractive-looking facade of this hotel is mirrored by the 21 comfortable rooms inside. The rustic restaurant is good and has many fish dishes.

Getting There & Away

Constance has trains to Offenburg via Triberg in the Black Forest (€29, 2¼ hours, hourly). There are good connections into Switzerland (which is 200m south!) including Zurich (€17, 1¼ hours, hourly).

Lindau has trains to Munich (€38, 2¼ hours, every two hours) and direct to Zurich (€25, four times daily). Trains to nearby Bregenz (€4.20, nine minutes, two hourly) let you connect to the rest of Austria and Switzerland.

WESTERN GERMANY

The western section of Germany mixes natural beauty with industry. The popular Rhine River offers boat rides amid castles and wineries – what more do you want? The Moselle River offers more of the same but with smaller tourist crowds. Very un-German Frankfurt is a major transport hub with some good nightlife that you're bound to encounter. The northwest, with industrial states like North Rhine-Westphalia, is home to a quarter of Germany's population and little beauty. Beautiful exceptions such as the cities of Cologne and Aachen are *big* exceptions.

MOSELLE VALLEY

Exploring the vineyards and wineries of the Moselle (Mosel) Valley is an ideal way to get a taste of German culture and people – and, of course, the wonderful wines. Take the time to slow down and savour a glass or two.

The Moselle is bursting at the seams with historical sites and picturesque towns built along the river below steep rocky cliffs planted with vineyards (they say locals are born with one leg shorter than the other so that they can easily work the vines). It's one of the country's most romantically scenic regions, with stunning views rewarding the intrepid hikers who brave the hilly trails.

Many winemakers have their own small pensions but accommodation is hard to find in May, on summer weekends or during the local wine harvest (mid-September to mid-October). Note also that much of the region – like the vines themselves – goes into a deep slumber from November to March, albeit after an autumn explosion of colour.

The most scenic part of the Moselle Valley runs 195km northeast from Trier to Koblenz; it's most practical to begin your Moselle Valley trip from one of these places.

Two good information sources for the valley are Koblenz's **tourist office** (☎ 0261-303 880; www.koblenz.de; Bahnhofsplatz 7; 🕑 9am-6pm Mon-Sat year-round, 10am-6pm Sun Apr-Oct), across from the train station, and Cochem's **tourist office** (☎ 02671-600 40; www.cochem.de; Endertplatz; 🕑 9am-5pm Mon-Sat, 10am-noon Sun, less often in winter), next to the Moselbrücke.

Koblenz is much more transit hub than tourist stop. **Cochem** is a deserving if often crowded stop. For a great view, head up to the **Pinnerkreuz** with the chairlift (€5) on Endertstrasse. The stunning **Reichsburg Castle** (☎ 02671-255; 🕑 9am-5pm mid-Mar–mid-Nov) is just a 15-minute walk up the hill from town. There are regular daily tours (€4.50).

A great itinerary for the Moselle (good in either direction) would be as follows: by boat Koblenz to Cochem, by train Cochem to Bullay and then by Moselbahn bus to Trier, stopping at any of the little villages along the way that grab you.

You'll find lots of sleeping options in all towns big and small. **Campingplatz Am Freizeitszentrum** (☎ 02671-44 09; Stadionstrasse, Cochem; camp sites per person/tent/car €5/5/6) is downstream from the northern bridge, alongside the river. **Moseltal-Jugendherberge** (☎ 02671-8633; www.djh.de; Klottener Strasse 9, Cochem; dm/s/d €19/31/48; 💻 ☒) is beautifully situated on the banks of the river. The 148 beds are mostly in spotless four-bed rooms with wi-fi.

Getting There & Around

Trains fan out in all directions from Koblenz. Up the Moselle to Trier (€20, 1½ hours, hourly) via Cochem, north along the Rhine to Cologne (€20, one hour, two hourly) and south on the Rhine to Mainz (€20, one hour, two hourly).

Between May and early October, **Köln-Düsseldorfer (KD) Line** (☎ 0221-208 8318; www.k-d.com) ferries sail daily between Koblenz and Cochem (€24 one way, 5¼ hours upstream, 4¼ hours downstream). Various smaller ferry companies also operate on the Moselle from some of the towns. Eurail and

German Rail passes are valid for all normal KD Line services.

Trains run twice hourly Cochem to Bullay (€5, 10 minutes) where you can pick up the bus.

Moselbahn (☎ 0651 147 750; www.moselbahn.de) runs buses between the train stations in Bullay and Trier (three hours each way), a very scenic route following the river's winding course and passing through numerous quaint villages.

The Moselle is a popular area among cyclists, and for much of the river's course there's a separate 'Moselroute' bike track. Most towns have a rental shop or two; ask at the tourist offices. Many of the Moselbahn buses also carry bikes.

TRIER

☎ 0651 / pop 100,000

Trier is touted as Germany's oldest town and you'll find more Roman ruins here than anywhere else north of the Alps. Its proximity to France can be tasted in its cuisine, while its large student population injects life among the ruins.

From the main train station head west along Bahnhofstrasse and Theodor-Heuss-Allee to the Porta Nigra, where you'll find Trier's **tourist office** (☎ 978 080; www.trier.de; 9am-6pm Mon-Sat, 10am-5pm Sun May-Oct; reduced hours winter).

Sights

The town's chief landmark is the **Porta Nigra** (admission €2.10; 9am-6pm Apr-Sep, to 5pm Mar & Oct, to 4pm Nov-Feb), the imposing city gate on the northern edge of the town centre, which dates back to the 2nd century AD. Nearby, **Städtisches Museum** (☎ 718 1459; Simeonstrasse 60; admission €5; 9.30am-5.30pm Tue-Sun) fills a renovated 11th-century Trier monastery with two millennium of Trier history.

Trier's massive (and massively restored) Romanesque **Dom** (www.dominformation.de; Liebfrausenstrasse 12; 6.30am-6pm Apr-Oct, to 5.30pm Nov-Mar) has a 1600-year history.

Additional Roman sites include the **Amphitheater** (admission €2.10; Olewigerstrasse; 9am-6pm Apr-Sep, to 5pm Mar & Oct, to 4pm Nov-Feb) and the gloomy underground caverns of the **Kaiserthermen** (admission €2.10; Im Palastgarten; same as Amphitheater).

The **Karl Marx Haus** (☎ 970 680; Brückenstrasse 10; admission €3; 10am-6pm Apr-Oct, to 5pm Tue-Sun Nov-Mar) is the suitably modest birthplace of the man. The walls are lined with manifestos.

Sleeping & Eating

The narrow and historic Judengasse, near the Markt, has several small bars and clubs. There's also a cluster of stylish places on Viehmarktplatz. The **Markthalle** (9am-10pm Mon-Sat), set back from Palaststrasse, has places selling fresh produce and wines from the region, as well as numerous small delis and cafes where you can eat in or take away.

Camping Treviris (☎ 869 21; Luxemburger Strasse 81; camp sites per person/tent/car €6/5/5; Apr-Oct) This camping ground is central and beside the Moselle River.

Hille's Hostel (☎ 710 2785; www.hilles-hostel-trier.de; Gartenfeldstrasse 7; dm €15-18, s/d €40/50; P) The rooms here are furnished with Ikea bunk beds and are set back from the road amidst some hardy palms.

Warsberger Hof (☎ 975 250; www.warsberger-hof.de; Dietrichstrasse 42; dm/s/d €23/30/50) A foundation-run hotel aimed at young people, the 150 beds are scattered about a vintage building that's ideally located. Bathrooms are shared and there's a fine outdoor cafe in the courtyard.

Astarix (☎ 722 39; Karl-Marx-Strasse 11; mains from €5) Popular student hang-out with good pizza and hot specials. The bar out front sometimes has live jazz.

Walderdorff's (☎ 9946 9212; Domfreihof 1A; mains €8-16) A high-concept wine bar and cafe across from the Dom. Score one of the dozens of tables out front or inside in the stylish surrounds.

Getting There & Away

Trier has a train service to Koblenz (€20, 1½ hours, hourly) via Bullay and Cochem, as well as to Luxembourg (€16, 50 minutes, hourly).

RHINE VALLEY – KOBLENZ TO MAINZ

A trip along the Rhine is on the itinerary of most travellers, as it should be. The section between Koblenz and Mainz offers ever-changing vistas of steep vineyard-covered mountains punctuated by scores of castles. It's really rather magical. Spring and autumn are the best times to visit; in summer it's overrun and in winter most towns go into hibernation. Mainz, like most of the other towns, has a good **tourist office** (☎ 286 210; www.indo-mainz.de; Brückenturm am Rathaus; 9am-6pm Mon-Fri, 10am-3pm Sat).

Every town along the route offers cute little places to stay or camp, and atmospheric places to drink and eat.

Sights & Activities

There are dozens of towns along this prime stretch of the Rhine. Details of some of the more notable follow. All have train and boat services.

Assmannshausen (right bank) is a small, relatively untouristed village with nice hotels, sweeping views and good hikes.

Bacharach is a medieval walled village where everyone looks up to the great **Jugendherberge** (☎ 1266; www.djh.de; dm €19) in a castle. **Boppard** (left bank) features Roman walls and ruins, while **Oberwesel** (left bank) has numerous towers and walkable walls of a ruined castle. The towns of **St Goar** and **St Goarshausen** are on opposite sides of the Rhine. St Goar is on the left bank and has one of the most impressive castles on the river: **Burg Rheinfels** (☎ 383; admission €5; 9am-6pm Apr-Oct, 11am-5pm Sat & Sun in good weather Nov-Mar). Across the river, just south of St Goarshausen, is the Rhine's most famous sight, the Loreley Cliff. Avoid **Rüdesheim**, an overrated and over-visited town of trinkets and hype.

The Koblenz-to-Mainz section of the Rhine is great for **wine tasting**, with Bacharach, 45km south of Koblenz, being one of the top choices for sipping. For tastings in other towns just follow your instincts.

Though the trails here may be a bit more crowded with day-trippers than those along the Moselle, **hiking** along the Rhine is also excellent. The slopes and trails around Bacharach are justly famous.

Getting There & Around

Koblenz and Mainz are the best starting points. The Rhine Valley is also easily accessible from Frankfurt on a very long day trip, but it could drive you to drink.

Each mode of transport on the Rhine has its own advantages and all are equally enjoyable. Try combining several of them. The **Köln-Düsseldorfer (KD) Line** (☎ 0221-208 83 18; www.k-d.com) runs several slow and fast boats daily between Koblenz and Mainz (as well as the less-interesting stretch between Cologne and Koblenz). The journey takes about four hours downstream and about 5½ hours upstream (€45, free with rail pass). Boats stop at various riverside towns along the way.

Frequent train services operate on both sides of the Rhine River, but are more convenient on the left bank. You can travel nonstop on IC/EC trains or travel by slower regional RB or RE services. The ride is amazing. Sit on the right heading north and on the left heading south. Note that most small stations don't have lockers.

Trains along the Rhine to Koblenz (€20, one hour) run twice hourly. Heidelberg (€20, one hour, hourly) is an easy trip as is Frankfurt via Frankfurt airport (€10, 40 minutes, several per hour).

FRANKFURT-AM-MAIN

☎ 069 / pop 643,000

Called 'Mainhattan', 'Bankfurt' and much more, Frankfurt is on the Main (pronounced 'mine') River, and after London it is Europe's centre of finance. Both sobriquets also refer to the city's soaring skyline of skyscrapers, a profile found nowhere else on the continent.

But while all seems cosmopolitan, Frankfurt is often just a small town at heart. Things get quiet in the evenings and the many museums are devoid of any real stars. It has cute old pubs you'd only find in a small town. However, when a major trade fair is in town, it feels as bustling as any metropolis.

Frankfurt is also Germany's most important transport hub for air, train and road connections so you'll probably end up here at some point. Note that it is generally referred to as Frankfurt-am-Main, or Frankfurt/Main, since there is another Frankfurt (Frankfurt-an-der-Oder) near the Polish border.

The area between the former prison/police station (Hauptwache) and the Römerberg, in the tiny vestige of Frankfurt's original old city, is the centre of Frankfurt. The Main River flows just south of the Altstadt, with several bridges leading to one of the city's livelier areas, Sachsenhausen.

Information

BOOKSHOPS

The Hauptbahnhof is an excellent place to go book shopping. Stores near tracks 7 and 17 have scores of English-language books and periodicals, as well as guidebooks and maps.

INTERNET ACCESS

The underground forecourt of the Hauptbahnhof has places for net access and cheap calls, as does the first block of the Kaiserstrasse.

LAUNDRY

Miele Wash World (Moselstrasse 17; wash/dry €4/1; 6am-11pm)

MEDICAL SERVICES

Doctor Referral Service (☎ 192 92; 🕑 24hr)

Uni-Klinik (☎ 630 10; Theodor Stern Kai, Sachsenhausen; 🕑 24hr)

MONEY

Reisebank Airport (Terminal 1, arrival hall B; 🕑 6am-11pm); Train station (🕑 7am-9pm) The train station branch is at the head of platform 1.

TOURIST INFORMATION

Tourist office (☎ 212 388 00; www.frankfurt-tourismus.de) Hauptbahnhof (Main hall of train station; 🕑 8am-9pm Mon-Fri, 9am-6pm Sat & Sun); Römer (Römerberg 27; 🕑 9.30am-5.30pm Mon-Fri, 10am-4pm Sat & Sun) In the northwest corner of Römerberg square. The Hauptbahnhof is the main office and has an efficient room-finding service (€3). The Frankfurt-am-Main Card (one/two days €9/13) gives 50% off admission to important attractions and unlimited travel on public transport.

Sights

About 80% of the old city was wiped off the map by two Allied bombing raids in March 1944, and postwar reconstruction was subject to the demands of the new age. Rebuilding efforts were more thoughtful, however, in the **Römerberg**, the old central area of Frankfurt west of the cathedral, where reconstructed 14th- and 15th-century buildings provide a glimpse of the beautiful city this once was. The old town hall, or **Römer**, is in the northwestern corner of Römerberg and consists of three 15th-century houses topped with Frankfurt's trademark stepped gables.

East of Römerberg is the **Frankfurter Dom**, the coronation site of Holy Roman emperors from 1562 to 1792. It's dominated by the elegant 15th-century Gothic **tower** (completed in the 1860s) – one of the few structures left standing after the 1944 raids.

Anyone with an interest in German literature should visit **Goethe Haus** (☎ 138 800; Grosser Hirschgraben 23-25; admission €5; 🕑 10am-6pm Mon-Sat, to 5.30pm Sun), where the writer was born in 1749.

Museum für Moderne Kunst (☎ 2123 0447; Domstrasse 10; admission €8; 🕑 10am-8pm Tue-Sun), north of the cathedral, features works of modern art by Joseph Beuys, Claes Oldenburg and many others. Also on the north bank there's the **Jüdisches Museum** (Jewish Museum; ☎ 2123 5000; Untermainkai 14-15; admission €4; 🕑 10am-5pm Tue-Sun, to 8pm Wed), a huge place with exhibits on the city's rich Jewish life before WWII.

Numerous museums line the south bank of the Main River along the so-called *Museumsufer* (Museum Embankment). The pick of the crop is the **Städelsches Kunstinstitut** (☎ 605 0980; Schaumainkai 63; admission €10; 🕑 10am-5pm Tue & Fri-Sun, to 9pm Wed & Thu), with a world-class collection of paintings by artists from the Renaissance to the 20th century, including Botticelli, Dürer, Van Eyck, Rubens, Rembrandt, Vermeer, Cézanne and Renoir.

Sleeping

Predictably, most of Frankfurt's budget accommodation is in the grotty Bahnhofsviertel, which surrounds the station. Check a room before committing. The streets between here and the Messe (convention centre) are convenient for early departures or meetings. During large trade fairs the town is booked out months in advance and rates soar.

City Camp Frankfurt (☎ 570 332; www.city-camp-frankfurt.de; An der Sandelmühle 35; camp sites per site/person/car €5/6/5; P 💻) This camping ground is in the Heddernheim district northwest of the city centre. It's a 15-minute ride on the U1, U2 or U3 from the Hauptwache U-Bahn station to Heddernheim.

Frankfurt Hostel (☎ 247 5130; www.frankfurt-hostel.com; Kaiserstrasse 74; dm €18-22, s/d from €50/60; 💻) A good indie hostel in a grand old building. Rooms have private bathrooms and there's a lively international crowd.

Haus der Jugend (☎ 610 0150; www.djh.de; Deutschherrnufer 12; dm from €22) Within walking distance of the city and Sachsenhausen's nightspots, this HI hostel is a good choice. From the train station take bus 46 to Frankensteinerplatz, or take S-Bahn lines S3, S4, S5 or S6 to Lokalbahnhof, then walk north for 10 minutes. Check-in begins at 1pm, curfew is 2am.

Pension Backer (☎ 747 992; Mendelssohnstrasse 92; s/d from €25/50; P) The Backer has 25 basic rooms with shared bathrooms; it's in a nice residential neighbourhood.

Hotel Am Berg (☎ 660 5370; www.hotel-am-berg-ffm.de; Grethenweg 23; r €35-100; ⊠) Located in a sandstone building in the quiet backstreets of Sachsenhausen, this hotel close to Südbahnhof has large rooms (some sharing bathrooms) that could have been sets for a '70s porn movie.

Eating

Known to the locals as Fressgasse (Munch-Alley), the Kalbächer Petrolse and Grosse

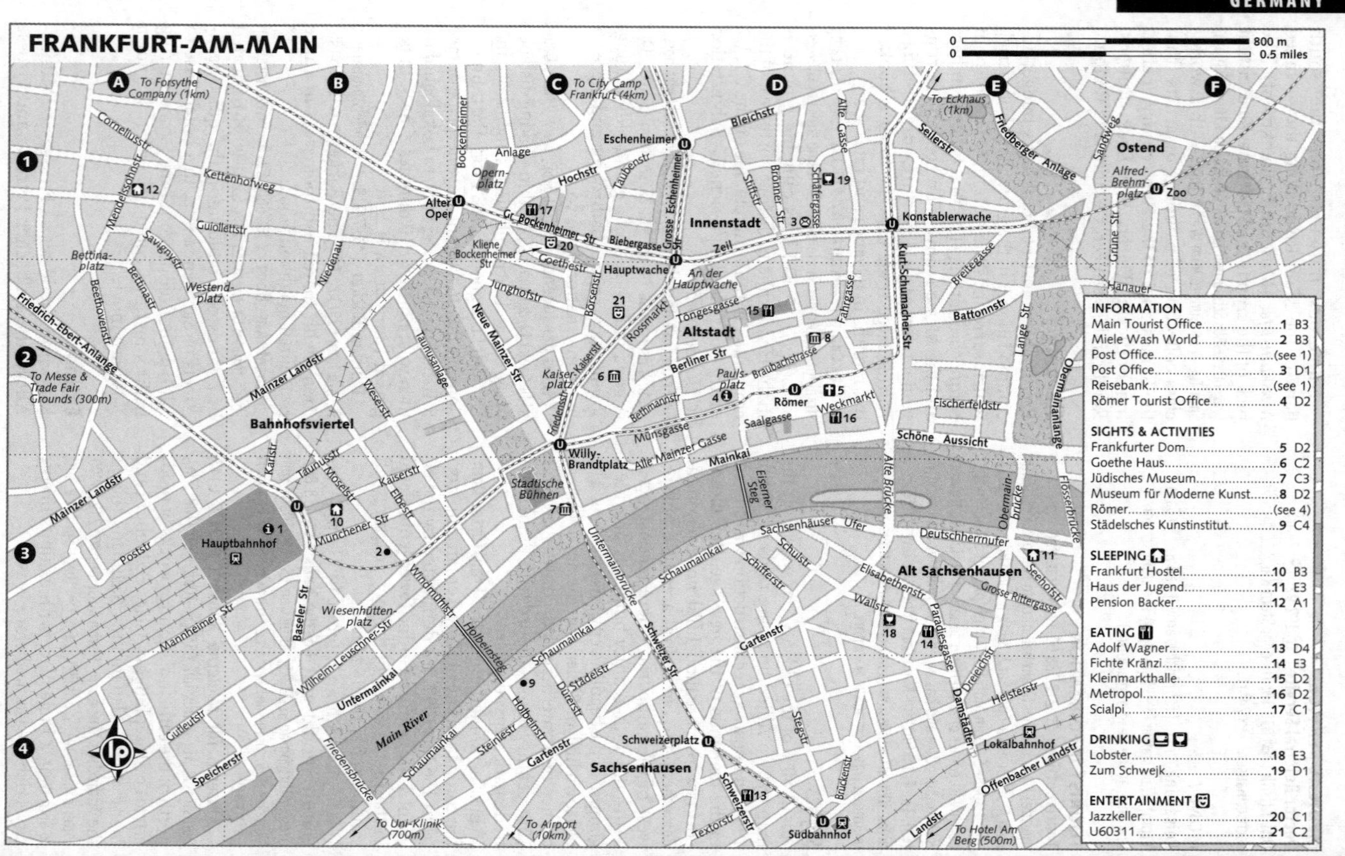
FRANKFURT-AM-MAIN
0 800 m
0 0.5 miles
INFORMATION
Main Tourist Office 1 B3
Miele Wash World 2 B3
Post Office (see 1)
Post Office 3 D1
Reisebank (see 1)
Römer Tourist Office 4 D2
SIGHTS & ACTIVITIES
Frankfurter Dom 5 D2
Goethe Haus 6 C2
Jüdisches Museum 7 C3
Museum für Moderne Kunst 8 D2
Römer (see 4)
Städelsches Kunstinstitut 9 C4
SLEEPING
Frankfurt Hostel 10 B3
Haus der Jugend 11 E3
Pension Backer 12 A1
EATING
Adolf Wagner 13 D4
Fichte Kränzi 14 E3
Kleinmarkthalle 15 D2
Metropol 16 D2
Scialpi 17 C1
DRINKING
Lobster 18 E3
Zum Schwejk 19 D1
ENTERTAINMENT
Jazzkeller 20 C1
U60311 21 C2
Innenstadt
Altstadt
Bahnhofsviertel
Ostend
Sachsenhausen
Alt Sachsenhausen
Main River
Hauptbahnhof
To Forsythe Company (1km)
To City Camp Frankfurt (4km)
To Eckhaus (1km)
To Messe & Trade Fair Grounds (300m)
To Uni-Klinik (700m)
To Airport (10km)
To Hotel Am Berg (500m)

GETTING INTO TOWN

S-Bahn lines S8 and S9 run every 15 minutes between the airport and Frankfurt Hauptbahnhof (€3.60, 4.15am to 1am, 11 minutes), usually continuing via Hauptwache and Konstablerwache. Taxis (about €35) take 30 minutes without traffic jams.

The airport train station has two sections: platforms 1 to 3 (below Terminal 1, hall B) handle S-Bahn connections, while IC and ICE connections are in the long-distance train station *(Fernbahnhof)* 300m distant.

Bockenheimer Strasse area has some medium-priced restaurants and fast-food places with outdoor tables in summer. Wallstrasse and the surrounding streets in Alt Sachsenhausen also have lots of lively midpriced restaurants.

Look for a plethora of outdoor stands serving food and drinks to gregarious crowds during April to October in the streets south of the Zeil.

APPLE-WINE TAVERNS

Apple-wine taverns are Frankfurt's great local tradition. They serve *Ebbelwoi* (Frankfurt dialect for Apfelwein), an alcoholic apple cider, along with local specialities such as *Handkäse mit Musik* (literally, 'hand-cheese with music'). This is a round cheese soaked in oil and vinegar and topped with onions; your bowel supplies the music. Some good taverns that serve *Ebbelwoi* are situated in Sachsenhausen.

our pick **Fichte Kränzi** (☎ 612 778; Wallstrasse 5; mains €7-15) Just superb. A smallish place down an alley with a large, shady tree outside. The schnitzels are tops as is the patter from the waiters.

Adolf Wagner (☎ 612 565; Schweizer Strasse 71; meals €8-15; ⏰) This old place has one of the most atmospheric interiors in Sachsenhausen. The garden is appealing as well.

RESTAURANTS

Metropol (☎ 288 287; Weckmarkt 13-15; mains €7) Near the Dom, this popular cafe serves up standard fare until late. Savour a coffee for hours with a book.

Eckhaus (☎ 491 197; Bornheimer Landstrasse 45; mains €8-14) The smoke-stained walls, the iron fan above the door and those ancient floorboards all suggest an inelegant, long-toothed past. Take the U-4 to Merianplatz.

Scialpi (☎ 282 226; Hochstrasse 51; mains €8-16) Excellent Italian fare. The pizzas are as thin as Milan models and as tasty…er, they are delicious. Tables outside vie with the stylish interior for your favour.

SELF-CATERING

Off Hasenpetrolse, **Kleinmarkthalle** (Hasengasse 5-7; ⏰ 7.30am-6pm Mon-Fri, to 3pm Sat) is a great produce market with loads of fruit, vegetables, meats and hot food.

Drinking & Clubbing

The apple-wine joints listed under Eating are great for a drink. Wander the streets of Alt Sachsenhausen to hear the echoes of the millions of American military personnel who drank at the gaudy bars here during the Cold War.

Lobster (☎ 612 920; Wallstrasse 21) A scenester bar in the heart of Sachsenhausen. Tables out front give smokers freedom while the techno tunes beat away in the intimate interior.

Zum Schwejk (☎ 293 166; Schäfergasse 20) This is a popular gay bar and one of several on this street.

Jazzkeller (☎ 288 537; Kleine Bockenheimer Strasse 18a) This club attracts top acts.

U60311 (☎ 297 060 311; Rossmarkt 6) A top club for techno, U60311 draws the best talent from around Europe. It's underground, literally, and often still going at noon from the night before.

Entertainment

Ballet, opera and theatre are strong features of Frankfurt's entertainment scene. Free *Frizz* has good listings (in German) of what's on in town.

Forsythe Company (☎ 2123 7586; www.theforsythecompany.de; Bockenheimer Depot, Carlo-Schmid-Platz 1) Easily the world's most talked-about dance company; the work of William Forsythe is often on tour.

Getting There & Away

AIR

Germany's largest airport is **Frankfurt airport** (FRA; ☎ 6901; www.frankfurt-airport.com), a vast labyrinth with connections throughout the world. It's served by most major airlines, although not many budget ones.

Only cynics like Ryanair would say that Frankfurt has another airport. **Frankfurt-Hahn airport** (HHN; www.hahn-airport.de) is 70km west of Frankfurt. Buses from Frankfurt's Hauptbahnhof take about 2¼ hours. It's fitting the bus company is called **Bohr** (☎ 06543-501 90; www.bohr-omnibusse.de; tickets €12; hourly).

BUS

The Deutsche-Touring Romantic Rd bus (see p478) leaves from the south side of the Hauptbahnhof.

TRAIN

The Hauptbahnhof handles more departures and arrivals than any other station in Germany. Among the myriad of services: Berlin (€111, four hours, hourly), Hamburg (€106, 3½ hours, hourly) and Munich (€89, 3¼ hours). For Cologne take the fast (€63, 75 minutes) ICE line or the slower and more scenic line along the Rhine (€41, 2½ hours, hourly).

Many long-distance trains also serve the airport. This station, Fernbahnhof, is beyond the S-Bahn station under Terminal 1.

Getting Around

Both single or day tickets for Frankfurt's excellent **transport network** (RMV; www.traffiq.de) can be purchased from automatic machines at almost any train station or stop. The peak period single tickets cost €2.20 and a *Tageskarte* (24-hour ticket) costs €5.60 (€8.90 with the airport).

COLOGNE

☎ 0221 / pop 1 million

Cologne (Köln) seems almost ridiculously proud to be home to Germany's largest cathedral; the twin-tower shape of its weather-beaten Gothic hulk adorns the strangest souvenirs, from egg cosies to expensive jewellery. However, this bustling Rhine-side metropolis has much more to offer than its most recognisable and ubiquitous symbol. As early as the 1st century AD, Colonia Agrippinensis was an important Roman trading settlement. Today it's one of Germany's most multicultural spots, with a vibrant nightlife only partly fuelled by the local *Kölsch* beer.

Orientation

The cathedral (Dom) and tourist information office are both on the doorstep of the main train station. The nightlife hubs of the Belgisches Viertel (tram 3, 4 or 5 to Friesenplatz) and the Zülpicher Viertel (tram 8 or 9 to Zülpicher Viertel/Bahnhof Süd) are several kilometres southwest.

Information

Several no-name internet cafes line Marzellenstrasse, minutes from the station.

Köln Welcome Card (per 24/48/72hr €9/14/19) Free public transport (including Bonn) and discounted museum admission.

Tourist office (Map p497; ☎ 2213 0400; www.koelntourismus.de; Unter Fettenhennen 19; 9am-8pm Mon-Sat, 10am-5pm Sun & hols)

Via Phone (Map p497 ☎ 1399 6200; Marzellenstrasse 3-5; per hr €1; 9am-midnight Mon-Sat, from 10am Sun)

Sights & Activities

DOM

As easy as it is to get church-fatigue in Germany, the huge **Kölner Dom** (Map p497; www.koelner-dom.de; admission free; 6am-7.30pm, no visitors during services) is one you shouldn't miss. Blackened with age, this gargoyle-festooned Gothic cathedral has a footprint of 12,470 sq metres, with twin spires soaring to 157m. Although its ground stone was laid in 1248, stop-start construction meant it wasn't finished until 1880, as a symbol of Prussia's drive for unification. Just over 60 years later it escaped WWII's heavy night-bombing largely intact.

The interior is dimly lit and moody, while behind the altar lies the most precious reliquary, the **Shrine of the Three Magi** (c 1150–1210). The shrine reputedly contains the bones of the Three Wise Men, brought here from Milan in the 12th century. It can be glimpsed through the gates to the inner choir, but for a closer look, take a **guided tour** (adult/concession €6/4; 10.30am & 2.30pm Mon-Sat, 2.30pm Sun in English).

Alternatively, you can embark on the seriously strenuous endeavour of climbing the 509 steps of the Dom's **south tower** (adult/concession €2.50/1; 9am-6pm May-Sep, to 5pm Oct, Mar & Apr, to 4pm Nov-Feb). You pass the 24-tonne **Peter Bell**, the world's largest working clanger, before emerging at 98.25m to magnificent views.

MUSEUMS

South along the riverbank is the glass-walled **Chocolate Museum** (Map p497; ☎ 931 8880; www.schokoladenmuseum.de; Am Schokoladenmuseum 1a; adult/concession €7.50/5; 10am-6pm Tue-Fri, 11am-7pm Sat &

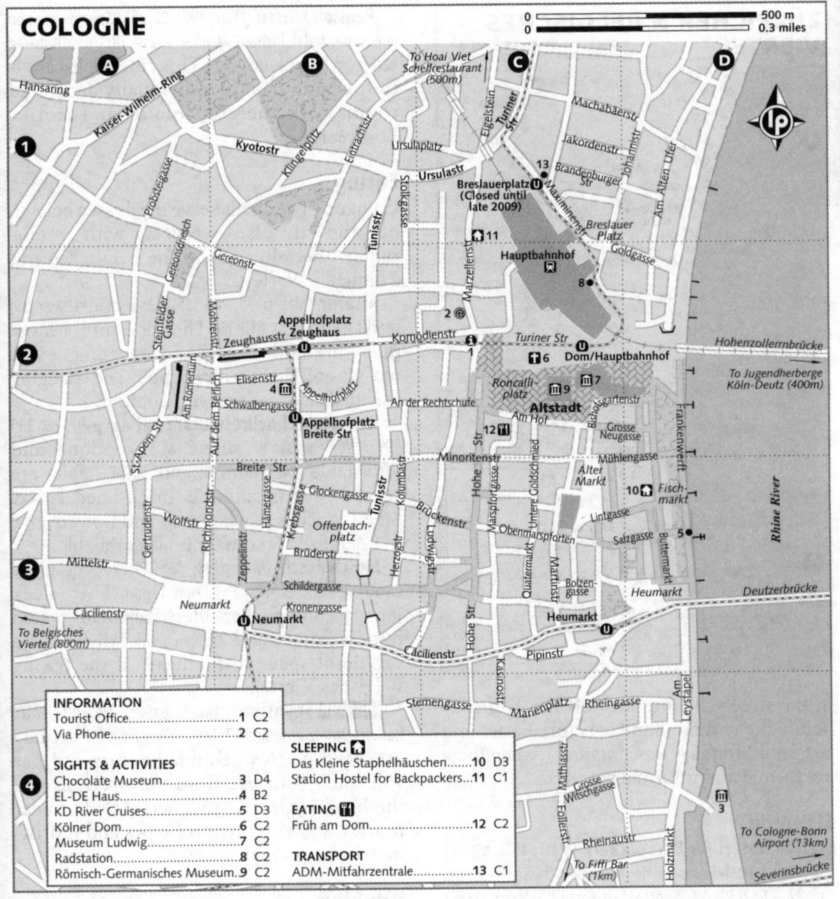

Sun, last entry 1hr before closing), where you nibble on samples while learning the history and process of chocolate-making. Don't miss the 'Cult chocolate' floor.

Two prominent museums sit next to the cathedral. The **Römisch-Germanisches Museum** (Map p497; Roman Germanic Museum; ☎ 2212 2304; www.museenkoeln.de; Roncalliplatz 4; adult/concession €5/3; 🕑 10am-5pm Tue-Sun) displays artefacts from the Roman settlement of Colonia Agrippinensis. The **Museum Ludwig** (Map p497; ☎ 2212 6165; www.museenkoeln.de; Bischofsgartenstrasse 1; adult/concession €9/6, 50% off after 5pm first Thu of each month; 🕑 10am-6pm Tue-Sun, to 10pm first Thu of each month) has an astoundingly good collection of pop art, German expressionism and Russian avant-garde painting, as well as photography.

Elsewhere, the sombre **EL-DE Haus** (Map p497; ☎ 2212 6331; www.nsdok.de, in German; Appellhofplatz 23-25; adult/concession €3.60/1.50; 🕑 10am-4pm Tue, Wed & Fri, to 6pm Thu, 11am-4pm Sat & Sun) documents Cologne's Nazi era.

TOURS

Rhine river trips are operated by **KD River Cruises** (Map p497; ☎ 208 8318; www.k-d.com; Frankenwerft 35). Day trips (10am, noon, 2pm and 6pm) cost €7.20.

Festivals & Events

Held just before Lent in late February or early March, Cologne's **Carnival** (Karneval) rivals Munich's Oktoberfest for exuberance, as people dress in creative costumes and party

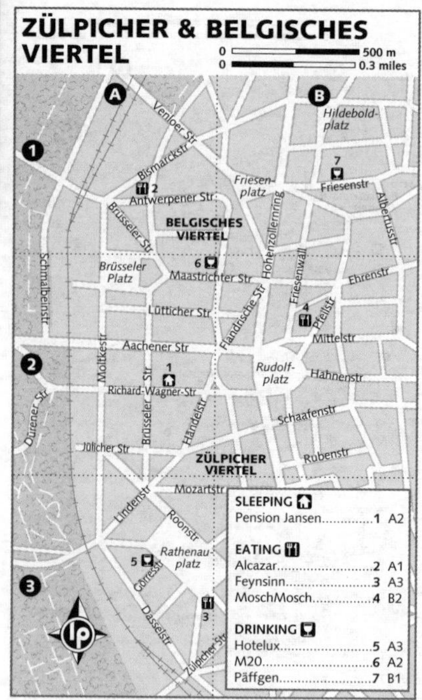

in the streets. Things kick off the Thursday before the seventh Sunday before Easter and last until Monday *(Rosenmontag)*, when there are formal and informal parades.

Sleeping

Station Hostel for Backpackers (Map p497; ☎ 912 5301; www.hostel-cologne.de; Marzellenstrasse 44-56; dm €17-22, s €32-39, d €55, breakfast €3; 💻) You can't get more convenient than this friendly six-floor hostel around the corner from the train station.

Jugendherberge Köln-Deutz (Map p497; ☎ 814 711; www.jugendherberge.de; Siegesstrasse 5a; dm/s €25/42) This is a behemoth of a hostel and while there's not much character in its green-grey rooms, those on the top floors have great views. Plus, everything feels clean and spanking new. It's a relatively easy 15-minute walk east from the main train station over the Hohenzollernbrücke.

Das Kleine Stapelhäuschen (Map p497; ☎ 272 7777; www.köln-altstadt.de/stapelhaeuschen; Fischmarkt 1-3; s/d from €40/67; 💻) A small, friendly hotel housed in a historic 12th-century building in the centre of old town, just off the riverbank.

Pension Jansen (Map p498; ☎ 251 85; www.pensionjansen.de; 2nd fl, Richard-Wagner-Strasse 18; s/d with shared bathroom from €45/65; ⊠) This cute, well-cared-for pension has six individually decorated rooms with cheerful colours and motifs. Book early.

Eating

Cologne's beer halls serve meals (see below), but the city also overflows with restaurants, especially around the Belgisches and Zülpicher Viertels.

Alcazar (Map p498; ☎ 515 733; Bismarckstrasse 39; snacks €4-9, mains €10-15) The food and atmosphere are both hearty and warming at this old-school, slightly hippie pub. The changing menu always has one vegie option.

Hoai Viet Schnellrestaurant (off Map p497; ☎ 139 3093; Weidengasse 68; mains €5-8) Exceptional and affordable Vietnamese and Thai staples are served in this sublime, brick-lined space. Small touches like bamboo and flowers give it a Zen feel. Take away is also available.

MoschMosch (Map p498; ☎ 965 7767; Pfeilstrasse 25-27; dishes €7-10; ⏲ 11am-11pm) This sleek Japanese noodle bar offers flavourful ramen noodle soups and teppanyaki dishes in a candle-lit space in the heart of the trendy Belgishes Viertel.

our pick **Feynsinn** (Map p498; ☎ 240 9210; Rathenauplatz 7; mains €7-18) The glint of artfully arranged glasses behind the mirrored bar will catch your eye from the street, as will the broken-glass chandeliers. Inside under murals, students, creative types and tourists tuck into seasonal cuisine.

Drinking

As in Munich, beer reigns supreme here. Local breweries produce a variety called *Kölsch*, which is relatively light and slightly bitter. In the beer halls, it's served in skinny 200mL glasses. You can get food too.

Früh am Dom (Map p497; ☎ 258 0394; Am Hof 12-14) This three-storey beer hall and restaurant (including cellar bar) is the most central, with black-and-white flooring, copper pans and tiled ovens keeping it real, despite the souvenir shop. It's open for breakfast.

Päffgen (Map p498; ☎ 135 461; Friesenstrasse 64-66) Another favourite, this thrumming wood-lined room has its own beer garden. It's not far from the bars of the Belgisches Viertel.

Hotelux (Map p498; ☎ 241 136; Rathenauplatz 22) Red walls, red booths and red lights; Hotelux serves cocktails and more than 30 types of 'Soviet water' (ie vodka) to students and intellectual types.

M20 (Map p498; ☎ 519 666; Maastrichter Strasse 20) This popular retro cocktail bar sports cube-shaped lights and brown leather sofas. Regular DJ evenings favour indie guitar rock, but some live acts play more laid-back Latin music.

Getting There & Away

AIR

Budget airline German Wings (www.germanwings.com) uses **Cologne-Bonn Airport** (CGN; www.airport-cgn.de) as its hub. Other scheduled flights go to widespread destinations.

CAR

The city is on a main north–south autobahn route and is easily accessible for drivers and hitchhikers. The **ADM-Mitfahrzentrale** (Map p497; ☎ 194 40; www.citynetz-mitfahrzentrale.de; Maximinen Strasse 2) is near the train station.

TRAIN

There are frequent RE services operating to Düsseldorf (€10.50 to €16, 30 minutes) and Aachen (€13.80, one hour). Frequent EC, IC, or ICE trains go to Hanover (€61, three hours), Frankfurt-am-Main (€39 to €61, one to 2¼ hours, three hourly) and Berlin (€102, 4¼ hours, hourly). Frequent Thalys high-speed services connect Cologne to Paris (€91, four hours) via Brussels and ICE trains go to Amsterdam (€56, 2½ hours).

Getting Around

Buses and trams serve the inner city, with local trains handling trips up to 50km away, including Bonn. Single city trips cost €1.60, while 1½-hour two-zone tickets are €2.

Cologne is flat and cycle-friendly. Bicycle hire is available next to the main train station at **Radstation** (Map p497; ☎ 139 7190; www.radstationkoeln.de; am Hauptbahnhof/Breslauerplatz; per 3hr €5, per 1/3/7 days €10/20/40; 🕒 5:30am-10:30pm Mon-Fri, 6:30am-8pm Sat, 8am-8pm Sun).

BONN

☎ 0228 / pop 315,000

Bonn is not only the birthplace of musical genius Ludwig van Beethoven – its brief tenure as capital of West Germany (from 1949) and as the home of German government departments (until 1999) has also left it with an excellent collection of museums.

The **tourist office** (☎ 775 000; www.bonn-regio.de; Windeckstrasse 1; 🕒 9am-6.30pm Mon-Fri, to 4pm Sat, 10am-2pm Sun) is a three-minute walk along Poststrasse from the Hauptbahnhof.

Music fans will head straight to the **Beethoven-Haus** (☎ 981 7525; www.beethoven-haus-bonn.de; Bonngasse 24-26; adult/concession €5/4; 🕒 10am-6pm Mon-Sat, 11am-6pm Sun Apr-Oct, to 5pm Nov-Mar), where the composer was born in 1770. The house contains memorabilia concerning his life and compositions.

Elsewhere, the **Haus der Geschichte der Bundesrepublik Deutschland** (FRG History Museum; ☎ 916 50; www.hdg.de; Willy-Brandt-Allee 14; admission free; 🕒 9am-7pm Tue-Sun) engagingly presents Germany's postwar history.

From Cologne, it's quicker to take an RE train to Bonn (€6.30, 20 minutes) than a tram (€8.40 day pass, 55 minutes each way). For river trips, see (p497).

DÜSSELDORF

☎ 0211 / pop 571,000

'D-Town' or 'The City D', as local editors like to call Düsseldorf, is Germany's fashion capital. But that means Jil Sander and Wolfgang Joop rather than cutting-edge streetwear, as you'll soon discover observing fur-clad *mesdames* with tiny dogs along the ritzy Königsallee.

Indeed, this elegant and wealthy town could feel stiflingly bourgeois if it weren't for its lively old-town pubs, its position on the Rhine and the postmodern architecture of its Mediahafen. Fortunately, those are more than enough to make up for its pretensions.

Information

Telesurf (Graf-Adolf-Strasse 102; per hr €2; 🕒 10am-2am Mon-Sat, to midnight Sun) Minutes left of the train station.

Tourist office (www.duesseldorf-tourismus.de) Altstadt (☎ 1720 2840; Marktstrasse/Ecke Rheinstrasse; 🕒 noon-6pm); Main office (☎ 172 0222; Immermannstrasse 65B; 🕒 9:30am-7pm Mon-Sat)

Sights & Activities

Düsseldorf has a lively **Altstadt** filled with enough restaurants and pubs to have earned it the slightly exaggerated title of the 'longest bar in the world'.

What really sets the city apart, however, is the contemporary architecture of its **Mediahafen**. Here, in the city's south, docks

GETTING INTO TOWN

From Düsseldorf International frequent S-Bahn services (1 & 7, €2.20) travel to the main train station. There's a coordinated bus service (€14, 1¼ hours) for Ryanair passengers from Niederrhein Airport (aka Weeze).

have been transformed into an interesting commercial park, most notably including the **Neuer Zollhof**, three typically curved and twisting buildings by Bilbão Guggenheim architect Frank Gehry.

On the street side of the red-brick building, there's a billboard with a map of the entire park. Alternatively, catch the lift 168m up the neighbouring **Rheinturm** (admission €3.50; 🕓 10am-11.30pm) for a bird's-eye view.

It's a pleasant stroll between the Mediahafen and the Altstadt along the riverside **Rheinuferpromenade**. Alternatively, you can join the city's elite window-shopping along **Königsallee**, or 'Kö' – Düsseldorf's answer to Rodeo Drive.

Recently reopened after renovations and featuring a brand new wing, **K20** (☎ 838 10; www.kunstsammlung.de; Grabbeplatz 5; adult/concession €6.50/4.50, combination ticket K20/K21 €10/8; 🕓 10am-6pm Tue-Fri, 11am-6pm Sat & Sun) contains early-20th-century masters.

Sleeping

Backpackers-Düsseldorf (☎ 302 0848; www.backpackers-duesseldorf.de; Fürstenwall 180; dm €22; 💻) This modern hostel adds bright colours and table football to soft beds and free wi-fi to come out a real winner. Near the Mediahafen, it's reached from the train station by bus 725 to Kirchplatz, from where there are several trams into town.

Jugendgästehaus (☎ 557 310; www.jugendherberge.de; Düsseldorfer Strasse 1; dm €22, s/d from €26/48; 💻) Situated in posh Oberkassel, recent renovations turned this 368-room hostel into a snazzy modern place that feels more like a boutique hotel. All rooms are en suite.

Eating & Drinking

Libanon Express (☎ 134 917; Berger Strasse 19-21; cafe €3-14, restaurant €10-19) Crammed with mirrors and tiles – and with recommendations stickered on the window – this cafe serves great kebabs, falafel and other Middle Eastern specialities.

Zum Uerige (☎ 866 990; Berger Strasse 1) In this noisy, cavernous place, the trademark Uerige Alt beer (a dark and semisweet brew typical of Düsseldorf) flows so quickly that the waiters just carry around trays and give you a glass whenever they spy one empty.

Lido (☎ 1576 8730; www.lido1960.de; Am Handelshafen 15) A glass and steel cube extends out over the water in the Mediahafen and its smooth outdoor lounge-deck is *the* place to see and be seen on a hot summer night.

Getting There & Around

Most airlines fly to **Düsseldorf International** (DUS; www.duesseldorf-international.de), but low-cost Ryanair uses **Niederrhein (Weeze) Airport** (NRN; www.flughafen-niederrhein.de).

The many train services from Düsseldorf include Cologne (€10.50 to €16, 25 to 30 minutes), Frankfurt-am-Main (€70, 1½ to 1¾ hours) and Berlin (€97, 4¼ hours).

The metro, trams and buses are useful to cover Düsseldorf's distances. A ticket for the centre costs €2.20 and for the greater city €4.30. Day passes start at €5.20.

AACHEN

☎ 0241 / pop 253,000

A spa-town with a hopping student population and tremendous amounts of character, Aachen's narrow cobbled streets, quirky fountains, shops full of delectable *Printen*, and pretty cathedral make for an excellent day trip from Cologne or Düsseldorf or a worthy overnight stay.

Orientation

Aachen's compact centre is contained within two ring roads roughly tracing the old city walls. The inner ring road, or Grabenring, changes names – most ending in 'graben' – and encloses the old city proper. To get to the tourist office from the Hauptbahnhof, cross Römerstrasse, follow Bahnhofstrasse north and then go left along Theaterstrasse to Kapuzinergraben.

Information

The Web (☎ 997 9210; Kleinmarschierstrasse 74-76; per 10min €0.50; 🕓 10am-3pm Mon-Thu, to 3am Fri & Sat, 11am-10pm Sun)

Tourist office (☎ 180 2960/1; www.aachen.de; Atrium Elisenbrunnen, Kapuzinergraben; 🕓 9am-6pm Mon-Fri year-round, to 2pm Sat Jan-Mar, to 3pm Sat & 10am-2pm Sun Apr-Dec)

Sights

OLD TOWN & FOUNTAINS

Next to the tourist office is the **Elisenbrunnen**. Despite its sulphuric 'rotten eggs' smell, you *can* drink it – it's supposedly good for the digestion.

In the far left-hand corner of the park behind the Elisenbrunnen is the **Geldbrunnen**, which represents the circulation of money. The comical figures around the pool clutch their coins or purses while the water is sucked down the central plughole (jokingly known as 'the taxman').

Head east along the top of the park here, towards Forum M, and turn left into Buchkremerstrasse. Soon you'll reach a fountain with a scary-looking creature. This is the mythological **Bahkauv**, rumoured to pounce on those returning late from the pub and demand a piggyback home.

Buchkremerstrasse becomes Büchel. Turn left just past Leo van den Daele restaurant, then right again and you'll come to Hühnermarkt, with its **Hühnerdiebbrunnen** (Chicken thief fountain). The hasty thief hasn't noticed one of his stolen chickens is a rooster and is about to unmask him by crowing.

From here, Aachen's main **Markt** is visible just to the northeast. The 14th-century **Rathaus** (adult/concession €2/1; 10am-5pm Mon-Fri, 10am-1pm & 2-5pm Sat & Sun) overlooks the Markt.

Head back down the hill along Krämerstrasse until you come to the **Puppenbrunnen** (Puppet fountain), where you're allowed to play with the movable bronze figures.

DOM

While Cologne's cathedral wows you with size and atmosphere, Aachen's similarly Unesco-listed **Dom** (Kaiserdom or Münster; www.aachendom.de; 7am-7pm Apr-Oct, to 6pm Nov-Mar) impresses with its shiny neatness. The small, Byzantine-inspired **octagon** at the building's heart dates from AD 805, but was refurbished in 2003 so its mosaics and marble gleam like new.

The building is significant not just because Charlemagne ordered it built, but also because 30 Holy Roman emperors were crowned here from 936 to 1531.

The brass **chandelier** in the centre was donated by Emperor Friedrich Barbarossa in 1165, while Charlemagne himself lies in the golden **shrine** behind the altar, a centuries-old magnet for pilgrims.

Multilingual leaflets in the antechamber provide a concise cathedral guide.

THERMAL BATHS

The 8th-century Franks were lured to 'Ahha' (water) for its thermal springs. And centuries later the state-of-the-art **Carolus Thermen** (Carolus Thermal Baths; ☎ 182 740; www.carolus-thermen.de; Stadtgarten/Passstrasse 79; without sauna from €10; 9am-11pm) is still reeling them in. The complex is part therapeutic spa and part swimming centre. Don't pay for the sauna; there's a steam room accessible to all. The baths are in the city garden, northeast of the centre.

Sleeping

Jugendgästehaus (☎ 711 010; www.jugendherberge.de; Maria-Theresia-Allee 260; dm €23.20, s €37; P) This modern DJH outpost sits on a hill overlooking the city, and gets lots of school groups. Take bus 2 to Ronheide.

Hotel Marx (☎ 375 41; www.hotel-marx.de; Hubertusstrasse 33-35; s/d from €54/79, with shared bathroom

THE DEVIL'S IN THE DETAIL

If the devil has all the best music, he also has the funniest myths. Aachen lore, for example, says you haven't really visited the town unless you've touched the thumb of hell's black prince.

The legend goes that a mysterious benefactor appeared when the town needed more money to finish its cathedral. Locals recognised him as Lucifer by his cloven hoofs, but being *lues* (cunning and crafty, in the local dialect) hatched a plan. When he asked to be repaid with the soul of the first being to enter the cathedral, they agreed, then released a wolf into the building. Satan pounced on the creature, but flew into a rage on realising he'd been cheated. Storming out of the cathedral, he slammed the door so hard he trapped his thumb.

Today, a statue of the wolf (or Roman bear) stands in the cathedral's antechamber, with a hole in its chest from where its soul was ripped. Meanwhile, 'the devil's thumb' remains stuck in the main cathedral doors – between the side doors currently used. Inside the lion's head on the right-hand door, you can feel, well, a digit-shaped something.

NOT QUITE GINGERBREAD

It comes in all shapes and sizes – a porcupine, a dog, Santa Claus or the Easter Bunny. It tastes like gingerbread, sort of. It's a little bit like *Lebkuchen,* but firmer. Window displays of **Aachener Printen** greet you all over town and we're certain you'll give in and buy a bag while you're here. The exact recipe is a closely guarded secret, but generally involves cinnamon, ginger, clove and allspice and makes a fantastic gift to bring home. Leo van den Daele (below) sells some of the best Printen in town.

from €37/70; 💻) There's a garden with pond out the back of this traditional family-run place. Inside the rooms are decent, even if the bathrooms are a little cramped.

Eating & Drinking

Aachen's students have their own 'Latin Quarter' along **Pontstrasse**, with dozens of bars and cheap eats. It heads northeast off the Markt and runs for nearly a kilometre. Laid-back sandwich king **Vitaminbar** (☎ 409 3912; Alexaniergraben 13-15; dishes €3-7) is an excellent budget choice.

Leo van den Daele (☎ 357 24; Büchel 18; dishes €5-9.50) A warren of 17th-century rooms linked by crooked stairs across four merchants' homes, this nationally renowned cafe specialises in gingerbread, or Printen. Yet you can also enjoy light meals – soups, sandwiches, quiches and *pastetchen* (vol au vents) – among its tiled stoves and antique knick-knacks.

Kaiser Wetter (☎ 9437 9950; www.kaiserwetter-aachen.de; Hof 5; mains €5-15) Stop by for a drink, a snack or a light meal of salads and pizzas at this restaurant-lounge in the centre of town. Relax at the outdoor tables under the shadow of giant roman pillars or step inside the modern interior.

Getting There & Around

There are frequent trains to Cologne (€13.80 to €19.50, 30 minutes to one hour) and twice-hourly service to Düsseldorf (€17.10, 70 minutes to 1½ hours). The high-speed Thalys train passes through regularly on its way to Brussels and Paris (€85, three hours).

Buses cost €1.50 (trip of a few stops), €2.20 (regular single) or €6.10 (day pass).

LOWER SAXONY

Lower Saxony (Niedersachsen) likes to make much of its half-timbered towns. Hamelin is certainly a true fairy-tale beauty, and leaning Lüneberg is quite unlike any other town you'll see. However, the state is also home to the famous Volkswagen car company, and even the business-minded capital, Hanover, has its diversions.

HANOVER

☎ 0511 / pop 523,000

German comedians – yes, they do exist – like to dismiss Hanover as 'the Autobahn exit between Göttingen and Walsrode'. However, the capital of Lower Saxony is really nowhere near that grim. While it's famous for hosting trade fairs, particularly the huge CEBIT computer show in March, it also boasts acres of greenery in the Versailles-like Herrenhäuser Gärten.

Parts of the central Altstadt look medieval, but few are. They're mostly clever fakes built after intense WWII bombing.

Information

Hannover Tourismus (☎ information 1234 5111, room reservations 1234 555; www.hannover.de; Ernst-August-Platz 8; 🕑 9am-6pm Mon-Fri, to 2pm Sat)

Teleklick Hannover (Schillerstrasse 23; 🕑 10am-11pm Mon-Sat, noon-10pm Sun) Internet access.

Sights

The enormous **Grosser Garten** (Large Garden; admission €3, free in winter) is the highlight of the **Herrenhäuser Gärten** (☎ 1684 7576; www.hannover.de/herrenhausen/start.htm; 🕑 9am-sunset). It has a small maze, Europe's tallest fountain and a popular beer garden. Check the website in summer for **Wasserspiele**, when fountains are synchronised, and the night-time **Illuminations**. The **Niki de Saint Phalle Grotto** is a magical showcase of the artist's work. She was French – her colourful figures adorn the famous Stravinsky fountain outside Paris's Centre Pompidou – but developed a special relationship with Hanover.

The **Neues Rathaus** was built between 1901 and 1913. Town models in the foyer reveal the extent of WWII devastation. Further east lies the Leine River where, since 1974, **Die Nanas** – three fluorescent-coloured, earth-mama sculptures by de Saint Phalle – have lived. They're best seen on Saturday, when there's a flea market at their feet.

GETTING INTO TOWN

The S-Bahn (S5) takes 16 minutes from the airport to the main train station (€3.50).

In summer, the **Machsee** (lake) has **ferries** (crossings €3, tours €6) and numerous boats for hire. There's a free public **swimming beach** on the southeastern shore.

Sleeping

The tourist office only finds private rooms during trade fairs but can arrange hotel bookings year-round for €7.

Jugendherberge (☎ 131 7674; www.jugendherberge.de; Ferdinand-Wilhelm-Fricke-Weg 1; dm €21; P 💻) This large space-lab looking structure houses a modern hostel with breakfast room and terrace bar overlooking the river in an area that feels more country than city. Take U3 or U7 to Fischerhof, cross the mini red suspension bridge and turn right.

GästeResidenz PelikanViertel (☎ 399 90; Pelikanstrasse 11; s €46-240, d €66-240, tr €92-300; P 💻) Upmarket student residence meets budget hotel, this huge complex (in the former Pelikan fountain-pen factory) has a wide range of Ikea-style rooms, all with kitchenettes. Prices skyrocket during trade-fair periods. Take U3, U7 or U9 to Pelikanstrasse.

Eating & Drinking

Markthalle (Karmarschstrasse 49; dishes €3.50-10; 🕑 7am-8pm Mon-Wed, to 10pm Thu & Fri, to 4pm Sat) This huge covered market of food stalls (sausages, sushi, tapas and more), gourmet delis and standing-only 'bars' is a no-nonsense, atmospheric place for a quick bite. It's also heaving each Friday evening with people proclaiming *Prost!* (Cheers!) to the start of the weekend.

Maestro (☎ 300 8575; www.maestro-hannover.de; Sophienstrasse 2; mains €7-14.50) This atmospheric subterranean restaurant offers an all-you-can-eat vegetarian buffet (€7) at lunch daily and surprises you with its hidden courtyard beer garden.

Café-Bar Celona (☎ 353 8576; Knochenhauerstrasse 42; mains €7-16) Latin-themed and plant-filled, this cafe-bar is fine any time of day (or night) for a bite, a drink, or both – but book ahead for its massive (and massively popular) all-you-can-eat Sunday brunch (€8.95).

Getting There & Around

Hanover's **airport** (HAJ; www.hannover-airport.de) has many connections, including on low-cost carrier **Air Berlin** (www.airberlin.com).

There are frequent ICE train services to Hamburg (€39, 1½ hours), Berlin (€58, 1½ hours), Cologne (€61, 2¾ hours) and Munich (€112, 4¼ hours), among others.

Most visitors only travel in the central 'Hannover' zone. Single tickets are €2.10 and day passes €4.10.

AROUND HANOVER

Hanover makes a good jumping-off point for day trips to the beautiful towns of Lower Saxony. By sticking to slower RE/ME trains, nonrail pass holders can travel all across the state on a daily €17 Niedersaschsen ticket.

Closest is quaint **Hamelin** (Hameln in German) of Pied Piper fame. With ornate architecture and lots of rat cakes, breads and souvenirs, it's a great place for kids big and small. The train station is about 800m east of the centre. To get to **Hameln Tourist Information** (☎ 957 823; www.hameln.de/touristinfo; Diesterallee 1; 🕑 9am-6pm Mon-Fri, 9.30am-4pm Sat, 9.30am-1pm Sun May-Sep, 9am-6pm Mon-Fri, 9.30am-1pm Sat Oct-Apr) take bus 2, 3, 4, 21 or 33.

The leaning town of **Lüneburg** is also immediately striking. Centuries of salt mining have resulted in widespread subsidence, leaving some of Lüneburg's pavements warped, while its gabled Hanseatic buildings twist and tilt. The **tourist office** (☎ 207 6620; www.lueneburg.de; 🕑 9am-5pm Mon-Fri, to 4pm Sat & Sun May-Sep, to 5pm Mon-Fri, to 2pm Sat Oct-Apr) is on the main market square. The city's easily reached from either Hanover (€23, one to 1¾ hours on ICE or ME services) or Hamburg (€11, 30 minutes on ICE).

Finally, **Wolfsburg** is home to Volkswagen's global headquarters and huge factory; the latter is as large as Monaco. At the attached theme park, **Autostadt** (Car City; ☎ 0800-2886 782 38; www.autostadt.de; Stadtbrücke; adult/concession €15/12; 🕑 9am-6pm), you can catch up on VW Beetle history, take a tour into the factory or test your driving skills. In town, there's also a separate **car museum** and a cutting-edge science centre, **Phaeno**. The **Wolfsburg tourist office** (☎ 899 930; www.wolfsburg.de; Willy Brandt-Platz 3; 🕑 9am-6pm Mon-Fri, 10am-3pm Sat & Sun) is in the train station. Frequent ICE services go to Hanover (€21, 30 minutes) and Berlin (€42, one hour).

BEWITCHING HARZ

The **Harz Mountains** constitute a mini-Alpine region straddling Saxony-Anhalt and Lower Saxony. Here, medieval castles overlook fairy-tale historic towns, while there are caves, mines and numerous hiking trails to explore.

The region's highest – and most famous – mountain is the Brocken, where one-time visitor Johann Wolfgang von Goethe set the 'Walpurgisnacht' chapter of his play *Faust*. His inspiration in turn came from folk tales depicting Walpurgisnacht, or *Hexennacht* (witches night) as an annual witches' coven. Every 30 April to 1 May it's celebrated enthusiastically across the Harz region.

Goslar

Goslar is a truly stunning 1000-year-old city with beautifully preserved half-timbered buildings and an impressive **Markt.** The town's **Kaiserpfalz** is a reconstructed Romanesque 11th-century palace. Just below there's the restored **Domvorhalle**, which displays the 11th-century 'Kaiserstuhl' throne, used by German emperors.

Brocken's summit is an easy day trip from Goslar. Take a bus (810) or train (faster) from Goslar to Bad Harzburg and then a bus (820) to Torfhaus, where the 8km Goetheweg trail begins.

If climbing a mountain is not your thing, a mere wander around town and a stroll along its circumference, a green space dotted with bucolic lakes and bits of the old city wall, makes for a fine day.

The **tourist office** (☎ 05321-780 60; www.goslar.de; Markt 7; ⏲ 9.15am-6pm Mon-Fri, 9.30am-4pm Sat, to 2pm Sun Apr-Oct, 9.15am-5pm Mon-Fri, 9.30am-2pm Sat Nov-Mar) can help with accommodation, which includes a **DJH Hostel** (☎ 05321-222 40; www.jugendherberge.de; Rammelsbergerstrasse 25; dm junior/senior €20.50/23.50; P) and hotels **Die Tanne** (☎ 05321-343 90; www.die-tanne.de; Bäringerstrasse 10; s €40-65, d €65-100; P) and the fancier **Kaiserworth** (☎ 05321-7090; www.kaiserworth.de; Markt 3; s €81-101, d €122-207, apt €182-252; 💻). For a special experience, don't miss **Fortezza** (☎ 05321-4803; Thomasstrasse 2; mains €8-17), a Spanish restaurant ensconced in a 16th-century tower attached to the old city wall.

As well as being serviced by buses (www.rbb-bus.de), Goslar is connected by train to Hanover (€15.20, one hour to 70 minutes).

Quedlinburg

The Unesco World Heritage town of Quedlinburg is best known for its spectacular castle district, perched on a 25m-high plateau above its historic half-timbered buildings. Originally established during the reign of Heinrich I (919–936), the present-day Renaissance **Schloss** dates from the 16th century. Its centrepiece is the restored baroque **Blauer Saal** (Blue Hall).

Contact **Quedlinburg-Tourismus** (☎ 03946-905 625; www.quedlinburg.de; Markt 2; ⏲ 9:30am-6:30pm Mon-Fri, to 4pm Sat, to 3pm Sun Apr-15 Oct; 9.30am-5pm Mon-Fri, to 2pm Sat 16 Oct-Mar) for more information. Lodgings include a **DJH hostel** (☎ 03946-811 703; www.jugendherberge.de; Neuendorf 28; dm junior/senior €16.50/19.50, bedding €3; P) and the hotels **Pension Zum Altstadtwinkel** (☎ 03946-91 9975; www.altstadtwinkel.de; Hohe Stasse 15; s/d/apt €35/66/120; P ⊠) and **Romantik Hotel Theophano** (☎ 03946-963 00; www.hoteltheophano.de; Markt 13-14; s/d from €69/79).

There are frequent trains to Hanover (€29, 2½ hours, hourly).

BREMEN

☎ 0421 / pop 547,000

Bremen is what Germans call *schön klein*, the equivalent of good things coming in small packages. You can easily travel on foot between its red-brick market place, art deco Böttcherstrasse and the dollhouse-sized Schnoor district.

Best known from the *Town Musicians of Bremen* fairy tale – about four animals who left home to find fame here – Bremen is predictably cute and pretty. But the waterfront promenade along the Weser River is a wonderful spot for a drink and the student district along Ostertorsteinweg is downright alternative.

Orientation

Head south (straight ahead) from the train station to reach the centre, on the banks of the Weser River. The Schlachte waterfront promenade is west of the centre; the

Schnoor district lies just east. The student and nightlife district is further east still along Ostertorsteinweg.

Information

Internet Café (☎ 168 440; Bahnhofstr 10; per hr €1; 🕑 10am-10pm Mon-Fri, 11am-10pm Sat, noon-10pm Sun).

Tourist office (☎ 01805-101030; www.bremen-tourism.de) Hauptbahnhof (🕑 9am-7pm Mon-Fri, 9:30-6pm Sat & Sun); Obernstrasse (Obernstrasse/Liebfrauenkirchhof; 🕑 10am-6.30pm Mon-Fri, to 4pm Sat & Sun) Organises daily city tours.

Sights & Activities

Bremen's **Markt** is striking, particularly its gabled **Rathaus**. In front stands a 13m-tall medieval statue of the knight **Roland**, Bremen's protector. On the building's western side, you'll find the **Town Musicians of Bremen** sculpture (1951). The animals are in their most famous pose, scaring the robbers who invaded their house, with the rooster atop the cat, perched on the dog, on the shoulders of the donkey.

Also on the Markt is the **Dom** and its slightly macabre **Bleikeller** (Lead Cellar; ☎ 365 0441; adult/concession €1.50/1; 🕑 10am-5pm Mon-Fri, 10am-2pm Sat, noon-5pm Sun Apr-Oct) Here, open coffins reveal eight corpses mummified in the dry air underground.

The nearby art-deco alley of **Böttcherstrasse** is unique. Through an arch with a striking golden relief, you enter a world of tall brick houses, shops, galleries, restaurants, a **Glockenspiel** and several (missable) museums.

A maze of narrow winding alleys, the **Schnoorviertel** was once the fishermen's quarter and then the red-light district. Now its dollhouse-sized cottages are souvenir shops and restaurants.

If you have time, visit **Beck's Brewery** (☎ 5094 5555; Am Deich 18-19; tours €8.50; 🕑 tours in German 10am-5pm Tue-Sat, to 3pm Sun, in English 11am Tue-Sun).

Sleeping

Bremer Backpacker Hostel (☎ 223 8057; www.bremer-backpacker-hostel.de; Emil-Waldmannstrasse 5-6; dm €17-23, s €28, bedding €3; 💻) A friendly place five minutes from the train station, where you'll find simply furnished but spotless rooms spread out over several levels (each floor is named after a continent), a full kitchen and living room.

DJH Hostel Bremen (☎ 163 820; www.jugendherberge.de; Kalkstrasse 6; dm junior/senior €23.50/26.50, s/d €33.50/38.50; ⊠ 💻) Like a work of art from the exterior, with a yellow and orange Plexiglas facade and slit rectangular windows, this refurbished building looks more like an art museum than a hostel. Comfortable dorms are all en suite and there's a rooftop terrace. Take tram 3 or 5 to Am Brill.

Eating

The student quarter in and around Ostertorsteinweg, **Das Viertel**, is full of restaurants and cafes and has a vaguely bohemian atmosphere. The waterfront promenade, **Schlachte**, is more expensive and mainstream. The Marktplatz is home to oodles of cheap snack stands.

Piano (☎ 785 46; Fehrfeld 64; mains €5.50-10.50) One of the most enduringly popular cafes in the student quarter, Piano serves pizza, pasta, steaks and veggie casseroles. Breakfast can also be enjoyed until 4pm.

Apadana (☎ 577 5997; Heinkenstrasse & Faulenstrasse; mains €6.50-13.50) This family-run, hospitable Persian restaurant serves lovingly prepared, traditional fare in a simple, quiet space.

Getting There & Away

Flights from **Bremen airport** (BRE: www.airport-bremen.de) include low-cost carrier Air Berlin (www.airberlin.com).

Frequent ICE trains go to Hamburg (€28, one hour) and Hanover (€30, one hour); ICE trains run hourly from Cologne (€62, three hours).

Getting Around

Trams and buses crisscross the city. With single tickets costing €2.20, a €5.90 day pass is excellent value.

> **GETTING INTO TOWN**
>
> Tram 6 leaves the airport frequently, heading to the centre (€2.20, 16 minutes).

NORTHERN GERMANY

Flat, sparse northwestern Germany features two very different gems. Hamburg might be the country's second-largest city, but its port has also made it the richest. With an outward-looking multicultural population, it features a nightlife and dining-out scene to rival Berlin's.

By contrast, the historic town of Lübeck trades on its absolutely stunning picture-postcard looks.

HAMBURG

☎ 040 / pop 1.76 million

Water, water everywhere – Germany's biggest port city has always been outward-looking. Its wealth, dynamism, multiculturalism and hedonistic red-light district, the Reeperbahn, all arise from its maritime history.

Joining the Hanseatic League trading bloc in the Middle Ages, Hamburg has been enthusiastically doing business with the world ever since. In the 1960s it nurtured the Beatles' musical talent. Today designer-clad residents cycle to their media jobs with a self-assurance unmatched by any other German city.

The Alster lakes, the Elbe River and the canals between the Speicherstadt warehouses are all perfect for leisure cruises. Haggling at the rowdy fish market early on Sunday is also an unrivalled experience.

Orientation

The sprawl of the city means you will probably be using public transport regularly. The Hauptbahnhof is central, near the Alster Lakes, but the Speicherstadt warehouses and port lie southwest, on the Elbe River. The nightlife districts of St Pauli (including the Reeperbahn) and Schanzenviertel are further west again.

Information

Hamburg Card (per 1/3/5 days €9/19/35) Free public transport and museum discounts.

Hamburg Tourismus Airport (☎ 5075 1010; 🕒 6am-11pm); Hauptbahnhof (☎ information 3005 1200, hotel bookings 3005 1300; www.hamburg-tourismus.de; Kirchenallee exit; 🕒 8am-9pm Mon-Sat, 10am-6pm Sun); Landungsbrücken (btwn piers 4 & 5, 🕒 8am-6pm Apr-Oct, 10am-6pm Nov-Mar; Ⓜ Landungsbrücken)

Internet Café (☎ 2800 3898; Adenauerallee 10; per hr €1.50; 🕒 10am-midnight Mon-Sat, to 1pm Sun; Ⓜ Hauptbahnhof)

Police Hauptbahnhof (Kirchenallee exit); St Pauli (Davidwache, Spielbudenplatz 31; Ⓜ Reeperbahn)

Tele-Time (☎ 4131 4730; Schulterblatt 39, behind the hookah lounge; per hr €2; 🕒 10am-midnight; Ⓜ Feldstrasse/Sternschanze) Internet access.

Dangers & Annoyances

Although safe, Hamburg contains several red-light districts around the train station and Reeperbahn. The Hansaplatz in St Georg can feel a bit dicey after dark. Fortunately, there's a strong police presence in these areas.

Sights & Activities

OLD TOWN

Hamburg's medieval **Rathaus** (☎ 4283 120 10; tours €3; 🕒 tours in English hourly 10.15am-3.15pm Mon-Thu, to 1.15pm Fri, to 5.15pm Sat, to 4.15 Sun; Ⓜ Rathausmarkt/Jungfernstieg) is one of Europe's most opulent. North of here, you can wander through the **Alsterarkaden**, the elegant Renaissance-style arcades sheltering shops and cafes alongside a canal or 'fleet'.

For many visitors, however, the city's most memorable building is south in the Merchant's District. The 1920s, brown-brick **Chile Haus** (cnr Burchardstrasse & Johanniswall; Ⓜ Mönckebergstrasse/Messberg) is shaped like an ocean liner, with remarkable curved walls meeting in the shape of a ship's bow and staggered balconies looking like decks.

LAKE & RIVER CRUISES

Hamburg is surrounded by water, so cruising on its many lakes, canals, harbour or river is one of the best ways to appreciate the city. Most boat tours cost around €10 to €12 per adult.

The **Inner and Outer Alster Lakes** (Binnenalster and Aussenalster) demonstrate the city's elegant side. Ships leave in summer from Jungfernstieg.

Port and Elbe River cruises start in summer at the St Pauli Landungsbrücken (Ⓜ Landungsbrücken). **Hadag** (☎ 311 7070; www.hadag.de; Brücke 2; 1hr harbour trip from €9) offers some of the best deals and cruises.

Cruises along the canals of the Speicherstadt (see below) also leave from the Landungsbrücken.

Better yet, hire your own rowboat or canoe. Opposite the Atlantic Hotel you'll find **Segelschule Pieper** (☎ 247 578; www.segelschule-pieper.de; An der Alster; per hr from €13; 🕒 Apr-Oct; Ⓜ Hauptbahnhof).

SPEICHERSTADT & HARBOUR

The beautiful red-brick, neo-Gothic warehouses lining the Elbe archipelago south of the Altstadt once stored exotic goods from all over the world. Now this so-called **Speicherstadt** (Warehouse city; Ⓜ Messberg/Baumwall) is full of visitors taking boat rides up its canals.

(Some operators leave from opposite the archipelago, as well as the Landungsbrücken.) Alternatively, you can just wander around its streets. Many of the warehouses have been turned into museums. Most of them are missable, but check out the Hamburg Tourismus website for whatever takes your fancy.

Further west, at the Landungsbrücken, there's a famous ship museum, **Rickmer Rickmers** (☎ 319 5959; www.rickmer-rickmers.de; Brücke No 1; adult/concession €3/2.50; ⏰ 10am-6pm).

REEPERBAHN

No discussion of Hamburg is complete without mentioning St Pauli, home of the **Reeperbahn** (Ⓜ Reeperbahn), Europe's biggest red-light district. Sex shops, peep shows, dim bars and strip clubs line the streets, which generally start getting crowded after 8pm or 9pm. This is also where the notorious **Herbertstrasse** is located (a block-long street lined with brothels that's off-limits to men under 18 and to women of all ages) as well as the **Erotic Art Museum** (☎ 317 4757; www.eroticartmuseum.de; Bernhard-Nocht-Strasse 69; adult/concession €8/5; ⏰ noon-10pm, to midnight Fri & Sat), and the **Condomerie** (☎ 319 3100; www.condomerie.de; Spielbudenplatz 18; ⏰ noon-midnight), with its extensive collection of prophylactics and sex toys.

FISCHMARKT

Here's the perfect excuse to stay up all Saturday night. Every Sunday between 5am and 10am, curious tourists join locals of every age and walk of life at the famous Fischmarkt in St Pauli. The market has been running since 1703, and its undisputed stars are the boisterous *Marktschreier* (market criers) who hawk their wares at full volume. Live bands also entertainingly crank out cover versions of ancient German pop songs in the adjoining *Fischauktionshalle* (Fish Auction Hall). Take bus 112 to Hafentreppe.

MUSEUMS

Of Hamburg's dozens of museums, the **Hamburger Kunsthalle** (☎ 428 131 200; www.hamburger-kunsthalle.de; Glockengiesserwall; adult/concession €8.50/5; ⏰ 10am-6pm Tue, Wed, Fri-Sun, to 9pm Thu; Ⓜ Hauptbahnhof) is a a standout. It consists of two buildings – an old one housing old masters and 19th-century art, and a new white concrete cube of contemporary works.

The **International Maritime Museum** (☎ 300 93 300; www.internationales-maritimes-museum.de; Koreastrasse 1; adult/concession €10/7; ⏰ 10am-6pm Tue, Wed, Fri-Sun, to 8pm Thu; Ⓜ Messberg) is the newest addition to Hamburg's **Hafen City**. This nine-floor, enormous space examines 3000 years of maritime history through displays of model ships, naval paintings, navigation tools and educational exhibits.

Sleeping

A & O City Hauptbahnhof Hostel(☎ 644 2104 5600; www.aohostel.com; Amsinkstrasse 6-10; dm €13-16, s/d from €29/32, breakfast €5, bedding €3; 💻 Ⓟ ⊠; Ⓜ Hauptbahnhof) New, clean, but rather sterile and characterless, this huge hostel is nevertheless excellent value and convenient. It also offers bike hire (€10 per day).

our pick **Superbude Hotel, Hostel & Lounge** (☎ 380 8780; www.superbude.de; Spaldingstrasse 152; dm €16-22, d €59-89, q €91-133; 💻 ⊠; Ⓜ Berliner Tor) This new addition near St Georg is just about the snazziest hotel-hostel we've seen. Housed in a former printing press, the modern, spacious dorms and rooms feel like trendy loft spaces. Breakfast is €7.

Jugendherberge-Auf dem Stintfang (☎ 313 488; www.jugendherberge.de; Alfred-Wegener-Weg 5; dm €20-23, d €59; 💻 Ⓟ ⊠; Ⓜ Landungsbrücken) Modern, clean and convenient (head out of the U-Bahn station and up the steps to the massive modern complex at the top of the hill), this DJH hostel overlooks the Elbe and the harbour. With lots of large, noisy school groups, however, it's very keen on rules, and you're locked out part of the day.

Kogge (☎ 312 872; www.kogge-hamburg.de; Bernhard-Nocht-Strasse 59; s/d/q from €29.50/49.50/78; 💻; Ⓜ Landungsbrücken/Reeperbahn) This friendly, fun rock'n'roll bar and hotel sits on a quiet street around the corner from the noisy Reeperbahn territory; all rooms share shower and toilet facilities. Popular with musicians and perfect for travellers planning to party all night and sleep until late (standard checkout is 2pm).

Hotel Pension Annenhof (☎ 243 426; www.hotelannenhof.de; Lange Reihe 23; s/d from €40/65; Ⓜ Hauptbahnhof) The Annenhof's attractive, cheerful rooms have polished wooden floorboards and clean, simple furnishings. There's no breakfast but plenty of cafes nearby.

Hotel Village (☎ 480 6490; www.hotel-village.de; Steindamm 4; s €50-75, d €65-100; 💻; Ⓜ Hauptbahnhof) A former bordello going straight, its boudoirs feature various mixes of red velvet,

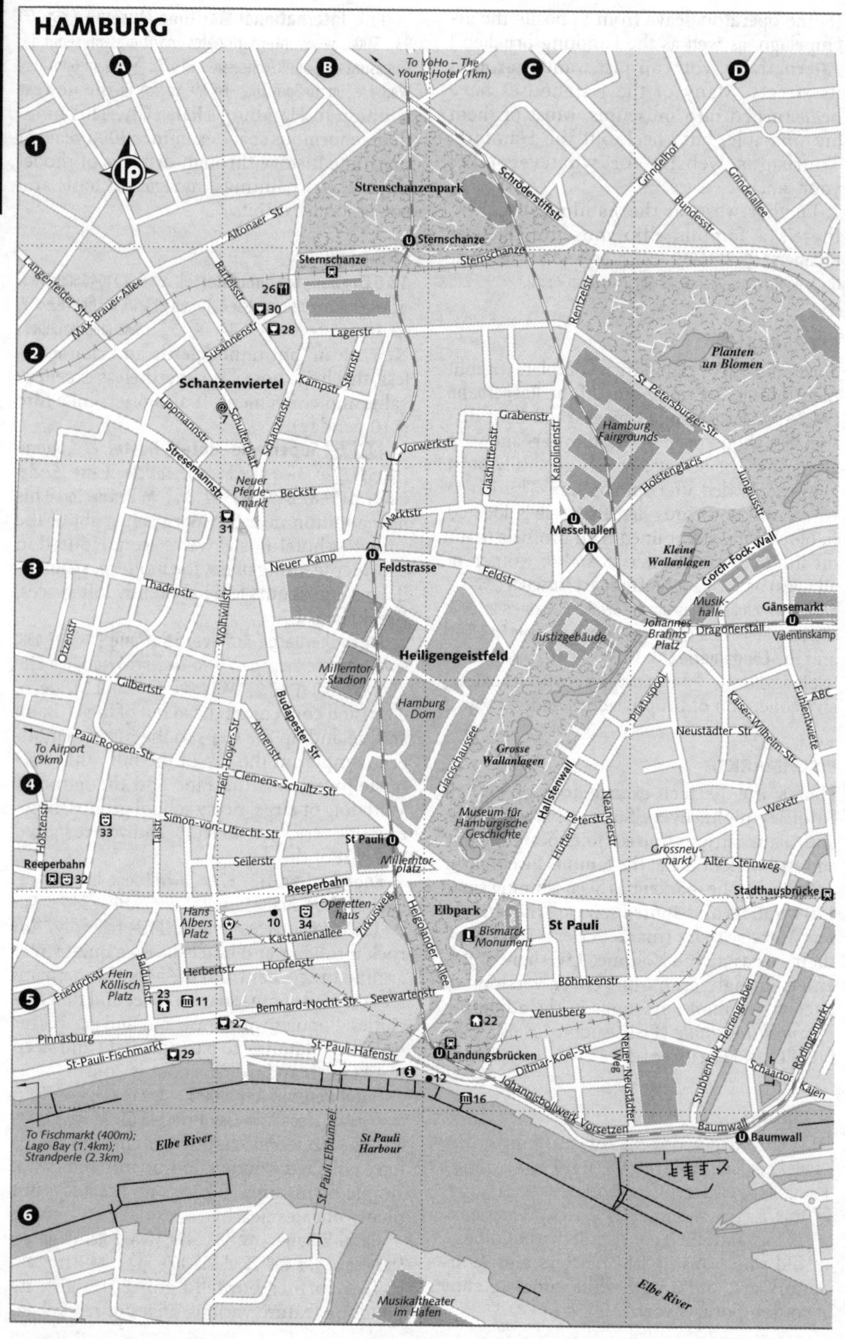
HAMBURG
To YoHo – The Young Hotel (1km)
Strenschanzenpark
Schröderstiftstr
Sternschanze
Altonaer Str
Langenfelder Str
Max-Brauer-Allee
Bartelsstr
Susannenstr
Schanzenviertel
Kampstr
Sternstr
Lagerstr
Planten un Blomen
St Petersburger-Str
Hamburg Fairgrounds
Grabenstr
Karolinenstr
Glashüttenstr
Vorwerkstr
Lippmannstr
Schulterblatt
Schanzenstr
Stresemannstr
Neuer Pferdemarkt
Beckstr
Marktstr
Messehallen
Holstenglacis
Jungiusstr
Kleine Wallanlagen
Gorch-Fock-Wall
Neuer Kamp
Feldstrasse
Feldstr
Thadenstr
Musikhalle
Gänsemarkt
Johannes Brahms Platz
Dragonerstall
Valentinskamp
Justizgebäude
Heiligengeistfeld
Millerntor-Stadion
Otzenstr
Wohlwillstr
Gilbertstr
Hamburg Dom
Budapester Str
Pilatuspool
Kaiser-Wilhelm-Str
Fuhlentwiete
ABC
Neustädter Str
To Airport (9km)
Paul-Roosen-Str
Hein-Hoyer-Str
Annenstr
Glacischaussee
Grosse Wallanlagen
Hallstenwall
Clemens-Schultz-Str
Neanderstr
Wexstr
Holstenstr
Simon-von-Utrecht-Str
Talstr
Museum für Hamburgische Geschichte
Peterstr
Hütten
St Pauli
Grossneumarkt
Alter Steinweg
Reeperbahn
Seilerstr
Millerntorplatz
Stadthausbrücke
Operettenhaus
Elbpark
Hans Albers Platz
Kastanienallee
Zirkusweg
Helgoländer Allee
Bismarck Monument
Herbertstr
Hopfenstr
Böhmkenstr
Friedrichstr
Hein Köllisch Platz
Balduinstr
Bernhard-Nocht-Str
Seewartenstr
Venusberg
Stubbenhuk
Herrengraben
Rödingsmarkt
Pinnasburg
St-Pauli-Hafenstr
Landungsbrücken
Ditmar-Koel-Str
Neuer Neustädter Weg
St-Pauli-Fischmarkt
Johannisbollwerk
Vorsetzen
Schaartor
Kajen
Baumwall
To Fischmarkt (400m); Lago Bay (1.4km); Strandperle (2.3km)
Elbe River
St Pauli Elbtunnel
St Pauli Harbour
Musikaltheater im Hafen
Elbe River
A
B
C
D
1
2
3
4
5
6
1
4
7
10
11
12
16
22
23
26
27
28
29
30
31
32
33
34

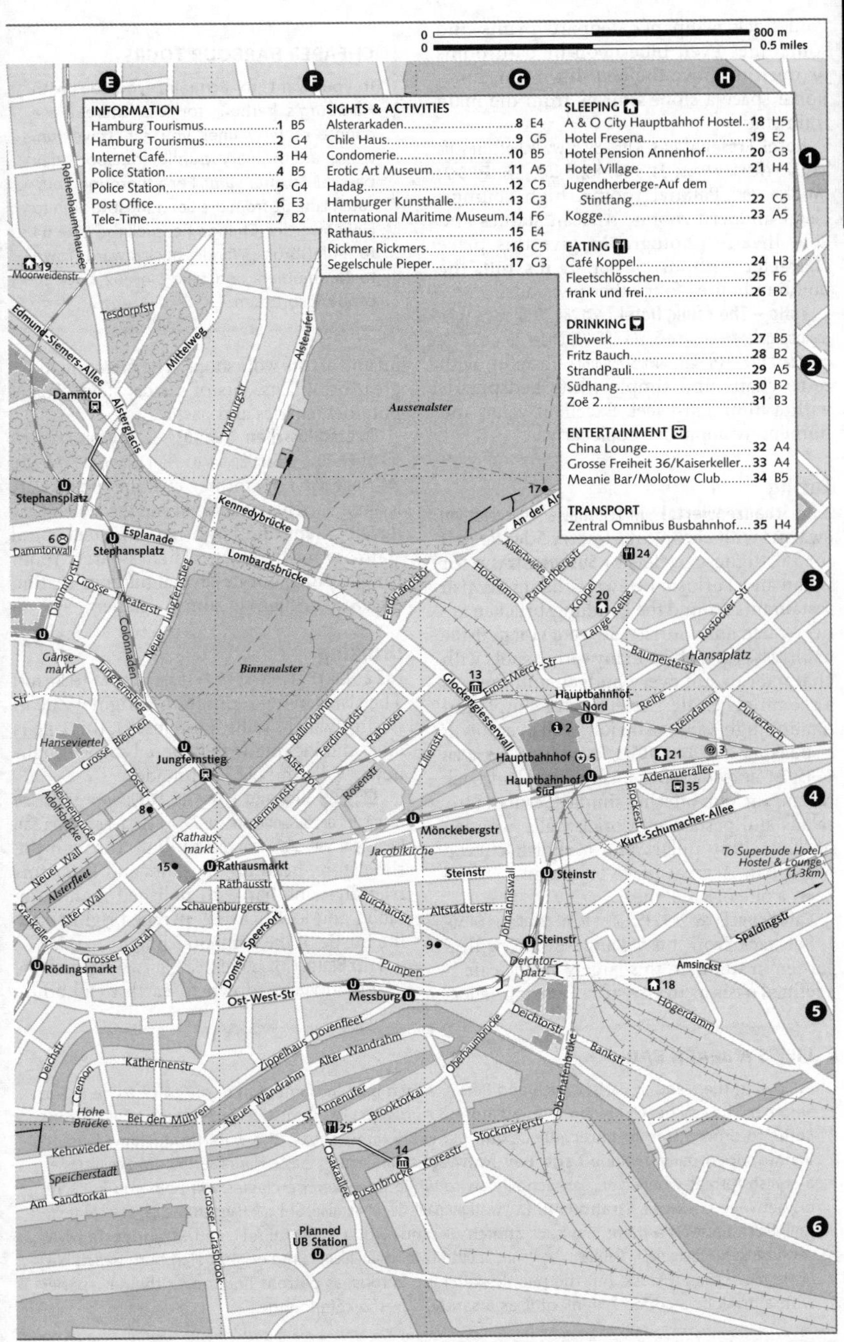
0 800 m
0 0.5 miles
E
F
G
H
1
2
3
4
5
6
INFORMATION
Hamburg Tourismus....1 B5
Hamburg Tourismus....2 G4
Internet Café....3 H4
Police Station....4 B5
Police Station....5 G4
Post Office....6 E3
Tele-Time....7 B2
SIGHTS & ACTIVITIES
Alsterarkaden....8 E4
Chile Haus....9 G5
Condomerie....10 B5
Erotic Art Museum....11 A5
Hadag....12 C5
Hamburger Kunsthalle....13 G3
International Maritime Museum....14 F6
Rathaus....15 E4
Rickmer Rickmers....16 C5
Segelschule Pieper....17 G3
SLEEPING
A & O City Hauptbahhof Hostel....18 H5
Hotel Fresena....19 E2
Hotel Pension Annenhof....20 G3
Hotel Village....21 H4
Jugendherberge-Auf dem Stintfang....22 C5
Kogge....23 A5
EATING
Café Koppel....24 H3
Fleetschlösschen....25 F6
frank und frei....26 B2
DRINKING
Elbwerk....27 B5
Fritz Bauch....28 B2
StrandPauli....29 A5
Südhang....30 B2
Zoë 2....31 B3
ENTERTAINMENT
China Lounge....32 A4
Grosse Freiheit 36/Kaiserkeller....33 A4
Meanie Bar/Molotow Club....34 B5
TRANSPORT
Zentral Omnibus Busbahnhof....35 H4
Rothenbaumchausee
Moorweidenstr
Tesdorpfstr
Edmund-Siemers-Allee
Mittelweg
Alsterufer
Dammtor
Alsterglacis
Warburgstr
Aussenalster
Stephansplatz
Kennedybrücke
An der Alster
Esplanade
Dammtorwall
Lombardsbrücke
Alstertwiete
Rautenbergstr
Holzdamm
Koppel
Lange Reihe
Ferdinandstor
Dammtorstr
Grosse Theaterstr
Neuer Jungfernstieg
Colonnaden
Gänsemarkt
Jungfernstieg
Binnenalster
Glockengiesserwall
Ernst-Merck-Str
Baumeisterstr
Rostocker Str
Hansaplatz
Hauptbahnhof-Nord
Reihe
Steindamm
Pulverteich
Hanseviertel
Grosse Bleichen
Ballindamm
Ferdinandstr
Raboisen
Lilienstr
Hauptbahnhof
Adenauerallee
Hauptbahnhof-Süd
Poststr
Alstertor
Hermannstr
Rosenstr
Brockestr
Bleichenbrücke
Adolfsbrücke
Mönckebergstr
Kurt-Schumacher-Allee
Rathausmarkt
Jacobikirche
Neuer Wall
Alsterfleet
Steinstr
To Superbude Hotel, Hostel & Lounge (1.3km)
Rathausstr
Alter Wall
Schauenburgerstr
Burchardstr
Altstädterstr
Johanninswall
Graskeller
Grosser Burstah
Speersort
Domstr
Spaldingstr
Rödingsmarkt
Pumpen
Deichtorplatz
Amsinckst
Messburg
Ost-West-Str
Högerdamm
Deichtorstr
Zippelhaus
Dovenfleet
Alter Wandrahm
Oberbaumbrücke
Bankstr
Deichstr
Katharinenstr
Cremon
Neuer Wandrahm
Oberhafenbrücke
Hohe Brücke
Bei den Mühren
St Annenufer
Brooktorkai
Kehrwieder
Stockmeyerstr
Osakaallee
Koreastr
Speicherstadt
Busanbrücke
Am Sandtorkai
Grosser Grasbrook
Planned UB Station

 Book your stay at lonelyplanet.com/hotels

gold flock wallpaper, leopard prints and sometimes even blue-neon-lit bathrooms or mirrors above the bed. It's a fun, functional space a stone's throw from the main train station.

Hotel Fresena (☎ 410 4892; www.hotelfresena.de; Moorweidenstrasse 34; s €65-85, d €88; 💻 P ⊠; M Dammtor) Palatial rooms, high ceilings, clean, modern rooms, African statues and cool theatre photographs give this place character without clutter. If it's full, the building houses four other pensions.

YoHo – The Young Hotel (☎ 284 1910; www.yoho-hamburg.de; Moorkamp 5; s/d €85/99, under 26yr €62/75, breakfast €12; P 💻; M Schlumpf) Tasteful, with retro chairs and simple white bedspreads with a minimalist feel. Excellent value and immensely popular – book early.

Eating

The **Schanzenviertel** (M Feldstrasse/Schanzenstern) swarms with cheap eateries; try **Schulterblatt** for Portuguese outlets or **Susanenstrasse** for Asian and Turkish. Be aware that many fish restaurants around the Landungsbrücken are over-rated and touristy. **St Georg's Lange Reihe** (M Hauptbahnhof) offers many eating spots with character to suit every budget, and there is a seemingly endless selection of simple but quality, high-value sushi joints all over town.

frank und frei (☎ 430 0573; Schanzenstrasse 93; mains €4-15; M Sternschanze) Big, bustling and laid-back restaurant-pub offering simple German fare, salads and pastas, with brick walls, wooden booths, shiny pillars and a stylish curved wood bar. A great place to unwind with a beer, a bite or a full meal.

Café Koppel (☎ 249 235; Lange Reihe 66; dishes €4.50-9) Set back from busy Lange Reihe, with a garden in summer, this largely veggie cafe is a refined oasis in an airy space housing galleries and artists workshops. The menu includes great breakfasts, lots of salads, stews, jacket potatoes, curries and pasta.

Fleetschlösschen (☎ 3039 3210; Brooktorkai 17; snacks €7-10; ⏰ 8am-8pm Mon-Fri, 11am-6pm Sat & Sun; M Messburg) This former customs post overlooks a Speicherstadt canal and the Hafen City development and has a narrow, steel spiral staircase to the toilets. There's barely room for 20 inside, but its several outdoor seating areas are brilliant in sunny weather.

CHEAPER HARBOUR TOURS

If you want to acquaint yourself with Hamburg's harbour for less, there are a couple of ferry lines you can travel on, using an ordinary public transport day pass (€5.50 after 9am). For a thorough 'tour' catch Line 62 from the Landungsbrücken to Finkenwerder. Change here for the Line 64 to Teufelsbrück. Wander back towards town to Neumühlen, and take Line 62 back to Landungsbrücken.

Drinking

Zoë 2 (Neuer Pferdemarkt 17; ⏰ from noon; M Feldstrasse) The sister living room to the original Zoë in Berlin (which, sadly, has closed), this one is alive and kicking with battered sofas, rough-hewn walls and old lampshades.

our pick **Südhang** (☎ 4309 9099; www.suedhang-hamburg.de; Susannenstrasse 29; ⏰ from noon Mon-Sat, from 4pm Sun; M Sternschanze) Walk through the shoe store, head up the stairs and enter this friendly wine bar with polished mahogany tables and low-lighting, perched right above the hustle of the neighbourhood.

Fritz Bauch (☎ 430 0194; Bartelstrasse 6; ⏰ from 5pm; M Sternschanze) A down-to-earth neighbour-

LIFE'S A BEACH BAR

Following the trend in Paris, Zurich and Berlin, beach bars in Hamburg are *the* place to be in the summer. The city beach season kicks off around April and lasts until at least September, as patrons come to drink, listen to music, dance and generally hang out on the waterfront. A few leading venues, open daily, include **Lago Bay** (www.lago.cc, in German; Grosse Elbstrasse 150; M Königstrasse), a stylish retreat where you can actually swim while free exercise classes will help you keep fit, er, between cocktails. **StrandPauli** (www.strandpauli.de, in German; St-Pauli Hafenstrasse 84; bus 112 to St-Pauli-Hafenstrasse) is a more laid-back stretch of sand with a youthful feel, and **Strandperle** (www.strandperle-hamburg.de, in German; Övelgönne 1; bus 112 to Neumühlen) is the original Hamburg beach bar. Little more than a kiosk, but the people-watching is tops, as patrons linger over the newspaper with a drink or a coffee – think of it as a sandy, alfresco cafe-lounge.

GETTING INTO TOWN

The **Airport Express** (☎ 227 1060; www.jasper-hamburg.de) runs between the Hauptbahnhof and airport (€5, 25 minutes, every 10 to 20 minutes) between 5:45am and midnight. You can also take the U1 or S1 to Ohlsdorf, then change to bus 110.

hood bar in the middle of the Schanzenviertel with yellow and pale-pink walls; wooden arched ceilings; basic, no-nonsense drinks; and hopping music.

Elbwerk (☎ 6579 1420; Bernhard-Nocht-Strasse 68; 🕑 from 11am; Ⓜ Landungsbrücken) Although this swanky cafe-lounge serves lite bites, this place is best for a cocktail at sunset and to admire its exceptional view over the Elbe River.

Clubbing

Meanie Bar/Molotow Club (☎ 310 845; www.molotowclub.com; Spielbudenplatz 5; 🕑 from 6pm; Ⓜ Reeperbahn) One of the few venues along the Reeperbahn with real local cred, the retro Meanie Bar sits above the Molotow Club, where an alternative, independent music scene thrives.

Grosse Freiheit 36/Kaiserkeller (☎ 3177 7811; Grosse Freiheit 36; 🕑 from 10pm Tue-Sat; Ⓜ Reeperbahn) Wedged between live sex theatres and peep shows, this is popular for live rock and pop, particularly as the Beatles played in the basement Kaiserkeller.

China Lounge (☎ 3197 6622; www.china-lounge.de; Nobistor 14; 🕑 from 11pm Wed, Fri & Sat, from 10pm Thu; Ⓜ Reeperbahn) This leading club has four areas playing electro, house, hip-hop and R&B – the main floor is under a huge laughing Buddha. Thursdays students pay no cover charge.

Getting There & Away

AIR

Hamburg's **airport** (HAM; www.flughafen-hamburg.de) has frequent flights to domestic and European cities, including on low-cost carrier **Air Berlin** (www.airberlin.com).

BUS

The **Zentral Omnibus Busbahnhof** (ZOB, central bus station; ☎ 247 5765; www.zob-hamburg.de; Adenauer Allee 78) is most popular for services to central and eastern Europe. **Eurolines** (☎ 4024 7106; www.eurolines.com) has buses to Prague (€64) and Vilnius (€84).

TRAIN

When reading train timetables, remember that there are two main train stations: Hamburg Hauptbahnhof and Hamburg-Altona. There are frequent RE trains to Lübeck (€11.50, 45 minutes), as well as various services to Hanover (€40, 1¼ hours) and Bremen (€28, 1¼ hours). In addition there are ICE trains to Berlin (€65, 1½ hours), Cologne (€78, four hours) and Munich (€127, 5½ hours) as well as Copenhagen (€79, 4¾ hours).

Getting Around

There's an integrated system of buses and U-Bahn and S-Bahn trains. Day tickets, bought from machines before boarding, cost €6, or €5.10 after 9am.

LÜBECK

☎ 0451 / pop 213,800

Two pointed cylindrical towers of Lübeck's Holstentor (gate) greet you upon arrival – if you think they're a tad crooked, you're not seeing things: they lean towards each other across the stepped gable that joins them. Right behind them, the streets are lined with medieval merchants' homes and spired churches forming the city's so-called 'crown'. It's hardly surprising that this 12th-century gem is on Unesco's World Heritage list.

Orientation & Information

Lübeck's old town is set on an island ringed by the canalised Trave River, a 10-minute walk east of the main train station. Leaving the station, head through the bus station and veer left along Hansestrasse. The tourist office is just across the Puppenbrücke (Doll Bridge), near the Holstentor.

Lübeck Travemünde Tourismus (☎ 01805 882 233; www.lubeck-tourism.de; Holstentorplatz 1; 🕑 10am-6pm Apr-Dec, 11am-7pm Tue-Sun Jan-Mar) Staff can organise city tours and sell discount cards.

Sights

The cute city gate or **Holstentor** (☎ 122 4129; adult/concession €5/2.50; 🕑 10am-5pm Tue-Sun Apr-Sep, to 4pm Tue-Sun Oct-Mar) is Lübeck's museum as well as its symbol. It's been under renovation, but should be out of its *trompe l'oeil* wraps by now. The six gabled brick buildings east of the Holstentor are the **Salzspeicher**, once used to store the salt that was pivotal to Lübeck's Hanseatic trade.

GETTING INTO TOWN

To head into town, catch scheduled bus 6 to the Hauptbahnhof and the neighbouring central bus station (one way €2.40, 20 minutes).

Behind these warehouses, the Trave River forms a moat around the old town, and if you do one thing in Lübeck in summer, it should be a boat tour. From April to September, **Maak-Linie** (☎ 706 3859; www.maak-linie.de) and **Quandt-Linie** (☎ 777 99; www.quandt-linie.de) depart regularly from either side of the Holstentorbrücke. Trips cost €8.

Each of Lübeck's churches offers something different. The shattered bells of the **Marienkirche** (Schüsselbuden 13; 10am-6pm Apr-Oct, to 5pm Tue-Sun Nov-Mar) still lie on the floor where they fell after a bombing raid. There's also a little devil sculpture outside, with an amusing fairy tale (in English). The tower lift in the **Petrikirche** (☎ 397 730; Schüsselbuden 13; adult/concession €3/2; 9am-9pm Apr-Sep, 10am-7pm Oct-Mar) affords superb views.

Have a look at the **Rathaus** before heading to **JG Niederegger** (Breite Strasse 89) opposite. This is Lübeck's mecca of chocolate-coated marzipan, with toothsome sweets and an adjoining cafe.

Lübeck has 90 *Gänge* (walkways) and *Höfe* (courtyards) tucked away behind its main streets, the most famous being the **Füchtingshof** (Glockengiesserstrasse 25; 9am-noon & 3-6pm); the delightful **Glandorps Gang** (Glockengiesserstrasse 41-51) was under renovation at press time but should be finished by 2010.

Fans of *The Tin Drum (Die Blechtrommel)* shouldn't miss the **Günter Grass-Haus** (☎ 122 4192; www.guenter-grass-haus.de; Glockengiesserstrasse 21; adult/concession €5/2.50, 'Kombi' card with Buddenbrookhaus €7/3; 10am-5pm Apr-Dec, 11am-5pm Jan-Mar), which includes a fine collection of manuscripts and sculptures. Fellow Nobel Prize–winning author Thomas Mann *(Death in Venice)* was born in Lübeck and he's commemorated in the award-winning **Buddenbrookhaus** (☎ 122 4190; www.buddenbrookhaus.de; Mengstrasse 4; adult/concession €5/2.50; 10am-6pm Apr-Dec, 11am-5pm Jan-Mar).

Sleeping

DJH Hostel Vor dem Burgtor (☎ 334 33; www.jugendherberge.de; Am Gertrudenkirchhof 4; dm junior/senior €16.40/18.40; P) Those fussy about their furnishings might like the huge, modern Vor dem Burgtor, though it's popular with school groups and outside the old town – just.

DJH Hostel Altstadt (☎ 702 0399; www.jugendherberge.de; Mengstrasse 33; dm junior/senior €18.70/21.70) Standard hostel in the old town – it isn't particularly new, but it's cosy and central.

Hotel zur Alten Stadtmauer (☎ 737 02; www.hotelstadtmauer.de; An der Mauer 57; s/d €42/70, with shared bathroom from €37/60; P) With pine furniture and splashes of red or yellow, this simple 25-room hotel is bright and cheerful. The wooden flooring means sound carries, and customers tend not to be quieter types. Back rooms overlook the river.

If none of the above appeal, two very cheap and basic places are **Sleep-Inn** (☎ 719 20; www.cvjm-luebeck.de; Grosse Petersgrube 11; dm €12.50) and the **Hotel Am Dom** (☎ 399 9430; www.cvjm-luebeck.de; Dankwartsgrube 43; s/d €36/68).

Eating

Suppentopf (☎ 400 8136; Fleischerstrasse 36; soups €3.50; 11am-4pm Mon-Fri) Always bustling, join Lübeck's office workers for a stand-up lunch of delicious, often spicy soup.

Tipasa (☎ 706 0451; Schlumacherstrasse 12-14; mains €5-16) Pizzas, curries and other budget meals are served below the faux caveman frescos of animals and Australian Aboriginal dot paintings.

Schiffergesellschaft (☎ 767 76; www.schiffergesellschaft.de; Breite Strasse 2; mains €10.50-23) The fact it's a tourist magnet can't detract from this 500-year-old guildhall's thrilling atmosphere. Seafood-heavy Frisian specialities and local beer are the way to go here.

Getting There & Around

Lübeck's **airport** (LBC; www.flughafen-luebeck.de) is linked to London by budget carriers Ryanair (www.ryanair.com) and easyJet (www.easyjetcom).

Trains head to Hamburg at least once an hour (€11.50, 45 minutes).

GERMANY DIRECTORY

ACCOMMODATION

Germany's accommodation is well organised. Some cities are short on budget hotels but private rooms are a good option in such situations. Accommodation usually includes breakfast. Look for signs saying *Zimmer frei* (rooms available) or *Fremdenzimmer* (tourist rooms). Most tourist offices offer a *Zimmervermittlung* (room-finding service), sometimes at a small charge.

Camping

There are more than 2000 organised camping grounds in Germany. Most are open April to September, but several hundred stay open all year round. Make sure you get permission before camping on private property. The best source of information is local tourist offices.

Hostels

Deutsches Jugendherbergswerk (DJH; www.djh.de) coordinates the official Hostelling International (HI) hostels in Germany. Rates in gender-segregated dorms or in family rooms range from €13 to €25 per person, including linen and breakfast. People over 27 are charged an extra €3 or €4.

Unless you're a member of your home country's HI association, you need to buy a Hostelling International Card for €15.50 (valid for one year) when you check in.

Indie hostels are more relaxed and can be found in Berlin, Munich, Frankfurt etc.

Pensions & Hotels

Pensions offer the basics of hotel comfort without asking hotel prices. Many are private homes, often a bit out of the centre of town. It's easiest to arrange bookings through tourist offices.

Cheap hotel rooms are hard to find during summer. Average budget prices are €35 to €60 for a room (without bathroom). Rates sometimes include a filling breakfast.

ACTIVITIES

Germany is ideal for hiking and mountaineering; popular areas include the Black Forest, the Harz Mountains, Saxon Switzerland, the Thuringian Forest and the Bavarian Alps. Good sources of information on hiking and mountaineering are **Verband Deutscher Gebirgs- und Wandervereine** (Federation of German Hiking Clubs; ☎ 0561-938 730; www.wanderverband.de) and **Deutscher Alpenverein** (German Alpine Club; ☎ 089-140 030; www.alpenverein.de).

The Bavarian Alps have the most extensive area for winter sports. Cross-country skiing is also good in the Black Forest and Harz Mountains. Local tourist offices are the best sources of information.

Eastern Germany has much to offer cyclists in the way of lightly travelled back roads, especially in the flat and less-populated north. There's also an extensive cycling trail along the Elbe River.

BUSINESS HOURS

Shops are generally open from 8am or 9am to 6pm (or in cities 8pm) Monday to Friday and usually 9am to 2pm (again as late as 8pm in cities) on Saturdays, but closed on public holidays. Except for a few rebels around train stations, by law everything retail is shut on Sunday – and many a charming town can seem utterly dead and deserted as a result. Don't expect to find the German equivalent of a 7-Eleven outside petrol and train stations.

Other businesses are generally open at the following times:

Banks 8.30am to 1pm and 2.30pm to 4pm Monday to Friday and until 5.30pm on Thursday, banks close on public holidays.
Bars around 6pm, while most nightclubs kick off at 11pm.
Museums closed on Monday or Tuesday.
Restaurants 11am to midnight, often closing from 3pm to 6pm.

DANGERS & ANNOYANCES

Although the usual precautions should be taken, crimes against travellers are rare in Germany. Africans, Asians and southern Europeans may encounter racial prejudice, especially in eastern Germany. The animosity is generally directed against immigrants, not tourists.

DISCOUNT CARDS

Many tourist offices offer local discount cards, generally including free public transport and free or discounted entry to attractions.

EMBASSIES & CONSULATES

The following embassies are all in Berlin. Many countries also have consulates in cities such as Frankfurt-am-Main and Munich.

Australia (Map pp454-5; ☎ 030-880 0880; www.australian-embassy.de; Wallstrasse 76-79)
Canada (Map pp454-5; ☎ 030-203 120; www.kanada-info.de; Leipziger Platz 17)
France (Map pp454-5; ☎ 030-590 039 000; www.botschaft-frankreich.de; Pariser Platz 5)

Ireland (Map pp454-5; ☎ 030-220 720; www.botschaft-irland.de; Friedrichstrasse 200)
Netherlands (Map pp454-5; ☎ 030-209 560; www.dutchembassy.de; Klosterstrasse 50)
New Zealand (Map pp454-5; ☎ 030-206 210; www.nzembassy.com; Friedrichstrasse 60)
UK (Map pp454-5; ☎ 030-204 570; www.britischebotschaft.de; Wilhelmstrasse 70)
USA (Map pp454-5; ☎ 030-238 5174; www.us-botschaft.de; Pariser Platz 2)

FESTIVALS & EVENTS

January & February

Karneval/Fasching (Carnival) The pre-Lent season is celebrated with costumed street partying, parades, satirical shows and general revelry, mostly in cities that are located along the Rhine such as Düsseldorf, Cologne and Mainz, but also in the Black Forest and Munich.

April

Walpurgisnacht Celebrated on 30 April throughout the Harz, this festival of pagan origin has villages roaring to life; young and old dress up as witches and warlocks and parade through the streets.

May

Maifest (May Festival) Villagers celebrate the end of winter by chopping down a tree *(Maibaum)*, painting, carving and decorating it, and staging a merry revelry with traditional costumes.
Rhein in Flammen (Rhine in Flames) Huge fireworks festival in Rhine villages; May to September.

June

Christopher Street Day (www.csd-germany.de) Major gay celebration with wild street parades and raucous partying, especially in Berlin, Cologne and Hamburg but also in Dresden, Munich, Stuttgart and Frankfurt.

July

B-Parade (www.b-parade.eu) Held each July, Berlin's huge techno street parade is the Loveparade's successor.

September, October & November

Oktoberfest (www.oktoberfest.de) Legendary beer-swilling party, enough said. Actually starts in mid-September; Munich (p475).
Frankfurt Book Fair (Frankfurter Buchmesse; www.buchmesse.de) October sees the world's largest book fair, with 1800 exhibitors from 100 countries.

December

Christmas Markets Popular across the country (see right).
Silvester The German New Year's Eve is called Silvester in honour of the 4th-century pope under whom the Romans adopted Christianity as their official religion; there's partying all night long.

> **CHRISTMAS MARKETS**
>
> Beginning in late November every year, central squares across Germany – especially in Bavaria – are transformed into Christmas markets or *Christkindlmarkts* (also known as *Weihnachtsmärkte*). Folks stamp about between the wooden stalls perusing seasonal trinkets (from treasures to schlock) while warming themselves with tasty *glühwein* (mulled, spiced red wine) and treats such as sausages and potato pancakes. They are popular with tourists but locals love 'em too, bundling up and carousing for hours. Nuremberg's market (www.chriskindlesmarkt.de) fills much of the centre and attracts two million people.

FOOD & DRINK

Germany is a meat-and-potatoes kind of country, although vegetarians shouldn't go hungry. Students can often eat quite cheaply at *mensas* (university cafeterias). Other popular cheap options are the ubiquitous doner kebab (Germany's favourite fast food) or a take away *China-Pfanne* (a noodle dish). Asian restaurants are generally quite fast-food oriented and will usually do vegetarian dishes on demand. Sunday brunch buffets are a great institution at many cafes and restaurants.

Wurst (sausage), in its many hundred of forms, is by far the most universal main dish in Germany. Regional favourites include *Bratwurst* (spiced sausage), *Weisswurst* (veal sausage), *Blutwurst* (blood sausage) and of course the Berlin *Currywurst*. Other popular main dishes include *Rippenspeer* (spare ribs), *Sauerbraten* (roast pork) and many forms of *Schnitzel* (breaded pork, chicken or veal cutlet).

Potatoes feature prominently in German meals, often as *Bratkartoffeln* (fried), *Kartoffelpüree* (mashed) or Swiss *Rösti* (grated, then fried). Salads, pasta and sandwiches are increasingly a part of the menu at even the most stalwart German restaurants and cafes.

Popular desserts include *Schwarzwälder Kirschtorte* (Black Forest cherry cake), as well as endless varieties of *Apfeltasche* (apple pastry).

At the liquid end of things, German beer is a cultural phenomenon that must be fully appreciated. *Helles Bier* is light, *Schwarzbier* or *Dunkles Bier* is dark, and *Pils* is slightly more bitter than normal lager, while *Alt* is darker and more full-bodied. A speciality is *Weizenbier,* made with wheat instead of barley malt and served either as *Kristall* (filtered) or *Hefe* (with yeast).

German wines are fairly inexpensive and are typically white and light and range from dry to very fruity. The Rhine and Moselle Valleys are the classic German wine-growing regions.

GAY & LESBIAN TRAVELLERS

Overall, Germans are tolerant of gays *(Schwule)* and lesbians *(Lesben)* although, as elsewhere in the world, cities (Berlin!) are more liberal than rural areas, and younger people tend to be more open-minded than older generations. Discrimination is more likely in eastern Germany and in the conservative south where gays and lesbians tend to keep a lower profile.

HOLIDAYS

Germany observes eight religious and three secular holidays nationwide. Shops, banks, government offices and post offices are closed on these days. States with predominantly Catholic populations, such as Bavaria and Baden-Württemberg, also celebrate Epiphany (6 January), Corpus Christi (10 days after Pentecost), Assumption Day (15 August) and All Saints' Day (1 November). Reformation Day (31 October) is only observed in eastern Germany.

The following are *gesetzliche Feiertage* (public holidays):

Neujahrstag (New Year's Day) 1 January

Ostern (Easter) March/April – Good Friday, Easter Sunday and Easter Monday

Christi Himmelfahrt (Ascension Day) 40 days after Easter

Maifeiertag/Tag der Arbeit (Labour Day) 1 May

Pfingsten (Whit/Pentecost Sunday & Monday) May/June; 50 days after Easter

Tag der Deutschen Einheit (Day of German Unity) 3 October

Weihnachtstag (Christmas Day) 25 December

2 Weihnachtstag (Boxing Day) 26 December

INTERNET ACCESS

More and more regular cafes, hostels and hotels offer wi-fi access – usually called WLAN in Germany.

LANGUAGE

The official language, *Hochdeutsch* (High German), is universally understood. English is widely understood by young or educated Germans, but less so outside big cities, especially in eastern Germany. See the Language chapter (p1262) for pronunciation guidelines and useful words and phrases.

LEGAL MATTERS

Germany's federal ban on smoking in public places is really a lot of smoke. In 2008 the federal court overturned the ban in small bars and restaurants and left final determination and enforcement up to individual states. Although a majority of cafes and nightspots remain nonsmoking, you'll encounter a few where smokers can light up.

MONEY

Germany's currency is the euro. See the Europe Directory (p1225) for a full discussion of all things monetary in Europe.

The easiest places to change cash in Germany are the banks or foreign exchange counters at airports and train stations, particularly those of the Reisebank. The main banks in larger cities generally have money-changing machines for after-hours use, although they don't often offer reasonable rates.

There are international ATMs virtually everywhere in Germany. Travellers cheques can be cashed at any bank. A percentage commission (usually a minimum of €5) is charged by most banks on any travellers cheque, even those issued in euros.

Tipping

Restaurant bills always include a service charge *(Bedienung)* but most people add 5% or 10% unless the service was truly abhorrent. At hotels it's nice to leave a few euros for the room cleaners. Tip bartenders about 5% and taxi drivers around 10%.

POST

Standard post office hours are 8am to 6pm weekdays and until noon on Saturday. Many train station post offices stay open later or offer limited services outside these hours.

Letters sent within Germany take one to two days for delivery; those addressed to destinations within Europe or to North America take four to six days and those to Australasia five to seven days.

TELEPHONE

See the Europe Directory (p1228) for a full discussion of using phones in Europe.

Deutsche Telekom directory assistance (☎ 118 37 for an English-speaking operator) charges a ridiculous €1.39 per minute for numbers within Germany and €1.99 for numbers outside Germany (☎ 118 34). Get the same information for free at www.telefonbuch.de.

Mobile Phones

Mobile phones ('handies') are ubiquitous in Germany; the main operators are T-Mobile, Vodafone, O2 and E-Plus. You can pick up a prepay SIM card for around €30; top-up cards are available from kiosks, various shops and vending machines. Mobile numbers generally begin with a ☎ 016 or ☎ 017 prefix.

Phone Codes

The country code for Germany is ☎ 49. To ring abroad from Germany, dial ☎ 00 followed by the country code, area code and number.

An operator can be reached on ☎ 0180-200 1033.

Phonecards

Most pay phones in Germany accept only phonecards, available for €5, €10 and €20 at post offices, news kiosks, tourist offices and banks. One call unit costs a little more than €0.06 from a private telephone and €0.10 from a public phone.

TOURIST INFORMATION

Before you even leave for Germany, you can consult the **German National tourist office** (Deutsche Zentrale für Tourismus, DZT; www.visits-to-germany.com).

TRAVELLERS WITH DISABILITIES

Germany caters reasonably well to the needs of *Behinderte* (disabled) travellers, with access ramps or lifts where necessary in most public buildings. Assistance is usually required when boarding public transport. If travelling on Deutsche Bahn distance services, you can arrange this when buying your ticket.

VISAS

Germany is part of the Schengen visa scheme (p1230). See the Europe Directory (p1229) for a full discussion about visas in Europe.

Greece Ελλάδα

HIGHLIGHTS

- **Acropolis** Savour your first glimpse of one of the most important monuments of the ancient world in Athens (p526)
- **Santorini** Experience the dramatic volcanic caldera of Santorini, arguably the most stunning Greek dot on the map (p544)
- **Rhodes** Meander through the atmospheric streets of the largest inhabited medieval town in Europe (p550)
- **Olympia** Dash off a quick 100m at the evocative birthplace of the games (p535)
- **Samaria Gorge** Trek through the most famous of Crete's spectacular gorges, then swim in the Libyan Sea (p549)
- **Mykonos** Party hard and lose yourself in the maze of white-walled streets originally designed to confuse pirates (p540)

FAST FACTS

- **Area** 131,944 sq km
- **Budget** €50 to €60 per day
- **Capital** Athens
- **Country code** ☎ 30
- **Famous for** ancient ruins, beautiful beaches
- **Language** Greek
- **Money** euro (€); A$1 = €0.55; C$1 = €0.60; ¥100 = €0.78; NZ$1 = €0.43; UK£1 = €1.12; US$1 = €0.74
- **Phrases** *yasas* (hello), *andio* (goodbye), *parakalo* (please), *efharisto* (thank you), *ne* (yes), *ohi* (no)

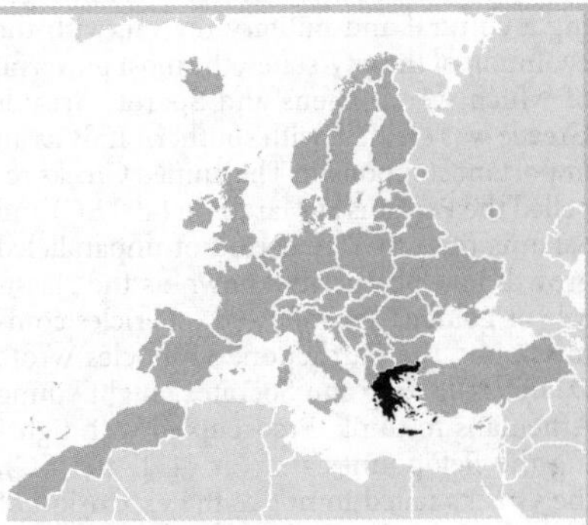

- **Population** 11.1 million
- **Visas** most travellers don't need one (p559)

TRAVEL HINTS

Remember sunglasses and sunscreen. *Gyro pita* (Greek version of doner kebab) are the best in cheap eats. Retsina may be an acquired taste, but it will suit your budget.

ROAMING GREECE

Explore Athens' museums and ancient sites before heading to the Peloponnese, visiting Nafplio, Mycenae and Olympia; ferry to the Cyclades and enjoy Mykonos and spectacular Santorini. Head further south to Crete, then on to Rhodes and its atmospheric Old Town.

There *is* something mystical and magical about Greece that makes it one of the most popular destinations on the planet. The alluring combination of history and hedonism attracts all sorts. Within easy reach of magnificent archaeological sites are breathtaking beaches lapped by amazingly clear waters. Throw in welcoming locals with an enticing culture, captivating music, tasty local cuisine and beverages, and it's easy to see why most visitors head home vowing to come back.

Adrenalin-focused travellers can mountain climb, hike, windsurf, dive and even hit the ski slopes. Party types can enjoy pulsating nightlife in Greece's vibrant modern cities and on islands such as Mykonos and Ios. And if all you're after is a peaceful holiday on a perfect beach, there are countless spots to enjoy your Greek dream.

Among the myriad attractions, travellers to Greece inevitably end up with a favourite site they long to return to – get out there and find yours.

HISTORY

With its strategic position at the crossroads of Europe and Asia, Greece has endured a long and turbulent history. During the Bronze Age (3000–1200 BC in Greece), the advanced Cycladic, Minoan and Mycenaean civilisations flourished. The Mycenaeans were swept aside in the 12th century BC by the warrior-like Dorians, who introduced Greece to the Iron Age.

By 800 BC, when Homer's *Odyssey* and *Iliad* were first written, Greece was undergoing a cultural and military revival, with the evolution of the city-states, the most powerful of which were Athens and Sparta. Greater Greece was created, with southern Italy as an important component. The unified Greeks repelled the Persians at Marathon (490 BC) and Salamis (480 BC). A period of unparalleled growth and prosperity known as the classical (or golden) age followed – Pericles commissioned the Parthenon, Sophocles wrote *Oedipus the King* and Socrates taught young Athenians to think. Preoccupied with fighting the Peloponnesian War (431–404 BC), the Greeks failed to notice the expansion of Macedonia under King Philip II, who easily conquered the war-weary city-states.

By 146 BC Greece and Macedonia had become Roman provinces. After the subdivision of the Roman Empire into Eastern and Western Empires in AD 395, Greece became part of the Eastern (Byzantine) Empire, based at Constantinople. In the centuries that followed, Venetians, Franks, Normans, Slavs, Persians, Arabs and, finally, Turks took turns chipping away at the Byzantine Empire. In 1453, when Constantinople fell to the Turks, most of Greece became part of the Ottoman Empire. By the 19th century the Ottoman Empire was in decline, and the Greeks fought the War of Independence (1821–32). In January 1833 Otho of Bavaria was installed as king, until 1862 when he was peacefully ousted and George I, a Danish prince, was chosen as king.

Greece fell to Germany in 1941 and resistance movements, polarised into royalist and communist factions, staged a bloody civil war lasting until 1949. This was a trigger for a mass exodus that saw almost one million Greeks head off to places such as Australia, Canada and the USA.

An army coup d'état in 1967 led to a period of brutality, repression and political incompetence. The 1974 Turkish occupation of North Cyprus became (and remains) one of the most contentious issues in Greek politics. The junta had little choice but to hand back power to the people.

In 1981 Greece entered the European Community (now the EU) and in 2002 it adopted the euro; prices have been on the rise ever since. Greece hosted a successful 2004 Olympics, but is still counting the cost.

During the long hot summer of 2007, the world watched as forest fires threatened Athens and caused untold damage in the western Peloponesse, Epiros and Evia.

Greece's foreign policy is dominated by a perceptibly warming, yet still sensitive relationship with Turkey – with Greece continuing to support Turkey's bid to join the EU.

THE CULTURE

Greece's population has exceeded 11.1 million, with around one-third of the people living in the Greater Athens area and more than two-thirds living in cities. Less than 15% live on the islands. Greece has an ageing population and declining birth rate, with big families a thing of the past. Population growth over the last couple of decades is due to a flood of migrants, both legal and illegal. Previously, Greece had been a nation of emigrants and

TIME YOUR VISIT

Spring and autumn are the best times to visit Greece – the weather is fine, temperatures are pleasant, beaches are uncrowded and off-season prices are in effect. Turn up in midsummer and you'll be battling the heat, crowds, accommodation that's booked solid and high-season prices.

there are an estimated 5 million people of Greek descent living around the world.

RELIGION

About 95% of the Greek population belongs to the Greek Orthodox Church. While older Greeks and those in rural areas tend to be deeply religious, most young people are decidedly more secular. The Greek year is centred on the saint's days and festivals of the church calendar. Name days (celebrating your namesake saint) are celebrated more than birthdays.

Orthodox Easter is usually at a different time than Easter celebrated by the Western churches, though generally in April/May.

ARTS

The arts have been integral to Greek life since ancient times, with architecture having had the most profound influence. Greek temples, seen throughout history as symbolic of democracy, were the inspiration for architectural movements such as the Italian Renaissance.

The first and greatest Ancient Greek writer was Homer, author of *Iliad* and *Odyssey*, telling the story of the Trojan War and the subsequent wanderings of Odysseus. The great love poets were Sappho (6th century BC) and Alcaeus (5th century BC), both of whom lived on Lesvos. Sappho's poetic descriptions of her affections for women gave rise to the term 'lesbian'. Nikos Kazantzakis, author of *Zorba the Greek* and numerous novels, plays and poems, is the most famous of 20th-century Greek novelists.

Greece's most famous painter was a young Cretan called Domenikos Theotokopoulos, who moved to Spain in 1577 and became known as the great El Greco.

Music has been a facet of Greek life since ancient times. The bouzouki is one of the main instruments of *rembetika* music – which is in many ways the Greek equivalent of the American blues and has its roots in the sufferings of the refugees from Asia Minor in the 1920s.

Greek film has for many years been associated with the work of film-maker Theo Angelopoulos, who won Cannes' Palme d'Or in 1998 with *An Eternity and One Day*. Since the late '90s, Greek cinema has witnessed a minor renaissance, with films such as *Safe Sex* (2000) luring Greek movie-goers back to the cinema.

ENVIRONMENT

Greece sits at the southern tip of the Balkan Peninsula. Of its 1400 islands only 169 are inhabited. The land mass is 131,944 sq km and Greek territorial waters cover a further 400,000 sq km. Around 80% of the land is mountainous, with less than a quarter of the country suitable for agriculture. In one of the most seismically active regions in the world, Greece has had more than 20,000 earthquakes in the last 40 years, most very minor.

The variety of flora in Greece is unrivalled in Europe, with a dazzling array of spectacular wild flowers. Lake Mikri Prespa in Macedonia has the richest colony of fish-eating birds in Europe, while the Dadia Forest Reserve in Thrace is home to the golden eagle and the giant black vulture. The brown bear still survives in very small numbers in the mountains of northern Greece. About half the population of Europe's rarest mammal, the monk seal, live in Greek waters. Zakynthos is home to Europe's last large sea turtle colony. The **Sea Turtle Protection Society of Greece** (☎/fax 21052 31342; www.archelon.gr) runs monitoring programs and is always on the look out for volunteers.

Greece is belatedly becoming environmentally conscious but, regrettably, it's too late for some regions. Deforestation and soil erosion are problems that go back thousands of years, with olive cultivation and goats being the main culprits. Forest fires are also a major problem. 2007 was a particularly devastating year for fires, many of which are thought to have been lit deliberately.

General environmental awareness remains at a depressingly low level, especially where litter is concerned.

TRANSPORT

GETTING THERE & AWAY

Air

Eleftherios Venizelos International Airport (ATH; ☎ 21035 30000; www.aia.gr), near Athens, handles the vast majority of international flights and has regular scheduled flights to all the European capitals. Other international airports with scheduled flights are **Macedonia airport** (SKG; ☎ 23104 73700), serving Thessaloniki; **Nikos Kazantzakis airport** (HER; ☎ 28102 28401), serving Iraklio; and **Diagoras airport** (RHO; ☎ 22410 83222), serving Rhodes.

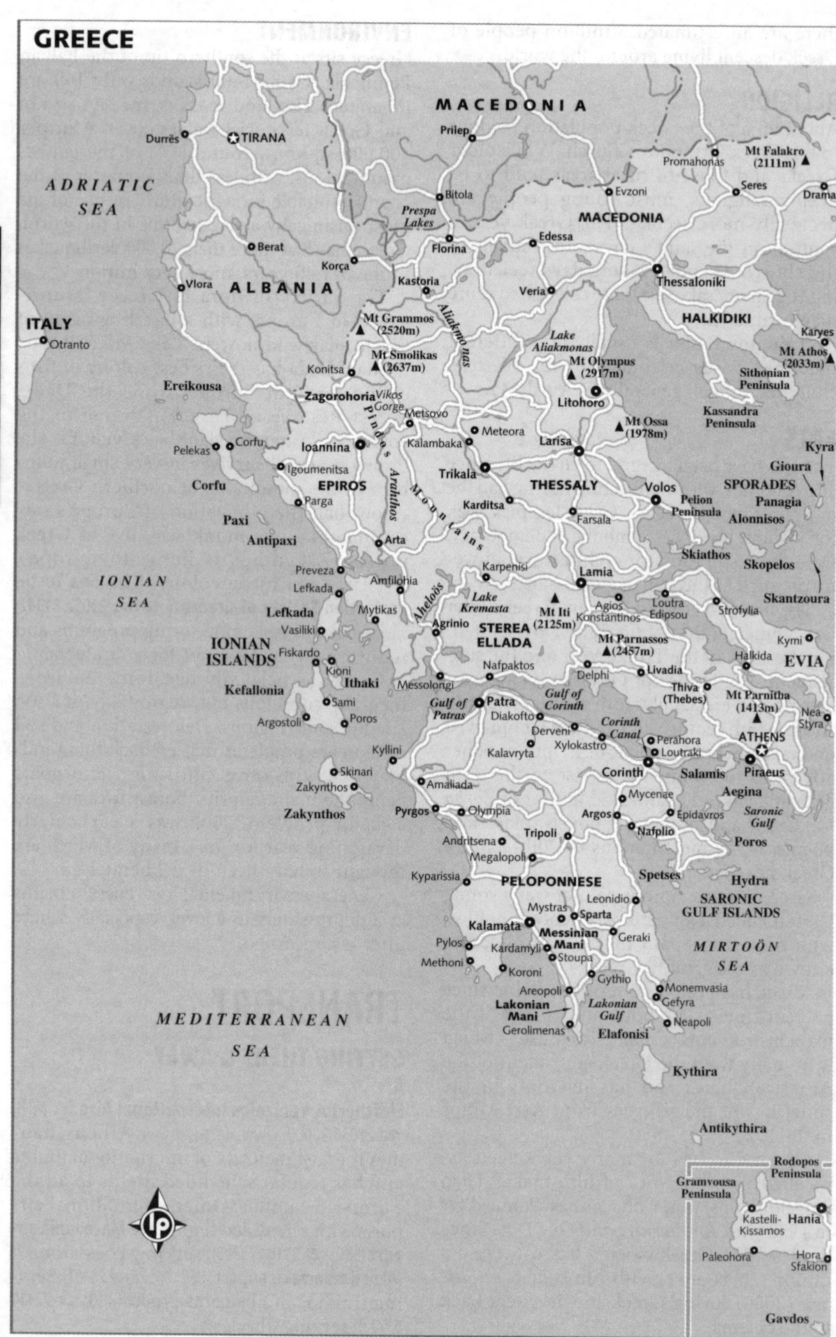
GREECE
MACEDONIA
ADRIATIC SEA
ALBANIA
ITALY
Otranto
Durrës
TIRANA
Prilep
Bitola
Prespa Lakes
Promahonas
Mt Falakro (2111m)
Evzoni
Seres
Drama
MACEDONIA
Berat
Korça
Florina
Edessa
Vlora
Kastoria
Veria
Thessaloniki
HALKIDIKI
Mt Grammos (2520m)
Aliakmonas
Lake Aliakmonas
Karyes
Mt Athos (2033m)
Mt Smolikas (2637m)
Mt Olympus (2917m)
Sithonian Peninsula
Konitsa
Ereikousa
Zagorohoria
Vikos Gorge
Litohoro
Kassandra Peninsula
Pindos Mountains
Metsovo
Mt Ossa (1978m)
Meteora
Kalambaka
Larisa
Kyra
Pelekas
Corfu
Ioannina
Giouri
Igoumenitsa
Trikala
Corfu
EPIROS
THESSALY
Volos
SPORADES
Parga
Arahthos
Karditsa
Pelion Peninsula
Panagia
Paxi
Farsala
Alonnisos
Antipaxi
Arta
Skiathos
Skopelos
Preveza
Karpenisi
Lamia
IONIAN SEA
Amfilohia
Lefkada
Aheloös
Lake Kremasta
Agios Konstantinos
Loutra Edipsou
Strofylia
Skantzoura
Lefkada
Mytikas
Mt Iti (2125m)
Vasiliki
Agrinio
STEREA ELLADA
Kymi
IONIAN ISLANDS
Mt Parnassos (2457m)
Fiskardo
Halkida
EVIA
Kioni
Nafpaktos
Delphi
Livadia
Ithaki
Kefallonia
Messolongi
Thiva (Thebes)
Mt Parnitha (1413m)
Sami
Gulf of Patras
Patra
Gulf of Corinth
Nea Styra
Argostoli
Poros
Diakofto
Derveni
Corinth Canal
Perahora
ATHENS
Xylokastro
Kalavryta
Loutraki
Kyllini
Corinth
Salamis
Piraeus
Skinari
Zakynthos
Amaliada
Mycenae
Aegina
Pyrgos
Olympia
Argos
Epidavros
Saronic Gulf
Zakynthos
Nafplio
Tripoli
Poros
Andritsena
Megalopoli
Spetses
Kyparissia
PELOPONNESE
Hydra
Leonidio
SARONIC GULF ISLANDS
Mystras
Sparta
Kalamata
Messinian Mani
Geraki
Pylos
Kardamyli
MIRTOÖN SEA
Stoupa
Methoni
Koroni
Gythio
Areopoli
Monemvasia
Lakonian Mani
Lakonian Gulf
Gefyra
Neapoli
Gerolimenas
Elafonisi
MEDITERRANEAN SEA
Kythira
Antikythira
Rodopos Peninsula
Gramvousa Peninsula
Kastelli-Kissamos
Hania
Paleohora
Hora Sfakion
Gavdos

GREECE

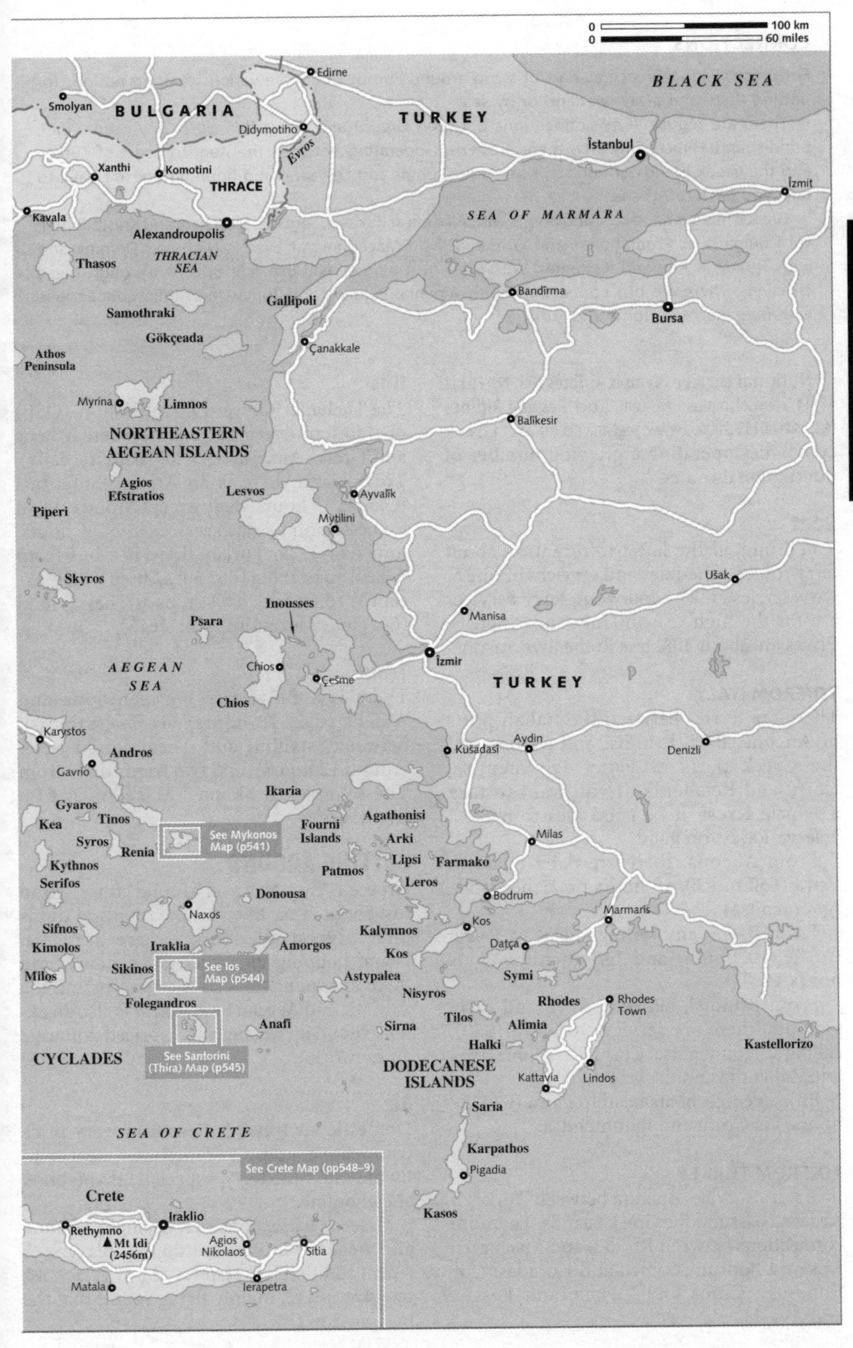
0 100 km
0 60 miles
BLACK SEA
BULGARIA
TURKEY
Edirne
Smolyan
Didymotiho
Evros
Îstanbul
İzmit
Xanthi
Komotini
THRACE
Kavala
Alexandroupolis
SEA OF MARMARA
THRACIAN SEA
Thasos
Samothraki
Gallipoli
Bandîrma
Bursa
Gökçeada
Athos Peninsula
Çanakkale
Myrina
Limnos
NORTHEASTERN AEGEAN ISLANDS
Balîkesir
Agios Efstratios
Lesvos
Ayvalîk
Piperi
Mytilini
Skyros
Uşak
Inousses
Psara
Manisa
İzmir
AEGEAN SEA
Chios
Çeşme
TURKEY
Chios
Karystos
Andros
Gavrio
Kuşadasî
Aydin
Denizli
Ikaria
Gyaros
Kea
Tinos
Agathonisi
Fourni Islands
Arki
Syros
Renia
See Mykonos Map (p541)
Lipsi
Farmako
Milas
Kythnos
Patmos
Serifos
Leros
Donousa
Bodrum
Naxos
Marmaris
Sifnos
Kalymnos
Kos
Kimolos
Iraklia
Amorgos
Kos
Datça
Milos
Sikinos
See Ios Map (p544)
Astypalea
Symi
Nisyros
Rhodes
Rhodes Town
Folegandros
Anafi
Sirna
Tilos
Alimia
Halki
Kastellorizo
CYCLADES
See Santorini (Thira) Map (p545)
DODECANESE ISLANDS
Kattavia
Lindos
Saria
SEA OF CRETE
Karpathos
See Crete Map (pp548–9)
Pigadia
Crete
Kasos
Iraklio
Rethymno
Mt Idi (2456m)
Agios Nikolaos
Sitia
Matala
Ierapetra
GREECE

CONNECTIONS

For those visiting Greece as part of a trip around Europe, there are various exciting options for getting there and away overland or by sea.

There are regular ferry connections between Greece and the Italian ports of Ancona, Bari, Brindisi and Venice. Similarly, there are ferries operating between the Aegean coast of Turkey and the Greek islands of Rhodes, Kos, Samos, Chios and Lesvos. Island-hopping doesn't have to take you back to Athens.

Greece has overland crossing points with Albania at Kakavia, Sagiada, Mertziani and Krystallopigi; with Bulgaria at Promahonas and Ormenio; with Macedonia at Evzoni, Niki, and Doïrani; and with Turkey at Kipi and Kastanies. With your own wheels, you can ride or drive through these crossings. There are bus connections with Albania, Bulgaria and Turkey, and train connections with Bulgaria, Macedonia and Turkey.

National carrier **Olympic Airlines** (OA; ☎ 80111 44444; www.olympicairlines.com) and **Aegean Airlines** (A3; ☎ 80111 20000; www.aegeanair.com) are Greek companies operating a growing number of international routes.

Boat

You'll find all the latest information about ferry routes, schedules and services online at www.ferries.gr. The following ferry services are for the high season (July and August). Prices are about 30% less in the low season.

TO/FROM ITALY

There are ferries between the Italian ports of Ancona, Bari, Brindisi and Venice and the Greek ports of Patra, Igoumenitsa, Corfu and Kefallonia. If you want to take a vehicle across, it's a good idea to make a reservation beforehand.

From Ancona, there are daily boats to Patra (€60 to €70, 19 hours or 21 hours via Igoumenitsa).

From Bari, daily sailings head to Patra, Corfu (10 hours) and Igoumenitsa (11½ hours, €53).

From Brindisi, between April and early October, there are services to Patra (€50), calling at Igoumenitsa, Corfu, Kefallonia, Paxi and Zakynthos on the way.

From Venice, boats head to Patra (€75, 29 hours) via Corfu and Igoumenitsa.

TO/FROM TURKEY

Five ferry services operate between Turkey's Aegean coast and the Greek Islands. There are connections between Rhodes and Marmaris; Kos and Bodrum; Samos and Kuşadası (for Ephesus); Chios and Çeşme; and Lesvos and Ayvalik.

Bus

The Hellenic Railways Organisation (OSE) operates an overnight bus between Athens and Tirana, Albania (€35.20, 16 hours, daily). To Bulgaria there is an Athens–Sofia bus (€45.50, 15 hours, daily except Monday) and a Thessaloniki–Sofia service (€19, 7½ hours, four daily). To Turkey there is a bus from Athens to İstanbul (€67.50, 22 hours, daily except Wednesday). This stops at Thessaloniki (€44) and Alexandroupolis (€15).

Train

There is a daily train between Sofia and Athens (€32, 18 hours) via Thessaloniki; between İstanbul and Thessaloniki (€48, around 12 hours); and two trains daily from Thessaloniki to Skopje (Macedonia; €14, five hours).

GETTING AROUND

Greece is easy to travel around. Buses go to just about every town on the map and trains offer a good alternative where available. Island-hopping in Greece is legendary, and there are countless ferries criss-crossing the Adriatic and Aegean Seas. There is also an extensive and increasingly well-priced domestic air network.

Air

Domestic air travel is becoming very price competitive, and it's sometimes cheaper to fly than take the ferry, especially if you book ahead online.

Greece's national carrier, Olympic Airlines, and Aegean Airlines are the big players. A recent addition is **Sky Express** (SEH; ☎ 28102 23500; www.skyexpress.gr), mainly flying routes that the big two don't.

Bicycle

With hilly terrain and stifling summer heat, cycling is not that popular a way to see the country. You can hire bicycles at most tourist centres, but these are generally for pedalling around town rather than for serious riding. Prices generally range from €10 to €12 per day. Bicycles are carried for free on ferries.

Boat

Island-hopping by boat in the Greek islands is great fun. Sea travel options are constantly changing. Operations are highly seasonal and changes to schedules can take place at the last minute. Check out www.ferries.gr for schedules, costs and links to company websites.

Most islands have a ferry service of some sort, although in winter these are pared back. Services pick up from April, and during July and August Greece's seas are a mass of wake and wash. The cheapest way to go is 'deck class' on a slow boat. The newer high-speed ferries, catamarans and hydrofoils are slashing travel times but usually cost much more.

Generally, tickets can be bought at the last minute at the dock, but in the high season some boats may be full – plan ahead.

The hub of the vast ferry network is Piraeus, the main port of Athens. It has ferries to the Cyclades, Crete, the Dodecanese, the Saronic Gulf Islands and the Northeastern Aegean Islands. Patra is the main port for ferries to the Ionian Islands, while Volos

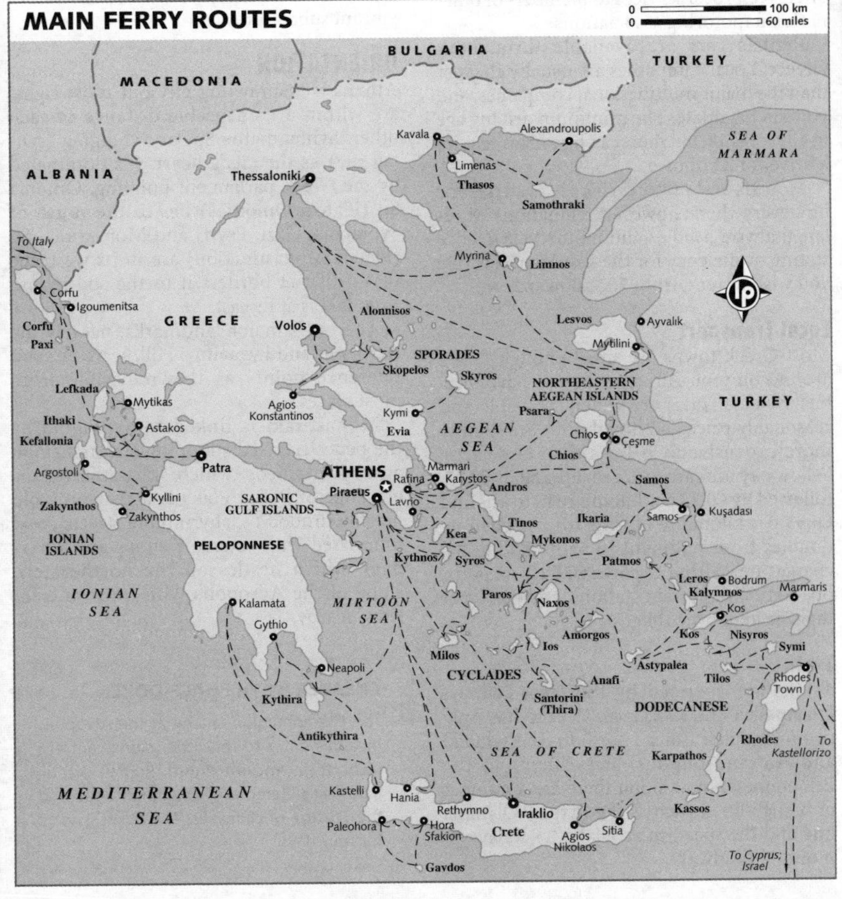

and Agios Konstantinos are the ports for the Sporades.

Bus

All long-distance buses are operated by regional collectives known as **KTEL** (www.ktel.org). Fares are fixed by the government and service routes can be found on the website. Buses are comfortable, generally run on time and are reasonably priced.

Car & Motorcycle

A great way to explore areas in Greece that are off the beaten track is by car. Almost all islands are served by car ferries, but they are expensive. Greece recognises all national driving licences and the International Driving Permit. The automobile club, **ELPA** (www.elpa.gr), offers reciprocal services to members of other national motoring associations.

Rentals cars are available throughout Greece. Local companies are usually cheaper than the major multinational companies, and you can negotiate. The minimum driving age in Greece is 18, but most car-hire firms require a driver of 21 or over.

Mopeds and motorcycles are available for hire everywhere; however, regulations stipulate that you need a valid motorcycle licence stating proficiency for the size of motorcycle you wish to rent, from 50cc upwards.

Local Transport

Most Greek towns are small enough to get around on foot. All major towns have local bus systems. Taxis are widely available and reasonably priced, although they are slightly more expensive in Athens than elsewhere. Yellow city cabs are metered. Flag fall is €0.75, followed by €0.28 per kilometre in towns and €0.53 per kilometre outside towns. The rate doubles from midnight to 5am. Additional charges are €3 from airports; €0.80 from ports, bus stations and train stations; and €0.30 per luggage item over 10kg.

Train

Trains are operated by the **Greek Railways Organisation** (OSE; www.ose.gr). Greece has only two main lines: Athens north to Thessaloniki and Alexandroupolis, and Athens to the Peloponnese. In addition there are a number of branch lines, such as the Pyrgos–Olympia line and the spectacular Diakofto–Kalavryta mountain railway.

Inter-Rail and Eurail passes are valid in Greece, but you still need to make a reservation.

ATHENS ΑΘΗΝΑ

pop 3.7 million

Stroll around a corner in Athens and come face to face with breathtaking archaeological treasures, reminders of the city's enormous historical influence on Western civilisation. With the makeover that accompanied the 2004 Olympics, Athens also debuted its cosmopolitan, chic side on the world stage. Though the city still suffers from traffic congestion, pollution and urban sprawl, take the time to look beneath her skin and you will discover a complex metropolis full of vibrant subcultures.

ORIENTATION

Athens is a sprawling city but most sights are within a manageable distance of each other. Syntagmatos Sq, or Syntagma (*syn-tag-ma*), is the city's heart. It's dominated by the Greek parliament building. Omonia Sq (Plateia Omonias) lies to the north of Syntagma; Gazi, Psyrri and Monastiraki Sq (Plateia Monastirakiou) are to its west; the Plaka district borders it to the south; and Kolonaki is at its east.

The city's major landmarks, namely the Acropolis and Lykavittos Hill, serve as good reference points as they're visible from most places.

Monastiraki is linked to Syntagma by the pedestrianised shopping streets Ermou and Mitropoleos, which skirts the northern edge of Plaka. Plaka is a charming old neighbourhood of labyrinthine streets (now inundated with souvenir shops and tavernas), which nestles on the northeastern slope of the Acropolis with most ancient sites nearby.

CHEAPER BY THE HALF-DOZEN

The €12 admission charge at the Acropolis includes entry to the other significant ancient sites: Ancient Agora, Roman Agora, Keramikos, Temple of Olympian Zeus and the Theatre of Dionysos. The ticket is valid for four days.

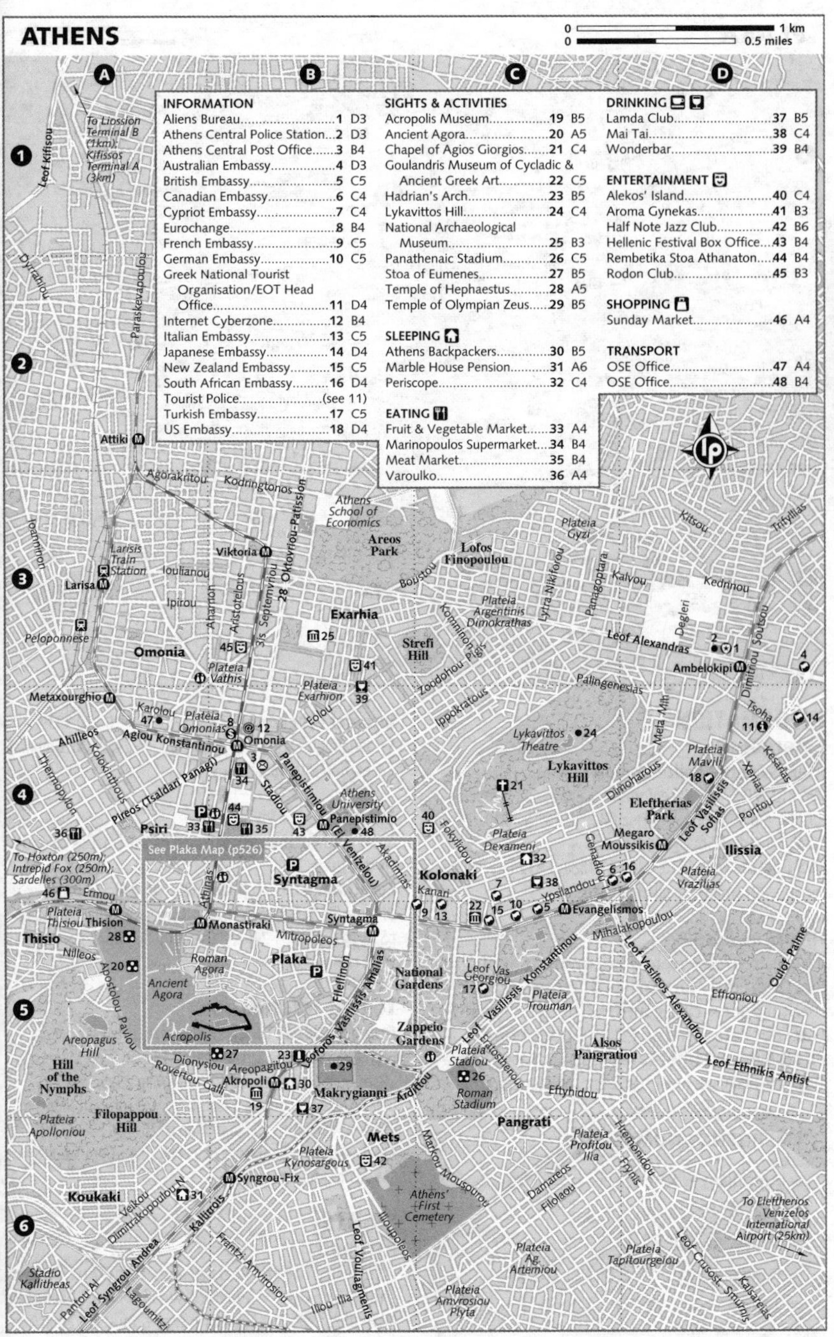
ATHENS
0 1 km
0 0.5 miles
A
B
C
D
1
2
3
4
5
6
INFORMATION
Aliens Bureau....1 D3
Athens Central Police Station....2 D3
Athens Central Post Office....3 B4
Australian Embassy....4 D3
British Embassy....5 C5
Canadian Embassy....6 C4
Cypriot Embassy....7 C4
Eurochange....8 B4
French Embassy....9 C5
German Embassy....10 C5
Greek National Tourist Organisation/EOT Head Office....11 D4
Internet Cyberzone....12 B4
Italian Embassy....13 C5
Japanese Embassy....14 D4
New Zealand Embassy....15 C5
South African Embassy....16 D4
Tourist Police....(see 11)
Turkish Embassy....17 C5
US Embassy....18 D4
SIGHTS & ACTIVITIES
Acropolis Museum....19 B5
Ancient Agora....20 A5
Chapel of Agios Giorgios....21 C4
Goulandris Museum of Cycladic & Ancient Greek Art....22 C5
Hadrian's Arch....23 B5
Lykavittos Hill....24 C4
National Archaeological Museum....25 B3
Panathenaic Stadium....26 C5
Stoa of Eumenes....27 B5
Temple of Hephaestus....28 A5
Temple of Olympian Zeus....29 B5
SLEEPING
Athens Backpackers....30 B5
Marble House Pension....31 A6
Periscope....32 C4
EATING
Fruit & Vegetable Market....33 A4
Marinopoulos Supermarket....34 B4
Meat Market....35 B4
Varoulko....36 A4
DRINKING
Lamda Club....37 B5
Mai Tai....38 C4
Wonderbar....39 B4
ENTERTAINMENT
Alekos' Island....40 C4
Aroma Gynekas....41 B3
Half Note Jazz Club....42 B6
Hellenic Festival Box Office....43 B4
Rembetika Stoa Athanaton....44 B4
Rodon Club....45 B3
SHOPPING
Sunday Market....46 A4
TRANSPORT
OSE Office....47 A4
OSE Office....48 B4
To Liossion Terminal B (1km); Kifissos Terminal A (3km)
Leof Kifisou
Dyrahiou
Paraskevapoulou
Attiki
Agorakritou
Kodringtonos
Oktovriou-Patission
28
Athens School of Economics
Areos Park
Lofos Finopoulou
Plateia Gyzi
Kitsou
Trifyllias
Ioannirou
Larisis Train Station
Larisa
Viktoria
Ioulianou
Ipirou
Aharnon
Aristotelous
3is Septemvriou
Boustou
Kalvou
Kedrinou
Panagoptara
Lytra Nikiforou
Plateia Argentinis Dimokratias
Komninon
Exarhia
Strefi Hill
Degleri
Leof Alexandras
Soutsou
Peloponnese
Omonia
Plateia Vathis
Plateia Exarhion
Zoodohou Pigis
Palingenesias
Ambelokipi
Dimitriou Soutsou
Metaxourghio
Karolou
Plateia Omonias
Eolou
Ippokratous
Tsoha
Lykavittos Theatre
Meta Mili
Ahilleos
Kolokinthous
Agiou Konstantinou
Thermopylon
Panepistimiou
Stadiou
Lykavittos Hill
Dimoharous
Plateia Mavili
Kesarias
Xenias
Pireos (Tsaldari Panagi)
Athens University
Panepistimio
(El Venizelou)
Akadimias
Fokylidou
Plateia Dexameni
Eleftherias Park
Vasilissis Sofias
Pontou
Psiri
To Hoxton (250m); Intrepid Fox (250m); Sardelles (300m)
See Plaka Map (p526)
Syntagma
Kolonaki
Kanari
Gennadiou
Megaro Moussikis
Ilissia
Plateia Vrazilias
Ermou
Athinas
Ypsilandou
Evangelismos
Plateia Thisiou
Thision
Monastiraki
Thisio
Mitropoleos
Mihalakopoulou
Nilleos
Apostolou Pavlou
Roman Agora
Plaka
Filellinon
Vasilissis Amalias
National Gardens
Leof Vas Georgiou
Vasilissis Konstantinou
Plateia Trouman
Leof Vasileos Alexandrou
Oulof Palme
Effroniou
Ancient Agora
Acropolis
Zappeio Gardens
Areopagus Hill
Hill of the Nymphs
Dionysiou Areopagitou
Rovertou Galli
Akropoli
Leoforos
Plateia Stadiou
Eratosthenous
Alsos Pangratiou
Leof Ethnikis Antist
Makrygianni
Ardittou
Roman Stadium
Eftyhidou
Plateia Apolloniou
Filopappou Hill
Pangrati
Mets
Plateia Kynosargous
Markou Mousourou
Plateia Profitou Ilia
Hremonidou
Frynis
Koukaki
Syngrou-Fix
Veikou
Dimitrakopoulou
Kallirrois
Athens' First Cemetery
Damareos
Filolaou
Iliou Ilia
Leof Vouliagmenis
Plateia Ag Artemiou
Plateia Tapitourgeiou
Leof Crusost. Smyrnis
Kalisareias
To Eleftherios Venizelos International Airport (25km)
Stadio Kallitheas
Pantou Al
Leof Syngrou Andrea
Lagoumitzi
Frantzi Amvrosiou
Plateia Amvrosiou Plyta
Iliou Ilia

GREECE

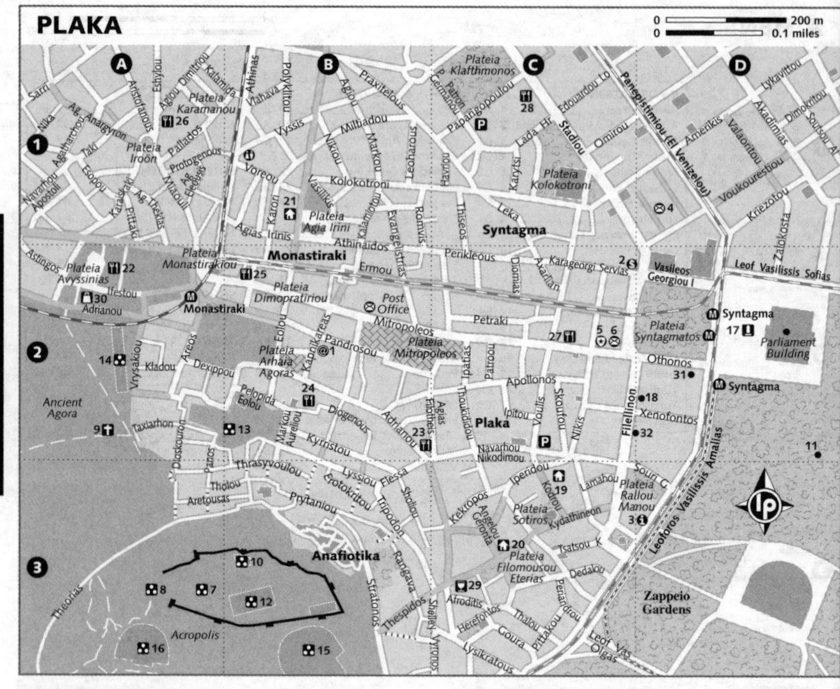

INFORMATION

Emergency

Athens Central Police Station Ambelokipi (Map p525; ☎ 210 770 5711/17; Leoforos Alexandras 173, Ambelokipi; Ⓜ Ambelokipi); Syntagma (Map p526; ☎ 210 725 7000; Syntagma Sq; Ⓜ Syntagma)

SOS Doctors (☎ 1016, 210 821 1888; ⏲ 24hr) Pay service with English-speaking doctors.

Internet Access

There are free wireless hot spots at Syntagma Sq, Gazi and the port of Piraeus, as well as in Starbucks cafes and some McDonald's. Internet cafes charge €2 to €4 per hour.

Bits & Bytes Internet Café (Map p526; Kapnikareas 19, Monastiraki; per hr €3; ⏲ 24hr; Ⓜ Monastiraki)

> **EMERGENCY NUMBERS**
>
> - Ambulance ☎ 166
> - Fire ☎ 199
> - Police ☎ 100
> - Roadside Assistance (ELPA) ☎ 104
> - Tourist Police ☎ 171

Internet Cyberzone (Map p525; ☎ 210 520 3939; Satovriandou 7, Omonia; per hr €2; ⏲ 24hr; Ⓜ Omonia) Prices drop after midnight.

Money

You will find branches of most banks around Syntagma Sq.

Eurochange Omonia (Map p525; ☎ 210 552 0314; Omonia Sq; ⏲ 9am-9pm; Ⓜ Omonia); Syntagma (Map p526; ☎ 210 331 2462; Karageorgi Servias 2; ⏲ 8am-9pm; Ⓜ Syntagma)

Tourist Information

Greek National Tourist Organisation/EOT airport (☎ 210 353 0445; arrivals hall; ⏲ 9am-7pm Mon-Fri, 10am-4pm Sat & Sun); head office (Map p525; ☎ 210 870 7000; www.gnto.gr; Tsoha 7; ⏲ 9am-2pm Mon-Fri; Ⓜ Ambelokipi); Syntagma (Map p526; ☎ 210 331 0392; Amalias 26; ⏲ 9am-7pm Mon-Fri, 10am-6pm Sat & Sun; Ⓜ Syntagma)

SIGHTS

Acropolis

Arguably the most important ancient monument in the Western world, the **Acropolis** (Map p526; ☎ 210 321 0219; sites & museum adult/con-

INFORMATION
Bits & Bytes Internet Café 1 B2
Eurochange 2 C2
Greek National Tourist Organisation / EOT Tourist Office 3 D3
Parcel Post Office 4 D1
Police Station Syntagma 5 C2
Syntagma Post Office 6 C2

SIGHTS & ACTIVITIES
Acropolis 7 A3
Beule Gate 8 A3
Church of the Holy Apostles 9 A2
Erechtheion 10 B3
National Gardens 11 D2
Parthenon 12 B3
Roman Agora 13 B2
Stoa of Attalos 14 A2
Theatre of Dionysos 15 B3
Theatre of Herodes Atticus 16 A3
Tomb of the Unknown Soldier (Changing of the Guard) 17 D2
Trekking Hellas 18 D2

SLEEPING
Hotel Adonis 19 C3
Student & Travellers' Inn 20 C3
Tempi Hotel 21 B1

EATING
Café Avyssinia 22 A2
Eat 23 B2
O Platanos 24 B2
Savas 25 B2
Taverna tou Psyrri 26 A1
Tzitzikas & Mermingas 27 C2
Vasilopoulou 28 C1

DRINKING
Brettos 29 C3

SHOPPING
Monastiraki Flea Market 30 A2

TRANSPORT
Aegean Airlines 31 D2
Olympic Airlines 32 C2

cession €12/6; 8am-7pm Apr-Oct, to 5.30pm Nov-Mar; M Akropoli) attracts multitudes of tourists.

Enter near the **Beule Gate** (Map p526), a Roman arch added in the 3rd century AD. Beyond this lies the **Propylaia**, the enormous, columned gate that was the city's entrance in ancient times.

But it's the **Parthenon** (Map p526) that epitomises the glory of ancient Greece. Completed in 438 BC, it's unsurpassed in grace and harmony. To achieve the appearance of perfect form, columns become narrower towards the top and the bases curve upward slightly towards the ends – effects that make them look straight.

To the north, lies the **Erechtheion** (Map p526) and its much-photographed Caryatids, the six maidens who support its southern portico. These are plaster casts; the originals are in the new, superb **Acropolis Museum** (Map p525; ☎ 210 321 0219; Makrigianni 2-4; 8am-7pm Apr-Oct, to 5pm Nov-Mar; M Akropoli) on the southern base of the hill.

South of the Acropolis

The importance of theatre in the everyday lives of Athenians is evident from the dimensions of the enormous **Theatre of Dionysos** (Map p526; ☎ 210 322 4625; 8am-7pm Apr-Oct, to 5.30pm Nov-Mar; M Akropoli). Built between 340 BC and 330 BC, it held 17,000 people. The **Stoa of Eumenes** (Map p525), built as a shelter and promenade for theatre audiences, runs west to the **Theatre of Herodes Atticus** (Map p526), built in Roman times.

Ancient Agora

The marketplace of early Athens, the **Ancient Agora** (Map p525; ☎ 210 321 0185; Adrianou 24; adult/concession €4/2; 8am-6.30pm Apr-Oct, to 5pm Nov-Mar; M Monastiraki) was the focal point of civic and social life. Socrates spent time here expounding his philosophy. The main monuments are the well-preserved **Temple of Hephaestus** (Map p525), the 11th-century **Church of the Holy Apostles** (Map p526) and the reconstructed **Stoa of Attalos** (Map p526), which houses the site's excellent museum.

Roman Agora

The Romans built their **agora** (Map p526; ☎ 210 324 5220; cnr Pelopida Eolou & Markou Aureliou; adult/concession €2/1; 8am-7pm Apr-Oct, to 5pm Nov-Mar; M Monastiraki) just east of the ancient Athenian agora. The well-preserved Tower of the Winds was built in the 1st century BC by Syrian astronomer Andronicus. This octagonal monument of marble is an ingenious construction that functioned as a sundial, weather vane, water clock and compass, in one.

Temple of Olympian Zeus & Panathenaic Stadium

Begun in the 6th century BC, Greece's largest **temple** (Map p525; ☎ 210 922 6330; adult/concession €2/1; 8am-7pm Apr-Oct, to 5pm Nov-Mar; M Akropoli), behind **Hadrian's Arch** (Map p525), took more than 700 years to build, with Emperor Hadrian overseeing its completion in AD 131. It's impressive for the sheer size of its Corinthian columns – 17m high with a base diameter of 1.7m. East of the temple, the Panathenaic Stadium (Map p525), built in the 4th century

 Book your stay at lonelyplanet.com/hotels

ATHENS FOR FREE

A simple wander through the streets brings eye candy galore, or take in:

- **National Gardens** (right)
- **Changing of the Guard** (below)
- **Monastiraki Flea Market** (p530)
- **Sunday Market** (p530)
- **Lykavittos Hill** (below)

BC as a venue for the Panathenaic athletic contests, hosted the first modern Olympic Games in 1896.

National Archaeological Museum

One of the world's great museums, the **National Archaeological Museum** (Map p525; ☎ 210 821 7717; www.culture.gr; Patission 44; adult/concession €7/3; 🕑 1-7.30pm Mon, 8am-7.30pm Tue-Sun Apr-Oct, 1-7.30pm Mon, 8.30am-3pm Tue-Sun Nov-Mar; Ⓜ Viktoria) contains significant finds from major archaeological sites throughout Greece. The vast collections include exquisite gold artefacts from Mycenae, spectacular Minoan frescoes from Santorini and intricate Cycladic figurines.

Goulandris Museum of Cycladic & Ancient Greek Art

This wonderful private **museum** (Map p525; ☎ 210 722 8321; www.cycladic-m.gr; Neofytou Douka 4, Kolonaki; adult/concession €5/2.50; 🕑 10am-4pm Mon & Wed-Fri, to 3pm Sat; Ⓜ Evangelismos) was custom-built to display its extraordinary collection of Cycladic art, with an emphasis on the early Bronze Age. It's easy to see how the graceful marble statues influenced the art of Modigliani and Picasso.

Lykavittos Hill

Pine-covered **Lykavittos** (Hill of Wolves; Map p525; Ⓜ Evangelismos) is the highest of the eight hills dotted around Athens. Climb to the summit for stunning views. The little **Chapel of Agios Giorgios** is floodlit at night and looks like a vision from a fairy tale from the streets below.

The main path to the summit starts at the top of Loukianou, or you can take the **funicular railway** (Map p525; €5.50; 🕑 9.15am-11.45pm) from the top of Ploutarhou.

Changing of the Guard

The traditionally costumed *evzones* (guards) guarding the **Tomb of the Unknown Soldier** (Map p526), in front of the parliament building on Syntagma Sq, change every hour on the hour. On Sundays at 11am, a whole platoon marches down Vasilissis Sofias to the tomb, accompanied by a band.

National Gardens

The **National Gardens** (Map p526; entrances on Leoforos Vasilissis Sofias & Leoforos Vasilissis Amalias, Syntagma; 🕑 7am-dusk; Ⓜ Syntagma) are a delightful, shady refuge during summer and have a relaxing cafe.

FESTIVALS & EVENTS

The annual **Hellenic Festival** (www.greekfestival.gr; ☎ 210 928 2900), the city's most important cultural event, runs from mid-June to August. International music, dance and theatre go on at venues across the city. Check the program and book tickets online, by phone (☎ bookings 210 327 2000), or at the **festival box office** (Map p525; Panepistimiou 39; Ⓜ Omonia).

SLEEPING

Book well ahead for July and August.

Athens Backpackers (Map p525; ☎ 210 922 4044; www.backpackers.gr; Makri 12, Makrigianni; dm €25, 2-/4-person studio with kitchen €80/120, 3-day min stay; Ⓜ Akropoli; ❄ 💻) This excellent, popular hostel boasts a rooftop party bar with Acropolis views, cafe, kitchen and daily movies. Breakfast and non-alcoholic drinks are included, and long-term storage, laundry, airport pick-up and tours are available.

Student & Travellers' Inn (Map p526; ☎ 210 324 4808; www.studenttravellersinn.com; Kydathineon 16, Plaka; dm €26, 4-person dm/d with shared bathroom €26/68, with private bathroom €28/73; Ⓜ Akropoli; ❄ 💻) Travellers like to chill in the courtyard of this well-situated hostel. Rooms may be spartan and housekeeping a bit lean, but extras (laundry, left luggage, travel service and tours) make up for this.

Marble House Pension (Map p525; ☎ 210 922 8294; www.marblehouse.gr; Zini 35, Koukaki; d/tr with shared bathroom €46/52, s/d/tr with private bathroom €46/52/59; Ⓜ Syngrou-Fix; ❄) This long-standing Athens favourite lies on a quiet cul-de-sac 10 minutes' walk from Plaka. Step through the garden pergola to quiet, spotless rooms with fridges, ceiling fans and safety boxes. For air-con add €9.

Tempi Hotel (Map p526; ☎ 210 321 3175; www.tempihotel.gr; Eolou 29, Monastiraki; s/d with shared bathroom €43/57, d/tr with private bathroom €64/78; Ⓜ Monastiraki) No-frills rooms may be tiny, but some have balconies overlooking Plateia Agia Irini. A communal kitchen and nearby markets make it ideal for self-caterers.

Hotel Adonis (Map p526; ☎ 210 324 9737; www.hotel-adonis.gr; Kodrou 3, Plaka; s/d/tr incl breakfast from €66/92/120; Ⓜ Syntagma; ❄) Stroll up the peaceful, pedestrianised street to this immaculate wee hotel. Guests return for the friendly welcome, great location and super Acropolis views from the roof garden.

Periscope (Map p525; ☎ 210 729 7200; www.periscope.gr; Haritos 22, Kolonaki; r from €160; Ⓜ Evangelismos; ⊠ ❄ 💻) A hip hotel with a cool edgy look (and Mini Cooper seats for chairs in the ground-floor cafe-bar), this place has comfortable minimalist rooms with all the mod cons and a quiet location in chic Kolonaki.

EATING

In addition to the mainstay tavernas, Athens has developed a flock of bistros, swank eateries, and high-end *mezedhes* (literally 'tastes') bars.

Savas (Map p526; Mitropoleos 86-88, Monastiraki; gyros €2; Ⓜ Monastiraki) This joint serves enormous grilled-meat plates (€8.50) and the tastiest *gyros* (pork, beef or chicken) in Athens. Take away or sit down in what becomes one of the city's busiest eat streets late at night.

Tzitzikas & Mermingas (Map p526; ☎ 210 324 7607; Mitropoleos 12-14, Syntagma; mezedhes €6-8; Ⓜ Syntagma) Greek merchandise lines the walls of this cheery, modern *mezedhopoleio* (*mezedhes* restaurant). The great range of delicious and creative *mezedhes* draws a bustling local crowd.

Taverna tou Psiri (Map p526; ☎ 210 321 4923; Eshylou 12, Psyrri; mains €6-11; Ⓜ Monastiraki) This atmospheric taverna is popular with locals who come for the daily specials menu. It's tucked away off Plateia Iroon; look for the apt mural of a drunk leaning against a lamp post.

O Platanos (Map p526; ☎ 210 322 0666; Diogenous 4, Monastiraki; mains €7-9; Ⓜ Monastiraki) Laid-back O Platanos (Plane Tree) serves tasty, home-cooked-style Greek cuisine. The lamb dishes are delicious and we love the leafy courtyard.

Eat (Map p526; ☎ 210 324 9129; Adrianou 91; mains €8-17; Ⓜ Syntagma) A sleek alternative to the endless traditional tavernas, Eat serves interesting salads and pastas and modern interpretations of Greek classics like shrimp dolmas with sun-dried tomatoes (€9).

Café Avyssinia (Map p526; ☎ 210 321 7407; Kynetou 7, Monastiraki; mains €8.50-14.50; Ⓜ Monastiraki) Hidden away on the edge of grungy Plateia Avyssinias in the middle of the flea market, this *mezedhopoleio* gets top marks for atmosphere and the food is not far behind.

You'll find the best selection of fresh produce at the **fruit and vegetable market** (Map p525; Athinas, Psiri; Ⓜ Omonia), opposite the **meat market** (Map p525; Athinas, Psiri; Ⓜ Omonia). Decent supermarkets in central Athens include **Marinopoulos** (Map p525; Athinas 60, Omonia; Ⓜ Omonia) and **Vasilopoulou** (Map p526; Stadiou 19, Syntagma; Ⓜ Panepistimio). They are closed Sundays.

SPLURGE

Varoulko (Map p525; ☎ 210 522 8400; www.varoulko.gr; Pireos 80, Gazi; mains €22-30; 🕑 closed Sun; Ⓜ Keramikos) For a magical Greek dining experience, you can't beat the winning combination of Acropolis views and delicious seafood by celebrated Greek chef Lefteris Lazarou. This Michelin-starred seafood restaurant remains popular with Athenian celebrities and food tourists who sup on sublime crayfish dolmas wrapped in sorrel leaves, squid-ink soup and smoked swordfish, all served up on simple minimalist white linen in an airy glass-fronted dining room.

DRINKING & ENTERTAINMENT

Athenians know how to party. Everyone has their favourite *steki* (hang-out), but expect people to show up after midnight.

Intrepid Fox (off Map p525; ☎ 210 346 6055; Triptolemou 30, Gazi; Ⓜ Keramikos) Drop in to the new It place for the artistic younger set. Plastered with posters from the Misfits to the Who, the place rocks out unlike any other in Athens. Occasional live bands play in a cage.

Mai-Tai (Map p525; Ploutarhou 18, Kolonaki; Ⓜ Evangelismos) Jam-packed with well-heeled young Athenians, this is just one in a group of happening spots in the middle of Kolonaki.

Brettos (Map p526; ☎ 210 323 2110; Kydathineon 41, Plaka; Ⓜ Syntagma) This distillery, bottle shop and bar is back-lit by an eye-catching collection of coloured bottles.

Wonderbar (Map p525; ☎ 210 381 8577; Themistokleous 80, Exarhia; Ⓜ Omonia) Relaxed by day, packed by night, this lounge bar attracts hip young Athenians who come for some of Athens' best DJs.

Akrotiri (☎ 210 985 9147; Vasileos Georgiou B 5, Agios Kosmas; admission €10; 🕑 10pm-5am) This massive beach club has a capacity for 3000, bars and lounges over different levels, and hosts great party nights with top DJs.

ourpick **Half Note Jazz Club** (Map p525; ☎ 210 921 3310; Trivonianou 17, Mets; Ⓜ Akropoli) Jazz buffs won't be disappointed – this dark, smoky club is the main venue for serious jazz.

Rodon Club (Map p525; ☎ 210 524 7427; Marni 24, Omonia; Ⓜ Omonia) You'll either love or hate this grungy club – the city's main venue for rock and metal – but die-hard fans swear by it.

Rembetika Stoa Athanaton (Map p525; ☎ 210 321 4362; Sofokleous 19, Psiri; ⌚ 3.30-6pm & midnight-late Mon-Sat Oct-May; Ⓜ Omonia) Located above the meat market, this is still *the* place to listen to *rembetika*.

Gay & Lesbian Venues

The greatest number of gay bars cluster in Makrigianni, south of the Temple of Olympian Zeus. Check out www.gay.gr or a copy of the *Greek Gay Guide* booklet at *periptera* (street kiosks).

Lamda Club (Map p525; ☎ 210 942 4202; Lembesi 15, Makrigianni) Athens' best gay dance club gets crowded late.

Alekos' Island (Map p525; Sarri 41, Psyrri) This long-standing gay bar is popular with a mellow older crowd.

SHOPPING

Athens is *the* place to shop for cool jewellery, chic clothes and shoes, as well as souvenirs such as backgammon sets, hand-woven textiles, olive oil–based skin-care products, worry beads and colourful ceramics. You'll find boutiques on Ermou; designer brands and cool shops in Kolonaki; and souvenirs, folk art and leather in Plaka and Monastiraki.

The enthralling **Monastiraki flea market** (Map p526; Ⓜ Monastiraki) starts at Plateia Monastirakiou. On weekends, visit the jam-packed **Sunday market** (Map p525; ⌚ 7am-2pm; Ⓜ Thision) at the end of Ermou, towards Gazi.

GETTING THERE & AWAY

Air

Athens is serviced by **Eleftherios Venizelos International Airport** (ATH; ☎ 210 353 0000; www.aia.gr) at Spata, 27km east of Athens. Facilities are excellent, with a 24-hour information desk.

Domestic flights are handled by **Olympic Airlines** (OA; Map p526; ☎ 210 926 4444; www.olympicairlines.com; Filellinon 15, Syntagma; Ⓜ Syntagma) and Crete-based **Aegean Airlines** (A3; Map p526; ☎ 210 626 1000; www.aegeanair.com; Othonos 10, Syntagma; Ⓜ Syntagma).

Bus

Athens has two main intercity **KTEL** (www.ktel.org) bus stations, one 5km, and one 7km to the north of Omonia. Timetables are available at EOT offices (see p526).

Kifissos Terminal A (☎ 210 512 4910; Kifissou 100) has buses running to the Peloponnese, Igoumenitsa, Ionian Islands, Florina, Ioannina, Kastoria, Edessa and Thessaloniki, among other destinations. Taxis from Syntagma cost about €6.

Liossion Terminal B (☎ 210 831 7153; Liossion 260) has departures to Trikala (for Meteora), Delphi, Larissa, Thiva, Volos and other destinations. To get here take bus 024 from out-

---

GETTING INTO TOWN

The 24-hour airport information desks at Eleftherios Venizelos airport are loaded with transport information. Bus X95 operates between the airport and Syntagma Sq (60 to 90 minutes, every 30 minutes, 24 hours). The Syntagma stop is on Othonos St. Bus X96 operates between the airport and Plateia Karaiskaki in Piraeus (60 to 90 minutes, every 20 minutes, 24 hours). Tickets for these services cost €3.20.

Line 3 of the metro links the airport to the city centre in around 30 minutes; it operates from Monastiraki from 5.50am to 10.50pm, and from the airport from 6.30am to 11.30pm. Tickets cost €6 and are valid for all forms of public transport for 90 minutes.

Taxi fares vary according to the time of day and level of traffic, but you should expect to pay from €25 to €30 from the airport to the city centre, and €30 from the airport to Piraeus, depending on traffic conditions. Both trips can take up to an hour. Expect to pay €50 in the wee hours.

If you arrive in Piraeus by ferry, the easiest way into the city is by metro (€80, 25 minutes) between 5am and midnight.

side the main gate of the National Gardens on Amalias. Get off the bus at Liossion 260, turn right onto Gousiou and you'll see the terminal.

Train

For information or bookings, call or visit an **OSE office** Omonia (Map p525; ☎ 210 524 0647; Karolou 1, Omonia; 8am-3pm Mon-Fri; Ⓜ Omonia); Syntagma (Map p525; ☎ 210 362 4402; Sina 6; 8am-3:30pm Mon-Fri, to 3pm Sat; Ⓜ Panepistimio).

GETTING AROUND

The metro system makes getting around central Athens and to Piraeus easy, but Athens' road traffic is still horrendous. A 24-hour travel pass (€3) is valid for all forms of public transport.

Bus & Trolleybus

Blue-and-white suburban buses and yellow trolleybuses operate from 5am to midnight. Route numbers and destinations are listed on the free EOT map. Get timetables at EOT tourist offices or the **Athens Urban Transport Organisation** (OASA; ☎ 210 883 6076; www.oasa.gr).

Special buses to Piraeus operate 24 hours. Bus 040 leaves from the corner of Syntagma and Filellinon, and bus 049 leaves from the Omonia end of Athinas. Tickets for all services cost €0.50 and must be purchased before boarding from a ticket booth or a *periptero*.

Metro

The metro operates from 5am to midnight. For metro timetables visit www.ametro.gr. Travel within one section costs €0.70 and a journey covering two or more sections costs €0.80. Tickets must be validated before travelling.

Taxi

Athenian taxis are yellow. The flag fall is €1 with an additional surcharge of €1 from ports and train and bus stations, and a €3.20 surcharge from the airport. After that, the day rate (tariff 1 on the meter) is €0.30 per kilometre. The rate doubles between midnight and 5am (tariff 2 on the meter). Baggage is charged at the rate of €0.30 per item over 10kg.

AROUND ATHENS

PIRAEUS ΠΕΙΡΑΙΑΣ

pop 175,700

Greece's main port and ferry hub is Piraeus. It takes around 25 minutes to get here from the centre of Athens by metro (avoid taking a bus or taxi – the streets are even more clogged than they are in Athens), so there's no reason to stay in shabby Piraeus.

Orientation & Information

Piraeus consists of a peninsula surrounded by harbours. The largest is the Megas Limin (Great Harbour) on the western side, from where all the ferries leave, along with hydrofoils and catamarans to the Saronic Gulf and the Cyclades. Check email at **Internet Center** (Akti Poseidonos 24; per hr €3.50; 10am-11pm) on the main road, across from the main harbour.

Stock up on supplies before a ferry trip at the general **market** (6am-4pm Mon-Fri) on Dimosthenous.

Getting There & Away

BUS

Two 24-hour bus services operate between central Athens and Piraeus. Bus 049 runs from Omonia to the bus station at the Great Harbour, and bus 040 runs from Syntagma to the Great Harbour bus station. The fare is €0.50 for each service. The X96 Piraeus–Athens Airport Express buses leave from the southwestern corner of Plateia Karaïskaki.

FERRY

The following information is a guide to ferry departures between June and mid-September. There are fewer ferries running in April, May and October, and they are radically reduced in winter – especially to smaller islands. The main branch of EOT in Athens (p526) has a reliable schedule, updated weekly. All ferry companies make timetables available online (see www.ferries.gr).

Crete There are two boats a day to Hania and Iraklio, a daily service to Rethymno, and three a week to Agios Nikolaos and Sitia.

Cyclades There are daily ferries to Amorgos, Folegandros, Ios, Kimolos, Kythnos, Milos, Mykonos, Naxos, Paros, Santorini, Serifos, Sifnos, Sikinos, Syros and Tinos; two or three ferries a week to Iraklia, Shinoussa, Koufonisi, Donoussa and Anafi; and none to Andros or Kea.

Dodecanese There are daily ferries to Kalymnos, Kos, Leros, Patmos and Rhodes; three a week to Karpathos and Kassos; and weekly services to the other islands.

Northeastern Aegean Islands Daily ferries to Chios, Lesvos (Mytilini), Ikaria and Samos; twice weekly to Limnos.

Saronic Gulf Islands Daily ferries head to Aegina, Poros, Hydra and Spetses year-round.

HYDROFOIL & CATAMARAN

Hellenic Seaways (www.hellenicseaways.gr) operates high-speed hydrofoils and catamarans to the Cyclades from early April to the end of October, and year-round services to the Saronic Gulf Islands.

METRO

The fastest and most convenient link between the Great Harbour and Athens is the metro (€0.80, 25 minutes). The station is close to the ferries, at the northern end of Akti Kalimassioti. Trains run every 10 minutes from 5am to midnight.

TRAIN

At the time of research, all services to the Peloponnese from Athens started and terminated at the Piraeus train station, although this may change.

GETTING AROUND

Local bus 904 runs between the bus stop beside the metro to the Great Harbour and Zea Marina near the Maritime Museum.

THE PELOPONNESE ΠΕΛΟΠΟΝΝΗΣΟΣ

The Peloponnese encompasses a breathtaking array of landscapes, villages and ruins. Home to Olympia, birthplace of the Olympic Games; the ancient archaeological sites of magical Epidavros, Mycenae and Corinth; the fairy-tale Byzantine city of Mystras; and ancient Sparta, much Greek history has played out here.

PATRA ΠΑΤΡΑ

pop 185,700

Greece's third-largest city, Patra is the principal ferry port for the Ionian Islands and Italy. Laid out on a grid stretching uphill from the port to the old *kastro* (castle), Patra is easy to negotiate. The tourist office, ports, train and bus stations are all along the waterfront and within easy walking distance of each other.

The friendly **Tourist office** (☎ 26104 61741; www.infocenterpatras.gr; Othonos Amalias 6; ⏰ 8am-10pm) has multilingual staff with plentiful information on transport and free stuff to do in town, free bicycles and internet access. Head to **Cyberia** (☎ 26012 79790; Gerokostopoulou 5; per hr €2.40; ⏰ 24hr) for internet access.

Pension Nicos (☎ 26106 23757; cnr Patreos 3 & Agiou Andreou 121; s/d with shared bathroom €23/33, s/d/tr with private bathroom €28/38/45) has marble stairs that lead to spotlessly clean rooms, smack in the city centre. Scores of stylish cafes and fast-food eateries lie between Kolokotroni and Ermou, while drinking hot spots cluster on Agios Nikolaos and Radinou (off Riga Fereou). **Mythos** (☎ 26103 29984; cnr Trion Navarhon 181 & Riga; mains €6-9; ⏰ 7pm-late) has friendly waiters serving excellent home-cooked Greek classics in a chandelier-strewn town house. Provision for your journey at **Dia Discount Supermarket** (Agiou Andreou 29; ⏰ closed Sun).

There are trains to Athens via Corinth, terminating at Piraeus or the airport. Trains run south daily to Pyrgos and Kalamata. Regular buses go to Athens via Corinth, and to Ioannina, Thessaloniki, Pyrgos (for Olympia) and Kalamata. Ferries depart for Zakynthos, Kefallonia, Ithaki, Corfu and Italy. The tourist office provides timetables and ticket agencies line the waterfront.

CORINTH ΚΟΡΙΝΘΟΣ

pop 29,800

Drab, modern Corinth (*ko*-rin-thoss) is an uninspiring town. Seven kilometres southwest are the ruins of **ancient Corinth** (☎ 27410 31207; site & museum €6; ⏰ 8am-7.30pm Apr-Oct, to 3pm Nov-Apr), which was one of ancient Greece's wealthiest cities. Earthquakes and invasions have left little standing. The only Greek monument remaining is the imposing **Temple of Apollo**; the others are Roman. **Acrocorinth**, the ruins of a citadel built on a massive outcrop of limestone, looms majestically over the site.

The great-value digs at **Tasos Taverna & Rooms** (☎ 27410 31225; fax 27410 31183; s/d/q €30/40/50;), in the centre of town, are spotlessly clean and above an excellent eatery serving home-style Greek classics. At Lecheon, about 4km west of Corinth, **Blue Dolphin Camping** (☎ 27410 25766; www.camping-blue-dolphin.gr; per adult/tent €6.50/6;) has a beach and decent facilities and offers tours. Buses from Corinth to Lecheon stop here.

There are buses to Athens (€6, 1½ hours), Lecheon, Ancient Corinth and Nafplio. It's more convenient to take the train to Patra and Athens. A handy new train service (the *proastiako*) runs between Corinth and Athens airport (€8, one hour, eight daily). Trains also head to Kalamata via Argos (for Nafplio).

NAFPLIO ΝΑΥΠΛΙΟ

pop 14,500

Elegant Venetian houses and neoclassical mansions dripping with crimson bougainvillea cascade down Nafplio's hillside to the azure sea.

The not-particularly-helpful **Municipal tourist office** (☎ 27520 24444; 25 Martiou; 9am-1pm & 4-8pm) is in Fillenon Sq. **Echorama** (☎ 27520 26050; Vas Alexandrou 9; per hr €3; 10am-10pm) has internet terminals in the heart of the old town.

Enjoy spectacular views of the town and surrounding coast from the magnificent hilltop **Palamidi Fortress** (☎ 27520 28036; admission €4; 8.30am-6.45pm Jun-Aug, to 2.45pm Sep-May), built by the Venetians between 1711 and 1714.

The old town is *the* place to stay, with plenty of pensions, but limited budget options. **Pension Dimitris Bekas** (☎ 27520 24594; Efthimiopoulou 26; s/d/tr €28/28/39) is the only good, central budget option. Clean, homey rooms have a top-value location, and the owner has a killer baseball-cap collection. **Kapodistrias** (☎ 27520 29366; www.hotelkapodistrias.gr; Kokinou 20; s/d incl breakfast €50/75;) has beautiful rooms, many with elegant canopy beds.

Nafplio's old-town streets are loaded with restaurants; the tavernas on Staïkopoulou and those overlooking the port on Bouboulinas get jam-packed on weekends. **Taverna Aeolos** (☎ 27520 26828; V Olgas 30; mains €5-13) is a boisterous taverna lined with copper pans that gets packed with locals sharing generous mixed-grill plates (€8.50).

There are buses to Athens (€11.30, 2½ hours) via Corinth. Buses also head to Argos (for Peloponnese connections), Mycenae and Epidavros.

MYCENAE ΜΥΚΗΝΕΣ

Although settled as early as the 6th millennium BC, **Ancient Mycenae** (☎ 27510 76585; admission €8; 8.30am-7pm Jun-Oct, to 3pm Nov-May) was at its most powerful from 1600 to 1200 BC. Mycenae's entrance, the **Lion Gate**, is Europe's oldest monumental sculpture. Homer accurately described Mycenae as being 'rich in gold' and excavations of **Grave Circle A** by Heinrich Schliemann in the 1870s uncovered magnificent gold treasures, such as the Mask of Agamemnon, now on display at the National Archaeological Museum (p528).

Most people visit on day trips from Nafplio, but the bare **Belle Helene Hotel** (☎ 27510 76225; Christou Tsounta; s/d incl breakfast €35/50), on the main street, is where Schliemann lived during the excavations.

Three buses go daily to Mycenae from Argos and Nafplio.

SPARTA ΣΠΑΡΤΗ

pop 19,600

Cheerful, unpretentious modern Sparta (*spar*-tee) is at odds with its ancient Spartan image of discipline and deprivation. Although there's little to see, the town makes a convenient base from which to visit Mystras.

Camping Paleologou Mystras (☎ 27310 22724; per adult/tent €6.50/3.50;), 2km west of Sparta on the road to Mystras, has basic facilities, but a gorgeous setting. Buses to Mystras will drop you there. In a cheery yellow building, **Hotel Cecil** (☎ 27310 24980; fax 27310 81318; Palaeologou 125; s/d €35/45;) has austere rooms with balconies overlooking the quiet end of the strip.

Locals chill out at **Café Ouzeri** (☎ 27310 081565; Palaeologou; mains €2-6). Next door, the sweet smell of spices inundates **Restaurant Elysse** (☎ 27310 29896; Palaeologou 113; mains €4.50-12), run by a friendly Greek-Canadian family.

There are buses to Athens (€16.80, 3½ hours) via Corinth, Gythio, Monemvasia and Mystras.

MYSTRAS ΜΥΣΤΡΑΣ

Magical **Mystras** (☎ 27310 83377; adult/concession €6/3; 8am-7.30pm Apr-Oct, to 3.30pm Nov-Mar) was once the effective capital of the Byzantine Empire. Ruins of palaces, monasteries and churches, most of them dating from between 1271 and 1460, nestle at the base of the Taÿgetos Mountains, and are surrounded by verdant olive and orange groves. Allow half a day to explore the site. While only 7km from Sparta, staying in the village nearby allows you to get there early before it heats up. Enjoy exquisite views and a beautiful swimming pool at **Hotel Byzantion** (☎ 27310 83309; www.byzantionhotel.gr; s/d €40/65;), near the main square.

GEFYRA & MONEMVASIA
ΓΕΦΥΡΑ & ΜΟΝΕΜΒΑΣΙΑ

pop 1,320

Slip out along a narrow causeway, up around the edge of a towering rock rising dramatically from the sea and arrive at the exquisite, walled village of Monemvasia. Enter the *kastro,* which was separated from mainland Gefyra by an earthquake in AD 375, through a narrow tunnel on foot, and emerge into an exquisite (carless) warren of cobblestone streets and stone houses.

Signposted steps lead up to the ruins of a **fortress** built by the Venetians in the 16th century, and the Byzantine **Church of Agia Sophia**, perched precariously on the edge of the cliff. Views are spectacular, and wildflowers shoulder-high in spring.

Hotel Aktaion (☎ 27320 61234; s/d €30/40), a clean, sunny hotel on the Gefyra end of the causeway, has balconies and views of the sea and 'the rock'. Spot the cluster of checked tablecloths just down the wharf a bit, and you'll come to **Taverna O Botsalo** (☎ 27320 61491; Port, Gefyra; mains €4-9), a tiny bistro serving savoury meals.

Buses travel daily to Athens (€25.40, 5½ hours) via Corinth and Sparta.

GYTHIO ΓΥΘΕΙΟ

pop 4490

Gythio (*yee*-thih-o) was once the port of ancient Sparta. Now it's an earthy fishing town on the Lakonian Gulf and gateway to the rugged, much more beautiful Mani Peninsula. Pretty **Marathonisi Islet**, linked to the mainland by a causeway, is said to be ancient Cranae, where Paris (prince of Troy) and Helen (the wife of Menelaus of Sparta) consummated the love affair that sparked the Trojan War.

Three kilometres south of Gythio, **Camping Meltemi** (☎ 27330 22833; www.campingmeltemi.gr; per adult/tent €5.50/5; 🅿) has its own beach, swimming pool and summer beauty contests! The Areopoli bus stops here. Friendly owner Voula keeps clean rooms and offers kitchen access at **Xenia Karlaftis Rooms** (☎ 27330 22719; opposite Marathonisi islet; s/d/tr €25/35/45).

The waterfront areas on the harbour and port are packed with fish tavernas and cafes. At **I Gonia** (☎ 27330 24024; Vassilis Pavlou; mains €6-15) you can watch all the action while supping on delectable taverna standards. It's on the corner, opposite the port.

Buses to Athens (€30.50, 4½ hours), Sparta, Areopoli and the Diros Caves depart regularly. There are ferries to Kissamos, Crete, via Kythira in summer.

THE MANI Η ΜΑΝΗ

The exquisite Mani completely lives up to its reputation for rugged beauty, abundant wildflowers in spring, and dramatic juxtapositions of sea and the Taÿgetos Mountains (threaded with wonderful walking trails). The Mani occupies the central peninsula of the southern Peloponnese and is divided into two regions: the arid Lakonian (inner) Mani in the south and the verdant Messinian (outer) Mani in the northwest near Kalamata.

Lakonian Mani

For centuries the Maniots were a law unto themselves, renowned for their fierce independence and their spectacularly murderous internal feuds. To this day, bizarre tower settlements built as refuges during clan wars dot the rocky slopes of Lakonian Mani.

Areopoli, some 30km southwest of Gythio, is a warren of cobblestone and ancient towers. **Tsimova Rooms** (☎ 27330 51301; Kapetan Matepan; s/d €55/60) is in a renovated tower tucked behind the Church of Taxiarhes. Step behind the counter to choose from the scrumptious specials at **Nicola's Corner Taverna** (☎ 27330 51366; Plateia Athanaton; mains €4-9), on the central square.

Buses go to Gythio, Itilo (for the Messinian Mani) and the Diros Caves.

Eleven kilometres south, the extensive, though touristy **Diros Caves** (☎ 27330 52222; adult/concession €12/7; 🕑 8.30am-5.30pm Jun-Sep, to 3pm Oct-May), contain a subterranean river.

Messinian Mani

Stone hamlets dot aquamarine swimming coves. Silver olive groves climb the foothills to the snowcapped Taÿgetos Mountains. Explore the splendid meandering roads and hiking trails from Itilo to Kalamata.

The people of the enchanting seaside village of **Kardamyli**, 37km south of Kalamata, know how good they've got it. Sir Patrick Leigh Fermor famously wrote about his rambles here in *Mani: Travels in the Southern Peloponnese.* Trekkers come for the magnificent **Vyros Gorge**. Walks are well organised and colour coded.

Olympia Koumounakou Rooms (☎ 27210 73623; r €30) is basic but clean and popular with backpackers who like the communal kitchen and courtyard. **Lela's Rooms** (☎ 27210 73541; s/d/f €55/65/70;

), run by the former housekeeper to Patrick Leigh Fermor, has basic, charming rooms on the sea, while the adjoining **Lela's Taverna** (mains €10) serves up tasty home-style Greek cuisine under pergolas on the water's edge.

Kardamyli is on the main bus route from Itilo to Kalamata (€2.50, one hour) and two to three buses stop daily at the central square.

OLYMPIA ΟΛΥΜΠΙΑ

pop 1000

Tucked along the Klados River, in fertile delta country, the modern town of Olympia supports the extensive ruins of the same name. The first Olympics were staged here in 776 BC, and every four years thereafter until AD 394 when Emperor Theodosius I banned them. During the competition the city-states were bound by a sacred truce to stop fighting and take part in athletic events and cultural exhibitions.

The folks at the **Olympia Municipal Tourist Office** (☎ 26240 23100; Praxitelous Kondyli) don't speak much English but have transport schedules. Check email at the excellent wireless **Ep@thlon C@fé** (☎ 26240 23894; Stefanopoulou 2; per 30min €2; 10am-late).

Ancient Olympia (☎ 26240 22517; adult/concession €6/3, site & museum €9/5; 8am-7pm May-Oct, to 5pm Nov-Apr) is dominated by the immense ruined **Temple of Zeus**, to whom the games were dedicated. Don't miss the statue of **Hermes of Praxiteles**, a classical sculpture masterpiece, at the exceptional **museum** (adult/concession €6/3; 10.30am-7pm Mon, 8am-7pm Tue-Sun May-Oct, to 5pm Nov-Apr).

Pitch your tent in the leafy grove at **Camping Diana** (☎ 26240 22314, fax 26240 22425; per adult/tent €8/6;), 250m west of town. Sparkling clean **Pension Posidon** (☎ 26240 22567; www.pensionposidon.gr; Stefanopoulou 9; s/d/tr €35/45/60;) offers the best value in the centre.

Tucked beneath the trees, **Taverna Gefsis Melathron** (☎ 26240 22916; George Douma 3; mains €5-8) is by far the best place to eat delicious traditional cuisine, including scrumptious vegetarian options, such as fried baby zucchini balls.

Catch buses at the stop on the north end of town. All northbound buses go via Pyrgos where you connect to buses for Athens, Corinth and Patra. Two buses go east from Olympia to Tripoli. Trains run daily to Pyrgos where you can switch for Athens, Corinth and Patra.

NORTHERN GREECE ΒΟΡΕΙΑ ΕΛΛΑΔΑ

Northern Greece is stunning, graced as it is with magnificent mountains, thick forests, tranquil lakes and archaeological sites. Most of all, it's easy to get off the beaten track and experience aspects of Greece noticeably different to other mainland areas and the islands.

THESSALONIKI ΘΕΣΣΑΛΟΝΙΚΗ

pop 800,800

Dodge cherry sellers in the street, smell spices in the air and enjoy waterfront breezes in Thessaloniki (thess-ah-lo-*nee*-kih), also known as Salonica (Saloniki). The second city of Byzantium and of modern Greece boasts countless Byzantine churches, a smattering of Roman ruins, engaging museums, shopping to rival Athens, fine restaurants and a lively cafe scene and nightlife.

Orientation

Laid out on a grid system, the main thoroughfares of Tsimiski, Egnatia and Agiou Dimitriou run parallel to Leof Nikis, on the waterfront. Plateias Eleftherias and Aristotelous, both off Leof Nikis, are the main squares.

Information

E-global Internet (Vas Irakliou 40; per hr €2.50; 24hr)
Tourist information office (☎ 23102 21100; the-info_office@gnto.gr; Tsimiski 136; 8am-2.45pm Mon-Fri, to 2pm Sat)
Tourist police (☎ 23105 54871; 5th fl, Dodekanisou 4; 7.30am-11pm)

Sights

Check out the seafront **White Tower** (☎ 231 026 7832; Lefkos Pyrgos; adult €2; 8am-7pm Tue-Sun, 12.30-7pm Mon) and wander the churches and *hammams* (Turkish baths) before stopping in at the award-winning **Museum of Byzantine Culture** (☎ 23108 68570; Leoforos Stratou 2; admission €4; 1-7.30pm Mon, 8am-3pm Tue-Fri), one of Greece's best, with splendid sculptures, mosaics, icons and other intriguing artefacts beautifully displayed. The exquisite finds at the **Archaeological Museum** (☎ 23108 30538; Manoli Andronikou 6; admission €4; 8.30am-3pm) include Macedonian gold from Alexander the Great's time.

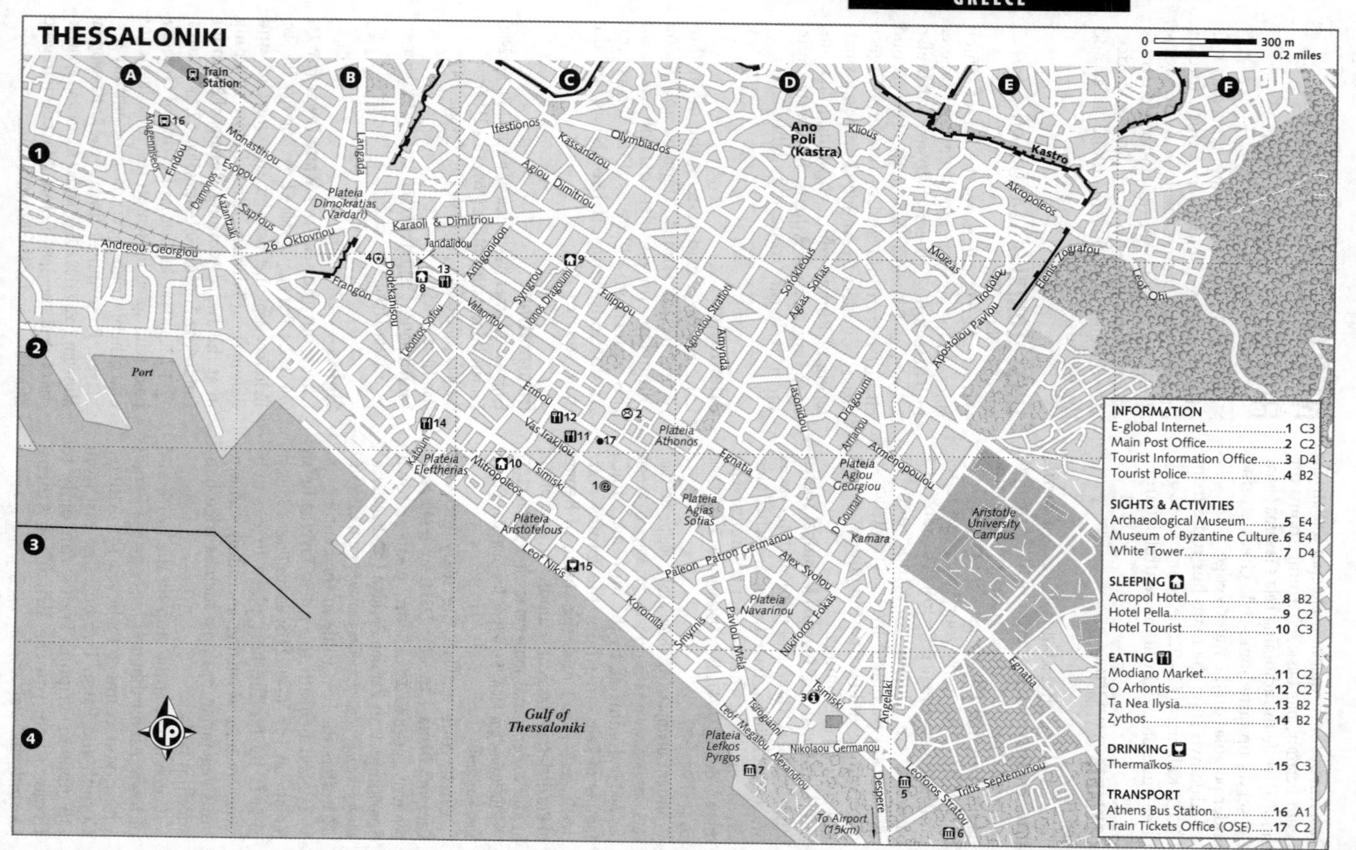
THESSALONIKI
0 300 m
0 0.2 miles
INFORMATION
E-global Internet 1 C3
Main Post Office 2 C2
Tourist Information Office 3 D4
Tourist Police 4 B2
SIGHTS & ACTIVITIES
Archaeological Museum 5 E4
Museum of Byzantine Culture 6 E4
White Tower 7 D4
SLEEPING
Acropol Hotel 8 B2
Hotel Pella 9 C2
Hotel Tourist 10 C3
EATING
Modiano Market 11 C2
O Arhontis 12 C2
Ta Nea Ilysia 13 B2
Zythos 14 B2
DRINKING
Thermaïkos 15 C3
TRANSPORT
Athens Bus Station 16 A1
Train Tickets Office (OSE) 17 C2
Train Station
Port
Gulf of Thessaloniki
Ano Poli (Kastra)
Kastro
Aristotle University Campus
Plateia Dimokratias (Vardari)
Plateia Eleftherias
Plateia Aristotelous
Plateia Athonos
Plateia Agias Sofias
Plateia Agiou Georgiou
Plateia Navarinou
Plateia Lefkos Pyrgos
To Airport (15km)
Egnatia
Tsimiski
Leof Nikis
Leof Megalou Alexandrou
Leoforos Stratou
Tritis Septemvriou
Nikolaou Germanou
Pavlou Mela
Agias Sofias
Langada
26 Oktovriou
Monastiriou
Andreou Georgiou
Anagenniseos
Akropoleos
Leof Ohi
Elenis Zografou
Olymbiados
Kassandrou
Agiou Dimitriou
Karaoli & Dimitriou
Ermou
Vas Irakliou
Mitropoleos
Filippou
Amynda
Iasonidou
Kamara
Angelaki
Despere

Sleeping

Acropol Hotel (☎ 23105 36170; Tandalidou 4; s/d with shared bathroom €20/25) A bit worse for wear, it's still the best budget option.

Hotel Pella (☎ 23105 24221; pellahot@otenet.gr; Ionos Dragoumi 63; s/d €36/52;) Tidy, quiet and family run with spotless rooms.

Hotel Tourist (☎ 23102 70501; www.touristhotel.gr; Mitropoleos 21; s/d incl breakfast €55/70;) Spacious rooms in a charming, central, neoclassical building are maintained by friendly staff.

Eating & Drinking

Tavernas dot Plateia Athonos, funky bars line Plateia Aristotelous and cafes and bars pack Leof Nikis.

O Arhontis (☎ 23102 80202; Ermou 26; mains €5; 11am-5pm) Eat delicious grilled sausages and potatoes off butcher's paper at this popular working-class eatery in Modiano market.

Zythos (☎ 23105 40284; Katouni 5; mains €5-10) Popular with locals, the friendly staff at this excellent taverna serve up delicious traditional Greek food, interesting regional specialities, good wines by the glass and beers on tap.

Ta Nea Ilysia (☎ 23105 36996; Leontos Sofou 17; mains €6) This no-nonsense taverna serves enormous portions of traditional dishes.

Thermaikos (☎ 23102 39842; Leof Nikis 21) This retro-cool bar plays funk, jazz and alternative music, and attracts a young arty crowd.

Head to **Modiano Market** for fresh fruit and vegetables, olives and bread.

Getting There & Away

Thessaloniki's **Makedonia airport** (SKG; ☎ 23104 73700) is 16km southeast of the centre. There are several flights a day to Athens, and to Ioannina, Lesvos, Limnos, Corfu, Iraklio, Mykonos, Chios, Hania, Samos, Crete, Rhodes and Santorini. From the airport to town, take bus 78 (€0.50, one hour, 5am to 10pm) or a taxi (€20, 20 minutes).

The **main bus station** (☎ 23105 95408; Monastiriou 319) services Athens (€35, seven hours, 12 daily) and Ioannina (€25, six hours, five daily), among other destinations.

The **train station** (☎ 23105 17517; Monastiriou) has seven daily express services to Athens (€36, 5½ hours) and two to Alexandroupolis (€10, six hours). All international trains from Athens (to Belgrade, Sofia, İstanbul etc) stop at Thessaloniki. Get schedules from the **train ticket office** (OSE; ☎ 23105 98120; Aristotelous 18) or the station.

Ferries go to, among others, Limnos, Lesvos and Chios throughout the year. One per week heads down through the Cyclades to Crete.

MT OLYMPUS ΟΛΥΜΠΟΣ ΟΡΟΣ

Greece's highest mountain, Mt Olympus, was the ancient home of the gods. The highest of its eight peaks is Mytikas (2918m), popular with trekkers, who use Litohoro (5km inland from the Athens–Thessaloniki highway) as their base. The main route to the top takes two days, with a stay overnight at one of the refuges (open May to October). Good protective clothing is essential, even in summer. The **EOS office** (☎ 23520 84544; Plateia Kentriki; 9.30am-12.30pm & 6-8pm Mon-Sat, Jun-Sep) has information on treks.

Olympos Beach Camping (☎ 23520 22111/2; www.olympos-beach.gr; Plaka Litohoro; per adult/tent €6/7; Apr-Oct) has decent bungalows, a good taverna, a funky waterfront lounge bar and a pleasant beach. The romantic guest house **Xenonas Papanikolaou** (☎ 23520 81236; xenpap@otenet.gr; Nikolaou Episkopou Kitrous 1; s/d €40/45) sits in a flowery garden up in the backstreets, a world away from the tourist crowds.

One of Greece's best country restaurants, **Gastrodromio El Olympio** (☎ 23520 21300; Plateia Kentriki; mains €7-11) serves up local specialities, an impressive regional wine list and gorgeous Olympus views.

From the bus stop, there are several buses daily to Thessaloniki (€8, 1½ hours) via Katerini, and three to Athens (€25, 5½ hours). Litohoro's train station, 9km away, gets daily trains on the Athens–Volos–Thessaloniki train line.

METEORA ΜΕΤΕΩΡΑ

Meteora (meh-*teh*-o-rah) should be a certified Wonder of the World with its magnificent late-14th-century monasteries perched dramatically atop enormous rocky pinnacles. Meteora's stunning rocks are also a climbing mecca.

While there were once monasteries on all 24 pinnacles, only six are still occupied: **Megalou Meteorou** (Grand Meteoron; 9am-5pm Wed-Mon), **Varlaam** (9am-2pm & 3.20-5pm Fri-Wed), **Agiou Stefanou** (9am-2pm & 3.30-6pm Tue-Sun), **Agias Triados** (Holy Trinity; 9am-12.30pm & 3-5pm Fri-Wed), **Agiou Nikolaou Anapafsa** (9am-3.30pm Sat-Thu) and **Agias Varvaras Rousanou** (9am-6pm). Admission is €2 for each monastery and strict dress codes apply (no bare shoulders or knees

GREECE

and women must wear skirts; borrow a long skirt at the door if you don't have one). Walk the footpaths between monasteries or drive the back road.

The tranquil village of **Kastraki**, 2km from Kalambaka, is the best base for visiting Meteora. **Vrachos Camping** (☎ 24320 22293; camping-kastraki@kmp.forthnet.gr; per adult/tent €5/5;) has great views, a good taverna, a barbecue and a pool, and is a short stroll from Kastraki.

our pick Gregarious hosts Thanassis and Toula Nakis' **Doupiani House** (☎ 24320 75326; doupiani-house@kmp.forthnet.gr; s/d/tr €30/45/55), 500m from the town square, is a comfy home from which to explore or simply sit and enjoy the panoramic views.

Taverna Gardenia (Kastrakiou St; mains €3-8) serves up the freshest Greek food with aplomb. The owners also have good-value and spacious rooms at **Plakjas** (☎ 24320 22504; s/d/tr €30/40/50), behind the restaurant.

Local buses shuttle between Kalambaka and Kastraki, some of which go to Moni Megalou Meteoron. Hourly buses from Kalambaka go to the transport hub of Trikala, from where there are buses to Ioannina and Athens (€23, 5½ hours). From Kalambaka, there are also express trains to Athens (€20, five hours, two daily) and Thessaloniki (€17, four hours, two daily).

IOANNINA ΙΩΑΝΝΙΝΑ

pop 61,700

Charming Ioannina (ih-o-*ah*-nih-nah), on the western shore of Lake Pamvotis at the foot of the Pindos Mountains, was a major intellectual centre during Ottoman rule. Today it's a thriving university town with a lively waterfront cafe scene.

The main streets meet in the town centre, around Plateia Dimokratias. Access the internet at **Web** (☎ 26510 26813; Pyrsinella 21; per hr €2.50; 24hr) and regional tourist information at **EOT** (☎ 26510 41142; Dodonis 39; 7.30am-2.30pm).

The narrow stone streets of the **old town** sit on a small peninsula jutting into the lake. Within its impressive fortifications, the **kale**, an inner citadel with lovely grounds and lake views, is home to the splendid **Fetiye Cami** (Victory Mosque), built in 1611, and the gem-like **Byzantine Museum** (☎ 26510 25989; admission €3; 8am-5pm). The serene **nisi** (island) shelters four monasteries among its trees. Ferries (€1.80, half-hourly summer, hourly winter) to the island leave from near the waterfront cafes and Plateia Mavili.

Pitch a tent at tree-lined **Limnopoula Camping** (☎ 26510 20541; Kanari 10; per adult/tent €8/4; May-Oct), splendidly set on the edge of the lake 2km northwest of town. In the old town, popular **Filyra** (☎ 26510 83560; alley off Andronikou Paleologou 18; r €65;) has rooms with kitchens and fills fast. Join local families along the flower-filled Kale wall at **Taberna To Manteio** (☎ 26510 25452; Plateia Georgiou 15; mains €7-8) for deliciously simple *mezedhes,* salads and grills. Scores of cafes and restaurants line the waterfront.

There are two flights a day to Athens. Buses head to Athens (€35, 7½ hours), Thessaloniki (€28, seven hours), Igoumenitsa (€8.20, 2½ hours, eight daily) and Trikala.

ZAGOROHORIA & VIKOS GORGE ΤΑ ΖΑΓΟΡΟΧΩΡΙΑ & ΧΑΡΑΔΡΑ ΤΟΥ ΒΙΚΟΥ

Do not miss the spectacular Zagori region, with its deep gorges, raging rivers, dense forests and snowcapped mountains. Some 46 charming villages, famous for their grey-slate architecture, and known collectively as the Zagorohoria, are sprinkled across a large expanse of the Pindos Mountains north of Ioannina. Formerly connected by stone paths and arching footbridges, paved roads now wind between these beautifully restored gems.

Delightful **Monodendri**, known for its special *pitta* bread, is a popular departure point for treks through dramatic **Vikos Gorge**, with its sheer limestone walls. It's a strenuous 7½-hour walk along well-marked paths from here to the remote (but popular) twin villages of **Megalo Papingo** and **Mikro Papingo**. Get cosy at quaint **Archontiko Zarkada** (☎ 26530 71305; www.monodendri.com; s/d incl breakfast €35/45), one of Greece's best-value small hotels.

Infrequent buses run from Monodendri (€3.10, one hour, twice weekly) and the Papingos (€5, two hours, three weekly) to Ioannina.

IGOUMENITSA ΗΓΟΥΜΕΝΙΤΣΑ

pop 9110

Though tucked beneath verdant hills and lying on the sea, this characterless west-coast port is little more than a ferry hub – keep moving.

If you must stay the night, look for *domatia* signs or have a '70s flashback at **Hotel Oscar** (☎ 26650 23338; Agios Apostolon 149; s/d €30/40), across from the Corfu ticket booths. **Taverna Emily Akti** (☎ 26650 23763; Podou 13; mains

HELLENIC WILDLIFE REHABILITATION CENTRE

While some Greeks may not appear too environmentally minded, others are making a sterling effort to face the country's ecological problems head on. The **Hellenic Wildlife Rehabilitation Centre** (☎ 22970 31338; www.ekpaz.gr; 10am-7pm) is one such place on the island of Aegina. The centre tackles the damage caused to wild birds and animals due to hunting and pollution, and runs projects such as the release of raptors into the wilds of Crete and Northern Greece. You can visit the centre for free, though donations are appreciated. Better yet, the centre welcomes volunteers and accommodation is supplied.

€6-8) manages to eke out some character, and tasty food, under a pergola near the Corfu ferry quay.

The **bus station** (☎ 26650 22309; Kyprou 29) services Ioannina (€8.20, 2½ hours, eight daily) and Athens (€33, eight hours, five daily).

Several companies operate ferries to Corfu (person/car €7/33, 1½ hours, hourly) between 5am and 10pm, and hydrofoils in summer. International services go to the Italian ports of Ancona, Bari, Brindisi, Trieste and Venice. Ticket agencies line the port.

SARONIC GULF ISLANDS ΝΗΣΙΑ ΤΟΥ ΣΑΡΩΝΙΚΟΥ

Scattered about the Saronic Gulf, these islands offer authentic and rewarding Greek island experiences within easy reach of Athens. The Saronics are named after the mythical King Saron of Argos, a keen hunter who drowned while chasing a deer that had swum into the gulf to escape.

AEGINA ΑΙΓΙΝΑ

pop 10,500

Once a major player in the Hellenic world, thanks to its strategic position at the mouth of the gulf, Aegina (*eh*-yee-nah) now enjoys its position as Greece's premier producer of pistachios. Pick up a bag before you leave!

Bustling **Aegina Town**, on the west coast, is the island's capital and main port. There is no official tourist office, but there are plenty of booking agencies along the waterfront. **Surf and Play** (☎ 22970 29096; Afeas 42; per 30min €2; 9am-late) provides internet access.

The impressive **Temple of Aphaia** (☎ 22970 32398; adult/concession €4/2; 8am-6.30pm), a well-preserved Doric temple 12km east of Aegina Town, is said to have served as a model for the construction of the Parthenon.

In Aegina Town, at the northern end of the waterfront, **Hotel Plaza** (☎ 22970 25600; s/d/tr €35/40/60) is a popular budget choice and has enthusiastic owners.

A flotilla of ferries (€8.20, 70 minutes) and hydrofoils (€13, 35 minutes) plies the waters between Aegina and Piraeus with great regularity. There is a good public bus service on the island.

HYDRA ΥΔΡΑ

pop 2900

The showcase of the Saronics, Hydra (*ee*-drah) is considered the most stylish destination of the group. Hydra Town has a picturesque horseshoe-shaped harbour with gracious white and pastel stone mansions stacked up the rocky hillsides that surround it.

A major attraction is Hydra's tranquillity. There are no motorised vehicles – apart from sanitation and construction vehicles – and the main forms of transport are by foot and donkey.

Hydra Town is on the island's north coast. There is no tourist office, but **Satis Tours** (☎ 22980 52184) on the waterfront is helpful, while just around the corner on Tombazi, **Flamingo Internet Café** (☎ 22980 53485; per 15min €3; 8.30am-10pm) has internet access.

Pension Erofili (☎ 22980 54049; www.pensionerofili.gr; Tombazi; s/d/tr €45/55/65;), tucked away in the inner town, has clean, comfortable rooms and an attractive courtyard.

There are two ferry (€12.50, 3½ hours) and six hydrofoil (€24, 1½ hours) services daily between Hydra and Piraeus. The ferries go via Aegina, while the hydrofoils mostly go via Poros.

SPETSES ΣΠΕΤΣΕΣ

pop 4000

Spetses is an attractive island that is packed with visitors in summer. **Spetses Town**, the main port, sprawls along half the northeast coast of the island. **1800 Net Café** (☎ 22980 29498; per 30min €2.50; 9am-midnight) provides internet access.

GREECE

Book your stay at lonelyplanet.com/hotels

There is no tourist office, but **Mimoza Travel** (☎ 22980 75170) on the waterfront can help with accommodation and other services.

Opposite the small town beach to the east of the ferry quay, **Villa Marina** (☎ 22980 72646; s/d €40/56; ❄) is a welcoming place with tidy rooms containing a fridge. Ask for a sea view.

A daily ferry connects Spetses to Piraeus (€15.30, four hours) via Hydra and Aegina. There are at least six hydrofoils daily to Piraeus (€37, 2½ hours). There are also boats to Kosta, Ermioni and Porto Heli on the Peloponnese mainland.

GREECE

CYCLADES ΚΥΚΛΑΔΕΣ

The Cyclades (kih-*klah*-dez) are Greek Islands to dream about. Rugged outcrops of rock in the azure Aegean, they are speckled with white cubist buildings and blue-domed Byzantine churches. Throw in sun-blasted golden beaches, a dash of hedonism and a fascinating culture, and it's easy to see why many find the Cyclades irresistible.

MYKONOS ΜΥΚΟΝΟΣ

pop 9700

Sophisticated Mykonos glitters happily under the Aegean sun, shamelessly surviving on tourism. The island has something for everyone, with marvellous beaches, romantic sunsets, chic boutiques, excellent restaurants and bars, and its long-held reputation as a mecca for gay travellers.

Orientation & Information

Angelo's Internet Café (☎ 22890 24106; Xenias, Hora; per hr €4.50) is on the road between the southern bus station and the windmills.

The **Tourist Information Office** (☎ 22890 25250; www.mykonos.gr; 🕑 9am-9pm Jul & Aug, 10am-5pm Easter-Jun, Sep & Oct) is at the western end of the waterfront. **Island Mykonos Travel** (☎ 22890 22232; www.discovergreece.org), on Taxi Sq, where the port road meets Hora town, is helpful for travel information.

Sights & Activities

A stroll around Mykonos Town, shuffling through snaking streets with blinding white walls and balconies of flowers, is a must for any visitor. **Little Venice**, where the sea laps up to the edge of the restaurants and bars, and Mykonos' famous hilltop row of **windmills** should be included in the spots-to-see list. You're bound to run into one of Mykonos' famous resident pelicans on your walk.

The island's most popular beaches are on the southern coast. **Platys Gialos** has wall-to-wall sun lounges, while nudity is not uncommon at **Paradise Beach**, **Super Paradise**, **Agrari** and gay-friendly **Elia**.

Sleeping

Paradise Beach Camping (☎ 22890 22852; www.paradisemykonos.com; per person/tent €9/5; 💻 🏊) There are lots of options here at Paradise Beach on the south coast, including camping, beach cabins and apartments, as well as bars, a swimming pool, games etc. It is skin-to-skin mayhem in summer. Minibuses meet ferries and buses go regularly into town.

Hotel Apollon (☎ 22890 22223; s/d with shared bathroom €50/65) Prepare for some old-world Mykonian charm in the middle of the main waterfront. Rooms are traditional and well kept, and the owner is friendly.

Hotel Philippi (☎ 22890 22294; chriko@otenet.gr; 25 Kalogera; s €60-90, d €75-120; ❄) In the heart of the *hora* (village), Philippi has spacious, bright, clean rooms that open onto a railed verandah overlooking a lush garden.

WORTH THE TRIP: DELOS ΔΗΛΟΣ

Southwest of Mykonos, the island of **Delos** (☎ 22890 22259; sites & museum €5; 🕑 9am-3pm Tue-Sun) is the Cyclades' archaeological jewel. According to mythology, Delos was the birthplace of Apollo, the god of light, poetry, music, healing and prophecy. The island flourished as an important religious and commercial centre from the 3rd millennium BC, reaching its apex of power in the 5th century BC.

Clambering among the ruins is an opportunity not to be missed, and the climb up **Mt Kynthos** (113m), the island's highest point, is a highlight.

Overnighting on Delos is forbidden. Numerous boat companies offer trips from Mykonos to Delos (€12.50 return, 30 minutes one way).

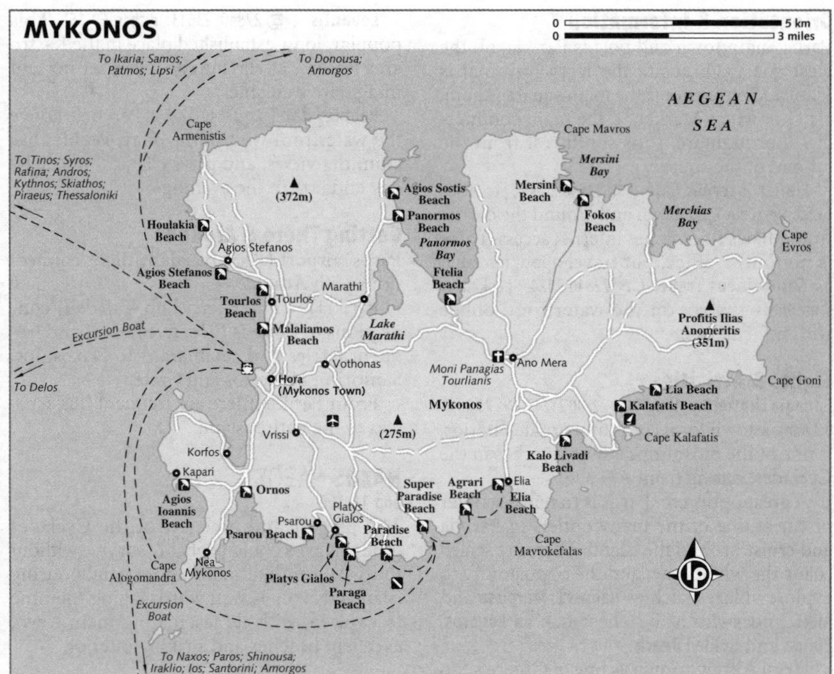

Eating & Drinking

There is no shortage of places to eat and drink in Mykonos Town. If you're on a budget, steer clear of the waterfront and head into the back of the maze that is Mykonos Town where there are plenty of cheap eats.

Paraportiani (☎ 22890 23531; dishes from €7) Just above the western end of the waterfront, Paraportiani does superb seafood and benefits from having the town's top tout, one of Mykonos' resident pelicans.

Fato a Mano (☎ 22890 26256; Meletopoulou Sq; dishes €8-15) In the back of the maze, Fato a Mano is worth taking the effort to find, serving up tasty Mediterranean and traditional Greek dishes.

Long feted as a gay travel destination, Mykonos has plenty of gay-centric clubs and hang-outs. In Little Venice, **Kastro** (☎ 22890 23072; Agion Anargion) is the spot to start the night with cocktails as the sun sets. **Pierro's** (☎ 22890 22177), just near Taxi Sq, is a popular dance club for rounding off the night.

Cavo Paradiso (☎ 22890 27205; www.cavoparadiso.gr) For those who want to go the whole hog, this club 300m above Paradise Beach picks up around 2am and boasts a pool the shape of Mykonos.

Getting There & Around

There are daily flights connecting Mykonos (JMK) to Athens.

Daily ferries arrive from Piraeus (€25, six hours). From Mykonos, there are daily ferries and hydrofoils to most major Cycladic islands, daily services to Crete, and less-frequent services to the northeastern Aegean Islands and the Dodecanese.

The southern bus station, a 300m walk up from the windmills, serves Agios Ioannis, Psarou, Platys Gialos and Paradise Beach. In summer, *caïques* (small fishing boats) from Mykonos Town and Platys Gialos go to Paradise, Super Paradise, Agrari and Elia Beaches.

PAROS ΠΑΡΟΣ

pop 13,000

Paros is a friendly, attractive, laid-back island that has long been prosperous, thanks to an abundance of pure white marble from which the *Venus de Milo* and Napoleon's tomb were sculpted.

Orientation & Information

Paros' main town and port is Parikia, on the west coast. Opposite the ferry terminal is Plateia Mavrogenous, the main square. Agora, also known as Market St, the main commercial thoroughfare, runs southwest from the far end of the square.

Planet Internet Café (☎ 22840 25060; per 30min €1.50; 🕑 10am-2am) down and around the corner from Mike's Rooms, has internet access. There is no tourist office, but travel agencies such as **Santorineos Travel** (☎ 22840 24245; bookings@santorineos-travel.gr), on the waterfront, oblige with information.

Sights & Activities

Panagia Ekatontapyliani (☎ 22840 21243; 🕑 7.30am-9.30pm), known for its beautiful ornate interior, is one of the most impressive churches in the Cyclades, dating from AD 326.

A great option on Paros is to rent a scooter or car at one of the many outlets in Parikia and cruise around the island. There are sealed roads the whole way, and the opportunity to explore villages such as **Naoussa**, **Marpissa** and **Aliki**, and swim at beaches such as **Logaras**, **Punda** and **Golden Beach**.

Hrysi Akti is known as one of Greece's top windsurfing spots.

Sleeping

The **Rooms Association** (☎ 22840 22722; 🕑 9am-1am) has a helpful kiosk on the quay. There's loads of camping around Paros, with charges of around €6 per person and €4 per tent.

Rooms Mike (☎ 22840 22856; www.roomsmike.com; s/d/tr €30/40/50) A popular and friendly place, Mike's offers a good location and local advice. There are options of rooms with shared facilities through to fully self-contained units with kitchens. Mike's sign is easy to spot from the quay.

Rooms Rena (☎ 22840 22220; www.cycladesnet.gr/rena; Epitropakis; s/d/tr €30/40/50; ❄) The quiet and well-kept rooms here are excellent value. Turn left from the pier then right at the ancient cemetery and follow the signs.

Eating & Drinking

Happy Green Cows (☎ 22840 24691; dishes from €5; 🕑 7pm-midnight) Just off the back of the main square, this place is popular with vegetarians. The menu and meal names are both creative, and the bar stays open after the kitchen closes.

Levantis (☎ 22840 23613; dishes €9-15) This popular, long-established place in the Kastro area features a relaxing courtyard setting and imaginative cuisine.

Pebbles Bar (☎ 22840 22283) Perched above the waterfront west of the quay, Pebbles has stunning views, and plays classical music by day and jazz in the evenings.

Getting There & Around

Paros' airport (PAS) has daily flight connections with Athens.

Parikia is a major ferry hub with daily connections to Piraeus (€30, five hours) and frequent ferries and catamarans to Naxos, Ios, Santorini, Mykonos and Crete.

From Parikia there are frequent bus services to the entire island.

NAXOS ΝΑΞΟΣ

pop 18,200

The biggest and greenest of the Cyclades group, Naxos could probably survive without tourism – unlike many of its neighbouring islands. Naxos is well worth taking the time to explore, with its fascinating main town, excellent beaches and striking interior.

Orientation & Information

Naxos Town, on the west coast, is the island's capital and port. The ferry quay is at the northern end of the waterfront, with the bus terminal out front.

Naxos Tourist Information Centre (NTIC; ☎ 22850 25201; www.naxostownhotels.com; 🕑 8am-midnight), a privately owned organisation just opposite the port, offers help with accommodation, tours, luggage storage and laundry. Next door, **Zas Travel** (☎ 22850 23330; 🕑 8am-midnight) sells ferry tickets and offers internet access for €4 an hour.

Sights & Activities

The hilltop 13th-century **kastro**, where the Venetian Catholics lived, looks out over the town and has a well-stocked **archaeological museum** (☎ 22850 22725; admission €3; 🕑 8.30am-3pm Tue-Sun).

The beach of **Agios Georgios** is a 10-minute walk south from the main waterfront. Beyond it, wonderful sandy beaches stretch as far south as **Pyrgaki Beach**. **Agia Anna Beach**, 6km from town, and **Plaka Beach** are lined with accommodation and packed in summer.

Rental wheels will help reveal Naxos' dramatic landscape. The **Tragaea region** has tranquil villages, churches atop rocky crags and huge olive groves. **Filoti**, the largest inland settlement, perches on the slopes of **Mt Zeus** (1004m), the highest peak in the Cyclades.

Sleeping

Camping Maragas (☎ 22850 42552; www.maragascamping.gr/naxos-camping.htm; camping/d/studio €9/45/70) On Agia Anna Beach to the south of town, this place has all sorts of options, including camping, rooms and studios, and there is a restaurant and minimarket on site.

our pick **Pension Sofi** (☎ 22850 23077; www.pensionsofi.gr; s, d & tr €30-75;) and **Studios Panos** (☎ 22850 26078; www.studiospanos.com; Agios Georgios Beach; d & tr €30-60; Apr-Oct;) are both run by members of the friendly Koufopoulos family. Sofi's is in town, while Panos is a 10-minute walk away near Agios Georgios Beach. All guests are met with a glass of family-made wine or ouzo, and rooms are immaculate, with bathroom and kitchen. They're highly recommended; rates at both places halve out of the high season. Call ahead for a pick-up at the port. Sofi is open year-round.

Eating & Drinking

Naxos Town's waterfront is lined with eating and drinking establishments.

To Smyrneiko (☎ 22850 24443; dishes from €5) A top pick among many restaurants along the waterfront, this place is popular with locals and does seafood well.

Picasso Mexican Bistro (☎ 22850 25408; dishes from €5) This is a stylish and popular place that does sensational Tex-Mex 20m off Court Sq, a few minutes' walk south of the main waterfront. Receives rave reviews.

Lemon (☎ 22850 24734; Protopapadaki) A cool cocktail bar and cafe right in the middle of the waterfront. Relax with a drink and watch the world go by.

Getting There & Around

Naxos airport (JNX) has daily flight connections with Athens.

There are daily ferries (€30, five hours) and catamarans (€45, 3¾ hours) to Piraeus, and good ferry and hydrofoil connections to most Cycladic islands and Crete. There are also ferries to Thessaloniki and Rhodes weekly.

Buses travel to most villages regularly from the bus terminal in front of the port.

IOS ΙΟΣ

pop 1850

Ios has long held a reputation as 'Party Island'. There are wall-to-wall bars and nightclubs in *hora* (also known as 'the village') that thump all night, and fantastic fun facilities at Milopotas Beach that entertain all day.

Orientation & Information

Ios' three population centres are all close on the west coast. Ormos is the port where ferries arrive. Two kilometres inland and up from the port is *hora,* while 2km to the southeast is Milopotas Beach. The young tend to stay in 'the village' or Milopotas, and the others at Ormos.

Double Click Internet (☎ 22860 92155; hora; per hr €4) is one of dozens of places providing internet access. There is no tourist office, but **Acteon Travel** (☎ 22860 91343; www.acteon.gr) has offices in Ormos, the village and Milopotas and is helpful.

Sights & Activities

The village has an intrinsic charm with its labyrinth of white-walled streets, and it's very easy to get lost, even if you haven't had one too many.

It's not only the nightlife, but also the beaches that lure travellers to Ios. **Milopotas** has everything a resort beach could ask for and parties hard. **Meltemi Water Sports** (☎ 22860 91680; www.meltemiwatersports.com), at the beach's far end, has rental windsurfers, sailboats and canoes.

Isolated **Manganari** on the south coast is known as Ios' most beautiful beach and is reached by bus or excursion boat in summer.

Sleeping

Far Out Camping & Beach Club (☎ 22860 91468; www.faroutclub.com; Milopotas; camping per person €12, bungalows €12-20, studios €90;) Right on Milopotas Beach, this place has tons of options. Facilities include camping, bungalows and hotel rooms, and its pools are open to the public.

Francesco's (☎ 22860 91223; www.francescos.net; hora; dm/s/d €15/35/45;) A lively meeting place in the village with superlative views from its terrace bar, Francesco's is convenient for party-going and rates halve out of the high season. The party spirit rules here, especially in the new 'giant Jacuzzi'.

GREECE

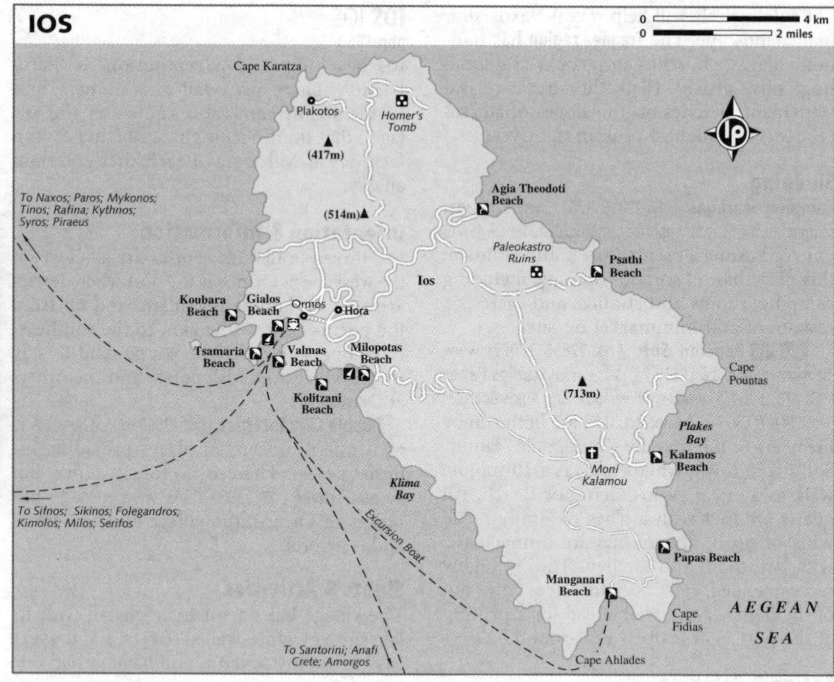

Eating & Drinking

There are numerous places to get cheap eats in the village.

Ali Baba's (☎ 22860 91558; hora; dishes from €6) Long an Ios favourite, Ali Baba's parties until late. Upbeat service complements the funky ambience, and the Thai dishes make for a change.

our pick **Pithari** (☎ 22860 92440; hora; dishes from €8) Behind the cathedral at the entrance to *hora*, Pithari offers an excellent array of tasty dishes. The seafood spaghetti is especially good.

At night, the compact little village just about erupts with bars. Its tiny central square gets so packed that come midnight you won't be able to fall over even if you wanted to.

Getting There & Around

Ios has daily ferry connections with Piraeus (€25, taking seven hours) and there are frequent hydrofoils and ferries to the major Cycladic islands and Crete. There are regular buses every 15 minutes between the port, the village and Milopotas Beach until early morning, and two to three a day to Manganari Beach.

SANTORINI (THIRA)
ΣΑΝΤΟΡΙΝΗ (ΘΗΡΑ)

pop 13,500

Stunning Santorini is unique and should not be missed. The startling sight of the submerged caldera almost encircled by sheer lava-layered cliffs – topped off by clifftop towns that look like a dusting of icing sugar – will grab your attention and not let it go.

Orientation & Information

Fira, the main town, perches on top of the caldera, with the new port of Athinios, where most ferries dock, 10km south by road. The old port of Fira Skala, used by cruise ships and excursion boats, is directly below Fira and accessed by cable car (€4 one way), donkey (€4; up only) or by foot (588 steps).

Internet access is available at **PC World** (☎ 22860 25551; Central Sq; per 30min €2.10). **Dakoutros Travel** (☎ 22860 22958; www.dakoutrostravel.gr; 8.30am-10pm), opposite the taxi station, is extremely helpful.

Sights & Activities

FIRA

The exceptional **Museum of Prehistoric Thira** (☎ 22860 23217; admission €3; ⏲ 8.30am-3pm Tue-Sun), which has wonderful displays of artefacts predominantly from ancient Akrotiri, is two blocks south of the main square. **Megaron Gyzi Museum** (☎ 22860 22244; admission €3.50; ⏲ 10.30am-1pm & 5-8pm Mon-Sat, 10.30am-4.30pm Sun) houses local memorabilia, including fascinating photographs of Fira before and after the 1956 earthquake (see the boxed text, p546).

AROUND THE ISLAND

Santorini's black-sand **beaches** of **Perissa** and **Kamari** sizzle in summer – beach mats are essential.

Excavations in 1967 uncovered the remarkably well-preserved Minoan settlement of **Akrotiri** at the south of the island. A section of the roof collapsed in 2005 killing one visitor, and at the time of research the site's future as a visitor attraction was up in the air.

On the north of the island, the flawless village of **Oia** (ee-ah), famed for its postcard sunsets, is less hectic than Fira and a must-visit. There's a path from Fira to Oia along the top of the caldera that takes three to four hours to walk.

Of the surrounding islets, only **Thirasia** is inhabited. Visitors can clamber around on volcanic lava on **Nea Kameni** then swim into warm springs in the sea at **Palia Kameni**; there are various excursions available to get you there.

Sleeping

Fira has spectacular views, but is miles from the beaches. Perissa has a great beach but is on the southeast coast, away from the caldera views.

Santorini Camping (☎ 22860 22944; www.santorinicamping.gr; per person €9; P 💻 🏊) This place, 500m east of Fira's main square, is the cheapest option. There is a restaurant, bar, minimarket and swimming pool, but no caldera views.

Pension Petros (☎ 22860 22573; www.astirthira.gr/petros; s & d €30-60; ❄) Three hundred metres east of the square in Fira, Petros' offers decent rooms at good rates, free airport and port trans-

GREECE

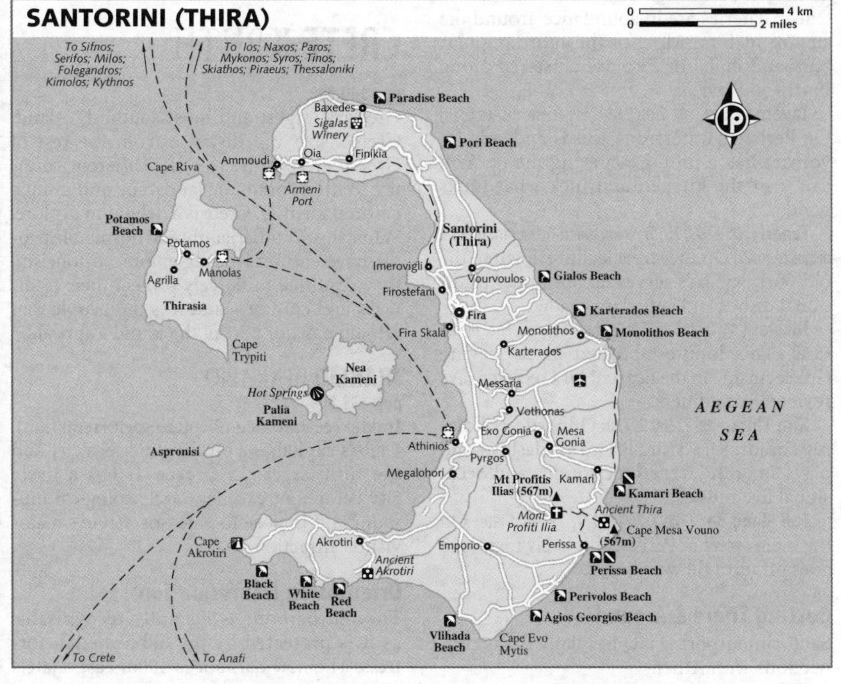

SANTORINI'S BIG BANGS

Santorini's violent volcanic past is visible everywhere, and through the centuries eruptions have regularly changed the shape of the island.

First inhabited around 3000 BC, the island was circular and known as Strongili (the Round One). About 1650 BC a massive volcanic explosion – speculated to be the biggest such explosion in recorded history – caused the centre of the island to sink, producing a caldera that the sea quickly filled in. The explosion generated a huge tsunami that is widely believed to have caused the demise of Crete's powerful Minoan culture.

The islet of Palia Kameni appeared in the caldera in 197 BC, while an eruption created the islet of Nea Kameni in 1707. In 1956 a savage earthquake measuring 7.8 on the Richter scale killed scores of people and destroyed most of the houses in Fira and Oia.

One thing is for certain – it isn't over yet. Minor tremors are fairly common. Santorini is incomparable when it comes to a sense of impermanence and precariousness.

fers, but no caldera views. It's a good budget option. The family also has other hotels.

Stelio's Place (☎ 22860 81860; www.steliosplace.com; Perissa; d, tr & q €30-80; P) Stelio's is an excellent option just back from Perissa's black-sand beach on the southeast coast. There's a refreshing pool, very friendly service, and free port and airport transfers. Rates halve out of the high season.

Eating & Drinking

Cheap eateries are in abundance around the square in Fira. Most of the more popular bars and clubs in Fira are clustered along Erythrou Stavrou.

Taverna Lava (☎ 22860 81776; Perissa; dishes €3-8) On Perissa's waterfront, this islandwide favourite has a mouth-watering menu. You can visit the kitchen and pick what looks good.

Fanari (☎ 22860 25107; www.fanari-restaurant.gr; Fira; dishes from €5) On the street leading down to the old port, Fanari's serves up both tasty traditional dishes and superlative views.

Nikolas (☎ 22860 24550; Erythrou Stavrou, Fira; dishes €5-10) This long-established place serving Greek cuisine in the heart of Fira receives rave reviews from diners.

Kira Thira (☎ 22860 22770) Opposite Nikolas restaurant, Kira Thira is Fira's oldest bar and plays smooth jazz, ethnic sounds and occasional live music.

Full Moon Bar (☎ 22860 81177; 9pm-late) On the main street in Perissa, this lively nightspot goes off until the wee hours.

Getting There & Around

Santorini airport (JTR) has daily flight connections with Athens.

There are daily ferries (€28, nine hours) and fast boats (€45, 5¼ hours) to Piraeus; daily connections in summer to Mykonos, Ios, Naxos, Paros and Iraklio; and ferries to the smaller islands in the Cyclades.

Buses go frequently to Oia, Kamari, Perissa and Akrotiri from Fira. Port buses usually leave Fira, Kamari and Perissa one to 1½ hours before ferry departures. A rental car or scooter is a great option on Santorini.

CRETE ΚΡΗΤΗ

pop 540,000

Greece's largest and most southerly island, Crete's size and distance from the rest of Greece gives it the feel of a different country. With its dramatic landscape and unique cultural identity, Crete is a delight to explore. While the proud, friendly and hospitable people have enthusiastically embraced tourism, they continue to fiercely protect their traditions and culture – and it is the people that remain a major part of the island's appeal.

IRAKLIO ΗΡΑΚΛΕΙΟ

pop 131,000

Iraklio (ee-*rah*-klee-oh; often spelt Heraklion), Crete's capital, is a bustling modern city and the fifth-largest in Greece. It has a lively city centre, an excellent archaeological museum and is close to Knossos, Crete's major visitor attraction.

Orientation & Information

The old harbour is instantly recognisable as it is protected by the old Venetian fortress. The new harbour is 400m east. Plateia

Venizelou, known for its Lion Fountain, is the heart of the city, 400m south of the old harbour up 25 Avgoustou.

Gallery Games (☎ 28102 82804; Korai 14; per hr €1.50; 24hr) and a host of other places have high-speed internet access.

The **tourist office** (☎ 28102 46299; Xanthoudidou 1; 8.30am-8.30pm Apr-Oct, to 3pm Nov-Mar) is opposite the archaeological museum.

Skoutelis Travel (☎ 28102 80808; www.skoutelis.gr; 25 Avgoustou 20), between Plateia Venizelou and the old harbour, handles airline and ferry bookings, and rents cars.

Sights

Iraklio's **archaeological museum** (☎ 28102 79000; Xanthoudidou 2; adult/student €6/3; 12.30-7pm Mon, 8am-7pm Tue-Sun) has an outstanding Minoan collection, second only to the national museum in Athens.

Protecting the old harbour is the impressive **Koules Venetian Fortress** (☎ 28102 46211; adult/student €2/1; 9am-6pm Tue-Sun), also known as Rocca al Mare, which, like the city walls, was built by the Venetians in the 16th century.

The **Battle of Crete Museum** (☎ 28103 46554; cnr Doukos Beaufort & Hatzidaki; admission free; 8am-3pm) chronicles the historic WWII battle with photographs, letters, uniforms and weapons.

Sleeping

Rent Rooms Hellas (☎ 28102 88851; Handakos 24; dm/d/tr with shared bathroom €11/30/42) A popular budget choice, this place has a lively atmosphere, packed dorms, a rooftop bar and a bargain breakfast (from €2.50).

Hotel Mirabello (☎ 28102 85052; www.mirabello-hotel.gr; Theotokopoulou 20; s/d €35/44;) A pleasant, relaxed budget hotel on a quiet street in the centre of town, this place is run by an ex–sea captain who has travelled the world. A good-value option. Check out the excellent website.

Eating & Drinking

There's a congregation of cheap eateries in the Plateia Venizelou and El Greco Park area, as well as a bustling, colourful market all the way along 1866.

Giakoumis Taverna (☎ 28102 80277; Theodosaki 5-8; dishes €2.50-8; closed Sun) With its full menu of Cretan specialities, Giakoumis is the best of a bunch of cheap tavernas in the market area. Take the first left heading inland up 1866.

Samaria Delizioso (☎ 28102 86203; Kantanoleon 11) The people running this place have real pride in the quality of their coffees, pastries, cakes and chocolates. Kick back streetside and watch the locals pass by.

Guernica (☎ 28102 82988; Apokoronou Kritis 2; 10am-late) In a rambling old building with a delightful terrace garden, Guernica combines traditional decor and contemporary music exquisitely.

Getting There & Around

There are many flights daily from Iraklio's Nikos Kazantzakis airport (HER) to Athens and, in summer, regular flights to Thessaloniki, Mykonos, Santorini and Rhodes.

Daily ferries service Piraeus (€30, seven hours), and most days boats go to Santorini and continue on to other Cycladic islands.

The bus station, with departures to Crete's major cities, is just inland from the new harbour.

KNOSSOS ΚΝΩΣΣΟΣ

Five kilometres south of Iraklio, **Knossos** (☎ 28102 31940; admission €6; 8am-7pm Jun-Oct, to 5pm Nov-May) was the capital of Minoan Crete.

Knossos (k-nos-*os*) is the most famous of Crete's Minoan sites and is the inspiration for the myth of the Minotaur. According to legend, King Minos of Knossos was given a magnificent white bull to sacrifice to the god Poseidon, but decided to keep it. This enraged Poseidon, who punished the king by causing his wife Pasiphae to fall in love with the animal. The result of this odd union was the Minotaur – half-man and half-bull – who lived in a labyrinth beneath the king's palace, munching on youths and maidens.

In 1900 Arthur Evans uncovered the ruins of Knossos. Although archaeologists tend to disparage Evans' reconstruction, the buildings – incorporating an immense palace, courtyards, private apartments, baths, lively frescoes and more – give a good idea of what a Minoan palace might have looked like.

Arrive early to avoid the crowds. Take local bus 2 from Iraklio (€1.15, three per hour).

RETHYMNO ΡΕΘΥΜΝΟ

pop 29,000

Rethymno (*reth*-im-no), Crete's third-largest town, is one of the island's architectural

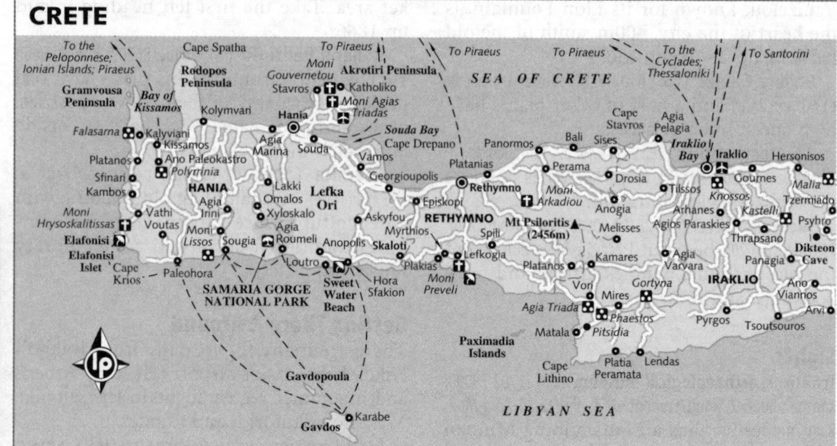

treasures, due to its stunning fortress and mix of Venetian and Turkish houses in the old quarter. It's on the north coast of Crete, west of Iraklio.

Galero Café (☎ 28310 54345; per hr €3), beside the Rimondi fountain with its spouting lion heads, has internet access. The **municipal tourist office** (☎ 28310 29148; www.rethymno.gr; Eleftheriou Venizelou; 🕑 9am-8.30pm Mar-Nov), on the beach side of the main drag, El Venizelou, is convenient and helpful. **Ellotia Tours** (☎ 28310 24533; www.rethymnoatcrete.com; Arkadiou 155) will answer all transport, accommodation and tour inquiries.

Rethymno's 16th-century **Venetian fortress** (fortezza; ☎ 28310 28101; Paleokastro Hill; admission €3; 🕑 8am-8pm) is the site of the city's ancient acropolis and affords great views across the town and mountains.

Happy Walker (☎ 28310 52920; www.happywalker.com; Tombazi 56) runs an excellent program of daily walks in the countryside (€25 per person), and also longer walking tours.

Rethymno Youth Hostel (☎ 28310 22848; www.yhrethymno.com; Tombazi 41; dm €9) is a well-run place with crowded dorms, free hot showers and no curfew.

Sea Front (☎ 28310 51981; www.rethymnoatcrete.com; Arkadiou 159; d €35-45; ❄) has all sorts of options and is ideally positioned with beach views and spacious rooms.

Restaurant Symposium (☎ 28310 50538; www.symposium-kriti.gr; dishes from €5), near the Rimondi fountain, takes its food seriously (check out the website) but has good prices.

There are regular ferries between Piraeus and Rethymno (€29, nine hours), and a high-speed service in summer. Buses depart regularly to Iraklio and Hania.

HANIA XANIA

pop 53,500

Crete's most romantic, evocative and alluring town, Hania (hahn-*yah;* often spelt Chania), west of Rethymno, is the former capital and the island's second-largest city. There is a rich mosaic of Venetian and Ottoman architecture, particularly in the area of the old harbour, which lures tourists in droves.

Orientation & Information

Connect to the internet at **Triple W Internet Café** (☎ 28210 93478; cnr Validinon & Halidon; per 30 minutes €1; 🕑 24hr). The **tourist information office** (☎ 28210 36155; Kydonias 29; 🕑 8am-2.30pm), located under the town hall, is helpful and provides practical information as well as maps. **Tellus Travel** (☎ 28210 91500; www.tellustravel.gr; Halidon 108; 🕑 8am-11pm) can help with schedules and ticketing, and also rents out cars.

Sights & Activities

A stroll around the **old harbour** is a must for any visitor to Hania. It is worth the 1.5km walk around the sea wall to get to the Venetian **lighthouse** at the entrance to the harbour.

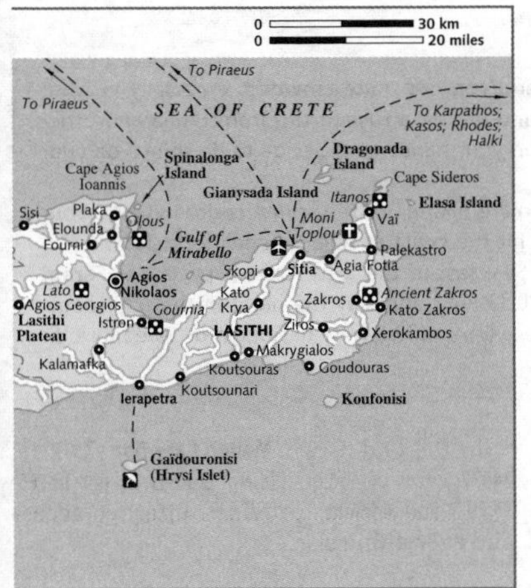

The **archaeological museum** (☎ 28210 90334; Halidon 30; admission €2; ⏲ 8.30am-3pm Tue-Sun) is in a 16th-century Venetian Church that the Turks made into a mosque.

Hania's covered **food market**, in a massive cross-shaped building, is definitely worth an inspection.

Sleeping

Camping Hania (☎ 28210 31138; per person/tent €5/4) Take the Kalamaki Beach bus from the east corner of Plateia 1866 (every 15 minutes) to get to this camping ground, which is located 3km west of town on the beach. There is a restaurant, bar and minimarket.

Pension Lena (☎ 28210 86860; www.lenachania.gr; Ritsou 5; s/d €35/55; ❄) For some real character in where you stay, Lena's pension, in an old Turkish building near the mouth of the old harbour, is where to go. Help yourself to one of the appealing rooms if Lena isn't there – pick from the available ones on the list on the blackboard.

Vranas Studios (☎ 28210 58618; www.vranas.gr; Agion Deka 10; studios €40-70; ❄ 💻) At the back of the cathedral, this place has immaculately maintained studios with kitchenettes. It also runs the internet cafe downstairs.

Eating & Drinking

The entire waterfront of the old harbour is lined with restaurants and tavernas, many of which qualify as tourist traps. Watch out for touts trying to reel you in.

our pick **Michelas** (☎ 28210 90026; mains €5-7; ⏲ 10am-4pm Mon-Sat) For some authentic Cretan specialities at reasonable prices head to Michelas in the eastern wing of the food market. This family-run place uses only Cretan ingredients and cooks up a great selection each day that you can peruse, then choose from.

Café Kriti (☎ 28210 58661; Kalergon 22; ⏲ 8pm-late) Away from the waterfront, Café Kriti is the best place in Hania to hear live Cretan music. It's rough-and-ready and a great place to drink and dance.

Synagogi (☎ 28210 96797; Skoufou 15) In a roofless Venetian building that was once a synagogue, this atmospheric spot offers up juices and coffee by day, and is a popular lounge bar by night.

Getting There & Away

There are several flights a day between Hania airport (CHQ) and Athens, and five flights a week to Thessaloniki. The airport is 14km east of town on the Akrotiri Peninsula.

Daily ferries sail between Piraeus (€30, nine hours) and the port of Souda, 9km southeast of Hania. Frequent buses run along Crete's northern coast to Iraklio, Rethymno and Kissamos-Kastelli; buses run less frequently to Paleohora, Omalos and Hora Sfakion.

SAMARIA GORGE

ΦΑΡΑΓΓΙ ΤΗΣ ΣΑΜΑΡΙΑΣ

The **Samaria Gorge** (☎ 28250 67179; admission €5; ⏲ 6am-3pm May–mid-Oct) is one of Europe's most spectacular gorges and a superb hike. Walkers should take rugged footwear, food, drinks and sun protection for this strenuous five- to six-hour trek.

You can do the walk as part of an excursion tour, or do it independently (see the boxed text, p550, for information) by taking the Omalos bus from the main bus station in Hania (€5.90, one hour) to the head of the gorge at Xyloskalo (1230m) at 6.15am, 7.30am, 8.30am or 2pm. It's a 16.7km walk out (all downhill) to Agia Roumeli on the coast, from where you take a boat to Hora Sfakion (€7.5, 1¼ hours, three daily) and then a bus back to Hania (€5.40, two hours, four daily). You are not allowed to spend the night in the gorge, so you need to complete the walk in a day.

GREECE

BEAT THE CROWDS AT SAMARIA

The Samaria Gorge walk is extremely popular and can get quite crowded, especially in summer. Most walkers have given the gorge a day and are on a rushed trip from Hania and other northern-coast cities. If you've got a bit of time on your hands, and decide to do things on your own, there's a much better option.

Leave from Hania in the morning, but once you're hiking, let the sprinters go and take your time through this stupendous gorge. When you hit the coast at Agia Roumeli (pop 125), down a cool beer, take a dip in the refreshing Libyan Sea, savour the tasty Cretan specials at **Faragi Restaurant & Rooms** (☎ 28250 91225; s/d/tr €20/30/35; ❄) and stay the night in the tidy rooms above the restaurant. The next day you can take a ferry either west to Sougia or Paleohora, or east to Loutro or Hora Sfakion.

DODECANESE ΔΩΔΕΚΑΝΗΣΑ

Strung out along the coast of western Turkey, the 12 main islands of the Dodecanese have suffered a turbulent past of invasions and occupations that has endowed them with a fascinating diversity.

RHODES ΡΟΔΟΣ

pop 98,000

Rhodes (Rodos in Greek) is the largest island in the Dodecanese. According to mythology, the sun god Helios chose Rhodes as his bride and bestowed light, warmth and vegetation upon her. The blessing seems to have paid off, for Rhodes produces more flowers and sunny days than most Greek islands.

Rhodes Town

pop 56,000

Rhodes' capital is Rhodes Town, on the northern tip of the island. Its World Heritage–listed Old Town, the largest inhabited medieval town in Europe, is enclosed within massive walls and is a joy to explore. To the north is New Town, the commercial centre.

INFORMATION

The **tourist information office** (EOT; ☎ 22410 35226; cnr Makariou & Papagou, New Town; 🕑 8am-2.45pm Mon-Fri) has brochures, maps and *Rodos News*, a free English-language newspaper.

In the New Town, **Triton Holidays** (☎ 22410 21690; www.tritondmc.gr; Plastira 9, Mandraki) is exceptionally helpful, handling accommodation bookings, ticketing and rental cars.

In the Old Town, **Mango Café Bar** (☎ 22410 24877; www.mango.gr; Plateia Dorieos 3; per hr €5; 🕑 9.30am-midnight) provides internet access and everything else.

SIGHTS & ACTIVITIES

The Old Town is reputedly the world's finest surviving example of medieval fortification. The Knights of St John lived in the Knights' Quarter in the northern end of the Old Town. The cobbled **Odos Ippoton** (Ave of the Knights) is lined with magnificent medieval buildings, the most imposing of which is the **Palace of the Grand Masters** (☎ 22410 23359; admission €6; 🕑 8.30am-7.30pm Tue-Sun). The 15th-century Knight's Hospital now houses the **archaeological museum** (☎ 22410 27657; Plateia Mousiou; admission €3; 🕑 8am-4pm Tue-Sun).

SLEEPING

Mango Rooms (☎ 22410 24877; www.mango.gr; Plateia Dorieos 3, Old Town; s/d/tr €36/46/56; ❄ 💻) A good-value one-stop shop near the back of the Old Town, Mango has a restaurant, bar and internet cafe down below, well-kept rooms above, and a superb sun terrace on top.

Hotel Spot (☎ 22410 34737; www.spothotelrhodes.com; Perikleous 21, Old Town; s/d/tr incl breakfast €45/60/80; ❄) Convenient and exceptionally clean, the Spot offers a small book exchange, internet facilities and attractive rooms.

Hotel Andreas (☎ 22410 34156; www.hotelandreas.com; Omirou 28d, Old Town; s/d €50/75; ❄) Tasteful, with individually decorated rooms and terrific views from its roof-terrace. Check it all out online, and choose your room before you go.

EATING & DRINKING

There is food and drink every way you look in Rhodes. Outside the city walls, there are a lot of cheap places in the New Market, at the southern end of Mandraki Harbour.

our pick **To Meltemi** (☎ 22410 30480; Kountourioti 8; mains €5-12) Gaze out on Turkey from this beachside taverna at the northern end of Mandraki Harbour. The seafood is superb. Try the grilled calamari stuffed with tomato and feta, and inspect the old photos of Rhodes.

Kafe Besara (☎ 22410 30363; Sofokleous 11, Old Town) This Aussie-owned establishment is one of the Old Town's liveliest bars and a great spot to hang out.

Mango Café Bar (☎ 22410 24877; Plateia Dorieos 3, Old Town) Mango claims to have the cheapest drinks in town and is the preferred haunt of local expats and die-hard travellers.

GETTING THERE & AROUND

There are plenty of flights daily between Rhodes airport (RHO) and Athens, two daily to Karpathos and one daily to Iraklio.

Rhodes is the main port of the Dodecanese and there is a complex array of departures. There are daily ferries from Rhodes to Piraeus (€40, taking 15 to 18 hours). At least three times a week there is a service via Karpathos to Crete. Hydrofoils travel daily to Symi and on to Kos. There are boats between Rhodes and Marmaris in Turkey (www.marmarisinfo.com; one way/return €50/70; 1¼ hours).

The west-side bus station, next to the New Market, serves the airport, Kamiros and the west coast. The **east-side bus station** (Plateia Rimini) serves the east coast, Lindos and the inland southern villages.

Around the Island

The **Acropolis of Lindos** (☎ 22440 31258; admission €6; 8.30am-6pm Tue-Sun), 47km from Rhodes Town, is an ancient city spectacularly perched atop a 116m-high rocky outcrop. Below is the town of **Lindos**, a tangle of streets with elaborately decorated 17th-century houses.

The extensive ruins of **Kamiros** (admission €4; 8am-5pm Tue-Sun), an ancient Doric city on the west coast, are well preserved and worth a visit.

KOS ΚΩΣ

pop 17,900

Captivating Kos, only 5km from the Turkish peninsula of Bodrum, has its own legion of fans. Popular with history buffs as the birthplace of Hippocrates (460–377 BC), the father of medicine, Kos also attracts an entirely different crowd – sun-worshipping beach lovers from northern Europe.

Orientation & Information

Kos Town is based around a circular harbour at the eastern end of the island. Akti Koundourioti is the main drag around the harbourfront.

Café Del Mare (☎ 22420 24244; www.cybercafe.gr; Megalou Alexandrou 4; per 30min €2; 9am-1am) is a well-equipped internet cafe near the harbour.

The **municipal tourist office** (☎ 22420 24460; www.kosinfo.gr; Vasileos Georgiou 1; 8am-2.30pm & 3-10pm Mon-Fri, 9am-2pm Sat) is on the waterfront directly south of the port and provides maps and accommodation information. **Exas Travel** (☎ 22420 28545; www.exas.gr) handles schedules, ticketing and excursions.

Sights & Activities

The focus of the **archaeological museum** (☎ 22420 28326; Plateia Eleftherias; adult/student €3/2; 8am-2.30pm Tue-Sun) is sculpture from excavations around the island. Not far off is is the **Hippocrates Plane Tree**, under which the man himself is said to have taught his pupils.

The **Castle of the Knights** (☎ 22420 27927; admission €4; 8am-2.30pm Tue-Sun), built in the 14th century to protect the old harbour, was originally separated from town by a moat. That moat is now Finikon, a major street.

On a pine-clad hill, 4km southwest of Kos Town, stand the extensive ruins of the renowned healing centre of **Asklipieion** (☎ 22420 28763; adult/student €4/3; 8.30am-6pm Tue-Sun), where Hippocrates practised medicine. Groups of doctors come from all over the world to visit.

If the history is all too much, wander around and relax at the town **beach** past the northern end of the harbour.

Sleeping

Pension Alexis (☎ 22420 28798, fax 22420 25797; Irodotou 9; s/d €25/30;) This highly recommended place has long been a budget favourite with travellers. It has large rooms with shared facilities, and a relaxing verandah and garden.

Hotel Afendoulis (☎ 22420 25321; www.afendoulishotel.com; Evripilou 1; s/d €35/50;) In a pleasant,

GREECE

Book your stay at lonelyplanet.com/hotels

quiet area about 500m south of the ferry quay, this well-kept hotel won't disappoint. Run by the charismatic English-speaking Alexis, this is a great place to relax and enjoy Kos.

Eating & Drinking

Restaurants line the central waterfront, but you might want to hit the backstreets for value.

Barbas (☎ 22400 27856; Evripilou 6; mains €3-5) Opposite Hotel Afendoulis, Barbas specialises in grills and has a mouth-watering chicken souvlaki. Sit at the streetside tables and watch the locals pass by.

Angelica's Beach Taverna (☎ 22420 24825; Antimachou 2; mains from €3) Right on the beach to the north of the harbour, Angelica, or Mama as she is better known, serves up succulent Greek dishes you can tuck into while still in your bathing suit.

Kalua (☎ 22420 24938; Akti Zouroudi 3) Just along the beach from Angelica's, Kalua is a popular outdoor venue with a swimming pool.

Getting There & Around

There are daily flights to Athens from Kos' Ippokratis airport (KGS).

There are frequent ferries from Rhodes to Kos that continue on to Piraeus (€45, 12 hours). Daily fast-boat connections head north to Patmos and Samos, and south to Symi and Rhodes. In summer, ferries depart daily for Bodrum in Turkey (€25 return, one hour).

There is a good public bus system on Kos, with the bus station on Kleopatras, near the ruins at the back of town.

PATMOS ΠΑΤΜΟΣ

pop 3050

Patmos has a sense of 'spirit of place', and with its great beaches and relaxed atmosphere, is a superb place to unwind. Orthodox and Western Christians have long made pilgrimages to Patmos, for it was here that John the Divine ensconced himself in a cave and wrote the Book of Revelations.

Orientation & Information

The main town and port of Skala is about halfway down the east coast of Patmos. Towering above Skala to the south is the *hora*, crowned by the immense Monastery of St John the Theologian.

Blue Bay Internet Café (☎ 22470 31165; per hr €4; ⌚ 9am-2pm & 5-8pm) is 200m south from the port in the Blue Bay Hotel. The **tourist office** (☎ 22470 31666; ⌚ 8am-6pm Mon-Fri Jun-Sep), post office and police station are in the white building opposite the port in Skala. **Apollon Travel** (☎ 22470 31324; apollontravel@stratas.gr), on the waterfront, handles schedules and ticketing.

Sights & Activities

The **Cave of the Apocalypse** (☎ 22470 31234; admission free, treasury €6; ⌚ 8am-1.30pm daily & 4-6pm Tue, Thu & Sun), where St John wrote his divinely inspired *Book of Revelations*, is halfway between the port and *hora*. Take a bus from the port or hike up the **Byzantine path**, which starts from a signposted spot on the Skala–*hora* road.

The **Monastery of St John the Theologian** (☎ 22470 31398; admission free; ⌚ 8am-1.30pm daily & 4-6pm Tue, Thu & Sun) looks more like a castle than a monastery and tops Patmos like a crown. It exhibits all kinds of monastic treasures.

Patmos' coastline provides secluded coves, mostly with pebble beaches. **Lambi Beach**, on the north coast, is a pebble beach–lover's dream come true.

Sleeping & Eating

Katina's Rooms (☎ 22470 31327, 69734 17241; s/d €35/50) The smiling Katina meets most boats and is happy to provide a ride to her four immaculately clean rooms at the northern end of the harbour.

Yvonni Studios (☎ 22470 33066; www.12net.gr/yvonni; s/d €35/50) On the western side of Skala, these exceptionally clean and pleasant studios are fully self-contained and big on privacy. Call ahead for a booking or drop into Yvonni's gift shop in Skala and ask for Theo.

Girovolies tou Magou (☎ 22470 33226; dishes from €3) Meat lovers will just croon over this place about 100m south of the port. There are tables on the beach, and the speciality of the house is rotisseried and skewered meats.

Getting There & Away

Patmos is well connected, with ferries to Piraeus (€35, 8 hours) and south to Rhodes. In summer, daily Flying Dolphin hydrofoils head south to Kos and Rhodes, and north to Samos.

GREECE

NORTHEASTERN AEGEAN ISLANDS
ΤΑ ΝΗΣΙΑ ΤΟΥ ΒΟΡΕΙΟ-ΑΝΑΤΟΛΙΚΟ ΑΙΓΑΙΟΥ

One of Greece's best-kept secrets, these far-flung islands are strewn across the northeastern corner of the Aegean, closer to Turkey than mainland Greece.

SAMOS ΣΑΜΟΣ

pop 32,800

A lush mountainous island with beautiful beaches only 3km from Turkey, Samos has a glorious history as the legendary birthplace of Hera, wife and sister of god-of-all-gods Zeus. Samos was an important centre of Hellenic culture, and the mathematician Pythagoras and storyteller Aesopus are among its sons.

Samos has two main ports: Vathy (Samos Town) in the northeast and Pythagorio on the southeast coast.

Pythagorio Πυθαγόρειο

pop 1300

Pretty Pythagorio, where you'll disembark if you've come from Patmos, is a small, enticing town with a yacht-lined harbour and a holiday atmosphere.

On the waterfront, **Pythagoras Internet Café** (☎ 22730 62722; per hr €2.50; 9am-2am) provides internet access. The cordial **municipal tourist office** (☎ 22730 61389; deap5@otenet.gr; 8am-9.30pm) is two blocks from the waterfront on the main street, Lykourgou Logotheti.

The excellent **statue of Pythagoras** and his triangle, on the waterfront opposite the ferry quay, should have you recalling his theorem from your high-school maths days. The 1034m-long **Evpalinos Tunnel** (☎ 22730 61400; adult/student €4/2; 8.45am-2.45pm Tue-Sun), built in the 6th century BC, was dug by political prisoners and used as an aqueduct to bring water from the springs of Mt Ampelos (1140m).The legendary birthplace of the goddess Hera, **Ireon** (☎ 22730 95277; adult/student €4/3; 8.30am-3pm Tue-Sun), is 8km west of Pythagorio. The temple at this World Heritage site was enormous – four times the Parthenon – though only one column remains.

Hotel Labito (☎ 22730 61086; www.labito.gr; s/d incl breakfast €45/55), a block back from the waterfront, is a friendly hotel with cosy rooms, most with a balcony. **Poseidon Restaurant** (☎ 22730 62530; mains from €5), on the small town beach, past the jetty with the Pythagoras statue on it, offers superb seafood.

Vathy (Samos) Βαθύ (Σάμος)

pop 2030

Busy Vathy, 25 minutes north of Pythagorio by bus, is an attractive working port town. Most of the action is along Themistokleous Sofouli, the main street that runs along the waterfront.

Pythagoras Hotel (☎ 22730 28601; Kallistratou 12; per hr €2.50) offers internet access. The rarely open and hard-to-find **tourist office** (☎ 22730 28582; Jun-Sep) is in a side street one block north of the main square. **ITSA Travel** (☎ 22730 23605; www.itsatravel.com), opposite the quay, is helpful with travel inquiries, excursions, accommodation and luggage storage.

The **archaeological museum** (☎ 22730 27469; adult/student €3/2; 8.30am-3pm Tue-Sun), by the municipal gardens, is first rate. The highlight is a 5.5m *kouros* (an ancient Greek statue of a young man).

our pick **Pythagoras Hotel** (☎ 22730 28601; www.pythagorashotel.com; Kallistratou 12; s/d €20/35; P) is a friendly, great-value place with a convivial atmosphere run by English-speaking Stelio. There is a restaurant serving home-cooked meals, a bar, satellite TV and internet access on site. Call ahead for free pick-up on arrival. **Garden Taverna** (☎ 22730 24033; Manolis Kalomiris; mains €4-9) serves good Greek food in a lovely garden setting; it's up to the left behind the main square.

Getting There & Around

There are daily flights to Athens.

A maritime hub, Samos offers daily ferries to Piraeus (€35, 13 hours), plus ferries heading north to Chios, west to the Cyclades and south to the Dodecanese. Daily hydrofoils ski south to Patmos, carrying on to Leros, Kalymnos and Kos. There are daily ferries to Kuşadası (for Ephesus) in Turkey (€37/47 one way/return plus €10 port taxes).

You can get to most of the island's villages and beaches by bus.

LESVOS (MYTILINI) ΛΕΣΒΟΣ (ΜΥΤΙΛΗΝΗ)

pop 93,500

Lesvos, or Mytilini as it is often called, tends to do things in a big way. The third-largest of the Greek islands after Crete and Evia,

SAPPHO, LESBIANS & LESVOS

Sappho, one of Greece's great ancient poets, was born on Lesvos during the 7th century BC. As most of her work was devoted to love and desire, and the objects of her affection were often female, Sappho's name and birthplace have come to be associated with female homosexuality.

These days, Lesvos is visited by many lesbians paying homage to Sappho. The island is very gay-friendly, in particular the southwestern beach resort of Skala Eresou, which is built over ancient Eresos where Sappho was born. The village is well set up to cater to lesbian needs and has a 'Women Together' festival held annually in September. Check out www.sapphotravel.com for details.

There is an excellent statue of Sappho in the main square on the waterfront in Mytilini.

Lesvos produces half the world's ouzo and is home to over 11 million olive trees. Lesvos has always been a centre of philosophy and artistic achievement, and to this day is a spawning ground for innovative ideas in the arts and politics.

The two main towns on the island are the capital of Mytilini on the southeast coast, and attractive Mithymna on the north coast.

Mytilini Μυτιλήνη

pop 27,250

The capital and main port, Mytilini has a large university campus and is lively year-round.

At the southern end of the harbour, **InSpot** (☎ 22510 45760; Hristougennon 12; per hr €2.40) has impressive internet access. The **tourist office** (☎ 22510 42511; 6 Aristarhou; 9am-1pm Mon-Fri), 50m up Aristarhou inland from the quay, offers brochures and maps, but its opening hours are limited. **Zoumboulis Tours** (☎ 22510 37755; Kountourioti 69), on the waterfront, handles flights, boat schedules, ticketing and excursions to Turkey.

SIGHTS & ACTIVITIES

Mytilini's excellent neoclassical **archaeological museum** (☎ 22510 22087; 8 Noemvriou; admission €3; 8am-7.30pm) has a fascinating collection from Neolithic to Roman times.

A superb place for a stroll or a picnic is the pine forest surrounding Mytilini's impressive **fortress** (adult/student €2/1; 8am-2.30pm Tue-Sun), which was built in early Byzantine times and enlarged by the Turks.

SLEEPING

Pension Thalia (☎ 22510 24640; Kinikiou 1; s/d €25/30) This pension has clean, bright rooms in a large house. It is about a five-minute walk north of the main square, up Ermou, the road that links the south and north harbours. Follow the signs from the corner of Ermou and Adramytiou.

Hotel Sappho (☎ 22510 22888; Kountourioti 31; s/d/tr €35/55/66) On the waterfront, rooms here are simple but clean. It's easy to find, and has the attraction of a 24-hour reception as ferries into Mytilini tend to arrive at nasty hours.

EATING & DRINKING

our pick Diavlos (☎ 22510 22020; Ladadika 30; mains from €4) Head straight to Diavlos for the best in both local cuisine and art; paintings by local artists line the walls.

Kalderimi (☎ 22510 46577; Thasou 3; mains from €6) Popular with locals, Kalderimi has an excellent ambience with tables in a vine-covered pedestrian street just back from the Sappho statue on the main harbour.

Ocean Eleven Bar (☎ 22510 27030; Kountourioti 17) In the corner on the waterfront, this is a superb spot to relax with a drink and partake in some Mytilini people-watching.

GETTING THERE & AROUND

Written up on flight schedules as Mytilene, Lesvos' Odysseas airport (MJT) has daily connections with Athens and Thessaloniki, and two a week to Chios.

In summer, there are daily boats to Piraeus (€40, 9 hours) via Chios, and one boat a week to Thessaloniki. There are four ferries a week to Ayvalik in Turkey (one way/return €30/45). Buses can take you to all parts of the island.

Mithymna Μήθυμνα

pop 1500

The gracious, preserved town of Mithymna (known by locals as Molyvos) is 62km north of Mytilini. Cobbled streets canopied by flowering vines wind up the hill below the impressive castle.

The helpful **municipal tourist office** (☎ 22530 71347; www.mithymna.gr; 8am-9pm Mon-Fri, 9am-7pm Sat & Sun), which has good maps, is 100m up from the bus stop. Some 50m further on, the cobbled main thoroughfare of 17 Noemvriou heads up to the right. Going straight at this point will take you to the colourful fishing port.

The noble **Genoese castle** (☎ 22530 71803; admission €2; 8am-7pm Tue-Sun) perches above the town like a crown and affords tremendous views out to Turkey.

Eftalou hot springs (☎ 22530 71245; public/private bath per person €3.50/5; public bath 10am-2pm & 4-8pm, private bath 9am-6pm), 4km from town on the beach, is a superb bathhouse complex with a whitewashed dome and steaming, pebbled pool. There are also private baths where you don't need a bathing suit.

Nassos Guest House (☎ 22530 71432; www.nassosguesthouse.com; Arionis; d & tr €20-35) is an airy, friendly place with shared facilities and a communal kitchen, in an old Turkish house oozing with character. It's easy to spot as it's the only blue house below the castle.

Betty's Restaurant (☎ 22530 71421; Agora; mains from €5) has superb home-style Greek food, views and atmosphere in a building that was once a notorious bordello. Betty also has a couple of **cottages** (☎ 22530 71022; www.bettyscottages.molivos.net) with kitchens in her garden that sleep up to four for €50.

Buses to Mithymna (€5) take 1¾ hours from Mytilini, though a hire car is a good option. There are a lot of outlets around the waterfront in Mytilini.

SPORADES ΣΠΟΡΑΔΕΣ

Scattered to the southeast of the Pelion Peninsula, to which they were joined in prehistoric times, the Sporades islands have mountainous terrain, dense vegetation and are surrounded by scintillatingly clear seas.

The main ports for the Sporades are Volos and Agios Konstantinos on the mainland.

SKIATHOS ΣΚΙΑΘΟΣ

pop 6150

Lush and green, Skiathos has a beach-resort feel about it. Skiathos Town and excellent beaches are on the hospitable south coast, while the north coast is precipitous and less accessible.

Skiathos Town's main thoroughfare is Papadiamanti, running inland opposite the quay. **Enter Internet** (☎ 69984 24460; per hr €3; 9am-1am) is one block back from the port with heaps of signage. There's a **tourist information booth** (☎ 24270 23172) at the port, but it opens irregularly. **Heliotropio Travel** (☎ 24270 22430; helio@skiathos.gr), opposite the ferry quay, handles ticketing and rents cars and scooters.

Skiathos has superb beaches, particularly on the south coast. **Koukounaries** is popular with families. A stroll over the headland, **Big Banana Beach** is stunning, but if you want an all-over tan, head a tad further to **Little Banana Beach**. At the Old Port in Skiathos Town, there are all sorts of offerings in terms of **boat excursions** – around-Skiathos trips (€25), and full-day trips that take in Skopelos, Alonnisos and the Marine Park (€35).

The **Rooms to Let** (☎ 24270 22990) bookings kiosk on the waterfront opens when ferries and hydrofoils arrive. **Camping Koukounaries** (☎ 24270 49250; per person/tent €8/4) is 30 minutes away from town by bus at beautiful Koukounaries Beach, with good facilities, a minimarket and a taverna. **Pension Pandora** (☎ 24270 24357, 69441 37377; www.skiathos.gr/html/advert/pans_pandora; s, d & q €30-70; P) is run by the effervescent Georgina. 10 minutes' walk north of the quay, the spotless rooms have TV, kitchens and balconies.

Skiathos Town is brimming with eateries. **Piccolo** (☎ 24270 22780; mains from €7), up from the Old Port in the tiny square behind the church, does exquisite pizzas and pastas in a lovely setting. Just off Plateia Papadiamanti, **Kentavros** (☎ 24270 22980) is popular with locals and expats alike for its mellow ambience and mixture of rock, jazz and blues.

In summer there is a daily flight from Athens to Skiathos. There are frequent daily hydrofoils to/from the mainland ports of Volos and Agios Konstantinos as well as cheaper ferries. The hydrofoils head to and from Skopelos and Alonnisos. Buses ply the south-coast road between Skiathos Town and Koukounaries stopping at all the beaches along the way.

SKOPELOS ΣΚΟΠΕΛΟΣ

pop 4700

A mountainous island, Skopelos is covered in pine forests, vineyards, olive groves and fruit orchards. The island's main port and

ECOTOURISM ON THE RISE

In a country not noted for its ecological long-sightedness, locals (especially the fishermen) initially struggled with the idea of the National Marine Park of Alonnisos when it was established in 1992 to protect the highly endangered Mediterranean monk seal and to promote the recovery of fish stocks.

These days though, the people of the Sporades have caught on to the advantages of having such a park on their doorstep. Ecotourism is on the rise, with daily excursions into the park from Skiathos, Skopelos and Alonnisos. Though your odds of seeing the shy monk seal aren't great – it's on the list of the 20 most endangered species worldwide – the chances of cruising among pods of dolphins (striped, bottlenose and common) are high.

capital of Skopelos Town is on the east coast. The crew of *Mamma Mia* recently took over Skopelos Town's accommodation for a month and filmed at Agnontas and Kastani beaches on the western coast.

In Skopelos Town there is no tourist office, but **Thalpos Holidays** (☎ 24240 29036; www.holidayislands.com) on the waterfront is handy for accommodation and tours. Along Doulidi, the street heading left off Souvlaki Sq, is the **Skopelos Internet Café** (☎ 24240 23093; per hr €3; 9am-midnight), post office and a stack of popular nightspots.

Pension Sotos (☎ 24240 22549; www.skopelos.net/sotos; s & d €20-55;), in the middle of the waterfront, has big rooms in an enchanting old Skopelete building. Check out individual rooms and their different prices online before you go.

Head to Souvlaki Sq, 100m up from the dock, for cheap eats such as *gyros* and souvlaki. The top spot in town to chill out is under the huge plane tree at **Platanos Jazz Bar** (☎ 24240 23661) on the waterfront. It's open all day, plays wicked jazz and blues until the late hours, and is the ideal place to recover from, or prepare for, a hangover.

Flying Dolphin hydrofoils dash several times a day to Skiathos, Alonnisos, Volos and Agios Konstantinos. There is also a daily ferry along the same route that costs less but takes longer. Frequent buses from Skopelos Town to Glossa stop at all beaches along the way.

ALONNISOS ΑΛΟΝΝΗΣΟΣ

pop 2700

Green, serene, attractive Alonnisos is at the end of the line and the least visited of the Sporades' main islands.

The port village of Patitiri was slapped together in 1965 after an earthquake destroyed the hilltop capital of Alonnisos Town. **Play Internet** (☎ 24240 66119; per hr €3; 9am-2pm & 6-9pm) can get you online. There is no tourist office, but **Alonnisos Travel** (☎ 24240 66000; www.alonnisostravel.gr) on the waterfront handles boat scheduling and ticketing.

The tiny *hora*, **Old Alonnisos**, is a few kilometres inland. Its streets sprout a profusion of plant life, alluring villas of eclectic design and dramatic vistas.

The **Rooms to Let service** (☎ 24240 66188, fax 24240 65577; 10am-2pm & 6-10pm), opposite the quay, books accommodation all over the island. **Camping Rocks** (☎ 24240 65410; per person €6) is a shady, basic camping ground. It is a steep hike about 1.5km from the port; go up Pelasgon and take the first road on your left. **Pension Pleiades** (☎ 24240 65235; www.pleiadeshotel.gr; s/d/tr €25/35/50;) looks out over the harbour and is visible from the quay. The rooms are immaculate, balconied, bright and cheerful.

Ferries with varying regularity connect Alonnisos to Volos and Agios Konstantinos via Skopelos and Skiathos. Flying Dolphin makes the most regular trips between the islands, travelling several times a day to Skopelos Town, Skiathos, Volos and Agios Konstantinos.

The local bus (€1.20) runs to the *hora* every hour.

IONIAN ISLANDS ΤΑ ΕΠΤΑΝΗΣΑ

The idyllic cypress- and fir-covered Ionian Islands stretch down the western coast of Greece from Corfu in the north to Kythira, off the southern tip of the Peloponnese. Mountainous, with dramatic cliff-backed beaches, soft light and turquoise water, they're more Italian in feel, offering a contrasting experience to other Greek islands.

CORFU ΚΕΡΚΥΡΑ

pop 114,000

Many consider Corfu to be Greece's most beautiful island, with the unfortunate consequence that it is often overrun with crowds.

Built on a promontory and wedged between two fortresses, Corfu's old town is a tangle of narrow walking streets through gorgeous Venetian buildings. Ferries dock at the new port, just west of the Neo Frourio. The **tourist police** (☎ 26610 30265; 3rd fl, Samartzi 4) provide helpful info. Check email at **Netoikos** (Kaloheretou 14; per hr €3), behind the Church of Agios Spyridon.

The **Archaeological Museum** (☎ 26610 30680; P Vraïla 5; admission €3; 8.30am-3pm Tue-Sun) houses a collection of finds from Mycenaean to classical times. The richly decorated **Church of Agios Spiridon** (Agios Spiridonos) displays the remains of St Spiridon, paraded through town four times a year.

Accommodation prices fluctuate wildly depending on season; book ahead. Recently renovated **Hotel Astron** (☎ 26610 39505; hotel_astron@hol.gr; Donzelot 15, Old Port; s €45-55, d €55-65) has some sea views, and light-filled rooms are managed by friendly staff. Good beaches surround the tiny town of **Agios Gordios**. Backpackers should head to low-key **Sunrock** (☎ 26610 94637; Pelekas Beach; dm/r per person €18/24) for its full-board hostel and genial atmosphere.

Old 45 *rembetika* records line the walls at **To Tsipouzadiko** (☎ 26610 82240; mains €5-8; dinner) and the gregarious owner serves up generous portions of fresh (cheap) Greek food. Every detail is cared for at **La Cucina** (☎ 26610 45029; Guilford 17; mains €10-15), from the hand-rolled *tortelloni* (pasta) to the inventive pizzas and muraled walls.

Daily flights link Corfu to Athens. Hourly ferries go to Igoumenitsa (€7, 1½ hours). In summer daily ferries and hydrofoils go to Paxi, and international ferries head to Patra. There are good bus services on the island.

KEFALLONIA ΚΕΦΑΛΛΟΝΙΑ

pop 45,000

Tranquil cypress- and fir-covered Kefallonia has fortunately not succumbed to package tourism to the extent some of the other Ionian islands have, despite being thrust under the spotlight following its starring role in *Captain Corelli's Mandolin*.

Pretty Fiskardo, with its pastel-coloured Venetian buildings set around a picturesque bay, was the only Kefallonian village not to be destroyed by the 1953 earthquake. Splendid **Myrtos Beach** is spellbinding from both above, where the postcard views from the precarious roadway are breathtaking, and below, where you'll think you've discovered the perfect beach.

Regina's Rooms (☎ 26740 41125; d €50-70), overlooking the village, is a budget bargain, ideal for self-caterers. All of its colourful breezy rooms have TV, fridge and balconies, some with gorgeous bay views or kitchenettes. Unassuming but famous **Tassia** (☎ 26740 41205; mains €8-18) serves up excellent Greek dishes.

Daily flights go to Athens from **Keffalonia airport** (EFL; ☎ 26710 41511). In high season, ferries go from Pesada to Agios Nikolaos (Zakynthos). Daily ferries operate from Sami to Patra, Pisaetos and Vathy (Ithaki), and from Argostoli and Poros to Kyllini (the Peloponnese).

GREECE DIRECTORY

ACCOMMODATION

Greece has a good range of budget accommodation, subject to strict price controls. By law, a notice must be displayed in every room stating the category of the room and the seasonal price. If you think there's something amiss, contact the tourist police.

Greece has around 340 camping grounds, though generally they are only open from April to October. The **Panhellenic Camping Association** (www.panhellenic-camping-union.gr) has detailed information. Standard facilities include hot showers, kitchens, restaurants and minimarkets – and often a swimming pool. Prices vary according to facilities, but reckon on €8 per adult, €5 for a small tent and €8 for a large one.

You'll find youth hostels in most major towns and on some islands. Most hostels throughout Greece are affiliated with the **Greek Youth Hostel Organisation** (☎ 21075 19530; y-hostels@otenet.gr). Most charge around €12 for a dorm bed, and you don't have to be a member to stay.

Domatia are the Greek equivalent of a bed and breakfast – minus the breakfast. Expect to pay about €25 to €35 for a single and €40 to €50 for a double. Don't worry about finding them – owners will find you as they greet ferries and buses shouting 'room!'.

Hotels in Greece are classified as deluxe, or A, B, C, D or E class. The ratings seldom seem to have much bearing on the price, which is determined more by season and location.

ACTIVITIES

Diving & Snorkelling

Snorkelling can be enjoyed just about anywhere along Greece's magnificent coastlines. Corfu, Mykonos and Santorini are just some of the good areas to snorkel. Diving, however, must take place under the supervision of a diving school to protect the antiquities still in the deep.

Hiking

Greece is a trekkers' paradise. Outside the main popular routes, though, the trails are generally overgrown and poorly marked. Several companies run organised treks; **Trekking Hellas** (Map p526; ☎ 21033 10323; www.outdoorsgreece.com; Filellinon 7, Athens) has options throughout Greece. **Cretan Adventures** (☎ 28103 32772; www.cretanadventures.gr; Evans 10, Iraklio) specialises in activities on Crete.

Windsurfing & Kitesurfing

Greece is a fantastic windsurfing destination and sailboards are widely available for hire, priced at €12 to €15 per hour. The top spots for windsurfing are Hrysi Akti on Paros, and Vasiliki on Lefkada, which is a popular place to learn. Kitesurfers should contact the **Greek Wakeboard & Kitesurf Association** (www.gwa.gr).

BUSINESS HOURS

Banks are open from 8am to 2pm Monday to Thursday, and to 1.30pm Friday. Some banks in the larger cities and towns are also open from 3.30pm to 6.30pm and on Saturday (8am to 1.30pm). Post offices are open from 7.30am to 2pm Monday to Friday; in major cities they're open until 8pm and also open from 7.30am to 2pm on Saturday.

In summer shops are generally open from 8am to 1.30pm and 5.30pm to 8.30pm on Tuesday, Thursday and Friday, and 8am to 2.30pm on Monday, Wednesday and Saturday. *Periptera* (kiosks) will often be your saviour: open from early morning to late at night, they sell everything from beer to bus tickets.

Restaurants in tourist areas generally open at 11am and stay open through to midnight; normal restaurant hours are 11am to 2pm and from 7pm to midnight or 1am. Cafes tend to open between 9am and 10am and stay open until midnight. Bars open around 8pm and close late, and while discos might open at 10pm, you'll drink alone until midnight. Nightclubs generally close around 4am, but many go through to dawn during summer.

EMBASSIES & CONSULATES

All foreign embassies in Greece are in Athens and its suburbs.

Australia (Map p525; ☎ 210 870 4000; Leoforos Alexandras & Kifisias, Ambelokipi)
Canada (Map p525; ☎ 210 727 3400; Genadiou 4)
Cyprus (Map p525; ☎ 210 723 7883; Irodotou 16)
France (Map p525; ☎ 210 361 1663; Leof Vasilissis Sofias 7)
Germany (Map p525; ☎ 210 728 5111; cnr Karaoli & Dimitriou 3, Kolonaki)
Italy (Map p525; ☎ 210 361 7260; Sekeri 2)
Japan (Map p525; ☎ 210 775 8101; Athens Tower, Leoforos Messogion 2-4)
New Zealand (Map p525; ☎ 210 687 4701; Kifissias 268, Halandri)
South Africa (Map p525; ☎ 210 680 6645; Kifissias 60, Maroussi)
Turkey (Map p525; ☎ 210 724 5915; Vasilissis Georgiou 8)
UK (☎ 210 723 6211; Ploutarhou 1, GR-106 75)
USA (Map p525; ☎ 210 721 2951; Leoforos Vasilissis Sofias 91, GR-115 21)

FESTIVALS & EVENTS

In Greece, it is probably easier to list the dates when festivals and events are *not* on! Some festivals are religious, some cultural and others seemingly just an excuse to party. Check out www.cultureguide.gr.

GAY & LESBIAN TRAVELLERS

While there is no legislation against homosexual activity, it is wise to be discreet and to avoid open displays of togetherness. Greece is a popular destination for gay travellers. Athens has a busy gay scene that packs up and heads to the islands for summer. Mykonos has long been famous for its bars, beaches and hedonism, and a visit to Eresos on Lesvos has become something of a pilgrimage for lesbians.

HOLIDAYS

New Year's Day 1 January
Epiphany 6 January
First Sunday in Lent February
Greek Independence Day 25 March
Good Friday/Easter Sunday March/April
May Day (Protomagia) 1 May
Feast of the Assumption 15 August
Ohi Day 28 October
Christmas Day 25 December
St Stephen's Day 26 December

INTERNET RESOURCES

Culture Guide (www.cultureguide.gr) Plenty of information about contemporary culture and the arts.

Greek National Tourist Organisation (www.gnto.gr) Concise tourist information.

Greek Travel Pages (www.gtp.gr) Useful directory for travel businesses.

Ministry of Culture (www.culture.gr) Information on ancient sites, art galleries and museums.

MONEY

Greece adopted the euro in 2002. Banks, post offices and currency-exchange offices are all over the place and will exchange all major currencies. ATMs are located everywhere except the smallest villages.

Greece is still a cheap destination by northern European standards, but it's no longer dirt cheap. A daily budget of €40 would entail staying in youth hostels or camping, staying away from bars, and only occasionally eating in restaurants or taking ferries. Allow at least €80 per day if you want your own room and plan to eat out regularly and see the sights. Your money will go a lot further if you travel in the quieter months, as accommodation is generally much cheaper outside the high season when there are more opportunities to negotiate better deals.

In restaurants the service charge is included on the bill, but it is the custom to leave a small tip – just round up the bill.

POST

Tahydromia (post offices) are easily identified by the yellow sign outside. Regular post boxes are yellow; red post boxes are for express mail. The postal rate for postcards and airmail letters within the EU is €0.60, to other destinations it's €0.65.

TELEPHONE

The Greek telephone service is maintained by Organismos Tilepikoinonion Ellados, always referred to by its acronym OTE (o-*teh*). Public phones are easy to use and pressing the 'i' button brings up the operating instructions in English. Public phones are everywhere and all use phonecards, which are sold at kiosks. Local calls cost €0.30 for three minutes. Telephone codes are part of the 10-digit number within Greece. The landline prefix is 2 and for mobiles it's 6. The international access code is ☎ 00 and the country code is ☎ 30.

If you have a compatible GSM phone from a country with a global roaming agreement with Greece, you will be able to use your phone there. You can purchase a Greek SIM card for around €20 and cards are available everywhere to recharge the SIM card.

VISAS

Visitors from most countries don't need a visa for Greece. The list of countries whose nationals can stay in Greece for up to three months includes Australia, Canada, all EU countries, Iceland, Israel, Japan, New Zealand and the USA. For longer stays, apply at a consulate abroad or at least 20 days in advance to the **Aliens Bureau** (Map p525; ☎ 210 770 5711; Leoforos Alexandras 173, Athens; 🕑 8am-1pm Mon-Fri) at the Athens Central Police Station. Elsewhere in Greece, apply to the local authority.

Hungary

HIGHLIGHTS

- **Budapest** Hungary's capital city will excite you with its excellent nightlife, history, culture…and thermal baths (p564)
- **Eger** Learn about the defiance this city showed to Turkish invaders, and how its Bull's Blood wine got its name (p578)
- **Lake Balaton** Party until dawn on the lively beaches of this vast lake, or take a pleasure cruise from one of its attractive towns (p575)
- **Kiskunság National Park** Watch the cowboys ride at Bugac, in the heart of the Hungarian Plain (p577)
- **Pécs** Absorb the Mediterranean climate and historic architecture of this southern city, including its intriguing Mosque Church (p576)
- **Danube Bend** Explore this stretch of the mighty river, dotted with attractive small towns and historic monuments (p573)

FAST FACTS

- **Area** 93,000 sq km (similar size to Portugal)
- **Budget** 10,000-20,000Ft per day
- **Capital** Budapest
- **Country code** ☎ 36
- **Famous for** paprika, tokay wine, goose-liver pâté and *csardas* music
- **Language** Hungarian (Magyar)
- **Money** Hungarian forint (Ft); A$1 = 159Ft; C$ = 181Ft; €1 = 286Ft; ¥100 = 225Ft; NZ$1 = 124Ft; UK£1 = 323Ft; US$1 = 213Ft
- **Phrases** *jo napot kivanok* (Good day/hello), *szia* (hi/bye), *köszönöm* (thank you)
- **Population** 9.94 million

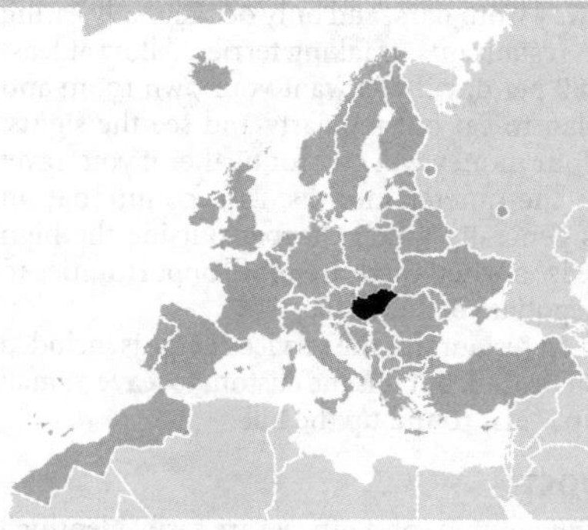

- **Visas** no visa required for most nationalities if you stay less than 90 days; see p580

TRAVEL HINTS

Look out for shops with the word *pék* (baker) in their name: they sell inexpensive fresh sweet and savoury pastries.

ROAMING HUNGARY

Most shoestringers base themselves in Budapest and take day trips around the country. Nothing is more than five hours away from Budapest by train.

Where else but Hungary can you laze about in an open-air thermal spa in midwinter, while snow patches glisten around you? Following that, it's *de rigueur* to head to a local bar where a Romani band yelps while a crazed crowd whacks its boot heels, as commanded by Hungarian tradition. Or go clubbing in an ancient bathhouse, where all dance in swimsuits, waist-deep in the healing waters.

If these pursuits don't appeal, there are always Roman ruins, ancient castles and Turkish minarets in baroque cities. In the countryside you can experience the joy of seeing cowboys riding, storks nesting on streetlamps, and a sea of apricot trees blooming.

Not that urban pleasures are neglected. Cosmopolitan Budapest is packed with world-class operas, monumental historical buildings, and the mighty Danube River flowing through its centre. Prices here are somewhere in the middle: not nearly as high as Austria nor as inexpensive as Ukraine. Having established itself as a state in the year 1000, Hungary has a long history, a rich culture and strong folk traditions that are well worth exploring.

HISTORY

By the 3rd century BC, the Roman Empire had extended its influence far enough to include Pannonia, all of today's Hungary west of the Danube (Transdanubia). By 441 the Huns, under Attila and his brother Bleda, had ended Roman rule in the area. However, the Huns' short-lived empire didn't long outlast Attila's death, leaving space for Avars, Franks and Slavs.

Historians usually date the Magyar (Hungarian) conquest to around 896, when Árpád led an alliance of seven tribes in the region. In the year 1000, Hungary's first king and patron saint, Stephen (István), was crowned, marking the foundation of the Hungarian state.

Medieval Hungary was powerful until 1526, when the Turks defeated the Hungarian army and occupied lands that included Budapest for 150 years. After the Turks' expulsion from Buda in 1686, the Austrian Habsburgs annexed the lands that had been under Turkish rule. An 1848 revolt for independence led by Transylvanian princes failed, but unrest eventually led to Hungarian autonomy as half of the Austro-Hungarian empire in 1867.

After WWI ended, with Hungary on the losing side, the 1920 Trianon Treaty stripped the country of more than two-thirds of its territory. Hungary's ambition to recover its loss drew the nation into WWII on the Axis side. When leftists tried to negotiate a separate peace in 1944, the Germans occupied Hungary and brought the fascist Arrow Cross Party to power. The Arrow Cross immediately began deporting hundreds of thousands of Jews to Auschwitz. By early April 1945, Hungary had been liberated by the Soviet army. In 1947 the communists took complete control of the government.

On 23 October 1956 anti-Soviet student demonstrations prompted Soviet tanks to move into Budapest, and by the end of the fighting, more than 25,000 people had died. Still, Soviet control was not as tight in Hungary as in its Slavic satellite states, and the ruling system that emerged was nicknamed 'Goulash Communism'.

Hungary began moving towards full democracy in 1989. The Republic of Hungary was proclaimed in October, and democratic elections were scheduled for March 1990. The last Soviet troops left the country in June 1991. Hungary became a full member of NATO in 1999 and joined the EU on 1 May 2004.

The painful transition to a market economy resulted in declining living standards for most people, but the late 20th and early 21st centuries saw astonishing economic growth. However, in 2008, reeling from the fallout of the global financial crisis, Hungary was forced to approach the International Monetary Fund for economic assistance.

THE CULTURE

Just over 93% of Hungary's population is ethnically Magyar. Non-Magyar minorities include Germans (2.6%), Serbs and other South Slavs (2%), Slovaks (0.8%) and Romanians (0.7%). The number of Roma is officially put at 1.9% of the population (or 193,800 people), though some sources estimate the figure as high as 4%.

ARTS

As you will see from the street names in every Hungarian town and city, the country celebrates and reveres its most influential musician, composer and pianist, Franz (or Ferenc) Liszt (1811–86). Béla Bartók (1881–1945) and Zoltán Kodály (1882–1967) made the first systematic study of Hungarian folk music; both integrated some of their findings into their compositions.

Romani (Gypsy) music, found in restaurants in its schmaltzy form (best avoided), has become a fashionable thing among the young, with Romani bands playing 'the real thing' in trendy bars till the wee hours. Klezmer music (traditional Eastern European Jewish music)

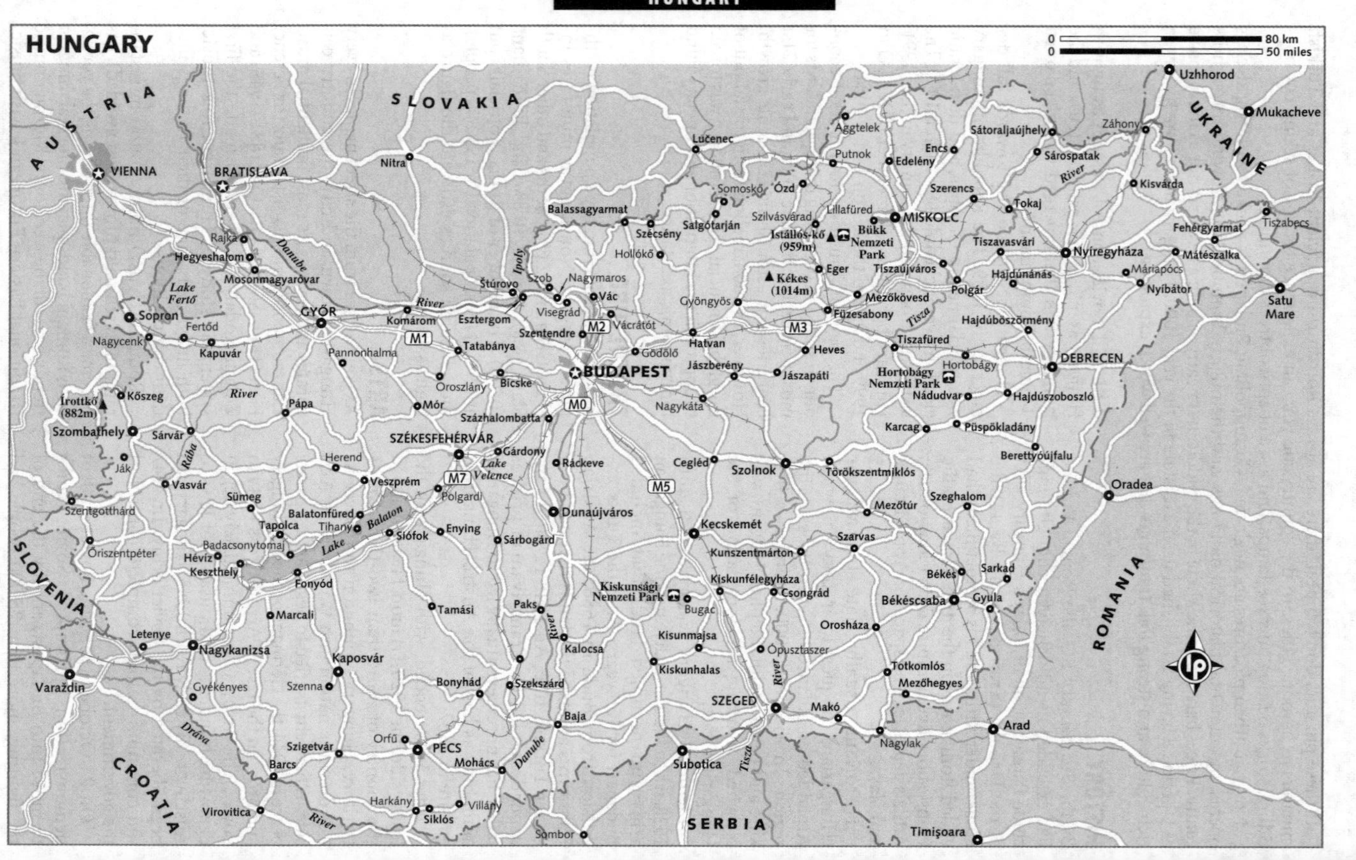
HUNGARY
0 80 km
0 50 miles
AUSTRIA
SLOVAKIA
UKRAINE
ROMANIA
SERBIA
CROATIA
SLOVENIA
VIENNA
BRATISLAVA
BUDAPEST
DEBRECEN
MISKOLC
SZEGED
PÉCS
GYŐR
SZÉKESFEHÉRVÁR
Uzhhorod
Mukacheve
Satu Mare
Tiszabecs
Fehérgyarmat
Mátészalka
Máriapócs
Nyírbátor
Kisvárda
Záhony
Nyíregyháza
Sárospatak
Sátoraljaújhely
Tokaj
Szerencs
Tiszavasvári
Hajdúnánás
Hajdúböszörmény
Hajdúszoboszló
Berettyóújfalu
Oradea
Püspökladány
Nádudvar
Hortobágy
Hortobágy Nemzeti Park
Karcag
Polgár
Tiszaújváros
Encs
Edelény
Aggtelek
Putnok
Lillafüred
Bükk Nemzeti Park
Mezőkövesd
Tiszafüred
Eger
Füzesabony
Szilvásvárad
Istállós-kő (959m)
Kékes (1014m)
Heves
Jászapáti
Ózd
Somoskő
Salgótarján
Lučenec
Gyöngyös
Hatvan
Jászberény
Nagykáta
Szécsény
Hollókő
Balassagyarmat
Vácrátót
Gödöllő
Nagymaros
Vác
Szob
Visegrád
Szentendre
Esztergom
Štúrovo
Ipoly
Tatabánya
Bicske
Oroszlány
Mór
Komárom
Nitra
Pannonhalma
Mosonmagyaróvár
Rajka
Hegyeshalom
Lake Fertő
Fertőd
Kapuvár
Sopron
Nagycenk
Kőszeg
Szombathely
Írottkő (882m)
Ják
Sárvár
Vasvár
Szentgotthárd
Őriszentpéter
Pápa
Sümeg
Herend
Veszprém
Balatonfüred
Tihany
Tapolca
Badacsonytomaj
Hévíz
Keszthely
Lake Balaton
Fonyód
Siófok
Polgárdi
Enying
Lake Velence
Gárdony
Százhalombatta
Ráckeve
Dunaújváros
Sárbogárd
Tamási
Paks
Kalocsa
Szekszárd
Bonyhád
Mohács
Villány
Siklós
Harkány
Orfű
Kaposvár
Szenna
Marcali
Szigetvár
Barcs
Nagykanizsa
Gyékényes
Letenye
Varaždin
Virovitica
Dráva
River
Rába
Danube
Tisza
Baja
Sombor
Subotica
Kiskunhalas
Kisunmajsa
Kiskunsági Nemzeti Park
Bugac
Kecskemét
Cegléd
Kiskunfélegyháza
Kunszentmárton
Csongrád
Ópusztaszer
Szolnok
Törökszentmiklós
Mezőtúr
Szarvas
Szeghalom
Orosháza
Békéscsaba
Békés
Gyula
Sarkad
Tótkomlós
Mezőhegyes
Makó
Nagylak
Arad
Timişoara
M0
M1
M2
M3
M5
M7

READING UP

National poetry taught in schools has a huge influence on the Hungarian psyche. The overall mood in the renowned 18th- and 19th-century poems is one of *honfibú*, literally 'patriotic sorrow', which amounts to a penchant for the blues. You can read a sample in the bilingual anthology *The Lost Rider* by Corvina Books. The 2002 Nobel prize winner, Imre Kertész, writes about the Holocaust and its after-effects in the novels *Fatelessness* and *Kaddish for an Unborn Child*.

For an easy introduction to the nation's past, check out *An Illustrated History of Hungary* by István Lázár or László Kontler's *A History of Hungary*.

has also made a comeback onto the playlists of the young and trendy.

Favourite painters from the 19th century include realist Mihály Munkácsy (1844–1900), the so-called painter of the plains, and Tivadar Kosztka Csontváry (1853–1919). Győző Vásárhelyi (1908–97), who changed his name to Victor Vasarely when he emigrated to Paris, is considered the 'father of op art'. The traditional embroidery, weavings and ceramics of the nation's *népművészet* (folk art) also endure, and there is at least one handicraft store in every town.

For details of Hungarian literature, see the boxed text on above.

ENVIRONMENT

Hungary occupies the Carpathian Basin to the southwest of the Carpathian Mountains. The Danube River (Duna) divides the Great Plain (Nagyalföld) in the east from Transdanubia (Dunántúl) in the west. Hungary has hundreds of small lakes and is riddled with thermal springs. Its 'mountains' to the north are merely hills, with the country's highest peak being Kékes (1014m) in the Mátra Range.

Although there are some rare animals in Hungary (wild cats, lake bats and Pannonian lizards), around 75% of the country's 480 known vertebrates are birds, for the most part waterfowl attracted by the rivers, lakes and wetlands.

In the past decade there has been a marked improvement in awareness of environmental issues. Many inefficient coal-fired power plants have been shut down, and the government has introduced lead- and sulphur-free petrol.

To travel responsibly and cut down your carbon emissions, consider travelling to Hungary by train (p564) or bus (p564), rather than flying. Once in the country, it's easy to avoid the large, generic hotel chains and opt for smaller, family-run establishments, therefore ensuring your *forints* go directly to the local community.

TRANSPORT

GETTING THERE & AWAY

Air

The vast majority of international flights land at **Ferihegy Airport** (☎ 1-296 7000; www.bud.hu) on the outskirts of Budapest. **Balaton Airport** (☎ 83-354 256; www.flybalaton.hu) receives Ryanair flights from Düsseldorf, Frankfurt and London Stansted, and is located 15km southwest of Keszthely near Lake Balaton. Hungary's national carrier is **Malév Hungarian Airlines** (MA; ☎ 06 40 212121; www.malev.hu). Low-cost airlines flying to Hungary:

Air Berlin (☎ 06 800 17 110; www.airberlin.com)
EasyJet (www.easyjet.com)
Germanwings (☎ 1-526 7005; www.germanwings.com)
Ryanair (www.ryanair.com)
Wizz Air (☎ 06 90 181 181; www.wizzair.com)

Boat

International hydrofoil services traverse the Danube daily from April to early October between Budapest and Vienna (€89, 5½ to 6½ hours), stopping in Bratislava with advance notice (€79, four hours). Students with ISIC cards receive a €10 discount.

CONNECTIONS

Hungary's landlocked status ensures plenty of possibilities for onward travel overland. There are direct train connections from Budapest to major cities in all of Hungary's neighbours. International buses head in all directions, including localities across the border in Serbia and Romania. And in the warmer months, you can take a ferry along the Danube to reach Bratislava or Vienna.

Boats leave from the International Ferry Pier (Nemzetközi Hajóállomás), next to the **Mahart PassNave Ticket Office** (Map p570; ☎ 1-484 4013; www.mahartpassnave.hu; Belgrád rakpart).

Bus

Most international buses arrive at the Népliget Bus Station in southeast Budapest. **Eurolines** (www.eurolines.com), in conjunction with its Hungarian affiliate, **Volánbusz** (☎ 1-382 0888; www.volanbusz.hu), is the international carrier. Two of the closest destinations from Budapest are Vienna (5900Ft, 3½ hours, five daily) and Bratislava (Pozsony in Hungarian; 3700Ft, four hours, one daily).

Car & Motorcycle

Third-party car insurance is compulsory for driving in Hungary. If your car is registered in the EU, it's assumed you have it. Other motorists must show a Green Card or buy insurance at the border.

Train

The Hungarian State Railways, **MÁV** (☎ 1-371 9449; www.mav.hu), links up with international rail networks in all directions and its schedule is available online. Eurail passes are valid in Hungary, as are **Inter Rail** (www.interrailnet.com) Global Passes. EuroCity (EC) and Intercity (IC) trains require a seat reservation and payment of a supplement. Sample destinations from Budapest include Vienna (€26, three hours); Bratislava (€16, 2½ hours); Prague (€38, seven hours); and Bucharest (€82, 13 to 15 hours). Most of the larger train stations have left-luggage rooms open at least 9am to 5pm.

GETTING AROUND

Air

Hungary does not have any scheduled internal flights.

Bus

Volánbusz (☎ 1-382 0888; www.volanbusz.hu) might sometimes be the only option if you are travelling outside the capital. Timetables are posted at stations and stops. Common footnotes you might see are *naponta* (daily) and *munkanapokon* (on work days). A few large bus stations have luggage rooms, but they generally close by 6pm.

Car & Motorcycle

All the big international car-hire firms have offices in Budapest. In general, you must be at least 21 years old and have had your licence for at least a year to hire a car. Note that there's a 100% ban on alcohol when you are driving, and this rule is strictly enforced.

Hitching

In Hungary, hitchhiking is legal except on motorways. Hitchhiking is never an entirely safe way to travel and we don't recommend it, but if you're willing, **Kenguru** (Map p570; ☎ 1-266 5837; www.kenguru.hu; VIII Kőfaragó utca 15, Budapest; 🕑 10am-2pm Mon-Fri) is an agency that matches riders with drivers.

Local Transport

Public transport is efficient and extensive, with city bus and, in many towns, trolleybus services. Budapest and Szeged also have trams, and there's an extensive metro and a suburban commuter railway in Budapest. Purchase tickets at newsstands before travelling and validate them once aboard. Inspectors do check tickets, especially on the metro lines in Budapest.

Train

MÁV (☎ 06 40 494 949; www.mav.hu) operates reliable train services on its 8000km of track. Second-class domestic train fares range from 125Ft for a journey of less than 5km, to 3830Ft for a 300km trip. IC trains are the most comfortable and modern. *Gyorsvonat* (fast trains) take longer and use older cars; *személyvonat* (passenger trains) stop at every village along the way. Seat reservations *(helyjegy)* are required on IC and some fast trains, which is indicated on the timetable by an 'R' in a box or a circle.

BUDAPEST

☎ 1 / pop 1.7 million

There's no other Hungarian city like Budapest in terms of size and importance. However, it's the beauty of Budapest – both natural and artificial – that makes it stand apart. Straddling a gentle curve in the Danube, the city is flanked by the Buda Hills on the west bank and the beginnings of the Great Plain to the east. Architecturally, it's a gem, with enough baroque, neoclas-

HUNGARY

sical, eclectic and art nouveau elements to satisfy anyone.

In recent years, Budapest has taken on the role of the region's party town, with plenty of nightlife. Though you need not venture out for fun; the city's scores of hostels offer some of the best facilities and most convivial company in Europe.

ORIENTATION

Budapest was built around a curve in the Danube (Duna) River, with hilly residential Buda to the west, suburban Óbuda to the northwest and flat, commercial Pest across the river to the east. The most central square in Pest is Deák Ferenc tér, where the three metro lines meet. Buda is dominated by Castle Hill and Gellért Hill; its main square is Moszkva tér.

The city is divided into 23 districts; a Roman numeral before or after the street address indicates the district. The Castle Hill district in Buda is district I, and the central pedestrian area of Pest is district V.

INFORMATION

Discount Card

The **Budapest Card** (☎ 266 0479; www.budapestinfo.hu; 48/72hr card 6500/8000Ft) offers access to many museums, unlimited public transport and discounts on tours and other services. Buy it at hotels, travel agencies, large metro station kiosks and tourist offices.

Internet Access

Most year-round hostels offer internet access.

Electric Café (Map p570; VII Dohány utca 37; per hr 200Ft; 9am-midnight)

Plastic Web (Map p570 ; V Irány utca 1; per hr 390Ft; 9.30am-11.30pm)

Medical Services

FirstMed Centers (Map p566; ☎ 224 9090; I Hattyú utca 14, 5th fl; 8am-8pm Mon-Fri, 9am-2pm Sat) On call 24/7 for emergencies.

Money

ATMs are quite common, especially on the ring roads and large arteries. Most banks have both an ATM and an exchange service.

K&H Bank (Map p570; V Váci utca 40)

OTP Bank (Map p570; V Nádor utca 6)

EMERGENCY NUMBERS

- Central emergency number (English spoken) ☎ 112
- Ambulance ☎ 104
- Fire ☎ 105
- Police ☎ 107
- 24-hour car assistance ☎ 188

Tourist Office

Tourinform Main Office (Map p570; ☎ 438 8080; V Sütő utca 2; 8am-8pm); Liszt Ferenc tér (Map p570; ☎ 322 4098; VI Liszt Ferenc tér 11; 10am-6pm Mon-Fri); Castle Hill (Map p566; ☎ 488 0475; I Szentháromság tér; 9am-7pm May-Oct, 10am-6pm Nov-Apr)

Travel Agencies

Discover Budapest (Map p570; ☎ 269 3843; VI Lázár utca 16; 9.30am-6.30pm Mon-Fri, 10am-4pm Sat & Sun) Helpful advice, accommodation bookings, internet access, and cycling and walking tours.

Express (Map p570; ☎ 327 7298; www.express-travel.hu; VII Dohány utca 30/a & Kazinczy utca 3/b; 8.30am-5pm Mon-Fri, 9am-1pm Sat) This youth-orientated agency can book accommodation in Budapest, particularly in hostels and colleges, and sells transport tickets.

Ibusz (Map p570; ☎ 501 4910; www.ibusz.hu; V Ferenciek tere 10; 9am-6pm Mon-Fri, 9am-1pm Sat) The main branch of this national agency offers an exchange office, books accommodation and sells train tickets.

SIGHTS & ACTIVITIES

Buda

Most of what remains of medieval Budapest is on **Castle Hill** (Várhegy; Map p566), perched above the Danube. Start at Moszkva tér metro station and continue up Várfok utca, or board bus 16A to reach it. You can't miss the neo-Gothic **Matthias Church** (Mátyás Templom; Map p566; www.matyas-templom.hu; I Szentháromság tér 2; adult/concession 700/480Ft; 9am-5pm Mon-Sat, 1-5pm Sun), which has a colourful, tiled roof and lovely murals inside. Across the square is **Fishermen's Bastion** (Halászbástya; Map p566; I Szentháromság tér; adult/concession 330/160Ft; 8.30am-11pm), a neo-Gothic arcade built in 1905. To the southeast is the entrance to the **Funicular** (Sikló; Map p566; I Szent György tér; one-way/return 800/1400Ft; 7.30am-10pm, closed 1st & 3rd Mon of month) in Szent György tér, which can take you back down the hill to Clark Adam tér.

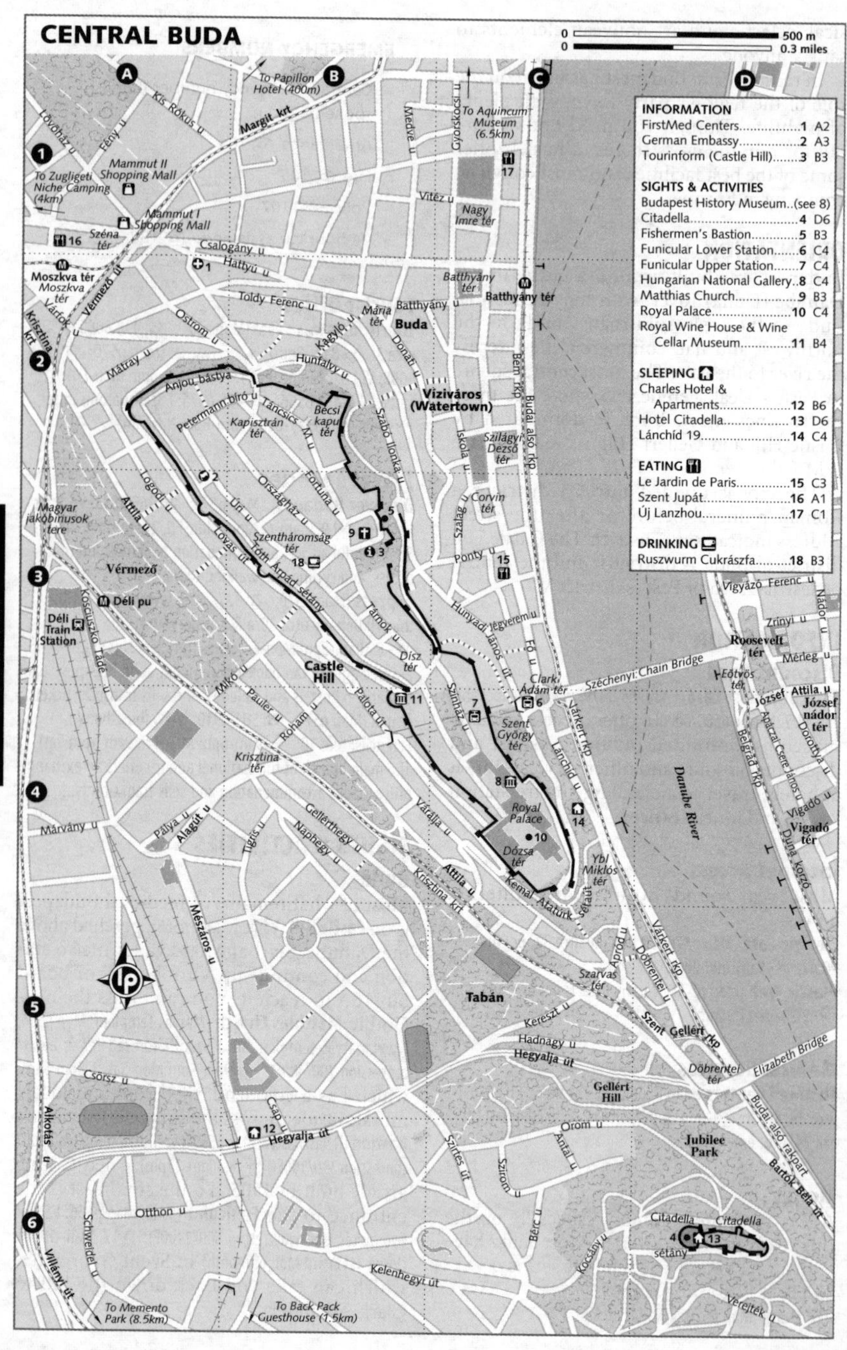
CENTRAL BUDA
0 500 m
0 0.3 miles
INFORMATION
FirstMed Centers....................1 A2
German Embassy....................2 A3
Tourinform (Castle Hill).......3 B3
SIGHTS & ACTIVITIES
Budapest History Museum..(see 8)
Citadella....................4 D6
Fishermen's Bastion....................5 B3
Funicular Lower Station.......6 C4
Funicular Upper Station.......7 C4
Hungarian National Gallery..8 C4
Matthias Church....................9 B3
Royal Palace....................10 C4
Royal Wine House & Wine Cellar Museum....................11 B4
SLEEPING
Charles Hotel & Apartments....................12 B6
Hotel Citadella....................13 D6
Lánchíd 19....................14 C4
EATING
Le Jardin de Paris....................15 C3
Szent Jupát....................16 A1
Új Lanzhou....................17 C1
DRINKING
Ruszwurm Cukrászfa..........18 B3
To Papillon Hotel (400m)
To Aquincum Museum (6.5km)
To Zugligeti Niche Camping (4km)
Mammut II Shopping Mall
Mammut I Shopping Mall
Moszkva tér
Batthyány tér
Buda
Víziváros (Watertown)
Vérmező
Déli pu
Déli Train Station
Castle Hill
Royal Palace
Dózsa tér
Széchenyi Chain Bridge
Danube River
Roosevelt tér
József nádor tér
Vigadó tér
Tabán
Gellért Hill
Elizabeth Bridge
Jubilee Park
Citadella
To Memento Park (8.5km)
To Back Pack Guesthouse (1.5km)

HUNGARY

The massive **Royal Palace** (Királyi Palota; Map p566) occupies the far end of Castle Hill; inside are the **Hungarian National Gallery** (Magyar Nemzeti Galéria; www.mng.hu; I Szent György tér 6; adult/concession 800/400Ft; 🕑 10am-6pm Tue-Sun) and the **Budapest History Museum** (Budapesti Történeti Múzeum; www.btm.hu; I Szent György tér 2; adult/concession 900/450Ft; 🕑 10am-6pm mid-Mar–mid-Sep, 10am-4pm Wed-Mon mid-Sep–mid-Mar).

Nearby is the **Royal Wine House & Wine Cellar Museum** (Borház és Pincemúzeum; Map p566; www.kiralyiborok.com; I Szent György tér, Nyugati sétány; adult/concession 900/500Ft; 🕑 noon-8pm), situated in former royal cellars dating back to the 13th century. Tastings cost 1350/1800/2700Ft for three/four/six wines.

The city's most famous thermal spa is the magnificent **Gellért Baths** (Gellért Fürdő; Map p570; ☎ 466 6166; Danubius Hotel Gellért, XI Kelenhegyi út; admission 3400Ft; 🕑 6am-7pm May-Sep, 6am-7pm Mon-Fri, 6am-5pm Sat & Sun Oct-Apr), south of Castle Hill. On Gellért Hill above the baths is the **Citadella** (Map p566; www.citadella.hu; admission free; 🕑 24hr), a fortress built by the Habsburgs after the 1848 revolt. Excellent views, exhibits, a restaurant and a hotel can be enjoyed here.

Many of the statues that once commemorated Soviet liberators, socialist ideals and communist leaders are now on display at **Memento Park** (off Map p566; www.mementopark.hu; XXII Balatoni út 16; adult/concession 1500/1000Ft; 🕑 10am-dusk) in far southwest Buda. Take tram No 19 from Clark Adam tér to the XI Etele tér terminus, then catch bus 150 to the park. Alternatively, a direct bus goes from Deák tér in Pest at 11am daily (adult/concession return 3950/2450Ft, including admission).

Aquincum Museum (Aquincumi Múzeum; www.aquincum.hu; III Szentendre út 139; adult/concession 900/450Ft; 🕑 10am-6pm May-Sep, 10am-5pm Tue-Sun Oct-Apr) contains the most complete 2nd-century Roman civilian town ruins left in Hungary. Catch the HÉV train out to Aquincum station.

BUDAPEST FOR FREE

Take advantage of these no-cost Budapest attractions:

- Stroll through the historic Castle Hill area (p565).
- Investigate the heroic monuments of Heroes' Sq (below).
- Take in the impressive views from the Citadella (left).
- Go people-watching in the attractive surrounds of City Park (below).
- Enjoy the bustle while browsing the Great Market (p571).

Pest

Start at **Heroes' Sq** (Hősök tere; off Map p570), above the metro station of the same name, to see the monument constructed to honour the 1000th anniversary (in 1896) of the Magyar conquest of the Carpathian Basin. The **Museum of Fine Arts** (Szépművészeti Múzeum; off Map p570; www.mfab.hu; XIV Dózsa György út 41; adult/concession 1200/600Ft; 🕑 10am-5.30pm Tue, Wed & Fri-Sun, 10am-10pm Thu), across the street, houses a collection of foreign art, including an impressive selection of El Grecos. To the north, in **City Park** (Városliget; off Map p570), is the 19th-century **Széchenyi Baths** (Széchenyi Fürdő; off Map p570; ☎ 363 3210; XIV Állatkerti út 11; admission 2600Ft; 🕑 6am-10pm), which has a dozen indoor and outdoor pools.

If you walk southwest from Heroes' Sq on Andrássy út, you'll pass many grand, World

GETTING INTO TOWN

The cheapest way to get into the city centre from Ferihegy Airport's Terminal 2 is to catch bus 200 (270Ft, or 350Ft on the bus), which terminates at the Kőbánya-Kispest metro station. From here, take the M3 metro line into the city centre. The total cost is 540Ft to 620Ft.

Bus 93 runs from Terminal 1 to Kőbánya-Kispest metro station for 270Ft (350Ft on the bus). Trains also link Terminal 1 with Nyugati station between 4am and 11pm, and cost 300Ft (or 520Ft if you board the hourly IC train).

However, the simplest way to get to town is to take the **Airport Minibus** (☎ 296 8555; www.airportshuttle.hu; one way/return 2990/4990Ft) directly to the place you're staying. An alternative is travelling with **Zóna Taxi** (☎ 365 5555), which has the monopoly on picking up taxi passengers from the airport. Fares to most central locations range from 5100Ft to 5700Ft.

If arriving in Budapest at a train or bus station, getting into the centre is simple. All stations are quite central, with connecting metro stations signposted, so it's easy to find your way.

Book your stay at lonelyplanet.com/hotels

Heritage-listed, 19th-century buildings on the way to **Terror House** (Terror Háza; Map p570; www.terrorhaza.hu; VI Andrássy út 60; adult/concession 1500/750Ft; 10am-6pm Tue-Fri, 10am-7.30pm Sat & Sun), a museum of spying and atrocities located in the former headquarters of the dreaded ÁVH secret police. The ornate, neo-Renaissance **Hungarian State Opera House** (Magyar Állami Operaház; Map p570; ☎ 332 8197; www.operavisit.hu; VI Andrássy út 22; tours adult/concession 2800/1400Ft; 3pm & 4pm), further along, was completed in 1884.

Váci utca (Map p570), in Pest's touristy centre, is an extensive pedestrian shopping street. It begins at the southwest terminus of the yellow line, Vörösmarty tér.

The huge, riverfront **Parliament** (Parlament; Map p570; ☎ 441 4904; www.parlament.hu; V Kossuth Lajos tér 1-3; adult/concession 2520/1260Ft; 8am-6pm Mon & Wed-Fri, 8am-4pm Sat, 8am-2pm Sun May-Sep, 8am-4pm Mon & Wed-Sat, 8am-2pm Sun Oct-Apr), apparently modelled on London's Westminster with the bonus of crazy spires, dominates Kossuth Lajos tér.

Northeast of the Astoria metro stop is what remains of the Jewish quarter. The twin-towered, 1859 **Great Synagogue** (Nagy Zsinagóga; Map p570; VII Dohány utca 2; synagogue & museum adult/concession 1600/750Ft; 10am-6.30pm Mon-Thu, 10am-2pm Fri, 10am-5.30pm Sun mid-Apr–Oct, 10am-3pm Mon-Thu, 10am-2pm Fri, 10am-4pm Sun Nov–mid-Apr) has a museum with a harrowing exhibit on the Holocaust. A few blocks south along the *kis körút* (little ring road) is the **Hungarian National Museum** (Magyar Nemzeti Múzeum; Map p570; www.hnm.hu; VIII Múzeum körút 14-16; adult/concession 1000/500Ft; 10am-6pm Tue-Sun), with historic relics from archaeological finds to coronation regalia.

HUNGARY

FESTIVALS & EVENTS

Spring Festival (www.springfestival.hu) Classical concerts and performances during March.

Sziget Music Festival (Óbudai hajógyár-sziget; www.sziget.hu) A week-long international sound-fest in late July or early August.

Hungarian Formula One Grand Prix (www.hungaroring.hu) Held at Mogyoród, 24km northeast of Budapest, in mid-August.

Budapest International Wine Festival (www.winefestival.hu) In September.

SLEEPING

Accommodation prices and standards are pretty reasonable in Budapest. Come summer (July to late August), basic student dormitories at colleges and universities open to all travellers. The Tourinform offices (p565) can help you locate them.

Private rooms in Budapest are plentiful. Costs range from 6000Ft to 7500Ft for a single, 7000Ft to 8500Ft for a double, and 9000Ft to 13,000Ft for a small apartment. Check the listing of travel agencies (p565) for places that can find you a room.

Buda

Zugligeti Niche Camping (off Map p566; ☎ 200 8346; www.campingniche.hu; XII Zugligeti út 101; camp sites per person/small tent/big tent/campervan 1800/1500/2000/3200Ft) An excellent option for mixing a city break with a hiking holiday: the camp's location is in the Buda Hills at the bottom station of a chairlift. Take bus 158 from Moszkva tér to the terminus.

our pick **Back Pack Guesthouse** (off Map p566; ☎ 385 8946; www.backpackbudapest.hu; XI Takács Menyhért utca 33; bed in yurt 2500Ft, large/small dm 3000/3500Ft, d 9000Ft;) A hippy-ish, friendly place, though relatively small, with a lush garden. Take bus 7 from Elizabeth Bridge (Erzsébet híd) or Keleti train station in Pest, tram 49 from the *kis körút* in central Pest, or tram 19 from Batthyány tér in Buda.

Hotel Citadella (Map p566; ☎ 466 5794; www.citadella.hu; XI Citadella sétány, Gellért Hill; dm 3200Ft, r from 10,500Ft) What could be better than sleeping in a historic old fortress? Well, OK, this hotel is pretty threadbare, though the dozen guestrooms are large and each has its own shower. Take bus 27 from XI Móricz Zsigmond körtér in Buda, then hike.

Martos Hostel (off Map p570; ☎ 209 4883; http://hotel.martos.bme.hu; XI Sztoczek utca 5-7; s/d/tr/q from 4000/6000/9000/12,000Ft, apt 15,000Ft;) Primarily student accommodation, Martos is open year-round to all. It's a few minutes' walk from Petőfi Bridge (or take tram 4 or 6).

SPLURGE

Lánchíd 19 (Map p566; ☎ 419 1900; www.lanchid19hotel.hu; I Lánchíd utca 19; s/d/ste from €120/140/300;) This new boutique number facing the Danube won the European Hotel Design Award for best architecture in 2008. Its facade features changing images derived from the movement of the Danube, and its rooms are equally impressive, containing distinctive artwork and unique chairs designed by art students.

Papillon Hotel (Map p566; ☎ 212 4750; www.hotelpapillon.hu; II Rózsahegy utca 3/b; s/d/tr/apt from €31/41/56/72;) This small 20-room hotel in Rózsadomb has a delightful back garden with a small swimming pool, and some rooms have balconies. There are also four apartments available in the same building.

Charles Hotel & Apartments (Map p566; ☎ 212 9169; www.charleshotel.hu; I Hegyalja út 23; d/tr/apt from €45/60/75;) Somewhat on the beaten track (a train line runs right past it), the Charles has inexpensive rooms with tiny kitchens and weary-looking furniture, as well as two-room apartments. Bike hire is available for 2000Ft per day.

Pest

Home-Made Hostel (Map p570; ☎ 302 2103; www.homemadehostel.com; VI Teréz körút 22; dm/d/q from €8/40/56;) This cosy, extremely welcoming hostel is decorated with recycled tables hanging upside down from the ceiling, and old valises serving as lockers.

Hostel Marco Polo (Map p570; ☎ 413 2555; www.marcopolohostel.com; VII Nyár utca 6; dm/s/d/tr/q from 3000/10,000/12,000/15,000/18,000;) Very central flagship hostel with swish, powder-blue rooms. There's a lovely courtyard.

Unity Hostel (Map p570; ☎ 413 7377; www.unityhostel.com; VI Király utca 60; dm/d from €12/36;) Located in the heart of party town, and has a roof terrace with breathtaking views of the Liszt Music Academy.

Gingko Hostel (Map p570; ☎ 266 6107; www.gingko.hu; V Szép utca 5; dm/d/q 3500/11,000/18,000Ft;) This very green hostel is one of the best kept in town, and so clean you could eat off its floor. There are books to share and bikes to hire (per day 2500Ft).

Red Bus Hostel (Map p570; ☎ 266 0136; www.redbusbudapest.hu; V Semmelweiss utca 14; dm/s/d/tr 3900/9900/9900/13,000Ft;) Central and well-managed place, with large and airy dorms as well as five private rooms. It's a quiet place with a fair number of rules – the full 16 are listed in reception – so don't expect to party here.

Central Backpack King Hostel (Map p570; ☎ 06 30 200 7184; centralbpk@freemail.hu; V Október 6 utca 15; dm/d/tr/q from €15/54/66/84;) This upbeat place has a small but scrupulously clean kitchen, and a large and very bright common room.

Boat Hotel Fortuna (off Map p570; ☎ 288 8100; www.fortunahajo.hu; XIII Szent István Park, Pesti alsó rakpart; s/d/tr from €20/30/40;) Sleeping on this one-time river ferry anchored in the Danube is a unique experience. The best choices on this 'boatel' are the air-conditioned rooms with shower and toilet at water level.

Garibaldi Guesthouse (Map p570; ☎ 302 3457; garibaldiguest@hotmail.com; V Garibaldi utca 5; s/d €28/36, apt per person €25-45) This old building belongs to a gregarious owner who has many apartments available over several floors, as well as private rooms.

Connection Guest House (Map p570; ☎ 267 7104; www.connectionguesthouse.com; VII Király utca 41; s/d from €45/50;) This central gay-friendly pension above a leafy courtyard attracts a young crowd due to its proximity to nightlife venues.

Hotel Medosz (Map p570; ☎ 3753 1700; www.medoszhotel.hu; VI Jókai tér 9; s/d/tr/ste from €49/59/69/89) Well priced for its central location, the Medosz is opposite the restaurants and bars of Liszt Ferenc tér. Its rooms are well worn, but slated for a revamp at the time of research.

Leo Panzió (Map p570; ☎ 266 9041; www.leopanzio.hu; V Kossuth Lajos utca 2/a; s/d from €49/76;) Just steps from Váci utca, this B&B with a lion motif is in the middle of everything. However, rooms have double-glazing and are quiet.

EATING

Ráday utca and Liszt Ferenc tér are the two most popular traffic-free streets. The moment the weather warms up, tables and umbrellas spring up outside the eateries along them.

To keep prices down, look for a *grill* (generally serving gyros and other grilled meats at self-service counters), an *étkezde* (literally 'eating place', where workers lunch; can be sit-down service), an *önkiszolgáló* (self-service canteen), a *kinai gyorsbüfé* (a Chinese 'fast' buffet), or a *szendvicsbar* (selling open-faced sandwiches to go).

Buda

Új Lanzhou (Mp p566; ☎ 201 9247; II Fő utca 71; mains 1190-3290Ft; noon-11pm) Many diners think this is the most authentic Chinese restaurant in Budapest. Make up your own mind while sampling the excellent soups, the relatively

SPLURGE

Bagolyvár (off Map p570; ☎ 468 3110; XIV Állatkerti út 2; mains 2850-4250Ft; noon-11pm) Serving imaginatively reworked Hungarian classics, the 'Owl's Castle' attracts the Budapest foodie cognoscenti. It's staffed entirely by women – in the kitchen, at table and front of house.

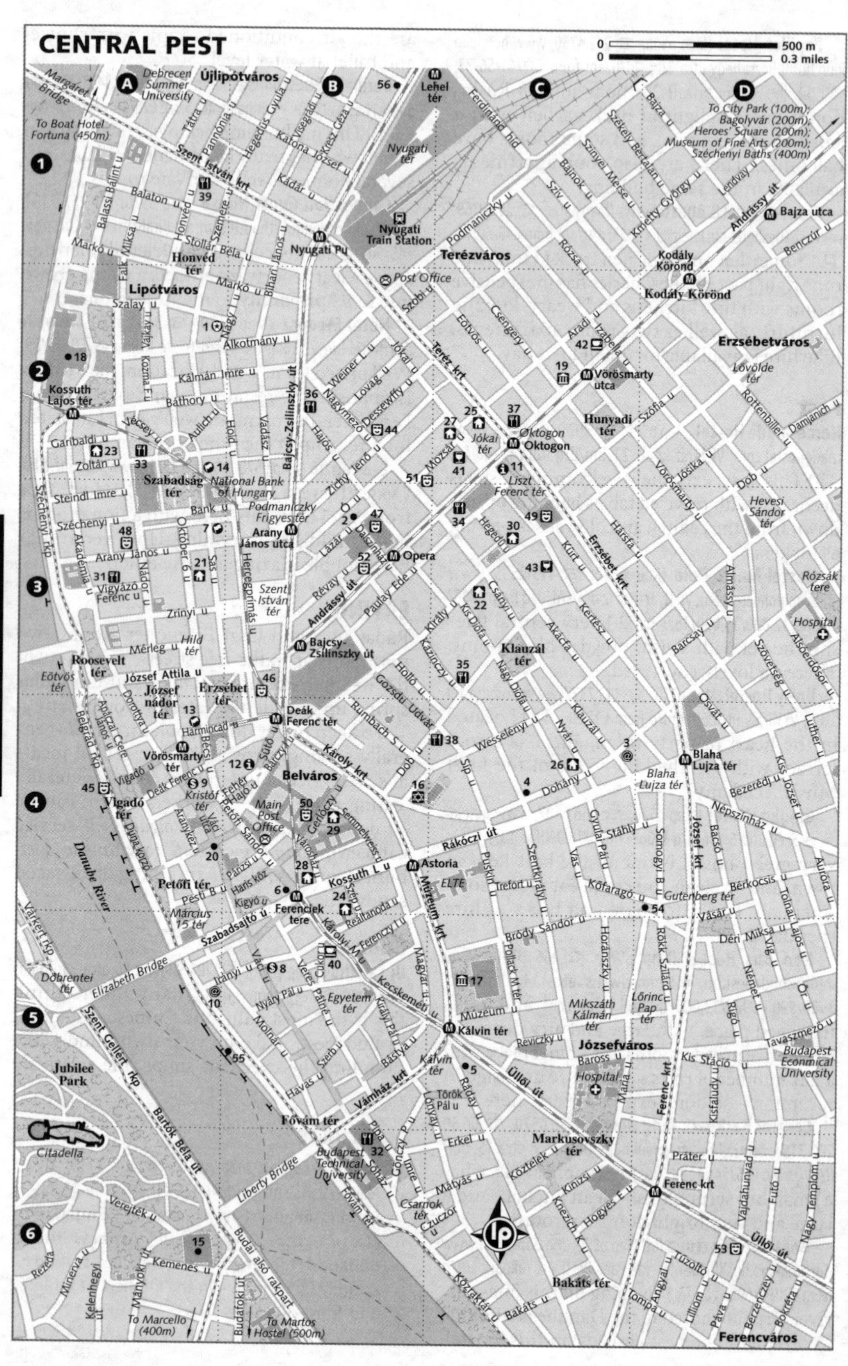
CENTRAL PEST
0 500 m
0 0.3 miles
To Boat Hotel Fortuna (450m)
To City Park (100m); Bagolyvár (200m); Heroes' Square (200m); Museum of Fine Arts (200m); Széchenyi Baths (400m)
Újlipótváros
Debrecen Summer University
Nyugati Train Station
Nyugati Pu
Terézváros
Post Office
Kodály Körönd
Lipótváros
Honvéd tér
Erzsébetváros
Kossuth Lajos tér
Szabadság tér
National Bank of Hungary
Oktogon
Liszt Ferenc tér
Podmaniczky Frigyes tér
Arany János utca
Opera
Szent István tér
Bajcsy-Zsilinszky út
Klauzál tér
Roosevelt tér
József nádor tér
Erzsébet tér
Deák Ferenc tér
Vörösmarty tér
Belváros
Vigadó tér
Main Post Office
Blaha Lujza tér
Astoria
Petőfi tér
Ferenciek tere
Március 15 tér
Danube River
Elizabeth Bridge
Döbrentei tér
Egyetem tér
Kálvin tér
Józsefváros
Hospital
Budapest Econmical University
Jubilee Park
Citadella
Fővám tér
Budapest Technical University
Liberty Bridge
Markusovszky tér
Ferenc krt
Bakáts tér
Ferencváros
To Marcello (400m)
To Martos Hostel (500m)

INFORMATION
Belváros-Lipótváros Police Station....1 A2
Discover Budapest....2 B3
Electric Café....3 C4
Express....4 C4
Hungarian Equestrian Tourism Association....5 C5
Ibusz....6 B4
Irish Embassy....7 A3
K&H Bank....8 B5
OTP Bank....9 A4
Plastic Web....10 A5
Tourinform (Liszt Ferenc tér)....11 C2
Tourinform (Main Office)....12 B4
UK Embassy....13 A4
US Embassy....14 A2

SIGHTS & ACTIVITIES
Gellért Baths....15 A6
Great Synagogue....16 B4
Hungarian National Museum....17 C5
Parliament....18 A2
Terror House....19 C2
Váci utca....20 A4

SLEEPING
Central Backpack King Hostel....21 A3
Connection Guest House....22 C3
Garibaldi Guesthouse....23 A2
Gingko Hostel....24 B4
Home-Made Hostel....25 C2
Hostel Marco Polo....26 C4
Hotel Medosz....27 C2
Leo Panzió....28 B4
Red Bus Hostel....29 B4
Unity Hostel....30 C3

EATING
Govinda....31 A3
Great Market....32 B6
Iguana....33 A2
Klassz....34 C3
Köleves....35 C3
Marquis de Salade....36 B2
Rothschild Supermarket....37 C2
Spinoza....38 C4
Szeráj....39 A1

DRINKING
Centrál Kávéház....40 B5
Kiadó Kocsma....41 C2
Lukács....42 C2
Szimpla....43 C3

ENTERTAINMENT
Alter Ego....44 B2
Columbus Jazzklub....45 A4
Gödör Klub....46 B3
Hungarian State Opera House....47 B3
Kalamajka Táncház....48 A3
Liszt Academy of Music....49 C3
Merlin....50 B4
Symphony Ticket Office....51 B2
Ticket Express....52 B3
Trafó Bar Tango....53 D6

TRANSPORT
Kenguru....54 D4
Mahart PassNave Ticket Office....55 B5
MÁV Start Passenger Service Centre....56 B1

large choice of vegetarian dishes, and the stylish surrounds.

Szent Jupát (Map p566; ☎ 212 2923; II Dékán utca 3; mains 1490-3380Ft; noon-2am Sun-Thu, noon-4am Fri & Sat) This is the classic late-night choice for solid Hungarian fare. It's just north of Moszkva tér and opposite the Fény utca market – enter from II Retek utca 16.

Marcello (off Map p570; ☎ 466 6231; XI Bartók Béla út 40; mains 2000Ft; noon-10pm Mon-Sat) Popular with students from the nearby university, this family-owned eatery has good Italian food at affordable prices.

Le Jardin de Paris (Map p566; ☎ 201 0047; II Fő utca 20; mains 2200-4700Ft; noon-midnight) A regular haunt of staff from the French Institute across the road, the Parisian Garden is located in a wonderful old townhouse with a delightful back garden. Set lunch is 1500Ft.

Pest

Govinda (Map p570; ☎ 269 1625; V Vigyázó Ferenc utca 4; mains 230-490Ft; 11.30am-8pm Mon-Fri, noon-9pm Sat) This vegetarian restaurant northeast of the Chain Bridge serves wholesome salads, soups and desserts.

Szeráj (Map p570; ☎ 311 6690; XIII Szent István körút 13; mains 450-1400Ft, 9am-4am Mon-Thu, 9am-5am Fri & Sat, 9am-2am Sun) A very inexpensive self-service Turkish place dishing up *lahmacun* (Turkish pizza), felafel and kebabs.

Köleves (Map p570; ☎ 322 1011; Kazinczy utca 35 & Dob utca 26; mains 1280-3680Ft; noon-midnight) Always buzzing, 'Stone Soup' attracts a young crowd with its delicious matzo-ball soup, tapas, lively decor and reasonable prices.

Iguana (Map p570; ☎ 331 4352; V Zoltán utca 16; mains 1390-3990Ft; 11.30am-12.30am) Decent-enough Mexican, but it's hard to say whether the pull is the *fajitas* or the frenetic party atmosphere.

our pick **Klassz** (Map p570; ☎ 413 1545; www.klassz.eu; VI Andrássy út 41; mains 1490-3490Ft; 11.30am-11pm Mon-Sat, 11.30am-6pm Sun) Klassz is focused on wine, but the food is also of a high standard. Varieties of *foie gras* and native *mangalica* pork are permanent stars on the menu.

Spinoza (Map p570; ☎ 413 7488; VII Dob utca 15; mains 1690-2490Ft) Attractive cafe-restaurant in the Jewish district, which hosts an art gallery and theatre that holds concerts and other live events. The cuisine is mostly Hungarian/Jewish nonkosher comfort food.

Marquis de Salade (Map p570; ☎ 302 4086; VI Hajós utca 43; mains 2400-3400Ft; noon-midnight) This basement restaurant is a strange hybrid of a place, with dishes from Russia and Azerbaijan as well as Hungary. There are lots of quality vegetarian choices on the menu.

Stock up on picnic supplies at the **Great Market** (Nagycsarnok; Map p570; IX Vámház körút 1-3; 6am-5pm Mon, 6am-6pm Tue-Fri, 6am-2pm Sat), Budapest's biggest market. A nonstop supermarket in Pest is **Rothschild Supermarket** (Map p570; VI Teréz körút 19; 24hr), near Oktogon.

DRINKING & CLUBBING

Budapest has a nightlife that can keep you up for days on end – and not just because the techno beat from the club next to your hotel is keeping you awake. There are plenty of lively nightclubs, pubs and summer *kerteks* (outdoor entertainment zones). However, the most pleasant place to imbibe might be in a *kávéház* (coffee house).

Bars & Cafes

Szimpla (Map p570; VII Kertész utca 48; 10am-2am Mon-Fri, noon-2am Sat, noon-midnight Sun) This distressed-looking, very down-to-earth place remains one of the city's most popular drinking venues. There's live music in the evenings from Tuesday to Thursday.

Kiadó Kocsma (Map p570; VI Jókai tér 3; 10am-2am Mon-Fri, noon-2am Sat & Sun) The 'Pub for Rent' is a great place for a swift pint, and is just a stone's throw from Liszt Ferenc tér.

Centrál Káveház (Map p570; V Károlyi Mihály utca 9; 8am-midnight) One of the finest coffee houses in the city, with high, decorated ceilings, lace curtains, pot plants, elegant coffee cups and professional service.

Lukács (Map p570; VI Andrássy út 70; 8.30am-8pm Mon-Fri, 9am-8pm Sat, 9.30am-8pm Sun) Station yourself where Hungary's dreaded ÁVH secret police once had its HQ.

On the Buda side of the river, drop into popular student pub **Kisrabló** (XI Zenta utca 3; 11am-2am Mon-Sat) by taking tram 19 or 49 one stop past Danubius Hotel Gellért; or enjoy coffee and cake at **Ruszwurm** (Map p566; I Szentháromság utca 7; 10am-7pm) on Castle Hill.

Nightclubs

Popular clubs include **Merlin** (Map p570; www.merlinbudapest.org; V Gerlóczy utca 4; 10am-midnight Sun-Thu, 10am-5am Fri & Sat), with everything from jazz and breakbeat to techno and house; **Gödör Klub** (Map p570; V Erzsébet tér; 9am-late), offering a mix of folk, world, rock and pop; the arty **Trafó Bár Tangó** (Map p570; IX Lilliom utca 41; 6pm-4am); and gay venue **Alter Ego** (Map p570; www.alteregoclub.hu; VI Dessewffy utca 33; 10pm-5am Fri & Sat).

To experience jazz and the Danube River simultaneously, head to **Columbus Jazzklub** (Map p570; ☎ 266 9013; www.majazz.hu; V Pesti alsó rakpart at Lánchíd bridgehead; 4pm-midnight), moored just off the northern end of V Vigadó tér. Music starts at 8pm nightly.

And for something completely different, **Cinetrip** (www.cinetrip.hu) is an amazing club night hosted inside the city's thermal spas. Check the website for upcoming locations.

ENTERTAINMENT

Tickets for concerts, performances and operas are quite reasonably priced. Tourinform (p565) can help you find out what's playing, as can the free *Budapest Funzine*, available at tourist spots. The free weekly *Pesti Est* (available at restaurants and clubs) lists live-music acts and guest DJs for clubs, and *Pesti Műsor* lists everything from clubs and films to art exhibits and classical music.

Hungarian State Opera House (Magyar Állami Operaház; Map p570; ☎ 331 2550; www.opera.hu; VI Andrássy út 22) Take in a performance while admiring the incredibly rich interior decoration. The ballet company performs here as well.

Liszt Academy of Music (Liszt Ferenc Zeneakadémia; Map p570; ☎ 342 0179; VI Liszt Ferenc tér 8) This magnificent venue hosts classical music concerts.

Kalamajka Táncház (Map p570; ☎ 354 3400; V Arany János utca 10; 8.30pm-midnight Sat) An excellent place to hear authentic Hungarian music, and dance to it!

A useful ticket broker, with outlets across town, is **Ticket Express** (Map p570; ☎ 312 0000; www.tex.hu; VI Andrássy út 18; 10am-6.30pm Mon-Fri, 10am-3pm Sat), while **Symphony Ticket Office** (Szimfonikus Jegyiroda; Map p570; ☎ 302 3841; VI Nagymező utca 19; 10am-6pm Mon-Fri, 10am-2pm Sat) specialises in classical music events.

GETTING THERE & AWAY

Air

There is no domestic air service in Hungary. See p563 for international flights.

Boat

In addition to its hydrofoils that travel internationally to Bratislava and Vienna (p563), **Mahart PassNave** (Map p570; ☎ 484 4005; www.mahartpassnave.hu; Vigadó tér Pier) ferries depart at least daily for Szentendre (one-way/return 1490/2235Ft, 1½ hours) from April to October, going on to Visegrád (one-way/return 1590/2385Ft, 3½ hours) in May and September.

Visegrád (one-way/return 2690/3990Ft; one hour) and Esztergom (one-way/return 3290/4990Ft, 1½ hours) can be reached by fast hydrofoil at weekends in May and September (and also on Friday from June to August).

There are also slower, cheaper daily ferries from Budapest to Visegrád (one-way/return 1590/2385Ft, 3½ hours), and Esztergom (one-

HUNGARY

way/return 1990/2985Ft, 5½ hours) between June and August. Services run on Friday and weekends in May, and weekends only in September.

When day tripping to these towns by ferry, remember to check the return departure time when you arrive at your destination. Most sail to Budapest between 4.30pm and 6.45pm.

Bus

Volánbusz (☎ 382 0888; www.volanbusz.hu) is the national bus line. All international buses and some buses to/from southern Hungary arrive at and depart from **Népliget bus station** (IX Üllői út 131). **Stadionok bus station** (XIV Hungária körút 48-52) generally serves places to the east of Budapest. Most buses to the northern Danube Bend arrive at and leave from the **Árpád híd bus station** (off XIII Róbert Károly körút). All three stations are on metro lines, and are in Pest. If the ticket office is closed, you can buy your ticket on the bus.

Car & Motorcycle

Most big international car-hire chains have branches at the airports. A standard daily rate is €60 per day with unlimited kilometres. Petrol costs about 245Ft per litre.

Train

The **MÁV-Start passenger service centre** (Map p570; ☎ 512 7921; www.mav-start.hu; V József Attila utca 16) provides information and sells domestic and international train tickets and seat reservations. You can also buy tickets at the stations.

Keleti train station (VIII Kerepesi út 2-4) handles international trains from Vienna and most other points east, plus domestic trains to/from the north and northeast. For some Romanian destinations, as well as domestic ones to/from the northwest and the Danube Bend, head for **Nyugati Train Station** (Map p570; VI Nyugati tér). For trains bound for Lake Balaton and the south, go to **Déli Train Station** (Map p566; I Krisztina körút 37). All three train stations are on metro lines.

GETTING AROUND

Public transport

Public transport is run by **BKV** (☎ 461 6500; www.bkv.hu). The three underground metro lines – M1 yellow, M2 red and M3 blue – meet at Deák tér in Pest. The HÉV above-ground suburban railway runs north from Batthyány tér in Buda. There's also an extensive network of buses, trams and trolleybuses. Public transport runs from 4.30am until 11.30pm. There are also 35 night buses that run along main roads. A single ticket for all forms of transport is 270Ft (60 minutes of uninterrupted travel, no metro line changes). The three-day *turista* ticket (3400Ft) makes things easier as it allows unlimited travel inside the city. Keep your ticket handy; the fine for 'riding black' is 6000Ft.

Taxis

Overcharging is common. Never get into a taxi that does not have a yellow licence plate, the logo of a taxi firm and a posted table of fares.

AROUND BUDAPEST

North of Budapest, the Danube breaks through the Pilis and Börzsöny Hills in a sharp bend before continuing along the Slovak border. The Roman Empire had its northern boundary here, and medieval kings ruled Hungary from majestic palaces overlooking the river at Esztergom and Visegrád. Today the area lures many day trippers from Budapest.

SZENTENDRE

☎ 26 / pop 24,000

Once an artists' colony, now a popular one-day trip from Budapest, pretty little Szentendre (*sen*-ten-dreh) has narrow, winding streets, and is a favourite with souvenir shoppers. It can be packed at weekends.

The **Tourinform** (☎ 317 965; szentendre@tourinform.hu; Dumtsa Jenő utca 22; 🕑 9.30am-4.30pm Mon-Fri year-round, also 10am-2pm Sat & Sun mid-Mar–Oct) has information about the many small museums and galleries in Szentendre. Outside the town is the enormous **Open-Air Ethnographic Museum** (Szabadtéri Néprajzi Múzeum; www.skanzen.hu; Sztaravodai út; adult/concession 1000/500Ft; 🕑 9am-5pm Tue-Sun late Mar-Oct). Walking through reassembled homes and villages from around the country in this *skansen* (village museum), you can see what life was – and sometimes still is – like in rural Hungary. Take the Skansen bus from stand 7 (20 minutes) at the bus station.

To get to Szentendre, take the commuter HÉV from Buda's Batthyány tér metro station to the end of the line (370Ft, 45 minutes, every 10 to 15 minutes). For ferry services from Budapest, see opposite.

VISEGRÁD

☎ 26 / pop 1700

The spectacular vista from the ruins of Visegrád's (*vish*-eh-grahd) 13th-century citadel, high on a hill above a curve in the Danube, is what pulls the visitors to this sleepy town. After the 13th-century Mongol invasions, Hungarian kings built the mighty **Visegrád Citadel** (Visegrád Cittadella; adult/concession 1400/700Ft; 9.30am-5.30pm mid-Mar–mid-Oct, 9.30am-5.30pm Sat & Sun mid-Oct–mid-Mar) high on the hilltop. It's a bit of a climb, but the views are well worth it. The **Royal Palace** (Királyi Palota; Fő utca 29; adult/concession 1000/500Ft; 9am-5pm Tue-Sun) stands on the flood plain at the foot of the hills.

Buses arrive from Budapest's Árpád híd bus station (525Ft, 1¼ hours, at least hourly), the Szentendre HÉV station (375Ft, 45 minutes, every 45 minutes) and Esztergom (375Ft, 45 minutes, hourly). For ferry services from Budapest, see p572.

ESZTERGOM

☎ 33 / pop 28,900

It's easy to see the attraction of Esztergom, even from a distance. The city's massive basilica, sitting high above the town and Danube River, is an incredible sight, rising magnificently from its rural setting.

The 2nd-century Roman-emperor-to-be Marcus Aurelius wrote his famous *Meditations* while he camped here. Stephen I, founder of the Hungarian state, was born here and crowned at the cathedral, and Esztergom was the royal seat from the late-10th to the mid-13th centuries.

Gran Tours (☎ 502 001; Rákóczi tér 25; 8am-5pm Mon-Fri, 9am-noon Sat Jun-Aug, 8am-4pm Mon-Fri Sep-May) is the best source of information in town. Hungary's largest church is the **Esztergom Basilica** (Esztergomi Bazilika; www.bazilika-esztergom.hu; Szent István tér 1; 6am-6pm). At the southern end of the hill is the extensive **Castle Museum** (Vár Múzeum; adult/concession 800/400Ft; 10am-6pm Tue-Sun Apr-Oct, 10am-4pm Tue-Sun Nov-Mar), with archaeological remnants from the 2nd and 3rd centuries.

Buses run to/from Budapest's Árpád híd Bus Station (675Ft, 1½ hours) and to/from Visegrád (375Ft, 45 minutes) at least hourly. Trains to Esztergom depart from Budapest's Nyugati Train Station (900Ft, 1½ hours, at least hourly). For ferry services from Budapest, see p572.

WESTERN HUNGARY

A visit to this region is a boon for anyone wishing to see remnants of Hungary's Roman legacy, medieval heritage and baroque splendour. Prominent here is vast Lake Balaton (600 sq km), Hungary's inland 'seaside', offering swimming, sailing, sunbathing and fishing during the warmer months.

SOPRON

☎ 99 / pop 56,400

Sopron (*shop*-ron) is one of Hungary's most beautiful towns, with a Gothic centre enclosed by medieval walls and filled with narrow streets and mysterious passages. The Mongols and Turks never got this far, so many medieval structures remain intact.

From the main train station, walk north on Mátyás király utca, which becomes Várkerület, part of a loop following the line of the former city walls. **Tourinform** (main branch ☎ 517 560; sopron@tourinform.hu; Liszt Ferenc utca 1; 9am-6pm mid-Jun–Aug, 9am-5pm Mon-Fri, 9am-noon Sat Sep–mid-Jun; southern branch ☎ 505 438; Deák tér 45; 9am-5pm Mon-Fri, 9am-noon Sat Apr-Oct) offers free internet access and plenty of tourist information.

The 60m-high **Fire Tower** (Tûztorony; Fő tér; adult/concession 700/350Ft; 10am-8pm May-Aug, 10am-6pm Tue-Sun Apr, Sep & Oct) rises above the old town's northern gate. You can climb the 154 steps for views as far as the Alps. There are several museums, monuments and churches worth checking out around Fő tér.

Outside Sopron, in Fertőd, is one of the country's most impressive palaces, the 126-room, Versailles-like, baroque **Esterházy Palace** (Esterházy Kasthély; Joseph Haydn utca 2; Palace Museum tour adult/concession 1500/750Ft, Great Palace tour 2500/2000Ft; 10am-6pm Tue-Sun mid-Mar–Oct, 10am-4pm Fri-Sun Nov–mid-Mar). It's easily accessible by bus (450Ft, 40 minutes, hourly).

Sleeping & Eating

Vákació Vendégház (☎ 338 502; www.vakacio-vendeghazak.hu; Ady Endre út 31; dm 2800Ft) Cheap and cheerful lodgings west of the town centre; bus 10 will drop you off right outside the door.

Jégverem Pension (☎ 510 113; www.jegverem.hu; Jégverem utca 1; s/d 6900/8900Ft) This is an excellent and central bet, located in an 18th-century ice cellar. The restaurant comes highly recommended.

You can eat while revisiting the Wild West at **Papa Joe's Saloon & Steak House** (☎ 340 933; Várkerület 108; mains 2000Ft; 11am-midnight Sun-Wed, 11am-2am Thu-Sat). A good old-fashioned cafe is the colourful **Zwinger** (Várkerület 92; 8am-7pm). For self-catering supplies, head for the **Match supermarket** (Várkerület 100; 6.30am-7pm Mon-Fri, 6.30am-3pm Sat).

For entertainment, check out upcoming events at the **Ferenc Liszt Conference & Cultural Centre** (Liszt Ferenc Kulturális Központ; ☎ 517 517; Liszt Ferenc tér), a concert hall, cafe and exhibition space rolled into one.

Getting There & Away

There are two buses a day to Budapest (3010Ft, 3¾ hours). Trains run to Budapest's Keleti train station (3390Ft, 2¾ hours, eight daily) and Vienna's Südbahnhof station (3750Ft, 1¼ hours, up to 15 daily).

KESZTHELY

☎ 83 / pop 21,800

At the very western end of Lake Balaton sits Keszthely (*kest*-hay). Its amazing Festetics Palace and popular public beach are reasons enough to make a trip here worth it. The town lies about 1km northwest of the lake, and stays open year-round. Summer activity centres on paid-admission beaches, waterfront parks, beer gardens and cafes near the ferry pier. **Tourinform** (☎ 314 144; keszthely@tourinform.hu; Kossuth Lajos utca 28; 9am-8pm Mon-Fri, 9am-6pm Sat mid-Jun–mid-Sep, 9am-5pm Mon-Fri, 9am-12.30pm Sat mid-Sep–mid-Jun) offers excellent information on the whole Balaton area.

At the northern end of pedestrian Kossuth Lajos utca is the glimmering, white, 1745 **Festetics Palace** (Festetics Kastély; Kastély utca 1; adult/concession 1650/800Ft; 9am-6pm Jul & Aug, 10am-4pm Sep-Jun). Part of the former residence has been turned into a museum.

A short walk north of the palace is the new **Ambient Hostel** (☎ 06 30 460 3536; hostel-accommodation.fw.hu; Sopron utca 10; dm/d from 2900/6800Ft;) with basic, cheap dorms. The big, simple rooms, with shared kitchens, at **Párizsi Udvar** (☎ 311 202; parizsiudvar@freemail.hu; Kastély utca 5; d/tr/apt 9400/11,400/15,000Ft) used to be part of the Festetics Kastély complex.

Grab healthy vegetarian choices in the pleasant **Vegetárius** (☎ 311 023; Rákóczi tér 3; mains 800-1000Ft; 11am-4pm Mon-Fri), down the hill from the palace; or enjoy the good fish selection, grill/roast specialities and leafy back garden of **Lakoma** (☎ 313 129; Balaton utca 9; mains 1000-2600Ft).

At the southern end of the main square, **Pelso Café** (Fő tér; 9am-9pm) does decent coffee, cake and cocktails. Shop for groceries while admiring the beautiful stained-glass windows of **CBA supermarket** (Kossuth Lajos utca 35) on the main street.

Balaton Airport (☎ 354 256; www.flybalaton.hu), 15km southwest of Keszthely at Sármellék, receives Ryanair flights from Düsseldorf, Frankfurt and London Stansted. There's no public transport between the airport and Keszthely, but transfers can be arranged with **FlyBalaton Airport Transfer** (☎ 554 055; www.balatonairporttransfer.com; one-way/return €6/10).

Buses run to Budapest (2780Ft, three hours, seven daily), while trains head to Budapest's Déli train station (2780Ft, four hours, six daily). Ferries link Keszthely with other towns on the lake from April to September.

SIÓFOK

☎ 84 / pop 23,900

Siófok is officially known as 'Hungary's summer capital' – unofficially it's called 'Hungary's Ibiza'. In July and August, nowhere in the country parties as hard or stays up as late as this lakeside resort, which attracts an ever-increasing number of international DJs and their avid followers.

The bus and train stations are in Millennium Park just off Fő utca, the main drag. **Tourinform** (☎ 310 117; tourinform@siofokportal.hu; Szabadság tér; 8am-7pm Mon-Fri, 10am-7pm Sat & Sun mid-Jun–mid-Sep, 8am-4pm Mon-Fri, 9am-noon Sat mid-Sep–mid-Jun) is located in the old wooden **Water Tower** (Szabadság tér; adult/concession 200/100Ft; 8am-7pm Mon-Fri, 10am-7pm Sat & Sun mid-Jun–mid-Sep, 8am-4pm Mon-Fri, 9am-noon Sat mid-Sep–mid-Jun). Climb it for views of the town and lake.

Nagy Strand (adult/concession 750/500Ft), Siófok's 'Big Beach', is centre stage on Petőfi sétány; there are often free concerts here on summer evenings. There are many more managed swimming areas along the lakeshore that cost around the same as Nagy Strand.

There are rowing boats and sailing **boats** for hire at various locations along the lake, and regular **lake cruises**.

Sleeping & Eating

Prices quoted here are for the high season in July and August. Tourinform can help find you a private room (€12 to €20 per person), or an apartment for slightly more.

 Book your stay at lonelyplanet.com/hotels

Siófok Város College (☎ 312 244; www.siofokvaroskollegiuma.sulinet.hu; Petőfi sétány 1; dm 2530Ft) Situated close to the action in central Siófok, it's hard to beat this basic college accommodation for price.

Hotel Yacht Club (☎ 311 161; www.hotel-yachtclub.hu; Vitorlás utca 14; s/d €58/92;) Overlooking the harbour is this excellent little hotel, with cosy rooms and a new wellness centre. Bicycles can be hired.

Roxy (☎ 506 573; Szabadság tér; mains 990-3000Ft) This pseudo-rustic restaurant-pub serves a wide range of international cuisine and surprisingly imaginative Hungarian mains.

Drinking & Entertainment

The turnover rate of bars and clubs is high, but the following manage to attract punters year after year:

Flőrt (www.flort.hu; Sió utca 4) Well-established club with trippy light shows.

Palace (www.palace.hu; Deák Ferencutca 2) Hugely popular club. Accessible by free bus from outside Tourinform between 9pm and 5am daily from May to mid-September.

Renegade (Petőfi sétány 9) Wild pub near the beach where table dancing and live music are commonplace.

Getting There & Away

From April to October, four daily ferries run between Siófok and other lake towns. There are also eight daily train connections to/from Budapest (1770Ft, two hours).

HUNGARY

SOUTHERN HUNGARY

South Hungary is a region of calm with a hint of the Mediterranean, a place to savour life at a slower pace. It's only marginally touched by tourism, and touring through the countryside is like travelling back in time.

PÉCS

☎ 72 / pop 156,000

Blessed with a mild climate, an illustrious past and a number of fine museums and monuments, Pécs (pronounced *paich*) is one of Hungary's most pleasant and interesting cities to visit.

From the train station, 1km south of the old town centre, walk up Jókai Mór utca to the central Széchenyi tér. **Tourinform** (☎ 213 315; baranya-m@tourinform.hu; Széchenyi tér 9; 8am-6pm Mon-Fri, 10am-8pm Sat & Sun Jun-Aug, 8am-5.30pm Mon-Fri, 10am-2pm Sat May, Sep & Oct, 8am-4pm Mon-Fri Nov-Apr) has internet access (per hour 100Ft) and tons of local info, including a list of museums. The **main post office** (Jókai Mór utca 10) is in a beautiful art nouveau building (1904) with a colourful Zsolnay porcelain roof.

Sights

The curiously named **Mosque Church** (Mecset Templom; Széchenyi tér; 10am-4pm Mon-Sat, 11.30am-4pm Sun mid-Apr–mid-Oct, 10am-noon Mon-Sat, 11.30am-2pm Sun mid-Oct–mid-Apr), which dominates the city's central square, is a striking old mosque-turned-church without a minaret. The city's beautifully preserved 19th-century **synagogue** (zsinagóga; Kossuth tér; adult/concession 500/300Ft; 10am-noon & 12.45-5pm Sun-Fri May-Oct), with its peach-coloured walls, is on the southern side of town. To the north, climb Szepessy Ignéc utca and turn west on Káptalan utca, a street lined with museums. Famous ceramics can be seen at the **Zsolnay Porcelain Museum** (Zsolnay Porcélan Múzeum; Káptalan utca 2; adult/concession 700/350Ft; 10am-5pm Tue-Sun).

Continue west to Dóm tér and the walled bishopric complex containing the four-towered **Saint Peter Basilica** (Szent Péter Bazilika; Dóm tér; adult/concession 800/500Ft; 9am-5pm Mon-Sat, 1-5pm Sun Apr-Oct; 10am-4pm Mon-Sat, 1-4pm Sun Nov-Mar). The oldest part of the building is the 11th-century crypt. The 1770 **Bishop's Palace** (Püspöki Palota; adult/concession 1500/700Ft; tours 2pm, 3pm & 4pm Thu late Jun–mid-Sep) stands in front of the cathedral. Nearby is a 15th-century **barbican**, the only stone bastion to survive from the old city walls.

Other attractions in town include the dreamy paintings at the **Csontváry Museum** (Csontváry Múzeum; Janus Pannonius utca 11; adult/concession 700/350Ft; 10am-6pm Tue-Sun Apr-Oct, 10am-4pm Tue-Sun Nov-Mar), which displays works by Tivadar Kosztka Csontváry (1853–1919), Hungary's answer to Van Gogh. The 16th-century **Hassan Jakovali Mosque** (Hassan Jakovali mecset; adult/concession 500/250Ft; 9.30am-5.30pm Wed-Sun late Mar-Oct) holds a small museum of Ottoman history.

Sleeping & Eating

Ibusz (☎ 211 011; www.ibusz.hu; Király utca 11; 8am-5pm Mon-Fri, 8am-noon Sat) arranges private rooms from 3500Ft per person.

Nap Hostel (☎ 950 684; www.naphostel.com; Király utca 23-25, enter from Szent Mór utca; dm/d from 2400/9600Ft;) A welcome addition to Pécs's budget accommodation scene, this place is situated on the 1st floor of a former bank.

Hotel Főnix (☎ 311 682; www.fonixhotel.hu; Hunyadi János út 2; s/d 7790/12,590Ft;) Odd angles and sloping eaves characterise the asymmetrical Hotel Főnix. Rooms on the top floor have skylights.

Ábrahám Kishotel (☎ 510 422; www.abrahamhotel.hu; Munkácsy Mihály utca 8; s/d/tr 9100/12,000/14,000Ft;) Excellent little guest house with a friendly welcome. It's owned by a religious establishment, so head elsewhere if you're looking for a party.

Hotel Diana (☎ 328 594; www.hoteldiana.hu; Tímár utca 4/a; s/d/tr/q from 9500/13,000/18,300/20,000Ft;) This very central pension offers spotless rooms, comfortable kick-off-your-shoes decor and a warm welcome.

Minaret (☎ 311 338; Ferencesek utcája 35; mains 1200-2100Ft; noon-4pm Sun & Mon, noon-9pm Tue-Thu, noon-11pm Fri & Sat) Boasting one of the loveliest gardens in the city, this eatery serves tasty Hungarian favourites.

our pick **Áfium** (☎ 511 434; Irgalmasok utca 2; mains 1400-1900Ft; 11am-1am) With Croatia and Serbia so close, it's a wonder that more restaurants don't offer cuisine from south of the border. Don't miss the bean soup with trotters.

The outrageously popular tavern **Korhely** (Boltív köz 2; 11am-midnight) has peanuts on the table, shells on the floor, a half dozen beers on tap and a sort of 'retro socialist meets Latin American' decor. For caffeine with views, visit **Coffein Café** (Széchenyi tér 9; 8am-midnight Mon-Thu, 8am-2am Fri & Sat, 10am-10pm Sun). Get self-catering supplies at **Interspar supermarket** (Bajcsy-Zsilinszky utca 11; 7am-9pm Mon-Thu & Sat, 7am-10pm Fri, 8am-7pm Sun) in the basement of the Árkád shopping centre.

Bóbit Puppet Theatre (Bóbita Bábszínház; ☎ 210 301; www.bobita.hu; Mária utca 18) is a cool puppet theatre, while the **Cyrano Lounge** (Czindery utca 6; 8pm-5am Fri & Sat) nightclub is popular with the in-crowd.

Getting There & Away

At least five buses a day travel between Pécs and Budapest (3010Ft, 4½ hours), three head to Siófok (2040Ft, three hours) and eight reach Szeged (3010Ft, 4½ hours). Pécs is on a main rail line to Budapest's Déli train station (3230Ft, 3½ hours, nine daily). Three daily trains run from Pécs to Osijek (two hours) in Croatia, with one continuing to the Bosnian capital, Sarajevo (nine hours).

GREAT PLAIN

Like the Outback for Australians or the Old West for Americans, the Great Plain (Nagy Alföld) holds a romantic appeal for Hungarians. Images of cowboys riding across the *puszta* (prairie) are scattered throughout the nation's poetry and painting. Beyond its 'big sky' appeal, the region is also home to cities of graceful architecture, winding rivers and easy-going afternoons.

KECSKEMÉT

☎ 76 / pop 103,000

Kecskemét is a green, pedestrian-friendly city, about halfway between Budapest and Szeged. It's famous for potent *barackpálinka* (apricot brandy), *libamaj* (goose liver), fine architecture and nearby horse farms, as well as a national park.

Tourinform (☎ 481 065; kecskemet@tourinform.hu; Kossuth tér 1; 8am-7pm Mon-Fri, 10am-8pm Sat & Sun Jul & Aug, 8am-6pm Mon-Fri Sep-Jun) is on the west side of the terracotta-coloured town hall, bang in the middle of the central square. It has a list of colleges offering accommodation and provides information on day trips to the horse show in **Kiskunság National Park** (Kiskunság Nemzeti Park; www.knp.hu) at Bugac, 30km southwest of Kecskémet.

Walk around the adjacent parklike squares, Kossuth tér and Szabadsag tér, and admire the eclectic building styles, including Technicolor art nouveau at the **Ornamental Palace** (Cifrapalota; Rákóczi út 1). Check out the folk theme at the **Hungarian Naive Art Museum** (Magyar Naive Müvészek; Gáspár András utca 11; adult/concession 200/100Ft; 10am-5pm Tue-Sun mid-Mar–Oct), southwest of Cifrapalota.

Take bus 1 to get to **Autós Camping** (☎ 329 398; Csabay Géza körút 5; camp sites per person/tent 800/700Ft, bungalows 5000-8000Ft; May-Sep) southwest of town, packed with simple tents and bungalows. **Teachers' College** (Tanítóképzö Kollégium; ☎ 486 977; loveikollegium@tfk.kefo.hu; Piaristák tere 4; s/d 2500/5000Ft; mid-Jun–Aug) is a good central choice among the academic accommodation options. For a place that feels better than home – flowery courtyard, homemade sweets with breakfast – choose **Fábián Pension** (☎ 477 677; www.panziofabian.hu; Kápolna utca 14; s/d from 8800/11,000Ft;).

Grab a quick self-service bite at **Aranyhomok Gyorsétterem** (☎ 503 730; Kossuth tér 3; mains 300-600Ft; 24hr), or an excellent Hungarian meal at **Liberté Étterem** (☎ 509 175; Szabadság tér 2; mains

HUNGARY

1200-2000Ft). Have a drink at the Western-themed pub **Wanted Söröző** (Csányi János körút 4; ⌚ 10am-midnight Mon-Sat, from 4pm Sun), and dance at **Bling Bling Nights** (www.blingblingnights.hu; Korona tér 2), a nightclub atop Malom Shopping Centre.

Hourly buses connect Kecskemét with Budapest's Népliget (1350Ft, 1½ hours) and with Szeged (1350Ft, 1¾ hours). Trains head to Budapest's Nyugati train station (1770Ft, 1½ hours, hourly) and Szeged (1350Ft, one hour, hourly).

SZEGED

☎ 62 / pop 177,000

It's hard to decide what's most appealing about Szeged (*seh*-ged): its shady green main square, the abundant sidewalk cafe seating in its pedestrian zone, or its stimulating architecture.

The train station is south of town via tram 1; the bus station is to the west within easy walking distance. Pedestrian Kárász utca is lined with cafes and stores, leading northwest to the parklike square, Széchenyi tér. **Tourinform** (☎ 488 699; http://tip.szegedvaros.hu; Dugonics tér 2; ⌚ 9am-5pm Mon-Fri, 9am-1pm Sat) is tucked away in a quiet courtyard off the southwest end of Kárász. East, along the Tisza River, is the huge, neoclassical **Ferenc Móra Museum** (Móra Ferenc Múzeum; www.mfm.u-szeged.hu; Roosevelt tér 1; adult/concession 600/300Ft; ⌚ 10am-5pm Tue-Sun). There are exhibits on the Avar people (5th to 8th centuries) and archaeological finds, as well as displays on folk life and art.

Especially worth visiting are the 1778 **Serbian Orthodox Church** (Szerb Ortodox Templom; adult/concession 200/150Ft; ⌚ 8am-4pm) for its fantastic gold iconostasis, and the **New Synagogue** (Új Zsinagóga; www.zsinagoga.szeged.hu; Gutenberg utca 13; adult/concession 300/150Ft; ⌚ 10am-noon & 1-5pm Sun-Fri Apr-Sep, 10am-2pm Sun-Fri Oct-Mar) for its ornate, painted interior.

Just north of the Old Town ring road is the **Pick Salami & Szeged Paprika Museum** (Pick Szalámi és Szegedi Paprika Múzeum; Felső Tisza-part 10; adult/concession 350/250Ft; ⌚ 3-6pm Mon, 9am-5pm Tue-Fri, 9am-noon Sat). Two floors of exhibits and old photos show traditional methods of salami production, and you can buy some to take away.

Partfürdő Camping (☎ 430 843; Közép-kikötő sor; camp sites per person/tent 990/350Ft, r 4600-6900Ft, bungalows 8,000-12,000Ft; ⌚ mid-May–Sep;) is a green, grassy camping ground across the river in New Szeged, with bungalows sleeping up to four people. The comfortable **Illes Panzió** (☎ 315 641; www.illespanzio-vadaszetterem.hu; Maros utca 37; r 9900-12,900Ft;) is north of the centre, not far from the Tisza River. **Chili Grill** (☎ 317 344; Nagy Jenő utca 4; mains 600-1000Ft; ⌚ 11am-10pm Mon-Fri, 11am-6pm Sat) is a great place for cheap eats such as turkey, bean and chilli wraps, while **Port Royal Étterem** (☎ 547 988; Stefánia 4; mains 1300-2200Ft) is a colourful tropical-themed place turning out tasty traditional dishes, international faves and veggie options.

There's a vast array of bars, clubs and other nightspots, especially around Dugonics tér. Cafe-bar **Virág** (Klauzál tér 1; ⌚ 8am-10pm) is a good place to linger over coffee or something harder, while **Sing Sing** (Mars tér C pavilion; ⌚ 11pm-5am Wed, Fri & Sat) stages huge warehouse rave parties.

Buses run to Budapest (2780Ft, 4¼ hours) seven times a day, and you can also catch daily buses to Arad in Romania, and Novi Sad and Subotica in Serbia. Szeged is on the main rail line to Budapest's Nyugati train station (2780Ft, 2¾ hours, hourly), stopping halfway along in Kecskemét (1770Ft, 1¼ hours, hourly).

NORTHEASTERN HUNGARY

If ever a Hungarian wine were world-famous, it would be tokay. And this is where it comes from, a region containing microclimates conducive to wine production. The chain of wooded hills in the northeast constitutes the foothills of the Carpathian Mountains, which stretch along the Hungarian border with Slovakia.

EGER

☎ 36 / pop 58,300

Filled with wonderfully preserved baroque architecture, Eger (*egg*-air) is a jewel box of a town containing gems aplenty, including wine-tasting opportunities. Eger Bull's Blood (Egri Bikavér) is a famous full-bodied red wine produced in the surrounding hills; it took its name from the wine-stained beards of the town's successful defenders against a Turkish attack in 1552. The friendly staff at **Tourinform** (☎ 517 715; eger@tourinform.hu; Bajcsy-Zsilinszky utca 9; ⌚ 9am-5pm Mon-Fri, 9am-1pm Sat & Sun mid-Jun–mid-Sep, 9am-5pm Mon-Fri, 9am-1pm Sat mid-Sep–mid-Jun) can supply all the information you need.

HUNGARY

Eger Castle (Egri Vár; www.egrivar.hu; Vár 1; adult/concession 1200/600Ft; 9am-5pm Tue-Sun Apr-Oct, 10am-4pm Tue-Sun Nov-Mar), up the hill off Dósza tér, was erected in the 13th century after a Mongol invasion. Inside the walled complex are several museums. A surprise awaits you east of the castle hill: a 40m-high **minaret** (Knézich Károly utca; admission 200Ft; 10am-6pm Apr-Oct), minus the mosque, is allegedly Europe's northernmost reminder of the Ottoman invasion of the 16th century. If you suffer from claustrophobia, don't climb the 97 narrow spiral steps to the top.

Step into the covered **market** (piac; Katona István tér; 6am-6pm Mon-Fri, 6am-1pm Sat, 6-10am Sun) to buy fruit, vegetables, meat and bread. A great place for pancakes and drinks is **Palatscintavár** (☎ 413 986; Dobó István utca 9; mains 1400-1600Ft), with a lovely bar.

A 15-minute walk southwest of the town centre, **Valley of the Beautiful Women** (Szépasszony völgy; off Király utca; 10am-5pm) is home to dozens of small wine cellars that produce Bull's Blood and other regional wines. Stop at any cellar door that strikes your fancy and ask to taste their wares (100Ft per decilitre). Bring an empty bottle and it will be filled up for about 350Ft per litre.

Tourinform can help you locate student accommodation in the summer. **Retur Panzió** (☎ 416 650; www.returvendeghaz.hu; Knézich Károly utca 18; s/d 4000/6000Ft) is an excellent central pension with a cheery shared kitchen/eating area and a huge garden.

Buses head from Eger to Kecskemét (2060Ft, 4½ hours, three daily) and Szeged (3220Ft, 5¾ hours, two daily). Trains run between Eger and Budapest's Keleti train station (2290Ft, 2½ hours) up to seven times a day.

HUNGARY DIRECTORY

ACCOMMODATION

Camping

Hungary has more than 400 camping grounds, listed in Tourinform's *Camping Hungary* map/brochure (www.camping.hu).

Hostels & Student Dormitories

From July to August the cheapest rooms are in vacant student accommodation. Local Tourinform offices can help you locate these. The **Hungarian Youth Hostels Association** (MISZSZ; www.miszsz.hu) keeps a list of year-round hostels throughout Hungary. Having a HI card may get you a 10% discount.

WORTH THE TRIP: TOKAJ

Another worthwhile wine destination is the smaller village of Tokaj, 43km northeast of Eger, which has long been celebrated for its sweet dessert wines. **Tourinform** (☎ 552 070; www.tokaj.hu; Serház utca 1; 9am-6pm Mon-Fri, 10am-7pm Sat & Sun Jun-Aug, 9am-5pm Mon-Fri Sep-May) is just off Rákóczi út, and can help with accommodation. Up to 16 trains a day link Tokaj directly to Budapest's Keleti (3750Ft; 2½ hours).

Pensions & Hotels

Quaint, often family run, *panziók* (pensions) are abundant and usually less expensive than hotels. Some hotels *(szállók* or *szállodák)* have less expensive room options, if you're willing to share the bathroom down the hall.

Private Rooms

Stick to travel agencies and avoid individuals at train stations in Budapest offering private rooms. Outside Budapest, you can look for houses with signs that read *'szoba kiadó'* or the German *'Zimmer frei'*; expect to pay between 3000Ft and 6000Ft per person per night.

ACTIVITIES

For locations of public thermal baths, ask Tourinform for the *Spa & Wellness* booklet. A booklet on equestrian tourism is also available, or you could contact the **Hungarian Equestrian Tourism Association** (Map p570; MLTSZ; ☎ 1-456 0444; www.equi.hu; IX Ráday utca 8, Budapest).

Hungary's flat terrain makes it ideal for cycling. **Velo-Touring** (☎ 1-319 0571; www.velo-touring.hu) has a great selection of seven-night trips in all regions. For canoeists, **Ecotours** (☎ 1-361-0438; www.ecotours.hu) leads seven-day Danube River canoe-camping trips.

BUSINESS HOURS

Opening hours are posted on front doors. *Nyitva* means 'open' and *zárva* means 'closed'. The majority of grocery stores are open from 7am to 6pm Monday to Friday, and to 1pm on Saturday. Most towns have a 'nonstop' convenience store, and many have hyper-supermarkets that are open 24 hours. Main post offices open 8am to 6pm weekdays, to noon Saturday. Bank hours are generally from 8am to 4pm weekdays.

EMBASSIES & CONSULATES

Embassies in Budapest include the following:

Australia (☎ 01-457 9777; XII Királyhágó tér 8-9)
Canada (☎ 01-392 3360; II Ganz utca 12-14)
France (☎ 01-374 1100; VI Lendvay utca 27)
Germany (Map p566; ☎ 01-488 3505; I Úri utca 64-66)
Ireland (Map p570; ☎ 01-301 4960; V Szabadság tér 7-9)
Netherlands (☎ 01-336 6300; II Füge utca 5-7)
South Africa (☎ 01-392 0999; II Gárdonyi Géza út 17)
UK (Map p570; ☎ 01-266 2888; V Harmincad utca 6)
US (Map p570; ☎ 01-475 4164; V Szabadság tér 12)

FESTIVALS & EVENTS

For Budapest events, see p568.
Balaton Festival Based in Keszthely, in May.
Sopron Festival Weeks (www.prokultura.hu) Late June to mid-July.
Szeged Open-Air Festival (www.szegediszabadteri.hu) July to August.

FOOD & DRINK

The omnipresent seasoning in traditional Hungarian cooking is paprika. *Pörkölt,* a paprika-infused stew, can be made from different meats, including *borju* (veal), but usually has no vegetables. *Galuska* (gnocchi-like dumplings) are the usual accompaniment. *Halászlé* (fisherman's soup) is a rich mix of several kinds of poached freshwater fish, tomatoes, green peppers and (you guessed it) paprika. Although served as a stew outside the country, inside Hungary *gulyás* (goulash) is a beef soup prepared with a paprika roux.

For dessert try the cold *gyümölcs leves* (fruit soup) or *palincsinta* (crêpes) with jam, sweet cheese or chocolate sauce. A good food-stand snack is *lángos,* fried dough that can be topped with cheese and/or *tejföl* (sour cream).

Two Hungarian wines are known internationally: the sweet, dessert wine Tokaji Aszú (see boxed text, p579) and the full-bodied red, Egri Bikavér (Eger Bull's Blood, see p578). For the harder stuff, try *pálinka,* a strong, firewaterlike brandy most commonly made out of plums or apricots.

INTERNET RESOURCES

Hungarian National Tourism Organisation (www.hungary.com)
Inside Hungary (www.insidehungary.com)
Lonely Planet (www.lonelyplanet.com) Includes travellers trading the latest information on the Thorn Tree message boards.

HOLIDAYS

New Year's Day 1 January
1848 Revolution Day 15 March
Easter Monday March/April
International Labour Day 1 May
Whit Monday May/June
St Stephen's Day 20 August
1956 Remembrance Day 23 October
All Saints' Day 1 November
Christmas Holidays 25-26 December

MONEY

The Hungarian forint (Ft) comes in coins of five, 10, 20, 50 and 100Ft, and notes of 200, 500, 1000, 2000, 5000, 10,000 and 20,000Ft. Some businesses quote prices in euros. Hungarians routinely tip waiters, hairdressers and taxi drivers.

POST

A *légiposta* (airmail) postcard within Hungary costs 70Ft, within Europe 150Ft, and to the rest of the world 170Ft.

TELEPHONE

Hungary's country code is ☎ 36. To make an outgoing international call, dial ☎ 00 first. To dial city-to-city (and all mobile phones) within the country, first dial ☎ 06, then the city code.

If you have a GSM mobile phone, consider buying a rechargeable SIM card from a local provider. Otherwise, the best place to make international calls is from a phone box with a phone card, which you can buy at newsstands in a variety of denominations.

VISAS

EU citizens do not need visas to visit Hungary and can stay indefinitely. Citizens of the USA, Canada, Israel, Japan, New Zealand and Australia do not require visas to visit Hungary as part of a stay of up to 90 days within the Schengen zone (p1230) of European nations.

South Africans do still require a visa. Check with the **Ministry for Foreign Affairs** (www.mfa.gov.hu) for an up-to-date list of which country nationals require visas.

Visas are issued at Hungarian consulates or missions, most international highway border crossings, Ferihegy airport and the International Ferry Pier in Budapest. However, visas are never issued on trains and rarely on buses.

Iceland

HIGHLIGHTS

- **Reykjavík runtur** Party till dawn on the city's Friday-night pub crawl (p590).
- **Blue Lagoon** Swim through steam clouds at Iceland's world-famous spa (p591).
- **Whale-watching** Come face-to-face with placid ocean giants (p585).
- **Vikings** Explore the world of those hairy Norsemen at Reykjavík's excellent museums (p585).

FAST FACTS

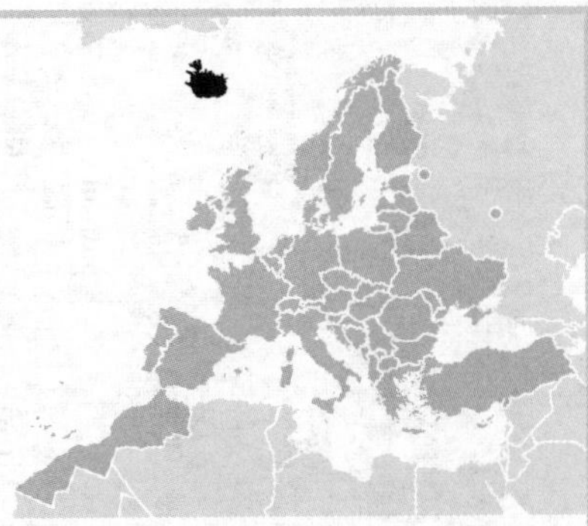

- **Area** 103,000 sq km (89 Icelands would fit into mainland USA)
- **Budget** Minimum Ikr9000 per day
- **Capital** Reykjavík
- **Country code** ☎ 354
- **Famous for** Björk, Blue Lagoon, Sigur Rós
- **Language** Icelandic
- **Money** Icelandic króna (Ikr); A$1 = Ikr94; C$1 = Ikr107; €1 = Ikr170; ¥100 = Ikr133; NZ$1 = Ikr74; UK£1 = Ikr192; US$1 = Ikr126
- **Phrases** *halló* (hello), *takk fyrir* (thanks), *skál!* (cheers!)
- **Population** 313,000
- **Visas** not required for visitors from Scandinavia, EU countries, the USA and the Commonwealth for stays of up to 90 days. See p593.

TRAVEL HINTS

Take a sleeping bag for discounted accommodation. Buy beer from Vín Búð (state alcohol shop) and start Friday night at home.

ROAMING ICELAND

Go wild on Reykjavík's Friday-night *runtur* (pub crawl), then sober up with a soak in the unearthly Blue Lagoon.

A land of troll-inhabited mountains and black-sand beaches, where calling seabirds are more common than a human voice – it sounds like a fairytale, but Iceland is only a hop away from the rest of Europe. Icelandic nature is exceptional: you'll never forget coming eye-to-eye with whales on a boat trip, or horse-trekking under the midnight sun. It's also a vast volcanic laboratory, where mighty forces make the land do loopy things. Admire thundering waterfalls, glittering-white glaciers, geysers, volcanoes and spouting mud pools; and bathe in the Blue Lagoon, the world's biggest hotpot, in the middle of a lava field. In winter, eerie Northern Lights streak the sky with flickering colours.

The same earth-shaking energy animates the inhabitants of Iceland's only city. Fuelled by coffee, sex and beer, Reykjavík's fashion-conscious crowds party like mad on the city's high-spirited weekend pub-crawl *(runtur)*. Music bursts from every seam – especially during the Iceland Airwaves festival in October.

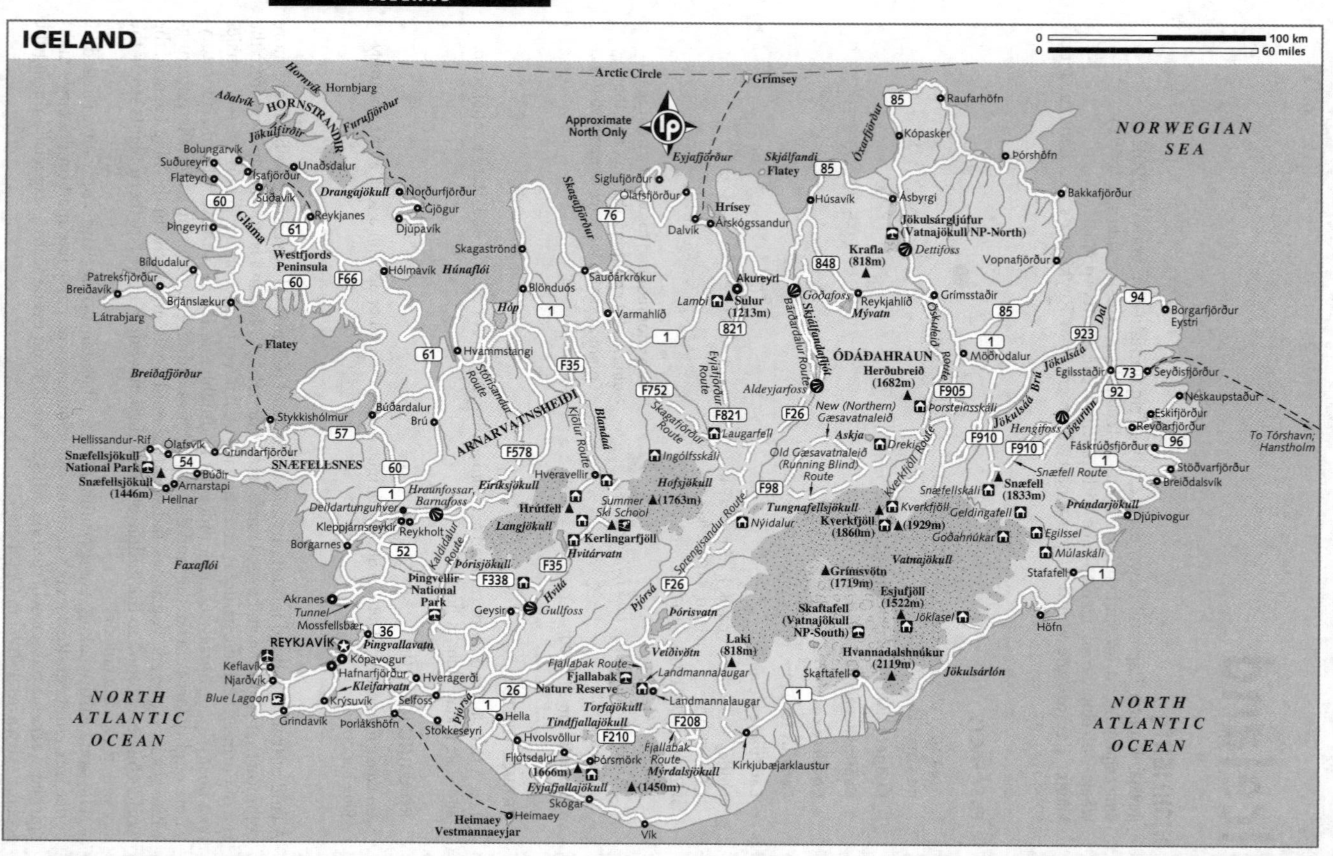
ICELAND
0 100 km
0 60 miles
Arctic Circle
Grímsey
Approximate North Only
NORWEGIAN SEA
NORTH ATLANTIC OCEAN
NORTH ATLANTIC OCEAN
To Tórshavn; Hanstholm
Hornvík
Hornbjarg
Aðalvík
HORNSTRANDIR
Furufjörður
Jökulfirðir
Bolungarvík
Suðureyri
Ísafjörður
Unaðsdalur
Flateyri
Súðavík
Drangajökull
Norðurfjörður
Gjögur
Reykjanes
Djúpavík
Gláma
Þingeyri
Westfjords Peninsula
Bíldudalur
Patreksfjörður
Breiðavík
Brjánslækur
Látrabjarg
Hólmavík
Húnaflói
Flatey
Breiðafjörður
Skagaströnd
Blönduós
Hóp
Hvammstangi
Stórisandur Route
Skagafjörður
Sauðárkrókur
Varmahlíð
Siglufjörður
Ólafsfjörður
Eyjafjörður
Dalvík
Hrísey
Árskógssandur
Akureyri
Lambi
Súlur (1213m)
Eyjafjörður Route
Goðafoss
Reykjahlíð
Mývatn
Skjálfandafljót
Bárðardalur Route
Aldeyjarfoss
Skjálfandi
Flatey
Húsavík
Öxarfjörður
Kópasker
Raufarhöfn
Þórshöfn
Bakkafjörður
Ásbyrgi
Jökulsárgljúfur (Vatnajökull NP-North)
Krafla (818m)
Dettifoss
Vopnafjörður
Grímsstaðir
Öskuleið Route
Möðrudalur
ÓDÁÐAHRAUN
Herðubreið (1682m)
Þorsteinsskáli
New (Northern) Gæsavatnaleið
Askja
Dreki
Kverkfjöll Route
Old Gæsavatnaleið (Running Blind) Route
Borgarfjörður Eystri
Dal
Jökulsá á Brú
Egilsstaðir
Seyðisfjörður
Neskaupstaður
Eskifjörður
Reyðarfjörður
Hengifoss
Lögurinn
Fáskrúðsfjörður
Stöðvarfjörður
Breiðdalsvík
Snæfell Route
Snæfellsskáli
Snæfell (1833m)
Þrándarjökull
Djúpivogur
Kverkfjöll
Tungnafellsjökull
Kverkfjöll (1860m)
(1929m)
Geldingafell
Goðahnúkar
Egilssel
Múlaskáli
Vatnajökull
Grímsvötn (1719m)
Esjufjöll (1522m)
Stafafell
Höfn
Jöklasel
Skaftafell (Vatnajökull NP-South)
Hvannadalshnúkur (2119m)
Jökulsárlón
Skaftafell
Laki (818m)
Kirkjubæjarklaustur
Nýidalur
Sprengisandur Route
Þjórsá
Þórisvatn
Veiðivötn
Fjallabak Route
Landmannalaugar
Fjallabak Nature Reserve
Landmannalaugar
Torfajökull
Tindfjallajökull
Fjallabak Route
Mýrdalsjökull
(1450m)
Þórsmörk
(1666m)
Eyjafjallajökull
Fljótsdalur
Hvolsvöllur
Hella
Skógar
Vík
Heimaey
Heimaey Vestmannaeyjar
Stokkseyri
Þorlákshöfn
Selfoss
Hveragerði
Kleifarvatn
Krýsuvík
Grindavík
Blue Lagoon
Njarðvík
Keflavík
Hafnarfjörður
Kópavogur
REYKJAVÍK
Þingvallavatn
Mossfellsbær
Tunnel
Akranes
Faxaflói
Borgarnes
Kleppjárnsreykir
Reykholt
Deildartunguhver
Hraunfossar, Barnafoss
Kaldidalur Route
Þórisjökull
Þingvellir National Park
Geysir
Gullfoss
Hvítá
Langjökull
Hrútfell
Kerlingarfjöll
Hvítárvatn
Summer Ski School
Hofsjökull
(1763m)
Ingólfsskáli
Skagafjörður Route
Laugafell
Hveravellir
Kjölur Route
Blandaá
Eiríksjökull
ARNARVATNSHEIÐI
Búðardalur
Brú
Stykkishólmur
Hellissandur-Rif
Ólafsvík
Grundarfjörður
SNÆFELLSNES
Snæfellsjökull National Park
Snæfellsjökull (1446m)
Búðir
Arnarstapi
Hellnar

HISTORY

Iceland's solitude was shattered by the Age of Settlement (AD 871–930), when a wave of Vikings crashed in from Norway. The settlers rejected monarchy in favour of the world's first democratic parliament, the Alþing, established in 930 at Þingvellir (Parliament Plains; see p592).

In the early 13th century, violent blood feuds among Icelandic chieftains led to periods of first Norwegian (1262) then Danish (1397) rule. For the next six centuries, Iceland was devastated by a Dark Age of famine, disease and disastrous volcanic eruptions.

Despite never-ending catastrophes, a sense of nationalism slowly grew. By 1874 Iceland had drafted its own constitution. The Republic of Iceland was established on 17 June 1944.

During WWII Iceland serviced British and US troops stationed at Keflavík. The war marked a dramatic leap forward, as subsistence farming gave way to frenzied building and prosperity.

Iceland may have prospered, but its apparent wealth was based on high borrowing, and the 2008 global financial crisis hit it especially hard. The króna lost half its value overnight, and the country was only saved from bankruptcy by a US$2.1 billion IMF loan.

Following four months of furious protests in Reykjavík, the government resigned at the end of January 2009. Jóhanna Sigurðardóttir was voted in as Iceland's first female prime minister in the April 2009 elections.

THE CULTURE

Most Icelanders are descended from early Scandinavian settlers and their Celtic slaves. Almost half of Iceland's 313,000 inhabitants live in Reykjavík. Icelanders are individualists, with a live-and-let-live attitude. Despite a love of extreme partying, Icelanders have one of the world's highest life expectancies – 79.4 years for men and 82.9 for women! Eight-four percent of the population is Lutheran.

ARTS

Bloody and powerful, Iceland's 13th-century sagas are its greatest cultural achievement – try *Egils Saga,* about a poet, murderer and grandson of a werewolf. *Independent People,* a blackly humorous novel about early-20th-century Iceland, won its author Halldór Laxness the Nobel Prize.

Björk and Sigur Rós are Iceland's most famous musical exports. New bands surface all the time: listen out for Leaves, FM Belfast, Seabear and Celestine. The music documentary *Screaming Masterpiece* (2005) is a fun introduction to Icelandic music.

ENVIRONMENT

Iceland is a young country with an active volcanic zone running southwest to northeast, responsible for all those lava flows, geysers, hot springs and volcanoes.

The only indigenous land mammal is the Arctic fox. Iceland compensates for this shortage with huge numbers of birds and 17 species of whale.

Whaling is an emotional topic. In 2006, Iceland resumed commercial whale-hunting: 25 nations issued a formal protest. Many restaurants serve *hval* (whalemeat).

TRANSPORT

GETTING THERE & AWAY

Air

Keflavík airport (KEF; ☎ 425 0600, flight times 425 0777; www.keflavikairport.com), 48km west of Reykjavík, is Iceland's main gateway. Flights to Greenland and the Faroe Islands use **Reykjavík domestic airport** (REK) in the city centre.

Internet-based airline **Iceland Express** (HW; ☎ 550 0600; www.icelandexpress.com) has the cheapest flights from Keflavík to London and Copenhagen. With increased competition, Icelandair (see p1234) often has equally cheap fares.

In summer, **Flugfélag Islands** (Air Iceland; NY; ☎ 570 3030; www.airiceland.is) flies from Reykjavík to the Faroe Islands, and to Kulusuk and Narsarsuaq (Greenland).

Boat

Between March and mid-October **Smyril Line's** (www.smyril-line.com) weekly car ferry *Norröna* sails from Denmark to Seyðisfjörður (eastern Iceland), via Tórshavn (Faroe Islands). Prices and schedules vary according to season; check the website for details.

GETTING AROUND

Air

The extensive domestic flight network is heavily dependent on the weather. Iceland's

WARNING: POST-CRASH PRICES

Iceland's economic problems have resulted in soaring inflation and wildly fluctuating exchange rates. In this chapter, we have given prices for summer 2009, but the financial uncertainty means that prices may look very different by the time you get here.

main domestic airline, **Flugfélag Íslands** (Air Iceland; ☎ 570 3030; www.airiceland.is), offers four-/five-/six-sector air passes (Ikr43,420/50,000/57,780) which must be bought outside Iceland. There's also a Fly-As-You-Please ticket, giving 12 days of unlimited travel (Ikr59,220). Domestic airport tax (Ikr1180) must be paid on every departure.

Bicycle

Rough roads and wild weather make cycling a challenge! Go prepared, and remember, you can always put your bike on a bus.

In several areas, including Reykjavík, bikes can be hired for around Ikr3500 per day.

Bus

BSÍ (Bifreiðastöð Íslands; Map pp586-7; ☎ 562 1011; www.bsi.is; BSÍ bus terminal, Vatnsmýrarvegur 10, Reykjavík) operates long-distance buses and sells money-saving passes. Many buses only run from June to August.

Car & Motorcycle

Transporting or renting a vehicle is expensive. The Reykjavík tourist office has details of special offers, but booking a car before you arrive is usually cheaper – see p1241.

You must be at least 20 years old to hire a car.

CONNECTIONS

Out on the edge of nothing, Iceland is nevertheless connected by regular flights from Keflavík airport to Denmark (Copenhagen), Finland (Helsinki), Norway (Bergen, Oslo and Stavanger) and Sweden (Göteborg and Stockholm) – see p583 for details.

For a more romantic arrival, take the ferry from Denmark (p583) along the jaw-dropping fjord to Seyðisfjörður.

Hitching

In summer hitching is possible in Iceland, but you may have to wait a long time in rural areas.

Local Transport

Reykjavík has a good local bus service. Taxis with English- or German-speaking drivers are available in most towns.

REYKJAVÍK

pop 116,992

Cute and coffee-fuelled, Iceland's eccentric capital is a tiny city with tremendous soul. You'll find rich Viking history, state-of-the-art geothermal pools, cosy cafes, super-stylish bars and a fizzing music scene, all teetering on the brink of the Arctic Circle.

The first settler, Ingólfur Arnarson, landed here in 871, naming the place Reykjavík (Smoky Bay) after steam rising from nearby fissures. Since then, Reykjavík has become a buzzing city while retaining its small-town charm.

ORIENTATION

Reykjavík's heart lies between Tjörnin (the Pond) and the harbour, with nearly everything else within walking distance.

INFORMATION

Discount Cards

Reykjavík Tourist Card (24/48/72 hr Ikr1400/1900/2400) Available at tourist offices, this gives free entry to galleries, museums and swimming pools, and includes a bus pass.

Internet Access

Aðalbókasafn (Reykjavík City Library; Map p588; ☎ 563 1717; www.borgarbokasafn.is; Tryggvagata 15; per hr Ikr200; 🕒 10am-9pm Mon, 10am-7pm Tue-Thu, 11am-7pm Fri, 1-5pm Sat & Sun) Libraries have the cheapest internet access.

Medical Services

Health Centre (Map p588; ☎ 585 2600; Vesturgata 7) Doctor's appointment for European/non-European visitors Ikr2600/8000.

Landspítali University Hospital (Map pp586-7; ☎ 543 2000; Fossvogur) 24-hour casualty department.

Lyfja Apótek (Map p588; ☎ 552 4045; Laugavegur 16; 🕒 9am-6pm Mon-Fri, 11am-4pm Sat) Central pharmacy.

EMERGENCY NUMBERS

- Police, ambulance and fire services ☎ 112.

Lyfja Apótek (Map pp586-7; ☎ 533 2300; Lágmúli 5; 8am-midnight) Late-night pharmacy. Take bus S2, 15, 17 or 19.

Money

Banks, clustered round Austurstræti and Bankastræti, offer the best exchange rates.

Landsbanki Íslands (Map p588; Austurstræti) Has no commission charges.

Telephone

There are public coin/cardphones at the main tourist office and Kringlan shopping centre (Map pp586–7).

Tourist Information

The excellent English-language newspaper *Grapevine* (www.grapevine.is), widely distributed, is an irreverent introduction to Reykjavík.

Main tourist office (Upplýsingamiðstöð Ferðamanna; Map p588; ☎ 590 1500; www.visitreykjavik.is; Aðalstræti 2; 8.30am-7pm Jun–mid-Sep, 9am-6pm Mon-Fri, 9am-4pm Sat, 9am-2pm Sun mid-Sep–May) There's also a desk at the Raðhús (City Hall).

SIGHTS & ACTIVITIES

The immense concrete church **Hallgrímskirkja** (Map p588; ☎ 510 1000; www.hallgrimskirkja.is; Skólavörðuholt; 9am-5pm mid-Aug–mid-Jun, 9am-7pm mid-Jun–mid-Aug), designed to resemble basalt columns, is Reykjavík's most famous building. For unmissable views, take an elevator trip up the 75m **tower** (adult Ikr400).

Iceland is terrific for whale-spotting: minkes often swim right up to the boats. Between April and October, **Elding Whale Watching** (Map p588; ☎ 555 3565; www.elding.is; adult Ikr7600) runs three-hour trips from the harbour.

Reykjavík's outdoor swimming pools, heated by volcanic water, are the city's social hubs. The biggest and best is **Laugardalslaug** (Map pp586-7; ☎ 553 4039; Sundlaugavegur 30; adult Ikr360, swimsuit/towel hire Ikr350/350; 6.30am-10pm Mon-Fri, 8am-10pm Sat & Sun, to 8pm Oct-Mar), with indoor and outdoor pools, seven Jacuzzi-like 'hot pots' and a five-star health resort next door. Take bus 14.

Bringing the Riviera to Reykjavík, the Blue-Flag **Nauthólsvík Hot Beach** (Ýlströndin; Map pp586-7; ☎ 511 6630; admission free; 10am-8pm mid-May–mid-Sep) is a dinky crescent of golden sand warmed by 18°C to 20°C geothermal water. Take bus 19.

Eccentric eruption-chaser Villi Knudsen screens his footage at the awesome **Volcano Show** (Map p588; ☎ 845 9548; vknudsen2000@yahoo.com; Red Rock Cinema, Hellusund 6a; adult Ikr1200). One-hour shows in English begin at 11am, 3pm and 8pm in July and August (less frequently outside high season).

The **National Museum** (Map p588; ☎ 530 2200; www.natmus.is; Suðurgata 41; adult/concession Ikr600/300, admission free Wed; 10am-5pm daily May–mid-Sep, 11am-5pm Tue-Sun mid-Sep-Apr, to 9pm first Thu of month) gives a fine overview of Iceland's culture and history. Its most treasured artefact is a stunning carved 13th-century church door.

The excellent **Saga Museum** (Map pp586-7; ☎ 511 1517; www.sagamuseum.is; adult/concession Ikr1500/1000; 10am-6pm Apr-Sep, noon-5pm Oct-Mar) brings Iceland's history to life with silicon models and bloodcurdling screams. It's inside the tourist complex **Perlan** (the Pearl), which also boasts two **artificial geysers** and a 360-degree **viewing deck** with tremendous mountain and city vistas. Take bus 18.

The city's newest museum is **Reykjavík 871+/-2** (Settlement Exhibition; Map p588; ☎ 411 6370; www.reykjavik871.is; Aðalstræti 16; adult Ikr600; 10am-5pm), based around a single Viking longhouse. It's a unique combination of archaeology, technology and imagination – go and see!

Þjóðmenningarhúsið (Culture House; Map p588; ☎ 545 1400; www.thjodmenning.is; Hverfisgata 15; adult/concession Ikr300/200, admission free Wed; 11am-5pm) offers intelligent displays about the sagas; darkened rooms contain the vellums themselves. Guided tours are available.

The **National Gallery** (Map p588; ☎ 515 9600; www.listasafn.is; Fríkirkjuvegur 7; admission free; 11am-5pm

GETTING INTO TOWN

From the BSÍ bus terminal, walk left along Vatnsmýrarvegur, then turn right along Njarðargata. Cross the ring road, then take the first road on the left, Sóleyjargata, which takes you to the city centre (1km). Alternatively, take a taxi.

From Keflavík airport the **Flybus** (☎ 562 1011; www.re.is) meets all incoming flights (Ikr1500, 50 minutes). Credit cards are accepted.

REYKJAVÍK

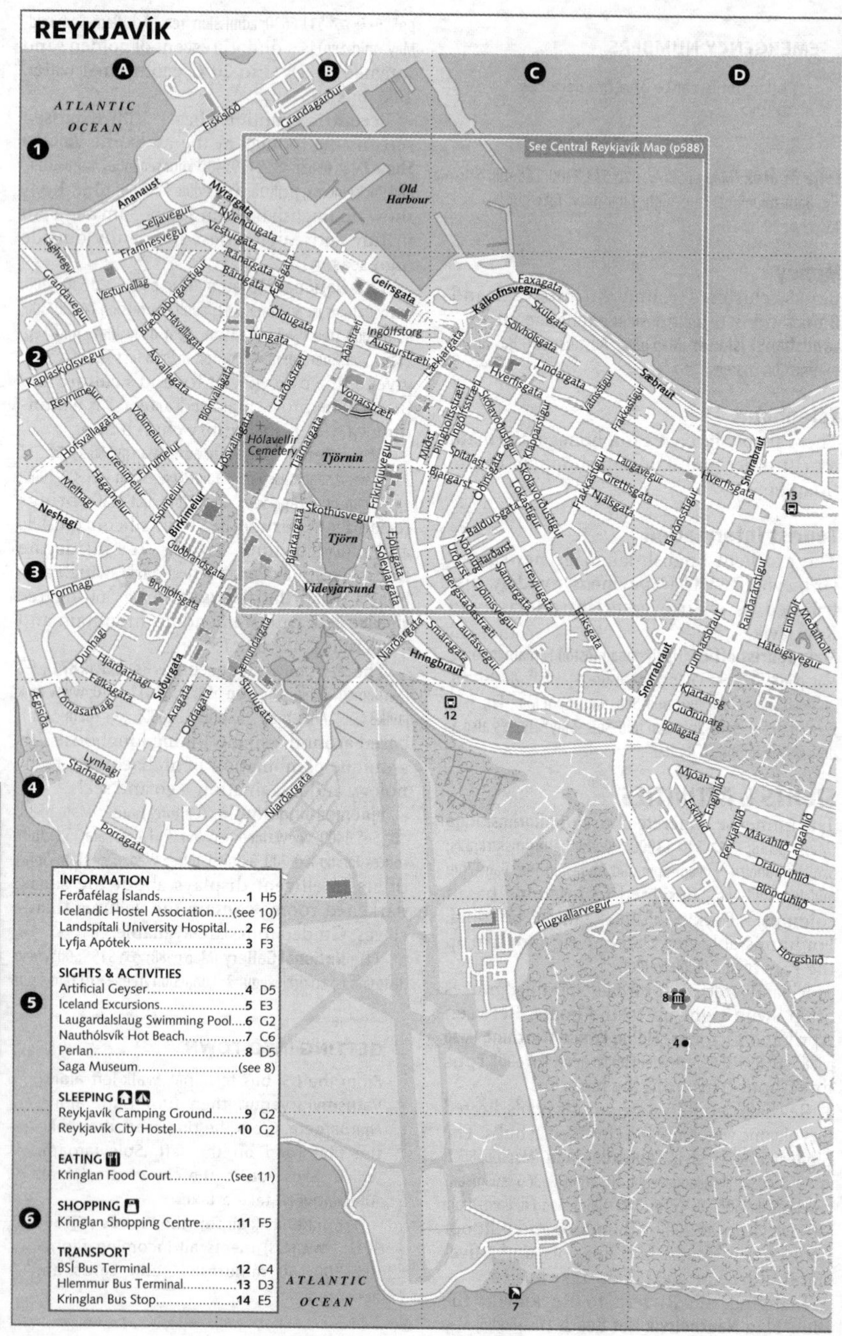

ICELAND

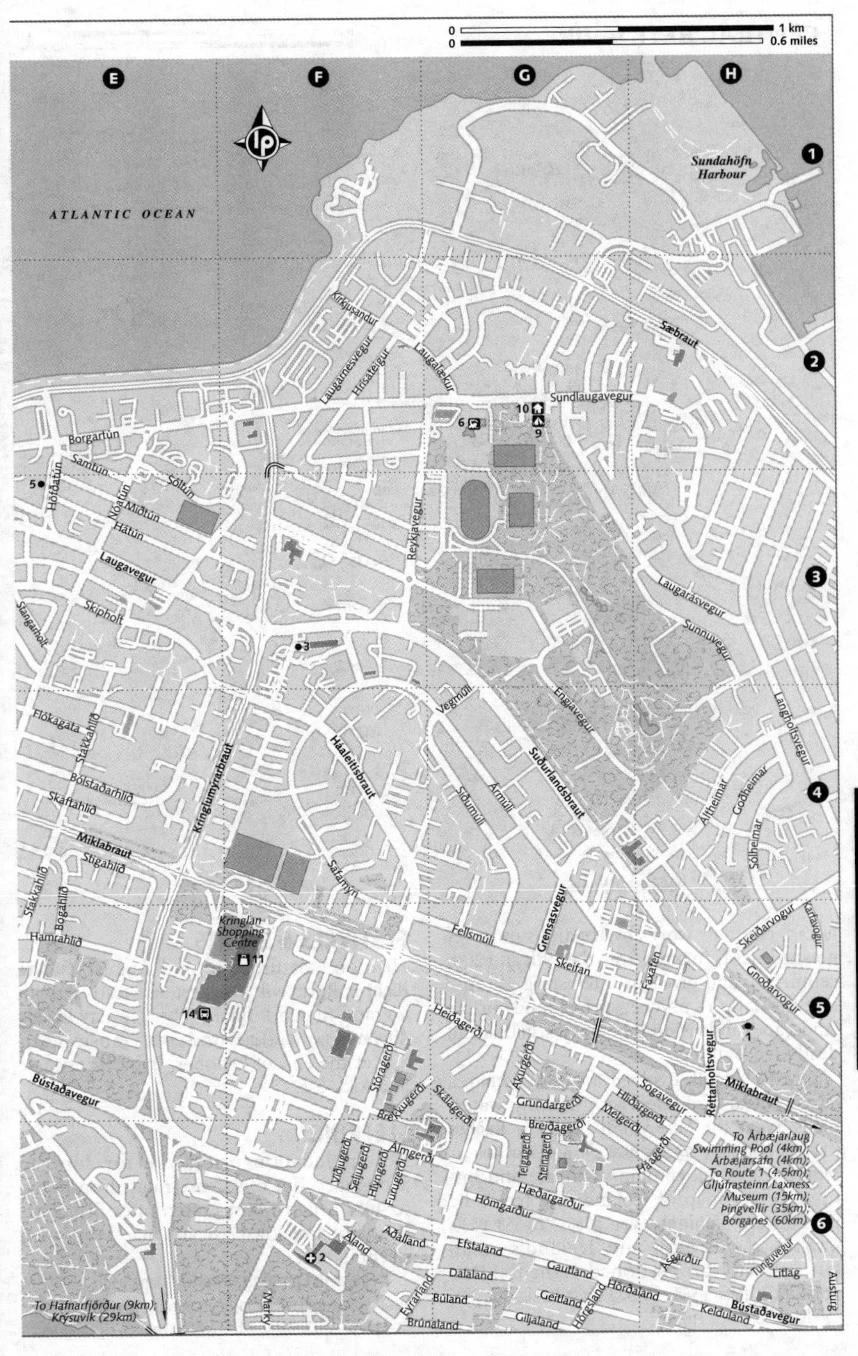

0 1 km
0 0.6 miles
E
F
G
H
1
2
3
4
5
6
ATLANTIC OCEAN
Sundahöfn Harbour
Kirkjusandur
Laugarnesvegur
Hrísateigur
Laugalækur
Sæbraut
Sundlaugavegur
Borgartún
Samtún
Sóltún
Höfðatún
Nóatún
Miðtún
Hátún
Laugavegur
Reykjavegur
Laugarásvegur
Sunnuvegur
Stangarholt
Skipholt
Engjavegur
Langholtsvegur
Vegmúli
Flókagata
Stakkahlíð
Háaleitisbraut
Suðurlandsbraut
Bólstaðarhlíð
Kringlumýrarbraut
Síðumúli
Ármúli
Álfheimar
Goðheimar
Skaftahlíð
Miklabraut
Stigahlíð
Safamýri
Sólheimar
Stakkahlíð
Bogahlíð
Grensásvegur
Kringlan Shopping Centre
Hamrahlíð
Fellsmúli
Skeiðarvogur
Karfavogur
Skeifan
Faxafen
Gnoðarvogur
Heiðagerði
Réttarholtsvegur
Bústaðavegur
Stóragerði
Akurgerði
Sogavegur
Miklabraut
Grundargerði
Hlíðargerði
Brekkugerði
Skálagerði
Melgerði
Breiðagerði
Viðjugerði
Seljugerði
Álmgerði
Teigagerði
Steinagerði
Hlyngerði
Furugerði
Hágerði
To Árbæjarlaug Swimming Pool (4km); Árbæjarsafn (4km); To Route 1 (4.5km); Gljúfrasteinn Laxness Museum (15km); Þingvellir (35km); Borganes (60km)
Hæðargarður
Hólmgarður
Áland
Aðalland
Efstaland
Ásgarður
Tunguvegur
Gautland
Dalaland
Litlag
Hörðaland
Austurg
Geitland
Búland
Hörgsland
Bústaðavegur
Markv
Eyrarland
Kelduland
Giljaland
Brúnaland
To Hafnarfjörður (9km); Krýsuvík (29km)
ICELAND

Book your stay at lonelyplanet.com/hotels

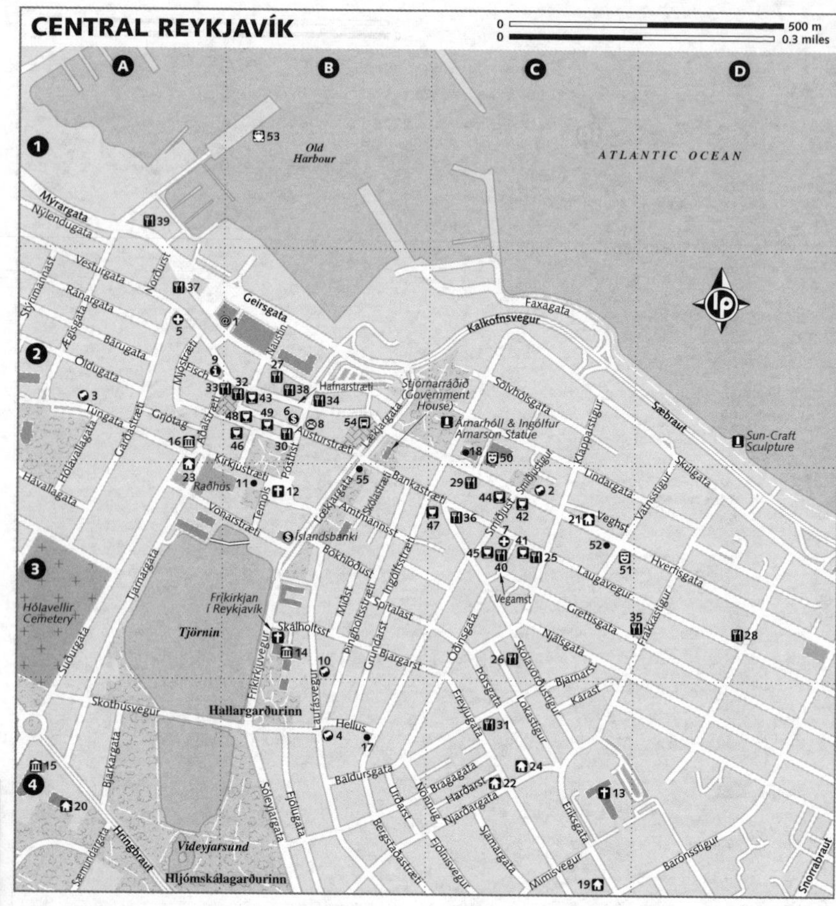

Tue-Sun) contains works by Iceland's most renowned artists (mainly from the 19th and 20th centuries), and gives an interesting glimpse into the nation's psyche: surreal mud-purple landscapes and visions of ogresses, giants and dead men walking.

Old Reykjavík evolved around **Tjörnin**, a large central lake filled with hooting waterbirds. Near the lake you'll find: the **Raðhús** (City Hall; Map p588; ☎ 563 2000; 🕑 8am-7pm Mon-Fri, noon-6pm Sat & Sun), containing a cafe and impressive 3D map of Iceland; the Icelandic parliament **Alþingi** (Map p588; ☎ 563 0500; www.althingi.is; Túngata); and Iceland's small but perfectly proportioned cathedral, the **Dómkirkja** (Map p588; ☎ 520 9700; Lækjargata 14a; 🕑 10am-5pm Mon-Fri).

FESTIVALS & EVENTS

Held on a Saturday in mid-August, **Culture Night** is Reykjavík's biggest arts festival, with a grand firework finale. The five-day **Iceland Airwaves** (www.icelandairwaves.com) music festival, at the end of October, is both intimate and kick-ass.

SLEEPING

Accommodation prices are for June to September; out of season, rates drop by up to 40%. Guest houses often offer discounts (but not breakfast) if you use your own sleeping bag.

Reykjavík Camping Ground (Map pp586-7; ☎ 568 6944; www.reykjavikcampsite.is; Sundlaugavegur 32; camp sites per person Ikr1000, 2-bed cabins Ikr6000; 🕑 mid-May–

INFORMATION
Aðalbóksafn (City Library)....1 B2
Danish Embassy....2 C3
French Embassy....3 A2
German Embassy....4 B4
Health Centre....5 A2
Landsbanki Íslands....6 B2
Lyfja Apótek....7 C3
Main Post Office....8 B2
Main Tourist Office....9 A2
UK Embassy....(see 4)
US Embassy....10 B3

SIGHTS & ACTIVITIES
Alþingi....11 B3
Domkirkja....12 B3
Elding Whale Watching....(see 53)
Hallgrímskirkja....13 C4
National Gallery....14 B3
National Museum....15 A4
Reykjavík 871 +/-2....16 A2
Volcano Show....17 B4
Þjóðmenningarhúsið....18 C2

SLEEPING
Eric the Red Guesthouse....19 C4
Garður Inn....20 A4
Gistiheimilið Domus....21 C3
Guesthouse Andrea....22 C4
Salvation Army Guesthouse....23 A2
Sunna Guesthouse....24 C4

EATING
Á Næstu Grösum....25 C3
Babalú....26 C3
Bæjarins Beztu....27 B2
Bónus Supermarket....28 D3
Café Cultura....29 C3
Café Paris....30 B2
Eldsmiðjan....31 C4
Emmessís og Pylsur....32 B2
Hlölla Bátar....33 B2
Hornið....34 B2
Indian Mango....35 D3
Kofi Tómasar Frænda....36 C3
Krua Thai....37 A2
Nonnabiti....38 B2
Sjávarkjallarinn....(see 9)
Sægreifinn....39 A1
Vegamót....40 C3

DRINKING
Café Oliver....41 C3
Celtic Cross....42 C3
Dubliner....43 B2
Grand Rokk....(see 42)
Hverfisbarinn....44 C3
Kaffibarinn....45 C3
NASA....46 B2
Q-Bar....47 C3
Thorvaldsen....48 B2
Vín Búð....49 B2

ENTERTAINMENT
National Theatre....50 C2
Regnboginn Cinema....51 C3

TRANSPORT
Borgarhjól SF (Bicycle Hire)....52 C3
Jetty for Whale Watching Tours....53 B1
Lækjartorg Bus Terminal....54 B2
Taxi Rank....55 B3

mid-Sep;) Reykjavík's well-equipped camping ground gets very busy in summer. It holds 650 people, though, so you'd be unlucky not to find a space. Bus 14.

Reykjavík City Hostel (Map pp586-7; ☎ 553 8110; www.hostel.is; Sundlaugavegur 34; per person 6-/4-/2-bed dm Ikr2100/3000/4300, bed linen Ikr800, breakfast Ikr1000;) This award-winning hostel is environmentally friendly, with helpful staff and excellent facilities (24-hour reception, large-screen TV room, bike rental etc), and it's perfect for meeting other travellers. The only drawback is the trek into town, but the soon-to-open central annexe will fix that. Bus 14.

Garður Inn (Map p588; ☎ 562 4000, 551 5900; www.inns-of-iceland.com; Hringbraut; sleeping-bag dm €30, sleeping-bag tw €40, s/d €95/115; Jun-Aug) The university campus, about 1km from the centre, rents out students' rooms in summer. The cheapest sleeping-bag accommodation is in 16-person dorms.

Salvation Army Guesthouse (Map p588; ☎ 561 3203; www.herinn.is; Kirkjustræti 2; sleeping-bag dm Ikr3000, s/d/tr/q Ikr7100/9900/14,000/17,500) The tiny rooms are frill-free, but their location couldn't be better. There's a bustling backpackery atmosphere, guest kitchen and lounging area.

Guesthouse Andrea (Map p588; ☎ 552 5515; www.aurorahouse.is; Njarðargata 43; sleeping bag dm Ikr4000, s/d Ikr9000/12,000; mid-May-Sep) Friendly Siggi runs this hidden guest house down a quiet side street. Its five private rooms (with sink, cooker, fridge) are ideal for self-caterers. Sleeping-bag accommodation is in a small-but-spruce bunk-bedded room.

Eric the Red Guesthouse (Map p588; ☎ 552 1940; www.eric.is; Eiríksgata 6; s/d Ikr8400/12,400, with bathroom Ikr10,400/13,400;) A modest little guest house in a handy location near Hallgrímskirkja. Rooms are plain, but kettles are provided and there's an excellent breakfast buffet.

Gistiheimilið Domus (Map p588; ☎ 561 1200; www.domusguesthouse.is; Hverfisgata 45; sleeping-bag dm Ikr3900; s/d Ikr9900/12,900, breakfast Ikr1500) Once the Norwegian embassy, Domus has a stately exterior and great location, although its rooms are a mixed lot. There's space for 22 sleeping-baggers in a dormitory annexe.

our pick **Sunna Guesthouse** (Map p588; ☎ 511 5570; www.sunna.is; Þórsgata 26; s/d from Ikr10,100/12,800;) Rooms here are simple, sunny and honey-coloured. Those at the front have good views of Hallgrímskirkja. The eight neat studio apartments (for one to four people, Ikr16,100 to Ikr32,000) suit small groups.

EATING

Icelandic food (from hot dogs to gourmet dishes) is all high quality, while prices are hair-raising. The thriving cafes are good for light lunches (most turn into bars at night); restaurants tend to be pricey places for dressed-up evening dining. Most eateries are on Laugavegur, Austurstræti and Ingólfstorg.

Restaurants

Krua Thai (Map p588; ☎ 561 0039; www.kruathai.is; Tryggvagata 14; mains Ikr1200-1900; noon-9.30pm Mon-Sat, 6-9.30pm Sun) Genuine Thai recipes are served

SPLURGE

Sjávarkjallarinn (Map p588; ☎ 511 1212; www.sjavarkjallarinn.is; Aðalstræti 2; Ikr3500-6000; 🕒 11.30am-2pm & from 6pm daily) The best dining experience in Reykjavík. The atmospheric Seafood Cellar combines shimmering fish and succulent crustaceans with the unexpected (pomegranate, coconut, lychee and chili) to form miniature works of art.

here. A glossy photo-menu shows what you'll get (spicy salads, curries and stir-fries), you order at the counter and tasty, fresh-cooked dishes magically appear.

Á Næstu Grösum (First Vegetarian; Map p588; www.anaestugrosum.is; ☎ 552 8410; Laugavegur 20b; daily special Ikr1490; 🕒 noon-10pm Mon-Sat, 5-10pm Sun) A first-rate veggie/organic restaurant, in a cheerful orange room overlooking Laugavegur, with inventive daily specials. There's extra spice on Indian nights (Friday and Saturday).

Sægreifinn (Map p588; ☎ 553 1500; Geirsgata 9; mains Ikr1000-2300; 🕒 10am-10pm) Eccentric Sægreifinn serves fresh seafood in what looks like a 1950s English chip shop…except for the stuffed seal. The sprightly, elderly owner specialises in lobster soup and smoked fish.

Indian Mango (Map p588; ☎ 551 7722; cnr Frakkastígur & Grettisgata; mains Ikr2200-3400; 🕒 from 5pm Mon-Sat) Focusing on Goan-Icelandic fusion food. Their bestselling creation is *svartfugl* (guillemot) marinaded in Indian spices.

Hornið (Map p588 ; ☎ 551 3340; Hafnarstræti 15; 9in pizza Ikr1360-2440, mains Ikr2300-4000; 🕒 11.30am-11pm) This bright, easygoing art-deco bistro serves large plates of grub. Choose freshly made pizzas or traditional Icelandic fish dishes.

Cafes

Babalú (Map p588; ☎ 552 2278; Skólavörðustígur 22a) More inviting than your own living room, Babalú is way-cute. It only sells tea, coffee, hot chocolate and crepes, but it's just ridiculously snug.

Kofi Tómasar Frænda (Koffin; Map p588; ☎ 551 1855; Laugavegur 2; snacks around Ikr800; 🕒 10am-1am Mon-Thu, 10am-5.30am Fri & Sat, 11am-1am Sun) Subterranean Koffin is a favourite student hang-out. Relax with magazines and a snack (nachos, cakes) and watch people scurrying along Laugavegur. At night, it's a candlelit bar with DJs.

Café Paris (Map p588; ☎ 551 1020; Austurstræti 14; snacks Ikr900-1500; 🕒 9am-1am Sun-Thu, 9am-5am Fri & Sat) A prime people-watching spot, particularly in summer when outdoor seating spills out onto Austurvöllur square. Start your day with a lazy breakfast and watch the world go by.

Café Cultura (Map p588; ☎ 530 9314; www.cultura.is; Hverfisgata 18; snacks & light meals Ikr990-2900; 🕒 11.30am-1am Mon-Thu, 11.30am-4am Fri & Sat, 1pm-1am Sun) This arty intercultural cafe has mosaic tables, well-priced nosh (felafel, spicy meatballs and couscous) and funky weekend DJs.

Vegamót (Map p588; ☎ 511 3040; www.vegamot.is; Vegamótstígur 4; snacks & light meals Ikr1300-2200; 🕒 11am-1am Mon-Thu, 11am-5am Fri & Sat, noon-1am Sun) A clubby place to eat, drink, gossip, see and be seen. The 'global' menu includes Mexican salad, seafood quesadilla and blackened chicken. At night it's packed with fashion-conscious drinkers.

Quick Eats

Icelanders swear by hot dogs from **Bæjarins Beztu** (Map p588; Tryggvagata): use the vital sentence *Eina með öllu* ('One with everything'!).

Late-opening snack bars and kiosks include: **Hlölla Bátar** (Map p588; Ingólfstorg; 🕒 11am-2am Sun-Thu, 10am-7am Fri & Sat) and **Emmessís og Pylsar** (Map p588; Ingólfstorg), selling ice cream and hot dogs; and **Nonnabiti** (Map p588; ☎ 551 2312; Hafnarstræti 9; snacks Ikr350-800; 🕒 to 2am).

The wood-fired pizzas at **Eldsmiðjan** (Map p588; ☎ 562 3838; Bragagata 38a; 10in pizza Ikr900-1500; 🕒 11am-11pm) are the best in town…no, you didn't imagine the snail topping.

The food court at Kringlan shopping centre (Map pp586–7) contains fast-food franchises.

Self-Catering

Bónus (Map p588; Laugavegur 59; 🕒 noon-6.30pm Mon-Thu, 10am-7.30pm Fri, 10am-6pm Sat) The cheapest supermarket in town.

DRINKING

Reykjavík is renowned for its weekend *runtur*, when hard-working Icelanders get sozzled at home, then hit the town from midnight onwards. Reykjavík is dressy, but there are pub-like places where you can get away with jeans. Usually the only difference between cafes and bars is the time of day: see also left.

Café Oliver (Map p588; ☎ 552 2300; www.cafeoliver.is; Laugavegur 20a) Oliver is the most in-vogue place for brunch, and for partying late in super-style. DJs pump out tunes on Thursdays, Fridays and Saturdays; queues to get in are l-o-n-g.

Kaffibarinn (Map p588; ☎ 551 1588; Bergstaðastræti 1) Damon Albarn of Blur and Gorillaz fame

TASTY TITBITS

Traditional Icelandic dishes reflect a nightmarish need to eat every last scrap: but you'll rarely see *svið* (singed sheep's head), *súrsaðir hrútspungar* (pickled ram's testicles) and *hákarl* (putrefied shark meat) for sale.

More palatable offerings include *harðfiskur* (dried strips of haddock with butter) and delicious yogurt-like *skyr*. The traditional alcoholic brew *brennivín* is schnapps made from potatoes and caraway seeds. It's fondly known as *svarti dauði* (black death).

owns part of this trendy bar. It's popular with celebs: at weekends you'll need a famous face or a battering ram to get in.

Grand Rokk (Map p588; ☎ 551 5522; www.grandrokk.is; Smiðjustígur 6) You'll feel as though you've known this down-to-earth pub all your life. Chess enthusiasts play during the day and live bands blow the roof off at night.

Celtic Cross (Map p588; ☎ 511 3240; Hverfisgata 26) and the **Dubliner** (Map p588; ☎ 511 3233; Hafnarstræti 4; 🕑 to 1am Sun-Thu, to 5am Fri & Sat) are fun, cosy Irish pubs favoured by travellers. Both have similar opening hours and regular live music.

Q-Bar (Map p588; ☎ 578 7868; Ingólfsstræti 3; 🕑 Sun-Thu 4pm-1am, Fri & Sat 4pm-5am) The only bar in Iceland that styles itself as gay, although it's really pretty mixed. Frequent gigs.

Hverfisbarinn (Map p588; ☎ 511 6700; www.hverfisbarinn.is; Hverfisgata 20; 🕑 to 1am Thu, to 5.30am Fri & Sat) A trendy bar and club with the queues to prove it! It's popular with (immaculately dressed) students, who come for live music on Thursdays and weekend DJs.

Thorvaldsen (Map p588; ☎ 511 1413; Austurstraeti 8-10) One of the hottest weekend clubs with DJs from Thursday to Saturday – dress well or you won't get in, and after midnight be prepared to queue. There's a tiny dance floor.

NASA (Map p588; ☎ 511 1313; nasa@nasa.is; Austurvöllur; admission Ikr1500-3500) Reykjavík's biggest nightclub, NASA plays chart music and club anthems. It's also the city's main venue for live bands – email for upcoming gigs.

ENTERTAINMENT

Reykjavík's **National Theatre** (Map p588; ☎ 585 1200; www.leikhusid.is; Lindargata 7; admission Ikr3400; 🕑 box office 12.30-6pm Mon & Tue, to 8pm Wed-Sun, theatre closed Jul & Aug) puts on around 12 plays, musicals and operas per year. The most central cinema is **Regnboginn** (Map p588; ☎ 551 9000; Hverfisgata 54; Ikr800). Listings can be found in daily newspapers, or click the 'Í Bíó' tab at www.kvikmyndir.is.

GETTING AROUND

Bicycle

Hire bikes from **Borgarhjól SF** (Map p588; ☎ 551 5653; www.borgarhjol.net; Hverfisgata 50; 🕑 8am-6pm Mon-Fri, 10am-2pm Sat) or Reykjavík City Hostel (p589) for Ikr3600 per day.

Bus

Reykjavík's excellent **Straetó** (☎ 551 2700; www.straeto.is/english) city bus system runs from 7am to 11pm or midnight (from 10am Sundays), with limited night buses at weekends. The two central terminals are Hlemmur (Map pp586–7) and Lækjartorg (Map p588). Bus stops are marked with the letter 'S'.

The fare is Ikr280 (no change given). The Reykjavík Tourist Card (see p584) includes a bus pass.

Taxi

There are usually taxis outside the bus stations and youth hostel, as well as bars on weekend nights. Alternatively, call **Borgarbíll** (☎ 552 2440), **BSR** (☎ 561 0000) or **Hreyfill-Bæjarleiðir** (☎ 588 5522).

AROUND REYKJAVÍK

BLUE LAGOON (BLÁA LÓNIÐ)

Iceland's most famous attraction is the **Blue Lagoon** (Bláa Lónið; ☎ 420 8800; www.bluelagoon.is; adult Ikr3400, towel/swimsuit/robe hire Ikr650/650/1200, spa treatments from Ikr2000; 🕑 8am-9pm Jun–Aug, 10am-8pm Sep–May), a milky-blue spa set in a massive black lava field, 50km southwest of Reykjavík. The futuristic Svartsengi geothermal plant provides an off-the-planet backdrop, as well as the spa's water – at a perfect 38°C and at Blue-Flag standards. Daub yourself in a silica-mud facepack, and loll in the hot pots with an ice-blue cocktail – it's so relaxing, you'll never want to leave. Bring plenty of conditioner to stop your hair going solid.

Between 10am and 6pm daily, there are six **Reykjavík Excursions** (☎ 562 1011; www.bsi.is) buses from the BSÍ bus terminal in Reykjavík. The Ikr4400 cost includes lagoon admission and return fare to Reykjavík (or onward journey to Keflavík airport).

THE GOLDEN CIRCLE

Marvel at Iceland's 'big three' destinations – Gullfoss, Geysir and Þingvellir National Park – on one day-long circular tour.

Gullfoss is a spectacular rainbow-tinged double waterfall, which drops 32m before thundering away down a vast rift. Ten kilometres down the road is **Geysir**, after which all spouting hot springs are named. The **Great Geysir** was plugged by rubble in the 1950s, thrown in by tourists trying to set it off. Luckily, the world's most reliable geyser **Strokkur** (Butter Churn) is right next door, spouting up to 30m every six minutes.

Þingvellir National Park is Iceland's most important historical location, and a Unesco World Heritage site. The Vikings established the world's first democratic parliament, the Alþing, here in AD 930. They certainly had a sense of drama – Þingvellir is inside an immense rift valley, caused by the separating North American and Eurasian tectonic plates.

The cheapest day trip (Ikr9800) is with **Iceland Excursions** (Gray Line; Map pp586-7; ☎ 540 1313; www.icelandexcursions.is; Höfðatún 12); you're usually collected from your accommodation.

ÞÓRSMÖRK

The Woods of Thor is a stunning glacial valley, full of weird rock formations, twisting gorges, a singing cave, mountain flowers and icy streams. Its proximity to Reykjavík (130km) makes it popular in summer, when tents pile up and camping grounds become partyville.

Wild camping is prohibited, but there are three huts – **Þórsmörk** (Ferðafélag Íslands; ☎ 568 2533; www.fi.is; sleeping-bag dm Ikr3300), **Básar** (Útivist; ☎ 562 1000; www.utivist.is; sleeping-bag dm Ikr2300) and **Húsadalur** (Reykjavík Excursions; ☎ 580 5400; www.thorsmork.is; sleeping-bag dm Ikr2800) – which have tent sites (per person Ikr800) around them. Reservations are strongly advised.

From mid-June to mid-September buses run between Reykjavík and Húsadalur (over the hill from Þórsmörk) at 8.30am daily. A second service runs from mid-June to August at 5pm daily (Ikr5200, 3½ hours).

ICELAND DIRECTORY

ACCOMMODATION

In Iceland, all hostels and some guesthouses and hotels offer a discount if guests use their own sleeping bags. We have given prices for sleeping-bag accommodation in each review where this service is available.

Due to Iceland's recent economic troubles, many hotels chose to give us their prices in euros, as the euro was more stable than the króna at the time of writing.

Camping

You're free to camp anywhere in Iceland, apart from on private land and in national parks and reserves.

Guest houses

Gistiheimilið (guest houses) range from private homes to purpose-built motels. Some offer sleeping-bag accommodation – a godsend if you're on a tight budget. Many places only open mid-May to August. Some offer a cheaper rate if you have your own sleeping bag.

Mountain Huts

Ferðafélag Íslands (Icelandic Touring Club; Map pp586-7; ☎ 568 2533; www.fi.is; Mörkin 6, IS-108 Reykjavík) maintains a system of *sæluhús* (mountain huts).

Summer Hotels

There are 13 summer-only **Edda Hotels** (☎ 444 4000; www.hoteledda.is), based in schools or conference centres. Some offer sleeping-bag accommodation in dorms.

Youth Hostels

Iceland's 25 superb youth hostels are administered by the **Icelandic Hostel Association** (Bandalag Íslenskra Farfugla; Map pp586-7; ☎ 553 8110; www.hostel.is; Sundlaugavegur 34, IS-105 Reykjavík). All have hot showers, cooking facilities, sheet hire, luggage storage and sleeping-bag accommodation.

ACTIVITIES

There is stunning **hiking** and **mountaineering** all over the country, especially in national parks and nature reserves. July, August and September are the best months for walking. For details, see www.outdoors.is or contact Ferðafélag Íslands (above).

For **horse-riding**, you can hire sturdy, sweet-natured little Icelandic horses at farms and tourist offices throughout the country. A two-hour/one-day ride costing about €60/100.

The best **rafting** in Iceland is at Varmahlíð in the north. **Activity Tours** (Ævintýraferðir; ☎ 453 8383; www.rafting.is; ⏲ May-Sep) runs an exhilarating, six-hour, white-water trip (Ikr9800, minimum age 18).

There are daily **scuba-diving** tours year-round with **Dive.is** (☎ 663 2858; www.dive.is; 2 dives at Þingvellir €199) from Reykjavík to Lake Þingvellir, which has astonishing 100m visibility.

Every town has at least one geothermal public **swimming** pool. See p585 for Reykjavík.

Iceland is great for **whale**- and **dolphin-watching** from mid-May to September. Regular sailings depart from Reykjavík (p585), although northern Húsavík is the 'whale-watching capital'.

BUSINESS HOURS

Usual business hours in Iceland:

Banks 9.15am-4pm Mon-Fri
Cafes & Bars 10am-6pm as cafes, then as bars to 1am Mon-Fri, to 3am or 6am at weekends
Post offices 9am-4.30pm Mon-Fri
Restaurants generally close by 10pm
Shops 9am-6pm Mon-Fri, 10am-noon or 4pm Sat, closed Sunday

CUSTOMS

See www.tollur.is for Icelandic customs regulations.

EMBASSIES & CONSULATES

A full list of Icelandic embassies and consulates is available at www.mfa.is. See right for information on visas.

Denmark (Map p588; ☎ 575 0300; www.ambreykjavik.um.dk; Hverfisgata 29)
France (Map p588; ☎ 575 9600; www.ambafrance.is; Túngata 22)
Germany (Map p588; ☎ 530 1100; embager@internet.is; Laufásvegur 31)
UK (Map p588; ☎ 550 5100; www.britishembassy.gov.uk; Laufásvegur 31)
USA (Map p588; ☎ 562 9100; www.usa.is; Laufásvegur 21)

FESTIVALS & EVENTS

For Reykjavík-only events, see p588.

Sumardagurinn Fyrsti (First Day of Summer) Arrives optimistically early on the first Thursday after 18 April, with Reykjavík holding the biggest carnival bash.
Independence Day The largest nationwide festival commemorates the founding of the republic in 1944 with parades and merriment on 17 June.
Midsummer Celebrated around 24 June, but less fervently than on the Scandinavian mainland.

HOLIDAYS

The following public holidays are observed in Iceland.

New Year's Day 1 January
Maundy Thursday Thursday before Easter
Good Friday to Easter Monday March/April
First Day of Summer First Thursday after 18 April
Labour Day 1 May
Ascension Day May
Whit Sunday & Whit Monday May
Independence Day 17 June
Shop & Office Workers' Holiday First Monday in August
Christmas Eve 24 December
Christmas Day 25 December
Boxing Day 26 December
New Year's Eve 31 December

INTERNET RESOURCES

Icelandic Tourist Board (www.icetourist.is)

MONEY

The unit of currency is the Icelandic króna (Ikr), which is divided into 100 aurar. Coins come in denominations of one, five, 10, 50 and 100 króna, and notes in 500, 1000, 2000 and 5000 króna.

Icelandic VAT *(söluskattur)* is included in marked prices: if you spend over Ikr4000 in a shop offering 'Iceland Tax-Free Shopping', you'll get a tax-refund coupon.

You can withdraw cash from banks using MasterCard, Visa or Cirrus ATM cards. MasterCard and Visa are accepted everywhere; Diners Club and Amex are less commonly used. Exchange travellers cheques and banknotes for Icelandic currency commission-free at Landsbanki Íslands banks.

Tipping isn't required.

POST

An airmail letter or postcard to Europe costs Ikr95/105 for economy/priority mail; to places outside Europe it costs Ikr105/140.

TELEPHONE

The international access code is ☎ 00, Iceland's country code is ☎ 354, and there are no area codes. Most Icelandic mobile phone numbers begin with the digit '8'.

For international directory assistance, and for assistance with reverse-charge (collect) calls, dial ☎ 1811.

VISAS

Schengen Agreement countries (see p1230) can enter Iceland with a valid identity card. Citizens of the European Economic Area (EEA), including Ireland and the UK, and the USA and Commonwealth countries can visit without a visa on a valid passport.

Ireland

HIGHLIGHTS

- **Dublin** Meander through the city's many museums, pubs and literary haunts, and ask a local, 'Where's the *craic*?' (fun) (p599)
- **Galway** Hang out in bohemian Galway with its hip cafes and live-music venues (p616)
- **Causeway Coast** Hike along the spectacular Causeway Coast and clamber across the Giant's Causeway (p625)
- **Off the beaten track** Take a boat trip to the 6th-century monastery perched atop the wild rocky islet of Skellig Michael (p615)

FAST FACTS

- **Area** 84,421 sq km
- **Budget** €65 per day
- **Capitals** Dublin (Republic of Ireland), Belfast (Northern Ireland)
- **Country codes** ☎ 353 (Republic of Ireland), 44 28 (Northern Ireland)
- **Famous for** U2, St Patrick, Guinness
- **Languages** English, Irish Gaelic
- **Money** euro (€) Republic/pound sterling (£) NI; A$1 = €0.55/£0.49; C$1 = €0.60/£0.56; €1 = £0.88; ¥100 = €0.78/£0.70; NZ$1 = €0.43/£0.39; £1 = €1.12; US$1 = €0.74/£0.66
- **Phrases** *Sláinte!* (cheers!), *dia duit* (hello), *go raibh* (thank you)

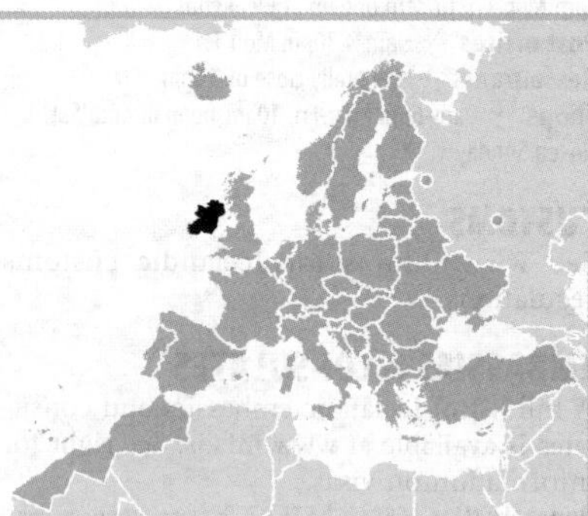

- **Populations** 3.9 million (Republic of Ireland), 1.7 million (Northern Ireland)
- **Visas** not necessary for EU, Australian, Canadian, New Zealand or USA citizens; see p629

TRAVEL HINTS

Keep an umbrella with you at all times, dress in layers and always stop to chat.

ROAMING IRELAND

Take in Dublin before swinging through Kilkenny and Cork. Hike around the west coast on your way to Galway, then head North to Derry, the Causeway Coast and Belfast.

Few countries have an image so plagued by cliché as Ireland's. From shamrocks and shillelaghs to leprechauns and lovable rogues, there's a plethora of platitudes to wade through before you scramble ashore on the real Ireland. But it's well worth looking beyond the tourist tat, for the Emerald Isle (oops, there we go again) is one of Western Europe's gems, a scenic extravaganza of lakes, mountains, sea and sky. From the lonely, wind-lashed wilderness of Donegal to the picture-postcard villages of County Cork, there are countless opportunities to get outdoors and explore, whether it's surfing the beach breaks of Bundoran or hiking the hills of Kerry and Connemara.

There are cultural pleasures too, of course, in the land of Joyce and Yeats, U2 and the Undertones. Dublin, Cork and Belfast all have top-notch restaurants, party-on pubs and a foot-stomping live-music scene. And there's a wealth of history to discover, from medieval castles and early Christian monasteries to the powerful political murals of Belfast and Derry. So enjoy your Guinness by all means, but push aside the forest of shamrocks for a bit and try to get a glimpse of the real Ireland.

HISTORY

Celtic warriors reached Ireland around 300 BC. Christian monks, including St Patrick, arrived around the 5th century AD, and from the end of the 8th century the rich monasteries were targets of raids by Vikings, who were followed by Anglo-Norman forces in 1169.

Oppression of the Catholic Irish got seriously underway in the 1500s when Henry VIII and his successor Elizabeth I attempted to impose a new Protestant church. Land confiscated from Catholic nobles was given to Protestant settlers from Scotland and England, a policy known as 'the Plantation', sowing the seeds of today's divided Ireland.

By the 18th century, Ireland's Catholics held less than 15% of the land and suffered brutal civil restrictions. Irish movements for civil rights alarmed the Protestant gentry, and in 1800 the Act of Union joined Ireland with Britain.

Successive failures of potato crops between 1845 and 1851 brought about the Great Famine – thousands starved while the British and Irish ruling classes profited from inflated food prices. About one million people died from disease or starvation, and another million emigrated.

At the turn of the century the British Parliament began to contemplate Irish home rule, but WWI interrupted the process. Ireland might still have moved, peacefully, towards some sort of accommodation but for a bungled uprising in 1916. Though it is now celebrated as a glorious bid for freedom, the Easter Rising was heavy on rhetoric and light on planning on both sides. After the insurrection was put down, a series of trials and executions (15 in all) transformed the ringleaders into martyrs and roused international support for Irish independence.

In the 1918 election, Irish republicans stood under the banner of Sinn Féin (Ourselves Alone) and won a majority of the Irish seats. Ignoring London's Parliament, the newly elected Sinn Féin deputies declared Ireland independent and formed the Dáil Éireann (Irish assembly), led by Eamon de Valera.

The resulting Anglo-Irish War (1919–21) pitted Sinn Féin and its military wing, the Irish Republican Army (IRA), against the British. During this period Michael Collins masterminded the IRA's campaign of violence (while serving as finance minister in the new Dáil). After months of negotiations, he and Arthur Griffith led the delegation that signed the Anglo-Irish Treaty in 1921, giving 26 of Ireland's 32 counties their independence; six largely Protestant counties in Ulster chose to remain part of the UK, as the province of Northern Ireland.

Under the Anglo-Irish Treaty, the British monarch remained the (nominal) head of the new Irish Free State. To de Valera and many Irish Catholics, the compromise was a betrayal of republican principles and a brief civil war ensued. A new 1937 constitution abolished fealty to Britain and claimed sovereignty over the six counties of Ulster. In 1948 the Irish government declared the country a republic.

In Northern Ireland, the Protestant majority had systematically excluded Catholics from power. In January 1969 civil rights marchers walking from Belfast to Derry were attacked by a Protestant mob outside Derry. British troops were sent to Derry and Belfast in August to maintain law and order. The peaceful civil rights movement foundered and an armed independence struggle began, led by the IRA.

Thus the so-called Troubles thundered through the 1970s and 1980s. Passions exploded in 1972 when 13 unarmed Catholics were shot dead by British troops in Derry on 'Bloody Sunday' (30 January), then again in 1981 when 10 IRA prisoners fasted to death.

In August 1994 a 'permanent cessation of violence' by the IRA was announced, to be matched by a Protestant ceasefire two months later. After setbacks, the peace process regained momentum with the May 1997 victory of Britain's Labour Party, and in July 1997, the IRA declared another ceasefire.

In April 1998 all-party talks produced the Good Friday Agreement, which allowed the people of Northern Ireland to decide their future by majority vote, committed its signatories to 'democratic and peaceful means of resolving differences on political

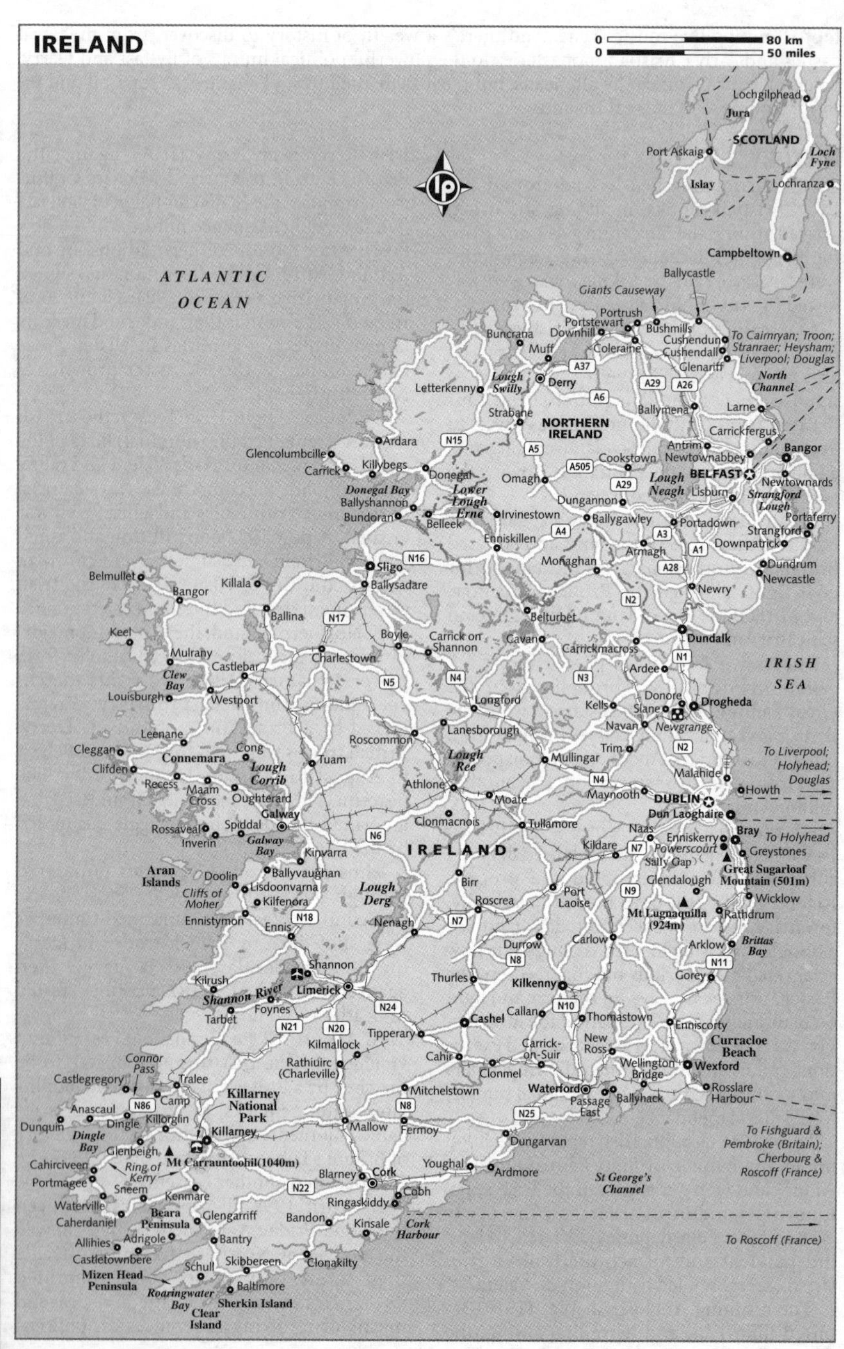
IRELAND
0 80 km
0 50 miles
ATLANTIC OCEAN
IRISH SEA
St George's Channel
North Channel
SCOTLAND
NORTHERN IRELAND
IRELAND
Lochgilphead
Jura
Port Askaig
Islay
Loch Fyne
Lochranza
Campbeltown
Ballycastle
Giants Causeway
Portrush
Portstewart
Bushmills
Downhill
Buncrana
Muff
Coleraine
Cushendun
Cushendall
Glenariff
To Cairnryan; Troon; Stranraer; Heysham; Liverpool; Douglas
Lough Swilly
Derry
Letterkenny
Strabane
Ballymena
Larne
Carrickfergus
Antrim
Newtownabbey
Bangor
BELFAST
Newtownards
Lough Neagh
Lisburn
Strangford Lough
Portaferry
Strangford
Downpatrick
Dundrum
Newcastle
Ardara
Glencolumbcille
Carrick
Killybegs
Donegal
Donegal Bay
Ballyshannon
Bundoran
Lower Lough Erne
Belleek
Irvinestown
Omagh
Cookstown
Dungannon
Ballygawley
Portadown
Enniskillen
Armagh
Monaghan
Newry
Sligo
Ballysadare
Belmullet
Killala
Bangor
Ballina
Keel
Boyle
Carrick on Shannon
Belturbet
Cavan
Carrickmacross
Dundalk
Mulrany
Castlebar
Clew Bay
Charlestown
Ardee
Louisburgh
Westport
Longford
Donore
Slane
Drogheda
Kells
Navan
Newgrange
Lanesborough
Leenane
Cleggan
Connemara
Cong
Roscommon
Lough Corrib
Tuam
Lough Ree
Mullingar
Trim
Clifden
Recess
Maam Cross
Oughterard
Athlone
Moate
Maynooth
Malahide
DUBLIN
Howth
To Liverpool; Holyhead; Douglas
Dun Laoghaire
Galway
Clonmacnois
Tullamore
Rossaveal
Spiddal
Inverin
Galway Bay
Naas
Bray
To Holyhead
Enniskerry
Powerscourt
Greystones
Kildare
Sally Gap
Kinvarra
Aran Islands
Doolin
Ballyvaughan
Glendalough
Great Sugarloaf Mountain (501m)
Cliffs of Moher
Lisdoonvarna
Kilfenora
Lough Derg
Birr
Port Laoise
Wicklow
Roscrea
Mt Lugnaquilla (924m)
Rathdrum
Ennistymon
Ennis
Nenagh
Carlow
Arklow
Brittas Bay
Durrow
Shannon
Gorey
Kilrush
Thurles
Kilkenny
Shannon River
Limerick
Foynes
Tarbet
Callan
Thomastown
Cashel
Tipperary
Kilmallock
Enniscorty
Curracloe Beach
Carrick-on-Suir
New Ross
Cahir
Rathluirc (Charleville)
Clonmel
Wellington Bridge
Wexford
Connor Pass
Castlegregory
Tralee
Camp
Killarney National Park
Mitchelstown
Waterford
Passage East
Ballyhack
Rosslare Harbour
Anascaul
Dingle
Killorglin
Dunquin
Dingle Bay
Killarney
Mallow
Fermoy
To Fishguard & Pembroke (Britain); Cherbourg & Roscoff (France)
Glenbeigh
Mt Carrauntoohil (1040m)
Dungarvan
Cahirciveen
Ring of Kerry
Youghal
Ardmore
Portmagee
Blarney
Cork
Sneem
Kenmare
Cobh
Ringaskiddy
Waterville
Caherdaniel
Beara Peninsula
Glengarriff
Bandon
Kinsale
Cork Harbour
To Roscoff (France)
Allihies
Adrigole
Bantry
Castletownbere
Schull
Skibbereen
Clonakilty
Mizen Head Peninsula
Baltimore
Roaringwater Bay
Sherkin Island
Clear Island
N15
N16
N17
N5
N4
N3
N2
N1
N6
N7
N9
N18
N8
N11
N10
N24
N21
N20
N86
N25
N22
A37
A29
A26
A6
A5
A505
A4
A3
A1
A28

IRELAND

> **READING UP**
>
> Interested in Irish history? Check out *A Traveller's History of Ireland* by Peter Neville. Frank McCourt's *Angela's Ashes* and Seamus Heaney's *The Spirit Level* are good glimpses into Irish culture. Another must-read is the hilarious *McCarthy's Bar* by Pete McCarthy.

issues', and established a new Northern Ireland Assembly.

The new assembly was beset by divisions from the outset – largely over acts of violence and wrangles about how and when the IRA should 'decommission' its weapons – which resulted in no less than four suspensions, the latest from 2002 until 2007. After five years of direct rule from London, a deal hammered out between the Democratic Unionist Party and Sinn Féin saw the assembly members finally take their seats in Stormont on 8 May 2007.

Today a cautious optimism prevails and, despite lingering animosity and occasional flare-ups of sectarian violence, most agree that the 'war' is finally over.

THE CULTURE

Prior to the 1845–51 Great Famine, Ireland's population was around eight million; death and emigration reduced it to around six million, and emigration continued at a high level for the next 100 years. It wasn't until the 1960s that the population began to recover.

Thanks to the EU and a strong economy, Ireland has seen a modest influx of immigrants, mostly from Eastern Europe, within the past five years. However, the global financial crisis of 2008 hit Ireland's economy hard, especially the once-thriving construction sector, and rising unemployment has seen many recent immigrants heading back home.

RELIGION

Religion has always played a pivotal role in Ireland. About 90% of people in the Republic are Roman Catholic, followed by 3% Protestant, 0.1% Jewish and the rest with no professed religious belief. In the North the breakdown is about 53% Protestant and 44% Catholic.

ARTS

Literature

The Irish have made an enormous impact on world literature. Important writers include Jonathan Swift, Oscar Wilde, WB Yeats, George Bernard Shaw, James Joyce, Sean O'Casey, Samuel Beckett and Roddy Doyle. The Ulster-born poet Seamus Heaney was awarded the Nobel Prize for Literature in 1995. Earlier Irish Nobel laureates include Shaw (1925), Yeats (1938) and Beckett (1969). Frank McCourt became a world favourite with his autobiographical, Pulitzer Prize–winning *Angela's Ashes*.

Music

Traditional Irish music – played on instruments such as the *bodhrán* (a flat, goatskin drum), *uilleann* (elbow) pipes, flute and fiddle – is an aspect of Irish culture that's impossible to miss. Of the Irish music groups, perhaps the best-known are the Chieftains, the Dubliners and the Pogues. Among popular Irish singers and musicians who have made it on the international stage are Van Morrison, Thin Lizzy, Sinéad O'Connor, Bob Geldof, U2, the Cranberries, the Corrs and Damien Rice.

ENVIRONMENT

Ireland is divided into 32 counties: 26 in the Republic and six in Northern Ireland. The island covers 84,421 sq km (about 83% is the Republic) and stretches 486km north to south and 275km east to west. At 259km, the Shannon River is the longest in Ireland, and Carrauntuohill (1040m) in County Kerry is the highest summit.

While Ireland's population density is among Europe's lowest, the population is rising. More people are settling in new suburban developments and buying holiday homes – 75,000 new houses have been built every year since 2000, leading to worries about over-development, environmental damage, and a property bubble that burst spectacularly in 2008.

Ireland is hardly in the vanguard of the environmental movement, but it did lead the way in 2002 with the much-publicised plastic bag tax, dubbed the 'plastax', which resulted in a 90% drop in bag waste. Beyond that, the government isn't pushing the environmental agenda much beyond ratifying EU agreements.

TRANSPORT

GETTING THERE & AWAY

Air

The Fáilte Ireland **online tourist office** (www.ireland.ie) has information on getting to Ireland from a number of countries. International departure tax is normally included in the price of your ticket.

There are nonstop flights from Britain, Continental Europe and North America to Dublin and Shannon, and nonstop connections from Britain and Continental Europe to Cork.

International airports in the Republic include the following:

Cork (ORK; ☎ 021-431 3131; www.corkairport.com)
Dublin (DUB; ☎ 01-814 1111; www.dublinairport.com)
Kerry (KIR; ☎ 066-976 4644; www.kerryairport.ie; Farranfore)
Knock (NOC; ☎ 094-67222; www.knockairport.com)
Shannon (SNN; ☎ 061-712000; www.shannonairport.com)
Waterford (WAT; ☎ 051-875589; www.flywaterford.com)

International airports in Northern Ireland include the following:

Belfast City (BHD; ☎ 028-9093 9093; www.belfastcityairport.com) Serves Britain.
Belfast International (BFS; ☎ 028-9448 4848; www.belfastairport.com) Serves Britain, Europe and the USA.
Derry (LDY; ☎ 028-7181 0784; www.cityofderryairport.com) Serves Britain.

See p1232 for details of air travel from outside Western Europe. Airlines, including budget airlines, flying to and from Ireland from within Western Europe include the following:

Aer Arann (RE; ☎ 0818 210210; www.aerarann.ie) A small carrier that operates flights within Ireland and also to Britain.
Aer Lingus (EI; ☎ 0818 365000; www.aerlingus.com) The Irish national airline, with direct flights to Britain, Continental Europe and the USA.
BMI British Midland (BD; ☎ 01-407 3036; www.flybmi.com)
easyJet (EZY; ☎ 0871 244 2366; www.easyjet.com)
Flybe (BEE; ☎ in the UK 01392-268500; www.flybe.com)
Iberia (IB; ☎ 0818 462000; www.iberia.com, in Spanish)
Jet2 (LS; ☎ 0818-200017; www.jet2.com)
Ryanair (FR; ☎ 0818 303030; www.ryanair.com) Ireland's budget carrier, flying to Britain and Continental Europe.

CONNECTIONS

Ireland is as just about as far as you can go in Western Europe – next stop to the west, North America. But Ireland can still serve as a stepping stone between mainland Europe and the UK. Ferry services run from Roscoff and Cherbourg in northern France to Rosslare (near Wexford) in southeast Ireland, from where you can continue your trip from Dublin to Wales, or from Belfast to Scotland or the Isle of Man.

Sea

There's a variety of ferry services from Britain and France to Ireland. Prices vary depending on season, time of day, day of the week and length of stay. One-way fares for an adult foot passenger can be as little as £25, but can exceed £75 in summer. For a car plus driver and up to four adult passengers, prices can cost £150 to £300.

Keep an eye out for special deals, discounted return fares and other money savers. And plan ahead – some services are booked up months in advance. **DirectFerries** (www.directferries.co.uk) lists all the available ferry routes and operators.

TO/FROM BRITAIN

Regular ferry services run to ports in the Republic and Northern Ireland from Scotland (Cairnryan–Larne, Stranraer–Belfast and Troon–Larne), England (Fleetwood–Larne, Liverpool–Belfast and Liverpool–Dublin), Wales (Fishguard–Rosslare Harbour, Holyhead–Dublin, Holyhead–Dun Laoghaire, and Pembroke–Rosslare Harbour) and from the Isle of Man (Douglas–Dublin and Douglas–Belfast).

Irish Ferries (☎ 0818-300 400, in the UK 0870 517 1717; www.irishferries.com) For ferry and fast-boat services from Holyhead to Dublin (two or 3¼ hours), and ferry services from Pembroke to Rosslare Harbour (3¾ hours).
Isle of Man Steam Packet Company (☎ 1800 805055, in the UK 0870 222 1333; www.steam-packet.com) Ferry and fast-boat services from Douglas (Isle of Man) to Belfast (2¾ hours, Easter to September) and Dublin (2¾ hours, Easter to September).
Norfolkline Irish Sea Ferries (☎ 01-819 2999, in the UK 0844 499 0007; www.norfolkline.com) Ferries from Liverpool to Belfast (eight hours) and Dublin (seven hours).
P&O Irish Sea (☎ 01-407 3434, in the UK 0871 66 44 999; www.poirishsea.com) Ferry and fast-boat services

from Cairnryan to Larne (one or 1¾ hours), Troon to Larne (1¾ hours, March to October) and Liverpool to Dublin (eight hours).

Stena Line (☎ 01-204 7777, in the UK 08705 707070; www.stenaline.co.uk) Ferry and fast-boat services from Holyhead to Dublin (three hours) and Dun Laoghaire (1¾ hours); Fishguard to Rosslare Harbour (1¾ or 3½ hours); Fleetwood to Larne (eight hours) and Stranraer to Belfast (1¾ or 3¼ hours).

TO/FROM FRANCE

Ferries run between Roscoff and Cherbourg to Rosslare Harbour and Cork.

Brittany Ferries (☎ in Ireland 021-427 7801, in France 0825 828 828; www.brittanyferries.com) Services from Roscoff to Cork once weekly (13 hours, April to September).

Celtic Link Ferries (☎ in Ireland 040-238084, in France 02 33 43 23 87; www.celticlinkferries.com) Twice weekly passenger-only service from Cherbourg to Rosslare Harbour (19 hours).

Irish Ferries (☎ in Ireland 0818-300 400, in France 01 56 93 43 40) Ferries from Roscoff/Cherbourg to Rosslare Harbour (17½ or 20½ hours, April to December).

GETTING AROUND

In Ireland public transport can be expensive (particularly trains), infrequent or both. For these reasons having your own transport – car or bicycle – can be a major advantage.

Bicycle

Ireland is great for cycling, despite inconsistent roads and weather. Typical rental costs for bicycles are €10 to €20 a day or around €50 to €100 a week. There are **Raleigh Rent-a-Bike** (www.raleigh.ie) agencies all over Ireland; like many local bike shops, they offer one-way hire for an extra charge.

Bicycles can be transported by bus if there's enough room; it costs €10 per trip. By train, costs are €3 to €10 for a one-way journey.

PASSES & DISCOUNTS

Eurail passes are valid for train travel in the Republic of Ireland, but not in Northern Ireland, and will get you a 50% discount on Irish Ferries crossings to France. InterRail passes give you a 50% reduction on train travel within Ireland and on Irish Ferries and Stena Line services. Both Bus Éireann and Iarnród Éireann offer discounts to International Student Identity Card (ISIC) holders.

Bus Éireann and Iarnród Éireann and their northern counterparts, Ulsterbus and Northern Ireland Railways, offer various flavours of unlimited-travel tickets. For more information, contact **Bus Éireann** (☎ 01-836 6111; www.buseireann.ie) or **Iarnród Éireann** (☎ 1850-360 222, 01-836 6222; www.irishrail.ie).

Bus

Bus Éireann (☎ 01-836 6111; www.buseireann.ie) operates services all over the Republic and into Northern Ireland. Fares are much cheaper than the train. Returns are only slightly more expensive than one-way fares and special deals are often available. Most intercity buses in Northern Ireland are operated by **Ulsterbus** (☎ 028-9066 6630; www.translink.co.uk).

Car & Motorcycle

People under 21 cannot hire a car; for most rental companies you must be at least 23 and have had a valid driving licence for one year. Your own local licence is usually sufficient to hire a car for up to three months.

Train

Iarnród Éireann (☎ 1850-360 222, 01-836 6222; www.irishrail.ie) has routes fanning out from Dublin. Tickets can be twice as expensive as the bus, but travel times may be dramatically reduced. A midweek return ticket sometimes costs just a bit more than the single fare but fares may be significantly higher on Friday or Sunday.

Northern Ireland Railways (☎ 028-9066 6630; www.translink.co.uk) has four lines from Belfast, one of which links up with the Republic's rail system.

DUBLIN

☎ 01 / pop 1.1 million

Sitting in a tapas bar on Great George's St, nursing a Guinness or a hangover (or both), you think about what your favourite experience has been in Dublin so far. Was it drinking in Temple Bar with people from dozens of other countries or was it buying fresh vegies at the Asian food market? Was it admiring the Georgian houses along St Stephen's Green or was it wandering the grounds of Trinity College? You never come to an answer, but you do realise that, just as the waters on the banks of the Liffey River seem to rise every day, so does your affection for this city.

EMERGENCY NUMBERS

- Ambulance, fire & police ☎ 999 or 112

Despite the economic downturn, Dublin is still in the list of Europe's top 10 most visited cities. Visitors swarm in droves like moths to a light bulb – for the historic museums, top-class attractions and Georgian architecture, while immigrants from Eastern Europe, Asia and Africa set up new lives for their families, adding even more depth and complexity to an already rich cultural tapestry. Add a hard-partying nightlife to this mixture and what you get is a city that's constantly changing, and having a rare ould time as it does so.

ORIENTATION

Dublin is neatly divided by the Liffey River into the more affluent 'south side' and the less prosperous 'north side'.

North of the river, important landmarks are O'Connell St, with its needle-shaped Monument of Light, and Gardiner St, with its B&Bs and guest houses. Henry St, the main shopping precinct, runs west off O'Connell. Busáras, the main bus station, and Connolly station, one of the main train stations, are near the southern end of Gardiner.

Immediately south of the river is the bustling Temple Bar district, Dame St, Trinity College and, just below it, the lovely St Stephen's Green. Pedestrianised Grafton St and its surrounding streets and lanes are crammed with shops and restaurants. About 2km west is Heuston station, the city's other main train station.

INFORMATION

Bookshops

Eason's (Map p604; ☎ 873 3811; 40 O'Connell St) One of the biggest magazine stockists in Ireland.

Hodges Figgis (Map p604; ☎ 677 4754; 56-8 Dawson St) Has a large selection of books on things Irish.

Sinn Féin Bookshop (Map p604; ☎ 872 7096; West 44 Parnell Sq)

Discount Cards

Dublin Pass (www.dublinpass.ie) Allows entrance into over 30 of Dublin's attractions as well as tours and special offers.

Internet Access

Dublin has more internet cafes than you can shake a stick at; Dorset St (Map pp602–3) and Temple Bar (Map p604) are full of them.

Internet Café & Call Shop (Map p604; ☎ 855 2560; 43 Lower Gardiner St; per hr €2) Wi-fi too.

Internet Exchange (Map p604; ☎ 670 3000; 3 Cecilia St; per hr €5; 🕑 9am-11pm)

Medical Services

Doctors on Call (☎ 453 9333; 🕑 24hr) Request a doctor to come to your accommodation (€60 to €75).

O'Connell's Pharmacy (Map p604; ☎ 873 0427; 55-6 O'Connell St; 🕑 7.30am-10pm Mon-Fri, 8am-10pm Sat, 10am-10pm Sun)

St James's Hospital (Map pp602-3; ☎ 410 3000; James's St) Dublin's main 24-hour accident and emergency department.

Well Woman Clinic (Map p604; ☎ 872 8051, 688 3714; www.wellwomancentre.ie; 35 Lower Liffey St; 🕑 9.30am-7.30pm Mon, Thu & Fri, 8am-7.30pm Tue & Wed, 10am-4pm Sat, 1-4pm Sun) Handles women's health issues and can supply contraception.

Money

The Dublin airport and Dublin Tourism Centre have currency-exchange counters, and numerous banks around the city centre have exchange facilities. The central bank offers the best exchange rates, while airport and ferry terminal bureaux offer the worst. ATMs are everywhere.

Post

Dublin's famous **General Post Office** (GPO; Map p604; ☎ 705 7000; O'Connell St; 🕑 8am-8pm Mon-Sat) is north of the river. South of the river there are post offices on South Anne St and St Andrew's St.

Tourist Information

All Dublin tourist offices provide walk-in services only – no phone inquiries.

Dublin Tourism Centre (Map p604; ☎ 605 7700; www.visitdublin.com; St Andrew's Church, 2 Suffolk St; 🕑 9am-7pm Mon-Sat, 10.30am-3pm Sun Jul & Aug, 9am-5.30pm Mon-Sat, 10.30am-3pm Sun Sep-Jun) Tourist information, accommodation bookings, car hire, maps and tickets for tours, concerts and Dublin Pass sales. Branches at City Centre (Map p604; 14 O'Connell St; 🕑 9am-5pm Mon-Sat) and Dun Laoghaire (off Map pp602-3; Dun Laoghaire ferryport; 🕑 10am-1pm & 2-6pm).

Fáilte Ireland (off Map pp602-3; ☎ 1850 230 330; www.ireland.ie; Baggot St; 🕑 9am-5pm Mon-Fri) Tourist information for the whole Republic of Ireland.

Northern Ireland Tourist Board (NITB; Map p604; ☎ 679 1977; www.discovernorthernireland.com; 16 Nassau St; ⏰ 9.15am-5.30pm Mon-Fri, 10am-5pm Sat) Information and accommodation booking services.

SIGHTS

Trinity College & Book of Kells

Ireland's premier university was founded by Elizabeth I in 1592. Its full name is the University of Dublin, but **Trinity College** (Map p604; College Green) is the institution's sole college. Until 1793 the students were all Protestants, but today most of them are Catholic. Women were admitted in 1903.

Student-guided **walking tours** (per person €10) take place twice an hour from 10.45am to 3.40pm Monday to Saturday and 10.45am to 3.15pm Sunday from mid-May to September, departing from inside the main gate on College St. The tour is a good deal since it includes admission to the *Book of Kells*, an elaborately illuminated manuscript dating from around AD 800, and one of Dublin's prime attractions. It's displayed in the **Old Library** (Map p604; ☎ 896 2320; www.tcd.ie/Library/heritage; admission €9; ⏰ 9.30am-5pm Mon-Sat year-round, 9.30am-4.30pm Sun May-Sep, noon-4.30pm Sun Oct-Apr), together with the 9th-century *Book of Armagh*.

Museums

Among the highlights of the impressive **National Museum** (Map p604; ☎ 667 7444; www.museum.ie; Kildare St; admission free; ⏰ 10am-5pm Tue-Sat, 2-5pm Sun) are its superb collection of prehistoric gold objects, including the exquisite 12th-century Ardagh Chalice, the world's finest example of Celtic art. Other exhibits focus on the Viking period, the 1916 Easter Rising and the struggle for Irish independence.

The **Chester Beatty Library** (Map p604; ☎ 407 0750; www.cbl.ie; Dublin Castle; admission free; ⏰ 10am-5pm Mon-Fri, 11am-5pm Sat, 1-5pm Sun, closed Mon Oct-Apr) houses a breathtaking collection of more than 20,000 manuscripts, rare books, miniature paintings, clay tablets, costumes and other objects spread across two floors. The 270 illuminated Qur'ans are just one draw.

Dublin Writers Museum (Map pp602-3; ☎ 872 2077; www.writersmuseum.com; 18-19 Parnell Sq; admission €7.25; ⏰ 10am-5pm Mon-Sat & 11am-5pm Sun year-round, to 6pm Mon-Fri Jun-Aug), north of the river, celebrates the city's long role as a literary centre, with displays on Joyce, Swift, Yeats, Wilde, Beckett and others.

Galleries

The **National Gallery** (Map pp602-3; ☎ 661 5133; www.nationalgallery.ie; West Merrion Sq; admission & guided tours free; ⏰ 9.30am-5.30pm Mon-Wed, Fri & Sat, 9.30am-8.30pm Thu, noon-5.30pm Sun, guided tours at 3pm Sat & 2pm, 3pm & 4pm Sun) has a fine collection, strong in Irish art. The Millennium wing has a small collection of contemporary Irish works.

North of the river on Parnell Sq, **Dublin City Gallery, The Hugh Lane** (Map pp602-3; ☎ 222 5550; www.hughlane.ie; admission free; ⏰ 10am-6pm Tue-Thu, 10am-5pm Fri & Sat, 11am-5pm Sun) has works by French impressionists and 20th-century Irish artists.

In Temple Bar, around Meeting House Sq, are the **National Photographic Archives** (Map p604; ☎ 603 0374; www.nli.ie; admission free; ⏰ 10am-5pm Mon-Fri, to 2pm Sat) and the **Gallery of Photography** (Map p604; ☎ 671 4654; www.irish-photography.com; admission free; ⏰ 11am-6pm Tue-Sat, 1-6pm Sun).

Christ Church Cathedral & Around

Christ Church Cathedral (Map p604; ☎ 677 8099; www.cccdub.ie; Christ Church Pl; adult/concession €6/4; ⏰ 9am-6pm Jun-Aug, 9.45am-5pm Sep-May) was a simple structure of wood until 1169, when the present stone church was built. In the southern aisle is a monument to the 12th-century Norman warrior Strongbow. Note the church's precariously leaning northern wall (it's been that way since 1562).

St Patrick's Cathedral & Around

As early as the 5th century, a church occupied the site of **St Patrick's Cathedral** (Map

DUBLIN FOR FREE

Dublin is no cheap city, but there are plenty of attractions that won't bust your budget.

- **Trinity College grounds** (left) Dublin's oldest and most beautiful university.
- **National Museum** (left) World's finest collection of prehistoric gold artefacts.
- **Chester Beatty Library** (left) Collection of oriental and religious art.
- **National Gallery** (above) Irish and European paintings.
- **St Stephen's Green** (Map pp602–3) The city's most picturesque public park.

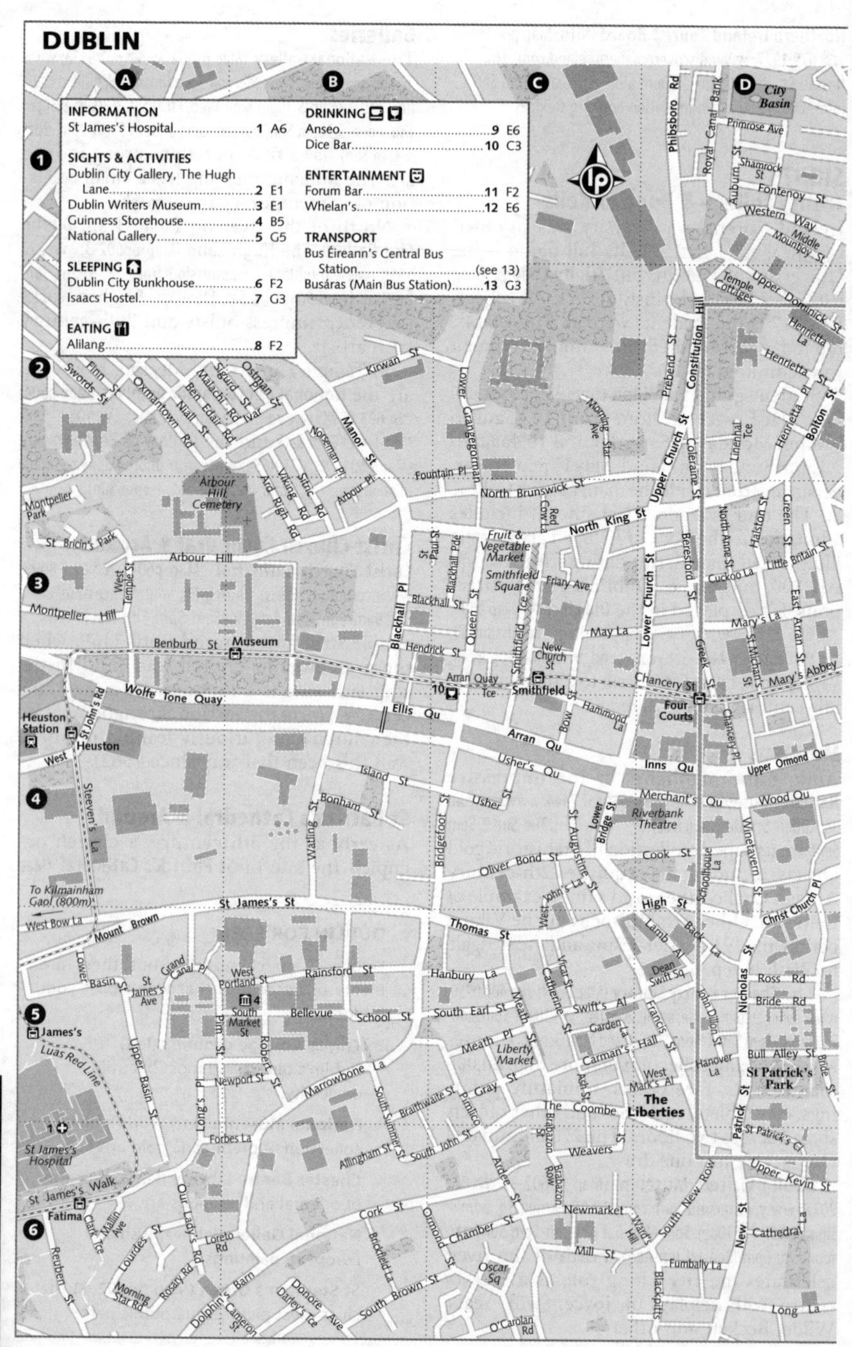
DUBLIN
A
B
C
D
1
2
3
4
5
6
INFORMATION
St James's Hospital 1 A6
SIGHTS & ACTIVITIES
Dublin City Gallery, The Hugh Lane 2 E1
Dublin Writers Museum 3 E1
Guinness Storehouse 4 B5
National Gallery 5 G5
SLEEPING
Dublin City Bunkhouse 6 F2
Isaacs Hostel 7 G3
EATING
Alilang 8 F2
DRINKING
Anseo 9 E6
Dice Bar 10 C3
ENTERTAINMENT
Forum Bar 11 F2
Whelan's 12 E6
TRANSPORT
Bus Éireann's Central Bus Station (see 13)
Busáras (Main Bus Station) 13 G3
City Basin
Phibsboro Rd
Royal Canal Bank
Primrose Ave
Auburn St
Shamrock St
Fontenoy St
Western Way
Middle Mountjoy St
Temple Cottages
Upper Dominick St
Henrietta La
Henrietta St
Henrietta Pl
Bolton St
Linenhall Tce
Constitution Hill
Prebend St
Morning Star Ave
Lower Grangegorman
Kirwan St
Manor St
Finn St
Swords St
Oxmantown Rd
Niall St
Ben Edair Rd
Malachi Rd
Sigurd Rd
Ostman Pl
Ivar St
Norseman Pl
Fountain Pl
Arbour Pl
Sitric Rd
Viking Rd
Ard Righ Rd
Arbour Hill Cemetery
Montpellier Park
St Bricin's Park
Arbour Hill
West Temple St
Montpellier Hill
North Brunswick St
Red Cow La
North King St
Upper Church St
Coleraine St
Beresford St
North Anne St
Halston St
Green St
Little Britain St
Cuckoo La
Fruit & Vegetable Market
Smithfield Square
Friary Ave
St Paul St
Blackhall Pde
Blackhall St
Blackhall Pl
Queen St
Smithfield Tce
New Church St
May La
Lower Church St
Mary's La
East Arran St
St Michan's St
Mary's Abbey
Benburb St
Museum
Hendrick St
Arran Quay Tce
Smithfield
Chancery St
Greek St
Wolfe Tone Quay
Ellis Qu
Arran Qu
Bow St
Hammond La
Four Courts
Chancery Pl
Heuston Station
Heuston
St John's Rd West
Island St
Usher's Qu
Usher St
Inns Qu
Upper Ormond Qu
Merchant's Qu
Wood Qu
Riverbank Theatre
Bonham St
Steeven's La
Watling St
Bridgefoot St
St Augustine St
Lower Bridge St
Schoolhouse La
Winetavern St
Cook St
Oliver Bond St
John's La West
To Kilmainham Gaol (800m)
St James's St
West Bow La
Mount Brown
Thomas St
High St
Lamb Al
Back La
Christ Church Pl
Dean Swift Sq
Lower Basin St
St James's Ave
Grand Canal Pl
West Portland St
Rainsford St
Hanbury La
Vicar St
Catherine St
Swift's Al
Ross Rd
Bride Rd
South Market St
Bellevue
School St
South Earl St
Meath St
Francis St
John Dillon St
Nicholas St
James's
Luas Red Line
Upper Basin St
Pim St
Robert St
Meath Pl
Liberty Market
Garden La
Hall
Carman's Hall
Bull Alley St
Bride St
St Patrick's Park
Newport St
Marrowbone La
South Summer St
Braithwaite St
Gray St
Pimlico
Ash St
West Mark's Al
Hanover La
The Liberties
Patrick St
The Coombe
Brabazon St
Long's Pl
Forbes La
Allingham St
South John St
Weavers
St Patrick's Cl
St James's Hospital
Ardee St
Brabazon Row
Upper Kevin St
South New Row
St James's Walk
Fatima
Our Lady's Rd
Mallin Ave
Clark Tce
Cork St
Ormond St
Newmarket
Ward's Hill
New St
Cathedral La
Lourdes St
Loreto Rd
Chamber St
Mill St
Brickfield La
Fumbally La
Reuben St
Morning Star Rd
Rosary Rd
Oscar Sq
Blackpitts
Dolphin's Barn
Cameron St
Donore Ave
Darley's Tce
South Brown St
O'Carolan Rd
Long La

IRELAND

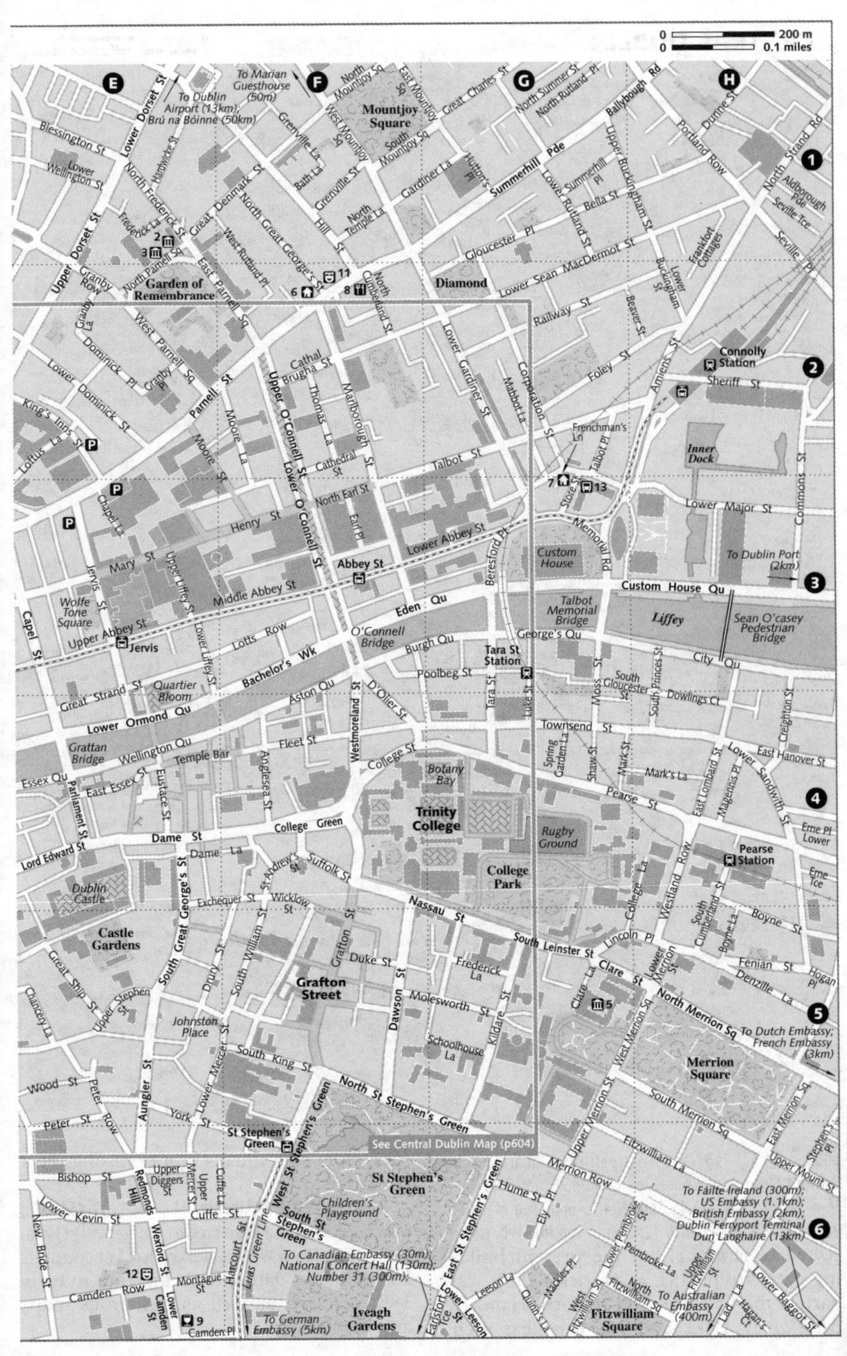
0 200 m
0 0.1 miles
E
F
G
H
1
2
3
4
5
6
To Dublin Airport (13km); Brú na Bóinne (50km)
To Marian Guesthouse (50m)
Lower Dorset St
Blessington St
Lower Wellington St
Hardwicke St
North Frederick St
Frederick La
Upper Dorset St
Granby Row
Granby La
North Parnell Sq
Garden of Remembrance
Great Denmark St
North Great George's St
West Rutland Pl
East Parnell Sq
Grenville La
Bath La
Grenville St
Hill St
North Mountjoy Sq
East Mountjoy Sq
West Mountjoy Sq
South Mountjoy Sq
Mountjoy Square
Great Charles St
Gardiner La
North Temple La
Hutton's Pl
North Cumberland St
Diamond
North Summer St
North Rutland Pl
Ballybough Rd
Summerhill Pde
Lower Rutland St
Summerhill Pl
Upper Buckingham St
Bella St
Gloucester Pl
Lower Sean MacDermot St
Lower Buckingham St
Frankfort Cottages
Portland Row
Dunne St
North Strand Rd
Aldborough Pde
Seville Tce
Seville Pl
Railway St
Beaver St
Foley St
Amiens St
Connolly Station
Sheriff St
West Parnell Sq
Dominick Pl
Lower Dominick St
Granby Pl
Parnell St
King's Inns St
Loftus La
Moore La
Moore St
Upper O'Connell St
Lower O'Connell St
Cathal Brugha St
Thomas La
Marlborough St
Cathedral St
Lower Gardiner St
Mabbot La
Corporation St
Frenchman's Ln
Talbot Pl
Talbot St
Store St
Inner Dock
Commons St
Lower Major St
Memorial Rd
Chapel La
Henry St
North Earl St
Earl Pl
Lower Abbey St
Beresford Pl
Custom House
To Dublin Port (2km)
Mary St
Upper Liffey St
Jervis St
Abbey St
Middle Abbey St
Wolfe Tone Square
Upper Abbey St
Jervis
Capel St
Lower Liffey St
Lotts Row
Eden Qu
O'Connell Bridge
Custom House Qu
Talbot Memorial Bridge
Liffey
Sean O'casey Pedestrian Bridge
George's Qu
City Qu
Burgh Qu
Tara St Station
Poolbeg St
Bachelor's Wk
Quartier Bloom
Great Strand St
Aston Qu
D'Olier St
Westmoreland St
Tara St
Luke St
Moss St
South Gloucester St
South Princes St
Dowlings Ct
Creighton St
Townsend St
Lower Ormond Qu
Grattan Bridge
Wellington Qu
Fleet St
Temple Bar
Essex Qu
East Essex St
Parliament St
Eustace St
Anglesea St
College St
Botany Bay
Trinity College
Spring Garden La
Shaw St
Mark St
Mark's La
East Lombard St
Magennis Pl
Lower Sandwith St
East Hanover St
Pearse St
Rugby Ground
Erne Pl Lower
Pearse Station
Erne Tce
Lord Edward St
Dame St
College Green
Dame La
St Andrew's St
Suffolk St
College Park
College La
Westland Row
Dublin Castle
Exchequer St
Wicklow St
Nassau St
South Leinster St
Lincoln Pl
South Cumberland St
Boyne La
Boyne St
Castle Gardens
South Great George's St
Drury St
South William St
Grafton St
Duke St
Frederick La
Clare St
Lower Merrion St
Fenian St
Hogan Pl
Denzille La
Great Ship St
Chancery La
Upper Stephen St
Grafton Street
Dawson St
Molesworth St
Kildare St
Clare La
North Merrion Sq
To Dutch Embassy; French Embassy (3km)
Johnston Place
Lower Mercer St
Schoolhouse La
West Merrion Sq
Merrion Square
South King St
Wood St
Peter Row
Aungier St
North St Stephen's Green
South Merrion Sq
East Merrion Sq
Peter St
York St
St Stephen's Green
See Central Dublin Map (p604)
Upper Merrion St
Fitzwilliam La
Upper Mount St
Bishop St
Upper Diggers St
Redmonds Hill
Upper Mercer St
Cuffe La
West St Stephen's Green
St Stephen's Green
East St Stephen's Green
Merrion Row
Hume St
Ely Pl
Children's Playground
Lower Kevin St
Cuffe St
South St Stephen's Green
Lower Pembroke St
To Fáilte Ireland (300m); US Embassy (1.1km); British Embassy (2km); Dublin Ferryport Terminal Dun Laoghaire (13km)
New Bride St
Wexford St
Harcourt St
Luas Green Line
To Canadian Embassy (30m); National Concert Hall (130m); Number 31 (300m)
Pembroke La
Upper Fitzwilliam St
Leeson La
Mackies Pl
Quinn's La
West Fitzwilliam Sq
North Fitzwilliam Sq
Camden Row
Montague St
Lower Camden St
Camden Pl
To German Embassy (5km)
Iveagh Gardens
Earlsfort Tce
Lower Leeson St
Fitzwilliam Square
To Australian Embassy (400m)
Lad La
Hagan's Ct
Lower Baggot St
IRELAND

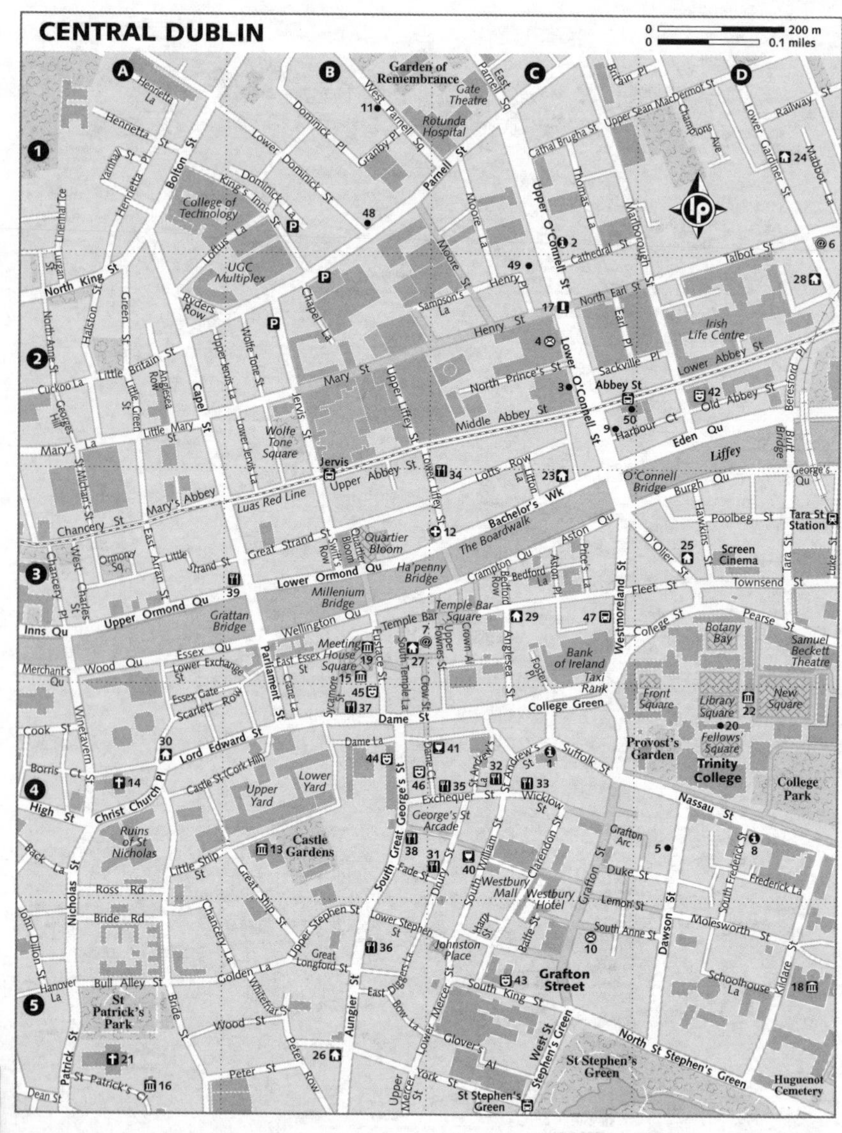

p604; ☎ 475 4817; www.stpatrickscathedral.ie; St Patrick's Close; adult/concession €5.50/4.20; 🕒 9am-6pm Mon-Sat, 9-11am, 12.45-3pm & 4.15-6pm Sun Mar-Oct, 9am-5pm Sat, 10-11am & 12.45-3pm Sun Nov-Feb, closed during times of worship) but the present building dates from 1191. St Patrick's choir was part of the first group to perform Handel's *Messiah* in 1742, and you can hear their successors sing the 5.45pm evensong most weeknights.

Nearby **Marsh's Library** (Map p604; ☎ 454 3511; www.marshlibrary.ie; adult/concession €2.50/1.50; 🕒 10am-1pm & 2-5pm Mon & Wed-Fri, 10.30am-1pm Sat) contains 25,000 books dating from the 16th to early 18th century, as well as numerous maps and manuscripts.

INFORMATION	Old Library......20 D4	Gruel......37 B4
Dublin Tourism Centre......1 C4	St Patrick's Cathedral......21 A5	Simon's Place......38 B4
Dublin Tourism Centre......2 C1	Trinity College......22 D4	Soup Dragon......39 B3
Eason's......3 C2		
General Post Office......4 C2	**SLEEPING**	**DRINKING**
Hodges Figgis......5 D4	Abbey Court Hostel......23 C3	Grogan's Castle Lounge......40 C4
Internet Café & Call Shop......6 D1	Abraham House......24 D1	Stag's Head......41 C4
Internet Exchange......7 B3	Ashfield House......25 D3	
Northern Ireland Tourist Board...8 D4	Avalon House......26 B5	**ENTERTAINMENT**
O'Connell's Pharmacy......9 C2	Barnacles Temple Bar House......27 B3	Abbey Theatre......42 D2
Post Office......10 C5	Globetrotters Tourist Hostel......28 D2	Gaiety Theatre......43 C5
Sinn Féin Bookshop......11 B1	Gogarty's Temple Bar Hostel......29 C3	George......44 B4
Well Woman Clinic......12 C3	Kinlay House......30 A4	Irish Film Institute (IFI)......45 B4
		Peacock Theatre......(see 42)
SIGHTS & ACTIVITIES	**EATING**	Rí Rá......46 B4
Chester Beatty Library......13 B4	Asia Market......31 C4	
Christ Church Cathedral......14 A4	Cedar Tree......32 C4	**TRANSPORT**
Gallery of Photography......15 B3	Cornucopia......33 C4	Aircoach Bus Stop......47 C3
Marsh's Library......16 A5	Epicurean Food Hall......34 C3	Cycleways......48 B1
Monument of Light......17 C2	Fallon & Byrne......35 C4	Dublin Bus......49 C2
National Museum......18 D5	Govinda's......36 B5	Iarnród Éireann Travel Centre......50 C2
National Photographic Archives..19 B3		

Kilmainham Gaol

The threatening **Kilmainham Gaol** (off Map pp602-3; ☎ 453 5984; Inchicore Rd; admission €5.30; 9.30am-6pm Apr-Sep, 9.30am-5.30pm Mon-Sat, 10am-6pm Sun Oct-Mar) played a key role in Ireland's struggle for independence and was the site of mass executions following the 1916 Easter Rising. An excellent audiovisual introduction to the building is followed by a thought-provoking tour. Catch bus 79, 78A or 51B from Aston Quay.

O'Connell St

During the 1916 Easter Rising, the Irish Volunteers used the **General Post Office** (GPO; Map p604; ☎ 705 7000; O'Connell St; 8am-8pm Mon-Sat) as a base for attacks against the British. Upon surrendering, the leaders of the Irish rebellion and 13 others (15 in all) were taken to Kilmainham Gaol and executed.

The nearby **Monument of Light** (Map p604), better known as 'The Spire', soars 120m over O'Connell St. The world's tallest sculpture, it occupies the site of Nelson's Pillar (like London's Nelson's Column, a monument to Horation, Lord Nelson), which was blown up by former IRA members in 1966.

Guinness Brewery

The **Guinness Storehouse** (Map pp602-3; ☎ 408 4800; www.guinness-storehouse.com; Market St; admission €15; 9.30am-7pm Jul-Aug, to 5pm Sep-Jun) sits in the malty fug of the mighty Guinness brewery. The tour is overpriced but at the end you get the best-tasting Guinness of your life for free. Take bus 51B or 78A from Aston Quay, or bus 123 from O'Connell St.

SLEEPING

Dublin is *always* bustling, so call ahead to book accommodation. Dublin Tourism offices can book accommodation for €4 plus a 10% deposit for the first night.

North of the Liffey

Isaacs Hostel (Map pp602-3; ☎ 855 6215; www.isaacs.ie; 2-5 Frenchman's Lane; dm/d from €16/66;) This busy, grungy hostel in a 200-year-old wine vault has loads of character. The lounge area is where it all happens, from summer BBQs to live music, and the easygoing staff are on hand 24/7 for advice and help.

GETTING INTO TOWN

Dublin Bus runs a frequent Airlink Express service to/from the airport, Busáras bus station, Heuston train station and various points around the city for €5 (30 to 40 minutes). Alternatively, take the slower bus 16A, 230 or 746 (€2, one hour). A taxi from the airport should cost around €22.

Buses 53 and 53A go to Busáras from the Dublin Ferryport terminal after all ferry arrivals (€3.30). From Dun Laoghaire's ferry terminal, take bus 46A to Fleet St in Temple Bar, bus 7 to Eden Quay or the Dublin Area Rapid Transport (DART) rail service to Pearse station (for south Dublin) or Connolly station (for north Dublin).

Globetrotters Tourist Hostel (Map p604; ☎ 878 8088; www.globetrottersdublin.com; 46-8 Lower Gardiner St; dm/tw incl breakfast €24/58; P) Funky decor and a little patio garden at the rear for that elusive sunny day make this city-centre place a good choice – it has 94 beds in a variety of dorms, all with handy, under-bed storage.

our pick **Abbey Court Hostel** (Map p604; ☎ 878 0700; www.abbey-court.com; 29 Bachelor's Walk; dm/d €22/88;) What this place lacks in physical charm, it makes up for in *craic*. Many of its residents are long-termers, giving the joint a community feel, and its two large common rooms and fantastic staff make this one of our favourite hostels in Dublin.

Also recommended:

Abraham House (Map p604; ☎ 855 0600; www.abraham-house.ie; 83 Lower Gardiner St; dm €15-36, d €38-46, all incl breakfast;) Friendly is an understatement at this large and lively hostel; close to the train station.

Dublin City Bunkhouse (Map pp602-3; ☎ 814 6255; www.thebunkhousedublin.com; 146 Parnell St; dm from €22;) Brand new, boutique-style hostel close to the city centre, which is getting rave reviews from travellers. Bicycle hire, cafe and free wi-fi.

South of the Liffey

Avalon House (Map p604; ☎ 475 0001; www.avalon-house.ie; 55 Aungier St; dm/d from €20/74;) This grand old Victorian building near St Stephen's Green houses a megahostel with four-, 12- and 20-bed mixed dorms on two levels, and en-suite singles and doubles offering some privacy.

Barnacles Temple Bar House (Map p604; ☎ 671 6277; www.barnacles.ie; 19 Temple Lane; dm/d from €19/80;) Plenty bright and immaculately clean, Barnacles' location in the heart of Temple Bar makes it a great place to stay if you don't mind the sound of drunken revellers outside your window; rooms at the back are quieter.

> **SPLURGE**
>
> **Number 31** (off Map pp602-3; ☎ 676 5011; www.number31.ie; 31 Leeson Close; s/d/tr from €120/175/230; P) The coach house and former dwelling of architect Sam Stephenson (of Central Bank fame) still feels like a 1960s designer pad with sunken sitting room, leather sofas, mirrored bar and floor-to-ceiling windows. A hidden oasis of calm, five minutes' walk from St Stephen's Green. Children under 10 are not allowed.

Ashfield House (Map p604; ☎ 679 7734; www.ashfieldhouse.ie; 19-20 D'Olier St; dm/d/q from €16/94/140;) Housed in a converted church a stone's throw from Temple Bar and O'Connell Bridge, this hostel feels more like a small hotel, with a good range of private en-suite rooms as well as four-, six- and eight-bed dorms.

Also recommended:

Kinlay House (Map p604; ☎ 679 6644; www.kinlayhouse.ie; 2-12 Lord Edward St; dm/d from €15/52;) Big, bustling and always busy, this is not a place for shrinking violets.

Gogarty's Temple Bar Hostel (Map p604; ☎ 671 1822; www.gogartys.ie/hostel; 58-9 Fleet St; dm/d from €23/76) Lively, party-atmosphere hostel right in the middle of the Temple Bar action.

EATING

Dubliners' new spending power has encouraged many excellent restaurants to take root, while the city's influx of immigrants has stimulated the market for ethnically diverse eateries.

North of the Liffey

Epicurean Food Hall (Map p604; Lower Liffey St; mains €3-12; 9.30am-5.30pm Mon-Sat) You'll be spoilt for choice in this bustling arcade that houses more than 20 food stalls. The quality can be hit and miss, but good choices include Itsabagel (for bagels), El Corte (for coffee) and Istanbul House (for kebabs).

Soup Dragon (Map p604; ☎ 872 3277; 168 Capel St; soups €5-10; 8am-5.30pm Mon-Fri, 11am-5pm Sat) Eat in or take away one of 12 tasty varieties of homemade soups, including shepherd's pie or spicy vegetable gumbo. Bowls come in three different sizes, and prices include fresh bread and a piece of fruit.

Alilang (Map pp602-3; ☎ 874 6766; 102 Parnell St; mains €10-13; noon-2.30pm & 5.30-11.30pm Mon-Fri, 12.30pm-midnight Sat & Sun) With Parnell St quickly becoming a Chinatown of sorts, Alilang's delicious mix of Chinese, Japanese and Korean cuisine gives it a leg up on the competition.

South of the Liffey

Simon's Place (Map p604; ☎ 679 7821; cnr George's St Arcade & South Great George's St; sandwiches €4-5; 9am-5.30pm Mon-Sat) Simon hasn't had to change his menu of doorstep sandwiches and wholesome vegetarian soups since he first opened shop two decades ago – the grub here is as heartening and legendary as he is.

PORTRAIT OF THE WRITER

Anyone who tells you that James Joyce (1882–1941) is an easy and enjoyable read is a rotten liar and should not be trusted. That said, no-one can doubt that Joyce's dense, often incomprehensible, work revolutionised the way stories are told. Beginning with *A Portrait of the Artist as a Young Man,* Joyce used stream-of-consciousness narratives to wander within a story's timeline, instead of telling it chronologically. Consider him an earlier, more Catholic Quentin Tarantino.

Joyce perfected this technique in his masterpiece, *Ulysses,* which focuses on a day in the life of two Irishmen – one a Catholic, the other a Jew – and in his last major work, *Finnegans Wake,* he went a step further, often using entirely nonsensical terms and disregarding plot completely.

While understanding Joyce's work may be out of the question, understanding his inspirational environment isn't. Next time you see a pub displaying a 'James Joyce Authentic Irish Pub Award' stop in, have a pint, and if anyone asks, tell them that *yer man* James is an easy and enjoyable read.

Govinda's (Map p604; ☎ 475 0309; 4 Aungier St; mains €6-11; 🕑 noon-9pm Mon-Sat) The soup at this branch of the Hare Krishna chain is so subtle and flavourful you'll think Krishna cooked it himself. The place is totally vegetarian, with a wholesome mix of salads and Indian-influenced hot daily specials.

Gruel (Map p604; ☎ 670 7119; 68a Dame St; mains €7-13; 🕑 7am-9.30pm Mon-Fri, 10.30am-10.30pm Sat & Sun) The best budget eatery in town, whether it's for the superfilling lunchtime roast-in-a-roll – a rotating list of slow-roasted organic meats stuffed into a bap and flavoured with homemade relishes – or the exceptional evening menu, where pasta, fish and chicken are given an exotic once-over.

Cedar Tree (Map p604; ☎ 677 2121; 11a St Andrew St; mains €8-12; 🕑 noon-midnight) Mosaic art on the walls and table-tops lend a Mediterranean air to this attractive little Lebanese restaurant – authentic mezze platters include tasty hummus, falafel and spinach-filled pastries.

Cornucopia (Map p604; ☎ 677 7583; 19 Wicklow St; mains €8-13; 🕑 8.30am-9pm Mon-Fri, 8.30am-8pm Sat, noon-7pm Sun) For those seeking escape from the Irish cholesterol habit, Cornucopia is a popular, mostly vegan cafe turning out scrumptious healthy goodies. There's even a hot vegetarian breakfast as an alternative to muesli.

Other recommendations:

Asia Market (Map p604; ☎ 677 9764; 18 Drury St; 🕑 10am-7pm) Fresh produce, dried goods and stir-fry sauces for self-caterers.

Fallon & Byrne (Map p604; ☎ 472 1000; Exchequer St; mains €6-9; 🕑 deli 9am-8pm Mon-Sat, 11am-6pm Sun) Queue for delicious sandwiches at the deli counter in this trendy New York–style food hall.

DRINKING & CLUBBING

Temple Bar, Dublin's 'party district', is almost always packed with raucous stag and hen parties, scantily clad girls, and loud guys from Ohio wearing Guinness T-shirts. If you're just looking to get smashed and hook-up with someone from another country, there's no better place in Ireland. If that's not your style, there's plenty to enjoy beyond Temple Bar. In fact, most of the best old-fashioned pubs are outside the district.

Grogan's Castle Lounge (Map p604; ☎ 677 9320; 15 South William St) A city-centre institution, Grogan's has long been a favourite haunt of Dublin's writers and painters, as well as others from the bohemian, alternative set. Drinks are marginally cheaper in the stone-floored public bar than in the lounge.

Stag's Head (Map p604; ☎ 679 3701; 1 Dame Ct) Built in 1770, and remodelled in 1895, the Stag's Head is possibly the best traditional pub in Dublin (and therefore the world). You may find yourself philosophising in the ecclesiastical atmosphere, as James Joyce once did. Some of the fitters that worked on this pub probably also worked on churches in the area, so the stained-wood-and-polished-brass similarities are no accident.

Whelan's (Map pp602-3; ☎ 478 0766; www.whelanslive.com; 25 Wexford St) A Dublin institution, providing a showcase for Irish singer-songwriters and other lo-fi performers.

Rí Rá (Map p604; ☎ 671 1220; www.rira.ie; Dame Ct; 🕑 Mon-Sat) One of the friendlier clubs in the city centre, Rí Rá is full nearly every night with a diverse crowd who come for the mostly funk music downstairs, or more laid-back lounge tunes and movies upstairs.

George (Map p604; ☎ 478 2983; 89 South Great George's St) The patriarch of Dublin's gay bars, and an excellent cruising venue, the venerable George has club nights Wednesday to Saturday, and stand-up comedy on Sunday.

Hipster spots include **Dice Bar** (Map pp602-3; ☎ 674 6710; 79 Queen St), the laid-back **Anseo** (Map pp602-3; ☎ 475 1321; 28 Lower Camden St) and the hip-hop **Forum Bar** (Map pp602-3; ☎ 878 7084; 144 Parnell St).

ENTERTAINMENT

For events, reviews and club listings, pick up a copy of the bimonthly freebie **Event Guide** (www.eventguide.ie) or the weekly *In Dublin*, available at cafes and hostels. Thursday's *Irish Times* has a pull-out section called 'The Ticket' that has reviews and listings of all things arty.

Cinemas

Irish Film Institute (IFI; Map p604; ☎ 679 5744; www.irishfilm.ie; 6 Eustace St) The fantastic IFI has two screens showing classic and art-house films.

Theatre & Classical Music

Abbey Theatre (Map p604; ☎ 878 7222; www.abbeytheatre.ie; Lower Abbey St) The famous Abbey Theatre is Ireland's national theatre, putting on new Irish works as well as revivals of Irish classics.

Peacock Theatre (Map p604; Lower Abbey St) The smaller and less expensive Peacock is committed to new plays and contemporary dramas, and is part of the same complex as the Abbey.

Gaiety Theatre (Map p604; ☎ 677 1717; www.gaietytheatre.com; South King St) This popular theatre – which famously staged the 1971 Eurovision Song Contest – hosts, among other things, a program of classical concerts, operas and musicals.

National Concert Hall (off Map pp602-3; ☎ 417 0000; www.nch.ie; Earlsfort Tce) Just south of the city centre, Ireland's premier orchestral hall hosts a variety of concerts year-round, including a series of lunch-time concerts from 1.05pm to 2pm on Tuesday from June to August.

GETTING THERE & AWAY

Air

Dublin airport (off Map pp602-3; ☎ 814 1111; www.dublinairport.com), about 13km north of the city centre, is Ireland's major international gateway airport, with direct flights from Europe, North America and Asia. Budget airlines like Ryanair and Flybe land here. See p598 for more details.

Boat

There are two direct ferries from Holyhead on the northwestern tip of Wales – one to Dublin Port and the other to Dun Laoghaire at the southern end of Dublin Bay. Boats also sail direct to Dublin Port from Liverpool and from Douglas, on the Isle of Man. See p598 for more details.

Bus

Busáras (Map pp602-3; ☎ 836 6111; www.buseireann.ie; Store St), Dublin's main bus station, is just north of the Liffey. Standard one-way fares from Dublin include Belfast (€15, three hours, 16 daily), Cork (€12, 3½ hours, six daily), Galway (€15, 3¾ hours, 16 daily) and Killarney (€16, three hours, 13 daily).

The private company **Citylink** (☎ 626 6888; www.citylink.ie) has daily services from Dublin (departing from both airport and city centre) to Galway for €15.

Aircoach (Map p604; ☎ 844 7118; www.aircoach.ie) can be caught at the airport and will take you to Belfast for €14. It can also be caught from in front of Boyle Sports on Westmoreland St and will take you to Cork, for the same price.

Train

North of the Liffey is **Connolly station** (Map pp602-3; ☎ 703 2358), for trains to Belfast, Derry, Sligo, other points north and Wexford. **Heuston station** (Map pp602-3; ☎ 703 3299), south of the Liffey and west of the city centre, is the station for Cork, Galway, Killarney, Limerick, Waterford, and most other points to the south and west. For travel information and tickets, contact the **Iarnród Éireann Travel Centre** (Map p604; ☎ 836 6222, bookings 703 4070; www.irishrail.ie; 35 Lower Abbey St). Regular one-way fares from Dublin include Belfast (€38, 2¼ hours, up to eight daily),

> **GETTING INTO TOWN**
>
> To get to the centre from the bus station, walk west along the river or south to Oliver Plunkett St. The train station, about 1.5km northeast of town, is a little further, but you can easily walk it via MacCurtain St, if you're staying on Wellington Rd. Frequent buses head from the airport (€5.50, 40 minutes), where there are direct budget flights to major cities all over Europe. See left for more details. Buses run from the ferry terminal (€3.30, 25 minutes) to the bus station.

Cork (€20, 2¾ hours, up to nine daily) and Galway (€15, 2¾ hours, five daily).

GETTING AROUND

Bicycle

Most rental places open during high season only, and rental costs are around €20 per day. Try **Cycleways** (Map p604; ☎ 873 4748; www.cycleways.com; 185-6 Parnell St).

Public Transport

Dublin Bus local buses cost from €1.50 to €2 for a single journey. You must pay the exact fare when boarding; drivers don't give change.

One-day passes cost €6 for bus services only (including Airlink), or €9.30 for travel on both bus and DART. Late-night Nitelink buses (€5) operate from the College St/Westmoreland St/D'Olier St triangle, south of the Liffey, until 4.30am on Thursday, Friday and Saturday nights.

Dublin Area Rapid Transport (DART; www.irishrail.ie) provides quick rail access as far north as Howth and south to Bray; Pearse station is handy for central Dublin.

The **Luas** (www.luas.ie) tram system runs on two (unconnected) lines; the green line runs from the eastern side of St Stephen's Green southeast to Sandyford, and the red line runs from Tallaght to Connolly station, with stops at Heuston station, the National Museum and Busáras. Single fares range from €1.50 to €2.20 depending on how many zones you travel through.

Taxis in Dublin are expensive, and flag fall costs €3.80, plus €1.50 per kilometre. For taxi service, call **National Radio Cabs** (☎ 677 2222).

AROUND DUBLIN

BRÚ NA BÓINNE

☎ 041

A thousand years older than Stonehenge, the Neolithic necropolis known as Brú na Bóinne (the Boyne Palace) is an extraordinary site. Its tombs date from about 3200 BC, roughly six centuries before Egypt's great pyramids. The complex, including the Newgrange and Knowth passage tombs can only be visited on a guided walk run by the **Brú na Bóinne visitor centre** (☎ 988 0300; Donore; visitor centre €2.90, visitor centre & Newgrange €5.80, visitor centre & Knowth €4.50; 🕑 9am-7pm Jun–mid-Sep, 9am-6.30pm May & late Sep, 9.30am-5.30pm Mar, Apr & Oct, 9.30am-5pm Nov-Feb). At 8.20am during the winter solstice, the rising sun's rays shine directly down Newgrange's passage and illuminate the chamber for a magical 17 minutes. Arrive early in summer as tours tend to fill it up.

Guided day tours from Dublin by **Mary Gibbons** (☎ 01-283 9973; www.newgrangetours.com; tour incl admission fees €35; 🕑 Mon-Sat) are excellent.

The site is 50km north of Dublin. The easiest transport option is the **Newgrange Shuttlebus** (☎ 1-800 424252; www.overthetoptours.com; €18 return).

SOUTHEASTERN IRELAND

KILKENNY

☎ 056 / pop 26,500

Medieval Kilkenny (Cill Chainnigh) is impossible to forget. Nestled in lush grounds overlooking the river, Kilkenny Castle stains itself upon your mind, while the town's excellent selection of pubs and eateries tantalises the tastebuds. Kilkenny is also renowned for its devotion to the arts, and hosts several world-class festivals throughout the year.

Most places of interest are on or close to Parliament St and its continuation High St, which runs parallel to the River Nore, and along Rose Inn St, which becomes John St as it leads away from the river to the northeast.

Information

Kilkenny e.centre (☎ 776 0093; 26 Rose St; per hr €6; 🕑 9am-9pm) Internet access, comfy and central.

Tourist office (☎ 775 1500; www.kilkennytourism.ie; Rose Inn St; 🕑 9.15am-1pm & 2-5pm Mon-Sat Sep-Jun, 9am-7pm Mon-Sat, 11am-5pm Sun Jul & Aug) Near the castle.

Sights

Stronghold of the Butler family, **Kilkenny Castle** (☎ 770 4100; www.kilkennycastle.ie; admission incl tour €5.30; 🕑 9.30am-7pm Jun-Aug, 10am-6.30pm Sep, 10.30am-5pm Apr-May, 10.30am-12.45pm & 2-5pm Oct-Mar) has a history dating back to 1172, when legendary Anglo-Norman Strongbow erected a wooden tower on the site. Highlights of the guided tour include the painted roof-beams of the **Long Gallery**, and the collection of Victorian antiques.

The approach on foot to **St Canice's Cathedral** (☎ 776 4971; www.stcanicescathedral.ie; adult/concession €3/2; 9am-6pm Mon-Sat, 2-6pm Sun Jun-Aug, 10am-1pm & 2-5pm Mon-Sat, 2-6pm Sun Apr-May & Sep, 10am-1pm & 2-4pm Mon-Sat, 2-4pm Sun Oct-Mar) from Parliament St leads over Irishtown Bridge and up **St Canice's Steps**, which date from 1614. Outside stands a 30m-tall **round tower** (admission €2; Apr-Oct) which you can climb – if you're over 12 – for a grand view of the town.

Sleeping

Tree Grove Caravan & Camping Park (☎ 777 0302; www.treegrovecamping.com; tent & 2 adults €15-20, car €2 extra; Mar–mid-Nov) This site is 1.5km south of Kilkenny, off the New Ross (R700) road; you can walk into town along a riverside footpath.

Kilkenny Tourist Hostel (☎ 776 3541; www.kilkennyhostel.ie; 35 Parliament St; dm/tw €17/42;) Centrally located, within a few steps of half a dozen clubs and restaurants, this hostel has a large kitchen and an atmospheric sitting room with sofas and a turf fire. Free wi-fi.

Rafter Dempsey's (☎ 772 2970; www.accommodationkilkenny.com; 4 Friary St; r €45-130) This place offers basic B&B accommodation in 16 rooms above a simple pub of the same name just off High St.

Eating

Gourmet Store (☎ 777 1727; 56 High St; sandwiches €4; 9am-6pm Mon-Sat) This classy deli is a good option for picnickers and hostellers.

Halal Centre (☎ 778 6389; 6 Irishtown; mains €6-12; 10am-11pm Sun-Wed, to midnight Thu-Sat) Boasting a menu of more than 100 items including vegie options, this tandoori take-away-delivery joint is one of the best and unnoticed places in town. It also doubles as a newsagent and corner store.

Marble City Bar (☎ 776 1143; 66 High St; lunch €7-10, dinner €10-15; 10am-9pm) Usual pub grub standards such as sausage with mash and fish and chips are raised above the norm here through the use of top-notch ingredients; a lower-level cafe facing St Kieran's St offers breakfasts, coffees and outdoor tables.

Drinking & Entertainment

John Cleere's (☎ 776 2573; 22 Parliament St) Cleere's often has good alternative bands – and the occasional poetry reading – in its theatre out the back.

Kyteler's Inn (☎ 772 1064; 27 St Kieran's St) The old house of Dame Kyteler (aka the Witch of Kilkenny) is a tourist magnet, but an atmospheric pub all the same.

Watergate Theatre (☎ 776 1674; www.watergatetheatre.com; Parliament St) The Watergate hosts musical and theatrical productions throughout the year.

Getting There & Away

McDonagh train station (☎ 772 2024; Dublin Rd) is east of the town centre along John St. At least four trains daily travel from Dublin's Heuston station to Kilkenny (€23, 1¾ hours) and then on to Waterford (€10, 50 minutes). Fares are higher on Friday and Saturday.

Bus Éireann (☎ 776 4933) operates from the train station. There are five buses a day to Dublin (€10, 2¼ hours), two to Cork (€15, three hours), and a couple to Wexford, Waterford and Rosslare Harbour.

SOUTHWESTERN IRELAND

CORK

☎ 021 / pop 119,400

There's a reason the locals call Cork (Corcaigh) 'The Real Capital' or 'The People's Republic of Cork' – something special is going on here. The city has long been dismissive of Dublin and with a burgeoning arts, music and restaurant scene, it's now gaining a cultural reputation to rival the capital's. The flurry of urban renewal that began with the city's stint in 2005 as European Capital of Culture continues apace, with new buildings, bars and arts centres springing up all over town. The best of the city is still happily traditional though – snug pubs with live-music sessions most of the week, excellent local produce in an ever-expanding list of restaurants, and a genuinely proud welcome from the locals.

Orientation

The city centre is an island between two channels of the Lee River. Oliver Plunkett St and the curve of St Patrick's St are the main shopping areas. North and south of St Patrick's St lie the city's most entertaining quarters: webs of narrow streets crammed with pubs, cafes, restaurants and shops. The train station and several hostels are north of the river.

Information

Main post office (Oliver Plunkett St)

Tourist office (☎ 425 5100; www.corkkerry.ie; Grand Pde; 9am-6pm Mon-Sat, 10am-3.40pm Sun Jul & Aug, 9.15am-5pm Mon-Fri & 9.30am-4.30pm Sat Sep-Jun)

Webworkhouse.com (☎ 427 3090; www.webworkhouse.com; 8a Winthrop St; per hr €1.50-3; 24hr)

There are also plenty of other internet cafes all over Cork.

Sights

Cork City Gaol (☎ 430 5022; www.corkcitygaol.com; Convent Ave; admission €7; 9.30am-6pm Mar-Oct, 10am-5pm Nov-Feb) closed down in 1923 and is now a terrific museum about a terrifying subject. Restored cells, mannequins representing prisoners and guards, and an impressive 35-minute audio tour bring home the horrors of 19th-century prison life.

Crawford Municipal Art Gallery (☎ 490 7855; www.crawfordartgallery.com; Emmet Pl; admission free; 10am-5pm Mon-Sat) combines the 18th-century Cork Customs House with 21st-century Dutch design, and is a must-see for anyone who enjoys art and architecture. Pieces by Irish artists like Jack Yeats and Cork's own James Barry sit among a fine permanent collection that features artists from Continental Europe as well.

Built in 1879, the Protestant **St Finbarre's Cathedral** (☎ 496 3387; www.cathedral.cork.anglican.org; Bishop St; admission €3; 9.30am-5.30pm Mon-Sat & 12.30-5pm Sun Apr-Sep, 10am-12.45pm & 2-5pm Mon-Sat Oct-Mar) is a Gothic Revival structure whose notable features include a Golden Angel, whose job is to blow her horn at the onset of the Apocalypse.

Sleeping

Kinlay House Shandon (☎ 450 8966; www.kinlayhouse.ie; Bob & Joan's Walk; dm €13-19, s/d from €38/46;) This labyrinthine hostel is in a quiet spot near St Anne's Church in Shandon. The decor has seen better days but the place has a fun, laid-back atmosphere.

Sheila's Hostel (☎ 450 5562; www.sheilashostel.ie; 4 Belgrave Pl; dm €15-18, d €48-52;) The sauna, cinema room, coffee shop and super-friendly staff make up for the occasionally cramped atmosphere in this always-heaving hostel.

Cork International Hostel (☎ 454 3289; www.corkinternationalhostel.com; 1-2 Redclyffe, Western Rd; dm €16-20, tw €44;) The cheerful staff at this bright and busy An Óige hostel do a great job coping with the constant flow of young travellers. It's 2km from the centre; bus 8 stops outside.

Brú Bar & Hostel (☎ 455 9667; www.bruhostel.com; 57 MacCurtain St; dm €17-23, d €50-60; P) Cork's funkiest hostel also has a popular bar and an internet cafe on the premises. This clean and friendly triple treat can be a rocking good time, especially on the weekends.

SPLURGE

Garnish House (☎ 427 5111; www.garnish.ie; Western Rd; s €60-80, d €90-140; P) With charming rooms (think flowers and fresh fruit), gourmet breakfasts and hosts who are eager to please, Garnish House is possibly the perfect B&B. From the moment you arrive and are greeted with tea and goodies, until the moment you leave, you will experience nothing short of absolute hospitality.

Eating

Wildways (☎ 427 2199; 21 Princes St; mains €3-6; 8am-5pm Mon-Fri, 9am-4.30pm Sat & Sun) Cork's first organic soup and sandwich bar serves such a variety of delicious and healthy food that even the pickiest of eaters can find something scrumptious. If you're around for breakfast, make sure to try the excellent chocolate-chip pancakes.

Quay Co-op (☎ 431 7026; 24 Sullivan's Quay; mains €8-11; 9am-9pm Mon-Sat) Flying the flag for alternative Cork, this place offers a range of self-service vegie options, all organic, including big breakfasts, rib-sticking soups and casseroles. It also caters for gluten-, dairy- and wheat-free needs.

Farmgate Café (☎ 427 8134; English Market; mains €10-15; 8.30am-10pm Mon-Sat) An unmissable Cork experience at the heart of the English Market, the Farmgate is perched on a balcony overlooking the market below, the source of all that fresh local produce on your plate.

For self-catering, head for the well-stocked food stalls at the **English Market** (9am-5.30pm Mon-Sat).

Drinking

Cork's pub scene is cracking, easily rivalling Dublin's. Locally brewed Murphy's is the stout of choice here, not Guinness. Check www.corkgigs.com for pubs with live music.

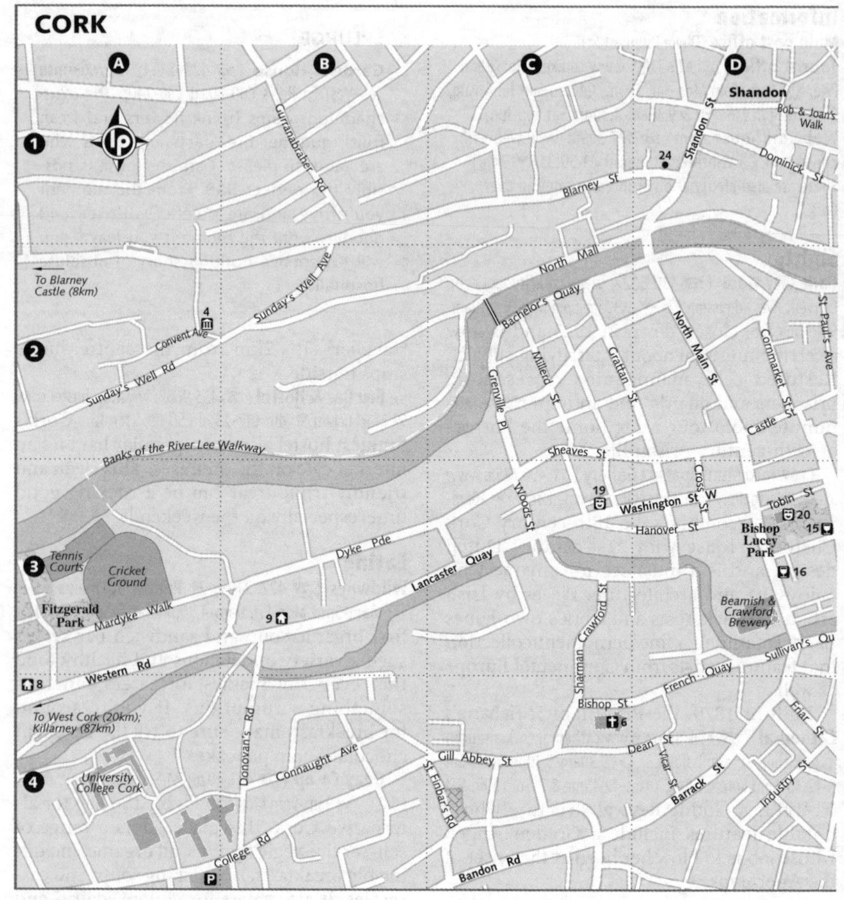

Mutton Lane Inn (☎ 427 3471; 3 Mutton Lane) With Victorian wallpaper, rock and roll posters, and a covered outdoor area for drinking and smoking, Cork's oldest pub is the type of place that you'll wish you had in your home town.

An Spailpín Fánach (☎ 427 7949; 28 S Main St) The 'wandering labourer' hosts trad sessions almost every night.

An Bróg (☎ 427 0074; 72 Oliver Plunkett St) This is *the* spot for Cork's 20-something crowd. Excellent live indie music and/or DJs every night of the week.

Entertainment

Cork's cultural life is generally of a high calibre. To see what's happening, grab **WhazOn?** (www.whazon.com), a free monthly publication available from the tourist office, newsagencies, shops, hostels and B&Bs.

Cork Opera House (☎ 427 0022; www.corkoperahouse.ie; Emmet Pl) Staging everything from opera and ballet to stand-up and puppet shows. It has wheelchair access.

Half Moon Theatre (☎ 427 0022; www.halfmoontheatre.ie; Emmet Pl) Located behind Cork Opera House, this theatre stages drama, comedy and live music.

Triskel Arts Centre (☎ 427 2022; www.triskelart.com; Tobin St) This is an important venue for contemporary art, film, theatre, music and photography.

Kino Cinema (☎ 427 1571; www.kinocinema.net; Washington St) The very cool Kino is Cork's only independent art-house cinema.

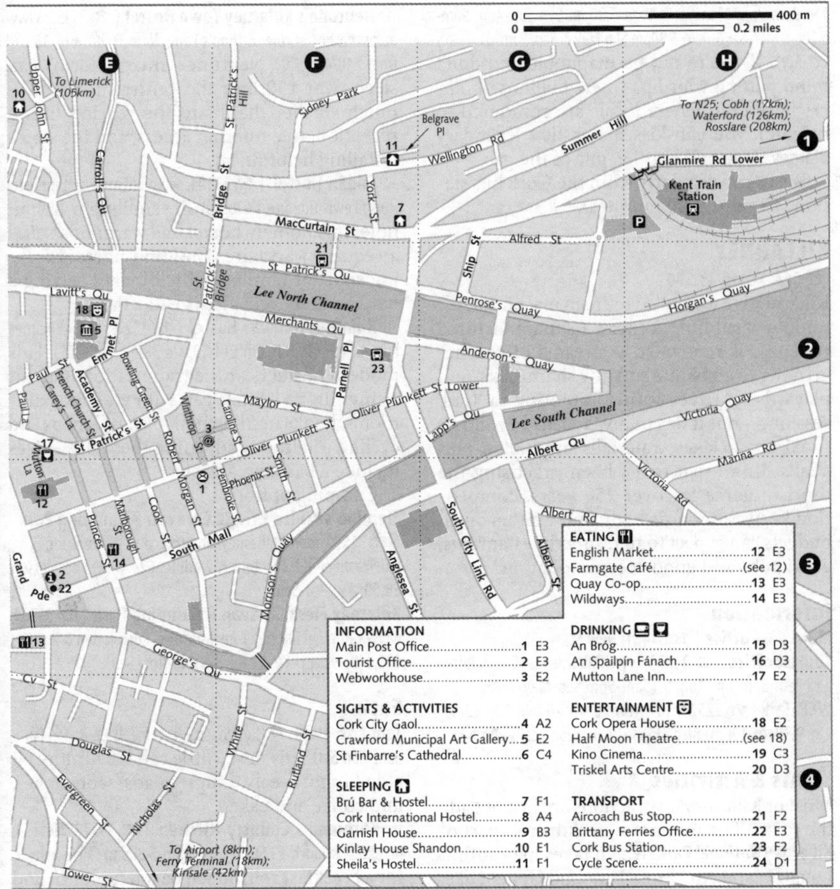

Getting There & Around

The **Cork bus station** (☎ 450 8188; cnr Merchants Quay & Parnell Pl) is just east of the city centre. You can get to most places in Ireland from Cork: Dublin (€12, taking 4½ hours, six daily), Killarney (€14, 1¾ hours, 14 daily), Waterford, Wexford and more. For a frequent direct bus service to Dublin city and the airport, take **Aircoach** (www.aircoach.ie) from St Patrick Quay, right behind the Gresham Metropole hotel (€14, four hours, eight daily).

Cork's **Kent train station** (☎ 450 4777; Glanmire Rd Lower) is across the river. Trains go to Dublin (€60, 2¾ hours, hourly), Galway (€60, five to six hours, seven daily) and Killarney (€24, 1½ to two hours, nine daily).

Brittany Ferries (☎ 427 7801; www.brittany-ferries.com; 42 Grand Pde) has regular sailings from Cork to Roscoff (France). The ferry terminal is at Ringaskiddy, about 15 minutes by car southeast of the city centre along the N28. See p599 for more details.

Cycle Scene (☎ 430 1183; www.cyclescene.ie; 396 Blarney St) has bikes for hire from €15/80 per day/week.

AROUND CORK

Blarney

☎ 021

Lying northwest of Cork, the village of Blarney (An Bhlarna) receives a gazillion visitors a year for one sole reason: **Blarney Castle** (☎ 438 5252; www.blarneycastle.ie; admission €10;

Book your stay at lonelyplanet.com/hotels

(🕒 9am-7pm Mon-Sat & 9am-5.30pm Sun Jun-Aug, 9am-6.30pm Mon-Sat & 9am-5.30pm Sun May & Sep, 9am-dusk daily Oct-Apr). If you're not germaphobic and don't mind putting your lips where millions of others have (and where locals are rumoured to urinate), you can kiss the castle's legendary **Blarney Stone** and get the 'gift of the gab'.

Buses run regularly from the Cork bus station (€5 return, 30 minutes).

KILLARNEY

☎ 064 / pop 13,500

Killarney is a well-oiled tourism machine in the middle of sublime scenery. Its manufactured tweeness is renowned – streams of coaches arriving to consume soft-toy shamrocks, and placards on street corners pointing to 'trad' sessions – but it has many charms beyond its proximity to lakes, waterfalls and 1000m-plus peaks. In a town that's been practising the tourism game for over 250 years, competition keeps standards high, and visitors on all budgets can expect to find superb restaurants, great pubs and good accommodation.

Information

Main post office (☎ 31461; New St)
Tourist office (☎ 31633; www.killarney.ie; Beech Rd; 🕒 9am-8pm Jun-Aug, 9.15am-5pm Sep-May)
WEB-Talk (☎ 22523; 107 New St; per 20 min/1 hr €2/5; 🕒 9.30am-10pm) Also offers cheap phone calls abroad.

Sights & Activities

Most of Killarney's attractions are just outside the town. The mountain backdrop is part of **Killarney National Park**, which takes in beautiful Lough Leane, Muckross Lake and Upper Lake. Besides Ross Castle and Muckross House, the park also has much to explore by foot, bike or boat. The *Killarney Area Guide* (€2 at the tourist office) has some ideas.

In summer the **Gap of Dunloe**, a scenic mountain pass squeezed between Purple Mountain and Carrauntouhill (at 1040m, Ireland's highest peak), is a tourist bottleneck. Rather than join the tourist hordes taking pony-and-trap rides, **O'Connors Tours** (☎ 30200; www.gapofdunloetours.com; 7 High St, Killarney) can arrange a bus, bike and boat circuit taking in the Gap.

Sleeping

Book ahead for accommodation from June to August. Hostels often rent out bikes and offer discounted tours. The tourist office books rooms for €4.

Neptune's Killarney Town Hostel (☎ 35255; www.neptuneshostel.com; Bishop's Lane, New St; dm €14-18, s/d from €40/44; 💻) Neptune's mixed dorms can sleep over 150, but the central hostel feels much smaller thanks to the roaring fire in reception, free internet access, and the staff's unfailing helpfulness.

Súgán Hostel (☎ 33104; www.killarneysuganhostel.com; Lewis Rd; dm/d €16/50) Resembling a hobbit hole, this homely hostel has warm hosts and an equally warm fire. The atmosphere is nothing short of familial, which makes leaving a hard task. Bicycle hire is €12 a day.

Killarney Railway Hostel (☎ 35299; www.killarneyhostel.com; Fair Hill; dm €14-19, s/d 38/52; P 💻) This modern hostel near the train station is about as inviting as hostels get, with en-suite bathrooms, bunks nestling in nooks, and maps and cycling itineraries adorning the walls. Prices include a basic breakfast.

Camping options:

Fleming's White Bridge Caravan & Camping Park (☎ 31590; www.killarneycamping.com; White Bridge, Ballycasheen Rd; car, tent & 2 adults €24, hikers per person €8.50; 🕒 Apr-Sep)
Killarney Flesk Caravan & Camping Park (☎ 31704; www.campingkillarney.com; Muckross Rd; car, tent & 2 adults €26, hikers per person €10; 🕒 mid-Apr–Sep)

Eating

Jam (☎ 31441; 77 High St; snacks & meals €2-8; 🕒 8am-6pm Mon-Sat) This funky little caff is a healthy pit stop for hot meals, soups, salads, sandwiches, and coffee and cake.

Kathleen's Country Kitchen (☎ 33778; New St; breakfast & lunch €3.50-11; 🕒 9am-5.30pm) The place for a breakfast roll, boiled bacon for lunch and no-nonsense service.

Revive Café & Wine Bar (☎ 266519; New St; mains €4-9; 🕒 9.30am-6pm) This comfortable modern cafe – think chocolate-brown leather armchairs – serves Illy-brand Italian espresso, freshly made sandwiches and delicious, home-baked rhubarb pie.

Scéal Eile (☎ 35066; 73 High St; mains €7-13; 🕒 9.30am-10pm May-Oct, 9.30am-6pm Mon-Sat Nov-Apr) There's a coffee shop crammed with delectable home baking on the ground floor, while upstairs there's a smart à la carte restaurant with Irish literary memorabilia decorating the walls, which serves traditional Irish cuisine.

For self-caterers, there is a **Tesco** (☎ 28530; New St; 🕒 8.30am-9pm Mon-Fri, 8.30am-7pm Sat, 10am-6pm Sun) across from the tourist office.

Drinking & Entertainment

Killarney Grand (☎ 31159; Main St) A great place for authentic music, if you can hear it over the boisterous crowd, the Grand has interesting takes on the traditional thing from 9pm. At 11pm modern bands take over (€6 cover).

O'Connor's (☎ 30200; 7 High St) This tiny but hugely popular pub stages a mix of trad, stand-up comedy, readings and pub theatre.

Granary (☎ 20075; Touhills Lane) Hidden down the alley next to the Killarney Grand, this bar/restaurant is one of the coolest hang-outs in town, with low lighting, exposed stone walls, and leather sofas. Bands and DJs play at weekends.

Getting There & Around

Operating from the **train station** (☎ 31067), **Bus Éireann** (☎ 30011) has regular services to Cork (€14, 1¾ hours, 14 daily), Galway via Limerick (€21, seven hours, eight daily), Dublin (€16, three hours, 13 daily) and Rosslare Harbour (€24, seven hours, two or three daily). Travelling by train to Cork (€23, 2¼ hours, three daily) or Dublin (€62, six hours, three daily) usually involves changing at Mallow.

O'Sullivan's (☎ 31282; 18 New St) hires out bikes for €15/80 per day/week.

THE RING OF KERRY

☎ 066

The Ring of Kerry, a 179km circuit around the Iveragh Peninsula with dramatic coastal scenery, is one of Ireland's premier tourist attractions. Most travellers tackle the Ring by bus on guided day trips from Killarney but you could spend days wandering here.

Sights

The **Ballaghbeama Pass** cuts across the peninsula's central highlands and has spectacular views and little traffic, while the shorter **Ring of Skellig**, at the end of the peninsula, has fine views of the Skellig Rocks and is less touristy. You can forgo roads completely by walking the **Kerry Way**, which winds through the Macgillycuddy's Reeks mountains past Carrauntuohill (1040m), Ireland's highest mountain.

Political hero Daniel O'Connell was born near **Cahirciveen**, one of the Ring's larger towns. The excellent **Barracks Heritage Centre** (☎ 947 2777; adult/student €4/2; 🕒 10am-4pm Mon-Sat Mar-May & Oct-Dec, 10am-6pm Mon-Sat, 1-5pm Sun Jun-Sep) has exhibits on Daniel O'Connell and moving material on the famine's local impact.

South of Cahirciveen the R565 branches west to **Valentia Island**, a jumping-off point for the unforgettable **Skellig Rocks**, two tiny islands 12km off the coast. The vertiginous climb up uninhabited Skellig Michael inspires an awe that monks could have clung to life in the meagre beehive-shaped stone huts that stand on the tiny strip of level land on top.

Calm seas permitting, boats run from spring to late summer from Portmagee, just before the bridge to Valentia, to Skellig Michael. The standard fare is around €40 return. Advance booking is essential; there are half-a-dozen boat operators, including **Casey's** (☎ 947 2437; www.skelligislands.com) and **Sea Quest** (☎ 947 6214; www.skelligsrock.com).

Sleeping

There are plenty of hostels and B&Bs along the Ring. It's wise to book your next night as you make your way around.

Travelling around the Ring at your own pace there's friendly **O'Shea's B&B** (☎ 947 2402; www.osheasbnb.com; Church St; s/d €45/70; Ⓟ) in the centre of Cahirciveen; the basic **Skellig Hostel** (☎ 947 9942; www.skellighostel.com; dm €15, d €52; Ⓟ) in Ballinskelligs; and the good-value **Royal** (☎ 947 6144; www.theroyalvalentia.com; r per person from €20; Ⓟ), a B&B on Valentia Island.

Getting There & Around

If you're not up to cycling, **Bus Éireann** (☎ 064-30011) runs a daily Ring of Kerry bus service from June to mid-September. Buses leave Killarney at 1.15pm and stop at Killorglin, Glenbeigh, Cahirciveen, Waterville, Caherdaniel and Moll's Gap, returning to Killarney at 5.40pm.

Travel agencies in Killarney, including **Destination Killarney** (☎ 064-32638; Scott's Gardens) and **O'Connor's Tours** (☎ 32456; 7 High St), offer daily tours of the Ring for about €25. Hostels in Killarney arrange tours for around €20.

THE WEST COAST

THE BURREN

The Burren of northern County Clare is a harsh and haunting landscape of bare rock, softened with a sprinkling of rare wildflowers; *Boireann* is Irish for 'Rocky Country', and the name is no exaggeration. The rugged limestone plateau is littered with ancient dolmens, ring forts, round towers, high crosses and a surprisingly diverse range of flora, while rocky foreshores and splendid cliffs line its coast.

If you're stuck for transport, multiple bus tours leave the Galway tourist office every morning for the Burren and Cliffs of Moher, including **O'Neachtain Tours** (☎ 091-553188; www.galway.net/pages/oneachtain-tours); they all cost around €25. **Burren Hill Walks** (☎ 065-707 7168; http://homepage.eircom.net/~burrenhillwalks) offers half-day guided walks for €15 to €25 per person.

Cliffs of Moher

The towering 200m-high Cliffs of Moher are one of Ireland's most famous features. In summer the cliffs are overrun by day-trippers, so consider staying in nearby Doolin and hiking or biking along the Burren's quiet country lanes, where the views are superb and crowds are never a problem. Be careful along these cliffs, especially in wet or windy weather.

The **Cliffs of Moher tourist centre** (☎ 065-708 1171; www.cliffsofmoher.ie; car park per vehicle €8, exhibition €4; 🕑 8.30am-7.30pm Jun-Aug, 9am-6pm Mar-May, Sep & Oct, 9am-5pm Nov-Feb) has exhibitions about the cliffs and the environment. You can avoid the crowds by visiting after the tourist centre closes.

GALWAY

☎ 091 / pop 72,400

Arty and bohemian, Galway (Gaillimh) is legendary around the world for its entertainment scene. Students make up a quarter of the city's population, and brightly painted pubs heave with live music on any given night. Cafes spill out onto cobblestone streets filled with a frenzy of fiddles, banjos, guitars and *bodhráns* (hand-held goatskin drums), and jugglers, painters, puppeteers and magicians in outlandish masks enchant passers-by.

Galway's city centre is tightly packed between the east bank of the Corrib River and Eyre Sq. The bus and train stations are within a stone's throw of Eyre Sq.

Information

Main post office (Eglington St)

net@ccess (☎ 569772; Old Malt Shopping Arcade, High St; per hr €3; 🕑 10am-10pm Mon-Fri, 10am-8pm Sat, noon-6pm Sun)

Tourist office (☎ 537700; www.irelandwest.ie; Forster St; 🕑 9am-5.45pm Jun-Oct, 9am-5.45pm Mon-Fri, 9am-12.45pm Sun Nov-May) Northeast of Eyre Sq.

Sights

Little remains of Galway's old city walls apart from the **Spanish Arch**, right beside the river. Nearby **Galway City Museum** (☎ 532460; Spanish Pde; admission free; 🕑 10am-5pm daily Jun-Sep, 10am-5pm Tue-Sat Oct-May) has exhibits on the city's history from 1800 to 1950, including an iconic Galway Hooker fishing boat, and a controversial statue of Galway-born writer and hell-raiser Pádraic O'Conaire (1883–1928), which was previously in Eyre Sq.

Parts of **Lynch Castle**, now a bank, date back to the 14th century. Lynch, so the story goes, was a mayor of Galway in the 15th century who, when his son was condemned for murder, personally acted as hangman. The stone facade that is the **Lynch Memorial Window** (Market St) marks the spot of the deed.

Across the road, in the Bowling Green area, is the **Nora Barnacle House Museum** (☎ 564743; www.norabarnacle.com; 8 Bowling Green; admission €3; 🕑 10am-5pm mid-May–mid-Sep or by appointment), the former home of the wife and lifelong muse of James Joyce. The small museum is dedicated to the couple.

Festivals

Galway Arts Festival (www.galwayartsfestival.com) A huge event held in July.

Galway Oyster Festival (www.galwayoysterfest.com) Has been going strong for over 50 years and draws thousands every autumn.

Sleeping

Salthill Caravan Park (☎ 523972; www.salthillcaravanpark.com; camp site per person €8-10; 🕑 Easter-Sep; Ⓟ) Just west of Salthill, off Salthill Rd, is this scenic spot right on the water. A bus runs the 4km into the city centre every half-hour.

Barnacle's Quay Street House (☎ 568644; www.barnacles.ie; 10 Quay St; dm €13-30, d €56-71; 💻) Set in a medieval townhouse with a modern extension, Barnacle's is at the heart of the action, surrounded by all the pubs, cafes and restaurants you came to Galway for.

Kinlay House (☎ 565244; www.kinlayhouse.ie; Merchant's Rd; dm €16-28, d €52-66; 💻) The modern, large, wheelchair-accessible Kinlay House is a convenient base half a block off Eyre Sq. It has clean, spacious rooms and a huge eating/lounge area, which can see all-night revelry. You can book discounted bus tours and Aran Island ferries at reception.

Griffin Lodge (☎ 589440; griffinlodge@eircom.net; 3 Father Griffin Pl; s €35-50, d €55-70; Ⓟ) You'll be welcomed like a long-lost friend at this completely

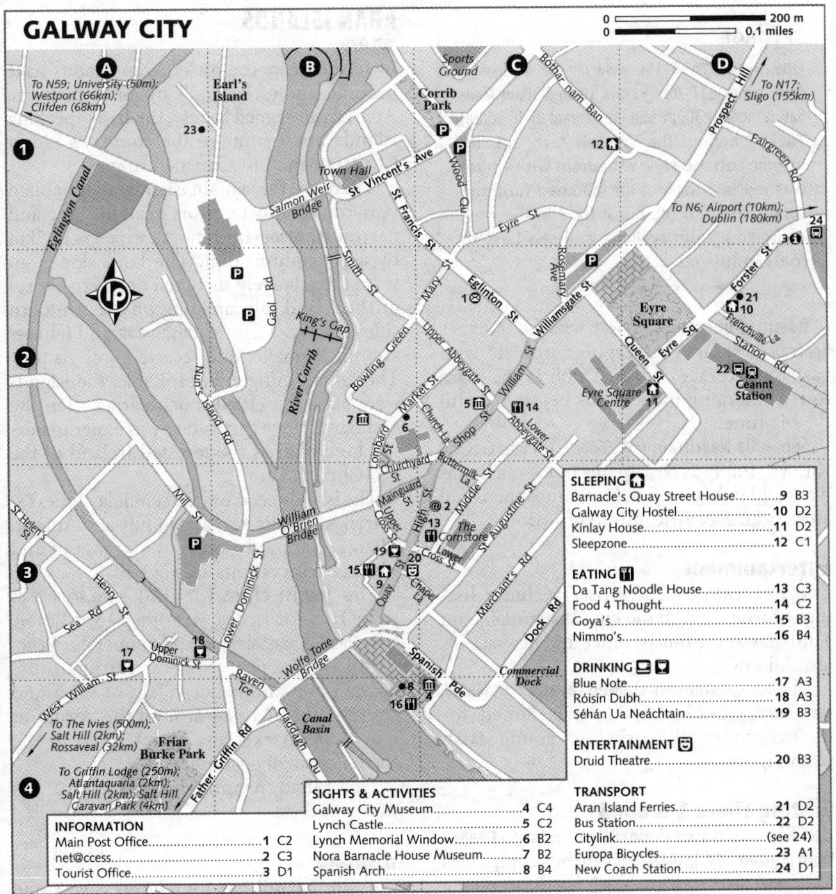

renovated B&B, which has eight immaculate rooms in soothing shades of spearmint and moss green.

Also recommended:

Galway City Hostel (☎ 566959; www.galwaycityhostel.com; Frenchville Lane; dm €16-26, d €50-75; 💻) A no-frills but friendly place to stay, right across from the bus station.

Sleepzone (☎ 566999; www.sleepzone.ie; Bóthar nam Ban, Wood Quay; dm €15-29, d €50-76, f €60-85; P 💻) Big, busy backpacker base with free internet and wi-fi, a bureau de change, pool table and BBQ terrace. Party-goers beware: no alcohol is allowed on the premises.

Eating & Drinking

Food 4 Thought (☎ 565854; Lower Abbeygate St; mains €5-6; 🕑 7.30am-6pm Mon-Fri, 8am-6pm Sat, 11.30am-4pm Sun) This New Agey cafe serves organic and vegetarian sandwiches, savoury scones, and wholesome dishes such as cashew-nut roast and moussaka made with textured vegetable protein.

Goya's (☎ 567010; 2 Kirwan's Lane; mains €5-10; 🕑 9.30am-6pm Mon-Sat) Goya's is a Galway treasure hidden down a narrow back alley, with cool pale blue decor, Segafredo coffee, superb cakes and hot lunchtime specials (12.30pm to 3pm).

Da Tang Noodle House (☎ 561443; Middle St; mains €11-17; 🕑 noon-3pm & 5.30-10pm Mon-Sat, 5.30-10.30pm Sun) This place on Middle St does light, healthy Chinese stir-fries and satays in a stylish paper-lantern-lit interior.

Blue Note (☎ 589116; 3 West William St) This jazzy pub-cum-dance-bar has a great summer beer garden and usually no cover charge.

SPLURGE

Nimmo's (☎ 561114; www.nimmos.ie; Spanish Arch; mains €17-26; ⏰ cafe 10am-3.30pm Mon-Sat & noon-3.30pm Sun, restaurant 6-10.30pm) Tucked behind the Spanish Arch, this informal, cottage-style restaurant with whitewashed interior and mismatched furniture serves some of the finest food in the west of Ireland, from scallops and sea bass to roast Irish lamb.

Róisín Dubh (☎ 586540; www.roisindubh.net; Upper Dominick St) A superpub complete with vast roof terrace, Róisín Dubh is *the* place to see emerging indie bands before they hit the big time.

Séhán Ua Neáchtain (☎ 568820; 17 Upper Cross St) Known simply as Neáchtains (*nock*-tans), this dusty old pub has a fabulous atmosphere and attracts an eccentric, mixed crowd.

Entertainment

The free *Galway Advertiser* includes listings of what's on in the city. It's available on Thursday at the tourist office and newsstands around town.

The long-established **Druid Theatre** (☎ 568660; www.druidtheatre.com; Chapel Lane) is famed for its experimental works by young Irish playwrights.

Getting There & Around

Bus Éireann buses depart from next to **Ceannt train station** (☎ 561444). Private bus companies use a **new coach station** a block northeast on the corner of Forster St and Fairgreen Rd.

Bus Éireann (☎ 562000) operates services to Doolin (€13, 1½ hours, seven daily Monday to Saturday in summer, twice on Sunday), Dublin (€13, 3¾ hours, hourly), Killarney (€20, 4¾ hours, three daily), Limerick, Sligo and beyond. **Citylink** (☎ 564163; www.citylink.ie) runs buses to Dublin (€15, three hours, hourly), and Clifden (€11) in Connemara.

Trains run to and from Dublin (€15, 2¾ hours, five daily). You can connect with other trains at Athlone.

Europa Bicycles (☎ 588830; www.westirelandcycling.com; Hunters Bldg, Earl's Island), opposite Galway Cathedral, rents out bikes from €12/60 per day/week, and can organise cycling tours of Connemara, the Burren and the Aran Islands.

ARAN ISLANDS

☎ 099

In recent years the rocky Aran Islands have become one of Ireland's major attractions. Apart from rugged beauty, the Irish-speaking islands boast some of the country's oldest Christian and pre-Christian ruins.

There are three main islands, all inhabited year-round. Most visitors head for long and narrow **Inishmór** (Inishmore), which is 14.5km by a maximum 4km. The land slopes up from the relatively sheltered northern shores of the island, plummeting on the southern side into the Atlantic. **Inishmaan** and **Inisheer** are much smaller and receive fewer visitors. Though seemingly inhospitable, the islands were actually settled much earlier than the mainland, since agriculture was easier to pursue here than in the forested Ireland of the pre-Christian era.

The islands get crowded at holiday times (St Patrick's Day, Easter) and in July and August, when accommodation is at a premium and advance reservations are advised.

The **tourist office** (☎ 61263; www.aranislands.ie; ⏰ 11am-7pm Jun-Sep, 11am-1pm & 2-5pm Mon-Fri, 10am-1pm & 2-5pm Sat & Sun Oct-May) operates year-round on the waterfront at Kilronan, the arrival point and major village of Inishmór. There's an ATM just around the corner at Spar Supermarket and about 150m to the north is a small post office.

The Ionad Árann heritage centre has internet access.

Inishmór

The 'Big Island' has four impressive stone forts thought to be 2000 years old. Halfway down the island and about 8km west of Kilronan, semicircular **Dún Aengus** (☎ 61008; admission €2.10; ⏰ 10am-6pm Mar-Oct, to 4pm Nov-Feb), perched on the edge of the sheer cliffs, is the best known.

About 1.5km north is **Dún Eoghanachta**, while halfway back to Kilronan is **Dún Eochla**; both are smaller, perfectly circular ring forts. Directly south of Kilronan and dramatically perched on a promontory is **Dún Dúchathair**, which is surrounded on three sides by cliffs.

SLEEPING & EATING

Kilronan Hostel (☎ 61255; www.kilronanhostel.com; Kilronan; dm/tw from €17/42; 💻) Perched above Tí Joe Mac's pub, this friendly hostel is just a two-minute walk away from the ferry; staff lend out fishing rods for free and can teach you to play hurling on the beach.

Mainistir House (☎ 61169; www.mainistirhousearan.com; dm/d €17/50; 💻) A quirky and colourful 60-bed hostel on the main road north of Kilronan, Mainistir caters for both backpackers and families. Book ahead for the great-value organic, largely vegetarian buffet dinners (€15; served at 8pm in summer, 7pm in winter).

Man of Aran Cottage (☎ 61301; www.manofarancottage.com; s/d from €45/74; 🕑 Mar-Oct) Built for the 1930s film of the same name, this thatched B&B has authentic stone-and-wood interiors with a genuinely homely feel. It also has a restaurant (lunch/dinner from €6/35; open lunch and dinner June to September, dinner only March to May and October) that serves fresh local fish and organic vegies and herbs from the owners' garden (dinner bookings are essential).

Inishmaan & Inisheer

The least visited of the three islands is Inishmaan (Inis Meáin, or 'Middle Island'), with a jagged coastline of startling cliffs and empty beaches. The main archaeological site is **Dún Chonchúir**, a massive stone fort built on a high point and offering views of the island.

The smallest island, only 8km off the coast from Doolin, is Inisheer (Inis Oírr, or 'Eastern Island'). The 15th-century **O'Brien Castle** (Caislea'n Uí Bhriain) overlooks the beach and harbour.

Getting There & Away

All three islands are served year-round by **Aran Island Ferries** (☎ 091-568903; www.aranislandferries.com; 4 Forster St, Galway); the trip takes around 40 minutes (€25 return). The boat leaves from Rossaveal, 32km west of Galway – it's an extra €7 return to catch an Island Ferries bus from Kinlay House Hostel in Galway. Buses leave 1½ hours before ferry departure times and are scheduled to meet arriving ferries. If you have a car, you can go straight to Rossaveal and leave it in the car park there for free.

Aran Direct (☎ 091-566535; www.arandirect.com) runs a nearly identical operation; at the time of research there were plans to introduce a high-speed catamaran ferry offering a one-hour crossing direct from Galway city to the Aran Islands – check the website for details.

Another option is to leave from Doolin in County Clare. **Doolin Ferries** (☎ 065-707 4455, 091-567676; www.doolinferries.com) runs to Inishmór (55 minutes) and Inisheer (40 minutes) for €40 return.

Inisheer and Inishmaan are small enough to explore on foot, but on larger Inishmór, bikes are definitely the way to go. **Aran Cycle Hire** (☎ 61132), just up from Kilronan's pier, is one of many bike shops that charge €10 per day.

Small operators offer island bus tours for around €10.

NORTHWESTERN IRELAND

SLIGO

☎ 071 / pop 17,900

William Butler Yeats (1865–1939) was born in Dublin and educated in London, but his poetry is infused with the landscapes, history and folklore of his mother's native Sligo (Sligeach). He returned many times and reminders of his presence in this lovely town are plentiful.

The **North West Regional Tourism office** (☎ 916 1201; www.sligotourism.ie; Temple St; 🕑 9am-5pm Mon-Sat Jun-Aug, 9am-5pm Mon-Fri Sep-May) is just south of the town centre. The **main post office** (Wine St) is east of the train and bus station. **Café Online** (☎ 914 4892; Stephen St; per hr €3.50; 🕑 10am-11pm Mon-Sat, noon-11pm Sun), across from the library, has internet access.

Sligo's two major attractions are outside town. **Carrowmore**, 5km to the southwest, is the site of a **megalithic cemetery** (☎ 916 1534; www.heritageireland.ie; admission €2.10; 🕑 10am-6pm Easter-Oct), which is one of the largest Stone Age necropolises in Europe.

In the churchyard at **Drumcliff**, 8km north of Sligo, is the **grave of WB Yeats**. Also in the churchyard is an extraordinary 11th-century **high cross**, carved with intricate biblical scenes. In summer the church shows a 15-minute audiovisual on Yeats and St Colmcille. The island of **Innisfree**, immortalised in Yeats' poem *The Lake Isle of Innisfree,* is in Lough Gill, southeast of Sligo town.

The basic but conveniently located **White House Hostel** (☎ 914 5160; Markievicz Rd; dm €14; Ⓟ) is just north of the town centre. For more comfort head to the excellent **Harbour House** (☎ 917 1547; www.harbourhousehostel.com; Finisklin Rd; dm/d €20/44; Ⓟ), which offers a little budget luxury.

Osta (☎ 914 4639; Garavogue Weir View, Stephen St; mains €5-10; 🕑 8am-7pm Mon-Wed, 8am-8pm Thu-Sat) is a superb cafe and wine bar with a prime location overlooking the river. **Fiddler's Creek** (☎ 914 1866; Rockwood Pde; mains €9-23; ⌚ food served noon-3pm & 5.30-10pm), on the opposite side of the river, serves excellent pub grub.

Getting There & Around

Bus Éireann (☎ 916 0066) has four services daily to/from Dublin (€16, four hours) and two to Westport (€15, two hours). The Galway–Sligo–Donegal–Derry service runs three times daily (twice on Sundays); it's €14 and 2½ hours to Galway, and €17 and 2½ hours to Derry.

The bus terminal is below the **train station** (☎ 916 9888), which is just west of the town centre along Lord Edward St. There are three trains daily to Dublin (€29, three hours).

BUNDORAN

☎ 071 / pop 1700

Surfers from all over the world come to Bundoran (Bun Dobhráin) to seek out some of Europe's best beach breaks. Pass by the tacky arcades, fast-food stalls and souvenir shops in the town centre and head for Tullan Strand, on the northern edge of town, the focal point of Bundoran's beach scene.

The seasonal **tourist office** (☎ 984 1350; www.irelandnorthwest.ie; Main St; ⌚ 10am-5pm Mon-Fri mid-Mar–Sep, 10am-4pm Fri & Sat Oct–mid-Mar) is opposite the Holyrood Hotel. The post office is a further 120m south.

Bundoran Surf Co (☎ 984 1968; www.bundoransurfco.com; ⌚ 9.30am-7pm) offers surfing lessons for beginners for €35 (three hours, including equipment). Surf and accommodation packages can also be arranged. If you prefer riding a horse to riding a wave, **Donegal Equestrian Holidays** (☎ 984 1288; www.donegalequestrianholidays.com; Bayview Ave) can provide anything from a one-hour hack (€30) to full day's trail ride (€110).

Once the holiday home of Viscount Enniskillen, the 300-year-old building housing the **Homefield Hostel** (☎ 984 1288; www.homefieldbackpackers.com; Bayview Ave; dm/d €20/50; P 💻) now hosts world travellers year-round. A good B&B option is **Bay View** (☎ 984 1237; Main St; s/d €40/64; P), a stately Edwardian town house with a view of the ocean.

Bus Éireann (☎ 074-912 1309) buses stop on Main St. There are direct daily services to Sligo (€9, 45 minutes), Galway (€18, 2¼ hours), Donegal (€7, 40 minutes) and more. **Ulsterbus** (☎ 028-9066 6630; www.ulsterbus.co.uk) has one daily service Monday to Friday to Belfast via Enniskillen. **Feda O'Donnell** (☎ 074-954 8114) buses stop two to three times daily, en route to Galway, at the Holyrood Hotel (Main St).

NORTHERN IRELAND

☎ 028

When you cross from the Republic into Northern Ireland you notice a couple of changes: the accent is different, the road signs are in miles, and the prices are in pounds sterling. But there's no border checkpoint, no guards, not even a sign to mark the crossing point – the two countries are in a customs union, so there's no passport control, no customs declarations. All of a sudden, you're in the UK.

Dragged down for decades by the violence and uncertainty of the Troubles, Northern Ireland today is a nation rejuvenated. The 1998 Good Friday Agreement laid the groundwork for peace and raised hopes for the future, and since then the province has seen a huge influx of investment and redevelopment. Belfast has become a happening place with a famously wild nightlife, while Derry is coming into its own as a cool, artistic city, and the stunning Causeway Coast gets more and more visitors each year.

There are still plenty of reminders of the Troubles – notably the 'peace lines' that still divide Belfast – and the passions that have torn Northern Ireland apart over the decades still run deep. But despite occasional setbacks there is an atmosphere of determined optimism.

BELFAST

pop 277,000

Once lumped with Beirut, Baghdad and Bosnia as one the four 'B's for travellers to avoid, Belfast has pulled off a remarkable transformation from bombs-and-bullets pariah to hip-hotels-and-hedonism party town. The city's skyline is in a constant state of flux as redevelopment continues apace. The old shipyards are giving way to the luxury waterfront apartments of the Titanic Quarter, and Victoria Sq, Europe's biggest urban regeneration project, has added a massive city-centre shopping mall to a list of tourist attractions that includes Victorian architecture, a glittering waterfront lined with modern art, foot-stomping music in packed-out pubs and the UK's second-biggest arts festival. The tourists have started to trickle back – get here before it becomes a flood.

Orientation

The city centre is compact, with the imposing City Hall in Donegall Sq as the central landmark. The principal shopping district is north of the square. North again, around Donegall St and St Anne's Cathedral, is the bohemian Cathedral Quarter.

South of the square, the so-called Golden Mile stretches for 1km along Great Victoria St, Shaftesbury Sq and Botanic Ave to Queen's University and the leafy suburbs of South Belfast; this area has dozens of restaurants and bars and most of the city's budget and midrange accommodation.

Information

Belfast Welcome Centre (☎ 9024 6609; www.gotobelfast.com; 47 Donegall Pl; 9am-7pm Mon-Sat, 11am-4pm Sun Jun-Sep, 9am-5.30pm Mon-Sat, 11am-4pm Sun Oct-May) Tourist information, accommodation booking, left luggage, and internet access for £1 per 20 minutes.

Fáilte Ireland (☎ 9032 7778; www.ireland.ie; 53 Castle St; 9am-5pm Mon-Fri year-round, 9am-12.30pm Sat Jun-Aug) Tourist information for the Irish Republic.

Hostelling International Northern Ireland (HINI; ☎ 9032 4733; www.hini.org.uk; 22-32 Donegall Rd) At the Belfast International Youth Hostel.

Main Post Office (12-16 Bridge St; 9am-5.30pm Mon-Sat) There are branches at Shaftesbury Sq and on University Rd.

Mega-Bite (☎ 9031 1423; Great Northern Mall, Great Victoria St; per 15min £1; 8.30am-8pm Mon-Fri, 10am-8pm Sat, 11am-8pm Sun) Convenient internet cafe.

Sights

The Renaissance-style **City Hall** (☎ 9027 0456; Donegall Sq; admission free; guided tours 11am, 2pm & 3pm Mon-Fri, 2pm & 3pm Sat), completed in 1906, is a testament to the city's industrial prosperity (closed for renovations till summer 2009). City Hall is fronted by an especially dour statue of Queen Victoria; her consort, Prince Albert, is commemorated in the **Albert Memorial Clocktower** (1867), which leans slightly to one side – Belfast's equivalent of Pisa's leaning tower.

The famed **Crown Liquor Saloon** (☎ 9027 9901; 46 Great Victoria St; 11.30am-11pm Mon-Sat, 12.30-10pm Sun) was built in 1885 and displays Victorian architecture at its most extravagant. The snugs are equipped with bells that once connected to a board behind the bar, enabling customers to order drinks without leaving their seats, and the original gas lamps are still in use.

Belfast's Harland & Wolff shipyards – whose famous yellow cranes **Samson and Goliath** dominate the city's eastern skyline – were the birthplace in 1911 of the *Titanic,* the 'unsinkable' ocean liner that struck an iceberg and sank in 1912. The Lagan Boat Company's excellent **Titanic Tour** (☎ 9033 0844; www.laganboatcompany.com; tour £10; 12.30pm & 2pm Fri-Mon Mar-Oct, Sat & Sun only Nov & Dec, also 3pm Fri-Mon May-Sep) shows you the main sights.

The **Ulster Folk & Transport Museums** (☎ 9042 8428; www.uftm.org.uk; admission per museum £5.50, both museums £7; 10am-6pm Mon-Sat, 11am-6pm Sun Jul-Sep, 10am-5pm Mon-Fri, 10am-6pm Sat, 11am-6pm Sun Mar-Jun, 10am-4pm Mon-Fri, 10am-5pm Sat, 11am-5pm Sun Oct-Feb), one of Northern Ireland's top attractions, is 11km northeast of the city centre on the Bangor road. The open-air Folk Museum has buildings ranging from traditional terrace houses to thatched-roof farm cottages, while the Transport Museum contains various Ulster-related vehicles, including a prototype of the DeLorean DMC sports car (of *Back to the Future* fame), and a display on the *Titanic.* From Belfast take Ulsterbus 1, or any Bangor-bound train that stops at Cultra station.

WEST BELFAST

The Catholic Falls Rd and the Protestant Shankill Rd have been battlefronts in Belfast's sectarian conflict since the 1970s. Even so, these areas are now quite safe and well worth visiting, if only to see the famous **murals** expressing local political and religious passions, and the infamous **Peace Line** – a 4km long barrier that divides Catholic and Protestant districts, and which has now been standing longer than the Berlin Wall.

Official Black Taxi Tours (☎ 9064 2264; www.belfasttours.com) and **Original Belfast Black Taxi Tours** (☎ 9058 6996) offer taxi tours of West Belfast, with an even-handed commentary on the Troubles. Running daily, prices are £8 per person based on a group of three to six sharing.

If you don't fancy an organised tour, pick up a map of the murals from the Belfast Welcome Centre and explore on foot.

Festivals

Cathedral Quarter Arts Festival (☎ 9023 2403; www.cqaf.com) This fantastic festival, in early May, attracts

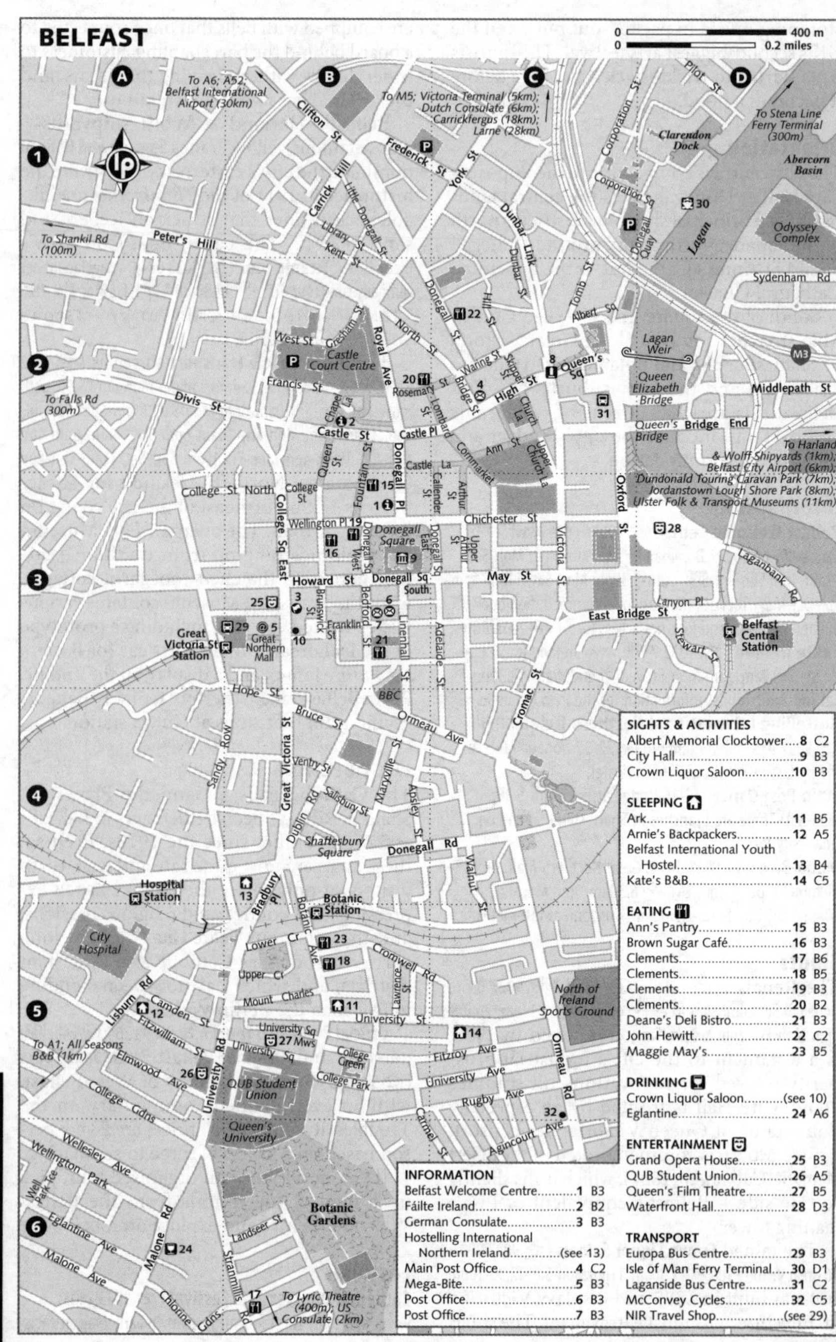
BELFAST
0 400 m
0 0.2 miles
To A6; A52; Belfast International Airport (30km)
To M5; Victoria Terminal (5km); Dutch Consulate (6km); Carrickfergus (18km); Larne (28km)
To Stena Line Ferry Terminal (300m)
To Shankil Rd (100m)
To Falls Rd (300m)
To Harland & Wolff Shipyards (1km); Belfast City Airport (6km); Dundonald Touring Caravan Park (7km); Jordanstown Lough Shore Park (8km); Ulster Folk & Transport Museums (11km)
To A1; All Seasons B&B (1km)
To Lyric Theatre (400m); US Consulate (2km)
Clifton St
Frederick St
York St
Carrick Hill
Little Donegall St
Library St
Kent St
Peter's Hill
Dunbar Link
Dunbar St
Corporation St
Corporation Sq
Pilot St
Clarendon Dock
Abercorn Basin
Donegall Quay
Lagan
Odyssey Complex
Sydenham Rd
Tomb St
Albert Sq
Lagan Weir
Queen Elizabeth Bridge
Queen's Bridge
Bridge End
Middlepath St
M3
Queen's Sq
High St
Waring St
Skipper St
Church La
Hill St
Donegall St
North St
Royal Ave
Gresham St
West St
Castle Court Centre
Francis St
Divis St
Rosemary St
Bridge St
Lombard St
Chapel La
Castle St
Castle Pl
Cornmarket
Ann St
Upper Church La
Queen St
Fountain St
Donegall Pl
Castle La
Callender St
Arthur St
College St North
College St
College Sq East
Wellington Pl
Donegall Square
Donegall Sq West
Donegall Sq East
Donegall Sq South
Upper Arthur St
Chichester St
Victoria St
Oxford St
May St
Howard St
Brunswick St
Bedford St
Franklin St
Linenhall St
Adelaide St
Lanyon Pl
East Bridge St
Laganbank Rd
Stewart St
Belfast Central Station
Great Victoria St Station
Great Northern Mall
Hope St
BBC
Bruce St
Ormeau Ave
Cromac St
Sandy Row
Great Victoria St
Ventry St
Salisbury St
Dublin Rd
Maryville St
Apsley St
Shaftesbury Square
Donegall Rd
Walnut St
Hospital Station
City Hospital
Bradbury Pl
Botanic Station
Botanic Ave
Lower Cr
Upper Cr
Cromwell Rd
Lawrence St
Mount Charles
University St
North of Ireland Sports Ground
Lisburn Rd
Camden St
Fitzwilliam St
University Rd
University Sq
University Sq Mws
Elmwood Ave
College Gdns
QUB Student Union
Queen's University
College Green
College Park
Fitzroy Ave
University Ave
Rugby Ave
Carmel St
Agincourt Ave
Ormeau Rd
Wellesley Ave
Wellington Park
Well Park Tce
Eglantine Ave
Malone Ave
Malone Rd
Landseer St
Stranmillis Rd
Chlorine Gdns
Botanic Gardens
SIGHTS & ACTIVITIES
Albert Memorial Clocktower....8 C2
City Hall....9 B3
Crown Liquor Saloon....10 B3
SLEEPING
Ark....11 B5
Arnie's Backpackers....12 A5
Belfast International Youth Hostel....13 B4
Kate's B&B....14 C5
EATING
Ann's Pantry....15 B3
Brown Sugar Café....16 B3
Clements....17 B6
Clements....18 B5
Clements....19 B3
Clements....20 B2
Deane's Deli Bistro....21 B3
John Hewitt....22 C2
Maggie May's....23 B5
DRINKING
Crown Liquor Saloon....(see 10)
Eglantine....24 A6
ENTERTAINMENT
Grand Opera House....25 B3
QUB Student Union....26 A5
Queen's Film Theatre....27 B5
Waterfront Hall....28 D3
TRANSPORT
Europa Bus Centre....29 B3
Isle of Man Ferry Terminal....30 D1
Laganside Bus Centre....31 C2
McConvey Cycles....32 C5
NIR Travel Shop....(see 29)
INFORMATION
Belfast Welcome Centre....1 B3
Fáilte Ireland....2 B2
German Consulate....3 B3
Hostelling International Northern Ireland....(see 13)
Main Post Office....4 C2
Mega-Bite....5 B3
Post Office....6 B3
Post Office....7 B3

GETTING INTO TOWN

Belfast's two bus stations – Laganside Bus Centre, near the river, and the bigger Europa Bus Centre, next to Great Victoria St train station – are both central, within five minutes' walk of Donegall Sq. Local trains connect Belfast Central (which, ironically, is *not* central) with Great Victoria St station via Botanic station. Most local bus services depart from Donegall Sq, near the City Hall, where there's a ticket and information kiosk.

Airport Express 300 buses link Belfast international airport with the Europa Bus Centre every 30 minutes (£7, 30 minutes). A taxi costs about £25. See p624 for details on getting into town from ferry ports.

pioneering writers, comedians, musicians and artists, and theatre productions.

Festival at Queen's (☎ 9066 7687; www.belfastfestival.com) For three weeks in late October and early November, Belfast hosts the second largest arts festival in the UK, in and around Queen's University.

Sleeping

Jordanstown Lough Shore Park (☎ 9034 0058; cshane@newtownabbey.gov.uk; camp sites £9) Basic camping ground in lovely seaside location in Newtownabbey, 8km north of town on Shore Rd (A2). Only two tent spaces so booking is essential.

Dundonald Touring Caravan Park (☎ 9080 9100; www.theicebowl.com; 111 Old Dundonald Rd; tent & 2 people £10; Mar-Oct) Larger camping ground next to the Dundonald Icebowl, 7km east of the city centre (take bus 19 from Donegall Sq West).

Ark (☎ 9032 9626; www.arkhostel.com; 44 University St; dm £11, s/d £20/32;) Bang in the heart of Queens student quarter, Ark is a small, convivial hostel with its own internet cafe. Note there's a 2am curfew.

Arnie's Backpackers (☎ 9024 2867; www.arniesbackpackers.co.uk; 63 Fitzwilliam St; dm £9-12;) More cosy than cramped, this small-scale hostel has a relaxed, down-home vibe, and Arnie manages to have a kindly disposition even when faced with Estonian football fans who've been drinking vodka for 12 hours straight.

Belfast International Youth Hostel (☎ 9032 4733, 9031 5435; www.hini.org.uk; 22-32 Donegall Rd; dm £10-14, s £19-29, tw £28-39; P) HINI's somewhat sterile 112-bed Belfast International is conveniently sited on the Golden Mile, which means it can be a bit noisy at night when the pubs and clubs empty.

Kate's B&B (☎ 9028 2091; katesbb127@hotmail.com; 127 University St; s/d £25/50) Kate's is a homely kind of place, from the window boxes bursting with colourful flowers to the cute dining room crammed with bric-a-brac. The bedrooms are basic but comfortable, and only a few minutes' walk from Botanic Ave.

Eating

Clements (☎ 9033 1827; 62 Botanic Ave; snacks £2-5, drinks £1.50-3; 7.30am-10.30pm) With loads of comfy seating and excellent cappuccinos, coffee chain Clements is Belfast's home-grown answer to Starbucks. Other branches are located on Donegall Sq West, Rosemary St and Stranmillis Rd.

Ann's Pantry (☎ 9024 9090; 29-31 Queen's Arcade; mains £1.50-5; 9am-5.30pm Mon-Sat) A tiny bakery with a next-door coffee shop, Ann's serves superb homemade soups, pies (try the steak and Guinness), cakes and choose-your-own sandwiches to take away or sit in.

Brown Sugar Café (☎ 9024 6097; 48 Upper Queen St; mains £3-5; 7.30am-4.30pm Mon-Fri, 9am-3.30pm Sat) A cool cafe with a scatter of snazzy cushions along its bench seats, Brown Sugar serves up all-day breakfasts, homemade soups, burgers, bagels and pancakes.

Maggie May's (☎ 9032 2662; 50 Botanic Ave; mains £4-6; 8am-10.30pm Mon-Sat, 10am-10.30pm Sun) This is a classic little caff with cosy wooden booths, murals of old Belfast, and a host of hungover students wolfing down huge Ulster fries at lunchtime. The all-day breakfast menu runs from tea and toast to eggy bread and maple syrup, while lunch can be soup and a sarnie or steak-and-Guinness pie.

John Hewitt (☎ 9023 3768; 51 Donegall St; mains £7-9; food served noon-3pm Mon-Sat) Named for the Belfast poet and socialist, this is a modern pub with a traditional atmosphere and a well-earned reputation for excellent food. The menu changes weekly.

Drinking & Clubbing

Crown Liquor Saloon (☎ 9024 9476; 46 Great Victoria St) Belfast's most famous bar has a wonderfully ornate Victorian interior. Despite being a tourist attraction it still fills up with crowds of locals at lunchtime and in the early evening.

Eglantine (☎ 9038 1994; 32 Malone Rd) The 'Eg' is a local institution, and widely reckoned to be the best of Belfast's student pubs. It serves good beer and good food, and there are DJs spinning most nights.

The **QUB Student Union** (☎ 0870 241 0126; www.qubsu-ents.com; Mandela Hall, Queen's Student Union, University Rd) has various bars and music venues hosting club nights, live bands and stand-up comedy. The monthly **Shine** (www.shine.net; admission £17-20; 1st Sat of month) is one of the city's best club nights.

Entertainment

Whatabout? is a free monthly guide to Belfast events issued by the Belfast Welcome Centre. Another useful guide is **The Big List** (www.thebiglist.co.uk).

Queen's Film Theatre (QFT; ☎ 9097 1097; www.queensfilmtheatre.com; 20 University Sq) The QFT is a two-screen art-house cinema, close to the university, and a major venue for the Belfast Film Festival in March.

Waterfront Hall (☎ 9033 4455; www.waterfront.co.uk; Lanyon Pl) The impressive 2235-seat Waterfront is Belfast's flagship concert venue, hosting local, national and international performers from pop stars to symphony orchestras.

Grand Opera House (☎ 9024 1919; www.goh.co.uk; 2-4 Great Victoria St) This grand old venue plays host to a mixture of opera, popular musicals and comedy shows.

Getting There & Away

For all Ulsterbus, city bus and Northern Ireland Railways (NIR) information, contact **Translink** (☎ 9066 6630; www.translink.co.uk). The **NIR Travel Shop** (☎ 9024 2420; Great Victoria St station; 9am-5pm Mon-Fri, 9am-12.30pm Sat) can book and provide information on trains, buses and ferries.

AIR

There are flights from some regional airports in Britain to the **George Best Belfast City Airport** (BHD; ☎ 9093 9093; www.belfastcityairport.com; Airport Rd), 6km northeast of the city centre. Everything else, including flights from the Republic, Britain, Amsterdam, Brussels and New York, goes to **Belfast International Airport** (BFS; ☎ 9448 4848; www.belfastairport.com), 30km northwest of the city.

BOAT

There are ferries to Belfast from Stranraer, Liverpool and the Isle of Man. For details on ferries to/from Northern Ireland, see p598.

Isle of Man Steam Packet Company (☎ 0870 222 1333; www.steam-packet.com) car ferries dock at Donegall Quay, a short walk north of the city centre.

Norfolkline Irish Sea Ferries (☎ 0844 499 0007; www.norfolkline.com) to Liverpool leave from Victoria terminal, 5km north of central Belfast; take a bus from Europa Bus Centre or catch a taxi. The terminal for **Stena Line** (☎ 0870 570 7070; www.stenaline.co.uk) services from Stranraer dock is 2km north of the city centre.

Other car ferries to and from Scotland dock at Larne, 28km north of Belfast.

BUS

Belfast has two bus stations. The main **Europa Bus Centre** (☎ 9066 6630), behind the Europa Hotel and next door to Great Victoria St train station, is reached via the Great Northern Mall beside the hotel. It's the main terminus for buses to Derry, Dublin and destinations in the west and south of Northern Ireland. The smaller **Laganside Bus Centre** (☎ 9066 6630; Oxford St), near the river, is mainly for buses to County Antrim and eastern County Down.

Ulsterbus has hourly Belfast–Dublin buses (£10, three hours) and a half-hourly service to Derry (£9, 1¾ hours). **Aircoach** (☎ 0870 225 7555; www.aircoach.ie) leaves from outside Jury's Hotel on College Sq East, Belfast, for Dublin airport (£10, 2½ hours, hourly).

TRAIN

Belfast has two main train stations: **Great Victoria St** (Great Northern Mall, Great Victoria St), next to the Europa Bus Centre, and **Belfast Central** (East Bridge St), east of the city centre.

Destinations served from Belfast Central include Derry (£10, 2¼ hours, seven or eight daily) and Dublin (£24, two hours, eight daily Monday to Saturday, five on Sunday). If you arrive by train at Central Station, your rail ticket entitles you to a free bus ride into the city centre. A local train also connects with Great Victoria St.

Great Victoria St station has services to Derry (£10, 2¼ hours, seven or eight daily) and Larne Harbour (£5, one hour, hourly).

Getting Around

A short trip on a city bus costs £1.20 to £1.80. Most local bus services depart from Donegall Sq, near the City Hall, where there's a ticket kiosk; otherwise, buy a ticket from the driver.

McConvey Cycles (☎ 9033 0322; www.mcconveycycles.com; 182 Ormeau Rd) hires out bikes for £15/60 per day/week. A deposit is required.

THE CAUSEWAY COAST

Ireland isn't short of scenic coastlines, but the Causeway Coast between Portstewart and Ballycastle – climaxing in the spectacular rock formations of the Giant's Causeway – is as magnificent as they come.

The **Ulsterbus** (☎ 9066 6630; www.translink.co.uk) Antrim Coaster (bus 252) links Belfast with Coleraine (£10, four hours, two daily Monday to Saturday) via Larne, Ballycastle, the Giant's Causeway, Bushmills, Portrush and Portstewart; a Sunday service operates from July to September only.

From July to mid-September the Causeway Rambler (bus 402) links Bushmills and Carrick-a-Rede (£5, 25 minutes, seven daily) via the Giant's Causeway and Ballintoy. The ticket allows unlimited travel in both directions for one day. Bus 172 runs year-round between Ballycastle and Portrush.

There are several hostels along the coast, including the following:

Sheep Island View Hostel (☎ 2076 9391; www.sheepislandview.com; 42a Main St, Ballintoy; camp sites/dm £5/10; P 💻) Offers dorm beds, shared accommodation in the camping barn, or a place to pitch a tent. It's on the B15 coast road 1km west of Carrick-a-Rede.

Ballycastle Backpackers (☎ 2076 3612; www.ballycastlebackpackers.net; 4 North St, Ballycastle; dm/tw £13/30; P) Near the waterfront and the main bus stop.

Mill Rest Hostel (☎ 2073 1222; 49 Main St; dm/tw £16/37; 🕑 daily Mar-Oct, Fri-Sun only Nov-Feb; 💻) Modern hostel, just 2.5 miles from the Giant's Causeway.

Carrick-a-Rede Island

The 20m-long **rope bridge** (☎ 2076 9839; £3.70; 🕑 10am-7pm Jun-Aug, 10am-6pm Mar-May, Sep & Oct) that connects Carrick-a-Rede Island to the mainland, swaying some 30m above the pounding waves, is a classic test of nerve. The island is the site of a salmon fishery and is a scenic 1.25km walk from the car park. Note that the bridge is closed in high winds.

Giant's Causeway

This spectacular rock formation – Northern Ireland's only Unesco World Heritage site – is one of Ireland's most impressive and atmospheric landscape features. When you first see it you'll understand why the ancients thought it wasn't a natural feature – the vast expanse of regular, closely packed, hexagonal stone columns looks for all the world like the handiwork of giants.

The more prosaic explanation is that the columns are simply contraction cracks caused by a cooling lava flow some 60 million years ago. The phenomenon is explained in an audiovisual (£1) at the **Causeway Visitors Centre** (☎ 2073 1855; www.giantscausewaycentre.com; 🕑 10am-6pm Jul-Aug, 10am-5pm Mar-Jun, Sep & Oct, 10am-4.30pm Nov-Feb).

It costs nothing to visit the site, but car parking is an exorbitant £5. It's an easy 10- to 15-minute walk downhill to the Causeway itself, but a more interesting approach is to follow the clifftop path northeast for 2km to the Chimney Tops headland, then descend the Shepherd's Steps to the Causeway.

DERRY

pop 83,700

Derry or Londonderry? The name you use for Northern Ireland's second-largest city can be a political statement, but today most people just call it Derry, whatever their politics. The 'London' prefix was added in 1613 in recognition of the Corporation of London's role in the 'plantation' of Ulster with Protestant settlers.

In the '60s resentment at the long-running Protestant domination of the city council boiled over in the (Catholic-dominated) civil rights marches of 1968. In August 1969 fighting between police and local youths in the poor Catholic Bogside district prompted the UK government to send British troops into Derry. In January 1972 'Bloody Sunday' resulted in the deaths of 13 unarmed Catholic civil rights marchers in Derry at the hands of the British army, an event that marked the beginning of the Troubles in earnest.

Today Derry is as safe to visit as anywhere else in Northern Ireland, while the Bogside and the inner city have been redeveloped. The city's long, dramatic history is still palpable – in the 17th-century city walls, in the captivating Bogside murals – but it's also a laid-back place with a well-founded reputation for musical excellence, from traditional to cutting-edge contemporary, and a lively arts scene that thrives in the city's many innovative venues.

Orientation

The centre of old Derry is the walled city on the western bank of the River Foyle. The bus

Book your stay at lonelyplanet.com/hotels

GETTING INTO TOWN

A free shuttle bus connects Derry's Waterside train station with the bus station. From there, follow Foyle St towards the Guildhall and edge along the outside of the town walls towards pedestrianised Waterloo Pl. Bear right down Strand Rd; the hostels and B&Bs all have their check-in points on Great James St, off Strand Rd.

station is just outside the walls at its north end; the modern city centre stretches north from here along Strand Rd. The train station is on the east bank of the River Foyle, across Craigavon Bridge, in a district known as the Waterside. The Bogside lies to the west of the walled city.

Information

Café Calm (☎ 7126 8228; 4 Shipquay St; per 15min £1; 🕑 8.30am-5pm Mon-Sat) Net access and excellent coffee.

Derry Visitor & Convention Bureau (☎ 7126 7284; www.derryvisitor.com; 44 Foyle St; 🕑 9am-7pm Mon-Fri, 10am-6pm Sat, 10am-5pm Sun Jul-Sep, 9am-5pm Mon-Fri & 10am-5pm Sat Mar-Jun & Oct, 9am-5pm Mon-Fri Nov-Feb) Tourist info for all of Northern Ireland and the Republic, as well as Derry. Also currency exchange and accommodation booking service.

Main Post Office (Custom House St) Just north of the walled city.

Sights

Derry's **city walls** (www.derryswalls.com), built between 1613 and 1618, were the last to be constructed in Europe, and are Ireland's only city walls to survive almost intact. They provide a fantastic walk, and offer a grandstand view of the Bogside (itself worth a closer look on foot) and the **People's Gallery**, a series of murals that decorate the gable ends of houses along Rossville St. Painted between 1997 and 2001 by the Bogside Artists (www.bogsideartists.com), they commemorate key events in the Troubles, including the Battle of the Bogside, Bloody Sunday, and the 1981 hunger strike.

The **Museum of Free Derry** (☎ 7136 0880; www.museumoffreederry.org; 55-61 Glenfada Park; adult/concession £3/2; 🕑 9am-4.30pm Mon-Fri year-round, 1-4pm Sat Apr-Sep, 1-4pm Sun Jul-Sep), just off Rossville St, chronicles the history of the Bogside, the civil rights movement and the events of Bloody Sunday.

O'Doherty's Tower, inside the northern corner of the city walls, is home to the **Tower Museum** (☎ 7137 2411; www.derrycity.gov.uk; admission £4; 🕑 10am-5pm Mon-Sat & 11am-3pm Sun Jul & Aug, 10am-5pm Mon-Sat Sep, 10am-5pm Tue-Sat Oct-Jun), which traces the story of Derry from the days of St Columbcille to the present, and has an excellent exhibition telling the story of *La Trinidad Valenciera* – a ship of the Spanish Armada that was wrecked at Kinnagoe Bay in Donegal in 1588.

Sleeping

Derry City Independent Hostel (☎ 7128 0542; www.derryhostel.com; 44 Great James St; dm £11-16, d or tw £36; 💻) Every hostel should strive to engender the warm atmosphere that Steve and Kylie have created here. It's a little cramped but it's funky and fun, with an eating nook covered in Indian paintings and pillows.

Merchant's House (☎ 7126 9691; www.thesaddlershouse.com; 16 Queen St; s/d £35/50) This historic, Georgian-style townhouse has an elegant lounge and dining room with marble fireplaces and antique furniture, TV and coffee-making facilities in all rooms, and homemade marmalade at breakfast. Call at the Saddler's House first to pick up a key.

Saddler's House (☎ 7126 9691; www.thesaddlershouse.com; 36 Great James St; s/d £35/55; P) Everything in this centrally located Victorian townhouse, from the sharp-witted hosts to their bulldog Bertie, is a joy.

Eating

Café Artisan (☎ 7128 2727; 18-20 Bishop St Within; mains £2-5; 🕑 9.30am-5.30pm Mon-Sat) This cool little cafe is tucked away at the back of the Bookworm bookshop and serves delicious homemade soups, deli sandwiches, *panini* and excellent cappuccinos.

Sandwich Co (☎ 7137 2500; The Diamond; sandwiches & salads £3-5; 🕑 9am-5pm Mon-Sat) White bread, brown bread, baguettes, *panini*, ciabatta – this place offers good-value, choose-your-own sandwiches and salads.

Encore Brasserie (☎ 7137 2492; Millennium Forum, Newmarket St; mains lunch £6, dinner £10-13; 🕑 noon-4pm & 5-9pm) Set in the lobby of the city's main cultural venue, the Encore is a stylish little place with friendly, efficient service and a crowd-pleasing menu of perennial favourites from homemade lasagne to slow-braised lamb shank.

For self-caterers, **Tesco** (Strand Rd) has a large supermarket in the Quayside Shopping Centre.

Drinking & Entertainment

Peadar O'Donnell's (☎ 7126 2318; 63 Waterloo St) Peadar's goes for traditional music sessions nightly and often on weekend afternoons too.

Sandino's (☎ 7130 9297; www.sandinos.com; 1 Water St) From the posters of Ché to the Free Palestine flag, this relaxed cafe-bar exudes a liberal, left-wing vibe. There are live bands on Friday nights, DJ sessions on Saturdays, and occasional jazz, folk or comedy gigs – check the website for what's on.

Nerve Centre (☎ 7126 0562; www.nerve-centre.org.uk; 7-8 Magazine St) The Nerve Centre was set up in 1990 as a multimedia arts centre to encourage young, local talent in the fields of music and film. It has a performance area, a theatre, an art-house cinema, a bar and a cafe.

Getting There & Away

The **bus station** (☎ 7126 2261) is just northeast of the city walls, on Foyle St. Ulsterbus service 212, the *Maiden City Flyer*, is the fastest service between Belfast and Derry (£10, 1¾ hours, every half-hour, less on Sunday). Bus 234 goes to Coleraine (£6, one hour, five daily Monday to Friday, two Sunday), where you can connect with the 252 Antrim Coaster service (p625). Bus 274 goes from Derry to Dublin (£16, four hours, every two hours).

Airporter (☎ 7126 9996; www.airporter.co.uk) buses run direct from Derry's Quayside Shopping Centre to Belfast International (one-way/return £18/28, 1½ hours) and George Best Belfast City (same fare, two hours) airports every 90 minutes Monday to Friday, and every two hours at weekends.

Derry's **Waterside train station** (☎ 7134 2228) lies across the River Foyle from the city centre, but is connected to it by a free Rail Link bus. Trains to Belfast (£10, 2¼ hours, seven or eight daily Monday to Saturday, four on Sunday) run via Coleraine, where you can change for Portrush (£9, 1¼ hours).

IRELAND DIRECTORY

ACCOMMODATION

Sleeping reviews in this chapter include the high-season price; low-season rates can be 15% to 25% lower.

Book ahead in peak season. **Fáilte Ireland** (off Map p602-3; ☎ 1850 230 330; www.ireland.ie; Baggot St; 9am-5pm Mon-Fri) books accommodation for a 10% room deposit and a fee of €4. The **Northern Ireland Tourist Board** (NITB; www.discovernorthernireland.com) books accommodation for free with a 10% room deposit. Accommodation for the Republic and the North may also be booked online, via the **Gulliver booking service** (www.gulliver.ie). A deposit of 10% and a €4 fee is payable.

Commercial camping grounds typically charge €12 to €18 for a tent and two people, and some hostels have space for tents. Unless indicated otherwise, prices given in this chapter for 'camp sites' are for a tent plus two people.

Hostels in Ireland can be heavily booked in summer, although there are hundreds of backpacker hostels and about 40 official youth hostels. From June to September most hostels cost from €15 to €20 a night, except for the more expensive hostels in Dublin, Belfast and a few other places.

Typical B&Bs cost around €20 to €40 per person a night (sharing a double room), though more-luxurious B&Bs can cost upwards of €55 per person. Most B&Bs fill up quickly in summer.

The following contacts are useful:

An Óige (☎ 01-830 4555; www.anoige.ie)
Hostelling International Northern Ireland (HINI; ☎ 028-9032 4733; www.hini.org.uk)
Independent Holiday Hostels (IHH; ☎ 01-836 4700; www.hostels-ireland.com)
Independent Hostel Owners in Ireland (IHO; ☎ 074-973 0130; www.independenthostelsireland.com)
Irish Caravan and Camping Council (www.camping-ireland.ie)

ACTIVITIES

Ireland is great for outdoor activities, and tourist offices have a wide selection of information sheets covering bird-watching (County Donegal and County Wexford), surfing (great along the west coast), scuba diving (West Cork), rock climbing, fishing, horse riding, sailing, canoeing and many other activities.

Walking is particularly popular, although you must come prepared for wet weather. There are now well over 20 way-marked trails throughout Ireland, one of the most popular being the 132km Wicklow Way.

BUSINESS HOURS

Offices are open 9am to 5pm Monday to Friday, shops a little later. Thursday and/or Friday shops stay open later. Many also open on Saturday. In winter, some tourist attractions open less often or may be shut completely. In Northern Ireland some tourist attractions are closed on Sunday morning.

Restaurants north and south tend to close around 9pm or 10pm. In the Republic, pubs close at 11.30pm Monday to Thursday, 12.30am Friday and Saturday and 11pm on Sunday; some pubs have licences allowing them to stay open till 2.30am Thursday to Saturday. In the North, pubs close at 11pm Monday to Saturday and 10pm on Sunday; those with late licences stay open until 1am Monday to Friday and to midnight on Sunday.

EMBASSIES & CONSULATES

The following countries have diplomatic offices in Dublin:

Australia (off Map pp602-3; ☎ 01-664 5300; www.ireland.embassy.gov.au; 2nd fl, Fitzwilton House, Wilton Tce, Dublin 2)
Canada (off Map pp602-3; ☎ 01-234 4000; www.canada.ie; 7-8 Wilton Tce, Dublin 2)
France (off Map pp602-3; ☎ 01-277 5000; www.ambafrance.ie; 36 Ailesbury Rd, Dublin 4)
Germany (off Map pp602-3; ☎ 01-269 3011; www.dublin.diplo.de; 31 Trimleston Ave, Booterstown, Co Dublin)
Netherlands (off Map pp602-3; ☎ 01-269 3444; www.netherlandsembassy.ie; 160 Merrion Rd, Dublin 4)
New Zealand Contact the NZ High Commission in London.
UK (off Map pp602-3; ☎ 01-205 3700; www.britishembassy.ie; 29 Merrion Rd, Ballsbridge, Dublin 4)
USA (off Map pp602-3; ☎ 01-668 8777; http://dublin.usembassy.gov; 42 Elgin Rd, Ballsbridge, Dublin 4)

In Northern Ireland, nationals of most countries should contact their embassy in London. Consulates in the North include the following:

Germany (☎ 028-9269 8356; german.consul@northernirelandchamber.com; 22 Great Victoria St, Belfast BT2 7BJ)
Netherlands (☎ 028-9037 0223; www.netherlands-embassy.org.uk; 14-16 West Bank Rd, Belfast BT3 9JL)
New Zealand (☎ 028-9264 8098; The Ballance House, 118A Lisburn Rd, Glenavy BT29 4NY)
USA (☎ 028-9038 6104; www.americanembassy.org.uk; Danesfort House, 223 Stranmillis Rd, Belfast BT9 5GR)

FESTIVALS & EVENTS

St Patrick's Day A cacophony of parades, fireworks and light shows for three days around 17 March in Dublin; Cork, Armagh and Belfast also have parades.
Dublin International Film Festival In April; also a highlight.
Bloomsday In Dublin, Leopold Bloom's Joycean journey around the city is marked by various events on 16 June.
Marching season In Northern Ireland every Orangeman in the country hits the streets on 'the 12th' (of July).
Galway Arts Festival (p616) A great regional cultural event in late July.
Kilkenny Arts Festival In late August.
All-Ireland hurling In Dublin in September.
Football finals In Dublin in September.
Galway Oyster Festival In September.
Belfast Festival At Queen's in November.

HOLIDAYS

Public holidays in the Republic and/or Northern Ireland:

New Year's Day 1 January
St Patrick's Day 17 March
Easter (Good Friday to Easter Monday inclusive) March/April
May Holiday 1st Monday in May
Christmas Day 25 December
St Stephen's Day (Boxing Day) 26 December

Northern Ireland

Spring Bank Holiday Last Monday in May
Orangemen's Day 12 July (following Monday if 12th is at weekend).
August Bank Holiday Last Monday in August.

Republic

June Holiday First Monday in June
August Holiday First Monday in August
October Holiday Last Monday in October

INTERNET RESOURCES

CIE Group (www.cie.ie) Handy for planning transport in the republic.
Entertainment Ireland (www.entertainmentireland.ie) Countrywide listings for clubs, theatres, festivals, cinemas, museums and much more.
Irish Tourist Board (www.ireland.ie) The Republic's tourist information site has heaps of practical info. It features a huge accommodation database with photos.
Northern Ireland Tourism (www.discovernorthernireland.com) Northern Ireland's official tourism information site is particularly strong on activities and accommodation.
Translink (www.translink.co.uk) Handy for planning transport in Northern Ireland.

MONEY

The Republic uses the euro, while Northern Ireland uses the British pound sterling (£). Banks offer the best exchange rates; exchange bureaux, open longer, have worse rates and higher commissions. Post offices generally have exchange facilities and open on Saturday morning.

In Northern Ireland several banks issue their own Northern Irish pound notes, which are equivalent to sterling but not readily accepted in Britain. Many hotels, restaurants and shops in the North accept euros.

Fancy hotels and restaurants usually add 10% or 15% service charge onto bills. Simpler places usually don't add service; if you decide to tip, just round up the bill (or add 10% at most). Taxi drivers do not have to be tipped.

POST

Post offices (An Post) throughout the Republic are generally open from 9am to 5.30pm Monday to Friday, and from 9am to 1pm Saturday; smaller offices close for lunch.

Letters weighing less than 50g cost €0.60 to Britain, and €0.65 to continental Europe and the rest of the world.

Post-office hours and postal rates in Northern Ireland are the same as in Britain.

TELEPHONE

To call Northern Ireland from the Republic, you do not use ☎0044 as for the rest of the UK. Instead, you dial ☎048 and then the local number. To dial the Republic from the North, however, use the full international code ☎00353, then the local number.

Local calls from a public phone in the Republic cost €0.50 for around three minutes (around €0.60 to a mobile phone). In Northern Ireland a local call costs at least £0.30. Some payphones in the North take euros. Prepaid phonecards work from all payphones.

You can dial direct to your home country operator and then reverse charges (collect) or charge the call to a local phone-credit card. From the Republic, dial the following codes, then the area code and number you want. Your home-country operator will come on the line before the call goes through.

Australia ☎ 1800 550061
France ☎ 1800 551033
New Zealand ☎ 1800 550064
UK (BT) ☎ 1800 550044
USA (AT&T) ☎ 1800 550000
USA (MCI) ☎ 1800 551001
USA (Sprint) ☎ 1800 552001

Reverse-charge calls can also be made from the North, using the same numbers as from the UK.

The mobile (cell) phone network in Ireland runs on the GSM 900/1800 system compatible with the rest of Europe and Australia, but not the USA. Mobile numbers in the Republic begin with 085, 086 or 087. A local pay-as-you-go SIM for your mobile will cost from around €10, but may work out free after the standard phone-credit refund.

VISAS

Citizens of the EU, Australia, Canada, New Zealand and the US don't need a visa to visit either the Republic or Northern Ireland. EU nationals are allowed to stay indefinitely, while other visitors can usually remain for three to six months. UK nationals born in Britain or Northern Ireland don't need a passport to visit the Republic, but should carry one anyway as identification.

Italy

HIGHLIGHTS

- **Rome** Hurl yourself into the maelstrom that is modern-day Rome (p636), a highly charged cocktail of culture, chaos and history
- **Venice** There's no better place to get lost than the haunting alleyways of Venice (p665), Italy's unforgettable canal city
- **Syracuse** Archimedes famously forgot to dress before leaping round the beautiful streets of Syracuse (p704) shouting *Eureka*! *Eureka*!
- **Lecce** Join the party at Lecce (p699), Puglia's coolest capital with its hip bars and opulent baroque architecture
- **Urbino** Long overshadowed by the Tuscan heavyweights, Urbino (p690) is a medieval gem in the heart of Italy's green centre

FAST FACTS

- **Area** 301,230 sq km (around half the size of Ukraine)
- **Budget** €60-150 per day
- **Capital** Rome
- **Country code** ☎ 39
- **Famous for** long lunches, ancient ruins, Tuscany, dodgy driving
- **Language** Italian
- **Money** euro (€); A$1 = €0.55; C$1 = 0.60; ¥100 = €0.78; NZ$1 = €0.43; UK£1 = €1.12; US$1 = €0.74
- **Phrases** *buon giorno* (hello), *arrivederci* (goodbye), *per favore* (please), *grazie* (thanks), *mi scusi* (excuse me)
- **Population** 58.13 million
- **Visas** EU citizens don't need a visa to enter Italy. Nationals of Australia, Canada, Israel, Japan, New Zealand, Switzerland and the USA don't need a visa for stays of up to 90 days. Non-EU citizens need a *permesso di soggiorno* (permit to stay) to work, study or live in Italy. See p711 for more details.

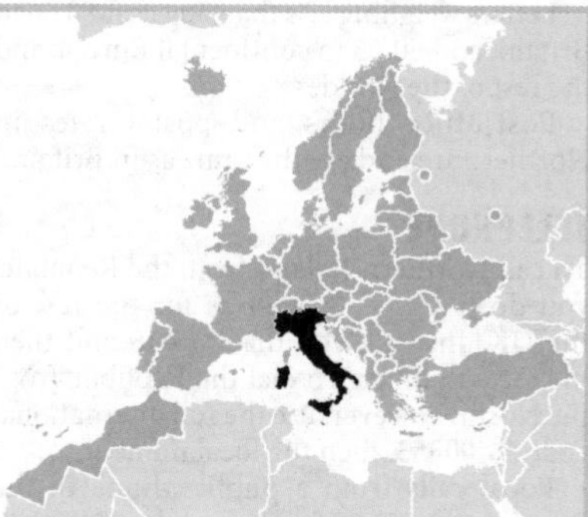

TRAVEL HINTS

Save money by drinking wine not beer; carry ID to claim student discounts; pack a smart set of clothes.

ROAMING ITALY

From Venice make south for Tuscany en route to Rome. With more time, visit Naples and the Amalfi Coast.

The world's love affair with Italy continues. The *bel paese* (beautiful country) might no longer be a blushing bride but this most beguiling of countries still has the power to thrill, to throw up surprises and excite emotion.

A tourist destination since the 18th century, Italy is still one of Europe's holiday hot spots. And it's not difficult to see why. Rome's grand monuments, Florence's Renaissance glories and the drama of the Amalfi Coast – these are all well known. Less famous is the red-blooded hedonism of Italy's foodie capital, Bologna, or the edgy atmosphere of Naples' high-voltage historic centre. Much of southern Italy is mountainous and remote, its forbidding landscape largely overlooked by foreign visitors.

In the country you'll find a wealth of outdoor opportunities. You can ski in the Alps, hike the Dolomites or dive off Sardinia's golden coast. Adrenalin junkies can catch fireworks on Sicily's volatile volcanoes.

But as much as the sights or the sport, a trip to Italy is about lapping up the lifestyle. It's about idling over a coffee at a streetside cafe or lingering over a long lunch; it's about looking good and putting your problems on hold.

HISTORY

The Etruscans were the first major force to emerge on the Italian peninsula. By the 7th century BC they dominated central Italy, rivalled only by the Greeks from the southern colony of Magna Graecia. Both groups thrived until the 3rd century BC when Rome's rampaging legionnaires crashed in.

Founded in 753 BC – possibly by Romulus, possibly not – Rome became a republic in 509 BC. Expansion followed and by the turn of the millennium it ruled much of Western Europe and the Mediterranean. After Caesar's death in 44 BC, his great-nephew Octavian defeated rivals Mark Antony and Cleopatra, and took the top job as Augustus Caesar, the first Roman emperor.

The empire's golden age came in the 2nd century AD but a century later it was in decline. Emperor Constantine legalised Christianity, and in AD 330 founded Constantinople in Byzantium, leaving Rome and its Western Empire to invading Germanic barbarians in 476.

The Middle Ages witnessed the development of Italy's powerful city-states, particularly in the centre and north. Of these, it was Florence under the Medici that made the biggest impact, giving rise to the 15th-century Renaissance.

By the early 16th century much of Italy was in foreign hands – the Austrian Habsburgs in the north and the Spanish Bourbons in the south. Not much changed until the mid-19th century when the Risorgimento (unification movement) culminated in the 1861 unification of Italy.

Italy's brief fascist interlude was a low point. Mussolini gained power in 1925 and in 1940 entered WWII on Germany's side. Defeat ensued and Il Duce was killed by partisans in April 1945.

Italy's postwar era has been largely successful. A founding member of the European Economic Community, it survived a period of domestic terrorism in the 1970s and enjoyed sustained economic growth in the 1980s.

The 1990s heralded a period of crisis as national bribery scandals rocked the nation, paving the way for Silvio Berlusconi's entry into politics. After a short period as PM in 1994, the billionaire media-magnate took the reins again in 2001, going on to become Italy's longest serving postwar PM. In 2008 he returned to power after a two-year period in opposition.

Nature has also played a role in Italy's history. As one of the world's most earthquake-prone countries, Italy has a long history of natural disasters. Italy's deadliest ever earthquake struck in 1908, razing the Sicilian town of Messina to the ground and claiming up to 200,000 lives. The latest earthquake struck the central region of Abruzzo on 6 April 2009, killing some 294 people and leaving up to 17,000 people homeless. The epicentre was near regional capital L'Aquila, but shock waves were felt as far away as Rome, 90 km to the southwest. Much of L'Aquila's medieval centre was destroyed.

THE CULTURE

Italian stereotypes are two-a-penny: Italians are volatile, charming, rakish and enviably uninhibited. What's more they all drive like loons, dress with finesse and love their *mamma*. Needless to say, the reality is far more complex: they can be deeply cynical (it's no coincidence that Machiavelli was Italian); ruthlessly efficient (the 2006 Turin Winter Olympics went off without a hitch); and surprisingly offbeat (Roberto Benigni's Oscar-winning film *Life is Beautiful* was a comedy about the Holocaust). On the whole, though,

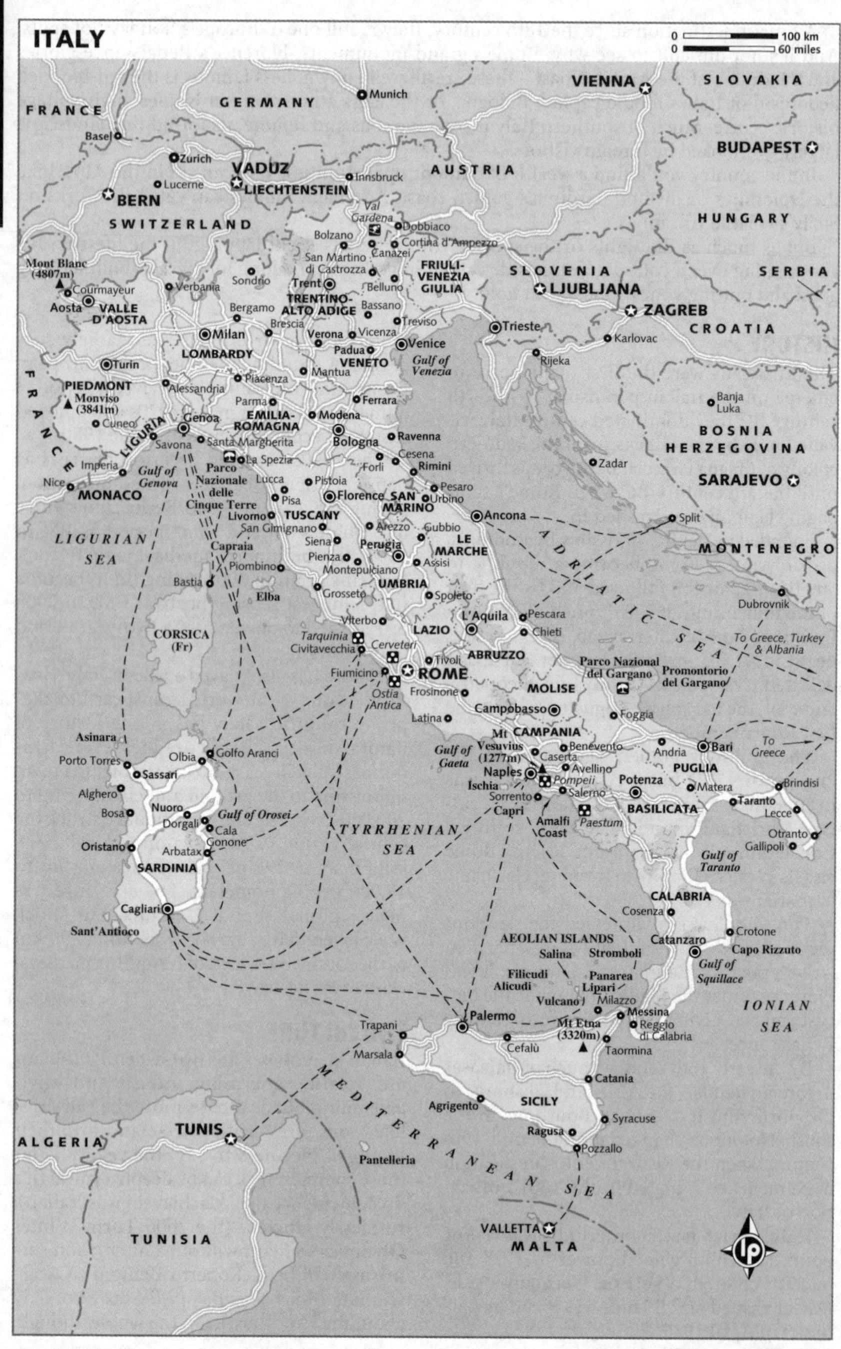
ITALY
0 100 km
0 60 miles
FRANCE
GERMANY
Munich
VIENNA
SLOVAKIA
Basel
Zurich
VADUZ
LIECHTENSTEIN
Innsbruck
AUSTRIA
BUDAPEST
Lucerne
BERN
SWITZERLAND
HUNGARY
Val Gardena
Dobbiaco
Bolzano
Cortina d'Ampezzo
San Martino di Castrozza
Canazei
Mont Blanc (4807m)
Sondrio
Trent
FRIULI-VENEZIA GIULIA
SLOVENIA
SERBIA
Courmayeur
Verbania
Belluno
LJUBLJANA
Aosta
VALLE D'AOSTA
TRENTINO-ALTO ADIGE
Bassano
ZAGREB
Bergamo
Brescia
Treviso
Trieste
CROATIA
Milan
Verona
Vicenza
Venice
Karlovac
LOMBARDY
Padua
Gulf of Venezia
Rijeka
Turin
VENETO
Mantua
PIEDMONT
Alessandria
Piacenza
Monviso (3841m)
Parma
Ferrara
Banja Luka
EMILIA-ROMAGNA
Modena
Cuneo
Genoa
LIGURIA
Bologna
Ravenna
BOSNIA HERZEGOVINA
Savona
Santa Margherita
Cesena
La Spezia
Forlì
Rimini
Imperia
Gulf of Genova
Parco Nazionale delle Cinque Terre
Zadar
Nice
MONACO
Lucca
Pistoia
Pesaro
SARAJEVO
Pisa
Florence
SAN MARINO
Urbino
Livorno
TUSCANY
Ancona
Split
San Gimignano
Arezzo
Gubbio
LIGURIAN SEA
Siena
LE MARCHE
Capraia
Perugia
MONTENEGRO
Pienza
Piombino
Montepulciano
Assisi
Bastia
Elba
Grosseto
UMBRIA
Spoleto
Dubrovnik
ADRIATIC SEA
Pescara
Viterbo
L'Aquila
CORSICA (Fr)
LAZIO
Chieti
Tarquinia
Cerveteri
To Greece, Turkey & Albania
Civitavecchia
Tivoli
ABRUZZO
Parco Nazional del Gargano
Promontorio del Gargano
Fiumicino
ROME
Ostia Antica
Frosinone
MOLISE
Campobasso
Foggia
Latina
Asinara
Mt Vesuvius (1277m)
CAMPANIA
Porto Torres
Olbia
Golfo Aranci
Gulf of Gaeta
Benevento
Andria
Bari
To Greece
Caserta
Sassari
Naples
Avellino
Pompeii
PUGLIA
Alghero
Ischia
Sorrento
Potenza
Matera
Brindisi
Salerno
Bosa
Nuoro
Gulf of Orosei
Capri
BASILICATA
Taranto
Dorgali
Lecce
Cala Gonone
TYRRHENIAN SEA
Amalfi Coast
Paestum
Oristano
Otranto
Arbatax
Gallipoli
SARDINIA
Gulf of Taranto
CALABRIA
Cagliari
Cosenza
Sant'Antioco
Crotone
AEOLIAN ISLANDS
Catanzaro
Capo Rizzuto
Salina
Stromboli
Gulf of Squillace
Filicudi
Panarea
Alicudi
Lipari
Vulcano
Milazzo
IONIAN SEA
Messina
Trapani
Palermo
Reggio di Calabria
Mt Etna (3320m)
Cefalù
Marsala
Taormina
Catania
MEDITERRANEAN SEA
Agrigento
SICILY
Syracuse
TUNIS
Ragusa
ALGERIA
Pozzallo
Pantelleria
VALLETTA
TUNISIA
MALTA

they tend to be conformist and fiercely protective of their region, a phenomenon known as *campanilismo* (literally, an attachment to the local bell tower). Family ties are also important. It's not unusual to find three generations living together and even if times are changing, most children stay at home until they marry.

SPORT

Football *(calcio)* rules. Juventus, AC Milan and Inter dominate the domestic game and often do well in European competitions. In 2006 Italy's World Cup victory was an operatic affair, marked by a pre-tournament corruption scandal and Zinedine Zidane's headbutt of Marco Materazzi in the final. Fortune has not favoured the national team since and they made a pretty poor showing at the 2008 European Championship.

Motor sports are also fanatically supported. In the wake of Michael Schumacher's retirement from Formula One, Ferrari has struggled to retain its aura of invincibility, although Kimi Raikkonen did win the 2007 F1 Drivers' Championship. On two wheels, Valentino Rossi won his eighth MotoGP World title in 2008. The Italian F1 Grand Prix is held at Monza in September.

RELIGION

Italians have an ambiguous relationship with religion. More than 80% of the country professes to be Catholic but only about a third regularly attend church. Still, first Communions, church weddings and regular feast days remain an integral part of life.

There are no official figures but it's estimated that there are about 1.3 million Muslims in Italy, making Islam Italy's second religion. There are also about 400,000 evangelical Protestants, 350,000 Jehovah's Witnesses and smaller numbers of Jews and Buddhists.

ARTS

Literature

Italian literature runs the gamut from Virgil's *Aeneid* to the chilling war stories of Primo Levi and the fantastical tales of Italo Calvino.

Dante, whose *Divina commedia* (Divine Comedy) dates to the early 1300s, was one of three 14th-century greats alongside Petrarch and Giovanni Boccaccio.

Then, in the early 16th century Machiavelli taught would-be despots how to manipulate power in *Il principe* (The Prince), and 300 years later 19th-century scribe Alessandro Manzoni wrote of star-crossed lovers in *I promessi sposi* (The Betrothed).

Italy's southern regions provide rich literary pickings. Giuseppe Tomasi di Lampedusa depicts Sicily's wary mentality in *Il gattopardo* (The Leopard), a theme that Leonardo Sciascia later returns to in *Il giorno della civetta* (The Day of the Owl), and Carlo Levi denounces southern poverty in *Cristo si é fermato a Eboli* (Christ Stopped at Eboli). More recently, Andrea Camilleri's Sicilian-based Montalbano detective stories have enjoyed great success.

> **READING UP**
>
> Bone up with *A Concise History of Italy* by Christopher Duggan, and Tomasi di Lampedusa's Sicilian classic *The Leopard*. Conspiracy theorists will enjoy *The Dark Heart of Italy*, Tobias Jones' personal exploration of Italy's modern underbelly. That is nothing, however, compared to the terrifying reality described by Roberto Saviano in his exposé of the Neapolitan Camorra, *Gomorrah* – a must for mafia junkies.
>
> On a lighter note, acclaimed Italian journalist Beppe Severgnini engagingly explains his country's foibles in *La Bella Figura*, an easy beach read.

Music

Emotional and highly theatrical, opera has always appealed to Italians. Performances of Verdi and Puccini are regularly staged at legendary theatres such as Milan's Teatro alla Scala (p662) and Naples' Teatro San Carlo (p695).

On the classical front, Antonio Vivaldi created the concerto in its present form and wrote *Le Quattro Stagione* (The Four Seasons). In more recent times, Neapolitan dub and techno outfit Almamegretta have achieved international success.

Architecture, Painting & Sculpture

Ancient ruins, Renaissance *palazzi* and baroque churches all stand testament to the central role that the arts have played in Italy's past.

Europe's most famous artistic movement, the Renaissance, took off in 15th-century Italy.

ITALY FOR FREE

- Get spiritual in Italy's legendary churches – St Peter's Basilica in Rome (p642), Venice's Basilica di San Marco (p667), the Duomo in Florence (p680) and Milan's Duomo (p659) are all free.
- Marvel at the ancient Romans greatest architectural achievement – the Pantheon (p644) in Rome.
- Get down to the Vatican Museums (p643) on the last Sunday of the month.
- Check out the rooftop views from Piazzale Michelangelo in Florence (p680).
- Jack up your adrenalin levels dodging Vespas in Naples' *centro storico* (historic city centre; p691).

Under the Medici in Florence and the Roman papacy, Leonardo da Vinci, Michelangelo Buonarrotti and Raphael set new standards of artistic expression.

Controversial and highly influential, Michelangelo Merisi da Caravaggio dominated the late 16th century. His realism contrasted with the exuberant style of the 17th-century baroque rivals Gianlorenzo Bernini and Francesco Borromini.

Signalling a return to classical sobriety, neoclassicism was the rage in the late 18th and early 19th centuries, producing sculptor Canova.

Of Italy's modern artists, Amedeo Modigliani is the most famous. Carrying contemporary Italy's architectural mantle are superstar architects Renzo Piano, author of the Georges Pompidou centre in Paris, Osaka airport and the New York Times building in NY, and Massimiliano Fuksas, who has designed flagship stores for Giorgio Armani in New York, Hong Kong and Tokyo and who recently designed the Zenith Music Hall in Strasbourg.

ENVIRONMENT

Bound by the Adriatic, Ligurian, Tyrrhenian and Ionian Seas, Italy has more than 8000km of coastline. Inland, about 75% of the peninsula is mountainous – the Alps curve 966km round the country's northern border while the Apennines extend 1350km from north to south.

Italy has 21 national parks, covering about 5% of the country, and more than 400 nature reserves, natural parks and wetlands. It also boasts over 40 Unesco World Heritage sites, more than any other country.

But Italy is not without its environmental problems. The two most obvious are air pollution and waste disposal. Heavy industry and high levels of car ownership have combined to produce dense smog, particularly in the industrialised north. Inadequate waste disposal has also led to pollution as illegal, sometimes toxic, refuse is pumped out to sea or buried in illegal dumps by organised crime outfits. Other problems include unfettered coastal development, erosion and forest fires.

TRANSPORT

GETTING THERE & AWAY

Air

You shouldn't have many problems finding a decent fare into Italy, particularly if flying from another European country. Low-cost airlines include:

Air Berlin (AB; ☎ 199 400 737; www.airberlin.com)
easyJet (U2; ☎ 899 234 589; www.easyjet.com)
Hapag-Lloyd Express (X3; ☎ 199 192 692; www.hlx.com)
Jet2 (LS; ☎ 199 404 023; www.jet2.com)
Ryanair (FR; ☎ 899 678 910; www.ryanair.com)
Vueling (VY; ☎ 800 78 77 88; www.vueling.com)

TREAD LIGHTLY

As a visitor, there's not a huge amount you can do to affect Italy's environmental problems, but you can try to tread more lightly. Practical tips:

- Save water by refilling plastic water bottles at drinking fountains – Italy's water is drinkable.
- Turn off the air-con when you leave your hotel/hostel room.
- Use trains, buses and ferries rather than flying – they're usually cheaper anyway.
- Respect barriers at archaeological sites.
- Keep your camera under wraps where (flash) photography is banned.

CONNECTIONS

Milan and Venice are northern Italy's two main transport hubs. From Milan, trains run to cities across Western Europe, including Barcelona, Paris, Amsterdam, Zürich, Munich and Vienna. Venice is better placed for Eastern Europe with rail connections to Prague, Ljubljana, Zagreb, Belgrade, Budapest and Bucharest. You can also pick up ferries in Venice for Corfu, Igoumenitsa and Patras (see p673). Down the east coast, there are ferries from Bari to various Greek ports, as well as to Durrës, Bar and Dubrovnik (see p699). At the other end of the country, Genoa has ferries to Barcelona, Tangiers and Tunis (see p657). You can also pick up ferries to Tunisia and Malta from Sicily (see p700).

The national airline is **Alitalia** (AZ; ☎ 06 22 22; www.alitalia.it); domestic airlines are **Air One** (AP; ☎ 199 207 080; www.flyairone.it) and **Meridiana** (IG; ☎ 89 29 28; www.meridiana.it).

Italy's main intercontinental gateway is Rome's **Leonardo da Vinci airport** (FCO; www.adr.it), better known as Fiumicino, but flights also serve Milan's **Malpensa** (MXP; www.sea-aeroportomilano.it). Low-cost carriers generally fly into Italy's regional airports, including Rome's **Ciampino** (CIA; www.adr.it), Pisa's **Galileo Galilei** (PSA; www.pisa-airport.com) and Venice's **Marco Polo** (VCE; www.veniceairport.it).

For further information on air travel see p1232.

Boat

Ferries connect Italy to Spain, Croatia, Greece, Turkey, Tunisia, Albania, Malta and Corsica. For details of routes, companies and online booking log onto **Traghettionline** (www.traghettionline.net).

Holders of Eurail and Inter-Rail passes should check with the ferry company if they are entitled to a discount or even a free passage.

For further details see Bari (p699), Genoa (p657), Sicily (p700) and Venice (p673).

Bus

A consortium of 32 European coach companies, **Eurolines** (☎ 055 35 70 59; www.eurolines.com) operates across Europe with offices in all major European cities. Italy-bound buses head to Ancona, Florence, Rome, Siena and Venice.

Train

You can catch international trains from:

Milan To/from Barcelona, Nice, Paris, Amsterdam, Zürich, Munich, Frankfurt and Vienna.
Rome To/from Monaco, Munich and Vienna.
Venice To/from Paris, Zürich, Munich, Vienna, Prague, Ljubljana, Zagreb, Belgrade, Budapest and Bucharest.

There are also international departures from Genoa, Turin, Verona, Bologna, Florence and Naples. Details are available at www.trenitalia.com.

In the UK, the **Rail Europe Travel Centre** (☎ 0870 848 848; www.raileurope.co.uk) can provide fare information on journeys to/from Italy.

For details of Eurail and Inter-Rail passes, both valid in Italy, see p1243.

GETTING AROUND

Bicycle

Bikes are available for rent in many Italian towns (from about €10 a day). They can be taken on any train carrying the bike logo on payment of a supplement (€3.50 on regional trains, €5 on Intercity and Eurostar, €10 on international trains), valid for 24 hours. Bikes travel free on most ferries.

Boat

Navi (large ferries) service Sicily and Sardinia; *traghetti* (smaller ferries) and *aliscafi* (hydrofoils) cover the smaller islands, including Elba, the Aeolian Islands, Capri, Ischia and Procida. The main embarkation points for Sardinia are Genoa, Livorno, Civitavecchia and Naples; for Sicily, Naples and Villa San Giovanni in Calabria. Most long-distance ferries travel overnight.

Major domestic ferry companies:

Grandi Navi Veloci (☎ 010 209 45 91; www.gnv.it)
Moby (☎ 199 30 30 40; www.mobylines.it)
Sardinia Ferries (☎ 199 400 500)
SNAV (☎ 081 428 55 55; www.snav.it)
Tirrenia (☎ 892 123; www.tirrenia.it)

Bus

Italy boasts an extensive and largely reliable bus network. Buses are not necessarily cheaper than trains, but in hilly areas such as Umbria, Sicily and Sardinia they are often the only choice. In larger cities companies have ticket offices or operate through agencies but in most villages and small towns tickets are sold in bars or on the bus itself. Reservations are usually only necessary on long-haul trips in high season.

Car & Motorcycle

Roads are generally good and there's an excellent system of toll *autostrade* (motorways). Petrol prices are high.

Many cities have traffic restrictions in their historical centres, although these don't apply to foreign-registered vehicles, mopeds or scooters.

To hire a car you'll need a valid driving licence (plus an International Driving Permit if required) and credit card. Age restrictions vary but generally you'll need to be 21 or over.

If driving your own car, carry proof of ownership and an international insurance certificate, known as a Carta Verde (Green Card), available from your insurance company.

Wearing a helmet is compulsory on all two-wheeled vehicles.

Train

Trenitalia (☎ 89 20 21; www.trenitalia.com) operates most trains in Italy. There are several types of train: local *regionale* or *interregionale* trains; faster InterCity (IC) services; and quickest of all, Eurostar (ES) trains. Regional trains are cheaper than InterCity and Eurostar services, both of which require a supplement determined by the distance to travel. Eurostar ticket prices include a compulsory reservation fee. Generally, it's cheaper to buy all local train tickets in Italy.

Unless otherwise stated, train prices quoted in this chapter are for an InterCity, one-way 2nd-class ticket.

Tickets must be validated – in the yellow machines at the entrance to platforms – before boarding trains.

The Carta Verde is available at all major train stations to anyone between 12 and 26. It costs €40 and is valid for a year, entitling holders to discounts of 10% on national trains and up to 25% on international trains.

For detailed information on using Italy's trains see www.seat61.com/Italy-trains.htm.

ROME

☎ 06 / pop 2.7 million

An epic, monumental metropolis, Rome has been in the spotlight for close on 3000 years. As the showcase centre of the Roman Empire, it was the all-powerful *caput mundi* (capital of the world). Later, as the Renaissance capital of the Catholic world, its name sent shivers of holy terror through believers and infidels alike. Some 500 years on and its name still exerts a powerful hold. Fortunately, the reality is every bit as enticing as the reputation. With its architectural and artistic treasures, its romantic corners and noisy markets, Rome is a city that knows how to impress.

ORIENTATION

Rome is surprisingly small, especially the *centro storico* (historic centre), focused on Piazza Navona and the Pantheon. The transport hub is Roma Termini (sometimes called Stazione Termini), the city's main train station. City buses leave from Piazza dei Cinquecento, just in front, and metro lines A and B run from under the station.

INFORMATION

Emergency

Police station (Questura; Map pp646-7; ☎ 06 468 61; Via San Vitale 15)

Internet Access

Splashnet (Map p640; Via Varese 33; per hr €1.50; 🕑 8.30am-11pm) Also has a laundry and left-luggage storage (€2 per bag per day).

Telephone Center International (Map p640; Via Volturno 52; per hr €2; 🕑 7am-midnight) Also good rates on international calls.

Medical Services

24-hour Pharmacy (Map p640; ☎ 06 488 00 19; Piazza dei Cinquecento 49/50/51)

EMERGENCY NUMBERS

- Ambulance ☎ 118
- Carabinieri/police ☎ 112/113
- Fire ☎ 115
- Roadside assistance ☎ 803 116

GETTING INTO TOWN

From Fiumicino

The *Leonardo Express* train service runs to Stazione Termini (the city's main train station) every half-hour between 6.35am and 11.35pm. It costs €11 and takes about 30 minutes.

During the night, **Cotral** (www.cotralspa.it) runs a bus from Fiumicino to Termini and then on to Stazione Tiburtino, departing at 1.15am, 2.15am, 3.30am and 5am. Tickets, available on the bus, cost €7.

From Ciampino

The easiest way is by bus. **Terravision** (☎ 06 454 41 345; www.terravision.eu) buses depart soon after flight arrivals for Via Marsala, just outside Stazione Termini. Get tickets (€8) online, on board, or at Ciampino airport.

Alternatively, **SIT** (☎ 06 591 68 26; www.sitbusshuttle.com) covers the same route, with regular departures from Ciampino between 8.30am and midnight. Buy tickets (€6) on board.

To make the return journey from Termini to Ciampino catch buses from the bus stops on Via Marsala.

Cotral runs two night buses, departing Ciampino at 11.50pm and 12.15am. Tickets (€5) are available on the bus.

Regular Cotral buses connect Ciampino with Anagnina metro station (€1.20, about 15 minutes) from where you can get the metro direct to Stazione Termini. Another option is to get a local orange bus to Ciampino train station (€1) from where regular trains connect with Termini.

Ospedale Bambino Gesù (Map pp638-9; ☎ 06 685 92 351; Piazza di Sant'Onofrio 4) For paediatric assistance.
Ospedale Santo Spirito (Map pp642-3; ☎ 06 6 83 51; Lungotevere in Sassia 1)

Tourist Information

Centro Servizi Pellegrini e Turisti (Map pp642-3; ☎ 06 698 81 662; St Peter's Sq; ⏰ 8.30am-4.15pm Mon-Sat) The Vatican tourist office.
Enjoy Rome (Map p640 ☎ 06 445 68 90; www.enjoyrome.com; Via Marghera 8a; ⏰ 8.30am-7pm Mon-Fri, to 2pm Sat) A private tourist office with a free hotel-reservation service.

The Comune di Roma runs a **multilingual tourist infoline** (☎ 820 59 127; ⏰ 9am-7pm) and information points across the city:
Castel Sant'Angelo (Map pp642-3; ☎ 06 688 09 707; Piazza Pia; ⏰ 9.30am-7pm)
Fiumicino airport (Terminal C, International Arrivals; ⏰ 9am-7pm)
Imperial Forums Visitor Centre (Map pp646-7; ☎ 06 699 24 307; Via dei Fori Imperiali; ⏰ 9.30am-6.30pm)
Piazza delle Cinque Lune (Map pp646-7; ☎ 06 688 09 240; ⏰ 9.30am-7pm) Near Piazza Navona.
Piazza Sonnino (Map pp646-7; ☎ 06 583 33 457; ⏰ 9.30am-7pm) In Trastevere.
Santa Maria Maggiore (Map p640; ☎ 06 474 09 55; Via dell'Olmata; ⏰ 9.30am-7pm) Near the basilica.
Stazione Termini (Map p640; ☎ 06 478 25 194; ⏰ 8am-9pm) In the hall parallel to platform 24.
Via Marco Minghetti (Map pp646-7; ☎ 06 678 29 88; ⏰ 9.30am-7pm) Near the Trevi Fountain.
Via Nazionale (Map pp646-7; ☎ 06 478 24 525; ⏰ 9.30am-7pm)

SIGHTS & ACTIVITIES

If you plan to blitz the sights, consider the Roma Pass (€20; valid for three days), which gives free admission to two museums or sites, free public transport and discounts on entry to other sites. It's available at all participating sites and tourist information points.

Note that EU citizens aged between 18 and 25, and students from countries with reciprocal arrangements, usually qualify for a discount at galleries and museums. In all cases you'll need proof of your age, ideally a passport or ID card.

Colosseum

Rome's iconic monument is a thrilling site. The 50,000-seater **Colosseum** (Map pp646-7; ☎ 06 399 67 700; admission incl Palatine Hill €11; ⏰ 9am-1hr before sunset; Ⓜ Colosseo) was ancient Rome's most feared arena and is today one of Italy's top tourist attractions. Queues are inevitable but

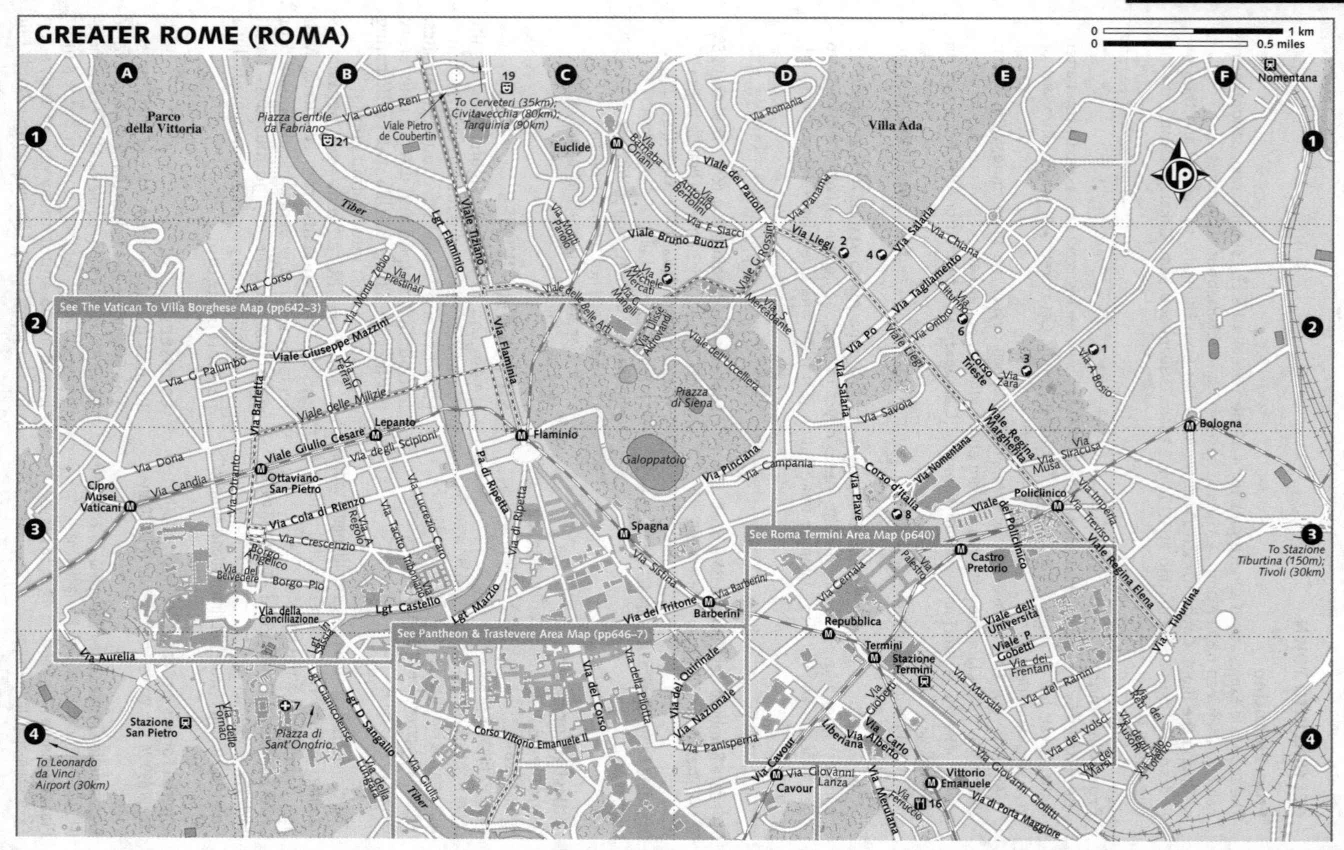
GREATER ROME (ROMA)
0 1 km
0 0.5 miles
Parco della Vittoria
Villa Ada
Piazza Gentile da Fabriano
Viale Pietro de Coubertin
Via Guido Reni
To Cerveteri (35km); Civitavecchia (80km); Tarquinia (90km)
Nomentana
To Stazione Tiburtina (150m); Tivoli (30km)
To Leonardo da Vinci Airport (30km)
Euclide
Flaminio
Spagna
Barberini
Repubblica
Termini
Stazione Termini
Castro Pretorio
Policlinico
Bologna
Vittorio Emanuele
Cavour
Lepanto
Ottaviano-San Pietro
Cipro Musei Vaticani
Stazione San Pietro
Piazza di Sant'Onofrio
Piazza di Siena
Galoppatoio
Tiber
Viale Tiziano
Via Flaminia
Lgt Flaminio
Pa di Ripetta
Via di Ripetta
Lgt Marzio
Via del Corso
Via della Pilotta
Corso Vittorio Emanuele II
Via Giulia
Lgt D Sangallo
Lgt Gianicolense
Via della Lungara
Via delle Fornaci
Via Aurelia
Via della Conciliazione
Borgo Pio
Via Crescenzio
Via Cola di Rienzo
Viale Giulio Cesare
Via Otranto
Via Barletta
Viale Giuseppe Mazzini
Viale delle Milizie
Via Candia
Via Doria
Via Tacito
Via Lucrezio Caro
Lgt Castello
Via Salaria
Via Piave
Via Po
Via Tagliamento
Corso Trieste
Corso d'Italia
Via Nomentana
Viale Regina Margherita
Viale Regina Elena
Viale del Policlinico
Via Tiburtina
Viale Liegi
Via Liegi
Viale dei Parioli
Viale Bruno Buozzi
Viale delle Belle Arti
Via Pinciana
Via Sistina
Via del Tritone
Via Nazionale
Via del Quirinale
Via Cavour
Via Merulana
Via Carlo Alberto
Via Marsala
Via Giovanni Giolitti
Via di Porta Maggiore
Via Panisperna
See The Vatican To Villa Borghese Map (pp642–3)
See Roma Termini Area Map (p640)
See Pantheon & Trastevere Area Map (pp646–7)

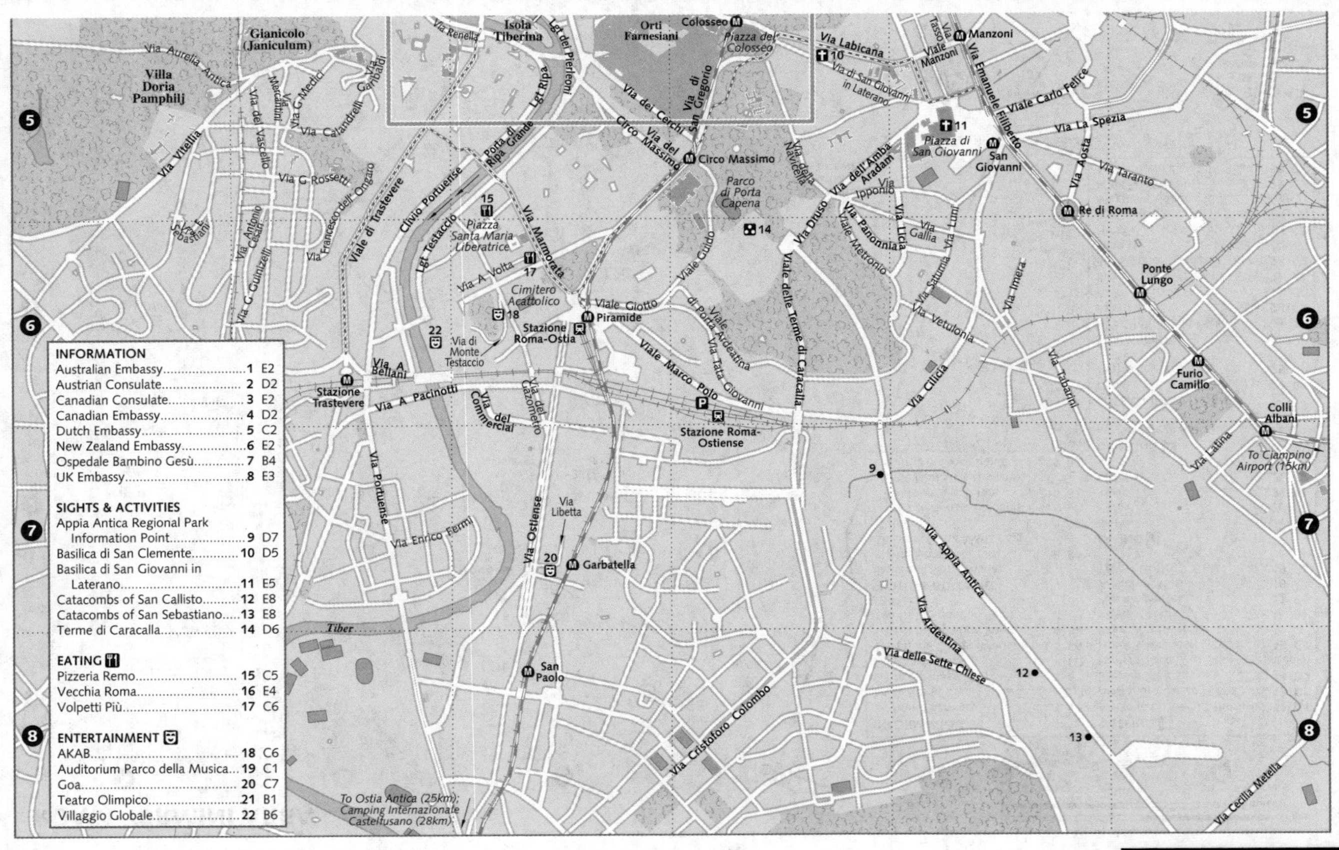

INFORMATION
Australian Embassy 1 E2
Austrian Consulate 2 D2
Canadian Consulate 3 E2
Canadian Embassy 4 D2
Dutch Embassy 5 C2
New Zealand Embassy 6 E2
Ospedale Bambino Gesù 7 B4
UK Embassy 8 E3
SIGHTS & ACTIVITIES
Appia Antica Regional Park Information Point 9 D7
Basilica di San Clemente 10 D5
Basilica di San Giovanni in Laterano 11 E5
Catacombs of San Callisto 12 E8
Catacombs of San Sebastiano 13 E8
Terme di Caracalla 14 D6
EATING
Pizzeria Remo 15 C5
Vecchia Roma 16 E4
Volpetti Più 17 C6
ENTERTAINMENT
AKAB 18 C6
Auditorium Parco della Musica 19 C1
Goa 20 C7
Teatro Olimpico 21 B1
Villaggio Globale 22 B6
Gianicolo (Janiculum)
Villa Doria Pamphilj
Isola Tiberina
Orti Farnesiani
Colosseo
Piazza del Colosseo
Via Labicana
Manzoni
Via Emanuele Filiberto
Viale Carlo Felice
Via La Spezia
Piazza di San Giovanni
San Giovanni
Via Aosta
Via Taranto
Re di Roma
Circo Massimo
Parco di Porta Capena
Viale delle Terme di Caracalla
Piramide
Stazione Roma-Ostia
Stazione Roma-Ostiense
Viale Marco Polo
Via Marmorata
Piazza Santa Maria Liberatrice
Cimitero Acattolico
Via di Monte Testaccio
Stazione Trastevere
Viale di Trastevere
Via Portuense
Via Ostiense
Garbatella
San Paolo
Tiber
Via Cristoforo Colombo
Via Appia Antica
Via Ardeatina
Via delle Sette Chiese
Via Cecilia Metella
Ponte Lungo
Furio Camillo
Colli Albani
Via Latina
To Ciampino Airport (15km)
To Ostia Antica (25km); Camping Internazionale Castelfusano (28km)

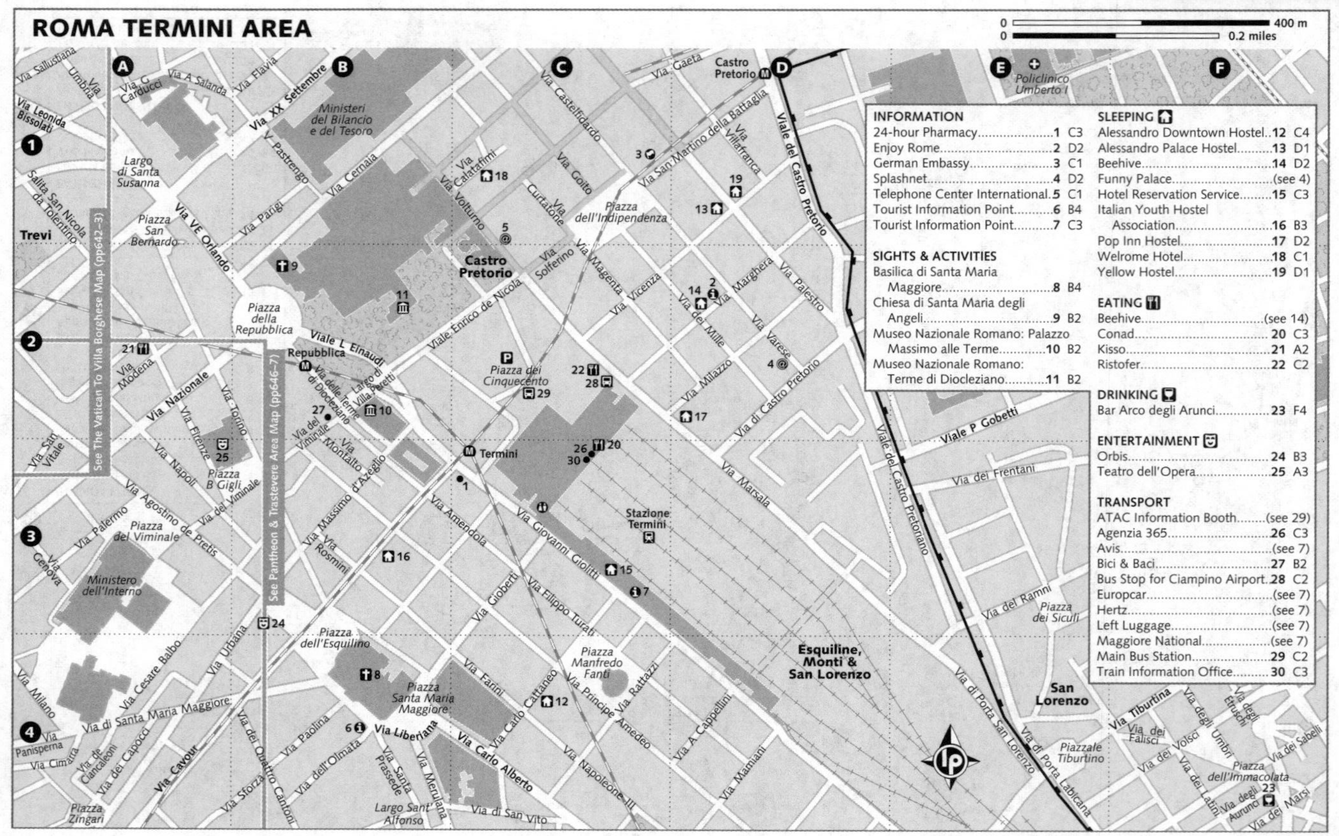
ROMA TERMINI AREA
0 400 m
0 0.2 miles
INFORMATION
24-hour Pharmacy....1 C3
Enjoy Rome....2 D2
German Embassy....3 C1
Splashnet....4 D2
Telephone Center International....5 C1
Tourist Information Point....6 B4
Tourist Information Point....7 C3
SIGHTS & ACTIVITIES
Basilica di Santa Maria Maggiore....8 B4
Chiesa di Santa Maria degli Angeli....9 B2
Museo Nazionale Romano: Palazzo Massimo alle Terme....10 B2
Museo Nazionale Romano: Terme di Diocleziano....11 B2
SLEEPING
Alessandro Downtown Hostel....12 C4
Alessandro Palace Hostel....13 D1
Beehive....14 D2
Funny Palace....(see 4)
Hotel Reservation Service....15 C3
Italian Youth Hostel Association....16 B3
Pop Inn Hostel....17 D2
Welrome Hotel....18 C1
Yellow Hostel....19 D1
EATING
Beehive....(see 14)
Conad....20 C3
Kisso....21 A2
Ristofer....22 C2
DRINKING
Bar Arco degli Arunci....23 F4
ENTERTAINMENT
Orbis....24 B3
Teatro dell'Opera....25 A3
TRANSPORT
ATAC Information Booth....(see 29)
Agenzia 365....26 C3
Avis....(see 7)
Bici & Baci....27 B2
Bus Stop for Ciampino Airport....28 C2
Europcar....(see 7)
Hertz....(see 7)
Left Luggage....(see 7)
Maggiore National....(see 7)
Main Bus Station....29 C2
Train Information Office....30 C3
See The Vatican To Villa Borghese Map (pp642–3)
See Pantheon & Trastevere Area Map (pp646–7)
Trevi
Castro Pretorio
Esquiline, Monti & San Lorenzo
San Lorenzo
Termini
Stazione Termini
Repubblica
Piazza della Repubblica
Piazza dei Cinquecento
Piazza dell'Indipendenza
Piazza dell'Esquilino
Piazza Santa Maria Maggiore
Piazza Manfredo Fanti
Piazza del Viminale
Ministero dell'Interno
Ministeri del Bilancio e del Tesoro
Policlinico Umberto I
Via XX Settembre
Via Nazionale
Via Cavour
Via Marsala
Via Giovanni Giolitti
Viale del Castro Pretorio
Via Tiburtina
Via Carlo Alberto

you can usually avoid them by buying your ticket at the nearby Palatine Hill. Alternatively, join a walking tour (€9 on top of ticket price) and use the shorter ticket line.

Originally known as the Flavian Amphitheatre, the Colosseum was started by Emperor Vespasian in AD 72 and finished by his son Titus in AD 80. It was clad in travertine and covered by a huge canvas awning, held aloft by 240 masts. Inside, tiered seating encircled the sand-covered arena, itself built over underground chambers where animals were caged. Games generally involved gladiators fighting wild animals or each other.

To the west of the Colosseum, the **Arco di Costantino** (Map pp646–7) was built to celebrate Constantine's victory over Maxentius at the battle of Milvian Bridge in AD 312.

Roman Forum & Palatine Hill

Rome's most famous ruins are what's left of the **Roman Forum** (Map pp646-7; ☎ 06 399 67 700; admission free; ⏲ 9am-1hr before sunset Mon-Sat; Ⓜ Colosseo), the social, political and commercial hub of the Roman Republic.

As you enter at Largo Romolo e Remo, ahead to your left is the **Tempio di Antonino e Faustina** (Map pp646–7), built by the senate in AD 141 and transformed into a church in the 8th century. To your right, the **Basilica Aemilia** (Map pp646–7), built in 179 BC, was 100m long with a two-storey porticoed facade lined with shops. At the end of the short path, **Via Sacra** traverses the Forum from northwest to southeast. Opposite the basilica stands the **Tempio di Giulio Cesare** (Map pp646–7), erected by Augustus in 29 BC on the site where Caesar's body had been burned.

Head right up Via Sacra and you reach the **Curia** (Map pp646–7), once the meeting place of the Roman senate and later converted into a church. In front of the Curia is the **Lapis Niger** (Map pp646–7), a large piece of black marble that purportedly covered Romulus' grave.

At the end of Via Sacra, the **Arco di Settimo Severo** (Map pp646–7) was erected in AD 203 to honour Emperor Septimus Severus and celebrate victory over the Parthians. It is considered one of Italy's major triumphal arches. Nearby, the **Millarium Aureum** (Map pp646–7) marked the centre of ancient Rome.

Southwest of the arch, eight granite columns are all that remain of the **Tempio di Saturno** (Map pp646–7), one of ancient Rome's most important temples. To the southeast, the Piazza del Foro, the Forum's main market and meeting place, is marked by the 7th-century **Colonna di Foca** (Column of Phocus; Map pp646–7). To your right are the foundations of the **Basilica Giulia** (Map pp646–7), a law court built by Julius Caesar in 55 BC. At the end of the basilica is the **Tempio di Castore e Polluce** (Map pp646–7), built in 489 BC in honour of the Heavenly Twins, Castor and Pollux. It is easily recognisable by its three remaining columns. Southeast of the temple, and closed to the public, is the **Chiesa di Santa Maria Antiqua** (Map pp646–7), the Forum's oldest Christian church.

Back towards Via Sacra, the **Casa delle Vestali** (Map pp646–7) was home to the virgins employed to keep the sacred flame alight in the adjoining **Tempio di Vesta** (Map pp646–7).

Continuing up Via Sacra, you pass the vast **Basilica di Costantino** (Map pp646–7), also known as the Basilica di Massenzio, en route to the **Arco di Tito** (Map pp646–7), built in AD 81 to celebrate the victories of the emperors Titus and Vespasian against Jerusalem.

From here, you can climb the **Palatine** (Map pp646-7; ☎ 06 399 67 700; entrances Via di San Gregorio 30 or Piazza Santa Maria Nova 53; admission incl Colosseum €11; ⏲ 9am-1hr before sunset; Ⓜ Colosseo). Ancient Rome's poshest neighbourhood, this is where Romulus is said to have founded the city in 753 BC.

Most of the Palatine is covered by the ruins of Emperor Domitian's vast 1st-century complex. Divided into the **Domus Flavia** (imperial palace; Map pp646–7), **Domus Augustana** (the emperor's private residence; Map pp646–7) and a **stadio** (stadium; Map pp646–7), it served as the main imperial residence for 300 years.

Among the best-preserved buildings on the Palatine is the frescoed **Casa di Livia** (Map pp646–7), home to Augustus' wife Livia, and the **Tempio della Magna Mater** (Map pp646–7), built in 204 BC.

Vatican City

pop 830

The world's smallest sovereign state, the Vatican is the jealous guardian of one of the world's greatest artistic and architectural patrimonies.

Covering just 0.44 sq km, the Vatican is all that's left of the Papal States. For more than a thousand years, the Papal States encompassed Rome and much of central Italy, but after

THE VATICAN TO VILLA BORGHESE

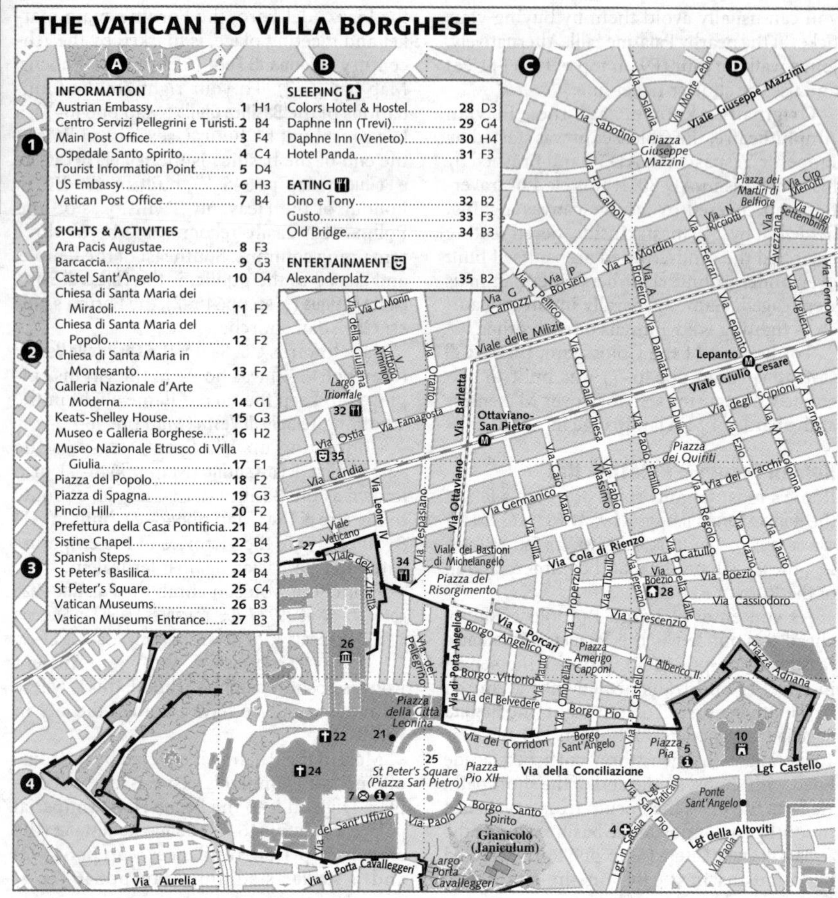

Italian unification in 1861 the pope was forced to give up his territorial possessions. Relations between Italy and the landless papacy remained strained until 1929 when Mussolini and Pius XI signed the Lateran Treaty and formally established the Vatican State.

ST PETER'S BASILICA & SQUARE

Italy's biggest, richest, and most spectacular church, **St Peter's Basilica** (Map pp642-3; ☎ 06 698 85 518; St Peter's Sq; admission free; 🕑 7am-7pm Apr-Sep, to 6.30pm Oct-Mar; Ⓜ Ottaviano-SanPietro) towers over the grandiose St Peter's Sq.

Built over the spot where St Peter was buried, the first basilica was consecrated by Constantine in the 4th century. In 1503, Bramante designed a new basilica, which took more than 150 years to complete. Michelangelo took over the project in 1547, designing the grand dome, which soars 120m above the altar. The cavernous 187m-long interior contains numerous treasures, including two of Italy's most celebrated masterpieces: Michelangelo's *Pietà*, the only work to carry his signature; and Bernini's 29m baldachin over the high altar.

Dress rules and security are stringently enforced at the basilica – no shorts, miniskirts or sleeveless tops.

Entrance to the **dome** (🕑 8am-6pm Apr-Sep, to 5pm Oct-Mar) is to the right as you climb the stairs to the basilica's atrium. Make the climb on foot (€5) or by lift (€7).

St Peter's Sq was designed by Bernini and laid out in the 17th century. The vast

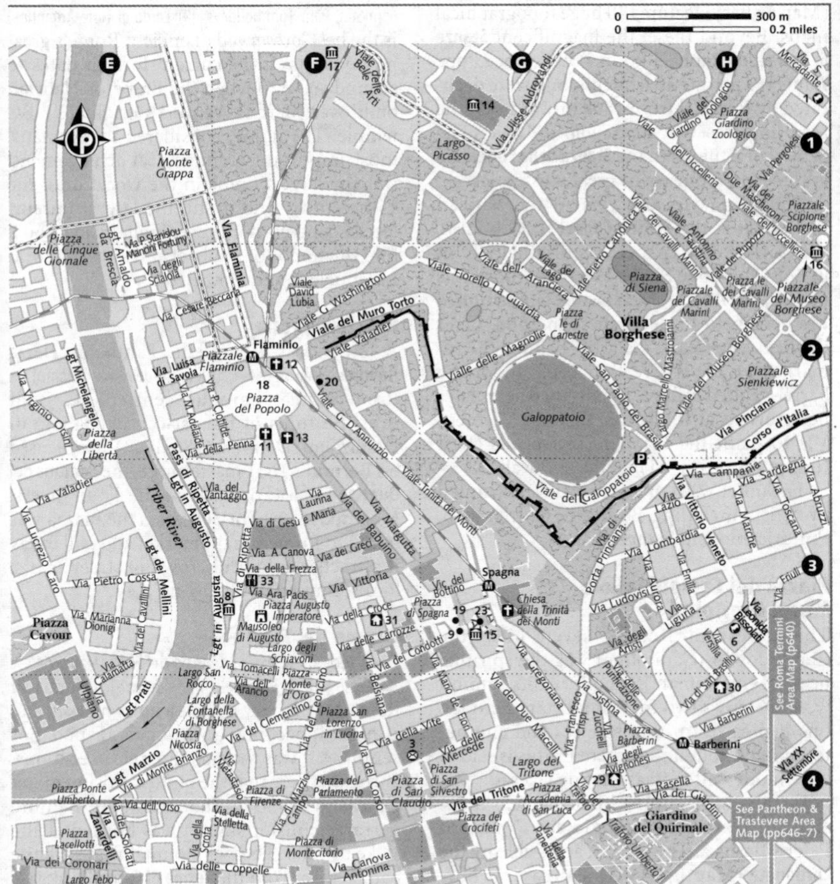

piazza is bound by two semicircular colonnades, each comprising four rows of Doric columns, and in its centre stands an obelisk brought to Rome by Caligula from Heliopolis (in ancient Egypt).

Each Wednesday at 11am, the pope addresses his flock at the Vatican (in July and August in Castel Gandolfo near Rome). For free tickets, contact the **Prefettura della Casa Pontificia** (Map pp642-3; ☎ 06 698 84 857; fax 06 698 85 863; 🕑 9am-1pm), through the bronze doors under the colonnade to the right of St Peter's.

VATICAN MUSEUMS

Boasting one of the world's great art collections, the **Vatican Museums** (Map pp642-3; adult/concession €14/8, free last Sun of month; 🕑 8.30am-4pm Mon-Sat, to 12.30pm last Sun of month; Ⓜ Ottaviano-San-Pietro) are housed in the Palazzo Apostolico Vaticano. Every inch of this vast 5.5-hectare complex is crammed with art, and you'll need several hours just for the highlights. There are four colour-coded itineraries, each of which finishes at the Sistine Chapel, so if you want you can walk straight there, although bear in mind that you can't backtrack once you're there. Audioguides are available for €6.

Home to some spectacular classical statuary, the **Museo Pio-Clementino** is to the left of the entrance complex. Highlights include the *Apollo Belvedere* and the 1st-century *Laocoön*, both in the Cortile Ottagono. Further on, the 175m-long **Galleria delle Carte Geografiche**

(Map Gallery) features 40 huge topographical maps. Beyond these, the magnificent **Stanze di Raffaello** (Raphael Rooms) were once Pope Julius II's private apartments, and were decorated by Raphael from 1508 onwards. Of the resulting frescoes, *La Scuola d'Atene* (The School of Athens) in the **Stanza della Segnatura** is considered one of his great masterpieces.

The climax to any visit to the Vatican Museums is the **Sistine Chapel** (Cappella Sistina; Map pp642-3). The chapel was originally built in 1484 for Pope Sixtus IV, after whom it is named, but it was Julius II who commissioned Michelangelo to decorate it in 1508. Over the next four years, the artist painted the remarkable *Genesis* (Creation; 1508–12) on the barrel-vaulted ceiling. Twenty-two years later he returned at the behest of Pope Clement VII to paint the *Giudizio Universale* (Last Judgement; 1534–41) on the end wall.

The other walls of the chapel were painted by artists including Botticelli, Ghirlandaio, Pinturicchio and Signorelli.

Piazza del Campidoglio & Musei Capitolini

The lowest of Rome's seven hills, the Campidoglio (Capitoline) was the spiritual heart of the Roman Republic. At its summit were the city's two most important temples: one dedicated to Juno Moneta and another to Jupiter Capitolinus, where Brutus is said to have hidden after assassinating Caesar.

In the 16th century Michelangelo redesigned Piazza del Campidoglio to face St Peter's Basilica. The square, accessible by the **Cordonata** (Map pp646–7) staircase, is bordered by **Palazzo Nuovo** (Map pp646–7) to the left, **Palazzo dei Conservatori** (Map pp646–7) on the right, and straight ahead **Palazzo Senatorio** (Map pp646–7), seat of city government since 1143. In the centre, the bronze **statue of Marcus Aurelius** (Map pp646–7) is a copy; the original is in Palazzo Nuovo.

Together, Palazzo Nuovo and Palazzo dei Conservatori house the **Musei Capitolini** (Capitoline Museums; Map pp646-7; ☎ 06 96 74 00; adult/concession €6.50/4.50; 🕑 9am-8pm Tue-Sun; 🚌 Piazza Venezia), the world's oldest public museums, dating to 1471.

Pantheon

A striking 2000-year-old temple, now church, the **Pantheon** (Map pp646-7; ☎ 06 683 00 230; Piazza della Rotonda; admission free; 🕑 8.30am-7.30pm Mon-Sat, 9am-6pm Sun, 9am-1pm holidays; 🚌 Largo di Torre Argentina) is the best-preserved of ancient Rome's great monuments. In its current form it dates to around AD 120 when the Emperor Hadrian built over Marcus Agrippa's original 27 BC temple. The dome, considered the Romans' most important architectural achievement, was the largest dome in the world until the 15th century and is still the largest unreinforced concrete dome ever built. Inside, you'll find the tombs of Raphael and kings Vittorio Emanuele II and Umberto I.

Piazza Navona

A few blocks west of the Pantheon, **Piazza Navona** (Map pp646-7; 🚌 Corso del Rinascimento) is Rome's great baroque centrepiece. Built over the ruins of the 1st-century Stadio di Domiziano (Domitian's Stadium), it is focused on Bernini's 1651 masterpiece, the **Fontana dei Quattro Fiumi** (Fountain of the Four Rivers; Map pp646–7). For 300 years the piazza was home to Rome's main market and still today it attracts a colourful crowd of street artists, locals, tourists and pigeons.

Campo de' Fiori

Dubbed 'il Campo', **Campo de' Fiori** (Map pp646-7; 🚌 Corso Vittorio Emanuele II), is a major focus of Roman life: by day it hosts a noisy market, and at night it becomes a vast open-air pub. For centuries it was the site of public executions, and it was here that the philosophising monk Giordano Bruno (the hooded figure in Ettore Ferrari's sinister statue) was burned at the stake in 1600. The twin fountains are granite baths taken from the **Terme di Caracalla** (Baths of Caracalla; Map pp638-9; ☎ 06 39 96 77 00; Via delle Terme di Caracalla 52; admission €6; 🕑 9am-1hr before sunset Tue-Sun, to 2pm Mon; Ⓜ Circo Massimo), whose vast ruins are an awe-inspiring sight. The 10-hectare baths' complex was inaugurated in AD 217 and included richly decorated pools, gymnasiums, libraries, shops and gardens.

Villa Borghese

Once the estate of Cardinal Scipione Borghese, this park, known as **Villa Borghese** (Map pp642-3; 🚌 Porta Pinciana), is a good spot for a breath of fresh air. Bike hire is available at various points, typically costing about €4 per hour. There are also several museums, including the fabulous **Museo e Galleria Borghese** (Map pp642-3; ☎ 06 3 28 10; www.galleriaborghese.it; Piazzale del Museo Borghese; adult/concession €8.50/5.50, plus obligatory booking fee €2; 8.30am-7.30pm Tue-Sun; Via Pinciana). With works by Caravaggio, Bernini, Botticelli and Raphael, this is arguably Rome's finest art gallery.

In the north of the park, the **Galleria Nazionale d'Arte Moderna** (Map pp642-3; 06 32 29 81; Viale delle Belle Arti 131; admission €6.50; 8.30am-7.30pm Tue-Sun; Viale delle Belle Arti) has an interesting collection of 19th- and 20th-century paintings. Nearby, the **Museo Nazionale Etrusco di Villa Giulia** (Map pp642-3; 06 320 05 62; Piazzale di Villa Giulia; admission €4; 8.30am-7.30pm Tue-Sun; Viale delle Belle Arti) displays Italy's finest Etruscan collection.

Trevi Fountain

Immortalised by Anita Ekberg in *La Dolce Vita*, the **Trevi Fountain** (Fontana di Trevi; Map pp646-7; Piazza di Trevi; M Barberini) was designed by Nicola Salvi in 1732 and depicts Neptune's chariot being led by Tritons, with sea horses representing the moods of the sea. The custom is to throw a coin over your shoulder into the fountain, thus ensuring your return to Rome. On an average day about €3000 is chucked away.

Piazza di Spagna & Spanish Steps

A hang-out for flirting adolescents and footsore tourists, Piazza di Spagna (Map pp642–3) and the Spanish Steps (Scalinata della Trinità dei Monti) have been a magnet for foreigners since the 18th century. Built with a legacy from the French in 1725, but named after the Spanish embassy to the Holy See, the steps were constructed to link the piazza with the well-heeled folks living above it.

To the right as you face the steps is the **Keats-Shelley House** (Map pp642-3; 06 678 42 35; Piazza di Spagna 8; 9am-1pm & 3-6pm Mon-Fri, 11am-2pm & 3-6pm Sat; M Spagna), where the poet Keats spent the last three months of his life. At the foot of the steps, the sinking boat fountain, the 1627 **Barcaccia** (Map pp642–3), is believed to be by Pietro Bernini, father of the more famous Gian Lorenzo. Opposite, **Via dei Condotti** is Rome's poshest shopping strip.

Piazza del Popolo & Around

One of Rome's landmark squares, **Piazza del Popolo** (Map pp642-3; M Flaminio) was laid out in 1538 at the point of convergence of three roads – Via di Ripetta, Via del Corso and Via del Babuino – known as Il Tridente. Guarding the piazza's southern approach are the twin 17th-century churches **Chiesa di Santa Maria dei Miracoli** (Map pp642–3) and **Chiesa di Santa Maria in Montesanto** (Map pp642–3). On the other side of the square, the **Chiesa di Santa Maria del Popolo** (Piazza del Popolo 12; 7am-noon & 4-7pm Mon-Sat, 8am-1.30pm & 4.30-7.30pm Sun; M Flaminio) houses two magnificent Caravaggio paintings: the *Conversione di San Paolo* (Conversion of St Paul) and the *Crocifissione di San Pietro* (Crucifixion of St Peter). Rising above the square is the Pincio Hill (Map pp642–3).

South of the piazza on Via di Ripetta, the **Ara Pacis Augustae** (Altar of Peace; Map pp642-3; 06 671 03 887; admission €6.50; 9am-7pm Tue-Sun; M Flaminio) is considered one of the most important works of ancient Roman sculpture. Today it's controversially housed in a white, glass pavilion designed by US architect Richard Meier.

Museo Nazionale Romano

Spread over five sites, the Museo Nazionale Romano (National Roman Museum) houses Rome's vast collection of classical art and statuary. A combined ticket covering each of the sites costs €7 and is valid for three days.

Lovers of ancient sculpture should make a beeline for **Palazzo Altemps** (Map pp646-7; 06 683 37 59; Piazza Sant'Apollinare 44; 9am-7.45pm Tue-Sun; Corso del Rinascimento), a lovely 15th-century *palazzo* which holds the best of the museum's classical sculpture.

Up near Termini, **Palazzo Massimo alle Terme** (Map p640; 06 399 67 700; Largo di Villa Peretti 1; 9am-7.45pm Tue-Sun; M Termini) features yet more sculpture, although the highlights are the amazing frescoes and wall paintings on the 2nd floor.

Nearby, the **Terme di Diocleziano** (Baths of Diocletian; Map p640; 06 488 05 30; Viale Enrico de Nicola 79; 9am-7.45pm Tue-Sun; M Termini) are a sight in themselves. Built at the turn of the 3rd century, they were Rome's largest baths complex, covering 13 hectares and capable of accommodating 3000 people. Nowadays, they are home to a large selection of archaeological artefacts, sarcophagi and terracotta objects.

Trastevere

The happening neighbourhood in central Rome, Trastevere is an old working-class area made good. It's a beautiful area at any time of the day, but it really comes into its own after dark when crowds of high-spirited revellers descend on its medieval, bar-strewn streets.

Don't miss the **Basilica di Santa Maria in Trastevere** (Map pp646-7; 06 581 48 02; Piazza Santa Maria in Trastevere; 7.30am-12.30pm & 3.30-7.30pm; Viale di Trastevere) in the lovely piazza of the

PANTHEON & TRASTEVERE AREA

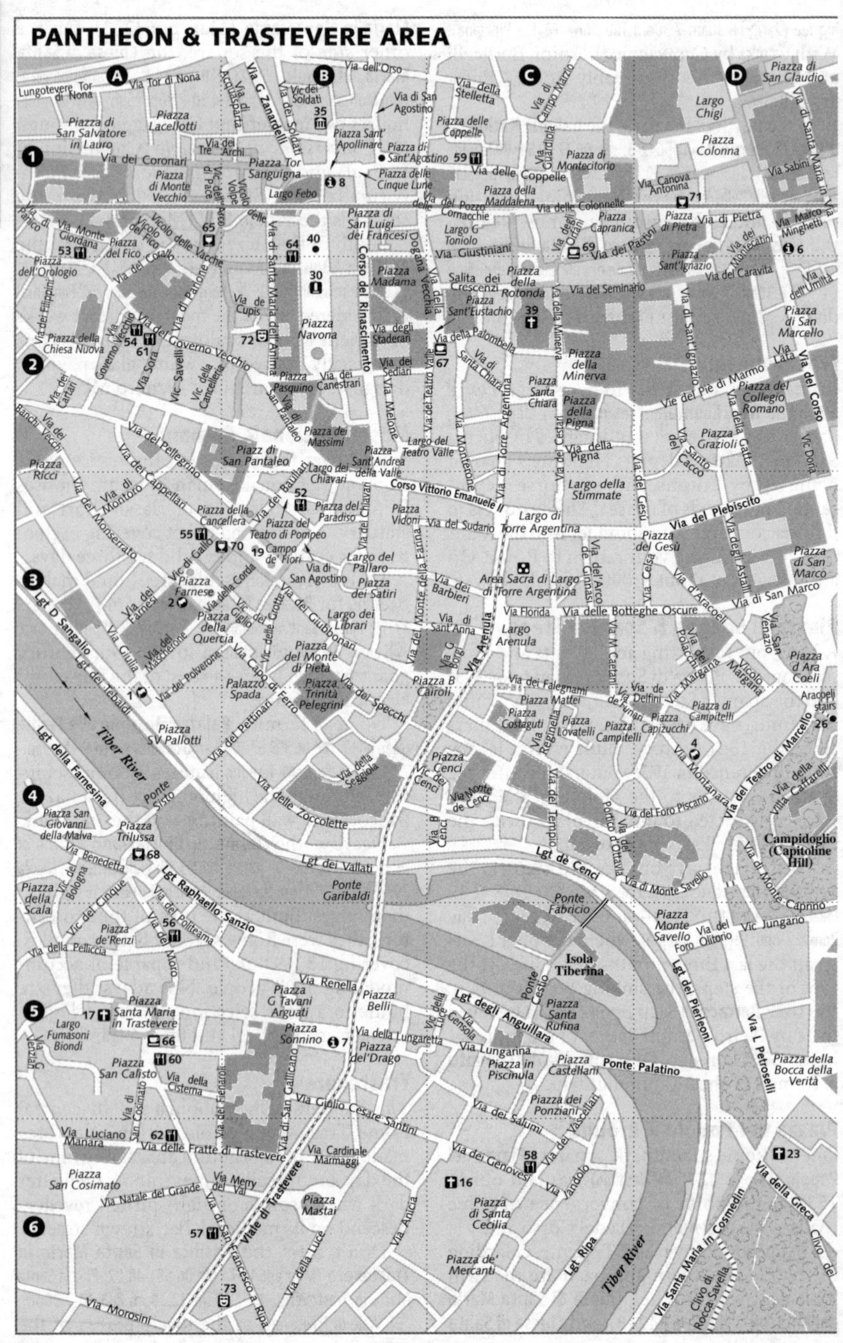

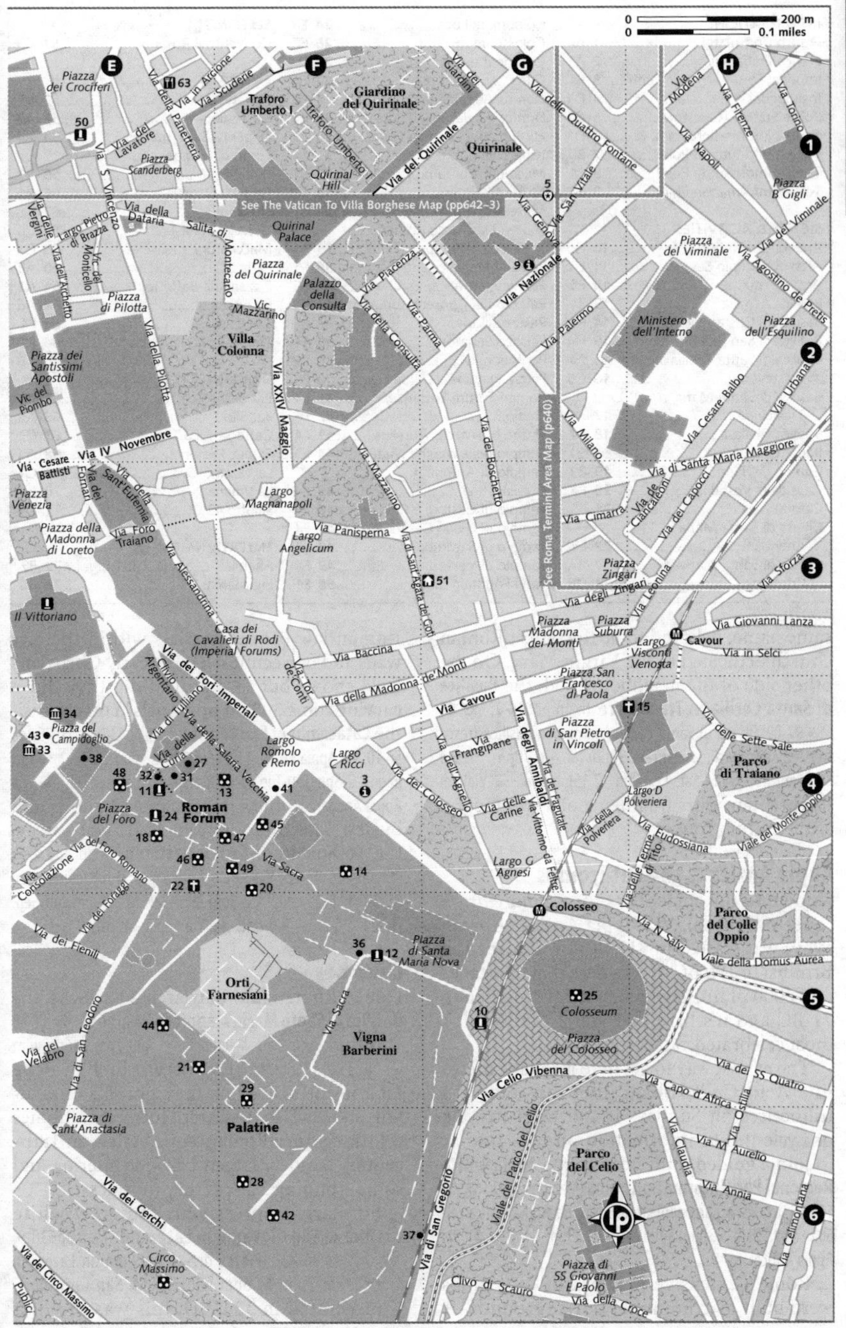

0 200 m
0 0.1 miles
See The Vatican To Villa Borghese Map (pp642–3)
See Roma Termini Area Map (p640)
Giardino del Quirinale
Quirinale
Quirinal Hill
Quirinal Palace
Villa Colonna
Ministero dell'Interno
Roman Forum
Orti Farnesiani
Vigna Barberini
Palatine
Colosseum
Parco di Traiano
Parco del Colle Oppio
Parco del Celio
Circo Massimo
Il Vittoriano
Casa dei Cavalieri di Rodi (Imperial Forums)
Via Nazionale
Via Cavour
Via dei Fori Imperiali
Via IV Novembre
Via XXIV Maggio
Via degli Annibaldi
Via di San Gregorio
Via dei Cerchi
Via Celio Vibenna
Cavour
Colosseo

INFORMATION
French Consulate....1 A4
French Embassy....2 A3
Imperial Forums Visitor Centre....3 F4
Irish Embassy....4 D4
Police Station (Questura)....5 G1
Tourist Information Point....6 D1
Tourist Information Point....7 B5
Tourist Information Point....8 B1
Tourist Information Point....9 G2

SIGHTS & ACTIVITIES
Arco di Costantino....10 G5
Arco di Settimio Severo....11 E4
Arco di Tito....12 F5
Basilica Aemilia....13 F4
Basilica di Costantino....14 F4
Basilica di San Pietro in Vincoli..15 H4
Basilica di Santa Cecilia in Trastevere....16 C6
Basilica di Santa Maria in Trastevere....17 A5
Basilica Giulia....18 E4
Bocca della Verità....(see 23)
Campo de' Fiori....19 B3
Casa delle Vestali....20 F4
Casa di Livia....21 E5
Chiesa di Santa Maria Antiqua....22 E4
Chiesa di Santa Maria in Cosmedin....23 D6
Colonna di Foca....24 E4
Colosseum....25 G5
Cordonata....26 D4
Curia....27 E4
Domus Augustana....28 F6
Domus Flavia....29 F5
Fontana dei Quattro Fiumi....30 B2
Lapis Niger....31 E4
Millarium Aureum....32 E4
Musei Capitolini....33 E4
Musei Capitolini....34 E4
Museo Nazionale Romano: Palazzo Altemps....35 B1
Palatine Entrance....36 F5
Palatine Entrance....37 F6
Palazzo dei Conservatori....(see 33)
Palazzo Nuovo....(see 34)
Palazzo Senatorio....38 E4
Pantheon....39 C2
Piazza Navona....40 B1
Roman Forum Entrance....41 F4
Stadio....42 F6
Statue of Marcus Aurelius....43 E4
Tempio della Magna Mater....44 E5
Tempio di Antonino e Faustina....45 F4
Tempio di Castore e Polluce....46 E4
Tempio di Giulio Cesare....47 F4
Tempio di Saturno....48 E4
Tempio di Vesta....49 F4
Trevi Fountain....50 E1

SLEEPING
Convento Il Rosario....51 G3

EATING
Baffetto 2....52 B3
Da Tonino....53 A2
Di per Di Supermarket....54 A2
Forno di Campo de' Fiori....55 A3
Forno la Renella....56 A5
Frontoni....57 A6
Le Mani in Pasta....58 C6
Maccheroni....59 C1
Paris....60 A5
Pizzeria da Baffetto....61 A2
Pizzeria Ivo....62 A6
San Crispino....63 E1
Tre Scalini....64 B1

DRINKING
Bar della Pace....65 A1
Bar San Calisto....66 A5
Caffè Sant'Eustachio....67 C2
Freni e Frizioni....68 A4
La Tazza d'Oro....69 C1
La Vineria....70 B3
Salotto 42....71 D1

ENTERTAINMENT
Anima....72 B2
Big Mama....73 B6

same name, believed to be the oldest Roman church dedicated to the Virgin Mary. On the other side of the neighbourhood, the **Basilica di Santa Cecilia in Trastevere** (Map pp646-7; ☎ 06 589 92 89; Piazza di Santa Cecilia; admission basilica/fresco free/€2; basilica 9am-12.30pm & 4-6.30pm, fresco 10.15am-noon Mon-Sat, 11.15am-12.15pm Sun; Viale di Trastevere) harbours fragments of a spectacular 13th-century fresco.

Appia Antica & the Catacombs

Known to the ancients as the *regina viarum* (queen of roads), Via Appia Antica (Appian Way) was started in 312 BC and finished in Brindisi in 190 BC. It was here that Spartacus and 6000 of his slave rebels were crucified in 71 BC and it's here that you'll find Rome's most celebrated catacombs.

The easiest way to get here is to take metro line A to Colli Albani, then bus 660. It's traffic-free on Sundays if you want to walk or cycle it. For information on bike hire or to join a guided tour, head to the **Appia Antica Regional Park Information Point** (Map pp638-9; ☎ 06 513 53 16; www.parcoappiaantica.org; Via Appia Antica 58-60; 9.30am-5.30pm summer, to 4.30pm winter; Via Appia Antica).

Rome's extensive network of catacombs were built as communal burial grounds. A Roman law banned burials within the city walls and persecution left the early Christians little choice but to dig. And dig they did – carving some 300km of tunnels. You can visit the **Catacombs of San Callisto** (Map pp638-9; ☎ 06 446 56 10; Via Appia Antica 110; adult/concession €5/3; 9am-noon & 2-5pm Thu-Tue, to 5.30pm Jun-Sep, closed Feb; Via Appia Antica), Rome's largest, most famous and busiest catacombs, and, a short walk away, the **Catacombs of San Sebastiano** (Map pp638-9; ☎ 06 785 03 50; Via Appia Antica 136; adult/concession €5/3; 9am-noon & 2-5pm Mon-Sat, to 5.30pm Jun-Sep, closed mid-Nov–mid-Dec; Via Appia Antica).

Churches

One of Rome's four patriarchal basilicas, the **Basilica di Santa Maria Maggiore** (Map p640; ☎ 06 48 31 95; Piazza Santa Maria Maggiore; 7am-7pm, to 6pm winter; Piazza Santa Maria Maggiore) was built by Pope Liberius in AD 352 on the sight of a miraculous snowfall. In its current form, it combines a 14th-century Romanesque belfry, an 18th-century facade, a largely baroque interior, and some stunning 5th-century mosaics.

Similarly impressive is the great white **Basilica di San Giovanni in Laterano** (Map pp638-9; ☎ 06 698 86 433; Piazza di San Giovanni in Laterano 4; 7am-7pm, to 6pm winter; M San Giovanni). Consecrated in 324 AD, this was the first

Christian basilica to be built in Rome and, until the late 14th century, was the pope's principal residence.

Just off Via Cavour, the **Basilica di San Pietro in Vincoli** (Map pp646-7; Piazza di San Pietro in Vincoli; 8am-12.30pm & 3-7pm; Ⓜ Cavour) is home to Michelangelo's magnificent *Moses*, as well as the chains worn by St Peter before his crucifixion.

The **Basilica di San Clemente** (Map pp638-9; ☎ 06 774 00 21; Via di San Giovanni in Laterano; 9am-12.30pm & 3.30-6.30pm; Ⓜ Colosseo), east of the Colosseum, is a multilayered affair. The 12th-century church at street level was built over a 4th-century church that was, in turn, built over a 1st-century Roman house with a temple dedicated to the pagan god Mithras.

Considered one of the finest medieval churches in Rome, the **Chiesa di Santa Maria in Cosmedin** (Map pp646-7; ☎ 06 678 14 19; Piazza della Bocca della Verità 18; 9am-1pm & 2.30-6pm; Via dei Cerchi) is most famous for the **Bocca della Verità** (Mouth of Truth; Map pp646–7) in its portico. Legend has it that if you put your right hand into the stone mouth and tell a lie, it will bite your hand off.

Facing onto Piazza della Repubblica, the hulking **Chiesa di Santa Maria degli Angeli** (Map p640; Piazza della Repubblica; 7am-6.30pm Mon-Sat, to 7.30pm Sun; Ⓜ Repubblica) occupies the central hall of Diocletian's enormous baths complex (see p645). Its most interesting feature is the double meridian in the transept.

SLEEPING

There's no point beating around the bush, Rome is expensive. Most of the hostels and budget *pensioni* (guest houses) are in the area around Termini train station – the best on the northeast side (take the Via Marsala exit). Always try to book ahead, even if it's just for the first night. The Rome Tourist Board website (www.romaturismo.it) has a full accommodation list. For B&Bs or longer-term accommodation try www.cross-polinate.com.

If you need help finding somewhere, there's a **hotel reservation service** (Map p640; ☎ 06 699 10 00; booking fee €3; 7am-10pm) at Stazione Termini.

Camping Internazionale Castelfusano (off Map pp638-9; ☎ 06 562 33 04; www.romacampingcastelfusano.it; per person/tent/car €9.50/4/5, 2-person bungalows €32-48;) On the seafront near Ostia, this is a well-equipped camping ground with tent pitches, bungalows and a mini-market. Take bus 061 from Via Cristoforo Colombo near Fermi metro station.

Pop Inn Hostel (Map p640; ☎ 06 495 98 87; www.popinnhostel.com; Via Marsala 80; dm €16-31, s with shared bathroom €40-85, with private bathroom €46-105, d with shared bathroom €42-104, with private bathrooom €52-120) A backpacker favourite, the Pop Inn is relaxed, lively and no-frills. Of the various sleeping options the six-bed mixed dorms are the best value.

Alessandro Palace (Map p640; ☎ 06 446 19 58; www.hostelsalessandro.com; Via Vicenza 42; dm €18-24, d €66-120, tr €58-144;) This buzzing spot offers spick-and-span hotel rooms, as well as four- to six-person dorms. It's run by a friendly international crew and its brick-vaulted bar is a great place to catch up with travellers. On the other side of Termini, Alessandro Downtown (Map p640) offers more of the same.

Yellow Hostel (Map p640; ☎ 06 493 82 682; www.the-yellow.com; Via Palestro 44; dm €18-38;) The Yellow is a hardcore hostel for a young, fit crowd. Dorms are mixed and, while clean and reasonably sized, can be noisy. There's no common room but most people hang out in the bar. There's free internet, wi-fi and left luggage.

Beehive (Map p640; ☎ 06 447 04 553; www.the-beehive.com; Via Marghera 8; dm €20-25, d €70-80;) A brilliant boutique hostel run by an environmentally conscious American couple. Rooms are spotless and there's a vegetarian cafe and small walled garden. Environmental touches include homemade soap and recycling bins.

Colors Hotel & Hostel (Map pp642-3; ☎ 06 687 40 30; www.colorshotel.com; Via Boezio 31; dm €20-27, d with shared bathroom €65-110, with private bathroom €80-130, tr with shared bathroom €75-120, with private bathroom €100-145;) A laid-back hostel-cum-hotel near the Vatican, Colors has spotless, multicoloured dorms, snazzy private rooms and a superhelpful staff. Hostel-stayers can cook in the fully equipped kitchen.

Funny Palace (Map p640; ☎ 06 447 03 523; www.funnyhostel.com; Via Varese 33; dm €20-30, d €79-89;) To find this popular hostel head for the Splashnet laundry, which doubles as the reception and internet point. Upstairs, the mixed dorms are big, sleeping up to 14 people, but are clean and well maintained. No credit cards.

Convento Il Rosario (Map pp646-7; ☎ 06 679 23 46; irodopre@tin.it; Via di Sant'Agata dei Goti 10; s/d €55/98) In the cobbled Monti area, this is a quiet, convent-run guest house. It's fairly basic but the location is good, rates are excellent and the

Book your stay at lonelyplanet.com/hotels

SPLURGE

Daphne Inn (Map pp642-3; ☎ 06 874 50 086; www.daphne-rome.com; Via di San Basilio 55 & Via degli Avignonesi 20; s €110-160, d with shared bathroom €90-150, with private bathroom €90-200, ste €320-550;) One of Rome's standout accommodation options, this inn is a star, offering value for money, exceptional service and fashionably attired rooms. It's spread over two sites, both within easy walking distance of Piazza Barberini, but the look is similar throughout – modern with cooling earth tones, leather chairs and linear, unfussy furniture. Particularly eye-catching are the suites at the Daphne Trevi.

rooms are perfectly comfortable. Note the 11pm curfew and cash-only payment.

Welrome (Map p640; ☎ 06 478 24 343; www.welrome.it; Via Calatafimi 15-19; s €50-100, d €50-110) Owner Mary takes great pride in looking after her guests and her seven rooms provide welcome respite from Rome's relentless streets.

Hotel Panda (Map pp642-3; ☎ 06 678 01 79; www.hotelpanda.it; Via della Croce 35; s €63-75, d €98-108, tr €130-140, q €170-180;) A budget bolthole near the Spanish Steps, the Panda is deservedly popular. Its superb position, attractive high-ceilinged rooms and honest rates ensure a year-round stream of travellers. Air-con costs €6.

EATING

The best places to eat are in the *centro storico* and Trastevere, but there are also excellent choices in San Lorenzo and Testaccio. The Termini area is best avoided although you'll find some decent takeaways, particularly around Piazza Vittorio Emanuele II.

Quick Eats & Self-Catering

Foragers will have their hands full in Rome's produce markets, which generally operate from 7am to 1.30pm. They include: Campo de' Fiori; the Nuovo Mercato Esquilino, near Piazza Vittorio Emanuele; Piazza San Cosimato in Trastevere; and Piazza Testaccio.

Supermarkets are thin on the ground, but you'll find a **Conad** (Map p640; 6am-midnight) at Termini station, and a **Di per Di** (Map pp646-7; Via del Governo Vecchio 119; 8am-9pm) near Piazza Navona.

For quick eats, head to **Frontoni** (Map pp646-7; Viale di Trastevere 52-56) or **Forno la Renella** (Map pp646-7; Via del Moro 15-16), both in Trastevere. On Campo de' Fiori, **Forno di Campo de' Fiori** (Map pp646-7; Campo de' Fiori 22) is famous for its pizza *bianca* (white pizza).

Ice Cream

Arguably Rome's best *gelateria* (ice-cream shop), **San Crispino** (Map pp646-7; Via della Panetteria 42) serves tubs of natural, seasonal flavours such as *crema* with honey. Near the Vatican Museums, **Old Bridge** (Map pp642-3; Viale dei Bastioni di Michelangelo 5) is perfect for a postmuseum pick-me-up, while **Tre Scalini** (Map pp646-7; Piazza Navona 30) is famous for its €10 *tartufo nero* (black truffle).

Restaurants, Trattorias & Pizzerias

CITY CENTRE

Pizzeria da Baffetto (Map pp646-7; ☎ 06 686 16 17; Via del Governo Vecchio 114; pizzas €8; 6.30pm-1am) For the full-on Roman pizza experience get down to this local institution. Meals are loud, chaotic and fast, but the thin-crust pizza's good and the vibe is fun. There's now a Baffetto 2 (Map pp646–7; ☎ 06 682 10 807; Piazza del Teatro di Pompeo 18; closed Tuesday) near Campo de' Fiori.

Gusto (Map pp642-3; ☎ 06 322 62 73; Piazza Augusto Imperatore 9; pizzas €8) A lunchtime favourite with office workers, this big 90s-style warehouse operation serves everything from thick-crust pizza to cheese platters, salads and overpriced fusion food. At lunch the €9 salad buffet is a good bet.

Da Tonino (Map pp646-7; ☎ 06 687 70 02; Via del Governo Vecchio 18; meals €18; Mon-Sat) This low-key neighbourhood trattoria sits among the bohemian boutiques on Via del Governo Vecchio. It's old school so don't expect frills, just filling Roman cooking served fast and served cheap.

Maccheroni (Map pp646-7; ☎ 06 683 07 895; Piazza delle Coppelle 44; meals €35) Popular with locals and tourists alike, this is the archetypal *centro storico* trattoria. It's boisterous, busy and fancy-free with a classic Roman menu and an attractive setting near the Pantheon.

TRASTEVERE, TESTACCIO & THE VATICAN

Pizzeria Remo (Map pp638-9; ☎ 06 574 62 70; Piazza Santa Maria Liberatice 44; pizzas €6) One of Rome's most popular pizzerias, this rowdy Testaccio spot is a favourite with Saturday-nighters.

Queues are the norm but the large, thin-crust pizzas and delicious bruschetta make the chaos bearable.

Pizzeria Ivo (Map pp646-7; ☎ 06 581 70 82; Via di San Francesco a Ripa 158; pizzas €6; ⏰ Wed-Mon) A perennially popular Trastevere pizzeria, Ivo fits the bill. With the TV on in the corner and waiters skilfully manoeuvring plates over the noisy hordes, diners chow down on classic thin-crust pizzas.

Volpetti Più (Map pp638-9; ☎ 06 574 43 06; Via A Volta 8; meals €10-15) A sumptuous *tavola calda* (a 'hot table' where pre-prepared pasta, meats and vegies are served canteen-style), this is one of the few places in town where you can sit down and eat well for less than €15. Choose from pizza, pasta, soup, meat, vegetables and fried nibbles.

our pick **Dino e Tony** (Map pp642-3; ☎ 06 397 33 284; meals €25; ⏰ Mon-Sat) Something of a rarity, Dino e Tony is an authentic trattoria in the Vatican area. Famous for its *amatriciana* (a spicy pasta sauce made with tomatoes, pancetta and pecorino cheese), it serves a monumental antipasto, which might well see you through to dessert.

Le Mani in Pasta (Map pp646-7; ☎ 06 581 60 17; Via dei Genovesi 37; meals €32; ⏰ Tue-Sun) This tasty Trastevere *osteria* (neighbourhood inn) specialises in pasta and grilled mains. Try *fettucine con ricotta e pancetta* (ribbon pasta with ricotta cheese and bacon) followed by grilled scampi.

AROUND ROMA TERMINI

Ristofer (Map p640; Via Marsala 13; meals €7.50) Huge helpings for hungry workers. Rome's railway workers' canteen serves the cheapest full meals in Rome and although the food is hardly cordon bleu, it does the job.

Kisso (Map p640; ☎ 06 478 24 677; Via Firenze 30; meals €12-35; ⏰ Mon-Sat) An affordable and popular Japanese restaurant just off Via Nazionale. Sushi and sashimi range from €13.50 to €48, making the €12 lunchtime menu the obvious choice.

Beehive (Map p640; ☎ 06 447 04 553; Via Marghera 8; meals €20) In the hostel of the same name (see p649), this small organic cafe serves delicious vegetarian food. The menu changes daily but staples include fresh homemade pasta, quiches, veggie burgers and couscous.

Vecchia Roma (Map pp638-9; ☎ 06 446 71 43; Via Ferruccio 12; meals €20; ⏰ Mon-Sat) Good, filling food at reasonable prices is what you get at this brick-vaulted trattoria near Piazza Vittorio Emanuele. The buffet antipasto sets you off well, whetting the appetite for classic pastas and traditional main courses.

SPLURGE

Paris (Map pp646-7; ☎ 06 581 53 78; Piazza San Calisto 7; meal €50; ⏰ Tue-Sat & lunch Sun) This elegant, old-fashioned restaurant with wooden beams and outdoor seating on a cobbled square serves the best Roman-Jewish cooking outside of the Jewish Ghetto. Dishes include an outstanding *carciofi alle giudia* (deep-fried artichoke) and crispy *fritto misto con baccalà* (fried vegetables with salted cod).

DRINKING

Drinking in Rome is all about looking the part and enjoying the atmosphere. Hardcore boozing does take place, mainly on Campo de' Fiori, but Rome is not really a heavy drinking town. There are an inordinate number of bars and cafes across the city, as well as a growing number of pubs.

Cafes

Caffè Sant'Eustachio (Map pp646-7; Piazza Sant'Eustachio 82) This unassuming cafe makes the best coffee in Rome. Served sugared and with a layer of froth, the espresso is a smooth, creamy blend with a reassuringly strong kick.

La Tazza d'Oro (Map pp646-7; Via degli Orfani 84-6) Not only does this busy, stand-up bar serve superb coffee, but it also does a mean *granita di caffè*, a crushed-ice concoction served with a big dollop of cream.

Bars & Pubs

Bar San Calisto (Map pp646-7; Piazza San Calisto; ⏰ Mon-Sat) Drug dealers, drunks, slumming uptowners, foreign students – they all flock to this Trastevere landmark for the cheap beer and laid-back atmosphere. It's famous for its chocolate, drunk hot or eaten as ice cream.

Bar della Pace (Map pp646-7; Via della Pace 3-7) Style hounds looking for the archetypal dolce vita bar can stop their search here. With its art nouveau interior, ivy-clad facade and well-dressed customers, it's the epitome of Italian style.

La Vineria (Map pp646-7; Campo de' Fiori 15) A good spot to watch the nightly Campo de' Fiori circus, this is the hippest of the squareside bars. It has a small, bottle-lined interior and several outside tables.

Bar Arco degli Arunci (Map p640; Via degli Arunci 42) On a car-free piazza in San Lorenzo, this attractive modern bar is a cool spot for a drink or light meal. Come between 7pm and 9pm and you can combine the two with an *aperitivo* (€7, including buffet).

Salotto 42 (Map pp646-7; Piazza di Pietra; 4pm-2am Tue-Sat, to midnight Sun) A laid-back lounge-bar on a picturesque *centro storico* piazza, Salotto 42 is hip yet unpretentious with soft sofas, coffee-table books and an excellent *aperitivo* spread.

Freni e Frizioni (Map pp646-7; Piazza Trilussa) This kicking bar is one of Trastevere's 'in' spots. Housed in a former garage (hence the name – 'brakes and clutches'), it attracts a young, fashionable crowd.

CLUBBING

Rome's clubbing scene is centred on Testaccio and the Ostiense area, although you'll also find places in Trastevere and the *centro storico*. You'll need to dress the part to get into the big clubs, which rarely get going much before midnight. Admission is sometimes free but drinks are expensive, typically €10 to €15.

AKAB (Map pp638-9; Via di Monte Testaccio 68-9) One of the most popular clubs on the Testaccio clubbing strip, Akab serves a steady supply of house, R & B and techno. Sweat to the tunes in the underground cellar or chill in the Zen garden.

Anima (Map pp646-7; Via Santa Maria dell' Anima 57) Romans and tourists squeeze into this cool *centro storico* bar to get close over a cocktail and high-octane hip-hop. Come early for a drink or drop by late to dance.

Goa (Map pp638-9; Via Libetta 13) Top DJs whip the floor into a house-induced frenzy at Rome's top mega-club. Last Sunday of the month is Venus Rising lesbian night.

ENTERTAINMENT

The best listings guide is *Roma C'è* (www.romace.it, in Italian), with an English-language section, published on Wednesdays (€1.50). Another useful guide is *Trova Roma*, a free insert with Thursday's *La Repubblica* newspaper. Rome's entertainment schedule heats up in summer, with numerous alfresco concerts and performances.

Two good ticket agencies are: **Orbis** (Map p640; ☎ 06 48 27 403; Piazza dell'Esquilino 37; 9.30am-1pm & 4-7.30pm Mon-Fri, 9.30am-1pm Sat) and the online agency **Hello** (☎ 800 90 70 80; www.helloticket.it, in Italian).

Live Music

Alexanderplatz (Map pp642-3; ☎ 06 397 42 171; www.alexanderplatz.it; Via Ostia 9) Rome's top jazz joint attracts international performers and a passionate, knowledgable crowd. In July and August the club transfers to Villa Celimontana park.

Big Mama (Map pp646-7; ☎ 06 581 24 51; www.bigmama.it; Via San Francesco a Ripa 18) This Trastevere basement is Rome's self-styled home of blues. It plays host to the world's top bluesmen and stages soul, jazz and funk.

Villaggio Globale (Map pp638-9; Lungotevere Testaccio) This alternative venue is housed in Rome's ex-slaughterhouse. The scene is cheap beer, spliff and dreadlocks, and the gigs are great.

Opera & Classical Music

Rome's premier concert complex is the **Auditorium Parco della Musica** (Map pp638-9; ☎ 06 802 41 281; www.auditorium.com; Viale Pietro de Coubertin 34). With its three concert halls and 3000-seater open-air arena, it stages everything from Beethoven to Bjork. The Auditorium is also home to Rome's top classical music organisation, the **Accademia di Santa Cecilia** (☎ box office 06 808 20 58; www.santacecilia.it), which organises a world-class symphony season.

The **Accademia Filarmonica Romana** (☎ 06 320 17 52; www.filarmonicaroma.org) concentrates on classical and chamber music at the **Teatro Olimpico** (Map pp638-9; ☎ 06 326 59 91; www.teatroolimpico.it; Piazza Gentile da Fabriano 17).

Rome's opera season runs from December to June. The main venue is the **Teatro dell'Opera** (Map p640; ☎ 06 481 601; www.operaroma.it; Piazza Beniamino Gigli 7). Ticket prices tend to be steep. In summer opera is performed outdoors at the spectacular Terme di Caracalla.

GETTING THERE & AWAY

Air

Rome's main international airport **Leonardo da Vinci** (FCO; off Map pp638-9; ☎ 06 6 59 51; www.adr.it), better known as Fiumicino, is 30km west of the city. The much smaller **Ciampino airport** (CIA; off Map pp638-9; ☎ 06 6 59 51; www.adr.it), 15km southeast of the city centre, is the hub for low-cost carriers including **Ryanair** (www.ryanair.com) and **easyJet** (www.easyjet.com).

Boat

Rome's port is at Civitavecchia (off Map pp638–9), about 80km north of Rome. The main ferry companies are:

Corsica Sardinia Ferries (☎ 199 400 500; www.sardiniaferries.com) For Golfo Aranci.

SNAV (☎ 081 428 55 55; www.snav.it) For Palermo and Olbia.

Tirrenia (☎ 892 123; www.tirrenia.it) For Arbatax, Cagliari and Olbia.

Bookings can be made at the Termini-based **Agenzia 365** (Map p640; 🕑 8am-8pm), at travel agents, or online at www.traghettionline.net. You can also buy directly at the port.

Half-hourly trains depart from Roma Termini to Civitavecchia (€4.50 to €8.50, one hour). On arrival, it's about a 15-minute walk to the port (to your right) as you exit the station.

Bus

Long-distance national and international buses use the terminus on Piazzale Tiburtina, in front of Stazione Tiburtina. Take metro line B from Termini to Tiburtina.

You can get tickets from the offices next to the bus terminus or at travel agencies. National companies include:

ARPA (☎ 199 166 952; www.arpaonline.it) For L'Aquila and Abruzzo.

Cotral (www.cotralspa.it, in Italian) For the Lazio region.

Interbus (☎ 0935 56 51 11; www.interbus.it, in Italian) For destinations in Sicily, including Messina, Catania and Palermo.

Marozzi (☎ 080 579 01 11; www.marozzivt.it, in Italian) To/from Sorrento, Bari, Matera and Lecce.

SAIS (☎ 091 616 60 28; www.saisautolinee.it, in Italian) For Sicily.

SENA (☎ 0577 20 82 82; www.senabus.it) To/from Siena, Milan and Bologna.

Sulga (☎ 800 099 661; www.sulga.it) For Perugia, Assisi and Ravenna.

Car & Motorcycle

Rome is circled by the Grande Raccordo Anulare (GRA) to which all *autostrade* (motorways) and main Rome-bound roads connect, including the A1 north–south artery (the Autostrada del Sole), and the A12, which connects Rome to Civitavecchia and Fiumicino airport.

Car-hire offices at Stazione Termini include **Avis** (Map p640; ☎ 06 481 43 73; www.avis.com), **Europcar** (Map p640; ☎ 06 488 28 54; www.europcar.com), **Hertz** (Map p640; ☎ 06 474 03 89; www.hertz.com) and **Maggiore National** (Map p640; ☎ 06 488 00 49; www.maggiore.com). All have offices at both airports as well.

Near Termini **Bici & Baci** (Map p640; ☎ 06 482 84 43; www.bicibaci.com; Via del Viminale 5; 🕑 8am-7pm) rents out scooters from €19 per day and motorbikes from €95.

Train

Almost all trains arrive at and depart from Stazione Termini. There are regular connections to all major Italian cities and many smaller towns. On the main concourse, the **train information office** (Map p640; 🕑 7am-9.45pm) is helpful (English is spoken) but often very busy. To avoid the queues, you can get information online at www.trenitalia.com or, if you speak Italian, by calling ☎ 89 20 21.

Facilities at Termini include telephones, ATMs, tourist information, post office, an underground shopping mall and **left luggage** (Map p640; 1st 5 hours €3.80, 6-12 hours per hr €0.60, 13 hours & over per hr €0.20; 🕑 6am-midnight).

Rome's second train station is Stazione Tiburtina, on metro line B.

GETTING AROUND

Car & Motorcycle

Driving in Rome is exhilarating, terrifying, fun and often pointless, given the perpetual gridlock. Riding a scooter is hairier but gives you more freedom and makes parking easier.

Most of the historic centre is closed to normal traffic. You're not allowed to drive in the centre from 6.30am to 6pm Monday to Friday and from 2pm to 6pm Saturday unless you're a resident or have special permission.

Parking is no fun. Blue lines denote pay-and-display spaces with tickets available from meters (coins only) and *tabacchi* (tobacconists). If your car gets towed away, check with the **traffic police** (☎ 06 6 76 91).

Public Transport

Rome has an integrated public-transport system, so the same ticket is valid for all modes of transport: bus, tram, metro and suburban railway. You can buy tickets at *tabacchi*, newsstands and from vending machines at main bus stops and metro stations. Single tickets cost €1 for 75 minutes, during which time you can use as many buses or trams as you like but only go once on the metro. Daily tickets cost €4 and give you unlimited trips; a three-day ticket costs €11; and a weekly ticket

€16. Tickets must be purchased before you get on the bus/train and validated in the yellow machine, or at the entrance gates for the metro. Ticketless riders risk an on-the-spot €50 fine.

Rome's buses and trams are run by **ATAC** (☎ 06 5 70 03; www.atac.roma.it). The **main bus station** (Map p640; Piazza dei Cinquecento) is in front of Stazione Termini, where there's an **information booth** (🕑 7.30am-8pm). Largo di Torre Argentina, Piazza Venezia and Piazza San Silvestro are also important hubs. Buses generally run from about 5.30am until midnight, with limited services throughout the night.

The Metropolitana has two lines, A and B, which both pass through Termini. Take line A for the Trevi Fountain (Barberini), Spanish Steps (Spagna), and Vatican (Ottaviano-San Pietro); and line B for the Colosseum (Colosseo). Trains run on line B between 5.30am and 11.30pm (1.30am on Friday and Saturday) and to 10pm on line A. From 10pm until 11.30pm (1.30am on Friday and Saturday) two temporary bus lines substitute metro line A: MA1 from Battistini to Arco di Travertino, and MA2 from Viale G Washington (off Piazzale Flaminio) to Anagnina.

Taxi

To minimise the risk of being ripped off make sure your taxi is licensed and metered, and always go with the metered fare, never an arranged price (the set fares to and from the airports are exceptions to this rule). Official rates are posted in taxis.

You can't hail a taxi, but there are major taxi ranks at the airports, Stazione Termini and Largo di Torre Argentina. To phone try:

Cosmos (☎ 06 8 81 77)
La Capitale (☎ 06 49 94)
Pronto Taxi (☎ 06 66 45)
Radio Taxi (☎ 06 35 70)
Samarcanda (☎ 06 55 51)
Tevere (☎ 06 41 57)

AROUND ROME

OSTIA ANTICA

An easy day trip from Rome, Ostia Antica is well worth a visit. Ostia was ancient Rome's port, and the clearly discernible ruins of restaurants, laundries, shops, houses and public meeting places give a good impression of what life must once have been like. Ostia was founded in the 4th century BC and thrived until the 5th century, when barbarian invasions and an outbreak of malaria led to its eventual abandonment and its slow burial in river silt, thanks to which it has survived so well.

Highlights in the **ruins** (☎ 06 563 58 099; adult/concession €6.50/3.25; 🕑 8.30am-6pm Apr-Oct, to 5pm Mar, to 4pm Nov-Feb) include the **Terme di Nettuno** (Baths of Neptune) and adjacent **amphitheatre**, built by Agrippa and later enlarged to hold 3000 people. Behind it, the **Piazzale delle Corporazioni** (Forum of the Corporations) is decorated with well-preserved mosaics.

To get to Ostia Antica from Rome take metro line B to Piramide, then the Ostia Lido train (25 minutes, half-hourly). The journey is covered by standard public-transport tickets (see p653).

TIVOLI

pop 51,900

A Roman resort and playground for the Renaissance rich, hilltop Tivoli is home to two Unesco-listed sites: Villa Adriana and Villa d'Este. Information is available at the **tourist information kiosk** (☎ 0774 31 35 36; Piazzale delle Nazioni Unite; 🕑 10am-2pm & 3-6pm Tue-Sun, morning only Aug) near the Cotral bus stop at the top of the hill.

Five kilometres from Tivoli proper, **Villa Adriana** (☎ 0774 38 27 33; admission with/without exhibition €10/6.50; 🕑 9am-6pm summer, to 3.30pm winter) was Emperor Hadrian's summer residence. One of the largest and most sumptuous villas in the Roman Empire, it was subsequently plundered for building materials, although enough remains to convey its magnificence.

The Renaissance **Villa d'Este** (☎ 0774 33 34 04; Piazza Trento; admission with/without exhibition €9/6.50; 🕑 8.30am-6.45pm Tue-Sun summer, to 4pm winter) was built in the 16th century for Cardinal Ippolito d'Este. But more than the villa, it's the elaborate gardens and their spectacular fountains that draw the crowds.

Tivoli is 30km east of Rome and accessible by Cotral bus (€2, one hour, every 20 minutes) from outside Ponte Mammolo station on metro line B.

To get to Villa Adriana from Tivoli town centre, take CAT bus 4X (€1, 10 minutes, hourly) from Largo Garibaldi.

TARQUINIA

pop 16,200

Some 90km northwest of Rome, Tarquinia is the most famous of Lazio's Etruscan centres. Founded in the 12th century BC, it reached its prime in the 4th century BC when it was a serious rival to Athens. Decline set in a century later and in 204 BC it surrendered to Rome.

The **tourist information office** (☎ 0766 84 92 82; Piazza Cavour 1; 🕑 8am-2pm Mon-Sat) is just inside the town's medieval gate (Barriera San Giusto).

Although the Etruscans were dominant in pre-Roman Italy, little of their culture remains. Much of what scholars know comes from findings in Tarquinia, many of which are displayed at the **Museo Nazionale Tarquiniense** (☎ 0766 85 60 36; Piazza Cavour; admission €6, incl necropolis €8; 🕑 8.30am-7.30pm Tue-Sun). You'll find rooms full of painted friezes, sarcophagi, jewellery and some plates decorated with Etruscan porn. Apparently the Etruscans were famous for their sexual dexterity and the words 'Etruscan' and 'prostitute' were used interchangeably.

Many findings came from the 7th-century BC **necropolis** (☎ 0766 85 63 08; Via Ripagretta; admission €6, incl museum €8.50; 🕑 8.30am-6.30pm Tue-Sun summer, to 2pm winter), 2km outside of town. Almost 6000 tombs have been excavated since the first digs in 1489, of which 60 are painted. To get to the necropolis take bus D (€0.60, seven daily) from outside the tourist office.

The easiest way to get to Tarquinia from Rome is by train; take the Pisa train from Termini (€6.20, 1¼ hours, seven daily). At Tarquinia station take bus BC (€0.60, every 30 to 50 minutes) to the town centre.

CERVETERI

pop 33,400

With its hilltop *centro storico* and haunting Etruscan tombs, Cerveteri makes a rewarding day trip from Rome. Cerveteri was one of the most important commercial centres in the Mediterranean from the 7th to the 5th century BC, but as Roman power grew so Cerveteri's fortunes faded, and in 358 BC the city was annexed by Rome.

The superhelpful tourist **tourist office** (☎ 06 995 51 971; Piazza Risorgimento 19; 🕑 9.30am-12.30pm & 5-7.30pm Tue-Sat) can provide information on local sights, accommodation and transport.

Cerveteri's Etruscan tombs are concentrated in the Unesco-listed **Necropoli di Banditaccia** (☎ 06 994 00 01; Piazzale Moretti; admission €6; 🕑 8.30am-6.30pm Tue-Sun summer, 8.30am-3.30pm Tue-Sun winter). The tombs are built into grassy *tumoli* (mounds of earth with carved stone bases), laid out in the form of a town. To get to the necropolis take bus G from the town centre.

Cerveteri is accessible from Rome by Cotral bus (€2.50, 1¼ hours, every 45 minutes) from outside Cornelia station on metro line A.

NORTHERN ITALY

Italy's well-heeled north is an alluring area of historical wealth and natural diversity. Bordered by the northern Alps and boasting some of the country's most spectacular coastline, it also encompasses Italy's largest lowland area, the decidedly non-picturesque Po valley plain. Of the cities it's Venice that hogs the limelight, but in their own way Turin, Genoa and Bologna offer plenty to the open-minded traveller. Verona is one of Italy's most beautiful cities, and the medieval centres of Padua, Ferrara and Ravenna all reward the visitor.

GENOA

pop 615,700

Genoa (Genova) is a city of aristocratic *palazzi* and malodorous alleyways, of Gothic architecture and industrial sprawl. You need only walk the labyrinthine, sometimes seedy streets of the *centro storico* to feel its raw energy. Birthplace of Christopher Columbus (1451–1506) and home to Europe's largest aquarium, it was once a powerful maritime republic known as La Superba; nowadays it's a fascinating port city that's worth a stopover, particularly as it's the gateway to the magnificent Cinque Terre National Park.

Orientation & Information

Central Genoa is concentrated between the two main train stations: Stazione Brignole and Stazione Principe. The central shopping

GETTING INTO TOWN

From Cristoforo Colombo aiport, the **Volabus** (☎ 010 558 24 14; 🕑 6.05am-11.20pm) airport shuttle goes to Stazione Principe (€4, 20 minutes, hourly). Bus 35 links Stazione Principe with Piazza de Ferrari in the city centre.

strip, Via XX Settembre, starts a short walk southwest of Stazione Brignole and leads up to Piazza de Ferrari. From adjacent Piazza Giacomo Matteotti, Via San Lorenzo leads to the waterfront and historic centre.

For information, head to the **tourist office** (☎ 010 868 74 52; www.apt.genova.it; Piazza Giacomo Matteotti; 9.30am-7.45pm). For information about the port, go to its **information booth** (10am-7pm).

Sights & Activities

Genoa's central square, Piazza de Ferrari, is a good place to start. Grandiose and impressive, it's flanked by imposing *palazzi*, including **Palazzo Ducale** (☎ 010 557 40 04; www.palazzoducale.genova.it, in Italian; entrance Piazza Giacomo Matteotti 9; admission varies according to exhibition; 9am-6.30pm Tue-Sun), once the seat of the city government, now Liguria's main exhibition space.

A short walk away, the 12th-century **Cattedrale di San Lorenzo** (Piazza San Lorenzo; 8-11.45am & 3-6.45pm) is notable for its stunning Gothic facade.

Down at the **Porto Antico** (Old Port; ☎ information 010 248 57 10; www.portoantico.it), interest centres on the **Acquario di Genova** (☎ 010 234 56 78; www.acquariodigenova.it; Ponte Spinola; admission €16; 9am-7.30pm Mon-Fri, 8.45am-8.30pm Sat & Sun Mar-Jun & Sep-Oct, 8.30am-10pm Jul & Aug, 9.30am-7.30pm Mon-Fri, 9.30am-8.30pm Sat & Sun Nov-Feb), Europe's largest aquarium. Designed by architect Renzo Piano, it houses 5000 animals in 6 million litres of water.

Genoa's main museums are on Via Garibaldi. The three most important, known collectively as the **Musei di Strada Nuova** (☎ 010 247 63 51; admission €8; 9am-7pm Tue-Fri, from 10am Sat & Sun), are housed in **Palazzo Bianco** (www.museopalazzobianco.it; Via Garibaldi 11), **Palazzo Rosso** (www.museopalazzorosso.it; Via Garibaldi 18) and **Palazzo Doria-Tursi** (www.museopalazzotursi.it; Via Garibaldi 9). The first two feature works by Flemish, Dutch, Spanish and Italian old masters, while the third displays the personal effects of Niccolò Paganini, Genoa's legendary violinist. Tickets, valid for all three museums, are available from the bookshop in Palazzo Doria-Tursi.

Sleeping

Ostello di Genova (☎ 010 242 24 57; www.ostellogenova.it; Via Costanzi 120; dm/s/d €16.50/25/46; closed Jan) Genoa's HI hostel is a functional, modern affair that makes little lasting impression, apart from its panoramic city views. Take bus 40 or 640 from Stazione Brignole; 35 and then 40 or 640 from Stazione Principe.

Albergo Carola (☎ 010 839 13 40; www.pensionecarola.it; Via Gropallo 4; s with shared bathroom €28-35, d with shared bathroom €46-60, with private bathroom €56-70) Conveniently close to Stazione Brignole, this is a classic old-school *pensione* (guest house). The 3rd-floor rooms and shared bathrooms are simple, small and spotless.

Hotel Bel Soggiorno (☎ 010 54 28 80; www.belsoggiornohotel.com; Via XX Settembre 19; s €60-85, d €70-107; P) An endearing mix of the modern and the antique, the Bel Soggiorno offers comfortable rooms with amenities such as satellite TV. It's in an excellent location and has a friendly owner.

Eating

Ligurian specialities include *pesto* (a sauce of basil, garlic, pine nuts and Parmesan) served with *trofie* (pasta curls), *pansoti* (ravioli in ground walnut sauce) and focaccia (flat bread made with olive oil). Look out for *friggitore* (stalls selling fritters made with chickpea flour or *baccalà*).

Panarello (☎ 010 56 10 37; Via Galata 67r) Come to this branch of the popular local chain to sample *pandolce Genovese*, a delicious cake made with raisins, candied fruit and pine nuts. It's bar service only.

Ristorante Pizzeria Piedigrotta (☎ 010 58 05 53; Piazza Savonarola 27; pizzas €5-7.50) If you like your pizzas huge, cheap and tasty, you'll love Piedigrotta. Enormously popular with locals, it has a welcoming interior and friendly staff.

Antica Cantina i Tre Merli (☎ 010 247 40 95; Vico dietro il Coro Maddalena 26r; meals €35; closed Sat lunch & Sun) An atmospheric option just off Via Garibaldi, 'The Three Crows' serves Ligurian cuisine with an emphasis on fish.

Drinking & Entertainment

Action centres on the *centro storico*, with a number of good bars clustered around Piazza delle Erbe.

Il Clan (☎ 010 254 10 98; www.ilclan.biz; Salita Pallavinci 16r, off Via XXX Aprile; 6.30pm-2am Tue-Sun) The city's most stylish bar-nightclub is conveniently located just off Piazza de Ferrari. Enjoy an *aperitivo* or rock up later, when fashion parades or photography exhibitions are regular occurrences.

Mentelocale Café (☎ 010 595 96 48; Piazza Giacomo Matteotti 9; 8am-10pm Mon-Thu, to 1am Fri, 10am-1am Sat & Sun) This swish cafe is by the entrance to the Palazzo Ducale. Sit on the Dalì-inspired red sofas and sip on something cool as you eye up fellow drinkers.

Storico Lounge Café (☎ 010 247 45 48; Piazza de Ferrari 34/36r; 🕒 6am-3am) The *aperitivo* buffet here is a favourite with the city's fashionable young things, who love congregating at the pavement tables overlooking Teatro Carlo Felice.

Getting There & Away

Cristoforo Colombo airport (GOA; ☎ 010 601 54 10; www.airport.genova.it; Sestri Ponente) is 6km west of the city.

The main bus terminal is on Piazza della Vittoria, south of Stazione Brignole. Book tickets at **Geotravels** (☎ 010 58 71 81; Piazza della Vittoria 57; 🕒 9am-12.30pm & 3-7pm Mon-Fri, 9am-12.30pm Sat).

Ferries sail from the **ferry terminal** (☎ 010 24 11; www.porto.genova.it; Via Milano 51), west of the city centre. Ferry companies include:

Grandi Navi Veloci (☎ 010 209 45 91; www2.gnv.it) To/from Sardinia (Porto Torres €29 to €139, 11 hours; Olbia €29 to €45, nine to 10 hours), Sicily (Palermo €133, 20 hours), Barcelona (€137 to €156, 18 hours), Tangiers (€295, 46 hours) and Tunis (€74, 24 hours).

Moby Lines (☎ 010 254 15 13; www.mobylines.it) To/from Corsica (Bastia €5 to €12, five hours) and Sardinia (Porto Torres €16 to €139, 10 hours; Olbia €18 to €139, 9½ hours).

Tirrenia (☎ 800 82 40 79; www.tirrenia.it) To/from Sardinia (Porto Torres €35 to €124, 10 hours; Olbia €52 to €144, 9¾ hours; Arbatax €53 to €179, 14½ hours).

There are direct trains to Milan (€15.50, 1½ hours, up to 25 daily), Pisa (€15, two hours, half-hourly), Rome (€36.30, 5½ hours, eight daily) and Turin (€15, 1¾ to 2¼ hours, up to 20 daily). Regional trains to La Spezia service the Cinque Terre (€5.30, 2 hours 20 minutes, half-hourly).

It generally makes little difference whether you leave from Brignole or Principe.

CINQUE TERRE

Liguria's eastern Riviera boasts some of Italy's most dramatic coastline, the highlight of which is the Parco Nazionale delle Cinque Terre (Cinque Terre National Park), just north of La Spezia. Summer gets very crowded, so try to visit in spring or autumn. You can either visit on a day trip from Genoa, or stay overnight in one of the five villages.

Online information about the park is available at www.parconazionale5terre.it. The park's main information office is to the right as you exit the train station at **Riomaggiore** (☎ 0187 92 06 33; 🕒 8.30am-7.30pm Mon-Fri, to 9.30pm Sat & Sun), and there are other offices in the train stations at Manarola, Corniglia, Vernazza, Monterosso and La Spezia (most open 7am to 8pm).

Sights & Activities

Named after its five tiny villages (Riomaggiore, Manarola, Corniglia, Vernazza and Monterosso), the Unesco-listed **Parco Nazionale delle Cinque Terre** encompasses some of Italy's most picturesque and environmentally sensitive coastline. The villages are linked by the 12km **Blue Trail** (Sentiero Azzurro), a magnificent, mildly challenging 9km (five-hour) trail. To walk it, you'll need to buy a Cinque Terre Card (per day/two days €5/8), available in all of the park offices. If you prefer, you can buy a Cinque Terre Treno Card (per day/two days €8.50/14.70), which covers the walk and unlimited train travel between Levanto, just north of the villages, and La Spezia to the south, including all five villages.

The Blue Trail is just one of a network of footpaths and cycle trails that crisscross the park. If water sports are more your thing, you can hire snorkelling gear (€10 per day) and kayaks (€7 per hour) at the **Diving Center 5 Terre** (☎ 0187 92 00 11; www.5terrediving.com; Via San Giacomo) in Riomaggiore. It also offers a snorkelling boat tour for €14.

Sleeping & Eating

Ostello 5 Terre (☎ 0187 92 02 15; www.cinqueterre.net/ostello; Via B Riccobaldi 21, Manarola; dm €20-23, d €55-65; 🕒 closed Nov-Feb; 💻) A popular eco-hostel with beds in clean single-sex dorms or private rooms. Extras include a restaurant offering well-priced set meals, and laundry facilities. Book ahead.

Hotel Ca' d'Andrean (☎ 0187 92 00 40; www.cadandrean.it; Via Doscovolo 101, Manarola; s €55-70, d €70-96; ❄) A excellent small hotel in the upper part of Manarola village, Ca' d'Andrean has modern rooms with satellite TV and private bathrooms. Breakfast costs €6.

L'Eremo Sul Mare (☎ 346 0195 880; www.eremosulmare.com; Sentiero Azzurro, Vernazza; r €80-110; ❄) This attractive B&B has only three rooms, all of which come with private bathrooms. There's a panoramic terrace, a kitchen and two large living rooms with fireplace. Cash only.

Focacceria Enoteca Antonia (☎ 0187 82 90 39; Via Fegina 124, Monterosso; foccacia per slice around €2.50; 🕒 9am-8pm Fri-Wed Mar-Oct) A great place to pick up picnic provisions of foccacia and the local DOC (see p710) wine.

Marina Piccola (☎ 0187 92 01 03; www.hotelmarinapiccola.com; Via Birolli 120, Manarola; meals €27) In Manarola, this welcoming place has an outdoor terrace with a lovely water view. Specialities include *zuppa di pesce* (fish soup) and *antipasto di mare* (seafood antipasto). It also offers small but comfortable air-conditioned rooms (s/d €87/105).

Getting There & Around

Regional train services from Genoa to Riomaggiore stop at each of the Cinque Terre villages (€4.40, two to 2½ hours). These services run every one to two hours between 4.53am and 10.20pm; the last train back to Genoa is at 11.19pm.

Trains run between La Spezia and Levanto every 30 to 60 minutes between 4.30am and 11.10pm, stopping at all of the villages en route.

Consorzio Marittimo Turistico 5 Terre (☎ 0187 81 84 40) runs ferries between four of the villages (not Corniglia) every day in summer (single/return €8/12.50). In summer **Golfo Paradiso** (☎ 0185 77 20 91; www.golfoparadiso.it) runs ferries between Genoa's Porto Antico and Vernazza (single/return €20/29). Check schedules at the Porto Antica information booth in Genoa (p656).

TURIN

pop 900,600

Much more than Fiat and smoking factories, Turin (Torino) is a dynamic, cosmopolitan city full of royal *palazzi*, baroque piazzas and world-class museums. If they fail to impress, the thriving cafe culture and vibrant nightlife are sure to win you over. There's also the added interest of the city's occult position. According to believers of magic, Turin is linked to Lyon and Prague by mystical lines of energy to form a so-called 'white magic triangle', and to London and San Francisco by lines of malevolent energy in a 'black magic triangle'.

Orientation & Information

At the time of research Stazione Porta Nuova was the main point of arrival, but most trains will be using the revamped Stazione Porta Susa in the future. From Porta Nuova cross Piazza Carlo Felice and follow Via Roma to reach Turin's two focal piazzas: San Carlo and Castello.

Maps, free walking-tour brochures and city information are available from the incredibly helpful **'Torino & You' Tourist Booths** (🕑 9am-7pm) on Via Giuseppe Verdi near the Mole Antonelliana and on Piazza San Carlo.

Sights & Activities

Consider the Torino & Piedmont Card (48-hour card €18), available at tourist offices and valid for all public transport (not the metro) and discounts or entry to 140 museums, monuments and castles.

Turin's grandest square is **Piazza Castello**, dominated by **Palazzo Madama**, and the mid-17th century **Palazzo Reale** (Royal Palace; ☎ 011 436 14 55; Piazza Castello; adult/concession €6.50/3.25; 🕑 8.30am-7.30pm Tue-Sun), whose **Giardino Reale** (Royal Garden; admission free; 🕑 9am-1hr before sunset) was designed in 1697 by Louis le Nôtre, noted for his work at Versailles.

Nearby, **Piazza San Carlo**, known as Turin's drawing room, is famous for its cafes and its twin baroque churches, **San Carlo** and **Santa Cristina**.

The **Cattedrale di San Giovanni Battista** (☎ 011 436 15 40; Piazza San Giovanni; 🕑 7am-noon & 3-7pm Mon-Sat, from 8am-Sun) is home to the Holy Shroud (Sindone), a copy of which is on display in front of the altar (the real thing is kept in a vacuum-sealed box and rarely revealed). Believers claim the linen cloth was used to wrap the crucified Christ.

Turin's **Museo Egizio** (Egyptian Museum; ☎ 011 440 69 03; www.museoegizio.it; Via Accademia delle Scienze 6; adult/concession €7/3.50; 🕑 8.30am-7.30pm Tue-Sun) boasts the world's most important collection of ancient Egyptian art outside of Cairo and London.

Towering 167m over the city, the **Mole Antonelliana** (Via Montebello 20) houses the fabu-

GETTING INTO TOWN

Sadem (☎ 011 300 01 66; www.sadem.it, in Italian) runs an airport shuttle (€5.50, 40 minutes, every 45 minutes) to Porta Nuova/Porta Susa train stations. It operates between 5.15am and 11.15pm; tickets are €0.50 more expensive if purchased on the bus.

There's also a train from the airport to Stazione Dora between 8am and 5pm Monday to Friday. It takes 30 minutes and costs €3.30.

lous **Museo Nazionale del Cinema** (☎ 011 813 85 60; www.museocinema.it; admission €6.50; ⌚ 9am-8pm Tue-Fri & Sun, to 11pm Sat). Don't miss the glass **Panoramic Lift** (€4.50), which whisks you up 85m in 59 seconds. Joint tickets for the museum and lift cost €8.

There are a number of top-notch private galleries and contemporary art museums in Turin, including the **Pinacoteca Giovanni e Marella Agnelli** (☎ 011 006 27 13; www.pinacoteca-agnelli.it; Via Nizza 262; admission €4-7; ⌚ 10am-7pm Tue-Sun), whose permanent collection features works by Canaletto, Canova, Picasso and Matisse, and the **Castello di Rivoli Museo d'Arte Contemporanea** (☎ 011 956 52 20; www.castellodirivoli.org; Piazza Mafalda di Savoia, Rivoli; admission €6.50; ⌚ 10am-5pm Tue-Thu, to 9pm Fri-Sun), which charts the development of Italian and international contemporary art from the 1950s onwards.

Sleeping & Eating

Ostello Torino (☎ 011 660 29 39; www.ostello.torino.it; Via Alby 1; dm/s with shared bathroom €15/21, d €80; ⌚ closed mid-Dec–mid-Jan; P 💻) Turin's HI hostel is quiet, comfortable and clean with three- or eight-person dorms and a variety of rooms. Catch bus 52 from Porta Nuova (64 on Sunday), otherwise it's a steep 2km walk.

L'Orso Poeta (☎ 011 517 89 96; www.orsopoeta-bed-and-breakfast.it; Corso Vittorio Emanuele II 10; s/d from €70/110; P ❄) Everyone will feel welcome at this B&B in an historic apartment building by the river. Its two small rooms have private bathroom and lots of character.

Alpi Resort Hotel (☎ 011 812 96 77; www.hotelalpiresort.it; Via A Bonafous 5; s/d from €80/90; P ❄) This excellent option is just off Piazza Vittorio Veneto. Impeccably clean and well-equipped rooms are quiet and comfortable; some even have jacuzzis. The breakfast spread is both lavish and delicious.

Da Ciro (☎ 011 53 19 25; Corso Vinzaglio 17; pizzas €5-8; ⌚ closed Sat lunch & Sun) The thin-crust pizzas that emerge from the wood-fired oven here are quite delicious. Decor is unpretentious and service is jovial – great stuff.

Otto Etre Quarti (8¼; ☎ 011 517 63 67; www.ottoetrequarti.it; Piazza Solferino 8c; lunch/dinner €15/30) Do as the locals do: claim a table in one of the high-ceilinged dining rooms or on the front terrace and order from the simple yet scrumptious menu. Otto Etre Quarti's ambience is casual chic and its prices are right – particularly at lunchtime.

Getting There & Around

In Caselle, 16km northwest of the city centre, **Turin airport** (TRN; ☎ 011 567 63 61; www.turin-airport.com) serves flights to/from European and national destinations.

Trains connect with Milan (€13.50, two hours, up to 30 daily), Venice (€35.25, five hours, five daily), Genoa (€15, 1¾ to 2¼ hours, up to 20 daily), Florence (€32, five hours, three daily) and Rome (€76, seven hours, seven daily).

MILAN

☎ 02 / pop 1.3 million

Italy's financial and fashion capital, Milan (Milano) is polluted, sophisticated and expensive. Its designer shops, vibrant cultural scene and wicked nightlife are the big draws but they don't come cheap, making the city a challenge for budget travellers.

Originally founded by Celtic tribes in the 7th century BC, Milan was conquered by the Romans in 222 BC and developed into a major trading and transport centre. From the 13th century it flourished under the rule of two powerful families, the Visconti and the Sforza.

Orientation

From Stazione Centrale train station, take the yellow MM3 underground (Metropolitana Milanese) line to Piazza del Duomo. The city's main attractions are concentrated in the area between the piazza and Castello Sforzesco.

Information

Mondadori (Piazza del Duomo; per hr €3; ⌚ 7am-11pm) Bookshop with internet access.

Pharmacy (☎ 02 669 07 35; Stazione Centrale; ⌚ 24hr)

Police station (Questura; ☎ 02 622 61; Via Fatebenefratelli 11)

Tourist offices (www.milanoinfotourist.com) Piazza del Duomo (☎ 02 774 04 343; Piazza Duomo 19a; ⌚ 8.45am-1pm & 2-6pm Mon-Sat, 9am-1pm & 2-5pm Sun); Stazione Centrale (☎ 02 774 04 318; ⌚ 9am-6pm Mon-Sat, 9am-1pm & 2-5pm Sun) Pick up the free guides *Hello Milano* and *Milanomese*.

Sights

With a capacity of 40,000, Milan's landmark **Duomo** (Piazza del Duomo; ⌚ 7am-7pm) is the world's largest Gothic cathedral. Commissioned in 1386 to a florid French-Gothic design and finished nearly 600 years later, it's a fairy-tale ensemble of 3400 statues, 135 spires and 155

GETTING INTO TOWN

Malpensa Shuttle (☎ 02 585 98 31 85; www.malpensashuttle.it) coaches run to Piazza Luigi di Savoia next to Stazione Centrale every 20 minutes. Tickets for the 50-minute journey cost single/return €7/12. The **Malpensa Bus Express** (☎ 02 339 10 794) covers the same route, departing half-hourly; tickets cost €7.50 and the trip takes 50 minutes.

By train, take the **Malpensa Express** (☎ 02 851 14 382; www.malpensaexpress.it) to Cadorna underground station – there are hourly or half-hourly departures. The 50-minute journey costs €11.

From Linate, half-hourly **Starfly** (☎ 02 585 87 237) buses run to Piazza Luigi di Savoia; tickets cost €4.50, journey time is 30 minutes. Alternatively, use local bus 73 to Piazza San Babila (€1, 20 minutes).

Autostradale (☎ 035 31 84 72; www.autostradale.it) runs half-hourly buses from Orio al Serio to Piazza Luigi di Savoia; the journey lasts one hour and tickets cost €8.90.

gargoyles. Climb to the **roof** (stairs/elevator €5/7; 9am-5.20pm most of the year, to 8.30pm - lift only - in summer) for memorable city views.

Nearby, the elegant **Galleria Vittorio Emanuele II** shopping arcade leads towards the famous **Teatro alla Scala** (☎ 02 720 03 744; www.teatroallascala.org; Piazza delle Scala; tour €5; 9am-12.30pm & 1.30-5.30pm when no performances are scheduled).

Milan's most famous tourist attraction – Leonardo da Vinci's mural of the *Last Supper* – is in the **Cenacolo Vinciano** (☎ 02 894 21 146; www.cenacolovinciano.org; Piazza Santa Maria delle Grazie 2; booking compulsory, admission €6.50 plus booking fee of €1.50; 8.15am-6.45pm Tue-Sun), just west of the city centre.

Back towards the centre, the 15th-century **Castello Sforzesco** (☎ 02 884 63 700; www.milanocastello.it; Piazza Castello 3; admission free; 9am-5.30pm Tue-Sun) was the Renaissance residence of the Sforza dynasty. It now shelters the **Musei del Castello** (☎ 02 884 63 703; adult/concession €3/1.50; 9am-5.30pm), a group of museums dedicated to art, sculpture, furniture, archaeology and music. Entry is free on Fridays between 2pm and 5.30pm and from Tuesday to Sunday between 4.30 and 5.30pm.

Art wonks shouldn't miss the **Pinacoteca di Brera** (☎ 02 894 21 146; www.brera.beniculturali.it; Via Brera 28; adult/concession €5/2.50; 8.30am-7.15pm Tue-Sun), the heavyweight collection of which includes Andrea Mantegna's masterpiece, the *Dead Christ*, and Raphael's *Betrothal of the Virgin*.

Sleeping

Prepare yourself for a budget blow-out when booking here – everything is ridiculously expensive, particularly when trade fairs are on (which is often). Booking is essential at all times of the year.

Ostello Piero Rotta (☎ 02 392 67 095; milano@ostellionline.org; Via Martino Bassi 2; dm €19) Milan's HI hostel is in the San Siro neighbourhood, not far from the football stadium. Low on atmosphere, it's cheap, clean and not a lot else.

Hotel De Albertis (☎ 02 738 34 09; www.hoteldealbertis.it; Via De Albertis 7; s €50-100, d €50-160;) This small, family-run two-star choice is in a leafy residential street 20 minutes' walk from the Duomo (or catch tram 27). Rooms are clean, cheerful and attractive.

Hotel Nuovo (☎ 02 864 64 444; www.hotelnuovomilano.com; Piazza Beccaria 6; r €60-150) In a city where 'cheap' is an ugly word, the Nuovo is a bastion of budget accommodation. Rooms are basic but clean, and the location, just off Corso Vittorio Emanuele II, is a winner. No breakfast.

Eating

Premiata Pizzeria (☎ 02 894 00 648; Via Alzaia Naviglio Grande 2; pizzas €5-10) Right on the canal in trendy Navigli, perennially busy Premiata serves up huge thick-crust pizzas that are perfect fodder after a few hours spent in surrounding bars.

Peck Italian Bar (☎ 02 869 30 17; Via Cesare Cantù 3; meals €40; 11.30am-8pm) This place truly encapsulates Milan – chic and sleek surrounds, top-quality produce and a glamorous clientele. The delicious Milanese menu features classics such as *cotolleto* (breaded veal cutlet) and risotto.

After dinner, think about a gelato at **Rinomata** (☎ 02 581 13 877; Ripa di Porta Ticinese).

Self-caterers can shop at the two supermarkets at Stazione Centrale (one on the upper level and one on the western side), at nearby **Di per Di** (Via Felice Casati 30; 8.30am-8pm Mon-Sat) or at the expensive but utterly irresistible **Peck Delicatessan** (☎ 02 802 31 61; Via Spadari 9; 3.30-7.30pm Mon, 9.15am-7.30pm Tue-Fri, 8.45am-7.30pm Sat).

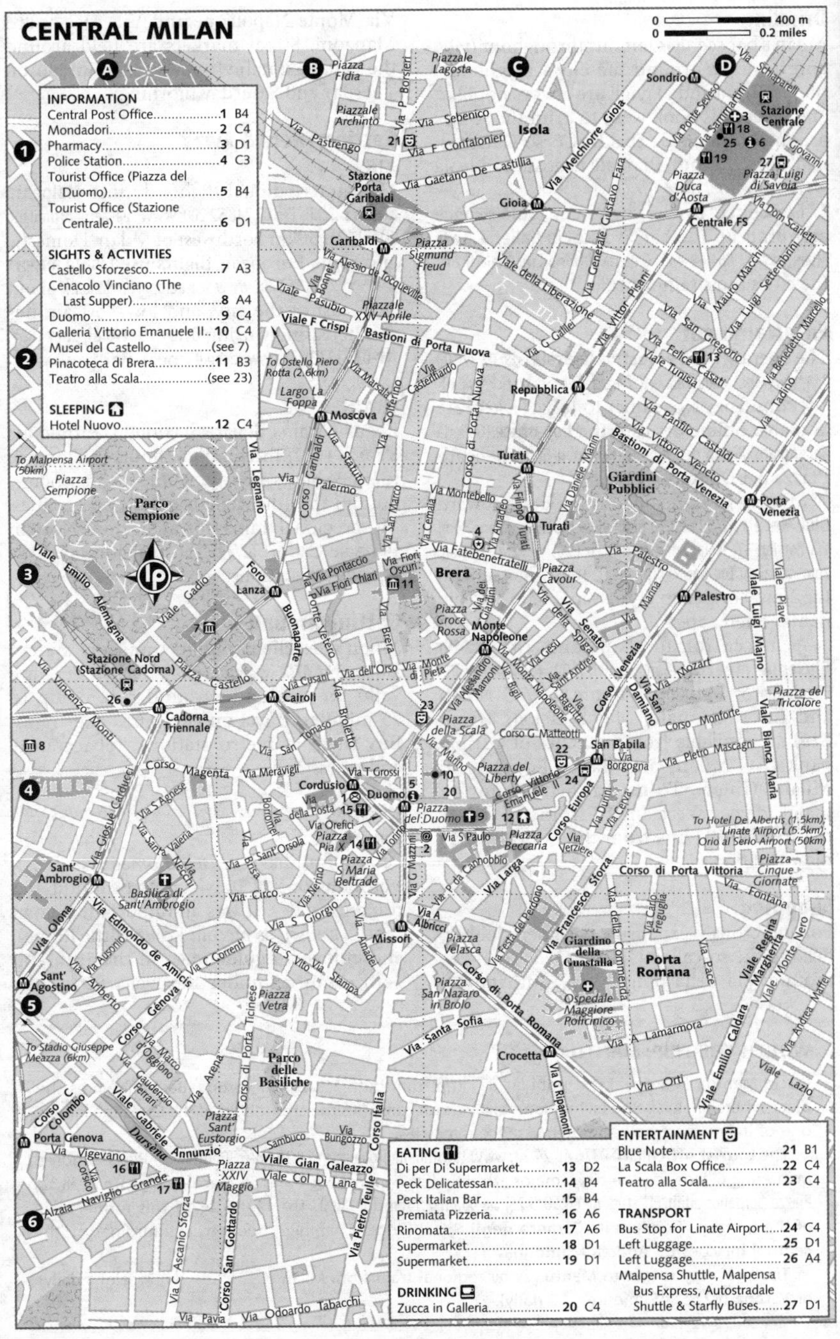
CENTRAL MILAN
0 400 m
0 0.2 miles
INFORMATION
Central Post Office....................1 B4
Mondadori....................2 C4
Pharmacy....................3 D1
Police Station....................4 C3
Tourist Office (Piazza del Duomo)....................5 B4
Tourist Office (Stazione Centrale)....................6 D1
SIGHTS & ACTIVITIES
Castello Sforzesco....................7 A3
Cenacolo Vinciano (The Last Supper)....................8 A4
Duomo....................9 C4
Galleria Vittorio Emanuele II..10 C4
Musei del Castello....................(see 7)
Pinacoteca di Brera....................11 B3
Teatro alla Scala....................(see 23)
SLEEPING
Hotel Nuovo....................12 C4
EATING
Di per Di Supermarket....................13 D2
Peck Delicatessan....................14 B4
Peck Italian Bar....................15 B4
Premiata Pizzeria....................16 A6
Rinomata....................17 A6
Supermarket....................18 D1
Supermarket....................19 D1
DRINKING
Zucca in Galleria....................20 C4
ENTERTAINMENT
Blue Note....................21 B1
La Scala Box Office....................22 C4
Teatro alla Scala....................23 C4
TRANSPORT
Bus Stop for Linate Airport....24 C4
Left Luggage....................25 D1
Left Luggage....................26 A4
Malpensa Shuttle, Malpensa Bus Express, Autostradale Shuttle & Starfly Buses....27 D1
Piazza Fidia
Piazzale Lagosta
Piazzale Archinto
Isola
Sondrio
Stazione Centrale
Piazza Duca d'Aosta
Piazza Luigi di Savoia
Centrale FS
Stazione Porta Garibaldi
Gioia
Garibaldi
Piazza Sigmund Freud
Piazzale XXV Aprile
Viale F Crispi
Bastioni di Porta Nuova
To Ostello Piero Rotta (2.6km)
Largo La Foppa
Moscova
Repubblica
Turati
Bastioni di Porta Venezia
Giardini Pubblici
Porta Venezia
To Malpensa Airport (50km)
Piazza Sempione
Parco Sempione
Brera
Piazza Cavour
Lanza
Palestro
Piazza Croce Rossa
Monte Napoleone
Stazione Nord (Stazione Cadorna)
Cairoli
Cadorna Triennale
Piazza della Scala
San Babila
Piazza del Tricolore
Cordusio
Duomo
Piazza del Duomo
Piazza del Liberty
Piazza Beccaria
To Hotel De Albertis (1.5km); Linate Airport (5.5km); Orio al Serio Airport (50km)
Piazza Pia X
Piazza S Maria Beltrade
Sant' Ambrogio
Basilica di Sant'Ambrogio
Corso di Porta Vittoria
Piazza Cinque Giornate
Missori
Piazza Velasca
Giardino della Guastalla
Porta Romana
Sant' Agostino
Piazza Vetra
Piazza San Nazaro in Brolo
Ospedale Maggiore Policlinico
To Stadio Giuseppe Meazza (6km)
Crocetta
Parco delle Basiliche
Piazza Sant' Eustorgio
Porta Genova
Piazza XXIV Maggio
Darsèna
Viale Gian Galeazzo
Corso Buenos Aires
Corso Venezia
Corso Magenta
Corso Europa
Via Larga
Corso di Porta Romana
Corso Genova
Corso Italia
Corso San Gottardo
Corso di Porta Ticinese
Viale Gabriele d'Annunzio
Alzaia Naviglio Grande
Via Vigevano
Via Odoardo Tabacchi
Via Pavia

Drinking

Milan's bar scene is famous throughout Italy, and it moves around the city's neighbourhoods. Brera and Navigli are always popular, and when this book went to print the scenes around Stazione Garibaldi (Corso Garibaldi and Corso Como), Piazzale Lagosta and Isola were hot, hot, hot.

For coffee, bypass the pricey table service and prop up the bar at **Zucca in Galleria** (Caffè Miani; ☎ 02 864 64 435; Galleria Vittorio Emanuele II 21), the city's most famous cafe.

Entertainment

The opera season at **Teatro alla Scala** (☎ 02 720 03 744; www.teatroallascala.org; Piazza delle Scala; tickets €10-110) runs from November to July. Tickets are available online or from the **box office** (Galleria del Sagrato, Piazza del Duomo; 🕑 noon-6pm) beneath Piazza del Duomo.

Milan's jazz aficionados gravitate toward **Blue Note** (☎ 02 690 16 888; www.bluenotemilano.com; Via Borsieri 37, Isola; admission from €20; 🕑 2-7pm Mon, 2pm-midnight Tue-Sat, 7-11pm Sun). It's affiliated with the New York Club of the same name, so big names often appear.

A mecca for football fans, the **Stadio Giuseppe Meazza** (San Siro; ☎ 02 404 24 32; Via Piccolomini 5; Ⓜ Lotto) is home to AC Milan and Internazionale. Match tickets (from €15) are available from branches of Cariplo bank (AC Milan) and Banca Popolare di Milano (Inter). To get to the stadium on match days, take tram 16 from Orefici or the free shuttle bus from the Lotto (MM1) metro station.

Shopping

For ludicrously expensive designer clobber, head to the so-called Golden Quad, the area around Via della Spiga, Via Sant'Andrea, Via Monte Napoleone and Via Alessandro Manzoni. Street markets are held around the canals, notably on Viale Papiniano on Tuesday and Saturday mornings.

Getting There & Away

AIR

Most international flights fly into **Malpensa airport** (MXP; 🕑 02 748 52 200; www.sea-aeroportimilano.it), about 50km northwest of Milan. Domestic and some European flights use **Linate airport** (LIN; 🕑 02 748 52 200 www.sea-aeroportimilano.it), about 7km east of the city; and low-cost airlines are increasingly using **Orio al Serio airport** (BGY; ☎ 035 32 63 23; www.sacbo.it), near Bergamo.

TRAIN

Regular trains depart Stazione Centrale for Venice (€22, three hours, hourly), Florence (€26, 3½ hours, hourly), Rome (€45, six hours, hourly) and other Italian and European cities. Most regional trains stop at Stazione Nord in Piazzale Cadorna. There is left-luggage storage at both stations.

Getting Around

Milan's excellent public transport system is run by **ATM** (www.atm-mi.it). Tickets (€1) are valid for one underground ride or up to 75 minutes' travel on city buses and trams. Buy them at metro stations, tobacconists and newsstands.

VERONA

pop 260,800

Setting for Shakespeare's *Romeo and Juliet*, Verona is one of Italy's most beautiful and romantic cities. It was an important Roman centre, known as *piccola Roma* (little Rome), and enjoyed a golden age in the 13th and 14th centuries under the Della Scala (aka

WORTH THE TRIP: MANTUA

Placid Mantua (Mantova) is a popular day trip from both Milan and Verona. Best known as the place where Shakespeare exiled Romeo, it was for centuries the stronghold of the Gonzaga family, one of Italy's most powerful Renaissance dynasties.

The **tourist office** (☎ 0376 43 24 32; www.turismo.mantova.it; 🕑 9.30am-6.30pm) is on Piazza Andrea Mantegna 6, close to the city's major attraction, the enormous **Palazzo Ducale** (☎ 0376 22 48 32; Piazza Sordello; adult/EU student €6.50/3.25; h8.45am-7.15pm Tue-Sun). The highlight of this former seat of the Gonzaga family is its **Camera degli Sposi** (Bridal Chamber), home to extraordinary 15th-century frescoes by Andrea Mantegna.

The best way to get to Mantua is by regional train from Milan (€8.55, 2¼ hours, eight daily) or Verona (€2.55, 45 minutes, 16 daily).

GETTING INTO TOWN

There are regular buses between Valerio Catullo airport and the main train station (€4.50, 15 minutes, every 20 minutes between 5.40am and 11.10pm).

If you're flying with Ryanair you'll be landing at Brescia airport, from where a CGA shuttle bus (€11, one hour, one daily) connects to Verona train station.

From the bus terminal in front of the train station buses 72 and 73 go to Piazza Brà, Verona's central square.

Scaligeri) family, a period noted for the savage family feuding on which Shakespeare based his tragedy.

Information is available at the three **tourist offices** (www.tourism.verona.it) Airport (☎ 045 861 91 63; 🕑 9am-5pm Mon-Tue, 9am-6pm Wed-Sat, 10am-4pm Sun); City Centre (☎ 045 806 86 80; Piazza Brà; 🕑 9am-7pm Mon-Sat, to 4pm Sun); Train Station (☎ 045 800 08 61; 🕑 8am-7pm Mon-Sat, to 3pm Sun).

Internet access is available at **Internet Etc** (Via Quattro Spade 3b; per hr €5.50; 🕑 2.30-7.45pm Mon, 9.30am-7.45pm Tue-Fri, 10.30am-7.45pm Sat, 3.30-7.45pm Sun).

The Verona Card (1/3 days €8/12) covers city transport and the main monuments. It's available from tourist offices and most sights.

Sights & Activities

In Piazza Brà, the 1st-century **amphitheatre** (☎ 045 800 03 60; www.arena.it; Piazza Brà; adult/concession €6/4.50; 🕑 8.30am-7.15pm Tue-Sun, 1.30-7.15pm Mon Oct-Jun, 8am-3.30pm end Jun-start Sep), known as the Arena, is the third-largest Roman amphitheatre in existence, with a capacity of 20,000. These days it's most famous as Verona's summer opera house (see p664).

From the Arena, walk along Via Mazzini, Verona's premier shopping strip, to Via Cappello and the **Casa di Giulietta** (Juliet's House; ☎ 045 803 43 03; Via Capello 23; courtyard free, museum admission €6; 🕑 8.30am-7.30pm Tue-Sun, 1.30-7.30pm Mon). Its pretty balcony is a much-loved happy-snap spot, and romantic superstition suggests that rubbing the right breast of Juliet's statue will bring you a new lover. Further along the street is **Porta Leoni**, one of the city's Roman gates; the other, **Porta Borsari**, is north of the Arena.

Set over the city's Roman forum, **Piazza delle Erbe** is lined with sumptuous palaces and filled with touristy market stalls. Through the **Arco della Costa**, **Piazza dei Signori** is flanked by the **Loggia del Consiglio**, the medieval town hall and Verona's finest Renaissance structure, and **Palazzo degli Scaligeri**, the former residence of the Della Scala family.

The tourist office at the train station offers free **bike hire**. There are 10 bikes available (first come, first served); leave ID as security.

Sleeping

High-season prices apply during the opera season (late June to the end of August), when it's absolutely essential to book ahead.

Ostello Villa Francescatti (☎ 045 59 03 60; www.villafrancescatti.com, in Italian; Salita Fontana del Ferro 15; dm €17.50-19, d €36) This beautiful hostel is housed in a 16th-century villa set in extensive grounds. To save yourself a steep uphill walk, take bus 73 from the train station (90 on Sundays). There's a strict 11.30pm curfew.

Hotel Torcolo (☎ 045 800 75 12; www.hoteltorcolo.it; Vicolo Listone 3; s €50-103, d €70-150; P ⊠) Not 50m from Piazza Brà, the homely Torcolo is ideally located. Its comfortable midsized rooms have double glazing and satellite TV. If weather permits, breakfast (included in high-season prices only) is served in the small piazza in front of the hotel.

L'Ospite (☎ 045 803 69 94; www.lospite.com; Via XX Settembre 3; apt for 3 €110-160, for 4 €125-180; ⊠) Over the river from the *centro storico*, L'Ospite has six self-contained flats for up to four people. Simple and bright with wood-beamed ceilings and fully equipped kitchens, they come with wi-fi and are ideal for longer stays.

Eating & Drinking

Boiled meats are a Veronese speciality, as is crisp Soave white wine.

Hosteria All'Orso (☎ 045 597214; Via Sottoriva 3/c; meals €30; 🕑 closed Sun & Mon lunch) A charming spot in Verona's trendy riverside district. Grab a table under the timber-beamed porticoes or in the rustic-chic interior and order from the menu of tempting north Italian staples.

For excellent pizza takeaway, get down to **Pizza Doge** (☎ 045 59 68 53; Via Roma 21b), a popular takeaway.

The drinking scene is centred on Via Sottoriva. Hot spots include **square** (☎ 045 59 71 20; Via Sottoriva 15; 🕑 6.30pm-2am Tue-Sat, 5pm-1am Sun), a cool, contemporary bar where you can drink cocktails, have a shiatsu massage and surf the net.

Book your stay at lonelyplanet.com/hotels

SPLURGE

Antica Bottega del Vino (☎ 045 800 45 35; Via Scudo di Francia 3; meal €50; ⏰ closed Tue) Established in 1890, this is a fabulous wine bar-cum-restaurant. You can enjoy a glass of wine (€1 to €11) from a mind-boggling array of choices while standing at the bar, or book a table for a meal. The food is rustic and delicious – freshly made *bigoli all'anatra* (pasta with a duck *ragù*), soupy *risotto all'Amarone* (rice cooked with Amarone wine) and a variety of perfectly cooked meat dishes. The surrounds couldn't be more atmospheric.

Entertainment

The opera season at the Roman **Arena** (☎ 045 800 51 51; www.arena.it; tickets €22.50-198) runs from late June to the end of August. Tickets are available online.

Getting There & Around

Verona's main **Valerio Catullo airport** (VRN; ☎ 045 809 56 66; www.aeroportoverona.it) is 12km outside the city. Ryanair flies to **Brescia airport** (VBS; ☎ 030 965 65 99), about an hour from Verona's city centre.

From the main bus terminal in front of the train station, buses 72 and 73 leave Stand F going to Piazza Erbe. Buses 11, 12 and 13 leave Stand A going to the Arena. Tickets cost €1.20 on the bus or €1 at the station's *tabacci*.

Verona is directly linked by rail to Milan (€12.50, two hours, half-hourly), Venice (€13.50, 1½ hours, half-hourly), Bologna (€15, 1¾ hours, hourly) and Rome (Eurostar €48.50, six hours, hourly).

PADUA

pop 210,300

Home to one of the world's oldest universities, Padua (Padova) is a fun place to hang out. But what really makes a visit worthwhile are the stunning Giotto frescoes in the Cappella degli Scrovegni.

From the train station, follow Corso del Popolo and its continuation Corso Garibaldi until you see a park on your right – the *cappella* (chapel) is here. Continue on Corso Garibaldi and its extension Via VII Febbraio to reach the *centro storico*.

Information is available at the three **tourist offices** Galleria Pedrocchi (☎ 049 876 79 27; ⏰ 9am-1.30pm & 3-7pm Mon-Sat); Piazza Del Santo (☎ 049 875 30 87; ⏰ 9am-1.30pm & 3-6pm Mon-Sat, 10am-1pm & 3-6pm Sun Apr-Oct only) Train Station (☎ 049 875 20 77; www.turismopadova.it; ⏰ 9am-7pm Mon-Sat, 9am-12.30pm Sun).

Sights & Activities

The **PadovaCard** (☎ 049 876 79 27; www.padovacard.it; €15), available from tourist offices and participating sights, provides free public transport and entry to many sights, including the Cappella degli Scrovegni (plus €1 booking fee).

Padua's biggest drawcard, the **Cappella degli Scrovegni** (☎ 049 201 00 20; www.cappelladegliscrovegni.it; Piazza Eremitani 8; admission incl Musei Civici agli Eremitani adult/concession €12/8; ⏰ 9am-7pm), is covered from floor to ceiling with frescoes by Giotto. Divided into 38 colourful panels (c1304–06), they boldly depict episodes from Christ's life. Visits, for which you'll need to book at least 24 hours in advance, are limited to 15 minutes.

In the adjacent **Musei Civici agli Eremitani** (☎ 049 820 45 51; Piazza Eremitani 8; ⏰ 9am-7pm Tue-Sun) you can peruse a small collection of Veneto art.

On the other side of the *centro storico*, the **Basilica di Sant'Antonio** (Basilica del Santo; ☎ 049 824 28 11; Piazza del Santo; ⏰ 6.30am-7.45pm) is an important place of pilgrimage. Each year thousands of visitors come to file past the surprisingly gaudy **tomb** of St Anthony, Padua's patron saint.

In the square outside the basilica, the bronze equestrian statue, the *Gattamelata* (Honeyed Cat), is by the Renaissance sculptor Donatello.

Sleeping & Eating

Ostello della Città di Padova (☎ 049 875 22 19; www.ostellopadova.it; Via Aleardo Aleardi 30; dm incl breakfast from €16.50) Functional and friendly, Padua's HI hostel has beds in large single-sex dorms and four- or six-person family rooms. Take the tram (€1) from the railway station to Via Cavalletto, turn right into Via Marin and then left at the Torresino church.

Albergo Verdi (☎ 049 836 41 63; www.albergoverdipadova.it; Via Dondi dall'Orologio 7; s €40-100, d €40-150; ❄) This stylish, modern choice offers quiet rooms with bright colour schemes and installed mod cons. An excellent location just off Piazza del Capitaniato completes the welcoming package.

Hotel Sant'Antonio (☎ 049 875 13 93; www.hotelsantantonio.it; Via San Fermo 118; s with shared bathroom €39-43, with private bathroom s €63-67, d €84-94; ❄) On the edge of the historic centre, the three-star Sant'Antonio is a safe, if rather staid, option. Breakfast costs an extra €7.50.

L'Anfora (☎ 049 65 66 29; www.osterianfora.it; Via dei Sconcin 13; meals €27; ⏰ closed Sun) A typical old-school *osteria* with bare wooden tables and racked wine bottles, L'Anfora serves hearty meals such as *pasta e fagioli* (pasta and beans) or *fegato alla veneziana con polenta* (liver and onions served with polenta).

Trattoria San Pietro (☎ 049 876 03 03; Via San Pietro 95; meals €32; ⏰ closed Sun Jun & Aug-Sep, all of Jul) The unassuming facade here gives no clue as to the excellence of the restaurant within. Dishes from the Veneto join specialities from Lombardy.

Getting There & Away

SITA buses (☎ 049 820 68 44; www.sitabus.it, in Italian) arrive from Venice (€3.55, 45 minutes, hourly) at Piazzale Boschetti, next to the Cappella degli Scrovegni.

There are regional trains to/from Venice (€2.90, 45 minutes, every 20 minutes) and direct services to Verona (€8.50, 50 minutes, every 20 minutes) and Bologna (€13, 1½ hours, every 45 minutes).

VENICE

pop 269,000

Arriving in Venice (Venezia) is like stepping into a surreal never-never land. Where most cities have car-choked roads and impenetrable one-way systems, Venice has gondolas, *vaporetti* (water buses) and a labyrinthine network of canals. But the beauty comes at a price. Both for you (Venice is Italy's most expensive city) and for the city itself (Venice's frequently flooded alleyways simply weren't designed for up to 20 million visitors a year).

Surprisingly, though, it's still possible to escape the crowds. Away from Piazza San Marco and the main monuments, there are parts of the city that rarely see many tourists. Make for the back lanes of the Dorsoduro and Castello *sestieri* (districts) for a glimpse of Venice's beguiling and melancholic nature.

History

Venice's origins date to the 5th and 6th centuries, when barbarian invasions forced the Veneto's inhabitants to seek refuge on the lagoon's islands. The city was initially ruled by the Byzantines from Ravenna, but in AD 726 the Venetians elected their first *doge* (duke).

Over successive centuries the Venetian Republic grew into a great merchant power, dominating half the Mediterranean, the Adriatic and the trade routes to the Levant – it was from Venice that Marco Polo set out for China in 1271. Decline began in the 16th century and in 1797 the city authorities opened the gates to Napoleon who, in turn, handed the city over to the Austrians. In 1866 Venice was incorporated into the Kingdom of Italy.

Orientation

Everybody gets lost in Venice. With 117 islands, 150-odd canals and 400 bridges (only three of which – the Rialto, the Accademia and, at the train station, the Scalzi – cross the Grand Canal) it's impossible not to.

It gets worse. Instead of a street and civic number, local addresses often consist of no more than the *sestiere* (Venice is divided into six districts: Cannaregio, Castello, San Marco, Dorsoduro, San Polo and Santa Croce) followed by a long number. Some, however, do have street names and where possible we've provided them. You'll still need to know that a street can be a *calle, ruga* or *salizzada;* beside a canal it's a *fondamenta*. A canal is a *rio,* a filled canal-turned-street a *rio terrà,* and a square a *campo* (Piazza San Marco is Venice's only piazza).

The most helpful points of reference are Santa Lucia train station and Piazzale Roma in the northwest, and Piazza San Marco (St Mark's Sq) in the south. The signposted path from the train station *(ferrovia)* to Piazza San Marco (the nearest Venice has to a main drag) is a good 40- to 50-minute walk.

Information

DISCOUNT CARDS

The Rolling Venice Card (€4) is for visitors aged 14 to 29; it offers discounts on food, accommodation, shopping, transport and museums. You can get it at tourist offices, and at HelloVenezia offices. You'll need ID.

The **Venice Card** (www.venicecard.it; under 30yr 3/7 days €53.50/76, 30yr & over €62/85) entitles holders to free entry to all of Venice's civic museums, the 16 Chorus churches, unlimited use of ACTV public transport, and use of public toilets. It doesn't always represent a saving, so check before buying.

GETTING INTO TOWN

From Marco Polo airport, take an **ATVO** (☎ 041 520 55 30; www.atvo.it, in Italian) bus (€3, 20 minutes, half-hourly) or ACTV bus 5d (€2, 25 minutes, half-hourly) to Piazzale Roma. Alternatively, **Alilaguna** (Map pp668-9; www.alilaguna.com) operates a fast ferry service from near Piazza San Marco (€12, 70 minutes, approximately hourly).

From Treviso airport, catch the ATVO **Ryanairbus** (€5, 70 minutes, 16 daily) to Piazzale Roma. To get to Piazza San Marco (St Mark's Sq) from Piazzale Roma take *vaporetto* (water bus) 1 or 3.

To visit the museums on Piazza San Marco you'll need to buy either a **Museum Pass** (☎ 041 240 52 11; www.museicivicveneziani.it; adult/EU citizen 15-59yr €18/12), which gives entry to the museums on Piazza San Marco and six other civic museums; or a San Marco Plus Ticket (€13/7.50), which gives entry to the San Marco Museums and your choice of one other civic museum. Both passes are available at participating museums.

The **Chorus Pass** (☎ 041 275 04 62; www.chorusvenezia.org; adult/student 29yr & under €9/6) covers admission to 16 of Venice's major churches. Otherwise entry to each church is €3.

EMERGENCY

Police station (Questura; Map pp668-9; ☎ 041 274 70 70; Fondamenta di San Lorenzo, Castello 5053)

INTERNET ACCESS

There are lots of internet cafes in Venice, none cheap.

botteg@internet (Map pp668-9; Calle delle Botteghe, San Marco 2970; per 15 min €3; 🕑 7am-midnight) Also an art gallery and secondhand English bookshop.

Libreria Mondadori (Map pp668-9; Salizzada San Moisè 1345, San Marco; per 10 min €1; 🕑 10am-8pm Mon-Sat, 11am-7.30pm Sun)

Planet Internet (Map pp668-9; Rio Terà San Leonardo, Cannaregio 1520; per 15 min €3; 🕑 9am-midnight)

LAUNDRY

Speedy Wash (Map pp668-9; Rio Terà San Leonardo, Cannaregio 1520; 8kg wash/dry €6/3; 🕑 8am-11pm) Next to Planet Internet.

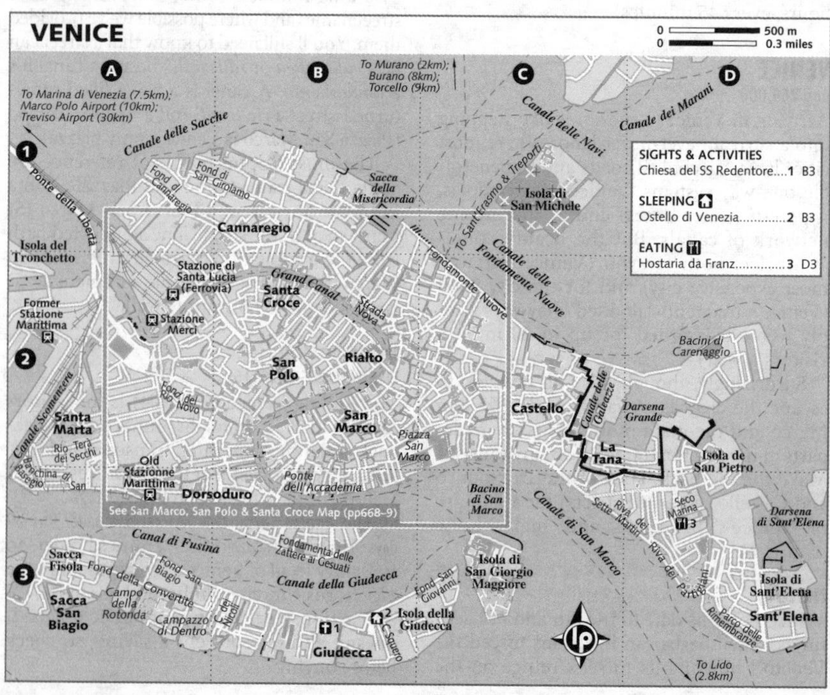

MEDICAL SERVICES

Twenty-four-hour pharmacies are listed in *Un Ospite a Venezia* (A Guest in Venice), a free guide available in many hotels.

Ospedale Civile (Hospital; Map pp668-9; ☎ 041 529 41 11; Campo SS Giovanni e Paolo 6777)

TOURIST INFORMATION

Pick up the free *Shows & Events* guide at tourist offices. It contains comprehensive city listings and a useful public transport map on the inside back cover. The tourist offices also sell a useful map of the city (€2.50).

Azienda di Promozione Turistica (Venice Tourist Board; ☎ central information line 041 529 87 11; www.turismovenezia.it) Lido (Gran Viale Santa Maria Elisabetta 6a; 9am-noon & 3-6pm Jun-Sep); Marco Polo airport (Arrivals Hall; 9am-9pm); Piazzale Roma (Map pp668-9; 9.30am-4.30pm Jun-Sep) In the basement of the car park over the road from the bus ticket office; Train Station (Map pp668-9; 8am-6.30pm); Piazza San Marco (Map pp668-9; Piazza San Marco 71f; 9am-3.30pm) The Piazza San Marco branch is the main tourist office.

Sights

A good way to whet your sightseeing appetite is to take *vaporetto* 1 along the **Grand Canal**, which is lined with rococo Gothic, Moorish and Renaissance palaces. Alight at Piazza San Marco, itself Venice's most famous sight.

PIAZZA SAN MARCO

Piazza San Marco beautifully encapsulates the splendour of Venice's past and its tourist-fuelled present. Flanked by the arcaded **Procuratie Vecchie** (Map pp668–9) and **Procuratie Nuove** (Map pp668–9), it's filled for much of the day with tourists, pigeons, balloon-vendors and police officers. While you're taking it all in, you might see the bronze *mori* (Moors) strike the bell of the 15th-century **Torre dell'Orologio** (clock tower; Map pp668–9).

But, it's to the remarkable **Basilica di San Marco** (St Mark's Basilica; Map pp668-9; ☎ 041 522 52 05; Piazza San Marco; admission free; 9.45am-5pm Mon-Sat, 2-5pm Sun Easter-Oct, 9.45am-5pm Mon-Sat, 2-4pm Sun Nov-Easter) that all eyes are drawn. Sporting spangled spires, Byzantine domes, luminous mosaics and lavish marblework, it was originally built to house the remains of St Mark. According to legend, the Evangelist's body was stolen from Alexandria in Egypt and smuggled to Venice in a barrel of pork. He's since been buried several times, his body now resting under the high altar. The original chapel was destroyed by fire in AD 932 and a new basilica was consecrated in its place in 1094. For the next 500 years it was a work in progress as successive *doges* added mosaics and embellishments looted from the East. The bronze horses above the entrance are replicas of statues 'liberated' from Constantinople in the Fourth Crusade (1204). Behind the main altar is the **Pala d'Oro** (Map pp668-9; admission €2; 9.45am-5pm Mon-Sat, 2-4.30pm Sun Apr-Sep, to 4pm Oct-Apr), a stunning gold altarpiece decorated with priceless jewels.

The basilica's 99m freestanding **campanile** (bell tower; Map pp668-9; admission €8; 9am-7pm Apr-Jun & Sep-Oct, to 9pm Jul-Aug, 9.30am-4.15pm Nov-Mar) dates from the 10th century, although it suddenly collapsed on 14 July 1902 and had to be rebuilt.

PALAZZO DUCALE

The official residence of the *doges* from the 9th century and the seat of the Republic's government, **Palazzo Ducale** (Doge's Palace; Map pp668-9; ☎ 041 271 59 11; Piazzetta di San Marco; admission with Museum Pass or San Marco Plus Ticket; 9am-7pm Apr-Oct, to 5pm Nov-Mar) also housed Venice's prisons. On the 2nd floor, the massive **Sala del Maggiore Consiglio** (Map pp668–9) is dominated by Tintoretto's *Paradiso* (Paradise), one of the world's largest oil paintings, which measures 22m by 7m.

The **Ponte dei Sospiri** (Bridge of Sighs; Map pp668–9) connects the palace to an additional wing of the city dungeons. It's named after the sighs that prisoners – including Giacomo Casanova – emitted en route from court to cell.

GALLERIA DELL'ACCADEMIA

One of Venice's top galleries, the **Galleria dell'Accademia** (Map pp668-9; ☎ 041 522 22 47; Dorsoduro 1050; adult/EU citizens 18-25yr €6.50/3.50; 8.15am-2pm Mon, to 7.15pm Tue-Sun) traces the development of Venetian art from the 14th to the 18th century. You'll find works by Bellini, Titian, Carpaccio, Tintoretto, Giorgione and Veronese.

COLLEZIONE PEGGY GUGGENHEIM

For something more contemporary, visit the **Collezione Peggy Guggenheim** (Map pp668-9; ☎ 041 240 54 11; www.guggenheim-venice.it; Palazzo Venier dei Leoni, Dorsoduro 701; adult/concession €10/5; 10am-6pm Wed-Mon). Housed in the American heiress' former home, the spellbinding collection

SAN MARCO, SAN POLO & SANTA CROCE

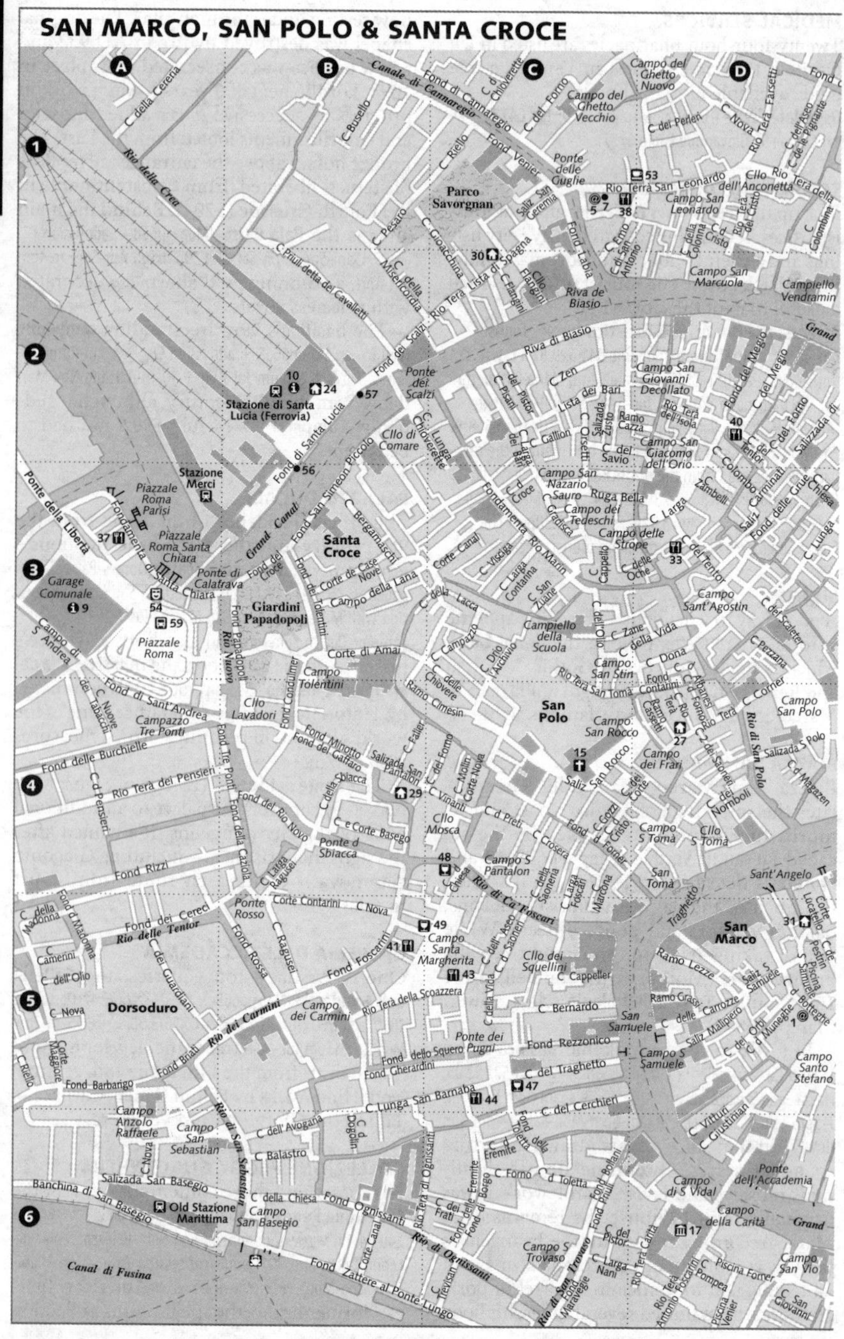

INFORMATION		
botteg@internet	1	D5
Libreria Mondadori	2	F5
Main Post Office	3	F3
Ospedale Civile (Hospital)	4	H3
Planet Internet	5	C1
Police Station	6	H4
Speedy Wash	7	C1
Tourist Office (Piazza San Marco)	8	F5
Tourist Office (Piazzale Roma)	9	A3
Tourist Office (Train Station)	10	B2
SIGHTS & ACTIVITIES		
Basilica di San Marco	11	G5
Campanile	12	G5
Chiesa dei SS Giovanni e Paolo	13	H3
Chiesa di Santa Maria della Salute	14	F6
Chiesa di Santa Maria Gloriosa dei Frari	15	C4
Collezione Peggy Guggenheim	16	E6
Galleria dell'Accademia	17	D6
Pala d'Oro	(see 11)	
Palazzo Ducale	18	G5
Piazza San Marco	19	G5
Ponte dei Sospiri (Bridge of Sighs)	20	G5
Procuratie Nuove	21	G5
Procuratie Vecchie	22	F5
Sala del Maggiore Consiglio	(see 18)	
Torre dell'Orologio	23	G5
SLEEPING		
Associazione Veneziana Albergatori Hotel Booking Service	24	B2
Ca' Riccio	25	G3
Foresteria Valdese	26	H4
Hotel Alex	27	D4
Hotel Bernardi	28	F2
Hotel Dalla Mora	29	B4
Hotel Minerva & Nettuno	30	C2
Locanda Antico Fiore	31	D5
Ostello Santa Fosca	32	E1
EATING		
Ae Oche	33	D3
All'Arco	34	E3
Antica Adelaide	35	F2
Billa (Supermarket)	36	E2
Coop	37	A3
Fish & Produce Market	38	C1
Osteria da Baco	39	H5
Osteria La Zucca	40	D2
Pizza al Volo	41	B5
Produce Market	42	F3
Punto Sma (Supermarket)	43	C5
Ristorante La Bitta	44	C5
Riva Reno	45	G4
Rosa Salva	46	H3
DRINKING		
Caffé Bar Ai Artisti	47	C5
Chet Bar	48	C4
Il Caffè	49	C5
La Cantina	50	E2
Muro Vino e Cucina	51	F3
Paradiso Perduto	52	E1
Torrefazione Costarica	53	D1
ENTERTAINMENT		
HelloVenezia Ticket Outlet	(see 57)	
HelloVenezia Ticket Outlet	54	A3
Teatro La Fenice	55	E5
TRANSPORT		
ACTV Booth	56	B3
ACTV Booth	57	B2
Alilaguna Fast Ferry to Airport	58	G6
Bus Station	59	A3

runs the gamut of modern art with works by Bacon, Pollock, Picasso and Dalí.

CHURCHES

Venice's churches harbour innumerable treasures; unusually, though, you have to pay to get into many of them. See p665 for details of the Chorus Pass.

Scene of the annual Festa del Redentore (opposite), the **Chiesa del SS Redentore** (Church of the Redeemer; Map p666; Campo del SS Redentore 194; admission €3; 10am-5pm Mon-Sat, 1-6pm Sun), on the island of Giudecca, was built by Palladio to commemorate the end of the great plague in 1577. Take *vaporetto* 41, 42 or 82 from the train station, alighting at Zitelle.

Guarding the entrance to the Grand Canal, the 17th-century **Chiesa di Santa Maria della Salute** (Map pp668-9; ☎ 041 522 55 58; Campo della Salute 1/b; admission sacristy €2; 9am-noon & 3.30-6pm) contains works by Tintoretto and Titian. Arguably the greatest of Venice's artists, Titian's celebrated masterpiece the *Assunta* (Assumption; 1518) hangs in the **Chiesa di Santa Maria Gloriosa dei Frari** (Map pp668-9; Campo dei Frari, San Polo 3004; admission €3; 9am-6pm Mon-Sat, 1-6pm Sun), the same church in which he's buried.

The vast Gothic **Chiesa dei SS Giovanni e Paolo** (Map pp668-9; ☎ 041 523 59 13; Campo SS Giovanni e Paolo; admission €3; 9.30am-7pm Mon-Sat, 1-6pm Sun) is famous for its glorious 15th-century stained-glass window, the largest in Venice.

THE LIDO

A thin strip of an island about a 15-minute *vaporetto* ride from Venice proper, the Lido (off Map p666) hosts the Venice Film Festival and boasts the city's best beach. Be warned, though, that it's almost impossible to find space on the sand in summer. It's accessible by *vaporetti* 1, 2, LN, 51, 52, 61 and 62.

ISLANDS

Murano (off Map p666) is the home of Venetian glass, and **Burano** (off Map p666), with its cheery pastel-coloured houses, is renowned for its lace. **Torcello** (off Map p666), the republic's original island settlement, was abandoned due to malaria and now counts no more than 80 residents. Torcello's Byzantine cathedral, **Santa Maria Assunta** (☎ 041 270 24 64; Piazza Torcello; admission €4; 10.30am-6pm Mar-Oct, to 5pm Nov-Feb), is Venice's oldest.

Vaporetto 41 (and *vaporetto* 5 in summer only) services Murano from the San Zaccaria *vaporetto* stop. *Vaporetto* LN services all three islands from the *vaporetto* stop at Fondamente Nuove in the northeast of the city. *Vaporetto* T connects Burano and Torcello.

Activities

If you gotta go, be prepared to pay – official rates per gondola (maximum six people) start at €80 (€100 at night) for a short trip including the Rialto but not the Grand Canal, and €120

(€150 at night) for a 50-minute trip including the Grand Canal.

Festivals & Events

Carnevale Masked ribaldry in the 10 days before Ash Wednesday.

Palio delle Quattro Repubbliche Marinare Venice, Amalfi, Genoa and Pisa take turns to host this historic regatta. It's in Venice in June 2011.

Festa del Redentore Held on the third weekend in July; celebrations climax with a spectacular fireworks display.

Regata Storica Costumed parades precede gondola races on the Grand Canal; held on the first Sunday in September.

Venice Biennale A major, year-long exhibition of international visual arts staged every even-numbered year from June to November.

Venice International Film Festival Italy's top film fest is held in late August to September at the Lido's Palazzo del Cinema.

Sleeping

Ouch! Prices in Venice hurt. It's always advisable to book ahead but essential at weekends, in May and September, and during Carnevale and other holidays. At the train station, the **Associazione Veneziana Albergatori** (Map p666; ☎ 800 843 006; Stazione di Santa Lucia; 8am-10pm Easter-Oct, to 9pm Nov-Easter) will book you a room for a small fee.

Marina di Venezia (off Map p666; ☎ 041 530 25 11; www.marinadivenezia.it; Via Montello 6, Punta Sabbioni; per person/tent €8.50/24.80; mid-Apr–end Sep;) On the Litorale de Cavallino, this big, brassy camping ground offers a long list of facilities including its own aquapark. Take the *vaporetto* from Punta Sabbioni to Fondamenta Nuove.

Ostello Santa Fosca (Map pp668-9; ☎ 041 71 57 75; www.santafosca.it; Cannaregio 2372; dm €20, d with shared bathroom €50) Here you can sunbathe in an enclosed garden near the Rialto before retiring to your dormitory for the night. There's a kitchen for guests to use (summer only). With a Rolling Venice Card rates are €2 cheaper. Breakfast isn't included.

Ostello di Venezia (Map p666; ☎ 041 523 82 11; www.ostellovenezia.it; Fondamenta delle Zitelle 86; dm €21) Venice's cheap but charmless HI hostel is over the water from Piazza San Marco on the island of Giudecca. Take *vaporetto* 41, 42 or 82 from the train station, alighting at Zitelle. There's an 11.30pm curfew.

Foresteria Valdese (Map pp668-9; ☎ 041 528 67 97; www.diaconiavaldese.org/venezia; Centro Culturale P Cavagnis, Castello 5170; dm €24-26, d €82-86;) Run by the Waldensian and Methodist Church and housed in a rambling old mansion, this well-run hostel is deservedly popular. Follow Calle Lunga Santa Maria Formosa from Campo Santa Maria Formosa.

Hotel Bernardi (Map pp668-9; ☎ 041 522 72 57; www.hotelbernardi.com; SS Apostoli Calle dell'Oca, Cannaregio 4366; s with shared/private bathroom €35/55, d with shared bathroom €55-70, with private bathroom €80-110) Comfortable rooms, hospitable owners and keen prices mean that this top choice is always heavily booked.

Hotel Alex (Map pp668-9; ☎ 041 523 13 41; www.hotelalexinvenice.com; Rio Terà, San Polo 2606; s with shared bathroom €35-50, d with shared bathroom €40-80, with private bathroom €60-108) The welcoming Alex is in a quiet spot near Campo dei Frari. Spread over three floors (no lift), most of the rooms are a decent size and all are decorated with simple efficiency.

Hotel Minerva & Nettuno (Map pp668-9; ☎ 041 71 59 68; www.minervaenettuno.it; Lista di Spagna, Cannaregio 230; s/d with shared bathroom €45/70, with private bathroom €65/110;) Stay at this place near the train station and do your bit for the environment. All the mod cons in the antique-laden rooms are fired by electricity produced from renewable sources.

Hotel Dalla Mora (Map pp668-9; ☎ 041 71 07 03; www.hoteldallamora.it; Salizada San Pantalon, Santa Croce 42a; s €70, d with shared bathroom €80-83, with private bathroom €100) This family-run one-star choice has small but clean and airy rooms in two buildings, some of which overlook a canal. There's a pleasant terrace, too.

Locanda Antico Fiore (Map pp668-9; ☎ 041 71 51 80; www.anticofiore.com; Corte Lucatello, San Marco 3486; r €70-145;) Warm colours and an overload of chintz are the decorative hallmarks of this comfortable hotel, just off the Grand Canal.

Ca'Riccio (Map pp668-9; ☎ 041 52 82 334; www.cariccio.com; Campo dei Miracoli, Cannaregio 5394a; s €77-99, d €99-154;) Located behind the magnificent Chiesa dei Miracoli, this 14th-century residence offers beautifully restored rooms overlooking a pretty courtyard.

Eating

At Venetian prices you'll be glad of the many affordable self-catering/snack options. For a sit-down meal, avoid the obvious tourist traps and duck down the side streets.

Venetian specialities include *risi e bisi* (pea soup thickened with rice), *sarde di saor* (fried sardines marinated in vinegar and onions) and *fragolino* (a fragrant strawberry-flavoured wine).

QUICK EATS

Osteria da Baco (Map pp668-9; ☎ 041 522 28 87; Calle delle Rasse, Castello 6672) A friendly local bar where gondoliers like to relax between trips, Osteria da Baco offers a range of tasty *tremezzini* (sandwiches, €1.30) that can be washed down with a beer (€3) or glass of *fragolino* (fragrant strawberry wine, €2).

All'Arco (Map pp668-9; ☎ 041 520 56 66; Calle dell'Arco, San Polo 436; chiceti €1.50-4, panini €4; 🕑 7.30am-9pm Mon-Sat) Popular with locals, this tiny *osteria* serves wonderful, fresh *panini*, a range of *cicheti* (bar snacks) and wine by the glass.

Pizza al Volo (Map pp668-9; ☎ 041 522 54 30; Campo Santa Margherita, Dorsoduro 2944; pizza slice from €2.50) In need of a pizza pit stop? Here's your opportunity. You'll be in the company of a steady stream of interns from the Guggenheim.

Riva Reno (Map pp668-9; ☎ 041 2411821; Salizada San Lio, Castello 5662) This sleek branch of the excellent national gelato chain is conveniently located between the Rialto and Piazza San Marco.

Rosa Salva (Map pp668-9; ☎ 041 522 79 49; Campo SS Giovanni e Paolo, Castello 6779; 🕑 closed Wed) Stop by this historic cafe for sensational *fritalle* (fried pastry puffs filled with zabaglione or cream).

RESTAURANTS

Ae Oche (Map pp668-9; ☎ 041 524 11 61; Calle del Tentor, Santa Croce 1552a/b; pizzas €7-10) Students adore the Tex-Mex decor and huge pizza list at this bustling place. It's on the main path between the *ferrovia* and San Marco.

Antica Adelaide (Map pp668-9; ☎ 041 523 26 29; Calle Priuli, Cannaregio 3728; meals €30) The ancient Adelaide was in the food business as far back as the 18th century. You can pop in for a drink and *cicheti* or tuck into a hearty bowl of pasta or full meal.

Osteria La Zucca (Map pp668-9; ☎ 041 524 15 70; Calle del Tentor, Santa Croce 1762; meals €32; 🕑 closed Sun) A wonderful, unpretentious little restaurant in an out-of-the-way spot, 'The Pumpkin' serves a range of innovative Mediterranean dishes prepared with fresh, seasonal ingredients.

Ristorante La Bitta (Map pp668-9; ☎ 041 523 05 31; Calle Lunga San Barnaba, Dorsoduro 2753a; meals €40; 🕑 closed Sun) The bottle-lined dining room and attractive internal courtyard are a lovely setting in which to enjoy your choice from a small, meat-dominated menu that changes with the season. No credit cards.

SPLURGE

Hostaria da Franz (Map p666; ☎ 041 522 70 24; Calle del Pestrin, Castello 3886; meal €70-90) Expensive? Yes. Elegant? Excessively. Delicious? You said it! This is one of the best seafood restaurants in the city, and it's also world renowned for its creamy tiramisu. On a quiet canal away from any tourist action, it's where the arty glitterati love to eat when they come for the Biennale.

SELF-CATERING

Head for the markets near the Rialto bridge, or on the Rio Terrà San Leonardo. There are also several supermarkets: **Punto Sma** (Map pp668-9; Campo Santa Margherita), **Billa** (Map pp668-9; Strada Nova, Cannaregio 3660) and **Coop** (Map pp668-9; Fondamenta di Santa Chiara, Piazzale Roma 506a).

Drinking

Venice harbours hundreds of bars and cafes, but the highest concentration is in the area around Campo Santa Margherita.

Caffè Bar Ai Artisti (Map pp668-9; ☎ 041 523 89 44; Fondamenta della Toletta, Dorsoduro 1169a) On Campo S Barnaba, this welcoming place is good for coffee during the day, but even better for a drink or two at night.

Chet Bar (Map pp668-9; ☎ 041 523 87 27; Campo Santa Margherita, Dorsoduro 3684) Late at night, patrons at this laid-back drinking den spill out of the bar and sit on the steps of the nearby bridge.

Il Caffè (Map pp668-9; ☎ 041 528 79 98; Campo Santa Margherita, Dorsoduro 2963) Popular with foreign and Italian students, this is one of Venice's historic drinking spots. Known to locals as Café Rosso because of its red frontage, it's got outdoor seating and great *sprizze* (a type of aperitif).

La Cantina (Map pp668-9; ☎ 041 522 82 58; Campo San Felice 3689, Cannaregio; 🕑 closed Mon, 2 weeks Jul-Aug & 2 weeks Jan) Sit at one of the outdoor tables at this *enoteca* (wine bar) and watch the passing traffic promenade up and down the Strada Nuova.

Paradiso Perduto (Map pp668-9; ☎ 041 72 05 81; Fondamenta della Misericordia, Cannaregio 2540; 🕑 closed Mon) Queer-friendly and flamboyant, this restaurant-cum-club heats up late, but when the DJs pump up the decibels it jives. There's live music most weekends.

Muro Vino e Cucina (Map pp668-9; ☎ 041 523 47 40; Campo Cesare Battisti, San Polo 222; 🕑 closed Sun) The centre of a happening nightlife scene in the market squares of the Rialto, Muro joins a number of bars in attracting huge gaggles of swarming drinkers.

Torrefazione Costarica (Map pp668-9; ☎ 041 71 63 71; Rio Terrá San Leonardo, Cannaregio 1337) Connoisseurs come here for Venice's best coffee. Espressos are smooth yet charged with flavour, cappuccinos exactly as they should be, warm and creamy.

Entertainment

Tickets for most events in Venice are available from **HelloVenezia ticket outlets** (www.hellovenezia.it), run by the ACTV transport network. You'll find them in front of the train station and at Piazzale Roma.

Teatro La Fenice (Map pp668-9; ☎ 041 24 24 for guided tours; www.teatrolafenice.it; Campo San Fantin, San Marco 1977; tickets from €15) is one of Italy's most important opera houses.

Shopping

Classic Venetian gifts include Murano glass, lace from Burano, Carnevale masks and *carta marmorizzata* (marbled paper). There are any number of shops selling these items, but if you want the best deal go to the source. Be warned that genuine Burano lace is expensive; much of the cheaper stuff sold round town is imported from the Far East.

The main shopping area is between San Marco and the Rialto, although if you're after designer clobber you should head to the area west of Piazza San Marco.

Getting There & Away

Most European and domestic flights land at **Marco Polo airport** (VCE; off Map p666; ☎ 041 260 92 60; www.veniceairport.it), 12km outside Venice. Ryanair flies to **Treviso airport** (TSF; off Map p666; ☎ 0422 31 51 11; www.trevisoairport.it), about 30km from town.

Minoan Lines (☎ 041 240 71 01; www.minoan.gr) runs ferries to Corfu (€69 to €91, 23½ hours), Igoumenitsa (€69 to €91, 22 hours) and Patras (€69 to €182, 36 hours) daily in summer and four times per week in winter.

ACTV (☎ 041 24 24; www.actv.it) buses service surrounding areas, including Mestre, Padua and Treviso. Tickets and information are available at the bus station in Piazzale Roma.

Venice's train station, Stazione di Santa Lucia, is directly linked by regional trains to Padua (€2.90, 45 minutes, every 20 minutes), Verona (€13.50, 1½ hours, half-hourly) and Ferrara (€6.15, two hours, half-hourly). It is easily accessible from Bologna, Milan, Rome and Florence. You can also reach points in France, Germany, Austria, Switzerland, Slovenia and Croatia from here.

Getting Around

The city's main mode of public transport is the *vaporetto*. Useful routes:

LN From Fondamenta Nuove to Murano, Burano and Torcello.
T Runs between Burano and Torcello.
1 From Piazzale Roma to the train station and down the Grand Canal to San Marco and the Lido.
2 From San Zaccaria (near San Marco) to the Lido via Giudecca, Piazzale Roma, the train station and the Rialto.
3 From Piazzale Roma to San Marco via the Rialto and Accademia.

Tickets, available from ACTV booths at the major *vaporetti* stops, are expensive: €6.50 for a single trip; €14 for 12 hours; €16 for 24 hours; €21 for 36 hours; €26 for 48 hours and €31 for 72 hours (€18 if you have a Rolling Venice card).

To cross the Grand Canal where there's no nearby bridge take a *traghetti* (public gondola; €0.50 per crossing).

FERRARA

pop 133,300

Surrounded by foggy plains, Ferrara is a quiet and well-to-do city that retains much of the austere splendour of its Renaissance heyday, when it was the seat of the powerful Este family (1260–1598). Overshadowed by the menacing Castello Estense, the compact medieval centre is atmospheric and lively.

Information is available from the **tourist office** (☎ 0532 29 93 03; www.ferrarainfo.com; 🕑 9am-1pm & 2-6pm Mon-Sat, 9.30am-1pm & 2-5.30pm Sun) inside Castello Estense. For internet, try **Sun Rise Internet Point** (Via Garibaldi 37, int 13/15; per hr €4; 🕑 9am-9.30pm).

Sights & Activities

If you're planning to visit the major monuments, buy a Museum Card (€14), which gives free entry to all municipal museums. They're available from both the Cathedral Museum and Palazzo Schifanoia.

Easily explored on foot, Ferrara's *centro storico* lies to the south of **Castello Estense** (☎ 0532 29 92 33; www.castelloestense.it; Viale Cavour; admission €7, plus Lion's Tower €1; 9.30am-5.30pm, closed Mon Jun-Feb). Complete with moat and drawbridges, the castle was begun by Nicolò II d'Este in 1385 and became the Este family's residence.

Nearby, the pink-and-white 12th-century **Duomo** (0532 20 74 49; Piazza Cattedrale; 7.30am-noon & 3-6.30pm Mon-Sat, 7.30am-12.30pm & 3.30-7.30pm Sun) is notable for its superb three-tiered marble facade with a Gothic depiction of the Last Judgement.

Fresco fans won't want to miss **Palazzo Schifanoia** (0532 24 49 49; Via Scandiana 23; admission €5; 9am-6pm Tue-Sun), one of Ferrara's earliest Renaissance buildings and another of the Este palaces. In the **Sala dei Mesi** (Room of the Months), the 15th-century frescoes are among the best examples of their type in Italy. Sadly, though, they're not in great nick.

Sleeping

You won't need to overnight to see Ferrara's sights, but it's a cheap alternative to Bologna, and a viable base for Venice.

Pensione Artisti (0532 76 10 38; Via Vittoria 66; s/d with shared bathroom €28/48, d with private bathroom €60) Put simply, this is the best budget option in town. Its scrubbed white rooms sparkle, the location is excellent, there are kitchen facilities for guests, and the owners are superfriendly.

Hotel de Prati (0532 24 19 05; www.hoteldeprati.com; Via Padiglioni 5; s €49-85, d €75-120;) The large, individually decorated and extremely comfortable rooms here sport features such as satellite TV and wi-fi. Downstairs, the yellow and orange walls stage contemporary art exhibitions. Great location.

Eating & Drinking

Trattoria Il Mandolino (0532 76 00 80; Via Carlo Mayr 83; meals €25; Wed-Sun, lunch Mon) This charmingly cluttered trattoria is a memorable place to dine on Ferrarese food. Menu staples include the house speciality, *salama da sugo con purè* (salty braised salami on a bed of mashed potato).

Messisbugo (0532 76 40 60; Via Carlo Mayr 79; 7pm-2am Tue-Sun) Despite a name that suggests Tex-Mex tack, Messisbugo is actually a cool, brick-vaulted bar favoured by bohemians and students, with friendly staff, great wines and a laid-back vibe.

Getting There & Around

Ferrara is easy to reach by train. There are regional trains to Bologna (€3.10, 35 minutes, every 30 to 60 minutes), Venice (€6.15, two hours, half-hourly) and nearby Ravenna (€4.50, 1¼ hours, 10 daily).

From the station take bus 1 or 9 for the historic centre.

BOLOGNA

pop 373,100

Boasting one of the country's great medieval cityscapes, Italy's culinary capital is an attractive, animated city. Its large student population and active gay scene ensure a cosmopolitan vitality, and with hundreds of bars, cafes and trattorias to choose from, you'll soon find somewhere to hang out.

Nicknamed *la rossa* (the red – as much a political moniker as reference to its colourful buildings), Bologna has long had a reputation for left-wing militancy. Passions have cooled since students faced down tanks in 1977 but the city remains highly political and the university, Europe's oldest, is still a source of student agitation.

Orientation & Information

Via dell'Indipendenza, the main north–south artery, leads from the train and bus stations into Piazza del Nettuno and Piazza Maggiore, the heart of the city.

Iperbole (051 219 31 84; URP, Piazza Maggiore 6; 9.30am-6.30pm Mon-Fri, 9.30am-1.30pm & 3.30-6.30pm Sat) Free internet access.

Lava e Asciuga (Via Irnerio 35b; wash/dry €3/1.50; 7am-midnight) Self-service launderette.

Liong@te Internet Point (www.liongate.it; 1st fl, Via Rizzoli 9; per hr €2; 10am-midnight)

Ospedale Maggiore (Hospital; 051 647 81 11)

Police station (Questura; 051 640 11 11; Piazza Galileo 7)

Tourist information (051 23 96 60; www.bolognaturismo.info) Airport (8am-8pm); Piazza Maggiore 1 (9.30am-7.30pm); Train Station (9am-7pm Mon-Sat, to 3pm Sun) Ask for a copy of the free 'what's on' booklet.

> **GETTING INTO TOWN**
>
> Every 20 minutes an Aerobus shuttle (€5, 30 minutes) runs from Guglielmo Marconi airport to the train station. From Forlì airport, **Ebus** (199 11 55 77) buses leave for Bologna train station shortly after Ryanair flights land. The trip takes 1½ hours and costs €10.
>
> To get to the centre from the train station take bus 25 or 30 (€1).

Sights & Activities

Bologna's porticoed *centro storico* is an atmospheric place to explore. Start in pedestrianised **Piazza Maggiore** and adjoining **Piazza del Nettuno**. Here you'll find the **Fontana del Nettuno** (Neptune's Fountain), sculpted by Giambologna in 1566 and featuring an impressively muscled Neptune. On the western flank of Piazza Maggiore is the **Palazzo Comunale** (Town Hall; ☎ 051 20 31 11; admission free), home to the **Collezioni Comunali d'Arte** (Civic Art Collection; admission free; 🕑 9am-3pm Tue-Fri, 10am-6.30pm Sat & Sun) and a museum dedicated to the work of artist **Giorgio Morandi** (admission free; 🕑 as above).

To the south, the Gothic **Basilica di San Petronio** (☎ 051 22 54 22; Piazza Maggiore; 🕑 7.45am-12.30pm & 3-6pm) is the world's fifth-largest basilica. Note the partially complete facade and, inside, the 17th-century brass sundial along the eastern aisle.

It's a short walk to **Piazza di Porta Ravegnana** and Bologna's two leaning towers, the **Due Torri**. The taller of the two, the 97m **Torre Asinelli** (admission €3; 🕑 9am-6pm, to 5pm winter), was built between 1109 and 1119 and is now open to the public. Climb the 498 steps for some superb city views.

The recently opened **Museo d'Arte Moderna do Bologna** (MAMBO; Museum of Modern Art; ☎ 051 649 66 11; Via Don Minzoni 14; admission free; 🕑 10am-6pm Tue-Wed & Fri-Sun, to 10pm Thu) is located in a converted bakery in Bologna's new – and very impressive – arts and culture precinct.

Sleeping & Eating

Accommodation is expensive (particularly during trade fairs) and can be difficult to find unless you book ahead. For a cheap bite, the university area around Via Rizzoli has hundreds of trattorias and restaurants.

Ostello Due Torri/San Sisto 2 (☎ 051 50 18 10; hostelbologna@hotmail.com; Via Viadagola 5; dm/s/d €16/25/38; 💻) Some 6km north of the city centre, Bologna's two HI hostels, barely 100m apart, are modern, functional and cheap. Take bus 93 (Monday to Saturday daytime), 301 (Sunday) or 21b (daily after 8.30pm) from Via Irnerio or Via Marconi. Mind the 11pm curfew.

Albergo delle Drapperie (☎ 051 22 39 55; www.albergodrapperie.com; Via delle Drapperie 5; s €60-105, d €75-140; ❄) In the heart of the happening Quadrilatero district, this place offers clean and comfortable rooms with good bathrooms. Breakfast costs an extra €5.

Pizzeria Belle Arti (☎ 051 22 55 81; Via Belle Arti 14; pizzas from €4.50, meals €25) This sprawling place near the university serves delicious thin-crust pizzas that deserve the descriptor 'the best in Bologna'. You'll find it next to the Odeon cinema.

Trattoria Mariposa (☎ 051 22 56 56; Via Bertiera 12; meals €20; closed Sun & Mon, dinner Thu) A genial, laid-back trattoria, the Mariposa serves a menu of simple homemade favourites such as tortellini with *ragù* or *burro e salvia* (butter and sage).

Two of the best *gelaterie* in Italy can be found in Bologna: **Gelateria Stefino** (Via Galleria 49b; 🕑 noon-12.30am) and **La Sorbetteria Castiglione** (Via Castiglione 44; 🕑 8.30am-10.30pm Tue-Fri, 9am-midnight Sat, 9am-10.30pm Sun).

Stock up at **Mercato delle Erbe** (Via Ugo Bassi 27; 🕑 Mon-Sat), Bologna's main covered market. Otherwise, there's a **Pam** (☎ 051 52 04 04; Via Marconi 28a) supermarket west of the centre, and the Quadrilatero area east of Piazza Maggiore harbours a **produce market** (Via Clavature 12; 🕑 Mon-Sat) and some of the city's best-known delis.

Drinking & Clubbing

Popular drinking areas include the Quadrilatero, east of Piazza Maggiore, where you'll find uberfashionable **Café de Paris** (☎ 051 23 49 80; www.cafedeparisbologna.org; Piazza del Francia 1c), **Rosa Rose** (☎ 051 22 50 71; Via Clavature 18b) and **Bar Calice** (☎ 051 26 45 06; Via Clavature 13a). Other popular bars are scattered around Piazza Verdi; jazz-focussed **Cantina Bentivoglio** (☎ 051 26 54 16; www.cantinabentivoglio.it; Via Mascarella 4b) and bohemian **La Scuderia** (☎ 051 656 96 19; www.lascuderia.bo.it; Piazza Verdi 2) are both hot. Most of these places also serve good food.

For somewhere to dance, **Cassero** (☎ 051 649 44 16; www.cassero.it; Via Don Minzoni 18), home of Italy's Arcigay organisation, is a top spot, hosting big DJs and gay and lesbian (and mixed) nights. In the university district, **Corto Maltese** (☎ 051 22 97 46; Via Borgo San Pietro 9/2a) is a popular student hang-out.

Getting There & Around

European and domestic flights arrive at Bologna's **Guglielmo Marconi airport** (BLQ; ☎ 051 647 96 15; www.bologna-airport.it), 6km northwest of the city. Ryanair flies to **Forlì** (FRL; ☎ 0543 47 49 21; www.forli-airport.it), 70km southeast of Bologna.

Bologna is a major rail hub. From the main **train station** (Piazza delle Medaglie d'Oro), trains run to Venice (€15.10, two hours, half-hourly), Florence (€10.75, one hour, every 20 minutes) and Rome (Eurostar, €37.20, 2¾ hours, hourly). National and international coaches depart from the main **bus station** (Piazza XX Settembre).

RAVENNA

pop 151,100

Most people visit Ravenna to see its remarkable Unesco-protected mosaics. Relics of the city's golden age as capital of the Western Roman and Byzantine Empires, they are described by Dante in his *Divine Comedy*, much of which was written here. Easily accessible from Bologna, this refined and polished town is easily covered in a day.

The city's **main tourist office** (☎ 0544 354 04; www.turismo.ravenna.it; Via Salara 8/12; ⌚ 8.30am-7pm Mon-Sat, 10am-6pm Sun summer, 8.30am-6pm Mon-Sat, 10am-4pm Sun winter) is in the *centro storico*. There's another office in **Classe** (Via Romea Sud 266; ⌚ 9.30am-12.30pm & 2.30-5.30pm).

Sights

You'll find Ravenna's main mosaics in the 6th-century **Basilica di San Vitale** (☎ 0544 21 51 93; Via Fiandrini; ⌚ 9am-7pm Apr-Sep, 9am-5.30pm Mar & Oct, 9.30am-5pm Nov-Feb), **Mausoleo di Galla Placidia** (☎ 0544 21 51 93; Via Fiandrini; ⌚ 9am-7pm Apr-Sep, 9am-5.30pm Mar & Oct, 9.30am-5pm Nov-Feb), **Battistero Neoniano** (Via Battistero; ⌚ 9am-7pm Apr-Sep, 9.30am-5.30pm Mar & Oct, 10am-5pm Nov-Feb) and the **Basilica di Sant'Apollinare Nuovo** (☎ 0544 21 95 18; Via di Roma; ⌚ 9am-7pm Apr-Sep, 9.30am-5.30pm Mar & Oct, 10am-5pm Nov-Feb), which was being restored at the time of research.

These four sites, plus the **Museo Arcivescovile** (☎ 0544 21 52 91; Piazza Arcivescovado; ⌚ 9am-7pm Apr-Sep, 9.30am-5.30pm Mar & Oct, 10am-5pm Nov-Feb), are covered by a single ticket (adult/concession €8.50/7.50), available at any one of the five monuments and valid for seven days. In summer there's an extra €2 booking fee for the Mausoleo di Galla Placida. Get details at www.ravennamosaici.it.

Some of the best mosaics are in the **Basilica di Sant'Apollinare in Classe** (☎ 0544 47 35 69; Via Romea Sud, Classe; adult/concession €3/1.50; ⌚ 8.30am-7.30pm), 5km out of town. Take bus 4 or 44 (€1) from Piazza Caduti per la Libertà.

Dante spent the last 19 years of his life in Ravenna after he was expelled from Florence. As a perpetual act of penance Florence supplies the oil for the lamp that burns in his **tomb** (Via Dante Alighieri 9; admission free; ⌚ 9am-7pm).

Eating & Drinking

Ostello Dante (☎ 0544 42 11 64; www.hostelravenna.com; Via Nicolodi 12; dm/s/d €14/22/40; 💻) Ravenna's vibrant HI youth hostel is in a modern building 1km east of the train station. There's wi-fi in the lobby. Take bus 1.

Naif (☎ 0544 42 23 15; Via Candiano 34; pizzas from €5, meals €25) A bright, brash place near the train station, this place is good for pizza as well as hearty pastas and filling mains.

Getting There & Away

Regional trains connect the city with Bologna (€5, 1½ hours, 13 daily) and Ferrara (€4.50, 1¼ hours, 11 daily).

In town, cycling is popular. The tourist office has 20 bikes that it makes available to visitors aged 18 or over at no charge.

THE DOLOMITES

Stretching across Trentino-Alto Adige and into the Veneto, the stabbing sawtooth peaks of the Dolomites provide some of Italy's most thrilling scenery. With their jagged silhouettes and colourful tints, they are popular all year – in winter for the skiing, in summer for the superb hiking.

Resorts range from exclusive Cortina d'Ampezzo to more budget-friendly places in the Val Gardena (opposite). Ski passes cover either single resorts or a combination of slopes; the most comprehensive is the **Superski Dolomiti pass** (www.dolomitisuperski.com; high season 3/6 days €125/220), which accesses 464 lifts and 1220km of runs in 12 valleys.

Hiking opportunities run the gamut from gentle strolls to hardcore mountain treks. Recommended areas include the Alpe di Siusi, a vast plateau above the Val Gardena; the area around Cortina; and Pale di San Martino, accessible from San Martino di Castrozza.

Information

Information on Trentino Alto-Adige can be obtained in Trent at the **tourist office** (☎ 0461 98 38 80; www.apt.trento.it; Via Manci 2; ⌚ 9am-7pm). Bolzano's **tourist office** (☎ 0471 30 70 00; www.bolzano-bozen.it; Piazza Walther 8; ⌚ 9am-6.30pm Mon-Fri, to 12.30pm Sat) can also help.

For activities and accommodation in the Veneto, ask at the **tourist office** (☎ 0436 32 31; www.infodolomiti.it; Piazzetta San Francesco 8; ⌚ 9am-12.30pm & 3.30-6.30pm) in Cortina.

The best online resource option is www.dolomiti.org, which has a great deal of useful information.

Getting There & Around

In Trentino-Alto Adige, **Bolzano airport** (BZO; ☎ 0471 25 52 55; www.abd-airport.it) is served by ski charter flights from the UK in the winter and daily year-round flights from Rome and Milan. Otherwise the nearest airports are in Verona (see p664) or Bergamo (Orio al Serio airport, p662).

On terra firma, the area's excellent bus network is run by **Trentino Trasporti** (☎ 0461 82 10 00; www.ttspa.it, in Italian) in Trentino; **SAD** (☎ 800 84 60 47; www.sii.bz.it) in Alto Adige; and **Dolomiti Bus** (www.dolomitibus.it, in Italian) in the Veneto. During winter, most resorts offer 'ski bus' services.

The main towns and the many ski resorts can be reached directly from cities such as Rome, Florence, Venice, Bologna, Milan and Genoa. Information is available from tourist offices and regional bus stations.

CANAZEI

One of the best-known resorts in the Val di Fassa, Canazei is a great spot for serious skiers. It has got 120km of downhill and cross-country runs and is linked to the challenging Sella Ronda ski network. There's even summer skiing on the Marmolada glacier, the stunning 3342m summit of which marks the highest point in the Dolomites.

Spend a cheap night at the Marmolada **camping ground** (☎ 0462 60 16 60, fax 0462 60 17 22; Strèda de Parèda 60; per person/tent €9.50/9.50; 🕑 year-round), or contact the **tourist office** (☎ 0462 60 96 00; www.fassa.com; Piazza Marconi 5; 🕑 8.30am-12.15pm & 3-7pm Mon-Sat, 10am-12.30pm Sun) for accommodation lists. The resort is accessible by **Trentino Trasporti bus** (www.ttspa.it, in Italian) from Trent (€5.50, 2½ hours, three daily).

VAL GARDENA

Branching northeast off the Val di Fassa, the Val Gardena is a popular skiing area with great facilities and accessible prices. In summer hikers head to the Sella Group and the Alpe di Siusi for rugged, high-altitude treks and to the Vallunga for more accessible walks.

The valley's main towns are Ortisei, Santa Cristina and Selva, all offering plenty of accommodation and easy access to runs. Further information is available online at www.gardena.org, or from the towns' tourist offices:

Ortisei (☎ 0471 77 76 00; Via Rezia 1; 🕑 8.30am-12.30pm & 2.30-6.30pm Mon-Sat, 10am-noon & 5-6.30pm Sun)
Santa Cristina (☎ 0471 77 78 00; Via Chemun 9; 🕑 8am-noon & 2.30-6.30pm Mon-Sat, 9.30am-noon Sun)
Selva (☎ 0471 77 79 00; Via Mëisules 213; 🕑 8am-noon & 3-6.30pm Mon-Sat, 9am-noon & 5-6.30pm Sun)

The Val Gardena is accessible from Bolzano by SAD bus and from Canazei in summer.

SAN MARTINO DI CASTROZZA

At the foot of the imposing Pale di San Martino range, San Martino di Castrozza acts as a gateway to the Parco Naturale Paneveggio – Pale di San Martino. The **tourist office** (☎ 0439 76 88 67; www.sanmartino.com; Via Passo Rolle 165; 🕑 9am-noon & 3-7pm Mon-Sat, 9.30am-12.30pm Sun) can provide skiing information and help with accommodation.

Trentino Trasporti buses run to/from Trent (€5.80, 2½ hours, four daily).

CENTRAL ITALY

Encompassing three regions, Tuscany, Umbria and Le Marche, central Italy is a green, hilly area peppered with rural villages and historic towns. Tuscany's fabled rolling landscape has long been considered the embodiment of rural chic and Florence harbours a significant portfolio of the world's Renaissance art collection. But venture off the beaten path, and it's still possible to lose yourself down a medieval side street in Umbria and lesser-known Le Marche.

FLORENCE

pop 366,000

One of the most written about cities in Italy, Florence (Firenze) has a strange effect on visitors. Travellers who normally loathe art galleries queue for hours to get into them, and people with no interest in Renaissance architecture start raving about tiered facades and frescoed apses. But break the spell and you'll find that Florence can be disheartening. Much of the centre has been surrendered to tourism and in summer the heat, pollution and crowds can be stifling. That said, it remains a charismatic city you'd be sorry to miss. The list of its famous sons reads like a Renaissance *Who's Who* – under M alone you'll find

ITALY

GETTING INTO TOWN

From Pisa's Galileo Galilei airport **Terravision** (☎ 06 321 20 011; www.terravision.it) runs buses to the train station (€8, 70 minutes, 12 daily). Otherwise there are regular trains (€5.10, 1½ hours, hourly).

Volainbus (☎ 800 42 45 00; www.ataf.net) runs a shuttlebus (€4.50, 25 minutes, half-hourly 5.30am to 11pm) connecting Florence airport with the SITA bus station.

Medici, Machiavelli and Michelangelo – and its celebrated cityscape lingers in the memory long after you've left town.

History

Many hold that Florentia was founded around 59 BC, but archaeological evidence suggests an earlier village, possibly established by the Etruscans around 200 BC. A rich merchant city by the 12th century, Florence grew into a powerful city-state under the Medici family, its cultural, artistic and political fecundity culminating in the 15th-century Renaissance.

The Medici were succeeded in the 18th century by the French House of Lorraine, which ruled until 1860 when the city was incorporated into the Kingdom of Italy. From 1865 to 1870, Florence was, in fact, capital of the fledgling kingdom.

During WWII parts of the city were destroyed by bombing, including all of its bridges except for Ponte Vecchio. In 1966 a devastating flood destroyed or severely damaged many important works of art. More recently, in 1993, the Mafia exploded a massive car bomb, killing five people and destroying part of the Uffizi Gallery.

Orientation

From Santa Maria Novella train station, it's a 550m walk along Via de' Panzani and Via de' Cerretani to the Duomo. From there, Via Roma leads down to Piazza della Repubblica and Via de' Calzaiuoli connects with Piazza della Signoria. Most major sights are within comfortable walking distance of the Duomo.

Information

BOOKSHOPS

Feltrinelli International (Map p681; ☎ 055 21 95 24; Via Cavour 12r; 9am-7.30pm Mon-Sat) Great selection of books in English.

EMERGENCY

Police station (Questura; Map p679; ☎ 055 497 71; Via Zara 2)

INTERNET ACCESS

Cyber Link (Map p681; Via Del Giglio 29r; per hr €4, students €3; 9.30am-12.30am) Also offers a left-luggage service (€5 per 24 hours).

Internet Train (per hr €4.30, students €3.20; 9.30am-midnight Mon-Sat, 10am-midnight Sun) Beneath Stazione di Santa Maria Novella (Map p679); Borgo San Jacopo 30r (Map p681); Via dell'Oriuolo 40r (Map p681); Via Guelfa 24a (Map p679); Via Porta Rossa 38 (Map p681) Opening times are for the Via Porta Rossa branch; others may vary.

LAUNDRY

Wash & Dry Lavarapido (☎ 800 23 11 72; 8kg wash/dry €3.50/3.50; 8am-10pm) Via de' Serragli 87r (Map p679); Via dei Servi 105r (Map p679); Via del Sole 29r (Map p681); Via della Scala 52-54r (Map p679); Via Nazionale 129r (Map p679)

MEDICAL SERVICES

Farmacia Comunale (Map p679; ☎ 055 28 94 35; Stazione di Santa Maria Novella; 24hr)

Misericordia di Firenze (Map p681; ☎ 055 21 22 22; Vicolo degli Adimari 1, Piazza del Duomo; 2-6pm Mon-Fri Mar-Oct) Fee-paying medical service.

Tourist Medical Service (Map p679; ☎ 055 47 54 11; Via Lorenzo il Magnifico 59; 24hr)

POST & TELEPHONE

Telecom office (Map p679; Via Cavour 21r; 7am-11pm) Public payphones.

TOURIST INFORMATION

Tourist offices airport (☎ 055 31 58 74; 8.30am-8.30pm); Borgo Santa Croce 29r (Map p681; ☎ 055 234 04 44; 9am-7pm Mon-Sat, to 2pm Sun Mar–mid-Nov, 9am-5pm Mon-Sat, to 2pm Sun mid-Nov–Feb); Piazza della Stazione 4 (Map p681; ☎ 055 21 22 45; www.comune.fi.it; 8.30am-7pm Mon-Sat, to 2pm Sun); Via Cavour (Map p679; ☎ 055 29 08 32; www.firenzeturismo.it; Via Cavour 1r; 8.30am-6.30pm Mon-Sat, to 1.30pm Sun) The Via Cavour branch is the main office.

Sights & Activities

You'll never avoid queuing in Florence, but by prebooking museum tickets you'll save time. For €4 extra per museum you can book tickets for the Uffizi, Palazzo Pitti, Galleria dell'Accademia and Cappelle Medicee through **Firenze Musei** (☎ 055 29 48 83; www.firenzemusei.it; booking service 8.30am-7pm Tue-Sun). Buy

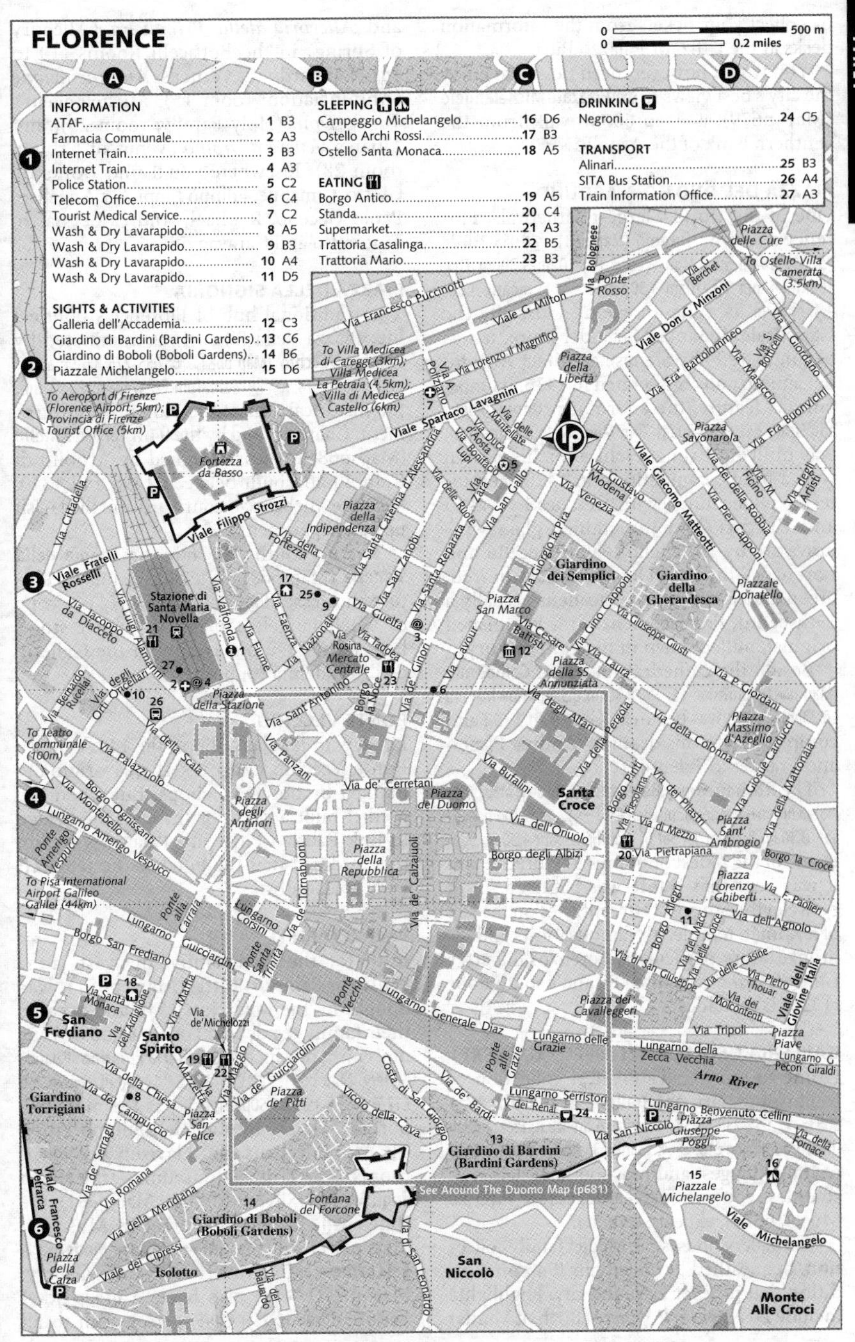
FLORENCE
0 500 m
0 0.2 miles
A
B
C
D
1
2
3
4
5
6
INFORMATION
ATAF 1 B3
Farmacia Communale 2 A3
Internet Train 3 B3
Internet Train 4 A3
Police Station 5 C2
Telecom Office 6 C4
Tourist Medical Service 7 C2
Wash & Dry Lavarapido 8 A5
Wash & Dry Lavarapido 9 B3
Wash & Dry Lavarapido 10 A4
Wash & Dry Lavarapido 11 D5
SIGHTS & ACTIVITIES
Galleria dell'Accademia 12 C3
Giardino di Bardini (Bardini Gardens) 13 C6
Giardino di Boboli (Boboli Gardens) 14 B6
Piazzale Michelangelo 15 D6
SLEEPING
Campeggio Michelangelo 16 D6
Ostello Archi Rossi 17 B3
Ostello Santa Monaca 18 A5
EATING
Borgo Antico 19 A5
Standa 20 C4
Supermarket 21 A3
Trattoria Casalinga 22 B5
Trattoria Mario 23 B3
DRINKING
Negroni 24 C5
TRANSPORT
Alinari 25 B3
SITA Bus Station 26 A4
Train Information Office 27 A3
To Aeroport di Firenze (Florence Airport; 5km); Provincia di Firenze Tourist Office (5km)
To Villa Medicea di Careggi (3km); Villa Medicea La Petraia (4.5km); Villa di Medicea Castello (6km)
To Ostello Villa Camerata (3.5km)
To Teatro Communale (100m)
To Pisa International Airport Galileo Galilei (44km)
Fortezza da Basso
Viale Filippo Strozzi
Viale Spartaco Lavagnini
Viale Fratelli Rosselli
Stazione di Santa Maria Novella
Piazza della Stazione
Piazza della Indipendenza
Piazza della Libertà
Piazza delle Cure
Piazza Savonarola
Viale Giacomo Matteotti
Viale Don G Minzoni
Giardino dei Semplici
Giardino della Gherardesca
Piazzale Donatello
Piazza San Marco
Piazza della SS Annunziata
Mercato Centrale
Piazza Massimo d'Azeglio
Piazza del Duomo
Piazza degli Antinori
Piazza della Repubblica
Santa Croce
Piazza Sant' Ambrogio
Piazza Lorenzo Ghiberti
Piazza dei Cavalleggeri
Piazza Piave
Arno River
Ponte Amerigo Vespucci
Ponte alla Carraia
Ponte Santa Trinità
Ponte Vecchio
Ponte alle Grazie
Lungarno Generale Diaz
Lungarno delle Grazie
Lungarno della Zecca Vecchia
Lungarno Serristori
Lungarno Benyenuto Cellini
Piazza Giuseppe Poggi
San Frediano
Santo Spirito
Piazza de' Pitti
Piazza San Felice
Giardino Torrigiani
Giardino di Bardini (Bardini Gardens)
Giardino di Boboli (Boboli Gardens)
Fontana del Forcone
Isolotto
San Niccolò
Piazzale Michelangelo
Viale Michelangelo
Piazza della Calza
Viale Francesco Petrarca
Monte Alle Croci
See Around The Duomo Map (p681)

or collect your tickets from the information desks at the Uffizi or Palazzo Pitti.

You won't, however, need tickets to enjoy the city's best views from **Piazzale Michelangelo** (Map p679), a steep 600m walk from the southern bank of the Arno River.

PIAZZA DEL DUOMO & AROUND

One of the world's largest cathedrals, Florence's Gothic **Duomo** (Map p681; ☎ 055 230 28 85; 🕑 10am-5pm Mon-Wed & Fri, 10am-3.30pm Thu, 10am-4.45pm Sat, 10am-3.30pm 1st Sat of month, 1.30-4.45pm Sun) is quite an eyeful. Officially the Cattedrale di Santa Maria del Fiore, it was begun in 1294 by Sienese architect Arnolfo di Cambio and consecrated in 1436. Its most famous feature, the enormous **cupola** (dome; admission €6; 🕑 8.30am-7pm Mon-Fri, to 5.40pm Sat), was built by Brunelleschi after his design won a public competition in 1420. The interior is decorated with frescoes by Vasari and Zuccari, and the stained-glass windows are by Donatello, Paolo Uccello and Lorenzo Ghiberti. The characteristic red, green and white marble facade is actually a 19th-century replacement of the unfinished original, pulled down in the 16th century.

Beside the cathedral, the 82m **Campanile** (Map p681; admission €6; 🕑 8.30am-6.50pm Nov-May, to 10.20pm Jun-Oct) was begun by Giotto in 1334 and completed after his death by Andrea Pisano and Francesco Talenti.

The Romanesque **Battistero** (baptistry; Map p681; Piazza di San Giovanni; admission €3; 🕑 12.15-6.30pm Mon-Sat, 8.30am-1.30pm 1st Sat of month, 8.30am-1.30pm Sun) is one of the oldest buildings in Florence and it was here that Dante was baptised. Built between the 5th and 11th centuries on the site of a Roman temple, it's famous for its gilded-bronze doors, particularly Lorenzo Ghiberti's *Gate of Paradise*. Andrea Pisano's south door (1336) is the oldest.

GALLERIA DEGLI UFFIZI (UFFIZI GALLERY)

Home to the world's greatest collection of Renaissance art, the **Galleria degli Uffizi** (Map p681; ☎ 055 238 86 51; www.uffizi.firenze.it; Piazza degli Uffizi 6; admission €10; 🕑 8.15am-6.35pm Tue-Sun) is one of Italy's biggest and most popular galleries, so unless you've booked a ticket (see Firenze Musei, p678), expect to queue.

The gallery houses the Medici family collection, bequeathed to the city in 1743 on condition that it never leave the city. Highlights include *La Nascita di Venere* (Birth of Venus) and *Allegoria della Primavera* (Allegory of Spring) in the Botticelli Rooms (10 to 14); Leonardo da Vinci's *Annunciazione* (Annunciation; room 15); Michelangelo's *Tondo Doni* (Holy Family; room 25); and Titian's *Venere d'Urbino* (Venus of Urbino; room 28). Elsewhere you'll find works by Giotto, Cimabue, Filippo Lippi, Fra Angelico, Paolo Uccello, Raphael, Andrea del Sarto, Tintoretto and Caravaggio.

PIAZZA DELLA SIGNORIA

The traditional hub of Florence's political life, Piazza della Signoria is dominated by **Palazzo Vecchio** (Map p681; ☎ 055 276 82 24; adult/concession €6/4.50; 🕑 9am-7pm Fri-Wed, to 2pm Thu), the historical seat of the Florentine government. Characterised by the 94m **Torre d'Arnolfo** (Map p681), it was designed by Arnolfo di Cambio and built between 1298 and 1340. Visit the Michelozzo courtyard and the lavish upstairs apartments.

To the south, the famous **Loggia della Signoria** (Map p681) is a 14th-century sculpture showcase. The statue of *David* is a copy of Michelangelo's original, which stood here until 1873 but is now in the Galleria dell'Accademia (opposite).

PONTE VECCHIO

Lined with jewellery shops, the 14th-century Ponte Vecchio (Map p681) was originally flanked by butchers' shops. But when the Medici built a corridor through the bridge to link Palazzo Pitti with Palazzo Vecchio, they ordered that the butchers be replaced with goldsmiths.

PALAZZO PITTI

Built for the Pitti family, the vast 15th-century Palazzo Pitti (Map p681) was bought by the Medici in 1549 and became their family residence. Today it houses four museums, of which the **Galleria Palatina** (Palatine Gallery; Map p681; ☎ 055 238 86 14; adult/concession €12/6; 🕑 8.15am-6.50pm Tue-Sun) is the most important. Works by Raphael, Filippo Lippi, Titian and Rubens adorn lavishly decorated rooms. Three other museums – the **Museo degli Argenti** (Silver Museum; Map p681), the **Museo delle Porcellane** (Porcelain Museum; Map p681) and the **Galleria d'Arte Moderna & del Costume** (Modern Art & Costume Gallery; Map p681) – are also here. A **group ticket** (adult/EU citizen 18-25yr €10/5) gets you in to all

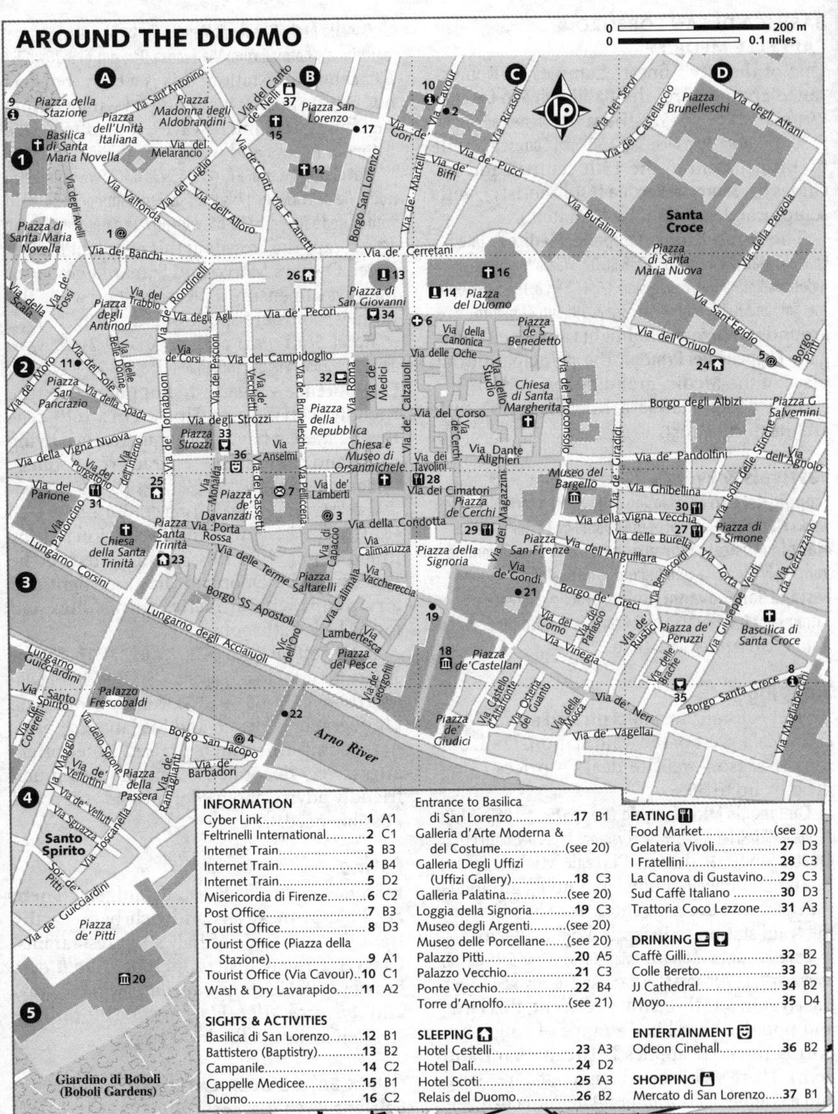

three as well as the Renaissance **Giardino di Boboli** (Boboli Gardens; Map p679) and **Giardino Bardini** (Bardini Gardens; Map p679). All sights covered by the ticket are open from 8.15am to 7.30pm between June and August, to 6.30pm from March to May and in September, to 5.30pm in October, and to 4.30pm in November and February.

GALLERIA DELL'ACCADEMIA

The **Galleria dell'Accademia** (Map p679; ☎ 055 238 86 09; Via Ricasoli 60; adult/concession €6.50/3.25; ⏰ 8.15am-6.50pm Tue-Sun) is where you'll find *David*, arguably the Western world's most famous sculpture. Michelangelo carved the giant figure from a single block of marble, finishing it in 1504 when he was just 29.

BASILICA DI SAN LORENZO & CAPPELLE MEDICEE

One of the city's finest examples of Renaissance architecture, the **Basilica di San Lorenzo** (Map p681; ☎ 055 264 51 84; Piazza San Lorenzo; admission €2.50; ⏲ 10am-5pm Mon-Sat, 1.30-5pm Sun) was built by Brunelleschi in the 15th century and includes his **Sagrestia Vecchia** (Old Sacristy), with sculptural decoration by Donatello.

The sumptuous **Cappelle Medicee** (Medici Chapels; Map p681; ☎ 055 238 86 02; Piazza Madonna degli Aldobrandini; adult/concession €6/4; ⏲ 8.15am-5.50pm Tue-Sat, 2nd & 4th Mon & 1st, 3rd & 5th Sun of month) are around the corner. Highlights are the extravagant **Cappella dei Principi**, the principal burial place of the Medici grand dukes, and the incomplete **Sagrestia Nuova**, Michelangelo's first architectural effort.

Festivals & Events

Scoppio del Carro (Explosion of the Cart) A cart full of fireworks is exploded in front of the Duomo on Easter Sunday.

Maggio Musicale Fiorentino (www.maggiofiorentino.com) Italy's longest-running music festival; April to June.

Festa di San Giovanni (Feast of St John) Florence's patron saint is celebrated on 24 June with costumed soccer matches on Piazza di Santa Croce.

Sleeping

Budget *pensioni* are concentrated around Via della Scala, west of the train station. Look out for off-season website deals – prices often drop by up to 50%.

Campeggio Michelangelo (Map p679; ☎ 055 681 19 77; Viale Michelangelo 80; www.ecvacanze.it; per person/tent/car €10.30/5.50/5.50; Ⓟ) Just off Piazzale Michelangelo, this large and well-equipped camping ground is the nearest to the city centre. Take bus 12 from the train station to Piazzale Michelangelo.

Ostello Santa Monaca (Map p679; ☎ 055 26 83 38; www.ostello.it; Via Santa Monaca 6; dm €16-20; 💻) Over the river in a 15th-century convent, this large and popular hostel has a range of single-sex dorms (lockout applies between 10am and 2pm). There's a kitchen, launderette, free wi-fi and a couple of computers. The 2am curfew is enforced and breakfast isn't included.

Ostello Villa Camerata (Map p679; ☎ 055 60 14 51; www.ostellofirenze.it; Viale Augusto Righi 2-4; dm €17.50-20; 💻) Housed in a beautiful 17th-century villa 5km northeast of the train station, Florence's HI hostel has 322 beds in various room combinations. Take bus 17A or 17B from the train station. Reservations are essential in summer.

Ostello Archi Rossi (off Map p679; ☎ 055 29 08 04; ostelloarchirossi@hotmail.com; Via Faenza 94r; dm €20-26; 💻) Near the train station, this is a busy, boisterous private hostel. It's equipped with washing machines and microwaves, and offers free internet access and walking tours.

Hotel Dalì (Map p681; ☎ 055 234 07 06; www.hoteldali.com; Via dell'Oriuolo 17; s with shared bathroom €34-40, d with shared bathroom €56-65, with private bathroom €68-80; Ⓟ) Escape the crowds at this excellent budget hotel. Owners Marco and Samanta go out of their way to ensure a pleasant stay, while the homey rooms are spotless and sunny.

Hotel Scoti (Map p681; ☎ 055 29 21 28; www.hotelscoti.com; Via de' Tornabuoni 7; s €45-75, d €75-125) On Florence's smartest shopping strip, the friendly Scoti is a gem. Housed in a 16th-century *palazzo*, it has an amazing frescoed living room and comfortable, characterful rooms.

Relais del Duomo (Map p681; ⏲ 055 21 01 47; www.relaisdelduomo.it, in Italian; Piazza dell'Olio 2; s €50-80, d €60-120; ❄ 💻) Florentine B&Bs don't come much better than this one. Located in the shadow of the Duomo, it has four light and airy rooms with attractive furnishings and lovely little bathrooms.

Hotel Cestelli (Map p681; ☎ 055 21 42 13; www.hotelcestelli.com; Borgo SS Apostoli 25; s with shared bathroom €60-80, d €50-115; Ⓟ ❄) Run by Florentine photographer Alessio and his Japanese partner Asumi, this much-praised hotel offers attractively decorated rooms and as much friendly advice about Florence as you could possibly need.

Eating

Florence caters well to all budgets. There are hole-in-the-wall sandwich bars, earthy trattorias and some of Italy's top restaurants. Classic Tuscan dishes include *ribollita*, a heavy vegetable soup, *canellini* (white beans) and *bistecca alla Fiorentina* (Florentine steak). Chianti is the local tipple.

QUICK EATS & SELF-CATERING

Gelateria Vivoli (Map p681; ☎ 055 29 23 34; Via Isola delle Stinche 7; ⏲ closed Mon & mid Aug) Ice-cream aficionados rate the gelati here the city's best. No cones, just a fabulous array of fresh flavours served in cups.

I Fratellini (Map p681; ☎ 055 239 60 96; Via dei Cimatori 38r; panini €2-3; ⏲ 8am-8pm, closed Sat & Sun Jul & Aug) Although no more than a hole-in-the-wall *panino* bar, I Fratellini is a city institution. Locals flock to its tiny counter for fresh-filled *panini* chased down with a glass of robust red wine.

Fresh produce is available at the central **food market** (Map p681; Piazza San Lorenzo; ⌚ 7am-2pm Mon-Sat). Alternatively, there's a **supermarket** (Map p679; Stazione di Santa Maria Novella) at the train station, and a **Standa** (Map p679; Via Pietrapiana 94) east of Piazza del Duomo.

RESTAURANTS

Borgo Antico (Map p679; ☎ 055 21 04 37; Piazza Santo Spirito 6r; pizzas €7-10, meals €25) On a vibrant piazza, this trendy eatery is great for whiling away a summer evening over a pizza and glass of something cool. Select from the menu of leafy salads, wood-fired pizzas and Tuscan specialities.

Sud Caffè Italiano (Map p681; ☎ 055 28 93 68; Via della Vigna Vecchia; pizza €9.50, pasta €8-10.50; ⌚ closed Sun & Mon) An ode to southern Italian casual chic, this place is perfect for a simple meal of pasta or pizza washed down by your choice from an impressive wine list.

Trattoria Casalinga (Map p679; ☎ 055 21 86 24; Via de' Michelozzi 9r; meals €15; ⌚ closed Sun) If you're after a filling meal at rock-bottom prices, look no further. Family-run and refreshingly unpretentious, it's always full of locals.

Trattoria Mario (Map p679; Via Rosina 2r; meals €18; ⌚ lunch Mon-Sat) Lunch at Mario's is fun, filling and frenetic. A noisy, cheerful place full of market workers and tourists, it serves hearty pastas and meaty main courses at keen prices.

La Canova do Gustavino (Map p681; ☎ 055 239 98 06; Via della Condotta 29r; meals €20) There aren't too many opportunities to enjoy a delicious cheap meal in stylish surrounds in Florence, which is why this friendly *enoteca* is such a find. Crunchy bruschetta, hearty soups and excellent pasta dishes are constant features on the small menu.

Trattoria Coco Lezzone (Map p681; ☎ 055 28 71 78; Vai Parioncino 26r; meals €25; ⌚ closed Sun) The name means 'the slovenly chef', but there's nothing slovenly about this Florentine institution. Classic Tuscan fare such as *ribollita, arista di maiale* (roasted pork loin) and *papa al pomodoro* (tomato and bread soup) take centre stage. No credit cards and no coffee.

Drinking

Colle Bereto (Map p681; ☎ 055 28 31 56; Piazza degli Strozzi 5r) Slip into something Dolce & Gabbana and join the fashionistas at this glam bar. It's known for excellent cocktails and a lavish *aperitivo* spread.

Caffè Gilli (Map p681; ☎ 055 21 38 96; Piazza della Repubblica 39r; ⌚ closed Mon & Tue) Save yourself an arm and a leg by standing at the art nouveau bar at this, Florence's grandest cafe.

JJ Cathedral (Map p681; ☎ 055 265 68 92; Piazza di San Giovanni 4r) JJ's is a magnet for vacationing foreign students, who come here to swill beer and admire the views of the Duomo. Try to snaffle the upstairs balcony table.

Moyo (Map p681; ☎ 055 247 97 38; Via de' Benci 23r) A mixed crowd of young locals and foreign students drink at this funky modern bar. It's good for coffee and free wi-fi during the day, drinks and upbeat music at night.

Negroni (Map p679; ☎ 055 24 36 47; Via dei Renai 17r) The famous Florentine cocktail gives its name to this popular bar in the trendy San Nicolò district. It's known for its art exhibitions, excellent *aperitivo* spread and cheap lunch buffet.

Entertainment

Florence's definitive monthly listings guide *Firenze Spettacolo* is sold at newsstands (€1.80).

Concerts, opera and dance are performed year-round at the **Teatro Comunale** (off Map p679; ☎ 800 11 22 11; Corso Italia 16), which is also the venue for events organised by the Maggio Musicale Fiorentino (opposite).

English-language films are screened at the **Odeon Cinehall** (Map p681; ☎ 055 21 40 68; www.cinehall.it, in Italian; Via Sassetti 1; tickets €7.50).

Shopping

Shopping is concentrated between the Duomo and the Arno. Just north of the Duomo, **Mercato di San Lorenzo** (Map p681; Piazza San Lorenzo; ⌚ Tue-Sun) is the place for leather goods, clothing and jewellery, although quality and prices vary.

Getting There & Away

The main airport serving Florence is Pisa's **Galileo Galilei airport** (PSA; off Map p679; ☎ 050 84 93 00; www.pisa-airport.com). There's also a small city airport 5km north of Florence, **Aeroporto di Firenze** (Aeroporto Vespucci; FLR; off Map p679; ☎ 055 306 13 00; www.aeroporto.firenze.it).

From the **SITA bus station** (Map p679; ☎ 800 37 37 60; www.sita-on-line-it, in Italian; Via Santa Caterina da Siena 17), buses leave for Siena (€6.80, 1½ hours, every 30 to 60 minutes) and San Gimignano (€6, 1¼ hours, 14 daily).

There are regular trains to/from Pisa (Regional €5.60, 1¼ hours, every 10 to 30 minutes), Rome (Eurostar AV, €36.10, one hour 40 minutes, hourly), Bologna (Eurostar AV, €16.20, one hour, hourly), Venice (Eurostar €32.30, 2¾ hours, 10 daily) and Milan (Eurostar AV, €39.90, two hours 10 minutes, hourly). Check times at the **train information office** (Map p679; ☎ 7am-9pm) in the station's main foyer.

Getting Around

ATAF (☎ 800 42 45 00; www.ataf.net) buses service the city centre. The most useful terminal is just outside the train station's eastern exit (see Map p679). Take bus 12 or 13 for Piazzale Michelangelo. Tickets (70 minute/24 hour €1.20/5) are sold at tobacconists and newsstands; you can also buy a 70-minute ticket on board the bus (€2).

Alinari (Map p679; ☎ 055 28 05 00; www.alinarirental.com; Via San Zanobi 38r; 9.30am-1pm & 2.45-6pm Mon-Sat, 10am-1pm Sun) rents out bikes for €7/12/24 per five hours/day/weekend and scooters for €35/55/125.

PISA

pop 87,200

One of Italy's most recognisable monuments, the Leaning Tower of Pisa (Torre Pendente) is a genuinely astonishing sight. Tower aside, Pisa is an unassuming university town that while pleasant enough, won't claim your attention for long.

Pisa's heyday came in the 12th and 13th centuries when it was a maritime power rivalling Genoa and Venice. It was eventually defeated by the Genoese in 1284 and, in 1406, fell to Florence. Under the Medici, the arts and sciences flourished and Galileo Galilei (1564–1642) taught at the university.

Orientation & Information

From Piazza Vittorio Emanuele II, just north of the train station, the Leaning Tower is a straightforward 1.5km walk: follow Corso Italia to the Arno, cross the river and continue down Borgo Stretto. At the end of Via G Carducci, bear left down Via Cardinale Pietro Maffi. You could also take bus 3 or shuttle A from the train station.

For city information, check www.pisaturismo.it or ask at one of the three **tourist offices** Airport (☎ 050 50 37 00; noon-10pm); City Centre (☎ 050 4 22 91; Piazza Vittorio Emanuele II 16; 9am-7pm Mon-Fri, to 1.30pm Sat); Leaning Tower (☎ 050 56 04 64; Piazza del Duomo 1; 10am-7pm).

Go online at **Internet Planet** (☎ 050 83 07 02; Piazza Cavallotti 3-4; per hr €3.50; 9am-midnight Mon-Fri, 10am-10pm Sat & Sun).

Sights & Activities

Undoubtedly one of the world's most beautiful squares, the **Campo dei Miracoli** (Field of Miracles) is home to Pisa's main sights: the cathedral, baptistry and Leaning Tower. Depressingly, it's also full of hawkers. You can purchase group tickets for the sights (not including the Leaning Tower); these cost €6 for the cathedral and baptistry and €10 for the cathedral, baptistry and cemetery.

The centrepiece of the Campo's Romanesque trio, the 11th-century candy-striped **cathedral** (☎ 050 56 09 21; admission €2; 10am-1pm & 2-5pm Nov-Feb, 10am-10pm Apr-Sep, to 7pm Oct, 6pm Mar) has a graceful tiered facade and cavernous interior.

To the west, the cupcake **battistero** (baptistry; admission €5; 10am-5pm Nov-Feb, 9am-6pm Mar, 8am-8pm Apr-Sep, 9am-7pm Oct) was started in 1153 and completed by Nicola and Giovanni Pisano in 1260.

But it's the campanile, better known as the **Leaning Tower** (Torre Pendente; www.opapisa.it; admission €15 plus booking fee €2; 10am-7pm Nov-Feb, 9am-6pm Mar, 8.30am-8.30pm Apr-Sep, 9am-7pm Oct), that's the big draw. Bonanno Pisano began building in 1173, but almost immediately his plans came a cropper in a layer of shifting soil. Only three of the tower's seven tiers were completed before it started tilting – continuing at a rate of about 1mm per year. By 1990 the lean had reached 5.5 degrees – beyond the critical point established by computer models. Stability was only ensured in 1998 when a combination of biased weighting and soil drilling forced the tower into a safer position. Today it's almost 4.1m off the perpendicular.

GETTING INTO TOWN

From Galileo Galilei airport regular trains (€1.10, five minutes, 15 daily) run to the city centre. Alternatively, take bus 1 (€0.95, 10 minutes, every 10 minutes) which drops you off at the train station.

Visits are limited to groups of 30; entry times are staggered and queuing is predictably inevitable. It is wise to book ahead. Note also that entry times change frequently; call ☎ 050 387 22 10 or log onto www.opapisa.it for confirmation.

Sleeping & Eating

Camping Torre Pendente (☎ 050 56 17 04; Via delle Cascine 86; www.campingtorrependente.it; per person/tent €8.50/12.50) Just under a kilometre from the Leaning Tower, this is a functional camping ground with decent facilities, including a supermarket, restaurant and small pool.

Hotel Francesco (☎ 050 55 54 53; www.hotelfrancesco.com; Via Santa Maria 129; r €70-150;) The best of the hotels lining busy Via Santa Maria (just off Campo dei Miracoli), the family-run Francesco offers a warm welcome and bright, mod-conned rooms. It also hires out bikes (€10 per day).

Caffetteria Betsabea (Piazza Dante Alighieri 7; pastas about €7; 7.30am-7.30pm Mon-Sat) This modest cafe does brisk business feeding students from the nearby political-science faculty. Choose from pastas, *panini*, and meal-sized salads.

Trattoria della Faggiola (☎ 050 55 61 79; Via della Faggiola 1; meals €20; lunch Mon-Thu, lunch & dinner Fri & Sat) This much-loved local eatery offers a limited menu of well-cooked, seasonal specialities.

Getting There & Away

The city's **Galileo Galilei airport** (PSA; ☎ 050 50 07 07; www.pisa-airport.com) is linked to the centre by train and bus (see opposite).

VAI (☎ 050 462 88; www.lazzi.it, in Italian) buses depart from the airport to Florence (€7.80, two hours, hourly) via Lucca. **Train SpA** (www.trainspa.it) buses go to Siena (€14, two daily).

Regular trains run to Florence (Regional €5.60, 1¼ hours, every 10 to 30 minutes), Rome (Regional €17.15, four hours, five daily) and Genoa (€15, two hours, half-hourly).

SIENA

pop 53,900

Famous for its crazy horse race (Il Palio), Siena is one of Italy's most enchanting medieval towns. Its walled centre, a beautifully preserved warren of dark lanes punctuated by Gothic *palazzi*, piazzas and eye-catching churches, is a lovely place to get lost. The action centres on Piazza del Campo (known as Il Campo), the sloping scallop that serves as a communal sunbed to scores of day trippers.

According to legend, Siena was founded by the sons of Remus, although it was the Middle Ages that heralded the city's golden age. Between the 13th and 15th centuries, painters of the Sienese School produced significant works of art, and Sts Catherine and Benedict called Siena home.

Orientation

The centre's main streets – the Banchi di Sopra, Via di Città and Banchi di Sotto – curve around Il Campo.

Information

Internet Train (Via di Città 121 & Via di Pantaneto 57; per hr €4; 10am-10pm)
Left Luggage (per day €5.50) At the bus station.
Police station (Questura; ☎ 0577 20 11 11; Via del Castoro 23)
Tourist office (☎ 0577 28 05 51; www.terresiena.it; Piazza del Campo 56; 9am-7pm)
Wash & Dry (Via di Pantaneto 38; 8am-10pm)

Sights & Activities

Ever since the 14th century, **Piazza del Campo** has been the city's focus. Forming the base of the piazza, the **Palazzo Pubblico** (or Palazzo Comunale) is a magnificent example of Sienese Gothic architecture. Inside, the **Museo Civico** (☎ 0577 29 26 14; adult/concession €7.50/4.50; 10am-7pm mid-Mar–end Oct, to 6pm Nov–mid-Mar) houses some extraordinary frescoes. Soaring above the *palazzo* is the 102m **Torre del Mangia** (admission €7; 10am-7pm mid-Mar–end Oct, to 4pm Nov–mid-Mar), which dates from 1297. A combined ticket to the two costs €12 and is only available at the Torre del Mangia ticket office.

The spectacular **Duomo** (☎ 0577 473 21; Piazza del Duomo; admission €3; 10.30am-7.30pm Mon-Sat, 1.30-5.30pm Sun Mar-end May, 10.30am-8pm Mon-Sat, 1.30-6.30pm Sun Jun-end Aug, 10.30am-7.30pm daily Sep-end Oct, 10.30am-6pm Mon-Sat Nov-end Feb) is another Gothic masterpiece. Begun in 1196, it was completed

GETTING INTO TOWN

From the train station take bus 8, 9 or 10 (€0.95) to Piazza Gramsci, from where Il Campo is a short, signposted walk away. From the bus station it's a 10-minute walk up Via La Lizza and Via delle Terme.

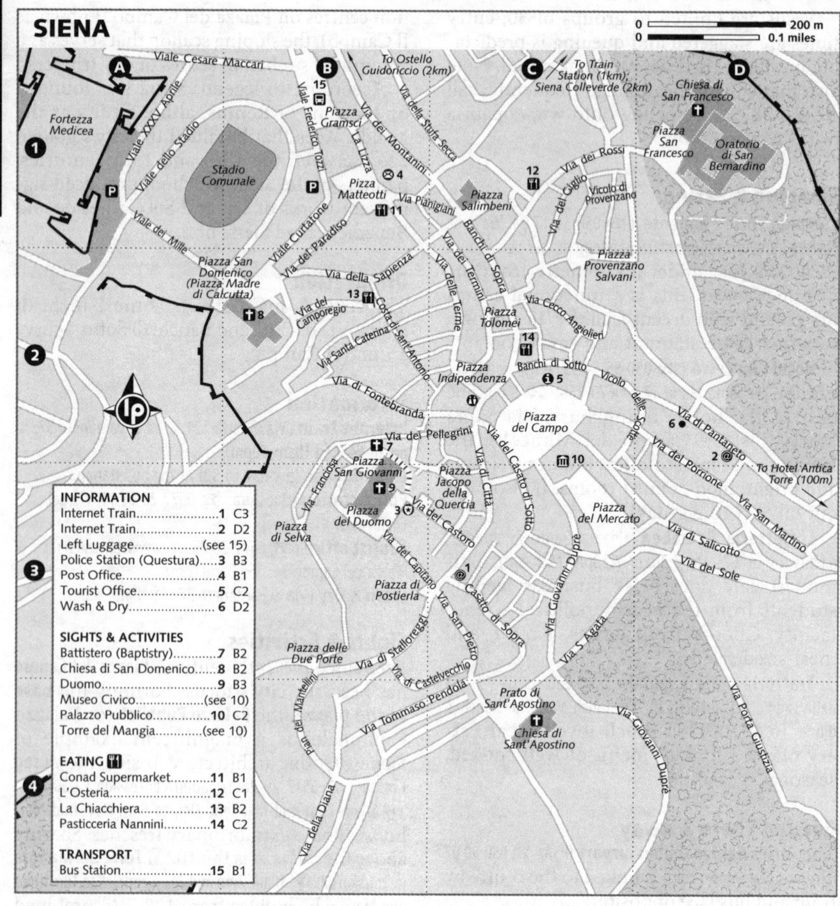

in 1215, although work continued well into the 13th century. Inside, it's the 14th-century **inlaid-marble floor** (floor viewing €6; 10.30am-7.30pm mid-Aug–late Oct) that's the highlight. Other noteworthy features include Donatello's bronze of St John the Baptist, and statues of St Jerome and Mary Magdalene by Bernini.

Behind the cathedral and down a flight of stairs, the **battistero** (baptistry; Piazza San Giovanni; admission €3; 9.30am-8pm Mar-Sep, to 7.30pm Oct, 10am-5pm Nov-Feb) has a Gothic facade and a rich frescoed interior.

On the western edge of the walled city, the **Chiesa di San Domenico** (Piazza San Domenico 1; admission free; 7.30am-1pm & 3-6.30pm) is the last resting place of St Catherine's head and thumb.

Festivals & Events

Siena's great annual event is the **Palio** (2 July and 16 August), a pageant culminating in a bareback horse race round Il Campo. The city is divided into 17 *contrade* (districts), of which 10 are chosen annually to compete for the *palio* (silk banner). The only rule in the three-lap race is that jockeys can't tug the reins of other horses.

Sleeping

Booking is essential for August and the Palio.

Colleverde Camping Ground (0577 33 25 45; www.campingcolleverde.com; Strada di Scacciapensieri 47; per person/tent/car €9/5.50/5.50; Mar-mid Oct;) Some 2.5km north of the historic centre (1.5km from the train station), this is

ITALY

WORTH THE TRIP: SAN GIMIGNANO

Dubbed the medieval Manhattan, San Gimignano is a tiny hilltop town deep in the Tuscan countryside. A mecca for day trippers from Florence and Siena, it owes its nickname to the 11th-century towers that soar above its pristine *centro storico*. To avoid the worst of the crowds try to visit midweek, preferably in deep winter.

The **tourist office** (☎ 0577 94 00 08; www.sangimignano.com; Piazza del Duomo 1; 🕑 9am-1pm & 3-7pm Mar-Oct, 9am-1pm & 2-6pm Nov-Feb) is a short walk from the bus stops on Piazza dei Martiri di Montemaggio. On the southern edge of Piazza del Duomo, the **Palazzo Comunale** (☎ 0577 99 03 12; Piazza del Duomo; admission €5; 🕑 9.30am-7pm Mar-Oct, 10am-5.30pm Nov-Feb) houses San Gimignano's art gallery (the **Pinacoteca**) and tallest tower, the **Torre Grossa**.

Regular buses link San Gimignano with Florence (€6, 1¼ hours, 14 daily) and Siena (€5.30, 1¼ hours, hourly). Most require a change at Poggibonsi.

a well set-up camping ground in the hills outside of town. Take bus 3 (€0.80) from Piazza Gramsci.

Ostello Guidoriccio (☎ 0577 522 12; siena@ostellionline.org; Via Fiorentina 89; per person €14.45; P 💻) An inconvenient 20-minute bus ride from the town centre, Siena's HI hostel has 46 neat but dark two-bed rooms and one single-sex eight-bed dorm. Take bus 10 or 15 from Piazza Gramsci, or 77 from the train station and tell the driver you're after the *ostello* (hostel).

Hotel Antica Torre (☎ 0577 22 22 55; www.anticatorresiena.it; Via di Fiera Vecchia 7; s €65-90, d €90-120; ❄) Three-star facilities meet two-star prices at this excellent choice. Eight pretty rooms with Tuscan-style decor are on offer in a restored 16th-century tower.

Eating

Pasticceria Nanini (☎ 0577 23 60 09; 24 Via Banchi di Sopra) For the finest *cenci* (fried sweet pastry), *panforte* (dense fruit-and-nut cake) and *ricciarelli* (almond biscuits) in town, you need go no further than this Sienese institution.

La Chiacchiera (☎ 0577 28 06 31; Costa di Sant'Antonio 4; meals €18) With its rustic wooden tables and stone walls, this is an atmospheric spot serving earthy, filling seasonal food. In summer, there's outdoor seating on a quiet pedestrian street.

L'Osteria (☎ 0577 28 75 92; Via dei Rossi 79-81; meals €25) Great food, big portions, no-nonsense red wine – the ideal recipe for a memorable meal. Service at L'Osteria is efficient and prices are right for this touristy neck of the woods.

For self-caterers, there's a handy **Conad supermarket** (☎ 0577 27 77 15; Piazza Matteotti 17) in the town centre.

Getting There & Away

Siena is not on a main train line so it's easier to take a bus. From the bus station on Piazza Gramsci, **Train SpA** (www.trainspa.it) and SITA buses run to/from Florence (€6.80, 1½ hours, every 30 to 60 minutes), Pisa airport (€14, two daily) and San Gimignano (€5.30, 1¼ hours, hourly), either direct or via Poggibonsi.

Sena (☎ 0577 28 32 03; www.sena.it) operates services to/from Rome (€18.50, three hours, 10 daily).

Both Train SpA and Sena have ticket offices underneath the piazza.

LUCCA

☎ 0583 / pop 82,300

Lucca is a love-at-first-sight type of place. Hidden behind monumental Renaissance walls, its historic centre is chock-full of handsome churches, excellent restaurants and tempting *pasticcerie* (pastry shops). Founded by the Etruscans, it became a city state in the 12th century and stayed that way for 600 years.

Get city information from one of the three **tourist offices** (☎ 0583 355 51 00; www.turislucca.com) Piazza Ducale (🕑 10am-1pm & 2-6pm Mon-Sat); Piazza Santa Maria (🕑 9am-8pm); Piazza Verdi (🕑 9am-7pm).

Sights

Lucca's 12m-high **city walls** were built around the old city in the 16th and 17th centuries and were once defended by 126 cannons. Today they are crowned by a wide, tree-lined footpath, accessible from Piazzale Verdi or Piazza Santa Maria.

The predominantly Romanesque **Cattedrale di San Martino** (☎ 0583 95 70 68; www.museocattedralelucca.it, in Italian; Piazza San Martino; 🕑 9.30am-5.45pm Mon-Fri, to 6.45pm Sat, 9-10.45am & noon-6pm Sun Mar-Oct,

9.30am-4.45pm Mon-Fri, to 6.45pm Sat, 11.20-11.50am & 1-4.45pm Sun Nov-Feb) dates to the 11th century. Inside, there's a magnificent *Last Supper* by Tintoretto.

Sleeping & Eating

Ostello San Frediano (☎ 0583 46 99 57; www.ostellolucca.it; Via della Cavellerizza 12; dm €18-19.50, d €50; P 💻) Comfort and service levels are high at this HI-affiliated hostel. There are 141 rooms, a bar and a restaurant. Breakfast costs €3.

Giurlani (☎ 0583 46 76 36; Via Fillungo 239) The best way to enjoy a Lucchese lunch is to picnic on the wall, particularly if you buy delectable provisions from this artisan produce shop.

Trattoria da Leo (☎ 0583 49 22 36; Via Tegrimi 1; meals €20; 🕑 Mon-Sat) A terrific trattoria greatly beloved of locals, da Leo serves delicious and well-priced meals. Choose from the colourful antipasto buffet (€8 per plate) or order a pasta, risotto or *secondo* from a large list.

Getting There & Away

From the bus station near Piazzale Guiseppe Verdi, buses run to/from Florence (€5, 80 minutes, hourly), Pisa airport (€2.80, 30 minutes, hourly Monday to Saturday and every two hours Sunday) and Pisa (€2.80, 30 minutes, half-hourly).

Regional trains run to/from Florence (€5, 1½ hours, hourly) and Pisa (€2.40, 30 minutes, half-hourly).

PERUGIA

pop 162,000

The lively student city of Perugia boasts a beautiful medieval centre and sweeping views of the Umbrian landscape. The presence of the University for Foreigners and a year-long calendar of cultural events, climaxing in the July Umbria Jazz Festival, ensure a buzz that's not always apparent in the region's rural hinterland.

Perugia has a bloody past. In the Middle Ages the Baglioni and Oddi families clashed, while later as a papal satellite the city fought with its neighbours. All the while art and culture thrived: Perugino and Raphael, his student, both worked here.

Orientation & Information

The historic centre is on top of the hill, the train station is at the bottom and the regional bus station, Piazza Partigiani, is halfway between the two. From Piazza Partigiani there are *scale mobili* (escalators) going up to Piazza Italia, where local buses terminate. From Piazza Italia, pedestrianised Corso Vannucci runs up to Piazza IV Novembre, the city's focal point. City maps are available at the **tourist office** (☎ 075 573 64 58; www.perugia.umbria2000.it; Piazza Matteotti 18; 🕑 8.30am-6.30pm).

To check your email try **Tempo Reale** (Via del Forno 17; per hr €1.50; 🕑 10am-11.30pm) in the historic centre.

> **GETTING INTO TOWN**
>
> From the train station, take bus G, R, TD or 24 (€1) to get up to the historic centre. Bus C leaves from outside the UPIM building opposite the station and goes to Piazza Cavallini, near the Duomo. From the intercity bus station on Piazza dei Partigiani, take the free *scala mobila* (escalator).

Sights

Flanking Piazza IV Novembre, the austere 14th-century **Duomo** (☎ 075 572 38 32; Piazza IV Novembre; 🕑 7am-12.30pm & 4-6.45pm Mon-Sat, 8am-12.45pm & 4-6.45pm Sun) has an unfinished two-tone facade and, inside, an altarpiece by Signorelli and sculptures by Duccio.

In the centre of the piazza, the stolid **Fontana Maggiore** was designed by Fra Bevignate and carved by Nicola and Giovanni Pisano between 1275 and 1278.

The 13th-century **Palazzo dei Priori** houses Perugia's best museums, including the **Galleria Nazionale dell'Umbria** (☎ 075 586 681; www.gallerianazionaleumbria.it; Corso Vannucci 19; adult/concession €6.50/3.25; 🕑 8.30am-7.30pm Tue-Sun), the collection of which contains works by local heroes Perugino and Pinturicchio. Close to the *palazzo*, the impressive **Nobile Collegio del Cambio** (Exchange Hall; ☎ 075 572 85 99; Corso Vannucci 25; adult/concession €4.50/2.60; 🕑 9am-12.30pm & 2.30-5.30pm Mon-Sat, 9am-1pm Sun) is home to impressive frescoes by Perugino.

Courses

The **Università per Stranieri** (University for Foreigners; ☎ 075 57 46 1; www.unistrapg.it; Piazza Fortebraccio 4) runs hundreds of courses in language, art, history, music and architecture.

Sleeping

Centro Internazionale per la Gioventù (☎ 075 572 28 80; www.ostello.perugia.it; Via Bontempi 13; dm €15, sheets €2; 🕑 closed mid-Dec–mid-Jan; 💻) A private hostel with decent four- to six-bed dorms, a frescoed TV room, a kitchen for guests' use and great views from the terrace. The lockout (10am to 4pm) and 1am curfew are strictly enforced. The price doesn't include breakfast.

Bed & Breakfast Spagnoli (☎ 075 573 51 27; www.perugiaonline.com/bbspagnoli; Via Cesare Caporali 17; s with shared bathroom €30-40, d with shared bathroom €45-60) The motto here is *semplice* (simple), and the three spacious rooms in this family home near Piazza Italia offer great value.

Primavera Mini Hotel (☎ 075 572 16 57; www.primaveraminihotel.com; Via Vincioli 8; s €42-65, d €65-75;) On the top floor of a 16th-century *palazzo,* this intimate two-star has spruce modern rooms decorated with understated style. Not all rooms have air-con, and breakfast costs an extra €3 to €6.

Eating

Don't leave town without trying Perugia's famous chocolate.

Caffè Morlacchi (☎ 075 572 17 60; Piazza Morlacchi 6/8; Mon-Sat) The local literati adore this effortlessly hip cafe. It has a laid-back vibe during the day, but revs up at night.

Pizzeria Mediterranea (☎ 075 572 13 22; Piazza Piccinino 11/12; pizzas €3.70-12; Wed-Mon) The wood-fired oven in the middle of the dining room is put to excellent use at this busy pizzeria. You can opt for a simple topping or lash out and order delectable *mozzarella di bufala* (fresh buffalo-milk mozzarella) to go on top for a small surcharge.

Ristorante dal Mi'Cocco (☎ 075 573 25 11; Corso Giuseppe Garibaldi 12; set menu €13; Tue-Sun) Loads of fun and long communal tables are on offer at this ebullient eatery. The three-course meals are dished up at set times – lunch 1pm, dinner 8.15pm – and change daily. It's wildly popular, so book ahead.

Self-caterers can shop at the **Coop supermarket** (Piazza Matteotti 15; 9am-8pm Mon-Sat) or, next door, at the **Covered Market** (7am-1.30pm Mon-Sat & 4.30-7.30pm Sat).

Getting There & Away

From the bus station on Piazza dei Partigiani, **Sulga** (☎ 800 09 96 61; www.sulga.it, in Italian) buses depart for Florence (€10.50, two hours, one daily) and Rome (€21, three hours, two daily), continuing onto Fiumicino airport (€21, four hours). **Sena** (☎ 800 93 09 60; www.sena.it, in Italian) serves Siena (€12, 1½ hours, three daily), while **APM** (☎ 800 51 21 41; www.apmperugia.it, in Italian) buses head up to Assisi (€3.10, one hour, 13 daily).

Regional trains connect with Rome (€10.50, 2¾ hours, 20 daily), Florence (€8.75, 2¼ hours, 14 daily) and Assisi (€2.05, 20 minutes, hourly).

ASSISI

pop 26,800

Seen from afar, the only clue to Assisi's importance is the imposing form of the Basilica di San Francesco jutting over the hillside. Thanks to St Francis, born here in 1182, this quaint medieval town is a major destination for millions of pilgrims.

The **tourist office** (☎ 075 81 25 34; www.assisi.umbria2000.it; Piazza del Comune 22; 8am-2pm & 3-6pm Mon-Sat, 10am-1pm Sun) can provide practical information.

Sights & Activities

Dress rules are applied rigidly at the main religious sights, so no shorts, miniskirts, low-cut dresses or tops. To book guided tours (in English) of the Basilica di San Francesco, email its **information office** (☎ 075 81 90 84; AssisiSanFrancesco@libero.it; Piazza San Francesco; 9am-noon & 2-5.30pm Mon-Sat).

The **Basilica di San Francesco** (www.sanfrancescoassisi.org; Piazza di San Francesco) comprises two churches. The **upper church** (8.30am-6.45pm Easter-Nov, to 5.45pm Nov-Easter) was damaged during a severe earthquake in 1997, but has since been restored to its former state. Built between 1230 and 1253 in the Italian Gothic style, it features superb frescoes by Giotto and works by Cimabue and Pietro Cavallini.

Downstairs in the dimly lit **lower church** (6am-6.45pm Easter-Nov, to 5.45pm Nov-Easter), constructed between 1228 and 1230, you'll find a series of colourful frescoes by Simone Martini, Cimabue and Pietro Lorenzetti. The crypt where St Francis is buried is below the church.

The 13th-century **Basilica di Santa Chiara** (☎ 075 81 22 82; Piazza Santa Chiara; 6.30am-noon & 2-7pm Apr-Oct, to 6pm Nov-Mar) contains the remains of St Clare, friend of St Francis and founder of the Order of Poor Clares.

Sleeping & Eating

You'll need to book ahead during peak times: Easter, August and September, and the Feast of St Francis (3 and 4 October).

Ostello della Pace (☎ 075 81 67 67; www.assisihostel.com; Via Valecchie 177; dm €16-18; 💻) In a pretty and quiet location between the train station and the old town, this family-run HI hostel offers a bar, restaurant, laundry room and bikes for hire.

Camere Santa Chiara (☎ 075 81 34 67; camere.santachiara@yahoo.it; Vicolo Sant'Antonio 1; s/d €50/60) This place has atmosphere and services in spades. There are only six rooms, but all are well equipped and one even has a private terrace.

Trattoria Pallotta (☎ 075 81 26 49; Vicolo della Volta Pinta 2; meals €25; 🕑 closed Tue) Duck under the frescoed Volta Pinta (Painted Vault) off Piazza del Comune to this brick-vaulted, wood-beamed trattoria. The menu is unapologetically local, featuring homemade *strangozzi* (like tagliatelle), roast pigeon and rabbit stew.

Getting There & Away

It is better to travel to Assisi by bus rather than train, as the train station is 4km from Assisi proper in Santa Maria degli Angeli. Buses arrive at and depart from Piazza Matteotti in the *centro storico*.

APM buses connect Assisi with Perugia (€3.10, one hour, 13 daily). Sulga operates buses to Rome (€17.50, three hours, two daily) and Florence (€12, 2½ hours, one daily).

If you arrive by train, a bus (Linea C, €1, half-hourly) runs between Piazza Matteotti and the station. Regional trains run to Perugia (€2.05, 20 minutes, hourly).

URBINO

pop 15,400

If you visit only one town in Le Marche, make it Urbino. It's a pain to get to, but as you wander its steep, Unesco-protected streets you'll be glad you made the effort. Birthplace of Raphael and Bramante, and a university town since 1564, it's still a bustling centre of culture and learning.

To get to the centre from the bus terminal on Borgo Mercatale, head up Via Mazzini or take the *ascensore* (lift) up to Via Garibaldi (€0.50).

Information and accommodation listings are available at the town's two **tourist offices** (☎ 0722 26 13; www.urbinoculturaturismo.it) Bus Terminus (🕑 9am-6pm Mon-Sat, to 1pm Sun); Centre (Via Puccinoti 35; 🕑 9am-1pm Mon, 9am-1pm & 3-6pm Tue-Sat, 9am-1pm Sun summer, closed Sun & Sat afternoon winter).

Urbino's centrepiece is the Renaissance **Palazzo Ducale** (☎ 0722 32 26 25; Piazza Duca Federico; adult/concession €8/4; 🕑 8.30am-7.15pm Tue-Sun, to 2pm Mon), designed by Laurana and completed in 1482. Inside, the **Galleria Nazionale delle Marche** features works by Raphael, Paolo Uccello, della Francesca and Verrocchio.

Right in the heart of the walled town, **Albergo Italia** (☎ 0722 27 01; www.albergo-italia-urbino.it; Corso Garibaldi 32; s €47-70, d €70-120; P ✇ 💻) has a bland modern interior offset by helpful staff, a pleasant garden terrace and comfortable rooms.

For a taste of local Marchigiani food, **La Trattoria del Leone** (☎ 0722 32 98 94; Via Cesare Battisti; meals €16-20; 🕑 dinner daily, lunch Sat & Sun) is an unassuming trattoria on the main square. There are well-priced set meals or you can order à la carte.

Trains don't run to Urbino. **Autolinee Ruocco** (☎ 800 90 15 91, 0975 790 33) runs a daily bus to Perugia (€13, 1¾ hours), for which it is essential to book in advance. **Autolinee Bucci** (☎ 0721 324 01; www.autolineebucci.com) runs two daily buses to Rome (€20.80, 4½ hours).

SOUTHERN ITALY

A sun-bleached land of spectacular coastlines, silent, windswept hills and proud towns, *il mezzogiorno* (the midday sun, as southern Italy is known) has a lot to offer. Centuries of foreign dominion have led to a fruitful fusion of architectural, artistic and culinary styles, evident throughout the area's four regions. Nature has done her bit too, dealing the area a dramatic topography that for centuries caused isolation and tribulation. It was only with the onset of 20th-century tourism that the Amalfi Coast, Matera and Sardinia began to escape grinding poverty.

NAPLES

pop 975,200

A raucous hell-broth of a city, Naples (Napoli) is loud, anarchic, dirty and edgy. Its Dickensian streets and in-your-face energy leave you disorientated, bewildered and hungry for more. Founded by Greek colonists, it became a thriving Roman city and was later the Bourbon capital of the Kingdom of the Two Sicilies. In the 18th century it was one of Europe's great cities, something you'll readily believe as you marvel at its imperious palaces. Many of Naples finest *palazzi* now house museums and art galleries, the best of

GETTING INTO TOWN

From Capodichino airport, you can either take the orange city bus 3S (€1.10, 30 minutes, half-hourly) to Piazza Garibaldi, or the Alibus airport shuttle (€3.10, 20 minutes, half-hourly) to Piazza Municipio or Stazione Centrale.

which is the Museo Archeologico Nazionale, one of Italy's premier museums and reason enough for a city stopover.

Orientation

A convenient point of reference is Stazione Centrale, which forms the eastern flank of Piazza Garibaldi, Naples' ugly transport hub. From Piazza Garibaldi, Corso Umberto I skirts the *centro storico,* which is centred on two parallel roads: Via San Biagio dei Librai and its continuation Via Benedetto Croce (together known as Spaccanapoli); and Via dei Tribunali. West of the *centro storico,* Via Toledo, Naples' main shopping strip, leads down to the city's grandest square, Piazza del Plebiscito.

Information

DISCOUNT CARDS

Campania ArteCard (☎ 800 600 601; www.campaniaartecard.it; 3 days Naples/3 days Campania/7 days Campania €13/25/28) Free or discounted admission to dozens of museums, plus free public transport. Available at train stations, newsagents, participating museums, online, or through the call centre.

EMERGENCY

Police station (Questura; ☎ 081 794 11 11; Via Medina 75)

INTERNET ACCESS

Navig@ndo (Via Santa Anna di Lombardi 28; per hr €2; 🕑 9am-8.30pm Mon-Fri, to 2pm Sat)

LEFT LUGGAGE

Stazione Centrale (1st 5 hours €3.80, 6-12 hours per hr €0.60, 13 hours & over per hr €0.20; 🕑 7am-11pm)

MEDICAL SERVICES

Ospedale Loreto-Mare (Hospital; ☎ 081 20 10 33; Via Amerigo Vespucci 26) On the waterfront, near the train station.

Pharmacy (☎ 081 26 88 81; Stazione Centrale; 🕑 7am-9.30pm) At the main train station.

TOURIST INFORMATION

Pick up a copy of *Qui Napoli,* a useful bilingual monthly publication with details of sights, transport, accommodation, and major events.

Tourist office Piazza del Gesù Nuovo 7 (☎ 081 552 33 28; www.inaples.it; 🕑 9.30am-1.30pm & 2.30-6pm Mon-Sat, 9am-1.30pm Sun); Stazione Centrale (☎ 081 20 66 66; main concourse; 🕑 9am-7pm); Via San Carlo 9 (☎ 081 40 23 94; opposite Teatro San Carlo; 🕑 9.30am-1.30pm & 2.30-6pm Mon-Sat, 9am-1.30pm Sun)

Dangers & Annoyances

Despite Naples' notoriety as a mafia hot spot, the city is pretty safe. That said, you should be careful about walking alone late at night near Stazione Centrale and Piazza Dante.

Petty crime is widespread. Be especially vigilant for pickpockets and moped bandits, many of whom target out-of-towners with expensive watches. And never ever buy electronic gear on Piazza Garibaldi – you'll be ripped off.

Sights

CENTRO STORICO & AROUND

Be sure to visit the **Museo Archeologico Nazionale** (☎ 081 442 21 49; Piazza Museo Nazionale 19; adult/concession €6.50/3.25; 🕑 9am-7.30pm Wed-Mon), home to one of the world's most important collections of Graeco-Roman antiquities. Highlights include the colossal *Toro Farnese* (Farnese Bull), *Ercole* (Hercules) and, on the mezzanine floor, *La Battaglia di Alessandro Contro Dario* (The Battle of Alexander against Darius), one of many awe-inspiring mosaics from Pompeii. On the same floor, the **Gabinetto Segreto** (Secret Room) boasts some majestic phalluses.

A short walk south of the museum, Piazza del Gesù Nuovo is flanked by the ashlar facade of the **Chiesa del Gesù Nuovo** (☎ 081 557 81 11; 🕑 7am-12.30pm & 4-7.30pm) and the **Basilica di Santa Chiara** (☎ 081 552 62 09; Via Santa Chiara 49; 🕑 7.30am-1pm & 4-8pm Mon-Sat), a hulking Gothic complex, the main attraction of which is the **Chiostro delle Clarisse** (Nuns' Cloisters; admission €5; 🕑 9.30am-5.30pm Mon-Sat, to 1pm Sun).

Naples' spiritual heart is the **Duomo** (☎ 081 44 90 97; Via Duomo; 🕑 8am-12.30pm & 4.30-7pm Mon-Sat, 8.30am-1.30pm & 5-7.30pm Sun). Built in the 13th century, it has a 19th-century neo-Gothic facade and a largely baroque interior. Inside, the holy of holies is the 17th-century **Cappella di San Gennaro**, containing the head of St Januarius (the city's patron saint) and

two vials of his congealed blood. The saint is said to have saved the city from disasters on various occasions.

PIAZZA DEL PLEBISCITO & AROUND

At the bottom of Via Toledo, Piazza Trieste e Trento leads onto **Piazza del Plebiscito**, Naples' grandest piazza. Forming one side of the square, the rusty-red **Palazzo Reale** (☎ 081 794 40 21; Piazza del Plebiscito I; admission €4; 🕑 9am-8pm Thu-Tue) was the official residence of the Bourbon and Savoy kings and now houses a rich collection of furniture, statues and paintings.

Overlooking the seafront, **Castel Nuovo** is one of Naples' landmark sites, a brooding

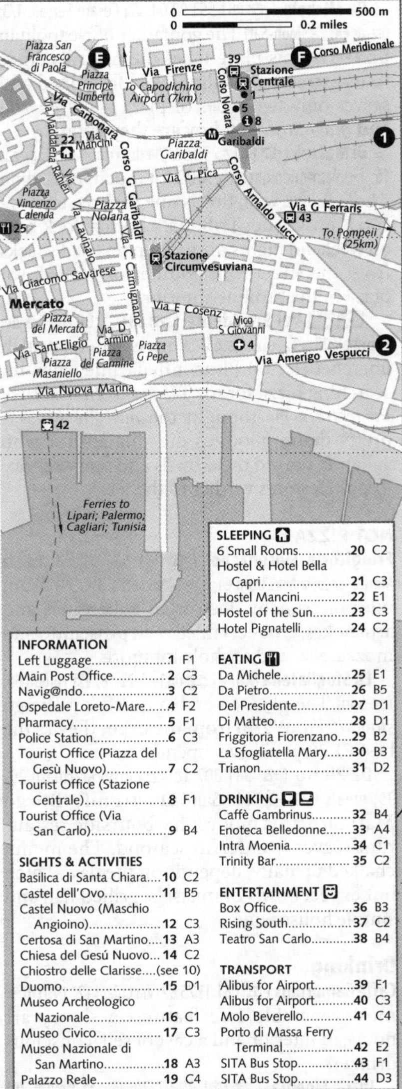

13th-century castle known to locals as the Maschio Angioino (Angevin Keep). Inside, the **Museo Civico** (☎ 081 795 20 03; adult/concession €5/4; 9am-7pm Mon-Sat, to 2pm Sun) displays some interesting 14th- and 15th-century frescoes and sculptures.

A second castle, the improbably named **Castel dell'Ovo** (Castle of the Egg; ☎ 081 24 00 055; Borgo Marinaro; admission free; 8am-6pm Mon-Sat, to 2pm Sun) marks the eastern end of the *lungomare* (seafront). Standing on the **Borgo Marinaro**, a small fishing village now given over to restaurants and bars, it was originally a Norman castle and then an Angevin fortress.

CERTOSA DI SAN MARTINO

The high point (quite literally) of Neapolitan baroque, the stunning **Certosa di San Martino** is one of Naples' must-see sights. Originally a 14th-century Carthusian monastery, it was given a 17th-century facelift by baroque maestro Cosimo Fanzago, and now houses the **Museo Nazionale di San Martino** (☎ 081 558 64 08; Largo San Martino 5; admission €6; 8.30am-7.30pm Thu-Tue). Highlights include the main church, the Chiostro Grande (Great Cloister) and the Sezione Presepiale, dedicated to rare 18th- and 19th-centrury *presepi* (nativity scenes).

CAPODIMONTE

A bus ride from the city centre, the colossal 18th-century Palazzo Reale di Capodimonte is home to the **Museo di Capodimonte** (☎ 081 749 91 11; Parco di Capodimonte; admission €7.50; 8.30am-7.30pm Thu-Tue), where you'll find works by Bellini, Botticelli, Caravaggio, Titian and Andy Warhol.

Take bus R4 to reach Capodimonte.

Festivals & Events

The **Festa di San Gennaro** honours the city's patron saint and is held three times a year (first Sunday in May, 19 September and 16 December). Thousands fill the Duomo to witness the saint's blood liquefy, a miracle said to save the city from disaster.

Sleeping

Most of the budget accommodation is in the ugly area around Stazione Centrale and down near the port. The *centro storico* has some good places, most hidden in centuries-old *palazzi*.

Hostel & Hotel Bella Capri (☎ 081 552 92 65; www.bellacapri.it; Via Melisurgo 4; dm €16-21, s €55-70, d €60-80, tr €80-100, q €90-110;) A hybrid hotel-cum-hostel, this is an excellent portside choice. The hotel rooms are smallish but comfy and the 7th-floor hostel is colourful and welcoming. Cheaper rooms with shared bathrooms are also available.

Hostel Mancini (☎ 081 553 67 31; www.hostelpensionemancini.com; Via Mancini 33; dm €18, s €45-55, d €50-65, tr €80-90, q €80-90) Near Stazione Centrale, this no-frills hostel/*pensione* was about to be given a facelift when we passed. If everything went according to plan it should now have a kitchen, a spacious communal area, and the dorms should all be en suite.

Hostel of the Sun (☎ 081 420 63 93; www.hostelnapoli.com; Via Melisurgo 15; dm €20, s/d/tr/q with shared bathroom €45/56/70/80, d/tr/q with private bathroom €70/90/100;) This award-winning hostel has the lot – great facilities, a young, helpful staff, and a breezy, inclusive vibe. Adding to the atmosphere is a vibrant colour scheme that extends to the dorms and hotel-quality private rooms. Just make sure you have €0.05 for the lift.

6 Small Rooms (☎ 081 790 13 78; www.6smallrooms.com; Via Diodato Lioy 18; dm/d €22/45;) In a dark *centro storico* street, this is a bright hostel with a homey, laid-back atmosphere. Once you've climbed six flights of treacherous stairs, you'll find an inviting living room, a fully equipped kitchen and three mixed dorms.

Hotel Pignatelli (☎ 081 658 49 50; www.hotelpignatellinapoli.com; Via San Giovanni Maggiore Pignatelli 16; s €35-50, d €70-90) One of the best bargains in the *centro storico*, the Pignatelli is on the 2nd floor of a historic *palazzo*. Rooms are decorated in a rustic Renaissance style with brass beds, terracotta floors, and wood-beamed ceilings.

Eating

Pizza was created in Naples and nowhere will you eat it better. There are any number of toppings but locals favour *margherita* (tomato, mozzarella and basil) or *marinara* (tomato, garlic, oregano and olive oil), cooked in a wood-fired oven.

Snacking is popular too. *Misto di frittura* – deep-fried vegetables – are available at takeaways called *friggatorie* all over town. For something sweet try a *sfogliatella* (a flaky pastry filled with cinnamon ricotta).

PIZZA

Trianon (☎ 081 553 94 26; Via Pietro Colletta 46; pizzas €4) A city institution, this marble-clad pizzeria has been on the dough since 1923. Queues wait to tuck into the usual range of pizzas prepared with practised flair by the hardworking *pizzaioli* (pizza makers).

Da Michele (☎ 081 553 92 04; Via Cesare Sersale 1/3; pizzas €4; Mon-Sat) The godfather of Neapolitan pizzerias, this place takes the no-frills ethos to its extremes. It's dingy, old fashioned and serves only two types of pizza – *margherita* and *marinara*. But, boy are they good!

Di Matteo (☎ 081 45 52 62; Via dei Tribunali 94; pizzas €5; 9am-midnight Mon-Sat) Not much more than a hole in the wall, this is one of three top pizzerias on Via dei Tribunali. Locals flock here on weekend nights to stock up on fried snacks from the streetfront counter or wolf down pizza in the broiling interior.

our pick **Del Presidente** (☎ 081 21 09 03; Via dei Tribunali 120/121; pizzas €5) This is where British uberchef Heston Blumenthal came when researching pizza for his TV series *In Search of Perfection*. He thought the *margherita* was pretty damn good, as did this author who valiantly braved the crowds and scary service to put Heston's verdict to the test.

NOT PIZZA

Friggitoria Fiorenzano (☎ 081 551 27 88; Piazza Montesanto; snacks from €1; Mon-Sat) Choose from piles of crunchy deep-fried aubergines and artichokes, croquets filled with prosciutto and mozzarella, and a whole lot more.

La Sfogliatella Mary (☎ 081 40 22 18; Via Toledo 66; Tue-Sun) The place to grab a quick, on-the-go *sfogliatella*. Warm from the oven, they're the best €1.20 you'll ever spend.

Da Pietro (☎ 081 807 10 82; Borgo Marinaro 29-30; meals €23; Tue-Sun) On trendy Borgo Marinaro, this modest harbourside restaurant serves wonderful seafood. The menu, chalked up daily, depends on the day's catch but expect bowls of mussels, grilled fish and simple house wine.

Drinking

Caffè Gambrinus (☎ 081 41 75 82; Via Chiaia 12) Naples' most venerable cafe features a showy art nouveau interior and a cast of self-conscious drinkers.

Intra Moenia (☎ 081 29 07 20; Piazza Bellini 70) Attracting a bohemian crowd, this arty cafe-cum-bookshop is beautifully located on Piazza Bellini.

Enoteca Belledonne (☎ 081 40 31 62; Vico Belledonne a Chiaia 18) Exposed brick walls, ambient lighting and bottle-lined shelves set the scene at this much-loved Chiaia wine bar.

Trinity Bar (☎ 081 551 45 69; Calata Trinita Maggiore 5) The most popular of the bars around Piazza del Gesù Nuovo. Grab a beer and kick back with the students.

Entertainment

For listings pick up *Qui Napoli* at tourist offices. You can buy tickets for most sporting and cultural events at **Box Office** (☎ 081 551 91 88; www.boxofficenapoli.it; Galleria Umberto I 15-16).

During May free concerts and cultural events are often held at weekends. Ask at the tourist offices for details.

Opera fans will enjoy an evening at **Teatro San Carlo** (☎ box office 081 797 23 31; www.teatrosancarlo.it; Via San Carlo 98; tickets from €25), one of Italy's top opera houses, which has a year-round program of opera and ballet. For something more contemporary, **Rising South** (Via San Sebastiano 19) is a kicking *centro storico* club.

Getting There & Away

AIR

Capodichino airport (NAP; ☎ 848 88 87 77; www.gesac.it), 7km northeast of the city centre, is southern Italy's main airport. Flights operate to most Italian cities and up to 30 European destinations, as well as New York.

BOAT

Naples is a major ferry port. Hydrofoils leave from Molo Beverello and Megellina; ferries depart from the Porta di Massa ferry terminal.

The major companies out of Naples:

Alilauro (☎ 081 761 10 04; www.alilauro.it) To/from Sorrento (hydrofoil €11.50, 35 minutes), Ischia (hydrofoil €17, 45 minutes).

Caremar (☎ 081 551 38 82; www.caremar.it) To/from Capri (ferry €8.70-9.60, 1¼ hours), Ischia (hydrofoil €14, 55 minutes), Procida (hydrofoil €9.25, 45 minutes).

Metro del Mare (☎ 199 600 700; www.metrodelmare.com) To/from Amalfi (ferry €15, 1½ hours), Positano (ferry €14, 55 minutes), Sorrento (ferry €6.50, 45 minutes).

NLG (☎ 081 552 07 63; www.navlib.it) To/from Capri (hydrofoil €17, 30 minutes).

Siremar (☎ 081 89 21 23; www.siremar.it) To/from Lipari (ferry €12.60, 10½ hours).

SNAV (☎ 081 428 55 55; www.snav.it) To/from Capri (hydrofoil €17, 45 minutes), Palermo (ferry €46, 10½ hours).

Tirrenia (☎ 081 89 21 23; www.tirrenia.com) To/from Palermo (ferry €48, 10¼ hours), Cagliari (€45, 16¼ hours).

BUS

Most buses leave from Piazza Garibaldi. **SITA** (☎ 199 73 07 49; www.sitabus.it, in Italian) runs buses to Pompeii (€2.40, 40 minutes, hourly), Sorrento (€3.30, one hour 20 minutes, three daily), Positano (€3.30, two hours, three daily), Amalfi (€3.30, two hours, eight daily) and Bari (€19.50, three hours, one daily).

Miccolis (☎ 081 200 380) serves Lecce (€28, 5½ hours) and Brindisi (€25.60, five hours).

TRAIN

Most trains stop at Stazione Centrale or underneath the main station at Stazione Garibaldi. There are up to 30 trains daily to Rome (€19.50 to €27.60, two hours) and some 20 to Salerno (€6.50, 35 minutes).

Ferrovia Circumvesuviana (☎ 800 05 39 39; www.vesuviana.it), accessible from Stazione Centrale, operates trains to Sorrento (€3.30, one hour 10 minutes) via Pompeii (€2.40, 40 minutes) and other towns along the coast. There are about 40 trains daily running between 5am and 10.40pm.

Getting Around

You can travel Naples by bus, metro and funicular. Journeys are covered by the Unico Napoli ticket, which comes in various forms: the standard ticket, valid for 90 minutes, costs €1.10; a daily pass is €3.10; and a weekend daily ticket is €2.60. Campania ArteCards (p691) are also valid on all forms of public transport.

POMPEII

An ancient town frozen in its 2000-year-old death throes, Pompeii was a thriving commercial town until Mt Vesuvius erupted on 24 August AD 79, burying it under a layer of *lapilli* (burning fragments of pumice stone) and killing some 2000 people. The skeletal, Unesco-listed **ruins** (☎ 081 857 53 47; www.pompeiisites.org; adult/concession €11/5.50, audioguides €6.50; 🕒 8.30am-7.30pm Apr-Oct, to 5pm Nov-Mar, last entry 1½hr before closing) provide a remarkable model of a working Roman city. Dotted around the 44-hectare site are a number of creepy body casts, made in the late 19th century by pouring plaster into the hollows left by disintegrated bodies.

Get information from the **tourist office** (☎ 081 536 32 93; pompeiturismo@email.it; Piazza Porta Marina Inferiore 12; 🕒 9am-3.30pm Mon-Sat) just outside the excavations at Porta Marina.

The easiest way to get to Pompeii is by the Ferrovia Circumvesuviana from Naples (€2.40, 35 minutes, half-hourly) or Sorrento (€1.90, 30 minutes, half-hourly). Get off at

Pompeii Scavi-Villa dei Misteri; the Porta Marina entrance is nearby.

CAPRI

pop 7260

Get beyond the glamorous veneer of Capri's chichi piazzas and designer boutiques and you'll discover an island of rugged seascapes, desolate Roman ruins and a surprisingly unspoiled rural interior.

The island is easily reached from Naples and Sorrento. Hydrofoils and ferries dock at Marina Grande, from where it's a short funicular ride up to Capri, the main town. A further bus ride takes you up to Anacapri.

Information is available online at www.capri.it, www.capritourism.it, or from one of the three **tourist offices** Anacapri (☎ 081 837 15 24; Via G Orlandi 59; 9am-3pm Mon-Sat); Capri Town (☎ 081 837 06 86; Piazza Umberto I; 8.30am-8.30pm Mon-Sat, 9am-3pm Sun summer, 9am-1pm & 3.30-6.45pm Mon-Sat winter); Marina Grande (☎ 081 837 06 34; 9am-1pm & 3.30-6.45pm Mon-Sat).

Sights & Activities

Capri's most famous attraction is the **Grotta Azzurra** (Blue Grotto; admission €4; 9am-1hr before sunset), a stunning sea cave illuminated by an other-worldly blue light. Boats leave from Marina Grande and the all-in round trip costs €21; allow a good hour.

When you're done exploring Capri Town's dinky whitewashed streets, head over to the **Giardini di Augusto** (Gardens of Augustus) for some breathtaking views. From here **Via Krupp** zigzags vertiginously down to Marina Piccola.

An hour's walk along Via Tiberio, **Villa Jovis** (admission €2; 9am-1hr before sunset) is what's left of Tiberius' main Capri residence. Double back and follow Via Matermània, for the **Arco Naturale**, a huge natural rock arch.

Up in Anacapri, **Villa San Michele** (☎ 081 837 14 01; Via Axel Munthe; admission €5; 9am-6pm May-Sep, to 5pm Oct-Apr, to 4.30pm Mar, to 3.30pm Nov-Feb) boasts some Roman antiquities and beautiful, panoramic gardens. For the best views on the island, take the **seggiovia** (chair lift; single/return €6/8; 9.30am-5pm Mar-Oct, 10.30am-3pm Nov-Feb) up from Piazza Vittoria to the summit of **Mt Solaro** (589m), Capri's highest point.

Sleeping & Eating

Capri has few genuinely budget sleeping options. Always book ahead.

Hotel La Tosca (☎ 081 837 09 89; www.latoscahotel.com; Via Dalmazio Birago 5; s €60-90, d €80-140; Apr-Oct;) La Tosca is one of the island's top budget hotels. With 11 sparkling white rooms, a central location, and a genial manager, it presses all the right buttons.

Hotel Bussola (☎ 081 838 20 10; www.bussolahermes.com; Trav La Vigna 14; d €70-140, tr €90-165, q €130-200;) A hospitable outpost on a quiet Anacapri lane, the year-round Bussola offers a warm welcome and attractive, sunny rooms. Depending on availability, there are also one or two rooms for students (€35 to €40 per person).

Trattoria Il Solitario (☎ 081 837 13 82; Via G Orlandi 96; pizzas from €5, meals €20; Apr-Oct) Just off Anacapri's main strip, this is a good, honest trattoria serving tasty local food. There are no surprises but you won't be disappointed with the large helpings and below-average prices.

Verginiello (☎ 081 837 09 44; Via Lo Palazzo 25; meals €20; daily Apr-Oct, Wed-Mon Dec-Mar) Offering straight-up Italian food and great views, this bustling restaurant is as near to a budget diner as you'll get in Capri Town. There's a good range of pastas and traditional main courses, including some fine grilled steaks.

In Capri Town, **Deco supermarket** (Via Roma; 8am-8pm Mon-Sat, 9am-1pm Sun) is a good place to load up with picnic provisions.

Getting There & Around

There are year-round hydrofoils and ferries to Capri from Naples and Sorrento. Timetables and fare details are available online at www.capritourism.com/en/timetable-and-prices.

From Naples, tickets cost €17 (hydrofoil), €14.50 (fast ferry) and €8.70 to €9.60 (ferry); see p695 for further details. When sailing from Naples you'll need to add another €0.40 harbour dues to these ticket prices.

From Sorrento, there are more than 25 sailings a day (less in winter). You'll pay €14.50 for the 20-minute hydrofoil crossing, €9.80 for the 25-minute fast ferry trip.

On the island, regular buses run from Capri Town up to Anacapri. Single tickets cost €1.40 on all island bus routes and on the funicular which links Marina Grande with Capri Town.

Contact **Rent a Scooter** (☎ 081 837 58 63; Via Roma 70; per hr €12) if you want to…well, you know, rent a scooter.

SORRENTO

pop 16,600

Overlooking the Bay of Naples and Mt Vesuvius, Sorrento is southern Italy's main package-holiday resort. Despite this, and despite the lack of a decent beach, it's an appealing place whose laid-back charm defies all attempts to swamp it in souvenir tat. There are few must-see sights but the *centro storico* is lively and the town makes a good jumping-off point for the Amalfi Coast, Pompeii and Capri.

There's an excellent **tourist office** (☎ fax 081 807 40 33; www.sorrentotourism.com; Via Luigi de Maio 35; 9am-6.30pm Mon-Sat summer, to 4pm winter) near Piazza Tasso, the town's focal square.

In town, the two main swimming spots are **Marina Piccola** and **Marina Grande**, although neither is especially appealing. Nicer by far is **Bagni Regina Giovanna**, a rocky beach set among the ruins of a Roman villa, 2km west of town. To get there take the SITA bus for Massalubrense.

Sleeping & Eating

Nube d'Argento (☎ 081 878 13 44; www.nubedargento.com; Via del Capo 21; per person/tent/car €11/10/5, 2-person bungalows €50-85; Mar-Dec) A popular camping ground 1km west of the town centre with shady pitches and excellent facilities.

our pick Ulisse Deluxe Hostel (☎ 081 877 47 53; www.ulissedeluxe.com; Via del Mare 22; dm/d/tr/q €25/70/105/140) Masquerading as a three-star hotel, this recently opened hostel is quite something. With its vast reception hall, smart modern rooms, en suite dorms and air of quiet efficiency, it's a cut above most town centre hotels, let alone hostels.

Hotel Linda (☎ 081 878 29 16; Via degli Aranci 125; s with shared bathroom €30, with private bathroom €35-38, d with shared bathroom €50, with private bathroom €60-70) A 10-minute walk from the train station, this is a classic, family-run *pensione*. It's a homey affair with comfortable modern rooms on the 2nd floor of an unappealing block of flats. No breakfast.

La Fenice (☎ 081 878 16 52; Via degli Aranci 11; pizzas €5, meals €30; Tue-Sun) This bustling restaurant is good place to try *gnocchi alla sorrentina* (potato gnocchi baked in tomato sauce with mozzarella), a traditional Sorrento speciality. If not, there's seafood, pizzas and meaty main courses.

Pizzeria Da Franco (☎ 081 877 20 66; Corso Italia 265; pizzas €6; 8am-2am) Don't expect frills at this laid-back pizzeria, just queues and the best pizza in town. Grab a spot at one of the rustic wooden tables and tuck into magnificent pizza, served on a metal tray with plastic cutlery.

Sisa Supermercato (☎ 081 807 44 65; Via degli Aranci 157) A supermarket on the eastern edge of town.

Getting There & Away

Circumvesuviana trains run half-hourly between Sorrento and Naples (€3.30, 1¼ hours) via Pompeii (€1.90 to Sorrento, €2.40 to Naples). Regular SITA buses leave from the train station for the Amalfi Coast, stopping in Positano (€3, 50 minutes) and Amalfi (€6, 1½ hours).

Sorrento is the main jumping-off point for Capri and ferries/hydrofoils run year-round from Marina Piccola. Tickets cost €14.50 (hydrofoil) or €9.80 (fast ferry).

AMALFI COAST

Stretching 50km along the southern side of the Sorrentine Peninsula, the Amalfi Coast (Costiera Amalfitana) is a postcard vision of Mediterranean beauty. Against a shimmering blue backdrop, whitewashed villages and terraced lemon groves cling to vertiginous cliffs backed by the craggy Lattari mountains. This Unesco-protected area is one of Italy's top tourist destinations, attracting hundreds of thousands of visitors each year, 70% of them between June and September.

Getting There & Away

Regular SITA buses run from Sorrento to Positano (€3, 50 minutes) and Amalfi (€6, 1½ hours); and from Salerno to Amalfi (€3, 1¼ hours).

Between April and September, **Metrò del Mare** (☎ 199 600 700; www.metrodelmare.com) runs boats from Naples to Sorrento (€6.50, 45 minutes), Positano (€14, 55 minutes), and Amalfi (€15, 1½ hours).

Positano

pop 3940

The best way to approach Positano, the coast's most expensive and glamorous town, is by boat. As you come into dock, feast your eyes on the unforgettable sight of colourful, steeply stacked houses packed onto the near-vertical green slopes.

The **tourist office** (☎ 089 87 50 67; Via del Saracino 4; 9am-1.30pm & 3.30-8pm Mon-Sat) can provide information on walking in these verdant peaks.

Hostel Brikette (☎ 089 87 58 57; www.brikette.com; Via Marconi 358; dm €22-27, d with shared bathroom €65-70, with private bathroom €90-110; Easter-Oct;) Near a bus stop at the top of town, this hostel is decidedly no-frills with six- to 20-person dorms and modest private rooms.

Hotel Continentale & La Tranquilita (☎ 089 87 40 84; www.continental.praiano.it; Via Roma 21, Praiano; 2-person tent €40, s €45-65, d €70-90; Apr-Oct) A welcoming hotel with a few tent pitches, the Continentale is by a bus stop on the road between Positano and Amalfi.

Da Costantino (☎ 089 87 57 38; Via Montepertuso; pizzas from €6, meals €25; Thu-Tue) About 300m above Hostel Brikette, this is one of the few authentic trattorias in town. Expect honest, down-to-earth Italian grub, pizza, chargrilled steaks, and fabulous views.

Amalfi

pop 5440

An attractive tangle of souvenir shops, dark alleyways and busy piazzas, Amalfi is the coast's main hub. Looming over the central piazza is the town's landmark **Duomo** (☎ 089 87 10 59; Piazza del Duomo; 7.30am-7.30pm), one of the few relics of Amalfi's past as an 11th-century maritime superpower. Between 10am and 5pm entry is through the adjacent Chiostro del Paradiso and costs €2.50.

Four kilometres west of town, the **Grotta dello Smeraldo** (admission €5; 9am-4pm) is a haunting sea cave. Boat trips from Amalfi cost €10 return.

Get details of these and other activities from the **tourist office** (☎ 089 87 11 07; www.amalfitouristoffice.it; Corso delle Repubbliche Marinare; 9am-1pm & 4-7pm Mon-Fri, to noon Sat).

Popular budget operation **A'Scalinatella Hostel** (☎ 089 87 14 92; www.hostelscalinatella.com; Piazza Umberto I 5, Atrani; dm €21, d/q with shared bathroom €60/100, with private bathroom €83/120;), in Atrani, has 10-bed dorms, rooms and apartments scattered across the village. Extras don't run to frills but there's internet, a washing machine and kitchen.

Housed in a 14th-century building on a petite piazza, **Hotel Lidomare** (☎ 089 87 13 32; www.lidomare.it; Largo Duchi Piccolomini 9; s €50-65, d €70-135;) is a lovely family-run hotel. The spacious rooms are full of character with majolica tiles and fine old antiques.

OUR PICK **Pizzeria Donna Stella** (☎ 338 358 84 83; Salita Rascica 2; pizzas from €5, mains €8; Tue-Sun) is a delightful back-alley pizzeria well worth searching out. Not only does it serve superb pizza but it also boasts one of Amalfi's loveliest settings – a delightful summer garden enclosed by jasmine-clad walls.

Self-caterers can stock up at **Supermercato Deco** (Salita dei Curiali; 8am-1.30pm & 5-8.30pm Mon-Sat).

MATERA

pop 57,400

Set atop two rocky gorges, Matera is famous for its *sassi* (cave dwellings), where up to half the town's population lived in abject poverty until the late 1950s. Ironically, the *sassi* are now Matera's fortune, attracting visitors from all over the world, and inspiring Mel Gibson to film *The Passion of the Christ* here.

The **tourist office** (☎ 0835 33 18 17; www.aptbasilicata.it; Via Spine Bianche 22; 8.30am-1pm & 4-7.30pm Mon-Sat, 8.30am-1pm Sun) can provide *sassi* maps.

Sights & Activities

Inhabited since the Paleolithic age, the *sassi* were brought to public attention by Carlo Levi's book *Cristo si é fermato a Eboli* (Christ Stopped at Eboli; 1954). His description of the area shamed the authorities into action and about 15,000 people were forcibly relocated in the late 1950s. In 1993 the *sassi* were declared a Unesco World Heritage site. Today the area is a fashionable spot for a second home.

The older of the two *sassi* areas, **Caveoso** is the more evocative (the other is **Barisano**). Highlights include the churches of **Santa Maria d'Idris** (9am-1pm & 3-7pm summer, 9.30am-1.30pm & 2.30-4.30pm winter) and **Santa Lucia alle Malve** (9am-1pm & 3-7pm summer, 9.30am-1.30pm & 2.30-4.30pm winter) with their well-preserved 13th-century Byzantine frescoes. Both are part of the *circuito urbano delle chiese rupestri*, a group of five churches in the *sassi* area. Tickets to individual churches cost €2.50; admission to all five is €6.

The **Casa-Grotta di Vico Solitario** (☎ 0835 31 01 18; off Via Bruno Buozzi; admission €1.50; 9.30am-8.30pm summer, to 5.30pm winter) has been set up to show family life 40 years ago, when a family of 10 might have shared a cave with their animals, but with no running water or electricity.

Sleeping & Eating

Le Monacelle (☎ 0835 34 40 97; www.lemonacelle.it; Via Riscatto 9/10; dm/s/d/tr/q €16/55/86/105/135; 💻) A former monastery, this hostel-cum-hotel is excellent value. Rooms are housed in the former cells and retain an air of elegant austerity, while outside the terrace offers unforgettable *sassi* views.

Sassi Hotel (☎ 0835 33 10 09; www.hotelsassi.it; Via san Giovanni Vecchio 89; s/d/ste €65/95/120; ❄) In the Barisano *sassi*, this is a friendly hotel housed in a rambling 18th-century *palazzo*. Rooms are bright with tasteful, modern furniture, terraces and panoramic views.

Ginger Caffè (☎ 0835 33 53 07; Via Lucana 54) Get down to this neighbourhood cafe for an early evening *aperitivo* – buy a €6 (€4 if nonalcoholic) drink and dig into a meal's worth of savoury snacks.

Il Terrazzino (☎ 0835 33 25 03; Vico San Giuseppe 7; meals €18; 🕑 Tue-Sun) Just off Piazza Vittorio Veneto, this teeming trattoria does a roaring trade in filling, no-nonsense pastas and simple meat dishes. Get into the mood with a rustic antipasto of olives, salami and cheese.

Fresh-produce market (Via A Persio) Daily market, just south of Piazza Vittoria Veneto.

Getting There & Away

The best way to reach Matera is by bus. From Rome's Stazione Tiburtina, **Marozzi** (☎ 06 225 21 47; www.marozzivt.it, in Italian) runs three daily buses (€33, 6½ hours). Matera's bus terminus is north of Piazza Matteotti near the train station.

By train, the **Ferrovie Appulo Lucano** (☎ 0835 572 52 29; www.fal-srl.it) runs regular services to Bari (€4, 1¼ hours, 14 daily).

BARI

pop 325,100

A bustling commercial city, Puglia's capital is best known for its ferry connections. And while it's not southern Italy's most appealing city, it's not without interest, particularly in the old town, *bari vecchia*. Get the low-down at the **tourist information point** (☎ 080 990 93 41; www.infopointbari.com; Piazza Aldo Moro; 🕑 9am-7pm Mon-Sat, to 1pm Sun) in front of the train station.

Bari's most important sight is the **Basilica di San Nicola** (☎ 080 573 71 11; Piazza San Nicola; 🕑 7am-1pm & 6-8pm Mon-Fri), the first great Norman church in the south and the last resting place of St Nicholas, aka Father Christmas.

If you need to stop over, **Hotel Pensione Giulia** (☎ 080 521 66 30; www.hotelpensionegiulia.it; Via Crisanzio 12; s €50-60, d €65-75; ❄) is an old-fashioned, family-run *pensione*, with clean, basic rooms. For a bite, **Al Pescatore** (☎ 080 523 70 39; Piazza Federico di Svevia II; meals €28) serves great seafood.

Ferries run from Bari to Greece (Corfu, Igoumenitsa, Patras), Albania (Durazzo), Croatia (Dubrovnik) and Montenegro (Bar). Ferry companies have offices at the port, accessible by bus 20 (€0.90) from the train station. You can also get tickets at **Morfimare Travel Agency** (☎ 080 578 98 11; Corso Antonio de Tullio 36-40) opposite the port.

There are regular trains to/from Rome (€36, up to 6½ hours), Brindisi (€6.80, one hour 20 minutes) and Lecce (€15, two hours), as well as many smaller towns in Puglia.

LECCE

pop 93,600

An urbane university town with a vibrant bar scene and a graceful historic centre, the 'Florence of the South' is well worth a stopover. Its bombastic displays of jaw-dropping baroque architecture (known as *barocco leccese* – Lecce baroque) are one of southern Italy's highlight sights.

Information is available from the **tourist office** (☎ 0832 24 80 92; Corso Vittorio Emanuele 24; 🕑 9am-1pm & 4-8pm Mon-Sat summer, to 7pm winter) in the historic centre.

The most celebrated example of Lecce's baroque architecture is the eye-popping **Basilica di Santa Croce** (☎ 0832 24 19 57; Via Umberto I; 🕑 9.30am-noon & 5-8pm). It took a team of 16th- and 17th-century craftspeople more than a hundred years to create the swirling facade that you see today. A short walk away, **Piazza del Duomo** is a further orgy of architectural extravagance. The 12th-century **cathedral** (☎ 0832 30 85 57; admission free; 🕑 7am-noon & 5-7.30pm) was completely restored by baroque master Giuseppe Zimbalo, who also fashioned the 68m-high **bell tower**. Facing the cathedral is the 15th-century **Palazzo Vescovile** (Bishop's Palace) and the 17th-century **Seminario**.

Lecce's social hub, **Piazza Sant'Oronzo** is built round the remains of a 2nd-century **Roman amphitheatre**, once the largest in Puglia.

Sleeping

Centro Storico (☎ 0832 24 27 27; www.bedandbreakfast.lecce.it; Via Vignes 2/b; s/d €40/57, ste €70-100; ❄) A modest B&B in a historic *palazzo*. The 2nd-floor rooms are bright and airy, decked out with parquet, wrought-iron beds and plain furniture. Upstairs, there's a sun terrace.

B&B Centro Storico Prestige (☎ 0832 24 33 53; www.bbprestige-lecce.it; Via S Maria del Paradiso 4; s €50-60, d €70-90; 💻) This is a cracking little B&B. The irrepressible Renata ushers guests into her lovingly tended 2nd-floor flat where sunlight floods into understated white guestrooms.

Eating & Drinking

Trattoria Le Zie (☎ 0832 24 51 78; Via Colonello Costadura 19; meals €25; ⏲ closed Sun dinner & Mon) Also known as 'Cucina Casareccia' (Homestyle Cooking), this family-run trattoria serves exactly what you hope – tasty, filling, *nonna*-style cooking.

Alle due Corti (☎ 0832 24 22 23; www.alleduecorti.com; Corte dei Giugni 1; meals €25) This popular restaurant is a fine place to get to grips with Salento's gastronomic heritage. Go for *ricchietelle cule rape* (orecchiette pasta with turnip tops) for a real taste of tradition.

Of the many bars in the centre, the **Caffè Letterario** (☎ 0832 24 23 51; www.caffeletterario.org, in Italian; Via Paladini 48) is a happening spot.

Getting There & Away

Lecce is the end of the main southeastern train line and there are direct trains to Brindisi (€5.30, 35 minutes), Bari (€15, two hours), and Rome (€51.30, six hours), as well as to points throughout Puglia.

SICILY

The Mediterranean's largest island, Sicily is a hotbed of southern excess. Everything about the place is extreme, from the beauty of its rugged landscape to its hybrid cuisine and flamboyant architecture. Over the centuries Sicily has seen off a catalogue of foreign invaders, from the Phoenicians and ancient Greeks to the Spanish Bourbons and WWII Allies. All have contributed to the island's complex and fascinating cultural landscape.

GETTING THERE & AWAY

Air

Flights from Italy's mainland cities and a number of European destinations land at Sicily's two main airports: **Palermo** (PMO; www.gesap.it; ☎ 091 702 01 11) and **Catania** (CTA; ☎ 095 723 91 11; www.aeroporo.catania.it).

Boat

Regular car and passenger ferries cross to Sicily (Messina) from Villa San Giovanni in Calabria. The island is also accessible by ferry from Genoa, Livorno, Naples and Cagliari, as well as Malta and Tunisia. The main companies:

Grandi Navi Veloci (☎ 091 587 801; www.gnv.it) Palermo to/from Genoa and Tunis.

Grimaldi Lines (☎ 091 611 36 91; www.grimaldi-ferries.com) Palermo to/from Salerno and Tunis.

SNAV (☎ 091 631 79 00; www.snav.com) Palermo to/from Naples and Civitavecchia.

Tirrenia (☎ 892 123; www.tirrenia.it) Palermo to/from Naples and Cagliari.

Timetables are seasonal, so check with a travel agent or online at www.traghettionline.net. Book well in advance during summer.

Bus

Direct bus services between Rome and Sicily are operated by **SAIS** (☎ 091 616 60 28; www.saisautolinee.it, in Italian) and **Interbus** (☎ 0935 56 51 11; www.interbus.it, in Italian), departing from Rome's Piazza Tiburtina. There are daily buses to Messina (€41, nine hours), Catania (€46, 11 hours), Palermo (€44, 12¾ hours) and Syracuse (€47, 12 hours).

Train

Direct trains run from Milan, Florence, Rome, Naples and Reggio di Calabria to Palermo and Catania. For further information contact **Trenitalia** (☎ 89 20 21; www.trenitalia.com).

PALERMO

pop 666,600

Still bearing the bruises of its WWII battering, Palermo is a compelling and chaotic city. It takes a little work, but once you've acclimatised to the frenetic streets you'll be rewarded with some of southern Italy's most exotic buildings. In among chaotic street markets and bombed-out *palazzi*, you'll find palaces, castles and churches, as well as some fabulous restaurants and tempting cafes.

Orientation

Palermo's centre is large but manageable on foot. The main street is Via Maqueda, which runs parallel to Via Roma, the busy road running north from the train station. Corso Vittorio Emanuele crosses Via Maqueda at a

GETTING INTO TOWN

A half-hourly bus service run by **Prestia e Comandé** (☎ 091 58 63 51) connects the airport with the train station. Tickets for the 50-minute journey cost €5.30 and are available on the bus. There's also the hourly Trinacria Express train service (€4.50, 45 minutes) to Stazione Centrale.

The ferry port is about 15 minutes' walk from the city centre.

junction known as the Quattro Canti (Four Corners). Most sights and hotels are within easy walking distance of this intersection.

Information

Aboriginal Café (Via Spinuzza 51; per hr €3.50; ⌚ 6pm-3am) Popular Australian-style pub with internet access.

Left Luggage (1st 5 hours €3.80, 6-12 hours per hr €0.60, 13 hours & over per hr €0.20; ⌚ 7am-11pm) At the train station.

Lo Cascio Pharmacy (☎ 091 616 21 17; Via Roma 1) All-night chemist.

Police station (Questura; ☎ 091 21 01 11; Piazza della Vittoria)

Tourist office Airport (☎ 091 59 16 98; ⌚ 8.30am-7.30pm Mon-Sat); Piazza Castelnuovo 34 (☎ 091 60 58 351; www.palermotourism.com; ⌚ 8.30am-2pm & 2.30-6pm Mon-Fri); Stazione Centrale (☎ 091 616 99 69; Piazza Giulio Cesare; ⌚ closed at time of research but due to reopen) Pick up *Agenda Turismo*, a useful booklet with loads of practical information.

Sights

A good starting point is the **Quattro Canti**, a road junction where Palermo's four central districts converge. Nearby, Piazza Pretoria is dominated by the ostentatious **Fontana Pretoria**, whose nude nymphs caused outrage when it was bought from Florence in 1573.

Around the corner in Piazza Bellini, **La Martorana** (Chiesa di Santa Maria dell'Ammiraglio; ☎ 091 616 16 92; ⌚ 8.30am-1pm & 3.30-7pm Mon-Sat, 8.30am-1pm Sun) is celebrated for its 12th-century bell tower and stunning Byzantine mosaics. Next door, the red-domed **Chiesa di San Cataldo** (admission €1; ⌚ 9am-2pm & 3.30-7pm Mon-Sat, 9am-2pm Sun) is of interest more for the Arab-Norman exterior than its surprisingly bare interior.

Palermo's extraordinary **cathedral** (☎ 091 33 43 73; Corso Vittorio Emanuele; admission free; ⌚ 9.30am-5.30pm Mon-Sat, 8am-1.30pm & 4.30-6pm Sun) is a visual riot of arches, cupolas and crenellations. Modified many times, it's a superb example of Sicily's unique Arab-Norman architecture. Barely less dramatic is **Palazzo Reale** (Palazzo dei Normanni; ☎ 091 626 28 33; Piazza Indipendenza; admission incl Cappella Palatina €6; ⌚ 8.30am-noon & 2-5pm Mon-Sat, 8.30am-12.30pm Sun), the theatrical seat of the Sicilian parliament. Downstairs, the 12th-century **Cappella Palatina** (Palatine Chapel; ☎ 091 626 28 33; admission €6; ⌚ 8.30am-noon & 2.30-5pm Mon-Sat, 8.30am-2pm Sun) is lavishly decorated with exquisite mosaics.

Palermo's musical heart beats at the neoclassical opera house **Teatro Massimo** (☎ 091 609 08 31; www.teatromassimo.it, in Italian; guided tours adult/concession €5/3; ⌚ 10am-2.30pm Tue-Sun), which was used as a backdrop for the closing scene of *The Godfather III*.

Southwest of the city centre, the macabre **Catacombe dei Cappuccini** (Capuchin Catacombs; ☎ 091 21 21 17; Piazza Cappuccini 1; admission €1.50; ⌚ 9am-noon & 3-5.30pm) hold the mummified bodies of some 8000 Palermitans who died between the 17th and 19th centuries. Take bus 327 from Piazza Indipendenza.

Sleeping

Trinacria (☎ 091 53 05 90; www.campingtrinacria.it; Via Barcarello 25; per person/tent/car €7/7/4) About 12km northwest of Palermo, this camping ground is by the sea at Sferracavallo. Catch bus 616 from Piazzale Alcide de Gasperi, reached by bus 101, or 107 from the train station.

Hotel Regina Palermo (☎ 091 611 42 16; www.hotelreginapalermo.com; Corso Vittorio Emanuele 316; s with shared bathroom €28, d with shared bathroom €40-54, with private bathroom €50-64) This friendly, family-run *pensione* is a great budget option, offering good-value digs near the Quattro Canti.

Hotel Cortese (☎ 091 33 17 22; www.hotelcortese.net; Via Scarparelli 16; s/d with shared bathroom €33/56, s/d/tr with private bathroom €38/66/80; ❄ 💻) This welcoming haven is a stone's throw from the chaotic Ballaró markets. Rooms are not the largest, but they are tastefully decorated with period furniture. Breakfast costs €4.

our pick **B&B Panormus** (☎ 091 617 58 26; www.bbpanormus.com; Via Roma 72; s €35-45, d €70-80, tr €90-100; ❄) Large airy rooms, a convenient location near the train station, a friendly young owner, and bargain rates – this excellent B&B ticks all the right boxes.

Eating

Traditional yet spicy, Palermo's food marries the island's superb produce with recipes imported by the Arab Saracens in the 9th century. Two specialities to try are *arancini* (deep-fried rice balls) and *cannoli* (pastry tubes filled with ricotta and candied fruit).

Panificio Tutto Il Mondo (Via Trabia 49; snacks from €1.20; 8.30am-2.30pm & 4.30-8.30pm Mon-Sat) A small bakery near Teatro Massimo, this is the place to try *sfincioni*, a Palermitan pizza topped with tomato, onion and chunks of *caciocavallo* cheese.

Antica Focacceria di San Francesco (091 32 02 64; Via Paternostro 58; set menus €6-12; Tue-Sun) A city institution, this frenetic eatery serves huge portions of filling Palermitan classics. Ignore the restaurant and eat in the canteen, where you can choose from various menus of pastas, fried snacks and *cannoli*.

For an adrenalin-charged food experience, dive into one of Palermo's legendary markets: **Capo** (Mon-Sat) on Via Sant'Agostino, or **Il Ballaró** (daily), in the Albergheria quarter off Via Maqueda. Easier but less fun is the **GS supermarket** (Via Salità Partanna 1) off Piazza Marinara.

Getting There & Away

National and international flights serve **Falcone-Borsellino airport** (PMO; www.gesap.it; 091 702 01 11), 35km west of Palermo.

The ferry terminal is northeast of the historic centre, off Via Francesco Crispi. Ferries for Cagliari (€51, 14½ hours) and Naples (€48, 10¼ hours) leave from Molo Vittorio Veneto; for Genoa (€96, 20 hours) from Molo S Lucia.

The main bus station is near Via Paolo Balsamo, next to the train station. Buses leave for Catania (€13.20, 2¾ hours, 14 daily), Messina (€14.10, 2¾ hours, six daily), Syracuse (€14, 3¼ hours, five daily) and Agrigento (€7.70, two hours, nine daily).

Trains leave from the Stazione Centrale for Messina (€18, 3½ hours, half-hourly) via Milazzo (€9.65), the jumping-off point for the Aeolian Islands. Long-distance trains go to Reggio di Calabria (€30, six hours, four daily), Naples (€47.50, nine to 10 hours, four daily) and Rome (€58, 11 to 12 hours, seven daily).

Getting Around

Walking is the best way to get around Palermo's centre but if you want to take a bus, most stop outside or near the train station. Tickets cost €1.10 and are valid for two hours.

AEOLIAN ISLANDS

Rising out of the cobalt blue seas off Sicily's northeastern coast, the Unesco-protected Aeolian Islands (Isole Eolie) have been seducing visitors since Odysses' time. With their wild, windswept mountains, hissing volcanoes and rich waters, they form a beautiful outdoor playground, ideal for divers, sun-seekers and adrenalin-junkies.

Lipari is the biggest of the seven islands (Lipari, Salina, Vulcano, Stromboli, Alicudi, Filicudi and Panarea), and the main transport hub. From there you can pick up connections to the other islands, including Vulcano, famous for its therapeutic mud, and Stromboli, whose active volcano supplies spectacular fire shows.

The islands' only **tourist office** (090 988 00 95; www.aasteolie.191.it, in Italian; Corso Vittorio Emanuele 202; 8.30am-1.30pm & 4.30-7.30pm Mon-Fri) is on Lipari.

Sights & Activities

On **Lipari**, learn about the islands' volcanic history at the **Museo Archeologico Eoliano** (090 988 01 74; admission €6; 9am-1pm & 3-7pm Mon-Sat) in the Aragonese **citadel**. For sunbathing, head to Canneto and the Spiaggia Bianca or Spiaggia Papesca at Porticello. Snorkelling and diving are popular; contact **Diving Center La Gorgonia** (090 981 26 16; www.lagorgoniadiving.it; Salita San Giuseppe; dives from €31) for equipment and guided dives. For tours of the islands, **Da Massimo** (338 369 44 04; www.damassimo.it; Via Maurolico 2) offers various packages, ranging from a €15 tour of Lipari and Vulcano to a €80 summit climb of Stromboli.

Vulcano is a malodorous and largely unspoilt island. Most people visit to make the hour-long trek up the **Fossa di Vulcano**, the island's active volcano (€3 for crater entrance), or to wallow in the **Laghetto di Fanghi** mud baths (€2.50).

Famous for its spectacular fireworks, **Stromboli** is the most active volcano in the region. To make the tough seven-hour ascent to the 920m summit you are legally required to hire a guide. At the top you're rewarded with incredible views of the Sciara del Fuoco (Trail of Fire). **Magmatrek** (090 986 57 68; www.magmatrek.it) organises afternoon climbs for €25 per person (minimum 10 people).

Sleeping & Eating

Most accommodation is on Lipari. Always try to book ahead as summer is always busy and many places close over the winter.

LIPARI

Don't dismiss outright offers by touts at the port as they're often genuine.

Baia Unci (☎ 090 981 19 09; www.baiaunci.it; Marina Garibaldi 2; per person/tent €10/12, 4-person bungalow €52-100) The island's shady camping ground is on the sea at Canneto, 2km out of Lipari town. On-site facilities include a restaurant, bar and diving centre.

Diana Brown (☎ 090 981 25 84; www.dianabrown.it; Vico Himera 3; s €30-80, d €40-100; ❄) Down a tiny back lane, Diana has comfortable rooms decorated in cheerful summery style. Kettles and fridges are provided and the darker downstairs rooms have a small kitchenette. Breakfast (€5) is served on the solarium.

our pick **Osteria Mediterranea** (☎ 090 981 25 11; Corso Vittorio Emanuele; meals €20) Offering excellent value for money, prompt, friendly service, and delicious food, this is an excellent choice. Large juicy olives arrive with the wine, whetting your appetite for wonderful seafood dishes, such as grilled catch of the day with almonds and sun-dried tomatoes.

The main drag, Corso Vittorio Emanuele, is lined with eateries, takeaways and bars. Next to the tourist office there's a **Sisa supermarket** (Corso Vittorio Emanuele 230; 🕑 8am-9pm Mon-Sat) and, further down, at No 150, a takeaway where you can pick up a snack and beer for €2.50.

VULCANO

Campers can down tents at **Camping Togo Togo** (☎ 090 985 21 28; www.campingvulcano.it; Porto Ponente; per person & tent €12; 🕑 Apr-Sep), a tranquil camping ground near Spiaggia Sabbia Nera. Another budget option is **Hotel Torre** (☎ 090 985 23 42; www.hoteltorrevulcano.it; Via Favaloro 1; d €40-80; ❄), with large, functional rooms near the port.

Getting There & Around

Ferries and hydrofoils leave for the islands from Milazzo. If arriving in Milazzo by train, you'll need to catch a bus (€1) or taxi (€10) to the port, 4km from the station.

Ustica Lines (☎ 0923 87 38 13; www.usticalines.it) and **Siremar** (☎ 892 123; www.siremar.it) run hydrofoils to Vulcano (€15, 40 minutes) and onto Lipari (€15.80, 55 minutes). Between June and September departures are almost hourly from 7am to 8pm. Siremar also runs ferries to the same destinations.

From Lipari, there are regular services to Vulcano (€5.80), Stromboli (€17.80), Filicudi (€15.80), Alicudi (€18.85) and the other islands.

TAORMINA

pop 11,100

Spectacularly perched on a clifftop terrace, Taormina is Sicily's glitziest resort, a sophisticated town with a pristine medieval core and grandstand coastal views. It was made famous by Goethe and DH Lawrence, who both lived here, but in the 9th century it was Sicily's Byzantine capital.

The **tourist office** (☎ 0942 2 32 43; www.gate2taormina.com; Piazza Santa Caterina; 🕑 8.30am-2pm & 4-7pm Mon-Thu, 8.30am-2pm Fri) can provide information and help with booking accommodation. Head to **Net Point** (Via Jallia Bassia 34; per 20 min €2; 🕑 9am-9pm) for internet access.

Take time to visit the stunning **Teatro Greco** (☎ 0942 2 32 20; Via Teatro Greco; adult/concession €6/3; 🕑 9am-7pm summer, to 4.30pm winter), a noble 3rd-century-BC theatre overlooking the sea.

For a swim, take the **cable car** (€3.50 return; 🕑 8am-8.15pm) down to the beach, **Lido Mazzarò**, and the tiny **Isola Bella** set in its own picturesque cove.

Sleeping & Eating

Taormina's Odyssey (☎ 0942 2 45 33; www.taorminaodyssey.com; Trav A – Via G Martino 2; dm €17-20, d €45-60) Taormina's sole hostel is a friendly, year-round affair about 10 minutes' walk from the centre (follow signs for Hotel Andromaco). Space is tight but there's still a well-stocked kitchen and convivial common room.

Pensione Casa Diana (☎ 0942 2 38 98; Via Di Giovanni 6; s/d €45/50) Yards from the main strip, this old-school *pensione* has clean, spartan rooms that while fine for a night or two can be noisy. No breakfast.

Vecchia Taormina (☎ 0942 62 55 89; Vico Ebrei 3; pizzas €6.50, meals €25) An unpretentious trattoria that serves no-nonsense local food, including classic *caponata* (sweet-and-sour aubergine and tomato ratatouille) and excellent wood-fired pizzas.

Ristorante Luraleo (☎ 0942 62 01 64; Via Bagnoli Croce 27/31, meals €25) Hanging copper pots, tacky stained glass and a vine-draped terrace set the stage for some pretty spot-on food.

Getting There & Away

Taormina is best reached by bus. From the bus terminus on Via Pirandello, Interbus runs to/from Messina (€3.50, 1¾ hours, hourly), and **Etna Trasporti** (☎ 095 53 27 16; www.etnatrasporti.it) connects with Catania (€4.40, 1½ hours, hourly).

MT ETNA

The dark silhouette of Mt Etna (3320m) broods ominously over the east coast, more or less halfway between Taormina and Catania. One of Europe's highest and most volatile volcanoes, it erupts frequently, spewing out lava and ash from four summit craters and fissures on the mountain's slopes.

By public transport the best way to get to there is to take the daily AST bus from Catania. This departs from in front of the main train station at 8.30am (returning at 4.30pm, €5.15 return) and drops you at the Rifugio Sapienza (1923m) where you can pick up the **Funivia dell'Etna** (cable car, bus & guide €49; 9am-5pm summer, to 3.30pm winter) to 2500m. From there buses courier you up to the official crater zone (2920m). If you want to walk, allow up to four hours for the round trip. Also make sure to have a sweater and coat to hand as it can get very cold up top, even in summer.

Gruppo Guide Alpine Etna Sud (☎ 095 791 47 55; www.etnaguide.com) is one of hundreds of outfits offering guided tours, typically involving 4WD transport and a guided trek. Reckon on at least €60 for a summit excursion.

Further Etna information is available from the **tourist office** (☎ 0975 730 62 55; 8am-8pm) at Catania train station.

If you want to overnight in Catania, the **Agora Hostel** (☎ 095 723 30 10; www.agorahostel.com; Piazza Curro 6; dm €21, s €30-35, d €50-55;) is a sociable spot with its own pub and restaurant.

SYRACUSE

pop 123,400

With its gorgeous *centro storico* and gritty ruins, Syracuse (Siracusa) is a baroque beauty with an ancient past. Archimedes' home town and one of Sicily's most visited cities, it was founded in 734 BC by Corinthian settlers and became the dominant Greek city-state on the Mediterranean. It eventually fell to the Romans in 212 BC.

Orientation & Information

From the train station, it's a 20-minute walk to Ortygia, the historic centre; take Via Francesco Crispi to Piazzale Marconi and then follow Corso Umberto I down to the bridge. Alternatively, jump on one of the regular shuttle buses which connect Ortygia with the station.

The **tourist office** (☎ 0931 46 42 55; Via Maestranza 33; 8.30am-1.45pm & 2.30-3.30pm Mon-Fri) is in Ortygia.

Sights

ORTYGIA

Connected to the town by bridge, the island of Ortygia is an atmospheric warren of elaborate baroque *palazzi,* lively piazzas and busy trattorias. Just off Via Roma, the 7th-century **cathedral** (Piazza del Duomo; 9am-7pm) was built over a pre-existing 5th-century BC Greek temple, incorporating most of the original columns in its three-aisled structure. South of Piazza del Duomo is the **Fontana Aretusa**, where fresh water has been bubbling up since ancient times.

PARCO ARCHEOLOGICO DELLA NEAPOLIS

Syracuse's main attraction is the **Parco Archeologico della Neapolis** (☎ 0931 6 50 68; Viale Paradiso; adult/concession €8/4; 8am-7pm summer, to 4pm winter), home to the city's ancient ruins. Hewn out of solid rock, the 5th-century-BC **Greek theatre** is where Aeschylus premiered many of his tragedies. Nearby, the **Orecchio di Dionisio** is an ear-shaped grotto, the perfect acoustics of which allowed Syracuse's tyrant Dionysius to eavesdrop on his prisoners. On the other side of Via Paradiso is the impressive 2nd-century **Roman amphitheatre.**

To get to the park take bus 1 or 4 to Corso Gelone. On foot, it's about 20 minutes from the train station.

About 500m east of the archaeological zone, the **Museo Archeologico Paolo Orsi** (☎ 0931 46 40 22; Viale Teocrito 66/a; adult/concession €8/4; 9am-6pm Tue-Sat, to 1pm Sun) houses Sicily's most extensive archaeological collection.

Sleeping & Eating

Lol Hostel (☎ 0931 46 50 88; www.lolhostel.com; Via Francesco Crispi 94; dm/d €20/58;) A terrific modern hostel near the train station. Accommodation is in mixed and girl-only dorms and sunny, cheerfully furnished private rooms.

Casa Mia (☎ 0931 46 33 49; www.bbcasamia.it; Corso Umberto 112; d €60-75;) On the principal mainland strip, this is a small, homey hotel. Its characterful, old-fashioned rooms are furnished with family heirlooms and imperious beds.

Castello Fiorentino (☎ 0931 2 10 97; Via del Crocifisso 6, trav Via Roma; pizza €5, meals €15) This place has all the hallmarks of a classic Italian pizzeria – the pizza is excellent, the atmosphere is raucous, and the pace is quick.

Sicilia in Tavola (☎ 392 461 08 89; Via Cavour 28; meals €22; ⌚ Tue-Sun) Come here for delicious home-made pasta and fresh-off-the-boat seafood. Try the prawn ravioli served with tomato, mint and parsley followed by *polpette in mucca* (fried fish cakes).

Getting There & Away

In general buses are more convenient than trains. Both **Interbus** (☎ 091 617 54 11; www.interbus.it, in Italian) and **AST** (☎ 0931 46 48 20; www.aziendasicilianatrasporti.it) run to/from Catania (€4.70, 1½ hours, hourly) and Palermo (€14, 3¼ hours, 10 daily).

Trains head to Taormina (€11.60, one hour, nine daily), Messina (€14.50, three hours, nine daily) and Catania (€7.50, 1¼ hours, 11 daily).

AGRIGENTO

pop 59,100

Agrigento enjoys fame and notoriety in equal measure – fame for its awe-inspiring Greek temples; notoriety for the rampant *abusivismo* (illegal building) that has overrun the medieval hilltop town. Founded around 581 BC by Greek settlers, Agrigento became an important trading centre under the Romans and Byzantines.

Intercity buses arrive on Piazzale Rosselli, where you can catch local bus 1, 2 or 3 to the Valley of the Temples. Up in the main town, the **tourist office** (☎ 800 31 55 55; Piazzale Aldo Moro; ⌚ 8am-2pm & 3-7pm Mon-Fri, 8am-1pm Sat) has limited information.

Sights

One of the most compelling archaeological sites in southern Italy, the **Valley of the Temples** is a Unesco-listed complex of temples and walls from the ancient city of Akragas, founded here in 581 BC. The **archaeological park** (☎ 0922 49 72 26; adult/concession €8/4, incl museum €10/5; ⌚ 8.30am-7pm) is divided into eastern and western zones. In the eastern zone, the 6th-century-BC **Tempio di Ercole** was originally as big as the Parthenon. Continuing east, the intact **Tempio della Concordia** was transformed into a Christian church in the 6th century and the **Tempio di Giunone** boasts an impressive sacrificial altar.

Over the road in the western zone, the 5th-century-BC **Tempio di Giove** originally covered an area of 112m by 56m with 20m-high columns interspersed with *telamoni* (giant male statues), one of which now stands in the **Museo Archeologico** (☎ 0922 40 15 65; adult/concession €8/4, incl park €10/5; ⌚ 9.30am-7pm Tue-Sat, to 1pm Sun & Mon) on the road up to Agrigento.

Sleeping & Eating

Campeggio Internazionale San Leone (☎ 0922 41 11 15; www.campingvalledeitempli.com; Viale Emporium 192, San Leone; per person/tent/car €7/7/3; Ⓟ 💻 🏊) This well-equipped camping ground is on the sea in the small town of San Leone. Take bus 2 from Agrigento train station.

B&B Atenea 191 (☎ 0922 59 55 94; www.atenea191.com; Via Atenea 191; s/d/tr/q €50/80/120/160) A labour of love for the artist owner, the seven rooms at this welcoming B&B are decorated with original paintings and exuberant floral stencils. Breakfast is served on the rooftop patio.

Café Girasole (Via Atenea 68-70; panino €2.50) A great little wine bar popular with lunching locals. You can prop up the bar or sit on the small terrace, shrouded in a mist of cooling water spray.

Trattoria Pizzeria Manhattan (☎ 0922 2 09 11; Salita M Angeli 9; set menu €15-18; ⌚ Mon-Sat) Good for straightforward Sicilian cooking, this modest trattoria is halfway up a staircase off Via Ateneo, Agrigento's main strip.

Getting There & Away

The bus is the easiest way to get to and from Agrigento. **Cuffaro** (☎ 091 616 15 10; www.cuffaro.info) runs buses to Palermo (€7.70, two hours, nine daily) and **SAIS** (☎ 091 616 60 28; www.saisautolinee.it, in Italian) serves Catania (€11.60, three hours, 14 daily).

SARDINIA

Celebrated for its spectacular beaches and VIP resorts, Sardinia is far more than it's made out to be. If you can drag yourself away from the gorgeous coastline and transparent waters, you'll discover a haunting and often spectacular interior of impenetrable granite gorges, forbidding peaks, and silent cork forests. Adding a sense of mystery are the 7000 *nuraghi* (circular stone towers) which pepper the landscape, all that's left of Sardinia's prehistoric past.

You can get round Sardinia on public transport but you'll discover much more with your own wheels.

GETTING THERE & AWAY

Air

Flights from Italian and European cities serve Sardinia's three main airports: **Elmas** (CAG; ☎ 070 21 12 11; www.sogaer.it) in Cagliari; Alghero's **Fertilia** (AHO; ☎ 079 93 52 82; www.algheroairport.it); and the **Aeroporto Olbia Costa Smeralda** (OLB; ☎ 0789 56 34 44; www.geasar.it) in Olbia.

Boat

Car and passenger ferries sail year-round from various Italian ports, including Civitavecchia, Genoa, Livorno, Naples and Palermo. The following is a brief rundown of the major routes and the companies that operate them:

Civitavecchia To/from Olbia (Moby Lines, Sardinia Ferries, Tirrenia); Cagliari (Tirrenia); Golfo Aranci (Sardinia Ferries).
Genoa To/from Porto Torres (Grandi Navi Veloci, Tirrenia); Olbia (Moby Lines, Tirrenia); Arbatax (Tirrenia).
Livorno To/from Olbia (Moby Lines); Golfo Aranci (Sardinia Ferries).
Naples To/from Cagliari (Tirrenia).
Palermo To/from Cagliari (Tirrenia).

Online, you can get sailing information and book tickets at www.traghettionline.net.

CAGLIARI

pop 159,400

Sardinia's capital and largest city is a far cry from Sardinia's celebrity-laden coastal resorts. A busy working port, it has not been prettified for the benefit of tourists and is all the more interesting for it. With its landmark citadel, great restaurants and popular, sandy beach, Cagliari is very much its own city.

Orientation

The main bus and train stations and port are near Piazza Matteotti, where you'll find the tourist office. The busy seafront road Via Roma connects with Largo Carlo Felice, which heads north to Piazza Yenne, the centre's focal square. Rising above everything is the historic Castello (castle) district.

Information

Lamarù (Via Napoli 43; per hr €3; ⌚ 9am-8pm Mon-Sat) Internet cafe.

GETTING INTO TOWN

From Elmas airport, half-hourly ARST buses run to the bus station on Piazza Matteotti; the 10-minute journey costs €2.

The port is an easy 10-minute walk to the city centre.

Ospedale Brotzu (Hospital; ☎ 070 53 91; Via Peretti)
Police station (Questura; ☎ 070 6 02 71; Via Amat Luigi 9)
Tourist office (☎ 070 66 92 55; Piazza Matteotti; ⌚ 8.30am-1.30pm & 2-8pm)

Sights & Activities

The most interesting part of town is the Castello district, the medieval citadel which towers over the city. Housed in Cagliari's former arsenal is the city's main museum complex, the **Citadella dei Musei**. Of its four museums, the most impressive is the **Museo Archeologico Nazionale** (☎ 070 68 40 00; Piazza dell'Arsenale; admission €4; ⌚ 9am-8pm Tue-Sun); its fascinating prehistoric bronzes provide one of the few clues to the island's mysterious *nuraghic* culture.

At the other end of Castello, past the 13th-century **Cattedrale di Santa Maria** (Piazza Palazzo 4; ⌚ 8.30am-12.30pm & 5.30-8pm) and its imposing Romanesque pulpits, is the monumental **Bastione San Remy** (Piazza Costituzione). This was formerly a strong point in the defensive walls and commands huge views over the city and distant lagoons.

To the west of the centre, the 2nd-century **Anfiteatro Romano** (Roman Amphitheatre; Vile Fra Ignazio; admission €4.30; ⌚ 9.30am-1.30pm Tue-Sat, 9.30am-1.30pm & 3.30-5.30pm Sun) provides a spectacular setting for summer concerts.

A short bus ride from the centre, Cagliari's vibrant beach, **Spiaggia di Poetto**, boasts inviting blue waters and a happening summer scene.

Festivals & Events

The annual **Festival of Sant'Efisio**, a colourful celebration mixing the secular and the religious, is held for four days from 1 May.

Sleeping

B&B La Marina (☎ 070 67 00 65; www.la-marina.it; Via Porcile 23; s €40, d €70-75; ❄) A good-value B&B in the atmospheric Marina district with four white, wood-beamed rooms. There are also a couple of communal breakfast rooms with fridges for guest use.

Albergo Aurora (☎ 070 65 86 25; www.hotelcagliariaurora.it; Salita Santa Chiara 19; s with shared bathroom €32-37, with private bathroom €41-46, d with shared bathroom €48-55, with private bathroom €60-68; ❄) A welcoming budget hotel just off buzzing Piazza Yenne. The ageing rooms are spacious and bright with pastel walls and exposed brickwork.

Hotel A&R Bundes Jack (☎/fax 070 66 79 70; www.hotelbjvittoria.it; Via Roma 75; s €48-58, d €76-88; ❄) The best budget hotel on the seafront, this old-fashioned *pensione* has large, high-ceilinged rooms decorated with robust furniture and sparkling chandeliers. Breakfast is not included.

Eating

Il Fantasma (☎ 070 65 67 49; Via San Domenico 94; pizzas €6.50; 🕒 Mon-Sat) A bit of a hike from the centre, this local favourite serves Cagliari's best pizza. If you haven't booked you'll need to arrive early to get a table in the cheerful, brick-lined interior.

Trattoria Gennargentu (☎ 070 67 20 21; Via Sardegna 60; meals €20) It doesn't look much from outside but this no-frills trattoria serves excellent food. There's a full menu of pastas and meaty mains but the seafood is the thing to go for.

Also worth a mention is **Antico Caffè** (☎ 070 65 82 96; Piazza Costituzione), an elegant cafe where you can get a pasta lunch for around €10.

Getting There & Around

Cagliari's **Elmas airport** (CAG; ☎ 070 211 211; www.sogaer.it) is 6km northwest of the city. The airport is served by a number of airlines, including easyJet, Ryanair and several other buget carriers, with routes to/from mainland Italian cities and destinations across Europe. In summer, there are additional charter flights.

Cagliari's ferry port is just off Via Roma. **Tirrenia** (☎ 892 123; www.tirrenia.it; Via dei Ponente 1; 🕒 8.30am-12.20pm & 3.30-6.50pm Mon-Sat) is the main ferry operator, with year-round services to Civitavecchia (€48, 16½ hours), Naples (€45, 16¼ hours) and Palermo (€51, 14½ hours). Book tickets at the port or at travel agencies.

From the bus station, ARST runs buses to/from Oristano (€6.50, 1½ hours, four daily) and Nuoro (€14.50, 3½ hours, four daily), as well as destinations on the Costa del Sud and Costa Rei. Get tickets from the McDonalds on the square. FdS buses link with Sassari (€17, 3¼ hours, three daily), and **Turmo Travel** (☎ 0789 2 14 87; www.gruppoturmotravel.com) runs a daily bus to Olbia (€18, 4¼ hours).

Down by the port, you can rent cars, bikes and scooters from **CIA Rent a Car** (☎ 070 65 65 03; www.ciarent.it; Via Molo Sant'Agostino 13; car per day from €39).

Trenitalia trains run from the station on Piazza Matteotti to Oristano (€5.15, up to two hours, hourly) and Sassari (€13.65, 4¼ hours, five daily).

ALGHERO

pop 50,600

A favourite of holidaying Brits, Alghero is the main resort on Sardinia's northwest coast. Surprisingly, though, it's not entirely given over to tourism and it is still an important fishing port. Interest is centred on the medieval *centro storico* with its robust stone ramparts and tight-knit lanes.

Alghero was founded in the 11th century by the Genovese and later became an important outpost of the Aragonese Catalans. Still today the local dialect is a form of Catalan, and the town retains something of a Spanish atmosphere.

Orientation & Information

Alghero's historic centre is on a small promontory jutting into the sea, with the new town radiating out behind and north along the coast.

On the eastern fringe of the *centro storico*, the superhelpful **tourist office** (☎ 079 97 90 54; www.comune.alghero.ss.it, in Italian; Piazza Porta Terra 9; 🕒 8am-8pm Mon-Sat, 10am-1pm Sun) can answer every imaginable question.

Sights & Activities

The *centro storico* is a charming mesh of narrow cobbled alleys hemmed in by Spanish Gothic *palazzi*. Of the various churches, the most interesting is the **Chiesa di San Francesco** (Via Carlo Alberto; 🕒 7.30am-noon & 5-8.30pm), with its mix of Romanesque and Gothic styles. Not far away, the cathedral's landmark **campanile** (bell tower; admission €2; 🕒 7-9.30pm Tue, Thu & Sat Jul-Aug, 5-8pm Sep, by appointment rest of year) is a fine example of Gothic-Catalan architecture.

From the port you can take a boat trip to **Capo Caccia** and the **Grotte di Nettuno** (☎ 079 94 65 40; adult/concession €10/5; 🕒 9am-7pm Apr-Sep, to 5pm Oct, to 4pm Jan-Mar, Nov & Dec), a mesmerising sea cave. The cheapest boat is the **Navisarda**

ferry (☎ 079 95 06 03; return €14), which departs hourly between 9am and 5pm from June to September, and four times daily the rest of the year. Allow 2½ hours for the round trip. Cheaper still, you can get a bus from Via Catalogna (€3.50 return, 50 minutes, three times daily summer, once winter).

Ten kilometres west of Alghero on the road to Porto Conte, the **Nuraghe di Palmavera** (☎ 079 95 32 00; admission €3; 9am-7pm summer, shorter hours winter) is a 3500-year-old *nuraghe* village, well worth a visit.

Sleeping & Eating

There's plenty of accommodation in Alghero but you'll need to book between June and September.

Camping La Mariposa (☎ 079 95 03 60; www.lamariposa.it; Via Lido 22; per person/tent/car €11/13/4, 4-person bungalows €47-78; ; Apr-Oct) About 2km north of the centre, this popular camping ground is on the beach amid pine and eucalyptus trees.

Hostal de l'Alguer (☎ /fax 079 93 20 39; www.alguerohostel.com; Via Parenzo 79; dm €18, s/d/tr/q per person €30/25/22/20; P) A characterless hostel near the airport in Fertilia. Although nothing special, it's clean and cheap. Meals are available (€9.50).

Hotel San Francesco (☎ 079 98 03 30; www.sanfrancescohotel.com; Via Ambrogio Machin 2; s €45-70, d €70-105;) The only hotel in Alghero's *centro storico*, this ex-convent has comfortable rooms.

Il Ghiotto (☎ 079 97 48 20; Piazza Civica 23; meals €10-15; Tue-Sun) One of the few places in Alghero where you can sit down and eat for as little as €10. There's a fantastic canteen serving a daily spread of *panini*, pastas, salads and mains.

Trattoria Maristella (☎ 079 97 81 72; Via Fratelli Kennedy 9; meals €27) Visitors and locals flock to this bustling little trattoria for reliable seafood and Sardinian specialities at honest prices.

Getting There & Away

Alghero's airport **Fertilia** (AHO; ☎ 079 93 52 82; www.algheroairport.it) is served by a number of low-cost carriers, including Ryanair and Air One, with connections to mainland Italy and European destinations.

> **GETTING INTO TOWN**
>
> Up to 10 daily FdS buses (€0.70, 20 minutes) connect the airport with Piazza Mercede in the town centre.

> **WORTH THE TRIP: BOSA**
>
> As much for the getting there as the town itself, a trip to Bosa is well worth it. The 46km road from Alghero is one of Sardinia's great coastal rides with unforgettable vistas at every turn. Bosa doesn't disappoint either, with its picturesque old town rising up from the Temo River.
>
> For the journey, you can rent cars, motorcycles and bikes from **Cicloexpress** (☎ 079 98 69 50; www.cicloexpress.com; Via Garibaldi, Alghero) from €65/55/8 per day.

Logudoro Tours (☎ 079 28 17 28) runs two daily buses from the airport to Cagliari (€20, 3½ hours). For Sassari, there are up to 15 daily buses (€3, one hour) from Via Catalogna, or you can catch a train (€2.20, 35 minutes, 10 daily) from the station about 1km southeast of the historic centre.

ITALY DIRECTORY

ACCOMMODATION

The bulk of Italy's accommodation consists of *alberghi* (hotels) and *pensioni*. Expect to pay high-season rates at Easter, in summer (mid-June to August), and over the Christmas–New Year period. Peak season in the ski resorts runs from December to March. Note also that many city hotels offer discounts in August and that many coastal hotels shut up for the winter, typically between November and March. Tourist offices have listings for all local accommodation.

As a rough guide, reckon on at least €55 for a double room in a budget hotel. The prices quoted in this chapter are for rooms with a private bathroom and, unless otherwise stated, include breakfast.

Under Italian law, smoking is banned in all public areas in hotels (receptions, lobbies, bars, dining rooms etc). Some hotels also ban it in guest rooms, although they are not legally obliged to do so.

Agriturismo & B&Bs

Dotted around the countryside *agriturismi* (farm stays) are all the rage, although you'll usually need your own transport. Accommodation varies from spartan billets on working farms to palatial rural retreats.

For information and lists check out www.agriturist.it or www.agriturismo.com.

Bed and breakfasts (B&B) are also popular. Prices are typically between €70 and €150 for a room. Good online resources include www.bbitalia.it and www.cross-pollinate.com.

Camping

Campers are well catered to in Italy. Lists of camping grounds are available from local tourist offices or online at www.campeggi.com, www.camping.it and www.touringclub.it. In high season rates can reach €15 per person and a further €10 to €15 for a tent pitch. Independent camping is not permitted in many places.

Hostels

Ostelli per la gioventù (youth hostels) are run by the **Italian Youth Hostel Association** (Associazione Italiana Alberghi per la Gioventù; Map p640; ☎ 06 487 11 52; www.ostellionline.org; Via Cavour 44, Rome), affiliated with **Hostelling International** (HI; www.hihostels.com). An HI card is required, which you can get in your home country or at many hostels. Dorms range from €15 to €30, often including breakfast. Many places also offer dinner for around €10.

There's also an increasing number of private hostels, many of which offer hotel-standard rooms alongside dorm accommodation.

Mountain Refuges

Italy boasts an extensive network of mountain *rifugi* (refuges). Open from July to September, they offer basic dorm-style accommodation, although some have double rooms. Reckon on €17 to €26 per person per night with breakfast included. **Club Alpino Italiano** (CAI; www.cai.it, in Italian) runs many of the refuges.

Religious Accommodation

Religious accommodation is a reliable money-saver, typically costing about €85 for a double room. The **Chiesa di Santa Susanna** (www.santasusanna.org) has a list of convents and monasteries throughout Italy. You can also try www.monasterystays.com, an online booking service.

ACTIVITIES

Cycling

Italy offers everything from teeth-rattling mountain biking to gentle valley rides. Tourist offices can usually provide details on trails and guided rides. Tuscany and Umbria are favourite spots, and there's excellent mountain-biking in the Dolomites, Sardinia and Sicily.

Hiking & Walking

Thousands of kilometres of *sentieri* (marked trails) criss-cross Italy, ranging from hardcore mountain treks to gentle lakeside ambles. In season (the end of June to September), the Dolomites are a favourite destination. Other hot spots include the Cinque Terre, Amalfi Coast and Mt Etna in Sicily.

Useful websites include www.cai.it (in Italian) and www.parks.it.

Skiing

Most of the country's top resorts are in the Alps, although there are excellent facilities throughout the Apennines. Skiing isn't cheap, and high-season costs (applicable December to March) will hurt. You'll save a bit buying a *settimana bianca* (literally 'white week') package, covering accommodation, food and ski passes.

See p676 for further details.

BUSINESS HOURS

Although many variations exist, the following are standard hours:

Banks (🕒 8.30am-1.30pm & 2.45-4.30pm Mon-Fri)
Bars & cafes (🕒 7.30am-8pm) Many open earlier and some stay open until the small hours.
Discos & clubs (🕒 10pm-4am) Action rarely starts much before midnight.
Pharmacies (🕒 9am-1pm & 4-7.30pm Mon-Fri, to 1pm Sat) Outside of these hours, pharmacies open on a rotation basis. All are required to post a list of other places open in the vicinity.
Post offices branch offices (🕒 8.30am-1.50pm Mon-Fri, to 11.50am Sat); major offices (🕒 8.30am-6.50pm Mon-Fri, to 1.15pm Sat)
Restaurants (🕒 noon-3pm & 7.30-11pm, later in summer) Most restaurants close one day a week.
Shops (🕒 9am-1pm & 3.30-7.30pm, or 4-8pm Mon-Sat) In larger cities many chain stores and supermarkets open from 9am to 7.30pm Monday to Saturday; some also open Sunday mornings, typically 9am to 1pm. Food shops are generally closed on Thursday afternoons; some other shops are closed on Monday mornings.

Many museums, gallery and archaeological sites operate summer and winter opening hours. Typically, winter hours apply between November and late March/early April.

DRIVING LICENCE

All EU driving licences are recognised in Italy. Holders of non-EU licences must get an International Driving Permit (IDP) to accompany their national licence.

EMBASSIES & CONSULATES

Listed are contact details for embassies and consulates in Rome. There are also British and US consulates in many major cities.

Australia (Map pp638-9; ☎ 06 85 27 21, emergencies 800 87 77 90; www.italy.embassy.gov.au; Via Antonio Bosio 5; 8.30am-5pm Mon-Fri)

Austria Consulate (Map pp638-9; ☎ 06 855 28 80; Viale Liegi 32; 9am-noon Mon-Fri); Embassy (Map pp642-3; ☎ 06 844 01 41; www.bmeia.gv.at/it/ambasciata/roma; Via Pergolesi 3)

Canada Consulate (Map pp638-9; ☎ 06 85 44 41; Via Zara 30; 8.30am-noon & 2-4pm Mon-Fri); Embassy (Map pp638-9; ☎ 06 85 44 41; www.international.gc.ca/canada-europa/italy; Via Salaria 243)

France Consulate (Map pp646-7; ☎ 06 68 60 11; Via Giulia 251; 9am-12.30pm Mon-Fri); Embassy (Map pp646-7; ☎ 06 68 60 11; www.ambafrance-it.org; Piazza Farnese 67)

Germany (Map p640; ☎ 06 49 21 31; www.rom.diplo.de; Via San Martino della Battaglia 4; 8.30-11.30am Mon-Fri)

Ireland (Map pp646-7; ☎ 06 697 91 21; www.ambasciata-irlanda.it; Piazza di Campitelli 3; 10am-12.30pm & 3-4.30pm Mon-Fri)

Netherlands (Map pp638-9; ☎ 06 322 86 001; www.olanda.it; Via Michele Mercati 8; 9am-noon Mon, Tue, Thu & Fri)

New Zealand (Map pp638-9; ☎ 06 853 75 01; www.nzembassy.com; Via Clitunno 44; 8.30am-12.45pm & 1.45-5pm Mon-Fri)

UK (Map pp638-9; ☎ 06 422 00 001; www.britishembassy.gov.uk/italy; Via XX Settembre 80a; 9am-5pm Mon-Fri)

USA (Map pp642-3; ☎ 06 4 67 41; www.usis.it; Via Vittorio Veneto 119a; 8.30am-12.30pm Mon-Fri)

FESTIVALS & EVENTS

Italy's most famous festivals and events:

Carnevale Many towns stage carnivals in the period before Ash Wednesday. The best known is in Venice (see p671).

Settimana Santa Holy Week is celebrated with processions and Passion plays.

Scoppio del Carro Fireworks display in Florence's Piazza del Duomo on Easter Saturday (see p682).

Palio delle Quattro Antiche Repubbliche Marinare (Regatta of the Four Ancient Maritime Republics) Boat races between the four historical maritime republics – Pisa, Venice, Amalfi and Genoa. The event rotates between the towns and is usually held in June.

Il Palio On 2 July and 16 August, Siena stages its crazy horse race (see p686).

Natale In the run-up to Christmas many churches set up elaborate cribs or nativity scenes known as *presepi* – Naples is famous for these.

FOOD & DRINK

Despite the ubiquity of pasta and pizza, Italian cuisine is highly regional. Local specialities abound and traditions are proudly maintained, so expect pesto in Genoa, pizza in Naples, and *ragù* (bolognese sauce) in Bologna. It's the same with wine: Piedmont produces Italy's great reds – Barolo, Barbaresco and Dolcetto – while Tuscany is famous for its Chianti, Brunello and white Vernaccia.

Vegetarians will find delicious fruit and veg in the hundreds of daily markets. Few restaurants cater specifically to vegetarians, although most serve vegetable-based *antipasti* (starters), pastas, *contorni* (side dishes) and salads.

A full Italian meal consists of an antipasto, a *primo piatto* (first course), *secondo piatto* (second course) with *insalata* (salad) or *contorno* (vegetable side dish), and a *dolce* (sweet). When eating out it's perfectly acceptable to order, say, a *primo* followed by an *insalata* or *contorno*.

Italian wines run the gamut from world-class reds to crisp whites and sparkling spumante. You'll get some idea of the quality by checking out the classification on the label – if you see the initials DOCG *(denominazione di origine controllata e garantita)*, you know you're onto a good thing. DOCG wines are made in a specific area according to strict rules and then tested by a special tasting committee. DOC *(denominazione di origine controllata)* wines have to meet similar but slightly less stringent criteria, while the ICG *(indicazione geografica tipica)* designation simply means that the wine was produced in a certain area. At the bottom of the barrel is *vino da tavola* (table wine).

Restaurants are usually open from noon to 3pm and 7.30pm to 11pm, later in summer. Most restaurants close one day a week.

GAY & LESBIAN TRAVELLERS

Discretion is the key. Although homosexuality is legal and tolerated in major cities, attitudes remain conservative and overt displays of affection could attract unwelcome attention, particularly in the more traditional south. Gay hotspots include Rome, Milan, Bologna, Florence and Padua, all of which boast active gay scenes. In summer, Taormina in Sicily and Tuscany's Torre del Lago offer gay action.

Italy's main gay rights association, Arcigay (www.arcigay.it), is a good source of information, as is Circolo Mario Mieli (www.mariomieli.org), a Rome-based organisation that produces the free monthly magazine AUT. A good online resource is www.gayfriendlyitaly.com.

HOLIDAYS

Public holidays:

New Year's Day (Capodanno) 1 January
Epiphany (Epifania) 6 January
Easter Monday (Pasquetta) March/April
Liberation Day (Giorno delle Liberazione) 25 April
Labour Day (Festa del Lavoro) 1 May
Republic Day (Festa della Repubblica) 2 June
Feast of the Assumption (Ferragosto) 15 August
All Saint's Day (Ognisanti) 1 November
Feast of the Immaculate Conception (Immacolata Concezione) 8 December
Christmas Day (Natale) 25 December
Boxing Day (Festa di Santo Stefano) 26 December

Individual towns also have holidays to celebrate their patron saints:

St Mark (Venice) 25 April
St John the Baptist (Florence, Genoa and Turin) 24 June
Sts Peter and Paul (Rome) 29 June
St Rosalia (Palermo) 15 July
St Janarius (Naples) First Sunday in May, 19 September and 16 December
St Ambrose (Milan) 7 December

INTERNET RESOURCES

Ferrovie dello Stato (www.trenitalia.it) Plan your train trips.
Italian Government Tourist Board (www.enit.it) Not always up-to-date site of the Italian tourist board.
Lonely Planet (www.lonelyplanet.com) Exchange tips with folk who've been to Italy.
Traghetti Web (www.traghettionline.net) Timetables and links to ferry companies.
Vatican (www.vatican.va) The Vatican's official website.

MONEY

Italy's currency is the euro. The best way to manage funds is to use your debit/credit cards while keeping a fistful of travellers cheques as backup. Visa and MasterCard are widely recognised, as are Cirrus and Maestro; American Express is accepted but is less common. Credit and debit cards can be used in *bancomat* (ATMs) displaying the appropriate sign – you'll need a four-digit PIN, though. If you don't have a PIN, some (but not all) banks will advance cash over the counter.

Visa, Travelex and Amex are the most widely accepted travellers cheques, although changing even these in smaller cities can be difficult. You'll find exchange offices at major airports and train stations.

You're not expected to tip on top of restaurant service charges, but if you think the service warrants it feel free to leave a little extra – 10% is fine. In bars, Italians often leave small change (€0.10 or €0.20).

POST

Italy's **Poste** (☎ 803 160; www.poste.it, in Italian) is improved but still not a model of efficiency. The standard service is *posta prioritaria* (priority mail). Registered mail is known as *raccomandato,* insured mail as *assicurato* and express post as *postacelere*.

Stamps *(francobolli)* are available at post offices and tobacconists *(tabacchi)*.

TELEPHONE

The international access code for Italy is ☎ 00; the country code is ☎ 39. Mobile phone numbers begin with a three-digit prefix such as 330 or 339. You must always dial the area code in Italy, even when calling locally. Toll-free (freephone) numbers are known in Italy as *numeri verdi* and usually start with 800.

Long-distance calls can easily be made from public phones – you'll need a *scheda telefonica* (telephone card), available from tobacconists and newsstands. Peak rates apply from 8am to 6.30pm Monday to Friday and until 1pm on Saturday.

You'll save a bit by calling from a cut-price call centre, which you'll find in many big cities. Alternatively, some internet cafes have Skype.

To make a reverse-charge (collect) international call, dial ☎ 170. All operators speak English.

VISAS

EU citizens do not need a visa to enter Italy. Nationals of Australia, Canada, Israel, Japan, New Zealand, Switzerland and the USA do not need a visa for stays of up to 90 days.

Non-EU nationals who stay in Italy longer than three months require a *permesso di soggiorno* (permit to stay). In theory, you should apply for this within eight days of arriving in Italy.

Non-EU citizens who want to study in Italy must obtain a study visa from their nearest Italian embassy or consulate.

Kosovo

HIGHLIGHTS

- **Prizren** In Prizren (p716), walk up to Kaljaja Fort for far-reaching views and a heart-wrenching perspective
- **Pristina** Pristina has all the chaos and cosmopolitanism of a newly declared capital (p714)
- **Gračanica Monastery** A timeless, revered piece of Serbian Orthodoxy that has stood its hallowed ground for centuries (p716)

FAST FACTS

- **Area** 10,887 sq km
- **Budget** €50 per day
- **Capital** Pristina
- **Country code** ☎ 381
- **Famous for** its controversial status
- **Languages** Albanian, Serbian
- **Money** euro (€); A$1 = €0.55; C$1 = €0.60; ¥100 = €0.78; NZ$1 = €0.43; UK£1 = €1.12; US$1 = €0.74
- **Phrases** *po* (yes), *jo* (no), *faleminderit* (thank you)
- **Population** 1.8 to 2.4 million

- **Visas** not required for up to 90 days for EU, UK, Australian, New Zealand, Canadian and US citizens

TRAVEL HINTS

Don't be lured into timeworn hotels on main roads; newer gems hide down laneways.

ROAMING KOSOVO

From Pristina to Peja for Serbian Orthodox sights and a Turkish-style bazaar. Back to Pristina via strongly Ottoman Prizren.

Kosovo doesn't leap to mind as a travel destination; it has the weakest economy in Europe and wounds of the past still show. But the future is coming on quickly. Though not universally recognised, Kosovo declared itself independent in early 2008.

Pristina is a montage of everywhere that's had a hand in its past, and it vies to play a role in its own future. Incongruous images abound: burgers on Bill Clinton Boulevard, İstanbul hair salons, and blood-red Albanian flags flapping next to the benign blue of those belonging to the UN and EU.

Nothing is more than a couple of hours from Pristina. It's possible to visit Unesco-recognised Serbian Orthodox monasteries in Prizren or barter for goat cheese in Peja's Turkish-style bazaar, and be back in Pristina for an unexpectedly decadent dinner.

HISTORY

In the 12th century, Kosovo was the heart of the Serbian empire. This Serbian golden age under Stefan Dušan saw construction of many Orthodox churches until the Turkish triumph at the pivotal 1389 Battle of Kosovo ushered in 500 years of Ottoman rule. The number of Serbs fell drastically, and Albanians and Muslims came to dominate the region's ethnic and religious make-up.

In 1989 the autonomy that Kosovo had gained in 1974 was suspended by Slobodan Milošević. Ethnic Albanian leaders declared independence in 1990 and war erupted in 1992.

A US-backed plan to return Kosovo's autonomy was rejected by Serbia in March 1999. After Serbia refused to desist from emptying the province of non-Serbians, NATO unleashed a bombing campaign. In June, Milošević withdrew troops and Kosovo became a UN-NATO protectorate.

Hashim Thaci became president in November 2007 and declared Kosovo independent on 17 February 2008. Several countries recognised its independence; Serbia wasn't one of them.

TRANSPORT

GETTING THERE & AWAY

Air

Pristina International Airport (☎ 038-5958 123; www.airportpristina.com) is 18km from Pristina.

Land

International bus routes from Pristina include Belgrade (€19, six hours), Novi Pazar (€5, three hours) – also reachable from Peja (€5, three hours) or Prizren (€10, six hours) – Skopje

TRAVEL ADVISORY

At the time of writing, unrest in border areas between Serbia and Kosovo following Kosovo's declaration of independence made travelling overland between them ill advised. Check travel advisories before attempting to do so.

There is a heavy KFOR presence in Serbian enclaves and sites of potential tension; carry your passport to present when requested.

Book your stay at lonelyplanet.com/hotels

VISITING KOSOVO FIRST

Serbia doesn't consider Kosovo's entry and exit points as part of an international border. So unless you initially entered Kosovo from Serbia itself, attempting to enter Serbia for the first time from Kosovo may be futile.

(€5, 1½ hours), Linz (€50, 14 hours) and İstanbul (€30, 20 hours).

GETTING AROUND

Bus

Services linking towns and villages are excellent. Buses stop at stations or can be flagged down anywhere.

Car

Rental car agencies include **Europcar** (☎ 038-138 594 101; www.auto-shkodra.com). Potholes make road conditions far from safe. It's unwise to bring in Serbian-plated cars.

Train

The train system is stretching to routes including Pristina to Peja (€3, 1½ hours) and Pristina to Skopje (€4, three hours). Locals generally take the bus.

PRISTINA

☎ **038 / pop 200,000**

Pristina, a great base for day trips to Peja and Prizren, looks like a torn-apart town crudely reassembled by differences of opinion. Look closer and you'll notice its pride at being a newly declared capital.

ORIENTATION & INFORMATION

Bulevardi Nëna Terezë converges with Agim Ramadani. Parallel is Luan Haradinaj. Bil Klinton Bulevardi runs southwest past the bus station and airport (18km) towards Peja.

Banks, travel agents and other shops line Bulevardi Nëna Terezë. **Barnatorja Pharmacy** (☎ 224 245; Bulevardi Nëna Terezë; 7.30am-8pm Mon-Sat, 9am-5pm Sun) is north of the Grand Hotel. Next door, **Library Dukagjini** (☎ 248 143; Bulevardi Nëna Terezë 20; 8am-8pm Mon-Sat) has maps and books.

EMERGENCY NUMBERS

- Ambulance ☎ 94
- Fire service ☎ 93
- Police ☎ 92
- Emergency ☎ 541 644 (from Vala phones ☎ 112)

Get **Pristina in Your Pocket** (www.inyourpocket.com/city/pristina.html) online or at Library Dukagjini.

SIGHTS

In Pristina's bustling bazaar area, **Kosovo Museum** (☎ 249 964; Sheshi Adam Jashari; admission €1; 9.30am-5.30pm Tue-Fri, 11am-3pm Sat & Sun) has an orange Austro-Hungarian exterior and more or less arbitrary opening hours. If it's open when you're there, take some time to see local artefacts (minus the 1247 that are yet to return from Belgrade after being moved there for safekeeping in 1998). **Sultan Mehmet Fatih Mosque** (the 'Big Mosque'), built by its namesake around 1461, was converted to Catholicism during the Austro-Hungarian era and refurbished again during WWII. Next to the 26m-high **Clock Tower**, vibrant interiors in the **Jashar Pasha Mosque** exemplify Turkish baroque style.

In the centre, check out the mechanomad **National Library** (www.biblioteka-ks.org) completed in 1982 by Croatian architect Andrija Mutnjakovic.

SLEEPING

Velania Guesthouse (Guesthouse Professor; ☎ 531 742, 044 16 74 55; www.guesthouse-ks.com; Velania 4/34; s/d €13/18;) Run by a jovial professor, Velania is the choice for anyone missing hostel socialising or their grandad. Kitchens have complimentary coffee. Private rooms have TVs and cable internet.

READING UP

Noel Malcolm's authoritative *Kosovo: A Short History* is widely available. *Three Elegies for Kosovo*, by Ismail Kadare, has been critically acclaimed and is one of the few works of fiction about Kosovo.

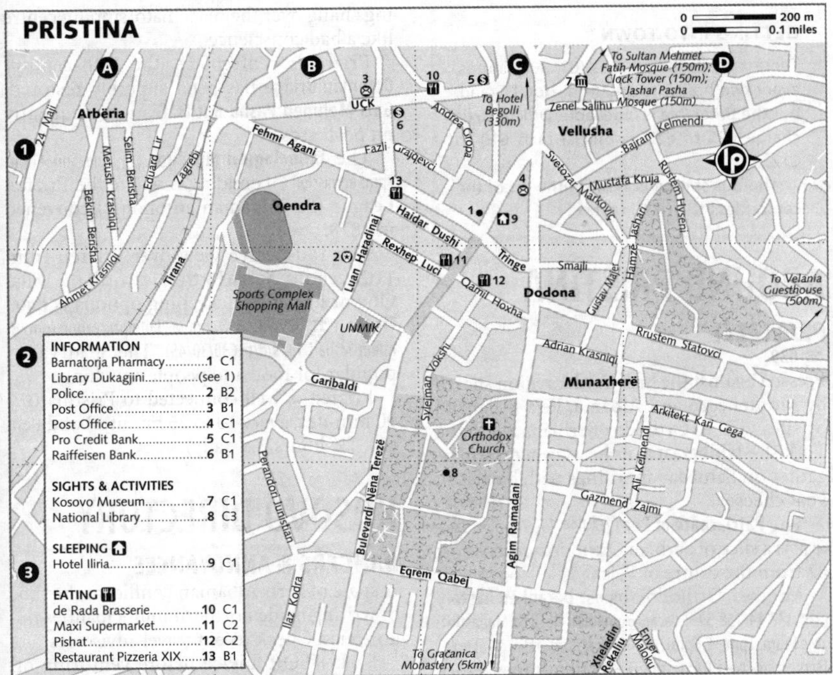

ourpick Hotel Begolli (☎ 044-308 093, 049-308 093; www.hotel-begolli.piczo.com; Rr Maliq pash Gjinolli 8; s/d €30/35, ste €50/60, apt €80/100;) This good-value hotel offers twice what you need and charges half what it could (the catch: no internet and dull breakfast). Opt for one of the front rooms rather than the smaller windowless rear ones.

Hotel Ileria (☎ 224 275; Bulevardi Nëna Terezë; s/d with bathroom €25/50, s/d without bathroom €20/40) Dated but central.

EATING

Quick, cheap fare is available in local eateries along Bulevardi Nëna Terezë, south of Garibaldi.

de Rada Brasserie (☎ 222 622; Rr UÇK 50; mains €7; 8am-midnight Mon-Sat, 6pm-midnight Sun) This is the sort of place you'd normally find in Paris, except here it's affordable.

Pishat (☎ 245 333; Rr Qamil Hoxha 11; mains €6; 8am-11pm Mon-Sat, noon to 11pm Sun) Popular with expats and discerning locals, here you can sample Albanian dishes.

Restaurant Pizzeria XIX (☎ 044-300 022; www.xixonline.com; Rr Luan Haradinaj 2; pizzas €2.50-6; 7am-midnight Sun-Thu; 7am-2am Fri & Sat) A rugged restaurant with a hard-working pizza oven.

Head to **Maxi Supermarket** (Rexhep Luci; 7am-midnight) for groceries.

GETTING THERE & AWAY

The **bus station** (Stacioni I Autobusëve; ☎ 038- 550 011; Rr Lidja e Pejes), 2km southwest of the centre, off Bil Klinton Bulevardi, serves all of Kosovo.

GETTING AROUND

Kombis (minibuses; from €0.30 to €0.50) are ubiquitous.

Local taxi trips cost a few euros. Unofficial taxis (ie blokes with cars) must be negotiated with.

CONNECTIONS

Only a few hours on the bus from Pristina will get you to Macedonia, Montenegro, Albania or Serbia. Long-haul buses head to Central Europe and even as far east as İstanbul.

GETTING INTO TOWN

There are allegedly buses (€3, 30 minutes, every two hours) to and from Hotel Grand, but the timetable is unreliable. Official taxis charge €20 to €25, unofficial taxis €10 to €12.

The bus station is 2km southwest of the centre; less than €2 in a taxi.

AROUND PRISTINA

PEJA (PEĆ)

☎ 039

Pressed against the lush border region shared by Montenegro and Albania, Peja is flanked by sites vital to Orthodox Serbians and has a Turkish-style **bazaar** at its heart, where farmers gather on Saturday mornings with barrels of goat cheese.

The **Patriachate of Peć** (☎ 044-150 755; 9am-6pm) is a slice of Serbian Orthodoxy. Taxis cost €2 from the centre of Peja.

Another Orthodox oasis, **Decani Monastery** (☎ 377 44 158 326; decani@gmx.net; Rl Ul St Manastirit; 11am-1pm, 4-6pm), is 15km south of Peja. Buses go to Decani (€0.80, 30 minutes, every 20 minutes) on their way to destinations such as Gjakovë.

Sleep at **Hotel Gold** (☎ 434 571; Eliot Engl 122/2; s/d €40/50,) or cosy **Hotel Peja** (☎ 044-406 777; hotel_peja@hotmail.com; Pjetro Marko; s/d €30/40,). Enjoy sky-high views (but average food) at the rooftop restaurant on the **Semitronix Centre** (☎ 432 754; Mbretëresha Teutë; 7am-11pm; meals €4).

There are regular buses from Pristina to Peja (€3, 90 minutes, every 15 to 20 minutes).

PRIZREN

☎ 029 / pop 70,000

Picturesque Prizren shines with post-independence euphoria, but burnt-out buildings hang over the macchiato-sipping centre like a bad conscience.

Prizren's centrepiece, the 15th-century **Ottoman Bridge** has been superbly restored. **Gazi Mehmed Pasha Baths** feature frequently on postcards.

The **Ethnological Museum** (Tue-Sun 11am-7pm; admission €1) building is where the Prizren League (for Albanian autonomy) convened in 1878.

The 180-degree view over Prizren from 11th-century **Kalaja Fortress** is worth the walk. One of few central sleeping options is **Hotel Tirana** (☎ 029-230 818; tirana_hotelpz@yahoo.com; Rr Adem Jashari 14; s/d/tr €30/30/45). The Shadrvan is popular for food and people-watching.

Prizren is well connected to Pristina (€3, 90 minutes, every 10 to 25 minutes) and Peja (€3, 1½ hours, six daily).

WORTH THE TRIP

Dusty fingers of sunlight pierce the darkness of **Gračanica Monastery** (6am-5pm), completed in 1321 by Serbian King Milutin. The enchanting monastery is guarded by KFOR soldiers. Take a Gjilan-bound bus (50c, 15 minutes, every 30 minutes) and get out in Gračanica.

KOSOVO DIRECTORY

DANGERS & ANNOYANCES

A spate of Serb-Albanian conflict at the time of writing made northern municipalities no-go zones. Check recent travel advisories.

Seek KFOR advice before venturing off beaten tracks; there are still some unexploded ordnance (UXO).

Make sure your insurance covers you in Kosovo.

EMBASSIES & CONSULATES

In the absence of consular representation, contact embassies in Skopje (p771).

Albania (☎ 248 208; www.mfa.gov.al; Qyteza Pejton, Rruga Mujo Ulqinaku 18)

Germany (☎ 254 500; www.konsulate.de/kosovo_e.php; Azem Jashanica 17)

Switzerland (☎ 248 088, 248 089, 248 090; www.eda.admin.ch/pristina; Adrian Krasniqi 11; 8.15am-noon, 2-3pm Mon-Fri)

UK (☎ 254 700; www.britishembassy.gov.uk; Ismail Qemajli 6; 8.30am-5pm Mon-Thu, 8.30am-1.30pm Fri)

US (☎ 5959 3119; http://pristina.usembassy.gov; Arberia, Nazim Hikmet 30; 8am-5pm Mon-Fri)

MONEY

Arrive with small denominations of euros. ATMs are common. Established businesses accept credit cards.

VISAS

Upon arrival, you get a 90-day entry stamp.

Latvia

HIGHLIGHTS

- **Rīga** Click your camera at the capital's shimmering church spires, devilish art nouveau gargoyles, and cobbled lanes hidden behind gingerbread trim (p720)
- **Sigulda** Trek through this Never-Never-Land, chronicling its vivid history with stops at rambling Livonian castles and top-secret Soviet bunkers (p728)
- **Cape Kolka** Close your eyes and listen to the waves crash over the crown of the desolate Kurzeme coastline (p727)

FAST FACTS

- **Area** 64,589 sq km
- **Budget** 20Ls to 25Ls per day
- **Capital** Rīga
- **Country code** ☎ 371
- **Famous for** ballet dancer Mikhail Baryshnikov and the jaw-dropping Song and Dance Festival
- **Languages** Latvian, Russian, English
- **Money** Lats (Ls); A$1=0.39Ls; C$ = 0.44Ls; €1=0.70Ls; ¥100=0.55Ls; NZ$1=0.30Ls; UK£1=0.79Ls; US$1=0.52Ls
- **Phrases** *labdien* (hello), *paldies* (thank you), *lūdzu* (please/you're welcome)
- **Population** 2.25 million

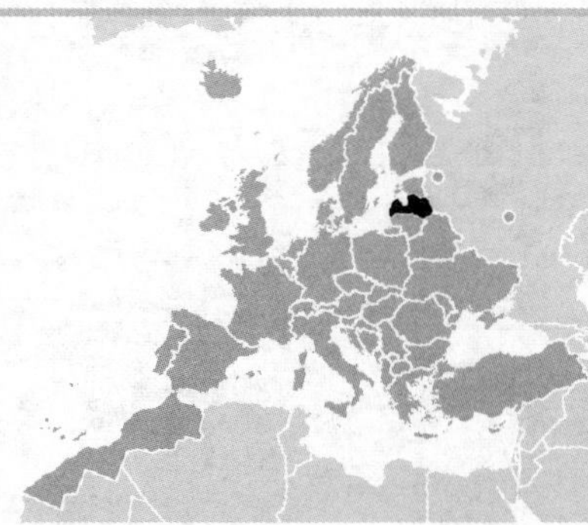

- **Visas** none required for stays of up to 90 days for Australian, Canadian, EU, New Zealand or US citizens.

TRAVEL HINTS

Market produce is almost always cheaper (and fresher) than the food at the grocery store.

ROAMING LATVIA

After sampling Rīga's nightlife, swing through Jūrmala for a spa session, then head up the coast to the stunning tip of Cape Kolka.

Tucked between Estonia to the north and Lithuania to the south, Latvia is the meat of the Baltic sandwich. We're not implying that the neighbouring nations are slices of white bread, but Latvia is the savoury middle, loaded with colourful fixings. Thick greens take the form of Gauja Valley pine forests peppered with castle ruins. Onion-domed Orthodox cathedrals cross the land from salty Liepāja to sweet Sigulda. Cheesy Russian pop blares along the beach in Jūrmala. And spicy Rīga adds an extra zing as the country's cosmopolitan nexus, and unofficial capital of the entire Baltic region.

The next few years will prove to be quite interesting as this hearty hinterland approaches the 20th birthday. No more are the days of teenage growing pains – big things are in store for this little country…

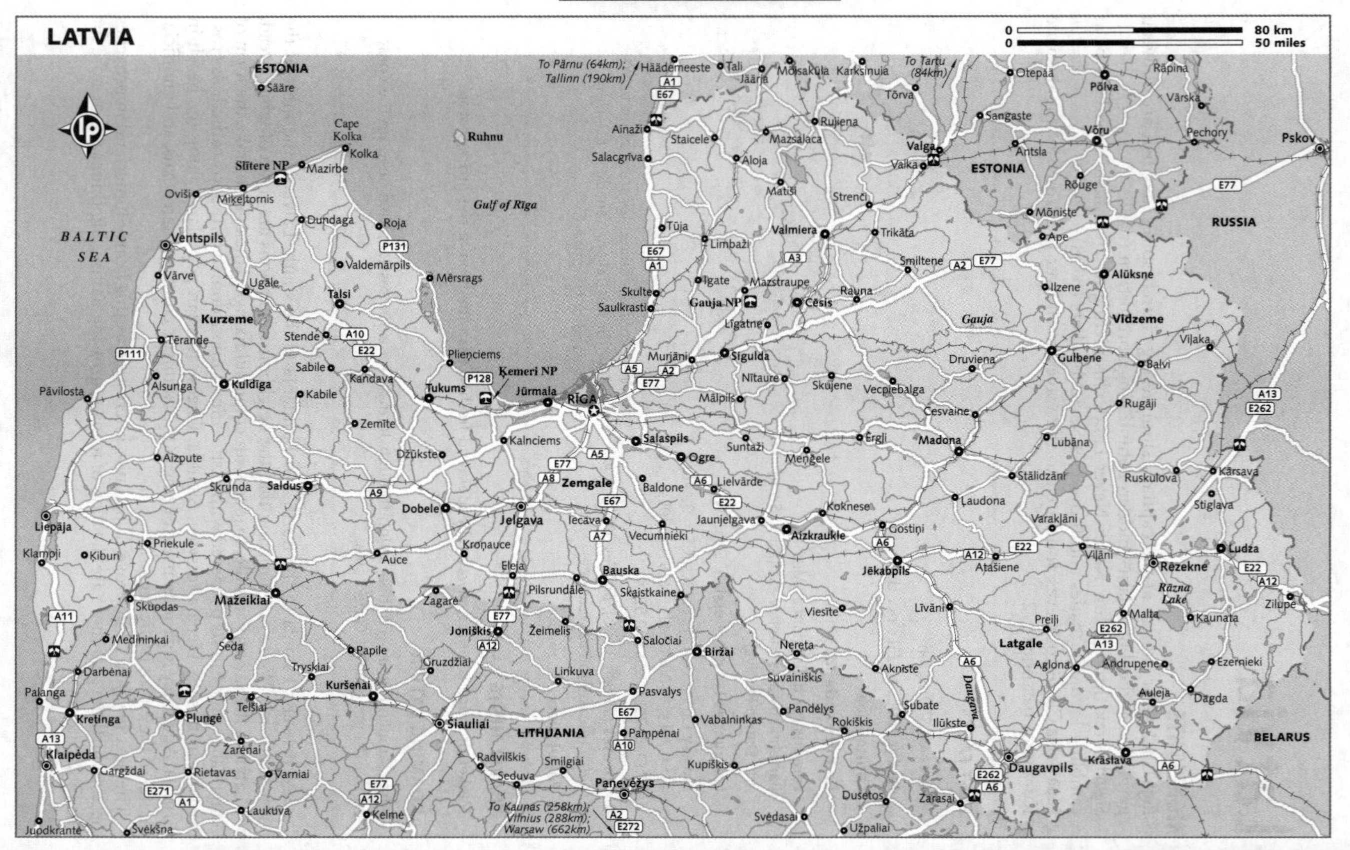
LATVIA
0 80 km
0 50 miles
BALTIC SEA
Gulf of Rīga
ESTONIA
RUSSIA
BELARUS
LITHUANIA
Ruhnu
Kurzeme
Zemgale
Vidzeme
Latgale
Gauja
Daugava
Rāzna Lake
RĪGA
Jūrmala
Ķemeri NP
Gauja NP
Slītere NP
Cape Kolka
Kolka
Mazirbe
Ventspils
Liepāja
Kuldīga
Talsi
Tukums
Jelgava
Dobele
Saldus
Bauska
Salaspils
Ogre
Sigulda
Cēsis
Valmiera
Valga
Valka
Alūksne
Gulbene
Madona
Aizkraukle
Jēkabpils
Rēzekne
Ludza
Daugavpils
Krāslava
Pāvilosta
Aizpute
Skrunda
Kandava
Sabile
Stende
Roja
Mērsrags
Salacgrīva
Ainaži
Limbaži
Saulkrasti
Skulte
Līgatne
Smiltene
Balvi
Viļaka
Kārsava
Zilupe
Preiļi
Aglona
Līvāni
Ilūkste
Šiauliai
Panevėžys
Klaipėda
Palanga
Mažeikiai
Biržai
Pskov
Võru
Põlva
Otepää
Pechory
To Pärnu (64km); Tallinn (190km)
To Tartu (84km)
To Kaunas (258km); Vilnius (288km); Warsaw (662km)
A1
A2
A3
A5
A6
A7
A8
A9
A10
A12
A13
E22
E67
E77
E262
P111
P128
P131

HISTORY

The first signs of modern humans in the region date back to the Stone Age, although Latvians descended from tribes that migrated to the region around 2000 BC.

In 1201, at the behest of the pope, German crusaders conquered Latvia, founded Rīga, and started the Knights of the Sword. Rīga became the major city in the German Baltic, thriving from trade between Russia and the West, and joining the Hanseatic League (a medieval merchant guild) in 1282.

The 15th, 16th and 17th centuries were marked with battles and disputes about how to divvy up what would one day become Latvia. After a period of Swedish rule, the Russians barged in and gobbled everything up during the Great Northern War (1700–21).

Out of the post-WWI confusion and turmoil arose an independent Latvian state, declared on 18 November 1918. By the 1930s, Latvia had achieved one of the highest standards of living in all of Europe. Initially, the Soviets were the first to recognise Latvia's independence, but the honeymoon didn't last long. Soviet occupation began in 1939 with the Molotov–Ribbentrop Pact. Latvia was seized by Nazi Germany from 1941 to 1945, and when WWII ended, the Soviets marched back in claiming to save Latvia from the Nazis.

The first public protest against Soviet occupation was on 14 June 1987, when 5000 people rallied at Rīga's Freedom Monument (p724) to commemorate the 1941 Siberia deportations. The country was finally able to declare independence on 21 August 1991, and on 17 September of that year, Latvia, along with its Baltic brothers, joined the UN. After a devastating crash of the country's economy, Vaira Vīķe-Freiberga won the election in 1999 with the promise of propelling the country towards EU membership. It was a tough uphill battle as the nation shook off its antiquated Soviet fetters, but on 1 May 2004 the EU opened its doors to the fledgling nation. Once the Baltic laggard, Latvia has registered the highest economic growth in the EU for the last four years.

THE CULTURE

Casual hellos on the street aren't common, but Latvians are a friendly and welcoming bunch. Some will find that there is a bit of guardedness in the culture, but this caution, most likely a response to centuries of foreign rule, has helped preserve the unique language and culture through changing times.

Of Latvia's population of 2.25 million, just 58.8% are ethnically Latvian. Russians (28.7%), Belarusians (3.8%), Ukrainians (2.6%), and Poles (2.5%) round out the demographics.

ARTS

The traditional importance of song as Latvia's greatest art form is shown in the 1.4 million *dainas* (folk songs) identified and collected by Krišjānis Barons (1835–1923). The Song & Dance Festival (p730), held every five years, was inscribed on Unesco's list of 'Oral and Intangible Heritage of Humanity' masterpieces in 2003.

Of Latvia's spectrum of visual arts, visitors will be most awestruck by the collection of art nouveau architecture in Rīga (p724).

ENVIRONMENT

Latvians love nature, so it's no surprise that almost half of the nation is covered with thick patches of forest. Much of this leafy terrain falls under protected jurisdiction, which continues to grow as Soviet industrial relics are eradicated.

The Latvian Sustainable Development Strategy was conceived in 2002, which is a broad-reaching scheme uniting environmental, social and economic structures to increase the longevity and viability of the Latvian land.

TRANSPORT

GETTING THERE & AWAY

Air

Rīga Airport (Lidosta Rīga; ☎ 6720 7009; www.riga-airport.com), about 10km southwest of the city centre, houses Latvia's national carrier, **AirBaltic** (☎ 6720 7886; www.airbaltic.com), which offers direct (and cheap!) flights to over 50 international destinations (most in Europe). **Ryanair** (www.ryanair.com) runs discount flights to a dozen European cities, including London (Stansted), Milan (Bergamo), Stockholm (Skavsta) and Dublin.

Boat

Rīga's passenger **ferry terminal** (☎ 6703 0800; www.rop.lv; Eksporta iela 3a) offers services to

Stockholm aboard **Tallink** (☎ 6709 9700; www.tallink.lv). **DFDS Tor Line** (☎ 2735 3523; www.dfdstorline.lv; Zivju iela 1), near the mouth of the Daugava River, goes to/from Lübeck, Germany (from 45Ls, 34 hours, two weekly). **Scandlines** (☎ 6360 0173; www.scandlines.lv) runs seasonal ferries five times weekly from Ventspils' **ferry terminal** (Dārza iela 6) to Nynashamn, Sweden (60km from Stockholm) and Rostock, Germany. **SSC Ferries** (☎ 6360 7184; www.sscf.lv) runs a ferry service (also from Ventspils) four to five times per week to Montu harbour on Saaremaa in Estonia.

Bus

Ecolines (☎ 6721 4512; www.ecolines.lv; 7am-9.30pm) has an office at the bus station in Rīga and additional offices in Daugavpils and Liepāja. **Eurolines Baltic** (☎ 6721 4080; www.eurolines.lv) is also based at Rīga bus station. International destinations include Warsaw, Berlin, Brussels, Kyiv, London, Moscow, St Petersburg, Paris and Prague. See the websites for full information.

Car & Motorcycle

Rental cars are allowed to travel around Latvia at no extra fee. There is no border control at the Estonian or Lithuanian borders.

Train

Rīga is linked by direct train to Moscow (from 20Ls, 17 hours, twice daily) and St Petersburg (from 16Ls, 13 hours, daily). Visit www.ldz.lv and www.1188.lv for updated international train schedules.

GETTING AROUND

Air

AirBaltic (☎ 6720 7886; www.airbaltic.com) offers government-subsidised domestic flights from Rīga twice daily (Monday to Friday) to/from Ventspils and five daily (all week) to/from Liepāja. One-way tickets start at 1Ls if purchased in advance. Flights are seasonal (summer only).

Bus

Buses are much more convenient than trains. Updated timetables are available at www.1188.lv. There are at least two buses hourly from Rīga to Sigulda (1Ls, one hour) and Liepāja (4.50Ls, 3½ hours).

CONNECTIONS

Latvia is the link in the Baltic chain, making Rīga a convenient connecting point between Tallinn and Vilnius. Long distance buses connect the capital to St Petersburg, Moscow, Kyiv, Warsaw, Prague and Berlin, and a ferry goes to and from Stockholm. Rīga is the hub of AirBaltic, which offers direct (and cheap!) services to a variety of Europe cities.

Car & Motorcycle

Though driving is undoubtedly the best way to get around the countryside, Latvians tend to be aggressive drivers.

Rīga's airport hosts the usual assortment of international car rental companies, although you can save a fair bit of cash by asking at your ho(s)tel about local agencies. Be prepared to pay cash.

Headlights must be on at all times while driving. Be sure to ask for *benzene* when looking for a petrol station – *gāze* means 'air'.

Train

Suburban trains are the best way to get from Rīga to Jūrmala (0.65Ls, 35 minutes, at least two hourly). Trains are also a reasonable option to get from Rīga to Sigulda (1.11Ls, one hour, hourly).

RĪGA

pop 717,371

'The Paris of the North', 'The Second City That Never Sleeps' – everyone's so keen to tack on qualifying superlatives to Latvia's capital, but regal Rīga does a hell of a job of holding its own. For starters, the city has the largest and most impressive showing of art nouveau architecture in Europe. Nightmarish gargoyles and praying goddesses adorn over 750 buildings along the stately boulevards radiating out from Rīga's castle core. The heart of the city – Old Rīga – is a fairy-tale kingdom of winding wobbly lanes and gingerbread trim that beats to the sound of a bumpin' discotheque.

ORIENTATION

Old Rīga (Vecrīga), which straddles the Daugava River, is separated from Central Rīga

EMERGENCY NUMBERS

- EU-wide emergency number ☎ 112
- Police ☎ 02
- Fire ☎ 01
- Ambulance ☎ 03

(Centrs) by an emerald necklace of lush parkland. The bus and train stations are located in the southeastern part of Central Rīga near the Old Rīga walls.

INFORMATION

Discount Cards

Prices for one-/two-/three-day **Rīga cards** are 10/14/18Ls. These are available at the Tourism Information Centres and offer large discounts for sights, tours, museums and accommodation, and maps.

Internet Access

Almost every hotel and hostel has wireless access (usually free of charge), as do a large percentage of restaurants (including the dozens of Double Coffee cafes peppered around the city centre).

Elik Kafe (☎ 6722 7079; www.elikkafe.lv; Merķela iela 1; per 30min 0.35Ls; 24hr) Located near the train station above the McDonalds.

net.café (☎ 6781 4440; Peldu iela 17; per hr 1Ls; 24hr) A chilled spot to update your blog. Full-service bar.

Media & Maps

City Spy (www.cityspy.info) Pocket-sized *City Spy* was the best map we found in town. Available at most budget accommodation.

Riga In Your Pocket (www.inyourpocket.com/latvia/city/riga.html; 2Ls) Handy city guide published every other month. Download a PDF version or pick up a copy at most hotels and tourist offices.

Riga This Week (www.rigathisweek.lv) An excellent (and free!) city guide available at virtually every sleeping option in town. Published every other month.

Medical Services

ARS Clinic (☎ 6720 1001, emergency 6720 1003; Skolas iela 5; 24hr) is an English-speaking service and an emergency home service.

Money

There are scores of ATMs scattered around the capital. Withdrawing cash is easier than trying to exchange travellers cheques or foreign currencies. **Marika** (Brīvības iela 30; 24hr) offers currency exchange services with reasonable rates.

Tourist Information

Rīga Tourism Information Centre (www.rigatourism.com) Main Office (☎ 2703 7900; Rātslaukums 6; 10am-7pm); Bus Station (☎ 2722 0555; 9am-7pm); Train Station (☎ 6730 7900; 10am-6.30pm) gives out free maps and has loads of information. Staff can arrange accommodation and book walking, bus or boat tours from a variety of operators.

SIGHTS

Old Rīga (Vecrīga)

Touristy Rātslaukums is home to the picture-worthy **Blackheads' House** (Rātslaukums 6; admission 1.50Ls; 10am-5pm Tue-Sun), built in 1344 as a veritable fraternity house for the Blackheads guild of unmarried German merchants. Facing the Blackheads' House across the square is the **Town Hall**. Both buildings were destroyed in WWII and rebuilt from scratch in recent years. The **Museum of Occupation in Latvia** (www.occupationmuseum.lv; Latviesu Strēlnieku laukums 1; admission free; 11am-6pm May-Sep, 11am-5pm Tue-Sun Oct-Apr) ironically inhabits a Soviet bunker, and carefully details Latvia's Soviet and Nazi occupations between 1939 and 1991.

Rīga's skyline centrepiece is Gothic **St Peter's Lutheran Church** (www.peterbaznica.lv; Skārņu iela 19; admission 2Ls; 10am-5pm Tue-Sun). Don't miss the view from the spire.

A colourful row of 18th-century buildings lines **Livu Laukums** – most of which have been turned into rowdy restaurants and beer halls. Don't miss the **Cat House** (Miestaru iela 10), named for the spooked black cat sitting on the roof.

The centrepiece of expansive Doma Laukums is Rīga's enormous **Dome Cathedral** (admission 0.50Ls; 11am-6pm Tue-Fri, 10am-2pm Sat). Founded in 1211 as the seat of the Rīga diocese, it is

GETTING INTO TOWN

Both the bus and train stations are located just beyond Old Rīga in the southeast corner of the city centre.

The airport is about 10km west of the city centre. Take bus 22 or 22a (0.40Ls, 30 minutes) into town. AirBaltic runs lime green vans (3Ls) to the hotel of your choice (in Central Rīga only). Taxis to Old Town cost about 7Ls.

still the largest church in the Baltics. The huge, 6768-pipe organ was the world's largest when it was completed in 1884 (it's now the fourth largest). Located behind Doma Laukums, away from the cathedral, are the **Three Brothers** (Mazā Pils iela 17, 19 & 21), exemplifying Old Rīga's diverse collection of old architectural styles (and echoing Tallinn's 'Three Sisters').

Latvia's first Lutheran services were held in nearby **St Jacob's Cathedral** (Klostera iela), which has an interior dating back to 1225. Today it is the seat of Rīga's Roman Catholic archbishopric.

Verdant Pils Laukums sits at the doorstep of **Rīga Castle** (Pils laukums 3). Originally built as the headquarters for the Livonian Order, the

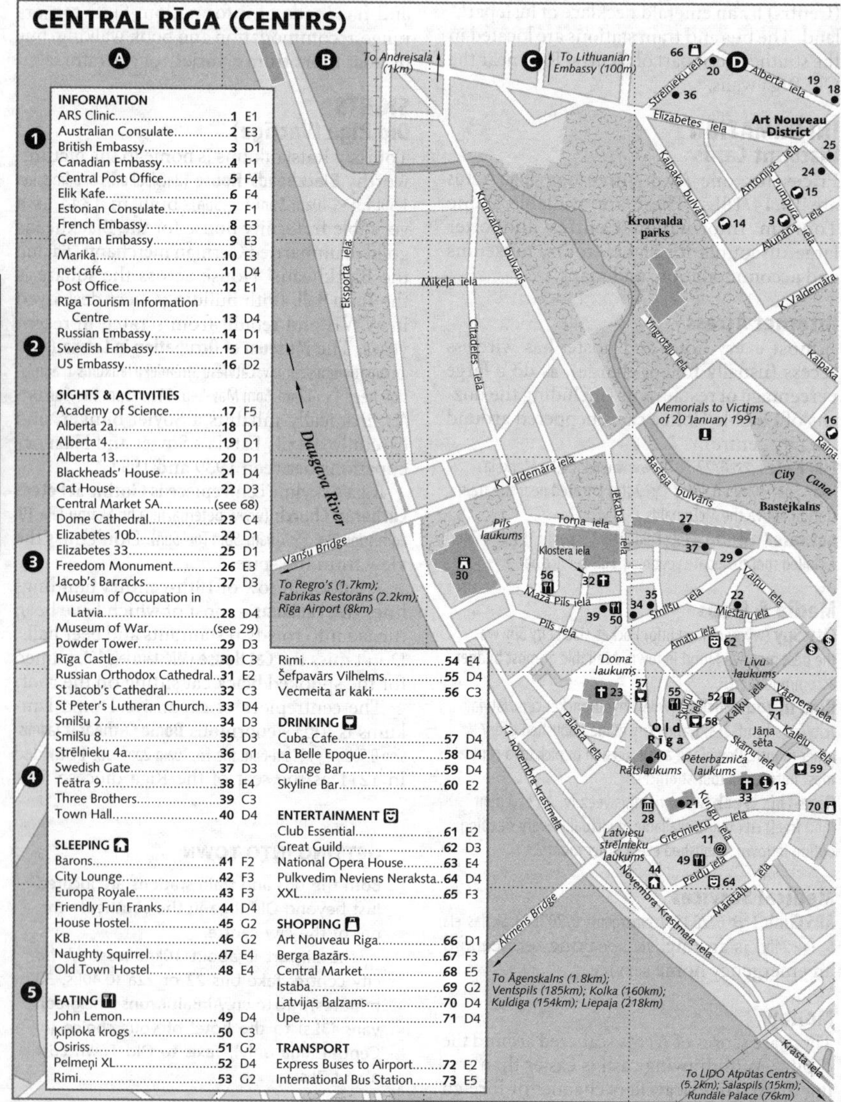

foundation of the castle dates to 1330 and served as the residence of the order's grand master. This canary yellow bastion boasts an art and history museum, and is also the home to Latvia's president (currently Valdis Zatlers).

The entire north side of Torņa iela is flanked by the custard-coloured **Jacob's Barracks** (Torna iela 4), now inhabited by cafes. Find **Trokšnu iela** nearby – Old Rīga's narrowest *iela* (street) – and the **Swedish Gate** (Torņu iela 11), which was built in 1698. The cylindrical **Powder Tower** (Smilšu iela 20) dates back to the 14th century. Today it is the **Museum of War** (www.karamuzejs.gov.lv; Smilšu iela 20; admission free; 10am-6pm Wed-Sun May-Sep, to 5pm Wed-Sun Oct-Apr).

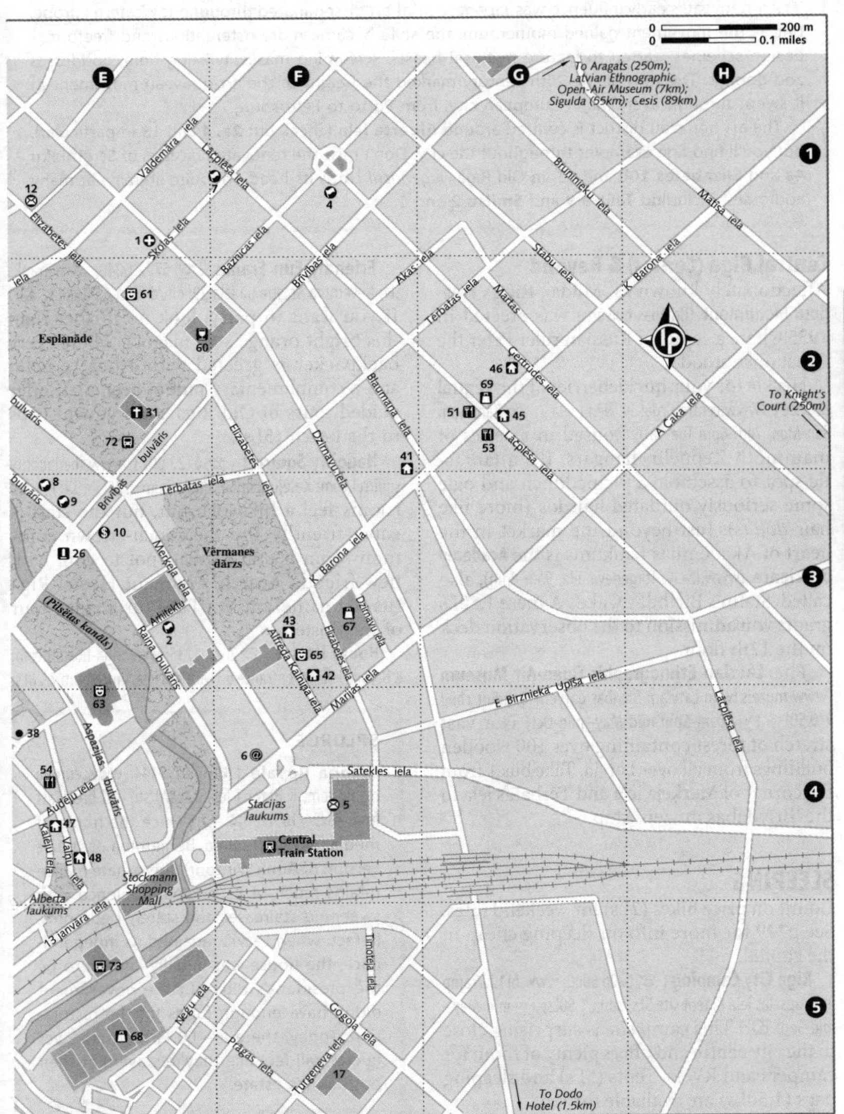

ART NOUVEAU IN RĪGA

If you ask any Rīgan where to find the city's world-famous art nouveau architecture, you will always get the same answer: 'look up!' Over 750 buildings in Rīga (more than any other city in Europe) boast this flamboyant and haunting style, and the number continues to grow as myriad restoration projects get underway. Art nouveau is also known as *Jugendstil,* meaning 'youth style', named after a Munich-based magazine called *Die Jugend,* which popularised the design on its pages.

Art nouveau's early influence was Japanese print art disseminated throughout Western Europe, but as the movement gained momentum, the style became more ostentatious and freeform – design schemes started to feature mythical beasts, screaming masks, twisting flora, goddesses and goblins. The turn of the 20th century marked the height of the art nouveau movement as it swept through every major European city, from Porto to Petersburg.

The art nouveau district is centred around **Alberta iela** (check out **2a, 4** and **13** in particular), but you'll find fine examples throughout the city. Don't miss the renovated facades of **Strēlnieku 4a** and **Elizabetes 10b** and **33**. In Old Rīga, *Jugendstil* crops its head up (quite literally) at many addresses, including **Teātra 9** and **Smilšu 2** and **8**.

Central Rīga (Centrs) & Beyond

Affectionately known as 'Milda', Rīga's **Freedom Monument** (Brīvības bulvāris) was erected in 1935 where a statue of Russian ruler Peter the Great once stood.

Heckle for your huckleberries at the **Central Market** (www.centraltirgus.lv; Nēgu iela 7; ⌚ 7am-5pm Sun-Mon, 7am-6pm Tue-Sat), housed in a series of mammoth Zeppelin hangars. It's a fantastic spot to assemble a picnic lunch and ogle some seriously outdated hairdos (more like hair-*don'ts*). Just beyond the market in the heart of Akadēmijas Laukums is the **Academy of Science** (www.lza.lv; Turgeņeva iela; 9am-8pm), also called 'Stalin's Birthday Cake'. A mere 1.50Ls grants you admission to the observation deck on the 17th floor.

The **Latvian Ethnographic Open-Air Museum** (www.muzejs.lv, in Latvian; Brīvības gatve 440; adult/child 1/0.50Ls; ⌚ 10am-5pm mid-May–mid-Oct) is a vast stretch of forest containing over 100 wooden buildings from all over Latvia. Take bus 1 from the corner of Merķeļa iela and Tērbatas iela to the 'Brīvdabas muzejs' stop.

SLEEPING

Count on price hikes (2Ls) for weekend rates. See p729 for more info on sleeping cheap in the capital.

Riga City Camping (☎ 6706 5000; www.bt1.lv/camping; Kīpsalas iela 8; tent site 5Ls, adult 1.50Ls; ⌚ mid-May–mid-Sep; 💻) This camp site is surprising close to the city centre and offers plenty of room for campers and RVers. Tents (5Ls) and sleeping bags (1.50Ls) are available for rent.

Friendly Fun Franks (☎ 6722 0040; www.franks.lv; Novembra Krastmala iela 29; dm/d from 6.90/40Ls; 💻) If you want to party, look no further than this bright orange stag-magnet, where every backpacker is greeted with a hearty hello and a complimentary pint of beer. Staff offer guided tours of Old Rīga and frequent trips to the beach (5Ls).

Naughty Squirrel (☎ 6722 0073; www.thenaughtysquirrel.com; Kalēju iela 50; dm/d from 7/28Ls; 💻) The rooms feel a bit worn-out, but the staff is super-friendly and the couch-strewn common room is still a great spot to chill with new friends. Search Argonaut Hostel Riga (its old name) on YouTube for a video tour of the hostel.

House Hostel (☎ 2649 1235; www.riga-hostels.com; K Barona iela 44, entrance on Lāčplēša iela; dm/d from 7/28Ls;

SPLURGE

Europa Royale (☎ 6707 9444; www.europaroyale.com; K Barona iela 12; s/d/ste incl breakfast from 83/94/105Ls; ❄ 💻) Once the home of media mogul Emilija Benjamiņa (Latvia's version of Anna Wintour), this ornate manse retains much of its original opulence with sweeping staircases and stately bedrooms. In fact, when Latvia regained its independence, the house was initially chosen to be the president's digs but the government didn't have enough funds for the restoration. Today, there are 60 large rooms, yet guests will feel like they're staying at their posh aunt's estate.

LATVIA

(💻) Warning: if you stay at 'The House', you probably won't see any of Rīga's sights – the ultrachilled common space is both effortlessly stylish and a veritable backpacker black hole (you'll never want to leave). The hostel doubles as the office for Riga Out There, a reputable tour operator.

our pick **City Lounge** (☎ 2935 8958; www.citylounge.lv; Alfrēda Kalniņa iela 4; dm/d from 11/36Ls; 💻) Guests will need a sherpa to climb the 128 stairs, but once you get to the top you'll find a fantastic hostel that's both spotless and hip (in an 'Orient-meets-Ikea' kinda way). Guests staying in the London room can store their luggage in the iconic red telephone booth, and in the Rīga room there's a giant city map on the ceiling so you can plan tomorrow's itinerary while lying in bed. Book nooks and electrical outlets are conveniently found beside every pillow.

KB (☎ 6731 2323; www.kbhotel.lv; K Barona iela 37; s/d/tr from 27/32/38Ls; 💻) This great B&B is located in a rather opulent building with a sweeping marble staircase taking travellers up to the top-floor hotel. The rooms are simple but well-appointed, and there's a modern communal kitchen.

Dodo Hotel (☎ 6724 0220; www.dodohotel.com; Jersikas iela 1; r from 27Ls; 💻) This new cheapie, located beyond the Central Market, is a fantastic find if you don't mind being removed from the action. Savvy designers have feng shui-ed the small rooms with stylish details like a scarlet accent wall and a mini plasma TV.

Other recommended hostels:

Barons (☎ 2910 5939; www.baronshostel.com; K Barona iela 25; dm/s/d 11/30/35Ls; 💻) Barons has a bit more personality than the other low-key hostels in central Rīga. Guests can cook in the spacious kitchen, or relax in front of the plasma TV.

Old Town Hostel (☎ 6722 3406; www.rigaoldtownhostel.lv; Valņu iela 43; dm/d 7/35Ls; 💻) The brick-lined pub on the ground floor doubles as the hostel's hang-out space. Spacious dorms have chandeliers and plenty of sunlight.

Knight's Court (☎ 6784 6400; www.knightscourt.lv; Bruņinieku iela 75b; dm/s/d incl breakfast from 7/25/32Ls; 💻) Furnishings are a bit outdated but everything is squeaky clean.

EATING

For centuries in Latvia, food equalled fuel, energising peasants as they worked the fields, and warming their bellies during bone-chilling Baltic winters. Today the era of boiled potatoes and pork gristle has begun to fade, but backpackers should still pack a sandwich if they don't want to pack an artery.

RĪGA FOR FREE

Three free things to do in the capital that will save you lots of Lats:

- Going click-crazy at the hundreds of **art nouveau facades** (opposite)
- Viewing the cityscape on a 26-floor elevator ride at the **Hotel Reval Latvija** (p726)
- Snooping around the Zeppelin hangars at the **Central Market** (p724)

Pelmeņi XL (Kaļķu iela 7; dumpling bowl 0.90-2.50Ls) A Rīga institution for backpackers and undiscerning drunkards, this extra-large cafeteria stays open extra-late (4am), serving up huge bowls of *pelmeņi* (Russian dumplings) to hungry mobs.

Šefpavārs Vilhelms (Šķūņu iela 6; pancake rolls 0.65Ls) Every time we visited, customers of every ilk were eagerly queuing for a quick nosh. Three blintzlike pancakes smothered in sour cream and jam equals the perfect backpacker's breakfast.

John Lemon (Peldu iela 21; mains 2.50-5Ls) This trendy spot attracts bleary-eyed partiers from Pulkvedis (across the street; see p726) for cheap, late-night munchies. Take your pick of three stylish rooms: an orange realm with '60s space-station sofa seating, the trellis-lined courtyard, or a small nook drenched in hot, lipstick reds and disco lights.

Osiriss (K Barona iela 31; mains 3-7Ls) Despite Rīga's fickle cafe culture where establishments come and go like the seasons, Osiriss continues to be a local mainstay. The green faux-marble tabletops haven't changed since the mid-'90s and neither has the clientele: angsty artsy types scribbling in their moleskines over a glass of red wine. Wi-fi available.

LIDO Atpūtas Centrs (LIDO Recreation Centre; Krasta iela 76; mains 3-7Ls) If Latvia and Disney World had a lovechild it would be the LIDO Atpūtas Centrs – an enormous wooden palace dedicated to the country's coronary-inducing cuisine. Servers dressed like Baltic milkmaids bounce around as patrons hit the rows of buffets for classics like pork tongue, potato pancakes and cold beet soup. Take tram 3, 7 or 9, or bus 17E, and get off at the 'LIDO' stop. There are a handful of miniature LIDO restaurants dotted around the city centre for those who don't have time to make it out to the mothership.

Vecmeita Ar Kaki (The Spinster & Her Cat; Mazā Pils iela 1; mains 3-7.50Ls) This cosy spot across from the president's palace specialises in cheap Latvian cuisine. Menus have been crafted from old-fashioned newspaper clippings and patrons dine on converted sewing-machine tables.

Ķiploka Krogs (Garlic Bar; Jēkaba iela 3/5, entrance from Mazā Pils; mains 4-11Ls) Vampires beware – *everything* at this joint contains garlic, even the ice cream. The menu is pretty hit or miss (though you can't go wrong with the pasta), but no matter what, it's best to avoid the garlic pesto spread – it'll taint your breath for days (trust us).

Rimi (www.rimi.lv; 9am-10pm) has two central supermarkets: Audēju iela 16, and K Barona iela 46. Fresh produce can also be purchased at the Central Market (see p724).

DRINKING & CLUBBING

If you want to party like a Latvian, assemble a gang of friends and pub-crawl your way through the city, stopping at colourful haunts for rounds of beers, belly laughter and, of course, black balsām. On summer evenings, nab a spot at one of the beer gardens in rowdy Livu Laukums.

Cuba Cafe (Jaun iela 15) An authentic mojito and a table overlooking Doma laukums is just what the doctor ordered after a long day of sightseeing. On colder days, swig your caipirinha inside amid dangling Cuban flags, wobbly stained-glass lamps, and the subtle murmur of trumpet jazz. Wi-fi available.

La Belle Epoque (French Bar; Mazā Jaunavu iela 8) Students flock to this basement bar to power down its trademark 'apple pie' shots (go for their 'ten shots for nine lats' deal if you're with friends.) The Renoir mural and kitsch *Moulin Rouge* posters seem to successfully ward off stag parties.

Orange Bar (Jāņa sēta 5) An alternative spot slathered in jet-black paint and splashes of neon orange light, this edgy alternative joint attracts hipsters of every ilk for some late-night carousing on the bar top.

Skyline Bar (Elizabetes iela 55) A must for anyone visiting Rīga, glitzy Skyline Bar sits on the 26th floor of the Hotel Reval Latvija. The sweeping views are the city's best, and the mix of glam spirit-sippers make for great people-watching under the retro purple lighting. Wi-fi available.

Club Essential (www.essential.lv; Skolas iela 2; 10pm-6am Thu, to 8am Fri & Sat, to 5am Sun) Rīga's hottest club is a spectacle of beautiful people boogying to some of Europe's top DJ talent. Overzealous security aside, there's no safer bet if partying till dawn is your mission.

Pulkvedim Neviens Neraksta (No One Writes to the Colonel; www.pulkvedis.lv; Peldu iela 26/28; admission weekend/weekday 3Ls/free; 8pm-3am Mon-Thu, to 5am Fri & Sat) The atmosphere at Pulkvedis is 'warehouse chic', with pumping '80s tunes on the ground floor, and trance beats down below. There's no such thing as a dull night at this old favourite.

XXL (Kalniņa iela 1; admission 1-10Ls; 6pm-7am) 'Tom of Finland-esque' porno adorns the walls and disco music blares on weekends at this gay club. A dark labyrinth and video screening room are also available. Sunday is men only.

ENTERTAINMENT

In Your Pocket (see p721) lists movie venues and full opera, ballet and classical music schedules. Check www.livas.lv for movie listings.

National Opera Theatre (6707 3777; www.opera.lv; Aspazijas bulvāris 3; tickets 5-30Ls; box office 10am-7pm) The pride of Latvia, boasting some of the finest opera in all of Europe (and for a fraction of the price of other countries). Mikhail Baryshnikov got his start here.

Great Guild (6722 7105; www.hbf.lv; Amatu iela 6; box office noon-6pm Tue-Sat) Home to the acclaimed Latvian National Symphonic Orchestra.

Dome Cathedral (6721 3213; www.hbf.lv; Doma laukums; box office noon-6pm Tue-Sat) Excellent acoustics and a massive organ make the twice-weekly evening concerts (Wednesday and Friday) well worth attending.

SHOPPING

Street sellers peddle their touristy wares outside St Peter's Church (p721). Check out **Berga Bazārs** (www.bergabazars.lv; Dzirnavu iela 84), a maze of upmarket boutiques orbiting the five-star Hotel Bergs, and keep an eye out for the beautiful Nameju rings worn by Latvians around the world as a way to recognise one another.

Art Nouveau Riga (Strēlnieku iela 9) Purchase a variety of art nouveau–related souvenirs, ranging from guidebooks to postcards and even stone gargoyles.

Istaba (K Barona iela 31a) A wee gallery displaying the works of local artisans mixed with kitsch trinkets and souvenirs. The loft 2nd floor doubles as a trendy cafe.

LATVIA

WORTH THE DETOUR: RUNDĀLE PALACE

If you only have time for one day trip out of Rīga, make it **Rundāle Palace** (Rundāles pils; ☎ 6396 2197; www.rundale.net; garden 1Ls, palace 2.50Ls, combined ticket 5Ls, guided group tour 32Ls; 🕑 10am-7pm Jun-Aug, to 6pm Sep-Oct, to 5pm Nov-Apr), 76km south of the capital near the tiny town of Bauska. The architect of this sprawling monument to aristocratic ostentatiousness was the Italian baroque genius Bartolomeo Rastrelli, best known for designing the Winter Palace in St Petersburg. About 40 of the palace's 138 rooms are open to visitors, as are the wonderfully landscaped gardens.

To reach the palace, take a bus from Rīga to Bauska (1.90Ls, 70 minutes to 1½ hours), then switch to one of the nine daily buses (0.35Ls) connecting Bauska to the palace, 12km away.

Latvijas Balzams (Audēju iela 8) A chain of liquor stores selling the trademark Latvian Black Balzāms.

Upe (Vāgnera iela 5) Classical Latvian music wafts through the air as customers peruse traditional instruments and CDs of local folk, rock and experimental artists.

GETTING THERE & AWAY

For information on arriving in Rīga, see p720.

GETTING AROUND

Public Transport

Tickets cost 0.40Ls (0.50Ls if you buy your tram or trolleybus ticket from the driver – exact change is necessary.) Tram and trolleybus tickets can also be purchased at Narvesen superettes. City transport runs daily from 5.30am to midnight. Some routes have an hourly night service. For Rīga public transport routes and schedules, visit www.rigassatiksme.lv.

Taxi

Officially, taxis charge 0.30Ls per kilometre (0.40Ls between 10pm and 6am), but don't be surprised if you get ripped off. Insist on the meter running before you set off. Meters usually start running at 0.50Ls to 1.50Ls. Don't pay more than 3Ls for short journeys.

AROUND RĪGA

JŪRMALA

pop 55,580

The Baltics' version of the French Riviera, Jūrmala is a long string of townships with stately wooden beach estates belonging to Russian oil tycoons and their supermodel trophy wives. Even during the height of communism, Jūrmala was always a place to *sea* and be seen. Today, on summer weekends, vehicles clog the roads when jetsetters and day-tripping Rīgans flock to the resort town for some serious fun in the sun.

The **Tourism Information Centre** (☎ 6714 7902; www.jurmala.lv; Lienes iela 5; 🕑 9am-7pm Mon-Fri, 10am-5pm Sat, 10am-3pm Sun) offers pamphlets detailing local **spas**, museums, and themed walking tours (the **wooden houses** trip is particularly interesting). Staff can also hook you up with a **bike rental** (per day 6Ls), and help you find accommodation (although if penny-pinching's your game, do a day trip to Jūrmala and sleep in Rīga.)

Campers can pitch a tent at **Kempings Nemo** (☎ 6773 2350; www.nemo.lv; Atbalss iela 1; cottages 8-32Ls, per camp site/person 2/2Ls, parking 2Ls; 🅿). From sushi to sausages, tastebuds will be satisfied along Jomas iela.

Two to three trains per hour go to/from Rīga (0.65Ls, 30 to 35 minutes); disembark at Majori station. Motorists driving the 15km into Jūrmala must pay a 1Ls toll per day, even if they are just passing through. Keep an eye out for the self-service toll stations.

WESTERN LATVIA

Just when you thought that Rīga was the only star of the show, in comes Western Latvia from stage left, dazzling audiences with a whole different set of talents. While the capital wows the crowd with intricate architecture and metropolitan majesty, Kurzeme (Courland in English) takes things in the other direction: miles and miles of jaw-dropping natural beauty.

Enchantingly desolate and hauntingly beautiful, a journey to **Cape Kolka** (Kolkasrags) feels like a trip to the end of the earth. During Soviet times the entire peninsula was zoned off as a high-security military base. The region's development was subsequently stunted, and today the string of remote coastal villages feels as though they've been locked away in a time capsule. The not-to-be-missed windswept moonscape at the waning edge of the cape (just 500m away) will have you daydreaming for days. Five daily buses link Rīga and the cape (3.85Ls to 4.85Ls, 3½ to 4¾ hours).

South of Cape Kolka, the quiet medieval town of **Kuldīga** wins hearts with its cobbled lanes and trickling waterfall (Europe's widest). A constellation of surfer towns dots the Kurzeme coast: **Ventspils**, a sleek shipping town; **Pāvilosta**, a quiet haven for windsurfers and beach bums; and **Liepāja**, a bustling burg in the south with a rough-around-the-edges garage-band scene.

In Liepāja, the **Tourist Information Office** (☎ 6348 0808; www.liepaja.lv/turisms; Rožu laukums 3/5; 9am-7pm Mon-Fri, to 4pm Sat, 10am-3pm Sun Jun-Aug, 9am-5pm Mon-Sat Sep-May) can give you directions to **Karosta Prison**, where tourists can have a 'prison experience' tour that involves donning prisoner garb, and being harassed by armed guards. Masochists can spend the night.

You'll either adore or abhor staying at **Hotel Fontaine** (☎ 6342 0956; www.fontaine.lv; Jūras iela 24; r from 20Ls;), a funky hostelry that feels like a second-hand store with its kitschy knick-knack shop used as the reception. Tighter budgets should try **Traveller's Hostel** (☎ 2869 0106; www.liepajahostel.com; Republikas iela 25; dm 10Ls;), a friendly spot with five bright rooms and oodles of common space.

Fontaine Palace (Dzirnavu iela 4) is a never-closing rock house luring loads of live acts and crowds of sweaty fanatics. Pablo, the roaring basement club at **Latvia's 1st Rock Café** (www.pablo.lv; Stendera iela 18/20; admission free-5Ls), features live music every night, and rave parties on the weekends.

There are daily flights connecting Rīga and Liepāja during the busier summer months. There are several buses (4.30Ls, 3¼ hours) and one early-morning train (3.40Ls, 3¼ hours) to/from Rīga.

EASTERN LATVIA

When Rīga's urban hustle fades into a pulsing hum of chirping crickets, you've entered Eastern Latvia. Known as Vidzeme or 'the Middle Land' to locals, the country's largest region is an excellent sampler of what Latvia has to offer. Most tourists head to **Gauja National Park** (Gaujas Nacionālais Parks; www.gnp.gov.lv; admission free), the country's oldest preserve, where forest folks hike, bike or paddle through the thicketed terrain, and history buffs ogle at the generous sprinkling of castles throughout.

For those with a little extra time to spare, consider a visit to **Cēsis**. 'Latvia's most Latvian town' offers daytrippers a mosaic of quintessential country life – a stunning Livonian castle, soaring church spires, cobbled roads and a lazy lagoon – all wrapped up in a bow like an adorable adult Disneyland. Stop by the **Cēsis Tourist Information Centre** (☎ 6412 1815; www.tourism.cesis.lv; Pils laukums; 9am-7pm Jun-Aug, to 6pm Sep-May) for maps, bike rentals, internet access and general information about the adorable town.

SIGULDA

pop 10,700

With a name that sounds like a mythical ogress, the gateway to the Gauja is an enchanting little spot with delightful surprises tucked behind every dappled tree. Locals proudly call their pine-peppered town the 'Switzerland of Latvia', but if you're expecting the majesty of a mountainous snow-capped realm, you'll be rather disappointed. Instead, Sigulda mixes its own exciting brew of scenic trails, extreme sports and 800-year-old castles steeped in colourful legends.

Information

Ask about the Sigulda Spiekis discount card at the **Sigulda Tourism Information Centre** (☎ 6797 1335; www.sigulda.lv; Valdemāra iela 1a; 10am-7pm Jun-Sep, to 5pm Oct-May). There's also an internet kiosk available.

Sights & Activities

Start at **Sigulda New Castle**, built in the 18th-century during the reign of German aristocrats. The **Sigulda Medieval Castle** (now ruins), around the back, was constructed in 1207 by the Order of the Brethren of the Sword. Take the **cable car** (☎ 6797 2531; www.lgk.lv; Poruka iela 14; one-way ride 1Ls; 10am-7.30pm Jun-Aug, 10am-5pm Sat & Sun May-Sep) over the scenic river valley to Krimulda Manor, currently used as a rehabilitation clinic.

Daredevils can try a 43m **bungee jump** (☎ 2644 0660; www.bungee.lv; Poruka iela 14; Friday/weekend jump 20/25Ls; 7.30pm to last jump Fri-Sun May-Sep) from the moving cable car. Check out the ruins of **Krimulda Medieval Castle** nearby, then follow the serpentine road to **Gūtmaņa Cave**. Immortalised by the legend of The Rose of Turaida (learn about her heartbreaking story at Turaida), it's the largest erosion cave in the Baltic. Take some time to read the myriad inscriptions carved into the cave walls, then head up to the **Turaida Museum Reserve** (☎ 6797 1402; www.turaida-muzejs.lv; admission 3Ls; ⏰ 10am-9pm May-Oct, 10am-5pm Nov-Apr) and its beautiful medieval castle, erected in the 13th century for the Archbishop of Rīga.

The one-of-a-kind **aerodium** (☎ 2838 4400; www.aerodium.lv; 2min weekday/weekend 15/18Ls, additional min weekday/weekend 5/6Ls; ⏰ 4-10pm Mon-Fri, noon-8pm Sat & Sun May-Sep) is a giant wind tunnel that propels participants up into the sky as though they were flying.

Sigulda's 1200m artificial **bobsled track** (☎ 6797 3813; Sveices iela 13) was built for the former Soviet bobsleigh team. In winter you can fly down the 16-bend track at 80km/h in a five-person **Vučko tourist bob** (per person 6Ls; ⏰ noon-7pm Sat & Sun Oct-Mar), or try the real Olympian experience on the hair-raising **winter bob** (per person 35Ls). Summer speed fiends can ride a wheeled **summer sled** (per person 6Ls; ⏰ 11am-6pm Sat & Sun May-Sep) without booking in advance.

Sleeping & Eating

Kempings Siguldas Pludmale (☎ 2924 4948; www.makars.lv; Peldu iela 2; person/tent/car/caravan 3/1.50/1.50/6Ls; ⏰ 15 May-15 Sep) Pitch your tent beside the sandy beach along the Gauja. The location is perfect, but there's only one bathroom for each sex.

Līvkalns (☎ 6797 0916; www.livkalns.lv; Pēteralas iela; s/d from 25/30Ls) No place is more romantically rustic than this idyllic retreat next to a pond on the forest's edge. The rooms are pine-fresh and sit among a campus of adorable thatch-roof manors. The cabin-in-the-woods-style restaurant is fantastic.

Kaķu Māja (Pils iela 8; mains 3-5Ls) A restaurant, canteen, bakery and nightclub all rolled into one charming gingerbread house.

Getting There & Around

It's easy to get to Sigulda from Rīga via train (1.10Ls, one hour, hourly) or bus (1Ls, one hour).

Sigulda's attractions are quite spread out; bus No 12 links all of the sights, and plies the route seven times daily (more on weekends).

LATVIA DIRECTORY

ACCOMMODATION

Cheap airfares and warmer weather lures the crowds during summer, so it's best to book your bed in advance. Prices drop by more than 30% in the colder months. Visit www.hotels.lv for detailed accommodation information; backpackers should check out **Hostelworld** (www.hostelworld.com) for additional info on Rīga's budget digs. Figure between 6Ls to 12Ls for a dorm bed throughout the country. There are loads of places to pitch a tent as well. If you want a bit more privacy, expect to spend between 35Ls and 60Ls for a double room in Rīga (high season).

ACTIVITIES

Latvia's miles and miles of forested acreage are tailor-made for nature enthusiasts. For an intense adrenaline fix, like bungee jumping, bobsledding, mountain biking and skydiving, head to the town of Sigulda (opposite). Water sports and spa enthusiasts should spend the day in Jūrmala (p727).

BUSINESS HOURS

Most bars and restaurants open roughly from 11am to 11pm. On weekends they stay open until 2am or later. Nightclubs usually go all night between Thursday and Sunday. Shops tend to be open from 11am to 7pm and post offices are generally open between 7.30am and 8pm. Banks operate from 9am to 5pm, but 24-hour ATMs are available all over.

EMBASSIES & CONSULATES

The following embassies are in Rīga:

Australia (☎ 6722 4251; australia@apollo.lv; Arhitektu iela 1-305)

Canada (☎ 6781 3945; www.dfait-maeci.gc.ca/canada-europa/baltics; Baznīcas laukums 4)

Estonia (☎ 6781 2020; www.estemb.lv; Skolas iela 13)

France (☎ 6703 6600; www.ambafrance-lv.org; Raiņa bulvāris 9)

Germany (☎ 6708 5100; www.riga.diplo.de; Raiņa bulvāris 13)

Lithuania (☎ 6732 1519; lt@apollo.lv; Rūpniecības iela 24)

New Zealand The New Zealand consulate for Latvia (p920) is in Warsaw, Poland.

Russia (☎ 6733 2151; www.latvia.mid.ru; Antonijas iela 2)

Spain (☎ 6732 0281; Elizabetes iela 11)
Sweden (☎ 6768 6600; www.swedenabroad.com/riga; Pumpura iela 8)
UK (☎ 6777 4700; http:ukinlatvia.fco.gov.uk; Alunāna iela 5)
USA (☎ 6703 6200; www.usembassy.lv; Raiņa bulvāris 7)

FESTIVALS & EVENTS

Līgo During this midsummer celebration on the night of June 23 (St John's Eve), the entire country retreats to feast on country food, jump over fires and re-enact other Pagan rituals.
Song & Dance Festival (www.dziesmusvetki2008.lv) Undoubtedly Latvia's biggest festival, held every five years. The 24th festival was held in 2008.

HOLIDAYS

The Latvia Institute website (www.li.lv) has a page devoted to special Latvian Remembrance Days. National holidays:

New Year's Day 1 January
Easter March/April
Labour Day 1 May
Restoration of Independence of the Republic of Latvia 4 May
Mothers' Day Second Sunday in May
Whitsunday Sunday in May or June
Līgo Eve (Midsummer festival) 23 June
Jāņi (St John's Day & Summer Solstice) 24 June
National Day 18 November; anniversary of proclamation of Latvian Republic, 1918
Christmas (Ziemsvētki) 25 December
Second Holiday 26 December
New Year's Eve 31 December

INTERNET RESOURCES

www.li.lv The Latvian Institute's official website offering an overview of Latvian culture and history.
www.1188.lv A magical website listing virtually every establishment in Latvia. The Latvian language setting yields the most search results. The search engine also provides up-to-date information on nightlife and traffic.
www.rigaoutthere.com Features a handy travel planner on the right-hand column.

MONEY

The national currency is the lats (Ls). Latvia is not expected to adopt the euro until at least 2012. Withdrawing cash and swiping plastic is easier than trying to exchange travellers cheques or foreign currencies. For detailed information and exchange rates, visit www.bank.lv.

A 10% gratuity is common in the capital, and many restaurants are now tacking the tip onto the bill.

POST

Postcard stamps for international addresses cost between 0.36Ls and 0.58Ls; see www.post.lv for more information.

TELEPHONE

Telephone rates are posted on the website of **Lattelekom** (www.lattelekom.lv). Phone cards (*telekarte*) for public phones are sold at post offices, newspaper stands and superettes. If your phone is GSM900/1800-compatible, you can purchase a SIM-card package from **Okarte** (www.lmt.lv) for 3Ls, available at any superette or Rimi grocery store.

VISAS

Holders of EU passports don't need a visa to enter Latvia; nor do Australian, Canadian, New Zealand or US citizens if staying for less than 90 days.

Liechtenstein

HIGHLIGHTS

- **Vaduz** Snap a picture of the royal castle with its stunning mountain backdrop in this tiny village masquerading as a capital (p732)
- **Malbun** Hit the slopes in this little resort to brag you've skied the Liechtenstein Alps (p735)
- **Hiking trails** Check out the country's 400km of trails through stunning alpine scenery – this can be accomplished anywhere in the tiny principality (p734)

FAST FACTS

- **Area** 150 sq km (2½ Liechtensteins would fit into Andorra!)
- **Budget** Sfr60-120 per day
- **Capital** Vaduz
- **Country code** ☎ 423
- **Famous for** dentures, sending postcards home stamped by the country's postal service
- **Language** German
- **Money** Swiss franc (Sfr); A$1 = Sfr0.84; C$1 = Sfr0.95; €1 = Sfr1.51; ¥100 = Sfr1.18; NZ$1 = Sfr0.66; UK£1 = Sfr1.70; US$1 = Sfr1.12
- **Phrases** *guten tag* (good day), *danke* (thanks), *auf wiedersehen* (goodbye), *sprechen Sie Englisch?* (do you speak English?)

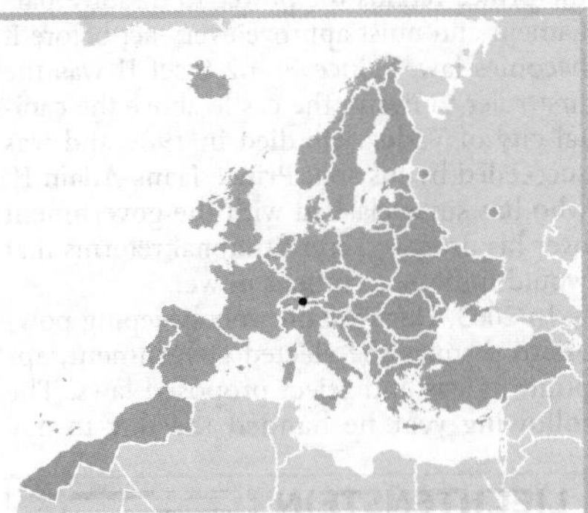

- **Population** 35,365
- **Visas** none required for citizens of the EU, USA, Australia, Canada, New Zealand and South Africa

TRAVEL HINTS

The compact size of this principality means that you can stay outside Vaduz and still reach all the attractions easily.

ROAMING LIECHTENSTEIN

Tour the entire country in a day or spend a night in Vaduz and another in Malbun to sink your teeth into the real Liechtenstein.

If Liechtenstein didn't exist, it would have been invented. A tiny mountain principality in the heart of 21st-century Europe, it certainly has novelty value. *Did you know it was the sixth smallest country?... It's still governed by an iron-willed monarch who lives in a Gothic castle on a hill... Yes, it really is the world's largest producer of dentures...* But if you're visiting this pocket-sized principality solely for the cocktail-party bragging rights, keep it hush. This exceedingly prosperous, theme-park micronation takes its independence seriously and would much rather be known for its stunning natural beauty than its false teeth. Notching up just 25km in length and 6km in width, barely larger than Manhattan with no international airport of its own, Liechtenstein is an easy day-trip saunter by public bus from Switzerland.

Vaduz is not the most soulful place on earth, but if you've come this far – coach-loads do for the souvenir passport stamp – it's worth venturing away from the capital for lovely Liechtenstein's spectacular riot of hiking and cycling trails, craggy cliffs, quaint villages and lush green forests.

HISTORY

A merger of the domain of Schellenberg and the county of Vaduz in 1712 by the powerful Liechtenstein family created the country. A principality under the Holy Roman Empire from 1719 to 1806, it achieved full sovereign independence in 1866. A modern constitution was drawn up in 1921, but even today the prince retains the power to dissolve parliament and must approve every act before it becomes law. Prince Franz Josef II was the first ruler to live in the castle above the capital city of Vaduz. He died in 1989 and was succeeded by his son, Prince Hans-Adam II, who has since clashed with the government over his proposed constitutional reforms that would limit government power.

In 2003, Hans-Adam won sweeping powers to dismiss the elected government, appoint judges and reject proposed laws. The following year he handed the day-to-day running of the country to his son Alois, although he remains titular head of state.

Scandal rocked the principality in 2008 when it was discovered that more than 1000 high-flying Germans had evaded tax by depositing large sums of money in trusts run by a Liechtenstein bank partly owned by the princely family. Liechtenstein didn't dispute that such money could have wound up in its banks (the principality doesn't consider tax evasion a crime) but accused Germany of spying.

TRANSPORT

GETTING THERE & AWAY

The nearest airports are Friedrichshafen (Germany) and Zürich, with train connections to the Swiss border towns of Buchs and Sargans. From each of these towns there are usually three daily buses to Vaduz (Sfr2.40/3.60 from Buchs/Sargans). Buses run every 30 minutes from the Austrian border town of Feldkirch; you sometimes have to change at Schaan to reach Vaduz.

A few Buchs–Feldkirch trains stop at Schaan (bus tickets are valid).

By road, the N16 from Switzerland passes through Liechtenstein via Schaan and ends at Feldkirch. The A13 follows the Rhine along the border; minor roads cross into Liechtenstein at each motorway exit.

GETTING AROUND

Buses (www.lba.li, in German) – cheap and reliable – traverse the country. Single fares (buy tickets on the bus) are Sfr2.40/3.60 for two/three zones, while a weekly bus pass costs Sfr13/6.50 per adult/child. Swiss travel passes are valid on all main routes. Timetables are posted at stops or grab one at the tourist office.

VADUZ

pop 5160

Vaduz is the kind of capital city where the butcher knows the baker; with tidy, quiet streets, lively patio cafes and a big Gothic-looking castle on a hill, it feels more like a village than anything else. It's also all most visitors to Liechtenstein see and at times it can feel like its soul has been sold to cater to the whims of tourist hordes who alight for 17 minutes on guided bus tours. Souvenir shops, tax-free luxury goods stores and cube-shaped concrete buildings dominate the small, somewhat bland town centre enclosed, which is by Äulestrasse and the pedestrian-only Städtle.

INFORMATION

Liechtenstein Center (☎ 239 63 00; www.tourismus.li; Städtle; ⌚ 9am-5pm) Tourist office; sells souvenir passport stamps for Sfr3.

SIGHTS & ACTIVITIES

Although the **Schloss Vaduz** (Vaduz Castle) is not open to the public, the exterior graces many a photograph and it is worth climbing up the hill. At the top, there's a magnificent vista of Vaduz with a spectacular mountain backdrop. There's also a network of walking trails along the ridge. For a peek inside the castle grounds, arrive on 15 August, Liechtenstein's **National Day**, when there are magnificent fireworks and the prince invites the entire country over to his place for a glass.

The well-designed **Liechtensteinisches Landesmuseum** (National Museum; ☎ 239 68 20; www.landesmuseum.li; Städtle 43; adult/concession Sfr8/5, combined with Kunstmuseum Sfr18/8; ⌚ 10am-5pm Tue-Sun, to 8pm Wed) provides an interesting romp through the principality's history, from medieval witch trials and burnings to the manufacture of false teeth.

The mainstay of the **Kunstmuseum Liechtenstein** (☎ 235 03 00; www.kunstmuseum.li; Städtle 32; adult/concession Sfr12/8, combined with Landesmuseum Sfr18/8; ⌚ 10am-5pm Tue-Sun, to 8pm Thu) is contemporary art, not the prince's collection of old masters, which has been relocated to the Liechtenstein Museum in Vienna. The **Post Museum** (☎ 236 61 05; Städtle 37; admission free; ⌚ 10am-noon & 1-5pm), on the 1st floor, is mildly diverting. It showcases all national stamps issued since 1912.

To see how Vaduz once looked, head northeast from the pedestrian zone to **Mitteldorf**, a charming quarter of traditional houses and verdant gardens.

IT'S LIECHTENSTEIN TRIVIA TIME!

- Liechtenstein is the only country in the world named after the people who purchased it.
- In its last military engagement in 1866, none of its 80 soldiers was killed. In fact, 81 returned, including a new Italian 'friend'. The army was disbanded soon afterwards.
- Low business taxes mean around 8000 firms, many of them so-called 'letterbox companies' with nominal head offices, are registered here – about twice the number of the principality's inhabitants.
- Liechtenstein is Europe's fourth smallest nation (only the Vatican, Monaco and San Marino are smaller).
- If you ever meet the prince in the pub, make sure he buys a round. The royal family is estimated to be worth €3.5 billion.

EMERGENCY NUMBERS

- Ambulance ☎ 144
- Fire ☎ 118
- Police ☎ 117

SLEEPING

Ask the tourist office for a list of private rooms and chalets outside Vaduz.

Camping Mittagspitze (☎ 392 36 77, 392 23 11; camp sites per adult/car Sfr9/5, tents Sfr6-8; ⌚ year-round;) A well-equipped ground in a leafy spot with a restaurant, TV lounge, playground and kiosk. Find it outside Vaduz, south of Triesen.

SYHA hostel (☎ 232 50 22; www.youthhostel.ch/schaan; Untere Rütigasse 6; dm/s/d Sfr33/57/84; ⌚ Mar-Oct, reception closed 10am-5pm) Renovated a few years ago, this hostel caters particularly to cyclists and families. Halfway between Schaan

SPLURGE

Gasthof Löwen (☎ 238 11 41; www.hotel-loewen.li; Herrengasse 35; s Sfr199-249, d Sfr299-349; P) Historic and creakily elegant, this six-centuries-old guest house has eight spacious rooms with antique furniture and modern bathrooms. There's a cosy bar, fine-dining restaurant and a rear outdoor terrace overlooking grapevines.

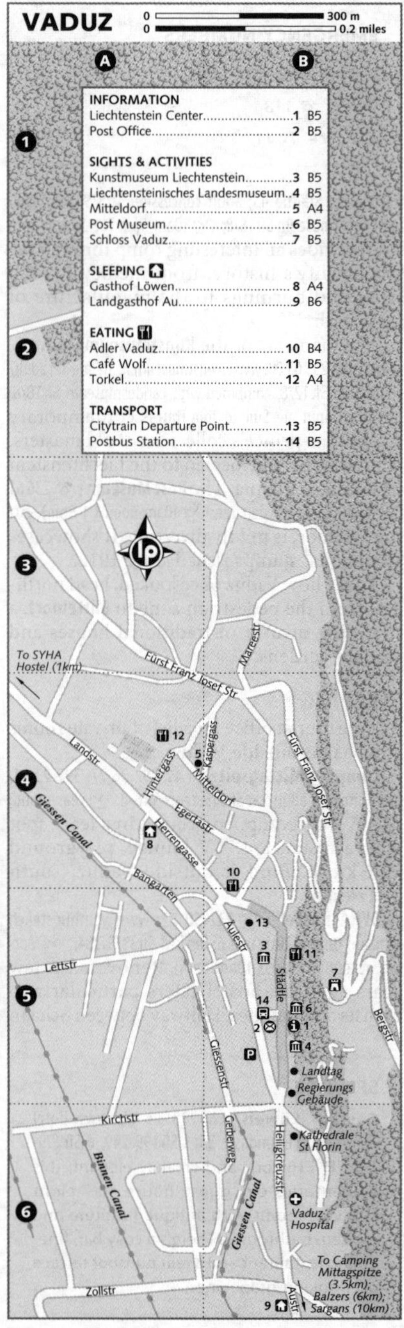

and Vaduz, it's within easy walking distance of either.

Landgasthof Au (☎ 232 11 17; Austrasse 2; s/d Sfr68/110, s/d with bathroom Sfr90/140; P) A couple of bus stops south of Vaduz town centre (about a 10-minute walk), this simple, family-run place is a reasonable budget option. Note it only accepts cash. The garden restaurant (mains Sfr18 to Sfr35, open Wednesday to Sunday) has a good name for local grub, anything from a ham omelette to a couple of vegetarian dishes.

EATING & DRINKING

Pedestrian-only Städtle has a clutch of pavement restaurants and cafes.

Café Wolf (☎ 232 23 21; Städtle 29; mains Sfr12.50-19.50) This relaxed cafe and restaurant has pavement tables in summer and a menu that mixes Swiss and international cuisine – anything from pizza to pseudo-Asian dishes.

Adler Vaduz (☎ 232 21 31; Herrenstrasse 2; dishes Sfr17.50-46; Mon-Fri) A pleasant restaurant in the Hotel Adler, this place offers a broad selection, from pasta to *Rindsfilet vom Grill auf Steinpilzrisotto mit Trüffel-Rotweinsauce nappiert* (beef steak fillet with mushroom risotto and a truffle–red wine sauce).

Torkel (☎ 232 44 10; Hintergass 9; dishes Sfr42-58) Just above the prince's vineyards sits His Majesty's ivy-clad restaurant. The garden terrace enjoys a wonderful perspective of the castle above, while the ancient, wood-lined interior is cosy in winter. Food mixes classic with modern. The set lunch menu (Sfr64) gives a good overview.

AROUND VADUZ

Outside Vaduz the air is crisp and clear with a pungent, sweet aroma of cow dung and flowers. The countryside, dotted with tranquil villages and enticing churches set to a craggy Alps backdrop, is about as idyllic and relaxing as it gets.

Triesenberg (bus 21 from Vaduz), on a terrace above Vaduz, commands excellent views over the Rhine valley. It has a pretty onion-domed church and the **Walsermuseum** (☎ 262 19 26; www.triesenberg.li; Jonaboda 2; adult/concession Sfr2/1; 7.45-11.45am & 1.30-5.45pm Mon-Fri, 7.45-11am & 1.30-5pm Sat) devoted to the Walser community, whose members came from Switzerland's Valais in the 13th century to settle.

There are 400km of **hiking trails** in Liechtenstein (see www.wanderwege.llv.li, in

LIECHTENSTEIN DIRECTORY

Liechtenstein and Switzerland share almost everything – currency, airports – so for more information about Liechtenstein basics, check out the Switzerland Directory (p1172). Liechtenstein has its own postal system.

German), along with loads of well-marked **cycling routes** (look for signs with a cycling symbol; distances and directions will also be included). The most famous hiking trail is the **Fürstensteig**, a rite of passage for nearly every Liechtensteiner. You must be fit and not suffer from vertigo, as in places the path is narrow, reinforced with rope handholds and/or falls away to a sheer drop. The hike, up to four hours, begins at the **Berggasthaus Gaflei** (bus 22 from Triesenberg). Travel light and wear good shoes.

MALBUN

pop 35

Welcome to Liechtenstein's one and only ski resort: at the end of the road from Vaduz, the 1600m-high resort of Malbun feels – in the nicest possible sense – like the edge of the earth.

The road from Vaduz terminates at Malbun. There is an ATM by the lower bus stop. The **tourist office** (☎ 263 65 77; www.malbun.li; ⏰ 9am-noon & 1.30-5pm Mon-Sat, closed mid-Apr–May & Nov–mid-Dec) is on the main street, not far from Hotel Walserhof.

Although limited, skiing is inexpensive for this part of the world and offers some bragging rights. Skiing is aimed at beginners, with a few intermediate and cross-country runs thrown in. Indeed, older British royals like Princes Charles learnt to ski here. A one-day/week ski pass (including the Sareis chairlift) costs Sfr45/205 and a day's ski rental from **Malbun Sport** (☎ 263 37 55; www.malbunsport.li; ⏰ 8am-6pm Mon-Fri, also Sat & Sun in high season) costs Sfr58 including boots and poles.

Hotel Walserhof (☎ 264 43 23; d Sfr140) is a simple mountain house with four doubles and cheerful outdoor dining. For gobsmacking mountain views over dinner, it's hard to beat **Bergrestaurant Sareiserjoch** (☎ 268 21 01; www.sareis.li; mains Sfr20-35; ⏰ Jun–mid-Oct & mid-Dec–Apr), at the end of the Sareis chairlift. Order *Käsknöpfli* (cheese-filled dumplings).

Lithuania

HIGHLIGHTS

- **Vilnius** Beautifully baroque, with its cobbled streets and skyline of church spires (p740)
- **Trakai** Its stunning island castle is the home of the rare Karaite people (p747)
- **Hill of Crosses** On the outskirts of Šiauliai is this devotional mound of thousands of crosses (p749)
- **Off the beaten track** The high sand dunes, pure air and fragrant pine forests of the enchanting Curonian Spit (p749)

FAST FACTS

- **Area** 65,300 sq km
- **Budget** 90Lt to 130Lt per day
- **Capital** Vilnius
- **Country code** ☎ 370
- **Famous for** causing the USSR to collapse, baroque churches, *cepelinai* (dough stuffed with meat and potato)
- **Languages** Lithuanian, Russian, English, German
- **Money** litas (Lt); A$1 = 1.92Lt; C$1 = 2.17Lt; €1 = 3.45Lt; ¥100 = 2.71Lt; NZ$1 = 1.50Lt; UK£1 = 3.89Lt; US$1 = 2.57Lt
- **Phrases** *labas* (hello), *ačiū* (thanks), *prašau* (please/you're welcome), *taip* (yes), *ne* (no), *viso gero* (goodbye)

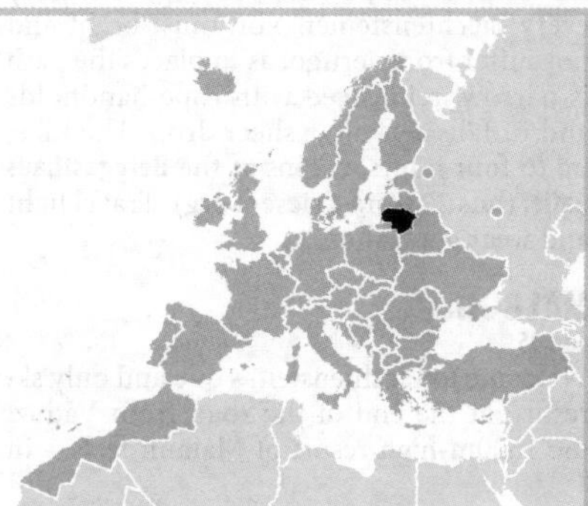

- **Population** 3.4 million
- **Visa** none required for Australian, Canadian, EU, New Zealand or US citizens for stays of up to 90 days (see p751)

TRAVEL HINTS

Even in fancy restaurants, Lithuanian specialities like *cepelinai* (dough stuffed with meat and potato) are dirt cheap. Wander into Vilnius' courtyards for glimpses of local life.

ROAMING LITHUANIA

After exploring Vilnius' treasures, head north to the Hill of Crosses then west to cycle or hike on Curonian Spit.

The Baltics have a reputation for their dour ways, but this image fades upon entering rebellious Lithuania. It's a country blessed with boundless energy and studded with reminders of its colourful history that date back to the time when amber first gained the moniker 'Baltic Gold'.

In Lithuania, a country favoured by Mother Nature where pagan roots run deep and Catholic passion lives on, travellers aren't short of things to see and do. For starters, there's effortlessly charming Vilnius and its skyline of baroque spires. Witnessing the eerie Hill of Crosses near Šiauliai is a truly unique experience. In the west thousands of migratory birds make the unique Curonian Spit their primary port of call, while the coastal capital Klaipėda combines a German heart with a Lithuanian soul. More and more tourists are stopping in Lithuania, but don't let that scare you away – there are enough delights to go around in this Baltic beauty.

HISTORY

Lithuania's history is a story of riches to rags and back again. It all started when ancient tribes fanned out across the Baltics to take advantage of the region's amber deposits. In the mid-13th century Aukštaitiai leader Mindaugas unified these tribes to create the Grand Duchy of Lithuania.

The country's golden era was from the 14th to 16th centuries. Vilnius was settled and Lithuania became one of Europe's largest empires. But in the 18th century Lithuania, which had merged with Poland, was carved up by Russia, Austria and Prussia in the partitions of Poland.

Lithuanian nationalists declared independence on 16 February 1918 with Kaunas as the capital, as Polish troops had annexed Vilnius from the Red Army in 1920. Lithuania's first president, Antanas Smetona, ruled the country with an iron fist during this time.

During WWII the Nazis murdered up to 300,000 people, mostly Jews, in Lithuania – many of them at Paneriai. Between 1944 and 1952 under Soviet rule, 250,000 Lithuanians were killed or deported while armed partisans resisted Soviet rule from the forests. Vilnius' Genocide Museum (p740) chronicles the resistance.

In the late 1980s Lithuania was the first Soviet state to legalise noncommunist parties, and on 11 March 1990 the new majority party declared independence. Moscow responded by marching troops into Vilnius and in January 1991, Soviet troops stormed key buildings in Vilnius, killing 14 people. The Soviets recognised Lithuanian independence on 6 September 1991 and the first ex-USSR republic was born.

Lithuania joined NATO in April 2004, and entered the EU a month later. The country's enthusiasm for the EU continues unabated. In a mid-2008 poll, 70% of the population still viewed EU membership optimistically. Many are gagging for the euro, but the EU currency won't be introduced until at least 2010. As with everything, EU membership has its downside: the country's younger generation are leaving in droves for the greener pastures of the UK and Ireland.

THE CULTURE

Easily the most ethnically homogeneous population of the three Baltic countries, Lithuanians account for 85% of the total population. Poles form 6.3% and Russians 5.1%. The remaining 3.6% comprises various nationalities from Eastern Europe and further afield.

Lithuanians are an outgoing, cheeky bunch, especially compared to their reticent neighbours in Latvia and Estonia. That has led some to call them the 'Spanish of the Baltics'. Others call them the 'Italians of the Baltics', citing their fierce pride – a result of the many brutal attempts to eradicate their culture and of memories of their long-lost empire.

ENVIRONMENT

Lush forests and more than 4000 lakes mark the landscape of flat Lithuania. Forest covers a third of the country and contains creatures such as wild boar, wolves, deer and elk. However, you're much more likely to spot a stork, as Lithuania has Europe's highest concentration of storks. Come late summer and autumn, mushrooms and wild berries blanket the forest floor, creating not only a rich food source but also a means of income for many rural dwellers who sell them from roadside stores.

For years, the environmental hot potato has been the Ignalina Nuclear Power Plant, 120km northeast of Vilnius. One of two reactors similar in design to Chornobyl was closed in December 2004, and the final shutdown of the plant is scheduled for sometime in 2009 or 2010 at a massive cost of €3.2 billion.

TRANSPORT

GETTING THERE & AWAY

Air

Kaunas Airport (☎ 37-399 307; www.kaunasair.lt; Savanorių prospektas), to the northwest of the capital, Vilnius, is the destination for budget airlines. Most tourists landing in Kaunas don't linger there for long and immediately hop in a car, taxi or bus for the one-hour drive to Vilnius.

Air Lithuania (TT; www.flylal.lt) flies to/from Antalya once a week in summer, while no-frills airline **Ryanair** (1I; ☎ 37-750 195; www.ryanair.com) handles the bulk of the airport's traffic, operating flights to/from Birmingham, Liverpool, Dublin, Frankfurt, and London's Stansted Airport.

LITHUANIA

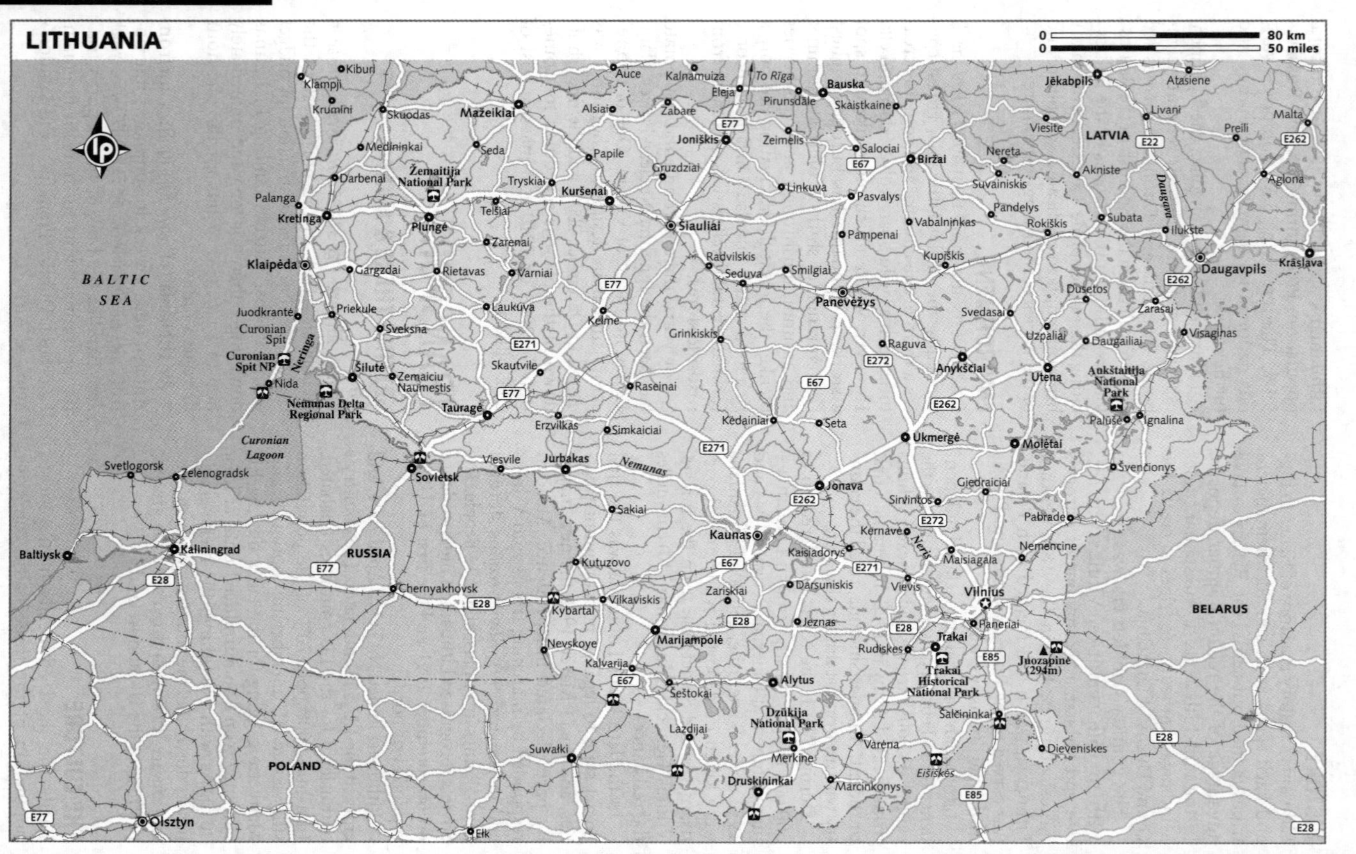

LITHUANIA

CONNECTIONS

Trains, buses and ferries provide travel options to Lithuania's neighbouring countries. From Vilnius, buses travel to Kaliningrad (Russia), Warsaw (Poland), Rīga (Latvia) and Minsk (Belarus); Kaliningrad can also be reached from Curonian Spit by bus. Trains also serve Kaliningrad, Warsaw and Minsk from the capital, but there are no connections to Rīga or Tallinn (Estonia). Denmark, Sweden and Germany can be reached by ferry from Klaipėda, Lithuania's international port.

Most international traffic to Lithuania still goes through **Vilnius International Airport** (☎ 5-273 9305; www.vno.lt; Rodūnė kelias 2). The schedule for **Air Baltic** (BT; www.airbaltic.com) and a list of other European airlines flying to Vilnius is on the airport's website.

Boat

From Klaipėda's **International Ferry Port** (Klaipėdos Nafta; ☎ 46-395 051; www.lisco.lt; Perkėlos gatvė 10), **Scandlines** (☎ 46-310 561; www.scandlines.lt; Naujoji Sodo gatvė 1) sails to Århus and Aabenraa (Denmark; with cabin, both €148, twice weekly). **Lisco Lines** (☎ 46-395 051; www.lisco.lt; Perkėlos gatvė 10) runs passenger ferries to/from Kiel (Germany; from €46, six weekly), Sassnitz (Germany; from €46, twice weekly) and Karlshamn (Sweden; from €52, daily).

Bus

The main international bus companies operating in Lithuania are **Eurolines** (www.eurolines.lt; Vilnius bus station Map pp742-3; ☎ 5-233 6666; Kaunas bus station ☎ 37-322 222; Klaipėda ☎ 46-415 555) and **Ecolines** (www.ecolines.net; Vilnius bus station Map pp742-3; ☎ 5-213 3300; Kaunas ☎ 37-202 022; Klaipėda ☎ 46-310 103).

Eurolines or Ecolines have buses between Vilnius and Rīga (55Lt, five hours, at least four daily), Kaliningrad (1100Lt, seven hours, two daily), Tallinn (from 108Lt, 10½ hours, up to five daily), Warsaw (106Lt, nine hours, three daily), Moscow (150Lt, 15 hours, daily), and St Petersburg (from 150Lt, 18½ hours, four daily).

There are a couple of buses that go weekly to a handful of Western European cities, including London and several German cities. There's a daily bus to Berlin (from 270Lt, 16 hours).

Car & Motorcycle

Coming from the south, you're looking at a 30-minute to one-hour wait at the two Polish border crossings (Ogrodniki and Budzisko). Lines at the Latvian border in the north are shorter.

Train

Vilnius is linked by regular direct trains to Moscow (from 170Lt, 15 to 18 hours, up to five daily), St Petersburg (from 130Lt, 13½ hours, daily), Kaliningrad (from 77Lt, 6½ hours, up to seven daily) and Minsk (65Lt, 4½ hours, up to eight daily). You'll need a Belarus visa for the Moscow train. For Warsaw (from 120Lt, eight to 10 hours, one daily), a change in Šeštokai is required.

GETTING AROUND

Bus

Timetables for local buses are displayed prominently in most stations. From Vilnius you can get to/from the following destinations by bus:

Destination	Cost	Duration	Frequency
Druskininkai	25Lt	2hr	10 daily
Kaunas	20Lt	1¾hr	2-3 hourly
Klaipėda	59Lt	4-5½hr	15 daily
Šiauliai	41Lt	3-4½hr	6 daily

Car & Motorcycle

You can drive across Lithuania in a couple of hours. Modern four-lane highways link Vilnius and Klaipėda (via Kaunas), and Vilnius and Panevėžys.

The big international rental-car agencies are well represented at Vilnius airport, but you'll save a ton of money by renting from a local operator. Charismatic **Rimas** (☎ 5-277 6213, 8-698-21662; rimas.cars@is.lt) rents older cars at the lowest rates in Vilnius.

Local Transport

Lithuanian cities are generously covered by networks of buses, trolleybuses and minibuses. In most towns you must punch your bus ticket or you'll risk a fine.

Train

You can lumber from Vilnius to a few domestic destinations on Lithuania's clunky suburban trains. Destinations include Kaunas (12Lt, 1¼ hours, up to 17 daily), Klaipėda (42.10Lt, five hours, three daily) and Šiauliai (28.70Lt, 2½ to three hours, three daily).

VILNIUS

☎5 / pop 542,800

Vilnius, the baroque bombshell of the Baltics, is a city of immense allure. As beautiful as it is bizarre, it easily tops the country's best-attraction bill, drawing tourists like moths to a flame with Europe's largest baroque old town, a spider web of cobbled streets and countless Orthodox and Catholic churches. And if that isn't enough, count on breakaway states, traditional artists' workshops and a healthy nightlife.

ORIENTATION

Most of the action in Vilnius is in Old Town. The northern border of Old Town merges with 'New Town' at Gedimino prospektas, a wide, part-time pedestrian avenue that runs west to east from parliament to Katedros aikštė (Cathedral Sq) – the spiritual, if not the geographical, heart of Vilnius.

INFORMATION

Internet Access & Telephone

A growing number of cafes, restaurants and hotels have free wi-fi zones; check www.wifi.lt for more information.

Collegium (Map pp744-5; Pilies gatvė 22-1; per hr 5Lt; 8am-midnight)

Interneto Kavinė (Map pp744-5; Pylimo gatvė 21; per hr 4Lt; 9am-midnight)

Media

Vilnius In Your Pocket (www.inyourpocket.com; 6Lt) Quality city guide published every two months and widely available; also downloadable from the website.

Medical Services

24-hour pharmacy (Gedimino Vaistinė; Gedimino prospektas 27)

Baltic-American Medical & Surgical Clinic (Map pp742-3; ☎234 2020; www.bak.lt; Nemenčinės gatvė 54a; 24hr) English-speaking health centre.

Money

Vilnius is littered with ATMs and banks, most offering currency and travellers-cheque exchange.

Keitykla Exchange (Map pp742-3; Parex Bankas; ☎213 5454; www.keitykla.lt; Geležinkelio gatvė 6; 24hr) Currency exchange with ATM. Parex Bankas is Lithuania's AmEx representative.

EMERGENCY NUMBERS

- Ambulance ☎03
- Fire ☎01
- Police ☎02

Tourist Information

Vilnius Tourist Information Centres (www.vilnius-tourism.lt; 9am-6pm Mon-Fri, 10am-4pm Sat & Sun) Town Hall (Map pp744-5; ☎262 6470; Didžioji gatvė 31); train station (Map pp742-3; ☎269 2091); Vilniaus gatvė (Map pp744-5; ☎262 9660; Vilniaus gatvė 22) Friendly centres with a wealth of glossy brochures and general information. It also arranges tour guides and books accommodation (a hotel reservation fee of 6Lt applies).

SIGHTS

Vilnius is a compact city, and most sights are easily reached on foot. Those visiting for a couple of days will scarcely move out of Old Town. Stay a couple more days and the New Town – with its museums, shops and riverside action – beckons.

Cathedral Square & New Town

Vilnius was founded on 48m-high Gediminas Hill, topped since the 13th century by the oft-rebuilt tower of ruined **Gediminas Tower** (Map pp744–5). There are amazing views of Old Town from the top of the tower, which houses the **Upper Castle Museum** (Map pp744-5; adult/child 4/2Lt; 10am-7pm May-Oct, 11am-5pm Tue-Sun Nov-Apr); reached by **funicular** (Map pp744-5; adult/child 2/1Lt; 10am-7pm May-Oct, 10am-5pm Nov-Apr), located at the rear of the Museum of Applied Arts.

At the base of Gediminas Hill sprawls Cathedral Sq (Katedros aikštė), dominated by **Vilnius Cathedral** (Map pp744-5; admission free; 7am-7.30pm, mass at 9am, 10am, 11am & 7pm Sun) and its 57m-tall **belfry** (Map pp744–5). The first wooden cathedral, built here in 1387–88, was in Gothic style, but has been rebuilt many times since then. The most important restoration was completed from 1783 to 1801, when the outside was redone in today's classical style. The interior's showpiece is baroque **St Casimir's Chapel** (Map pp744–5), with frescoes depicting the life of St Casimir (Lithuania's patron saint), whose silver coffin lies within.

At the square's eastern end is an **equestrian statue of Gediminas** (Map pp744–5), built on an ancient pagan site, and behind it stands the **Royal Palace** (Valdovų rumai; Map pp744–5).

Demolished by the Russians in the late 18th century, the palace has been reconstructed over the past few years and should be open again by the time you read this.

The **Museum of Applied Arts** (Map pp744-5; www.ldm.lt; Arsenalo gatvė 3a; admission 6Lt; 11am-6pm Tue-Sat, 11am-4pm Sun), in the old arsenal at the foot of Gediminas Hill, houses exhibitions showcasing 15th- to 19th-century Lithuanian sacred art. Next door, the **National Museum of Lithuania** (Map pp744-5; www.lnm.lt; Arsenalo gatvė 1; adult/child 4/2Lt; 10am-5pm Tue-Sat, 10am-3pm Sun) retells everyday Lithuanian life from the 13th century till WWII.

Gedimino prospektas, the main boulevard of Vilnius' 19th-century New Town, heads due west from Cathedral Sq all the way to the silver-domed Orthodox **Church of the Saint Virgin's Apparition** (Map pp744-5; A Mickevičiaus gatvė 1), 1.75km away. Roughly halfway is Lukiškių aikštė, formerly Lenin Sq. The Lenin Statue that once stood here is now in Druskininkai's Soviet sculpture park (see the boxed text, p748).

The building facing the square was the notorious KGB headquarters and prison, but is now the **Museum of Genocide Victims** (Map pp744-5; ☎ 249 6264; www.genocid.lt; Aukų gatvė 2a; admission 4Lt; 10am-5pm Tue-Sat, to 3pm Sun). Called the 'KGB Museum' by locals, it is Vilnius' most important and most popular museum. It is best taken in with a headphone audio tour (8Lt).

Old Town & Around

Eastern Europe's largest old town deserves its Unesco status. The area stretches 1.5km south from Cathedral Sq and the eastern end of Gedimino prospektas.

Cobbled **Pilies gatvė** (Map pp744–5) – the hub of tourist action and the main entrance to Old Town from Katedros aikštė – buzzes with life. Nearby is Eastern Europe's oldest university, the **Vilnius University** (Map pp744-5; ☎ 268 7001; www.vu.lt; Universiteto gatvė 3; adult/child 5/1Lt; 9am-6pm Mon-Sat), featuring 13 courtyards framed by 15th-century buildings and splashed with 300-year-old frescoes and **St John's Church** (Map pp744-5; 10am-5pm Mon-Sat), a baroque gem.

At the southern border of Old Town, the 16th-century **Gates of Dawn** (Aušros Vartai; Map pp744–5) is the only one of the town wall's original nine gates still intact. The gate houses the **Chapel of the Blessed Virgin Mary** (Map pp744-5; admission free; 6am-7pm) containing the black-and-gold 'miracle-working' **Virgin Mary icon**, one of the holiest icons in Polish Catholicism.

There are four famous churches near the Gates of Dawn: early baroque **St Teresa's Church** (Map pp744–5; built from 1635–50), the pink, domed 17th-century **Orthodox Church of the Holy Spirit** (Map pp744–5), the dilapidated **Holy Trinity Church** (Map pp744–5) and, further up Aušros Vartų gatvė, ravishing **St Casimir's Church** (Map pp744–5), the oldest of Vilnius' baroque masterpieces (1604–15).

Old Town's main commercial street, Vokiečių gatvė, offers fine views of several churches, including **St Catherine's Church** (Map pp744-5; Vilniaus gatvė 30) displaying Vilnius' trademark peach baroque style. This area used to be part of Vilnius' Jewish Quarter. Dubbed the 'Jerusalem of the north', Vilnius had one of Europe's most prominent Jewish communities until Nazi brutality virtually wiped it out.

Jewish Vilnius is far too rich a topic to adequately cover here, but there are several excellent resources available if you want to dig deeper into Lithuania's Jewish past. A good place to start your tour is the **Centre for Tolerance**

TOP FIVE QUIRKY ATTRACTIONS

Vilnius has an undeniable mischievous streak, as the following attest:

Frank Zappa memorial (Map pp744-5; Kalinausko gatvë 1) The world's first Zappa statue is in a graffiti-splashed courtyard.

Angel of Užupis statue (Map pp744-5; Užupio & Malūnro gatvė) The oddball symbol of Vilnius' strangest district.

Egg statue (Map pp744-5; cnr Šv Stepono & Raugyklos gatvė) Was in Užupis' main square until it 'hatched' the Angel of Užupis in 2002.

Žaliasis Tiltas (Green Bridge) statues (Map pp744-5) The communist-era sculptures here weren't torn down because the locals adore them.

Stebuklas (miracle) tile If you stand on this tile on Cathedral Sq and turn around clockwise, your wish will allegedly come true. But first you must find it!

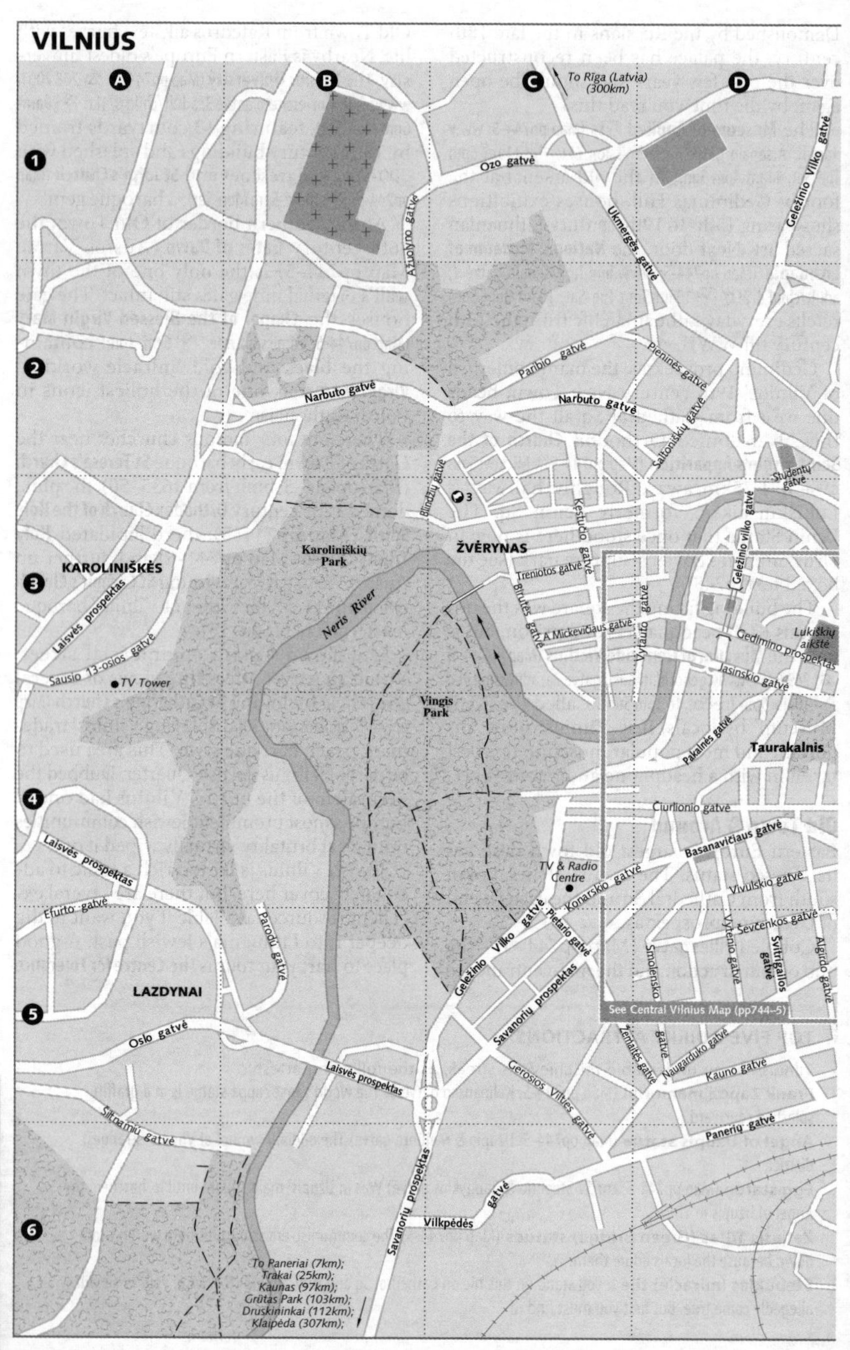
VILNIUS
To Rīga (Latvia) (300km)
Ozo gatvė
Ažuolyno gatvė
Ukmergės gatvė
Geležinio Vilko gatvė
Paribio gatvė
Pieninės gatvė
Narbuto gatvė
Narbuto gatvė
Saltoniškių gatvė
Studentų gatvė
Blindžių gatvė
3
Kęstučio gatvė
ŽVĖRYNAS
Karoliniškių Park
KAROLINIŠKĖS
Treniotos gatvė
Birutės gatvė
Geležinio vilko gatvė
Vytauto gatvė
A Mickevičiaus gatvė
Gedimino prospektas
Lukiškių aikštė
Jasinskio gatvė
Laisvės prospektas
Sausio 13-osios gatvė
TV Tower
Neris River
Vingis Park
Pakalnės gatvė
Taurakalnis
Čiurlionio gatvė
Basanavičiaus gatvė
Laisvės prospektas
TV & Radio Centre
Konarskio gatvė
Vivulskio gatvė
Efurto gatvė
Parodų gatvė
Geležinio Vilko gatvė
Pietario gatvė
Ševčenkos gatvė
Smolensko gatvė
Vytenio gatvė
Švitrigailos gatvė
Algirdo gatvė
LAZDYNAI
Savanorių prospektas
See Central Vilnius Map (pp744–5)
Oslo gatvė
Žemaitės gatvė
Naugarduko gatvė
Laisvės prospektas
Gerosios Vilties gatvė
Kauno gatvė
Siltnamių gatvė
Panerių gatvė
Savanorių prospektas
Vilkpėdės gatvė
To Paneriai (7km); Trakai (25km); Kaunas (97km); Grūtas Park (103km); Druskininkai (112km); Klaipėda (307km);
LITHUANIA

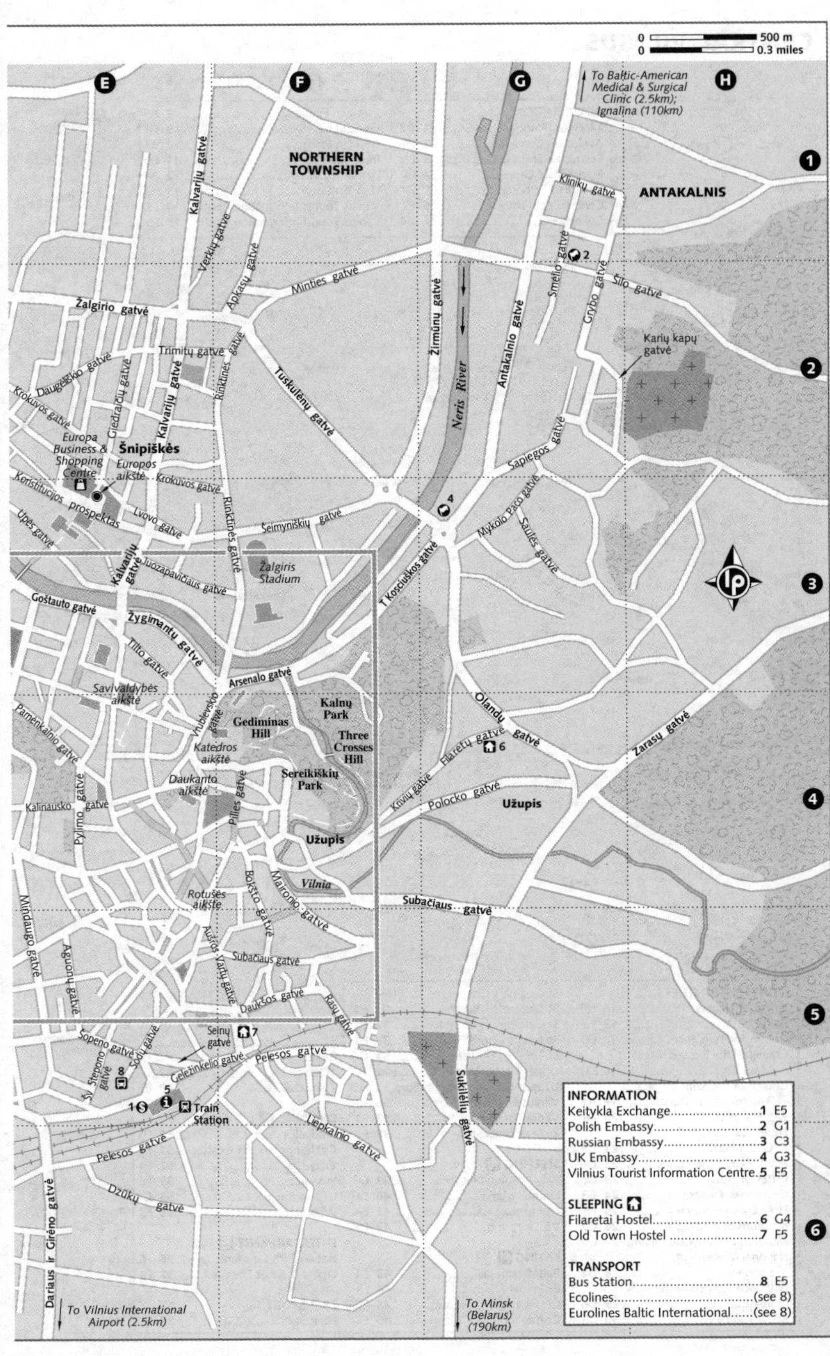
0 500 m
0 0.3 miles
To Baltic-American Medical & Surgical Clinic (2.5km); Ignalina (110km)
NORTHERN TOWNSHIP
ANTAKALNIS
Šnipiškės
Užupis
Europa Business & Shopping Centre
Europos aikštė
Žalgiris Stadium
Gediminas Hill
Kalnų Park
Three Crosses Hill
Sereikiškių Park
Katedros aikštė
Daukanto aikštė
Savivaldybės aikštė
Rotušės aikštė
Neris River
Vilnia
Train Station
Karių kapų gatvė
Seinų gatvė
Žalgirio gatvė
Kalvarijų gatvė
Verkių gatvė
Apkasų gatvė
Minties gatvė
Žirmūnų gatvė
Antakalnio gatvė
Klinikų gatvė
Šilo gatvė
Smėlio gatvė
Grybo gatvė
Tuskulėnų gatvė
Rinktinės gatvė
Trimitų gatvė
Giedraičių gatvė
Daugėliškio gatvė
Krokuvos gatvė
Konstitucijos prospektas
Upės gatvė
Lvovo gatvė
Šeimyniškių gatvė
Sapiegos gatvė
Mykolo Paco gatvė
Saulės gatvė
T Kosciuškos gatvė
Juozapavičiaus gatvė
Goštauto gatvė
Žygimantų gatvė
Tilto gatvė
Arsenalo gatvė
Vrublevskio gatvė
Olandų gatvė
Filaretų gatvė
Zarasų gatvė
Kreivių gatvė
Polocko gatvė
Pamėnkalnio gatvė
Kalinausko gatvė
Pylimo gatvė
Pilies gatvė
Bokšto gatvė
Maironio gatvė
Subačiaus gatvė
Aušros Vartų gatvė
Mindaugo gatvė
Aguonų gatvė
Daukšos gatvė
Rasų gatvė
Šopeno gatvė
Sodų gatvė
Šv Stepono gatvė
Geležinkelio gatvė
Pelesos gatvė
Liepkalnio gatvė
Sukilėlių gatvė
Dzūkų gatvė
Dariaus ir Girėno gatvė
To Vilnius International Airport (2.5km)
To Minsk (Belarus) (190km)
INFORMATION
Keitykla Exchange 1 E5
Polish Embassy 2 G1
Russian Embassy 3 C3
UK Embassy 4 G3
Vilnius Tourist Information Centre 5 E5
SLEEPING
Filaretai Hostel 6 G4
Old Town Hostel 7 F5
TRANSPORT
Bus Station 8 E5
Ecolines (see 8)
Eurolines Baltic International (see 8)

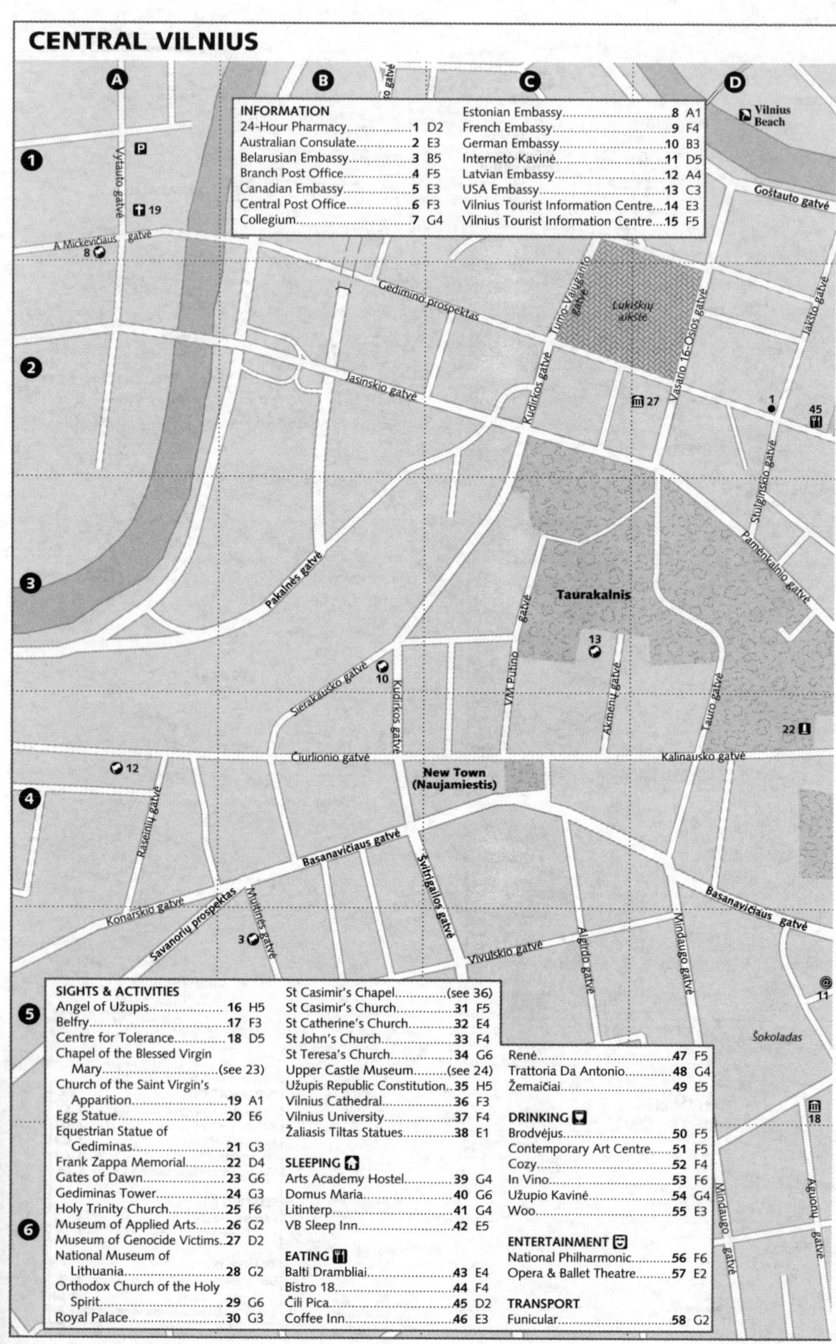
CENTRAL VILNIUS
A
B
C
D
1
2
3
4
5
6
INFORMATION
24-Hour Pharmacy 1 D2
Australian Consulate 2 E3
Belarusian Embassy 3 B5
Branch Post Office 4 F5
Canadian Embassy 5 E3
Central Post Office 6 F3
Collegium 7 G4
Estonian Embassy 8 A1
French Embassy 9 F4
German Embassy 10 B3
Interneto Kavinė 11 D5
Latvian Embassy 12 A4
USA Embassy 13 C3
Vilnius Tourist Information Centre 14 E3
Vilnius Tourist Information Centre 15 F5
Vilnius Beach
Vytauto gatvė
A Mickevičiaus gatvė
Goštauto gatvė
Gedimino prospektas
Jasinskio gatvė
Tumo-Vaižganto gatvė
Lukiškių aikštė
Kudirkos gatvė
Vasario 16-Osios gatvė
Jakšto gatvė
Stulginskio gatvė
Pamėnkalnio gatvė
Pakalnės gatvė
Taurakalnis
VM Putino gatvė
Sierakausko gatvė
Akmenų gatvė
Tauro gatvė
Čiurlionio gatvė
Kalinausko gatvė
New Town (Naujamiestis)
Raseinių gatvė
Basanavičiaus gatvė
Konarskio gatvė
Savanorių prospektas
Muitinės gatvė
Švitrigailos gatvė
Vivulskio gatvė
Algirdo gatvė
Mindaugo gatvė
Šokoladas
Aguonų gatvė
SIGHTS & ACTIVITIES
Angel of Užupis 16 H5
Belfry 17 F3
Centre for Tolerance 18 D5
Chapel of the Blessed Virgin Mary (see 23)
Church of the Saint Virgin's Apparition 19 A1
Egg Statue 20 E6
Equestrian Statue of Gediminas 21 G3
Frank Zappa Memorial 22 D4
Gates of Dawn 23 G6
Gediminas Tower 24 G3
Holy Trinity Church 25 F6
Museum of Applied Arts 26 G2
Museum of Genocide Victims 27 D2
National Museum of Lithuania 28 G2
Orthodox Church of the Holy Spirit 29 G6
Royal Palace 30 G3
St Casimir's Chapel (see 36)
St Casimir's Church 31 F5
St Catherine's Church 32 E4
St John's Church 33 F4
St Teresa's Church 34 G6
Upper Castle Museum (see 24)
Užupis Republic Constitution 35 H5
Vilnius Cathedral 36 F3
Vilnius University 37 F4
Žaliasis Tiltas Statues 38 E1
SLEEPING
Arts Academy Hostel 39 G4
Domus Maria 40 G6
Litinterp 41 G4
VB Sleep Inn 42 E5
EATING
Balti Drambliai 43 E4
Bistro 18 44 F4
Čili Pica 45 D2
Coffee Inn 46 E3
René 47 F5
Trattoria Da Antonio 48 G4
Žemaičiai 49 E5
DRINKING
Brodvėjus 50 F5
Contemporary Art Centre 51 F5
Cozy 52 F4
In Vino 53 F6
Užupio Kavinė 54 G4
Woo 55 E3
ENTERTAINMENT
National Philharmonic 56 F6
Opera & Ballet Theatre 57 E2
TRANSPORT
Funicular 58 G2

LITHUANIA

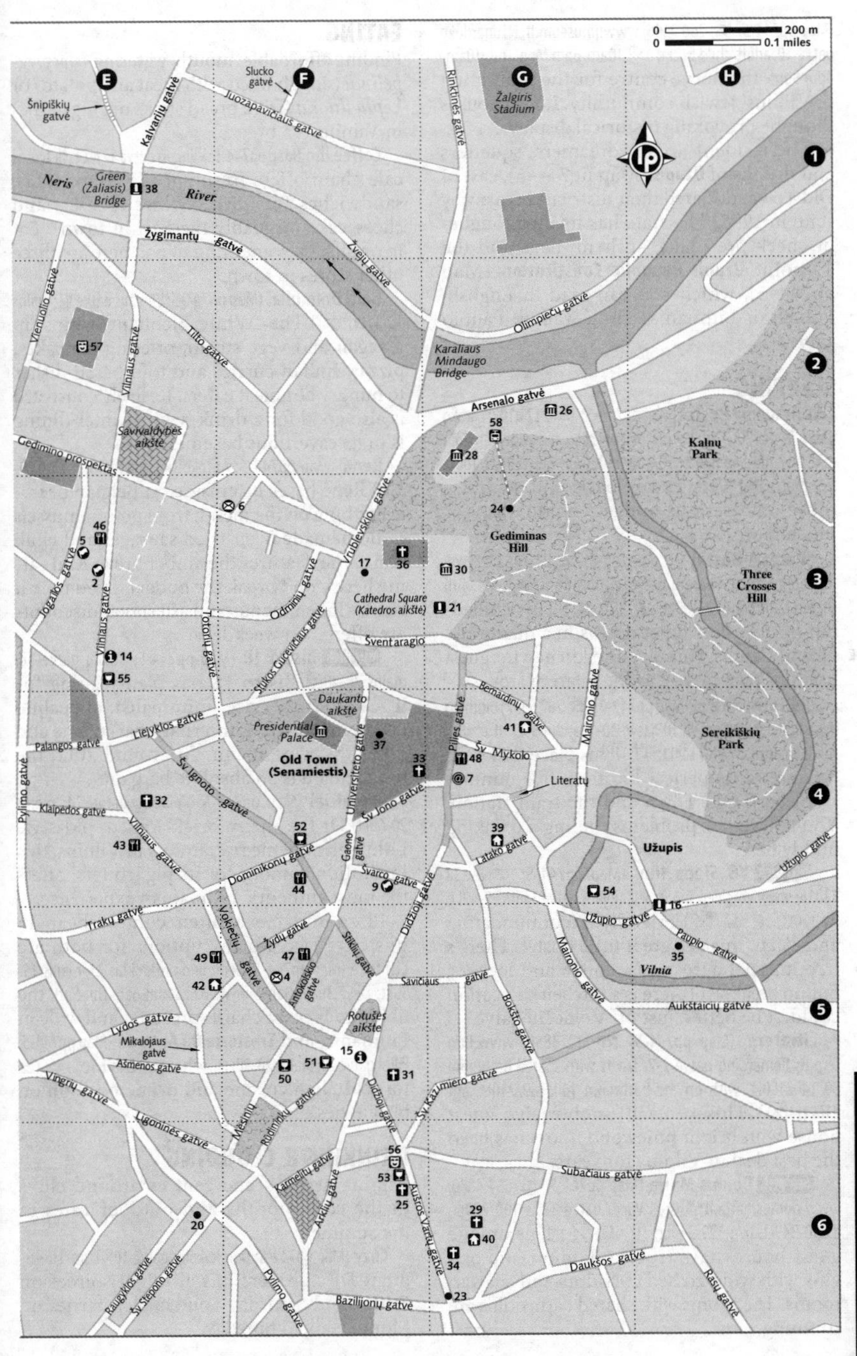

0 200 m
0 0.1 miles
E
F
G
H
1
2
3
4
5
6
Šnipiškių gatvė
Slucko gatvė
Kalvarijų gatvė
Juozapavičiaus gatvė
Rinktinės gatvė
Žalgiris Stadium
Neris
River
Green (Žaliasis) Bridge
38
Žygimantų gatvė
Žvejų gatvė
Olimpiečų gatvė
Karaliaus Mindaugo Bridge
Vienuolio gatvė
57
Vilniaus gatvė
Tilto gatvė
Arsenalo gatvė
26
58
28
Savivaldybės aikštė
Gedimino prospektas
Vrublevskio gatvė
Kalnų Park
6
24
Gediminas Hill
46
5
2
Jogailos gatvė
Odminių gatvė
17
36
30
Three Crosses Hill
Cathedral Square (Katedros aikštė)
21
Totorių gatvė
Šventaragio
14
55
Stuokos Gucevičiaus gatvė
Daukanto aikštė
Bernardinų gatvė
Maironio gatvė
Liejyklos gatvė
Presidential Palace
37
41
Sereikiškių Park
Palangos gatvė
Old Town (Senamiestis)
Universiteto gatvė
33
48
Šv Mykolo
Pilimo gatvė
Šv Ignoto gatvė
7
Literatų
32
Klaipėdos gatvė
Šv Jono gatvė
39
Užupis
52
Latako gatvė
Užupio gatvė
43
Vilniaus gatvė
Gaono gatvė
Dominikonų gatvė
Švarco gatvė
9
44
Didžioji gatvė
54
16
Užupio gatvė
Trakų gatvė
Vokiečių gatvė
Žydų gatvė
Stiklių gatvė
Paupio gatvė
35
49
47
4
Antokolskio gatvė
Vilnia
42
Savičiaus gatvė
Maironio gatvė
Bokšto gatvė
Aukštaičių gatvė
Rotušės aikštė
Lydos gatvė
Mikalojaus gatvė
15
Ašmenos gatvė
50
51
31
Vingrių gatvė
Šv Kazimiero gatvė
Ligoninės gatvė
Mėsinių
Rudininkų gatvė
Didžioji gatvė
56
Subačiaus gatvė
Karmelitų gatvė
53
25
Arklių gatvė
Aušros Vartų gatvė
29
20
40
34
Daukšos gatvė
Raugyklos gatvė
Šv Stepono gatvė
Pylimo gatvė
Rasų gatvė
23
Bazilijonų gatvė
LITHUANIA

(Map pp744-5; ☎ 266 9666; www.jmuseum.lt; Naugarduko gatvė 10; adult/child 5/2Lt; 🕑 10am-6pm Mon-Thu, 10am-4pm Sun), the nerve centre for the rebuilding of Vilnius' Jewish community. It also houses thought-provoking historical displays.

The resident artists, dreamers, squatters and drunks of **Užupis** (Map pp744–5), east of Old Town, declared their district a breakaway state in 1998. The state has its own tongue-in-cheek president, anthem, flags and the 41-point **Užupis Republic Constitution** (Map pp744–5), which you can read in English, French or Lithuanian on a wall on Paupio gatvė.

SLEEPING

Arts Academy Hostel (Map pp744-5; ☎ 212 0102; Latako gatvė 2; dm 20-22Lt, tw per person 30Lt, tr per person 26Lt mid-Jul–mid-Sep, s/d/tr 60/100/110Lt Apr-Sep, 50/90/100Lt Sep-Mar; P) Very cheap, basic and central – those on a serious budget couldn't ask for much more.

Filaretai Hostel (Map pp742-3; ☎ 215 4627; www.filaretaihostel.lt; Filaretų gatvė 17; dm from 34Lt, s/d with shared bathroom 70/100Lt; P 💻 ⊠) This chilled-out hostel offers quiet rooms in a quaint old villa in Užupis. Laundry and kitchen for guest use too. Take bus 34 to the Filaretų stop.

Old Town Hostel (Map pp742-3; ☎ 262 5357; oldtownhostel@lha.lt; Aušros Vartų gatvė 20-15a; dm 35Lt, d/tr with shared bathroom 110/144Lt; 💻) This place sticks out because of its perfect location, five minutes from both Old Town and the train station. You'll have few problems finding a drinking buddy here.

our pick **VB Sleep Inn** (Map pp744-5; ☎ 8-638 32818; www.vb-sleep-inn.lt; Mikalojaus gatvė 3; dm 39-42Lt, tw 110Lt; P 💻 ⊠) Friendly, accommodating and clean, this is a great little hostel. There's free internet access, tea, coffee and lockers, but no breakfast (there is a kitchen). Location couldn't be better, just off Vokiečių gatvė.

Litinterp (Map pp744-5; ☎ 212 3850; www.litinterp.lt; Bernardinų gatvė 7-2; s/d/tr with shared bathroom 80/140/180Lt, with private bathroom 100/160/210Lt, apt 210Lt; ⊠) This central, unobtrusive guest house with bright pinewood floors has been the best deal in Vilnius for years.

our pick **Domus Maria** (Map pp744-5; ☎ 264 4880; www.domusmaria.lt; Aušros Vartų gatvė 12; s 100-289Lt, d 150-349Lt, tr/q 329/369Lt; P 💻 ⊠) This unique guest house stays true to its monastic origins with wide arched corridors and spartan rooms. The rooms with shared bathrooms are stunning value.

EATING

Finding affordable, mouth-watering curry, *cepelinai* (dough filled with meat and potato) or *kepta duona* (fried bread sticks oozing garlic) in Vilnius is a breeze.

Coffee Inn (Map pp744-5; Vilniaus gatvė 17) This local cafe chain offers freshly made wraps (8Lt), sandwiches (6.50Lt), cookies (3.50Lt) and cheesecake (arguably the best in town). Eat in or pick up something to go; there are three other stores in town.

Balti Drambliai (Map pp744-5; Vilniaus gatvė 41; mains 10-17Lt; ⊠) The 'White Elephant' whips up a vegan and vege storm, offering pancakes, pizzas, Indian curries and tofu-based dishes to hungry nonmeat eaters. Its lively courtyard is also good for a drink, while winter dining is in its cavernous basement.

René (Map pp744-5; Antokolskio gatvė 13; mains 20-35Lt) René bases its cuisine on Belgian beer – everything on the menu, from pots of mussels to homemade oven-fried sausages and chilli con carne, features the amber brew. And eating here won't break the budget if you time it right – lunch menus and afternoon discounts are offered on weekdays.

our pick **Bistro 18** (Map pp744-5; Stiklių gatvė 18; mains 20-40Lt) Bistro 18 has plenty going for it – friendly service, minimalist, appealing decor, imaginative, international cuisine and a lengthy wine menu. At around 20Lt, the lunch menu is an absolute bargain.

Žemaičiai (Map pp744-5; Vokiečių gatvė 24; mains 20-60Lt) Of the many brick-walled, old-style Lithuanian theme restaurants in Vilnius, this institution, famous for its pig trotters, offers the most authentic Lithuanian experience.

Pizza and pasta often comes cheap in this city. Two worthy options for both are **Čili Pica** (Map pp744-5; Gedimino prospektas 23; mains 15-30Lt; 🕑 7.30am-3am Sun-Wed, 7.30am-6am Thu-Sat), the ubiquitous pizza chain spread far and wide in Lithuania, and **Trattoria Da Antonio** (Map pp744-5; Pilies gatvė 20; mains 20-30Lt), which wins local votes for its Italian cuisine and prime position on busy Pilies.

DRINKING & CLUBBING

Vilnius' party scene centres around clubs in the cold months and outdoor cafes in the summer.

Cozy (Map pp744-5; Dominikonų gatvė 10) The basement DJ club here has all-night soirées on Friday and Saturday and smaller parties on Monday and Thursday.

In Vino (Map pp744-5; Aušros Vartų gatvė 7) The bar of the moment, with one of the loveliest courtyards in the city. Excellent wines, expensive tapas, and a few mains.

Contemporary Art Centre (Map pp744-5; Vokiečių gatvė 2) This art centre has a smoky hideout bar filled with arty Lithuanian luvvies, and one of the most simple but hip summer terraces in town.

Užupio Kavinė (Map pp744-5; Užupio gatvė 2; mains 10-20Lt) This legendary spot is known for its arty clientele and good cheap breakfasts. Ask the bartender for a copy of the Užupis constitution in English.

Brodvėjus (Map pp744-5; ☎ 210 7208; Mėsinių 4; cover 10-15Lt; ⌚ nightly) Hordes of expats and pretty young things flock here night after night to dance to 'I Will Survive', 'Mambo No 5' and the same tired-but-innocuous soundtrack.

Woo (Map pp744-5; www.woo.lt; Vilniaus gatvė 22) Escape the mainstream at this basement club below Radvilos' Palace. Resident DJs spin drum 'n' bass, techno and house to a backdrop of VJ art. Jazz sessions occasionally fill the space.

ENTERTAINMENT

In Your Pocket publishes a list of movie theatres as well as listings for opera, theatre, classical music and other big events.

Opera & Ballet Theatre (Map pp744-5; ☎ 262 0727; www.opera.lt; Vienuolio gatvė 1) Classical productions in a grand, gaudy building near the river.

National Philharmonic (Map pp744-5; ☎ 266 5233; www.filharmonija.lt; Aušros Vartų gatvė 5) The country's most renowned orchestras perform here.

GETTING THERE & AWAY

See the information under the Transport section (p737).

GETTING AROUND

Public Transport

Unless you're heading well out of Old Town, you won't have much need for public transport in Vilnius, although the route from the train station to New Town via Pylimo gatvė is handy. It is serviced by trolleybuses 2 and 5, and by buses 26, 26a and 53. Tickets cost 1.10Lt at news kiosks and 1.40Lt direct from the driver; punch tickets on board in a ticket machine or risk a 20Lt on-the-spot fine.

> **GETTING INTO TOWN**
>
> From the Vilnius airport to the centre take bus 1, which runs every hour, to the train station (1.10Lt, 20 minutes). You can also take bus 2 to Lukiškių aikštė on Gedimino prospektas in New Town. A taxi from the airport to the city centre should cost between 40Lt and 50Lt.
>
> The adjacent train station and bus station are a five-minute walk from the southern edge of Old Town.

Taxi

Taxis officially charge 3Lt per kilometre (more at night) and must have a meter. Drivers often try to rip off tourists, especially if flagged down on the street. Order a cab by calling ☎ 261 6161, ☎ 240 0004 or ☎ 239 5539.

AROUND VILNIUS

PANERIAI

During WWII the Nazis – aided by Lithuanian accomplices – exterminated three-quarters of Vilnius' 100,000-strong Jewish population at this site, 10km southwest of central Vilnius. From the entrance a path leads to the small **Paneriai Museum** (Agrastų gatvė 15; ⌚ 11am-6pm Wed-Sat Jun-Sep, by appointment Oct-May). There are over two dozen trains daily from Vilnius to Paneriai station (1.30Lt, 15 minutes), from where it's about a 1km walk southwest along Agrastų gatvė to the site.

TRAKAI

☎ 528 / pop 5,400

With its red-brick fairy-tale castle, Karaite culture, quaint wooden houses and pretty lakeside location, Trakai is a must-see within easy reach of the capital.

The Karaites are named after the term *Kara*, which means 'to study the scriptures' in both Hebrew and Arabic. The sect originated in Baghdad and practises strict adherence to the Torah (rejecting the rabbinic Talmud). Grand Duke of Lithuania Vytautas brought about 380 Karaite families to Trakai from Crimea, in around 1400, to serve as bodyguards. Only 60 Karaites remain in Trakai today and their numbers – about 280 in Lithuania – are dwindling rapidly.

 Book your stay at lonelyplanet.com/hotels

This area has protected status as the **Trakai Historical National Park** (www.seniejitrakai.lt). The **tourist information centre** (☎ 51934; www.trakai.lt; Vytauto gatvė 69; 9am-5pm Mon, 8am-6pm Tue-Fri, 9am-3pm Sat & Sun May-Sep, 8am-5pm Oct-Apr) sells maps, books accommodation and has information on fishing, sailing, scuba diving, horse riding and a range of other activities.

Trakai's trophy piece is the fairy-tale **Island Castle**, occupying a small island in Lake Galvė. The painstakingly restored, red-brick Gothic castle dates to the late 14th century. Inside the castle, the **Trakai History Museum** (☎ 53946; www.trakaimuziejus.lt; adult/student 12/5Lt; 10am-7pm May-Sep, 10am-6pm Tue-Sun Oct, Mar & Apr, to 5pm Nov-Feb) charts the history of the castle.

Kempingas Slėnyje (☎ 53 380; www.camptrakai.lt; Slėnio gatvė 1; adult/car/tent 18/8/9Lt, summer houses for 3 people 90Lt, d/tr/q with shared bathroom 70/90/100Lt, cottage for 2-6 people 220-300Lt, d in guest house 140Lt) is a sublime complex 5km out of Trakai on the northern side of Lake Galvė, with tent sites by the lake, wooden cabins and a spectacular guest house.

Sample *kibinai* (meat-stuffed Karaite pastries similar to *empanadas*) at **Kibininė** (Karaimų gatvė 65; kibinai 3.80-5Lt) or **Kybynlar** (Karaimų gatvė 29; mains 15-30Lt).

Up to 10 trains daily (3.40Lt, 40 minutes) travel between Trakai and Vilnius.

CENTRAL LITHUANIA

KAUNAS

☎ 37 / pop 358,000

Lithuania's second city remains stubbornly provincial, but holds some appeal for those willing to scratch beneath its hard-edged surface. That appeal lies mainly in its attractive Old Town.

Information

Tourist office (☎ 323 436; www.kaunastic.lt; Laisvės alėja 36; 9am-7pm Mon-Fri, 10am-1pm & 2-6pm Sat, 10am-3pm Sun Jun-Aug, 9am-6pm Mon-Fri, 10am-3pm Sat May & Sep, 9am-6pm Mon-Fri Oct-Apr) Books accommodation, sells maps and guides, arranges bicycle rental (50Lt per day plus 5Lt for lock) and guided tours of the Old Town (35Lt, 4pm Thu mid-May–Sep).

Kavinė Internetas (www.cafenet.ot.lt; Vilniaus gatvė 24; per hr 5Lt; 9am-9pm) Internet.

Sights

Start any trip to Kaunas wandering through its lovely Old Town, where most streets lead to Rotušės aikštė (Central square), dominated by the 18th-century white, baroque former city hall, now the **Palace of Weddings**. On the northeastern corner of the square, **St Peter & Paul Cathedral** (Vilniaus gatvė 1) owes much to baroque reconstruction, but the early-15th-century Gothic shape of its windows remain. **Maironis' tomb** is outside the south wall of the cathedral.

Kaunas expanded east from the Old Town in the 19th century, giving birth to the modern New Town and its 1.7km-long pedestrian street, **Laisvės alėja**, which today is lined with bars, shops and restaurants. A handful of museums can be found close to the main street.

WORTH THE TRIP: GRŪTO PARKAS

Mildly controversial **Grūto Parkas** (☎ 313-55511; www.grutoparks.lt; adult/child 15/7Lt; 9am-8pm), 125km south of Vilnius near the spa town of Druskininkai, has been an enormous hit since it opened in 2001. The sprawling grounds, built to resemble a Siberian concentration camp, contain dozens of statues of Soviet heroes, exhibits on Soviet history and loudspeakers bellowing Soviet anthems. The statues once stood confidently in parks or squares across Lithuania.

There are up to 10 buses daily between Druskininkai and Vilnius, and hourly buses to/from Kaunas (both 25Lt, two hours). Ask to be let off at the park turn-off, then walk the final 1km to the park.

Sleeping

our pick Kauno Arkivyskupijos Svečių Namai (☎ 322 597; http://kaunas.lcn.lt/guesthouse; Rotušės aikštė 21; s/d/tr with shared bathroom 50/80/100Lt) This squeaky-clean jewel is enviably located in an old monastery wedged between two ancient churches. Rooms are Spartan but spacious; breakfast is not included.

Litinterp (☎ 228 718; www.litinterp.lt; Gedimino gatvė 28/7; s/d/tr from 120/160/210Lt; 8.30am-7pm Mon-Fri, 9am-3pm Sat; ☒) Not a lot of character, but rooms are cheap, clean and highly functional, and staff are superfriendly and knowledgable about the town.

Eating & Drinking

our pick Morkų Šelsmas (Laisvės alėja 78b; mains 10-12Lt; 8am-7pm Mon-Fri, 11am-7pm Sat, 11am-5pm

Sun) 'Carrot Party' specialises in imaginative vegetarian mains, tasty salads, home-baked muffins and carrot-based smoothies – all using local organic produce when available. Tucked away in a private courtyard.

Žalias Ratas (Laisvės alėja 36b; mains 7-30Lt) Hidden behind the tourist office is this pseudo-rustic inn where staff don traditional garb and bring piping-hot Lithuanian fare to eager customers.

BO (Muitinės gatvė 9) This laid-back bar attracts a student/alternative set and gets crammed to overflowing on weekends. Its own brew is a rather potent tasty offering.

Getting There & Away

There are direct buses between Kaunas and Vilnius (20Lt, 1¾ hours, up to three per hour), Klaipėda (44Lt, 2¾ hours, over 20 daily), Šiauliai (30Lt, three hours, 23 daily), Rīga (42Lt, five hours, one daily) and Tallinn (106Lt, nine hours, one daily).

There are 17 trains daily to/from Vilnius (12Lt, 1¼ hours). The airport is 10km north of the Old Town. Take minibus 120 (1.50Lt) to Old Town.

ŠIAULIAI

☎ 41 / pop 128,400

Lithuania's fourth-largest city is home to the country's most awe-inspiring sight, the legendary **Hill of Crosses** (Kryžių kalnas). It is a two-hump hillock blanketed by thousands of crosses. The sound of the evening breeze tinkling through the crosses that appear to grow on the hillock is indescribable and unmissable.

Some of the crosses are devotional, others are memorials (many for people deported to Siberia) and some are finely carved folk-art masterpieces. The crosses were bulldozed by the Soviets, but each night people crept past soldiers and barbed wire to plant yet more, risking their lives or freedom to express their national and spiritual fervour.

This strange place lies 12km north of Šiauliai – 10km north up highway A12, then 2km east from a well-marked turn-off (the sign says 'Kryžių kalnas 2'). You can rent a bike (5Lt per hour) from the **Tourist Information Centre** (☎ 523 110; www.tic.siauliai.lt; Vilniaus gatvė 213; ⏲ 9am-6pm Mon-Fri, 10am-4pm Sat, 10am-3pm Sun) and pedal out here, take a taxi (40Lt) or ride one of seven daily buses.

Šiauliai College Youth Hostel (☎ 523 764; www.jnn.siauliukolegija.lt; Tilžės gatvė 159; s/d/tr 50/70/90Lt; ⊠) takes care of all your lodging needs, with spick-and-span rooms at incredibly low prices.

To get here take a bus from Vilnius (41Lt, three to 4½ hours, six daily), Kaunas (30Lt, three hours, 23 daily), Klaipėda (30Lt, 3½ hours, five daily) or Rīga (28Lt, 2½ hours, four daily), or a train from Vilnius (29Lt, 2½ hours, three daily).

WESTERN LITHUANIA

KLAIPĖDA

☎ 46 / pop 186,000

Gritty Klaipėda is Lithuania's main port city and a gateway to the lush natural beauty of Curonian Spit. It boasts a fascinating history as the East Prussian city of Memel, and a few buildings from that era still stand. The city celebrates its nautical heritage each July with a flamboyant **Sea Festival**.

The **tourist office** (☎ 412 186; www.klaipedainfo.lt; Turgaus gatvė 7; ⏲ 9am-7pm Mon-Fri, 10am-4pm Sat & Sun Jun-Aug, 9am-6pm Mon-Fri, 10am-4pm Sat May & Sep, 9am-6pm Mon-Fri Oct-Apr) is exceptionally efficient, selling maps, arranging accommodation, renting bicycles (10/40Lt per hr/day plus €100/300Lt deposit) and providing free internet access.

Klaipėda Travellers Hostel (☎ 211 879; www.lithuanianhostels.org; Butkų Juzės gatvė 7/4; dm/d 44/88Lt; 💻) is poorly located near the bus station; consider forking out a bit more for the centrally located **Litinterp Guesthouse** (☎ 410 644; www.litinterp.lt; Puodžių gatvė 17; s/d/tr with shared bathroom 80/140/180Lt, with private bathroom 100/160/210Lt; ⊠).

There are buses to Klaipėda from Vilnius (59Lt, four to 5½ hours, 15 daily), Kaunas (44Lt, 2¾ hours, over 20 daily) and Šiauliai (30Lt, 3½ hours, five daily).

To get to Smiltynė on Curonian Spit, board a ferry at the **passenger terminal** (www.keltas.lt; Žvejų gatvė 8) due west of Old Town. Ferries leave every half-hour in the high season and cost 2Lt return (10 minutes). Vehicles must use the **new ferry terminal** (Nemuno gatvė 8), 2.5km south of the passenger terminal (per car 32Lt, at least hourly).

CURONIAN SPIT

pop 3100

This magical pigtail of land dangling off the western rump of Lithuania hosts some of the worlds' most precious sand dunes and a menagerie of elk, deer and avian wildlife. The fragile spit, which Unesco recognised as a World Heritage Site in 2000, is divided roughly evenly between Lithuania and Russia's Kaliningrad region in the south.

Lithuania's share of the spit is protected as the **Curonian Spit National Park** (www.nerija.lt), which has two **visitors centres** (Nida ☎ 469-51256; nidainfo@nerija.lt; Naglių gatvė 8; ⏰ 9am-noon & 1-5pm Mon-Thu, till 6pm Fri & Sat, till 4pm Sun May-Sep; Smiltynė ☎ 46-402 257; info@nerija.lt; Smiltynės plentas 11; ⏰ 9am-noon & 1-6pm Mon-Fri, 9am-6pm Sat, 9am-4pm Sun Jun-Aug, 8am-noon & 1-5pm Mon-Fri Sep-May), with abundant information on walking, cycling, boating and other activities.

Smiltynė, where the ferries from Klaipėda dock, is administratively part of Klaipėda and is jammed on summer weekends with city slickers flocking to its beaches. You're better off heading south to laid-back **Juodkrantė** or busier **Nida**, where there are fine guest houses and beaches. Both have **tourist information centres** (www.visitneringa.lt), which can help with accommodation and activities.

An excellent way to see the spit is on a bicycle. A flat cycling trail runs all the way from Nida to Smiltynė, and you stand a good chance of seeing elk, boar or other wildlife at any point along that path. Keep an eye out for one of Neringa's can't-miss attractions, a massive colony of grey herons and cormorants, about 1km south of Juodkrantė, where there's a breathtaking panorama of thousands of nests amid pine trees.

There are bicycles for hire in all towns; some allow you to leave your bike in Smiltynė and bus back to Nida.

Litinterp Guesthouse (p749) in Klaipėda can help arrange accommodation, as can the tourist offices. Private rooms are the cheapest option, going for around 80Lt per room.

Getting There & Away

To get to the spit you need to take a ferry from Klaipėda to Smiltynė (see p749). Buses and microbuses run throughout the day between Smiltynė and Nida (9Lt, one hour).

LITHUANIA DIRECTORY

ACCOMMODATION

Vilnius has a few hostels, but none are state of the art. Outside of Vilnius most hostels are grim Soviet affairs, but in rural areas you can find perfectly fine hotel rooms at hostel prices. Most camping grounds are cheap and basic (5Lt to 20Lt per camp site), but they are gradually improving.

Vilnius has a serious room crunch so book ahead in the high season. The city's tourist information offices can help in a pinch, but they tend to utilise unexceptional midrange hotels. Rooms at coastal locations such as Curonian Spit fill up months ahead in the summer.

In Your Pocket (www.inyourpocket.com) has comprehensive hotel listings for Vilnius, Kaunas, Šiauliai, Klaipėda and Curonian Spit.

ACTIVITIES

Lithuania is conducive to any activity revolving around its many forests: hiking, mushrooming, berrying, picnicking and birdwatching are at the top of the list. Lakes are also abundant, especially in the wilderness of Aukštaitija National Park (not covered in this book – see www.anp.lt for details).

Cycling is becoming more popular in flat Lithuania. Most towns and cities have several outlets that rent out bikes. A great place for an all-day ride is Curonian Spit (p749).

BUSINESS HOURS

Most shops open at 9am or 10am and close around 7pm on weekdays and Saturday. Banks are generally open between 9am and 5pm on weekdays. Restaurants tend to open around noon and close around 11pm, but many stay open much later on weekends.

EMBASSIES & CONSULATES

Australia (Map pp744-5; ☎ 5-212 3369, emergency 8-687 11117; australia@consulate.lt; Vilniaus gatvė 23)
Belarus (Map pp744-5; ☎ 5-213 2255; www.belarus.lt; Muitinės gatvė 41)
Canada (Map pp744-5; ☎ 5-249 0950; www.canada.lt; Jogailos gatvė 4)
Estonia (Map pp744-5; ☎ 5-278 0200; www.estemb.lt; A Mickevičiaus gatvė 4a)
France (Map pp744-5; ☎ 5-212 2979; www.amba france-lt.org; Švarco gatvė 1)
Germany (Map pp744-5; ☎ 5-210 6400; www.deutsche botschaft-wilna.lt; Sierakausko gatvė 24/8)
Latvia (Map pp744-5; ☎ 5-213 1260; www.latvia.lt; Čiurlionio gatvė 76)
Poland (Map pp742-3; ☎ 5-270 9001; www.wilno .polemb.net; Smėlio gatvė 20a)
Russia (Map pp742-3; ☎ 5-272 1763; www.rusemb.lt; Latvių gatvė 53/54)
UK (Map pp742-3; ☎ 5-246 2900; www.britain.lt; Antakalnio gatvė 2)

USA (Map pp744-5; ☎ 5-266 5500; www.usembassy.lt; Akmenų gatvė 6)

FESTIVALS & EVENTS

There's no better time to observe Lithuanian culture than during its stupendous Unesco-honoured **national song festival**, held every four years in July in Vilnius. The next one is scheduled for 2011.

The pan-Baltic **Baltika Folklore Festival** takes place all over Lithuania every three years. Lithuania is due to host the festival in 2011.

Vilnius' two main festivals are the **Vilnius Festival**, a summer festival of classical music in June; and **Capital Days** (September), a five-day celebration of carnivals, street theatre, dancing, masked parades and craft fairs.

HOLIDAYS

New Year's Day 1 January
Independence Day 16 February; anniversary of 1918 independence declaration
Lithuanian Independence Restoration Day 11 March
Easter Sunday
Easter Monday
International Labour Day 1 May
Feast of St John (Midsummer) 24 June
Statehood Day 6 July; commemoration of coronation of Grand Duke Mindaugas, 13th century
Assumption of Blessed Virgin 15 August
All Saints' Day 1 November
Christmas 25-26 December

INTERNET RESOURCES

Recommended sites pertaining to Lithuania include:

Bus Tickets (www.autobusubilietai.lt) Comprehensive national and international bus information.
Lithuania Travel Information (www.travel.lt) Precisely what its name says; set up by the Lithuanian Tourism Fund.
Litrail (www.litrail.lt) Train timetable and information by Lithuanian Railways.

MONEY

The Lithuanian litas (the plural is litai; Lt) will remain firmly in place until at least 2010, when Lithuania could possibly trade in its litai for the euro. All but the smallest Lithuanian towns usually have at least one bank with a functional ATM. Most big banks cash travellers cheques and exchange most major currencies. Credit cards are widely accepted.

Waiters and bartenders definitely appreciate a 10% tip.

POST

Sending a postcard/letter abroad costs 2.45/2.95Lt.

TELEPHONE

To call other cities within Lithuania, dial ☎ 8 followed by the city code and phone number. To make an international call dial ☎ 00 before the country code.

To call a mobile phone within Lithuania, dial ☎ 8 followed by the eight-digit number.

Payphones – increasingly rare given the widespread use of mobiles – only accept phonecards, sold in denominations of 9/13/16/30Lt at news stands.

VISAS

Citizens from the EU, Australia, Canada, Japan, New Zealand and the USA do not need visas for entry if staying for less than 90 days. For information on other countries and obtaining a visa, visit www.migracija.lt.

Luxembourg

HIGHLIGHTS

- **Luxembourg City** Sample seasonal fruit tarts at Brasserie l'Annexe then stroll the capital's famous Chemin de la Corniche (p754)
- **Echternach** Relive fairy tales while hiking the Müllerthal's enchanting forests from Echternach (p759)
- **Off the beaten track** Let your imagination reign from the lofty heights of Château de Bourscheid (p759)

FAST FACTS

- **Area** 2586 sq km (slightly smaller than Rhode Island, USA)
- **Budget** €55 to €60 per day
- **Capital** Luxembourg City
- **Country code** ☎ 352
- **Famous for** banking
- **Languages** French, German, Lëtzebuergesch
- **Money** Euro (€); A$1 = €0.55; C$1 = 0.60; ¥100 = €0.78; NZ$1 = €0.43; UK£1 = €1.12; US$1 = €0.74
- **Phrases** *Moien/bonjour* (Lëtzebuergesch/French) hello, *äddi/au revoir* (goodbye)
- **Population** 466,000

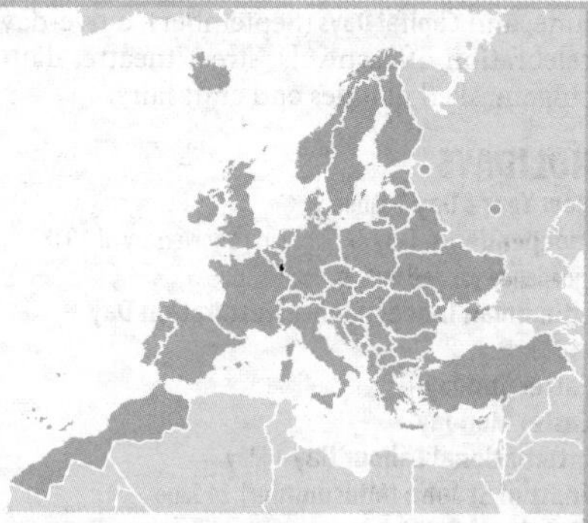

- **Visas** none required for most travellers to visit for up to three months (see p760)

TRAVEL HINTS

Stock up on alcohol, tobacco, perfume and petrol in Luxembourg – they're cheaper here than in neighbouring countries.

ROAMING LUXEMBOURG

Browse Luxembourg City's ancient core then move on to Echternach, Vianden, Diekirch or Remich – none is more than an hour away.

The Grand Duchy of Luxembourg (Luxemburg, Lëtzebuerg) is fairy-tale stuff. Go back in time to a land of counts and dynasties, wars and victories, fortresses and promontories – only the fire-breathing dragon is missing. Let your imagination reign from the top of mist-shrouded castles as you wander the pathways of enchanting forests, or while exploring old wine-making villages. If magic can happen anywhere in 21st-century Europe, it may well be here.

Just 57km wide and 82km long, the Grand Duchy is Europe's third-smallest country. Not that size is an issue. With one of Europe's healthiest economies and a generally high standard of living, Luxembourgers are proud to live in a seriously diminutive land – and a beautiful one to boot.

But a word of warning: keep imagination and stories at bay until you're firmly here. Drift off to sleep while en route and chances are you'll miss this tiny country altogether (and then it really will take on fairy-tale status).

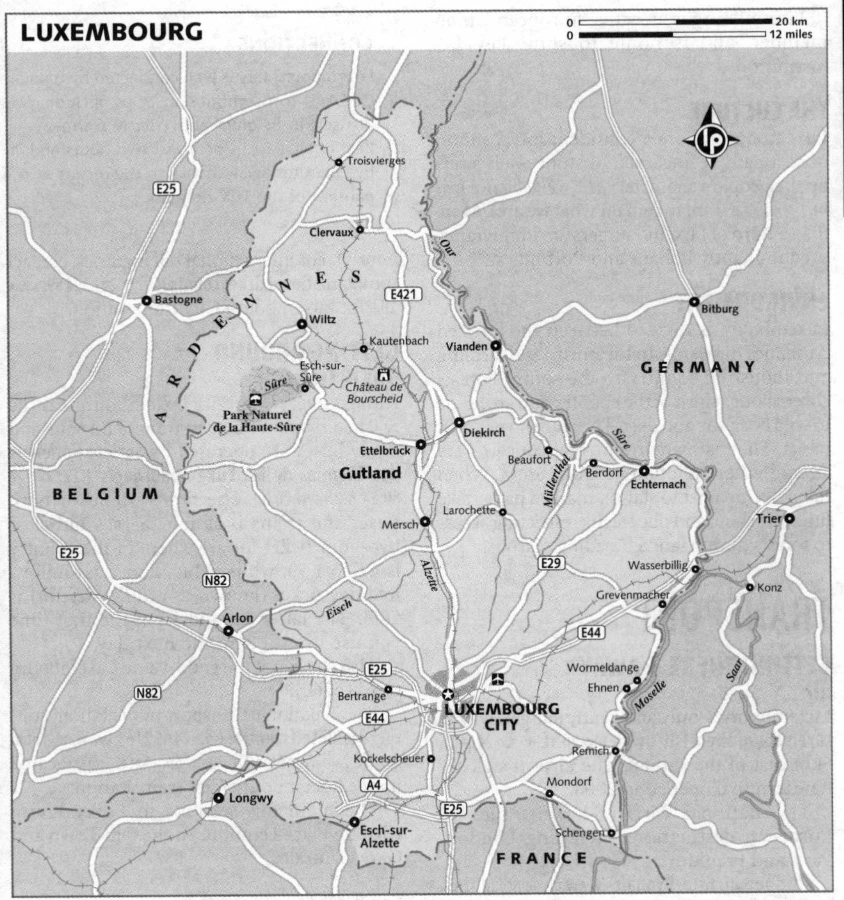

HISTORY

Once upon a time, more than 1000 years ago (in 963 to be exact), a count called Sigefroi (or Siegfried, Count of Ardennes) built a castle high on a promontory, laying the foundations for both the present-day capital and a dynasty that spawned rulers throughout Europe.

By the end of the Middle Ages the fortified city was much sought after. Besieged, devastated and rebuilt more than 20 times in 400 years, it became the strongest fortress in Europe after Gibraltar, hence its nickname 'Gibraltar of the north'.

The Duchy's current borders were set in 1839. Its delicate position between France and Germany led to the major European powers declaring the Duchy neutral in 1867. As a result, much of its historic fortifications were dismantled, though the damp galleries known as the Bock Casemates (p755) can still be visited.

When Germany invaded in 1914, Luxembourg's neutrality was quashed. It was occupied for the whole of WWI and again in WWII; for insight into the 1944 Battle of the Ardennes, visit the Musée National d'Histoire Militaire in Diekirch (p759).

Luxembourg rode out the depression in the iron and steel industries in the 1970s to become a noted financial centre and tax haven. But Luxembourg's strict laws on banking secrecy mean the system can be exploited for tax evasion and fraud. In 2008 the European Commission began revising legislation that could put an end to such secrecy.

Luxembourg is an active European Union member, and is home to some key EU institutions.

THE CULTURE

Luxembourgers are a confident lot. A motto occasionally seen carved in stone walls sums up the people's character: *Mir wëlle bleiwe wat mir sin* (We want to remain what we are). More than a third of Luxembourgers are immigrants, predominantly Italians and Portuguese.

ENVIRONMENT

Luxembourg is divided between the forested Ardennes highlands to the north, and farming and industrial country to the south. Forests cover about a third of the country and are home to wild boar, fox and deer. There are no national parks. The main environmental concerns are air and water pollution in urban areas. When hiking, remember to stay on marked paths, take litter with you, and obey signs restricting access to forests during fauna breeding seasons.

TRANSPORT

GETTING THERE & AWAY

Air

Luxembourg's only international gateway is **Luxembourg airport** (LUX; www.luxairport.lu; ☎ 24 64 1), 6km east of the capital. The airport's glossy new terminal opened in 2008.

The national carrier, Luxair, flies to European destinations including London, Paris and Frankfurt.

Budget airline **Ryanair** (www.ryanair.com) flies to Frankfurt/Hahn in Germany from where there's a bus connection to Luxembourg (one-way €17, 1¾ hours, 10 daily); check www.easybycoach.com.

For a list of major airlines, see the Transport chapter (p1235).

Car & Motorcycle

The main routes into Luxembourg are the E25 from Brussels, the A4 from Paris, the E25 from Metz in France and the E44 from Trier in Germany.

Train

International train services include: Brussels (€29 one way, 2¾ hours, hourly), Amsterdam (€50, 5½ hours, hourly), Paris (€65, two hours, four daily) and Trier (€8.40, 40 minutes, hourly). For international rail inquiries, contact the **international ticket counters** (☎ 24 89 24 89; www.cfl.lu) at Luxembourg City train station.

> **CONNECTIONS**
>
> Luxembourg City is well connected by train (see left) to neighbouring cities, including Brussels in Belgium and Trier in Germany. Best of all, Paris is now just two hours and five minutes away thanks to the recent expansion of the TGV network.

GETTING AROUND

Bus & Train

Almost everywhere in Luxembourg can be reached by either bus or train. All trains and many buses are operated by **Société Nationale des Chemins de Fer Luxembourgeois** (CFL; ☎ 24 89 24 89; www.cfl.lu). The fare system for both buses and trains is simple: a 1st-/2nd-class two-hour ticket for anywhere in the country is €2.30/1.50, while a 1st-/2nd-class unlimited day ticket (known as a *Billet Réseau*) is €6/4. The latter is valid from the first time you use it until 8am the next day.

Also check out the good-value Luxembourg Card (p760).

For all national transport information, contact **Mobiliteitszentral** (☎ 24 65 24 65; www.mobiliteit.lu; ⏲ 7am-7pm Mon-Fri, 10am-6pm Sat & Sun), located inside Luxembourg City train station.

The main bus stations in Luxembourg City are Place Hamilius in the Old Town and Gare Centrale.

Car & Motorcycle

Road rules are easy to understand and standard international signs are in use. The blood-alcohol limit for drivers is 0.05% and the speed limit on motorways is 130km. Fuel prices are among the cheapest in Western Europe: unleaded costs €1.32 per litre and diesel is €1.29.

LUXEMBOURG CITY

pop 136,000

Luxembourg City is a story-book beauty. This 1000-year-old city radiates a composed air of new and old: the former evident by state-of-the-art museums and a gleaming new art gallery; the latter by its striking position high on a promontory overlooking the Pétrusse and Alzette Rivers. Explore deep river gorges, admire skylines pierced by towers and turrets, and enjoy a relaxed pace of life in this most elegant of European capitals.

ORIENTATION

Luxembourg City is divided into four sections: the pedestrianised Old Town with its main squares, Place d'Armes and Place Guillaume II; the river valley neighbourhoods of Grund, Clausen and Pfaffenthal; the ever-evolving business district of Kirchberg northeast of the Old Town; and the train station quarter, an area of no appeal, south of the Old Town. Easy access to the Grund is provided by an elevator on Plateau du St Esprit.

INFORMATION

Clinique Ste Thérèse (☎ 49 77 61; 36 Rue Sainte Zithe) Central hospital providing emergency services.

Cyber Beach Place Guillaume II (☎ 20 40 17 50; 19 Place Guillaume II; per hr €3.60; 10am-6pm Mon-Fri) Rue de Bonnevoie (☎ 26 64 95 97; 8 Rue de Bonnevoie; per hr €3; 10am-10pm Mon-Fri, 2-8pm Sat, 3-8pm Sun) Both locations offer relaxed web surfing.

Luxembourg City Tourist Office (☎ 22 28 09; www.lcto.lu; Place Guillaume II; 9am-7pm Mon-Sat, 10am-6pm Sun Apr-Sep, 9am-6pm Mon-Sat, 10am-6pm Sun Oct-Mar)

Luxembourg National Tourist Office (☎ 42 82 82 20; www.visitluxembourg.lu; Place de la Gare; 8.30am-6.30pm Mon-Sat, 9.15am-12.30pm & 1.45-6pm Sun Jun-Sep, 9.15am-12.30pm & 1.45-6pm Oct-May)

SIGHTS

Start at the restaurant-lined **Place d'Armes**, Luxembourg's central pedestrianised square, from where it's an easy walk to the stately **Place Guillaume II**, lined with 19th-century buildings including the neoclassical **Hôtel de Ville** (City Hall).

The nearby **Musée National d'Histoire et d'Art** (☎ 47 93 30 1; www.mnha.lu; Marché-aux-Poissons; admission €5; 10am-5pm Tue-Sun), the country's principal museum, houses permanent collections of Roman and medieval relics, fortification models and art dating from the 13th century.

Next up is the **Bock Casemates** (☎ 22 28 09; Montée de Clausen; admission €1.75; 10am-5pm Mar-Oct), a honeycomb of rock galleries carved out under the Bock by the Spaniards in 1744.

Exit the casemates and wander the city's beautiful **Chemin de la Corniche**, a promenade that offers fabulous views over the Grund and leads up to Rue du St Esprit, home to the **Musée d'Histoire de la Ville de Luxembourg** (☎ 47 96 30 61; www.musee-hist.lu, in French; 14 Rue du St Esprit; adult/concession €5/3.70; 10am-6pm Tue-Sun, to 8pm Thu). Explore the city's history using a glass elevator that beautifully reveals the Old Town's rocky geology.

The Moorish-style **Palais Grand-Ducal** (Rue du Marché-aux-Herbes; admission €6; mid-Jul–early Sep, guided tours in English 4.30pm Mon-Fri & 1.30pm Sat) was built in the 1570s during Spanish rule. The royals, however, never resided here; it is used as the Grand Duke's office.

Over on Kirchberg, the **Musée d'Art Moderne Grand-Duc Jean** (Mudam; ☎ 45 37 85 1; www.mudam.lu; 3 Parc Dräi Eechelen; adult/concession €5/3; 11am-6pm Thu-Mon, 11am-8pm Wed), designed by Chinese-American architect Ieoh Ming Pei (responsible for the Louvre pyramid in Paris), opened in 2006. Take any bus marked 'Eurobus' from either Gare Centrale or the bus stop on Blvd Royal (just north of Place Hamilius) and get off at the Philharmonie.

Luxembourg's most-visited war cemetery is the **US Military Cemetery** (9am-5pm) at Hamm, 4km east of the capital. Here lie more than 5000 US war dead, including George S Patton Jr, the audacious general of the US Third Army who played a large part in Luxembourg's WWII liberation. Take bus 8 from opposite Gare Centrale

EMERGENCY NUMBERS

- Ambulance ☎ 112
- Police ☎ 113
- Roadside breakdown (Club Automobile de Luxembourg) ☎ 26 000

FOR FREE

- Stroll 'Europe's most beautiful balcony' – Luxembourg City's Chemin de la Corniche (right).
- Visit the capital's Musée d'Histoire de la Ville de Luxembourg (right) on Thursday evenings.
- Relive history at the US Military Cemetery (right) near Luxembourg City.
- Take in Gregorian chants at Clervaux (p758).

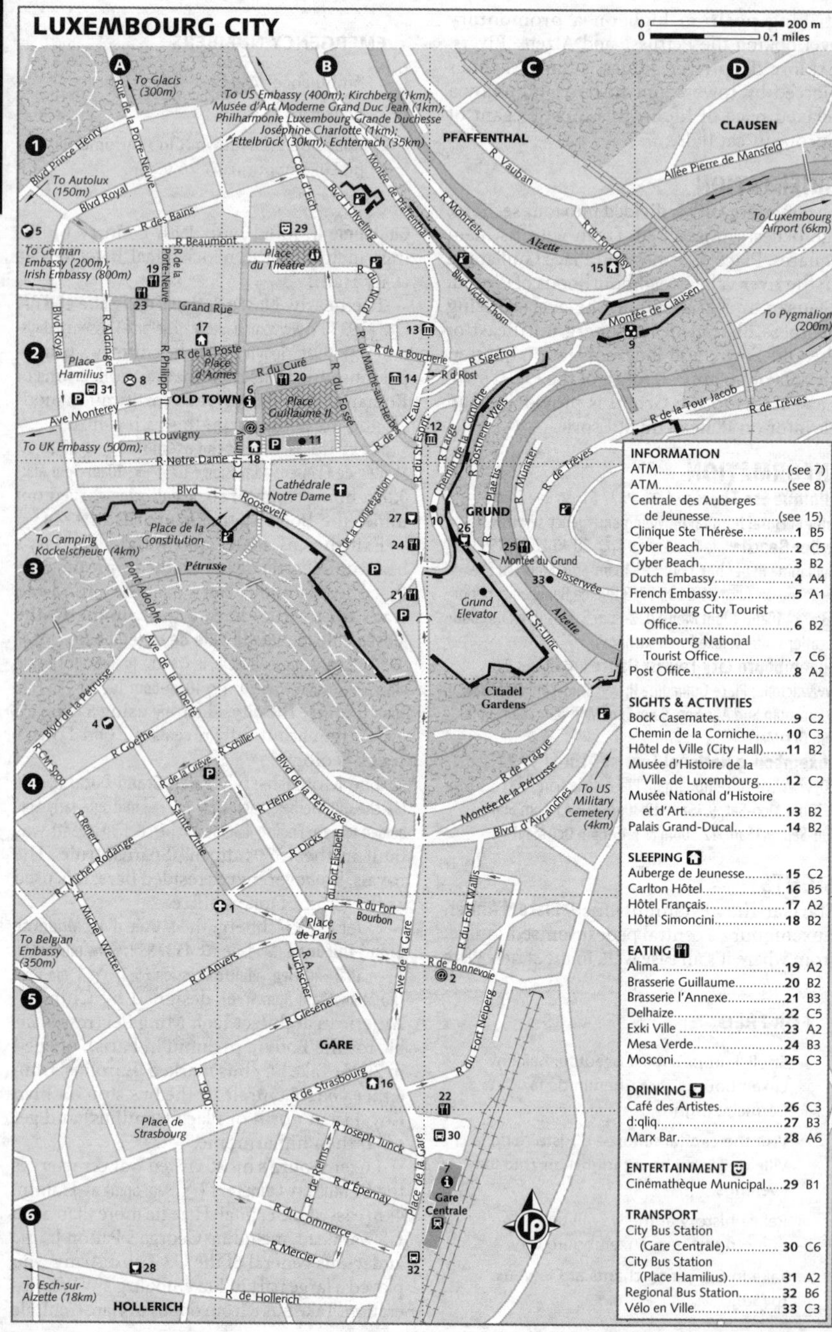
LUXEMBOURG CITY
0 200 m
0 0.1 miles
A
B
C
D
1
2
3
4
5
6
To Glacis (300m)
To US Embassy (400m); Kirchberg (1km); Musée d'Art Moderne Grand Duc Jean (1km); Philharmonie Luxembourg Grande Duchesse Joséphine Charlotte (1km); Ettelbrück (30km); Echternach (35km)
PFAFFENTHAL
CLAUSEN
Allée Pierre de Mansfeld
To Luxembourg Airport (6km)
To Autolux (150m)
To German Embassy (200m); Irish Embassy (800m)
To Pygmalion (200m)
Blvd Prince Henry
Blvd Royal
R des Bains
R Beaumont
Rue de la Porte-Neuve
R de la Porte-Neuve
Côte d'Eich
Bvd F D Ulveling
Montée de Pfaffenthal
R Vauban
R Mohrfels
Alzette
R du Fort Olisy
Blvd Victor Thorn
Place du Théâtre
R du Nord
Grand Rue
R Aldringen
R Philippe II
R de la Poste
Place d'Armes
Place Hamilius
R du Curé
R de la Boucherie
R Sigefroi
R d Rost
Montée de Clausen
OLD TOWN
Place Guillaume II
R du Fossé
R du Marché-aux-Herbes
R de l'Eau
Ave Monterey
R Louvigny
R Chimay
R Notre Dame
To UK Embassy (500m);
R de la Tour Jacob
R de Trèves
R du St Esprit
R Large
Chemin de la Corniche
R Sosthène Weis
Plaetis
R Münster
R de Trèves
Blvd Roosevelt
Cathédrale Notre Dame
Place de la Constitution
To Camping Kockelscheuer (4km)
Pétrusse
R de la Congrégation
GRUND
Montée du Grund
Bisserwée
Grund Elevator
R St-Ulric
Citadel Gardens
Pont Adolphe
Ave de la Liberté
Blvd de la Pétrusse
R CM Spoo
R Goethe
R de la Grève
R Schiller
R Sainte Zithe
R Heine
Blvd de la Pétrusse
R de Prague
Montée de la Pétrusse
To US Military Cemetery (4km)
Blvd d'Avranches
R Renert
R Michel Rodange
R Dicks
R du Fort Elisabeth
R du Fort Wallis
R Michel Welter
R du Fort Bourbon
Place de Paris
To Belgian Embassy (350m)
R d'Anvers
R A Duchscher
Ave de la Gare
R de Bonnevoie
R du Fort Neipperg
R Glesener
GARE
R 1900
R de Strasbourg
Place de Strasbourg
R Joseph Junck
R de Reims
R d'Épernay
R du Commerce
R Mercier
Place de la Gare
Gare Centrale
To Esch-sur-Alzette (18km)
HOLLERICH
R de Hollerich
INFORMATION
ATM (see 7)
ATM (see 8)
Centrale des Auberges de Jeunesse (see 15)
Clinique Ste Thérèse 1 B5
Cyber Beach 2 C5
Cyber Beach 3 B2
Dutch Embassy 4 A4
French Embassy 5 A1
Luxembourg City Tourist Office 6 B2
Luxembourg National Tourist Office 7 C6
Post Office 8 A2
SIGHTS & ACTIVITIES
Bock Casemates 9 C2
Chemin de la Corniche 10 C3
Hôtel de Ville (City Hall) 11 B2
Musée d'Histoire de la Ville de Luxembourg 12 C2
Musée National d'Histoire et d'Art 13 B2
Palais Grand-Ducal 14 B2
SLEEPING
Auberge de Jeunesse 15 C2
Carlton Hôtel 16 B5
Hôtel Français 17 A2
Hôtel Simoncini 18 B2
EATING
Alima 19 A2
Brasserie Guillaume 20 B2
Brasserie l'Annexe 21 B3
Delhaize 22 C5
Exki Ville 23 A2
Mesa Verde 24 B3
Mosconi 25 C3
DRINKING
Café des Artistes 26 C3
d:qliq 27 B3
Marx Bar 28 A6
ENTERTAINMENT
Cinémathèque Municipal 29 B1
TRANSPORT
City Bus Station (Gare Centrale) 30 C6
City Bus Station (Place Hamilius) 31 A2
Regional Bus Station 32 B6
Vélo en Ville 33 C3

(15 minutes, every 20 minutes Monday to Saturday, every 40 minutes Sunday).

SLEEPING

Camping Kockelscheuer (☎ 47 18 15; www.camp-kockelscheuer.lu; 22 Route de Bettembourg; adult/camp sites €3.75/4.50; Easter-Oct) Pleasantly situated between a forest and a sports centre, 4km southwest of the city. Take bus 5 from Gare Centrale or Place Hamilius.

Auberge de Jeunesse (☎ 22 68 89; luxembourg@youthhostels.lu; 2 Rue du Fort Olizy; dm/s €19.70/31.70;) The capital's only real budget option is fabulously located at the base of the Old Town. Modern no-fuss rooms, a terrace and a restaurant that does Luxembourg's cheapest (€9) four-course meal are the salient features. Bus 9 from the airport or Gare Centrale stops nearby. Alternatively it's a 40-minute walk from Gare Centrale.

Carlton Hôtel (☎ 29 96 60; www.carlton.lu; 9 Rue de Strasbourg; s/d Mon-Fri €95/120, Sat & Sun €65/85;) This atmospheric old gem, c 1920, has stained-glass windows in the foyer, modern rooms and incredibly welcoming staff. Inquire about discount rates in July and August.

Hôtel Français (☎ 47 45 34; www.hotelfrancais.lu; 14 Place d'Armes; s/d Mon-Fri €105/140, Sat & Sun €99/125;) This intimate hotel dotted with objets d'art has a prized location overlooking the Old Town's busy main square. The affable owner, Mr Simoncini, opened the new Hôtel Simoncini (☎ 22 28 44; www.hotelsimoncini.lu; 6 Rue Notre Dame) in late 2008.

EATING

The Old Town is the place to dine. In summer, the tree-lined squares and pedestrianised streets in this quarter turn into large open-air dining areas. Two supermarkets for self-caterers include **Alima** (Rue de la Porte-Neuve) and **Delhaize** (Place de la Gare).

Exki Ville (☎ 26 20 39 39; 72 Grand Rue; snacks & light meals €3-8; 7am-7pm;) Organic produce and wholesome snacks are the mainstay of this modern self-service cafe.

Brasserie l'Annexe (our pick; ☎ 26 26 25 07; 7 Rue du St Esprit; mains €12.50-15; lunch & dinner Mon-Fri;) This new brasserie has well and truly won the locals with beautifully presented food and a large terrace. No matter what, don't skip dessert – the seasonal fruit tarts are sublime.

Brasserie Guillaume (☎ 26 20 20 20; 12 Place Guillaume II; mains €13-25; 10am-1am;) Longstanding Old Town brasserie that's perfect for a late-night bite.

Mesa Verde (☎ 46 41 26; 11 Rue du St Esprit; mains veg €19.80, fish €23-26; lunch Wed-Fri Sep-Jul, dinner Tue-Sat year-round;) Imaginative vegetarian and seafood dishes are offered at this perennial favourite. It's often full, and deservedly so.

SPLURGE

Mosconi (☎ 54 69 94; 13 Rue Münster, Grund; mains €27-34; lunch & dinner Tue-Sat;) This was the first Italian restaurant in the Benelux (that's Belgium, the Netherlands and Luxembourg locally abbreviated) to be starred by Michelin – since 2006 it has had two twinkles. The location's fabulous – reservations essential.

DRINKING

The Old Town, Grund, Clausen and Hollerich are the most popular spots for a night out.

d:qliq (☎ 26 73 62; www.dqliq.lu; 17 Rue du St Esprit; 5pm-1am Tue-Sat, to 3am Fri) Intimate bar that's enlivened the Old Town's live-music scene. Spans three floors and offers hip and lesser-known bands from abroad.

Café des Artistes (☎ 46 13 27; 22 Montée du Grund; evenings Tue-Sun) This nostalgic Grund cafe has been around since 1968. Don't miss the piano soirée nights (Wednesday to Saturday).

Marx Bar (☎ 48 84 26; 42 Rue de Hollerich; from 5pm) A lively bar in the nightlife hub at Hollerich.

Pygmalion (☎ 42 08 60; 19 Rue de la Tour Jacob; 4pm-1am Sun-Thu, 4pm-3am Fri & Sat) This moody little Irish haunt is one of several pubs in Clausen, an area favoured by late-night revellers. Take bus 9 or night bus CN1 to get there.

ENTERTAINMENT

The weekly English-language magazine *352 Luxembourg News* has entertainment listings (including films in English). Also check out **Luxembourg Ticket** (☎ 47 08 95 1; www.luxembourgticket.lu, in French). The country's two biggest contemporary music venues – **Rockhal** (www.rockhal.lu) and **Kulturfabrik** (www.kulturfabrik.lu) are both in the town of Esch-sur-Alzette, a 20-minute train ride southwest of Luxembourg City.

GETTING INTO TOWN

From Luxembourg airport, bus 16 (€1.50, 20 minutes, every 15 minutes) stops at Place Hamilius close to Place d'Armes. Buses run from 5.30am to 9.30pm. Train travellers arriving at Gare Centrale can reach Place d'Armes by jumping on any bus departing from the platforms to the right as you exit the station, or by walking 1.25km (head up Ave de la Gare).

Philharmonie Luxembourg Grande-Duchesse Joséphine-Charlotte (☎ 26 32 26 32; www.philharmonie.lu; 1 Place de l'Europe) Luxembourg's new concert venue is a stunning oval job that brings life to the boring office blocks of Kirchberg.

Cinémathèque Municipal (☎ 47 96 26 44; 17 Place du Théâtre; adult/concession €4/2.80) The closest thing in Luxembourg to an art-house cinema, and cheap to boot.

SHOPPING

The pedestrianised streets around Place d'Armes offer chic boutiques and international chain stores – try Rue Philippe II and Grand Rue for starters.

On the second and fourth Saturday morning of each month, it's *brocante* (bric-a-brac) time on Place d'Armes.

GETTING AROUND

For bike rental there's **Vélo en Ville** (☎ 47 96 23 83; 8 Bisserwée; half/full day €12.50/20; 🕐 10am-noon & 1-8pm Apr-Oct).

AROUND LUXEMBOURG

Nowhere in Luxembourg is much more than an hour's drive from the capital, making day trips or nights away fabulously accessible.

VIANDEN

pop 1600

If Vianden's impeccably restored medieval castle doesn't bring back childhood tales of princes and princesses, baddies and beasts, nothing will. Hidden in verdant forests in the country's north, this immensely popular little town is accessed from Luxembourg City by train to Ettelbrück (30 minutes, half-hourly) and then bus 570 (30 minutes, hourly).

The **tourist office** (☎ 83 42 57 1; www.vianden.eu, in French; 1a Rue du Vieux Marché; 🕐 8am-6pm Mon-Fri, 10am-2pm Sat & Sun Apr-Aug, 9am-noon & 1-5pm Mon-Fri, 10am-2pm Sat Sep-Mar) is down by the Our River.

Looming over the town is the **château** (☎ 83 41 08 1; www.castle-vianden.lu; Grand Rue; adult/concession €5.50/4.50; 🕐 10am-6pm Apr-Sep, 10am-5pm Mar & Oct, 10am-4pm Nov-Feb). The oldest part dates from the 11th century.

Vianden's picturesque position can be photographed from the **télésiège** (chairlift; ☎ 83 43 23; 39 Rue du Sanatorium; admission €4.50; 🕐 10am-6pm Jun-Sep, closed Mon Easter-May & Oct).

The **Maison de Victor Hugo** (☎ 26 87 40 88; www.victor-hugo.lu, in French; 37 Rue de la Gare; admission €4; 🕐 11am-5pm Tue-Sun) was home to author Victor Hugo for three months during his 19-year exile from France.

Draped along the river bank to the south of town is **Camping de l'Our** (☎ 83 45 05; 3 Route de Bettel; adult/camp sites €4.50/5; 🕐 Easter-Oct).

The **Auberge de Jeunesse** (☎ 83 41 77; www.youthhostels.lu; 3 Montée du Château; dm/s €15.70/27.70; 🕐 early Jan-late Dec; 💻 ⊠) sits in the shadow of the chateau – a long 1km uphill walk from the bus station.

Hôtel/Restaurant Pétry (☎ 83 41 22; www.hotel-petry.com; 15 Rue de la Gare; s/d from €57/74; 🕐 mid-Feb–Dec; 💻 P ⊠) is a rambling riverside hotel with modern rooms offering either castle or river views, and good-value meals (mains €12-30).

CLERVAUX

pop 1800

Clervaux is best associated with a permanent photographic exhibition that draws visitors from far afield. Situated at Luxembourg's northern tip, the town is easily reached from the capital by train (one hour, departs hourly).

The **tourist office** (☎ 92 00 72; www.tourisme-clervaux.lu; 🕐 9.45-11.45am & 2-6pm Jul & Aug, 2-5pm Mon-Sat Easter-Jun, 9.45-11.45am & 1.30-5.30pm

A ROYAL AFFAIR

Luxembourgers love their royalty. In 1919, the Grand Ducal family was put up for referendum and after a resounding 'yes', their existence has never again been questioned. The current rulers, Grand Duke Henri and Grand Duchess Maria Teresa, came to the throne in 2000 and are as popular as their predecessors.

Mon-Sat Sep-Oct) is housed in a side turret of Clervaux's castle.

The **castle**, damaged in 1944, is visited mostly for Unesco's World Heritage–listed exhibition, **Family of Man** (☎ 92 96 57; admission €4.50; 10am-6pm Tue-Sun Mar-Dec), collated by Edward Steichen (1879–1973), a Luxembourg-born pioneer of American photography. Steichen compiled the 500 black-and-white photos in 1955 at the age of 76 and they travelled the world for years before coming to rest here.

Clervaux's turreted **Benedictine Abbey of St Maurice** pokes out of the forest high above the town and is accessible by a 1km track from behind the church above the castle. Time your visit to hear one of the beautiful **Gregorian masses** (10.30am daily, 6pm Mon-Fri, 5pm Sat & Sun).

Camping Clervaux (☎ 92 00 42; www.camping-clervaux.lu; 33 Klatzewee; adult/camp sites €5.30/5.50;) is along the river bank, 400m from the town centre.

Hôtel/Restaurant Koener (☎ 92 10 02; www.koener clervaux.lu; 14 Grand Rue; r Sun-Thu from €35, Fri & Sat from €40;) is a big, lemon-coloured hotel on the pedestrianised main street. The restaurant (mains €12-22) even has vegetarian offerings.

CHÂTEAU DE BOURSCHEID

Roughly halfway between Wiltz and Ettelbrück, a road winds up to the magnificent **Château de Bourscheid** (☎ 99 05 70; 1 Schlasswee; adult/concession €3.50/3; 9am-6pm Apr-Sep, 10am-5pm Oct, 10am-5pm Sat & Sun Nov-Mar). This 1000-year-old castle is one of the Grand Duchy's most beautiful and affords the best views. However, you'll need wheels to get here.

ECHTERNACH

pop 5100

Explore the Müllerthal region's evocative forests from the ancient town of Echternach. The **tourist office** (☎ 72 02 30; www.echternach-tourist.lu; Parvis de la Basilique; 9.30am-5.30pm Jul & Aug, 9.30am-5.30pm Mon-Fri Sep-Easter) is in a courtyard next to the town's huge basilica. The **basilica** (9.30am-6.30pm), the country's most important religious building, is the final resting place of St Willibrord, an Anglo-Saxon monk who founded Echternach's abbey in the 7th century.

Marked **hiking trails** begin at Rue Charly, a block south of the town's bus station. **E1** (11.7km, four hours), a circular path from Echternach to Berdorf and back, winds up via the **Gorge du Loup**, a sheer-sided canyon flanked by dramatic sandstone formations.

Rock climbers can head to the Auberge de Jeunesse for its **climbing wall** (free-climbing €3.50, 2hr lesson €10; 3-5pm Tue-Sun); **mountain bikes** (half/full day €8/15) can also be hired.

Camping Officiel (☎ 72 02 72; 5 Route de Diekirch; www.camping-echternach.lu; adult/camp sites €5/6; Easter-Oct;) is draped along the hillside 200m from the bus station.

The town's modern **Auberge de Jeunesse** (☎ 72 01 58; www.youthhostels.lu; Chemin vers Rodenhof; dm/s €17.70/29.70, 3-course meals €9;) is 2km from the bus station next to a lake. From Luxembourg City take bus 110 to the Nonnemillen/Lac stop (next to the Q8 petrol station), from where it's a 1km walk (in the direction of Rodenhof).

Hostellerie de la Basilique (☎ 72 94 83; www.hotel-basilique.lu; 7 Place du Marché; s/d/tr €91/110/150; Easter–mid-Nov;) is the best hotel/restaurant address (mains €11-25) in town.

Two bus services connect Luxembourg City with Echternach – bus 110 (45 minutes, every 45 minutes) and bus 111 (via Berdorf, 55 minutes, hourly).

DIEKIRCH

pop 6000

This pleasant town on the banks of the gushing Sûre River mainly attracts visitors interested in Luxembourg's wartime history. An excellent collection of memorabilia detailing the WWII Battle of the Bulge and the liberation of Luxembourg by US troops is housed at the **Musée National d'Histoire Militaire** (☎ 80 89

DETOUR: REMICH

Tickle your taste buds with fruity white wine or bottles of bubbly made in Luxembourg's **Moselle Valley**, one of Europe's smallest wine regions. Drop in at a dozen towns and hamlets draped along the **Route du Vin** (Wine Rd) southeast of the capital; the nicest is **Remich**.

Several *caves* (cellars) give tours. The best is at **St Martin** (☎ 23 69 97 74; 53 Route de Stadtbredimus, Remich; admission €3; 10am-noon & 1.30-5.30pm Apr-Oct), about 1.5km north of Remich. Bus 450 (four daily) from Remich to Grevenmacher stops in front of the winery.

From Luxembourg City, bus 175 runs to Remich (45 minutes, half-hourly).

08; 10 Rue Bamertal; admission €5; 10am-6pm Apr-Nov, 2-6pm Dec-Mar), a 10-minute walk north from Diekirch's train station. There are regular trains from Luxembourg City to Diekirch (40 minutes, half-hourly).

LUXEMBOURG DIRECTORY

ACCOMMODATION

Camping grounds are abundant, mainly in the central and northern regions.

Ten hostels are operated by **Centrale des Auberges de Jeunesse** (☎ 26 27 66 40; www.youthhostels.lu; 2 Rue du Fort Olisy, L-2261 Luxembourg), which is affiliated with Hostelling International (HI). Most hostels close irregularly throughout the year, so ring ahead.

B&Bs and cheap hotels are very light on the ground – most hotels are in the midrange and top-end brackets.

ACTIVITIES

With a 5000km network of marked walking paths, the Grand Duchy is hiking heaven. Tracks marked by white triangles connect the HI hostels. Local tourist offices stock regional walking maps. The Müllerthal region offers fascinating hiking tracks (see p759).

Cycling is a popular pastime but rental outfits are few – see Vélo en Ville (p758) or Echternach (p759). Bikes can be taken on trains for free.

BUSINESS HOURS

Standard opening hours:

Banks (8.30am-4.30pm Mon-Fri, Sat morning in Luxembourg City)
Clubs (10pm-3am)
Post offices (9am-5pm Mon-Fri, 9am-noon Sat)
Pubs & Bars (11am-1am)
Restaurants (noon-2 or 3pm & 7-11pm)
Shops (9am-6pm Mon-Sat) Some shops close for two hours at lunch.
Tourist information offices Hours vary – see the individual city/town sections.

DISCOUNT CARDS

The **Luxembourg Card** (1/2/3 days adult €10/17/24, family of 2 adults & 3 children €20/34/48, valid Easter-end Oct) gives free admission to many attractions plus unlimited use of public transport, and is available from tourist offices.

EMBASSIES & CONSULATES

The nearest Australian, Canadian and New Zealand embassies are in Belgium (p132). The following embassies are in Luxembourg City:

Belgium (☎ 44 27 46 1; 4 Rue des Girondins, L-1626)
France (☎ 45 72 71 1; 8 Blvd Joseph II, L-1840)
Germany (☎ 45 34 45 1; 20-22 Ave Émile Reuter, L-2420)
Ireland (☎ 45 06 10; 28 Route d'Arlon, L-1140)
Netherlands (☎ 22 75 70; 6 Rue Sainte Zithe, L-2763)
UK (☎ 22 98 64; 14 Blvd Joseph II, L-1840)
USA (☎ 46 01 23; 22 Blvd Emmanuel Servais, L-2535)

FESTIVALS & EVENTS

The **Luxembourg National Tourist Office** (www.ont.lu) lists festivals on its website. The country's biggest event is **Luxembourg National Day** (June 23) – make sure you're in the capital the day before to catch fireworks and the all-night party.

HOLIDAYS

New Year's Day 1 January
Easter Monday March/April
May Day 1 May
Ascension Day Fortieth day after Easter
Whit Monday Seventh Monday after Easter
National Day 23 June
Assumption 15 August
All Saints' Day 1 November
Christmas Day 25 December
School Holidays mid-July to mid-September; first week in November; two weeks around Christmas; one week at Carnival; two weeks at Easter; one week at Ascension

MONEY

Luxembourg uses euros. Banks are the best bet for exchange – you'll have no trouble finding one in Luxembourg. ATMs are also common. Tipping is not obligatory as service and VAT are included in hotel and restaurant prices.

POST

Letters (under 20g) cost €0.70 to EU countries and €0.90 to non-EU countries.

TELEPHONE

Luxembourg's country code is ☎ 352. To telephone abroad, the international access code is ☎ 00. To get an international operator, call ☎ 12410. Numbers prefixed with ☎ 0800 are toll-free numbers. Reverse charge (collect) calls can be made by dialling ☎ 80 02 00 first.

VISAS

Visa requirements are the same as for Belgium (see p133).

Macedonia Македонија

HIGHLIGHTS

- **Skopje** Macedonia's burgeoning capital has history, good eats and buzzing bars, and is a base for regional travel (p764)
- **Ohrid** Macedonia's spiritual heart, Ohrid overlooks a magnificent lake, with sublime churches, summer beaches and nightlife (p767)
- **Bitola** Set below the lush hills of Pelister National Park, stylish Bitola has old-world charm in its neoclassical architecture and laid-back cafe life (p770)

FAST FACTS

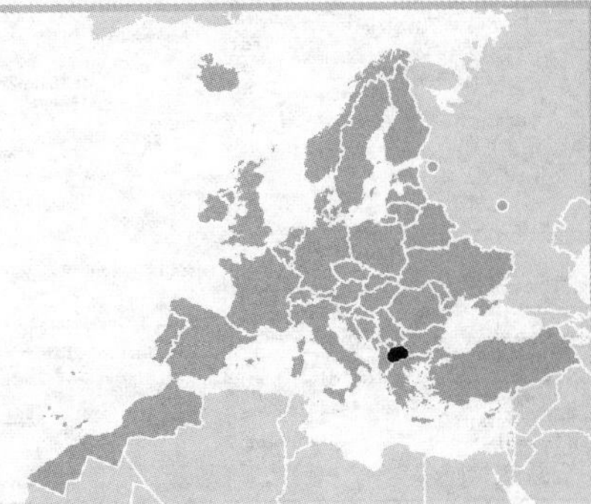

- **Area** 25,713 sq km
- **Budget** 1530MKD per day
- **Capital** Skopje
- **Country code** ☎ 389
- **Famous for** Lake Ohrid, Byzantine monasteries, name dispute with Greece
- **Language** Macedonian
- **Money** Macedonian denar (MKD); A$1 = 33.3MKD; C$1 = 37.8MKD; €1 = 60MKD; ¥100 = 47MKD; NZ$1 = 26MKD; UK£1 = 67.5MKD; US$1= 44.6MKD
- **Phrases** *zdravo* (hello), *blagodaram/fala* (thanks), *molam* (please), *prijatno* (goodbye)
- **Population** 2 million
- **Visas** unnecessary for many visitors; see p772

TRAVEL HINTS

Many street signs are in Cyrillic. People often give directions according to landmarks – maybe because many street addresses are listed as bb, meaning *bez broj* (without number).

ROAMING MACEDONIA

Enjoy Skopje's old-town attractions and cafe life for a day, then experience Ohrid's culture, churches and lake for two days.

Still largely unexplored, Macedonia retains an air of mystery, an ethos accentuated by its vast stretches of pristine mountain wilderness and a unique cultural legacy that combines ancient ruins, Byzantine churches, Ottoman mosques and concrete Yugoslav mementos.

Fun-loving Macedonia also offers genuine homegrown hospitality and roaring traditional festivals. Here food and drink are not only cheap by Western standards, but also delicious – many swear by Macedonia's tomatoes, sweet red peppers and robust wines.

One benefit of Macedonia's small size is that the most important places are well-connected and can be tackled quickly. The capital, Skopje, is a modernising metropolis with intriguing historical attractions, good restaurants and happening nightlife, while the most-visited destination, Ohrid, is marked by a medieval castle, atmospheric old town and its immense lake. Both Ohrid and Bitola (Macedonia's stylish second city) are flanked by mountains, so it's also perfect for off-the-beaten-track outdoor activities. For the adventurous traveller, Macedonia is hard to beat.

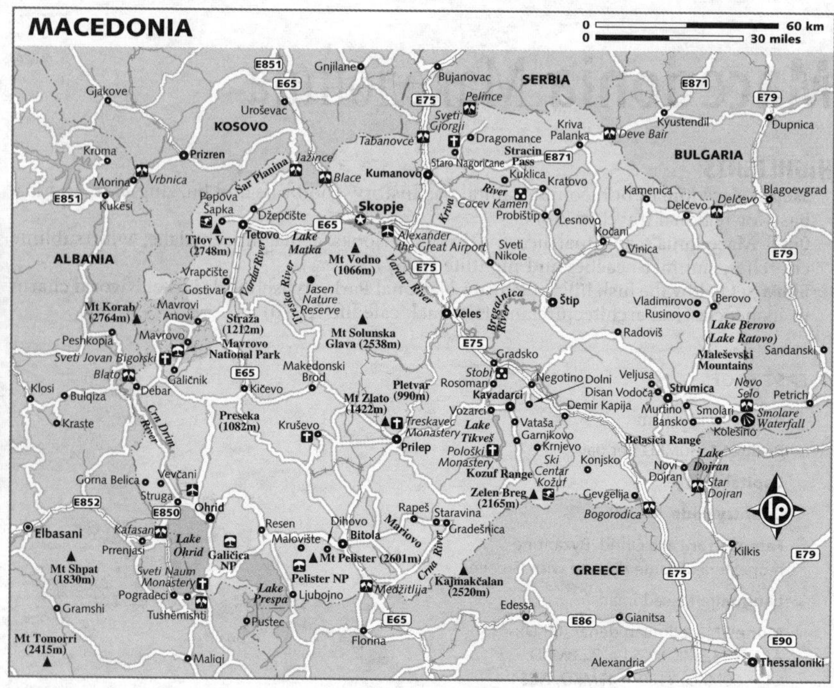

HISTORY

The historical and geographical Macedonia is divided between the Republic of Macedonia, Greece and Bulgaria. The ancient Macedonian empire developed by Phillip II and his son, Alexander the Great, spread Macedonian power to India in the 4th century BC. Their glorious legacy has been claimed by both modern-day Macedonians and Greeks, unsurprisingly fuelling enmity and nationalist rhetoric.

In 168 BC, Romans conquered Macedonia; when Rome split in 395AD, Macedonia was assigned to the Eastern (Byzantine) half. In the 7th century Slavic tribes arrived, and thereafter Macedonia passed between Byzantine, Bulgarian and Serbian rule, before Ottoman Turks conquered in 1389.

In 1913, after the two Balkan Wars, geographical Macedonia was divided between Greece, Bulgaria and Serbia. After WWI, the Serbs incorporated their share (essentially the present-day Macedonian state) into Royalist Yugoslavia. Assimilation programs were levied against the Macedonian populations in the three newly-enlarged states. During WWII, Macedonians largely joined Josip Broz Tito's communist partisans rather than the (then-occupying) Bulgarians.

Tito honoured his wartime promises by granting Macedonia full republic status within the new federal Yugoslavia. However, he also nationalised property and imposed communism, altering Macedonia's traditionally rural society. So, while Yugoslavia became relatively prosperous, Macedonia remained its poorest republic.

When Yugoslavia's republics disintegrated violently in the early 1990s, Macedonia alone separated peacefully, in 1992. However, Greece insisted that the new country had no right to the name 'Macedonia', claiming that it implied territorial claims against Greece, which has a province with the same name. Greek pressure meant that when Macedonia gained UN admission in 1993, it was under the 'provisional' title of Former Yugoslav Republic of Macedonia (FYROM). As in other 1990s-era 'transition' countries, an oligarchical system arose in Macedonia amid shady privatisations and deliberate bankrupting of state-owned firms.

Simultaneously, Macedonia's Albanian minority was voicing its displeasure at alleged ill-treatment. During NATO's 1999 Kosovo intervention to defend ethnic Albanians there, Macedonia sheltered over 400,000 Kosovar refugees. Nevertheless, Albanian separatists waged war in Macedonian areas bordering Kosovo in early 2001. Hostilities subsided with the internationally brokered Ohrid Framework Agreement in August 2001, granting minorities more rights and political participation.

Since then, ethnic tensions have dissipated. In December 2005, Macedonia won EU membership candidacy, though NATO membership was quashed in April 2008, when Greece vetoed the invitation. However, while Greece remained determined that Macedonia rename itself before joining NATO and the EU, Macedonians too remain determined to withstand pressure many consider unfair and chauvinistic.

THE CULTURE

Macedonia's population of 2 million people (in 2004) included Macedonians (66.6%), Albanians (22.7%), Turks (4%), Roma (2.2%), Serbs (2.1%) and others (2.4%). Most Macedonians (and Serbs) are Orthodox Christians, while most Albanians, Turks and Roma are Muslim. In shrines of either faith, it's best to dress modestly.

ARTS

Little Macedonia has a great many prominent artists. Ethno group Syntesis has performed Macedonian folk music before audiences worldwide, as have giants of classical and opera, like pianist Simon Trpčevski and singer Boris Trajanov.

Macedonians' favourite, however, is Toše Proeski, a charismatic singer who died tragically in 2007 at the age of 26. Wherever you go, you're bound to hear his songs. Listening to Macedonians explain why this humanitarian singer meant so much to them will help you understand the country and its people.

ENVIRONMENT

Macedonia's 25,713 sq km is mostly plateau (600m to 900m above sea level), though over 50 mountain peaks top 2500m. It's also where the Continental and Mediterranean climate zones converge. The Vardar River passes through Skopje en route to the Aegean Sea.

READING UP

Who Are the Macedonians? by Hugh Poulton offers useful historical background; Chris Delisio's *Hidden Macedonia* is an intriguing travelogue about the Ohrid and Prespa lake region.

Lakes Ohrid and Prespa, in southwestern Macedonia, are three-million-year-old tectonic lakes; at 300m, Ohrid is the Balkans' deepest, and shelters numerous endemic species – including the endangered Ohrid trout. Although fishing this trout is supposedly illegal, restaurants sell it – try one of Macedonia's three other, nonendangered trout varieties instead.

TRANSPORT IN MACEDONIA

GETTING THERE & AWAY

Air

Alexander the Great Airport (☎ 02-3148 651) is 23km from Skopje. Ohrid has little **St Paul the Apostle Airport** (☎ 046-252 820). See www.airports.com.mk for information. Numerous European airlines serve Skopje, but tickets are pricey. Alternatively, fly to Thessaloniki in Greece with a low-budget carrier, and continue by train or bus to Macedonia.

Macedonian Airlines (IN; www.mat.com.mk), **BH Airlines** (JA; www.bhairlines.ba) and **Helvetic** (2L; www.helvetic.com) are some of the international carriers serving Macedonia.

MOST USEFUL BORDER CROSSINGS

Macedonia's 14 border crossings access Albania, Bulgaria, Greece, Serbia and Kosovo.

The most used border crossing with Albania is Kafasan, 12km southwest of Struga on Lake Ohrid, leading to Tirana. For Bulgaria, Deve Bair (90km from Skopje), leads to Sofia. For Greece, the road/rail crossing at Bogorodica/Gevgelija accesses Thessaloniki. For Serbia and Kosovo, respectively, Tabanovce north of Kumanovo and Blace north of Skopje both have road/rail transport.

MACEDONIA

CONNECTIONS

Macedonia is well connected: from Skopje, buses serve Sofia, Belgrade, Pristina, Tirana, İstanbul and Thessaloniki in Greece. Thessaloniki is also the terminus of an international train line running through Skopje to Belgrade, Zagreb and Ljublana. Long-haul buses reach Austria and Germany.

Bus

From Skopje, buses serve Belgrade (1400MKD, nine hours, 13 daily), Prishtina (350MKD, two hours, eight daily), Sofia (850MKD, 5½ hours, three daily), Thessaloniki (1280MKD, four hours, three weekly), Tirana (1300MKD, seven hours, two daily), Zagreb (3150MKD, 12 hours, one daily), Ljubljana (3770MKD, 14 hours, one daily) and İstanbul (2560MKD, 12 hours, five daily), as well as further-flung destinations such as Budapest, Vienna and Stuttgart.

Car & Motorcycle

A green card (p1240) is required for entry.

Train

The north–south train line serving Macedonia starts in Thessaloniki. There are two daily Thessaloniki–Skopje trains (700MKD, five hours), continuing through Serbia to Belgrade (1300MKD, eight to 10 hours, two daily), and then Zagreb and Ljubljana. Another international line unites Skopje and Pristina (Kosovo).

For international-route timetables, see the **Macedonian Railways** (Makedonski Zheleznici; (www.mz.com.mk/patnichki/timetable.htm), and **Euro Railways** (www.eurorailways.com) websites. However the timetables aren't reliable, and trains are frequently late, so confirm at the time.

GETTING AROUND

Bus

The bus network offers frequent services from Skopje nationwide. Buses range from run-down to modern, but are safe and comfortable. Baggage fees (10MKD) are sometimes charged. If there's room, carry bags on inside to avoid paying.

Car & Motorcycle

Skopje has many car-rental agencies, from big names to local companies.

Train

Macedonia's railway services limited destinations, the furthest being Gevgelija and Bitola in the south (both trip cost around 200MKD). Macedonian Railways' website has timetables (www.mz.com.mk/patnichki/timetable.htm).

SKOPJE СКОПЈЕ

☎ 02 / pop 640,000

Don't let the drab Yugoslav-era architecture fool you – Skopje's a lively town, and one with history, culture and nightlife. Recent improvements on the budget accommodation scene mean it's fairly affordable, too.

Dramatically bisected by the Vardar River, Skopje's two parts are united by several bridges including the 15th-century Kamen Most (Stone Bridge), which leads into the Čaršija (old Turkish bazaar). Despite a destructive earthquake in 1963 (and resulting Yugoslav concrete experimentation), Ottoman mosques and Turkish baths renovated into art galleries still stand, interspersed with crafts shops and teahouses. Above them looms Tvrdina Kale (the city fort), offering great views.

Skopje also boasts great cafes, restaurants, bars and pumping clubs. While still vexed by potholes, begging and reckless drivers, Macedonia's capital is fun, with something for everyone.

ORIENTATION

The Vardar River divides Skopje. North of it is the Čaršija and south is the new town, and the main square, Ploštad Makedonija. Mt Vodno rises to the south.

INFORMATION

ATMs and *menuvačnici* (exchange offices) are plentiful.

EMERGENCY NUMBERS

- Ambulance ☎ 194
- Car emergency assistance ☎ 196
- Fire ☎ 193
- Highway & roadside assistance ☎ 15555
- Police ☎ 192

SKOPJE FOR FREE

Climb the Ottoman fortress **Tvrdina Kale**, (below) for panoramic views, and stroll the old Turkish bazaar, **Čaršija** (below). In summer, rollerblade or relax at the **City Park**.

City hospital (☎ 3130 111; 11 Oktomvri 53; 24 hr)
City of Skopje Bureau for Tourism and Information (070-812 882; www.skopje.mk; Vasil Adzilarski bb; 8.30am-4.30pm Mon-Fri) Informative city tourism office.
Contact Café (Gradski Trgovski Centar; per hr 120MKD)
Go Macedonia (☎ 3232 273; www.gomacedonia.com.mk; Trgovski Centar Beverly Hills lok 32, Naroden Front 19) Arranges hiking, biking, caving and winery tours.
Macedonia Travel (☎ 3112 408; www.macedoniatravel.com; Orce Nikolov 109/1, lok 3) Does numerous tours, and affordable flight/hotel combos.
Neuromedica private clinic (☎ 3133 313; 11 Oktomvri 25; 24 hr)
Skopje Online (www.skopjeonline.com.mk) Updated city info.

SIGHTS

From the main square, Ploštad Makedonija, cross the **Kamen Most** bridge and enter the **Čaršija**, where Skopje's Ottoman past lingers. The **Church of Sveti Dimitrija** (9am-6pm), just left, is a handsome, three-aisled Orthodox church from 1886. Across, note the double domes of the **Daud Paša Baths** (1466). The building houses the **City Art Gallery** (☎ 3133 102; Kruševska 1a; admission 100MKD; 9am-3pm Tue-Sun), with modern art exhibits. Also see the other old-bath-turned-art-gallery, **Čifte Amam** (Bitpazarska bb; admission 50MKD; 9am-4.45pm Mon-Fri, to 3pm Sat, to 1pm Sun).

Further on, the **Museum of Macedonia** (☎ 3116 044; Čurčiska 86; admission 50MKD; 9am-3pm Tue-Sun) documents neolithic through communist times, plus ethnographical items, icons and iconostases. Archaeological items decorate **Kuršumli An** (1550), once an Ottoman caravanserai (inn).

The underground **Church of Sveti Spas** (admission 100MKD; 8am-3pm Tue-Sun) has a stunning wood-carved iconostasis from the early 19th century. It hosts the **Tomb and Museum of Goce Delčev**, a nationalist leader killed by Turks in 1903.

Above it, the 1492 **Mustafa Paša mosque** (Samoilova bb) exemplifies magnificent Ottoman architecture.

Opposite is the Ottoman **Tvrdina Kale** fortress, offering great views from above.

Back on Ploštad Makedonija cross Dimitrije Čupovski to embrace the cafe life of pedestrianised Makedonija. This street ends at the **City Museum** (☎ 3114 742; Mito Hadživasilev Jasmin bb; admission free; 9am-3pm Tue-Sun), with interesting temporary exhibitions. The city's former train station, it's fronted by a stone clock, its fingers frozen in time at 5.17am on 27 July 1963, when the great Skopje earthquake struck.

Framing Skopje to the south, **Mt Vodno** is topped by the 66m-high **Millenium Cross**, the world's largest, illuminated at night.

Further west along Vodno, in the Gorno Nerezi suburb-village, the **Sveti Pantelejmon monastery** (1164) has important Byzantine frescoes. Take a taxi (20 minutes, 120MKD).

FESTIVALS & EVENTS

The October **Skopje Jazz Festival** (☎ 3131 090; www.skopjejazzfest.com.mk; Maksim Gorki 5) always features a world-renowned headliner. The **International Film Festival – OSFAF** (www.osfaf.org.mk) also occurs in October. In December, the ever-more-popular **Taxirat Festival** (☎ 2775 430; www.lithiumrecords.com.mk; Gradski Trgovski Centar) rocks Skopje.

SLEEPING

Websites like www.allmacedoniahotels.com book hotel rooms. Macedonia Travel (see left) offers good-value flight/hotel combos.

Art Hostel (☎ 070-233 336; www.art-hostel.com.mk; Tome Arsovski 14; dm/s/d €12/25/40) is a 20-minute walk from both the central square and the bus/train stations. There are slightly cramped six-bed dorms and small private rooms. The shared bathrooms are clean and new, and there's a billiards table and low-lit outdoor balcony.

Hostel Hostel (☎ 3222 321; Ognjen Pricev 18; d/s/d €12/25/40) A five-minute walk from Art Hostel, this hostel has fewer amenities and smaller rooms.

Hotel Square (☎ 3225 090; 6th fl, Nikola Vapčarov 2; s/d/tr incl breakfast €45/50/75) Overlooking the Ploštad, this little place offers great value for the location it's in. The cosy rooms are

SPLURGE

Hotel TCC Plaza (☎ 3111 807; Vasil Glavinov 12; s/d/ste €95/115/144) Ideal for weary travellers seeking some pampering, this central five-star hotel offers spacious, nicely lit rooms and suites. The spa centre includes a relaxing swimming pool, fitness centre and a variety of massage treatments (from 600MKD).

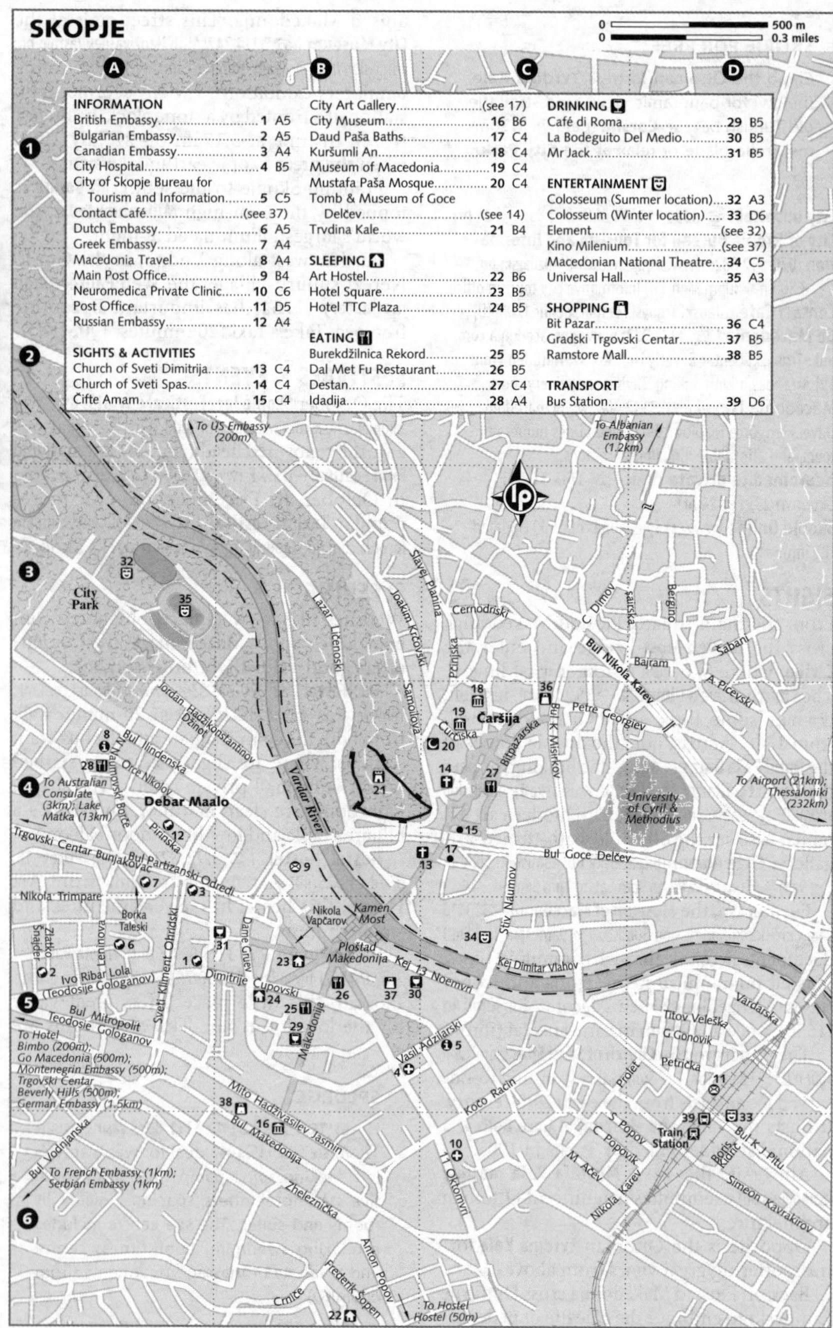

SKOPJE
0 500 m
0 0.3 miles
INFORMATION
British Embassy 1 A5
Bulgarian Embassy 2 A5
Canadian Embassy 3 A4
City Hospital 4 B5
City of Skopje Bureau for Tourism and Information 5 C5
Contact Café (see 37)
Dutch Embassy 6 A5
Greek Embassy 7 A4
Macedonia Travel 8 A4
Main Post Office 9 B4
Neuromedica Private Clinic 10 C6
Post Office 11 D5
Russian Embassy 12 A4
SIGHTS & ACTIVITIES
Church of Sveti Dimitrija 13 C4
Church of Sveti Spas 14 C4
Čifte Amam 15 C4
City Art Gallery (see 17)
City Museum 16 B6
Daud Paša Baths 17 C4
Kuršumli An 18 C4
Museum of Macedonia 19 C4
Mustafa Paša Mosque 20 C4
Tomb & Museum of Goce Delčev (see 14)
Trvdina Kale 21 B4
SLEEPING
Art Hostel 22 B6
Hotel Square 23 B5
Hotel TTC Plaza 24 B5
EATING
Burekdžilnica Rekord 25 B5
Dal Met Fu Restaurant 26 B5
Destan 27 C4
Idadija 28 A4
DRINKING
Café di Roma 29 B5
La Bodeguito Del Medio 30 B5
Mr Jack 31 B5
ENTERTAINMENT
Colosseum (Summer location) 32 A3
Colosseum (Winter location) 33 D6
Element (see 32)
Kino Milenium (see 37)
Macedonian National Theatre 34 C5
Universal Hall 35 A3
SHOPPING
Bit Pazar 36 C4
Gradski Trgovski Centar 37 B5
Ramstore Mall 38 B5
TRANSPORT
Bus Station 39 D6
To US Embassy (200m)
To Albanian Embassy (1.2km)
City Park
Vardar River
Čaršija
Debar Maalo
To Australian Consulate (3km); Lake Matka (13km)
To Airport (21km); Thessaloniki (232km)
University of Cyril & Methodius
To Hotel Bimbo (200m); Go Macedonia (500m); Montenegrin Embassy (500m); Trgovski Centar Beverly Hills (500m); German Embassy (1.5km)
To French Embassy (1km); Serbian Embassy (1km)
To Hostel Hostel (50m)
Kamen Most
Ploštad Makedonija
Train Station
Lazar Ličenoski
Joakim Krčovski
Slavej Planina
Samoilova
Cernodriski
Pčinjska
Curčiska
Bitpazarska
Bul K Misirkov
Bul Nikola Karev
C Dimov
Bajram
Bergino
Šabani
A Pićevski
Petre Georgiev
Bul Goce Delčev
Jordan Hadžikonstantinov Džinot
Bul Ilindenska
Orce Nikolov
N Naumovski Borče
Pirinska
Trgovski Centar Bunjakovac
Bul Partizanski Odredi
Nikola Trimpare
Borka Taleski
Zlatko Šnajder
Leninova
Svetii Kliment Ohridski
Dame Gruev
Nikola Vapčarov
Ivo Ribar Lola (Teodosije Gologanov)
Dimitrije Čupovski
Bul Mitropolit Teodosije Gologanov
Makedonija
Kej 13 Noemvri
Kej Dimitar Vlahov
Stiv Naumov
Vasil Adzilarski
Koco Racin
Mito Hadživasilev Jasmin
Bul Makedonija
Bul Vodnjanska
Zheleznička
Anton Popov
Frederik Šopen
Crniče
11 Oktomvri
Vardarska
Titov Veleška
G Gonovik
Petrička
Prolet
S Popov
C Popovik
M Ačev
Nikola Karev
Bul K J Pitu
Boris Kidrič
Simeon Kavrakirov

well-kept and modern, and the balcony cafe offers lovely views.

Hotel Bimbo (☎ 3214 517; 29 Noemvri 63; s/d incl breakfast €35/50) In a residential area near the centre, it offers clean, well-maintained rooms.

EATING

Skopje has numerous good and inexpensive eateries. Fruit and vegetable markets are cheaper (and better) than supermarkets.

The Čaršija has *kebapčilnici* (restaurants selling beef kebabs), like **Destan** (104 6; kebabs 120MKD). Try *burek* (flaky filo-dough pie with cheese or ground beef) for breakfast at places like **Burekdžilnica Rekord** (Dimitrije Čupovski 5; burek 45MKD).

Idadija (Rade Koncar 1; mains 250MKD) Nestled amidst other *skara* (grilled meats) places, Idadija does simple, nourishing grills.

Dal Met Fu Restaurant (Ploštad Makedonija; mains 280-350MKD) Ever-popular Dal Met Fu has great pastas and salads, cheerful waitresses and preening position behind big windows that look onto the square.

DRINKING & CLUBBING

Cafes and bars open until 1am on Fridays and Saturdays, till midnight other days. After that, only late-licence nightclubs operate. Skopje gets international DJs; see www.skopjeclubbing.com.mk.

Café di Roma (Makedonija) has Skopje's best espresso and a stylish clientele.

our pick **La Bodeguito Del Medio** (Kej 13 Noemvri) Known as 'the Cuban', this gregarious riverfront place serves Cuban food, and has a long bar lined with carousers and cocktails by night.

Mr Jack (bul Partizanski Odredi 3) A rockin' night bar with 50 whiskys, draught Guinness and live bands.

Colosseum (www.colosseum.com.mk; City Park summer, under train station winter) is Skopje's biggest, most popular club, along with **Element** (www.element.com.mk; City Park).

ENTERTAINMENT

Universal Hall (☎ 3224 158; bul Partizanski Odredi bb; tickets 100-200MKD) hosts classical, jazz, pop and kids' performances.

Macedonian National Theatre (☎ 3114 060; Kej Dimitar Vlahov bb; tickets 100-400MKD) hosts opera, ballet and classical music.

GETTING INTO TOWN

There are no airport buses, so arrange a taxi beforehand through your hotel, or take a waiting cab. Drivers sometimes charge exorbitant rates, but for the 23km drive to town, 800MKD to 1000MKD is normal. The train and bus stations are a 15-minute walk southeast of the city centre. Taxis here may attempt occasional rip-offs; remember the average in-town rate (50MKD to 100MKD), and that drivers should use meters.

Kino Milenium (☎ 3111 111; Gradski Trgovski Centar; tickets 60-120MKD) Skopje's largest modern cinema.

SHOPPING

The Čaršija sells jewellery, traditional carpets and clothing, while **Bit Pazar** sells fruit, vegetables and bric-a-brac. The **Gradski Trgovski Centar** (11 Oktomvri) is an open-air mall. **Ramstore** (Mito Hadživasilev Jasmin bb) by the City Museum is somewhat slicker.

GETTING THERE & AWAY

Skopje's **bus station** (☎ 2466 011; bul KJ Pitu) adjoins the **train station** (Zheleznička Stanica; ☎ 3164 255; bul KJ Pitu). At the former only, English is spoken, and there's an exchange office (both have ATMs). Buses cover international and domestic destinations including Bitola (480MKD, three hours, 10 daily) and Ohrid (450MKD, three hours, 11 daily). In summer, book ahead.

Trains serve several domestic destinations; the only international destinations are Serbia, Kosovo and Greece. The longest domestic rail journey is to Bitola (210MKD, four hours, three daily).

GETTING AROUND

Skopje is navigable on foot, and taxis are inexpensive. City buses cost 25MKD to 35MKD.

WESTERN MACEDONIA

OHRID ОХРИД

☎ 046 / pop 55,749

Ohrid is Macedonia's most popular destination, boasting an atmospheric old town with beautiful churches, topped by a medieval castle overlooking serene, 34km-long Lake Ohrid. In summer, there's great swimming on nearby beaches, nightlife and an excellent, month-long festival.

At 300m deep and three million years old, this lake, shared by Macedonia (two-thirds) and Albania (one-third), is one of Europe's deepest and most ancient.

Although human habitation here goes back 8000 years, Macedonians are proudest of Ohrid's role after the 9th century, when the Ohrid literary school, established by St Kliment and St Naum, developed the Cyrillic alphabet – still used by several Slavic nations today.

Orientation & Information

The compact Old Town is hemmed in south and west by the lake and by pedestrian mall, Sveti Kliment Ohridski in the east. The bus station is 1.5km east of centre.

Internet Café Inside (Amam Trgovski Centar; per hr 60MKD) Located in a mall near Ploštad Sveti Kliment Ohridski.

Itna Medicinska Sluzhba (☎ 266 217; Dimitar Vlahov bb; 24hr) Accident and emergency clinic.

Ohrid.com (www.ohrid.com.mk) Municipal website.

Tourist Bureau Biljana (☎ 070-684 428; www.beyondohrid.com; Car Samoil 38) Offers general info, accommodation assistance, bike rental and outdoors activities around Ohrid.

Sights

Most Ohrid churches charge 100MKD admission. On Mondays, museums are closed.

To see Ohrid's sites in the least exhausting way, work your way down from the top. Start at the old town's **Upper Gate** (Gorna Porta), about 80MKD from the centre by taxi.

Inside, turn left to the 13th-century church of **Sveta Bogorodica Perivlepta** (admission 100MKD; 9am-1pm & 4-8pm), which features vivid biblical frescoes and an **icon gallery** (9am-2pm & 5-8pm Tue-Sun).

Straight from the Gorna Porta, find Ohrid's impressive **Classical Amphitheatre**. Originally built for theatre, it now hosts the Summer Festival (see right).

From Gorna Porta, follow the signs right to the massive, 10th-century **Car Samoil's Castle** (admission 30MKD; 9am-6pmTue-Sun). Ascend the narrow stairs to the ramparts for fantastic views. Then follow the wooded path down to the church of **Sveti Kliment i Pantelejmon** (Plaošnik; 9am-6pm; admission free). Originally a 5th-century basilica, it was restored in 2002 according to Byzantine architectural designs. It houses St Kliment's relics, plus original foundations and mosaic under glass floor segments. Across lie 4th-century church foundations, with early Christian mosaics.

The path downhill culminates at the 13th-century **Church of Sveti Jovan at Kaneo**, rising majestically from a cliff over the lake. Continuing from here, Kočo Racin leads past lovely old houses, to a long staircase leading to its grandest church – the frescoed, 11th-century **Sveta Sofija Cathedral** (Car Samoil bb; 10am-8pm) lined with columns.

Continuing from here along Car Samoil you'll see the architecturally exquisite 1827 **National Museum** (Car Samoil 62; admission 50MKD; 9am-4pm & 7-11pm Tue-Sun). The Robev Residence houses an archaeological display, and the Urania Residence opposite has an ethnographic display.

Exiting the old town on Car Samoil, turn left onto the pedestrian mall, Sveti Kliment Ohridski, lined with cafes and shops. Follow it to the end and an enormous, 900-year-old plane tree, the **Činar**.

Festivals & Events

July kicks off both the **Balkan Festival of Folk Dances & Songs** and the **Ohrid Summer Festival** (☎ 262 304; www.ohridsummer.com.mk), featuring classical and opera concerts, theatre and dance. Ohrid's **swimming marathon**, covering 30km from Sveti Naum monastery to Ohrid, occurs in June.

Sleeping

For **private rooms or apartments** (per person €5-10) look for the sign *sobi* (rooms), or inquire at Tourist Bureau Biljana (left).

our pick **Villa Lucija** (☎ 265 608; lucija@mtnet.mk; Kosta Abraš 29; s/d/apt €15/25/40) The Old Town Lucija

WORTH THE TRIP

Only 30 minutes from Skopje, **Lake Matka** sits in lush tranquility beneath the steep Treska Canyon, and offers hiking, rock climbing, boating and caving.

Matka also features several grottoes and churches along wooded trails. In these caves hermits once meditated and Macedonian revolutionaries hid from Turks.

From Skopje drive, take a taxi (350MKD), or catch bus 60 along bul Partizanski Odredi (hourly, 40 minutes, 60MKD).

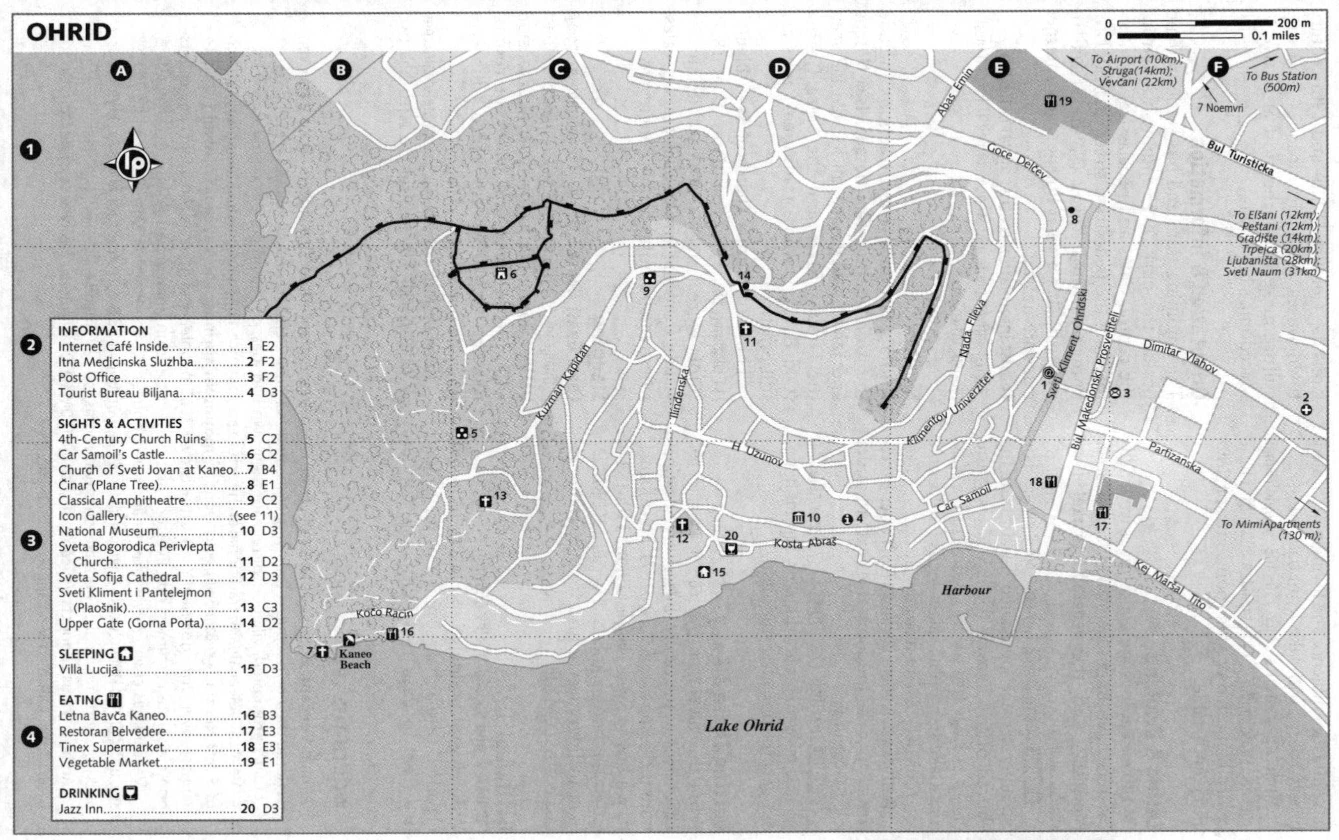
OHRID
0 200 m
0 0.1 miles
INFORMATION
Internet Café Inside....1 E2
Itna Medicinska Sluzhba....2 F2
Post Office....3 F2
Tourist Bureau Biljana....4 D3
SIGHTS & ACTIVITIES
4th-Century Church Ruins....5 C2
Car Samoil's Castle....6 C2
Church of Sveti Jovan at Kaneo....7 B4
Činar (Plane Tree)....8 E1
Classical Amphitheatre....9 C2
Icon Gallery....(see 11)
National Museum....10 D3
Sveta Bogorodica Perivlepta Church....11 D2
Sveta Sofija Cathedral....12 D3
Sveti Kliment i Pantelejmon (Plaošnik)....13 C3
Upper Gate (Gorna Porta)....14 D2
SLEEPING
Villa Lucija....15 D3
EATING
Letna Bavča Kaneo....16 B3
Restoran Belvedere....17 E3
Tinex Supermarket....18 E3
Vegetable Market....19 E1
DRINKING
Jazz Inn....20 D3
To Airport (10km); Struga(14km); Vevčani (22km)
To Bus Station (500m)
7 Noemvri
Bul Turistička
Goce Delčev
Abas Emin
To Elšani (12km); Peštani (12km); Gradište (14km); Trpejca (20km); Ljubaništa (28km); Sveti Naum (31km)
Dimitar Vlahov
Sveti Kliment Ohridski
Bul Makedonski Prosvetiteli
Nada Fileva
Klimentov Univerzitet
Partizanska
To MimiApartments (130 m);
Kej Maršal Tito
Car Samoil
H Uzunov
Ilindenska
Kuzman Kapidan
Kosta Abraš
Kočo Racin
Kaneo Beach
Harbour
Lake Ohrid

MACEDONIA

Book your stay at lonelyplanet.com/hotels

has fantastic ambience and lovingly decorated, breezy rooms with lake-front balconies.

Mimi Apartments (☎ 250 103; mimioh@mail.com.mk; Strašo Pinđur 2; r incl breakfast 800MKD) These centrally located private rooms are spacious and comfortable.

Eating & Drinking

Old town eateries are good but pricey. Self-caterers have **Tinex supermarket** (bul Makedonski Prosvetiteli), and the **vegetable market** (Sveti Kliment Ohridski).

our pick **Letna Bavča Kaneo** (Kočo Racin 43) The 'summer terrace' on Kaneo beach, near the church of Sveti Jovan (p768), is tasty and cheap. A huge fish fry-up of diminutive *plasnica* (lake fish), plus salad, feeds two people for 120MKD. Swim from the dock.

Restoran Belvedere (Kej Maršal Tito 2) does excellent *skara,* The outdoor tables extend under a leafy canopy.

our pick **Jazz Inn** (☎ 070-304 737; Kosta Abraš 74; 10.30pm-4am) This low-lit, jazzy hipster hangout gets roaring after midnight.

Getting There & Away

From the **bus station** (☎ 260 339; 7 Noemvri bb), 1.5km east of the centre, buses serve destinations including Skopje (see p767). For Albania, take a bus to Sveti Naum (29km, 110MKD). Cross the border and take a cab (300MKD) 6km to Pogradeci. Ohrid to Sveti Naum by taxi costs 900MKD.

BITOLA БИТОЛА

☎ 047 / pop 95,385 / elev 660m

With elegant buildings and beautiful locals, elevated Bitola has sophistication inherited from its days as the Ottoman 'City of Consuls'. Colourful 18th- and 19th-century townhouses, Ottoman mosques, and cafe culture make Bitola the most attractive of Macedonia's big towns.

Orientation & Information

The adjoining train and bus stations stand beside the park, a 15-minute walk from the centre. Cafes and neoclassical architecture line the pedestrian street, Maršal Tito, known as Širok Sokak ('Wide Street' in Turkish). It's a wi-fi hotspot, and internet cafes are nearby.

Tourist information centre (☎ 241 641; bitola-tourist-info@t-home.mk; Sterio Georgiev 1) Helpful local tourism office.

Sights

Bitola's Ottoman-era attractions include the 16th-century **Yeni Mosque**, **Isak Mosque** and **Yahdar-Kadi Mosque**, all located between the Dragor River and the Stara Čaršija (Old Bazaar), where traditional crafts are still practised.

The sumptuous **Church of Sveti Dimitrij** (11 Oktomvri bb; 7am-6pm) dates from 1830. Bitola's great neoclassical architecture is visible from the Širok Sokak's many cafes, where the beautiful people congregate.

Sleeping

Chola Guest House (☎ 224 919; guesthouse_chola@hotmail.com; Stiv Naumov 80; s/d €12/20) Bitola's best budget option lies in this quiet old mansion with pretty, clean and well-kept rooms. Ask the taxi driver for Video Club Dju (directly opposite).

Hotel De Niro (☎ 229 656; www.hotel-deniro.com; s/d/ste €35/50/80) The central De Niro has two

WORTH THE TRIP

Offbeat **Vevčani**, 22km northwest of Ohrid, is an independent-minded village: in fact, locals even declared their own republic following Macedonia's 1992 independence. Although secession wasn't actually attempted, villagers did create their own flag, passports and currency, now souvenirs.

Vevčani's clear air and traditional architecture are enhanced by its icon-rich 18th-century **Church of Sveti Nikola** (8am-5pm), and wooded **mountain springs**. The **Vevčani Carnival** (12 to 14 January, over Orthodox New Year), attracts over 3000 people, who gape as some fairly lit villagers don elaborate costumes, ride livestock and pontificate from homegrown floats.

Vevčani has cheap private rooms and guest houses like the **Pansion Kutmičevica** (☎ 046-798 399, 070-249 197; kutmicevica@yahoo.com.mk; d €30), a family-run B&B with traditional decor, lake views, and hearty rustic meals. There are only two rooms, so call ahead.

An hourly bus connects Vevčani with Struga (30MKD, 20 minutes), easily accessible from Ohrid. A taxi from Ohrid to Vevčani costs 600MKD.

locations: one with old Bitola-style rooms and Italian restaurant (on Kiril i Metodij 5), the other with slick minimalist fixtures and pub (on Rusveltova 1).

Eating & Drinking

El Greko (cnr Maršal Tito & Elipda Karamandi; mains 180-320MKD) This Sokak taverna and pizzeria has great beer-hall ambience.

Art Gallery-Café Van (Dalmatinska 29) This Čaršija cafe has eclectic decor like icons, oil paintings and photos of old Bitola.

Basa (Leninova) A darkly lit, happening bar off Leninova.

Getting There & Away

The **bus station** (☎ 231 420; Nikola Tesla) and the **train station** (☎ 237 110; Nikola Tesla) are adjacent, about 1km south of centre. Buses serve Skopje (480MKD, four hours, 10 daily), among other destinations. Trains also serve Skopje (210MKD, three hours, three daily).

For Greece, take a taxi to the border (450MKD), where you can seek a Greek cab; however, some Bitola cab driver will also go all the way to Florina for 3000MKD.

MACEDONIA DIRECTORY

ACCOMMODATION

City hotels are expensive, though cheaper options are starting to emerge. Affordable, quality private accommodation exists in holiday areas. Monastery dorms are another budget option. Book ahead for summer, Orthodox Christmas (7 January) and Orthodox Easter visits.

ACTIVITIES

Lake Matka near Skopje offers great hiking, as do Galičica (near Ohrid) and Pelister (near Bitola) National Parks. Swimming's good in Lake Ohrid.

BUSINESS HOURS

Businesses operate 8am to 8pm weekdays and 8am to 2pm on Saturdays. Post offices operate 6.30am to 4pm, and banks 7am to 5pm Monday to Friday.

DANGERS & ANNOYANCES

Young beggars along Skopje's main square and riverfront can vex; keep your hands firmly on your valuables.

EMBASSIES & CONSULATES

The following missions can all be found in Skopje.

Albania (off Map p766; ☎ 02-2614 636; ambshqip@mt.net.mk; HT Karpoš 94a)

Australia (off Map p766; ☎ 02-3061 114; austcon@mt.net.mk; Londonska 11b)

Bulgaria (Map p766; ☎ 02-3229 444; bgemb@unet.com.mk; Ivo Ribar Lola 40)

Canada (Map p766; ☎ 02-3225 630; honcon@unet.com.mk; bul Partizanski Odredi 17a)

France (off Map p766; ☎ 02-3118 749; www.ambafrance-mk.org; Salvador Aljende 73)

Germany (off Map p766; ☎ 02-3093 900; dt.boskop@mol.com.mk; Lerinska 59)

Greece (Map p766; ☎ 02-3219 260; grfyrom@unet.com.mk; Borka Taleski 6)

Montenegro (off Map p766; ☎ 02-3227 277; mail@montenegroembassy.org.mk; Vasil Stefanovski 7)

Netherlands (Map p766; ☎ 02-3129 319; www.nlembassy.org.mk; Leninova 69-71)

Russia (Map p766; ☎ 02-3117 160; embassy@russia.org.mk; Perinska 44)

Serbia (off Map p766; ☎ 02-3129-298; yuamb@unet.com.mk; Pitu Guli 8)

UK (Map p766; ☎ 02-3299 299; beskopje@mt.net.mkl; Dimitrie Čupovski 26)

US (Map p766; ☎ 02-3102 000; http://macedonia.usembassy.gov; Samoilova 21)

HOLIDAYS

New Year 1 and 2 January
Orthodox Christmas 7 January
International Women's Day 8 March
Orthodox Easter Week March/April
Labour Day 1 May
SS Cyril and Methodius Day 24 May
Ilinden Day 2 August
Republic Day 8 September
1941 Partisan Day 11 October

INTERNET RESOURCES

Culture in Macedonia (www.culture.in.mk) Cultural info and festival listings.

Exploring Macedonia (www.exploringmacedonia.com) Useful travel website.

Macedonia Loves You (www.macedonialovesyou.eu) An informative, photo-rich site.

MONEY

The Macedonian denar (MKD) comes in 10MKD, 50MKD, 100MKD, 500MKD, 1000MKD and 5000MKD notes, and one-, two- and five-denar coins and are nonconvertible abroad. Euros are usually accepted. Some hotels quote rates in euros.

Macedonian *menuvačnici* (exchange offices) work commission-free. ATMs are widespread, except in villages. Avoid travellers cheques. Credit cards aren't always accepted – carry cash.

POST

Mail services to and from Macedonia are efficient.

TELEPHONE & FAX

Internet cafes offer cheap international phone service. Public-telephone cards sold in kiosks or post offices in units of 100 (200MKD), 200 (300MKD), 500 (650MKD) or 1000 (1250MKD) offer good value for domestic calls. Drop the initial zero in city codes and mobile prefixes (the three-digit numbers starting with ☎ 07) when calling from abroad.

VISAS

Passport holders from Australia, Canada, the EU, Iceland, Israel, New Zealand, Norway, Switzerland, Turkey and the USA don't need visas, and can stay for three months. Visas are required for most others. Visa fees average US$30 for a single-entry visa and US$60 for a multiple-entry visa. Confirm at www.mfa.gov.mk.

Malta

HIGHLIGHTS

- **Valletta** Immerse yourself in the history and sights of the pint-sized capital (p776)
- **Beaches** Discover how Malta earned a reputation for beachside holidays (p783)
- **Festas** Toast a patron saint amid an infectious mix of music, food and fireworks (p783)
- **Mdina** Step back in time in the silent streets of this elegant town (p781)
- **Best journey** Head to Gozo to experience its slower pace, and maybe even learn to scuba dive (p781)

FAST FACTS

- **Area** 316 sq km (double the size of Liechtenstein)
- **Budget** €35 per day
- **Capital** Valletta
- **Country code** ☎ 356
- **Famous for** Knights of St John, WWII heroism, falcons
- **Languages** Maltese, English
- **Money** Euro (€); A$1 = €0.55; C$1 = 0.60; ¥100 = €0.78; NZ$1 = €0.43; UK£1 = €1.12; US$1 = €0.74
- **Phrases** *merħba* (hello), *saħħa* (goodbye), *grazzi* (thanks)

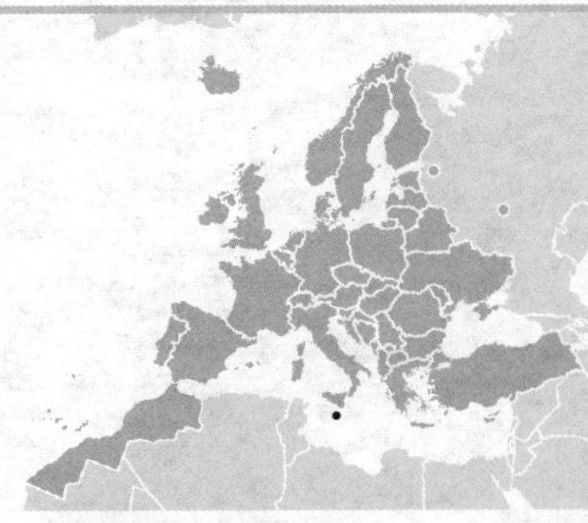

- **Population** 410,000
- **Visas** Not needed for most visitors for stays of up to three months (p784)

TRAVEL HINTS

Get around on the big old buses, and sate your hunger with cheap *pastizzi* (pastries filled with ricotta cheese or mushy peas).

ROAMING MALTA

Soak up the history of Valletta and Mdina, check out the ancient temples, and go diving and chill out on Gozo.

Despite being made up of three small islands on the very southern edge of Europe, Malta veritably groans under the weight of its rich and tumultuous history, dramatic and unusual geography and fascinating cultural influences.

From its historic North African and Arabic influences (listen carefully to the local language) to the Sicilian-inspired cuisine on its menus and the oddly 1950s British feel to much of the place, Malta will almost certainly surprise you. And while there has definitely been an eclectic mix of influences and a roll-call of rulers over the centuries, be in no doubt, Malta is not just a notional outpost of Italy or a relic of colonial Britain; this diminutive island nation has a quirky character all its own.

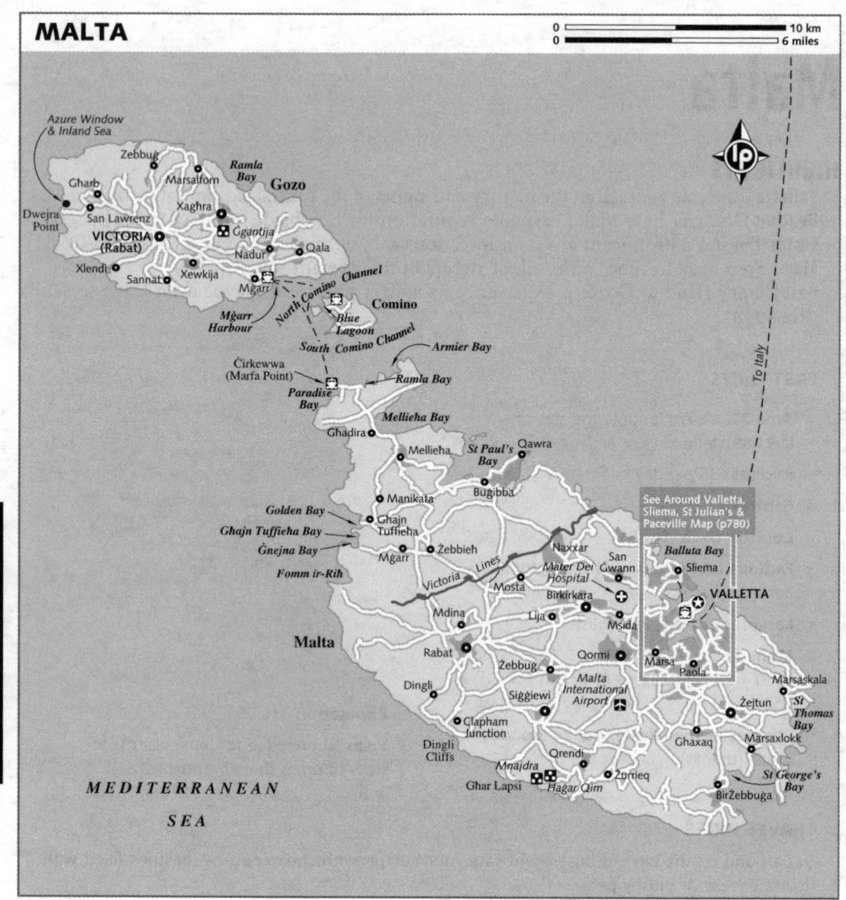

HISTORY

Malta's oldest monuments are the mysterious megalithic temples at Ġgantija near Xagħra on Gozo, and Ħaġar Qim and Mnajdra on the southwest coast of the main island. Built between 3800 and 2500 BC, they're the world's oldest surviving freestanding structures. From around 800 to 218 BC, Malta was colonised by the Phoenicians and Carthaginians, and then became part of the Roman Empire. In AD 60 St Paul was shipwrecked on the island, where (according to folklore) he converted the islanders to Christianity. Arabs arrived in 870 and had a considerable influence on agriculture and language. Then came a succession of Normans, Angevins (French), Aragonese and Castilians (Spanish).

In 1530 the islands were given to the Knights of the Order of St John, a religious crusader organisation founded in Jerusalem. The Knights expelled invading Turks in 1565 and were considered 'saviours of Europe'. Soon afterwards, though, the order declined and surrendered to Napoleon in 1798 without a fight. The British helped liberate the island in 1800 and began to develop Malta into a major naval base. The new member of the British Empire suffered greatly from WWII bombing.

In 1947 the devastated island was given a measure of self-government. The country gained independence in 1964, and became a republic in 1974. In 2004 Malta joined the EU, and introduced the euro as its currency in January 2008.

READING UP

Ernle Bradford writes well about Malta in crisis. *The Great Siege* is a page-turning account of the epic 1565 battle between the Ottoman Turks and the Knights of St John. In Bradford's *Siege: Malta 1940–1943*, the role of the bad guys is played by the bomb-dropping Italians and Germans in WWII.

THE CULTURE

Malta is Europe's most densely populated country. The population is around 410,000, with most living in the satellite towns around Valletta, Sliema and the Grand Harbour; approximately 31,000 live on Gozo, while Comino's permanent population is only four. More than 95% of the population is Maltese-born.

Despite an easy blend of Mediterranean and British culture, there's still a strong feeling of tradition. Around 98% of the population is Roman Catholic. Businesses are closed on Sunday, and abortion and divorce are illegal.

ENVIRONMENT

The Maltese archipelago consists of three inhabited islands: Malta, Gozo and Comino. They lie in the middle of the Mediterranean, south of Sicily, east of Tunisia and north of Libya. These densely populated islands feature no major hills and little greenery to soften the stony, sun-bleached landscape. There is virtually no surface water and no permanent creeks or rivers.

TRANSPORT

GETTING THERE & AWAY

Air

Malta is well connected to Europe and North Africa. All flights arrive at and depart from **Malta International Airport** (MLA; ☎ 2124 9600; www.maltairport.com) at Luqa, 8km south of Valletta. The Maltese national airline is **Air Malta** (☎ 2166 2211; www.airmalta.com; Misraħ-il-Ħelsien, Valletta).

Budget carriers **Easyjet** (www.easyjet.com), **Ryanair** (www.ryanair.com) and **Germanwings** (www.germanwings.com) all fly to Malta from their Western European hubs.

Boat

Malta has regular sea links with Italy. You can also sail from Tunis to Malta (but not from Malta direct to Tunis).

Virtu Ferries (www.virtuferries.com; ☎ in Malta 2206 9022, in Catania 095-535 711, in Pozzallo 0932-954 062) offers Malta–Sicily crossings with its catamaran service to/from Pozzallo and Catania. The Pozzallo–Malta crossing takes only 90 minutes and operates year-round. High-season passenger fares one way/return are €67/107.

Grimaldi Ferries (☎ 2122 6873; www.grimaldi-ferries.com) operates a weekly service year-round from Catania in Sicily as well as two other services from Genoa and Civitavecchia.

Grandi Navi Veloci (GNV; ☎ 2569 1600; www.gnv.it) operates a weekly Palermo–Malta service. GNV also offers a connection from Genoa to Malta via Tunis, which makes it possible to travel to Malta from Tunisia, but not vice versa. Check the website for details as departures are sporadic.

GETTING AROUND

Boat

Gozo Channel Company (www.gozochannel.com; ☎ in Ċirkewwa 2158 0435, in Mġarr 2156 1622) runs regular car ferry services between Ċirkewwa (Malta) and Mġarr (Gozo), with crossings every 45 to 75 minutes from 6am to around 10pm (and every two hours throughout the night). Bus 45 runs regularly from Valletta to Ċirkewwa to connect with the ferry to Gozo. Bus 25 runs between Victoria and Mġarr on Gozo.

The **Marsamxetto ferry service** (☎ 2146 3862) crosses frequently between Valletta and Sliema (€0.97, five minutes). Arrival and departure points are at the Strand in Sliema and the end of Triq San Marku in northwest Valletta.

CONNECTIONS

Malta is well connected to both Sicily and mainland Italy by sea and can be reached by an occasional ferry from Tunisia too. Catamarans to Pozzallo and Catania in Sicily are the fastest and most frequent connection, while other services link Malta to Palermo, Genoa and Civitavecchia. The ferries from Tunis only operate *to* Malta, they then return to Genoa, making onward travel to Tunisia by sea impossible.

Bus

Malta and Gozo are served by buses run by the **Malta Public Transport Association** (ATP; ☎ 2125 0007/8; www.atp.com.mt). Most of Malta's services originate from the chaotic City Gate terminus, just outside Valletta's fortifications. Fares are cheap – from €0.47 to €1.16 (be sure to have small change for the driver when you board). Services are regular and the more popular routes run till 11pm. Ask at an ATP kiosk or tourist office for a free timetable.

On Gozo, the bus terminus is in Victoria, just south of Triq ir-Reppublika. All services depart from here and cost €0.47.

Car & Motorcycle

With low rental rates it might make economic sense to hire a car, but unless you're a confident driver it might not be worth the aggravation. Road rules are often ignored, roads are confusingly signposted and parking can be difficult.

All the major international car-hire companies are at the airport, and there are dozens of local agencies. Shop around – rates depend on season, length of rental, and size and make of car. Daily rates for the smallest vehicles start from around €20.

Taxi

Official taxis are metered but generally expensive. **Wembley Motors** (☎ 2137 4141) offers a 24-hour service.

VALLETTA

pop 7000

The Maltese capital is a stunner. Whereas careless modern development has blighted much of the rest of Malta's coast, Valletta has retained its architectural unity and ancient charm. Activity bustles around Triq ir-Repubblika and Triq il-Merkanti, but walk the quiet, narrow backstreets to get a feel for everyday life. The city overlooks the impressive Grand Harbour to the southeast and Marsamxett Harbour to the northwest.

INFORMATION

Bank of Valletta (cnr Triq ir-Repubblika & Triq San Ġwann) Foreign-exchange machine and ATMs.

HSBC Bank (20 Triq ir-Repubblika) Foreign exchange and ATMs.

Mater Dei (☎ 158; Tal-Qroqq, Birkirkara) This brand new public hospital is located near the University of Malta.

> **EMERGENCY NUMBER**
>
> For all emergencies (police, fire, ambulance), call ☎ 112.

Police station (☎ 2122 5495; Triq Nofs in-Nhar)

Tourist office (☎ 2123 7747; Misraħ il-Ħelsien; 9am-7pm Mon-Sat, to 1pm Sun, closed public holidays) In the City Arcade on the right as you enter through City Gate.

Ziffa (☎ 2122 4307; 194 Triq id-Dejqa; per hr €5; 9am-11pm Mon-Sat, 10am-4pm Sun) Internet access, wi-fi and good rates for international phone calls.

SIGHTS

A walk around the bulky city walls features spectacular views – be sure to stop at the **Upper Barrakka Gardens** in the southwest for a vista that puts the grand in Grand Harbour.

Check out the breathtaking baroque interior of **St John's Co-Cathedral** (☎ 2122 0526; Triq ir-Repubblika; adult/student €5.82/1.50; 9.30am-4.30pm Mon-Fri, to 12.30pm Sat, closed Sun, public holidays & during services), built in the 1570s. Inside is the **Cathedral Museum**, which houses two magnificent works by the Italian painter Caravaggio.

The 16th-century **Grand Master's Palace** (Pjazza San Ġorġ) is the seat of the Maltese parliament. From the entrance on Triq il-Merkanti, it's possible to visit the **State Apartments** (☎ 2124 9349; adult/student €4.66/2.33; 10am-4pm Fri-Wed), full of works of art. The apartments are closed when official state visits take place.

At the **National Museum of Archaeology** (☎ 2122 1623; Triq ir-Repubblika; adult/student €2.33/1.16; 9am-7pm) you can admire beautiful objects that have been found at Malta's prehistoric sites – check out the intriguing female figurines (the so-called 'fat ladies').

At the furthest point of Valletta is **Fort St Elmo**, built in 1552 by the Knights of St John and generally closed to the public. Next to the fort, the informative **National War Museum** that commemorates Malta's heroic involvement in WWII was closed for renovations at the time of writing.

Built in 1731, the beautiful **Manoel Theatre** (☎ 2124 6389; www.teatrumanoel.com.mt; 115 Triq it-Teatru l-Antik; theatre tours €4; tours at least four times daily Mon-Sat) is one of the oldest theatres in Europe. There's a varied program of events October to May, or you can take a guided tour to see the baroque auditorium. The transformed 16th-century **St James' Cavalier Centre**

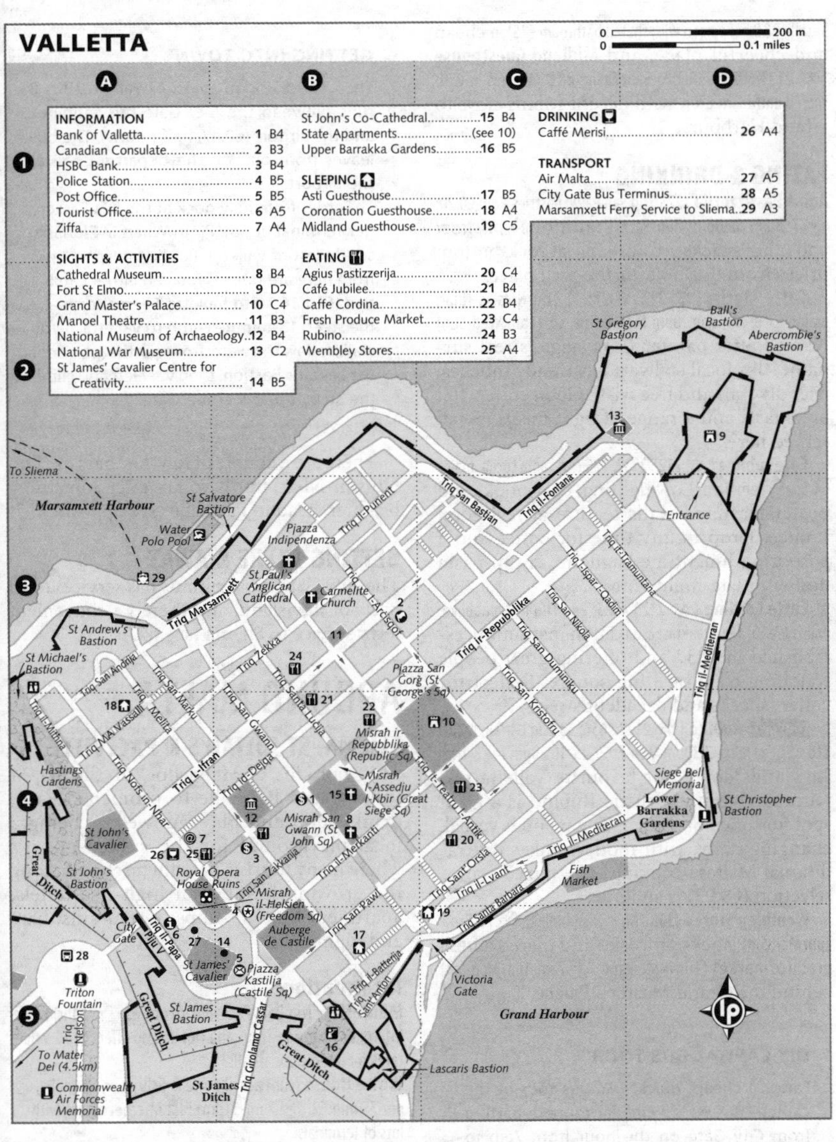

for Creativity (www.sjcav.org; Triq Nofs in-Nhar) now houses exhibition spaces, a theatre and an art-house cinema.

SLEEPING

our pick **Asti Guesthouse** (☎ 2123 9506; http://mol.net.mt/asti; 18 Triq Sant'Orsla; B&B per person with shared bathroom €17) You'll get a taste of old-school Valletta charm here in a 350-year-old building converted into a guest house that offers the best-value accommodation in town. Asti has a charming host, simple, spacious rooms and spotless shared bathrooms. Breakfast is served in a vaulted dining room under a chandelier.

Standby accommodation options include **Coronation Guesthouse** (☎ 2123 7652; 10E Triq MA

 Book your stay at lonelyplanet.com/hotels

Vasalli; B&B per person with shared bathroom €15), a cheap and cheerful place, and **Midland Guesthouse** (☎ 2123 6024; 255 Triq Sant'Orsla; B&B per person with shared bathroom €20), with decent rooms close to Grand Harbour.

EATING & DRINKING

Agius Pastizzerija (273 Triq San Pawl; pastries from €0.20; 7.30am-5.30pm Mon-Sat) Traditional *pastizzi* and other snacks are available at rock-bottom prices from this hole-in-the-wall place.

Caffé Merisi (☎ 2123 8027; 11 Triq Nofs in-Nhar; mains €3-8; 8am-8pm Mon & Tue, to 11pm Wed-Sun) Named after painter Caravaggio's real surname, this local stalwart has trendy touches, friendly staff and free wi-fi. Good coffee, full breakfasts and a range of light meals are all served here.

Café Jubilee (☎ 2125 2332; 125 Triq Santa Lucija; mains €4-8; 8am-1am) Low lighting, cosy nooks and poster-plastered walls feature at feel-good Jubilee. Drop in any time for coffee and a *pastizzi*, a lunchtime baguette, cheap pasta dinner or late-night vino.

Caffé Cordina (☎ 2123 4385; 244 Triq ir-Repubblika; mains €4-10; breakfast & lunch) An institution, established in 1837 and offering great people watching on a bustling square. Perfect for coffee, snacks and decadent sweets.

our pick **Rubino** (☎ 2122 4656; 53 Triq L-Ifran; mains €10-15; noon-2.30pm Mon-Fri, 7.45-10.30pm Tue & Thu-Sat) Hands down our favourite Valletta restaurant, charming, rustic Rubino is a great spot for lunch or dinner. The menu is verbal, changing daily, with modern takes on traditional Maltese cooking. The mixed starter selection (€8.95) is sublime.

Wembley Stores (305 Triq ir-Repubblika; 7.15am-7pm Mon-Sat) stocks groceries and there's a **fresh produce market** (Triq il-Merkanti; 7am-1pm Mon-Sat) behind the Grand Master's Palace.

DIY CAPITAL BUS TOUR

Fancy a cheap, quick, DIY bus tour of the capital? Bus 98 is a circular route departing from City Gate on the hour from 7am to 6pm. It does a clockwise loop around the bastions of Valletta and through Floriana, so you can take in harbour views, Fort St Elmo and the start of the new Valletta Waterfront area (encompassing Pinto Wharf). A complete circuit takes around 15 to 20 minutes; the fare is all of €0.35.

GETTING INTO TOWN

The airport is 8km south of Valletta. Bus 8 runs between the City Gate bus terminus and the airport (€0.47, half-hourly). The bus leaves from outside the departure hall at the airport.

Ferries from Italy dock at the Sea Passenger Terminal beside Pinto Wharf in Floriana, southwest of Valletta. Public transport links from here are poor – you can either catch a taxi (€10/16.30 to Valletta/Sliema) or make the steep 15-minute climb to Valletta. If you walk, follow the waterfront northeast, under the Lascaris Bastion, then veer left and climb the steps up at Victoria Gate.

There are a couple of low-key bars on Triq Nofs in-Nhar, but if you're after something brighter, head to Paceville (see opposite).

GETTING THERE & AWAY

The City Gate bus terminus has services to all parts of the island, and there's a convenient ferry service to Sliema (see p775).

AROUND MALTA

SLIEMA, ST JULIAN'S & PACEVILLE

The cool kids of Malta flock to Sliema, St Julian's and Paceville to promenade, eat, drink, shop and play. As well as being a local playground for the cashed-up, it's where many tourists base themselves, among the growing number of high-rise hotels, apartment blocks, shops, restaurants, bars and nightclubs.

Information

MelitaNet (Triq Ball, Paceville; per hr €2; 24hr) Large internet cafe inside Tropicana Hotel. Also offers good-value rates for international calls.

White House (cnr Paceville Ave & Schreiber, Paceville; per 75 min €2; 7am-11pm) Fast internet access with lots of terminals.

Sights & Activities

There are good views of Valletta from Triq ix-Xatt (The Strand), even if there's not much to see in Sliema itself. Triq ix-Xatt and Triq it-Torri (Tower Rd) make for a perfect waterfront stroll, with plenty of bars and cafes en route. **Beaches** in the area are mostly shelves

WORTH THE TRIP: HYPOGEUM

The town of Paola, about 4km south of Valletta, is home to the magnificent **Hal Saflieni Hypogeum** (☎ 2180 5018/9; Triq iċ-Ċimiterju; admission €9.32; tours hourly 9am-4pm), usually referred to simply as the Hypogeum, a complex of underground burial chambers thought to date from 3600 to 3000 BC. Excellent 50-minute tours of the complex are available, but the number of visitors has been restricted in order to preserve this fragile Unesco World Heritage–listed site. Prebooking is therefore absolutely *essential* (usually a couple of weeks before you wish to visit); tickets are available in person from the Hypogeum and the National Museum of Archaeology in Valletta (p776), or online at www.heritagemalta.org. Note that kids under six are not permitted to visit the Hypogeum.

of bare rock; there are better facilities at the private **lidos** along the coast, which include swimming pools, sun lounges, bars and water sports (admission costs around €5 to €7 per day).

Captain Morgan Cruises (☎ 2346 3333; www.captainmorgan.com.mt) operates from the waterfront area of Sliema known as The Ferries and has a boat trip for every traveller's taste and budget, including a popular tour of Grand Harbour (€15.75). Shop around – there are lots of competitors along the waterfront.

Sleeping

NSTS Hibernia Residence & Hostel (☎ 2133 3859/5450; www.nsts.org; Triq Mons G Depiro, Sliema; dm €8, low/high season s €27/49 d €28/50;) Malta's only hostel is perfect for those after quality budget accommodation. As well as the roll-call of facilities (laundry, kitchens, breakfast room/cafeteria, TV lounge, internet cafe, rooftop sun terrace), there are single-sex dorms, or twin studios with private bathroom and kitchenette. From Valletta, take bus 62, 64 or 67 to Balluta Bay and walk 300m up Triq Manwel Dimech; Triq Mons G Depiro is on the left. The hotel hires bicycles out for €13 per day.

Hotel Valentina (☎ 2138 2232; www.hotelvalentina.com; Triq Schreiber; d incl breakfast €46-106;) The colourful modern rooms at boutiquey Valentina aren't huge, but then neither are the prices. The party-central location is fab, and facilities include air-con and satellite TV. A bargain.

Eating

This area is Malta's gastronomic heartland. Fertile hunting grounds for top dining experiences include Spinola Bay and the sleek Portomaso complex.

Avenue (☎ 2135 1753; Triq Gort, Paceville; mains €5-9; lunch Mon-Sat, dinner daily) Multicoloured and multiroomed, the Avenue is a quiet escape from Paceville's traffic with a huge pizza and pasta menu, Murano glass and Venetian masks as decor and tonnes of outdoor tables.

Paparazzi (☎ 2137 4966; 159 Triq San Ġorġ, Spinola Bay; mains €8-12; 10am-midnight) The sunny terrace here is a prime people-watching spot, with a fine view of Spinola Bay. Fight your way through Paparazzi's hearty portions on the cheeky, crowd-pleasing menu. It's veg-friendly.

our pick **Olivers** (☎ 2138 0023; 19/21 Paceville Ave, Paceville; mains €14-21; 7-11pm Tue-Sun) This newcomer to Paceville's dining scene is a real boon. The classy, dark-red interior and discrete service immediately set it apart from the crowd, though the real draw is the excellent food. Try the braised rabbit on tomato fondue, the sea bass with almond and pesto gnocchi or the red king prawns, egg noodles and leaks. Mmmmm.

Self-caterers should head to **Arkadia Foodstore** (Triq il-Knisja, Paceville; 8am-8pm Mon-Sat) or **Tower Foods Supermarket** (46 Triq il-Kbira, Sliema; 8am-7.30pm Mon-Sat).

Drinking & Clubbing

Paceville is the place for partying, with wall-to-wall bars and clubs, especially around the northern end of Triq San Ġorġ, and it's jam-packed on weekends year-round (and nightly in summer).

BJ's (☎ 2137 7642; Triq Ball, Paceville) An offbeat club featuring live music nightly (primarily jazz) and drawing a more mature crowd than most of its neighbours.

Fuego (☎ 2138 6746; www.fuego.com.mt; Triq Santu Wistin, Paceville; admission free) Get hot and sweaty dancing up a storm at this popular salsa bar – head first to its free salsa-dancing classes (Monday to Wednesday from 8.30pm).

AROUND VALLETTA, SLIEMA, ST JULIAN'S & PACEVILLE

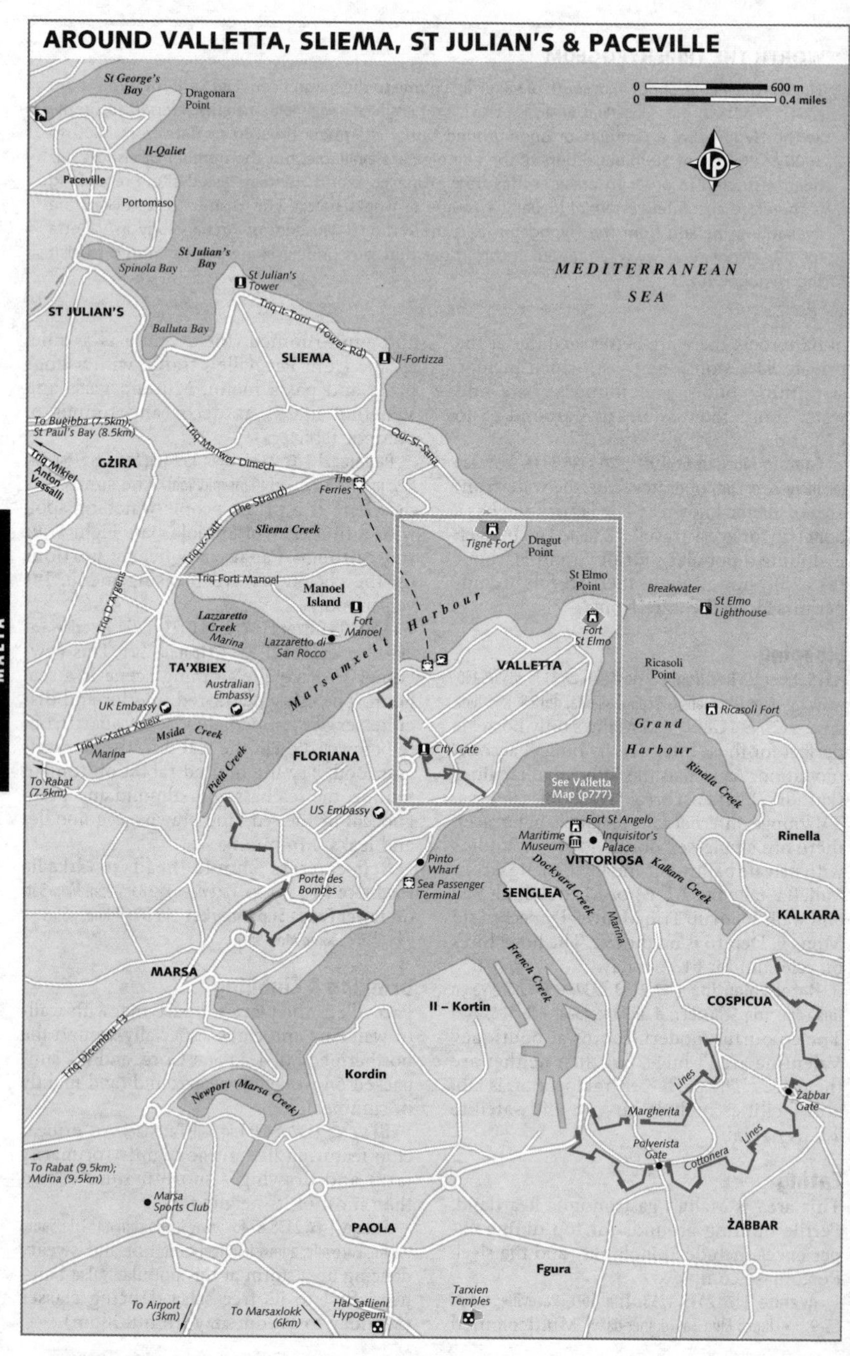
St George's Bay
Dragonara Point
Il-Qaliet
Paceville
Portomaso
St Julian's Bay
Spinola Bay
St Julian's Tower
ST JULIAN'S
Balluta Bay
Triq it-Torri (Tower Rd)
SLIEMA
Il-Fortizza
MEDITERRANEAN SEA
To Buġibba (7.5km); St Paul's Bay (8.5km)
Triq Mikiel Anton Vassalli
GŻIRA
Triq Manwel Dimech
Qui-Si-Sana
The Ferries
Triq ix-Xatt (The Strand)
Sliema Creek
Tigné Fort
Dragut Point
Triq Forti Manoel
Manoel Island
St Elmo Point
Breakwater
St Elmo Lighthouse
Triq D'Argens
Lazzaretto Creek Marina
Fort Manoel
Lazzaretto di San Rocco
Marsamxett Harbour
Fort St Elmo
VALLETTA
TA'XBIEX
Ricasoli Point
Australian Embassy
UK Embassy
Ricasoli Fort
Triq ix-Xatta Xbiex
Msida Creek Marina
Grand Harbour
Pietà Creek
FLORIANA
City Gate
To Rabat (7.5km)
See Valletta Map (p777)
Rinella Creek
US Embassy
Fort St Angelo
Maritime Museum
Inquisitor's Palace
Rinella
Pinto Wharf
VITTORIOSA
Dockyard Creek
Kalkara Creek
Porte des Bombes
Sea Passenger Terminal
SENGLEA
KALKARA
Marina
French Creek
MARSA
Il – Kortin
COSPICUA
Triq Diċembru 13
Kordin
Lines
Żabbar Gate
Newport (Marsa Creek)
Margherita
Polverista Gate
Cottonera
To Rabat (9.5km); Mdina (9.5km)
Marsa Sports Club
PAOLA
ŻABBAR
Fgura
To Airport (3km)
To Marsaxlokk (6km)
Hal Saflieni Hypogeum
Tarxien Temples
0 600 m
0 0.4 miles

Havana Bar (☎ 2137 4500; www.havanamalta.com; Triq San Ġorġ, Paceville; admission free) With three dance floors, six bars and an eclectic range of music from retro 1970s and '80s to soul and hip-hop, this place has something for everyone.

Axis (☎ 2138 2767; www.axis.com.mt; Triq San Ġorġ, Paceville) Malta's biggest and best nightclub (and one that's managed to stand the test of time) houses three separate clubs (Axis Main, The Matrix and Styx; usually serving up commercial house) and seven bars providing party space for more than 3000 punters. There's usually a cover charge.

Getting There & Away

Buses 62, 64 and 67 run regularly between Valletta and Sliema, St Julian's and Paceville (€0.47). There's also a ferry service between Sliema and Valletta (see p775).

MDINA & RABAT

Elegant, aristocratic Mdina (which is aptly nicknamed the Silent City) is perched on a rocky outcrop in the country's southwest. Fortified for more than 3000 years, it was Malta's old political centre; today visitors can spend hours wandering the quiet, narrow streets. Rabat is the town settlement outside the walls.

Mdina's main square is dominated by **St Paul's Cathedral** (Pjazza San Pawl; adult/student €2.50/1.75; 🕒 9.30-4.45pm Mon-Sat, 3-4.45pm Sun), worth visiting for the huge fresco of St Paul's shipwreck. The entry ticket is also valid for the **Cathedral Museum** (☎ 2145 4697; Pjazza San Pawl; adult/student €2.50/1.75; 🕒 9.30am-4.30pm Mon-Fri, 9.30am-3.30pm Sat) opposite, which is housed in a baroque 18th-century palace originally used as a seminary.

Sleeping & Eating

our pick Point de Vue Guesthouse & Restaurants (☎ 2145 4117; www.pointdevuemalta.com; 5 Saqqajja, Rabat; B&B per person €35; 💻) This century-old 12-room guesthouse is rightly popular, due to a combination of affordable rates and its position just metres from Mdina's town walls.

Fontanella Tea Gardens (☎ 2145 0204; Triq is-Sur; mains €3-7; 🕒 10am-6pm winter, 10am-11pm summer) With a dazzling array of cakes (€2.20 each) to accompany the wonderful views from the terrace, it's a real shame about the ordinary service.

Il Gattopardo (☎ 2145 1213; 20 Triq Villegaignon; mains €8-10; 🕒 11am-4pm Mon-Sat year-round, 7-9.30pm Thu, Fri & Sat summer) The name (meaning 'The Leopard') may be Italian, but this art bistro set in a lovely old house with a shady courtyard serves a Greek-inspired menu.

Getting There & Away

From Valletta, take bus 80 or 81 to reach Rabat (€0.54); from Sliema and St Julian's take bus 65 (€1.16); from Buġibba take bus 86 (€1.16). The bus terminus in Rabat is on Is-Saqqajja, 150m south of Mdina's Main Gate.

GOZO

The island of Gozo is much more tranquil than its big sister Malta. Fewer tourists venture over and, if they do, it's often on a day trip. The sights could indeed be packed into one day, but the island's real charm is best appreciated at a slower pace – visit the beaches, learn to dive, take a boat trip or simply relax.

VICTORIA (RABAT)

Victoria, also known as Rabat, is the chief town of Gozo and sits at the centre of the island, 6km from the ferry terminal at Mġarr. All bus routes originate and finish at the terminus on Triq Putirjal, about 10 minutes' walk from the Citadel.

Pjazza Indipendenza, the main square of Victoria, is a hive of activity, with open-air cafes, craft shops and traders peddling fresh produce.

Victoria is crowned by the **Citadel** (also known as Il-Kastell, or Citadella), a miniature version of Malta's Mdina. A stroll around the Citadel offers panoramic views across the island. The **Cathedral of the Assumption** (Misraħ il-Katidral; admission €3; 🕒 9am-5pm Mon-Sat) was built between 1697 and 1711. Entrance includes an audio guide. Call into nearby **Ta'Rikardu** (☎ 2155 5953; 4 Triq il-Fossos; 🕒 10am-6pm) for local produce chock-full of flavour. Order a platter (€8.75 for two people) and wash it down with Gozitan wine.

MARSALFORN

Marsalforn is built around a cove and is the favoured choice on Gozo for tourists in summer, so it has decent facilities despite there being nothing to see in the town itself. You can hike eastwards a couple of kilometres over the hill to Ramla Bay in about 45 minutes, or west to swimming holes and saltpans.

ourpick **Maria Giovanna Hostel** (☎ 2155 3630; www.tamariagozo.com/hostel.htm; 41 Triq ir-Rabat; s incl breakfast €20-40, d incl breakfast €40-60; 💻) is the top pick of budget accommodation on Gozo. This small, extremely welcoming guesthouse just back from the waterfront retains a loyal clientele who come back again and again. There are now 15 rooms following recent renovations, each charmingly decorated and with beautiful new bathrooms. All rooms have balconies, with one exception, and guests are free to use the kitchen.

Cool little **Il-Kartell** (☎ 2155 1965; Triq il-Port; mains €12) is an upmarket waterfront fish restaurant with lots of interesting dishes including braised rabbit in red wine and a superb *aljotta* (fish soup).

Marsalforn is a 4km walk from Victoria, or catch bus 21.

XAGĦRA

Xagħra conforms to the classic Mediterranean image of the tree-lined village square where old men sit and chat in the shade of oleanders. Close by are the megalithic temples of **Ġgantija** (☎ 2155 3194; access from Triq L-Imqades; adult/student €3.49/1.75; 🕐 9am-5pm), dating from 3600 BC. These temples are the oldest freestanding stone structures in the world, predating the pyramids of Egypt by more than 500 years. Their purpose is the subject of much debate; the best place to learn about them is at Valletta's National Museum of Archaeology (p776).

It's not far from here to one of Gozo's best beaches. **Ramla Bay** has a beautiful redsand strand perfect for sunbathing. Follow the signposts from town.

Xagħra Lodge (☎ 2156 2362; www.xaghralodge.com; Triq Dun Ġorġ Preċa; s/d incl breakfast €47/65; ❄ 🏊) is a friendly guest house with decent facilities, including air-con, bathroom, balcony and cable TV in all rooms, plus a swimming pool and adjacent bar, and vegetarian-friendly Chinese restaurant.

Buses 64 and 65 run between Victoria and Xagħra.

COMINO

Tiny Comino, once reportedly the hideout of pirates, now hosts boatloads of invaders of the sun-seeking variety. The island's biggest attraction is the photogenic **Blue Lagoon**, a sheltered cove with a whitesand seabed and clear turquoise waters. You can take a boat trip here from many resort areas in Malta and Gozo; hordes of day-trippers will sadly put paid to any desert-island fantasies.

Comino Hotel (☎ 2152 9821; www.cominohotel.com; half-board per person €30-70; 🕐 Apr-Oct; ❄ 💻 🏊) provides the only accommodation on the island, but its prices don't exactly cater for a shoestring budget. The hotel runs a ferry service from Ċirkewwa in Malta and Mġarr in Gozo (€8.15 return). Independent water taxis also operate regularly to the island from these two ports; from Mġarr it's usually €7 return; from Ċirkewwa it's €10 return.

MALTA DIRECTORY

ACCOMMODATION

Accommodation is plentiful and the **Malta Tourism Authority** (www.visitmalta.com) can provide listings. There is one camping ground, but its shadeless grounds and remote location render it unappealing. There is a handful of hostels and an array of guesthouses that offer great value. Rates are significantly reduced during off-peak periods. The high season is generally June to September, as well as the Christmas–New Year period.

ACTIVITIES

The website of the **Malta Tourism Authority** (www.visitmalta.com) showcases activities available in Malta. Click the 'What to See & Do' pages.

Diving

Water babies are well catered for. Diving conditions are excellent: visibility often exceeds 30m and there's a variety of marine life. The Mediterranean's warm temperatures mean that diving is possible year-round. There are more than 40 diving schools; the majority are members of the **Professional Diving Schools Association** (PDSA; www

.pdsa.org.mt). See also www.visitmalta.com/en/diving for details of dive sites, regulations and operators.

Swimming

The best sandy beaches on Malta are Ġnejna Bay, Għajn Tuffieħa Bay and Golden Bay, all in Malta's northwest (bus 47 from Valletta or bus 652 from Sliema); and Mellieħa Bay in the north (bus 44 or 45 from Valletta or bus 645 from Sliema/St Julian's). The best sandy beaches on Gozo are Ramla Bay (bus 42) and Xlendi Bay (bus 87).

There are some excellent rocky swimming spots on Comino (the Blue Lagoon) and in Malta's south (Għar Lapsi). Gozo has some good rocky sites too, including Dwejra in the west.

BUSINESS HOURS

Standard opening hours:

Banks 8.30am-12.30pm Mon-Fri & 8.30-11.30am Sat
Eating Noon-3pm & 7-11pm
Government museums 9am-5pm; closed major public holidays
Shopping 9am-1pm & 4-7pm Mon-Sat; closed Sun and public holidays. Some shops stay open all day in summer, especially in tourist areas.

CUSTOMS

If you're entering Malta from outside the EU, the duty-free allowance per person is 1L of spirits, 1L of wine and 200 cigarettes.

EMBASSIES & CONSULATES

Full lists of Maltese embassies abroad and foreign embassies in Malta can be found at www.foreign.gov.mt.

Countries with representation in Malta:

Australia (☎ 2133 8201; Villa Fiorentina, Rampa Ta'Xbiex, Ta'Xbiex)
Canada (☎ 2552 3233; 103 Triq l-Arċisqof, Valletta)
UK (☎ 2323 0000; www.ukinmalta.fco.gov.uk; Whitehall Mansions, Xatt Ta'Xbiex, Ta'Xbiex)
USA (☎ 2561 4000; http://valletta.usembassy.gov; 3rd fl, Development House, Triq Sant'Anna, Floriana)

FESTIVALS & EVENTS

Each village has an anual *festa* (feast day) honouring its patron saint, and you can't avoid getting caught up in the celebrations, even if you wanted to. The streets are illuminated and the festivities culminate in a huge procession, with fireworks, marching brass bands and a life-size statue of the patron saint. *Festa* season runs from May to September – but these aren't the only excuses to throw a party in Malta. The website www.maltafestivals.com lists what's on, where and when (including links to *festa* dates and locations).

HOLIDAYS

New Year's Day 1 January
St Paul's Shipwreck 10 February
St Joseph's Day 19 March
Freedom Day 31 March
Good Friday March/April
Labour Day 1 May
Commemoration of 1919 Independence Riots 7 June
Feast of Sts Peter and Paul (L-Imnarja Festival) 29 June
Feast of the Assumption 15 August
Victory Day 8 September
Independence Day 21 September
Feast of the Immaculate Conception 8 December
Republic Day 13 December
Christmas Day 25 December

INTERNET RESOURCES

About Malta (www.aboutmalta.com) Directory of Malta sites.
Gozo (www.gozo.com) Gozo-specific travel information.
Malta Tourism Authority (www.visitmalta.com) Huge official site.

MONEY

Malta adopted the euro in January 2008. To avoid stealth price hikes, the cost of all goods is legally required to be listed in the old Maltese Lira as well as euros, hence the often bizarre prices for museum tickets, public transport and other state-run services. Banks usually offer better currency exchange rates than hotels. There is a 24-hour exchange bureau and ATMs at the airport and at Valletta's Pinto Wharf. ATMs can be found in most towns.

It's a good idea to round up a taxi fare or restaurant bill to leave a small tip. Shops have fixed prices; hotels and car-hire agencies offer reduced rates in the low and shoulder seasons (October to May).

TELEPHONE

The international direct dialling code is ☎ 00. To call Malta from abroad, dial the international access code, ☎ 356 (Malta's country code) and the eight-digit number (there are no area codes). Local mobile numbers begin with 79 or 99. For overseas enquiries, call ☎ 1152.

Card-operated public telephones are widely available; buy phonecards at kiosks, post offices and souvenir shops.

VISAS

Visas are not needed for visits of up to three months by nationals of most Commonwealth countries (excluding South Africa, India and Pakistan), most European countries, the USA and Japan. Full details (and visa application forms) are on the website of Malta's **Ministry of Foreign Affairs** (www.foreign.gov.mt).

Moldova

HIGHLIGHTS

- **Chişinău** Stroll green backstreets and parks, enjoy the surprisingly fine eating options, then sample its religion-changing nightlife (p788)
- **Orheiul Vechi** Detox at the country's most visually stimulating sight: a sweeping valley with a fantastic cave monastery, burrowed by 13th-century monks (p793)
- **Around Chişinău** Designate a driver for tours of these legendary wine cellars, arguably the best-value wine tours on Earth (p792)
- **Transdniestr** Go *way* off the beaten path in this self-styled 'republic', a surreal, living homage to the Soviet Union (p793)

FAST FACTS

- **Area** 33,843 sq km
- **Budget** €30-40 (330-450 lei) per day
- **Capital** Chişinău
- **Country code** ☎ 373
- **Famous for** wine, folk art, breakaway regions
- **Languages** Moldovan, Russian; also Ukrainian in Transdniestr
- **Money** Moldovan lei; A$1 = 8.42 lei; C$1 = 9.56 lei; €1 = 15.14 lei; ¥100 = 11.89 lei; NZ$1 = 6.60 lei; UK£1 = 17.08 lei; US$1 = 11.27 lei
- **Population** 4.3 million
- **Phrases** *bună* (hello), *mulţumesc/merci* (thank you), *cum vă numiţi?* (what's your name?)

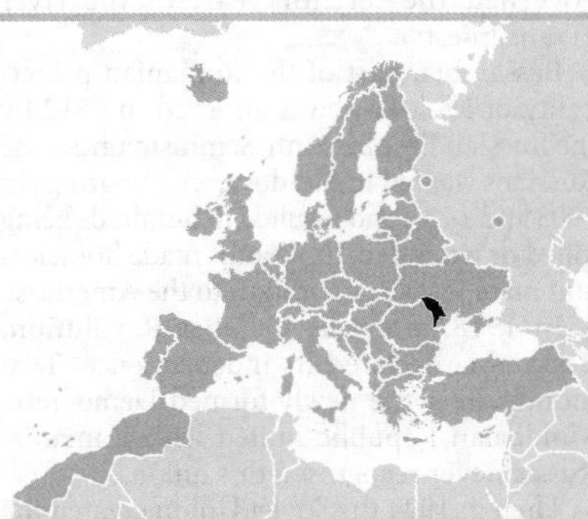

- **Visas** required for Australian and New Zealand passport holders; see p796 for details

TRAVEL HINTS

Enter Moldova via Romania, from where connections are frequent and easy, and then either return to Romania or continue eastward.

ROAMING MOLDOVA

Party in Chişinău, go to Orheiul Vechi, splurge for a big-name vineyard tour, then head to Transdniestr.

Moldo-who? Vaguely known in Europe, and all but anonymous to the rest of the world, travel blogs about Moldova are more often written by melancholy Peace Corps volunteers than tipsy revellers enjoying what is arguably the best wine drinking (ad)venture on the planet. More sober tourist attractions are few but outstanding, like the dramatic and beautiful setting of the Orheiul Vechi cave monastery or the breakaway republic of Transdniestr, still chugging along as one of Europe's top (and most notorious) idiosyncratic wonders. Chişinău's unexpectedly superb dining and clubbing options have been known to extend a few visits as well.

A veritable melee of cultural, political and economic turmoil ensued after the country's 1991 independence – eye-popping even by post-Soviet standards. As the former USSR collapsed, the Soviet-bent Transdniestr area declared independence. A bloody civil war ensued, leaving hundreds dead. Today, the cat-and-mouse politics and alleged transgressions of Transdniestr continue to aggravate Chişinău and unsettle the EU.

Though news briefs about Moldova's corruption, organised crime, arms dealing and human trafficking have subsided, alleged vote rigging in the April 2009 elections sparked anticommunist protests and violence, making the country's EU membership aspirations seem ever more remote.

HISTORY

Moldova today straddles two historic regions divided by the Nistru River. Historic Romanian Bessarabia incorporated the region west of the Nistru, while tsarist Russia governed the territory east of the river (Transdniestr).

Bessarabia, part of the Romanian principality of Moldavia, was annexed in 1812 by the Russian Empire. Anti-Semitism under the Russians was felt in Moldova, with pogroms in 1903 and 1905, and resulted in hundreds being killed or wounded, thousands made homeless and mass Jewish emigration to the Americas.

In 1918, after the October Revolution, Bessarabia declared its independence. Two months later the newly formed Democratic Moldavian Republic united with Romania. Russia never recognised this union.

Then in 1924 the Soviet Union created the Moldavian Autonomous Oblast on the eastern banks of the Nistru River, and incorporated Transdniestr into the Ukrainian Soviet Socialist Republic (SSR). A few months later the Soviet government renamed the oblast the Moldavian Autonomous Soviet Socialist Republic (Moldavian ASSR). During 1929 the capital was moved to Tiraspol from Balta (in present-day Ukraine).

In June 1940 the Molotov-Ribbentrop Pact meant Soviet troops occupied Romanian Bessarabia and joined it with the southern part, naming it the Moldavian Soviet Socialist Republic.

During 1941 allied Romanian and German troops attacked the Soviet Union. Bessarabia and Transdniestr fell into Romanian hands. Consequently, thousands of Bessarabian Jews were sent to labour camps and then deported to Auschwitz.

In August 1944 the Soviet army reoccupied Transdniestr and Bessarabia. In July 1949, 25,000 ethnic Moldovans (Romanians) were deported to Siberia, followed by another quarter of a million from 1950 to 1952.

It wasn't until February 1990 that the first democratic elections to the Supreme Soviet (parliament) were won by the Popular Front. In April 1990 the Moldovan national flag was reinstated – except in Transdniestr.

Moldova declared its full independence in August 1991. Today Vladimir Voronin is president of the republic, and also the president of the parliamentary Communist Party.

Widely regarded as the poorest nation in Europe and one of the most corrupt countries in the world, Moldova is endeavouring to shake these stigmas. In late 2005 the country signed agreements committing itself to combat corruption and human trafficking.

Romania's 2007 entrance into the EU made Moldova its eastern frontier. Moldovans now need difficult-to-get visas to enter Romania, causing newfound feelings of heightened isolation and dwindling opportunities.

The Russian–Georgian conflict of 2008 was deeply felt in Moldova due to its similar predicament with Russian-occupied Transdniestr.

THE CULTURE

Moldovans make up 78.2% of the total population, Ukrainians constitute 8.4%, Russians 5.8%, Gagauz 4.4%, Bulgarians 1.9%, 'other' 1.5%, and other nationalities such as Belarusians, Poles and Roma compose 1.3%.

In Transdniestr, Ukrainians and Russians make up 58% of the region's population; Moldovans make up 34%. It's one of the least urbanised countries in Europe.

Transdniestr and Gagauzia notwithstanding, much of Moldova's culture is Romanian by origin.

ARTS

There's a wealth of traditional folk art in Moldova; carpet making, pottery, weaving and carving predominate. The country also has prolific modern composers, painters and sculptors.

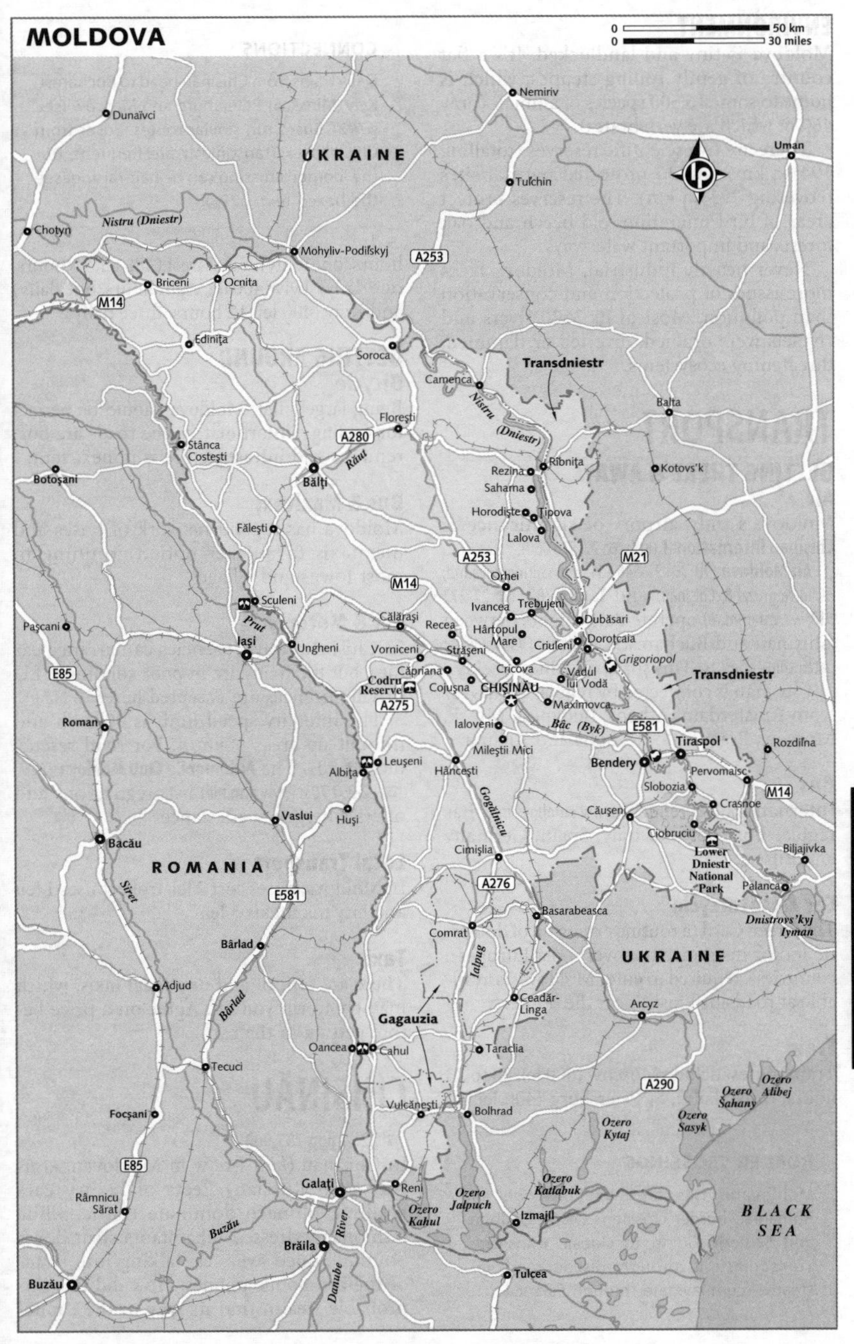
MOLDOVA
0 50 km
0 30 miles
UKRAINE
Nemiriv
Dunaïvci
Uman
Tuľchin
Nistru (Dniestr)
Chotyn
Mohyliv-Podiľskyj
A253
Briceni
Ocnita
M14
Edinița
Soroca
Transdniestr
Camenca
Nistru
(Dniestr)
Balta
Florești
A280
Stânca
Costești
Răut
Rîbnița
Kotovs'k
Botoșani
Bălți
Rezina
Saharna
Horodiște
Ţipova
Fălești
Lalova
A253
M21
Orhei
M14
Sculeni
Ivancea
Trebujeni
Prut
Pașcani
Călărași
Recea
Hârtopul
Mare
Dubăsari
Iași
Ungheni
Vorniceni
Strășeni
Criuleni
Dorotcaia
Grigoriopol
E85
Căpriana
Cricova
Vadul
lui Vodă
Transdniestr
Codru
Reserve
Cojușna
CHIȘINĂU
A275
Maximovca
Roman
Ialoveni
Bâc (Byk)
E581
Tiraspol
Rozdiľna
Mileștii Mici
Bendery
Albița
Leușeni
Hâncești
Pervomaisc
Slobozia
M14
Gogâlnicu
Crasnoe
Vaslui
Huși
Căușeni
Bacău
Ciobruciu
Lower
Dniestr
National
Park
Cimișlia
Biljajivka
ROMANIA
Siret
A276
Palanca
E581
Basarabeasca
Dnistrovs'kyj
Iyman
Comrat
Bârlad
Ialpug
UKRAINE
Adjud
Gagauzia
Ceadâr-
Linga
Arcyz
Bârlad
Oancea
Cahul
Taraclia
Tecuci
A290
Ozero
Alibej
Ozero
Šahany
Vulcănești
Bolhrad
Focșani
Ozero
Kytaj
Ozero
Sasyk
E85
Ozero
Katlabuk
Galați
Reni
Râmnicu
Sărat
Ozero
Kahul
Ozero
Jalpuch
Izmajil
BLACK
SEA
River
Buzău
Brăila
Danube
Tulcea
Buzău
MOLDOVA

ENVIRONMENT

Moldova is tiny and landlocked. It's a flat country of gently rolling steppes, which is home to some 16,500 species of animals (only 460 of which are vertebrates).

There are five scientific reserves (totalling 194 sq km) and 30 protected natural sites (covering 223 sq km). The reserves protect areas of bird migration, old beech and oak forests and important waterways.

Never heavily industrial, Moldova faces more issues of protection and conservation than pollution. Most of its 3600 rivers and rivulets were drained, diverted or dammed, threatening ecosystems.

TRANSPORT

GETTING THERE & AWAY

Air

Moldova's only airport of significance is **Chişinău International** (KIV; ☎ 22-526 060).

Air Moldova (9U; ☎ 22-546 464; www.airmoldova.md; B-dul Negruzzi 8, Chişinău) and **Tarom** (RO; ☎ 22-272 618; www.tarom.ro) operate daily flights between Chişinău and Bucharest. **Carpatair** (V3; www.carpatair.com) flies to Timişoara six times weekly.

Chişinău is connected by regular flights to/from Amsterdam, Athens, Budapest, Minsk, Moscow, Prague, Rome, Sofia and Vienna.

Bus

International **Eurolines** (www.eurolines.md) has regular bus routes to Italy, Spain, Germany and Russia.

Car & Motorcycle

The Green Card (a routine extension of domestic motor insurance to cover most European countries), required to enter Moldova, is available at roadside kiosks near the borders.

Train

Train routes include Moscow (600 lei, 28 to 33 hours, three daily), St Petersburg (400 lei, 40 hours, one daily), Bucharest (488 lei, 14 hours, one daily), Lviv (400 lei, eight hours, one daily) and Kyiv (400 lei, 12 hours, three daily).

> **BORDER CROSSINGS**
>
> Moldovan visas are available *only* at Romanian border crossings Oancea, Albiţa and Sculeni. Going to Odesa, transiting Transdniestr is strongly discouraged; instead circumnavigate through Palanca.

> **CONNECTIONS**
>
> Daily trains from Chişinău head to Bucharest, Kyiv, Minsk, St Petersburg and Moscow (see p792). Buses run similar routes. Buses from Chişinău to Transdniestr are frequent, but the 'border' crossing can be hair-raising (see the boxed text, p795).

GETTING AROUND

Bicycle

Being largely flat, Moldova should be perfect for cycling. Unfortunately, the roads are horrendous and infrastructure is nonexistent.

Bus & Maxitaxi

Moldova has a good network of buses and maxitaxis (a quicker option) running to most towns and villages.

Car & Motorcycle

In Chişinău, travel agencies can arrange car hire, but the roads are in poor condition. EU driving licences are accepted here.

The intercity speed limit is 90km/h and in built-up areas 60km/h. For road rescue, dial ☎ 901. The **Automobile Club Moldova** (ACM; ☎ 22-292 703; www.acm.md) lists regulations and offers emergency assistance.

Local Transport

In Moldova, buses cost 2 lei, trolleybuses 1 leu and city maxitaxis 3 lei.

Taxi

There are official and unofficial taxis, which may try to rip you off. Agree on a price before getting in the car.

CHIŞINĂU

☎ 22 / pop 785,000

In Chişinău (*kish*-i-now in Moldovan, *kish*-i-nyov in Russian) fleets of luxury cars rivalling Monaco dominate traffic, while fashionably dressed inhabitants strut down boutique-lined avenues, talking into state-of-the-art mobile phones. How did this improbable wealth find its way to the capital

> **READING UP**
>
> *Playing the Moldovans at Tennis* is Tony Hawks' hilarious account of visiting a much bleaker Moldova in the mid-'90s while satisfying a drunken bet to defeat the entire Moldovan football team at tennis. Moldova took a mild PR hit in *The Geography of Bliss*, by Eric Weiner, who recounts his visit to the alleged 'least happy nation on the planet'. *The Moldovans: Romania, Russia and the Politics of Culture* by Charles King is a more recent, textbook snapshot of this 'intriguing East Europe borderland'.

of Europe's poorest country? Answer: you don't wanna know and we ain't asking.

Sizable incoming cash flow from emigrants working abroad accounts for some of this dubious affluence, but the contrast between the merely well off and the truly well connected is eye-popping. While this above-the-law dodginess alarms visitors, citizens of this vibrant city have long since dismissed these oddities in favour of what really counts: having a good time.

First chronicled in 1420, Chişinău became a hotbed of anti-Semitism in the early 20th century (see p786). Later Chişinău was the headquarters of the USSR's southwestern military operations during Soviet rule. Between 1944 and 1990 the city was called Kishinev, its Russian name.

In 2007 Chişinău elected 28-year-old Liberal Party vice-president Dorin Chirtoacă as their mayor, a small victory for the anti-communist coalition.

ORIENTATION

Chişinău's layout is a typically Soviet grid system of straight streets. The main street, B-dul Ştefan cel Mare, crosses the city from southeast to northwest.

INFORMATION

Internet Access

Internet (Hotel Cosmos, Piaţa Negruzzi 2; per hr 7 lei; 24hr)

Medical Services

Contact the US embassy (p795) for a list of English-speaking doctors. A list of specialists is also available at http://moldova.usembassy.gov/medical-information.html.

Felicia (☎ 223 725; B-dul Ştefan cel Mare 62; 24hr) Well-stocked pharmacy.

Municipal Clinical Emergency Hospital (☎ 903; www.ournet.md/~scmu; Str Toma Ciorba 1; 24hr) Provides a variety of emergency services.

Money

There are ATMs all over the city centre, in all the hotels and in shopping centres. Currency exchanges are concentrated around the bus and train stations and along B-dul Ştefan cel Mare.

Eximbank (☎ 272 583; B-dul Ştefan cel Mare 6; 9am-5pm Mon-Fri) Can give cash advances in foreign currency.

Tourist Information

There's no tourist centre in Moldova but plenty of agencies provide information, including **Soleil Tours** (☎ 271 312; B-dul Negruzzi 5). Check out **Radu Sargu** (☎ 0691-389 53; www.moldova-travel.com) for apartment rentals, local information and assistance.

SIGHTS

City Centre

A good place to begin is smack in the city centre, where Chişinău's best-known parks diagonally oppose each other, forming two diamonds at the city's core. The highlights here are the **Holy Gates** (1841), more commonly known as Chişinău's Arc de Triomphe. To its east sprawls **Parcul Catedralei** (Cathedral Park), dominated by the city's main **Orthodox Cathedral** (1836).

Government House, where cabinet meets, is the gargantuan building opposite the Holy Gates. The parliament convenes in **Parliament House** (B-dul Ştefan cel Mare 123), further north. Opposite this is the **Presidential Palace**.

Grădina Publică Ştefan cel Mare şi Sfînt (Ştefan cel Mare Park) is the city's main strolling, cruising area. The park entrance is guarded by a **statue** (1928) of Ştefan, the greatest symbol of Moldova's brave past.

Museums

The **National Archaeology and History Museum** (☎ 240 426; Str 31 August 1989 121A; admission/photo/video

> **EMERGENCY NUMBERS**
>
> - Ambulance ☎ 903
> - Fire ☎ 901
> - Police ☎ 902

MOLDOVA

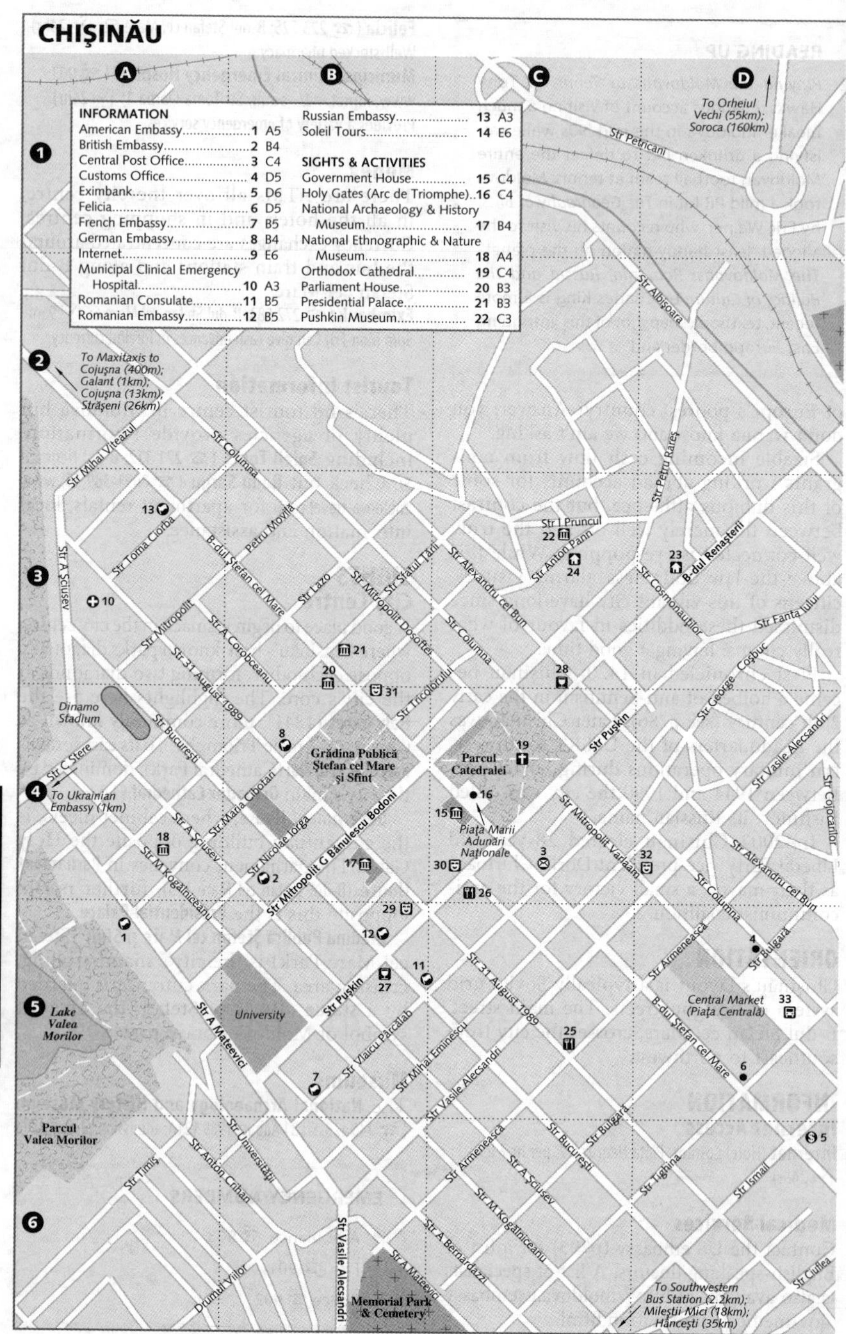
CHIŞINĂU
INFORMATION
American Embassy 1 A5
British Embassy 2 B4
Central Post Office 3 C4
Customs Office 4 D5
Eximbank 5 D6
Felicia 6 D5
French Embassy 7 B5
German Embassy 8 B4
Internet 9 E6
Municipal Clinical Emergency Hospital 10 A3
Romanian Consulate 11 B5
Romanian Embassy 12 B5
Russian Embassy 13 A3
Soleil Tours 14 E6
SIGHTS & ACTIVITIES
Government House 15 C4
Holy Gates (Arc de Triomphe) 16 C4
National Archaeology & History Museum 17 B4
National Ethnographic & Nature Museum 18 A4
Orthodox Cathedral 19 C4
Parliament House 20 B3
Presidential Palace 21 B3
Pushkin Museum 22 C3
To Orheiul Vechi (55km); Soroca (160km)
To Maxitaxis to Cojuşna (400m); Galant (1km); Cojuşna (13km); Străşeni (26km)
To Ukrainian Embassy (1km)
To Southwestern Bus Station (2.2km); Mileştii Mici (18km); Hânceşti (35km)
Str Petricani
Str Albişoara
Str Petru Rareş
Str I Pruncul
Str Anton Pann
B-dul Renaşterii
Str Cosmonauţilor
Str Fanta Iului
Str George Coşbuc
Str Vasile Alecsandri
Str Cojocarilor
Str Mihai Viteazul
Str Columna
Petru Movilă
Str Toma Ciorba
B-dul Ştefan cel Mare
Str A Şciusev
Str Lazo
Str Mitropolit Dosoftei
Str Statul Ţării
Str Alexandru cel Bun
Str Mitropolit
Str A Corobceanu
Str 31 August 1989
Str Tricolorului
Str Puşkin
Dinamo Stadium
Str C Stere
Str Bucureşti
Grădina Publică Ştefan cel Mare şi Sfînt
Parcul Catedralei
Piaţa Marii Adunări Naţionale
Str Mitropolit Varlaam
Str Maria Cibotari
Str Nicolae Iorga
Str Mitropolit G Bănulescu Bodoni
Str M Kogălniceanu
Str Armenească
Str Bulgară
Central Market (Piaţa Centrală)
Lake Valea Morilor
University
Str A Mateevici
Str Vlaicu Pârcălab
Str Mihai Eminescu
Str Vasile Alecsandri
Parcul Valea Morilor
Str Timiş
Str Anton Crihan
Str Universităţii
Str Tighina
Str Ismail
Str A Bernardazzi
Drumul Viilor
Memorial Park & Cemetery
Str Ciuflea
MOLDOVA

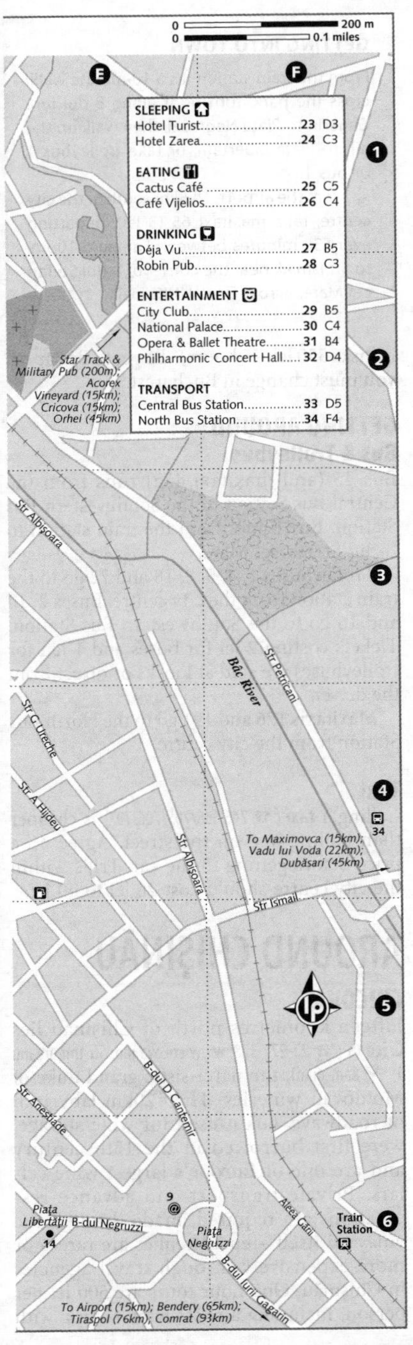

15/15/40 lei; 9am-6pm Tue-Sat) is the granddaddy of Chişinău's museums. There are archaeological artefacts from Orheiul Vechi, including Golden Horde coins, Soviet-era weaponry and a huge WWII diorama.

The highlight of the wonderful **National Ethnographic & Nature Museum** (244 002; Str M Kogălniceanu 82; admission 15 lei; 10am-6pm Tue-Sun) is a life-size reconstruction of a mammal skeleton, discovered in the Rezine region in 1966. Allow an hour to see the museum's pop art, taxidermied animals, and exhibits covering geology, botany and zoology. English-language tours – arranged in advance – cost 100 lei.

The **Pushkin Museum** (292 685; Str Anton Pann 19; admission 15 lei; 10am-4pm Tue-Sun) is housed in a cottage where Russian poet Alexandr Pushkin (1799–1837) spent an exiled three years between 1820 and 1823. Here he wrote *The Prisoner of the Caucasus* as well as a few other classics. English-language tours are 100 lei.

SLEEPING

Check out the **Adresa** (www.adresa.md) and **Marisha** (www.marisha.net) websites for cheap homestays and apartments.

Hotel Zarea (227 625; Str Anton Pann 4; s/d with shared bathroom 270/390 lei, d 'deluxe' 560-700 lei) This drab high-rise has dour, smoky rooms that are appropriately priced. Breakfast isn't included.

Hotel Turist (220 637; B-dul Renaşterii 13; s 500-700 lei, d 500 lei) For a kitsch blast of the Soviet past, try this friendly place: it overlooks a giant Soviet memorial to communist youth and sports a socialist mural on its facade. The low-end singles are in tatty condition.

EATING

For the cheapest eats, there are some kiosks and small cafes around the bus station/central market and the university.

Café Vijelios (Str Puşkin 22; mains 10-22 lei; 11am-11pm) This cafeteria serves surprisingly succulent food priced for the impoverished university crowd.

our pick Cactus Café (502 394; www.cactus.md; Str Armenească 41; mains 95-175 lei; 9am-11pm;) The Wild-West-meets-urban-bohemian interior decor here will stun wine-fogged patrons into thinking they've been zapped to Brooklyn during the night. Extravagant breakfasts, vegetarian meals and daring plates like 'turkey jam rolls wrapped in aubergines' don't help to dull the sensation.

DRINKING & CLUBBING

Chişinău parties in earnest every weekend, but in some of the larger clubs be prepared for body searches, metal detectors and tough-guy posturing from goonish doormen.

Déjà Vu (☎ 227 693; Str Bucureşti 67; ⏲ 11am-2am) This cocktail bar has a tantalising menu of drinks on offer.

Robin Pub (Str Alexandru cel Bun 83; ⏲ 11am-midnight) An ideal place to forget about the world in an unpretentious pub atmosphere.

City Club (Str 31 August 1989, 121; ⏲ 10pm-6am) In the alley next to the Licurici Puppet Theatre, this 2nd-floor club vies for the title of 'Hippest Place in Town'.

Galant (☎ 717 407; Calle Ieşilor 49; ⏲ 10pm-4am) In the Buiucani neighbourhood, Galant is for fans of dance music and charitable bartenders. The petit dance floor gets a little tight.

ENTERTAINMENT

Opera & Ballet Theatre (☎ 244 163; B-dul Ştefan cel Mare 152; ⏲ box office 10am-2pm & 5-7pm) Home to the esteemed national opera and ballet.

Philharmonic Concert Hall (☎ 224 505; Str Mitropolit Varlaam 78) Moldova's National Philharmonic is based here.

National Palace (Palatul Naţional; ☎ 213 544; Str Puşkin 21; ⏲ box office 11am-5pm) Various cabarets, musicals and local theatre group productions are performed here.

GETTING THERE & AWAY

Chişinău has three bus stations. Most domestic and international buses depart from the **North Bus Station** (Autogară Nord; ☎ 439 489), except Transdniestr-bound lines (which depart from the Central Bus Station). Domestic and international maxitaxis operate from the **Central Bus Station** (Autogara Centrală; ☎ 542 185; Str Mitropolit Varlaam). Maxitaxis go to Tiraspol (32 lei, 1½ hours) and Bendery (27 lei, 1½ hours) every 20 to 35 minutes from 6.30am to 6.30pm. Buses to/from southern destinations and Iaşi use the **Southwestern Bus Station** (Autogara Sud-vest; ☎ 723 983; cnr Şoseaua Hânceşti & Str Spicului), 2km from the city centre.

International routes departing from Chişinău's sparkling new **train station** (☎ 252 737; Aleea Gării) include three daily trains to Moscow (600 lei, 28 to 33 hours), three daily trains to Kyiv (400 lei, 12 hours), one each to St Petersburg (400 lei, 40 hours) and Bucharest (488 lei, 14 hours), and three to Lviv (400 lei, eight hours), and three weekly services to Minsk (550 lei, 25 hours). To get to Budapest, you must change in Bucharest.

> **GETTING INTO TOWN**
>
> From the train station it's a 10-minute walk: cross the park, turn right along B-dul Iurii Gagarin to Piaţa Negruzzi, then walk up the hill to Piaţa Libertăţii; or take trolleybus 1 or bus 1.
>
> From the airport, 14.5km south of the city centre, take maxitaxi 65 (3 lei), departing every 30 minutes between 5am and 10pm, to Str Ismail, near the corner of B-dul Ştefan cel Mare, across from UNIC mall.

GETTING AROUND

Bus & Trolleybus

Bus 45 (and maxitaxi 45a) runs from the Central Bus Station to the Southwestern Bus Station. Bus 1 goes from the train station to B-dul Ştefan cel Mare.

Trolleybuses 1, 4, 5, 8, 18 and 22 go to the train station from the city centre. Buses 2, 10 and 16 go to the Southwestern Bus Station. Tickets costing 2 lei for buses and 1 leu for trolleybuses are sold at kiosks or direct from the driver.

Maxitaxis 176 and 191 go to the North Bus Station from the city centre.

Taxi

Calling a **taxi** (☎ 746 565/705/706/707) is cheaper than hailing one on the street. Agree on a price before getting in the car. Trips within the city centre should cost 20 lei to 40 lei.

AROUND CHIŞINĂU

CRICOVA

Fifteen kilometres north of Chişinău lies **Cricova** (☎ 22-277 378; www.cricova.md; Str Ungureanu 1; ⏲ 8am-4pm), the narcissistic grand duke of Moldovan wineries. The 120km labyrinth of roadways, 60km used for wine storage, were first burrowed in the 15th century and are one of Europe's largest wine cellars. Private transport and advance reservations are required, made through the vineyard itself – email replies are rare – or more expensively through travel agencies in Chişinău. One-hour tours are 500 lei per person, including a short wine tasting with *placinte* (pastries) and gift bottles of wine and champagne.

MILEŞTII MICI

Arguably, **Mileştii Mici** (☎ 382 333; www.milestii-mici.md; 9am-5pm Mon-Fri), 18km south of Chişinău, has a superior-value tour. Two-hour tours, with tasting and lunch, are 500 lei per person. Also housed in a limestone mine, these are *the* largest cellars in Europe (over 200km of tunnels). They were recognised by Guinness in 2005 for having the largest wine collection in the world, 1.5 million bottles. The collection has now surpassed the 2-million-bottle mark.

COJUŞNA

In the village of Cojuşna, 12km northwest of Chişinău, **Cojuşna** (☎ 615 329; Str Lomtadze 4; 8am-6pm) is moribund in comparison with Cricova; however, the winery tours given here are down to earth and friendly.

ORHEIUL VECHI

The breathtaking **Orheiul Vechi Monastery Complex** (Complexul Muzeistic Orheiul Vechi; ☎ 235-34 242; adult/student 10/5 lei; 9am-6pm Tue-Sun), 10km southeast of Orhei and marked on maps as the village of Trebujeni, is arguably Moldova's nonwine tourist high point.

The **Cave Monastery** (Mănăstire în Peşteră), part of a series of precarious caves tunnelled into a dramatic limestone cliff, was dug by successive Orthodox monks beginning in the 13th century. Shorts are forbidden and women must cover their heads inside the monastery.

TRANSDNIESTR

pop 555,500

The self-declared republic of Transdniestr (Pridnestrovskaia Moldavskaia Respublica, or PMR in Russian), a narrow strip of land covering 3567 sq km on the eastern bank of the Nistru River is, according to its people, one of the world's last surviving bastions of communism.

Political jibba-jabba and historic ethnic boundaries aside, Moldova maintains that Transdniestr was illegally grabbed. With Russia's support, Transdniestr effectively won its 'independence' during a bloody civil war in the early 1990s. A tenuous, bitter truce has ensued ever since.

Travellers will be stunned by this idiosyncratic region that has developed its own currency, police force, army and borders, controlled by Transdniestran border guards. Transdniestrans boycott the Moldovan independence day and celebrate their own independence day on 2 September.

Although as recently as 2007 we were sternly informed that Western visitors are officially 'not welcome' in Transdniestr, its tourism website (www.visitpmr.com) paradoxically woos all comers, painting the area as 'Europe's hidden jewel' and giving a decidedly abridged version of the region's recent history and independence.

In truth, visits here can be quite pleasant, and the surreal atmosphere is admittedly unforgettable, though increasingly aggressive (and expensive) bribe shakedowns at the border leave many visitors too traumatised to notice.

INFORMATION

Money

The only legal tender is the Transdniestran ruble, though some taxi drivers, shopkeepers and market traders will accept payment in US dollars, Moldovan lei or Ukrainian hryvnia.

Post

Transdniestran stamps featuring General Suvorov can only be used for letters sent within Transdniestr and are not recognised anywhere else. For letters to Moldova, Romania and the West, you have to use Moldovan stamps (available here but less conveniently than in Moldova).

TIRASPOL

☎ 533 / pop 183,700

Tiraspol ('town on the Nistru' river in Greek), 70km east of Chişinău, is an open-air museum of Soviet-style communism and one of the most peculiar and distinctly memorable places in Europe. The city was founded in 1792 following Russian domination of the area.

The train and bus stations are next to each other at the end of ul Lenina.

Information

Central telephone office (cnr ul 25 Oktober & ul Kommunisticheskaya; 24hr) Through the far-left door, you can buy phonecards and use internet (per hour 3.50 rubles).

Gasprom Bank (ul 25 Oktober 76; 9am-8pm Mon-Sat) Changes money.

Internet (ul 25 October 76; per hr 4.5 rubles; 9am-11pm) Below Gasprom Bank.

Sights

At the western end of ul 25 Oktober stands a Soviet armoured tank, from which the Transdniestran flag flies. Behind is the Heroes' Cemetery with its **Tomb of the Unknown Soldier**, flanked by an eternal flame in memory of those who died on 3 March 1992 during the first outbreak of fighting.

The **Tiraspol National United Museum** (ul 25 Oktober 42; admission 4 rubles; 9am-5pm Sun-Fri) is the closest the city has to a local history museum, with an exhibit on poet Nikolai Dimitriovich Zelinskogo, who founded the first Soviet school of chemistry. Opposite is the **Presidential Palace**, from where Igor Smirnov rules his mini-empire.

The **House of Soviets** (Dom Sovetov), towering over the eastern end of ul 25 Oktober, has Lenin's angry-looking bust peering out from its prime location. Inside is a **memorial** to those who died in the 1992 conflict.

The **Kvint factory** (37 333; http://kvint.biz; ul Lenina 38) is one of Transdniestr's pride and joys. Since 1897 it's been making some of Moldova's finest brandies. There are no excursions, but you can buy its astonishingly inexpensive products here or at the **town centre store** (ul 25 Oktober 84; 24hr).

Sleeping & Eating

You must register at the **OVIR** (ul Kotovskogo No 2a; Mon-Fri) if you are staying more than 24 hours. Visit www.marisha.net to arrange a homestay.

Hotel Aist (73 776; per Naberezhnyi 3; d 240-300 rubles) Despite a derelict exterior, this is a decent hotel. More expensive rooms have hot water, private toilet and TV.

WORTH THE TRIP: BENDERY

Bendery is the greener, more aesthetically agreeable counterpart to Tiraspol. Despite civil-war bullet holes still decorating several buildings – Bendery was hardest hit by the 1992 military conflict with Moldova – the city centre is a breezy place. Trolleybus 19 and maxitaxis 19 and 20 cross the bridge over the Dniestr to Bendery.

SCAMS

Bucharest-style restaurant pricing scams are emerging. Never order anything, particularly wine, without confirming the price *in writing* (eg menu) to avoid surprises on the bill. If you've been victimised, keep all receipts and report it to the police.

Travellers are required to have their passports with them *at all times*. Cheeky police do random checks.

7 Fridays (92 210; ul 25 Oktober 112; mains 14-60 rubles; 11am-midnight) A popular cafe serving all manner of meat, salads and soups. Menus are Russian-only, but there are pictures to point at.

Getting There & Away

BUS

From Tiraspol there are five daily buses to Bălţi (71.60 rubles, six hours), 13 daily to Odesa (37.25 rubles, three hours), one daily to Kyiv (185 rubles, 14 hours) and one weekly to Berlin. Buses go to Chişinău nearly every half-hour from 5.50am to 8.50pm (26.70 rubles, 1½ hours), and maxitaxis run regularly from 6.30am to 6.10pm.

TRAIN

One daily train goes to Moscow, via Kyiv, leaving promptly at 2.06am (3rd/2nd class 700/1000 rubles, 26 hours). All other train services have been discontinued indefinitely.

MOLDOVA DIRECTORY

ACCOMMODATION

Chişinău has a good range of hotels, though many are criminally overpriced. Most towns have small hotels that have survived from communist days. Basic singles and doubles with a shared bathroom cost €25 to €35 per room, but outside the capital rooms will usually be €12 to €20. Unless noted otherwise, breakfast is included in the price.

Camping grounds *(popas turistic)* are practically nonexistent, but wild camping is possible unless explicitly prohibited.

BUSINESS HOURS

Banks (9am-3pm) Many banks close for an hour around noon.

Museums (9am-5pm Tue-Sun)
Post offices (8am-7pm Mon-Fri, to 4pm Sat)
Restaurants (to 11pm)
Shops (9am or 10am-6pm or 7pm) Some shops close on Sunday.

CUSTOMS

See **Welcome to Moldova!** (www.turism.md) for the latest changes in customs regulations.

You may have to prove that you have enough money to finance your stay. You're allowed to cross the border either way with 1L of alcohol, 2L of beer and up to 200 cigarettes. The **customs office** (22-569 460; Str Columna 65) is in Chişinău.

EMBASSIES & CONSULATES

The following countries have embassies or consulates in Chişinău:

France (22-200 400; www.ambafrance.md; Str Vlaicu Pârcălab 6)
Germany (22-200 600; ambasada-germana@riscom.md; Str Maria Cibotari 35)
Romania Consulate (22-237 622; Str Vlaicu Pârcălab 39); Embassy (22-228 126; ambrom@moldnet.md; Str Bucureşti 66/1)
Russia (22-234 942; www.moldova.mid.ru; B-dul Ştefan cel Mare 153)
UK (22-251 818; www.britishembassy.md; Str Nicolae Iorga 18)
Ukraine (22-582 151; www.mfa.gov.ua, in Ukrainian; Str V Lupu 17)
US (22-408 300; http://moldova.usembassy.gov; Str A Mateevici 103)

BORDERS SANS BOREDOM

We receive continuous reader feedback about the Transdniestran border, where organised intimidation is used to separate travellers from their money. Accusations of incomplete paperwork or invented transgressions lead to ludicrous 'fines' starting as high as €200.

It's recommended you travel in private transport with Moldovan plates. Also, you're advised to avoid the hectic, bribe-factory Bendery border crossing. The virtually deserted crossing at Grigoriopol is a comparative breeze, however you *cannot* transit Transdniestr to Ukraine using this crossing.

Entry permits are still 'officially' 12 lei, available *at the border* no matter what the guys on duty playfully tell you. For stays of less than 10 hours, you don't need to pay this fee.

FESTIVALS & EVENTS

The major festival is the **Wine Festival** on the second Sunday in October. The government has instituted a visa-free regime for this period. Chişinău's **City Day** is 14 October.

HOLIDAYS

New Year's Day 1 January
Orthodox Christmas 7 January
International Women's Day 8 March
Orthodox Easter April/May
Victory (1945) Day 9 May
Independence Day 27 August
National Language Day 31 August

INTERNET RESOURCES

Get everyday Moldovan news and information at **Moldova Azi** (www.azi.md).

MONEY

We've quoted most prices in this chapter in Moldovan lei, to make on-the-ground price references easier. Moldovan lei come in denominations of 1, 5, 10, 20, 50, 100, 200 and 500. There are coins for 1, 5, 10, 25 and 50 bani (there are 100 bani in a leu).

The breakaway Transdniestran republic in Moldova has its own currency, which is unexchangeable anywhere else in the world (see also p793).

Outside Chişinău, ATMs are sparse. It's near impossible to use travellers cheques in shops or restaurants. While credit cards won't get you anywhere in rural areas, they are widely accepted in larger department stores, hotels and most restaurants in cities and towns.

Tipping is gaining momentum, though still not an automatic practice for locals. Generally, leaving 10% will be considered generous.

POST

It costs 5 lei to 7 lei to send a postcard or letter under 20g to Western Europe, Australia and the USA.

DHL (www.dhl.com) has offices in Chişinău, Bălţi and Tiraspol.

TELEPHONE

Moldtelecom sells phonecards for domestic calls, available at any telephone centre. International calls require a prepaid card, like Treitelecom, sold at any Moldpressa newspaper stand.

Mobile phone service in Moldova is provided by Moldcell and the ubiquitous **Orange** (www.orange.md).

VISAS

Citizens of EU member states, the USA, Canada and Japan no longer need visas. Everyone else, including Australian and New Zealand citizens, are still on the hook for visas and may require letters of invitation, acquired from an accredited travel agency, a company, organisation or individual. The price of a single-/double-entry tourist visa valid for one month is US$60/75. Single-/double-entry transit visas valid for 72 hours are US$30/60.

Visas can be acquired on arrival at Chişinău airport or, if arriving by bus or car from Romania, the three border points: Sculeni (north of Iaşi), Albiţa (main Bucharest–Chişinău border) and Oancea. Those requiring an invitation must present the original document (copies/faxes not accepted) at the border if buying a visa there.

See **Welcome to Moldova!** (www.turism.md) and follow the links to check for the latest changes in the visa regime.

Montenegro Црна Гора

HIGHLIGHTS

- **Bay of Kotor** Explore historic towns hemmed in between majestic limestone cliffs and inky waters (p800)
- **Sveti Stefan** Enjoy the iconic island views while lazing on the sands (p802)
- **Durmitor National Park** Raft through a deep canyon, hike remote trails, or tackle some of Europe's cheapest ski slopes (p804)

FAST FACTS

- **Area** 13,812 sq km (half the size of Belgium)
- **Budget** €30 to €50 per day
- **Capital** Podgorica
- **Country code** ☎ 382
- **Famous for** being really beautiful
- **Language** Montenegrin
- **Money** euro (€); A$1 = €0.55; C$1 = 0.60; ¥100 = €0.78; NZ$1 = €0.43; UK£1 = €1.12; US$1 = €0.74
- **Phrases** *zdravo* (hello), *doviđenja* (goodbye), *hvala* (thanks)
- **Population** 678,000

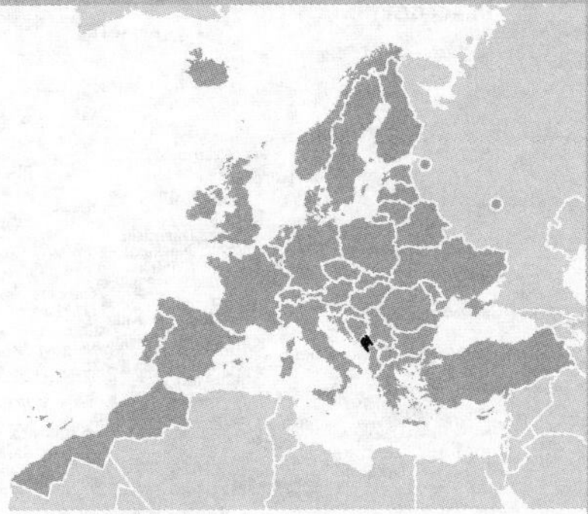

- **Visas** Australian, Canadian, New Zealand, US and all EU citizens do not require visas (p806)

TRAVEL HINTS

Private rooms are almost always the cheapest sleeping option.

ROAMING MONTENEGRO

Spend most of you time on the coast, then head through Cetinje and on to Durmitor National Park.

Imagine a place with sapphire beaches as spectacular as Croatia's, rugged peaks as dramatic as Switzerland's, canyons nearly as deep as Colorado's, *palazzi* as elegant as Venice's and towns as old as Greece's, and then wrap it up in a Mediterranean climate and squish it into an area two-thirds of the size of Wales. Then you start to get a picture of Montenegro.

Given its natural assets, tourism is vitally important to Montenegro's future. In that respect it's done spectacularly well in filling its tiny coast with Eastern European sunseekers for two months of each year, while serving up the rest of the country as bite-sized day trips. The upshot for intrepid travellers is that you can easily sidestep the hordes by heading to the rugged mountains. This is, after all, a country where wolves and bears still lurk in forgotten corners.

Montenegro, Crna Gora, Black Mountain: the name itself conjures up romance and drama. There are plenty of both on offer as you explore this perfumed land, bathed in the scent of wild herbs, conifers and Mediterranean blossoms. Yes, it really is as magical as it sounds.

HISTORY

Montenegro's history is one of dogged independence, facing greater forces that have ultimately crashed in failure against its rocky fastness. For 500 years Montenegro retained its independence against the Ottoman Turkish tide that flooded southeast Europe. During this time a distinct identity was born, which distinguished its people from the other Serbian tribes. While the size of its territory waxed and waned, it was always centred on Lovćen, the mountain expanse that contains Cetinje within its foothills. It's from this 'black mountain' that the country takes its name: Crna Gora in the local tongue and Montenegro in Italian.

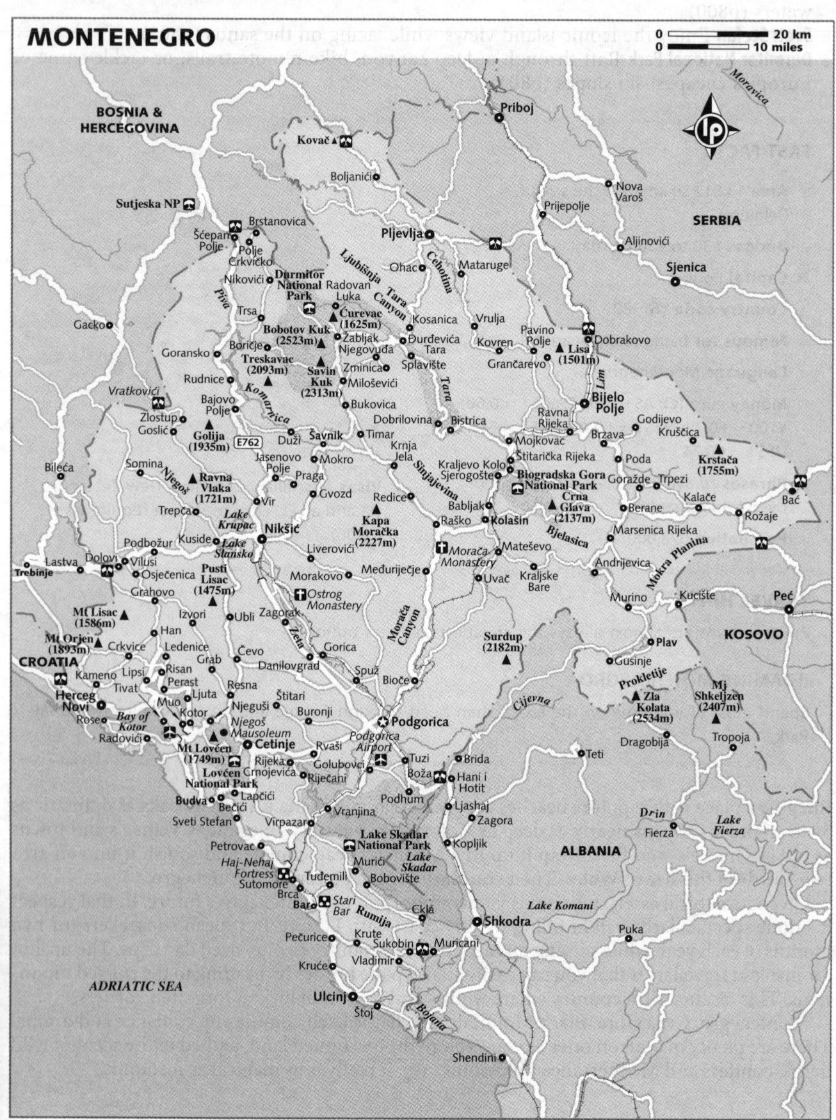

READING UP

- *Realm of the Black Mountain: A History of Montenegro* by Elizabeth Roberts (2007).
- *Montenegro: A Novel* by Starling Lawrence (1997) Turn-of-the-20th-century politics, bloodshed and romance.

Following emancipation from the Austrians, who invaded during WWI, Montenegro was incorporated into the first Yugoslavia under the Serbian king. As a reward for its support of the partisans during WWII, Socialist Federal Republic of Yuglosavia president Tito gave Montenegro republic status in the postwar Yugoslav federation. From then on Montenegro was a loyal member of all the Yugoslavian entities, culminating in the loose union of Serbia and Montenegro that came to an end with the proindependence vote in May 2006. Montenegro is now fully independent for the first time since 1916.

THE CULTURE

Montenegro's 2003 census revealed a population of 678,000, split into Montenegrins (43%), Serbs (32%), Bosniaks (8%), Albanians (5%) and others (12%). There are large Slavic Muslim and Albanian minorities, mostly in the east. The Bay of Kotor has strong historic links with Croatia's Dalmatian coast. Montenegrins are closely related to Serbs, with whom they share the same faith, Orthodox Christianity. Montenegrins are on average remarkably tall, making them ideal basketball players.

ENVIRONMENT

The country is characterised by a narrow coastal strip backed by a high alpine hinterland and an interior karst plain.

Deer, lynx, wolves and brown bears inhabit the mountains, while Lake Skadar is the biggest bird sanctuary in Europe and one of the Dalmatian pelican's last remaining habitats. There are four national parks (Durmitor, Lovćen, Biogradska Gora and Lake Skadar), and the Bay of Kotor and Durmitor are Unesco-recognised sites.

Montenegro has declared itself 'an ecological state' in its constitution, but still faces problems with pollution, rubbish dumping and safeguarding its water supply.

TRANSPORT

GETTING THERE & AWAY

Air

Many of the major European carriers service Montenegro's two international airports: Tivat and Podgorica. The budget airlines have yet to join them, although some fly into neighbouring Croatia; Dubrovnik's Čilipi airport is very close to the border. **Montenegro Airlines** (YM; ☎ 020-664 411; www.montenegroairlines.com), the national carrier, flies to many European cities.

See p1235 for more information.

Boat

Ferry services connect Montenegro with Italy.

Montenegro Lines (☎ 030-303 469; www.montenegrolines.net; ferry terminal, Bar) has boats from Bar to Bari (€60, 10 hours, at least three weekly) and Ancona (€72, 16 hours, twice weekly from July to early September).

Azzurra Line (☎ 39-80-592 8400; www.azzurraline.com) has weekly ferries between Bar and Bari (€48; ten hours) and Kotor and Bari (€55; nine hours) but only from June/July to September.

Note that cabins cost extra and that cars can be transported.

Bus

There's a well-developed bus network linking Montenegro with the rest of Europe. Podgorica is the main hub but buses stop at many coastal towns as well. From Herceg

BORDER CROSSINGS

Expect delays on the busy checkpoint leading to Dubrovnik, Croatia. Montenegro's longest land border is with Bosnia and Hercegovina (BiH). Two major checkpoints are at Dolovi and Šćepan Polje, with remote crossings at Vratkovići and in the Kovač Mountains.

For Serbia, the busiest crossing is north of Bijelo Polje, with others northeast of Rožaje and east of Pljevlja. There's only one crossing leading into Kosovo, between Rožaje and Peć. You can reach Albania from Ulcinj (Sukobin crossing) and Podgorica (Hani i Hotit).

CONNECTIONS

Many travellers make the most of the proximity of Dubrovnik's Čilipi airport to tie in Montenegro with a visit to Croatia. At the other end of the coast, Ulcinj is the perfect primer for exploring Albania. A train line and frequent bus connections make travelling through Serbia a breeze.

Novi, for example, there are buses to Dubrovnik (€8, taking two hours, departing twice daily), Sarajevo (€22, seven hours, four daily) and Belgrade (€30, 13 hours, nine daily). From Ulcinj there's a daily bus and two minibuses to Shkodra (€4.50, 90 minutes) and three buses to Pristina (€22.50, eight hours).

Car & Motorcycle

You'll need an International Driving Permit and a Green Card for your vehicle.

Train

Montenegro's only international rail connection starts from Bar and cuts through the centre of the country en route to Belgrade (Serbia). For onward connections see p1242.

GETTING AROUND

The bus network is extensive and reliable. Buses are usually comfortable, air-conditioned and rarely full.

The major European car-hire companies have a presence in various centres but **Meridian Rentacar** (☎ 033-454 105; www.meridian-rentacar.com), which has offices in Budva, Bar and Podgorica, is a reliable, cheap option. Cars are required to carry a first-aid kit, an emergency-stop warning triangle, spare tyre and spare bulbs.

Hitching, while never entirely safe, is very popular in Montenegro.

MONTENEGRO FOR FREE

- Kotor's historic lanes (right)
- The views over Sveti Stefan (p802)
- Velika Plaža (p803)
- Ostrog Monastery (p804)

COASTAL MONTENEGRO

Coming from Croatia and entering the mountain-framed folds of the Bay of Kotor, the beauty meter goes off the scale. It doesn't let up when you hit the Adriatic Coast, where you'll find a charismatic set of small settlements, set against clear waters and sandy beaches.

KOTOR КОТОР

☎ 032 / pop 13,510

Wedged between brooding mountains and a moody corner of the bay, this dramatically beautiful town combines historic grace with happening street culture. Its sturdy ancient walls arch steeply up the slopes behind it. From a distance they're barely discernable from the mountain's grey hide but at night they're spectacularly lit, reflecting in the water to give the town a golden halo. Within those walls lie labyrinthine marbled lanes where churches, boutiques, bars and restaurants on hidden piazzas take you by surprise.

Orientation & Information

The western flank of the funnel-shaped Stari Grad lies against Kotor fjord. An 18th-century gateway off Jadranski Put, which runs along the waterside, leads into the old pedestrian-only town. The bus station is 1km away on the Budva road.

Sights

The old town's most impressive building is 12th-century **St Tryphon's Cathedral** (Trg Sv Tripuna, Stari Grad; admission €1.50; 8.30am-7pm).

The **Maritime Museum** (☎ 069-045 447; Trg Bokeljske Mornarice, Stari Grad; admission €4; 8am-2pm Mon-Sat & 9am-1pm Sun), housed in an early 18th century palace, celebrates Kotor's proud naval history.

Energetic travellers can make the 1200m, 1350-step ascent up the **fortifications** (admission €2).

EMERGENCY NUMBERS

- Ambulance ☎ 124
- Fire service ☎ 123
- Police ☎ 122

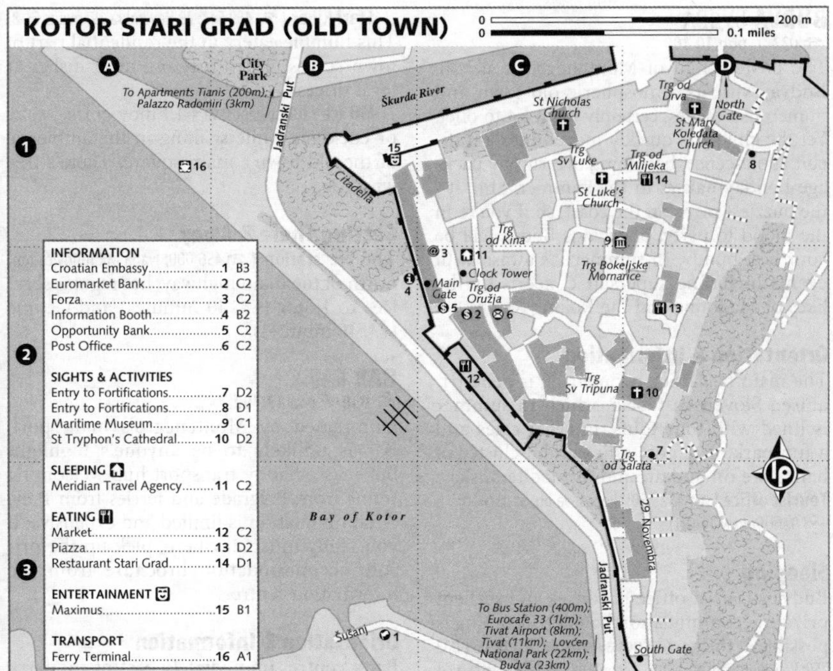

Sleeping

Enquire about private accommodation at the city's information booth. **Meridian Travel Agency** (☎ 323 448; www.tameridian.cg.yu; near Trg od Oružja, Stari Grad) also books private rooms (per person €15 to €30) and hotels.

Eurocafe 33 (☎ 069-047 712; lemaja1@cg.yu; Muo 33; r €20-25 per person; ❄) On the waterfront heading south from the town, this traditional stone building with its own concrete 'beach' offers a range of rooms, some of which share bathrooms.

Apartments Tianis (☎ 302 178; www.tianis.net; r/apt €50/70; ❄) This newish block offers large, clean apartments and rooms, some of which have a magical view to the old town.

SPLURGE

Palazzo Radomiri (☎ 333 172; www.palazzoradomiri.com; Dobrota; s €60-160, d €100-200, ste €60-280; ❄) Exquisitely beautiful, this honey-coloured early-18th-century *palazzo* has been transformed into a first-rate boutique hotel. It's worth the lengthy stroll into Kotor.

Eating

There are tons of small bakeries, takeaway joints and cafe-bars on Kotor's cobbled lanes. In the evening, speakers are dragged out onto the ancient squares and the techno cranked up.

Market (outside town walls; 🕑 7am-2pm) Inexpensive snacks and produce.

Piazza (☎ 069 205 720; Trg Bokeljske Mornarice; mains €2.50-7.50; 🕑 8am-late) Serves sandwiches, pancakes and excellent thin-based pizza.

Restaurant Stari Grad (☎ 322 025; Trg od Mlijeka; mains €8-18) Head straight through to the stone-walled courtyard, grab a seat under the vines and prepare to get absolutely stuffed full of fabulous food. Some vegetarian options are available.

Clubbing

Maximus (☎ 334 342; near Trg od Oružja; admission €2-5; 🕑 11pm-5am Thu-Sat, nightly in summer) Montenegro's most pumping club.

Getting There & Away

The **bus station** (☎ 325 809) has frequent services to Budva (€3, 40 minutes) and Podgorica (€7, two hours).

A taxi to Tivat airport costs around €8.

BUDVA БУДВА

☎ 033 / pop 10,100

The poster child of Montenegrin tourism, Budva, with its atmospheric old town and numerous beaches, certainly has a lot to offer. Yet the child has quickly moved into a difficult adolescence, becoming overrun by package holidaymakers in the summer. Still, it's the buzziest place on the coast, so if you're in the mood to party, bodacious Budva will be your best buddy. In summer it's awash with events including superstar concerts by the likes of Madonna and the Rolling Stones.

Orientation & Information

The main beachside promenade is pedestrianised Slovenska Obala, which in summer is lined with tour touts, internet cafes and a fun park. The post office and a cluster of banks are on and around ul Mediteranska.

Tourist office (☎ 452 750; Njegoševa bb, Stari Grad; 9am-9pm May-Oct)

Sleeping

Budva's tourist office produces an excellent private accommodation booklet. Camping is possible at the basic **Budva Autocamp** (☎ 069-062 759; Velji Vinogradi bb; tent & 2 people €8) in the centre of town and at swampy **Jaz Beach camp site** (☎ 463 545; tent & car €2.50).

Hotel Kangaroo (☎ 458 653; www.kangaroo.cg.yu; Velji Vinogradi bb; s €29-69, d €39-69, tr €59-104;) lets you bounce into a large clean room at this midsized hotel that's a quick hop to the beach.

Eating & Drinking

For cheap fast food and pumping beach bars, stroll along Slovenska Obala.

Fenix Caffe Pizzeria (Velji Vinogradi bb; sandwiches €2-2.50, pizza €4.50-6) The service can be brusque but the pizzas are excellent and substantial.

Stari Ribar (☎ 459 543; 29 Novembra 19; mains €3-8) This humble eatery in the residential part of town serves grilled fish and meat dishes at local prices.

MB Ice Club (Njegoševa 44) Enjoy coffee, cake or cocktails while soaking in the ambience of the old town's main square. There's free wi-fi too.

Getting There & Away

The **bus station** (☎ 456 000; Ivana Milutinovića bb), north of the main highway, has regular services to Kotor (€3, 40 minutes) and Cetinje (€3, 40 minutes).

BAR БАР

☎ 030 / pop 13,790

Dominated by Montenegro's main port, Bar is unlikely to be anyone's highlight but it is a handy transport hub welcoming trains from Belgrade and ferries from Italy. Accommodation is limited and expensive; if you really must stay here, pick up the private accommodation brochure from the information centre.

Orientation & Information

Bar's centre, immediately east of the ferry terminal, has a post office, shops and banks.

Tourist Information Centre (☎ 311 633; Obala 13 Jula bb; 7am-9pm Jul & Aug, 7am-2pm Mon-Fri Sep-Jun)

Sights

Impressive **Stari Bar** (admission €1; 9am-5pm Apr-Oct), dates back over a thousand years and stands on a bluff off the Ulcinj road. A steep cobbled hill takes you to a short dark passage through the fortifications, which pops you out into what seems to be a huge garden of vine-clad walls, abandoned streets and over 200 ruins overgrown with grass and wild flowers.

DETOUR: SVETI STEFAN

Impossibly picturesque **Sveti Stefan**, 5km south of Budva, provides the biggest 'wow' moment on the entire coast. From the 15th century to the 1950s this tiny island, connected to the shore by a narrow isthmus and crammed full of terracotta-roofed dwellings, housed a simple fishing community. Now the entire island is a luxury resort, but you can still enjoy the views from the sublime beaches on either side.

Overlooking it all, **Vila Drago** (☎ 468 477; www.viladrago.com; Slobode 32; d €34-68, tr €58-100, apt €103-170;) offers sublime views, super-comfy pillows and fully stocked bathrooms. Watch the sunset from the grapevine-covered terrace restaurant (mains €4-11) and enjoy local specialities such as roast suckling pig (€15/kg).

Buses marked Stari Bar depart from the centre of Bar every hour (€1).

Getting There & Away

The **bus station** (☎ 346 141) and adjacent **train station** (☎ 301 622; www.zeljeznica.cg.yu) are 1km southeast of the centre. Look for the street signs, grab a cab or ask a local for directions *(Gdje je stanica?)*. Bus destinations include Podgorica (€5, seven daily) and Ulcinj (€2.50, 30 minutes, six daily).

ULCINJ УЛЦИЊ

☎ 030 / 10,840

If you want a feel for Albania without actually crossing the border, buzzy Ulcinj's the place to go. The population is 72% Albanian and the elegant minarets of numerous mosques give Ulcinj a distinctly Eastern feel. For centuries Ulcinj had a reputation as a pirate's lair but now it's known for its fine beaches, including **Velika Plaža**, which stretches for 12 sandy kilometres.

Orientation & Information

You'll find banks, internet cafes, supermarkets, pharmacies and a post office on Rruga Hazif Ali Ulqinaku, the main road heading down to **Mala Plaža** (Small Beach). Velika Plaža starts 4km southeast of the town.

Sleeping & Eating

Real Estate Travel Agency (☎ 421 609; www.realestate-travel.com; Hazif Ali Ulqinaku bb) The obliging English-speaking staff can help you find private rooms (from €10 per person), apartments or hotel rooms.

Bonita Apartments (☎ 423 164; bonita-ul@cg.yu; Ivan Millutinoviqit 67; s/d/tr/q €20/30/45/60; ☒) Offers small but perfectly adequate apartments in a 2008-built block above Mala Plaža.

Casa Agata (☎ 455 025; Velika Plaža-Ada Bojana road, Štoj; apt €20-40; ☒) While the apartments here are literally a little rough around the edges, they're kept very clean and tidy. It's a good homely option and only 250m from Velika Plaža.

Hotel Dolcino (☎ 422 288; www.hoteldolcino.com; Hazif Ali Ulqinaku bb; s/d/q/ste €40/50/60/70; ☒) For a modern minihotel the prices are exceptionally reasonable, especially given the central location.

Market (Gjergj Kastrioti Skënderbeu bb) At the top end of town.

Restaurant Pizzeria Bazar (☎ 421 639; Hazif Ali Ulqinaku bb; mains €4-10) An upstairs restaurant that's a great idling place when the streets below are heaving with tourists.

Getting There & Away

The **bus station** (☎ 413 225) is on the northeastern edge of town just off Bulevar Vëllazërit Frashëri. Services head to Bar (€2.50, 30 minutes, six daily), Podgorica (€7, one hour, daily) and Shkodra (€4.50, 90 minutes, daily).

Minibuses head to Shkodra at 9am and 3pm (or when they're full) from the carpark beside Ulcinj's market (about €5).

CENTRAL MONTENEGRO

The heart of Montenegro – physically, spiritually and politically – is easily accessed as a day trip from the coast, but it's well deserving of a longer exploration. This really is the full Monte: soaring peaks, hidden monasteries, steep river canyons and historic towns. Podgorica, the nation's capital, serves as the transport hub and is worth a day's exploration, but it's elsewhere that your focus should lie.

CETINJE ЦЕТИЊЕ

☎ 041 / pop 15,140

Rising from a green vale surrounded by rough, grey mountains, Cetinje is an odd mix of former capital and overgrown village where single-storey cottages and stately mansions share the same street.

The **National Museum of Montenegro** (all museums €8; 🕘 9am-5pm) is actually a collection of five museums housed in a clump of important buildings. A joint ticket will get you into all of them or you can buy individual tickets. Best are the **History Museum** (☎ 230 310; Novice Cerovića 7; admission €3) and **Art Museum** (admission €3), housed in the former parliament (1910). The other three are set around the main square: **King Nikola Museum** (☎ 230 555; admission €5), **Njegoš Museum** (☎ 231 050; admission €3) and the **Ethnographic Museum** (admission €2).

Founded in 1484, **Cetinje Monastery** (☎ 231 021; 🕘 8am-6pm) has a spectacular **treasury** (€2; 🕘 8am-4pm). It's only open to groups but if you are persuasive enough, appropriately dressed and prepared to wait around, you may be able to get in.

The **bus station** (Trg Golootočkih Žeta) is two blocks from the main street. Buses leave every 30 minutes for Podgorica (€3) and hourly for Budva (€3).

WORTH THE TRIP: OSTROG MONASTERY

Resting on a cliff 900m above the Zeta valley, gleaming white **Ostrog Monastery** (1665) is a strangely affecting place. Dubbed 'Sv Vasilije's miracle' because no-one seems to understand how it was built, it gives the impression that it has grown out of the very rock. The **guest house** (☎ 067-405 258; dm €4) offers tidy single-sex dorm rooms. There's no public transport but numerous tour buses head here from the coast (€15 to €20).

DURMITOR NATIONAL PARK
ДУРМИТОР

☎ 052 / pop 4900

Magnificent scenery ratchets up to the stupendous in this national park, where ice and water have carved a dramatic landscape from the limestone. Some 18 glacial lakes dot the Durmitor Range, which has 48 peaks over 2000m. From December to March it is Montenegro's main ski resort, while in summer it's popular with hikers and rafters.

Orientation & Information

Žabljak, at the eastern edge of the range, is the park's principal gateway. It's not very big and nor is it attractive, but it has a supermarket, post office, bank, hotels and restaurants.

Durmitor National Park Visitor Centre (☎ 360 228; www.nparkovi.cg.yu; ⌚ 7am-2pm Autumn & Spring, 8am-6pm Winter & Summer) On the road to the Black Lake. It includes a wonderful micromuseum focussing on the park's flora and fauna.

Summit Travel Agency (☎ 361 502; anna.grbovic@cg.yu; Njegoševa bb, Žabljak) Can arrange private rooms (from €10 per person), jeep tours (€100 for up to three people), rafting trips (half-/one-/two-day tour €50/110/200) and mountain-bike hire (per hour/day €2/10).

Activities

RAFTING

Slicing through the mountains at the northern edge of the national park like they were made from the local soft cheese, the **Tara River** forms a canyon that at its peak is 1300m deep. The two-day raft along the river is the country's premier outdoor attraction (May to October only). Most of the day tours from the coast traverse only the last 18km of the river – this is outside the national park and hence avoids hefty fees.

If you've got your own wheels you can save a few bucks by heading directly to Šćepan Polje. **Tara Tour** (☎ 069-086 106; www.tara-tour.com) offers an excellent half-day trip (with/without breakfast and lunch €30/40) and has a cute set of wooden chalets with squat toilets and showers in a separate block. Accommodation, three meals and a half-day's rafting costs €55.

HIKING

Durmitor is one of the best marked mountain ranges in Europe for hikers (entry fee per day €2). Check the weather forecast, stick to the tracks and prepare for sudden drops in temperature.

SKIING

The three main ski centres are all accessible from Žabljak: **Savin Kuk** (advanced skiers), **Javorovača** (beginners) and **Mali Štuoc** (suits all levels of experience).

One of the big attractions for skiing here is the cost: day passes are around €15, weekly passes €70 and ski lessons between €10 and €20. You can rent ski and snowboard gear from **Sport Trade** (☎ 069-538 831; Vuka Karadžića 7, Žabljak) for €10 per day.

Sleeping & Eating

Autokamp Mlinski Potok Mina (☎ 069-497 625; camp site per person €3, bed €10) With a fabulously hospitable host, this camping ground above the National Park Visitors Centre is an excellent option. The owner's house can sleep twelve guests in comfortable wood-panelled rooms and he has another house by the Black Lake that sleeps eleven.

MB Hotel (☎ 361 601; www.mb-hotel.com; Tripka Đakovića bb, Žabljak; s/d/villa €30/57/100) This little hotel offers modern rooms, English-speaking staff, an attractive restaurant/bar and wi-fi.

Eko-Oaza Suza Evrope (☎ 067-511 755; eko-oaza@cg.yu; Dobrilovina; cottage €50) Situated at the beginning of the arm of the park that stretches along the River Tara, this 'eco oasis' has four comfortable wooden cottages, each sleeping five people.

National Eco Restaurant (☎ 361 337; Božidara Žugića 8, Žabljak; mains €3-10) A great place to try traditional mountain food, such as lamb or veal roasted 'under the pan' (€24 per kg).

Getting There & Away

The **bus station** (☎ 361 318) is at the southern end of Žabljak on the Nikšić road. Buses head to Belgrade (€25, 9 hours, two daily) and Podgorica (€9.50, 3½ hours, three daily).

MONTENEGRO DIRECTORY

ACCOMMODATION

Private accommodation is most affordable, often with rooms as good as hotels and certainly more personable; look for the '*sobe*', '*zimmer*' or 'rooms' signs all along the coast. There are summer camping grounds along the coast.

ACTIVITIES

Žabljak, in the Durmitor National Park (opposite), is the main activity centre for snow bunnies, hikers and rafters.

BUSINESS HOURS

The usual opening hours in Montenegro:

Banks 8am-5pm Mon-Fri, 8am-noon Sat
Cafe-bars 9pm-3am
Government offices 9am-5pm Mon-Fri
Restaurants 8am-midnight
Shops 8am-5pm or later Mon-Fri, to noon Sat; on the coast shops open till late every day in summer

DANGERS & ANNOYANCES

Montenegro is generally safe but the roads can be treacherous due to kamikaze-style driving habits. There are two species of venomous vipers but they'll try their best to keep out of your way.

EMBASSIES & CONSULATES

For a full list, see www.vlada.cg.yu/eng/mininos/. The following are all in Podgorica unless otherwise stated:

Albania (☎ 020-652 796; Zmaj Jovina 30)
Bosnia & Hercegovina (☎ 020-618 105; Atinska 58)
Croatia Podgorica (☎ 020-269 760; Vladimira Ćetkovića 2); Kotor (☎ 032-323 127; Šušanj 248)
France (☎ 020-655 348; Atinska 35)
Germany (☎ 020-667 285; Hercegovačka 10)
Italy (☎ 020-234 661; Bul Džordža Vašingtona 83)
Serbia (☎ 020-402 500; Hotel Podgorica, Bul Svetog Petra Cetinjskog 1)
UK (☎ 020-205 460; Bul Svetog Petra Cetinjskog 149)
USA (☎ 020-225 417; Ljubljanska bb)

FOOD & DRINK

Loosen your belt – you're in for a treat. Eating in Montenegro is generally an extremely pleasurable experience. By default, most of the food is local, fresh and organic, and hence very seasonal. The food on the coast is virtually indistinguishable from Dalmatian cuisine: lots of grilled seafood, garlic, olive oil and Italian dishes. Inland it's much more meaty and Serbian-influenced.

The village of Njeguši in the Montenegrin heartland is famous for its *pršut* (dried ham) and cheese. On the coast, be sure to try the fish soup, grilled squid (served plain or stuffed with *pršut* and cheese) and black risotto (made from squid ink).

Vranac (red) and Krstač (white) are the indigenous grapes, while Nikšićko Pivo (try saying that after a few) is the local beer. Many people distil their own *rakija* (brandy), made out of just about anything (grapes, pears, apples etc).

HOLIDAYS

Public holidays in Montenegro include:

New Year's Day 1 January
Orthodox Christmas 7 and 8 January
Orthodox Easter Monday date varies, usually April/May
Labour Day 1 May
Independence Day 21 May
Statehood Day 13 July

INTERNET RESOURCES

Montenegro Times (www.themontenegrotimes.com)
National Tourist Organisation (www.montenegro.travel)
Visit Montenegro (www.visit-montenegro.com)

LANGUAGE

Montenegrin is now the official name for the language of Montenegro, although it's little different from Serbian, Bosnian and Croatian. Both the Cyrillic and Latin alphabets are used. Albanian is widely spoken around Ulcinj. Most people speak some English.

MONEY

All prices quoted in this chapter are in euros (€), Montenegro's official currency (even though Montenegro is not part of the Eurozone). You'll find banks with ATMs in all major towns, most of which accept Visa, MasterCard, Maestro and

Cirrus. Don't rely on credit cards for restaurants, shops or smaller hotels.

Tipping isn't expected although it's common to round up to the nearest euro.

POST

Every town in the country has a post office but do be prepared to experience horrendous queues. Travellers can receive mail, addressed *poste restante,* in all towns for a small charge.

TELEPHONE

Post offices are the best places to make international calls. Local SIM cards are widely available.

VISAS

Visas are not required for citizens of all EU countries, Australia, New Zealand, Canada and the United States. In the majority of cases visas allow a stay of up to 90 days.

Morocco

HIGHLIGHTS

- **Fez medina** Get lost in the alleyways of Islam's greatest living medieval city (p822)
- **Marrakesh** Taste *1001 Nights* in the open-air spectacle of the Djemaa el-Fna square (p827)
- **Chefchaouen** Chill in the Rif Mountains in the dazzling blue town of Chefchaouen (p815)
- **Essaouira** Catch the sea breeze in Morocco's hippest resort (p820)

FAST FACTS

- **Area** 446,550 sq km
- **Budget** Dh350 to Dh700 per day
- **Capital** Rabat
- **Country code** ☎ 212
- **Famous for** Humphrey Bogart and *Casablanca*, Marrakesh, tajine and couscous, trendy riad hotels
- **Languages** Darija (Moroccan Arabic), French, Berber
- **Money** dirham (Dh); A$1 = Dh6.21; C$1 = Dh7.03; €1 = Dh11.17; ¥100 = Dh8.76; NZ$1 = Dh4.85; UK£1 = Dh12.59; US$1 = Dh8.31
- **Phrases** *ssalamu'lekum* (hello); *shukran* (thanks); *insh'allah* (God willing)

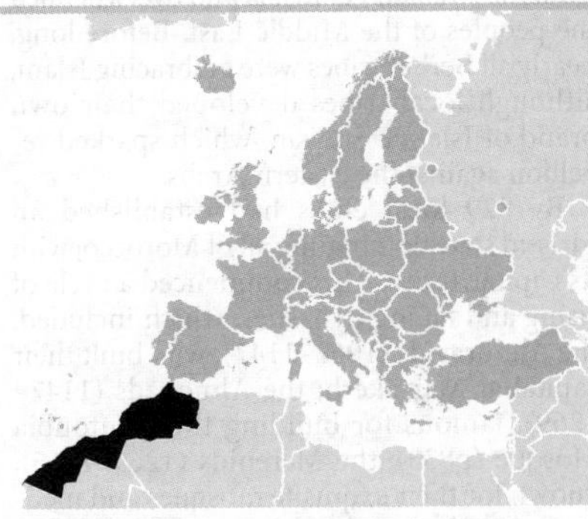

- **Population** 33.7 million
- **Visas** most visitors can enter Morocco for 90 days without a visa (p836)

TRAVEL HINTS

Guard your small change jealously and break big notes when you can for cafes, tips and taxis.

ROAMING MOROCCO

From the Tangier ferry, head to Fez via Chefchaouen. South to Marrakesh, the High Atlas and Sahara, finishing at Essaouira.

For many travellers, Morocco might just be a short hop away by ferry from Spain, or by one of the myriad budget airlines, but it's a much further distance to travel culturally. The regular certainties of Europe are suddenly swept away by the arrival in full technicolour of Africa and Islam. It's a complete sensory overload.

Tangier, that faded libertine on the coast, has traditionally been a first port of call, but the winds blow you quickly along the Atlantic coast to movie-star famous Casablanca, and white-washed fishing port gem Essaouira. Inland, the great imperial cities of Marrakesh and Fez attract visitors in droves as they have done for centuries. The winding streets of their ancient medinas have enough surprises around each corner to fill a dozen repeat trips.

If you really want to escape from everything, Morocco still has a couple of trump cards. The High Atlas mountains seem custom-made for hiking boots, or if you prefer someone else to do the walking, simply saddle up your camel and ride it straight into the Sahara, to watch the sun set over an ocean of sand.

HISTORY

Most present-day Moroccans are descendents of indigenous tribes that have inhabited the Maghreb hills for thousands of years. When the Romans arrived in North Africa in the 2nd century BC, they called the locals 'Berbers' (similar to the term 'Barbarian' ascribed to the northern European tribes) because of their incomprehensible tongue.

In the second half of the 7th century, the soldiers of the Prophet Mohammed set forth from the Arabian Peninsula and overwhelmed the peoples of the Middle East. Before long, nearly all Berber tribes were embracing Islam, although local tribes developed their own brand of Islamic Shi'ism, which sparked rebellion against the eastern Arabs.

By 829 local elites had established an Idrissid state dominating all of Morocco, with its capital at Fez. This commenced a cycle of rising and falling dynasties, which included: the Almoravids (1062–1147), who built their capital at Marrakesh; the Almohads (1147–1269), famous for building the Koutoubia Mosque (p830); the Merenids (1269–1465), known for their exquisite mosques and medersas (Qur'anic schools), especially in Fez; the Saadians (1524–1659), responsible for the Palais el-Badi in Marrakesh (p830); and the Alawites (1659–present).

France took control in 1912, establishing its capital at Rabat, with Spain holding a token zone in the north of the country. Opposition from Berber mountain tribes was crushed, but political resistance emerged with the development of the Istiqlal (independence) party.

Independence was finally granted in 1956. The Spanish also withdrew, retaining the coastal enclaves of Ceuta and Melilla. Sultan Mohammed V became king, and was succeeded by his son in 1961. Despite moves towards democracy and several coup attempts, Hassan II retained all effective power until his death in 1999. His biggest legacy has been Morocco's occupation and territorial claim of the former Spanish colony of Western Sahara. Despite de facto Moroccan control, Western Sahara's legal status is still subject to international dispute and UN monitoring.

The new king, Mohammed VI, has adopted a reformist agenda, especially in the area of social policy and women's rights. He has sought to tie Morocco closer to Europe and has overseen a tourism boom and economic liberalisation, but also the backwash of Islamist violence, with a small number of home-grown terrorist attacks.

THE CULTURE

People of Arab-Berber descent make up almost the entire Moroccan population, which although still mostly rural, is increasingly urbanised, and young to boot – 55% are under 25 years. High growth rates mean that the population is set to double almost every 25 years.

RELIGION

Morocco is a Muslim country. Muslims share their roots with Jews and Christians and respect these groups as *Ahl al-Kteb*, People of the Book. Fundamentalism is mostly discouraged but remains a presence, especially among the urban poor who have enjoyed none of the benefits of economic growth. That said, the majority of Muslims do not favour such developments and the popularity of fundamentalism is not as great as Westerners imagine.

Emigration to France, Israel and the USA has reduced Morocco's once robust Jewish community to about 7000 from a high of around 300,000 in 1948.

ENVIRONMENT

Morocco's three ecological zones – coast, mountain and desert – host more than 40 different ecosystems and provide habitat for many endemic species, including the iconic and sociable Barbary macaque (also known as the Barbary ape). Unfortunately, pressure from sprawling urban areas and the encroachment of industrialisation in Morocco's wilderness means that 18 mammals (a staggering 15% of the total) and a dozen bird species are considered endangered.

Pollution, desertification, overgrazing and deforestation are the major environmental issues facing the Moroccan government. Despite plantation programs and the development of new national parks, less than 0.5% of Moroccan territory is protected, one-third of Morocco's ecosystems are disappearing, 10% of vertebrates are endangered and 25,000 hectares of forest are lost every year.

Global warming has stolen valuable snowfall from mountain regions whose rivers depend upon the melt; in the south, most rivers

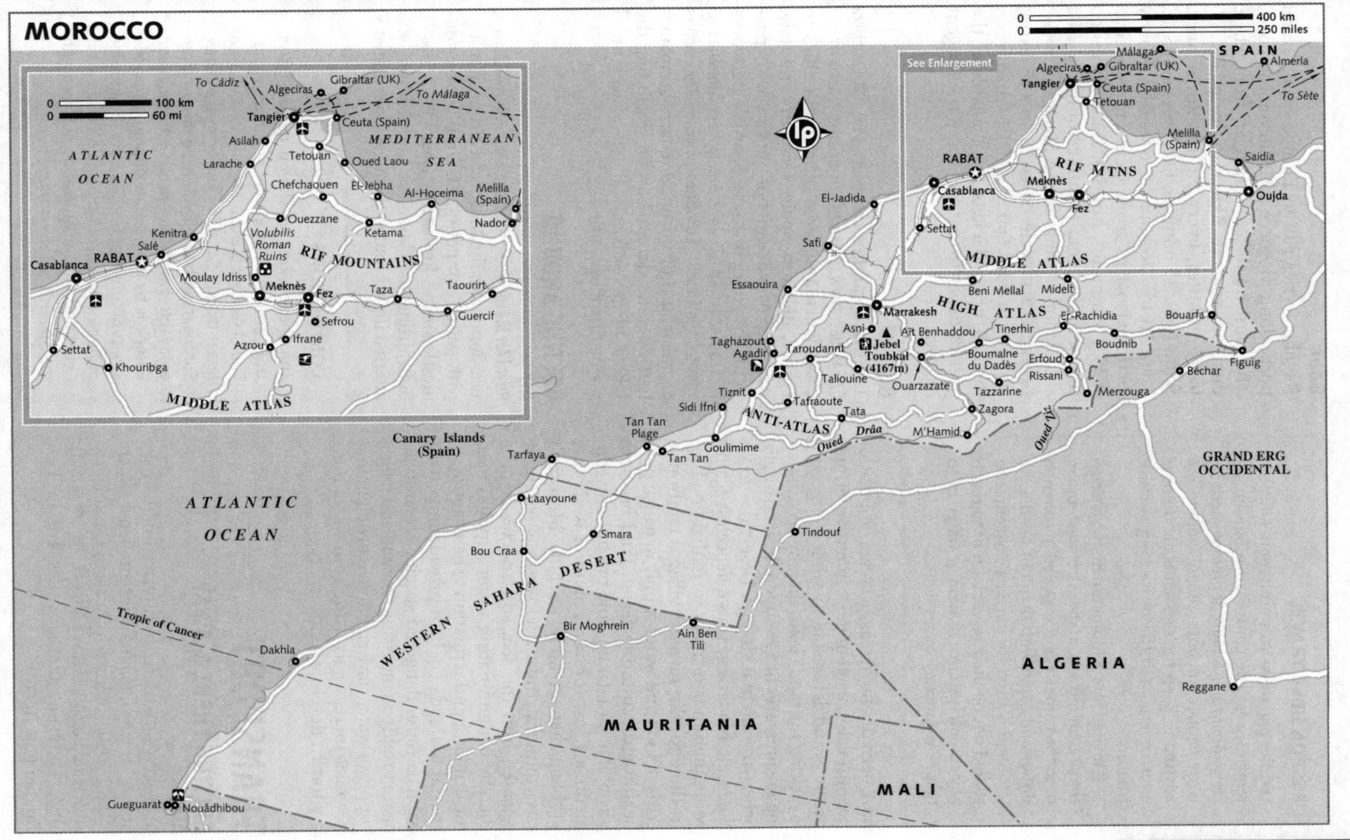
MOROCCO
0 400 km
0 250 miles
0 100 km
0 60 mi
To Cádiz
Algeciras
Gibraltar (UK)
To Málaga
Tangier
Ceuta (Spain)
MEDITERRANEAN
SEA
Asilah
Tetouan
Oued Laou
ATLANTIC
OCEAN
Larache
Chefchaouen
El-Jebha
Al-Hoceima
Melilla (Spain)
Nador
Ouezzane
Ketama
Kenitra
Volubilis Roman Ruins
Salé
RABAT
Casablanca
RIF MOUNTAINS
Moulay Idriss
Meknès
Fez
Taza
Taourirt
Guercif
Sefrou
Ifrane
Azrou
Settat
Khouribga
MIDDLE ATLAS
See Enlargement
Málaga
SPAIN
Almería
To Sète
Melilla (Spain)
Saidia
Oujda
RIF MTNS
El-Jadida
Safi
Essaouira
Beni Mellal
Midelt
Marrakesh
HIGH ATLAS
Er-Rachidia
Bouarfa
Asni
Aït Benhaddou
Tinerhir
Boudnib
Figuig
Taghazout
Agadir
Taroudannt
Jebel Toubkal (4167m)
Boumalne du Dadès
Erfoud
Rissani
Béchar
Taliouine
Ouarzazate
Tazzarine
Merzouga
Tiznit
Tafraoute
Sidi Ifni
Tata
Zagora
ANTI-ATLAS
M'Hamid
Oued Drâa
Oued Ziz
Tan Tan Plage
Tan Tan
Goulimime
Canary Islands (Spain)
Tarfaya
GRAND ERG OCCIDENTAL
Laayoune
ATLANTIC
OCEAN
Smara
Tindouf
Bou Craa
WESTERN SAHARA DESERT
Tropic of Cancer
Bir Moghrein
Aïn Ben Tili
Dakhla
ALGERIA
Reggane
MAURITANIA
MALI
Gueguarat
Nouâdhibou

RESPONSIBLE TRAVEL

Despite extensive Westernisation, Morocco remains a largely conservative Muslim society. As a rule, a high degree of modesty is demanded of both sexes. Women are advised to keep their shoulders and upper arms covered and to opt for long skirts or trousers.

If invited into a Moroccan home, it's customary to remove your shoes before stepping onto the carpet. Food is served in common dishes and eaten with the right hand – the left hand is used for personal hygiene and should not be used to eat with or to touch any common source of food or water, or to hand over money or presents.

have been dry for at least 10 years. Population pressures also result in more intensive farming practices and deforestation, while overgrazing is picking the land clean, thereby accumulating the pressures heaped upon the land by global environmental change. Desertification is the result, rendering crops defenceless against whipping sandstorms or torrential flooding. In the end, the ravaged villages confront a crisis of food and water supply in which poor health and sanitation fester, land becomes unsuitable for farming, and pristine environments are lost forever. Pollution is another problem that threatens to choke Morocco's environment. Industrial waste is routinely released into the sea, soil and waterways, thereby contaminating water supplies used for drinking and irrigation. The draining of coastal wetlands – which provide important habitats for endangered species – continues apace to address the rising demand and falling supply of water for irrigation, a problem that becomes increasingly acute with water-hungry tourist developments.

TRANSPORT

GETTING THERE & AWAY

Air

Morocco's two main international entry points are **Mohammed V international airport** (☎ 022 539040), 30km southeast of Casablanca; and Marrakesh's **Ménara Airport** (☎ 044 447865). Other international airports are in Fez, Tangier and Agadir.

Boat

Regular ferries run to Europe from several ports along Morocco's Mediterranean coast. The most trafficked is Tangier, from where there are boats to Algeciras, Spain (€31, 60 to 70 minutes, every 90 minutes), Tarifa, Spain (€40, 35 minutes, five daily) and Sete, France (€165, 36 hours, two weekly). Hourly ferries also run from Ceuta to Algeciras (€28, 35 minutes, hourly). Daily ferries go from Al-Hoceima (summer only), Melilla and Nador to Almería and Málaga in Spain. Bringing a bicycle costs €8 to €15 extra, while a car adds €60 to €80. Children travel for half price. Tickets are available at the port of departure or from any travel agent in town.

Bus

The Moroccan bus company **CTM** (☎ Casablanca 022 458080; www.ctm.co.ma) operates buses from Casablanca and most other main cities to France, Belgium, Spain, Germany and Italy. Another Moroccan bus service with particularly good links to Spanish networks is **Tramesa** (☎ 022 245274; http://perso.menara.ma/tramesa07, in French). **Eurolines** (www.eurolines.com) is a consortium of European coach companies that operates across Europe (including the UK) and to Morocco. It has offices in all major European cities.

GETTING AROUND

Air

Royal Air Maroc (RAM; ☎ 09000 0800; www.royalairmaroc.com) dominates the Moroccan airline industry, with paltry competition from one other domestic airline, **Regional Air Lines** (☎ 022 538080). Both airlines use Casablanca as their hub, with internal flights routed through Mohammed V

CONNECTIONS

The cheap-flight revolution has well and truly arrived in Morocco, and budget airlines link Casablanca, Marrakesh and, to a lesser extent, Fez and Tangier to the major European air hubs. If you have time, a more enjoyable way of connecting to mainland Europe is by ferry, either zipping across the Straits of Gibraltar from Tangier to Algeciras or Tarifa in Spain, or from Spain's enclaves of Ceuta and Melilla (above), to connect with the Spanish rail network.

International Airport. Student and under-26 youth discounts of 25% are available on all RAM domestic flights, but only if the ticket is bought in advance from one of its offices. For most routes, flying is an expensive and inconvenient option compared to road or rail.

Bus

A dense network of buses operates throughout Morocco, with many private companies competing for business alongside the comfortable and modern coaches of the main national carrier **CTM** (in Casablanca ☎ 022 45 80 80).

The **ONCF** (www.oncf.ma, in French) train company runs buses through Supratours to widen its train network, for example running connections from Marrekesh to Essaouira. Morocco's other bus companies are all privately owned and only operate regionally. It's best to book ahead for CTM and Supratours buses, which are slightly more expensive than those of other companies.

Car & Motorcycle

Taking your own vehicle to Morocco is straightforward. In addition to a vehicle registration document and an International Driving Permit (although many foreign licences, including US and EU ones, are also acceptable), a Green Card is required from the car's insurer. Not all insurers cover Morocco.

Renting a car in Morocco isn't cheap, with prices starting at Dh3500 per week or Dh500 per day for a basic car with unlimited mileage. International hire companies are well-represented, and booking in advance online secures the best deals. Most companies demand a returnable cash deposit (Dh3000 to Dh5000) unless you pay by credit card.

In Morocco you drive on the right-hand side. On a roundabout, give way to traffic entering from the right.

Local Transport

Cities and bigger towns have local *petits taxis*, which are a different colour in every city. They are not permitted to go beyond the city limits, are licensed to carry up to three passengers and are usually metered.

The old Mercedes vehicles you'll see belting along roads and gathered in great flocks near bus stations are *grands taxis* (shared taxis). They link towns to their nearest neighbours. *Grands taxis* take six extremely cramped passengers and normally only leave when full.

EMERGENCY NUMBERS

- Ambulance ☎ 15
- Fire ☎ 16
- Police ☎ 19

Train

Morocco's train network is run by **ONCF** (www.oncf.ma, in French). There are two lines that carry passengers: from Tangier in the north down to Marrakesh; and from Oujda in the northeast, also to Marrakesh, joining with the Tangier line at Sidi Kacem.

Trains are comfortable, fast and generally preferable to buses where available. There are different 1st- and 2nd-class fares on all these trains, but 2nd-class is more than adequate on any journey. Couchettes are available on the overnight trains between Marrakesh and Tangier.

Two types of rail discount cards are available in Morocco. The Carte Fidelité (Dh149) is for those aged over 26 and gives you 50% reductions on eight return or 16 one-way journeys in a 12-month period. If you're under 26, the Carte Jaune (Dh99) will give you the same discounts. To apply for the card you will need one passport-sized photo as well as a photocopy of your passport.

MEDITERRANEAN COAST & THE RIF

Bounded by the red crags of the Rif Mountains and the crashing waves of the Mediterranean, northern Morocco's wildly beautiful coastline conceals attractions as diverse as the cosmopolitan hustle of Tangier and the superbly relaxing town of Chefchaouen.

TANGIER

pop 650,000

Like the dynamic strait upon which it sits, Tangier is the product of 1001 currents, including Islam, Berber tribes, colonial masters, a highly strategic location, a vibrant port, the Western counterculture and the international jetset. Tangier has regularly passed between Moroccan and Western control – for half the 20th century it was under the dubious control of an international council, making it a byword for licentious behaviour and dodgy dealings.

Many travellers simply pass through, but if you take it head-on and learn to handle the hustlers, you'll find it a lively, cosmopolitan place with an energetic nightlife.

Orientation

Tangier's small medina climbs up the hill to the northeast of the city, while the ville nouvelle surrounds it to the west, south and southeast. The large, central square known as the Grand Socco (officially renamed Place du 9 Avril 1947) provides the link between the two.

Information

Blvds Pasteur and Mohammed V are lined with numerous banks with ATMs and *bureau de change* counters. Blvd Pasteur also has plenty of internet places.

Clinique du Croissant Rouge (Red Cross Clinic; ☎ 039 946976; 6 Rue al-Mansour Dahabi)

Espace Net (16 Ave Mexique; per hr Dh5; 🕒 9.30am-1am) Internet access.

ONMT (Office National Marocain du Tourisme; ☎ 039 948050; 29 Blvd Pasteur; 🕒 8.30am-4.30pm Mon-Fri).

Sights

The **Kasbah** sits on the highest point of Tangier, behind stout walls. Coming from the medina, you enter through Bab el-Aassa, the southeastern gate, to find the **Kasbah Museum** (☎ 039 932097; admission Dh10; 🕒 9am-12.30pm Wed-Mon, plus 3-5.30pm Wed, Thu & Sat-Mon), a worthwhile museum devoted to Moroccan arts, with pleasant gardens – as befits a part of the old Sultans' palace.

In the southwest corner of the medina, the **Old American Legation Museum** (☎ 039 935317; www.legation.org; 8 Rue d'Amerique; donations appreciated; 🕒 10am-1pm & 3-5pm Mon-Fri) is an intriguing relic of the international zone with a fascinating collection of memorabilia.

Heading uphill, you eventually emerge at **Bab Fass**, the keyhole-shaped gate that opens to the renovated plaza of **Grand Socco**. A short walk up Rue d'Angleterre brings you to one of the more charming oddities of Tangier, the Victorian-era **St Andrews Church** (🕒 services 8.30am & 11am Sun).

Sleeping

Youth Hostel (☎ 039 946127; 8 Rue al-Antaki; dm with/without HI card Dh30/40) Tangier's youth hostel is just off Ave d'Espagne, close to an area with plenty of bars. It's fair value as Moroccan youth hostels go – clean enough but a bit tired. A hot shower costs Dh5.

Hotel Mamora (☎ 039 934105; www.hotelmamora.site.voila.fr; 19 Rue des Postes; low season: s/d with sink Dh60/120, with toilet Dh100/150, with shower Dh200/230) With a variety of rooms at different rates, this is a good bet. It's a bit institutional, but clean, well run, and strong value for the money. The rooms overlooking the green-tiled roof of the Grande Mosquée are the most picturesque, if you don't mind the muezzin's call.

Hôtel Biarritz (☎ 039 932473; 102-4 Ave d'Espagne; s/d Dh150/200) This old place holds its age well – all rooms have showers and are nicely furnished (some have balconies), more than comfy enough to lay your head. The 1940s glazed-tile staircase adds a bit of character, plus there's a bar and handy restaurant.

Hôtel Ibn Batouta (☎ 039 939311; postmaster@ibn-batouta.com; 8 Rue Magellan; s/d Dh150/200, with bathroom Dh200/250) Perched on the steep lane opposite the similar El-Muniria Hotel, this is a hangover from the days when Beat writers like Kerouac, Burroughs and Ginsberg haunted the city. Rooms in the main building come with bathroom, they're airy with views to the sea, but hot in summer.

Marco Polo (☎ 039 941124; www.marco-polo.ma; 2 Rue al-Antaki; s/d from Dh330/400 low season, Dh420/560 high season, breakfast Dh35) This newly renovated hotel is the perfect choice if you aren't looking for local atmosphere. Lots of light, sparkling marble floors, and pastel walls make this bright and welcoming. Its location provides easy access to both the ville nouvelle and the medina.

Eating

In the medina there's a host of cheap eating possibilities around the Petit Socco and the adjacent Ave Mokhtar Ahardan, with rotisserie chicken, sandwiches and brochettes all on offer. In the ville nouvelle, try the streets immediately south of Place de France, which are flush with fast-food outlets, sandwich bars and fish counters.

Fast Food Brahim (16 Ave Mexique; sandwiches Dh15-18; 🕒 11am-midnight) Great made-to-order sandwiches. You can't go wrong here with half a baguette filled with *kefta* (seasoned minced lamb) and salad to eat on the hoof.

Mix Max (6 Ave du Prince Héritier; meals Dh20-45; 🕒 noon-2am) One of the newer and trendier fast-food joints, with great paninis, shawarmas, and other creative fast fare.

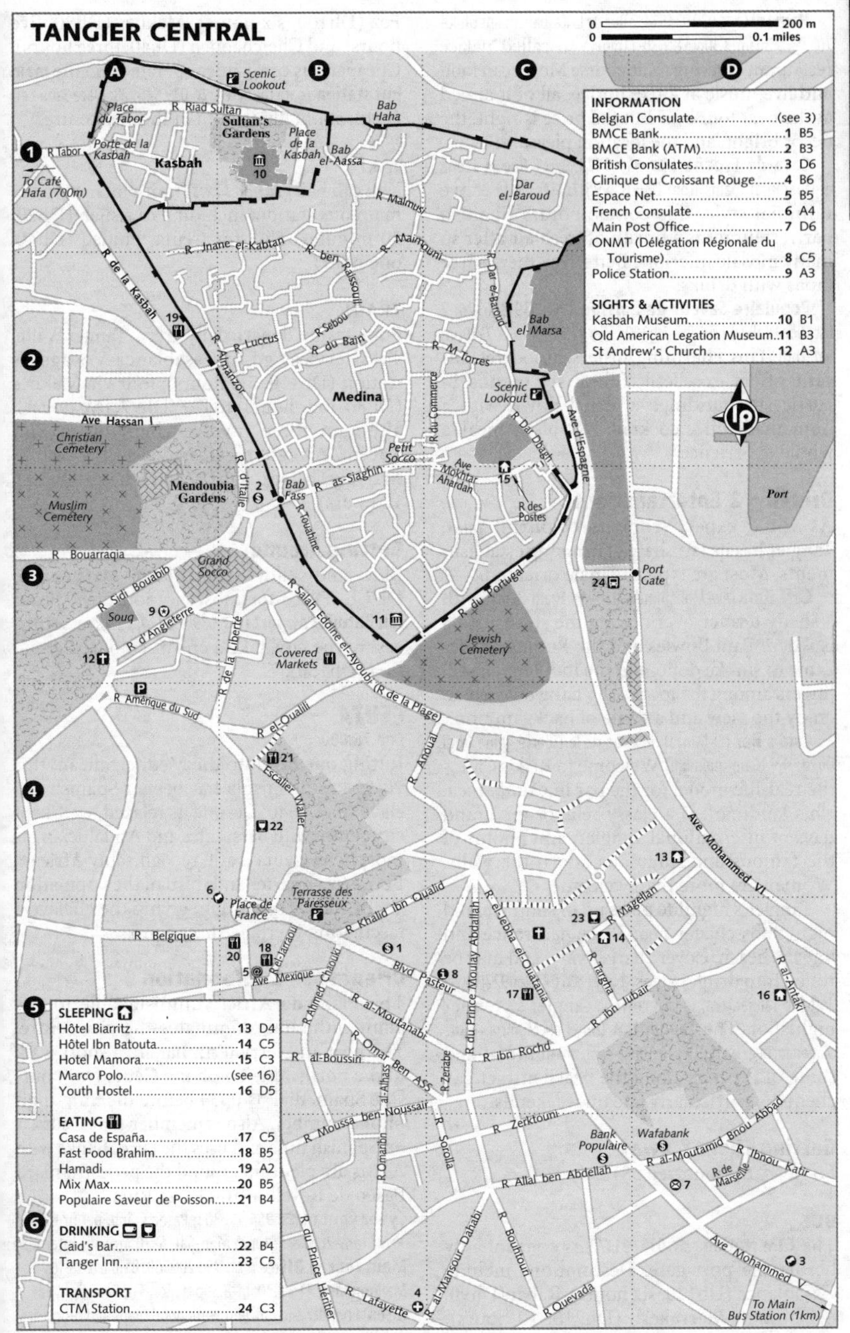
TANGIER CENTRAL
0 200 m
0 0.1 miles
INFORMATION
Belgian Consulate....................(see 3)
BMCE Bank....................1 B5
BMCE Bank (ATM)....................2 B3
British Consulates....................3 D6
Clinique du Croissant Rouge....................4 B6
Espace Net....................5 B5
French Consulate....................6 A4
Main Post Office....................7 D6
ONMT (Délégation Régionale du Tourisme)....................8 C5
Police Station....................9 A3
SIGHTS & ACTIVITIES
Kasbah Museum....................10 B1
Old American Legation Museum....................11 B3
St Andrew's Church....................12 A3
SLEEPING
Hôtel Biarritz....................13 D4
Hôtel Ibn Batouta....................14 C5
Hotel Mamora....................15 C3
Marco Polo....................(see 16)
Youth Hostel....................16 D5
EATING
Casa de España....................17 C5
Fast Food Brahim....................18 B5
Hamadi....................19 A2
Mix Max....................20 B5
Populaire Saveur de Poisson....................21 B4
DRINKING
Caid's Bar....................22 B4
Tanger Inn....................23 C5
TRANSPORT
CTM Station....................24 C3
Scenic Lookout
Place du Tabor
R Riad Sultan
Sultan's Gardens
Place de la Kasbah
Porte de la Kasbah
Kasbah
R Tabor
To Café Hafa (700m)
Bab Haha
Bab el-Aassa
Dar el-Baroud
R Malmusi
R Jnane el-Kabtan
R ben Raissouli
R Maimouni
R de la Kasbah
R Dar el-Baroud
Bab el-Marsa
R Lucus
R Sebou
R du Bain
R M Torres
R Almanzor
Medina
R du Commerce
Scenic Lookout
Ave Hassan I
Christian Cemetery
Muslim Cemetery
Mendoubia Gardens
R d'Italie
Bab Fass
R as-Siaghin
Petit Socco
Ave Mokhtar Ahardan
R Dar Dbagh
Ave d'Espagne
R des Postes
Port
R Bouarraqia
Grand Socco
R Touahine
Port Gate
R Sidi Bouabib
Souq
R d'Angleterre
R de la Liberté
R Salah Eddine el-Ayoubi (R de la Plage)
R du Portugal
Jewish Cemetery
Covered Markets
R Amérique du Sud
R el-Oualili
R Anoual
Escalier Waller
Ave Mohammed VI
Terrasse des Paresseux
Place de France
R Khalid Ibn Oualid
R el-Jebha el-Ouatania
R du Prince Moulay Abdallah
R Magellan
R Belgique
R el-Jarraoui
Ave Mexique
Blvd Pasteur
R Ahmed Chaouki
R al-Moutanabi
R Targha
R ibn Jubair
R al-Antaki
R Omar Ben ASS
R ibn Rochd
R al-Boussiri
R al-Alhass
R Zenabe
R Moussa ben-Noussair
R Sorolla
R Zerktouni
Bank Populaire
Wafabank
R al-Moutamid Bnou Abbad
R Ibnou Katir
R de Marseille
R Omarbn
R Allal ben Abdellah
R du Prince Héritier
R al-Mansour Dahabi
R Bouhtouri
Ave Mohammed V
R Lafayette
R Quevada
To Main Bus Station (1km)

Hamadi (☎ 039 934514; 2 Rue de la Kasbah; mains Dh40-70; ⏲ 9.30am-3.30pm & 7.30-11pm) A so-called 'palace restaurant' offering multicourse Moroccan food and live music at a fixed price, all of it aimed at the next tour bus. But the price is right, the decor bright, and the location pleasant.

Casa de España (☎ 039 947359; 11 Rue el-Jebha el-Ouatania; mains from Dh60) With its attractive minimal style, this contemporary Spanish bar/restaurant is a breath of fresh air after so many mosaic interiors. Better yet, there's free tapas with drinks.

Populaire Saveur de Poisson (☎ 039 336326; 2 Escalier Waller; prix fixe Dh150; ⏲ 12.30-4pm & 7-10pm Sat-Thu) This charming little seafood restaurant offers excellent, filling set menus in rustic surroundings, washed down with a homemade juice cocktail. Not just a meal, a whole experience.

Drinking & Entertainment

As you'd expect from its colourful past, Tangier has its fair share of drinking establishments. Most are typically male oriented.

Café Hafa (Ave Mohammed Tazi; ⏲ 10am-8pm) With a shady terrace overlooking the straits, Hafa is where Paul Bowles and the Rolling Stones came to smoke dope, and the indolent air still lingers among the locals who hang out here to enjoy the view and a game of backgammon.

Caid's Bar (El-Minzah, 85 Rue de la Liberté; wine from Dh20; ⏲ 10am-midnight) Welcome to Rick's Cafe – the real-life model for the bar in *Casablanca*. This landmark is a classy relic of the grand days of international Tangier, and photos of the famous and infamous adorn the walls. Women are more than welcome.

Tangier's nightlife picks up in summer, and nightclubs cluster near Place de France and line the beach. Cover charges vary, and may be rolled into drink prices. **Loft** (☎ 073 280927; www.loftclub-tanger.com) is currently Tangier's premier nightspot. The **Tanger Inn** (Hotel el- Muniria, 1 Rue Magellan; beer Dh10; ⏲ 10.30pm-1am, to 3am Fri & Sat) and some of the bars along the beach attract gay clientele, particularly late on weekends.

Getting There & Away

For ferry options, see p810.

BUS

The **CTM station** (☎ 039 931172) is conveniently beside the port gate. Destinations include Casablanca (Dh120, six hours), Rabat (Dh90, 4½ hours), Marrakesh (Dh210, 10 hours), Fez (Dh100, six hours), Meknés (Dh80, five hours) and Chefchaouen (Dh40, three hours). Cheaper bus companies operate from the **main bus station** (gare routière; ☎ 039 946928; Place Jamia el-Arabia), about 2km south of the city centre.

TAXI

You can hail *grands taxis* from a lot next to the main bus station, including to Asilah (Dh20, 30 minutes) and, for Ceuta, Fnideq (Dh40, one hour).

TRAIN

Four trains depart daily from Tanger Ville. Two services go to Casablanca-Voyageurs station (Dh118, 5½ hours); four via Meknès (Dh80, four hours) to Fez (Dh97, five hours), although three involve changing at Sidi Kacem. A night service goes all the way to Marrakesh (seat Dh197, couchette Dh350, 12 hours).

Getting Around

Blue- and yellow-striped *petits taxis* charge Dh7 to Dh10 for most city journeys. From **Ibn Batouta Airport** (☎ 039 393720), 15km southeast of the city, take a cream-coloured *grand taxi* (Dh150).

CEUTA

pop 76,000

Jutting out east into the Mediterranean, this 20-sq-km peninsula has been a Spanish enclave since 1640. Despite its relaxed, well-kept city centre with bars, cafes and Andalucian atmosphere, Ceuta is still recognisably African. Between a quarter and third of the population are of Rif Berber origin, giving the enclave a fascinating Iberian-African mix.

Orientation & Information

The Plaza de Africa, unmistakable for its giant cathedral, dominates the city centre. The port and ferry terminal are a short walk to the northwest. To phone Ceuta from outside Spain, dial ☎ 0034 before the nine-digit phone number. Also remember that Ceuta is on Spanish time and uses the euro. Banks with ATMs are plentiful around the pedestrianised Paseo de Revellin, and Plaza Ruiz.

Cyber Ceuta (☎ 956 512303; Paseo Colón; per hr €2.40; ⏲ 11am-2pm & 5-10pm Mon-Sat, 5-10pm Sun) Internet.

Main Tourist Office (☎ 956 200560; Baluarte de los Mallorquines; ⏲ 8.30am-8.30pm Mon-Fri, 9am-8pm Sat & Sun) Friendly and efficient, with good maps and brochures.

Sights

Ceuta's history is marked by the **Ruta Monumenta**, a series of excellent information boards in English and Spanish outside key buildings and monuments.

The impressively restored **royal city walls** (☎ 956 511770; Ave González Tablas; admission free incl gallery; 🕑 10am-2pm & 5-8pm) are worth a visit, and contain the striking **Museo de los Muralles Reales** art gallery tucked inside.

The most intriguing museum is the underground **Museo de la Basilica Tardorromana** (Calle Queipo de Llano; 🕑 10am-1.30pm & 5-7.30pm Mon-Sat, 10am-1.30pm Sun) integrated into the architectural remains of an ancient basilica discovered during street work in the '80s, and including a bridge over open tombs, skeletons included.

Sleeping

Ceuta is home to plenty of *pensiónes* or *casas de huéspedes* (guest houses), some of which are identifiable only by the large blue-and-white 'CH' plaque.

Pensión La Bohemia (☎ 956 510615; 16 Paseo de Revellín; s/d €25/35) A charming, little place with potted plants, tiled floors and a surfeit of pictures of Marilyn Monroe. The rooms are fresh and clean with piping-hot communal showers.

Hostal Central (☎ 956 516716; www.hostalesceuta.com; Paseo del Revellín; s/d/tr €34/44/54; ❄) This good-value, centrally located hotel is the next step up from a *pension*. Bright rooms are small but spotless, and all come with bathroom and fridge. Low-season discounts can tip this place into the budget bracket.

Hostal Plaza Ruiz (☎ 956 516733; www.hostalesceuta.com; 3 Plaza Ruiz; low/high season s €34/45, d €44/60, tr €54/76; ❄) Sister hotel to the Central, this place has a similar, welcoming style and a charming location. Rooms are airy; the best have wrought-iron balconies overlooking the plaza cafes.

Eating

The Pablado Marinero (Seamen's Village) beside the yacht harbour is home to a variety of decent cheap restaurants. The best place to look for tapas bars is in the streets behind the post office and around Millán Astray to the north of Calle Camoens. Also try **Cala Carlota** (☎ 956 525061; Calle Edrisis; set menu from €7) for its three-course *menú del diá* (daily set menu).

Getting There & Away

Bus 7 runs up to the Moroccan border (*frontera*) every 10 minutes from Plaza de la Constitución (€0.60). The large *grands taxi* lot next to Moroccan border control has departures to Fnideq (Dh5, 10 minutes) – change there for Tangier.

The **estación marítima** (ferry terminal; Calle Muelle Cañonero Dato) is west of the town centre and from here there are several daily high-speed ferries to Algeciras (p810).

CHEFCHAOUEN

pop 45,000

Set beneath the striking peaks of the Rif Mountains, Chefchaouen (also known by its diminutive 'Chaouen') has long been charming travellers. One of the prettiest in Morocco, Chefchaouen's **medina** has blinding blue-white hues, red-tiled roofs and an unmistakeably Andalucian flavour. The heart of the medina is the shady, cobbled **Plaza Uta el-Hammam**, dominated by the red-hued walls of the **kasbah** (☎ 039 986343; admission Dh10; 🕑 9am-1pm & 3-6.30pm Wed-Mon) and the striking **Grande Mosquée**. Inside the kasbah's gardens is a modest **ethnographic museum** with photos of old Chefchaouen.

Trekking in the Rif Mountains is another of Chefchaouen's drawcards, especially **Jebel el-Kelaâ** (1616m), which towers over the town and can be easily climbed in one day.

Information

Banque Populaire Medina (Plaza Uta el-Hammam; 🕑 9.30am-1pm & 3.30-9pm Mon-Fri) ATM; Ciudad Nueva (Ave Hassan II)

Saadoune.net (Plaza Uta el-Hammam; per hr Dh10; 🕑 9am-2pm & 3pm-midnight) Internet access.

Sleeping

Even late into spring, Chefchaouen gets cold at night, so ask for an extra blanket.

Hotel Mauritania (☎ 039 986184; 15 Rue Qadi Alami; s/d Dh45/80) Rooms are simple here, but staff are helpful, there's a comfy courtyard lounge ideal for meeting other travellers, and the breakfasts (Dh20) are great.

Hostal Yasmina (☎ 039 883118; yasmina45@hotmail.com; 12 Calle Lalla Horra; r per person Dh70) For the price bracket, this place sparkles. Rooms are bright and clean, the location is a stone's throw from Plaza Uta el-Hammam, and the roof terrace is very welcoming.

Hostal Guernika (☎ 039 987434; 49 Onssar; r Dh200) This is a warm and charming place, with a very caring and attentive owner, not too far from the Plaza Uta el-Hammam. There are several great streetside rooms—large and bright, facing the mountains—but others are dark. All have showers.

Dar Terrae (☎ 039 987598; darterrae@hotmail.com; Ave Hassan I; s/d/tr incl breakfast Dh250/350/450) These funky, cheerfully painted rooms are individually decorated, have their own bathroom and fireplace, and are hidden up and down a tumble of stairs and odd corners. Breakfasts are fantastic. It's poorly signed – if in doubt ask for the 'Hotel Italiano'.

Eating

Plaza Cafe-Restaurants (Plaza Uta el-Hamman; breakfast from Dh15, mains from Dh25; 8am-11pm) A popular eating option in Chefchaouen is to choose one of about a dozen cafe-restaurants on the main square. Menus are virtually identical – continental breakfasts, soups and salads, tajines and seafood – but the food is generally pretty good, and the ambience lively.

Restaurant Les Raisins (☎ 067 982878; 7 Rue Sidi Sifri; tajines Dh20, set menu from Dh40; 7am-9pm) A bit out of the way, this family-run place is a perennial favourite with locals and tourists alike, and known for its couscous royal.

Assaada (☎ 066 317316; Bab Ain; set menu Dh40) This reliable cheapie tries hard to please. Located on both sides of the alley just prior to Bab el-Ain, it offers the usual Moroccan menu, but also great fruit shakes, and a funky graffiti rooftop terrace. The staircase isn't for the faint-hearted.

Getting There & Away

Many bus services from Chefchaouen originate elsewhere and are often full on arrival, so buy your ticket a day in advance if possible. **CTM** (☎ 039 987669) services include Casablanca (Dh120, eight hours), Fez (Dh70, four hours) and Tangier (Dh40, three hours) and further destinations. *Grands taxis* heading to Tetouan (Dh30, one hour) leave from just below Plaza Mohammed V – change for Tangier or Ceuta.

ATLANTIC COAST

Morocco's Atlantic littoral is surprisingly varied, with sweeping beaches and lagoons, the urban sprawl around the political and economic capitals of Rabat and Casablanca, and the pretty fishing ports-cum-tourist drawcard of Essaouira.

CASABLANCA

pop 4 million

Casa, as Casablanca is popularly known, is a city of contradictions, offering a unique insight into modern Morocco. It's a sprawling, European-style city that's home to traffic racing along wide boulevards, public parks, imposing Hispano-Moorish and art deco buildings and simmering social problems. The city's rundown facades stand in sharp contrast to Casablanca's modernist landmark, the enormous and incredibly ornate Hassan II mosque.

Orientation

The relatively small medina sits in the north of the city close to the port. To the south of the medina is Place des Nations Unies, a large traffic junction that marks the heart of the city. The CTM bus station and Casa Port train station are in the city centre. Casa-Voyageurs train station is 2km east of the centre and the airport is 30km southeast of the city.

Information

There are banks – most with ATMS and foreign-exchange offices – on almost every street corner in the centre of Casablanca.

BMCE (Bank Marocaine du Commerce Extérieur; Hyatt Regency Hotel; 9am-9pm) Good for after-hours and weekend services.

Crédit du Maroc (☎ 022 477255; 48 Blvd Mohammed V) Separate bureau de change that is very central.

Gig@net (☎ 022 484810; 140 Blvd Mohammed Zerktouni; per hr Dh10; 24hr) Internet access.

LGnet (☎ 022 274613; 81 Blvd Mohammed V; per hr Dh6; 9am-midnight) Internet access.

Office National Marocain du Tourisme (ONMT; ☎ 022 271177; 55 Rue Omar Slaoui; 8.30am-4.30pm Mon-Fri)

Service d'Aide Médicale Urgente (SAMU; ☎ 022 252525; 24hr) Private ambulance service.

Sights

Rising above the Atlantic northwest of the medina, the **Hassan II Mosque** is the world's third-largest mosque, built to commemorate the former king's 60th birthday. The mosque rises above the ocean on a rocky outcrop reclaimed from the sea. It's a vast building that holds 25,000 worshippers and can accommodate a further 80,000 in the courtyards and squares around it. To see the interior of the mosque you must take a **guided tour** (☎ 022 482886; adult/student Dh120/60; 9am, 10am, 11am & 2pm Sat-Thu).

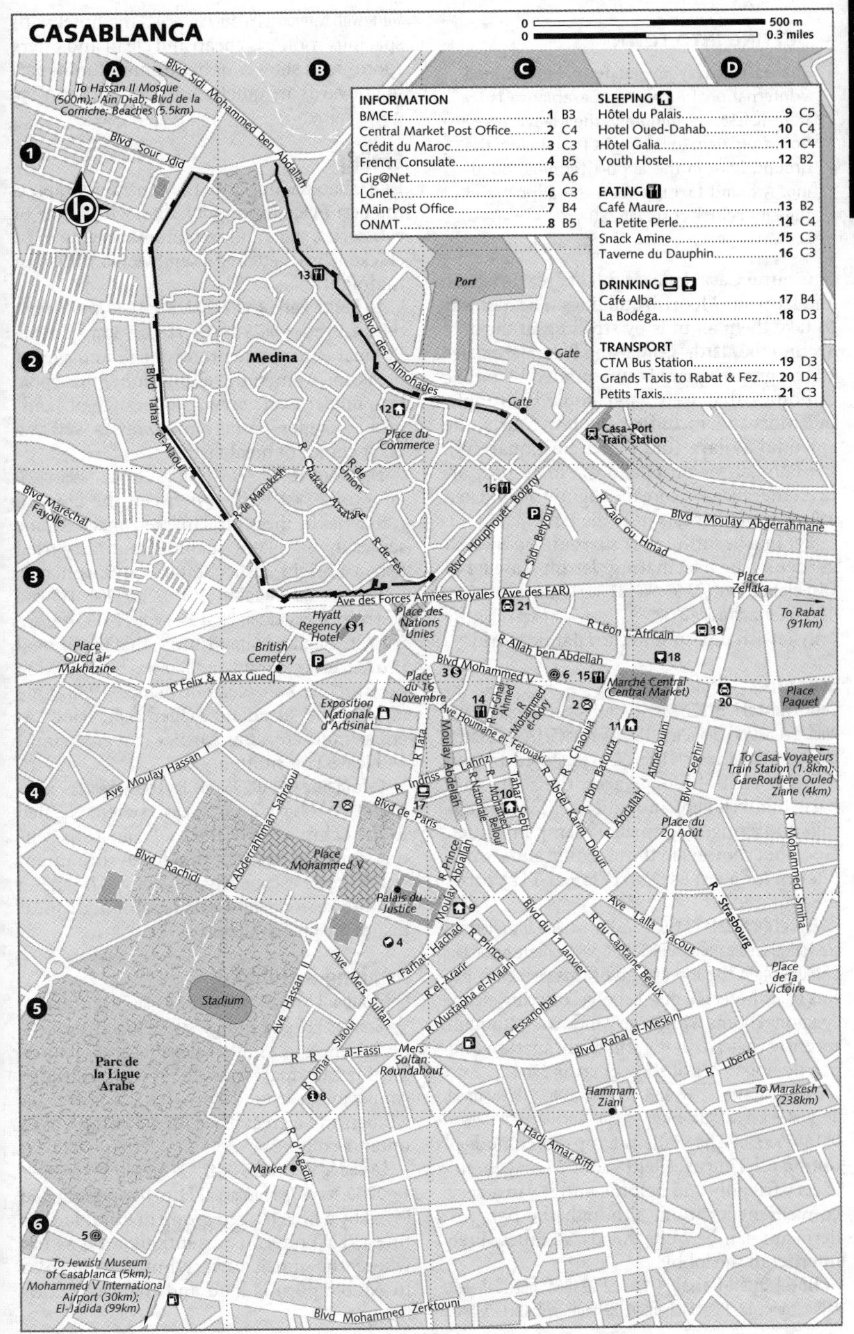
CASABLANCA
0 500 m
0 0.3 miles
A
B
C
D
1
2
3
4
5
6
INFORMATION
BMCE....1 B3
Central Market Post Office....2 C4
Crédit du Maroc....3 C3
French Consulate....4 B5
Gig@Net....5 A6
LGnet....6 C3
Main Post Office....7 B4
ONMT....8 B5
SLEEPING
Hôtel du Palais....9 C5
Hotel Oued-Dahab....10 C4
Hôtel Galia....11 C4
Youth Hostel....12 B2
EATING
Café Maure....13 B2
La Petite Perle....14 C4
Snack Amine....15 C3
Taverne du Dauphin....16 C3
DRINKING
Café Alba....17 B4
La Bodéga....18 D3
TRANSPORT
CTM Bus Station....19 D3
Grands Taxis to Rabat & Fez....20 D4
Petits Taxis....21 C3
To Hassan II Mosque (500m); 'Ain Diab; Blvd de la Corniche; Beaches (5.5km)
Blvd Sidi Mohammed ben Abdallah
Blvd Sour Jdid
Port
Medina
Gate
Gate
Blvd des Almohades
Blvd Tahar el-Alaoui
Place du Commerce
Casa-Port Train Station
R de Marrakesh
R Chakab Arsalane
R de Union
R de Fès
Blvd Houphouet Boigny
R Sidi Belyout
R Zaid ou Hmad
Blvd Moulay Abderrahmane
Blvd Maréchal Fayolle
Place Zellaka
Ave des Forces Armées Royales (Ave des FAR)
To Rabat (91km)
Hyatt Regency Hotel
Place des Nations Unies
R Léon L'Africain
Place Oued al-Makhazine
British Cemetery
R Allah ben Abdellah
Blvd Mohammed V
R Felix & Max Guedj
Place du 16 Novembre
Marché Central (Central Market)
Place Paquet
Exposition Nationale d'Artisinat
R el-Ghali Ahmed
R Mohammed el-Qory
Ave Houmane el-Fetouaki
R Chaouia
R Ibn Batouta
Almedouini
Blvd Seghir
To Casa-Voyageurs Train Station (1.8km); GareRoutière Ouled Ziane (4km)
Ave Moulay Hassan I
R Abderrahman Sahraoui
R Tata
R Indriss Lahrizi
Moulay Abdellah
R Nationale
R Mohammed Belloul
R Tahar Sebti
R Abdel Karim Diouri
R Abdallah
Place du 20 Août
Blvd de Paris
R Mohammed Smiha
Blvd Rachidi
Place Mohammed V
R Prince Moulay Abdallah
Palais du Justice
R Strasbourg
Ave Lalla Yacout
Blvd du 11 Janvier
R du Captaine Beaux
R Farhat Hachad
R Prince
Ave Mers Sultan
Ave Hassan II
Stadium
R el-Ararir
R Mustapha el-Maani
R Essanolbar
Place de la Victoire
Parc de la Ligue Arabe
R Omar Slaoui
R al-Fassi
Mers Sultan Roundabout
Blvd Rahal el-Meskini
R Liberté
To Marakesh (238km)
Hammam Ziani
R Hadj Amar Riffi
R d'Agadir
Market
To Jewish Museum of Casablanca (5km); Mohammed V International Airport (30km); El-Jadida (99km)
Blvd Mohammed Zerktouni

Book your stay at lonelyplanet.com/hotels

GETTING INTO TOWN

The easiest way to get from Mohammed V International Airport to Casablanca is by train (Dh35, 35 minutes); they leave every hour from 6am to midnight from below the ground floor in the airport terminal building. A grand taxi between the airport and the city centre costs Dh250.

Central Casablanca is full of great art-deco and Hispano-Moorish buildings. The best way to take them all in is by strolling in the area around the **Marché Central** and **Place Mohammed V**. The grand square is surrounded by public buildings that were later copied throughout Morocco, including the law courts, the splendid Wilaya (old police headquarters), the Bank al-Maghrib, and the main post office. After that, explore the slightly dilapidated 19th-century **medina** near the port.

Set in a beautiful villa surrounded by lush gardens, the fascinating **Jewish Museum of Casablanca** (☎ 022 994940; 81 Rue Chasseur Jules Gros, Oasis; Dh20, with guide Dh30; 🕑 10am-5pm Mon-Fri) is the only Jewish museum in the Islamic world.

Sleeping

Youth Hostel (☎ 022 220551; frmaj1@menara.com; 6 Place Ahmed el-Bidaoui; dm/d/tr incl breakfast Dh45/120/180, sheets Dh5; 🕑 8-10am & noon-11pm; 💻) Clustered around a bright central lounge area, the rooms are basic but well kept and quiet, with high ceilings and a lingering smell of damp in winter. Good hot showers in the morning and a small kitchen for guest use. No IYHF or YHA cards are required.

Hôtel du Palais (☎ 022 276191; 68 Rue Farhat Hachad; s/d with shared bathroom Dh80/120, with private bathroom Dh140/240) At the lower end of this price range, this basic hotel is a good choice, offering clean, spacious rooms with large windows. Although recently upgraded, it's still fairly spartan and can be noisy. A hot shower costs Dh10.

Hôtel Galia (☎ 022 481694; galia_19@hotmail.fr; 19 Rue Ibn Batouta; s/d/tr Dh150/220/300, with shower Dh170/250/330) The Galia is a top-notch budget option offering excellent value. Management is very friendly and helpful, and it's in a very convenient location, although the bar underneath can be quite rowdy at times. Free internet in the lobby.

Hôtel Oued-Dahab (☎ 022 223866; oueddahab@yahoo.com; 17 Rue Mohamed Belloul; s/d Dh120/180, s/d/tr with bathroom Dh150/250/295) This hotel with spacious rooms is cheap and clean and offers rooms with shower or bathroom. Rooms facing inwards are quieter but a bit darker. Very good value.

Eating

Rue Chaouia, opposite the central market, is the best place for a quick bite, with a line of rotisseries, stalls and restaurants serving roast chicken, brochettes and sandwiches until past midnight.

La Petite Perle (☎ 022 272849; 17-19 Ave Houmane el-Fetouaki; mains Dh25-45; 🕑 11.30am-3pm & 6-11pm) Popular with young professionals and a quiet break for women travelling alone, this spotless, modern cafe serves up a range of sandwiches, crêpes, pastas and pizzas as well as a great choice of breakfasts.

Snack Amine (☎ 022 541331; Rue Chaouia; mains Dh25-45; 🕑 noon-2am) Tucked between the chicken rotisseries by the central market, Snack Amine serves up big plates of simple but tasty fried fish in a bright, rather soulless atmosphere.

Taverne du Dauphin (☎ 022 221200; 115 Blvd Houphouet Boigny; mains Dh70-90, menu Dh110; 🕑 Mon-Sat) A Casablanca institution, this traditional Provencal restaurant and bar has been serving up *fruits de mer* (seafood) since 1958. One taste of the succulent grilled fish, fried calamari and *crevettes royales* (royal shrimp) will leave you smitten.

Café Maure (☎ 022 260960; Blvd des Almohades; mains Dh60-90; 🕑 10am-midnight, to 6pm in winter) Nestled in the ochre walls of the *sqala,* an 18th-century fortified bastion, this lovely restaurant is a tranquil escape from the city. The menu favours seafood and salads, although meat dishes are also available.

Drinking & Clubbing

Café Alba (☎ 022 227154; 59-61 Rue Indriss Lahrizi; 🕑 8am-1am) High ceilings, swish furniture, subtle lighting and a hint of elegant colonial times set this cafe apart from the more traditional smoky joints around town. It's hassle-free for women and a great place for watching Casa's up-and-coming.

La Bodéga (☎ 022 541842; 129 Rue Allah ben Abdellah; 🕑 12.30-3pm & 7pm-midnight) Hip, happening and loved by a mixed-aged group of Casablanca's finest, La Bodéga is essentially a tapas bar where the music (everything from Salsa to Arabic pop) is loud and the Rioja flows freely.

The beachfront suburb of Aïn Diab is the place for late-night drinking and dancing, with a strip of discos along the beachfront. Expect to pay at least Dh100 admission and as much again for drinks.

Getting There & Away

BUS

The modern **CTM bus station** (☎ 022 541010; 23 Rue Léon L'Africain) has daily CTM departures to Essaouira (Dh130, seven hours, three daily), Fez (Dh100, five hours, 12 daily), Marrakesh (Dh80, four hours, nine daily) and Tangier (Dh130, six hours, six daily). The modern **Gare Routière Ouled Ziane** (☎ 022 444470), 4km southeast of the centre, is the bus station for non-CTM services.

TAXI

Grands taxis to Rabat (Dh35), and some to Fez (Dh60), leave from Blvd Hassan Seghir, near the CTM bus station. However, the train is more convenient and comfortable.

TRAIN

All long-distance trains, as well as those to Mohammed V airport, depart from **Casa-Voyageurs train station** (☎ 022 243818). Destinations include Marrakesh (Dh84, three hours, nine daily), Fez (Dh103, 4½ hours, nine daily) via Meknès (Dh86, 3½ hours) and Tangier (Dh118, 5¾ hours, three daily). Trains to Rabat (Dh36, one hour) leave from **Casa-Port train station** (☎ 022 223011).

Getting Around

Expect to pay Dh10 in or near the city centre for a red *petit taxi* fare.

RABAT

pop 1.7 million

Relaxed, well kept and very European, flag-waving Rabat is as cosmopolitan as Casablanca, but lacks the frantic pace and grimy feel of its economic big brother. Its elegant tree-lined boulevards and imposing administrative buildings exude an unhurried, diplomatic and hassle-free charm that many travellers grow to like.

Orientation

The main administrative buildings and many of the hotels lie just off the city's main thoroughfare, the wide, palm-lined Ave Mohammed V. The entrance to the medina is at the northern end of the avenue, while the train station, Rabat Ville, is at the southern end.

Information

Numerous banks (with ATMs) are concentrated along Ave Mohammed V.

Librairie Livre Service (46 Ave Allal ben Abdallah; per hr Dh7; 9am-noon & 3-8pm Mon-Sat) Internet access.

Office National Marocain du Tourisme (ONMT; ☎ 037 673756; cnr Rue Oued El Makhazine & Rue Zalaka, Agdal; 8.30am-noon & 3-6.30pm Mon-Fri)

Sights & Activities

Barely 400 years old, Rabat's **medina** is tiny compared to Fez or Marrakesh, although it still piques the senses with its rich mixture of spices, carpets, crafts, cheap shoes and bootlegged DVDs. The **Kasbah des Oudaias** sits high up on the bluff overlooking the Oued Bou Regreg and contains within its walls the oldest **mosque** in Rabat, built in the 12th century and restored in the 18th. The southern corner of the kasbah is home to the **Andalucían Gardens** (sunrise-sunset), laid out by the French during the colonial period. The centrepiece is the grand 17th-century palace containing the **Musée des Oudaia** (☎ 037 731537; admission Dh10; 9am-noon & 3-5pm Oct-Apr, to 6pm May-Sep).

Towering above the Oued Bou Regreg is Rabat's most famous landmark, **Le Tour Hassan** (Hassan Tower). In 1195, the Almohad sultan Yacoub al-Mansour began constructing an enormous minaret, intending to make it the highest in the Muslim world, but he died before the project was completed. Abandoned at 44m, the beautifully designed and intricately carved tower still lords over the remains of the adjacent mosque.

The cool marble **Mausoleum of Mohammed V** (admission free; sunrise-sunset), built in traditional Moroccan style, lies opposite the tower. The present king's father (the late Hassan II) and grandfather are laid to rest here, surrounded by intensely patterned *zellij* mosaics from floor to ceiling.

Abandoned, crumbling and overgrown, the combined ancient Roman city of **Sala Colonia** and Merenid necropolis of **Chellah** (cnr Ave Yacoub al-Mansour & Blvd Moussa ibn Nassair; admission Dh10; 9am-5.30pm) is one of Rabat's most evocative sights. Rarely visited and overgrown with fruit trees and wild flowers, it's an atmospheric place to roam around.

Sleeping

Hôtel al-Maghrib al-Jadid (☎ 037 732207; 2 Rue Sebbahi; s/d Dh70/110, hot showers Dh7.50) Although the rooms at this hotel are fairly small and spartan, they are pristinely clean, and have shuttered windows that let in lots of light.

Hôtel Dorhmi (☎ 037 723898; 313 Ave Mohammed V; s/d Dh90/130, hot showers Dh10) Immaculately kept, very friendly and keenly priced, this family-run hotel is the best of the medina options. The simple rooms are bright and tidy and surround a central courtyard on the first floor above the Banque Populaire.

Hôtel Splendid (☎ 037 723283; 8 Rue Ghazza; s/d with shared bathroom Dh104/130, with private bathroom Dh130/190) Slap-bang in the heart of the medina, the spacious, bright rooms, with high ceilings, big windows, cheerful colours and simple wooden furniture, are set around a pleasant courtyard.

Hôtel Majestic (☎ 037 722997; www.hotelmajestic.ma; 121 Ave Hassan II; s/d Dh239/279) Though not as palatial as it sounds, this wonderfully modern place has smallish rooms with sleek, new furniture and fittings if not a lot of character. Despite the double glazing the rooms can be noisy, so it's best to forego the medina view for a room at the back.

Eating & Drinking

For quick eating, go to Ave Mohammed V just inside the medina gate, where you'll find a slew of hole-in-the-wall joints dishing out tajines, brochettes, salads and chips.

Restaurant de la Libération (256 Ave Mohammed V; mains Dh30) Cheap, cheerful and marginally more classy than the string of other eateries along this road (it's got plastic menus and tablecloths), this basic restaurant does a steady line in traditional favourites. Friday is couscous day when giant platters of the stuff are delivered to the eager masses.

Café Maure (Kasbah des Oudaias; 🕒 9am-5.30pm) Sit back, relax and just gaze out over the estuary to Salé from this chilled open-air cafe spread over several terraces in the Andalucían Gardens. Mint tea is the thing here, accompanied by little almond biscuits delivered on silver trays. It's an easy place to pass time writing postcards and a relaxed venue for women.

Le Ziryab (☎ 037 733636; 10 Zankat Ennajar; mains Dh90-140) This chic Moroccan restaurant is in a magnificent building just off Rue des Consuls. The blend of old-world character and stylish contemporary design is also reflected in the excellent menu of interesting variations on tajine, couscous, *pastilla* (a rich, savoury-sweet pie) and grilled meat and fish.

Getting There & Away

BUS

The main **gare routière** (☎ 037 795816) and the less chaotic **CTM station** (☎ 037 281488) are 5km southwest of the city centre. CTM has services to Casablanca (D35, 1½ hours, eight daily), Essaouira (Dh115, three hours, three daily), Fez (Dh68, 3½ hours, seven daily), Marrakesh (Dh120, five hours, three daily) and Tangier (Dh90, 4½ hours, five daily).

GRANDS TAXIS

Grands taxis leave for Casablanca (Dh35) from just outside the intercity bus station. Other grands taxis leave for Fez (Dh65) and Meknès (Dh50) from a lot off Ave Hassan II behind the Hôtel Bouregreg.

TRAIN

Rabat Ville train station (☎ 037 736060) is right in the centre of town, and not to be confused with Rabat Agdal train station to the west. Trains run every 30 minutes until 10.30pm to Casa-Port train station in Casablanca (Dh36, one hour), with services to Fez (Dh76, 3½ hours, eight daily) via Meknès (Dh60, 2½ hours), Tangier (Dh91, 4½ hours, seven daily) and Marrakesh (Dh112, 4½ hours, eight daily).

Getting Around

Rabat's blue *petits taxis* are plentiful and quick. A ride around the centre of town will cost about Dh10.

ESSAOUIRA

pop 70,000

Perennially popular Essaouira has long been a favourite of the travellers' trail: laid-back and artsy with sea breezes and picture-postcard ramparts that all conspire to extend trips longer than expected. It's the kind of place where you'll sigh deeply and relax enough to shrug off your guarded attitude and just soak up the atmosphere.

Sights

Essaouira's walled, late-18th-century **medina** was added to Unesco's World Heritage list in 2001. The mellow atmosphere, narrow winding streets lined with colourful shops, whitewashed houses and heavy old wooden doors make it a wonderful place to stroll. The easiest place to access the ramparts is at **Skala de la Ville**. Down by the harbour, the **Skala du Port** (adult/child Dh10/3; 8.30am-noon & 2.30-6pm) offers picturesque views over the fishing port and **Île de Mogador**.

Océan Vagabond (024 783934; www.oceanvagabond.com, in French; 8am-8pm) rents out water-sports equipment and offers instruction along Essaouira's wide sandy beach. Be aware of strong Atlantic currents.

The **Gnaoua and World Music Festival** (held over the third weekend in June) is a four-day musical extravaganza with concerts on Place Moulay Hassan.

Sleeping

Dar Afram (024 785657; www.dar-afram.com; 10 Rue Sidi Magdoul; s Dh150, d Dh300-400 Oct-May, s Dh250, d Dh400-450 Jun-Sep) This extremely friendly guest house has simple, spotless rooms with shared bathrooms and a funky vibe. The Aussie-Moroccan owners are musicians and an impromptu session often follows the evening meals shared around a communal table. It also has a lovely tiled hamam.

Hotel Beau Rivage (024 475925; beaurivage@menara.ma; 14 Place Moulay Hassan; d with shared bathroom Dh200, s/d/tr with private bathroom Dh250/350/450, breakfast Dh20) A long-time backpacker's favourite, this cheery hotel on the central square could hardly be better located. Ensuite rooms are clean, comfy and airy, with a few facing onto a rooftop terrace with views over the town that make it ideal for lazy late-morning breakfasts.

Riad Nakhla (/fax 024 474940; www.essaouiranet.com/riad-nakhla; 2 Rue Agadir; s/d Dh225/325, ste Dh400-500) A beautiful courtyard, with elegant stone columns and trickling fountain, lifts this place above the standard budget hotel. The well-appointed bedrooms are simple but comfortable and immaculately kept. Breakfast on the stunning roof terrace is another treat.

Hôtel Les Matins Bleus (024 785363, 066 308899; www.les-matins-bleus.com; 22 Rue de Drâa; Oct-May s/d/ste Dh275/420/840, Jun-Sep Dh300/460/920) This charming hotel has bright, traditionally styled rooms surrounding a central courtyard painted in cheerful colours. The rooms all have plain white walls, local fabrics and spotless bathrooms. Breakfast is served on the sheltered terrace from where you'll get good views over the medina.

Eating

Place Moulay Hassan offers plenty of sandwich stands and cafes for lazy breakfasts and lunches, plus snack stands and hole-in-the-wall type places line Ave Sidi Mohammed ben Abdallah, Ave Zerktouni and just inside Bab Doukkala.

Outdoor fish grills (port end of Place Moulay Hassan; around Dh40) These unpretentious stands offer one of the definitive Essaouira experiences. Just choose what you want to eat from the colourful displays of freshly caught fish and shellfish at each grill and wait for it to be cooked on the spot and served with a pile of bread and salad.

Restaurant Ferdaous (024 473655; 27 Rue Abdesslam Lebadi; mains Dh60-80, set menu Dh105; closed Mon) A delightful Moroccan restaurant, and one of the few places in town that serves real, traditional Moroccan food (like home cooking).

Getting There & Away

The **bus station** (024 785241) is about 400m northeast of the medina, an easy walk during the day but better in a petit taxi (Dh10) if you're arriving/leaving late at night. **CTM** (024 784764) has several buses daily for Casablanca (Dh125, six hours), and one to Marrakesh (Dh75, 2½ hours).

Supratours (024 475317) runs buses to Marrakesh train station (Dh80, 2½ hours, four daily) to connect with trains to Casablanca. Book in advance.

IMPERIAL CITIES

From green hills and wooded mountains to historic cities and holy shrines, this region lays a strong claim to being the most diverse in the country. Whether in grand old Fez or the clamour of Marrakesh, this could be the part of Morocco where you spend most of your time.

FEZ

pop 1 million

Fez is 1400 years old and Morocco's spiritual beating heart. Its medina (Fez el-Bali) is the largest living medieval Islamic city in the world, and the world's largest car-free

Book your stay at lonelyplanet.com/hotels

urban environment. A first visit can be overwhelming, an assault on the eyes, ears and nose through covered bazaars, winding alleys, mosques, workshops, past people and pack animals that seem to take you out of the 21st century and back to an imagined *Arabian Nights*.

Orientation

Fez is neatly divided into three parts: Fez el-Bali (the core of the medina, entered through Bab Bou Jeloud gate) in the east; Fez el-Jdid (containing the *mellah*, or Jewish quarter, and Royal Palace) in the centre; and the Ville Nouvelle, the administrative area constructed by the French, to the southwest.

Information

INTERNET ACCESS

Cyber Club (Map p825; Blvd Mohammed V; per hr Dh6; 9am-10pm)

Cyber Batha (Map p823; Derb Douh; per hr Dh10; 9am-10pm) Has English as well as French keyboards.

MEDICAL SERVICES

Hôpital Ghassani (off Map p825; ☎ 055 622777) One of the city's biggest hospitals; located east of the ville nouvelle in the Dhar Mehraz district.

Night Pharmacy (Map p825; ☎ 035 623493; Blvd Moulay Youssef; 9pm-6am) Located in the north of the ville nouvelle; staffed by a doctor and a pharmacist.

MONEY

There are plenty of banks (with ATMs) in the Ville Nouvelle along Blvd Mohammed V. In the medina, there's **Société Générale** (Map p823; Ave des Français; 8.45am-noon & 2.45-6pm Mon-Thu, 8.45-11am Fri, 8.45am-noon Sat), outside Bab Bou Jeloud.

TOURIST INFORMATION

There is no tourist information in the medina, but there is the **Tourist Information Office** (Syndicat d'Initiative; Map p825; ☎ 035 623460; Place Mohammed V).

Dangers & Annoyances

Fez has long been notorious for its *faux guides* (unofficial guides) and carpet shop hustlers. Walking alone late at night in the medina is also not advisable, as knife-point robberies aren't unknown.

Festivals & Events

Every June the **Fès Festival of World Sacred Music** (☎ 035 740535; www.fesfestival.com) brings together music groups and artists from all corners of the globe, and has become an established favourite on the world music festival circuit.

Sights

MEDINA (FEZ EL-BALI)

Within the old walls of Fez el-Bali lies an incredible maze of twisting alleys, blind turns and hidden souqs. Navigation can be confusing and getting lost at some stage a certainty, but this is part of the medina's charm: you never quite know what discovery lies around the next corner.

Outside the medina walls, the **Merenid tombs** (Map p823) are dramatic in their advanced state of ruin. The views over Fez are spectacular and well worth the climb. Look for the black smoke in the southern part of the city, marking the potteries.

FEZ EL-JDID (NEW FEZ)

Only in a city as old as Fez could you find a district dubbed 'New' because it's only 700 years old. It's home to the **Dar el-Makhzen** (Royal Palace; Map p825; Pl des Alaouites), whose entrance is a stunning example of modern restoration, but the 80 hectares of palace grounds are not open to the public.

In the 14th century, Fez el-Jdid became a refuge for Jews, thus creating a **mellah**. The *mellah's* southwest corner is home to the fascinating **Jewish Cemetery & Habarim Synagogue** (Map p825; admission free, donations appreciated; 7am-7pm).

Sleeping

MEDINA

Pension Kawtar (Map p823; ☎ 035 740172; pension_kaw@yahoo.fr; Derb Taryana, Talaa Seghira; dm Dh60, s/d with shared bathroom Dh200/300, d with private bathroom Dh350, breakfast Dh25) Well-signed off Talaa Seghira, the Kawtar is a family-run concern, as much a home as a hostel. Amazingly, there are 10 rooms tucked into the place – those on the ground floor are a bit gloomy, but they get better the closer you get to the roof terrace. Great value for the price.

Hôtel Cascade (Map p823; ☎ 035 638442; 26 Rue Serrajine, Bab Bou Jeloud; dm Dh80, r Dh160, breakfast Dh20) One of the grand-daddies of the Morocco shoestring hotels, the Cascade still keeps drawing them in. You don't expect much for the price and you don't really get it either – it's all pretty basic – but if you're up for stretching budgets and meeting plenty of like-minded travellers then this might be the place for you.

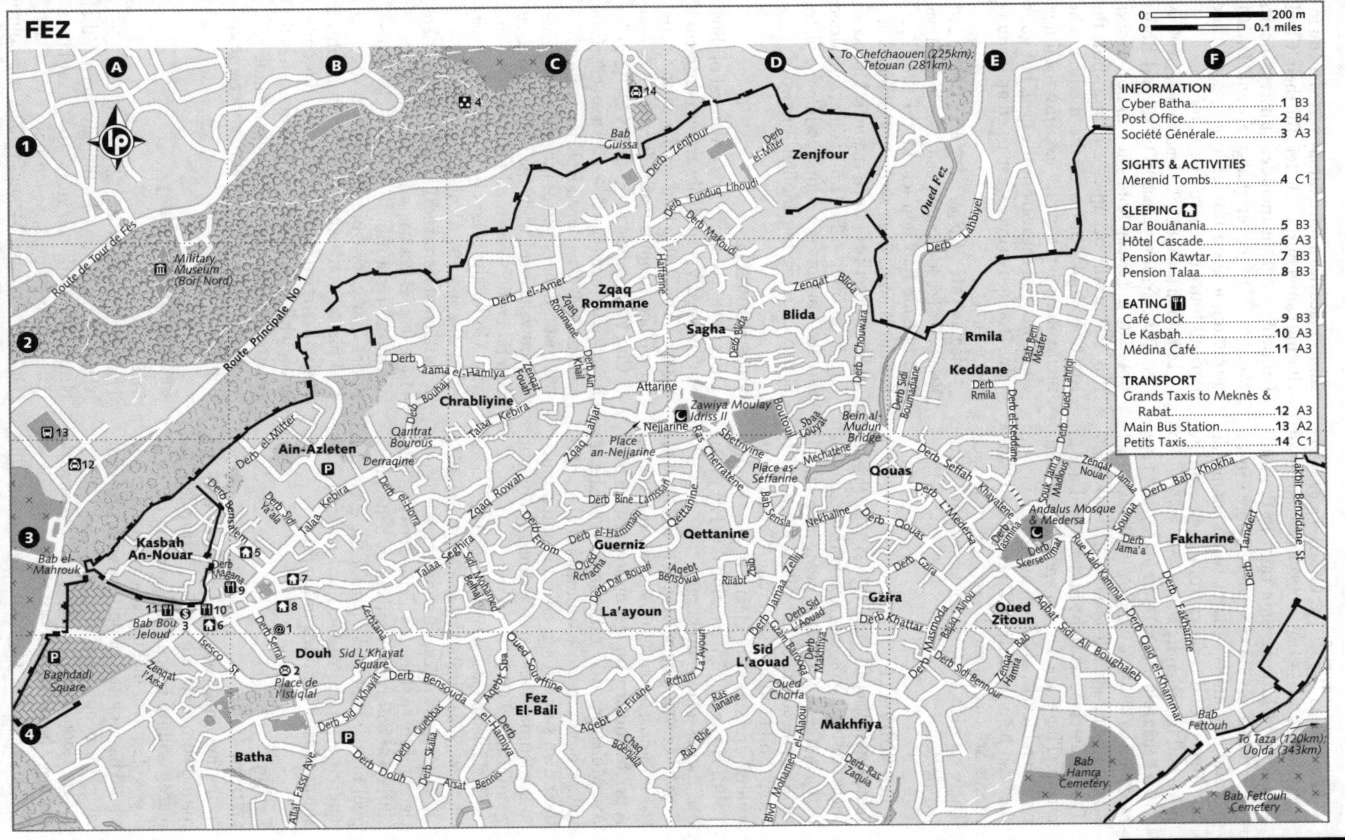
FEZ
0 200 m
0 0.1 miles
INFORMATION
Cyber Batha 1 B3
Post Office 2 B4
Société Générale 3 A3
SIGHTS & ACTIVITIES
Merenid Tombs 4 C1
SLEEPING
Dar Bouânania 5 B3
Hôtel Cascade 6 A3
Pension Kawtar 7 B3
Pension Talaa 8 B3
EATING
Café Clock 9 B3
Le Kasbah 10 A3
Médina Café 11 A3
TRANSPORT
Grands Taxis to Meknès & Rabat 12 A3
Main Bus Station 13 A2
Petits Taxis 14 C1
To Chefchaouen (225km); Tetouan (281km)
To Taza (120km); Oujda (343km)
Military Museum (Borj Nord)
Route Principale No 1
Route de Tour de Fes
Oued Fez
Zenjfour
Blida
Sagha
Zqaq Rommane
Chrabliyine
Ain-Azleten
Kasbah An-Nouar
Bab Bou Jeloud
Bab el-Mahrouk
Baghdadi Square
Place de l'Istiqlal
Douh
Batha
Fez El-Bali
La'ayoun
Guerniz
Qettanine
Sid L'aouad
Makhfiya
Gzira
Qouas
Keddane
Rmila
Fakharine
Oued Zitoun
Andalus Mosque & Medersa
Zawiya Moulay Idriss II
Place as-Seffarine
Place an-Nejjarine
Bein al-Mudun Bridge
Bab Guissa
Bab Fettouh
Bab Fettouh Cemetery
Bab Hamra Cemetery
Lakbir Benzidane St
Allal Fassi Ave
Blvd Mohamed el-Alaoui
Talaa Kebira
Talaa Seghira
Derb el-Mitter
Derb Bensalem
Isesco St
Derb Serraj

Pension Talaa (Map p823; ☎ 035 633359; pacohicham@hotmail.com; 14 Talaa Seghira; s/d Dh90/120) A small but well-formed little *pension* right in the middle of things on Talaa Seghira. There's just a handful of compact rooms so it's often full, but it gets good reviews from guests for the price and has friendly staff.

Dar Bouânania (Map p823; ☎ 035 637282; 21 Derb be Salem, Talaa Kebira; s/d Dh200/500, s/d Dh300/600 with shower, q with shared bathroom Dh400, breakfast Dh30) This is as close as tight budgets will get to a riad. There are several well-sized rooms on several levels, although as all face inward they can be quite dark at times. Shared bathrooms are clean, and there's a roof terrace. There's a high season supplement of Dh100 per person.

VILLE NOUVELLE

Youth Hostel (Map p825; ☎ 035 624085; 18 Rue Abdeslam Serghini; dm Dh45; 🕑 8-10am, noon-3pm & 6-10pm) One of the better youth hostels in Morocco, this is right in the centre of the ville nouvelle. Tidy rooms and facilities (including Western-style toilets) are superbly clean. If you're not a Youth Hostelling International (YHI) member, there's a Dh5 surcharge.

Hôtel Central (Map p825; ☎ 035 622335; 50 Rue Brahim Roudani; s/d Dh130/160, with shower Dh150/180) A bright and airy budget option just off busy Ave Mohammed V. All rooms have external toilets, but even those without a shower have their own sinks. It's good value and popular so sometimes there aren't enough rooms to go around.

Hôtel Splendid (Map p825; ☎ 035 622148; splendid@iam.net.ma; 9 Rue Abdelkarim el-Khattabi; s/d Dh318/412; ❄ 🏊) For the price, this hotel makes a good claim for three stars. It's all modern and tidy, with good bathrooms and comfy beds, plus a pool for the heat and a bar for the evenings. There's a dining room, but breakfast isn't automatically included in the price.

Eating

MEDINA

In the medina, you won't have to walk far to find someone selling food – tiny cell-like places grilling brochettes, cooking up cauldrons of soup or making sandwiches. Bab Bou Jeloud has a cluster of options with streetside tables for people-watching.

Café Clock (Map p823; ☎ 035 637855; www.cafeclock.com; 7 Derb el-Mergana, Talaa Kebira; mains Dh55-80; 🕑 9am-10pm) In a restored townhouse, this funky place has a refreshingly varied menu including camel burger. Better still, their 'Clock Culture' program includes sunset concerts every Sunday (cover charge around Dh20), attracting a good mix of locals, expats and curious tourists. There's wi-fi, too.

Le Kasbah (Map p823; Rue Serrajine; mains Dh40, set menu Dh70; 🕑 8am-midnight) On several floors opposite the cheap hotels at Bab Bou Jeloud, this restaurant occupies a prime spot: the top floor looks out over the medina. The menu itself isn't overly exciting – tajines, couscous and meat from the grill, but good value (though drinks are marked up if you're not eating).

Médina Café (Map p823; ☎ 035 633430; 6 Derb Mernissi Bab Bou Jeloud; mains Dh70-100; 🕑 8am-10pm) Just outside Bab Bou Jeloud, this small restaurant is an oasis of serenity, decorated in a traditional yet restrained manner. Moroccan fare is on offer – the lamb tajine with dried figs and apricots is a winner, while the plates of couscous are big enough for two.

VILLE NOUVELLE

There are a few cheap eats on or just off Blvd Mohammed V, especially around the central market. You'll also find sandwich and rotisserie places around Place Florence.

Chez Vittorio (Map p825; ☎ 035 624730; 21 Rue Brahim Roudani; mains from Dh80, salads from Dh30, pizza or pasta from Dh56) This dependable favourite covers the rustic Italian restaurant angle well. Food is good value, and while the initial service can be a bit creaky your meal tends to arrive in a trice. Go for the pizzas or steak, as the pasta often disappoints. Alcohol is served.

Restaurant Marrakech (Map p825; ☎ 035 930876; 11 Rue Omar el-Mokhtar; mains from Dh55; ❄) A charming restaurant behind thick wooden doors that goes from strength to strength. Red plaster walls and dark furniture plus a cushion-strewn salon at the back adds ambience, while the menu's variety refreshes the palette, with dishes like chicken tajine with apple and olive, or lamb with aubergine and peppers.

Getting There & Away

BUS

The **CTM bus station** (off Map p825; ☎ 035 732992) is near Place Atlas in the southern Ville Nouvelle, with services to Casablanca (Dh100, five hours, seven daily) via Rabat (Dh70, 3½ hours), Meknès (Dh20, one hour,

FEZ VILLE NOUVELLE

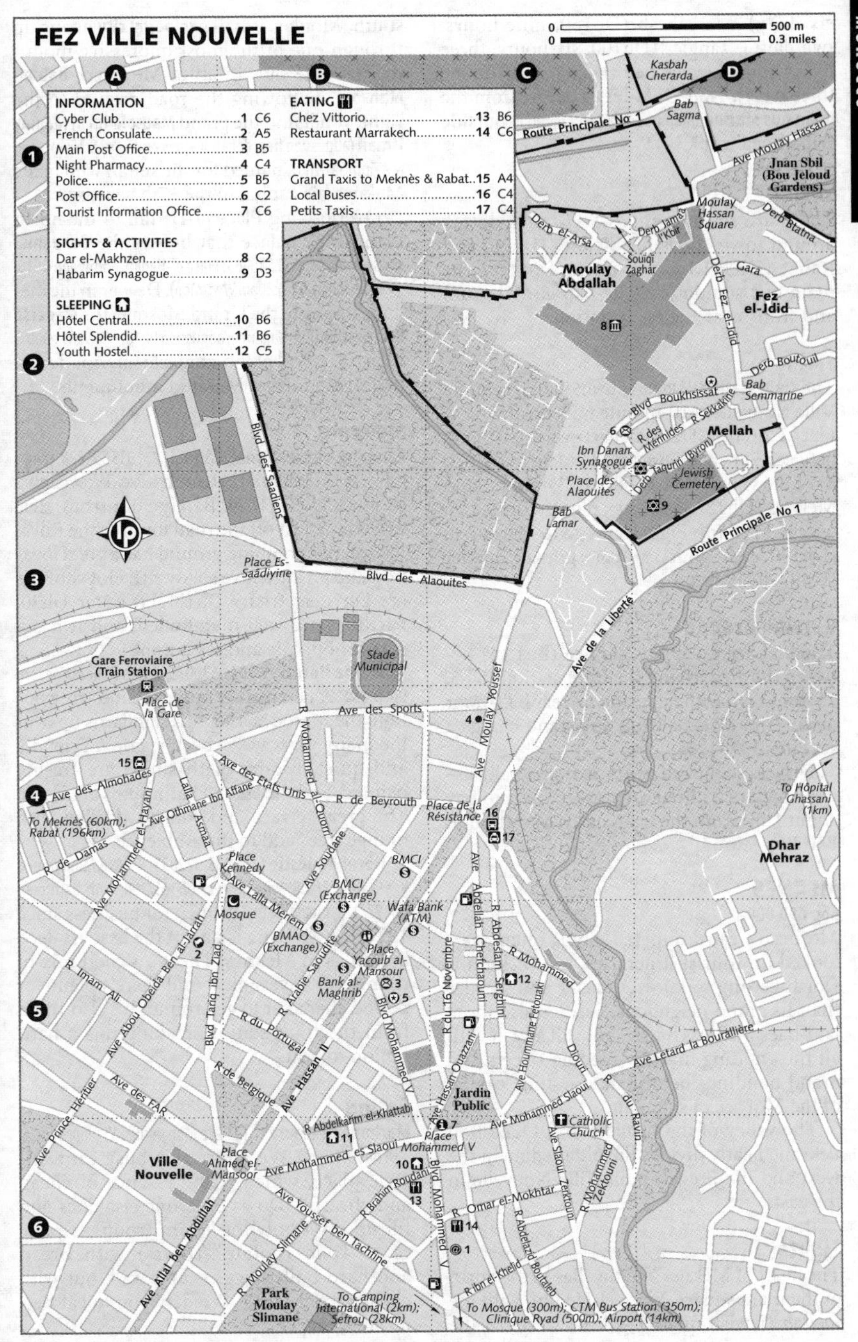

six daily), Marrakesh (Dh160, nine hours, two daily), Tangier (Dh100, six hours, three daily) and Chefchaouen (Dh700, four hours, three daily). Non-CTM buses depart from the **main bus station** (Map p823; ☎ 035 636032) outside Bab el-Mahrouk.

TAXI

There are several *grands-taxi* ranks dotted around town. Taxis for Meknès (Dh16) and Rabat (Dh59) leave from in front of the main bus station (outside Bab el-Mahrouk) and from near the train station.

TRAIN

The **train station** (Map p823 ☎ 035 930333) is in the Ville Nouvelle, a 10-minute walk northwest of Place Florence. Trains depart every two hours between 7am and 5pm to Casablanca (Dh103, 4½ hours), via Rabat (Dh76, 3½ hours) and Meknès (Dh18, one hour), plus there are two overnight trains. Eight trains go to Marrakesh (Dh180, eight hours) and one goes to Tangier (Dh97, five hours).

Getting Around

There is a regular bus service (bus 16) between the airport and the train station (Dh3, 25 minutes), with departures every half-hour or so. *Grands taxis* from any stand charge a set fare of Dh120.

Drivers of the red *petits taxis* generally use their meters without any fuss. Expect to pay about Dh9 from the train or CTM station to Bab Bou Jeloud.

MEKNÈS

pop 690,000

Morocco's third imperial city is often overlooked on tourist itineraries, but Meknès is worth getting to know. Quieter and smaller than its grand neighbour, Fez, it's also more laid-back and less hassle, but still awash with all the winding, narrow medina streets and grand buildings befitting a one-time capital of the Moroccan sultanate.

The valley of the (usually dry) Oued Bou Fekrane neatly divides the old medina in the west and the French-built Ville Nouvelle in the east.

Sights

The heart of Meknès' medina lies to the north of the main square, Place el-Hedim, with the *mellah* (Jewish quarter) to the west. To the south, Moulay Ismail's **imperial city** opens up through one of the most impressive monumental gateways in all of Morocco, **Bab el-Mansour**. Following the road around to the right, you'll find the grand **Mausoleum of Moulay Ismail** (admission free, donations welcome; 🕑 8.30am-noon & 2-6pm Sat-Thu), named for the sultan who made Meknès his capital in the 17th century.

Overlooking Place el-Hedim to the north is the 1882 palace that houses the **Dar Jamaï museum** (☎ 055 530863; Place el-Hedim; admission Dh10; 🕑 9am-noon & 3-6.30pm Wed-Mon). Deeper in the medina, opposite the Grand Mosque, the **Medersa Bou Inania** (Rue Najjarine; admission Dh10; 🕑 9am-noon & 3-6pm) is typical of the exquisite interior design that distinguishes Merenid monuments.

Sleeping

Camping International d'Agdal (☎ 035 551828; camping per adult/child Dh17/12, plus per tent/bicycle/car/caravan/camper Dh10/10/17/17/20) Barely 50m from Heri es-Souani, just off the road towards the Royal Palace, this camping ground has a great location and an attractive shady site. Hot showers are Dh7, electricity Dh15 and water Dh20. Facilities are well-maintained, and it has a small shop, cafe and restaurant.

Maroc Hôtel (☎ 035 530075; 7 Rue Rouamzine; s/d Dh90/180) A perennially popular shoestring option, the Maroc has kept its standards up over the many years we've been visiting. Friendly and quiet, rooms (with sinks) are freshly painted, and the shared bathrooms are clean. The great terrace and courtyard filled with orange trees add to the ambience.

Hôtel Majestic (☎ 035 522035; 19 Ave Mohammed V; s/d Dh127/168, with shower Dh165/198, with bathroom Dh197/229, breakfast Dh22) Open for business since 1937, the Majestic is one of the best art deco buildings in Meknès. There's a good mix of rooms (all have sinks), and there's plenty of period character to go around. It's also 100m from the train station, making this a hard option to beat.

Eating

Marhaba Restaurant (23 Ave Mohammed V; tajines Dh25; 🕑 noon-10pm) We adore this busy canteen-style place, which is the essence of cheap and cheerful. Do as everyone else does and fill up on a bowl of *harira* (soup), a plate of *makoda* (potato fritters) with bread and hard-boiled eggs – and walk out with change from Dh15. We defy you to eat better for cheaper.

NRJ (☎ 035 400324; 30 Rue Amir Abdelkader; breakfast from Dh22, salads Dh20-30, pizzas Dh35-60; 24hr) Importing a bit of big city laptop-friendly cool, NRJ is all glass-topped tables, under-lit seating, wi-fi and funky tunes on the stereo. Perfect for a light meal any time of day, the paninis and good range of juices are particularly good.

Sandwich stands (Place el-Hedim; sandwiches around Dh30; 7am-10pm) Take your pick of any one of the stands lining Place el-Hedim, and sit at the canopied tables to watch the scene as you eat. There are larger meals such as tajines, but the sandwiches are usually pretty quick and excellent, while a few places nearer the medina walls do a good line in sardines.

Restaurant Oumnia (☎ 035 533938; 8 Ain Fouki Rouamzine; set menu Dh80) Less a formal restaurant than a few rooms of a family home converted into dining salons, the emphasis here is on warm service and hearty Moroccan fare. There's just a three-course set menu, but it's a real winner, with delicious *harira* (lentil soup), salads and a choice of several tajines of the day.

Getting There & Away

Although Meknès has two train stations, head for the more convenient **El-Amir Abdelkader** (☎ 035 522763), two blocks east of Ave Mohammed V. There are nine daily trains to Fez (Dh18, one hour). Eight go to Casablanca (Dh86, 3½ hours) via Rabat (Dh59, 2¼ hours), with five for Marrakesh (Dh162, seven hours) and one for Tangier (Dh80, four hours) – or take a westbound train and change at Sidi Kacem.

The **CTM bus station** (☎ 035 522585; Ave des FAR) is about 300m east of the junction with Ave Mohammed V. The main bus station lies just outside Bab el-Khemis, west of the medina. CTM departures include Casablanca (Dh80, four hours, six daily) via Rabat (Dh50 2½ hours), Marrakesh (Dh120, eight hours, daily) and Tangier (Dh80, five hours, three daily).

The principal *grand taxi* rank is a dirt lot next to the bus station at Bab el-Khemis. There are regular departures to Fez (Dh16, one hour) and Rabat (Dh44, 90 minutes). *Grands taxis* for Moulay Idriss (Dh10, 20 minutes) leave from opposite the Institut Français – this is also the place to organise round trips to Volubilis.

AROUND MEKNÈS

The Roman ruins of **Volubilis** (admission Dh20, parking Dh5, guide Dh140; 8am-sunset) sit in the midst of a fertile plan about 33km north of Meknès. The city is the best-preserved archaeological site in Morocco. One of the country's most important pilgrimage sites, the relaxed whitewashed town **Moulay Idriss**, is only about 5km from Volubilis. A half-day outing by *grands taxi* from Meknès will cost around Dh350, including a stop at Moulay Idriss.

MARRAKESH

pop 2 million

Marrakesh grew rich on the camel caravans threading their way across the desert, but these days it's cheap flights from Europe bringing tourists to spend their money in the souqs that fatten the city's coffers. As many locals have taken the opportunity to move out of the medina into modern housing, so foreigners have arrived to transform those houses into style magazine–friendly guest houses.

But Marrakesh's old heart still beats strongly enough, from the time-worn ramparts that ring the city, to the nightly spectacle of the Djemaa el-Fna that cavorts like a medieval circus on the edge of the labyrinthine medina.

Like most Moroccan cities, Marrakesh is divided into new and old sections; it's a short taxi ride or a 30-minute walk from the centre of the ville nouvelle to Djemaa el-Fna.

Information

EMERGENCY

Ambulance (☎ 024 443724)

Brigade Touristique (☎ 024 384601; Rue Sidi Mimoun; 24hr)

INTERNET ACCESS

Cybercafes ringing the Djemaa el-Fna charge Dh8 to Dh12 per hour; just follow signs reading 'c@fe.'

Cyber Café in CyberPark (Ave Mohammed V; per hr Dh10; 9.30am-8pm)

Hassan Internet (☎ 024 441989; Immeuble Tazi, 12 Rue Riad el Moukha; per hr Dh8; 7am-1am)

MEDICAL SERVICES

Pharmacie de l'Unité (☎ 024 435982; Ave des Nations Unies, Guéliz; 8.30am-11pm)

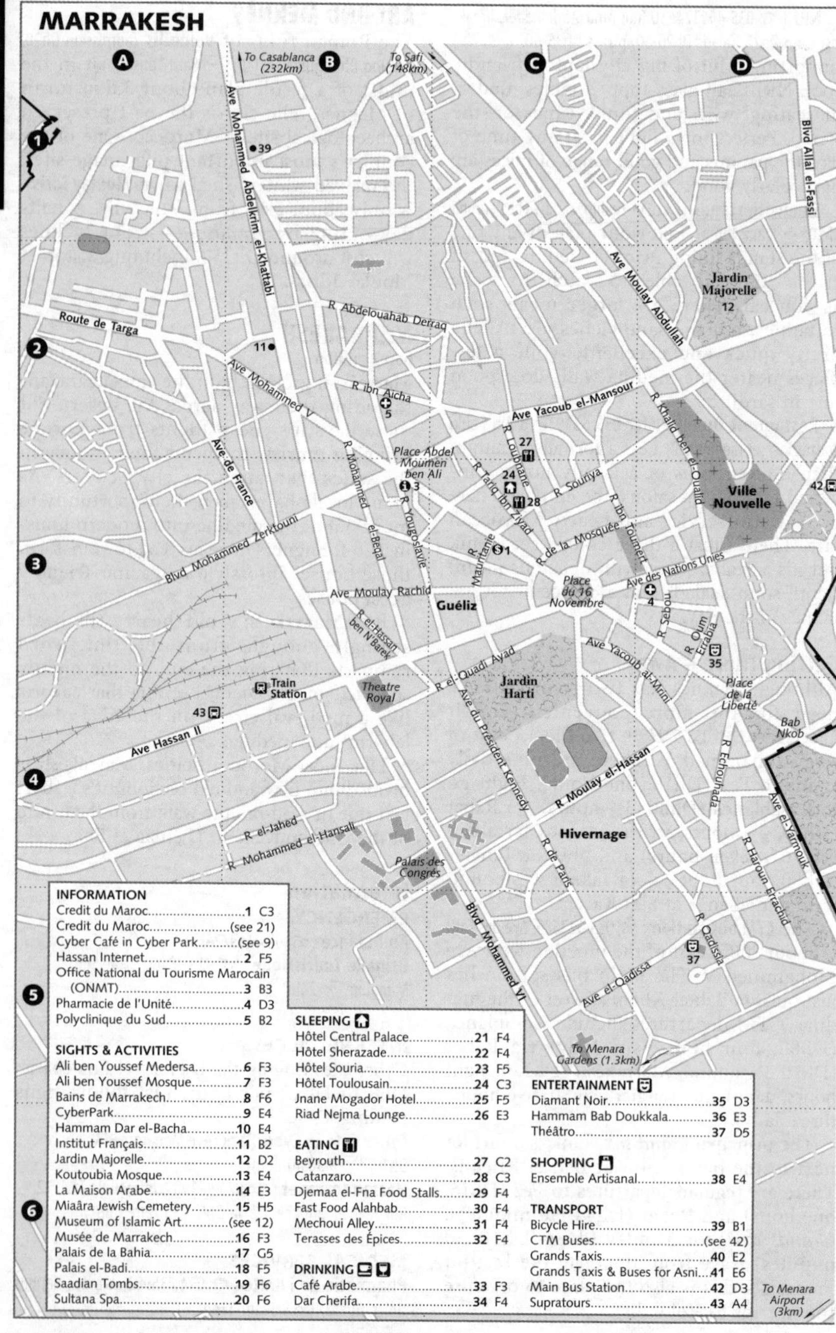
MARRAKESH
To Casablanca (232km)
To Safi (148km)
Ave Mohammed Abdelkrim el-Khattabi
Blvd Allal el-Fassi
Jardin Majorelle
12
Ave Moulay Abdullah
R Abdelouahab Derraq
Route de Targa
Ave Mohammed V
R ibn Aicha
Ave Yacoub el-Mansour
R Khalid ben el-Oualid
Place Abdel Moumen ben Ali
R Loubnane
R Tariq Ibn Ziyad
R Souriya
Ville Nouvelle
Ave de France
R Mohammed el-Beqal
R Yougoslavie
Blvd Mohammed Zerktouni
R Mauritanie
R de la Mosquée
R Ibn Toumert
Ave des Nations Unies
Place du 16 Novembre
Ave Moulay Rachid
Guéliz
R Sebou
R Oum Errabia
R el-Hassan ben N'Barek
Ave Yacoub al-Mrini
R el-Quadi Ayad
Jardin Harti
Train Station
Theatre Royal
Ave du Président Kennedy
Place de la Liberté
Bab Nkob
Ave Hassan II
R Moulay el-Hassan
R Echouhada
Ave el-Yarmouk
Hivernage
R el-Jahed
R Mohammed el-Hansali
Palais des Congrés
R de Paris
R Haroun Errachid
Blvd Mohammed VI
R Oadissia
Ave el-Qadissa
To Menara Gardens (1.3km)
To Menara Airport (3km)
INFORMATION
Credit du Maroc....1 C3
Credit du Maroc....(see 21)
Cyber Café in Cyber Park....(see 9)
Hassan Internet....2 F5
Office National du Tourisme Marocain (ONMT)....3 B3
Pharmacie de l'Unité....4 D3
Polyclinique du Sud....5 B2
SIGHTS & ACTIVITIES
Ali ben Youssef Medersa....6 F3
Ali ben Youssef Mosque....7 F3
Bains de Marrakech....8 F6
CyberPark....9 E4
Hammam Dar el-Bacha....10 E4
Institut Français....11 B2
Jardin Majorelle....12 D2
Koutoubia Mosque....13 E4
La Maison Arabe....14 E3
Miaâra Jewish Cemetery....15 H5
Museum of Islamic Art....(see 12)
Musée de Marrakech....16 F3
Palais de la Bahia....17 G5
Palais el-Badi....18 F5
Saadian Tombs....19 F6
Sultana Spa....20 F6
SLEEPING
Hôtel Central Palace....21 F4
Hôtel Sherazade....22 F4
Hôtel Souria....23 F5
Hôtel Toulousain....24 C3
Jnane Mogador Hotel....25 F5
Riad Nejma Lounge....26 E3
EATING
Beyrouth....27 C2
Catanzaro....28 C3
Djemaa el-Fna Food Stalls....29 F4
Fast Food Alahbab....30 F4
Mechoui Alley....31 F4
Terasses des Épices....32 F4
DRINKING
Café Arabe....33 F3
Dar Cherifa....34 F4
ENTERTAINMENT
Diamant Noir....35 D3
Hammam Bab Doukkala....36 E3
Théâtro....37 D5
SHOPPING
Ensemble Artisanal....38 E4
TRANSPORT
Bicycle Hire....39 B1
CTM Buses....(see 42)
Grands Taxis....40 E2
Grands Taxis & Buses for Asni....41 E6
Main Bus Station....42 D3
Supratours....43 A4

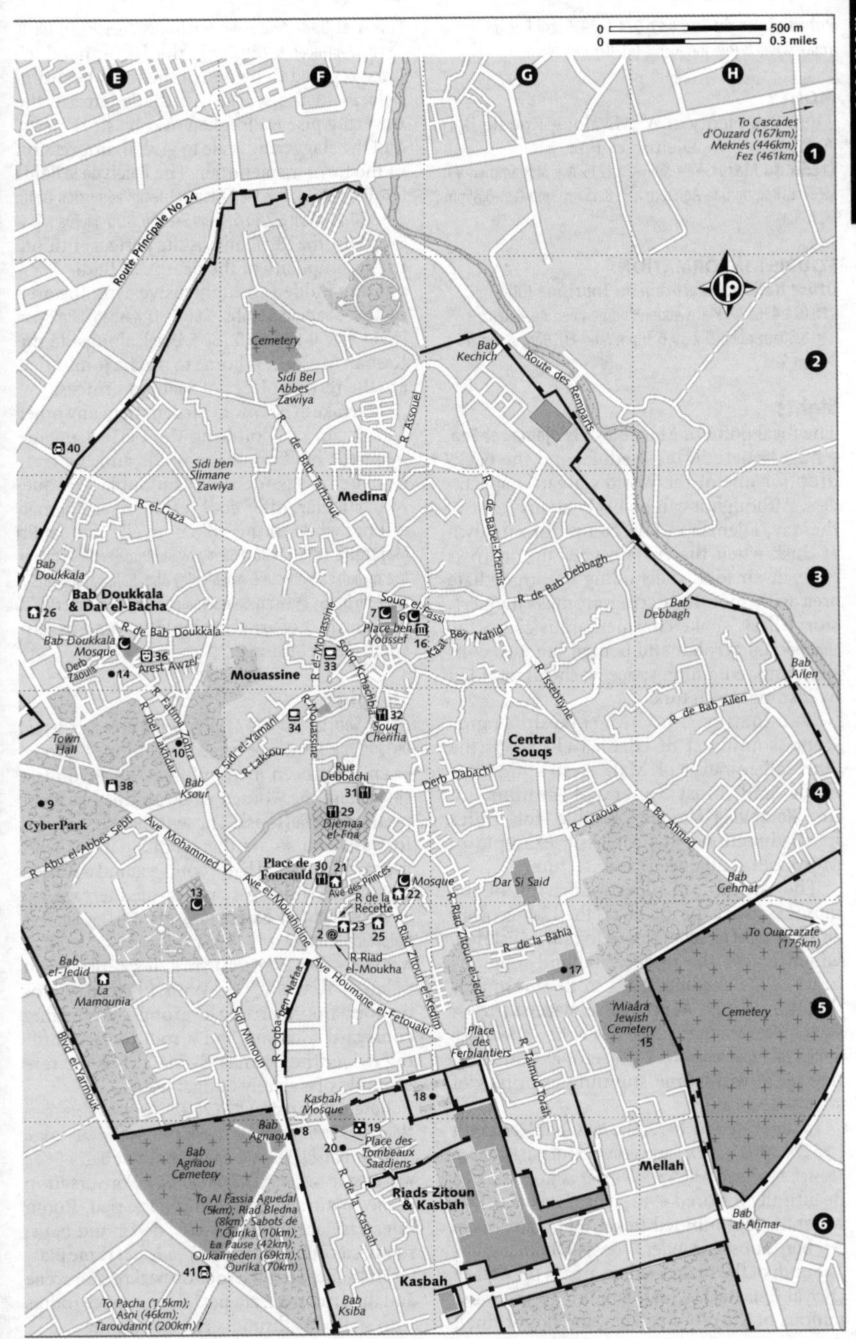
0 500 m
0 0.3 miles
E
F
G
H
To Cascades d'Ouzard (167km); Meknés (446km); Fez (461km)
Route Principale No 24
Cemetery
Sidi Bel Abbes Zawiya
Bab Kechich
Route des Remparts
R Assouel
R de Bab Tarhzout
Sidi ben Slimane Zawiya
Medina
R el-Gaza
R de Babel-Khemis
Bab Doukkala
Bab Doukkala & Dar el-Bacha
R de Bab Doukkala
Bab Doukkala Mosque
Derb Zaouia
Arest Awzel
Mouassine
R el-Mouassine
Souq Kchachbia
Souq el-Fassi
Place ben Youssef
Kâat Ben Nahid
R de Bab Debbagh
Bab Debbagh
R Issebtiyne
Bab Ailen
R de Bab Ailen
R Fatima Zohra
R Ibel Lakhdar
Town Hall
R Sidi el-Yamani
R Laksour
R Mouassine
Souq Cherifia
Central Souqs
Rue Debbachi
Derb Dabachi
Bab Ksour
CyberPark
Djemaa el-Fna
R Graoua
R Ba Ahmad
R Abu el-Abbes Sebti
Ave Mohammed V
Place de Foucauld
Ave des Princes
Mosque
Dar Si Said
Bab Gehmat
Ave el-Mouahidine
R de la Recette
R Riad Zitoun el-Kedim
R Riad Zitoun el-Jedid
R de la Bahia
To Ouarzazate (175km)
R Riad el-Moukha
Bab el-Jedid
La Mamounia
Ave Houmane el-Fetouaki
R Oqba ben Nafaa
R Sidi Mimoun
Place des Ferblantiers
R Talmud Torah
Miaâra Jewish Cemetery
Cemetery
Blvd el-Yarmouk
Kasbah Mosque
Bab Agnaou
Place des Tombeaux Saadiens
Bab Agnaou Cemetery
R de la Kasbah
Riads Zitoun & Kasbah
Mellah
Bab al-Ahmar
To Al Fassia Aguedal (5km); Riad Bledna (8km); Sabots de l'Ourika (10km); La Pause (42km); Oukaimeden (69km); Ourika (70km)
Kasbah
Bab Ksiba
To Pacha (1.5km); Asni (46km); Taroudannt (200km)
1
2
3
4
5
6
2
6
7
8
9
10
13
14
15
16
17
18
19
20
21
22
23
25
26
29
30
31
32
33
34
36
38
40
41

Polyclinique du Sud (☎ 024 447999; cnr Rue de Yougoslavie & Rue Ibn Aicha, Guéliz; 🕑 24hr)

MONEY

There are plenty of ATMs along Rue de Bab Agnaou off the Djemaa el-Fna.

Crédit du Maroc Ville Nouvelle (215 Ave Mohammed V); Medina (Rue de Bab Agnaou; 🕑 8.45am-1pm & 3-6.45pm Mon-Sat)

TOURIST INFORMATION

Office National Marocain du Tourisme (ONMT; ☎ 024 436179; Place Abdel Moumen ben Ali, Guéliz; 🕑 8.30am-noon & 2.30-6.30pm Mon-Fri, 9am-noon & 3-6pm Sat)

Sights

The focal point of Marrakesh is **Djemaa el-Fna**, a huge square in the medina, and the backdrop for one of the world's greatest spectacles. Although it can be lively at any hour of the day, Djemaa el-Fna comes into its own at dusk when the curtain goes up on rows of open-air food stalls filling the immediate area with mouthwatering aromas. Jugglers, storytellers, snake charmers, musicians, the occasional acrobat and benign lunatics consume the remaining space, each surrounded by jostling spectators.

Dominating the Marrakeshi landscape, southwest of Djemaa el-Fna, is the 70m-tall minaret of Marrakesh's most famous and most venerated monument, the **Koutoubia Mosque**. Visible for miles in all directions, it's a classic example of Moroccan-Andalucían architecture.

The largest and oldest-surviving of the mosques inside the medina is the 12th-century **Ali ben Youssef Mosque** (closed to non-Muslims), which marks the intellectual and religious heart of the medina. Next to the mosque is the 14th-century **Ali ben Youssef Medersa** (☎ 024 441893; Place ben Youssef; admission Dh40; 🕑 9am-6pm winter, 9am-7pm summer), a peaceful and meditative place with some stunning examples of stucco decoration.

Inaugurated in 1997, the **Musée de Marrakesh** (☎ 024 390911; www.museedemarrakech.ma; Place ben Youssef; admission Dh30; 🕑 9am-7pm) is housed in a beautifully restored 19th-century palace, Dar Mnebhi. A combined ticket that also covers Ali ben Youssef Medersa costs Dh60.

South of the main medina area is the **Kasbah** (Royal Quarter), which is home to the most famous of the city's palaces, the now-ruined **Palais el-Badi** (Place des Ferblantiers; admission Dh10; 🕑 8.30am-noon & 2.30-6pm), 'the Incomparable', once reputed to be one of the most beautiful palaces in the world. All that's left are the towering pisé walls taken over by stork nests, and the staggering scale to give an impression of the former splendour. The **Palais de la Bahia** (☎ 024 389564; Rue Riad Zitoun el-Jedid; admission Dh10; 🕑 8.30-11.45am & 2.30-5.45pm Sat-Thu, 8.30-11.30am & 3-5.45pm Fri), the 'Brilliant', is the perfect antidote to the simplicity of the nearby el-Badi.

Long hidden from intrusive eyes, the area of the **Saadian Tombs** (Rue de la Kasbah; admission Dh10; 🕑 8.30-11.45am & 2.30-5.45pm), alongside the Kasbah Mosque, is home to ornate tombs that are the resting places of Saadian princes.

Marrakesh has more gardens than any other Moroccan city, offering the perfect escape from the hubbub of the souqs and the traffic. The rose gardens of Koutoubia Mosque, in particular, offer cool respite near Djemaa el-Fna, while in the ville nouvelle, the **Jardin Majorelle** (☎ 024 301852; www.jardinmajorelle.com; cnr Ave Yacoub el-Mansour & Ave Moulay Abdullah; garden Dh30, museum Dh15; 🕑 8am-6pm summer, 8am-5pm winter) is a sublime mix of art-deco buildings and psychedelic desert mirage.

Sleeping

Hôtel Souria (☎ 024 445970; 17 Rue de la Recette; s/d Dh130/170) 'How are you? Everything's good?' Even if it's been mere minutes since you last saw them, the women who run this place expertly never fail to ask. The sentiment is straightforward and so are the rooms – 10 no-frills rooms with shared bathrooms around a garden courtyard, with a patchwork-tiled terrace.

Hôtel Central Palace (☎ 024 440235; hotelcentralpalace@hotmail.com; 59 Derb Sidi Bouloukat; d Dh155, with shower/bath Dh205/305) Sure, it's central, but palatial? Actually, yes. With 40 clean rooms on four floors arranged around a burbling courtyard fountain and a roof terrace lording it over the Djemaa el-Fna, this is the rare example of a stately budget hotel.

Hôtel Sherazade (☎ 024 429305; www.hotelsherazade.com; 3 Derb Djemaa, Riad Zitoun el-Kedim; s/d with shared bathroom Dh180/230, s with en-suite bathroom Dh220-640, d with en-suite bathroom Dh270-690; ❄) Conversation comes naturally in this laid-back riad. Room rates vary according to A/C, decor and bathroom – a couple have slinky *tadelakt* (lime plaster) tubs. Between the rooftop backpacker scene and the gruff muezzin next door, terrace rooms with shared bathrooms call for earplugs.

Hôtel Toulousain (☎ 024 430033; www.geocities.com/hotel_toulousain; 44 Rue Tariq ibn Ziyad; s/d with shared shower & toilet Dh140/190, with private shower & shared toilet Dh150/200, with private bathroom Dh180/230, incl breakfast) An easygoing budget hotel run by a kindly Moroccan-American family in Guéliz in the Ville Nouvelle. Some rooms get stuffy in summer, so guests hang out in the tranquil patios under the banana trees. or head for the nearby inexpensive restaurants.

Jnane Mogador (☎ 024 426323; www.jnanemogador.com; Derb Sidi Bouloukat, 116 Riad Zitoun el-Kedim; s/d/tr/q Dh360/480/580/660; 💻) An authentic 19th-century riad with all the 21st-century guest-house fixings: prime location, in-house hamam, double-decker roof terraces, and owner Mohammed's laid-back hospitality. Perennially popular, book in advance.

Riad Nejma Lounge (☎ 024 382341; www.riad-nejmalounge.com; 45 Derb Sidi M'Hamed el-Haj, Bab Doukkala; d incl breakfast Dh495-795; ❄ 💻 🏊) Lounge lizards chill on hot-pink cushions in the whitewashed courtyard, and graphic splashes of colour make wood-beamed guestrooms totally mod, though the rustic showers can be temperamental. Handy for ville nouvelle restaurants and shops.

Eating

The cheapest and most exotic place to eat in town remains the food stalls on Djemaa el-Fna, piled high with fresh meats and salads, goats' heads and steaming snails. Bargain dining for less than Dh50, or head for the roof-terrace restaurants overlooking the square.

Fast Food Alahbab (Rue de Bab Agnaou; salads Dh15-25, sandwiches Dh20-30; 🕒 7am-11pm) The awning boasting 'recommended by Lonely Planet' must be 25 years old now, and still we stand by our initial assessment of the Dh35 shawarma accompanied by four sauces and just-right French fries, though the avocado milkshake is best avoided.

Mechoui Alley (east side of Souq Ablueh; olive souq; quarter-kilo lamb with bread Dh30-50; 🕒 11am-2pm) Just before noon, the vendors at this row of stalls start carving up sides of *mechoui* (slow-roasted lamb). Point to the best-looking cut of meat, and ask for a *'nuss'* (half) or *'rubb'* (quarter) kilo. Some haggling might ensue, but you'll procure a baggie of falling-off-the-bone delicious lamb with fresh-baked bread, cumin and olives.

Catanzaro (☎ 024 433731; 42 Rue Tariq ibn Ziyad, Guéliz; pizzas or pasta Dh60-80, mains Dh80-120; 🕒 noon-2.30pm & 7.30-11pm Mon-Sat; ❄) Where are we, exactly? The thin-crust, wood-fired pizza says Italy, the wooden balcony and powerful air-con suggest the Alps, but the spicy condiments and spicier clientele are definitely mid-town Marrakesh. Grilled meat dishes are juicy and generous, but the Neapolitan pizza with capers, local olives and Atlantic anchovies steals the show.

Beyrouth (☎ 024 423525; 9 Rue Loubnane; mains Dh80-150) Bright, lemony Lebanese flavours, with a mix-and-match *mezze* (starters) that's a feast for two with tabouleh, spinach pies and felafel for Dh160. The smoky, silky *baba ghanoush* (aubergine dip) here gives Moroccan eggplant caviar serious competition for best Middle Eastern spread.

Terrasse des Épices (☎ 024 375904; 15 Souq Cherifia; set meal Dh100-150) Head to the roof for lunch on top of the world in a mud-brick *bhou* (booth). Check the chalkboard for the Dh100 fixed-price special: Moroccan salads followed by scrawny but scrumptious chicken-leg tajine with fries, then strawberries and mint. Reservations handy in high season.

Drinking

The number one spot for a cheap and delicious drink is right on Djemaa el-Fna, where orange juice is freshly squeezed around the clock for just Dh4. Rooftop cafes overlook the square. As elsewhere in Morocco, the traditional bars in Marrakesh are mostly dire beer- and male-oriented places.

Dar Cherifa (☎ 024 426463; 8 Derb Cherfa Lakbir, near Rue Mouassine; tea/coffee Dh15-25; 🕒 noon-7pm) Revive souq-sore eyes at this serene late-15th-century Saadian riad, where tea and saffron coffee is served with contemporary art and literature downstairs or terrace views upstairs.

Café Arabe (☎ 024 429728; www.cafearabe.com; 184 Rue Mouassine, Medina; 🕒 10am-midnight; ❄) Gloat over souq purchases with cocktails on the roof at sunset or a glass of wine next to the Zen-zellij courtyard fountain. The food is mixed.

Entertainment

Sleeping is overrated in a city where the nightlife begins around midnight. Most of the hottest clubs are in the Hivernage district of the ville nouvelle. Admissions range from Dh150 to Dh350 including the first drink. Each drink thereafter costs at least Dh50. Dress to impress. Options include super-club **Pacha** (☎ 024 388405; www.pachamarrakech.com; Complexe Pacha Marrakech, Blvd

Mohammed VI, Hivernage; admission Mon-Fri before/after 10pm free/Dh150-200, Sat & Sun Dh200-300; 8pm-5am); **Diamant Noir** (024 434351; Hôtel Marrakech, cnr Ave Mohammed V & Rue Oum Errabia, Guéliz; admission from Dh100; 10pm-4am), which is gay-friendly on weeknights and has a seedy charm on weekends; and the lively house and R&B tunes of **Théâtro** (024 448811; Hôtel es Saadi, Rue Qadissia, Hivernage; admission Dh200; 11.30pm-5am).

Getting There & Away

BUS

Most buses arrive and depart from the main **bus station** (024 433933; Bab Doukkala) just outside the city walls. A number of companies run buses to Fez (from Dh130, 8½ hours, at least six daily) and Meknès (from Dh120, six hours, at least three daily). **CTM** (024 434402; Window 10, Bab Doukkala bus station) operates daily buses to Fez (Dh160, 8½ hours, one daily). There are also daily services to Agadir (Dh90, four hours, nine daily), Casablanca (Dh85, four hours, three daily) and Essaouira (Dh80, 2½ hours).

Supratours (024 435525; Ave Hassan II), west of the train station, operate three daily coaches to Essaouira (Dh65, 2½ hours).

TRAIN

For the **train station** (024 447768; cnr Ave Hassan II & Blvd Mohammed VI, Guéliz), take a taxi or city bus (3, 8, 10 and 14, among others, Dh3) from the centre. There are trains to Casablanca (Dh84, three hours, nine daily), Rabat (Dh112, four hours), Fez (Dh180, eight hours, eight daily) via Meknès (Dh162, seven hours) and nightly trains to Tangier (Dh190).

Getting Around

A *petit taxi* to Marrakesh from the airport (6km) should cost no more than Dh60. Alternatively, bus 11 runs irregularly to Djemaa el-Fna. The creamy-beige *petits taxis* around town cost anywhere between Dh5 and Dh15 per journey.

HIGH ATLAS MOUNTAINS & DESERT

Morocco is about far more than its historical cities. When you can't stand another souq, head for the open spaces of the High Atlas Mountains and the sands of the Sahara.

HIGH ATLAS

The highest mountain range in North Africa, the High Atlas run diagonally across Morocco, from the Atlantic coast northeast of Agadir all the way across to northern Algeria, a distance of almost 1000km. In Berber it's called Idraren Draren (Mountain of Mountains) and it's not hard to see why.

Although wild and harsh, the area has long been inhabited by the Atlas Berbers. Their flat-roofed, earthen villages cling tenaciously to the mountainsides, while irrigated, terraced gardens and walnut groves flourish below. The entire area is crisscrossed by well-used mule trails – some of which once undoubtedly carried trade caravans and pilgrims between the Sahara and the northern plains.

Hiking

The Moroccan tourist office, Office National Marocain du Tourisme (ONMT), publishes the useful booklet *Morocco: Mountain and Desert Tourism* (2005), with lists of guides and other useful information. Treks of longer than a couple of days will almost certainly require a guide (Dh300 per day) and pack mule (Dh100).

Jebel Toubkal

One of the most popular trekking routes in the High Atlas is the ascent of Jebel Toubkal (4167m), North Africa's highest peak. The Toubkal area is just two hours' drive south of Marrakesh and easily accessed by local transport.

The usual starting point is the picturesque village of **Imlil**, 17km from Asni off the Tizi n'Test road between Marrakesh and Agadir. Most trekkers stay overnight in Imlil. There is a *bureaux des guides* (guide office) in Imlil, where you should be able to pick up a trained, official guide (with ID cards).

There is plenty of accommodation in Imlil. Try **Hôtel el-Aïne** (024 485625; rooftop beds Dh30, r per person Dh45) or **Dar Adrar** (06 70 726809, http://toubkl.guide.free.fr/gite; d incl breakfast/half-board Dh220/330), at the top of the village. Imlil is also well-stocked for shops with trekking supplies.

Frequent local buses (Dh15, 1½ hours) and *grands taxis* (Dh30, one hour) leave south of Bab er-Rob in Marrakesh to Asni, where you change for the final 17km to Imlil (Dh15 to Dh20, one hour).

DRÂA VALLEY

A ribbon of technicoloured *palmeraies*, earth-red kasbahs and stunning Berber villages, the Drâa Valley is a special place. The valley eventually seeps out into the sands of the desert near M'hamid, which played a key role in controlling the ancient trans-Saharan trade routes that Marrakesh's wealth was built on.

Zagora

The iconic 'Tombouktou, 52 jours' (Timbuktu, 52 days) signpost was recently taken down in an inexplicable government beautification scheme, but Zagora's fame as a desert outpost is indelible. Although the town is drab, it has a large market on Wednesday and Sunday selling produce, hardware and livestock, and is the base for trips to the dunes.

If you don't want to head direct to M'hamid, agencies in Zagora running day and camping trips to the desert include **Caravane Dèsert et Montagne** (☎ 024 846898, 066 122312; www.caravanedesertetmontagne.com; 112 Blvd Mohammed V) and **Découverte Sud Maroc** (☎ 024 846115; www.geocities.com/decousudma). Bank on paying around Dh350 per day.

SLEEPING & EATING

Hôtel la Rose des Sables (☎ 024 847274; Ave Allal Ben Abdallah; s/d Dh50/60, with bathroom Dh60/90) Off-duty desert guides unwind in these basic, tidy rooms right off the main drag, and you might be able to coax out stories of travellers gone wild over tasty tajine meals at the sidewalk cafe (set menu Dh40 to Dh50).

Auberge Restaurant Chez Ali (☎ 024 846258; www.chezali.prophp.org; Ave de l'Atlas Zaouiate El Baraka, Zagora; garden tents per person Dh40, showers Dh5, rooms per person incl breakfast/full-board Dh100/260, with terrace Dh200/360) The peacocks stalking the garden can't be bothered, but otherwise the welcome here is very enthusiastic. The skylit rooms upstairs have new pine furnishings and tiled floors though some mattresses are a tad lumpy. Meals are down-home Berber cooking.

All hotels have their own restaurants and will provide set meals (Dh100 to Dh150) to nonguests by prior reservation. Moroccan fare with less flair can be had at cheap, popular restaurants along Blvd Mohammed V.

GETTING THERE & AWAY

The **CTM bus station** (☎ 024 847327) is at the southwestern end of Blvd Mohammed V, and the main bus and *grands taxi* lot is at the northern end. CTM has a daily service to Marrakesh (Dh100) and Casablanca (Dh175). There are also minibuses (Dh25) and *grands taxis* (Dh30) to M'hamid.

M'hamid

Once it was a lonesome oasis, but these days M'Hamid is a wallflower no more. Today the road is flanked with hotels to accommodate travellers lured here by the golden dunes of the Sahara. M'Hamid Bali, the old town, is 3km away across the Oued Drâa. It has an impressive and very well-preserved kasbah.

M'hamid's star attraction is **Erg Chigaga**, a mind-boggling 40km stretch of golden Saharan dunes that's the equal of Erg Chebbi near Merzouga. It's 56km away – a couple of hours by 4WD or several days by camel. A closer alternative is Erg Lehoudi, but it's in bad need of rubbish collection. **Sahara Services** (☎ 061 776766; www.saharaservices.info), 300m on right after M'Hamid entry, and **Zbar Travel** (☎ 068 517280; www.zbartravel.com) are both reliable agencies offering tours – an overnight camel trek should start at about Dh380.

If you're not sleeping with your camel in the desert, try **Camping Hammada du Drâa** (☎ 024 848080; camping per person Dh15 plus per car Dh20, Berber tents per person Dh50), which offers simple but still decent fare.

There's a daily CTM bus at 4.30pm to Zagora (Dh25, two hours), Ouazazarte (Dh70, seven hours), Marrakesh (Dh120, 11 to 13 hours) and Casablanca (Dh205, 15 hours), plus an assortment of private buses, minibuses and *grands taxis.*

MOROCCO DIRECTORY

ACCOMMODATION

Camping facilities are available around or near most Moroccan cities, while *auberges de jeunesses* (youth hostels) operate in Casablanca, Fez, Marrakesh, Meknès, Rabat and Tangier. Medina hotels certainly have their share of grim places, but there are budget gems out there too. In most budget hostels and hotels you'll be required to share toilet and shower facilities. Prices throughout this chapter are, therefore, for rooms with shared bathroom facilities unless stated otherwise. The prices listed in this chapter are for the high season and include tax; always check the price you are quoted is TTC (all taxes included).

Advance reservations are highly recommended for all places listed in this chapter, especially in summer.

ACTIVITIES

Hamams

Visiting a *hamam* (traditional bathhouse) is a ritual at the centre of Moroccan society and a practical solution for those who don't have hot water at home (or in their hotel). Every town has at least one public *hamam*. A visit usually costs Dh10, with a massage costing an extra Dh15 or so.

Hiking

Morocco's many mountain ranges offer a wide array of trekking opportunities. Most travellers head straight for the highest peaks of the High Atlas – treks can be organised from Marrakesh or from the nearby village of Imlil (p832). Chefchaouen (p815) is the place to start treks through the Rif Mountains. Spring and autumn are the best times for trekking.

Surfing & Windsurfing

With thousands of kilometres of Atlantic coastline, Morocco has some great surfing spots. Highlights are the beaches in Essaouira (p820) for windsurfing.

BUSINESS HOURS

Cafes 7am-11pm.
Restaurants noon-3pm & 7-11pm.
Shops 9am-12.30pm & 2.30-8pm Mon-Sat (often closed longer at noon on Fri).
Tourist offices 8.30am-12.30pm & 2.30-6.30pm Mon-Thu.

DANGERS & ANNOYANCES

Morocco's era as a hippy paradise is long past. Plenty of fine *kif* (dope) is grown in the Rif Mountains, but drug busts are common and Morocco isn't a good place to investigate prison conditions.

A few years ago the *brigade touristique* was set up in the principal tourist centres to clamp down on Morocco's notorious *faux guides* (false guides) and hustlers. Anyone convicted of operating as an unofficial guide faces jail time and/or a huge fine. This has reduced but not eliminated the problem of *faux guides*. You'll still find plenty of these touts hanging around the entrances to medinas and outside train stations, especially at Tangier port. Remember that their main interest is the commission gained from certain hotels or on articles sold to you in the souqs.

If possible, avoid walking alone at night in the medinas of the big cities as knife-point muggings aren't unknown.

A certain level of sexual harassment is the norm for women travellers in Morocco. It comes in the form of nonstop greetings, leering and other unwanted attention, but it's rarely dangerous. It's best to avoid overreacting and to ignore this attention. Where a would-be suitor is particularly persistent, threatening to go to the police or the *brigade touristique* is amazingly effective. Women will save themselves a great deal of grief by avoiding eye contact and dressing modestly (covering knees and shoulders).

EMBASSIES & CONSULATES

For details of all Moroccan embassies abroad and foreign embassies in Morocco, go to www.maec.gov.ma.

The following are in Rabat:

Belgium (☎ 037 268060; info@ambabel-rabat.org.ma; 6 Ave de Marrakesh)

Canada (☎ 037 687400; fax 037 687430; 13 Rue Jaafar as-Sadiq, Agdal)

France (☎ 037 689700; www.ambafrance-ma.org; 3 Rue Sahnoun, Agdal)

Germany (☎ 037 709662; www.amballemagne-rabat.ma; 7 Rue Madnine)

Ireland (☎ 022 660306; gb@copragri.co.ma; 7 Rue Madnine) In Casablanca, honorary consul only.

Italy (☎ 037 706598; ambaciata@iambitalia.ma; 2 Rue Idriss el-Azhar)

Japan (☎ 037 631782; fax 037 750078; 39 Ave Ahmed Balafrej Souissi)

Mauritania (☎ 037 656678; ambassadeur@mauritanie.org.ma; 7 Rue Thami Lamdaouar, Soussi I)

Netherlands (☎ 037 219600; nlgovrab@mtds.com; 40 Rue de Tunis)

Spain (☎ 037 633900; emb.rabat@mae.es; Rue Ain Khalouiya, Route des Zaers km 5.300, Souissi)

UK (☎ 037 238600; www.britain.org.ma; 17 Blvd de la Tour Hassan) Provides consular support for New Zealand.

USA (☎ 037 762265; www.usembassy.ma; 2 Ave de Marrakesh)

FESTIVALS & EVENTS

Religious festivals are significant for Moroccans. Local *moussems* (saints days) are held all over the country throughout the year and some draw big crowds.

Major festivals:

Gnaoua & World Music Festival (Essaouira; www.festival-gnaoua.co.ma) Held in June.

Festival of World Sacred Music (Fez; www.fesfestival.com) Every June.

Marrakesh Popular Arts Festival (www.maghrebarts.ma, in French) Held in July

International Cultural Festival (Asilah) July/August.

Moussem of Moulay Idriss II (Fez) September/October.

HOLIDAYS

All banks, post offices and most shops are shut on the main public holidays, including the following:

New Year's Day 1 January
Independence Manifesto 11 January
Labour Day 1 May
Feast of the Throne 30 July
Allegiance of Oued-Eddahab 14 August
Anniversary of the King's and People's Revolution 20 August
Young People's Day 21 August
Anniversary of the Green March 6 November
Independence Day 18 November

In addition to secular holidays there are many national and local Islamic holidays and festivals, all tied to the lunar calendar, including the following:

Eïd al-Adha Marks the end of the Islamic year. Most things shut down for four or five days.

Eïd al-Fitr Held at the end of the month-long Ramadan fast, which is observed by most Muslims. The festivities last four or five days, during which Morocco grinds to a halt.

Mawlid an-Nabi (Mouloud) Celebrates the birthday of the Prophet Mohammed.

INTERNET RESOURCES

The Lonely Planet website (www.lonelyplanet.com) has up-to-date news and the Thorn Tree bulletin board, where you can post questions.

Al-Bab (www.al-bab.com/maroc) Also called The Moroccan Gateway, Al-Bab has excellent links, especially for current affairs, news and good books about Morocco.

Maghreb Arts (www.maghrebarts.ma, in French) Up-to-the-minute coverage of theatre, film, music, festivals and media events in Morocco.

Maroc Blogs (http://maroc-blogs.com) Useful blog aggregator pulling in feeds from the entire Moroccan blogging community.

Tourism in Morocco (www.tourism-in-morocco.com/index_en.php) Morocco's official tourist information site; user-friendly, with guided tours, links and news.

MONEY

The Moroccan currency is the dirham (Dh), which is divided into 100 centimes. There is no black market, although it's forbidden to take dirhams out of the country. The Spanish enclaves of Ceuta and Melilla use the euro.

ATMs *(guichets automatiques)* are widespread and generally accept Visa, MasterCard, Electron, Cirrus, Maestro and InterBank cards. Major credit cards are widely accepted in the main tourist centres, although their use often attracts a surcharge of around 5% from Moroccan businesses. Amex, Visa and Thomas Cook travellers cheques are also widely accepted for exchange by banks. Australian, Canadian and New Zealand dollars are not quoted in banks and are not usually accepted.

Tipping

Tipping and bargaining are integral parts of Moroccan life. Practically any service can warrant a tip, and a few dirham for a service willingly rendered can make your life a lot easier. Tipping between 5% and 10% of a restaurant bill is appropriate.

POST

Post offices are distinguished by the 'PTT' sign or the 'La Poste' logo. You can sometimes buy stamps at *tabacs*, the small tobacco and newspaper kiosks you see scattered about the main city centres.

The postal system is fairly reliable, but not terribly fast. It takes about a week for letters to get to their European destinations, and two weeks or so to get to Australia and North America. Sending post from Rabat or Casablanca is quicker.

The parcel office, indicated by the sign '*colis postaux*', is generally in a separate part of the post office building. Take your parcel unwrapped for customs inspection. Some parcel offices sell boxes.

TELEPHONE

A few cities and towns still have public-phone offices, often next to the post office, but more common are privately run *téléboutiques,* which can be found in every town and village on almost every corner. Most public payphones are card-operated, with *télécartes* (phonecards) sold in general stores and news kiosks.

All domestic phone calls in Morocco require a nine-digit number, which includes the three-digit area code (or GSM code). When calling overseas from Morocco, dial ☎ 00, the country code and then the city code and number. Morocco's country code is ☎ 212.

Morocco has three GSM mobile phone networks, Méditel, Maroc Telecom and Wana, which cover 90% of the population. Moroccan mobile numbers start with ☎ 01, ☎ 06 or ☎ 07. A local sim card costs around Dh30 and top-up scratch cards are sold everywhere.

TOILETS

Outside the major cities, public toilets are rare and you will usually need to bring your own paper *(papier hygiénique),* a tip for the attendant (Dh2 to Dh3), stout-soled shoes and often a nose clip. Toilets are mostly of the Asian-style squat variety (referred to as 'Turkish toilets').

VISAS

Most visitors to Morocco do not require visas and are allowed to remain in the country for 90 days on entry. Exceptions to this include nationals of Israel, and most sub-Saharan African countries (including South Africa). Moroccan embassies have been known to insist that you get a visa from your country of origin. Should the standard 90-day stay be insufficient, it is possible (but difficult) to apply at the nearest police headquarters (Préfecture de Police) for an extension – it's simpler to leave the country and return. The Spanish enclaves of Ceuta and Melilla have the same visa requirements as mainland Spain.

The Netherlands

HIGHLIGHTS

- **Amsterdam** One of Europe's most beautiful cities – plus hash, hedonism and more (p841)
- **Rotterdam** Cutting-edge architecture and unique nightlife (p851)
- **Maastricht** Heady, cosmopolitan and stylish (p856)
- **Best Journey** Anywhere – the Netherlands is a small country, and it's all good
- **Off-the-beaten track** Groningen (p855) – thousands of students, dozens of tourists

FAST FACTS

- **Area** 41,526 sq km
- **Budget** €40 to €75 per day
- **Capital** Amsterdam
- **Country code** ☎ 31
- **Famous for** extraordinary paintings, bikes everywhere, cheese, tolerance, not drowning under the North Sea, dikes
- **Languages** Dutch, Frisian
- **Money** euro (€); A$1 = €0.55; C$1 = 0.60; ¥100 = €0.78; NZ$1 = €0.43; UK£1 = €1.12; US$1 = €0.74
- **Phrases** *hallo* (hello), *dag* (goodbye), *bedankt* (thanks), *sorry/excuses* (sorry)
- **Population** 16.6 million

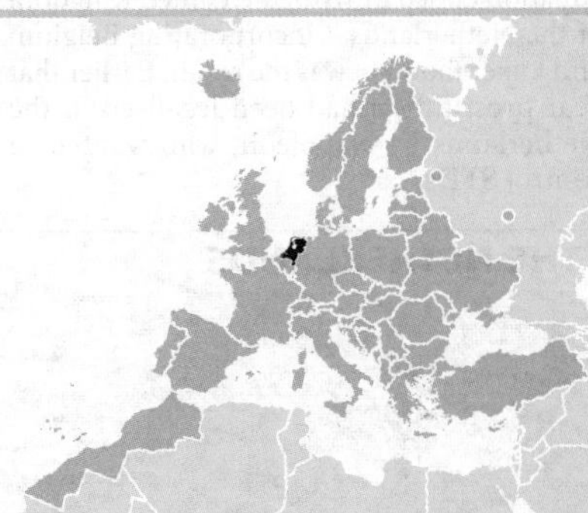

- **Visas** none required for passport holders from Australia, Canada, New Zealand, USA and most of Europe (see p860)

TRAVEL HINTS

Eighty-thousand bicycles are stolen here annually – always lock up. (You can almost always rent a replacement at a train station.)

ROAMING THE NETHERLANDS

Try the Randstad belt – including Amsterdam, Den Haag (The Hague), Delft and Rotterdam – for a classic slice of Dutch life.

Many think they know the Netherlands. Amsterdam is among the most distinctive of European cities; it's certainly one of the most beautiful. It may very well be the most eccentric. But it's not the Netherlands' only claim to fame. Den Haag (The Hague), Leiden, Haarlem and Delft are intriguing historical cities. Maastricht is a hybrid of European influences. Edgy Rotterdam always seems to be a century ahead of the rest of the country.

The Netherlands isn't the most budget-conscious option, but there's still an immense concentration of cafes and pubs everywhere, where you can nurse a coffee or beer (cheap and bountiful) and watch the world. Best of all, transport is efficient and well priced (this country is a day-tripper's paradise), the nightlife is pumping and the Dutch are wryly welcoming.

HISTORY

Early Dutch history was bound with Belgium and Luxembourg – the three were known as the Low Countries until the 16th century.

The Netherlands' Golden Age lasted from about 1580 to 1740. The era's wealth was generated by the Dutch East India Company, which travelled to the Far East for spices and other exotic goods, colonised the Cape of Good Hope and Indonesia, and established trading posts throughout Asia.

In 1795 the French invaded. When the occupation ended in 1815, the United Kingdom of the Netherlands – incorporating Belgium and Luxembourg – was the result. Earlier that year prostitution had been legalised in the Netherlands by Napoleon, who wanted to control STDs.

In 1830 the Belgians rebelled and became independent, and Luxembourg followed nine years later.

The Netherlands stayed neutral in WWI and tried to repeat the feat in WWII, only to be invaded by the Germans. The country was devastated and most of its Jewish population was murdered.

In 1953 a high spring tide and severe storm breached Zeeland's dikes, drowning 1835 people. A massive engineering project (Delta Project, p848) was built to prevent the tragedy from ever happening again.

In the '60s Amsterdam became Europe's radical heart, giving rise to the squatter's movement and the promiscuity that lingers still.

Cannabis was decriminalised in 1976, and in 2003 the Netherlands became the first

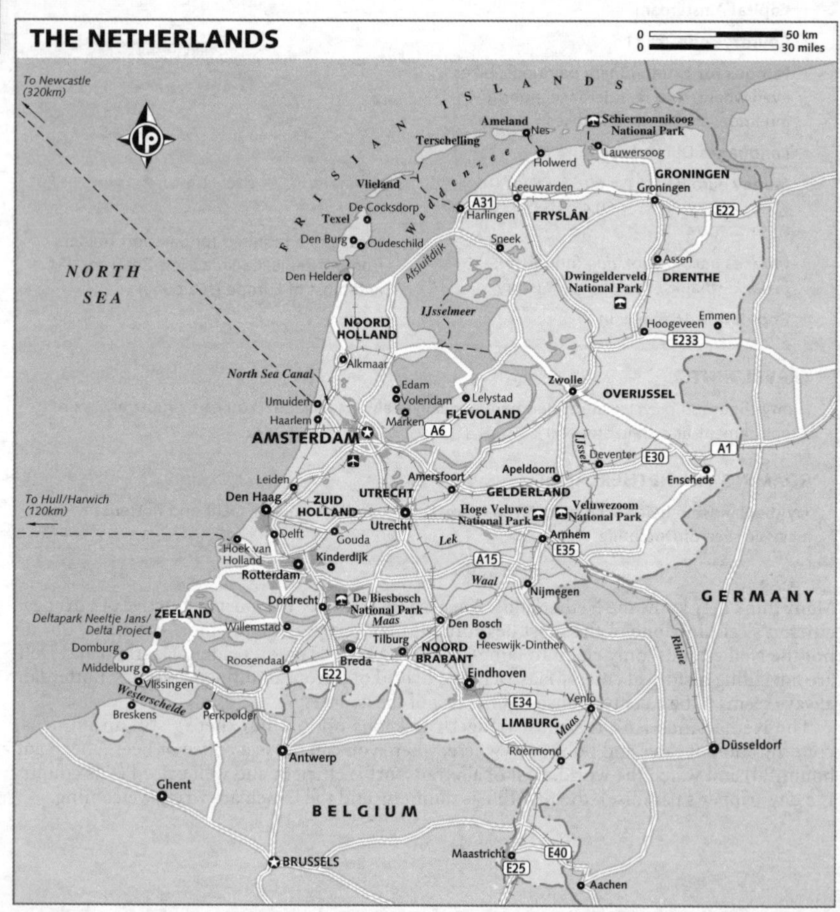

READING UP

Diary of Anne Frank, by Anne Frank, is a moving account of a Jewish girl's thoughts while hiding from the occupying Germans. The classic 1972 novel *The Happy Hooker,* by Xaviera Hollander, is an unapologetic, upbeat look at the world of a Dutch sex worker. *Amsterdam: A Traveller's Literary Companion,* edited by Manfred Wolf, contains 20 stories arranged by neighbourhood from contemporary Amsterdam writers. *Netherland* is the acclaimed 2008 novel by the Irish-born, Dutch-raised author Joseph O'Neill. In it, a Dutch narrator explores life in New York and London after 9/11.

country in the world to legalise prescriptions of medicinal cannabis.

In 1992 members of the European community assembled in Maastricht to sign the treaty that created the EU.

A year later, the Netherlands regulated doctor-assisted euthanasia, and in 2000 it was legalised under stringent guidelines – again, the first country to do so. That year the Netherlands also became the first nation to legalise same-sex marriages.

As the Netherlands has become more crowded, immigration has become a political hot potato. In 2002 politician Pim Fortuyn, an advocate of zero immigration, was shot dead a few days before the Dutch general election.

In 2004 there was another high-profile assassination. Theo van Gogh, an inflammatory filmmaker and columnist was shot repeatedly in Amsterdam. The murderer was an Islamic Moroccan; when he died, Van Gogh was completing a film about Pim Fortuyn.

Van Gogh was known for his controversial statements about Muslims, and he had received death threats after he made a short film, *Submission* (written by ex-Muslim Hirsi Ali), detailing the abuse of Muslim women.

Meanwhile Den Haag stays in the news as war-crimes trials move forward for people such as Radovan Karadzic in the city's various international courts. Meanwhile Amsterdam has announced controversial plans to limit pot-selling coffee shops and prostitution.

THE CULTURE

Nine-tenths of the population are of Dutch stock. Around 400,000 people in the northern Fryslân province speak their own language. People from the former colonies of Indonesia, Surinam and the Netherlands Antilles, along with recent arrivals from Turkey and Morocco, account for about 6% of the population.

ARTS

The Netherlands has spawned a realm of celebrated painters, including Bosch, Rembrandt, Vermeer and Van Gogh. The Dutch are world leaders in modern dance and the Netherlands is home to many orchestras. The Dutch have won three Best Foreign Language Film Academy Awards.

ENVIRONMENT

The Netherlands' land mass now encompasses 41,526 sq km; half of it lies at or below sea level in the form of polders (stretches of land reclaimed from the sea). The danger of floods is most acute in Zeeland.

The Netherlands' highest point – just 321m – is the Vaalserberg, in the province of Limburg.

Billions spent on sewage treatment means that Amsterdam's canals are now fairly clean, and agriculture and industry have been forced to reduce run-off and pollution. Recycle your trash, just like the locals do.

TRANSPORT

GETTING THERE & AWAY

Air

Huge **Schiphol airport** (AMS; ☎ 0900 01 41; www.schiphol.nl) is the Netherlands' main international airport. It is only 18km southwest of Amsterdam.

Rotterdam airport (RTM; ☎ 010 446 34 44; www.rotterdam-airport.nl) is very small.

The following airlines are among the many serving Schiphol:

Aer Lingus (EI; ☎ 0900 265 82 07; www.aerlingus.com)
BMI (BD; ☎ 020-346 92 11; www.flybmi.com)
British Airways (BA; ☎ 020-346 95 59; www.britishairways.com)
Cathay Pacific (CX; ☎ 020-653 20 10; www.cathaypacific.com)
Delta Air Lines (DL; ☎ 020-201 35 36; www.delta.com)
easyJet (EZY; ☎ 0900 265 80 22; www.easyjet.com)
KLM (KL; ☎ 020-474 77 47; www.klm.nl)
Lufthansa (LH; ☎ 0900 123 47 77; www.lufthansa.com)

Singapore Airlines (SQ; ☎ 020-548 88 88; www.singaporeair.com)
United Airlines (UA; ☎ 020-201 37 08; www.unitedairlines.nl)

Boat

Several companies operate car/passenger ferries between the Netherlands and the UK:
Stena Line (☎ in UK 08705 707070; www.stenaline.co.uk) Sails between Harwich and Hoek van Holland.
P&O Ferries (☎ in UK 08705 202020; www.poferries.com) Operates an overnight ferry every evening between Hull and Europoort (near Rotterdam).
DFDS Seaways (☎ in UK 08702 520524; www.dfds.co.uk) Sails between Newcastle and IJmuiden, which is close to Amsterdam.

Bus

Eurolines (☎ in UK 08705 143219; www.eurolines.com) serves the Netherlands. It offers a variety of passes with prices that vary by time of year.

Busabout (☎ in UK 020-7950 1661; www.busabout.com) is a UK-based budget alternative. It runs coaches on circuits in Continental Europe including one through Amsterdam; passes are available in a variety of flavours.

Car & Motorcycle

You'll need the vehicle's registration papers, third-party insurance and an international drivers' permit in addition to your domestic licence. The national auto club, **ANWB** (www.anwb.nl, in Dutch) has offices across the country and will provide info if you can show an auto-club card from your home country (eg AAA in the US and AA in the UK).

Train

The Netherlands has good train links to Germany, Belgium and France. All Eurail, Inter-Rail, Europass and Flexipass tickets are valid on the Dutch national train service, **Nederlandse Spoorwegen** (Netherlands Railways, NS; ☎ international inquiries 0900 9296; www.ns.nl). Many international services, including those on the highspeed line to Belgium, are operated under the Hispeed brand (www.nshispeed.nl). In addition, Thalys (www.thalys.com) fast trains serve Brussels and Paris.

When it finally opens (years late and over budget), the high-speed line from Amsterdam (via Schiphol and Rotterdam) will shorten travel times to Antwerp (70 minutes), Brussels (1¾ hours) and Paris (three hours).

CONNECTIONS

Train connections to neighbouring countries are good. Amsterdam is linked to Cologne (2½ hours) and south to Brussels (2¾ hours; 1¾ hours after the new high-speed line opens), where you can connect with Eurostar to London. Maastricht is right on the Belgian and German borders. Connections to Cologne and Brussels take 90 minutes from Maastricht.

GETTING AROUND

Bicycle

The Netherlands has 20,000km of cycling paths. Tourist offices have numerous routes and suggestions.

More than 100 train stations throughout the country have bicycle facilities for rental, protected parking, repair and sales. To hire, in most cases you'll need to show your passport and leave an imprint of your credit card or a deposit. Private operators charge €6 to €8 per day, and €30 to €35 per week. Many hostels and hotels offer bike rental.

Boat

Ferries connect the mainland with Texel and the other islands off the north coast.

Bus & Tram

The national *strippenkaart* (strip card) used for transport fares nationwide is history. These practical and simple paper tickets have been replaced by the *OV-chipkaart*, a credit card–sized card that you load with credit. When you board public transport, you'll use the card on gates or card readers which will deduct the value of the ride. Most rides will cost €2.50, although various deals can lower this.

The rollout of the *OV-chipkaart* in 2009 was rather rocky. The best thing you can do is ask how to buy one at tourist offices when you arrive in the country. Vending machines accepting coins and some ATM cards are meant to be common.

Car & Motorcycle

Petrol and car hire tends to be expensive. You'll need to show a valid driving licence when hiring a car in the Netherlands. You must be at least 23 years of age to hire a car.

EMERGENCY NUMBER

- Police, fire, ambulance ☎ 112

Train

The train network is run by **Nederlandse Spoorwegen** (NS; ☎ national inquiries 0900 9296; www.ns.nl). Trains are fast and frequent and serve most places of interest. Distances are short.

Tickets can be bought at the window (for an extra €0.50 for one ticket, €1 for two or more). Ticket machines have an English option and accept coins and some ATM cards. Credit cards are not accepted.

Consider a one-year *Voordeelurenabonnement* (€55) for a 40% discount on travel weekdays after 9am, on weekends and public holidays, and all of July and August. Nationwide rail passes are a bad deal given the low fares and short distances.

Most train stations have lockers operated by credit cards (average daily cost €4).

AMSTERDAM

☎ 020 / pop 747,000

If Amsterdam were a staid place it would still be one of Europe's most beautiful and historic cities, right up there with Venice and Paris. But add the qualities that make it Amsterdam: the funky and mellow bars, brown cafes full of characters, pervasive irreverence, whiffs of pot and an open-air marketplace for sleaze and sex and you have a literally intoxicating mix.

Amsterdam has always been a liberal place, ever since the Golden Age, when it led European art and trade. Centuries later, in the 1960s, it again led the pack – this time in the principles of tolerance, with broad-minded views on drugs and same-sex relationships taking centre stage.

Wander the 17th-century streets, tour the iconic canals, stop off to enjoy a masterpiece, discover a funky shop and choose from food from around the world. Walk or ride a bike around the concentric rings of the centre and bask in the many worlds-within-worlds where nothing ever seems the same twice.

ORIENTATION

From Centraal Station the streets radiate across the network of canals. The Dam is the heart, a 10-minute walk from Centraal Station. Leidseplein is the centre of (mainstream) Amsterdam nightlife, and Nieuwmarkt is a vast cobblestone square with open-air markets and popular pubs.

INFORMATION

Discount Card

I Amsterdam Card (per 24/48/72hr €33/43/53) Available at tourist offices (VVV) and some hotels. It gives admission to most museums, canal boat trips, and discounts at shops, attractions and restaurants, and also includes a transit pass. It's good if you plan to do a lot, otherwise, see p847 for transit-only passes.

Internet Access

Most places to stay have internet access for guests. Cafes and coffee shops also often have computers and/or wi-fi.

Internet City (☎ 620 12 92; Nieuwendijk 76; per hr €2; 🕑 9am-midnight)

Medical Services

Centrale Doktersdienst (Central Doctors Service; ☎ 592 34 34; 🕑 24hr) Doctor, dentist or pharmacy referrals.

Onze Lieve Vrouwe Gasthuis (☎ 599 91 11; Oosterparkstr 1) A 24-hour public hospital.

Money

GWK Travelex (Grenswisselkantoor; ☎ 0900 0566; Centraal Station; 🕑 8am-10pm Mon-Sat, 9am-10pm Sun) Converts travellers cheques and makes hotel reservations; also at Schiphol.

Tourist Information

Joho (☎ 517 13 57; www.joho.nl; Taksteeg 8; 🕑 10am-6pm Mon-Sat) Sells travel services, guidebooks and offers advice on work and volunteering.

Tourist office (VVV; ☎ 0900 400 40 40; www.vvvamsterdam.nl) Centraal Track 2 (Centraal Station; 🕑 8am-8pm Mon-Sat, 9am-5pm Sun); Stationsplein 10 (🕑 7am-9pm Mon-Fri, 8am-9pm Sat & Sun)

SIGHTS & ACTIVITIES

Rijksmuseum (☎ 674 70 00; www.rijksmuseum.nl; Stadhouderskade 42; admission €10; 🕑 9am-6pm Sat-Thu, to 8.30pm Fri) boasts a collection valued in the billions, but until renovations finish in 2013 (or later) there are only a few masterpieces displayed, including a couple of Vermeers and the crowning glory, Rembrandt's *Nightwatch* (1650). On most days crowds make the entire experience unpleasant. Some of the rooms have low ceilings and you'll find the Louvre's

CENTRAL AMSTERDAM

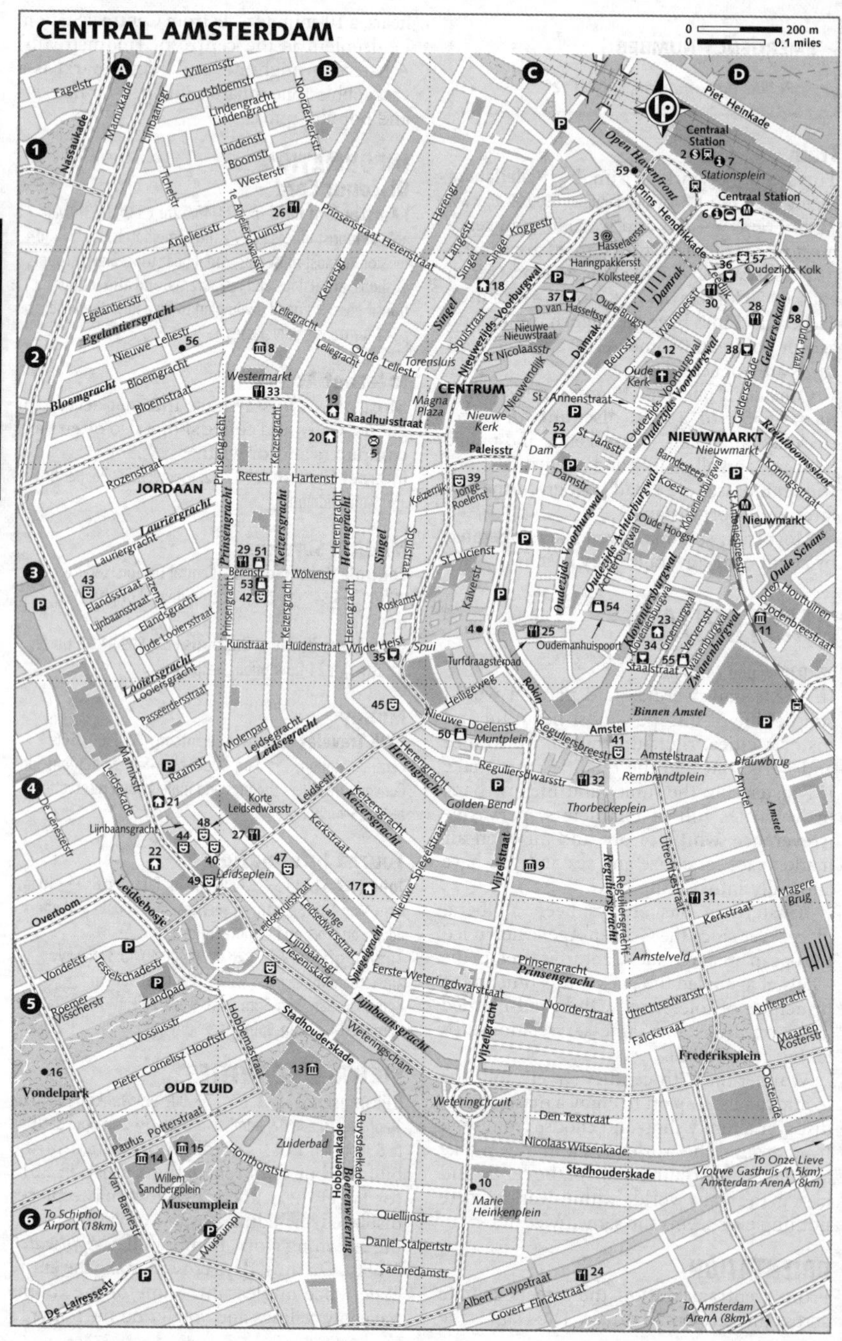

INFORMATION		
GVB	1	D1
GWK Travelex	2	D1
Internet City	3	C1
Joho	4	C3
Post Office	5	B2
Tourist Office	6	D1
Tourist Office	7	D1
SIGHTS & ACTIVITIES		
Anne Frank Huis	8	B2
FOAM	9	C4
Heineken Experience	10	C6
Museum Het Rembrandthuis	11	D3
Prostitution Information Centre	12	D2
Rijksmuseum	13	B5
Stedelijk Museum	14	A6
Van Gogh Museum	15	A6
Vondelpark	16	A5
SLEEPING		
Hans Brinker Budget Hotel	17	B4
Hotel Brouwer	18	C2
Hotel Nadia	19	B2
Hotel Pax	20	B2
International Budget Hostel	21	A4
Quentin Hotel	22	A4
Stayokay Stadsdoelen	23	D3
EATING		
Albert Cuypmarkt	24	C6
Crea	25	C3
De Bolhoed	26	B1
Febo	27	B4
Hofje van Wijs	28	D2
Pancakes!	29	B3
'Skek	30	D2
Tempo Doeloe	31	D4
Van Dobben	32	C4
Wil Graanstra Friteshuis	33	B2
DRINKING		
Doelen	34	C3
Hoppe	35	B3
In 't Aepjen	36	D2
In De Wildeman	37	C2
't Mandje	38	D2
ENTERTAINMENT		
Abraxas	39	C3
Boom Chicago	40	A4
Escape	41	C4
Felix Meritis	42	B3
Maloe Melo	43	A3
Melkweg	44	A4
Odeon	45	B4
Paradiso	46	B5
Rokerij	47	B4
Sugar Factory	48	A4
Uitburo	49	A4
SHOPPING		
Bloemenmarkt	50	C4
Boekie Woekie	51	B3
Condomerie	52	C2
Mendo	53	B3
Oudemanhuispoort Book Market	54	D3
Puccini	55	D3
TRANSPORT		
Bike City	56	A2
Canal Bus	57	D2
Orangebike	58	D2
Rederij Lovers Boat Terminal	59	C1

Mona Lisa mobs snapping pics with abandon. Save one queue by buying your ticket online.

The outstanding **Van Gogh Museum** (☎ 570 52 00; www.vangoghmuseum.nl; Paulus Potterstraat 7; adult/12-21 yr €10/2.50; 🕑 10am-6pm Sat-Thu, to 10pm Fri) houses the world's largest Van Gogh collection. Trace the artist's life from his tentative start though to his Japanese phase, and on to depression and the black cloud that descended over him and his work.

When open, the **Stedelijk Museum** (☎ 573 29 11; www.stedelijkindestad.nl; Museumplein; 🕑 10am-6pm) features around 100,000 pieces including Impressionist works from Monet, Picasso and Chagall, and pop art from Warhol and Lichtenstein. Until renovations are complete (possibly early 2010) a few select works are on display around town; check the website for details.

Vondelpark (www.vondelpark.nl, in Dutch) is an English-style park with free concerts, ponds, lawns, thickets, winding footpaths and three outdoor cafes. It was named after the poet and playwright Joost van den Vondel, the 'Dutch Shakespeare', and is popular with joggers, skaters, buskers and lovers.

The **Red Light District** (aka the Wallen; see p844) with its cacophony of sex shops, coffee shops, souvenir vendors and more retains the power to bewilder, even if near-naked prostitutes propositioning passers-by from black-lit windows is the oldest Amsterdam cliché. The Red Light District is bound by Zeedijk, Nieuwmarkt and Kloveniersburgwal in the east; Damstraat, Oude Doelenstraat and Oude Hoogstraat in the south; and Warmoesstraat in the west.

You almost expect to find the master himself at the **Museum Het Rembrandthuis** (Rembrandt House Museum; ☎ 520 04 00; www.rembrandthuis.nl; Jodenbreestraat 4; admission €8; 🕑 10am-5pm), the house where Rembrandt van Rijn ran his painting studio, only to lose the lot when profligacy set in, enemies swooped and bankruptcy came knocking. The museum has scores of etchings and sketches.

The streets around the Rembrandt House are prime wandering territory; a vibrant mix of old Amsterdam, canals, and quirky shops and cafes.

The **Anne Frank Huis** (Anne Frank House; ☎ 556 71 00; www.annefrank.org; Prinsengracht 267; admission €8.50; 🕑 9am-9pm Apr-Aug, to 7pm Sep-Mar), where Anne wrote her diary, lures almost a million visitors annually with its secret annexe, reconstruction of Anne's melancholy bedroom, and her actual diary, with its optimistic writing tempered by quiet despair. Crowds are lightest in the early morning or evening. Look for the newly added photo of Peter Schiff, her 'one true love'.

GETTING INTO TOWN

Trains from Schiphol airport to Centraal Station leave every few minutes, take 15 to 20 minutes, and cost €3.80/6.40 per single/return.

THE NETHERLANDS

RED LIGHTS & GREEN CIGARETTES: WHEN LESS IS MORE

Amsterdam's city government caused a stir in 2008 when it unveiled a plan to reduce by roughly half the number of windows used by prostitutes for self-marketing in the Red Light District. It also announced plans to close half of the coffee shops in the same area, or about 20% of the total city-wide. Needless to say these plans aroused considerable controversy. Many mocked the city's claim that organised crime controls much of these businesses and expressed fear that it was really a scheme to make Amsterdam's sleazy heart 'upscale'.

However, the latest announcement is merely part of a process that has been going on for years. The city has already bought and closed some brothels on Oudekerksplein, replacing them with small artist-run boutiques.

Meanwhile, you can learn all you ever wanted to know about the Red Light District on a **Prostitute Information Centre walking tour** (☎ 420 73 28; www.pic-amsterdam.com; Enge Kerksteeg 3; tour €12.50; ⌚ varies). Tours are led by former prostitutes and proceeds go to the centre, which assists the women to find new work.

FOAM (Fotografie Museum Amsterdam; ☎ 551 65 00; www.foam.nl; Keizersgracht 609; admission €7; ⌚ 10am-5pm Sat-Wed, to 9pm Thu & Fri) is an airy gallery devoted to painting with light. Two storeys of changing exhibitions feature world-renowned photographers such as Sir Cecil Beaton, Annie Leibovitz and Henri Cartier-Bresson.

New for 2009, the **Heineken Experience** (☎ 523 94 36; www.heinekenexperience.com; Stadhouderskade 78; admission €15; ⌚ 11am-7pm) is the much-gussied up reincarnation of the brewer's old brewery tour. Now there are multimedia displays, rides and plenty of gift shops in the old brewery. It's Amsterdam's most popular attraction; acolytes enjoy samples of the beer, which (like Stella Artois et al) is dismissed as an 'old man's beer' at home and sold at a premium abroad.

SLEEPING

Book ahead for weekends and in summer. Many places cater specifically to party animals with booze flowing, pot smoking and general mayhem around the clock. Others exude Old World charm. Wi-fi is near universal but elevators are not.

Stayokay Stadsdoelen (☎ 624 68 32; www.stayokay.com; Kloveniersburgwal 97; dm €18-28, s €45-60, d €50-80; 💻 ☒) Efficient Stadsdoelen is always bustling with backpackers and we can understand why. The staff are friendly and the mix of 11 ultraclean, single-sex and mixed rooms (each with up to 17 beds and free lockers) offer a modicum of privacy. There's a big TV room, a great smoke-free bar, a pool table and laundry facilities.

Hans Brinker Budget Hotel (☎ 622 06 87; www.hans-brinker.com; Kerkstraat 136; dm/d from €25/40; 💻) The lobby is a circus, rooms have all the ambience of a public hospital, and the 538 beds are almost always filled with school groups and backpackers. But the bar is merry, the disco pulsates, the restaurant serves cheap meals and rooms have shower and toilet. The 'eco-features' are a hoot.

International Budget Hostel (☎ 624 27 84; www.internationalbudgethostel.com; Leidsegracht 76; dm €28-32, tw from €70; 💻 ☒) The former warehouse in a canalside location is close to nightlife. There's a four-person limit in rooms and a cool mix of backpackers from around the world lounging in the common areas. It's clean and the staff have charm that's greater than the prices.

Hotel Pax (☎ 624 97 35; Raadhuisstraat 37; r €30-80) This budget choice – run by two cheery brothers – on the hotel-lined Raadhuisstraat has an art-student vibe. All 11 rooms have TV and each is individually decorated (some share bathrooms). The larger rooms have views of the Westerkerk and Keizersgracht.

Quentin Hotel (☎ 626 21 87; www.quentinhotels.com; Leidsekade 89; r €45-100) The Quentin, decorated with colourful murals, rock-star art and contemporary handmade furniture, offers a variety of rooms: some with balconies and canal views, others small and cramped. It's popular with actors and musicians performing at nearby venues.

Hotel Nadia (☎ 620 15 50; www.nadia.nl; Raadhuisstraat 51; r €55-150; ❄ 💻 ☒) This handsome building has a precipitous set of stairs (go figure) but the energetic staff will tote your luggage up them. Rooms are immaculate, with linens that will bounce coins. Rooms to the front have great views of the Westerkerk.

Hotel Brouwer (☎ 624 63 58; www.hotelbrouwer.nl; Singel 83; r €60-95; ☒) The eight rooms in this house dating back to 1652 are named after Dutch painters, simply furnished and boast canal views. There's a mix of Delft-blue tiles and early-20th-century furniture, and a tulip-sized elevator. Breakfast is included; no credit cards.

EATING

Amsterdam abounds in food choices. Happy streets for hunting include Utrechtsestraat, Spuistraat and any of the little streets lining and connecting the west canals such as Berenstraat.

Restaurants

Pancakes! (☎ 528 97 97; Berenstraat 38; mains from €3; 🕑 10am-7pm) A great place to sample Dutch pancakes in an atmosphere free of clogs and other kitsch – and there are just as many locals here as tourists.

our pick **Van Dobben** (☎ 624 42 00; Korte Reguliersdwarsstraat 5; mains from €4) Open since the 1940s, the venerable Van Dobben has white-tiled-walls and white-coated counter men who specialise in snappy banter. Trad Dutch fare is the speciality: try the *pekelvlees* (something close to corned beef) and the best *kroketten* (croquettes) and pea soup in town.

De Bolhoed (☎ 626 18 03; Prinsengracht 60-62; mains from €8) An old-school vegie eatery, De Bolhoed has been dishing up generous helpings of Italian, Mexican and Middle Eastern dishes to Amsterdammers for decades. Enjoy the tables among plants by the canal.

'Skek (☎ 427 05 51; Zeedijk 4-8; mains from €13; 🕑 noon-1am Sun-Thu, to 3am Fri & Sat) Run by students for students (ID gets you one-third off), this friendly, fun cafe-bar is a nice place to get some tasty Mediterranean fare. Bands occasionally perform at night.

Tempo Doeloe (☎ 625 67 18; www.tempodoeloerestaurant.nl; Utrechtsestraat 75; mains from €18; 🕑 dinner) One of the most respected Indonesian restaurants in the city, this tiny place is also more formal than most. It's the place to go if you've never enjoyed a *rijsttafel* (rice table).

Cafes

Hofje Van Wijs (☎ 624 04 36; Zeedijk 43; mains €4-8) The 200-year-old coffee and tea vendor Wijs & Zonen maintains this oasis of a courtyard cafe. Many of the teas are from Indonesia and you can get excellent coffees, cakes and meals. The place runs a weekly walking tour (3pm Sunday), which covers this once blighted area.

Crea (☎ 525 14 23; Turfdraagsterpad 17; mains €4-10) Walking along Grimburgwal, you can't help but notice the prime cafe chairs across the canal. They're part of the University of Amsterdam's cultural centre, a laid-back spot that's a superb urban escape.

Quick Eats

Febo (☎ 620 86 15; Leidsestraat 94) Insert a few coins in the machine and live the legend. The *bami* (noodle) rolls are hot as napalm, the *frikadel* (skinless sausage) frightening and the *kaassoufflé* (cheese snack) utterly unsoufflélike. But plucking a treat from the automat windows is a drunken Dutch tradition.

Wil Graanstra Friteshuis (☎ 624 40 71; Westermarkt 11) This little stall near the Anne Frank Huis has been serving up delectably light and crispy fries with mayo since 1956. Nearby stalls offer local staples such as herring on a stick.

Self-Catering

Albert Heijn supermarkets are found all over town. **Albert Cuypmarkt** (www.decuyp.nl; Albert Cuypstraat; 🕑 10am-5pm Mon-Sat) is Amsterdam's largest, busiest market – it's 100 years old. Food of every description can be found here, plus flowers, souvenirs, clothing, hardware and household goods.

DRINKING

Doelen (☎ 624 90 23; Kloveniersburgwal 125) On a busy crossroad between the Amstel and the Red Light District, this cafe dates back to 1895 and looks it: carved wooden goat's head, stained-glass lamps, sand on the floor. During fine weather the tables spill across the street for picture-perfect canal views.

our pick **Hoppe** (☎ 420 44 20; Spuistraat 18) This gritty *bruin café* (brown cafe) has been luring drinkers for more than 300 years. Journalists, bums, socialites and raconteurs toss back brews amidst the ancient wood panelling. Most months the energetic crowd spews from the dark interior and onto the Spui.

In De Wildeman (☎ 638 23 48; Kolksteeg) An oasis in the otherwise grim tourist ghetto south of the station. There are seats outside on the quiet street and a good selection of beers inside.

In 't Aepjen (☎ 626 84 01; Zeedijk 1) Candles burn even during the day at this bar in a 15th-century house, one of two remaining wooden buildings in the city. The name allegedly comes from the bar's role in the 16th and

COFFEE SHOPS

'Café' means 'pub' throughout the Netherlands; 'coffee shops' are where one procures pot. Note that new smoking regs mean you can puff pot but not tobacco.

Abraxas (☎ 625 57 63; Jonge Roelensteeg 12) The Abraxas management knows what stoners want: mellow music, comfy sofas, rooms with different energy levels, and thick milkshakes. The considerate staff and relaxed clientele make this a great place for coffee-shop newbies. Get stoned and send strange emails from the computers.

Rokerij (☎ 422 66 43; Lange Leidsedwarsstraat 41) Behind the black hole of an entrance you'll find Asian decor and candlelight for those tired of the Rastafarian vibe. One of several locations.

17th centuries as a crash pad for sailors from the Far East, who often toted *aapjes* (monkeys) with them.

't Mandje (☎ 622 53 75; Zeedijk 63) Amsterdam's – and perhaps the world's – oldest gay bar opened in 1927, then shut in 1982, when the Zeedijk grew too seedy. But its trinket-covered interior was lovingly dusted every week until it reopened in 2008. There's live jazz and a retro DJ spinning 78s on a Victrola.

CLUBBING

Escape (☎ 622 11 11; www.escape.nl; Rembrandtplein 11) Amsterdam's biggest, glitziest club has managed to keep the bass pumping since the '80s; it got a recent major tech revamp. Long lines get longer when a big-name DJ mixes.

Odeon (☎ 521 85 55; www.odeontheater.nl; Singel 460) Set in a skinny canal house, the Odeon has been a creative party spot for decades. Glam but accessible, its club nights cater to a veteran crowd.

Sugar Factory (☎ 626 50 06; www.sugarfactory.nl; Lijnbaansgracht 238) One night it's Balkan beats; another, it's a 10-piece soul band – the Sugar Factory has all kinds of live entertainment. Equally important, the vibe is always welcoming and creative. It's an excellent midsize space, with a smoking lounge upstairs.

ENTERTAINMENT

Live Music

Maloe Melo (☎ 420 45 92; Lijnbaansgracht 163) Home to Amsterdam's blues scene, this dingy venue is rowdy and casual, and often adds bluegrass and soul to the calendar.

Melkweg (☎ 531 81 81; www.melkweg.nl; Lijnbaansgracht 234a) The 'Milky Way' – it's housed in a former dairy – must be Amsterdam's coolest club-gallery-cinema-cafe-concert hall. Its vibrant program of events is so full and varied that it's impossible not to find something you want to go to, from international DJ club nights to live Brazilian jazz.

Paradiso (☎ 626 45 21; www.paradiso.nl, in Dutch; Weteringschans 6) This converted church has been a premier rock venue since the '60s. Expect interesting dance music, anything from Finnish DJs spinning jazz to Afro New Wave from New York and tech-hop from Detroit.

Sport

Four-times European champion Ajax is the Netherlands' most famous football team. Ajax plays in the **Amsterdam ArenA** (☎ 311 13 33; www.amsterdamarena.nl; Arena Blvd 11), usually on Saturday evenings and Sunday afternoons August to May. Enjoy a 'World of Ajax' tour.

Theatre

Boom Chicago (☎ 423 01 01; www.boomchicago.nl; Leidseplein 12) Hosting English-language stand-up and improv comedy year-round. See it over dinner and a few drinks. Inspiration is culled from Chicago's legendary Second City.

Felix Meritis (☎ 626 13 11; www.felixmeritis.nl, in Dutch; Keizersgracht 324) This wonderful arts and culture space, established in 1777, occasionally hosts experimental European theatre, along with innovative music, dance, lectures and readings. The cafe here, with its huge open windows, is great.

SHOPPING

The real pleasure of shopping in Amsterdam is finding some tiny shop selling something you'd find nowhere else.

The big department stores cluster around the Dam. Chains line the pedestrian (in more ways than one) Kalverstraat.

The Red Light District buzzes with vibrating latex creations. **Condomerie** (☎ 627 41 74; Warmoesstraat 141) puts the 'pro' back in prophylactic: rarely can you shop for a condom in such a tasteful setting and grapple with so many choices.

GET 'UIT' AND ABOUT

Not sure how to spend your evening? Head to the last-minute ticket desk at the **Uitburo** (☎ 621 13 11; www.aub.nl; Leidseplein 26; 10am-7.30pm Mon-Sat, noon-7.30pm Sun), in the corner of the Stadsschouwburg. Comedy, dance, concerts, even club nights are all potentially available at a significant discount – and handily marked 'LNP' (language no problem) if the event doesn't hinge on understanding Dutch to have fun.

Nieuwmarkt has several good streets for typically eccentric local stores. **Puccini** (☎ 626 54 74; Staalstr 17) will have you singing arias about the amazing range of house-made chocolates.

Just as the stores themselves brim with surprises, several streets along the western canals brim with surprising little shops. You can easily lose a day wandering Reestraat and Hartenstraat and the blocks south to Runstraat and Huidenstraat. For example, **Mendo** (☎ 612 12 16; Berenstraat 11) has a striking combination of visually stunning books, art, candy and even umbrellas. Nearby, **Boekie Woekie** (☎ 639 05 07; Berenstraat 16) sells books by artists, whether that means a self-published monograph or an illustrated story that's handcrafted right down to the paper. Buy a 'Two Lips from Amsterdam' T-shirt.

Markets

Bloemenmarkt (Singel; 9am-5pm, closed Sun Dec-Feb) 'Floating' flower market that's actually on pilings. Traders can advise on import regulations. Notorious for pickpockets.

Oudemanhuis Book Market (Oudemanhuispoort; 11am-4pm Mon-Fri) A favourite with academics, this moody old covered alleyway connecting two streets is lined with second-hand booksellers.

GETTING THERE & AWAY

Some train fares: Den Haag (€10, 50 minutes), Rotterdam (€13.60, one hour), Utrecht (€6.80, 35 minutes), Groningen (€36.70, two hours 20 minutes), Maastricht (€28.70, 2½ hours).

GETTING AROUND

Bicycle

For bicycle rental, try **Bike City** (☎ 626 37 21; www.bikecity.nl; Bloemgracht 68-70; per day/week €15/62), where there's no advertising on the bikes – you might pass for a local – or **Orangebike** (☎ 528 99 90; www.orangebike.nl; Geldersekade 37; per 3 hr/day/week €6/10/43), which offers a range of city tours (from €20). Both companies require a passport or other ID and a credit-card or cash deposit.

Boat

Amsterdam's canal boats are, understandably, popular ways to tour the town but most are actually a bit claustrophobic, with steamed-up glass windows surrounding the passengers. Look for a boat with an open seating area.

Canal Bus (☎ 623 98 86; www.canalbus.nl; day pass €18) does several circuits between Centraal Station and the Rijksmuseum between 10am and 8pm. The day pass is valid until noon the next day. The same company rents canal bikes (pedal boats) for €10 per person per hour (€7 per person if there are more than two people per canal bike). They can be found at docks by Leidseplein and near the Anne Frank Huis.

Rederij Lovers (☎ 530 10 90; www.lovers.nl; Prins Hendrikkade 25-27; 1hr tour per person €11) offers a variety of night-time cruises.

Public Transport

Services – including the iconic trams – are run by the local transit authority, the GVB; national railway (NS) tickets are not valid on local transport. The GVB has a highly useful **information office** (☎ 0900 80 11; www.gvb.nl; Stationsplein 10; 7am-9pm Mon-Fri, 8am-9pm Sat & Sun) across the tram tracks from the Centraal Station main entrance.

Public transport in Amsterdam, like the rest of the Netherlands, has switched to the *OV-chipkaart* (p840). You can buy one-ride cards for €2.50 from machines at major transit points or on trams and buses. A better deal are the unlimited-ride tickets sold by the GVB (from machines and the office), which are good for 24/48/72/96 hours and cost €7/11.50/14.50/17.50.

Night buses take over shortly after midnight when the trams and regular buses stop running.

Taxi

Amsterdam taxis are expensive, even over short journeys. Try **Taxicentrale Amsterdam** (☎ 677 77 77).

SMALL TOWNS & DAY TRIPS

Oodles of cute small Dutch towns can be reached from Amsterdam in under 1½ hours by train. Here are a few to consider:

- **Alkmaar** is massively touristy, but its cheese ceremony dates back to the 17th century.
- **Delta Project** (www.deltawerken.com; best visited by car) shows you how the Dutch tamed the North Sea.
- **Deventer** is a sleepy Hanseatic League town with over 1000 16th- and 17th-century buildings.
- **Gouda** is the perfect little Dutch town, replicated in many places across the Netherlands.
- **Haarlem** has cobblestone streets, canals and the excellent Frans Hals Museum.
- **Keukenhof Gardens** (www.keukenhof.nl) shows off millions, maybe billions of tulips in spring, and is close to Leiden.

Get more info at the tourist office across from Amsterdam Centraal Station, p841, or online at www.1000dutchdelights.com. For train details to these towns, see www.ns.nl.

RANDSTAD

The Randstad (literally 'Rim City') is the Netherlands' most densely populated region (and among the world's densest), containing almost half the country's population. It's in the west, stretching from Amsterdam to Rotterdam, including cities most iconically Dutch: Den Haag, Utrecht, Leiden and Delft.

LEIDEN

☎ 071 / pop 118,000

Lovely Leiden is a refreshing, vibrant town, patterned with canals and attractive old buildings. It also has a few claims to fame: it's Rembrandt's birthplace, and it's home to the Netherlands' oldest university (and 20,000 students), the alma mater of René Descartes.

Joho (☎ 516 12 77; www.joho.nl; Stille Rijn 8-9) Has travel books, maps, travel gear and supplies, and internet access.

Tourist office (☎ 0900 222 23 33; www.leidenpromotie.nl; Stationsweg 2d; 🕒 11am-5.30pm Mon, 9.30am-5.30pm Tue-Fri, 10am-4.30pm Sat year-round, 11am-3pm Sun Jun-Aug) Good maps and historic info.

Sights & Activities

The 17th-century **Lakenhal** (Cloth Hall; ☎ 516 53 60; www.lakenhal.nl; Oude Singel 28-32; admission €4; 🕒 10am-5pm Tue-Fri, noon-5pm Sat & Sun) houses the Municipal Museum, with an assortment of works by old masters, as well as period rooms and temporary exhibits.

The **Rijksmuseum van Oudheden** (National Museum of Antiquities; ☎ 516 31 63; www.rmo.nl; Rapenburg 28; admission €8.50; 🕒 10am-5pm Tue-Sun) has a classy collection of hieroglyphs and 94 mummies.

Cultural achievements by civilisations worldwide – especially Indonesia – are on show at the **Museum Volkenkunde** (Museum of Ethnology; ☎ 516 88 00; www.volkenkunde.nl; Steenstraat 1; admission €7.50; 🕒 10am-5pm Tue-Sun).

Leiden's carefully restored windmill, **De Valk** (Falcon; ☎ 516 53 53; http://home.wanadoo.nl/molenmuseum; 2e Binnenvestgracht 1; admission €3; 🕒 10am-5pm Tue-Sat, 1-5pm Sun), explains wind-blown technology; the upper levels afford an inspired view of the old town.

Rent a canoe or kayak from **Botenverhuur 't Galgewater** (☎ 514 97 90; www.galgewater.nl; per hr from €5; 🕒 11am-6pm mid-Apr–Oct) and explore the canals.

Sleeping & Eating

De Noordduinen (☎ 402 52 95; Campingweg 1; camp sites from €18; 🕒 Apr-Oct) The closest camping ground, 8km west of town. Take bus 31 or 41; call first.

Stayokay Noordwijk (☎ 0252-37 29 20; www.stayokay.com; Langevelderlaan 45, Noordwijk; dm from €25) The hostel is next to popular Noordwijk beach. Take buses 57 or 90 (last bus at 11pm) 45 minutes to Sancta Maria hospital and walk for 10 minutes.

Pension Witte Singel (☎ 512 45 92; www.pension-ws.demon.nl; Witte Singel 80; r €49-95; 💻) Seven bright rooms (some sharing bathrooms) with large windows overlook most agreeable scenery: the perfectly peaceful Singel canal in front and a typically Dutch garden out back. Free wi-fi.

Annie's (☎ 512 57 37; Hoogstraat 1a; mains from €8; 🕑 11am-1am) At the confluence of canals and pedestrian zones, Annie's has a prime water-level location with dozens of tables on a floating pontoon. This classy cafe is good for a drink or a casual meal.

Brasserie FYN (☎ 512 60 66; www.brasseriefyn.nl; Nieuwe Rijn 37; dishes €9; 🕑 dinner daily, lunch Sat year-round & Wed-Fri Apr-Sep) This cute little bistro is right on a canal and has tables outside when the Dutch weather allows. Dishes have a tapas style, with a fusion of flavours from Holland to the Med to Indonesia.

Surakarta (☎ 512 35 24; Noordeinde 51-53; mains from €12; 🕑 dinner;) Javanese art lines the walls at this neighbourhood Indonesian place which does a busy take-away service in addition to its elegant *rijsttafel* service. Several more ethnic places are nearby.

Entertainment

Jazzcafé the Duke (☎ 566 15 85; www.jazzcafetheduke.nl; Oude Singel 2) No windows, but loads of yellowing, vintage jazz posters on the walls. The motto is, 'If we don't have it, you don't need it'. It's true: you don't need windows to enjoy this atmospheric den, with its fine live jazz every night. Several coffee shops are nearby.

Getting There & Away

Sample train fares: Amsterdam (€8, 35 minutes, six per hour) and Den Haag (€3.20, 10 minutes, six per hour). Regional and local buses leave from the bus station directly in front of Centraal Station.

DEN HAAG (THE HAGUE)

☎ 070 / pop 476,000

Den Haag, officially known as 's-Gravenhage (the Count's Hedge), is the Dutch seat of government (although Amsterdam's the capital). Home to the royal family, it's a stately, regal place filled with palatial embassies and mansions, green boulevards and parks, prestigious art galleries, a mouth-watering culinary scene, a clutch of tasty museums and some throbbing nightlife.

Stanley & Livingstone (☎ 365 73 06; Schoolstraat 21) Grab the latest Lonely Planet at this excellent travel bookshop.

Tourist office (☎ 0900 340 35 05; www.denhaag.com; Hofweg 1; 🕑 10am-6pm Mon-Fri, to 5pm Sat, noon-5pm Sun) Sells tickets for local events, has internet access and a good reading area.

Sights

For a painless introduction to Dutch and Flemish Art, visit the **Mauritshuis** (☎ 302 34 56; www.mauritshuis.nl; Korte Vijverberg 8; admission €12; 🕑 10am-5pm Tue-Sat, 11am-5pm Sun), a small museum in a jewel-box of an old, 17th-century palace. Highlights include the Dutch *Mona Lisa:* Vermeer's *Girl with a Pearl Earring*. The Rembrandts include a wistful self-portrait from the year of his death, 1669. Even if you're just passing Den Haag on the train, it's well worth hopping off to visit.

Adjoining the Mauritshuis, the **Binnenhof** (☎ 364 61 44; 🕑 10am-4pm Mon-Sat) is surrounded by parliamentary buildings that have long been at the heart of Dutch politics. The sterile central courtyard was once used for executions.

The **Grote Kerk** (☎ 302 86 30; Rond de Grote Kerk 12), dating from 1450, has a fine pulpit that was constructed 100 years later. The neighbouring 1565 **old town hall** is a splendid example of Dutch Renaissance architecture.

Admirers of De Stijl and Piet Mondrian mustn't miss the HP Berlage–designed **Gemeentemuseum** (Municipal Museum; ☎ 338 11 20; Stadhouderslaan 41; www.gemeentemuseum.nl; admission €8.50; 🕑 11am-5pm Tue-Sun). It also houses extensive exhibits of applied arts, costumes and musical instruments. Mondrian's unfinished *Victory Boogie Woogie* takes pride of place. There are also a few Picassos and some Eschers.

Madurodam (☎ 355 39 00; www.madurodam.nl; George Maduroplein 1; admission €14; 🕑 9am-8pm) is a miniaturised Netherlands, complete with 1:25 scale versions of Schiphol, Amsterdam, windmills and tulips, Rotterdam harbour, the Delta dikes, and so on. It's yet another example of the Dutch passion for recreating their reality artificially.

The long beach at **Scheveningen** (www.scheveningen.nl) attracts 9 million visitors per year. On warm days the sands get over-subscribed but there's commercial relief to be found in a slew of diversions that would warm the cockles of any Blackpool or Atlantic City huckster. Escape the madness on paved bike paths that run for miles through desolate dunes. Most streets heading west reach Scheveningen but the beach is more pleasantly approached at the end of a 15- to 20-minute (4km) bike ride that will take you past the lush homes of some of Den Haag's most well-heeled residents.

Book your stay at lonelyplanet.com/hotels

Sleeping

Duinhorst (☎ 324 22 70; www.duinhorst.nl; Buurtweg 135; camp sites per person/tent €5/5; ⏰ Apr-Sep) Camping ground set among the dunes east of Scheveningen. Take bus 28 from Den Haag HS station or 29 from Centraal Station to the end of the line, from where it's about 1km west.

Stayokay Den Haag (☎ 315 78 88; www.stayokay.com/denhaag; Scheepmakerstraat 27; dm from €23; 💻) This branch of the Stayokay hostel chain has all the usual facilities including a bar, a restaurant, internet and games. It's around 15 minutes' walk from Den Haag HS station.

Hotel 't Centrum (☎ 346 36 57; www.hotelhetcentrum.nl; Veenkade 5-6; r €40-85) The 13 rooms here are the best deal close to the centre. Things are basic white but spotless and comfortable; some rooms share bathrooms. Apartments have basic cooking facilities and there's a small cafe. Book ahead.

Eating & Drinking

Café De Oude Mol (☎ 345 16 23; Oude Molstraat 61; snacks from €3) Some of the old National Geographics piled in the window actually predate the crusty yet genial characters arrayed around the bar. Pass through the ivy covered door and you'll find Den Haag without the pretence.

our pick **De Zwarte Ruiter** (The Black Rider; ☎ 364 95 49; Grote Markt 27; snacks from €4) The Rider faces off with the competing Boterwaag across the Markt like rival Kings of Cool. We call this one the winner, with its terrace and deco mezzanine – light-filled, split-level and cavernous – and boisterous crowds of commoners, diplomats and, no doubt, the odd international jewel thief.

Zebedeüs (☎ 346 83 93; Rond de Grote Kerk 8; meals from €7) Built right into the walls of the Grote Kerk, this bright cafe is a day-tripper's dream, with huge, fresh sandwiches served all day. Grab one of many tree-shaded tables outside or relax with a coffee and a newspaper at the big tables within.

Cloos (☎ 363 97 86; Plein 12a; mains from €8) One of a gaggle of swank cafes on the vast Plein. Rest your gentrified butt on the comfy wicker chairs and watch the pigeons bedevil the solemn statue of Willem de Eerste, hero of the Spanish war. Who knows what the famous nationalist would have thought about Cloos' Italian menu.

Getting There & Around

Most Den Haag trains start/stop their journeys from Den Haag Centraal Station. But some through-trains only stop at Den Haag HS (Holland Spoor) station just south of the centre.

Sample train fares: Amsterdam (€10, 50 minutes, four per hour), Delft (€2.50, 12 minutes, four per hour), Rotterdam (€4.30, 25 minutes, four per hour) and Schiphol (€7.30, 30 minutes). Tram 1 links to both Scheveningen and Delft.

DELFT

☎ 015 / pop 96,300

Ah, lovely Delft: compact, charming, relaxed. Founded around 1100, it maintains tangible links to its romantic past despite the pressures of modernisation and hordes of day-trippers. Many of the canalside vistas seem taken right from *Girl with a Pearl Earring*, the novel about Golden Age painter Jan Vermeer which was made into a movie (and partially shot here) in 2003. Vermeer's *View of Delft* is an enigmatic, nonrealist vision of the town (it hangs in the Mauritshuis, p849, in Den Haag). Delft is also famous for its 'delftware', the distinctive blue-and-white pottery originally duplicated from Chinese porcelain by 17th-century artisans.

Tourist office (☎ 0900 515 15 55; www.delft.nl; Hippolytusbuurt 4; ⏰ 10am-4pm Sun & Mon, 9am-6pm Tue-Fri, 10am-5pm Sat) Free internet and a highly recommended range of thematic walking guides.

Sights & Activities

The 14th-century **Nieuwe Kerk** (☎ 212 30 25; www.nieuwekerk-delft.nl; Markt; admission €3.20; ⏰ 9am-6pm Apr-Oct, 11am-4pm Nov-Apr, closed Sun) houses the crypt of the Dutch royal family. The fee includes entrance to the **Oude Kerk** (☎ 212 30 15; www.oudekerk-delft.nl; Heilige Geestkerkhof; ⏰ 9am-6pm Apr-Oct, 11am-4pm Nov-Mar, closed Sun) – and vice versa. The latter, 800 years old, is a surreal sight: its tower leans 2m from the vertical. Among the tombs inside is Vermeer's.

The nonprolific painter (only 35 works are firmly attributed to him) is the star of the **Vermeer Centre Delft** (☎ 213 85 88; Voldersgracht 21; admission €6; ⏰ 10am-5pm), which looks at his artistry and life in detail but actually has none of his paintings.

Municipal Museum Het Prinsenhof (☎ 260 23 58; www.gemeentemusea-delft.nl; St Agathaplein 1; admission €6; ⏰ 10am-5pm Tue-Sat, 1-5pm Sun), a former convent, is where Willem the Silent was assassinated in 1584. The museum displays various objects telling the story of the 80-year war with Spain.

The **Museum Nusantara** (☎ 260 23 58; www.nusantara-delft.nl, in Dutch; St Agathaplein 4; admission €3.50; 10am-5pm Tue-Sat, 1-5pm Sun) shines a light on the Netherlands' colonial past. There's a collection of furniture and other lifestyle artefacts from 17th-century Batavia (now Jakarta).

See Delft on a **canal boat tour** (☎ 212 63 85; www.rondvaartdelft.nl; admission €6; 11am-5pm Apr-Oct) departing from Koornmarkt 113.

Sleeping

Quiet Delft would make a good base for exploring much of Holland, with frequent and fast train services putting towns from Leiden to Rotterdam less than 20 minutes away. The usual array of cafes surround the Markt.

Hotel de Kok (☎ 212 21 25; www.hoteldekok.nl; Houttuinen 15; r €66-125) The 30 rooms here are simple but very conveniently located near the train station and with a sweet garden terrace.

Hotel Coen (☎ 214 59 14; www.hotelcoen.nl; Coenderstraat 47; r from €70;) Just behind the train station, this family-run hotel has 55 beds in a variety of rooms, from budget singles as thin as your wallet to grander doubles. There's wi-fi throughout.

Eating & Drinking

our pick **'t Walletje** (☎ 214 04 23; Burgwal 7; mains €7-12) Tables front this small bistro on a pedestrian street near the centre. Lunch features good smoothies, sandwiches and salads. At night three-course specials (€20) are artfully prepared and feature nice accents like pesto sides with seafood and steaks.

Locus Publicus (☎ 213 46 32; Brabantse Turfmarkt 67) Glowing from within, this beer cafe has more than 200 brews. It's charming and filled with cheery locals who've found their new candy store.

Getting There & Away

Sample train fares: Den Haag (€2.50, 12 minutes), Rotterdam (€3.20, 12 minutes) and Amsterdam (€11.60, one hour). Tram 1 makes the run to Den Haag.

ROTTERDAM

☎ 010 / pop 605,000

Rotterdam, the second-largest Dutch city, was bombed flat during WWII. The following decades were spent rebuilding the harbour and the centre, often with eye-popping architecture that's unique in Europe. Today, Rotterdam has a crackling energy, with vibrant nightlife, a diverse, multi-ethnic community, an intensely interesting maritime tradition and a wealth of top-class museums. It also has a long-standing, edgy rivalry with Amsterdam. When local football team Feyenoord meets Ajax of Amsterdam, the fur *always* flies. And when Rotterdam unleashed its extreme form of techno, gabber, on the world in the early '90s, one of its most enduring targets was Amsterdam: an early gabber single was memorably titled 'Amsterdam, Waar Lech Dat Dan?' ('Amsterdam, Where the Hell is That?').

Information

The Rotterdam Welcome Card offers discounts on sights, hotels and restaurants; it's €5. Buy it from the tourist office.

Tourist office (☎ 271 01 28; www.rotterdam.info; Stationsplein 45; 9am-6pm Mon-Fri, to 5pm Sat & Sun) The VVV Rotterdam Info Café offers free internet, paid wi-fi; excellent cafe with rooftop views. Pick up the essential *R Zine*.

Use-It (☎ 240 91 58; www.use-it.nl; Schaatsbaan 41-45; 9am-6pm Tue-Sun mid-May–mid-Sep, to 5pm Tue-Sat mid-Sep–mid-May) Offbeat independent tourist organisation all but lost amidst the station construction. Has free wi-fi, books cheap accommodation and publishes the useful *Simply the Best* local booklet.

Sights

Museum Boijmans van Beuningen (☎ 441 94 00; www.boijmans.nl; Museumpark 18-20; admission €9, Wed free; 11am-5pm Tue-Sun) is among Europe's very finest museums and has a permanent collection taking in Dutch and European art (Bosch, Van Eyck, Rembrandt, Tintoretto, Titian and Bruegel's *Tower of Babel*). The surrealist wing features ephemera, paraphernalia and famous works from Dalí, Man Ray and more.

The **Nederlands Architectuur Instituut** (NAI; ☎ 440 12 00; www.nai.nl; Museumpark 25; admission €8; 10am-5pm Tue-Sat, 11am-5pm Sun & holidays) offers a full overview of Dutch architecture. The NAI is a worthy monument in a city that celebrates built space like no other.

The **Overblaak development** (1978–84), designed by Piet Blom, is marked by its pencil-shaped tower and arresting upended, cube-shaped apartments. One unit, the **Kijk-Kubus Museum-House** (☎ 414 22 85; www.kubuswoning.nl; admission €2.50; 11am-5pm), lets you see what it's like to live at odd angles.

A shimmy up Rotterdam's soaring 185m **Euromast** (☎ 436 48 11; www.euromast.com; Parkhaven 20;

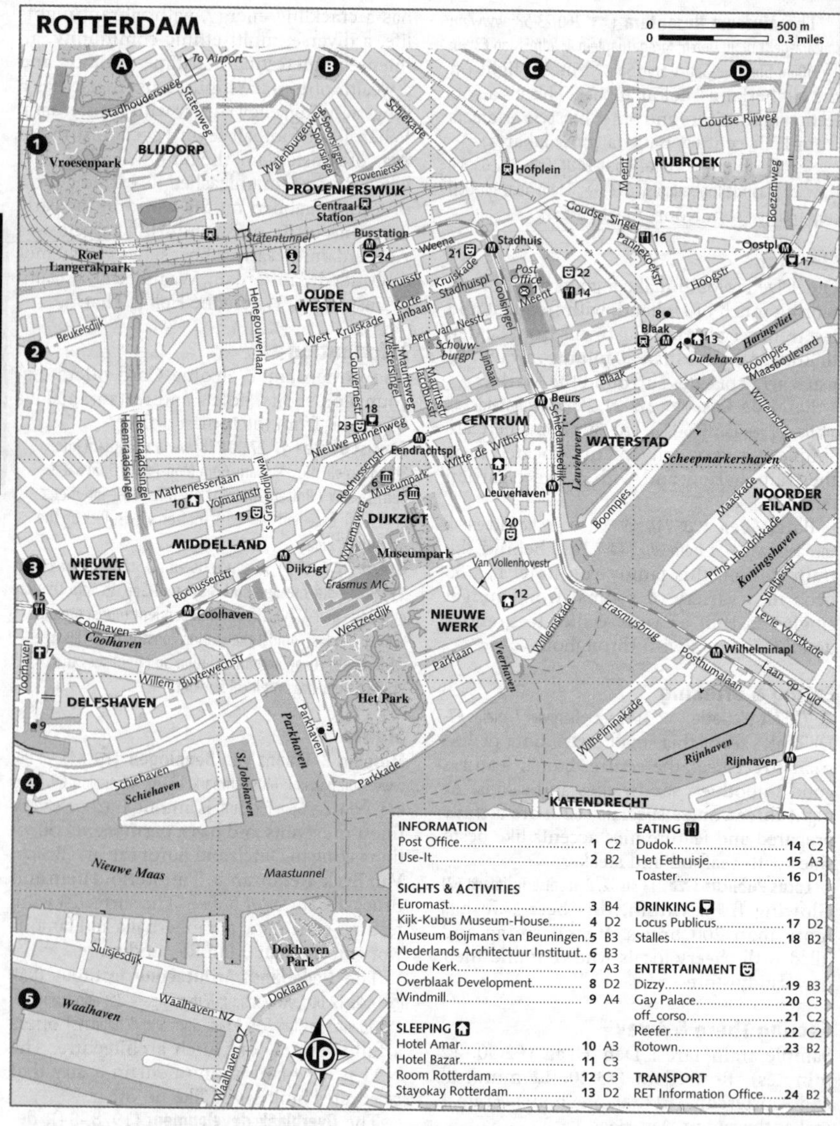

admission €8.30; 10am-11pm) is a must. It offers unparalleled 360-degree views of Rotterdam, with its rotating, glass-walled 'Euroscope' contraption ascending to near the summit.

Delfshaven was once the main seaport for the city of Delft and today is a lively bit of Rotterdam's past. A reconstructed 18th-century **windmill** (Voorhaven 210; 1-5pm Wed, 10am-4pm Sat) still grinds flour, while the **Oude Kerk** on Voorhaven is where the Pilgrim Fathers prayed for the last time before leaving the city on 22 July 1620.

Sleeping

The tourist office and Use-It (p851) make reservations for a small fee.

BLOWING IN THE WIND

In 1740 a series of windmills were built to drain a polder about 12km southeast of Rotterdam. Today 19 of the Dutch icons survive at **Kinderdijk** (www.kinderdijk.nl), which is a Unesco monument. You can wander the dikes for over 3km amidst the spinning sails and visit inside one of the **windmills** (admission €3.50; 🕑 9.30am-5.30pm). It's a good bicycle ride (ask at Use-It) or you can go on a three-hour boat tour (get details from the tourist office).

Room Rotterdam (☎ 282 72 77; www.roomrotterdam.nl; Van Vollenhovenstraat 62; dm from €15; 💻) A popular hostel with 16 dorm rooms with two to 10 beds. Each has its own decor, ranging from 'Dutch Delight' to 'Love'. It's a lively, young place and rocks much of the night.

Stayokay Rotterdam (☎ 436 57 63; www.stayokay.com/rotterdam; Overblaak; dm from €20.50; 💻) In 2009, Rotterdam's Stayokay hostel moved to the landmark Overblaak development, with its crazy shaped units. The 46 rooms boast a new and spiffy decor.

Hotel Amar (☎ 425 57 95; www.amarhotel.nl; Mathenesserlaan 316; s/d €30/60; 💻) This friendly, small place is in a leafy neighbourhood close to Delfshaven, Museumplein and good nightlife. Rooms are simple but comfy, and the ones at the back overlook a large and peaceful garden. All share bathrooms.

Hotel Bazar (☎ 206 51 51; www.hotelbazar.nl; Witte de Withstraat 16; r €60-120) Bazar is deservedly popular for its 27 Middle Eastern-, African- and South American–themed rooms: lush, brocaded curtains, exotically tiled bathrooms and more. Top-floor rooms have balconies and views. Breakfast is spectacular: Turkish breads, international cheeses, yoghurt, pancakes and coffee. The ground-floor bar and restaurant is justifiably popular.

Eating

Delfshaven is a vibrant, multi-ethnic neighbourhood with many cafes and bars, especially along the canal near the Oude Kerk. Look for lots of ethnic snack bars.

Toaster (☎ 413 70 81; Pannekoekstraat 38a; meals €6-12; 🕑 closed Mon) Take time out from cruising the trendy shops and little lanes in and around Pannekoekstraat at this neighbourhood hangout. Although the name refers to the many toasted sandwiches, there are also tapas and all-day breakfasts. Some nights you can enjoy live music from the sofas.

Dudok (☎ 433 31 02; Meent 88; dishes €6-20) There are always crowds at this sprawling brasserie near the centre. Inside it's all high ceilings and walls of glass, outside, you have your pick of an array of tables lining the street. Meals range from breakfast to snacks to cafe fare like soups and pasta.

Het Eethuisje (☎ 425 49 17; Mathenesserdijk 436; mains €8-10) Trad Dutch food is served from this little storefront near the canal. Tuck into meaty fare served with rib-sticking starchy sides. Utterly tourist-free.

Drinking

Stalles (☎ 436 16 55; Nieuwe Binnenweg 11a) This classic *bruin café* is on a great stretch of road near plenty of good shops, cafes and bars. It has an extensive range of single-malt whiskies.

Locus Publicus (☎ 433 17 61; Oostzeedijk 364) The listings of the more than 200 beers on offer cover the panelled walls at this outstanding specialist beer cafe.

Coffee Shop

Reefer (☎ 412 26 13; Oppert 1) This is the funky coffeehop of your dreams – or delirium. Grab a joint from the vending machine and mellow out to house, techno and other modish tunes.

Clubbing

Dizzy (☎ 477 30 14; www.dizzy.nl; 's-Gravendijkwal 127) Live concerts Monday and Tuesday nights and Sunday afternoons. The evening performances are scorching: everything from hot jazz to fast and funky Brazilian and salsa. There are regular jazz jam sessions.

Gay Palace (☎ 414 14 86; www.gay-palace.nl; Schiedamsesingel 139) Every Saturday night, Rotterdam's gay nightclub has four floors of throbbing action, with different scenes on each floor (including a 'lesbian corner').

off_corso (☎ 411 38 97; www.off-corso.nl; Kruiskade 22) This is where it's at: bleeding-edge local and international DJs mashing up a high-fibre electronic diet of bleeps 'n' beats. Art displays provide diversions at this prototypical Rotterdam club.

Rotown (☎ 436 26 69; www.rotown.nl; Nieuwe Binnenweg 17-19) A smooth bar, a dependable live rock venue, an agreeable cafe, a popular meeting place. The musical program features new local talent, established international acts and crossover experiments.

Getting There & Away

The area around Rotterdam Centraal Station is one big construction site until the stunning new station – above and below ground – is completed in 2012. The high-speed train to Belgium will stop here – travel time to Brussels will be one hour when everything is open. Sample train fares: Amsterdam (€13.60, one hour, four every hour) and Utrecht (€9.30, 40 minutes, two every hour).

Getting Around

Rotterdam's trams, buses and metro are provided by **RET** (☎ 447 69 11; www.ret.nl). Most converge in front of CS, where there is an **information office** (🕑 6am-11pm Mon-Fri, 8am-11pm Sat & Sun) that also sells tickets. Day passes are €6.

Rent bikes from Use-it (p851) for €6 per day.

UTRECHT CITY

☎ 030 / pop 283,000

Utrecht is one of the Netherlands' oldest cities – not that you'd know it when you step off the train and find yourself lost in the maze that is the Hoog Catharijne shopping centre. The Hoog is huge…and it's attached to the station…and it seemingly goes on forever…and ever. But fight your way through and you'll emerge starry-eyed into a beautiful, vibrant, old-world city centre, ringed by striking 13th-century canal wharves. The wharves, well below street level, are unique to Utrecht and the streets alongside brim with chic shops, restaurants and cafes. The city's student community of 40,000 is the largest in the country.

Information

Municipal library (☎ 286 18 00; Oudegracht 167; per hr €3; 🕑 10am-9pm Mon, 11am-6pm Tue-Fri, 10am-5pm Sat) Internet access.

Tourist office (☎ 0900 128 87 32; www.utrecht.nl; Domplein 9; 🕑 10am-6pm Mon-Fri, to 5pm Sat, noon-5pm Sun) Sells maps and organises tours of the nearby Domtoren.

Sights & Activities

The tourist office has a good booklet that covers Utrecht's myriad small museums that feature everything from waste water to old trains.

One of Utrecht's favourite sons, Dick Bruna, is honoured at the **Dick Bruna Huis** (☎ 236 23 62; www.dickbrunahuis.nl; Agnietenstraat 2; admission €8; 🕑 11am-5pm Tue-Sun). Bruna is the creator of beloved cartoon rabbit Miffy, and she naturally takes pride of place, along with an extensive overview of Bruna's career.

Admission to Dick Bruna Huis also includes entry to the nearby **Centraal Museum** (☎ 236 23 62; www.centraalmuseum.nl; Nicolaaskerkhof 10; admission €8; 🕑 11am-5pm Tue-Sun), which has a wide-ranging collection of applied arts dating back to the 17th century as well as paintings by some of the Utrecht School artists. There's even a 12th-century boat that was dug out of the local mud.

The **Domtoren** (Cathedral Tower; ☎ 233 30 36; www.domtoren.nl; Domplein; admission €7.50; 🕑 11am-4pm Mon-Sat, noon-4pm Sun) is 112m high, with 465 steps. It's a tough haul to the top but well worth the exertion: the tower gives unbeatable city views. The guided tour in Dutch and English is detailed; buy tickets at the tourist office.

Sleeping

our pick **Strowis Budget Hostel** (☎ 238 02 80; Boothstraat 8; www.strowis.nl; dm from €15, r €58; 💻) This 17th-century building is near the town centre and has been lovingly restored and converted into a hostel. It's open 24 hours a day, has a cosy bar and is run by a bunch of ex-hippies. Highly recommended.

B&B Utrecht (☎ 06 5043 4884; www.hostelutrecht.nl; Lucas Bolwerk 4; dm/r from €19/55; 💻) Straddling the border between hostel and hotel, this spotless inn in an elegant old building has an internal Ikea vibe. Breakfast and internet access is free as is use of a huge range of musical instruments.

Eating & Drinking

When Utrecht groans with visiting mobs, you can escape down to the waterside canal piers with a picnic.

Oudaen (☎ 231 18 64; www.oudaen.nl; Oudegracht 99; mains €8-22) The best choice on this busy stretch of the canal. Set in a restored 14th-century banquet hall, it has a varied menu of salads, steaks and seafood. Best of all, it brews its own beer, which you can enjoy under the high ceilings or outside on the canal.

our pick **Blauw** (☎ 234 24 63; Springweg 64; set menu from €20; 🕑 dinner) Blauw is *the* place for stylish Indonesian food in Utrecht. Young and old alike enjoy superb rice tables amidst the stunning red decor that mixes vintage art with hip minimalism.

Café Ledig Erf (☎ 231 75 77; Tolsteegbrug 3) This classy pub overlooks a confluence of canals (and other cafes) at the southern tip of town. The terrace vies with the beer list in offering the most joy. The autumn bock-beer fest is a winner.

't Oude Pothuys (☎ 231 89 70; Oudegracht 279) Small and dark, this totally refurbished basement pub has nightly music – jam sessions with locals trying their hand at rock and jazz. Enjoy drinks on the canalside pier.

Getting There & Away

Utrecht is easily walked (once you escape the shopping mall). Its train station is a major connection point and is the Netherlands' busiest. It is on the line linking Amsterdam to Cologne. Sample train fares: Amsterdam (€6.80, 35 minutes), Maastricht (€25, two hours) and Rotterdam (€9.30, 40 minutes).

NORTHERN NETHERLANDS

This region includes independently minded Fryslân province, which used to incorporate regions of the Netherlands, northern Germany and Denmark until it became part of the united Netherlands. Although the Frisian language is similar to Dutch, pronunciation is entirely different.

GRONINGEN CITY

☎ 050 / pop 178,000

It may be a long way from Amsterdam, but Groningen's a vibrant, youthful city, boasting all you'd expect of a progressive Dutch metropolis – its 20,000-strong student population (which has been around since 1614 when the university opened) sees to that. There are also the requisite art museums, theatre and classical concerts, as well as gabled houses reflected in silent canals.

Tourist office (☎ 313 97 41; www.toerisme.groningen.nl; Grote Markt 25; ⌚ 9am-6pm Mon-Sat year-round, 11am-3pm Sun Jun-Aug) As lively as the city itself.

Sights

The striking, polymorphous **Groninger Museum** (☎ 366 65 55; www.groninger-museum.nl; Museumeiland 1; admission €10; ⌚ 10am-5pm Tue-Thu, Sat & Sun, to 10pm Fri) occupies three islands in the middle of the canal in front of the station and hosts contemporary design and photography exhibitions alongside classic Golden Age Dutch paintings.

The 16th-century **Martinikerk** (☎ 311 12 77; Grote Markt; ⌚ noon-5pm Tue-Sat mid-April–mid-Nov), at the northern corner of the Grote Markt, is eye-catching. Its tower, the Martinitoren, is 96m tall and is considered to have one of the most finely balanced profiles in the country. A climb to the top (€3; purchase ticket at tourist office) yields sweeping views.

Sleeping

Stadspark Camping (☎ 525 16 24; www.stadscampings.nl; Campinglaan 4; camp sites per 2 adults & tent €16; ⌚ mid-Mar–mid-Oct) From the train station, take bus 4 about 3km west to the Stadspark stop.

Hotel Garni Friesland (☎ 312 13 07; www.hotelfriesland.nl; Kleine Pelsterstraat; s/d €40/65) The Garni is bare bones, but it's in a good location on a street with several cafes and the prices are unbeatable. Service is friendly and amenable; the 17 rooms unadorned.

Eating & Drinking

Groningen has no fixed opening hours for cafes and bars, which means that some people are stumbling off to work as others are stumbling home from a night out.

't Feithhuis (☎ 3135335; www.restaurant-feithhuis.nl; Martinikerkhof 10; mains €8-16) In a leafy pedestrian quarter just off the Grote Markt, this stylish grand cafe has a wide terrace outside and a stark, woodsy decor inside. The walls are lined with posters and floral arrangements abound. The food ranges from bagels to complex sandwiches and Mediterranean-flavoured mains.

De Pintelier (☎ 318 51 00; Kleine Kromme Elleboog 9) Step back to the 1920s at this cosy bar where the selection of beer and *jenever* (ginlike drink) reads like an encyclopaedia. Its long wooden bar and thicket of tables are timeless.

Entertainment

Vera (☎ 313 46 81; www.vera-groningen.nl; Oosterstraat 44; ⌚ Tue-Sat) A legendary venue that bills itself as the 'club for the international pop underground', Vera mixes it up with art-house films, deejays, club nights and a constant stream of bands, many hoping to repeat the success of U2 and Nirvana, who both played here in the nascent days.

Jazz Café de Spieghel (☎ 312 63 00; Peperstraat 11) This one's a perennial favourite, with

THE NETHERLANDS

Book your stay at lonelyplanet.com/hotels

nightly live jazz, blues or funk (Monday is open-mic). Candles add to the smooth, sultry atmosphere.

Getting There & Away

Sample train fares: Amsterdam (€26.70, two hours 20 minutes, two per hour), Leeuwarden (€8.30, 50 minutes, two per hour), Rotterdam (€29.60, 160 minutes, two per hour) and Utrecht (€24.50, two hours, two per hour).

TEXEL

☎ 0222 / pop 13,500

Texel (*tes*-sel) is a natural playground of broad white beaches, lush nature reserves, forests and picture-book villages. Now 25km long and 9km wide, it consisted of two islands until 1835, when a spit of land to Eyerland Island was pumped dry. The island, just 3km off the coast of Noord Holland province, makes a superb getaway from the mainland rush, with beauty and isolation in abundance – except in mid-June, when spectators line the beaches for the largest catamaran race in the world, the Round Texel Race (www.roundtexel.com).

Tourist office (☎ 31 47 41; www.texel.net; Emmalaan 66, Den Burg; 🕑 9am-5.30pm Mon-Fri, to 5pm Sat) Can book rooms and has internet access. It has loads of advice for hikers, bikers and nude sunbathers.

Sights & Activities

Duinen van Texel National Park is a patchwork of varied dunescape along the entire western coast of the island. Salt fens and heath alternate with velvety, grass-covered dunes. Much of the area is a bird sanctuary and accessible only on foot.

Just near the windswept beach is **De Dennen**, a dark and leafy forest. Originally planted as a source of lumber, today it has an enchanting network of walking and cycling paths. In springtime the forest floor is carpeted with snowdrops first planted in the 1930s.

Sleeping

Although Texel has an astounding 46,000 beds, book ahead, especially in July and August. Eating opportunities abound in season.

Stayokay Texel (☎ 31 54 41; www.stayokay.com; Haffelderweg 28, Den Burg; dm €25, d €65; 💻 ⊠) Bright and airy, this hostel could be an upscale resort – if it weren't for the bunk beds. It's close to the town centre and 6km from the beach. Rent a bike and pedal to the shore.

't Anker (☎ 31 62 74; www.t-anker.texel.com; Kikkertstraat 24, De Cocksdorp; s/d from €43/85) This small, family-run hotel is full of charm and cheer, and has eight basic yet comfy rooms in quiet De Cocksdorp. There's wi-fi.

Getting There & Around

Trains from Amsterdam to Den Helder (€12.90, 75 minutes) are met by a bus that connects with the **car ferry** (☎ 36 96 00; www.teso.nl; adult/car return €4/38; 🕑 6.30am-9.30pm), which then makes the crossing in 20 minutes. Local busses criss-cross Texel.

SOUTHERN NETHERLANDS

MAASTRICHT

☎ 043 / pop 122,000

Talk about a diamond in the rough. The Netherlands' other great city couldn't be further from Amsterdam and the pearls of the Randstad and still be in the country. Granted Maastricht sits on a little geographic appendage dangling down like an appendix but it is well worth the time to journey here from the northwest (and you can easily continue to Belgium and Germany).

Amidst the 1650 listed historic buildings, look for Spanish and Roman ruins, French and Belgian twists in the architecture, splendid food and small-town cosmopolitan flair that made Maastricht a natural location for the signing of the namesake treaty, which created the modern EU in1992.

Information

Centre Ceramique Library (☎ 350 56 00; Ave Céramique 50; internet access free; 🕑 10.30am-8.30pm Tue & Thu, 10.30am-5pm Wed & Fri, 10am-5pm Sat, 1-5pm Sun) A multifaceted cultural centre.

Grand Net Internet Café (81 Boschstraat; per hr €2) One of several here.

Tourist office (☎ 325 21 21; www.vvvmaastricht.nl; Kleine Straat 1; 🕑 9am-6pm Mon-Sat, 11am-3pm Sun). In the 15th-century Dinghuis; offers excellent walking tour brochures.

Sights & Activities

The postmodern **Bonnefantenmuseum** (☎ 329 01 90; www.bonnefantenmuseum.nl; Ave Céramique 250; admission €7.50; 🕑 11am-5pm Tue-Sun) features a striking 28m tower that houses various provocative exhibits. The collection combines Flemish masterpieces from the 16th and 17th centuries with controversial modern works.

The large square of Vrijthof is surrounded by lively cafes and cultural institutions. It's dominated by **Sint Servaasbasiliek** (admission €2; 10am-5pm), a pastiche of architecture dating from AD 1000. The most beautiful carving dates from the 15th century.

Much of Maastricht is riddled with defensive tunnels dug into the soft sandstone during the many sieges over the centuries. The best place to see the tunnels is on a tourist office–led tour of **Fort St Pieter** (321 78 78; admission €5; tour times vary by season), a Roman fort on St Pietersberg, 2km south of Helpoort (an old town gate).

The Romans built tunnels throughout the hills over a period of 2000 years; at one stage, they even extended under the Netherlands–Belgium border. The tourist office leads spooky and thrilling **cave tours** (321 78 78; admission €5; tour times vary by season). Tours are in Dutch but some guides speak English and the chills know no language barrier.

Sleeping

Stayokay Maastricht (750 17 90; www.stayokay.com/maastricht; Maasboulevard 101; dm/r from €18/50;) A stunner of a hostel with a large terrace right on the Maas River. Choose from one of the 199 beds in dorms and private rooms. It's just south of the centre in a park.

Hotel Holla (321 35 23; www.hotelholla.nl; Boschstraat 104-106; r €42-80;) In an elegant 1855 building, the 24 rooms here are freshly redone with wi-fi, flat-screen TV and stylish linen. Adding to the great value is the ground-floor cafe which serves excellent coffee in smart surrounds.

Hotel la Colombe (321 57 74; www.hotellacolombe.nl; Markt 30; r €45-90) On the Markt, in a simple, white building, la Colombe has rooms that are equally unadorned, but all have TV and bath. This unassuming but friendly hotel has a decent cafe and it rents out scooters and bikes.

Hotel Sansa (323 33 21; Stationstraat 26; s/d from €50/60) Close to the station, this simple place adjoins a cheap eatery that's good for anything deep-fried. The 16 rooms are basic and clean; the cheapest share showers.

Eating

Excellent restaurants are even more common in Maastricht than old fortifications.

Reitz (321 57 06; Markt 75; chips €2) Join the queues for this iconic French fry stall which has been serving perfectly scrumptious *frites* (chips/fries) under the classic neon sign for decades.

our pick **Bisschopsmolen** (327 06 13; Stenebrug 1-3; meals €4-10; 9.30am-6pm Tue-Sat, 11am-5pm Sun) How cool is this? A working water wheel powers a vintage flour mill which supplies an adjoining bakery. The loafs come in many forms and are joined by other tasty treats (direct from the ovens on view out the back). The cafe has sandwiches and other in-house creations. Finally, you can self-tour the mill and see how flour's been made for eons.

Cafe Ut Mooswief (325 40 44; Markt 66; mains €6-15) Closest to the daily market stalls on the Markt, this unassuming cafe stands out from the plethora of competition by giving you ultracomfy seats for your bum while providing superb fare for your tum. Among the Dutch classics, the pea soup is a standout.

Drinking

our pick **Take One** (321 64 23; www.takeonebiercafe.nl, in Dutch; Rechtstraat 28) Cramped and narrow from the outside, this 1930s tavern has well over 100 beers from the most obscure parts of the Benelux. It's run by a husband-and-wife team who help you select the beer most appropriate to your tastes. The Bink Blonde is sweet, tangy and very good.

In Den Ouden Vogelstruys (321 48 88; www.vogelstruys.nl; Vrijthof 15) Overlooking the cathedral across the square, this antique bar is a little bit naughty and a little bit nice.

Getting There & Away

Regular trains link Maastricht to Brussels (€28, 1½ hours) and with connections Cologne is two hours away (€23). Sample Dutch train fares: Amsterdam (€28.70, 2½ hours, hourly) and Utrecht (€25, two hours, hourly).

THE NETHERLANDS DIRECTORY

ACCOMMODATION

Always book accommodation ahead, especially during high season; note that many visitors choose to stay in Amsterdam even if travelling elsewhere. The tourist offices operate booking services; when booking for two, make it clear whether you want two single (twin) beds or a double bed.

In cities you should expect to pay at least €50 for a double room in a budget hotel, up to €125 in a midrange hotel and from €125 for the top end. Prices are higher in Amsterdam.

Many Dutch hotels have steep, perilous stairs but no lifts, although most top-end and many midrange hotels are exceptions.

Accommodation in B&Bs is mostly found in the country – local tourist offices can help.

In this chapter, breakfast is not included in rates unless otherwise specified; shared bathrooms are noted.

Lists of camping grounds are available from tourist offices. Expect to pay roughly €10 to €20 for two people and a tent overnight, plus €3 to €6 for a car. The camping grounds have plenty of caravan hook-ups.

Stayokay (☎ 020-501 31 33; www.stayokay.com) is the Dutch hostelling association. A youth hostel card costs €15 at the hostels; non-members pay an extra €2.50 per night and after six nights you're a member. The usual HI discounts apply.

ACTIVITIES

Skating, windsurfing, sailing, boating and hanging out at the beach are popular Dutch pastimes. Check the tourist offices for further information. Cycling is a religion.

BUSINESS HOURS

Usual business hours in the Netherlands:

Banks (⏲ 9am-4pm or 5pm Mon-Fri)

Bars (⏲ 11am-midnight or 2am)

Nightclubs (⏲ 9pm or 10pm-3am or later)

Museums Many are closed on Monday.

Post offices (⏲ 9am-5pm Mon-Fri, 10am-1pm Sat)

Restaurants (⏲ 11am-2.30pm or 3pm & 5.30-10pm or 11pm)

Shops (⏲ noon-5.30pm Mon, 9am-5.30pm or 6pm Tue-Fri, 9am-5pm Sat) Most towns have late-night shopping (until 9pm) on either Thursday or Friday. In Amsterdam and tourist centres you will find many shops open on Sunday. Supermarkets often have extended trading hours.

DISCOUNT CARDS

Available from the museums themselves, a *Museumkaart* gives access to 400 museums across the country for €30 (€17 for under-25s).

The Euro<26 Card, or **Cultureel Jongeren Paspoort** (Cultural Youth Passport, CJP; www.cjp.nl; €15), available from tourist offices and hostels, gives people aged under 30 discounts to museums and cultural events around the Netherlands and Europe.

EMBASSIES & CONSULATES

Australia (☎ 070-310 82 00; www.netherlands.embassy.gov.au; Carnegielaan 4, Den Haag)

Belgium (☎ 070-312 34 56; www.diplomatie.be/thehague; Alexanderveld 97, Den Haag)

Canada (☎ 070-311 16 00; www.netherlands.gc.ca; Sophialaan 7, Den Haag)

France (www.ambafrance.nl) Amsterdam (☎ 020-530 69 69; Vijzelgracht 2); Den Haag (☎ 070-312 58 00; Smidsplein 1)

Germany (☎ 020-574 77 00; Honthorststraat 36-8, Amsterdam)

Ireland (☎ 070-363 09 93; www.irishembassy.nl; Dr Kuyperstraat 9, Den Haag)

New Zealand (☎ 070-346 93 24; www.nzembassy.com/netherlands; Eisenhowerlaan 77/N, Den Haag)

UK (www.britain.nl) Amsterdam (☎ 020-676 43 43; Koningslaan 44); Den Haag (☎ 070-427 04 27; Lange Voorhout 10)

USA (http://thehague.usembassy.gov) Amsterdam (☎ 020-575 53 30; Museumplein 19); Den Haag (☎ 070-310 22 09; Lange Voorhout 102)

FESTIVALS & EVENTS

February & March

Carnaval Celebrated with greater vigour in Maastricht than anywhere else in Europe, save Venice (Italy) and Sitges (Spain). The orgy of partying and carousing begins the Friday before Shrove Tuesday and lasts until the last person collapses some time on the following Wednesday.

TEFAF Maastricht Art & Antiques Show (www.tefaf.com) Held annually in mid-March.

April

Amsterdam Fantastic Film Festival (www.afff.nl) European and international fantasy, horror and science fiction movies held in late April.

Koninginnedag (Queen's Day) On 30 April it's celebrated countrywide, but especially so in Amsterdam, which becomes awash in orange costumes and fake afros, beer, balloon animals, beer, dope, Red Bull, beer, leather boys, skater dikes, temporary roller coasters, clogs, clothes horses, fashion victims, grannies and grandpas…

May

Herdenkingsdag (Remembrance Day) Held 4 May.

Bevrijdingsdag (Liberation Day) Held 5 May.

Nationale Molendag (National Windmill Day) On the second Saturday in May, nearly every working windmill in the country opens its doors to visitors.

June

Holland Festival (www.hollandfestival.nl) For all of June the country's biggest music, drama and dance extravaganza centres on Amsterdam. Highbrow and pretentious meet lowbrow and silly.

July

North Sea Jazz Festival (www.northseajazz.nl) The world's largest jazz festival, held in Rotterdam in mid-July.

August

Gay Pride Canal Parade First Saturday.
Fit For Free Dance Parade (www.fitforfreedance parade.nl) Rotterdam goes sick, mate, inna-urban funky techno style in mid-August.
Uitmarkt (www.uitmarkt.nl) The reopening of Amsterdam's cultural season for three days in late August.

September

Open Monument Day (www.openmonumentendag .nl) Every second weekend in September more than 3000 historic buildings and monuments normally closed to the public are opened for free.

November

Sinterklaas intocht The Dutch Santa Claus arrives on a boat 'from Spain' with his staff in mid-November.

December

Sinterklaas On 5 December, families exchange small gifts ahead of Christmas religious celebrations.

GAY & LESBIAN TRAVELLERS

Amsterdam is Europe's gay capital – enough said. The further you get from the capital, though, the more hidden are gay and lesbian bars, except in Rotterdam and the university towns. The age of consent in the Netherlands is 16. Attitudes towards gays and lesbians are among the most progressive in the world.

The best source for information is the **Gay & Lesbian Switchboard** (☎ 020-623 65 65; www.switch board.nl) and **COC** (☎ 020-626 30 87; www.coc.nl), the national gay and lesbian organisation, with branches throughout the country.

HOLIDAYS

Public Holidays

Nieuwjaarsdag New Year's Day.
Goede Vrijdag Good Friday.
Eerste Paasdag Easter Sunday.
Tweede Paasdag Easter Monday.
Koninginnedag (Queen's Day) 30 April.
Bevrijdingsdag (Liberation Day) 5 May.
Hemelvaart Ascension Day.
Eerste Pinksterdag Whit Sunday (Pentecost).
Tweede Pinksterdag Whit Monday.
Eerste Kerstdag (Christmas Day) 25 December.
Tweede Kerstdag (Boxing Day) 26 December.

LEGAL MATTERS

Dutch cops are helpful, with a sense of humour. One of their leaflets urges foreigners to seek help if they find themselves in trouble, like falling into a canal stoned: 'Don't be embarrassed', they say, 'we've seen it all before'. They can hold you for six hours for questioning if you break the law.

Drugs are actually illegal in the Netherlands. Possession of soft drugs up to 5g is tolerated but larger amounts can get you jailed. Hard drugs are treated as a serious crime.

Smoking is banned in all public places, including bars. In a uniquely Dutch solution, you can still smoke pot in coffee shops as long as there's no tobacco mixed in.

MONEY

See p1225 for a full discussion of all things monetary in Europe.

The easiest places to change cash in the Netherlands are the banks or foreign exchange counters at airports and train stations.

There are international ATMs virtually everywhere in the Netherlands. Travellers cheques can be cashed at any bank. A percentage commission (usually a minimum of €5) is charged by most banks on any travellers cheque, even those issued in euros.

The *chipknip* card is mainly used for small cashless payments. A prepaid version (www .interegi.nl) is available for those without a Dutch bank account. With a Maestro-compatible card you should be fine, too.

Tipping

Restaurant bills include a service charge but most people add 5% to 10% unless the service is truly abhorrent. At hotels it's nice to leave a few euros for the room cleaners. Tip taxi drivers around 10%. Tipping in bars is not expected.

TELEPHONE

Most public phones will accept credit cards as well as various phonecards. The official KPN-Telecom public phone boxes charge

€0.10 per 20 seconds for national calls. The cost of international calls varies depending on the destination, and will change frequently as a result of competition.

Mobile Phones

The Netherlands uses GSM 900/1800, compatible with the rest of Europe and Australia but not with some North American phones. Prepaid mobile phones are widely available at mobile-phone shops starting from around €30, as are SIM cards.

Phone Codes

To ring abroad, dial ☎00 followed by the country code for your target country, the area code (you usually drop the leading 0 if there is one) and the subscriber number. The country code for calling the Netherlands is ☎31 and the area code for Amsterdam is ☎020; again, drop the leading 0 if you're calling from outside the Netherlands. When using a land line, do not dial the city code if you are in the area covered by it.

Phonecards

For public telephones, cards are available at post offices, train station counters, VVV and GWK offices and tobacco shops for €5, €10 and €20. Train stations have Telfort phone booths that require a Telfort card (available at GWK offices or ticket counters), although there should be KPN booths nearby.

VISAS

The Netherlands is part of the Schengen visa scheme. See p1229 for a full discussion about visas in Europe.

Norway

HIGHLIGHTS

- **Bergen** For a picturesque coastal locale and charming wooden buildings, you can't beat this lively city and its proximity to fjords (p877)
- **Lofoten Islands** Hike spectacular mountain-islands rising from fishing villages so postcard-perfect that they look fake (p885)
- **Best journey** The Oslo–Bergen train boggles eyeballs as it rushes past snowy plateaus, spectacular fjords and spotless wilderness (p877)
- **Off the beaten track** Hike from Fjærland's farm valley to blue-ice glacier, and admire the fjord below (p882)

FAST FACTS

- **Area** 385,200 sq km
- **Budget** Nkr500 per day (excluding transport costs)
- **Capital** Oslo
- **Country code** ☎ 47
- **Famous for** canned fish, Vikings, whaling
- **Languages** Norwegian and Sami
- **Money** Norwegian krone (Nkr); A\$1 = Nkr4.92; C\$1 = Nkr5.58; €1 = Nkr8.84; ¥100 = Nkr6.94; NZ\$1 = Nkr3.85; UK£1 = Nkr9.96; US\$1 = Nkr6.57
- **Phrases** *Hei* (hello), *takk* (thanks), *ya* (yes), *nei* (no), *stengt* (closed)

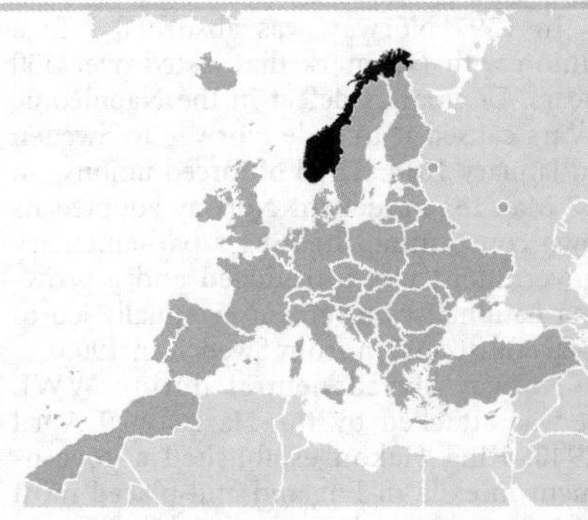

- **Population** 4.7 million
- **Visas** not required for most visitors for stays up to 90 days.

TRAVEL HINTS

Pack booze before arrival. Student ID equals big discounts on transport and attractions. Bring hip clothes. Buy *minipris* (p866) rail tickets.

ROAMING

Train from Oslo to Bergen, stopping to ski in Geilo. Ogle fjords. Head for Trondheim. Take Hurtigruten to Lofoten, then Tromsø.

There's a reason why 19th-century landscape painters obsessed over Norway: at almost every corner staggeringly beautiful wilderness lurked to overwhelm their artistic sensibilities. Today that wilderness, various and downright sublime, remains shockingly intact, offering terrain for some of the world's most scenic skiing and hiking. Enjoy fjords, glaciers and mountains, all linked by a massive network of trails, dotted with scenic huts that provide some of Norway's cheapest lodging. Along the way, Europe's most expensive country will compel you to eat a lot of fish. Much of Norway lies above the Arctic Circle, home to the Midnight Sun's ceaseless light, the Polar Night's gloomy darkness or the ghost-like, swirling aurora borealis. Set amid these phenomena are Lofoten's remote fishing villages and Tromsø, a lively university town that makes a convenient polar gateway. A country of just 4.7 million people, Norway's few cities are picturesque with districts of old wooden buildings, harbours of fishing boats and plenty of cafes, whose outdoor terraces fill with overeager Norwegians from the moment winter ends. Oslo and Bergen are the biggest cities, and each enjoys esoteric museums (think Viking ships and leprosy), lively nightlife and public transport that takes you straight into the wilderness.

HISTORY

Norway's greatest impact on world history was during the Viking Age, usually dated from the plundering of England's Lindisfarne monastery by Nordic pirates in 793. Over the next century, the Vikings made raids throughout Europe. The Viking leader Harald Hårfagre (Fairhair) unified Norway in 872. Their power ended when Alexander III, King of Scots, defeated a Viking force at the Battle of Largs in 1263.

In 1397 Norway was absorbed into a union with Denmark that lasted over 400 years. Denmark's defeat in the Napoleonic Wars caused it to cede Norway to Sweden in January 1814. Tired of forced unions, on 17 May 1814 a defiant Norway adopted its own constitution. In 1884 a parliamentary government was introduced and a growing nationalist movement eventually led to peaceful secession from Sweden in 1905.

Norway stayed neutral during WWI. It was attacked by the Nazis on 9 April 1940. King Håkon established a government in exile in England and placed most of Norway's merchant fleet under the command of the Allies. Although Norway remained occupied until the end of the war, it had an active resistance movement. The royal family returned in June 1945.

Norway joined the European Free Trade Association (EFTA) in 1960, but has since been reluctant to forge closer bonds with other European nations. During 1994, a national referendum on joining the EU was held and rejected. Norway has lead many contemporary environmental initiatives, such as the creation of the Svalbard Global Seed Vault (2008) and the recently declared goal of becoming carbon neutral by 2030, largely by purchasing offsets from developing countries. In 1993 Norway resumed commercial whaling in defiance of an international ban. The government, which supports the protection of threatened species, contends that minke whales, with an estimated population of 100,000, can sustain a limited harvest. For more information, see the websites of the **International Whaling Commission** (www.iwcoffice.org), **World Wide Fund for Nature** (www.wwf.org) and **Greenpeace** (www.greenpeace.org).

THE CULTURE

With only 4,700,000 people, Norway has one of the lowest population densities in Europe and one of the world's highest standards of living. The largest cities are Oslo with 550,000 residents, then Bergen, Trondheim and Stavanger.

Most Norwegians are of Nordic origin, thought to have descended from central and northern European tribes who migrated northwards around 8000 years ago. In addition, there are about 40,000 Sami (formerly known as Lapps), the indigenous people of Norway's far north who make up the country's largest ethnic minority. Many still live a traditional nomadic life, herding reindeer in Finnmark.

SPORT

'Ski' is a Norwegian word and Norway makes a credible claim to having invented the sport. Other spectator sports include speed skating and football (soccer). Empathetic winter visitors will experience displaced vertigo as they witness ski jumping at, amongst other places, Holmenkollen (p869).

ARTS

Norway's best known artists include Edvard Munch, landscape painter JC Dahl, classical composer Edvard Grieg, sculptor Gustav Vigeland and playwright Henrik Ibsen.

Norway's stave churches are some of the oldest wooden buildings on Earth. Named for their vertical supporting posts, these structures are distinguished by dragon-headed gables resembling ornately carved prows of Viking ships. Other significant architectural features in the country include the romantic 'dragon style', found in some historic hotels, and art nouveau, best observed in Ålesund.

Norwegians Sigrid Undset and Knud Hamsun (a Nazi collaborator) won the Nobel Prize for Literature in 1928 and 1920, respectively. Undset is best known for *Kristin Lavransdottir,* while Hamsun won the Nobel Prize for *The Growth of the Soil.* Angar Mykle's *Lasso Round the Moon* (1954) might be the best book you've never read. Per Petterson's haunting *Out*

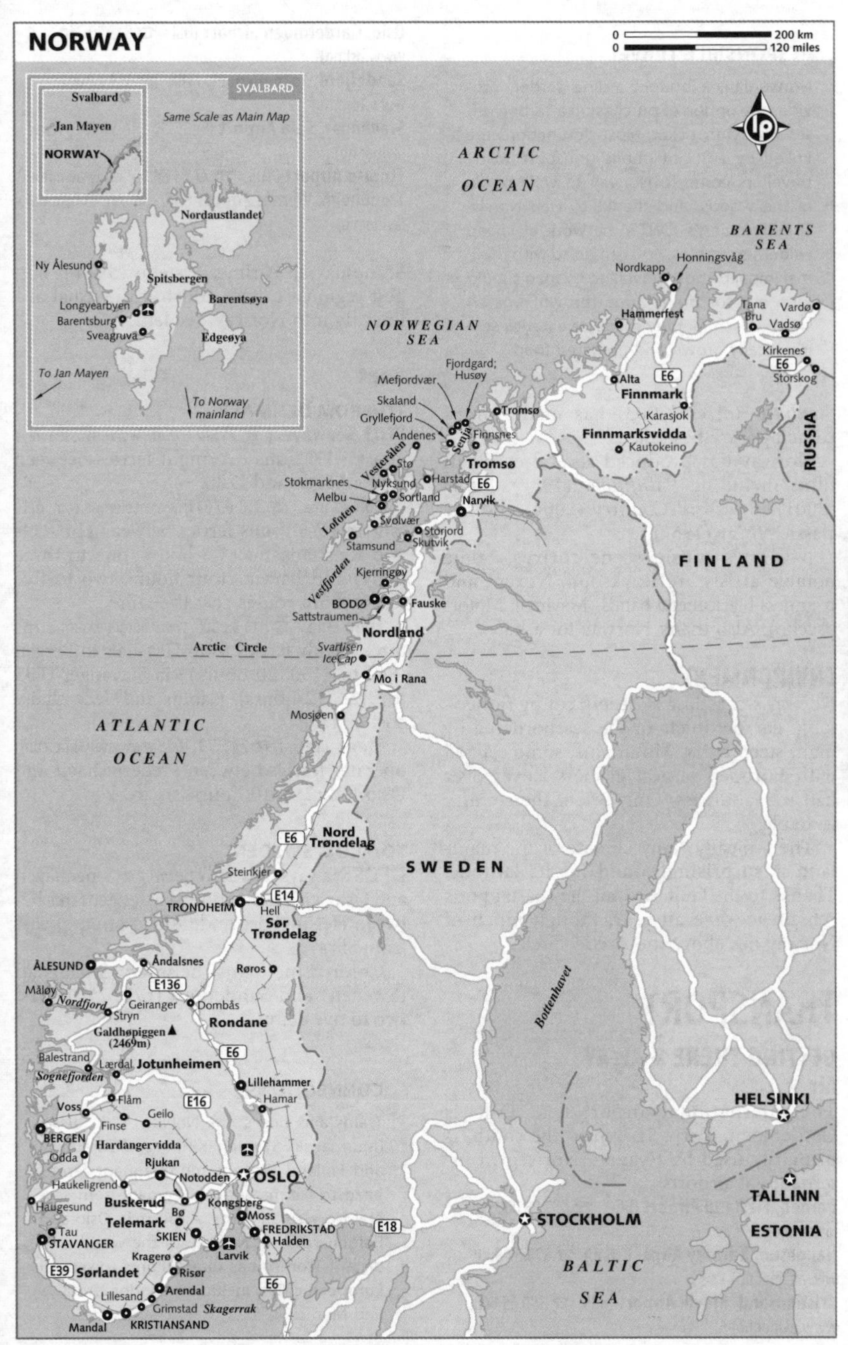
NORWAY
0 200 km
0 120 miles
SVALBARD
Svalbard
Jan Mayen
NORWAY
Same Scale as Main Map
Nordaustlandet
Ny Ålesund
Spitsbergen
Longyearbyen
Barentsburg
Barentsøya
Sveagruva
Edgeøya
To Jan Mayen
To Norway mainland
ARCTIC OCEAN
BARENTS SEA
NORWEGIAN SEA
Nordkapp
Honningsvåg
Hammerfest
Tana Bru
Vardø
Vadsø
Kirkenes
Storskog
Alta
Finnmark
Karasjok
Finnmarksvidda
Kautokeino
RUSSIA
Fjordgard; Husøy
Mefjordvær
Skaland
Gryllefjord
Tromsø
Andenes
Senja
Finnsnes
Vesterålen
Stø
Nyksund
Harstad
Stokmarknes
Sortland
Melbu
Narvik
Lofoten
Svolvær
Storjord
Skutvik
Stamsund
Vestfjorden
Kjerringøy
BODØ
Fauske
Sattstraumen
Nordland
FINLAND
Arctic Circle
Svartisen IceCap
Mo i Rana
Mosjøen
ATLANTIC OCEAN
Nord Trøndelag
SWEDEN
Steinkjer
TRONDHEIM
Hell
Sør Trøndelag
ÅLESUND
Åndalsnes
Røros
Måløy
Nordfjord
Geiranger
Dombås
Stryn
Rondane
Galdhøpiggen (2469m)
Bottenhavet
Balestrand
Lærdal
Jotunheimen
Sognefjorden
Lillehammer
Flåm
Hamar
Voss
Geilo
Finse
BERGEN
Hardangervidda
HELSINKI
Odda
Rjukan
Notodden
OSLO
Haukeligrend
TALLINN
Haugesund
Buskerud
Kongsberg
Bø
Moss
Telemark
FREDRIKSTAD
STOCKHOLM
Tau
STAVANGER
SKIEN
Halden
ESTONIA
Larvik
Kragerø
Sørlandet
Risør
BALTIC SEA
Arendal
Lillesand
Grimstad
Skagerrak
Mandal
KRISTIANSAND
E6
E14
E136
E16
E18
E39

RESPONSIBLE TRAVEL

Norwegian, a budget airline carrier, provides the option of purchasing a carbon offset with your ticket. Most destinations are linked by efficient public transport. Many travellers come to Norway to walk or ski in the woods, and thanks to Den Norske Turistforening's (DNT's) network of cheap wilderness cabins, you can do so with minimal impact. Those travelling by road should look out for *brune hane* (brown rooster) signs, which identify roadside eateries selling locally grown and prepared food.

Stealing Horses (2003) has made him a contemporary bestseller.

Norway has produced several excellent films including *Pathfinder* (1987), *Elling* (2001), *Beautiful Country* (2004) and the classic *Ni Liv* (1957).

Norway's music scene thrives. Some notable artists are Røyksopp, Noxagt and countless black metal bands (Mayhem, Motorpsycho). Also thank Norway for a-ha.

ENVIRONMENT

Norway's coastline is deeply cut by fjords – long, narrow inlets of the sea bordered by high, steep cliffs. Mountains, some capped with Europe's largest glaciers, cover over half the landmass. Only 3% of the country is arable.

The typically rainy climate of the mainland is surprisingly mild for its latitude. Thanks to the Gulf Stream, the coastal ports remain ice-free all year, though much of Norway lies above the Arctic Circle.

TRANSPORT

GETTING THERE & AWAY

Air

The international airport near Oslo is Gardemoen. Torp, 123km to the south, is primarily used by Ryanair. Norwegian international airports:

Bergen, Flesland Airport (BGO; ☎ 559 98 000; www.avinor.no)

Haugesun, Karmøy Airport (HAU; ☎ 528 57 900; www.avinor.no)

Kristiansand, Kjevik Airport (KRS; ☎ 380 65 600; www.avinor.no)

Oslo, Gardermoen airport (OSL; ☎ 815 50 250; www.osl.no)

Sandefjord, Torp Airport, (TRF; ☎ 334 27 002; www.torp.no)

Stavanger, Sola Airport (SVG; ☎ 516 58 000; www.avinor.no)

Tromsø Airport (TOS; ☎ 77 64 84 00; www.avinor.no)

Trondheim, Værnes airport (TRD; ☎ 748 43 000; www.avinor.no)

Scandinavian Airlines Systems (SAS) is biggest regional carrier. Most of the usual airlines fly into Norway, see left.

Boat

TO/FROM DENMARK

DFDS Seaways (☎ 216 21 000, www.dfdsseaways.com; €53-300) runs overnight ferries between Copenhagen and Oslo.

Color Line (☎ 810 00 811; www.colorline.com; deck passenger €26-62) runs ferries between Hirtshals and Kristiansand (3¼ hours, one to three daily) and Larvik (four hours, two to five daily). Both routes cost the same.

Fjord Line (☎ 815 33 500; www.fjordline.com) runs three weekly ferries from Hirtshals to Bergen (€44 to €130, 20 hours) via Stavanger (€35 to €128, 12 hours). Cabins and deck chairs cost extra.

Stena Line (☎ 231 79 100; www.stenaline.com) operates ferries between Frederikshavn and Oslo (Nkr210, 10 hours, six weekly).

TO/FROM SWEDEN

DFDS Seaways sails daily between Copenhagen and Oslo, via Helsingborg. Passenger fares between Helsingborg and Oslo (14 hours) cost from Skr475.

Color Line runs between Strömstad (Sweden) and Sandefjord (€22, 2½ hours, two to five daily).

CONNECTIONS

Trains and buses link Norway with Russia (Murmansk), Sweden (Kiruna and Göteborg) and Finland (Rovaniemi). Frequent ferries head to Germany and Denmark from several Norwegian ports. Airports in Oslo and Bergen connect Norway to the world, and distant Tromsø has direct flights to several European cities, including London, Antalya and Munich.

Bus

TO/FROM DENMARK

Säfflebussen (☎ 0771-151515 in Sweden; www.safflebussen.se) runs from Copenhagen via Malmö in Sweden to Oslo (Nkr224, eight hours, three daily).

Swebus Express (☎ 0200-218218 in Sweden; www.swebusexpress.se) also runs to/from Copenhagen (Skr357, 8½ hours, three daily).

TO/FROM FINLAND

Eskelisen Lapin Linjat (☎ 016-3422 160 in Finland; www.eskelisen-lapinlinjat.com) runs daily summer buses from Rovaniemi (Finland) to Nordkapp (€127, 11 hours) and Tromsø (€95, eight hours).

TO/FROM SWEDEN

Säfflebussen runs from Stockholm to Oslo (Skr425, 7½ hours, fives times daily) via Karlstad, and from Göteborg to Oslo (Skr265, four hours, seven daily). Swebus Express has the same routes with similar prices.

Train

TO/FROM SWEDEN

Sveriges Järnväg (☎ 0771-757575 in Sweden; www.sj.se) sends daily trains from Stockholm to Oslo (Skr500 to Skr706, six to seven hours) and other points; book discounted tickets at least seven days in advance. **Connex** (☎ 0771-260000 in Sweden; www.connex.se) links Narvik to Stockholm (Skr700 to Skr820, 20 hours, two daily) via Kiruna.

GETTING AROUND

Norway's public transport is efficient, with trains, buses and ferries timed to link effectively. The *NSB Togruter* has rail schedules and information on connecting buses. Boat and bus departures vary daily and are seasonal, so pick up the latest *ruteplan* (timetable) from regional tourist offices. Most buses, boats and some trains have student discounts – always ask, *'Er der en student tilbud/rebatt?'*.

Air

Norway has 50 airports, most listed on www.avinor.no. Air travel is worth considering due to the great distances involved in overland travel. The following fly domestic routes:

Norwegian (DY; ☎ 815 21 815; www.norwegian.no)
SAS (SK; ☎ 915 05 400; www.sas.no)
Widerøe (WF; ☎ 751 11 111; www.wideroe.no)

Bicycle

Given its geography, Norway is not ideally suited for extensive bicycle touring. The *Sykkelguide* series of booklets (Nkr120), available at larger tourist offices, has maps and English text.

Boat

A comprehensive network of ferries and express boats links Norway's islands, coastal towns and fjord districts; see specific destinations for details.

HURTIGRUTEN COASTAL STEAMER

For more than a century Norway's **Hurtigruten** (☎ 810 30 000; www.hurtigruten.no) has been the lifeline for villages scattered along the remote coast. One ship heads north from Bergen each night, pulling into 35 ports on its six-day journey to Kirkenes. With good weather, expect spectacular scenery.

The ships accommodate deck-class travellers, and on most you may sleep in public areas (free, but uncomfortable and noisy). Most passengers rent cabins for overnight trips. Students receive 50% discount. Sample fares from Bergen include Nkr1951 to Trondheim, Nkr3348 to Svolvær and Nkr4300 to Tromsø. Shorter port-to-port trips are often the easiest and cheapest way to get from one coastal city to another (for example, the fare from Svolvær to Tromsø is Nkr1055).

From September to April, prices are greatly reduced with return journeys at a further 50% reduction on the return portion of the ticket.

Bus

Nor-Way Bussekspress (☎ 815 44 444; www.nor-way.no), the main carrier, has routes connecting every main town. There's a host of local buses companies; most of them operate within a single county. Fares are based on distance travelled and average Nkr160 for the first 100km.

In Nordland, several Togbuss (train-bus) routes offer half-price fares to Eurail passholders. It runs between Fauske and Bodø, Narvik, Tromsø, Svolvær and Harstad.

Car & Motorcycle

The **Road User Information Centre** (☎ 175) tells you the latest road conditions throughout Norway.

For a full list of ferry schedules, fares and reservation phone numbers, grab *Rutebok for Norge*, available in larger bookshops. For motoring information, contact the national automobile club, **Norges Automobil-Forbund** (NAF;

☎ 926 08 505; www.naf.no). For 24-hour breakdown assistance call the NAF on ☎ 08505.

Major car-rental companies have offices at airports and in city centres. Rates include insurance, though if you get in an accident you are responsible for the first Nkr5000 in damages.

Hitching

Hitching is legal and relatively safe, but uncommon.

Train

Norway has an excellent, though limited, national rail system. **Norges Statsbaner** (NSB; ☎ 815 00 888; www.nsb.no) operates most lines. 'Ordinary'-class travel is great. Komfort-class travel isn't worth the extra Nkr90. Hugely discounted *minipris* tickets are sometimes available. These tickets are only available online, at least a day in advance. Buy early – these sell out. High-standard sleeping compartments cost Nkr850 and have two beds.

All stations have luggage lockers for Nkr15 to Nkr50 per 24 hours.

TRAIN PASSES

Eurail's (www.eurail.com) Norway Pass (US$265/289/319/359/405 for three/four/five/six/eight days' travel within one month) allows unlimited train travel for three to eight days within Norway. Purchase before or after you arrive in Norway. The Flåm line isn't covered (there's a 30% discount). There's a 50% discount on Bergen–Stavanger ferries

OSLO

pop 550,000

Norway's capital is easily the country's most cosmopolitan city, offering diverse nightlife options, an array of cafes and bars and some excellent museums, not least the Nasjonalgalleriet and Vikingskipshuset. While not as picturesquely stunning as Bergen, Oslo contains famous Vigeland Park is eminently strollable, particularly along the banks of the Akerselva. What distinguishes Oslo from many other capitals is its immediate proximity to expansive wilderness areas. It lies at the head of a fjord (not as impressive as those on the west coast, but a fjord all the same) and a mountainous forest penetrates the city's boundary. The pleasant result is that you can take a subway to ski lifts and an extensive network of trails.

EMERGENCY NUMBERS

- Ambulance (☎ 113)
- Fire (☎ 110)
- Police (☎ 112)

ORIENTATION

Oslo's central train station (Oslo Sentralstasjon, also known as 'Oslo S') is at the eastern end of the city centre. From there the main street, Karl Johans gate, runs through the heart of the city. Reach the Grünerløkka neighbourhood by taking Storgata northwestward across the Akerselva River. The Grønland immigrant district is east of Oslo S.

Most central city sights are within a 15-minute walk of Karl Johans gate.

INFORMATION

Bookshops

Nomaden (Map pp870-1; ☎ 221 31 415; Uranienborgveien 4; 🕑 closed Sun) Travel guides, maps and gear.

Discount Cards

Oslo Card (1/2/3 days Nkr220/320/410) Provides entry to most attractions and travel on public transport. Students, who get half-price entry at most sights, usually do better buying a public-transport pass (or walking) and paying separate admissions.

Internet Access

Artic Internet Café (Map pp870-1; ☎ 221 71 940; Oslo S; per 30/60min Nkr35/60; 🕑 8am-midnight)

Deichmanske Bibliotek (Map pp870-1; Henrik Ibsens gate 1) Free internet access limited to an hour, unlimited wi-fi.

Use-it (opposite; free access if younger than 28)

Medical Services

Jernbanetorget Apotek (Map pp870-1; ☎ 224 12 483; Fred Olsens gate; 🕑 24hr) Pharmacy opposite Oslo S.

Oslo Kommunale Legevakten (Map pp870-1; ☎ 229 32 293; Storgata 40) Medical clinic with 24-hour emergency services.

Money

Change money at the **airport bank** (Gardemoen; 🕑 from 5.30am Sat, 6.30am-8pm Sun). ATMs are everywhere. The tourist office and post office exchange money at a less-advantageous

NORWAY

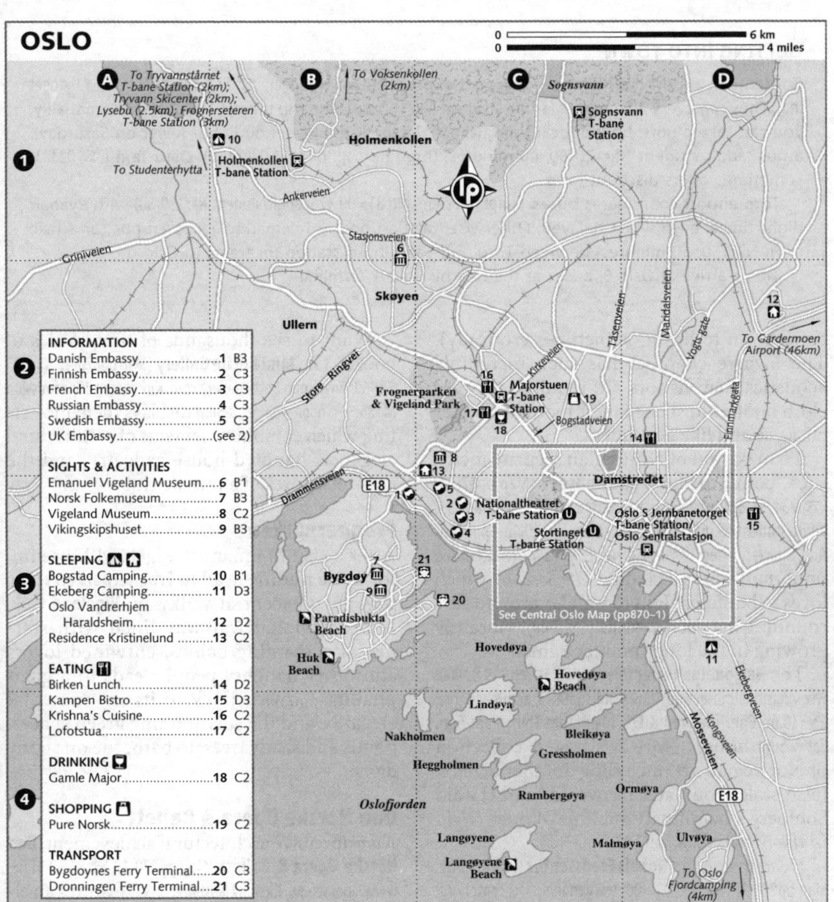

rate than banks. **Forex** (Map pp870-1; ☎ 224 13 060; Fridtjof Nansens plass 6 & Oslo S; 🕑 9am-6pm Mon-Fri) is the largest foreign-exchange service in Scandinavia.

Tourist Information

Den Norske Turistforening (DNT; Map pp870-1; ☎ 228 22 822; www.dntoslo.no; Storgata 3; 🕑 10am-4pm Mon-Wed & Fri, 10am-6pm Thu, 10am-2pm Sat, open 1hr earlier in summer) Book wilderness huts and get info on hiking.

Oslo Promotion (Map pp870-1; ☎ 815 30 555; www.visitoslo.com; Fridjtof Nansens plass 5; 🕑 9am-7pm Jun-Aug, 9am-5pm Mon-Sat Apr-May & Sep, 9am-4pm Mon-Fri Oct-Mar) Get the free *Oslo Guide*.

Use-It (Map pp870-1; ☎ 224 15 132; www.use-it.no; Møllergata 3; 🕑 9am-6pm Mon-Fri Jul & Aug, 11am-5pm Mon-Fri Sep-Jun) Exceptionally savvy advice. Dispenses *Streetwise*, an invaluable and free guide to Oslo on the cheap.

SIGHTS

In addition to those mentioned below, Oslo also has museums dedicated to skating, mail, and architecture. See the *Oslo Guide* or *Streetwise*.

Museums & Galleries

For a sensory overload, enter the **Emanuel Vigeland Museum** (Map p867; ☎ 221 45 788; www.emanuelvigeland.museum.no; Grimelundsveien 8; admission Nkr30; 🕑 noon-4pm Sun), the life work and mausoleum of Gustav's brother. As you adjust to the dark of the windowless nave, you'll discern enormous frescoes depicting human life from

GETTING INTO TOWN

Gardemoen airport has high-speed **airport express trains** (FlyToget; ☎ 177, 815 00 777; www.flytoget.no). They run every 20 minutes (adult/student Nkr160/80). The trip takes 19 minutes. Alternatively, you can take a northbound local train (Nkr94, 26 to 40 minutes, hourly but fewer on Saturday), a bus (adult/student Nkr120/80, 40 minutes, three hourly) or taxi (Nkr450). **Oslo Taxi** (☎ 02323) sometimes offers discount rates.

Torp airport coordinates **buses** (TorpExpressen; ☎ 815 00 176; adult/student Nkr150/80) with Ryanair flight times, even when delayed. Otherwise, take an hourly Telemarksekspressen bus (or a taxi; from Nkr150, 10 minutes) between Torp and Sandefjord station for trains to Oslo.

Trains arrive at Oslo S; buses at the nearby Galleri Terminal.

conception to death (sometimes erotically). The bizarre chamber has such incredible acoustics that visitors are required to wear cloth booties to silence their footfalls. Finger clicks sound like gunshots.

To make fun of Norwegian security measures, come to the **Munchmuseet** (Map pp870-1; ☎ 234 93 500; www.munch.museum.no; Tøyengata 53; adult/student Nkr65/35, free Oct-Mar; 🕑 10am-6pm Jun-Aug, shorter hr rest of year) where you can admire important works including *The Scream*, which loves to be stolen. Exit to wander around surrounding **botanical gardens** (🕑 24hr), vibrantly growing in the long summer light.

NORWAY

The **Nasjonalgalleriet** (Map pp870-1; ☎ 219 82 000; www.nasjonalmuseet.no; Universitetsgata 13; admission free; 🕑 10am-6pm Tue Wed & Fri, 10am-7pm Thu, 11am-5pm Sat & Sun) houses Norway's largest collection of Norwegian art, including another *Scream* (also stolen, but later recovered) and Harald Sohlberg's hauntingly sublime *Winter Night in the Mountains* (1914).

Head inside the **Nobels Fredssenter** (Peace Centre; Map pp870-1; ☎ 483 01 000; www.nobelpeacecenter.org; Rådhusplassen 1; adult/student Nkr80/55; 🕑 10am-6pm Tue-Sun) for flashy high-tech screens exploring themes of peace and conflict. View exhibits on Nobel Peace Prize winners from 1901 to the present.

For explorations of a medieval fortress, visit **Akershus Festning** (Map pp870-1; admission free; 🕑 6am-9m), begun under King Håkon in 1299 with excellent views of the Oslofjord from a strategic position on the eastern side of the harbour. Within the park-like grounds, find **Akershus Slott** (Map pp870-1; ☎ 224 12 521; adult/student Nkr65/45; 🕑 10am-4pm Mon-Sat, 12.30-4pm Sun May–mid-Sep) a medieval palace with Renaissance modifications. In its dungeons you'll find dark cubby-holes where outcast nobles languished, while the upper floors have banquet halls and staterooms.

Want to see thousands of tiny bottles of booze? The **Mini Bottle Gallery** (Map pp870-1; ☎ 233 57 960; www.minibottlegallery.com; Kirkegaten 10; admission Nkr85; 🕑 noon-4pm Sat & Sun) displays them in a setting which combines elements of architectural elegance, haunted-house gadgetry, and the crass overtures of a puerile club.

Frognerparken

After a visit to Emanuel Vigeland Museum, for more nudity, head to **Frognerparken's** (Map p867; 🕑 24hr) central walkway, **Vigeland Park**. A processional walkway lined with statues of screaming babies, entwined lovers and other naughty people leads to a giant phallus. Crowds flock to its monumental elegance and the surrounding green spaces, ponds and shady trees, to barbecue on sunny days.

Den Norske Opera & Ballett

An impressive architectural achievement, **Den Norske Opera & Ballett** (Map pp870-1; ☎ 815 444 88; www.operaen.no; Kirsten Flagstads plass 1) features an elegant wooden performance space set dramati-

OSLO FOR FREE

- Stroll past blasting waterfalls and old factories along the Akerselva (right).
- Play king of the mountain atop the National Opera (above).
- Eat a picnic amid the fabulous sculptures of Vigeland Park (above).
- Enjoy stunning views of Oslo from the Nordic ski trails around Frognerseteren (above).
- Admire *The Scream* in the Nasjonalgalleriet (left).

cally in a translucent cube. The roof, though, might be the best treat. Essentially an urban promenade, its large, sloping plans extend down to the sidewalk. Follow the crowds up to scramble around and look out over the fjord. It feels like a playground for adults that happens to host ballets.

Bygdøy

The Bygdøy peninsula holds excellent attractions, particularly the **Vikingskipshuset** (Viking Ship Museum; Map p867; ☎ 221 35 280; Huk Aveny 35; adult/student/child Nkr50/35/30; ⏲ 9am-6pm May-Sep, 11am-4pm Oct-Apr), which houses three 9th-century ships excavated from the Oslofjord region, two of them shockingly intact. These were drawn ashore and used as tombs for nobility, who were buried in blue clay with everything they needed in the hereafter (jewels, furniture, food and servants).

Nearby, the **Norsk Folkemuseum** (Map p867; ☎ 221 23 700; Museumsveien 10; adult/student/child Nkr95/70/25; ⏲ 10am-6pm mid-May–mid-Sep, shorter hr rest of year) displays 140 buildings clustered according to region, mostly from the 17th and 18th centuries. Dirt paths wind past sturdy barns, *stabbur* (storehouses on stilts) and sod-roofed farmhouses sprouting wildflowers. On summer Sundays, there's usually folk music and dancing at 2pm.

Ferries run to Bygdøy (Nkr22, 15 minutes, every 30 to 40 minutes) from mid-April to early October, leaving from Rådhusbrygge 3. Bus 20 also runs to Bygdøy from the National Theatre.

Islands & Beaches

Ferries to half a dozen islands in the Oslofjord leave from Vippetangen quay. These islands make great scenic excursions for cook-outs and swimming. **Hovedøya**, the closest island, has a rocky coastline, but its southwestern side is a popular sunbathing area. Boats to Hovedøya leave from Vippetangen once or twice hourly between 6am and midnight from late May to mid-August, with fewer runs the rest of the year.

Further south, the undeveloped island of **Langøyene** offers far better swimming. Boats to Langøyene depart daily late May to mid-August.

Bygdøy (above) has two popular beaches, **Huk** and **Paradisbukta**, which are reached by taking bus 30 from Jernbanetorget to its last stop.

ACTIVITIES

A network of ski and hiking trails leads into Nordmarka from Frognerseteren, northwest of the city at the end of T-bane line 1. One fairly strenuous walk is from Frognerseteren to Lake Sognsvann, where you can take T-bane line 5 back to the city. If you're interested in wilderness hiking, contact the **DNT office** (p867).

Oslo's ski season is roughly December to March. The downhill slopes at **Tryvann Skicenter** (p867; ☎ 404 62 700; www.tryvann.no; day/half-day lift ticket Nkr310/225; alipine/nordic rentals Nkr310/200; ⏲ 10am-10pm Mon-Fri, 10am-5pm Sat & Sun) are near Voksenkollen Station. Cross-country trails are free.

For a particularly good **urban walk**, follow the Akerselva River's banks to find several waterfalls and the converted factory buildings that comprise the edge of the trendy Grünerløkka district, where you'll undoubtedly spend your time drinking.

FESTIVALS & EVENTS

Inferno Metal Festival (www.infernofestival.net; ⏲ April) Best to wear black.

17 May Constitution Day Oslo's most festive annual event is the celebration, when city residents descend on the royal palace in traditional garb.

Holmenkollen Ski Festival (☎ 229 23 200; www.skiforeningen.no; ⏲ mid-Mar) Attracts ski jumpers from around the world.

Oslo International Jazz Festival (☎ 224 29 120; www.oslojazz.no; ⏲ Aug) Six days of amazing gigs.

Øya Festival (www.oyafestivalen.com; ⏲ Aug) Over 200 bands play everywhere, including medieval ruins.

SLEEPING

When things get hopeless, **Use-It** (p867) can usually help. They book double rooms in private homes for Nkr300 to Nkr500 (excluding breakfast). There's no fee. **Oslo Promotion** (p867) books such rooms for Nkr35. Visit www.bbnorway.com for a dozen B&Bs in the city.

Hostel

Anker Hostel (Map pp870-1; ☎ 229 97 200; www.ankerhostel.no; Storgata 55; 4-/6-bed dm Nkr215/240, d Nkr560, breakfast Nkr85) A utilitarian hostel on a cheerless intersection of wide streets in close proximity to Grünerløkka.

Oslo Vandrerhjem Haraldsheim (Map p867; ☎ 222 22 965; www.haraldsheim.no; Haraldsheimveien 4; dm/s/d Nkr245/415/540; 💻 🅿) Big and busy, this modern

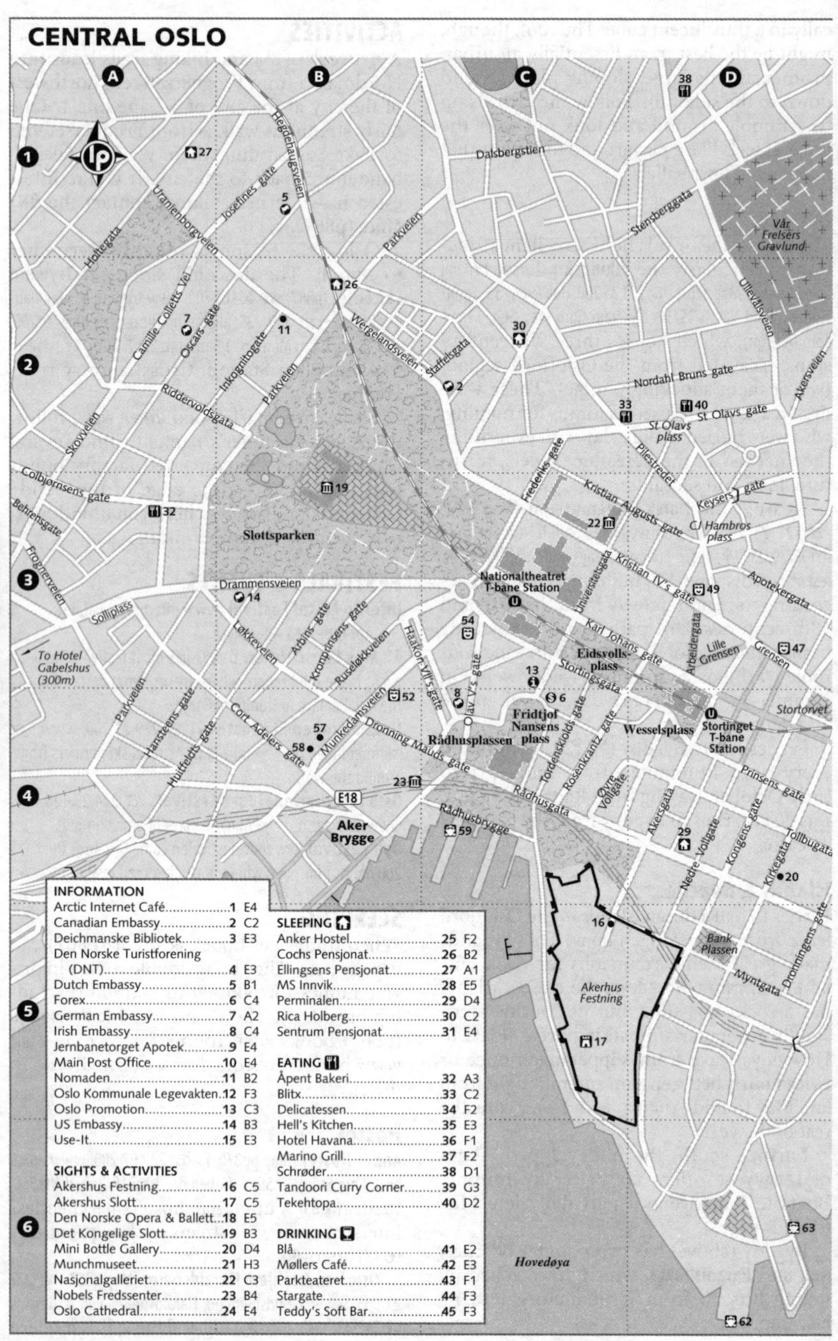
CENTRAL OSLO
A
B
C
D
1
2
3
4
5
6
Dalsbergstien
Stensberggata
Vår Frelsers Gravlund
Ullevålsveien
Akersveien
Heggehaugsveien
Josefines gate
Uranienborgveien
Holtegata
Parkveien
Camille Colletts Vei
Oscars gate
Inkognitogate
Wergelandsveien
Staffelsgata
Nordahl Bruns gate
St Olavs gate
St Olavs plass
Pilestredet
Riddervoldsgata
Skovveien
Colbjørnsens gate
Behrensgate
Frognerveien
Fredriks gate
Kristian Augusts gate
Keysers gate
CJ Hambros plass
Slottsparken
Nationaltheatret T-bane Station
Universitetsgata
Kristian IV's gate
Apotekergata
Drammensveien
Solliplass
To Hotel Gabelshus (300m)
Løkkeveien
Arbins gate
Kronprinsens gate
Ruseløkkveien
Haakon VII's gate
Olav V's gate
Karl Johans gate
Eidsvolls-plass
Stortingsgata
Arbeidergata
Lille Grensen
Grensen
Stortorvet
Fridtjof Nansens plass
Rådhusplassen
Tordenskiolds gate
Rosenkrantz gate
Wesselsplass
Stortinget T-bane Station
Hansteens gate
Huitfeldts gate
Cort Adelers gate
Munkedamsveien
Dronning Mauds gate
Rådhusgata
Prinsens gate
Øvre Vollgate
Akersgata
Nedre Vollgate
Kongens gate
Kirkegata
Tollbugata
E18
Aker Brygge
Rådhusbrygge
Akerhus Festning
Bank Plassen
Myntgata
Dronningens gate
Hovedøya
INFORMATION
Arctic Internet Café 1 E4
Canadian Embassy 2 C2
Deichmanske Bibliotek 3 E3
Den Norske Turistforening (DNT) 4 E3
Dutch Embassy 5 B1
Forex 6 C4
German Embassy 7 A2
Irish Embassy 8 C4
Jernbanetorget Apotek 9 E4
Main Post Office 10 E4
Nomaden 11 B2
Oslo Kommunale Legevakten 12 F3
Oslo Promotion 13 C3
US Embassy 14 B3
Use-It 15 E3
SIGHTS & ACTIVITIES
Akershus Festning 16 C5
Akershus Slott 17 C5
Den Norske Opera & Ballett 18 E5
Det Kongelige Slott 19 B3
Mini Bottle Gallery 20 D4
Munchmuseet 21 H3
Nasjonalgalleriet 22 C3
Nobels Fredssenter 23 B4
Oslo Cathedral 24 E4
SLEEPING
Anker Hostel 25 F2
Cochs Pensjonat 26 B2
Ellingsens Pensjonat 27 A1
MS Innvik 28 E5
Perminalen 29 D4
Rica Holberg 30 C2
Sentrum Pensjonat 31 E4
EATING
Åpent Bakeri 32 A3
Blitx 33 C2
Delicatessen 34 F2
Hell's Kitchen 35 E3
Hotel Havana 36 F1
Marino Grill 37 F2
Schrøder 38 D1
Tandoori Curry Corner 39 G3
Tekehtopa 40 D2
DRINKING
Blå 41 E2
Møllers Café 42 E3
Parkteateret 43 F1
Stargate 44 F3
Teddy's Soft Bar 45 F3

NORWAY

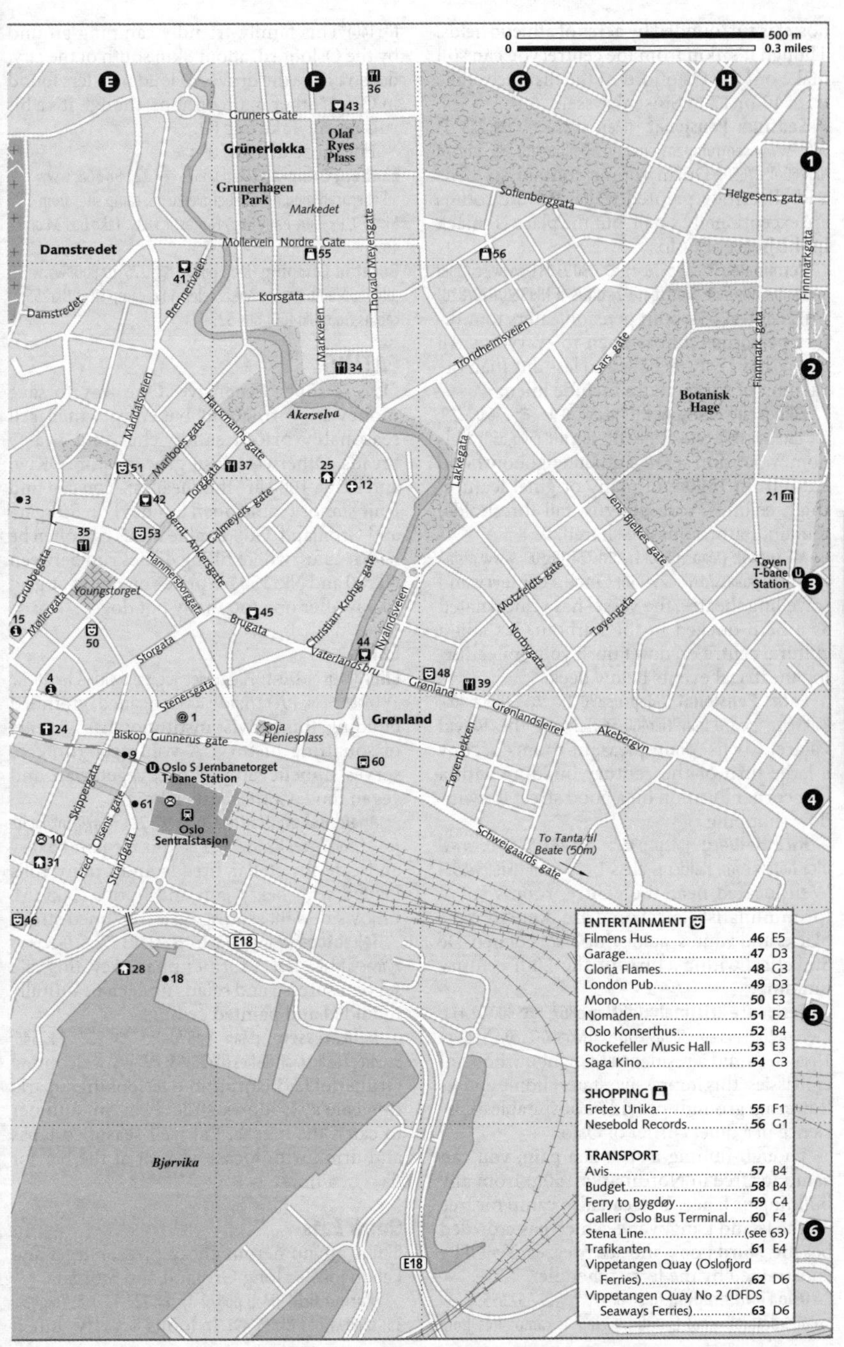

ENTERTAINMENT

Filmens Hus	46	E5
Garage	47	D3
Gloria Flames	48	G3
London Pub	49	D3
Mono	50	E3
Nomaden	51	E2
Oslo Konserthus	52	B4
Rockefeller Music Hall	53	E3
Saga Kino	54	C3

SHOPPING

Fretex Unika	55	F1
Nesebold Records	56	G1

TRANSPORT

Avis	57	B4
Budget	58	B4
Ferry to Bygdøy	59	C4
Galleri Oslo Bus Terminal	60	F4
Stena Line	(see 63)	
Trafikanten	61	E4
Vippetangen Quay (Oslofjord Ferries)	62	D6
Vippetangen Quay No 2 (DFDS Seaways Ferries)	63	D6

hostel is surrounded by acres of athletic fields. Though it's 4km from the centre, you can still make out the Oslofjord in the distance. Take tram 13 or 17 to Sinsenkrysset.

Sentrum Pensjonat (Map pp870-1; ☎ 223 35 580; www.sentrumpensjonat.no; Tollbugata 8; dm/s/d Nkr260/450/650) Dorm rooms contain six beds and cheerfully painted walls. Private rooms are exceptionally small, but the place is smack in the heart of Oslo.

Perminalen (Map pp870-1; ☎ 230 93 081; www.sentrumpensjonat.no; Øvre Slottsgate 2; dm/s/d Nkr360/620/820) This central 55-room pension caters to military personnel, but is open to everyone. All rooms have private bath and less dirt than the vacuum of space. Rates include linen.

Ellingsen's Pensjonat (Map pp870-1; ☎ 226 00 359; ep@tiscal.no; Holtegata 25; s Nkr330-460, d Nkr540-650) This homey pension set in a quiet neighbourhood dates from 1890 and many original features (high ceilings, rose designs, tall thresholds) remain. Bathrooms are shared.

MS Innvik (Map pp870-1; ☎ 224 19 500; www.msinnvik.no; Langkaia; s/d Nkr425/750) Once a car ferry and travelling theatre, the vessel has reincarnated as a B&B docked in the harbour. It's still a cultural centre, so don't flush your toilet during theatrical events below deck.

Cochs Pensjonat (Map pp870-1; ☎ 233 32 400; Parkveien 25; s/d from Nkr460/560) Near the Royal Palace, Cochs' plain pleasant rooms occupy a large turn-of-the-century building with a fine corner location on a good street for window shopping.

Rica Holberg (Map p867; ☎ 231 57 200; www.rica-hotels.com; Holbergs plass 1; s/d from Nkr695/895) Well located near the centre, rooms strive for minimalist flair. Some are done in reds, blacks and whites, achieving a sort of neo-De Stijl effect within a turn-of-the-20th-century building.

Residence Kristinelund (Map p867; ☎ 400 02 411; www.kristinelund.no; s Nkr690-1070, d Nkr890-1180; 8am-11pm) Set amid a residential neighbourhood of embassies, this impressive stately home and its flowering grounds provide a hospitable experience in a quiet corner of Oslo.

Though finding a spot is a pain, you can camp for free in Nordmarka 150m from any building or fence. You can also camp for free on the Island Langøyene, which has crowded beaches, bird poop and sea breezes. You'll be constrained by the ferry schedule.

Oslo Fjordcamping (Map p867; ☎ 227 52 055; www.oslofjordcamping.no; Ljansbrukveien 1; camp sites from Nkr140) This family-friendly camping ground by the Oslofjord, about 8km south of the city, doesn't have the droves of loud revellers found in Oslo's other main options, though it's a bit run down. Take bus 83.

For those droves, try:

Ekeberg Camping (Map p867; ☎ 221 98 568; www.ekebergcamping.no; Ekebergveien 65; camp sites from Nkr170; Jun-early Sep) Fantastic view. Take bus 34 or 46.

Bogstad Camping (Map p867; ☎ 225 10 800; www.bogstadcamping.no; Ankerveien 117; camp sites Nkr255, cabins from Nkr460) Bus 32.

EATING

Oslo is super expensive. One way to save money is to frequent bakeries, which sell reasonably priced sandwiches and hearty breads. Otherwise, visit grocery stores: Kiwi and Rema 1000 are the cheapest. You can find fruit stands (some open Sunday) on Storgata and Grønland. Good-value meals can often be had at cafes, where filling dishes run between Nkr80 and Nkr150 – a price you might be glad to pay after one too many hot dogs.

Cafes

Blitx (Map pp870-1; Pilestredet 30c; sandwiches Nkr10-20; noon-6pm; V) Inside a barricaded, graffitied building, this activist institution has 30 years of squatting history. A volunteer-run cafe serves unbelievably cheap vegetarian and vegan food. Coffee costs Nkr5.

Åpent Bakeri (Map pp870-1; ☎ 224 49 470; Inkognito Tce 1; sandwiches Nkr55-75) Try this elegant bakery and cafe for stellar breads and grainy rolls loaded with berry jam and butter (Nkr15). Enjoy sidewalk seating on a tree-lined street.

Tekehtopa (Map pp870-1; ☎ 222 03 352; St Olav plass 2; mains Nkr85-135) A former pharmacy, this cafe serves espresso and salads under a beautifully moulded and painted ceiling.

Delicatessen (Map pp870-1; ☎ 227 14 546; Søndregate 8; small dishes Nkr38-66; V) A welcoming Grünerløkka institution overlooking a park, this cafe's windows slide away in summer to catch the breeze. Eat well-seasoned tapas and drink with locals who sit at the bar for days at a time.

Quick Eats

There are numerous cheap pizza, burger and kebab joints along Grøland and Storgata.

Marino Grill (Map pp870-1; ☎ 221 13 018; Torggata 35; sandwiches Nkr35-49) It looks scruffy, but it also turns out delicious kebabs stuffed with flavourful lamb on fresh pita (most shops in Norway use processed meat, but not this one). It's absolutely packed after last call.

Birken Lunch (Map p867; ☎ 227 16 230; Thorvald Meyersgate 33; mains Nkr40-100) Grab a filling spinach and cheese *bolle* or some meat and boiled potatoes at this remnant of an eatery that recalls Grünnerløkka's blue-collar roots.

Tandoori Curry Corner (Map pp870-1; ☎ 221 79 906; Grønland 22; mains Nkr55-65; V) It might look like misery from the street, but you'll find it well worth entering this dive for excellent curries and Indian specialities.

Hotel Havana (Map pp870-1; ☎ 232 30 323; Thorvald Meyersgate 36; dishes Nkr50-100; ⏲ 10am-6pm Mon-Sat) A Grünerløkka delicatessen serving great takeaway food; try substantial fish burgers with homemade aioli.

Restaurants

Frognerseteren (Map p867; ☎ 229 24 040; Holmenkollveien 200; snacks Nkr40-100;) On a mountainside overlooking the city, this 19th-century eatery has big fireplaces and kick-arse apple cake in a building combining rusticity with the delicacy of 'dragon-style' ornamentation. Take T-Bane 1 to Frognerseteren.

Krishna's Cuisine (Map p867; ☎ 226 92 269; Sørkendalsveien 10b; lunch/dinner Nkr85/125; ⏲ noon-8pm Mon-Sat) Krishna's serves daily vegetarian meals where you might eat corn soup, cucumber salad and a pile of broccoli in yellow curry. Portions are so huge that most just buy a plate of the hot dish.

Tanta til Beate (off Map pp870-1; ☎ 226 84 613; Schweigaards gate 56; breakfast Nkr55-80, dinner mains Nkr115-170) For hearty egg-and-bacon breakfasts (served until 4pm), many of Oslo's recovering night owls make their way to this find on the east side of town. At night, eat curries, many of them vegetarian.

Schrøder (Map pp870-1; ☎ 226 05 183; Waldemar Thranes gate 8; soup Nkr59, mains Nkr99-129) Enjoy steaming plates of farm food such as *fårikål* (layers of lamb and cabbage) in a sometimes rowdy restaurant typified by cheap tablecloths and free-flowing beer. Definitely haunted by locals, not tourists.

Hell's Kitchen (Map pp870-1; Møllergata 23; pizza Nk100-150) Eat pizza in this bar favoured by the cool kids. A good-looking place, sit in a padded booth dimly lit by designy electric orbs with illuminated bottles of booze beaconing through the dark. Packed at night.

SPLURGE

Kampen Bistro (Map p867; ☎ 221 97 708; Bøgata 21; soup Nkr110, mains Nkr235) Way off the beaten track in a traditionally working-class neighbourhood, select exactingly prepared dishes (rosemary cod with lentil pureé) from a limited blackboard menu at one of Oslo's finest restaurants. High end, pretty and thoroughly casual, it attracts droves, from the stodgy to the cool. Reservations needed.

Lofotstua (Map p867; ☎ 224 69 396; Kirkeveien 40; mains Nkr180-255; ⏲ 3-10pm Mon-Fri) Run by a family from the Lofoten islands, this restaurant turns out a changing menu of fantastic fish dishes (including whale in season) and looks like a dive bar revived as a sea shanty. Nice!

DRINKING

Many thrifty backpackers just drink the bottle they brought from home. Hip bars are concentrated around Grünerløkka and Youngstorget. Since the line between cafe and bar is blurry, also consider Hell's Kitchen (left) and Delicatessen (opposite). If you're under 20, places serving anything other than beer and wine can't let you through the door. Use-it's *Streetwise* (p867) outlines numerous spots friendly to the young.

Blå (Map pp870-1; ☎ 400 04 277; Brenneriveien 9; beer Nkr52) Enjoy covered outdoor seating under coloured lights inches from the swirling Akerselva. Find it amid a beautifully crumbling, graffiti-covered factory complex. Weekends host incredibly cool bands and club nights.

Parkteateret (Map pp870-1; ☎ 223 56 300; Olaf Ryes plass 11; beer Nkr52) The yellow-and-black foyer of this theatre and performance space serves espresso and beer to big crowds taking advantage of outdoor seating overlooking an English-style square.

Teddy's Soft Bar (Map pp870-1; ☎ 221 73 650; Brugata 3a; beer Nkr52) This place provides a view into the 1950s via its thoroughly unchanged interior and ancient Wurlitzer. While good burgers are served, most come for the suds.

Møllers Café (Map pp870-1; Mariboesgata 9; beer Nkr44) Come inside for a rough-around-the-edges bar with wooden art-deco booths, hard rock jukebox and pool table. It only sells beer, so those aged 18 and 19 especially love it.

Gamle Major (Map p867; ☎ 224 62 904; Bogstadveien 66; beer Nkr58) Enter an old pub (dating from 1921) with wainscotting, brass lamps and a neon sign drolly advertising 'prescriptions'. Look further to discover you've ventured into an illusionist's parlour, one with secret chambers.

Stargate (Map pp870-1; Grønland 2; beer Nkr38) Low prices at this ugly watering hole attract youthful cheapskates, immigrants and guys with too-red noses.

For booze and bands, try Blå and:

Garage (Map pp870-1; ☎ 553 21 980; www.garage.no; Grensen 9)

Mono (Map pp870-1; ☎ 224 14 166; www.cafemono.no; Pløensgata 4)

CLUBBING

Anytime Blå (p873) has a DJ, be there. Covers costs around Nkr100.

Nomaden (Map pp870-1; ☎ 908 21 354; www.nomadenclub.com; Bernt Ankers gate 17) A diverse crowd overflows in this casual basement-level club. The floor throbs on account of nearly everyone dancing, with far fewer wallflowers than other spots.

Gloria Flames (Map pp870-1; ☎ 221 71 600; Grønland 18) DJs, such as the highly regarded Alv Gustavsen, play a heavy mix of rock, indie and esoteric in a room done up with oversized comics.

NORWAY

Gay & Lesbian Venues

There are few strictly queer clubs in Oslo. Several attract mixed crowds and some venues offer a weekly gay night. For details, pick up the free *Pink Planet* at the tourist office or look in *Streetwise*. **Fire Club Oslo** (www.fireoslo.no) hosts monthly club nights and masquerades at various spots around town.

London Pub (Map pp870-1; ☎ 227 08 700; CJ Hambros plass 5; 🕒 3pm-3am) This is Oslo's largest hangout for the studs, where you can dance every night. Upstairs tends to attract bigger crowds and younger guys (and to have a cover). Downstairs is mellower.

ENTERTAINMENT

The tourist office's *What's On in Oslo* lists concerts, theatre and special events.

Cinemas

Filmens Hus (Map pp870-1; ☎ 224 74 500; Dronningens gate 16) Art house.

Saga Kino (Map pp870-1; ☎ 415 19 000; Stortingsgata 28) Mainstream Hollywood.

Live Music

Den Norske Opera & Ballett (p868)

Oslo Konserthus (Map pp870-1; ☎ 231 13 110; www.oslokonserthus.no; Munkedamsveien 14) Emphasises fine jazz and classical music.

Rockefeller Music Hall (Map pp870-1; ☎ 222 03 232; www.rockefeller.no; Torggata 16) Books big-name contemporary rock (Bloc Party, Morrissey), jazz and more.

SHOPPING

For fashionable clothes, independent booksellers, record shops and plastic eyeglass frames, head to **Bogstadveien** (Map p867), a retail thoroughfare. Try poking around Grünnerløkka's boutiques, where you'll also find **Fretex Unika** (Map pp870-1; Markveien 53). Oslo's various Salvation Army shops separate their stuff into categories and this branch is where all the trendy clothes go.

Pure Norsk (Map p867; ☎ 224 64 045; www.purnorsk.no; Theresesgate 14) sells a discerning selection of Norwegian-designed items, such as stylish umbrellas, thick wool blankets or a life-sized luminous moose head of glowing plastic.

A cadaver with a nosebleed greets visitors entering **Nesebold Records** (Map pp870-1; ☎ 227 17 822; www.neseblodrecords.com; Rathkesgate 7), a cramped shop selling all things metal: CDs, obscure records and collectors' items. If you ever wanted leather gauntlet's worn by *Mayhem's* Blasphemer, you're in luck.

GETTING THERE & AWAY

Air

Most flights land at Gardemoen, 50km north of the city. Oslo Torp is a secondary airport, 123km south of the city.

Boat

DFDS Seaways runs to/from Copenhagen Stena Line and use the docks off Skippergata.

Color Line boats to/from Hirtshals (Denmark) and Kiel (Germany) dock at Hjortneskaia.

Bus

Long-distance buses use a terminal at Galleri Oslo, just east of Oslo S.

Car & Motorcycle

You'll have to pay a Nkr15 to Nkr25 toll each time you drive into Oslo.

All major car-rental companies have booths at Gardemoen airport. In the city centre, find:

Avis (Map pp870-1; ☎ 815 69 044; Munkedamsveien 27)
Budget (Map pp870-1; ☎ 220 17 610; Oslo Spektrum)

Train

All trains arrive and depart from Oslo S. Some stop at Nationaltheatret.

GETTING AROUND

Boat

Ferries to Bygdøy leave from Rådhusbrygge every 30 to 40 minutes, while ferries to the islands in the Oslofjord leave from Vippetangen.

Public Transport

Oslo has an efficient public-transport system. A ticket on any service costs Nkr22 if you buy it from a station agent or kerbside machines. You can also buy your ticket from drivers for Nkr30. An unlimited *dagskort* (day ticket) costs Nkr60, but can't be used between 1am and 4am. **Trafikanten** (Map pp870-1; ☎ 815 00 176; Jernbanetorget; ⏲ 7am-8pm Mon-Fri, 8am-6pm Sat & Sun) provides schedules and transit maps.

Bus and tram lines extend to the suburbs. Most converge at Jernbanetorget in front of Oslo S. Most westbound buses, including those to Bygdøy and Vigeland Park, also stop on the southern side of the National Theatre.

The T-Bane, Oslo's five-line metro train network, underground in the city centre, is faster and goes further than most bus lines.

Service frequency drops dramatically at night but, on weekends only, *Nattlinjer* night buses 200 to 218 follow the tram routes until 4am (tickets Nkr50; passes not valid).

Taxi

Taxis charge up to Nkr90 at flagfall and from Nkr12 to Nkr18 per kilometre. Any taxi with a lit sign is available for hire. Otherwise, phone **Taxi2** (☎ 02202) or **Oslo Taxi** (☎ 02323). Meters start running at the point of dispatch, adding to what will become a gigantic bill.

SOUTHERN NORWAY

The curving south coast exists as a magnet for vacationing Norwegian families, who come to the area for its beaches, offshore islands and sailing opportunities. Unless they're here to pilot masted vessels, first-time foreign travellers generally visit the coast's sleepy wooden towns (Mandal and Grimstad, for example) as a pit stop en route to more exciting locales. The notable exception is Stavanger, a lively international city conveniently positioned for explorations of surrounding fjords and surfing spots.

STAVANGER & AROUND

pop 120,5700

Don't be misled by Stavanger's title 'Oil Capital of Norway' – this is a picturesque city of narrow cobbled streets and small white houses. The centre is lively, containing a fine stock of bars, cafes and places to stroll. It's an excellent point from which to begin exploring the Lysefjord.

The adjacent bus and train stations are a 10-minute walk from the harbour. The **tourist office** (☎ 518 59 200; www.visitstavanger.com; Rosenkildetorget 1; ⏲ 9am-8pm Jun-Aug, shorter hr rest of year) is near the church.

Sights & Activities

The most popular outing is the two-hour hike to the top of the incredible **Preikestolen** (Pulpit Rock), 25km east of Stavanger. You can inch up to the edge of its flat top and peer 600m straight down to the Lysefjord. The tourist office details public transit to the trailhead.

Rønde Fjord Cruise (☎ 518 95 270; www.rodne.no; daily tours mid-May–Aug, weekend tours Oct-Apr; adult Nkr340) sightseeing boats cruise the lovely steep-walled Lysefjord, passing fish farms, waterfalls, goats and seals along the way. Discount on internet booking or purchase at the tourist office.

Purists are attracted to Stavanger's unpopulated (and C-O-L-D) surf breaks. For rentals (Nkr400 per day), lessons and advice, visit **Surf Centrum** (☎ 228 37 873; Breigata 4; ⏲ 10am-7pm Mon-Fri, 10am-5pm Sat). The closest surfable spot is 15km to the south.

A fun quarter for strolling about is **Gamle Stavanger** where cobblestone walkways lead through rows of very well-preserved, 18th-century, whitewashed wooden houses.

The cool **Norsk Oljemuseum** (☎ 519 39 300; www.norskolje.museum.no; Kjeringholmen; adult/child Nkr80/40; ⏲ 10am-7pm Jun-Aug, 10am-4pm Mon-Sat, 10am-6pm Sun Sep-May) nicely balances the technical side of oil exploration with archive footage of significant moments in the history of Norwegian oil

Visit the fishy **Canning Museum** (☎ 518 42 700; Øvre Strandgate 88a; admission Nkr60; ⏲ 11am-4pm mid-Jun–mid-Aug) to learn about soul-destroying jobs of the 19th century.

Sleeping

Stavanger Camping Mosvangen (☎ 515 32 971; www.mosvangencamping.no; Tjensvoll 1B; camp sites without/with car Nkr80/110, dm Nkr120, 2-/4-person huts Nkr350/550; ⏰ mid-May–mid-Sep) In a clearing near lake Mosvangen, you'll find a large field with minimal shade trees and some mass-produced cabins. There's also a dormitory. Nearby trails lead to town (3km).

Stavanger Vandrerhjem Mosvangen (☎ 515 32 971; www.mosvangencamping.no; Tjensvoll 1B; camp sites without/with car Nkr80/110, dm Nkr120, 2-/4-person huts Nkr350/550; ⏰ mid-May–mid-Sep) Lakeside and private, two- and four-bed rooms enjoy access to trails around lake Mosvagen.

Preikestolhytta (☎ 971 65 551; www.preikestolhytta.no; dm/d Nkr250/670; ⏰ Jun-Aug;) Trees grow from this isolated turf-roofed hostel, 25km out of the city within walking distance of Pulpit Rock and other amazing hikes. The cafeteria works with a local culinary school.

Tone's B&B (☎ 515 24 207; www.tones-bb.net; Peder Claussøns gate 22; s/d 350/500) Sleep in one of three comely rooms in this pleasant B&B on a quiet street up the hill from Gamble. The shared bathroom is well kept.

Rogalandsheimen Gjestgiveri (☎ 515 20 188; www.rogalandsheimen.no; Muségata 18; s/d Nkr600/725; 💻) Paintings cover every surface of this charming 19th-century guest house. Rooms share bath and attract artists and musicians.

Eating & Drinking

Kult Kafeen (☎ 518 91 600; Sølvberggata; plates Nkr78-135) In the culture house, this cafe serves daily meals (including plates of salmon and asparagus) that are a relative bargain.

Resept (☎ 515 53 980; Østervåg 43; mains Nkr79-139) This cafe's decor involves minimal couches and solid coloured walls recalling the supergraphics of the '70s. Enjoy vegetarian pasta and noodles with shrimp.

Café Sting (☎ 518 93 878; Valberggata 3; mains Nkr148-169) With a hill-top position next to the Valberg Tower, Sting serves flank steak on garlic bread and good salads. The clientele is mostly gay on Friday and Saturday nights when there is often a DJ.

Cementen (☎ 515 67 800; Nedre Strandgate 2) Bartenders play quality tunes. Bands and DJs frequently perform in a back room. Pick up a used book (Nkr10) and Sunday beer special.

Taket (☎ 518 43 701; Nedre Strandgata 15) Stavanger's biggest disco plays pop hits to a crowd space whose sense of decor is lost in blackness. Sticky floors.

A **fish market** at the harbour sells hot fish cakes (Nkr10). **Våland Dampbakeri & Conditori** (☎ 51 86 19 23; Nygaten 24) bakes flaky pastry. Nearby, a pile of bars on Skagen attract boisterous crowds with outdoor, waterside terraces and cheesy songs ('Dancing Queen') playing at top volume.

Getting There & Away

The train runs to Oslo (Nkr871, eight hours, two to four daily) via Kristiansand (Nkr418, 3¼ hours, three to seven daily). Nor-Way Bussekspress offers connecting services to Oslo (Nkr650, 10½ hours, one to three daily) and direct to Bergen (Nkr470, 5½ hours, approximately hourly). **Flaggruten** (☎ 518 68 780) runs boats to Bergen (Nkr800, 4¼ hours, one to four daily).

KRISTIANSAND

pop 80,000

Summertime Kristiansand offers urban life and a small bathing beach right in the town centre. Strollers will enjoy poking around Posebyen, a district containing a large concentration of white houses from the 17th and 18th centuries. It's a busy seaside holiday resort for Norwegians, but foreign tourists with limited time generally prefer Oslo, Bergen and Stavanger. The exception is when Kristiansand hosts the week-long **Quart Festival** (☎ 381 46 969; www.quart.no), when dozens of bands play daily.

The train, bus and ferry terminals are together on the west side of the city centre near the **tourist office** (☎ 381 21 314; www.sorlandet.com; Rådhusgaen 6; ⏰ 8.30am-6pm Mon-Fri, 9am-6pm Sat, noon-6pm Sun mid-Jun–late Aug, 8.30am-3.30pm Mon-Fri rest of year).

Roligheden Camping (☎ 380 96 722; www.roligheden.no; camp sites from Nkr140, 4-person cabins from Nkr750; Ⓟ) lies near a small, crowded beach 3km east of town, while **Frosbusdal Rom** (☎ 911 29 906; www.gjestehus.no; Frobusdalen 2; s Nkr400-500, d Nkr600-800;) comes with stained glass and period character in a romantic home from 1917.

Find **Generalen Cafe** (☎ 380 90 791; www.ravnedalen.no in Norwegian; in Ravendalen Park; ⏰ May-Aug), hidden in a forested park, on a promenade encircling a swan-filled pond. Visit the little red cabin to enjoy burgers (Nkr150) and beer. Bands play many nights.

NORWAY

Trains run to Stavanger (Nkr418, three hours) and Oslo (Nkr619, 4¾ hours) three to seven times daily. Nor-Way Busseksress goes to: Stavanger (Nkr380, four hours, two to four daily), Oslo (Nkr340, 5¼ hours, seven to nine daily) and Bergen (Nkr650, 12 hours, one daily). Regional buses depart hourly for towns along the south coast. Color Line boats depart for Hirtshals (Denmark) p864.

BERGEN & THE WESTERN FJORDS

The Western Fjords' steep crystalline walls drop with sublime force straight into blue water, often decorated with waterfalls and small farms that harmoniously blend into the natural landscape. Summer hiking opportunities exist along the fjord walls and on the enormous Jostedalsbreen glacier. Bergen with its 15th-century waterfront, is pleasing to behold, and contains fine nightlife and restaurants. For regional information, contact **Fjord Norge** (www.fjordnorway.com).

OSLO TO BERGEN

The Oslo–Bergen railway line provides a seven-hour journey past forests, alpine villages, and the starkly beautiful **Hardangervidda** plateau.

Midway is **Geilo**, a ski centre where you can practically walk off the train and onto a lift. There's good summer **hiking** in the mountains around Geilo, which has a **hostel** (☎ 320 87 060; www.oenturist.no; Lienvegen 137; dm/s/d Nkr275/470/650) near the centre.

From Geilo the train climbs 600m through a tundra-like landscape of high lakes and snow-capped mountains to the tiny village of **Finse**, near the **Hardangerjøkulen** ice cap. Finse has year-round **skiing** and is in the midst of a network of summer **hiking trails**. One of Norway's most frequently trodden trails winds from the Finse station down to the fjord town of **Aurland**, a four-day trek. There's breathtaking mountain scenery along the way as well as a series of DNT mountain huts a day's walk apart – the nearest is Finsehytta, 200m from Finse station.

Myrdal, further west along the railway line, is the connecting point for the spectacularly steep Flåm railway, which twists and turns its way down 20 splendid kilometres to **Flåm** (p881).

Tours

Train stations sell the **Norway in a Nutshell** (☎ 815 68 222; www.fjordtours.com) ticket combining morning trains from Bergen to Flåm, a ferry along the spectacular Aurlandsfjorden and Nærøyfjorden to Gudvangen, a bus to Voss and a train back to Bergen (Nkr935) in time for a late dinner, or you can continue on to Oslo (Nkr1295).

BERGEN

pop 250,000

Norway's second-largest city might be its most beautiful. Set on a peninsula surrounded by mountains and the sea, the compact centre offers a tangle of crooked streets, picturesque wooden neighbourhoods and hilltop views. Bergen provides ample opportunities to linger in cafes and bars, while a large university population helps to secure Bergen's claim as western Norway's cultural capital, supporting theatres, a philharmonic orchestra and notable rock scene. Drawback: expect rain 275 days of the year.

Orientation & Information

The bus and train stations lie a block apart on Strømgaten, a 10-minute walk from the Express Boats (ferry terminals). Most of the restaurants, hotels and sites cluster around Vågen, the inner harbour.

INTERNET ACCESS

Cyberhouse (Hollendergaten 9; per hr Nkr60 🕒 9am-11pm)

Library (☎ 555 68 500; Strømgaten 6) Free, time-limited access.

MEDICAL SERVICES

Legevakt Medical Clinic (☎ 555 68 700; Vestre Strømkaien 19; 🕒 emergencies 24hr)

Pharmacy (☎ 552 18 384; Bergen Storsenter near bus station; 🕒 8am-11pm Mon-Sat, 10am-11pm Sun)

TOURIST INFORMATION

DNT office (☎ 553 35 810; www.bergen-turlag.no; Tverrgaten 4; 🕒 10am-4pm Mon-Wed & Fri, 10am-6pm Thu, 10am-2pm Sat)

Tourist Office (☎ 555 52 000; www.visitbergen.com; Vågsallmenningen 1; 🕒 8.30am-10pm Jun-Aug, 9am-8pm May & Sep, 9am-4pm Mon-Sat Oct-Apr)

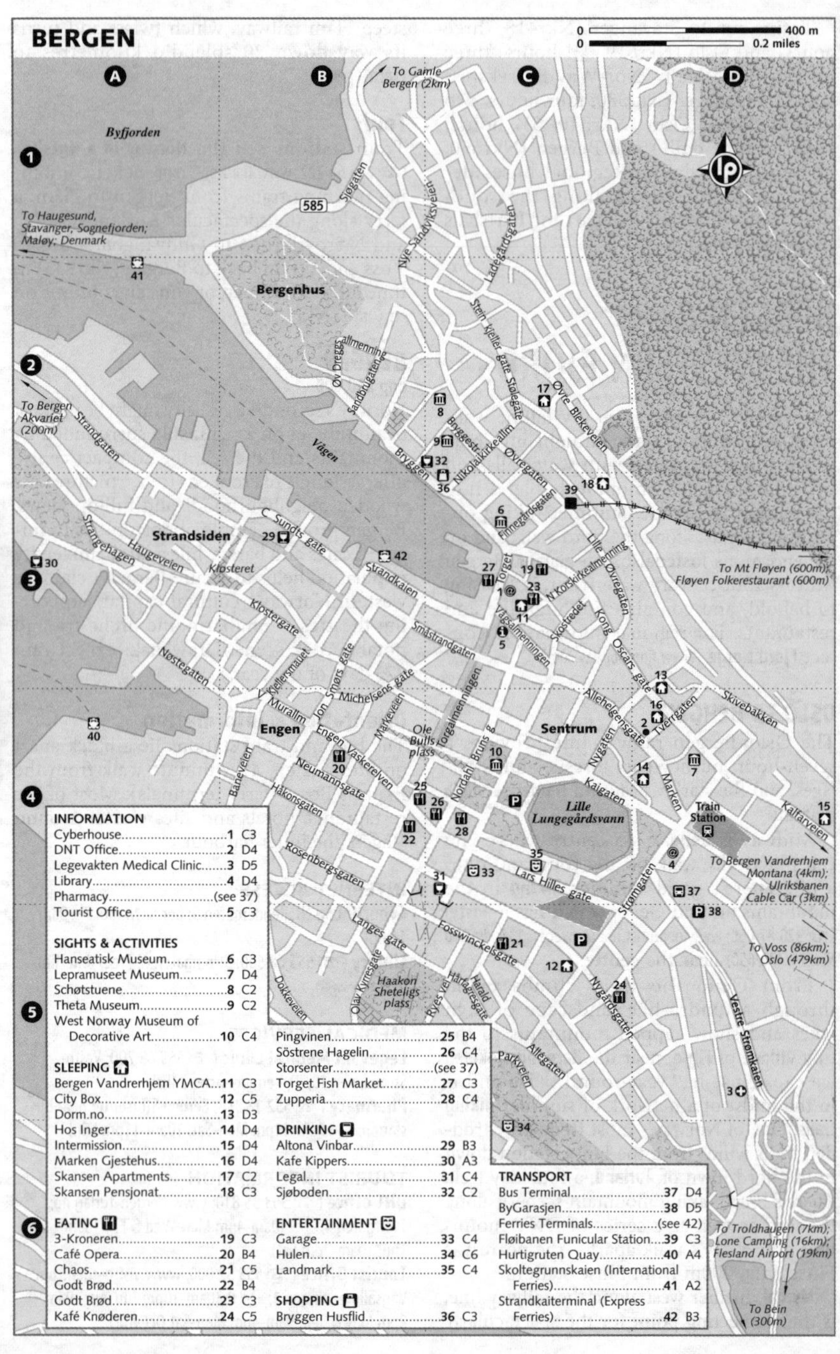
BERGEN
0 400 m
0 0.2 miles
A
B
C
D
1
2
3
4
5
6
To Gamle Bergen (2km)
Byfjorden
To Haugesund, Stavanger, Sognefjorden; Måløy; Denmark
585
Sjøgaten
Nye Sandviksveien
Ladegårdsgaten
Bergenhus
Stein Kjeller gate
Stølegate
Øv Dreggsallmenning
Sandbrugaten
Øvre Blekeveien
To Bergen Akvariet (200m)
Strandgaten
Vågen
Bryggen
Bryggestr
Nikolaikirkeallm
Øvregaten
Finnegårdsgaten
Strangehagen
Haugeveien
Strandsiden
C Sundts gate
Klosteret
Strandkaien
Torget
Lille Øvregaten
N Korskirkealmenning
To Mt Fløyen (600m); Fløyen Folkerestaurant (600m)
Klostergate
Smastrandgaten
Vågsallmenningen
Skostredet
Kong Oscars gate
Nøstegaten
V Kjellersmauet
Jon Smørs gate
Michelsens gate
Allehelgensgate
Tverrgaten
Skivebakken
Murallm
Engen
Engen Vaskerelven
Markeveien
Ole Bulls plass
Torgalmenningen
Nordahl Bruns g
Sentrum
Nygaten
Marken
Baneveien
Neumannsgate
Håkonsgaten
Kaigaten
Lille Lungegårdsvann
Train Station
Kalfarveien
Rosenbergsgaten
Lars Hilles gate
Strømgaten
To Bergen Vandrerhjem Montana (4km); Ulriksbanen Cable Car (3km)
Langes gate
Fosswinckelsgate
To Voss (86km); Oslo (479km)
Dokkeveien
Olav Kyrresgate
Haakon Shetheligs plass
Ryes vei
Harald Hårfagresgate
Nygårdsgaten
Vestre Strømkaien
Parkveien
Allégaten
To Troldhaugen (7km); Lone Camping (16km); Flesland Airport (19km)
To Bein (300m)
NORWAY

INFORMATION
Cyberhouse 1 C3
DNT Office 2 D4
Legevakten Medical Clinic 3 D5
Library 4 D4
Pharmacy (see 37)
Tourist Office 5 C3

SIGHTS & ACTIVITIES
Hanseatisk Museum 6 C3
Lepramuseet Museum 7 D4
Schøtstuene 8 C2
Theta Museum 9 C2
West Norway Museum of Decorative Art 10 C4

SLEEPING
Bergen Vandrerhjem YMCA 11 C3
City Box 12 C5
Dorm.no 13 D3
Hos Inger 14 D4
Intermission 15 D4
Marken Gjestehus 16 D4
Skansen Apartments 17 C2
Skansen Pensjonat 18 C3

EATING
3-Kroneren 19 C3
Café Opera 20 B4
Chaos 21 C5
Godt Brød 22 B4
Godt Brød 23 C3
Kafé Knøderen 24 C5
Pingvinen 25 B4
Söstrene Hagelin 26 C4
Storsenter (see 37)
Torget Fish Market 27 C3
Zupperia 28 C4

DRINKING
Altona Vinbar 29 B3
Kafe Kippers 30 A3
Legal 31 C4
Sjøboden 32 C2

ENTERTAINMENT
Garage 33 C4
Hulen 34 C6
Landmark 35 C4

SHOPPING
Bryggen Husflid 36 C3

TRANSPORT
Bus Terminal 37 D4
ByGarasjen 38 D5
Ferries Terminals (see 42)
Fløibanen Funicular Station 39 C3
Hurtigruten Quay 40 A4
Skoltegrunnskaien (International Ferries) 41 A2
Strandkaiterminal (Express Ferries) 42 B3

FRYKT OG FRYD

If you've decided to avoid the crowds and visit Bergen in the winter, why not avoid them further and join **Frykt og Fryd** (Fear & Joy) a small group of cold-water enthusiasts who go swimming in the harbour every Sunday at 1pm near the USF building (Kafe Kippers). A Portuguese hymn to the ocean is sung right before the plunge to better fortify the group's collective resolve.

Sights & Activities

The old medieval quarter and World Heritage site of **Bryggen** contains long, timber buildings housing museums, restaurants and shops. The alleys that run along their less-restored sides offer an intriguing view into the stacked-stone foundations and rough-plank construction of centuries past.

The **Hanseatisk Museum** (☎ 555 44 690; Finnegårdsgaten 1a; adult/child Nkr50/free; ⏲ 9am-5pm mid-May–mid-Sep, 11am-2pm Tue-Sat 11am-4pm Sun mid-Sep–mid-May) occupies a timber building (1704) with some of Norway's creakiest floors. Its character and beds give a glimpse of the austere living conditions of Hanseatic merchants. Entry tickets are also valid for **Schøtstuene** (Øvregaten 50) where the Hanseatic merchants once met for business and beer guzzling.

The eclectic collection of the **West Norway Museum of Decorative Art** (☎ 553 36 633; www.vk.museum.no; Nordahl Brunsgate 9; adult/student Nkr50/40; ⏲ 11am-5pm mid-May–mid-Sep, noon-4pm Tue-Sun mid-Sep–mid-May) includes a Lego set, an armchair shaped like a tarantula, Edvard Grieg's table setting and a quilt made from children's raincoats.

A one-room reconstruction of a clandestine Resistance headquarters, uncovered by the Nazis in 1942, the **Theta Museum** (☎ 555 52 080; Enhjørningsgården; admission Nkr20; ⏲ 2-4pm Tue, Sat & Sun mid-May–mid-Sep) is hidden in an upper storey at the rear of the Bryggen warehouse with the unicorn figurehead.

Wash your hands before and after visiting the **Lepramuseet** (Leprosy Museum; ☎ 559 61 155; Kong Oscars gate 59; adult/student Nkr40/20; ⏲ 11am-4pm mid-May–Aug), an enclosed wooden complex (1754) whose wards, church and kitchen appear tranquil from a cobbled, tree-shaded interior court.

For an unbeatable city view, take the **Fløibanen funicular** (admission Nkr35; ⏲ from 8am) to Mt Fløyen (320m) and its restaurant. Well-marked hiking trails lead into the forest.

The **Ulriksbanen cable car** (admission Nkr50) up Mt Ulriken (642m) offers a panoramic view of the city, fjords and mountains. Many take the cable car one way and walk (about three hours) across a well-beaten trail to the funicular station at Mt Fløyen.

Sleeping

The tourist office books single/double rooms in private homes from Nkr300/500 (plus Nkr50 booking fee); it sometimes finds last-minute hotel discounts.

Bergen Vandrerhjem YMCA (☎ 556 06 055; www.bergenhostel.com; Nedre Korskirkealmenning 4; budget/4-/6-person dm Nkr155/210/230, d Nkr750; ⏲ reception 7am-midnight) A perfectly central hostel where dorm dwellers reside in plain, linoleum-floored bunk rooms sleeping four to six, or in windowless caverns (it gets noisy here) sleeping 15 or 32. Rooftop decks provide views over surrounding garrets.

Intermission (☎ 553 00 400; Kalfarveien 8; Nkr180; ⏲ mid-Jun–mid-Aug) This old white house has 37 beds, where the hospitable Christian Student Fellowship serves waffles to guests many nights.

Dorm.no (☎ 982 38 600; www.dm.no; Kong Oscars gate 44; dm Nkr220; 💻) Offers 16 beds in an attractive dormitory with linen included. There's a lively cafe/pub and pleasant terrace.

Marken Gjestehus (☎ 553 14 404; www.marken-gjestehus.com; Kong Oscars gate 45; 4-/6-/8-person dm Nkr220/195/175, s/d Nkr450/600) Rooms have wooden floors, spiffy furniture of recent vintage, and big windows, often with a decent view. No breakfast.

SPLURGE

Kvikne's Hotel (☎ 576 94 200; www.kviknes.no; d in historic bldg Nkr2210, s/d in modern bldg Nkr1080/1660; ⏲ Apr-Sep) This pristinely preserved, 19th-century timber hotel boasts a fabulous collection of art and superb craftwork in its 'dragon-style' lounges. As you sit in a chair once owned by JC Dahl, staring at the summer-lit fjord, your mind will struggle to comprehend vast interior and exterior beauty. Many rooms have lovely, fjord-oriented balconies – you want one of these. Avoid the newer concrete wing.

Skansen Pensjonat (☎ 553 19 080; www.skansen-pensjonat.no; Vetrlidsalmenningen 29; s/d Nkr400-450/650-750) Trudge up steep cobbled streets through a pretty neighbourhood to this hilltop house from 1918.

City Box (☎ 553 12 500; www.citybox.no; Nygårdsgaten 31; s Nkr400-500, d 500-600) For tasteful rooms with no frills, this place offers low prices by providing no amenities. It's near some of Bergen better cafes.

Hos Inger (☎ 553 21 241; inyg@hib.no; Grønnevollen 14m; s/d Nkr500/700, breakfast Nkr100) Sleep in a wooden house (over 110 years old) on a quiet pedestrian street near the train station. Rooms share a cheerful common kitchen.

Skansen Apartments (☎ 412 01 780; Nedre Blekvei 6; http://home.broadpark.no/~ggrin/; 1/2 people in apt Nkr500/800) Located up a hill in a maze of pretty, cobbled streets, this small operation lets out a handful of apartments with private kitchens and shared bath. Very quiet with views over the harbour.

Also try:

Bergen Vandrerhjem Montana (☎ 552 08 070; www.montana.no; Johan Blyttsvei 30; 20-/4-person dm Nkr200/265, s/d Nkr650/780) A large hostel 5km from the centre of town by bus 31. Mountainside view.

Lone Camping (☎ 553 92 960; www.lonecamping.no; Hardangerveien 697, Haukeland; camp sites Nkr150, 2-person cabins Nkr610) Tent sites on a grassy lakeshore,19km east of Bergen by bus 900.

NORWAY

Eating

Godt Brød (☎ 553 28 000; Nedre Korskirkealmenningen 12 or Veste Torggata 2) This bakery does organic breads, pastries and delicious herb-dough pizzas topped with marinated vegetables (Nkr35).

3-Kroneren (Kong Oscars gate 3; sausage Nkr45) Enjoy a selection of glistening, fantastic sausages including bratwurst, reindeer and lamb.

Söstrene Hagelin (☎ 553 26 949; Olav Kyrres gate 33; dishes Nkr35-100; 🕑 9am-6pm Mon-Fri, 10am-3pm Sat) Eat fish pudding, fish casserole and other staples. Filling takeaway fish balls (Nkr35) come with potatoes.

Chaos (☎ 553 21 550; Fosswinckels gate 16; light meals Nkr50-80) This neighbourhood cafe and its thrift-store assortment of tables and lamps serve coffee, beer and snacks to chatting students.

Kafé Knøderen (☎ 416 60 357; Lydeer Sagens gate 22; snacks & food Nkr15-78) Enjoy coffee and light pancakes with crystallised sugar and good sandwiches in this lovely casual cafe filled with light, wooden furniture of greens, blues and greys. Turntables play Janis Joplin.

Zupperia (☎ 555 58 144; Nordahl Bruns gate; soup Nkr50-100) From fish to gazpacho, Zupperia serves 11 kinds of soups such as *husenottsuppe* (ox tail boiled with vegetables).

Pingvinen (☎ 556 04 646; Vaskerelven 20; mains Nkr120-149; 🕑 to 3.30am) This brick-walled pub's blackboard announces the day's offerings. Cooks embrace traditional cuisine, preparing hearty meals (meatloaf with leeks, fish with macaroni) with finesse.

Café Opera (☎ 552 30 315; Engen 18; sandwiches Nkr40-60, mains Nkr85-140,) A continental vibe permeates this early-20th-century cafe, serving salads, reindeer and sandwiches with brie walnuts and cherries. Big corner windows stare at the opera house. Top DJs on weekends.

our pick **Bein** (☎ 555 911 00; Fjøsangerveien 30; sandwiches Nkr75, mains Nkr105-160; 🕑 to 1.30am Sun-Thu, to 2.30am Fri & Sat) For authentic, exactingly prepared Norwegian cuisine, track down this old art-deco pharmacy. Eat squash, cod and sausages from a butcher around the corner in a room that crosses a bar with an informal diner far from where the tourists roam.

Storsenter, at the bus station, has fast-food outlets, a Vinmonopolet, and **Rimi** and **Spar** supermarkets. Torget's **fish market** sells fresh fruit and seafood snacks to droves of tourists, including salmon rolls for Nkr20; or plates of fish from Nkr60 to Nkr100. It's fun, but prices are slightly inflated.

Drinking & Entertainment

You might also drink at the cafes listed above.

Legal (Christies gate at Nygårdsgaten) The design theme comes from the 1960s English rock scene. Find red lighting, retro flooring, period lamps and tattooed university graduates.

Altona Vinbar (☎ 553 04 072; Strandgaten 81) A taverna since the 16th century, the small, cell-like rooms of this wine bar create a subterranean maze connected by incredibly short openings (duck through a hole 1m high).

Sjøboden (☎ 553 16 777; Bryggen 29) In a Hanseatic-era building, squeeze through crowds, dodge ceiling-suspended barrels and bump into a bad two-piece passionately playing County Roads. Expensive beer, but no cover.

Kafe Kippers (☎ 553 10 060; Georgernes Verft) Part of a cultural centre and former sardine cannery; enjoy outdoor, harbourside tables in the sunshine. Jazz many nights.

Landmark (☎ 553 17 755; Rasmus Meyers Alle 5; 🕑) This place hosts readings, experimental bands, and DJs. A white room of high modernist design becomes transformed at night with eerie lighting. Weekdays, grab a subdued drink and attend an event (often no cover). Many weekends, dance with Bergen's coolest.

Garage (☎ 553 21 980; www.garage.no; Christies gate 14; ⏰ from 6pm) Norway's rock headquarters consistently books top bands, including international acts. Concerts are held in a big, black basement.

Hulen (☎ 553 33 838; www.hulen.no in Norwegian; Olaf Ryes vei 47) Carved into the bowels of a hill, the renowned club occupies a former bomb shelter.

Shopping

Intimate **Skostredet** provides two blocks of independent boutiques, many selling goods made by hip designers from Bergen. For that reindeer sweater you desperately crave, try **Bryggen Husflid** (☎ 553 28 803; Bugården).

Getting There & Away

BOAT

Daily Fjord1 (www.fjord1.no) boats run to Balestrand (Nkr420, four hours) and Flåm (Nkr560, 5½ hours). A southbound express boats goes to Stavanger (Nkr620/710 one-way/return, four hours, two daily). These leave from Strandkaiterminalen on the western side of Vågen.

The *Hurtigruten* docks at the terminal east of Nøstegaten.

International ferries dock north of Rosenkrantztårnet.

BUS

Buses run to Ålesund (Nkr596, 10 hours, two daily), Trondheim (Nkr783, 14¼ hours, one daily), Stavanger (Nkr470, five hours, eight daily) and destinations in the Western Fjords.

TRAIN

Trains run to Oslo (Nkr761, 6½ to 7¾ hours, three to five daily).

Getting Around

Flybussen (www.flybussen.no) runs between the airport and Bergen's bus station (Nkr75, 45 minutes, at least twice hourly), stopping at many large hotels.

City buses cost Nkr20.

SOGNEFJORDEN

Sognefjorden, Norway's longest and deepest fjord, cuts a slash across western Norway. In some places sheer lofty walls rise more than 1000m above the water, while in others there is a gentler shoreline with farms, orchards and small towns.

The broad main waterway is impressive, but by cruising into the fjord's narrower arms, such as the lovely Nærøyfjorden (so pristine and archetypical that it's a Unesco site) to Gudvangen, you'll have idyllic views of sheer cliff faces and cascading waterfalls.

Tourist information is available at www.sognefjorden.no.

Getting There & Away

Fjord1 (☎ 559 07 070; www.fjord1.no) operates year-round express boats between Bergen and 10 Sognefjord towns.

There are numerous local ferries linking the fjord towns and a network of buses. They're detailed at www.ruteinfo.net and in timetables available at tourist offices.

Flåm

pop 500

A village of orchards and buildings scenically set at the head of Aurlandsfjorden, Flåm sees 500,000 visitors every summer. It's a jumping-off spot for travellers taking the Gudvangen or Sognefjorden boats, a turnaround point for the 'Norway in a Nutshell' tour and the base station for the dramatic Flåm railway. Adventurous visitors arrive from Finse by mountain bike. It's five or six hours downhill – obscenely picturesque – and you can return your rental in Flåm's centre. The **tourist office** (☎ 576 33 313; www.alr.no; ⏰ 8.30am-8pm Jun-Aug, 8.30am-4pm May & Sep) has details.

Friendly **Flåm Camping & Hostel** (☎ 576 32 121; www.hihostels.no; dm/s/d Nkr2655/330/570; ⏰ May-Sep) has just 31 beds – book early. If full, they might install you in a large dollhouse.

The Flåm railway runs between Myrdal and Flåm (Nkr230) numerous times daily, in sync with the Oslo–Bergen service. At Flåm, buses and boats head out to towns around Sognefjord.

Balestrand

pop 800

This genteel farming community enjoys a mountain backdrop, fjord views and eerie summer light. The road that runs south along

DETOUR: FJÆRLAND

This farming village on beautiful Fjærlandsfjorden, near two arms of the **Jostedalsbreen** ice cap, is a supremely inviting destination. Roads pass within 300m of two arms of the glacier: the **Supphellebreen** and the creaking, blue-iced **Bøyabreen**.

To avoid crowds, a three-hour hike leads you past waterfalls and wildflowers onto a ridge of moss-covered boulders and finally to **Flatbreehytta**, a pair of wind-beaten, DNT huts near the summit (1000m) with the glacier immediately behind. Find the trailhead 2km north on Rv5. Turn at signs for Suppehellebreen and then Flatbreehytta.

The **tourist office** (☎ 576 93 233; www.fjaerland.org) has irregular hours. Also find the **Norwegian Glacier Museum** (☎ 576 93 288; www.bre.museum.no; admission Nkr110) and **Bøyum Camping** (☎ 576 93 252; www.fjaerland.org/boyumcamping; camp sites Nkr125, dm/s/d/cabins Nkr150/270/340/690), which offers simple turf-roofed cabins and camp sites.

Between May and September, ferries run to/from Balestrand (Nkr175, 1¼ hours, two daily). The morning departure connects in Balestrand with the boat to Flåm and links with Bergen-bound ferries

the fjord has little traffic and is a pleasant place to stroll. It's lined with orchards, gardens and Viking burial mounds. One is topped by a statue of the legendary King Bele, erected by Germany's Kaiser Wilhelm II who spent his holidays here regularly until WWI.

The **tourist office** (☎ 576 91 255; www.sognefjord.no; 🕒 8am-6pm Mon-Sat, 10am-5pm Sun Jun-Aug, 10am-5pm Mon-Sat May & Sep) rents bikes.

At **Sjøtun Camping** (☎ 576 91 223; www.sjotun.com; camp sites from Nkr35, cabins Nkr250; 🕒 Jun-Sep), a 15-minute walk south along the fjord, you can pitch a tent or rent a rustic four-bunk cabin. **Balestrand Hostel** (☎ 576 91 303; www.kringsja.no; dm/s/d Nkr255/00/790; 🕒 late Jun–mid-Aug) is a pleasant lodge-style place perched near the water.

There's a supermarket and cafe near the dock. You can enjoy Kvikne's beauty by grabbing an aquavit from its hotel bar and nursing it on a balcony.

Daily express boats run to/from Bergen (Nkr420, four hours) and Flåm (Nkr210, 1¾ hours).

ÅNDALSNES

pop 2500

Åndalsnes, by the Romsdalsfjord, is the northern gateway to the western fjords. Most visitors arrive by train from Dombås, a scenic route descending through a deeply cut valley with dramatic waterfalls. Just before Åndalsnes, the train passes **Trollveggen**, a sheer 1500m-high rock face whose jagged and often cloud-shrouded summit is considered the ultimate challenge among Norwegian climbers.

The town itself is nondescript, but the scenery is top notch. Contact the **tourist office** (☎ 712 21 622; www.visitandalsnes.com; 🕒 9am-6pm Mon-Fri, 11am-6pm Sat & Sun mid-Jun–mid-Aug, 8am-2.30pm Mon-Fri rest of year) about **hiking** in surrounding mountains and valleys.

The turf-roofed **Åndalsnes Vandrerhjem Setnes** (☎ 712 21 382; www.aandalsnesvandrerhjem.no; dm/s/d Nkr260/470/680; 🕒 late May-early Sep) offers rustic accommodation 2km from town – just far enough to be surrounded by idyllic flowering pastures and mountain views.

The train from Dombås runs to Åndalsnes (Nkr212, 1½ hours, two to four daily), in sync with Oslo–Trondheim trains. Buses to Ålesund (Nkr245, 2¼ hours, two to four daily) meet the trains.

ÅLESUND

pop 42,000

Lucky for you, this pretty coastal town burned to the ground in 1904. The amazing rebuilding created a fantastical downtown unlike anything else in Norway – a harmonious collection of pastel buildings almost entirely designed in the art-nouveau tradition, well-staged on the end of a hilly peninsula.

The **tourist office** (☎ 701 57 600; www.visitalesund.com; 🕒 8am-7pm Mon-Fri, 8am-6pm Sat & Sun late Jun–mid-Aug, shorter hr rest of year) books excursions to coastal islands covered with nesting birds.

In town, puff up **Aksla's** 418 steps up for a splendid view of Ålesund and the surrounding islands or visit the brilliant **Art Nouveau Centre** (☎ 701 04 970; www.jugendstilsenteret.no; Apotekergata 16; adult/student Nkr60/30; 🕒 10am-5pm Jun-Aug, shorter hr rest of year), occupying a splendid Jugenstil pharmacy. It presents the work of well-known conti-

NORWAY

nental art-nouveau masters alongside their Norwegian counterparts.

The tourist office keeps lists of **private rooms** that start at around Nkr300 per person.

Tidy and central, **Ålesund Hostel** (☎ 701 15 830; www.hihostels.no; Parkgata 14; dm/s/d Nkr225/550/675, 💻) offers dorms that sleep 12. Enjoy an impressive vaulted common space and a breakfast better than many other Norwegian hostels.

There are several cafes and bakeries. If you fancy a hip drink, visit **Lille Løvenvold** (☎ 701 25 400; Løvenvoldgata 2), which feels like a red-light district.

The bus to Åndalsnes (Nkr245, 2¼ hours, two to four daily) is timed to meet arriving and departing trains. The *Hurtigruten* docks at Skansekaia Terminal.

NORTHERN NORWAY

From barren tundra to Lofoten's jagged islands, the arctic north offers remote terrain enlivened by the supernatural Midnight Sun and aurora borealis. Tromsø, the world's Northernmost university town, parties year round, while medieval Trondheim, Norway's third-largest city, provides plenty of culture and charm. On some freezing inland mountains you'll find Rorøs, a Unesco-protected copper-mining town.

An interesting travel alternative is the *Hurtigruten,* which pulls into every sizable port passing some of the best coastal scenery in Scandinavia. A good thing, too, since Norwegian trains only run as far as Bodø.

RØROS

pop 5600

Røros is an old copper-mining town with a Unesco-protected historic district. The first mine opened in 1644, but in 1977, after 333 years of operation, the company went bankrupt. Røros' main attractions are turf-roofed **miners' cottages** as well as other centuries-old timber buildings, a prominent 1784 **church** with an excellent baroque interior, **slag heaps**, and the old smelting works, part of the **Rørosmuseet** (☎ 724 06 170; Malmplassen; adult/student/child Nkr60/50/30; 🕑 10am-7pm mid-Jun–mid-Aug, shorter hr rest of year). The **tourist office** (☎ 72 41 11 65; Peder Hiortsgata 2; 🕑 9am-3.30pm Mon-Fri, 10.30am-12.30pm Sat) advises on fishing, hiking and subterranean tours of the defunct **Olavsguva mine** (☎ 724 10 000; www.rorosinfo.com; Peder Hiortsgata 2; 🕑 9am-6pm Mon-Sat, 10am-2pm Sun mid-Jun–mid-Aug), 13km northeast of town.

Family-run **Idrettsparken Hotell** (☎ 724 11 089; Øra 25; www.idrettsparken.no; camp sites Nkr100, cabins from Nkr420, hotel s/d from Nkr665/990; 🅿) occupies a modern building surrounded by soccer pitches. Head to **Thomasgården Kafe-Galleri** (☎ 724 12 470; Kjerkgata 48; snacks Nkr35-50) for apple cake and a nice read in a rustic room filled with ceramics.

Røros is 46km west of the Swedish border, via highway Rv31. Trains run between Oslo (Nkr679, five hours, two to six daily) and Trondheim (Nkr228, 2½ hours, three daily). Buses run to Trondheim (Nkr245, three hours, two to four daily) and overnight to Oslo (Nkr395, six hours, daily).

TRONDHEIM

pop 145,000

Trondheim, Norway's third-largest city and its original capital, is a lively university town with a rich medieval history. It was founded at the estuary of the winding Nidelva River in 997 by the Viking king Olav Tryggvason. After a fire razed most of the city in 1681, Trondheim was redesigned, with wide streets and a Renaissance flair, by General Caspar de Cicignon. The steeple of the medieval Nidaros Cathedral dominates the city centre.

The train station and coastal steamer quay are across the canal, a few minutes' north of the centre.

Internet (www.tradlosetrondheim.no; per 3/24 hr Nkr10/29) A city-sponsored wireless signal covers the central peninsula.

Library (Kongens gate; 🕑 9am-4pm Mon-Fri, 10am-3pm Sat Jul–mid-Aug, 9am-7pm Mon-Thu, 9am-4pm Fri, 11am-4pm Sat rest of year) Free internet.

Tourist office (☎ 738 07 660; www.trondheim.no; Torvet; 🕑 8.30am-10pm Mon-Fri, 10am-4pm Sat & Sun Jul-Aug, 9am-6pm Mon-Fri, 10am-4pm Sat & Sun mid-May–Jun, 9am-4pm Mon-Fri, 10am-2pm Sat & Sun Sep–mid-May)

Sights

Nidaros Cathedral (☎ 735 39 160; www.nidarosdomen.no; Kongsgårdsgata; admission Nkr50; 🕑 from 9am Mon-Sat, 1-4pm Sun May–mid-Sep; shorter hr otherwise) is Scandinavia's largest medieval building. The oldest wing dates from the 12th century, and popular belief holds that the altar lies over the grave of St Olav, the Viking king who replaced the worship of Nordic gods with Christianity. From July to August, visitors

 Book your stay at lonelyplanet.com/hotels

can climb the cathedral tower for a splendid view of the city. Also view the Norwegian **crown jewels**.

The **Ringve Museum** (☎ 738 70 280; www.ringve.no; Lade Allé 60; adult/student/child Nkr75/50/25; 11am-3pm or 5pm mid-May–mid Sep, 11am-4pm Sun mid-Sep–mid-May) is a music-history museum set in an 18th-century manor and **botanical garden**. Music students give tours, demonstrating the antique instruments on display. Take bus 3 or 4.

Trøndelag Folk Museum (☎ 738 90 100; Sverresborg Allé; adult/student/child Nkr80/55/30; 11am-6pm Jun-Aug, shorter hr otherwise) set around the ruins of a medieval castle, displays 60 period buildings, including a small, 12th-century stave church (visit in winter to understand how dark and miserable services must have been). Catch bus 8 or 9 from Dronningens gate.

Sleeping

The tourist office books **rooms** in private homes, mostly on the city outskirts and averaging Nkr300/450 for singles/doubles, for a Nkr30 fee.

Trondheim InterRail Centre (☎ 738 99 538; www.tirc.no; Elgesetergate 1; dm Nkr150; Jul–mid-Aug;) University students operate this crash pad. Yeah, you'll sleep on an assortment of military cots with 15 to 40 others, but the place attracts convivial people. The cafe sometime offers backpackers beer specials.

Singsaker Sommerhotel (☎ 738 93 100; Rogertsgata 1; dm/s/d with shared bathroom Nkr200/410/620) In a building originally built as a club for occupying German officers, it's set on a hill amid a grassy neighbourhood of beautiful homes. Sleep either privately or in a dark, 12-person bunkroom.

Trondheim Hostel (☎ 738 74 450; www.trondheim-vandrerhjem.no; Weidemannsvei 41; dm/s/d from Nkr230/490/620; P) On a hillside 2km east of the train station, this hostel's underwhelming rooms could use renovation. Internet costs Nkr2 per minute.

Åse Andersen (☎ 735 11 540; Nedre Møllenberg Gate 27; s/d Nkr350/500; mid-Jun–Aug) Wood-panelled rooms and comfortable furniture fill this cheerful ochre-coloured house on a quiet residential street. Linen costs Nkr50. Shared bathroom.

Eating & Drinking

There's a **Rema 1000** (Torvet) and the **Ravnkloa fish market.** For baguette sandwiches and pastries, try **Godt Brøt** (Thomas Angells Gate 16).

Uffa (www.uffa.no; Innherredsveien 69c; noon-4pm Tue-Thu & during events; food Nkr20) Long ago, the Sex Pistols played in this centre for activists. Uffa still organises six to eight punk shows per month in a squat white house with interiors covered in graffiti. It also hosts many informal political meetings and operates a mostly vegan cafe. Find it east on E6 opposite a green-steepled church.

Lyche (☎ 738 99 500; Elgesetergate 1; dinner Nkr45; from 5pm Sun-Fri, from 3pm Sat) Volunteers prepare a filling daily meal. It's one of many enterprises inside the Studentersamfundet.

Mormor's Stue (☎ 735 22 022; Nedre Enkeltskillingsveita 2; mains Nkr75-99; 10am-11.30 Mon-Sat, 1-11.30pm Sun) Eat sandwiches and pasta in a cosy house full of lace, parlours and dusty pictures of grandma. On Sundays a calorifically evil cake and coffee buffet (Nkr54) fills every seat, as does an evening beer special (from 5pm pay Nkr35).

Ramp (Strandveien at Gregus gate; dishes Nkr80-140) This neighbourhood cafe serves 'ecological' fair (meaning organic and/or vegetarian). Well furnished with vintage furniture, the bohemian joint often books experimental bands. Follow E6 east. Pass the Scandic Hotel and pick up Strandveien on the left side of the rotary.

Vertshuset Tavern (☎ 738 78 070; Sverresborg Allé 11; mains Nkr100-320) Dating from 1739 and blessed with enormous fireplaces, the menu features traditional, superbly prepared items such as roast elk and herring with beets. For atmosphere on a budget, eat pancakes with jam and bacon.

Baklandet Skydsstation's (☎ 739 21 044; Øvre Baklandet 33; dishes Nkr110-200) Set on a charming street, this cafe's wood-burning stove and fish soup keep people warm in the winter.

Den Gode Nabo (☎ 738 74 240; Øvre Bakklandet; pub fare Nkr59-130) This bar occupies the lower level of an ancient warehouse. Admire several centuries of patchwork carpentry.

Trondheim Mikrobryggeri (☎ 735 17 515; Prinsens gate 39) Enjoy brews by the glass or pitcher amid pleasant brick walls and varnished wooden surfaces. It's bright enough inside to read a book.

Studentersamfundet (☎ 738 99 500; Elgeseter-gate 1; from 5pm) The ideal student centre features a maze of bars and an excellent calendar of film screenings, DJs and bands – during the school year.

Getting There & Away

The airport is in Værnes, 32km east of Trondheim. Airport buses cost Nkr80.

Trains go to Oslo (Nkr837, 6½ to 7½ hours, two to six daily), Bodø (Nkr924, 10 hours, two daily) and Røros (Nkr228, 2½ hours, three daily). If you're in a hurry to get north, consider taking the overnight train from Oslo, tossing your gear into a locker and spending the day exploring Trondheim before continuing on an overnight train to Bodø.

Nor-Way Bussekspress services run to and from Ålesund (Nkr500, 7 hours, one to two daily), Bergen (Nkr783, 14½ hours, one daily), Oslo (Nkr495, nine hours, one to two daily) and Røros (Nkr232, three hours, two to four daily).

The *Hurtigruten* docks in Trondheim.

BODØ

pop 46,000

In addition to being the terminus for the northern railway line, Bodø is Nordland's largest town and is mostly visited as a jumping-off point for Lofoten. Because the town was flattened during WWII air raids and completely rebuilt in the 1950s, Bodø is really quite ordinary in appearance – but it does have a lovely mountain backdrop.

The **tourist office** (☎ 755 48 000; www.visitbodo.com; Sjøgata 3; ⌚ 9am-8pm Mon-Fri, 10am-6pm Sat, noon-8pm Sun Jun-Aug, shorter hr Sep-May) is near the waterfront.

Three kilometres from town via bus 12, waterside **Bodøsjøen Camping** (☎ 755 63 680; Kvernhusveien; camp sites from Nkr130; cabins Nkr250-500) offers a grassy field for tenters. The grounds have worthwhile cabins, modern amenities and fine views over sea and mountain.

A 2nd floor cafeteria above a fishers' outfitter, **Løvold's** (☎ 755 20 261; Tollbugata 9; dishes Nkr40-120) bustles at lunch time, offering daily specials of traditional Norwegian grub to a crowd of sea dogs and old-timers.

Kafé Kafka (☎ 755 23 550; Sandgata 5B; food Nkr92-140) serves marinated vegetable sandwiches and light fare to people reading on upholstered couches. Bands play some weekends.

Bodø is the northern terminus of the Norwegian train network, with a service to Trondheim (Nkr924, 10 hours, twice daily).

The *Hurtigruten* travels to/from Lofoten. Car ferries and express boats also travel to Lofoten. See the tourist office for schedules.

LOFOTEN

These spectacular glacier-carved mountains soar straight out of the sea. From a distance they appear as an unbroken line known as the Lofoten Wall. Up close, their dramatically scenic fishing villages prove excellent bases from which to climb, cycle and fish. Fishing is particularly good in winter when the warming Gulf Stream draws spawning Arctic cod from the Barents Sea, followed by migrating farmer-fisherman.

The four main islands are all linked by bridge or tunnel. See www.lofoten-info.no for bus and ferry schedules.

Svolvær

pop 4500

A compact town of old wooden buildings and modern concrete blocks, the principle seat of Lofoten might be two notches less picturesque than its brothers, but it's still a pretty spot from which to base your explorations. **Destination Lofoten** (☎ 760 69 800; www.lofoten.info; Torget; ⌚ 9am-9.30pm Mon-Fri, 9am-8pm Sat, 10am-9.30pm Sun mid-Jun–mid-Aug, shorter hr rest of year) can tell you about the incredible bird islands of Værøy and Røst and fishing excursions.

Daredevil mountaineers like to scale **Svolværgeita** (Svolvær Goat), a distinctive, two-pronged peak visible from the harbour, and jump from one horn to the other. A graveyard at the bottom awaits those who miss. There's also a rough route from the Goat over to the extraordinary **Devil's Gate**. Or ride a boat (Nkr350) into the **Trollfjord**, so spectacularly steep and narrow that you might experience the kind of terror and awe associated with the Romantic Sublime.

On stilts sticking and projecting over the water, the 100-year-old **Svolvær Sjøhuscamping** (☎ 760 70 336; www.svolver-sjohuscamp.no; Parkgata 12; r Nkr440-490) has small rooms with bunks and pleasant views. Guests share bathrooms and a kitchen. You'll also find bakeries and a handful of pubs and restaurants.

Buses run to Å (Nkr215, 3½ hours, two to four daily). Express buses runs to/from Narvik (Nkr433, 4½ hours, two daily).

OVDS's boats run to/from Bodø (adult Nkr297, 3½ hours, one daily) and the *Hurtigruten* stops here.

Kabelvåg

If you got off the boat and thought Svolvær's blend of traditional and modern wasn't cute enough, this pleasing village lies only 5km west and is connected by the E10 and a paved walking trail. Narrow channels lined with old warehouses lead to the circular cobbled torget, whose pattern of paving recalls the hulls of small fishing boats themselves docked nearby. **Præstenbrygga** (☎ 760 78 060; Torget; mains Nkr75-140), a cosy pub, serves pizza (toppings include cod and smoked whale), and has live music.

Stamsund

pop 1000

The quiet fishing hamlet of Stamsund makes a fine destination largely because of its dockside hostel, **Justad HI Hostel/Rorbuer** (☎ 760 89 334; fax 760 89 739; dm/s/d Nkr125/300/400, cabins Nkr600-800; mid-Dec–mid-Oct). It attracts many repeat customers drawn by the old beach house, friendly manager (ask about hiking routes) and free loans of fishing gear and rowing boats.

The *Hurtigruten* stops en route between Bodø (Nkr261, 4½ hours) and Svolvær (Nkr132, 1½ hours). In July and August, buses run to/from Leknes (Nkr30, 25 minutes, up to eight times daily) where you can make connections.

Å

A preserved fishing village, Å's shoreline is lined with red-painted *rorbu* (fishing cabins), many sticking out into the sea, perched on forbidding rocks connected by wooden footbridges. Racks of drying cod are placed nearly everywhere and picture-postcard scenes of haunting beauty occur at every turn.

The **Tørrefiskmuseum** (Stockfish Museum ☎ 911 50 560; adult/student Nkr40/25; 10am-5pm mid-Jun–mid-Aug, 11am-5pm Mon-Fri early Jun & late Aug), inside a 1920s cod plant, details the history of the stockfish industry. Many of Å's 19th-century buildings are set aside as the **Norwegian Fishing Village Museum** (☎ 760 91 488; admission Nkr50; 10am-5pm late Jun-late Aug, 11am-3pm Mon-Fri Sep–mid-Jun), complete with old boats and boat houses, a bakery from 1844 and Europe's oldest cod-liver oil factory.

Moskenesstraumen Camping (☎ 760 91 344; camping for 1/2/3 persons Nkr90/110/130, cabins Nkr400-700) sits near a cliff with good views of Værøy island, which lies on the other side of **Moskenesstraumen**, the swirling maelstrom that inspired the fictional tales of Jules Verne and Edgar Allen Poe.

Å-Hamna Rorbuer (☎ 760 91 211; www.lofotenferie.com dm/d Nkr110/450, rorbuer Nkr650-1000;) has pleasant dorms in a restored 1860s home and cosy *rorbu,* usually with magnificent views, containing four to eight beds each. Off-season you can get the best *rorbuer* for around Nkr450, firewood included.

You can buy fresh fish from local fishers, visit a small **food shop**, and drink beer in **Brygga Restaurant.**

Up to three daily buses run to Leknes (Nkr107, 1¾ hours), Svolvær (Nkr200, 3¼ hours) and Sortland (Nkr312 plus Nkr30 for a ferry, 5¼ hours).

OVDS runs car ferries from Bodøto Moskenes (Nkr561/155 for car and driver/passenger, 3¼ hours, five to six daily), 5km north of Å.

TROMSØ

pop 52,000

Tromsø, at latitude 69°40'N, is the world's northernmost university town. In contrast to some of the more sober communities dotting the north coast of Norway, it's a spirited place with street music, cultural happenings and more pubs per capita than any other Norwegian town. A backdrop of snow-topped peaks provides spectacular scenery, excellent hiking in summer and great skiing and dogsledding December to April. The **tourist office** (☎ 776 10 000; www.destinasjontromso.no; Kirkegata 2; 9am-4pm Mon-Fri, 10am-4pm Sat) can help.

Take a midnight sun stroll through the 1.6-hectare **botanical garden** (Breivika; bus 20; admission free; 24hr), which blooms brightly despite its northern locale. Visit the creepy wax figures beating seals in the **Polar Museum** (☎ 776 84 373; Søndre Tollbugata 11; adult/student/child Nkr50/45/10; 10am-7pm mid-Jun–mid-Aug, shorter hr rest of year) or tour **Mack Brewery** (☎ 776 24 500; Storgata 5; tours Nkr130; 9am-5pm Mon-Wed, 9am-6pm Fri, 9am-3pm Sat), established in 1877, at 1pm from Monday to Thursday.

Sleeping

Tromsø Camping (☎ 776 38 037; www.tromsocamping.no; camp sites Nkr150, cabins Nkr450-1000; P) Grounds are so overcrowded with cabins that you might have trouble breathing. It's on the mainland, 2km away.

Tromsø HI Hostel (☎ 776 57 628; www.hihostels.no; Åsgårdveien 9; dm/s/d Nkr170/300/400; mid-Jun–mid-Aug) A university student house the rest of the year, this short concrete tower contains rooms with bunk beds. It's 1.5km west of the city centre.

Ami Hotel (☎ 776 82 208; www.amihotel.no; Skolegata 24; s/d Nkr550/650, s/d with shared bathroom Nkr450/590; 💻) Ami's plain rooms vary in quality: some are bright and cheery, others worn and drab, with bathrooms that look like utility closets.

Eating & Drinking

Aunegården (☎ 776 51 234; Sjøgata 29; cake Nkr65, dishes Nkr115-155; 🕑 to midnight) Serving amazing cakes (try chocolate truffle with meringue and syrupy hazelnut crust), this cafe operates out of a former general store dating from 1830. Good salads.

Driv (☎ 776 00 776; Tollbugata 3; dishes Nkr75-125) This student culture house occupies an old warehouse and serves pizza, burgers and beer. It books bands and sometimes operates a disco. There's a harbourside hot tub in winter.

Le Mirage (☎ 776 85 234; Storgata 42; mains Nrk85-165) Sit in brown overstuffed faux-leather chairs in this trendy cafe/bar long favoured by Tromsø's fashionably dressed. Not loud, it's a good place for conversation. Supports more drinking than eating.

Blå Rock Café (☎ 776 10 020; Strandgata 14) Live bands and DJs (playing rock, naturally) cause hearing damage in a black-coloured club with Elvis pinball and 50 kinds of beer spilling on the floor. Good burgers.

Skarven (☎ 776 00 720; Strandtorget 1; 🕑 Tue-Sat) This well-dressed pub offers an ample wooden room with extensive terrace seating right on the water. Superior bar food is served.

Verdensteateret (☎ 777 53 090; Storgata 93b) This small, stylish cafe occupies part of a lovely art-nouveau cinema from 1915. The bar vends wine, beer and light snacks. Small bands and DJs perform most weeks.

Getting There & Away

Tromsø is the main airport for northern Norway. Airport buses (Nkr55) depart from the Radisson SAS Hotel.

Express buses run to Alta (Nkr484, 6½ hours, one daily), and to Narvik (Nkr370, 4¼ hours, three daily), some of them timed to continue to Bodø and Svolvær.

The *Hurtigruten* stops here.

NORDKAPP

Nordkapp (North Cape), a high rugged coastal plateau at latitude 71°10′21"N, claims to be the northernmost point in Europe and is the main destination for most visitors to the far north. The sun never drops below the horizon from mid-May to the end of July. To many visitors, Nordkapp, with its steep cliffs and stark scenery, emanates a certain spiritual aura. Long before other Europeans took an interest in the area, Nordkapp was considered a power centre by the Sami people.

Nowadays, there's a rip-off Nkr195 entrance fee and a touristy complex. If you want to really appreciate Nordkapp, take a walk out along the cliffs.

The continent's real northernmost point, **Knivskjelodden** (latitude 71°11'08"N) can't be reached by vehicles, but you can hike 18km return (five hours) to this promontory from a car park, 9km south of Nordkapp.

Depending on snow conditions, the toll road to Nordkapp is usually open from May to mid-October; the **Road User Information Centre** (☎ 177) gives opening dates.

The closest town of any size is **Honningsvåg**, 35km from Nordkapp with a population of 3500. Here you'll find a **tourist office** (☎ 784 77 030; www.nordkapp.no; Fiskeriveien 4B; 🕑 8.30am-8pm Mon-Fri, noon-8am Sat & Sun mid-Jun–mid-Aug, 8.30am-4pm Mon-Fri rest of year), the cheery hostel **Northcape Guesthouse** (☎ 47 25 50 63; www.northcapeguesthouse.com; Elvebakken 5a; dm/s/d Nkr250/300/600) and, unbelievably, a **microbrewery**.

From June to August, local buses run at least twice daily between Honningsvåg (a stop for the Hurtigruten) and Nordkapp (Nkr90, 45 minutes).

NORWAY DIRECTORY

ACCOMMODATION

During summer, it's wise to reserve all accommodation, particularly at hostels.

Camping & Cabins

Tent space costs from Nkr80 at the most basic sites to Nkr255 in Oslo. Many camping grounds rent simple cabins from about Nkr300 a day, usually with cooking facilities. Bedding is rarely provided.

Norway has an *allemannsretten* (Right of Common Access) dating back 1000 years. This lets you pitch a tent anywhere in the wilderness for two nights, at least 150m from the nearest house or cottage and leave no trace of your stay. From 15 April to 15

September, lighting a fire in the proximity of woodlands is forbidden.

DNT (p867) maintains an extensive network of staffed and unstaffed huts, a day's hike apart, in much of Norway's mountain country. At unstaffed huts (dm members/nonmembers Nkr165/265), keys must be picked up in advance at DNT offices in nearby towns (deposit Nkr150); at staffed huts hikers simply show up – no-one is turned away, even if there's only floor-space left. At staffed huts, nightly fees for members/nonmembers in a room with one to three beds are Nkr205/270; rooms with four to six beds Nkr165/235; dormitories Nkr105/170. Breakfast (members/nonmembers Nkr85/110), sandwiches (Nkr10/15), dinner (Nkr125/145) and snacks are served, though members might do better by ordering a full-board option with their room. Basic membership for one calendar year costs Nkr465/265 adult/student.

Hostels

Norway has 53 *vandrerhjem* (hostels) affiliated with Hostelling International (HI) and several dozen that are not. Many operate in summer only. Most hostels have private rooms at higher prices. Bring your own sleeping sheet and pillowcase, or hire linen for around Nkr50. Nearly all hostels have kitchens for guests and provide breakfast. The Norwegian hostelling association is **Norske Vandrerhjem** (☎ 231 24 310; www.hihostels.no).

Hotels

Although normal hotel prices are high, many substantially reduce their rates in the summer and on Friday and Saturday. Many chains offer passes which give discounts, such as **Choice Club** (www.choicehotels.no) and **Fjord Pass** (www.fjordpass.no).

Pensions & Private Rooms

Private rooms, usually bookable through tourist offices, average Nkr350/500 for singles/doubles. Breakfast isn't normally included. Along highways, you may see *Rom* signs, indicating informal accommodation for around Nkr350 (without breakfast).

ACTIVITIES

Fishing

No licence is required for saltwater fishing. In freshwater, a national licence (available from post offices for Nkr225) is mandatory and often a local licence (available from tourist offices, hotels and camping grounds for Nkr60 to Nkr375 per day) is required.

Hiking

Norway has unsurpassable hiking, ranging from easy trails in the forests around the cities to long treks through the mountains. Due to deep winter snows, hiking in many areas is seasonal; in the highlands, it's often limited to the period of late June to September. Popular wilderness hiking areas are Jotunheimen, Rondane and Hardangervidda, but stunning walks are everywhere. For more information contact **DNT** (p867) .

Skiing

Norway has thousands of kilometres of maintained cross-country ski trails and scores of resorts with excellent downhill runs. The Geilo, Finse, Narvik, Lillehammer and Holmenkollen area near Oslo are some of the more popular spots.

BUSINESS HOURS

Shops open 10am to 5pm weekdays, 10am to 2pm on Saturday; post offices 9am to 5pm weekdays, 10am to 2pm on Saturdays; banks 8.15am to 3pm weekdays; supermarkets 9am to 9pm weekdays, 9am to 6pm on Saturday; and restaurants 8am to 11am, noon to 3pm and 6pm to 11pm.

Many museums have short hours (11am to 3pm is common). On Sunday most stores – including bakeries and supermarkets, and some restaurants – are closed.

CLIMATE

The typically rainy climate of mainland Norway is surprisingly mild for its latitude – thanks to the Gulf Stream, all coastal ports remain ice free throughout the year.

Average July temperatures are 16°C in the Oslo area and 11°C in the north. In January, the average maximum temperature is 1°C in the south and -3°C in the north. However, it can get much colder, especially in areas away from the coast.

EMBASSIES & CONSULATES

Australia The nearest Australian embassy is in Copenhagen; contact the British embassy in an emergency.

Canada (Map pp870-1; ☎ 229 95 300; www.canada.no; Wergelandsveien 7, 0244 Oslo)

Denmark (Map p867; ☎ 225 40 800; www.amboslo.um.dk; Olav Kyrres gate 7, 0244 Oslo)
Finland (Map p867; ☎ 221 24 900; www.finland.no Thomas Heftyes gate 1, 0244 Oslo)
France (Map p867; ☎ 232 84 600; www.ambafrance-no.org; Drammensveien 69, 0244 Oslo)
Germany (Map pp870-1; ☎ 232 75 400; www.oslo.diplo.de; Oscars gate 45, 0244 Oslo)
Ireland (Map pp870-1; ☎ 220 17 200; osloembassy@dfa.ie; Haakon VII's gate 1, 0212 Oslo)
Netherlands (Map pp870-1; ☎ 233 33 600; www.netherlands-embassy.no; Oscars gate 29, 0244 Oslo)
New Zealand The British embassy handles consular affairs; the nearest New Zealand embassy is in The Hague.
Russia (Map p867; ☎ 225 53 278; www.norway.mid.ru; Drammensveien 74, 0244 Oslo)
Sweden (Map p867; ☎ 241 14 200; www.swedenabroad.com; Nobels gate 16, 0244 Oslo)
UK (Map p867; ☎ 231 32 700; www.britishembassy.gov.uk; Thomas Heftyes gate 8, 0244 Oslo)
USA (Map pp870-1; ☎ 224 48 550; www.usa.no; Henrik Isbens gate 48, 0255 Oslo)

FESTIVALS & EVENTS

Norway is chock-a-block with special festivals, which take place in every city, town and village. Most of these occur during the summer. For information about the country's biggest festivals, check out www.norwayfestivals.com.

HOLIDAYS

Constitution Day, 17 May, is Norway's biggest holiday, with many Norwegians dressing in traditional folk costumes. The biggest celebration is in Oslo – marching bands and thousands of schoolchildren parade to Det Kongelige Slott to be greeted by the royal family.

Norway practically shuts down during Christmas and Easter weeks, when you'll be fortunate to find an open bar or grocery store.

New Year's Day 1 January
Maundy Thursday Thursday before Easter
Good Friday March/April
Easter Monday March/April
Labour Day 1 May
Constitution Day 17 May
Ascension Day The 40th day after Easter
Whit Monday The eighth Monday after Easter
Christmas Day 25 December
Boxing Day 26 December

INTERNET RESOURCES

www.fjordnorway.com All about the star attraction.
www.norwaypost.no News in English.
www.visitnorway.com Comprehensive tourist site.

LEGAL MATTERS

The legal drinking age is 18 years to drink beer and wine, 20 years for spirits. Penalties for possessing drugs and controlled substances are severe. The age of consent is 16 years. It is illegal to smoke in public spaces, including bars.

MONEY

The Norwegian krone is written NOK in international money markets, Nkr in northern Europe and kr within Norway. One krone equals 100 øre. Coins come in denominations of 50 øre and one, five, 10 and 20 kroner, and bills in denominations of 50, 100, 200, 500 and 1000 kroner.

ATMs are available in every town mentioned in this chapter.

All banks will exchange major foreign currencies and accept all travellers cheques, which command a better exchange rate than cash. You can also change money in hotels and at post offices, but the rate won't be as good.

Tipping is not required or expected.

POST

Cards and letters up to 20g cost Nkr7 within Norway, Nkr9 to elsewhere in Europe and Nkr11 to the rest of the world. Mail can be received poste restante at almost all post offices in Norway.

TELEPHONE

To make international calls from Norway, dial ☎ 00 than the country code and phone number. The country code for calling Norway from abroad is ☎ 47. Norway has no telephone area codes; domestic numbers consist of eight digits.

Most pay phones accept Nkr1, Nkr5, Nkr10 and Nkr20 coins, and will return unused coins but won't give change, so only insert the minimum amount (Nkr5 for all calls) to ensure a connection. Directory assistance (☎ 180) costs Nkr9 per minute. A peak-rate national call costs Nkr8, then Nkr0.65 per minute. It is more expensive to call a mobile phone than a landline. Using a hotel room's phone carries prohibitive charges.

Telekort (phone cards) are sold in Nkr40, Nkr90 ad Nkr140 denominations and work out cheaper than coins. Find them at post offices and 7-Eleven stores.

Mobile Phones

GSM mobile telephone networks cover over 90% of Norway's populated areas. There are two main service providers: **Telenor Mobil** (☎ 810 70 700; www.telenor.com) and **NetCom** (☎ 238 88 000; www.netcom.no in Norwegian).

Purchased SIM cards from any 7-Eleven and from some Narvesen Kiosks. As the connection instructions are entirely in Norwegian, you're better off purchasing the card from a Telehuset outlet, where they'll help you connect on the spot. Cards start at Nkr200, which includes Nkr100 worth of calls.

VISAS

Citizens of the USA, Canada, the UK, Ireland, Australia and New Zealand need valid passports to visit Norway, but do not need visas for stays of less than three months. The same is true for EU and European Economic Area (EEA – essentially EU and Scandinavia) countries, most of Latin America and most Commonwealth countries.

Poland

HIGHLIGHTS

- **Wawel Hill** Experience the beauty and history of Kraków's magnificent castle (p902)
- **Wrocław** Get into the bar, club and restaurant scene of this lively student city (p909)
- **Warsaw Rising Museum** Discover Warsaw's tragic wartime history (p898)
- **Off the beaten track** Enjoy the skiing or hiking life in the Tatra Mountains (p909)

FAST FACTS

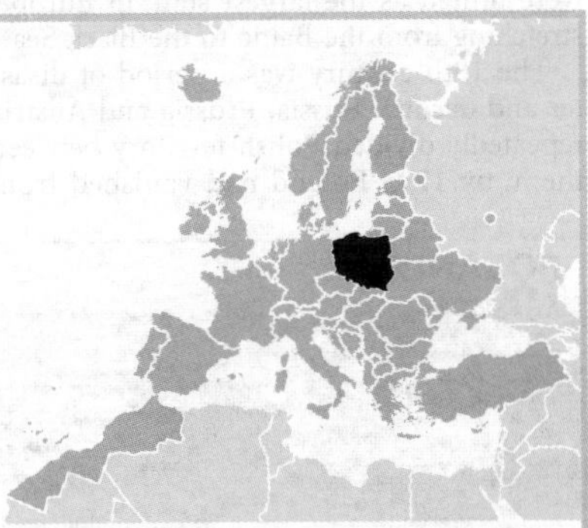

- **Area** 312,685 sq km
- **Budget** 150zł per day
- **Capital** Warsaw
- **Country code** ☎ 48
- **Famous for** Chopin, Copernicus, Marie Curie, solidarity, vodka
- **Language** Polish
- **Money** złoty (zł); A$1 = 2.48zł; C$1 = 2.81zl; €1 = 4.45zł; ¥100 = 3.49zł; NZ$1 = 1.94zł; UK£1 = 5.02zł; US$1 = 3.31zł
- **Phrases** *dzień dobry* (good day), *Ile to kosztuje?* (how much is it?), *dziękuję* (thank you)
- **Population** 38 million
- **Visas** no visa needed for citizens of the EU, Australia, New Zealand, the US and Canada; see p920

TRAVEL HINTS

Hotel weekend rates are often less expensive. It's also worth asking if a hotel has cheaper rooms than the posted rate.

ROAMING POLAND

From Warsaw, head to Kraków. Take a day trip to Zakopane, before continuing to Wrocław. Finish up at seaside Gdańsk.

If they were handing out prizes for 'most eventful history', Poland would be sure to get a gong. The nation has spent centuries at the pointy end of history, grappling with war, invasion and foreign occupation. Nothing, however, has succeeded in suppressing the Poles' strong sense of nationhood and cultural identity, as exemplified by the ancient royal capital of Kraków, with its breathtaking castle, and bustling Warsaw, with the painstaking postwar reconstruction of its devastated Old Town.

Other lively regional centres such as urbane Gdańsk, cultured Wrocław and bustling Poznań exude a sophisticated energy that's a heady mix of old and new. Away from the cities, Poland is a diverse land, from its northern sandy beaches to its magnificent southern mountains.

Although prices are rising as its economy gathers strength, Poland is still good value for travellers and has a transport system that makes it easy to get around. As the Polish people work on combining their distinctive national identity with their place in the heart of Europe, it's a fascinating time to visit this beautiful country.

HISTORY

Poland's history started in the early Middle Ages with the Polanians (People of the Plains). Mieszko I, Duke of the Polanians, adopted Christianity in 966 and embarked on a successful campaign of conquest.

Encroachment from Germanic peoples led to the relocation of the royal capital from Poznań to Kraków in 1038. The kingdom prospered under Kazimierz III 'the Great' (1333–70), and in 1569 Poland and Lithuania were united as the largest state in Europe, stretching from the Baltic to the Black Sea.

The 18th century was a period of disaster and decline. Russia, Prussia and Austria repeatedly divided Polish territory between them; by 1795 Poland had vanished from the map of Europe. Finally, upon the end of WWI the old imperial powers dissolved, and a sovereign Polish state was restored.

On 1 September 1939, a Nazi blitzkrieg rained down from the west; soon after, the Soviets invaded Poland from the east. The Germans then used Poland as a base for invading the Soviet Union. By the time the Nazi regime was finally ousted at the end of WWII, 6 million Poles had died, including the country's 3 million Jews, who were brutally annihilated in death camps.

After WWII, Poland endured four decades of Soviet-dominated communist rule. Finally, in 1990 Solidarity leader Lech Wałęsa became Poland's first postwar democratically elected president.

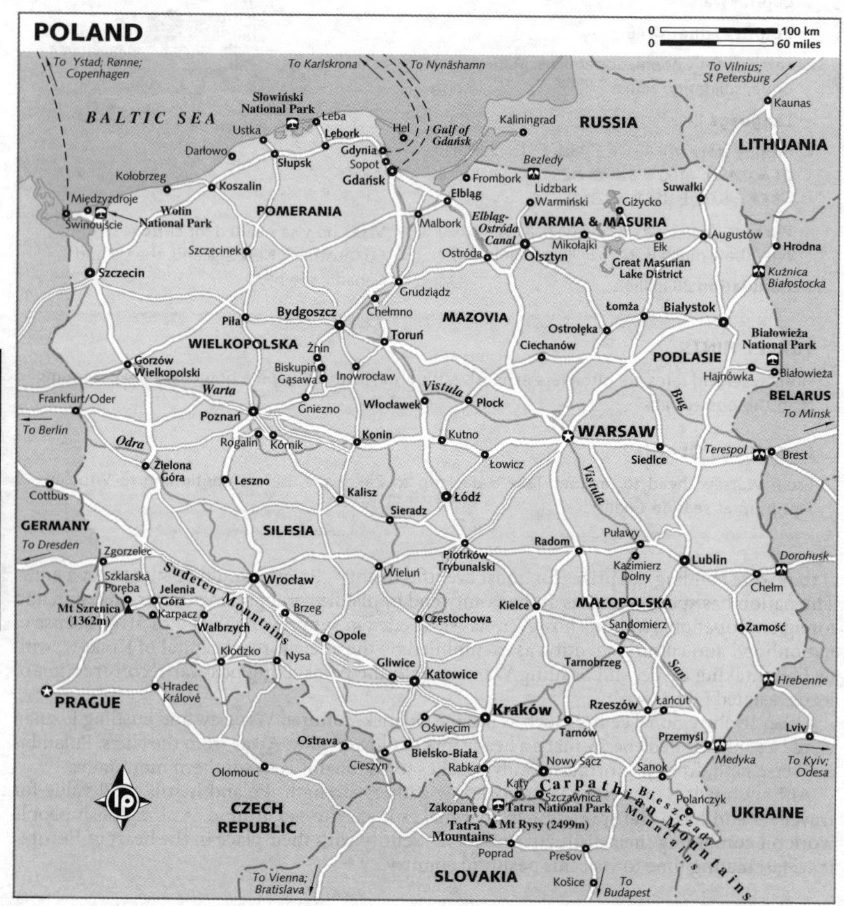

The postcommunist transition brought radical changes, but within a decade Poland had rebuilt the foundations of a market economy. Poland joined the EU in May 2004.

In the 2007 parliamentary elections, Poles decisively rejected the eccentric Eurosceptic policies of the government headed by identical twin Kaczyński brothers, president Lech and prime minister Jarosław. The new Civic Platform government of prime minister Donald Tusk is steering a probusiness, pro-EU course.

THE CULTURE

Due to Nazi genocide and the forced resettlements that followed WWII, Poland became an ethnically homogeneous country. Some 98% of the population are ethnic Poles.

Poles are friendly and polite, but not overly formal. The way of life in large urban centres increasingly resembles Western styles and manners. In the countryside, however, a more conservative culture dominates, with traditional gender roles, and strong religious convictions and family ties.

When greeting, Polish men are passionate about shaking hands. Polish women, too, often shake hands with men, but the man should always wait for the woman to extend her hand first.

Outside the big towns, knowledge of foreign languages is limited. To polish your Polish, see p1274.

ARTS

Poland has inherited a rich literary tradition dating from the 15th century, though its modern voice was shaped during the long period of foreign occupation in the 19th century.

At the turn of the 20th century, the avant-garde 'Young Poland' movement in art and literature developed in Kraków. Among its most notable representatives were the writer Stanisław Wyspiański (1869–1907).

The most famous Polish musician was undoubtedly Frédéric Chopin (1810–49), whose music displays the melancholy and nostalgia that became hallmarks of the national style. Present-day Polish musicians you might catch live in concert include the controversial Doda (pop singer), Feel (pop-rock band), Łzy (pop-rock band), Indios Bravos (reggae band) and Kasia Cerekwicka (pop singer).

Poland's most renowned painter was Jan Matejko (1838–93), whose monumental historical paintings hang in galleries throughout the country.

Poland has produced several world-famous film directors including Roman Polański, who directed hits such as *Rosemary's Baby* and *Chinatown*, and Krzysztof Kieślowski, best known for the *Three Colours* trilogy.

READING UP

God's Playground: A History of Poland, by Norman Davies, offers an in-depth analysis of Polish history, and his *Rising '44* vividly covers the wartime Warsaw Rising. Also check out Timothy Garton Ash's *The Polish Revolution: Solidarity 1980–82*. *Jews in Poland,* by Iwo Cyprian Pogonowski, is a comprehensive work. Also of interest is Alan Furst's spy thriller *The Polish Officer*.

ENVIRONMENT

Though Poles have become more environmentally conscious since the communist days, there's still some distance to travel. You can help by using recycling bins wherever possible (currently only found in the centres of some larger cities), and by minimising the amount of packaging you use. Polish supermarket staff are quick to whip out a flimsy plastic bag the moment you step up to the checkout; treat it as a personal challenge to have your own reusable bag ready before they can do so.

TRANSPORT

GETTING THERE & AWAY

Air

The majority of international flights to Poland arrive at Warsaw's Okęcie airport, while other well-serviced airports include Kraków and Gdańsk. International flights also reach other destinations including Poznań, Wrocław, Łódź, Bydgoszcz and Szczecin.

The national carrier **LOT** (☎ 801 703 703, from mobile 22 9572; www.lot.com) flies to major European cities, and to some North American cities during the summer months. Another Polish airline, **Jet Air** (☎ 22 846 8661; www.jetair.pl) connects Berlin, Copenhagen and Vienna with regional Polish airports.

A vast array of budget carriers fly into Poland from airports across Europe, including a range of regional airports in Britain and Ireland. There are budget flights to all of the Polish airports mentioned above. For more information on low-cost airlines, see p1235.

Boat

Any travel agency in Scandinavia will sell tickets for the following services. In Warsaw, inquire at **Orbis Travel** (☎ 22 827 7265; ul Bracka 16) or its branches in other cities.

Polferries (www.polferries.pl) Runs every second day between Gdańsk and Nynäshamn (18 hours) in Sweden. Also operates from Świnoujście to Ystad (eight hours, daily) in Sweden; Rønne (5¼ hours, Saturday) in Denmark; and Copenhagen (nine to 10½ hours, five weekly).

Stena Line (www.stenaline.com) Between Gdynia and Karlskrona (10½ hours) in Sweden.

Unity Line (www.unityline.pl) From Świnoujście to Ystad (6¾ hours).

Bus

International bus services are cheaper than trains, but not as comfortable or fast.

The Polish national bus company **PKS** (☎ 22 652 2321; www.pekaesbus.com.pl) runs dozens of buses each week from Warsaw to major cities in Germany.

From Warsaw, **Eurolines** (☎ 32 351 2020; www.eurolinespolska.pl) operates regular buses to and from Cologne (20¾ hours, one daily), London (29 hours, three weekly), Paris (29 hours, one daily), Rome (28 hours, three weekly) and Vienna (12 hours, five weekly).

Eurolines also has three weekly services (more in summer) from Olsztyn to Paris, via Gdańsk (38 hours); and three weekly from Lublin to Paris, via Kraków, Wrocław and Częstochowa (39 hours).

Eurolines also runs links to eastern cities such as Minsk, Brest, Vilnius, Tallinn and Riga. Check the website for times and prices.

BORDER CROSSINGS

Since Poland joined the Schengen zone in late 2007, there have been no border posts or border crossing formalities between Poland and fellow EU members Germany, the Czech Republic, Slovakia and Lithuania.

Belarus Terespol and Kuźnica Białostocka

Russia Gronowo and Bezledy

Ukraine Medyka, Hrebenne and Dorohusk

From Przemyśl, regular buses run to Lviv (95km) in Ukraine.

Car & Motorcycle

To drive a car into Poland, EU citizens need their driving licence, while other nationalities must obtain an International Driving Permit in their home country. Vehicle registration papers and liability insurance are also required.

Train

Domestic trains in Poland are significantly cheaper than international services, so you'll save money if you buy a ticket to a Polish border destination, then take a local train.

Note that some international trains to/from Poland have become notorious for theft. Keep a grip on your bags, particularly on the Berlin–Warsaw, Prague–Warsaw and Prague–Kraków overnight trains, and on any train travelling to/from Gdańsk. If possible, sleep in a compartment with others.

Several trains serve the Warsaw–Berlin route every day (via Frankfurt/Oder and Poznań), including EuroCity express services (six hours, three daily). It's easy to transfer to other German destinations once in Berlin, though there's also a direct service between Warsaw and Cologne. Other useful trains run between Kraków and Berlin, via Wrocław; and between Gdańsk and Berlin, via Poznań.

Trains to/from Prague serve Warsaw (nine to 10 hours, two daily) and Kraków (8½ hours, one daily). To/from Vienna, trains connect with Warsaw (eight to nine hours, three daily) and Kraków (seven to eight hours, two daily).

Trains travel between Budapest and Warsaw (12 hours, two daily): one travels via Bratislava, the other via Kraków and Košice in eastern Slovakia.

Warsaw has direct train links with Kyiv (Ukraine), Minsk (Belarus) and Moscow. There are also trains running between Gdańsk and Kaliningrad (five hours, one daily) in Russia.

Trains run twice daily from Kraków via Przemyśl to Lviv in Ukraine (6½ to 9½ hours).

If you're heading to Russia and your train passes through Belarus, be aware that you need a Belarusian transit visa and you must obtain it in advance; see p111 for details.

CONNECTIONS

Due to its central position, Poland offers plenty of possibilities for onward travel. The country is well connected by train (opposite) to neighbouring nations. International buses head in all directions (opposite), including eastward to the Baltic States, Belarus and Ukraine. From southern Zakopane, it's easy to hop to Slovakia via bus or even minibus. And from the Baltic coast ports of Gdańsk and Świnoujście, ferries head to various ports in Denmark and Sweden (opposite).

GETTING AROUND

Bus

Buses can be useful on short routes and through the southern mountains, but usually trains are quicker and more comfortable, and private minibuses are quicker and more direct.

Most buses are operated by the state bus company PKS, which provides two kinds of service from its bus terminals *(dworzec autobusowy PKS)*: ordinary buses (marked in black on timetables) and fast buses (marked in red), which ignore minor stops.

Tickets for buses are usually bought at the terminal, but sometimes can be purchased from drivers.

Car & Motorcycle

Major international car rental companies such as **Avis** (www.avis.pl), **Hertz** (www.hertz.pl) and **Europcar** (www.europcar.com.pl) have offices in larger cities and at airports. Prices are comparable to rental in Western Europe.

Car theft is a problem in Poland, so consider paying for guarded parking.

Train

Trains will be your main means of transport, especially for long distances. They are cheap, reliable and rarely overcrowded.

InterCity trains operate on major routes out of Warsaw, including Gdańsk, Kraków, Wrocław and Poznań. They only stop at major cities and are the fastest way to travel.

Express trains *(pociąg ekspresowy)* are also quick, as are the similar but cheaper TLK trains *(pociąg TLK)*. Fast trains *(pociąg pospieszny)* are a bit slower and cheaper still, and are the most common type of train between cities. Slow passenger trains *(pociąg osobowy)* should only be used for short trips.

Most trains offer two classes: 2nd *(druga klasa)* and 1st *(pierwsza klasa)*, which is 50% more expensive.

WARSAW (WARSZAWA)

pop 1.7 million

Warsaw (Warszawa in Polish, var-*shah*-va) may not be the prettiest of Poland's cities, but this bustling business centre is home to a dazzling array of dining and nightlife options.

It's true that the city can be hard work, its traffic-choked streets lined with uninspiring massive concrete buildings. However, look at Warsaw with a historic perspective – as a city that's survived everything fate could throw at it – and you'll see the capital in an entirely new light.

When you factor in its entertainment options, the beauty of its reconstructed Old Town and Royal Way, and the history represented by its former Jewish district and the Warsaw Rising Museum, what emerges is a complex city that well repays a visit.

ORIENTATION

The area west of the Vistula River includes the city centre, including the historic Old Town. Almost all tourist attractions and facilities are located in this zone.

INFORMATION

Bookshops

American Bookstore (☎ 22 827 4852; ul Nowy Świat 61) Books, including guidebooks, and maps.

EMPiK Galeria Centrum (ul Marszałkowska 116/122); Royal Way (ul Nowy Świat 15/17) Foreign books, newspapers and magazines.

Internet Access

Expect to pay around 5zł per hour in Warsaw.

Casablanca (ul Krakowskie Przedmieście 4/6; 9am-1am Mon-Fri, 10am-2am Sat, to midnight Sun)

EMERGENCY NUMBERS

- Ambulance ☎ 999
- Fire ☎ 998
- Police ☎ 997 (☎ 112 from mobile phones)
- Roadside Assistance ☎ 981 or 022 9637

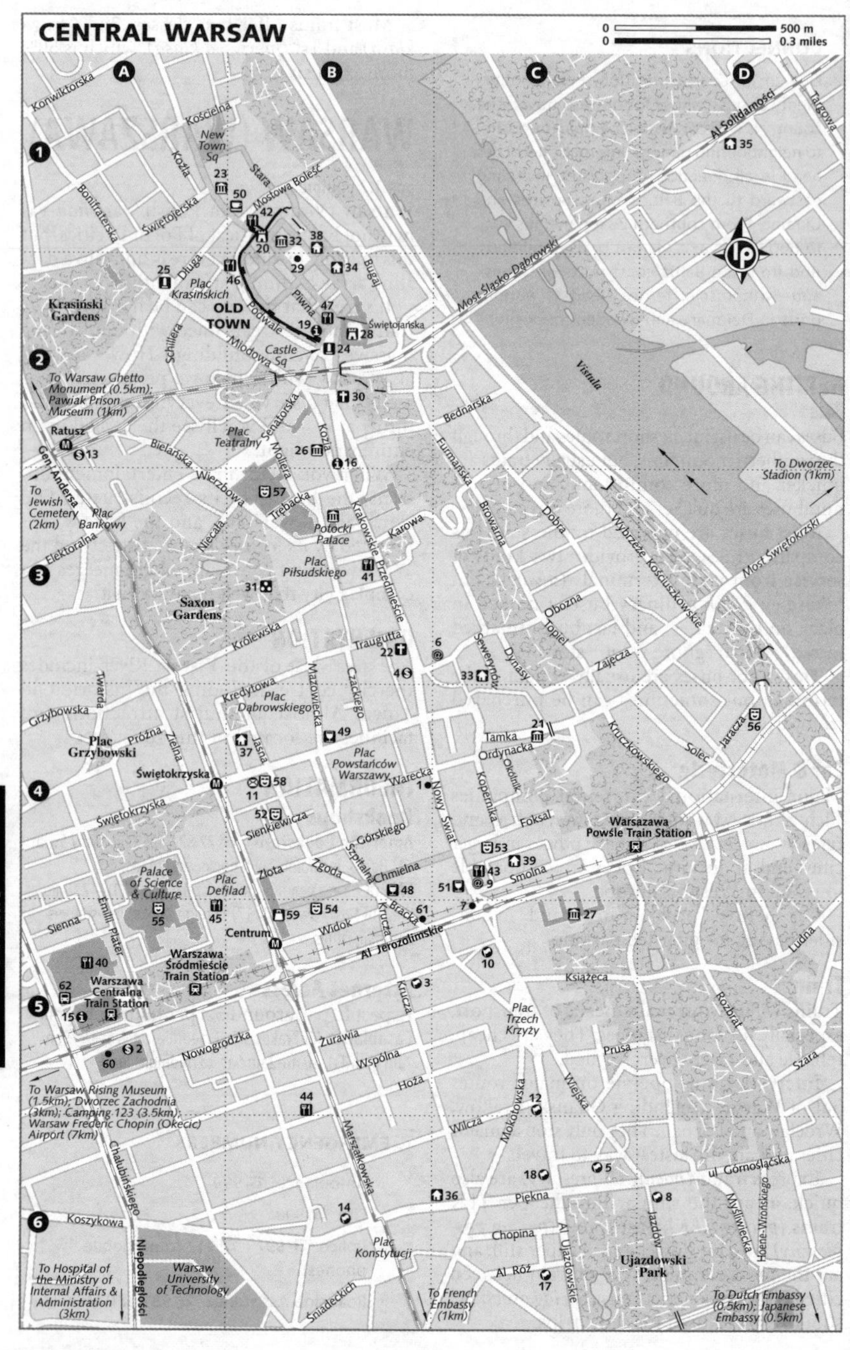
CENTRAL WARSAW
0 500 m
0 0.3 miles
New Town Sq
OLD TOWN
Plac Krasińskich
Krasiński Gardens
Castle Sq
To Warsaw Ghetto Monument (0.5km); Pawiak Prison Museum (1km)
Ratusz
Plac Teatralny
To Jewish Cemetery (2km)
Plac Bankowy
Potocki Palace
Plac Piłsudskiego
Saxon Gardens
Plac Dąbrowskiego
Plac Grzybowski
Świętokrzyska
Plac Powstańców Warszawy
Palace of Science & Culture
Plac Defilad
Centrum
Warszawa Śródmieście Train Station
Warszawa Centralna Train Station
Warsazawa Powśle Train Station
Plac Trzech Krzyży
To Warsaw Rising Museum (1.5km); Dworzec Zachodnia (3km); Camping 123 (3.5km); Warsaw Frederic Chopin (Okecic) Airport (7km)
Plac Konstytucji
Warsaw University of Technology
To Hospital of the Ministry of Internal Affairs & Administration (3km)
To French Embassy (1km)
Ujazdowski Park
To Dutch Embassy (0.5km); Japanese Embassy (0.5km)
To Dworzec Stadion (1km)
Vistula
Most Śląsko-Dąbrowski
Most Świętokrzyski
Al Solidarności
Wybrzeże Kościuszkowskie
Al Jerozolimskie
Krakowskie Przedmieście
Nowy Świat
Marszałkowska
Konwiktorska
Kościelna
Kozła
Bonifraterska
Świętojerska
Długa
Stara
Mostowa
Bolesć
Bugaj
Piwna
Podwale
Świętojańska
Miodowa
Schillera
Senatorska
Kozia
Moliera
Bielańska
Gen Andersa
Wierzbowa
Trębacka
Niecała
Elektoralna
Karowa
Bednarska
Furmańska
Browarna
Dobra
Królewska
Traugutta
Czackiego
Mazowiecka
Kredytowa
Sewerynów
Dynasy
Topiel
Obozna
Zajęcza
Twarda
Grzybowska
Próżna
Zielna
Jasna
Tamka
Ordynacka
Okólnik
Kopernika
Warecka
Kruczkowskiego
Solec
Jaracza
Sienkiewicza
Górskiego
Foksal
Smolna
Złota
Zgoda
Szpitalna
Chmielna
Bracka
Krucza
Widok
Sienna
Emilii Plater
Książęca
Ludna
Rozbrat
Żurawia
Nowogrodzka
Wspólna
Hoża
Prusa
Szara
Wiejska
Mokotowska
Wilcza
Chałubińskiego
ul Górnośląska
Myśliwiecka
Hoene-Wrońskiego
Piękna
Koszykowa
Niepodległości
Chopina
Al Róż
Al Ujazdowskie
Jazdów
Śniadeckich
Targowa
A
B
C
D
1
2
3
4
5
6
1
2
3
4
5
6
7
8
9
10
11
12
13
14
15
16
17
18
19
20
21
22
23
24
25
26
27
28
29
30
31
32
33
34
35
36
37
38
39
40
41
42
43
44
45
46
47
48
49
50
51
52
53
54
55
56
57
58
59
60
61
62

POLAND

INFORMATION
- American Bookstore 1 B4
- American Express 2 A5
- Apteka Grabowskiego .... (see 15)
- Australian Embassy 3 B5
- Bank Pekao 4 B3
- Canadian Embassy 5 C6
- Casablanca 6 C3
- EMPiK .... (see 59)
- EMPiK 7 C5
- German Embassy 8 D6
- Internet Café 9 C4
- Irish Embassy 10 C5
- Main Post Office 11 B4
- New Zealand Embassy 12 C5
- PKO Bank 13 A2
- South African Embassy 14 B6
- Tourist Office 15 A5
- Tourist Office 16 B2
- UK Embassy 17 C6
- US Embassy 18 C6
- Warsaw Tourist Information Centre 19 B2

SIGHTS & ACTIVITIES
- Barbican 20 B1
- Chopin Museum 21 C4
- Church of the Holy Cross 22 B3
- Maria Skłodowska-Curie Museum 23 A1
- Monument to Sigismund III Vasa 24 B2
- Monument to the Warsaw Rising 25 A2
- Museum of Caricature 26 B2
- National Museum 27 C5
- Royal Castle 28 B2
- Rynek Starego Miasta 29 B2
- St Anne's Church 30 B2
- Tomb of the Unknown Soldier 31 B3
- Warsaw Historical Museum 32 B1

SLEEPING
- Hostel Helvetia 33 C3
- Hostel Kanonia 34 B2
- Hotel Praski 35 D1
- Nathan's Villa Hostel 36 C6
- Oki Doki Hostel 37 B4
- Old Town Apartments 38 B1
- Smolna Youth Hostel 39 C4

EATING
- Albert Supermarket 40 A5
- Bar Bistro Bez Kantów 41 B3
- Bar Pod Barbakanem 42 B1
- Cô Tú 43 C4
- Green Way 44 B5
- MarcPol Supermarket 45 A5
- Podwale Piwna Kompania 46 B2
- Restauracja Przy Zamku 47 B2

DRINKING
- Między Nami 48 B4
- Paparazzi 49 B4
- Pożegnanie Z Afryką 50 B1
- Sense 51 C4

ENTERTAINMENT
- Filharmonia Narodowa 52 B4
- Foksal 19 .... 53 C4
- Kino Atlantic 54 B5
- Kinoteka 55 A5
- Teatr Ateneum 56 D4
- Teatr Wielki 57 B3
- Underground Music Café 58 B4

SHOPPING
- Galeria Centrum 59 B5

TRANSPORT
- LOT Office 60 A5
- Orbis Travel 61 B5
- Polski Express Ticket Kiosk & Bus Stop 62 A5

Internet Café (ul Nowy Świat 18/20; 9am-11pm Mon-Fri, 10am-10pm Sat & Sun)

Medical Services

Apteka Grabowskiego (☎ 22 825 6986; Warszawa Centralna train station) An all-night pharmacy.

Hospital of the Ministry of Internal Affairs & Administration (☎ 22 508 2000; ul Wołoska 137) A hospital preferred by government officials and diplomats.

Money

American Express (Marriott Hotel, Al Jerozolimskie 65/79)

Bank Pekao (ul Krakowskie Przedmieście 1)

PKO Bank (Plac Bankowy 2)

Tourist Information

Each tourist office provides free city maps and booklets (look out for *Warsaw in Short* and the *Visitor*), and helps book hotel rooms.

Tourist office (☎ 9431; www.warsaw tour.pl) Airport (8am-8pm May-Sep, to 6pm Oct-Apr); Royal Way (ul Krakowskie Przedmieście 39; 9am-8pm May-Sep, to 6pm Oct-Apr); Warszawa Centralna train station (main hall; 8am-8pm May-Sep, to 6pm Oct-Apr)

Warsaw Tourist Card (1/3 days 35/65zł) Discounts on attractions and transport. Buy it from tourist offices.

Warsaw Tourist Information Centre (☎ 22 635 1881; www.wcit.waw.pl; pl Zamkowy 1/13; 9am-6pm Mon-Fri, 10am-6pm Sat, 11am-6pm Sun) In the Old Town.

SIGHTS & ACTIVITIES

Old Town

Plac Zamkowy (Castle Sq) is the main gateway to the Old Town. All the buildings here were superbly rebuilt from their foundations after destruction in WWII. Within the square stands the **Monument to Sigismund III Vasa**, who moved the capital from Kraków to Warsaw in 1596.

On the square is the massive 13th-century **Royal Castle** (Plac Zamkowy 4; adult/concession 20/13zł, free Sun Sep-May, free Mon Jun-Aug; 11am-4pm Mon, 10am-4pm Tue-Sat, 11am-4pm Sun, closed Mon Oct-Apr), featuring sumptuously decorated rooms including the Senators' Antechamber, with its landscapes of 18th-century Warsaw by Bernardo Bellotto (Canaletto's nephew).

From the castle, walk down ul Świętojańska to the magnificent **Rynek Starego Miasta** (Old Town Market Sq). Off the square is the **Warsaw Historical Museum** (Rynek Starego Miasta 42; adult/concession 6/3zł, free Sun; 11am-6pm Tue & Thu, 10am-3.30pm Wed & Fri, 10.30am-4.30pm Sat & Sun). At noon it shows an English-language film depicting the wartime destruction of the city.

Walk west for one block to the **Barbican**, part of the medieval city walls. North along ul Freta is the **Marie Skłodowska-Curie Museum** (ul Freta 16; adult/concession 6/3zł; 10am-4pm Tue-Sat, to 3pm Sun), with displays about the great scientist and her discoveries regarding radioactivity.

GETTING INTO TOWN

Bus 175 leaves every 10 to 15 minutes from the airport to the Old Town, via ul Nowy Świat and the Warszawa Centralna train station. If you arrive in the wee hours, night bus N32 links the airport with Warszawa Centralna every 30 minutes.

The taxi fare between the airport and the city centre is about 35zł to 40zł. Beware unmarked 'Mafia' cabs, which charge astronomical rates.

If arriving by train, Warszawa Centralna train station is in the city centre. If you arrive by bus at either major PKS bus station, you can take a train from an adjoining station into the centre.

Heading southwest, you'll reach the **Monument to the Warsaw Rising** (cnr ul Długa & ul Miodowa). This striking set of statuary honours the heroic Polish revolt against German rule in 1944.

Royal Way (Szlak Królewski)

This 4km route connects the Old Town with the modern city centre, and is served by bus 180.

Just south of the Royal Castle is the ornate 15th-century **St Anne's Church** (ul Krakowskie Przedmieście 68), with impressive views from its **tower** (adult/concession 3/2zł; 10am-6pm Tue-Sun).

Along nearby ul Kozia is the quirky **Museum of Caricature** (www.muzeumkarykatury.pl; ul Kozia 11; adult/concession 5/3zł, free Sat; 11am-5pm Tue-Sun), exhibiting numerous original works by Polish and foreign caricaturists.

About 300m further south, at the entrance to the Saxon Gardens, is the poignant **Tomb of the Unknown Soldier**. It's not open to the public, but be here at noon on Sunday to see the Changing of the Guard.

Back along the Royal Way is the 17th-century **Church of the Holy Cross** (ul Krakowskie Przedmieście 3). Chopin's heart is preserved in the second pillar on the left-hand side of the main nave; it was brought from Paris, where he died of tuberculosis aged only 39. If you want to know more, head along ul Tamka towards the river to the small **Chopin Museum** (ul Okólnik 1; adult/concession 8/4zł, free Wed; 10am-6pm Tue-Sat). On show are letters, handwritten musical scores and his last piano.

East of the junction of ul Nowy Świat and Al Jerozolimskie is the **National Museum** (Al Jerozolimskie 3; adult/concession 12/7zł, incl temporary exhibitions 17/10zł, museum free Sat; 10am-4pm Tue-Fri, to 5pm Sat & Sun), with an impressive collection of Greek and Egyptian antiquities, Coptic frescoes, medieval woodcarvings and Polish paintings; look out for the surrealistic fantasies of Jacek Malczewski.

Warsaw Rising Museum

This impressive **museum** (ul Grzybowska 79; adult/concession 4/2zł, free Sun; 8am-6pm Mon, Wed & Fri, 10am-8pm Thu, to 6pm Sat & Sun) commemorates Warsaw's insurrection against its Nazi occupiers in 1944, which ended in the destruction of much of the city and its population. The moving story of the Rising is retold via photographs, exhibits and audiovisual displays, with captions in English. Catch tram 8, 22 or 24 west from Al Jerozolimskie.

Jewish Warsaw

The suburbs northwest of the Palace of Culture & Science were once predominantly inhabited by Jewish Poles. During WWII the Nazis established a Jewish ghetto in the area, but razed it after crushing the Warsaw Ghetto Uprising in April 1943. Roman Polański's moving 2002 film *The Pianist* was set here.

The **Warsaw Ghetto Monument** (cnr ul Anielewicza & ul Zamenhofa) remembers the Nazis' victims via pictorial plaques. The nearby **Pawiak Prison Museum** (ul Dzielna 24/26; admission free; 10am-4pm Wed-Sun) was a Gestapo prison during the Nazi occupation. Exhibits include letters and other personal items.

The most striking remainder is Europe's largest **Jewish Cemetery** (ul Okopowa 49/51; admission 4zł; 10am-5pm Mon-Thu, 9am-1pm Fri, 9am-4pm Sun). Founded in 1806, it has over 100,000 gravestones. Visitors must wear a head-covering to enter, and it's accessible from the Old Town on bus 180.

FESTIVALS & EVENTS

Mozart Festival (www.operakameralna.pl) June/July.
Warsaw Summer Jazz Days (www.adamiakjazz.pl) July.
Art of the Street Festival (www.sztukaulicy.pl) July.
Warsaw Autumn International Festival of Contemporary Music (www.warsaw-autumn.art.pl) September.
Warsaw Film Festival (www.wff.pl) October.

SLEEPING

Not surprisingly, Warsaw is the most expensive Polish city for accommodation, though there are several reasonably priced hostels around town.

Camping 123 (☎ 22 822 9121; www.astur.waw.pl; ul Bitwy Warszawskiej 1920r 15/17; per person/tent 24/10zł, cabins 90zł;) Set in extensive grounds near the Dworzec Zachodnia bus station. There's a tennis court nearby.

Smolna Youth Hostel (☎ 22 827 8952; www.hostelsmolna30.pl; ul Smolna 30; dm/s/d 36/65/120zł) These popular basic budget digs are handy for shops and restaurants, the bathrooms are clean and there's a kitchen. Note the midnight curfew (2am in July and August) and dorms separated by gender.

Hostel Helvetia (☎ 22 826 7108; www.hostel-helvetia.pl; ul Kopernika 36/40; dm 45-65zł, r 150-190zł) Bright hostel with an attractive combined lounge and kitchen. Dorms have lockers available, there's one small women-only dorm, and the hostel hires out bikes. Enter from the street behind, ul Sewerynów.

Nathan's Villa Hostel (☎ 22 622 2946; www.nathansvilla.com; ul Piękna 24/26; dm 45-65zł, r 170-180zł, apt 220zł) A sunlit courtyard leads to well-organised dorms and comfortable private rooms. The kitchen is well set up, and there's a free laundry and book exchange.

Hostel Kanonia (☎ 22 635 0676; www.kanonia.pl; ul Jezuicka 2; dm 50zł, r 190-240zł) Housed in a historic building in the heart of the Old Town. Some rooms have picturesque views onto the cobblestone streets, and there's a dining room with basic kitchen facilities.

Oki Doki Hostel (☎ 22 826 5112; www.okidoki.pl; Plac Dąbrowskiego 3; dm 55-73zł, s/d 142/220zł) Each dorm is decorated thematically using the brightest paints available; try the red 'Communist'. The hostel also has a bar, free washing machine and kitchen, and hires out bikes.

Hotel Praski (☎ 22 818 4989; www.praski.pl; Al Solidarności 61; s 147-210zł, d 160-230zł) The rooms of this inexpensive hotel have attractive high ceilings and comfortable beds. Red carpets add old-fashioned charm, and some rooms have views of Praski Park.

Premiere Classe (☎ 22 624 0800; www.campanile.com.pl; ul Towarowa 2; r 189zł) Rooms are small but bright, and neatly set up with modern furnishings. Friendly staff are a definite bonus. Guests can use the restaurant, bar and fitness centre in the neighbouring sister hotels.

Old Town Apartments (☎ 22 887 9801; www.warsawshotel.com; Rynek Starego Miasta 12/14; apt from €70) These renovated apartments can house up to six people. Most have washing machines and all have kitchens. Check the website for cheap last-minute offers.

EATING

Warsaw's eateries cover diverse cuisines and price ranges; a good selection can be found in the Old Town and around ul Nowy Świat.

Bar Pod Barbakanem (ul Mostowa 27/29; mains 5-8zł; 8am-5pm Mon-Fri, 9am-5pm Sat & Sun) A former milk bar that survived the fall of the Iron Curtain and continues to serve cheap, unpretentious food. Fill up while peering through the lace curtains at the passing tourist hordes.

Green Way (☎ 22 696 9321; ul Hoża 54; mains 10-13zł; 10am-8pm Mon-Fri, 11am-7pm Sat & Sun) Slicker than the usual outlet of this chain, with a cafe ambience and a good outdoor dining zone. Take your pick of the international menu, which includes goulash, curry, samosas and enchiladas.

our pick **Cô tú** (Hadlowo-Usługowe 21; mains 10-14zł; 10am-9pm Mon-Fri, 11am-7pm Sat & Sun) The wok at this simple Asian diner never rests, and the menu is enormous, covering seafood, vegetables, beef, chicken and pork. Duck through the archway at Nowy Świat 26 to find it.

Bar Bistro Bez Kantów (☎ 22 892 9800; ul Krakowskie Przedmieście 11; mains 15-45zł; 6am-11pm) Informal, sunlit eatery on the Royal Way, serving dishes involving pork, duck, veal and fish. It also offers breakfast.

Podwale Piwna Kompania (☎ 22 635 6314; ul Podwale 25; mains 21-49zł; 11am-1am Mon-Sat, noon-1am Sun) The menu at 'The Company of Beer' features lots of grilled items and dishes such as roast duck, Wiener schnitzel, pork ribs and steak. There's a courtyard as well.

Most convenient for groceries are the **MarcPol Supermarket** (Plac Defilad) in front of the Palace of Culture & Science, and the **Albert Supermarket** (ul Złota 59) in the Złote Tarasy shopping centre behind Warszawa Centralna train station.

SPLURGE

Restauracja Przy Zamku (☎ 22 831 0259; Plac Zamkowy 15; mains 38-85zł) An attractive, old-fashioned kind of place with hunting trophies on the walls and attentive, white-aproned waiters. The top-notch Polish menu includes fish and game and a bewildering array of starters – try the excellent hare pâté served with cranberry sauce.

DRINKING & CLUBBING

There's no shortage of good bars and clubs in Warsaw. Explore ul Mazowiecka, ul Sienkiewicza and the area around ul Nowy Świat for more action.

Sense (ul Nowy Świat 19; noon-late) A very modern, mellow bar. Comfortable banquettes sit beneath strings of cube-shaped lights, and some drinks are measured in a 'Palace of Culture' (a tall scientific beaker).

Między Nami (ul Bracka 20) Cafe-bar 'Between You and Me' attracts a trendy set with its designer furniture and whitewashed walls. There's no sign over the door; look for the white awnings and chilled crowd.

Paparazzi (ul Mazowiecka 12) Big, roomy venue where you can sip a bewildering array of cocktails under blown-up photos of Hollywood stars. There's comfortable seating around the central bar.

Pożegnanie Z Afryką (ul Freta 4/6; 11am-9pm) 'Out of Africa' offers little beyond coffee – but it's a memorable brew. Choose from dozens of varieties, and a range of tempting cakes.

Foksal 19 (ul Foksal 19; bar 5pm-1am Mon-Thu, to 3am Fri & Sat, nightclub 11pm-5am Fri & Sat) Downstairs is a backlit bar, subdued golden lighting and comfy couches. Upstairs is a blue-lit nightclub, with DJs playing a variety of sounds.

Underground Music Café (www.under.pl in Polish; ul Marszałkowska 126/134) Students and backpackers pour into this basement club for its cheap beer, dark lighting and music that varies from '70s and '80s to house, R & B and hip hop. Enter via the staircase facing the McDonald's.

ENTERTAINMENT

To discover what's on, check out the *Visitor* and the cheeky but comprehensive *Warsaw in Your Pocket* (5zł), available from tourist offices or via free download (www.inyourpocket.com/poland/city/warsaw.html).

Teatr Ateneum (☎ 22 625 7330; www.teatrateneum.pl, in Polish; ul Jaracza 2) leans towards contemporary Polish-language productions. **Teatr Wielki** (☎ 22 692 0200; www.teatrwielki.pl; Plac Teatralny 1) hosts opera and ballet. **Filharmonia Narodowa** (☎ 22 551 7111; www.filharmonia.pl; ul Jasna 5) is the venue for classical music concerts.

Free jazz concerts also take place in the Old Town Market Square on Saturday at 7pm in July and August.

Catch a film at the central **Kino Atlantic** (ul Chmielna 33), or **Kinoteka** (Plac Defilad 1) within the Palace of Culture & Science.

SHOPPING

Galeria Centrum (ul Marszałkowska 104/122) is a central modern shopping mall. There are also plentiful antique, arts and crafts shops around Rynek Starego Miasta in the Old Town, so brandish your credit card and explore.

GETTING THERE & AWAY

Air

Frederic Chopin Airport (www.lotnisko-chopina.pl) is more commonly called Okęcie airport. Flights can be booked at the **LOT office** (☎ 801 703 703; www.lot.com; Al Jerozolimskie 65/79). See p893 for details on air travel to and from Warsaw.

Bus

Warsaw has two major bus terminals for PKS buses. **Dworzec Zachodnia** (Western Bus Station; Al Jerozolimskie 144) handles domestic buses heading south, north and west of the capital, including nine daily to Częstochowa (41zł, four hours), 10 to Gdańsk (50zł, six hours), nine to Kraków (43zł, six hours), five to Toruń (37zł, four hours), four to Wrocław (51zł, seven hours) and five to Zakopane (57zł, eight hours).

Dworzec Stadion (Stadium Bus Station; ul Sokola 1) handles domestic buses to the east and southeast, including 20 daily to Lublin (26zł, three hours) and three to Zamość (35zł, 4¾ hours).

Polski Express (www.polskiexpress.net) sells tickets from a kiosk along Al Jana Pawła II, next to Warszawa Centralna train station. Its buses travel to Częstochowa (46zł, five hours, one daily), Kraków (73zł, eight hours, one daily), Lublin (31zł, 3½ hours, five daily) and Toruń (41zł, 3½ hours, eight daily).

International buses depart from and arrive at Dworzec Zachodnia or, occasionally, outside Warszawa Centralna.

Train

The train station that most travellers will use is **Warszawa Centralna** (Warsaw Central; Al Jerozolimskie 54). However, it's not always where trains start or finish, so make sure you get on or off promptly; and guard your belongings against pickpocketing and theft at all times.

GETTING AROUND

Public Transport

The standard ticket (2.80zł) is valid for one ride only on a bus, tram or metro train travelling anywhere in the city. Warsaw is the only place in Poland where holders of International

Student Identity Cards (ISIC) get a public-transport discount (48%).

Tickets are also available for 60/90 minutes (4/6zł), one day (9zł), three days (16zł), one week (32zł) and one month (78zł). Buy tickets from kiosks (including those marked RUCH) before boarding, and validate them on board.

Taxi

Taxis are a quick and easy way to get around. Beware of unauthorised 'Mafia' taxis parked in front of top-end hotels, at the airport, outside Warszawa Centralna train station and in the vicinity of most tourist sights.

MAŁOPOLSKA

Małopolska (literally 'lesser Poland') is a beautiful area, within which the visitor can spot plentiful remnants of traditional life amid green farmland and historic cities. The region covers a large swathe of southeastern Poland, from the former royal capital, Kraków, to the eastern Lublin Uplands.

KRAKÓW

pop 756,000

While many Polish cities are centred on an attractive Old Town, none can compare with Kraków for sheer effortless beauty. Miraculously escaping from destruction in WWII, the city seems to have led a lucky existence. As it was the royal capital of Poland until 1596, Kraków is packed with attractive historic buildings and streetscapes. The city's centrepiece is the stunning Wawel Castle and Cathedral.

Just outside the Old Town lies Kazimierz, the former Jewish quarter, its silent synagogues reflecting the tragedy of the recent past. The district's tiny streets and low-rise architecture make it an interesting place to explore.

Information

INTERNET ACCESS

Greenland Internet Café (ul Floriańska 30; per hr 4zł; 9am-midnight)

Klub Garinet (ul Floriańska 18; per hr 4zł; 9am-midnight)

MONEY

Foreign-exchange offices and ATMs are common. Most foreign-exchange offices close on Sunday, and areas near Rynek Główny and the main train station offer poor exchange rates.

Bank Pekao (Rynek Główny 32)

TOURIST INFORMATION

Two free magazines, *Welcome to Craców & Małopolska* and *Visitor: Kraków & Zakopane*, are available at tourist offices. The useful *Kraków in Your Pocket* booklet (5zł) can be downloaded for free (www.inyourpocket.com/poland/city/krakow.html). The Kraków Tourist Card (www.krakowcard.com) costs 50/65zł for two/three days and gives discounts on sights and transport.

Małopolska Tourism Information Centre (☎ 12 421 7706; www.mcit.pl; Rynek Główny 1/3; 9am-8pm May-Sep, to 5pm Oct-Apr) Centrally located in the Cloth Hall.

Tourist office Kazimierz (☎ 12 422 0471; ul Józefa 7; 10am-6pm May-Sep, 11am-5pm Oct-Apr); ul Św Jana (☎ 12 421 7787; www.karnet.krakow.pl; ul Św Jana 2; 10am-6pm Mon-Sat); ul Szpitalna (☎ 12 432 0110; ul Szpitalna 25; 9am-7pm May-Oct, to 5pm Nov-Apr); Town Hall tower (☎ 12 433 73 10; Rynek Główny 1; 9am-7pm Apr-Sep, to 5pm Oct-Mar).

POLAND

GETTING INTO TOWN

From the airport, take a shuttle bus to the nearby train station, from the sign marked 'PKP' outside the terminal building. A conductor on the train will sell you a ticket (8zł) for the short journey to Kraków Główny train station. The train operates from 4am to midnight, departing every 30 minutes between 7.30am and 9pm (hourly outside these times).

The taxi fare between the airport and the centre is about 60zł, but avoid unmarked unofficial cabs, which charge like wounded bulls.

If arriving by train, walk out of the main train station, then through the nearby road underpass and you're in the Old Town. The main bus station is on the other side of the tracks from the train station, connected by another underpass.

Sights & Activities

OLD TOWN

The Old Town is focused on **Rynek Główny** (Main Market Sq), Europe's largest medieval town square (200m by 200m). At its centre is the 16th-century Renaissance **Cloth Hall** (Sukiennice), housing a large **souvenir market**.

The huge main altarpiece of the 14th-century **St Mary's Church** (Rynek Główny 4; adult/concession 6/4zł; 11.30am-6pm Mon-Sat, 2-6pm Sun) is the finest Gothic sculpture in Poland, and is opened ceremoniously each day at 11.50am.

Just south of St Mary's, the **English Language Club** (ul Sienna 5; admission 1.50zł; 6-8pm Wed) has met weekly since the 1980s. The meetings are a fun way to meet a mixed bunch of Poles, expats and tourists in a relaxed setting.

West of the Rynek is the **Collegium Maius** (ul Jagiellońska 15; adult/concession 12/6zł, Sat 6zł; 10am-2.20pm Mon-Fri, to 1.20pm Sat), the oldest surviving university building in Poland. Guided tours run half-hourly and there's usually a couple in English, at 11am and 1pm. Even if you don't go on a tour, step into the magnificent arcaded courtyard for a glimpse of the beautiful architecture.

From St Mary's Church, walk northeast up ul Floriańska to the 14th-century **Florian Gate**. Beyond it is the **Barbican** (adult/concession 6/4zł; 10.30am-6pm Apr-Oct), a defensive bastion built in 1498. Nearby, the **Czartoryski Museum** (ul Św Jana 19; adult/concession 10/5zł, free Sun May-Oct, free Thu Nov-Apr; 10am-6pm Tue-Sat, to 4pm Sun May-Oct, to 3.30pm Tue-Sun Nov-Apr) features an impressive collection of European art, including Leonardo da Vinci's *Lady with an Ermine*.

South of Rynek Główny, along ul Grodzka, is the early-17th-century Jesuit **Church of SS Peter & Paul** (ul Grodzka 64; dawn-dusk), Poland's first baroque church.

WAWEL HILL

Wawel Hill (grounds admission free; 6am-dusk) is Kraków's main draw for tourists, and its castle and cathedral are iconic symbols of Poland. There are several attractions within the castle, each requiring a separate ticket.

Within the magnificent **Wawel Castle** (☎ 12 422 5155; www.wawel.krakow.pl) are the **State Rooms** (adult/concession 15/8zł, free Mon Apr-Oct, free Sun Nov-Mar; 9.30am-1pm Mon, to 5pm Tue-Fri, 11am-6pm Sat & Sun Apr-Oct, 9.30am-4pm Tue-Sat Nov-Mar) and the **Royal Private Apartments** (adult/concession 20/15zł; 9.30am-5pm Tue-Fri, 11am-6pm Sat & Sun Apr-Oct, 9.30am-4pm Tue-Sun Nov-Mar). Entry to the latter is only allowed on a guided tour. If you want to hire a guide who speaks English, French or German, contact the on-site **guides office** (☎ 12 422 1697).

The 14th-century **Wawel Cathedral** (adult/concession 10/5zł; 9am-5pm Mon-Sat, 12.15-5pm Sun) was long the coronation and burial place of Polish royalty, and houses **Royal Tombs**, including that of King Kazimierz the Great. The bell tower of the golden-domed **Sigismund Chapel** (1539) contains the country's largest bell (11 tonnes).

KAZIMIERZ

Founded by King Kazimierz the Great in 1335, Kazimierz later became home to Jews fleeing persecution from all corners of Europe.

During WWII the Nazis relocated Jews to a walled ghetto in Podgórze, just south of the Vistula River. They were exterminated in the nearby **Płaszów Concentration Camp**, as portrayed in Steven Spielberg's haunting film *Schindler's List*. If you want to learn more, **Jarden Tourist Agency** (☎ 12 421 71 66; www.jarden.pl; ul Szeroka 2; tours 60zł) runs related tours.

The eastern Jewish quarter is dotted with synagogues. The 15th-century **Old Synagogue** houses the **Jewish Museum** (ul Szeroka 24; adult/concession 7/5zł; 10am-2pm Mon, 9am-5pm Tue-Sun Apr-Oct, 10am-2pm Mon, 9am-4pm Wed-Sun Nov-Mar), with exhibitions on Jewish traditions.

Not far away, the **Galicia Museum** (www.galiciajewishmuseum.org; ul Dajwór 18; adult/concession 12/6zł; 9am-7pm Mar-Oct, 10am-6pm Nov-Feb) displays modern-day photographic traces of south-eastern Poland's once-thriving Jewish community.

Festivals & Events

Organ Music Festival March.
Krakow International Film Festival (www.cracowfilmfestival.pl) May.
Jewish Culture Festival (www.jewishfestival.pl) June/July.
International Festival of Street Theatre (www.teatrkto.pl) July.
Summer Jazz Festival (www.cracjazz.com) July.

Sleeping

Kraków is unquestionably Poland's major tourist destination, with prices to match. Booking ahead is recommended.

Cracow Hostel (☎ 12 429 1106; www.cracowhostel.com; Rynek Główny 18; dm 35-80zł, ste 300zł) Budget accommodation perched high above the Rynek, with an amazing view of St Mary's Church

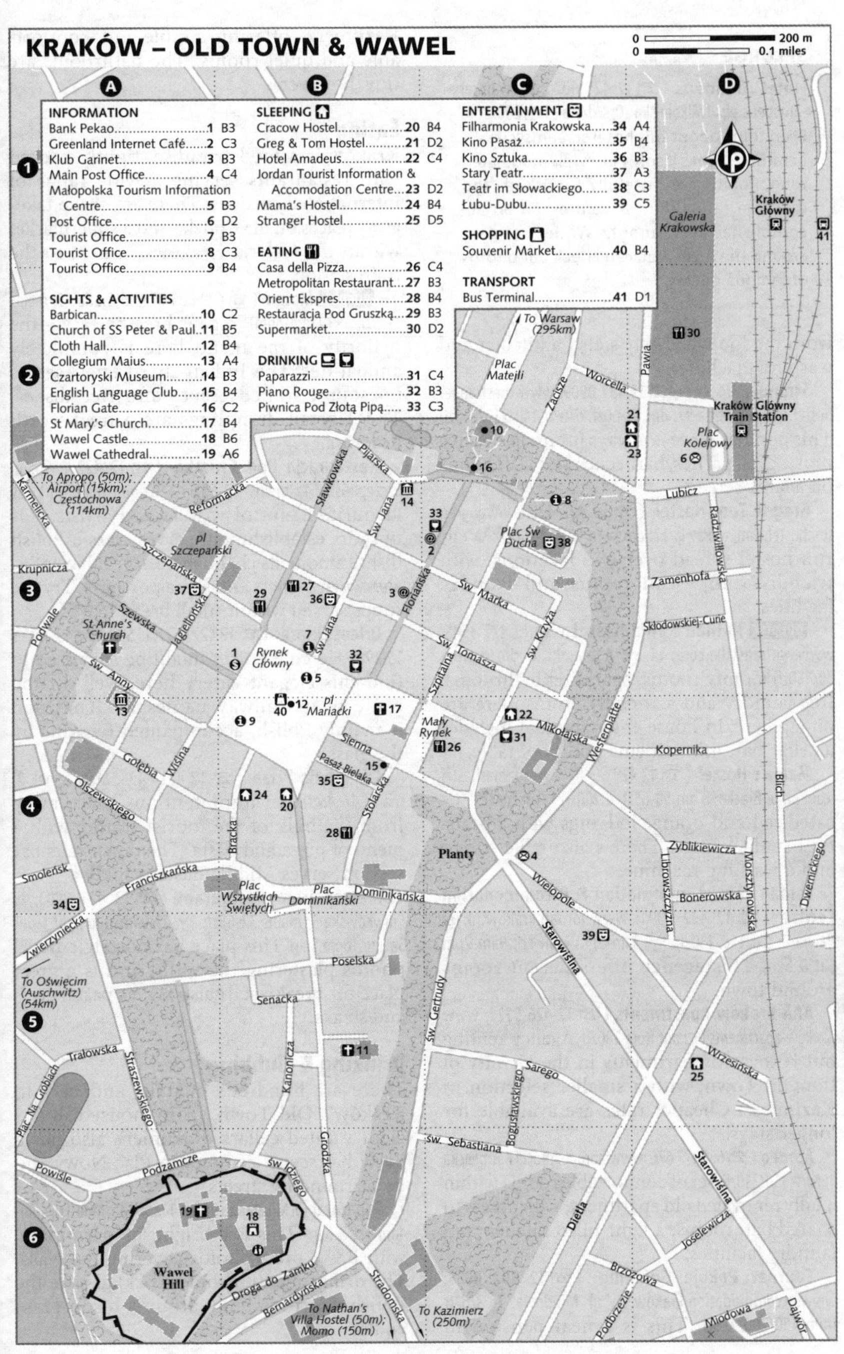
KRAKÓW – OLD TOWN & WAWEL
0 200 m
0 0.1 miles
A
B
C
D
1
2
3
4
5
6
INFORMATION
Bank Pekao....1 B3
Greenland Internet Café....2 C3
Klub Garinet....3 B3
Main Post Office....4 C4
Małopolska Tourism Information Centre....5 B3
Post Office....6 D2
Tourist Office....7 B3
Tourist Office....8 C3
Tourist Office....9 B4
SIGHTS & ACTIVITIES
Barbican....10 C2
Church of SS Peter & Paul....11 B5
Cloth Hall....12 B4
Collegium Maius....13 A4
Czartoryski Museum....14 B3
English Language Club....15 B4
Florian Gate....16 C2
St Mary's Church....17 B4
Wawel Castle....18 B6
Wawel Cathedral....19 A6
SLEEPING
Cracow Hostel....20 B4
Greg & Tom Hostel....21 D2
Hotel Amadeus....22 C4
Jordan Tourist Information & Accomodation Centre....23 D2
Mama's Hostel....24 B4
Stranger Hostel....25 D5
EATING
Casa della Pizza....26 C4
Metropolitan Restaurant....27 B3
Orient Ekspres....28 B4
Restauracja Pod Gruszką....29 B3
Supermarket....30 D2
DRINKING
Paparazzi....31 C4
Piano Rouge....32 B3
Piwnica Pod Złotą Pipą....33 C3
ENTERTAINMENT
Filharmonia Krakowska....34 A4
Kino Pasaż....35 B4
Kino Sztuka....36 B3
Stary Teatr....37 A3
Teatr im Słowackiego....38 C3
Łubu-Dubu....39 C5
SHOPPING
Souvenir Market....40 B4
TRANSPORT
Bus Terminal....41 D1
Galeria Krakowska
Kraków Główny
Kraków Główny Train Station
Plac Kolejowy
To Warsaw (295km)
Plac Matejki
Worcella
Pawia
Zacisze
Lubicz
To Apropo (50m); Airport (15km); Częstochowa (114km)
Karmelicka
Reformacka
Pijarska
Sławkowska
Św Jana
Floriańska
Plac Św Ducha
pl Szczepański
Szczepańska
Krupnicza
Radziwiłłowska
Zamenhofa
Św Marka
Skłodowskiej-Curie
Podwale
St Anne's Church
Szewska
Jagiellońska
Rynek Główny
Św Tomasza
Szpitalna
Św Krzyża
Św. Anny
pl Mariacki
Mały Rynek
Mikołajska
Westerplatte
Kopernika
Sienna
Pasaż Bielaka
Stolarska
Gołębia
Wiślna
Olszewskiego
Bracka
Planty
Blich
Zyblikiewicza
Librowszczyzna
Morsztynowska
Dwernickiego
Bonerowska
Smoleńsk
Franciszkańska
Plac Wszystkich Świętych
Plac Dominikański
Dominikańska
Wielopole
Starowiślna
Zwierzyniecka
To Oświęcim (Auschwitz) (54km)
Poselska
Senacka
Św. Gertrudy
Kanonicza
Grodzka
Tralowska
Straszewskiego
Plac Na Groblach
Sarego
Wrzesińska
Bogusławskiego
Św. Sebastiana
Powiśle
Podzamcze
Św Idziego
Wawel Hill
Droga do Zamku
Bernardyńska
Stradomska
To Nathan's Villa Hostel (50m); Momo (150m)
To Kazimierz (250m)
Dietla
Józefińska
Joselewicza
Brzozowa
Podbrzezie
Miodowa
Dajwór

POLAND

SPLURGE

Hotel Amadeus (☎ 12 429 6070; www.hotel-amadeus.pl; ul Mikołajska 20; s/d/ste €190/200/300) Everything about this hotel screams 'class' – or rather, speaks it softly in a well-modulated tone. Rooms are tastefully furnished, and there's a sauna, fitness centre and an accomplished restaurant. While hanging around the foyer, you can check out photos of famous guests.

from the lounge. There's also a kitchen and washing machine.

Stranger Hostel (☎ 12 432 0909; www.thestrangerhostel.com; ul Dietla 97; dm 45-60zł, d/tr/q 140/210/240zł) This popular place is always jumping, via live music gigs, parties, barbecues and DVD films on a large screen.

Greg & Tom Hostel (☎ 12 422 4100; www.gregtomhostel.com; ul Pawia 12; dm from 50zł, d 150zł) Well-run hostel spread over two locations, with friendly staff, clean rooms and laundry facilities.

our pick **Nathan's Villa Hostel** (☎ 12 422 3545; www.nathansvilla.com; ul Św Agnieszki 1; dm/d from 50/160zł) Comfy rooms, sparkling bathrooms, free laundry and a friendly atmosphere are on tap here. In-house entertainment includes a cellar bar, mini-cinema and pool table.

Mama's Hostel (☎ 12 429 5940; www.mamashostel.com.pl; ul Bracka 4; dm 50-65zł, d 200zł) Centrally located red-and-orange lodgings with a beautiful sunlit lounge. There's also table soccer and a washing machine.

Jordan Tourist Information & Accommodation Centre (☎ 12 422 6091; www.jordan.krakow.pl; ul Pawia 8; s/d 110/130zł; 🕑 8am-6pm Mon-Fri, 9am-2pm Sat & Sun) This agency offers decent rooms around town.

AAA Kraków Apartments (☎ 12 426 5121; www.krakow-apartments.biz; apt from 180zł) Agency renting out renovated apartments in the vicinity of the Old Town, with a smaller selection in Kazimierz. Cheaper rates are available for longer stays.

Apropo (☎ 665 277 676; www.apropo.info; ul Karmelicka 36; d/tr 150/210zł) Set of comfortable rooms within a fully renovated old apartment, with access to shared bathrooms, a light-filled kitchen and laundry facilities.

Tournet Pokoje Gościnne (☎ 12 292 0088; www.accommodation.krakow.pl; ul Miodowa 7; s/d/tr from 150/200/220zł) This is a neat pension in Kazimierz, offering simple but comfortable and quiet rooms. The bathrooms are tiny, however.

Eating

Kraków is a food paradise, tightly packed with restaurants serving a wide range of international cuisines. There are cheap takeaway places on ul Grodzka and a supermarket within the Galeria Krakowska, next to the train station.

our pick **Momo** (☎ 609 685 775; ul Dietla 49; mains 4-13zł; 🕑 11am-8pm) Vegans breathe easy – the majority of the menu here is completely animal-free. This Indian-styled eatery serves up soups, stuffed crepes and rice dishes. The Tibetan dumplings are a treat worth ordering.

Restauracja Pod Gruszką (☎ 12 422 8896; ul Szczepańska 1; mains 12-55zł; 🕑 noon-midnight) A favourite haunt of writers and artists, this upstairs establishment serves classic Polish dishes among its chandeliers, lace tablecloths, age-worn carpets and sepia portraits. Try the soups served within small bread loaves.

Orient Ekspres (☎ 12 422 6672; ul Stolarska 13; mains 15-39zł) Hercule Poirot might be surprised to find this elegant eatery here, well off the route of its railway namesake. The food is mainly Polish, accompanied by wine by the glass.

Casa della Pizza (☎ 12 421 6498; Mały Rynek 2; mains 16-46zł) An unpretentious place away from the bulk of the tourist traffic, with a menu of pizza and pasta. The downstairs bar section serves Middle Eastern food.

Metropolitan Restaurant (☎ 12 421 9803; ul Sławkowska 3; mains 22-68zł; 🕑 7.30am-midnight Mon-Sat, to 10pm Sun) This place has nostalgic B&W photos plastering the walls, and is a great place for breakfast. It also serves pasta, grills and steaks.

Drinking & Clubbing

There are hundreds of pubs and bars in Kraków's Old Town, many housed in ancient vaulted cellars. Kazimierz also has a lively bar scene, centred on Plac Nowy and its surrounding streets.

Paparazzi (ul Mikołajska 9; 🕑 11am-1am Mon-Fri, 4pm-4am Sat & Sun) This is a bright, modern place, with B&W press photos covering the walls. The drinks menu includes cocktails like the Polish Martini, built around bison-grass vodka.

Singer (ul Estery 20; 9am-4am Sun-Thu, to 5am Fri & Sat) This relaxed Kazimierz cafe-bar's moody candlelit interior is full of character. Alternatively, sit outside and converse over a sewing machine affixed to the table.

Piwnica Pod Złotą Pipą (ul Floriańska 30; noon-midnight) Less claustrophobic than other cellar bars, with lots of tables for eating or drinking. Decent bar food and international beers on tap.

Piano Rouge (Rynek Główny 46; noon-3am) A sumptuous cellar venue decked out with billowing lengths of colourful silk, hosting live jazz nightly.

Łubu-Dubu (ul Wielopole 15; 6pm-late) This grungy upstairs nightclub features garish colours and a collection of objects from 1970s Poland. A series of rooms creates spaces for talking or dancing.

Alchemia (ul Estery 5; 9am-3am) In Kazimierz, Alchemia exudes a shabby-is-the-new-cool look and hosts regular live music gigs and theatrical events through the week.

Entertainment

The monthly Polish-English booklet *Karnet* (4zł) lists almost every event in the city.

Stary Teatr (12 422 4040; www.stary-teatr.pl, in Polish; ul Jagiellońska 5) Offers quality theatre.

Teatr im Słowackiego (12 422 4022; Plac Św Ducha 1) Built in 1893, this theatre focuses on Polish classics and large productions.

Filharmonia Krakowska (12 422 9477; www.filharmonia.krakow.pl; ul Zwierzyniecka 1) Hosts one of the best orchestras in the country; concerts are usually held on Friday and Saturday.

Two central cinemas are **Kino Sztuka** (cnr ul Św Tomasza & Św Jana) and the tiny **Kino Pasaż** (Rynek Główny 9).

Getting There & Away

The John Paul II International airport (www.lotnisko-balice.pl) is accessible by train (8zł, 16 minutes, half-hourly) from Kraków Główny station.

LOT flies between Kraków and Warsaw several times a day, and there are also daily domestic flights via Jet Air to Poznań. Budget operators connect Kraków to various European cities, including an array of destinations across Britain and Ireland. Check the airport's website for schedules.

The modern main **bus terminal** (ul Bosacka 18) is conveniently located on the other side of the main train station from the Old Town, but its services are of limited interest.

Kraków Główny train station (Plac Dworcowy), on the northeastern outskirts of the Old Town, handles all international trains and most domestic rail services. Each day from Kraków, 22 trains head to Warsaw (48zł, three hours). There are also nine trains daily to Częstochowa (31zł, 2½ hours), 14 to Wrocław (45zł, 4½ hours), 11 to Poznań (53zł, 7½ hours), two to Lublin (49zł, 5¼ hours) and 11 to Gdynia via Gdańsk (62zł, 8¾ hours).

OŚWIĘCIM

pop 40,800

Few place names have more impact than **Auschwitz**, which is seared into public consciousness as the location of history's most extensive experiment in genocide. Every year hundreds of thousands visit Oświęcim (osh-*fyen*-cheem) to learn about the infamous Nazi death camp's history, and to pay respect to the dead.

Established within disused army barracks in 1940, Auschwitz was expanded into the largest centre for the extermination of European Jews. Two more camps were subsequently established nearby: Birkenau (Brzezinka), also known as Auschwitz II, and Monowitz (Monowice). In the course of their operation, between 1 and 1.5 million people were murdered in these death factories.

Many of Auschwitz's original buildings remain, serving as a bleak document of the camp's history. A dozen surviving prison blocks house sections of the **State Museum Auschwitz-Birkenau** (33 844 8100; www.auschwitz.org.pl; admission free; 8am-7pm Jun-Aug, to 6pm May & Sep, to 5pm Apr & Oct, to 4pm Mar & Nov, to 3pm Dec-Feb).

The murder of huge numbers of Jews and other inmates took place at **Birkenau** (admission free; 8am-7pm Jun-Aug, to 6pm May & Sep, to 5pm Apr & Oct, to 4pm Mar & Nov, to 3pm Dec-Feb). Although much of the camp was destroyed by retreating Nazis, the size of the place provides some idea of the scale of this heinous crime.

English-language tours (adult/concession 39/30zł, 3½ hours) of Auschwitz and Birkenau leave at 10am, 11am, 1pm and 3pm daily. About every half-hour, the cinema in the visitors centre at the entrance to Auschwitz shows a 15-minute documentary film (adult/concession 3.50/2.50zł) about the liberation of the camp by Soviet troops on 27 January 1945.

Some basic explanations in Polish, English and Hebrew are provided on site, but you'll understand more if you buy the *Auschwitz*

WORTH THE TRIP

It's not every day you get to meet a miracle worker. However, in the pilgrimage town of Częstochowa, 114km northwest of Kraków, you can come face to face with the Black Madonna. Since the 15th century, this religious portrait has been credited with miracles, from the summoning forth of spring water to the protection of the monastery during the Swedish sieges of the 1650s. To view the Black Madonna, head along the main street, Al Najświętszej Marii Panny, to the graceful Jasna Góra monastery atop a hill in the city centre. In addition to the holy painting, this attractive complex also houses three museums. Częstochowa has regular bus and train connections with Warsaw, Kraków, Gdańsk and Wrocław; check those cities' transport sections for more details.

Birkenau Guide Book (translated into about 15 languages) from the visitors centre.

Getting There & Away

Buses run approximately hourly from the bus station in Kraków to Oświęcim (11zł, 1½ hours), either passing by or terminating at the museum.

Every half-hour from 11.30am to 4.30pm between 15 April and 31 October, free buses run between the visitors centres at Auschwitz and Birkenau (operating to 5.30pm in May and September, and to 6.30pm from June to August). Otherwise, follow the signs for an easy walk (3km) between both places.

LUBLIN

pop 353,000

If the crowds are becoming too much in Kraków, you could do worse than jump on a train to Lublin. This attractive eastern city has many of the same attractions – a beautiful Old Town, a castle, good bars and restaurants – but is less visited by international tourists.

It's also remembered for an important moment in Polish history: in 1569 the Lublin Union was signed here, uniting Poland and Lithuania. Today its beautifully preserved Old Town is an attractive blend of Gothic, Renaissance and baroque architecture.

Information

Bank Pekao City centre (ul Krakowskie Przedmieście 64); Old Town (ul Królewska 1)

Net Box (ul Krakowskie Przedmieście 52; per hr 4.50zł; 9am-9pm Mon-Fri, 10am-9pm Sat, 2-9pm Sun) Internet access in a courtyard off the street.

Tourist office (81 532 4412; www.lublin.pl; ul Jezuicka 1/3; 9am-6pm Mon-Fri, 10am-4pm Sat, 10am-3pm Sun May-Sep, 9am-5pm Mon-Fri, 10am-3pm Sat Oct-Apr) Lots of free brochures, including the city walking-route guide *Tourist Routes of Lublin*.

Sights

The compact historic quarter is centred on the **Rynek**, the market square surrounding the neoclassical **Old Town Hall** (1781). From here you can access the **Underground Route** (Rynek 1; adult/concession 6/4zł; 10am-4pm Wed-Fri, noon-5pm Sat & Sun May-Oct), a 280m trail through connected cellars beneath the city streets, with historical exhibitions along the way.

The **Historical Museum of Lublin** (Plac Łokietka 3; adult/concession 3.50/2.50zł; 9am-4pm Wed-Sat, to 5pm Sun), displaying documents and photos, is inside the 14th-century **Kraków Gate**, a remnant of medieval fortifications.

For an expansive view of the Old Town, climb to the top of the **Trinitarian Tower** (1819), which houses the **Religious Art Museum** (Plac Katedralny; adult/concession 7/5zł; 10am-5pm Tue-Sun Apr-Oct, to 3pm Sat & Sun Nov-Mar). Nearby is the 16th-century **cathedral** (Plac Katedralny; dawn-dusk) and its impressive baroque frescoes.

The substantial 14th-century **castle**, standing on a hill northeast of the Old Town, has a dark history. During the Nazi occupation, over 100,000 people passed through its doors before being deported to the death camps. Its major occupant is now the **Lublin Museum** (www.zamek-lublin.pl; ul Zamkowa 9; adult/concession 6.50/4.50zł; 9am-4pm Wed-Sat, to 5pm Sun). On display are paintings, silverware, porcelain, woodcarvings and weaponry, mostly labelled only in Polish. Check out the alleged 'devil's paw print' on the 17th-century table in the foyer, linked to an intriguing local legend.

MAJDANEK

About 4km southeast is the **State Museum of Majdanek** (www.majdanek.pl; admission free; 9am-4pm). It commemorates one of the largest Nazi death camps, where some 235,000 people were massacred. Barracks, guard towers and barbed-wire fences remain in place; even more chilling are the crematorium and gas chambers.

Trolleybus 156 and bus 23 leave from a stop near the Bank Pekao on ul Królewska, running to the entrance of Majdanek.

Sleeping

Youth Hostel (☎ 81 533 0628; ul Długosza 6; dm/d/tr 32/72/108zł) Simple rooms are decorated with potted plants, and there's a kitchen and a pleasant courtyard area with seating. It's 100m up a poorly marked lane off ul Długosza; take the second left turning when walking down from ul Racławickie.

Lubelskie Samorządowe Centrum Doskonalenia Nauczycieli (☎ 81 532 9241; www.lscdn.pl; ul Dominikańska 5; dm 52zł) In an atmospheric old building, offering rooms with between two and five beds.

Dom Nauczyciela (☎ 81 533 8285; www.oupislublin.republika.pl; ul Akademicka 4; s/d/tr from 90/110/195zł) Value-packed accommodation in the heart of the university quarter, west of the Old Town. Rooms are clean, with good bathrooms. There are bars and eateries nearby.

Motel PZM (☎ 81 533 4232; ul Prusa 8; s/d from 120/160zł) The PZM is housed in an uninspiring concrete pile, but the rooms are decent enough and it's handy for the bus station.

our pick **Hotel Waksman** (☎ 81 532 5454; www.waksman.pl; ul Grodzka 19; s/d 200/220zł, ste from 260zł) Small gem within the Old Town, containing elegantly appointed rooms and an attractive lounge with tapestries on the walls.

Eating & Drinking

Pueblo Desperados (☎ 81 534 6179; Rynek 5; mains 6-24zł; 9am-10pm Mon-Thu, to midnight Fri & Sat, 10am-10pm Sun) Takes a reasonable stab at Mexican cuisine in its tiny sombrero-decorated premises, presenting Tex-Mex favourites and so-called Mexican pizzas.

Pizzeria Acerna (☎ 81 532 4531; Rynek 2; mains 11-41zł) The Acerna is a popular eatery on the main square, serving cheap pizzas and pasta in dazzling variations.

Magia (☎ 81 532 3041; ul Grodzka 2; mains 16-70zł; noon-midnight) Charming, relaxed restaurant with a large outdoor courtyard. Dishes range from tiger shrimps and snails to deer and duck, with every sort of pizza, pasta and pancake in between.

Caram'bola Pub (ul Kościuszki 8; 10am-late Mon-Fri, noon-late Sat & Sun) This pub is a pleasant place for a beer or two, and it also serves inexpensive bar food.

There's a supermarket close to the bus terminal.

Getting There & Away

From the **bus terminal** (Al Tysiąclecia), opposite the castle, hourly services head to Kraków (38zł) and Zamość (15zł). From the same terminal, Polski Express offers five daily buses to Warsaw (31zł, three hours).

Private minibuses to a variety of destinations, including Warsaw (30zł, every half-hour), leave from bus stops north and west of the bus terminal.

The **train station** (Plac Dworcowy) is 1.2km south of the Old Town and accessible by bus 1 or 13. Services go to Warsaw (34zł, 2½ hours, 12 daily) and Kraków (49zł, 5¼ hours, two daily).

ZAMOŚĆ

pop 66,500

While most Polish cities date from the Middle Ages, Zamość (*zah*-moshch) is pure Renaissance. It was founded in 1580 by nobleman Jan Zamoyski and designed by an Italian architect, and was intended to become a prosperous trading settlement. The splendid architecture of Zamość's Old Town escaped destruction in WWII, and was added to Unesco's World Heritage List in 1992.

Information

Bank Pekao (ul Grodzka 2)

K@fejka Internetowa (Rynek Wielki 10; per hr 3zł; 7.30am-5pm Mon-Fri, 9am-2pm Sat) Internet access.

Tourist office (☎ 84 639 2292; Rynek Wielki 13; 8am-6pm Mon-Fri, 10am-5pm Sat & Sun May-Sep, 8am-5pm Mon-Fri, 9am-2pm Sat Oct-Apr)

Sights

The **Rynek Wielki** (Great Market Sq) is an impressive Italianate Renaissance square, dominated by the lofty pink **Town Hall** and surrounded by colourful arcaded burghers' houses. The **Museum of Zamość** (ul Ormiańska 30; adult/concession 6/3zł; 9am-4pm Tue-Sun) is based in two of the loveliest buildings on the Rynek and houses interesting displays, paintings, folk costumes and archaeological finds.

Southwest of the square is the mighty 16th-century **cathedral** (ul Kolegiacka; dawn-dusk, except during services), which holds the tomb of Zamoyski. The **belfry** (admission 1.50zł; May-Sep) can be climbed for good views of the historic cathedral bells and the Old Town.

Before WWII, Jewish citizens accounted for 45% of the town's population. The most significant Jewish architectural relic is the

 Book your stay at lonelyplanet.com/hotels

Renaissance **synagogue** (ul Pereca 14; adult/concession 5/2zł; 9am-5pm Tue-Sat). It's awaiting transformation into a cultural centre, but you can visit and see its original wall and ceiling decoration, and a simple photo exhibition of Jewish life in the region.

On the eastern edge of the Old Town is the antiquated **Market Hall** (Hala Targowa), closed until 2010 due to a major renovation under way at the time of research. Behind it is the best surviving **bastion** from the original wall that encircled Zamość.

Sleeping & Eating

Pokoje Gościnne OSiR (84 638 6011; ul Królowej Jadwigi 8; dm/s/d/tr 24/90/125/150zł) Located in a sprawling sporting complex a 15-minute walk west of the Old Town. Rooms are plainly furnished but clean, although the bathrooms fall short of ideal.

Camping Duet (84 639 2499; ul Królowej Jadwigi 14; s/d/tr/q 75/90/120/150zł;) West of the Old Town, Camping Duet has neat bungalows, tennis courts, a restaurant, sauna and Jacuzzi. Larger bungalows sleep up to six.

Hotel Jubilat (84 638 6401; www.hoteljubilat.pl; ul Kardynała Wyszyńskiego 52; s/d/ste from 136/177/292zł) A reasonable, if slightly drab, place to spend the night, right beside the bus station. It's a long way from anywhere else.

Hotel Arkadia (84 638 6507; www.arkadia.zamosc.pl; Rynek Wielki 9; s/d/tr/ste from 140/160/200/250zł) With just nine rooms, this is a compact place with a pool table and restaurant. It's shabby but charming, with an unbeatable position on the Rynek.

Bar Asia (ul Staszica 10; mains 5-9zł; 8am-5pm Mon-Fri, to 4pm Sat) For hungry but broke travellers, this cafeteria-style place serves cheap and tasty Polish food, including several variants of *pierogi* (dumplings).

Restauracja Muzealna (84 638 7300; ul Ormiańska 30; mains 10-25zł; 11am-10pm Mon-Sat, to 9pm Sun) Atmospheric cellar restaurant below the main square, serving a better class of Polish cuisine at reasonable prices. Has a well-stocked bar.

For self-caterers, there's the handy **Lux mini-supermarket** (ul Grodzka 16; 7am-8pm Mon-Sat, 8am-6pm Sun) near the Rynek.

Getting There & Away

Buses are more convenient and quicker than trains. The **bus terminal** (ul Hrubieszowska) is 2km east of the Old Town and reached by city buses 0 and 3. Daily buses go to Kraków (40zł, seven hours, five daily), Warsaw (35zł, 4¾ hours, three daily) and Lublin (15zł, two hours, hourly).

Quicker and cheaper are the minibuses that travel every 30 minutes between Lublin and Zamość (10zł, 1½ hours). They leave from the minibus stand opposite the bus terminal in Zamość, and from a corner northwest of the bus terminal in Lublin. Check the changeable timetable for departures to other destinations, including Warsaw and Kraków.

From the **train station**, about 1km southwest of the Old Town, one train heads to Lublin (28zł, 1½ hours) every day, and one to Warsaw (48zł, 5½ hours).

CARPATHIAN MOUNTAINS

The Carpathians (Karpaty) stretch from the southern border with Slovakia into Ukraine, and their wooded hills and snowy mountains are a beacon for hikers, skiers and cyclists. The most popular destination here is the mountain resort town of Zakopane.

ZAKOPANE

pop 27,300

Zakopane is Poland's major winter sports centre, located at the foot of the Tatra Mountains. It may resemble a tourist trap, with its overcommercialised, overpriced exterior, but it has a relaxed, laid-back vibe that makes it a great place to chill out for a few days, even if you don't want to ski or hike.

The **tourist office** (18 201 2211; ul Kościuszki 17; 9am-5pm Jul-Aug, 9am-5pm Mon-Fri Sep-Jun) is helpful. Several foreign-exchange offices and banks line the main streets. **Widmo** (ul Galicy 6; per hr 5zł; 7.30am-midnight Mon-Fri, 9am-midnight Sat & Sun) is a convenient place to surf the internet.

Centrum Przewodnictwa Tatrzańskiego (Tatra Guide Centre; 18 206 3799; ul Chałubińskiego 42a; 9am-3pm) is able to arrange English- and German-speaking mountain guides.

Mt Gubałówka (1120m) has great views over the Tatras. A **funicular** (adult/concession one way 10/8zł, return 16/12zł; 8am-10pm Jul-Aug, 8.30am-

POLAND

7.20pm Apr-Jun & Sep, 8.30am-6pm Oct-Nov) covers the 1388m-long route in less than five minutes, climbing 300m from its base station just north of ul Krupówki.

Sleeping

Accommodation prices fluctuate considerably between low season and high season (the latter includes December to February, and July to August). Always book in advance.

Some travel agencies in Zakopane can arrange private rooms. Expect a double room to cost about 70zł in the peak season in the town centre, and about 50zł for somewhere further out.

Locals offering private rooms may approach you at the bus or train stations; alternatively, just look out for signs posted in front of private homes – *noclegi* and *pokoje* both mean 'rooms available'.

Youth Hostel Szarotka (☎ 18 201 3618; www.szarotkaptsm.republika.pl; ul Nowotarska 45; dm/d/tr 40/100/150zł) This friendly, homey place gets packed out in the high season. There's a kitchen and washing machine on site.

Carlton (☎ 18 201 4415; www.carlton.pl; ul Grunwaldzka 11; s/d/tr 100/200/300zł) Good-value pension in a grand old house, featuring light-filled rooms with modern furniture. There's an impressive shared balcony, and a big comfy lounge lined with potted plants.

Eating

The main street, ul Krupówki, is lined with all sorts of eateries.

Pstrąg Górski (☎ 18 206 4163; ul Krupówki 6; mains 16-30zł; 9am-10pm) This self-service fish restaurant, overlooking a narrow stream, serves some of the freshest trout, salmon and sea fish in town. It's excellent value.

Stek Chałupa (☎ 18 201 5918; ul Krupówki 33; mains 18-40zł; 8am-midnight) This big, friendly barn of a place has waiters in traditional garb. The menu features meat dishes, particularly steaks, though there are vegetarian choices.

Getting There & Away

From the **bus terminal** (ul Chramcówki), PKS buses run to Kraków every 45 to 60 minutes (16zł, two hours). Private companies Trans Frej and Szwagropol also run Kraków-bound buses (18zł) at the same frequency.

The **train station** (ul Chramcówki) has services to Kraków (33zł, 3½ hours) every two hours or so. Three trains a day go to Gdynia via Gdańsk (64zł, 13 hours), two to Poznań (56zł, 12 hours) and six to Warsaw (53zł, nine hours).

TATRA MOUNTAINS

The Tatras, 100km south of Kraków, form the highest range of the Carpathian Mountains, stretching across the Polish–Slovakian border. A quarter is in Poland and is mostly part of the Tatra National Park (about 212 sq km).

The **cable car** (adult/concession return 38/28zł; 7am-9pm Jul-Aug, 7.30am-5pm Apr-Jun & Sep-Oct, 8am-4pm Nov) trip from Kuźnice (3km south of Zakopane) to the summit of Mt Kasprowy Wierch (1985m) is a classic tourist experience enjoyed by Poles and foreigners alike. At the end of the trip, you can get off and stand with one foot in Poland and the other in Slovakia. Another popular destination is the emerald-green **Lake Morskie Oko** (Eye of the Sea), among the loveliest in the Tatras.

If you're doing any hiking in the Tatras, get a copy of the *Tatrzański Park Narodowy* map (1:25,000), which shows all hiking trails in the area.

Zakopane boasts four major ski areas, and **Mt Kasprowy Wierch** and **Mt Gubałówka** offer the best conditions and most challenging slopes. The ski season extends until early May.

Camping isn't allowed, but **PTTK** (Polish Tourist Country Lovers Society; http://english.pttk.pl) maintains eight mountain refuges and hostels, which provide simple accommodation. Check availability at the **Dom Turysty PTTK** (☎ 18 206 3281; ul Zaruskiego 5) in Zakopane.

SILESIA (ŚLĄSK)

Silesia (Śląsk) is a fascinating mix of landscapes. Though the industrial zone around Katowice has limited attraction for visitors, beautiful Wrocław is a historic city with lively nightlife, and the Sudeten Mountains draw hikers and other nature lovers.

The region's history is similarly diverse, having been governed by Polish, Bohemian, Austrian and German rulers. After two centuries as part of Prussia and Germany, the territory was largely included within Poland's new borders after WWII.

WROCŁAW

pop 640,000

When citizens of beautiful Kraków enthusiastically encourage you to visit Wrocław (*vrots*-wahf), you know you're onto something good. The city's beautiful Old Town is a gracious mix of Gothic and baroque styles, and its large student population ensures a healthy number of restaurants, bars and nightclubs.

Wrocław has been traded back and forth between various rulers over the centuries, having begun life in the year 1000. Upon its return to Poland from Germany in 1945, Wrocław was a shell of its former self, having sustained massive damage in WWII. Sensitive restoration has since returned the historic centre to its former splendour.

Information

Bank Pekao (ul Oławska 2)

Tourist office (☎ 71 344 3111; www.wroclaw.pl; Rynek 14; 🕑 9am-9pm Apr-Oct, to 8pm Nov-Mar)

W Sercu Miasta (ul Przejście Żelaźnicie 4; per hr 4zł; 🕑 9am-midnight Mon-Sat, noon-midnight Sun) Internet cafe down a laneway in the middle of the Rynek.

Sights

In the centre of the Old Town is the attractive **Rynek** (Market Sq). The beautiful **Town Hall** (built from 1327 to 1504) on the southern side plays host to the **City Dwellers' Art Museum** (adult/concession 7/5zł, free Wed; 🕑 11am-5pm Tue-Sat, 10am-6pm Sun), with stately rooms on show, and exhibits featuring the art of gold and the stories of famous Wrocław inhabitants.

In the northwestern corner of the Rynek are two attractive small houses linked by a baroque gate. They're called **Jaś i Małgosia** (ul Św Mikołaja), a couple better known to English speakers as Hansel and Gretel. See if you can spot the diminutive statue of a gnome at ground level, just to the west of these houses. He's one of the many **Gnomes of Wrocław** scattered through the city, attributed to the symbol of the Orange Alternative, a communist-era dissident group.

Behind gate and gnome is the monumental 14th-century **St Elizabeth's Church** (ul Elżbiety 1; admission 5zł; 🕑 9am-7pm Mon-Fri, 11am-5pm Sat, 1-6pm Sun May-Oct, 10am-5pm Mon-Sat, 1-5pm Sun Nov-Apr) with its 83m-high tower, which you can climb for city views.

East of the Old Town you'll find Wrocław's pride and joy, the giant **Panorama of Racławicka** (www.panoramaraclawicka.pl; ul Purkyniego 11; adult/concession 20/15zł; 🕑 9am-5pm Tue-Sun May-Oct, to 4pm Tue-Sun Nov-Apr). It's a 360-degree painting of a 1794 battle, in which the Polish peasant army, led by Tadeusz Kościuszko, defeated Russian forces intent on partitioning Poland. Created for the centenary of the battle in 1894, the painting is an immense 114m long and 15m high. Obligatory tours (with audio in English and other languages) run every 30 minutes between 9am and 4.30pm from April to November, and from 10am to 3pm from December to March. The ticket also allows entry to the National Museum on the same day.

Located nearby, the **National Museum** (www.mnwr.art.pl; Plac Powstańców Warszawy 5; adult/concession 15/10zł, free Sat; 🕑 9am-4pm Wed-Fri & Sun, 10am-6pm Sat) exhibits Silesian medieval art, and a fine collection of modern Polish painting.

North of the river is **Ostrów Tumski** (Cathedral Island), a picturesque area full of churches. Here you'll find the Gothic **Cathedral of St John the Baptist** (Plac Katedralny; 🕑 10am-6pm Mon-Sat except during services). Uniquely, there's a lift to whisk you to the top of the **tower** (adult/concession 5/4zł; 🕑 10am-6pm Mon-Sat) for superb views. Nearby are the charming **Botanical Gardens** (ul Sienkiewicza 23; adult/concession 7/5zł; 🕑 8am-6pm Apr-Oct).

To the south of the Old Town, on the corner of ul Świdnicka and ul Piłsudskiego, is a fascinating sculpture called **Passage** (Przejście), which depicts a group of pedestrians being swallowed by the pavement, only to re-emerge on the other side of the street.

Festivals & Events

Musica Polonica Nova Festival (www.musicapolonicanova.pl, in Polish) February.

Jazz on the Odra International Festival (www.jnofestival.pl) June.

Wrocław Non Stop (www.wroclawnonstop.pl) June/July.

Castle Party (www.castleparty.com) July/August.

Wratislavia Cantans (www.wratislavia.art.pl) September.

Wrocław Marathon (www.wroclawmaraton.pl) September.

Sleeping

MDK Youth Hostel (☎ 71 343 8856; www.mdk.kopernik.wroclaw.pl; ul Kołłątaja 20; dm/d from 22/29zł) This is a basic, tidy place, located in a grand mustard-coloured building. Some dorms are huge and beds are packed close together.

Stranger Hostel (☎ 71 344 1206; www.thestrangerhostel.com; ul Kołłątaja 16; dm 40-55zł) A tatty old staircase leads to attractive dorms with ornate lamps and decorative ceilings. Guests have access to a kitchen, washing machine, games console and DVD projector.

Nathan's Villa Hostel (☎ 71 344 1095; www.nathansvilla.com; ul Świdnicka 13; dm/r from 45/150zł) This comfortable 96-bed place is conveniently placed 150m south of the Rynek. However, it also accepts noisy Polish school groups in addition to backpackers, so check before you check in.

Bursa Nauczycielska (☎ 71 344 3781; www.dodn.wroclaw.pl/bursa; ul Kotlarska 42; s/d/tr/q 65/110/105/120zł) A basic but clean hostel with shared bathrooms, located just one block northeast of the Rynek. There's a lot of brown in the colour scheme, but the rooms are quite cosy.

Hotel Zaułek (☎ 71 341 0046; www.hotel.uni.wroc.pl; ul Garbary 11; s/d from 260/330zł) Old-fashioned guest house run by the university. The 1pm checkout is a plus for heavy sleepers, and discounted weekend prices are a steal. Half and full board are available.

Hotel Europejski (☎ 71 772 1000; www.silfor.pl; ul Piłsudskiego 88; s/d/ste 269/309/349zł) The formerly drab Europejski has recently been transformed into a smart business hotel. Rooms are clean and bright, and very handy for the train station.

Eating & Drinking

Bar Wegetariański Vega (☎ 71 344 3934; Rynek 1/2; mains 5-6zł; 🕑 8am-7pm Mon-Fri, 9am-5pm Sat) This cheap cafeteria in the centre of the Rynek offers vegetarian dishes in a light green space. Upstairs there's a vegan section, open from noon.

Bazylia (Plac Uniwersytecki; mains 5-10zł; 🕑 8am-8pm) Bustling student eatery with huge plate-glass windows. The menu has Polish standards such as *bigos* (cabbage and meat stew) and *gołąbki* (cabbage rolls), and a decent range of salads and other vegetable dishes.

Mexico Bar (☎ 71 346 0292; ul Rzeźnicza 34; mains 13-38zł; 🕑 noon-midnight) Compact, warmly lit restaurant featuring sombreros, backlit masks and a chandelier made of beer bottles. All the Tex-Mex standards are on the menu; book ahead at weekends.

Pub Guinness (Plac Solny 5; 🕑 noon-2am) A lively, fairly authentic Irish pub. The ground-floor bar buzzes with student and traveller groups getting together, and there's a restaurant and beer cellar as well.

PRL (Rynek Ratusz 10; 🕑 noon-late) The dictatorship of the proletariat is alive and well in this venue inspired by communist nostalgia. Disco lights play over a bust of Lenin, and 'red menace' memorabilia is scattered through the maze of rooms.

Entertainment

Check out the (free and in English) bimonthly the *Visitor* for details of what's on in this important cultural centre.

Teatr Polski (☎ 71 316 0777; www.teatrpolski.wroc.pl, in Polish; ul Zapolskiej 3) Theatrical venue staging classic Polish and foreign drama.

Filharmonia (☎ 71 342 2001; www.filharmonia.wroclaw.pl; ul Piłsudskiego 19) Hosts classical music concerts, mostly on Friday and Saturday nights.

Kino Helios (www.heliosnet.pl; ul Kazimierza Wielkiego 19a) Modern multiplex screening English-language films.

Getting There & Away

From **Copernicus Airport** (www.airport.wroclaw.pl), LOT flies between Wrocław and Warsaw, Brussels, Frankfurt and Munich. Tickets can be purchased at the **LOT office** (☎ 801 703 703; ul Piłsudskiego 36). Various budget carriers connect Wrocław with other European cities, including a number of British and Irish regional destinations. Consult the airport's website for details and schedules. The half-hourly bus 406 and night bus 249 link the airport with Wrocław Główny train station.

If you're travelling to/from Wrocław at the weekend by bus or train, you'll be in competition with thousands of itinerant university students, so book your ticket as early as possible.

The **bus terminal** (ul Sucha 11) is south of the main train station, and offers four daily buses to Warsaw (51zł, seven hours). For most other travel, however, the train is more convenient.

From **Wrocław Główny train station** (ul Piłsudskiego 105), trains to Kraków (45zł, 4½ hours) depart every one or two hours, with similarly frequent services to Warsaw (102zł, 5¾ hours). Wrocław is also linked by train to Poznań (34zł, 2½ hours, at least hourly) and Częstochowa (34zł, three hours, four daily).

WIELKOPOLSKA

Wielkopolska (Greater Poland) is the region in which Poland came to life in the Middle Ages. As a result of this ancient eminence, its cities and towns are full of historic and cultural attractions. The region's historic significance didn't save it from international conflict, however, and it became part of Prussia in 1793. The battles of WWII later caused widespread destruction throughout the area, though Poznań has since been restored to its prominent economic role.

POZNAŃ

pop 565,000

No one could accuse Poznań of being too sleepy. Between its regular trade fairs, student population and visiting travellers, it's a vibrant city with a wide choice of attractions. There's a beautiful Old Town at its centre, with a number of interesting museums and a range of lively bars, clubs and restaurants. The surrounding countryside is also good for cycling and hiking.

Information

Bank Pekao Old Town (ul 23 Lutego); ul Św Marcin (ul Św Marcin 52/56)

E24 (ul Półwiejska 42; per hr 4.50zł; 24hr) Internet access within the massive Stary Browar shopping centre.

Tourist office (61 852 6156; Stary Rynek 59; 9am-8pm Mon-Sat, 10am-6pm Sun May-Sep, 9am-5pm Mon-Fri Oct-Apr)

Sights

If you're in the attractive **Stary Rynek** (Old Market Sq), look aloft. Every noon two metal goats above the Renaissance **Town Hall** clock butt their horns together 12 times, in accordance with an old legend. Inside the building, the **Poznań Historical Museum** (adult/concession 5.50/3.50zł, free Sat; 9am-4pm Tue, Thu & Fri, 11am-6pm Wed, 10am-3pm Sat & Sun) displays splendid period interiors.

Nearby is the **Museum of Musical Instruments** (Stary Rynek 45; adult/concession 5.50/3.50zł, free Sat; 11am-5pm Tue-Sat, 10am-3pm Sun). The **Archaeological Museum** (ul Wodna 27; adult/concession 6/3zł, free Sat; 10am-4pm Tue-Fri, to 6pm Sat, to 3pm Sun) contains Egyptian mummies and displays on the prehistory of western Poland.

The 17th-century **Franciscan Church** (ul Franciszkańska 2; 8am-8pm), one block west of the Rynek, has an ornate baroque interior, complete with wall paintings and rich stucco work.

The nearby **National Museum: Paintings & Sculpture Gallery** (Al Marcinkowskiego 9; adult/concession 10/6zł, free Sat; 10am-6pm Tue, 9am-5pm Wed, 10am-4pm Thu, 10am-5pm Fri & Sat, 10am-3pm Sun) displays mainly 19th- and 20th-century Polish paintings.

In a park in the area west of the Rynek, the moving **Monument to the Victims of June 1956** commemorates the dead and injured of the massive 1956 strike by the city's industrial workers. Next door in the Cultural Centre, there's more detail in the **Museum of Poznań June 1956** (ul Św Marcin 80/82; adult/concession 4/2zł, free Sat; 10am-6pm Tue-Fri, to 4pm Sat & Sun).

Some 2.5km east of the Old Town is **Lake Malta**. A fun way to visit the lake is to take tram 3, 4 or 8 from Plac Wielkopolski to the Rondo Śródka stop on the other side of Ostrów Tumski. From the nearby terminus you can catch a miniature train along the **Malta Park Railway** (ul Jana Pawła II; adult/concession 4.50/3zł; 10am-6.45pm Mon-Fri, to 6pm Sat & Sun May-15 Oct), which follows the lake's shore to the **New Zoo** (ul Krańcowa 81; adult/concession 9/6zł; 9am-7pm Apr-Sep, to 4pm Oct-Mar).

Festivals & Events

The largest trade fairs take place in January, June, September and October.

Poznań Jazz Festival (www.jazz.pl) March.

St John's Fair Cultural event in June.

Malta International Theatre Festival (www.malta-festival.pl) June.

Sleeping

During Poznań's regular trade fairs (see above), accommodation rates increase dramatically. A room may also be difficult to find, so it pays to book ahead. Prices given here are for outside the trade-fair periods.

Youth Hostel No 3 (61 866 4040; ul Berwińskiego 2/3; dm 30zł) This is a 15-minute walk southwest of the train station along ul Głogowska, adjacent to Park Wilsona. It's a basic 'no frills' option, and there's a 10pm curfew.

Biuro Zakwaterowania Przemysław (61 866 3560; www.przemyslaw.com.pl; ul Głogowska 16; s/d/apt from 53/85/170zł; 8am-6pm Mon-Fri, 10am-2pm Sat) Accommodation agency near the train station; rates for weekends and stays of more than three nights are cheaper.

Frolic Goats Hostel (61 852 4411; www.frolicgoatshostel.com; ul Wrocławska 16/6; dm/d/tr from 50/140/250zł)

Hostel aimed squarely at the international backpacker. There's a washing machine on the premises, bike hire is available, and room rates are unaffected by trade fairs. Enter from ul Jaskółcza.

Mini Hotelik (☎ 61 633 1416; Al Niepodległości 8a; r 129-161zł) Like it says on the label, this is a small place, in an old building between the train station and the Old Town. It's basic but clean. Enter from ul Taylora.

Hotel Lech (☎ 61 853 0151; www.hotel-lech.poznan.pl; ul Św Marcin 74; s/d/tr 172/264/366zł) Hotel Lech has standard three-star decor, but rooms are relatively spacious and the bathrooms are modern. Flash your ISIC card for a discount.

our pick **Rezydencja Solei** (☎ 61 855 7351; www.hotel-solei.pl; ul Szewska 2; s/d/ste 199/299/389zł) Close to the Rynek, this tiny hotel offers small but cosy rooms in an old-fashioned residential style. The attic suite is amazingly large and can accommodate up to four people.

Eating & Drinking

Bar Wegetariański (☎ 61 821 1255; ul Wrocławska 21; mains 5-10zł; 11am-6pm Mon-Fri, to 3pm Sat) Cheap vegetarian place in a cellar off the main road, bedecked with plant life about its walls.

Deserovnia (☎ 61 852 5029; ul Świętosławska 12; mains 19-55zł) One side of this split-personality venue is a sporty bar, all dark timber, beer and photos of sports stars. The other side is a gracious restaurant serving classy Polish cuisine. Heads or tails?

Sioux (☎ 61 851 6286; Stary Rynek 93; mains 20-100zł; noon-11pm) Cowboy-themed place, with bizarrely named dishes such as 'Scoundrels in Uniforms from Fort Knox' (chicken legs).

Tapas Bar (☎ 61 852 8532; Stary Rynek 60; mains 32-62zł; noon-midnight) Atmospheric place dishing up authentic tapas and Spanish wine. Most tapas dishes are 14zł to 22zł, so forget the mains and share with friends.

Proletaryat (ul Wrocławska 9; 1pm-2am Mon-Sat, 3pm-2am Sun) A small red communist nostalgia bar. Play 'spot the communist leader' while sipping a local boutique beer.

Czarna Owca (ul Jaskółcza 13; noon-2am Mon-Fri, 5pm-2am Sat) Literally 'Black Sheep', this is a popular nightclub with nightly DJs playing a mix of genres including R & B, house, rock, Latin, soul and funk.

Entertainment

Teatr Wielki (☎ 61 659 0280; www.opera.poznan.pl; ul Fredry 9) is the venue for opera and ballet, while the **Filharmonia** (☎ 61 853 6935; www.filharmonia.poznan.pl; ul Św Marcin 81) offers classical concerts at least weekly.

Getting There & Away

From **Poznań airport** (www.airport-poznan.com.pl), LOT flies regularly to Warsaw, Frankfurt and Munich. Tickets are available from the **LOT office** (☎ 801 703 703; airport) or from **Orbis Travel** (☎ 61 851 2000; Al Marcinkowskiego 21). There are also daily domestic flights via Jet Air to Kraków. A vast array of other European cities are serviced by budget airlines, including London, Dublin and Copenhagen. Check the airport's website for schedules. The airport is accessible by buses 59 and L.

The **bus terminal** (ul Towarowa 17) is located about 600m east of the train station. However, most destinations can be reached more comfortably and frequently by train. The busy **Poznań Główny train station** (ul Dworcowa 1) offers services to Kraków (53zł, 7½ hours, 11 daily), Gdańsk and Gdynia (48zł, 5½ hours, seven daily), Toruń (33zł, 2½ hours, six daily) and Wrocław (34zł, 2½ hours, at least hourly). Nearly 20 trains a day head to Warsaw (95zł, 3½ hours).

POMERANIA (POMORZE)

Pomerania (Pomorze) is an attractive region with diverse drawcards, from beautiful beaches to architecturally pleasing cities. The region's sandy coastline is a popular destination for holidaymakers in summer. The historic port city of Gdańsk is situated at the region's eastern extreme, while the attractive Gothic city of Toruń lies inland, within a belt of forests and lakes.

GDAŃSK

pop 457,000

Port cities are usually lively places with distinctive personalities, and Gdańsk is no exception. From its lively riverside waterfront to the Renaissance splendour of its charming narrow streets, there's plenty to like about this coastal city.

After being tussled over by Germans and Poles for centuries, Gdańsk suffered immense damage in WWII. In the 1980s it achieved international fame as the home of the Solidarity trade union, whose rise helped precipitate the fall of communism in Europe.

Information

Bank Pekao (ul Garncarska 23)
Jazz 'n' Java (ul Tkacka 17/18; per hr 5zł; 10am-10pm) Internet cafe.
PTTK office (58 301 1343; www.pttk-gdansk.pl; ul Długa 45; 9am-6pm Mon-Fri, 8.30am-4.30pm Sat & Sun) This tourist office is opposite the Main Town Hall.

Sights

MAIN TOWN

The beautiful ul Długa (Long Street) and Długi Targ (Long Market) form the historic **Royal Way**. Polish kings traditionally paraded through the **Upland Gate** (built in the 1770s on a 15th-century gate), onward through the **Foregate** (which once housed a torture chamber) and **Golden Gate** (1614), and proceeded east to the Renaissance **Green Gate** (1568).

Following the royal lead and starting from the Upland Gate, walk east to the Foregate. Within this structure, you can visit the **Amber Museum** (www.mhmg.gda.pl/bursztyn; adult/concession 10/5zł, free Tue; 10am-2.30pm Tue, to 3.30pm Wed-Sat, 11am-3.30pm Sun).

Proceed to the **Gdańsk History Museum** (ul Długa 47; adult/concession 8/5zł, free Tue; 10am-3pm Tue, to 4pm Wed-Sat, 11am-4pm Sun), inside the towering Gothic **Main Town Hall**. Outside is **Neptune's Fountain** (1633). Nearby, the **Golden House** (1618) has a strikingly rich facade.

North of the Green Gate is the 14th-century **St Mary's Gate**, through which lies picturesque **ul Mariacka** (St Mary's St), lined with 17th-century burgher houses and amber shops.

At the end of ul Mariacka is the gigantic 14th-century **St Mary's Church** (admission free; 8.30am-6pm except during services). Watch little figures troop out at noon from its 14m-high astronomical clock, which is adorned with zodiacal signs. Climb the 405 steps of the **tower** (adult/concession 4/2zł) for a giddy view over the town.

Further north along the waterfront, the **Central Maritime Museum** (ul Ołowianka 9-13; 1 section adult/concession 6/4zł, all 4 sections 15/9zł; 10am-6pm May-Oct, to 4pm Tue-Sun Nov-Apr) offers a fascinating insight into Gdańsk's seafaring past. The museum is split into two sections on opposite sides of the river, linked by a regular ferry service. Adjacent to the eastern section on Ołowianka Island is the **Sołdek Museum Ship**, built here just after WWII.

OLD TOWN

Almost totally destroyed in 1945, the Old Town has never been completely rebuilt. However, among its gems are **St Catherine's Church** (ul Wielke Młyny; 8am-6pm Mon-Sat), Gdańsk's oldest church (begun in the 1220s). Opposite the church is the **Great Mill** (ul Wielke Młyny), which was built by the Teutonic Knights around 1350. It used to produce 200 tonnes of flour per day and continued to operate until 1945.

At the north end of the Old Town is the evocative **Roads to Freedom Exhibition** (ul Wały Piastowskie 24; adult/concession 6/4zł; 10am-4pm Tue-Sun), an excellent museum charting the decline and fall of Polish communism. Further north, the soaring **Monument to the Shipyard Workers** (Plac Solidarności), erected in 1980, stands at the entrance to the Gdańsk Shipyards.

OLD SUBURB

The **National Museum's Department of Early Art** (ul Toruńska 1; adult/concession 10/6zł; 10am-5pm May-Sep, 9am-4pm Oct-Apr) is famous for its Dutch and Flemish paintings, especially Hans Memling's 15th-century *Last Judgment*.

Festivals & Events

International Organ Music Festival (www.gdanskie-organy.com) June to August.
International Street & Open-Air Theatre Festival (www.feta.pl) July.
Sounds of the North Festival (www.nck.org.pl) July/August.
International Shakespeare Festival (www.teatr-szekspir.gda.pl) August.
St Dominic's Fair (www.mtgsa.pl) August.

Sleeping

Camping Nr 218 Stogi (58 307 3915; www.camping-gdansk.pl; ul Wydmy 9; per person/tent 12/6zł, cabins 60-110zł; May-Sep) This camping ground is only 200m from the beach in the seaside holiday centre of Stogi, about 5.5km northeast of the Main Town. Take tram 8 or 13 from the main train station in Gdańsk.

Youth Hostel (58 301 2313; www.mokf.com.pl; ul Wałowa 21; dm/s/d/tr/q 18/31/62/63/84zł) Old-style hostel on the doorstep of the Gdańsk Shipyards. Rooms are brown and basic, but clean. Smoking and drinking are strictly forbidden, and there's a midnight curfew.

Dom Harcerza (58 301 3621; www.domharcerza.prv.pl; ul Za Murami 2/10; dm/s/d/tr/q 34/50/120/150/160zł) The rooms are small but cosy, and the bathrooms are clean at this busy budget accommodation. There's a charming old-fashioned restaurant on the ground floor.

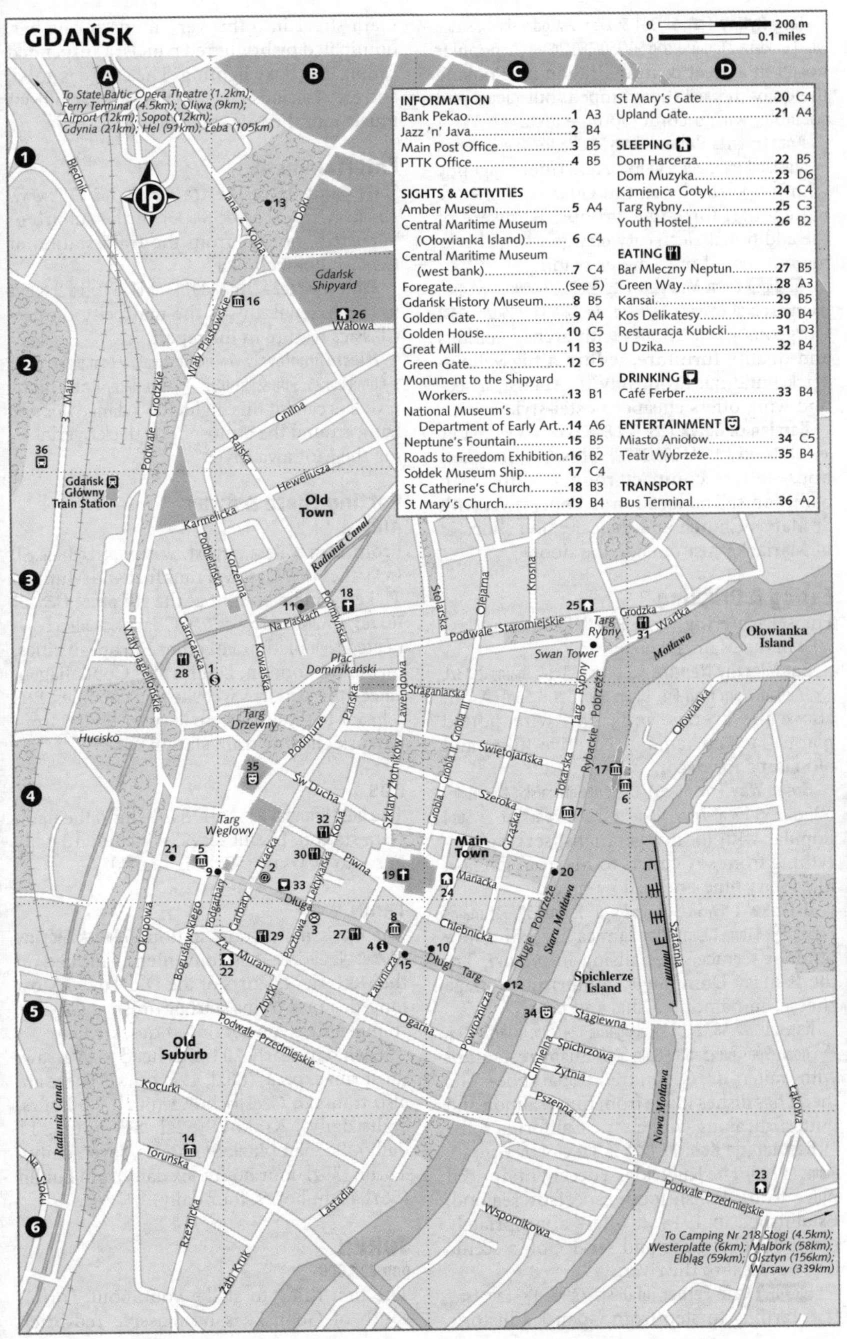
GDAŃSK
0 200 m
0 0.1 miles
To State Baltic Opera Theatre (1.2km); Ferry Terminal (4.5km); Oliwa (9km); Airport (12km); Sopot (12km); Gdynia (21km); Hel (91km); Łeba (105km)
INFORMATION
Bank Pekao 1 A3
Jazz 'n' Java 2 B4
Main Post Office 3 B5
PTTK Office 4 B5
SIGHTS & ACTIVITIES
Amber Museum 5 A4
Central Maritime Museum (Ołowianka Island) 6 C4
Central Maritime Museum (west bank) 7 C4
Foregate (see 5)
Gdańsk History Museum 8 B5
Golden Gate 9 A4
Golden House 10 C5
Great Mill 11 B3
Green Gate 12 C5
Monument to the Shipyard Workers 13 B1
National Museum's Department of Early Art 14 A6
Neptune's Fountain 15 B5
Roads to Freedom Exhibition 16 B2
Sołdek Museum Ship 17 C4
St Catherine's Church 18 B3
St Mary's Church 19 B4
St Mary's Gate 20 C4
Upland Gate 21 A4
SLEEPING
Dom Harcerza 22 B5
Dom Muzyka 23 D6
Kamienica Gotyk 24 C4
Targ Rybny 25 C3
Youth Hostel 26 B2
EATING
Bar Mleczny Neptun 27 B5
Green Way 28 A3
Kansai 29 B5
Kos Delikatesy 30 B4
Restauracja Kubicki 31 D3
U Dzika 32 B4
DRINKING
Café Ferber 33 B4
ENTERTAINMENT
Miasto Aniołów 34 C5
Teatr Wybrzeże 35 B4
TRANSPORT
Bus Terminal 36 A2
Błędnik
Jana z Kolna
Doki
Gdańsk Shipyard
Wałowa
Wały Piastowskie
3 Maja
Podwale Grodzkie
Gnilna
Rajska
Heweliusza
Gdańsk Główny Train Station
Old Town
Karmelicka
Podbielańska
Korzenna
Radunia Canal
Stolarska
Olejarna
Krosna
Targ Rybny
Grodzka
Wartka
Na Piaskach
Podmłyńska
Podwale Staromiejskie
Swan Tower
Motława
Ołowianka Island
Wały Jagiellońskie
Garncarska
Kowalska
Plac Dominikański
Lawendowa
Straganiarska
Ołowianka
Targ Drzewny
Pańska
Grobla I
Grobla II
Grobla III
Świętojańska
Tokarska
Rybackie Pobrzeże
Hucisko
Podmurze
Św Ducha
Szklary Złotników
Szeroka
Grząska
Targ Węglowy
Kozia
Tkacka
Piwna
Main Town
Mariacka
Stara Motława
Podgarbary
Garbary
Długa
Lektykarska
Chlebnicka
Szafarnia
Okopowa
Bogusławskiego
Pocztowa
Za Murami
Ławnicza
Długi Targ
Długie Pobrzeże
Spichlerze Island
Zbytki
Ogarna
Powroźnicza
Stągiewna
Old Suburb
Podwale Przedmiejskie
Chmielna
Spichrzowa
Żytnia
Kocurki
Pszenna
Nowa Motława
Łąkowa
Radunia Canal
Toruńska
Na Stoku
Lastadia
Wspornikowa
Rzeźnicka
Żabi Kruk
To Camping Nr 218 Stogi (4.5km); Westerplatte (6km); Malbork (58km); Elbląg (59km); Olsztyn (156km); Warsaw (339km)
POLAND

Targ Rybny (☎ 58 301 5627; www.gdanskhostel.com.pl; ul Grodzka 21; dm/d/tr/q 50/150/180/240zł) A popular hostel in a great central location overlooking the quay. It's a little cramped, but clean and sociable, with a comfy lounge area.

Apartments Poland (☎ 58 346 9864; www.apartmentpoland.com; apt €30-65) Apartment agency with properties in central Gdańsk. Some are big enough for larger groups. Be aware of the additional electricity charge when checking out, based on a meter reading.

our pick **Dom Muzyka** (☎ 58 326 0600; www.dom-muzyka.pl; ul Łąkowa 1/2; s/d/ste 220/310/460zł;) Gorgeous white rooms with arched ceilings and quality furniture, within a big yellow-brick building. From July to August, a second wing offers cheaper hostel-style beds.

Kamienica Gotyk (☎ 602 844 535; www.gotykhouse.eu; ul Mariacka 1; s/d 280/310zł) This Gothic guest house offers compact rooms, with clean bathrooms. The location is impressive, with St Mary's Church and the cafes and shops of ul Mariacka just outside the door.

Eating & Drinking

For self-catering, visit **Kos Delikatesy** (ul Piwna 9/10) in the Main Town.

Bar Mleczny Neptun (ul Długa 33/34; mains 2-13zł; 7.30am-7pm Mon-Fri, 10am-6pm Sat & Sun) A cut above the average milk bar, with potted plants, lace curtains, decorative tiling and old lamps for decor.

Green Way (☎ 58 301 4121; ul Garncarska 4/6; mains 7-10zł; 10am-7pm Mon-Fri, noon-7pm Sat & Sun) Popular with local vegetarians, serving everything from soy cutlets to Mexican goulash in a folksy blue-and-yellow space.

U Dzika (☎ 58 305 2676; ul Piwna 59/61; mains 7-39zł; 11am-10pm) Pleasant eatery with a nice outdoor terrace, specialising in *pierogi*. Try the Fantasy Dumplings, comprising cottage cheese, cinnamon, raisins and peach.

Kansai (☎ 58 324 0888; ul Ogarna 124/125; mains 8-99zł; noon-9pm Tue-Sat, to 8pm Sun) Sushi restaurant with waiters dressed in traditional robes. The menu has dishes made from tuna, salmon and butterfish, along with classic California rolls.

Restauracja Kubicki (☎ 58 301 0050; ul Wartka 5; mains 24-80zł) The Kubicki is a decent midpriced place to try Polish food, especially seafood. Established in 1918, it offers appropriately old-fashioned decor and service off a scenic laneway next to the river.

our pick **Café Ferber** (ul Długa 77/78; 8am-late) It's startling to step from Gdańsk's historic main street into this very modern cafe-bar, dominated by bright red panels, a suspended ceiling and boxy lighting. The coffee is good, and on weekends DJs spin house and chill-out music into the wee small hours.

Entertainment

State Baltic Opera Theatre (☎ 58 763 4912; www.operabaltycka.pl; Al Zwycięstwa 15) In the suburb of Wrzeszcz, not far from the train station at Gdańsk Politechnika.

Teatr Wybrzeże (☎ 58 301 1328; ul Św Ducha 2) Next to the Arsenal, this is the main city theatre. Classics feature in the repertoire.

Miasto Aniołów (www.miastoaniolow.com.pl, in Polish; ul Chmielna 26; admission 10zł; 9pm-late) Late-night revellers can hit this nightclub's dance floor or hang around the atmospheric deck overlooking the Motława River.

Getting There & Away

AIR

From **Lech Wałęsa airport** (www.airport.gdansk.pl), LOT flies to Warsaw, Frankfurt and Munich. Tickets can be bought at the **LOT office** (☎ 801 703 703; ul Wały Jagiellońskie 2/4). Gdańsk is also connected to a plethora of other European cities, including London, Dublin and Copenhagen. Check the airport's website for schedules. Bus B heads to the airport up to twice hourly from Gdańsk Główny train station.

BUS

The **bus terminal** (ul 3 Maja 12) is behind the main train station. Useful services include 10 daily buses to Warsaw (50zł, six hours).

TRAIN

The city's main train station, **Gdańsk Główny** (ul Podwale Grodzkie 1), is conveniently located on the western outskirts of the Old Town. Most long-distance trains start or finish at Gdynia, so make sure you get on/off quickly here.

Each day nearly 20 trains head to Warsaw; most run express (88zł, 4½ hours). There are also trains to Częstochowa (60zł, 9½ hours, eight daily), Kraków (62zł, 8¾ hours, 11 daily), Poznań (48zł, 5½ hours, seven daily), Toruń (39zł, four hours, six daily) and Lublin (56zł, eight hours, four daily).

TORUŃ

pop 207,000

The first thing to strike you about Toruń, south of Gdańsk, is its massive red-brick

WORTH THE TRIP

The magnificent **Malbork Castle** makes a great day trip from Gdańsk. It's the largest Gothic castle in Europe, and was once known as Marienburg, headquarters of the medieval Teutonic Knights. Its sinister form looms over the relatively small town and the Nogat River – grab a sneak preview by looking right as your train crosses the river. Trains run regularly from Gdańsk Głowny station (50 minutes). Once you get to Malbork station, turn right, cross the highway and follow ul Kościuszki to the castle. Compulsory tours are usually in Polish, but ask about English-language options. There are places to eat at the castle and in the town.

churches, looking more like fortresses than places of worship. The city is a pleasant place to spend a few days, offering a nice balance between a relaxing slow pace and engaging entertainment diversions.

Toruń is also famous as the birthplace of Nicolaus Copernicus, who revolutionised the field of astronomy in 1543 by asserting that the earth travelled around the sun. He's a figure you will not be able to escape – you can even buy gingerbread men in his likeness.

Toruń was fortunate to escape major damage in WWII, and as a result is the best-preserved Gothic town in Poland.

Information

Ksero Uniwerek (ul Franciszkańska 5; per hr 3zł; 8am-7pm Mon-Fri, 9am-4pm Sat) Internet access.
PKO Bank (ul Szeroka)
Tourist office (56 621 0931; www.it.torun.pl; Rynek Staromiejski 25; 9am-4pm Mon & Sat, to 6pm Tue-Fri, to 1pm Sun)

Sights

The starting point for any exploration is the **Rynek Staromiejski** (Old Town Sq). The **Regional Museum** (www.muzeum.torun.pl; Rynek Staromiejski 1; adult/concession 10/6zł; 10am-6pm Tue-Sun May-Sep, to 4pm Tue-Sun Oct-Apr) sits within the massive 14th-century **Old Town Hall**, featuring a fine collection of Polish art, medieval stained glass and religious paintings. Climb the 40m-high **tower** (adult/concession 10/6zł; 10am-4pm Tue-Sun Apr, to 8pm Tue-Sun May-Sep) for great views.

In front of the Old Town Hall is an elegant **statue of Copernicus**. Look for other interesting items of statuary around the square, including a dog and umbrella from a famous Polish comic strip, a donkey that once served as a punishment device, and a fabled violinist who saved Toruń from a plague of frogs.

On the square, the richly decorated 15th-century **House Under the Star** contains the **Far Eastern Art Museum** (Rynek Staromiejski 35; adult/concession 7/4zł; 10am-6pm Tue-Sun May-Sep, to 4pm Tue-Sun Oct-Apr).

In 1473 Copernicus was born in the brick Gothic house that now contains the fairly dull **Museum of Copernicus** (ul Kopernika 15/17; adult/concession 10/7zł; 10am-6pm Tue-Sun May-Sep, to 4pm Tue-Sun Oct-Apr), with replicas of the great astronomer's instruments. More engaging exhibits in the same building include an **audiovisual presentation** (adult/concession 12/7zł) about Copernicus' life in Toruń and the extravagantly titled **World of Toruń's Gingerbread** (adult/concession 10/6zł).

One block east is the **Cathedral of SS John the Baptist & John the Evangelist** (ul Żeglarska; adult/concession 3/2zł; 9am-5.30pm Mon-Sat, 2-5.30pm Sun Apr-Oct), with its massive **tower** (adult/concession 6/4zł) and bell.

Further east, beyond the old city wall, are the ruins of the **Teutonic Castle** (ul Przedzamcze; adult/concession 4/2zł, free Mon; 10am-6pm), destroyed in 1454 by angry townsfolk protesting the Teutonic Knights' oppressive regime.

Sleeping

Camping Nr 33 Tramp (56 654 7187; www.tramp.mosir.torun.pl; ul Kujawska 14; camping per person 8.50zł, tents 5.50-11zł, d/tr/q 50/70/90zł; May-Sep) Camping ground on the edge of the train line, with an on-site snack bar. It's a five-minute walk west of the main train station.

Orange Hostel (56 652 0033; www.hostelorange.pl; ul Prosta 19; dm/s/d/tr 30/50/90/120zł) This cheerful international backpackers' joint is in a handy location, and its kitchen is an impressive place to practise the gentle art of self-catering.

Hotel Trzy Korony (56 622 6031; www.hotel3korony.pl; Rynek Staromiejski 21; s/d/tr/ste from 100/140/180/260zł) This budget hotel is by no means luxurious, but the simple rooms are neatly furnished with pine furniture, blue sofas and sunny yellow wallpaper.

Hotel Pod Orłem (56 622 5024; www.hotel.torun.pl; ul Mostowa 17; s/d/apt from 120/150/215zł) Great-value hotel, although the rooms are smallish and some contain poky bathrooms. The corridors

 Book your stay at lonelyplanet.com/hotels

are fun with their jumble of framed pop-art images and old photos.

Hotel Pod Czarną Różą (☎ 56 621 9637; www.hotelczarnaroza.pl; ul Rabiańska 11; s/d/tr/ste 170/210/250/320zł) Hotel spread between a historic inn and a new wing facing the river. Some doubles come with small but functional kitchens.

Eating & Drinking

Bar Mleczny Pod Arkadami (ul Różana 1; mains 3-8zł; 9am-7pm Mon-Fri, to 4pm Sat) Classic milk bar with low-cost dishes and a takeaway window serving super-cheap *zapiekanki* (toasted rolls with cheese, mushrooms and ketchup) and sweet waffles.

Sułtan (☎ 56 621 0607; ul Mostowa 7; mains 8-12zł; noon-midnight) Middle Eastern cuisine in a cheerful venue decorated with colourful lanterns and Arabic script. Serves up kebabs, along with soups and salads.

Gospoda Pod Modrym Fartuchem (☎ 56 622 2626; Rynek Nowomiejski 8; mains 10-35zł; 10am-10pm) Folksy 15th-century pub once visited by Polish kings and Napoleon, located on the New Town Sq. Polish dishes and Indian cuisine are on the menu.

Manekin (☎ 56 621 0504; Rynek Staromiejski 16; mains 11-13zł) Vaguely Wild West decor adorns this inexpensive central restaurant specialising in *naleśniki* (crepes). It offers a variety of filled pancakes, including vegetarian options.

Tantra (ul Ślusarska 5) Colourful New Town bar done out in an Indian and Tibetan theme, and layered with cloth and other artefacts from the subcontinent.

Jazz God (ul Rabiańska 17; 5pm-2am Sun-Thu, to 4am Fri & Sat) A lively cellar bar with rock DJs every night from 9pm.

Entertainment

Teatr im Horzycy (☎ 56 622 5222; Plac Teatralny 1) presents theatre performances, while **Dwór Artusa** (Artus Court; ☎ 56 655 4929; Rynek Staromiejski 6) offers classical music.

Nasze Kino (www.naszekino.pl, in Polish; ul Podmurna 14; admission 12zł) A cool little art-house cinema embedded within part of the old city wall.

Getting There & Away

The **bus terminal** (ul Dąbrowskiego) is about 1km north of the Old Town. Polski Express has eight buses a day to Warsaw (41zł, 3½ hours).

The main **Toruń Główny train station** (Al Podgórska) is on the opposite side of the Vistula River and linked to the Old Town by buses 22 and 27. Some trains stop and finish at the more convenient Toruń Miasto train station, about 500m east of the New Town.

From Toruń Główny there are trains to Poznań (33zł, 2½ hours, six daily), Gdańsk and Gdynia (39zł, four hours, six daily), Kraków (53zł, 7½ hours, three daily), Wrocław (48zł, 5½ hours, three daily) and Warsaw (41zł, three hours, nine daily).

WARMIA & MASURIA

GREAT MASURIAN LAKES

The dominant feature of Warmia and Masuria is its beautiful postglacial landscape dominated by thousands of lakes. The largest lake is **Lake Śniardwy** (110 sq km). About 200km of canals connect these bodies of water, so the area is a prime destination for yachties and canoeists, as well as those who prefer to hike, fish and mountain-bike.

The detailed *Wielkie Jeziora Mazurskie* map (1:100,000) is essential for anyone exploring the region by water or hiking trail. The *Warmia i Mazury* map (1:300,000), available at regional tourist offices, is perfect for more general use.

Mikołajki (mee-ko-*wahy*-kee) is a picturesque base for exploring the lakes. The **tourist office** (☎ 87 421 5507; www.mikolajki.pl; Plac Wolności 3; 9am-8pm Jul-Aug, to 5pm Tue-Sun May-Jun & Sep-Oct) is in the town centre. There are *kantors* (see opposite) and *bankomats* (ATMs) nearby.

From the bus terminal, next to the bridge at Plac Kościelny, six buses go to Olsztyn each day (15zł, two hours), from where you can connect to major cities. Several daily buses also head northeast to Giżycko (10zł, one hour), and four to Warsaw (38zł, 4½ hours). From the sleepy train station, two slow trains shuttle daily to Olsztyn (14zł, two hours).

The remains of Hitler's wartime headquarters, called the **Wolf's Lair** ('Wolfsschanze' in German), is a local bus ride from Kętrzyn (reached via Giżycko or Olsztyn), about 30km north of Mikołajki. In 1944 a group of high-ranking German officers tried to assassinate Hitler here. The leader of the plot, Claus von Stauffenberg, entered a meeting with a bomb in his briefcase, and placed it near the dictator. Although the explosion killed and wounded several people, Hitler suffered only minor injuries. Stauffenberg and some 5000 people involved in the plot were subsequently executed. These dramatic events were reprised in the 2008 Tom Cruise movie *Valkyrie*. To reach the eerie ruins of the complex, catch one of several daily PKS buses (3.50zł, 15 minutes) from Kętrzyn to Węgorzewo (via Radzieje, not Srokowo) and get off at the entrance.

POLAND DIRECTORY

ACCOMMODATION

Camping & Mountain Refuges

Poland has hundreds of camping grounds, and many offer good-value cabins and bungalows. Most open May to September, but some only open their gates between June and August.

PTTK runs a chain of mountain refuges *(schroniska górskie)* for trekkers. The more-isolated refuges are obliged to accept everyone, so can be crowded in the high season. Refuges are normally open all year, but confirm with the nearest PTTK office.

Private Rooms, Hostels and Hotels

Some destinations have agencies – usually called a *biuro zakwaterowania* or *biuro kwater prywatnych* – which arrange accommodation in private homes. Rooms cost about 80/110zł for singles/doubles. During the high season, home owners also directly approach tourists, and private homes in smaller resorts and villages have signs outside their gates or doors offering a *pokoje* (room) or *noclegi* (lodging).

Youth hostels *(schroniska młodzieżowe)* in Poland mostly open only in July and August; the year-round hostels have more facilities. These hostels are open to all, with no age limit. Curfews are common.

Privately operated hostels operate in the main cities, geared towards international backpackers. They offer more modern facilities, though prices are higher. These hostels usually offer free use of washing machines, in response to the absence of laundromats in Poland. A dorm bed can cost anything from 15zł to 75zł per person per night. Single/double rooms, if available, cost from about 80/100zł.

Hotel prices often vary according to season, and are posted at hotel reception desks. Top-end hotels sometimes quote prices in euros, and discounted weekend rates are often available.

Two reliable companies can arrange accommodation over the internet: www.poland4u.com and www.hotelspoland.com.

The following websites might be useful:

Polish Camping and Caravanning Federation (www.pfcc.eu)
Polish Youth Hostels Association (www.ptsm.org.pl)
PTTK (www.pttk.pl) Runs mountain hostels and other budget lodgings.

ACTIVITIES

Hikers can enjoy marked trails across the Tatra and Sudeten Mountains, and the Great Masurian Lakes district. Trails are easy to follow, and detailed maps are available from most larger bookshops. Poland is fairly flat and ideal for cyclists. Zakopane will delight skiers from December and March.

BUSINESS HOURS

Supermarkets and larger stores often have longer opening hours than other shops. Banks have shorter hours in smaller towns. *Kantors* (foreign currency exchange agents) generally follow shop hours. Nightclubs are often open from 9pm to the wee small hours.

Typical business hours in Poland:

Banks (🕙 8am-5pm Mon-Fri, sometimes 8am-2pm Sat)
Cafes & Restaurants (🕙 11am-11pm)
Shops (🕙 10am-6pm Mon-Fri, 10am-2pm Sat)

DANGERS & ANNOYANCES

Poland is relatively safe, but be alert for pickpockets around major train stations, such as Warszawa Centralna. Robberies have become a problem on night trains, especially on international routes. Try to share a compartment with other people if possible.

Smoking is common in most public places, especially pubs and restaurants.

EMBASSIES & CONSULATES

The following embassies are in Warsaw.

Australia (☎ 22 521 3444; www.australia.pl; ul Nowogrodzka 11)
Canada (☎ 22 584 3100; www.canada.pl; ul Matejki 1/5)
France (☎ 22 529 3000; www.ambafrance-pl.org; ul Puławska 17)
Germany (☎ 22 584 1700; www.ambasadaniemiec.pl; ul Jazdów 12)
Ireland (☎ 22 849 6633; www.irlandia.pl; ul Mysia 5)
Japan (☎ 22 696 5000; www.pl.emb-japan.go.jp; ul Szwoleżerów 8)

Netherlands (☎ 22 559 1200; www.nlembassy.pl; ul Kawalerii 10)
New Zealand (☎ 22 521 0500; www.nzembassy.com; Al Ujazdowskie 51)
South Africa (☎ 22 625 6228; warsaw.consular@foreign.gov.za; ul Koszykowa 54)
UK (☎ 22 311 0000; www.britishembassy.pl; Al Róż 1)
USA (☎ 22 504 2000; http://poland.usembassy.gov; Al Ujazdowskie 29/31)

GAY & LESBIAN TRAVELLERS

Since the change of government in 2007, overt homophobia from state officials has declined; though with the Church remaining influential in social matters, gay acceptance in Poland is still a work in progress. As a result, the Polish gay and lesbian scene is fairly discreet.

Warsaw and Kraków are the best places to find bars and clubs. The best sources of information on gay Warsaw and Kraków are online at www.gayguide.net and www.gaypoland.pl. **Lambda** (☎ 22 628 5222; www.lambda.org.pl) is a national gay rights and information service.

HOLIDAYS

Poland's official public holidays are:
New Year's Day 1 January
Easter Sunday March or April
Easter Monday March or April
State Holiday 1 May
Constitution Day 3 May
Pentecost Sunday Seventh Sunday after Easter
Corpus Christi Ninth Thursday after Easter
Assumption Day 15 August
All Saints' Day 1 November
Independence Day 11 November
Christmas 25 and 26 December

INTERNET ACCESS

Internet access is near-universal in Polish accommodation. In the unlikely event that your lodgings are offline, you'll likely find an internet cafe nearby; expect to pay between 3zł and 5zł per hour. Also, some forward-thinking city councils have set up wireless access in their main market squares (eg Warsaw's Rynek Starego Miasta).

INTERNET RESOURCES

Poland Tourism Portal (www.poland.travel) Useful travel site.
Poland.pl (www.poland.pl) News and a website directory.
Polska (www.poland.gov.pl) Comprehensive government portal.

MONEY

The official Polish currency is the złoty (*zwoti*), abbreviated to zł. The złoty is divided into 100 groszy, abbreviated as gr. The Polish government has set 2012 as the date it will adopt the euro, though various regulatory hurdles may yet delay that event.

Private foreign-exchange offices – called *kantors* – are *everywhere*. The most widely accepted currencies are the euro, the US dollar and the pound sterling (in that order). Foreign-exchange offices rarely cash travellers cheques. Not all banks do either, and most charge a commission.

ATMs *(bankomats)* are common in all sizeable towns. Banks without an ATM might give cash advances over the counter on credit cards, which are widely accepted.

Tipping isn't common in Poland, but feel free to leave 10% extra for waiters or taxi drivers if you've had good service.

POST

Most cities have several post offices. The *poczta główna* (main post office) has the widest range of facilities.

TELEPHONE

Phone numbers throughout Poland have nine digits (the zero at the start was recently dropped). To call from abroad, dial the country code ☎ 48, then the local number. The international access code for overseas calls from Poland is ☎ 00.

Most public telephones use magnetic phonecards, available at post offices and kiosks in units of 15 (9zł), 30 (15zł) and 60 (24zł).

VISAS

EU citizens do not need visas to visit Poland and can stay indefinitely. Citizens of Australia, Canada, Israel, New Zealand, Switzerland and the USA can stay in Poland up to 90 days without a visa. Other nationals should check with Polish embassies in their countries.

Note that, since Poland's entry into the Schengen zone of European countries in December 2007, the 90-day visa-free entry period has been extended to all the Schengen countries; so if you're travelling from Poland through Germany and France, for example, you can't exceed 90 days in total. Once your 90 days is up, you must leave the Schengen zone for a minimum 90 days before you can once again enter it visa-free.

Portugal

HIGHLIGHTS

- **Lisbon** Wander the picturesque lanes of the old-fashioned Alfama before heading to the nightlife mayhem of Bairro Alto (p928)
- **Lagos** Join the nightly party in carnivalesque Lagos, while soaking up lovely beaches by day (p938)
- **Best Journey** Catch the train from Porto along the Douro river, with dramatic views of craggy, terraced vineyards (p948)
- **Off the beaten track** Parque Nacional da Peneda Gerês offers exceptional hiking through forests and over high plateaus dotted with ancient stone villages and archaeological sites (p950)

FAST FACTS

- **Area** 92,389 sq km (twice the size of Switzerland as a comparison)
- **Budget** €40 to €60
- **Capital** Lisbon
- **Country code** ☎ 351
- **Famous for** *fado* (melancholic singing), football, port, *azulejos* (tiles), salted cod
- **Language** Portuguese
- **Money** euro (€); A$1 = €0.55; C$1 = 0.60; ¥100 = €0.78; NZ$1 = €0.43; UK£1 = €1.12; US$1 = €0.74
- **Phrases** *bom dia* (hello), *obrigado/a* (thank you), *desculpe* (excuse me), *adeus* (goodbye), *faz favor* (please)

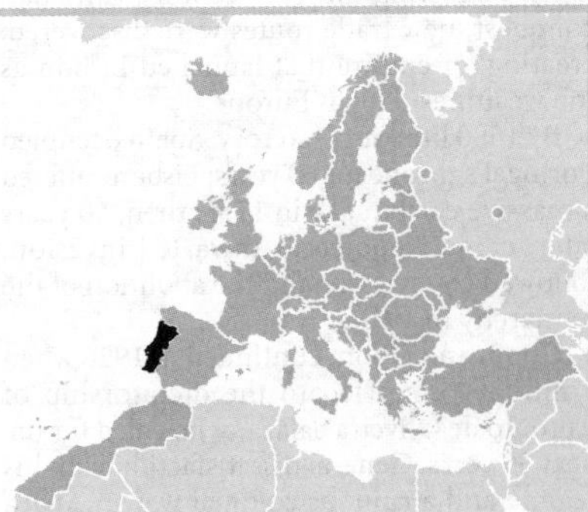

- **Population** 10.7 million
- **Visas** None required for most visitors for stays up to 90 days.

TRAVEL HINTS

Be wary of the *couvert* (nibbles) provided at the start of a meal as they usually cost and you *can* send them back.

ROAMING PORTUGAL

From the north, take in Porto before heading south to Coímbra and Lisbon. From there explore nearby Sintra, then head east to Évora and south to the Algarve.

The once-great seafaring empire of Portugal today straddles two worlds. Portugal is still a land of old-fashioned charm, where medieval castles and picture-perfect villages lie scattered over meandering coastlines and flower-covered hillsides. Meanwhile, cities like Lisbon and Porto offer more modern enticements. Both are magical places for the wanderer, with riverside views, cobblestone streets and rattling trams framed by looming cathedrals. Narrow lanes hide old book stores, tiny boutiques and an eclectic mix of restaurants, bars and nightclubs, giving new life to the timeworn setting.

Outside the cities, rambling vineyards and cork groves roll off into the distance, towards jagged peaks in the north and gentler slopes in the south. More famous is Portugal's comely shoreline, which has long enchanted visitors. Stretching along the Atlantic are dramatic, end-of-the-world cliffs, wild dune-covered beaches, protected coves and long, sandy islands fronting calm blue seas.

For the traveller, Portugal's dual nature presents rewarding opportunities to see both sides of the coin, from visiting old-fashioned wine estates to gallery-hopping, overnighting in medieval stone villages to people-watching at trendy beach resorts. Sometimes Portugal is a country happily in conflict with itself and, while the scales are even, there's no better time to visit.

HISTORY

Early settlers of the Iberian Peninsula included the Celts, Phoenicians, Greeks, Romans and Visigoths. The Moors conquered Portugal in the 8th century, and their influence lingers in the culture, architecture and dark looks of the people. This is particularly noticeable in the Algarve, where the Moors established their capital in Silves (see p939 for more information). Following the 12th-century Christian conquest, new trade routes were discovered, creating an empire that launched Lisbon as the wealthiest city in Europe.

By 1580 life wasn't so rosy: Spain occupied Portugal's throne for 60 years; Lisbon suffered a massive earthquake in 1755; then, 50 years later, came Napoleon's thwarted invasion, followed by civil war and the abolition of the monarchy in 1910.

Doom and gloom continued in 1926 when a military coup led to the dictatorship of António de Oliveira Salazar who ruled for the next 36 years. General dissatisfaction with his regime and a ruinous colonial war in Africa led to a peaceful military coup on 25 April 1974. The subsequent granting of independence to Portugal's African colonies led to the arrival of nearly one million refugees.

The 1970s and early '80s saw extreme swings between the political right and left, but Portugal's entry into the EU in 1986 secured, at last, a measure of stability, and Expo '98 also gave the country an ego boost. This was furthered by Porto's status as a European Capital of Culture in 2001 followed, in 2004, by Portugal's playing host to the European Football Championships.

Parliamentary elections in 2005 brought to power socialist legislator José Sócrates, who promised to revitalise the economy and tackle unemployment. He's had moderate success, while earning a few enemies by slashing pensions and privatising public services.

Sócrates, a former environment minister, has set ambitious goals for Portugal in the realm of renewable energy. Under his government, enormous wind farms and solar power plants have opened, along with experimental technologies such as a wave power plant (harnessing the ocean's energy). There are also plans to build a nationwide network of recharging stations for electric cars by 2012.

THE CULTURE

Portugal has a population of 10.7 million, with an estimated three million Portuguese living abroad. Since May 2004 African and Brazilian immigrants have been joined by new immigrants from central and Eastern Europe.

Portugal has a strong Catholic influence and remains a conservative country. In general, the Portuguese are congenial, with an unhurried approach to life that can translate into lack of efficiency and tardiness. Speaking Portuguese, however clumsily, will earn you lots of points.

ARTS

The best-known form of Portuguese music is the melancholic, nostalgic songs called *fado* (literally 'fate'), said to have originated from troubadour and African slave songs. The late Amália Rodrigues was the Edith Piaf of Portuguese *fado*. Today it is Mariza who has captured the public's imagination with her extraordinary voice and fresh contemporary image. Her 2005 release *Transparente* was a big worldwide seller, while her latest album *Terra* (2008) brings a more global sound to her music. Lisbon's Alfama district has plenty of *fado* houses (p933) to hear the good stuff.

Unique to Portugal is Manueline architecture, named after its patron King Manuel I (1495–1521). It symbolises that era's zest for discovery and is hugely flamboyant with spiralling columns and elaborate ornamentation.

The most striking Portuguese visual art are the stunning painted *azulejo* tiles, covering everything from houses to churches. Lisbon has its own *azulejo* museum (p928).

ENVIRONMENT

Portugal has 25 natural parks, nature reserves and protected landscape areas. These areas total approximately 6500 sq km – just over 7% of Portugal's land area. There are 13 World

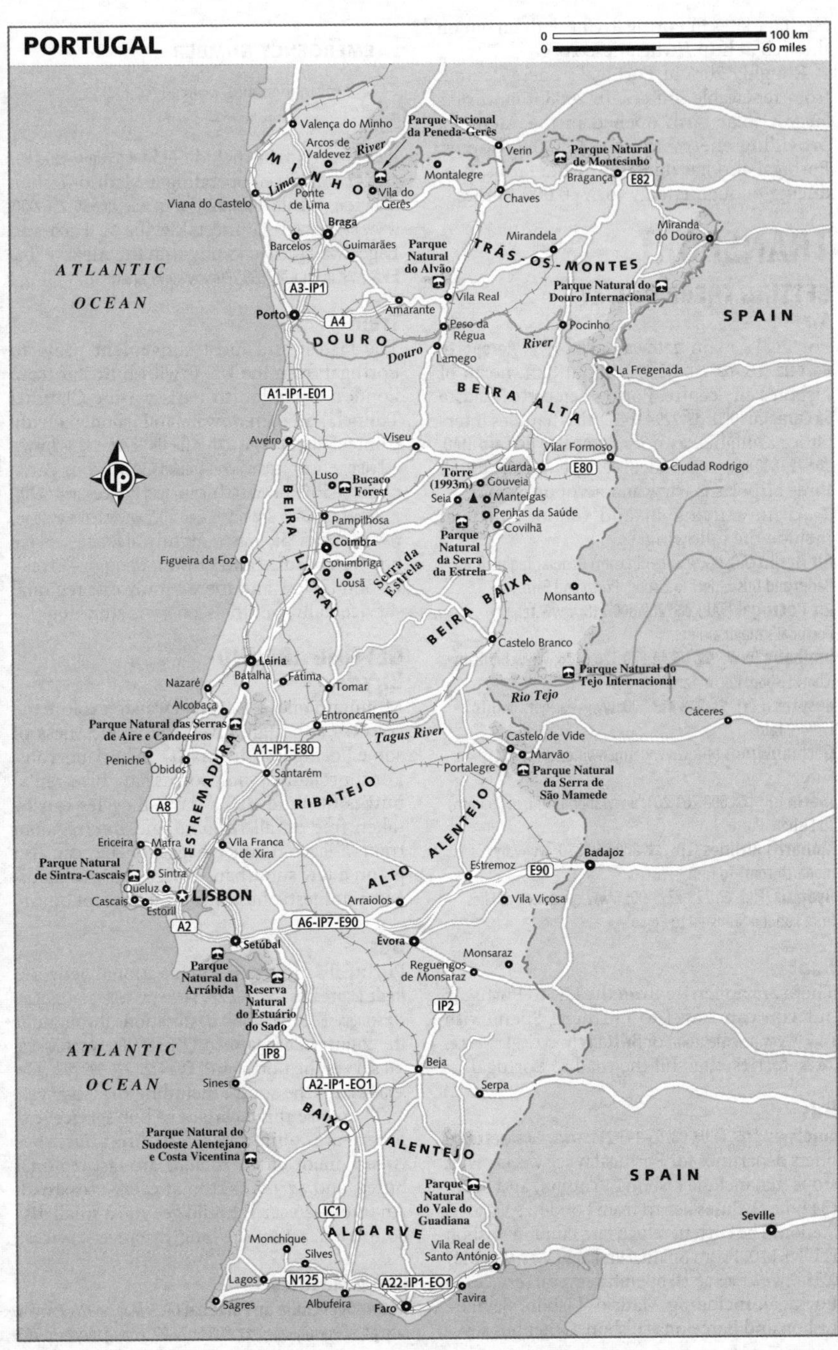
PORTUGAL
0 100 km
0 60 miles
ATLANTIC OCEAN
SPAIN
Valença do Minho
Parque Nacional da Peneda-Gerês
Arcos de Valdevez
River
Lima
MINHO
Vila do Gerês
Ponte de Lima
Viana do Castelo
Verin
Parque Natural de Montesinho
Montalegre
Bragança
E82
Chaves
Braga
Barcelos
Guimarães
Parque Natural do Alvão
TRÁS-OS-MONTES
Mirandela
Miranda do Douro
Parque Natural do Douro Internacional
A3-IP1
Vila Real
Amarante
Porto
A4
Peso da Régua
Pocinho
DOURO
Douro
River
Lamego
La Fregenada
A1-IP1-E01
BEIRA ALTA
Aveiro
Viseu
Vilar Formoso
Guarda
E80
Ciudad Rodrigo
Luso
Buçaco Forest
Torre (1993m)
Gouveia
Seia
Manteigas
Penhas da Saúde
BEIRA LITORAL
Pampilhosa
Covilhã
Parque Natural da Serra da Estrela
Coimbra
Figueira da Foz
Conimbriga
Lousã
Serra da Estrela
BEIRA BAIXA
Monsanto
Castelo Branco
Leiria
Parque Natural do Tejo Internacional
Nazaré
Batalha
Fátima
Tomar
Rio Tejo
Alcobaça
Cáceres
Entroncamento
Parque Natural das Serras de Aire e Candeeiros
Tagus River
Castelo de Vide
Marvão
Peniche
A1-IP1-E80
Óbidos
Portalegre
Parque Natural da Serra de São Mamede
Santarém
RIBATEJO
ESTREMADURA
A8
ALTO ALENTEJO
Ericeira
Mafra
Vila Franca de Xira
Badajoz
Parque Natural de Sintra-Cascais
Sintra
Estremoz
E90
Queluz
LISBON
Cascais
Estoril
Arraiolos
Vila Viçosa
A2
A6-IP7-E90
Setúbal
Évora
Parque Natural da Arrábida
Monsaraz
Reserva Natural do Estuário do Sado
Reguengos de Monsaraz
IP2
IP8
Beja
Sines
A2-IP1-EO1
Serpa
BAIXO ALENTEJO
Parque Natural do Sudoeste Alentejano e Costa Vicentina
Parque Natural do Vale do Guadiana
IC1
ALGARVE
Seville
Monchique
Vila Real de Santo António
Silves
Lagos
N125
A22-IP1-EO1
Tavira
Sagres
Albufeira
Faro

PORTUGAL

Heritage sites in Portugal. Check them out on the web at http://whc.unesco.org.

Roughly 20% of Portugal's energy comes from renewable sources. In 2008, the world's largest solar farm opened in the Alentejo, providing energy to power 30,000 homes. Portugal also has numerous wind farms, producing enough energy for 750,000 homes.

TRANSPORT

GETTING THERE & AWAY

Air

Portugal's main gateway airport is **Aeroporto Portela** (LIS; ☎ 218 413 500), about 8km north of Lisbon's city centre. Porto's **Aeroporto Francisco Sá Carneiro** (OPO; ☎ 229 432 400) also handles international flights, as does **Aeroporto de Faro** (FAO; ☎ 229 800 800) in the Algarve. The website for all three airports is www.ana-aeroportos.pt.

Airlines flying in and out of Portugal include the following:

Air Berlin (AB; www.airberlin.com) Regular flights from Berlin and Dusseldorf to Lisbon, Porto and Faro.
Air Portugal (TAP; ☎ 289 800 218; www.tap.pt) Portugal's major airline.
bmibaby (WW; ☎ UK 44 870 126 6726; www.bmibaby.com) Lisbon, Porto, Faro.
easyJet (EZY; ☎ 218 413 700; www.easyjet.com) To Lisbon, Faro.
GermanWings (4U; www.germanwings.com) To Lisbon, Faro.
Iberia (IB; ☎ 808 261 261; www.iberia.com, in Spanish) To Lisbon, Porto.
Monarch Airlines (ZB; ☎ 800 860 270; www.flymonarch.com) To Faro.
Ryanair (FR; ☎ 229 432 400; www.ryanair.com) Flies from London Stansted to Porto.

Boat

There are no ferries from the UK to Portugal, but you can travel to northern Spain with **P&O** (www.poferries.com) or **Brittany** (www.brittanyferries.co.uk) ferries, then hit the road to Portugal.

Bus

Eurolines (☎ in UK 08705-143 219; www.eurolines.co.uk) offers departures for Portugal twice weekly with stops that include Lisbon (36 hours) and Porto (34 hours). Buses depart from London's Victoria Station. The current return fare London–Lisbon is UK£110. From Spain, **Eurolines** (☎ in Madrid 915 063 360; www.eurolines.es) operates several services to Portugal, including Madrid–Lisbon, Seville–Lisbon and Barcelona–Lisbon. Other bus services from Spain include **ALSA** (☎ in Madrid 902 422 242; www.alsa.es) operating a Madrid–Lisbon service, while **Damas** (☎ in Huelva 959 256 900; www.damas-sa.es) connects Seville to Faro and Lagos via Huelva, jointly with the Algarve line **EVA** (☎ in Faro 289 899 700; www.eva-bus.com).

EMERGENCY NUMBER

- Ambulance, fire, police (☎ 112)

Train

The fastest and most convenient route to Portugal from the UK is with Eurostar from London Waterloo to Paris via the Channel Tunnel, and then onward to Lisbon via Irún. Contact **Rail Europe** (☎ in the UK 08705-848 848; www.raileurope.co.uk; return ticket around €300). From Paris, contact **SNCF** (www.sncf.com; return ticket around €210).

Renfe (☎ in Spain 902 240 202; www.renfe.es; one-way ticket from €56) has a nightly sleeper service between Madrid and Lisbon. Badajoz–Elvas–Lisbon is slow and there is only one regional service daily, but the scenery is stunning.

GETTING AROUND

Bicycle

Mountain biking is a great way to explore the country although, given the recklessness of some Portuguese drivers, it can be dangerous. For short jaunts, some towns have bike-rental outfits (around €10 a day). Bicycles can be taken free on all *regional* and *interregional* trains as accompanied baggage. They can also go on a few suburban services on weekends. Most domestic bus lines won't accept bikes.

Bus

Portugal's most important national network, **Rede Expressos** (☎ 707 223 344; www.rede-expressos.pt, in Portuguese), serves 300 destinations throughout the country. **Rodonorte** (☎ 259 340 710; www.rodonorte.pt) serves the north, and **Eva** (☎ 289 899 700; www.eva-bus.com) the south, including the Algarve.

There are three classes of bus service: *expressos* are comfortable, fast, direct buses between major cities; *rápidas* are fast regional buses; and *carreiras* stop at every crossroad. An under-26 card should get you a small discount, at least on the long-distance services.

Car & Motorcycle

Automóvel Clube de Portugal (ACP; Map pp926-7; www.acp.pt, in Portuguese; ☎ 808 502 502, emergency help 707

509 510; www.acp.pt) provides medical, legal and breakdown assistance and has a reciprocal arrangement with major foreign automobile clubs, such as AA and RAC.

To hire a car in Portugal you must generally be at least 25 and have held your home licence for a year minimum. To hire a scooter of up to 50cc you must be 18-plus with a driving licence. For more powerful motorbikes you must have a driving licence covering these vehicles from your home country.

Speed limits for cars and motorcycles are 50km/h in cities and public centres, 90km/h on normal roads and 120km/h on motorways. Drivers and front passengers in cars must wear seat belts. Motorcyclists and passengers must wear helmets, and motorcycles must have headlights on day and night. Using a mobile phone while driving could result in a fine.

Drink-driving laws are strict with a maximum legal blood-alcohol level of 0.05%.

Local Transport

Outside Lisbon or Porto there's little reason to take a municipal bus. For Lisbon and Porto's metros pick up route maps at the respective tourist offices.

Taxis are plentiful, but don't miss the trams (an endangered species in Lisbon and Porto), or the funiculars and lifts of Lisbon.

Train

Caminhos de Ferro Portugueses (CP; ☎ 808 208 208; www.cp.pt) is the state-wide train network and is generally efficient, although it can be slower than long-distance buses. Most trains are *regionais* (R) or *suburbanos*, stopping at stations en route. The more costly *intercidades* (IC) trains are faster, while the most luxurious and pricey are the *alfa pendulares* (AP) trains. Both the IC and AP lines require seat reservations in advance.

LISBON

pop 580,000

Lisbon is a city of steep hills, candy-bright houses, twisting alleys and grand plazas where locals relax in the sunshine. Add to that, swirly Manueline turrets, ivory-white domes and a Moorish castle on the hillside, and you have one of Europe's under-appreciated masterpieces.

Yet Lisa, as locals nickname their city, is no superficial beauty. Retrospective and innovative, Lisbon is a twilight zone between past and future: dodgem-like trams screech through cobbled streets and Afro-Brazilian beats pulsate in the graffiti-slashed Bairro Alto, Zen-style sushi bars sidle up to one-pan family taverns, and thimble-sized haberdasheries abut eco-cool design stores. Neither time- nor trend-obsessed, Portugal's capital is refreshingly authentic.

ORIENTATION

North of Rossio train station in Central Lisbon is Praça dos Restauradores, at the bottom of Av da Liberdade. West of the Rossio it's a steep climb to the Bairro Alto district, a youthful neighbourhood packed with bohemian bars and restaurants. East of the Rossio, it's yet more climbing up to Castelo de São Jorge and the Alfama district with its tangle of ancient lanes. Several kilometres to the west of Rossio is Belém, with its not-to-be missed attractions. Parque das Nações, the former Expo '98 site and the Oceanarium lie on the revamped waterfront, located to the northeast of the city centre.

INFORMATION

Bookshop

Livraria Bertrand (Map pp930-1; ☎ 213 421 941; Rua Garrett 73) Bertrand has excellent selections amid 18th-century charm.

Discount Cards

Lisboa Card (24/48/72 hr €15/26/32) Good for unlimited travel on most city transport (and includes the admission to 28 museums, historic buildings and other places of interest). You can buy the Lisboa Card at Ask Me Lisboa tourist offices (p928).

Emergency

Tourist police post (Map pp930-1; ☎ 213 421 634; Palácio Foz, Praça dos Restauradores; 🕑 24hr)

Internet Access

Cyber Bica (Map pp930-1; ☎ 213 225 004; Rua Duques de Bragança; per hr €3; 🕑 noon-midnight Mon-Fri)

Web Café (Map pp930-1; ☎ 213 421 181; Rua do Diário de Notícias 126; per hr €3; 🕑 7pm-2am)

Medical Services

Hospital Britânico (British Hospital; Map pp926-7; ☎ 213 943 100, 213 929 360; Rua Saraíva de Carvalho 49) English-speaking staff, plus dental care.

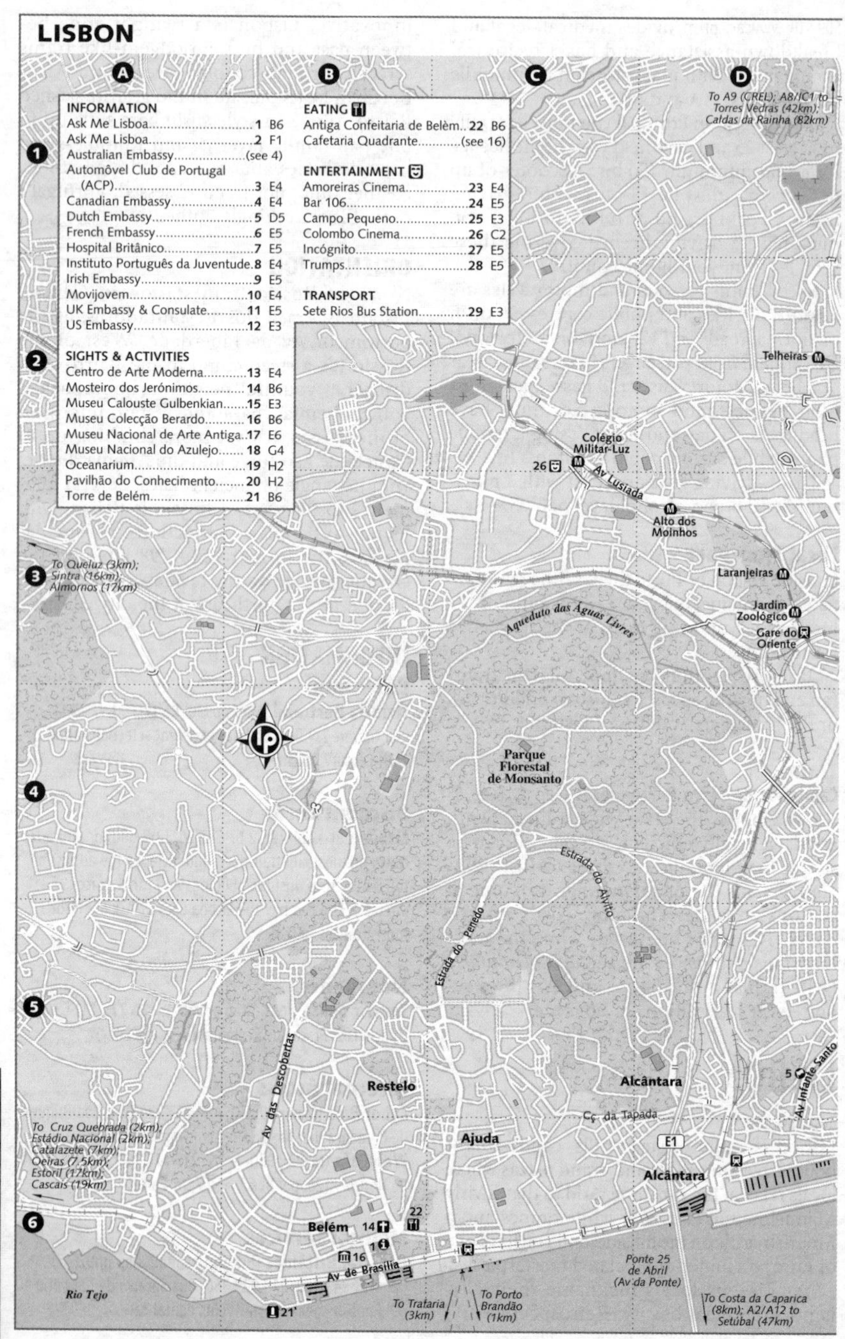
LISBON
A
B
C
D
INFORMATION
Ask Me Lisboa.......1 B6
Ask Me Lisboa.......2 F1
Australian Embassy.......(see 4)
Automôvel Club de Portugal (ACP).......3 E4
Canadian Embassy.......4 E4
Dutch Embassy.......5 D5
French Embassy.......6 E5
Hospital Britânico.......7 E5
Instituto Português da Juventude.......8 E4
Irish Embassy.......9 E5
Movijovem.......10 E4
UK Embassy & Consulate.......11 E5
US Embassy.......12 E3
SIGHTS & ACTIVITIES
Centro de Arte Moderna.......13 E4
Mosteiro dos Jerónimos.......14 B6
Museu Calouste Gulbenkian.......15 E3
Museu Colecção Berardo.......16 B6
Museu Nacional de Arte Antiga.......17 E6
Museu Nacional do Azulejo.......18 G4
Oceanarium.......19 H2
Pavilhão do Conhecimento.......20 H2
Torre de Belém.......21 B6
EATING
Antiga Confeitaria de Belèm.......22 B6
Cafetaria Quadrante.......(see 16)
ENTERTAINMENT
Amoreiras Cinema.......23 E4
Bar 106.......24 E5
Campo Pequeno.......25 E3
Colombo Cinema.......26 C2
Incógnito.......27 E5
Trumps.......28 E5
TRANSPORT
Sete Rios Bus Station.......29 E3
To A9 (CREL); A8/IC1 to Torres Vedras (42km); Caldas da Rainha (82km)
1
2
3
4
5
6
Telheiras
Colégio Militar-Luz
26
Av Lusíada
Alto dos Moinhos
Laranjeiras
Jardim Zoológico
Gare do Oriente
To Queluz (3km); Sintra (16km); Almornos (17km)
Aqueduto das Águas Livres
Parque Florestal de Monsanto
Estrada do Alvito
Estrada do Penedo
Av das Descobertas
Restelo
Alcântara
5
Av Infante Santo
Cç da Tapada
E1
Ajuda
Alcântara
To Cruz Quebrada (2km); Estádio Nacional (2km); Catalazete (7km); Oeiras (7.5km); Estoril (17km); Cascais (19km)
22
Belém
14
1
16
Av de Brasília
Rio Tejo
21
To Trafaria (3km)
To Porto Brandão (1km)
Ponte 25 de Abril (Av da Ponte)
To Costa da Caparica (8km); A2/A12 to Setúbal (47km)

PORTUGAL

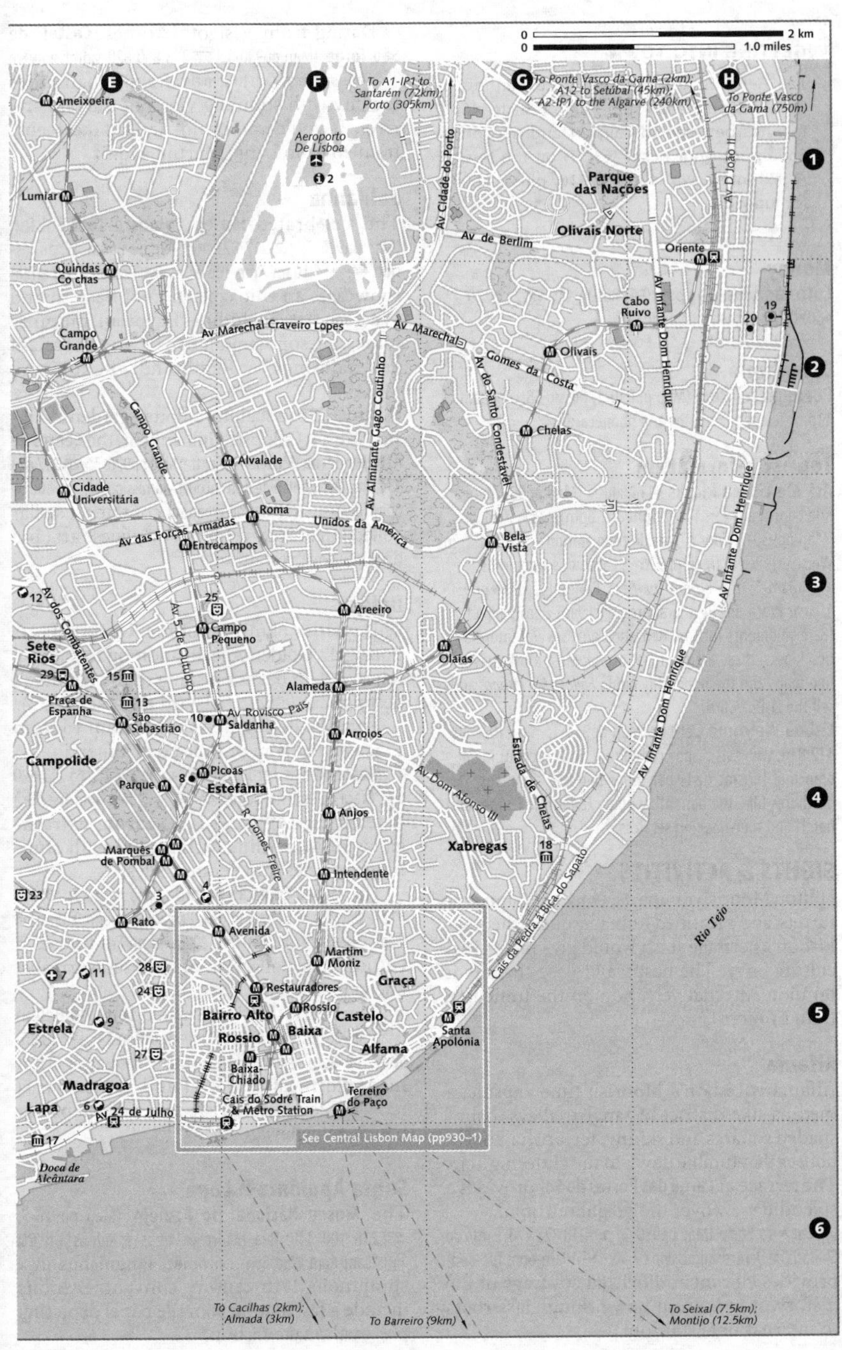
0 2 km
0 1.0 miles
To A1-IP1 to Santarém (72km); Porto (305km)
To Ponte Vasco da Gama (2km); A12 to Setúbal (45km); A2-IP1 to the Algarve (240km)
To Ponte Vasco da Gama (750m)
Ameixoeira
Aeroporto De Lisboa
Lumiar
Parque das Nações
Olivais Norte
Av de Berlim
Av Cidade do Porto
Av D João II
Oriente
Quindas Co chas
Cabo Ruivo
Av Marechal Craveiro Lopes
Av Marechal Gomes da Costa
Campo Grande
Olivais
Av do Santo Condestável
Av Infante Dom Henrique
Chelas
Alvalade
Av Almirante Gago Coutinho
Cidade Universitária
Roma
Unidos da América
Av das Forças Armadas
Entrecampos
Bela Vista
Av dos Combatentes
Av 5 de Outubro
Campo Pequeno
Areeiro
Sete Rios
Olaias
Praça de Espanha
Alameda
São Sebastião
Av Rovisco Pais
Saldanha
Arroios
Campolide
Picoas
Estefânia
Parque
Av Dom Afonso III
Estrada de Chelas
Anjos
R Gomes Freire
Marquês de Pombal
Xabregas
Intendente
Rato
Avenida
Cais da Pedra à Bica do Sapato
Rio Tejo
Martim Moniz
Restauradores
Graça
Bairro Alto
Rossio
Castelo
Baixa
Santa Apolónia
Estrela
Alfama
Baixa-Chiado
Madragoa
Terreiro do Paço
Lapa
Av 24 de Julho
Cais do Sodré Train & Metro Station
See Central Lisbon Map (pp930–1)
Doca de Alcântara
To Cacilhas (2km); Almada (3km)
To Barreiro (9km)
To Seixal (7.5km); Montijo (12.5km)

GETTING INTO TOWN

The AeroBus (91) runs every 20 minutes from 7.45am to 8.15pm, taking 30 to 45 minutes between the airport and Cais do Sodré; buy your ticket (€3.35) on the bus. A taxi into town is about €10, plus €1.60 for luggage.

Money

Cota Câmbios (Map pp930-1; Rossio 41; ☎ 213 220 480) Offers a good exchange rate.

Telephone

Portugal Telecom (Map pp930-1; Rossio 68; 🕑 8am-11pm) Telephone booths and phonecards.

Tourist Information

Ask Me Lisboa kiosks Rua Augusta (Map pp930-1; near Rua Conceição; 🕑 10am-1pm & 2-6pm); Santa Apolónia (Map pp930-1; door 47, inside train station; 🕑 8am-1pm Wed-Sat); Belém (Map pp926-7; Largo dos Jerónimos; 🕑 10am-1pm & 2-6pm Tue-Sat); Palácio Foz (Map pp930-1; near Praça dos Restauradores; 🕑 9am-8pm); airport (8am-midnight) Turismo de Lisboa runs several information kiosks; these are the most useful. Most kiosks have free maps and the bimonthly guide *Follow Me Lisboa,* and sell the Lisboa Card.

Lisboa Welcome Center (Map pp930-1; ☎ 210 312 810; www.visitlisboa.com; Praça do Comércio) Main branch of Turismo de Lisboa, providing free city maps, brochures (like the bimonthly guide *Follow Me Lisboa*) and hotel- and tour-booking services.

SIGHTS & ACTIVITIES

Hilltop Moorish ramparts, twirling Manueline turrets, and a fortified Romanesque cathedral – Lisbon's heritage stash would give most cities culture envy. The best way to see the city is on foot. Alternatively, hop on the funicular, tram or metro.

Alfama

Alfama is Lisbon's Moorish time capsule: a medina-like district of tangled alleys, palm-shaded squares and skinny, terracotta-roofed houses that tumble down to the glittering Tejo. The terrace at **Largo das Portas do Sol** provides a splendid view over the neighbourhood.

Casa do Fado (Map pp930-1; ☎ 218 823 470; Largo do Chafariz de Dentro; admission €2.50; 🕑 10am-6pm Tue-Sun) provides vibrant audiovisual coverage of the history of *fado* from its working-class roots to international stardom.

Dating from Visigothic times, **Castelo de São Jorge** (Map pp930-1; ☎ 218 800 620; admission €5; 🕑 9am-9pm Mar-Oct, to 6pm Nov-Feb) sits high above the city with stunning views of the city and river. If you'd rather not walk, take scenic tram 28 from Largo Martim Moniz.

Saldanha

The celebrated **Museu Calouste Gulbenkian** (Map pp926-7; ☎ 217 823 461; Ave de Berna 45; admission €4; 🕑 10am-6pm Tue-Sun; Ⓜ Praça de Espanha) showcases an epic collection of Eastern and Western art, including Egyptian mummy masks, Mesopotamian urns, Qing porcelain and paintings by Rembrandt, Renoir and Monet.

Situated in a sculpture-dotted garden alongside Museu Calouste Gulbenkian, the **Centro de Arte Moderna** (Modern Art Centre; Map pp926-7; ☎ 217 823 474; Rua Dr Nicaulau de Bettencourt; admission €4; 🕑 10am-6pm Tue-Sun; Ⓜ Praça de Espanha) contains a stellar collection of 20th-century Portuguese art (and an excellent restaurant).

Belém

This quarter 6km west of the Rossio reflects Portugal's Golden Age. In addition to cultural relics, Belém bakes up some of the country's best *pastéis de nata* (custard tarts; see p932).

To reach Belém, hop aboard tram 15 from Praça da Figueira or Praça do Comércio.

Mosteiro dos Jerónimos (Map pp926-7; ☎ 213 620 034; Praça do Império; admission €6; 🕑 10am-5pm Tue-Sun) dates from 1496 and is a soaring extravaganza of Manueline architecture with stunning carvings and ceramic tiles.

The **Museu Colecção Berardo** (Map pp926-7; ☎ 213 612 400; www.museuberardo.pt; Praça do Império; admission free; 🕑 10am-7pm Sat-Thu, 10am-10pm Fri) houses a cutting-edge collection of abstract, surrealist and pop art.

The World Heritage–listed **Torre de Belém** (Map pp926-7; ☎ 213 620 034; admission €4; 🕑 10am-5pm Tue-Sun) symbolises the voyages that made Portugal powerful and is *the* tourist icon of Portugal. Brave the tiny steps for panoramic views.

Santa Apolónia & Lapa

The **Museu Nacional do Azulejo** (Map pp926-7; ☎ 218 100 340; Rua Madre de Deus 4; admission €4; 🕑 10am-6pm Wed-Sun, 2-6pm Tue) languishes in a sumptuous 17th-century convent. Exhibits include a fascinating 36m tile panel depicting pre-earthquake Lisbon.

The **Museu Nacional de Arte Antiga** (Ancient Art Museum; Map pp926-7; ☎ 213 912 800; Rua das Janelas Verdes; admission €4; 🕒 10am-6pm Wed-Sun, 2-6pm Tue) is in Lapa, Lisbon's moneyed diplomatic quarter, and houses a ripping collection of works by European and Asian artists.

Parque das Nações

The former Expo '98 site, a revitalised 2km-long waterfront area in the northeast, includes the enormous **Oceanarium** (Map pp926-7; ☎ 218 917 002; www.oceanario.pt; admission €11; 🕒 10am-7pm; Ⓜ Oriente) and the **Pavilhão do Conhecimento** (Map pp926-7; Living Science Centre; ☎ 218 917 100; admission €7; 🕒 10am-6pm Tue-Fri, 11am-7pm Sat & Sun; Ⓜ Oriente), with over 300 interactive exhibits for kids of all ages.

Alcântara

The old wharves have been slickly revamped into a row of bars and restaurants with tables sprawling out onto the promenade. After drinks or a bite under the faux Golden Gate Bridge, take a waterfront stroll to Belém.

FESTIVALS & EVENTS

The **Festa do Santo António** (Festival of Saint Anthony), from 12 to 13 June, culminates the three-week **Festas de Lisboa**, with processions and dozens of street parties.

SLEEPING

Lisbon has many inexpensive *pensões* (guest houses) throughout the centre along with upmarket backpacker digs. For atmosphere, book a room near the Alfama; for nightlife, check into Bairro Alto.

our pick **Poets Hostel** (Map pp930-1; ☎ 213 461 058; www.lisbonpoetshostel.com; Rua Nova da Trindade 2; dm €20; 💻) The 17th-century town house has been lovingly reincarnated as a charming hostel with high-ceilinged, light-flooded dorms.

Lounge Hostel (Map pp930-1; ☎ 213 462 061; www.lisbonloungehostel.com; Rua de São Nicolau 41; dm/d €20/60; 💻) These ultrahip Baixa digs have a party vibe. Bed down in immaculate dorms and meet like-minded travellers in the hip lounge.

Goodnight Hostel (Map pp930-1; ☎ 213 430 139; http://goodnighthostel.com; Rua dos Correiros 113; dm/d €20/50; 💻) This glam hostel rocks with its fab location, retro design and friendly owner. The high-ceilinged dorms offer vertigo-inducing views over Baixa.

Travellers House (Map pp930-1; ☎ 210 115 922; http://travellershouse.com; Rua Augusta 89; dm from €22; 💻) This super-friendly hostel is set in a converted 250-year-old house and offers cosy dorms, a lounge with beanbags, an internet corner and a communal kitchen.

Pensão Imperial (Map pp930-1; ☎ 213 420 166; Praça dos Restauradores 78; s/d with shower €25/40) Cheery Imperial has a terrific location over the main square. The high-ceilinged rooms with rickety '70s-style furniture are nothing flash, but some have flower-draped balconies overlooking the *praça*.

Pensão Ninho das Águias (Map pp930-1; ☎ 218 854 070; Costa do Castelo 74; s/d/tr with shared bathroom €30/40/60) It isn't called 'eagle's nest' for nothing: this guest house has a Rapunzel-esque turret affording magical 360-degree views over Lisbon. Book well ahead.

Pensão Globo (Map pp930-1; ☎ 213 462 279; pensaoglobo@hotmail.com; Rua do Teixeira 37; s/d €30/50; 💻) Run by friendly English-speaking folk, Globo is a no-frills cheapie. Go for rooms 301, 302 or 303 with large windows overlooking the leafy street.

Pensão São João da Praça (Map pp930-1; ☎ 218 862 591; 218862591@sapo.pt; 2nd fl, Rua de São João da Praça 97; d with shared/private bathroom €35/50) So close to the *sé* you can almost touch the gargoyles, this 19th-century guest house has a mix of clean, sunny rooms; the best have river-facing verandas.

Anjo Azul (Map pp930-1; ☎ 213 478 069; www.anjoazul.com; Rua Luz Soriano 75; d €50-80; 💻) Adorned with homoerotic artwork, this gay-friendly hotel has rooms that range from scarlet-and-black love nests with heart pillows to chocolate-caramel numbers. All have squeaky-clean bathrooms and teeny balconies.

Sé Guesthouse (Map pp930-1; ☎ 218 864 400; 1st fl, Rua de São João da Praça 97; d with shared bathroom €70) This shrine to wanderlust brims with the owners' worldly knick-knacks, from pharaohs to Bolivian throws. The bright rooms have karma-chameleon red, gold and green colours and technicolour lights; many feature little balconies facing the *sé*.

EATING

New-generation chefs at the stove, first-rate raw ingredients and a generous pinch of world spice have put the Portuguese capital back on the gastro map.

The city's best food market is **Mercado da Ribeira** (Map pp930-1; Av da 24 de Julho; 🕒 5am-2pm Mon-Sat), near Cais do Sodré station. A good central supermarket is **Pingo Doce** (Map pp930-1;

CENTRAL LISBON

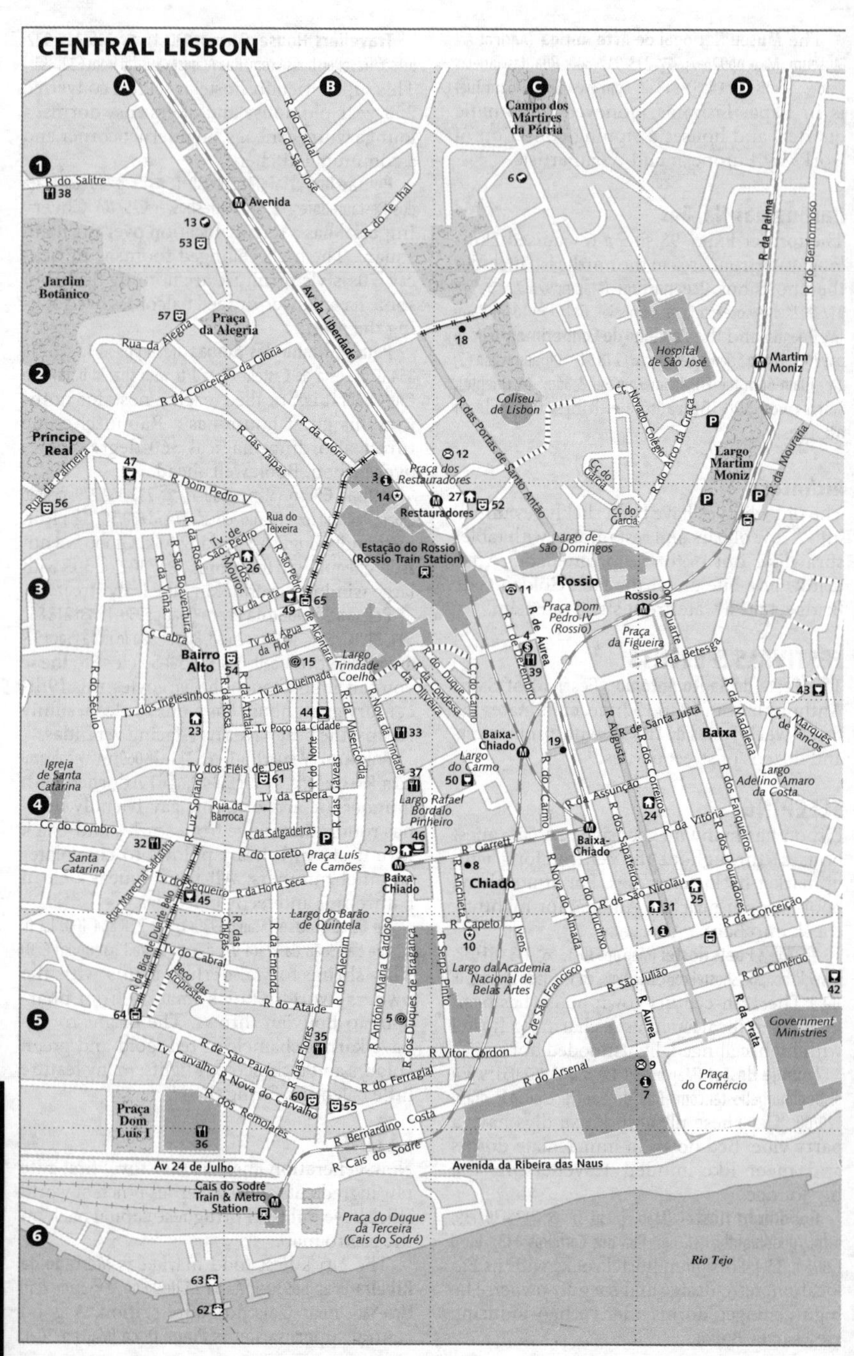

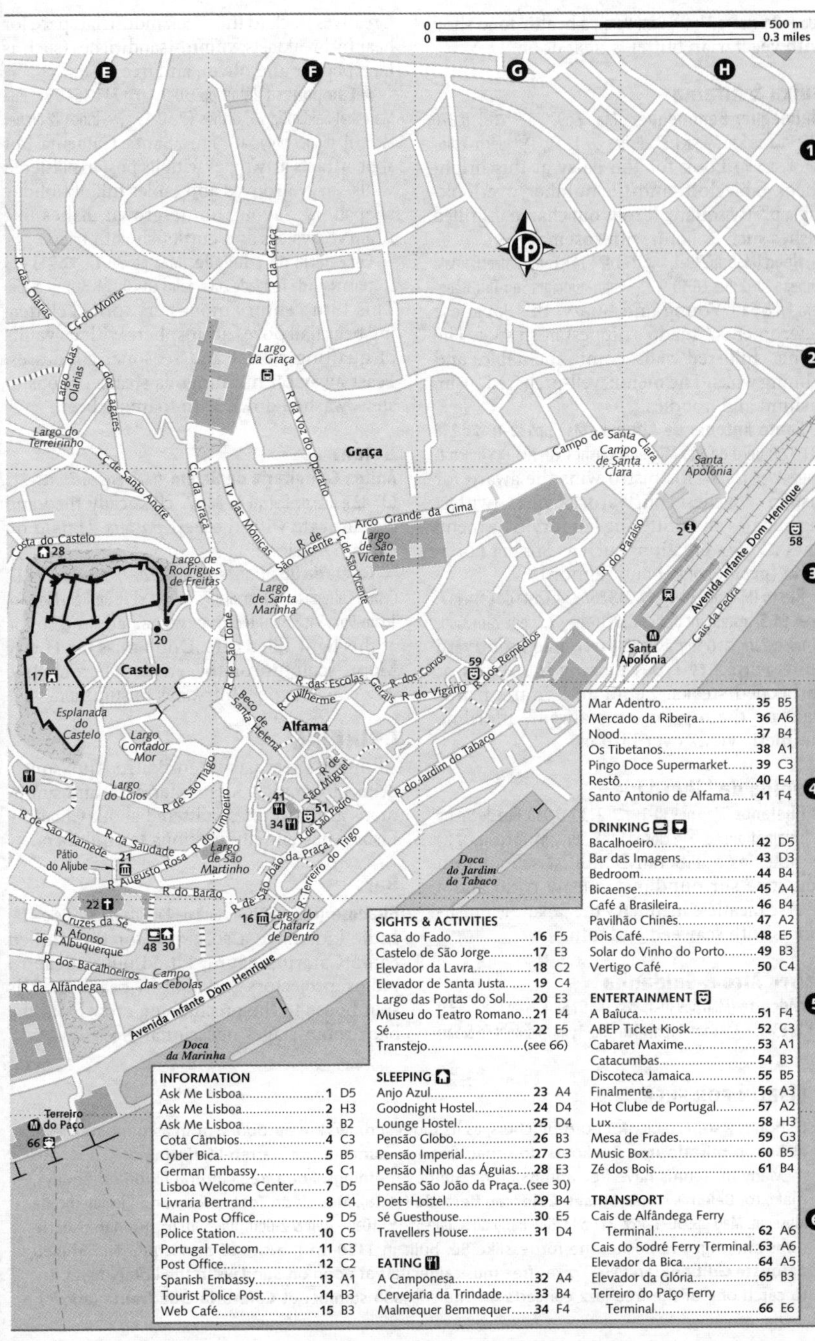
0 500 m
0 0.3 miles
E
F
G
H
1
2
3
4
5
6
R das Olarias
Cç do Monte
Largo das Olarias
R dos Lagares
Largo do Terreirinho
Cç de Santo André
R da Graça
Largo da Graça
R da Voz do Operário
Graça
Cç da Graça
Tv das Mónicas
R de São Vicente
Cç de São Vicente
Arco Grande da Cima
Largo de São Vicente
Campo de Santa Clara
Campo de Santa Clara
Santa Apolónia
R do Paraíso
Avenida Infante Dom Henrique
Cais da Pedra
Santa Apolónia
Costa do Castelo
28
Largo de Rodrigues de Freitas
Largo de Santa Marinha
20
17
Castelo
R de São Tomé
Beco de Santa Helena
R das Escolas Gerais
R dos Corvos
R do Vigário
R dos Remédios
59
R Guilherme
Alfama
Esplanada do Castelo
Largo Contador Mor
R de São Miguel
R do Jardim do Tabaco
40
Largo do Loios
R de São Tiago
R do Limoeiro
41
34
51
R de São Pedro
R de São Mamede
R da Saudade
Largo de São Martinho
Pátio do Aljube
21
R Augusto Rosa
R de São João da Praça
R Terreiro do Trigo
Doca do Jardim do Tabaco
22
R do Barão
16
Largo do Chafariz de Dentro
Cruzes da Sé
R Afonso de Albuquerque
48 30
R dos Bacalhoeiros
Campo das Cebolas
R da Alfândega
Avenida Infante Dom Henrique
Doca da Marinha
Terreiro do Paço
66
2
58

INFORMATION
Ask Me Lisboa 1 D5
Ask Me Lisboa 2 H3
Ask Me Lisboa 3 B2
Cota Câmbios 4 C3
Cyber Bica 5 B5
German Embassy 6 C1
Lisboa Welcome Center 7 D5
Livraria Bertrand 8 C4
Main Post Office 9 D5
Police Station 10 C5
Portugal Telecom 11 C3
Post Office 12 C2
Spanish Embassy 13 A1
Tourist Police Post 14 B3
Web Café 15 B3

SIGHTS & ACTIVITIES
Casa do Fado 16 F5
Castelo de São Jorge 17 E3
Elevador da Lavra 18 C2
Elevador de Santa Justa 19 C4
Largo das Portas do Sol 20 E3
Museu do Teatro Romano 21 E4
Sé 22 E5
Transtejo (see 66)

SLEEPING
Anjo Azul 23 A4
Goodnight Hostel 24 D4
Lounge Hostel 25 D4
Pensão Globo 26 B3
Pensão Imperial 27 C3
Pensão Ninho das Águias 28 E3
Pensão São João da Praça (see 30)
Poets Hostel 29 B4
Sé Guesthouse 30 E5
Travellers House 31 D4

EATING
A Camponesa 32 A4
Cervejaria da Trindade 33 B4
Malmequer Bemmequer 34 F4
Mar Adentro 35 B5
Mercado da Ribeira 36 A6
Nood 37 B4
Os Tibetanos 38 A1
Pingo Doce Supermarket 39 C3
Restô 40 E4
Santo Antonio de Alfama 41 F4

DRINKING
Bacalhoeiro 42 D5
Bar das Imagens 43 D3
Bedroom 44 B4
Bicaense 45 A4
Café a Brasileira 46 B4
Pavilhão Chinês 47 A2
Pois Café 48 E5
Solar do Vinho do Porto 49 B3
Vertigo Café 50 C4

ENTERTAINMENT
A Baîuca 51 F4
ABEP Ticket Kiosk 52 C3
Cabaret Maxime 53 A1
Catacumbas 54 B3
Discoteca Jamaica 55 B5
Finalmente 56 A3
Hot Clube de Portugal 57 A2
Lux 58 H3
Mesa de Frades 59 G3
Music Box 60 B5
Zé dos Bois 61 B4

TRANSPORT
Cais de Alfândega Ferry Terminal 62 A6
Cais do Sodré Ferry Terminal 63 A6
Elevador da Bica 64 A5
Elevador da Glória 65 B3
Terreiro do Paço Ferry Terminal 66 E6

Rua de Dezembro 73; 9am-9pm); a health-food shop with vegetarian buffet is next door.

Baixa & Alfama

Malmequer Bemmequer (Map pp930-1; ☎ 218 876 535; Rua de São Miguel 23; dishes €6-12.50; lunch & dinner Wed-Sun) Look for the daisy at this bright check-tablecloth-and-tile number, overlooking a pretty square. It rolls out charcoal-grilled dishes such as lamb with rosemary.

Nood (Map pp930-1; ☎ 213 474 141; Largo Rafael Bordalo Pinheiro 20; dishes €6.50-9; noon-midnight Sun-Thu, noon-2am Fri & Sat) Young and buzzy, this Japanese newcomer is Chiado's hippest nosh spot. The scene: chilli-red walls, communal tables and flaming woks. The menu: well-prepared sushi, sashimi and noodles.

Santo Antonio de Alfama (Map pp930-1; ☎ 218 881 328; Beco de São Miguel 7; dishes €8-16; lunch & dinner Wed-Mon) This bistro wins the award for Lisbon's loveliest courtyard: all vines, twittering budgies and fluttering laundry. The menu stars its own creations such as Sophia Loren salad (pesto, rocket and salmon).

Restô (Map pp930-1; ☎ 218 867 334; Costa do Castelo 7; tapas €4-5, restaurant dishes €10-16; 7.30pm-2am Mon-Fri, noon-2am Sat & Sun) Restô's tree-filled courtyard hums with arty types tucking into tapas or barbecued steaks. Zebra and giraffe prints glam up the top-floor restaurant, affording mesmeric views over Lisbon.

Avenida da Liberdade

Os Tibetanos (Map pp930-1; ☎ 213 142 038; Rua do Salitre 117; mains from €6; closed Sat & Sun; M Avenida;) Doubles as a Tibetan Buddhist school with Zen-style surroundings, a leafy patio and a diverse meatless menu; try the Japanese mushrooms with seaweed and tofu.

Bairro Alto & Saldanha

Mar Adentro (Map pp930-1; ☎ 346 91 58; Rua do Alecrim 35; snacks €3-5; 10am-11pm Mon-Thu, 1pm-midnight Fri & Sat) Creatives flock to this sleek industrial space for healthy breakfasts, yummy sandwiches (such as feta, pepper and olive), and free wi-fi.

A Camponesa (Map pp930-1; ☎ 213 464 791; Rua Marechal Saldanha 23; dishes €7.50-15; lunch & dinner Mon-Fri, dinner only Sat) This Santa Catarina hot spot attracts arty types with its poster-plastered walls, jazzy grooves and tables full of holiday snapshots. Savour home-grown dishes like Algarve oysters and cuttlefish with fried egg.

Cervejaria da Trindade (Map pp930-1; ☎ 213 423 506; Rua Nova da Trindade 20C; mains €8-20; M Baixa-Chiado) This 13th-century monastery turned clattering beer hall oozes atmosphere with its vaults of quaffing clerics and seasonal goddesses. Feast away on humungous steaks or lobster stew, washed down with foaming beer.

Belém

Antiga Confeitaria de Belém (Map pp926-7; ☎ 213 637 423; Rua de Belém 86-88) A classically tiled and elegant cafe with the best *pastéis de nata* on earth. Delicious!

Cafetaria Quadrante (Map pp926-7; ☎ 213 622 722; Centro Cultural de Belém; dishes €5-8; 10am-8pm Mon-Fri, 10am-9pm Sat & Sun) Revive over salads and soups at this light-filled cafe. Don't miss the Henry Moore sculpture on the terrace. There are free jazz concerts on Thursdays in summer.

DRINKING

All-night street parties in Bairro Alto, sunset drinks from high Alfama terraces, and sumptuous art deco cafes scattered about Chiado – Lisbon has enticing options for imbibers.

Bars

Bicaense (Map pp930-1; Rua da Bica de Duarte Belo 42A) Indie kids have a soft spot for this chilled Santa Catarina haunt, kitted out with retro radios, projectors and squishy beanbags. DJs spin house to the preclubbing crowd and the back room stages occasional gigs.

LISBON FOR FREE

Lisbon is a superb city for euro-pinchers, as its biggest draws are outdoors: from astounding views at hilltop **miradouros** (lookouts) to urban treasure hunts in the warren-like **Alfama**.

Many museums have free admission on Sunday mornings. For a free cultural fix on other days, make for Belém's iconic **Museu Colecção Berardo** (p928), **Museu do Teatro Romano** (Roman Theatre Museum; Map pp930-1; ☎ 217 513 200; Pátio do Aljube 5; 10am-1pm & 2-6pm Tue-Sun) for Roman theatre ruins and, right opposite, the fortresslike **Sé**, built in 1150 on the site of a mosque. The **Museu Calouste Gulbenkian** (p928) gives free musical recitals at noon on Sundays in the library foyer. Try to catch one of the free jazz concerts on Thursdays in summer at **Cafetaria Quadrante** (above).

PORTUGUESE SOUL

Bluesy, bittersweet *fado* encapsulates the Lisbon psyche like nothing else. The melancholic, uniquely Portuguese singing style was born in the Alfama – still one of the world's best places to hear it live.

- **A Baîuca** (Map pp930-1; ☎ 218 867 284; Rua de São Miguel 20; minimum €25; 🕑 dinner Thu-Mon) On a good night, walking into A Baîuca is like gatecrashing a family party. It's a special place with *fado vadio,* where locals take a turn and spectators hiss if anyone dares to chat during the singing. Reserve ahead.
- **Clube de Fado** (Map pp930-1; ☎ 218 852 704; www.clube-de-fado.com; Rua de São João da Praça; minimum €10; 🕑 9pm-2.30am Mon-Sat) Clube de Fado hosts the cream of the *fado* crop in vaulted, dimly lit surrounds. Big-name *fadistas* perform here alongside celebrated guitarists.
- **Mesa de Frades** (Map pp930-1; ☎ 917 029 436; Rua dos Remédios 139A; minimum €15; 🕑 dinner Wed-Mon) A magical place to hear *fado,* tiny Mesa de Frades used to be a chapel. It's tiled with exquisite *azulejos* and has just a handful of tables. The show begins around 11pm.

Bedroom (Map pp930-1; Rua do Norte 86) It's a bedroom, but these beauties aren't sleeping. Join them on the dance floor for electro and hip-hop, or recline on the beds in the lounge shimmering with gold wallpaper and chandeliers.

Bar das Imagens (Map pp930-1; Calçada Marquês de Tancos 1; 🕑 11am-2am Tue-Sat, 3-11pm Sun) With a terrace affording vertigo-inducing views over the city, this cheery bar serves potent cuba libres and other well-prepared cocktails.

Bacalhoeiro (Map pp930-1; ☎ 218 864 891; Rua dos Bacalhoeiros 125; 💻) Nonconformist, laid-back Bacalhoeiro shelters a cosy bar and hosts everything from alternative gigs to film screenings, salsa nights and themed parties. Free wi-fi.

Vertigo Café (Map pp930-1; ☎ 213 433 112; Travessa do Carmo 4; snacks €4-7; 🕑 10am-midnight) Artists lap up the boho vibe at this glam Chiado cafe, where they can relax, read the papers and play draughts.

Pavilhão Chinês (Map pp930-1; Rua Dom Pedro V 89-91) Pavilhão Chinês is an old curiosity shop of a bar with oil paintings and model spitfires dangling from the ceiling, and cabinets brimming with glittering Venetian masks and Action Men. Play pool or bag a comfy armchair with (pricey) cocktail in hand.

Solar do Vinho do Porto (Map pp930-1; ☎ 213 475 707; Rua São Pedro de Alcântara 45; 🕑 11am-midnight Mon-Sat) Part of an 18th-century mansion, the low-lit, beamed cavern is ideal for nursing a glass of fine port.

Cafes

Café a Brasileira (Map pp930-1; ☎ 213 469 547; Rua Garrett 120; 🕑 8am-2am; Ⓜ Baixa-Chiado) An historic watering hole for Lisbon's 19th-century greats, with warm wooden innards and a busy counter serving daytime coffees and pints at night.

Pois Café (Map pp930-1; ☎ 218 862 497; Rua de São João da Praça 93; dishes €4-12; 🕑 11am-8pm Tue-Sun) Boasting a laid-back boho vibe, Pois Café has creative salads, sandwiches and tangy juices. Its sofas invite lazy afternoons spent reading novels and sipping coffee.

CLUBBING

Music Box (Map pp930-1; www.musicboxlisboa.com; Rua Nova do Carvalho 24) Under the brick arches on Rua Nova do Carvalho lies one of Lisbon's hottest clubs. Music Box hosts loud and sweaty club nights with music shifting from electro to rock, plus ear-splitting gigs by rising bands.

Incógnito (Map pp926-7; Rua Poiais de São Bento 37) No-sign, pint-sized Incógnito offers an alternative vibe and DJs thrashing out indie rock and electropop. Work it out with a fun crowd on the tiny basement dance floor, or breathe more easily in the loft bar upstairs.

Lux (Map pp930-1; ☎ 218 820 890; www.luxfragil.com; Armazém A, Cais da Pedra; 🕑 11pm-6am Thu-Sat) Hollywood actor John Malkovich helped bankroll this super-cool club with its peacocking beauty crowd.

Discoteca Jamaica (Map pp930-1; Rua Nova do Carvalho; 🕑 11pm-4am) Gay and straight, black and white, young and old – everyone has a soft spot for this offbeat club. It gets going around 2am at weekends with DJs pumping out reggae, hip-hop and retro.

Cabaret Maxime (Map pp930-1; www.cabaret-maxime.com; Praça da Alegria 58) Young Lisboetas flock to this former strip club for DJ nights of old-school tunes, or loud, sweaty gigs of established and upcoming local bands.

Live Music

Hot Clube de Portugal (Map pp930-1; ☎ 213 467 369; www.hcp.pt; Praça da Alegria 39; 🕑 10pm-2am Tue-Sat; Ⓜ Avenida) This small, poster-plastered cellar has staged top-drawer jazz acts since the 1940s. Shows are at 11pm and 12.30am.

Catacumbas (Map pp930-1; Travessa da Água da Flor 43) Moodily lit and festooned with portraits of legends like Miles Davis, this den is jam-packed when it hosts live jazz on Thursday night.

Zé dos Bois (Map pp930-1; ☎ 213 430 205; www.zedosbois.org; Rua da Barroca 59) Focusing on tomorrow's performing arts and music trends, Zé dos Bois is an experimental venue with a graffitied courtyard for chilling. The edgy space has hosted bands like Black Dice and Animal Collective.

Gay & Lesbian Venues

Lisbon has a relaxed yet flourishing gay scene. Visit www.portugalgay.pt for more listings.

Bar 106 (Map pp926-7; www.bar106.com; Rua de São Marçal 106) Young and fun with an upbeat, preclubbing vibe and crazy events such as Sunday's message party.

Finalmente (Map pp930-1; Rua da Palmeira 38) This popular club has a tiny dance floor, nightly drag shows and wall-to-wall crowds.

Trumps (Map pp926-7; www.trumps.pt; Rua da Imprensa Nacional 104B) Lisbon's hottest gay club with cruisy corners and a sizeable dance floor.

ENTERTAINMENT

Pick up the free bimonthly *Follow me Lisboa*, the *Agenda Cultural Lisboa* or quarterly *Lisboa Step By Step* from the tourist office for what's on. Check out www.visitlisboa.com (Lisbon tourist office website) and www.lisboacultural.pt (for cultural events).

Cinemas

Lisbon has dozens of cinemas, including the multiscreen **Amoreiras** (Map pp926-7; ☎ 213 878 752; Av Eng Duarte Pacheco) and **Colombo** (Map pp926-7; ☎ 217 113 222; Av Lusíada; Ⓜ Colégio Militar-Luz), both located within shopping centres.

Sport

Lisbon's football teams are Benfica, Belenenses and Sporting. Euro 2004 led to the upgrading of the 65,000-seat Estádio da Luz and the construction of a new 54,000-seat Estádio Nacional. Bullfights are staged on Thursday from May to October at **Campo Pequeno** (Map pp926-7; ☎ 217 932 442; Av da República; tickets €10-75). Tickets for both sports are available at **ABEP ticket kiosk** (Map pp930-1; ☎ 213 475 824; Praça dos Restauradores; Ⓜ Restauradores).

GETTING THERE & AWAY

Air

Lisbon is connected by daily flights to Porto, Faro and many European cities; see p924 for details.

Bus

Lisbon's long-distance bus terminal is **Sete Rios** (Map pp926-7; Rua das Laranjeiras; Ⓜ Jardim Zoológico). From here, big carriers like **Rede Expressos** (☎ 213 581 460; www.rede-expressos.pt) run frequent services to destinations all over Portugal, while **Eva/Mundial Turismo** (☎ 213 581 466; www.eva-bus.com) runs buses to Faro, Lagos and other Algarve destinations.

The other major terminal is **Gare do Oriente** (Map pp926–7), concentrating on services to the north and to Spain. The biggest companies operating from here are **Renex** (☎ 218 956 836; www.renex.pt) and Spanish operator **Avanza** (☎ 218 940 250; www.avanzabus.com).

Train

Santa Apolónia station (Map pp930-1; ☎ 808 208 208) is the terminus for northern and central Portugal. You can catch trains from Santa Apolónia to **Gare do Oriente** (Map pp926–7), which has departures to the Algarve and international destinations. **Cais do Sodré station** (Map pp930–1) is for Belém, Cascais and Estoril. Newly reopened **Rossio station** (Map pp930–1) is the terminal to Sintra via Queluz.

For fares and schedules, visit www.cp.pt.

GETTING AROUND

Car & Motorcycle

On the outskirts of the city there are cheap (or free) car parks near Parque das Nações or Belém. The most central underground car park is at Praça dos Restauradores. On Saturday afternoons and Sunday, parking is normally free in pay-and-display areas.

Public Transport

BUS & TRAM

A one-day Bilhete Carris/Metro (€3.70) gives unlimited travel on all buses, trams, metros and funiculars. Pick it up from Carris kiosks and metro stations. The Lisboa Card is good for unlimited travel on nearly all city transport (see p925).

A single ticket costs €1.35 on board or €0.81 if you buy a *bilhete único de coroa* (BUC; a one-zone city-centre ticket) beforehand at a Carris kiosk (there's one in Praça da Figueira).

Don't leave the city without riding tram 28 from Largo Martim Moniz or tram 12 from Praça da Figueira through the narrow streets of the Alfama.

Buses and trams generally run from 6am to 1am.

FERRY

Car, bicycle and passenger ferries leave frequently from the Cais do Sodré ferry terminal (Map pp930–1) to Cacilhas (€0.81, 10 minutes), a transfer point for some buses to Setúbal. From Terreiro do Paço terminal, catamarans zip across to Monijo (€2.10, every 30 minutes) and Seixal (€1.75, every 30 minutes).

METRO

The **metro** (www.metrolisboa.pt; 1-zone single/return €1.25/1.55, 2-zone €1.95/2.45; 6.30am-1am) is useful for hops across town and to the Parque das Nações. Buy a *caderneta* (10-ticket booklet; one-/two-zone caderneta €7.40/10.35) if you'll be using the metro often.

AROUND LISBON

SINTRA

pop 26,400

Lord Byron called this hilltop town a 'glorious Eden' and, although best appreciated at dusk when the coach tours have left, it *is* a magnificent place. Less than an hour west of Lisbon, Sintra was the traditional summer retreat of Portugal's kings. Today it's a fairytale setting of stunning palaces and manors surrounded by rolling green countryside.

Orientation & Information

The Estefânia train station is a 1.5km scenic walk northeast of the centre. Sintra's bus station, and another train station, are a further 1km east in the new-town district of Portela de Sintra. Frequent shuttle buses run to the historic centre.

The **tourist office** (☎ 219 231 157; www.cm-sintra.pt; Praça da República 23; 9am-7pm) has useful maps and can help with accommodation.

Sights & Activities

Although the whole town resembles a historical theme park, there are several compulsory sights. Most are free or discounted with the Lisboa Card (see p925).

The **Palácio Nacional de Sintra** (☎ 219 106 840; Largo Rainha Dona Amélia; admission €5; 10am-5.30pm Thu-Tue) is a dizzy mix of Moorish and Gothic architecture with twin chimneys that dominate the town.

The **Museu de Arte Moderna** (☎ 219 248 170; www.berardocollection.com; Av Heliodoro Salgado; admission €3; 10am-6pm Tue-Sun) hosts rotating exhibitions covering the entire modern-art spectrum, from kinetic and pop art to surrealism and expressionism.

An energetic 3km greenery-flanked hike from the centre, the 8th-century ruined ramparts of **Castelo dos Mouros** (☎ 219 107 970; admission €5; 10am-6pm, to 8pm May–mid-Sep) provide fine views.

Trudge on a further 20 minutes to the exuberantly kitsch **Palácio da Pena** (☎ 219 105 340; admission €6; 10am-6.30pm Tue-Sun, to 5pm Nov-May), where every room is crammed with fascinating treasures.

Monserrate Gardens (☎ 219 237 116; www.parquedesintra.pt; admission €5; 9am-7pm, to 8pm Jun-Sep) are fabulously lush botanical gardens 4km from town. A manicured lawn sweeps up to the whimsical, Moorish-inspired **palácio** (guided visits 10am-1pm & 2pm-6.30pm), a 19th-century romantic folly that can be visited by advance appointments.

En route to the gardens is **Quinta da Regaleira** ☎ 219 106 650; Rua Barbosa du Bocage; admission €6; 10am-8pm), a magnificent World Heritage site and, as an early 20th-century neo-Manueline extravaganza, one of Sintra's highlights.

Cabra Montêz (☎ 917 446 668; www.cabramontez.com; Rua D Mafalda, Belas) arranges all kinds of adventurous pursuits including trekking/rafting/canyoning trips.

Sleeping & Eating

Casa de Hóspedes Dona Maria da Parreirinha (☎ 219 232 490; Rua João de Deus 12-14; d €40-45; P) This small, homely guest house is run by a charming elderly couple. Doubles are old-fashioned but spotless, with big windows, dark-wood furnishings and floral fabrics.

Vila Marquês (☎ 219 230 027; www.vilamarques.net; Rua Sotto Mayor 1; s/d with shared bathroom €35/50, with private bathroom €50/60) Fabulous tiled pictures adorn this traditional manor house with its grand staircase, grandmotherly rooms and an outside terrace with duck-pond views.

Village Café (☎ 219 213 013; Rua Gil Vicente 21; mains around €6; ⏲ daily) Popular with a young crowd, the laid-back, barn-style cafe makes a great pit stop for inexpensive lunch specials, salads and pastries.

Tulhas (☎ 219 232 378; Rua Gil Vicente 4; mains €9-14; ⏲ closed Wed) Set in a converted grain warehouse, Tulhas is dark, tiled and quaint, with twisted chandeliers and a remarkable *bacalhau com natas* (shredded cod with cream and potato).

Xentra (☎ 219 240 759; Rua Consiglieri Pedroso 2A) This cellar bar has a vaguely medieval feel with stone walls and an arched ceiling.

Getting There & Around

Train services (€1.70, 40 minutes) run every 15 minutes between Sintra and Lisbon's Rossio station. Buses run regularly between Sintra and Cascais (€3.35, 60 minutes).

Unless you fancy an uphill hike, it's worth buying the Scotturb *Bilhete Diário Circuito da Pena* (€4.50), a hop-on, hop-off day pass for bus 434 (every 15 minutes, 9.15am to 7.50pm), which runs from the train station via Sintra-Vila to Castelo dos Mouros (10 minutes), Palácio da Pena (15 minutes) and back.

CASCAIS

pop 33,400

Cascais is a crowded summer seaside resort with elegant buildings, an atmospheric old town, and a happy abundance of bars and restaurants.

The **tourist office** (☎ 214 868 204; www.visiteestoril.com; Rua Visconde de Luz 14; ⏲ 9am-7pm Mon-Sat, 10am-6pm Sun) has accommodation lists and bus timetables.

Sights & Activities

Cascais' three sandy bays – **Praia da Conceição**, **Praia da Rainha** and **Praia da Ribeira** – are great for a sunbake or a tingly Atlantic dip, but attract crowds in summer.

The once high-class resort of **Estoril**, 2km east of Cascais, feels more like Florida than Monaco, though it still boasts a large **casino** (☎ 214 667 700; www.casino-estoril.pt; ⏲ 3pm-3am, floor show 11pm).

The sea roars into the coast at **Boca do Inferno** (Hell's Mouth), 2km west of Cascais. Spectacular **Cabo da Roca**, Europe's westernmost point, is 16km from Cascais and Sintra (served by buses from both towns). Wild **Guincho** beach, 3km from Cascais, is a popular surfing venue.

Sleeping & Eating

Cascais Beach Hostel (☎ 309 906 421; www.cascaisbeachostel.com; Rua da Vista Alegre 10; dm/d €20/49; 🖳 🏊) This funky newcomer is central for Cascais' beaches and nightlife. Dorms and doubles sport shiny wood floors and citrus hues. There's a lounge, bike rental, free wi-fi and a small pool in the garden.

Residencial Avenida (☎ 214 864 417; Rua da Palmeira 14; d €30) Sparkling-clean, well-placed accommodation efficiently run by English-speaking owners.

Tanya's Palace (☎ 214 846 332; Sebastião Carvalho e Melo 15; mains €7) If you're suffering from hot-and-spicy withdrawal, Tanya's serves decent Indian and Thai dishes.

Getting There & Around

Trains run frequently to Cascais, via Estoril (€1.70, 40 minutes), from Cais do Sodré station in Lisbon. **Transrent** (☎ 214 864 566; www.transrent.pt; Centro Commercial Cisne, Av Marginal) rents out cars, bicycles and motorcycles.

SETÚBAL

pop 115,000

Unsurprisingly, Portugal's third-largest port is famous for its excellent seafood restaurants. Other draws are a stunning Manueline church and an easy-going pedestrianised centre lined with shops and cafes. Setúbal is also a fine base for exploring the aquatic wonders of the Sado estuary.

Pick up info at either the **municipal tourist office** (☎ 936 515 845; www.mun-setubal.pt; Av Luísa Todi 486; ⏲ 9am-9pm) or the **regional tourist office** (☎ 265 539 130; www.costa-azul.rts.pt; Travessa Frei Gaspar 10), which has Roman ruins beneath its glass floor.

Sights & Activities

Portugal's first Manueline building, the **Igreja de Jesus** (Praça Miguel Bombarda; admission free; ⏲ 9am-1pm & 2-5.30pm Tue-Sun), has maritime motifs and twisted pillars that resemble coiled ropes. The **Galeria da Pintura Quinhentista** (Rua do Balneă Rio Paula Borba; admission €1.10; ⏲ 9am-noon & 1.30-5.30pm Tue-Sat), around the corner, has a renowned collection of 16th-century paintings.

Good **beaches** west of town include Praia da Figuerinha (accessible by bus in summer). Across the estuary at Tróia is a more developed beach, plus' the ruins of a Roman settlement. On the ferry trip across you may see some of the estuary's 30 or so bottle-nosed dolphins.

SAL (☎ 265 227 685; www.sal.pt, in Portuguese) organises walks from €6 per person. For jeep safaris, hiking and biking in the Serra da Arrábida, or canoe trips through the Reserva Natural do Estuário do Sado, contact **Planeta Terra** (☎ 919 471 871; www.planetaterra.pt; Praça General Luís Domingues 9). **Vertigem Azul** (☎ 265 238 000; www.vertigemazul.com; Av Luísa Todi 375) offers canoe and dolphin-spotting excursions. There are wine-cellar tours of **José Maria da Fonseca** (☎ 212 198 940; www.jmf.pt; Rua José Augusto Coelho 11; per person €2.50-3.50; 🕒 10am-12.30pm & 2-5pm Mon-Fri), the oldest Portuguese producer of table wine.

Sleeping

Parque de Campismo (☎ 265 238 318; Outão; adult/tent/car €3.60/4.40/5.90) Situated 4km west of Setúbal, this green and shady site is right on the coast, perfect for those who want to snorkel or windsurf. It's accessible by regular bus (25 minutes).

Pousada da Juventude (☎ 265 534 431; setubal@movijovem.pt; Largo José Afonso; dm/d €9/32; 🕒 curfew 11pm-7am) Near the busy fishing harbour, this hostel has tidy dorms.

Residencial Todi (☎ 265 220 592; Av Luísa Todi 244; s/d with shared bathroom €20/30, with private bathroom €25/35) If street noise doesn't affect your shut-eye, this is a decent and clean cheapie on the main drag.

Residencial Bocage (☎ 265 543 080; www.residencialbocage.com; Rua de São Cristóvão 14; s/d incl breakfast €38/50; ❄) Centrally located Bocage has renovated rooms with parquet floors, comfy beds and squeaky-clean bathrooms.

Eating

Head to the western end of Avenida Luísa Todi for tasty, fresh-from-the-Atlantic seafood. The simple, buzzy restaurants with alfresco seating are a great place to sample local specialities like *caldeirada,* a fish stew prepared in a brass pot.

For self-caterers there's the supermarket **Pingo Doce** (Av Luísa Todi 149; 🕒 8am-9pm) and the large **mercado municipal market** next door, selling fresh fish and produce.

Duarte dos Frangos (☎ 265 522 603; Av Luísa Todi 285; roast chicken for 1/2 people €5.50/8.50; 🕒 lunch Fri-Wed, dinner Fri-Tue) This cosy spot just south of the old town whips up succulent roast chicken.

Casa Santiago (☎ 265 221 688; Av Luísa Todi 92; mains €7-12; lunch & dinner Mon-Sat) The scent of sizzling fish on the grill may reel you into this local favourite, where hungry lunchtime crowds feast on huge portions of *choco frito* (fried cuttlefish).

Getting There & Away

Buses leave at least hourly from Lisbon's Praça de Espanha (€4, one hour). Ferries shuttle across the estuary to Tróia approximately every 45 minutes (€1.30, 15 minutes).

THE ALGARVE

Love it or loathe it, it's easy to see the allure of the Algarve: breathtaking cliffs, golden sands, scalloped bays and long sandy islands. Although overdevelopment has blighted parts of the coast, head inland and you'll find lovely Portuguese countryside once again. Algarve highlights include the forested slopes of Monchique, the pretty riverside town of Tavira and windswept, historic Sagres. Underrated Faro is the regional capital.

You can travel the Algarve via the rail line running from Lagos to the Spanish border; local tourist offices have timetables.

FARO

pop 58,000

Faro is an attractive seaside town and makes a good base to explore the rest of this coastal strip. It has an attractive marina, well-maintained parks and plazas and an historic old town full of pedestrian lanes and outdoor cafes. To avoid the crowds, visit out of season.

The bus and train terminals are on Av da República just north of the marina. The **tourist office** (☎ 289 803 604; www.cm-faro.pt; Rua da Misericórdia) has informative leaflets. Go online at pleasant **Café Aliança** (Rua Dr Francisco Gomes; per hr €2.50; 🕒 10am-11.45pm).

Sights & Activities

The small picturesque **Cidade Velha** (Old Town) is an intriguing place to wander, with its winding, peaceful cobbled streets

Book your stay at lonelyplanet.com/hotels

and squares. The palm-clad **waterfront** has pleasant kick-back cafes. Faro's beach, **Praia de Faro** (Ilha de Faro), is 6km southwest of town; take bus 16 from opposite the bus station. Less crowded is unspoilt **Ilha Deserta**, reachable by ferry (five departures daily from May to September) for €5 one way.

Sleeping & Eating

Pousada da Juventude (☎ 289 826 521; www.pousadasjuventude.pt; Rua da Polícia de Segurança Pública 1; dm €13, d with shared/private bathroom €30/38; reception ⌚ 24hr) Adjoining a small park, this hostel offers basic, clean rooms with no frills but is a good budget option.

Pensão Residencial Oliveira (☎ 289 812 154; Rua Horta Machado 28; s/d/tr with shared bathroom from €20/30/45) This place's nine well-worn rooms are cluttered and have flowery bedspreads and floral odours.

Residencial Dandy (☎ 289 824 791; Rua Filipe Alistão 62; d with shared/private bathroom €40/50) The best rooms at this bohemian-chic place have antique furniture, high ceilings and wrought-iron balconies. Smaller, tile-floored rooms are in the back.

Residencial Adelaide (☎ 289 802 383; www.adelaideresidencial.com; Rua Cruz dos Mestres 7; s/d incl breakfast €45/50; ❄) This modern, pleasant guest house is good value for its clean and light rooms, some with terraces.

Adega Nova (☎ 289 813 433; Rua Francisco Barreto 24; mains €6-12; ⌚ lunch & dinner) This long-time favourite serves tasty meat and fish dishes amid country charm.

Restaurante A Taska (☎ 289 824 739; Rua do Alportel 38; mains €6-13; ⌚ lunch & dinner Mon-Sat) Popular with locals, this cosy trattoria-style restaurant serves delicious regional fare.

Getting There & Away

Faro airport has both domestic and international flights (see p924). Buses 14 and 16 (€1.55) run into town until 9pm. A taxi costs about €12.

There are six daily express buses to Lisbon (€16, four hours) and frequent buses to other coastal towns. Five trains run daily to Lisbon (€18, four hours).

TAVIRA

pop 12,500

Set on either side of the meandering Rio Gilão, Tavira is a charming town. The ruins of a hilltop castle, an old Roman bridge and a smattering of Gothic and Renaissance churches are among the historic attractions.

The **tourist office** (☎ 281 322 511; Rua da Galeria 9) can help with accommodation and the **town hall** (Praça da Republica; ⌚ 9am-9pm Mon-Fri, 10am-1pm Sat) provides free internet access.

One of the town's 30-plus churches, the Renaissance façade of the **Igreja da Misericórdia** is the most striking in the Algarve. Tavira's ruined **castle** (Rua da Liberdade; admission free; ⌚ 9am-5pm Mon-Fri, 10am-5pm Sat & Sun) dominates the town. Nearby, the 16th-century **Palácio da Galeria** (☎ 281 320 540; Calçada da Galeria; admission €2; ⌚ 10am-noon & 4-7.30pm Tue-Sat) holds occasional exhibitions.

Ilha de Tavira is an island beach connected to the mainland by a ferry (€1.80 return) at Quatro Águas. Walk the 2km or take the (summer only) bus from the bus station.

Enjoy pedal power with a rented bike from **Casa Abilio** (☎ 281 323 467; Rua Goao Vaz C Real 23a). Rent kayaks for a paddle along the river at **Sport Nautica** (☎ 281 324 943; Rua Jacques Pessoa 26).

Camping de Tavira (☎ 281 324 455; www.campingtavira.com; Ilha da Tavira; camp sites per 1/2 people incl tent €9/14; ⌚ May-Oct) is a summer-only camping option on the Ilha de Tavira. **Pensão Residencial Lagôas** (☎ 281 322 252; Rua Almirante Cândido dos Reis 24; s/d from €20/30) has bright rooms around a twee flowery patio. **Residencial Princesa do Gilão** (☎/fax 281 325 171; Rua Borda d'Água de Aguiar 10; s/d/tr €45/55/65; ❄) has tight but neat rooms, some with river views.

For a tasty bang-up meal, try **Restaurante Bica** (☎ 281 323 843; Rua Almirante Cândido dos Reis 24; mains €6-16), where fresh grilled fish go nicely with inexpensive Borba wine.

Frequent trains and buses run daily between Faro and Tavira (€3, one hour).

LAGOS

pop 25,400

In summer the pretty fishing port of Lagos has a party vibe; its picturesque cobbled streets and comely nearby beaches pack with revellers and sunseekers. The municipal **tourist office** (☎ 282 764 111; www.lagosdigital.com, in Portuguese; Largo Marquês de Pombal) is in the centre of town. Sip coffee over email at **Café Gélibar** (Rua Lançarote de Freitas 43A; internet access per hr €3; ⌚ 9am-11pm Mon-Sat, to 8pm Sun).

The **municipal museum** (☎ 282 762 301; Rua General Alberto da Silveira; admission €2; ⌚ 9.30am-12.30pm & 2-5pm Tue-Sun) houses archaeological finds and ecclesiastical treasures.

The best beach scene is at **Meia Praia** to the east, and **Praia da Luz** and reclusive **Praia do Pinhão** to the west.

Blue Ocean (☎ 964 665 667; www.blue-ocean-divers.de) organises diving, kayaking and snorkelling safaris. On the promenade, fishermen offer motorboat jaunts to nearby grottoes. **Kayak Adventures** (☎ 913 262 200) offers kayaking trips. Rent windsurfing gear from **Windsurf Point** (☎ 282 792 315, www.windsurfpoint.com).

Campismo da Trindade (☎ 282 763 893; camp sites per adult/tent/car €3.10/4.80/4.50) doesn't have much tent-peg space in summer; it's 200m south of the town walls. **Pousada da Juventude** (☎ 282 761 970; www.pousadasjuventude.pt; Rua Lançarote de Freitas 50; dm €16, d with shared/private bathroom €35/43; 24hr;) is a well-run hostel and good place to meet other travellers. Laid-back **Carlos House** (☎ 916 594 225; carloshousez@yahoo.com; Rua Jogo da Bola 8; dm from €19.50;) is uphill from the centre with a guest kitchen and rooftop terrace. A party atmosphere prevails at **Rising Cock Hostel** (☎ 969 411 131; Travessa do Forno 14; dm €28;), with a lounge, terrace and free internet.

Backpacker-favourite **Casa Rosa** (☎ 966 884 317; Rua do Ferrador 22; dishes €3-7; 5pm-midnight) serves up simple, good-value mains such as veggie stir-fry, chilli con carne and fajitas.

Adega da Marina (☎ 282 764 284; Av dos Descobrimentos 35; mains €6-9; lunch & dinner) is a barnlike place dishing out generous portions of grilled chicken and seafood favourites.

Bus and train services depart frequently for other Algarve towns and around eight times daily to Lisbon (€18.50, 4½ hours).

SILVES

pop 10,800

The one-time capital of Moorish Algarve, Silves is a pretty town of jumbled orange rooftops scattered above the banks of the Rio Arade. Clamber around the ramparts of its fairy-tale castle for superb views.

Silves train station is 2km from town with a connecting bus. The **tourist office** (☎ 289 442 255; www.cm-silves.pt; Rua 25 de Abril) can help with accommodation. Get online at **It-Connect** (Rua Pintor Bernardo Marques; per hr €1.50).

Residencial Ponte Romana (☎ 282 443 275; d €30) has an ace location beside a Roman bridge with views of the castle and surrounding orchards. Rooms are comfortable, and there's a welcoming bar-restaurant downstairs.

Café Ingles (☎ 282 442 585; mains €7-14), below the castle, is an English-owned, funky place serving up vegetarian dishes, homemade soups and wood-fired pizza, plus live music at weekends.

Nine trains run daily from Lagos (€2.10, 35 minutes), and are met by local buses. Eight buses run daily to Silves from Albufeira (€3.60, 40 minutes).

SAGRES

pop 1940

The small, elongated village of Sagres has an end-of-the-world feel with its sea-carved cliffs and empty, wind-whipped fortress high above the ocean. There is a central **tourist office** (☎ 282 624 873; Rua Comandante Matoso; Tue-Sat).

The **fort** (admission €3; ☎ 10am-8.30pm May-Sep, 10am-6.30pm Oct-Apr) offers breathtaking views over the seaside cliffs; according to legend, this is where Henry the Navigator established his navigation school and primed the early Portuguese explorers.

Visit Europe's southwestern-most point, the **Cabo de São Vicente** (Cape St Vincent), 6km to the west. A solitary lighthouse stands on this barren cape (there's one bus on weekdays).

This coast is ideal for surfing; hire windsurfers at sand dune–fringed **Praia do Martinhal**. You can sign up for surfing lessons, hire bikes and arrange canoe trips with **Sagres Natura** (☎ 282 624 072; www.sagresnatura.com; Rua São Vicente).

DiversCape (☎ 965 559 073; www.diverscape.com; Porto da Baleeira) organises diving trips.

Orbitur Sagres (☎ 282 624 371; camp sites per adult/tent €3.50/4), 2km from town, is off the Cabo de São Vicente road. **Casa de Pasto A Grelha** (☎ 282 624 193; Rua Comandante Matoso; mains €4) is an informal spot with superb spit-roasted chicken.

Frequent daily buses run from Lagos (€3.40, 50 minutes).

CENTRAL PORTUGAL

The vast centre of Portugal is a rugged swath of rolling hillsides, whitewashed villages and olive groves and cork fields. Richly historic, it is scattered with prehistoric remains and medieval castles. It's also home to one of Portugal's most architecturally intriguing towns, Évora, as well as several spectacular walled villages. There are fine local wines and plenty of outdoor exploring in the dramatic Beiras region.

ÉVORA

pop 56,500

Évora is an enchanting place to delve into the past. Inside 14th-century walls, narrow, winding lanes lead to a striking medieval cathedral, a Roman temple, and a picturesque town square. These old-fashioned good looks are the backdrop to a lively student town surrounded by wineries and dramatic countryside.

Orientation & Information

The train station is 1km southeast of the centre. The bus station is 500m west of the centre.

The **tourist office** (☎ 266 777 071; www.cm-evora.pt, in Portuguese; Praça do Giraldo 73) has an excellent city map. Log on at the **town hall** (Praça de Sertório; internet access free; 9am-12.30pm & 2-5pm Mon-Fri).

Sights & Activities

Évora's cathedral, **Sé** (Largo do Marquês de Marialva; admission €1; 9am-noon & 2-5pm), has fabulous cloisters and a museum jam-packed with ecclesiastical treasures.

The **Temple of Diana** (Largo do Conde de Vila Flor) was once part of the Roman Forum and is a magnificent relic dating back almost 1800 years.

Capela dos Ossos (☎ 266 744 307; Largo Conde de Vila Flor; admission €1.50; 9am-1pm & 2.30-6pm) provides a real Addams family day out. This ghoulish Chapel of Bones is constructed from the bones and skulls of several thousand people.

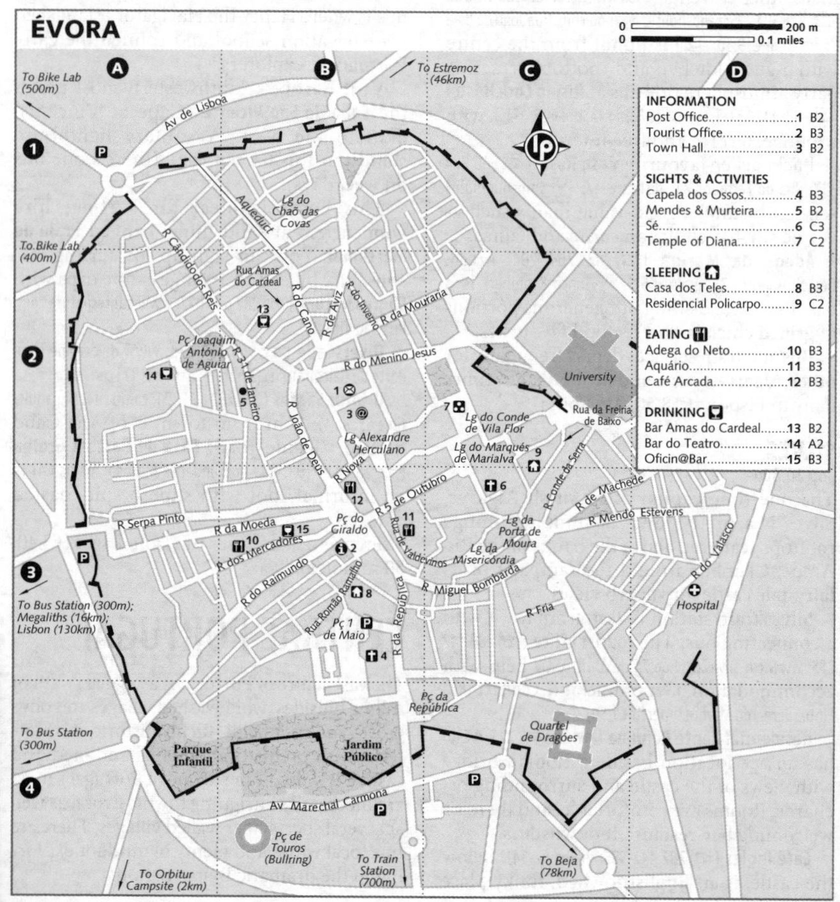

WORTH THE TRIP: CASTELO DE VIDE

A worthy detour north of Évora, is the hilltop, story-book town **Castelo de Vide**, noted for its picturesque houses with Gothic doorways. Highlights are the **Judiaria** (Old Jewish Quarter), the medieval backstreets and castle-top views. Try to spend a night here before heading skywards to **Marvão**, a striking mountain-top walled village (population 190), 12km from Castelo de Vide. The **tourist offices** Castelo de Vide (☎ 245 901 361; www.cm-castelo-vide.pt; Praça Dom Pedro V); Marvão (☎ 245 909 131; Largo de Santa Maria) can help with accommodation.

On weekdays, three buses run from Portalegre to Castelo de Vide (€5, 20 minutes). Three buses daily connect Portalegre with Evora (€11, 2 hours).

Mendes & Murteira (☎ 266 739 240; www.evora-mm.pt; Rua 31 de Janeiro 15a) offers half-day tours of surrounding megaliths or around the city itself.

Sleeping & Eating

Orbitur Campsite (☎ 266 705 190; camp sites per adult/tent/car €4.80/5.40/4.70) A grassy, tree-shaded, well-equipped camping ground 2km southwest of town on the N380. Bus 5 or 8 (€1.20) goes close by.

Casa dos Teles (☎ 266 702 453; Rua Romão Ramalho 27; s with shared bathroom €25, d €30-35, r with private bathroom €40; ❄) These 10 mostly light and airy rooms are a decent value; quieter back rooms overlook a pretty courtyard.

Residencial Policarpo (☎ 266 702 424; www.pensaopolicarpo.com; Rua da Freiria de Baixo 16; s/d with shared bathroom €30/35, with private bathroom €52/57) This former 16th-century home is charming and atmospheric if somewhat faded.

Aquário (☎ 266 785 055; Rua de Valdevinos 7; mains €6-8) Vibrant little vegetarian restaurant with just a few daily choices, including a vegan option.

Adega do Neto (☎ 266 209 916; Rua dos Mercadores 46; mains €6-7) This cheap and cheerful eatery has good daily specials such as fried chicken or *feijoada* (pork and bean casserole).

Café Arcada (Praça do Giraldo 10; meals €6.50-10; ⌚ breakfast, lunch & dinner) An Évora institution, serving up coffee, crêpes and cakes, with outdoor tables on the plaza.

Drinking & Entertainment

Bar do Teatro (Praça Joaquim António de Aguiar; ⌚ 8pm-2am) This small, inviting bar has high ceilings, old-world decor and a friendly mixed crowd.

Oficin@Bar (Rua da Moeda 27; ⌚ 8pm-2am Mon-Sat) Attracting all ages, this is a small, relaxed bar with jazz and blues playing in the background.

Bar Amas do Cardeal (☎ 266 721 133; Rua Amas do Cardeal 4a; ⌚ 10pm-3am) This darkly lit bar attracts an eclectic crowd for post-1am drinking, and weekend dancing on the small dance floor.

Getting There & Away

Évora has six to 12 buses daily to Lisbon (€11.50, two hours) and three to Faro (€15, five hours). Three daily trains run from Lisbon (€10, 2½ hours).

MONSARAZ

pop 977

In a dizzy setting, high above the plain, this walled village has a moody medieval feel and magnificent views. The **tourist office** (☎ 266 557 136; Praça Dom Nuno Álvares) can advise on accommodation. Eat before 8pm as the town tucks up early to bed.

Museu de Arte Sacra (Praça Dom Nuno Álvares; admission €1; ⌚ 10am-1pm & 2-6pm) has a display of religious artefacts; the 15th-century fresco is superb. Three kilometres north of town is **Menhir of Outeiro**, one of the tallest megalithic monuments ever discovered.

Up to four buses daily connect Monsaraz with the larger town of Reguengos de Monsaraz (€2.50, 35 minutes), from which there are onward connections to Évora.

ÓBIDOS

pop 11,000

This walled village was a wedding gift from Dom Dinis to his wife Dona Isabel (beats a fondue set), and its historic centre is a delightful place to wander. Located some 88km north of Lisbon (and 17km from the coast), Óbidos is one of the iconic attractions of Estremadura, a region of extremely fertile farmland set amid rolling hills and valleys running from the mouth of the Rio Tejo almost to the Rio Mondego. Highlights include the **Igreja de Santa Maria** (Rua Direita), with fine *azulejos*, and views from the town walls. The **tourist office** (☎ 262 955 060; www.cm-obidos.pt, in Portuguese; Rua Direita) has a brochure of walks in the area.

Óbido Sol (☎ 262 959 188; Rua Direita 40; d €40) is a neatly kept old town house, with comfortable rooms surrounding a snug living room.

There are direct buses Monday to Friday from Lisbon (€7, 70 minutes) or via Caldas da Rainha, 10 minutes away.

NAZARÉ & AROUND

pop 16,000

With a warren of narrow cobbled lanes running down to a wide cliff-backed beach, Nazaré is Estremadura's most picturesque coastal resort. The town centre is jammed with seafood restaurants, bars and local women in traditional dress hawking rooms for rent. The **tourist office** (☎ 262 561 194) is at the end of Av da República.

Beaches are the main attraction here; swimmers should beware of dangerous currents. Climb or take the funicular to cliff-top **Sítio** with its cluster of fishermen's cottages and technicolour views.

Two of Portugal's big-time architectural masterpieces are close by. Follow the signs to **Alcobaça** where, right in the centre of town, is the immense **Mosteiro de Santa Maria de Alcobaça** (☎ 262 505 120; admission €5, church admission free; 9am-7pm) dating from 1178; don't miss the colossal former kitchen.

Batalha's massive Gothic **Mosteiro de Santa Maria de Vitória** (☎ 244 765 497; admission to cloisters & unfinished chapels €5; 9am-6pm), dating from 1388, is home to the tomb of Henry the Navigator.

Uphill a few blocks from the beach in Nazaré, **Vila Conde Fidalgo** (☎ 262 552 361; http://condefidalgo.planetaclix.pt; Av da Independência Nacional 21a; 2-/4-person apt €45/75) is a pretty little complex built around a series of flower-filled courtyards Rooms all have kitchenettes.

The popular family tavern **A Tasquinha** (☎ 262 551 945; Rua Adrião Batalha 54; mains €6.50-10; Tue-Sun) serves high-quality seafood at reasonable prices.

Nazaré has numerous bus connections to Lisbon (€8.60, two hours). There are several buses daily to Alcobaça (€2, 20 minutes).

TOMAR

pop 17,000

A charming town straddling a river, Tomar is the famed home of the Knights Templar; check out their headquarters, the outstanding monastery **Convento de Cristo** (☎ 249 313 481; admission €5; 9am-6pm Jun-Sep, 9am-5pm Oct-May). Other rarities include a magnificent 17th-century **Aqueduto de Pegões** (aqueduct) and a medieval **synagogue** (Rua Dr Joaquim Jacinto 73; admission free; 10am-1pm & 2-6pm). The town is backed by the dense greenery of the **Mata Nacional dos Sete Montes** (Seven Hills National Forest). Tomar's **tourist office** (☎ 249 322 427; turismo.tomar@sapo.pt; Av Dr Cândido Madureira) dispenses town and forest maps.

Dutch-run **Camping Redondo** (☎ 249 376 421; www.campingredondo.com; camp sites per adult/car/tent €3.50/2.10/2.80, 4-person bungalow €60-75;) is a well-equipped camping ground 10km northeast at Poço Redondo.

Tomar's most atmospheric budget choice, **Residencial União** (☎ 249 323 161; residencialuniao@oninet.pt; Rua Serpa Pinto 94; s/d/q €25/38/45;), features sizeable rooms with antique furniture and fixtures.

Tomar's best-known restaurant, **Bela Vista** (☎ 249 312 870; Rua Fonte do Choupo 6; mains €6-10) serves tasty traditional plates (like roast kid) with a riverside terrace.

At least four express buses go daily to Lisbon (€8, two hours) and there are even more frequent trains (€8.20, two hours).

COIMBRA

pop 150,000

Coimbra is a dynamic yet comfortably lived-in city, with a student life centred on the magnificent 13th-century university. Aesthetically eclectic, there are elegant shopping streets, ancient stone walls and backstreet alleys with hidden *tascas* (taverns) and *fado* bars.

Coimbra's annual highlight is Queima das Fitas, a boozy week of revelry when students celebrate the end of the academic year (begins the first Thursday in May).

Orientation & Information

There are three train stations: Coimbra A, Coimbra B and Coimbra Parque. Most trains arrive at Coimbra A, a short walk from the centre. The main bus station is 15 minutes' walk northwest of the centre.

Casa Municipal da Cultura (☎ 239 702 630; Rua Pedro Monteiro; 10am-7.30pm Mon-Fri, 2-6.30pm Sat) offers free internet access near the youth hostel.

For town info, visit the **tourist office** (☎ 239 859 884; coimbraviva@cm-coimbra.pt; Praça da Porta Férrea).

WORTH THE TRIP: CONIMBRIGA

Conimbriga, 16km south of Coimbra, is the site of the well-preserved ruins of a **Roman town** (9am-8pm mid-Mar–mid-Sep, 10am-6pm mid-Sep–mid-Mar), including mosaic floors, baths and fountains. There's a good **museum** (admission €4; 9am-8pm Tue-Sun summer, 10am-6pm Tue-Sun winter) here with a restaurant. Frequent buses run to Condeixa, 2km from the site; direct buses (€2) depart at 9am and 9.35am (only 9.35am at weekends) from the **AVIC terminal** (Rua João de Ruão 18, Coimbra), returning at 1pm and 5pm (only 5pm at weekends).

Sight & Activities

Igreja de Santa Cruz (239 822 941; Praça 8 de Maio; admission €2.50; 9am-noon & 2-5pm) has a fabulous ornate pulpit and medieval royal tombs. Get here via the lift (one way €1.50) by the market.

Velha Universidade (Old University; 239 822 941; www.uc.pt/sri; admission €6; 10am-noon & 2-5pm) is unmissable in its grandeur. You can visit the library with its gorgeous book-lined hallways and the Manueline chapel dating back to 1517.

Capitão Dureza (239 918 148; www.capitaodureza.com, in Portuguese; Barcouça) organises rafting, canoeing, biking and hiking trips.

Sleeping

Pousada da Juventude (239 822 955; coimbra@movijovem.pt; Rua António Henriques Seco 12-14; dm/d €11/28) A solid, efficiently run hostel, but avoid the gloomy basement dorms; take northbound bus 6, 7 or 29 from Coimbra A station.

Pensão Kanimambo (239 827 151; fax 239 828 408; Av Fernão de Magalhães 484; s/d from €12/22;) Near the bus station, this '70s concrete apartment block offers clean, basic rooms.

Pensão Residencial Larbelo (239 829 092; residencialarbelo@sapo.pt; Largo da Portagem 33; s/d €30/40;) Bang in the centre, Larbelo boasts high-ceilinged rooms with wooden-floors and modern furnishings. Front rooms opening onto the Largo da Portagem are especially nice.

Pensão-Restaurante Flôr de Coimbra (239 823 865; flordecoimbrahr@sapo.pt; Rua do Poço 5; s/d/tr from €30/35/40) This once-grand 19th-century home with its own restaurant offers loads of character in a great location.

Eating

Head to the lanes west of Praça do Comércio, especially Rua das Azeiteiras, for cheap eats. Self-caterers should stop by the modern **Mercado Municipal Dom Pedro V** (Rua Olímpio Nicolau Rui Fernandes; Mon-Sat) for fruit, vegetables and more.

Café Santa Cruz (239 833 617; Praçca 8 de Maio; Mon-Sat) A former chapel that has been resurrected into one of Portugal's most atmospheric cafes.

Restaurante Jardim da Manga (239 829 156; Rua Olímpio Nicolau Rui Fernanda; mains €5-7.50; closed Sat) A student favourite, this cafeteria-style restaurant serves up tasty meat and fish dishes, with pleasant outdoor seating beside the Jardim da Manga fountain.

Zé Manel (239 823 790; Beco do Forno 12; mains €7-10; Mon-Sat) There's great food, huge servings and a zany atmosphere, with walls papered with diners' comments, cartoons and poems. Vegetarian choices.

Clubbing

Via Latina (916 433 432; Rua Almeida Garrett 1; midnight-6am Tue-Sat) Students swear by the DJs at this simple, sweaty, excellent dance club.

Vinyl (Avenida Afonso Henriques 43; midnight-4am Tue-Sat) Another perennial favourite, where a mostly student crowd does the soft shake to predictable pop tunes.

Entertainment

Coimbra-style *fado* is more cerebral than the Lisbon variety, and its adherents staunchly protective. **our pick** **Á Capella** (239 833 985; www.acapella.com.pt; Rua Corpo de Deus; admission €10 incl one drink; 10pm-2am), housed in a fabulous 14th-century former chapel, and **Bar Diligência** (239 827 667; Rua Nova 30; 6pm-2am) are good spots to catch live *fado*.

Getting There & Away

At least 12 buses and as many trains run daily from Lisbon (€12, 2½ hours) and Porto (€11, 1½ hours), plus frequent buses from Faro and Évora, via Lisbon. Other useful connections include eight daily buses to Luso/Buçaco (from Coimbra A; €3, 45 minutes).

LUSO & THE BUÇACO FOREST

pop 2000

This sylvan region harbours a lush forest of century-old trees surrounded by countryside dappled with heather, wildflowers and leafy ferns. There's even a fairy-tale palace here, a 1907 neo-Manueline extravagance, where visitors can dine or stay overnight. Buçaco was chosen as a retreat by 16th-century monks and surrounds the lovely spa town of Luso.

The **tourist office** (☎ 231 939 133; Av Emídio Navarro 136; ⌚ Mon-Sat) has maps and leaflets about the forest and trails, plus free internet access. The **Termas** (thermal baths; ☎ 231 937 910; Av Emídio Navarro; admission free; ⌚ May-Oct) offers a range of treatments.

Just above town, **Casa de Hóspedes Familiar** (☎ 231 939 612; paulcoelho@sapo.pt; Rua Ernesto Navarro 34; d/tr €35/40) is a homey late-Victorian country house with simple cosy rooms, some with little verandas and views.

Palace Hotel do Buçaco (☎ 231 930 101; www.almeidahotels.com; s/d from €150/180; ❄) provides the fairy-tale overnight in an ostentatious palace complete with gargoyles, ornamental garden and turrets. The elegant restaurant offers seven-course menus for around €45.

Buses to/from Coimbra (€3, 45 minutes) run four times daily each weekday and twice daily on weekends. IR trains run four times daily from Coimbra-A to Luso/Buçaco station (€1.61, 30 minutes).

SERRA DA ESTRELA

The forested Serra da Estrela has a raw natural beauty and offers some of the country's best hiking. This is Portugal's highest mainland mountain range (1993m), and the source of its two great rivers: Mondego and Zêzere. The town of **Manteigas** makes a good base for hiking and exploring the area. The **main park office** (☎ 275 980 060; pnse@icn.pt; Rua 1 de Maio 2; Manteigas; ⌚ Mon-Fri) provides details of popular walks in the Parque Natural de Serra da Estrela; additional offices are at Seia, Gouveia and Guarda.

The park publishes *Discover the Region of the Serra da Estrela,* a walking guide in English with maps and narratives (€4.25).

Sleeping

Parque Municipal de Campismo (☎ 271 221 200; Rua do Estádio Municipal, Guarda; camp sites per adult/tent/car €2/1.50/2) Basic tent-peg space, southwest of Guarda's town centre.

Pousada da Juventude (☎ 275 335 375; penhas@movijovem.pt; Penhas da Saúde; dm/d from €10/25) Located 10km above Covilhã, this first-rate mountaintop hostel is a good excursion base, providing meals and kitchen facilities.

Pensão Serradalto (☎ 275 981 151; Rua 1 de Maio 15, Manteigas; s/d/ste €35/45/60) In a renovated stone house, the Serradalto offers wood-floored rooms with simple antique furnishings, plus fine valley views from a sunny upstairs terrace.

Getting There & Around

Two regular weekday buses connect Manteigas with Guarda, from which there are onward services to Coimbra and Lisbon. Several buses run daily from Coimbra along the park's perimeter to Seia, Gouveia, Guarda or Covilhã.

NORTHERN PORTUGAL

Beneath Spanish Galicia, northern Portugal is a land of lush river valleys, sparkling coastline, granite peaks and virgin forests. This region is also gluttony for wine-lovers: it's the home of refreshing *vinho verde* wine and ancient vineyards along the dramatic Rio Douro. Gateway to the north is Porto, a beguiling riverside city blending both medieval and modern attractions. Smaller towns and villages also offer cultural allure, from majestic Braga, the country's religious heart, to the seaside beauty Viana do Castelo.

PORTO

pop 300,000

At the mouth of the Rio Douro, the hilly city of Porto presents a jumble of styles, eras and attitudes: narrow medieval alleyways, extravagant baroque churches, prim squares, and wide boulevards lined with beaux-arts edifices. A lively city with chatter in the air and a tangible sense of history, Porto's old-world river-frontage district is a World Heritage site. Across the water twinkle the neon signs of Vila Nova de Gaia, the headquarters of the major port manufacturers.

Orientation

Porto centre is small enough to cover mainly by foot. The city clings to the north bank of the Douro River, spanned by five bridges to Vila Nova de Gaia, home to the port-wine lodges. The picturesque Ribeira district lies along the waterfront.

Information

Branch tourist office (☎ 222 057 514; Praça Dom João I 43) Smaller than main office but equally helpful.

Main tourist office (☎ 223 393 472; www.portoturismo.pt; Rua Clube dos Fenianos 25) Next door to the tourist police office.
On web (Praça General Humberto Delgado 291; internet access per hr €1.80; 10am-2am Mon-Sat, 3pm-2am Sun)
Santo António Hospital (☎ 222 077 500; Largo Prof Abel Salazar) English-speaking staff.
Telephone office (Praça da Liberdade 62; 10am-10pm)

Sights & Activities

Head for the riverfront **Ribeira** district for an atmospheric stroll and check out the gritty local bars, superb restaurants and river cruises.

Torre dos Clérigos (Rua dos Clérigos; admission €2; 10am-noon & 2-5pm) rewards climbers of the 225 steep steps with the best panorama of the city.

The **Sé** (☎ 222 059 028; Terreiro da Sé; cloisters admission €2; 8.45am-12.30pm & 2.30-7pm) dominates Porto and is worth a visit for its architecture and vast ornate interior.

Many of the port-wine lodges in Vila Nova de Gaia run daily tours and tastings, including **Taylor's** (☎ 223 742 800; www.taylor.pt; Rua do Choupelo 250; 10am-6pm Mon-Fri).

The **Museu de Arte Contemporânea** (☎ 226 156 500; www.serralves.pt; Rua Dom João de Castro 210; admission €5; 10am-7pm) has works by some of Portugal's best modern artists.

Museu do Vinho (Wine Museum; ☎ 222 076 300; museuvinhoporto@cm-porto.pt; Rua de Monchique 45-52; admission €2; 11am-7pm Tue-Sun) traces the history of wine and port with informative films, exhibits and tastings.

Porto's best art museum, the **Soares dos Reis National Museum** (☎ 223 393 770; Rua Dom Manuel II 44; admission €3; 10am-6pm Wed-Sun, 2-6pm Tue) exhibits Portuguese painting and sculpture masterpieces from the 19th and 20th centuries.

Festivals & Events

Porto's big festivals are the **Festa de São João** (St John's Festival), from 20 to 24 June, and the international film festival **Fantasporto** in February. Also worth catching are the **Celtic music festival** in April/May, and the **rock festival** in August.

Sleeping

Campismo Marisol (☎ 227 135 942; fax 227 126 351; Rua Alto das Chaquedas 82, Praia de Canide; adult/tent/car €2/3.50/2.75) One of three camp sites near the sea, Marisol is 6km south of Porto. Other options (all get packed in summer) include **Campismo Madalena** (☎ 227 122 520; www.orbitur.com; Rua do Cerro, Praia da Madalena; adult/tent/car €4.80/5.40/4.70), 7km south of Porto, and **Campismo Angeiras** (☎ 229 270 571; www.orbitur.com; Rua de Angeiras, Lavra; adult/tent/car €4.80/5.40/4.70), 20km north of Porto.

Pousada da Juventude (☎ 226 177 257; www.pousadasjuventude.pt; Rua Paulo da Gama 551; dm/d €14/38; 24hr;) A tastefully spruced-up hostel 4km west of the centre. Reservations essential. Take bus 500 from Aliados.

Pensão Duas Nações (☎ 222 081 616; www.duasnacoes.com.pt; Praça Guilherme Gomes Fernandes 59; s/d/tr from €14/23/36;) A backpacker favourite with walls washed in bright primary colours and comfortable clean rooms.

Pensão Astória (☎ 222 008 175; Rua Arnaldo Gama 56; s/d from €20/30) In a town house above the Rio Douro, this spotless place has old-world charm; several rooms have superb views. Reservations recommended.

Pensão do Norte (☎ 222 003 503; Rua de Fernandes Tomás 579; s/d/tr from €30/40/55) Newly opened in 2008, the Pensão do Norte has simple but attractive rooms with wood floors and windows opening onto the brilliant azulejo-covered Capela das Almas.

Pensão Cristal (☎ 222 002 100; Rua Galeria de Paris 48; s/d/tw/tr €35/45/50/60;) The new budget favourite in town, Pensão Cristal lies on a quiet street near a few galleries and bars. Rooms are clean and cosy with tile floors and simple wood furnishings.

Eating

Casa Filha da Mãe Preta (☎ 222 055 515; Cais da Ribeira 40; mains €6-9; Mon-Sat) On Ribeira's riverfront, this is the most congenial of a long line of touristy restaurants. Go early to bag an upstairs front table for prime Douro views.

O Caçula (☎ 222 055 937; Travessa do Bonjardim 20; mains €7-9; Mon-Sat) Tucked down a narrow lane, O Caçula serves tasty vegetarian and grilled dishes in a trim, contemporary space.

Praia da Luz (Av Brasil; mains €7-14; 9am-2am) Beautifully set along the rocky beach in Foz do Douro, trendy Praia da Luz serves up delightful grilled seafood and bistro dishes and plenty of cocktails. Sit outside on a wooden deck facing crashing waves (but bring a sweater).

Simbiose (☎ 222 030 398; Rua Infante Dom Henrique 133; mains €9-13; Tue-Sun) On two floors in an airy, quayside town house, Simbiose cooks up decent traditional dishes and lovely river views.

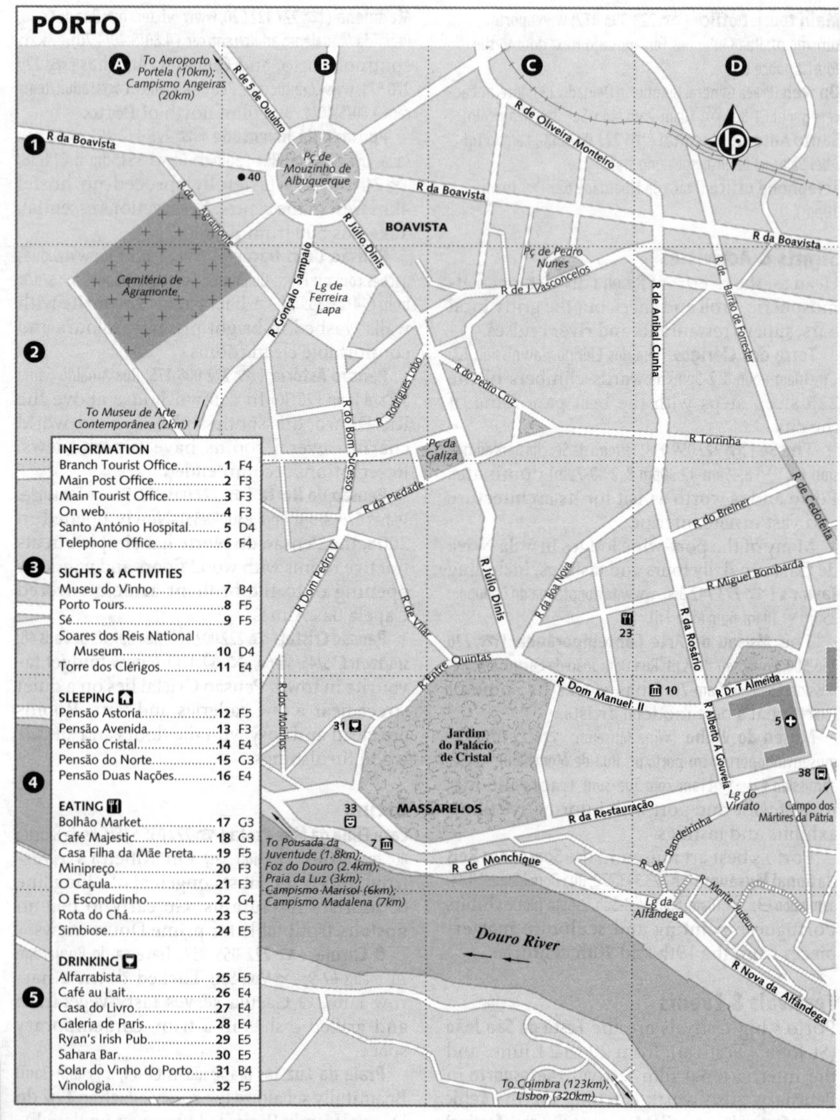

O Escondidinho (☎ 222 001 079; Rua Passos Manuel 144; mains €13-20) Amid *azulejos*, dark wood furnishings and starched white place settings, O Escondidinho serves nicely flavoured traditional fare.

Some cafes and self-catering options:

Bolhão market (Rua Formosa; 8am-5pm Mon-Fri, 8am-1pm Sat) Fruit, veggies, cheese and deli goodies in a 19th-century wrought-iron building. Further east along Rua Formosa are equally enticing old-fashioned food shops.

Café Majestic (☎ 222 003 887; Rua Santa Catarina 112; 9.30am-midnight Mon-Sat) An art-nouveau extravagance where old souls linger over afternoon tea.

Minipreço (Rua Sá da Bandeira 355; 9am-8pm Mon-Sat) A well-stocked central supermarket.

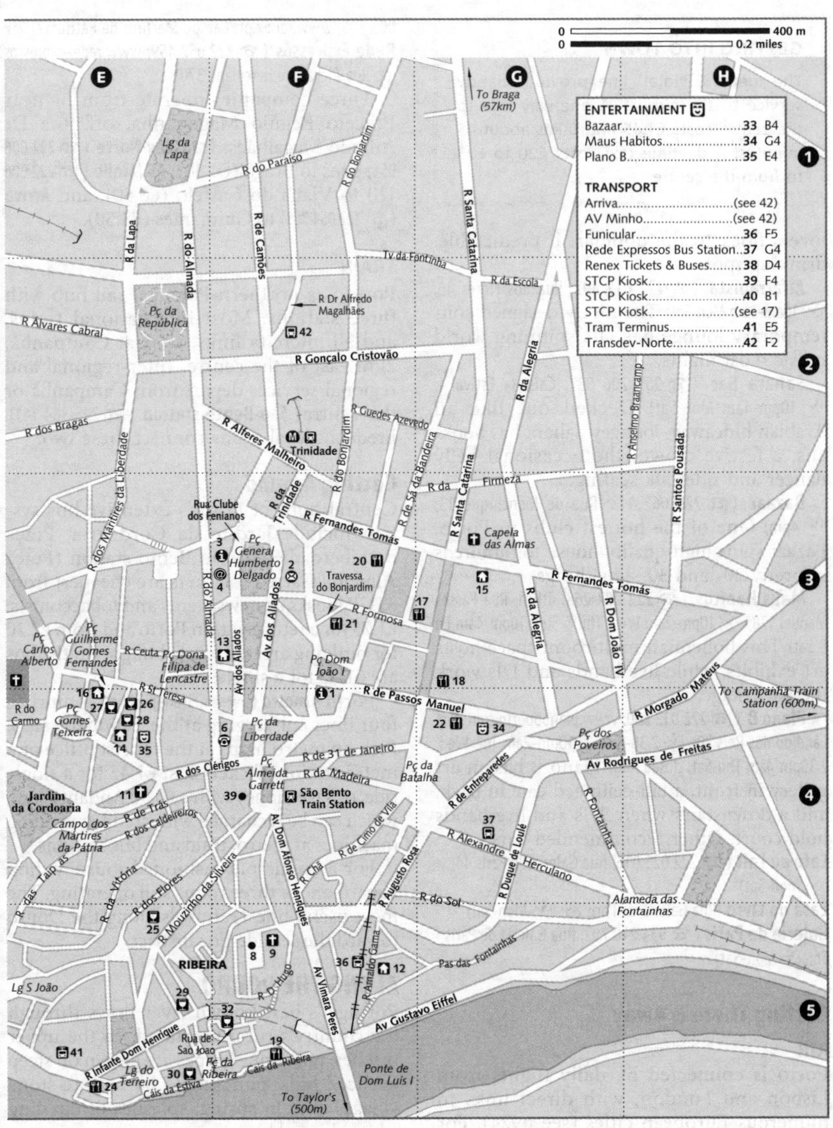

Rota do Chá (Rua Miguel Bombarda 457; tea €2) This proudly bohemian cafe has a verdant, rustic back garden and a magnificent tea selection.

Drinking & Clubbing

Solar do Vinho do Porto (☎ 226 097 749; Rua Entre Quintas 220; 🕑 4pm-midnight Mon-Sat) A converted 19th-century manor with hundreds of ports available – best enjoyed in the picturesque garden overlooking the Douro.

Vinologia (☎ 936 057 340; www.lamaisondesporto.com; Rua de São João 46; 🕑 4-9pm Mon-Wed, 4pm-midnight Thu-Sat, 6-9pm Sun) In the Ribeira, this wine bar stocks over 200 different ports.

Ryan's Irish Pub (☎ 222 005 366; Rua Infante Dom Henrique 18; 🕑 6pm-2am) Expats and whisky

GETTING INTO TOWN

The metro's 'violet' line provides handy service to the airport. A one-way ride to the centre costs €1.45 and takes about 45 minutes. A daytime taxi costs €20 to €25 to/from the centre.

lovers flock to the popular, if predictable, drinking spot.

Alfarrabista (☎ 222 012 892; Rua dos Flores 46; 🕑 10am-2am Mon-Sat) The nicely designed contemporary lounge has DJs spinning world music most nights.

Sahara Bar (☎ 969 206 037; Caís da Estiva 4; 🕑 10pm-4am Mon-Sat) Decked out like an Arabian hideaway, loungey Sahara has hookahs, a festive crowd, the occasional belly dancer and sidewalk seating.

Bazaar (☎ 226 062 113; Rua de Monchique 13; 🕑 4pm) One of the hottest clubs in Porto, Bazaar spins high-quality house to hundreds of pretty 20- and 30-somethings.

Maus Habitos (☎ 222 087 268; 4th fl, Rua Passos Manuel 178; 🕑 10pm-2am Wed, Thu & Sun, 10pm-4am Fri & Sat) This bohemian multiroom space hosts art exhibits, while live bands and DJs work the back stage.

Plano B (☎ 222 012 500; www.planobporto.com; Rua Cândido dos Reis 30; 🕑 2.30-8pm & 10pm-2am Tue-Wed, 2.30pm-4am Thu-Sat, closed Aug) Plano B has an art gallery in front, a tall-ceilinged cafe in back, and a downstairs where DJs and live bands hold court. Other recommended bars:

Café au Lait (☎ 222 025 016; Rua Galeria de Paris 44; 🕑 Mon-Sat)

Casa do Livro (Rua Galeria de Paris 85; 🕑 Mon-Sat)

Galeria de Paris (☎ 934 210 792; Rua Galeria de Paris 56; 🕑 Mon-Sat)

Getting There & Away

AIR

Porto is connected by daily flights from Lisbon and London, with direct links to numerous European cities (see p924). For flight information, call ☎ 229 432 400.

BUS

Porto has a baffling number of private bus companies leaving from different terminals; the main tourist office can help with transport queries. In general, for Lisbon (€16.50) and the Algarve, the choice is **Renex** (☎ 222 003 395; www.renex.pt; Campo Mártires de Pátria 37) or **Rede Expressos** (☎ 222 052 459; www.rede-expressos.pt; Rua Alexandre Herculano 370).

Three companies operate from or near Praceto Régulo Magauanha, off Rua Dr Alfredo Magalhães: **Transdev-Norte** (☎ 222 006 954) goes to Braga (€4.30); **AV Minho** (☎ 222 006 121) to Viana do Castelo (€6.50); and **Arriva** (☎ 222 051 383) to Guimarães (€4.50).

TRAIN

Porto is a northern Portugal rail hub with three stations. Most international trains, and all intercity links, start at Campanhã, 2km east of the centre. Inter-regional and regional services depart from Campanhã or the central **São Bento station** (☎ 225 364 141). Frequent local trains connect these two.

Getting Around

Central hubs of Porto's extensive bus system include Jardim da Cordoaria, Praça da Liberdade and São Bento station (Praça Almeida Garrett). Tickets are cheapest from STCP kiosks or newsagents and tobacconists: €1.75 for a return within Porto and from €2.20 for outlying areas. Tickets bought on the bus are €1.45 for a single.

Porto's **metro** (www.metrodoporto.pt) comprises four lines converging at the Trinidade stop. Pick up metro maps at the tourist office or a metro station. Tickets cost €1.45 for a single ride, or save money with a €0.50 Andante card, which can be recharged with credit at vending machines at metro, train and bus stations.

For a scenic old-fashioned journey, hop aboard one of three trams still operating. The most useful line 1E travels along the Douro toward the seaside Foz district.

ALONG THE DOURO

Portugal's best-known river flows through the country's rural heartland. In the upper reaches, port-wine grapes are grown on steep terraced hills, punctuated by remote stone villages and, in spring, splashes of dazzling white almond blossom.

The Douro River is navigable right across Portugal. Highly recommended is the train journey from Porto to Pinhão (€9.05, 2½ hours, five trains daily), the last 70km clinging to the river's edge; trains continue to Pocinho (from Porto €10.75, 3½ hours). **Porto Tours** (☎ 222 000 073; www.portotours.com; Torre Medieval, Calçada Pedro Pitões 15), situated next to Porto's cathedral, can arrange tours, including idyllic Douro cruises. Cyclists and drivers can choose river-hugging roads along either bank, and visit wineries along the way (check out www.rvp.pt for an extensive list of wineries open to visitors). You can also stay overnight in scenic wine lodges among the vineyards.

VIANA DO CASTELO

pop 37,500

The jewel of the Costa Verde (Green Coast), Viana do Castelo has both an appealing medieval centre and lovely beaches just outside the city. In addition to its natural beauty, Viana do Castelo whips up some excellent seafood and hosts some magnificent traditional festivals, including the spectacular **Festas da Nossa Senhora da Agonia** (see p952) in August. The **tourist office** (☎ 258 822 620; www.rtam.pt; Rua Hospital Velho) is handily located in the old centre.

Sights & Activities

The stately heart of town is Praça da República, with its delicate fountain and grandiose buildings, including the 16th-century **Misericórdia**, a striking Renaissance building, its upper storeys supported by ornate caryatids.

Atop Santa Luzia Hill, the **Templo do Sagrado Coração de Jesus** (Temple of the Sacred Heart of Jesus; ☎ 258 823 173; admission free; 8am-7pm Apr-Sep, 8am-5pm Oct-Mar) offers a grand panorama across the river. It's a steep 2km climb; you can also catch a ride on the newly restored funicular railway (one-way/return €2/3).

Viana's enormous arcing beach, **Praia do Cabedelo**, is one of the Minho's best, with little development to spoil its charm. It's across the river from town, best reached by ferry (adult €1.10; hourly 8.15am to 7pm) from the pier south of Largo 5 de Outubro.

Sleeping

Pousada da Juventude Gil Eannes (☎ 258 821 582; www.pousadasjuventude.pt; Gil Eannes; dm €8) This hostel is located in the bowels of a former naval hospital ship. Plush? Not exactly, but the novelty factor is high.

Residencial Viana Mar (☎/fax 258 828 962; Av dos Combatentes da Grande Guerra 215; s/d from €30/40) This well-worn place has thin carpeting, tall ceilings and simple furnishings. Rooms in the back are gloomy; front rooms are brighter with balconies.

Dolce Vianna (☎ 258 824 860; pizzariadolcevianna@gmail.com; Rua do Poço 44; d €40;) Above a popular pizzeria in the town centre, these quiet rooms are spick-and-span, with tile floors and sturdy furnishings.

Eating & Drinking

The newest destination for dining or drinking is the waterfront Praça da Liberdade, with its open-air cafes and restaurants.

Restaurant O Pescador (☎ 258 826 039; Largo de São Domingos 35; mains €9-13) A friendly, family-run restaurant admired by locals for its good seafood.

our pick **Taberna do Valentim** (☎ 258 827 505; Rua Monsignor Daniel Machado 180; mains €12-14; Mon-Sat) In the old fishermen's neighbourhood, this fantastic seafood restaurant serves grilled fish by the kilo and rich seafood stews – *arroz de tamboril* (monkfish rice) and *caldeirada* (fish stew).

Caffe del Rio (☎ 258 822 963; Rua da Bandeira 179-185; 1pm-2am Sun-Thu, 1pm-4am Fri & Sat) The sleek glass-and-chrome, '60s-style bar upstairs has great river views. On weekends, DJs spin house and hip hop here. It's located on the river, a short stroll east along the promenade.

Getting There & Away

Five to 10 trains go daily to Porto (€8, two hours). There are also express buses to Porto (€6.50, 2¼ hours) and Lisbon (€17, 5½ hours).

BRAGA

pop 120,000

Braga boasts an astounding array of churches, their splendid baroque facades looming above the old plazas and narrow lanes of the historic centre. Lively cafes, trim little boutiques and some excellent restaurants add to the appeal.

Orientation & Information

Arriving at the train station, it's a 15-minute walk to the old town via Rua Andrado Corvo. The main bus station is a 10-minute walk north of town. The **tourist office** (☎ 253 262 550; www.cm-braga.pt; Praça da República 1) can help with accommodation and maps.

Sights & Activities

In the centre of Braga is the **Sé** (Rua Dom Paio Mendes; admission free; 8.30am-6.30pm), one of Portugal's most extraordinary cathedrals, with roots dating back a thousand years. Within the cathedral you can also visit the **treasury** (admission €2) and **choir** (admission €2).

At Bom Jesus do Monte, a hilltop pilgrimage site 5km from Braga, is an extraordinary stairway, the **Escadaria do Bom Jesus**, with allegorical fountains, chapels and a superb view. City bus 2 (€1.30) runs frequently from Braga to the site, where you can climb the steps (pilgrims sometimes do this on their knees) or ascend by funicular railway (€1.20).

It's an easy day trip to **Guimarães** with its medieval town centre and a palace of the dukes of Bragança. It's also a short jaunt to **Barcelos**, a town famed for its enormous Thursday market.

Sleeping

Pousada da Juventude (☎ 253 616 163; www.pousadasjuventude.pt; Rua de Santa Margarida 6; dm/d €7/22) This bland but lively hostel is a 10-minute walk from the centre.

Grande Residência Avenida (☎ 253 609 020; www.residencialavenida.net; 2nd fl, Av da Liberdade 738; s/d from €26/33; ❄) Rooms at this friendly, family-run place have frilly decor and vary widely in size and light; some have verandas.

Residencial São Marcos (☎/fax 253 277 177; Rua de São Marcos 80; s/d from €30/35; ❄) In a fine old town house, São Marcos offers large, comfortable, recently refurbished rooms with high ceilings and parquet floors.

Eating & Drinking

Livraria Café (☎ 253 267 647; Av Central 118; mains €4; 🕑 9am-7.30pm Mon-Sat) Tucked inside the bookshop Centésima Página, this charming cafe serves tasty quiches, salads and desserts. There are outdoor tables in the pleasantly rustic garden.

Cozinha da Sé (☎ 253 277 343; Rua Dom Frei Caetano Brandão 95; mains €7-10; 🕑 Tue-Sun) A handsome Braga newcomer, Sé serves traditional, high-quality dishes.

Taberna do Felix (☎ 253 617 701; Praça Velha 17; mains €7-10; 🕑 dinner Mon-Sat) Near the Arco da Porta Nova, this country-style tavern prepares delightful Franco-Portuguese dishes. Next door are several other excellent restaurants, including a vegetarian one.

Taperia Palatu (☎ 253 279 772; Rua Dom Afonso Henrique 35; mains €8-12; 🕑 Mon-Sat) A Spanish/Portuguese couple serves up delectable Spanish tapas and classic Portuguese dishes on an airy courtyard.

Getting There & Away

Trains arrive twice daily from Lisbon (€22 to €30, four hours), Coimbra (€12 to €22, 2¼ hours) and Porto (€2.15, 1¼ hours), and there are daily connections north to Viana do Castelo. Daily bus services link Braga to Porto (€4.50, 1¼ hours) and Lisbon (€18, five hours). Car hire is available at **AVIC** (☎ 253 203 912; Rua Gabriel Pereira de Castro 28; 🕑 Mon-Fri), with prices starting at €30 per day.

PARQUE NACIONAL DA PENEDA-GERÊS

Spread across four impressive granite massifs, this vast park encompasses boulder-strewn peaks, precipitous valleys, gorse-clad moorlands and forests of oak and pine. It also shelters more than 100 granite villages that, in many ways, have changed little since Portugal's founding in the 12th century. For nature lovers the stunning scenery is unmatched in Portugal for camping, hiking and other outdoor adventures. The park's main centre is at at the sleepy, hot-spring village of Vila do Gerês (also called Caldas do Gerês and simply Gerês – though Campo do Gerês is another town altogether).

Information

The head park office is **Adere-PG** (☎ 258 452 250; www.adere-pg.pt; 🕑 Mon-Fri) in Ponte de Barca. Obtain park information and reserve cottages and other park accommodation through them. Gerês' **tourist office** (☎ 253 391 133; fax 253 391 282; 🕑 closed Thu) can provide information on activities and accommodation.

Activities

HIKING

There are trails and footpaths through the park, some between villages with accommodation. Leaflets detailing these are available from the park offices.

Day hikes around the region are popular. An adventurous option is the old Roman road from Mata do Albergaria (10km up-valley from Gerês by taxi or hitching), past the **Vilarinho das Furnas** reservoir to Campo do Gerês. More distant destinations include **Ermida** and **Cabril**, both with simple accommodation.

CYCLING & HORSE RIDING

Mountain bikes can be hired in Campo do Gerês (15km northeast of Vila do Gerês) from **Equi Campo** (☎ 253 357 022, www.equicampo.com; per hr/day €5/17; 🕑 10am-7pm). Guides here also lead horse-riding trips, hikes and combination hiking/climbing/rappelling excursions.

WATER SPORTS

Rio Caldo, 8km south of Gerês, is the base for water sports on the Caniçada reservoir. English-run **AML** (Água Montanha e Lazer; ☎ 253 391 779, 968 021 142; www.aguamontanha.com; Lugar de Paredes, Rio Caldo) rents out kayaks, plus pedal boats, rowing boats and small motorboats. It also organises kayaking trips along the Albufeira de Salamonde.

Sleeping & Eating

Vila do Gerês has plenty of *pensões,* though many are block-booked by spa patients in summer.

Parque Campismo de Cerdeira (☎ 253 351 005; www.parquecerdeira.com; camp sites per adult/tent/car €4.60/3.90/4.30, 2-/4-person bungalows €63/85;) In Campo de Gerês, this place has oak-shaded sites, eco-friendly bungalows, a pool, mini-market and a particularly good restaurant.

Pousada da Juventude de Vilarinho das Furnas (☎ 253 351 339; www.pousadasjuventude.pt; dm/d €13/38, bungalows €80;) This former dam workers' camp has bungalows, dorms and a cafeteria, all amid woodlands.

Pensão Flôr de Moçambique (☎ /fax 253 391 119; d from €30) The best budget option in Vila do Gerês, this guest house offers modern rooms, most with verandas and nice views.

Getting There & Away

From Braga, at least five coaches run daily to Rio Caldo and Vila do Gerês, and three to Campo do Gerês (fewer at weekends). Because of the lack of transport within the park, it's a good place to have your own wheels. You can rent in Braga (opposite).

PORTUGAL DIRECTORY

ACCOMMODATION

Most tourist offices have lists of accommodation to suit all budgets, and can help with reservations.

Camping is always the cheapest option, although some camping grounds close out of season. The multilingual, annually updated *Roteiro Campista* (www.roteiro-campista.pt; €6), sold in larger bookshops, lists Portugal's camping grounds.

The most common types of guest house are the *residencial* and the *pensão*, which are usually family owned and comfortable; many have cheaper rooms with shared bathroom.

Portugal has 36 *pousadas da juventude* (youth hostels; www.pousadasjuventude.pt) within the Hostelling International (HI) system.

Another cheaper option is a *quarto particular* (private room); ask at tourist offices.

Pousadas are government-run former castles, monasteries or palaces, often in spectacular locations. Contact tourist offices or **Pousadas de Portugal** (www.pousadas.pt).

ACTIVITIES

Off-road cycling and bike trips are growing in popularity in Portugal; good starting points are Tavira (p938) in the Algarve, Sintra (p935) and Setúbal (p936) in central Portugal and Parque Nacional da Peneda-Gerês (opposite) in the north.

Popular water sports include surfing, windsurfing, canoeing, white-water rafting and water skiing. For local specialists, see Lagos (p938), Sagres (p939), Évora (p940), Tavira (p938), Coimbra (p942) and Parque Nacional da Peneda-Gerês (opposite).

BUSINESS HOURS

Banks 8.30am to 3pm Monday to Friday.
Bars & Clubs 8pm to midnight Monday to Thursday, to 3am or 4am on Friday and Saturday; hours vary and they're generally closed on Sunday or Monday.
Internet cafes 10am to 10pm; hours vary.
Post offices 8.30am to 6.30pm Monday to Friday, 8.30am to 1pm Saturday.
Restaurants lunch noon to 2.30pm, dinner 7pm to 10pm.
Shops 9am to 7pm Monday to Friday, 9am to 1pm Saturday.
Tourist offices 9am to 7pm Monday to Saturday; in smaller towns they close for lunch between noon and 2.30pm.

EMBASSIES & CONSULATES

Australia (Map pp926-7; ☎ 213 101 500; www.portugal.embassy.gov.au; 2nd fl, Av da Liberdade 200)
Canada (Map pp926-7; ☎ 213 164 600; http://geo.international.gc.ca/canada-europa/portugal; 3rd fl, Av da Liberdade 196)
France (Map pp926-7; ☎ 213 939 100; www.ambafrance-pt.org; Rua de Santos-o-Velho 5)
Germany (Map pp930-1; ☎ 218 810 210; www.lissabon.diplo.de; Campo dos Mártires da Pátria 38)
Ireland (Map pp926-7; ☎ 213 929 440; www.embassyofireland.pt; Rua da Imprensa, Estrela)
Netherlands (Map pp926-7; ☎ 213 914 900; www.emb-paisesbaixos.pt; Av Infante Santo 43)

Spain (Map pp926-7; ☎ 213 472 381; embesppt@correo.mae.es; Rua do Salitre 1, 1269-052 Lisbon)
UK (Map pp926-7; ☎ 213 924 000; www.britishembassy.gov.uk/portugal; Rua de São Bernardo 33)
USA (Map pp926-7; ☎ 217 273 300; http://portugal.usembassy.gov; Av das Forças Armadas)

FESTIVALS & EVENTS

Holy Week Festival Easter week in Braga features colourful processions, including Ecce Homo, with barefoot penitents carrying torches.
Festas das Cruzes Held in Barcelos in May, the Festival of the Crosses is known for processions, folk music and dance, and regional handicrafts.
Feira Nacional da Agricultura In June Santarém hosts the National Agricultural Fair, with bullfighting, folk singing and dancing.
Festa do Santo António The Festival of St Anthony fills the streets of Lisbon on 13 June.
Festas de São João Porto and Braga's big street bash is the St John's Festival, building up to 23 and 24 June.
Festas da Nossa Senhora da Agonia Viana do Castelo's Our Lady of Suffering Festival runs for three days, including the weekend nearest to 20 August, and is famed for folk arts, parades and fireworks.

HOLIDAYS

New Year's Day 1 January
Carnival Shrove Tuesday February/March
Good Friday and the following Saturday March/April
Liberty Day 25 April (commemorating the 1975 revolution)
Labour Day 1 May
Corpus Christi May/June (the ninth Thursday after Easter)
Portugal Day 10 June
Feast of the Assumption 15 August
Republic Day 5 October
All Saints' Day 1 November
Independence Day 1 December (celebrating independence from Spain in 1640)
Immaculate Conception 8 December
Christmas Day 25 December

MONEY

There are numerous banks with ATMs located throughout Portugal. Credit cards are accepted in many hotels, restaurants and shops.

If you are satisfied with the service, tip 5% to 10%. Taxi drivers are generally not tipped.

POST

Stamps can be bought over the counter from post office or alternatively from any automatic dispensing machine *(Correio de Portugal – Selos)*. Postcards and letters up to 20g cost €0.54/0.67/0.77 within Portugal/within Europe/outside Europe.

TELEPHONE

To call Portugal from abroad, call the international access code (☎ 00), then Portugal's country code (☎ 35 1), then the number. All Portuguese phone numbers have nine digits. These include area codes, which always need to be dialled. For general information dial ☎ 118, for international inquiries dial ☎ 179, and for reverse-charge (collect) calls dial ☎ 120.

Phonecards are the most reliable and the cheapest way of calling from a telephone booth. They can be purchased at post offices, newsagents and tobacconists in denominations of €5 and €10.

VISAS

EU nationals need only a valid passport or identity card for entry to Portugal, and may stay indefinitely. Citizens of Australia, Canada, New Zealand and the USA can stay for up to 90 days in any half-year without a visa. Citizens of other countries should check out the www.travisa.com website for more information.

Romania

HIGHLIGHTS

- **Braşov** Scale castles and mountains using this Gothic, medieval centrefold as a base (p964)
- **Cluj-Napoca** A lively student town with Romania's most laid-back clubs and bars (p969)
- **Sighişoara** Dracula's birthplace has a lovely medieval citadel, hostels and torture museums (p967)
- **Off-the-beaten track** Southern Bucovina's painted monasteries live on in this bucolic paradise (p972)

FAST FACTS

- **Area** 237,500 sq km (about the size of Britain)
- **Budget** €25 to €35 (92 lei to 128 lei) per day
- **Capital** Bucharest
- **Country code** ☎ 40
- **Famous for** Transylvania, Dracula, beautiful scenery
- **Language** Romanian
- **Money** nou leu (lei); A$1 = 2.33 lei; C$1 = 2.64 lei; €1 = 4.18 lei; ¥100 = 3.28 lei; NZ$1 = 1.82 lei; UK£1 = 4.71 lei; US$1 = 3.11 lei; see p973 for details on the changed currency
- **Phrases** *bună* (hello); *da* (yes); *nu* (no); *mulţumesc* (thank you)

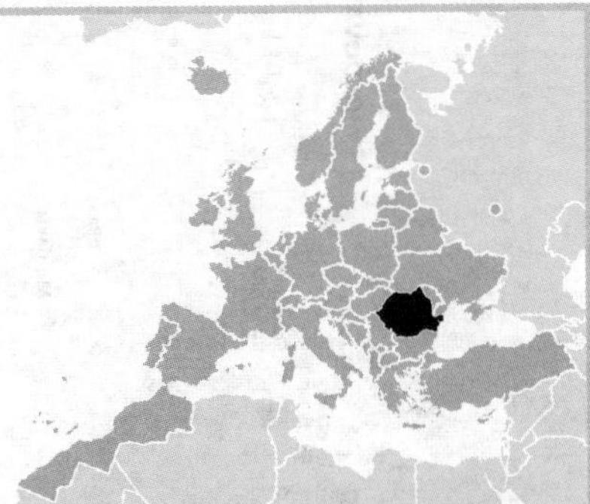

- **Population** 22.3 million
- **Visa** none required for citizens of the EU, US, Canada, UK, Australia or New Zealand; see p974

TRAVEL HINTS

Hire a car and stay in family *pensiune* (pensions) in small villages. Getting on the backroads, even just 2km off the highways, unveils a deeper, more traditional world. Cars are cheaper from Cluj-Napoca or Bucharest.

ROAMING ROMANIA

If you're coming from Budapest, stop in Cluj-Napoca, before touring Transylvania (Sighişoara, Braşov, Sinaia) and fly out of Bucharest.

After decades, centuries in some cases, of an unseen hand leaning on Romania's 'pause' button, breathtaking change and development are underway. Formerly the 'wild west of Eastern Europe', EU membership has ushered in repaired roads, reliable utilities and economic reform. Unfortunately, it's also brought stupefying inflation and troubling horse-cart rules. Outside the big cities, however, it's business as usual. Romania's singular beauty, beguiling simplicity and fascinating history remain untouched. Hand-ploughed fields, sheep stampedes and homemade plum brandy endure. The Carpathian mountains offer exceptional hiking, cycling and skiing options. Towns like Braşov, Sibiu and Sighişoara are time-warp strolling grounds for fans of Gothic architecture, Austro-Hungarian legacy and Dracula shtick. Unesco World Heritage–listed painted monasteries dot Southern Bucovina and big cities like Cluj and Timişoara are a blast too.

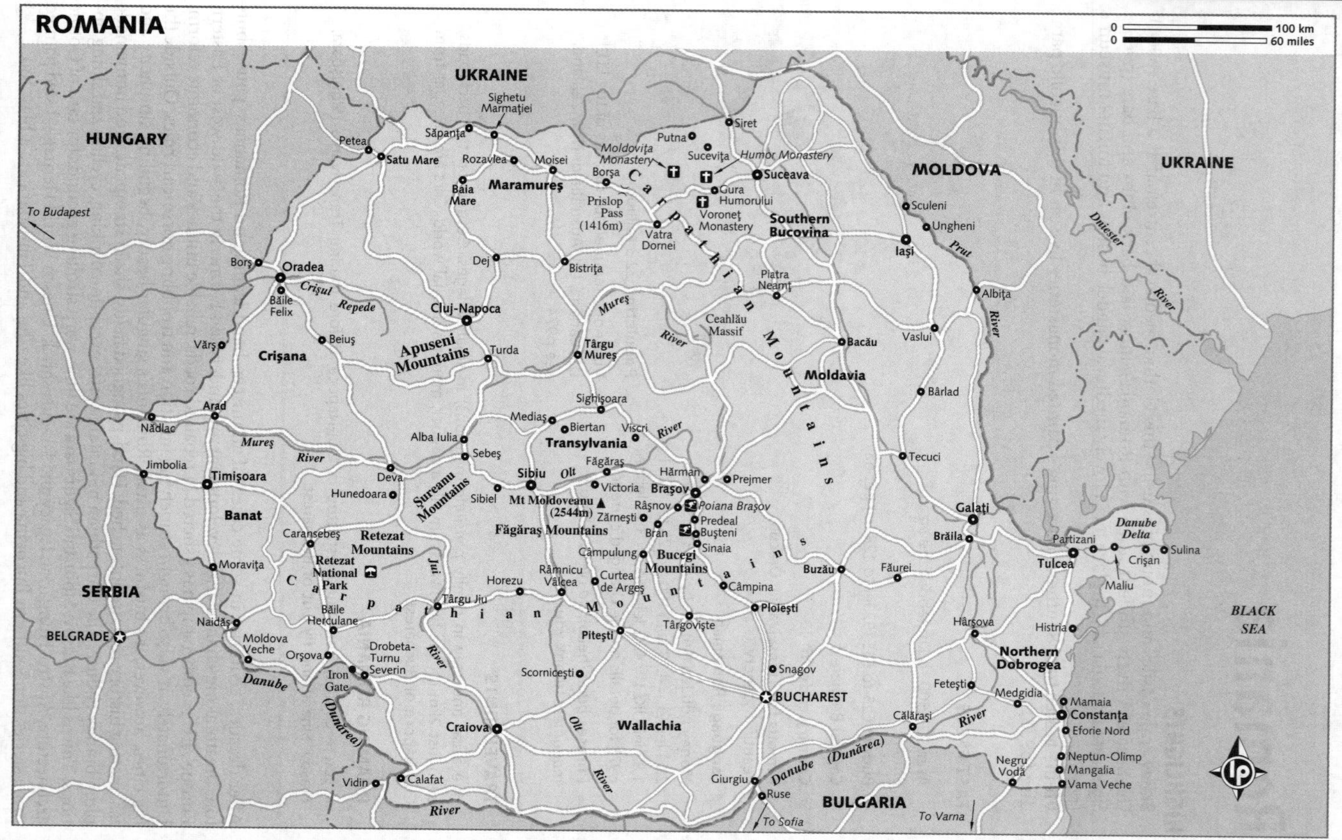
ROMANIA
0 100 km
0 60 miles
UKRAINE
HUNGARY
MOLDOVA
UKRAINE
SERBIA
BULGARIA
BLACK SEA
To Budapest
Sighetu Marmaţiei
Săpânţa
Petea
Satu Mare
Rozavlea
Moisei
Baia Mare
Maramureş
Borşa
Moldoviţa Monastery
Putna
Suceviţa
Siret
Humor Monastery
Suceava
Gura Humorului
Voroneţ Monastery
Southern Bucovina
Prislop Pass (1416m)
Vatra Dornei
Carpathian Mountains
Sculeni
Ungheni
Iaşi
Prut
Dniester
River
Albiţa
River
Borş
Oradea
Băile Felix
Crişul Repede
Cluj-Napoca
Dej
Bistriţa
Mureş
River
Piatra Neamţ
Ceahlău Massif
Bacău
Vaslui
Vârş
Beiuş
Crişana
Apuseni Mountains
Turda
Târgu Mureş
Moldavia
Bârlad
Sighişoara
Arad
Nădlac
Mediaş
Biertan
Viscri
River
Alba Iulia
Transylvania
Mureş
River
Sebeş
Tecuci
Jimbolia
Timişoara
Deva
Făgăraş
Hărman
Prejmer
Sibiu
Olt
Hunedoara
Şureanu Mountains
Sibiel
Victoria
Braşov
Mt Moldoveanu (2544m)
Râşnov
Poiana Braşov
Banat
Zărneşti
Predeal
Făgăraş Mountains
Bran
Buşteni
Galaţi
Brăila
Caransebeş
Retezat Mountains
Sinaia
Câmpulung
Bucegi Mountains
Partizani
Danube Delta
Sulina
Crişan
Tulcea
Maliu
Moraviţa
Retezat National Park
Jui
Buzău
Făurei
Râmnicu Vâlcea
Curtea de Argeş
Horezu
Câmpina
Târgu Jiu
Ploieşti
Băile Herculane
Târgovişte
Hârşova
Histria
Naidăş
Piteşti
BELGRADE
Moldova Veche
Orşova
Drobeta-Turnu Severin
Northern Dobrogea
River
Snagov
Iron Gate
Danube
Scorniceşti
Feteşti
(Dunărea)
BUCHAREST
Medgidia
Mamaia
Constanţa
Eforie Nord
Wallachia
Craiova
Olt
Călăraşi
River
Negru Vodă
Neptun-Olimp
Mangalia
Vama Veche
Vidin
Calafat
Giurgiu
Danube (Dunărea)
Ruse
River
To Sofia
To Varna

HISTORY

Ancient Romania was inhabited by Thracian tribes, also known as Dacians. From the 7th century BC the Greeks established trading colonies along the Black Sea, and the Romans conquered the area in AD 105–06.

From the 10th century the Magyars expanded into Transylvania, and by the 13th century all of Transylvania was under the Hungarian crown.

Prince Vlad, ruler of Wallachia in 1448, 1456–62 and 1476–77, gained the name Ţepeş (Impaler) after the punishment he used against enemies – driving a wooden stake through the victim's backbone without touching any vital nerve, ensuring at least 48 hours of suffering before death. He was called 'Dracula', meaning 'son of the dragon', after his father, Vlad Dracul.

After the Russian defeat in the Crimean War (1853–56) Romanian nationalism grew, and in 1859 Alexandru Ioan Cuza was elected to the thrones of Moldavia and Wallachia, creating a national state, which took the name Romania in 1862.

In 1916 Romania entered WWI on the Allied side. As Romania began losing land in WWII, General Ion Antonescu imposed a fascist dictatorship and joined Hitler, sending 400,000 Romanian Jews and 36,000 Roma to grisly deaths at Auschwitz and other camps. But in 1944 Romania changed sides, declaring war on Nazi Germany. In 1947 the monarchy was abolished and the Romanian People's Republic proclaimed.

In 1960 Romania adopted an independent foreign policy under two leaders, Gheorghe Gheorghiu-Dej (leader from 1952–65) and his protégé Nicolae Ceauşescu (1965–89). Ceauşescu's domestic policy was chaotic and megalomaniacal, famously exporting food to finance his schemes while citizens starved.

On 15 December 1989 ethnic-Hungarian Father Lászlo Tökés publicly condemned the dictator, prompting the Reformed Church of Romania to remove him from his post. Police attempts to arrest demonstrators failed and civil unrest quickly spread. Ceauşescu dispatched troops to crush the rebellion. On 21 December in Bucharest, an address by Ceauşescu was cut short by booing demonstrators, who were crushed by police gunfire and armoured cars. The following morning thousands more took to the streets. By the next day Ceauşescu and his wife were arrested. On 25 December they were executed by firing squad.

In 1990 Romania held its first democratic elections, but internal disagreements hampered economic reform.

Romania joined the Council of Europe in 1993 and NATO in 2002. Chumming up with the USA, Romania allowed Iraq-bound military to set up bases and granted lucrative construction projects to American companies – something some EU members weren't happy with. At the last minute in 2006, the EU granted Romania membership in 2007 – though Brussels warned it will continue to monitor progress in fighting corruption and organised crime. Romania has since been threatened with EU sanctions after reviews in both 2007 and 2008 for lack of progress, though at the time of writing none had been handed down.

THE CULTURE

Romanians make up 89% of the population; Hungarians are the next largest ethnic group (7%), followed by Roma (2%), and smaller populations of Ukrainians, Germans, Russians and Turks. Germans and Hungarians live almost exclusively in Transylvania, while Ukrainians and Russians live mainly near the Danube Delta, and Turks along the Black Sea Coast.

The government estimates that only 400,000 Roma live in Romania, although other sources estimate between 1.5 and 2.5 million.

ARTS

Romania has a strong tradition of rural crafts, music and dance. Religious icon painting was widely practised, particularly between the 17th and 19th centuries.

Artist Nicolae Grigorescu (1838–1907) is known for adapting impressionism to Romanian peasant themes. Sculptor Constantin Brancusi (1876–1957) was a central figure of the modernist movement and one of the early pioneers of abstractionism.

New regard for Romanian cinema has emerged, starting with hits like Nae Caranfil's comedy *Filantropica* (2002) and Cristi Puiu's *The Death of Mr Lăzărescu* (2005). In 2007, director Cristian Mungiu won the Cannes Film Festival's top prize with *4 Months, 3 Weeks and 2 Days*, while Cristian Nemescu's film *Un Certain Regard* also took honours.

READING UP

One of the best history books on Romania, Lucian Boia's excellent *Romania* surveys Romania's past and present in a colourful, if philosophical, way. Robert Kaplan's *Balkan Ghosts* devotes a couple of key chapters to postrevolutionary Romania. Some of Isabel Fonseca's fascinating *Bury Me Standing* follows the Roma population in Romania. Of course, the most famous 'Romanian' book is Bram Stoker's *Dracula*.

ENVIRONMENT

Oval-shaped Romania is made up of three main geographical regions. The mighty Carpathian Mountains form the shape of a scythe sweeping down through the country's centre from Ukraine and then curling northwards.

East of the mountains are low-lying plains that end at the Black Sea and Europe's second-largest delta region, where the Danube spills into the Black Sea.

Rural Romania has thriving animal populations in its parks and mountains, including lynxes, foxes, wolves, bears and badgers.

Romania has nearly 600 protected areas, including 13 national parks, three biosphere reserves and one World Natural Heritage site (the Danube Delta), totalling over 1.2 million hectares.

TRANSPORT

GETTING THERE & AWAY

Air

Romania's national airline is **Tarom** (Transporturile Aeriene Române; RO; www.tarom.ro). Bucharest's **Henri Coanda International Airport** (formerly Otopeni; OTP; ☎ 021-201 4050; www.otp-airport.ro) is the country's largest.

Some international flights – with direct services to Paris, London, Amsterdam, Germany, Italy, Greece, Budapest and other destinations in Eastern Europe – originate from Timişoara, Cluj-Napoca, Sibiu and Târgu Mureş.

Carpatair (V3; ☎ 256 300 900; www.carpatair.com) connects Timişoara with Italy, France and Germany; it also flies from Budapest to Cluj-Napoca. **Air Moldova** (9U; ☎ 021-312 1258; www.airmoldova.md) and Tarom together operate daily flights between Chişinău and Bucharest.

The following budget carriers fly out of Bucharest, Cluj, Timişoara, Sibiu, Târgu Mureş and Constanţa to London, Italy, Germany, France, Spain, Belgium, Portugal, Austria, Poland, Hungary, Bulgaria, Sweden and Cyprus:

Blue Air (www.blueair-web.com)
easyJet (www.easyjet.com)
germanwings (www.germanwings.com)
Myair (www.myair.com)
Ryanair (www.ryanair.com)
Wizz Air (www.wizzair.com)

Bus

International **Eurolines** (www.eurolines.ro) has a flurry of buses linking numerous cities in Romania with Western Europe. Buses to Germany cost €125 one way, while buses to Paris and Rome cost about €90 to €110.

Most large cities have a weekly bus to İstanbul. Maxitaxis go from Bucharest and Constanţa to Sofia, some stopping in Ruse. Several daily buses connect Suceava in Moldavia with Chernivtsi, Ukraine.

Car & Motorcycle

The best advice here is to make sure all your documents (personal ID, insurance, registration and visas, if required) are in order before crossing into Romania. The Green Card (a routine extension of domestic motor insurance to cover most European countries) is valid in Romania. Extra insurance can be bought at the borders.

Expect long queues at Romanian checkpoints, particularly on weekends.

Train

International train tickets are sometimes sold at train stations, but mostly at Romanian State Railways (CFR) offices in town (look for the Agentia de Voiaj CFR signs) or Wasteels offices. Tickets must be bought at least two hours prior to departure.

Those travelling on an Inter-Rail or Eurail pass still need to make seat reservations (€4, €15 if using a couchette) on express trains within Romania, but cheap train prices hardly justify the cost of using a rail pass here.

There are four daily trains between Bucharest and Budapest's Keleti station (13 to 16 hours), three of which pick up passengers in Braşov. Two daily trains run between Sofia and Bucharest (11 hours); both stop in Ruse.

There's an overnight connection from Bucharest to İstanbul (20 hours) on the *Bosfor*. There's also an overnight service between Bucharest and Chişinău (12 hours); the daily train to Moscow (47 hours) stops in Kiev, Ukraine (31 hours).

GETTING AROUND

Air

State-owned airline **Tarom** (Transporturile Aeriene Române; RO; www.tarom.ro) is Romania's main carrier. **Carpatair** (V3; www.carpatair.com) runs domestic routes from its hub in Timişoara.

Bicycle

There are generally bike and bike-repair shops in most major towns, but bike hire is not that widespread. A good place to hire one is Sinaia (p963).

Bus

A mix of clunky buses, microbuses and maxitaxis combine to form the seriously disorganised Romanian bus system. Schedules, companies and even 'stations' (sometimes lots) change often. The most useful route to take a maxitaxi – essentially a van with minimal storage space – is between Bucharest and Sighişoara, stopping in Sinaia and Braşov.

Car & Motorcycle

Even if you're on a budget, it's well worth splitting the costs for a car – sometimes as low as €25 per day – and getting out into rural areas. **Autonom** (www.autonom.ro) often has the best rates. Car-hire rates are cheaper in Cluj-Napoca and Bucharest than Braşov. Daewoo Matiz is the cheapest model. Factor in a lot of extra time when driving (road construction is booming), and get a road map from city bookshops or petrol stations.

Your country's driving licence will be recognised here. There is a 0% blood-alcohol tolerance limit. Seat belts are compulsory in the front and back; children under 12 years are forbidden to sit in the front.

Speed limits are 90km/h on major roads and 70km/h inside highway villages and towns unless otherwise noted.

Local Transport

Buses, trams and trolleybuses provide transport within most towns and cities in Romania, although many are crowded. They usually run from about 5am to midnight, although services can get thin on the ground after 7pm in more remote areas. Purchase tickets at street kiosks marked *'bilete'* or *'casă de bilete'* before boarding, and validate them once onboard.

In many rural parts, the only vehicle that passes will be horse-powered. Bucharest is the only city in Romania to boast a metro system.

Train

The national train timetable *(mersul trenurilor)* is sold for €3 (10 lei) at **Căile Ferate Române** (CFR; Romanian State Railways; www.cfr.ro) offices, or check the website.

The cheapest trains are local *personal* trains. *Accelerat* trains are faster, and *rapid* faster still, hence a tad more expensive and less crowded. Seat reservations are obligatory and automatic when you buy your ticket; pricier intercity trains are the most comfortable.

Advance tickets are sold at stations or from an Agentia de Voiaj CFR in every city centre.

Note that *sosire* means 'arrivals' and *plecare* is 'departures'.

Sleepers *(vagon de dormit)* are available between Bucharest and Arad, Cluj-Napoca, Oradea, Suceava and Timişoara.

BUCHAREST

☎ 021/031 / pop 2.1 million

Many Romanians slam it, some travellers depart shell-shocked after a couple of days, but Bucharest is an intriguing and evolving mix of eras. Wide boulevards with century-old villas mingle with (deviously hidden) 18th-century monasteries, unsightly communist-built housing blocks and statement-making government headquarters. The country's top museums are here, and there's plenty of green parks providing escape from the repellent effects of newly available personal car loans. Ongoing development and gentrification of the crumbling historic centre is encouraging and hints at a modernised return to classiness.

ORIENTATION

The main boulevard of Bucharest runs between Piaţa Victoriei, Piaţa Romană, Piaţa Universităţii and Piaţa Unirii. The main

EMERGENCY NUMBERS

- Police, Fire and Ambulance ☎ 112

train station, Gara de Nord, is a few kilometres northwest of central Bucharest.

INFORMATION

Bookshops

Librărie Noi (Map p961; ☎ 311 0700; B-dul Nicolae Bălcescu 18; 9.30am-8.15pm Mon-Sat, 11am-6.45pm Sunday) Super bookshop with antiques, Lonely Planet guidebooks and maps.

Internet Access

Nearly all hotels and hostels have internet access. Cafes with wi-fi are common.

Access Internet (Map p959; ☎ 317 4153; B-dul Lascăr Catargiu 6; per hr 4 lei; 24hr) International calls start at 0.12 lei per minute.

Internet & Games (Map p961; ☎ 0721-877 886; B-dul Regina Elisabeta 25; per hr 4 lei; 24hr)

Left Luggage

Train Station (Map p959; Piaţa Gara de Nord 1; per day small/large bag 3/6 lei; 24hr) At the train station, to the right in the hallway leading to the front exit.

Medical Services

Emergency Clinic Hospital (Map p959; ☎ 230 0106; Calea Floreasca 8; 24hr)

Money

Currency exchanges and ATMs are everywhere. Changing money at banks is better. Avoid the currency-exchange counters at the airport; there are ATMs in the arrivals hall.

Banca Comercială Română (Map p961; B-dul Regina Elisabeta 5; 8.30am-5.30pm Mon-Fri, 8.30am-12.30pm Sat)

Telephone

RomTelecomm cards (from 10 lei) are available from newsstands. Most phone booths are neglected, but they're still working. You'll have no problem finding a shop selling Orange or Vodaphone SIM cards for your mobile phone – try a central street such as B-dul General Magheru.

Tourist Information

Bucharest continues to ignore its baffling absence of tourism resources. Travel agencies in the centre focus primarily on getting you *out* of the country. Hostels and hotels are your best bet for domestic information.

Wasteels (Map p959; ☎ 317 0370; www.wasteelstravel.ro; Gara de Nord; 8am-7pm Mon-Fri, to 2pm Sat) On the left side of the exit hallway of the train station, Wasteels can rent cars and help with train reservations.

DANGERS & ANNOYANCES

Bucharest's abundant stray dogs are largely docile, but occasionally bite. If bitten, go to a hospital for antirabies injections within 36 hours.

Taxi drivers sometimes charge extortionately high prices. Worst are those outside Gara de Nord. Legit taxis have prices written on the side, ranging from 1.7 to 3.3 lei per kilometre.

SIGHTS & ACTIVITIES

Piaţa Unirii

Strangely inspired by trips to Pyongyang and Beijing in the 1980s, Nicolae Ceauşescu had an entire suburb of historic buildings smashed to create **B-dul Unirii**, Romania's 'Champs Elysées', a chaotic, fountain-lined 3.2km boulevard – deliberately pipping Paris' by a resounding 6m (take that Frenchies!).

Anchoring B-dul Unirii is the mother of all white elephants, the **Palace of Parliament** (Palatul Parlamentului; Map p959; ☎ 311 3611; B-dul Naţiunile Unite; adult/student 22 lei/free with ID; 10am-4pm), the world's second-largest administrative building (after the Pentagon). Built in 1984 (and still 10% unfinished), the building's 12 storeys and 3100 rooms cost an estimated €3.3 billion. The hourly 45-minute tours are the only way to see a handful of the opulent marble rooms. Enter from the north side. Around the other side (access from the southwest) is the superb **National Museum of Contemporary Art** (Muzeul Naţionalde Arta Contemporana; Map p959; ☎ 318 9137; www.mnac.ro; Calea 13 Septembrie; adult/student 8 lei/free; 10am-6pm Wed-Sun), with temporary, edgy modern-art exhibits.

Historic Centre

Just northwest of Piaţa Unirii you can see what Ceauşescu ruined in Bucharest's humble historic heart. The busted-up **Curtea Veche** (Old Princely Court; Map p961; Str Franceza 21-23; admission 3 lei; 10am-5pm) dates from the 15th century. Nearby is **Hanul lui Manuc** (Map p961) – an active hotel and one-time shelter for merchants.

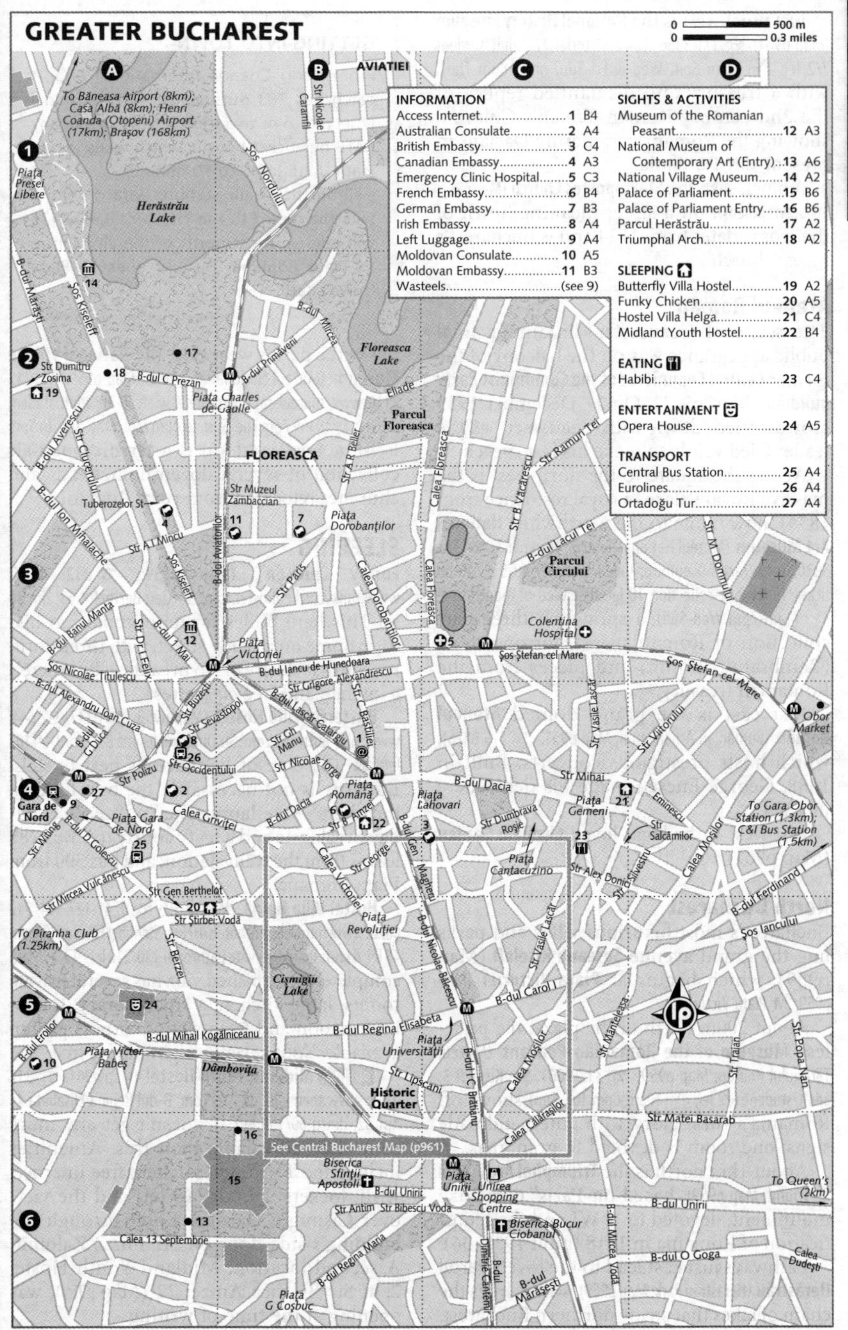
GREATER BUCHAREST
0 500 m
0 0.3 miles
INFORMATION
Access Internet 1 B4
Australian Consulate 2 A4
British Embassy 3 C4
Canadian Embassy 4 A3
Emergency Clinic Hospital 5 C3
French Embassy 6 B4
German Embassy 7 B3
Irish Embassy 8 A4
Left Luggage 9 A4
Moldovan Consulate 10 A5
Moldovan Embassy 11 B3
Wasteels (see 9)
SIGHTS & ACTIVITIES
Museum of the Romanian Peasant 12 A3
National Museum of Contemporary Art (Entry) 13 A6
National Village Museum 14 A2
Palace of Parliament 15 B6
Palace of Parliament Entry 16 B6
Parcul Herăstrău 17 A2
Triumphal Arch 18 A2
SLEEPING
Butterfly Villa Hostel 19 A2
Funky Chicken 20 A5
Hostel Villa Helga 21 C4
Midland Youth Hostel 22 B4
EATING
Habibi 23 C4
ENTERTAINMENT
Opera House 24 A5
TRANSPORT
Central Bus Station 25 A4
Eurolines 26 A4
Ortadoğu Tur 27 A4
AVIATIEI
To Băneasa Airport (8km); Casa Albă (8km); Henri Coanda (Otopeni) Airport (17km); Braşov (168km)
Piaţa Presei Libere
Herăstrău Lake
Floreasca Lake
Parcul Floreasca
FLOREASCA
Piaţa Charles de Gaulle
Piaţa Dorobanţilor
Parcul Circului
Colentina Hospital
Piaţa Victoriei
Obor Market
Gara de Nord
Piaţa Gara de Nord
Piaţa Română
Piaţa Lahovari
Piaţa Gemeni
Piaţa Cantacuzino
To Gara Obor Station (1.3km); C&I Bus Station (1.5km)
To Piranha Club (1.25km)
Piaţa Revoluţiei
Cişmigiu Lake
Piaţa Universităţii
Historic Quarter
Piaţa Victor Babeş
Dâmboviţa
See Central Bucharest Map (p961)
Biserica Sfinţii Apostoli
Piaţa Unirii
Unirea Shopping Centre
Biserica Bucur Ciobanul
To Queen's (2km)
Piaţa G Coşbuc
Şos Kiseleff
B-dul C Prezan
B-dul Aviatorilor
Şos Ştefan cel Mare
B-dul Dacia
B-dul Carol I
B-dul Regina Elisabeta
B-dul Mihail Kogălniceanu
B-dul Unirii
Calea Victoriei
Calea Floreasca
Calea Dorobanţilor
Calea Griviţei
Calea Moşilor
Calea 13 Septembrie
Str Lipscani
Str Matei Basarab

Just northwest is the **National History Museum** (Map p961; ☎ 311 3356; Calea Victoriei 12; adult/student 7/2 lei; 🕑 10am-6pm Wed & Fri-Sun, noon-8pm Thu), with a treasury and dismantled replica of the 2nd-century Roman Trajan's Column, showing the Romans conquering Dacians in present-day Romania.

A block east, the **Stavropoleos Church** (Map p961; Str Stavropoleos), on a street meaning 'town of the cross', dates from 1724 and is Bucharest's nicest church.

Ateneul Român

The scene of Ceauşescu's infamous final public appearance was on the balcony of the former **Central Committee of the Communist Party building** (Map p961). On 21 December 1989 crowds cried 'down with Ceauşescu' as the leader tried vainly to make his last speech.

Across the square to the northwest is the massive Royal Palace (a royal residence from 1834), now home to the worthwhile **National Art Museum** (Muzeul Naţional de Artă; Map p961; ☎ 313 3030; http://art.museum.ro; Calea Victoriei 49-53; combo ticket 15 lei, one collection 10 lei, first Wed of month free; 🕑 11am-7pm Wed-Sun), a sprawling three-part collection of Romanian art, European art (Rembrandt, Rodin) and pieces from the Romanian treasury.

Just east is the grand domed **Ateneul Român** (Romanian Athenaeum; Map p961; ☎ 315 6875), which hosts prestigious concerts. Built in 1888, George Enescu made his debut here in 1898.

Just west is the local-loved **Cişmigiu Garden** (Map p961).

North Bucharest

Bucharest's most luxurious villas and parks hug the grand avenue **Şoseaua Kiseleff** (Map p959), which begins at **Piaţa Victoriei** (Map p959; Ⓜ Piaţa Victoriei).

About 200m north of the plaza, the priceless **Museum of the Romanian Peasant** (Muzeul Tăranului Român; Map p959; ☎ 317 9661; Şos Kiseleff 3; adult/student 6/2 lei; 🕑 10am-6pm Tue-Sun) shows off Romania's rural glory with cute handmade signs; one room is devoted to grandmas.

About 1km north is the **Triumphal Arch** (Arcul de Triumf; Map p959), based on Paris' namesake monument, devoted to WWI and the reunification of Romania in 1918 (built 1935–36).

Pathways just east lead to the lovely **Parcul Herăstrău** (Herăstrău Park; Map p959), which hugs the chain of lakes that stripe northern Bucharest.

GETTING INTO TOWN

From Henri Coanda international airport catch bus 783 outside the main terminal (7 lei return or two trips one-way, from any RATB bus-ticket booth), which takes you to Piaţa Unirii in 40 to 50 minutes.

From the train station, Gara de Nord, take the metro to the city centre. Bus 133 will take you just north of the city centre to Piaţa Romană; bus 85 goes to Piaţa Universităţii.

On the park's west side, the **National Village Museum** (Muzeul Naţional al Satului; Map p959; ☎ 317 9110; www.muzeul-satului.ro; Şos Kiseleff 28-30; adult/student 6/3 lei; 🕑 9am-7pm Tue-Sun, to 4pm Mon May-Sep, to 5pm Tue-Fri, to 4pm Mon Oct-Apr) is a terrific open-air collection of several dozen homesteads and churches relocated from rural Romania.

SLEEPING

Funky Chicken (Map p959; ☎ 312 1425; www.funkychickenhostel.com; Str Gen Berthelot 63; dm 30 lei) This bare-bones hostel occupies an historic home on a shady street, with three dorm rooms that sleep 18. No breakfast, but there's a kitchen and free cigarettes.

Butterfly Villa Hostel (Map p959; ☎ 0747-032 644; www.villa-butterfly.com; Str Dumitru Zosima 82; dm/d 44/103 lei; ❄ 💻) One of Bucharest's best hostels. Butterfly is not necessarily the best located, but there's free laundry, a roof terrace, all-day breakfasts and a leafy courtyard. Bus 282 leaves from the train station, and bus 300 from Piaţa Romana.

Hostel Villa Helga (Map p959; ☎ 0741-127 514, 212 0828; www.rotravel.com/hotels/Helga; Str Mihei Einescu 184; dm 45 lei, d with shared/private bathroom 130/210 lei; 💻) This completely refurbished villa has several private rooms, large kitchen, a small library, tourist information and train station/airport pickup available. Your seventh night here is free.

our pick **Midland Youth Hostel** (Map p961; ☎ 317 0362; www.themidlandhostel.com; B-dul Regina Elisabeta 44 Apt 32; dm/d 60/150 lei) It doesn't get any more central or affordable than this. Amenities include the TV room, kitchen, free internet/wi-fi, lockers, laundry (5 lei) and the view over Cişmigiu Garden. Enter through the building's side door on Str Ion Z Zalomit. A second location, Midland Youth Hostel 2, at Str Biserica Amzei 22 (Map p959), was opening at the time of writing.

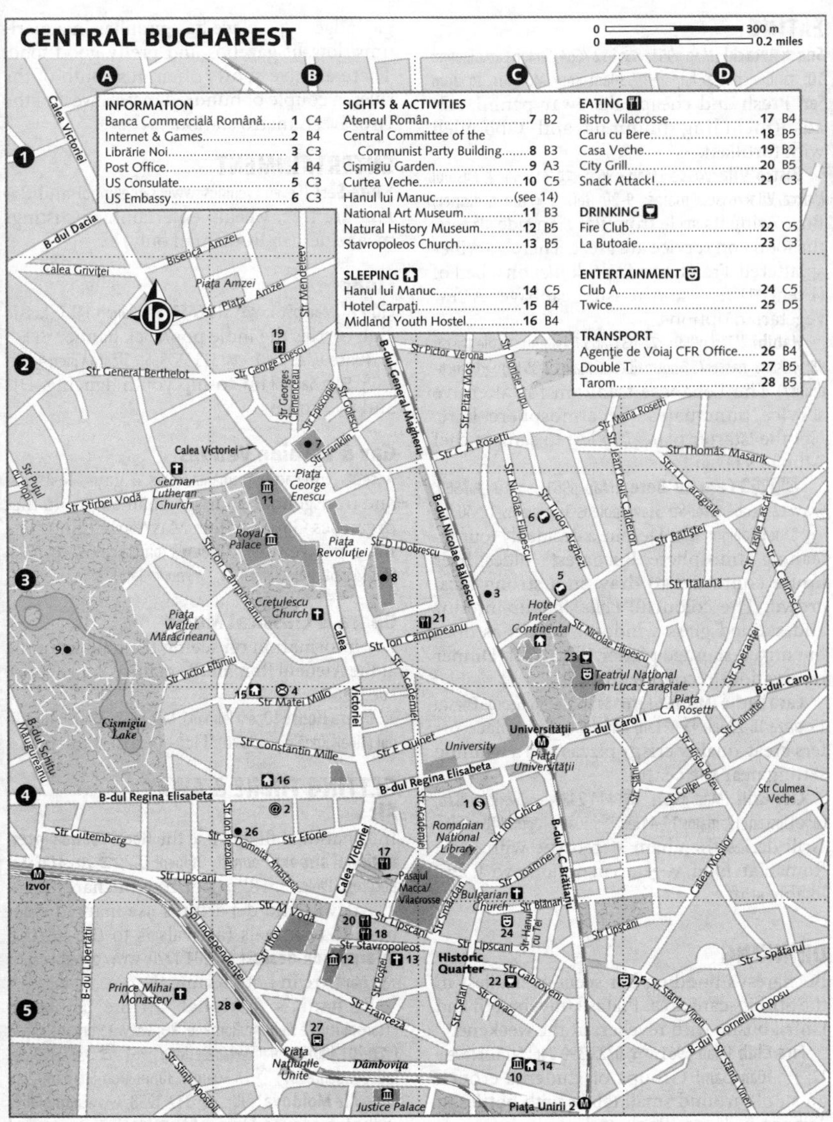

Hotel Carpaţi (Map p961; ☎ 315 0140; www.hotelcarpatibucuresti.ro; Str Matei Millo 16; s/d with shared bathroom 118/180 lei, d with private bathroom 220-261 lei; 💻) This popular central option has 40 recently renovated rooms – some rather tiny and creaky – and a great breakfast served with a little pomp in the Paris-style lobby lounge. Lobby wi-fi only.

Hanul lui Manuc (Manuc's Inn; Map p961; ☎ 313 1415; hmanuc@rnc.ro; Str Franceză 62-64; s/d 162/260 lei) This 19th-century merchants' inn *(caravanserai)* was under renovation during our visit. It's one of the city's oldest buildings with a colourful guest list from its past including prostitutes, criminals and Lonely Planet authors. Expect notably higher prices when it reopens.

EATING

Snack Attack! (Map p961; ☎ 312 7664; Str Ion Câmpineanu 10; sandwiches 8 lei; 🕒 7.30am-8pm Mon-Fri, to 2pm Sat) Fresh and cheap take-away panini, salads (including hummus and tabbouleh with tortillas).

Bistro Vilacrosse (Map p961; ☎ 315 4562; Pasajul Macca/Vilacrosse; mains 9-20 lei; 🕒 lunch-dinner) Borrowing its style from Parisian side streets, the food and service are great. There's a wine-splattered Transylvania pork *filet* on a bed of (French!) fries and roasted cabbage. A few vegetarian options.

Habibi (Map p959; ☎ 031-805 5498; Str. Vasile Lascăr 98; wissam_nasser75@hotmail.com; mains 9-35 lei; 🕒 lunch-dinner) The Lebanese tradition for attentive service punctuates the atmosphere here. Get the 'starter plate' (30 lei) to sample chef Ahmad's favs.

our pick **Caru cu Bere** (Map p961; ☎ 313 7560; www.carucubere.ro; Str Stavropoleos 3-5; mains 12-40 lei; 🕒 8am-midnight; 💻) Despite a decidedly tourist-leaning atmosphere, Bucharest's oldest beer house continues to draw in a strong local crowd. The colourful *belle epoque* interior and stained-glass windows dazzle, as does the mixed sausage platter (for two!). Dinner reservations recommended.

Casa Veche (Map p961; ☎ 312 5816; Str George Enescu 15; pizza 16-23 lei; 🕒 11am-midnight) This place offers great-quality crispy pizzas and a winning setting near the centre.

City Grill (Map p961; ☎ 314 2489; www.citygrill.ro; Calle Lipscani 12; mains 16-44 lei; 🕒 10am-10pm; 💻) City Grill defies the chain stereotype with great Romanian food, vegetarian options, wi-fi and likable staff.

DRINKING

Bucharest's budding bar scene is liveliest in the Str Lipscani area. Piaţas Universităţii and Unirii bustle with revellers at the weekend.

Fire Club (Map p961; ☎ 0722-390 946; Str Gabroveni 12; 🕒 10am-5am) Groups of students crouch on stools around small tables with bottles of Tuborg in hand. Rock and punk shows are staged in the basement.

La Butoaie (Map p961; B-dul Nicolae Bălcescu 2) Huge with uni students, this open-deck bar on the 5th floor of the Ion Luca Caragiale National Theatre fits hundreds.

Piranha Club (off Map p959; ☎ 315 9129; www.clubpiranha.ro; Spl Independenţei 313; 🕒 10am-late) About 2.5km west of the centre, this unique jungle lodge–type place has piranhas in aquariums, low-lit gazebos and pretty good food. There are live shows often. It's south of the river, a couple of hundred metres west of the Grozăveşti metro station.

ENTERTAINMENT

Şapte Seri (Seven Evenings; www.sapteseri.ro) and *24-Fun* are free, weekly entertainment listings magazines (in Romanian only).

Clubs

Club A (Map p961; ☎ 315 6853; Str Blănari 14) Classic club carries the indie pop/rock banner.

Twice (Map p961; ☎ 313 5593; Str Sfânta Vineri 4, Sect 3; 🕒 9pm-5am) Hip-to-hip youth dancing, DJs and two rooms.

Gay & Lesbian Venues

Accept (www.accept-romania.ro) is a gay-, lesbian- and transgender-rights Romanian group that organises GayFest (late May/early June). The main gay venue is **Queen's** (off Map p959; ☎ 0722-988 541; Str Juliu Barach 13; 🕒 noon-3am).

Opera & Classical Music

For information on seeing the philharmonic at the Ateneul Român (Romanian Atheneum), see p960.

Opera House (Opera Română; Map p959; ☎ 313 1857; B-dul Mihail Kogălniceanu 70) Tickets cost 8 to 16 lei.

GETTING THERE & AWAY

Air

International flights use the **Henri Coanda international airport** (formerly Otopeni; OTP; ☎ 201 4788; Şos Bucureşti-Ploieşti), 18km north of Bucharest.

Arrivals and departures use marked side-by-side terminals (arrivals is to the north). **Information desks** (☎ 204 1220; www.otp-airport.ro; 🕒 24hr) are in both terminals.

Romania's national airline is **Tarom** (Transporturile Aeriene Române; RO; www.tarom.ro) Airport (☎ 201 400); Central Bucharest (Map p961; ☎ 337 0400; Spl Independenţei 17; 🕒 8.30am-7.30pm Mon-Fri, 9am-2pm Sat). **Air Moldova** (9U; ☎ 312 1258; www.airmoldova.md) also serves Henri Coanda international airport.

Băneasa airport (BBU; ☎ 232 0020; Şos Bucureşti-Ploieşti 40), 8km north of the city centre, is used for some internal and charter flights.

Bus

Bucharest's bus companies come and go and change departure points frequently. Travelling by train is preferable. The most popular routes are the maxitaxis to Braşov (21 lei, 2½ hours), which stop in Sinaia, Buşteni and Predeal on the way. Some continue on to Sighişoara (35 lei, five hours). **C&I** (☎ 256 8039; Str Ritmului 35) runs these from its office 3.25km east of Piaţa Romana – from metro Piaţa Iancului, go south one block on Şoseaua Mihei Bravu (toward Maxbet Casino) then right on B-dul Ferdinand, from where it's up two blocks on the left. Buses 69 and 85 go there from Gara de Nord.

The biggest name in international buses is **Eurolines** (Map p959; ☎ 316 3661; www.eurolines.ro; Str Buzeşti 44; 24hr), which links many Western European destinations with Bucharest.

Maxitaxis to Sofia, Bulgaria (66 lei, daily at 3.44pm) depart from **Double T** (Map p961; ☎ 313 3642; Calea Victoriei 2; 6am-9pm).

The Turkey-bound have several options to İstanbul (150 lei, 12 hours) around Gara de Nord, including **Ortadoğu Tur** (Map p959; ☎ 318 7538; Str Gara de Nord 6-8).

Every 45 minutes or so, maxitaxis head for Costanţa (33 lei) from the so-called **Central Bus Station** (Autogara; Map p959), about 350m east of the train station.

Car

Major car-hire agencies can be found at the Henri Coanda international airport arrivals hall. Cheapest are **C&V** (☎ 201 4611, 0788-998 877; www.dvtouring.ro) and **Autonom** (www.autonom.com), offering Daewoo Matiz for 72 lei per day if you hire for over a week.

Train

The central train station is **Gara de Nord** (Map p959; ☎ 319 9539; Piaţa Gara de Nord 1). Call ☎ 021-9521 or ☎ 021-9522 for telephone reservations. Buy advance tickets here or at **Agentia de Voiaj CFR office** (Map p961; ☎ 313 2643; www.cfr.ro; Str Domnita Anastasia 10-14; 7.30am-7.30pm Mon-Fri, 9am-1.30pm Sat). The Wasteels agency located at Gara de Nord (see p958) can help.

Check the latest schedules on **CFR** (www.cfr.ro), or the reliable **Die Bahn** (www.bahn.de, in German).

Sample direct daily services are in the following table.

Destination	Price (lei)	Duration (hr)	Daily Departures
Braşov	36.4	2½	hourly
Cluj-Napoca	68.4	7½	6
Sighişoara	52.6	4½	9
Timişoara	85.2	8	8

Daily international service includes trains to Belgrade (12 hours), Budapest (13 to 15 hours), İstanbul (19 hours) and Sofia (11 hours).

GETTING AROUND

At the time of writing, in long awaited response to the increasingly slow and unpredictable journey by road, train service to Henri Coanda airport had just begun, leaving hourly from Gara de Nord from 5am to 11pm. The journey (6 lei, 45 minutes) includes a short shuttle bus ride from the train terminus to the airport.

For buses, trams and trolleybuses buy tickets (1.30 lei) at any RATB street kiosk, marked *'casa de bilete'* or simply *'bilete'*. Punch your ticket onboard. Public transport runs roughly from 5am to 11pm Monday to Saturday (less on Sunday).

Bucharest's metro (two-ride/10-ride tickets 2.20/8 lei) runs frequently on four lines from 5.30am to 11.30pm.

The taxis outside Gara de Nord are not recommended. Call for a reputable company, such as **Cobalcescu** (☎ 021-9451), **CrisTaxi** (☎ 021-9461) and **Taxi Sprint** (☎ 021-9495).

TRANSYLVANIA

After a century of being name-checked in literature and cinema, the word 'Transylvania' enjoys instant, worldwide recognition. The mere mention of it conjures waves of imagery: mind-bending mountains, Gothic castles, fortified churches, dusty peasant villages, spooky moonlight and a role-call of bloodthirsty, shape-shifting creatures with wicked overbites.

Unexplained puncture-wounds to the neck notwithstanding, Transylvania is all those things and more. There's hiking and skiing, cited as being second only to Switzerland, valleys with Saxon towns, fortified churches, Bran and Peleş Castles and, yes, Dracula's face will stare back at you from a variety of coffee mugs and T-shirts.

SINAIA

☎ **0244 / pop 14,600**

Sinaia is set among an exquisite, fir-clad scrap of the towering Bucegi Mountains, offering ski runs and hiking trails for year-round fun. It developed into a major

Book your stay at lonelyplanet.com/hotels

BUCEGI MOUNTAINS

Sinaia and Buşteni, 5km north, are the principal gateways to this stunning (and popular) mountain range of dizzying skiing, mountain biking and hiking fun on a plateau situated high up on the border of Transylvania and Wallachia. Hikes are well marked – some make for great cycling. There are cabanas up here, but most visitors go for a day trip.

From Sinaia, the 30-person **cable-car station** (☎ 311 764, 311 872; to Cota 1400m/2000m one way 13/23.50 lei, return 26/47 lei; 🕑 8.30am-4pm or 5pm Tue-Sun) leaves half-hourly with two station points marked by elevation. Lines stack for a couple of hours in summer.

Snow (☎ 311 198; Str Cuza Voda 2a; 🕑 9am-6pm), near the cable car in Sinaia, hires skis/snowboards for 35 lei per day, bikes for 60 lei.

resort after King Carol I selected the area for his summer residence in 1870 and built the sinfully lavish Peleş Castle, now one of Romania's primary tourist destinations.

Orientation

From the train station climb up the stairway across the street to busy B-dul Carol I, where maxitaxis between Bucharest and Braşov stop. From the train station, the cable car is located to the left and the palace is uphill to the right.

Information

Banks are along B-dul Carol I.

Dracula's Land (☎ 311 441; mihneasutu@yahoo.com; B-dul Carol I 14; 🕑 9am-5pm or 6pm) Signed simply 'Tourist Office', with chummy blokes that find villa rooms or arrange guides.

Eco Laundry (☎ 0788-660 788; B-dul Carol I 31; 🕑 7am-4pm) Drop-off laundry behind the big grey building. It's 3 lei to 10 lei per article of clothing.

Salvamont (☎ 313 131, nationwide 0-SALVAMONT; Primărie, B-dul Carol I) Inside the Tourism Information Centre, also at Cota 2000 chairlift station.

Sinaia Tourism Information Centre (☎ 315 656; www.info-sinaia.ro; B-dul Carol I 47; 🕑 8.30am-4.30pm Mon-Fri) Lots and lots of information and brochures and maps, but can't book rooms.

Sights

Romania's new monarchy debuted in a blaze of pomp with **Peleş Castle** (☎ 310 205; compulsory tour 15 lei; 🕑 11am-5pm Tue, 9am-4.15pm Wed-Sun). King Carol I's vision of fairy-tale turrets rising above acres of green meadows and grand reception halls with heavy wood-carved ceilings and gilded pieces is still awe-inspiring a century later. Worthwhile tours take in the 1st floor only – note the ground-breaking central vacuuming system.

About 100m uphill is Queen Marie's less-fussy art nouveau–style home, the **Pelişor Palace** (☎ 310 918; compulsory tour 10 lei; 🕑 9am-5pm Wed-Sun).

Sleeping

Travel agencies can help find rooms in *pensiunes* and villas in the area.

Hotel Economat (☎ 311 151; srpsinaia@apps.ro; Aleea Peleşului 2; s/d 90/180 lei) Just outside the Peleş gate, these are decent rooms in a setting lovely enough that first-time visitors have been known to mistake it for the castle!

Hotel Caraiman (☎ 313 551; B-dul Carol I 4; palace@rdslink.ro; s/d/apt 135/180/235 lei; 💻) Of all the faded-glory century-old hotels, this 1881 red-and-white Caraiman is less royal ball and more rustic and laid-back.

Eating

There are a few fast-food stands and pizza places along B-dul Carol I.

Irish House (☎ 310 060; www.irishhouse.ro; B-dul Carol I 80; mains 10-30 lei; 🕑 8am-midnight) Guinness on tap (9 lei) and Irish dishes are on offer, including an 'Irish Breakfast' (11 lei), but this place fills for its good Romanian food and pizzas.

Getting There & Away

Sinaia is on the Bucharest–Braşov rail line – 126km from the former and 45km from the latter – so jumping on a train to Bucharest (24 lei, 1½ hours) or Braşov (16.1 lei, one hour) is a cinch.

Buses and maxitaxis run every 45 minutes between roughly 7am and 10pm from the central bus stop on B-dul Carol I to Bucharest or Braşov.

BRAŞOV

☎ **0268/0368 / pop 284,600**

Braşov is Romania's ground-zero tourist destination for very good reason. Ringed by perfect mountains and verdant hills, the city is adorned with baroque facades, bohemian outdoor cafes, the lovely Piaţa Sfatului and agreeable locals. Innumerable day trips can be launched from here: hiking/skiing in the Bucegi Mountains, castling in Bran, Râşnov and Sinaia and more.

Orientation

Several brick pedestrian lanes lead from central Piaţa Sfatului, including Str Republicii, which leads north to B-dul Eroilor and Parcul Central. B-dul Eroilor also links two other main thoroughfares, Str Mureşenilor to the west and Str Nicolae Bălcescu to the east.

The train station is 3km northeast of the city centre. Braşov has a few bus stations – Autogara 1, next to the train station, is the most active.

Information

You'll find numerous ATMs, banks and exchange offices on and around Str Republicii and B-dul Eroilor.

Aventours (☎ 472 718; www.discoveromania.ro; Str Paul Richter 1; ⏰ 10am-3pm Mon-Fri) Great tailor-made tours (particularly mountain-based) and oodles of information on the area.

County Hospital (☎ 333 666; Calea Bucareşti 25-27; ⏰ 24hr) Northwest of the city centre.

Raiffeisen Bank (Piaţa Sfatului; ⏰ 9am-6.30pm Mon-Fri, 10am-2pm Sat) Gives cash advances on Visa or MasterCard.

Tibi Internet (☎ 410 185; Str Gheorghe Bariţa 8; per hr 3 lei; ⏰ 24hr)

Tourist Information Centre (☎ 419 078; www.brasovcity.ro; Piaţa Sfatului 30; ⏰ 9am-5pm) English-speaking staff can point you to tour services and track down hotel vacancies.

Sights

Though sorely lacking in decent museums, drifting through Braşov's medieval glory is arresting enough. A good starting point for a walk is central **Piaţa Stafalui**, where prisoners were once tortured in the gold **Council House** (Casa Sfatului), which dates from 1420. The building also houses the tourist information centre and unremarkable **Braşov Historical Museum** (☎ 472 350; adult/student 5/1 lei; ⏰ 10am-6pm Tue-Sun Jun-Sep, 9am-5pm Tue-Sun Oct-May).

Looming from the south, the Gothic **Black Church** (Biserica Neagră; admission 4 lei; ⏰ 10am-5pm Mon-Sat), built between 1384 and 1477, gained its name after a 1689 fire blackened its walls. Inside the church you can see apse statues moved from outside and 120 fabulous Turkish rugs. Recitals are held in summer on the 4000-pipe organ (5 lei).

A couple of blocks east, cobbled **Str Sforii** is one of Europe's narrowest 'streets'. Looming above on Mt Tâmpa is the 'Hollywood'-style Braşov sign; to reach it (and hiking trails), take the **Tâmpa cable car** (Telecabina; ☎ 478 657; one-way/return 10/20 lei; ⏰ 9.30am-5pm Tue-Sun).

Good vantage points of the city from the west side are at the **Black Tower** (Turnul Negru) and **White Tower** (Turnul Alba) – both rather white actually – reached on a creekside promenade alongside the city's original walls. A side road leads to the promenade from about 200m south of the Black Church.

Sleeping

Gabriel Hostel (☎ 0744-844 223; Str Vasile Saftu 41-A; dm/d 35/100 lei; 💻) This 50-bed place was preparing for a major overhaul during our visit. Take bus 51 to the last stop, the door's across the street.

Rolling Stone Hostel (☎ 0744-816 970; www.rollingstone.ro; Str Piatra Mare 2A; dm/r from 36/120 lei; 💻) Run by the high-energy Bolea family, the Stone is a welcoming hostel spot, with an on-site bar and bike rental.

Kismet Dao Villa (☎ 514 296; www.kismetdao.ro; Str Democratiei 2B; dm/d 40/130 lei; 💻) This four-floor villa offers a DVD library, playful staff and one free beer/soda to get your evening started.

Hotel Aro Sport (☎ 478 800; Str Sfântu Ioan 3; s/d 56/78 lei) These boxy rooms evoke classic Eastern European travel – a sink in the corner and a shower down the hall. They're surprisingly clean and bright though. No breakfast.

Eating & Drinking

Hard Discount (Str Nicolae Bălcescu; ⏰ 24hr) Fully stocked supermarket next to the fruit and vegetable market.

Ando's (Str B-dul 15 Noiembrie 4; mains 6-11 lei; ⏰ 10am-10pm) Big shawarma and sandwiches at low prices – and zero character.

Pizza Pasta Venezia (☎ 470 511; Str Hirscher 2; pastas & pizza 10-24 lei; ⏰ 10am-10pm) Identical menu as next door, but wall-sized Venetian paintings and soft lighting help this cosy Italian restaurant fill before its neighbours.

Bistro de l'Arte (☎ 0722-219 980; www.bistrodelarte.ro; Piaţa Enescu 11; mains 12-28 lei; ⏰ 9am-1am Mon-Sat, noon-midnight Sun; 💻) On the ground floor of a cosy 15th-century building, the Bistro serves small meals – sandwiches, fish, spaghetti and breakfasts.

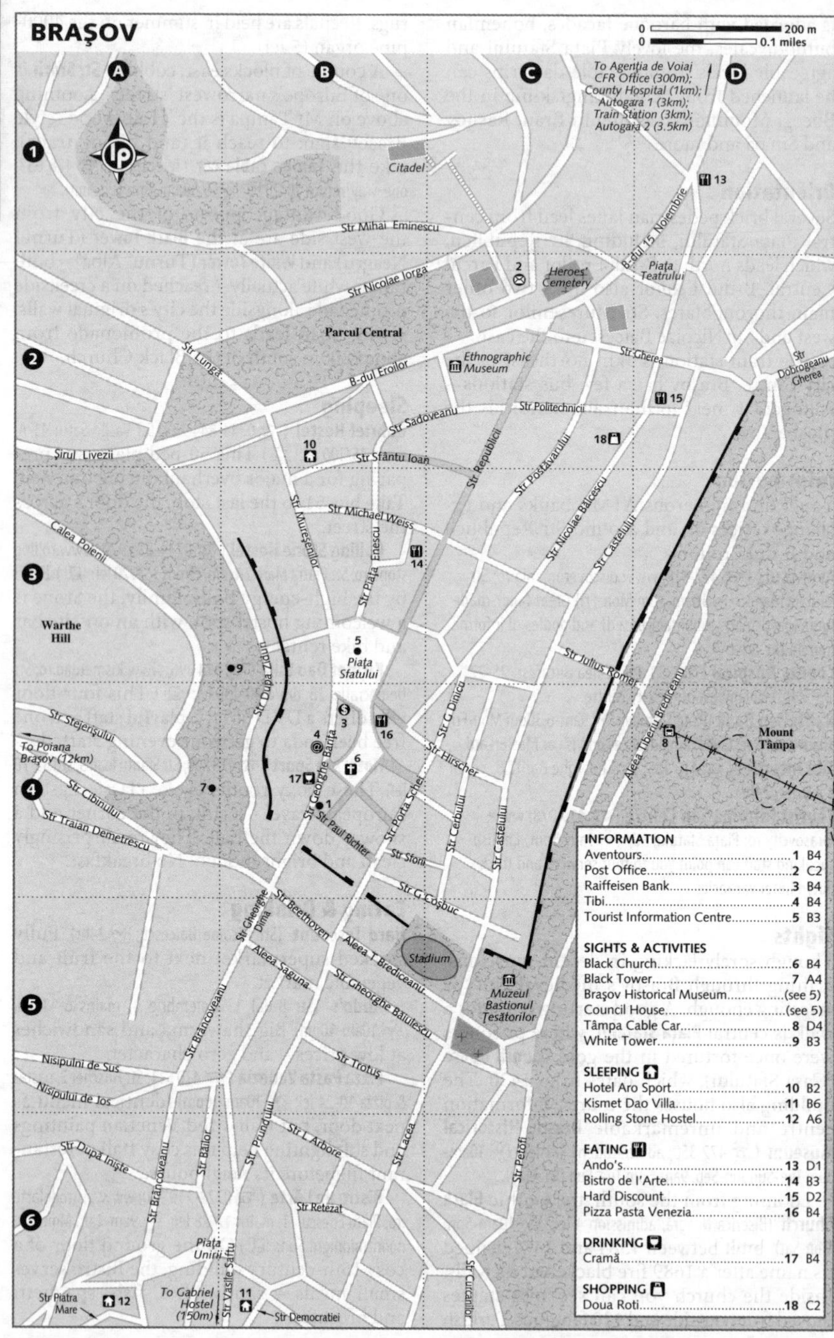
BRAŞOV
0 200 m
0 0.1 miles
A
B
C
D
1
2
3
4
5
6
To Agenţia de Voiaj CFR Office (300m); County Hospital (1km); Autogara 1 (3km); Train Station (3km); Autogara 2 (3.5km)
Citadel
Str Mihai Eminescu
B-dul 15 Noiembrie
Piaţa Teatrului
Heroes' Cemetery
Str Nicolae Iorga
Parcul Central
Str Lunga
B-dul Eroilor
Ethnographic Museum
Str Gherea
Str Dobrogeanu Gherea
Str Politechnicii
Str Sadoveanu
Şirul Livezii
Str Sfântu Ioan
Str Republicii
Str Poştăvarului
Str Michael Weiss
Str Mureşenilor
Str Piaţa Enescu
Str Nicolae Bălcescu
Str Castelului
Calea Poienii
Warthe Hill
Piaţa Sfatului
Str După Ziduri
Str Julius Romer
Str Stejerişului
To Poiana Braşov (12km)
Str G Dinicu
Str Hirscher
Aleea Tiberiu Brediceanu
Mount Tâmpa
Str Cibinului
Str Traian Demetrescu
Str Gheorghe Bariţiu
Str Paul Richter
Str Porta Schei
Str Cerbului
Str Castelului
Str Sforii
Str G Coşbuc
Str Gheorghe Dima
Str Beethoven
Aleea T Brediceanu
Stadium
Aleea Saguna
Str Gheorghe Baiulescu
Muzeul Bastionul Ţesătorilor
Str Brâncoveanu
Nisipului de Sus
Nisipului de Jos
Str Troţuş
Str După Inişte
Str Bailor
Str Prundului
Str L Arbore
Str Lacea
Str Petőfi
Str Retezat
Piaţa Unirii
Str Vasile Saftu
Str Curcanilor
Str Piatra Mare
To Gabriel Hostel (150m)
Str Democratiei
INFORMATION
Aventours 1 B4
Post Office 2 C2
Raiffeisen Bank 3 B4
Tibi 4 B4
Tourist Information Centre 5 B3
SIGHTS & ACTIVITIES
Black Church 6 B4
Black Tower 7 A4
Braşov Historical Museum (see 5)
Council House (see 5)
Tâmpa Cable Car 8 D4
White Tower 9 B3
SLEEPING
Hotel Aro Sport 10 B2
Kismet Dao Villa 11 B6
Rolling Stone Hostel 12 A6
EATING
Ando's 13 D1
Bistro de l'Arte 14 B3
Hard Discount 15 D2
Pizza Pasta Venezia 16 B4
DRINKING
Cramă 17 B4
SHOPPING
Doua Roti 18 C2

Cramă (Str Gheorghe Bariţa 20; 9.30am-8pm Mon-Fri, 9am-2pm Sat) A well-hidden alley/basement joint, selling wine starting at 5 lei per litre for red, and 4.5 lei for white. *Ţuică* (60-proof plum brandy) is 29.5 lei for one litre – enough to flatten the whole hostel.

Shopping

Doua Roti (470 207; Str Nicolae Bălcescu 55; 8.30am-5pm Mon-Fri, 9am-1pm Sat) Bike shop selling used bikes from 200 lei.

Getting There & Away

BUS

Braşov's most active bus 'station' is **Autogara 1** (427 267), a ramshackle lot next to the train station. Maxitaxis go hourly to-and-fro on the Târgu Mureş–Sighişoara–Braşov–Buşteni–Bucharest route.

Autogara 2 (Bartolomeu; 426 332; Str Avram Iancu 114), 1km west of the train station, sends half-hourly buses from roughly 6.30am to 11.30pm to Râşnov (2.5 lei, 25 minutes) and Bran (4 lei, 40 minutes). All buses to Braşov stop each way at Râşnov. Take bus 12 to reach the station.

TRAIN

Advance tickets are sold at the **Agentia de Voiaj CFR office** (477 015; Str 15 de Noiembrie 43; 8am-7.30pm Mon-Fri), north of the city centre. Hourly trains go daily to Bucharest (32 lei, 2½ hours), a dozen daily to Sighişoara (34 lei, 2½ hours) and five daily to Cluj-Napoca (36 lei, six hours). International links include three daily trains to Budapest (144/194 lei seat/sleeper, 14 hours).

The train station has left-luggage facilities.

Getting Around

Bus 51 reaches the city centre from the train station (prebuy your ticket). From the city centre, hail a bus in Piaţa Unirii or anywhere on Str Nicolae Bălcescu.

BRAN & RÂŞNOV

0268 / pop 5300

It isn't really Dracula's castle – oh, he may have defecated here once – but it's hard to skip **Bran Castle** (238 333; www.brancastlemuseum.ro; adult/student 12/6 lei; 9am-7pm Tue-Sun, noon-7pm Mon May-Sep, 9am-5pm Tue-Sun Oct-Apr), a real, mountain-cradled, spooky castle. Tour groups and Dracula T-shirts take away a little from the experience.

Visitors to Bran can easily make a dual-castle day trip from Braşov by stopping in Râşnov to visit the mountain-top ruins of the interesting 13th-century **Râşnov Fortress** (Cetatea Râsnov; 230 255; admission 12 lei; 9am-8pm May-Oct, to 6pm Nov-Apr).

Overnighting in either town is pricey. **Vila Bran** (236 866; www.vilabran.ro; Str Principală 238; r 100-160 lei;) is unflinchingly touristy, but the view of the hills is worth it (no breakfast). In Râşnov, **Pensiunea Stefi** (0721-303 009; www.hotelstefi-ro.com; Piaţa Unirii 5; r 100 lei;) has carpeted rooms, sauna, fitness centre and a wading pool (breakfast 14 lei).

See Braşov (left) for information on transport.

SIGHIŞOARA

0265 / pop 32,300

Where Vlad 'Ţepeş' Dracula first scampered about, when skewered Turks were just a twinkle in his eye, Sighişoara is a dreamy, compact, medieval citadel town. Brightly coloured, half-a-millennium-old townhouses border hilly cobbled streets, church bells clang atmospherically in the early hours, and overloaded tour buses jockey for parking space.

Orientation & Information

The bus and train stations are about a 15-minute walk north of the (visible) citadel.

Banca Transilvania, between Piaţa Cetătii and Muzeulul, has an ATM in the citadel.

Café International & Family Centre (Piaţa Cetătii 8; per hr 3 lei; 8am-8pm Mon-Sat Jun-Sep, 1-7pm Mon-Sat Oct-May) Nonprofit agency doubles as a tourist office; also runs year-round internet cafe.

Tourist Information (770 415; Str O Goga; 10am-4pm Mon-Fri, 9am-1pm Sat) Can book beds.

Sights

Most of Sighişoara's sights are clustered in the delightfully medieval **citadel** – perched on a hillock and fortified with a 14th-century wall. Entering the citadel, which is on the Unesco World Heritage list, you pass under the massive **clock tower** (Turnul cu Ceas), dating from 1280. Inside is the great little **History Museum** (771 108; Piaţa Muzeului 1; admission 5 lei; 10am-4.30pm Mon, 9am-6.30pm Tue-Fri, 9am-4.30pm Sat & Sun mid-May–mid-Sep, 9am-3.30pm Tue-Fri, 10am-3.30pm Sat & Sun mid-Sep–mid-May), with small rooms off the winding steps that terminate at the 7th-floor lookout.

A combo ticket (10 lei) includes entrance to the small, dark **Torture Room Museum** (admission 3 lei; same as History Museum) under the clock tower, and the small **collection of medieval arms** (adult/student 4/2 lei; same as History Museum), towards Piaţa Cetăţii.

The renovated **Casa Dracula** (now a restaurant, serving 3 lei glasses of wine in the moody dining room) is where Vlad Ţepeş reputedly lived until the age of four.

Sleeping

Burg Hostel (778 489; www.ibz.ro; Str Bastionului 4-6; dm 30 lei, s/d with shared bathroom 50/78 lei, s/d with private bathroom 70/86 lei;) This slightly sterile hostel has functional rooms of various bed counts. Breakfast is 12 lei. Net extra, wi-fi free.

Gia Hostel (772 486; hotelgia@gmail.com; Str Libertăţii 41; dm from 35 lei, r 95-99 lei;) Backing the railway line (about a 15-minute walk to the citadel), these rooms recently enjoyed a thoughtful redecoration. Services include bike rental, bar, an hour's free internet and kitchen/grill access.

Nathan's Villa (772 546; www.nathansvilla.com; Str Libertăţii 8; dm/d 37/85 lei;) This popular choice (with free laundry and a bar) is usually the best (and only) nightlife in town. It stays open from April to November only.

our pick Bed & Breakfast Coula (777 907; Str Tâmplarilor 40; per person 54 lei) This homey, unsigned 400-year-old home in the citadel has large rooms with classic ceramic wood-fire heaters. Run by a heart-breakingly kind English-speaking family, they can help arrange Saxon church trips and rent you bikes (25 lei). There are six rooms (only one's in use in winter). Dinner available with advance notice.

Eating

Rustic (Str Decembrie 1, 7; mains 6-18 lei; 8am-midnight Mon-Sat, noon-midnight Sun) This wood-and-brick 'man's man' bar-restaurant is down from the citadel. The *ciorba ţaraneasca de porc* (countryside pork soup) will erase the hangover acquired at Nathan's Villa. Eggs served all day.

Getting There & Away

About a dozen daily trains connect Sighişoara with Braşov (27 lei, two hours), nine of which go on to Bucharest (55 lei, 4½ hours). Five daily trains go to Cluj-Napoca (46 lei, 3½ hours). Buy tickets at the **train station** (771 886) or at the central **Agentia de Voiaj CFR** (771 820; Str Goga 6A; 8.30am-3.30pm Mon-Fri).

Next to the train station, the **bus station** (771 260; Str Libertăţii) sends buses to Budapest (72 lei, eight hours, two weekly) and Sibiu (15 lei, 2½ hours, five daily).

SIBIU

0269/0369 / pop 154,900

Pealing, crumbling, car-rattling old Sibiu, despite being the capital and most culturally active of the Transylvanian Saxon towns, was frequently overshadowed by Braşov, Sighişoara and Cluj. Then the EU designated it as a 'Capital of Culture' for 2007. Now freshly scrubbed, painted and cobblestoned, the pedestrian areas are frame-worthy from any angle and every third building has been declared a historic monument. Some locals liked the old Sibiu better, falling roof tiles, ankle-twisting cobblestones and all, but there's no arguing that new Sibiu is ready to dance in the spotlight.

Orientation

The adjacent bus and train stations are near the centre of town. Exit the station and stroll up Str General Magheru four blocks to Piaţa Mare, the historic centre.

Information

Banca Comercială Română (Str Nicolae Bălcescu 11; 8.30am-5.30pm Mon-Fri, to 12.30pm Sat)

Internet (Str Nicolae Bălcescu 29; per hr 2.5 lei; 24hr)

Salvamont (0745-140 144, 0-SALVAMONT; 8am-4pm Mon-Fri) For 24-hour mountain rescue.

Tourist Information Centre (208 913; www.sibiu.ro; Piaţa Mare 2; 9am-5pm Mon-Sat) On the ground floor of the new city hall.

Sights

The expansive Piaţa Mare was the very centre of the old walled city. The **Brukenthal Museum** (217 691; www.brukenthalmuseum.ro; Piaţa Mare 5; adult/student 12/3 lei; 10am-6pm) is the oldest and likely finest art gallery in Romania, with excellent collections of 16th- and 17th-century art including a giant 1808 painting of Sibiu. The square's most impressive building is the **Banca Agricola** (Piaţa Mare 2), now housing the town hall and Tourist Information Centre. Just west is the newly redesigned **History Museum** (Str Mitropoliei 2; all three exhibitions 17 lei; 10am-5pm), featuring copious new displays starting at the Palaeolithic age and sweeping through all the epochs.

Nearby, on Piaţa Huet, is the Gothic **Biserica Evanghelică** (Evangelical Church; 9am-3pm Mon-Fri, 9am-8pm Sat, 11am-8pm Sun), built from 1300 to 1520, under partial renovation lasting until 2011.

It's worth walking along the 16th-century **city walls** and watchtowers, a few blocks southeast of Piaţa Mare.

Sibiu's highlight is the sprawling **Museum of Traditional Folk Civilization** (Muzeul Civilizaţiei Populare Tradiţionale Astra; 242 599; Calea Răşinarilor 14; admission 15 lei; 10am-6pm Tue-Sun, to 8pm depending on the weather), an open-air museum 5km from the centre with more than 120 traditional dwellings, mills and churches brought from around the country. Trolleybus 1 from the train station goes there (get off at the last stop and keep walking; it's less than 1km).

Sleeping

our pick Flying Time Hostel (0369-730 179; www.sibiuhostel.ro; Str Gheorghe Lazar 6; dm 40-45 lei, d 145 lei;) In an 18th-century building designed to stay naturally cool, there's great beds, a flowery inner courtyard cafe and pub with live music.

Chess Hostel (0740-096 920; www.chesshostelsibiu.ro; Ştefan Cel Mare 6; dm 40-50 lei; P) The airy dorms have lockers, clothes hooks, hangers and lights on every bed. No breakfast, but there's a kitchen for self-caterers.

Pensiune Halemadero (212 509; Str Măsarilor 10; s/d/tr 40/80/120 lei) Family-run four-room deal in the lower town. Rooms are old-school, with TV and shared bathroom. No breakfast.

Eating

Grand Plaza (210 427; Str 9 Mai 60; mains 9-13 lei; 9am-10.30pm) No-nonsense Romanian cuisine at great prices. The *ciolan de porc pe varză călită* (pig knee with beans) is quite the spectacle.

Crama Sibiul Vechi (Str Ilarian; mains 14-28 lei; noon-midnight) This popular brick cellar reels in locals for its tasty Transylvanian armoury of *ciorba* (soup), mutton, sausages, beef and fish.

La Piazzetta (230 879; Piaţa Mică 15; pizza & pasta 16-22 lei) This square pizza shop is livelier than most.

Entertainment

Sibiu's International Astra Film Festival is held in May. The **Philharmonic** (210 264; www.filarmonicasibiu.ro; Str Cetatii 3-5) had been a big cultural player since 1949.

Getting There & Around

Tarom (211 157; Str Nicolae Bălcescu 10; 9am-12.30pm & 1.30-5pm Mon-Fri) has daily flights to Bucharest (from 169 lei one-way), Munich (683 lei) and Vienna (1349 lei). **Carpatair** (229 161; www.carpatair.com) flies to Germany and Italy via Timişoara. Budget airline **Blue Air** (www.blueair-web.com) flies to Madrid, Cologne and Stuttgart. Trolleybus 8 runs between the airport and the train station.

Daily bus and maxitaxi service includes four to Braşov (20 lei, 2½ hours), five to seven to Bucharest (48 lei, 5½ hours), nine to Cluj-Napoca (28 lei, 3½ hours), and two to Timişoara (43 lei, six hours).

There are 10 daily direct trains to Braşov (29 lei, 2½ hours), four to Bucharest (44 lei, five hours) and three to Timişoara (44 lei, five hours). Buy tickets at the station or **Agentia de Voiaj CFR office** (216 441; Str Nicolae Bălcescu 6; 7am-8pm Mon-Fri).

CLUJ-NAPOCA

0264 / pop 318,000

Aka 'Club-Napoca', this city isn't as picturesque as its Saxon neighbours, but it's famed for its dozens of cavernous, unsnooty discos filled with agreeable students. Even outside the clubs, Cluj is one of Romania's most energised and welcoming cities.

Orientation & Information

The *Gara* (train station) is 1.5km north of the central Piaţa Unirii (bordered on the north by Str Regele Ferdinand, on the south by B-dul Eroilor), reached by tram 101 down Str Horea. Three blocks east of Piaţa Unirii is Piaţa Avram Iancu. City information and an excellent interactive map are at www.cluj4all.com.

Banca Comercială Română (Str Gheorghe Bariţiu 10-12; 8.30am-6pm Mon Fri, 8.30am-12.30pm Sat) Changes travellers cheques.

Blade Net (Str Iuliu Maniu 17; per hr 2.4 lei; 8am-midnight) Two blocks east of Piaţa Unirii.

Diverta (Str Universităţii 1; 8am-8pm Mon-Fri, 9am-4pm Sat) Has contemporary titles in English.

Pan Travel (420 516; www.pantravel.ro; Str Grozavescu 13; 9am-5pm Mon-Fri) This top-notch outfit can book accommodation, car rental (from 108 lei per day) and arrange Maramureş trips. It's best to make contact ahead of time.

Sights

The vast 14th-century **St Michael's Church** dominates Piaţa Unirii. The neo-Gothic tower (1859) topping the Gothic hall church creates a great landmark. Outside is a huge equestrian statue (1902) of the famous Hungarian king Matthias Corvinus (r 1458–90), who was born in the city.

Facing Piaţa Unirii is the interesting **National Art Museum** (☎ 496 952; Piaţa Unirii 30; admission 4.6 lei; ⌚ 10am-5pm Wed-Sun), housed inside the baroque Banffy Palace (1791).

The memorably fun, three-room **Pharmaceutical Museum** (☎ 597 567; Str Regele Ferdinand 1; admission 5 lei; ⌚ 10am-4pm Mon-Sat) features ground mummy dust, 18th-century aphrodisiacs and medieval alchemy symbols.

In the 'student ghetto' west of the city centre, inside the wooded **Biology and Geology Faculty**, you'll find the surprisingly rewarding **Museum of Zoology** (☎ 595 739; Str Clinicilor 5-7; admission 2 lei; ⌚ 9am-3pm Mon-Fri, 10am-2pm Sat & Sun), an L-shaped lab that looks like it hasn't changed in five decades. From Str Clinicilor, veer left through the brick gate.

Just south, head past fast-food joints up Str Bogdan P Haşdeu to Str Pasteur to reach the fragrant 1930 **Alexandru Borza Botanic Gardens** (☎ 592 152; Str Republicii 42; adult/student 4/2 lei; ⌚ 9am-6pm).

For an overall view of Cluj-Napoca, climb up the **cetatea** (citadel; 1715) northwest of the city centre.

Courses

Access (☎ 420 476; www.access.ro; Str Ţebei 21, 3rd fl; ⌚ 10am-6pm Mon & Thu, 2-8pm Tue & Wed, 2-6pm Fri) offers Romanian-language courses.

Sleeping

Camping Făget (☎ 596 227; camp sites 28 lei, 2-person huts 58 lei) This hilltop collection of OK cabanas and tent spots is 7km south of the centre. Take bus 35 to the end of the line, from where it's a 2km marked hike.

our pick **Retro Hostel** (☎ 450 452; www.retro.ro; Str Potaissa 13; dm from 39 lei, s/d/tr 77/116/165 lei; 💻) On a quiet lane amid 16th-century citadel wall fragments, the newly expanded Retro is one of Romania's best hostels. Dorms are a little tight and there's only a couple of bathrooms. The chatty and tirelessly helpful staff offer good-value day trips. Breakfast 14 lei.

Pensiunea Junior (☎ 432 028; www.pensiune-junior.ro; Str Căi Ferate 12; s/d 100/130 lei; 💻) This unholy red-coloured building with simple rooms is on a loud, unappealing street 100m east of the train station. Rooms 1 and 7 are away from traffic noise. Free wi-fi. No breakfast.

Vila 69 (☎ 591 592; vila69@email.ro; Str Haşden 69; s/d 115/150 lei; 💻) Seventeen rather simple but modern rooms in a happy little place near university action. Take Str Clinicilor, turn left on Str Piezişă – it's 200m up the street. Free wi-fi.

Eating

There are heaps of good pizza, hamburger and kebab options on Piaţa Lucian Blaga and Str Napoca, just west of Piaţa Unirii.

Speed/Alcatraz (Str Napoca 4-6; pizza 13 lei, sandwiches 5 lei; ⌚ 24hr) is a busy fast-food option with good seating choices, including some in the 'Al Capone' jail cages.

For fresh produce, stroll through the central market, northwest of Piaţa Unirii on Piaţa Mihai Viteazul, which also houses supermarket **Oncos** (⌚ 7am-9pm Mon-Sat, 8am-8pm Sun).

Drinking

Diesel Bar (☎ 493 043; Piaţa Unirii 17) Walk past the hipsters in the all-glass entry and go downstairs into a towering, cavernous room, with red-spotlit tables and 15 lei gin and tonics.

Music Pub (☎ 432 517; Str Horea 5; ⌚ 9am-3am Mon-Fri, noon-5am Sat, 5pm-5am Sun) A little wild west up front, the sprawling pub is a great, casual place. Live music Saturday and Sunday.

The 'student ghetto', southwest of Cluj-Napoca's centre (on and off Str Piezişă, reached by Str Clinicilor about 300m from Piaţa Lucian Blaga), teams with lively open-air bars, including **La Solas** (Str Piezişă; ⌚ 10am-2am).

Getting There & Away

AIR

Tarom has at least three daily direct flights to Bucharest (one-way/return from 202/352 lei). Tickets can be bought at the airport (8km east of town, reached by bus 8) or at the **Tarom city office** (☎ 432 669; Piaţa Mihai Viteazul 11; ⌚ 8am-6pm Mon-Fri, 9am-1pm Sat). Budget carrier **Wizz Air** (www.wizzair.com) flies to London, Paris, Rome, Barcelona and more.

BUS

Daily bus service from **Autogara 2** (Autogara Beta; ☎ 455 249), 350m northwest of the train station (take the overpass), includes two buses to Braşov (37 lei), two to Bucharest (48 lei) and several to Budapest (70 lei). Note: there is no Autogara 1.

CAR

Cluj has some of the best car-hire rates in the country. **Pan Travel** (☎ 420 516; www.pantravel.ro; Str Grozavescu 13; ⏲ 9am-5pm Mon-Fri) and **Autonom** (☎ 590 588; www.autonom.ro; Str Victor Babes 10) offer Dacias and Matiz for 108 lei per day.

TRAIN

The **Agentia de Voiaj CFR** (☎ 432 001; Piaţa Mihai Viteazul 20; ⏲ 7am-7pm Mon-Fri) sells domestic and international train tickets in advance. Sample fares for *accelerat* trains include Braşov (44 lei, four hours), Bucharest (53 lei, 7½ hours), Budapest (110 lei, five hours) and Timişoara (44 lei, seven hours).

Note there's no left-luggage service at the train station.

CRIŞANA & BANAT

Until 1918, the areas of Crişana (north of the Mureş River) and Banat (to the south) were governed jointly with Vojvodina (Serbia) and Hungary's Great Plain. This legacy can still be appreciated in spirit and in the weathered Habsburg architecture in Oradea, Arad and Timişoara, the latter still brimming with pride after lighting the fuse that ignited the 1989 revolution.

Zigzag between urban refinement, mountain activities and hot-spring resorts, all within a few hours' drive.

TIMIŞOARA

☎ 0256 / pop 321,900

Tenacious Timişoara stunned the world – not to mention the Ceauşescus – as the birthplace of the 1989 revolution. Beaming residents refer to it as '*Primul Oraş Liber*' (First Free Town). A charming Mediterranean air pervades here, accentuated by regal Habsburg buildings and a thriving cultural and sports scene.

Orientation

Confusingly, Gara Timişoara-Nord (the northern train station) is west of the city centre. Walk east along B-dul Republicii to the Opera House and Piaţa Victoriei. Further north is Piaţa Libertăţii. Piaţa Unirii, the Old Town square, is two blocks further north. Timişoara's bus station is beside the Idsefin Market, three blocks from the train station.

Information

Farmado Pharmacy (Piaţa Victoriei 7; ⏲ 8am-9pm Mon-Fri, 9am-9pm Sat & Sun)

Info Centru Turistic (☎ 437 973; http://infocentru.onepoint.ro; Str Alba Iulia 2; ⏲ 9am-8pm Mon-Fri, 9am-5pm Sat) This new tourism office explodes with accommodation and train assistance, maps and Banat regional info.

Telephone office (Str N Lenau; ⏲ 9am-6pm Mon-Fri, 9am-1pm Sat) Has fax facilities and free internet points!

Volksbank (☎ 406 101; Str Piatra Craiului 2; ⏲ 9am-5.30pm)

Sights

Begging to be photographed with your widest lens is **Piaţa Victoriei**, a beautifully landscaped pedestrian mall lined with shops and cafes and the **Teatrul Naţional şi Opera Română** (National Theatre & Opera House; ☎ 201 284; Str Mărăşeşti 2) at its head (see p972).

Towering over the mall's southwestern end is the Romanian Orthodox **Metropolitan Cathedral** (1946). Next to the cathedral is **Central Park**, and just south of it the **Bega Canal** runs along tree-lined banks.

The 1989 revolution ignited on 15 December 1989 at the **Biserica Reformată Tőkés** (Tőkés Reformed Church; ☎ 492 992; Str Timotei Cipariu 1), where Father Lászlo Tőkés spoke out against the dictator.

Piaţa Libertăţii and the **Primăria Veche** (Old Town Hall), built in 1734, lie to the north. **Piaţa Unirii** is Timişoara's most picturesque square, featuring a baroque **Roman Catholic cathedral** (1754) and the **Serbian Orthodox cathedral** (1754).

Sleeping & Eating

Camping International (☎ 208 925; campinginternational@yahoo.com; Aleea Pădurea Verde 6; camp sites 20 lei, chalets with central heating s/d/q 92/126/220 lei) Nestled in the Green Wood forest on the opposite side of town from Timişoara-Nord train station. The main entrance to this excellent camping ground is on Calea Dorobanţilor. From the station catch trolleybus 11 to the end of the line, stopping 50m from the camping ground. The site has a restaurant.

Hotel Moara cu Noroc (☎ 214 203; Str Lirei 4; d 60 lei) Timişoara's only budget option. No frills in a noncentral, residential neighbourhood. Take trolleybus 14 (from centre about 10 minutes, from the train station about 20 minutes), alight at the first stop with a blue 'Melinda Impex steel' sign after passing two consecutive cemeteries on the left. Cross the street and

SOUTHERN BUCOVINA

The painted churches of Southern Bucovina are among the greatest artistic monuments of Europe – in 1993 they were collectively designated a World Heritage site by Unesco. Erected at a time when northern Moldavia was threatened by Turkish invaders, the Orthodox monasteries were surrounded by strong defensive walls. Biblical stories were portrayed on the church walls in colourful pictures possibly for mere aesthetics or so illiterate worshippers could better understand the stories, but more likely in reaction to encroaching Protestantism from Western Europe. The exteriors of many of the churches are covered with these magnificent 16th-century frescoes. Remarkably, most of the intense colours have been preserved despite five centuries of punishing weather.

Bucovina's monasteries are generally open 9am to 5pm or 6pm daily. The monasteries of **Voroneţ**, **Humor** and **Moldoviţa**, all accessible by bus and train, provide a representative sample of what Bucovina has to offer. The gateway to the painted churches is **Suceava**. **Gura Humorului**, a small logging town 37km west of Suceava, is an alternative base from which to visit some of the monasteries, but transport connections are weak.

Getting to Suceava, six trains go daily from Bucharest (71 lei, six hours), four from Cluj (42 lei, 6½ hours) and one overnight from Braşov (eight hours).

walk 100m down alley Str Lirei to the white and blue building. No breakfast.

Hotel Cina Banatul (☎ 490 130; B-dul Republicii 3-5; s/d 120/140 lei) Still the best-value pad in the centre. No breakfast.

Java Coffee House (☎ 432 495; Str Pacha 6; ⏲ 24hr) A dark, cosy coffee shop. Hot sandwiches (6 lei) available across the street at Java Snack House.

Entertainment

Movies are screened in their original language at **Cinema Timis** (☎ 491 290; Piaţa Victoriei 7; tickets 6 lei).

The **Teatrul Naţional şi Opera Română** (National Theatre & Opera House; ☎ 201 284; Str Mărăşeşti 2; tickets from 40 lei) is highly regarded. Buy tickets in its **Agenţia Teatrală** (☎ 499 908; ⏲ 10am-1pm & 5-7pm Tue-Sun).

Classical concerts are held most evenings at the **Filharmonia de Stat Banatul** (State Philharmonic Theatre; ☎ 492 521; B-dul CD Loga 2). Tickets can be bought at the box office inside the Filharmonia or from the Agenţia Teatrală.

Getting There & Away

Tarom (☎ 200 003; B-dul Revoluţiei 1989 3-5; ⏲ 8am-8pm Mon-Fri, 7am-1pm Sat) has four daily direct flights to Bucharest (starting at 212 lei) and several weekly international flights.

Timişoara is the hub of **Carpatair** (www.carpatair.ro), with direct service to nine key Romanian cities as well as a growing list of international destinations.

Maxitaxis run daily to Oradea and Arad from the **bus station** (Autogara; ☎ 493 471; B-dul Maniu Iuliu 54; ⏲ 6am-8pm Mon-Fri).

International buses leave from the east bus station, outside the east train station, where you'll find **Atlasib** (☎ 226 486) and **Eurolines** (☎ 288 132; timisoara.ag@eurolines.ro). Call **Murat** (☎ 0744-144 326, no English) for bus tickets to İstanbul.

All major train services depart from the **Gara Timişoara-Nord** (☎ 491 696; Str Gării 2). The **Agenţia de Voiaj CFR** (☎ 491 889; cnr Str Măcieşilor & Str Babeş; ⏲ 7am-8pm Mon-Fri, international tickets 9am-7pm) sells tickets as well.

Daily fast trains include five to Bucharest (82 lei), one to Cluj-Napoca (64 lei), five to Baile Herculane (38 lei), one to Baia Mare via Arad (12 lei), three to Budapest (95 lei) and one to Belgrade (64 lei).

ROMANIA DIRECTORY

ACCOMMODATION

Look out for homey *pensiune* (pensions), which cost about €25 to €35 (an extra €7 to €10 per person for full board), a little more in cities. The best online resource is **Rural Tourism in Romania** (www.ruraltourism.ro); otherwise contact **Antrec** (National Association of Rural, Ecological & Cultural Tourism; www.antrec.iiruc.ro).

Hostels usually run around €12 to €14 for a dorm bed; sometimes private rooms (with shared bathroom) are available for €20 to €30.

Hostels vary in quality, with Bucharest's at the top in terms of travel-savvy hang-outs. **Youth Hostels Romania** (www.hihostels-romania.ro) has information on HI hostels.

Prices for hotels have risen in recent years, but they tend to offer the most privacy and comfort. Some old stalwarts have been scrubbed up. Midrange hotels cost from €30 to €60, more so in Bucharest.

In-town camping is often in less-than-ideal locations, and conditions are sometimes quite shoddy. In most mountain areas there's a network of *căsuţe* (wooden huts) with restaurants and dormitories. Prices are much lower than those of hotels and no reservations are required.

Apă caldă (hot water) is finally ubiquitous, though air-conditioning is still rare in budget places.

ACTIVITIES

Most outdoor fun sticks to Romania's Carpathians, which stripe the country impressively. Emergency rescue is provided by **Salvamont** (☎ 0725-826 668; www.salvamont.org, in Romanian), a voluntary mountain rescue organisation with 21 stations countrywide.

Hiking is the top activity, and mountain biking is getting more popular. A great place to go for both is into the Bucegi Mountains from Sinaia (p963), where you can hire a bike and take it to the plateau atop the mountains by lift - from where hiking trails can be reached, too. Hiking trails in Romania are well marked, with a series of huts along trails. Guided hikes are offered by www.alpineguide.ro and www.greenmountainholidays.ro.

Clubul de Cicloturism Napoca (office@ccn.ro; Cluj-Napoca) can offer bike-hire advice. **Transylvania Adventure** (www.adventuretransylvania.com) offers eight-day trips from mid-May though mid-October for about €800.

Skiing and snowboarding are popular in winter. Sinaia (p963) has slopes, but most Braşov kids take day trips to Poiana Braşov, about 15km southwest. Hire costs about €10 to €12, five-trip lift tickets about €34.

CUSTOMS

Officially, you're allowed to import hard currency up to a maximum of €10,000. Valuable goods and foreign currency over €10,000 should be declared upon arrival. For foreigners, duty-free allowances are 4L of wine, 2L of spirits and 200 cigarettes. For more information check www.customs.ro.

EMBASSIES & CONSULATES

Unless stated otherwise, the following foreign embassies are in Bucharest.

Australia (Map p959; ☎ 021-316 7558; Str Buzeşti 14-18, 5th fl)
Canada (Map p959; ☎ 021-307 5000; bucst@dfait-maeci.gc.ca; Str Tuberozelor 1-3)
France (Map p959; ☎ 021-303 1000; www.ambafrance-ro.org; Str Biserica Amzei 13-15)
Germany Bucharest (Map p959; ☎ 021-202 9830; www.bukarest.diplo.de; Str Gheorghe Demetriade 6-8); Sibiu (☎ 0269-211 133; Str Lucian Blaga 15-17); Timişoara (☎ 0256-309 800; www.temeswar.diplo.de; Spl Vladimirescu 10, Timişoara)
Ireland (☎ 021-310 2131; www.embassyofireland.ro; Str Buzeşti 50-52)
Moldova Bucharest (Map p959; ☎ 021-230 0474; consulat.bucuresti@msa.md; Aleea Alexandru 40); Bucharest (Map p959; ☎ 021-410 9827; B-dul Eroilor 8)
UK (Map p959; ☎ 021-201 7200; www.ukinromania.fco.gov.uk; Str Jules Michelet 24)
USA Bucharest (Map p961; ☎ 021-200 3300; www.usembassy.ro; Str Tudor Arghezi 7-9); Bucharest (Map p961; ☎ 021-200 3300; Str Nicolae Filipescu 26)

FESTIVALS & EVENTS

A few favourite festivals are listed (also watch out for horse trades and shepherd cheese measurement celebrations):

Juni Pageant During April in Braşov.
Bucharest Carnival Held late May to early June in Bucharest.
Medieval Festival of the Arts During July in Sighişoara.
International Folk Music & Dance Festival of Ethnic Minorities in Europe During August in Cluj-Napoca.
Sâmbra Oilor During September in Bran.
Iaşi Days Held mid-October in Iaşi.
De la Colind la Stea During December in Braşov.

HOLIDAYS

New Year 1 & 2 January
Catholic & Orthodox Easter Mondays March/April
Labour Day 1 May
Romanian National Day 1 December
Christmas 25 & 26 December

MONEY

From January 2007, the old lei was taken out of circulation, and the new lei (abbreviated 'RON') – with four fewer zeroes – took over. If someone offers an old note (say a 500,000-lei note instead of a 50 RON note), don't take it. The new lei notes come in denominations of one, five, 10, 50, 100, 200 and 500 – try to avoid the 200s and 500s as no one outside of hotels will give change for them. Coins ('bani') come in one, five, 10, 20 and 50. People sometimes still quote prices in old lei, giving hapless travellers sticker-shock.

We've quoted most prices in this chapter in Romanian lei to make on-the-ground price references easier.

ATMs are everywhere, compatible with Cirrus, Plus, Visa, MasterCard and Eurocard. Some banks give cash advances on credit cards in your home currency.

Dodgy moneychangers are everywhere, subtly disguising a '9' as a '0', etc. Count your money carefully. You should change at banks whenever possible. Dollars and euros are easiest to exchange, though British pounds are widely accepted. You must show a passport to change money.

Cashing travellers cheques is becoming increasingly difficult. Credit cards won't get you anywhere in rural areas, but they are widely accepted in larger department stores, hotels and most restaurants in cities and towns.

POST

A postcard or letter under 20g to Europe from Romania costs 2.70 lei and takes seven to 10 days. The postal system is reliable, if slow.

TELEPHONE

As of 2008, you must use area codes, provided under our destination headings, when dialling any landline in Romania, even if you're just down the road. This goes for nonemergency three- and four-digit short numbers as well. Emergency numbers are still only three digits.

Cellphone numbers are 10 digits, beginning with 07.

Phonecards (10 lei) can be purchased at newsstands and used in phone booths for domestic or international calls.

European cellphones with roaming work in Romania; otherwise you can get a Romania number from Orange or Vodaphone. SIM cards cost about 18 lei including credit; calls are about 0.35 to 0.50 lei per minute.

Dial ☎ 971 for Romania's international operator.

VISAS

Your passport's validity must extend to at least six months beyond the date you enter the country in order to obtain a visa.

Citizens of USA, Canada, Australia, New Zealand, Japan and many other countries may travel visa-free for 90 days. EU citizens, obviously, may stay indefinitely. Check for the latest details at the **Ministry of Foreign Affairs** (www.mae.ro) before departure.

Romania issues two types of visas to tourists: transit or single-entry. Transit visas (for those from countries other than the ones mentioned above) are for stays of no longer than three days, and cannot be bought at the border.

Make sure you check your visa requirements for Serbia and Montenegro, Hungary, Bulgaria and Ukraine if you plan to cross those borders. If you are taking the Bucharest–St Petersburg train, you need Ukrainian and Belarusian transit visas on top of the Russian visa.

Russia Россия

HIGHLIGHTS

- **The Hermitage** The imperial splendour of St Petersburg's Winter Palace and the incredible art collection in the Hermitage are unmissable (p987)
- **The Kremlin and Red Square** The spires of the Kremlin (p980), Lenin's embalmed body and fabulous St Basil's Cathedral (p980) are the ultimate Russian experience
- **A Trip to the Theatre** Experience a sophisticated evening's entertainment at the world famous Bolshoi (p986) or Mariinsky Theatres and (p991)
- **Kurshskaya Kosa** This World Heritage site, a slender spit of sand and pine forests shared between Russia and Lithuania, boasts some of Europe's highest dunes (p995)

FAST FACTS

- **Area** 16,995,800 sq km
- **Budget** US$80 per day
- **Capital** Moscow
- **Country code** ☎ 7
- **Famous for** vodka, communism, oil, billionaires
- **Language** Russian
- **Money** rouble (R); A$1 = R24; C$1 = R27; €1 = R43; ¥100 = R34; NZ$1 = R19; UK£1 = R49; US$1 = R32;
- **Phrases** *privyet* (hi), *do svidaniya* (goodbye), *spasiba* (thanks), *izvinitye* (excuse me), *mozhno yesho stakanchik?* (may I have another little glassful?)

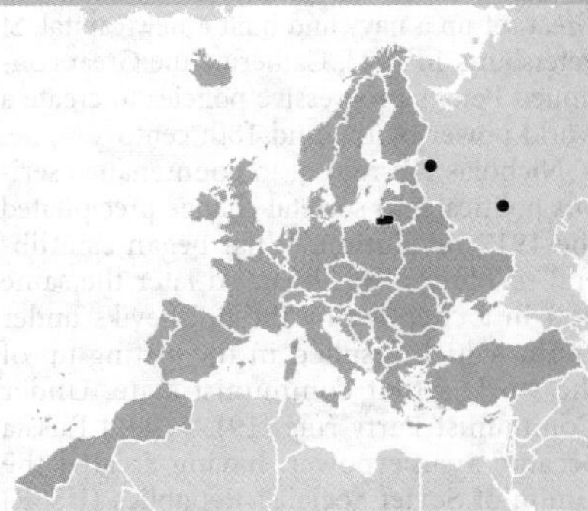

- **Population** 141.4 million
- **Visas** required by all – begin preparing well in advance of your trip! For more details, see p997

TRAVEL HINTS

Don't lose your immigration card. Keep a photocopy of your visa and passport on you at all times.

ROAMING RUSSIA

Devote a couple of days to dynamic Moscow, then head north to St Petersburg for a taste of tsarist splendour.

Like a musclebound henchman guarding the door to an exclusive club, Russia casts a threatening yet tantalising shadow over its European neighbours. Stay in the EU if you want things easy and hassle-free, but venture east for one of the last truly adventurous and unpredictable destinations on the continent. Moscow's long history, amazing Kremlin, arresting architecture and frenzied pace of development makes it a must on any trip to Eastern Europe. Awash with the financial proceeds of Russia's great mineral wealth, Moscow not only offers an amazing restaurant, bar and shopping scene but is increasingly a place of exciting artistic and creative experimentation. It's a similar deal in St Petersburg, with its colourful, crumbling Italianate mansions, beautifully wending canals and mind-blowing cultural treasures. For something totally different, drop into friendly little Kaliningrad, up until 1945 the German Kingdom of Prussia. This verdant exclave of Russia wedged between Poland and Lithuania, and probably the least visited area in this book.

HISTORY

Russia has its cultural origins in Kyivan Rus, the kingdom located in what is today Ukraine and Belarus. From here the Slavs expanded into modern European Russia. It was during the Romanov dynasty (1613–1917) that Russia began to develop into the vast nation it is today: territorial expansion from the 17th to 19th centuries saw the country gobble up Siberia, the Arctic, the Russian Far East, Central Asia and the Caucasus. Peter the Great set up a navy and built a new capital, St Petersburg, in 1703. Catherine the Great continued Peter's progressive policies to create a world power by the mid-18th century.

Nicholas II's refusal to countenance serious political and societal change precipitated the 1917 revolution. What began as a liberal revolution was hijacked later the same year in a coup led by the Bolsheviks under Lenin, which resulted in the setting up of the world's first communist state. Under Communist Party rule (1917–1991) Russia became a superpower, having created the Union of Soviet Socialist Republics (USSR) and absorbing some 14 neighbouring states between 1922 and 1945. The terror of Stalin, the reforms of Khrushchev and the stagnation during the Brezhnev era finally led to Mikhail Gorbachev's period of reform known as *perestroika* in 1985. Within six years the USSR had collapsed alongside communism and reformer Boris Yeltsin led Russia into a new world of cutthroat capitalism.

On New Year's Eve 1999, Yeltsin resigned in favour of Vladimir Putin, a steely-faced ex-KGB officer and then prime minister. Putin's policy of steering a careful course between reform and centralisation (plus an economy booming off the back of oil and gas exports) made him popular. But his tightening of control over the media and political opponents, as well as Russia's brutal clampdown on the independence movement in Chechnya, caused concern among liberals around the world.

Having served his two-term limit as president, Putin was succeeded in March 2008 by heir apparent Dmitry Medvedev. Non-Russian observers worried about how 'democratic' this practically pre-ordained election really was, and fretted even more in August of the same year when Russia came to blows with Georgia over the breakaway regions of Abkhazia and South Ossetia. Medvedev presides over a strong economy growing at an average 7% per year and a nation awash with US$ billionaires that has become the world's number-one luxury-goods market – Lenin is surely spinning in his mausoleum!

THE CULTURE

While the vast majority of people you meet will describe themselves as Russian, ethnic homogeneity is far from that simple. Over the centuries Russia has absorbed people from a huge number of nationalities including the Mongols, the Tatars, Siberian peoples, Ukrainians, Jews and Caucasians. Soviet rulers did their best to mould a common culture but differences in ways of life do exist.

At the individual level, Russians have a reputation for being dour, depressed and unfriendly. In fact, most Russians are anything but, yet find constant smiling indicative of idiocy, and ridicule pointless displays of happiness commonly seen in Western culture. And even though some Russians can be unfriendly – even downright rude – when you first meet them, their warmth as soon as the ice is broken is quite astounding. Just keep working at it.

ARTS

Russian literature is one of the world's greatest: the nineteenth century poet Alexander Pushkin is the national bard, while other greats include Mikhail Lermontov, Leo Tolstoy, Anton Chekhov and Fyodor Dostoyevsky. Russia's musical heritage is equally illustrious: Tchaikovsky, Prokofiev and Shostakovich have all had a huge influence on the development of modern classical music.

ENVIRONMENT

While Russia encompasses almost every conceivable type of landscape, European Russia is characterised by flat fields and forests. You can take the train from one city to the other and barely pass a hill or a valley. However, the Kaliningrad region sports half of the sandy Kurshskaya Kosa (Curonian Spit), the

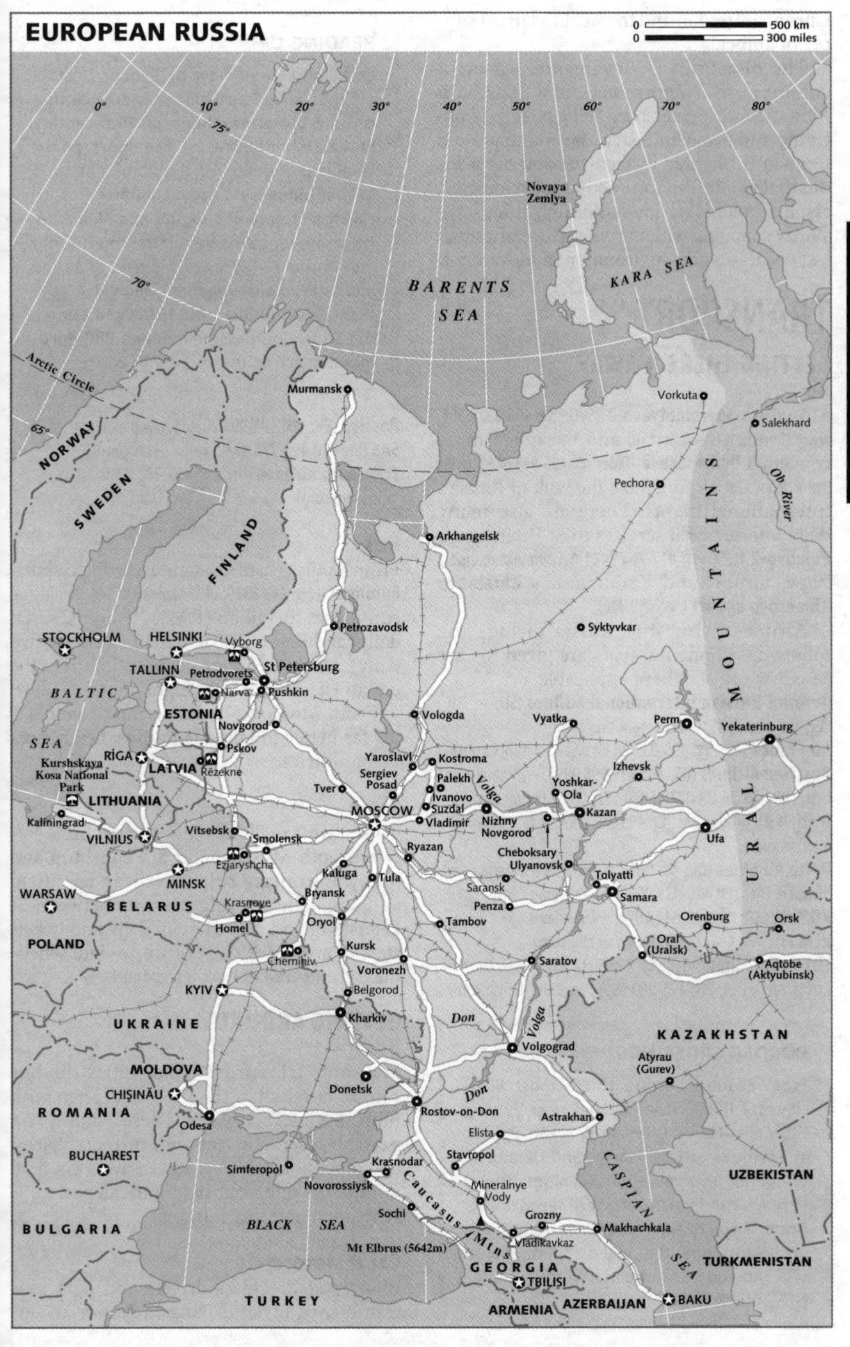
EUROPEAN RUSSIA
0 500 km
0 300 miles
BARENTS SEA
KARA SEA
Novaya Zemlya
Arctic Circle
NORWAY
SWEDEN
FINLAND
Murmansk
Vorkuta
Salekhard
Pechora
Arkhangelsk
Ob River
URAL MOUNTAINS
Petrozavodsk
Syktyvkar
STOCKHOLM
HELSINKI
Vyborg
St Petersburg
TALLINN
Petrodvorets
Narva
Pushkin
BALTIC SEA
ESTONIA
Novgorod
Vologda
Vyatka
Perm
Yekaterinburg
RIGA
Pskov
LATVIA
Rēzekne
Kurshskaya Kosa National Park
LITHUANIA
Kaliningrad
VILNIUS
Yaroslavl
Kostroma
Sergiev Posad
Palekh
Ivanovo
Suzdal
Vladimir
Tver
MOSCOW
Volga
Nizhny Novgorod
Yoshkar-Ola
Izhevsk
Kazan
Ufa
Vitsebsk
Smolensk
Ezjaryshcha
MINSK
Ryazan
Kaluga
Tula
Cheboksary
Ulyanovsk
Tolyatti
Samara
Saransk
Penza
WARSAW
BELARUS
Bryansk
Krasnoye
Homel
Oryol
Tambov
POLAND
Orenburg
Orsk
Oral (Uralsk)
Aqtöbe (Aktyubinsk)
Chernihiv
Kursk
Voronezh
Saratov
KYIV
Belgorod
Kharkiv
Don
UKRAINE
KAZAKHSTAN
Volgograd
MOLDOVA
Atyrau (Gurev)
Donetsk
CHIŞINĂU
Rostov-on-Don
ROMANIA
Odesa
Astrakhan
Elista
BUCHAREST
Simferopol
Krasnodar
Stavropol
Novorossiysk
Mineralnye Vody
CASPIAN SEA
UZBEKISTAN
Sochi
Caucasus Mtns
Grozny
Makhachkala
BULGARIA
BLACK SEA
Vladikavkaz
Mt Elbrus (5642m)
GEORGIA
TURKMENISTAN
TBILISI
TURKEY
ARMENIA
AZERBAIJAN
BAKU
0° 10° 20° 30° 40° 50° 60° 70° 80°
75° 70° 65°

Curonian Lagoon and the world's largest supply of amber.

The disastrous environmental legacy of communism is enormous. As well as both Moscow and St Petersburg being polluted from traffic and heavy industry, the countryside is frequently blighted by factories and other industrial plants. Environmental consciousness remains relatively low, although things are slowly changing with the emergence of a small but vocal Russian environmental movement.

TRANSPORT

GETTING THERE & AWAY

Air

Moscow's **Sheremetyevo-2** (SVO; ☎ 495-232 6565; www.sheremetyevo-airport.ru) and the much more congenial **Domodedovo** (DME; ☎ 495-933 6666; www.domodedovo.ru) airports host the bulk of Russia's international flights. There are also many daily international services to St Petersburg's **Pulkovo-2** (LED; ☎ 812-704 3444; www.pulkovoairport.ru/eng) airport and Kaliningrad's **Khrabrovo Khrabrovo airport** (☎ 459 426).

Airlines flying into Russia include the following. Phone numbers are given for the Moscow office, where applicable.

Aeroflot Russian International Airlines (SU; ☎ 495-223 5555; www.aeroflot.ru/eng)
Air France (AF; ☎ 495-937 3839; www.airfrance.com)
Austrian Airlines (OS; ☎ 495-995 0995; www.aua.com)
bmi (BD; ☎ in UK 0870 6070 555; www.flybmi.com)
British Airways (BA; ☎ 495-363 2525; www.britishairways.com)
Delta Air Lines (DL; ☎ 800-700 0990; www.delta.com)
Finnair (AY; ☎ 495-933 0056; www.finnair.com)
KD Avia (KD; ☎ 495-641 1074; www.kdavia.eu)
KLM (KL; ☎ 495-258 3600; www.klm.com)
LOT Polish Airlines (LO; ☎ 800-5082 5082; www.lot.com)
Lufthansa (LH; ☎ 495-980 9999; www.lufthansa.com)
Rossiya (FV; ☎ 495-995 2025; www.pulkovo.ru/en/)
SAS (SK; ☎ 495-775 4747; www.flysas.com)
Transaero Airlines (UN; ☎ 495-788 8080; www.transaero.com)

BORDER CROSSINGS

From Eastern Europe you're most likely to enter Russia from Finland near Vyborg, Estonia at Narva, Latvia at Rēzekne, Belarus at Krasnoye or Ezjaryshcha, and Ukraine at Chernihiv. You can enter Kaliningrad from Lithuania and Poland at any of seven border posts. If you're travelling to or from Russia via Belarus, note that you do need a transit visa and you must obtain it in advance; see p111 for details.

READING UP

Crime and Punishment by Fyodor Dostoyevsky is an existentialist masterpiece that is superbly atmospheric of 19th-century St Petersburg. One of the most popular Russian writers of the 20th century is Mikhail Bulgakov – read his fantastical satirical masterpiece *The Master and Margarita*. For a revealing snapshot of the country, dip into *Russia: A Journey to the Heart of a Land and its People* by Jonathan Dimbleby – the hefty side product of a 16,000km journey the British journalist made for a BBC documentary across the country in 2007.

Bus

From Baltiiskaya metro station in St Petersburg, **Eurolines** (☎ 449 8370; ul Shkapina 10; Ⓜ Baltiiskaya) runs buses to Tallinn (R900, 7½ hours, seven daily) and Rīga (R700 to R1050, 11 hours, two daily). There are also regular services from the city to Helsinki (R1400, eight hours).

From Moscow – considering distances – it's far better to take the train to neighbouring countries.

Train

There are excellent daily connections between both Moscow and St Petersburg and many European cities, even as far afield as Paris. The overnight trains between St Petersburg and Moscow run daily and tickets start at around R950. For up-to-date schedules, see **Poezda.net** (www.poezda.net).

GETTING AROUND

Bus

For short trips from major cities the bus can be faster than the train and often with more frequent services. There's almost no need to reserve a seat and, in most places, it's impossible anyway. Just arrive a good 30 minutes to one hour before the departure is scheduled and buy a ticket.

Car & Motorcycle

Poor roads, reckless drivers and rapacious traffic cops make driving in Russia an unappetising prospect. Thankfully, public transport is very good. However, if you do drive in Russia, you must have a valid International Driving Permit, your passport and insurance documentation for your vehicle.

Train

Long-distance services need to be booked at least 24 hours in advance. *Platskartny* (3rd class) compartments, while cheaper, have open bunk accommodation so are not ideal for those who value privacy. *Kupeyny* (coupé; 2nd class) carriages contain four fold-down beds per compartment. Prices between Moscow and St Petersburg in 2nd class begin at R2060.

You'll need to present your passport (or a photocopy) to buy tickets. At stations queues can be very long and move with interminable slowness. Far preferable is to use one of the generally queue-free service centres that exist in all big train stations, or a travel agency – at either you'll typically pay a surcharge of around R200 per ticket. Hostels can also usually book tickets for you and have them delivered for a small fee.

CONNECTIONS

Bordering Belarus, Estonia, Latvia, Lithuania, Poland and Ukraine, Russia has excellent train and bus connections with the rest of Eastern Europe. With all your various visas in order, a wide variety of itineraries is possible. Interesting routes linking Kaliningrad (p995) with St Petersburg will take you through the Baltic countries, while trains from Kaliningrad to Moscow head first to Minsk in Belarus and then on to the Russian capital via Smolensk. Trains from Kharkiv in Ukraine transit via Kursk, Oryol and Tula to terminate in Moscow.

MOSCOW МОСКВА

pop 10 million

Intimidating in its scale, but also exciting and unforgettable, Moscow is many things to many people, a place that inspires extreme passion or loathing. History, power and wild capitalism hang in the air, alongside an explosion of creative energy throwing up edgy art galleries and a dynamic restaurant, bar and nightlife scene with something for everyone. Tchaikovsky and Chekhov are well represented at the city's theatres, but you can also see world premiers by up-and-coming composers and choreographers. Although much of its architectural heritage has been destroyed, the sturdy stone walls of the Kremlin continue to occupy the founding site of Moscow, and remains of the Soviet state are scattered all around the city.

EMERGENCY NUMBERS

- Ambulance ☎ 03
- Fire ☎ 01
- Police ☎ 02

ORIENTATION

The medieval centre of the city, the Kremlin, is a triangle on the northern bank of the Moscow River. The modern city centre radiates around it – the main streets being Tverskaya ul and ul Novy Arbat. The eight-lane highway known as the 'garden ring' encloses Moscow's central district.

INFORMATION

American Medical Centre (☎ 495-933 7700; www.amcenter.ru; Grokholsky per 1; Ⓜ Prospekt Mira) Offers 24-hour emergency service, consultations and a full range of medical specialists, including paediatricians and dentists. Also has an on-site pharmacy with English-speaking staff.

Cafemax Tverskoy (☎ 495-741 7571; Novoslobodskaya ul 3; per hr R120; 🕑 24hr; Ⓜ Novoslobodskaya); Zamoskvorechie (☎ 495-950 6050; Pyatnitskaya ul 25; per hr R50-90; 🕑 24hr; Ⓜ Novokuznetskaya) Discounts available for late-night and early-morning hours.

Central telegraph (Tverskaya ul 7; 🕑 post 8am-10pm, telephone 24hr; Ⓜ Okhotny Ryad) This convenient office offers telephone, fax and internet services.

Maria Travel Agency (☎ 495-725 5746; ul Maroseyka 13; Ⓜ Kitay-Gorod) Offers visa support, apartment rental and some local tours, including the Golden Ring.

Moscow City Tourist Information Centre (☎ 495-232 5657; www.moscow-city.ru; ul Ilynka 4; 🕑 9am-6pm Mon-Fri; Ⓜ Kitay-Gorod)

Time Online Komsomolskaya (☎ 495-266 8351; Komsomolskaya pl 3; per hr R70-100; 🕑 24hr; Ⓜ Komsomolskaya); Okhotny Ryad (☎ 495-988 6426; per hr R70-100; 🕑 24hr; Ⓜ Okhotny Ryad) Offers copy and photo services, as well as over 100 zippy computers or free wi-fi access.

RUSSIA FOR FREE

Russia's booming economy has sent prices soaring but some of the best things to do here cost nothing, or very little:

- Marching across Moscow's **Red Square** and paying your respects to Lenin (below)
- Riding Moscow's **metro** – for R19 you could spend all day checking out magnificent stations
- Window-shopping and architecture-spotting along St Petersburg's **Nevsky Prospekt** (p987)
- Communing with nature in the forests and on the pristine beaches of the **Kurshskaya Kosa National Park** (p995)

Unifest Travel (☎ 495-234 6555; www.unifest.ru; Komsomolsky pr 13; Ⓜ Park Kultury) On-the-ball travel company offering rail and air tickets, visa support, and trans-Siberian and Central Asian packages. It's south of the centre.

SIGHTS

Red Square

Entering massively impressive Red Sq (or Krasnaya pl) through the **Resurrection Gate** (Voskresenskiye Vorota), you'll emerge with a superb view of the magnificently flamboyant **St Basil's Cathedral** (Sobor Vasilia Blazhennogo; ☎ 495-698 3304; adult/student R100/50; ⏲ 11am-5pm Wed-Mon; Ⓜ Ploshchad Revolyutsii) on the far side. This ultimate symbol of Russia was created between 1555 and 1561 (replacing an existing church on the site) to celebrate the capture of Kazan by Ivan the Terrible. Built over the grave of the barefoot holy fool Vasily (Basil) the Blessed, who predicted Ivan's damnation, its design is the culmination of a wholly Russian style that had been developed through the building of wooden churches and it's definitely worth going inside to see the stark medieval wall paintings.

At the square's northwestern corner is **Lenin's Tomb** (☎ 495-623 5527; admission free; ⏲ 10am-1pm Tue-Thu, Sat & Sun; Ⓜ Ploshchad Revolyutsii). Visit it while you can, since the former leader may eventually end up beside his mum in St Petersburg. For now, the embalmed leader remains as he has been since 1924 (apart from a retreat to Siberia during WWII). Before joining the queue, drop your camera at the left-luggage office in the State History Museum (see following), as you will not be allowed to take it with you. After trooping past the embalmed, oddly waxy figure, emerge from his red and black stone tomb and inspect where Stalin, Brezhnev and many of communism's other heavy hitters are buried along the Kremlin wall.

The **State History Museum** (☎ 495-692 3731; www.shm.ru; adult/student R150/60, audio guide R110; ⏲ 10am-5pm Wed-Sat & Mon, 11am-7pm Sun; Ⓜ Ploshchad Revolyutsii) has an enormous collection covering the whole Russian empire from the Stone Age on. The building, dating from the late 19th century, is itself an attraction – each room is in the style of a different period or region. A joint ticket (adult/student R230/115) allowing access to the State History Museum and St Basil's Cathedral is available at either spot.

Finally, drop into **GUM** (☎ 495-788 4343; www.gum.ru; Krasnaya pl 3; ⏲ 10am-10pm; Ⓜ Ploshchad Revolyutsii) to see the showpiece Soviet shopping centre turned designer mall for the new rich, with its stunning glass roof and centrepiece fountains.

The Kremlin

The apex of Russian political power and once the centre of the Orthodox Church, the **Kremlin** (☎ 495-202 3776; www.kremlin.museum.ru; adult/student R300/50, audio guide R200; ⏲ 9.30am-4pm Fri-Wed; Ⓜ Aleksandrovsky Sad) is not only the kernel of Moscow but of the whole country. It's from here that autocratic tsars, communist dictators and democratic presidents have done their best – and worst – for Russia.

Occupying a roughly triangular plot of land covering Borovitsky Hill on the north bank of the Moscow River, the Kremlin is enclosed by high walls 2.25km long, with Red Sq outside

GETTING INTO TOWN

All airports are accessible by a convenient **Aeroexpress train** (☎ 8-800-700 3377; www.aero-express.ru); services leave from different stations depending on the airport they serve. If you wish to take a taxi, it is highly recommended to book in advance (see p986) to take advantage of fixed rates offered by most companies (usually R1000 to R1500 to/from any airport). All of Moscow's many train stations are in the city centre and have their own metro stations with direct access from the concourse.

the east wall. The best views of the complex are from Sofiyskaya nab across the river.

Before entering the Kremlin, deposit bags at the **left-luggage office** (per bag R60; 9am-6.30pm Fri-Wed), beneath the Kutafya Tower near the main ticket office. The main ticket office is in the Alexandrovsky Garden, just off Manezhnaya pl. The ticket to the 'Architectural Ensemble of Cathedral Sq' covers entry to all five church-museums, as well as Patriarch's Palace and exhibits in the Ivan the Great Bell Tower. It does not include the Armoury or the Diamond Fund Exhibition. You can and should buy tickets for the Armoury here.

Photography is not permitted inside the Armoury or any of the buildings on Sobornaya pl (Cathedral Sq). Visitors wearing shorts will be refused entry.

SOUTHWEST BUILDINGS

From the Kutafya Tower, which forms the main visitors' entrance, walk up the ramp and pass through the Kremlin walls beneath the **Trinity Gate Tower** (Troitskaya Bashnya). The lane to the right (south) passes the 17th-century **Poteshny Palace** (Poteshny Dvorets), where Stalin lived. The horribly out of place glass and concrete **State Kremlin Palace** (Kremlyovksy Dvorets Syezdov) houses a concert and ballet auditorium, where many Western pop stars play when they are in Moscow.

ARMOURY & DIAMOND FUND

In the Kremlin's southwestern corner is the **Armoury** (adult/student R350/70, audio guide R200; 10am, noon, 2.30pm, 4.30pm), a numbingly opulent collection of treasures accumulated over time by the Russian State and Church. Tickets specify entry times. Highlights include Fabergé eggs and cartloads of royal regalia.

If the Armoury doesn't sate your diamond lust, there are more in the separate **Diamond Fund Exhibition** (Vystavka Almaznogo Fonda; ☎ 495-629 2036; admission R500; 10am-1pm & 2-5pm Fri-Wed; M Aleksandrovsky Sad), in the same building. The lavish collection includes the largest sapphire in the world.

SOBORNAYA PLOSHCHAD

On the northern side of Sobornaya pl, with five golden helmet domes and four semicircular gables facing the square, is the **Assumption Cathedral** (Uspensky Sobor), built between 1475 and 1479. As the focal church of pre-revolutionary Russia, it's the burial place of most heads of the Russian Orthodox Church from the 1320s to 1700.

The delicate little single-domed church beside the west door of the Assumption Cathedral is the **Church of the Deposition of the Robe** (Tserkov Rizopolozheniya), built between 1484 and 1486 by masons from Pskov.

With its two golden domes rising above the eastern side of Sobornaya pl, the 16th-century **Ivan the Great Bell Tower** (Kolokolnya Ivana Velikogo) is the Kremlin's tallest structure. Beside the bell tower stands the **Tsar Bell**, a 202-tonne monster that cracked before it ever rang. North of the bell tower is the mammoth **Tsar Cannon**, cast in 1586, but never shot.

The 1508 **Archangel Cathedral** (Arkhangelsky Sobor), at the square's southeastern corner, was for centuries the coronation, wedding and burial church of tsars. The tombs of all of Russia's rulers from the 1320s to the 1690s are here bar one (Boris Godunov, who was buried at Sergiev Posad).

Finally, the **Annunciation Cathedral** (Blagoveshchensky Sobor), at the southwest corner of Sobornaya pl and dating from 1489, contains the celebrated icons of master-painter Theophanes the Greek. He probably painted the six icons at the right-hand end of the diesis row, the biggest of the six tiers of the iconostasis. *Archangel Michael* (the third icon from the left on the diesis row) and the adjacent *St Peter* are ascribed to Russian master Andrei Rublev.

Pushkin Museum of Fine Arts

Moscow's premier foreign-art museum is the **Pushkin Museum of Fine Arts** (☎ 495-203 7998; www.museum.ru/gmii; ul Volkhonka 12; adult/student R300/150, audio tour R200; 10am-6pm Tue-Sun; M Kropotkinskaya), showing off a broad selection of European works, mostly appropriated from private collections after the revolution. The collection includes Dutch and Flemish masterpieces from the 17th century, several Rembrandt portraits, as well as the ancient and impressive Treasures of Troy. The Pushkin's amazing collection of Impressionist and post-Impressionist paintings is housed next door at the new **Gallery of European & American Art of the 19th & 20th Centuries** (☎ 495-203 1546; ul Volkhonka 14; adult/student R300/150; 10am-6pm Tue-Sun, to 8pm Thu; M Kropotkinskaya).

Cathedral of Christ the Saviour

Dominating the skyline along the Moscow River, the gargantuan **Cathedral of Christ the**

CENTRAL MOSCOW

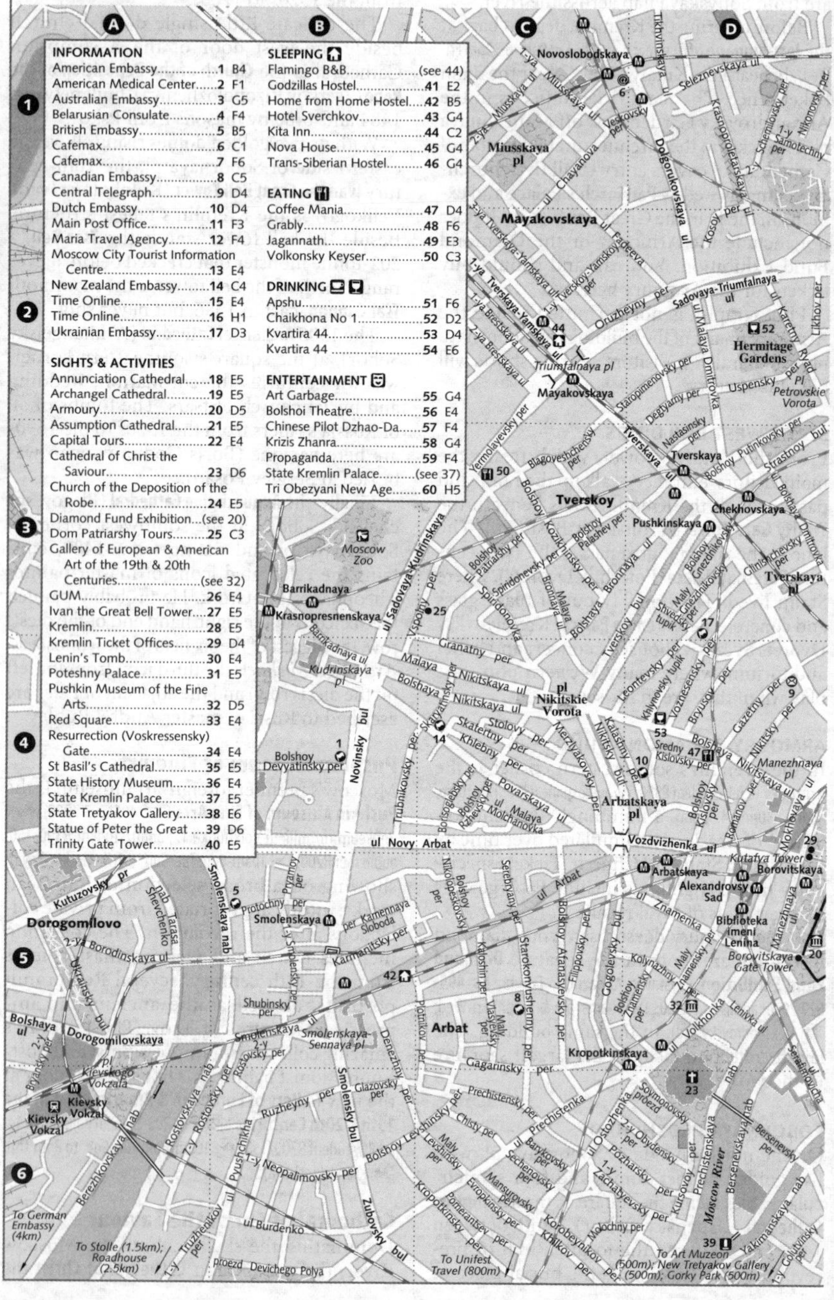

INFORMATION

- American Embassy......1 B4
- American Medical Center......2 F1
- Australian Embassy......3 G5
- Belarusian Consulate......4 F4
- British Embassy......5 B5
- Cafemax......6 C1
- Cafemax......7 F6
- Canadian Embassy......8 C5
- Central Telegraph......9 D4
- Dutch Embassy......10 D4
- Main Post Office......11 F3
- Maria Travel Agency......12 F4
- Moscow City Tourist Information Centre......13 E4
- New Zealand Embassy......14 C4
- Time Online......15 E4
- Time Online......16 H1
- Ukrainian Embassy......17 D3

SIGHTS & ACTIVITIES

- Annunciation Cathedral......18 E5
- Archangel Cathedral......19 E5
- Armoury......20 D5
- Assumption Cathedral......21 E5
- Capital Tours......22 E4
- Cathedral of Christ the Saviour......23 D6
- Church of the Deposition of the Robe......24 E5
- Diamond Fund Exhibition......(see 20)
- Dom Patriarshy Tours......25 C3
- Gallery of European & American Art of the 19th & 20th Centuries......(see 32)
- GUM......26 E4
- Ivan the Great Bell Tower......27 E5
- Kremlin......28 E5
- Kremlin Ticket Offices......29 D4
- Lenin's Tomb......30 E4
- Poteshny Palace......31 E5
- Pushkin Museum of the Fine Arts......32 D5
- Red Square......33 E4
- Resurrection (Voskressensky) Gate......34 E4
- St Basil's Cathedral......35 E5
- State History Museum......36 E4
- State Kremlin Palace......37 E5
- State Tretyakov Gallery......38 E6
- Statue of Peter the Great......39 D6
- Trinity Gate Tower......40 E5

SLEEPING

- Flamingo B&B......(see 44)
- Godzillas Hostel......41 E2
- Home from Home Hostel......42 B5
- Hotel Sverchkov......43 G4
- Kita Inn......44 C2
- Nova House......45 G4
- Trans-Siberian Hostel......46 G4

EATING

- Coffee Mania......47 D4
- Grably......48 F6
- Jagannath......49 E3
- Volkonsky Keyser......50 C3

DRINKING

- Apshu......51 F6
- Chaikhona No 1......52 D2
- Kvartira 44......53 D4
- Kvartira 44......54 E6

ENTERTAINMENT

- Art Garbage......55 G4
- Bolshoi Theatre......56 E4
- Chinese Pilot Dzhao-Da......57 F4
- Krizis Zhanra......58 G4
- Propaganda......59 F4
- State Kremlin Palace......(see 37)
- Tri Obezyani New Age......60 H5

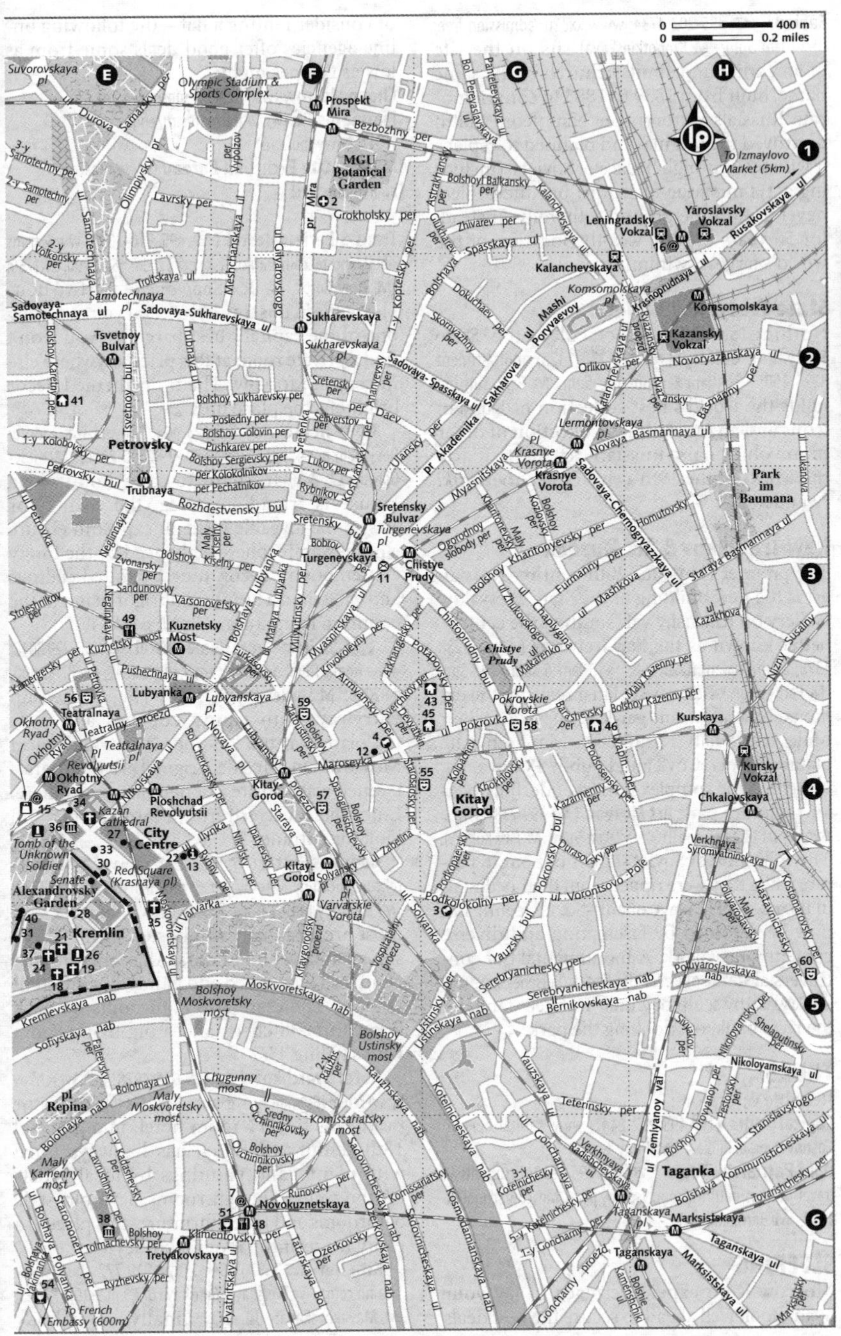
0 400 m
0 0.2 miles
To Izmaylovo Market (5km)
Olympic Stadium & Sports Complex
Prospekt Mira
MGU Botanical Garden
Leningradsky Vokzal
Yaroslavsky Vokzal
Kalanchevskaya
Komsomolskaya
Kazansky Vokzal
Sukharevskaya
Tsvetnoy Bulvar
Petrovsky
Trubnaya
Sretensky Bulvar
Turgenevskaya
Chistye Prudy
Krasnye Vorota
Lermontovskaya
Park im Baumana
Kuznetsky Most
Lubyanka
Teatralnaya
Okhotny Ryad
Ploshchad Revolyutsii
Kitay-Gorod
Kitay Gorod
City Centre
Kazan Cathedral
Tomb of the Unknown Soldier
Red Square (Krasnaya pl)
Senate
Alexandrovsky Garden
Kremlin
Chistye Prudy
Kurskaya
Kursky Vokzal
Chkalovskaya
Taganka
Marksistskaya
Taganskaya
Novokuznetskaya
Tretyakovskaya
pl Repina
To French Embassy (600m)

Book your stay at lonelyplanet.com/hotels

Saviour (☎ 495-202 4734; www.xxc.ru; admission free; ⏲ 10am-5pm; Ⓜ Kropotkinskaya) sits on the site of an earlier and similar church of the same name, built from 1839 to 1883 to commemorate Russia's victory over Napoleon. Stalin destroyed the original and planned to replace it with a 315m-high 'Palace of Soviets' (including a 100m statue of Lenin) but the project never got off the ground – literally. Instead, for 50 years the site was the location of the world's largest swimming pool.

State Tretyakov Gallery

Nothing short of spectacular, the **State Tretyakov Gallery** (☎ 499-238 1378; adult/student R225/150; ⏲ 10am-6.30pm Tue-Sun; Ⓜ Park Kultury) holds the world's best collection of Russian icons and an outstanding collection of other prerevolutionary Russian art, particularly the works of the 19th-century *peredvizhniki* (wanderers).

New Tretyakov & Art Muzeon

The premier venue for 20th-century Russian art is the new building of the State Tretyakov Gallery on Krymsky val (south of the centre), better known as the **New Tretyakov** (☎ 499-238 1378; adult/student R225/150; ⏲ 10am-6.30pm Tue-Sun; Ⓜ Park Kultury). Besides socialist realism, the exhibits showcase avant-garde artists like Kasimir Malevich, Vasily Kandinsky, Marc Chagall, Natalia Goncharova and Lyubov Popova.

Behind the complex is the wonderful, open-air sculpture park **Art Muzeon** (☎ 499-238 3396; ul Krymsky val 10; admission R100; ⏲ 9am-9pm; Ⓜ Park Kultury). The collection of Soviet statues put out to pasture when they were ripped from their pedestals in the post-1991 wave of anti-Soviet feeling has now been joined by fascinating and diverse contemporary work. A monumental but controversial **statue of Peter the Great** (Bersenevskaya nab; Ⓜ Polyanka) by sculptor Zurab Tsereteli stands on the river bank, overlooking the park.

TOURS

Reliable operators:

Capital Tours (☎ 495-232 2442; www.capitaltours.ru; Gostiny Dvor, ul Ilinka 4; Ⓜ Kitay-Gorod)

Dom Patriarshy Tours (☎ 495-795 0927; http://russiatravel-pdtours.netfirms.com; Vspolny per 6, Moscow school No 1239; Ⓜ Barrikadnaya).

SLEEPING

Moscow is an expensive place to lay your head. Book well ahead to secure the best deals or consider renting a flat – the following online agencies offer good deals some from as low as €62 per night:

Cheap Moscow (www.cheap-moscow.com)

Flatmates.Ru (www.flatmates.ru/eng)

HOFA (www.hofa.ru)

Moscow City Excursion Bureau (www.moscowapartments.net)

Trans-Siberian Hostel (☎ 495-916 2030; www.transsiberianhostel.com; Barashevsky per 12; dm R630-700, d R1750; Ⓜ Kitay-Gorod; 💻 ☒) Snag one of the two double rooms in this tiny hostel, and you're getting one of the capital's best bargains: you won't find a private room at this price anywhere else in central Moscow. The train-themed decor brightens the place up.

Nova House (☎ 495-623 4659; novahostel@nm.ru; Devyatkin per 4, apt 6; dm R680, d R2600-2800; Ⓜ Kitay-Gorod; 💻 ☒) It's hard to say who at Nova House is friendlier: Oleg, the owner, or Vasya, the loveable resident cat. Both ensure a homey atmosphere, enhanced by the funky contemporary decor, mural-painted ceilings and walls, and a beautiful upright piano in the common living room. Bonus: bikes!

our pick **Home from Home Hostel** (☎ 495-229 8018; www.home-fromhome.com; apt 9, ul Arbat 49; dm R700-800, d R2000; Ⓜ Smolenskaya; ☒ 💻) The spruced-up entryway, with comfy couches and potted plants on the landing, is rare indeed in Moscow! Once inside, original art and mural-painted walls create a bohemian atmosphere. Enter the courtyard from Plotnikov per and look for entrance 2.

Godzillas Hostel (☎ 495-699 4223; www.godzillashostel.com; Bolshoy Karetny per 6; dm/d/tr R725/1740/2175; Ⓜ Tsvetnoy bul; 💻 ☒) Moscow's biggest and most professionally run hostel, with 90 beds spread out over four floors. All rooms are spacious and light-filled and painted in different colours. There are also bathrooms on each floor, three kitchens and a big living room with satellite TV.

Hotel Sverchkov (☎ 495-625 4978; per Sverchkov 8; sverchkov8@mail.ru s/d from R3800/4400; Ⓜ Chistye Prudy) This tiny 11-room hotel, in a graceful 18th-century building, has hallways lined with plants, and paintings by local artists on the walls. Though rooms have old-style bathrooms and faded furniture, this place is a rarity for its intimacy and homeyness.

Kita Inn (☎ 8 926 664 4118, 8 919 772 4002; www.kitainn.com; 2-ya Tverskaya-Yamskaya 6/7, apt 9-10; r R3325; Ⓜ Mayakovskaya; 💻 ☒) Finally, somebody opened a proper pension in Moscow. The private rooms are simple and sweet – Ikea beds, posters on the wall and windows overlooking a shady courtyard. The owner has a few flats in the neighbourhood all offering similar facilities; see also Flamingo B&B (www.flamingobed.com).

EATING

For snacks on the run, there are plenty of street stands selling hot dogs, *chebureki* (Caucasian meat pasties) and blini around metro stations and on many central avenues. For self-catering, supermarkets are your best bet; they're all over central Moscow and carry a decent range of pasta and other easy-to-prepare dishes.

Grably (☎ 495-545 0830; Pyatnitskaya ul 27; meals R200-300; 10am-11pm; M Novokuznetskaya) The big buffet features an amazing array of fish, poultry and meat, plus salads, soups and desserts. After you run the gauntlet and pay the bill, take a seat in the elaborate winter-garden seating area.

Volkonsky Keyser (☎ 495-699 4620; Bolshaya Sadovaya ul 2/46; meals R200-400; M Mayakovskaya) The queue often runs out the door as loyal patrons wait their turn for the city's best fresh-baked breads, pastries and pies. It's worth the wait, especially if you decide on a fruit-filled croissant or to-die-for olive bread.

Stolle (☎ 499-246 0589; Malaya Pirogovskaya ul 16; meals R200-500; 9am-9pm; M Sportivnaya) The selection of sweets and savoury 'stolle' pies sit on the counter, fresh from the oven. It may be difficult to decide (mushroom or meat; apricot or apple?) but you really can't go wrong.

Jagannath (☎ 495-628 3580; Kuznetsky most 11; meals R300-500; 10am-11pm; M Kuznetsky Most) If you are in need of vitamins, this is a funky vegetarian cafe, restaurant and shop with free wi-fi. Its Indian-theme decor is more New Agey than ethnic. Service is slow but sublime, and the food is worth the wait.

Coffee Mania (☎ 495-775 4310; Moscow Conservatory, Bolshaya Nikitskaya ul 13; meals R600-800; 24hr; M Aleksandrovsky Sad) This friendly, informal cafe (one of a chain) is beloved for its homemade soups, fresh-squeezed juices and steaming cappuccino, not to mention its summer terrace overlooking the leafy courtyard of the conservatory.

DRINKING

Kvartira 44 (☎ 495-291 7503; Bolshaya Nikitskaya ul 22/2; noon-2am Sun-Thu, to 6am Fri & Sat; M Okhotny Ryad) Somebody had the brilliant idea to convert an old Moscow apartment into a crowded, cosy bar, with tables and chairs tucked into every nook and cranny. There is another apartment near the Tretyakov (☎ 495-238 8234; ul Malaya Yakimanka 24/8; M Polyanka).

Apshu (☎ 495-953 9944; Klimentovsky per 10; 24hr; M Tretyakovskaya;) This trendy basement place, a magnet for artists and other creative types, offers inexpensive food and drinks, board games, art exhibitions, concerts…basically something for everyone.

Chaikhona No 1 Gorky Park (☎ 495-778 1756; M Frunzenskaya); Hermitage Garden (☎ 495-971 6842; 2pm-last guest; M Chekhovskaya) Housed in an inviting, exotic tent, laid with Oriental rugs and plush pillows, this cool Uzbek lounge and cafe is one of the best chill-out spots in the city. If you are hungry, there is *plov* (rice pilaf) and *shashlyk* (meat kebab) on the menu.

Gravitate toward the **Hermitage Gardens** (M Pushkinskaya Tverskaya) or the **Aleksandrovsky Garden** (M Okhotny Ryad) during the summer months for relaxed beer drinking amid the greenery.

CLUBBING

Propaganda (☎ 495-624 5732; www.propagandamoscow.com; Bolshoy Zlatoustinsky per 7; meals R500-700; noon-6am; M Kitay-gorod) This long-time favourite, with exposed brick walls and pipe ceilings, is a cafe by day, but at night they clear the dance floor and let the DJ do his stuff. This is a gay-friendly place, especially on Sunday nights.

Krizis Zhanra (☎ 495-623 2594; www.kriziszhanra.ru; ul Pokrovka 16/16; concerts 9pm daily, 11pm Fri & Sat; M Chistye Prudy) Everybody has something good to say about Krizis and what's not to love? Good cheap food, copious drinks and rockin' music every night, all of which inspires the gathered to get their groove on.

Tri Obezyani New Age (☎ 495-916 3555; www.gaycentral.ru, in Russian; Nastavnichesky per 11/1; 10pm-7am Thu-Sun; M Chkalovskaya) The biggest and best club on the gay scene, but go in a group or take a taxi from the metro: there have been reports of attacks on the surrounding streets.

Check **Gay.Ru** (www.gay.ru) for gay-friendly listings.

ENTERTAINMENT

To find out what's on, see the weekly magazine *element* (www.elementmoscow.ru) and the entertainment section in Friday's *Moscow Times* (www.themoscowtimes.com).

Classical Music, Opera & Ballet

Bolshoi Theatre (☎ 495-250 7317, hot line 8-800-333 1333; www.bolshoi.ru; Teatralnaya pl 1; tickets R200-2000; Ⓜ Teatralnaya) An evening at the Bolshoi is still one of Moscow's most romantic options. Both the ballet and opera companies perform a range of Russian and foreign works. At the time of research, the Bolshoi was preparing to re-open its main stage after a multiyear renovation. In the meantime, the smaller New Stage (Novaya Stsena) has been hosting performances.

Kremlin Ballet Theatre (☎ 495-620 7729; www.kremlin-gkd.ru; ul Vozdvizhenka 1; Ⓜ Alexandrovsky Sad) Leading dancers also appear with the Kremlin Ballet which performs in the State Kremlin Palace (inside the Kremlin).

Live Music

For major concerts, the main venues are the Olimpiisky Sports Complex (Ⓜ Tsvetnoy Bulvar) and the Kremlin Palace (p981). More intimate smaller venues:

Art Garbage (☎ 495-628 8745; www.art-garbage.ru; Starosadsky per 5; 🕑 noon-6am; Ⓜ Kitay-gorod)

Chinese Pilot Dzhao-Da (☎ 495-623 2896; www.jao-da.ru, in Russian; Lubyansky proezd 25; cover R300-500; 🕑 concerts 10pm Thu, 11pm Fri & Sat; Ⓜ Kitay-Gorod)

Roadhouse (☎ 499-245 5543; www.roadhouse.ru; ul Dovatora 8; 🕑 noon-midnight, concerts 9pm; Ⓜ Sportivnaya)

SHOPPING

GUM (p980) is packed with designer labels and good souvenir shops. Alternatively jump on the metro to reach **Izmaylovo market** (admission R15; 🕑 9am-6pm Sat & Sun; Ⓜ Partizanskaya), a sprawling area packed with art, handmade crafts, antiques, Soviet paraphernalia and just about anything you might want for a souvenir.

GETTING AROUND

Metro

The **Moscow metro** (www.mosmetro.ru) is the easiest, quickest and cheapest way of getting around. The stations are marked outside by 'M' signs. Magnetic tickets (R19) are sold at ticket booths. To save queuing every time buy a multiple-ride ticket (10 rides for R155, 20 for R280).

Taxi

The standard way to hail an unofficial 'taxi' is simply to hold out your hand – when a car stops, state your destination, wait for the driver to give you a price, and then either shut the door, negotiate or get in. Expect to pay R150 to R200 for a ride around the city centre. Official taxis – which can be recognised by the chequerboard logo on the side and/or a small green light in the windscreen – charge higher rates. To book a cab by phone, call the **Central Taxi Reservation Office** (Tsentralnoe Byuro Zakazov Taxi; ☎ 495-627 0000; www.cbz-taxi.ru).

ST PETERSBURG САНКТ ПЕТЕРБУРГ

☎ **812 / pop 4.6 million**

Elegant, enchanting and hedonistic, Russia's one-time capital is a fascinating hybrid of traditional Russia and contemporary Europe, where one moment you can be clapping along to a fun Russian folk-music show in a baroque hall or sniffing incense inside a mosaic-covered Orthodox church, the next grooving on the dance floor of an underground club or posing at a contemporary art event in a renovated bakery. Above all, the city is a visual delight. The Neva River and surrounding canals reflect unbroken facades of handsome 18th- and 19th-century buildings, housing a spellbinding collection of cultural storehouses, culminating in the incomparable Hermitage.

ORIENTATION

St Petersburg is spread out across many different islands, some real and some created through the construction of canals. The central street is Nevsky Prospekt, which extends for some 4km from the Alexander Nevsky Monastery (Lavra Alexandra Nevskogo) to the Hermitage.

INFORMATION

American Medical Clinic (☎ 740 2090; www.amclinic.ru; nab reki Moyki 78; Ⓜ Sadovaya)

Cafemax (☎ 273 6655; www.cafemax.ru; Nevsky pr 90/92; per hr R40; 🕑 24hr; Ⓜ Mayakovskaya) Wi-fi available here. Also has a branch in the Hermitage.

City Realty (☎ 570 6342; www.cityrealty.ru; Muchnoy per 2; tourist visas from US$25; Ⓜ Nevsky Pr) Can arrange all types of visa including business ones, as well as accommodation and transport tickets.

City Tourist Information Centre (☎ 310 8262; www.visit-petersburg.com; Sadovaya ul 14/52; 🕑 10am-7pm Mon-Sat; Ⓜ Gostiny Dvor) The English-speaking staff are vague about most things but will do their best to help. There are also branches outside the Hermitage (Dvortsovaya pl 12; 10am-7pm daily; Nevsky Prospekt) and at the Pulkova 1 and 2 air terminals (10am-7pm Mon-Fri).

Medem International Clinic & Hospital (336 3333; www.medem.ru; 6 Marata ul; Mayakovskaya) International clinic and hospital.

Ost-West Kontaktservice (327 3416; www.ostwest.com; Nevsky pr 105; 10am-6pm Mon-Fri; Ploshchad Vosstaniya) Here can find you an apartment to rent, and organise tours and tickets.

Quo Vadis? (333 0708; www.quovadis.ru; Nevsky pr 66; per hr R100; 24hr; Gostiny Dvor) Internet cafe. Enter from Liteyny pr.

SIGHTS

The Hermitage & Dvortsovaya Ploshchad

Mainly set in the magnificent Winter Palace, the **State Hermitage** (571 3465; www.hermitagemuseum.org; Dvortsovaya pl 2; admission R350, ISIC cardholders free; 10.30am-6pm Tue-Sat, to 5pm Sun) is stacked with treasures, ranging from Egyptian mummies and Scythian gold to early-20th-century European art by Matisse and Picasso. Avoid ticket queues by booking online (US$17.95) through the Hermitage's website.

The museum's main entrance is from **Dvortsovaya ploshchad** (Palace Sq), one of the city's most impressive and historic spaces. Stand back to admire the palace and the central 47.5m **Alexander Column**, named after Alexander I and commemorating the 1812 victory over Napoleon. Enclosing the square's south side is the **General Staff Building**, which in its east wing has a much less crowded but just as worthy branch of the **Hermitage** (314 8260; www.hermitagemuseum.org/html_En/03/hm3_11.html; Dvortsovaya pl 6-8; adult/student R200/free; 10am-6pm Tue-Sun; Nevsky Pr).

Church of the Saviour on Spilled Blood

This multidomed dazzler of a **church** (Spas na Krovi; 315 1636; http://eng.cathedral.ru/saviour; Konyushennaya pl; adult/student R300/150; 10am-8pm Thu-Tue May-Sep; 11am-7pm Thu-Tue Oct-Apr; Nevsky Pr), partly modelled on St Basil's in Moscow, was built between 1883 and 1907 on the spot where Alexander II was assassinated in 1881 (hence its gruesome name). The interior's 7000 sq metres of mosaics fully justify the entrance fee.

Russian Museum

The former Mikhailovsky Palace, now the **Russian Museum** (Russky Muzey; 595 4248; www.rusmuseum.ru; Inzhenernaya ul 4; adult/student R350/150; 10am-5pm Mon, to 6pm Wed-Sun; Gostiny Dvor), houses one of the country's finest collections of Russian art. After the Hermitage you may feel you have had your fill of art, but try your utmost to make some time for this gem of a museum.

> **GETTING INTO TOWN**
>
> From Moskovskaya metro, bus 39 runs to Pulkovo-1, the domestic terminal, and bus 13 runs to Pulkovo-2, the international terminal. There are also plenty of *marshrutky* (minibuses). The trip takes about 15 minutes and costs just R16 to R22, or you can take the buses and *marshrutky* K3 all the way from the airport to Sennaya pl in the city centre or K39 to pl Vosstaniya (R35). Buses stop directly outside each of the terminals. By taxi it should be around R600 to get to the city (R400 from the city to the airport).

St Isaac's Cathedral

The golden dome of this **cathedral** (Isaakievsky Sobor; 315 9732; http://eng.cathedral.ru; Isaakievskaya pl; adult/student R300/150; 10am-8pm Thu-Mon, closed last Mon of the month; Sadovaya or Sennaya Pl) dominates the city skyline. Its lavish interior is open as a museum, but the real attraction here is the panoramic view from the **colonnade** (adult/student R150/100; 10am-7pm Thu-Mon, closed last Mon of the month) around the dome's drum and reached by 262 steps.

Nevsky Prospekt

You can't leave St Petersburg without having walked at least part of Nevsky Pr, Russia's most famous street. Highlights along it include the **Kazan Cathedral** (Kazansky Sobor; 571 4826; Kazanskaya pl 2; admission free; 10am-7pm, services 10am & 6pm; Nevsky pr) with its curved arms reaching out towards the avenue. Opposite is the **Singer Building**, a Style Moderne beauty recently restored to all its splendour from when it was the headquarters of the sewing machine company; inside is the bookshop Dom Knigi.

Further along you'll pass the covered arcades of historic department store **Bolsoy Gostiny Dvor** (www.bgd.ru; Nevsky pr 35; Gostiny Dvor), a Rastrelli creation dating from 1757–85. An enormous **statue of Catherine the Great** stands at

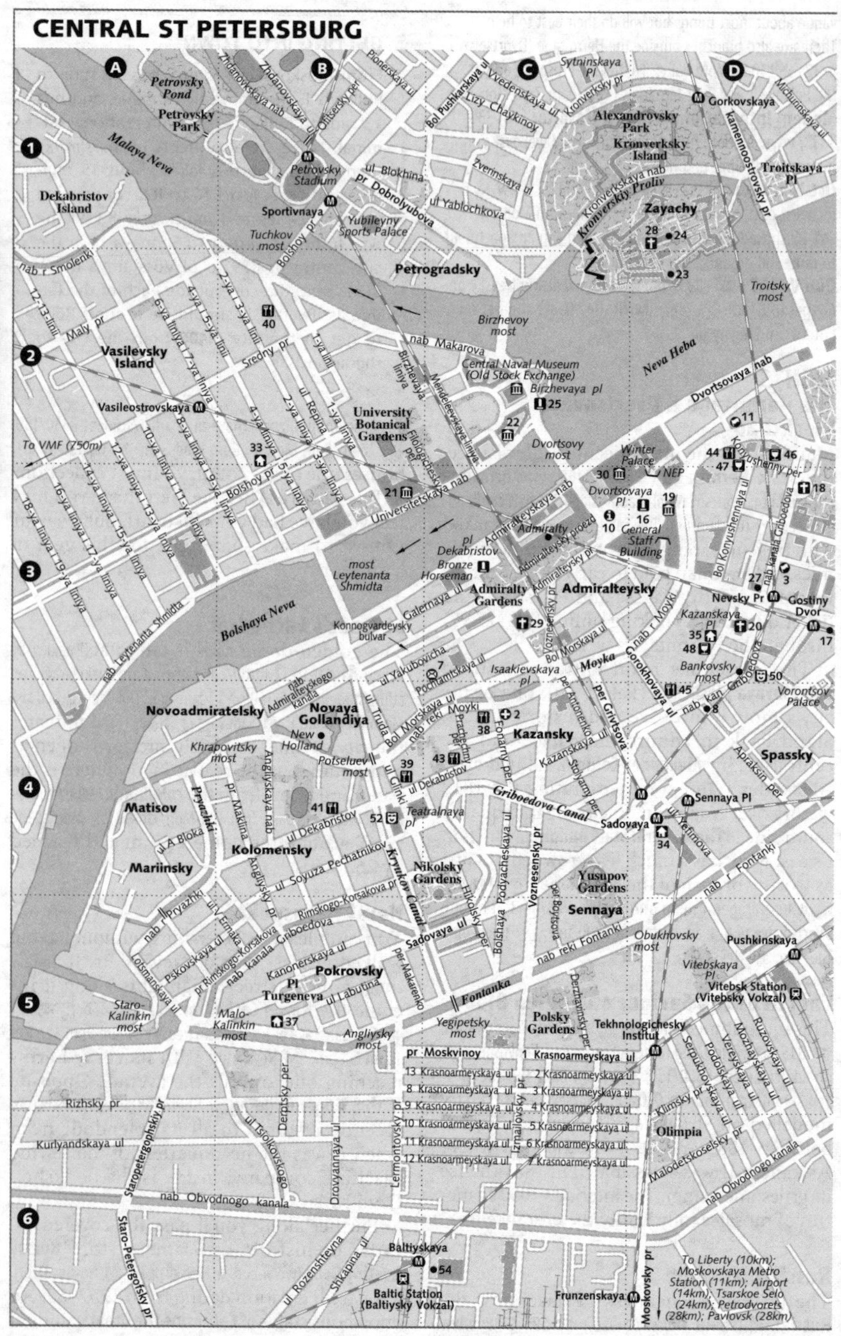
CENTRAL ST PETERSBURG
Petrovsky Pond
Petrovsky Park
Malaya Neva
Dekabristov Island
Petrovsky Stadium
Sportivnaya
Tuchkov most
Yubileyny Sports Palace
Petrogradsky
Alexandrovsky Park
Kronverksky Island
Zayachy
Gorkovskaya
Troitskaya Pl
Troitsky most
Birzhevoy most
Vasilevsky Island
Vasileostrovskaya
To VMF (750m)
Central Naval Museum (Old Stock Exchange)
Birzhevaya pl
University Botanical Gardens
Dvortsovy most
Neva Heba
Winter Palace
NEP
Dvortsovaya Pl
General Staff Building
Admiralty
Pl Dekabristov
Bronze Horseman
most Leytenanta Shmidta
Bolshaya Neva
Admiralty Gardens
Admiralteysky
Nevsky Pr
Gostiny Dvor
Kazanskaya Pl
Bankovsky most
Vorontsov Palace
Konnogvardeysky bulvar
Isaakievskaya pl
Novoadmiratelsky
Novaya Gollandiya
New Holland
Kazansky
Khrapovitsky most
Potseluev most
Spassky
Matisov
Teatralnaya pl
Griboedova Canal
Sennaya Pl
Sadovaya
Kolomensky
Mariinsky
Nikolsky Gardens
Yusupov Gardens
Sennaya
Obukhovsky most
Pushkinskaya
Vitebskaya Pl
Vitebsk Station (Vitebsky Vokzal)
Pokrovsky
Pl Turgeneva
Staro-Kalinkin most
Malo-Kalinkin most
Angliysky most
Yegipetsky most
Polsky Gardens
Tekhnologichesky Institut
Fontanka
Olimpia
Baltiyskaya
Baltic Station (Baltiysky Vokzal)
Frunzenskaya
To Liberty (10km); Moskovskaya Metro Station (11km); Airport (14km); Tsarskoe Selo (24km); Petrodvorets (28km); Pavlovsk (28km)
Moskovsky pr
nab Obvodnogo kanala
Rizhsky pr
Kurlyandskaya ul
Staropetergofsky pr
Staro-Petergofsky pr

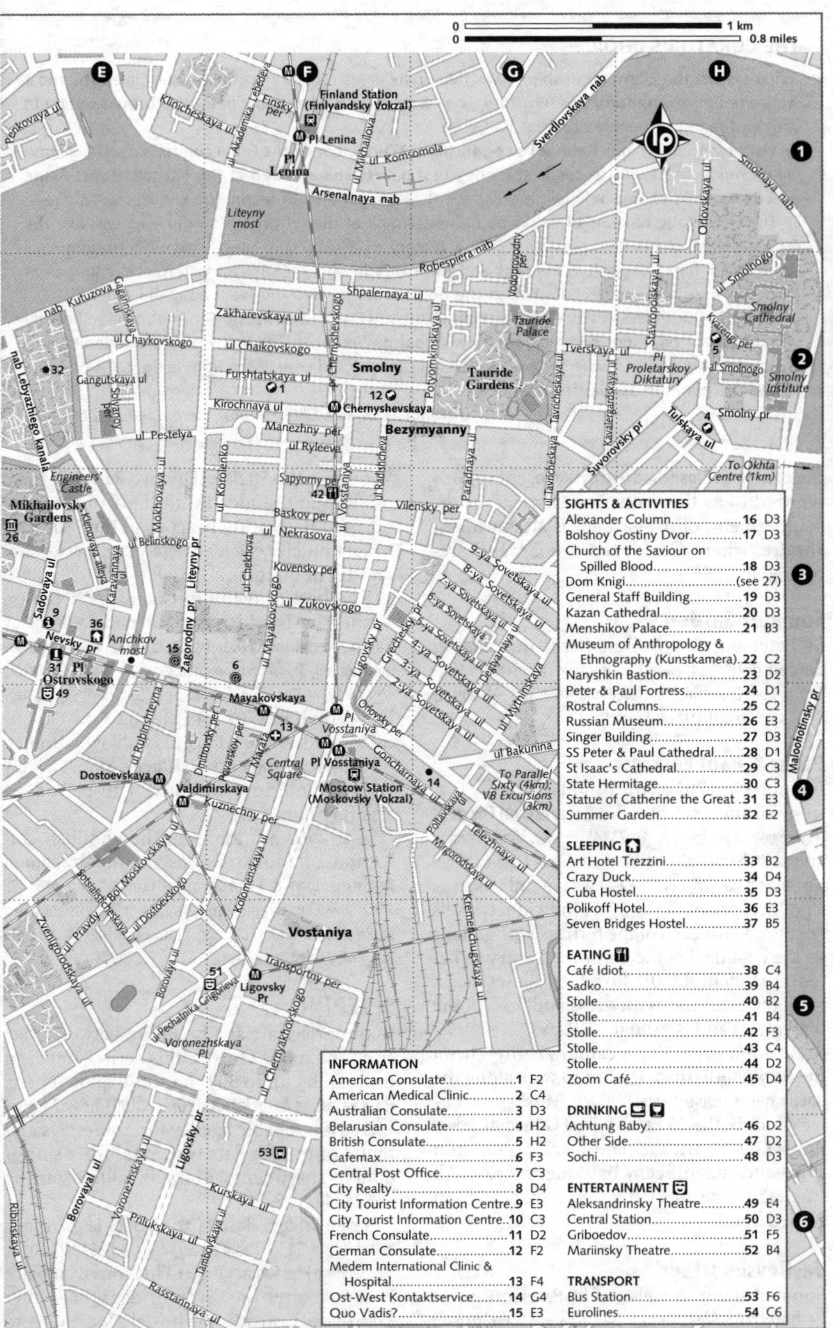
0 1 km
0 0.8 miles
E
F
G
H
1
2
3
4
5
6
Finland Station (Finlyandsky Vokzal)
Pl Lenina
Pl Lenina
Klinicheskaya ul
ul Akademika Lebedeva
Finsky per
ul Mikhailova
ul Komsomola
Arsenalnaya nab
Sverdlovskaya nab
Smolnaya nab
Penkovaya ul
Liteyny most
Robespiera nab
Orlovskaya ul
ul Smolnogo
Smolny Cathedral
Smolny Institute
Shpalernaya ul
Vodoprovodny per
Stavropolskaya ul
Kvarengi per
nab Kutuzova
Gagarinskaya
Zakharevskaya ul
ul Chaykovskogo
ul Chaikovskogo
Potyomkinskaya ul
Tauride Palace
Tauride Gardens
Tverskaya ul
Pl Proletarskoy Diktatury
al Smolnogo
Smolny pr
Tulskaya ul
Suvorovsky pr
Kavalergardskaya ul
Tavricheskaya ul
To Okhta Centre (1km)
nab Lebyazhiego kanala
Gangutskaya ul
Solyanoy per
Furshtatskaya ul
pr Chernyshevskogo
Smolny
Chernyshevskaya
Kirochnaya ul
Manezhny per
Bezymyanny
ul Pestelya
ul Ryleeva
Engineers' Castle
Mikhailovsky Gardens
Mokhovaya ul
ul Korolenko
Sapyorny per
ul Radishcheva
Paradnaya ul
Vilensky per
Baskov per
ul Nekrasova
Klenovaya alleya
ul Belinskogo
Liteyny pr
ul Chekhova
Kovensky per
ul Mayakovskogo
ul Vosstaniya
ul Zhukovskogo
Karavannaya ul
Sadovaya ul
9-ya Sovetskaya ul
8-ya Sovetskaya ul
7-ya Sovetskaya ul
6-ya Sovetskaya ul
5-ya Sovetskaya ul
4-ya Sovetskaya ul
3-ya Sovetskaya ul
2-ya Sovetskaya ul
Ligovsky pr
Grechesky pr
Degtyarnaya ul
ul Mytninskaya
Nevsky pr
Anichkov most
Zagorodny pr
Pl Ostrovskogo
Mayakovskaya
Pl Vosstaniya
Orlovsky per
ul Bakunina
ul Rubinshteyna
Dmitrovsky per
Povarskoy per
ul Marata
Central Square
Pl Vosstaniya
Goncharnaya ul
To Parallel Sixty (4km); VB Excursions (3km)
Dostoevskaya
Valdimirskaya
Moscow Station (Moskovsky Vokzal)
Kuznechny per
Poltavskaya ul
Telezhnaya ul
Mirgorodskaya ul
Sotsialisticheskaya ul
Bol Moskovskaya ul
ul Dostoevskogo
ul Pravdy
Kolomenskaya ul
Kremenchugskaya ul
Vostaniya
Zvenigorodskaya ul
Borovaya ul
ul Pechatnika Grigorieva
Transportny per
Ligovsky Pr
Voronezhskaya Pl
ul Chernyakhovskogo
Ligovsky pr.
Borovaya ul
Voronezhskaya ul
Kurskaya ul
Prilukskaya ul
Tambovskaya ul
Rasstannaya ul
Ribinskaya ul
Maloohotinsky pr
RUSSIA

INFORMATION
American Consulate....1 F2
American Medical Clinic....2 C4
Australian Consulate....3 D3
Belarusian Consulate....4 H2
British Consulate....5 H2
Cafemax....6 F3
Central Post Office....7 C3
City Realty....8 D4
City Tourist Information Centre....9 E3
City Tourist Information Centre....10 C3
French Consulate....11 D2
German Consulate....12 F2
Medem International Clinic & Hospital....13 F4
Ost-West Kontaktservice....14 G4
Quo Vadis?....15 E3

SIGHTS & ACTIVITIES
Alexander Column....16 D3
Bolshoy Gostiny Dvor....17 D3
Church of the Saviour on Spilled Blood....18 D3
Dom Knigi....(see 27)
General Staff Building....19 D3
Kazan Cathedral....20 D3
Menshikov Palace....21 B3
Museum of Anthropology & Ethnography (Kunstkamera)..22 C2
Naryshkin Bastion....23 D2
Peter & Paul Fortress....24 D1
Rostral Columns....25 C2
Russian Museum....26 E3
Singer Building....27 D3
SS Peter & Paul Cathedral....28 D1
St Isaac's Cathedral....29 C3
State Hermitage....30 C3
Statue of Catherine the Great..31 E3
Summer Garden....32 E2

SLEEPING
Art Hotel Trezzini....33 B2
Crazy Duck....34 D4
Cuba Hostel....35 D3
Polikoff Hotel....36 E3
Seven Bridges Hostel....37 B5

EATING
Café Idiot....38 C4
Sadko....39 B4
Stolle....40 B2
Stolle....41 B4
Stolle....42 F3
Stolle....43 C4
Stolle....44 D2
Zoom Café....45 D4

DRINKING
Achtung Baby....46 D2
Other Side....47 D2
Sochi....48 D3

ENTERTAINMENT
Aleksandrinsky Theatre....49 E4
Central Station....50 D3
Griboedov....51 F5
Mariinsky Theatre....52 B4

TRANSPORT
Bus Station....53 F6
Eurolines....54 C6

 Book your stay at lonelyplanet.com/hotels

THE CURATOR'S CHOICE

'I first visited the Hermitage when I was five or six years old. At that time what I liked the most were the **Egyptian mummies** (Rm 100). They were displayed at a low height so I could see them well and read their names such as Pa De Ist.

Visitors shouldn't miss **Raphael's Loggia** (Rm 227) – Catherine the Great commissioned Giacomo Quarrengi in the 1780s to create this copy of a gallery she admired at the Vatican. It was made exactly to scale so not only is it a great event of art but also of technique and design.

The Hermitage has lots of works by Rubens, many of them from his studio – he was like the Damien Hirst of his day, presiding over a factory of artists. One piece that undoubtedly was done by his hand, though, is **Perseus and Andromeda** (Rm 246). It's a masterpiece. You look at Medusa's eyes and you feel afraid and the horse looks so real you feel you could touch it.

From the 20th-century works I recommend Matisse's **Dance and Music** (Rm 344), a magnificently vibrant pair of paintings commissioned by his patron Sergei Shchukin. Originally the genitalia of the nude male dancers were shown, but [were later] painted over. If the light is right, it's possible to see the painting as Matisse intended.'

Dr Dimitri Ozerkov, Chief Curator, Hermitage 20/21 Project

the centre of **Ploshchad Ostrovskogo**, commonly referred to as the Catherine Gardens; at the southern end of the gardens is **Aleksandrinksy Theatre**, where Chekhov's *The Seagull* premiered in 1896.

Summer Garden

St Petersburg's loveliest park, the **Summer Garden** (Letny Sad; admission free; 10am-10pm May-Sep, to 8pm Oct–mid-Apr, closed mid–late-Apr; M Gostiny Dvor) is a great place to relax.

Peter & Paul Fortress

Founded in 1703 as the original military fortress for the new city, the **Peter & Paul Fortress** (Petropavlovskaya krepost; ☎ 238 4550; www.spbmuseum.ru/peterpaul; grounds 6am-10am, exhibitions 11am-6pm Thu-Mon, to 5pm Tue; M Gorkovskaya) was mainly used as a political prison up to 1917. Individual tickets are needed for each of the fortress's attractions so the best deal is the combined entry ticket (adult/student R250/130) which allows access to all the exhibitions on the island (except the bell tower) and is valid for 10 days.

At noon every day a cannon is fired from the **Naryshkin Bastion**. It's fun to walk along the **battlements** (adult/student R100/60). Most spectacular of all is the **SS Peter & Paul Cathedral** (adult/student R170/80), with its landmark needle-thin spire and magnificent baroque interior. All Russia's tsars since Peter the Great have been buried here.

Vasilevsky Island

Some of the best views of St Petersburg can be had from Vasilevsky Island's eastern 'nose', known as the **Strelka**. The two **Rostral Columns** on the point, studded with ships' prows, were oil-fired navigation beacons in the 1800s; on some holidays, such as **Victory Day**, gas torches are still lit on them.

The best of many museums gathered on Vasilevsky Island is the riverside **Menshikov Palace** (Menshikovsky Dvorets; ☎ 323 1112; www.hermitagemuseum.org; Universitetskaya nab 15; adult/student R200/100; 10.30am-6pm Tue-Sat, to 5pm Sun; M Vasileostrovskaya), built in 1707 for Peter the Great's confidant Alexander Menshikov. Now a branch of the Hermitage, the palace's impressively restored interiors are filled with period art and furniture.

Also worth a look are the ghoulish collection of monstrosities in the **Museum of Anthropology & Ethnography** (Kunstkamera; ☎ 328 1412; www.kunstkamera.ru; entrance on Tamozhenny per; adult/student R200/100; 11am-6pm Tue-Sat, to 5pm Sun; M Vasileostrovskaya).

SLEEPING

Room prices are at a premium between May and September. Outside this period, rates can drop up by up to 30% on those quoted here. **Host Families Association** (HOFA; ☎ 901 305 8874; www.hofa.ru) is a reliable agency for homestays and rental of private flats with rates for a single/double/apartment without breakfast starting at €29/44/118.

Seven Bridges Hostel (☎ 572 5415; http://7bridges.night.lt; apt 34, ul Labutina 36; dm/s/d US$18/23.50/26; M Sennaya Pl or Sadovaya;) This convivial place is named after the seven bridges that tether Pokrovsky Ostrov – the hostel's location – to the rest of St Petersburg. The two dorm rooms have four beds each and there's a very comfy lounge well stocked with books and videos.

Cuba Hostel (☎ 921 7115, 315 1558; www.cubahostel.ru; Kazanskaya ul 5; dm R550; Ⓜ Nevsky Pr; 🖳) This funky hang-out presses all the right buttons in terms of atmosphere, friendliness, price and location. Each of the dorms – holding from four to 10 beds – is painted a different colour, and arty design is used throughout.

Crazy Duck (☎ 310 1304; www.crazyduck.ru; apt 4, Moskovsky pr 4; dm from R750; Ⓜ Sadovaya or Sennaya Pl; 🖳) A cheery newcomer to the city's hostel scene offering plenty of home comforts to supplement its dorms, including a fab lounge, kitchen with top-notch facilities and jacuzzi bath.

our pick **Art Hotel Trezzini** (☎ 332 1035; www.trezzini-hotel.com; Bolshoy pr 8; s/d incl breakfast from R2500/3360; Ⓜ Vasileostrovskaya; ❄ 🖳) All the rooms are very appealing, even the compact economy singles, at this arty hotel. Stand outs are rooms 201 and 214, which have little balconies and overlook the neighbouring St Andrew's Cathedral.

Polikoff Hotel (☎ 314 7925; www.polikoff.ru; Nevsky pr 64/11; r incl breakfast from R3000; Ⓜ Gostiny Dvor; ❄ 🖳) Tricky to find (the entrance is through the brown door on Karavannaya ul, where you'll need to punch in 26 for reception), the Polikoff Hotel is worth hunting out for its rooms brimming with contemporary cool decor, quiet but central location and pleasant service.

EATING

St Petersburg is one of the best place to eat in Russia. Those on a budget should look out for blini kiosks throughout the city where a quick snack will not cost you more than R50.

Stolle (www.stolle.ru; pies R60-100; 🕑 8am-10pm); Konyushennaya per (Konyushennaya per 1/6; Ⓜ Nevsky Pr); ul Dekabristov 19 & 33 (Ⓜ Sadovaya or Sennaya Ploshchad); ul Vosstaniya (ul Vosstaniya 32; Ⓜ Chernyshevskaya); Vasilyevsky Island (Syezdovskaya & 1-ya linii 50; Ⓜ Vasileostrovskaya) We can't get enough of the traditional Russian savoury and sweet pies at this expanding chain of cafes and we guarantee you'll also be back for more. It's easy to make a meal of it with soups and other dishes that can be ordered at the counter.

Zoom Café (www.cafezoom.ru; Gorokhovaya ul 22; mains R200-400; ⊠; Ⓜ Nevsky Prospekt) Popular boho/student hang-out with regularly changing art exhibitions on its walls. Serves unfussy tasty European and Russian food, has wi-fi access, a very relaxed ambience, and a no-smoking zone.

Café Idiot (☎ 315 1675; nab reki Moyki 82; meals R400; 🕑 11am-1am; ⊠; Ⓜ Sennaya Ploshchad) This long-running vegetarian cafe charms with its pre-evolutionary atmosphere. It's an ideal place to visit for a nightcap or late supper. It also has free wi-fi.

SPLURGE

Sadko (☎ 920 8228; www.probka.org; ul Glinki 2; mains R260-650; Ⓜ Sadovaya or Sennaya Pl) The impressive decor here applies traditional floral designs to a slick contemporary style. Serving all the Russian favourites, it has a great children's room and is ideal as a pre- or post-Mariinsky Theatre dining option. The waiters, many music students at the local conservatory, give impromtu vocal performances.

DRINKING

our pick **Achtung Baby** (Konyushennaya pl 2; entry after 10pm Fri & Sat R300; 🕑 6pm-6am; Ⓜ Nevsky Pr) The best of several bars and clubs that have taken over the old tsarists-era stables makes great use of the vast, high-ceiling space. We love the furry globes that hang over the bar.

Sochi (Kazanskaya ul 7; 🕑 6pm-6am; Ⓜ Nevsky Pr) Occupying one half of the same building as the microbrewery Tinkoff is this new venture by the woman who launched St Petersburg's DJ-bar scene. Prop yourself at the long bar or groove along with the hipsters to bands and eclectic selections from the DJs.

Other Side (www.theotherside.ru; Bolshaya Konyushennaya ul 1; 🕑 noon-last customer, concerts 8pm Sun-Thu, 10pm or 11pm Fri & Sat; Ⓜ Nevsky Pr) There's live music most nights at this fun and funky bar as well as decent food (mains R200 to R500) but most people turn up to enjoy its seven beers on tap.

ENTERTAINMENT

Check out Friday's edition of the free newspaper *St Petersburg Times* (www.sptimes.ru) for the latest listings.

Mariinsky Theatre (☎ 326 4141; www.mariinsky.ru; Teatralnaya pl 1; 🕑 box office 11am-7pm; Ⓜ Sadovaya or Sennaya Pl) Home to the world-famous Kirov Ballet and Opera company. A visit here is a must, if only to wallow in the sparkling glory of the interior. Book tickets in advance on the website for here and for its acoustically splendid new concert hall (ul Pisareva 20) which is nearby.

Griboedov (☎ 764 4355; www.griboedovclub.ru; Voronezhskaya ul 2A; cover R100-400, free noon-8pm; cafe noon-8pm, club 5pm-6am; M Ligovsky Pr) This eternally hip club in an artfully converted bomb shelter is a fun place most nights. They've recently extended above ground with the groovy cafe-bar Griboedov Hill, which hosts live music performance in the evenings.

The main gay club is the slick **Central Station** (☎ 312 3600; www.centralstation.ru; ul Lomonosova 1/28; admission before midnight free, after midnight R100-300; 6pm-6am; M Gostiny Dvor). For other gay-friendly options check out **Excess** (www.xs.gay.ru).

GETTING AROUND

The metro (flat fare R17) is best for covering the large distances across the city. The four lines cross over in the city centre and go out to the suburbs. Around the city centre, *marshrutka* (shared minibuses) are a good alternative. Costs vary on each route, but the average fare is R20, and is displayed prominently inside each van. To stop a *marshrutka*, simply hold out your hand and it will stop. Jump in, sit down, pass your cash to the driver (a human chain operates if you are not seated nearby), and then call out *'ostanovityes pozhalusta!* ('astano-vit-yes pa-zhal-sta') when you want to get out and the driver will pull over.

To book a taxi in advance try **Peterburgskoe taksi 068** (Petersburg Taxi; ☎ 068 324 7777; www.taxi068.spb.ru, in Russian).

KALININGRAD REGION КАЛИНИНГРАДСКАЯ ОБЛАСТЬ

pop 955,300

Sandwiched by Poland to the south and Lithuania to the east and north, and with 148km of Baltic coastline to the west, the Kaliningrad region is a Russian exclave that's intimately attached to the Motherland yet also a world apart. In this 'Little Russia' – only 15,100 sq km – you'll find plenty of fine hotels and restaurants, a youthful outlook plus all the traditions of the big parent, wrapped up in a manageable package of beautiful countryside, splendid beaches and fascinating historical sights.

> **GETTING INTO TOWN**
>
> Take bus 138 from Kaliningrad's Khrabrovo airport to the bus station (R30, one hour, hourly). The bus station is next to the South train station. Taxis ask at least R700 for the ride from the airport.

KALININGRAD КАЛИНИНГРАД

☎ 4012 / pop 423,000

A fascinating, affluent city that's clearly going places, Kaliningrad is an excellent introduction to Russia's most liberal region. Interesting museums and historical sights sprout in between the shiny new shopping centres and multitude of leafy parks that soften vast swathes of brutal Soviet architecture. Plentiful transport options and good hotels mean you can use the city as a base to see the rest of the region.

Founded as a Teutonic fort in 1255, Königsberg joined the Hanseatic League in 1340, and from 1457 to 1618 was the residence of the grand masters of the Teutonic order and their successors, the dukes of Prussia. The first king of Prussia Frederick I was crowned here in 1701. For the next couple of centuries the city flourished, producing citizens such as the 18th-century philosopher Emmanuel Kant.

Old photos attest that the former Königsberg was once an architectural gem equal to Prague or Krakow. The combined destruction of WWII and the Soviet decades put paid to all that. However, there are lovely prewar residential suburbs that evoke the Prussian past, and following the successful reconstruction of the war-damaged cathedral (mainly thanks to donations from Germany) the authorities also have big plans to remodel Kaliningrad with a mix of futuristic and heritage-inspired building projects.

Orientation

Leninsky pr, a north–south avenue, is the city's main artery, running over 3km from the bus and main train station, Yuzhny vokzal (South Station) to Severny vokzal (North Station). About halfway it crosses the Pregolya

River and passes the cathedral, the city's major landmark. The city's modern heart is further north, around pl Pobedy.

Information

Baltma Tours (☎ 931 931; www.baltma.ru; 4th fl, pr Mira 94) Can arrange visas, hotel accommodation, tailored city tours and a wide array of excursions.

Kaliningrad Regional Informative Educational Centre of Tourism (☎ 655 055; www.tourismkaliningrad.ru; Fish Village, 2 Oktyabrskaya ul; 10am-8pm) Staffed by helpful, English-speaking staff; you can buy guides to the region here.

King's Castle (☎ 350 782; www.kaliningradinfo.ru; Hotel Kaliningrad, Leninskiy pr 81; 8am-8pm Mon-Fri, 9am-4pm Sat) A private tourist agency that also operates as a very efficient tourist information centre. Offers internet access, city tours and ones to the Kurshskaya Kosa.

Telekom (ul Teatralnaya 13; internet per hr R50; 9am-7pm) For long-distance calls, fax and internet access.

Sights

Striking Gothic **Kaliningrad Cathedral** (☎ 646 868; adult/student R100/50; 9am-5pm) was the geographical and spiritual heart of old Königsberg. Founded in 1333, it was almost destroyed during WWII, but has been undergoing restoration since 1992. The showpiece main hall, with fabulous vaulted ceilings, serves as a concert hall. Upstairs a museum has displays of old Königsberg, objects from archaeological digs and a shrine to Immanuel Kant, who was born, studied and died in Königsberg.

Along the river west of the cathedral is the fascinating **World Ocean Museum** (☎ 538 915; www.vitiaz.ru; nab Petra Velikogo 1; adult/student R200/120, individual vessels R120/80; 11am-6pm Wed-Sun Apr-Oct, 10am-5pm Wed-Sun Nov-Mar), where you can learn about sea and space exploration aboard a B-413 submarine and two giant Soviet research ships

Just north of the cathedral is Tsentralnaya ploshchad (Central Sq), on which sits one of the ugliest of Soviet creations, **Dom Sovetov** (House of Soviets). Kaliningrad's magnificent castle (1255) stood here before it was damaged in WWII then dynamited out of existence by narrow-minded Soviet planners in 1967–68.

At the northern terminus of Leninsky pr lies ploshchad Pobedy (Victory Sq), dominated by the newly built **Church of Christ the Saviour**. Extending west of the square is pr Mira, a pleasant, shop-lined artery leading to bustling Central Park (Tsentralny Park). Walks through the linden-scented, tree-lined old German neighbourhood of **Amalienau** around here is the best way to experience old Königsberg.

The Kaliningrad region produces some 90% of the world's amber. View some of the treasures made from this petrified resin at the **Amber Museum** (☎ 466 888; www.ambermuseum.ru; pl Vasilevskogo 1; admission R90; 10am-6pm Tue-Sun) located within **Dohna Tower**, which served as a fortress to protect adjacent **Rossgarten Gate** (pl Vasilevskogo 3), one of the old city gates. Beyond that another one of the gates, **King's Gate** (☎ 581 272; ul Frunze 112; adult/student R80/40; 11am-6pm Wed-Sun) houses a small but well-presented history museum.

Sleeping

Kaliningrad is crying out for a decent hostel or budget accommodation.

Komnaty Otdykha (☎ 586 447; pl Kalinina; s & d R800) Inside the south train station, the resting rooms are surprisingly quiet and clean, with OK shared bathrooms. Find them by turning right down the corridor after the ticket hall and walking up to the 3rd floor.

our pick **Villa Severin** (☎ 365 373; www.villa-severin.ru; ul Leningradskaya 9a; s/d from R950/1900) There's a very homely atmosphere at this pretty villa, set back from the Prud Verkny, with nine comfortably furnished rooms including simple student rooms.

Moskva (☎ 352 300; www.hotel.kaliningrad.ru; pr Mira 19; s/d from R1950/2400) Kaliningrad's oldest hotel has been reborn after extensive renovations and boasts bright, spacious rooms, friendly atmosphere and a good location. Under the same management are the Hotel Kaliningrad and Chaika Hotel.

Eating & Drinking

our pick **Croissant Café** (pr Mira 24; meals R100; 9am-11pm Sun-Thu, 24hr Fri & Sat) A chic baked goods heaven. Indulge in flaky pastries, quiches, muffins, biscuits and cakes, as well as omelettes and blini for breakfast.

Don Chento (☎ 937 672; www.donchento.ru; Sovetsky pr 9-11; meals R100-200) No need to endure depressing Soviet throwback *stolovaya* (canteen) for budget meals when you can dig in at the self-serve salad bar or pick a slice of pizza at this stylish chain with several branches across the city. It sponsors a jazz festival each August.

First Café (☎ 644 829; www.first-cafe.ru; ul Yepronovskaya 21) Kaliningrad's answer to Starbucks has three other locations in the city

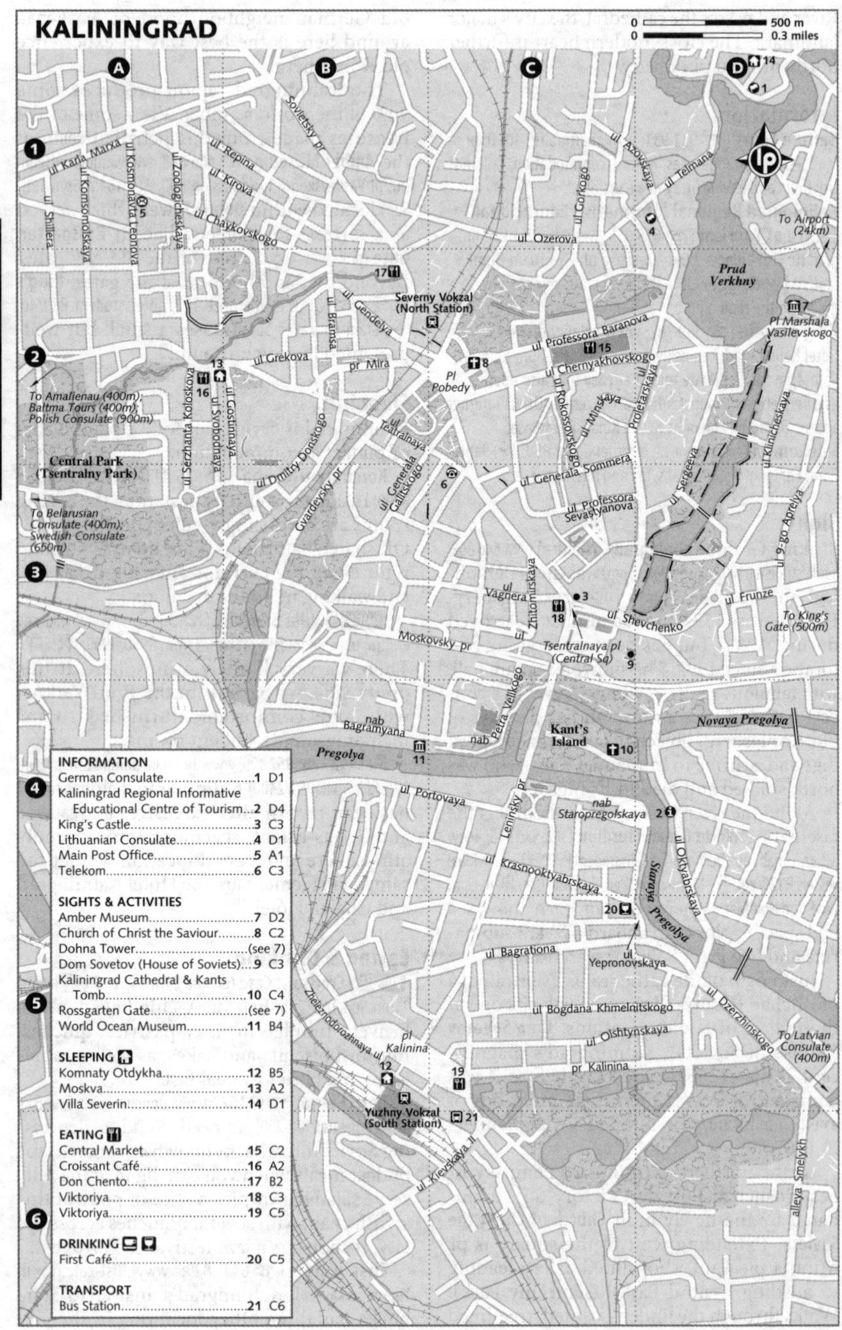
KALININGRAD
0 500 m
0 0.3 miles
A
B
C
D
1
2
3
4
5
6
ul Karla Marxa
ul Shillera
ul Komsomolskaya
ul Kosmonavta Leonova
ul Zoologicheskaya
ul Repina
ul Kirova
ul Chaykovskogo
Sovietsky pr
ul Azovskaya
ul Telmana
ul Gorkogo
ul Ozerova
To Airport (24km)
Prud Verkhny
Severny Vokzal (North Station)
ul Gendelya
ul Bramsa
ul Grekova
pr Mira
Pl Pobedy
ul Professora Baranova
ul Chernyakhovskogo
Pl Marshala Vasilevskogo
To Amalienau (400m); Baltma Tours (400m); Polish Consulate (900m)
ul Serzhanta Koloskova
ul Gostinnaya
ul Svobodnaya
ul Rokossovskogo
ul Minskaya
Proletarskaya
ul Teatralnaya
Central Park (Tsentralny Park)
ul Dmitry Donskogo
Gvardeysky pr
ul Generala Galitskogo
ul Generala Sommera
ul Professora Sevastyanova
ul Sergeeva
ul Klinicheskaya
ul 9-go Aprelya
To Belarusian Consulate (400m); Swedish Consulate (650m)
ul Vagnera
Zhitomirskaya
ul Shevchenko
ul Frunze
To King's Gate (500m)
Moskovsky pr
Tsentralnaya pl (Central Sq)
nab Bagramyana
nab Petra Velikogo
Kant's Island
Novaya Pregolya
Pregolya
ul Portovaya
Leninsky pr
nab Staropregolskaya
ul Oktyabrskaya
ul Krasnooktyabrskaya
Staraya Pregolya
ul Yepronovskaya
ul Bagrationa
ul Bogdana Khmelnitskogo
ul Dzerzhinskogo
Zheleznodorozhnaya ul
pl Kalinina
ul Olshtynskaya
pr Kalinina
To Latvian Consulate (400m)
Yuzhny Vokzal (South Station)
ul Kievskaya
alleya Smelykh
INFORMATION
German Consulate 1 D1
Kaliningrad Regional Informative Educational Centre of Tourism 2 D4
King's Castle 3 C3
Lithuanian Consulate 4 D1
Main Post Office 5 A1
Telekom 6 C3
SIGHTS & ACTIVITIES
Amber Museum 7 D2
Church of Christ the Saviour 8 C2
Dohna Tower (see 7)
Dom Sovetov (House of Soviets) 9 C3
Kaliningrad Cathedral & Kants Tomb 10 C4
Rossgarten Gate (see 7)
World Ocean Museum 11 B4
SLEEPING
Komnaty Otdykha 12 B5
Moskva 13 A2
Villa Severin 14 D1
EATING
Central Market 15 C2
Croissant Café 16 A2
Don Chento 17 B2
Viktoriya 18 C3
Viktoriya 19 C5
DRINKING
First Café 20 C5
TRANSPORT
Bus Station 21 C6

RUSSIA

WORTH THE TRIP: KURSHSKAYA KOSA NATIONAL PARK

Tall, windswept sand dunes and dense pine forests teaming with wildlife lie along the 98km-long Curonian Spit, a Unesco World Heritage site that divides the tranquil Curonian lagoon from the Baltic Sea. The 50km of the spit that lie in Russian territory are protected within the **Kurshskaya Kosa National Park** (www.kurshskayakosa.ru; admission per person R30, per car R200) and it's a fascinating place to explore or to relax on pristine beaches. Highlights include the spectacular views of the dunes from raised platforms at **Vistota Efa** (42km mark; free), and the **Dancing Forest** (Tantsuyushchiy Les; 37km mark; free) where wind-sculpted pines do indeed appear to be frozen mid-boogie.

Four buses a day from Kaliningrad (via Zelenogradsk) head up the Spit en route to Klaipėda in Lithuania. For more flexibility rent a car or arrange a tour in either Kaliningrad or Zelenogradsk, from where a car and driver for half a day should cost around R1500.

other than this branch opposite Fish Village. It's a stylish cafe-bar operation with a wide range of drinks, snacks and free wi-fi.

Self-caterers should visit the lively central market on ul Chernyakhovskogo or **Viktoriya** (Kaliningrad Plaza, Leninsky pr 30; 10am-10pm), a large Western-style supermarket that also has a handy branch opposite the bus and train station at pl Kalinina.

Getting There & Away

You can get to Kaliningrad by direct bus from Klaipėda (R240, three hours, four daily), Kaunas/Vilnius (R465/640, six/eight hours, twice daily), Riga (R660, nine hours, twice daily), Tallinn (R1192, 14 hours, daily), Olshtyn/Gdansk (R350/500, four/five hours, twice daily) and Warsaw (R650, nine hours, daily). **König Auto** (☎ 460 304) has several buses weekly to Berlin (R2300) and many other German cities.

International trains services include Vilnius (R1700, six hours, four daily), Berlin (R2900, 14 hours, daily), Moscow (R2700, 23 hours, three dails), St Petersburg (R3000, 26 hours, daily), and Kyiv (R2500, 25 hours, every other day).

RUSSIA DIRECTORY

ACCOMMODATION

Both Moscow and St Petersburg have a number of well-established and reliable hostels, although they are significantly more expensive than in most other countries (budget around R750 per night). Hotel rooms start from about R500, although these are invariably shabby Soviet relics; R800 to R1500 is a more realistic minimum. Booking ahead is always advised. Camping is not possible in either Moscow or St Petersburg.

ACTIVITIES

Taking a traditional Russian *banya* is a must. These wet saunas are a social hub and a fantastic experience for any visitor to Russia. Leave your inhibitions at home and be prepared for a beating with birch twigs (far more pleasant than it sounds). Russians swear there's no better way of getting clean – ask at your hostel or hotel for the nearest public *banya* where entry can be as low as R100.

BUSINESS HOURS

Usual business hours in Russia:

Banks (8am or 9am-5pm or 6pm Mon-Fri)
Offices (8am or 9am-5pm or 6pm Mon-Fri)
Restaurants (noon-11am) Many are in fact virtually 24-hour establishments

DANGERS & ANNOYANCES

Watch out for pickpockets in Moscow and St Petersburg. Also bear in mind that some police officers and other uniformed officials are on the take. Never allow them to go through your wallet or pockets; carry a photocopy of your passport, so if you're asked for identification you can hand this over rather than the real thing. If you feel you are being unfairly treated or the police try to make you go somewhere with them, pull out your mobile phone and threaten to call your embassy *('ya pozvonyu svoyu posolstvu')*.

Never drink tap water in St Petersburg as it may contain *Giardia lamblia,* a parasite that can cause horrific stomach cramps and nausea. Bottled water is available to purchase everywhere.

Sadly, racism is a problem in Russia. Be vigilant on the streets around Hitler's birthday (20 April), when bands of right-wing thugs have been known to roam around spoiling for a fight with anyone who doesn't look Russian. It's a sure thing that if you look like a foreigner you'll be targeted with suspicion by many (the police, in particular). Moscow and St Petersburg have all seen violent attacks on non-Russians, particularly people from the Caucasus.

EMBASSIES & CONSULATES

Check out www.russianembassy.net for a full list of Russian embassies and consulates overseas.

Australia Moscow (☎ 495-956 6070; www.russia.embassy.gov.au; Podkolokolny per 10A/2; Ⓜ Kitay Gorod); St Petersburg (☎ 812-315 1100; ul Italyanskaya 1; Ⓜ Nevsky pr)
Belarus Kaliningrad (☎ 4012-214 412; ul Dm Donskogo 35a); Moscow (☎ 495-924 7031; www.embassybel.ru; Maroseyka ul 17/6, 101000; Ⓜ Kitay Gorod); St Petersburg (☎ 812-274 7212; ul Bonch-Bruevicha 3a; Ⓜ Chernyshevskaya)
Canada Moscow (☎ 495-925 6000; www.dfait-maeci.gc.ca; Starokonyushenny per 23; Ⓜ Kropotkinskaya)
France Moscow (☎ 495-937 1500; www.ambafrance.ru; ul Bolshaya Yakimanka 45; Ⓜ Oktyabrskaya); St Petersburg (☎ 812-332 2270; nab reki Moyki 15; Ⓜ Nevsky Pr)
Germany Kaliningrad (☎ 4012-326 923; www.kaliningrad.diplo.de; ul Demyana Bednogo 13a); Moscow (☎ 495-937 9500; www.moskau.diplo.de; Mosfilmovskaya ul 56; Ⓜ Universitet, then bus No 119); St Petersburg (☎ 812-320 2400; Furshtatskaya ul 39; Ⓜ Chernyshevskaya)
Latvia Kaliningrad (☎ 4012-706 755; Englesa ul 52a)
Lithuania Kaliningrad (☎ 4012-959 486; Proletarskaya ul 133)
Netherlands Moscow (☎ 495-797 2900; www.netherlands-embassy.ru; Kalashny per 6; Ⓜ Arbatskaya)
New Zealand Moscow (☎ 495-956 3579; www.nzembassy.msk.ru; Povarskaya ul 44; Ⓜ Arbatskaya)
Poland Kaliningrad (☎ 4012-950 419; www.polkon-kaliningrad.ru; Kashtanovaya Alleya 51)
Sweden Kaliningrad (☎ 4012-959 400; Kutuzova ul 29)
UK Moscow (☎ 495-956 7200; http://ukinrussia.fco.gov.uk/en/; Smolenskaya nab 10; Ⓜ Smolenskaya); St Petersburg (☎ 812-320 3200; pl Proletarskoy Diktatury 5; Ⓜ Chernyshevskaya)
Ukraine Moscow (☎ 495-629 9742; www.mfa.gov.ua; Leontevsky per 18; Ⓜ Pushkinskaya)
USA Moscow (☎ 495-728 5000; www.moscow.usembassy.gov; Bol Devyatinsky per 8; Ⓜ Barrikadnaya); St Petersburg (☎ 812-331 2600; Furshtatskaya ul 15; Ⓜ Chernyshevskaya)

HOLIDAYS

Following are Russia's main public holidays:

New Year's Day 1 January
Russian Orthodox Christmas Day 7 January
Defender of the Fatherland Day 23 February
International Women's Day 8 March
International Labour Day/Spring Festival 1 May
Victory Day (1945) 9 May
Russian Independence Day When the Russian republic of the USSR proclaimed its sovereignty in June 1991; 12 June
Unity Day 4 November

Many businesses are also closed from 1 to 7 January. Other widely celebrated holidays are Defenders of the Motherland Day (23 February) and Easter Monday.

MONEY

The Russian currency is the rouble, written as 'рубль' and abbreviated as 'ру' or 'р'. There are 100 kopecks in a rouble and these come in coin denominations of one (rarely seen), five, 10 and 50. Also issued in coins, roubles come in amounts of one, two, five and 10, with banknotes in values of 10, 50, 100, 500, 1000 and 5000 roubles.

You can use all major credit and debit cards in ATMs, and in good restaurants and hotels. It's possible to exchange travellers cheques, although at a price. Euro or US dollar cash is the best to bring, and should be in pristine condition – crumpled or old notes are often refused. Most major currencies can be exchanged at change booths all over any town in Russia. Look for the sign *obmen valyut*.

POST

The Russian post service **Potcha Rossia** (www.russianpost.ru/portal/en/home/posta) gets an unfair rap. Postcards, letters and parcels sent abroad usually arrive within a couple of weeks, but there are occasional lapses. To send a postcard or letter up to 20g anywhere in the world by air costs R19 or R16.10, respectively.

TELEPHONE

The international code for Russia is ☎ 7. The international access code from land lines in Russia is ☎ 8, followed by 10 after the second tone, followed by the country code. From mobile phones, just dial + before the country code to place an international call. To call a mobile phone (typically 10-digit numbers starting with 9) from a land line or vice versa dial ☎ 8 plus the number.

At the time of research Moscow had two area codes: ☎ 495 and ☎ 499. Over the next few years many ☎ 495 numbers will change to the ☎ 499 code (with a slight change of number in several cases).

VISAS

Everyone needs a visa to visit Russia – allow yourself at least a month before you travel to secure one. For most travellers a tourist visa, valid for 30 days from the date of entry, will be fine. The process has three stages – invitation, application and registration.

Invitation

To obtain a visa, you first need an invitation. Hotels and hostels will usually issue anyone staying with them an invitation (or 'visa support') free or for a small fee (typically around €20 to €30). Visa invitation fees are similar if you apply via a travel agent or online through:

Express to Russia (www.expresstorussia.com)
Russian Business Visa (www.russian-business-visa.com)
Russia Direct (www.russiadirect.co.uk)
Visa Able (www.visaable.com)
Way to Russia (http://waytorussia.net)
Zierer Visa Services (☎ 1-866 788 1100; www.zvs.com)

Application

Invitation in hand you can then apply for a visa at a Russian embassy. Costs vary – anything from US$50 to US$450 – depending on the type of visa needed, how quickly you need it and which embassy you use (each have different fees and slightly different application rules). We highly recommended applying for your visa in your home country rather than on the road – indeed the rule is that you're supposed to do this although we know from experience that some embassies and consulates can be more flexible than others.

Registration

On arrival, you should fill out an immigration card; these are often given out in advance on your flight. You surrender one half of the form immediately to the passport control, while the other you keep for the duration of your stay and give up only on exiting Russia. Take good care of this as you'll need it for registration and could face problems while travelling in Russia – and certainly will on leaving – if you cannot produce it.

You must register your visa within three working days of arrival. If you're staying at a hostel or hotel, they should be able to do this for you for free or a small fee (typically around €20). Once registered, you should receive a separate slip of paper confirming the dates you'll be staying at that particular hotel. Keep this safe – that's the document that any police who stop you will need to see.

If staying in a homestay or rental apartment, you'll either need to pay a travel agency (anything from €20 to €70) to register your visa for you or make arrangements with the landlord or a friend to register you through the post office. See http://waytorussia.net/RussianVisa/Registration.html for how this can be done as well as a downloadable form that needs to be submitted at post offices.

Serbia Србија

HIGHLIGHTS

- **Kalemegdan Citadel** Explore the citadel that dominates Belgrade with its cannons and tanks, and sets the city's tone (p1002)
- **Novi Sad** Relax in atmospheric cafes and take a wander around Petrovaradin Citadel, host of the annual Exit Festival in July (p1007)
- **Subotica** Admire gorgeous art nouveau architecture at every turn and travel back to another era in timeless cafes (p1008)

FAST FACTS

- **Area** 102,350 sq km
- **Budget** 2600DIN per day
- **Capital** Belgrade
- **Country code** ☎ 381
- **Famous for** tennis (Ana Ivanovic, Monica Seles, Novak Djokovic, Jelena Jankovic…)
- **Language** Serbian
- **Money** dinar (DIN); A$1 = 52DIN; C$1 = 59DIN; €1 = 93DIN; ¥100 = 73DIN; NZ$1 = 41DIN; UK£1 = 105DIN; US$1 = 69DIN
- **Phrases** *zdravo* (hello), *dovidjenja* (goodbye), *molim* (please), *hvala* (thanks)
- **Population** 7.5 million

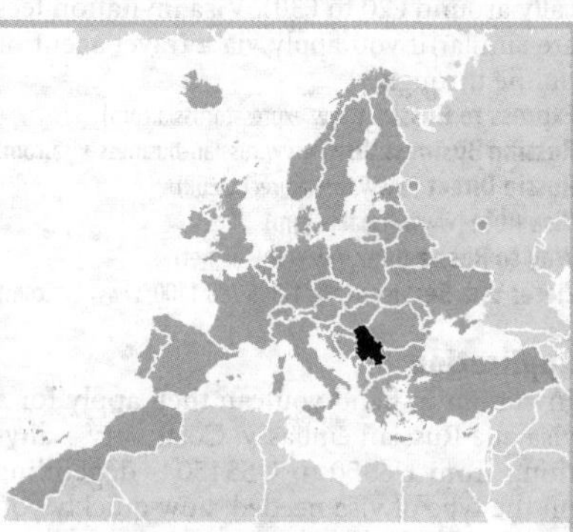

- **Visa** no visa needed for citizens of the EU, Australia, New Zealand, the US and Canada; see p1010

TRAVEL HINTS

Negotiate discounted accommodation by staying more than a few days, and explore the region by day-tripping. Fuel yourself at local markets and bakeries.

ROAMING SERBIA

Cultural and culinary exploration in Belgrade, day trips into Fruška Gora from Novi Sad, then on to Hungary via Subotica.

Independent travellers to this misunderstood state will be surprised by Serbia. Art nouveau Hungarian influences cross the border into the Vojvodinian region. Novi Sad, presided over by the Petrovarian Citadel, hosts the edgy Exit festival which reverberates through Europe, except perhaps the nearby Fruška Gora, where monastic life has endured for generations.

Travellers looking for authenticity will find it here; villages have maintained their age-old hospitality and offer glimpses into rural life that is fast fading elsewhere in the world. Serbs welcome you as an opportunity for cross-cultural engagement over a drink or five.

Beating at Serbia's heart is Belgrade, once dismissed as drab but now hailed a partygoer's playground and culture-junkie's overdose. Vivid museums, innovative restaurants and nightlife of every pace for every taste make this all-hours town a visitor's playground.

After years of isolation and repression, this soulful state has emerged bruised but determined to launch itself into a future with Europe.

HISTORY

The region's original Illyrian inhabitants were augmented by Celts and then Slavs in the 6th century AD. The assignation of Serbia to the Byzantine Empire in AD 395, and then the conversion of the population to orthodoxy in 879, wedded Serbia to Eastern Europe.

The Ottoman Turks defeated Serbia at the pivotal 1389 Battle of Kosovo; independence from Turkish rule wasn't achieved until 500 years later in 1815.

After WWI, Serbia joined Croatia, Slovenia, Vojvodina and Macedonia to form Yugoslavia, which during WWII was partitioned between Germany, Italy, Hungary and

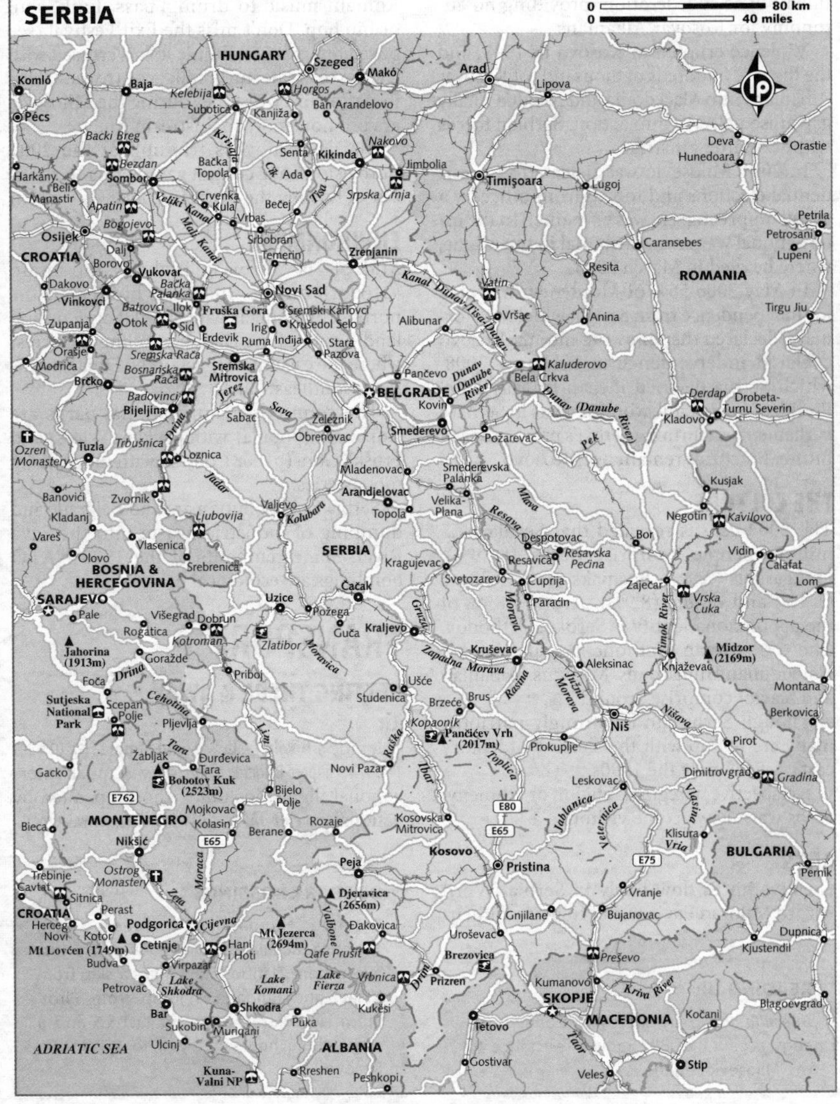

Bulgaria. Tito, a communist partisan resistance leader, became leader of the Federal Republic of Yugoslavia in 1945, of which Serbia became a republic.

In 1986 communist leader Slobodan Milošević espoused an image of a 'Greater Serbia', horrifying Slovenia and Croatia. Through bloody war, the federation collapsed. In 1992 Serbia and Montenegro formed a third Yugoslav federation, providing no autonomy for Kosovar Albanians.

Violence erupted in Kosovo in 1998, and the flight of hundreds of thousands of Kosovar Albanians into Macedonia and Albania finally galvanised NATO into action. Serbian forces withdrew after air strikes.

In 2001 Milošević was defeated in presidential elections and forced from office by a popular uprising. He was extradited to the international war crimes tribunal in the Hague, where he died in March 2006.

In May 2006 55% of Montenegrins voted for independence from Serbia, which was formally declared the following month. Kosovo declared independence in February 2008, which Serbia deemed illegal. In May 2008 President Boris Tadić won 102 seats in Serbia's parliament, reaffirming Serbia's pro-European future. Fractures remain over Kosovo.

THE CULTURE

The 2002 census revealed that Serbia's 7.5 million people comprise Serbs (82.9%), Hungarians (3.9%), Bosniaks (1.8%), Roma (1.4%) and others (8.9%). Around 85% of the population identify as Serbian Orthodox. The 5% Roman Catholic population are Vojvodinian Hungarians. Muslims (Albanian and Slavic) comprise around 3%.

Though Serbs can be strongly patriotic, many are fed up with the shadow of history cast over them by the 1990s.

Irrespective of region, religion or ethnicity, Serbs warmly welcome visitors.

ARTS

Creative juices flow freely in Serbia. Word wizard Milorad Pavić writes in many dimensions; *The Inner Side of the Wind* can be read from the back or the front.

Director Emir Kusturica sets the bar on Serbian cinema with his raucous approach to storytelling. Look for *Underground* (1995), the surreal tale of seemingly never-ending Balkan conflicts, *Black Cat, White Cat* (1998), *Zavet* (2007) and *Life is a Miracle* (2004).

Modern music means anything from wild Romani music to drum'n'bass, funk, soul or hip hop. Don't miss the Exit Festival (see boxed text, p1008). Ethnic folk is crossed with techno to create 'turbofolk', controversial for its nationalist overtones during the Milošević era but now more mainstream fun.

Marija Šerifović's triumph at the 2007 Eurovision Song contest gave Serbia the honour of hosting the event in 2008.

READING UP

Guerrilla Radio by Matthew Collin is an edgy account of B92 radio's resistance to the Milošević regime.

ENVIRONMENT

Midzor is Serbia's highest mountain (2169m), on the Bulgarian border. In the north, Vojvodina is pancake-flat agricultural land. South of the Danube, rolling hills crest where the eastern outpost of the Dinaric Alps slices southeastwards.

The country's major national parks are Kopaonik (popular with package skiers) and Fruška Gora (p1008), dotted with functioning monasteries.

Serbia faces pollution around Belgrade and dumping of industrial waste into the Sava River. Some remnants of the 1999 NATO bombings are ecological hazards.

TRANSPORT

GETTING THERE & AWAY

Air

Belgrade's **Nikola Tesla Beograd airport** (☎ 011-209 444; www.airport-Belgrade.co.yu) serves most international flights, including those operated by national carrier **JAT** (☎ 011-311 4222; www.jat.com).

BORDER CROSSINGS

Entering Hungary is a breeze from Subotica, Bosnia and Hercegovina are just a hop from Zlatibor, Romania's a skip from Vršac, and Bulgaria a jump from Pirot. From Novi Pazar, a fare of just €5 and a spare three hours get you to Pristina in Kosovo.

CONNECTIONS

Belgrade is well connected to neighbours near and far. Bucharest, Budapest, Ljubljana, Moscow, Sofia and Zagreb are a train ride away, while buses serve Banja Luka, Ljubljana, Sarajevo and Split. Popular connections are buses to France and Germany, and trains from Belgrade to Budapest or Zagreb.

Bus

Bus services travel as far north as Sweden and as far east as Turkey.

Car & Motorcycle

Drivers need an International Driving Permit and vehicles need a Green Card.

Train

Daily train services from Belgrade include the following (prices include sleeper): Budapest (2780DIN, seven hours), İstanbul (5190DIN, 26 hours), Ljubljana (4150DIN, 10 hours), Moscow (10,000DIN, 50 hours), Munich (9000DIN, 17 hours), Thessaloniki (4200DIN, 16 hours), Vienna (6950DIN, 11 hours) and Zagreb (3100DIN, seven hours). Visit www.serbianrailways.com for more details.

The route to Bar (1000DIN plus three-/six-berth couchette 1000/564DIN, 11½ hours) along the Montenegrin coast is popular.

GETTING AROUND

Bicycle

Vojvodina is relatively flat but main roads make for dull days. Picturesque winding roads down south have narrow shoulders.

Bicycle paths are improving in larger cities.

Bus

Connections can be sporadic outside major hubs, particularly in southern Serbia.

Reservations are only worthwhile for international routes and during festivals. Receipts are given for stowed luggage (20DIN to 50DIN).

Car & Motorcycle

Major car hire companies are ubiquitous. Small car hire typically costs €50 per day; check where you *can't* take the car.

The **Automobile & Motorcycle Association of Serbia** (www.amss.org.yu) provides roadside assistance (☎ 987).

Train

Serbian Railways (☎ 011-361 4811; www.serbianrailways.com; 6 Nemanjina St, Belgrade) serves Novi Sad, Subotica and Niš from Belgrade.

BELGRADE БЕОГРАД

☎ 011 / pop 1.58 million

Edgy, adventurous, audacious Belgrade evolves before your eyes. Beograd means 'White City' but this colourful capital is anything but bland.

Here the Sava River meets the Danube, east meets west, and old-world culture gives way to new-world nightlife. Socialist blocks are squeezed between art-nouveau masterpieces, and remnants of the Habsburg legacy contrast with Ottoman relics. Grand restaurants, funky bars and smoky dens line Knez Mihailova, overlooked by the ancient Kalemegdan Citadel crowning the city. Deeper in the heart of Belgrade, museums guard the country's heritage, where Tito and other ghosts of the past have been laid to rest.

Young Serbs are shaking off the past, almost on a nightly basis when they shake and groove into the early hours. Young or old, day or night, bustling Belgraders keep this eclectic city alive.

ORIENTATION

The central train station and two adjacent bus stations are on the southern side of the city centre. A couple of blocks northeast, Terazije runs to Trg Republike, from where Knez Mihailova, Belgrade's pedestrian boulevard, leads to Kalemegdan Citadel.

INFORMATION

Bookshops & Internet Access

Mamut (Map pp1004-5; ☎ 0645 152248; cnr Knez Mihailova & Sremska; per hr 100DIN; 9am-10pm Mon-Sat, noon-10pm Sun) An expansive book and stationary shop with a top-floor internet cafe. Wi-fi is free if you BYO laptop.

EMERGENCY NUMBERS

- Ambulance ☎ 94
- Fire ☎ 93
- Police ☎ 92
- Roadside assistance inside/outside Belgrade ☎ 987/011-9800

SERBIA

Internet Resources

Belgrade City (www.beograd.org.yu)
Belgrade in Your Pocket (www.inyourpocket.com/serbia/city/Belgrade.html)
Tourist Organisation of Belgrade (www.tob.co.yu)

Medical Services

Boris Kidrič Hospital Diplomatic Section (Map pp1004-5; ☎ 643 839; Miloša Porcerca Pasterova 1; ⏲ 7am-7pm Mon-Fri)
Klinički Centar (Map pp1004-5; ☎ 361 7777; Miloša Porcerca Pasterova 2; ⏲ 24hr) Medical clinic.
Prima 1 (Map pp1004-5; ☎ 361 0999; Nemanjina 2; ⏲ 24hr) All-hours pharmacy.

Tourist Information

Tourist Organisation of Belgrade (Map pp1004-5; www.tob.co.yu) Central Railway Station (☎ 361 2732; ⏲ 9am-8pm Mon-Fri, 9am-5pm Sat, 10am-4pm Sun); Makedonska 5 (☎ 334 3460; ⏲ 9am-9pm Mon-Fri, 10am-4pm Sat & Sun); Terazije Underpass (☎ 635 622; ⏲ 9am-8pm Mon-Fri, 9am-5pm Sat) Brochures, maps and events listings.

SIGHTS

Some 115 battles have been fought over **Kalemegdan Citadel** (Map pp1004–5), fortified since Celtic times. Much of what stands today is the product of 18th-century Austro-Hungarian and Turkish reconstructions. Through **Stambol Gate** (Map pp1004–5), built by the Turks in around 1750, you'll find yourself in the firing line of cannons and tanks as you enter the **Military Museum** (Map pp1004-5; ☎ 334 4408; admission 100DIN; ⏲ 10am-5pm Tue-Sun), presenting a complete military history of former Yugoslavia up to the 1999 NATO bombings. Captured Kosovo Liberation Army (KLA) weapons are on display.

The 1831 **Palace of Princess Ljubica** (Map pp1004-5; ☎ 2638 264; Kneza Sime Markovića 8; admission 100DIN; ⏲ 10am-5pm Tue & Wed, noon-8pm Thu, 10am-5pm Fri & Sat, 10am-2pm Sun), with an authentic *hamam* (Turkish bath), was the domain of Prince Miloš' wife.

The **National Museum** (Map pp1004-5; ☎ 330 6000; www.narodnimuzej.org.yu; Trg Republike 1a) was closed for renovations at the time of writing. A few blocks away, the **Ethnographical Museum** (Map pp1004-5; ☎ 328 1888; Studentski Trg 13; admission 60DIN; ⏲ 10am-5pm Tue-Sat, 9am-2pm Sun) contains traditional costumes, tools and handicrafts.

The **Gallery of Frescoes** (Map pp1004-5; ☎ 2621 491; www.narodnimuzej.org.yu; Cara Uroša 20; admission free; ⏲ 10am-5pm Tue, Wed, Fri & Sat, noon-8pm Thu, 10am-2pm Sun) contains full-size replicas of church and monastery paintings, exact down to reproduced scratches.

The **Museum of Automobiles** (Map pp1004-5; ☎ 303 4625; Majke Jevrosime 30; admission 100DIN; ⏲ 11am-7pm) is a compelling collection of vehicles including Tito's '57 Cadillac convertible.

Meet the man on the 100DIN note at the wondrously interactive **Nikola Tesla Museum** (Map pp1004-5; ☎ 2433 886; www.tesla-museum.org; Krunska 51; admission 200DIN; ⏲ 10am-6pm Tue-Fri, 10am-1pm Sat & Sun).

Behind the central post office, the church of **Sveti Marko** (Map pp1004-5; ☎ 323 1940; Bulevar Kralja Aleksandra 17) was modelled on Gračanica Monastery in Kosovo (see p716), and contains the grave of Emperor Dušan (1308–55). Behind it is the tiny white **Russian church** (Map pp1004–5) erected by Russian refugees who fled the October Revolution.

South down Kralja Milana and across Trg Slavija, **Sveti Sava** (Map p1003; Svetog Save) is the world's biggest Orthodox church, a fact entirely obvious from under its dome. The church is built where the Turks apparently burnt relics of St Sava (the founder of the independent Serbian Orthodox Church).

Maršal Tito's grave (Kuća Cveća, House of Flowers; Map p1003; ☎ 367 1485; Bulevar Mira; admission free; ⏲ 10am-5pm Tue-Sat, 10am-1pm Sun) displays gifts presented to Tito, including a Rolls-Royce from Queen Elizabeth II, a writing set from JFK and a bowl given 'with great admiration and affection' by Elizabeth Taylor and Richard Burton. Take trolleybus 40 or 41 at the south end of Parliament on Kneza Miloša.

The **Aviation Museum** (off Map p1003; ☎ 267 0992; admission 400DIN; ⏲ 8.30am-7pm summer, 9am-3.30pm winter, closed Mon) at the airport in Suračin contains rare planes, a WWII collection, and bits of the American stealth fighter shot down in 1999.

GETTING INTO TOWN

Nikola Tesla Beograd airport is 18km west of Belgrade. **JAT bus** (☎ 675 583; one way 160DIN; ⏲ 5am-9pm airport-town, 7am-10pm town-airport) connects the airport hourly with Trg Slavija and the train station. Alternatively, bus 72 connects the airport with Zeleni Venac (60DIN, every 30 minutes) in the centre of Belgrade. Ignore prowling taxi sharks; ask the tourist office in the arrivals hall to call a taxi for you. A taxi from the airport to Knez Mihailova should be around 1100DIN.

SERBIA

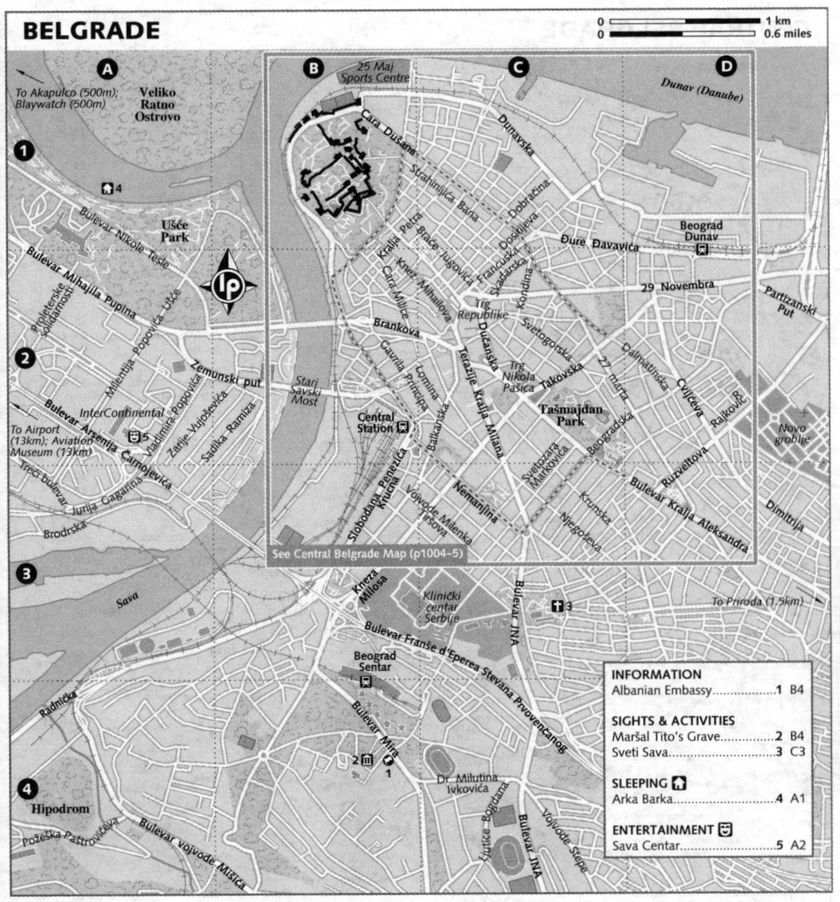

Skadarska (Map pp1004–5), Belgrade's bohemian answer to Montmartre, is worth exploring. East of Trg Republike, this cobblestoned strip was where Belgrade's creative community gathered in cafes and restaurants.

SLEEPING

The **Youth Hostel Organisation** (Ferijalni Savez Beograd; Map pp1004-5; ☎ 324 8550; www.hostels.org.yu; 2nd fl, Makedonska 22; 9am-5pm) does deals with local hotels for HI members and international student card holders.

UniTurs Hostel (Map pp1004-5; ☎ 3346 241; www.uni-turs.com; Andrićev Venac 12/3; dm 800-960DIN, tw 1200DIN;) A well-equipped sparkling surprise in an otherwise dingy building.

Hostel City Center (Map pp1004-5; ☎ 264 4055; www.hostelcitycenterbelgrade.com; Savski trg 7; dm 850-1020DIN, s/d with shared bathroom from 1890/2520DIN, with private bathroom from 2460/3280DIN, apt 3925DIN) Hotel/hostel hybrid opposite the train station. Airy rooms sans toilets have sinks.

Yellowbed Hostel (Map pp1004-5; ☎ 2628 220; info@yellowbed.net; Višnjićeva 3; dm from 1000DIN;) A terrace, good-humoured staff and a central location behind Studentski Trg.

our pick **Arka Barka** (Map p1003; ☎ 064 200 4445; www.arkabarka.net; Bulevar Nikole Tesle bb; per person €15;) Floating on the Danube (within stumbling distance of barges), Ikea-fresh Arka Barka hostel has a breezy verandah and a couple of private rooms. Walk or take bus 15 or 84.

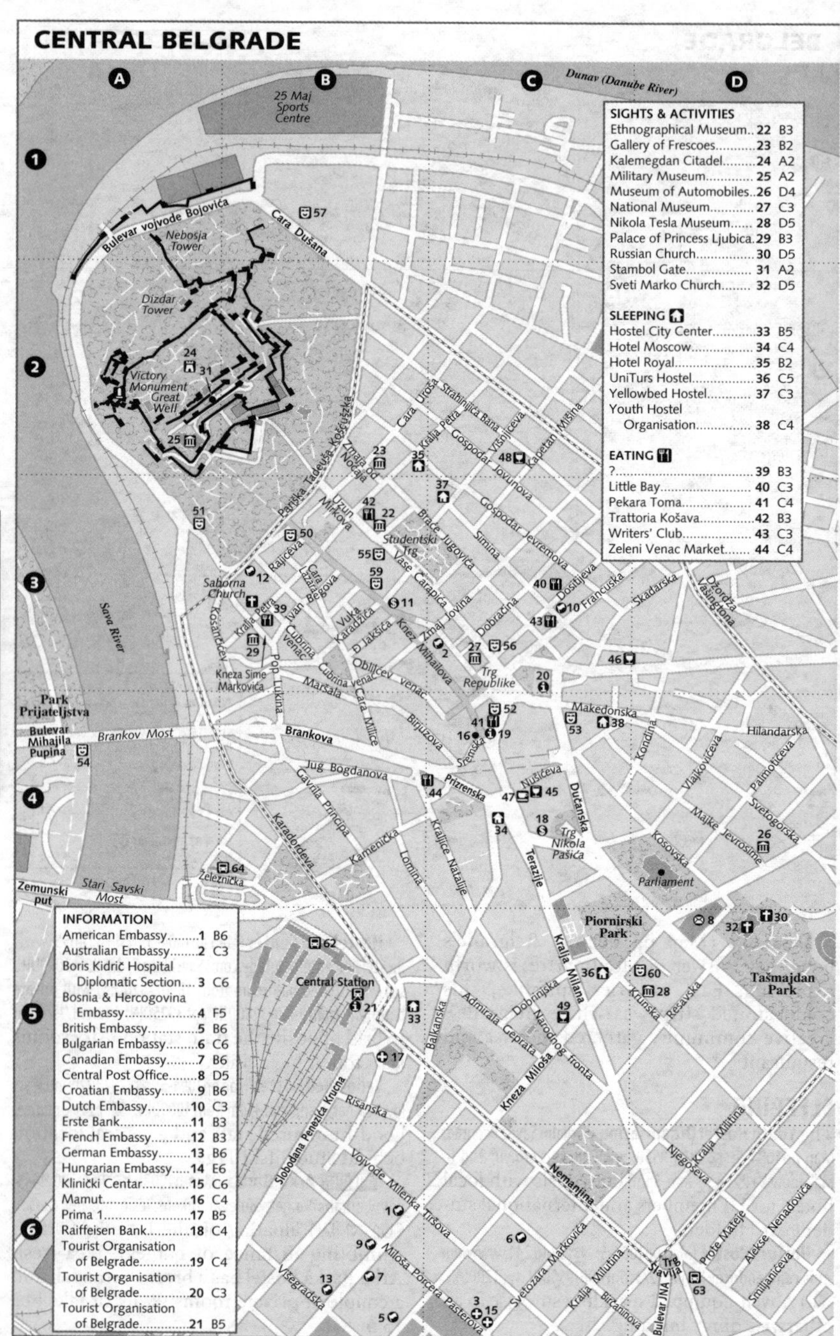
CENTRAL BELGRADE
A
B
C
D
1
2
3
4
5
6
SIGHTS & ACTIVITIES
Ethnographical Museum..22 B3
Gallery of Frescoes...........23 B2
Kalemegdan Citadel.........24 A2
Military Museum.............25 A2
Museum of Automobiles..26 D4
National Museum............27 C3
Nikola Tesla Museum......28 D5
Palace of Princess Ljubica.29 B3
Russian Church...............30 D5
Stambol Gate..................31 A2
Sveti Marko Church........32 D5
SLEEPING
Hostel City Center...........33 B5
Hotel Moscow.................34 C4
Hotel Royal......................35 B2
UniTurs Hostel.................36 C5
Yellowbed Hostel............37 C3
Youth Hostel Organisation...............38 C4
EATING
?.......................................39 B3
Little Bay.........................40 C3
Pekara Toma...................41 C4
Trattoria Košava.............42 B3
Writers' Club...................43 C3
Zeleni Venac Market.......44 C4
INFORMATION
American Embassy..........1 B6
Australian Embassy.........2 C3
Boris Kidrič Hospital Diplomatic Section.....3 C6
Bosnia & Hercogovina Embassy.....................4 F5
British Embassy..............5 B6
Bulgarian Embassy.........6 C6
Canadian Embassy..........7 B6
Central Post Office.........8 D5
Croatian Embassy...........9 B6
Dutch Embassy..............10 C3
Erste Bank.....................11 B3
French Embassy.............12 B3
German Embassy...........13 B6
Hungarian Embassy.......14 E6
Klinički Centar...............15 C6
Mamut..........................16 C4
Prima 1..........................17 B5
Raiffeisen Bank.............18 C4
Tourist Organisation of Belgrade.............19 C4
Tourist Organisation of Belgrade.............20 C3
Tourist Organisation of Belgrade.............21 B5
Dunav (Danube River)
25 Maj Sports Centre
Bulevar vojvode Bojovića
Cara Dušana
Nebosja Tower
Dizdar Tower
Victory Monument
Great Well
Sava River
Park Prijateljstva
Bulevar Mihajila Pupina
Brankov Most
Brankova
Zemunski put
Stari Savski Most
Saborna Church
Central Station
Piornirski Park
Parliament
Tašmajdan Park
Trg Republike
Studentski Trg
Trg Nikola Pašića
Trg Slavija
Pariška
Tadeuša Košćuszka
Cara Uroša
Strahinjića Bana
Kralja Petra
Višnjićeva
Kapetan Mišina
Gospodar Jovunova
Gospodar Jevremova
Zmaja od Nočaja
Uzun Mirkova
Braće Jugovića
Simina
Rajićeva
Cara Lazara
Ivan Begova
Vasé Čarapića
Zmaj Jovina
Dobračina
Dositjeva
Francuska
Skadarska
Džordža Vašingtona
Kosančićev
Vuka Karadžića
Knez Mihailova
Đ Jakšića
Čubrina venac
Obilićev venac
Kneza Sime Markovića
Pop Lukina
Maršala
Cara Milice
Birjuzova
Makedonska
Kondina
Hilandarska
Vlajkovićeva
Palmotićeva
Svetogorska
Majke Jevrosime
Kosovska
Sremska
Nušićeva
Dučanska
Jug Bogdanova
Prizrenska
Gavrila Principa
Karađorđeva
Kamenička
Lomina
Kraljice Natalije
Terazije
Železnička
Kralja Milana
Dobrinjska
Admirala Geprata
Narodnog fronta
Krunska
Resavska
Balkanska
Risanska
Kneza Miloša
Slobodana Penezića Krcuna
Vojvode Milenka
Tiršova
Nemanjina
Njegoševa
Kralja Milutina
Prote Mateje
Alekse Nenadovića
Smiljanićeva
Svetozara Markovića
Miloša Pocera
Pasterova
Višegradska
Kralja Milutina
Birčaninova
Bulevar JNA
SERBIA

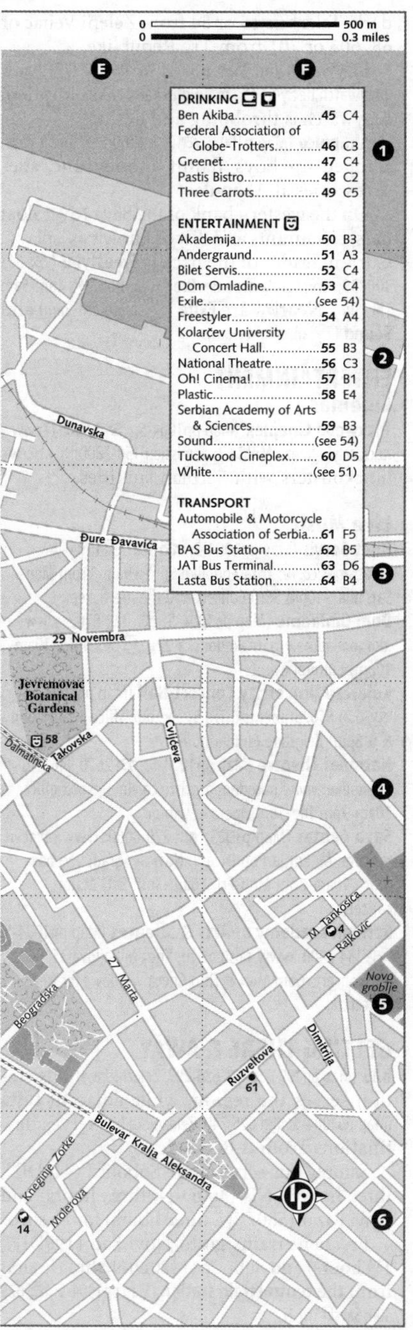

> **SPLURGE**
>
> **Hotel Moscow** (Hotel Moskva; Map pp1004-5; ☎ 268 6255; hotelmoskva@absolutok.net; Balkanska 1; s/d from €100/143;) A source of pride since opening in 1906, the art-nouveau Hotel Moscow has not made a move to modernise. Despite some single rooms persecuting you for not being a double, and prices that mock the common man, this is *the* place to scribble your memoirs at a big old desk.

Hotel Royal (Map pp1004-5; ☎ 2634 222; www.hotelroyal.co.yu; Kralja Petra 56; s 2640-3600DIN, d 3600DIN;) Perpetually buzzing Royal hits three Cs: cheap, clean, central. Consequently crowded.

EATING

Priroda (off Map p1003; ☎ 2411 890; sneskapriroda@yahoo.com; Batutova 11; meals 25-400DIN; noon-7pm) Even carnivores will appreciate the break from Serbian staples at vegetarian Priroda, about 6km east of the central train station.

? (Map pp1004-5; ☎ 635 421; Kralja Petra 6; meals 250-500DIN; 8am-midnight) An essential albeit hit-and-miss dining experience, this timeworn tavern offers lamb *ispod saća,* or even young bull's sex glands. Its quizzical name is the result of the adjacent church objecting to the tavern initially naming itself Cathedral Cafe, saying it 'desecrated the name of God's temple'. Baffled, the tavern relabelled with a '?'.

our pick **Little Bay** (Map pp1004-5; ☎ 328 4163; www.little-bay.co.uk; Dositijeva 9a; meals 400DIN; 9am-1am) Inexplicably cheap and one of the best in town. Enjoy a roast (295DIN) and live opera from a private opera box.

Writers' Club (Klub Književnika; Map pp1004-5; ☎ 2627 931; Francuska 7; meals 400-600DIN; 8pm-2am) A culinary and literary institution. Solid staples include the stuffed courgettes and roast lamb with potatoes.

Trattoria Košava (Map pp1004-5; ☎ 2627 344; www.trattoriakosova.com; Kralja Petra 36; meals 400-800DIN; 8am-1am Mon-Fri, noon-1am Sat & Sun) Choose between Italian and Serbian mains or just massacre berry pancakes (250DIN) in wholesome lamp-lit nostalgic surrounds.

Pekara Toma (Map pp1004-5; Kolarčeva 10; 24hr) To satiate post or pre-clubbing munchies, follow your nose for freshly baked pick-me-ups.

Zeleni Venac Market (Map pp1004-5; cnr Brankova Prizrenska & Narodnog Fronta; 7am-4pm) DIY scrounging ground for fresh food and quick take-away snacks.

DRINKING & CLUBBING

Bars & Cafes

Greenet (Map pp1004-5; ☎ 323 8474; Nušićeva 3; ⏰ 8am-midnight) Greenet is *the* place for coffee connoisseurs. You can take away your hot beverage, but it's better enjoyed in the green and brown tones draped over the width of Nušićeva. Linger over a mocha – the local favourite.

our pick **Federal Association of Globe-Trotters** (Map pp1004-5; ☎ 324 2303; www.aur.org.yu; Bul Despota Stefana 7/1; ⏰ 1pm-midnight Mon-Fri, 3pm-late Sat & Sun) Through the black gate, past the lazy cats and down the dingy staircase is an oasis of eclectic cool. Trust us.

Ben Akiba (Map pp1004-5; ☎ 323 7775; Nušićeva 8; ⏰ 9am-late) Belgrade's worst-kept secret: a converted 1st-floor flat where the city's chic come for cocktails and conversation.

Three Carrots (Map pp1004-5; ☎ 683 748; www.threecarrots.co.yu; Kneza Miloša 16; ⏰ 9am-1am) Fast-flowing Guinness plus occasional live music equals Belgrade's Irish offering.

Pastis Bistro (☎ 328 8188; Strahinjića Bana 52b; ⏰ 8am-late) Mild mood, smooth tunes, suave clientele.

Clubs

Belgrade's ever-changing club scene is limited only by imagination and hours in the day. Ask locals for latest hot spots.

Andergraund (Underground; Map pp1004-5; ☎ 063 407070; www.andergraund.com; Pariška 1a; ⏰ 10am-4am) Sweaty crowds gyrate about the citadel.

White (Map pp1004-5; ☎ 063 308039; Pariška 1a; ⏰ 11am-4am) Next to Andergraund, White pulls a colourful crowd of disco and house fans.

Akademija (Art Kafe 'Fleka'; Map pp1004-5; ☎ 627 846; www.akademija.net, in Serbian; Rajićeva 10; ⏰ 10pm-4am Mon-Sat, noon-2am Sun) Any type of alternative music can happen in the bowels of this place.

Enjoy the views on the summer-only terrace at **Oh! Cinema!** (Map pp1004-5; ☎ 328 4000; Kalemegdan Citadel; ⏰ 11pm-4am) and the pace of **Plastic** (Map pp1004-5; ☎ 064 640 3956; www.club-plastic.com; cnr Dalmatinska & Takovska; ⏰ 10pm-late Thu-Sat).

RIVER BARS & CLUBS

Adjacent to Hotel Jugoslavija in Novi Belgrade, west of the city centre, are the Danube river barges (most closed in winter), which morph from floating bars to thumping clubs after dark. Take bus 15 or 84 from Zeleni Venac or 68, 603 or 701 from Trg Republike.

Blaywatch (off Map p1003; ☎ 064 477771; www.blaywatch.net.yu; ⏰ midnight-4am) As implied, Blaywatch is throbbing and fleshy.

Akapulco (Map p1003; ☎ 778 4760; ⏰ noon-3am) Blinged-up boys flaunt money and she-accessories at Akapulco.

On the western bank of the Sava River float bars, restaurants and discos known as 'splavs'. Current leader of the pack is **Freestyler** (☎ 063 300839; www.splavfree.rs; Brodaska bb; ⏰ 1am-5am Thu-Sun). Nearby are **Exile** (⏰ midnight-3am) and **Sound** (⏰ midnight-3am).

ENTERTAINMENT

Cinemas

Tuckwood Cineplex (Map pp1004-5; ☎ 323 6517; www.tuck.co.yu; Kneza Miloša 7; admission 150-280DIN) shows blockbusters with Serbian subtitles.

Live Music

Bilet Servis (Map pp1004-5; ☎ 303 3311; www.biletservis.co.yu; Trg Republike 5; ⏰ 9am-11pm Mon-Sat, noon-10pm Sun) Concert and theatre tickets.

Dom Omladine (Map pp1004-5; ☎ 324 8202; www.domomladine.org; Makedonska 22; ⏰ box office 10am-10pm) Cultural events.

Kolarčev University Concert Hall (Map pp1004-5; ☎ 630 550; Studentski Trg 5; ⏰ box office 10am-noon & 6-8pm) Belgrade Philharmonia.

National Theatre (Map pp1004-5; ☎ 2620 946; Trg Republike; www.narodnopozoriste.co.yu; ⏰ box office 10am-2pm Tue-Sun) Opera in winter.

Sava Centar (Map p1003; ☎ 220 6060; www.savacentar.com; Milentija Popovića 9, Novi Beograd; ⏰ box office 10am-8pm Mon-Fri, 10am-3pm Sat) Major concerts.

Serbian Academy of Arts & Sciences (Map pp1004-5; ☎ 334 2400; www.saisu.ac.yu; Knez Mihailova 35; ⏰ concerts 6pm Mon & Thu) Check windows for free concerts.

GETTING THERE & AWAY

BAS (Map pp1004-5; ☎ 636 299; Železnička 4) bus station serves the region, while adjacent **Lasta** (Map pp1004-5; ☎ 625 740; Železnička bb) serves destinations around Belgrade.

Sample bus services are Subotica (440DIN, three hours), Niš (460DIN, three hours) and Novi Pazar (580DIN, three hours) for Kosovo.

Frequent trains go to Novi Sad (199DIN, 1½ hours) and Subotica (420DIN, three hours) from the **central train station** (Map pp1004-5; ☎ 629 400; Savski Trg 2).

GETTING AROUND

Bus tickets cost 29DIN from a street kiosk or 40DIN from the driver.

Tram 2 usefully connects bus and train stations with Kalemegdan Citadel.

Wave down distinctly labelled cruising cabs; a 5km trip costs around 200DIN.

VOJVODINA
ВОЈВОДИНА

Serbian highlights spring forth from the level plains of Vojvodina: Subotica is an art-deco dream and Novi Sad hosts Exit (see boxed text, p1008), one of the freshest music festivals in the Balkans. For more information, visit www.vojvodinaonline.com.

NOVI SAD НОВИ САД

☎ 021 / pop 299,000

Cafes spill onto Novi Sad's main thoroughfare (Zmaj Jovina) and atmospheric alleyways become social centres after dark. A 2.5km walk from the bus or train station (or bus 11A) gets you to the centre, where you can pick up info at the **tourist information centre** (☎ 421 811; www.novisadtourism.org.yu; Mihajla Pupina 9; ⏲ 8.30am-8pm Mon-Thu, 7.30am-8pm Fri, 7.30am-2pm Sat).

Sights

Novi Sad's **Petrovaradin Citadel** sits atop a mighty volcanic rock. In the 88 years it took to build (1692–1780), the daily death toll is estimated to have been 70 to 80 of the prisoners who were 'earning their purgatory' building it. Inside is a **museum** (muzgns@eunet.yu; admission 100DIN; ⏲ 9am-5pm Tue-Sun).

Building 35 of the **Museum of Vojvodina** (Muzej Vojvodine; ☎ 420 566; www.muzejvojvodine.org.yu; Dunavska 35-37; admission 100DIN; ⏲ 9am-5pm Tue-Sun) covers Vojvodinian history from Palaeolithic times to the late 19th century. Building 37 takes the story to 1945 with harrowing emphasis on WWI and WWII.

Sleeping

Brankovo Kolo (☎ /fax 528 623; www.hostelns.com; Episkopa Visariona 3; d/tr/q per person €8/7/6; ⏲ 1 Jul-25 Aug; P 💻) An efficient but homey hostel.

Downtown (☎ 64 192 0342; www.hotelsnovisad.com; Njegoševa 2; €10 per person) Book ahead at chilled

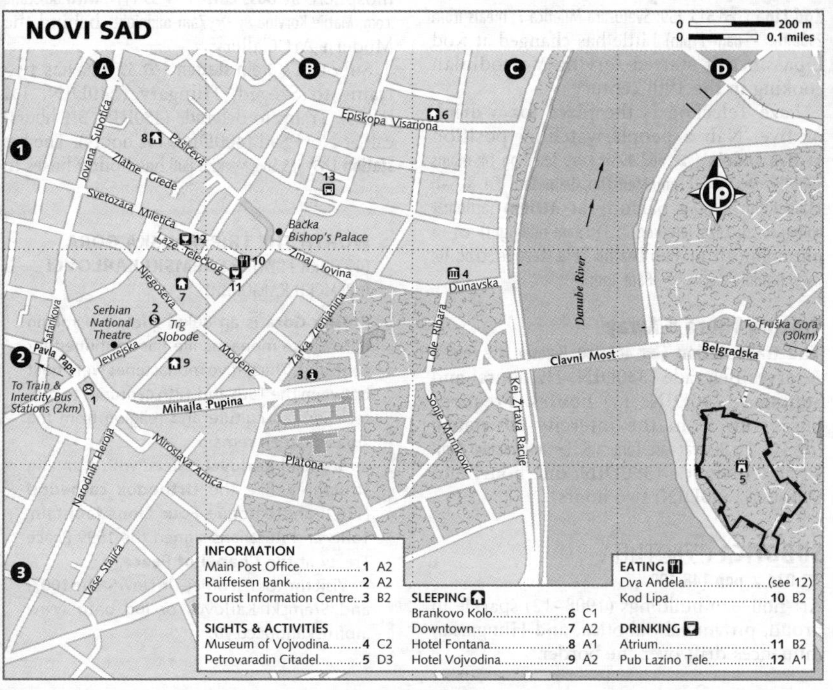

Book your stay at lonelyplanet.com/hotels

ENTERING THE STATE OF EXIT

Each July people unite around Petrovaradin Citadel in Novi Sad for the epic **Exit Festival** (www.exitfest.org). The first, held in 2000, is remembered for having energised a generation against Milošević. In 2006, rather than tickets, revellers were issued with passports to the State of Exit – the 'newest Balkan State' and a decidedly peaceful one. In 2008 the likes of Manu Chau, Primal Scream, the Sex Pistols and the Hives attended…along with around 100,000 people from around the world.

but glistening Downtown, or rock up with fingers crossed.

Hotel Fontana (☎ 621 779; www.fontana-ns.com; Pašićeva 27; s/d/tr 2800/3300/4000DIN; P ✿) Well-sized rustic rooms overlooking the popular courtyard restaurant (www.restoranfontana.com).

Hotel Vojvodina (☎ 622 122; www.hotelvojvodina.co.yu; Trg Slobode 2; s/d from 3100/4400DIN) The atmosphere at this state-run(down) hotel dates back to 1854.

Eating & Drinking

Kod Lipa (☎ 615 259; Svetozara Miletića 7; meals from 250DIN; 8am-11pm) Little has changed at Kod Lipa since it started serving Vojvodinian cooking in the 19th century.

Laze Telečkog is the place for a drink or five. Nab a people-watching position at **Dva Anđela** (☎ 662 4989; Laze Telečkog 14; mains 500DIN; 9am-11pm Mon-Thu, 9am-1am Fri & Sat, 11am-11pm Sun), a balcony at **Atrium** (atrium@bomar.co.yu; Laze Telečkog 2; 9am-midnight) or a phonebooth at **Pub Lazino Tele** (Laze Teleckog 16; www.lazinotele.com; 8am-1am).

Getting There & Away

The **train station** (☎ 443 200; Bulevar Jaše Tomića 4) serves Belgrade (330DIN, 1½ hours) and Subotica (290DIN, 1½ hours). Frequent buses run from the intercity **bus station** (☎ 442 021; Bulevar Jaše Tomića 6; information 6am-11pm) to Belgrade (590DIN, one hour) and Subotica (690DIN, two hours).

SUBOTICA СУБОТИЦА

☎ 024 / pop 148,400

Art-nouveau buildings (1908–12) sparkle in proud, provincial Subotica, and Hungarian influences drift over the border.

The **Tourist information office** (☎ 670 350; ticsu@subotica.net; 8am-8pm Mon-Sat, to noon Sun) is at the town hall. Most sights are nearby along the Korzo and the main square, Trg Republike.

The **Modern Art Gallery** (☎ 552 651; liksus@tippnet.co.yu; Trg Lenjina 5; admission 50DIN; 8am-6pm weekdays, 9am-noon Sat), located opposite the train station, is one of Serbia's most stunning buildings.

The 1910 **town hall** (Trg Republike) also houses a **historical museum** (admission 50DIN; 10am-2pm Tue-Fri, 10am-1pm Sat). The 1854 Romanesque **National Theatre building** on the main square houses Serbia's oldest theatre.

The **synagogue**, Subotica's very first art-nouveau building, is undergoing much-needed renovations.

Well-hidden **Hostel Bosa Milećević** (☎ 548 290; 7 Marije Vojnić Tošinice br 7; per person 930DIN), behind the Ekonomski Fakultet at Segedinksi put 11, saves tidy rooms for budget travellers.

Take tea at time-frozen **Ravel** (☎ 554 670; Nušićeva 2; cakes 50-100DIN; 9am-10pm Mon-Sat, 11am-10pm Sun) or enjoy a meal and art-nouveau atmosphere at **Boss Caffe** (☎ 55 1111; www.bosscaffe.com; Matije Korvina 8; 7am-midnight) behind the Modern Art Gallery.

Subotica's **train station** (☎ 555 606) has two trains to Szeged, Hungary (240DIN, 1¾ hours). Trains to Belgrade (480DIN, 3½ hours) call at Novi Sad (400DIN, 1½ hours). The **bus station** (☎ 555 566; Marksov Put) has hourly buses to

WORTH THE TRIP: FRUŠKA GORA (ФРУШКА ГОРА) & SREMSKI KARLOVCI (СРЕМСКИ КАРЛОВЦИ)

Fruška Gora is an 80km stretch of rolling hills where monastic life has continued for centuries. Thirty-five monasteries were built between the 15th and 18th centuries to protect Serbian culture and religion from the Turks. Sixteen remain.

Sremski Karlovci is lined with stunning structures, like the **Orthodox cathedral** (1762) and baroque **Four Lions fountain**. Turks and Austrians signed the 1699 Peace Treaty at the **Chapel of Peace**.

Visit the tourist offices in Novi Sad (p1007) and Sremski Karlovci, or log onto www.npfruskagora.co.yu.

WORTH THE TRIP: ZLATIBOR (ЗЛАТИБОР)

Zlatibor is a special region of rolling plains, prophecies, traditions and hospitality.

Quirky adventures await in Mokra Gora village. Colourful **Drvengrad** (Küstendorf; ☎ 31-800 686; www.mecavnik.info; Mećavnik hill; admission 180DIN; ⏰ 9am-9pm) was built in 2002 by enigmatic filmmaker Emir Kusturica for his film *Life is a Miracle*. Take Bruce Lee St past the church for prime panoramas.

Delightfully disorienting **Šargan 8 railway** (☎ 31-510 288; www.zeleznicesrbije.com; 2½hr trip 500DIN; ⏰ 10.30am & 1.25pm Apr-Sep, 8am & 4.10pm when required) tourist train was once part of a narrow-gauge railway linking Belgrade with Sarajevo and Dubrovnik.

Reach these sights via bus from Užice or tour with **Zlateks** (☎ 31-841 244; www.zlateks.co.yu; Tržni centar bus station; ⏰ 7am-8pm).

Novi Sad (650DIN, two hours) and Belgrade (900DIN, 3½ hours).

SERBIA DIRECTORY

ACCOMMODATION

A key website for hostel bookings is www.hostelworld.com; it may charge a surcharge but is generally reliable.

More backpacker hostels are opening in urban hubs, but in rural towns private rooms and apartments offer value unheard of elsewhere in Europe; ask at tourist offices.

ACTIVITIES

The more interesting slopes of Kopaonik are used mostly by package ski tourists. The mild gradients of Zlatibor (see boxed text, above) offer hiking and idyllic village explorations in summer months.

BUSINESS HOURS

Usual business hours in Serbia (to be taken with a grain of salt):

Banks (⏰ 8am-5am Mon-Fri, 8am-2pm Sat)
Bars (⏰ 9pm-3am)
Restaurants (⏰ 8am-11pm or midnight)
Shops (⏰ 8am-6pm Mon-Fri, some to early afternoon Sat)

DANGERS & ANNOYANCES

Serb–Albanian tensions remain at the Kosovo border. Check the situation before attempting to cross overland.

EMBASSIES & CONSULATES

Visit www.mfa.gov.yu/Worldframe.htm for a list of Serbian diplomatic missions. The following embassies and consulates are in Belgrade:

Albania (Map p1003; ☎ 011-306 6642; embassy.belgrade@mfa.gov.al; Bulevar Mira 25a)
Australia (Map pp1004-5; ☎ 011-330 3400; belgrade.embassy@dfat.gov.au; Čika Ljubina 13)
Bosnia and Hercegovina (Map p1003; ☎ 011-329 1995; ambasadabih@sbb.co.yu; Milana Tankosića 8)
Bulgaria (Map pp1004-5; ☎ 011-361 3980; bulgamb@eunet.yu; Birčaninova 26)
Canada (Map pp1004-5; ☎ 011-306 3000; bgrad@international.gc.ca; Kneza Miloša 75)
Croatia (Map pp1004-5; ☎ 011-367 9150; crobg@mvpei.hr; Kneza Miloša 62)
France (Map pp1004-5; ☎ 011-302 3500; ambafr_1@eunet.yu; Pariška 11)
Germany (Map pp1004-5; ☎ 011-306 4300; germany@sbb.co.yu; Kneza Miloša 74-6)
Hungary (Map pp1004-5; ☎ 011-244 0472; mission.blg@kum.hu; Krunska 72)
Netherlands (Map pp1004-5; ☎ 011-2023 900; bel@minbuza.nl; Simina 29)
UK (Map pp1004-5; ☎ 011-264 5055; ukembbg@eunet.yu; Resavska 46)
USA (Map pp1004-5; ☎ 011-361 9344; belgrade.usembassy.gov; Kneza Miloša 50)

FESTIVALS & EVENTS

Factor in Novi Sad's **Exit Festival** (www.exitfest.org) in July (see boxed text, opposite) and **International Festival of Street Musicians** (www.cekans.org.yu) held in June.

For full-on festivity, try **Dragačevo Trumpet Festival** (www.guca.co.yu) held in August in Guča.

FOOD & DRINK

A staple snack is *burek*, pastry pie made with *sir* (cheese), *meso* (meat), *krompiruša* (potato) or occasionally *pecurke* (mushrooms); add yoghurt for breakfast. Serbia is famous for grilled meats; *ćevapčići* (grilled kebab) can make a filling meal.

Pivo (beer) is ubiquitous. Many people distil their own *rakija* (brandy) from plums and other fruit.

HOLIDAYS

New Year 1 and 2 January
Orthodox Christmas 7 January
Constitution Day 15 February
International Labour Days 1 and 2 May

LANGUAGE

Serbian is the common language. Many people know some English and German. Vojvodinian Hungarians use the Latin alphabet, Serbs use both Latin and Cyrillic.

MONEY

Serbia retains the dinar though some hotels may require payment in euros. Exchange offices readily change hard currencies into dinars and back again.

ATMs are widespread and cards are accepted by established businesses.

You can tip by rounding up restaurant bills or taxi fares. If a round-up doesn't amount to much, add some coins or think 10%.

POST

Parcels should be taken unsealed to the main post office for inspection.

You can receive poste restante for a small charge.

TELEPHONE

Press *i* on public phones for dialling commands in English. Calls to Europe/Australia/North America cost around 50/100/80DIN a minute. Phonecards (from post offices and tobacco kiosks) don't last long for long distances; it's better to call from post offices.

TOURIST INFORMATION

Tourist offices in major towns are useful starting points.

National Tourist Office of Serbia (www.serbia.travel)
Tourist Organisation of Belgrade (www.tob.co.yu)

VISAS

Tourist visas for less than 90 days aren't required by citizens of most European countries, Australia, New Zealand, Canada and the USA. See the **Ministry of Foreign Affairs** (www.mfa.gov.yu/Visas/VisasR.htm).

SERBIA

Slovakia

HIGHLIGHTS

- **High Tatras** Hike between super cheap mountain huts beneath the crests of one Europe's smallest alpine mountain ranges (p1021)
- **Spiš Castle** Explore the sprawling 4 hectares of fortress ruins high atop a picturesque hillside (p1023)
- **Bratislava** Spend a day wandering the rabbit warren of old town streets, hopping from cafe to cafe at your whim (p1015)

FAST FACTS

- **Area** 49,035 sq km (two-thirds the size of England)
- **Budget** €50 per day in Bratislava
- **Capital** Bratislava
- **Country code** ☎ 421
- **Famous for** Ice hockey (Slovakia makes more ice-hockey pucks than any other country), beautiful women and *slivovice* (firewater-like plum brandy)
- **Languages** Slovak
- **Money** euro (€); A$1 = €0.55; C$1 = 0.60; ¥100 = €0.78; NZ$1 = €0.43; UK£1 = €1.12; US$1 = €0.74
- **Phrases** *Ahoj* (hello), *Dovidenia* (Goodbye), *Ďakujem* (Thank you), *Este pivo prosím* (Another beer please), *Kde je WC (veyt-say)?* (Where's the toilet?)

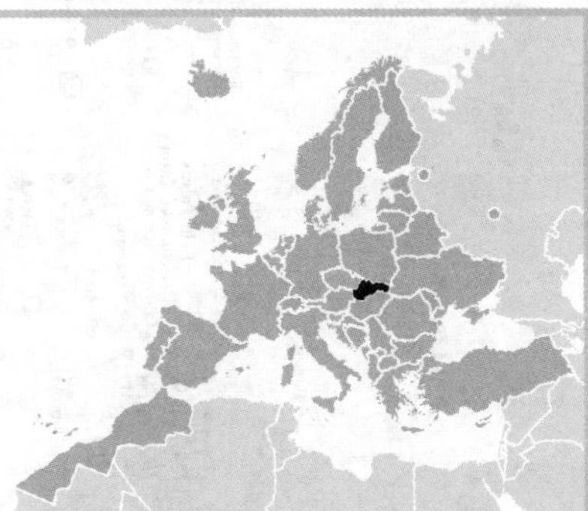

- **Population** 5.4 million
- **Visas** citizens of the UK, USA, Canada, Australia, New Zealand and Japan can enter Slovakia for 90 days without a visa. Nationals of EU member states can travel freely (p1026)

TRAVEL HINTS

Buy a detailed map, locate a castle-ruin symbol and start hiking; there are dozens of fortress remains on public trails.

ROAMING SLOVAKIA

Bratislava is the first point of entry for most travellers. A lucky few sneak in through the back door – through Zakopane, Poland, to the rugged Belá Tatras.

Slov-what-ia? Once famously confused with Slovenia to the south, this wee country has been put on the map – for better or worse – by low-cost carriers and bachelor parties in the capital. The winding streets and countless sidewalk cafes of Bratislava are worth enjoying for a night or two. Just make sure you also venture outside the city to the ancient castles, traditional villages and national parks. Trails criss-cross the country, from the dense, low-hilled forests to the rocky peaks of the High Tatra mountains. And while it's true the communist past left an ugly, modern-concrete mark in places, you'll also find romantic hilltop castles and medieval walled cities to explore. Besides, since prices in Bratislava have risen close to rivalling those in Vienna, you have another reason to head into the countryside – staying and dining there is still a pittance.

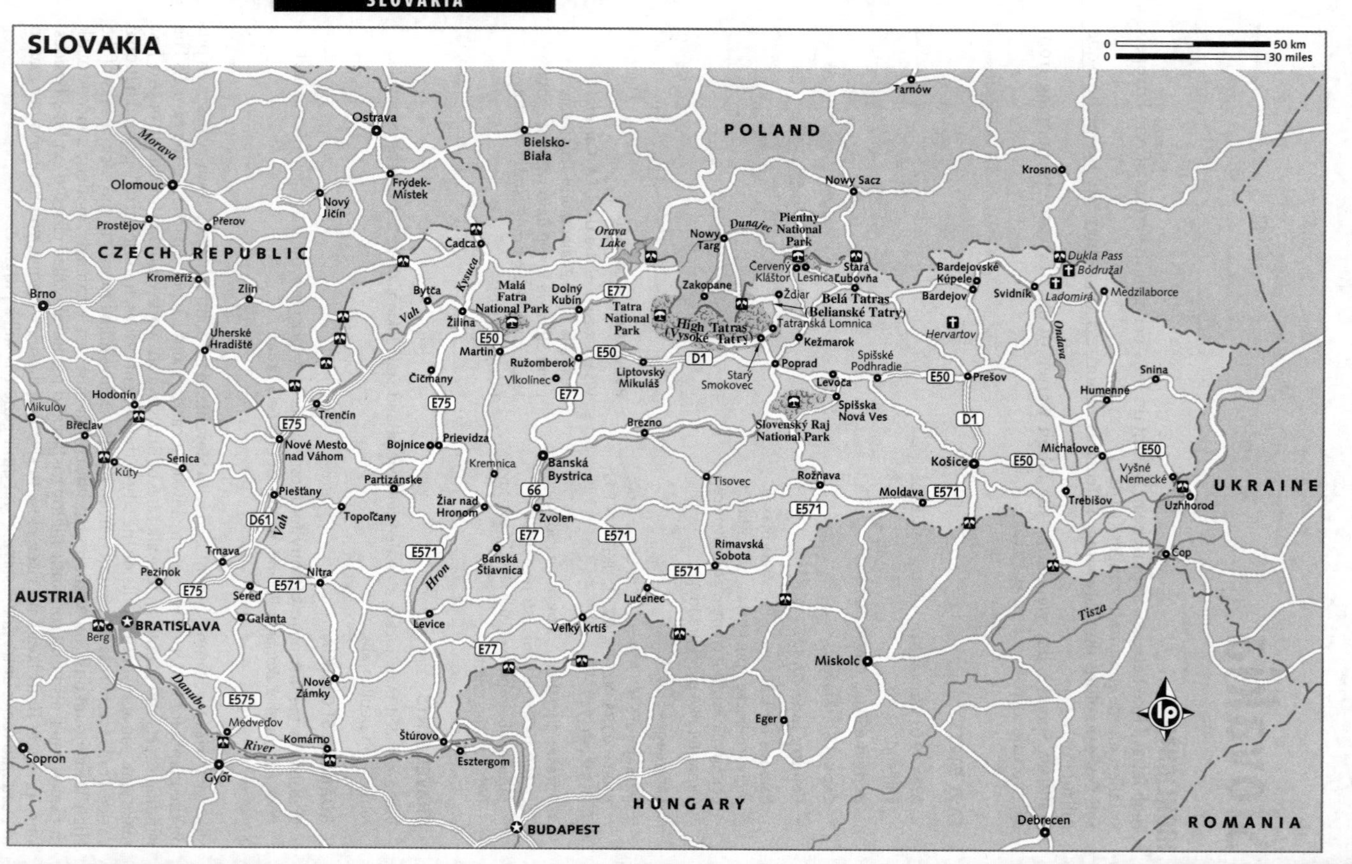
SLOVAKIA
0 50 km
0 30 miles
POLAND
UKRAINE
ROMANIA
HUNGARY
CZECH REPUBLIC
AUSTRIA
BRATISLAVA
BUDAPEST
Brno
Mikulov
Břeclav
Hodonín
Kúty
Senica
Berg
Pezinok
Trnava
Sereď
Galanta
Medveďov
Győr
Sopron
Danube
River
Komárno
Nové Zámky
Nitra
Váh
Piešťany
Nové Mesto nad Váhom
Trenčín
Topoľčany
Partizánske
Bojnice
Prievidza
Čičmany
Bytča
Žilina
Čadca
Kysuca
Martin
Malá Fatra National Park
Ružomberok
Vlkolínec
Dolný Kubín
Orava Lake
Liptovský Mikuláš
Tatra National Park
Zakopane
High Tatras (Vysoké Tatry)
Nowy Targ
Dunajec
Pieniny National Park
Červený Kláštor
Lesnica
Ždiar
Tatranská Lomnica
Belá Tatras (Belianske Tatry)
Starý Smokovec
Poprad
Kežmarok
Levoča
Spišska Nová Ves
Slovenský Raj National Park
Spišské Podhradie
Stará Ľubovňa
Nowy Sacz
Tarnów
Bardejov
Bardejovské Kúpele
Hervartov
Prešov
Svidník
Ladomirá
Dukla Pass
Bódružal
Medzilaborce
Krosno
Ondava
Humenné
Snina
Michalovce
Trebišov
Vyšné Nemecké
Uzhhorod
Cop
Tisza
Debrecen
Košice
Moldava
Miskolc
Rožňava
Eger
Tisovec
Rimavská Sobota
Lučenec
Veľký Krtíš
Brezno
Banská Bystrica
Zvolen
Kremnica
Žiar nad Hronom
Banská Štiavnica
Hron
Levice
Štúrovo
Esztergom
Ostrava
Frýdek-Místek
Nový Jičín
Olomouc
Prostějov
Přerov
Kroměříž
Zlín
Uherské Hradiště
Morava
Bielsko-Biała
E50
E75
E77
E571
E575
D1
D61
66

HISTORY

Slavic tribes wandered west into what would become Slovakia around the 5th century; by the 9th, the territory was part of the short-lived Great Moravian Empire. Subsequently the Magyars (Hungarians) moved in next door and laid claim to the whole territory for the next 800 or so years.

In the 19th century Slovak intellectuals cultivated ties with the Czechs, and after WWI took the nation into the united Czechoslovakia. The day before Hitler's troops invaded Czech territory in March 1939, a fascist puppet state set up the first independent Slovakia as a German ally. It was not a populist move, however, and in August 1944 Slovak partisans instigated the ill-fated Slovak National Uprising (Slovenské Národné Povstanie, or SNP), inspiring countless future street names.

After 1948, power was centralised in Prague until the 1989 Velvet Revolution brought down the curtain on communism. Vladimír Mečiar and the Movement for a Democratic Slovakia (HZDS) came to power in 1992 along with a zealous nationalism, and the Czechoslovak federation dissolved peacefully on 1 January 1993. Slovakia became an independent nation and the balance of power shifted from left to right and back again. In May 2004, the country entered NATO and the EU, and in January 2009 adopted the euro as the official currency.

THE CULTURE

A deeply religious (84% claim religious affiliation, 82% of which are Catholic) and familial people, Slovaks have strong social ties and a deep sense of folk traditions. Young people are generally warm and open, often speaking English, but there can be a reserve about the older generations. So many long faces on public buses! If you're able to break through (asking for help often works), the shell cracks to reveal amazing generosity and hospitality. Thankfully, surly service is now the exception rather than the rule in the tourist industry.

Government statistics estimate that Slovakia's population is 86% Slovak, 10% Hungarian, 0.8% Czech and 1.7% Roma (though some nongovernmental groups estimate the Roma population as high as 4%). The Roma are still viewed with uncompromising suspicion and some live in eastern Slovakian settlements with substandard conditions.

SPORT

Wander into any bar or restaurant during puck-pushing season (September to April) and 12 large men and an ice rink will never be far from the TV screen. Local club rivalries are heated, but the Olympic team showing has flagged in recent years. The news that Slovakia will host the 2011 World Championships, and that Bratislava will get a snazzy new stadium, surely perked up fans.

Football (soccer) fills the summer months, SK Slovan Bratislava being the nation's most successful team.

ARTS

Traditional folk arts, from music to architecture, are at the heart of Slovakia's charm. Uľuv is the national folk-art collective, with stores all over the country. The nation has some striking examples of religious art and architecture, including the sculpted altar at the Church of St Jacob in Levoča (p1022), the Cathedral of St Elizabeth in Košice (p1023) and the nail-less wooden churches in far eastern Slovakia (p1024).

ENVIRONMENT

Culminating in the icy peaks of the High Tatras, Slovakia is a crescendo of forested hills and jagged mountains. With all this natural beauty it's not surprising that more than 20% of the country is designated as protected parkland and weekend walks in nature are a national obsession.

Watchdog groups like the International Union for the Conservation of Nature have protested that more and more development in the High Tatras has put national park status in question.

TRANSPORT

GETTING THERE & AWAY

Air

MR Štefánika Airport (BTS; www.airportbratislava.sk) receives flights from across Western Europe. British destinations are particularly well served from Bratislava by **Ryanair** (FR; ☎ 353-1 249 7791; www.ryanair.com) and **SkyEurope Airlines** (NE; ☎ 02-4850 1000; www.skyeurope.com). SkyEurope also flies to London from Košice and Poprad. **Czech Airlines** (OK; ☎ 02-5720 0710; www.czechairlines.com) shuttles between Prague and both Bratislava and Košice. To get here from beyond

READING UP

Stanislav Kirschbaum's *A History of Slovakia – The Struggle for Survival* is a very readable history. Martin Šimečka's *Year of the Frog* is an interesting portrayal of life in the communist '80s. For more in-depth travel information about Slovakia, don't mind if we recommend Lonely Planet's *Czech & Slovak Republics*.

the European continent, use **Vienna International Airport** (VIE; www.viennaairport.com), 60km from Bratislava, which is connected by hourly buses.

Boat

Plying the waters is a cruisey way to get to Bratislava from neighbouring Danube cities Vienna (one way €22 to €28, 1½ hours) and Budapest (one way €79, four hours). **Slovenská plavba a prístavy** (☎ 02-5293 2226; www.lod.sk; Hydrofoil Terminal, Fajnorovo nábr 2; ⌚ Apr-Sep) runs one or two daily hydrofoils to each. **Twin City Liner** (☎ 0903610716; www.twincityliner.com; Propeller Terminal, Rázusovo nábr; ⌚ Jun-Oct) operates up to six boats a day between Bratislava and Vienna only.

Bus

Eurolines (☎ 02-5556 7349; www.eurolines.sk) runs direct buses between Bratislava and Prague (€12, four hours, one daily), Budapest (€19, 3½ hours, one daily) and Western European cities.

Car & Motorcycle

All foreign drivers' licences with photo ID are valid in Slovakia. As well as your vehicle's registration papers, you need a Green Card (which proves drivers travelling through Europe have insurance that complies with the minimum requirements of the places that they drive through) – for more information, see p1240. Your vehicle must display a nationality sticker and carry a first-aid kit and warning triangle.

Train

Direct trains connect Bratislava with Prague (€27, 4½ hours, six daily), Budapest (€21, three hours, seven daily) and Vienna (€9, one hour, 30 daily). One nightly departure links Bratislava with Kraków (€36, 7½ hours, one daily) and Warsaw (€40, 8¼ hours, one daily) in Poland. A sleeper train leaves Košice every evening for Moscow (€57, 36 hours – *ugh!*).

CONNECTIONS

You can fly from Europe into Slovakia itself, but Bratislava is just 60km from the well-connected Vienna International Airport. By train from Bratislava, Budapest (three hours) and Prague (five hours) are easy to reach. You can connect to Zakopane, Poland (2½ hours) from Poprad near the Tatra Mountains, and to Uzhhorod, Ukraine (2½ hours) through Košice.

GETTING AROUND

Checking nationwide bus, train and plane schedules is easiest at http://cp.atlas.sk.

Bicycle

Roads are often narrow and in towns cobblestones and tram tracks can be a dangerous combination. Theft is a problem, so a lock is a must. The cost of transporting a bicycle by rail is usually 10% of the train ticket, but not all trains have bicycle compartments.

Bus

National buses run by **Slovenská autobusová doprava** (SAD; www.sad.sk) are comparably priced to trains, but less convenient for most cities in this chapter.

Car & Motorcycle

To use Slovakia's motorways (denoted by green signs), vehicles must have a motorway sticker displayed on the windshield. Rental cars already have them. You can buy these at petrol stations (€6 for a week, €11 for a month; for vehicles up to 1.5 tonnes).

Parking restrictions are eagerly enforced: always buy a ticket from a machine, or the person wandering around with a satchel, and display it on your dashboard.

Hitching

Hitchhiking is not unheard of in rural areas. If you do hitch, it is safer to travel in pairs.

Local Transport

City buses and trams operate from around 4.30am to 11.30pm daily. Tickets are sold at public transport offices, at newsstands and from ticket machines, and must be validated once you're aboard.

Train

Slovak Republic Railways (Železnice Slovenskej republiky; www.zsr.sk) provides a cheap and efficient national service. Most of the places covered in this chapter are on or near the main railway line between Bratislava and Košice.

BRATISLAVA

☎ 02 / pop 426,100

A charming old town lies across the river from communist concrete block housing estates, and an age-old castle shares the skyline with the 1970s, UFO-like New Bridge – the capital city is nothing if not a host of contrasts. Still, narrow pedestrian streets, pastel 18th-century rococo buildings and sidewalk cafes galore make for a supremely strollable – if miniscule – historic centre. Chic wannabe bars and restaurants continue to pop up and the old town buzzes with more and more European visitors in the wake of euro conversion. You could say the city's been discovered.

ORIENTATION

The old town centre is bounded by Hodžovo nám to the north, the castle to the west, Šafariková nám to the east and Hviezdoslavovo nám and the Danube to the south.

INFORMATION

Bookshops

Next Apache (Panenská 28; 9am-10pm Mon-Fri, 10am-10pm Sat & Sun) Loads of used English books and a comfy cafe.

Discount Cards

The Bratislava Culture & Information Centre sells the Bratislava City Card (one/two/three days for €6/10/12), which includes city transport and provides discounted museum admissions.

Emergency

Main Police Station (☎ 159; Gunduličova 10)

Internet Access

Internet Kaviaren (☎ 095248208; 1st fl, Kamenné nám 1; per 15 min €1; 9am-9pm Mon-Fri, 9am-7pm Sat & Sun) Ten terminals hidden behind the garden department in Tesco.

Wifi Café (Ground fl, Tatracentrum, Hodžovo nám 2; per hr €3.50; 8am-10pm Mon-Fri, 11am-10pm Sat & Sun) Six flat-screen terminals; wi-fi for the cost of a beverage.

> **EMERGENCY NUMBERS**
>
> - Ambulance, fire & police ☎ 112

Medical Services

Poliklinika Ruzinov (☎ 4823 4113; Ružinovská 10) Hospital and 24-hour pharmacy.

Money

Old town has an excess of banks and ATMs, with several convenient branches on Poštova and around Kamenné nám. Bus, plane and train stations all have ATMs.

Tourist Information

Bratislava Culture & Information Centre (BKIS; ☎ 16 186; www.bkis.sk; Klobučnícka 2; 8.30am-7pm Mon-Fri, 10am-5pm Sat) Brusque, official city office.

Bratislava Tourist Service (BTS; ☎ 2070-7501; www.bratislava-info.sk; Ventúrska 9; 10am-8pm) Tiny space, but more helpful staff.

City website (http://visit.bratislava.sk)

SIGHTS & ACTIVITIES

Lording over the west side of town, the winding ramparts and grounds of **Bratislava Castle** (Bratislavský hrad; grounds admission free; 9am-8pm Apr-Sep, to 6pm Oct-Mar) are great for a walk overlooking the city. During the Turkish occupation of Budapest, this was the seat of Hungarian royalty. A fire devastated the fortress in 1811 and most of what you see today is a reconstruction from the 1950s. Except for a small archaeology exhibit on the castle, most of the interiors that make up the **Historical Museum** (Historické múzeum; ☎ 5441 1441; www.snm.sk; adult/concession €3/1.50; 9am-5pm Tue-Sun) are closed for reconstruction until 2011.

Moving displays about the city's former Jewish community are exhibited at the **Museum of Jewish Culture** (Múzeum židovskej kultúry; ☎ 5441 8507; Židovská 17; adult/concession €6.70/3; 11am-5pm Sun-Fri). Across the street, a relatively modest interior belies the elaborate history of **St Martin's Cathedral** (Dóm sv Martina; ☎ 5443 1359; Rudnayovo nám; admission €1.50; 8-11.30am & 1.30-4.30pm Mon-Sat). Eleven ruling Hungarian

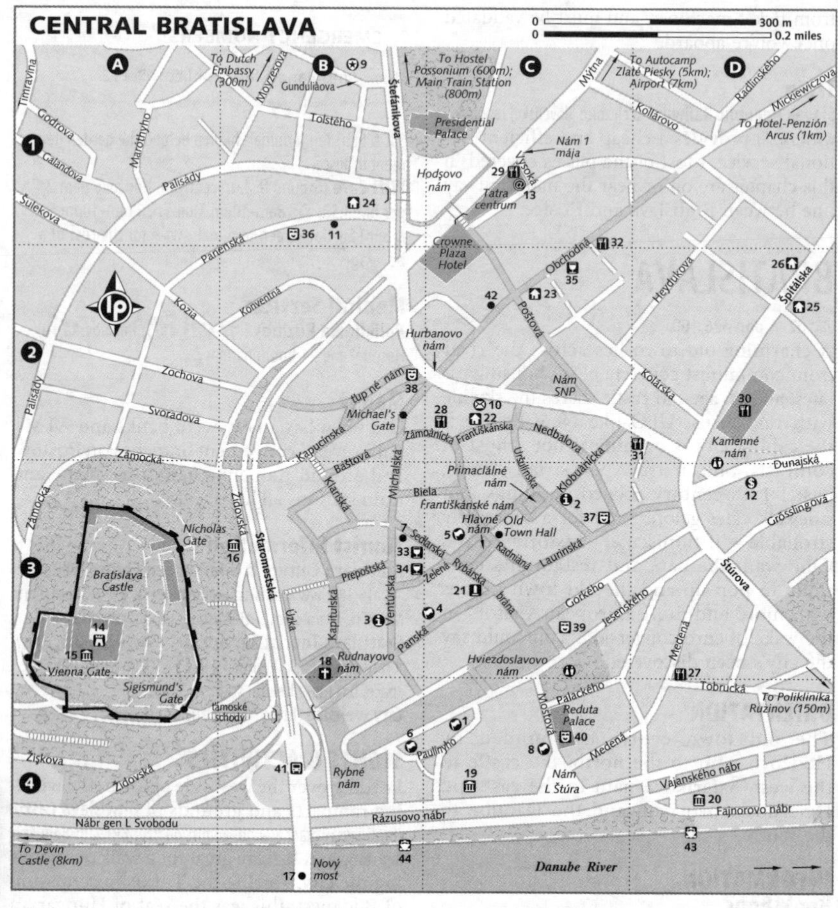

monarchs were crowned here between 1563 and 1830. The busy highway almost touching St Martin's follows the moat outside former city walls. To construct the road and the UFO-like **New Bridge** (Nový most; ☎ 6252 0300; www.u-f-o.sk; Viedenská cesta; observation deck adult/concession €6.70/3.30; ⏰ 10am-11pm) in the 1970s, an ancient synagogue and other old buildings were destroyed. The multicoloured lights flashing from the spaceship after dark come from a sky-high disco, not aliens.

Further along the Danube, check out the first-floor exhibits of the **Slovak National Museum** (Slovenské národné múzeum; ☎ 5934 9122; www.snm.sk; Vajanského nábrežie 2; adult/concession €3.30/1.70; ⏰ 9am-5pm Tue-Sun) for an overview of folk cultures and customs countrywide.

An 18th-century palace and a Stalinist-modernist building make interesting co-hosts for the **Slovak National Gallery** (Slovenská národná galéria; ☎ 5443 4587; www.sng.sk; Rázusovo nábrežie 2; adult/concession €3.30/1.70; ⏰ 10am-5pm Tue-Sun) and its eclectic collection – from Gothic art to graphic design.

FESTIVALS & EVENTS

Bratislava's best events are music-related. Classical music takes centre stage at the **Bratislava Music Festival** (Bratislavské hudobné slávnosti; ☎ 5443 4546; www.bhsfestival.sk), which runs from late September to mid-October. **Bratislava Jazz Days** (Bratislavských jazzových dní; ☎ 5293 1572; www.bjd.sk) swings for a long weekend in September.

INFORMATION
- American Embassy........1 C4
- Bratislava Culture & Information Centre........2 C3
- Bratislava Tourist Service........3 B3
- British Embassy........4 C3
- French Embassy........5 C3
- German Embassy........6 B4
- Internet Kaviaren........(see 30)
- Interpress Slovakia........7 B3
- Irish Embassy........8 C4
- Main Police Station........9 B1
- Main Post Office........10 C2
- Next Apache........11 B1
- Tatra Banka........12 D3
- Wifi Café........13 C1

SIGHTS & ACTIVITIES
- Bratislava Castle........14 A3
- Historical Museum........15 A3
- Museum of Jewish Culture........16 B3
- New Bridge........17 B4
- St Martin's Cathedral........18 B3
- Slovak National Gallery........19 C4
- Slovak National Museum........20 D4
- The Watcher Statue........21 C3

SLEEPING
- Arcadia Hotel........22 C2
- City Hostel........23 C2
- Downtown Backpackers........24 B1
- Hostel Blues........25 D2
- Patio Hostel........26 D2

EATING
- Pizza Mizza........27 D3
- Prašná Bašta........28 C2
- Presto........29 C1
- Tesco Department Store........30 D2
- U Jakubu........31 D2
- U Remeselníka........32 C1

DRINKING
- Dubliner........33 B3
- Greenwich Cocktail Bar........34 B3
- Kréma Gurmánov Bratislavy........35 C2

ENTERTAINMENT
- Apollon Club........36 B1
- Café Štúdio Club........37 C3
- Channels........38 B2
- Slovak National Theatre........39 C3
- Slovak Philharmonic........40 C4

TRANSPORT
- Bus to Devín Castle........41 B4
- DPB Office........42 C2
- Hydrofoil Terminal........43 D4
- Propeller Terminal........44 B4

SLEEPING

The Bratislava Culture & Information Service has a list of the many college dormitories open to all in summer. Hostels listed here have free wi-fi, kitchens, laundries, and beer and wine for sale.

Autocamp Zlaté Piesky (☎ 4425 7373; www.intercamp.sk; Senecká cesta 2; camp site per person/tent €3.50/2.50, bungalow €19-32; ⏲ May-Sep; ♿) The facilities are old but abundant – two restaurants, food stands, playground, minigolf, lake swimming and boat rental. Tents gather here and there on a shady lawn. Take tram 2 from the train station to the terminus here (7km northeast of centre).

Hostel Possonium (☎ 2072 0007; www.possonium.sk; Šancová 20; dm €17-18, d €51; ☒ 🖳) Drawbacks at one of Blava's newer hostels include street noise seeping into the cramped six- to 10-bed rooms and a 2km walk to the centre, but you are across from the train station.

Hostel Blues (☎ 09204020; www.hostelblues.sk; Špitálska 2; dm/d/apt €20/63/108; ☒ 🖳) Friendly, professional staff not only help you plan your days, they offer free sight-seeing tours weekly. Jazz bands play occasional nights in the large coffeehouse-like communal space (with free internet computers). Choose from clean, modern single sex or co-ed dorms, or those with double bunk beds.

Downtown Backpackers (☎ 5464 1191; www.backpackers.sk; Panenská 31; dm €20-25, d €66; ☒ 🖳) Still a boozy (you enter through the bar) Bohemian classic. Red brick walls and tapestries add character to this place, as does the fact you have to walk through some dorm rooms to get to others.

Hotel-Penzión Arcus (☎ 5557 2522; www.hotelarcus.sk; Moskovská 5; s/d incl breakfast €68/100; 🖳) Because this hotel was once an apartment building, dated rooms are quite varied in size and shape (some with balcony, some with courtyard views); bathrooms are new and sparkly. Communal kitchen is available, and some rooms have internet access.

Patio Hostel (☎ 5292 5797; www.patiohostel.com; Špitálska 35; dm €23-28; ☒ 🖳) Much like a college dorm (100 beds, concrete walls); tiny kitchenettes on various floors.

City Hostel (☎ 5263 6041; www.cityhostel.sk; Obchodná 38; s/d €40/60; 🖳) More hotel than hostel, with cubicle-like singles and doubles that have private bathrooms and TV.

GETTING INTO TOWN

The main train station, Hlavná stanica, is about 1km north of the centre. To get there walk down to Šancová, veer right and cross over the pedestrian bridge, then continue south down Štefánikova. You can also take bus 93 to Hodžovo nám or tram 13 to Nám L Štúra.

The bus station *(autobusová stanica)* is 1.5km east of the old town. Turn left out of the main doors and then right to follow Mlynské nivy (which becomes Dunajská) into the centre. Bus 206 connects the bus and train stations, stopping centrally at Hodžovo nám.

Bratislava's MR Štefánika Airport is 7km northeast of the centre. Bus 61 links it to the train station.

EATING

The best meal deals in town are at the worker-oriented (daytime-only) self-service cafeterias called *samoobsluha, bufet* or *jedáleň*. Student-oriented cheap eats line Obchodná.

U Jakubu (☎ 5441 7951; Nám SNP 24; mains €2-5; 🕑 8am-6pm Mon-Fri) Pile on the hearty fried and stewed classics in standard Slovak cafeteria style.

Presto (☎ 5464 8057; ground fl, Tatra Centrum, Hodžovo nám 3; mains €3-6; 🕑 8am-3pm Mon-Fri) Owned by the upscale Italian restaurant next door, this modern cafeteria has an international flavour – and loads of vegetables.

U Remeselníka (☎ 5273 1357; Obchodná 64; mains €4-10) A great, folksy sit-down restaurant; perfect for trying *halušky*, the national dish of dumplings topped with sheep's cheese and bacon.

Prašná Bašta (☎ 5443 4957; Zámočnicka 11; mains €8-15) The round, vaulted interior and hidden courtyard ooze old Bratislava charm. Dishes range from traditional (potato dough–crusted schnitzel) to modern Eastern European (pork medallions with cream, leek and mustard sauce).

And then there are these options:

Tesco (☎ 4446 4057; Kamenné nám 1; 🕑 8am-9pm Mon-Fri, 9am-7pm Sat & Sun) Big basement supermarket for self catering.

Pizza Mizza (☎ 5296 5034; Tobrucká 5; mains €5-11) Long list of wood-fired pizzas; pastas, too.

DRINKING & CLUBBING

Kréma Gurmánov Bratislavy (☎ 5273 1279; Obchodná 52; 🕑 10am-2am Mon-Fri, 4pm-3am Sat, 4pm-midnight Sun) Drink a dark and smoky toast to a statue of Stalin under the Soviet flag at the KGB bar.

Channels (☎ 0911447323; Župné nám 2; 🕑 9.30am-4am) Each of this club's two stories has a bar and a dance floor for grooving to a techno beat.

SPLURGE

Arcadia Hotel (☎ 5949 0500; www.arcadia-hotel.sk; Františkánska 3; s/d incl breakfast €250/280; ⊠ ✱ 🅿) Ornate stained-glass skylights top the interior courtyard, hand-painted designs grace the dining room's vaulted arches…pains have clearly been taken to make sure you know this five-star hotel is a former 13th-century palace. Cuddle into the luxe robe and relax on the red-and-gold silk settee before you dress for a decadent dinner.

WORTH THE TRIP

Fortress lovers should head 8km west of Bratislava to **Devín Castle** (☎ 6573 0105; Muranská; adult/concession €3/1.50; 🕑 10am-5pm Tue-Fri, to 6pm Sat & Sun mid-Apr–Oct), the onetime military plaything of 9th-century warlord Prince Ratislav. Peer at the older bits that have been unearthed and tour a reconstructed palace museum. Bus 29 links the castle with Bratislava's Nový most stop, under the bridge.

Apollon Club (☎ 091548031; Panenská 24; 🕑 6pm-3am Mon-Thu & Sun, 6pm-5am Fri & Sat) The only gay disco in town has two bars and three stages. Monday is karaoke; Sunday, boys only.

Café Štúdio Club (☎ 5443 1796; Laurinská 13; 10am-1am Mon-Wed, to 3am Thu & Fri, 4pm-3am Sat) Bop to the oldies or chill out to jazz – most nights there's live music of some sort here.

To meet rowdy English speakers (and for no other reason), proceed to the **Dubliner** (☎ 5441 0706; Sedlárska 6; 🕑 11-3am Mon-Sat, to 1am Sun); nearby **Greenwich Cocktail Bar** (☎ 0910760222; Zelená 10; 🕑 4pm-2am) has a more mixed Slovak-to-visitor ratio.

ENTERTAINMENT

Slovak National Theatre (Slovenské národné divadlo; www.snd.sk; Hviezdoslavovo nám; 🕑 ticket office 8am-5.30pm Mon-Fri, 9am-1pm Sat) Enjoy opera, ballet and concerts on a budget (€15 to €30 per seat; discount for students with ID). Buy tickets around the back side of the building.

Slovak Philharmonic (Slovenská Filharmónia; ☎ 5920 8233; www.filharmonia.sk; cnr Nám L Štúra & Medená; 🕑 ticket office 1-7pm Mon, Tue, Thu & Fri, 8am-2pm Wed) Listen to classical music in gilt splendour at the philharmonic's Reduta Palace theatre home.

You can buy tickets for Bratislava's hallowed ice hockey team, **HC Slovan** (☎ 4445 6500; www.hcslovan.sk in Slovak; Stadium, Odbojárov 3), online at www.eventim.sk.

GETTING THERE & AWAY

Check bus and train timetables at http://cp.atlas.sk.

Air

For more on flying to Bratislava from abroad, see p1013. **SkyEurope** (NE; ☎ 4850 1000; www.skyeurope.com) has up to five daily flights to Košice

BRATISLAVA FOR FREE

- Search the old town streets for a number of statues like *The Watcher* who peeps out of an imaginary manhole at the intersection of Panská and Rybárska, below a Men at Work sign. See if you can't find *The Frenchman* on a park bench, and *The Photographer* stalking his subject paparazzi-style.
- Browse the crafts market on Hlavné nám; even more food and shopping booths fill the square around Christmas and Easter holidays.
- Log on to the free wi-fi when you're not people-watching in Hviezdoslavovo square.

(50 minutes); book three weeks or more ahead for the best deals.

Boat

From April to September you can cruise to Vienna and Budapest by hydrofoil (see p1014).

Bus

The **main bus station** (☎ reservations 5556 7349; www.eurolines.sk) is 1.3km east of Hlavné nám. Locals call it *Mlynské nivy*, because of the street it's on. Buses leave from here heading to towns across Slovakia, but trains have similar prices, and more convenient schedules.

Train

At least 12 daily trains depart from the **main train station** (Hlavná stanica; www.zsr.sk), 1km north of the centre, for Košice (€19, 5½ hours), most via Trenčín (€6, two hours), Žilina (€10, 2¾ hours) and Poprad (€14, 4¾ to eight hours). Intercity (IC) and Eurocity (EC) trains are the fastest, and require supplements and seat reservations.

GETTING AROUND

Bus & Tram

Dopravný Podnik Bratislava (DPB; ☎ 5950 5950; www.dpb.sk) runs an extensive tram, bus and trolleybus network. You can buy tickets (€0.50/0.60/0.75 for 10/30/60 minutes) at newsstands and at the **DPB office** (Obchodná 14; 9am-5.30pm Mon-Fri). One-/two-/three-/seven-day *turistické cestovné lístky* (tourist travel passes) cost €3/6/7/10 and are sold at the office and train and bus stations. Validate on board. Check routes and schedules at www.imhd.sk.

Taxi

Bratislava's taxis have meters, but there still seems to be a slight English-speaking surcharge. Within the old town a trip should usually cost no more than €10. You'll save money if you have someone who speaks Slovak call a company like **Fun Taxi** (☎ 16 777) ahead instead of picking up a cab on the street.

WESTERN & CENTRAL SLOVAKIA

TRENČÍN

☎ 032 / pop 56,850

What's not to like about a place with a mighty clifftop castle, pretty Renaissance buildings and a lively university population? Roman legionnaires were the first tourists to arrive, establishing a garrison outpost in the 2nd century.

From the bus and train stations walk west through the city park and under the highway past the Tatra Hotel, where a street bears left uphill to Mierové nám, the main square. The **Cultural Information Centre** (☎ 161 86; www.trencin.sk; City Office, Sládkovičova; 10am-5pm Mon-Fri, 10am-noon Sat) has very helpful staff. There are several banks and ATMs on the main square, quite close to **Mike Studio** (Mierové nám 25; internet per hr €2; 9am-10pm Mon-Sat, 10am-10pm Sun), where you can check email.

The reconstructed **Trenčín Castle** (Trenčiansky hrad; ☎ 7435 657; www.muzeumtn.sk; off Matušova; adult/concession €4/2; 9am-5.30pm May-Oct, to 3.30pm Nov-Apr) dates from around the 15th century. You can wander the ramparts after paying admission, but visiting the palace rooms requires taking an included 75-minute tour. Minstrels and sword fighters bring medieval times to life during night tours in July and August. Carved in the rock below the castle is a Roman inscription from AD 179 that recalls the 2nd Legion's victory over the Germanic Kvad tribes. To see it you have to ask at the reception inside the **Hotel Tatra** (Gen MR Štefánika 2).

SLOVAKIA

A line of neat little log cabins lines up riverside at **Autocamping na Ostrove** (☎ 7434 013; http://web.viapvt.sk/autocamping.tn; Ostrov; camp site per person/tent €1.50/2, bungalow per person €7; ⌚ May-15 Sep), on an island in the middle of the Vah River. **Penzión Svorad** (☎ 743 03 22; www.svorad-trencin.sk; Palackého 4; dm €19-26; ☒), a dormlike hostel in a grammar school, is faded at best, but the price – and the castle views – are just right.

For a late-night meal, **Bistro Central** (Štúrovo nám 10; mains €2-5; ⌚ 9am-7pm Mon-Thu, 9am-4am Fri, 7pm-4am Sat) food stand is convenient. Chicken and risotto dishes are quite good at the **Cinema Movie Club Restaurant** (☎ 0902898533; Palackého 33; mains €5-8), but the real steal is the weekday lunch set menu for under €4. Free wi-fi, too.

Numerous cafes, perfect for a drink, line the pedestrian plazas. Check out **Steps Bar & Pub** (☎ 7446 252; Sládkovičova 4-6; ⌚ 10.30am-1am Sun-Thu, to 4am Fri & Sat), which has imports on tap downstairs and a college-age crowd on the dance floor upstairs.

World music, jazz, hip-hop, alternative: Slovakia's largest music festival, **Bazant Pohoda Festival** (www.pohodafestival.sk), rocks the whole town one weekend in July.

Most trains from Bratislava (€6, two hours, seven daily) continue on from here to Košice (€14, four hours) via Žilina (€6, one to two hours).

MALÁ FATRA NATIONAL PARK

☎ 041

A 200-sq-km swathe of its namesake mountain range is incorporated into Malá Fatra National Park (Národný Park Malá Fatra), where pine-clad slopes are topped with eerie, sentinel-like formations. From **Vrátna Valley** (Vrátna dolina; www.vratna.sk), 25km east of Žilina, you can access the trailheads and ski lifts. A **cable car** (kabínkova lanovka; ☎ 5993 049; Chata Vrátna; adult/concession round-trip €10/7; ⌚ 8am-4pm) ride carries you from the top of the valley to the mountain saddles. The long, one-street town of Terchová sits at the lower end of the valley. **Terchová Tourist Information Centre** (☎ 5695 307; www.ztt.sk; Sv Cyrila a Metoda 96, Terchová; ⌚ 8am-5pm Mon-Fri, 9am-4pm Sat, 10am-3pm Sun) can help with accommodation and bike rental; there's an ATM next door.

Buses link Žilina with Terchová (€1.40, 45 minutes) and Chata Vrátna (€1.60, one hour), at the top of the valley, at least every two hours. Žilina is on the main railway line with 12 daily connections between Bratislava (€9, 2¾ hours, 12 daily) and Košice (€10, three hours, 12 daily), via Trenčín (€6, one hour).

EASTERN SLOVAKIA

Alpine peaks, old towns and even older castles: eastern Slovakia's mountains are a must-see for anyone visiting the country.

HIGH TATRAS

☎ 052

Photo opportunities at upper elevations in the High Tatras (Vysoké Tatry) might get you fantasising about a career with *National Geographic* – pristine snowfields, ultramarine mountain lakes, crashing waterfalls. Lower elevations will be recovering for a generation from the 2004 wind storm that uprooted trees and turned a once-dense pine forest into a stubbly meadow. Gerlachovský štít, the highest peak, rises to 2654m, but this isn't exactly Switzerland – the massif is only 25km wide and 78km long. Thank goodness, since prices in the three main mountain villages are still low in comparison to Switzerland. Hint: if you really want to save money, check out the Belá Tatras (p1022) to the east.

Starý Smokovec, a 20th-century resort town, is roughly central, with peaceful Tatranská Lomnica 11km east and overdeveloped, lakeside Štrbské Pleso 16km west. A comprehensive network of tourist trails and ski tows, lifts and runs covers the range. Since 1949 most of this jagged mountain range has been part of **Tatra National Park** (Tanap; www.tanap.sk), complementing a similar park in Poland. To protect the environment, higher trails are officially closed when snow lingers from November to mid-June. August and September are the best months for high-altitude hiking; July can be rainy. For the latest weather and advice, contact the **Mountain Rescue Service** (Horská služba; ☎ 18 300; http://his.hzs.sk/; Starý Smokovec 23).

Information

Tatra Information Office (TIK; www.tatry.sk) Starý Smokovec (☎ 4423 440; Starý Smokovec 23; ⌚ 8am-8pm Mon-Fri, to 1pm Sat); Tatranská Lomnica (☎ 4468 118; Cesta Slobody; ⌚ 10am-6pm Mon-Fri, 9am-1pm Sat); Štrbské Pleso (☎ 4492 391; Hotel Toliar; ⌚ 8am-4pm) The Štrbské Pleso branch is best for trail information, Smokovec has the largest office and, overall, the staff in Lomnica are the most accommodating.

T-Ski Travel (☎ 4423 200; www.slovakiatravel.sk; Starý Smokovec 46; 🕑 9am-4pm Mon-Thu, to 5pm Fri-Sun) Books lodging, including some hikers' huts; at the funicular station.

Activities

More than 600km of hiking trails stretch across alpine valleys and up to some peaks, with hikers' huts to stop at along the way. From Starý Smokovec a **funicular railway** (☎ 4467 618; www.vt.sk; adult/concession return €7/5.50; 🕑 7.30am-7pm) takes you up to **Hrebienok** (1280m) on the 65km-long **Magistrála Trail**. An extremely popular gondola links Tatranská Lomnica with the bustling lake, winter sports and fun park area of **Skalnaté pleso** (1751m; www.vt.sk; adult/concession return €12/6; 🕑 8.30am-7pm Jul-Aug, to 3.30pm Sep-Jun); a smaller cable car continues from there to the precipitous 2634m summit of **Lomnický štít** (adult/concession return €20/16; 🕑 8.30am-7pm Jul-Aug, to 3.30pm Sep-Jun).

Sleeping

A hiker's *chata* (mountain hut) along the upper altitude trails may be anything from a communal cabin to a chalet. Rates range from about €15 to €20 per person whether it's a dorm bed or a twin room with a bathroom down the hall; some sort of food is always available. Book private rooms ahead of time over the internet (see www.tatry.sk and www.tanap.sk/homes.html). Hotel prices drop by a third from October to May.

STARÝ SMOKOVEC & AROUND

Pension Vesna (☎ 4422 774; vesna@stonline.sk; Nový Smokovec 69; s/d €32/54) Family-run and friendly. The seven rooms in this simple guest house are all spacious; some have three beds and a separate living area.

Bilíkova chata (1220m; ☎ 4422 439; www.bilikovachata.sk in Slovak; r with shared bathroom €53) Though called a *chata*, this log chalet five minutes from the upper terminus of the funicular station has private rooms and a full restaurant.

Other mountain huts above the village:

Zamkovského chata (1475m; ☎ 4422 636; www.zamka.sk) 28 beds in two- to four-bed rooms; full board available. Between the funicular upper station and Skalnaté pleso.

Zbojnícka chata (1960m; ☎ 0903638000; www.zbojnickachata.sk) Sixteen dorm-style beds, self-service eatery and small kitchen. One-hour hike east of the funicular.

TATRANSKÁ LOMNICA & AROUND

Eurocamp FICC (☎ 4467 741; www.eurocamp-ficc.sk; camp site per person/tent/car €4/3/3.50, bungalows €40-53; 🕑 year-round; 🏊) Party central, capacity 1500. Eurocamp has restaurants, bars, a pool and ball courts. Five minutes northeast of the Lomnica-Eurocamp train station.

Penzión Encian (☎ 4467 520; www.tatry.sk/encian; s/d €33/66) This big half-timber house is central in the village. Cosy up by the restaurant's fireplace. Rear-facing rooms have great views of Lomnický štít.

From the top of the cable car you can hike to the huts above Starý Smokovec, or you can make the strenuous 2½-hour trek from Skalnaté pleso east to lakeside **Chata pri Zelenom plese** (1540m; ☎ 4467 420; www.zelenepleso.sk), a 50-bed mountain hiker's lodge.

Eating & Drinking

Each of the three main villages has a *potraviny* (grocery store).

Samoobslužná Reštaurácia (☎ 4781 011; Hotel Toliar, Štrbské Pleso 21; mains €2.50-6; 🕑 7am-10pm) This self-service cafeteria in Štrbské Pleso serves one-pot meals (goulash, chicken stir-fry) and a few vegetarian options.

Reštaurácia Stará Mama (☎ 4467 216; Shopping centre Sintra, Tatranská Lomnica; mains €5-12) A rustic fave; substantial soups and homemade *pirohy* (like Polish pirogies, half moon-shaped dumplings served with sheep's cheese and bacon) here are hearty dishes priced right.

In Starý Smokovec, **Pizzéria Albas** (☎ 4423 460; Starý Smokovec; pizzas €3-7) comes recommended by every second resident under 30; the rest are drinking at **Tatry Pub** (☎ 442 2448; Starý Smokovec; 🕑 1-11pm Mon-Thu, 11am-midnight Fri-Sun), the official watering hole of the Mountain Guide Club.

Getting There & Away

To get to and from most destinations by public transport you'll have to switch in Poprad (p1022). Buses from Poprad travel to Starý Smokovec (€0.80, 20 minutes, every 30 minutes), Tatranská Lomnica (€1.20, 35 minutes, every 60 minutes) and Štrbské Pleso (€1.50, 50 minutes, every 45 minutes). At least every 1½ hours buses connect Tatranská Lomnica with Ždiar (€1, 25 minutes) in the Belá Tatras.

A main train line runs through Poprad. From there switch to narrow-gauge electric trains that run hourly between Poprad and Štrbské Pleso (one hour), via Starý Smokovec (30 minutes). Change at Starý Smokovec to get to Tatranská Lomnica (15 minutes). A third route runs from Tatranská Lomnica through Studeny Potok (15 minutes) to Poprad (25 minutes). A €1.50 ticket covers up to a 29km ride, but it's easier to buy a one-/three-/seven-day pass for €3.30/6.70/12. If there's not a ticket window, purchase from the conductor; validate on board.

Getting Around

Local buses run between the resort towns every 20 minutes and tend to be quicker than the train: Starý Smokovec to Tatranská Lomnica costs €0.30 and takes 10 minutes, to Štrbské Pleso costs €1 and takes 33 minutes.

BELÁ TATRAS

☎ 052

Travel east over the High Tatra mountain ridges and you start to hear a Slovak spoken with a Polish accent. The Goral folk culture and wooden cottages give tiny Ždiar, the main settlement in the Belá Tatras (*Belianské Tatry*), a rustic, laid-back quality that the larger resort villages lack. From here it's an easy day trip or journey on to Poland; heck, you can walk there.

Several hiking trails lead off from the rural village lined with decorated timber cottages. The tiny **Ždiar House Museum** (Ždiarsky dom; ☎ 4498 142; adult/concession €3/1.50; ⏰ 10am-4pm Tue-Sun) showcases colourful local folk costumes and has a restaurant attached.

our pick Ginger Monkey Hostel (☎ 4498 0844; www.gingermonkey.eu; Ždiar 294; dm/d €13/30; ⊠ 💻) is housed in a great old Goral house with even more amazing mountain views. Ex-pat hosts often get a group together at a local restaurant for dinner, where conversations range from life's purpose to which superhero could whoop who. Free wi-fi and communal kitchen with complimentary tea, coffee and light breakfast.

There are up to six buses daily between Ždiar and Poprad (€1.80, 50 minutes). At least four daily buses travel between Ždiar and the Polish border, Tatranská Javorina, Lysá Poľana stop (€1, 30 minutes). From there you can walk across the bridge to the Polish side, where there are regular public buses and private minibuses to Zakopane (26km).

POPRAD

☎ 052 / pop 55,200

Poprad is an important transport transfer point, and is otherwise known mainly for its giant thermal water park, **Aqua City** (☎ 7851 222; www.aquacitypoprad.sk; Športová 1397; per day from €18; ⏰ 9am-9pm). **SkyEurope** (☎ 02-4850 1000; www.skyeurope.com) flies between London and the **Poprad-Tatry International Airport** (☎ 7763 875; www.airport-poprad.sk; Na Letisko 100) three times a week.

Intercity (IC) or Eurocity (EC) trains are the quickest way to get in and out of Poprad; four a day run to Bratislava (€16, four hours) and Košice (€6.50, one hour). To reach Poland, you can take a bus to Tatranská Javorina, Lysá Poľana stop (€2.50, 1½ hours, four daily) and walk to the Polish buses waiting to take you to Zakopane.

LEVOČA

☎ 053 / pop 14,700

So this is what Slovakia looked like in the 14th century. Fairly complete medieval walls still protect the age-old centre from onslaught and, so far, international chain stores have been held at bay. The Gothic Church of St Jacob and its fabulous altar are the pride of the Slovak nation's religious art collection.

To get to the centre, walk 1km north of the train and bus stations via Michala Hlaváčka. The **tourist information office** (☎ 4513 763; www.levoca.sk; Nám Majstra Pavla 58; ⏰ 9am-6pm daily May-Sep, 9am-4pm Mon-Fri, 10am-2pm Sat Oct-Apr) has a handy free photocopied map that you have to ask for. Check email at **Levonet Internet Café** (Nám Majstra Pavla 38; per hr €2.50; ⏰ 10am-10pm).

Nám Majstra Pavla, Levoča's central square, is chock-a-block with superb Gothic and Renaissance buildings. But everyone comes to see the spindles-and-spires **Church of St Jacob** (Chrám sv Jakuba; ☎ 4512 347; www.chramsvjakuba.sk; adult/concession €2/1; ⏰ by tour at least 1-4pm yr round) and its 16m-high wooden altar (1517) carved by renowned Master Pavol of Levoča. Purchase tickets for your allotted time in the Municipal Weights House opposite the north door. Next to the Gothic town hall *(radnica)*, also centre square, stands a 16th-century **cage of shame** for naughty boys and girls.

Two- to four-bed rooms in the hostel-like guest house **Oáza** (☎ 4514 511; www.ubytovanieoaza.sk; Nová 65; r with shared bathroom per person €10) surround a central, shared garden, complete with chickens. For meat-free dishes head to no-fuss **Vegetarián** (☎ 451 4576; Uhoľná 137; mains €3-5; ⏰ 10am-3.15pm Mon-Fri). **Reštaurácia Slovenka** (☎ 4512 339; Nám Majstra Pavla 66; mains €3-7) is the only place in town to get homemade *pirohy* and other traditional Slovak sheep's cheese dishes.

Bus travel is most practical from here to Spišská Nová Ves (€0.80, 20 minutes, every 30 minutes), Košice (€4, two hours, five daily) and Poprad (€1.60, 30 minutes, 21 daily), where you can switch to the main Bratislava–Košice train line.

SPIŠSKÉ PODHRADIE

☎053 / pop 3830

The 4-hectare ruins of Unesco World Heritage site **Spiš Castle** (Spišský hrad; ☎053-4541 336; www.spisskyhrad.com; Spišské Podhradie; adult/concession €4.50/2.50; ⏰9am-6pm May-Oct) are eerie enough. Just imagine how imposing the fortress complex crowning the ridge on the eastern side of Spišské Podhradie was in full form. Historic chronicles first mention Spiš Castle in 1209, and the central residential tower, at the highest elevation, is thought to date from that time. A Romanesque palace contains weaponry exhibits upstairs and torture chambers below.

A kilometre west of Spišské Podhradie is the still-active **Spiš Chapter** (Spišská kapitula; ☎0907388411; adult/concession €2/1; ⏰11.15am-2.45pm), a 13th-century Catholic complex encircled by a 16th-century wall.

Buses connect with Levoča (€1, 20 minutes) and Poprad (€2.20, 50 minutes) at least hourly, making this an easy full-day trip from Levoča or the Tatras. Buses stop 1km west of the castle and 1km east of Spiš Chapter in the village centre.

KOŠICE

☎055 / pop 235,300

Ok, it's not the snazziest in Europe, but an eclectic mix of ancient to art nouveau architecture – arranged around a pretty, garden-filled pedestrian square chock-a-block with cafes – makes Slovakia's second city eminently agreeable. Plus, with so many locals out and about, you get a real sense of community here. Košice received its city coat of arms in 1369 and, skipping forward, in the 18th and 19th century was a stronghold for anti-Habsburg (Austrian) sentiment. Though industry rings the city's outskirts today (US Steel is the town's main employer), the old-town heart is alive and well.

Orientation & Information

The adjacent bus and train stations are a spit east of the old town. Walking five minutes along Mlynské brings you onto Hlavná, the main square.

City Information Centre (☎6258 888; www.kosice.sk; Hlavná 59; ⏰9am-6pm Mon-Fri, 9am-1pm Sat) Loads of maps and books; internet access (per 15 minutes €0.50).

Ľudová Banka (Mlynská 29) ATM and exchange.

Sights & Activities

The architecture and musical fountain on Hlavná are quite pleasant. But it's the dark and brooding 14th-century **Cathedral of St Elizabeth** (Dóm sv Alžbety; ☎0908667093; Hlavná nám; adult/concession €4/2; ⏰1-5pm Mon, 9am-5pm Tue-Fri, 9am-1pm Sat), centre square, that wins the prize for sight most likely to grace your Košice postcard home. Descend to the crypt of Duke Ferenc Rákóczi, who led a failed 18th-century Hungarian revolt against Austria, or climb to the heights in the tower. To the north, the interesting Urban Tower (built in the 14th century, rebuilt in the 1970s) building contains a cheesy **Wax Museum** (Muzéum voskoyvy figurín; ☎6232 534; www.waxmuseum.sk; Hlavná 3; adult/concession €4/2.60; ⏰11am-3pm Mon-Fri, noon-3pm Sat, 1-3pm Sun). Explore the defence chambers and waterways of medieval Košice in the mazelike **archaeological excavations** (☎6228 393; Hlavná; adult/concession €1/0.60; ⏰10am-6pm Tue-Sun), discovered nearby during city building work in 1996.

More buried treasure is displayed at the **East Slovak Museum** (Východoslovenské múzeum; ☎622 0309; Hviezdoslavovo 3; adult/concession €2/1; ⏰9am-5pm Tue-Sat, 9am-1pm Sun): a secret stash of thousands of 15th- to 18th-century gold coins was unearthed during the 1935 renovation of a local house. Anyone have a shovel?

Sleeping & Eating

The City Information Centre has a list of student dorms open in summer.

K2 (☎6230 909; Štúrova 32; s/d with shared bathroom €18/26) It's just an ageing tourist hostel room with a bed. But what more do you want for this price in the old town? No common room, no kitchen, no laundry.

Kosmalt Hostel (☎6423 572; kosmalt@kosmalt.sk; Kysucká 16; s/d €20/26; 💻) This huge former student dorm (capacity 1000) is outside the centre, but has a game room, bar and restaurant. Catch tram 6 from the train/bus station to the Kino Družba stop.

Penzión Grand (☎6337 546; www.penzionslovakia.sk; Kováčska 65; s/d/tr €46/52/66) Oddly mismatched furnishings decorate 2nd- and 3rd-floor rooms that ring an interior courtyard with skylights. Wi-fi in some rooms.

WORTH THE TRIP

In 2008, Unesco added a number of eastern Slovakia's mostly Greek Catholic (Uniate) and Orthodox nail-less **wooden churches** to the World Heritage list. Interiors often have elaborate icon screens. For more information, buy the colour booklet *Wooden Churches Around Bardejov* at the Bardejov tourist office, or go online to www.grkatpo.sk/drevenecerk.

Dargov Department Store (Hlavná 2; mains €2-5; 7am-7pm Mon-Fri, 9am-5pm Sat, 9am-3pm Sun) Dig into sausages and stuffed cabbage at the store's ground-floor cafeteria. There's a supermarket, too.

Karczma Mlyn (6220 547; Hlavná 82; mains €4-8 11am-midnight Sun-Thu, until 1am Sun) Locals frequent this pub for heaping portions of hearty food as well as for a pint. Set lunch menus are a bargain.

Piano Café (0915517339; Hlavná 92; pizzas €5-6; 10am-midnight Mon-Thu, 10am-1am Fri, 3pm-1am Sat, 3pm-midnight Sun) Enjoy pizza with your piano music at street level; in the cellar bar you can get down to more of a disco beat.

Getting There & Away

AIR

Košice International Airport (KSC; 622 1093; www.airportkosice.sk) is 6km southeast of the centre. **SkyEurope** (NE; Bratislava 02-4850 1000; www.skyeurope.com) has up to five daily flights to/from Bratislava (50 minutes), and connects with London weekly. **Austrian Airlines** (OS; 02-4940 2100; www.austrianairlines.com) flies to Vienna and **Czech Airlines** (OK; 6782 490; www.czechairlines.com) wings its way to Prague.

BUS

Buses are most efficient for getting to Levoča (€4, two hours, eight daily) or Bardejov (€3.60, two hours, 12 daily). By bus is also the best way to travel to Uzhhorod in Ukraine (€6, 2½ hours), once daily at 12.40pm (a second, early morning bus runs from Friday to Sunday).

TRAIN

Up to 10 express trains a day run to/from Poprad (€6.50, 1¼ hours). To Bratislava, an Intercity or Eurocity train (€19, five hours, four daily) is your quickest option.

You can also ride the rails from Košice to Budapest (€25, four hours, four daily), Hungary, and Kraków (€25, six hours, one daily), Poland. A sleeper train leaves Košice every night for Moscow (€57, 36 hours), stopping in Kyiv (€32, 22½ hours), Ukraine.

Getting Around

Transport tickets (€0.60, one zone) are good for buses and trams in most of the city; buy them from newsstands and validate them on board. Bus 23 between the airport and the train station requires a two-zone ticket (€1).

BARDEJOV

054 / pop 33,400

All steep roofs and flat fronts, pastel hues and paint-and-plaster details, Bardejov's 15th-century Gothic-Renaissance town square has been enthusiastically well-preserved (Unesco thinks so, too). The **tourist information centre** (4723 013; www.bardejov.sk; Radničné nám 21; 9am-5pm Mon-Fri, 9am-4pm Sat, 1-4pm Sun) provides free maps of the main square, which has a few small museums. The excellent **Icon Exposition** (Expozícia ikony; Radničné nám 27; adult/concession €2/1; 8am-noon & 12.30-4pm Tue-Sun) has more than 130 dazzling icons, from the 16th to 19th centuries, which shed light on the region's eastern Christian religions. Nearby **Bardejovské Kúpele**, 3km north, is a spa town with a rustic village museum. Bunk out in one of the five bright rooms that share a communal kitchen and laundry in family-run **Penzión Semafor** (0905830984; www.penzionsemafor.sk; Kellerova 13; s/d €24/38, apt s/d €28/38); two 'apartments' have small kitchens of their own. There are no trains to Bardejov, but buses make the run to/from Košice (€4, 1¾ hours, eight daily), Poprad (€5, 2½ hours, eight daily) and beyond.

SLOVAKIA DIRECTORY

ACCOMMODATION

In this chapter we've quoted main season rates (May to September); prices rise during Christmas and Easter holidays and drop 10% to 50% from October to April.

Camping

Most camping grounds open May to September and are accessible by public transport. They'll usually have a snack bar and small cabins that are cheaper than a hotel. Camping wild in national parks is prohibited.

Hostels

Outside Bratislava, only tiny Ždiar in the Belá Tatras has a backpacker-style hostel. Student dormitories throughout the country open to tourists in July and August. For cheap sleeps in other months, *ubytovňa* is the word to know. These are local-oriented worker or tourist hostels with no common spaces.

Hotels & Pensions

Sleeping in Bratislava costs considerably more than in the rest of the country. *Penzión* (guest house) rooms start at €60/75 for singles/doubles there, and top-end hotels top out at more than €175. Outside the capital, guest house rooms start at €35 for a single, €50 for a double, and there are no four-stars to be found.

ACTIVITIES

The High Tatras (p1020) have just about every outdoor activity you can think of: mountain biking, mountain climbing, downhill skiing, cross-country skiing, snowboarding and hiking.

BUSINESS HOURS

Most museums and castles are closed on Monday and tourist attractions outside the capital may only open from May to September.

Banks (🕑 8am-5pm Mon-Thu, to 4pm Fri)
Bars (🕑 noon-midnight or 1am)
Post offices (🕑 8am-7pm Mon-Fri, to 11am Sat)
Restaurants (🕑 11am-10pm)
Shops (🕑 9am-5pm Mon-Fri, 9am-noon Sat) Department stores have longer hours.

DANGERS & ANNOYANCES

The crime rate is low compared with Western Europe, but pickpocketing does happen. Never leave anything on the seat of an unattended vehicle, even a locked one. That's just advertising you don't want it any more.

EMBASSIES & CONSULATES

Australia and New Zealand do not have embassies in Slovakia; the nearest are in Vienna and Berlin respectively. The following are all in Bratislava:

France (☎ 02-5934 7111; www.france.sk; Hlavné nám 7)
Germany (☎ 02-5920 4400; www.pressburg.diplo.de; Hviezdoslavovo nám 10)
Ireland (☎ 02-5930 9611; www.dfa.ie; Carlton Savoy Bldg, Mostová 2)
Netherlands (☎ 02-5262 5081; www.holandskoweb.com; Frana Krála 5)
UK (☎ 02-5998 2000; www.britishembassy.sk; Panská 16)
USA (☎ 02-5443 0861; http://slovakia.usembassy.gov; Hviezdoslavovo nám 4)

FESTIVALS & EVENTS

Folk festivals take place all over Slovakia in June and August; the biggest is the **Východná Folklore Festival**, 32km west of Poprad.

HOLIDAYS

New Year's & Independence Day 1 January
Three Kings Day 6 January
Good Friday and Easter Monday March/April
Labour Day 1 May
Victory over Fascism Day 8 May
Cyril and Methodius Day 5 July
SNP Day 29 August
Constitution Day 1 September
Our Lady of Sorrows Day 15 September
All Saints' Day 1 November
Christmas 24 to 26 December

INTERNET RESOURCES

The website of the **Slovak Tourism Board** (www.slovakia.travel) has loads of information on the country's attractions. **What's On Slovakia** (www.whatsonslovakia.com) lists events.

MONEY

As of January 2009, Slovakia's currency is the euro. You'll still hear reference to the former currency, the Slovak crown (Sk).

Almost all banks have exchange desks and there are usually branches in or near a city's old town square. ATMs are quite common, even in smaller places. Visa and MasterCard are widely accepted in Bratislava, less so in the rest of the country.

Your Slovak friends will likely complain you're spoiling the waiters if you don't just round up to the next 10 digit, but tips of 5% to 10% are appreciated in restaurants.

POST

Slovenská pošta (www.posta.sk) service is fairly efficient; stamps for international airmail letters and postcards cost €0.80.

TELEPHONE

Slovakia's country code is ☎ 421. When dialling from abroad, drop the initial 0 from the area code. To dial internationally from inside Slovakia, dial ☎ 00, the country code and then the number. International phone cards such as **EZ Phone** (www.ezcard.sk; per min to UK & USA €0.60) are the easiest and cheapest way to reach out and touch home. Some internet cafes even have web cams and/or headsets for Skype calling.

TOURIST INFORMATION

The **Association of Information Centres of Slovakia** (AiCES; ☎ 16 186; www.aices.sk) has an extensive network of city information centres helping you find your way around.

VISAS

Citizens of other EU countries do not require visas to enter Slovakia. Visitors from Australia, New Zealand, Canada, Japan and the United States can enter the country visa-free for up to 90 days. South Africans need a visa. For a full list of nationalities that do not require visas, see www.mzv.sk (under 'Ministry' and then 'Travel'). If you do require a visa, it must be bought in advance – they are not issued on arrival.

Slovenia

HIGHLIGHTS

- **Ljubljana** Slovenia's 'Beloved' capital with a hilltop castle, green spaces and vibrant nightlife (p1031)
- **Škocjan Caves** A vast underground cavern straight out of Jules Verne with a raging river running through it (p1040)
- **Bovec** Probably the best outdoor activities centre in all of Slovenia (p1040)
- **Bled** An impossibly beautiful lake with an island and a hilltop castle as a backdrop (p1037)
- **Piran** Strolling through the romantic Venetian port and enjoying an alfresco seafood meal (p1042)

FAST FACTS

- **Area** 20,273 sq km
- **Budget** €35 to €60 per day
- **Capital** Ljubljana
- **Country code** ☎ 386
- **Famous for** hiking and skiing, Lipizzaner horses, *pršut* (air-dried ham)
- **Language** Slovene
- **Money** euro (€); A$1 = €0.55; C$1 = 0.60; ¥100 = €0.78; NZ$1 = €0.43; UK£1 = €1.12; US$1 = €0.74
- **Phrases** *dober dan* (hello), *živijo* (hi), *prosim* (please), *hvala* (thank you), *oprostite* (excuse me), *nasvidenje* (goodbye)
- **Population** 2.018 million

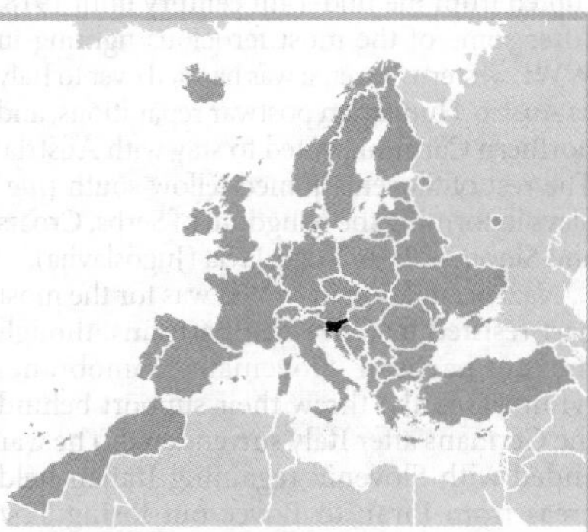

- **Visas** not required by most visitors (not including South Africans) for up to 90 days (p1045)

TRAVEL HINTS

Start with www.slovenia.info. Make use of low-cost bicycles in Ljubljana. Bring black tea; it's not that easy to find.

ROAMING SLOVENIA

Travel north from Ljubljana to Bled and Bovec and, via Kranjska Gora, over the stunning Vršič Pass down into the Soča Valley, the Karst and the coast.

It's a tiny place, about half the size of Switzerland, and counts just over 2 million people. But 'good things come in small packages' and never was that old chestnut more appropriate than in describing Slovenia (Slovenija), a pint-sized republic bordering Italy, Austria, Hungary, Croatia and the Adriatic Sea.

Soaring peaks are hemmed by forests and deep valleys, offering an unparalleled choice of affordable active sports; indeed, in recent years Slovenia really has become Europe's activities playground. Lowland hills are covered with vines and riddled with awesome caves. The short coastline offers beaches and superb Venetian architecture at Koper and Piran. Many towns have picturesque old quarters, including Ljubljana, with important sights, atmospheric cafes and stylish shops.

Slovenia is safe, compact, friendly and multilingual, with an up-to-date infrastructure and many attractions. It may not be bargain-basement but it's fabulously good value. And with more than half of its total area covered in forest, Slovenia truly is one of the greenest countries in the world.

HISTORY

Slovenes played a key role in the development of democracy. By the early 7th century their Slavic forebears had founded the Duchy of Carantania (now Karnburg in Austria), where ruling dukes were elected by ennobled commoners. This model was noted by Thomas Jefferson when drafting the American Declaration of Independence.

Austria controlled Slovenia almost uninterrupted from the mid-14th century until 1918. After some of the most ferocious fighting in WWI, western Slovenia was handed over to Italy as Austro-Hungarian postwar reparations, and northern Carinthia voted to stay with Austria. The rest of Slovenia joined fellow south *(jug)* Slavs in forming the Kingdom of Serbs, Croats and Slovenes, later Yugoslavia (Jugoslavija).

Nazi occupation in WWII was for the most part resisted by Slovenian partisans, though the antipartisan Slovenian Domobranci (Home Guards) threw their support behind the Germans after Italy surrendered. The war ended with Slovenia regaining Italian-held areas from Piran to Bovec but losing Trst (Trieste) and Gorica (Gorizia).

Slovenia represented only 8% of the national population of Yugoslavia but was its economic powerhouse, producing up to 20% of the GDP. By the 1980s the federation was becoming increasingly Serb-dominated and Slovenes feared losing their political autonomy. After free elections, Slovenia broke away from Yugoslavia on 25 June 1991. A 10-day war that left 66 people dead followed; Yugoslavia swiftly signed a truce in order to concentrate on regaining control of coastal Croatia instead. Slovenia was admitted to the UN in May 1992 and joined the EU in May 2004. It shared the presidency of the EU Council with France in 2008.

THE CULTURE

The population of Slovenia is largely homogeneous. More than 87% are ethnic Slovenes, with the remainder being Croats, Serbians, Bosnians and Roma; there are also small enclaves of Italians and Hungarians. Slovenes are ethnically Slavic, typically multilingual and extroverts, and Roman Catholic (58%).

ARTS

Slovenia's most beloved writer is the Romantic poet France Prešeren (1800–49), whose lyric poetry helped to raise Slovenian national consciousness.

Many of Ljubljana's most characteristic architectural features were added by Jože Plečnik (1872–1957).

Slovenia's vibrant music scene embraces rave, techno, jazz, punk, thrash-metal and *chansons* (eg torch songs from Vita Mavrič); the most popular local rock group is Siddharta. There's also a folk-music revival: listen for the groups Katice and Katalena.

ENVIRONMENT

Slovenia is amazingly green; indeed, just under 57% of its total surface area is covered in forest. Triglav National Park (p1037) is particularly rich in native flowering plants. Among endemic fauna is a blind salamander called *Proteus anguinus* (see p1040), which lives deep in karst caves and can survive for years without eating.

TRANSPORT

GETTING THERE & AWAY

Air

Slovenia's national airline, **Adria Airways** (JP; ☎ 080 13 00, 01-369 10 10; www.adria-airways.com) flies to 28 European cities. With the inauguration of nonstop daily flights from London's Stansted airport by **easyJet** (EZY; ☎ 04-206 16 77;

READING UP

The Making of Slovenia, edited by Marko Štepec, is a succinct illustrated history of Slovenia in the 20th century. *Slovenia 1945: Memories of Death and Survival after World War II,* by John Corsellis and Marcus Ferrar, is the harrowing story of the forced return to Slovenia and execution of thousands of members of the anti-Communist Domobranci after WWII. The best overall sourcebook for the country is Lonely Planet's *Slovenia.*

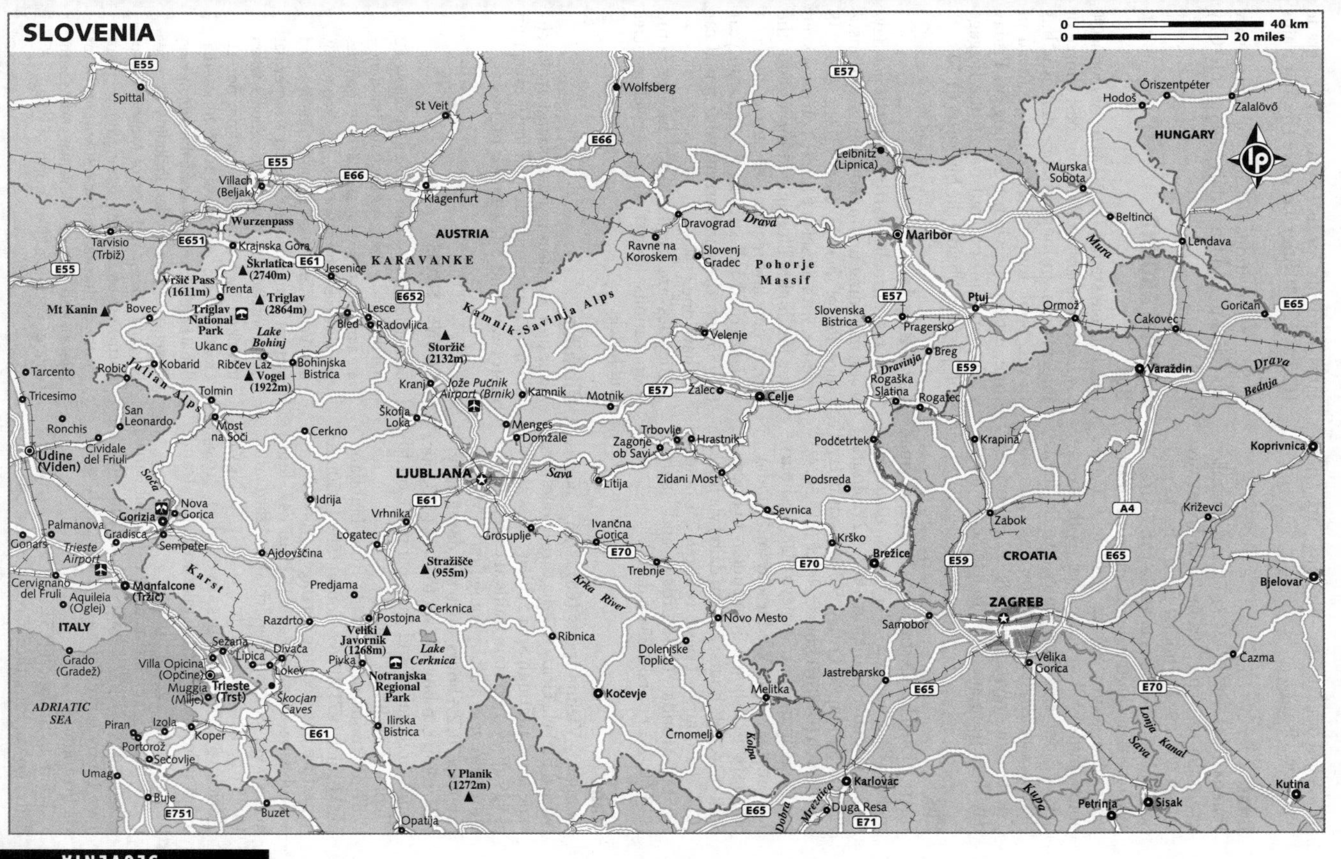
SLOVENIA
0 40 km
0 20 miles
HUNGARY
AUSTRIA
CROATIA
ITALY
ADRIATIC SEA
LJUBLJANA
ZAGREB
KARAVANKE
Kamnik Savinja Alps
Pohorje Massif
Julian Alps
Karst
Triglav National Park
Notranjska Regional Park
Lake Bohinj
Lake Cerknica
Škocjan Caves
Drava
Mura
Sava
Soča
Krka River
Kolpa
Kupa
Lonja Kanal
Dravinja
Bednja
Mrežnica
Dobra
Mt Kanin
Škrlatica (2740m)
Triglav (2864m)
Vogel (1922m)
Vršič Pass (1611m)
Storžič (2132m)
Stražišče (955m)
Veliki Javornik (1268m)
V Planik (1272m)
Jože Pučnik Airport (Brnik)
Trieste Airport
Wurzenpass
E55
E651
E61
E652
E66
E57
E59
E65
E70
E71
E751
A4
Spittal
Villach (Beljak)
Klagenfurt
St Veit
Wolfsberg
Leibnitz (Lipnica)
Tarvisio (Trbiž)
Bovec
Kranjska Gora
Trenta
Jesenice
Lesce
Radovljica
Bled
Bohinjska Bistrica
Ukanc
Ribčev Laz
Kobarid
Tolmin
Most na Soči
Cerkno
Škofja Loka
Kranj
Kamnik
Mengeš
Domžale
Motnik
Idrija
Logatec
Vrhnika
Predjama
Postojna
Cerknica
Pivka
Ilirska Bistrica
Ajdovščina
Nova Gorica
Šempeter
Gorizia
Gradisca
Razdrto
Divača
Lokev
Lipica
Sežana
Trieste (Trst)
Villa Opicina (Opčine)
Muggia (Milje)
Koper
Izola
Piran
Portorož
Sečovlje
Umag
Buje
Buzet
Opatija
Monfalcone (Tržič)
Aquileia (Oglej)
Grado (Gradež)
Cervignano del Friuli
Palmanova
Gonars
Udine (Viden)
Cividale del Friuli
San Leonardo
Robič
Ronchis
Tarcento
Tricesimo
Grosuplje
Ivančna Gorica
Ribnica
Kočevje
Trebnje
Dolenjske Toplice
Novo Mesto
Črnomelj
Metlika
Litija
Zagorje ob Savi
Trbovlje
Hrastnik
Zidani Most
Sevnica
Krško
Brežice
Podsreda
Podčetrtek
Žalec
Celje
Velenje
Slovenj Gradec
Dravograd
Ravne na Koroškem
Slovenska Bistrica
Rogaška Slatina
Rogatec
Pragersko
Breg
Maribor
Ptuj
Ormož
Murska Sobota
Beltinci
Lendava
Hodoš
Őriszentpéter
Zalalövő
Goričan
Čakovec
Varaždin
Koprivnica
Krapina
Zabok
Križevci
Bjelovar
Čazma
Kutina
Velika Gorica
Samobor
Jastrebarsko
Karlovac
Duga Resa
Sisak
Petrinja

SLOVENIA

www.easyjet.com), many Britons are now weekend visitors.

Boat

Venezia Lines (☎ 05-674 71 61; www.venezialines.com) sails to Venice from Piran (one way/return €46/89, 2¼ hours) from May to mid-September. The **Prince of Venice** (☎ 05-617 80 00; www.kompas-online.net) catamaran from nearby Izola also serves Venice (€47 to €70, 2½ hours) mid-April to September. Both operate between one and three times a week. **Trieste Lines** (www.triestelines.it) ferries now link Piran and Trieste (one-way/return €6.80/12.60) twice a day daily from late April to late September.

Bus

International bus destinations from Ljubljana include Belgrade (€35, 7¾ hours, 10am and 10.25pm daily; Frankfurt (€83, 12½ hours, 7.30pm Sunday to Friday, 9.30pm Saturday) via Munich (€48, 6¾ hours); Poreč (€17.50, 4½ hours, 1.45pm daily), Sarajevo (€38, 9½ hours, 3.15pm daily, 4pm Wednesday and Sunday); Skopje (€50, 15 hours, 3pm Sunday to Friday); Split (€44, 10½ hours, 7.40pm daily) via Rijeka (€17, 2½ hours); Trieste (€11.60, 2¾ hours, 2.25pm Monday to Saturday); and Zagreb (€13.60, 2½ hours, 2.25am daily).

Train

Ljubljana–Vienna trains (€61.80, 6¼ hours, twice daily) via Graz (€31.40, three hours) are expensive, although Spar Schiene fares as low as €29 apply on certain trains at certain times. Otherwise save a bit by going first to Maribor (from €7.70, 2½ hours, up to two dozen daily), where you can buy a ticket to Graz (€13, one hour, three daily) and then continue on to Vienna (€31.40, 2¾ hours).

Three trains depart daily from Ljubljana for Munich (€71.40, 6½ hours). The 11.50pm departure has sleeping carriages available.

Ljubljana–Venice trains (€25 to €47, four hours) via Sežana depart at 2.22am and 10.35am. It's cheaper to go first to Nova Gorica (€7.75, 3½ hours, five daily), cross over to Gorizia and then take an Italian train to Venice (€8.75, 2¼ hours).

There are seven trains daily from Ljubljana to Zagreb (€12.20, 2½ hours) via Zidani Most. Two trains serve Rijeka (€12.60, 2½ hours) via Postojna.

Trains to Budapest (€57.80, 8¾ hours, twice daily) go via Ptuj; there are Budapest Spezial fares available for as low as €29. Belgrade (€25 to €44, 10 hours) is served by four trains a day.

Seat reservations (€3.50) are compulsory on trains to and from Italy and on InterCity (IC) trains.

GETTING AROUND

Bus

Ljubljana bus station (☎ 234 46 00, information 090 934 230; www.ap-ljubljana.si) is your best source of information on long-distance domestic bus travel. Book long-distance buses ahead of time, especially when travelling on Friday afternoon. Putting your bag in the luggage compartment below the bus costs €1.50.

Car & Bicycle

Daily rates usually start at €40/210 per day/week including unlimited mileage and insurance. Petrol *(bencin)* costs €1.212 to €1.248 per litre, with diesel at €1.311. You must keep your headlights illuminated throughout the day. A new law requires all cars to display a *vinjeta* (road-toll sticker; per half/full year €35/55) on the windscreen; your rental car will have one.

Bicycles are available for hire at some train stations, tourist offices, travel agencies and hotels.

Hitching

Although we don't recommend it, hitch-hiking is fairly common and legal, except on motorways and a few major highways.

CONNECTIONS

Border formalities with Slovenia's fellow EU neighbours – Italy, Austria and Hungary – are almost nonexistent, and all three countries are accessible by train and, less frequently, bus. Venice and Trieste can also be reached by boat from the coast. Expect a somewhat closer inspection of your documents when travelling by train or bus to/from non-EU Croatia. There are upwards of 20 international border crossings along the 670km-long Slovenia–Croatia border, including Obrežje/Bregana (3km southeast of Mokrice/26km northwest of Zagreb); Jelšane/Rupa (10km south of Ilirska Bistrica/30km north of Rijeka); and Sečovlje/Plovanija (7km southeast of Portorož/80km north of Pula).

EMERGENCY NUMBERS

- Ambulance (☎ 112)
- Fire brigade (☎ 112)
- Police (☎ 113)
- Road emergency or towing (☎ 1987)
- SOS Women's Helpline (☎ 080-11 55; open from noon to 10pm Monday to Friday, from 6pm Saturday and Sunday)

Train

Buy tickets on **Slovenske Železnice** (Slovenian Railways; ☎ 01-291 33 32; www.slo-zeleznice.si) before boarding or you'll incur a €2.50 supplement. Be aware that EuroCity (EC) and InterCity (IC) trains carry a surcharge of €1.50 while InterCity Slovenia ones cost €5.70 extra in 2nd class. Unusually, trains in Slovenia are usually cheaper than buses.

LJUBLJANA

☎ 01 / pop 216,200

Charming Ljubljana has a small but delightful Old Town, a vibrant street-cafe culture and a large student community. Add some excellent museums and galleries, atmospheric bars and varied, accessible nightlife and the Slovenian capital can sometimes feel like a mini-Prague or a Lilliputian Kraków.

ORIENTATION

Prešernov trg, on the left bank of the Ljubljanica River, is the heart of Ljubljana. Just across Triple Bridge is the Old Town below Castle Hill.

INFORMATION

Bookshops

Geonavtik (☎ 252 70 27; www.geonavtik.com; Kongresni trg 1; ⌚ 8.30am-8.30pm Mon-Fri, 8.30am-4pm Sat) Guides to and books on Slovenia.

Kod & Kam (☎ 200 27 32; www.gzs-dd.si/kod&kam; Trg Francoske Revolucije 7; ⌚ 8am-8pm Mon-Fri, 8am-1pm Sat) Map specialist.

Discount Card

Ljubljana Card (per 72 hr €12.50) This excellent-value discount card, valid for three days and available from tourist offices, offers unlimited admission to museums and city buses, and myriad discounts.

Internet Access

Internet is available at virtually all hostels and hotels as well as the STIC (below, per half-hour €1) and the following:

Cyber Café Xplorer (☎ 430 19 91; Petkovškovo nabrežje 23; per 30 €2.50, 5hr €12; ⌚ 10am-10pm Mon-Fri, 2-10pm Sat & Sun) Cheap international phone connections too.

Portal.si Internet (☎ 234 46 00; Trg OF 4; per hr €3.80; ⌚ 7am-8.30pm) In the bus station (go to window No 4).

STA Travel Café (☎ 439 16 90; www.staljubljana.com; 1st fl, Trg Ajdovščina 1; per 20min €1; ⌚ 8am-midnight Mon-Sat) Part of the travel agency.

Left Luggage

Bus station (Trg OF 4; per day €2; ⌚ 5.30am-10.30pm Sun-Fri, 5am-10pm Sat) Window No 3.

Train station (Trg OF 6; per day €2-3; ⌚ 24hr) Lockers on platform No 1.

Medical Services

University Medical Centre Ljubljana (☎ 522 50 50; www3.kclj.si; Zaloška c 2; ⌚ A&E service 24hr)

Money

ATMs are everywhere. At both the train and bus stations you'll find **bureaux de change** (⌚ 7am-8pm) that change cash (no commission) but not travellers cheques.

Abanka (☎ 300 15 00; Slovenska c 50; ⌚ 9am-5pm Mon-Fri)

Nova Ljubljanska Banka (☎ 476 39 00; Trg Republike 2; ⌚ 8am-6pm Mon-Fri)

Tourist Information

Ljubljana Tourist Information (TIC; ☎ 306 12 15; www.visitljubljana.si; Kresija Bldg, Stritarjeva ul; ⌚ 8am-9pm Jun-Sep, to 7pm Oct-May); train station (☎ 433 94 75; Trg OF 6; ⌚ 8am-10pm Jun-Sep, 10am-7pm Oct-May)

Slovenia Tourist Information Centre (STIC; ☎ 306 45 76; www.slovenia.info; Krekov trg 10; ⌚ 8am-9pm Jun-Sep, to 7pm Oct-May) Internet and bicycle hire also available.

Travel Agencies

Erazem (☎ 430 55 37; www.erazem.net; basement, Miklošičeva c 26; ⌚ 10am-5pm Mon-Fri Jun-Sep, noon-5pm Mon-Fri Oct-May) Flight and train bookings, student and hostel cards sold.

STA Ljubljana (☎ 439 16 90; www.staljubljana.com; 1st fl, Trg Ajdovščina 1; ⌚ 10am-1pm & 2-5pm Mon-Fri) Discount airfares for students.

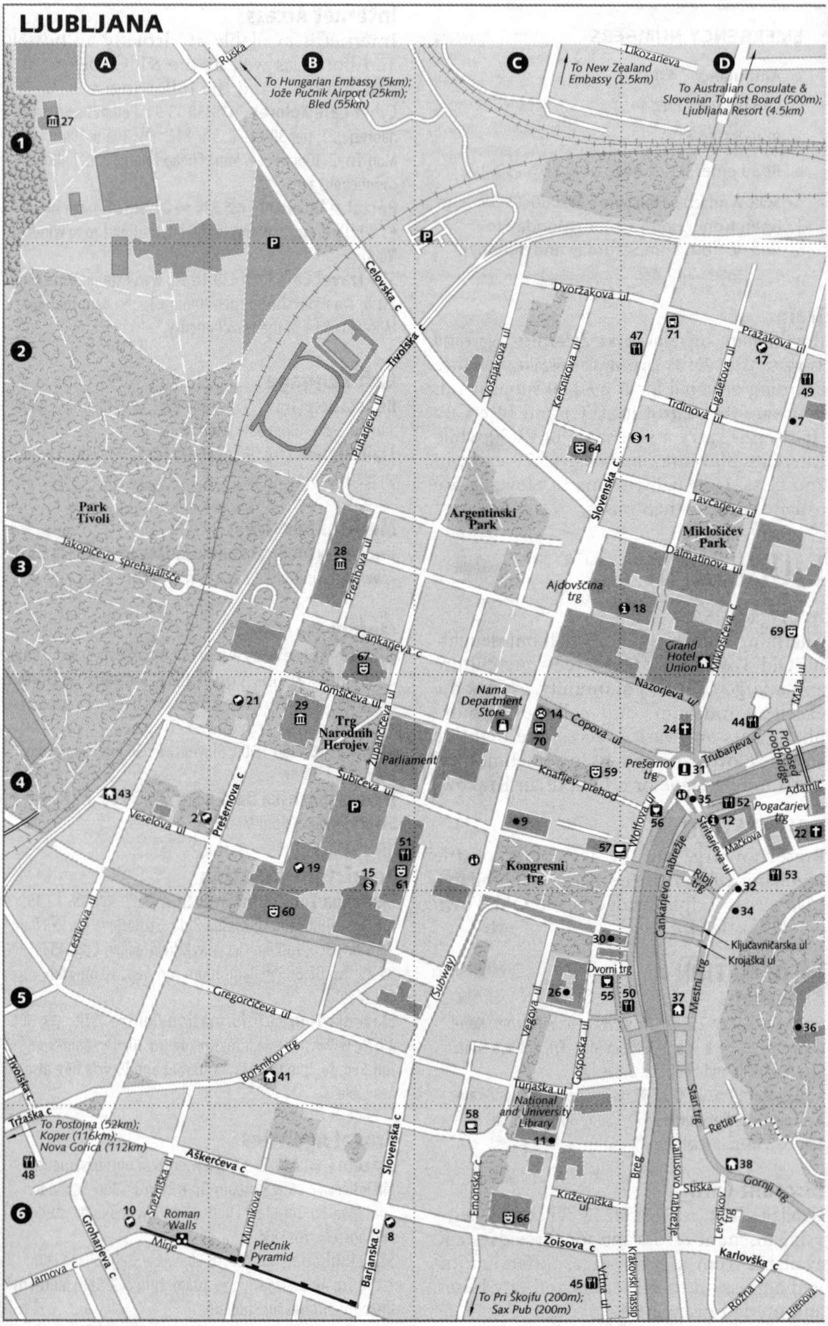

LJUBLJANA

To Hungarian Embassy (5km); Jože Pučnik Airport (25km); Bled (55km)
To New Zealand Embassy (2.5km)
To Australian Consulate & Slovenian Tourist Board (500m); Ljubljana Resort (4.5km)
To Postojna (52km); Koper (116km); Nova Gorica (112km)
To Pri Škofju (200m); Sax Pub (200m)

Park Tivoli
Argentinski Park
Miklošičev Park
Ajdovščina trg
Grand Hotel Union
Nama Department Store
Trg Narodnih Herojev
Parliament
Prešernov trg
Kongresni trg
Dvorni trg
National and University Library
Roman Walls
Plečnik Pyramid
Proposed Footbridge
(Subway)

Ruska, Likozarjeva, Celovska c, Tivolska c, Dvoržakova ul, Pražakova ul, Trdinova ul, Cigaletova ul, Vošnjakova ul, Kersnikova ul, Slovenska c, Puharjeva ul, Tavčarjeva ul, Dalmatinova ul, Jakopičevo sprehajališče, Prežihova ul, Cankarjeva c, Miklošičeva c, Nazorjeva ul, Tomšičeva ul, Župančičeva ul, Čopova ul, Trubarjeva c, Mala ul, Adamič, Prešernova c, Šubičeva ul, Knafljev prehod, Wolfova ul, Veselova ul, Pogačarjev trg, Mačkova, Stritarjeva ul, Ribji trg, Cankarjevo nabrežje, Ključavničarska ul, Krojaška ul, Mestni trg, Lestikova ul, Gregorčičeva ul, Vegova ul, Gosposka ul, Borštnikov trg, Tivolska c, Tržaška c, Turjaška ul, Stari trg, Retler, Aškerčeva c, Snežniška ul, Murnikova, Emonska c, Breg, Gallusovo nabrežje, Križevniška ul, Stiška, Levstikov trg, Gornji trg, Grohar jeva c, Mirje, Jamova c, Barjanska c, Zoisova c, Krakovski nasip, Vrtna ul, Karlovška c, Rožna ul, Hrenova

A B C D
1 2 3 4 5 6

1, 2, 7, 8, 9, 10, 11, 12, 14, 15, 17, 18, 19, 21, 22, 24, 26, 27, 28, 29, 30, 31, 32, 34, 35, 36, 37, 38, 41, 43, 44, 45, 47, 48, 49, 50, 51, 52, 53, 55, 56, 57, 58, 59, 60, 61, 64, 66, 67, 69, 70, 71

SLOVENIA

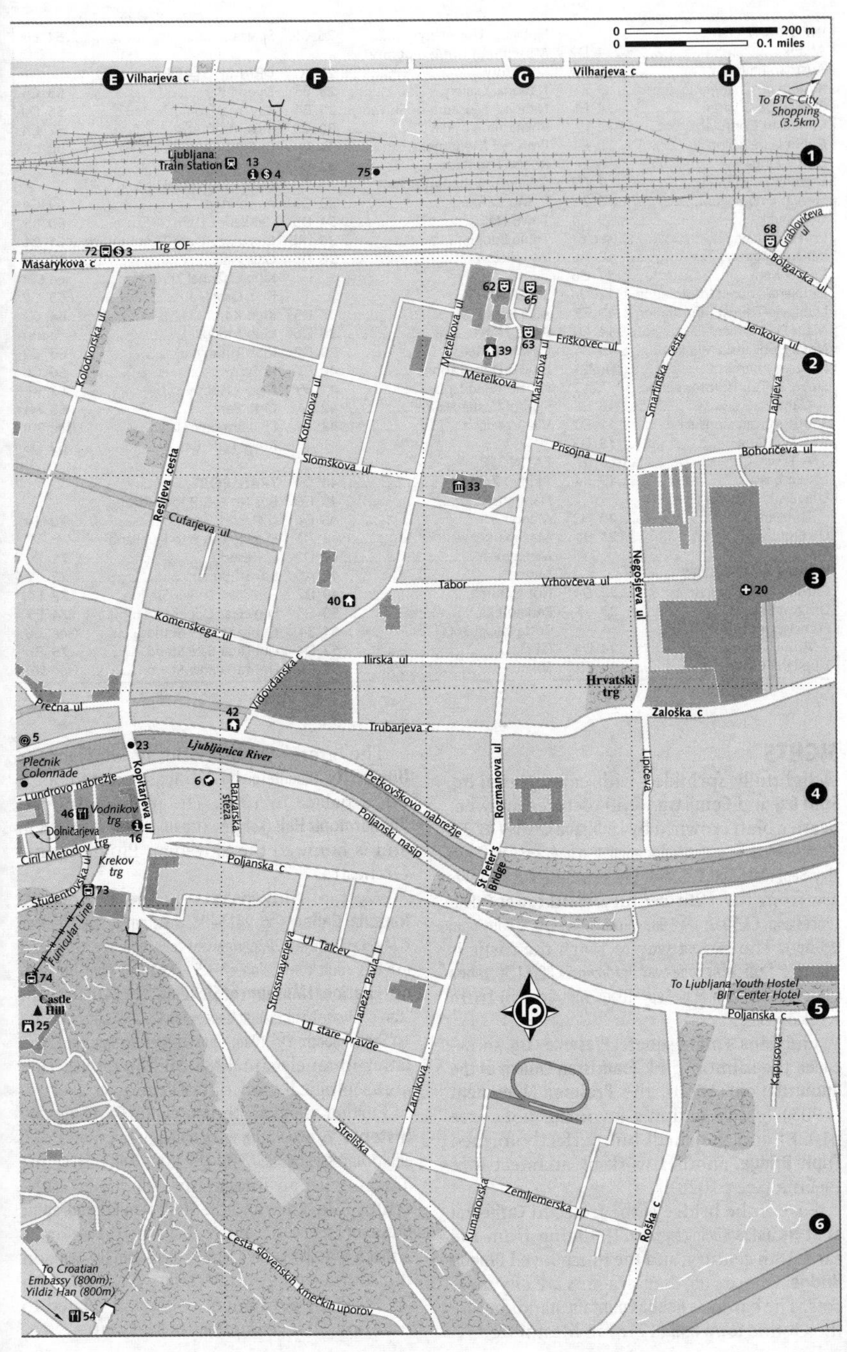

0 200 m
0 0.1 miles
Vilharjeva c
To BTC City Shopping (3.5km)
Ljubljana Train Station
Trg OF
Masarykova c
Metelkova ul
Metelkova
Friškovec ul
Maistrova ul
Šmartinska cesta
Jenkova ul
Japljeva
Grablovičeva ul
Bolgarska ul
Kolodvorska ul
Kotnikova ul
Slomškova ul
Prisojna ul
Bohoričeva ul
Resljeva cesta
Cufarjeva ul
Tabor
Vrhovčeva ul
Negošijeva ul
Komenskega ul
Vidovdanska c
Ilirska ul
Hrvatski trg
Prečna ul
Zaloška c
Trubarjeva c
Ljubljanica River
Plečnik Colonnade
Lundrovo nabrežje
Kopitarjeva ul
Barvarska steza
Petkovškovo nabrežje
Poljanski nasip
Rozmanova ul
Lipičeva
Vodnikov trg
Dolničarjeva
Ciril Metodov trg
Krekov trg
Poljanska c
St Peter's Bridge
Študentovska ul
Funicular Line
Ul Talcev
Strossmayerjeva
Janeza Pavla II
Castle Hill
Ul stare pravde
Žarnikova
To Ljubljana Youth Hostel BIT Center Hotel
Poljanska c
Kapusova
Streliška
Zemljemerska ul
Kumanovska
Roška c
Cesta slovenskih kmečkih uporov
To Croatian Embassy (800m); Yildiz Han (800m)

INFORMATION		
Abanka	**1**	D2
Austrian Embassy	**2**	A4
Bureau de Change	**3**	E1
Bureau de Change	**4**	F1
Canadian Consulate	(see 19)	
Cyber Café Xplorer	**5**	E4
Dutch Embassy	**6**	E4
Erazem	**7**	D2
French Embassy	**8**	B6
Geonavtik	**9**	C4
Irish Embassy	(see 6)	
Italian Embassy	**10**	A6
Kod & Kam	**11**	C6
Ljubljana Tourist Information	**12**	D4
Ljubljana Tourist Information	**13**	F1
Main Post Office	**14**	C4
Nova Ljubljanska Banka	**15**	B4
Portal.si Internet	(see 72)	
Slovenia Tourist Information Centre	**16**	E4
South African Consulate	**17**	D2
STA Ljubljana	**18**	D3
STA Travel Café	(see 18)	
UK Embassy	**19**	B4
University Medical Centre Ljubljana	**20**	H3
US Embassy	**21**	B4
SIGHTS & ACTIVITIES		
Cathedral of St Nicholas	**22**	D4
Dragon Bridge	**23**	E4
Franciscan Church of the Annunciation	**24**	D4
Ljubljana Castle	**25**	E5
Ljubljana University	**26**	C5
Museum of Contemporary History	**27**	A1
National Gallery	**28**	B3
National Museum of Slovenia	**29**	B4
Philharmonic Hall	**30**	C5
Prešeren Monument	**31**	D4
Robba Fountain	**32**	D4
Slovenian Ethnographic Museum	**33**	G3
Town Hall	**34**	D5
Triple Bridge	**35**	D4
Watchtower	**36**	D5
SLEEPING		
Alibi Hostel	**37**	D5
Antiq Hotel	**38**	D6
Celica Hostel	**39**	G2
Dijaški Dom Tabor	**40**	F3
Penzion Pod Lipo	**41**	B5
Simbol Castle Hostel	**42**	F4
Vila Veselova	**43**	A4
EATING		
Ajdovo Zrno	**44**	D4
Harambaša	**45**	C6
Market	**46**	E4
Maximarket	(see 51)	
Mercator	**47**	D2
Mirje	**48**	A6
Nobel Burek	**49**	D2
Paninoteka	**50**	D5
Restavracija 2000	**51**	B4
Ribca	**52**	D4
Sokol	**53**	D4
Špajza	**54**	E6
DRINKING		
Dvorni Bar	**55**	C5
Kavarna Tromostovje	**56**	D4
Kavarna Zvezda	**57**	C4
Le Petit Café	**58**	C6
ENTERTAINMENT		
As Lounge	**59**	C4
Cankarjev Dom	**60**	B5
Cankarjev Dom Ticket Office	**61**	B4
Gala Hala	**62**	G2
Klub Channel Zero	(see 62)	
Klub Gromka	**63**	G2
Klub K4	**64**	C2
Klub Monokel	(see 65)	
Klub Tiffany	**65**	G2
Križanke	**66**	C6
Opera House	**67**	B3
Orto Bar	**68**	H1
Philharmonic Hall	(see 30)	
Roxly Café Bar	**69**	D3
TRANSPORT		
Bus No 6 & 8 to Ljubljana Resort	**70**	C4
Bus No 6 & 8 to Ljubljana Resort	**71**	D2
Bus Station	**72**	E1
Funicular Lower Station	**73**	E4
Funicular Upper Station	**74**	E5
Ljubljana Bike Stand	(see 39)	
Ljubljana Bike Stand	**75**	F1
Ljubljana Bike Stand	(see 16)	

SIGHTS

Delightfully sprinkled with cafes, **Mestni trg**, **Stari trg** and **Gornji trg** wend picturesquely beneath a bluff crowned by **Ljubljana Castle** (☎ 232 99 94; www.ljubljanafestival.si; admission free; 9am-11pm May-Sep, 10am-9pm Oct-Apr). Up here the best views are from the 19th-century **Watchtower** (adult/concession €3.50/2; 9am-9pm May-Sep, 10am-6pm Oct-Apr). The fastest way to reach the castle is via the **funicular** (one-way up/down €1.80/€1.50, return €3; 9am-11pm May-Sep, 10am-9pm Oct-Apr) from Krekov trg.

Ljubljana's main square, **Prešernov trg**, showcases the salmon-pink **Franciscan Church of the Annunciation** (1660), the **Prešeren Monument** (1905) to the nation's favourite poet (see p1028) and the small but perfectly formed **Triple Bridge**, another work by architect Jože Plečnik (see p1028).

East of the bridge is the frescoed **Cathedral of St Nicholas** (Dolničarjeva ul 1), dating from the early 18th century, and the much loved **Dragon Bridge**, whose guardian dragons are city mascots. The baroque **Robba Fountain** stands before the Gothic **town hall** (1718) in Mestni trg.

The grand main building of **Ljubljana University** (Kongresni trg 12) was erected as a ducal palace in 1902. The more restrained **Philharmonic Hall** (Kongresni trg 10) dates from 1898 and is home to the Slovenian Philharmonic Orchestra.

West of Slovenska c is the impressive **National Gallery** (☎ 241 54 18; www.ng-slo.si; Prešernova c 24 & Cankarjeva c 20; permanent collection free, temporary exhibits adult/concession €7/3.5; 10am-6pm Tue-Sun) and **National Museum of Slovenia** (☎ 241 44 00; www.nms.si; Muzejska ul 1; adult/concession €3/2.50, admission free 1st Sun of month; 10am-6pm Fri-Wed, to 8pm Thu), the latter in an elegant 1888 building, with rich archaeological and coin collections.

Further afield are the **Museum of Contemporary History** (☎ 300 96 10; www.muzej-nz.si; Celovška c 23; adult/concession €3.35/2.50; 10am-6pm), in Park Tivoli, with an imaginative glance at 20th-century Slovenia, and the **Slovenian Ethnographic Museum** (☎ 300 87 00; www.etno-muzej.si; Metelkova ul 2; adult/concession €4.50/2.50; 10am-6pm Tue-Sun), on the southern edge of Metelkova Mesto, with an excellent permanent collection related to traditional Slovenian trades and crafts.

GETTING INTO TOWN

The bus and train stations are 800m north of central Prešernov trg; to reach the square walk south along Miklošičeva cesta, with its wonderful art nouveau buildings.

The cheapest way to/from Ljubljana's **Jože Pučnik Airport** (www.lju-airport.si) at Brnik, 27km north of the city, is by city bus from stop 28 (€4.10, 50 minutes, 27km). These run at 5.20am and hourly from 6.10am to 8.10pm Monday to Friday; at the weekend there's a bus at 6.10am and then one every two hours from 9.10am to 7.10pm. A **shuttle van** (☎ 041-792 865) links the bus station with the airport up to 10 times daily between 5.20am and 10.30pm (€5, 30 minutes).

SLEEPING

Ljubljana Resort (☎ 568 39 13; www.ljubljanaresort.si/eng; Dunajska c 270; camp sites per adult €7.50-13.50; year-round) It's got a pretty grandiose name, but wait till you see the facilities at this attractive six-hectare camping ground-cum-resort 4km north of the centre (bus 6 or 8).

Dijaški Dom Tabor (☎ 234 88 40; www.d-tabor.lj.edus.si; Vidovdanska c 7; dm/s/d €10/26/38; late Jun-late Aug) In summer, five colleges open their dormitories *(dijaški dom)* to visitors, but only this 300-bed one is really central. Enter from Kotnikova ul.

Simbol Castle Hostel (☎ 041-720 825; www.simbol.si; Petkovškovo nabrežje 47; dm/d/tr/q €16/50/54/68) A new favourite, this hostel with five rooms, each with their own kitchen, wraps around a tiny courtyard bordering the Ljubljanica. One room has views of the castle.

Alibi Hostel (☎ 251 12 44; www.alibi.si; Cankarjevo nabrežje 27; dm/d €20/50) This well-situated 106-bed hostel right on the Ljubljanica has brightly painted, airy dorm rooms with four to 12 wooden bunks and five doubles.

our pick **Celica Hostel** (☎ 230 97 00; www.hostelcelica.com; Metelkova ul 8; dm €21, s/d/tr cell €47/54/66, per person 4- to 5-bed €27, 6- to 7-bed €22) This stylish former prison (1882) in Metelkova has 20 'cells', complete with bars, nine rooms and apartments with three to seven beds and a popular 12-bed dorm. There are also three cafes and a gallery where everyone can show their own work.

SPLURGE

Antiq Hotel (☎ 421 35 60; www.antiqhotel.si; Gornji trg 3; s €61-164, d €77-204) Ljubljana's first boutique hotel has 16 spacious rooms and apartments in the Old Town, a small wellness centre next door and a multitiered back garden. The decor is kitsch with a smirk, and there are fabulous little touches throughout. The two cheapest rooms (Nos 2 and 9) have their own dedicated bathrooms on the corridor.

Vila Veselova (☎ 059-926 721; www.v-v.si; Veselova ul 14; dm €21, d/q €68/102) This attractive canary-yellow villa with garden and 42 beds opposite Park Tivoli offers mostly hostel accommodation in three colourful rooms with four to eight beds, but there's also a double and two apartments with attached facilities.

Penzion Pod Lipo (☎ 031-809 893; www.penzion-podlipo.com; Borštnikov trg 3; d/tr/q €59/72/96) Atop a venerable old *gostilna* (inn), this 10-room inn offers excellent value right in the centre. We love the communal kitchen, original hardwood floors and sunny, east-facing terrace.

EATING

Self-Catering

Handy supermarkets include **Mercator** (Slovenska c 55; 7am-9pm) and the enormous **Maximarket** (☎ 476 68 00; basement, Trg Republike 1; 9am-9pm Mon-Fri, 8am-5pm Sat). The colourful **market** (Pogačarjev trg & Vodnikov trg; 6am-6pm Mon-Fri, 6am-4pm Sat Jun-Sep, 6am-4pm Mon-Sat Oct-May) is north and east of the cathedral.

Quick Eats

Nobel Burek (Miklošičeva c 30; snacks €1.40-2; 24hr) This hole in the wall serves *burek* (flaky pastry sometimes stuffed with meat, cheese or apple) and pizza round the clock.

Ajdovo Zrno (☎ 041-690 478; Trubarjeva c 7; soups & sandwiches €1.80-2, set lunch €6; 10am-7pm Mon-Fri) This simple vegetarian cafe serves soups, sandwiches, fried vegetables and salads (self-service €3 to €6).

Restavracija 2000 (☎ 476 69 25; Trg Republike 1; dishes €1.50-3, set lunch €6.50; 9am-7pm Mon-Fri, to 3pm Sat) Upbeat self-service eatery in the basement of the Maximarket department store.

Paninoteka (☎ 041 529 824; Jurčičev trg 3; soups & toasted sandwiches €2.40-6; 8am-1am Mon-Sat, 9am-11pm Sun) Healthy sandwich creations on a lovely little square by the river.

Ribca (☎ 425 15 44; Adamič-Lundrovo nabrežje 1; dishes €3-7.50; 8am-4pm Mon-Fri, to 2pm Sat) Below the Plečnik Colonnade, this basement seafood place serves generous set lunches to hungry market-goers.

Restaurants

Harambaša (☎ 041-843 106; Vrtna ul 8; dishes €3.50-6; 10am-10pm Mon-Fri, noon-10pm Sat, to 6pm Sun) Authentic Bosnian cuisine (mostly grilled things) served at low tables in a charming cottage.

Mirje (☎ 426 60 15; Tržaška c 5; pizza €4-8.50; 10am-10pm Mon-Fri, noon-5pm Sat) The pick of the crop of Ljubljana's many pizzerias, this place southwest of the city centre also does excellent pasta and more elaborate Italian dishes.

Pri Škofju (☎ 426 45 08; Rečna ul 8; mains €7-15, set lunch €5.30-6.90; 10am-midnight Mon-Fri, from noon Sat & Sun) This wonderful little place with an ever-changing menu in tranquil Krakovo serves some of the best local dishes and salads in town.

Sokol (☎ 439 68 55; Ciril Metodov trg 18; mains €7-20; noon-11pm) In this old vaulted house, traditional Slovenian food is served on heavy tables by costumed waiters. Both the quality and quantity will please.

Yildiz Han (☎ 426 57 17; Karlovška c 19; mains €8.50-15, set lunch €5; noon-midnight Mon-Sat) If Turkish is your thing, head for authentic (trust us) 'Star House', which features belly dancing on Friday night.

our pick **Špajza** (☎ 425 30 94; Gornji trg 28; mains €14.60-22, set lunch €10; noon-11pm Mon-Sat, to 10pm Sun) The 'Pantry' is a lovely decorated restaurant in the Old Town with rough-hewn tables and chairs, wooden floors, frescoed ceilings and nostalgic bits and pieces. Come here for the 'Špajza filet' (€22), which is actually horseflesh, or a taste of oven-roasted kid (€14.60). Wines are sourced from a dozen different Slovenian producers.

DRINKING

Kavarna Zvezda (☎ 421 90 90; Kongresni trg 4 & Wolfova ul 14; 7am-11pm Mon-Sat, 10am-8pm Sun) The 'Star Cafe' is celebrated for its cakes, especially its legendary *skutina pečena* (€2.60), an eggy cheesecake.

Le Petit Café (☎ 251 25 75; Trg Francoske Revolucije 4; 7.30am-midnight) Just opposite the Križanke, this pleasant place offers great coffee and breakfast (€2.60 to €6.50).

Kavarna Tromostovje (☎ 430 12 18; Prešernov trg 1; 7am-1am Apr-Oct) On the southern side of Prešernov trg, this roped-off cafe-bar is one of the most popular places in the city for a drink if you just want to sit outside and watch the passing parade.

Dvorni Bar (☎ 251 12 57; Dvorni trg 2; 8am-1am Mon-Sat, to midnight Sun) This wine bar is an excellent place to taste Slovenian vintages; it stocks more than 100 varieties.

Sax Pub (☎ 283 14 57; Eipprova ul 7; noon-1am Mon, from 10am Tue-Sat, 4-10pm Sun) Decorated with colourful murals and graffiti inside and out, this Trnovo mainstay has live or canned jazz depending on the day of the week and time of year.

CLUBBING

Orto Bar (☎ 232 16 74; www.orto-bar.com; Grablovičeva ul 1; 8am-4am Mon-Wed, to 5am Thu-Sat, 6-9pm Sun) A popular bar-club for late-night drinking and dancing, with occasional live music, Orto is just five minutes' walk from Metelkova.

Roxly Café Bar (☎ 430 10 21; www.roxly.si; Mala ul 5; 7am-2am Mon-Wed, to 3am Thu & Fri, 10am-3am Sat) New venue north of the Ljubljanica features live rock music from 10pm two or three nights a week.

As Lounge (☎ 425 88 22; www.gostilnaas.si; Čopova ul 5a; 9pm-3am Wed-Sat) DJs transform this candle-lit basement bar into a pumping, crowd-pulling nightclub four nights a week. Enter from Knafljev prehod.

Klub K4 (☎ 438 02 61; www.klubk4.org; Kersnikova ul 4; 8pm-2am Tue, to 4am Wed & Thu, 9pm-6am Fri & Sat, 10pm-4am Sun) This evergreen venue in the basement of the student union features rave-electronic music Friday and Saturday and a popular gay-and-lesbian night on Sunday.

Metelkova Mesto (www.metelkova.org; Masarykova c 24) 'Metelkova Town', an ex-army garrison taken over by squatters after independence, is an alternative-lifestyle centre with a dozen idiosyncratic venues coming to life generally after midnight daily in summer and at the weekend the rest of the year. They include **Gala Hala** (www.galahala.com), with live bands and club nights; **Klub Channel Zero** (www.ch0.org), with punk and hardcore; and **Klub Gromka** (www.metelkova.org/gromka), with folk music, theatre and live concerts. To the left of the main entrance, **Klub Tiffany** (www.ljudmila.org/siqrd/tiffany) and **Klub**

Monokel (www.klubmonokel.com) are for gay men and lesbians respectively.

ENTERTAINMENT

The quarterly *Ljubljana Life* (www.ljubljanalife.com) has practical information and listings and is free, but **Ljubljana in Your Pocket** (www.inyourpocket.com; €2.90), another quarterly, is much more useful. The TIC's *Where to? in Ljubljana* lists cultural and sporting events.

The most active cultural venue is **Cankarjev Dom** (☎ 241 71 00; www.cd-cc.si; Prešernova c 10), whose **ticket office** (☎ 241 72 99; 11am-1pm & 3-8pm Mon-Fri, to 1pm Sat & 1hr before performance) is in the subway below the Maximarket supermarket.

Check for classical concerts at the **Philharmonic Hall** (☎ 241 08 00; www.filharmonija.si; Kongresni trg 10) and for opera and ballet at the **Opera House** (☎ 241 17 40; www.opera.si; Župančičeva ul 1). The **Križanke** (☎ 241 60 00, box office 241 60 26; Trg Francoske Revolucije 1-2) hosts events during the Ljubljana Festival (p1044) in an erstwhile monastic complex dating from the 13th century.

GETTING THERE & AWAY

Bus

Ljubljana's **bus station** (☎ 234 46 00, information 090 93 42 30; www.ap-ljubljana.si; Trg OF 4; 5.30am-10.30pm Sun-Fri, 5am-10pm Sat) has multilingual info-phones; just pick one up and wait for the connection. Frequent buses serve Bohinj (€8.30, two hours, hourly) via Bled (€6.30, 1¼ hours). Most buses to Piran (€12, three hours, up to seven daily) go via Koper (€11.10, 2½ hours, up to 16 daily) and Postojna (€6, one hour, up to 36 daily).

Train

The **train station** (☎ 291 33 32; www.slo-zeleznice.si; Trg OF 6; 5am-10pm) has daily services to Koper (€7.75 to €13, 2½ hours, up to five daily). Alternatively you can take one of the more frequent Sežana-bound trains and change at Divača (€6.25 to €7.75, 1¾ hours). For international services, see p1030.

GETTING AROUND

Ljubljana has an excellent network of city buses but you'll need them only if you're staying out of town. Buy little metal tokens (*žetoni;* €0.80) from newsstands or pay €1 when boarding.

Ljubljana Bike (per 2hr/day €1/5; 8am-7pm or 9pm Apr-Oct) has two-wheelers available from some 10 locations around the city, including the train station, STIC (p1031), Celica Hostel (p1035) and Antiq Hotel (p1035).

JULIAN ALPS

The Julian Alps – named in honour of Mr Caesar – form Slovenia's dramatic northwest frontier with Italy. Triglav National Park, established in 1924, includes almost all of the alps lying within Slovenia. The centrepiece of the park is, of course, triple-peaked Mt Triglav (2864m), Slovenia's highest mountain. Along with an embarrassment of fauna and flora, the area offers a wide range of adventure sports.

BLED

☎ 04 / pop 5515

With its emerald-green lake, picture-postcard church on a tiny island, medieval castle clinging to a rocky cliff and some of the country's highest peaks as backdrops, Bled seems to have been designed by the very god of tourism. It's small, convenient and a delightful base from which to explore.

Information

À Propos Bar (☎ 574 40 44; Bled Shopping Centre, Ljubljanska c 4; per 15/30min €1.25/2.10; 8am-midnight) Internet access.

Gorenjska Banka (C Svobode 15; 9-11.30am & 2-5pm Mon-Fri, 8-11am Sat)

Kompas (☎ 572 75 00; www.kompas-bled.si; Bled Shopping Centre, Ljubljanska c 4; 8am-8pm Mon-Sat, to noon & 4-8pm Sun Jul & Aug, 8am-7pm Mon-Sat Sep-Jun) Rents private rooms and bicycles.

Tourist Information Centre Bled (☎ 574 11 22; www.bled.si; C Svobode 10; 8am-9pm Mon-Sat, 9am-5pm Sun Jul & Aug, 8am-7pm Mon-Sat, 11am-5pm Sun Mar-Jun, Sep & Oct, 9am-6pm Mon-Sat, noon-4pm Sun Nov, 8am-6pm Mon-Fri, 8am-1pm Sun Dec-Feb) Internet access is free for 15 minutes, then €2.50/4 for 30/60 minutes.

Sights

On its own romantic tiny island is the baroque **Church of the Assumption**. Reach it by piloted **gondola** (pletna; ☎ 041-427 155; €12); prices are standard from any jetty and it's a 1½-hour trip. Row-yourself **boats** for three to four people cost €10 to €13 per hour.

Perched atop a 100m-cliff, **Bled Castle** (☎ 572 97 80; Grajska c 25; adult/concession €7/6; 8am-8pm May-Oct, to 5pm Nov-Apr) is the perfect backdrop to the lake. A footpath leads up from behind the Bledec Hostel.

Activities

The 6km stroll around the lake shouldn't take more than a couple of hours, including the short (but steep) climb to the **Osojnica viewing point**. An easy walk is to **Vintgar Gorge** (adult/concession €4/3; ⏲ 8am-7pm mid-May–Oct), 3km to the northwest. In summer, a bus (€3.50) leaves Bled bus station daily for Vintgar at 10am.

For something more adrenalin-raising, ask **Adventure Rafting Bled** (☎ 574 40 41, 051-676 008; www.adventure-rafting.si; Grajska c 21; ☎ Apr-Oct), based at the Bled Backpackers Rooms hostel, or **3glav adventures** (☎ 041-683 184; www.3glav-adventures.com; Ljubljanska c 1; ⏲ 9am-7pm Apr-Oct) about their rafting or kayaking trips (€25 to €44).

Sleeping

Private rooms are available though Kompas (p1037), with singles/doubles starting at €24/38.

Camping Bled (☎ 575 20 00; www.camping.bled.si; Kidričeva c 10c; camp sites per adult €8.50-11.50; ⏲ Apr–mid-Oct) This popular 6.5-hectare site fills a small valley at the western end of the lake.

Bledec Hostel (☎ 574 52 50; www.mlino.si; Grajska c 17; dm low/high season from €16/18, d per person low/high season €22/24; 💻) Well-organised official (read institutional) hostel has dorms with four to seven beds with attached bathrooms, a bar and inexpensive restaurant.

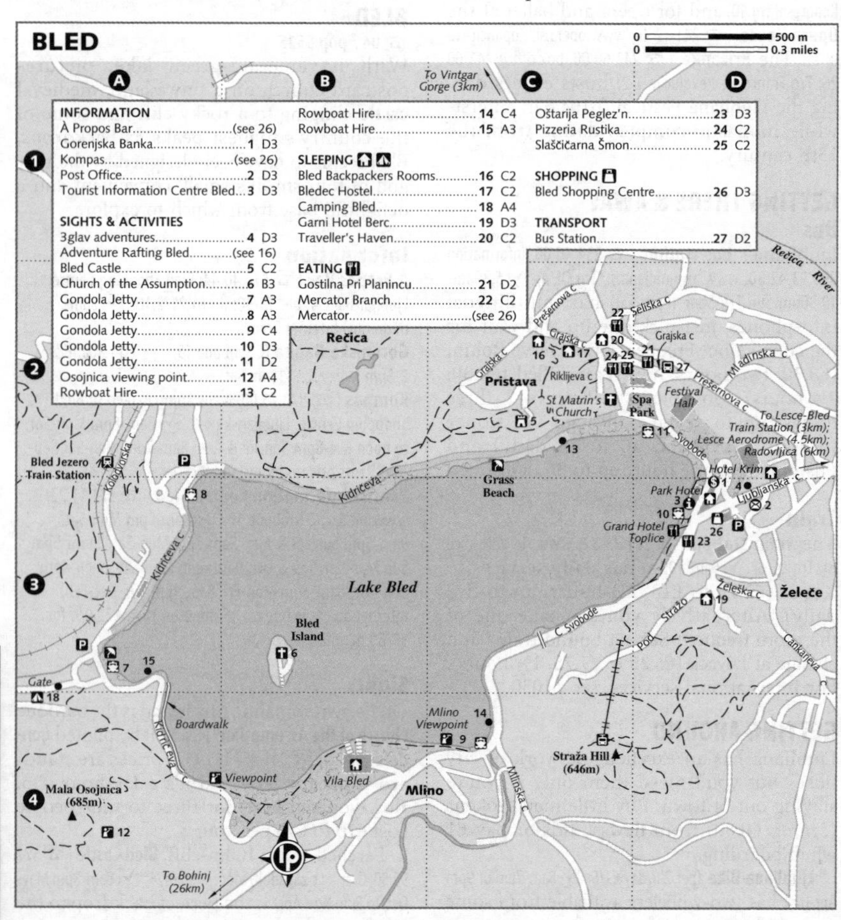

Bled Backpackers Rooms (☎ 574 40 41, 051-678 008; www.bled-backpackersrooms.com; Grajska c 21; r per person €17; 💻) This five-room place with 20 beds and the George Best Bar below has become Bled's party hostel.

Traveller's Haven (☎ 031-704 455, 041-396 545; www.travellers-haven.com; Riklijeva c 1; r per person €19; 💻) Stunning six-room facility in a converted old villa (c 1909) with between two and six beds, a great kitchen, free internet and laundry and a chilled vibe.

Garni Hotel Berc (☎ 576 56 58; www.berc-sp.si; Pod Stražo 13; s €40-45, d €65-70; 💻) Purpose-built and vaguely recalling a Swiss chalet, this small hotel has 15 rooms on two floors in a quiet location above the lake.

Eating

Slaščičarna Šmon (☎ 574 16 16; Grajska c 3; 🕒 7.30am-10pm) Bled's culinary speciality is *kremna rezina* (cream cake; €2.20), a layer of vanilla custard topped with whipped cream and sandwiched neatly between two layers of flaky pastry. This is the best place to try it.

Gostilna Pri Planincu (☎ 574 16 13; Grajska c 8; mains €5-20.50; 🕒 noon-10pm) A cosy pub-restaurant just down the hill from the three hostels, with simple Slovenian mains and grilled Balkan specialities.

Pizzeria Rustika (☎ 576 89 00; Riklijeva c 13; pizza €5.70-9.50; 🕒 noon-midnight Tue-Sun) A marble-roll down the hill from the hostels, Rustika has its own wood-burning oven and an outside terrace.

Ostarija Peglez'n (☎ 574 42 18; C Svobode 19a; mains €8.50-22; 🕒 11am-midnight) The best restaurant in Bled, the 'Iron Inn' has attractive retro decor and serves some of the best fish dishes in town.

You'll find a **Mercator** (Ljubljanska c 4; 🕒 7am-8pm Mon-Sat, 8am-noon Sun) at the eastern end of Bled Shopping Centre. There's a **Mercator branch** (Prešernova c 48; 🕒 7am-8pm Mon-Sat, 8am-4pm Sun) close to the hostels.

Getting There & Around

Buses to Bohinj (€3.60, one hour, hourly) and Ljubljana (€6.30, 1¼ hours, hourly) depart from the central bus station. Trains for Bohinjska Bistrica (€1.50, 20 minutes, seven a day) and Nova Gorica (€5.35, two hours, seven a day) use Bled Jezero station, which is 2km west of the centre. Trains for Ljubljana (€4.10 to €7.60, 45 minutes, up to 17 a day) use Lesce-Bled station, 4km to the east of town.

BOHINJ

☎ 04 / pop 5275

Bohinj, a larger and much less developed glacial lake 26km to the southwest of Bled, is a world apart from Bled. Mt Triglav itself is visible from the Bohinj and there are activities galore – from kayaking and mountain biking to trekking up Triglav via one of the southern approaches.

Bohinjska Bistrica, the area's largest village, is 6km east of the lake and useful for its train station. The minuscule tourist centre at the lake's eastern end is **Ribčev Laz**, containing a supermarket, a post office that changes money and has an ATM, and the **Bohinj Tourist Office** (☎ 574 60 10; www.bohinj-info.com; Ribčev Laz 48; 🕒 8am-8pm Mon-Sat, to 6pm Sun Jul & Aug, 8am-6pm Mon-Sat, 9am-3pm Sun Sep-Jun).

Sights & Activities

Central **Alpinsport** (☎ 572 34 86; www.alpinsport.si; Ribčev Laz 53; 🕒 9am-7pm Jun-Aug, 10am-6pm Sep-May) organises a range of activities and rents kayaks, canoes, mountain bikes and other equipment from a kiosk near the stone bridge. Next door is the **Church of St John the Baptist**, which contains splendid 15th- and 16th-century frescoes but is undergoing a protracted renovation.

The nearby village of **Stara Fužina** has an appealing little **Alpine Dairy Museum** (☎ 041-564 904; Stara Fužina 181; adult/concession €2.10/1.60; 🕒 11am-7pm Tue-Sun Jul & Aug, 10am-noon & 4-6pm Tue-Sun Jan-Jun, Sep & Oct). Just 2km east is **Studor**, a village famed for its *kozolci* and *toplarji*, Slovenia's unique single and double hayracks.

Sleeping

The TIC has private rooms (per person €10 to €15) and apartments are available (doubles €33 to €44, quads €48.50 to €70).

Avtokamp Zlatorog (☎ 572 34 82; www.aaturizem.com; Ukanc 2; camp sites per person €7-12; 🕒 May-Sep) This pine-shaded 2.5-hectare site accommodating 500 guests is at the lake's western end.

Hostel Pod Voglom (☎ 572 34 61; www.hostel-podvoglom.com; Ribčev Laz 60; dm €16-18, per person r with private bathroom €22-24, shared bathroom €19-21; 💻) This recently revived budget accommodation has 119 beds in 46 somewhat frayed rooms in two buildings. The so-called Hostel Building has doubles, triples and dormitory accommodation with shared facilities; rooms in the Rodica Annexe, with between one and four beds, are en suite.

Penzion Gasperin (☎ 572 36 61; www.bohinj.si/gasperin; Ribčev Laz 36a; r per person €22-33;) This positively spotless chalet-style guesthouse with 20 rooms (nine of which are spanking new) is 350m east of the tourist office and run by a friendly British/Slovenian couple.

Getting There & Around

Buses run from Ukanc ('Bohinj Zlatorog' on most schedules) to Ljubljana (€8.70, two hours, hourly) via Ribčev Laz, Bohinjska Bistrica and Bled (€4.10, one hour), with another six daily buses direct to Bohinjska Bistrica (€2.70 20 minutes). From Bohinjska Bistrica, trains to Nova Gorica (€4.70, 1¼ hours, up to seven daily) make use of a century-old tunnel under the mountains that provides the only direct option for reaching the Soča Valley.

SOČA VALLEY

The Soča Valley region is defined by the 96km-long Soča River coloured a deep, almost artificial turquoise. The valley has more than its share of historical sights, most of them related to WWI, but most visitors are here for rafting, hiking, skiing and other active sports.

BOVEC

☎ 05 / pop 1760

The best alpine views are at Bovec, which lies in the shadow of Mt Kanin, Slovenia's highest ski resort. The compact village square, Trg Golobarskih Žrtev, has everything you need, including the **Tourist Information Centre Bovec** (☎ 389 64 44; www.bovec.si; Trg Golobarskih Žrtev; 8.30am-8.30pm Jul & Aug, 9am-5pm Mon-Fri, 9am-noon & 4-6pm Sat, 9am-noon Sun Sep-Jun) and a half-dozen adrenalin-raising adventure-sports companies, including **Avantura** (☎ 041-718 317; www.avantura.org) and **Bovec Rafting Team** (☎ 388 61 28, 041-338 308; www.bovec-rafting-team.com).

The TIC has a list of private rooms (per person €15 to €30). Camping facilities are generally better in nearby Kobarid but **Kamp Polovnik** (☎ 388 60 69; www.kamp-polovnik.com; Ledina 8; camp sites per adult €5-7; Apr–mid-Oct), about 500m southeast of the centre, is convenient. The 103-room **Alp Hotel** (☎ 388 40 40; www.alp-chandler.si; Trg Golobarskih Žrtev 48; s €48-60, d €66-90;) is fairly good value and as central as you are going to find here.

Getting There & Away

Buses to Nova Gorica (€7.50, two hours, up to five a day) go via Kobarid (€3.10, 30 minutes). A service to Kranjska Gora (€6.70, two hours) via the spectacular Vršič Pass departs five times daily (six on Sunday) in July and August, and on Saturday and Sunday at 3.35pm in June and September.

KARST & COAST

Slovenia's short coast (47km) is not renowned for its fine beaches, though the southernmost resort of Portorož has some decent ones. Koper and Piran, two important towns full of Venetian Gothic architecture, are the main drawcards here. En route from Ljubljana or the Soča Valley, you'll cross the Karst, a huge limestone plateau and a land of olives, ruby-red Teran wine, *pršut* (air-dried ham) and deep caves.

POSTOJNA & ŠKOCJAN CAVES

☎ 05

Two kilometres northwest of the town of Postojna (population 8850), **Postojna Cave** (☎ 700 01 00; www.postojnska-jama.si; Jamska c 30; adult/concession €19/16; tours hourly 9am-6pm Jul & Aug, to 5pm May, Jun & Sep, 10am, noon, 2pm & 4pm Apr & Oct, 10am, noon & 3pm Nov-Mar) is home to the endemic *Proteus anguinus* – cute, eyeless salamanders nicknamed 'human fish'. The cave is filled with endless stalagmites, stalactites and almost as many tourists. Visits (1½ hours) involve an underground train ride as well as a 1.7km walk with gradients but no steps. Dress warmly or rent a shawl as it's 8°C to 10°C down there.

The quieter and more remote **Škocjan Caves** (☎ 708 21 00; www.park-skocjanske-jame.si; Škocjan 2; adult/concession €14/10; tours hourly 10am-5pm Jun-Sep, 10am, 1pm & 3.30pm Apr, May & Oct, 10am & 1pm Mon-Sat, 10am, 1pm & 3pm Sun Nov-Mar) are 4km southeast of Divača (population 1330). Staff at the train station ticket office can provide you with a photocopied route map for walking to the caves. Alternatively, a courtesy van meets incoming trains at 10am, 11.04am, 2pm and 3.35pm and will transport those with bus or train tickets to the caves.

Sleeping & Eating

Kompas Postojna (☎ 721 14 80; www.kompas-postojna.si; Titov trg 2a; 8am-7pm Mon-Fri, 9am-1pm Sat Jun-Aug,

SLOVENIA

8am-6pm Mon-Fri, 9am-1pm Sat May, Sep & Oct, 8am-5pm Mon-Fri, 9am-1pm Sat Nov-Apr) has private rooms (per person €18 to €20).

Hotel Sport (☎ 720 22 44; www.sport-hotel.si; Kolodvorska c 1; dm €20, s €55-65, d €70-90, tr €96-125, q €120-160; 💻) The Sport offers reasonably good value for money, with 32 spick-and-span and very comfortable rooms, including 40 hostel beds. It's just 300m north of the centre of Postojna and rents mountain bikes (per half/full day €9/15) for exploring nearby Notranjska Regional Park.

Gostilna Malovec (☎ 763 12 25; Kraška 30a; r per person €20) In Divača, you'll find half a dozen basic but comfortable renovated rooms in a building beside a popular traditional restaurant (mains €5 to €15, open 8am to 10pm).

Getting There & Around

Buses from Ljubljana to Koper, Piran and Nova Gorica all stop in Postojna (€6, one hour, half-hourly) and Divača (€8, 1½ hours, half-hourly). The train is good for Divača (€6.25, 1½ hours, hourly) but less useful for Postojna.

KOPER

☎ 05 / pop 24,630

Coastal Slovenia's largest town, Koper (Capodistria in Italian) at first glance appears to be a workaday city that scarcely gives tourism a second thought. Yet its medieval core is delightfully quiet and far less overrun than its ritzy cousin Piran, 17km down the coast.

The **Tourist Information Centre Koper** (☎ 664 64 03; www.koper.si; Titov trg 3; 🕒 9am-9pm Jul & Aug, 9am-5pm Mon-Fri, to 7pm Sat & Sun Sep-Jun) is within the restored Renaissance **Praetorian Palace** (admission free), which also houses an old pharmacy. Opposite, the splendid 1463 **loggia** is now the elegant **Loggia Café** (☎ 621 32 13; Titov trg 1; 🕒 7.30am-10pm Mon-Sat, from 10am Sun). The **Koper Regional Museum** (☎ 663 35 70; Kidričeva ul 19; admission €2.50; 🕒 9am-1pm & 6-9pm Tue-Sun Jul & Aug, 10am-6pm Tue-Fri, 9am-1pm Sat & Sun Sep-Jun) inside the Belgramoni-Tacco Palace has an Italianate sculpture garden.

Sleeping & Eating

The **Palma Travel Agency** (☎ 663 36 60; Pristaniška ul 21; 🕒 8am-7pm Mon-Fri, 9am-noon Sat) can arrange private rooms (per person €20 to €31) and apartments (for two people €32 to €40, for four people €56 to €70).

Motel Port (☎ 639 32 60; www.port-turizem.si; Ankaranska c 7; dm €15-17, s €29-40, d €43-48, tr €54-60; ❄ 💻) Hidden on the 2nd floor of a shopping centre southeast of the Old Town, this place has 30 rooms, some of them en suite and air-conditioned and others dorm rooms with four to six beds.

Museum Hostel (☎ 626 18 70, 041-504 466; bozic .doris@siol.net; Mladinska ul 7; apt per person €20-25) This excellent-value place is more a series of bright apartments with modern kitchens and bathrooms than a hostel. Reception is at the little Bife Museum, a cafe-bar at Muzejski trg 6.

Istrska Klet Slavček (☎ 627 67 29; Župančičeva ul 39; dishes €2.50-14; 🕒 7am-10pm Mon-Fri) This 'Istrian Cellar' in an 18th-century palace is one of the most colourful places for a meal in Koper's Old Town. Filling set lunches go for under €7.

Getting There & Away

Buses run to Piran (€3.10, 30 minutes) every 20 minutes on weekdays and half-hourly on weekends. Up to nine buses daily head for Ljubljana (€11.10, 1¾ to 2½ hours), though the five daily trains (€7.75 to €13, 2¼ hours) are more comfortable.

WORTH THE TRIP

Slovenia's second city, **Maribor**, has no unmissable sights but oozes with charm thanks to its delightfully patchy Old Town. Pedestrianised central streets buzz with cafes and student life, and in late June/early July the riverside Lent district hosts a major arts festival. The **Tourist Information Centre Maribor** (☎ 234 66 10; www.maribor.si; Partinzanska c 6a; h9am-7pm Mon-Fri, to 6pm Sat & Sun Jul & Aug, 9am-6pm Mon-Sat, to 1pm Sun Sep-Jun) has a list of places to stay, but for budget accommodation try the new **Alibi C2** (☎ 051 663 555; www.alibi.si; Cafova ul 2; dm €17-20, d per person €20-25; 💻), a super-swanky hostel in a beautifully restored 19th-century building. From Ljubljana reach Maribor by bus (€12, three hours, two to four a day) or by train (€7.75, 2½ hours), with up to two dozen daily departures. Consider a quick bus trip to picture-postcard **Ptuj** (€3.60, 45 minutes, hourly), which is just down the road.

PIRAN

☎ 05 / pop 4430

Little Piran (Pirano in Italian) sits on the tip of a narrow peninsula, the westernmost point of Slovenian Istria. Piran Bay and Portorož (population 2900), Slovenia's largest beach resort, lie to the south. Piran's Old Town is a gem of Venetian Gothic architecture and full of picturesque narrow streets.

Sergej Mašera Maritime Museum (☎ 671 00 40; Cankarjevo nabrežje 3; adult/concession €3.50/2.50; 9am-noon & 6-9pm Tue-Sun Jul & Aug, 9am-noon & 3-6pm Tue-Sun Sep-Jun) and the new **Museum of Underwater Activities** (☎ 041-685 379; Župančičeva ul 24; adult/concession €3/2; 9.30am-10pm Jun-Sep) are on the harbour on the way to central Tartinijev trg, where you'll find the **Tourist Information Center Piran** (☎ 673 44 40; www.portoroz.si; Tartinijev trg 2; 9am-7pm Jul-Sep, 9am-5pm Oct-Jun).

Piran is dominated by the **Cathedral of St George** (Adamičeva ul 2), whose soaring **bell tower** (1608) was modelled on the campanile of St Mark's Cathedral in Venice. The nearby **Minorite monastery** (☎ 673 44 17; Bolniška ul 30) has a delightful cloister.

Sleeping

Maona Tourist Agency (☎ 673 45 20; www.maona.si; Cankarjevo nabrežje 7; 9am-8pm Mon-Sat, 10am-1pm & 5-7pm Sun) rents private rooms (singles €15.85 to €25, doubles €23 to €35).

Kamp Fiesa (☎ 674 62 30; autokamp.fiesa@siol.net; camp sites per adult €8.50-10; May-Sep) The closest camping ground to Piran is this tiny site at Fiesa, 4km by road but less than 1km if you follow the coastal trail *(obalna pešpot)* east of the Church of St George.

Val Hostel (☎ 673 25 55; www.hostel-val.com; Gregorčičeva ul 38a; r per person €22-25; Sep-May;) This central, partially renovated hostel has 22 rooms, with two to four beds, shared shower, kitchen and washing machine. It's a great favourite with backpackers.

Alibi B11 (☎ 673 01 41, 031-363 666; www.alibi.si; Bonifacijeva ul 11; r per person €20-22;) The newest addition to the ever-expanding Alibi stable has mostly doubles in eight rooms over four floors in an ancient (and rather frayed) townhouse on a narrow street. Reception for all three hostels is here.

Diagonally opposite is **Alibi B14** (Bonifacijeva ul 14; dm per person €20-22), an upbeat and colourful four-floor party place with six rooms, each with two to six beds, bath and kitchenette. There's also a washing machine here. More subdued is **Alibi T60** (Trubarjeva ul 60; r per person €25-27.50;) to the east with a fully equipped double on each of five floors.

Eating

Flora (☎ 673 12 58; Prešernovo nabrežje 26; pizza €4-7.50; 10am-1am Jul & Aug, 10am-10pm Sep-Jun) The terrace of this simple pizzeria east of the Punta lighthouse has uninterrupted views of the Adriatic.

Pri Mari (☎ 673 47 35, 041-616 488; Dantejeva ul 17; mains €7.50-16; 10am-11pm Tue-Sun Jul & Aug, noon-10pm Tue-Sat, to 6pm Sun Sep-Jun) This stylish Italian-owned restaurant, located south of the bus station, serves up the most inventive Mediterranean and Slovenian dishes in town.

Galeb (☎ 673 32 25; Pusterla ul 5; mains €8-11; 11am-4pm & 6-11pm or midnight Wed-Mon) This excellent family-run restaurant with seafront seating is east of the Punta lighthouse.

There's a small **Mercator** (Levstikova ul 5; 7am-8pm Mon-Sat, 8am-noon Sun) supermarket in the Old Town behind the town hall.

Getting There & Away

From the bus station, buses run every 20 to 30 minutes to Koper (€3.10, 30 minutes) via Izola. Five buses head for Trieste (€10, 1¾ hours) between 6.45am and 6.55pm Monday to Saturday. Between three and five daily buses go to Ljubljana (€12, 2½ to three hours) via Divača and Postojna. From the southern end of Tartinijev trg, a shuttle bus (€1) goes every 15 minutes to Lucija via Portorož.

SPLURGE

Riva (☎ 673 221 80; Prešernovo nabrežje; mains €8-24; h11.30am-midnight) If you want to treat yourself to a seafront seafood meal while in Piran, choose this place – the only one of a slew of seafood restaurants along Prešernovo nabrežje that we patronise. It's classier than most, has the strip's best decor and the most romantic sea views. The food takes no risks but like so many other things in this short and mostly happy life we prefer our seafood *au naturel*.

SLOVENIA DIRECTORY

ACCOMMODATION

Camping grounds generally charge per person. Most sites close from mid-October to mid-April.

Slovenia's growing stable of hostels includes Ljubljana's trendy Celica and the Alibi hostels found in the capital, Piran and Maribor. Throughout the country there are student dorms moonlighting as hostels in July and August.

Tourist information offices can help you access private rooms, apartments and tourist farms, or they can recommend private agencies that will. Be aware that there are usually surcharges of 30% to 50% on stays of fewer than three nights.

Guesthouses, known as a *penzion, gostišče* or *prenočišča,* are often cosy and better value than full-blown hotels; in any case, it can be difficult to find a double room in a hotel for under €50. A tourist tax of between €0.50 and €1 is levied per person per day in most communities.

ACTIVITIES

Skiing is a national passion, with slopes particularly crowded over the Christmas holidays and early in February. See www.slovenia.info/skiing for much more information.

Hiking is extremely popular, with around 7000km of waymarked trails and 170 mountain huts; book these via tourist offices. Check out the website of the **Alpine Association of Slovenia** (www.pzs.si).

Bovec (p1040) is a magnet for fans of extreme sports, notably paragliding and canyoning. The nearby Soča River offers Slovenia's best white-water rafting. The Sava River at Bohinj (p1039) is a great base for fly-fishing.

Mountain bikes are available for rent from travel agencies at Bled, Bohinj, Bovec and Postojna between May and October.

BUSINESS HOURS

All businesses post their opening times *(delovni čas)* on the door. Many shops close Saturday afternoons and only a handful of grocery stores open on Sunday, including some branches of the Mercator chain. Most museums close on Monday. Banks often take lunch breaks from 12.30pm to 2pm and only a few open on Saturday morning.

Restaurants typically open for lunch and dinner until at least 10pm, and bars until midnight, though they may have longer hours on the weekend and shorter ones on Sunday.

Usual business hours in Slovenia include the following:

Banks Open 8am or 8.30am to 5pm weekdays (often with a lunchtime break from 12.30pm to 2pm) and 8am until noon or 1pm on Saturday.

Main post offices Open 8am to 7pm weekdays and 8am until noon or 1pm on Saturday.

Restaurants From 10am or 11am to 10pm or 11pm daily.

Shops Open 10am to 6pm Monday to Friday, to 1pm on Saturday.

Supermarkets Open from 8am to 7pm on weekdays and to 1pm on Saturday.

EMBASSIES & CONSULATES

Following are some of the embassies and consulates in Ljubljana.

Australia (☎ 01-425 42 52; Dunajska c 50; 9am-1pm Mon-Fri)

Austria (☎ 01-479 07 00; Prešernova c 23; 8am-noon Mon-Thu, to 11am Fri)

Canada (☎ 01-252 44 44; 12th fl, Trg Republike 3; 9am-noon Mon-Fri)

Croatia (☎ 01-425 62 20; Gruberjevo nabrežje 6; 9am-1pm Mon-Fri)

France (☎ 01-479 04 00; Barjanska c 1; 8.30am-12.30pm Mon-Fri)

Hungary (☎ 01-512 18 82; ul Konrada Babnika 5; 8am-5pm Mon-Fri)

Ireland (☎ 01-300 89 70; Palača Kapitelj, Poljanski nasip 6; 9.30am-12.30pm & 2.30-4pm Mon-Fri)

Italy (☎ 01-426 21 94; Snežniška ul 8; 9-11am Mon-Fri)

Netherlands (☎ 01-420 14 61; Palača Kapitelj, Poljanski nasip 6; 9am-noon Mon-Fri)

New Zealand (☎ 01-580 30 55; Verovškova ul 57; 8am-3pm Mon-Fri)

South Africa (☎ 01-200 63 00; Pražakova ul 4; 3-4pm Tue) In Kompas building.

UK (☎ 01-200 39 10; 4th fl, Trg Republike 3; 9am-noon Mon-Fri)

USA (☎ 01-200 55- 00; Prešernova c 31; 9-11.30am & 1-3pm Mon-Fri)

FESTIVALS & EVENTS

Major cultural and sporting events are listed under 'Events' on the website of the **Slovenian Tourist Board** (www.slovenia.info) and in its comprehensive *Calendar of Major Events in Slovenia.*

The most important and/or colourful include the following:

Kurentovanje (www.kurentovanje.net) A 'rite of spring' celebrated in Ptuj for 10 days leading up to Shrove Tuesday (February or early March).

Festival Lent (http://lent.slovenija.net) A two-week extravaganza of folklore and culture in Maribor's Old Town in late June/early July.

Ljubljana Festival (www.ljubljanafestival.si) The nation's premier cultural event (music, theatre and dance) held from early July to late August.

Cows' Ball (www.bohinj.si) A zany weekend of folk dance and music at Bohinj in September marking the return of the cows from their high pastures to the valleys.

FOOD & DRINK

It's relatively hard to find such archetypal Slovenian foods as *žlikrofi* ('ravioli' filled with cheese, bacon and chives), *brodet* (fish soup) from the coast, *ajdovi žganci z ocvirki* (buckwheat 'porridge' with savoury pork crackling/scratchings) and salad greens doused in *bučno olje* (pumpkin seed oil); generally these are dishes eaten at home. A *gostilna* or *gostišče* (inn) or *restavracija* more frequently serves *rižota* (risotto), *klobasa* (sausage), *zrezek* (cutlet/steak), *golaž* (goulash) and *paprikaš* (piquant chicken or beef 'stew').

Also popular are such Balkan specialities as *cevapčiči* (spicy meatballs of beef or pork), *pljeskavica* (spicy meat patties) and *ražnjiči* (shish kebabs).

You can snack cheaply on takeaway slices of pizza or *burek* (€2 to €3). Alternatives include *štruklji* (cottage-cheese dumplings) and *palačinke* (thin sweet pancakes).

Distinctively Slovenian wines *(vino)* include peppery red Teran made from Refošk grapes in the Karst region, Cviček, a dry light red – almost rosé – wine from eastern Slovenia, and Malvazija, a straw-coloured white wine from the coast that is light and dry.

Beer *(pivo)*, whether *svetlo* (lager) or *temno* (dark), is best on draught *(točeno)*.

There are dozens of kinds of *žganje* (brandy) available, made from all manner of fruit.

GAY & LESBIAN TRAVELLERS

Roza Klub (☎ 01-430 47 40; Kersnikova ul 4) in Ljubljana is made up of the gay and lesbian branches of ŠKUC (Študentski Kulturni Center or Student Cultural Centre).

GALfon (☎ 01-432 40 89; 🕑 7-10pm Mon-Fri) is a hotline and source of general information for gays and lesbians. The websites of **Slovenian Queer Resources Directory** (www.ljudmila.org/siqrd) and **Out In Slovenia** (www.outinslovenija.com) are both extensive and partially in English.

Slovenia has no sodomy laws. A national gay rights law bans discrimination in employment and other areas on the basis of sexual preference, and homosexuals are allowed in the military. Outside Ljubljana, however, there is little evidence of a gay presence, much less a lifestyle.

HOLIDAYS

Slovenia celebrates 14 holidays *(prazniki)* a year.

New Year 1 & 2 January
Prešeren Day (Slovenian Culture Day) 8 February
Easter & Easter Monday March/April
Insurrection Day 27 April
Labour Days 1 & 2 May
National Day 25 June
Assumption Day 15 August
Reformation Day 31 October
All Saints' Day 1 November
Christmas Day 25 December
Independence Day 26 December

INTERNET ACCESS

Virtually every hostel and hotel now has internet access – a computer for guests' use, wi-fi or both. Most cities and towns have at least one cybercafe but they usually have only a handful of terminals.

INTERNET RESOURCES

The website of the **Slovenian Tourist Board** (www.slovenia.info) is tremendously useful. Most Slovenian towns and cities have a website accessed by typing www.town.si or sometimes www.town-tourism.si (eg www.ljubljana.si or www.ptuj-tourism.si).

LANGUAGE

Closely related to Croatian and Serbian, Slovene *(slovenščina)* is written in the Roman alphabet. On toilets an 'M' *(Moški)* indicates 'men' and 'Ž' *(Ženske)* is 'women'. Virtually everyone in Slovenia speaks at least one other language. For more, see p1282.

MONEY

Slovenia adopted the euro as its national currency in January 2007, and was the first of the 10 new EU states to do so. Exchanging foreign currency is simple at banks, major post offices, travel agencies and *menjalnice* (bureaux de change), although do note that some of the latter don't accept travellers cheques. Major credit and debit cards are accepted almost everywhere, and ATMs are ubiquitous.

POST

Local mail costs €0.27 for letters up to 20g, while an international airmail stamp costs €0.45. Poste restante is free; pick it up from the main post office at Slovenska c 32, 1101 Ljubljana.

TELEPHONE

Public telephones require a phonecard (*telefonska kartica* or *telekartica*), available at post offices and some newsstands. The cheapest card (€4, 25 units) gives about 20 minutes' calling time to other European countries. Mobile phones generally have the prefix 031, 040, 041 or 051. SIM cards with €5 credit are available for €12 from **SiMobil** (www.simobil.si) and €15 from **Mobitel** (www.mobitel.si).

TOURIST INFORMATION

The Ljubljana-based **Slovenian Tourist Board** (☎ 01-589 18 40; www.slovenia.info; Dunajska c 156) has dozens of tourist information centres (TICs) in Slovenia and branches in a half-dozen European countries.

VISAS

Citizens of European countries as well as Australia, Canada, Israel, Japan, New Zealand and the USA do not require visas for stays of up to 90 days. Those who do require visas (including South Africans) can get them at any Slovenian embassy or consulate; see the website of the **Ministry of Foreign Affairs** (www.mzz.gov.si/en) for a full listing. They cost €35 and you'll need confirmation of a hotel booking plus a photo.

Spain

HIGHLIGHTS

- **La Sagrada Família** Fanciful yet packed with serious symbolism, Gaudí's masterpiece in Barcelona is one of the country's most interesting creations (p1075)
- **Seville** Soak up orange-blossom scents and surrender to the party atmosphere in Spain's fiery southern metropole (p1088)
- **Segovia** Amble under the aqueduct and around the Alcázar (p1065)
- **Best Journey** Follow the pilgrims along the Camino de Santiago (p1111)
- **Mallorca** Relax on splendid beaches and take to the hills for some spectacular hiking around Deià (p1082)

FAST FACTS

- **Area** 504,782 sq km
- **Budget** At least €50 per day
- **Capital** Madrid
- **Country code** ☎ 34
- **Famous for** sunshine, late nights, bull-fighting, *gazpacho* (cold tomato soup), *Don Quixote*, Pedro Almodóvar films
- **Languages** Spanish (Castilian or Castellano), Catalan (Català), Basque (Euskera), Galician (Galego)
- **Money** euro (€); A$1 = €0.55; C$1 = 0.60; ¥100 = €0.78; NZ$1 = €0.43; UK£1 = €1.12; US$1 = €0.74
- **Phrases** *hola* (hello), *gracias* (thanks), *adiós* (goodbye)

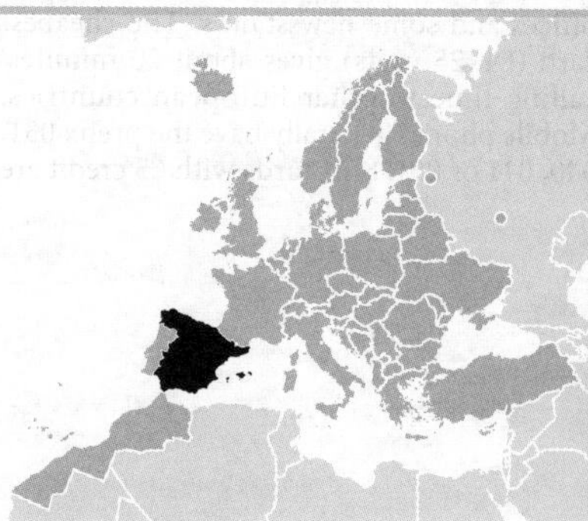

- **Population** 45 million
- **Visas** none required for most visitors for stays up to 90 days (see p1115)

TRAVEL HINTS

Spanish *menús del día* (fixed-price lunches) are a godsend for the hungry. Load up on fresh food at city produce markets.

ROAMING SPAIN

From Madrid, take day trips to Toledo, Ávila and Segovia. Then head northeast to Barcelona, stopping in Zaragoza, or make the trip south to Seville via Córdoba.

The word Spain conjures up images of dark-haired flamenco dancers, proud bullfighters, pitchers of sangria and sun-drenched beaches. Get behind the clichés, however, and you'll find there's far more to Spain than immediately meets the eye.

From its Roman amphitheatres to Muslim palaces, from Gothic cathedrals to Modernista marvels, the country is a treasure chest of artistic and architectural gems across a matchless cultural palette. An army of contemporary architects has left a slew of daring signature buildings across Spain's cities.

Emerald green mountains seem to slide into the wild blue Atlantic in the north. Proud, solitary castles and medieval towns are strewn across the interior. White villages glitter in inland

Andalucía. Rugged mountain ranges like the Sierra Nevada (Europe's most southerly ski resort) are draped across the landscape.

Up and down the country, the local zest for life creates an intense, hedonistic vibe in its effervescent cities. Indeed, if there is one thing Spaniards love, it is to eat, drink and be merry, whether gobbling up tapas over fine wine in Madrid and the south, or sampling their elaborate Basque Country equivalent, *pintxos*, over cider in the north.

HISTORY

North Africans settled in the peninsula from around 8000 BC and, in the millennia that followed, Celtic tribes, Phoenician merchants, Greeks and Carthaginians trickled in. The Romans arrived in the 3rd century BC but by AD 410 they had been replaced by the Christian Visigoths. Three hundred years later, Muslim Berbers and Arabs from North Africa took over most of the Iberian peninsula.

The 8th century saw the beginning of the Christian Reconquista. By the mid-13th century, the Christians had taken most of the peninsula. In 1469, the kingdoms of Castile and Aragón were united by the marriage of Isabel, princess of Castile, and Fernando, heir to Aragón's throne. Known as the Catholic Monarchs, they united Spain and laid the foundations for the Spanish golden age. They also expelled and executed thousands of Jews and other non-Christians under the dark cloud of the Inquisition. In 1492, the Reconquista was completed when the last Muslim ruler of Granada surrendered to them.

That same year, Christopher Columbus stumbled on the Bahamas and claimed the Americas for Spain. This sparked a period of exploration and exploitation that yielded Spain enormous wealth, while destroying the ancient American empires. Spain's downfall began soon after. It would culminate with the disastrous Spanish-American War of 1898, which marked the end of the Spanish empire.

During the Spanish Civil War (1936–39), the Nationalists, led by General Francisco Franco, received heavy military support from Nazi Germany and fascist Italy, while the elected Republican government received support only from the Soviet Union and the International Brigades, made up of volunteer foreign leftists. By 1939 Franco had won and an estimated 350,000 Spaniards had died. Franco's 35-year dictatorship began with Spain isolated and crippled by recession. It wasn't until the 1950s and '60s that the country began to recover.

Franco died in 1975, having named Juan Carlos his successor. King Juan Carlos I is widely credited with having overseen Spain's transition from dictatorship to democracy. The first elections were held in 1977 and a new constitution was drafted in 1978. Spain joined the European Community in 1986.

The forward-thinking Spain of today is led by the Socialist Party of Spain (PSOE), under President José Luís Rodríguez Zapatero. Zapatero was elected in 2004, just days after the 11 March terrorist attacks in Madrid. He made waves immediately by withdrawing Spanish troops from Iraq. Under Zapatero, gay marriage was legalised and a massive amnesty legalised the presence of hundreds of thousands of illegal immigrants. Zapatero's attempts to reach a peace deal with ETA Basque terrorists, however, ended in failure.

Shortly after his re-election in March 2008, Zapatero was confronted with an economy that suddenly came juddering to a halt after years of enviable growth figures. Unemployment exploded from 8.3% to 11.3% in the 12 months to October 2008. Amid the growing fears of recession, Zapatero pushed through a law on 'historic memory' that provoked sharp debate. Aimed at investigating the crimes and executions of the Franco years, it represented the first official attempt to deal with the country's dictatorial past.

THE CULTURE

Spain has a population of 45 million, descended from the many peoples who have settled here over the millennia, among them Iberians, Celts, Romans, Jews, Visigoths, Berbers, Arabs and 20th-century immigrants from across the globe. The biggest cities are Madrid (3.13 million), Barcelona (1.59 million), Valencia (805,000) and Seville (700,000).

Only about 20% of Spaniards are regular churchgoers, but Catholicism is deeply ingrained in the culture. As the writer Unamuno said, 'Here in Spain we are all Catholics, even the atheists.'

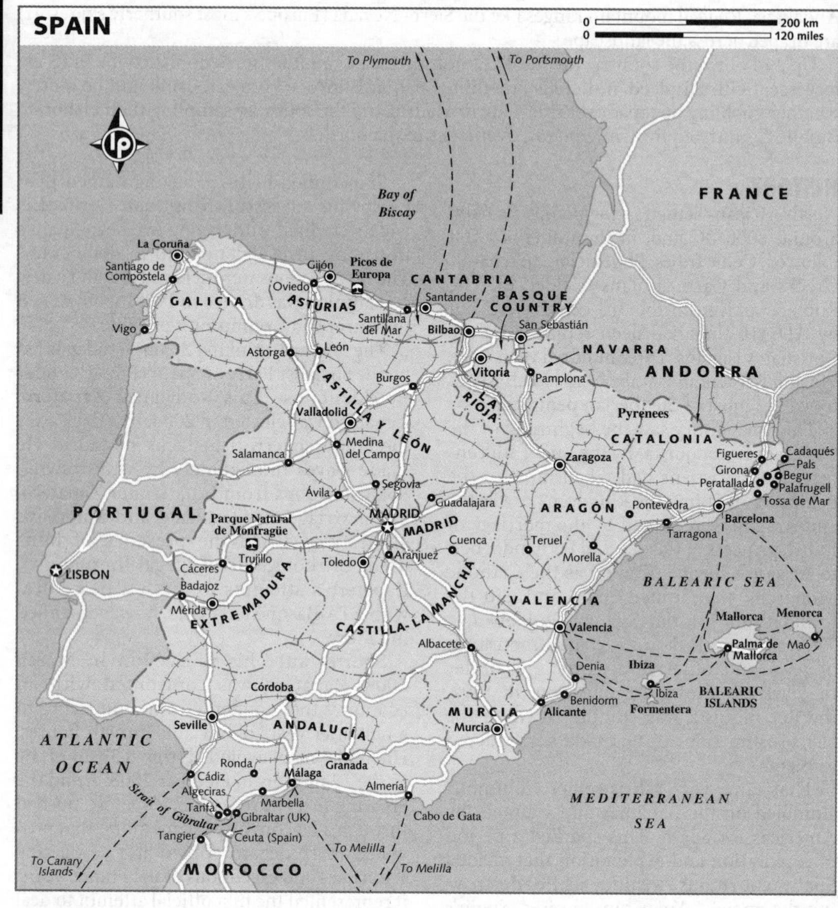

SPORT

Spain's national sport is football (soccer). While every city has at least one team with its loyal band of followers, the greatest rivalry is between Real Madrid and FC Barcelona (Barça), Spain's top two teams.

Bullfighting is also popular, especially around Madrid and in southern Spain, where it is present at all important festivals. Animal-rights groups argue, not without reason, that the taunting and slaughter of the bulls is painful and cruel. Supporters of this 'art' say that *toros bravos* (wild bulls) live like kings until the day of the slaughter. Whether or not you want to witness a *corrida* (bullfight) must be a personal decision.

ARTS

The giants of Spain's golden age (1550–1650) were Toledo-based El Greco (originally from Crete) and Diego Velázquez, perhaps Spain's most revered painter. Both excelled with insightful portraits. The genius of the late 18th and early 19th centuries was Francisco Goya, whose versatility ranged from unflattering royal portraits and anguished war scenes to bullfight etchings.

Catalonia was the powerhouse of early-20th-century Spanish art, claiming the hugely prolific Pablo Picasso (born in Andalucía), the colourful symbolist Joan Miró and surrealist Salvador Dalí. In architecture, the region and its capital, Barcelona, were adorned with the imaginative and at times plain wacky buildings of the *modernistas,* led by Antoni Gaudí.

Important 20th-century icons include Catalan abstract artist Antoni Tàpies and Basque sculptor Eduardo Chillida. Mallorca's Miquel Barceló is one of Spain's best-known artists working today.

ENVIRONMENT

The country covers 84% of the Iberian Peninsula and spreads over almost 505,000 sq km, more than half of which is high tableland, the *meseta*. Spain is Europe's second-hilliest country after Switzerland. Mountain ranges include the mighty Pyrenees, along the French border, and the Sierra Nevada in Andalucía. Principal rivers include the Ebro and Duero in the north, the Tajo across the centre and Guadalquivir in the south.

Intense debate on diverting water from these rivers to other, drier regions highlights Spain's growing problem of water scarcity. Prudent consumption remains the order of the day – reining in those long showers is good for everyone!

In parks and other protected areas, stick to established routes, obtain permits for restricted areas and don't damage vegetation or scare wildlife. Take extreme care to avoid starting fires, which every summer ravage large areas of Spain.

Giving your custom to local businesses, especially those with ecofriendly credentials, in and around parks and protected areas helps sustain rural economies.

You are what you eat! Seeking out better restaurants that use fresh local products or shopping at produce markets is a way of contributing to your well-being and the local economy.

Littering remains a big issue on crowded beaches. Bin your rubbish!

> **READING UP**
>
> *Ghosts of Spain*, by Giles Tremlett, looks at contemporary Spain, a country in overdrive trying to catch up with the rest of the West. *Between Hopes and Memories: A Spanish Journey*, by Michael Jacobs, is an amusing and personal reflection on contemporary Spain. Jacobs sets out from Madrid and criss-crosses the country, dipping into historical, literary and cultural themes. *Tuning Up At Dawn,* by Tomás Graves, looks at Mallorca (and Spain) since the Civil War, with emphasis on the music world in which he was caught up.

TRANSPORT

GETTING THERE & AWAY

Air

Spain has many international **airports** (☎ 902 40 47 04; www.aena.es), but if you're flying in from beyond Europe you'll land in Madrid (MAD) or Barcelona (BCN). From within Europe, a plethora of flag and low-cost carriers fly into airports around the country, including: Alicante (ALC), Almería (LEI), Bilbao (BIO), Girona (GRO), Ibiza (IBZ), Málaga (AGP), Menorca (MAH), Palma de Mallorca (PMI), Reus (REU), Santiago de Compostela (SCQ), Seville (SVQ), Valencia (VLC) and Zaragoza (ZAZ).

Among the low cost and other small carriers operating into Spain are the following:

Air Europa (UX; ☎ 902 40 15 01; www.aireuropa.com)
BMI (BD; ☎ 91 275 46 29; in UK 0870 607 0555; www.flybmi.com)
clickair (XG; ☎ 902 25 42 52; www.clickair.com)
easyJet (U2; ☎ 807 26 00 26; www.easyjet.com)
germanwings (4U; ☎ 91 625 97 04, in Germany 0900-1919100; www15.germanwings.com)
Jet2 (LS; ☎ 902 88 12 69, in UK 0871 226 1737; www.jet2.com)
Monarch (ZB; ☎ 800 09 92 60, in UK 0870 040 5040; www.flymonarch.com)
Ryanair (FR; ☎ 807 22 00 32; www.ryanair.com)
Spanair (JK; ☎ 902 13 14 15; www.spanair.com)
Vueling (VY; ☎ 902 33 39 33; www.vueling.com)

Boat

TO/FROM MOROCCO

Several companies run regular ferry services between Spain and Morocco. **Acciona Trasmediterránea** (☎ 902 45 46 45; www.trasmediterranea.es) operates routes including Algeciras–Tangier (from €42, up to 2½ hours). It also runs ferries to the Spanish enclaves of Ceuta and Melilla in northern Morocco, from Algeciras and Almería respectively.

Don't buy Moroccan currency until you reach Morocco, as you will get ripped off in Algeciras.

TO/FROM UK

If you drive your own car, a ferry is your best bet. **Brittany Ferries** (☎ in UK 0870 907 6103; www.brittany-ferries.co.uk) runs Plymouth–Santander ferries (24 hours) twice-weekly from mid-March to mid-November. Two people travelling with a car in August might pay £454 one-way.

P&O Ferries (☎ in UK 0871 664 5645; www.poferries.com) runs Portsmouth–Bilbao ferries (35 hours) two or three times weekly year-round. A typical fare is €190 per passenger with cabin and €400 per car (with two passengers).

TO/FROM ITALY

Grandi Navi Veloci (☎ 902 41 02 00; www1.gnv.it) runs a daily ferry service from Genoa to Barcelona (18 hours). An economy-class airline-style seat can cost as little as €16 in winter. **Grimaldi Ferries** (☎ 902 53 13 33, in Italy 081 496444; www.grimaldi-ferries.com) has a similar service between Barcelona and Civitavecchia (for Rome, 20 hours) and Livorno (Tuscany, 19½ hours) up to six days a week.

TO/FROM ALGERIA

Acciona Trasmediterránea runs daily ferries from Alicante to Oran (nine hours, leaving at 11pm or noon, late June to early September).

Bus

There are regular bus services to Spain from European cities such as Lisbon, London and Paris. From London, the popular mega-company **Eurolines** (www.nationalexpress.com/eurolines) offers regular services to Barcelona (24 to 26 hours), Madrid (25 to 30 hours) and other cities. Advance bookings and student ID cards can get you deep discounts.

Train

Unless you're simply hopping over the border from France or you already have a rail pass, travelling to Spain by train will usually be more expensive than by air. That said, rail travel for slow travellers can be a pleasant (and ecologically friendlier) alternative.

For details on long-distance rail travel, contact the **Rail Europe Travel Centre** (☎ in UK 08448 484064; www.raileurope.co.uk) in London. See p1242 for more on rail passes and train travel through Europe.

CONNECTIONS

The typical overland route leads many travellers from France over the Pyrenees into Spain. Options include following the Camino de Santiago via Roncesvalles (Navarra) or heading down the green Val d'Aran in Catalonia. Similarly, there is nothing to stop you carring on to Portugal. Numerous roads and the Madrid–Lisbon rail line connect the two countries.

The obvious sea journey leads across the Strait of Gibraltar to Morocco. The most common routes connect Algeciras with Tangier and the Spanish North African enclave of Ceuta. From both there is plenty of transport deeper on into Morocco.

GETTING AROUND

Students and seniors are eligible for discounts of 30% to 50% on almost all types of transport within Spain.

Air

Spain's major domestic airline, **Iberia** (www.iberia.com), has an extensive network covering all of Spain. Competing with Iberia are Spanair and Air Europa, as well as the low-cost companies clickair (an Iberia subsidiary) and Vueling. Between them, they cover a host of Spanish destinations. The busiest route by far, in spite of strong competition from the high-speed AVE train, is the Barcelona–Madrid *puente* (bridge). EasyJet has a hub in Madrid and offers domestic flights to Oviedo, Ibiza and A Coruña. Ireland's Ryanair also runs a handful of domestic Spanish flights.

Boat

Regular ferries connect the Spanish mainland with the Balearic Islands. For ferry details, see p1081. The main companies are **Baleària** (☎ 902 16 01 80; www.balearia.com), **Iscomar** (☎ 902 11 91 28; www.iscomar.com) and **Acciona Trasmediterránea** (☎ 902 45 46 45; www.trasmediterranea.es).

Bus

Spain's bus network is operated by countless independent companies and reaches into the most remote towns and villages. Many towns and cities have one main bus station where most buses arrive and depart. The best-known national company, under whose umbrella many smaller companies operate, is **Alsa** (☎ 902 42 22 42; www.alsa.es).

Bus ticket prices vary, depending on the popularity of the route and the comfort and speed of the service. Generally, fares are cheaper than on the faster, long-distance trains. The trip from Madrid to Barcelona costs around €27 one way. From Barcelona to Seville, one of the longest trips you could do (15 to 16 hours), you pay around €74.

It is not necessary, and often not possible, to make advance reservations for local bus journeys. It is, however, a good idea to turn up at least 30 minutes before the bus leaves to guarantee a seat. For longer trips, you can and should buy your ticket in advance.

Other bus companies:

Avanza (☎ 902 02 00 52; www.avanzabus.com)
Comes (☎ 902 19 92 08; www.tgcomes.es)
La Roncalesa (☎ 943 46 10 64)
Larrea/La Sepulvedana (☎ 902 22 22 82; www.lasepulvedana.es)
Los Amarillos (☎ 902 21 03 17; www.losamarillos.es)
PESA (☎ 902 10 12 10; www.pesa.net)
Portillo (☎ 902 14 31 44; www.ctsa-portillo.com)
Socibus/Secorbus (www.socibus.es)

Train

Trains are mostly modern and comfortable, and late arrivals are the exception rather than the rule. The high-speed network is in constant expansion.

Renfe (☎ 902 24 02 02; www.renfe.es), the national railway company, runs numerous types of trains. Travel times and fares vary greatly depending on the speed and comfort of the service, and in some cases on the day of travel.

Regionales are all-stops trains (think cheap and slow). *Cercanías* provide regular services from major cities to the surrounding suburbs and hinterland, sometimes even crossing regional boundaries. High-speed AVE trains link Madrid with Barcelona (via Zaragoza, Lleida and Tarragona), Burgos, Huesca (via Zaragoza), Málaga, Seville (via Córdoba), Valladolid (and in coming years Madrid–Valencia via Cuenca and Madrid–Bilbao).

Similar trains used on conventional Spanish tracks (which differs from the standard European gauge) connect Barcelona with Valencia and Alicante in the Euromed service.

A host of modern intermediate services (Alaris, Altaria, Alvia, Arco and Avant) offer speedy and comfortable service around the country on shorter distance runs like Madrid–Toledo and Barcelona–Lleida.

Some slow overnight services offer bed and couchette options.

You can buy tickets and make reservations online, at stations, at travel agencies displaying the Renfe logo and in Renfe offices in many city centres.

EMERGENCY NUMBERS

- EU-wide emergency number ☎ 112
- Fire department ☎ 080
- Medical emergencies ☎ 061
- Police ☎ 091

TRAIN PASSES

Rail passes are valid for all long-distance Renfe trains, but Inter-Rail users have to pay supplements on Talgo, InterCity and AVE trains. All passholders making reservations pay a small fee.

MADRID

pop 3.13 million

Spain's capital is a vibrant place, the hub of the country's government and commerce, and an exciting city bubbling over with creativity. Madrid may not have the effortless elegance of European capitals like Paris or Rome, but it has a raw energy that is infectious. Explore the old streets of the centre, relax in the plazas, soak up the culture in excellent art museums and experience the city's legendary nightlife.

HISTORY

Madrid was little more than a muddy, mediocre village when King Felipe II declared it Spain's capital in 1561. By the early 20th century Madrid finally began to look like a proper capital.

The 1940s and '50s were trying times for the capital, with rampant poverty. Nowhere was Franco's thumb as firmly pressed down as on Madrid. When the dictator died in 1975, the city exploded with creativity and life, giving Madrileños the party-hard reputation they still cherish.

Islamic terrorist bombs rocked Madrid in March 2004, just before national elections,

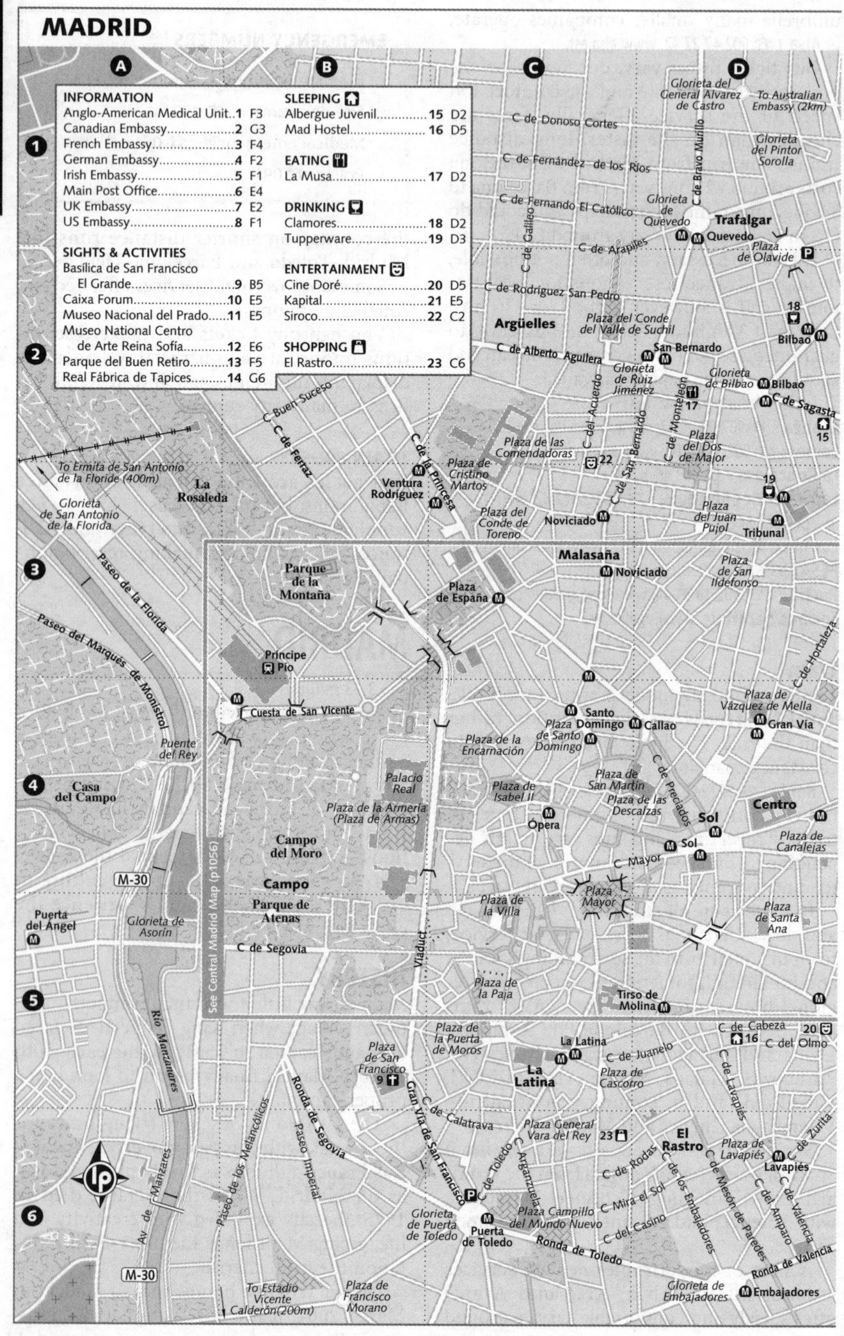
MADRID
A
B
C
D
1
2
3
4
5
6
INFORMATION
Anglo-American Medical Unit..1 F3
Canadian Embassy..................2 G3
French Embassy.....................3 F4
German Embassy....................4 F2
Irish Embassy........................5 F1
Main Post Office....................6 E4
UK Embassy..........................7 E2
US Embassy...........................8 F1
SIGHTS & ACTIVITIES
Basílica de San Francisco
El Grande...............................9 B5
Caixa Forum.........................10 E5
Museo Nacional del Prado......11 E5
Museo National Centro
de Arte Reina Sofía.............12 E6
Parque del Buen Retiro..........13 F5
Real Fábrica de Tapices..........14 G6
SLEEPING
Albergue Juvenil..................15 D2
Mad Hostel..........................16 D5
EATING
La Musa...............................17 D2
DRINKING
Clamores.............................18 D2
Tupperware.........................19 D3
ENTERTAINMENT
Cine Doré............................20 D5
Kapital................................21 E5
Siroco.................................22 C2
SHOPPING
El Rastro.............................23 C6
Glorieta del General Álvarez de Castro
To Australian Embassy (2km)
Glorieta del Pintor Sorolla
C de Donoso Cortes
C de Fernández de los Ríos
C de Bravo Murillo
C de Fernando El Católico
Glorieta de Quevedo
Trafalgar
Quevedo
Plaza de Olavide
C de Galileo
C de Arapiles
C de Rodríguez San Pedro
Argüelles
Plaza del Conde del Valle de Suchil
Bilbao
San Bernardo
C de Alberto Aguilera
Glorieta de Ruiz Jiménez
Glorieta de Bilbao
C de Sagasta
C Buen Suceso
C de Ferraz
C de la Princesa
Plaza de las Comendadoras
C del Acuerdo
C de San Bernardo
C de Monteleón
Plaza del Dos de Major
Plaza de Cristino Martos
Ventura Rodríguez
To Ermita de San Antonio de la Floride (400m)
La Rosaleda
Glorieta de San Antonio de la Florida
Plaza del Conde de Toreno
Noviciado
Plaza del Juan Pujol
Tribunal
Malasaña
Plaza de San Ildefonso
Parque de la Montaña
Plaza de España
Paseo de la Florida
Paseo del Marqués de Monistrol
Príncipe Pío
Cuesta de San Vicente
C de Hortaleza
Plaza de Vázquez de Mella
Santo Domingo
Callao
Gran Vía
Plaza de Santo Domingo
Plaza de la Encarnación
Puente del Rey
Casa del Campo
Palacio Real
Plaza de San Martín
C de Preciados
Plaza de Isabel II
Plaza de las Descalzas
Plaza de la Armería (Plaza de Armas)
Ópera
Sol
Centro
Plaza de Canalejas
Campo del Moro
C Mayor
M-30
Campo
Parque de Atenas
Plaza de la Villa
Plaza Mayor
Puerta del Ángel
Glorieta de Asorín
Plaza de Santa Ana
C de Segovia
See Central Madrid Map (p1056)
Viaduct
Plaza de la Paja
Tirso de Molina
Río Manzanares
Plaza de la Puerta de Moros
La Latina
C de Cabeza
C del Olmo
Plaza de San Francisco
C de Juanelo
Plaza de Cascotro
C de Lavapiés
Ronda de Segovia
Gran Vía de San Francisco
C de Calatrava
Paseo de los Melancólicos
Paseo Imperial
Plaza General Vara del Rey
El Rastro
Plaza de Lavapiés
Lavapiés
C de Zurita
C de Toledo
C Arganzuela
C de Rodas
C de los Embajadores
C de Mesón de Paredes
C del Amparo
C de Valencia
Av de Manzares
Plaza Campillo del Mundo Nuevo
C Mira el Sol
C del Casino
Glorieta de Puerta de Toledo
Puerta de Toledo
Ronda de Toledo
Ronda de Valencia
To Estadio Vicente Calderón (200m)
Plaza de Francisco Morano
Glorieta de Embajadores
Embajadores

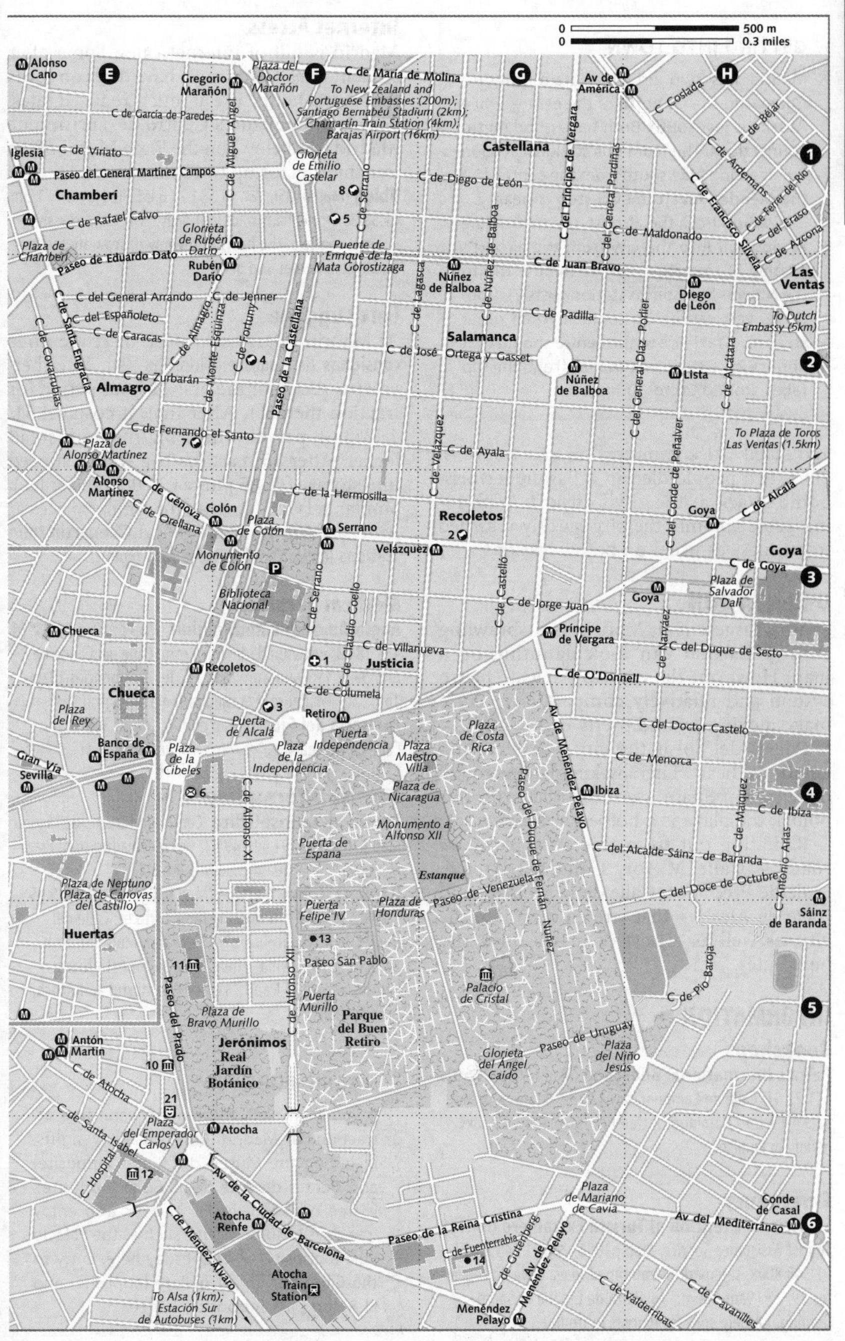
0 500 m
0 0.3 miles
E
F
G
H
1
2
3
4
5
6
Alonso Cano
Gregorio Marañón
Plaza del Doctor Marañón
C de María de Molina
Av de América
To New Zealand and Portuguese Embassies (200m); Santiago Bernabéu Stadium (2km); Chamartín Train Station (4km); Barajas Airport (16km)
C de García de Paredes
C de Miguel Ángel
C Coslada
C de Béjar
Castellana
C del Príncipe de Vergara
C del General Pardiñas
C de Ardemans
Iglesia
C de Viriato
Glorieta de Emilio Castelar
Paseo del General Martínez Campos
C de Diego de León
C de Francisco Silvela
C de Ferrer del Río
Chamberí
C de Serrano
C de Núñez de Balboa
C de Rafael Calvo
C de Maldonado
C del Eraso
C de Azcona
Glorieta de Rubén Darío
Plaza de Chamberí
Paseo de Eduardo Dato
Rubén Darío
Puente de Enrique de la Mata Gorostizaga
C de Lagasca
Núñez de Balboa
C de Juan Bravo
Las Ventas
Diego de León
C del General Arrando
C de Jenner
C de Santa Engracia
C del Españoleto
C de Almagro
C de Monte Esquinza
C de Fortuny
Paseo de la Castellana
C de Padilla
C del General Díaz Porlier
To Dutch Embassy (5km)
C de Caracas
Salamanca
C de Covarrubias
C de José Ortega y Gasset
C de Alcántara
C de Zurbarán
Almagro
Núñez de Balboa
Lista
C de Fernando el Santo
C de Velázquez
Plaza de Alonso Martínez
C de Ayala
C del Conde de Peñalver
To Plaza de Toros Las Ventas (1.5km)
Alonso Martínez
C de Génova
C de la Hermosilla
C de Orellana
Colón
Plaza de Colón
Recoletos
Goya
C de Alcalá
Serrano
Velázquez
Monumento de Colón
Goya
C de Goya
Plaza de Salvador Dalí
Biblioteca Nacional
C de Claudio Coello
C de Castelló
C de Jorge Juan
Goya
Chueca
Príncipe de Vergara
C de Narváez
C de Villanueva
C del Duque de Sesto
Justicia
Recoletos
C de O'Donnell
Chueca
C de Columela
Plaza del Rey
Retiro
Puerta de Alcalá
Plaza de Costa Rica
Av de Menéndez Pelayo
C del Doctor Castelo
Banco de España
Plaza de la Cibeles
Plaza de la Independencia
Puerta Independencia
Plaza Maestro Villa
Gran Vía
Sevilla
C de Menorca
C de Alfonso XI
Plaza de Nicaragua
Paseo del Duque de Fernán Núñez
Ibiza
C de Máiquez
C de Ibiza
Monumento a Alfonso XII
Puerta de España
C del Alcalde Sáinz de Baranda
Estanque
C Antonio Arias
Plaza de Neptuno (Plaza de Cánovas del Castillo)
Paseo de Venezuela
C del Doce de Octubre
Puerta Felipe IV
Plaza de Honduras
Sáinz de Baranda
Huertas
Paseo San Pablo
C de Pío Baroja
C de Alfonso XII
Paseo del Prado
Palacio de Cristal
Puerta Murillo
Plaza de Bravo Murillo
Parque del Buen Retiro
Antón Martín
Jerónimos
Real Jardín Botánico
Paseo de Uruguay
Plaza del Niño Jesús
Glorieta del Ángel Caído
C de Atocha
C de Santa Isabel
Plaza del Emperador Carlos V
Atocha
C Hospital
Av de la Ciudad de Barcelona
Plaza de Mariano de Cavia
Conde de Casal
Av del Mediterráneo
Atocha Renfe
Paseo de la Reina Cristina
C de Fuenterrabía
C de Gutenberg
Av de Menéndez Pelayo
C de Méndez Álvaro
Atocha Train Station
C de Valderribas
C de Cavanilles
To Alsa (1km); Estación Sur de Autobuses (1km)
Menéndez Pelayo

GETTING INTO TOWN

Madrid has two principal train stations: Chamartín sits far north of the centre, while Atocha is just south. Both have good metro connections. The main bus station, Estación Sur, is a long hike south from the centre, but the Méndez Álvaro metro stop is nearby.

Coming from the airport, the metro (line 8) zips you into the city from the airport's T2 and T4 terminals. The 12-minute trip to the Nuevos Ministerios station costs €1; from there, you can easily connect to all other stations. A taxi ride to the centre should cost about €25 (€35 from Terminal 4) and the trip takes around 20 to 30 minutes.

and killed 191 commuters on four trains. In 2007, two people died in a Basque terrorist bomb attack at the city's airport. With remarkable aplomb, the city quickly returned to business as usual on both occasions.

ORIENTATION

Spain's largest city, Madrid is a sprawling metropolis that can look daunting on a map. However, the easy-to-navigate metro system and relatively compact city centre make moving around pretty easy.

Puerta del Sol is the city's physical and emotional heart. Literally kilometre zero (all distances in Spain are measured from this point), the plaza is a hotbed of activity.

Radiating out from this busy plaza are roads – Calle Mayor, Calle del Arenal, Calle de Preciados, Calle de la Montera and Calle de Alcalá – that stretch deep into the city, as well as a host of metro lines and bus routes.

INFORMATION

Bookshops

Petra's International Bookshop (Map p1056; ☎ 91 541 72 91; Calle de Campomanes 13; ⏲ 11am-9pm Mon-Sat; Ⓜ Santo Domingo) A treasure trove of used books, mainly in English.

Emergency

Servicio de Atención al Turista Extranjero (Foreign Tourist Assistance Service; Map p1056; ☎ 91 548 85 37, 91 548 8008; satemadrid@munimadrid.es; Calle de Leganitos 19; ⏲ 9am-10pm; Ⓜ Plaza de España or Santo Domingo) A help spot for tourists in trouble.

Internet Access

Madrid is full of internet cafes. Some offer student rates, while most have deals on cards for several hours' use at much-reduced rates. The Ayuntamiento's Centro de Turismo de Madrid (see below) on the Plaza Mayor offers free internet for up to 15 minutes.

Bbigg (Map p1056; ☎ 91 531 23 64; Calle Mayor 1; 1/5hr €2.50/3; ⏲ 9.30am-midnight daily; Ⓜ Sol) A massive internet centre in the heart of town with separate sections for Skype, internet and games.

Left Luggage

At Madrid's Barajas Airport, there are three **consignas** (left-luggage offices; ⏲ 24hr). In either, you pay €3.60 for the first 24-hour period (or fraction thereof). After that, it costs €4.64/4.13/3.61 per day in a big/medium/small locker. After 15 days the bag will be moved into storage (€1.85 plus a €37.08 transfer fee). Similar services operate for similar prices at Atocha (Map pp1052–3) and **Chamartín train stations** (off Map pp1052-3; ⏲ 7am-11pm).

Medical Services

Anglo-American Medical Unit (Map pp1052-3; ☎ 91 435 18 23; www.unidadmedica.com; Calle del Conde de Aranda 1; ⏲ 9am-8pm Mon-Fri, for emergencies 10am-1pm Sat; Ⓜ Retiro) For medical help in English.

Farmacia del Globo (Map p1056; ☎ 91 369 20 00; Calle de Atocha 46; ⏲ 24hr; Ⓜ Antón Martín)

Tourist Information

Municipal Tourist Office (Centro de Turismo de Madrid; Map p1056; ☎ 91 429 49 51; www.esmadrid.com; Plaza Mayor 27; ⏲ 9.30am-8.30pm; Ⓜ Sol)

Regional tourist office (Map p1056; ☎ 91 429 49 51, 902 10 00 07; www.turismomadrid.es; Calle del Duque de Medinaceli 2; ⏲ 8am-8pm Mon-Sat, 9am-2pm Sun; Ⓜ Sevilla) There are also tourist offices at Barajas airport (T1 and T4), and Chamartín and Atocha train stations.

MADRID FOR FREE

If you plan well, there are several free attractions in Madrid. Entry to many sights, including the Museo del Prado (opposite) and Centro de Arte Reina Sofía (opposite), is free on Sundays. EU citizens also enjoy free days in some sights, such as the Palacio Real (opposite) – Wednesday here. Entry to the Caixa Forum art gallery (opposite) and El Retiro park (opposite) is free.

SIGHTS & ACTIVITIES

Get under the city's skin by walking its streets, sipping coffee and beer in its plazas and relaxing in its parks. Madrid de los Austrias, the maze of mostly 15th- and 16th-century streets surrounding the Plaza Mayor, is the city's oldest district. Working class, multicultural Lavapiés, alternative Chueca, bar-riddled Huertas and Malasaña, and chic Salamanca all reward pedestrian exploration.

Build in time for top art collections at the Prado, Reina Sofía and Thyssen-Bornemisza museums, as well as the Palacio Real.

Museo Nacional del Prado

Spain's premier museum, and one of the finest art collections in the world, the **Museo Nacional del Prado** (Map pp1052-3; ☎ 91 330 28 00; http://museoprado.mcu.es; Paseo del Prado s/n; adult/student/under 18yr & over 65yr €6/4/free, Sun free, headset guide €3.50; 9am-8pm Tue-Sun; M Banco de España) is a seemingly endless parade of priceless works from Spain and beyond. The collection is divided into eight major collections: Spanish paintings (1100–1850), Flemish paintings (1430–1700), Italian paintings (1300–1800), French paintings (1600–1800), German paintings (1450–1800), sculptures, decorative arts, and drawings and prints. There is generous coverage of Spanish greats, such as Goya, Velázquez and El Greco.

From the first floor of the Palacio de Villanueva, passageways lead to the Edificio Jerónimos, the Prado's modern extension. The main hall contains information counters, a bookshop and cafe. Rooms A and B (and Room C on the first floor) host temporary exhibitions.

Museo Thyssen-Bornemisza

Opposite the Prado, the **Museo Thyssen-Bornemisza** (Map p1056; ☎ 91 369 01 51; www.museothyssen.org; Paseo del Prado 8; adult/concession €6/4; 10am-7pm Tue-Sun; M Banco de España) is an eclectic collection of international masterpieces. Begin your visit on the 2nd floor, where you'll start with medieval art, and make your way down to modern works on the ground level, passing paintings by Titian, El Greco, Rubens, Rembrandt, Cézanne, Monet, Renoir, Van Gogh, Miró, Picasso, Gris and many others.

Centro de Arte Reina Sofía

A stunning collection of mainly Spanish modern art, the **Museo Nacional Centro de Arte Reina Sofía** (Map pp1052-3; ☎ 91 774 10 00; www.museoreinasofia.es; Calle de Santa Isabel 52; adult/student €6/4, 2.30-9pm Sat & 10am-2.30pm Sun free, audioguide €3; 10am-9pm Mon & Wed-Sat, 10am-2.30pm Sun; M Atocha) is home to Picasso's *Guernica* – his protest against the German bombing of the Basque town of Guernica during the Spanish Civil War in 1937. There are also important works by surrealist Salvador Dalí and abstract paintings by the Catalan artist Joan Miró.

Caixa Forum

The **Caixa Forum** (Map pp1052-3; ☎ 91 330 73 00; www.fundacio.lacaixa.es, in Spanish; Paseo del Prado 36; admission free; 10am-10pm; M Atocha), opened in 2008, seems to hover above the ground. On one wall is the *jardín colgante* (hanging garden), a lush vertical wall of greenery almost four storeys high. Inside are four floors of top-quality art exhibitions.

Palacio Real & Around

Madrid's 18th-century **Palacio Real** (Map p1056; ☎ 91 542 69 47; www.patrimonionacional.es; Calle de Bailén s/n; adult/student €10/3.50, EU citizens free Wed; 9am-6pm Mon-Sat, 9am-3pm Sun & holidays Apr-Sep, closed 1hr earlier Oct-Mar; M Ópera) is used mainly for important events. It's one of King Juan Carlos I's official residences and you can visit 50 of its 2800-plus rooms.

Outside the main palace, poke your head into the **Farmacia Real** (Map p1056; Royal Pharmacy), where apothecary-style jars line the shelves. Continue on to the **Armería Real** (Map p1056; Royal Armoury), where you'll be impressed by the shiny (and surprisingly tiny!) royal suits of armour, most of them from the 16th and 17th centuries.

The **Catedral de Nuestra Señora de la Almudena** (Map p1056; ☎ 91 542 22 00; Calle de Bailén; 9am-9pm; M Ópera) is just across the plaza from the Palacio Real. Finished in 1992 after a century of work, the cathedral has never really won a place in the hearts of Madrileños. It's worth a quick peek but is much less captivating than the imposing 18th-century **Basílica de San Francisco El Grande** (Map pp1052-3; ☎ 91 365 38 00; Plaza de San Francisco 1; admission €3; 8-11am Mon, 8am-1pm & 4-6.30pm Tue-Fri, 4-8.45pm Sat; M La Latina).

Parque del Buen Retiro

Popular with joggers, families out for a stroll, lovey-dovey couples and anyone else looking for a break from the chaos of the city, this **park** (Map pp1052-3; 7am-midnight May-Sep,

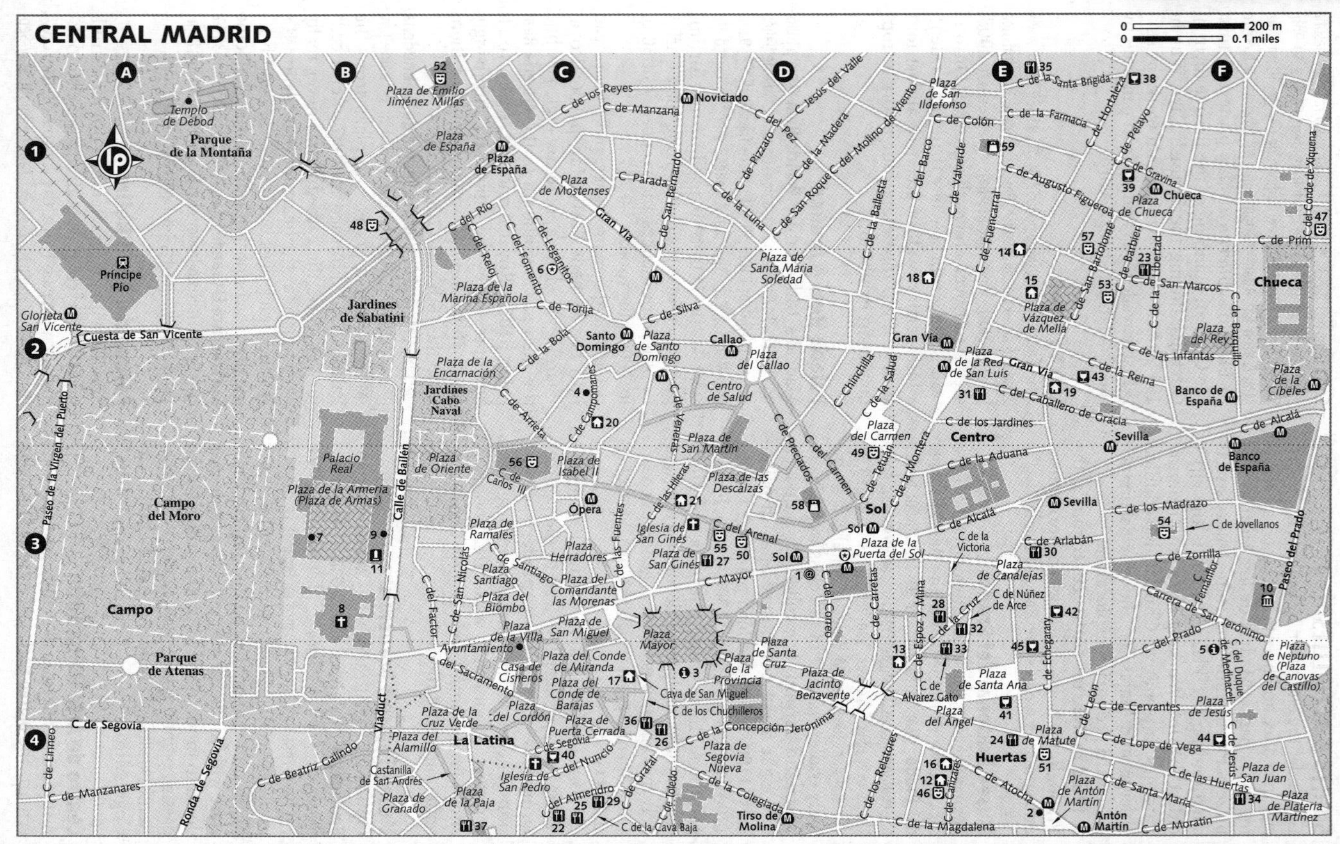
CENTRAL MADRID
0 200 m
0 0.1 miles
Templo de Debod
Parque de la Montaña
Príncipe Pío
Glorieta San Vicente
Cuesta de San Vicente
Paseo de la Virgen del Puerto
Campo del Moro
Campo
Parque de Atenas
C de Segovia
C de Linneo
C de Manzanares
Ronda de Segovia
C de Beatriz Galindo
Plaza de Emilio Jiménez Millas
Plaza de España
Jardines de Sabatini
Palacio Real
Plaza de la Armería (Plaza de Armas)
Calle de Bailén
Viaduct
Jardines Cabo Naval
Plaza de Oriente
Plaza de la Encarnación
Plaza de la Marina Española
Plaza de Isabel II
C de Carlos III
Ópera
Plaza de Ramales
Plaza Santiago
Plaza del Biombo
Plaza de la Villa
Ayuntamiento
Casa de Cisneros
Plaza de la Cruz Verde
Plaza del Alamillo
La Latina
Castanilla de San Andrés
Plaza de Granado
Plaza de la Paja
Iglesia de San Pedro
Plaza Mayor
Plaza de San Miguel
Plaza del Conde de Miranda
Plaza del Conde de Barajas
Plaza del Cordón
Plaza de Puerta Cerrada
Cava de San Miguel
C de los Chuchilleros
C de la Cava Baja
Plaza de Segovia Nueva
Tirso de Molina
C de Toledo
C de la Colegiata
Plaza de la Provincia
Plaza de Santa Cruz
Plaza de Jacinto Benavente
C de la Concepción Jerónima
Santo Domingo
Plaza de Santo Domingo
Callao
Plaza del Callao
Centro de Salud
Plaza de San Martín
Plaza de las Descalzas
Iglesia de San Ginés
Plaza de San Ginés
C del Arenal
C Mayor
Sol
Plaza de la Puerta del Sol
Plaza del Carmen
C de Preciados
C del Carmen
C de la Montera
Centro
C de los Jardines
C de la Aduana
Gran Vía
Plaza de la Red de San Luis
C del Caballero de Gracia
Plaza de Santa María Soledad
Noviciado
Plaza de Mostenses
Plaza de San Ildefonso
C de Fuencarral
C de Hortaleza
Plaza de Vázquez de Mella
Chueca
Plaza de Chueca
Plaza del Rey
Banco de España
Plaza de la Cibeles
C de Alcalá
Sevilla
C de los Madrazo
C de Jovellanos
C de Zorrilla
Paseo del Prado
Carrera de San Jerónimo
Plaza de Canalejas
C de la Victoria
C de Núñez de Arce
Plaza de Santa Ana
C de Álvarez Gato
Plaza del Ángel
C de Echegaray
C del Prado
C del Duque de Medinaceli
Plaza de Neptuno (Plaza de Cánovas del Castillo)
Plaza de Jesús
C de Cervantes
C de Lope de Vega
Plaza de Matute
Huertas
C de Atocha
Plaza de Antón Martín
Antón Martín
C de las Huertas
Plaza de San Juan
Plaza de Platería Martínez
C de Moratín
C de la Magdalena
C de los Relatores

INFORMATION			Los Amigos Backpackers' Hostel	20	C2	Café del Nuncio	40	C4
Bbigg	1	D3	Los Amigos Sol Backpackers' Hostel	21	D3	Cervecería Alemana	41	E4
Farmacia del Globo	2	E4	**EATING**			La Venencia	42	E3
Municipal Tourist Office	3	D4	Almendro 13	22	C4	Museo Chicote	43	E2
Petra's International Bookshop	4	C2	Bazaar	23	F2	Taberna de Dolores	44	F4
Regional Tourist Office	5	F4	Casa Alberto	24	E4	Viva Madrid	45	E4
Servicio de Atención al Turista Extranjero	6	C2	Casa Lucas	25	C4	**ENTERTAINMENT**		
SIGHTS & ACTIVITIES			Casa Revuelta	26	C4	Casa Patas	46	E4
Armería Real	7	B3	Chocolatería de San Ginés	27	D3	La Fulanita de Tal	47	F1
Catedral de Nuestra Señora de la Almudena	8	B3	La Casa del Abuelo	28	E3	Las Tablas	48	B1
Farmacia Real	9	B3	La Chata	29	C4	Localidades Galicia	49	D3
Museo Thyssen-Bornemisza	10	F3	La Finca de Susana	30	E3	Palacio Gaviria	50	D3
Palacio Real	11	B3	La Gloria de Montera	31	E2	Popular	51	E4
SLEEPING			La Trucha	32	E3	Princesa	52	B1
Cat's Hostel	12	E4	Las Bravas	33	E4	Sunrise	53	E2
Hostal Adriano	13	E4	Maceiras	34	F4	Teatro de la Zarzuela	54	F3
Hostal América	14	E2	Ribeira Do Miño	35	E1	Teatro Joy Eslava	55	D3
Hostal Don Juan	15	E2	Sobrino de Botín	36	C4	Teatro Real	56	C3
Hostal Horizonte	16	E4	Viva La Vida	37	C4	Why Not?	57	E1
Hostal La Macarena	17	C4	**DRINKING**			**SHOPPING**		
Hostal La Zona	18	E2	Areia	38	F1	El Corte Inglés	58	D3
Hotel de Las Letras	19	E2	Café Acuarela	39	F1	Mercado de Fuencarral	59	E1

7am-10pm Oct-Apr; Ⓜ Retiro) is as much a Madrid tradition as tapas and *terrazas* (terrace cafes). Come on a weekend for street performers, clowns, puppet shows and the occasional theatre performance.

Real Fábrica de Tapices

Founded in 1721, this **tapestry workshop** (Map pp1052-3; ☎ 91 434 05 51; www.realfabricadetapices.com; Calle de Fuenterrabía 2; admission €2.50; 🕑 10am-2pm Mon-Fri Sep-Jul; Ⓜ Menéndez Pelayo) still produces ornate tapestries and carpets by hand. Take one home for a mere €10,000 per square metre.

FESTIVALS & EVENTS

Madrid's social calendar is packed with festivals and special events. Check with the tourist office or in publications such as the *Guía del Ocio* to see what's on. Major holidays and festivals include the following:

Fiesta de San Isidro Street parties, parades, bullfights and other fun events honour Madrid's patron saint on and around 15 May.

Summer Festivals Small-time but fun, the neighbourhood summer festivals, such as San Cayetano in Lavapiés, and San Lorenzo and La Paloma in La Latina, allow hot and sweaty Madrileños to drink and dance the night away in the streets.

SLEEPING

During a major holiday or trade fair, prices can rise by 15% to 20%. During slower periods, you might find big discounts, especially in the top-end hotels. The streets of Huertas (around Plaza Santa Ana) and Malasaña (north of Gran Vía) are loaded with cheapies.

Los Austrias & Centro

Los Amigos Backpackers' Hostel (Map p1056; ☎ 91 547 17 07; www.losamigoshostel.com; Calle de Campomanes 6; dm €17-19; Ⓜ Ópera; 💻) Gregarious folk will be at home here – lots of students hang at Los Amigos, staff are savvy and there are bright dorm-style rooms for four to 12 people (with free lockers). A similar deal is available at nearby Los Amigos Sol Backpackers' Hostel (Map p1056; ☎ 91 559 24 72; 4th fl, Calle de Arenal 26; dorm bed €16 to €19).

Cat's Hostel (Map p1056; ☎ 91 369 28 07; www.catshostel.com; Calle de Cañizares 6; dm €19, d from €24; Ⓜ Antón Martín; 💻) The fine internal courtyard boasts lavish Andalucian tilework, a fountain, a spectacular glass ceiling and is surrounded by an open balcony. There's a super-cool basement bar.

Mad Hostel (Map pp1052-3; ☎ 91 506 48 40; www.madhostel.com; Calle de Cabeza 24; dm €20; Ⓜ Antón Martín; 💻) Mad Hostel's 1st-floor courtyard – with retractable roof – is a wonderful place to chill, while the four- to eight-bed rooms are smallish but clean.

our pick Hostal Horizonte (Map p1056; ☎ 91 369 09 96; www.hostalhorizonte.com; Calle de Atocha 28, 2nd fl; s with shared/private bathroom €29/40, d €44/55; Ⓜ Antón Martín) Billing itself as a *hostal* (small family-run hotel) run by travellers for travellers, Hostal Horizonte is well run. The rooms have

SPLURGE

Hotel de Las Letras (Map p1056; ☎ 91 523 79 80; www.hoteldelasletras.com; Gran Vía 11; d from €165; Ⓜ Gran Vía) Hotel de las Letras started the rooftop hotel bar trend in Madrid. The bar's wonderful, but the whole hotel is excellent with individually styled rooms.

far more character than your average *hostal*, with high ceilings, deliberately old-world furnishings and modern bathrooms.

Hostal La Macarena (Map p1056; ☎ 91 365 92 21; www.silserranos.com, in Spanish; Cava de San Miguel 8; s/d €60/74; Ⓜ Sol; 💻) On one of the old cobblestone streets that runs past Plaza Mayor, this *hostal* is loaded with old-style charm. The rooms are nicely spacious and decorated in warm colours.

Sol, Huertas & Atocha

Hostal Adriano (Map p1056; ☎ 91 521 13 39; www.hostaladriano.com; Calle de la Cruz 26, 4th fl; s/d/tr €49/63/83; Ⓜ Sol) They don't come any better than this bright and cheerful *hostal* wedged in the streets that mark the boundary between Sol and Huertas. Most rooms are well sized and each has its own colour scheme.

Malasaña & Chueca

Albergue Juvenil (Map pp1052-3; ☎ 91 593 96 88; www.ajmadrid.es; Calle de Mejía Lequerica 21; dm €18-24; Ⓜ Bilbao or Alonso Martínez; 💻) The Albergue's rooms are spotless, no dorm houses more than six beds (each has its own bathroom) and facilities include a gym, free internet, laundry and TV/DVD room.

Hostal Don Juan (Map p1056; ☎ 91 522 31 01; Plaza de Vázquez de Mella 1; s/d/tr €38/53/71; Ⓜ Gran Vía) Don John would have liked this elegant two-storey *hostal*. It's filled with art (each room has original works) and antique furniture. Rooms are simple but luminous and large.

Hostal América (Map p1056; ☎ 91 522 64 48; www.hostalamerica.net; Calle de Hortaleza 19; s/d €40/55; Ⓜ Gran Vía) A lovely mother-son-dog team preside over super-clean, spacious and IKEA-dominated rooms. As most rooms face on to the usual interior 'patio' of the building, you should get a good night's sleep.

Hostal La Zona (Map p1056; ☎ 91 521 99 04; www.hostallazona.com; Calle de Valverde 7; s/d/tr €50/60/85; Ⓜ Gran Vía; ❄ 💻) Catering primarily to a gay clientele, the stylish Hostal La Zona has exposed brickwork, wooden pillars and a subtle colour scheme.

Beyond the Centre

High Tech Madrid Aeropuerto (☎ 91 564 59 06; www.hthoteles.com; Calle Galeón 25; r €75-150; Ⓜ Aeropuerto; 🚭 ❄ 💻 🚗) With a free shuttle service to and from the airport, this stylish place can be a lifesaver for those with an early or late flight.

EATING

It's possible to find just about any kind of cuisine and eatery in Madrid, from ageless traditional to trendy fusion. Madrid is a focal point of cooking from around the country and is particularly renowned for seafood.

From the chaotic tapas bars of La Latina to countless neighbourhood favourites, you'll have no trouble tracking down specialities like *cochinillo asado* (roast suckling pig) or *cocido madrileño* (a hearty stew made of beans and various animals' innards).

Los Austrias & Centro

La Gloria de Montera (Map p1056; ☎ 91 523 44 07; Calle del Caballero de Gracia 10; meals €20-25; Ⓜ Gran Vía) Minimalist style, tasty Mediterranean dishes and great prices mean that you'll probably have to wait in line to eat here.

Sol, Huertas & Atocha

La Finca de Susana (Map p1056; ☎ 91 369 35 57; Calle de Arlabán 4; meals €20-25; Ⓜ Sevilla) A well-priced mix of Spanish and international fare makes this a popular choice with locals and tourists. The softly lit dining area is bathed in greenery and draws a hip young crowd.

our pick **Maceiras** (Map p1056; ☎ 91 429 15 84; Calle de Jesús 7; meals €20-25; 🕒 lunch & dinner Tue-Sun, dinner Mon; Ⓜ Antón Martín) Galician tapas (think octopus, green peppers etc) never tasted so good as in this agreeably rustic bar down the bottom

SPLURGE

Sobrino de Botín (Map p1056; ☎ 91 366 42 17; www.botin.es; Calle de los Cuchilleros 17; meals €35-45; Ⓜ La Latina or Sol) Reputedly opened in 1725, this is the oldest restaurant in Madrid. The secret of its staying power is fine *cochinillo* (suckling pig; €21.10) and *cordero asado* (roast lamb; €21.10) cooked in wood-fired ovens.

A TAPAS TOUR

Madrid's home of tapas is La Latina, especially along Calle de la Cava Baja and the surrounding streets. **Almendro 13** (Map p1056; ☎ 91 365 42 52; Calle de Almendro 13; meals €15-25; Ⓜ La Latina) is regularly voted among the top tapas bars in Madrid for traditional snacks. Nearby, **Casa Lucas** (Map p1056; ☎ 91 365 08 04; Calle de la Cava Baja 30; meals €20-25; 🕑 lunch & dinner Thu-Tue, dinner Wed; Ⓜ La Latina) and **La Chata** (Map p1056; ☎ 91 366 14 58; Calle de la Cava Baja 24; meals €25-30; 🕑 lunch & dinner Thu-Mon, dinner Wed; Ⓜ La Latina) are popular.

Good for *bacalao* (cod) is **Casa Revuelta** (Map p1056; ☎ 91 366 33 32; Calle de Latoneros 3; meals €10-15; 🕑 lunch & dinner Tue-Sat, lunch Sun; Ⓜ La Latina).

In Huertas, **La Casa del Abuelo** (Map p1056; ☎ 91 521 23 19; Calle de la Victoria 12; meals €15-25; 🕑 11.30am-3.30pm & 6.30-11.30pm; Ⓜ Sol) is famous for *gambas a la plancha* (grilled prawns) or *gambas al ajillo* (prawns sizzling in garlic). For *patatas bravas* (fried potatoes lathered in a spicy tomato sauce), **Las Bravas** (Map p1056; ☎ 91 532 26 20; Callejón de Álvarez Gato 3; meals €15; 🕑 10am-11.30pm; Ⓜ Sol) is the place, while **La Trucha** (Map p1056; ☎ 91 532 08 82; Calle de Núñez de Arce 6; 🕑 Tue-Sat; Ⓜ Sol) has a counter overloaded with enticing Andalucían tapas.

of the Huertas hill, especially when washed down with a crisp white Ribeiro.

Casa Alberto (Map p1056; ☎ 91 429 93 56; www.casaalberto.es; Calle de las Huertas 18; meals €20-25; 🕑 noon-1.30am Tue-Sat, noon-4pm Sun; Ⓜ Antón Martín) Casa Alberto has been around since 1827. The secret to its endurance is vermouth on tap, excellent tapas and fine sit-down meals.

La Latina & Lavapiés

Viva La Vida (Map p1056; ☎ 91 366 33 49; www.vivalavida.vg; Costanilla de San Andrés 16; veg buffet per 100g €1.80; 🕑 11am-midnight; Ⓜ La Latina) This organic food shop has as its centrepiece an enticing vegetarian buffet with hot and cold food that's always filled with flavour.

Malasaña & Chueca

This is the place for international food and creative, contemporary cuisine. Some of the city's best (and best-priced) eateries can be found along the side streets of the trendy Chueca district.

Ribeira Do Miño (Map p1056; ☎ 91 521 98 54; Calle de la Santa Brigida 1; meals €20-25; 🕑 Tue-Sat; Ⓜ Tribunal) The *mariscada de la casa* (€30 for two) is a platter of seafood so large that even the hungriest of visitors will leave satisfied.

Bazaar (Map p1056; ☎ 91 523 39 05; www.restaurantbazaar.com; Calle de la Libertad 21; meals €25-30; Ⓜ Chueca) Bazaar's pristine-white interior design with theatre lighting may draw a crowd that looks like it stepped out of the pages of *Hola!* magazine, but the food is extremely well-priced and innovative.

La Musa (Map pp1052-3; ☎ 91 448 75 58; www.lamusa.com.es; Calle de Manuela Malasaña 18; meals €25-30; Ⓜ San Bernardo) The fried green tomatoes with strawberry jam and great meat dishes are fun and filled with flavour.

DRINKING

Madrileños live life on the streets, and bar-hopping is a pastime enjoyed by young and old alike. If you're looking for a traditional bar, head to the Huertas district or La Latina. For an edgier feel and a gay-friendly crowd, hit Chueca. Malasaña is the place for alternative and grunge locales. In summer, the terrace bars that pop up all over the city are unbeatable.

Los Austrias, Centro & La Latina

Café del Nuncio (Map p1056; Calle de Segovia 9; Ⓜ La Latina) Lace curtains and red-wood panelling set the tone at this bustling bar. In summer, the outdoor terrace is divine.

Museo Chicote (Map p1056; www.museo-chicote.com; Gran Vía 12; 🕑 8am-4am Mon-Sat; Ⓜ Gran Vía) A timeless classic popular with socialites and film stars, the Museo Chicote has a lounge atmosphere late at night and a stream of famous faces all day.

Sol, Huertas & Atocha

Cervecería Alemana (Map p1056; Plaza de Santa Ana 6; 🕑 10.30am-12.30am Sun-Thu, 10.30am-2am Fri & Sat, closed August; Ⓜ Antón Martín or Sol) A classic and classy watering hole, this place is famous for its cold, frothy beers and delicious tapas. It was one of Hemingway's haunts.

Taberna de Dolores (Map p1056; Plaza de Jesús 4; Ⓜ Antón Martín) Here since 1908, this delightful little bar smothered in tiles has beer

SPAIN

MADRID'S FAVOURITE POST-CLUBBING MUNCHIES

Chocolatería de San Ginés (Map p1056; Pasadizo San Ginés 5; 9am-7am Wed-Sun, 6pm-7am Mon & Tue; M Sol) Join the sugar-searching throngs who end the night at this mythic bar (it doesn't close until 7am), famous for its freshly fried *churros* (fried sticks of dough) and syrupy hot chocolate.

and wine flowing freely, along with sea salty anchovies.

our pick **La Venencia** (Map p1056; Calle de Echegarary 7; M Sol) Your sherry (in several varieties) is poured straight from dusty wooden barrels and your tab literally chalked up on the bar itself.

Viva Madrid (Map p1056; www.barvivamadrid.com; Calle de Manuel Fernández y González 7; M Antón Martín or Sol) A landmark covered in beautiful coloured tiles, Viva Madrid does tapas earlier in the evening and drinks late into the night.

Malasaña & Chueca

Gay-friendly Chueca is packed with bars for punters of all persuasions, and Malasaña is known for its funky, alternative venues.

Areia (Map p1056; www.areiachillout.com, in Spanish; Calle de Hortaleza 92; M Chueca or Alonso Martínez) The ultimate lounge bar by day, Areia has groovy DJs take over at night with deep and chill house, nu jazz, bossa and electronica.

Tupperware (Map pp1052-3; Corredera Alta de San Pablo 26; 8pm-3.30am Sun-Wed, 9pm-3.30am Thu-Sat; M Tribunal) Unbelievably kitschy, with plastic dolls and pictures of old TV stars as decor, this fun bar plays danceable pop and '80s music every night of the week.

CLUBBING

You'll be dancing until dawn in Madrid's numerous clubs. Some big-name clubs are concentrated around Gran Vía, although Chueca, Malasaña and Huertas are good bets, too.

Palacio Gaviria (Map p1056; Calle del Arenal 9; M Sol) Special international student nights and other theme nights bring the big crowds to this converted mansion near the Puerta del Sol.

Teatro Joy Eslava (Map p1056; www.joy-eslava.com, in Spanish; Calle del Arenal 11; M Sol) Housed in a 19th-century neoclassical theatre, Joy hosts lots of theme parties and student nights. It's a megaclub, but can still be a good place to meet people.

Siroco (Map pp1052-3; www.siroco.es, in Spanish; Calle de San Dimas 3; 10pm-6am Thu-Sat; M Noviciado) One of the most eclectic nightclubs in Madrid, Siroco does everything from reggae to acid jazz, from 1970s pop to funk, house and hip-hop. It's a good place to hear local music, too.

Kapital (Map pp1052-3; www.grupo-kapital.com, in Spanish; Calle de Atocha 125; M Atocha) This massive seven-storey nightclub has something for everyone: from cocktail bars and dance music to karaoke, salsa, hip-hop and more chilled spaces for R&B and soul.

ENTERTAINMENT

The *Guía del Ocio* (€1) is the city's classic weekly listings magazine. Better are **Metropoli** (www.elmundo.es, in Spanish), *El Mundo*'s Friday listings supplement; and **On Madrid** (www.elpais.com, in Spanish), *El País*' version. **La Netro** (http://madrid.lanetro.com, in Spanish) is a comprehensive online guide.

Gay & Lesbian Venues

Chueca is Madrid's lively, gay-friendly neighbourhood, and you'll find lots of gay and lesbian bars and clubs in the area.

Café Acuarela (Map p1056; 91 522 21 43; Calle de Gravina 10; 2pm-3am; M Chueca) For something low-key, head to this quiet bar.

Why Not? (Map p1056; Calle de San Bartolomé 7; 10.30pm-6am; M Chueca) A hetero-friendly place where nothing's left to the imagination (things get pretty amorous here). Pop and chart music are the standard here.

Two of the more outrageous gay nightspots in Madrid are **Sunrise** (Map p1056; Calle de Barbieri 7; midnight-6am Thu-Sat; M Chueca) and **La Fulanita de Tal** (Map p1056; www.fulanitadetal.com, in Spanish; Calle del Conde de Xiquena 2; 10pm-3am Sun-Wed, 10pm-4am Thu-Sat; M Chueca).

Live Music

Populart (Map p1056; 91 429 84 07; www.populart.es; Calle de las Huertas 22; admission free; show 11pm; M Antón Martín or Sol) Get here early if you want a seat because this smoky, atmospheric bar is always packed with fans yearning for some soothing live jazz, blues or flamenco.

Clamores (Map pp1052-3; www.clamores.es, in Spanish; Calle de Alburquerque 14; admission €5-20; M Bilbao) Clamores is one of the most diverse live music stages in Madrid. Jazz is a staple, but world music, flamenco, soul fusion, singer-songwriter, pop and rock all make regular appearances.

Las Tablas (Map p1056; ☎ 91 542 05 20; www.lastablasmadrid.com, in Spanish; Plaza de España 9; admission €10-30; daily show at 10.30pm; M Plaza de España) Las Tablas has quickly earned a reputation for quality flamenco. Most nights you'll see a classic flamenco show, with plenty of throaty singing and soul-baring dancing.

Casa Patas (Map p1056; ☎ 91 369 04 96; www.casapatas.com; Calle de Cañizares 10; admission about €35; M Antón Martín) One of the best *tablaos* (flamenco venues) in the city, this is a great place to see passionate dancing, although it's one of the pricier options. Call or check the website for the latest showtimes.

Cinemas

Several movie theatres are huddled around Gran Vía and Calle de la Princesa.

Princesa (Map p1056; ☎ 91 541 41 00; Calle de la Princesa 3; M Plaza de España) Head here for a selection of flicks screened in their original language *(versión original)*, including English.

Cine Doré (Map pp1052-3; ☎ 91 369 11 25; Calle de Santa Isabel 3; Tue-Sun; M Antón Martín) The National Film Library offers fantastic classic and vanguard films for just €2.

Sport

Get tickets to football matches and bullfights from box offices or through agents like **Localidades Galicia** (Map p1056; ☎ 91 531 27 32; www.eol.es/lgalicia; Plaza del Carmen 1; 9.30am-1pm & 4.30-7pm Tue-Sat; M Sol).

FOOTBALL

Real Madrid plays at the **Santiago Bernabéu Stadium** (off Map pp1052-3; ☎ 91 398 43 00; www.realmadrid.com; Avenida de Concha Espina 1; tour €10; 10am-7pm Mon-Sat, 10.30am-6.30pm Sun, closed day of game; M Santiago Bernabéu). Fans can take an interesting tour through the presidential box, dressing room and the field.

BULLFIGHTING

Some of Spain's top *toreros* (bullfighters) swing their capes in **Plaza de Toros Las Ventas** (off Map pp1052-3; ☎ 91 356 22 00; www.las-ventas.com, in Spanish; Calle de Alcalá 237; M Las Ventas) . Fights are held every Sunday afternoon from mid-May to October. Get tickets (from €5 standing in the sun) at the plaza box office, **Localidades Galicia** (Map p1056; ☎ 91 531 27 32; www.eol.es/lgalicia; Plaza del Carmen 1; 9.30am-1pm & 4.30-7pm Tue-Sat; M Sol) or from official ticket agents on Calle Victoria.

> **STREET SMARTS**
>
> Madrid's street markets are great places to browse and, sometimes, to find a bargain. The most famous market is **El Rastro** (Map pp1052-3; Calle Ribera Curtidores; 8am-2pm Sun; M La Latina). A bustling flea market, this chaotic jumble of people and objects overflows with a bit of everything (much of it rubbish but, often, curious rubbish). The madness begins at the Plaza Cascorro and worms its way downhill. Watch your wallet.

Theatre & Opera

Madrid has a lively cultural scene, with concerts and shows going on throughout the city.

Teatro Real (Map p1056; ☎ 902 24 48 48; www.teatro-real.com, in Spanish; Plaza de Oriente; M Ópera) The Teatro Real is the city's grandest stage for elaborate operas and ballets. You'll pay as little as €15 for a spot so far away you will need a telescope, although the sound quality is consistent throughout.

Teatro de la Zarzuela (Map p1056; ☎ 91 524 54 00; http://teatrodelazarzuela.mcu.es; Calle de Jovellanos 4; M Banco de España) Come here for *zarzuela,* a very Spanish mixture of dance, music and theatre.

SHOPPING

Salamanca district is the home of upmarket fashions, with chic boutiques lining up to showcase the best that Spanish and international designers have to offer. Some of it spills over into Chueca, but Malasaña is Salamanca's true alter ego, home to fashion that's as funky as it is offbeat and ideal for that studied underground look that will fit right in with Madrid's hedonistic after-dark crowd. Central Madrid – Sol, Huertas or La Latina – offers plenty of individual surprises.

Mercado de Fuencarral (Map p1056; ☎ 91 521 41 52; www.mdf.es/madrid; Calle de Fuencarral 45; M Chueca) With shops like Fuck, Ugly Shop and Black Kiss, this reverse snobs' small is funky, grungy and filled to the rafters with torn T-shirts and more black leather and silver studs than you'll ever need.

El Corte Inglés (Map p1056; ☎ 902 22 44 11; www.elcorteingles.es; Calle de Preciados 1, 2, 3 & 9; M Sol)

Spain's enormous department store has branches all over the city and sells everything from food and furniture to clothes, appliances and toiletries. It's truly one-stop shopping.

GETTING THERE & AWAY

Madrid's international Barajas Airport (MAD; off Map pp1052–3), 16km northeast of the city, is a busy place, with flights coming in from all over Europe and beyond. See p1049 for more information.

Estación Sur de Autobuses (off Map pp1052-3; ☎ 91 468 42 00; www.estaciondeautobuses.com, in Spanish; Calle de Méndez Álvaro 83; Ⓜ Méndez Álvaro), just south of the M-30 ring road, is the city's principal bus station. It serves most destinations to the south and many in other parts of the country. Alsa has buses to Barcelona (€28 to €39, 7½ to 8½ hours, 27 daily), Zaragoza (€14.40 to €20, 3¾ to four hours, 28 daily) and many other destinations.

Renfe (www.renfe.es) trains connect Madrid with destinations throughout Spain. Long-distance and *cercanías* (local area) trains pass through Chamartín and Atocha stations.

High-speed AVE trains run to Barcelona (€105 to €124, 2¾ to three hours, up to 18 daily) and Seville (€67 to €74, 2½ hours, up to 20 daily).

GETTING AROUND

Madrid's 284km of **metro** (www.metromadrid.es) is Europe's second-largest metro system, after London. A single ride costs €1 and a 10-ride ticket is €6.70. You can also get a one-, two-, three-, five- or seven-day travel pass. The metro is quick, clean, relatively safe and runs from 6am until 2am.

The bus system is also good, but working out the maze of bus lines can be a challenge. Contact **EMT** (www.emtmadrid.es) for more information. Twenty-six night-bus *búhos* (owls) routes operate from midnight to 6am, with all routes originating in Plaza de la Cibeles.

CASTILLA Y LEÓN

The true heart of Spain, Castilla y León is littered with hilltop towns sporting magnificent Gothic cathedrals, monumental city walls and mouth-watering restaurants.

ÁVILA

pop 53,800 / elev 1130m

Ávila's romantic old town has a picture-postcard look and an open-museum feel. It's a perfect place to spend a day strolling down narrow laneways and soaking up history.

There's a **tourist office** (☎ 920 21 13 87; www.turismocastillayleon.com; Plaza de Pedro Dávila 4; ⏲ 9am-2pm & 5-8pm mid-Sep–Jun, 9am-8pm Sun-Thu, 9am-9pm Fri & Sat Jul–mid-Sep) near the Puerta del Rastro.

Sights & Activities

Don't even *think* of leaving town without enjoying the walk along Ávila's 12th-century **murallas** (walls; ☎ 920 21 13 87; admission €4; ⏲ 11am-6pm Tue-Sun Sep-Jun, 10am-8pm Jul & Aug). The two access points are at the **Puerta del Alcázar** (⏲ 11am-6pm Tue-Sun Oct-Apr, 11am-8pm Tue-Sun May-Sep) and the **Puerta de los Leales** (Casa de las Carnicerias; ⏲ 10am-6pm Tue-Sun Oct-Apr, 10am-8pm Tue-Sun May-Sep), which allow walks of 300m and 800m respectively.

Embedded in the eastern walls, the 12th-century **cathedral** (☎ 920 21 16 41; Plaza de la Catedral; admission €4; ⏲ 10am-7pm Mon-Fri, 10am-8pm Sat, noon-6pm Sun Jun-Sep, shorter hr rest of year) was the first Gothic-style church built in Spain. It boasts rich walnut choir stalls and a long, narrow central nave that makes the soaring ceilings seem all the more majestic.

Even more beloved by locals than the cathedral is the **Convento de Santa Teresa** (☎ 920 21 10 30; admission free; ⏲ 8.45am-1.30pm & 3.30-9pm Tue-Sun), built in 1636 at the birthplace of 16th-century mystic and ascetic, Santa Teresa. It's home to relics, including a piece of the saint's ring finger, as well as a small museum about her life.

Sleeping

Hostal San Juan (☎ 920 25 14 75; www.hostalsanjuan.es; Calle de los Comuneros de Castilla 3; s/d Nov-May from €24/38, Jun-Oct €30/48) With warm tones throughout, Hostal San Juan is pleasant, friendly and close to everything in Ávila. The rooms don't have a lot of character, but they're terrific value.

Hostal Arco San Vicente (☎ 920 22 24 98; www.arcosanvicente.com; Calle de López Núñez 6; s €45-50, d €60-70) Another terrific option, this engaging *hostal* has lovely, brightly painted rooms and friendly owners. The rooms at the back are quieter and have a private terrace.

Eating & Drinking

Posada de la Fruta (☎ 920 22 09 84; www.posadadelafruta.com, in Spanish; Plaza de Pedro Dávila 8; meals €10-18) Informal meals can be had here at the cafe-bar in a light-filled, covered courtyard, while the traditional *comedor* (dining room) serves *menús* (fixed-price meals) and à la carte dishes.

There are several good bars just outside the Puerta de los Leales, the best of which is the noisy, smoky and welcoming **Bodeguito de San Segundo** (☎ 920 22 59 17; www.vinoavila.com, in Spanish; Calle de San Segundo 19; 🕙 11am-midnight Thu-Tue).

Getting There & Away

The **bus station** (☎ 920 22 01 54; Avenida de Madrid 2) is a five-minute walk northeast from the cathedral. Up to nine buses daily (€7.10, one hour 20 minutes) connect with Madrid's Estación Sur. Avanza has buses to Segovia (€4.30, 55 minutes, five daily Monday to Friday, one to two on weekends) and Salamanca (€5.60, 1½ hours, four daily Monday to Friday, one to three on weekends).

From the **train station** (Paseo de la Estación), more than 30 trains run daily to Madrid (from €6.50, 1¼ to two hours) and a handful to Salamanca (€8.40, one to 1½ hours).

SALAMANCA

pop 155,900

This is a city of rare architectural splendour, awash with sandstone overlaid with Latin inscriptions in ochre and an extraordinary virtuosity of Plateresque and Renaissance styles. The monumental highlights are many, especially the Catedral Nueva and grand Plaza Mayor. King Alfonso XI founded what was long Spain's greatest university in 1218 and

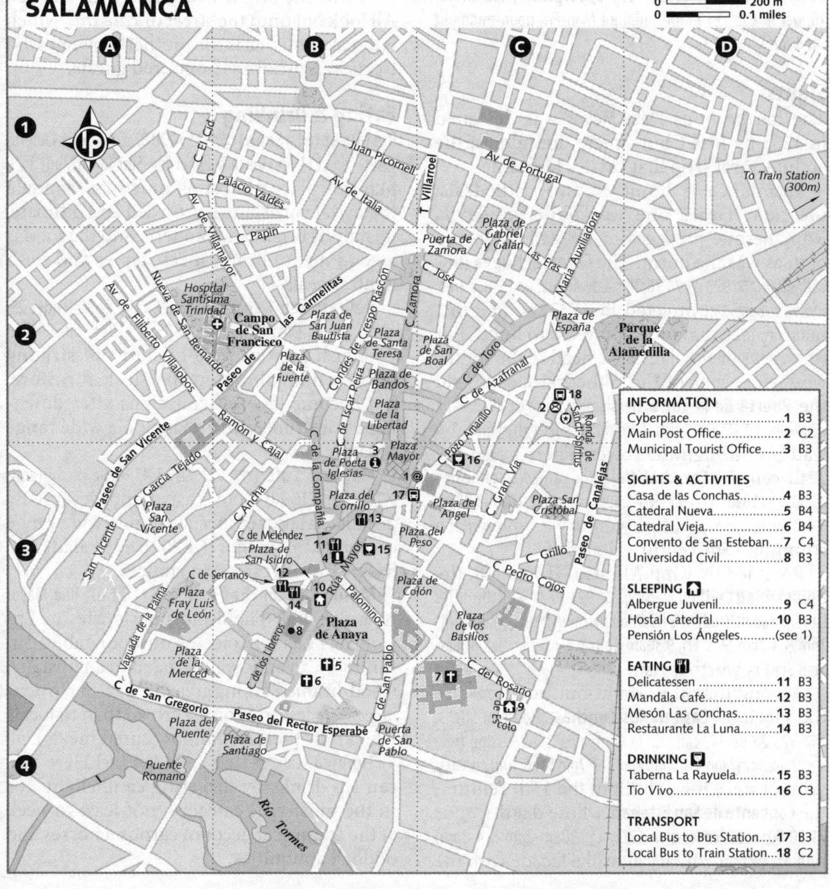

Book your stay at lonelyplanet.com/hotels

FIND THE FROG

The university's facade is an ornate mass of sculptures and carvings, and hidden among this 16th-century Plateresque creation is a tiny stone frog. Legend says that those who find the frog will have good luck in studies, life and love. A hint: it's sitting on a skull on the pillar that runs up the right-hand side of the facade.

this is still a university town. A favourite with young foreigners who come to learn Spanish, it can be quite a party town.

There's a helpful **tourist office** (☎ 923 21 83 42; www.salamanca.es; Plaza Mayor 14; 9am-2pm & 4.30-8pm Mon-Fri, 10am-8pm Sat, 10am-2pm Sun) in the centre of town. For internet, try **Cyberplace** (Plaza Mayor 10; per hr €1; 11am-midnight Mon-Fri, noon-midnight Sat & Sun).

Sights

The harmonious **Plaza Mayor** was designed in 1755 by José Churriguera, founder of the architectural style that carries his name.

Salamanca is home to two cathedrals: the new, larger one was built beside its Romanesque predecessor instead of on top of it, as was the norm. The **Catedral Nueva** (New Cathedral; ☎ 923 21 74 76; Plaza de Anaya; admission free; 9am-8pm), completed in 1733, is a Gothic masterpiece that took 220 years to build. For fine views over Salamanca, head to the southwestern corner of the cathedral facade and the **Puerta de la Torre** (Ieronimus; Plaza de Juan XXIII; admission €3.25; 10am-7.15pm), from where stairs lead up through the tower. There's also the 12th-century **Catedral Vieja** (Old Cathedral; admission €3.50; 10am-12.30pm & 4-5.30pm Oct-Mar, 10am-1.30pm & 4-7.30pm Apr-Sep), a 12th-century temple with a stunning 15th-century altarpiece.

Founded by King Alfonso XI in 1218, the **Universidad Civil** (university; ☎ 923 29 44 00; Calle de los Libreros; adult/student €4/2, Mon morning free; 9.30am-1pm & 4-7pm Mon-Fri, 9.30am-1pm & 4-6.30pm Sat, 10am-1pm Sun) is worth a visit.

Among the other stand-out buildings are the glorious **Casa de las Conchas** (House of Shells; ☎ 923 26 93 17; Calle de la Compañia 2; admission free; 9am-9pm Mon-Fri, 9am-2pm & 4-7pm Sat & Sun), a city symbol since it was built in the 15th century; the **Convento de San Esteban**, whose **church** (☎ 923 21 50 00; adult/concession €3/2; 10am-2pm & 4-8pm) has an extraordinary altarlike facade with the stoning of San Esteban (St Stephen) as its central motif.

Sleeping

Albergue Juvenil (☎ 923 26 91 41; www.alberguesalamanca.com; Calle de Escoto 13-15; dm €12.90, s/d €25/36) Salamanca's youth hostel is ideal for those looking for travel buddies as it's a popular, well-run place with large, clean dorms.

Pensión Los Ángeles (☎ 923 21 81 66; Plaza Mayor 10; s/d from €18/30) In a prime location on Plaza Mayor and with cheap prices to boot, this place is a winner. Those with balconies overlooking the plaza are for three to five people. It's a steep climb up to the *pension*.

Hostal Catedral (☎ 923 27 06 14; Rúa Mayor 46; s/d €30/48) Just across from the *catedrales*, this lovely *hostal* has a few extremely pretty, clean-as-a-whistle, bright bedrooms with shower. All look out onto the street or *catedral*, which is a real bonus, as is the motherly owner who treats her visitors as honoured guests.

Eating & Drinking

Restaurante La Luna (☎ 923 21 28 87; Calle de los Libreros 4; set menu €11; lunch & dinner Tue-Sun, lunch Mon) We like this place almost as much as Mandala (below). Downstairs is crowded and intimate, upstairs is bright and modern, and the food is a good mix of hearty meat staples and fresh lighter meals.

Delicatessen (☎ 923 28 03 09; Calle de Meléndez 25; menú del día €14.50, meals €20-25; 9am-late) The youngish patrons tend to start out striking poses while lolling on the sleek furniture, but become less self-conscious after downing a few drinks and grazing on a wide range of tapas.

Mandala Café (☎ 923 12 33 42; Calle de Serranos 9-11; meals €15-20) Cool, casual and deservedly popular, Mandala specialises in a wide range of *platos combinados* (€4.20 to €9), salads and has plenty of vegetarian choices.

Mesón Las Conchas (☎ 923 21 21 67; Rúa Mayor 16; meals €20-30) The atmospheric Mesón Las Conchas has a choice of outdoor tables (in summer), an atmospheric bar and an upstairs, wood-beamed dining area; the bar, in particular, caters less to a tourist crowd than to locals who know their *embutidos* (cured meats).

Tío Vivo (Calle de Clavel 3; 4pm-late) Here you can sip drinks by flickering candlelight. It's in the must-visit category, not least to peek at the whimsical decor of carousel horses and oddball antiquities.

Taberna La Rayuela (Rúa Mayor 19; 6pm-1am Sun-Thu, 6pm-2am Fri & Sat) This low-lit upstairs bar is an intimate place with a 20-something crowd.

Getting There & Away

The **bus station** (923 23 67 17; Avenida de Filiberto Villalobos 71-85) is northwest of the town centre. Avanza has hourly departures to Madrid (regular/express €11.80/17.40, 2½ to three hours) with other buses going to Valladolid (€7.40, 1½ hours), Ávila (€5.58, 1½ hours) and Segovia (€9.88, 2¾ hours).

Up to eight trains depart daily for Madrid's Chamartín station (€16.50, 2½ hours) via Ávila (€8.40, one hour). There are also frequent services to Valladolid (from €7.50, 1½ hours).

SEGOVIA

pop 56,050 / elev 1002m

This high and, in winter, chilly city, warms the traveller's heart with such extraordinary sights as the grand Roman aqueduct and fairytale Alcázar (castle), not to mention steaming serves of hearty suckling pig in many an old-town restaurant.

There's a **tourist office** (921 466 720; www.turismodesegovia.com; Plaza del Azoguejo 1; 10am-7pm Sun-Fri, 10am-8pm Sat) next to the aqueduct. For your internet fix, head to **InternetCaf** (921 42 51 58; Calle de Teodosio el Grande 10; per hr €2; 9am-11pm).

Sights

El Acueducto (the Roman aqueduct), an 894m-long engineering wonder that looks like an enormous comb plunged into the centre of Segovia, is 28m high and was built without a drop of mortar – just good old Roman know-how.

In the heart of town is the resplendent **Catedral** (cathedral; 921 46 22 05; Plaza Mayor; adult/concession €3/2, Sun 9.30am-1.15pm free; 9.30am-5.30pm Oct-Mar, 9.30am-6.30pm Apr-Sep), home to some exceptional artwork and a graceful Gothic cloister.

The fortified **Alcázar** (921 46 07 59; www.alcazardesegovia.com; Plaza de la Reina Victoria Eugenia; adult/concession €4/3, tower €2, admission free on 3rd Tue of month for EU citizens; 10am-6pm Oct-Mar, 10am-7pm Apr-Sep) is perched dramatically on the edge of town. Roman foundations are buried somewhere underneath, but what we see today is a 13th-century structure that burned down in 1862 and was subsequently rebuilt. Inside is a collection of armour and military gear, but even better are the ornate interiors of the reception rooms and the 360° views from the **Torre de Juan II**.

Sleeping

Pensión Ferri (921 46 09 57; Calle de Escuderos 10; s/d with shared bathroom €18/28) Occupying an old house in a superb location, the rooms are simple but quaint and incorporate some of the building's original wood and brick work.

Hostal Juan Bravo (921 46 34 13; Calle de Juan Bravo 12; d with washbasin/private bathroom €35/43) Another excellent choice, Hostal Juan Bravo has rooms at the back with stunning views of the Sierra de Guadarrama; the friendly owners round out a great package.

Eating & Drinking

La Almuzara (921 46 06 22; Calle Marqués del Arco 3; meals €15; lunch & dinner Tue-Sat, dinner Sun) If you're a vegetarian, you don't need to feel like an outcast in this resolutely carnivorous city. La Almuzara features lots of vegetarian dishes, pastas and salads and the ambience is warm and artsy.

Mesón José María (921 46 11 11; www.rtejosemaria.com in Spanish; Calle del Cronista Lecea 11; meals €30-40) Close to Plaza Mayor, this respected *mesón* offers great tapas in the bar and five dining rooms serving exquisite *cochinillo* (suckling pig, €21.35) and other local specialities.

Restaurante El Fogón Sefardí (921 46 62 50; www.lacasamudejar.com; Calle de Isabel La Católica 8; meals €30-40) This is one of the most original places in town, serving Sephardic cuisine (dishes like aubergine stuffed with vegetables, pine nuts and almonds).

Late-night action is concentrated near Plaza Mayor (especially along Calle de los Escuderos and Calle la Infanta Isabel).

La Tasquina (921 46 19 54; Calle de Valdeláguila 3; 9pm-late) This wine bar draws crowds large enough to spill out onto the pavement nursing their good wines, *cavas* (sparkling wines) and cheeses.

Getting There & Away

The **bus station** (92 142 77 07; Paseo Ezequiel González 12) is a 15-minute walk from the aqueduct. La Sepulvedana buses leave half-hourly from Madrid's Paseo de la Florida bus stop (€5.90, 1½ hours).

Up to nine normal trains run daily from Madrid to Segovia (one-way €5.90, two hours), leaving you at the main train station, 2.5km from the aqueduct. The high-speed AVE (€9, 35 minutes) deposits you at the Segovia-Guiomar station, 5km from the aqueduct.

LEÓN

pop 135,100 / elev 527m

León's stand-out attraction is the cathedral, one of the most beautiful in Spain. By day, this pretty city rewards long exploratory strolls. By night, the city's large student population floods into the narrow streets and plazas of the city's picturesque old quarter, the Barrio Húmedo.

The **tourist office** (☎ 987 23 70 82; Plaza de Regla; 🕑 9am-2pm & 5-8pm Mon-Fri, 10am-2pm & 5-8pm Sat & Sun Oct-Jun, 9am-8pm daily Jul-Sep) is opposite the cathedral. For internet access, try **Locutorio La Rua** (☎ 987 21 99 94; Calle de Varillas 3; 1/5 hr €2/5; 🕑 9.30am-9.30pm Mon-Fri, 10.30am-2.30pm & 5.30-9.30pm Sat).

Sights

León's breathtaking 13th-century **cathedral** (☎ 987 87 57 70; www.catedraldeleon.org, in Spanish; admission free; 🕑 8.30am-1.30pm & 4-7pm Mon-Sat, 8.30am-2.30pm & 5-7pm Sun Oct-Jun, 8.30am-1.30pm & 4-8pm Mon-Sat, 8.30am-2.30pm & 5-8pm Sun Jul-Sep) is a marvel of Gothic architecture. It's famous for its stained-glass windows, which give it an ethereal quality. Inside, there's a **museum** (admission incl cloister €3.50; 🕑 9.30am-1.30pm & 4-7pm Mon-Fri, 9.30am-1.30pm Sat Oct-Jun, 9.30am-1.30pm & 4-7.30pm Mon-Fri, to 7pm Sat Jul-Sep), which is entered through the **cloister** (admission €1).

Nearby is the **Real Basílica de San Isidoro**, a simple Romanesque church housing the **Panteón Real** (☎ 987 87 61 61; admission €4, Thu afternoon free; 🕑 10am-1.30pm & 4-6.30pm Mon-Sat, 10am-1.30pm Sun Sep-Jun, 9am-8pm Mon-Sat, 9am-2pm Sun Jul & Aug), where Leónese royalty lies buried beneath a canopy of fine Romanesque frescoes.

Sleeping

Hostal Bayón (☎ 987 23 14 46; Calle del Alcázar de Toledo 6; s/d with washbasin €15/28, with shower €25/35) The laid-back owner presides over cheerful, brightly painted rooms with pine floors. You're surrounded by modern León, but just a five-minute walk from the old town.

Eating & Drinking

Restaurante Luisón (☎ 987 25 40 29; Plaza Puerta Obispo 16; meals €15-20, menú del día €8; 🕑 daily) Offhand waiters sling out hearty food that keeps the locals fortified during cold winters. You'll need to book ahead, especially at lunchtime when locals can't get enough of the local *botillo berciano*, a succulent pork dish, or *cocido leónes* (León-style chickpea stew).

El Tizón (☎ 987 25 60 49; Plaza de San Martín 1; meals €25-30, menú del día €13; 🕑 lunch & dinner Fri, Sat & Mon-Wed, lunch Sun) The tapas are good here, but the small sit-down restaurant, with an abundant set lunch, is even better. House specialities include the local *embutidos* (cured meats).

The Barrio Húmedo's night-time epicentre is Plaza de San Martín and surrounding streets (especially Calle de Juan de Arfe and Calle de la Misericordia). A good night could begin at **Rebote** (Plaza de San Martín 9; 🕑 8pm-1am), then move on to funky **Delicatessen** (Calle de Juan de Arfe 10; 🕑 10pm-3am Wed-Sat), both bars.

Getting There & Away

Alsa has numerous daily buses from the bus station on Paseo del Ingeniero Sáez de Miera to Madrid (€20.74, 3½ hours) and Burgos.

Regular passenger trains travel to Burgos (from €17.90, two hours), Madrid (from €22.40, 4¼ hours) and Barcelona (from €43.20, 10 hours).

BURGOS

pop 174,100 / elev 861m

The legendary warrior El Cid was born just outside Burgos and is buried in its extraordinary Gothic cathedral. Pick up information at the **municipal tourist office** (☎ 947 28 88 74; www.aytoburgos.es, in Spanish; Plaza del Rey Fernando 2; 🕑 10am-2pm & 4.30-7.30pm Mon-Fri, 10am-1.30pm & 4-7.30pm Sat & Sun mid-Sep–Jun, 10am-8pm daily Jul–mid-Sep). For internet, try **Ciber-Café Cabaret** (Calle de la Puebla 21; per hr from €2.50; 🕑 noon-1am Sun-Thu, 7pm-4am Fri & Sat).

Sights

The World Heritage–listed **Cathedral** (☎ 947 20 47 12; Plaza del Rey Fernando; adult/pilgrim & student €4/2.50; 🕑 9.30am-7.30pm 19 Mar-Oct, 10am-7pm Nov-18 Mar) is a Gothic gem. El Cid lies buried beneath the central dome.

The **Monasterio de las Huelgas** (☎ 947 20 16 30; guided tours adult/student €5/4, Wed free; 🕑 10am-1pm & 3.45-5.30pm Tue-Sat, 10.30am-2pm Sun) was founded in 1187 by Eleanor of Aquitaine and is still home to Cistercian nuns. To see the monastery, guided tours (in Spanish) are compulsory; they leave the ticket office every 50 minutes or so. From the cathedral, it's a pleasant 30-minute walk west along the southern bank of the Río Arlanzón.

Sleeping & Eating

Pensión Peña (☎/fax 947 20 63 23; Calle de la Puebla 18; s/d with shared bathroom from €20/26) This impeccable place with a motherly owner has rooms with delightful individual touches, such as hand-painted washbasins. The central location is a plus.

Cervecería Morito (☎ 947 26 75 55; Calle de la Sombrerería; 🕒 1-3.30pm & 7.30pm-midnight) The king of Burgos tapas bars has its two floors that are usually full. A typical order is *alpargata* (lashings of cured ham with bread, tomato and olive oil; €2.70).

La Cabaña Arandino (Calle de la Sombrerería; 🕒 1-3.30pm & 7-11pm) Opposite Cervecería Morito, this place also does good tapas; locals love the *tigres* (mussels with spicy sauce).

Getting There & Away

From Burgos' **bus station** (Calle de Miranda 4), Alsa runs regular buses to Madrid (€15.65, 2¾ hours), Bilbao (€11.15, two hours), San Sebastián (€14.90, 3½ hours) and León (€13.30, 3¼ hours).

By train, Burgos is connected with Madrid (from €23.10, four hours, up to seven daily), Bilbao (from €16.60, three hours, five daily), León (from €17.90, two hours, four daily) and Salamanca (from €20.10, 2½ hours, three daily).

CASTILLA-LA MANCHA

Known as the stomping ground of Don Quijote and Sancho Panza, Castilla-La Mancha conjures up images of lonely windmills, medieval castles and bleak, treeless plains. The characters of Miguel de Cervantes provide the literary context, but the richly historic cities of Toledo and Cuenca are the most compelling reasons to visit.

TOLEDO

pop 55,100 / elev 655m

Toledo is a corker of a city. Commanding a hill rising above the Río Tajo, it's crammed with monuments that attest to the waves of conquerors and communities – Roman, Visigoth, Jewish, Muslim and Christian – that have called it home during its turbulent history.

Information

Locutorio Santo Tomé (☎ 925 21 65 38; Calle de Santo Tomé 1; per hr €2; 🕒 11am-10.30pm) Internet access.

Main tourist office (☎ 925 25 40 30; www.toledo-turismo.com; Plaza del Ayuntamiento s/n; 🕒 10.30am-2.30pm Mon, 10.30am-2.30pm & 4.30-7pm Tue-Sun)

Tourist office (☎ 925 22 08 43; fax 925 25 26 48; Puerta Nueva de Bisagra s/n; 🕒 9am-6pm Mon-Fri, 9am-7pm Sat, 9am-3pm Sun)

Sights

The **Catedral** (admission €7; 🕒 10.30am-6.30pm Mon-Sat, 2-6.30pm Sun) is Toledo's major landmark. There's loads to see within its hefty stone walls, including art by El Greco, Zurbarán, Crespi, Titian, Rubens and Velázquez.

The **Museo de Santa Cruz** (☎ 925 22 10 36; Calle de Cervantes 3; admission free; 🕒 10am-6pm Mon-Sat, 10am-2pm Sun) contains a large collection of furniture, faded tapestries and paintings. Upstairs is an impressive collection of El Greco's works.

In the southwestern part of the old city, the queues outside an unremarkable church, the **Iglesia de Santo Tomé** (☎ 925 25 60 98; www.santotome.org; Plaza del Conde; admission €1.90; 🕒 10am-6pm), betray the presence of El Greco's masterpiece, *El Entierro del Conde de Orgaz*.

The **Museo Sefardi** (☎ 925 22 36 65; www.museosefardi.net, in Spanish; Calle Samuel Leví s/n; adult/12-25yr €2.40/1.20, audioguides €3; 🕒 10am-6pm Tue-Sat, 10am-2pm Sun) is housed in the beautiful 14th-century **Sinagoga del Tránsito**.

Sleeping

Accommodation is often full, especially from Easter to September.

HI Albergue Juvenil en San Servando (☎ 925 22 45 54; ralberguesto@jccm.es; dm under/over 26yr €9.50/12) This youth hostel has a grand setting in a castle, no less, with fine views, plus an attractive interior with beamed ceilings in the communal room and modern sleeping quarters.

La Posada de Zocodover (☎ 925 25 58 14; Calle Cordonerías 6; r €40) There are just seven clean and acceptable rooms at this superbly located place near the city's main square – which can equal earplugs at weekends.

Hostal Alfonso XII (☎ 925 25 25 09; www.hostal-alfonso12.com; Calle de Alfonso XII; r €65; ⊠ ❄) A gingerbread cottage of a place with original beams, terracotta tiles and stylish, albeit small, rooms decorated with impeccable taste.

Eating & Drinking

Santa Fe (☎ 670 65 42 16; Calle Santa Fe 6; menú €8, tapas €2) You can eat here better and for half the price than the restaurants on nearby

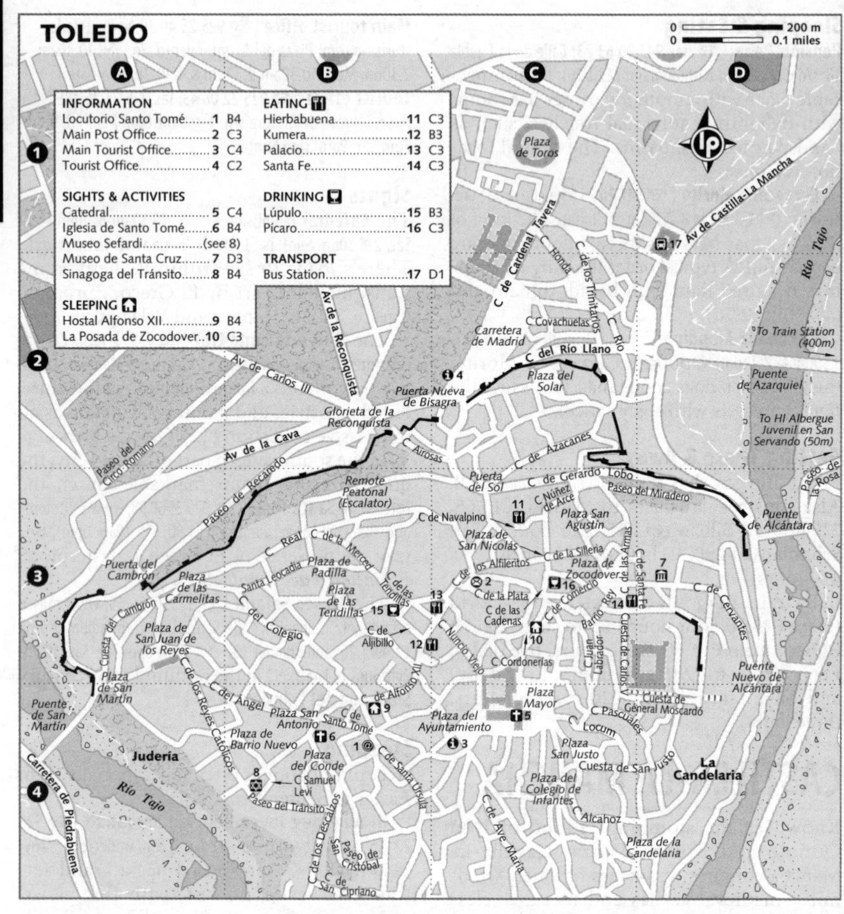

Zocodover. Sit down in the half-tiled dining room to enjoy tapas, tortilla with green pepper, homemade paella and *pollo al ajillo* (chicken in tomato and garlic sauce).

our pick **Palacio** (☎ 925 21 59 72; Calle Alfonso X el Sabio 3; meals €14-18, menú €13.90) An unpretentious place where stained glass, beams and efficient old-fashioned service combine with traditional no-nonsense cuisine. Hungry? Try a gut-busting bowl of *judias con perdiz* (white beans with partridge) for starters.

Kumera (☎ 925 25 75 53; Calle Alfonso X el Sabio 2; meals €18-25) The interior here is all golden brick and stone complemented by colourful artwork; the menu is similarly diverse with choices like tuna in soy sauce, crepes with salmon, spinach and cheese, and venison with roast peppers.

Hierbabuena (☎ 925 22 39 24; Calle de Navalpino 45; meals €18-25, menú €34.30; closed Sun night) A dress-for-dinner restaurant with tables set around a flower-filled patio dishing up classy cuisine like artichokes stuffed with Catalan sausages and creamed leeks.

Pícaro (☎ 925 22 13 01; Calle de las Cadenas 6) A popular cafe-*teatro* (theatre) serving an eclectic range of *copas* (drinks). From Monday to Thursday it's perfect for a quiet beverage, while the weekend ups the pace on Friday and Saturday nights when the disco ball starts spinning at 2.30am.

Lúpulo (☎ 925 25 71 36; Calle de Aljibillo 5) Serving a choice of over 50 Spanish and foreign beers, Lúpulo has a popular spill-over outside terrace.

Getting There & Away

Toledo's **bus station** (☎ 925 21 58 50; Avenida de Castilla-La Mancha) is northeast of the old town. Buses depart for Madrid every half-hour from about 6am to 10pm daily (8.30am to 11.30pm Sunday and holidays). Direct buses (€4.50, one hour) run hourly; other services (1½ hours) go via villages along the way. There are also services to Cuenca (€10.90, 2¼ hours).

Built in 1920, the **train station** (Paseo Rosa) is a pretty introduction to the city. The high-speed AVE service runs every hour or so to Madrid's Atocha station (€9, 30 minutes).

CUENCA

pop 53,000

Teetering on the edge of the Júcar and the Huécar gorges, Cuenca's *alta ciudad* (high town) is full of crumbling ancient buildings known as *casas colgadas* (hanging houses), which cling for dear life to the steep sides of the ravines.

The **tourist office** (☎ 969 32 31 19; www.aytocuenca.org in, Spanish; Plaza Mayor s/n; 9am-9pm Mon-Sat, 9am-2.30pm Sun May-Sep, 9am-2pm & 5-8pm Mon-Sat, 9am-2pm Sun Oct-Apr) is in the historic centre. For internet, try **La Repro 11** (☎ 969 23 14 40; Fray Luis de León 16; per hr €1.20; 10am-2pm & 5-8pm Mon-Sat).

Sights & Activities

Cuenca's 16th-century **casas colgadas** seem to tumble over a clifftop, their balconies projecting out over the gorge. To view them properly, walk over the **Puente San Pablo** (1902), an iron footbridge that crosses the ravine. Within one of the houses is the excellent **Museo de Arte Abstracto Español** (Museum of Abstract Art; ☎ 969 21 29 83; www.march.es; adult/12-25yr €3/1.50; 11am-2pm & 4-6pm Tue-Fri, 11am-2pm & 4-8pm Sat, 11am-2.30pm Sun), whose constantly evolving displays include works by Eduardo Chillida, Manuel Millares, Pablo Palazuelo, Eusebio Sempere and Antoni Tàpies.

The **Catedral** (☎ 96 922 46 26; Plaza Mayor; admission €2; 10am-2pm & 4-6pm Mon-Fri, 10am-7pm Sat, 10am-6.30pm Sun) is an odd pastiche of 16th-century Gothic experimentation and 20th-century restoration. The stained-glass windows look like they would be more at home in the abstract-art museum. Look out for the Chapter House and Deep Chapel.

Sleeping & Eating

Pensión Central (☎ 969 21 15 11; Calle de Alonso Chirino 7; s/d/tr with shared bathroom €14/24/31; ☒) This is a cheap sleep in a fresh and tidy *pensión* in the new town. Rooms are adequate and clean with TV and washbasin.

Pensión La Tabanqueta (☎ 969 21 12 90; Calle de Trabuco 13; s/d with shared bathroom €15/30) Room prices in this listed building are the best you'll find in the historic centre and some rooms have five-star views of Río Júcar. This place is plain but charming, and there's a popular bar-restaurant attached.

Posada de San José (☎ 969 21 13 00; www.posadasanjose.com; Ronda de Julián Romero 4; s/d with shared bathroom from €25/38, with views from €55/86) A 17th-century former choir school, this place retains an extraordinary monastic charm with its crumbling portal, uneven floors and original tiles. Enjoy spectacular views and fresh flowers in the room. The restaurant is recommended.

our pick **La Bodeguilla de Basilio** (☎ 969 23 52 74; Calle Fray Luis de León 3; raciones €10-13) Arrive here with an appetite as you are presented with a complimentary plate of tapas when you order a drink. The restaurant out the back has more good tucker.

Getting There & Away

Up to nine buses daily serve Madrid (€10.50, two hours). Other services include Valencia (€11.95, 2½ hours, up to three daily) and Toledo (€10.90, 2¼ hours, one to two daily).

Cuenca lies on the train line connecting Madrid and Valencia. Trains to Madrid's Atocha station depart six times on weekdays and four times on weekends (€10.65, 2½ hours).

CATALONIA

A triangular piece of territory in the northeast corner of the peninsula, Catalonia is a distinct region rich with possibilities. Home to stylish Barcelona, ancient Tarragona, romantic Girona, and countless alluring destinations along the coast, in the Pyrenees and in the rural interior, Catalonia (Catalunya in Catalan, Cataluña in Castilian) is a treasure box waiting to be opened.

BARCELONA

pop 1.59 million

Stylish Barcelona is a forward-thinking place, on the cutting edge of art, design and cuisine but with an equally rich past stretching back to Roman days. Whether you explore its medieval palaces and plazas, gawk at the *modernista* masterpieces, shop for designer duds along its stylish boulevards, sample its exciting nightlife or just soak up the sun on the city beaches, you'll be hard-pressed not to fall in love with this vibrant city.

Orientation

Central Plaça de Catalunya marks the divide between historic and modern Barcelona. From here, the long pedestrian boulevard La Rambla shoots southeast to the sea, with the busy old town Barri Gòtic (Gothic Quarter) and El Raval districts hugging it on either side. To the northwest of the plaza spreads L'Eixample, the vast gridlike district, laced with *modernista* marvels, endless shopping options and plenty of restaurants and bars mixed in with the turn-of-the-20th-century apartment and office blocks.

Information

BOOKSHOPS

Casa del Llibro (Map pp1072-3; ☎ 902 02 64 07; www.casadellibro.com; Passeig de Gràcia 62; Ⓜ Passeig de Gràcia) Good English section.

EMERGENCY

Guardia Urbana (City Police; Map p1074; ☎ 092; La Rambla 43; Ⓜ Liceu)

Mossos d'Esquadra (Catalan police; Map pp1072-3; ☎ 088; Carrer Nou de la Rambla 80; Ⓜ Parallel)

INTERNET ACCESS

Bornet (Map p1074; ☎ 93 268 15 07; www.bornet-bcn.com; Carrer de Barra de Ferro 3; per 1/10hr €2.80/20; 🕓 10am-11pm Mon-Fri, noon-11pm Sat, Sun & holidays; Ⓜ Jaume I)

easyInternetcafé (Map p1074; www.easyeverything.com; La Rambla 31; per hr €2.50; 🕓 8am-2.30am; Ⓜ Liceu)

LAUNDRY

Lavaxpress (Map p1074; www.lavaxpres.com; Carrer de Ferlandina 34; 🕓 8am-11pm; Ⓜ Sant Antoni) An 8kg wash costs €3.50; drying is €3.50 for 30 minutes. There are other branches around town.

MEDICAL SERVICES

24-hour Pharmacy La Rambla (Map p1074; La Rambla 98; Ⓜ Liceu); Passeig de Gràcia (Map pp1072-3; Passeig de Gràcia 26; Ⓜ Passeig de Gràcia) These are two of several 24-hour pharmacies in the city.

Hospital Clínic (Map pp1072-3; ☎ 93 227 54 00; www.hospitalclinic.org; Carrer Villarroel 170; Ⓜ Hospital Clínic) Modern hospital with good services.

TOURIST INFORMATION

Main tourist office (Map p1074; ☎ 93 285 38 32; www.barcelonaturisme.com; Plaça de Catalunya 17-S underground; 🕓 9am-9pm; Ⓜ Catalunya)

Sights & Activities

LA RAMBLA

Spain's most famous boulevard, the part-pedestrianised **La Rambla** explodes with life. Stretching from **Plaça de Catalunya** to the waterfront, it's lined with street artists, newsstands and vendors selling everything from mice to magnolias.

The colourful **Mercat de la Boqueria** (Map p1074; La Rambla; 🕓 8am-8pm Mon-Sat; Ⓜ Liceu), a fresh food market with a *modernista* entrance, is one of La Rambla's highlights. Nearby, stop for a tour of the **Gran Teatre del Liceu** (Map p1074; ☎ 93 485 99 00; www.liceubarcelona.com; La Rambla dels Caputxins 51-59; admission with/without guide €8.50/4; 🕓 guided tour 10am, unguided visits 11.30am, noon, 12.30pm & 1pm; Ⓜ Liceu), the city's opera house.

GETTING INTO TOWN

The main train station, Sants, is a hike from the centre of town, but is well connected by metro. Catch the green line (3) to reach La Rambla. The main bus station, Estació del Nord, is just northeast of the Barri Gòtic. Walk along the Ronda de Sant Pere for about 15 minutes to reach Plaça de Catalunya or hop on the metro at the nearby Arc de Triomf stop.

From the airport, you can take the A1 Aerobús (€4.05, 30 to 40 minutes depending on traffic, every six to 15 minutes) to Plaça de Catalunya and La Rambla. The C10 local train runs from the airport to Estació de França (handy for La Barceloneta and El Born) via Estació Sants (the main train station) and Passeig de Gràcia (for the centre). It runs twice an hour from 6am to 10.29pm and takes 35 minutes. A one-way ticket costs €2.60 (unless you have a multiride ticket for Barcelona public transport – see p1079).

Also stop at the **Plaça Reial**, a 19th-century square surrounded by arcades lined with restaurants and bars. At the waterfront end of La Rambla stands the **Monument a Colom** (Map pp1072-3; ☎ 93 302 52 24; Plaça del Portal de la Pau; lift €2.50; ⌚ 9am-8.30pm Jun-Sep, 10am-6.30pm Oct-May; Ⓜ Drassanes), a statue of Columbus atop a tall pedestal. A small lift takes you to the top for panoramic views.

Just west of La Rambla is the **Museu Marítim** (Map pp1072-3; ☎ 93 342 99 20; www.museumaritimbarcelona.org; Avinguda de les Drassanes; adult/student €6.50/3.25; ⌚ 10am-8pm; Ⓜ Drassanes), a gorgeous Gothic creation. Housed in the city's once mighty medieval shipyards, the museum takes an in-depth look at Catalonia's seafaring past. The full-scale replica of Don Juan of Austria's royal galley from the Battle of Lepanto is the highlight.

BARRI GÒTIC

Barcelona's Gothic **Catedral** (Map p1074; ☎ 93 342 82 60; Plaça de la Seu; admission free, special visit €5; ⌚ 8am-12.45pm & 5.15-8pm, special visit 1-5pm Mon-Sat, 2-5pm Sun & holidays; Ⓜ Jaume I) was built on top of the ruins of an 11th-century Romanesque church. The facade is a neo-Gothic addition tacked on in the 19th century. Highlights include the cool cloister, the crypt tomb of martyr Santa Eulàlia (one of Barcelona's two patron saints), the choirstalls (€2.20), the lift to the rooftop (€2.20) and the modest art collection in the **Sala Capitular** (chapterhouse; admission €2). You only pay the individual prices if you visit outside the special visiting hours.

Not far from the cathedral is pretty **Plaça del Rei** and the fascinating **Museu d'Història de la Ciutat** (Map p1074; ☎ 93 256 21 00; www.museuhistoria.bcn.cat; Carrer del Veguer; adult/student €6/4; ⌚ 10am-2pm & 4-7pm Tue-Sat, 10am-3pm Sun; Ⓜ Jaume I), where you can visit a 4000-sq-metre excavated site of Roman Barcelona under the plaza. The museum encompasses historic buildings including the **Palau Reial Major** (Main Royal Palace), once a residence of the kings of Catalonia and Aragón, and its **Saló del Tinell** (Great Hall). In summer, outdoor concerts are often held in Plaça del Rei.

EL RAVAL

To the west of La Rambla is El Raval district, a once-seedy, now-funky area overflowing with cool bars and shops. Visit the **Museu d'Art Contemporani de Barcelona** (Macba; Map p1074; ☎ 93 412 08 10; www.macba.es; Plaça dels Àngels 1; adult/concession €7.50/6, Wed €3.50; ⌚ 11am-8pm Mon & Wed, 11am-midnight Thu-Fri, 10am-8pm Sat, 10am-3pm Sun & holidays late Jun-late Sep, 11am-7.30pm Mon & Wed-Fri, 10am-8pm Sat, 10am-3pm Sun & holidays Oct-late Jun; Ⓜ Universitat), which has an impressive collection of international contemporary art.

LA RIBERA

Home to medieval Barcelona's bustling textile industry and to its wealthy merchants, La Ribera was once the city's most prosperous quarter. Now it's a trendy district exploding with boutiques, restaurants and bars.

A series of palaces where some of those wealthy merchants once lived now house the **Museu Picasso** (Map p1074; ☎ 93 256 30 00; www.museupicasso.bcn.es; Carrer de Montcada 15-23; adult/student €9/3, temporary exhibitions €5.80, 1st Sun of month free; ⌚ 10am-8pm Tue-Sun & holidays; Ⓜ Jaume I), home to more than 3000 Picassos, most from early in the artist's career.

The heart of the neighbourhood is the elegant **Església de Santa Maria del Mar** (Map p1074; Plaça de Santa Maria del Mar; admission free; ⌚ 9am-1.30pm & 4.30-8pm; Ⓜ Jaume I), a stunning example of Catalan Gothic.

The opulent **Palau de la Música Catalana** (Map p1074; ☎ 902 47 54 85; www.palaumusica.org; Carrer de Sant Francesc de Paula 2; adult/student incl guided tour €10/9; ⌚ 50min tours every 30min 10am-6pm Easter & Aug, 10am-3.30pm Sep-Jul; Ⓜ Urquinaona) is one of the city's most delightful modernist works. Designed by Lluís Domènech i Montaner in 1905, it hosts concerts daily.

La Ribera is bordered to the east by the sprawling **Parc de la Ciutadella** (Map pp1072-3; ⌚ 8am-6pm Nov-Feb, 8am-8pm Oct & Mar, 8am-9pm Apr-Sep; Ⓜ Barceloneta), a park ideal for strolling or picnics. It's home to a small **zoo** (Map pp1072-3; ☎ 93 225 67 80; www.zoobarcelona.com; Passeig de Picasso & Carrer de Wellington; admission €15.40; ⌚ 10am-7pm Jun-Sep, 10am-6pm mid-Mar–May & Oct, 10am-5pm Nov–mid-Mar; Ⓜ Barceloneta), which holds about 7500 living thingies, from gorillas to insects.

L'EIXAMPLE

Modernisme, the Catalan version of art nouveau, transformed Barcelona's cityscape in the early 20th century. Most *modernista* works were built in l'Eixample, the grid-plan district that was developed from the 1870s on.

Modernisme's star architect was the eccentric Antoni Gaudí (1852–1926), a devout Catholic whose work is full of references to nature and Christianity. His masterpiece, **La**

BARCELONA

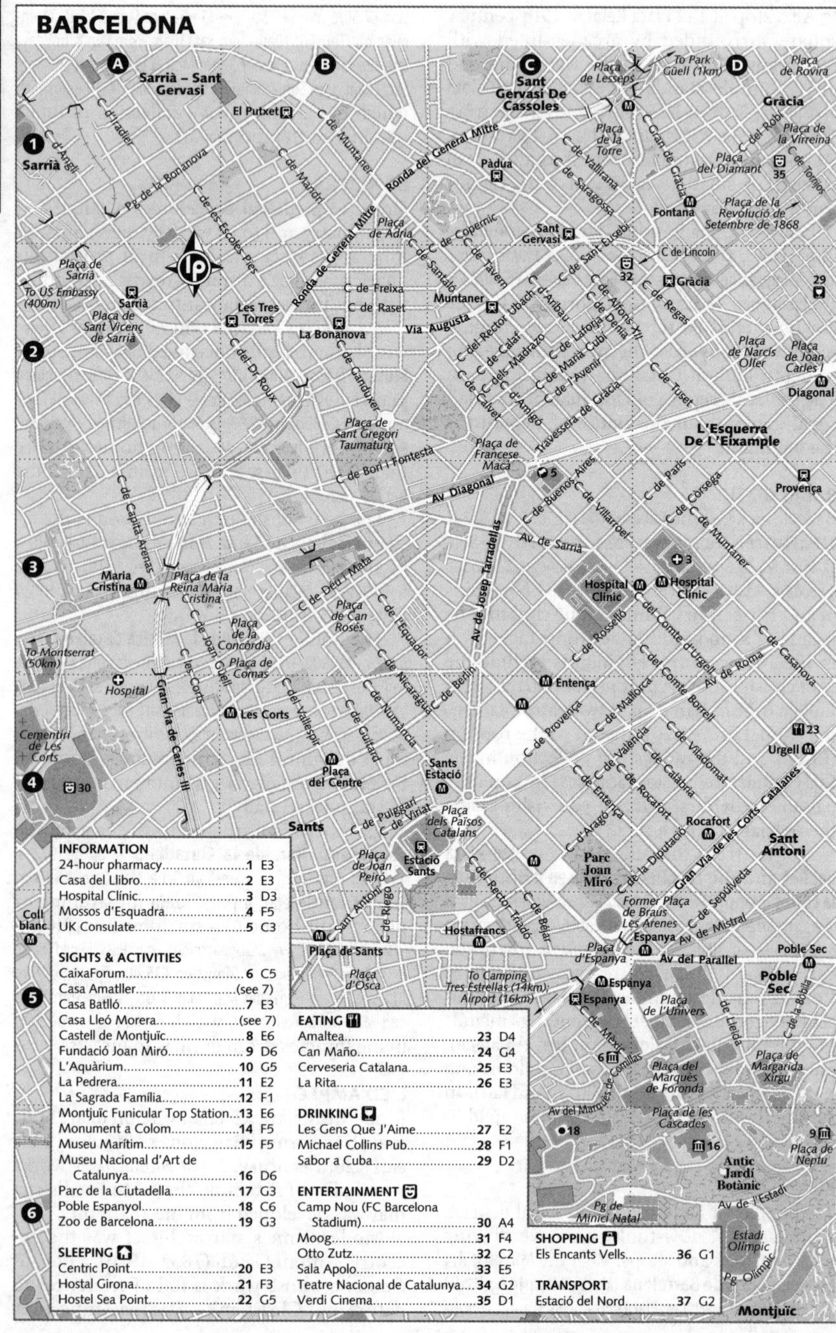
INFORMATION
24-hour pharmacy 1 E3
Casa del Llibro 2 E3
Hospital Clínic 3 D3
Mossos d'Esquadra 4 F5
UK Consulate 5 C3
SIGHTS & ACTIVITIES
CaixaForum 6 C5
Casa Amatller (see 7)
Casa Batlló 7 E3
Casa Lleó Morera (see 7)
Castell de Montjuïc 8 E6
Fundació Joan Miró 9 D6
L'Aquàrium 10 G5
La Pedrera 11 E2
La Sagrada Família 12 F1
Montjuïc Funicular Top Station 13 E6
Monument a Colom 14 F5
Museu Marítim 15 F5
Museu Nacional d'Art de Catalunya 16 D6
Parc de la Ciutadella 17 G3
Poble Espanyol 18 C6
Zoo de Barcelona 19 G3
SLEEPING
Centric Point 20 E3
Hostal Girona 21 F3
Hostel Sea Point 22 G5
EATING
Amaltea 23 D4
Can Maño 24 G4
Cerveseria Catalana 25 E3
La Rita 26 E3
DRINKING
Les Gens Que J'Aime 27 E2
Michael Collins Pub 28 F1
Sabor a Cuba 29 D2
ENTERTAINMENT
Camp Nou (FC Barcelona Stadium) 30 A4
Moog 31 F4
Otto Zutz 32 C2
Sala Apolo 33 E5
Teatre Nacional de Catalunya 34 G2
Verdi Cinema 35 D1
SHOPPING
Els Encants Vells 36 G1
TRANSPORT
Estació del Nord 37 G2
A
B
C
D
1
2
3
4
5
6
Sarrià – Sant Gervasi
Sant Gervasi De Cassoles
Gràcia
Sarrià
El Putxet
Pàdua
Fontana
Sant Gervasi
Muntaner
Les Tres Torres
La Bonanova
Plaça de Lesseps
To Park Güell (1km)
Plaça de Rovira
Plaça de la Torre
Plaça del Diamant
Plaça de la Virreina
Plaça de la Revolució de Setembre de 1868
C de Lincoln
Plaça de Sarrià
To US Embassy (400m)
Plaça de Sant Vicenç de Sarrià
Plaça de Adrià
Ronda del General Mitre
Pg de la Bonanova
Via Augusta
Av Diagonal
Travessera de Gràcia
Plaça de Narcís Oller
Plaça de Joan Carles I
Diagonal
L'Esquerra De L'Eixample
Provença
Plaça de Sant Gregori Taumaturg
Plaça de Francesc Macà
C de Bori i Fontestà
Av de Sarrià
Maria Cristina
Plaça de la Reina Maria Cristina
Hospital Clínic
To Montserrat (50km)
Hospital
Gran Via de Carles III
Les Corts
Cementiri de Les Corts
Plaça de la Concòrdia
Plaça de Comas
Plaça de Can Rosés
Av de Josep Tarradellas
Entença
Urgell
Plaça del Centre
Sants Estació
Sants
Plaça dels Països Catalans
Estació Sants
Plaça de Joan Peiró
Rocafort
Sant Antoni
Parc Joan Miró
Gran Via de les Corts Catalanes
Former Plaça de Braus Les Arenes
Coll blanc
Hostafrancs
Plaça de Sants
Plaça d'Espanya
Espanya
Av del Paral·lel
Av de Mistral
Poble Sec
Plaça d'Osca
To Camping Tres Estrelles (14km); Airport (16km)
Plaça de l'Univers
Plaça de Margarida Xirgu
Plaça del Marquès de Foronda
Av del Marquès de Comillas
Plaça de les Cascades
Antic Jardí Botànic
Plaça de Neptu
Av de l'Estadi
Pg de Minici Natal
Estadi Olímpic
Pg Olímpic
Montjuïc

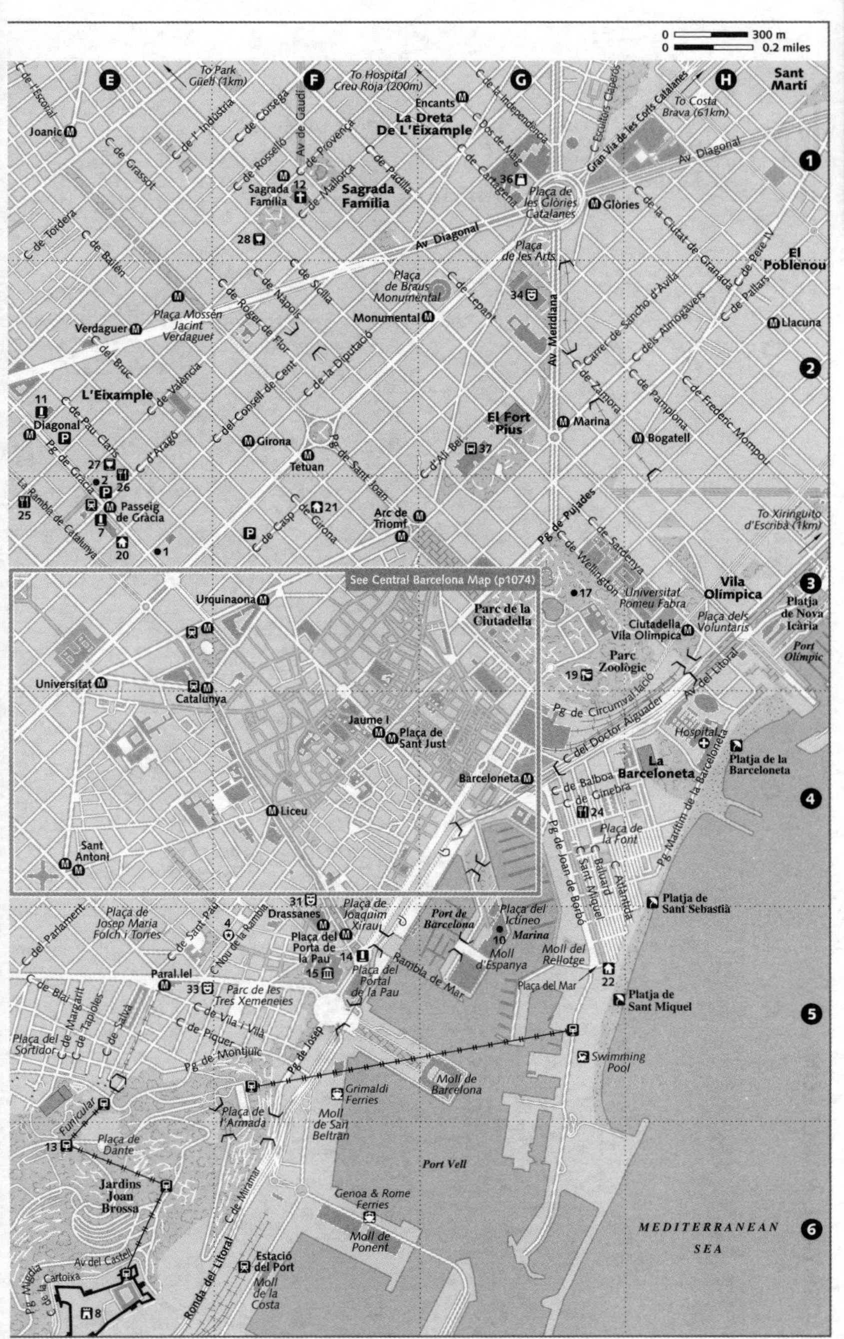

To Park Güell (1km)
To Hospital Creu Roja (200m)
To Costa Brava (61km)
Sant Martí
La Dreta De L'Eixample
Sagrada Família
L'Eixample
El Poblenou
El Fort Pius
Vila Olímpica
Parc de la Ciutadella
Parc Zoològic
La Barceloneta
See Central Barcelona Map (p1074)
To Xiringuito d'Escribà (1km)
Platja de Nova Icària
Port Olímpic
Platja de la Barceloneta
Platja de Sant Sebastià
Platja de Sant Miquel
Port de Barcelona
Port Vell
Moll de Barcelona
Grimaldi Ferries
Genoa & Rome Ferries
Estació del Port
Jardins Joan Brossa
MEDITERRANEAN SEA

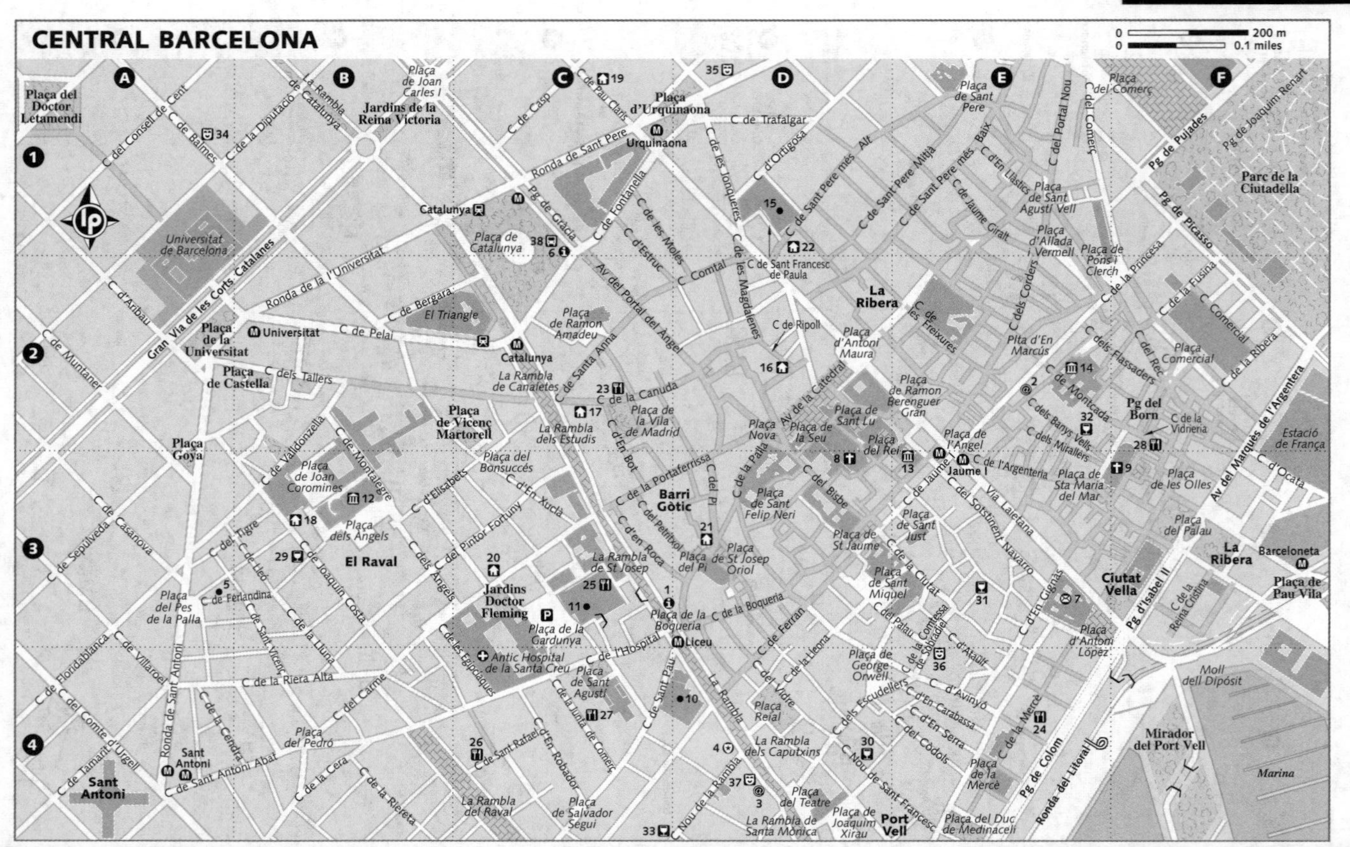
CENTRAL BARCELONA
200 m
0.1 miles
Plaça del Doctor Letamendi
Universitat de Barcelona
Gran Via de les Corts Catalanes
Plaça de la Universitat
Plaça de Castella
Plaça Goya
Jardins de la Reina Victoria
Plaça de Joan Carles I
Plaça de Catalunya
El Triangle
Catalunya
Universitat
Urquinaona
Plaça d'Urquinaona
Plaça de Vicenç Martorell
El Raval
Plaça dels Àngels
Plaça de Joan Coromines
Jardins Doctor Fleming
Antic Hospital de la Santa Creu
Plaça de la Gardunya
Plaça de Sant Agustí
Plaça del Pes de la Palla
Sant Antoni
Ronda de Sant Antoni
Plaça del Pedró
La Rambla del Raval
Plaça de Salvador Seguí
Liceu
Barri Gòtic
Plaça de Sant Felip Neri
Plaça Nova
Plaça de la Seu
Plaça del Rei
Plaça de St Jaume
Plaça Reial
La Rambla
Plaça del Teatre
La Rambla de Santa Mònica
Plaça de George Orwell
Port Vell
Plaça de la Mercè
Plaça del Duc de Medinaceli
Jaume I
Via Laietana
La Ribera
Plaça d'Antoni Maura
Plaça de Ramon Berenguer Gran
C de Montcada
Pg del Born
Plaça de Sta Maria del Mar
Ciutat Vella
Plaça d'Antoni López
Pg d'Isabel II
Pg de Colom
Ronda del Litoral
Mirador del Port Vell
Moll dell Dipòsit
Marina
Barceloneta
Plaça de Pau Vila
Estació de França
Av del Marquès de l'Argentera
Parc de la Ciutadella
Pg de Picasso
Pg de Pujades
Plaça de Sant Pere
Av del Portal del Àngel
Ronda de Sant Pere
Pg de Gràcia

INFORMATION
24-hour Pharmacy....1 C3
Bornet....2 E2
easyInternetcafé....3 D4
Guardia Urbana....4 D4
Lavaxpress....5 A3
Main Tourist Office....6 C1
Post Office....7 E3

SIGHTS & ACTIVITIES
Catedral....8 D3
Església de Santa Maria del Mar....9 F3
Gran Teatro del Liceu....10 D4
Mercat de la Boqueria....11 C3
Museu d'Art Contemporani de Barcelona....12 B3
Museu d'Història de la Ciutat....13 E3
Museu Picasso....14 E2
Palau de la Música Catalana....15 D1
Palau Reial Major....(see 13)
Saló del Tinell....(see 13)

SLEEPING
Alberg Hostel Itaca....16 D2
Hostal Campi....17 C2
Hostal Gat Raval....18 B3
Hostal Goya....19 C1
Hotel Aneto....20 C3
Hotel Jardí....21 D3
Pensió 2000....22 D1

EATING
Bagel Shop....23 C2
Bar Celta....24 E4
Bar Pinotxo....25 C3
Casa Leopoldo....26 C4
Organic....27 C4
Orígen 99.9%....28 F2

DRINKING
Casa Almirall....29 B3
Club Soul....30 D4
La Clandestina....31 E3
La Fianna....32 E2
London Bar....33 C4

ENTERTAINMENT
Arena Madre....34 A1
DBoy....35 D1
Harlem Jazz Club....36 E4
Tablao Cordobés....37 D4

TRANSPORT
A1 Aerobús....38 C1

Sagrada Família (Map pp1072-3; ☎ 93 207 30 31; www.sagradafamilia.org; Carrer de Mallorca 401; adult/student €10/8; 9am-8pm Apr-Sep, 9am-6pm Oct-Mar; M Sagrada Família), is a work in progress and Barcelona's most famous building. Construction began in 1882 and could be completed in 2020.

Eventually there'll be 18 towers, all more than 100m high, representing the 12 apostles, four evangelists and Mary, Mother of God, plus the tallest tower (170m) standing for Jesus Christ. Climb high inside some of the towers (or take the elevator, €2) for a different perspective.

Gaudí's **La Pedrera** (Map pp1072-3; ☎ 902 40 09 73; www.fundaciocaixacatalunya.es; Carrer de Provença 261-265; adult/student €8/4.50; 9am-8pm Mar-Oct, 9am-6.30pm Nov-Feb; M Diagonal) is his best-known secular creation. Inside, you can visit a museum about Gaudí and his work, a *modernista* apartment and the surreal rooftop with its bizarre chimneys.

Just down the street is the unique facade of the **Casa Batlló** (Map pp1072-3; ☎ 93 216 03 66; www.casabatllo.es; Passeig de Gràcia 43; adult/student €16.50/13.20; 9am-8pm, occasionally hrs shortened; M Passeig de Gràcia), an allegory for the legend of St George (Sant Jordi in Catalan) the dragon-slayer. On the same block are two other *modernista* gems, **Casa Amatller** (Map pp1072-3; Passeig de Gràcia 41) by Josep Puig i Cadafalch and the **Casa Lleó Morera** (Map pp1072-3; Passeig de Gràcia 35) by Lluís Domènech i Montaner. This mishmash of architectural styles gave the block its nickname, the *Manzana de Discordia* (Block/Apple of Discord, a play of words on an ancient Greek myth – *manzana* means both apple and block).

High up in the Gràcia district sits Gaudí's enchanting **Park Güell** (off Map pp1072-3; ☎ 93 413 24 00; Carrer d'Olot 7; admission free; 10am-9pm Jun-Sep, 10am-8pm Apr, May & Oct, 10am-7pm Mar & Nov, 10am-6pm Dec-Feb; M Lesseps or Vallcarca, 24), originally designed to be a self-contained community with houses, schools and shops. The project flopped, but we're left with a Dr Seuss–style playground filled with colourful mosaics and Gaudí-designed paths and plazas.

The website www.rutadelmodernisme.com is a great resource on modernisme in Barcelona.

WATERFRONT

Barcelona has two major ports, **Port Vell** (Old Port) at the base of La Rambla, and **Port Olímpic** (Olympic Port) 1.5km up the coast. Shops, restaurants and nightlife options are plentiful around both marinas, particularly Port Olímpic. Between the two ports sits the onetime factory workers' and fishermen's quarter, **La Barceloneta.** It preserves a delightfully scruffy appearance and abounds with crowded seafood eateries.

At the end of Moll d'Espanya in Port Vell is **L'Aquàrium** (Map pp1072-3; ☎ 93 221 74 74; www.aquariumbcn.com; Moll d'Espanya; admission €16; 9.30am-11pm Jul & Aug, 9.30am-9.30pm Jun & Sep, 9.30am-9pm Mon-Fri & 9.30am-9.30pm Sat & Sun Oct-May; M Drassanes), with its 80m-long shark tunnel.

Barcelona boasts 4km of city *platjas* (beaches), including the gritty **Platja de la Barceloneta** and continuing northeast, beyond Port Olímpic, with a series of cleaner, more attractive strands.

MONTJUÏC

A hill of gardens southwest of the centre, Montjuïc serves as a Central Park of sorts and is a great place for a stroll overlooking the city. It is dominated by the **Castell de Montjuïc** (Map pp1072–3), a onetime fortress. Buses 50,

55 and 61 all head up here. A local bus, the PM (Parc de Montjuïc) line, does a circle trip from Plaça d'Espanya to the *castell*. Cable cars and a funicular line also access the area.

Several city museums and attractions are here:

CaixaForum (Map pp1072-3; ☎ 93 476 86 00; www.fundacio.lacaixa.es in Spanish; Avinguda del Marquès de Comillas 6-8; admission free; 🕒 10am-8pm Tue-Fri & Sun, 10am-10pm Sat; M Espanya) Housed in a remarkable former *modernista* factory designed by Puig i Cadafalch; puts on major art exhibitions.

Fundació Joan Miró (Map pp1072-3; ☎ 93 443 94 70; www.bcn.fjmiro.es; Plaça de Neptu; admission €8; 🕒 10am-8pm Tue-Wed, Fri & Sat, 10am-9.30pm Thu, 10am-2.30pm Sun & holidays Jul-Sep) The definitive museum showcasing Joan Miró's works.

Museu Nacional d'Art de Catalunya (Map pp1072-3; ☎ 93 622 03 76; www.mnac.es; Mirador del Palau Nacional; adult/student €8.50/6; 🕒 10am-7pm Tue-Sat, 10am-2.30pm Sun & holidays) A broad panoply of Catalan and European art.

Poble Espanyol (Map pp1072-3; ☎ 93 508 63 30; www.poble-espanyol.com; Avinguda del Marquès de Comillas; adult/student €8/6; 🕒 9am-8pm Mon, 9am-2am Tue-Thu, 9am-4am Fri & Sat, 9am-midnight Sun) A showcase of typical Spanish architecture, with shops, restaurants and nightlife.

Festivals & Events

The **Festes de la Mercè** (www.bcn.cat/merce), around 24 September, are the city's biggest party, with four days of concerts, dancing, *castellers* (human castle-builders), fireworks and *correfocs* – a parade of firework-spitting dragons and devils. The evening before the **Dia de Sant Joan** (24 June) is a colourful midsummer celebration with bonfires and fireworks.

Sleeping

For cheaper accommodation close to the action, check out Barri Gòtic and El Raval.

CAMPING

Around the beachy town of Castelldefels, southwest of Barcelona, the C-31 highway is lined with camping grounds. **Tres Estrellas** (off Map pp1072-3; ☎ 93 633 06 37; www.camping3estrellas.com; Carretera C31, Km186.2, Viladecans; 2-person sites with car €33; 🕒 mid-Mar–mid-Oct; P 💻 🏊) is a good option. Catch bus L95 from Barcelona's Plaça de Catalunya or Plaça Espanya to get there.

LA RAMBLA & BARRI GÒTIC

The Ciutat Vella (Old City) is packed with budget *hostales* and *pensiones*.

Alberg Hostel Itaca (Map p1074; ☎ 93 301 97 51; www.jo-oh.com/itaca; Carrer de Ripoll 21; dm €18, d €50-55; M Jaume I; 💻) A bright option near La Catedral, Itaca has spacious dorms with parquet floors, pleasant spring colours and a couple of doubles with private bathroom.

Hostal Campi (Map p1074; ☎ 93 301 35 45; hcampi@terra.es; Carrer de la Canuda 4; s/d with shared bathroom €31/54, d with private bathroom €62; M Catalunya) An excellent bottom-end deal. The best rooms are the doubles with their own loo and shower.

Hotel Jardí (Map p1074; ☎ 93 301 59 00; www.hoteljardi-barcelona.com; Plaça de Sant Josep Oriol 1; d €79-106; M Liceu; ❄) The best rooms in this attractively located spot are the doubles with a balcony over one of the prettiest squares in the city.

LA RIBERA & WATERFRONT

Hostel Sea Point (Map pp1072-3; ☎ 93 231 20 45; www.seapointhostel.com; Plaça del Mar 1-4; dm €21.50; M Barceloneta; 💻) What this youth hostel lacks in charm it makes up for with position. Set in an ugly high-rise and with rather tight dorms, it is right on the beach.

Pensió 2000 (Map p1074; ☎ 93 310 74 66; www.pensio2000.com; Carrer de Sant Pere més Alt 6; s/d with shared bathroom €54/67, with private bathroom €66/86; M Urquinaona; 💻) This cheerful *pensión*, with its seven canary-yellow rooms, is conveniently located opposite the Palau de la Música Catalana (p1071).

our pick **Hotel Banys Orientals** (Map p1074; ☎ 93 268 84 60; www.hotelbanysorientals.com; Carrer de l'Argenteria 37; s/d €89/107; M Jaume I; ❄ 💻) Cool blues and aquamarines combine with dark-hued parquet floors to lend this boutique beauty an understated charm.

EL RAVAL

Hostal Gat Raval (Map p1074; ☎ 93 481 66 70; www.gataccommodation.com; Carrer de Joaquín Costa 44; s/d with shared bathroom €50/70, d with private bathroom €80; M Universitat; ❄ 💻) They've opted for a pea-green and lemon-lime colour scheme in this hip young 2nd-floor *hostal*, deep in El Raval. Rooms are pleasant and secure.

Hotel Aneto (Map p1074; ☎ 93 301 99 89; www.hotelaneto.com; Carrer del Carme 38; s/d €55/75; M Liceu; ❄) In one of the nicer parts of El Raval, the Aneto is a good-value, simple midrange base.

L'EIXAMPLE

Centric Point (Map pp1072-3; ☎ 93 215 65 38; www.centricpointhostel.com; Passeig de Gràcia 33; dm €21-27, d €50;

(M) Passeig de Gràcia;) Stay on Barcelona's snootiest boulevard without paying the commensurate rent! This hostel offers 400 beds in a *modernista* building.

Hostal Girona (Map pp1072-3; ☎ 93 265 02 59; www.hostalgirona.com; Carrer de Girona 24; r up to €66; (M) Arc de Triomf) A 2nd-floor, family-run *hostal*, the Girona is a basic but clean and friendly spot.

Hostal Goya (Map p1074; ☎ 93 302 25 65; www.hostalgoya.com; Carrer de Pau Claris 74; s €70, d €96-113; (M) Urquinaona;) The Goya is a gem of a place on the chichi side of l'Eixample and a short stroll from Plaça de Catalunya. Rooms have parquet floors and a light colour scheme.

Eating

Barcelona is foodie heaven. Although the city has a reputation for being the hot spot for 'new Spanish cuisine', dishes like shellfish paella, pigs' trotters, rabbit with snails and *butifarra* (a tasty local sausage) and other traditional dishes are still the backbone of many eateries.

LA RAMBLA & BARRI GÒTIC

Skip the over-priced traps along La Rambla and get into the winding lanes of the Barri Gòtic. Self-caterers should explore the Mercat de la Boqueria (p1070).

Bagel Shop (Map p1074; ☎ 93 302 41 61; Carrer de la Canuda 25; meals €10; 9.30am-9.30pm Mon-Sat, 11am-4pm Sun; (M) Liceu;) Top your bagel with anything from turkey and cheese to Mallorcan *sobrassada* (soft, tangy sausage) or *butifarra* at this informal cafe.

Bar Celta (Map p1074; ☎ 93 315 00 06; Carrer de la Mercè 16; meals €20; noon-midnight; (M) Drassanes) Bar Celta specialises in *pulpo* (octopus) and other seaside delights from Galicia. The waiters waste no time in serving up bottles of crisp white Ribeiro wine to wash down the *raciones* (large tapas serving).

LA RIBERA & WATERFRONT

La Barceloneta is the place to go for seafood; Passeig Joan de Borbó is lined with eateries but locals head for the back lanes.

Orígen 99.9% (Map p1074; ☎ 93 310 75 31; www.origen99.com; Carrer de la Vidrieria 6-8; meals €15-20; 12.30pm-1am; (M) Jaume I;) A shop-restaurant combo, Origins boasts that 99.9% of everything it sells is from Catalonia. The ever-changing daily *menú* features local specialities such as *escalivada* (roasted veggies on bread) and Catalan sausages.

> **SPLURGE**
>
> **Casa Leopoldo** (Map p1074; ☎ 93 441 30 14; www.casaleopoldo.com; Carrer de Sant Rafael 24; meals €50; lunch & dinner Tue-Sat, lunch Sun, Sep-Jul; (M) Liceu;) Several rambling dining areas with magnificent tiled walls and exposed timber-beam ceilings, make this a fine option. The seafood menu is extensive and the local wine list strong.

Can Maño (Map pp1072-3; ☎ 93 319 30 82; Carrer del Baluard 12; meals €15-20; Mon-Sat; (M) Barceloneta) You'll need to be prepared to wait, before being squeezed in at a packed table for a raucous night of *raciones* (posted on a board at the back) over a bottle of *turbio* – a cloudy white and pleasing plonk.

EL RAVAL

Organic (Map p1074; ☎ 93 301 09 02; www.antoniaorganickitchen.com; Carrer de la Junta de Comerç 11; meals €14-20; noon-midnight; (M) Liceu;) A long sprawl of a vegetarian diner, Organic is always full. Choose from a limited range of options that change from day to day, and tuck into the all-you-can-eat salad bar in the middle of the restaurant.

our pick Bar Pinotxo (Map p1074; ☎ 93 317 17 31; Mercat de la Boqueria; meals €15-20; 6am-5pm Mon-Sat Sep-Jul; (M) Liceu) Of the half-dozen or so tapas bars and informal eateries scattered about the market, this one near the Rambla entrance is the most popular. Dig into tapas and *raciones* of hearty market food.

L'EIXAMPLE

La Rita (Map pp1072-3; ☎ 93 487 23 76; Carrer d'Aragó 279; mains €6-10, menú €7.90; (M) Passeig de Gràcia) For a bit of style, this popular restaurant does the trick. Be prepared to wait in line for samples of its pastas, seafood and traditional dishes.

Cervesería Catalana (Map pp1072-3; ☎ 93 216 03 68; Carrer de Mallorca 236; mains €6-15; (M) Passieg de Gràcia) Arrive early to try the delicious tapas and *flautas* (long skinny sandwiches) at this classic tavern off Rambla de Catalunya.

Amaltea (Map pp1072-3; ☎ 93 454 86 13; www.restaurantamaltea.com; Carrer de la Diputació 164; meals €10-15; lunch Mon-Thu, Fri & Sat; (M) Urgell;) The weekday set lunch (€10) offers a series of dishes that change frequently with the seasons. Savour the *empanadillas* (pastry pockets stuffed with spinach or hiziki algae and tofu).

Drinking

You won't go thirsty in Barcelona. The city abounds with day-time cafes, laid-back lounges and lively night-time bars. Closing time is generally 2am Sunday to Thursday and 3am on Friday and Saturday.

BARRI GÒTIC

Club Soul (Map p1074; Carrer Nou de Sant Francesc 7; Ⓜ Drassanes) Club Soul is one of the hippest club-style hang-outs in this part of town. Each night the DJs change the musical theme, which could range from deep funk to deeper house.

La Clandestina (Map p1074; Baixada de Viladecols 2bis; 10am-10pm Sun-Thu, 9am-midnight Fri & Sat; Ⓜ Jaume I) Opt for tea, a beer or a Middle Eastern narghile (the most elaborate way to smoke). You can even get a head massage or eat cake in this chilled tea shop.

EL RAVAL

Casa Almirall (Map p1074; Carrer de Joaquín Costa 33; Ⓜ Universitat) In business since the 1860s, this corner drinkery is dark and intriguing, with *modernista* decor and a mixed clientele.

London Bar (Map p1074; ☎ 93 318 52 61; Carrer Nou de la Rambla 34; Ⓜ Drassanes) A popular hang-out and open since 1909, London Bar has *modernista* touches and the occasional music act way out back.

LA RIBERA

La Fianna (Map p1074; Carrer dels Banys Vells 15; Ⓜ Jaume I) There is something medieval-Oriental about this bar, with its bare stone walls, forged iron candelabras and cushion-covered lounges. As the night wears on, it's elbow room only.

L'EIXAMPLE & GRÀCIA

Les Gens Que J'Aime (Map pp1072-3; Carrer de València 286; Ⓜ Passeig de Gràcia) This intimate relic of the 1960s offers jazz music in the background and a cosy scattering of velvet-backed lounges around tiny dark tables.

Michael Collins Pub (Map pp1072-3; Plaça de la Sagrada Família 4; Ⓜ Sagrada Família) To be sure of a little Catalan-Irish craic, this barn-sized, storming pub is just the ticket.

Sabor a Cuba (Map pp1072-3; Carrer de Francisco Giner 32; Ⓜ Diagonal) A mixed crowd of Cubans and fans of the Caribbean island come to drink *mojitos* and shake their stuff in this home of *ron y son* (rum and sound).

Clubbing

Barcelona clubs are spread a little more thinly than bars across the city. They tend to open from around midnight until 6am. Entry can cost from nothing to €20 (one drink usually included).

Sala Apolo (Map pp1072-3; www.sala-apolo.com; Carrer Nou de la Rambla 113; Ⓜ Parallel) In this old theatre, the Nitsaclub team provides house, techno and break-beat sounds from Thursday to Sunday nights. Earlier in the evening, concerts generally take place.

Moog (Map pp1072-3; www.masimas.com/moog; Carrer de l'Arc del Teatre 3; Ⓜ Liceu) This fun, minuscule club is a downtown hit. In the main downstairs dance area, DJs dish out house, techno and electro, while upstairs you can groove to indie and occasional classic pop.

Otto Zutz (Map pp1072-3; www.ottozutz.es; Carrer de Lincoln 15; Ⓜ Fontana) Beautiful people only need apply for entry into this three-floor dance den. Head downstairs for house or upstairs for funk and soul.

Entertainment

GAY & LESBIAN VENUES

Barcelona's gay and lesbian scene is concentrated in the blocks around Carrers de Muntaner and Consell de Cent (dubbed Gayxample). Here you'll find ambience every night of the week in the bars, discos and drag clubs.

Party hard at classic gay discos such as **Arena Madre** (Map p1074; www.arenadisco.com; Carrer de Balmes 32; Ⓜ Universitat) and **Dboy** (Map p1074; www.dboyclub.com; Ronda de Sant Pere 19-21; Fri-Sun; Ⓜ Urquinaona).

LIVE MUSIC

Harlem Jazz Club (Map p1074; ☎ 93 310 07 55; Carrer Comtessa de Sobradiel 8; Ⓜ Liceu) Here you'll find a guaranteed dose of quality jazz and enough smoke to cook a sausage.

Tablao Cordobés (Map p1074; ☎ 93 317 57 11; www.tablaocordobes.com; La Rambla 35; show only €35, with dinner €68; Ⓜ Liceu) Although Barcelona is not the best place to see flamenco, you can catch a reasonable show here.

CINEMAS

A popular cinema for subtitled foreign films is **Verdi** (Map pp1072-3; ☎ 93 238 79 90; www.cines-verdi.com; Carrer Verdi 32; Ⓜ Fontana). There are plenty of places to kick on after the film here.

SPORT

Football fans can see FC Barcelona play at **Camp Nou** (Map pp1072-3; ☎ 902 18 99 00, from abroad +34 93 496 36 00; www.fcbarcelona.com; Carrer Arístides Maillol; Ⓜ Collblanc). Even if you can't score tickets, stop by for a peek at the **museum** (admission €8.50; ⏰ 10am-8pm Mon-Sat, 10am-2.30pm Sun & holidays mid-Apr–mid-Oct, 10am-6.30pm Mon-Sat, 10am-2.30pm Sun & holidays mid-Oct–mid-Apr).

THEATRE

Most theatre in the city is in Catalan. There are quite a few venues that stage vanguard drama and dance, including the **Teatre Nacional de Catalunya** (Map pp1072-3; ☎ 93 306 57 00; www.tnc.es; Plaça de les Arts 1; Ⓜ Glòries).

Shopping

Most mainstream fashion stores are along a shopping 'axis' that runs from Plaça de Catalunya along Passeig de Gràcia, then left (west) along Avinguda Diagonal.

The El Born area in La Ribera is awash with tiny boutiques, especially those purveying young, fun fashion. There are plenty of shops scattered throughout the Barri Gòtic (stroll Carrer d'Avinyò and Carrer de Portaferrissa). For secondhand stuff, head for El Raval, especially Carrer de la Riera Baixa.

Bargain hunters love **Els Encants Vells** (Map pp1072-3; ☎ 93 246 30 30; Carrer Dos de Maig 186; ⏰ 8.30am-6pm Mon, Wed, Fri & Sat; Ⓜ Glòries), a free-for-all flea market.

Getting There & Away

AIR

Barcelona's airport, El Prat de Llobregat (BCN; off Map pp1072–3), is 12km southwest of the city centre and Spain's second airport after Madrid. See p1049 for contact details.

BUS

The main terminal for domestic and international buses is the **Estació del Nord** (Map pp1072-3; ☎ 902 30 32 22; www.barcelonanord.com; Carrer d'Ali Bei 80; Ⓜ Arc de Triomf). Alsa goes to Madrid (€27, eight hours, 16 daily), Valencia (€24.50, 4½ to 6½ hours, 14 daily) and many other destinations.

TRAIN

Virtually all trains travelling to and from destinations within Spain stop at **Estació Sants** (Map pp1072-3; Ⓜ Sants-Estació). High-speed trains to Madrid via Lleida and Zaragoza take as little as two hours 40 minutes (€40 to €163 depending on conditions).

Getting Around

Information about Barcelona's public transport is available online at www.tmb.net and on ☎ 010.

Barcelona's metro system spreads its tentacles around the city in such a way that most places of interest are within a 10-minute walk of a station. Buses and suburban trains are needed only for a few destinations. A single metro, bus or suburban train ride costs €1.30, but a T-1 ticket, valid for 10 rides, costs only €7.20.

GIRONA

pop 92,200

Medieval Girona, built along the banks of the Onyar River, is an easy daytrip from Barcelona or a pleasant base in itself. The old city sits along the river's eastern bank. Get information at the **tourist office** (☎ 972 22 65 75; www.ajuntament.gi/turisme; Rambla de la Llibertat 1).

The **Catedral** (☎ 972 21 44 26; www.lacatedraldegirona.com; admission €4; ⏰ 10am-2pm & 4-7pm Tue-Sat Mar-Jun, 10am-8pm Tue-Sat Jul-Sep, 10am-2pm & 4-6pm Tue-Sat Oct-Feb, 10am-2pm Sun & holidays) boasts Europe's widest Gothic nave (23m), a lovely Romanesque cloister and a blustering baroque facade.

Wander the narrow streets of the nearby **Call** (onetime medieval Jewish Quarter) and visit the **Museu d'Història dels Jueus de Girona** (Jewish History Museum, aka the Centre Bonastruc Ça Porta; ☎ 972 21 67 61; Carrer de la Força 8; adult/student €2/1.50; ⏰ 10am-8pm Mon-Sat Jun-Oct, 10am-6pm Mon-Sat Nov-May, 10am-3pm Sun & holidays). You can also walk along the medieval **walls** (⏰ dawn-dusk) around the edge of the old quarter.

With just five rooms, the family-run **Bed & Breakfast Bells Oficis** (☎ 972 22 81 70; www.bellsoficis.com; Carrer dels Germans Busquets 2; r €35-85; ⊠ ❄ 💻) is perfectly placed just off Rambla de la Llibertat. The rooms are all very different. The two best ones have balconies overlooking the Rambla.

For a quick sandwich or simple hot dishes, **König** (☎ 972 22 57 82; Carrer dels Calderers 16; meals €8-15; ⏰ daily), or 'King', boasts a broad outdoor terrace shaded by thick foliage.

There are more than 20 trains per day to Figueres (€2.60 to €2.90, 30 to 40 minutes), some of which go on to France, and Barcelona (€5.90 to €6.70, 1½ hours).

FIGUERES

Figueres is home to the zany **Teatre-Museu Dalí** (☎ 972 67 75 00; www.salvador-dali.org; Plaça de Gala i Salvador Dalí 5; adult/student €11/8, entry includes Dalí Joies;

9am-8pm Jul-Sep, 10.30am-6pm Tue-Sun Oct-Jun), housed in a 19th-century theatre converted by Salvador Dalí (who was born here). It has a fascinating collection of his strange creations and is the site of his crypt.

TARRAGONA

pop 134,200

Barcelona's senior in Roman times and a lesser medieval city, Tarragona has some outstanding attractions: Catalonia's finest Roman ruins, a magnificent medieval cathedral in a pretty old town and some decent beaches.

Seek information at the **tourist office** (977 25 07 95; www.tarragonaturisme.cat; Carrer Major 39; 9am-9pm Mon-Sat, 10am-3pm Sun Jul-Sep, 10am-2pm & 4-7pm Mon-Sat Oct-Sun, 10am-2pm Sun & holidays year round).

Sights & Activities

Start at the **Museu Arqueològic** (977 23 62 09; www.mnat.es; Plaça del Rei 5; adult/student €2.40/1.20; 9.30am-8.30pm Tue-Sat, 10am-2pm Sun & holidays Jun-Sep, 9.30am-1.30pm & 3.30-7pm Tue-Sat, 10am-2pm Sun & holidays Oct-May), where you'll gain an understanding of Roman Spain.

Four major Roman sites around town, plus a 14th-century mansion, make up the **Museu d'Historia de Tarragona** (www.museutgn.com; adult/concession per site €2.45/1.25, ticket to all MHT elements €9.25/4.60; 9am-9pm Mon-Sat, 9am-3pm Sun Easter-Sep, 9am-7pm Mon-Sat, 10am-3pm Sun & holidays Oct-Easter). The **Pretori i Circ Romans** (Pretorium & Roman Circus; 977 23 01 71; Plaça del Rei) includes part of the vaults of the Roman circus, where chariot races were held. Near the beach is the well-preserved **Amfiteatre Romà** (Roman Amphitheatre; 977 24 25 79; Plaça d'Arce Ochotorena), where gladiators battled each other, or wild animals, to the death. Southeast of Carrer de Lleida are remains of the **Fòrum Romà** (Roman Forum; 977 24 25 01; Carrer del Cardenal Cervantes), dominated by several imposing columns. The **Passeig Arqueològic** is a peaceful walk around part of the perimeter of the old town.

The **Catedral** (977 23 86 85; Pla de la Seu; admission €3.50; 10am-1pm & 4-7pm Mon-Sat mid-Mar–May, 10am-7pm Mon-Sat Jun–mid-Oct, 10am-5pm Mon-Sat mid-Oct–mid-Nov, 10am-2pm Mon-Sat mid-Nov–mid-Mar) sits at the highest point of Tarragona. Some parts of the building date back to the 12th century.

The town beach, **Platja del Miracle**, is reasonably clean but can get terribly crowded. **Platja Arrabassada**, 1km northeast across the headland, is longer, and **Platja Llarga**, beginning 2km further out, stretches for about 3km.

Sleeping & Eating

Look for tapas bars and inexpensive cafes on the Plaça de la Font. The Moll de Pescadors (Fishermens' Wharf) is the place to go for seafood restaurants.

Hostal La Noria (977 23 87 17; Plaça de la Font 53; s/d €30/48) For a bargain basement position right on the old town's main square, you can't do much better than these corner digs.

Quim Quima (977 25 21 21; Carrer de les Coques 1bis; meals €35, menú del día €14.90; lunch Tue-Thu, Fri & Sat) This renovated medieval mansion makes a marvellous setting for a meal. Huddle up to a bare stone wall or opt for the shady little courtyard.

Getting There & Away

At least 38 regional and long-distance trains per day run to/from Barcelona's Passeig de Gràcia via Sants. The cheapest fares (for Regional and Catalunya Express trains) cost €5.15 to €5.80 and the journey takes one to 1½ hours. Faster trains cost more. High-speed Avant-class trains to Lleida and AVE trains on the Barcelona–Madrid line call at the new Camp de Tarragona station (about 20 minutes out of town by shuttle bus from the bus station).

The **bus station** (Avinguda Roma), just off Plaça Imperial Tarraco, has plenty of regional services.

BALEARIC ISLANDS

pop 1.07 million

The Balearic Islands (Illes Balears in Catalan) adorn the glittering Mediterranean waters off Spain's eastern coastline. Although they're beach tourism destinations *par excellence*, there's much more on offer than the mix of sun, sea and sangria – you'll also find simple fishing and farming villages, Gothic cathedrals and Stone Age ruins.

Check out websites such as www.illesbalears.es, www.baleares.com, http://abc-mallorca.com and www.newsmallorca.com.

GETTING THERE & AWAY

Air

If your main goal in Spain is to visit the Balearic Islands, there are plenty of direct flights from European cities to Mallorca and, to a lesser extent, Ibiza and Menorca.

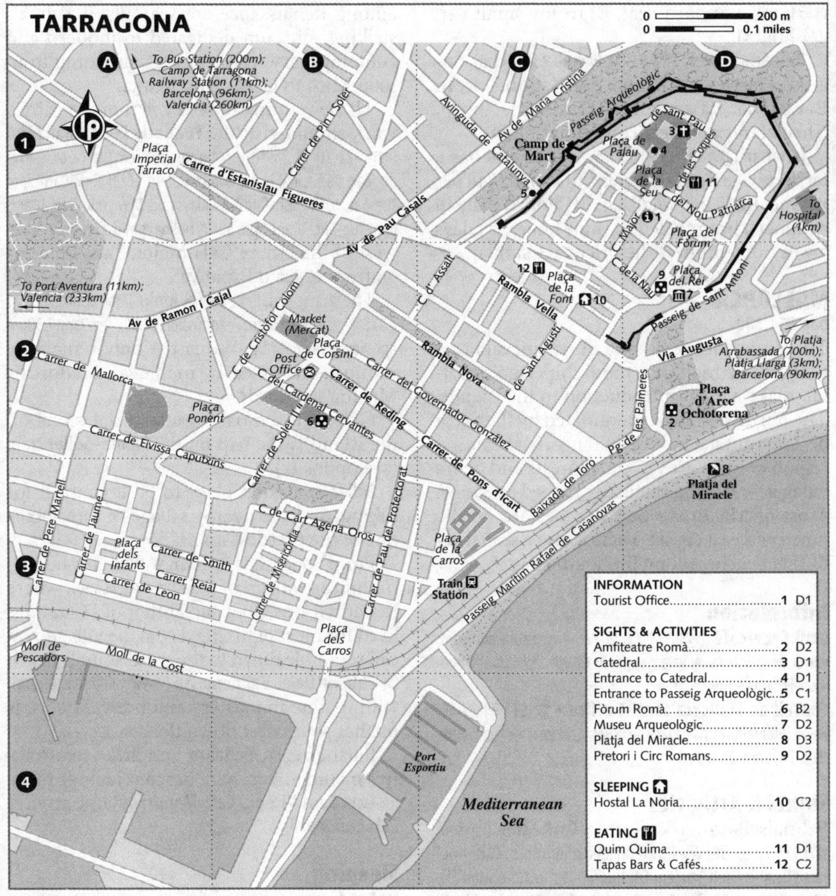

If already in Spain, scheduled flights from major cities are operated by Iberia, Air Europa, clickair, Spanair and Vueling.

Inter-island flights are expensive, with a trip from Palma de Mallorca to Ibiza or Maó (Menorca) easily costing up to €140.

Boat

The main ferry company, **Acciona Trasmediterránea** (www.trasmediterranea.es), runs services between Barcelona and Valencia on the mainland, and Ibiza City, Maó and Palma de Mallorca. Tickets can be purchased from any travel agency or online. Timetables and fares vary constantly.

From Barcelona, two daily services run to Palma de Mallorca from about Easter to late October. A high-speed catamaran leaves at 4pm (€90 for standard seat, €180 for small car; four hours), while an overnight ferry leaves at 11pm (€47 for standard seat, €154 for small car; 7¼ hours). All continue to Ibiza.

From Valencia, a high-speed catamaran leaves for Palma (six hours) via Ibiza (3½ hours) at 4pm and a direct overnight ferry at 11pm (7½ hours). The fast ferry operates Thursday to Tuesday and the overnight Monday to Saturday. Prices are similar to those from Barcelona.

Acciona Trasmediterránea runs two fast ferries or catamarans a day between Palma and Ibiza City (generally leaving Ibiza at 7am and 7.45pm, and Palma at 7.30am and 8.45pm) from Easter to the end of October

(€61 for standard seat, €116 for small car; 2¼ hours).

Baleària (☎ 902 16 01 80; www.balearia.com) operates ferries to Palma de Mallorca from Barcelona, Valencia and Denia (via Ibiza). Check fares and departure times online.

Iscomar (☎ 902 11 91 28; www.iscomar.com) has a ferry service from Barcelona to Palma (€48 per person, €140 per small car; 7½ hours, daily in summer). From Valencia (nine hours, six days a week in summer) the prices are similar.

MALLORCA

pop 814,300

The sunny, ochre hues of the medieval heart of Palma de Mallorca, the archipelago's capital, make a great introduction to the islands. The northwest coast, dominated by the Serra de Tramuntana mountain range, is a beautiful region of olive groves, pine forests and ochre villages, with a spectacularly rugged coastline. Most of Mallorca's best beaches are on the north and east coasts. There is also a scattering of fine beaches along the south coast.

Information

Azul Cybercafé (☎ 971 71 29 27; www.azulgroup.com; Carrer de la Soledat 4; internet per hr €2.90; 🕒 8.30am-8pm Mon-Fri, noon-6pm Sat)

Consell de Mallorca tourist office (☎ 971 71 22 16; www.infomallorca.net; Plaça de la Reina, Palma; 🕒 9am-8pm Mon-Fri, 9am-2pm Sat)

Sights & Activities

Palma's landmark Gothic **Cathedral** (La Seu; ☎ 971 72 31 30; www.catedraldemallorca.org; Carrer del Palau Reial 9; adult/student €4/3; 🕒 10am-6.30pm Mon-Fri, 10am-2.30pm Sat Jun-Sep, 10am-5.30pm Mon-Fri, 10am-2.30pm Sat Apr-May & Oct, 10am-2.30pm Mon-Fri, 10am-2.30pm Sat Nov-Mar) is home to some interesting *modernista* touches by Antoni Gaudí and the spectacular modern remake of the Capella del Santíssim i Sant Pere chapel by local artist Miquel Barceló.

Opposite the cathedral is the **Palau de l'Almudaina** (☎ 971 21 41 34; www.patrimonionacional.es; Carrer del Palau Reial s/n; adult/student €3.20/2.30; 🕒 10am-6pm Mon-Fri, 10am-2pm Sat Apr-Sep, 10am-2pm & 4-6pm Mon-Fri, 10am-2pm Sat Oct-Mar), a onetime Muslim fort turned into the residence of the Mallorcan monarchs.

Es Baluard (Museu d'Art Modern i Contemporani; ☎ 971 90 82 00; www.esbaluard.org; Porta de Santa Catalina 10; adult/student €6/4.50, temporary exhibitions €4/3; 🕒 10am-10pm Tue-Sun mid-Jun–Sep, 10am-8pm Tue-Sun Oct–mid-Jun), set among Renaissance-era seawalls, is Palma's striking museum dedicated to modern and contemporary works of art – anything from Joan Miró to Oskar Kokoschka.

Those wanting to see even more of Miró's work should visit the **Fundació Pilar i Joan Miró** (☎ 971 70 14 20; http://miro.palmademallorca.es; Carrer de Joan de Saridakis 29; adult/student €6/3; 🕒 10am-7pm Tue-Sat, 10am-3pm Sun & holidays mid-May–mid-Sep, 10am-6pm Tue-Sat, 10am-3pm Sun & holidays mid-Sep–mid-May), west of the city in Cala Major. Take bus 3 or 46 from Plaça d'Espanya.

The atmospheric **Banys Árabs** (Arab Baths; ☎ 971 72 15 49; Carrer de Serra 7; admission €1.50; 🕒 9am-7.30pm Apr-Nov, 9am-6pm Dec-Mar) is the only remaining monument to early medieval Mallorca's Muslim overlords.

One of the most popular excursions on the island is the trip on the **Palma–Sóller train** (see opposite).

Sóller is a good place to base yourself for hiking, and the nearby village of **Fornalutx** is one of the prettiest on Mallorca.

From Sóller, it is a 10km walk to the beautiful hilltop village of **Deià** (www.deia.info), where Robert Graves, poet and author of *I Claudius*, lived for most of his life. From the village, you can scramble down to the small shingle beach of **Cala de Deià**. **Valldemossa** (www.valldemossa.com), with its fine monastery and pretty streets, is further southwest down the coast.

Further east, **Pollença** and **Artà** are attractive inland towns. Nice beaches include those at **Cala Sant Vicenç**, **Cala Mondragó** and around **Cala Llombards**.

Sleeping

PALMA

Hostal Pons (☎ 971 72 26 58; Carrer del Vi 8; s/d with shared bathroom €25/45) This *hostal* seems unchanged since the 1880s. The downstairs chambers are cluttered with antiques and artworks, and the quaint bedrooms all have timber bedsteads.

Hostal Corona (☎ 971 73 19 35; www.hostal-corona.com; Carrer de Josep Villalonga 22; s €30, d €45-55) With its palm trees and plants, the hotel's courtyard has a far-away feel. The rooms are simple, with timber furnishings and old tiled floors. In the evening, the courtyard turns into a chilled-out bar (open 6pm to 1am Tuesday to Sunday). The nearest bus stop is at Avinguda de Joan Miró 24 (take buses 3 or 46 from Plaça d'Espanya).

Hostal Brondo (☎ 971 71 90 43; www.hostalbrondo.net; Carrer de Ca'n Brondo 1; s/d with shared bathroom

€40/55, d with private bathroom €70) Climb the courtyard stairs to arrive in a homey sitting room overlooking the narrow lane. High-ceilinged rooms (No 3 with a glassed-in gallery) furnished in varying styles (from Mallorcan to vaguely Moroccan) are atmospheric.

AROUND THE ISLAND

The **Consell de Mallorca tourist office** (☎ 971 71 22 16; www.infomallorca.net; Plaça de la Reina, Palma; 🕑 9am-8pm Mon-Fri, 9am-2pm Sat) can supply information on rural and other accommodation around the island.

Hostal Miramar (☎ 971 63 90 84; www.pensionmiramar.com; Carrer de Can Oliver s/n, Deià; d €84) Hidden up in what could almost be described as the jungle above the main road, this 19th-century stone house with gardens is a shady retreat.

Eating & Drinking

PALMA

If you're putting together a picnic, go to the **Mercat de l'Olivar** (Plaça del Olivar; 🕑 7am-2pm Mon-Sat), Palma's central produce market.

Sa Pastanaga (☎ 971 72 41 94; Carrer de Sant Elies 6b; meals €12.20; 🕑 lunch Mon-Fri; ⊠) Locals queue for vegetarian set lunches. Yellow walls and exposed beams lend an intimate feel to the place.

Bar España (☎ 971 72 42 34; Carrer de Ca'n Escurrac 12; meals €15-20; 🕑 6pm-midnight Mon, 10am-midnight Tue-Sat) Pick your *pintxos* (Basque Country tapas) at the bar (where you can't smoke) and sample with house wine. Or take them to a table (smoker-friendly).

The old quarter is the city's most vibrant nightlife zone – particularly along the narrow streets between Plaça de la Reina and Plaça de la Drassana. Look around the Santa Catalina (especially Carrer de Sant Magí) and Es Molinar districts. Palma's clubs are largely concentrated west of the city centre along Passeig Marítim, Avinguda de Joan Miró and Plaça de Gomila.

Getting Around

Sant Joan airport (PMI) is 10km east of Palma. Bus 1 runs every 15 minutes between Sant Joan airport and Plaça d'Espanya in central Palma (€1.85, 15 minutes) and on to the ferry terminal.

Most of the island is accessible by bus from Palma. All buses depart from (or near) the **bus station** (Estació d'Autobusos; Carrer d'Eusebi Estada). For information, contact **Transport de les Illes Balears** (TIB; ☎ 971 17 77 77; http://tib.caib.es).

The popular train to **Sóller** (☎ 971 75 20 51, 902 36 47 11; http//:trendesoller.com; one way/return €9/14) is a pretty ride.

IBIZA

pop 117,700

Ibiza (Eivissa in Catalan) is an island of extremes. Its formidable party reputation is completely justified, with some of the world's greatest clubs attracting hedonists from the world over. The interior and northeast of the island, however, are another world, with peaceful country drives, hilly green territory and laid-back beaches.

The **tourist office** (☎ 971 30 19 00; www.ibiza.travel; Passeig de Vara de Rei 1; 🕑 9am-8pm Mon-Fri, 9am-7pm Sat, 9am-3pm Sun) is in central Ibiza City. Check email at **Surf@Net** (☎ 971 19 49 20; Carrer de Riambau 8; per hr €2.40; 🕑 11am-11pm Mon-Fri, 3-11pm Sat).

Sights & Activities

Ibiza City's port area of **Sa Penya** is crammed with funky and trashy clothing boutiques and arty-crafty market stalls. From here, you can wander up into **D'Alt Vila**, the atmospheric old walled town. You can walk along the length of the walls – a stiff climb in parts but great for views. Along the perimeter walk is the **Museu d'Art Contemporani** (☎ 971 30 27 23; Ronda de Narcís Puget s/n; admission free; 🕑 10am-1.30pm & 5-8pm Tue-Fri, 10am-1.30pm Sat & Sun May-Sep, 10am-1.30pm & 4-6pm Tue-Fri, 10am-1.30pm Sat & Sun Oct-Apr). High up in the town is the 14th-century **cathedral** and adjoining **Museu Arqueològic** (☎ 971 30 17 71; Plaça de la Catedral 3; adult/student €2.40/1.20; 🕑 9am-3pm Tue-Sat, 10am-2pm Sun Oct-Mar, 10am-2pm & 6-8pm Tue-Sat, 10am-2pm Sun Apr-Sep).

The heavily developed **Platja de ses Figueretes** beach is a 20-minute walk southwest of Sa Penya, but you're better off heading south to the beaches at **Ses Salines**, a half-hour ride on bus 11 (€1.50).

Ibiza has numerous unspoiled and relatively undeveloped beaches. **Cala de Boix**, on the northeastern coast, is the only black-sand beach on the island, while further north are the lovely beaches of **S'Aigua Blanca**. Some of the country and inland villages of this corner of the island are worth exploring.

On the north coast near Portinatx, **Cala Xarraca** is in a secluded bay, and near Port de Sant Miquel is the attractive **Cala Benirrás**.

In the southwest, **Cala d'Hort** has a spectacular setting overlooking two rugged rock islets.

 Book your stay at lonelyplanet.com/hotels

LETTING LOOSE IN THE MEGACLUBS

In summer (late May to the end of September) the west of the island is a continuous party from sunset to sunrise and back again. In 2007, the International Dance Music Awards named three Ibiza clubs (Amnesia, Pacha and Space) among the top five in the world.

The clubs operate nightly from around 1am to 6am and each has something different. Theme nights, fancy-dress parties and foam parties (where you are half-drowned in the stuff) are regular features. Admission can cost anything from €25 to €60.

The best include: **Amnesia** (☎ 971 19 80 41; www.amnesia.es; 4km north of Ibiza on road to Sant Rafel; nightly early Jun-Sep); **Es Paradis** (☎ 971 34 66 00; www.esparadis.com; Carrer de Salvador Espriu 2, Sant Antoni de Portmany; nightly mid-May–Sep); **Pacha** (www.pacha.com; north side of Ibiza port; nightly Jun-Sep, Fri & Sat Oct-May); **Privilege** (☎ 971 19 81 60; www.privilegeibiza.com; 5km north of Ibiza on road to Sant Rafel); and **Space** (☎ 971 39 67 93; www.space-ibiza.es; Platja d'en Bossa; 4.30pm-6am Jun–mid-Oct).

A good website is **Ibiza Spotlight** (www.ibiza-spotlight.com).

The best thing about rowdy **Sant Antoni**, the island's second biggest town, is heading to the small rock-and-sand strip on the north shore to join hundreds of others for sunset drinks at a string of chilled bars.

our pick Café del Mar (☎ 971 34 25 16; www.cafedelmar.es; 5pm-4am) remains the best-known, but further north, along the pedestrian walkway, places such as **Coastline Café**, **Sun Beach Bar** and **Kanya** all have pools and attract plenty of punters. After the sun goes down all turn up the rhythmic heat and pound on until 4am, from about June to October.

Local **buses** (www.ibizabus.com) run to most destinations between May and October.

Sleeping

Camping Cala Nova (☎ 971 33 17 74; www.campingcalanova.com; sites per 2 people, tent & car €26.15) Close to a good beach and 12km northeast of Ibiza City, this is one of Ibiza's best camping grounds.

Casa de Huéspedes Navarro (☎ 971 31 07 71; Carrer de sa Creu 20; s/d €30/55) Right in the thick of things, this simple place has 10 rooms at the top of a flight of stairs. The front rooms have harbour views, the interior ones are quite dark (but cool in summer) and there's a sunny rooftop terrace.

Hostal La Marina (☎ 971 31 01 72; www.hostal-lamarina.com; Carrer de Barcelona 7; s €68, d €85-175;) Looking onto the waterfront and bar-lined Carrer de Barcelona, this mid-19th-century building has all sorts of brightly coloured rooms in different shapes and prices.

Hostal-Residencia Parque (☎ 971 30 13 58; www.hostalparque.com; Carrer de Vicent Cuervo 3; s with shared bathroom €60, d with private bathroom €110-170) The best doubles overlook pleasant Plaça del Parc from above the eponymous cafe. Doubles are comfortable but singles are predictably pokey.

Eating & Drinking

Croissant Show (☎ 971 31 76 65; Plaça de la Constitució s/n; light breakfast about €6; 6am-11pm) Opposite the food market, this is where *everyone* goes for an impressive range of pastries and other breakfast, post-partying goodies. It is quite a scene all on its own.

our pick Comidas Bar San Juan (☎ 971 31 16 03; Carrer de Guillem de Montgri 8; meals €15-20; Mon-Sat) A family-run operation with two small dining rooms, this simple eatery offers outstanding value, with fish dishes for around €10 and many small mains for €6 or less.

Ca' n'Alfredo (☎ 971 31 12 74; Passeig de Vara de Rei 16; meals €40-45; lunch & dinner Tue-Sat, lunch Sun) Locals love Alfredo's place for the freshest of seafood and other island cuisine. The food's so good it's essential to book. Try the *filetes de gallo de San Pedro en salsa de almendras* (filets of fine local white fish in almond sauce).

Sa Penya is the nightlife centre. Dozens of bars keep the port area jumping. Alternatively, various bars at Platja d'En Bossa combine sounds, sand, sea and sangria.

Getting Around

Buses between the airport (7km west of Ibiza City) and the central port area of Ibiza City via Platja d'En Bossa operate hourly between 6.30am and 11.30pm (€1.50, 20 to 25 minutes).

Plenty of ferries make the 25- to 35-minute trip between Ibiza City and the neighbouring island of Formentera each day. Tickets cost at least €21.50 each way.

FORMENTERA

pop 8440

For some the 20km-long island of Formentera is a legend. The coast is alternately fringed with jagged cliffs and beaches backed by low dunes. Except when the island is filled to capacity from mid-July to late August, it is a wonderful place to escape to. There is little to do but enjoy the crystal sea, zip around on a scooter, eat and then start all over again.

Formentera's **tourist office** (☎ 971 32 20 57; www.turismoformentera.com; 9am-7pm Mon-Fri, 9am-3pm Sat & Sun May-Sep) is in La Savina.

Hostal Pepe (☎ 971 32 80 33; Carrer Major 68, Sant Ferran de ses Roques; s/d with breakfast €46/60) is located on the pleasant (and on summer nights lively) main street near the village's old sandstone church. This whitewashed place with flashes of blue has 45 simple and breezy rooms with bathroom.

our pick **Fonda Rafalet** (☎ 971 32 70 16; Es Caló; s/d €64/107), overlooking a small rocky harbour in a diminutive fishing hamlet, has spacious rooms (many with sea views), and also incorporates a bar and popular seafood restaurant.

There are plenty of bars in Es Pujols. For a sundowner, try **Blue Bar** (☎ 971 18 70 11; www.bluebarformentera.com; Km8; noon-4am Apr-Oct). It is the south's chill-out bar *par excellence*.

MENORCA

pop 90,200

Renowned for its pristine beaches and archaeological sites, tranquil Menorca was declared a Biosphere Reserve by Unesco in 1993. The capital, Maó, is known as Mahón in Castilian.

Information

Tourist office airport (☎ 971 15 71 15; 8am-10pm daily Jul-Aug, 8am-10pm Mon-Fri, 8am-2pm Sat May-Jun & Sep-Oct); Ciutadella (☎ 971 38 26 93; Plaça de la Catedral 5; 9am-2pm & 4-9pm Mon-Fri, 9am-2pm Sat May-Sep, 9am-1pm & 5-7pm Mon-Fri Oct-Apr)

Sights & Activities

Maó and Ciutadella are both harbour towns, and from either place you'll have to commute to the beaches. **Maó** gets a lot of tourist traffic.

Ciutadella, with its smaller harbour and historic buildings, has a more distinctly Spanish feel to it and is more attractive than Maó. A narrow country road leads south of Ciutadella (follow the 'Platges' sign from the *ronda*, or ring road) and then forks twice to reach some of the island's loveliest beaches: (from west to east) **Arenal de Son Saura**, **Cala en Turqueta**, **Es Talaier**, **Cala Macarelleta** and **Cala Macarella**. As with most beaches, you'll need your own transport.

In the centre of the island, the 357m **Monte Toro** has great views of the whole island; on a clear day you can see as far as Mallorca.

On the northern coast, the picturesque town of **Fornells** is on a large bay popular with windsurfers.

Sleeping

Camping S'Atalaia (☎ 971 37 42 32; www.campingsatalaia.com; sites per 2 people, tent & car €23.20; P) Shaded by pine trees, this pleasant camping ground is two-thirds of the way down the Ferreries–Santa Galdana road.

Posada Orsi (☎ 971 36 47 51; Carrer de la Infanta 19, Maó; s/d with washbasin €30/49, d with private bathroom €60; ☒) Pastel colours are all the go here, and you may pick up the scent of incense. Rooms are equally bright (with lots of pink, hot orange and sky blue) and have mosquito nets (handy).

Hostal-Residencia Oasis (☎ 971 38 21 97; Carrer de Sant Isidre 33, Ciutadella; s/d €40/55) Set around a spacious garden courtyard, this quiet place close to the heart of the old quarter has pleasant rooms.

Eating & Drinking

The ports in both Maó and Ciutadella are lined with bars and restaurants.

MAÓ

Ses Forquilles (☎ 971 35 27 11; Carrer de Rovellada de Dalt 20; meals €30-35; lunch & dinner Thu-Sat, lunch Mon-Wed) This self-proclaimed 'gastronomic space' offers tasty snacks and a handful of dishes ranging from steak tartar to *fideuá de sépia negra* (a noodle and cuttlefish dish).

Akelarre (☎ 971 36 85 20; www.akelarrejazz.es; Moll de Ponent 41-43; 3pm-4am daily Jun-Sep, 7pm-4am Thu-Sat, 7pm-3am Sun-Wed Oct-May) Ambient and jazz dance music dominate the wee hours in this place.

CIUTADELLA

Café Balear (☎ 971 38 00 05; Placa de Sant Joan 15; meals €25-30; Mon-Sat) This long-standing favourite offers attractive outdoor seating and an excellent seafood-dominated menu.

Café des Museu (Carreró d'es Palau 4; 10pm-3.30am) A charming old-town cocktail bar tucked away down a tight lane and occasional host to live gigs – anything from acid jazz to bossanova.

Getting Around

Menorca's airport (MAH) is served by buses to the bus station in Maó (€1.55, 15 minutes) every half-hour from 5.55am to 10.25pm and then (June to September only) hourly to 12.25am.

You can catch **TMSA** (☎ 971 36 04 75; www.tmsa.es) buses from the bus station. In summer (May to October), at least eight go to Ciutadella (€4.40, one hour). Other destinations are served less regularly.

For car hire, try **Autos Valls** (☎ 971 35 42 44; www.autosvalls.com; Plaça d'Espanya 13) or **Autosmenorsur** (☎ 971 36 56 66; Moll de Llevant 35). The latter also have motorbikes.

VALENCIA & MURCIA

A warm climate, interesting cities and an abundance of seaside resorts make this a popular destination. The beaches of the Costa Blanca (White Coast) draw most of the visitors, but venture beyond the shore to get a real feel for the region.

VALENCIA

pop 805,300

Valencia is where paella first simmered over a wood fire. It's a vibrant, friendly, mildly chaotic place with two outstanding fine-arts museums, an accessible old quarter, Europe's newest cultural and scientific complex – and an exciting nightlife scene.

Information

Ono (☎ 96 328 19 02; Calle San Vicente Mártir 22; per hr €3.50; 🕑 10am-10pm) Internet access.

Regional tourist office (☎ 96 398 64 22; Calle Paz 48; 🕑 9am-2.30pm & 4.30-8pm Mon-Fri)

Turismo Valencia (VLC) tourist office (☎ 96 315 39 31; www.turisvalencia.es) Plaza de la Reina (Plaza de la Reina 19; 🕑 9am-7pm Mon-Sat, 10am-2pm Sun); Train Station (🕑 9am-7pm Mon-Sat, 10am-2pm Sun)

Sights & Activities

You'll see Valencia's best face by simply wandering around the **Barrio del Carmen**, strolling the **Jardines del Turia** (in what was once the city's river) or people-watching in one of the city's many plazas.

Valencia's Romanesque-Gothic-baroque-Renaissance **Catedral** (admission with audioguide €4; 🕑 10am-5.30pm/6.30pm Mon-Sat, 2-5.30pm Sun) is a one-off compendium of centuries of architectural history and home to the Capilla del Santo Cáliz, a chapel containing what they say is the Holy Grail.

The stunning **Ciudad de las Artes y las Ciencias** (City of Arts & Sciences; ☎ reservations 902 10 00 31; www.cac.es; Autovía a El Saler; combined ticket for all 3 attractions €30.60) is a complex of museums including the **L'Oceanográfic aquarium** (admission €23.30; 🕑 10am-6pm/8pm Sep–mid-Jul, 10am-midnight mid-Jul–Aug), the **Museo de las Ciencias Príncipe Felipe** (admission €7.50; 🕑 10am-7pm/9pm) interactive science museum, **L'Hemisfèric** (admission €7.50) planetarium and IMAX theatre and L'Umbracle covered garden. Also here is the shimmering, beetle-like **Palau de les Arts Reina Sofía** (☎ 902 20 23 83; www.lesarts.com; Autovía a El Saler) performing arts centre. Bus 35 goes from Plaza del Ayuntamiento.

Stretch your towel on broad **Playa de la Malvarrosa**, which runs into **Playa de las Arenas**, each bordered by the **Paseo Marítimo** promenade and a string of restaurants. One block back, lively bars and discos thump out the beat in summer. Take bus 1, 2 or 19, or the high-speed tram from Pont de Fusta or the Benimaclet Metro junction.

Sleeping & Eating

Hôme Backpackers (☎ 96 391 37 97; www.likeathome.net; Calle Santa Cristina s/n; dm €17.80; 💻) This, the simplest of the Hôme team's three excellent budget hostels, each with self-catering facilities, has 170 beds and a large roof terrace for chilling out or soaking up the sun. The owners also run Hôme Youth Hostel (www.homeyouthhostel.com) and rental flats.

Hostal Antigua Morellana (☎ 96 391 57 73; www.hostalam.com; Calle En Bou 2; s €45-55, d €55-65; ❄) In an elegant renovated 18th-century building, this helpful hotel has cosy, good-sized rooms with satellite TV and balconies.

La Tastaolletes (☎ 96 392 18 62; Calle Salvador Giner 6; tapas €5-9, mains €8-10; 🕑 Tue-Sat & dinner Mon) This tiny place does a creative range of vegetarian tapas using quality prime ingredients.

L'Hamadríada (☎ 96 326 08 91; www.hamadriada.com; Plaza Vicente Iborra 3; midday menú €10; 🕑 lunch daily, dinner Wed-Sat) Down a blind alley, this slim white rectangle of a place does an innovative midday menú, perfectly simmered rice dishes that change daily and great meat grills.

La Utielana (☎ 96 352 94 14; Plaza Picadero dos Aguas 3; meals around €15; 🕑 lunch & dinner Mon-Fri, lunch Sat)

BURN BABY BURN

In mid-March, Valencia hosts one of Europe's wildest street parties: **Las Fallas de San José.** For one week (12–19 March), the city is engulfed by an anarchic swirl of fireworks, music, festive bonfires and all-night partying. On the final night, giant *ninots* (effigies), many of political and social personages, are torched in the main plaza.

Tucked away off Calle Prócida, La Utielana packs in the crowds, drawn by wholesome fare and exceptional value for money.

At weekends, locals flock to Las Arenas, just north of the port, where a long line of restaurants overlooking the beach serve up paella. **La Pepica** (☎ 96 371 03 66; Playa de Levante 6; mains €8-20) is one of the locals' favourites.

Drinking & Entertainment

The Barrio del Carmen, university area (around Avenidas de Aragón and Blasco Ibáñez), the area around the Mercado de Abastos and, in summer, the new port area and Malvarrosa are all jumping with bars and clubs.

Café San Jaume (☎ 96 391 24 01; Calle Caballeros 51) This is a stalwart of Carmen's bar scene, with lots of room upstairs and a particularly fine terrace.

Cafe-Bar Negrito (Plaza del Negrito) At this bar, which traditionally attracts a more left-wing, intellectual clientele, the crowd spills out onto the square.

Xino Xano (Calle Alta 28) The genial owner, a well-known DJ in his own right, picks from his collection of dub, reggae and funk.

Getting There & Away

The **bus station** (☎ 96 346 62 66) is on Avenida Menéndez Pidal. There are regular services to/from Madrid (€23 to €29, four hours), Barcelona (€25.15 to €38.50, four to 5½ hours) and Alicante (€17.60 to €20, 2½ hours).

From Valencia's **Estación del Norte** (Calle Jativa), trains also go to/from Madrid, Barcelona and Alicante, among other destinations.

Getting Around

Metro line 5 connects the airport, downtown and port. Valencia has an integrated bus, tram and metro network. Tourist offices stock maps for both services. The high-speed tram leaves from the FGV tram station, 500m north of the cathedral, at the Pont de Fusta. This is a pleasant way to get to the beach, the paella restaurants of Las Arenas and the port.

ALICANTE

pop 322,700

With its elegant, palm-lined boulevards, lively nightlife scene and easy-to-access beaches, Alicante is the kind of all-in-one Spanish city that makes a great one- or two-day stopover.

The **municipal tourist office** (www.alicanteturismo.com) has branches at the bus station and train station. Get internet access at **Xplorer Cyber Café** (Calle San Vicente 46; per hr €1.20; 9am-midnight).

Sights

A multilevel fortress dating from the 12th century, the imposing **Castillo de Santa Bárbara** (admission free; 10am-9.30pm May-Sep, 9am-6.30pm Nov-Mar) affords magnificent views over the city and sea. To get here, cross the footbridge beside the **Playa del Postiguet** (the main city beach) and take the elevator to the top.

Sleeping & Eating

Camping Costa Blanca (☎ 96 563 06 70; www.campingcostablanca.com; Calle Convento, Campello; sites per person/tent/car €5.65/8.25/5.65;) This camping ground, 10km north of Alicante, has a poolside bar, restaurant and minilibrary. The tram passes right by.

our pick **Hostal Les Monges Palace** (☎ 96 521 50 46; www.lesmonges.net; Calle San Agustín 4; s €30-44, d €45-56; P) This agreeably quirky place is a treasure, with its winding corridors, tiles, mosaics and antique furniture.

Bíomenú (☎ 96 521 31 44; Calle Navas 17; 9.30am-7pm Mon-Sat, 9.30-11.30pm Sun) This ultracheap option is both a vegetarian buffet restaurant and shop specialising in organic produce.

El Trellat (☎ 965 20 62 75; Calle Capitán Segarra 19; menús lunch €11.50, dinner €17.50; lunch Mon-Sat, dinner Fri & Sat) Beside the covered market, this friendly place serves creative three-course *menús*.

Drinking & Entertainment

The old quarter around Catedral de San Nicolás is wall-to-wall bars. Down by the harbour, the Paseo del Puerto, tranquil by day, is a double-decker line of bars, cafes and night-time discos.

Getting There & Away

From the **bus station** (☎ 96 513 07 00; Calle Portugal 17), over 10 motorway buses go daily to Valencia (€17.60 to €20, 2½ hours), seven to Murcia (€5.20, one hour) and at least 10 to Madrid (€26.30, 5¼ hours).

Destinations from the main **Renfe Estación de Madrid** (Avenida de Salamanca) include Murcia (€4.30, 1¼ hours, hourly), Valencia (€26.30, 1¾ hours, 10 daily), Madrid (€41, 3¾ hours, seven daily) and Barcelona (€50.70, 4¾ hours, eight daily).

TRAM (☎ 900 72 04 72) runs a smart new tram to Benidorm (€4, every half hour) along a pretty coastal route.

MURCIA

pop 409,800

The capital of the rural Murcia region (see www.murciaturistica.es), Murcia City was founded in 825 as an Islamic settlement called Mursiya. Get more information at the **tourist office** (☎ 968 35 87 49; www.murciaciudad.com; Plaza del Cardenal Belluga; 🕒 10am-2pm & 5-9pm Mon-Sat, 10am-2pm Sun Jun-Sep, 10am-2pm & 4.30-8.30pm Mon-Sat, 10am-2pm Sun Oct-May).

Head to the **Catedral de Santa María** (Plaza Cardinal Belluga; 🕒 7am-1pm & 5-8pm) to marvel at its fabulously opulent baroque facade. The cathedral took four centuries to build and is a hodge-podge of architectural styles.

Sleeping & Eating

Pensión Murcia (☎ 968 21 99 63; Calle Vinadel 6; s/d with shared bathroom €43/25, with private bathroom €50/40; ❄) Tucked into a quiet elbow near bars and shops, this 16-room *pensíon* has tidy rooms with floral bedspreads, modern bathrooms and more space than most cheap sleeps in the city.

Figón de Alfaro (☎ 968 21 68 62; Calle Alfaro 7; meals €12-15; 🕒 lunch & dinner Mon-Sat, lunch Sun) Choose between the chaotic bar area or more sedate interconnecting dining room. Have a full meal or snack on juicy *montaditos* (minirolls) or innovative one-offs like *pastel de berejena con salsa de calabacín* (aubergine pie with a courgette sauce).

Los Arroces del Romea (☎ 968 21 84 99; Plaza Romea s/n; meals €20-25) Watch the speciality paella-style rice dishes being prepared in cartwheel-size pans over the flames while munching on circular *murciano* bread drizzled with olive oil. There are five rice dishes to choose from, including vegetarian.

Getting There & Away

Up to five trains travel daily to/from Madrid (€41.30, 4¼ hours). Hourly trains operate to/from Lorca (€14.50, one hour).

Alsa has buses to Granada (€18.75, 3½ hours, seven daily), Valencia (€14.50, 3¾ hours, four to six daily) and Madrid (€24, five hours, 10 daily).

ANDALUCÍA

The tapping feet and clapping hands of a passionate flamenco performance is an Andalucian signature that's as distinctive as the sweet aroma of orange blossom or the voluptuous flavour offered by a glass of chilled summer *gazpacho*. In the past, armies of Muslims and Christians fought over this sun-drenched part of Spain; these days, tourists are the only visitors to arrive in battalions.

SEVILLE

pop 699,100

A sexy, gutsy and gorgeous-looking city, Seville is home to two of Spain's most colourful festivals, fascinating and distinctive barrios and a local population that lives life to the fullest. A fiery place (as you'll soon see in its packed and noisy tapas bars!), it is also hot – try to avoid July and August.

Information

Internetia (Avenida Menéndez Pelayo 45; per hr €2; 🕒 11am-11pm) Internet access.

Municipal tourist office (☎ 954 22 17 14; Calle de Arjona 28; 🕒 9am-7.30pm Mon-Fri, 9am-2pm Sat & Sun)

Regional tourist offices Avenida de la Constitución 21 (☎ 954 22 14 04; otsevilla@andalucia.org; 🕒 9am-7pm Mon-Fri, 10am-2pm & 3-7pm Sat, 10am-2pm Sun, closed holidays); Estación Santa Justa (☎ 954 53 76 26; 🕒 9am-8pm Mon-Fri, 10am-2pm Sat & Sun, closed holidays)

Turismo Sevilla (☎ 954 21 00 05; www.turismosevilla.org; Plaza del Triunfo 1; 🕒 10.30am-7pm Mon-Fri)

Sights & Activities

The city's towering and lavishly decorated **Catedral** (☎ 954 21 49 71; adult/student €7.50/1.50, admission free Sun; 🕒 11am-6pm Mon-Sat, 2.30-7pm Sun Sep-Jun, 9.30am-4.30pm Mon-Sat, 2.30-7pm Sun Jul & Aug) was built on the site of Muslim Seville's main mosque between 1401 and 1507. The adjoining tower, **La Giralda**, was the mosque's minaret and dates from the 12th century. Climb to the top for the city views.

A residence of Muslim and Christian royalty for many centuries, Seville's **Alcázar** (☎ 954 50 23 23; adult/student €7/free; ⏲ 9.30am-8pm Tue-Sat, to 6pm Sun & holidays Apr-Sep, 9.30am-6pm Tue-Sat, to 2.30pm Sun & holidays Oct-Mar) was founded in 913 as a Muslim fortress. The Alcázar has been expanded and rebuilt many times in its 11 centuries of existence. The Catholic Monarchs, Fernando and Isabel, set up court here in the 1480s as they prepared for the conquest of Granada. Later rulers created the Alcázar's lovely gardens.

The **Museo de Bellas Artes** (☎ 954 78 65 00; Plaza del Museo 9; adult/student €1.50/free; ⏲ 2.30-8.30pm Tue, 9am-8.30pm Wed-Sat, 9am-2.30pm Sun, closed Mon) has an outstanding collection of Spanish art, focusing on local artists such as Bartolomé Esteban Murillo and Francisco Zurbarán.

WALKS & PARKS

Seville's medieval *judería* (Jewish quarter), the **Barrio de Santa Cruz**, east of the cathedral and Alcázar, is a tangle of quaint, winding streets and lovely plant-filled plazas perfumed with orange blossom. Its most characteristic plaza is **Plaza de Santa Cruz**.

A more straightforward walk is along the **river bank** and past Seville's famous bullring, the **Plaza de Toros de la Real Maestranza** (☎ 954 22 45 77; www.realmaestranza.es; Paseo de Cristóbal Colón 12; tours €5; ⏲ half-hourly 9.30am-7pm Nov-Apr, 9.30am-8pm May-Oct, 9.30am-3pm bullfighting days), one of the oldest in Spain. The tour is in English and Spanish.

South of the centre is **Parque de María Luisa**, with its maze of paths, tall trees, flowers, fountains and shaded lawns. Be sure to seek out the magnificent **Plaza de España** with its fountains, canal and a simply dazzling semicircle of *azulejo* (ceramic tile)-clad buildings.

Turismo Sevilla publishes an excellent booklet with self-guided walks.

Festivals & Events

Semana Santa During the week leading up to Easter Sunday, thousands of members of religious brotherhoods in penitents' garb with tall, pointed hoods *(capirotes)* join processions carrying sacred images through the city.

Feria de Abril Held in late April, the Feria involves six days of music, dancing, horse riding and traditional dress, plus daily bullfights.

Bienal de Flamenco The biggest of all Spain's flamenco festivals, held for a month in September during even-numbered years.

Sleeping

Note that prices over Semana Santa and Feria can be up to double the high-season rates cited here. The city's accommodation is often full on weekends and is always booked solid during festivals.

Oasis Backpackers' Hostel (☎ 954 29 37 77; www.oasissevilla.com; Plaza Encarnación 29; dm/d €20/46 incl breakfast; ❄ 💻) Seville's offbeat, buzzing backpacker central is in a narrow street behind the church of the Anunciación. Each dorm bed has a personal safe and there is a small rooftop pool.

Casa Sol y Luna (☎ 954 21 06 82; www.casasolyluna1.com; Calle Pérez Galdós 1A; s/d/tr with shared bathroom €22/38/60, d with private bathroom €45) This is a first-rate *hostal* in a beautifully decorated house dating from 1911, with embroidered white linen that makes you feel as if you're staying at your grandma's.

Pensión Córdoba (☎ 954 22 74 98; Calle Farnesio 12; s/d with shared bathroom €40/60, with private bathroom €55/75; ❄) Run for the past 30 years by a friendly older couple, Pensión Córdoba is on a quiet pedestrian street. Rooms are basic but spotless.

Hostal Museo (☎ 954 91 55 26; www.hostalmuseo.com; Calle Abad Gordillo 17; s/d €48/60; ❄ 💻) The immaculate rooms are endowed with solid wooden furniture and comfortable beds.

Hotel Simón (☎ 954 22 66 60; www.hotelsimonsevilla.com; Calle García de Vinuesa 19; s €60-70, d €95-110; ❄) A charming small hotel in a grand old 18th-century house, with spotless and comfortable rooms. Even the light filtering into the antique patio seems dipped in tea.

Eating

El Patio San Eloy (Calle San Eloy 9; tapas €1.50-3) Patches of old tiling remain at the always-busy Patio San Eloy, where you can sit on the tiled steps at the back and feast on a fine array of *burguillos* (small filled rolls).

Cervecería Giralda (☎ 954 22 82 50; Calle Mateos Gago 1; tapas €3.50-5) Exotic variations are merged with traditional dishes in this onetime Muslim bathhouse.

Restaurante La Cueva (☎ 954 21 31 43; Calle Rodrigo Caro 18; mains €11-24, menú €16) This popular bull's head–festooned eatery cooks up a storming fish *zarzuela* (casserole; €30 for two people) and a hearty *caldereta* (lamb stew; €14.90).

Restaurante Modesto (☎ 954 41 68 11; Calle Cano y Cueto 5; mains €11-34) This bustling, unpretentious place is famed for its lobster and monkfish stew.

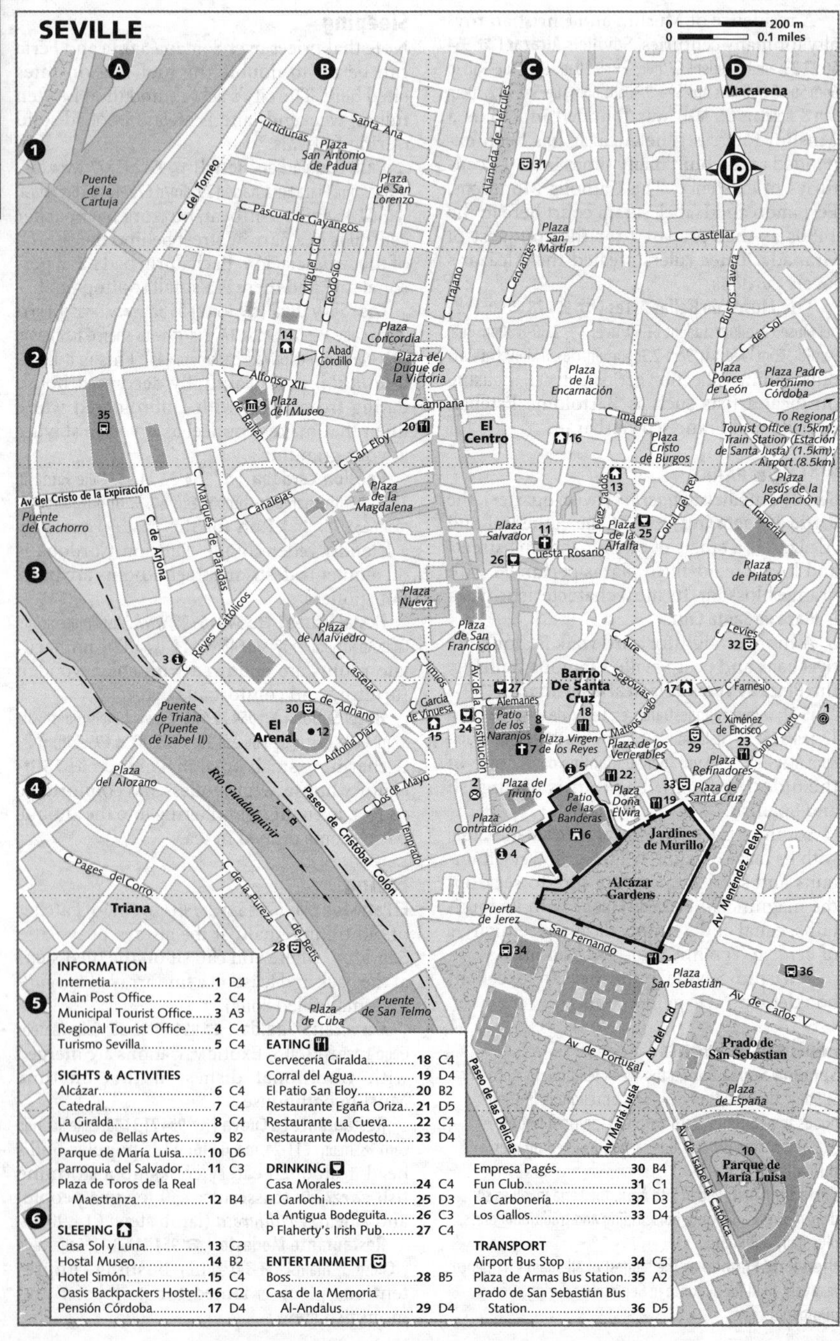
SEVILLE
0 200 m
0 0.1 miles
A
B
C
D
1
2
3
4
5
6
Macarena
Puente de la Cartuja
C Santa Ana
Curtidurías
Plaza San Antonio de Padua
Plaza de San Lorenzo
C del Torneo
Alameda de Hércules
C Pascual de Gayangos
Plaza San Martín
C Castellar
C Miguel Cid
C Teodosio
C Trajano
C Cervantes
C Bustos Tavera
C del Sol
Plaza Concordia
C Abad Gordillo
Plaza del Duque de la Victoria
C Alfonso XII
Plaza del Museo
C de Bailén
C Campana
Plaza de la Encarnación
C Imagen
Plaza Ponce de León
Plaza Padre Jerónimo Córdoba
To Regional Tourist Office (1.5km); Train Station (Estación de Santa Justa) (1.5km); Airport (8.5km)
El Centro
Plaza Cristo de Burgos
C San Eloy
Plaza Jesús de la Redención
Av del Cristo de la Expiración
C Marqués de Paradas
Plaza de la Magdalena
C Canalejas
Puente del Cachorro
C de Arjona
C Pérez Galdós
Plaza de la Alfalfa
Corral del Rey
C Imperial
Plaza Salvador
Cuesta Rosario
Plaza de Pilatos
Reyes Católicos
Plaza Nueva
Plaza de San Francisco
Plaza de Malviedro
C Castelar
C Jimios
Av de la Constitución
C Aire
C Levíes
Barrio De Santa Cruz
C Segovias
C Farnesio
C Alemanes
C García de Vinuesa
Puente de Triana (Puente de Isabel II)
C de Adriano
El Arenal
Patio de los Naranjos
Plaza Virgen de los Reyes
C Mateos Gago
C Ximénez de Enciso
Plaza de los Venerables
Plaza Refinadores
C Cano y Cueto
C Antonia Díaz
Plaza del Alozano
Río Guadalquivir
Paseo de Cristóbal Colón
C Dos de Mayo
C Temprado
Plaza del Triunfo
Patio de las Banderas
Plaza Doña Elvira
Plaza de Santa Cruz
Plaza Contratación
Jardines de Murillo
Av Menéndez Pelayo
C Pages del Corro
C de la Pureza
Alcázar Gardens
Triana
C del Betis
Puerta de Jerez
C San Fernando
Plaza San Sebastián
Av de Carlos V
Plaza de Cuba
Puente de San Telmo
Av del Cid
Av de Portugal
Prado de San Sebastian
Paseo de las Delicias
Plaza de España
Av María Lusia
Av de Isabel la Católica
Parque de María Luisa

INFORMATION
Internetia 1 D4
Main Post Office 2 C4
Municipal Tourist Office 3 A3
Regional Tourist Office 4 C4
Turismo Sevilla 5 C4

SIGHTS & ACTIVITIES
Alcázar 6 C4
Catedral 7 C4
La Giralda 8 C4
Museo de Bellas Artes 9 B2
Parque de María Luisa 10 D6
Parroquia del Salvador 11 C3
Plaza de Toros de la Real Maestranza 12 B4

SLEEPING
Casa Sol y Luna 13 C3
Hostal Museo 14 B2
Hotel Simón 15 C4
Oasis Backpackers Hostel 16 C2
Pensión Córdoba 17 D4

EATING
Cervecería Giralda 18 C4
Corral del Agua 19 D4
El Patio San Eloy 20 B2
Restaurante Egaña Oriza 21 D5
Restaurante La Cueva 22 C4
Restaurante Modesto 23 D4

DRINKING
Casa Morales 24 C4
El Garlochi 25 D3
La Antigua Bodeguita 26 C3
P Flaherty's Irish Pub 27 C4

ENTERTAINMENT
Boss 28 B5
Casa de la Memoria Al-Andalus 29 D4
Empresa Pagés 30 B4
Fun Club 31 C1
La Carbonería 32 D3
Los Gallos 33 D4

TRANSPORT
Airport Bus Stop 34 C5
Plaza de Armas Bus Station 35 A2
Prado de San Sebastián Bus Station 36 D5

GETTING INTO TOWN

Amarillos Tours (☎ 902 21 03 17) runs buses between the airport and the Puerta de Jerez (€2.20 to €2.50, 30 to 40 minutes, at least 15 daily). A taxi costs about €18.

Corral del Agua (☎ 954 22 48 41; Callejón del Agua 6; mains €16.50-22; Mon-Sat) Inventive Al-Andalus and traditional dishes are served in a semi-tropical courtyard under a twining canopy of vines and jacaranda.

Restaurante Egaña Oriza (☎ 954 22 72 11; Calle San Fernando 41; mains €22-32; Mon-Fri & dinner Sat) Regarded as one of the city's best restaurants, Egaña Oriza cooks up superb Andalucian-Basque cuisine, including lasagne with seafood, lobster and truffles.

Drinking & Clubbing

Bars usually open until 2am weekdays and 3am at the weekend. Drinking and partying really get going around midnight on Friday and Saturday. In summer, dozens of open-air late-night bars *(terrazas de verano)* spring up along the river.

P Flaherty's Irish Pub (☎ 954 21 04 17; Calle Alemanes 7; 11am-late) Sports fans tend to gravitate towards Flaherty's, which occupies a premium position opposite the cathedral.

Casa Morales (☎ 954 22 12 42; Garcia de Vinuesa 11) Casa Morales was founded in 1850, and not much has changed since in this defiantly old-world bar. Towering clay *tinajas* (wine storage jars) carry the chalked-up tapas choices of the day.

El Garlochi (Calle Boteros 4) Named after the *gitano* (Roma) word for 'heart', this deeply camp bar hits you with clouds of incense, Jesus and Virgin images on scarlet walls, and potent cocktails like Sangre de Cristo (Blood of Christ).

Plaza del Salvador is brimful of drinkers from mid-evening to 1am. Grab a drink from **La Antigua Bodeguita** (☎ 954 56 18 33) and sit on the steps of the Parroquia del Salvador. Calle Pérez Galdós, off Plaza de la Alfalfa, also has a handful of busy bars.

The Alameda de Hércules area, a former red-light district, has lots of offbeat bars. Some have live music.

With funk, Latino, hip-hop and jazz bands taking the stage, **Fun Club** (☎ 958 25 02 49; Alameda de Hércules 86; admission live-band nights €3-6, other nights free; 11.30pm-late Thu-Sun, from 9.30pm live-band nights) is a dance warehouse that is a music-lovers' favourite.

On Calle del Betis, on the far bank of the Guadalquivir, you'll find some good dance bars/discos, including **Boss** (Calle del Betis 67; admission free with flyer; 8pm-7am Tue-Sun), one of Seville's top dance spots.

Entertainment

La Carbonería (☎ 954 21 44 60; Calle Levíes 18; admission free; about 8pm-4am) The sprawling converted coal yard throngs every night of the week with tourists and locals who come to mingle and enjoy live flamenco.

Casa de la Memoria Al-Andalus (☎ 954 56 06 70; Calle Ximénez de Enciso 28; admission €14; 9pm & 10.30pm) Book a ticket here for nightly shows with a focus on medieval and Sephardic Al-Andalus styles of music, in a room of shifting shadows.

For flamenco, hotels and tourist offices tend to steer you towards *tablaos* (expensive, tourist-oriented flamenco venues). Of these, **Los Gallos** (☎ 954 21 69 81; www.tablaolosgallos.com; Plaza de Santa Cruz 11; admission incl 1 drink €30; 2hr shows 8-10pm & 10.30pm-12.30am) is a cut above the average.

Getting There & Away

AIR

A range of domestic and international flights lands in Seville's San Pablo airport (SVQ), 8.5km from the city centre.

BUS

Regular services run from the **Plaza de Armas bus station** (☎ 954 90 80 40; Avenida del Cristo de la

DEATH IN THE AFTERNOON

Seville's bullfight season runs from Easter to October, with fights about 7pm most Sundays, and every day during the Feria de Abril and the preceding week. Tickets cost between €32.50 and €110, depending on who's fighting. *Sol* (sun) seats are cheaper than *sombra* (shade) seats. Bullfighting can be gory and isn't for everyone; but if it is your thing, and you get a skilled matador, the atmosphere in the ring can be electrifying. Tickets can be purchased in advance from **Empresa Pagés** (☎ 954 50 13 82; Calle de Adriano 37) and from 4.30pm on fight days at the bullring.

Expiración). Destinations include Madrid (€18.65, six hours, 14 daily), Mérida (€11, three hours, 12 daily), Cáceres (€15, four hours, six daily) and northwestern Spain. This is also the station for buses to Portugal. **Alsa** (www.alsa.es) runs two daily buses to Lisbon (€41, seven hours).

Buses to other parts of Andalucía use **Prado de San Sebastián bus station** (☎ 954 41 71 11; Plaza San Sebastián). Twelve or more buses run daily to/from Córdoba (€9.40, two hours) and Granada (€18.60, 3½ hours), and five to Ronda (€10.50, 2½ hours) and Málaga (€14.75, 2¾ hours).

TRAIN

From Seville's **Estación de Santa Justa** (Avenida Kansas City), 1.5km northeast of the centre, there are super-fast AVE trains as well as regular trains to Madrid (€58.90 to €75.10, 2½ to 3½ hours, hourly). Other destinations include Barcelona (€57.50 to €88, 10½ to 13 hours, three daily), Cádiz (€9.80, 1¾ hours, 13 daily), Córdoba (€8.20 to €28.30, 40 minutes to 1½ hours, 21 or more daily) and Granada (€21.65, three hours, four daily).

Getting Around

Buses are run by Seville's urban transport authority, **Tussam** (☎ 902 45 99 54; www.tussam.es). The C1, C2, C3 and C4 buses do useful circular routes linking the main transport terminals and the city centre. Two new tram lines operate between Plaza Nueva (near the Ayuntamiento) and along Avenida de la Constitución to the Archivo de Indias and Puerta de Jerez, then down San Fernando to the bus station at Prado de San Sebastian. Tickets cost €1.10. A metro line is under construction.

SeVici (☎ 902 01 10 32; www.sevici.es; 🕑 7am-9pm) is a cycle hire network comprising almost 200 fully automated pick-up/drop-off points across the city. A one-week subscription costs €5. Your first 30 minutes cycling is free, the next hour costs €1, while second and subsequent hours are €2 per hour.

CÓRDOBA

pop 323,600

Córdoba pays graceful testament to its Moorish past. Its magnificent Mezquita (Mosque) has been described as the greatest visual representation of homesickness ever constructed, and is one of the highlights of any visit to Spain.

Information

Ch@t (Calle Claudio Marcelo 15; per hr €1.80; 🕑 9am-1.30pm & 4.30-8.30pm Mon-Fri Nov-Mar, 9.30am-1.30pm & 5.30-8.30pm Apr-Oct, 10am-1.30pm Sat) Internet.

Policía Nacional (☎ 95 747 75 00; Avenida Doctor Fleming 2)

Regional tourist office (☎ 957 35 51 79; Calle de Torrijos 10; 🕑 9am-7.30pm Mon-Fri, 9.30am-3pm Sat, Sun & holidays) Facing the western side of the Mezquita, this helpful office offers information on the city and the surrounding countryside.

Sights & Activities

The inside of the famous **Mezquita** (☎ 957 47 05 12; admission €8; 🕑 10am-7pm Mon-Sat Apr-Oct, to 6pm Mon-Sat Nov-Mar, 9-10.45am & 1.30-6.30pm Sun year-round), which was begun by emir Abd ar-Rahman I in 785 and enlarged by subsequent generations, is a mesmerising sequence of two-tier arches amid a thicket of columns. From 1236, the mosque was used as a church and in the 16th century a cathedral was built right in its centre – somewhat wrecking the effect of the original Muslim building.

The **Judería**, Córdoba's medieval Jewish quarter northwest of the Mezquita, is an intriguing maze of narrow streets, small plazas and traditional houses with flower-filled patios. Don't miss the beautiful little **Sinagoga** (Calle de los Judíos 20; admission €0.30, EU citizen free; 🕑 9.30am-2pm & 3.30-5.30pm Tue-Sat, 9.30am-1.30pm Sun & holidays).

Southwest of the Mezquita stands the **Alcázar de los Reyes Cristianos** (Fortress of the Christian Monarchs; ☎ 957 42 01 51; Campo Santo de Los Mártires s/n; adult/student €4/2, free Fri; 🕑 10am-2pm & 4.30-6.30pm Tue-Sat mid-Oct–Apr, 10am-2pm & 5.30-7.30pm Tue-Sat May-Jun & Sep–mid-Oct, 8.30am-2.30pm Tue-Sat Jul-Aug, 9.30am-2.30pm Sun & holidays year-round), with its large and lovely gardens.

Indulge your senses at the renovated **Hammam Baños Árabes** (Arab Baths; ☎ 957 48 47 46; www.hammamspain.com/cordoba; Calle Corregidor Luis de la Cerda 51; bath/bath & massage €12/16; 🕑 2hr sessions 10am, noon, 2pm, 4pm, 6pm, 8pm & 10pm) where you can enjoy an aromatherapy massage, with tea, hookah and Arabic sweets.

It's well worth the 8km trip west of Córdoba to the intriguing **Medina Azahara** (Madinat al-Zahra; ☎ 957 32 91 30; Carretera Palma del Río, Km 5.5; admission €1.50, EU citizen free; 🕑 10am-6.30pm Tue-Sat mid-Sep–May, to 8.30pm May–mid-Sep, to 2pm Sun year-round), a mighty Muslim city-palace from the 10th century. A taxi costs €37 for the return trip, with one hour to view the site, or you can

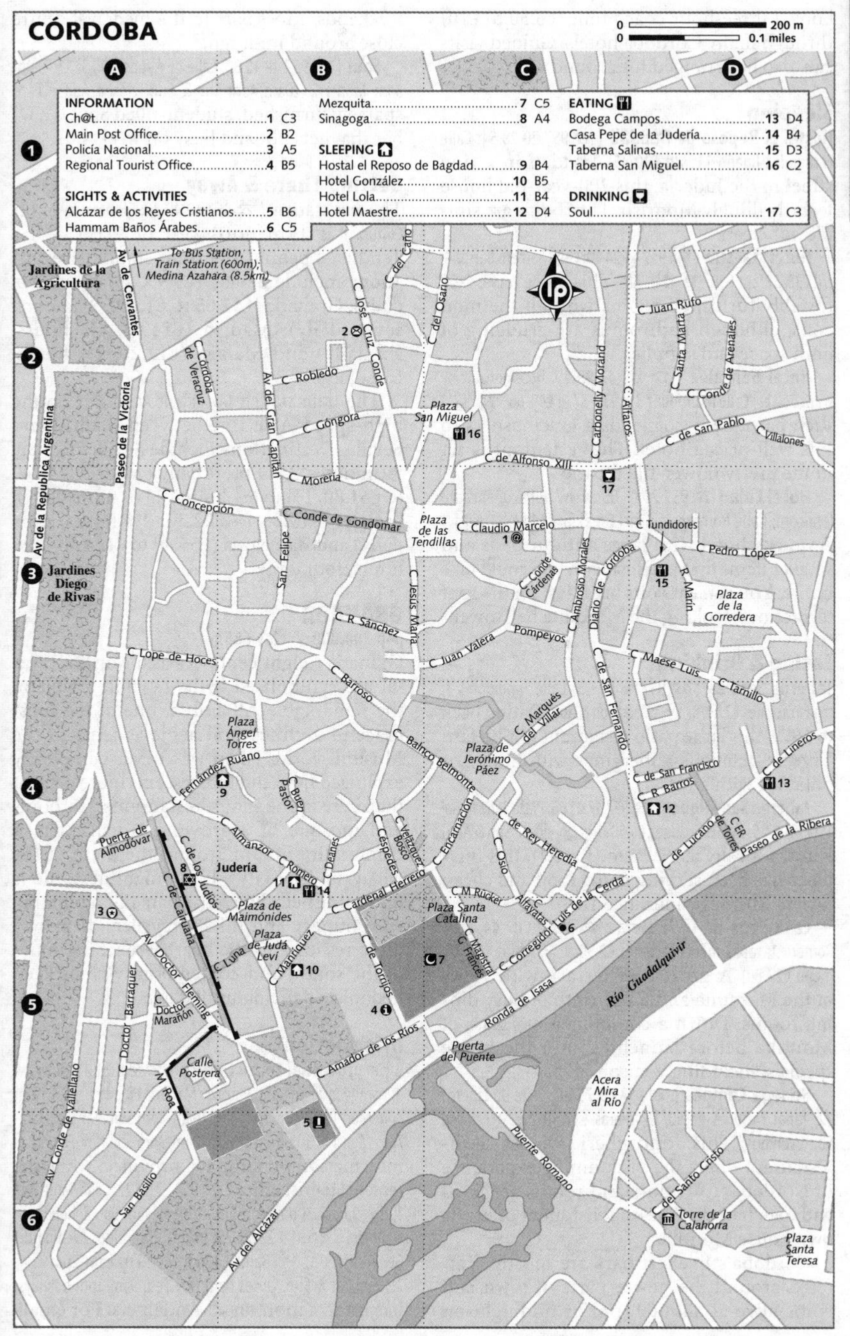
CÓRDOBA
0 200 m
0 0.1 miles
A
B
C
D
1
2
3
4
5
6
INFORMATION
Ch@t 1 C3
Main Post Office 2 B2
Policía Nacional 3 A5
Regional Tourist Office 4 B5
SIGHTS & ACTIVITIES
Alcázar de los Reyes Cristianos 5 B6
Hammam Baños Árabes 6 C5
Mezquita 7 C5
Sinagoga 8 A4
SLEEPING
Hostal el Reposo de Bagdad 9 B4
Hotel González 10 B5
Hotel Lola 11 B4
Hotel Maestre 12 D4
EATING
Bodega Campos 13 D4
Casa Pepe de la Judería 14 B4
Taberna Salinas 15 D3
Taberna San Miguel 16 C2
DRINKING
Soul 17 C3
To Bus Station, Train Station (600m); Medina Azahara (8.5km)
Jardines de la Agricultura
Jardines Diego de Rivas
Av de Cervantes
Paseo de la Victoria
Av de la República Argentina
C Córdoba de Veracruz
Av del Gran Capitán
C José Cruz Conde
C del Caño
C del Osario
C Robledo
C Góngora
C Morería
C Concepción
C Conde de Gondomar
Plaza San Miguel
Plaza de las Tendillas
C de Alfonso XIII
C Claudio Marcelo
C Carbonelly Morand
C Alfaros
C Juan Rufo
C Santa Marta
C Conde de Arenales
C de San Pablo
C Villalones
C Tundidores
C Pedro López
R Marín
Plaza de la Corredera
C Conde Cárdenas
C Ambrosio Morales
Diario de Córdoba
San Felipe
C Jesús María
C R Sánchez
Pompeyos
C Juan Valera
C Lope de Hoces
C Barroso
C Maese Luis
C Tarnillo
C de San Fernando
C Marqués del Villar
Plaza de Jerónimo Páez
Plaza Ángel Torres
C Fernández Ruano
C Buen Pastor
C Balnco Belmonte
C de Rey Heredia
C de San Francisco
C R Barros
C de Lineros
C de Lucano
C ER de Torres
Paseo de la Ribera
Puerta de Almodóvar
C de los Judíos
Judería
C Almanzor
C Romero
C Deanes
C Céspedes
C Velázquez Bosco
C Encarnación
C Osio
C Cardenal Herrero
C M Rücker
C Alfayatas
C Corregidor Luis de la Cerda
Plaza de Maimónides
Plaza Santa Catalina
C de Cairuana
C Luna
Plaza de Judá Leví
C Manríquez
C de Torrijos
C Magistral
C Frances
Río Guadalquivir
Av Doctor Fleming
C Doctor Barraquer
C Doctor Marañón
Ronda de Isasa
C Amador de los Ríos
Puerta del Puente
Calle Postrera
M Roa
Acera Mira al Río
Puente Romano
Av Conde de Vallellano
C San Basilio
Av del Alcázar
C del Santo Cristo
Torre de la Calahorra
Plaza Santa Teresa

book a three-hour coach tour (€6.50 to €10) through many Córdoba hotels. Guided visits can also be arranged for around €15.

Sleeping

Hostal El Reposo de Bagdad (☎ 957 20 28 54; Calle Fernández Ruano 11; s/d €30/45) Hidden in a tiny street in the Judería, this 200-year-old house feels thrillingly Moorish. The rooms are simple but clean.

Hotel Maestre (☎ 957 47 24 10; Calle Romero Barros 4; s/d €38/52, apt €58; P) This place has comfortably furnished rooms with all the mod cons, although bathrooms are grudging of both space and supplies.

Hotel González (☎ 957 47 98 19; hotelgonzalez@wanadoo.es; Calle Manríquez 3; s €35-37, d €49-66) Rich baroque decor lends a graciousness to this well-priced hotel. The restaurant is set in the pretty flower-filled patio.

Hotel Lola (☎ 957 20 03 05; www.hotelconencantolola.com; Calle Romero 3; d incl breakfast €114; P) A quirky hotel with large antique beds and smaller items that you just wish you could take home. You can eat your breakfast on the roof terrace overlooking the Mezquita bell tower.

Eating & Drinking

Taberna Salinas (☎ 957 48 01 35; Calle Tundidores 3; tapas/raciones €2.50/8; closed Sun & Aug) Dating back to 1879, this large patio restaurant fills up fast. Try the delicious aubergines with honey or potatoes with garlic.

Taberna San Miguel (☎ 957 47 01 66; Plaza San Miguel 1; tapas €2-5, media raciones €5.50-10; closed Sun & Aug) Known locally as *El Pisto* (Barrel), this busy place has been serving rustic food and cheap jugs of Moriles wine since 1880.

Casa Pepe de la Judería (☎ 957 20 07 44; Calle Romero 1; tapas/media raciones €2.50/9.50, mains €11-18, menu €27.80) A great roof-terrace with views of the Mezquita and a labyrinth of busy dining rooms. Down a complimentary glass of Montilla before launching into the house specials, including venison fillets.

Bodega Campos (☎ 957 49 75 00; Calle de Lineros 32; tapas/raciones €6.50/16, mains €17.50-29; closed Sun evenings) This atmospheric winery-slash-restaurant offers the peak dining experience in Córdoba. Corridors and rooms are lined with oak barrels. The establishment offers its own house Montilla.

Córdoba's liveliest bars are mostly scattered around the newer parts of town and come alive at about 11pm or midnight on weekends. Most bars in the medieval centre close around midnight.

Soul (☎ 957 49 15 80; Calle de Alfonso XIII 3; 9am-3am Mon-Fri, 10am-4am Sat & Sun, closed Aug) The sparsely furnished, student-filled Soul is a DJ bar that gets hot and busy on weekends.

Getting There & Away

The **bus station** (☎ 957 40 40 40; Glorieta de las Tres Culturas) is 1km northwest of Plaza de las Tendillas, behind the train station. Destinations include Seville (€9.95, 1¾ hours, six daily), Granada (€12.05 to €16.60, 2½ hours, seven daily), Madrid (€14.40, 4½ hours, six daily) and Málaga (€12.20, 2¾ hours, five daily).

The **train station** (Avenida de América) is on the high-speed AVE line between Madrid and Seville. Destinations include Seville (€27.80, 90 minutes, 23 or more daily), Madrid (€48.40 to €61.80, 1¾ to 6¼ hours, 23 or more daily), Málaga (€19.05 to €22.30, 2½ hours, nine daily) and Barcelona (€55.40 to €124.50, 10½ hours, four daily).

GRANADA

pop 300,000 / elev 685m

Granada's eight centuries as a Muslim capital are symbolised in its keynote emblem, the remarkable Alhambra, one of the most graceful architectural achievements in the Muslim world. Islam was never completely expunged here and today seems more present than ever in the shops, restaurants, tearooms and mosque of a growing North African community in and around the maze of the Albayzín. The city's lively nightlife scene is undiminished. The tapas bars fill to bursting with hungry and thirsty revellers, flamenco dives resound to the heart-wrenching tones of the south, and contemporary clubs keep hedonists dancing until dawn.

Information

The **provincial tourist office** (☎ 958 24 71 28; www.turismodegranada.org; Plaza de Mariana Pineda 10; 9am-8pm Mon-Fri, 10am-7pm Sat, 10am-3pm Sun Mar-Oct, 9am-7pm Mon-Fri, 10am-7pm Sat, 10am-3pm Sun Nov-Feb) has information on Granada province, while the **regional tourist office** (☎ 958 22 10 22; Calle Santa Ana 1; 9am-7.30pm Mon-Sat, 9.30am-3pm Sun & holidays); Alhambra (☎ 958 22 95 75; ticket-office bldg, Avenida del Generalife s/n; 8am-7.30pm Mon-Fri, 8am-2pm & 4-7.30pm Sat & Sun, closes 6pm Nov-Feb, 9am-1pm holidays) has information on all Andalucía. For email, try **Cyberlocutorio Alhambra** (Calle Joaquin Costa 40; per hr €1.50; 10.30am-midnight daily).

Sights & Activities

ALHAMBRA

The mighty **Alhambra** (902 44 12 21; www.alhambra.org; adult/student €12/9, Generalife only €6; 8.30am-8pm Mar-Oct, to 6pm Nov-Feb, closed 25 Dec & 1 Jan) is breathtaking. Much has been written about its fortress, palace, patios and gardens, but nothing can really prepare you for seeing the real thing.

The **Alcazaba**, the Alhambra's fortress, dates from the 11th to the 13th centuries. There are spectacular views from the tops of its towers. The **Palacio Nazaríes** (Nasrid Palace), built for Granada's Muslim rulers in their 13th- to 15th-century heyday, is the centrepiece of the Alhambra. The beauty of its patios and intricacy of its stuccoes and woodwork, epitomised by the Patio de los Leones (Patio of the Lions) and Sala de las Dos Hermanas (Hall of the Two Sisters), are stunning. The **Generalife** (Palace Gardens) is a great spot to relax and contemplate the complex from a little distance.

The Palacio Nazaríes is also open for **night visits** (10pm-11.30pm Tue-Sat Mar-Oct, 8pm-9.30pm Fri & Sat Nov-Feb). Tickets cost the same as daytime tickets: the ticket office opens 30 minutes before the palace's opening time, closing 30 minutes after it. You can book ahead for night visits in the same ways as for day visits (see below).

OTHER ATTRACTIONS

Exploring the narrow, hilly streets of the **Albayzín**, the old Moorish quarter across the river from the Alhambra, is highly enjoyable. When doing this, make sure you keep your wits about you, as muggings sometimes occur around here. Make sure you climb uphill to reach the **Mirador de San Nicolás** – a viewpoint with breathtaking vistas and a relaxed, hippy scene.

It's also well worth exploring the streets and lanes surrounding **Plaza de Bib-Rambla**, and visiting the **Capilla Real** (Royal Chapel; 958 22 92 39; www.capillarealgranada.com; Calle Oficios; admission €3.50; 10.30am-12.45pm & 4-7pm Mon-Sat, 11am-12.45pm & 4-7pm Sun Apr-Oct, 10.30am-12.45pm & 3.30-6.15pm Mon-Sat, 11am-12.45pm & 3.30-6.15pm Sun Nov-Mar), where Fernando and Isabel, the Christian monarchs who conquered Granada in 1492, are buried. The sacristy contains a small but impressive **museum** with Fernando's sword and Isabel's sceptre, silver crown and personal art collection, which is mainly Flemish but also includes Botticelli's *Prayer in the Garden of Olives*.

Next door to the chapel is Granada's **Catedral** (958 22 29 59; admission €3.50; 10.45am-1.30pm & 4-8pm Mon-Sat, 4-8pm Sun Apr-Oct, to 7pm Nov-Mar), which dates from the early 16th century.

ALHAMBRA TICKETS

It's advisable to book in advance (€1 extra per ticket). You can book up to a year ahead in two ways: **Alhambra Advance Booking** (902 88 80 01, from abroad +34 93 492 37 50; 8am-9pm daily); and **Servicaixa** (www.servicaixa.com), online booking in Spanish and English. You can also buy tickets in advance from Servicaixa cash machines, but only in the **Alhambra grounds** (8am-7pm Mar-Oct, 8am-5pm Nov-Feb). Alhambra tickets are only valid for half a day, so specify whether you wish to visit in the morning or afternoon.

Sleeping

our pick **Oasis Backpackers' Hostel** (958 21 58 48; www.oasisgranada.com; Placeta Correo Viejo 3; dm €18, d €40;) Oasis is seconds away from the bars on Calle Elvira. There's free internet access, a rooftop terrace and personal safes. The location is tricky – it's best to walk up Caldereria Nueva, then left down narrow Calle Correo Viejo into the *placeta* itself.

Pension Venecia (958 22 39 87; Cuesta de Gomérez 2; s/d/tr/q with shared bathroom €19/30/53/60) A lovely *hostal* with friendly hosts and flower- and picture-filled turquoise corridors, just off Plaza Nueva.

Hostal Britz (/fax 958 22 36 52; Cuesta de Gomérez 1; s/d with shared bathroom €25/36, with private bathrooom €36/48) The friendly, efficient Britz has 22 clean, functional rooms with double-glazing, gleaming wooden surfaces and central heating. There's also a lift.

Hostal La Ninfa (958 22 79 85; Campo del Príncipe s/n; s/d €46/70;) A rustic place covered inside and out with brightly painted ceramic stars and plates. It has clean, cosy rooms, friendly owners and an attractive breakfast room.

Eating

Granada is one of the last bastions of that fantastic practice of free tapas with every

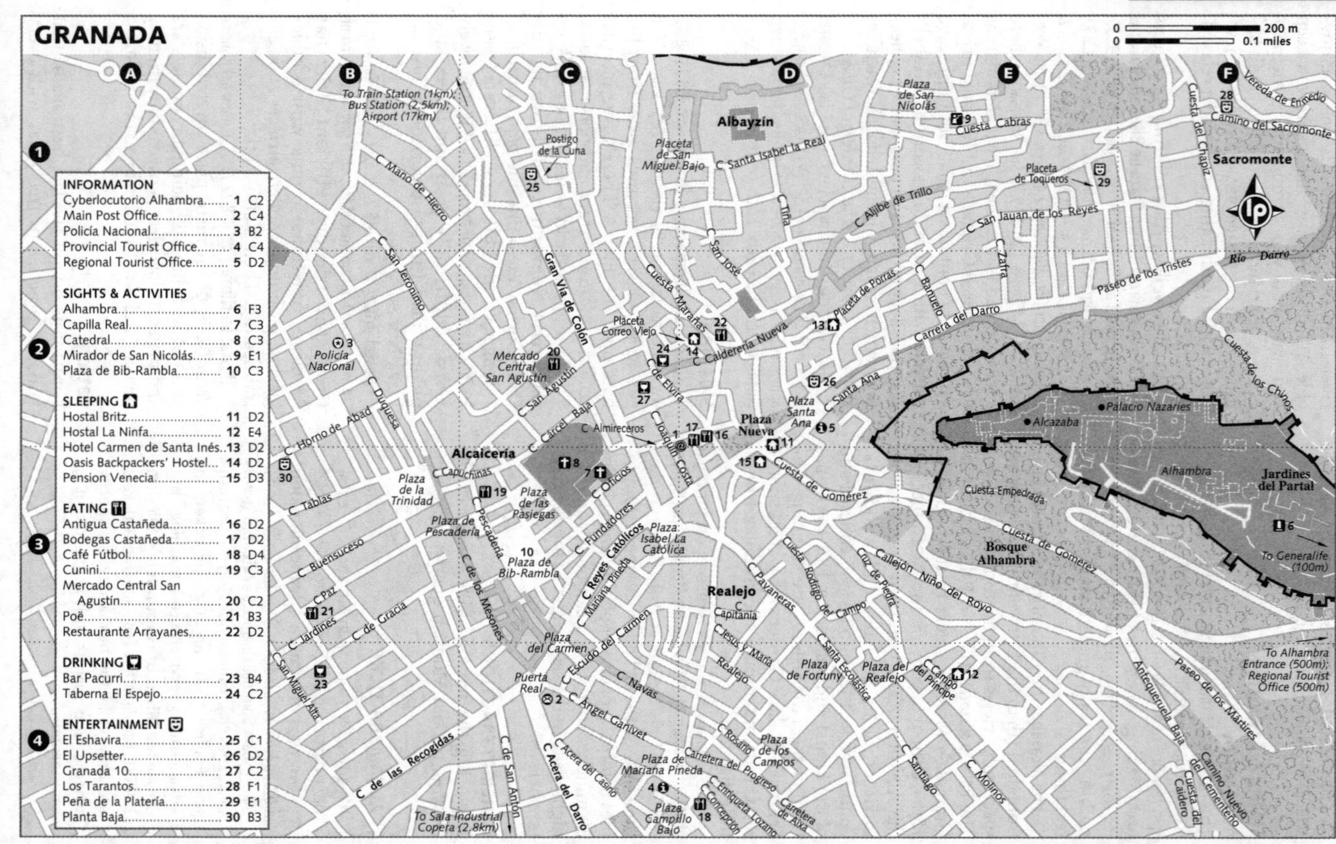
GRANADA
INFORMATION
Cyberlocutorio Alhambra 1 C2
Main Post Office 2 C4
Policía Nacional 3 B2
Provincial Tourist Office 4 C4
Regional Tourist Office 5 D2
SIGHTS & ACTIVITIES
Alhambra 6 F3
Capilla Real 7 C3
Catedral 8 C3
Mirador de San Nicolás 9 E1
Plaza de Bib-Rambla 10 C3
SLEEPING
Hostal Britz 11 D2
Hostal La Ninfa 12 E4
Hotel Carmen de Santa Inés 13 D2
Oasis Backpackers' Hostel 14 D2
Pension Venecia 15 D3
EATING
Antigua Castañeda 16 D2
Bodegas Castañeda 17 D2
Café Fútbol 18 D4
Cunini 19 C3
Mercado Central San Agustín 20 C2
Poë 21 B3
Restaurante Arrayanes 22 D2
DRINKING
Bar Pacurri 23 B4
Taberna El Espejo 24 C2
ENTERTAINMENT
El Eshavira 25 C1
El Upsetter 26 D2
Granada 10 27 C2
Los Tarantos 28 F1
Peña de la Platería 29 E1
Planta Baja 30 B3
Albayzín
Sacromonte
Alhambra
Palacio Nazaríes
Alcazaba
Jardines del Partal
Bosque Alhambra
Realejo
Alcaicería
Plaza Nueva
Gran Vía de Colón
To Train Station (1km); Bus Station (2.5km); Airport (17km)
To Generalife (100m)
To Alhambra Entrance (500m); Regional Tourist Office (500m)
To Sala Industrial Copera (2.8km)

> **SPLURGE**
>
> **Hotel Carmen de Santa Inés** (☎ 958 22 63 80; www.carmensantaines.com; Placeta de Porras 7; s/d €80/96, r with sitting room €140-222; ❄) This Islamic-era house, extended in the 16th and 17th centuries, offers a lovely breakfast patio in a garden of myrtles, fruit trees and fountains.

drink, and some have an international flavour. The labyrinthine Albayzín holds a wealth of eateries all tucked away in the narrow streets. Calle Calderería Nueva is a fascinating muddle of *teterías* (tea rooms) and Arabic-influenced takeaways.

Café Fútbol (Plaza de Mariana Pineda 6; 🕒 6am-midnight) This 1922 art nouveau cafe is a great choice for chocolate and *churros.*

Poë (Calle Paz; media ración €3) British-Angolan Poë offers Brazilian favourites such as *feijoada* (black bean and meat stew) or chicken stew with polenta, and has a trendy multicultural vibe.

our pick **Bodegas Castañeda** (Calle Almireceros; raciones from €6) An institution, and reputedly the oldest bar in Granada, this kitchen whips up traditional food in a typical *bodega* (traditional wine bar) setting. Their free tapa of *paella* is almost enough for a light lunch. Get a table before 2pm as it gets busy.

Antigua Castañeda (Calle de Elvira; raciones €8-16) Soak up potent 'Costa' wine from the Contraviesa with a few *montaditos* (small sandwiches; €5 to €6).

Restaurante Arrayanes (☎ 958 22 84 01; Cuesta Marañas 4; mains €8.50-19; 🕒 from 8pm) In the Albayzín, this intimate restaurant serves decent Moroccan dishes in a dining area strewn with brocade banquettes, rugs and brightly coloured cushions.

Cunini (☎ 958 25 07 77; Plaza de Pescadería 14; set menú €19, mains €11-23) Cunini dishes up first-class fish and seafood as tapas if you stand at the bar, or full meals out the back.

For fresh fruit and veg, head for the large covered **Mercado Central San Agustín** (Calle San Agustín; 🕒 8am-2pm Mon-Sat), a block west of the cathedral.

Drinking & Clubbing

The best street for drinking is rather scruffy Calle Elvira (try above-average **Taberna El Espejo** at number 40) but other chilled bars line Río Darro at the base of the Albayzín, and Campo del Príncipe attracts a sophisticated bunch.

Bodegas Castañeda (Calle Almireceros) and **Antigua Castañeda** (Calle de Elvira) are the most inviting and atmospheric, with out-of-the-barrel wine and generous tapas to keep things going.

Bar Pacurri (☎ 958 25 27 75; Calle de Gracia 21; tapas €2.50-5; 🕒 1pm-1am) Munch on above-average tapas with well-chosen wines at this small, arty bar.

Sala Industrial Copera (☎ 958 25 84 49; www.industrialcopera.net; Carretera Armilla, Calle la Paz, warehouse 7; admission varied; 🕒 midnight-late Fri & Sat) This warehouse club is where serious clubbers go for all-nighters, with a constantly changing schedule of live acts. You can count on lots of techno and hip-hop, and DJs from Ibiza, Madrid and Barcelona. Get a cab.

Granada 10 (Calle Cárcel Baja; admission €6; 🕒 from midnight, closed mid-Jul & Aug) A glittery converted cinema is now Granada's top club for the glam crowd, who recline on the gold sofas and go crazy to cheesy Spanish pop tunes.

Planta Baja (☎ 630 95 08 24; Calle Horno de Abad 11; www.plantabaja.net; admission €5; 🕒 12.30am-6am Tue-Sat) Planta Baja's popularity never seems to wane, and it's no wonder since it caters to a diverse crowd *and* has top DJs.

Entertainment

El Eshavira (☎ 958 29 08 29; Postigo de la Cuna 2; 🕒 from 10pm) Duck down a spooky alley to this shadowy haunt of flamenco and jazz. It is jam-packed on Thursday and Sunday, the performance nights.

El Upsetter (☎ 958 22 72 96; Carrera del Darro 7; admission for flamenco show €12; 🕒 10pm-late) The Upsetter has a decent nightly flamenco show from 10pm to midnight only, and doubles as a dreadlock-swinging reggae bar for the rest of the week.

Peña de la Platería (☎ 958 21 06 50; Placeta de Toqueros 7) Buried deep in the Albayzín warren, this is a genuine aficionados' club with a large outdoor patio. Catch a 9.30pm performance on Thursday or Saturday.

The Sacromonte caves harbour touristy flamenco haunts for which you can prebook through hotels and travel agencies, some of whom offer free transport. Try for a spot at the Friday or Saturday midnight shows at **Los Tarantos** (☎ day 958 22 45 25, night 958 22 24 92; Camino del Sacromonte 9; admission €24) for a lively experience.

Getting There & Away

Autocares J Gonzalez (☎ 95 849 01 64; www.autocaresjosegonzalez.com) runs a bus service between Granada's airport (GRX) and the city centre, 17km distant. A taxi costs €18 to €22.

The **bus station** (Carretera de Jaén) is 3km northwest of the centre. Bus 33 (€1.10) travels between the two. There are buses to Córdoba (€12 to €16.60, 2¾ hours direct, nine daily), Seville (€18.55, three hours direct, eight daily), Málaga (€9, 1½ hours direct, 16 daily) and Madrid (€15.65, five to six hours, 10 to 13 daily).

The **train station** (Avenida de Andaluces) is 1.5km northwest of the centre. Four trains run daily to/from Seville (€21.65, three hours), three to/from Ronda (€12.25, three hours) and Algeciras (€18.35, 4½ hours). One or two trains go to Madrid (€62.20, four to five hours) and Valencia (€46.10 to €72.30, 7½ to eight hours).

To reach the city centre from the train station, walk to Avenida de la Constitución and pick up bus 4, 6, 7, 9 or 11 going to the right (east). From the centre (Gran Vía de Colón) to the train station, take bus 3, 4, 6, 9 or 11.

COSTA DE ALMERÍA

The coast east of Almería in eastern Andalucía is perhaps the last section of Spain's Mediterranean coast where you can have a beach to yourself. This is Spain's sunniest region – even in late March it can be warm enough to strip off and take in the rays. For information, visit the **regional tourist office** (☎ 950 27 43 55; Parque de Nicolás Salmerón s/n; 9am-7pm Mon-Fri, 10am-2pm Sat & Sun) in Almería City.

Sights & Activities

The **Alcazaba** (☎ 950 17 55 00; Calle Almanzor s/n; admission €1.50, EU citizen free; 9am-8.30pm Apr-Oct & 9am-6.30pm Nov-Mar), an enormous 10th-century Muslim fortress, is the highlight of Almería City.

The best thing about the region is the wonderful coastline and semidesert scenery of the **Cabo de Gata** promontory. All along the 50km coast from El Cabo de Gata village to Agua Amarga, some of the most beautiful and empty beaches on the Mediterranean alternate with precipitous cliffs and scattered villages. Roads or paths run along or close to this whole coastline, which is a protected area. The main village is laid-back **San José**, with excellent beaches nearby, such as **Playa de los Genoveses** and **Playa de Mónsul**.

Sleeping & Eating

ALMERÍA

Hostal Sevilla (☎ 950 23 00 09; Calle de Granada 23; s/d €38/54;) This best budget bet is a cheerful and efficient place that offers clean rooms and a good central location. Bathrooms are miniscule but modern.

Hotel Torreluz (☎ 950 23 43 99; www.torreluz.com; Plaza de las Flores 2 & 3; s/d 2-star €39/64, 3-star €56/74; P) Burnt-plum walls, comfortable beds and good prices make this one of Almería's best-value places to stay.

Comidas Sol de Almería (Calle Circunvalación, Mercado Central; menú €10.50; 12.30pm-4pm, closed Sun) A jolly restaurant, opposite the busy covered market, with a large sunlit yet sheltered patio behind it. Hungry shoppers stream in for the extensive and hearty lunch *menú*.

CABO DE GATA

Hostal Sol Bahía (☎ 950 38 03 07; fax 950 38 03 06; Avenida de San José, San José; d €40-70;) The Sol Bahía and its sister establishment, Hostal Bahía Plaza, across the street, are in the centre of San José and have functional, clean rooms in bright, modern buildings.

MOJÁCAR

Hostal Arco Plaza (☎ 950 47 27 77; fax 950 47 27 17; Calle Aire Bajo 1, Plaza Nueva; s/d €36/52;) Bang in the centre of the village, the Arco Plaza has rooms in pretty pastel shades with spacious bathrooms and crisp, white linen. Management and staff seem incredibly friendly and efficient.

Restaurante El Viento del Desierto (Plaza Frontón; mains from €7.50; closed Sun & Jan) Good-value, long-established Moroccan-cum-Spanish eatery just by the church.

Getting There & Away

From Almería's **bus station** (☎ 95 026 20 98; Plaza de Barcelona), Alsina Graells travels to Granada (€10.10 to €12.25, 2½ to four hours, five daily), Málaga (€14.55, 3¼ hours, nine daily) and Seville (€27.70 to €28.60, 7½ to nine hours, three daily).

From the **train station** (Plaza de la Estación) there are services to Madrid (€33.90 to €38, seven hours, one daily), Granada (€13.40, 2¼ hours, four daily) and Seville (€32.10, 5½ hours, four daily).

MÁLAGA

pop 720,000

This exuberant port city suffers unfairly from its proximity to the overdeveloped Costa del Sol. Málaga is an enticing mix of pedestrianised streets, vibrant nightlife and great tapas, with a world-class gallery thrown in for good measure. It's got Andaluz charm in spades, particularly during Semana Santa and the August *feria*.

Information

Meeting Point (Plaza de la Merced 20; internet per min/hr €0.20/1-2; 10am-11pm Mon-Sat, 1.30-11pm Sun)

Municipal tourist office (www.malagaturismo.com, in Spanish) Plaza de la Marina (952 12 20 20; 9am-7pm Mon-Fri, 10am-7pm Sat & Sun Apr-Oct, 9am-6pm Mon-Fri, 10am-6pm Sat & Sun Nov-Mar); Casita del Jardinero (952 13 47 31; Avenida de Cervantes 1; same hr)

Sights & Activities

The fabulous **Museo Picasso Málaga** (902 44 33 77; www.museopicassomalaga.org; Palacio de Buenavista, Calle San Agustín 8; permanent collection €6, temporary exhibition €4.50, combined ticket €8, under-26 students half price; 10am-8pm Tue-Thu & Sun, to 9pm Fri & Sat) is set in the lovely 16th-century Palacio de Buenavista. The museum is stacked with more than 200 works covering the length of Picasso's astonishing career.

Málaga's **Catedral** (952 21 59 17; www.3planalfa.es/catedralmalaga; Calle Molina Lario, entrance Calle Císter; admission €3.50; 10am-5.30pm Mon-Fri, to 5pm Fri, closed Sun & holidays) has a peculiar lopsided look (the south tower was never completed) and a magnificent 18th-century baroque facade.

The **Alcazaba** (952 22 51 06; Calle Alcazabilla; admission €2, combined ticket incl Castillo de Gibralfaro €3.20; 9.30am-8pm Tue-Sun Apr-Oct, 8.30am-7pm Tue-Sun Nov-Mar, closed Mon & major holidays) fortress and palace dates from the 8th century. Above it rises the older **Castillo de Gibralfaro** (952 22 72 30; admission €2; 9am-9pm Apr-Sep, to 6pm Oct-Mar). Below the Alcazaba is a **Roman theatre**.

Sandy city beaches stretch several kilometres in each direction from the port. **Playa de la Malagueta**, handy to the city centre, has some excellent bars and restaurants close by. **Playa de Pedregalejo** and **Playa del Palo**, about 4km east of the centre, are popular and reachable by bus 11 from Paseo del Parque.

Sleeping

Hostal Derby (952 22 13 01; Calle San Juan de Dios 1, 4th fl; s/d €36/49;) A good-value *hostal* with spacious rooms and big windows, some overlooking the harbour.

Hostal Larios (952 22 54 90; www.hostallarios.com; Calle Marqués de Larios 9; s/d with shared bathroom €39/49, s/d/tr with private bathroom €48/58/78; P) This central *hostal* outclasses all others in the budget range. The 12 rooms are painted apricot and blue.

El Riad Andaluz (952 21 36 40; www.elriadandaluz.com; Calle Hinestrosa 24; s/d €70/90;) Colourful and exotic, this gorgeous restored monastery offers eight rooms with Moroccan decor set around an atmospheric patio.

Eating

La Rebaná (Calle Molina Lario 5; tapas €3, raciones €7-11.50) A great, noisy tapas bar near the Picasso Museum. Dark wood, tall windows and exposed brick walls create a minimal, laid-back space. Try the foie gras with salted nougat for a unique tapa.

Comoloco (Calle Denis Belgrano 17; salads €8-10 & pittas €5-6; 1pm-1am) Huge windows look on to the little street – or you can look in at the ravenous crowd inside. The menu features a vegetarian's delight of salads and generously filled pitta wraps amid industrial decor.

Gorki (952 22 14 66; Calle Strachan 6; platos combinados €7.50-16) This popular upmarket tapas bar has pavement tables and a modern interior full of wine-barrel tables and stools.

Café de Flores (952 60 85 24; Calle Madre de Dios 29; menu €9.50, mains €14-23; 1.30pm-late Tue-Sun) With plexiglass furniture, abstract art and a DJ, this haunt of smart young *malagueños* is a coffee bar and lunch stop by day. At night, good food comes with muted clubbing sounds.

At lunch, locals tend to gravitate towards the excellent fish restaurants at Playas de Pedregalejo and del Palo, a few kilometres east of the centre, which specialise in *fritura malagueña* (fried fish, anchovies and squid).

Drinking

On weekend nights, the web of narrow old streets north of Plaza de la Constitución comes alive. Look for bars around Plaza de la Merced, Plaza Mitjana and Plaza de Uncibay. Try also the venerable old **Antigua Casa de Guardia** (952 21 46 80; Alameda Central 18); **Bodegas El Pimpi** (952 22 89 90; Calle Granada 62; 7pm-2am), with a fun-loving crowd; and **Liceo** (Calle Beatas 21; 9pm-1am Thu-Sat), a grand old mansion turned young music bar.

Getting There & Away

Málaga's Pablo Ruiz Picasso Airport (AGP), the main international gateway to Andalucía, receives flights by dozens of airlines (budget and otherwise).

The Aeropuerto train station on the Málaga–Fuengirola line is a five-minute walk from the airport. Trains run about every half-hour from 6.49am to 11.49pm, to Málaga-Renfe station (€2, 11 minutes) and Málaga-Centro station.

Acciona-Trasmediterránea (Estación Marítima, Local E1) operates a fast ferry (four hours) and a slower ferry (7½ hours) daily year-round to/from Melilla (fast ferry/ferry per passenger €55/33.50, per car €174/156).

Málaga's **bus station** (952 35 00 61; Paseo de los Tilos) is 1km southwest of the city centre. Frequent buses travel to Seville (€16, 2½ hours, nine or more daily), Granada (€10, 1½ to two hours, 17 daily), Córdoba (€12.50, 2½ hours, five daily) and Ronda (€9.50, 2½ hours, nine or more daily). Nine buses also run daily to Madrid (€21.50, six hours).

The main station, **Málaga-RENFE** (Explanada de la Estación), is around the corner from the bus station. The super-fast AVE service runs to Madrid (€71.20 to €79.20, 2½ hours, six daily).

Trains also go to Córdoba (€19, one hour, 10 daily), Seville (€17.30 to €33, two to 2½ hours, five daily) and Barcelona (€58.40 to €129.40, 6½ to 13 hours, two daily). For Granada (€13.45, 2½ hours) and Ronda (€8.85, 1½ hours minimum), change at Bobadilla.

ALGECIRAS

pop 111,300

An unattractive industrial and fishing town between Tarifa and Gibraltar, Algeciras is the major port linking Spain with Morocco. Keep your wits about you, and ignore offers from the legions of moneychangers, drug-pushers and ticket-hawkers who hang out here. The **tourist office** (956 57 32 41; Calle Juan de la Cierva s/n; 9am-7.30pm Mon-Fri, 9.30am-3pm Sat & Sun) is near the port. Hopefully you won't need to seek help from the **Policía Nacional** (956 66 04 00; Avenida de las Fuerzas Armadas 6).

Companies such as **Acciona-Trasmediterránea** (902 45 46 45; www.trasmediterranea.es) and **EuroFerrys** (956 65 23 24; www.euroferrys.com) operate frequent ferries to/from Tangier, Morocco (passenger/car and passenger €42/160, 1¼ to 2½ hours) and Ceuta, the Spanish enclave on the Moroccan coast (passenger/car and passenger €39.50/146.10, 35 minutes). **Buquebus** (956 65 24 73) operates a similar Ceuta service at least six times daily.

The bus station is on Calle San Bernardo. Buses depart for La Línea (€1.85, 30 minutes) every 30 to 45 minutes. Up to 13 buses run to/from Tarifa (€1.85, 30 minutes) and Cádiz (€10.60, 2½ hours) and six to/from Seville (€16.50, 2½ hours). **Daibus** (956 58 78 97) runs four daily buses to Madrid (€27.55, eight to nine hours).

From the **station** (956 63 10 05), adjacent to Calle San Bernardo, trains run to/from Madrid (€38.10 to €63.50, six or 11 hours, two daily) and Granada (€18.35, four hours, three daily). All go through Ronda (€6.70 to €17.40, 1¾ hours).

CÁDIZ

pop 128,550

Cádiz is crammed onto the head of a promontory like an overcrowded ocean liner. Columbus sailed from here on his second and fourth voyages, and after his success in the Americas, Cádiz grew into Spain's richest and most cosmopolitan city in the 18th century. The best time to visit is during the February *carnaval* (carnival), which rivals Rio in terms of outrageous exuberance.

The **municipal tourist office** (956 24 10 01; Paseo de Canalejas s/n; 8.30am-6pm Mon-Fri, 9am-5pm Sat & Sun) has helpful staff.

Sights & Activities

The yellow-domed 18th-century **Catedral** (956 28 61 54; Plaza de la Catedral; adult/student €5/3, free during services; 10am-6.30pm Mon-Fri, 10am-4.30pm Sat, 1-6.30pm Sun, services 7-8pm Tue-Fri, 11am-1pm Sun) is the city's most striking landmark.

Get your bearings by climbing up the baroque **Torre Tavira** (956 21 29 10; Calle Marqués del Real Tesoro 10; adult/student €4/3.30; 10am-6pm, to 8pm 15 Jun-15 Sep), the highest of Cádiz' old watchtowers, which features sweeping views of the city.

The **Museo de Cádiz** (956 20 33 68; Plaza de Mina; admission €1.50, EU citizen free; 2.30-8.30pm Tue, 9am-8.30pm Wed-Sat, 9.30am-2.30pm Sun) has a magnificent collection of archaeological remains, as well as a fine-art collection.

Sleeping & Eating

Casa Caracol (☎ 956 26 11 66; www.caracolcasa.com; Calle Suárez de Salazar 4; dm/hammock incl breakfast €16/10; 💻) Casa Caracol is the only backpacker hostel in the old town. Friendly and crowded, it has bunk dorms for four and eight, a communal kitchen, free internet, and a roof terrace with hammocks. It's often full.

Hostal Fantoni (☎ 956 28 27 04; www.hostalfantoni.net; Calle Flamenco 5; s/d €45/70; ❄) The Fantoni offers a dozen elegant and spotless rooms in an attractively modernised 18th-century house. The roof terrace catches a breeze in summer.

La Gorda Te Da De Comer (tapas €2-2.40) Luque (Calle General Luque 1; 🕑 Mon-Sat); Rosario (cnr Calle Rosario & Calle Marqués de Valdeiñigo; 🕑 Tue-Sat) Incredibly tasty food at low prices amid trendy pop design. Try the *solomillo* in creamy mushroom sauce or the curried chicken strips with Marie-Rose dip.

Mesón Cumbres Mayores (☎ 956 21 32 70; Calle Zorrilla 4; tapas €1.50-2, mains €9-18) The wood-beamed Cumbres Mayores has an excellent tapas bar in the front and a small restaurant in the back.

Getting There & Away

From the Cádiz **bus station** (☎ 95 680 70 59; Plaza de la Hispanidad), buses head for Seville (€10.65, 1¾ hours, 10 daily), Tarifa (€7.90, two hours, five daily), Ronda (€12.60, three hours, two daily), Málaga (€19.60, four hours, six daily) and Granada (€27.90, five hours, four daily).

From the **train station** (Plaza Sevilla), services run to Seville (€9.80, two hours, 15 daily), Córdoba (€34 to €43, three hours, three daily) and Madrid (€63, five hours, two daily).

TARIFA

pop 17,600

Windy, laid-back Tarifa is so close to Africa that you can almost hear the call to prayer issuing from Morocco's minarets. The town is a bohemian haven of cafes and crumbling Moorish ruins. There's also a lively windsurfing and kitesurfing scene.

Stretching west are the long, sandy (and largely deserted) beaches of the Costa de la Luz (Coast of Light), backed by cool pine forests and green hills.

The town's **tourist office** (☎ 956 68 09 93; www.aytotarifa.com, in Spanish; Paseo de la Alameda; 🕑 10am-2pm daily year-round, 4-6pm Mon-Fri Oct-May, 6-8pm Mon-Fri Jun-Sep) has lots of information on the area. For internet, try **Pandora** (Calle Sancho IV El Bravo 13A; internet per hr €2; 🕑 10am-2.30pm & 5-9.30pm).

Sights & Activities

The **Castillo de Guzmán** (Calle Guzmán El Bueno), which dates from the 10th century, was closed for refurbishment at the time of writing. It may reopen in 2010.

On the isthmus leading out to Isla de las Palomas, **Playa Chica** is sheltered but a very small beach indeed. From here the spectacular **Playa de los Lances** stretches northwest to the huge sand dune at **Ensenada de Valdevaqueros**. Most of the **kite-surfing** and **windsurfing** action occurs between Tarifa and Punta Paloma, 11km northwest.

The Strait of Gibraltar is good **whale-** and **dolphin-watching** territory from spring to autumn. Excursions are available.

firmm (☎ 956 62 70 08; www.firmm.org; Calle Pedro Cortés 4; 🕑 Mar-Oct) Uses every trip to record data.

Turmares (☎ 956 68 07 41; www.turmares.com; Avenida Alcalde Juan Núñez 3; 🕑 Jan-Nov) Has the largest boats, holding 40 and 60 people (one with a glass bottom).

Whale Watch España (☎ 956 62 70 13; www.whalewatchtarifa.net; Avenida de la Constitución 6; 🕑 Apr-Oct)

Sleeping & Eating

Melting Pot (☎ 956 68 29 06; www.meltingpothostels.com; Calle Turriano Gracil 5; dm €22-25, d €54, incl breakfast; 💻) The Melting Pot is a friendly, well-equipped hostel just off the Alameda.

Hostal Africa (☎ 956 68 02 20; hostal_africa@hotmail.com; Calle María Antonia Toledo 12; s/d with shared bathroom €35/50, with private bathroom €50/65; 🕑 closed 24 Dec-31 Jan) Rooms are attractive and there's an expansive terrace with wonderful views.

Chilimoso (☎ 956 68 50 92; Calle Peso 6; dishes €4-6) This tiny place serves tasty vegan and vegetarian food with Oriental leanings.

Bodega La Casa Amarilla (☎ 956 68 19 93; Calle Sancho IV El Bravo 9; mains €14-18) With an attractive, flowery patio, this is a top place in town for local grilled meats and fish, good *revueltos* (scrambled egg dishes) and tapas.

Getting There & Away

Comes runs six or more daily buses to Cádiz (€7.90, 1¾ hours) and Algeciras (€1.90, 30 minutes), four to Seville (€15.30, three hours), two to Málaga (€12.45, two hours), and one to Zahara de los Atunes (€3.25, 40 minutes) on the Costa de la Luz.

FRS (☎ 956 68 18 30; www.frs.es; Estación Marítima) runs fast ferries between Tarifa and Tangier (passenger/car/motorcycle one-way €31/85/31, 35 minutes, eight daily).

GIBRALTAR

pop 27,900

The British colony of Gibraltar is like 1960s Britain on a sunny day, with double-decker buses, bobbies and the fried-egg-and-chip-style eateries. In British hands since 1713, it was the starting point for the Muslim conquest of Iberia a thousand years earlier. Spain has never fully accepted UK control of the island but, for the moment at least, talk of joint sovereignty seems to have gone cold. Inhabitants speak English and Spanish and signs are in English.

INFORMATION

To enter Gibraltar you must have a passport or EU national identity card. Gibraltar is outside the Schengen area, and visitors needing a Schengen-area visa who intend to enter from Spain should ensure that they have a double-entry visa if they wish to return to Spain. Nationals from certain countries require a visa to enter; contact the **Immigration Department** (☎ 46411; rgpimm@gibgibtelecom.net).

The currency is the Gibraltar pound. Change any unspent Gibraltar pounds before you leave. You can also use euros or pounds sterling.

To phone Gibraltar from Spain, the telephone code is ☎ 9567; from other countries dial the international access code, then ☎ 350 and the local number. To phone Spain from Gibraltar, just dial the nine-digit Spanish number.

There's internet access at **General Internet Business Centre** (☎ 44227; 36 Governor's St; per hr £3; 10am-10pm Tue-Sat, noon-9pm Sun & Mon).

There are a couple of **tourist offices** Main office (☎ 74950; www.gibraltar.gov.gi; Duke of Kent House, Cathedral Sq; 9am-5.30pm Mon-Fri); Casemates Sq (☎ 74982; 9am-5.30pm Mon-Fri, 10am-3pm Sat, 10am-1pm Sun).

SIGHTS & ACTIVITIES

The **Gibraltar Museum** (Bomb House Lane; admission £2; 10am-6pm Mon-Fri, to 2pm Sat), with its interesting historical collection and Muslim-era bathhouse, is worth a peek. Wander into the **Alameda Botanical Gardens** (Red Sands Rd; 8am-sunset) for some chill-out time.

The large **Upper Rock Nature Reserve** (admission incl attractions £8, vehicle £1.50, pedestrian excl attractions £1; 9.30am-7pm), covering most of the upper rock, has spectacular views. The rock's most famous inhabitants are its colony of Barbary macaques, the only wild primates in Europe. Some of these hang around the **Apes' Den** near the middle cable-car station; others can often be seen at the top station or Great Siege Tunnels. Other attractions include **St Michael's Cave**, a large natural grotto renowned for its stalagmites and stalactites, and the **Great Siege Tunnels**, a series of galleries hewn from the rock by the British to provide new gun emplacements during the Great Siege by the Spaniards (1779–83).

Dolphin-watching is an option from April to September. Boats head out to the Bahía de Algeciras from Watergardens Quay or adjacent Marina Bay.

SLEEPING & EATING

Cannon Hotel (☎ 51711; www.cannonhotel.gi; 9 Cannon Lane; s/d with shared bathroom £26.50/38.50, d with private bathroom £47, all incl breakfast) This is a small, budget-priced hotel right in the main shopping area.

Caleta Hotel (☎ 76501; www.caletahotel.gi; Sir Herbert Miles Rd; d/ste without/with sea view £110/150; P) Caleta has a wonderful location overlooking Catalan Bay, on the east side of the Rock, five minutes from town. Its cascading terraces have panoramic sea views, and there's a host of luxurious gym and spa facilities.

Clipper (☎ 79791; 78B Irish Town; mains £3.50-9) Most of Gibraltar's pubs serve British pub meals. The Clipper offers real pub grub and a genuine pub atmosphere.

House of Sacarello (☎ 70625; 57 Irish Town; daily specials £7-11.50; 9am-7.30pm Mon-Fri, 9am-3pm Sat, closed Sun) This chic place in a converted coffee warehouse serves light lunches, including pastas and salads. Linger over afternoon tea (£4) between 3pm and 7.30pm.

GETTING THERE & AWAY

Easyjet (www.easyjet.com), **Iberia** (www.iberia.com) and **Monarch** (www.flymonarch.com) fly daily to/from London Gatwick.

FRS (☎ in Tarifa, Spain 956 68 18 30; www.frs.es) operates one ferry a week between Gibraltar and Tangier (Morocco).

There are no regular buses to Gibraltar, but La Línea de la Concepción bus station is only a five-minute walk from the border.

EXTREMADURA

A sparsely populated stretch of vast skies and open plains, Extremadura is far enough from most beaten tourist trails to give you a genuine sense of exploration, something for which Extremeños themselves have always had a flair.

TRUJILLO

pop 9700

Trujillo is a delightful little town that can't be much bigger now than it was in 1529, when its most famous son, Francisco Pizarro, set off with his three brothers and a few buddies for an expedition that culminated in the bloody conquest of the Incan empire.

There's a **tourist office** (☎ 927 32 26 77; www.ayto-trujillo.com, in Spanish; Plaza Mayor s/n; 🕑 10am-2pm & 4-7pm Oct-May, 10am-2pm & 5-8pm Jun-Sep) in the centre. For internet, try **Ciberalia** (☎ 927 65 90 87; Calle Tiendas 18; per hr €2; 🕑 11am-midnight).

Sights

A **statue of Pizarro** dominates the splendid Plaza Mayor. On the plaza's southern side, the **Palacio de la Conquista** (closed to visitors) sports the carved images of Francisco Pizarro and the Inca princess Inés Yupanqui. The **Palacio Juan Pizarro de Orellana** (admission free; 🕑 10am-1.30pm & 4.30-6.30pm) and 16th-century **Palacio de los Duques de San Carlos** (admission €1; 🕑 10am-1pm & 4.30-6.30pm), now a convent, can also be visited.

Up the hill, the **Iglesia de Santa María la Mayor** (Plaza de Santa María) is an interesting hotchpotch of 13th- to 16th-century styles, with some fine paintings by Fernando Gallego of the Flemish school. At the top of the hill, Trujillo's Moorish **castillo** (☎ 927 32 26 77; Calle Convento de las Jerónimas 12) is an impressive structure commanding great views.

The **Museo del Queso** (Cheese Museum; ☎ 927 32 30 31; Calle Francisco Pizarro s/n; admission €2.30) is set in a former convent. The admission price includes a tasting of *Torta del Casar*, the local favourite, and some wine too.

Sleeping & Eating

Hostal Orellana (☎ 927 32 07 53; Calle Ruiz de Mendoza 2; s/d €30/45; ❄) The comfortable rooms in this 16th-century house have exposed stone, dark timber and warm decor with terracotta tiles and butter-coloured paintwork.

Posada Dos Orillas (☎ 927 65 90 79; www.dosorillas.com; Calle de Cambrones 6; d Sun-Thu €70-90, Fri & Sat €81-107; ❄ 💻) This tastefully renovated 16th-century mansion in the walled town once served as a silk-weaving centre. The rooms replicate Spanish colonial taste.

Restaurante La Troya (☎ 927 32 13 64; Plaza Mayor 10; set meals €15) The *menú* here is enormous – perfect for patrons who've just spent eight hours labouring in the fields, and overwhelming for anyone else.

Mesón Alberca (☎ 927 32 22 09; Calle de Cambrones 8; meals €30-40, menú €17.50; 🕑 Thu-Sun) Dark-timber tables laid with gingham cloths, or a pretty ivy-clad terrace, create a choice of warm atmospheres for sampling classic *extremeño* cooking. The speciality is oven roasts.

Getting There & Away

The **bus station** (Avenida de Miajadas) is 500m south of Plaza Mayor. There are services to/from Madrid (€15.20 to €19, three to 4¼ hours, up to 10 daily), Cáceres (€3.55, 45 minutes, eight daily) and Mérida (€7.35, 1½ hours, three daily).

CÁCERES

pop 89,050

Cáceres' *ciudad monumental* (old town), built in the 15th and 16th centuries, is perfectly preserved. The town's action centres on Plaza Mayor, at the foot of the old town, and busy Avenida de España, a short distance south. Get info at the **municipal tourist office** (☎ 927 24 71 72; Calle Ancha 7; 🕑 10am-2pm & 4.30-7.30pm or 5.30-8.30pm Tue-Sun) and email at **Yass** (Calle del General Ezponda 12; per hr €1; 🕑 10am-10pm).

Sights

Entering the *ciudad monumental* from Plaza Mayor, you'll see ahead the fine 15th-century **Concatedral de Santa María** (Plaza de Santa María; 🕑 10am-1pm & 5-8pm Mon-Sat, 9.30am-2pm & 5-8pm Sun).

Climb the 12th-century **Torre de Bujaco** (Plaza Mayor; admission €2; 🕑 10am-2pm & 5.30-8.30pm Mon-Sat, 10am-2pm Sun Apr-Sep, 10am-2pm & 4.30-7.30pm Mon-Sat, 10am-2pm Sun Oct-Mar) for great views.

Many of the old city's churches and imposing medieval mansions can be admired only from the outside, but you can visit the **Museo de Cáceres** (☎ 927 01 08 77; Plaza de las Veletas 1;

admission/EU citizens €1.20/free; 9am-2.30pm & 4-7.15pm Tue-Sat, 10.15am-2.30pm Sun), which is housed in a 16th-century mansion built over a 12th-century Moorish *aljibe* (cistern).

Sleeping & Eating

Hotel Iberia (927 24 76 34; www.iberiahotel.com, in Spanish; Calle de los Pintores 2; s/d €46/65;) Located in an 18th-century former palace, this 36-room hotel has plush, if quirky, public areas and more traditional rooms with parquet floors, cream walls and pale-grey tiled bathrooms.

El Corral de las Cigüeñas (Calle Cuesta de Aldana 6; 8am-1pm Mon-Fri, 7pm-3am Tue-Sat, 5-11pm Sun) The secluded courtyard, with its lofty palm trees, is perfect for one of the best-value breakfasts around: there are seven versions to choose from!

Mesón El Asador (927 22 38 37; Calle Moret 34; raciones €6-8, meals €18-25; closed Sun) Enter the dining room and you get the picture right away – one wall is covered with hung hams. You won't taste better roast pork (or lamb) in town.

Getting There & Away

From the **bus station** (927 23 25 50; Carretera de Sevilla), 1.5km southwest of Plaza Mayor, there are several runs to Trujillo (€3.55, 45 minutes) and Mérida (€4.80, 50 minutes).

Up to five trains per day run to/from Madrid (€17.80 to €24.50, four hours), Plasencia (€4.35, 1½ hours) and Mérida (€5.25, one hour).

MÉRIDA

pop 74,900

Once the biggest city in Roman Spain, Mérida is home to more ruins of that age than anywhere else in the country and is a wonderful spot to spend a few archaeologically inclined days.

Information is available at the **municipal tourist office** (924 33 07 22; Calle Santa Eulalia 64; 9.30am-2pm & 4-7pm or 5-8pm). For internet access, try **Friends on Line** (Calle Romero Leal 5; per hr €2; 11am-2pm & 4pm-midnight).

Sights

The awesome ruins of Mérida's **Teatro Romano & Anfiteatro** (Calle Alvarez S. de Buruaga; admission €7, admission incl Casa del Anfiteatro, Los Columbarios, Casa del Mitreo, Alcazaba, Zona Arqueológica de Morería, Basilica de Santa Eulalia & Circo Romano €10; 9.30am-1.45 & 5-7.15pm Jun-Sep, 9.30am-1.45 & 4-6.15pm Oct-May) shouldn't be missed. The theatre was built in 15 BC and the gladiators' ring, or Anfiteatro, seven years later. Combined, they could hold 20,000 spectators.

Other monuments of interest are the **Casa del Anfiteatro**, the **Casa del Mitreo**, the **Alcazaba** (Calle Graciano; admission €4), the **Basílica de Santa Eulalia** (Avenida de Extremadura; admission €4), remains of the 1st-century **Circo Romano** (Avenida Juan Carlos; admission €4), the only surviving hippodrome of its kind in Spain, and the **Museo Nacional de Arte Romano** (924 31 16 90; www.mnar.es; Calle de José Ramón Mélida; adult/18-25yr €2.40/1.20; 10am-2pm & 5-7pm Tue-Sat, 10am-2pm Sun Mar-Nov, 10am-2pm & 4-6pm Tue-Sat, 10am-2pm Sun Dec-Feb).

Opening hours for all except the museum are 9.30am to 1.45pm and 4pm to 6.15pm October to May, and 9.30am to 1.45pm and 5pm to 7.15pm June to September.

Other reminders of imperial days are scattered about town, including the **Puente Romano**. At 792m, it's one of the longest bridges the Romans ever built.

Sleeping & Eating

Hotel Cervantes (924 31 49 61; www.hotelcervantes.com; Calle Camilo José Cela 8; s €40-50, d €60-70; P) The best deal in this price bracket with attractive half-panelled rooms thath include marble floors, full baths and dark wood furniture. The bar-restaurant serves a bacon-and-egg breakfast.

Hotel Velada (924 31 51 10; www.veladahoteles.com; Avenida Reina Sofia s/n; r €60-85; P) The city's newest hotel is just 600m from the Teatro Romano and has a faux-temple exterior complete with columns. The rooms are modern, carpeted and comfortable with gleaming marble bathrooms.

Casa Benito (924 33 07 69; Calle San Francisco 3; tapas €2.60) Squeeze onto a tiny stool in the wood-panelled dining room, prop up the bar or relax on the sunny terrace for tapas at this bullfight enthusiasts' hang-out. The adjacent *Asador* specialises in roasts including *rabo de toro* (bull's tail).

Restaurante Nicolás (924 31 96 10; Calle Felix Valverde Lillo 15; meals €20-25; Mon-Sat, lunch Sun) Long admired as a local favourite, this is one of the classier city dining options. Its relaxing ground-floor bar serves *raciones* while upstairs the food is decidedly more exciting than the restaurant's rather drab decor.

Getting There & Away

The **bus station** (Avenida de la Libertad) is across the river. Destinations include: Seville (€11.95, 2½ hours), Cáceres (€4.80, 50 minutes), Trujillo (€7.35, 1¼ hours) and Madrid (€20.65 to €27, four to five hours).

From the **train station** (Calle Cardero), there are four trains to Madrid (€28.75 to €31.80, 4½ to 5½ hours) and two to Seville (€12.15, five hours). Up to six trains run to/from Cáceres (€5.25, one hour).

ARAGÓN, BASQUE COUNTRY & NAVARRA

This northeast area of Spain is brimming with fascinating destinations: from the arid hills and proud history of Aragón to the lush coastline and gourmet delights of the Basque Country (País Vasco) to the wine country and famous festivals of Navarra.

ARAGÓN

Zaragoza

pop 624,600 / elev 200m

Zaragoza is a busy regional capital with a seemingly voracious appetite for eating out and late-night revelry. The old centre, crowned by the majestic Basílica del Pilar, throws up echos of its Roman and Muslim past. The old town is also home to El Tubo (The Tube), a maze of streets with countless tapas bars and cafes.

INFORMATION

Conecta-T (☎ 976 20 59 79; Murallas Romanas 4; per hr €1.60; 🕑 10am-11pm Mon-Fri, 11am-11pm Sat & Sun) Internet access.

Oficina de Turismo de Aragón (☎ 976 28 21 81; www.turismodearagon.com; Avenida de César Augusto 25; 🕑 9am-2pm & 5-8pm Mon-Fri, from 10am Sat & Sun)

Zaragoza Turismo (☎ 902 14 20 08; www.zaragoza.es/ciudad/turismo) Main tourist office (Plaza del Pilar; 🕑 9am-9pm Easter-Oct, 10am-8pm Nov-Easter); Torreón de la Zuda (Glorieta de Pío XII; 🕑 10am-2pm & 4.30-8pm Nov-Easter, 9am-9pm Easter-Oct)

SIGHTS

The baroque **Basílica de Nuestra Señora del Pilar** (☎ 976 39 74 97; admission free; 🕑 6.45am-9.30pm) has long been a place of pilgrimage. The faithful flock to the **Capilla Santa** to kiss a piece of marble pillar. They believe the Virgin Mary appeared to St James atop this pillar in AD 40.

At Plaza del Pilar's southeastern end is Zaragoza's brooding 12th- to 17th-century cathedral, **La Seo** (☎ 976 29 12 38; Plaza de la Seo; admission €2.50; 🕑 10am-6pm Tue-Fri, 10am-2pm & 3-6pm Sat, 10-11.30am & 2.30-6pm Sun Jun-Sep, shorter hr rest of year). Its northwest facade is a Mudéjar masterpiece, and inside is an impressive 15th-century main altarpiece in coloured alabaster.

Begin a Roman tour of Zaragoza with a stop at the **Museo del Foro de Caesaraugusta** (☎ 976 39 97 52; Plaza de la Seo 2; admission €2; 🕑 10am-2pm & 5-8pm Tue-Sat, 10am-2pm Sun, last entry 1hr before closing time), an interesting museum about Roman life. Some 70m below lie the remains of the Roman town, brought to life by an audiovisual show (in Spanish).

The **Palacio de la Aljafería** (☎ 976 28 96 84; Calle de los Diputados; adult/concession €3/1, Sun free; 🕑 10am-2pm & 4-6.30pm Mon-Wed & Fri-Sat, 10am-2pm Sun Nov-Mar, 10am-2pm & 4.30-8pm Sat-Wed, 4.30-8pm Fri Apr-Jun & Sep-Oct, 10am-2pm & 4.30-8pm daily Jul & Aug) is Spain's most outstanding Muslim building outside Andalucía. Built as the palace of the Muslim rulers who held the city from 714 to 1118, it is now home to Aragón's parliament.

SLEEPING

On and around Plaza del Pilar and Avenida César Augusto you'll find most of the sleeping options.

Hostal El Descanso (☎ 976 29 17 41; Calle de San Lorenzo 2; s/d with shared bathroom €20/30) Simple, bright rooms, a family atmosphere and a central location overlooking a pretty plaza near the Roman theatre add up to a good budget deal.

Hotel Rio Arga (☎ 976 39 90 65; www.hotelrioarga.es; Contamina 20; s/d €43/60; P ❄ 💻) In a quiet location, yet ideal for all central needs, there are comfy rooms here. Most have been renovated with flat-screen TVs and a modern look.

Hotel Sauce (☎ 976 20 50 50; www.hotelsauce.com; Calle de Espoz y Mina 33; s/d €58.85/74.90; P ❄ 💻) This small hotel has good rooms with a mix of styles from traditional and cosy to pastel tones and a modern, classy look. Breakfast is €7.50.

EATING & DRINKING

Zaragoza has some terrific tapas bars, with dozens of places on or close to Plaza de Santa Marta and towards the southern end of Calle Heroísmo. Otherwise the narrow streets of El Tubo, north of Plaza de España, are tapas central.

Mercado Central (Plaza de Lanuza; 8am-2pm) Get your fresh fruit and vegies at Central, the main city market.

ourpick **Casa Pascualillo** (976 39 72 03; Calle de la Libertad 5; lunch & dinner Tue-Sat, lunch Sun) The bar groans under the weight of every tapas variety imaginable with seafood and meat in abundance, but the house speciality is El Pascualillo, a 'small' *bocadillo* of *jamón* (ham roll), mushrooms and onion.

Casa Juanico (976 29 50 88; Calle de Santiago 30-32; tapas from €2, menú del día €11; closed Tue) For cheap tapas and a friendly atmosphere, this place can't be beat, and the summer terrace is ideal.

El Rincón de Aragón (976 20 11 63; Calle de Santiago 3-5; menú del día €12.95, menú Aragonés €19.90) One house speciality among many in this knockabout place is *ternasco asado con patatas a la pobre* (roasted suckling lamb ribs with 'poor man's potatoes').

Calle del Temple, southwest of Plaza del Pilar, is the spiritual home of Zaragoza's roaring nightlife. This is where the city's students head out to drink. There are more bars lined up along this street than anywhere else in Aragón.

GETTING THERE & AWAY

High-speed AVE trains leave Zaragoza's futuristic **Estación Intermodal Delicias** (Calle Rioja 33) for Madrid (€50.90, 1½ hours, 17 daily) and Barcelona (€58.90, one hour).

Dozens of bus lines fan out across Spain from the bus station attached to the train station.

Rest of Aragón

Aragón is a land of stark contrast. The centre is largely barren, stretching south to the cold, wintry but greener territory around **Teruel** (tourist office 978 60 22 79; Calle Tomás Nogués 1), and north to Huesca and on to the pretty Pyrenees. Little visited Teruel is home to some stunning Mudéjar architecture.

In the north, the **Parque Nacional de Ordesa y Monte Perdido** (www.ordesa.net) and the **Parque Natural Posets-Maladeta** (www.cerler.es) are excellent for hiking. The village of **Torla** is the gateway to the Parque Nacional de Ordesa y Monte Perdido, while **Benasque** is a popular base for the Parque Natural Posets-Maladeta. Another enchanting base for exploration in the region is **Aínsa**, a valley town of stone houses an hour's bus ride from Torla.

South of the hamlet of **La Besurta** is the great Maladeta massif, a superb challenge for experienced climbers. This forbidding line of icy peaks, with glaciers suspended from the higher crests, culminates in **Aneto** (3404m), the highest peak in the Pyrenees. There are plenty of hiking and climbing options for all levels in these mountain parks bordering France.

BASQUE COUNTRY

The Basques, whose language is believed to be among the world's oldest, claim two of Spain's most interesting cities as their own – San Sebastián and Bilbao. Stately San Sebastián offers a slick seaside position and some of the best food Spain has to offer. The extraordinary Guggenheim Bilbao museum is that city's centrepiece.

San Sebastián

pop 183,300

Stylish San Sebastián (Donostia in Basque) has the air of an upscale resort, complete with an idyllic location on the shell-shaped Bahía de la Concha. The natural setting – crystalline waters, a flawless beach, green hills on all sides – is captivating, but the city itself has plenty to offer. Head to the buzzing Parte Vieja (Old Quarter) for tempting tapas bars and gourmet restaurants.

INFORMATION

Centro de Atracción y Turismo (943 48 11 66; www.sansebastianturismo.com; Calle Reina Regente 3; 8.30am-8pm Mon-Sat, 10am-7pm Sun Jun-Sep, 9am-2pm & 3.30-7pm Mon-Sat, 10am-2pm Sun Oct-May)

Donosti-Net (943 42 94 97; Calle de Narrica 3; per 10min/1hr €0.90/3.30; 9am-11pm) A one-stop travellers' service, with email, travel info and left luggage.

SIGHTS & ACTIVITIES

San Sebastián's beautiful city beaches, **Playa de la Concha** and **Playa de Ondarreta**, are popular spots year-round. East of the Urumea River is the somewhat less crowded **Playa de la Zurriola**, popular with surfers. To escape the crowds, take the small **boat** (10am-8pm Jun-Sep) to the **Isla de Santa Clara**, an island in the middle of the bay. From here you can enjoy pretty views of the seafront.

For more good views, take the 30-minute walk up to **Monte Urgull**, a hill topped by low castle walls and a statue of Christ. The walk begins at a stairway in Plaza de Zuloaga.

The best vista in San Sebastián is from **Monte Igueldo**. Drive up or catch the **funicular** (return trip €2.30; 10am-10pm Jul & Aug, 10/11am-6/9pm, depending on month through rest of year) from the western end of the seafront *paseo*.

San Sebastián's best museum is the **Museo Chillida Leku** (943 33 60 06; www.museochillidaleku.com; adult/student €8.50/6.50; 10.30am-3pm Wed-Mon Sep-Jun, 10.30am-8pm Mon-Sat, 10.30am-3pm Sun Jul & Aug), 10km outside the city centre. An outdoor sculpture garden featuring 40 large-scale works by the famed Basque artist Eduardo Chillida, this peaceful place is ideal for picnics. To get here, take the G2 bus (€1.25) for Hernani from Calle de Okendo in San Sebastián and get off at Zabalaga.

San Sebastián's **aquarium** (943 44 00 99; www.aquariumss.com; Paseo del Muelle 34; adult/student €10/8; 10am-9pm Jul & Aug, 10am-8pm Apr-Jun & Sep, 10am-7pm Mon-Fri & 10am-8pm Sat & Sun Oct-Mar) is home to more than 5000 tropical fish, morays, sharks and a variety of other finned creatures.

SLEEPING

our pick Urban House (943 42 81 54; www.enjoyeu.com; Alameda Blvd 24; dm/r €27/50;) Loud and colourful rooms set the tone for this superb party house where summer fun rules supreme. It's smack in the centre of the action.

Pensión La Perla (943 42 81 23; www.pensionlaperla.com; Calle de Loyola 10; s/d/tr €35/55/70) Brisk, old-fashioned service and clean, fairly plain rooms keep this well-located central digs busy. The no-nonsense woman who runs it is very helpful.

Pensión Edorta (943 42 37 73; www.pensionedorta.com; Calle del Puerto 15; r with shared/private bathroom €60/80;) A fine spot with rooms that are all tarted up in brash modern colours but with a salute to the past in the stone walls and ceilings.

Hotel de Londres e Inglaterra (943 44 07 70; www.hlondres.com; Calle de Zubieta 2; s/d from €175/225; P) Queen Isabel II set the tone for this hotel well over a century ago and things have stayed pretty regal ever since. It oozes class and some rooms have stunning views over Playa de la Concha.

EATING

Considered the birthplace of *nueva cocina española,* this area is home to some of the country's top chefs. Yet not all the good food is pricey. Head to the Parte Vieja for San Sebastián's *pintxos,* Basque-style tapas.

Pintxos

Pintxo etiquette is simple. Ask for a plate and point out what *pintxos* (bar snacks) you want. Accompany with *txakoli,* a cloudy white wine poured like cider to create a little fizz. When you're ready to pay, hand over your plate with all the *pintxo* toothpicks and tell bar staff how many drinks you've had. It's an honour system that has stood the test of time. Expect to pay €2.50 to €3.50 for a *pintxo* and *txakoli.*

Bar La Cepa (Calle de 31 de Agosto 7) The best *jamón jabugo* does not disappoint here and you eat beneath the blank eyes of a very large bull's head.

La Mejillonera (Calle del Puerto; mussels from €3) If you thought mussels came only with garlic sauce, come here and discover mussels by the thousand in all their glorious forms.

our pick Astelena (Plaza de la Constitución Calle Iñigo 1) The *pintxos* draped across the counter in this bar, tucked into the corner of the plaza, stand out as some of the best in the city. Many are a fusion of Basque and Asian inspirations.

Restaurants

Restaurante Alberto (943 42 88 84; Calle de 31 de Agosto 19; mains from €15; closed Tue) A charming old seafood restaurant with a fishmongers-style window display of the day's catch.

Arzak (943 27 84 65; Avenida Alcalde Jose Elosegui 273; meals €150-160) Three-Michelin-star chef Juan Mari Arzak is a national institution. Arzak is now assisted by his daughter Elena and they never cease to innovate. The restaurant is about 1.5km east of San Sebastián. Reservations are obligatory.

DRINKING

The Parte Vieja is a fun place any night of the week. Around 8pm the tapas bars start hopping as people enjoy a pre-dinner round of *pintxos.* The revelry lasts until midnight midweek, and until the cock crows on weekends. Another hot spot is the area around Calle de los Reyes Católicos, behind the Catedral del Buen Pastor.

GETTING THERE & AWAY

From San Sebastián airport (EAS), catch the Interbus that runs regularly to the Plaza de Gipuzkoa in town (€1.55, times vary).

The main **Renfe train station** (Paseo de Francia) is just across Río Urumea, on a line linking Paris to Madrid. There are several services daily to Madrid (from €37.20, six hours) and two to Barcelona (from €38.20, eight hours). ET/FV trains run from Amara train station west to Bilbao (€6.50, 2½ hours, hourly).

The **bus station** (Plaza Pío XII) is a 20-minute walk south of Parte Vieja. City bus 28 makes the run to and from the centre. PESA has frequent services to Bilbao (€9.20, one hour). La Roncalesa has up to 10 buses daily to Pamplona (€6.50, one hour).

Bilbao

pop 354,100

The commercial hub of the Basque Country, Bilbao (Bilbo in Basque) is best known for the magnificent Guggenheim Museum, designed by Canadian star architect Frank Gehry. Spend time exploring Bilbao's Casco Viejo (Old Quarter), a grid of elegant streets dotted with shops, cafes, *pintxos* bars and several small but worthy museums.

INFORMATION

L@zar (☎ 944 45 35 09; Sendeja 5; per min €0.06; 🕒 10.30am-1.30am Mon-Fri, 11am-1.30am Sat & Sun) For internet.

Tourist office (☎ 944 79 57 60; www.bilbao.net/bilbaoturismo; Plaza del Ensanche 11; 🕒 9am-2pm & 4-7.30pm Mon-Fri) Has other branches at the Teatro Arriaga, Museo Guggenheim and airport.

SIGHTS

The **Museo Guggenheim** (☎ 944 35 90 80; www.guggenheim-bilbao.es; Avenida Abandoibarra 2; adult/student €12.50/7.50; 🕒 10am-8pm Tue-Sun Sep-Jun, daily Jul & Aug) is an experience. For many, the building is more interesting than the exhibitions inside. With its undulating forms covered in titanium scales, the structure was inspired by the shapes of ships and fish. Many credit this creation with revitalising modern architecture and creating a new standard in vanguard design.

Nearby, the **Museo de Bellas Artes** (Fine Arts Museum; ☎ 944 39 60 60; www.museobilbao.com; Plaza del Museo 2; adult/student €5.50/4, Wed free; 🕒 10am-8pm Tue-Sun) often seems to exceed its more famous cousin for content.

The **Casco Viejo**, Bilbao's old quarter, is a compact area of charming streets, boisterous bars and plenty of quirky and independent shops.

The **Euskal Museoa** (Museum of Basque Archaeology, Ethnography & History; ☎ 944 15 54 23; www.euskal-museoa.org; Plaza Miguel Unamuno 4; adult/student €3/1.50, Thu free; 🕒 11am-5pm Tue-Sat, 11am-2pm Sun) gives a complete lesson in Basque history.

Take the metro to the **Puente Colgante** (Hanging Bridge; www.puente-colgante.com; Calle Barria 3, Las Arenas Getxo; 🕒 10am-sunset) to walk or, better yet, ride across on the gondola (€0.30 each way) that hangs from the world's oldest 'transporter bridge'.

SLEEPING

The Bilbao tourism authority has a useful **reservations department** (☎ 902 87 72 98; www.bilbaoreservas.com).

Pensión Mardones (☎ 944 15 31 05; www.pensionmardones.com; Calle Jardines 4; s/d €34/48; 💻) This well-kept number has nice carved wooden wardrobes in the rooms and lots of exposed wooden roof beams.

Pensión Iturrienea Ostatua (☎ 944 16 15 00; www.iturrieneaostatua.com; Calle de Santa María 14; d/tr €70/96) Easily the most eccentric hotel in Bilbao, this part farmyard/part old-fashioned toy shop is a work of art in its own right. Try to get a characterful room on the first floor.

EATING

Xukeia (☎ 944 15 97 72; Calle el Perro) Xukeia has something of the look of a small-town French bistro overlaid with raucous Spanish soul. The drool-inducing *pintxos* have won awards and are cheaper than elsewhere.

El Globo (☎ 944 15 42 21; Calle de Diputación 8) One of the best *pintxos* options in the modern Ensanche part of town, this popular bar has a terrific range, including *txangurro gratinado* (spider crab) and *morcilla rebozada* (blood sausage in light batter).

Abaroa (☎ 944 13 20 51; Campo Volantin 13; mains €7-12) This brightly furnished restaurant specialises in hearty countryside fare with a twist of today. Black pudding and a bowl of beans never tasted so good!

DRINKING

Las Siete Calles are transformed into one big street party at night. Bars and discos line the streets, especially rowdy Calle Barrenkale. For something a bit more low-key, take your pick of the cafes on Plaza Nueva.

GETTING THERE & AWAY

Bilbao's airport (BIO) is near Sondika, 12km northeast of the city. The airport bus Bizkaibus A3247 (€1.25, 30 minutes) runs to/from Termibus (bus station), where there is a tram stop and a metro station.

Two Renfe trains run daily to Madrid (from €39.80, six hours) and Barcelona (€39.80, nine hours) from the Abando train station. Slow **FEVE** (www.feve.es) trains run from Concordia station next door west into Cantabria and Asturias.

Bilbao's main bus station (Termibus) is southwest of town. Regular services operate to/from Madrid (€26.10, 4¾ hours), Barcelona (€40.60, seven hours), Pamplona (€12.85, 1¾ hours) and Santander (€9.25, 1½ hours).

NAVARRA

Navarra, historically and culturally linked to the Basque Country, is known for its fine wines and the San Fermines festival in Pamplona.

Pamplona

pop 195,800 / elev 456m

Immortalised by Ernest Hemingway in *The Sun Also Rises,* the pre-Pyrenean city of Pamplona (Iruña in Basque) is home of the wild Sanfermines (aka Encierro or Running of the Bulls) festival, but also an extremely pleasant and walkable city. The **tourist office** (☎ 848 42 04 20; www.navarra.es; Calle de Esclava 1; 🕑 10am-2pm & 4-7pm Mon-Sat, 10am-2pm Sun) has English-speaking staff.

SIGHTS

Pamplona's **Catedral** (☎ 948 22 29 90; Calle Dormitalería; guided tours admission €4.40; 🕑 10am-7pm Mon-Fri, 10am-2.30pm Sat mid-Jul–mid-Sep, 10am-2pm & 4-7pm Mon-Fri, 10am-2pm Sat mid-Sep–mid-Jul) stands on a rise just inside the city ramparts. It is a late-medieval Gothic gem with a beautiful cloister.

The walls and bulwarks of the grand fortified citadel, the star-shaped **Ciudadela** (Avenida del Ejército; admission free; 🕑 7.30am-9.30pm Mon-Sat, 9am-9.30pm Sun), lurk amid the greenery in what is now a charming park.

Around 9km northeast of Pamplona in Alzuza, the **Museo Oteiza** (☎ 948 33 20 74; www.museooteiza.org; Calle de la Cuesta 7; adult/student €4/2, Fri free; 🕑 11am-7pm Tue-Sun Jun-Sep, 10am-3pm Tue-Fri, 11am-7pm Sat & Sun Oct-May) contains almost 3000 pieces by the renowned Navarran sculptor, Jorge Oteiza. **Río Irati** (☎ 948 22 14 70) has at least one bus a day to Alzuza from Pamplona's bus station.

> **SURVIVING SANFERMINES**
>
> The Sanfermines festival is held on 6–14 July, when the city is overrun with thrill-seekers, curious onlookers and, oh yeah, bulls. The Encierro (Running of the Bulls) begins at 8am daily, when bulls are let loose from the Coralillos Santo Domingo. The 825m race lasts just three minutes, so don't be late. The safest place to watch the Encierro is on TV. If that's too tame for you, try to sweet-talk your way onto a balcony or book a room in a hotel with views.

SLEEPING

Accommodation is hard to come by during Sanfermines – book months in advance. Prices below don't reflect the huge (up to fivefold) mark-up you'll find in mid-July.

Habitaciones Mendi (☎ 948 22 52 97; Calle de las Navas de Tolosa 9; r €40) Creaky, wooden staircases and equally creaky, chintzy rooms make it just like being at your gran's.

Hostal Arriazu (☎ 948 21 02 02; www.hostalarriazu.com; Calle Comedias 14; s/d with breakfast €55/65; P 💻) Falling somewhere between a budget pension and a midrange hotel, there is superb value in this former theatre. The rooms are plain but the bathrooms are as good as you'll find.

Hotel Europa (☎ 948 22 18 00; www.hreuropa.com; Calle de Espoz y Mina 11; s/d €86.45/95.25; 💻) Wow! What a bizarre concoction of fake marble, equally fake gold-framed portraits of historical figures and photographs of the famous and not-so famous visitors to the hotel.

EATING & DRINKING

Central streets such as Calle San Nicolás and Calle Estafeta are lined with tapas bars, many of which morph into nightspots on weekends.

Sarasate (☎ 948 22 57 27; Calle de San Nicolás 21; menú del día Mon-Fri/Sat & Sun €10.50/16.50) This bright, uncluttered vegetarian restaurant on the 1st floor offers excellent vegie dishes and gluten-free options.

our pick Baserri (☎ 948 22 20 21; Calle de San Nicolás 32; menú del día €14) This place has won tons of food awards. As you'd expect from such a certificate-studded bar, the meals and the *pintxos* are superb. A *menú de degustación,* a sampler of *pintxos,* costs €24.

Café Iruña (☎ 948 22 20 64; Plaza del Castillo 44) This old Hemingway haunt was mentioned 14 times in *The Sun Also Rises*. It's a popular spot for breakfast, coffee, a light meal or some early evening tipples.

GETTING THERE & AWAY

Renfe trains run to/from Madrid (€51.80, three hours, three daily) and San Sebastián (from €14.70, two hours, three daily). Bus 9 connects the station with the centre.

From the **bus station** (☎ 948 22 38 54; Calle Conde Oliveto 8), buses leave for most towns throughout Navarra. Regular bus services travel to Bilbao (€12.50, 1¾ hours) and San Sebastián (€6.50, one hour).

CANTABRIA, ASTURIAS & GALICIA

With a landscape reminiscent of parts of the British Isles, 'Green Spain' offers great walks in national parks, seafood feasts in coastal towns and oodles of opportunities to plunge into the ice-cold waters of the Bay of Biscay.

SANTANDER

pop 181,800

Most of modern Santander stands in drab contrast to its pretty beaches. A huge fire raged through the city in 1941, but what's left of the 'old' centre is a lively source of entertainment for the palate and liver.

Information

Ciberlope (www.ciberlope.com; Calle de Lope de Vega 14; per 30min from €1.20; 10.30am-midnight Mon-Fri, 11.30am-midnight Sat, 5pm-midnight Sun)

Municipal tourist office (☎ 942 20 30 00; www.ayto-santander.es, in Spanish; Jardines de Pereda; 9am-9pm daily mid-Jun–mid-Sep, 8.30am-1.30pm & 4-7pm Mon-Fri, 10am-2pm Sat mid-Sep–Easter & 10am-7pm Sat Easter–mid-Jun)

Regional tourist office (☎ 942 31 07 08; www.turismodecantabria.com, in Spanish; Calle de Hernán Cortés 4; 9am-9pm Jul-Sep, 9.30am-1.30pm & 4-7pm Oct-Jun) In the Mercado del Este.

Sights & Activities

The **Catedral** (☎ 942 22 60 24; Plaza del Obispo José Eguino y Trecu s/n; ☎ 10am-1pm & 4-8pm Mon-Fri, 10am-1pm & 4.30-8pm Sat, 10am-1.30pm & 5-9pm Sun & holidays) is composed of two 13th-century Gothic churches, one above the other. Several other museums are dotted about town.

The beaches on the **Bahía de Santander** are more protected than **Playa del Sardinero**. The latter is a hike from the city centre, so catch bus 1, 2 or 3 from outside the post office. **Playa del Puntal**, a finger of sand jutting out from the eastern side of the bay, is idyllic on calm days. Boats sail there every 30 minutes between 10am and 8pm from June to late September, from the Estación Marítima Los Reginas (€3.90 return).

Sleeping

Hospedaje Botín (☎ 942 21 00 94; www.hospedajebotin.com; Calle de Isabel II No 1; s/d €38/54.50) The homey Botín has some spacious rooms with showers and *galerías* (glassed-in balconies).

Pensión La Corza (☎ 942 21 29 50; Calle de Hernán Cortés 25; r with washbasin/bathroom €42/55) The best deal around, La Corza is on pleasant Plaza de Pombo, with high-ceilinged, handsomely furnished rooms up on the 3rd floor, some with balconies overlooking the square.

Eating & Drinking

Bodega Cigaleña (☎ 942 21 30 62; Calle de Daoiz y Velarde 19; tapas from €2; Mon-Sat) A classic bar for tapas, wine and laughter, this is one of the most popular of its ilk in the old town.

Café de Pombo (☎ 942 22 32 24; Calle de Hernán Cortés 21) On the square of the same name, Pombo is an elegant spot for lingering breakfasts.

La Conveniente (☎ 942 21 28 87; Calle de Gómez Oreña 9; meals €15-20; dinner Mon-Sat) This cavernous *bodega* (wine cellar) has high stone walls, wooden pillars and beams, and more wine bottles than you may ever have seen in one place. You might go for a cheese *tabla* (platter) or other classic *raciones*. Servings are generous.

Plaza de Cañadío is home to several *bares de copas*, where you can enjoy an outdoor beer in the evening. Calle de Santa Lucía, along with Calle del Río de la Pila and its immediate neighbourhood, also teem with bars of all descriptions.

Getting There & Away

From Plymouth in the UK, **Brittany Ferries** (☎ UK 0870 9076103, Spain 942 36 06 11; www.brittany-ferries.co.uk) runs a twice-weekly car ferry to Santander (20½ hours) from mid-March to mid-November.

From the **bus station** (☎ 942 21 19 95; www.santandereabus.com), Alsa runs at least six buses daily to/from Madrid (€26.50 to €39, 5¼ to 6½ hours).

Renfe has three trains daily to/from Madrid (€43.90, 4½ to 5¼ hours). FEVE, next door, operates three to/from Bilbao (Basque Country).

AROUND SANTANDER

Some 34km west of Santander, **Santillana del Mar** (www.santillanadelmar.com) is a bijou medieval village and the obvious overnight base for visiting the nearby Cueva de Altamira.

The country's finest prehistoric art, found in the Cueva de Altamira, 2km southwest of Santillana del Mar, is off-limits to all but the scientific community. However, the **Museo Altamira** (☎ 942 81 80 05; http://museodealtamira.mcu.es; adult/student €2.40/1.20; 9.30am-8pm Tue-Sat, 9.30am-3pm Sun & holidays May-Oct, shorter hr Nov-Apr; P) allows you to view a fullsize replica of the Sala de Polícromos (Polychrome Hall), with its 14,500-year-old depictions of bison, horses and other beasts.

Buses run three to four times a day from Santander to Santillana del Mar.

SANTIAGO DE COMPOSTELA

pop 88,000 / elev 260m

The supposed burial place of St James (Santiago), Santiago de Compostela is a bewitching city. Christian pilgrims journeying along the Camino de Santiago often end up mute with wonder on entering its medieval centre. Fortunately, they usually regain their verbal capacities over a late-night foray into the city's lively bar scene.

Information

Cyber Nova 50 (☎ 981 56 41 33; Rúa Nova 50; per hr €1.20; 9am-midnight Mon-Fri, 10am-11pm Sat & Sun)

Municipal tourist office (☎ 981 55 51 29; www.santiagoturismo.com; Rúa do Vilar 63; 9am-9pm Jun-Sep, 9am-2pm & 4-7pm Oct-May)

Sights

The **Catedral del Apóstol** (www.catedraldesantiago.es; Plaza do Obradoiro; 7am-9pm), a superb Romanesque creation of the 11th to 13th centuries, is the heart and soul of Santiago. It's said that St James' remains were buried here in the 1st century AD and rediscovered in 813. Today, visitors line up to kiss his statue, which sits behind the main altar. The **Museo da Catedral** (☎ 981 56 05 27; Praza do Obradoiro; admission €5; 10am-2pm & 4-8pm Jun-Sep, 10am-1.30pm & 4-6.30pm Oct-May, closed Sun afternoon) includes the cathedral's cloisters, treasury and crypt.

To get a grasp on local culture, visit the **Museo do Pobo Galego** (Galician Folk Museum; ☎ 981 58 36 20; Rúa San Domingos de Bonaval; admission free; 10am-2pm & 4-8pm Tue-Sat, 11am-2pm Sun), housed in the attractive former Convento de San Domingos de Bonaval.

The **Museo das Peregrinacións** (☎ 981 58 15 58; Rúa de San Miguel 4; admission €2.40; 10am-8pm Tue-Fri, 10.30am-1.30pm & 5-8pm Sat, 10.30am-1.30pm Sun) explores the pilgrim culture that has so shaped Santiago. Look out for the fascinating illuminated map showing pilgrimage destinations across the world.

Sleeping

Hostal Suso (☎ 981 58 66 11; Rúa do Vilar 65; s/d €20/40) Stacked above a bar, this family-run *hostal* represents the best deal in town. Immaculate rooms have spick-and-span bathrooms, firm beds and modern wood furniture. Light sleepers should request an interior room.

Hostal Seminario Mayor (☎ 981 58 30 09; www.viajesatlantico.com/pinario; Praza da Inmaculada 5; s/d/tr incl breakfast €30/47/60; Jul-Sep) Rooms are basic, but this *hostal* offers the rare experience of staying inside a Benedictine monastery. With 126 rooms, it's a good bet when everywhere else is full.

our pick **Casa-Hotel As Artes** (☎ 981 55 52 54; www.asartes.com; Travesía de Dos Puertas 2; r €88-98;) On a quiet street near the Cathedral, these lovely stone-walled rooms exude a romantic rustic air. Breakfast (€9) is served in a homey dining room overlooking the street.

Eating & Drinking

O Gato Negro (☎ 981 58 31 05; Rúa da Raíña; raciones €3-9) Marked only with a green door and a black cat, this old-town haunt serves plates of seafood, ham, cheese or peppers on five sought-after tables.

Restaurante Ó Dezaseis (☎ 981 56 48 80; Rúa de San Pedro 16; mains €11-13, menú €11.50) Wood-beam ceilings and exposed stone walls give an invitingly rustic air to this popular tavern just beyond the touristy buzz. The mixed crowd tucks into specialities such as *caldo Gallego* (Galician soup).

O Beiro (☎ 981 58 13 70; Rúa da Raíña 3; mains €11-24) The house speciality are *tablas* (trays) of delectable cheeses and sausages, but you can also get tapas and *raciones* at this friendly two-storey tavern and *viñoteca* (wine bar).

If you're after tapas and wine, graze along Rúa do Franco and Rúa da Raíña. For people-watching, hit the cafes along Praza da Quinatana and Rúa do Vilar. The liveliest area lies east of Praza da Quintana, especially along Rúa de San Paio de Antealtares, known as a hotspot for live music.

Getting There & Around

Flights from various Spanish and European destinations (including Dublin, Frankfurt and London) land at Lavacolla airport (SCQ). Some 21 **Empresa Freire** (☎ 981 58 81 11) buses run daily between Lavacolla airport and the bus station (€1.70). About half continue to/depart from Rúa do Doutor Teixeiro, southwest of Praza de Galicia.

Services fan out from the **bus station** (☎ 981 54 24 16; Rúa San Caetano) to destinations all over Galicia and the rest of Spain.

From the **train station** (Avenida de Lugo), trains travel to/from Madrid (€45) on a daytime Talgo (seven hours) or an overnight Trenhotel (nine hours). Regional trains operate to A Coruña (€3.90 to €5.25, 45 to 70 minutes) and other destinations.

SPAIN DIRECTORY

ACCOMMODATION

In this chapter, budget options (doubles €60 and under) include everything from dorm-style youth hostels to family-style *pensiones* and slightly better heeled *hostales*. At the upper end of this category you'll find rooms with air-conditioning and private bathrooms. Midrange *hostales* and hotels (€61 to €180) are more comfortable and most offer standard hotel services. Business hotels, trendy boutique hotels and luxury hotels are in the top-end category (€181 and up). All prices quoted are for rooms with attached bathroom unless otherwise specified. Some hotels have non-smoking rooms or floors but this is far from common practice.

Always check room charges before putting down your bags, and remember that prices can and do change with time. The price of any type of accommodation varies with the season and accommodation prices listed in this book are a guide only.

Virtually all accommodation prices are subject to IVA, the Spanish version of value-added tax, which is 7%. This may or may not be included in the price. To check, ask: *Está incluido el IVA?* (Is IVA included?). In some cases you will be charged the IVA only if you ask for a receipt.

Camping

Spain's camping grounds vary greatly in service, cleanliness and style. They're rated from first to third class and priced accordingly. Camping grounds usually charge per person, per tent and per vehicle – typically €4 to €8.50 for each. There are lots of helpful online guides, including www.campingsonline.com/espana and www.campinguia.com.

Some camping grounds close from around October to Easter. With few exceptions, camping outside camping grounds is illegal, as is building fires. You'll need permission to camp on private land.

Hostels

Albergues juveniles (youth hostels) are cheap places to stay, especially for lone travellers. Expect to pay from €12 to €27 per night, depending on location, age and season. Spain's Hostelling International (HI) organisation, **Red Española de Albergues Juveniles** (REAJ; www.reaj.com), has more than 200 youth hostels throughout Spain. Official hostels require HI membership (buy a membership card at virtually all hostels) and most have curfews.

Hotels, Hostales & Pensiones

Most other options fall into the categories of hotels (one to five stars, full amenities), *hostales* (high-end guest houses with private bathroom; one to three stars) or *pensiones* (guest houses, usually with shared bathroom; one to three stars). Expect a double room at a *pensión* or *hostal* to cost €40 to €60 per night. A three-star hotel will generally cost from €80 up. Often, you can get great hotel deals online.

ACTIVITIES

Cycling

The Vuelta a España is one of Europe's great bike races (after the Tour de France and Giro d'Italia) and the country has produced many fine cyclists. They are confronted by all sorts of terrain, from vast plains to tough mountains. Cycling is especially popular among locals and tourists on the Balearic

Islands. Mountain biking is popular; areas such as Andalucía and Catalonia have many good tracks.

Skiing

Skiing is cheaper but less varied than in much of the rest of Europe. The season runs from December to mid-April. The best resorts are in the Pyrenees, especially in northwest Catalonia. The Sierra Nevada in Andalucía offers the most southerly skiing in Western Europe.

Surfing, Windsurfing & Kitesurfing

The Basque Country has good surf spots, including San Sebastián, Zarautz and the legendary left at Mundaka. Tarifa, with its long, deserted beaches and ceaseless wind, is generally considered to be the windsurfing capital of Europe. It is also a top spot for kitesurfing.

Walking

Spain is a trekker's paradise. Read about some of the best treks in Lonely Planet's *Walking in Spain*. Useful for hiking, especially in the Pyrenees, are maps by Editorial Alpina. The series combines information booklets with detailed maps. Buy them at bookshops, sports shops and sometimes at petrol stations near hiking areas.

Some of Spain's best walking is in its parks. Throughout Spain, you'll find GR (*Grandes Recorridos,* or long distance) trails. These are indicated with red-and-white markers. The Camino de Santiago (St James' Way, with several branches) is perhaps Spain's best-known long-distance walk.

BUSINESS HOURS

Banks (8.30am-2pm Mon-Fri, some also 4-7pm Thu or 9am-2pm Sat)
Bars Open from early evening, but there won't be much going on until after dinner. Closing time in Madrid and Barcelona 2am Sunday to Thursday and 3am Friday and Saturday.
Central post offices (8.30am-10pm Mon-Sat; others 8.30am to 2pm or 8.30pm Mon-Fri, 9am-1.30pm Sat)
Clubs (midnight-6am) Little happens before 2am.
Department stores (10am-10pm Mon-Sat)
Museums Variable opening hours; many museums close Monday.
Offices (9am-2pm & 4.30pm or 5pm-8pm Mon-Fri) Some people still follow the tradition of heading home for lunch and a siesta.
Restaurants (1pm-4pm & 8.30pm-midnight)
Shops (9am-2pm or 10am-2pm & 4-8pm or 5-8pm Mon-Sat) Some don't close for lunch.

EMBASSIES & CONSULATES

Some 70 countries have their embassies in Madrid. Most embassies' office hours are around 9am to 2pm Monday to Friday.

Australia (91 353 66 00; www.spain.embassy.gov.au; Plaza del Descubridor Diego de Ordás 3)
Canada (Map pp1052-3; 91 423 32 50; www.canada-es.org; Calle de Núñez de Balboa 35)
France (Map pp1052-3; 91 423 89 00; www.ambafrance-es.org; Calle de Salustiano Olózaga 9)
Germany (Map pp1052-3; 91 557 90 00; www.madrid.diplo.de; Calle de Fortuny 8)
Ireland (Map pp1052-3; 91 436 40 93; Paseo de la Castellana 46)
Netherlands (off Map pp1052-3; 91 353 75 00; www.embajadapaisesbajos.es; Avenida del Comandante Franco 32)
New Zealand (off Map pp1052-3; 91 523 02 26; www.nzembassy.com; Calle del Pinar 7)
Portugal (off Map pp1052-3; 91 782 49 60; www.embajadaportugal-madrid.org; Calle del Pinar 1)
UK Madrid (Map pp1052-3; 91 700 82 00; www.ukinspain.com; Calle de Fernando el Santo 16); Barcelona (Map pp1072-3; 93 366 62 00; Avinguda Diagonal 477)
USA Madrid (Map pp1052-3; 91 587 22 00; www.embusa.es; Calle de Serrano 75); Barcelona (off Map pp1072-3; 93 280 22 27; Passeig de la Reina Elisenda de Montcada 23-25)

FESTIVALS & EVENTS

January

Festividad de San Sebastián Held in San Sebastián (p1106) on 20 January; the whole town goes berserk.

February & March

Carnaval A time of fancy-dress parades and merrymaking celebrated around the country on the eve of the Christian Lent season (40 days before Easter). Among the wildest parties are those in Cádiz (p1100) and Sitges, near Barcelona.
Las Fallas Valencia's (p1086) mid-March party (www.fallas.es, in Spanish), with all-night dancing and drinking, mammoth bonfires, first-class fireworks and processions.

April

Semana Santa Parades of holy images and huge crowds, notably in Seville (p1088), during Easter week.
Feria de Abril A week-long party held in Seville (p1088; http://feriadesevilla.andalunet.com, in Spanish) in late April, a kind of counterbalance to the religious peak of Easter.

July

Sanfermines The highlight of this originally religious festival is the running of the bulls in Pamplona (p1109; www.sanfermin.com). It's held in early July.

August

Semana Grande A week of heavy drinking and hangovers all along the northern coast during the first half of August.

September

Festes de la Mercè Barcelona's (p1069; www.bcn.cat/merce) big annual party, held around 24 September.

HOLIDAYS

Spain has at least 14 official holidays a year, some observed nationwide, some very local. When a holiday falls close to a weekend, Spaniards like to make a *puente* (bridge), taking the intervening day off, too. The holidays following are observed virtually everywhere.

New Year's Day 1 January
Three Kings' Day (when children receive presents) 6 January
Good Friday Before Easter Sunday
Labour Day 1 May
Feast of the Assumption 15 August
National Day 12 October
All Saints' Day 1 November
Feast of the Immaculate Conception 8 December
Christmas 25 December

The two main periods when Spaniards go on holiday are Semana Santa (the week leading up to Easter Sunday) and the month of August. At these times accommodation in beachside resorts can be scarce and transport heavily booked.

LANGUAGE

Spanish, or Castilian (Castellano) as it is more precisely called, is spoken throughout Spain, but there are also three other important regional languages: Catalan (Català), another Romance language with close ties to French, is spoken in Catalonia, and dialects of it are spoken in the Balearic Islands and in Valencia; Galician (Galego), similar to Portuguese, is spoken in Galicia; and Basque (Euskera; of obscure, non-Latin origin) is spoken in the Basque Country and in Navarra.

LEGAL MATTERS

Spaniards no longer enjoy liberal drug laws. No matter what anyone tells you, it is not legal to smoke dope in public bars. There is a reasonable degree of tolerance when it comes to people having a smoke in their own home, but not in hotel rooms or guest houses.

If you are arrested in Spain, you have the right to an attorney and to know the reason you are being held. You are also entitled to make a phone call.

MONEY

Spain's currency is the euro (€). Banks tend to give better exchange rates than the currency-exchange offices. Travellers cheques attract a slightly better rate than cash. It's easy to withdraw money – ATMs are ubiquitous.

In restaurants, tipping is a matter of personal choice – the majority of people leave some small change; 5% is plenty, 10% is generous. It's common to leave small change in bars and cafes. Bargaining in Spain is not common, although you could ask for a discount for long-term room rental and the like.

POST

Stamps are sold at post offices and *estancos* (tobacco shops with the Tabacos sign in yellow letters on a maroon background). A postcard or letter weighing up to 20g costs €0.60 from Spain to other European countries, and €0.78 to the rest of the world.

Mail to/from Europe normally takes up to a week, and to North America, Australia or New Zealand around 10 days.

Poste-restante mail can be addressed to you at either poste restante or *lista de correos,* the Spanish name for it, at the city in question. It's a fairly reliable system.

TELEPHONE

Blue public payphones are common and fairly easy to use. They accept coins, phonecards and, in some cases, credit cards. Phonecards come in €6 and €12 denominations and, like postage stamps, are sold at post offices and tobacconists.

International reverse-charge (collect) calls are simple to make: dial ☎ 900 followed by the appropriate code. For example: ☎ 99 00 61 for Australia, ☎ 99 00 44 for the UK, ☎ 99 00 64 for New Zealand, ☎ 99 00 15 for Canada, and ☎ 99 00 11 (AT&T) for the USA.

Telephone codes in Spain are an integral part of the phone number. All numbers are nine digits and you just dial that nine-digit number. All numbers prefixed with ☎ 900 are toll-free numbers. Mobile phone numbers in Spain start with the number 6. The cost of calls to mobiles varies.

TOURIST INFORMATION

Most towns and large villages of any interest have a helpful *oficina de turismo* (tourist office) where you can get maps and brochures. **Turespaña** (www.spain.info, www.tourspain.es), the country's national tourism body, presents a variety of general information and links on the entire country in its web pages. You can also find their offices abroad listed there.

VISAS

Citizens of EU countries can enter Spain freely with their national identity card or passport. Non-EU nationals must take their passport.

Spain is one of the Schengen countries; see the boxed text (p1230). A standard visa for one Schengen country is generally valid for the others and valid for up to 90 days.

Nationals of Australia, Canada, Israel, Japan, New Zealand and the USA need no visa for stays of up to 90 days, but must have a passport valid for the whole visit.

Norwegian, Swiss, Icelandic and EU nationals planning to stay in Spain more than 90 days are supposed to register with the police and obtain a resident's number during their first month in the country.

South Africans are among the nationalities that do need a visa. You must obtain the visa in your country of residence. Multiple-entry visas will save you trouble if you plan to leave Spain for Gibraltar and/or Morocco, then re-enter. Visas are not renewable.

Sweden

HIGHLIGHTS

- **Stockholm** Touring the waterways, exploring top-notch museums and wandering the cobblestoned backstreets of Gamla Stan (p1123)
- **Göteborg** Explore cutting-edge style and the secrets of the underground in Sweden's 'second city' (p1140)
- **Ice Hotel** Enjoying a frosty beverage and a frozen bed at this ultracool jewel in the far north (p1145)
- **Malmö** Getting as close to the continent as possible without leaving the country in this multicultural city (p1136)
- **Off-the-beaten track** Doing a bicycle loop around the island of Gotland, the best budget destination in Sweden (p1135)

FAST FACTS

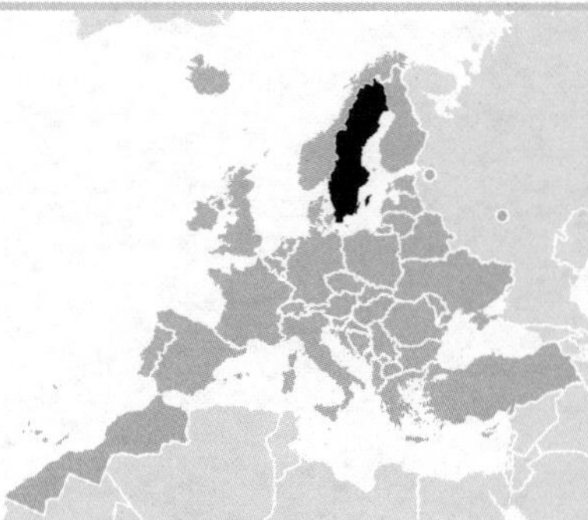

- **Area** 449,964 sq km
- **Budget** Skr700 to Skr1000 per day
- **Capital** Stockholm
- **Country code** ☎ 46
- **Famous for** Vikings, Volvos, blondes, ABBA, meatballs, Ikea
- **Languages** Swedish plus five official minority languages
- **Money** Swedish krona (Skr); A$1 = Skr5.95; C$1 = Skr6.75; €1 = Skr10.70; ¥100 = Skr8.40; NZ$1 = Skr4.66; UK£1 = Skr12.06; US$1 = Skr7.96
- **Phrases** *hej* (hello), *hej då* (goodbye), *ja* (yes), *nej* (no), *tack* (thanks)
- **Population** 9.02 million
- **Visas** not needed for most visitors for stays of up to three months

TRAVEL HINTS

Eat out at lunchtime, buy your alcohol duty-free, and take advantage of Sweden's excellent hostels and friendliness towards free camping.

ROAMING SWEDEN

Soak up Stockholm style, dig into Uppsala, Göteborg and Malmö, and explore some islands – big (Gotland) or small (Stockholm archipelago).

At first glance, Sweden might not seem like a terribly outlandish place. But the more time you spend here, the stranger and more wonderfully foreign it becomes. It's tempting to blame the country's out-there position on the map. But there's more at work here than geographical isolation. Sweden's literature and cinema favour a weighty, Gothic sense of drama blended with gallows humour and stark aesthetics – all of which, in some form, at some point, will confront the visitor. Alert travellers will notice a particular tone here that hints at many things: depth of feeling, awareness of doom, absence of sentimentality, strength of principle, avoidance of conflict, a sombre conviction that certain things matter. Of course, such intangibles won't likely make it into your post-trip slide show. But the mysterious Swedish sensibility enhances every aspect of a traveller's experience.

It's an exciting time to visit, too – the small country with its long history of consistent moderation just happens to be embracing rapid change. Swedish music, fashion, food and art couldn't be more vibrant. Even the usually dull world of politics is shaking things up. Don't miss the chance to get in while it's hot.

HISTORY

The Viking Age was getting under way by the 9th century; Vikings made their mark in Russia, as well as trading with (and pillaging) Byzantine territories. Along with pagan gods, the aristocrats and their chosen kings (many from Denmark) reigned. A century of Swedish nationalist grumblings erupted in rebellion under the young nobleman Gustaf Vasa, who was crowned Gustaf I in 1523. In 1809 a constitutional amendment divided legislative powers between king and parliament.

By 1900 almost one in four Swedes lived in cities and the level of industry was increasing. In this environment the working class was radicalised. Sweden declared itself neutral at the outbreak of WWI. The Social Democrats, in power since 1932, introduced a welfare state after the war.

The 1950s and '60s saw a rapid rise in the standard of living for ordinary Swedes. But the world recession of the early 1990s led to massive devaluation of the Swedish krona. Their economy and national confidence shaken, Swedes voted to join the EU.

Since 1995 Sweden's welfare state has undergone tough reforms and the economy has improved. A 2003 referendum on whether Sweden should adopt the euro resulted in a 'no' vote. The referendum was overshadowed by the murder just days before of Sweden's popular foreign minister, Anna Lindh.

In recent years Sweden has grown away from its homogeneous past, both culturally and economically. Immigration and a new reliance on the IT industry have corresponded with greater social diversity. Whether because of this new diversity or dissatisfaction with the status quo, in the general election of September 2006, control of Sweden's government shifted from the Social Democrats to the centre-right Alliance for Sweden, who remain in power.

THE CULTURE

Around nine million people call Sweden home, making it Scandinavia's most populous country. Most of those folks live in the urban centres of Stockholm, Göteborg and Malmö – only 12% of the population lives in Norrland, which takes up two-thirds of the country's geographical area.

There are about 17,000 Sami (the indigenous people of Scandinavia, sometimes called Lapps) in Sweden, largely concentrated in the north. More than 17% of Sweden's population are foreign-born. Most immigrants have come from other European countries, including Russia, the former Yugoslavia, Poland and Greece. The largest non-European ethnic group consists of Assyrian/Syriac people. Chile and Somalia also have a sizeable presence, and there are around 45,000 Roma.

Sweden's overall approach to family life is in line with its socially progressive tendencies. The extensive state-mandated maternity/paternity leave is shared equally between parents – it's as common to see fathers pushing strollers as it is to see mothers. Gay and lesbian couples have the same rights as heterosexual married couples under Swedish law, and have been able to adopt children since 2003.

Some 87% of the Swedish population is Lutheran, although only about 10% regularly attend church services.

SPORT

More than a million Swedes play football, the country's most popular sport. The most high-profile name in Swedish football is probably England's former national team coach, Sven-Göran Eriksson, famed for his scandalous love life. Eriksson left the job after the 2006 FIFA World Cup in Germany.

Ice hockey is another big sport in Sweden. There are amateur teams in most communities and 12 professional teams in the premier league. The handsome visage of Swedish hockey star Peter 'Foppa' Forsberg graces advertisements all over the country.

Tennis star Björn Borg has moved on to designing underpants, but the sport he dominated is still a popular one in Sweden. Golf, sailing and *bandy* (similar to ice hockey) are also common.

Alpine skiing competitions are held annually and the huge Nordic race called Vasaloppet takes place each year in March.

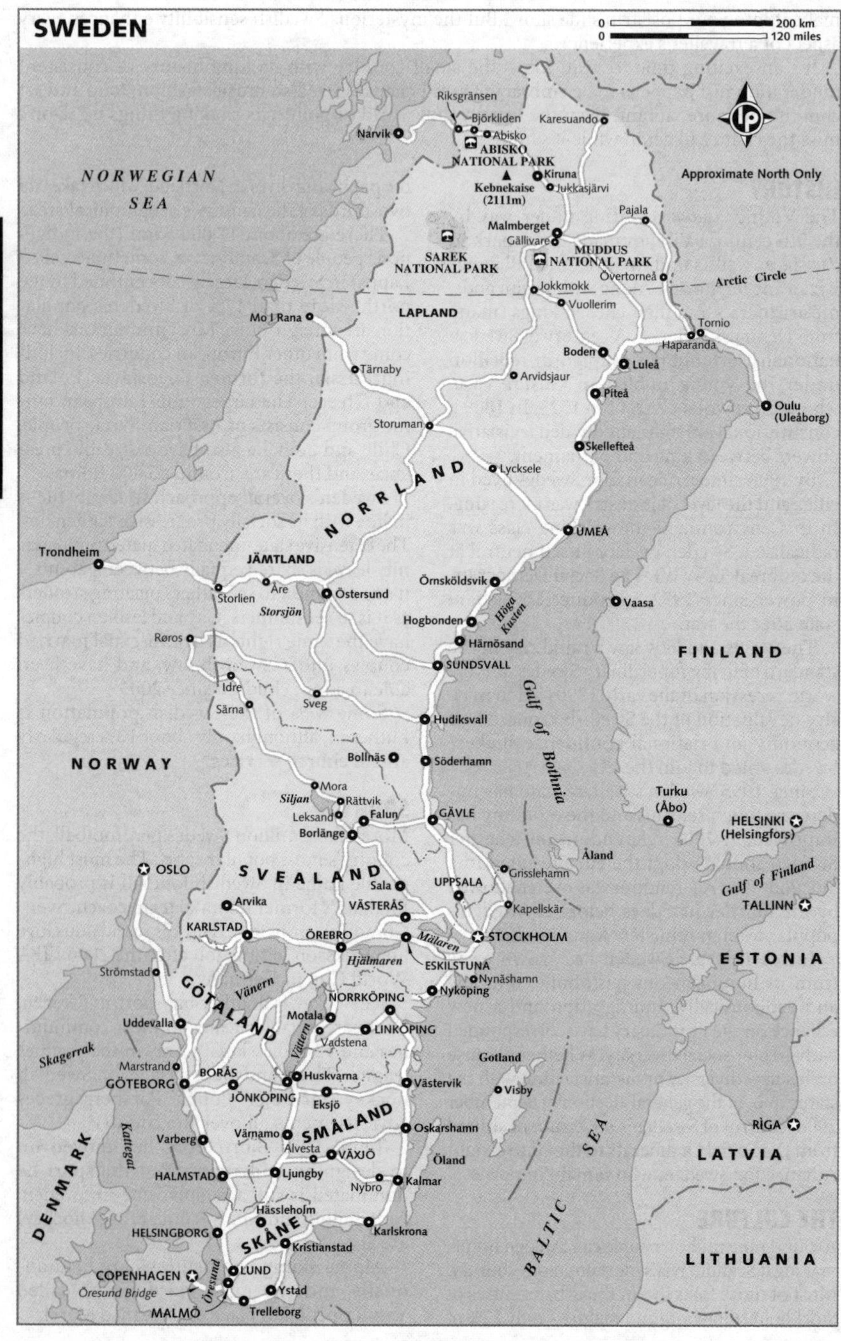
SWEDEN
0 200 km
0 120 miles
Approximate North Only
NORWEGIAN SEA
Riksgränsen
Björkliden
Abisko
Narvik
Karesuando
ABISKO NATIONAL PARK
Kiruna
Kebnekaise (2111m)
Jukkasjärvi
Pajala
Malmberget
Gällivare
SAREK NATIONAL PARK
MUDDUS NATIONAL PARK
Övertorneå
Arctic Circle
Jokkmokk
Vuollerim
Mo I Rana
LAPLAND
Tornio
Haparanda
Boden
Luleå
Tärnaby
Arvidsjaur
Piteå
Oulu (Uleåborg)
Storuman
Skellefteå
Lycksele
NORRLAND
UMEÅ
Trondheim
JÄMTLAND
Storlien
Åre
Östersund
Storsjön
Örnsköldsvik
Vaasa
Hogbonden
Höga Kusten
Härnösand
Røros
FINLAND
SUNDSVALL
Idre
Särna
Sveg
Gulf of Bothnia
Hudiksvall
NORWAY
Bollnäs
Söderhamn
Mora
Siljan
Rättvik
Leksand
Falun
GÄVLE
Borlänge
Turku (Åbo)
HELSINKI (Helsingfors)
Åland
OSLO
SVEALAND
Grisslehamn
Sala
UPPSALA
Gulf of Finland
Arvika
VÄSTERÅS
Kapellskär
TALLINN
KARLSTAD
ÖREBRO
Mälaren
STOCKHOLM
Hjälmaren
ESKILSTUNA
ESTONIA
Strömstad
Vänern
GÖTALAND
Nynäshamn
Nyköping
NORRKÖPING
Motala
Uddevalla
LINKÖPING
Vadstena
Vättern
Skagerrak
Gotland
Marstrand
BORÅS
Huskvarna
GÖTEBORG
Västervik
JÖNKÖPING
Eksjö
Visby
SMÅLAND
Kattegat
Oskarshamn
Värnamo
RIGA
DENMARK
Varberg
Alvesta
VÄXJÖ
LATVIA
Öland
HALMSTAD
Ljungby
Kalmar
Nybro
BALTIC SEA
Hässleholm
SKÅNE
Karlskrona
HELSINGBORG
Kristianstad
LITHUANIA
COPENHAGEN
LUND
Öresund Bridge
Öresund
Ystad
MALMÖ
Trelleborg

CONNECTIONS

Getting to the rest of Scandinavia and further into Europe from Sweden is easy. From Stockholm there are train and bus connections to London or Berlin (see p1121) as well as to Denmark (p1121 and p1121), Finland (p1121) and Norway (p1121 and p1122). Ferries are another option, with frequent connections between many Swedish ports and the rest of Europe (see right). Airports in Stockholm and Göteborg connect Sweden with the rest of the world (see right).

ARTS

Sweden's 19th-century artistic highlights include Carl Larsson (1853–1919), Anders Zorn (1860–1920), and Bruno Liljefors (1860–1939). Carl Milles (1875–1955) is Sweden's greatest sculptor, once employed as Rodin's assistant.

Well-known Swedish writers include the poet Carl Michael Bellman (1740–95), playwright August Strindberg (1849–1912) and children's writer Astrid Lindgren (1907–2002). Vilhelm Moberg (1898–1973) won international acclaim with *Utvandrarna* (The Emigrants; 1949) and *Nybyggarna* (The Settlers; 1956).

Swedish cinema is inextricably linked with the name of Ingmar Bergman. His deeply contemplative films (*The Seventh Seal; Through a Glass Darkly; Persona)* explore alienation, the absence of God, the certainty of death and other light-hearted themes. Recently, Trollhättan and Ystad have become filmmaking centres, the former thanks to wunderkind director Lukas Moodysson, whose *Lilja 4-Ever, Fucking Åmål* and *Tillsammans* have all been hits.

Any survey of Swedish music must at least mention ABBA, the iconic winners of the 1974 Eurovision Song Contest. More current Swedish successes are pop icon Robyn, indie melody-makers Peter Björn & John, and the exquisitely mellow José González, whose cover of The Knives' track 'Heartbeats' catapulted the Göteborg native to international stardom.

Sweden's inspired design includes Jonas Bohlin 'Tutu lamps' and Tom Hedquist milk cartons. While simplicity still defines the Nordic aesthetic, new designers are challenging Scandi functionalism with bold, witty work. Aesthetic prowess also fuels Sweden's thriving fashion scene. Since the late 1990s, local designers have roused global admiration: Madonna dons Patrik Söderstam trousers and Acne Jeans sell like hotcakes at LA's hip Fred Segal. Sweden now exports more fashion than pop.

ENVIRONMENT

Sweden covers an area of 449,964 sq km, and its maximum north–south extent is 1574km. Flat and open Skåne in the south is similar to Denmark, but further north the landscape is hillier and heavily forested. The coastline is notable for its small fjords and skerries.

Nature-loving Swedes led Europe in setting up national parks in the early 20th century; there are now 28 in Sweden (the biggest and best are in Lapland).

Ecological consciousness in Sweden is very high. Swedes are fervent believers in sorting and recycling household waste (paper, glass, plastic etc) – you'll be expected to do the same in hostels and camping grounds.

TRANSPORT

GETTING THERE & AWAY

Air

The major international airport is Stockholm's **Arlanda airport** (ARN; ☎ 08-797 6000; www.lfv.se), with direct flights linking the country to major Scandinavian towns, and European and North American cities. Göteborg's **Landvetter airport** (GOT; ☎ 031-941000) and Malmö's **Sturup airport** (MMX; ☎ 040-613 1000), as well as a few other minor airports, also have direct international flights.

The national carrier is **SAS** (SK; ☎ 0770-727727; www.scandinavian.net).

Boat

Ferry connections between Sweden and its neighbours are frequent and straightforward. Most lines offer substantial discounts for seniors, students and children, and many rail-pass holders also get reduced fares. Most prices quoted in this chapter are for single journeys at peak times (weekend travel, overnight crossings, mid-June to mid-August); at other times, fares may be up to 30% lower.

TO/FROM DENMARK

Helsingør–Helsingborg

This is the quickest route and has frequent ferries (crossing time around 20 minutes).

ACE Link (☎ 042-38 58 80; www.acelink.se, in Swedish) Regular passenger-only ferries to Helsingør from around 7am to 8pm daily. Pedestrian/bicycle Skr48/16.
HH-Ferries (☎ 042-19 80 00; www.hhferries.se) Twenty-four-hour service. Pedestrian/car and up to nine passengers Skr24/300.
Scandlines (☎ 042-18 63 00; www.scandlines.se) Similar service and prices.

Göteborg–Fredrikshavn

Stena Line (☎ 031-704 00 00; www.stenaline.se) Three-hour crossing. Up to six ferries daily. Pedestrian/car and five passengers/bicycle Skr185/1525/225.
Stena Line (Express) Two-hour crossing. Up to three ferries daily. Pedestrian/car and five passengers/bicycle Skr285/1795/275.

Varberg–Grenå

Stena Line (☎ 031-704 00 00; www.stenaline.se) Four-hour crossing. Three or four daily. Pedestrian/car and five passengers/bicycle Skr285/1595/280.

Ystad–Rønne

BornholmsTrafikken (☎ 0411-55 87 00; www.bornholmstrafikken.dk) Conventional (1½ hours) and fast (80 minutes) services, two to nine times daily. Pedestrian/car and five passengers/bicycle from €23/133/25.

TO/FROM EASTERN EUROPE

To/from Estonia, **Tallink** (☎ 08-666 60 01; www.tallink.ee, in Estonian) runs the routes Stockholm–Tallinn and Kapellskär–Paldiski.

Scandlines (☎ 08-52 06 02 90; www.scandlines.dk) operates Ventspils–Nynäshamn ferries around five times per week.

To/From Lithuania, **Lisco Line** (☎ 0454-336 80; www.lisco.lt) runs daily Karlshamn–Klaipėda.

To/From Poland, **Polferries** (☎ 040-12 17 00; www.polferries.se) and **Unity Line** (☎ 0411-55 69 00; www.unityline.pl) have daily Ystad–Swinoujscie crossings. Polferries also runs Nynäshamn–Gdańsk. **Stena Line** (☎ 031-704 00 00; www.stenaline.se) sails Karlskrona–Gdynia.

TO/FROM FINLAND

Helsinki is called Helsingfors in Swedish, and Turku is Åbo. Stockholm–Helsinki and Stockholm–Turku ferries run daily throughout the year via the Åland islands. **RG Line** (☎ 090-18 52 00; www.rgline.com) runs the routes Umeå–Vaasa and Sundsvall–Vaasa.

Stockholm–Helsinki

Silja Line (☎ 08-22 21 40; www.silja.com) Around 15 hours. Ticket and cabin berth from €122.
Viking Line (☎ 08-452 40 00; www.vikingline.fi) Operates the same routes with slightly cheaper prices.

Stockholm–Turku

Silja Line (☎ 08-22 21 40; www.silja.com) Eleven hours. Deck place €11, cabins from €49; prices are higher for evening trips. From September to early May, ferries also depart from Kapellskär (90km northeast of Stockholm): connecting buses operated by Silja Line are included in the full-price fare.
Viking Line (☎ 08-452 40 00; www.vikingline.fi) Operates the same routes with slightly cheaper prices. In high season it offers passage from both Stockholm and Kapellskär.

Stockholm–Åland Islands (Mariehamn)

Besides the Silja Line and Viking Line routes to Helsinki and Turku, two companies offer foot-passenger-only overnight cruises. Prices quoted are for return trips.
Ånedin-Linjen (☎ 08-456 22 00; www.anedinlinjen.com, in Swedish) Six hours, daily. Couchette Skr75, berth from Skr250.
Birka Cruises (☎ 08-702 72 00; www.birkacruises.com) A 22-hour round trip. One or two daily. Berth from Skr350. Prices include supper and breakfast.
Eckerö Linjen (☎ 0175-258 00; www.eckerolinjen.fi) Runs to the Åland Islands from Grisslehamn.

TO/FROM GERMANY

Trelleborg–Sassnitz

Scandlines (☎ 042-18 61 00; www.scandlines.se) A 3¾-hour trip. Two to five times daily. Pedestrian/car and up to nine passengers/passenger with bicycle Skr125/925/195. A fuel surcharge of Skr50 to Skr80 may be added.

Trelleborg–Rostock

Scandlines (☎ 042-18 61 00; www.scandlines.se) Six hours (night crossing 7½ hours). Two or three daily. Pedestrian/car and up to nine passengers/passenger with bicycle Skr195/1025/225. A fuel surcharge of Skr50 to Skr80 may be added.
TT-Line (☎ 0410-562 00; www.ttline.com) Same as Scandlines, with similar prices.

Trelleborg–Travemünde

TT-Line (☎ 0410-562 00; www.ttline.com) Seven hours. Two to five daily. Pedestrian/car and up to five passengers/passenger with bicycle from Skr290/1045/390. Berths are compulsory on night crossings.

Göteborg–Kiel

Stena Line (☎ 031-704 00 00; www.stenaline.se) Fourteen hours. One crossing nightly. Pedestrian/car and up to five passengers from Skr495/1760.

TO/FROM NORWAY

There's a daily overnight **DFDS Seaways** (☎ 031-65 06 80; www.dfdsseaways.com) ferry between Copenhagen and Oslo, via Helsingborg. Passenger fares between Helsingborg and Oslo (14 hours) cost from Skr1100, and cars Skr475, but the journey can't be booked online; you'll need to call. DFDS also sails from Göteborg to Kristiansand (Norway) three days a week (from seven hours); call for prices.

A **Color Line** (☎ 0526-620 00; www.colorline.com) ferry between Strömstad (Sweden) and Sandefjord (Norway) sails two to six times daily (2½ hours) year-round. Tickets cost from Nkr175 (rail passes get 50% discount).

TO/FROM UK

DFDS Seaways (www.dfdsseaways.com) Göteborg (☎ 031-65 06 50); UK (☎ 08705-33 30 00) has two crossings per week between Göteborg and Newcastle via Kristiansand (Norway). The trip takes 25 hours. Fares start from around £35 per person including economy berth; cars cost £75 and bicycles are free. Booking these trips online is somewhat maddening; it's best to call instead.

Bus

Eurolines (☎ 031-10 02 40; www.eurolines.com), the long-distance bus operator, has an office inside the bus terminals in Sweden's three largest cities: Stockholm, Göteborg and Malmö. Full schedules and fares are listed on the website.

Bus journeys are possible between Sweden and the Continent – these vehicles go directly to ferries.

TO/FROM CONTINENTAL EUROPE

Eurolines bus services run between Sweden and several European cities. The Stockholm to London service (Skr1250, 30 hours, one to four times weekly) goes via Malmö, Copenhagen, Hamburg and Amsterdam or Brussels. There are also services from Göteborg to Berlin (Skr710, 17 hours, three weekly).

TO/FROM DENMARK

Eurolines runs buses between Stockholm and Copenhagen (Dkr280, nine hours, at least three per week), and between Göteborg and Copenhagen (Dkr200, 4½ hours, daily). **Swebus Express** (☎ 0200-21 82 18; www.swebusexpress.se) and **Säfflebussen** (☎ 0771-15 15 15; www.safflebussen.se) both run regular buses on the same routes, and have discount fares for travel from Monday to Thursday. All companies offer student, youth (under 26) and senior discounts.

TO/FROM FINLAND

Tapanis Buss (☎ 0922-129 55; www.tapanis.se, in Swedish) runs express coaches from Stockholm to Tornio via Haparanda twice a week (Skr570, 15 hours).

There are regular regional services from Haparanda to Övertorneå (some continue to Pello, Pajala and Kiruna); you can walk across the border at Övertorneå or Pello and pick up a Finnish bus to Muonio, with onward connections from there to Kaaresuvanto and Tromsø (Norway).

TO/FROM NORWAY

Säfflebussen runs from Stockholm to Oslo (Skr425, 7½ hours, fives times daily) via Karlstad, and from Göteborg to Oslo (Skr265, four hours, seven daily). Swebus Express has the same routes with similar prices.

In the north, buses run once daily from Umeå to Mo i Rana (eight hours) and from Skellefteå to Bodø (nine hours, daily except Saturday); for details, contact **Länstrafiken i Västerbotten** (☎ 0771-10 01 10; www.tabussen.nu) and **Länstrafiken i Norrbotten** (☎ 0771-10 01 10; www.ltnbd.se), respectively.

Car & Motorcycle

Direct access to Sweden by land is possible from Norway, Finland and Denmark (from Denmark via the Öresund toll bridge). You can drive from Copenhagen to Malmö across the Öresund bridge on the E20 motorway. Tolls are paid at Lernacken, on the Swedish side, in either Danish (single crossing per car Dkr260) or Swedish (Skr325) currency, or by credit or debit card.

Train

Train and bus journeys are also possible between Sweden and the Continent – these vehicles go directly to ferries.

TO/FROM DENMARK

Öresund trains operated by **Skånetrafiken** (www.skanetrafiken.se) run every 20 minutes from 6am to midnight (and once an hour thereafter) between Copenhagen and Malmö (round trip Skr140, 35 minutes each way) via the bridge. The trains usually stop at Copenhagen airport.

From Copenhagen, it's necessary to change in Malmö for Stockholm trains. Six or seven services operate directly between Copenhagen and Göteborg (Skr327, four hours). Trains every hour or two connect Copenhagen, Kristianstad and Karlskrona. X2000 high-speed trains are more expensive.

TO/FROM NORWAY

Trains run daily between Stockholm and Oslo (Skr500 to Skr706, six to seven hours), and there's a night train from Stockholm to Narvik (Skr811, about 20 hours). You can also travel from Helsingborg to Oslo (Skr750, seven hours), via Göteborg.

GETTING AROUND

Bicycle

Skåne and Gotland are ideal for cycling. The best season is May to September in the south, and July and August in the north. You'll find bike-hire outlets and dedicated paths in most major towns.

Boat

An extensive boat network serves the Stockholm archipelago, and boat services on Lake Mälaren, west of Stockholm, are busy in summer. Regular ferries from Nynäshamn and Oskarshamn serve Gotland and, in summer, many small islands off the coast.

Bus

Swebus Express (☎ 0200 21 82 18; www.swebusexpress.se) has the largest network of express buses, but they only serve the southern half of the country (as far north as Mora in Dalarna). **Svenska Buss** (☎ 0771-67 67 67; www.svenskabuss.se, in Swedish) and **Säfflebussen** (☎ 0771-15 15 15; www.safflebussen.se, in Swedish, Danish & Norwegian) also connect many southern towns and cities with Stockholm; prices are often slightly cheaper than Swebus Express, but services are less frequent.

North of Gävle, regular connections with Stockholm are provided by several smaller operators, including **Ybuss** (☎ 0771-33 44 44; www.ybuss.se, in Swedish), which has services to Sundsvall, Östersund and Umeå.

Generally, it's cheaper to travel between Monday and Thursday, book online, and buy tickets more than 24 hours before departure. If you're a student or senior, it's worth asking about fare discounts, though many bus companies only give student prices to holders of Swedish student cards.

Car & Motorcycle

Sweden has good roads, and you usually only need your own driving licence and a credit card for car hire. International car-hire chains start at around Skr600 per day for smaller models, but shop around, as weekend or summer packages may be offered at discount rates. All the major firms (eg Avis, Hertz, Europcar) have offices in major cities. If bringing your own car, you'll need vehicle registration documents.

The Swedish national motoring association is **Motormännens Riksförbund** (☎ 020-21 11 11, 08-690 38 00; www.motormannen.se; Sveavägen 159, SE-10435 Stockholm).

Train

Sweden has an extensive and reliable railway network, and trains are certainly faster than buses. Many destinations in the northern half of the country, however, cannot be reached by train alone.

TRAIN OPERATORS

Travel on the superfast X2000 services is much pricier than on 'normal' trains. Full-price 2nd-class tickets for longer journeys are expensive (around twice the price of equivalent bus trips), but there are various discounts available, especially for booking a week or so in advance *(förköpsbiljet)*, or at the last minute (for youth and pensioner fares). Students and those under 26 get a 30% discount on the standard adult fare.

Inlandsbanan (☎ 0771-53 53 53; www.inlandsbanan.se) A slow and scenic 1300km route from Kristinehamn to Gällivare and one of the great rail journeys in Scandinavia. Several southern sections have to be travelled by bus, but the all-train route starts at Mora. It takes seven hours from Mora to Östersund (Skr395) and 15 hours from Östersund to Gällivare (Skr918). A pass allows two weeks' unlimited travel for Skr1450.

Sveriges Järnväg (SJ; ☎ 0771-75 75 75; www.sj.se) National network covering most main lines, especially in the southern part of the country.

Tågkompaniet (☎ 0771-44 41 11; www.tagkompaniet.se, in Swedish) Operates overnight trains from Göteborg and Stockholm north to Boden, Kiruna, Luleå and Narvik, and the lines north of Härnösand.

TRAIN PASSES

The Sweden Rail Pass, Eurodomino tickets and international passes, such as Inter-Rail and Eurail, are accepted on SJ services and most regional trains (but not on local services like Stockholm's *tunnelbana*). The **Eurail Scandinavia Pass** (www.eurail.com) entitles you to unlimited rail travel in Denmark, Finland, Norway and Sweden; it is valid in second-class only and is available for four, five, six, eight or 10 days of travel within a two-month period (prices start from youth/adult US$255/335). It also provides free travel on Scandlines' Helsingør to Helsingborg route, and 20% to 50% discounts on other ship routes.

STOCKHOLM

☎ 08 / pop 802,600

It's hard to imagine a city that makes better use of its natural assets than Stockholm. The capital city's famously clean, blue water sparkles under the midsummer sun, practically begging locals and visitors alike to take a dip (go ahead, it's allowed!). Winter is equally beautiful, as snowfall makes the big, square buildings look like frosted cakes. But the city is far from a museum piece. Just the opposite – its design and fashion industries race to be cutting edge, and its food scene is intensely hip.

ORIENTATION

Stockholm is built on 14 islands. The modern centre (Norrmalm) is focused on the square known as Sergels Torg. This business and shopping hub is linked by a network of subways to Centralstationen (Central Train Station); these subways also link with the *tunnelbana* (metro; or T) stations. The large, busy tourist office, Sweden House, is in the eastern part of Norrmalm.

Smack in the middle of Stockholm is Gamla Stan, the historic Old Town. To the east of Gamla Stan is the island of Djurgården, home to many of Stockholm's museums. The island of Skeppsholmen sits between Djurgården and Gamla Stan. Södermalm, the city's funky, bohemian area, inhabits the large island to the south of Gamla Stan. Arguably Sodermalm's coolest section is the area south of Folkungagatan, or SoFo.

INFORMATION

Discount Cards

SL Tourist Card (www.sl.se; per 24/72hr Skr100/200) Covers transport only.

Stockholm Card (www.stockholmtown.com; adult 24/48/72hr Skr330/460/580) Available from tourist offices, camping grounds, hostels, hotels and Storstockholms Lokaltrafik (SL) centres, the card gives free entry to about 75 attractions (including Skansen), free city parking in metered spaces, free sightseeing by boat and free travel on public transport.

> **EMERGENCY NUMBER**
>
> - Ambulance, fire, police ☎ 112

Emergency

Police station Kungsholmen (Map pp1126-7; ☎ 401 13 00; Kungsholmsgatan 37; 🕒 24hr); Södermalm (Map p1128; ☎ 401 01 00; Torkel Knutssonsgatan 20; 🕒 24hr)

Internet Access

Sidewalk Express (www.sidewalkexpress.se, in Swedish; per hr Skr19) A chain of roving internet kiosks at numerous central locations – Centralstationen, Cityterminalen, Arlanda and Bromma airports, inside some convenience stores and coffee shops.

Left Luggage

There are three sizes of **left-luggage boxes** (per 24hr from Skr40-90) at Centralstationen. Similar facilities exist at the neighbouring bus station and at major ferry terminals.

Medical Services

Apoteket CW Scheele (Map p1128; ☎ 454 81 30; Klarabergsgatan 64) 24-hour pharmacy.

CityAkuten (Map p1128; ☎ 412 29 00; Apelbergsgatan 48; 🕒 8am-8pm) Emergency health and dental care.

Södersjukhuset (Map pp1126-7; ☎ 616 10 00; Ringvägen 52) The most central hospital.

Money

ATMs are plentiful. The exchange company Forex has over a dozen branches in the capital and charges Skr15 per travellers cheque; the following are two handy locations:

Stockholm Arlanda airport (Terminal 2; 🕒 5.30am-10pm Sun-Fri, to 6pm Sat)

Sweden House (Map p1128; ☎ 820 03 89; Hamngatan 27; 🕒 10am-6pm Mon-Fri, 10am-5pm Sat, noon-4pm Sun)

Tourist Information

Sweden House (Map p1128; ☎ 50 82 85 08; www.stockholmtown.se; Hamngatan 27; 🕒 9am-7pm Mon-Fri, 10am-5pm Sat, 10am-4pm Sun May-Sep, 9am-6pm Mon-Fri, 10am-5pm Sat, 10am-4pm Sun Oct-Apr) The

GETTING INTO TOWN

If you arrive by train (into Centralstationen, the main train station) or bus (into Cityterminalen, the main bus terminal, neighbouring Centralstationen), you're walking distance to the modern shopping and business district of Stockholm, and well placed to get anywhere in the capital by *tunnelbana* (the local metro system), local bus or on foot.

If you arrive by ferry to any of the major harbours, jump on one of the shuttle buses provided by the ferry operators to get into Cityterminalen.

Stockholm's principal airport, Arlanda, is 45km north of the city centre. The **Arlanda Express** (☎ 020-22 22 24) train travels between Arlanda and Centralstationen (from Skr220, 20 minutes) at 15- to 20-minute intervals from around 5am to midnight. A cheaper option is the **Flygbussarna** (☎ 08-600 10 00; www.flygbussarna.se) bus service to/from Cityterminalen (Skr110, 40 minutes). A taxi from Arlanda to the city centre shouldn't cost more than Skr495.

main tourist office is just off Kungsträdgården across from the NK department store.

SIGHTS

Gamla Stan

Once you get over the armies of tourists wielding ice-cream cones and shopping bags, you'll discover that the oldest part of Stockholm is also its most beautiful. The city emerged here in the 13th century and grew with Sweden's power until the 17th century, when the castle of Tre Kronor, symbol of that power, burned to the ground.

The 'new' royal palace, **Kungliga Slottet** (Map p1128; ☎ 402 61 30; www.royalcourt.se; Slottsbacken; each attraction Skr90, combined ticket Skr130; most attractions 🕑 10am-4pm mid-late May & early–mid-Sep, 10am-5pm Jun-Aug, noon-3pm Tue-Sun mid-Sep–mid-May), is constructed on the ruins of Tre Kronor and is one of Stockholm's highlights. Its 608 rooms make it the largest royal palace in the world. The **Changing of the Guard** (12.15pm Monday to Saturday, 1.15pm Sunday and public holidays) takes place in the outer courtyard.

Near the palace, **Storkyrkan** (Map p1128; ☎ 723 30 09; Skr25; 🕑 9am-6pm mid-May–Oct, to 4pm rest of yr) is the Royal Cathedral of Sweden, consecrated in 1306. On the main square, Stortorget, is **Nobelmuseet** (Map p1128; ☎ 53 48 18 00; Stortorget; Skr60; 🕑 10am-5pm Wed-Mon, to 8pm Tue mid-May–mid-Sep, 11am-5pm Wed-Sun, to 8pm Tue mid-Sep–mid-May), presenting the history of the Nobel Prize and its recipients.

Djurgården

Leafy, attraction-rich Djurgården is a must-see. Take bus 47 from Centralstationen or the regular Djurgården ferry services from Nybroplan or Slussen. By the bridge you can hire bikes – the best way to explore the area. Beyond Djurgården's large tourist haunts are plenty of small gems, including some excellent art collections.

You could easily spend all day at **Skansen** (Map pp1126-7; ☎ 442 80 00; www.skansen.se; Skr60-145, depending on season; 🕑 10am-8pm May-late Jun, to 10pm late Jun-Aug, to 8pm Sep, to 4pm Mar, Apr & Oct, to 3pm Nov-Feb, to 4pm Christmas market weekends). This 'Sweden in miniature' was the world's first open-air museum (it opened in 1891); today over 150 traditional houses and exhibits from all over Sweden occupy the attractive hill top.

The flagship *Vasa* sank within minutes of being launched in 1628 and was resurrected from the mud some 300 years later. The acclaimed **Vasamuseet** (Map pp1126-7; ☎ 51954800; www.vasamuseet.se; Galärvarvsvägen 14; admission Skr95, 5-8pm Wed Sep-May Skr75; 🕑 8.30am-6pm Jun-Aug, 10am-5pm Thu-Tue, 10am-8pm Wed Sep-May) allows you to look into the lives of 17th-century sailors, plus appreciate a brilliant achievement in marine archaeology.

Nordiska Museet (National Museum of Cultural History; Map pp1126-7; ☎ 51 95 60 00; www.nordiskamuseet.se; Djurgårdsvägen 6-16; admission Skr60, from 4pm Wed Sep-May free; 🕑 10am-5pm Jun-Aug, 10am-4pm Mon-Fri, to 8pm Wed, 11am-5pm Sat & Sun Sep-May) is housed in an enormous Renaissance-style castle, with notable temporary exhibitions and vast Swedish collections.

Gröna Lund Tivoli (Map pp1126-7; ☎ 58 75 01 00; www.gronalund.com; admission Skr70; 🕑 noon-10pm Mon-Sat, to 8pm Sun Jun, 11am-10pm Sun-Thu, to 11pm Fri & Sat Jul-early Aug, varies May & early Aug–mid-Sep) is a fun park with dozens of rides and amusements; the Åkband day pass (Skr280) gives unlimited rides, or individual rides range from Skr20 to Skr60. Big-name concerts are often held here in summer.

Central Stockholm

Near Centralstationen is the vibrant but distinctly unbeautiful **Sergels Torg** (Map p1128), a public square that's actually round. **Kulturhuset** (Map p1128; ☎ 5083 1508; Sergels Torg; 🕑 11am-7pm Mon-Fri, to 5pm Sat & Sun, some sections closed Mon) is a huge, modern building containing galleries, a theatre, bookshop, design store, reading room, cafes, a comics library and a craft room for teens.

Not far away is the beloved public park **Kungsträdgården** (Map p1128), where locals gather in all weather. There's an outdoor stage, winter ice-skating rink, cafes and kiosks.

Sweden's largest art museum, the excellent **Nationalmuseum** (Map p1128; ☎ 51 95 44 10; www.nationalmuseum.se; Södra Blasieholmshamnen; admission Skr100; 🕑 11am-5pm Wed-Sun, to 8pm Tue Jun-Aug, 11am-5pm Wed & Fri-Sun, to 8pm Tue & Thu Sep-May) houses the national collection of painting, sculpture, drawings, decorative arts and graphics, from the Middle Ages to the present.

The main national historical collection is at the enthralling **Historiska Museet** (Museum of National Antiquities; Map pp1126-7; ☎ 51 95 56 00; www.historiska.se; Narvavägen 13; admission Skr60; 🕑 11am-5pm Tue, Wed & Fri-Sun, 11am-8pm Thu Oct-Apr, 10am-5pm May-Sep). Displays cover prehistoric, Viking and medieval archaeology and culture, and the incredible Gold Room's rare treasures include a seven-ringed gold collar.

Skeppsholmen

Across the bridge by the Nationalmuseum are more museums, including the sleek, impressive **Moderna Museet** (Map pp1126-7; ☎ 51 95 52 00; www.modernamuseet.se; Exercisplan 4; admission Skr80; 🕑 10am-8pm Tue, to 6pm Wed-Sun), which boasts a world-class collection of modern art, sculpture, photography and installations, temporary exhibitions and an outdoor sculpture garden. The adjacent **Arkitekturmuseet** (Museum of Architecture; ☎ 58 72 70 02; Exercisplan 4; www.arkitekturmuseet.se; Skr50, free admission 4-6pm Fri; 🕑 10am-8pm Tue, to 6pm Wed-Sun) has a permanent exhibition spanning 1000 years of Swedish architecture.

Kungsholmen

The main visitor sight here is the landmark **Stadshuset** (City Hall; Map p1128; ☎ 50 82 90 58; Hantverkargatan 1; entrance by tour only, Skr60; 🕑 tours in English 10am, 11am, noon, 2pm, 3pm & 4pm Jun-Aug, 10am, noon & 2pm rest of yr), resembling a large church, with two internal courtyards. Inside are the mosaic-lined Gyllene Salen (Golden Hall), Prins Eugen's own fresco re-creation of the lake view from the gallery, and the Blå Hallen (Blue Hall), where the annual Nobel Prize banquet is held. The **tower** (Skr20; 🕑 9am-5pm Jun-Aug, to 4pm May & Sep) offers stellar views and a great thigh workout.

Other Areas

Södermalm (Map p1128) is Stockholm's most striking neighbourhood, where artistic and alternative types hang out – if you're looking for, say, a straight-edge vegan all-ages punk club, this is the place. The street scene is scarcely less exciting than the gorgeous views over Stockholm from the island's northern cliffs (called the Söder Heights). Start at the top of **Katarinahissen** (Slussen; Map p1128), an old lift (Skr5) that goes up from Slussen. Or sneak onto the free elevator at McDonald's next door. Wooden stairs also snake up the hillside.

ACTIVITIES

From Djurgårdsbron's **Sjöcafe** (Map pp1126-7; ☎ 660 57 57; canoes per hr/day Skr75/300; 🕑 9am-9pm Apr-Sep), next to the bridge leading to Djurgården, you can rent bikes, in-line skates, kayaks, canoes, rowboats and pedalboats. Opposite, floating resto-bar **Strandbryggan** (Map pp1126-7; ☎ 660

STOCKHOLM FOR FREE

The heady days of multiple free-admission museums in Stockholm are past, but with a little manoeuvring of your schedule and adjustment of plans, you can still score freebies.

- Nordiska Museet (opposite) has free admission from 4pm to 8pm Wednesdays September to May.
- Parks in Stockholm never charge admission.
- Arkitekturmuseet (left) has free admission 4pm to 6pm Fridays.
- Save your legs and sneak onto the free elevator (above) at McDonald's to get a lift up the hill above Slussen.
- Pee for free at Östermalms Saluhall (p1131).
- Some shows at Dansens Hus are free – check the website for a schedule (p1132).

STOCKHOLM

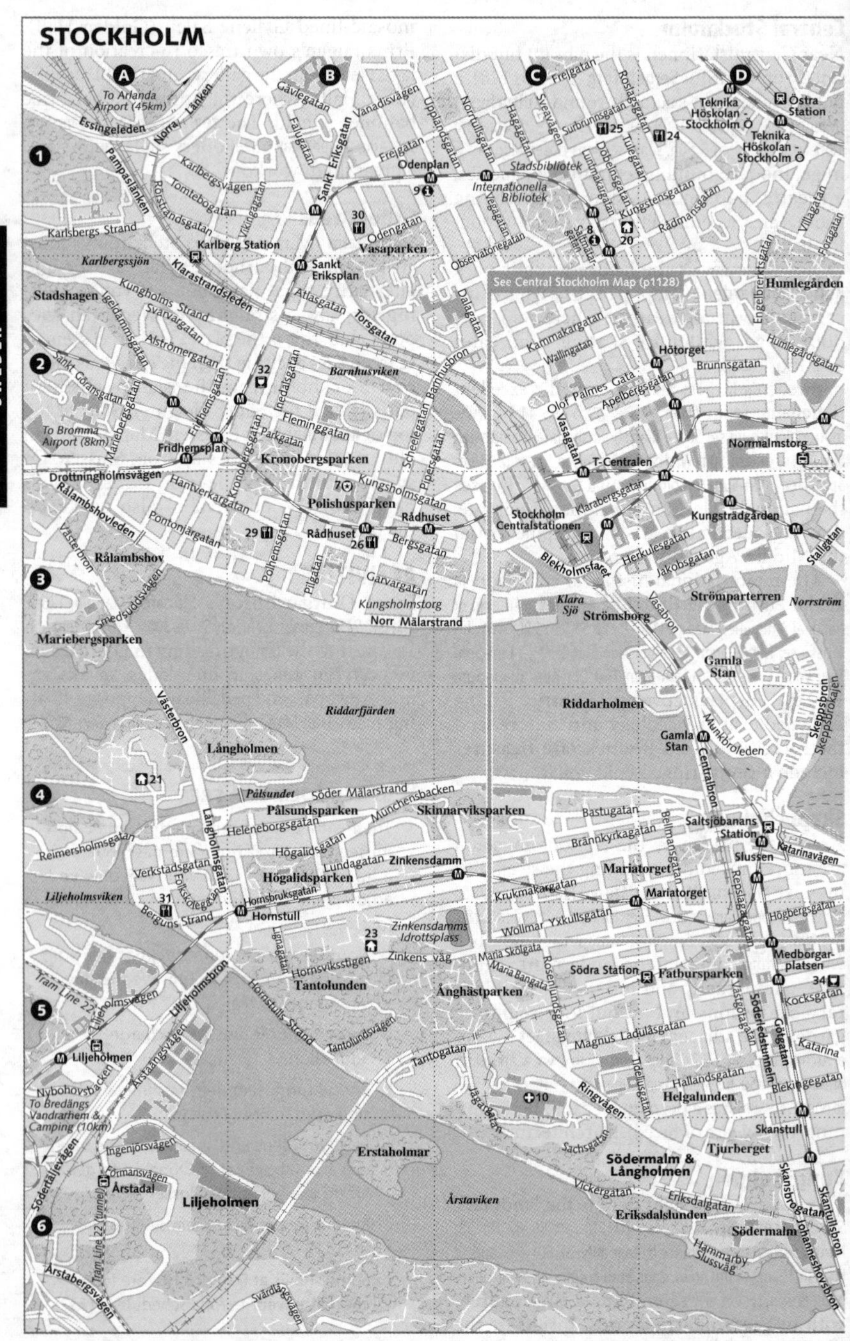

A
B
C
D
1
2
3
4
5
6
To Arlanda Airport (45km)
Essingeleden
Norra Länken
Pampaslänken
Gävlegatan
Falugatan
Sankt Eriksgatan
Vanadisvägen
Upplandsgatan
Norrtullsgatan
Hagagatan
Sveavägen
Frejgatan
Surbrunnsgatan
Roslagsgatan
Tulegatan
Döbelnsgatan
Luntmakargatan
Teknika Höskolan - Stockholm Ö
Östra Station
Karlbergsvägen
Tomtebogatan
Rörstrandsgatan
Vikingagatan
Odenplan
Stadsbibliotek
Internationella Bibliotek
Vegagatan
Kungstensgatan
Rådmansgatan
Villagatan
Karlbergs Strand
Karlberg Station
Karlbergssjön
Odengatan
Vasaparken
Sankt Eriksplan
Observatoriegatan
Saltmätargatan
Klarastrandsleden
Stadshagen
Kungsholms Strand
Igeldammsgatan
Svarvargatan
Alströmergatan
Atlasgatan
Torsgatan
Dalagatan
See Central Stockholm Map (p1128)
Humlegården
Engelbrektsgatan
Humlegårdsgatan
Kammakargatan
Wallingatan
Hötorget
Brunnsgatan
Sankt Göransgatan
Mariebergsgatan
Fridhemsgatan
Inedalsgatan
Barnhusviken
Barnhusbron
Fleminggatan
Parkgatan
Kronobergsgatan
Scheelegatan
Pipersgatan
Olof Palmes Gata
Apelbergsgatan
Vasagatan
To Bromma Airport (8km)
Fridhemsplan
Kronobergsparken
Norrmalmstorg
T-Centralen
Drottningholmsvägen
Hantverkargatan
Kungsholmsgatan
Polishusparken
Klarabergsgatan
Kungsträdgården
Rålambshovleden
Pontonjärgatan
Rådhuset
Stockholm Centralstationen
Stallgatan
Västerbron
Polhemsgatan
Bergsgatan
Herkulesgatan
Jakobsgatan
Rålambshov
Pilgatan
Garvargatan
Blekholmsfaret
Smedsuddsvägen
Kungsholmstorg
Klara Sjö
Strömsborg
Strömparterren
Norrström
Norr Mälarstrand
Vasabron
Mariebergsparken
Gamla Stan
Riddarfjärden
Riddarholmen
Skeppsbron
Skeppsbrokajen
Långholmen
Munkbroleden
Centralbron
Pålsundet
Söder Mälarstrand
Münchensbacken
Pålsundsparken
Skinnarviksparken
Bastugatan
Heleneborgsgatan
Brännkyrkagatan
Bellmansgatan
Saltsjöbanans Station
Reimersholmsgatan
Högalidsgatan
Katarinavägen
Långholmsgatan
Slussen
Verkstadsgatan
Lundagatan
Zinkensdamm
Mariatorget
Folkskolegatan
Högalidsparken
Krukmakargatan
Liljeholmsviken
Hornsbruksgatan
Repslagargatan
Högbergsgatan
Bergsunds Strand
Hornstull
Wollmar Yxkullsgatan
Lignagatan
Zinkensdamms Idrottsplass
Medborgarplatsen
Maria Skolgata
Maria Bangata
Hornsviksstigen
Zinkens väg
Rosenlundsgatan
Södra Station
Fatbursparken
Tram Line 22
Liljeholmsbron
Tantolunden
Ånghästparken
Kocksgatan
Liljeholmsvägen
Hornstulls Strand
Tantolundsvägen
Västgötagatan
Södermalmsleden
Södertunneln
Götgatan
Katarina
Magnus Ladulåsgatan
Liljeholmen
Årstaängsvägen
Tantogatan
Tideliusgatan
Nybohovsbacken
To Bredängs Vandrarhem & Camping (10km)
Jägargatan
Ringvägen
Hallandsgatan
Blekingegatan
Helgalunden
Skanstull
Sachsgatan
Tjurberget
Ingenjörsvägen
Erstaholmar
Södermalm & Långholmen
Södertäljevägen
Ormansvägen
Årstadal
Vickergatan
Liljeholmen
Årstaviken
Eriksdalsgatan
Eriksdalslunden
Skansbron
Johanneshovsbron
Skanstullsbron
Tram Line 22 (tunnel)
Södermalm
Hammarby Slussväg
Årstabergsvägen
Svärdlångsvägen

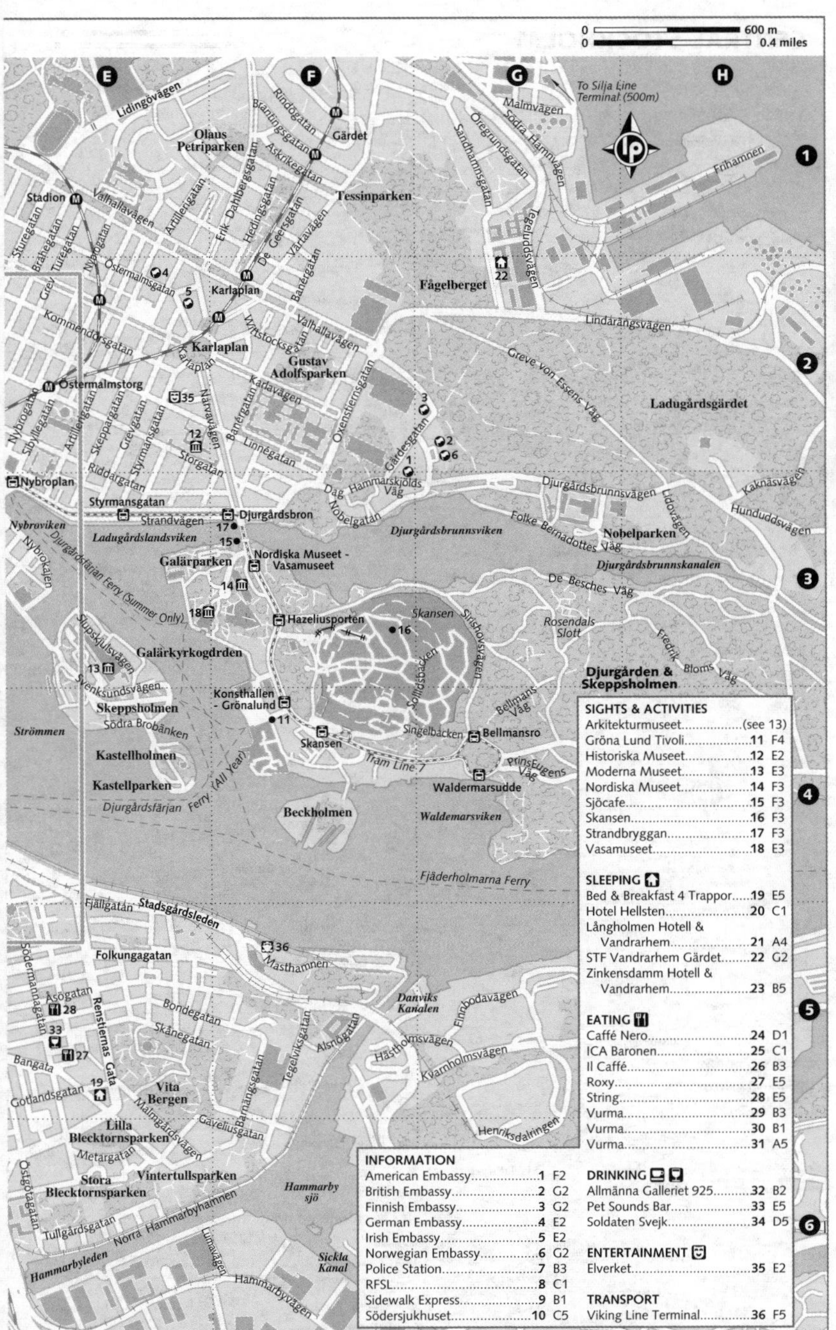
0 600 m
0 0.4 miles
E
F
G
H
1
2
3
4
5
6
To Silja Line Terminal (500m)
Djurgården & Skeppsholmen
Lidingövägen
Olaus Petriparken
Rindögatan
Brantingsgatan
Askrikegatan
Gärdet
Stadion
Valhallavägen
Artillerigatan
Erik Dahlbergsgatan
Hedingsgatan
De Geersgatan
Värtavägen
Tessinparken
Malmvägen
Södra Hamnvägen
Öregrundsgatan
Sandhamnsgatan
Tegeluddsvägen
Frihamnen
Sturegatan
Brahegatan
Turegatan
Nybrogatan
Grev
Östermalmsgatan
Karlaplan
Banérgatan
Fågelberget
Kommendörsgatan
Wittstocksgatan
Valhallavägen
Lindarängsvägen
Greve von Essens Väg
Gustav Adolfsparken
Östermalmstorg
Karlavägen
Oxenstiernsgatan
Ladugårdsgärdet
Nybrogatan
Sibyllegatan
Skeppargatan
Grevgatan
Styrmansgatan
Narvavägen
Linnégatan
Storgatan
Gärdesgatan
Riddargatan
Nybroplan
Dag Hammarskjölds Väg
Nobelgatan
Djurgårdsbrunnsvägen
Kaknäsvägen
Lidovägen
Hunduddsvägen
Styrmansgatan
Strandvägen
Djurgårdsbron
Nybroviken
Ladugårdslandsviken
Djurgårdsbrunnsviken
Folke Bernadottes Väg
Nobelparken
Nybrokajen
Djurgårdsfärjan Ferry (Summer Only)
Galärparken
Nordiska Museet - Vasamuseet
Djurgårdsbrunnskanalen
De Besches Väg
Hazeliusporten
Skansen
Sirishovsvägen
Rosendals Slott
Slupskjulsvägen
Galärkyrkogården
Solliden
Fredrik Bloms Väg
Svenksundsvägen
Konsthallen - Grönalund
Skeppsholmen
Strömmen
Södra Brobänken
Bellmans Väg
Kastellholmen
Singelbacken
Bellmansro
Skansen
Tram Line 7
Prins Eugens Väg
Kastellparken
Djurgårdsfärjan Ferry (All Year)
Waldermarsudde
Beckholmen
Waldemarsviken
Fjäderholmarna Ferry
Fjällgatan
Stadsgårdsleden
Folkungagatan
Masthamnen
Södermannagatan
Åsögatan
Renstiernas Gata
Bondegatan
Danviks Kanalen
Finnbodavägen
Skånegatan
Alsnögatan
Hästholmsvägen
Kvarnholmsvägen
Bangata
Tegelviksgatan
Gotlandsgatan
Vita Bergen
Barnängsgatan
Malmgårdsvägen
Gaveliusgatan
Lilla Blecktornsparken
Henriksdalringen
Metargatan
Östgötagatan
Stora Blecktornsparken
Vintertullsparken
Hammarby sjö
Tullgårdsgatan
Norra Hammarbyhamnen
Hammarbyleden
Sickla Kanal
Limavägen
Hammarbyvägen
SIGHTS & ACTIVITIES
Arkitekturmuseet (see 13)
Gröna Lund Tivoli 11 F4
Historiska Museet 12 E2
Moderna Museet 13 E3
Nordiska Museet 14 F3
Sjöcafe 15 F3
Skansen 16 F3
Strandbryggan 17 F3
Vasamuseet 18 E3
SLEEPING
Bed & Breakfast 4 Trappor 19 E5
Hotel Hellsten 20 C1
Långholmen Hotell & Vandrarhem 21 A4
STF Vandrarhem Gärdet 22 G2
Zinkensdamm Hotell & Vandrarhem 23 B5
EATING
Caffé Nero 24 D1
ICA Baronen 25 C1
Il Caffé 26 B3
Roxy 27 E5
String 28 E5
Vurma 29 B3
Vurma 30 B1
Vurma 31 A5
INFORMATION
American Embassy 1 F2
British Embassy 2 G2
Finnish Embassy 3 G2
German Embassy 4 E2
Irish Embassy 5 E2
Norwegian Embassy 6 G2
Police Station 7 B3
RFSL 8 C1
Sidewalk Express 9 B1
Södersjukhuset 10 C5
DRINKING
Allmänna Galleriet 925 32 B2
Pet Sounds Bar 33 E5
Soldaten Svejk 34 D5
ENTERTAINMENT
Elverket 35 E2
TRANSPORT
Viking Line Terminal 36 F5

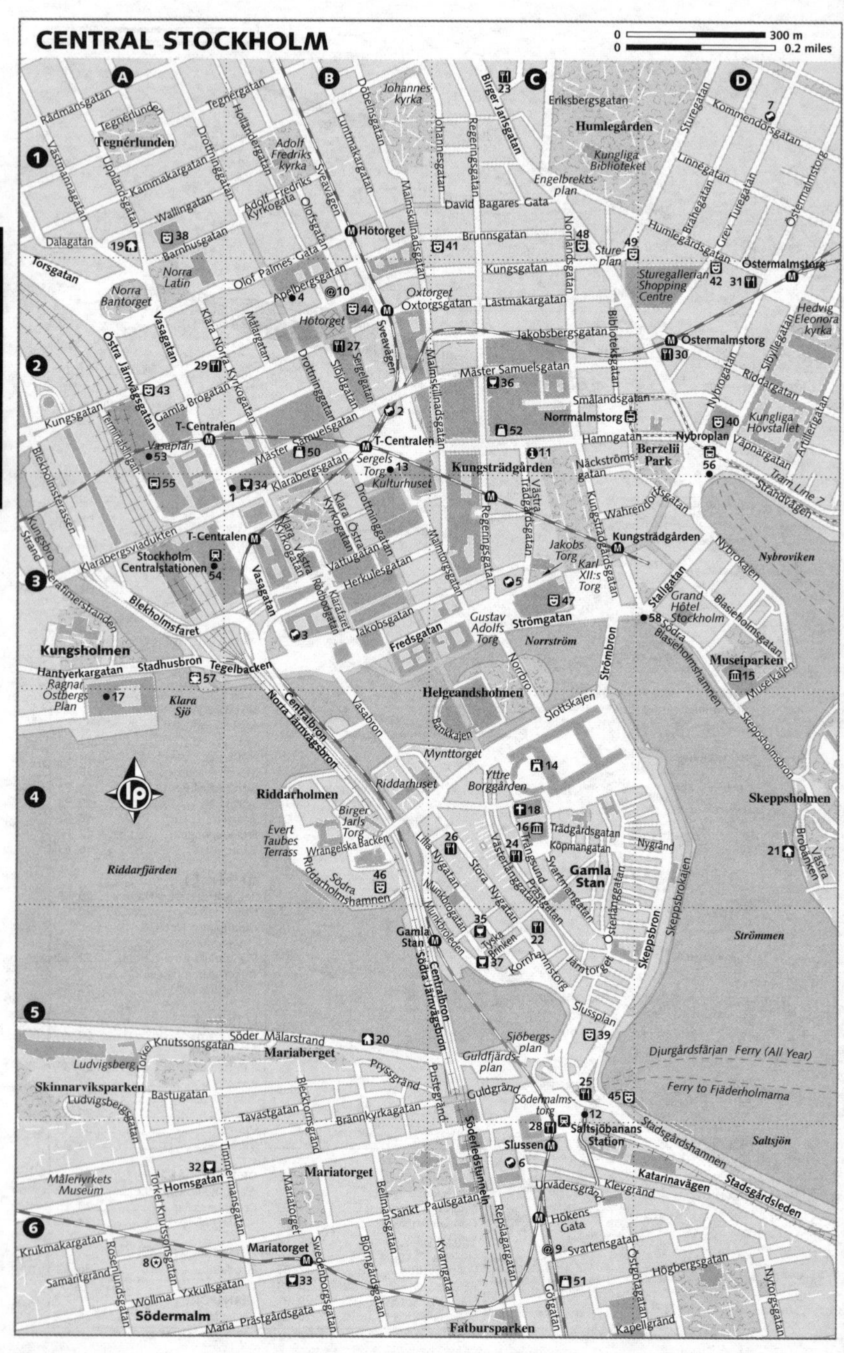
CENTRAL STOCKHOLM
300 m
0.2 miles
Tegnérlunden
Humlegården
Kungliga Biblioteket
Hötorget
Östermalmstorg
T-Centralen
Kungsträdgården
Norrmalmstorg
Nybroplan
Berzelii Park
Stockholm Centralstationen
Kungsholmen
Helgeandsholmen
Riddarholmen
Gamla Stan
Skeppsholmen
Museiparken
Riddarfjärden
Strömmen
Mariaberget
Skinnarviksparken
Mariatorget
Slussen
Saltsjöbanans Station
Södermalm
Fatbursparken
Djurgårdsfärjan Ferry (All Year)
Ferry to Fjäderholmarna
Saltsjön
Nybroviken
Norrström
Klara Sjö

INFORMATION
Apoteket CW Scheele....1 B3
Australian Embassy....2 B2
Canadian Embassy....3 B3
CityAkuten....4 B2
Danish Embassy....5 C3
Dutch Embassy....6 C6
Forex....(see 11)
French Embassy....7 D1
Police Station....8 A6
Sidewalk Express....9 C6
Sidewalk Express....10 B2
Sweden House....11 C2

SIGHTS & ACTIVITIES
Katarinahissen....12 C5
Kulturhuset....13 B2
Kungliga Slottet (Royal Palace)..14 C4
Nationalmuseum....15 D3
Nobelmuseet....16 C4
Stadshuset....17 A4
Storkyrkan....18 C4

SLEEPING
City Backpackers....19 A1
Den Röda Båten - Mälaren/Ran..20 B5
Vandrarhem af Chapman & Skeppsholmen....21 D4

EATING
Café Art....22 C5
Café Saturnus....23 C1
Chokladkoppen....24 C4
Coop Konsum....25 C5
Hemköp....(see 50)
Hermitage....26 C4
Hötorgshallen....27 B2
Nystekt Strömming....28 C6
Vetekatten....29 A2
Vivo T-Jarlen....30 D2
Östermalms Saluhall....31 D2

DRINKING
Marie Laveau....32 A6
Side Track....33 B6
Systembolaget....34 B3
Systembolaget....35 C5
Systembolaget....36 C2
Torget....37 C5

ENTERTAINMENT
Dansens Hus....38 A1
Debaser....39 C5
Dramaten....40 D2
Glenn Miller Café....41 C1
Grodan....42 D2
Jazzclub Fasching....43 A2
Konserthuset....44 B2
Lady Patricia....45 C5
Lino Club Sthlm....46 B4
Operan....47 C3
Spy Bar....48 C1
Sturecompagniet....49 C1

SHOPPING
Åhléns Department Store....50 B2
DesignTorget....51 C6
DesignTorget....(see 13)
NK Department Store....52 C2

TRANSPORT
Arlanda Express Terminal....53 A2
Centralstationen Ticket Office....54 A3
Cityterminalen....55 A3
Djurgården Boats....56 D2
Flygbussarna....(see 55)
Lake Mälaren Boats....57 A3
Silja and Tallink....(see 55)
Swebus Express....(see 55)
Waxholmsbolaget Office....58 D3
Ybuss....(see 55)

37 14; www.strandbryggan.se, in Swedish; Strandvägskajen 27; 10am-1am daily) rents sailing and motorboats from April to September. Sailing boats cost around Skr495 per hour, and all boats can be rented for a day, weekend or week.

FESTIVALS & EVENTS

Smaka På Stockholm Held in the first week of June, this festival in Kungsträdgården lets visitors taste from the menus of top local restaurants.

Stockholm Jazz Festival (www.stockholmjazz.com) Held 19-23 July.

SLEEPING

Most hotels give steep discounts on weekends and in summer (Midsummer's Day to mid-August), up to 50% off.

our pick **Vandrarhem af Chapman & Skeppsholmen** (Map p1128; ☎ 463 22 66; www.stfchapman.com; dm Skr185-230, tw from Skr530;) The legendary *af Chapman* is a storied vessel that has done plenty of travelling of its own. It's now well anchored in a superb, quiet location, swaying gently off Skeppsholmen. Bunks in dorms below decks have a nautical ambience, unsurprisingly. Staff members are friendly and knowledgeable about the city and surrounding areas. Apart from showers and toilets, all facilities are on dry land in the Skeppsholmen hostel, where you'll find a good kitchen with a laid-back common room and a separate TV lounge. Laundry facilities and 24-hour internet access are available.

Bredängs Vandrarhem (off Map pp1126-7; ☎ 97 62 00; mail@bredangvandrarhem.se; Stora Sällskapetsväg 51; camp sites Skr250, dm Skr200, 5-bed cabins Skr1450) A lakeside option 10km southwest of central Stockholm. It's well equipped, with a hostel and cabins. Take the metro to T-Bredäng, then walk 700m. If you're driving, it's well signposted from the E4/E20 motorway.

Långholmen Hotell & Vandrarhem (Map pp1126-7; ☎ 668 05 10; www.langholmen.com; dm Skr220, cell s/d Skr420/Skr540, hotel s/d Skr1435/1740;) Guests at this hotel/hostel, in a former prison on Långholmen island, sleep in bunks in a cell. The kitchen and laundry facilities are good, the restaurant serves meals all day, and Långholmen's popular summertime bathing spots are a towel flick away.

Zinkensdamm Hotell & Vandrarhem (Map pp1126-7; ☎ 616 81 00; www.zinkensdamm.com; Zinkens väg 20; dm Skr220, r with shared/private bathroom Skr530/730;) The Zinkensdamm STF is unabashedly fun. It's attractive and well equipped – complete with an ubersleek guest kitchen and personal lockers in each room – and caters for families with kids as well as pub-going backpackers. While the hostel breakfast buffet isn't spectacular, hostellers can buy the better hotel breakfast.

Den Röda Båten – Mälaren/Ran (Map p1128; ☎ 644 43 85; www.theredboat.com; Söder Mälarstrand, Kajplats 6; dm Skr230-260, s/d incl breakfast Skr700/1200;) 'The Red Boat' is a hotel and hostel on two vessels,

SWEDEN

SPLURGE

Hotel Hellsten (Map pp1126-7; ☎ 661 86 00; www.hellsten.se; Luntmakargatan 68; s/d Skr1990/2390; 💻) Hip Hellsten is owned by anthropologist Per Hellsten, whose slick slumber number features objects from his travels and life, including Congolese tribal masks and his grandmother's chandelier. Rooms are supremely comfortable and individually styled, with themes spanning rustic Swedish to Indian exotica; some even feature original tile stoves. The sleek bathrooms sport phones and hand-cut Greek slate. Hotel extras include a sauna and small fitness room, as well as live jazz in the ethno-chic lounge on Thursday evenings.

Mälaren and *Ran*. The hostel section is the cosiest of Stockholm's floating accommodations, thanks to lots of dark wood, nautical memorabilia and friendly staff. Hotel-standard rooms are also excellent.

City Backpackers (Map p1128; ☎ 20 69 20; www.citybackpackers.org; Upplandsgatan 2a; dm from Skr230; 💻) The closest hostel to Centralstationen has clean rooms, friendly staff, free bike hire and excellent facilities, including sauna, laundry and a kitchen (with a free stash of pasta). City tours are also offered.

STF Vandrarhem Gärdet (Map pp1126-7; ☎ 463 22 99; gardet@stfturist.se; Sandhamnsgatan 59; dm Skr270, s/d from Skr540/680; 💻) Located in quiet Gärdet, a quick metro ride from Östermalm, Stockholm's first 'designer hostel' ditches low-cost drab for smart, contemporary rooms featuring red Pin chairs, fluffy sheepskins, textured rugs and designer flat-screen TVs. All have a bathroom, some boast a small kitchenette, and towels and sheets are included. Take bus 1 from Centralstationen to Östhammarsgatan bus stop.

Bed & Breakfast 4 Trappor (Map pp1126-7; ☎ 642 3104, 0735-69 38 64; www.4trappor.se; Gotlandsgatan 78; apt s/d Skr650/800, with breakfast Skr700/900) For elegant slumming, it's hard to beat this apartment, complete with cosy, floorboarded bedroom (maximum two guests), modern bathroom and well-equipped kitchen (espresso machine included!). Breakfast is served in the owners' next-door apartment, and the SoFo address means easy access to Stockholm's coolest shops and hang-outs. There's a two-night minimum stay and a discounted rate for stays of over five nights. Book months ahead.

EATING

The sheer number of dining choices in Stockholm means it's usually possible to fill your belly without emptying your wallet. Don't miss coffee and cakes in an old-fashioned *konditori* (bakery cafe) or a visit to one of the dizzying market halls.

Look out for the daily lunch special called *dagens rätt* or *dagens lunch* at a fixed price (usually Skr65 to Skr75) between 11.30am and 2pm. For a quick, inexpensive snack, try a *grillad korv med bröd* – grilled hot dog on a bun (Skr12 to Skr25, available from countless stands and carts).

Gamla Stan

Chokladkoppen (Map p1128; ☎ 20 31 70; Stortorget; cakes & snacks Skr30-70) Arguably Stockholm's best-loved cafe, hole-in-the-wall Chokladkoppen sits slap bang on the Old Town's enchanting main square. It's a gay-friendly spot, with cute, gym-fit waiters, a look-at-me summer terrace and yummy grub like broccoli and blue cheese pie and scrumptious cakes.

Café Art (Map p1128; ☎ 411 76 61; Västerlånggatan 60; lunch Skr69) This atmospheric, barrel-vaulted cellar cranks up the cosy factor with its candlelit tables, snug nooks and art-slung walls. A perfect spot for *fika* (coffee and cake), it also makes a mean baguette and great shrimp salads.

Hermitage (Map p1128; ☎ 411 95 00; Stora Nygatan 11; lunch/dinner Skr80/95) Don't let the '80s-style coffee-shop decor put you off; herbivores love Hermitage for its simple, tasty vegetarian nosh. Salad, homemade bread, tea and coffee are included in the price.

Central Stockholm

Vetekatten (Map p1128; ☎ 21 84 54; Kungsgatan 55; tea, coffee & snacks from Skr25; 🕑 7.30am-8pm Mon-Fri, 9.30am-5pm Sat, noon-5pm Sun) A cardamom-scented labyrinth of cosy nooks, antique furnishings and oil paintings, Vetekatten is not so much a cafe as an institution. Wish back the old days over filling sandwiches, heavenly scrolls and warming cups of tea.

Caffé Nero (Map pp1126-7; ☎ 22 19 35; Roslagsgatan 4; coffee & pastries from Skr25; 🕑 7am-10pm Mon-Fri, 8am-10pm Sat, 8am-6pm Sun) Architect Tadao Ando would approve of the brutal (and brutally hip) concrete interiors at this Vasastan hang-out, where local hipsters down mighty caffé, grappa shots, salubrious panini and Italian home cooking, from sublime veal meatballs to a naughty tiramisu.

Hötorgshallen (Map p1128; Hötorget; 10am-6pm Mon-Thu, to 6.30pm Fri, to 4pm Sat Aug-May, 10am-6pm Mon-Fri, to 3pm Sat Jun & Jul) At this multicultural food-hall, stalls sell everything from fresh Nordic seafood to fluffy hummus and fragrant teas. Ready-to-eat options include Lebanese spinach parcels, kebabs and vegetarian burgers. Or squeeze into galley-themed dining nook Kajsas Fiskrestaurang for *fisksoppa* (fish stew) with mussels and aioli (Skr80).

Östermalm

Östermalms Saluhall (Map p1128; Östermalmstorg; 9.30am-6pm Mon-Thu, to 6.30pm Fri, to 4pm Sat) Stockholm's historic blue-ribbon market offers fresh fish, seafood, meat, fruits, vegetables and hard-to-find cheeses. The building is a Stockholm landmark, designed as a Romanesque cathedral of food in 1885. For a treat, book a table at Lisa Elmqvist (meals Skr140 to Skr310), one of the city's top seafood eateries (trust the staff's recommendations). There's a clean, free, well-hidden toilet in the corner opposite the market entrance.

Café Saturnus (Map p1128; ☎ 611 77 00; Eriksbergsgatan 6; pastries Skr55, baguettes Skr25; 7am-8pm Mon-Fri, 9am-7pm Sat & Sun) For velvety caffe latte, Gallic-inspired baguettes and perfect pastries, saunter into this casually chic bakery-cafe. Sporting a stunning mosaic floor, and a hit with everyone from yummy mummies to Swedish princesses, it's a fabulous spot to flick through the paper while devouring Stockholm's finest cinnamon bun.

Södermalm

Nystekt Strömming (Map p1128; Södermalmstorg; combo plates Skr30-50; varies, generally 10am-6pm Mon-Fri, 11am-4pm Sat & Sun) Get authentic Swedish fast food – fried *(stekt)* herring platters – at this humble cart outside the metro station at Slussen.

String (Map pp1126-7; ☎ 714 85 14; Nytorgsgatan 38; coffee & pastry around Skr45, salads Skr59-69; 9.30am-9pm Mon-Thu, 9.30am-7.30pm Fri, 10.30am-7pm Sat & Sun) This retro-funky SoFo cafe does a bargain weekend brunch buffet (Skr65, 10.30am-1pm). Load your plate with everything from cereals, yoghurt and fresh fruit to pancakes, toast and amazing homemade hummus. Fancy that '70s chair you're plonked on? Take it home; almost everything you see is for sale.

Kungsholmen

Vurma (Map pp1126-7; ☎ 650 93 50; Polhemsgatan 15; sandwiches Skr27-69, salads Skr73; 10am-6pm) Squeeze in among the chattering punters, fluff up the cushions and eavesdrop over a vegan latte at this kitsch-hip cafe-bakery. The scrumptious sandwiches and salads are inspired; try the chevre cheese, marinated chicken, tomato, cucumber, walnuts, apple and mustard salad. You'll find other branches in Vasastan (Gästrikegatan 2) and Södermalm (Bergsunds Strand 31).

Il Caffè (Map pp1126-7; ☎ 652 30 04; Bergsgatan 17; focaccia Skr47-95; 8am-6pm Mon-Fri, 10am-6pm Sat & Sun) Low-strung lights, edgy graphic murals and indie-cool regulars load this cafe with boho grit. The authentic focaccias are great, and best washed down with a jumbo-sized caffe latte.

Self-Catering

The handiest central supermarket is **Hemköp** (Map p1128; Klarabergsgatan 50; 7am-9pm Mon-Fri, 10am-9pm Sat & Sun), in the Åhléns department store. Others include:

ICA Baronen (Map pp1126-7; Odengatan 40; 8am-10pm)

Vivo T-Jarlen (Map p1128; inside the Östermalmstorg Tunnelbana station; 7am-9pm Mon-Fri, 10am-7pm Sat, 11am-7pm Sun) Enter from Grev Turegatan.

Coop Konsum (Map p1128; Katarinavägen 3-7; 7am-9pm Mon-Fri, 9am-9pm Sat & Sun)

DRINKING

Nightlife is the most varied in Södermalm, along Götgatan, Östgötagatan and Skånegatan and near Medborgarplatsen. For fashionable late-night bars and clubs brimful of the beautiful people, go to Stureplan. Beers are cheapest during after-work happy hours, usually 4pm to 6pm Monday to Friday.

Marie Laveau (Map p1128; ☎ 668 85 00; www.marielaveau.se, in Swedish; Hornsgatan 66; 5pm-midnight Tue & Wed, to 3am Thu-Sat) In an old sausage factory, this kicking Söder playpen draws a boho-chic crowd. The designer-grunge bar (think chequered floor and subway-style tiled columns) serves killer cocktails and contemporary nosh (Skr84 to Skr199), while the sweaty basement hosts thumping club night Bangers 'n' Mash on Saturdays.

Pet Sounds Bar (Map pp1126-7; ☎ 643 82 25; www.petsoundsbar.se, in Swedish; Skånegatan 80; from 5pm Mon-Sat) A SoFo favourite, this jamming bar pulls in music journos, indie culture vultures and the odd Goth rocker. While the restaurant serves decent Italo-French grub, the real fun happens in the basement. Head down for a mixed bag of live bands, release parties and DJ sets.

Allmänna Galleriet 925 (Map pp1126-7; ☎ 41 06 81 00; www.ag925.se; Kronobergsgatan 37; ⏲ from 5pm Tue-Sat, closed mid-Jun–Jul) AG925 has all the 'It kid' prerequisites: obscure urban location (ex-silver factory and anonymous facade), postindustrial fit-out (steel-plate floors, white-tiled walls, Tom Dixon lights) and edgy art slung on the walls.

Soldaten Svejk (Map pp1126-7; ☎ 641 33 66; Östgötagatan 35) There's great Czech beer on tap in this crowded, amber-windowed, wooden-floored pub, decorated with heraldic shields.

SWEDEN

Systembolaget

The state-owned alcohol monopoly is the only place to buy real booze to take away. A complete listing is given online; the following are some handy central branches:

Systembolaget (www.systembolaget.se) Lilla Nygatan (Map p1128; ☎ 411 65 06; Lilla Nygatan 11; ⏲ 10am to 6pm Mon to Wed, to 7pm Thu & Fri, to 3pm Sat); Klarabergsgatan (Map p1128; ☎ 21 47 44; Klarabergsgatan 62; ⏲ 10am to 8pm Mon-Fri, to 3pm Sat); Regeringsgatan (Map p1128; ☎ 796 98 10; Regeringsgatan 44; ⏲ 10am to 7pm Mon-Fri, to 3pm Sat)

CLUBBING

Stockholm is home to some mighty clubs, with DJ royalty regularly on the decks. You'll find the slickest spots in cash-flash Östermalm, especially on and around Stureplan. Expect an entry charge of Skr100 to Skr200 at the trendiest venues, not to mention notoriously picky door bitches (style up or opt out!). Södermalm offers a more varied scene, with club nights spanning local indie to salsa.

Spy Bar (Map p1128; ☎ 54 50 37 01; www.thespybar.com, in Swedish; Birger Jarlsgatan 20; admission Skr160; ⏲ 10pm-5am Wed-Sat) Set in a turn-of-the-century flat (spot the tiled stoves), this party stalwart pulls in a 20- and 30-something media crowd, as well as the odd American heiress (yes, Paris partied here). Expect three bars, electro, rock and hip-hop beats and no entry after 2am (unless you're well connected, darling).

Sturecompagniet (Map p1128; ☎ 611 78 00; www.sturecompagniet.se; Sturegatan 4; admission Skr120, after midnight Skr140; ⏲ 10pm-3am Thu-Sat) Swedish soap stars, flowing champagne and look-at-me attitude set a decadent scene at this glitzy, multilevel playpen. Dress to impress, and flaunt your wares to commercial house. Guest DJs have included Roger Sanchez.

Grodan (Map p1128; ☎ 679 61 00; www.grodannattklubb.se, in Swedish; Grev Turegatan 16; admission Skr120; ⏲ 10pm-3am Fri & Sat) At street level it's a packed bar and mock-baroque restaurant serving great mod nosh. In the cellar, A-list DJ talent from Stockholm, London and beyond (think Axwell, Özgur Can, Ben Watt) spin the vinyl, pumping out house and electro tracks for sweat-soaked clubbers.

ENTERTAINMENT

Concerts, Theatre & Dance

Stockholm is a theatre city, with outstanding dance, opera and music performances; for an overview, pick up the free *What's On Stockholm* guide from the tourist office. Ticket sales are handled by the tourist office at Sweden House, or you can buy direct from **Ticnet** (☎ 0771-70 70 70; www.ticnet.se). Tickets aren't cheap and often sell out, especially for Saturday shows, but you can occasionally get last-minute deals.

Konserthuset (Map p1128; ☎ 50 66 77 88; www.konserthuset.se; Hötorget; tickets Skr80-325) Head here for classical concerts and other musical marvels, including the Royal Philharmonic Orchestra.

Operan (Map p1128; ☎ 791 44 00; www.operan.se; Operahuset, Gustav Adolfs Torg; tickets Skr135-460) The Royal Opera is the place to go for thunderous tenors, sparkling sopranos and classical ballet. It also has some bargain tickets in seats with poor views for as little as Skr40, and occasional lunchtime concerts for Skr180 (including light lunch).

Dramaten (Map p1128; ☎ 667 06 80; www.dramaten.se; Nybroplan; tickets Skr190-320) The Royal Theatre stages a range of plays in a sublime art nouveau environment.

Elverket (Map pp1126-7; ☎ 667 06 80; www.dramaten.se; Linnégatan 69) Dramaten's experimental stage pushes the boundaries with edgier offerings performed in a converted power station.

Dansens Hus (Map p1128; ☎ 50 89 90 90; www.dansenshus.se; Barnhusgatan 12-14; tickets free-Skr300) The stomping ground of Mats Ek's Cullberg Ballet, this place is a must for contemporary dance fans.

Live Music

On any night you can catch anything from emerging indie acts to edgy rock, blues and Balkan pop. Jazz and blues have a particularly strong presence; an annual jazz festival is held in mid-July.

Debaser (Map p1128; ☎ 462 98 60; www.debaser.se, in Swedish; Karl Johanstorg 1, Slussen; ⏲ 7pm-1am, to

GAY & LESBIAN STOCKHOLM

Still glowing from EuroPride 2008, Stockholm is a dazzling spot for queer travellers. Sweden's legendary open-mindedness makes homophobic attitudes rare and party-goers of all persuasions are welcome in any bar or club. As a result, Stockholm doesn't do a 'gay ghetto', although you'll find most of the queercentric venues in Södermalm and Gamla Stan. For club listings and events, pick up a free copy of street-press magazine *QX*, found at many clubs, stores and cafes around town. Its website (www.qx.se) is more frequently updated. *QX* also produces a free, handy *Gay Stockholm Map*. **RFSL** (Map pp1126-7; ☎ 50 16 29 50; www.rfsl.se/stockholm, in Swedish; Sveavägen 57), the national organisation for gay and lesbian rights, is a good source of information, with a library and cafe to boot.

Roxy (Map pp1126-7; ☎ 640 96 55; www.roxysofo.se; Nytorget 6; closed Mon) In Södermalm, this is a chic resto-bar popular with lipstick lesbians, publishing types and SoFo's creative set, all of whom nibble on brilliant mod-Med nosh to sultry tango tunes.

Torget (Map p1128; ☎ 20 55 60; www.torgetbaren.com; Mälartorget 13) In Gamla Stan, this is Stockholm's premier gay bar-cum-restaurant, with eye-candy staff, mock-baroque touches and a civilised salon vibe.

Side Track (Map p1128; ☎ 641 16 88; www.sidetrack.nu; Wollmar Yxkullsgatan 7; Wed-Sat) A particular hit with down-to-earth guys, with a low-key, publike ambience and decent grub for peckish punters on the prowl.

Lino Club Sthlm (Map p1128; ☎ 411 69 76; www.linoclub.se; Södra Riddarholmshamnen 19; Sat) is Stockholm's hottest Saturday night gay club, with four bars, three dance floors and mingle-friendly outdoor terrace.

Lady Patricia (Map p1128; ☎ 743 05 70; Stadsgårdskajen 152; Sun) The perennial Sunday-night favourite with its superb seafood restaurant, two crowded dance floors, drag shows and Schlager-loving crowd. It's all aboard a docked old royal yacht.

3am club nights Sun-Thu, 8pm-3am Fri & Sat) The king of rock clubs hides away under the Slussen interchange. Emerging or bigger-name acts play most nights, while the killer club nights span anything from rock-steady to punk and electronica.

For jazz and blues, try the intimate, snob-proof **Glenn Miller Café** (Map p1128; ☎ 10 03 22; Brunnsgatan 21) or the reliable **Jazzclub Fasching** (Map p1128; ☎ 53 48 29 60; www.fasching.se; Kungsgatan 63).

SHOPPING

Non-EU residents are entitled to a duty-free refund of up to 17.5% on single purchases of more than Skr200 bought from tax-free shopping outlets (look for the 'Tax Free' sticker).

DesignTorget Götgatan (Map p1128; ☎ 462 35 20; Götgatan 31, Södermalm); Sergels Torg (Map p1128; ☎ 50 83 15 20; Basement, Kulturhuset, Sergels Torg) If you love good design but don't own a gold Amex, head to this clued-up chain, which sells the work of emerging designers alongside established denizens.

For all-in-one retail therapy, scour department store giant **Åhléns** (Map p1128; ☎ 676 60 00; Klarabergsgatan 50) or its upmarket rival **NK** (Map p1128; ☎ 762 80 00; Hamngatan 12-18).

GETTING THERE & AWAY

Air

Stockholm's main airport, **Arlanda** (ARN; ☎ 797 6000), is 45km north of the city centre. **Bromma airport** (BMA; ☎ 797 6874), 8km west of Stockholm, is a minor airport used for some domestic flights. Two airports are used by some low-cost carriers and sometimes labelled as 'Stockholm', despite being a fair distance from the capital: **Skavsta airport** (NYO; ☎ 0155-28 04 00) is 100km south of Stockholm, near Nyköping; and **Västerås airport** (VST; ☎ 021-805600) is near the town of Västerås, about 105km northwest of Stockholm. Transport connects all airports to Stockholm (see the boxed text, p1124).

Bus

Cityterminalen (Map p1128; 3.30am-midnight) is above and next door to Centralstationen (follow the signs inside the main station hall, or use the street entrance on Klarabergsviadukten). From Cityterminalen there are long-distance buses to most major towns in Sweden, eg to Malmö (Skr325, eight to 10 hours) and Göteborg (Skr193 to Skr277, 7 to 7½ hours) as well as international

SWEDEN

destinations, airport buses and buses to ferry ports. Cityterminalen has good facilities, including ATMs, foreign exchange, cafes, lockers and internet access.

Train

Stockholm is the centre for SJ's national services. Direct trains to/from Copenhagen, Oslo, Storlien (for Trondheim) and Narvik arrive and depart from **Centralstationen** (⏲ 5am-12.30am), as do the SL *pendeltåg* (commuter) services that operate within Stockholm county.

GETTING AROUND

Bicycle

Stockholm has an extensive network of bicycle paths, and top day trips include Djurgården; a loop going from Gamla Stan to Södermalm, Långholmen and Kungsholmen (on lakeside paths); and Drottningholm. See p1125 for bike-hire information.

Boat

Djurgårdsfärjan city ferries link Djurgården with Nybroplan and Slussen; ferries cost from Skr25 and run every 20 minutes in summer (less often in the low season).

Public Transport

Storstockholms Lokaltrafik (SL; www.sl.se) runs all *tunnelbana* (T or T-bana) metro trains, local trains and buses within the entire Stockholm county. There is an SL information office in the basement concourse at **Centralstationen** (⏲ 6.30am-11.15pm Mon-Sat, 7am-11.15pm Sun) and another near the Sergels Torg entrance (open until 6.30pm weekdays, 5pm weekends), which issues timetables and sells the SL Tourist Card and Stockholm Card. You can also call ☎ 600 10 00 for schedule and travel information.

The Stockholm Card (p1123) covers travel on all SL trains and buses in greater Stockholm. The 24-hour (Skr100) and 72-hour (Skr200) SL Tourist Cards are primarily for transport and give free entry to only a few attractions. The 72-hour SL Tourist Card (Skr260) is good value, especially if you use the third afternoon for transport to either end of the county: you can reach the ferry terminals in Grisslehamn, Kapellskär or Nynäshamn, as well as all of the archipelago harbours. If you want to explore the county in more detail, bring a passport photo and get yourself a 30-day SL pass (Skr690).

On Stockholm's public-transport system the minimum fare costs two coupons, and each additional zone costs another coupon (up to five coupons for four or five zones). Coupons cost Skr20 each (Skr15 from ticket machines at *tunnelbana* stations), but it's much better to buy strips of tickets for Skr180. Coupons are stamped at the start of a journey. Travelling without a valid ticket can lead to a fine of Skr600 or more. Coupons, tickets and passes can be bought at metro stations, Pressbyrån kiosks, SL railway stations and SL information offices. Tickets cannot be bought on buses.

International rail passes (eg Scanrail, Interrail) aren't valid on SL trains.

AROUND STOCKHOLM

Royal palaces, vintage villages and Viking traces: the greater Stockholm county is worth a venture or three. Handily, the SL Tourist Card or travel passes allow unlimited travel on all buses and local trains in the area.

STOCKHOLM ARCHIPELAGO

☎ 08

The Stockholm archipelago and its 24,000 islands is the favourite time-off destination for locals. The website **Stockholmtown** (www.stockholmtown.com) has a large section devoted to the archipelago and **Skärgårdsstiftelsen** (www.skargardsstiftelsen.se) is another great resource.

The main boat operator to the archipelago is **Waxholmsbolaget** (Map p1128; ☎ 679 5830; www.waxholmsbolaget.se); timetables are located at offices outside the Grand Hôtel on Strömkajen in Stockholm, and at the harbour in Vaxholm.

Each island has its own character, and while many can be visited on a day trip, staying overnight is recommended. **Finnhamn** has excellent swimming spots; book in advance to stay at the **STF hostel** (☎ 54 24 62 12; info@finnhamn.nu; dm Skr260; 💻), the largest hostel in the archipelago with 80 beds and boat-hire available.

Utö, far out in the southern archipelago, is popular among cyclists. Open from May to September, the **STF hostel** (☎ 50 42 03 15; reception@utovardshus.se; Gruvbyggan; dm Skr330), associated with the nearby *värdshus* (restaurant), is in a former summer house. Reception and meals are at the *värdshus*, which is also known for its gourmet **restaurant** (lunch Skr89-119, mains around Skr200; ⏲ closed Jan).

UPPSALA

☎ 018 / pop 182,000

Drenched in history but never stifled by the past, Uppsala has the party vibe of a university town to balance out its atmosphere of weighty cultural significance. It's a good combination, one that makes the town both fun and functional.

On the edge of the city is Gamla (Old) Uppsala, the original site of the town, once a flourishing 6th-century religious centre where humans made sacrifices to the Norse gods and home to an ancient burial ground.

The **tourist office** (☎ 727 48 00; www.uppsalatourism.se; Fyristorg 8; 10am-6pm Mon-Fri, 10am-3pm Sat, also noon-4pm Sun mid-Jun–mid-Aug) is close to the cathedral.

Sights & Activities

Uppsala began at the three great grave mounds at **Gamla Uppsala** (admission free; 24hr), 4km north of the modern city and well signposted (bus 2 from Stora Torget). The mounds are said to be the graves of pre-Viking kings and lie in a cemetery with about 300 smaller mounds and a great heathen temple. **Gamla Uppsala Museum** (☎ 23 93 00; www.raa.se/gamlauppsala; admission Skr50; 11am-5pm May-Aug, noon-3pm Wed, Sat & Sun Sep–mid-Dec & Jan-Apr) contains finds from the cremation mounds, a poignant mix of charred and melted beads, bones and buckles.

Originally constructed by Gustav Vasa in the mid-16th century, **Uppsala Slott** (Castle; ☎ 54 48 11; www.uppsalaslott.se; admission by guided tour only, Skr70; English tours 1pm & 3pm Tue-Sun Jun-Aug) features the state hall where kings were enthroned and a queen abdicated. It's open by guided tour only, but anyone is free to wander the **Botanic Gardens** (7am-9pm May-Aug, to 7pm Sep-Apr) below the castle hill, originally laid out by Carl von Linné (Linnaeus).

A wonder cabinet of wonder cabinets, the **Museum Gustavianum** (☎ 471 75 71; www.gustavianum.uu.se; Akademigatan 3; admission Skr40; 11am-4pm Tue-Sun) rewards appreciation of the weird and well organised. The shelves in the pleasantly musty building hold case after case of obsolete tools and preserved oddities: stuffed birds, astrolabes, alligator mummies, exotic stones and dried sea creatures. Don't miss the anatomical theatre tucked inside the dome.

Sleeping & Eating

Uppsala Vandrarhem & Hotell (☎ 24 20 08; www.uppsalavandrarhem.se; Kvarntorget 3; dm Skr170-200, s/d hostel Skr400/500, s/d hotel Skr795/895, weekends Skr650/800; P) This new hotel-hostel combo, located in a sort of minimall, is removed from the action but easily walkable from the train station. Hostel rooms are upstairs; hotel rooms on two levels face an enclosed courtyard that works as breakfast room. Breakfast is included in the hotel prices, Skr75 extra for hostellers.

Ofvandahls (☎ 13 42 04; Sysslomansgatan 3-5; cakes & snacks around Skr40) An Uppsala institution, this classy *konditori* dates back to the 19th century and is a cut above your average coffee-and-bun shop. It's endorsed by no less a personage than the king, and radiates old-world charm; somehow those faded red-striped awnings just get cuter every year.

Eko Caféet (☎ 12 18 45; Drottninggatan 5; snacks Skr50-70) This funky little place with retro and mismatched furniture serves some of the best coffee in town. It does Italian-style wholefood, turns into a tapas bar on Wednesday to Saturday evenings, and frequently hosts live jazz/folk, as well as changing art exhibits and general studenty goings-on. In summer it just opens for lunch Monday to Friday.

Getting There & Around

The bus station is outside the train station on Kungsgatan. Bus 801 departs at least twice an hour for nearby Arlanda airport. Swebus Express runs regularly to Stockholm (Skr52, one hour), as does SJ trains.

City buses to Gamla Uppsala leave from Stora Torget or on Dragarbrunnsgatan.

GOTLAND

☎ 0498 / pop 57,400

Gorgeous Gotland has much to brag about: a Unesco-lauded capital, truffle-sprinkled woods, A-list dining hot spots, talented artisans, and more hours of sunshine than anywhere else in Sweden. It's also one of the country's richest historical regions, with around 100 medieval churches and countless prehistoric sites, from stone-ship settings and burial mounds to hilltop fortress remains.

Getting There & Away

Destination Gotland (☎ 0771-22 33 00; www.destinationgotland.se) operates car ferries year-round between Visby and both Nynäshamn and Oskarshamn. Departures from Nynäshamn are from two to six times daily (five hours, or three hours by high-speed catamaran). From

Oskarshamn there are one or two daily departures (three hours).

Regular one-way tickets for the ferry cost from Skr180, but from mid-June to mid-August there is a more complicated fare system; some overnight, evening and early-morning sailings in the middle of the week are cheaper.

Getting Around

Gotlands Cykeluthyrning (☎ 214133; info@gotlandscykeluthyrning.com; ⏰ mid-May–Aug), behind Saluhall not far from Visby harbour, rents bikes (per day/week from Skr65/325) and tents (Skr100/400).

Kollektiv Trafiken (☎ 214112) runs buses to all corners of the island; tickets start at Skr12.

VISBY

☎ 0498 / pop 22,300

The port town of Visby is medieval eye candy and enough to warrant a trip to Gotland all by itself. A Unesco World Heritage site, Visby swarms with holidaymakers in the summer, and from mid-June to mid-August cars are banned in the old town. For many, the highlight of the season is the costumes, performances, crafts, markets and re-enactments of **Medeltidsveckan** (Medieval Week; www.medeltidsveckan.com), held during the first or second week of August. Finding accommodation during this time is almost impossible unless you've booked ahead.

The **tourist office** (☎ 20 17 00; www.gotland.info; Skeppsbron 4-6; ⏰ 8am-7pm summer, shorter hours rest of yr) is at the harbour.

Set aside enough time to stroll the perimeter (3.5km) along the **13th-century wall** with its 40 towers. The ruins of 10 medieval churches are all within the town walls and contrast with the old but sound **cathedral**, north of Stortorget. **Gotlands Fornsal** (☎ 29 27 00; www.lansmuseetgotland.se; Strandgatan 14; admission Skr75; ⏰ 10am-6pm Fri-Wed, to 7pm Thu Jun–mid-Sep, noon-4pm Tue-Sun mid-Sep–May) is one of the largest and best regional museums in Sweden, with a notable collection of runestones and early grave findings.

Sleeping

Moderately priced accommodation in and around Visby is in demand; book well in advance.

Norderstrands Camping (☎ 20 33 00; camp sites low/high season Skr85/145, cabins low/high season from Skr350/550; ⏰ late Apr–mid-Sep) The closest camping ground is this place by the sea, 800m north of Visby's ring wall (well connected by a walking and cycling path).

Fängelse Vandrarhem (☎ 20 60 50; Skeppsbron 1; dm/r from Skr180/240) As hard to get into as it once was to get out of, this hostel offers beds year-round in the small converted cells of an old prison. It's in a handy location, between the ferry dock and the harbour restaurants, and there's a cute terrace bar in summer. Reserve well in advance and always call ahead before arriving to ensure someone can let you in.

Gotlands Resor (☎ 20 12 60; info@gotlandsresor.se; Färjeleden 3) This travel agency, in Hamnhotellet, books stylish, fully equipped cottages (from Skr670 per night) in eastern and northern Gotland. Summer bookings should be made six months ahead.

Eating & Drinking

Sitting in cafes and bars facing the harbour or town square seems to be the chief pastime in Visby, and the choices are legion.

Vinäger (☎ 21 11 60; Hästgatan 3; sandwiches Skr49-68, salads Skr85-95; ⏰ outdoor restaurant 9am-10pm summer only) Sporting a slick, ethno-chic interior, this hip cafe-bar emphasises fresh food, whether it's a fetta and hummus wrap or lingonberry and cardamom muffins. Directly across the street, Vinäger's outdoor resto-bar cranks up the X-factor with a glam alfresco lounge.

Effes (☎ 21 06 22; snacks & meals Skr70-145) Gloriously grungy and packed with characters (rockers and Goths love the place), this pub-bar just off Adelsgatan is built into the town wall. There's an outdoor courtyard, pool tables and live music in summer.

ICA (Stora Torget; ⏰ 8am-8pm Mon-Sat, 10am-8pm Sun) This small supermarket is right on the main square; there are larger options outside Österport gate.

SOUTHERN SWEDEN

Sweden's southernmost county, Skåne (Scania) was Danish property until 1658 and still flaunts its differences. You can detect them in the strong dialect *(skånska)*, in the half-timbered houses, and in Skåne's hybrid flag: a Swedish yellow cross on a red Danish background.

MALMÖ

☎ 040 / pop 280,900

Once dismissed as crime-prone and tatty, Sweden's third-largest city has rebranded

GETTING INTO TOWN

Flygbussarna (☎ 0771-77 77 77; www.flygbussarna.com) runs from Centralstationen to Sturup airport (Skr99, 40 minutes) roughly every 40 minutes on weekdays, with six services on Saturday and seven on Sunday. Trains run directly from Malmö to Copenhagen's main airport (Skr95, 35 minutes, every 20 minutes), which has a much wider flight selection.

itself as progressive and downright cool. It's no coincidence that two of Stockholm's hippest icons – rock club Debaser and fashion-forward boutique Tjallamalla – have come to town.

Information

Forex (Centralstationen; 7am-9pm) There are several other branches scattered about town.

Malmö Card (per 1/2/3 days Skr130/160/190) Allows free bus transport, free entry to several museums and discounts at other attractions; available from the tourist office.

Sidewalk Express (Centralstationen; per hr Skr19) Internet access.

Tourist office (☎ 34 12 00; www.malmo.se; 9am-7pm Mon-Fri, 10am-4pm Sat & Sun mid-Jun–early Sep, 9am-6pm Mon-Fri, 10am-3pm Sat & Sun late May–mid-Jun, 9am-5pm Mon-Fri, 10am-3pm Sat & Sun rest of yr) Inside Centralstationen. Pick up the useful, free booklet *Malmö This Month*.

Sights & Activities

The cobblestone streets and appealing buildings around **Lilla Torg** are restored parts of the late-medieval town. The houses are now galleries, boutiques and restaurants.

The main museums of Malmö are based in and around **Malmöhus** (☎ 34 44 37; www.malmo.se/museer; Malmöhusvägen; combined entry Skr40; 10am-4pm Jun-Aug, noon-4pm Sep-May). You can walk through the royal apartments, see the **Stadsmuseum** with its Malmö collection, and see works by important Swedish artists like John Bauer and Sigrid Hjerten at the **Konstmuseum**. There's also an **aquarium** and **Naturmuseum**.

Ribersborg is a long, sandy beach backed by parkland about 2km west of the city centre. Out in Öresund, reached by a 200m-long pier, is the naturist **Ribersborgs Kallbadhus** (☎ 260366; www.ribban.se; admission Skr55; daily), dating from 1898. There's a cold, open-air saltwater pool and wood-fired sauna, and separate sections for men and women. Get there on bus 32.

Sleeping

Private rooms or apartments from about Skr375 per person are available through **City Room** (☎ 795 94; www.cityroom.se); bedsheets and towels cost an additional Skr100 per set. The agency has no office address but the phone is manned weekdays 9am to noon.

STF Vandrarhem Malmö (☎ 822 20; Backavägen 18; 2-/3-/4–6-bed dm from Skr190/150/150, s/d from Skr315/410;) Well-equipped, if rather large and impersonal, the STF hostel sits 3.5km south of the city centre, overlooking the E6 (take bus 2 from Centralstationen).

Bosses Gästvåningar (☎ 32 62 50; info@bosses.nu; Södra Förstadsgatan 110b; s/d/tr/q from Skr350/495/595/750;) The quiet, clean rooms in this SVIF hostel are like those of a budget hotel, with proper beds, TVs and shared bathrooms. Service is helpful and it's close to Möllevångstorget and opposite the town hospital (follow the signs for 'Sjukhuset' if arriving by car).

Eating & Drinking

For sheer atmosphere, head to the restaurant-bars on Lilla Torg.

Solde (☎ 692 80 87; Regementsgatan 3; panini Skr40; closed Sun) Malmö's coolest cafe is a grit-chic combo of concrete bar, white-tiled walls, art exhibitions and indie-hip regulars. The owner is an award-winning barista; watch him in action over lip-smacking Italian panini, biscotti and *cornetti* (croissants).

Glassfabriken (☎ 23 81 01; Kristianstadsgatan 16; meals around Skr50; closed Mon) Easy to miss, this grungy, alcohol-free cafe/cultural bolt-hole cranks out cheap, salubrious grub like vegan salads, ciabatta and freshly baked cakes. Play board games over mango milkshakes, check out the local art on display or catch the occasional music or theatre gig.

Krua Thai (☎ 12 22 87; Möllevångstorget 14; mains Skr79-95; 11am-3pm Mon, 11am-3pm & 5-10pm Tue-Fri, 1-10pm Sat, 2-10pm Sun) Down the southern end of town is this authentic, long-standing Thai joint. The family also runs a central takeaway (Södergatan 22).

Buy groceries at central **Mästerlivs supermarket** (Engelbrektsgatan; 7am-9pm). The best produce market is found on Möllevångstorget.

On Lilla Torg, hit **Victors** (☎ 12 76 70), **Moosehead** (☎ 12 04 23) and **Mello Yello** (☎ 30 45 25); they're all great spots, with alfresco summer seating (you may have to wait for a table), tasty meals and everything from Chilean whites to outrageous cocktails.

Getting There & Away

Sturup airport (☎ 613 10 00; www.malmoairport.se) is 33km southeast of Malmö. The low-cost carrier Ryanair flies between London and Sturup, from where there are frequent trains and buses to Copenhagen, making Malmö a cheap gateway to the Danish capital.

Long-distance buses depart from a terminal at the end of Skeppsbron, about 500m north of Centralstationen. Swebus Express travels daily to Stockholm, Göteborg and Oslo. Trains are best for trips across the Öresund bridge.

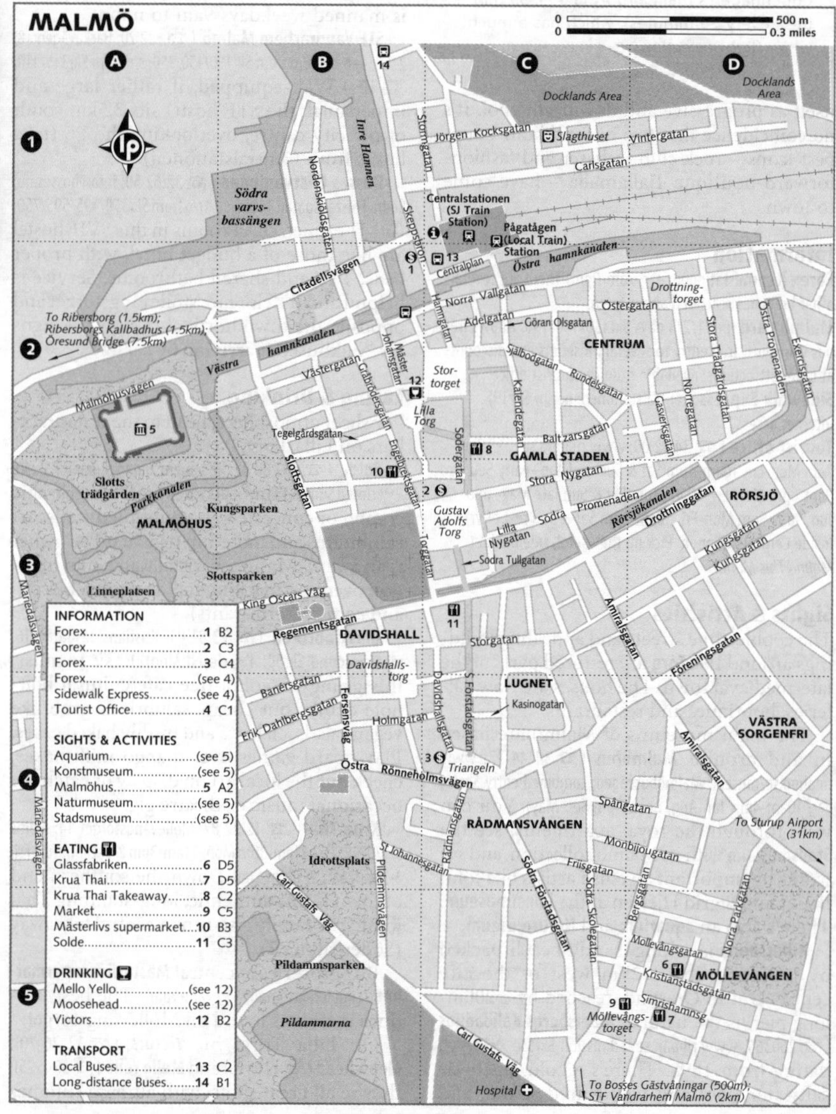

SJ services (including X2000) run regularly to/from Göteborg and Stockholm, all via Lund.

Skånetrafiken (☎ 0771-77 77 77; www.skanetrafiken.se) operates the local buses and trains in the southern region, and sells a variety of value cards and passes. Local buses depart from near Centralstationen. Local (purple) trains run to Helsingborg (two to three hours), Lund (15 minutes, Skr42), Ystad (48 minutes, Skr78) and other nearby destinations. International train passes are accepted.

LUND

☎ 046 / pop 105,300

Centred round a striking cathedral, Lund is a soulful blend of leafy parks, medieval abodes and coffee-sipping bookworms. Like most university hubs, however, it loses some of its buzz during the summer, when students head home for the holidays.

The **tourist office** (☎ 35 50 40; www.lund.se; Kyrkogatan 11; 10am-7pm Mon-Fri, 10am-3pm Sat, 11am-3pm Sun mid-Jun–Aug, 10am-5pm Mon-Fri, 10am-3pm Sat May–mid-Jun & Sep, 10am-5pm Mon-Fri Oct-Apr) is opposite the cathedral.

Construction on Lund's Romanesque **Domkyrka** (cathedral) began about 1100, when Lund became Europe's largest archbishopric. The cathedral is magnificent: visit at noon or 3pm (1pm and 3pm weekends and holidays) when the astronomical clock strikes up *In Dulci Jubilo*.

The spectacular **Kulturen** (☎ 35 04 00; www.kulturen.com; Tegnerplatsen; admission Skr70; 11am-5pm mid-Apr–Sep, noon-4pm Tue-Sun Oct–mid-Apr) claims to be the world's second-oldest open-air museum (it opened in 1892). Its impressive collection of about 40 buildings fills two blocks.

Sleeping & Eating

The tourist office can book private rooms from Skr300 per person plus a Skr50 fee.

STF Vandrarhem Lund Tåget (☎ 14 28 20; www.trainhostel.com; Vävaregatan 22; dm Skr150) This quirky hostel is based in old railway carriages in parkland behind the station. The triple bunks and tiny rooms are OK if you're cosying up with loved ones, but a little claustrophobic with strangers. Less novel are the hot-water vending machines in the showers (have a few Skr1 coins handy).

Hotel Ahlström (☎ 211 01 74; info@hotellahlstrom.se; Skomakaregatan 3; s/d with shared bathroom Skr729/895, d with private bathroom Skr1100) Lund's oldest hotel is friendly and affordable, and on a quiet, central street. Rooms have parquet floors, cool white walls and washbasins (most bathrooms are shared). Breakfast is brought to your door.

Ebbas Skafferi (☎ 13 41 56; Bytaregatan 5; lunch Skr65; 9am-7pm Mon-Fri, to 6pm Sat & Sun) Ebbas is the perfect cafe: think warm wooden tables, green plants and flowers, odd bits of artwork, a laid-back courtyard, and scrumptious coffee, tea and tasty grub.

Getting There & Away

There are frequent SJ services and local train departures from Lund to Malmö (15 minutes, Skr42); some trains continue to Copenhagen (one to 1½ hours, Skr130). Long-distance trains between Stockholm and Malmö stop in Lund. Buses leave from outside the train station.

HELSINGBORG

☎ 042 / pop 125,000

At its heart, Helsingborg is a sparkly showcase of rejuvenated waterfront, metro-glam restaurants, lively cobbled streets and lofty castle ruins. With Denmark looking on from a mere 4km across the Öresund, its flouncy, turreted buildings feel like a brazen statement.

The **tourist office** (☎ 10 43 50; www.helsingborg.se; Rådhuset, Stortorget; 9am-8pm Mon-Fri, 9am-5pm Sat & 10am-3pm Sun mid-Jun–Aug, 10am-6pm Mon-Fri, 10am-2pm Sat Sep–mid-Jun) can help with inquiries.

The eye-catchingly modern **Dunkers Kulturhus** (☎ 10 74 00; www.dunkerskulturhus.se; Kungsgatan 11; exhibitions Skr70; 10am-5pm Tue-Sun, to 8pm Thu), just north of the transport terminals, houses the **town museum** and **art museum** (combined entry Skr70), plus a concert hall, restaurant and cafe. Take a stroll along the northern waterfront from here to admire the sleek apartment buildings and restaurants, all part of a successful harbour redevelopment project.

You can access the square medieval tower **Kärnan** (☎ 10 59 91; admission Skr20; 10am-6pm Jun-Aug, closed Mon rest of yr) from steps near the tourist office. The tower is all that remains of a 14th-century castle; the view from the top (34m) overlooks Öresund to the Danish heartland.

Sleeping & Eating

Helsingborgs Vandrarhem (☎ 14 58 50; info@hbgturist.com; Järnvägsgatan 39; dm from Skr195) Despite the somewhat anonymous vibe, Helsingborg's only central hostel offers clean, comfortable rooms about 200m from Knutpunkten. Reception opens between 3pm and 6pm.

Villa Thalassa (☎ 38 06 60; www.villathalassa.com; Dag Hammarskjöldsväg; dm from Skr200, s/d Skr600/800) This SVIF option is a lovely early-20th-century villa situated in beautiful gardens. Hostel accommodation is in huts, but the hotel-standard rooms (with or without private bathroom) are a cut above if your budget will stretch. The villa lies 3km north of central Helsingborg in the Pålsjö area. Bus 219 stops 500m short, at the Pålsjöbaden bus stop.

Self-caterers should head to the **ICA supermarket** (Drottninggatan 48).

Getting There & Away

The main transport centre is Knutpunkten; the underground platforms serve SJ trains bound for Stockholm, Göteborg, Copenhagen and Oslo, plus regional trains. At ground level and a little south, but still inside the same complex, is the bus terminal. Daily long-distance services run to destinations including Göteborg and Oslo.

Knutpunkten is the terminal for frequent ferries to Denmark and Oslo; for details on sea travel from Helsingborg, see p1119.

GÖTEBORG (GOTHENBURG)

☎ 031 / pop 493,600

Often caught in Stockholm's shadow, gregarious Göteborg (Gothenburg in English) socks a mighty punch of its own. Some of the country's finest talent hails from its streets, including music icons José González and Soundtrack of Our Lives. Ornate architecture lines its tram-rattled streets, grit-hip cafes hum with bonhomie, and must-sees include Scandinavia's amusement-park heavyweight.

Information

Göteborg Pass (per 24/48hr Skr225/310) Gives free entry to Liseberg and some city attractions, city tours and public transport. Collect it at tourist offices, hotels and hostels.

Östra Sjukhuset (☎ 343 40 00) Large hospital near tram terminus 1, northeast of town.

Police station (☎ 739 20 00; Ernst Fontells Plats) Off Skånegatan, near Nya Ullevi stadium.

Sidewalk Express (www.sidewalkexpress.se; per hr Skr19) Internet kiosks at central locations (Centralstationen, Landvetter airport, inside the 7-Eleven store at Vasaplatsen).

Tourist offices (☎ 61 25 00; www.goteborg.com) branch tourist office (Nordstan; ⌚ 10am-6pm Mon-Fri, 10am-4pm Sat, noon-3pm Sun); main tourist office (Kungsportsplatsen 2; ⌚ 9am-6pm Jun-Aug, 9am-5pm Mon-Fri, 10am-2pm Sat Sep-May)

GETTING INTO TOWN

Göteborg-Landvetter airport is about 25km from the city centre. **Flygbuss** (www.flygbussarna.se) runs several times a day from the airport to Nils Ericsson terminal (Skr75, 30 minutes). Local **Tidpunkten Västtrafik buses** (☎ 0771-41 43 00) buses run daily from the airport to Göteborg central (Skr20).

Sights

Liseberg (☎ 40 01 00; www.liseberg.se; admission Skr70; ⌚ to 10pm or 11pm most days May-Aug, to 9pm or 10pm during Christmas period) fun park is dominated by its spaceport-like tower. The ride to the top, some 83m above the ground, climaxes in a spinning dance and a breathtaking view of the city. Leave your stomach at the gate. Each ride costs between one and four coupons (Skr20 each) per go, but it probably makes sense to buy a pass (one/two days Skr290/380). Opening hours are complex; check the website. Take tram 4 or 5.

By Liseberg is the striking **Universeum** (☎ 335 64 50; www.universeum.se; Södra Vägen 50; admission Skr165; ⌚ 10am-7pm late Jun-Aug, to 6pm Sep-late Jun), a huge and impressive 'science discovery centre' featuring everything from rainforests to a shark tank.

The **Stadsmuseum** (☎ 612770; Norra Hamngatan 12; admission Skr40; ⌚ 10am-5pm daily May-Aug, Tue-Sun Sep-Apr) has archaeological, local and historical collections, including Sweden's only original Viking ship.

The main art collections are at **Konstmuseet** (☎ 61 29 80; www.konstmuseum.goteborg.se; Götaplatsen; admission Skr40; ⌚ 11am-6pm Tue & Thu, to 9pm Wed, to 5pm Fri-Sun), with impressive collections of Nordic and European masters (notable for works by Rubens, Van Gogh, Rembrandt and Picasso) and touring exhibitions.

The excellent **Röhsska Museet** (☎ 61 38 50; www.designmuseum.se; Vasagatan 37; admission Skr40; ⌚ noon-8pm Tue, noon-5pm Wed-Fri, 11am-5pm Sat & Sun) covers modern Scandinavian design and decorative arts.

There are some great green oases, including **Trädgårdsföreningen** (entry on Nya Allén; admission Skr15 May-Aug, otherwise free), laid out in 1842 and home to pretty cafes, a rosarium and palm house.

Sleeping

STF Vandrarhem Stigbergsliden (☎ 24 16 20; www.hostel-gothenburg.com; Stigbergsliden 10; dm/d from

Skr150/350;) In a renovated 19th-century seaman's institute (tram 3, 9 or 11 to Stigbergstorget), this is a hostel with history. Staff are greatly helpful, and besides the usual stuff (big kitchen, laundry, TV room), perks include a sheltered garden and bike rental (Skr50 per day).

STF Vandrarhem Slottsskogen (42 65 20; www.sov.nu; Vegagatan 21; dm Skr185-210, s/d Skr345/490; P) Unlike many Swedish hostels, big, friendly Slottsskogen is a cracking place for meeting other travellers. For a small extra payment there's access to a laundry, sauna and sun bed, and the buffet breakfast (Skr55) is brilliant. Parking spaces can be booked for a fee; reception is closed between noon and 2pm. Take tram 1 or 6 to Olivedalsgatan.

Masthuggsterrassens Vandrarhem (42 48 20; www.mastenvandrarhem.com; Masthuggsterrassen 10h; dm/r Skr190/480;) If you're after a good night's sleep, try this clean, quiet, well-run place. Fine facilities include three lounges, three kitchens and a little library (mostly Swedish books), and it's handy if you're catching an early ferry to Denmark. Take tram 3, 9 or 11 to Masthuggstorget and follow the signs.

Lilleby Havsbad Camping (56 22 40; info@lillebycamping.se; Lillebyvägen; camp sites Skr220; Jun-Aug) This agreeable seaside spot lies 20km west of the city centre in Torslanda. Take bus 25 from Centralstationen to Lillebyvägen, then change to bus 23.

Lisebergs Camping & Stugbyar Kärralund (84 02 00; karralund@liseberg.se; Olbergsgatan 1; camp sites Skr375, cabins from Skr595) Liseberg fun park owns and operates a range of accommodation around Göteborg. This family-friendly camping ground is the closest one to town (tram 5 to Welandergatan), with 35 unreservable tent sites – so turn up early.

Kvibergs Vandrarhem & Stugby (43 50 55; www.vandrarhem.com; Kvibergsvägen 5; tr/q Skr550/690;) This sterling SVIF hostel, a few kilometres northeast of the city centre (tram 6, 7 or 11), boasts super amenities, including flat-screen TVs, wi-fi, sauna, sun beds, laundry, table tennis, two kitchens and two lounges. There are no dorms; you rent out the entire room. Hotel-style rooms and cabins are also available.

Hotel Flora (13 86 16; www.hotelflora.se; Grönsakstorget 2; s/d Skr1195/1495;) An extreme makeover has turned Flora from frumpy to fabulous, its uberslick rooms now flaunting black-and-white interiors, designer chairs, flat-screen TVs and sparkling bathrooms. Top-floor rooms have air-conditioning, several rooms offer river views and the chic split-level courtyard is perfect for sophisticated chilling.

Eating

Kungsportsavenyn is lined with restaurants, cafes and bars (although prices here can be higher than in other parts of town). Vasagatan is close to the student heartland and has excellent cafes. Linnégatan (close to most of the hostels) has more good options.

Alexandras (Kungstorget; 711 23 81; meals around Skr40) Located in the central Saluhallen, this famous bolthole dishes out excellent hearty soups and stews, particularly welcoming on a chilly day.

Andrum (13 85 04; Östra Hamngatan 19; large plate Skr69; 11am-9pm Mon-Fri, noon-8pm Sat & Sun) Vegetarians love this casual spot with its value-for-money, all-day lunch buffet. It's simple, tasty, wholesome stuff, and cheerfully recommended.

Solrosen (Kaponjärgatan 4; dinner mains Skr75-80; 11.30am-11pm Mon-Thu, 11.30am-midnight Fri, 11.30am-1am Sat, 2-8pm Sun, closed Sun summer) A 1970s survivor, this laid-back student favourite is a Haga institution (note the photos of passed-on regulars above the counter). Pay tribute over soulful vegetarian dishes and a bountiful salad buffet. For the best value, choose one of the hot dishes on the menu board, which include the salad buffet in the price.

Da Matteo (13 06 09; Vallgatan 5; pizzas Skr75-89, salads Skr79-95; 9am-7pm Mon-Fri, 10am-5pm Sat, 11am-4pm Sun) A mecca for coffee snobs, head here for wickedly fine espresso, mini *sfogliatelle* (Neapolitan pastries) and savouries like real-deal pizzas, panini and salads. There's a sun-soaked courtyard and a second branch on Viktoriapassagen.

Self-caterers should head to the **Hemköp supermarket** (8am-10pm) in the Nordstan complex.

Drinking

While Kungsportsavenyn brims with beer-downing tourists, try the following savvier options.

Lokal (13 32 00; Kyrkogatan 11; 4pm-1am Mon-Sat) Awarded Best Bar in Göteborg, this effortlessly cool hang-out pulls everyone from artists and media types to the odd punk rocker. The drinks are inspired (think kiwi and ginger

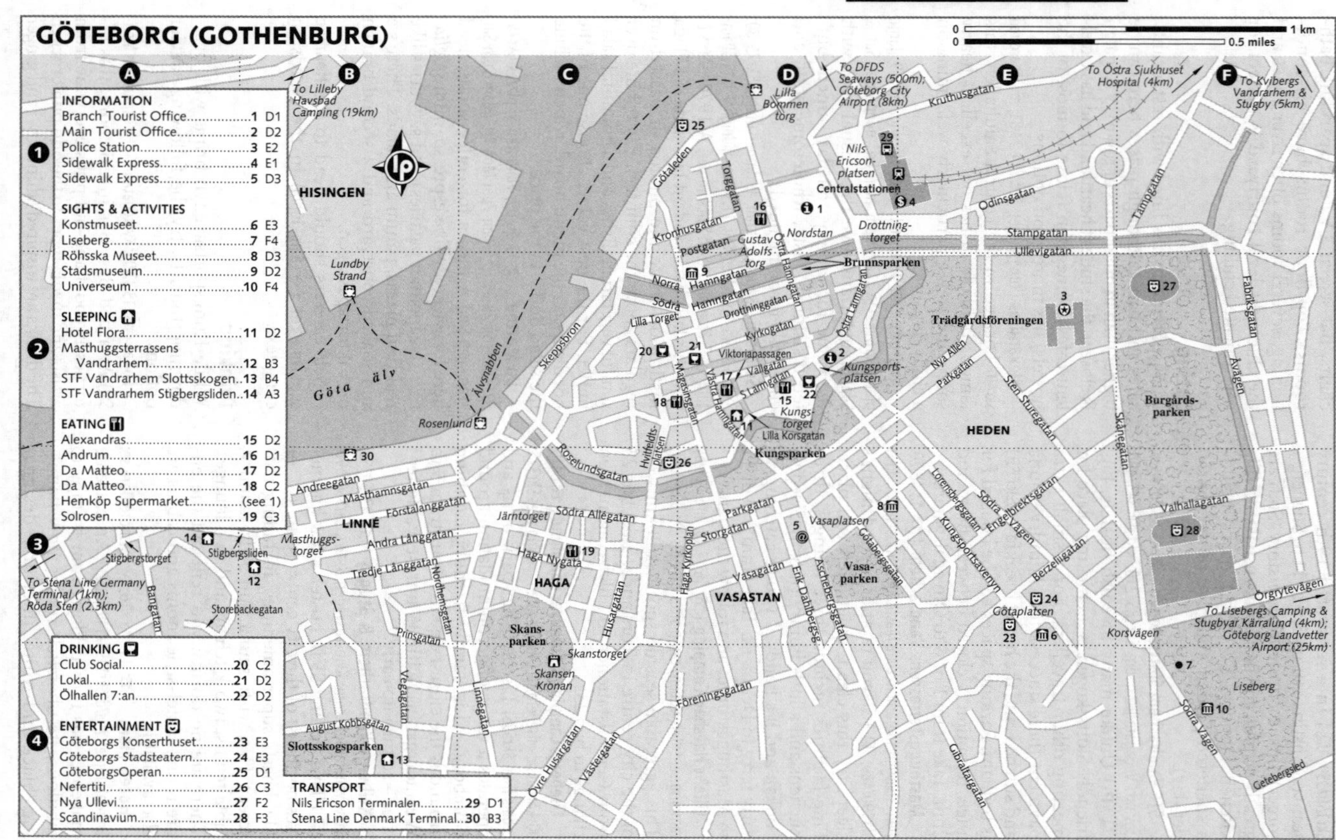
GÖTEBORG (GOTHENBURG)
INFORMATION
Branch Tourist Office 1 D1
Main Tourist Office 2 D2
Police Station 3 E2
Sidewalk Express 4 E1
Sidewalk Express 5 D3
SIGHTS & ACTIVITIES
Konstmuseet 6 E3
Liseberg 7 F4
Röhsska Museet 8 D3
Stadsmuseum 9 D2
Universeum 10 F4
SLEEPING
Hotel Flora 11 D2
Masthuggsterrassens Vandrarhem 12 B3
STF Vandrarhem Slottsskogen 13 B4
STF Vandrarhem Stigbergsliden 14 A3
EATING
Alexandras 15 D2
Andrum 16 D1
Da Matteo 17 D2
Da Matteo 18 C2
Hemköp Supermarket (see 1)
Solrosen 19 C3
DRINKING
Club Social 20 C2
Lokal 21 D2
Ölhallen 7:an 22 D2
ENTERTAINMENT
Göteborgs Konserthuset 23 E3
Göteborgs Stadsteatern 24 E3
GöteborgsOperan 25 D1
Nefertiti 26 C3
Nya Ullevi 27 F2
Scandinavium 28 F3
TRANSPORT
Nils Ericson Terminalen 29 D1
Stena Line Denmark Terminal 30 B3
0.5 miles
1 km
HISINGEN
HEDEN
VASASTAN
HAGA
LINNÉ
Göta älv
Centralstationen
Kungsparken
Trädgårdsföreningen
Burgårdsparken
Skansparken
Slottsskogsparken
Liseberg
To Lilleby Havsbad Camping (19km)
To DFDS Seaways (500m); Göteborg City Airport (8km)
To Östra Sjukhuset Hospital (4km)
To Kvibergs Vandrarhem & Stugby (5km)
To Lisebergs Camping & Stugbyar Kärralund (4km); Göteborg Landvetter Airport (25km)
To Stena Line Germany Terminal (1km); Röda Sten (2.3km)

daiquiri), the pick-and-mix menu brims with fusion flavours, and music spans soul, jazz and electro. Best of all, staff donate 10% of their tips to a Cambodian orphanage.

Club Social (☎ 13 87 55; Magasinsgatan 3; 🕑 4pm-2am Tue-Sat) A svelte black-and-white leather bar demands classic cocktails, which is just what this glam-cool newbie delivers. Join in-the-know locals for smooth Bellinis, a tapas-fuelled catch-up session or the petite selection of mains which change daily according to what looks best at the morning market.

Ölhallen 7:an (☎ 13 60 79; Kungstorget 7) For low-fuss, old-school soul, don't miss this well-worn Swedish beerhall, which hasn't changed in about 100 years. There's no food, wine or pretension, just beer, and plenty of choices.

Clubbing

Clubs have varying minimum-age limits, ranging from 18 to 25, and many may charge admission depending on the night.

Nefertiti (☎ 711 15 33; www.nefertiti.se, in Swedish; Hvitfeldtsplatsen 6; admission Skr90-320) A Göteborg institution, this cool venue is famous for its smooth live jazz, blues and world music, usually followed by kicking club nights spanning techno, deep house and soul to hip hop and funk. Times vary, so check the website.

Röda Sten (☎ 12 08 16; www.rodasten.com; Röda Sten 1; 🕑 Fri & Sat) Paging Berlin with its postindustrial look, this power station-turned-art gallery cranks up the party vibe with live bands on Friday nights and club nights on Saturdays. Expect indie pop the first Saturday of the month, followed by '80s tunes (complete with retro-clad punters), reggae, and techno each subsequent Saturday.

Entertainment

Göteborgs Stadsteatern (City Theatre; ☎ 61 50 50; www.stadsteatern.goteborg.se; Götaplatsen; tickets from Skr220; 🕑 closed May-Aug) Stages theatre productions in Swedish.

Göteborgs Konserthuset (Concert Hall; ☎ 726 53 10; www.gso.se; Götaplatsen; 🕑 closed May-Aug) Home to the local symphony orchestra, with top international guests and sterling performances.

GöteborgsOperan (☎ 13 13 00; www.opera.se, in Swedish; Christina Nilssons gata; tickets Skr90-565) At Lilla Bommen harbour; stages classical and modern ballet and opera and assorted musical performances in a striking contemporary building.

Gothenburghers are avid sports fans. Outdoor stadiums include **Nya Ullevi** (www.ullevi.se) for football matches and **Scandinavium** (www.scandinavium.se) for ice hockey, located at opposite ends of Burgårdsparken, east of the CBD. For details on both stadiums, contact **Skanegatan** (☎ 81 10 20).

Getting There & Away

AIR

Twenty-five kilometres east of the city, **Landvetter airport** (GOT; ☎ 94 10 00) has services to many European cities. **Gothenburg City airport** (GSE; ☎ 92 60 60; www.goteborgcityairport.se) is a minor airport 10km northwest of the city centre, used by Ryanair.

BOAT

Göteborg is a major entry point for ferries, with several terminals. For more details of ferry services and fares to Denmark, Germany and the UK, see p1119.

BUS

The modern bus station, Nils Ericson Terminalen, is next to Centralstationen. Eurolines and Swebus Express share an office here.

Swebus Express (☎ 0771-21 82 18; www.swebusexpress.com) has an office at the bus terminal and operates frequent buses to most major towns. Services to Stockholm (Skr420, seven hours) run five to seven times daily. Other direct destinations include Copenhagen (Skr300, four to five hours), Halmstad (Skr108, 1¾ hours), Helsingborg (Skr200, three hours), Jönköping (Skr140, 1¾ hours), Oslo (Skr220, four hours), Malmö (Skr281, three hours), and Örebro (Skr250, four hours).

Svenska Buss (☎ 0771-67 67 67; www.svenskabuss.se) has daily departures for Stockholm (Skr410, 7½ hours) via Jönköping (Skr130, 2¼ hours).

Prices can be considerably lower than those quoted here for advanced bookings, especially for Swebus Express and Säfflebussen.

TRAIN

Centralstationen serves SJ and regional trains, with direct trains to Malmö, Copenhagen, Oslo and Stockholm, plus other destinations in the southern half of Sweden. Direct train services to Stockholm depart approximately hourly.

Book your stay at lonelyplanet.com/hotels

Getting Around

Buses, trams and ferries make up the city's public-transport system; there are Tidpunkten information booths inside Nils Ericson Terminalen, on Drottningtorget and at Brunnsparken. The easiest way to cover lengthy distances in Göteborg is by tram. There are 11 lines, all converging near Brunnsparken, one block from Centralstationen. An individual transport ticket costs Skr20. 'Value cards' (Skr50 to Skr100) reduce the cost considerably. Holders of the Göteborg Pass travel free.

NORTHERN SWEDEN

Norrland is remote enough that travellers here aren't likely to see the tour-bus crowd – or, for that matter, much of anyone else. Reindeer outnumber cars on the roads, and much of the landscape consists of deep green forest. It's a paradise for nature lovers who enjoy hiking, skiing and other outdoor activities.

ÖSTERSUND

☎ 063 / pop 58,400

This pleasant town by Lake Storsjön, in whose chilly waters is said to lurk a rarely sighted monster, has good budget accommodation and is a relaxed and scenic place, and an excellent gateway town for further explorations of Norrland. The **tourist office** (☎ 14 40 01; www.turist.ostersund.se; Rådhusgatan 44; 🕑 9am-5pm daily Jun-Aug, Mon-Fri Sep-May) is opposite the town hall, one block from the bus station. Ask about monster-spotting **lake cruises** (Skr65 to Skr95) from June to September.

Don't miss **Jamtli** (☎ 15 01 00; www.jamtli.com; mid-Jun–Aug Skr110, rest of yr Skr60; 🕑 11am-5pm daily Jun-Aug, closed Mon rest of yr), 1km north of the town centre. It combines the lively exhibitions of the regional museum and a large museum village. Take bus 2.

An offshoot of Färgfabriken in Stockholm, the newly opened **Färgfabriken Norr** (☎ 390 00 00; Byggnad 33, Infanterigatan 30; www.fargfabriken.se; admission free; 🕑 noon-5pm Thu-Fri, to 4pm Sat & Sun) is a huge new art space across E14 from Jamtli. It's a cavernous room with an ambitious curatorial scope. Take bus 14 or 8.

Some attractions lie on the adjacent island of Frösön, reached by road or footbridge from the middle of Östersund.

Sleeping & Eating

STF Vandrarhem Jamtli (☎ 12 20 60; vandrarhemmet@jamtli.com; Museiplan; dm Skr140-160, s/d from Skr235/280) Take the chance to live among Östersund's major attraction: this small, quaint hostel is inside the Jamtli museum precinct. Take Bus 2.

Brunkullans (☎ 10 14 54; Postgränd 5; mains Skr115-149; 🕑 11am-2pm Mon-Fri, from 5pm Tue-Sat, from 4pm Fri) A local favourite for its outdoor patio, Brunkullans also has a wonderfully atmospheric, candlelit 19th-century interior space. The menu features Swedish classics and upscale versions of basic bar food.

Getting There & Away

Bus 63 runs northeast to Umeå (6 hours, two to four daily). Direct trains run from Stockholm (Skr923, six hours) via Uppsala and Gävle.

UMEÅ

☎ 090 / pop 112,000

With the vibrant feel of a college town (it has around 30,000 students), Umeå is a welcome outpost of urbanity in the barren north. It's one of the fastest-growing towns in Sweden and an agreeable place to hang out, wind down or stock up for an outdoor adventure. The **tourist office** (☎ 16 16 16; www.visitumea.se; Renmarkstorget 15) is central.

Gammlia (☎ 17 18 00; admission free; 🕑 10am-5pm mid-Jun–mid-Aug, 10am-4pm Tue-Fri, noon-4pm Sat, noon-5pm Sun rest of yr), a cluster of museums 1km east of the town centre, includes the cultural/historical exhibits and Sami collections of the regional **Västerbottens Museum**.

STF Vandrarhem Umeå (☎ 77 16 50; info@umeavandrarhem.com; Västra Esplanaden 10; dm Skr140, s/d from Skr240/280) has tiny but comfortable rooms and is one of the few youth hostels in the region actually occupied by youth.

The long-distance bus station is opposite the train station on Järnvägsallén, just north of the town centre. Umeå is the main centre for **Länstrafiken Västerbotten** (☎ 020-91 00 19), the regional bus network. Direct buses run to Mo i Rana in Norway; other daily destinations include Östersund.

KIRUNA

☎ 0980 / pop 23,500

A few years back, it became clear that years of iron-ore extraction was sucking the stability out of the bedrock underneath Kiruna. In

2007 the town voted to shift itself a couple of miles northwest; plans are to move the railway and about 450 homes by 2013, with the rest of the town centre to follow gradually.

The **tourist office** (☎ 188 80; www.lappland.se; Lars Janssonsgatan 17, in Folkets Hus; 8.30am-9pm Mon-Fri, to 6pm Sat & Sun Jun-Aug, Mon-Sat rest of yr), on the main square, has computers for internet access and can book mine tours and accommodation.

Every winter at Jukkasjärvi, 18km east of Kiruna, the amazing **Ice Hotel** (www.icehotel.com) is built from hundreds of tonnes of ice from the frozen local river. This custom-built 'igloo' has a chapel and a bar – you can drink from a glass made of ice – and ice-sculpture exhibitions. It also has 50 'hotel rooms' outfitted with reindeer skins and sleeping bags.

Near the church in Jukkasjärvi is **Gárdi** (adult Skr60; tours 10am-6pm mid-Jun–mid-Aug), a reindeer yard that you can tour with a Sami guide to learn about reindeer farming and Sami culture. Regular bus 501 runs between Kiruna and Jukkasjärvi (Skr29, 30 minutes, several daily).

Sleeping & Eating

Rådhusbyn Ripan Hotell & Camping (☎ 630 00; www.ripan.se; Campingvägen 5; camp sites Skr125, hotel s/d from Skr1200/1535, cabins from Skr995; P) In the northern part of town, this is a large and well-equipped camping ground with hotel-standard chalets in addition to its caravan and tent sites. Ask about the organised walk (Skr450, 1pm Fridays) to Samegården, the museum of Sami culture, and other activities.

SVIF Yellow House (☎ 137 50; www.yellowhouse.nu; Hantverkaregatan 25; dm from Skr150, s/d Skr300/400) The SVIF hostel also has budget hotel rooms; the excellent facilities include a sauna, kitchen and laundry, a TV in each room, and a nice, quiet enclosed garden.

Café Safari (☎ 174 60; Geologsgatan 4; meals Skr35-65) This is the nicest cafe in town, a long skinny room with good coffee, cakes and light meals such as sandwiches, quiche and baked potatoes.

Getting There & Away

The small **airport** (KRN; ☎ 68 000), 9km east of town, has flights to/from Stockholm.

Regional buses in this vast region are operated by **Länstrafiken Norrbotten** (☎ 020-47 00 47) from the bus station on Hjalmar Lundbohmsvägen, opposite the town hall. Buses serve all major settlements.

SWEDEN DIRECTORY

ACCOMMODATION

Cabins & Chalets

Daily rates for *stugor* (cabins and chalets, often found at camping grounds or in the countryside) offer good value for small groups and families, and range in both facilities and price (Skr350 to Skr800). Check www.stuga.nu for details.

Camping

Sweden has hundreds of camping grounds; the best time for camping is from May to August. Prices vary, from Skr150 for a basic site to Skr250 for the highest standards. Most camping grounds have kitchens and laundry facilities, and many are popular family holiday spots with the works: swimming pool, minigolf, bike and/or canoe hire, restaurant etc. Visit www.camping.se for information.

Hostels

Sweden has nearly 500 *vandrarhem* (hostels). Some 315 hostels are affiliated with **Svenska Turistföreningen** (STF; ☎ 08-463 21 00; www.svenskaturistforeningen.se), part of Hostelling International (HI). Holders of HI membership cards pay the same rates as STF members. Nonmembers can pay Skr50 extra (Skr100 at some mountain lodges), or join up at hostels. In this book we quote prices at STF hostels for members.

Around 190 hostels belong to **Sveriges Vandrarhem i Förening** (SVIF; ☎ 0413-55 34 50; www.svif.se). No membership is required and rates are similar to those of STF hostels. Pick up the free guide at tourist offices or SVIF hostels.

Hostels in Sweden are difficult to get into outside reception opening times. The secret is to phone and make a reservation during the (usually short) reception hours; they'll provide you with an entry code.

Hotels

There are few budget hotels in Sweden, but even upscale hotels provide good-value weekend and summer (mid-June to mid-August) rates, often up to 50% off regular prices, and many offer substantial discounts for early or online booking. All prices listed in this chapter are regular prices

SWEDEN

ACTIVITIES

Swedes are huge nature lovers and are active year-round, on bike paths, forest jogging tracks, rivers and lakes, mountain trails, and the snow and ice. The right of public access to the countryside (called *'allemansrätten'*) means that in Sweden, by law, you're allowed to walk, boat, ski or swim on private land as long as you stay at least 70m from houses and keep out of gardens, fenced areas and cultivated land. You can camp for more than one night in the same place, and fires may be set where safe (not on bare rocks) with fallen wood. Cars may not be driven across open land or on private roads. Close all gates. Do not disturb farm animals or reindeer.

Hiking

Hiking is popular everywhere in Sweden and the mountain challenge of the northern national parks is compelling. These parks are rarely snow-free, however, and the jewel, Sarek, is for experienced hikers only. Good equipment is vital.

For information on organised group walks and STF mountain huts, which are placed at intervals averaging about 20km along popular trails like Kungsleden, near Kiruna, contact **STF** (☎ 08-463 21 00; www.svenskaturistforeningen.se).

Skiing

Cross-country (Nordic) skiing opportunities vary depending on snow and temperatures, but the northwest usually has plenty of snow from December to April (but not a lot of daylight in December and January). Practically all town areas (except the far south) have marked skiing tracks, often illuminated. For resort reviews in English, visit www.goski.com and www.thealps.com.

BUSINESS HOURS

Bars (🕑 5pm-1am)
Restaurants (🕑 lunch 11.30am-2pm, dinner 6-10pm) Many restaurants are closed Sunday or Monday.
Shops (🕑 9am-6pm Mon-Fri, to 1pm Sat)

EMBASSIES & CONSULATES

The following diplomatic missions are in Stockholm.

Australia (Map p1128; ☎ 08-613 29 00; www.sweden.embassy.gov.au; 11th fl, Sergels Torg 12)
Canada (Map p1128; ☎ 08-453 30 00; www.canadaemb.se; Tegelbacken 4)
Denmark (Map p1128; ☎ 08-406 75 00; www.ambstockholm.um.dk, in Danish; Jakobs Torg 1)
Finland (Map pp1126-7; ☎ 08-676 67 00; www.finland.se/fi, in Finnish & Swedish; Gärdesgatan 9-11)
France (Map p1128; ☎ 08-459 53 00; www.ambafrance-se.org, in French & Swedish; Kommendörsgatan 13)
Germany (Map pp1126-7; ☎ 08-670 15 00; www.stockholm.diplo.de, in German & Swedish; Skarpögatan 9)
Ireland (Map pp1126-7; ☎ 08-661 80 05; irish.embassy@swipnet.se; Östermalmsgatan 97)
Netherlands (Map p1128; ☎ 08-55 69 33 00; www.netherlands-embassy.se; Götgatan 16a)
Norway (Map pp1126-7; ☎ 08-665 63 40; emb.stockholm@mfa.no; Skarpögatan 4)
UK (Map pp1126-7; ☎ 08-671 30 00; www.britishembassy.se; Skarpögatan 6-8)
USA (Map pp1126-7; ☎ 08-783 53 00; http://stockholm.usembassy.gov; Dag Hammarskjölds Väg 31)

FESTIVALS & EVENTS

Vasaloppet In Mora on the first Sunday in March, the Vasaloppet is an annual ski race commemorating King Gustav Vasa's historic trip along the same route.
Midsummer's Eve & Midsummer Day First Friday and Saturday after 21 June. The biggest party of the year, Midsummer's Day is when Swedes gather to celebrate the all-too-brief season by eating, drinking, singing and dancing around maypoles.

HOLIDAYS

Many businesses close early the day before and all day after official public holidays, including the following:

Nyårsdag (New Year's Day) 1 January
Trettondedag Jul (Epiphany) 6 January
Långfredag, Påsk, Annandag Påsk (Good Friday, Easter Sunday and Monday) March/April
Första Maj (Labour Day) 1 May
Kristi Himmelsfärds dag (Ascension Day) May/June
Pingst, Annandag Pingst (Whit Sunday and Monday) Late May or early June
Midsommardag (Midsummer's Day) First Saturday after 21 June
Alla Helgons dag (All Saints' Day) Saturday, late October or early November
Juldag (Christmas Day) 25 December
Annandag Jul (Boxing Day) 26 December

INTERNET RESOURCES

Stockholmtown (www.stockholmtown.com) A good trip-planning guide.
The Local (www.thelocal.se) Swedish news in English.

MONEY

The Swedish krona, usually called 'crown' by Swedes speaking English, is divided into 100 öre. Coins are 50 öre and one, five and

10 kronor, and notes are 20, 50, 100, 500 and 1000 kronor.

Service charges are usually included in restaurant bills and taxi fares, but it's common to tip about 10% in a restaurant or round up the taxi fare (particularly if there's luggage).

TELEPHONE

About 70% of Swedes own a mobile phone, so the number of public phones has dwindled. There are almost no coin phones; public telephones take Telia phonecards (available at most Pressbyrå shops).

For international calls dial ☎ 00 followed by the country code and the local area code. For international directory assistance dial ☎ 11 81 19 (not a free call). To call collect, dial ☎ 020-00 18.

VISAS

Citizens of EU countries can enter Sweden with a passport or a national identification card (passports are recommended) and stay up to three months. Nationals of Nordic countries (Denmark, Norway, Finland and Iceland) can stay and work indefinitely, but nationals of other countries require residence permits *(uppehållstillstånd)* for stays of between three months and five years; there is no fee for this permit for EU citizens.

Citizens of Australia, New Zealand, Canada and the US can enter and stay in Sweden without a visa for up to three months. Australian and New Zealand passport holders aged 18 to 30 can qualify for a one-year working-holiday visa.

Citizens of South Africa and many other African, Asian and some Eastern European countries require tourist visas for entry. These are only available in advance from Swedish embassies (allow two months); there's a nonrefundable application fee of Skr550 for most applicants.

Residence permits must be applied for before entering Sweden. Allow up to eight months. Foreign students are granted residence permits if they can prove acceptance by a Swedish educational institution and are able to guarantee that they can support themselves financially.

Migrationsverket (☎ 011-15 60 00; www.migrationsverket.se; SE-60170 Norrköping) is the Swedish migration board and it handles all applications for visas and work or residency permits.

SWEDEN

Switzerland

HIGHLIGHTS

- **Jungfrau Region** Gargantuan mountain vistas and white-knuckle adrenalin adventures abound (p1169)
- **Zürich** Party all night in one of Europe's hippest cities (p1163)
- **Geneva** Get wet with a free fountain dash beneath the Jet d'Eau (p1153)
- **Bern** Be wooed by medieval charm, folkloric fountains and a pulsating party scene in Switzerland's capital (p1159).
- **Best journey** Ride the cable car to the top of the Schilthorn (p1170), check out million-dollar views over lunch in its revolving restaurant then ski down the mountain to Mürren (p1170)
- **Off-the-beaten track** Sleep on a farm and eat carrot cheese in the clover-shaped Jura (p1157); warm your cockles with a shot of absinthe (p1157)

FAST FACTS

- **Area** 41,285 sq km
- **Budget** Sfr60 to Sfr100 per day, excluding transport
- **Capital** Bern
- **Country code** ☎ 41
- **Famous for** cheese, yodelling, the Matterhorn, cuckoo clocks, banking
- **Languages** German, French, Italian, Romansch
- **Money** Swiss franc (Sfr); A$1 = Sfr0.84; C$1 = Sfr0.95; €1 = Sfr1.51; ¥100 = Sfr1.18; NZ$1 = Sfr0.66; UK£1 = Sfr1.70; US$1 = Sfr1.12
- **Population** 7.59 million
- **Phrases** *gruezi* (hello, good day), *merci vielmal* (thank you very much), *adieu* (goodbye), *sprechen sie Englisch?* (do you speak English?)
- **Visas** No visa required for citizens of the UK, Ireland, the EU, USA, Canada, Australia, New Zealand, South Africa, Norway and Iceland; others need a Schengen Visa (see p1230)

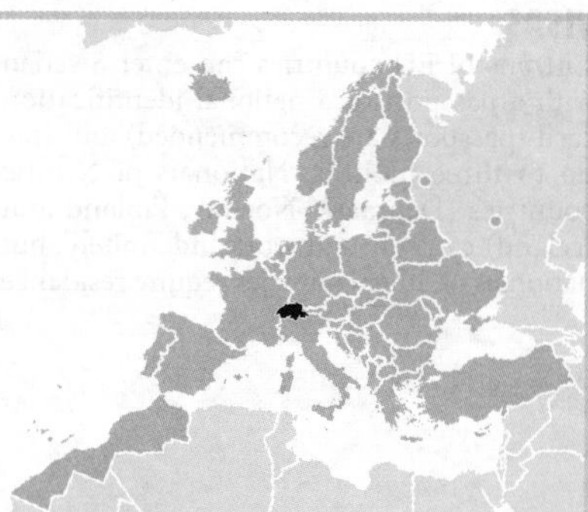

TRAVEL HINT

Drinking before a toast is unforgivable and will lead to seven years of bad sex…so superstition says.

ROAMING

Start in Geneva, saunter lakeside to Lausanne and Montreux then dive into the deep, dark Jura. Or hit Zermatt, Interlaken and the Jungfrau Region, Lucerne and Zürich.

In Europe's Heidi land of a trillion mountain scenes just begging to be made into a postcard, rosy-faced goat herders really do yodel to the clang of cowbells while cheesy fondues bubble inside snug chalets iced with snow. But there is far more to 21st-century Switzerland than heart-warming Alpine tradition: this smart, smug, truly ravishing enclave in Europe gave the world absinthe, LSD, secret bank accounts and the world wide web.

Switzerland is addictive: it has a natural beauty that Hollywood and Bollywood moviemakers drool over, a gargantuan cultural diversity (four official languages says it all), and enough adrenalin-pumping action to fuel inner-junkie cravings for months. Winter or summer, the fest rages: fly down some of the world's most famous ski slopes, hobnob off-piste with celebrities over cocktails served in ice-carved flutes, snowshoe to your igloo, hike past marmots, party until dawn with Züri-West's urban cool crowd and know *this* is Europe's land (…OK, a bijou one) of plenty.

HISTORY

In 1291 the forest communities of Uri, Schwyz and Nidwalden formed an alliance – the origin of the Swiss Confederation. The Swiss began seizing more land, but finally overreached themselves. Defeated by a superior force of French and Venetians, they declared neutrality. Swiss mercenaries continued to serve in other armies for centuries, earning an unrivalled reputation for skill and courage.

The French invaded in 1798, but following Napoleon's defeat at Waterloo, Switzerland gained full independence. In 1848 the Swiss agreed upon a new federal constitution. Having achieved political stability, Switzerland could concentrate on economic and social matters.

The Swiss carefully guarded their neutrality during the world wars, and emerged with a thriving commercial, financial and industrial base. Zürich developed as an international banking centre, and international bodies set up their headquarters in Geneva. However, an independent commission of historians has confirmed that tens of thousands of Jewish refugees were rejected from Switzerland's border during WWII and left to face their fate in Nazi Germany. Swiss banks were accused of banking Nazi plunder and Holocaust victims' accounts during WWII. After years of recriminations and a threatened lawsuit, two Swiss banks made a settlement of US$1.25 billion to Holocaust victims' families in 1998.

Switzerland's *annus horribilus* was 2001: national airline Swissair collapsed, a canyoning accident in the Bernese Oberland killed 21 tourists, and an unprecedented gun massacre in the Zug parliament and fatal fire in the Gotthard Tunnel prompted intense soul-searching. Switzerland became the 190th member of the UN in 2002 and in 2005 it joined Europe's 'Schengen' passport-free travel zone, effective at land borders since December 2008 and at airports from March 2009. The Swiss banned smoking on public transport in 2005 and in 2007 Ticino became the first canton to outlaw smoking in all public places. Others hope to do the same.

Switzerland's privileged banking sector was not immune to the global financial crisis. Switzerland's two largest banks, UBS and Crédit Suisse, both admitted heavy losses in 2008, prompting the government to wade in with a US$60-billion bail-out package for UBS.

THE CULTURE

Living quietly with your neighbours is a national obsession and there are strict rules about noise levels. Good manners infuse the national psyche and politeness is the cornerstone of all social intercourse. Always shake hands when being introduced to a Swiss, and kiss on both cheeks to greet and say goodbye to friends. Don't forget to greet shopkeepers when entering shops.

Most locals are of Germanic origin, and this is shown in the breakdown of the four national languages. German speakers account

WHERE THE WILD THINGS ARE

- Albert Einstein came up with his theories of relativity, including the $E=mc^2$ formula, in Bern.
- Switzerland gave birth to the world wide web at the acclaimed CERN research institute (www.cern.ch) in Geneva.
- Val de Travers, near Neuchâtel, claims to be the birthplace of the mythical green alcohol, absinthe.
- Chemist Albert Hofmann was using LSD to conduct migraine-cure tests in Basel in 1943 when he accidentally absorbed the compound through his fingertips and became the first man to trip on acid.

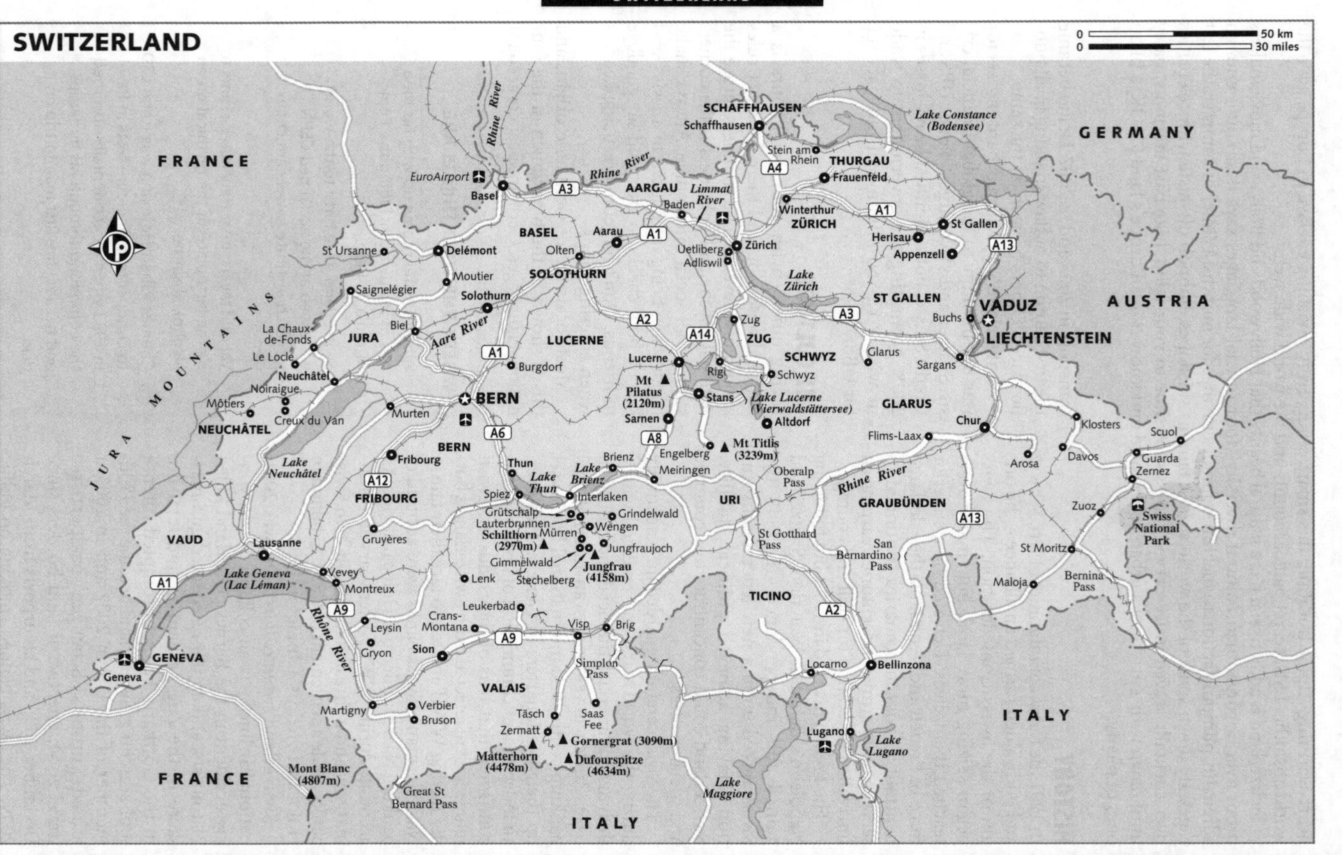
SWITZERLAND
0 50 km
0 30 miles
GERMANY
AUSTRIA
LIECHTENSTEIN
VADUZ
FRANCE
ITALY
JURA MOUNTAINS
Rhine River
Lake Constance (Bodensee)
Limmat River
Lake Zürich
Aare River
Lake Lucerne (Vierwaldstättersee)
Lake Brienz
Lake Thun
Lake Neuchâtel
Lake Geneva (Lac Léman)
Rhône River
Lake Maggiore
Lake Lugano
SCHAFFHAUSEN
THURGAU
AARGAU
ZÜRICH
BASEL
SOLOTHURN
JURA
LUCERNE
ZUG
SCHWYZ
ST GALLEN
GLARUS
GRAUBÜNDEN
URI
TICINO
VALAIS
BERN
FRIBOURG
NEUCHÂTEL
VAUD
GENEVA
Schaffhausen
Stein am Rhein
Frauenfeld
Winterthur
Zürich
Uetliberg
Adliswil
Baden
EuroAirport
Basel
Aarau
Olten
St Ursanne
Delémont
Moutier
Saignelégier
Solothurn
Biel
La Chaux-de-Fonds
Le Locle
Neuchâtel
Noiraigue
Môtiers
Creux du Van
Murten
BERN
Burgdorf
Fribourg
Gruyères
Thun
Spiez
Interlaken
Brienz
Meiringen
Grütschalp
Lauterbrunnen
Grindelwald
Wengen
Schilthorn (2970m)
Mürren
Jungfraujoch
Gimmelwald
Jungfrau (4158m)
Stechelberg
Lenk
Lausanne
Vevey
Montreux
Leukerbad
Crans-Montana
Leysin
Gryon
Sion
Visp
Brig
Simplon Pass
Martigny
Verbier
Bruson
Täsch
Saas Fee
Zermatt
Gornergrat (3090m)
Matterhorn (4478m)
Dufourspitze (4634m)
Mont Blanc (4807m)
Great St Bernard Pass
Geneva
Lucerne
Mt Pilatus (2120m)
Stans
Sarnen
Rigi
Zug
Schwyz
Altdorf
Engelberg
Mt Titlis (3239m)
Oberalp Pass
St Gotthard Pass
San Bernardino Pass
Locarno
Bellinzona
Lugano
Glarus
Sargans
Buchs
St Gallen
Herisau
Appenzell
Chur
Flims-Laax
Arosa
Klosters
Davos
Scuol
Guarda
Zernez
Zuoz
Swiss National Park
St Moritz
Maloja
Bernina Pass
A1
A2
A3
A4
A6
A8
A9
A12
A13
A14

for around 64% of the population, French 19%, Italian 8% and Romansch under 1%. Around 20% of the country's residents are non-Swiss citizens.

ENVIRONMENT

Mountains make up 70% of Switzerland's 41,285 sq km. The Dufourspitze (4634m) in the Monte Rosa Massif is the highest point, but the Toblerone-shaped Matterhorn (4478m) is way more famous.

The St Gotthard Mountains in central Switzerland are the source of many lakes and rivers, including the Rhine and the Rhône. The Jura Mountains straddle the border with France, and peak at around 1700m.

The ibex with its huge curved ridged horns is the most distinctive Alpine animal. Spot some of the 12,000 remaining in the country's only national park, the 169-sq-km Swiss National Park.

The Swiss are environmentally friendly: citizens produce less than 400kg of waste each per year (half the figure for the USA), are diligent recyclers and are fans of public transport.

Reinventing the Alps is a hot topic. Most pressing is not so much how to be ecological, how to burn clean energy – several Swiss mountain resorts do this already. Rather, it is what can be done to keep ski resorts sustainable as the globe warms. Switzerland's 1800 glaciers cover 2000 sq km but are melting rapidly, with the 23km-long Aletsch Glacier notably shrinking 114.6m in 2006 alone and slated to shrink 80% by 2100 if things don't change.

YODEL DOWNLOADS

The most traditional form of Swiss music, yodelling began in the Alps to communicate between peaks and is fast becoming the trendy thing to do in urban circles thanks to Swiss folk singers like Nadja Räss.

'Dr Schacher Seppli', a traditional song re-yodelled by Switzerland's best-known yodeller, farmer and cheese-maker **Rudolf Rymann** (1933–2008), is an iconic iPod download. The other big sound is **Sonalp** (www.sonalp.com), a nine-man band from the Gruyères region whose vibrant ethno-folk mix of yodelling, cow bells, musical saw, classical violin and didgeridoo is contagious.

TRANSPORT

GETTING THERE & AWAY

Air

Zürich (www.zurich-airport.com) and **Geneva** (www.gva.ch) are the two busiest international airports, served by dozens of international airlines. In addition loads of budget operators serve Switzerland:

Air Berlin (AB; www.airberlin.com)
Air Transat (TS; www.airtransat.com)
Atlas Blue (8A; www.atlas-blue.com)
Baboo (F7; www.flybaboo.com)
bmibaby (WW; www.bmibaby.com)
easyJet (EZS/EZY; www.easyjet.com)
Flybe (BE; www.flybe.com)
Flyglobespan (Y2; www.flyglobespan.com)
germanwings (4U; www.germanwings.com)
Helvetic (2L; www.helvetic.com)
Jet2.com (LS; www.jet2.com)
Ryanair (FR; www.ryanair.com)
Transavia.com (HV; www.transavia.com)

Car & Motorcycle

Roads into Switzerland are good. Some minor Alpine passes are closed November to May; check with the local tourist offices.

To use Swiss motorways buy a **vignette** (www.vignette.ch); it costs Sfr40, is valid for one year and must be stuck on your windscreen.

Train

Switzerland is a train-travel hub. Zürich is the busiest international terminus with two direct day trains and a night train to Vienna (book separate women-only compartments in advance) and plenty of Germany connections. Several daily trains run to Paris from Geneva, Lausanne, Bern and Basel. Most connections to/from Italy pass through Milan before branching off to Zürich, Lucerne, Bern or Lausanne.

GETTING AROUND

Bicycle

Hire wheels from many train stations (see www.rent-a-bike.ch; Sfr33/day) and return to any station with a rental office. Bikes can be transported on most trains; station-rented bikes travel free (maximum five bikes per train), otherwise buy a bike pass (Sfr15/day). Bern, Geneva and Zürich offer free bike loans from their train stations.

GO GREEN, TRAVEL SUSTAINABLE

- Sleep in B&Bs, on farms, in haylofts or at eco-places stamped with the Steinbock label (www.steinbock-label.ch), one to five Steinbock (capricorns) reflecting degrees of sustainability.
- Trade in four wheels for two with free bike-hire schemes in Geneva (p1156), Bern (p1161) and Zürich (p1167).
- Reduce your carbon snow-print with an environmentally friendly ski trip. Of the many Swiss resorts polishing their eco halos to offset the impact of skiing, our favourites are St-Moritz (p1163), Flims-Laax (p1163) and car-free Zermatt (p1158) and Mürren (p1170). Planning tools: **Save our Snow** (www.saveoursnow.com) and the **Association of Car-Free Swiss Resorts** (www.gast.org).
- Road-test **SwitzerlandMobility** (www.switzerlandmobility.ch), a pioneering green-travel network of the country's nonmotorised traffic routes – 22 national and 147 regional routes for walkers (6300km), cyclists (8500km), mountain bikers (3300km), rollerbladers/skaters (1000km) and canoeists (250km) – only the Swiss could dream up. Each perfectly signposted trail comes with suggested equipment-hire outlets, accommodation options, public-transport connections, digital maps, striking landscapes and nature spots en route, etc.

Bus

Yellow postal buses supplement the rail network, linking towns to the more inaccessible regions in the mountains. Services are regular; departures tie in with train arrivals.

Car & Motorcycle

The **Swiss Touring Club** (www.tcs.ch) is affiliated with Britain's AA.

Prebook for the best deals on car hire; competitive rates are often found on **Auto Europe** (www.autoeurope.com).

Switzerland is tough on drink-driving; if your blood alcohol level is over 0.05% you face a large fine or imprisonment.

Train

Trains are clean, reliable, frequent and as fast as the terrain allows. Prices are high but travel passes make them affordable. Major stations are connected by hourly departures, but services stop from around midnight to 6am. For train information surf **Swiss Federal Railways** (www.rail.ch, www.sbb.ch/en).

LAKE GENEVA REGION

Western Europe's biggest lake stretches like a liquid mirror between French-speaking Switzerland (north) and France (south). Known as Lake Geneva by most or Lac Léman to Francophones, the Swiss shore cosets palm-tree-studded Riviera resorts and emerald vines marching uphill.

GENEVA

pop 178,700

Supersleek, slick and cosmopolitan, Geneva (Genève in French, Genf in German) is a rare breed of city. It's one of Europe's priciest. Its people chatter in every language under the sun (184 nationalities comprise 45% of the city's population) and it's constantly thought of as the Swiss capital – which it isn't. This gem of a city superbly strung around the sparkling shores of Europe's largest Alpine lake is, in fact, only Switzerland's third-largest city. Yet the whole world is here – the UN, International Red Cross, International Labour Organization and World Health Organization included.

Orientation

The Rhône River divides Geneva into *rive droite* (right bank) – home to central train

CONNECTIONS

It's a doddle to move on from Switzerland, landlocked as it is between France, Germany, Austria, Liechtenstein and Italy. Some Geneva city buses cross into France and there are direct train connections from Geneva to Paris, Hamburg, Milan and Barcelona. Zürich enjoys daily trains to/from Stuttgart, Münich and Innsbruck. In northern Switzerland, European rail hub Basel has separate train stations serving France and Germany. Then of course, there is Italy, a hop and a skip from Locarno in Ticino.

EMERGENCY NUMBERS

- Police ☎ 117
- Fire ☎ 118
- Ambulance ☎ 144
- Motoring breakdown service ☎ 140
- Swiss Mountain Rescue ☎ 1414

station Gare de Cornavin and seedy Pâquis district – and *rive gauche* (left bank), where the old town overlooks Geneva's iconic Jet d'Eau pencil fountain.

Information

Glocals (www.glocals.com) Globals and locals share their tips.
Hospital (☎ 022 372 33 11, emergency 022 372 81 20; www.hug-ge.ch; Rue Micheli du Crest 24)
Internet Café de la Gare (☎ 022 731 51 87; Gare de Cornavin; per hr Sfr10; 🕒 7.30am-10.30pm Mon-Fri, 8.30am-10.30pm Sat & Sun) For a list of free wireless access points in Geneva see www.freespot.ch.
Police station (☎ 117; Rue de Berne 6)
Salon Lavoir (Rue du 31 Decembre 12; 🕒 6am-midnight) Laundromat.
SOS Médecins à Domicile (☎ 022 748 49 50; www.sos-medecins.ch) Home/hotel doctor calls.
Spotted by Locals (http://geneva.spottedbylocals.com) English-language blog.
Tourist office (☎ 022 909 70 00; www.geneve-tourisme.ch; Rue du Mont-Blanc 18; 🕒 10am-6pm Mon, 9am-6pm Tue-Sat)

Sights & Activities

Geneva's best-known landmark (spot it from the plane) is the 140m-tall **Jet d'Eau**. At any one time seven tonnes of water shoot in the air with incredible force – 200km/h, 1360 horsepower – to create a sky-high plume kissed by a rainbow on sunny days.

Other sights include the **Flower Clock** crafted from 6500 flowers in the **Jardin Anglais** (Quai du Général-Guisan); and **Île Rousseau**, an island pierced by a statue honouring the thinker born on the main street in the **old town** at Grand Rue 40, now a museum. Nearby is the part-Romanesque, part-Gothic **Cathédrale St Pierre**, where Protestant John Calvin preached from 1536 to 1564; trace his life in the **International Museum of the Reformation** (☎ 022 310 24 31; www.musee-reforme.ch; Rue du Cloître 4; adult/concession Sfr10/7; 🕒 10am-5pm Tue-Sun).

At the art deco **Palais des Nations** (☎ 022 907 48 96; Ave de la Paix 14; tours adult/student Sfr10; 🕒 10am-noon & 2-4pm Apr-Jun, Sep & Oct, 10am-5pm Jul & Aug, 10am-noon & 2-4pm Mon-Fri Nov-Mar), the European arm of the UN, see where decisions about world affairs are made on the hour-long tour (bring your passport). Don't miss its gardens and the towering grey titanium monument donated by the USSR to commemorate the conquest of space.

The **International Red Cross & Red Crescent Museum** (☎ 022 748 95 25; www.micr.org; Ave de la Paix 17; admission free; 🕒 10am-5pm Wed-Mon) is a compelling multimedia trawl through atrocities perpetuated by humanity.

TRAVEL PASSES & DISCOUNTS

Swiss public transport is efficient, fully integrated and incorporates trains, buses, boats and funiculars. Discount passes make the system even more appealing. Find more information at http://traintickets.myswitzerland.com.

The Swiss Pass offers unlimited travel on Swiss federal railways, boats, most alpine postal buses, and trams and buses in 38 towns. Reductions of 50% apply on funiculars, cable cars and private mountain railways such as Jungfrau Railways. These passes are available for four days (Sfr260), eight days (Sfr376), 15 days (Sfr455), 22 days (Sfr525) and one month (Sfr578). Under 26s can buy the Swiss Youth Pass equivalent, 25% cheaper in each instance. The Swiss Flexi Pass allows free, unlimited trips for three (Sfr249) to six days (Sfr397) within a month. With either pass, two people travelling together get 15% off. Passes also snag you free admission to all Swiss museums.

The Swiss Card (one month Sfr182) allows a free return journey from your arrival point to any destination in Switzerland, 50% off rail, boat and bus excursions, and reductions on mountain railways. The Half-Fare Card (one month Sfr99) is a similar deal minus the free return trip.

All these passes are best purchased before arrival at www.swisstravelsystem.com or in the UK from the **Swiss Travel Centre** (☎ 0207 420 49 00; 30 Bedford St, London WC2E 9ED). In Switzerland larger train-station offices sell them.

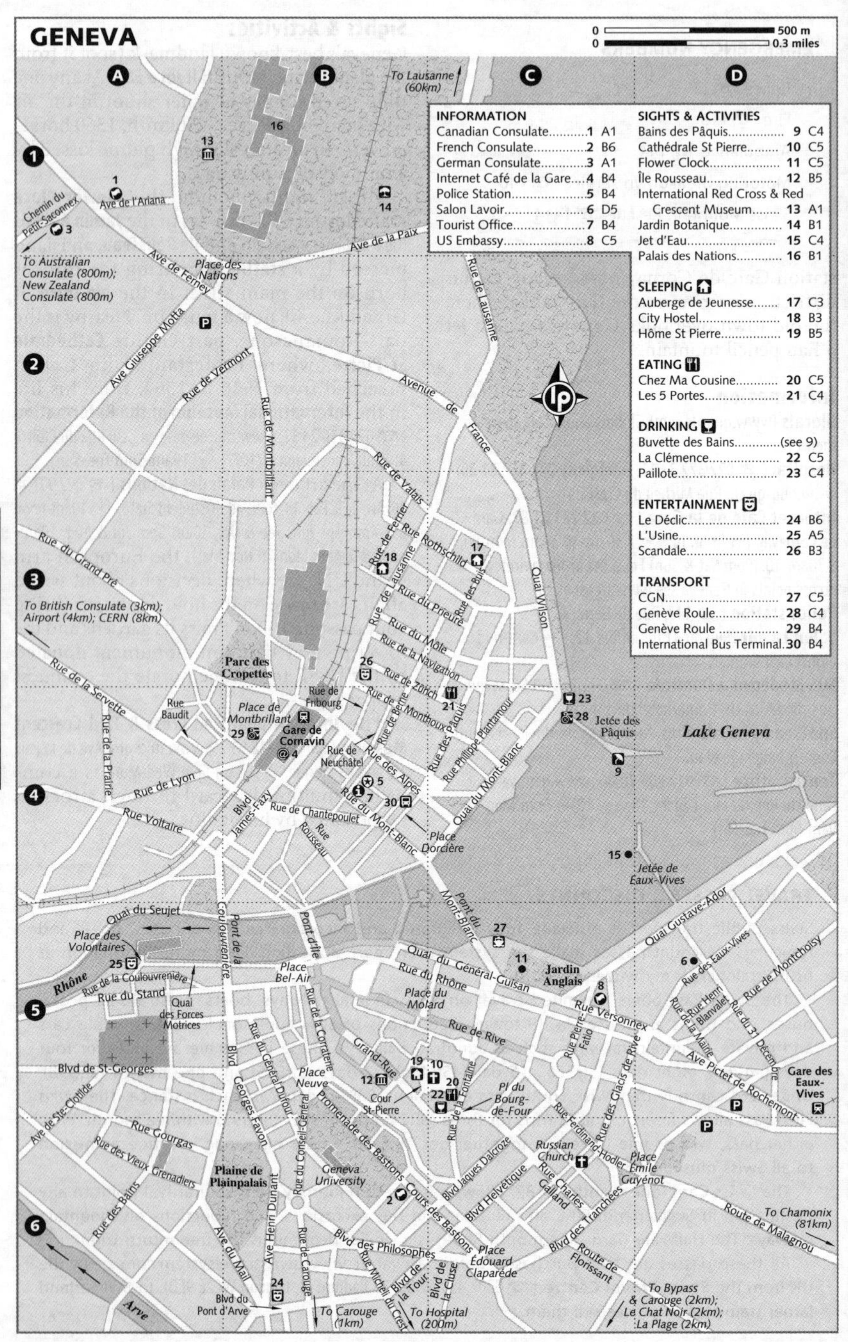
GENEVA
0 500 m
0 0.3 miles
A
B
C
D
1
2
3
4
5
6
INFORMATION
Canadian Consulate 1 A1
French Consulate 2 B6
German Consulate 3 A1
Internet Café de la Gare 4 B4
Police Station 5 B4
Salon Lavoir 6 D5
Tourist Office 7 B4
US Embassy 8 C5
SIGHTS & ACTIVITIES
Bains des Pâquis 9 C4
Cathédrale St Pierre 10 C5
Flower Clock 11 C5
Île Rousseau 12 B5
International Red Cross & Red Crescent Museum 13 A1
Jardin Botanique 14 B1
Jet d'Eau 15 C4
Palais des Nations 16 B1
SLEEPING
Auberge de Jeunesse 17 C3
City Hostel 18 B3
Hôme St Pierre 19 B5
EATING
Chez Ma Cousine 20 C5
Les 5 Portes 21 C4
DRINKING
Buvette des Bains (see 9)
La Clémence 22 C5
Paillote 23 C4
ENTERTAINMENT
Le Déclic 24 B6
L'Usine 25 A5
Scandale 26 B3
TRANSPORT
CGN 27 C5
Genève Roule 28 C4
Genève Roule 29 B4
International Bus Terminal 30 B4
To Lausanne (60km)
Chemin du Petit-Saconnex
Ave de l'Ariana
To Australian Consulate (800m); New Zealand Consulate (800m)
Ave de la Paix
Place des Nations
Ave de Ferney
Ave Giuseppe Motta
Rue de Vermont
Rue de Montbrillant
Avenue de France
Rue de Lausanne
Rue du Grand Pré
To British Consulate (3km); Airport (4km); CERN (8km)
Rue de Valais
Rue de Fernier
Rue Rothschild
Rue des Buis
Rue de Lausanne
Rue du Prieuré
Rue du Môle
Rue de la Navigation
Quai Wilson
Rue de la Servette
Parc des Cropettes
Rue de Zürich
Rue de Fribourg
Rue de Berne
Rue de Monthoux
Rue Baudit
Rue de la Prairie
Place de Montbrillant
Gare de Cornavin
Rue de Neuchâtel
Rue des Pâquis
Rue Philippe Plantamour
Quai du Mont-Blanc
Jetée des Pâquis
Lake Geneva
Rue de Lyon
Rue des Alpes
Rue du Mont-Blanc
Rue Voltaire
Blvd James-Fazy
Rue de Chantepoulet
Rue Rousseau
Place Dorcière
Jetée de Eaux-Vives
Quai du Seujet
Place des Volontaires
Pont de la Coulouvrenière
Pont de l'Île
Pont du Mont-Blanc
Quai Gustave-Ador
Rhône
Rue de la Coulouvrenière
Rue du Stand
Quai des Forces Motrices
Place Bel-Air
Quai du Général-Guisan
Rue du Rhône
Place du Molard
Jardin Anglais
Rue des Eaux-Vives
Rue de Montcholsy
Rue Versonnex
Rue de Rive
Rue Pierre-Fatio
Rue Henri Blanvalet
Rue de la Mairie
Rue du 31 Décembre
Rue de la Corraterie
Rue du Général-Dufour
Blvd de St-Georges
Blvd Georges Favon
Grand-Rue
Place Neuve
Cour St-Pierre
Rue de la Fontaine
Pl du Bourg-de-Four
Rue des Glacis de Rive
Ave Pictet de Rochemont
Gare des Eaux-Vives
Ave de Ste-Clotilde
Rue Gourgas
Rue des Vieux Grenadiers
Plaine de Plainpalais
Rue du Conseil-Général
Promenade des Bastions
Geneva University
Blvd Jaques Dalcroze
Russian Church
Rue Ferdinand-Hodler
Place Emile Guyénot
Blvd Helvétique
Rue Charles Galland
Cours des Bastions
Blvd des Tranchées
Route de Malagnou
To Chamonix (81km)
Rue des Bains
Ave Henri Dunant
Ave du Mail
Rue de Carouge
Blvd des Philosophes
Rue Micheli du Crest
Blvd de la Tour
Blvd de la Cluse
Place Édouard Claparède
Route de Florissant
Arve
Blvd du Pont d'Arve
To Carouge (1km)
To Hospital (200m)
To Bypass & Carouge (2km); Le Chat Noir (2km); La Plage (2km)

> **GETTING INTO TOWN**
>
> From the airport there are regular trains into Gare de Cornavin (Sfr2.60, six minutes), the central train station on the northern lake shore. Cross the Pont du Mont Blanc road bridge to reach the old town, a 10-minute walk away.

Flowers, art installations and soul-stirring views of Mont Blanc on clear days make the northern lakeshore promenade a pleasure to walk: pass hip **Bains des Pâquis** (☎ 022 732 29 74; www.bains-des-paquis.ch; Quai du Mont-Blanc 30; 9am-8pm mid-Apr–mid-Sep) where Genevans have frolicked in the sun since 1872. Further north, peacock-studded lawns ensnare the **Jardin Botanique** (admission free; 8am-7.30pm Apr-Oct, 9.30am-5pm Nov-Mar).

The web was born at the **European Organisation for Nuclear Research** (CERN; ☎ 022 767 84 84; visits-service@cern.ch; guided tour by advance reservation free; tours 9am & 2pm Wed & Sat; tram 14 or 16 to Avanchet, then bus 56), a laboratory for research into particle physics funded by 20 nations, 8km west. Book tours one month in advance and bring your passport.

Festivals & Events

The historical festival **L'Escalade**, held in Geneva on 11 December, celebrates deliverance from would-be conquerors.

Sleeping

When checking in, ask for your free public transport ticket covering unlimited bus travel for the duration of your hotel stay.

Hôme St-Pierre (☎ 022 310 37 07; www.homestpierre.ch; Cour St-Pierre 4; dm Sfr29, s/d with washbasin Sfr46/68; reception 9am-noon & 4-8pm Mon-Sat, 9am-noon Sat) Women are the primary clientele at this boarding house founded by the German Lutheran Church in 1874; just six dorm beds are up for grabs for six lucky guys. Magical rooftop terrace.

Auberge de Jeunesse (☎ 022 732 62 60; www.yh-geneva.ch; Rue Rothschild 28-30; dm Sfr29, d from Sfr85; 6.30-10am & 2pm-1am Jun-Sep, 6.30-10am & 4pm-midnight Oct-May) Dorms max out at 12 beds.

City Hostel (☎ 022 901 15 00; www.cityhostel.ch; Rue de Ferrier 2; dm Sfr32-36, s/d Sfr59/86; reception 7.30am-noon & 1pm-midnight; P) Spanking clean is the trademark of this hostel. Rates include sheets, towels and use of the kitchen, TV room and a free locker.

Eating

In the old town, terrace cafes and restaurants crowd Geneva's oldest square, medieval Place du Bourg-de-Four. Rue de Fribourg, Rue de Neuchâtel, Rue de Berne and the northern end of Rue des Alpes are loaded with kebab, falafel and other quick-eat joints.

Les 5 Portes (☎ 022 731 84 38; Rue de Zürich 5; brunch Sfr10, mains Sfr15-20; 9-2am Mon-Fri, 11-2am Sat, 11am-8pm Sun) The Five Doors is a fashionable Pâquis port of call that embraces every mood and moment.

Chez Ma Cousine (☎ 022 310 96 96; www.chezmacousine.ch; Place du Bourg-de-Four 6; lunch Sfr14.90; 11am-10pm) *'On y mange du poulet'* (we eat chicken!) is the strap line of this student institution, which appeals for its generously handsome portions of chicken, potatoes and salad at an unbeatable price.

Buvette des Bains (☎ 022 738 16 16; www.bains-des-paquis.ch; Quai du Mont-Blanc 30; mains Sfr15; 8am-10pm) Meet Genevans at this earthy beach bar at Bains des Pâquis. Dining is on trays and in summer alfresco.

Drinking & Clubbing

Events and live gigs are covered in the *Genéve Agenda* (free at the tourist office). Pâquis, the district between the train station and lake, is well endowed with bars.

> **FREEBIE THRILLS**
>
> Bags of fabulous things to see and do in Geneva don't cost a cent. Our favourite freebies:
>
> - Dashing like mad under the Jet d'Eau (p1153).
> - Getting lost in the old town (p1153).
> - Hobnobbing with big-bang scientists at CERN (left).
> - Going green in the Jardin Botanique (left).
> - Flopping on the beach astride the Bains des Pâquis (left) jetty or renting a pedalo, sailing to the middle of the lake and popping open a bottle of champers.
> - Cycling lakeside into France or to Lausanne (p1156).

Scandale (☎ 022 731 83 73; www.scandale.ch; Rue de Lausanne 24) Retro 1950s furnishings in a cavernous interior with comfy sofas ensures this lounge bar with Saturday-night DJs and bands stays full.

La Clémence (☎ 022 312 24 98; www.laclemence.ch; Place du Bourg-de-Four 20) Indulge in a glass of local wine or artisanal beer at this veritable cafe-bar on Geneva's loveliest square.

La Plage (☎ 022 342 20 98; Rue Vautier 19; 11-1am Mon-Thu, 10-2am Fri & Sat, 5pm-1am Sun) With its bare wood tables, checked lino floor, green wood shutters and tables outside, 'the Beach' in Carouge is one of Geneva's timeless drinking holes.

L'Usine (☎ 022 781 34 90; www.usine.ch; Place des Volontaires 4) This converted gold-roughing factory entertains its visitors with dance nights, art happenings, theatre, cabaret and club nights.

Le Chat Noir (☎ 022 343 49 98; www.chatnoir.ch, in French; Rue Vautier 13) Nightly jazz, rock, funk and salsa gigs.

Le Déclic (☎ 022 320 59 40; www.ledeclic.ch; Blvd du Pont d'Arve 28) Gay nightclub.

In summer the lakeside **paillote** (Quai du Mont-Blanc 30) gets rammed; tables are inches from the water.

SWITZERLAND

Getting There & Around

Geneva airport has frequent connections to most major European cities.

CGN (☎ 0848 811 848; www.cgn.ch) operates a steamer service from its Jardin Anglais jetty to other Lake Geneva villages. Most sail May to September, including those to/from Lausanne (Sfr37.60, 3½ hours).

International buses depart from the **bus station** (☎ 0900 320 320, 022 732 02 30; www.coach-station.com; Place Dorcière).

Trains connections include Lausanne (Sfr20.60, 40 minutes), Bern (Sfr46, 1¾ hours), Zürich (Sfr80, 2¾ hours), Paris (Sfr127, 3½ hours), Hamburg (Sfr276, 9½ hours), Milan (Sfr97, 4½ hours) and Barcelona (Sfr125, 10 hours).

Rent a bike at **Genève Roule** (☎ 022 740 13 43; www.geneveroule.ch; Place de Montbrillant 17; 8am-6pm Mon-Sat) or its seasonal Jetée des Pâquis pick-up point for Sfr12/20 per day/weekend. May to October, borrow a bike carrying publicity for free.

Public transport is excellent. A day pass costs Sfr7.

LAUSANNE

pop 119,200

In a fabulous location overlooking Lake Geneva, Lausanne is an enchanting beauty with several distinct personalities: the former fishing village, Ouchy, with its summer beach-resort feel; Place St-François, with stylish, cobblestone shopping streets; and Flon, a warehouse district of bars, galleries and boutiques. One of the country's grandest Gothic cathedrals dominates its medieval centre.

The **tourist office** (☎ 021 613 73 21; www.lausanne-tourisme.ch; Place de la Navigation 4; 9am-6pm Oct-Mar, to 8pm Apr-Sep) neighbours Ouchy metro station.

Sights

The **Musée de l'Art Brut** (www.artbrut.ch; Ave des Bergières 11-13; adult/student Sfr10/5, 1st Sat of month free; 11am-6pm Tue-Sun Sep-Jun, 11am-6pm daily Jul & Aug), with its fascinating amalgam of 15,000 works of art created by psychiatric patients, eccentrics and incarcerated criminals, is Switzerland's most alluring museum.

Another must is the Gothic **Cathédrale de Notre Dame** (7am-7pm Mon-Fri, 8am-7pm Sat & Sun Apr-Aug, 7am-5.30pm Sep-Mar).

Sleeping

Hotel guests get a Lausanne Transport Card covering unlimited public transport.

Camping de Vidy (☎ 021 622 50 00; www.campinglausannevidy.ch; Chemin du Camping 3; adult/car Sfr7.50/3, tent Sfr10-18) This camping ground is on the lake just west of the Vidy sports complex; take bus 2 to Bois de Vaux 50.

Lausanne GuestHouse (☎ 021 601 80 00; www.lausanne-guesthouse.ch; Chemin des Épinettes 4; dm Sfr33-38, s/d with shared bathroom Sfr85/95, with private bathroom Sfr94/115; P ⊠) An attractive mansion converted into quality backpacking accommodation near the train station. Many rooms have lake views and some of the building's energy is solar.

Hôtel du Port (☎ 021 612 04 44; www.hotel-du-port.ch; Place du Port 5; s/d Sfr180/230; ⊠) A perfect location in Ouchy, the best doubles peep at the lake and suites slumber on the 3rd floor.

Eating & Drinking

Lausanne is one of Switzerland's busier night-time cities. Look for the free listings booklet *What's Up* (www.whatsupmag.ch) in bars.

Café Romand (☎ 021 312 63 75; Place St François 2; mains Sfr18-28.50) Bankers to punks feast on traditional dishes – ranging from fine fondue to *cervelle au beurre noir* (brains in black butter) – cooked in the kitchen which operates all day. Follow the tatty sign into the arcade.

Café de Grancy (☎ 021 616 86 66; www.cafedegrancy.ch; Ave du Rond Point 1; mains Sfr18-35) An old-time bar resurrected with flair by young entrepreneurs, this is a hip hang-out with floppy lounges, wi-fi and weekend brunch.

Giraf Bar (☎ 021 323 53 90; Escaliers du Marché; 🕑 8.30pm-1am Tue-Thu, to 2am Fri & Sat) This tiny smoke-filled bar fills up on Friday and Saturday night; dig the giraffe-skin motif on the lampshades.

Le Bleu Lézard (☎ 021 321 38 30; www.bleu-lezard.ch; Rue Enning 10; 🕑 7am-1am Mon-Thu, 7am-2am Fri, 8am-2am Sat, 9.30am-1am Sun) An oldie but a goodie, this corner bar-eatery cooks up Sunday brunch, wi-fi, a chatty atmosphere and club-styled dance floor in the cellar.

Entertainment

MAD (☎ 021 340 69 69; www.mad.ch; Route de Genève 23; admission up to Sfr25) With five floors of entertainment and every sound going, MAD throbs. Dress snappy and be at least 25.

La Ruche (www.la-ruche.ch; Rue de la Tour 41; admission free-Sfr10) The Beehive is so hot even clubbers from Geneva trek here.

Getting There & Around

There are trains to Geneva (Sfr20.60, 33 to 51 minutes, up to six hourly), Geneva airport (Sfr25, 42 to 58 minutes, up to four hourly) and Bern (Sfr31, 70 minutes, one or two hourly). For boat services, see opposite.

MONTREUX

pop 23,200

In 1971 Frank Zappa was doing his thing in the casino here when the building caught fire, casting a pall of smoke over Lake Geneva and inspiring the members of Deep Purple to pen their classic rock number *Smoke on the Water*.

This Swiss Riviera showpiece has inspired writers, artists and musicians for centuries – and it's easy to see why: Montreux boasts stunning Alps views, tidy rows of pastel buildings and Switzerland's most extraordinary castle, 11th-century **Château de Chillon** (☎ 021 966 89 10; www.chillon.ch; Ave de Chillon 21; adult/student Sfr12/10; 🕑 9am-6pm Apr-Sep, 9.30am-5pm Mar & Oct, 10am-4pm Nov-Feb), a 45-minute walk from Montreux or a ride on trolley bus 1 (Sfr2.30).

Crowds throng to the two-week **Montreux Jazz Festival** (www.montreuxjazz.com) in early July. Free concerts take place daily, but big-name gigs cost Sfr40 to Sfr100.

On the waterfront, **Auberge de Jeunesse** (☎ 021 963 49 34; Passage de l'Auberge 8, Territet; dm from Sfr32; 🕑 mid-Feb–mid-Nov; 💻) is a chirpy hostel 30 minutes' walk along the lake clockwise from the tourist office (or take the local train to Territet or bus 1).

Café du Grütli (☎ 021 963 42 65; Rue du Grand Chêne 8; mains up to Sfr30) is a cheerful little eatery hidden in the old town that provides good home cooking.

There are trains to Geneva (Sfr28, 70 minutes, hourly) and Lausanne (Sfr10.20, 25 minutes, three hourly).

FRIBOURG, NEUCHÂTEL & THE JURA

A far cry from the staggering Alpine scenes more readily associated with Switzerland, this gentle corner in the west is a 'secret'. From the evocative medieval cantonal capitals of Fribourg and Neuchâtel to the mysterious green hills and deep forests of the Jura, it promises discovery off the beaten track.

Absinthe was first distilled in the **Val de Travers** (aka the Pays des Fées – Fairyland) in 1740 (although it was a Frenchman called Pernod who made the first-known bitter green liqueur a few kilometres across the border in France) and produced commercially in 1797. From 1910, following Switzerland's prohibition of the wickedly alcoholic, ruthlessly bitter aniseed drink, distillers of the 'devil in the bottle' moved underground. In 2005 Switzerland lifted its absinthe ban and the **Blackmint – Distillerie Kübler & Wyss** (☎ 032 861 14 69; www.blackmint.ch; Rue du Château 7, Môtiers) distilled its first true and authentic batch of the mythical *fée verte* (green fairy) from valley-grown wormwood. Mix one part crystal-clear liqueur with five parts water to make it green.

A green sleep in this valley is **L'Aubier** (☎ 032 732 22 11; www.aubier.ch; s/d from Sfr125/160), an eco-hotel on a biodynamic farm in Montézillon, 8km southwest of Neuchâtel. Light-flooded rooms overlook fields of grazing cows whose milk is mixed with carrot juice to make carrot cheese (sold in its ecoboutique).

VALAIS

Matterhorn country: an intoxicating land that seduces the toughest of critics with its endless panoramic vistas and breathtaking views. A century ago farmers in this earthy part of southern Switzerland didn't have two francs to rub together. Today celebrities sip Sfr10,000 champagne cocktails from ice-carved goblets in this jet-set land with a great outdoors so extraordinary it never goes out of fashion. Switzerland's 10 highest mountains, all over 4000m, are here.

ZERMATT

pop 5790

The Matterhorn: that unfathomable monolith synonymous with Switzerland that one simply can't quite stop looking at. And it's right here in Zermatt, indisputable skiing, mountaineering and hiking hot spot (and car-free to boot, yay!).

Electric taxis whisk guests about. Bahnhofstrasse is the main street. Surf for free or hook your laptop up to wi-fi at **Papperla Pub** (☎ 027 967 40 40; www.papperlapub.ch).

The **tourist office** (☎ 027 966 81 00; www.zermatt.ch; Bahnhofplatz 5; 🕒 8.30am-6pm Mon-Sat, 8.30am-noon & 1.30-6pm Sun mid-Jun–Sep, 8.30am-noon & 1.30-6pm Mon-Sat, 9.30am-noon & 4-6pm Sun rest of year) has all the bumph.

Activities

Views from the cable cars are uniformly breathtaking as is the cogwheel train to 3090m **Gornergrat** (Sfr38 one way, 35 to 45 minutes, two to three per hour). Sit on the right-hand side to gawp at Matterhorn. Alternatively, hike from Zermatt to Gornergrat in five hours.

Zermatt is cruising heaven with long red runs, a scattering of blues for ski virgins and knuckle-whitening blacks for experts. Free buses shuttle skiers between the three ski areas, **Rothorn**, **Stockhorn** and **Klein Matterhorn**. Snowboarders make for Klein Matterhorn's freestyle park and half-pipe, while mogul fans go wild over Stockhorn. Klein Matterhorn is topped by Europe's highest cable-car station (3820m), providing access to Europe's highest skiing and Switzerland's most extensive summer skiing. A day pass for all ski lifts in Zermatt (excluding Cervinia) costs Sfr67/57 per adult/student or Sfr75/64 including Cervinia.

Find the ski school and mountain guides office inside the **Alpin Center** (☎ 027 966 24 60; www.alpincenter-zermatt.ch; Bahnhofstrasse 58; 🕒 8.30am-noon & 3-7pm mid-Nov–Apr & Jul-Sep).

Sleeping & Eating

Many places close between seasons.

Hotel Bahnhof (☎ 027 967 24 06; www.hotelbahnhof.com; Bahnhofstrasse; dm/s/d Sfr43/78/98) Opposite the station, these spruce budget digs have lounge, snazzy open-plan kitchen and proper beds – a godsend after schussing down mountains all day. Free wi-fi.

Zermatt SYHA Hostel (☎ 027 967 23 20; Staldenweg 5; dm/d with half-board Sfr47.50/100; 💻) Question: how many hostels have Matterhorn peeking through the window in the morning? Answer: one.

our pick **Berggasthaus Trift** (☎ 079 408 70 20; dm/d with half-board Sfr63/150; 🕒 Jul-Sep) It's a trudge to this 2337m-high Alpine haven run by Hugo (a whiz on the alphorn) and Fabienne, but the hike is outstanding. Snap the sun setting over Monte Rosa.

DETOUR: ZEN OUT IN GRYON & LEYSIN

Trek off the beaten track to lap up Swiss Alpine charm in untouched Gryon (1130m), with meadow hiking trials and **Chalet Martin** (☎ 024 498 33 21; Chalet Martin; www.gryon.com; dm/d from Sfr25/70; P 💻), a Swiss-Australian-run hostel which travellers rave about. The vibe is laid-back and the place organises activities galore, paragliding, skiing and chocolate-tasting included. Train it from Lausanne to Bex (Sfr17.40, 40 minutes, hourly), then take the cogwheel train to Gryon (Sfr6.20, 30 minutes, hourly). The hostel is a five-minute signposted walk from the train stop.

Equally Zen is Leysin, a hub for skiers, boarders and hikers who can't get enough of **Hiking Sheep** (☎ 024 494 35 35; www.hikingsheep.com; dm/d Sfr30/80; P 🐾 💻). The tall, art-deco house has a kitchen, great communal facilities, a pine-forested backyard and breathtaking views from its balconies. Find it a two-minute walk from Leysin-Grand Hôtel train station. Ride the cogwheel train from Aigle (Sfr10.80, 30 minutes, hourly), in turn linked by train with Lausanne (Sfr14.80, 30 minutes, hourly).

Bayard Metzgerei (☎ 027 967 22 66; Bahnhofstrasse 9; sausages around Sfr6; 🕒 noon-6.30pm Jul-Sep, 4-6.30pm Dec-Mar) Follow your nose to this butcher's grill for to-go bratwurst, chicken and other carnivorous bites.

Drinking

Papperla Pub (☎ 027 967 40 40; Steinmattstrasse 34) Rammed with sloshed skiers, this pub blends pulsating music with lethal Jägermeister bombs and good vibes. Squeeze in, slam shots and shuffle downstairs to Schneewittchen club for more of the same.

Hennu Stall (☎ 027 966 35 10; Klein Matterhorn) Last one down to this snow-bound 'chicken run' is a rotten egg. Hennu is the wildest après-ski shack on Klein Matterhorn. Order a metre-long 'ski' of shots.

Igloo Bar (Gornergrat; www.iglu-dorf.ch; 🕒 10pm-4am) Subzero sippers sunbathe, stare at the Matterhorn and guzzle *Glühwein* (mulled wine) amid the ice sculptures at this igloo bar. It's on the run from Gornergrat to Riffelberg.

Getting There & Around

Trains depart roughly every 20 minutes from Brig (Sfr35, 1½ hours), stopping at Visp en route. Zermatt is also the starting point of the *Glacier Express* to Graubünden, one of the world's most spectacular train rides.

Motorists must park at Täsch (Sfr13.50 per day) and train (Sfr7.60, 12 minutes) it up to Zermatt.

BERN

pop 122,500

One of the planet's most underrated capitals, Bern is fabulous. With the genteel, old soul of a Renaissance man and the heart of a high-flying 21st-century gal, this riverside city is both medieval and modern. The 15th-century old town is gorgeous enough to sweep you off your feet and make you forget the century (it's definitely worthy of its Unesco World Heritage site protection order). But edgy vintage boutiques, artsy-intellectual bars and Renzo Piano's futuristic art museum crammed with Paul Klee pieces slams you firmly back into the present.

INFORMATION

Internet Café (☎ 031 311 9850; www.pokerhill.ch, in German; Aarbergergasse 46; per hr Sfr8-10; 🕒 9.30am-12.30am Mon-Fri, noon-12.30am Sat)

Stauffacher (☎ 031 311 24 11; Neuengasse 25; 🕒 9am-7pm Mon-Fri, to 9pm Thu, to 5pm Sat) English books on the 3rd floor.

Tourist Center (☎ 031 328 12 12; Bärengraben; 🕒 9am-6pm Jun-Sep, 10am-4pm Mar-May & Oct, 11am-4pm Nov-Feb) Tourist office by the bear pits.

Tourist Center Bahnhof (☎ 031 328 12 12; www.berninfo.com; Bahnhoftplatz; 🕒 9am-8.30pm Jun-Sep, 9am-6.30pm Mon-Sat, 10am-5pm Sun Oct-May) Street-level floor of the train station.

SIGHTS & ACTIVITIES

Old Town

Medieval Bern, with 6km of covered arcades and cellar shops/bars descending from the streets, is the sandstone city's prime attraction. Join the crowds congregating around the **Zytglogge** (clock tower) at four minutes before the hour to watch its revolving figures twirl; street-snack on hot chestnuts; and trip between decorative **fountains** (1545) depicting historical and folkloric characters…and a giant snacking on children at the **Kindlifresserbrunnen** on Kornhausplatz.

The dizzying climb up the lofty spire – Switzerland's tallest – of the Gothic, 15th-century **Cathedral** (audioguide Sfr5, tower admission Sfr4; 🕒 10am-5pm Tue-Sat, 11.30am-5pm Sun Easter-Nov, 10am-noon & 2-4pm Tue-Fri, to 5pm Sat, 11.30am-2pm Sun rest of year, tower closes 30 min earlier), is worth the 344-step hike.

The world's most famous scientist developed his theory of relativity in 1905 at what's now the **Einstein Museum** (☎ 031 312 00 91; www.einstein-bern.ch; Kramgasse 49; adult/student Sfr6/4.50; 🕒 10am-7pm Mon-Fri, to 4pm Sat Feb-Dec), housed in the humble apartment where Einstein lived while working as a clerk in the local patent office.

Across the Aare River, 28-year-old brown bear Pedro, who has spent his life in Bern's 3.5m-deep stone **Bärengraben** (bear pit; www.baerenpark-bern.ch; 🕒 9.30am-5pm), will move to a new, spacious riverside park in autumn 2009. Bears – the heraldic mascot of the city – have

GETTING INTO TOWN

Shuttle buses coordinated with flight arrivals/departures link **Bern-Belp airport** (www.alpar.ch), 9km southeast, with the train station (Sfr15, 20 minutes) on the western edge of the old town. The main sights are a few minutes' walk from here.

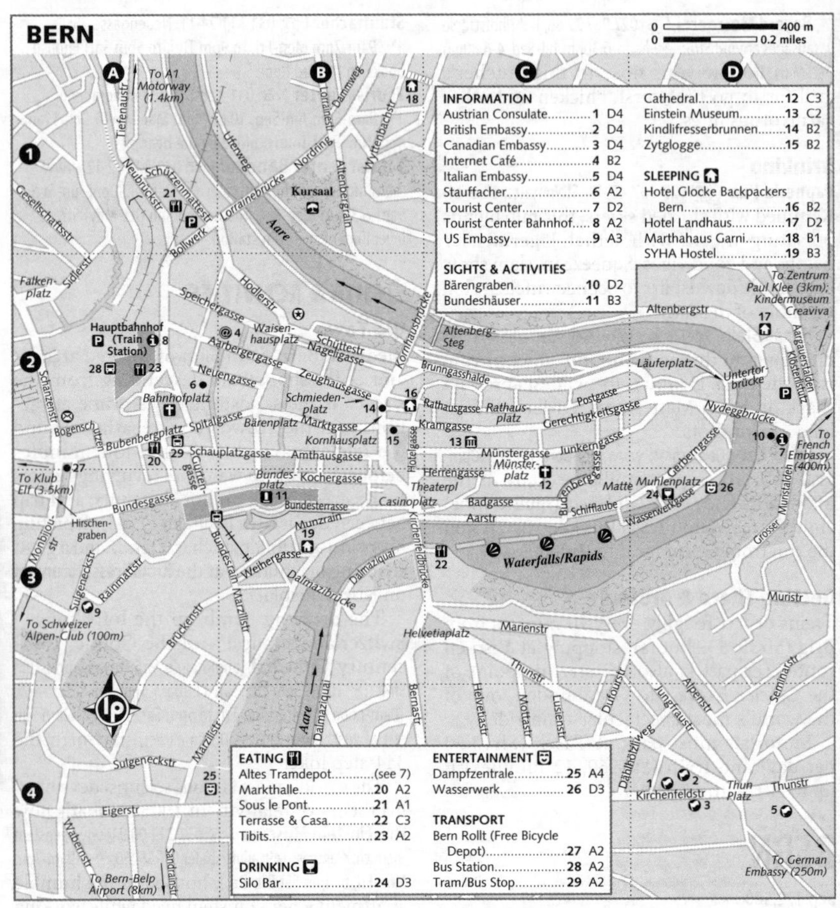

been here since 1857. Don't feed them; buy a paper cone of fresh fruit (Sfr3) from Walter, their keeper.

Paul Klee Centre

Forming a three-peak wave next to the Bern-Ostring exit of the A6, Renzo Piano's remarkable **Zentrum Paul Klee** (☎ 031 359 01 01; www.zpk.org; Monument in Fruchtland 3; adult/concession Sfr16/6; ⌚ 10am-5pm Tue-Sun) is Bern's Guggenheim. The exhibition space showcases 4000 rotating works from Paul Klee's prodigious and often playful career. Inspired music audio guides (which cost Sfr5) take visitors on one-hour DIY musical tours. In the grounds, a walk through fields will take you past a stream of sculptures, including some contemporary works by artists such as Yoko Ono and Sol LeWitt. To get here, take bus 12.

Houses of Parliament

The 1902 **Bundeshäuser** (☎ 031 332 85 22; www.parliament.ch; Bundesplatz; admission free; ⌚ hourly tours 9am-4pm Mon-Sat), home of the Swiss Federal Assembly, are impressively ornate. When the parliament is in recess you can tour the place; otherwise watch from the public gallery. Bring your passport.

FESTIVALS & EVENTS

Bern takes on a carnival atmosphere for the unique **Onion Market**, held on the fourth Monday of November.

SPLURGE

Hotel Landhaus (☎ 031 331 41 66; www.landhausbern.ch; Altenbergstrasse 4; dm Sfr30, dm without/with pillow & quilt Sfr33/38, d with shared/private bathroom Sfr120/160; P ⊠ 💻) The stall-like dorms are rather unappealing, but for the thrill of kipping in a classy hotel without the price tag, they're bearable. With more dough, this historic hotel is fantastic. Think stripped-back modern interior, spiral wooden stairs and individually renovated rooms with shared guest kitchen. The slick ground-floor restaurant-jazz bar is the icing on the cake.

SLEEPING

SYHA hostel (☎ 031 326 11 11; www.youthhostel.ch/bern; Weihergasse 4; dm Sfr33; 🕑 reception 7am-noon & 2pm-midnight; ⊠ 💻) This hostel sports a leafy terrace with ping-pong table across from the river. Free bike hire May to October.

Hotel Glocke Backpackers Bern (☎ 031 311 37 71; www.bernbackpackers.com; Rathausgasse 75; dm Sfr33-41; 🕑 reception 8-11am & 3-10pm; ⊠ 💻) Internet station and free wi-fi. Its old-town location makes this the top choice for many.

our pick **Marthahaus Garni** (☎ 031 332 41 35; www.marthahaus.ch; Wyttenbachstrasse 22a; dm Sfr45, s/d with shared bathroom Sfr69/99, with private bathroom Sfr110/135; ⊠ 💻) Plum in a leafy residential location, this five-storey building is like a friendly boarding house. Spotless rooms are white with a smattering of modern art.

EATING

Cafes and restaurants fill Bärenplatz and Theaterplatz.

Markthalle (Bubenbergplatz 9) Buzzing in quick-snack action, this covered market arcade is jam-packed with eateries from around the world. Eat curries, vegetarian, wok stir-fries, *bruschette*, noodles, pizza, south Indian, Turkish, Middle Eastern etc standing at bars or around plastic tables.

Tibits (☎ 031 312 91 11; Bahnhofplatz 10) This train-station vegetarian buffet restaurant is just the ticket for a quick, healthy meal any size, any time. Serve yourself, get it weighed, pay and eat.

Sous le Pont (☎ 031 306 69 55; Schützenmatte; mains Sfr5-15) Grab fries, falafel or a *schnitzel* from the graffiti-covered hole in the wall next to the Sous le Pont cafe-bar and dine at a graffiti-covered table in the graffiti-covered courtyard.

Altes Tramdepot (☎ 031 368 14 15; Am Bärengraben; mains Sfr16-20) Even locals recommend this cavernous microbrewery. Swiss specialities snug up to stir-fries, pasta and international dishes on the bistro menu.

Terrasse & Casa (☎ 031 350 50 01; www.schwellenmaetteli.ch; Dalmaziquai 11; mains Sfr28-45) 'Bern's Riviera', this twinset of classy hang-outs on the Aare is an experience. Terrasse is a glass shoebox with wooden decking and sun loungers overlooking a weir; Casa cooks Italian in a country-styled timber-framed house.

DRINKING & CLUBBING

For an earthy drink with old-generation locals, prop up the marble-topped bar inside Markthalle (left).

Silo Bar (☎ 031 311 54 12; www.silobar.ch, in German; Muhlenplatz 11) By the water, Bern's 19th-century corn house throbs with mainstream hits and a lively student set – *the* place to drink, dance and party.

Wasserwerk (☎ 031 312 12 31; www.wasserwerkclub.ch; Wasserwerkgasse 5) Bern's main techno venue with bar, club and occasional live music.

Klub Elf (www.klubelf.ch; Ziegelackerstasse 11a) House, techno, trance and minimal sound are the dance beat at this weekend club, west of the centre, where the real Saturday-night party kicks off after midnight and continues with an 'After' party on Sunday at 5am. Find flyers on MySpace.

Dampfzentrale (☎ 031 310 05 40; www.dampfzentrale.ch, in German; Marzilistrasse 47) This industrial red-brick riverside building hosts concerts, festivals, gigs, contemporary dance and a lovely riverside restaurant terrace.

GETTING THERE & AROUND

Hourly trains connect to most Swiss towns, including Geneva (Sfr46, 1¾ hours), Basel (Sfr37, 70 minutes) and Zürich (Sfr46, one hour).

Walk around or hop on a bus or tram; tickets cost Sfr2/3.80 for six stops/single journey within zones 1 and 2.

Cycle, skateboard or nip around on a microscooter with **Bern Rollt** (☎ 079 277 28 57; www.bernrollt.ch; train station; 1st 4 hours free, then per hr Sfr1).

Book your stay at lonelyplanet.com/hotels

TICINO

Heidi never mentioned this Switzerland: the summer air is rich and hot, the peacock-proud posers propel their scooters in and out of traffic – Italian weather, Italian style and yes, Italian ice cream, Italian pizza, Italian architecture and Italian language.

South of the Alps, Ticino (Tessin in German and French) fuses Swiss cool with Italian passion, as evidenced by a lusty love for Italian comfort food and full-bodied wines balanced by a healthy respect for rules and regulations.

LOCARNO

pop 14,700

A rambling red enclave of Mediterranean piazzas and arcades on the northern shore of Lake Maggiore, Locarno enjoys more sunshine than any other Swiss town. Enjoy.

Five minutes' walk west of the train station is its heart, Piazza Grande, and **tourist office** (☎ 091 791 00 91; www.maggiore.ch; Largo Zorzi 1; 9am-6pm Mon-Fri, 10am-6pm Sat, 10am-1.30pm & 2.30-5pm Sun mid-Mar–Oct, 9.30am-noon & 1.30-5pm Mon-Fri, 10am-noon & 1.30-5pm Sat Nov–mid-Mar).

The formidable **Madonna del Sasso**, with its panoramic views of the lake and town, features a church with 15th-century paintings and small museum.

In August 150,000-odd film buffs hit town for the two-week **International Film Festival** (www.pardo.ch). Cinemas are used during the day but at night films are shown in the open air on a giant screen in the Piazza Grande.

Camping Delta (☎ 091 751 60 81; www.campingdelta.com; Via Respini 7; camp sites Sfr47-57, plus per adult/student Sfr18/16; Mar-Oct), brilliantly located between the shores of Lago Maggiore and the Maggia River, is ab fab.

Rooms at **Vecchia Locarno** (☎ 091 751 65 02; www.hotel-vecchia-locarno.ch; Via della Motta 10; s/d Sfr55/100) are gathered around a sunny internal courtyard, evoking a Mediterranean mood. Digs are simple but comfy; bathrooms are shared.

Lake Maggiore has a great range of fresh tasty fish including *persico* (perch) and *corigone* (whitefish).

A huge hit with night owls, **Bar Sport** (Via della Posta 4; 8-1am Mon-Fri, 10-1am Sat, 2pm-1am Sun; ⊠) is a rough-and-tumble bar with a red-walled dance space out the back and a beer garden. A few other bars loiter nearby.

There are trains to/from Brig (Sfr51, 2½ hours, hourly).

LUGANO

pop 49,800

There is a distinct snappiness in the air in Switzerland's southernmost tourist town, where visitors unravel the spaghetti maze of cobblestone streets while locals toil behind counters – this is the country's third most important banking centre.

A sophisticated slice of Italian life with colourful markets, upmarket shops, interlocking piazza and lakeside parks, lucky Lugano lounges on Lake Lugano's northern shore, at the feet of Mounts San Salvatore and Bré. Read: a superb base for lake trips, water sports and hillside hikes.

The **tourist office** (☎ 091 913 32 32; www.lugano-tourism.ch; Riva Giocondo Albertolli; 9am-7pm Mon-Fri, 9am-5pm Sat, 10am-5pm Sun Apr-Oct, 9am-noon & 2-5.30pm Mon-Fri, 10am-12.30pm & 1.30-5pm Sat Nov-Mar) also runs a booth at the train station (open 2pm to 7pm Monday to Saturday), a 10-minute walk uphill from the old town.

Wander the porticoed lanes woven around the busy main square, Piazza della Riforma; pop into Romanesque **Chiesa di Santa Maria degli Angioli** (Piazza Luini) with two frescoes by Bernardino Luini; and chomp on chocolate at the **Museo del Cioccolato Alprose** (☎ 091 611 88 88; www.alprose.ch; Via Rompada 36, Caslano; adult Sfr3; 9am-5.30pm Mon-Fri, 9am-4.30pm Sat & Sun).

The **SYHA hostel** (☎ 091 966 27 28; www.luganoyouthhostel.ch; Via Cantonale 13, Savosa; dm/s/d Sfr26/68/96; mid-Mar–Oct;), housed in Villa Savosa, is one of Switzerland's more enticing youth hostels. To get there, take bus 5 to Crocifisso.

For pizza or overpriced pasta, any of the places around Piazza della Riforma are pleasant and lively enough. Lugano's lakeside beach restaurant **Al Lido** (☎ 091 971 55 00; Viale Castagnola; brunch 11am-6pm, dinner Wed-Sat) is hot for Sunday brunch and its Wednesday-evening version with DJ thrown in. Local Lugano beauties crowd around the long, orange-lit bar in **Soho Café** (☎ 091 922 60 80; Corso Pestalozzi 3; ⊠) where chilled DJ music creates a pleasant buzz.

Postal buses run to/from St Moritz (Sfr69, four hours, daily late June to mid-October and late December to early January). Reserve at the **bus station** (☎ 091 807 85 20; Via Serafino Balestra) or train-station information office.

SWITZERLAND

GRAUBÜNDEN

Don't be fooled by Graubünden's diminutive size on a map. This is topographic origami at its finest. Unfold the rippled landscape to find an outdoor adventurer's paradise riddled with walking trails, lakes and downhill ski slopes – including superswanky St Moritz and backpacker mecca Flims-Laax. Linguistically wired to flick from Italian to German to Romansch, locals keep you on your toes too.

ST MORITZ

pop 5060

Switzerland's original winter wonderland and the cradle of Alpine tourism, St Moritz (San Murezzan in Romansch) has been luring royals, the filthy rich and moneyed wannabes since 1864. With its smugly perfect lake, aloof mountains and Gucci set propping up the bars, the town looks a million dollars…and is – in the shape of superb carving on Corviglia (2486m), hairy black Diavolezza runs and endless hiking trails when the powder melts. See www.skiengadin.ch for the complete low-down.

The **tourist office** (☎ 081 837 33 33; www.stmoritz.ch; Via Maistra 12; 9am-6.30pm Mon-Fri, 9am-noon & 1.30-6pm Sat, 4-6pm Sun) is in St Moritz Dorf above the train station.

Budget beds are gold-dust rare in St Moritz, but you'll find one at **Jugendherberge St Moritz** (☎ 081 836 61 11; Stille Via Surpunt 60; www.youthhostel.ch/st.moritz; dm/d Sfr55/137;), edging the forest. The four-bed dorms and doubles are quiet and clean. There's a kiosk, games room and laundromat.

English-styled **Bobby's Pub** (☎ 081 834 42 83; Via dal Bagn 50a) and **Roo Bar** (☎ 081 837 50 50; Via Traunter Plazzas 7) are hot watering holes.

The **Palm Express postal bus** (☎ 058 386 31 66) runs to/from Lugano (Sfr69, four hours, daily summer, Friday, Saturday and Sunday winter); advance reservations are obligatory.

FLIMS-LAAX

They say if the snow ain't falling anywhere else, you'll surely find some around Flims-Laax. These two towns, along with tiny Falera, 20km west of Chur, form a single ski area known as the Weisses Arena (White Arena), with 220km of slopes catering for all levels. Laax in particular is known as a mecca for snowboarders, who spice up the local nightlife too. The resort is barely two hours by train and bus (less by car) from Zürich airport.

The main **tourist office** (☎ 081 920 92 00; www.flims.com summer, www.laax.com winter; Via Nova; 8am-6pm Mon-Fri, to noon Sat mid-Jun–mid-Aug, 8am-5pm Mon-Sat mid-Dec–mid-Apr) is in Flims-Dorf.

Mostly intermediate or easy ski slopes peak at 3000m although there are some 45km of more-challenging runs. A one-day ski pass (Sfr62 plus Sfr5 for KeyCard to access lifts) also covers ski buses.

Laax was the first Swiss resort to allow snowboarders to use the lifts back in 1985, and remains a mecca for snowsurfers, with two huge half-pipes (one said to be the biggest in the world) and a freestyle park huddled around the unfortunately named Crap Sogn Gion peak. The season starts in late October on the glacier and, depending on snowfalls, in mid-December elsewhere.

In summer try river rafting on a turbulent 17km stretch of the Vorderrhein between Ilanz and Reichenau. It will take you through the **Rheinschlucht** (Rhine Gorge), aka Switzerland's Grand Canyon. **Swissraft** (☎ 081 911 52 50; www.swissraft.ch) runs half-/full-day rafting expeditions (Sfr109/160).

Sleep? Dream on. It may resemble an oversized Rubik's cube, but **Riders Palace** (☎ 081 927 97 00; www.riderspalace.ch; Laax Murschetg; dm Sfr30-60, d Sfr180-280) is a curious slice of designer cool with bare concrete walls and fluorescent lighting. Choose between basic five-bed dorms, slick rooms with Philippe Starck tubs, or hi-tech suites complete with PlayStation and Dolby surround. Find it 200m from the Laax lifts.

Titillate tastebuds with the raw funk of **La Vacca** (☎ 081 927 99 62; Plaun Station, Laax-Murschetg lifts; mains Sfr40-70), a tepee where cowhide-draped chairs surround an open fire and the menu (think bison steak paired with full-bodied Argentine wine) is as exciting as the design.

After a day pounding powder, you can slam shots, check email and shimmy in your snow boots at **Crap Bar** (☎ 081 927 99 45; Laax-Murschetg lifts).

Postal buses run to Flims hourly from Chur (Sfr12.80 to Flims Dorf, 30 minutes).

ZÜRICH

pop 350,200

Switzerland's biggest city and finance centre is also the hippest. Why else would Google (whose employees, known as Zooglers, shimmy into work down a fire pole) have its European engineering centre here? This is a city where Berlin grunge meets swish posh,

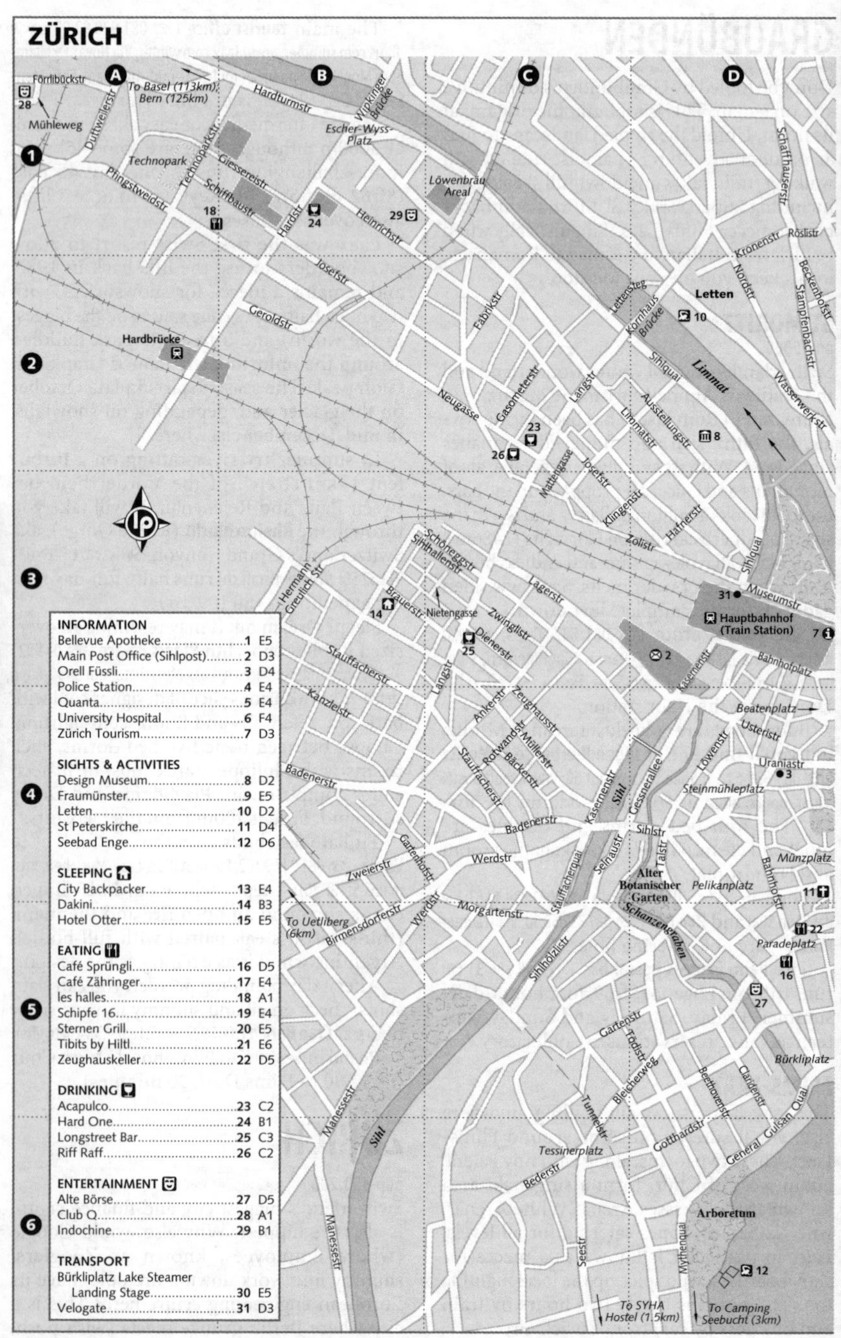
ZÜRICH
INFORMATION
Bellevue Apotheke....1 E5
Main Post Office (Sihlpost)....2 D3
Orell Füssli....3 D4
Police Station....4 E4
Quanta....5 E4
University Hospital....6 F4
Zürich Tourism....7 D3
SIGHTS & ACTIVITIES
Design Museum....8 D2
Fraumünster....9 E5
Letten....10 D2
St Peterskirche....11 D4
Seebad Enge....12 D6
SLEEPING
City Backpacker....13 E4
Dakini....14 B3
Hotel Otter....15 E5
EATING
Café Sprüngli....16 D5
Café Zähringer....17 E4
les halles....18 A1
Schipfe 16....19 E4
Sternen Grill....20 E5
Tibits by Hiltl....21 E6
Zeughauskeller....22 D5
DRINKING
Acapulco....23 C2
Hard One....24 B1
Longstreet Bar....25 C3
Riff Raff....26 C2
ENTERTAINMENT
Alte Börse....27 D5
Club Q....28 A1
Indochine....29 B1
TRANSPORT
Bürkliplatz Lake Steamer Landing Stage....30 E5
Velogate....31 D3
To Basel (113km); Bern (125km)
Förrlibuckstr
Mühleweg
Duttweilerstr
Hardturmstr
Wipkinger Brücke
Escher-Wyss-Platz
Technopark
Technoparkstr
Giessereistr
Schiffbaustr
Pfingstweidstr
Hardstr
Heinrichstr
Löwenbräu Areal
Josefstr
Geroldstr
Hardbrücke
Fabrikstr
Lettensteg
Kornhaus Brücke
Letten
Schaffhauserstr
Kronenstr
Röslistr
Nordstr
Beckenhofstr
Stampfenbachstr
Wasserwerkstr
Limmat
Sihlquai
Ausstellungstr
Limmatstr
Langstr
Gasometerstr
Neugasse
Mattengasse
Klingenstr
Hafnerstr
Zolistr
Schöneggstr
Sihlhallenstr
Hermann Greulich Str
Brauerstr
Nietengasse
Lagerstr
Museumstr
Hauptbahnhof (Train Station)
Zwinglistr
Dienerstr
Bahnhofplatz
Stauffacherstr
Kanzleistr
Kasernenstr
Ankerstr
Zeughausstr
Rotwandstr
Müllerstr
Bäckerstr
Beatenplatz
Usteristr
Uraniastr
Löwenstr
Steinmühleplatz
Gessnerallee
Badenerstr
Sihl
Sihlstr
Talstr
Münzplatz
Gartenhofstr
Werdstr
Stauffacherquai
Selnaustr
Alter Botanischer Garten
Pelikanplatz
Bahnhofstr
Zweierstr
Morgartenstr
Schanzengraben
Paradeplatz
To Uetliberg (6km)
Birmensdorferstr
Sihlhölzlistr
Gartenstr
Tödistr
Bürkliplatz
Claridenstr
Beethovenstr
Bleicherweg
Tunnelstr
Manessestr
Gotthardstr
General Guisan Quai
Tessinerplatz
Bederstr
Arboretum
Seestr
Mythenquai
To SYHA Hostel (1.5km)
To Camping Seebucht (3km)

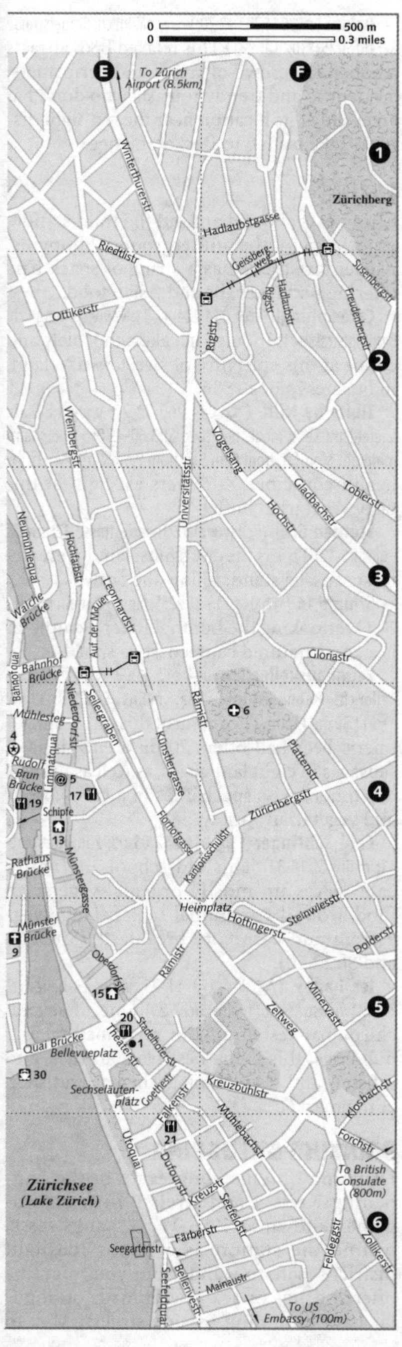

where fashion fiends flock to drink and club in once-industrial Züri-West, and where Europe's largest street party lets its hair down each August for an all-nighter to remember.

ORIENTATION

Compact and easy to navigate, Zürich is at the northern end of Lake Zürich with the city centre split by the Limmat River.

INFORMATION

Bellevue Apotheke (☎ 044 266 62 22; www.bellevue-apotheke.com; Theaterstrasse 14; ⏲ 24hr) Chemist.

Orell Füssli (☎ 044 211 04 44; www-books.ch; Bahnhofstrasse 70; ⏲ 9am-8pm Mon-Fri, to 6pm Sat) English-language bookshop.

Police station (☎ 044 216 71 11; Bahnhofquai 3)

Quanta (☎ 044 260 72 66; Limmatquai 94; per hr Sfr10; ⏲ 9am-midnight) Internet access.

University Hospital (☎ 044 255 11 11, 044 255 21 11; www.usz.ch; Rämistrasse 100) Casualty.

Zürich Tourism (☎ 044 215 40 00, hotel reservations 044 215 40 40; www.zuerich.com; train station; ⏲ 8am-8.30pm Mon-Sat, 8.30am-6.30pm Sun May-Oct; 8.30am-7pm Mon-Sat, 9am-6.30pm Sun Nov-Apr)

ZürichCard (per 24/72hr Sfr17/24) Available from the tourist office and airport train station; provides free public transport, free museum admission and more.

SIGHTS

Elegant **Bahnhofstrasse** is simply perfect for window-shopping and affluent Züricher-watching. On Sunday it seems as if all of Zürich takes an afternoon stroll around the **lake**: odd human traffic jam aside, it's worth the cultural experience.

The 13th-century **Fraumünster** (Cathedral; Münsterplatz; ⏲ 9am-6pm May-Sep, 10am-5pm Oct-Apr) has some of the world's most distinctive stained-glass windows, while the 13th-century tower of **St Peterskirche** (St Peter's Church; St-Peterhofstatt; ⏲ 8am-6pm Mon-Fri, 8am-4pm Sat, 11am-5pm Sun) has Europe's largest clock face (8.7m in diameter).

Exhibitions at Zürich's **Design Museum** (☎ 043 446 67 67; www.museum-gestaltung.ch; Ausstellungstrasse 60; adult/student Sfr9/6; ⏲ 10am-8pm Tue-Thu, to 5pm Fri-Sun) are impressive and wide-ranging – anything from Bollywood to photographic short stories.

ACTIVITIES

May to mid-September the city's green lake-shore parks buzz with bathers, sun-seekers, in-line skaters, footballers, lovers, picnickers, party animals, preeners and police patrolling

GETTING INTO TOWN

Between 6am and midnight up to nine trains an hour yo-yo between Zürich airport and the main train station, Hauptbahnhof (Sfr6, 9 to 14 minutes), on the western bank of the river near the old town.

on rollerblades. **Outdoor swimming areas** (admission Sfr6; 9am-7pm May & Sep, to 8pm Jun-Aug) – think rectangular wooden pier partly covered by pavilion – open both here and up the Limmat River. Favourites include trendy **Seebad Enge** (044 201 38 89; www.seebadenge.ch; Mythenquai 95) and **Letten** (044 362 92 00; Lettensteg 10), where hip Züri-Westers swim, barbecue, skateboard, play volleyball or just drink and hang on the grass and concrete.

FESTIVALS & EVENTS

Zürich lets its hair down on Saturday in the second week of August with an enormous techno **street parade** (www.street-parade.ch) with 30 lovemobiles and more than half a million excited ravers.

SLEEPING

Camping Seebucht (044 482 16 12; www.camping-zurich.ch; Seestrasse 559; 2 people, tent & car Sfr27; May-Sep) On the western shore of the lake, 4km from the city centre, this site has good facilities. Catch bus 161 or 165 from Bürkliplatz.

City Backpacker (044 251 90 15; www.city-backpacker.ch; Niederdorfstrasse 5; dm/s/d Sfr34/71/104;) Overcome any claustrophobia at this trifle-cramped party hostel by hanging out in summer on the roof terrace – the best spot in Zürich to wind down at sunset with a few cold beers.

Hotel Foyer Hottingen (044 256 19 19; www.hotel-foyer-hottingen.ch; Hottingerstrasse 31; dm Sfr40, s/d with shared bathroom Sfr110/145, s with private bathroom Sfr125-145, d with private bathroom Sfr165-185;) Rooms are clinical but startling value. Some have a balcony, each floor has showers and communal kitchen and the top floor is a dorm for women only.

SYHA hostel (043 399 78 00; www.youthhostel.ch; Mütschellenstrasse 114, Wollishofen; dm/s/d Sfr42/106.50/127;) This bulbous, purple-red hostel features a swish 24-hour reception/dining hall, flat-screen TVs and sparkling modern bathrooms. Take tram 7 to Morgental or S-Bahn to Wollishofen.

Dakini (044 291 42 20; www.dakini.ch; Brauerstrasse 87; s/d Sfr75/130;) This relaxed B&B attracts a bohemian crowd of artists and performers, academics and trendy tourists who don't bat an eyelid at its location near the red-light district. Take tram 8 to Bäckeranlange.

EATING

Cheap eats abound around the train station, especially in the underground Shopville. Niederdorfstrasse has a string of snack bars offering pizza, kebabs and Asian food.

Café Sprüngli (044 224 47 31; www.spruengli.ch; Bahnhofstrasse 21) Indulge in cakes, chocolate and coffee at this epicentre of sweet Switzerland, in business since 1836.

Tibits by Hiltl (044 260 32 22; www.tibits.ch; Seefeldstrasse 2; meals per 100g Sfr3.60-4.10; 6.30am-midnight Mon-Fri, from 8am Sat, from 9am Sun) With-it, health-conscious Zürichers eat light at this tasty vegetarian buffet.

Sternen Grill (Bellevueplatz/Theatrestrasse 22; snacks from Sfr5-12) This is the city's most famous grease-feast sausage stand; follow the crowds.

Schipfe 16 (044 211 21 22; Schipfe 16; menus Sfr16-20) Overlooking the Limmat River, Schipfe 16 is a good-natured canteen-style spot.

Zeughauskeller (044 211 26 90; www.zeughauskeller.ch; Bahnhofstrasse 28a; mains Sfr17.50-33.50; 11.30am-11pm) The menu at this huge, atmospheric beer hall offers 20 different kinds of sausages in eight languages, as well as numerous other Swiss specialities of a carnivorous and vegetarian variety.

Café Zähringer (044 252 05 00; Zähringerplatz 11; mains Sfr18-32) This old-school alternative cafe serves up mostly organic, vegetarian food around communal tables. Huge vegetarian and carnivore breakfasts (Sfr20.50 and Sfr22.50).

les halles (044 273 11 25; www.les-halles.ch; Pfingstweidstrasse 6; mains Sfr22-29) One of several chirpy bar-restaurants in revamped factory buildings, this is the best place to tuck into mussels and fries. Hang at the bar and shop at the market.

DRINKING & CLUBBING

Drinking options congregate in the happening Kreis 4 and Kreis 5 districts, together known as Züri-West. Langstrasse, behind the station, is a minor red-light district – safe to wander but you might be offered drugs or sex – with loads of popular bars humming in side streets. May to

September the trendy water bars at the lake baths (see opposite) are hot places to hang barefooted. Clubbers should dress well and be prepared to cough up Sfr15 to Sfr30 admission.

Longstreet Bar (☎ 044 241 21 72; www.longstreetbar.ch; Langstrasse 92) Run by the guy seemingly behind half Zürich's nightlife, this purple-felt-lined one-time cabaret is a throbbing music bar with DJs. Count light bulbs by the thousands.

Hard One (☎ 044 444 10 00; www.hardone.ch; Hardstrasse 260) The punters flock to this glass cube of a lounge bar for great views and weekend gigs.

our pick **Club Q** (☎ 044 444 40 50; www.club-q.ch; Förrlibückstrasse 151) In a car park, Club Q is for serious dancers only. Ibiza nights don't quite match the Spanish rave island's mega-club vibe, but for Zürich's club crowd it's the next best thing. The club's minor cousin, BBQ, is in the same car park.

Indochine (☎ 044 448 11 11; www.club-indochine.ch; Limmatstrasse 275) Zürich's answer to Paris' Buddha Bar. Models and rich kids mingle between the dimly lit fat Buddhas at this faux opium den.

Alte Börse (www.alteboerse.com; Bleicherweg 5) Hundreds of dance fanatics cram in to this recently opened club for intense electronic sessions with DJs from all over the world. Occasional live acts too.

Acapulco (☎ 044 272 66 88; Neugasse 56) is a retro hang-out, while the cinema-cum-bistro **Riff Raff** (☎ 044 444 22 05; Neugasse 57), is a counter-culture way to start the evening.

GETTING THERE & AWAY

Zürich airport (☎ 043 816 22 11; www.zurich-airport.com), 10km north of the centre, is a small international hub with two terminals.

Daily trains serve Stuttgart (Sfr76, three hours), Munich (Sfr104, 4½ hours) and Innsbruck (Sfr79, four hours) and many other international destinations. There are direct departures to most major Swiss towns including Lucerne (Sfr23, 46 to 50 minutes), Bern (Sfr46, 57 minutes) and Basel (Sfr31, 55 minutes).

GETTING AROUND

There is a comprehensive bus, tram and S-Bahn service. Short trips under five stops are Sfr2.40 and a 24-hour pass for the centre is Sfr7.80.

April to October **lake steamers** (☎ 044 487 13 33; www.zsg.ch) depart from Bürkliplatz.

City bikes (www.zuerirollt.ch) can be picked up at **Velogate** (train station; ⏰ 8am-9.30pm) for free if you bring the bike back after six hours or pay Sfr5/day.

CENTRAL SWITZERLAND & BERNER OBERLAND

This region should come with a health warning: caution – may cause trembling in the north face of Eiger, uncontrollable bouts of euphoria at the foot of Jungfrau, 007 delusions at Schilthorn and A-list fever in Gstaad. Indeed, the landscape here is such that electric-green spruce forests, mountains so big they'll swallow you up, surreal china blue skies, swirling glaciers and turquoise lakes seem hallucinatory.

LUCERNE

pop 58,400

Recipe for a gorgeous Swiss city: take a cobalt lake ringed by mountains of myth, add a medieval old town and sprinkle with covered bridges, sunny plazas, candy-coloured houses and waterfront promenades. Lucerne is bright, beautiful and has been little Miss Popular since the 19th century.

Don't miss the old town with medieval ramparts and towers, 15th-century buildings with painted facades, and its famous bridges, **Kapellbrücke** (Chapel Bridge; 1333), famously destroyed in part by a spectacular 1993 fire and subsequently rebuilt (fire damage is still obvious on the 17th-century pictorial panels under the roof), and the **Spreuerbrücke** (Spreuer Bridge) with darker but better-preserved *Dance of Death* panels.

Lucerne's blockbuster cultural attraction is the **Sammlung Rosengart** (☎ 041 220 16 60; www.rosengart.ch; Pilatusstrasse 10; adult/student Sfr18/16; ⏰ 10am-6pm Apr-Oct, 11am-5pm Nov-Mar), studded with masterpieces by Cézanne, Klee, Kandinsky, Miró, Matisse and Monet. Some 200 photographs capturing the last years of Picasso's life complement the main collection.

Lucerne's boisterous six-day **Fasnacht** party kicks off on 'Dirty Thursday' with the emergence of the character 'Fritschi' from the town hall and moves through raucous celebrations climaxing on Mardi Gras (Fat Tuesday). June's **Jodler Fest Luzern** (www.jodlerfestluzern.ch) is a classic Alpine shindig comprising 12,000 yodellers, alphorn players and flag throwers.

Travellers love the vibe at **Backpackers Lucerne** (☎ 041 360 04 20; www.backpackerslucerne.ch; Alpenquai 42; dm/d Sfr31/70; reception 7-10am & 4-11pm;), quite possibly backpacker heaven with its lake-facing balconies, art-slung walls and soulful lounge. Find it a 15-minute walk southeast of the train station.

SYHA hostel (☎ 041 420 88 00; www.youthhostel.ch/luzern; Sedelstrasse 12; dm/d Sfr32.50/82; check-in 2pm-midnight in summer, from 4pm in winter; P) is modern, well-run and clean, and value-for-money meals are available throughout the day. Take bus 18 from the train station to Jugendherberge.

Self-caterers head to Hertensteinstrasse where cheap eats are plentiful.

With its stainless-steel bar, sturdy wooden tables and chalkboard menus, **Jazzkantine** (☎ 041 410 73 73; Grabenstrasse 8; mains Sfr15-22) is an arty haunt. Go for tasty *bruschette* or more ambitious dishes like penne vodka. Saturday-night gigs follow week-night jazz workshops.

As well as a cracking sense of humour, **Schützengarten** (☎ 041 240 01 10; Bruchstrasse 20; mains Sfr18.50-45) has smiley service, wood-panelled surrounds, appetising vegetarian and vegan dishes and organic wine. Sit on the vine-strewn terrace in summer.

Destinations served by hourly trains include Zürich (Sfr23, one hour), Interlaken (Sfr33.40, two hours) and Bern (Sfr35, 1½ hours).

SWITZERLAND

INTERLAKEN

pop 5290

Catering to backpackers like nowhere else in the country, Interlaken is often the main Swiss destination for budget travellers. Interlaken is also a mecca for thrill seekers, and many a traveller leaves with a much lighter wallet after blowing mind-boggling amounts of cash on a range of white-knuckle, high-adrenalin sports. Most are not disappointed.

If you don't have loads of money, check out the myriad hiking trails in the area – the views are amazing and free!

Orientation & Information

Most of Interlaken lies between its two train stations, Interlaken Ost and West. The main shopping street, Höheweg, runs between the stations and you can walk from one to the other in 20 minutes.

Near Interlaken West is **Interlaken Tourismus** (☎ 033 826 53 00; www.interlakentourism.ch; Höheweg 37; 8am-7pm Mon-Fri, 8am-5pm Sat, 10am-noon & 5-7pm Sun Jul–mid-Sep, 8am-noon & 1.30-6pm Mon-Fri, 9am-noon Sat rest of year).

Activities

Some say leaping from an aeroplane over the Swiss Alps is a life-changing experience. Others argue that canyoning is, while some swear by night sledding or zorbing (Sfr95), the latest craze whereby you're strapped inside a giant plastic ball and flung down a hill. Whatever your adventure-sport taste, you'll find it in Interlaken.

Options include rock climbing (Sfr90), rafting or canyoning (Sfr110), bungee jumping (Sfr130), skydiving (Sfr430), paragliding (Sfr160) and hang-gliding (Sfr195). Most excursions are without incident, but there's always a small risk and it's wise to ask about safety records and procedures.

Major operators:

Alpin Center (☎ 033 823 55 23; www.alpincenter.ch; Hauptstrasse 16)

Alpinraft (☎ 033 823 41 00; www.alpinraft.ch; Hauptstrasse 7)

Outdoor Interlaken (☎ 033 826 77 19; www.outdoor-interlaken.ch; Hauptstrasse 15)

Swissraft (☎ 033 821 66 55; www.swissraft-activity.ch; Obere Jungfraustrasse 72)

Sleeping

RiverLodge & Camping TCS (☎ 033 822 44 34; Brienzstrasse 24; camp sites per adult/tent/car Sfr9/7/4, dm/s/d Sfr28/64/88; May–mid-Oct) Facing the Aare River and handy for Interlaken Ost train station, this camping ground and hostel duo offer first-class facilities including a kitchen, laundry and wi-fi. Rent bikes and kayaks here.

Schlaf im Stroh (☎ 033 822 04 31; www.uelisi.ch; Lanzenen 30; per person Sfr28 incl breakfast; May-Sep; P) Our readers sing the praises of this friendly farm. Bring your sleeping bag to snooze in

SPLURGE

Hotel Otter (☎ 044 251 22 07; www.wueste.ch; Oberdorfstrasse 7; s/d from Sfr115/150) A true gem, the Otter has 17 rooms variously decorated with pink satin sheets and plastic beads, raised beds, wall murals and, in one instance, a hammock. A popular bar, the Wüste, is downstairs.

the straw and wake up to a hearty breakfast. There are resident cats, goats and rabbits. It's 15 minutes' walk from Interlaken Ost station along the Aare River (upstream).

Balmer's Herberge (☎ 033 822 19 61; www.balmers.ch; Hauptstrasse 23; dm Sfr27-30, d Sfr74-80; P 💻) Adrenalin junkies hail Balmer's for its fun frat-house vibe. These party-mad digs offer beer-garden happy hours, wrap lunches, a pumping bar with DJs, and chill-out hammocks for nursing your hangover.

Funny Farm (☎ 033 828 12 81; www.funny-farm.ch; Hauptstrasse 36; dm Sfr30-38.50, s/d Sfr90/110; P 💻) Midway between squat and island shipwreck, this ramshackle art-nouveau house surrounded by makeshift bars and a swimming pool is patrolled by a dopey St Bernard called Spliff. Dorms are faded, but guests don't care; they're here for the party.

Backpackers Villa Sonnenhof (☎ 033 826 71 71; www.villa.ch; Alpenstrasse 16; dm/d Sfr37/98, Jungfrau view extra Sfr5; reception 7am-11pm; 💻) While most Interlaken hostels are charged with more energy than a Duracell bunny, this homely place recharges your batteries. The olive-fronted villa exudes Victorian flair with stucco and vintage steamer trunks, immaculate dorms, a well-equipped kitchen and leafy garden.

Eating & Drinking

Am Marktplatz is scattered with bakeries and bistros that have alfresco seating. The bars at Balmer's and Funny Farm are easily the liveliest drinking holes for revved-up 20-somethings.

Sandwich Bar (☎ 033 821 63 25; Rosenstrasse 5; snacks Sfr4-8; 7.30am-7pm Mon-Fri, 8am-5pm Sat) This snack bar is an untouristy gem. Choose your bread and get creative with fillings. Our favourite is *Bündnerfleisch* (air-dried meat), sundried tomatoes and parmesan). Otherwise try soups, salads and locally made ice cream.

Goldener Anker (☎ 033 822 16 72; www.anker.ch, in German; Marktgasse 57; mains Sfr18-38) This beamed restaurant, locals whisper in your ear, is the best in town. Globetrotters include everything from sizzling fajitas to red snapper and ostrich steaks. Live bands.

Getting There & Away

Trains to Grindelwald (Sfr10.20, 40 minutes, hourly), Lauterbrunnen (Sfr7, 20 minutes, hourly) and Lucerne (Sfr30, two hours, hourly) depart from Interlaken Ost. Trains to Brig (Sfr41, 1½ hours, hourly) and Montreux via Bern or Visp (Sfr57 to Sfr67, 2¼ hours, hourly) leave from either Interlaken West or Ost.

JUNGFRAU REGION

This is where your heart skips a beat. Presided over by glacier-encrusted monoliths Eiger, Mönch and Jungfrau (Ogre, Monk and Virgin), the scenery stirs the soul and strains the neck muscles. A magnet for skiers and boarders, a one-day ski pass costs Sfr59. Come summer, walk and walk and walk.

Grindelwald

pop 3810

Skiers and hikers cottoned onto the charms of this simple farming village nestled in a valley under the north face of the Eiger in the late 19th century, making it one of Switzerland's oldest resorts. Think archetypal Alpine chalets and verdant pastures set against an Oscar-worthy backdrop.

Grindelwald tourist office (☎ 033 854 12 12; www.grindelwald.ch; Dorfstrasse; 8am-noon & 1.30-6pm Mon-Fri, 9am-noon & 1.30-5pm Sat & Sun summer & winter, 8am-noon & 1.30-5pm Mon-Fri, 9am-noon Sat rest of year) is at the Sportzentrum, 200m from the train station.

First is the main **skiing area**, with runs stretching from Oberjoch at 2486m to the village at 1050m. In summer ride Europe's longest **cable car** (☎ 033 854 80 80; www.maennlichen.ch) from Grindelwald-Grund to Männlichen (single/return Sfr31/Sfr51) to revel in extraordinary views and soul-rousing hikes.

The cosy wooden chalet housing the excellent **SYHA hostel** (☎ 033 853 10 09; www.youthhostel.ch/grindelwald; Terrassenweg; dm Sfr31.50-38.50, d with shared bathroom

SLEEP SUSTAINABLE

Perched above Grindelwald village, eco-friendly chalet **Naturfreundehaus** (☎ 033 853 13 33; www.naturfreundehaeuser.ch; Terrassenweg; dm/s/d Sfr36/46/72; closed low season; P), whose name translates as the 'House of Friends of Nature', is a green gem. Most folk have a cat or dog; Vreni and Heinz have Mono, a six-year-old trout, as family pet. Creaking floors lead up to cute pine-panelled rooms, including a shoebox single – apparently Switzerland's smallest. Try an Eiger coffee with amaretto or a homemade mint cordial in the quirky cafe, downstairs. The garden has wonderful views to Eiger and Wetterhorn.

SWITZERLAND

Sfr80, with private bathroom Sfr108; reception 7.30-10am & 4-10pm;) is perched high on a hill with magnificent views. Avoid the 20-minute slog from the train station by taking the Terrassenweg-bound bus to the Gaggi Säge stop.

Near the Männlichen cable-car station, **Mountain Hostel** (033 854 38 38; www.mountainhostel.ch; dm Sfr37-42, d Sfr92-102;) is a good base for sports junkies. Cyclists are especially welcomed. Rates include free ice skating and swimming nearby.

Hourly trains link Grindelwald with Interlaken Ost (Sfr10.20, 40 minutes, hourly).

Lauterbrunnen

pop 2480

Bijou Lauterbrunnen, with its main street cluttered with Swiss chalet architecture, is friendly and down to earth. It's known largely for the crash-bang spectacle of the **Trümmelbach Falls** (033 855 32 32; www.truemmelbach.ch; adult Sfr11; 9am-5pm Apr-Jun & Sep-Nov, 8.30am-6pm Jul & Aug), 4km out of town, where up to 20,000L of water per second corkscrews through ravines and potholes inside the mountain. A bus from the train station (Sfr3.40) takes you to the falls.

The **tourist office** (033 856 85 68; www.wengen-muerren.ch; 9am-noon & 1-6pm daily May-Sep, 9am-noon & 1-6pm Mon-Fri rest of year) is opposite the train station. Two minutes away is **Valley Hostel** (033 855 20 08; www.valleyhostel.ch; dm/d Sfr25/70; reception 8am-noon & 3-10pm;), a chilled hostel with open-plan kitchen, garden with waterfall views, free wi-fi and internet, and chirpy team who organise activities.

A few minutes' walk south of the centre, near the Staubbach Falls, **Camping Jungfrau** (033 856 20 10; www.camping-jungfrau.ch; camp sites per adult/tent/car Sfr11.60/10/3.50, dm Sfr27-30;) is a Rolls-Royce of a camping ground with cosy dorms, huts, kitchen, bike rental, wi-fi and internet stations, and dog shower for messy pups.

On the food front, hit **Airtime** (033 855 15 15; www.airtime.ch; 9am-8pm summer, 9am-noon & 4-8pm winter;), a funky cafe, book exchange, laundry and extreme-sports agency inspired by Daniela and Beni's travels in New Zealand.

Gimmelwald

pop 120

Decades ago an anonymous backpacker scribbled these words in the Mountain Hostel's guest book: 'If heaven isn't what it's cracked up to be, send me back to Gimmelwald.' Enough said. When the sun is out in Gimmelwald, the place will take your breath away.

Surrounding hiking trails include one down from Mürren (30 to 40 minutes) and one up from Stechelberg (1¼ hours). Cable cars are also an option (Mürren or Stechelberg Sfr5.60).

After a long summer hike, bed down at **Pension Berggeist** (033 855 17 30; www.berggeist.ch; dm/d Sfr15/40), a dead-simple rustic place with bargain rooms, priceless views and sandwiches sold by the centimetre. Book all kinds of activities here, including skydiving and llama trekking.

Or there's backpacking legend **Mountain Hostel** (033 855 17 04; www.mountainhostel.com; dm Sfr20; reception 8.30am-noon & 6-11pm Apr-Nov;). A soak in its outdoor whirlpool with stunning views hits the spot every time.

Mürren

pop 440

Arrive on a clear evening when the sun hangs low on the horizon, and you'll think you've died and gone to heaven. Car-free Mürren *is* storybook Switzerland.

The **tourist office** (033 856 86 86; www.wengen-muerren.ch; 8.30am-7pm Mon-Sat, to 8pm Thu, to 6pm Sun high season, 8.30am-7pm Mon-Sat, to 5pm Sun shoulder seasons, 8.30am-noon & 1-5pm Mon-Fri low season) is in the sports centre.

Sleeping options include **Eiger Guesthouse** (033 856 54 60; www.eigerguesthouse.com; dm Sfr40-70, d with shared/private bathroom from Sfr120/160;), by the train station, with downstairs pub serving tasty grub.

Tham's (033 856 01 10; mains Sfr15-28; dinner) serves Asian food cooked by a former five-star chef who's literally taken to the hills to escape.

Schilthorn

There's a tremendous 360-degree panorama from the 2970m **Schilthorn** (www.schilthorn.ch). On a clear day, you can see from Titlis to Mont Blanc and across to the German Black Forest. This is where some scenes from *On Her Majesty's Secret Service* were shot in the 1960s, as the fairly tacky **Touristorama** below the **Piz Gloria** revolving restaurant reminds you.

Buy a Sfr116 excursion trip (Half-Fare Card and Eurail Pass 50% off, Swiss Pass 65% off) going to Lauterbrunnen, Grütschalp, Mürren, Schilthorn and returning through Stechelberg to Interlaken. A return from Lauterbrunnen (via Grütschalp) and Mürren costs about Sfr100, as does the return journey via the Stechelberg cable car.

Jungfraujoch

Sure, the world wants to see Jungfraujoch (3454m) and yes, tickets are expensive, but don't let that stop you. It's a once-in-a-lifetime trip. There's a reason why two million people a year visit this, Europe's highest train station.

Clear good weather is essential for the trip; check www.jungfrau.ch or call ☎ 033 828 79 31, and don't forget warm clothing, sunglasses and sunscreen. Up top, when you tire (is this possible?) of the view, dash downhill on a snow disc (free), zip across the frozen plateau on a flying fox (Sfr20), enjoy a bit of tame skiing or boarding (Sfr33), drive a team of Greenland dogs or do your best Tiger-Woods-in-moon-boots impersonation with a round of glacier golf. It isn't cheap at Sfr10 a shot, but get a hole in one and you win the Sfr100,000 jackpot (which, mysteriously, nobody has yet won).

From Interlaken Ost, the journey time is 2½ hours (Sfr177.80 return, Swiss Pass/Eurail Sfr133, cheaper early-morning tickets available).

NORTHERN SWITZERLAND

This region is left off most people's Switzerland itineraries – precisely why you should add it to yours! It's known for industry and commerce, but it has a healthy dose of grazing cows, green rolling hills, tiny rural towns and water (in the form of Lake Constance and the Rhine River on the German border).

BASEL

pop 163,100

Strangely, given its northerly location, Basel (Bâle) has some of Switzerland's hottest weather. And indeed, as the mercury rises the city sheds its notorious reserve and cuts loose as locals bob along the Rhine (Rhein) River, cool off in fountains, whiz around on scooters and dine and drink on overcrowded pavements. It could almost be Italy, not the dual border with France and Germany!

The **tourist office** (☎ 061 268 68 68; www.basel.com; Stadt-Casino, Barfüsserplatz, Steinenberg 14; ⌚ 8.30am-6.30pm Mon-Fri, 9am-5pm Sat, 9am-4pm Sun) has all the bumf on Basel's many art galleries.

Sights & Activities

With its cobbled streets, fountains (check the wacky one by Swiss sculptor Jean Tinguely on Theaterplatz) and medieval churches, the old town is wonderful to wander. In Marktplatz enjoy the rust-coloured **Rathaus** (town hall), with frescoed courtyard. Southeast, the 12th-century **cathedral** is another highlight.

> **GETTING INTO TOWN**
>
> Bus 50 links EuroAirport, 5km northwest in neighbouring France, with Basel's SBB train station (Sfr6.60, 20 minutes). The trip by **taxi** (☎ 061 691 77 88) costs around Sfr40.

Art lovers ogle at Switzerland's largest art collection inside the **Kunstmuseum** (Museum of Fine Arts; ☎ 061 206 62 62; www.kunstmuseumbasel.ch; St Alban-Graben 16; adult/student Sfr12/5, 1st Sun month free; ⌚ 10am-5pm Tue-Sun).

But the art space to really knock your socks off is the **Fondation Beyeler** (☎ 061 645 97 00; www.beyeler.com; Baselstrasse 101, Riehen; adult/student Sfr23/12, ⌚ 10am-6pm, to 8pm Wed). Of all the private Swiss collections made public, former art dealers Hildy and Ernst Beyeler's treasure chest of Miró and Max Ernst sculptures, tribal figures from Oceania, 19th- and 20th-century Picassos and Rothkos etc is the most remarkable. To get to the low, light-filled, open-plan building by leading Italian architect Renzo Piano, ride tram 6 to Riehen.

In summer, join the locals bobbing in the Rhine – the swim is spectacular, popular and free.

Sleeping

Hotel guests: when you check in, remember to ask for your mobility ticket entitling you to free public transport.

Basel Backpack (☎ 061 333 00 37; www.baselbackpack.ch; Dornacherstrasse 192; dm/s/d Sfr32/80/98; ☒ 💻) Converted from a factory, this independent hostel has colour-coded eight-bed dorms and sedate doubles.

SYHA Basel City Youth Hostel (☎ 061 365 99 60; www.youthhostel.ch/basel.city; Pfeffingerstasse 8; dm/s/d Sfr35.50/79/95; ⌚ reception 7am-noon & 3-11pm; 💻) In former post-office buildings across from the train station, this hostel touts rooms with up to four beds and space a plenty – including a summertime interior courtyard to hang out in.

Eating & Drinking

For a quick, cheap bite on the run, the daily market on Marktplatz has tasty bratwurst (Sfr5) and delicious breads (up to Sfr10). Steinenvorstadt has countless fast-food outlets, cafes and restaurants, and Barfüsserplatz teems with teens and 20-somethings on the weekends. A whiff of grunge floats around Kleinbasel (the area around Rheingasse and Utengasse) with a few bars and red-light zone to lend it edge.

Acqua (☎ 061 564 66 66; www.acquabasilea.ch; Binningerstrasse 14; dishes Sfr15-42; lunch & dinner Tue-Fri, dinner Sat) For a glam post-industrial experience, head to these converted waterworks. Cuisine is Tuscan and Basel's beautiful people drink in the attached lounge bar. Summer terrace.

Druck Punkt (☎ 061 261 50 22; St Johanns Vorstadt 19; set menus Sfr17.50 & 22.50; Mon-Fri) This converted print shop makes an unpretentious bistro, with chalky walls and heavy wooden tables.

Getting There & Around

EuroAirport (☎ 061 325 31 11; www.euroairport.com), 5km north in France, serves Basel (as well as Mulhouse, France and Freiburg, Germany).

Basel is a major European rail hub with two main train stations, the Swiss-French SBB (south bank) and the BBF (north bank) for trains to/from Germany. Destinations include Paris (Sfr91, 3¾ hours), Frankfurt (Sfr133, three hours, daily), Hamburg (Sfr214, 6½ to 7½ hours, daily), Geneva (Sfr69, 2¾ hours, twice hourly) and Zürich (Sfr31, 55 minutes to 1¼ hours, twice hourly).

If you're not staying in town, bus/tram tickets cost Sfr1.90/3/8 for up to four stops/central zone/day pass.

SWITZERLAND DIRECTORY

ACCOMMODATION

Switzerland has HI-affiliated hostels (see www.youthhostel.ch), where nonmembers pay an additional 'guest fee' of Sfr6, and independent hostels, which can be more charismatic. Alpine chalets and rural farmhouses offering hostel-style accommodation can be found through **Naturfreundehaus** (Friends of Nature; www.nfhouse.org). A dorm bed costs between Sfr30 and Sfr40, including sheets (sleeping bags have long been banished from Swiss hostels for fear of bed bugs).

Useful websites:

Aventure sur la paille/Schlaf im Stroh (www.abenteuer-stroh.ch) Camp on straw in a hay barn. For more on this novel experience unique to Switzerland, see p1215.

BnB (www.bnb.ch) Bed and breakfasts, budget to palatial.

Camping & Caravanning in Switzerland (www.camping-switzerland.ch) Swiss Camping Association.

MySwitzerland.com (www.myswitzerland.com) Great resource for tracking down all types of accommodation, including bunkers, igloos and so on.

Rural Tourism (www.tourisme-rural.ch) Rural sleeps.

Swiss Backpackers (www.swissbackpackers.ch) Private hostel group.

Swiss Holidays Farms (www.bauernhof-ferien.ch) Farm accommodation, including camping.

Swiss Youth Hostels (SYHA; www.youthhostel.ch)

ACTIVITIES

There are dozens of ski resorts throughout Switzerland. Equipment hire is available at resorts, and ski passes allow unlimited use of mountain transport.

There's no better way to enjoy the spectacular scenery than to walk through it. There is 50,000km of designated paths. Yellow trail signs make it difficult to get lost, and each gives an average walking time to the next destination. Slightly more strenuous mountain paths have white-red-white markers. You can waterski, sail and windsurf on most lakes, and there are over 350 lake beaches. Rafting is possible on many alpine rivers, including the Rhine and the Rhône.

Bungee jumping, paragliding, canyoning and other high-adrenalin sports are available throughout Switzerland, especially in the Interlaken area.

BUSINESS HOURS

Usual business hours in Switzerland:

Banks (8.30am-4.30pm Mon-Fri) Some local variations.

Post offices (7.30am-noon & 2-6.30pm Mon-Fri, 7.30-11am Sat)

Restaurants (noon-2pm & 6-10pm)

Shops (8am-6.30pm Mon-Fri, with 90min or 2hr break at noon)

EMBASSIES & CONSULATES

Embassies are in Bern while cities such as Zürich and Geneva have several consulates. Australia and New Zealand have no embassy in Switzerland, but each has a consulate in Geneva. For a comprehensive list of embassies in Switzerland and Swiss embassies abroad, see www.eda.admin.ch.

Australia (☎ 022 799 91 00; www.australia.ch; Chemin des Fins 2, CH-1121 Geneva)

Austria (☎ 031 356 52 52; www.aussenministerium.at/bern, in German; Kirchenfeldstrasse 77-79, Bern)

Canada Bern (☎ 031 357 32 00; www.canada-ambassade.ch; Kirchenfeldstrasse 88); Geneva (☎ 022 919 92 00; 5 Ave de l'Ariana)
France Bern (☎ 031 359 21 11; www.ambafrance-ch.org, in German & French; Schosshaldenstrasse 46); Geneva (☎ 022 319 00 00; www.consulfrance-geneve.org, in French; 2 Cours des Bastions)
Germany Basel (☎ 061 693 33 03; Schwarzwaldallee 200); Bern (☎ 031 359 41 11; www.bern.diplo.de, in German & French; Willadingweg 83); Geneva (☎ 022 730 11 11; Chemin du Petit-Saconnex 28c)
Italy (☎ 031 350 07 77; www.ambitalia.ch; Elfenstrasse 14, Bern)
New Zealand (☎ 022 929 03 50; Chemin des Fins 2, Grand-Saconnex, Geneva)
UK Bern (☎ 031 359 77 00; www.britain-in-switzerland.ch; Thunstrasse 50); Geneva (☎ 022 918 24 00; Ave Louis Casai 50)
USA Bern (☎ 031 357 70 11; http://bern.usembassy.gov; Sulgeneckstrasse 19); Geneva (☎ 022 840 51 60; Rue François Versonnex 7); Zürich (☎ 043 499 29 60; Dufourstrasse 101)

FESTIVALS & EVENTS

Find more events than we could possibly list on www.switzerland.com.
Fasnacht A lively spring carnival of wild parties and parades is celebrated countrywide in February, with particular enthusiasm in Basel and Lucerne.
Combats de Reines March to October, the lower Valais stages traditional cow fights known as the Combats de Reines.
National Day Fireworks mark the country's National Day on 1 August.
Vintage Festivals Early October, down a couple in wine-growing regions like Neuchâtel and Lugano.

HOLIDAYS

New Year's Day 1 January
Easter March/April; Good Friday, Easter Sunday and Monday
Ascension Day 40th day after Easter
Whit Sunday & Monday 7th week after Easter
National Day 1 August
Christmas Day 25 December
St Stephen's Day 26 December

INTERNET ACCESS

Surfing in internet cafes is expensive (Sfr5 to Sfr15 per hour) and often limited; you often can't open attachments. Public wireless access points are at major airports, 30-odd Swiss train stations and more and more hostels, hotels and cafes. Most are paying and cost around Sfr4 per hour on top of provider charges; track Swisscom's 1200 hot spots online at www.swisscom-mobile.ch.

MONEY

Swiss francs (Sfr, written CHF locally) are divided into 100 centimes (called *rappen* in German-speaking Switzerland). All major travellers cheques and credit cards are accepted. Virtually all train stations have money-exchange facilities open daily.

POST

Postcards and letters to Europe cost Sfr1.30/1.20 priority/economy; to elsewhere they cost Sfr1.80/1.40.

TELEPHONE

The country code for Switzerland is ☎ 41. Area codes don't exist in Switzerland. Numbers for a particular city or town share the same three-digit prefix (eg Bern 031, Geneva 022) but numbers must always be dialled in full, even when calling from next door – literally.

Mobile numbers start with 079. To find a phone number in Switzerland check the **digital phone book** (http://tel.local.ch/en), dial ☎ 1812 to speak to a machine or ☎ 1811 for a real person.

National telephone provider **Swisscom** (http://fr.swisscom.ch) operates the world's densest network of public phone booths (coin- and card-operated)! Minimum charge for a call is Sfr0.50 and phones accept euro coins too.

The normal/cheap tariff for international dialling to fixed-line phones is Sfr0.12/0.10 per minute for Australia, Britain, Canada, New Zealand and the USA; and Sfr0.25/0.20 to countries including Ireland, Japan and the Netherlands.

Save money by buying a prepaid Swisscom card worth Sfr10, Sfr20, Sfr50 and Sfr100. Or look for prepaid cards from rival operators such as **Mobile Zone** (www.mobilezone.ch, in German, French & Italian).

Prepaid local SIM cards (Sfr30 to Sfr100) are available from the three network operators: **Orange** (www.orange.ch), **Sunrise** (www.sunrise.ch) and **Swisscom Mobile** (www.swisscom-mobile.ch). You'll need your passport when you buy.

VISAS

For up-to-date visa info, go to www.eda.admin.ch and click 'Services'.

Visas aren't required for passport holders from the UK, EU, Ireland, the USA, Canada, Australia, New Zealand, South Africa, Norway and Iceland. Others need a Schengen Visa (see p1230).

Turkey

HIGHLIGHTS

- **İstanbul** The glorious one-time Byzantine and Ottoman capital is one of the world's truly great cities (p1179)
- **Cappadocia** Sleep in fairy chimneys and explore underground cities in this jaw-droppingly bizarre and beautiful region (p1198)
- **Selçuk** Kick back in the best *pensions* on the coast, near awesome Ephesus and the site of St John's tomb (p1189)
- **Antalya** Located on both the 'Turquoise Coast' and the 'Turkish Riviera', the stylish Mediterranean hub has a Roman-Ottoman old quarter (p1195)
- **Off-the-beaten track** At Mt Nemrut, decapitated stone heads litter a king's burial mound at 2150m above sea level (p1200)

FAST FACTS

- **Area** 779,452 sq km (six times the size of Greece)
- **Budget** €20 to €30 per day
- **Capital** Ankara
- **Country code** ☎ 90
- **Famous for** Turkish delight, *hamams* (Turkish baths), carpets, moustaches, ancient history
- **Language** Turkish
- **Money** Turkish Lira (TL); A$1 = TL1.17; CA$1 = TL1.32; €1 = TL2.10; ¥100 = TL1.65; NZ$1 = TL0.91; UK£1 = TL2.37; US$1 = TL1.57
- **Phrases** *merhaba* (hello), *tamam* (OK), *teşekkürler* (thank you), *bu akşam olmaz* (not tonight, thanks)

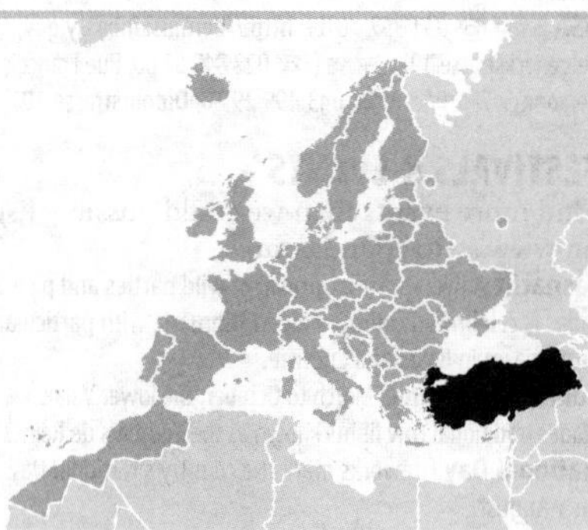

- **Population** 71.9 million
- **Visas** available on entry

TRAVEL HINTS

When haggling for a carpet, be prepared to pay repeat visits, question the price and drink gallons of çay (tea).

ROAMING TURKEY

Circle anticlockwise from İstanbul to see some historical highlights: Gallipoli, Troy, Ephesus, Olympos, Antalya, Konya, Cappadocia and Ankara.

Although most Turks see their country as European, Turkey packs in as many wailing minarets and spice-trading bazaars as neighbouring Iran, Iraq and Syria. This bridge between continents has absorbed Europe's modernism and sophistication, and Asia's culture and tradition. Travellers can enjoy historical hotspots, mountain outposts, expansive steppes and all the exoticism of the Middle East, without having to forego comfy beds and buses.

Turkey's charms range from sun-splashed beaches to İstanbul's mosques, and while these gems fit its reputation as a continental meeting point, the country can't be pigeonholed that easily. Areas like Cappadocia, a dreamscape dotted with fairy chimneys, are completely unlike anywhere else on the planet.

So many Turkish sights, such as Troy and Gallipoli, are familiar from history lessons and Hollywood blockbusters, that travelling here is like reading a historical thriller. When it's time to close the book and seek worldly pleasures, Turkey still shines as brightly as its red-and-white flag, being the land that introduced the world to the döner kebap. Vegetarians will prefer meze, ideally sampled with rakı (aniseed spirit) or a tulip-shaped glass of çay (tea). And that's before you lace up your hiking boots or pull on a dive mask...

HISTORY

The greatest early Anatolian civilisation was the Hittites, who were a force to be reckoned with from 2000 to 1200 BC. After the collapse of the Hittite empire, parts of the country were not reunited until the Greco-Roman period.

In AD 330 the Roman emperor Constantine founded an imperial city at Byzantium. Renamed Constantinople, it became the capital of the Eastern Roman Empire and was the Byzantine Empire's heart for a thousand years. However, invasion by the Seljuk Turks heavily reduced the empire's territory, and Constantinople was sacked during the Fourth Crusade (1202–04). The Byzantines eventually regained the ravaged city in 1261.

In 1453 Constantinople fell to Ottoman Turk Sultan Mehmet II (the Conqueror) and was renamed İstanbul. A century later, under Süleyman the Magnificent, the Ottoman Empire reached its zenith, spreading deep into Europe, Asia and North Africa.

By the 20th century European nationalism had led to widespread independence movements, and the Turks emerged from WWI stripped of their last non-Turkish provinces. Most of Anatolia itself was divided among the victorious Europeans, leaving virtually nothing for Turkey.

At this low point, Mustafa Kemal (later Atatürk), the father of modern Turkey, took over. Under his rule, the Turks won their War of Independence (1919–23), repelling the Greeks at Smyrna (İzmir), and founded a new secular Turkish republic.

Following Atatürk's death in 1938 and the introduction of full democracy in 1950, Turkey experienced considerable political turbulence, including the execution of Democratic Party leader Adnan Menderes. The army became a key force in national politics, stepping in roughly once a decade to restore national order and repair imbalances of power. The occupation and division of Cyprus became the major issue of the 1970s, while 1980 was marked by widespread civil unrest, a deadlocked parliament and a military coup.

During the 1980s and '90s Turkey was wracked by conflict with the Kurdistan Workers' Party (PKK), fighting for the creation of a Kurdish state in the southeast.

In February 2001 the Turkish economy collapsed spectacularly, and the events of 9/11 hit the previously resilient tourist sector hard. The International Monetary Fund (IMF) pumped in funds to refloat the economy, and with the 2002 landslide election of the Justice and Development Party (AKP), things started to look up for the country. So far Prime Minister Recep Tayyip Erdoğan's regime has proved moderate and has trodden a skilful path through Turkey's minefield of vested interests. However, many Turks are wary of the party's pro-Islamic leanings; the AKP's opponents mounted a legal campaign in 2008 to close down the ruling party for persuing a nonsecular agenda; political meltdown was averted when the Constitutional Court ruled against the closure.

Accession talks with the EU began in October 2005, and the resulting concessions and development have fostered a growing optimism, although many of the country's old tensions remain. Sporadic bombings by a breakaway group of Kurdish rebels throughout Turkey – including in İstanbul (in July 2008) and coastal tourist resorts – remind us that the Kurdish problem is far from resolved.

THE CULTURE

Turkey's population consists predominantly of Turks, with a large Kurdish minority (perhaps 14 million) and much smaller groups of Laz, Hemşin, Arabs, Jews, Greeks and Armenians. Arab influence is strongest in the Antakya (Hatay) area bordering Syria. Southeastern Turkey is solidly Kurdish.

Republican Turkey has predominantly adopted a Westernised lifestyle, at least on the surface. In smaller towns and villages, particularly in the east, you might encounter a more-conservative people.

TURKEY

Things may be changing but Turkish society is still basically sexually segregated by gender, especially once you get away from the big cities and tourist resorts. Although younger Turks are questioning the old ways and women do hold positions of authority (there has even been a female prime minister), foreign women can find themselves being harassed. It's mostly just catcalls and dubious remarks, but serious assaults do occasionally occur.

Travelling with companions usually improves matters and it's worth remembering that Turkish women ignore men who speak to them in the street. Dressing appropriately (see Responsible Tourism, p1203) will also reduce unwanted attention.

ENVIRONMENT

The Dardanelles, Sea of Marmara and Bosphorus strait divide Turkey between Asia and Europe, but Eastern Thrace (European Turkey) makes up only 3% of the total land area. The remaining 97% is Anatolia, a vast plateau rising eastward towards the Caucasus Mountains.

Large parts of Turkey's 8300km-long coastline are given over to tourism.

The Aegean and Mediterranean coasts have mild, rainy winters and hot, dry summers. The Anatolian plateau can be boiling in summer and freezing in winter. The Black Sea coast is mild and humid in summer, and chilly and wet in winter.

Mountainous eastern Turkey is icy cold and snowy in winter, and only pleasantly warm

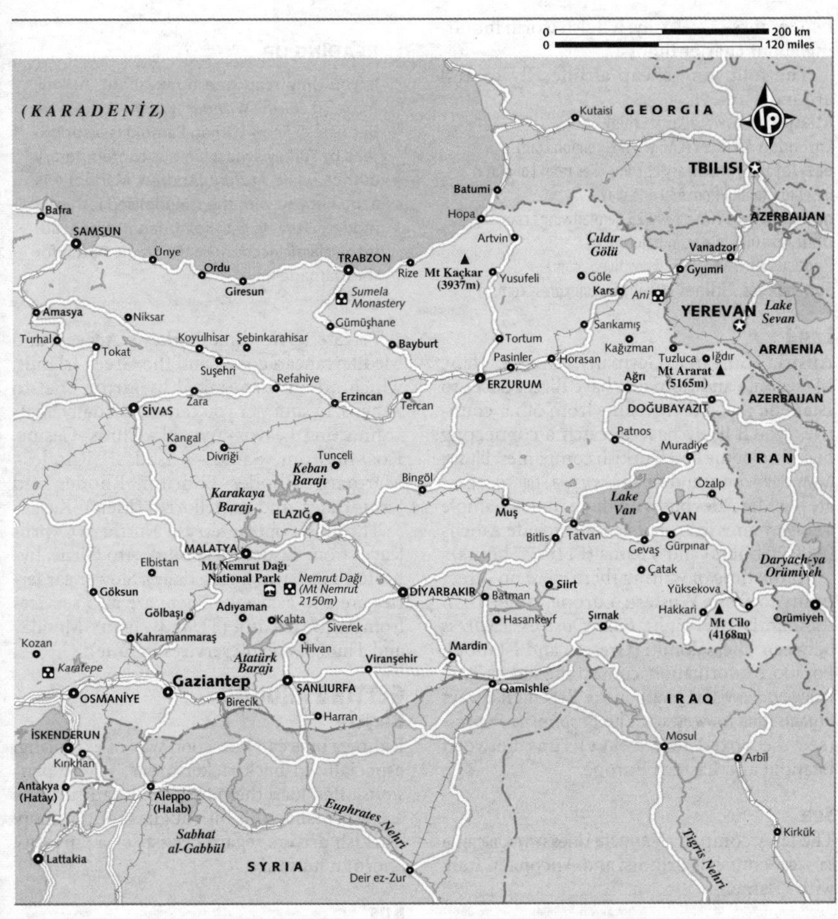

during high summer. The southeastern parts are dry and mild in winter and baking hot during summer.

There's a number of low-emission ways to get to and around Turkey, notably the train. Try an 'express' train trip like the 1000km-plus, 41-hour journey from İstanbul to Lake Van. A suggested train route from London to İstanbul is via Paris, Munich, Zagreb (Croatia) and Belgrade (Serbia), where you can join the *Bosphorus Express* (see the boxed text, p1178).

TURKEY FOR FREE

Turkey is such a richly cultural country that just wandering its streets, marvelling at the mosques and smelling the kebaps, is a great way to get a taste of the place. Top strolls are down İstanbul's vibrant Istiklal Caddesi (see p1183) and through Cappadocia's lunar valleys (see p1198).

TRANSPORT

GETTING THERE & AWAY

Air

The cheapest fares are almost always to İstanbul, but you can get cheap flights in summer to Antalya, İzmir, Bodrum and Dalaman. **Turkish Airlines** (TK; www.thy.com) and European carriers fly to İstanbul from most major European cities. If you're planning a two- or three-week stay, it's also worth inquiring about charter flights.

The following cheap airlines fly to and around Turkey:

Atlasjet (KK; www.atlastjet.com)
Corendon Airlines (CAI; www.corendon.com)
easyJet (EZY; www.easyjet.com) Flies from London & Basel to İstanbul from €30 one way.
germanwings (GWI; www25.germanwings.com)
Onur Air (OHY; www.onurair.com.tr)
Pegasus Airlines (PGT; www.flypgs.com)
Sun Express Airlines (XQ; www.sunexpress.com.tr)

Land

Austria, Bulgaria, Germany, Greece, Italy, Macedonia and Romania have direct buses to İstanbul; if you're travelling from other countries, you'll likely have to catch a connecting bus. Two of the best Turkish companies, **Ulusoy** (www.ulusoy.com.tr) and **Varan** (www.varan.com.tr), operate big Mercedes buses on these routes. Sample one-way fares to/from İstanbul include Athens (€68, 20 hours) and Vienna (€110, 27 hours).

At the time of writing there were no direct trains to/from Western Europe, other than the comfy overnight *Filia-Dostluk Express* between Thessaloniki (Greece) and İstanbul. For more information, contact the **Turkish State Railways** (www.tcdd.gov.tr) or the **Hellenic Railways Organisation** (www.ose.gr). The *Bosphorus Express* (see the boxed text, below) runs between İstanbul and Eastern Europe.

Sea

The ferry company **Marmara Lines** (www.marmaralines.com) connects Brindisi and Ancona in Italy with Çeşme.

CONNECTIONS

İstanbul is well connected to Europe. Buses leave the otogar (bus terminal) for countries including Austria, Bulgaria, Germany, Greece, Italy, Macedonia and Romania, but trains and ferries are more romantic. The most useful daily trains are the *Bosphorus Express* to Chişinău (Moldova) or Budapest (Hungary) via Bucharest (Romania), or to Belgrade (Serbia) via Bulgaria (Dimitrovgrad and Sofia); and the *Filia-Dostluk Express* to Thessaloniki (Greece). Ferries connect Turkey's Aegean and Mediterranean coasts with Greek islands, Northern Cyprus and Italy; and İstanbul with Ukraine.

READING UP

If you only read one book about Turkey, make it *Birds Without Wings (*Louis de Berniéres). *Snow* (Orhan Pamuk) is a superb read by Turkey's most famous contemporary author, while *Atatürk* (Andrew Mango) will acquaint you with the still-idolised father of modern Turkey. *Gallipoli* (Alan Moorehead) is the classic account of the tragic battle for the Dardanelles.

Private ferries link Turkey's Aegean and Mediterranean coasts and the Greek islands, which are in turn linked by air or boat to Athens. In summer you can expect daily boats connecting Lesvos–Ayvalık, Chios–Çeşme, Kos–Bodrum, Samos–Kuşadası, Rhodes–Marmaris, Rhodes–Bodrum, Rhodes and Simi–Datça, and Kastellorizo (Meis)–Kaş.

The most popular ferry to Northern Cyprus leaves from Taşucu, near Silifke (to Girne, hydrofoil TL69, two hours, daily). Slower car ferries are also available. There are also services from Alanya to Girne (TL90, 3½ hours, Monday and Thursday, extra services in June).

GETTING AROUND

Bicycle

Riding a bike can be a good way of exploring, especially in backpacker areas, where *pensions* often loan them for free. Road surfaces are acceptable, if a bit rough, though many Turkish drivers regard cyclists as a curiosity and/or a nuisance.

Bus

Turkish buses go almost everywhere, cheaply, frequently, comfortably and free of smoke. Kamil Koç, Metro, Ulusoy and Varan are the better companies, offering greater speed and comfort for slightly higher fares (plus better safety records than many rivals).

A town's otogar (bus terminal) is often outside the centre, but bus companies should offer a *servis* (free minibus) to the centre.

Local routes are usually operated by midibuses or dolmuşes (minibuses), which might run to a timetable or set off when full.

Fez Bus (Map p1184; ☎ 0212-516 9024; www.feztravel.com; Akbıyık Caddesi 15, Sultanahmet) is a hop-on, hop-off bus service linking the main resorts of the Aegean and the Mediterranean with İstanbul, Cappadocia and Nemrut Dağı.

EMERGENCY NUMBERS

Most emergency services have only Turkish-speaking operators, so your best bet is to find an English-speaking local to help.

- Ambulance ☎ 112
- Fire ☎ 110
- Police ☎ 155

Car & Motorcycle

Car hire in Turkey starts at €35 a day (insurance included). Driving can be hazardous; **Türkiye Turing ve Otomobil Kurumu** (Turkish Touring & Automobile Association; ☎ 0212-282 8140; www.turing.org.tr) can help with questions and problems. An International Driving Permit is handy, but not essential.

Hitching

Hitching is possible but not common among travellers in Turkey, and works better over short distances. Commercial vehicles are most likely to pick you up, but will expect payment. Please note Lonely Planet does not recommend hitchhiking, and women should never hitchhike alone.

Train

The **Turkish State Railways** (☎ 444 8233 nationwide; www.tcdd.gov.tr) runs services across the country. Although most people still opt for buses as train journey times are notoriously long, the system is being overhauled; the fast line between İstanbul and Ankara (6½ to 9¾ hours) is set to be followed by a similar service between the capital and Konya. The train network covers central and eastern Turkey fairly well, but doesn't travel along the coastlines at all, apart from a short stretch running between İzmir and Selçuk. The sleeper trains linking Ankara with İstanbul and İzmir are worth considering as an alternative to bus travel.

İSTANBUL

☎ 0212 / pop 16 million

İstanbul's populous neighbourhoods – dating from the Byzantine era, from the golden age of the Ottoman sultans and from recent, less-affluent times – form a dilapidated but ultimately cohesive mosaic. Here, you can retrace the steps of the Byzantine emperors when visiting Sultanahmet's monuments and museums; marvel at the magnificent Ottoman mosques on the city's seven hills; and wander the cobbled streets of ancient Jewish, Greek and Armenian neighbourhoods. Centuries of urban sprawl unfurl before your eyes on ferry trips up the Bosphorus or Golden Horn.

There has never been a better time to visit. As the possibility of a European-flavoured future is embraced in boardrooms and rooftop bars, the city's feeling of *hüzün* (melancholy) is being replaced with energy, innovation and optimism.

HISTORY

Late in the 2nd century AD the Roman Empire conquered the small city-state of Byzantium, which was renamed Constantinople in AD 330 after Emperor Constantine moved his capital there. The city walls kept out barbarians for centuries while the western part of the Roman Empire collapsed. When the city fell for the first time in 1204, it was ransacked by the loot-hungry Europeans of the misguided Fourth Crusade.

İstanbul regained its former glory only after 1453, when it was captured by Mehmet the Conqueror and made the capital of the Ottoman Empire. During the glittering reign of Süleyman the Magnificent (1520–66) the city was graced with many beautiful new buildings, and managed to retain much of its charm even during the empire's long decline.

Occupied by Allied forces after WWI, the city came to be regarded as the decadent playpen of the sultans, and when the Turkish Republic was proclaimed in 1923, Ankara became the new capital. Nevertheless, İstanbul remains a commercial, cultural and financial centre, and is still Turkey's number one city in all but name.

ORIENTATION

The Bosphorus strait, between the Black and Marmara Seas, divides European İstanbul from its Asian half. The European side is divided by the Golden Horn (Haliç) estuary into the 'newer' quarter of Beyoğlu in the north and Old İstanbul in the south; the Galata Bridge spans the two.

Sultanahmet, the heart of Old İstanbul, has the bulk of the tourist sites, exchange offices, cheap hotels and restaurants. Divan Yolu runs

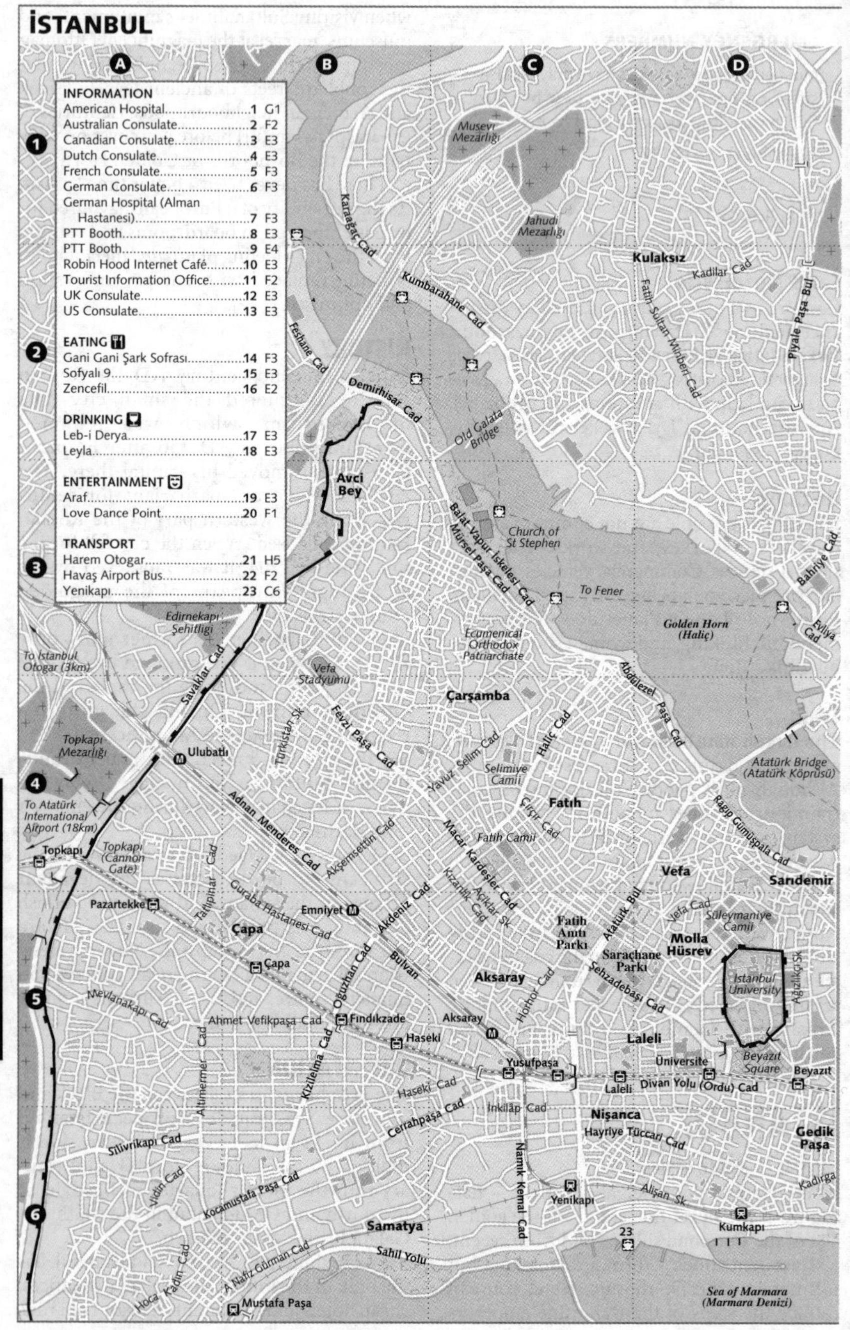
İSTANBUL
A
B
C
D
1
2
3
4
5
6
INFORMATION
American Hospital....1 G1
Australian Consulate....2 F2
Canadian Consulate....3 E3
Dutch Consulate....4 E3
French Consulate....5 F3
German Consulate....6 F3
German Hospital (Alman Hastanesi)....7 F3
PTT Booth....8 E3
PTT Booth....9 E4
Robin Hood Internet Café....10 E3
Tourist Information Office....11 F2
UK Consulate....12 E3
US Consulate....13 E3
EATING
Gani Gani Şark Sofrası....14 F3
Sofyalı 9....15 E3
Zencefil....16 E2
DRINKING
Leb-i Derya....17 E3
Leyla....18 E3
ENTERTAINMENT
Araf....19 E3
Love Dance Point....20 F1
TRANSPORT
Harem Otogar....21 H5
Havaş Airport Bus....22 F2
Yenikapı....23 C6
Musevi Mezarlığı
Jahudi Mezarlığı
Karaağaç Cad
Kumbarahane Cad
Kulaksız
Kadılar Cad
Fatih Sultan Minberi Cad
Piyale Paşa Bul
Feshane Cad
Demirhisar Cad
Old Galata Bridge
Avcı Bey
Balat Vapur İskelesi Cad
Mürsel Paşa Cad
Church of St Stephen
To Fener
Bahriye Cad
Golden Horn (Haliç)
Evliya Cad
Edirnekapı Şehitliği
To İstanbul Otogar (3km)
Savaklar Cad
Ecumenical Orthodox Patriarchate
Vefa Stadyumu
Çarşamba
Abdülezel Paşa Cad
Turkistan Sk
Feyzi Paşa Cad
Haliç Cad
Topkapı Mezarlığı
Ulubatlı
Yavuz Selim Cad
Selimiye Camii
Atatürk Bridge (Atatürk Köprüsü)
To Atatürk International Airport (18km)
Adnan Menderes Cad
Fatih
Çırçır Cad
Ragıp Gümüşpala Cad
Topkapı
Topkapı (Cannon Gate)
Akşemsettin Cad
Macar Kardeşler Cad
Fatih Camii
Kızanlık Cad
Açıklar Sk
Vefa
Sarıdemir
Pazartekke
Taftipınar Cad
Guraba Hastanesi Cad
Emniyet
Akdeniz Cad
Fatih Anıtı Parkı
Atatürk Bul
Vefa Cad
Süleymaniye Camii
Çapa
Oğuzhan Cad
Bulvarı
Saraçhane Parkı
Molla Hüsrev
İstanbul University
Ağızlıkçı Sk
Mevlanakapı Cad
Aksaray
Horhor Cad
Şehzadebaşı Cad
Ahmet Vefikpaşa Cad
Fındıkzade
Haseki
Laleli
Altımermer Cad
Kızılelma Cad
Yusufpaşa
Beyazıt Square
Üniversite
Beyazıt
Divan Yolu (Ordu) Cad
Haseki Cad
Cerrahpaşa Cad
İnkılâp Cad
Nişanca
Hayriye Tüccarı Cad
Gedik Paşa
Silivrikapı Cad
Namık Kemal Cad
Yıldız Cad
Kocamustafa Paşa Cad
Yenikapı
Alişan Sk
Kadırga
Samatya
23
Kumkapı
Sahil Yolu
A Nafiz Gürman Cad
Hoca Kadın Cad
Mustafa Paşa
Sea of Marmara (Marmara Denizi)

TURKEY

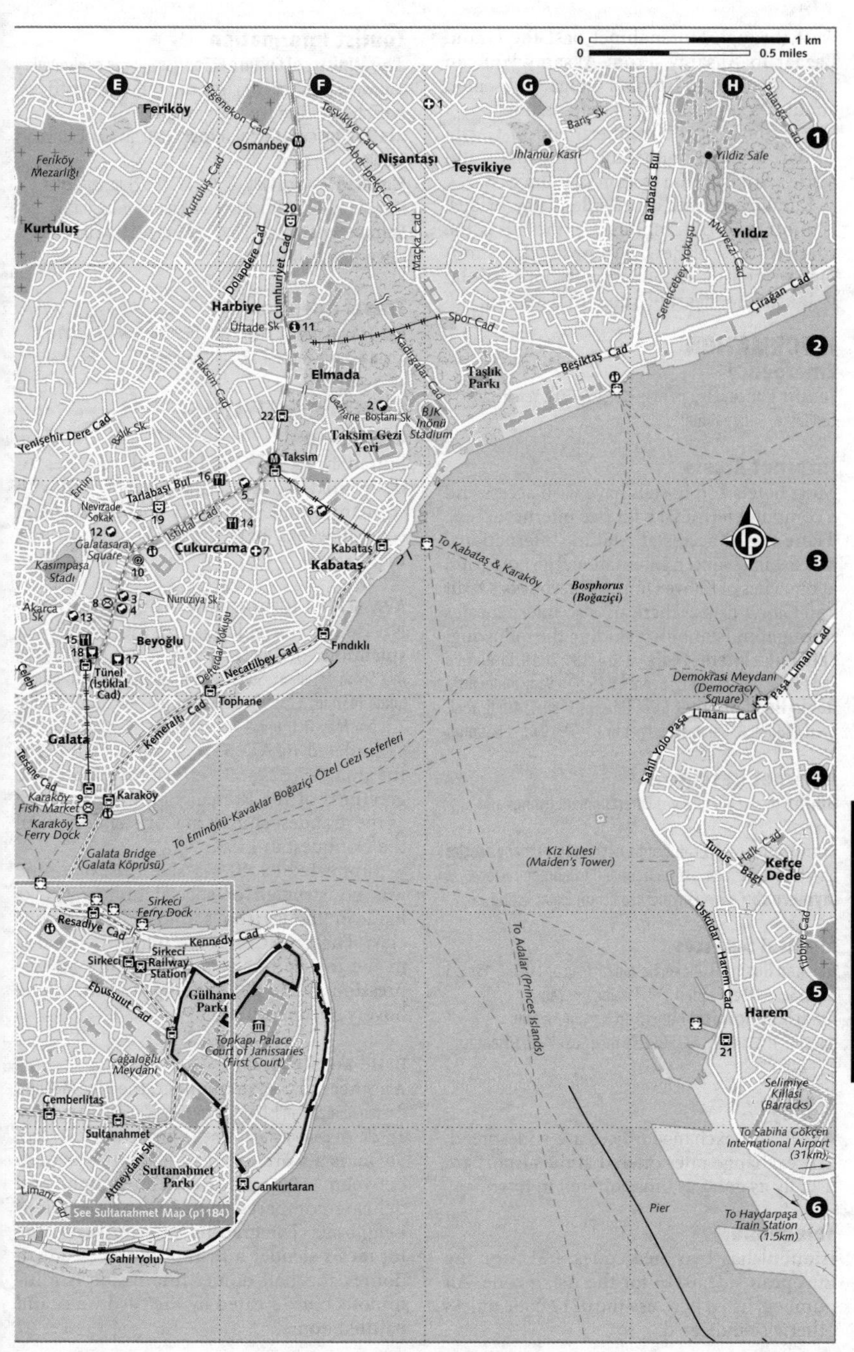
0 1 km
0 0.5 miles
E
F
G
H
1
2
3
4
5
6
Feriköy
Ergenekon Cad
Osmanbey
Teşvikiye Cad
Abdi İpekçi Cad
Nişantaşı
Teşvikiye
Barış Sk
Ihlamur Kasri
Palanga Cad
Yildiz Sale
Barbaros Bul
Yıldız
Müvezzi Cad
Serencebey Yokuşu
Feriköy Mezarlığı
Kurtuluş
Kurtuluş Cad
Dolapdere Cad
Cumhuriyet Cad
Maçka Cad
Harbiye
Üftade Sk
Spor Cad
Çırağan Cad
Kadırgalar Cad
Elmada
Taşlık Parkı
Beşiktaş Cad
Taksim Cad
Gazhane Bostanı Sk
BJK İnönü Stadium
Taksim Gezi Yeri
Yenişehir Dere Cad
Balık Sk
Taksim
Emin
Tarlabaşı Bul
Nevizade Sokak
İstiklal Cad
Galatasaray Square
Çukurcuma
Kabataş
To Kabataş & Karaköy
Kasimpaşa Stadı
Nuruziya Sk
Bosphorus (Boğaziçi)
Akarca Sk
Beyoğlu
Defterdar Yokuşu
Fındıklı
Tünel (İstiklal Cad)
Necatilbey Cad
Çelebi
Tophane
Kemeraltı Cad
Demokrasi Meydanı (Democracy Square)
Paşa Limanı Cad
Sahil Yolo Paşa Limanı Cad
Galata
Tersane Cad
To Eminönü-Kavaklar Boğaziçi Özel Gezi Seferleri
Karaköy
Karaköy Fish Market
Karaköy Ferry Dock
Galata Bridge (Galata Köprüsü)
Kiz Kulesi (Maiden's Tower)
Tunus Bagi
Halk Cad
Kefçe Dede
Sirkeci Ferry Dock
Resadiye Cad
Kennedy Cad
Sirkeci
Sirkeci Railway Station
Üsküdar - Harem Cad
Tıbbiye Cad
Ebussuut Cad
Gülhane Parkı
To Adalar (Princes Islands)
Harem
Topkapı Palace Court of Janissaries (First Court)
Cağaloğlu Meydanı
Selimiye Kilası (Barracks)
Çemberlitaş
Sultanahmet
To Sabiha Gökçen International Airport (31km)
Atmeydanı Sk
Sultanahmet Parkı
Cankurtaran
Limanı Cad
See Sultanahmet Map (p1184)
Pier
To Haydarpaşa Train Station (1.5km)
(Sahil Yolu)
TURKEY

west through Sultanahmet past the Grand Bazaar to Aksaray. From Aksaray you can catch the train to İstanbul Otogar at Esenler, about 10km northwest of Sultanahmet.

Eminönü, at the southern end of Galata Bridge, is the terminus for many buses and ferries. Sirkeci train station is 100m east.

Karaköy, on the other side of the bridge, is another ferry terminus. Up the hill is the southern end of Beyoğlu's pedestrian shopping street, İstiklal Caddesi; at its northern end is Taksim Sq, heart of 'modern' İstanbul.

INFORMATION

Emergency

Tourist Police (Map p1184; ☎ 527 4503; Yerebatan Caddesi 6, Sultanahmet)

Internet Access

Most hotels and hostels have wi-fi access and a computer terminal with free internet access. There's wi-fi access at Atatürk International and Sabiha Gökçen International airports, and at branches of Kahve Dünyası, Starbucks, Ozsüt and Gloria Jeans. There are also internet cafes throughout İstanbul, including the following:

Café Turka Internet Café (Map p1184; 2nd fl, Divan Yolu Caddesi 22, Sultanahmet; per hr €1.25; 9am-midnight)

Robin Hood Internet Café (Map pp1180-1; 4th fl, Yeni Çarşı Caddesi 8, Galatasaray; per hr €1; 9am-11.30pm)

Internet Resources

Biletix (www.biletix.com) Entertainment listings and tickets.

Cornucopia (www.cornucopia.net) Features many articles on İstanbul, including restaurant and exhibition reviews.

Mymerhaba (www.mymerhaba.com) Expat listings.

Medical Services

German Hospital (Alman Hastanesi; Map pp1180-1; ☎ 293 2150; Sıraselviler Caddesi 119, Taksim; 24hr)

American Hospital (Amerikan Hastanesi; Map pp1180-1; ☎ 444 3777; Güzelbahçe Sokak 20, Nişantaşı; 24hr)

Money

ATMs and exchange offices are widespread. The exchange rates offered at the airport are usually as good as those offered in town.

Telephone

İstanbul has two area codes: 0212 for the European side, 0216 for the Asian zone. All numbers listed here use the 0212 code unless otherwise indicated.

Tourist Information

The **Ministry of Culture & Tourism** (www.tourismturkey.org, www.turizm.gov.tr) runs the following offices, which provide free city maps:

Atatürk International Airport (International Arrivals Terminal; 24hr)

Elmadağ (Map pp1180-1; ☎ 233 0592) Just off Cumhuriyet Caddesi, a 10-minute walk north of Taksim Sq.

Sultanahmet (Map p1184; ☎ 518 8754) At the northeast end of the Hippodrome.

Travel Agencies

Fez Travel (Map p1184; ☎ 516 9024; www.feztravel.com; Akbıyık Caddesi 15, Sultanahmet)

SIGHTS & ACTIVITIES

Old İstanbul

Sultanahmet is 'Old İstanbul', a Unesco-designated World Heritage site packed with so many wonderful sights you could spend several weeks here and still only scratch the surface.

AYA SOFYA (CHURCH OF HOLY WISDOM)

No doubt you will gasp at the overblown splendour of **Aya Sofya** (Map p1184; ☎ 522 0989; Aya Sofya Meydanı, Sultanahmet; admission €10, official guide (45min) €25; 9am-5pm Tue-Sun Nov-Apr, until 7.30pm May-Oct, upper gallery closes 15-30min earlier). Completed in AD 537, as part of Emperor Justinian's (527–65) effort to restore the greatness of the Roman Empire, it reigned as the grandest church in Christendom until the Conquest in 1453.

Supported by 40 massive ribs, its dome was constructed of special hollow bricks made in Rhodes from a unique, light, porous clay. These rest on huge pillars concealed in the interior walls, which creates an impression inside the building that the dome hovers unsupported.

BLUE MOSQUE

Another striking monument, the **Blue Mosque** (Sultan Ahmet Camii; Map p1184; Hippodrome, Sultanahmet; closed during prayer times), just south of Aya Sofya, is a work of art in itself. It was built between 1606 and 1616, and is light and delicate compared with its squat, ancient neighbour. The graceful exterior is notable for its six slender minarets and a cascade of domes and half domes; the inside is a luminous blue, created by the tiled walls and painted dome.

TOPKAPI PALACE

Possibly the most iconic monument in İstanbul, the opulent **Topkapı Palace** (Topkapı Sarayı; Map p1184; ☎ 512 0480; www.topkapisarayi.gov.tr/eng; Babıhümayun Caddesi; admission palace/harem €10/7.50; ⏰ 9am-7pm Wed-Mon summer, 9am-5pm winter) is a highlight of any trip. The palace was begun by Mehmet shortly after the Conquest in 1453, and Ottoman sultans lived in this impressive environment until the 19th century. It consists of four massive courtyards and a series of imperial buildings, including pavilions, barracks, audience chambers and sleeping quarters. Make sure you visit the mind-blowing **harem**, the palace's most famous sight, and the **Treasury**, which features an incredible collection of precious objects.

GRAND BAZAAR

Just north of Divan Yolu is the **Grand Bazaar** (Kapalı Çarşı; Map p1184; ⏰ 9am-7pm Mon-Sat), a labyrinthine medieval shopping mall also known as the Covered Market. With some 4000 shops selling everything from carpets to clothing, including silverware, jewellery, antiques and belly-dancing costumes, it's a fun place to wander around and get lost – which you can bet your *arasta* you will!

BASILICA CISTERN

Across the tram lines from Aya Sofya is the entrance to this majestic Byzantine **Basilica Cistern** (Yerebatan Sarnıçı; Map p1184; ☎ 522 1259; Yerebatan Caddesi 13, Sultanahmet; admission €5; ⏰ 9am-6.30pm Apr-Sep, to 5.30pm Oct-Mar), built by Justinian in AD 532. This vast, atmospheric, column-filled cistern stored up to 80,000 cubic metres of water for regular summer use in the Great Palace, as well as for times of siege.

İSTANBUL ARCHAEOLOGY MUSEUM

Downhill from the Topkapı Palace, this superb **museum complex** (Arkeoloji Müzeleri; Map p1184; ☎ 520 7740; Osman Hamdi Bey Yokuşu, Gülhane; admission €5; ⏰ 9am-5pm Tue-Sun) is a must-see for anyone interested in the Middle East's ancient past. The main building houses an outstanding collection of Greek and Roman statuary, including the magnificent sarcophagi from the royal necropolis at Sidon in Lebanon. A separate building on the same site, the **Museum of the Ancient Orient**, houses Hittite relics and other older archaeological finds.

The Bosphorus

Don't leave the city without exploring the Bosphorus. Most day-trippers take the much-loved **Public Bosphorus Excursion Ferry** (one way/return €5/9; ⏰ 10.35am year-round, noon & 1.35pm mid-Apr-Oct), which ferries up its entire length. These depart from Eminönü (Map p1184) and stop at various points en route to Anadolu Kavağı (the turnaround point). The shores are sprinkled with sights, including the monumental Dolmabahçe Palace, the majestic Bosphorus Bridge, the waterside suburbs of Arnavutköy, Bebek, Kanlıca, Emirgan and Sarıyer, as well as lavish *yalıs* (waterfront wooden summer residences) and numerous mosques.

Beyoğlu

Beyoğlu (Map pp1180–1) is the heart of modern İstanbul, ground-zero for galleries, cafes and boutiques, with hip new restaurants opening almost nightly, and enough bars to quench a dedicated drinker's thirst. It's a showcase of cosmopolitan Turkey at its best – miss Beyoğlu and you haven't seen İstanbul.

Stretching from Tünel Sq to Taksim Sq, **Istiklal Caddesi** (Independence Ave; Map pp1180–1) was known in the late 19th century as the Grand Rue de Péra, carrying the life of the modern city up and down its lively promenade. It's still the life and soul of the party, and a stroll along its length is a must.

TOURS

Kirkit Voyage (Map p1184; ☎ 518 2282; www.kirkit.com; Amiral Tafdil Sokak 12, Sultanahmet; half- & full-day tours €23-50) specialises in small-group walking tours of the must-see sights.

SLEEPING

İstanbul's accommodation is becoming quite pricey, but the best area to stay remains Cankurtaran, where the quiet streets have moderate hotels and more-luxurious options,

SPLURGE

Hotel Empress Zoe (Map p1184; ☎ 518 2504; www.emzoe.com; Adliye Sokak 10, Cankurtaran; s €55-75, d €65-135, ste €120-240; ☒ ❄ 💻) Individually decorated rooms in adjoining buildings share a gorgeous flower-filled garden, where breakfast is served, and a rooftop lounge-terrace with terrific views. Book well ahead.

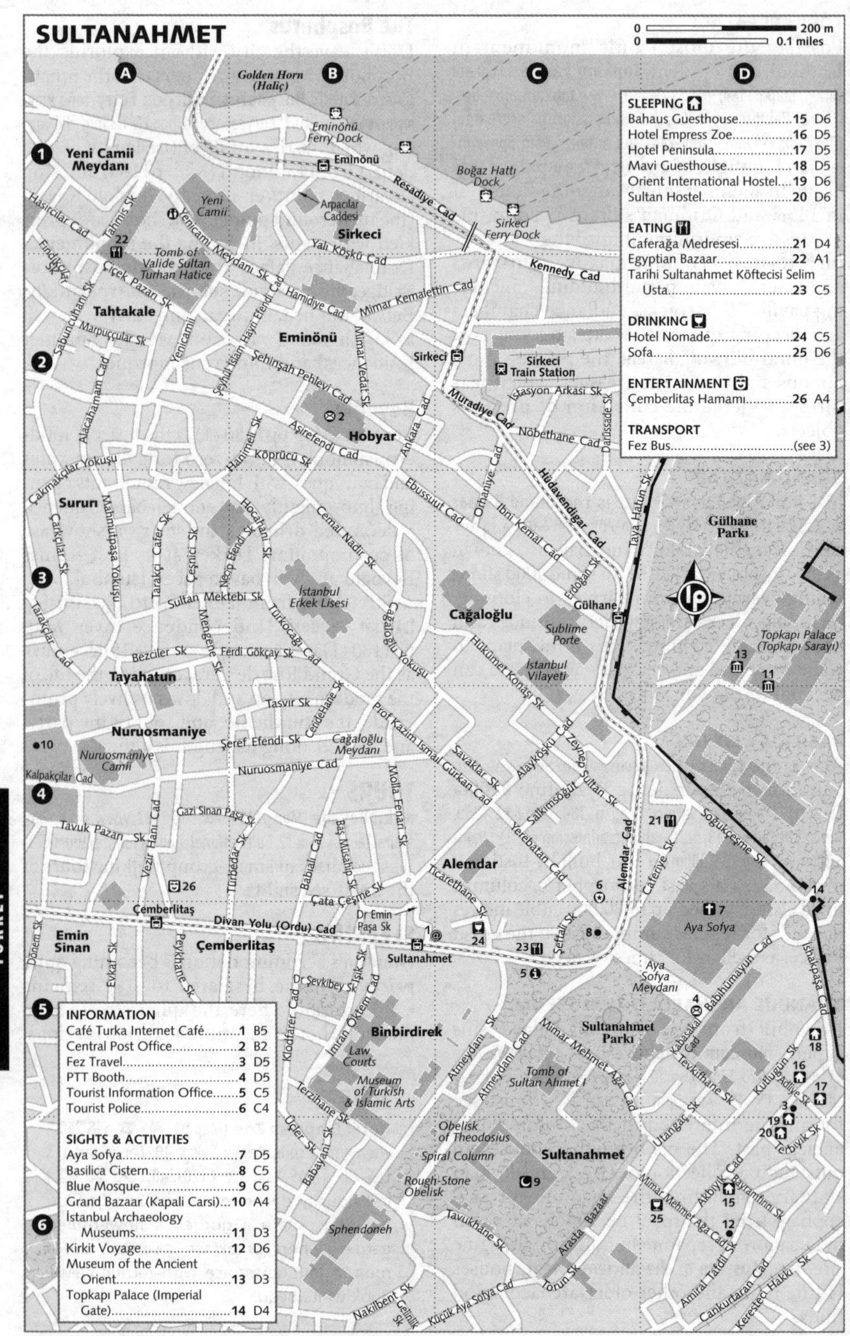
SULTANAHMET
0 200 m
0 0.1 miles
Golden Horn (Haliç)
Eminönü Ferry Dock
Eminönü
Boğaz Hattı Dock
Sirkeci Ferry Dock
Yeni Camii Meydanı
Yeni Camii
Arpacılar Caddesi
Sirkeci
Tomb of Valide Sultan Turhan Hatice
Tahtakale
Eminönü
Sirkeci
Sirkeci Train Station
Hobyar
Sururı
Gülhane Parkı
İstanbul Erkek Lisesi
Cağaloğlu
Sublime Porte
İstanbul Vilayeti
Gülhane
Topkapı Palace (Topkapı Sarayı)
Tayahatun
Nuruosmaniye
Nuruosmaniye Camii
Cağaloğlu Meydanı
Alemdar
Aya Sofya
Emin Sinan
Çemberlitaş
Sultanahmet
Aya Sofya Meydanı
Binbirdirek
Law Courts
Museum of Turkish & Islamic Arts
Sultanahmet Parkı
Tomb of Sultan Ahmet I
Obelisk of Theodosius
Spiral Column
Rough-Stone Obelisk
Sultanahmet
Sphendoneh
Divan Yolu (Ordu) Cad
Kennedy Cad
Reşadiye Cad
Hüdavendigar Cad
Muradiye Cad
Alemdar Cad
Arasta Bazaar
SLEEPING
Bahaus Guesthouse....15 D6
Hotel Empress Zoe....16 D5
Hotel Peninsula....17 D5
Mavi Guesthouse....18 D5
Orient International Hostel....19 D6
Sultan Hostel....20 D6
EATING
Caferağa Medresesi....21 D4
Egyptian Bazaar....22 A1
Tarihi Sultanahmet Köftecisi Selim Usta....23 C5
DRINKING
Hotel Nomade....24 C5
Sofa....25 D6
ENTERTAINMENT
Çemberlitaş Hamamı....26 A4
TRANSPORT
Fez Bus....(see 3)
INFORMATION
Café Turka Internet Café....1 B5
Central Post Office....2 B2
Fez Travel....3 D5
PTT Booth....4 D5
Tourist Information Office....5 C5
Tourist Police....6 C4
SIGHTS & ACTIVITIES
Aya Sofya....7 D5
Basilica Cistern....8 C5
Blue Mosque....9 C6
Grand Bazaar (Kapali Carsi)....10 A4
İstanbul Archaeology Museums....11 D3
Kirkit Voyage....12 D6
Museum of the Ancient Orient....13 D3
Topkapı Palace (Imperial Gate)....14 D4

GETTING INTO TOWN

Getting from the Atatürk International Airport (off Map pp1180–1) to Sultanahmet by public transport is cheap and easy. Take the LRT service from the airport six stops to Zeytinburnu (€0.70), from where you connect with the tram that takes you directly to Sultanahmet (€0.70) – about 50 minutes all up. Shuttle buses also operate, including the Havaş airport bus (€5, 35 minutes to one hour, half-hourly), which goes to Taksim Sq. Sultanahmet travel agencies and hostels book minibuses in the other direction for around €5 a head. A taxi between the airport and Sultanahmet or Taksim Sq costs about €17.50, more between midnight and 6am or if there's heavy traffic.

Sabiha Gökçen International Airport (off Map pp1180–1) is less convenient. The Havaş airport bus connects it to Taksim Sq (€5, one to 1½ hours, hourly); Sultanahmet travel agencies and hostels book minibuses to the airport for around €15 a head. A taxi to/from Sultanahmet costs at least €40.

with stunning views from their roof terraces. Unless otherwise stated, rates include breakfast and private bathrooms; the exception is hostel dorms, which have shared bathrooms. Private rooms are overpriced at some of these options.

Camping is inconvenient and costs about as much as staying in a cheap hotel, with transport fares on top.

Mavı Guesthouse (Map p1184; ☎ 517 7287; www.maviguesthouse.com; Kutlugün Sokak 3, Sultanahmet; rooftop mattress/dm/d €8/12/36; 💻) Tiny Mavi's management is very friendly, which is just as well since some of its rooms are cramped and windowless, with uncomfortable beds. There are 24 mattresses on the decrepit rooftop.

Sultan Hostel (Map p1184; ☎ 516 9260; www.sultanhostel.com; Akbıyık Caddesi 21, Cankurtaran; dm €14, d with shared/private bathroom €38/44; ☒ 💻) The Sultan offers freshly painted dorms with new bunks and good mattresses, and a 10% discount for HI cardholders.

Orient International Hostel (Map p1184; ☎ 518 0789; www.orienthostel.com; Akbıyık Caddesi 13, Cankurtaran; dm €14, s with shared bathroom €30, d with private bathroom €70; ☒ 💻) Bursting with backpackers, the Orient should only be considered if you don't care about creature comforts and are ready to party. There's a shower for every 12 guests and dorms range from light and quiet to dark and uncomfortable.

Bahaus Guesthouse (Map p1184; ☎ 638 6534; www.travelinistanbul.com; Akbıyık Caddesi, Bayramfırını Sokak No 11/13; dm €15, d with shared/private bathroom €40/50; ☒ 💻) Generating great word of mouth, Bahaus' friendly and knowledgeable staff run a professional operation that avoids the institutional feel of some of its nearby competitors. The rooftop terrace bar gets top marks.

our pick Hotel Peninsula (Map p1184; ☎ 458 6850; www.hotelpeninsula.com; Adliye Sokak 6, Cankurtaran; s/d €35/45; ☒ ❄) This unassuming, super-friendly hotel has 12 comfortable rooms with private bathrooms, plus a lovely terrace with sea views and comfortable hammocks.

EATING

Teeming with affordable fast-food joints, cafes and restaurants, İstanbul is a food-lover's paradise. Sultanahmet has the least impressive range of eating options in the city, so we recommend crossing the Galata Bridge to join the locals. For fresh and dried fruit, nuts and Turkish delight head to the **Egyptian Bazaar** (Mısır Çarşısı; Map p1184).

Caferağa Medresesi (Map p1184; ☎ 513 3601; Caferiye Sokak; soup €1.50, köfte €5) This teensy *lokanta* (restaurant) in the courtyard of a medrese near Topkapı Palace is a rare treat in Sultanahmet, allowing you to nosh in stylish surrounds without paying through the nose.

Tarihi Sultanahmet Köftecisi Selim Usta (Map p1184; ☎ 520 0566; Divan Yolu Caddesi 12) Beware the other *köfte* (meatballs) places along this strip purporting to be the *meşhur* (famous) *köfte* restaurant; No 12 is the real McCoy.

our pick Gani Gani Şark Sofrası (Map pp1180-1; ☎ 244 8401; www.naumpasakonagi.com; Taksim Kuyu Sokak 11; pides €3.50-4.75, kebaps €3.75-5) Young Turkish couples love lolling on the traditional Anatolian seating

SPLURGE

Sofyalı 9 (Map pp1180-1; ☎ 245 0362; Sofyalı Sokak 9, Tünel; meze €2-4, mains €5-8; 🕑 11am-1am Mon-Sat) Sample some of the city's best *meyhane* (tavern) food – notably the *Arnavut ciğeri* (Albanian fried liver), fried fish and meze – in surroundings as welcoming as they are attractive. Tables are hot property at weekends.

TURKEY

at this cheap and friendly eatery. Tables and chairs are also available to enjoy the kebaps, *mantı* (Turkish ravioli) and pide.

Zencefil (Map pp1180-1; ☎ 243 8234; Kurabiye Sokak 8; mains €5-6) Comfortable and quietly stylish, this popular vegetarian cafe offers crunchy-fresh organic produce, homemade bread and guilt-free desserts.

DRINKING & CLUBBING

The Sultanahmet bar scene is concentrated on Akbıyık Caddesi, catering to the denizens of the surrounding hostels. Dedicated bar- and club-goers should seek out the byways of Beyoğlu, where streets such as **Nevizade Sokak** (Map pp1180–1) are crammed with raucous, rakı-and-meze-serving *meyhanes* (taverns).

To check out the city's vistas and hipsters, head to Beyoğlu's rooftops. Although the bars and clubs here are cheaper than the superclubs along the Bosphorus, drinks average €7.50 to €10 and you should don your finest threads.

Note that some parts of Beyoğlu can be pretty seedy. Ignore 'friendly' locals who try to lure you into trouble with promises of free drinks etc.

Sofa (Map p1184; ☎ 458 3630; Mimar Mehmet Ağa Caddesi 32, Cankurtaran; 🕑 11am-11pm) Candlelit tables beckon patrons into this friendly cafe/bar just off Akbıyık Caddesi, with a daily happy hour between 5pm and 6.30pm.

Hotel Nomade (Map p1184; ☎ 513 8172; Ticarethane Sokak 15, Alemdar; 🕑 noon-11pm) This boutique hotel's terrace bar overlooks Aya Sofya and the Blue Mosque. Settle down in a comfortable chair to enjoy a glass of wine, beer or freshly squeezed fruit juice.

Leyla (Map pp1180-1; ☎ 245 4028; Tünel Sq 186A, Tünel; 🕑 7am-2am) With a great location opposite the Tünel entrance, trendy Leyla is a popular meeting place.

Leb-i Derya (Map pp1180-1; ☎ 244 1886; www.lebiderya.com; 7th fl, Kumbaracı Yokuşu 115, Tünel; 🕑 11am-2am Mon-Fri, 8.30am-3am Sat & Sun) This unpretentious place, on the top floor of a dishevelled building off İstiklal Caddesi, is an İstanbul favourite for its Bosphorus and Old City views.

Beyoğlu's nightclubs include **Araf** (Map pp1180-1; ☎ 244 8301; 5th fl, Balo Sokak 32; no cover charge; 🕑 5pm-4am), popular among English teachers and Turkish-language students for its in-house Gypsy band and cheap beer; and the gay club **Love Dance Point** (Map pp1180-1; ☎ 296 3357; www.lovedancepoint.com; Cumhuriyet Caddesi 349/1, Harbiye; admission €15 incl 1 drink; 🕑 11.30pm-4am Wed, 11.30pm-5am Fri & Sat).

ENTERTAINMENT

The city's most interesting historical *hamams* (Turkish baths) are pricey and touristy, but are worth visiting nonetheless. The Ottoman **Çemberlitaş Hamamı** (Map p1184; ☎ 522 7974; www.cemberlitashamami.com.tr; Vezir Hanı Caddesi 8, Çemberlitaş; bath services €14.50-39.50; 🕑 6am-midnight) is one of İstanbul's most atmospheric *hamams*.

GETTING THERE & AWAY

Air

İstanbul's busiest international airport is the **Atatürk International Airport** (off Map pp1180-1; IST; ☎ 465 5555; www.ataturkairport.com), 23km west of Sultanahmet. **Sabiha Gökçen International Airport** (off Map pp1180-1; SAW; ☎ 0216-585 5000; www.sgairport.com), some 50km east of Sultanahmet, on the Asian side of the city, is increasingly popular for cheap flights from Europe.

Boat

Yenikapı (Map pp1180–1), south of Aksaray Sq, is the dock for fast ferries across the Sea of Marmara to Yalova, Bursa and Bandırma.

Bus

At Esenler, İstanbul Otogar (off Map pp1180–1) is a monster, with 150-plus ticket offices and buses leaving for all parts of Turkey and beyond. Buses depart for Ankara (€12.50 to €22, six hours) about every 30 minutes; from dawn till dusk, you rarely have to wait longer than that for departures to other cities.

There is a much smaller bus station on the Asian shore at Harem (Map pp1180–1). If you're arriving by bus from anywhere in Anatolia (the Asian side of Turkey), it's quicker to get out at Harem and take the car ferry to Sirkeci/Eminönü (€0.70), which runs between 7am and 9.30pm daily.

Train

The train station for services to Edirne, Greece and Eastern Europe is Sirkeci (Map p1184). The twice-daily *Dostluk/Filia Express* is an excellent service between Thessaloniki (Greece) and İstanbul (from €50, 12 hours).

On the Asian shore, Haydarpaşa (off Map pp1180–1) is the terminus for trains to Anatolia, Syria and Iran. Several express trains a day run to Ankara (€4.50 to €36, seven to 10 hours), but the Turkish coast is not well served.

GETTING AROUND

Boat

The cheapest and pleasantest way to negotiate İstanbul is by ferry. Short ferry hops cost €0.70. The main ferry docks are located at the mouth of the Golden Horn (Map p1184; Eminönü, Sirkeci and Karaköy) and at Beşiktaş, a few kilometres northeast of the Galata Bridge, south of Dolmabahçe Palace.

Bus

İstanbul's efficient bus system has major stations at Taksim Sq, Beşiktaş, Aksaray, Rüstempaşa-Eminönü, Kadıköy and Üsküdar, with most services running between 6.30am and 11.30pm. You must have a ticket (€0.70) before boarding; stock up at the white booths near major stops, and at some shops.

Funicular Railway

The Tünel (Map pp1180–1), İstanbul's 19th-century funicular system, mounts the hill from Karaköy to Tünel Meydanı and İstiklal Caddesi (€0.70, 7am to 9pm).

A new funicular railway (Map pp1180–1) runs from the Bosphorus shore at Kabataş up the hill to Taksim Sq (€0.70, around every three minutes).

Light Rail Transit (LRT)

A LRT service connects Aksaray with the airport, stopping at 15 stations including the otogar along the way. It departs every 10 minutes or so from 5.40am until 1.40am and costs €0.70.

Taxi

İstanbul is full of yellow taxis, all of them with meters (although not every driver wants to run them). A trip from Sultanahmet to Taksim Sq costs around €5.

Train

Suburban trains from Sirkeci (€0.70) run along the southern walls of Old İstanbul and the Marmara shore at least twice an hour.

Outside the main entrance to Sirkeci station there is a convenient tram that runs up the hill to Sultanahmet, or over the Golden Horn to Kabataş, from which point you can travel by funicular rail to Taksim Sq. Haydarpaşa station is connected by ferry to Karaköy and Eminönü (€0.70, at least every half hour).

Tram

The excellent *tramvay* (tramway) service runs between Kabataş and Zeytinburnu (from where you can catch the LRT to Atatürk International Airport) via Karaköy, Eminönü and Sultanahmet. Tickets cost €0.70.

AEGEAN COAST

Turkey's Aegean coast can convincingly claim more ancient ruins per square kilometre than any other region in the world. Here you'll see the famous ruins of Troy, Ephesus and Bergama (Pergamum), and here you can contemplate the devastation of war at the battlefield sites of Gallipoli. Ruins aside, it isn't as scenic as the Med, but it doesn't have as many resort developments either – a definite plus for independent travellers.

GALLIPOLI (GELIBOLU)

To most Europeans Gallipoli (Gelibolu) is little more than a footnote in WWI events, but to generations of Turks, Australians and New Zealanders, the battle for the Dardanelles was one of the most poignant chapters in the war. On 25 April 1915 the first Anzac (Australia and New Zealand Army Corps), British and Indian troops landed on the Gallipoli peninsula, hoping for a quick victory against Turkish defences. However, strategic blunders turned the operation into a protracted stalemate, and after nine months of horrendous casualties the Allied forces withdrew.

The Turkish officer responsible for the defence of Gallipoli was none other than Mustafa Kemal, later Atatürk, and his success is commemorated in Turkey on 18 March. The big draw for most foreign travellers, however, is Anzac Day on 25 April, when a dawn service commemorates the anniversary of the Allied landings, attracting thousands of travellers from Australia and beyond.

The scenic peninsula is now a national park, scattered with moving memorials to the dead of the various nations that fought here. If time is tight, the easiest way to see the sights is on a minibus tour from Çanakkale with **Hassle Free Tours** (☎ 0286-213 5969; www.hasslefreetour.com; €22.50-27.50) or **Trooper Tours** (☎ 0286-217 3343; www.troopertours.com; €27.50). If you're less pressed, it's cheaper to take a ferry from Çanakkale to Eceabat across the strait and a dolmuş to the Kabatepe Information Centre & Museum (3.5km south of Anzac Cove), then follow the heritage trail.

You could also stay at Eceabat, on the Thracian (European) side of the strait. **TJs Hotel** (☎ 0286-814 2458; www.anzacgallipolitours.com; Cumhuriyet Meydanı 2/A; dm €7.50, s/d €25/35; P ✖ 💻) has rooms to suit every budget, and also runs its own highly rated tours.

Hourly car ferries cross the strait from Çanakkale to Eceabat (€1). In summer there are several dolmuşes daily from Eceabat to the ferry dock at Kabatepe (€1, 15 minutes). These can drop you at the Kabatepe Information Centre & Museum, or at the base of the road up to Lone Pine and Chunuk Bair.

ÇANAKKALE

☎ 0286 / pop 86,600

The liveliest settlement on the Dardanelles, this sprawling harbour town would be worth a visit for its sights, nightlife and overall vibe even if it didn't lie opposite the Gallipoli Peninsula. A good base for visiting Troy, it has become a popular destination for weekending Turks; if possible, visit midweek.

Information

Maxi Internet (Fetvane Sokak 51; per hr €0.75; 🕑 10am-1am)

Tourist office (☎ 217 1187; 🕑 8am-noon & 1-7pm Jun-Sep, to 5pm Oct-May) Near the ferry pier.

Sights

A park in the military zone at the southern end of the quay houses the **Military Museum** (Askeri Müze; admission €1.50; 🕑 9am-noon & 1.30-5pm Tue, Wed & Fri-Sun) and the Ottoman **Çimenlik Kalesi** (Meadow Castle). Just over 2km south of the ferry pier, on the road to Troy, the **Archaeological Museum** (Arkeoloji Müzesi; admission €2.50; 🕑 8am-5pm) holds artefacts found at Troy and Assos.

Sleeping & Eating

Çanakkale has hotels to suit all pockets, except on Anzac Day, when prices skyrocket. If you do intend to be in town around 25 April, you should book months in advance.

Anzac House Hostel (☎ 213 5969; www.anzachouse.com; 59-61 Cumhuriyet Meydanı; dm €8, s/d/tr with shared bathroom €14/20/27; 💻) Not to be confused with the three-star Anzac Hotel, central, cheap Anzac House is the main backpacker haunt.

Efes Hotel (☎ 217 3256; www.efeshotelcanakkale.com; Aralık Sokak 5; s/d €15/25; ⊠ ✖) An excellent budget choice, with cheery decor and a welcoming owner. The best rooms have open showers and orthopaedic mattresses. The breakfasts are great, and there's a little garden with a fountain.

Stalls along the *kordon* (esplanade) peddle simple fare such as *peynir helvaş*, a local speciality made with soft white village cheese, flour, butter and sugar.

Köy Evi (☎ 213 4687; Yalı Caddesi 13; menu €2.50; 🕑 8am-midnight) Proper home cooking rules in this tiny eatery, where local women make *mantı*, *börek* (filled pastry) and *gözleme* (savoury crepe).

Getting There & Away

There are regular buses to İstanbul (€15, six hours) and İzmir (€15, 5½ hours). Dolmuşes to Troy (€2, 35 minutes) leave from the station at the northern end of the bridge over the Sarı River.

TROY

Of all the ancient sites in Turkey, the remains of the great city of Troy are in fact among the least impressive. You'll have to work hard to imagine the fateful day when the Greeks tricked the Trojans by hiding soldiers inside a wooden horse. However, the ruins are an important stop for history buffs, and if you have read about the original Trojan horse in Virgil's *The Aeneid*, they have a romance few places on Earth can match.

To get the most out of a visit to the **site** (☎ 0286-283 0536; admission per person/car €7.50/1.50; 🕑 8.30am-7pm May-15 Sep, to 5pm 16 Sep-end Apr) it's worth hiring a guide (€50, 1½ hours). Inquire at the ticket booth or restaurants or email **Mustafa Askin** (thetroyguide@hotmail.com), author of one of the guidebooks sold at the souvenir shops.

Hassle Free Tours (☎ 0286-213 5969; www.hasslefreetour.com) and **Trooper Tours** (☎ 0286-217 3343; www.troopertours.com), amongst others, offer tours of Troy (around €25 per person).

Hourly dolmuşes run from Çanakkale (€2, 35 minutes).

BERGAMA

☎ 0232 / pop 58,210

A workaday market town, Bergama has become a major stop on the tourist trail because of its proximity to the remarkable ruins of Pergamum, site of Ancient Rome's preeminent medical centre. During Pergamum's

TURKEY

heyday (between Alexander the Great and the Roman domination of Asia Minor) it was one of the Middle East's richest and most powerful small kingdoms. The **tourist office** (☎ 631 2851; İzmir Caddesi 54) is on the main street, just north of the Archaeology Museum.

Pergamum **Acropolis** (admission €10; 🕒 8.30am-5.30pm), a windswept hilltop site 6km from central Bergama, is the part everyone comes to see, with its commanding location and spectacular sloping amphitheatre. The **Asclepion** (Temple of Asclepios; admission €7.50; 🕒 8.30am-5.30pm), 3.5km from the city centre, was a famous medical school with a library that rivalled that of Alexandria in Egypt. In Bergama, the **Red Basilica** (admission €2.50; 🕒 8.30am-5.30pm) is the imposing remains of a 2nd-century temple to the Egyptian gods Serapis, Isis and Harpocrates.

In the excellent **Archaeology Museum** (İzmir Caddesi; admission €2.50; 🕒 8.30am-5.30pm Tue-Sun), look out for the statues from Pergamum.

In a converted 180-year-old house with views of the Red Basilica, the **Odyssey Guesthouse** (☎ 653 9189; www.odysseyguesthouse.com; Abacihan Sokak 13; dm €5, s/d with shared bathroom €10/17.50) has seven rather sparse but clean and atmospheric rooms.

Buses run to İzmir (€5, two hours) every 45 minutes and to Ayvalık (€3.75, 1¼ hours) at least every hour.

İZMIR

☎ 0232 / pop 2.6 million

Though you may eventually fall for its hectic nightlife, great shopping and top-notch museums, İzmir can take some getting used to. Certainly nowhere else in the region can prepare you for the sheer size, sprawl and intensity of the place. The seafront is one of its main attractions, the wide, pleasant esplanade of Birinci Kordon providing eating, drinking and sunset-watching opportunities.

Inland, the ruins of the extensive 2nd-century AD Roman **agora** (admission €1.50; 🕒 8am-5pm) are just southeast of the chaotic, atmospheric bazaar. It's also worth taking bus 33 to the hilltop **Kadifekale** fortress, where women still weave kilims on horizontal looms and the views are breathtaking.

Information

Internet Café (1369 Sokak 9; per hr €0.83)
Tourist Information (☎ 483 5117; Akdeniz Mahallesi 1344, Sokak 2)

Sleeping & Eating

There are plenty of cheap and midpriced hotels around the train station. A number of establishments on 1296 Sokak, just southwest of the station, occupy restored Ottoman houses, although their interiors can be grungy and uninviting.

Otel Hikmet (☎ 484 2672; 945 Sokak 26; s/d €7.50/17.50, with shower €10/22.50) The sign outside says 'Hotel very good' and it's not wrong. Tucked away on cobbled streets off a cafe-lined square, this family-run house is full of character.

For fresh fruit, veg or freshly baked bread and delicious savoury pastries, head for the canopied market, just off Anafartalar Caddesi. In Alsancak's eateries, you lose the *kordon*'s sea views (and high prices) but gain on atmosphere; try 1453 Sokak (Gazi Kadinlar Sokağı).

Getting There & Around

Many bus companies have ticket offices in the Basmane-Çankaya area, near the train station. They usually provide a *servis* to the otogar, 6.5km from the city centre. Frequent buses serve Selçuk (€3, one hour), Çanakkale (€19, six hours) and many other destinations.

The pleasantest way to get around İzmir is by **ferry** (🕒 6.30am-1am). Frequent timetabled services link the piers at Konak, Pasaport, Alsancak and Karşiyaka. *Jetons* (travel tokens) cost €2 each.

SELÇUK

☎ 0232 / pop 27,280

Selçuk boasts the remains of one of the Seven Wonders of the Ancient World, an excellent museum, a fine basilica and mosque, a stork nest–studded aqueduct and, right on the town's doorstep, Ephesus. However, compared to the vast tourism factory of nearby Kuşadası, Selçuk's tourism industry is a small scale, workshop-sized affair.

The western side of Atatürk Caddesi, north of Ephesus Museum, is the quieter part of town and contains many *pensions;* the eastern side holds the otogar and plenty of shops and restaurants. The **tourist office** (☎ 892 6945; www.selcuk.gov.tr) is opposite the museum.

Sights & Activities

Even if you're not an architecture buff, you can't help but be dazzled by the sheer beauty of the ruins of **Ephesus** (admission €10; 🕒 8am-5pm

Oct-Apr, 8am-7pm May-Sep), the best-preserved classical city in the eastern Mediterranean. If you want to get a feel for what life was like in Roman times, Ephesus is an absolute must-see. Wandering down the former main street, you'll see the well-preserved (or restored) remains of structures such as the Temple of Hadrian, Terraced Houses (where the rich folk lived) and the Fountain of Trajan. The real photo ops, though, are the immense Great Theatre, which could hold 25,000 people; and the monumental facade of the Library of Celsus, which stored 12,000 scrolls in niches around its walls. An audioguide with brain-addling amounts of information can be hired for €2.50. Ephesus is a 3km, 45-minute walk west of Selçuk. Frequent dolmuşes to Pamucak and Kuţadası pass the turn-off (€0.50, five minutes).

In Selçuk, the main attraction is the excellent **Ephesus Museum** (Uğur Mumcu Caddesi; admission €2.50; 8am-5pm Oct-Apr, to 7pm May-Sep), with its priceless collection of artefacts from the Roman period. On the hill above Atatürk Caddesi, the **Basilica of St John** (admission €2.50; 8am-5pm Oct-Mar, to 7pm May-Sep) is said to be built over the apostle's tomb. Between Ephesus and Selçuk, the less-impressive ruins of the **Temple of Artemis** (admission free; 8am-5pm, to 7pm May-Sep) were once one of the Seven Wonders of the Ancient World.

Sleeping & Eating

Competition between Selçuk's many *pensions* is intense, and the standard of service and value offered by these places is higher than perhaps anywhere else.

Australia & New Zealand Guesthouse (892 6050; www.anzguesthouse.com; 1064 Sokak 12; dm €6.50, d with shared/private bathroom €15/22.50) Despite the rules posted in the rooms, this is a welcoming place with sofas and comfortable clutter in its courtyard, and a great covered roof terrace. Bikes are free or you can hire a motor-scooter.

Atilla's Getaway (892 3847; www.atillasgetaway.com; dm €8, bungalows with shared bathroom €8, r with private bathroom €16) An attractively laid-out camping and bungalow complex 2.5km south of Selçuk. Run by a welcoming Turkish-Australian, it's packed with facilities and has a fun, buzzing atmosphere.

There's no shortage of cheap eateries in Selçuk; those at the eastern end of Cengiz Topel Caddesi have neat views of the town's Byzantine aqueduct. **Ejder Restaurant** (892 3296; Cengiz Topel Caddesi 9/E; pide €2, kebap €3.50) is a favourite with locals and travellers alike.

Old House Restaurant & Bar (Eski Ev; 892 9357; 1005 Sokak 1/A; mains €3-4.50) Tables are set in a little courtyard amid grapefruit and pomegranate trees. Try the appetising speciality 'Old House Kebap' (€4.50), served sizzling on a platter.

Getting There & Away

While it's easy enough to get to Selçuk direct from İzmir (€3, one hour), coming from the south or east you generally have to change at Aydın, from where buses leave almost hourly to other destinations (such as Bodrum, Marmaris, Fethiye, Denizli and Antalya). Dolmuşes go to Aydın (€2.50, one hour, every 40 minutes), Kuşadası (€2, 30 minutes, every 20 minutes) and Pamucak (€1.25, 10 minutes).

KUŞADASI

0256 / pop 50,000

It's easy to sneer at Kuşadası's package hotels, fast-food restaurants, in-your-face bazaar, tattoo parlours, karaoke bars, and holiday crowds. But many locals are very proud of the place, seeing it as exemplifying a can-do, make-the-best-of-yourself spirit.

The stone **castle** on the island in the harbour, once a pirates' hideout, is the only major attraction here, but Kuşadası makes a good base for visiting the ancient cities of **Priene**, **Miletus** and **Didyma** to the south. Admission to each site is €1.50.

Most cheap accommodation is on the steep narrow streets just southwest of the bazaar. **Captain's House** (614 4754; www.captainshousepansiyon.com; İstiklal Caddesi 66; s/d €12.50/25) occupies a prime position on the seafront, next to a popular restaurant/cafe. **Sezgin's Guesthouse** (614 4225; www.sezginhotel.com; Aslanlar Caddesi 68; s/d €20/24), perhaps the top budget choice, offers large, wood-panelled rooms with comfortable beds, armchairs, TVs, fridges and small balconies.

Kuşadası's prime dining location is down by the picturesque marina, but for the cheapest options, head inland to the old quarter, Kaleiçi. **Avlu** (614 7995; Cephane Sokak 15; mains €2.50-4) is well worth seeking out, offering 1st-class mama-cooked meals.

Barlar Sokak (Bar St), chock-a-block with Irish-theme pubs, can be lots of fun after a few drinks.

TURKEY

DETOUR: PAMUKKALE

East of Selçuk (160km), Pamukkale's gleaming white ledges (travertines), with pools that flow over the plateau edge, used to be one of the most familiar images of Turkey. Sadly, the water supply has dried up and it is no longer possible to bathe in the pools. Next to this fragile wonder, you can tour the magnificent ruins of the Roman city of **Hierapolis** (admission €10; daylight), an ancient spa resort with a theatre, a colonnaded street, a latrine building and a necropolis.

Then swim amid sunken columns at Hierapolis' **Antique Pool** (adult/child €9/4.50; 9am-7pm), and visit the **Hierapolis Archaeology Museum** (admission €1.50; 9am-12.30pm & 1.30-7.15pm Tue-Sun).

There are several **camp sites** (camping per person about €3.50) and welcoming, family-run *pensions*. **Hotel Dört Mevsim** (0258-272 2009; www.hoteldortmevsim.com; Hasan Tahsin Caddesi 19; dm €5, s/d €10/17.50;) has simple, clean rooms in a quiet lane.

Frequent buses connect local hub Denizli with İzmir (€10, four hours) and Konya (€15, six hours). Buses run between Denizli and Pamukkale every 15 minutes (€1, 30 minutes).

Kuşadası's otogar is at the southern end of Kahramanlar Caddesi on the bypass highway. Out of season you'll probably have to change at İzmir (€7.50, 1¼ hours) or Söke (€2, 30 minutes) for most destinations. In summer, three buses run daily to Bodrum (€10, 2½ hours). For Selçuk (€2, 25 minutes) and Söke, pick up a minibus on Adnan Menderes Bulvarı.

From April to October boats depart daily to Samos (one way/same-day return €30/35); ferries do not operate in the winter.

BODRUM

0252 / pop 28,580

Some people will tell you Bodrum is an unsophisticated low-end resort town; they obviously haven't been to Kuşadası. In fact, Bodrum manages to welcome the summer hordes without diluting its character and charm. With laws in place restricting the height of buildings, the town has nice architectural uniformity and, out of season, its whitewashed houses and subtropical gardens can appear almost idyllic.

The Adliye Camii, a small white mosque, marks the town centre, separating Bodrum's two main bays. The otogar is 500m inland, along Cevat Şakir Caddesi.

Information

Cybernet Internet Café (Üçkuyular Caddesi 7; per hr €1; 24hr)

Tourist Office (316 1091; Kale Meydanı; 9am-6pm Mon-Fri, daily in summer)

Sights & Activities

The **Castle of St Peter** adorns about every brochure, postcard and flyer in Bodrum, and it's still an essential stop. Built in 1437 by the Crusaders, the castle houses the sensational **Museum of Underwater Archaeology** (admission €5; 9am-noon & 1-7pm Tue-Sun summer, 8am-noon & 1-5pm winter).

With its good visibility, clean water and pleasant temperatures, Bodrum is a good place for **diving** or **snorkelling**. The **Snorkel & Dive Center** (313 6017; Cevat Şakir Caddesi 5) is a good starting point. A full day's diving with two dives, boat, all equipment, insurance, hotel transfers and lunch per person costs €45. All-day snorkelling trips cost €20 per person.

Sleeping & Eating

There are plenty of budget hotels and *pensions*, particularly in the centre and along the Eastern Bay, although be aware that the closer you are to the front, the less chance you'll have of getting a good night's sleep. Thankfully there are also some quieter choices inland.

Sedan Pansiyon (316 0355; off Türkkuyusu Caddesi 121; s/d with shared bathroom €10/16, with private bathroom €12/24) This basic *pension* has rooms of varying sizes and states of repair arranged around a ramshackle but peaceful courtyard.

Sevin Pension (316 7682; www.sevinpension.com; Türkkuyusu Caddesi 5; dm €13, s €18-22, d €25-36;) It may be basic, but for the price, it offers a lot: a prime (albeit noisy) location, TV, free wi-fi, good breakfasts and helpful staff.

Cevat Şakir Caddesi and the bazaar harbour the best-value eateries – Turkish restaurants and *büfes* (snack bars), where you can pick up a döner wrapped in pide for €2. *Nargileh* (water pipe) fans should try the **Old Café** (Cumhuriyet Caddesi), while dedicated

TURKEY

Book your stay at lonelyplanet.com/hotels

clubbers will want to boogie on down to the mighty **Halıkarnas** (www.halikarnas.com.tr; Cumhuriyet Caddesi; admission week/weekend €15/17.50; 10pm-5am mid-May–Oct), an open-air club with kitschy Roman temple styling and beer/spirits from €5.

Getting There & Away

There are at least two buses a day from Bodrum to Antalya (€17.50, eight hours), Fethiye (€12.50, six hours), İzmir (€12.50, four hours), Kuşadası (€10, 2½ hours) and Marmaris (€10, three hours).

Daily ferries link Bodrum with Kos (from €25 same-day return). From June to September hydrofoils go to Rhodes (€60 same-day return, 2¼ hours). Contact the **Bodrum Ferryboat Association** (316 0882; Kale Caddesi Cümrük Alanı 22) for tickets and information.

MEDITERRANEAN COAST

The Western Mediterranean, known as the 'Turquoise Coast', is a glistening stretch of clear blue sea where Gods once played in pebble coves and spectacular ruins abound. The region's seamless mix of history and holiday inspires and enchants. In spots like Patara and Olympos, your sandcastles are humbled by vine-covered Corinthian temples and Lycian tombs; in Kaş, plunge into activities such as scuba diving and kayaking over underwater ruins.

MARMARIS

0252 / pop 35,160

An unashamedly brash harbour town that swells to more than 200,000 people during summer, Marmaris is heaven or hell depending which way your boat floats. It sports one of Turkey's swankiest marinas, and a stunning natural harbour where Lord Nelson organised his fleet for the attack on the French at Abukir in 1798. Not far away, the **Reşadiye and Hisarönü Peninsulas** hide bays of azure backed by pine-covered mountains and gorgeous fishing villages.

Iskele Meydanı, the main square, is by the harbour northwest of the castle; 39 Sokak, known as Bar St for instantly obvious reasons, runs northeast from here. The otogar is 3km north of town.

Information

Internet C@fe (Atatürk Caddesi, Huzur 30; per 30min €1; 10am-1am)

Tourist office (412 1035; Iskele Meydanı 2; 8am-noon & 1-5pm Mon-Fri, daily Jun–mid-Sep) Right near the castle.

Sights

The small **castle** (admission €1.50; 8am-noon & 1-5pm Tue-Sun) houses a modest museum and offers fine views of Marmaris.

Tours

Cruise-boats along the waterfront offer tours of outlying beaches and islands. A day's outing usually costs €25 to €40 per person; check carefully exactly what you'll get before agreeing to anything.

You'll usually visit Paradise Island, Aquarium, Phosphoros Cave, Kumlubuku, Amos, Turunç, Green Sea and İçmeler. Two- and three-day trips often take in **Dalyan** and **Kaunos**, and you can charter longer, more serious boat trips to **Datça** and the ruins at **Knidos**, or along the Hisarönü Peninsula.

Sleeping & Eating

Marmaris has hundreds of good-value sleeping options, especially for self-caterers. Off-season, expect serious discounts.

Interyouth Hostel (412 3687; interyouth@turk.net; 42 Sokak 45; dm or s with/without ISIC card €5/12.50, d €15;) Located inside the covered bazaar, this hostel is efficiently run and a great source of travel information. Bathrooms are shared.

Maltepe Pansiyon (412 1629; 66 Sokak 9; s/d €15/25;) The shady garden and free internet are the main attractions at this long-standing budget choice.

For cheap eats, try the bazaar area, the old town around the castle, and the stalls catering to ravenous late-night revellers on Bar St.

Two perennially popular nightspots are **Back Street** (412 4048; 39 Sokak 93) and **Areena** (412 2906; 39 Sokak 54), with its bar elevated above a large dance floor.

Getting There & Away

Frequent buses serve Fethiye (€7.50, three hours, half-hourly), Bodrum (€9, 3½ hours) and Dalyan (via Ortaca; €3.50, 1½ hours), and there are two daily services to Antalya (€17.50, six hours).

TURKEY

Catamarans sail daily to Rhodes from 15 April to 1 November only (same day/open return €50/75). Tickets can be bought from any travel agency, including **Yeşil Marmaris Travel & Yachting** (☎ 412 2290; www.yesilmarmaris.com).

DALYAN

☎ 0252 / pop 5000

Dalyan is a laid-back river-mouth community with a strong farming pedigree and a growing penchant for tourism. It makes an entertaining base for exploring the surrounding fertile waterways, in particular the loggerhead sea turtle nesting grounds at **Iztuzu Beach** and **Lake Köyceğiz**.

The main activity here is boating out of town. The most popular jaunt (about €10) takes you to Iztuzu beach, the ruins of **Kaunos** (admission €2.50; 8.30am-5.30pm) and the **Sultaniye hot springs** (admission €2) on the shores of Lake Köyceğiz, possibly with a mud bath thrown in. You can save money and ensure your lira is spread evenly around town by taking boats run by the **Dalyan Kooperatifi** (☎ 284 7843).

Dalyan Camping (☎ /fax 284 4157; Maraş Caddesi 144; per tent/caravan €7.50/12.50, 2-/3-/4-person bungalows €10/20/30; Apr-Oct) has a central location by the river. The eight pinewood bungalows are simple and clean. A revelation right in the heart of town, **Çınar Sahil Pension** (☎ 284 2402; www.cinarsahilpansiyon.com; Yalı Sokak 14; s/d €15/25) has a terrace with possibly the best views in Dalyan.

To get anywhere from Dalyan, you have to take a minibus from the stop behind the mosque to Ortaca (€0.75, hourly), and change.

FETHIYE

☎ 0252 / pop 50,700

In 1958 an earthquake levelled the old harbour city of Fethiye, sparing only the ancient remains of **Telmessos** (400 BC). Fifty years on, Fethiye is once again a prosperous and proud hub of the western Mediterannean. Its natural harbour, tucked away in the southern reaches of a broad bay scattered with pretty islands, is perhaps the region's finest.

Fethiye's otogar is 2.5km east of the town centre, with a separate station for minibuses 1km east of the centre. Dolmuşes run along the main street, Atatürk Caddesi, taking you past the government buildings, the PTT and several banks. The **tourist office** (☎ 614 1527; İskele Meydanı; 10am-noon & 1-5.30pm daily May-Sep, Mon-Sat Oct-Apr) is opposite the marina, just past the Roman theatre.

Sights & Activities

In central Fethiye, little remains of the original town of Telmessos other than a Roman **theatre** and several Lycian **sarcophagi**. The cliffs hold several rock-cut tombs, including the Ionic **Tomb of Amyntas** (admission €2.50; 8am-7pm). **Fethiye Museum** (505 Sokak; admission €2.50; 8.30am-5pm Tue-Sun) has some small statues and votive stones.

Most people enjoy the well-promoted **12-Island Boat Tours** (per person €12.50), the tours to **Butterfly Valley** (€10) via Ölüdeniz, the **Saklıkent Gorge Tour** (€20) and the **Dalyan Tour** (€20).

Dolmuşes run to the nearby evocative Ottoman Greek 'ghost town' of **Kayaköy** (admission €2.50; 9am-7pm), abandoned after the population exchange of 1923 when Greek-speaking peoples of Anatolia were shipped to Greece while Muslim residents of Greece were transferred to Turkey. These exchanges, designed to forestall ethnic violence by creating unified nation states on the Aegean, brought great disruption and the creation of such ghost villages. A little further over the mountains is **Ölüdeniz** (Dead Sea), with a tranquil **lagoon**, but an unfortunate packed belt of hotels behind the **beach**. Popular activities are paragliding and parasailing. You may prefer to catch a boat from Ölüdeniz to the beautiful **Butterfly Valley** (€6.25 return), with a handful of laid-back accommodation options. There are frequent dolmuşes to Ölüdeniz (€1.50, 25 minutes) from Fethiye.

Fethiye is the starting (or finishing) point for the 500km **Lycian Way** (see p1201), a superb scenic walking trail along the coast. The town also makes a good base for visiting the beautiful **Saklıkent Gorge** and the ruins at **Tlos** and **Pınara**.

Sleeping & Eating

Most budget places will have staff pick you up from the bus station; otherwise, dolmuşes marked 'Karagözler' run along Fevzi Çakmak Caddesi towards the *pensions*.

Ideal Pension (☎ 614 1981; www.idealpension.net; 26 Sokak 1; dm/s/d from €10/17.50/20;) Running for two decades, Ideal Pension provides high quality, cheap beds, a large terrace with bay views and generous breakfasts.

Tan Pansiyon (☎ 614 1584; fax 614 1676; 30 Sokak 43; s/d €15/25) When the backpacker grind wears thin, try this traditional Turkish *pension* run by a charming elderly couple.

One way to taste Fethiye's fabulous fish without losing too many Turkish lira is to bring your own! Buy your fish from the market, take it to one of the surrounding restaurants and ask them to cook it. A nominal charge of €2.75 will procure you a sauce to accompany your flipper, green salad, garlic bread, fruit and coffee. One such eatery is **Hilmi et Balık Restaurant** (☎ 612 6242; Hal ve Pazar Yeri 53), a firm local favourite.

Getting There & Away

Heading to Antalya, the inland bus route (€8, four hours) is shorter and cheaper, though less scenic, than the coastal route (€10, 7½ hours), which also serves Patara (€3, 1½ hours) and Kaş (€4, 2½ hours). For intermediate destinations, go to the minibus station near the mosque.

The 'blue cruise' has become a travellers' institution, and is still the most pleasant way to get between Fethiye and Olympos or Marmaris – you travel on a *gület* (wooden yacht), calling in at bays along the way for swimming, sunbathing and variable amounts of boozing. Depending on the season, the price for a three-night cruise per person is usually €100 to €180 for Fethiye and €180 for Marmaris.

PATARA

☎ 0242

Patara's main claim to fame is its superb 20km-long **beach** (admission €2.50), one of Turkey's best. It's a nesting ground for sea turtles and the resting place of extensive, overgrown **ruins**, which are good for a scramble.

Near Patara are two Unesco World Heritage sites: the **Letoön** (admission €2.50; 🕑 8.30am-5pm), which has excellent mosaics and a sacred pool; and impressive **Xanthos** (admission €1.50; 🕑 8.30am-5pm), which boasts a Roman theatre and Lycian pillar tombs.

Patara's amenities are in Gelemiş village, 2.5km inland from the beach. **Rose Pension** (☎ 843 5165; www.rosepensionpatara.com; s/d €10/17.50; ❄) offers garden-fresh produce, a stylish lounge and genuine hospitality.

Buses plying the Fethiye–Antalya main road will drop you at the Gelemiş turn-off, from where dolmuşes run to the village every 45 minutes.

KAŞ

☎ 0242 / pop 7700

The 500m-high mountain known as 'Sleeping Man' (Yatan Adam) has watched Kaş evolve from a beautiful place of exile for political dissidents, to a funky boutique shopping and cafe strip, to a seaside adventure playground.

Apart from enjoying the town's mellow ambience and small pebble beaches, you can walk a few hundred metres to the restored Roman **theatre**. Lycian **sarcophagi** are dotted about the streets, and the **tombs** cut into the cliffs above the town are beautifully lit at night.

The most popular **boat trip** (€12.50 to €15) is to Kekova Island and Üçağız, passing submerged Byzantine ruins. Other water-based fun includes some world-class scuba diving (about €30 per dive, PADI course available) and kayaking (about €25 per day), organised by local agencies such as **Bougainville Travel** (☎ 836 3737; www.bougainville-turkey.com; İbrahim Selin Caddesi 10).

Information

Net-C@fé (İbrahim Serin Caddesi 16/B; per hr €1; 🕑 9am-1am)
Tourist office (☎ 836 1238; 🕑 8am-noon & 1-7pm Mon-Fri May-Oct, to 5pm Nov-Apr) On the main square.

Sleeping & Eating

Cheap *pensions* are mostly west of Atatürk Bulvarı.

Kaş Camping (☎ 836 1050; Yaşar Yazici Caddesi; 2-person camp sites €10) Situated on an attractive rocky site 800m west of town, this has long been the most popular place for camping, with a lovely swimming area and bar.

Santosa Pension (☎ 836 1714; Recep Bilgin Caddesi 4; s/d €10/20; ❄ 💻) Rooms at this clean, quiet and cheap backpackers are bare and simple, but excellent for the price.

Kaş has a thriving restaurant scene. **Naturel** (☎ 836 2834; Gürsöy Sokak 6; meals €7.50-10) is one of the best, offering dishes cooked to old Ottoman recipes.

Drinking

There is a good choice of low-key, fun drinking holes. Try **Hi-Jazz Bar** (☎ 836 1165; Zümrüt Sokak 3) or, on the harbour, the hip new **Echo Bar** (Gürsoy Sokak).

Getting There & Away

Buses and dolmuşes depart from Kaş' central otogar for all local destinations. Regular services include Fethiye (€3.50, two hours), Patara (€2.50, 45 minutes), Olympos (€4, 2½ hours) and Antalya (€4.50, 3½ hours).

TURKEY

OLYMPOS

☎ 0242

Long beloved of hippies and New Age types, **ancient Olympos** (admission per day €1.50) was once a major port city; now it's a fantastically wild, abandoned place where ruins peek out from forest copses, rock outcrops and riverbanks. The deep, shaded valley containing the ruins opens onto the extensive **beach**.

According to legend, the nearby **Chimaera** (Yanartaş), a cluster of natural eternal flames, was the hot breath of a subterranean monster. Easily sighted by ancient mariners, it is now a mere glimmer of its former fiery self, but no less exotic. To find the Chimaera, follow the signs 7km from Olympos and climb the hill (staff from most *pensions* will run you there for around €5).

Sleeping & Eating

Most visitors come here to stay in the legendary treehouse camps, which line the track along the valley down to the ruins. All camps include breakfast and dinner in the price. Note that it's worth being extra attentive with personal hygiene and food while staying here; every year some travellers wind up ill. Don't swim around the point area.

Kadir's Yörük Top Treehouse (☎ 892 1250; www.kadirstreehouses.com; dm €10, bungalows €20;) Kadir's started the tree-living trend, and the fun has not gone away: there are three bars and a rock-climbing wall.

Şaban (☎ 892 1265; www.sabanpansion.com; dm/tree house €10/15, bungalows €17.50-20;) Şaban is not a party place, but sells itself on tranquillity, space, a family-feel and great home cooking.

Getting There & Away

Buses plying the main road between Antalya and Fethiye will drop you off at the roadside restaurant at the top of the hill. Minibuses leave for Çıralı (€1.10) and Olympos (€1.35) from the restaurant from roughly 8.30am to 6.30pm on the half-hour.

ANTALYA

☎ 0242 / pop 603,200

Once seen by travellers as the gateway to the 'Turkish Riviera', Antalya is generating a buzz among culture-vultures. Situated directly on the Gulf of Antalya (Antalya Körfezi), the largest Turkish city on the Mediterranean is both stylishly modern and classically beautiful. It boasts the creatively preserved Roman-Ottoman quarter of Kaleiçi, a pristine Roman harbour, plus stirring ruins in the surrounding Beydağları (Bey Mountains).

The otogar is 4km north of the city centre; the blue-and-white Terminal Otobusu 93 (€50) heads for the town centre every 20 minutes or so. Antalya's central landmark and symbol, the Yivli Minare (Grooved Minaret), stands near the main square, called Kale Kapısı (Fortress Gate). To get into Kaleiçi from the square, head south down the hill.

Information

Natural Internet Cafe (8am-11pm)

Owl Bookshop (Barbaros Mahallesi, Akarçeşme Sokak 21; 10am-7pm Mon-Sat)

Tourist office (☎ 241 1747; Yavuz Ozcan Parkı; 8am-7pm)

Sights & Activities

About 2km west of the city centre, **Antalya Müzesi** (Cumhuriyet Caddesi; admission €7.50; 9am-7.30pm Tue-Sun) houses spectacular finds from nearby Perge and Aspendos – it's one of Turkey's best museums. The *tramvay* (€0.50) takes you to the Müze stop.

Heading downhill from the clock tower you'll pass the **Yivli Minare** (Grooved Minaret), rising above an old mosque. Further into Kaleiçi, the **Kesik Minare** (Truncated Minaret) is built on the site of a ruined Roman temple.

Just off Atatürk Caddesi, the monumental **Hadrian's Gate** (Hadriyanüs Kapısı) was erected during the Roman emperor Hadrian's reign (AD 117–38).

The **Suna & İnan Kıraç Kaleiçi Museum** (Kocatepe Sokak 25; admission €1.50; 9am-noon & 1-6pm Thu-Tue) is a lovingly restored Ottoman mansion displaying rituals and milestones in typical Ottoman lives.

Need some hush and a cool place to rest your sightseeing-abused feet? Nothing beats **Karaalioğlu Parkı**, a large, attractive and flower-filled park that's good for a stroll. Alternatively, do some yoga at the **Association for the Unity of Mankind** (☎ 244 5807; Hesapçı Sokak 7).

Sleeping & Eating

There are *pensions* aplenty in Kaleiçi – most housed in renovated historic buildings.

White Garden Pansiyon (☎ 248 9115; www.xhost.co.uk/whitegarden; Hesapçı Geçidi 9; s/d €15/20;) The White Garden combines tidiness, discre-

TURKEY

Book your stay at lonelyplanet.com/hotels

tion and class beyond its price, not to mention impeccable service, in a beguiling restored building and courtyard.

Hotel Blue Sea Garden (☎ 248 8213; www.blueseagarden.com; Hesapçı Sokak 65; s/d with half board €20/30;) The pluses here are the extra-large swimming pool area, the go-getting management and the excellent restaurant. The elevated rooms are more peaceful.

An endless assortment of cafes and eateries is found around the harbour. For cheap eating, cross Atatürk Caddesi and poke around deep in the commercial district. **Can Can Pide Yemek Salonu** (☎ 243 2548; Hasim Iscan Mahallesi, Arik Caddesi 4A; Adana durum €3; 9am-11pm Mon-Sat), located diagonally across the street from Plaza Cinemas, serves fantastic *çorba* (soup), pide and Adana *durum* (lamb kebap). It's elbow room only, so go ahead and nudge right in.

Getting There & Away

From the otogar, regular buses head for Olympos (€4, 1½ hours), Konya (€9, six hours), Göreme (€19, 10 hours) and most major destinations.

CENTRAL ANATOLIA

On central Turkey's hazy plains, the sense of history is so pervasive that the average kebap chef can remind you that the Romans preceded the Seljuks. This is, after all, the region where the whirling dervishes first swirled, Atatürk began his revolution, Alexander the Great cut the Gordion Knot, King Midas turned everything to gold, and Julius Caesar uttered his famous line, *'Veni, vidi, vici'* (I came, I saw, I conquered).

ANKARA

☎ 0312 / pop 4.5 million

İstanbullus may quip that the best view in Ankara is the train home, but the Turkish capital has more substance than its reputation as a staid administrative centre suggests. The capital established by Atatürk offers a mellower, more manageable vignette of urban Turkey than İstanbul, and boasts two of the country's most important sights: the Anıt Kabir and the Anatolian Civilisations Museums.

Orientation

Ankara's *hisar* (citadel) crowns a hill 1km east of Ulus Meydanı (Ulus Sq), the heart of Old Ankara. Modern Ankara lies further south, around Kızılay Meydanı (Kızılay Sq), Kavaklıdere and Çankaya, the well-heeled residential neighbourhood that hosts many embassies.

Atatürk Bulvarı is the city's main north–south axis, running right through town. Ankara's mammoth otogar is 5.5km southwest of Ulus.

Information

There are many internet cafes in Ulus and Kızılay, particularly around Ulus Meydanı and Karanfil Sokak, and wi-fi is widely available.

Tourist office (☎ 310 8789/231 5572; Anafartalar Caddesi 67, Ulus; 9am-5pm Mon-Fri, 10am-5pm Sat) Plans are to move to a new office at the train station.

Sights & Activities

The **Anatolian Civilisations Museum** (☎ 324 3160; admission €7.50; 8.30am-5pm) is the perfect introduction to the complex weave of Turkey's chequered ancient past, housing artefacts cherry-picked from just about every significant archaeological site in Anatolia. It's a must, and provides a perfect excuse to wander inside the nearby **citadel**'s thick Byzantine walls.

The **Anıt Kabir** (Mausoleum of Atatürk; admission free; 9am-5pm mid-May–Oct, to 4pm Nov-Jan, to 4.30pm Feb–mid-May), 2km west of Kızılay, is the monumental tomb of modern Turkey's founder and a place of pilgrimage for many Turks.

Various Roman ruins are scattered around Ulus, including the **Column of Julian**, erected in AD 363, and the **Temple of Augustus & Rome**. Near the temple are remains of the **Roman Baths** (admission €1.50; 8.30am-12.30pm & 1.30-5.30pm).

If you have any energy left for more museums, the **Ethnography Museum** (Talat Paşa Bulvarı; admission €1.50; 8.30am-12.30pm & 1.30-5.30pm) and neighbouring **Painting & Sculpture Museum** (admission free; 9am-noon & 1-5pm) are worth a look.

Sleeping

Despite its general seediness, Ulus is handy if you want to visit the Anatolian Civilisations Museum and then move speedily on again.

Otel Mithat (☎ 311 5410; www.otelmithat.com.tr; Tavus Sokak 2; s/d/tr €11.50/16.50/21.50) Near Opera Meydanı, the Mithat's spartan rooms have tatty lino and small beds. On the plus side, there are TVs, phones, private bathrooms and wi-fi.

Kale Otel (☎ 311 3393; Şan Sokak 13; s/d €15/25) One of the closest hotels to the museum, the Kale is one of Ulus' more pleasant budget options behind its off-putting pink-and-red interior.

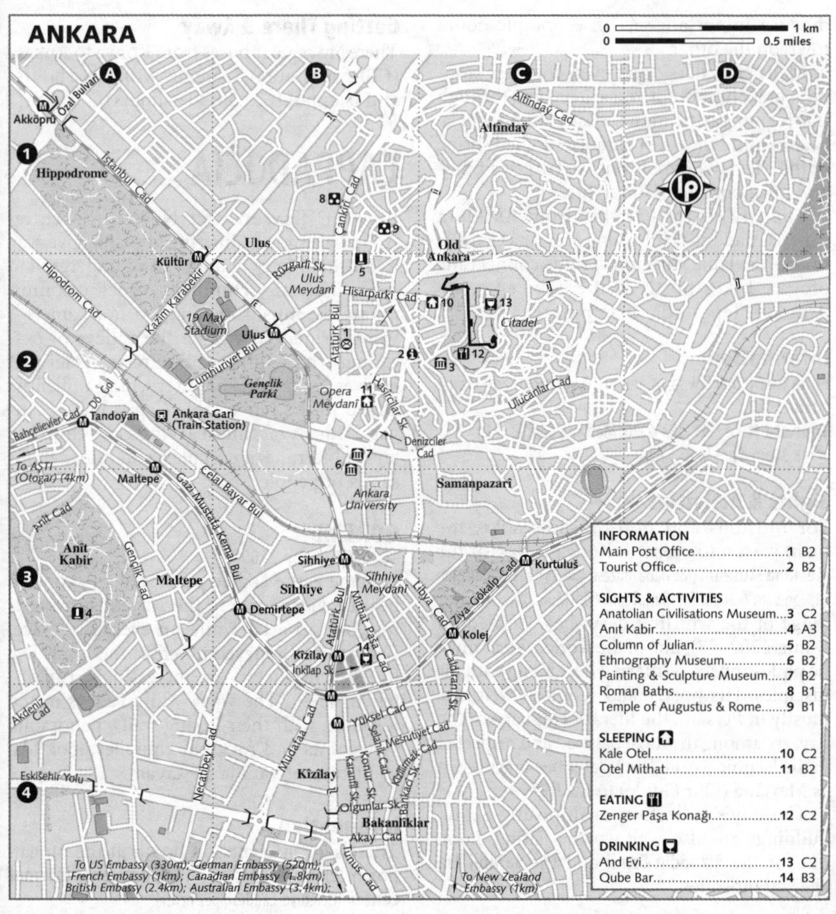

Eating & Drinking

You'll have no problems eating out in Ulus, although most restaurants stick to the tried-and-true (and popular) Turkish kebap'n'salad formula. For more choice, head to the pedestrian zone north of Ziya Gökalp Caddesi in Kızılay.

Zenger Paşa Konağı (☎ 311 7070; www.zengerpasa.com; Doyran Sokak 13, Ulus; mains €6-8.50; 🕑 noon-12.30am; ❄) Wonderful ethnographic displays liven up this restored old house, one of several atmospheric (if slightly touristy) restaurants up in the citadel

The best place for a tea is **And Evi** (İçkale Kapısı, Ulus), on the citadel walls. Kızılay is great for a night out, with buzzing hang-outs such as **Qube Bar** (Bayındır Sokak 16B).

Getting There & Around

Ankara's huge otogar (AŞTİ) dispatches passengers across the country all day and night. For İstanbul (€12.50 to €16.50, five to 6½ hours) buses depart every 30 minutes. Other useful services include those to Bursa (€14, six hours), Antalya (€15, eight hours), İzmir (€17.50, eight hours) and Göreme (€12.50, five hours).

KONYA

☎ 0332 / pop 762,000

Turkey's equivalent of the 'Bible Belt', conservative Konya treads a delicate path between its historical significance as the home town of the whirling dervish orders and a bastion of Seljuk culture on the one hand, and its modern importance as an economic boom town on the other.

Many travellers don't even consider stopping in Konya, but if you are passing through this region, say from the coast to Cappadocia, bear in mind that the turquoise-domed shrine of the Mevlâna here is one of Turkey's finest and most characteristic sights.

The city centre stretches from Alaaddin Tepesi (Aladdin's Hill) along Mevlâna Caddesi to the Mevlâna Museum. Trams connect the otogar, 14km north of the city centre, to Alaaddin Tepesi (€1, 30 minutes).

Information

Elma Net (Çinili Sokak 14; per hr €0.50; 🕒 10am-11pm) Internet cafe.

Tourist office (☎ 353 4020; Mevlâna Caddesi 21; 🕒 8.30am-5pm Mon-Sat)

Sights & Activities

For Muslims and non-Muslims alike, the main reason to come to Konya is to visit the **Mevlâna Museum** (Mevlâna Müzesi; ☎ 351 1215; admission €1; 🕒 9am-6.30pm Tue-Sun, 10am-6pm Mon), the former lodge of the whirling dervishes. Celaleddin Rumi (1207–73), one of the world's great mystic philosophers, is interred here along with his disciples. His poetry and religious writings, mostly in Persian, the literary language of the day, are among the most beloved and respected in the Islamic world. Rumi later became known as Mevlâna (Our Guide) to his followers.

The city's collection of imposing Seljuk buildings are also well worth visiting. Look out for the **Alaaddin Camii** and the **Sahib-i Ata Külliyesi** mosques.

Sleeping & Eating

Otel Mevlâna (☎ 352 0029; Cengaver Sokak 2; s/d/tr from €20/30/42.50) Across Mevlâna Caddesi from Otel Bera Mevlâna, this friendly central option is a good choice for backpackers of both sexes.

Mevlâna Sema Otel (☎ 350 4623; www.semaotel.com; Mevlâna Caddesi 67; s/d/tr €25/37.50/50; ❄) With a great position, some swanky decor and comfortable, beige rooms, the Mevlâna Sema has a lot going for it. Rooms at the rear are quieter.

Gülbahçesı Konya Mutfağı (☎ 351 0768; Gülbahçe Sokak 3; mains €2-4) One of Konya's best restaurants, mostly because of its upstairs terrace overlooking the Mevlâna Museum's gardens. Dishes include *yaprak sarma* (stuffed grape leaves) and Adana kebaps.

Getting There & Away

There are regular buses from Konya to Ankara (€10, four hours), Göreme (€10, three hours) and İstanbul (€22.50, 11½ hours).

CAPPADOCIA

Between Kayseri and Nevşehir, Central Anatolia's mountain-fringed plains give way to a land of fairy chimneys and underground cities. The fairy chimneys – rock columns, pyramids, mushrooms and a few camels – were formed, alongside the valleys of cascading white cliffs, when Erciyes Daği (Mt Erciyes) erupted. The intervening millennia added to the remarkable Cappadocian canvas, with Byzantines carving cave churches and subterranean complexes to house thousands of people.

GÖREME

☎ 0384 / pop 2100

Göreme is the archetypal travellers' utopia: a beatific village where the surreal surroundings spread a fat smile on everyone's face. Beneath the honeycomb cliffs, the locals live in fairy chimneys – or, increasingly, run hotels in them. The wavy white valleys in the distance, with their hiking trails, panoramic viewpoints and rock-cut churches, look like giant tubs of vanilla ice cream.

Information

There's an information booth at the otogar. For internet access, try the **Flintstones Internet Center** (Belediye Caddesi; per hr €1)

Sights & Activities

A World Heritage site, **Göreme Open-Air Museum** (admission €7.50; 🕒 8am-5pm) is Cappadocia's finest collection of rock-hewn cave churches. The churches are tiny, so avoid weekends and try and nip in between the many tour groups; go at midday, when the groups stop for lunch. The fresco-filled **Dark Church** (Karanlık Kilise; admission €4) is worth the extra charge; also don't miss the sizeable **Tokalı Church**, across the road from the main entrance.

Tours

Göreme is the main base for tours of Cappadocia's most popular sites (one-day trips about €30). Tours usually start at a lookout point with a view across the valleys, then continue to locations such as Ihlara Valley, a pottery in Avanos, the rock formations in Devrent Valley, Uçhisar's **rock citadel** (admission €1.50; 8am-8.15pm), and one of the fascinating underground cities at **Kaymaklı** or **Derinkuyu** (admission €7.50; 8am-5pm, last admission 4.30pm). Many companies also offer trips further afield, for example to eastern Turkish locations such as Nemrut Dağı (Mt Nemrut). We recommend the following:

Kapadokya Balloons (271 2442; www.kapadokyaballoons.com; Adnan Menderes Caddesi) The most respected hot-air balloon company in the region.

Middle Earth Travel (271 2559; www.middleearthtravel.com; Cevizler Sokak 20) The adventure travel specialist offers climbing and treks from one-day expeditions to one-week missions.

Yama Tours (271 2508; www.yamatours.com; Müze Caddesi 2) Local tours plus three-day trips to Nemrut Dağı (€150), leaving on Monday and Thursday.

Sleeping

On the hilly southern side of town are dozens of *pensions*, many offering rooms carved out of the natural rock. The information booth displays details of most options.

Kaya Camping Caravaning (343 3100; kayacamping@www.com; camp sites per adult/child €6.50/4.50;) This impressive camping ground is 2.5km from the centre of town, uphill from the Göreme Open-Air Museum.

Ufuk (271 2157; www.ufukpension.com.tr; off Müze Caddesi; dm €5, s/d/tr €12.50/20/27.50, breakfast €2.50;) Popular with Japanese and Korean travellers, Ufuk offers a terrace and rooms including a five-bed cave dorm, ranged around a scruffy courtyard with fruit trees.

Paradise Caves Hotel (271 2248; www.paradisecaveshotel.com; off Müze Caddesi; dm excl breakfast €5, s/d incl breakfast €15/25;) It's smarter than neighbouring Ufuk, even if its name is a generous description of the rooms with old carpets. Positive features include fairy chimney rooms, a fireplace in the three-bed dorm, and a multi-tiered terrace.

Köse Pension (271 2294; www.kosepension.com; dm €6, s with shared bathroom €10, tw hut €20, d & tw with private bathroom €30, tr with shared/private bathroom €30/37.50;) Köse Pension has the usual rough edges, but these are compensated for by a swimming pool in the garden and a terrace where communal meals are served. Run by Edinburgh-born Dawn and family, the cheerily painted backpacker institution has wooden huts and a 20-bed dorm on the roof.

Eating

There is a strip of good eateries on the quiet side of the dry canal, away from the busy Bilal Eroğlu Caddesi.

Point Café (Müze Caddesi; mains €5) Missing your favourite comfort foods? A Turkish-South African couple dishes up curries, burgers, fruit smoothies, filter coffee and homebaked cakes.

Dibek (271 2209; Hakkı Paşa Meydanı 1; mains €5-7.50) One of Göreme's best restaurants; try a *testi kebap* (kebap cooked in a terracotta pot, broken at the table to serve). You must give three hours' notice, so the dish can be slow-cooked in a stone oven.

Getting There & Away

As well as regular services to Ankara (€12.50, 4½ hours) and Konya (€10, three hours), night buses run to İstanbul (€20, 11 to 12 hours) and Antalya (€17.50, nine hours). Half-hourly dolmuşes connect Göreme with Nevşehir (€1.50, 30 minutes), a bigger transport hub.

IHLARA VALLEY

0382

The **Ihlara Valley** (admission €2.50; 8am-6.30pm) was a favourite retreat of Byzantine monks. Dozens of painted churches carved from the rock have survived, and hikers can follow the course of the river (Melendiz Suyu) as it flows for 13km from the wide, shallow valley at Selime to a narrow gorge at Ihlara village. It's an unforgettable experience, thanks to the sea of greenery – alive with birds – hugging the banks of the stream at the base of this beautiful canyon. Many people visit on day tours from Göreme, which allow only a few hours to walk the central part of the gorge, but to walk the whole way is likely to be a highlight of your trip to Turkey.

There are modest *pensions* at both ends (Ihlara village and Selime). You can also break your journey into two parts, with an overnight stay in Belisırma's camping grounds or lone *pension*. Note that all accommodation is closed out of season (December to March).

Ten dolmuşes a day travel from local transport hub Aksaray to Ihlara village (€2) via Selime and Belisırma. To travel in the opposite direction, you have to catch a taxi; between Ihlara village and Selime should cost about €12.50, and from Selime to Aksaray, about €22.50.

KAYSERI

☎ 0352 / pop 1.2 million

Mixing Seljuk tombs, mosques and modern developments, Kayseri is both Turkey's most Islamic city after Konya and one of the economic powerhouses nicknamed the 'Anatolian tigers'. It may not boast central Cappadocia's charms, but if you are passing through this transport hub, it's worth taking a look at a Turkish boomtown with a strong sense of its own history.

Now acting as an overflow valve for the nearby bazaar, the basalt-walled Seljuk **citadel** is Kayseri's centrepiece. Nearby are the **Ulu Cami** (Great Mosque), which has one of Anatolia's first brick minarets, and the Ottoman-style **Kurşunlu Cami** (Lead-Domed Mosque). The beautifully decorated **Güpgüpoğlu Konağı**, an 18th-century mansion, houses an interesting **Ethnographic Museum** (admission €1.50; 8am-5pm Tue-Sun).

Beyond the dark reception and institutional corridors at **Hotel Sur** (☎ 222 4367; Talas Caddesi 12; s/d/tr €20/30/37.50), rooms are bright and comfortable and some overlook the city walls. **Elif Hotel** (☎ 336 1826; elifotelkayseri@elifotelkayseri.com; Osman Kavuncu Caddesi 2; s/d/tr €20/35/45) is a bargain, with satellite TV and minibars in the rooms. The rear of the building is quieter.

Turkish Airlines and Onur Air have daily flights to/from İstanbul (from €27 one way, 1½ hours). Sun Express serves İzmir twice a week (€37 one way, 1½ hours). Buses serve all destinations, including Ürgüp (€3, 1¼ hours) and Göreme (€5, 1½ hours).

TURKEY

EASTERN TURKEY

Like a challenge? Eastern Turkey – vast, remote and culturally very Middle Eastern – is the toughest part of Turkey to travel in but definitely the most exotic, and certainly the part that feels least affected by mass tourism. Winter here can be bitterly cold and snowy.

Fighting between the Turkish military and the PKK (Kudistan Workers Party) separatist group has simmered down in southeastern Turkey, making the area much safer, but do seek local advice before travelling in the region.

MT NEMRUT NATIONAL PARK

Two thousand years ago, an obscure Commagene king chose to erect his own **memorial sanctuary** on top of a mountain. Today the highlight of the Mt Nemrut National Park is this sanctuary, an artificial summit strewn with the heads of gigantic statues of gods and kings. The stunning scenery, historical sights, and the undeniable sense of mystique and folly that emanate from the site make a visit here essential.

There are several bases for visiting Mt Nemrut. To the north is Malatya, where the **tourist office** (☎ 0422-323 2942) organises daily minibus tours (€40, minimum two people, May to September/October). The tours take in a sunset visit to the heads, a night at a hotel near the summit and a second visit at dawn. Alternatively you can visit the mountain from Kahta, which is a better option as you can tour all the sights on the southern side, although you need to be wary of what's on offer here (Kahta has always had a reputation as a rip-off town). Two recommended Kahta-based guides are **Mehmet Akbaba** (☎ 0535-295 4445; akbabamehmet@hotmail.com) and **Nemrut Tours** (☎ 0416-725 6881; Mustafa Kemal Caddesi), based at **Hotel Nemrut** (☎ 725 6881; www.hotelnemrut.net; Mustafa Kemal Caddesi; s/d €22.50/35; P).

Because of the transport difficulties, many people prefer to take tours from Göreme in Cappadocia (see p1198).

In high summer the most pleasant places to stay, especially if you have your own transport, are the camping grounds and village guest houses on the southern slopes of the mountain. The pretty village of Karadut, 12km from the summit, has a few small eateries.

VAN

☎ 0432 / pop 391,000

On the southeastern shore of vast Lake Van, the easygoing city of Van boasts a hilltop **castle** (admission €1.50, 9am-dusk), overlooking the foundations of **Eski Van** (the old city) and a fabulous **museum** (admission €1.50; 8am-noon & 1-5pm Tue-Sun), but the 10th-century Armenian church on **Akdamar Island** is the star attraction. Its biblical reliefs are jaw-dropping, not to mention its location on Lake Van, a vast expanse of water ringed by snowcapped mountains.

Thrifty backpackers rate **Otel Aslan** (☎ 216 2469; Özel İdare İş Merkezi Karşısı; s €7.50-10, d €10-17.50), a central hotel-cum-hostel, but don't leave valuables in your room. Much better is

Büyük Asur Oteli (☎ 216 8792; asur_asur2008@hotmail.com; Cumhuriyet Caddesi, Turizm Sokak; s/d €22.50/37.50; P), comfy, friendly and well set up for the needs of travellers.

There are several dolmuşes a day to Doğubayazıt (€5, three hours) and buses to Diyarbakır (€12.50, seven hours), from where you can continue on to Kahta (for Mt Nemrut National Park); there is one daily service to Kars (€15, six hours).

Minibuses run the 44km from near Beş Yol in Van to Akdamar harbour for €1.50 during the high season. At other times there's an hourly minibus to Gevaş (€1.50), 5km from the boat dock. Boats to the island run when traffic warrants it (minimum 10 people). Provided others are there to share the cost, a return ticket for the 20-minute voyage and admission to the island costs €2.50.

KARS

☎ 0474 / pop 78,500

The massive fortress and fine old Russian houses are well worth a look, but most people come to the setting of Orhan Pamuk's novel *Snow* to visit the dramatic ruins of **Ani** (admission €2.50; 8.30am-5pm), 45km east of the city. Formerly the capital of the Armenian kingdom, Ani was completely deserted in 1239 after a Mongol invasion. The ghost city, fronted by a hefty wall, now lies in fields overlooking the Arpaçay River, which forms the border with Armenia. The site exudes an eerie ambience that is simply unforgettable.

The central **Kent Otel** (☎ 223 1929; Hapan Mevkii; s/d €7.50/15) may have lumpy beds, plain decor and outdated facilities, but it's well taken care of and secure.

There are daily buses to locations including Ankara (€25, 16 hours) and Van (€15, six hours). Transport to Ani has always been sparse, so most people opt for the taxi minibuses (€15 with a minimum of six passengers; €50 private hire) organised by Kars' **tourist office** (☎ 212 6817; Lise Caddesi; 8am-noon & 1-5pm Mon-Fri).

TURKEY DIRECTORY

ACCOMMODATION

Camping grounds are dotted around Turkey, though not as frequently as you might hope. Some hotels and *pensions* will also let you camp on their grounds for a small fee (€2.50 to €7.50).

Turkey has no official hostel network, although there are plenty of hostels with dormitories in touristy destinations, where dorm beds usually cost about €5 to €7.50 per night.

Otherwise, small family-run *pensions* and hotels receive most of the traveller traffic and generally offer excellent value for money. Single/double prices in these options can be as low as €10/20 for a good, clean room with shared bathroom, with access to extras such as a choice of simple meals, laundry services and international TV channels. In the same bracket, the most you'll pay for a room with private bathroom is €20/35.

Note that virtually nowhere in Turkey is far from a mosque; light sleepers might want to bring earplugs for the early-morning call to prayer.

ACTIVITIES

Hiking and trekking, particularly in the national parks, are a great way to get to grips with the country. So far Turkey has two waymarked routes: the Lycian Way (Fethiye to Antalya) and St Paul Trail (Perge to Lake Eğirdir), both around 500km long.

Water sports from diving to kayaking are available in the Aegean and Mediterranean resorts. Those of a lazier (or drunker) disposition can take an extended boat trip along the coast. Skiing is becoming more popular, and some of the best facilities are at Uludağ, near Bursa, and Mt Erciyes, near Kayserı. The biggest and most renowned resort is Palandöken (near Erzurum) and the most scenic is Sarıkamış (near Kars), where snowboarders are also catered for. A dawn hot air balloon flight above Cappadocia's fairy chimneys is certainly a sublime start to the day.

BUSINESS HOURS

Typical business hours in Turkey:

Banks 8.30am-noon & 1.30-5pm Mon-Fri.

Bars from late afternoon until after midnight; in tourist areas they might also be open all day.

Internet cafes 9am-late.

Museums 9am-4.30pm Nov-Mar, 8.30am-6pm Apr-Oct; most museums close Mon.

Post offices 8.30am-12.30pm & 1.30-5.30pm Mon-Fri.

Restaurants 8am-10pm.

Shops 9am-6pm Mon-Fri; in tourist areas, food and souvenir shops are often open virtually around the clock.

DANGERS & ANNOYANCES

Although Turkey is in no way a dangerous country to visit, it's always wise to be a little cautious, especially if you're travelling alone. Be wary of pickpockets in buses, markets and other crowded places. Keep an eye out for anyone lurking near ATMs.

Turks are fast drivers and pedestrians should give way to cars and trucks in all situations – and be ready to dive out of the way.

In İstanbul single men are sometimes lured to bars by new Turkish 'friends', then made to pay an outrageous bill. Drugging is also a serious risk. Be a tad wary who you befriend, especially when you're new to the country.

At the time of writing, travelling in the southeast was safe, but you should check the current situation before setting out. Visitors should also note that sporadic bombings, including a double-bomb attack in İstanbul in 2008, target affluent areas frequented by tourists. Again, check advisories for the latest information.

EMBASSIES & CONSULATES

Most foreign embassies are in Ankara (see http://tinyurl.com/6ywt8a for more information). The following countries have embassies and consulates in Ankara and İstanbul:

Australia Ankara (Map p1197; ☎ 0312-459 9521; www.embaustralia.org.tr; 7th fl, Uğur Mumcu Caddesi 88, Gaziosmanpaşa); İstanbul (Map pp1180-1; ☎ 0212-243 1333; 2nd fl, Suzer Plaza, Asker Ocağı Caddesi 15, Elmadağ, Şişli)

Canada Ankara (Map p1197; ☎ 0312-409 2700; Cinnah Caddesi 58, Çankaya; 🕒 8.30am-5.45pm Mon-Thu, to 1pm Fri); İstanbul (Map pp1180-1; ☎ 0212-251 9838; 5th fl, İstiklal Caddesi 373, Beyoğlu)

France Ankara (Map p1197; ☎ 0312-409 2700; Cinnah Caddesi 58, Çankaya; 🕒 8.30am-5.45pm Mon-Thu, to 1pm Fri); İstanbul (Map pp1180-1; ☎ 0212-334 8730; Istiklal Caddesi 8, Taksim)

Germany Ankara (Map p1197; ☎ 0312-455 5100; Atatürk Bulvarı 114, Kavaklıdere); İstanbul (Map pp1180-1; ☎ 0212-334 6100; İnönü Caddesi 16-18, Taksim)

Netherlands Ankara (Map p1197; ☎ 0312-409 1800; Hollanda Caddesi 3, Yıldız); İstanbul (Map pp1180-1; ☎ 0212-393 2121; İstiklal Caddesi 393, Beyoğlu)

New Zealand (🕒 closes 1pm Fri May-Oct & 4.30pm Fri Nov-Apr) Ankara (Map p1197; ☎ 0312-467 9054; www.nzembassy.com/turkey; 4th fl, İran Caddesi 13, Kavaklıdere); İstanbul (Map pp1180-1; ☎ 0212-244 0272; İnönü Caddesi 48/3, Taksim)

UK Ankara (Map p1197; ☎ 0312-455 3344; fax 0312-455 3320; Şehit Ersan Caddesi 46a, Çankaya; 🕒 closes 4.15pm Mon-Fri); İstanbul (Map pp1180-1; ☎ 0212-334 6400; Meşrutiyet Caddesi 34, Tepebaşı, Beyoğlu)

USA Ankara (Map p1197; ☎ 0312-455 5555; fax 467 0019; Atatürk Bulvarı 110, Kavaklıdere); İstanbul (Map pp1180-1; ☎ 0212-335 9000; Kaplıcalar Mevkii 2, Istinye)

FESTIVALS & EVENTS

Camel Wrestling Hoof it to Selçuk on the last Sunday in January.

Anzac Day Held at Gallipoli on 25 April.

Oil-Wrestling Championships Held at Kırkpınar, late June or early July (www.kirkpinar.com).

International İstanbul Music Festival Every June, İstanbul hosts world-class classical concerts.

Aspendos Festival Opera and ballet in the Roman theatre, from mid-June to early July.

Mevlana Festival Held in Konya during December.

HOLIDAYS

New Year's Day 1 January
Children's Day 23 April
Youth & Sports Day 19 May
Victory Day 30 August
Republic Day 29 October

Turkey also celebrates all of the main Islamic holidays, the most important of which are the month-long **Ramazan** and, about two months later, **Kurban Bayramı**. Due to the fact that these holidays are celebrated according to the Muslim lunar calendar, they take place around 11 days earlier each year.

INTERNET RESOURCES

Mymerhaba (www.mymerhaba.com) Information site aimed at expats.

Tourism Turkey (www.tourismturkey.org) Government website with grab-bag of info.

Turkey Travel Planner (www.turkeytravelplanner.com) Regularly updated travel information.

Turkish Daily News (www.turkishdailynews.com) Newspaper home page.

MONEY

Turkey's currency, the Türk Lirası (Turkish Lira; TL), replaced the Yeni Türk Lirası (New Turkish Lira; YTL) in January 2009. Lira comes in notes of five, 10, 20, 50 and 100, and coins of one, five, 10, 25 and 50 kuruş and one lira. Prices in this chapter are quoted in more-stable euros.

Cash & Credit Cards
US dollars and euros are the easiest currencies to change, although many banks and exchange offices will change other major currencies, such as UK pounds and Japanese yen. You may find it difficult to exchange Australian or Canadian currency anywhere except at banks and offices in major cities.

Visa and MasterCard/Access are widely accepted by hotels, shops, bars and restaurants, although not by *pensions* and local restaurants outside main tourist areas. You can also get cash advances on these cards. Amex cards are rarely accepted.

Tipping & Bargaining
Waiters and bath attendants expect around 10% of the bill. You can also round up taxi fares if you wish. Hotel and transport prices may be negotiable, and you should always bargain for souvenirs, even if prices are 'fixed'.

POST
The Turkish postal service is known as the PTT. Turkish *postanes* (post offices) are indicated by black-on-yellow 'PTT' signs.

RESPONSIBLE TOURISM
Respecting Muslim sensibilities should be a point of principle. Women should keep their legs, upper arms and neckline covered, except on the beach. When entering a mosque, women should cover their heads and shoulders, and everyone should cover their legs and remove their shoes.

There's a number of low-emission ways to get to and around Turkey, notably the train. Try an 'express' train trip like the 1000km-plus, 41-hour journey from İstanbul to Lake Van.

TELEPHONE
Türk Telekom (www.telekom.gov.tr) has a monopoly on phone services, and service is efficient if costly. Almost all public telephones require Türk Telekom phonecards. If you're only going to make one call, look for signs saying *köntörlü telefon*, where the cost of your call will be metered. The cheapest option for international calls is with phone cards such as Bigalo.

To call the international operator in Turkey, dial ☎ 115.

VISAS
Nationals of the following countries don't need a visa to visit Turkey: Denmark, Finland, France, Germany, Ireland, Israel, Italy, Japan, New Zealand, Sweden and Switzerland. Although nationals of Australia, Austria, Belgium, Canada, the Netherlands, Norway, Portugal, Spain, the UK and the USA need a visa, this is just a stamp in the passport that you buy on arrival at the airport or at an overland border. How much you pay for your visa varies; at the time of writing, Australians and Americans paid US$20 (or €15), Canadians US$60 (or €45), and British citizens UK£10 (or €15 or US$20). Customs officers expect to be paid in one of these currencies, in hard cash, and may not accept Turkish lira. No photos are required.

The standard visa is valid for three months and, depending on your nationality, usually allows for multiple entries. See the **Ministry of Foreign Affairs** (www.mfa.gov.tr) for the latest information.

Ukraine Україна

HIGHLIGHTS

- **Kyiv** See the stunning churches of this ancient Slavic city and enjoy the vibe of the exciting modern capital all in one place (p1206)
- **Lviv** Sip a cappuccino with the caffeine-fuelled locals under the Gothic eaves of this haunting city (p1211)
- **Best journey** Board a night train in awesome Kyiv (p1206), and wake up in lovely Lviv (p1211), a totally different Ukrainian world

FAST FACTS

- **Area** 603,700 sq km (the biggest in Europe)
- **Budget** at least 300hry per day
- **Capital** Kyiv
- **Country code** ☎ 380
- **Famous for** the Orange Revolution, Chornobyl, chicken Kiev (or should that be Kyiv?)
- **Languages** Ukrainian (official), Russian
- **Money** Ukrainian hryvnia (hry); A$1 = 5.70hry; C$1 = 6.47hry; €1 = 10.24hry; ¥100 = 8.02hry; NZ$1 = 4.47hry; UK£1 = 11.54hry; US$1 = 7.61hry
- **Phrases** *doh-brih dyen* (hello), *ya nih rah-zoo-mee-yu* (I don't understand), *dya-koo-yoo* (thanks)

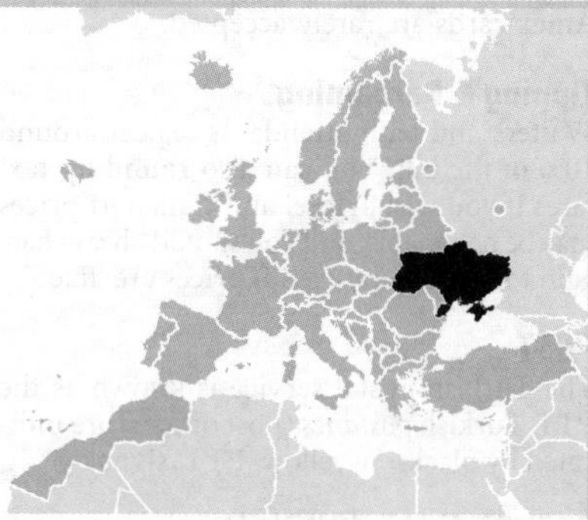

- **Population** 46.4 million
- **Visas** required for Australians and New Zealanders; see p1213

TRAVEL HINTS

Watch out for the heavy swinging doors to the Kyiv metro stations – they really pack a punch.

ROAMING UKRAINE

Kick around Kyiv for at least three days, and give lovely Lviv your lovin' for two or more.

Having thrown off the Soviet shackles in the exciting days of 2005's Orange Revolution, this latecomer to the European party has now opened its doors unreservedly to the West, and while progress has not been without its pitfalls, it's hard not to be broadly optimistic about Ukraine's future as it continues to emerge from Russia's shadow and looks forward to entering its third decade of independence.

'The land on the edge' is how Ukraine's name translates into English, and you'll immediately notice how the country is simultaneously familiar and foreign, predictable and surprising. It's the last stop on the continent before the great enigma of Russia. While many travellers stop off solely in Kyiv on their way through to the east, it's well worth taking your time to see the far more Ukrainian city of Lviv, long touted as 'the new Prague' and a staggeringly wealthy receptacle of architecture, history and art that amazingly survived WWII almost untouched. Ukraine is changing all the time so get here as soon as possible while it remains a land apart.

HISTORY

Before the 13th century, Ukraine was yanked back and forth by nogoodniks such as the Huns and Mongols before settling in the hands of Russian princes. By the 15th century, groups of fierce, wild fighters calling themselves Cossacks (sort of like punks on horseback) fought anyone who encroached upon their borders or belief system (Orthodoxy).

In 1932 and 1933, Stalin engineered a famine, killing millions in Ukraine. In WWII, an estimated 6 million Ukrainians died.

Ukraine declared independence from the USSR in August 1991, and Leonid Kuchma led the country during the late '90s and the early 21st century. Knowing Kuchma wouldn't be able to run in the October 2004 presidential elections, his close ally Viktor Yanukovych ran in his place, challenged by Viktor Yushchenko, an opposition leader who was allegedly poisoned a week before the elections.

Because no one carried more than 50% of the votes in the first round, there was a run-off, which showed Yanukovych as the winner. Suspecting foul play, the Ukrainian population came out en masse on 22 November to protest, with 500,000 people gathering on Kyiv's maydan Nezalezhnosti with tents and orange flags. They stayed on in the snow, sometimes numbering over a million, until 26 December 2004, when a repeat run-off forced by the so-called 'Orange Revolution' took place. Yushchenko won the election and was inaugurated in January 2005.

Since Yushchenko's victory, his popularity has declined vastly, with allegations of corruption and repeated energy crises rocking the nation due to disagreements with neighbouring Russia. One time Yushchenko ally, Yulia Tymoshenko, Ukraine's Prime Minister in 2005, and then again from 2007, is now Yushchenko's number one rival for power in the 2010 presidential elections. Having toned down her anti-Russian rhetoric, built bridges with Moscow over gas prices and been notably restrained in her criticism of the Russian invasion of Georgia in 2008, Tymoshenko has skilfully positioned herself as the Kremlin's favoured candidate for the Ukrainian presidency. But despite the divisive political culture of the country it's not all bad, especially when compared with neighbouring Belarus and Russia; Ukraine today enjoys a vibrant political scene, genuine debate and a largely free press.

THE CULTURE

The Ukrainian population is 78% Ukrainian and 17% Russian. The remainder includes Belarusians, Moldovans, Bulgarians, Poles, Hungarians, Romanians, Tatars and Jews. Almost all of the country's Tatar population (about 250,000) lives in Crimea.

Although most Ukrainians speak Russian, many people in Lviv will not use the language and the number of English-language speakers is growing.

RELIGION

Nearly 97% of Ukrainian believers are Christian. Central and southern Ukraine mostly follow the Moscow-based Ukrainian Orthodox Church, while the rest of the country follows the Kyiv-based Uniate Church (also known as the Ukrainian Catholic Church, and under the jurisdiction of the Vatican). There are some small Jewish minorities in cities. Muslim communities, primarily Tatars, live in Crimea.

ENVIRONMENT

On 26 April 1986, reactor No 4 at Chornobyl (Chernobyl in Russian) nuclear power station, 100km north of Kyiv, exploded and almost 9 tonnes of radioactive matter spewed into the sky. Roughly 4.9 million people living in northern Ukraine, southern Belarus and southwestern Russia were affected. Western monitors now figure that radioactivity levels at Chornobyl are negligible, so organised tours of the site and surrounding 'ghost' villages occur, if you dare.

TRANSPORT

GETTING THERE & AWAY

Air

AeroSvit, Ukrainian International Airlines and major European airlines fly to and from Kyiv's airports:

Boryspil International Airport (KBP; ☎ 044-490 4777; www.airport-borispol.kiev.ua) International flights, some domestic; 35km from centre.

Zhulyany Airport (☎ 044-242 2308; www.airport.kiev.ua; Povitroflotsky pr 92) Domestic and short international flights; 4km from Kyiv.

Bus

Apart from **Autolux** (www.autolux.ua) – a private company with comfortable domestic buses – train travel is far preferable.

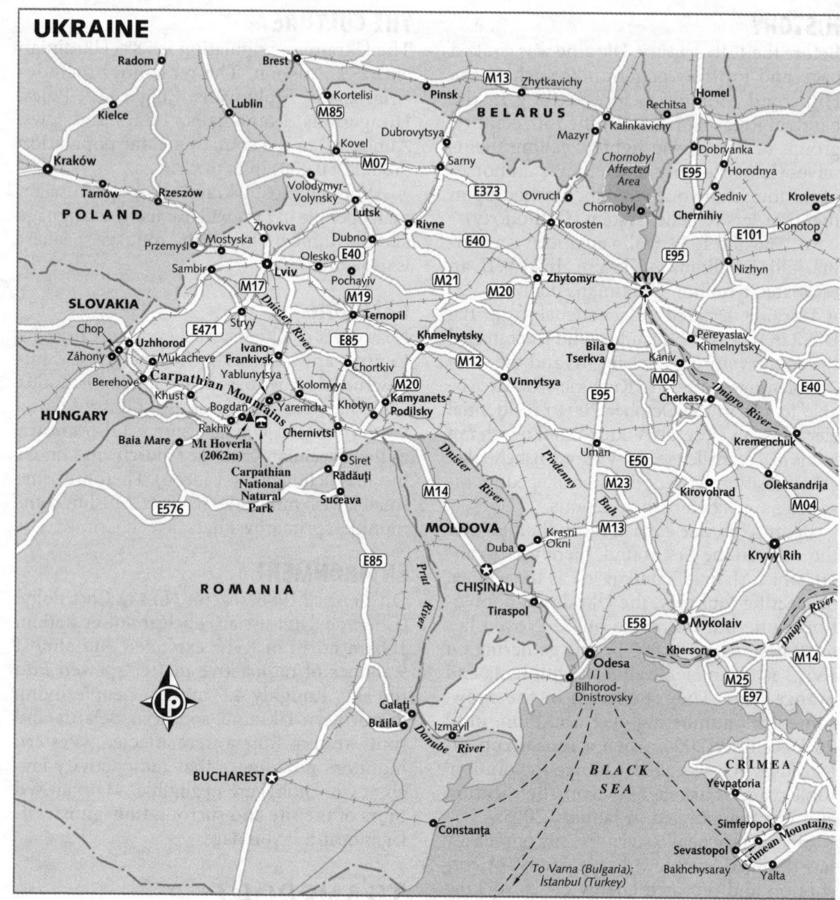

Train

Passports are required for ticket purchases in Kyiv. Kyiv is a good hub, with daily trains to all surrounding countries and Ukrainian cities.

GETTING AROUND

Air

Budget airline **Wizzair** (www.wizzair.com) flies regularly between Kyiv and Lviv.

Bus

There are six daily buses in each direction between Kyiv and Lviv (100hry, 11 hours).

Train

There are several daily trains in each direction between Kyiv and Lviv (70hry to 110hry, 6½ to 12 hours, six daily).

KYIV КИЇВ

☎ 044 / pop 2.7 million

Kyiv is a city changing fast. A national capital for less than two decades, it has taken on the role with aplomb and can comfortably compare to long-established seats of government elsewhere in Europe, with its extraordinary history, dramatic geography and developmental frenzy.

Home of Ukraine's still-fragile democracy and seat of the Orange Revolution, Kyiv is a busy, exciting party town. Take a walk down the Stalinist Khreshchatyk, now the city's premier shopping district, see centuries of faith at the Caves Monastery and join young Kyivans out at one of the city's hot nightspots –

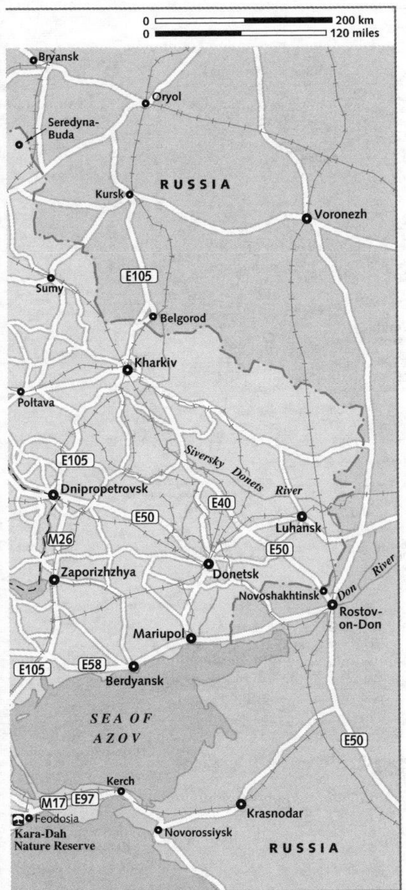

you won't be bored in this post-revolutionary boom town.

ORIENTATION

The main street, closed to motor traffic on Saturday and Sunday, is vul Khreshchatyk. The Dnipro River flows north–south just east of the centre. Although there are some nice sandy beach areas along the east side of the river (called the Left Bank), the area is generally devoid of interest.

INFORMATION

Hotels will do laundry at a reasonable rate. Many apartment rentals offer a washing machine. Left-luggage offices are at the train and bus stations.

ATMs and currency-exchange booths are ubiquitous. Rates offered by hotels are not necessarily worse, but always shop around. Larger banks will cash travellers cheques and give cash advances on credit cards.

American Medical Centre (☎ 490 7600; www.amcenters.com; vul Berdychivska 1) Handles routine and emergency medical and dental needs. Staff speak English.

Orbita (☎ 234 1693; 2nd fl, vul Khreshchatyk 29; per hr 6hry; 🕑 8am-1am) The handiest internet cafe in the city centre.

Sam Travel (☎ 238 6020; vul Ivana Franka 40-B) Organise tours throughout Ukraine, including to the Carpathians, Chernobyl and Crimea.

SIGHTS

With its underground labyrinths lined with mummified monks and extraordinary churches, the **Caves Monastery** (☎ 290 3071; www.lavra.kiev.ua, in Russian; vul Sichnevoho Povstannya 21; adult incl map 16hry; 🕑 upper monastery 9am-7pm May-Sep, 9.30am-6pm Ocy-Apr, lower monastery sunrise-sunset, caves 9am-4.30pm) is the spiritual heart of the Ukrainian people and the single most popular tourist site in the city.

St Sophia's Cathedral (☎ 278 2083; Sofiyivska pl; grounds 2hry, cathedral 22hry, bell tower 5hry; 🕑 grounds 9am-7pm, cathedral 10am-6pm Fri-Tue, to 5pm Wed) holds a monastery and the city's oldest church (built 1017–31). The entire complex is on Unesco's World Heritage List.

Your visit wouldn't be complete without a walk along steep, cobblestoned **Andriyivsky uzviz** (Andrew's descent), one of the oldest and definitely the quaintest street in town. Avoid the incline by taking the **funicular** (admission 50 kopeks; 🕑 6.30am-11pm) to the top, where you'll find **St Michael's Monastery** and, further down, the 1754 **St Andrew's Church**. From there, you can spend an hour or two shopping down Andriyivsky uzviz.

The best museums include the moving, must-see display at the **Chornobyl Museum** (☎ 417 5422; prov Khoryva 1; adult/student 10/3hry; 🕑 10am-6pm Mon-Sat, closed last Mon of month). Also try the **Bulgakov House-Museum** (☎ 425 3188;

READING UP

Everything Is Illuminated, by Jonathan Safran Foer, is the unforgettable, magical realist story of the author's trip to western Ukraine to find the woman who saved his grandfather from the Nazis.

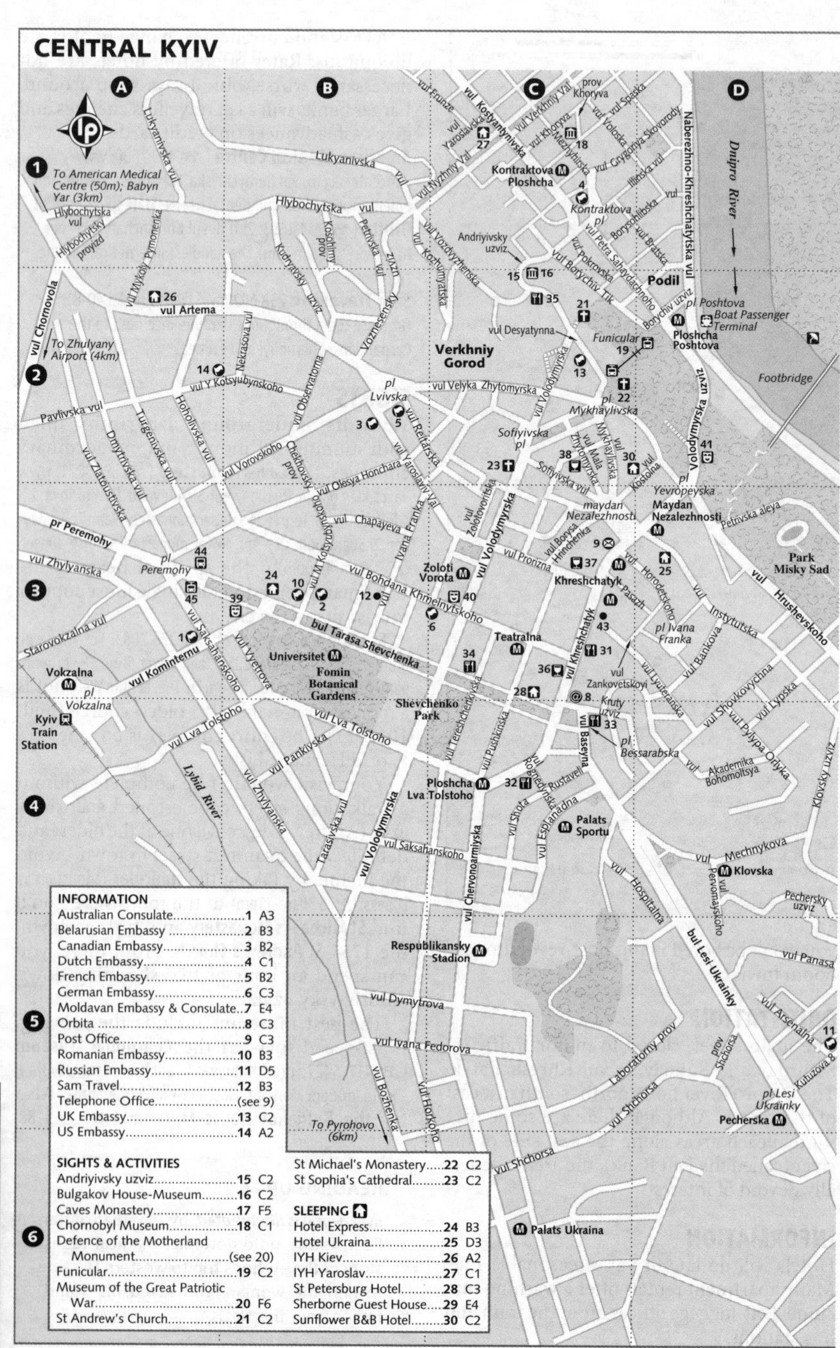
CENTRAL KYIV
To American Medical Centre (50m); Babyn Yar (3km)
To Zhulyany Airport (4km)
To Pyrohovo (6km)
Verkhniy Gorod
Podil
Dnipro River
Park Misky Sad
Fomin Botanical Gardens
Shevchenko Park
Kontraktova Ploshcha
Ploshcha Poshtova
Maydan Nezalezhnosti
Zoloti Vorota
Khreshchatyk
Teatralna
Universitet
Vokzalna
Kyiv Train Station
Ploshcha Lva Tolstoho
Palats Sportu
Klovska
Respublikansky Stadion
Pecherska
Palats Ukraina
Boat Passenger Terminal
Funicular
Footbridge
INFORMATION
Australian Consulate 1 A3
Belarusian Embassy 2 B3
Canadian Embassy 3 B2
Dutch Embassy 4 C1
French Embassy 5 B2
German Embassy 6 C3
Moldavan Embassy & Consulate 7 E4
Orbita 8 C3
Post Office 9 C3
Romanian Embassy 10 B3
Russian Embassy 11 D5
Sam Travel 12 B3
Telephone Office (see 9)
UK Embassy 13 C2
US Embassy 14 A2
SIGHTS & ACTIVITIES
Andriyivsky uzviz 15 C2
Bulgakov House-Museum 16 C2
Caves Monastery 17 F5
Chornobyl Museum 18 C1
Defence of the Motherland Monument (see 20)
Funicular 19 C2
Museum of the Great Patriotic War 20 F6
St Andrew's Church 21 C2
St Michael's Monastery 22 C2
St Sophia's Cathedral 23 C2
SLEEPING
Hotel Express 24 B3
Hotel Ukraina 25 D3
IYH Kiev 26 A2
IYH Yaroslav 27 C1
St Petersburg Hotel 28 C3
Sherborne Guest House 29 E4
Sunflower B&B Hotel 30 C2

UKRAINE

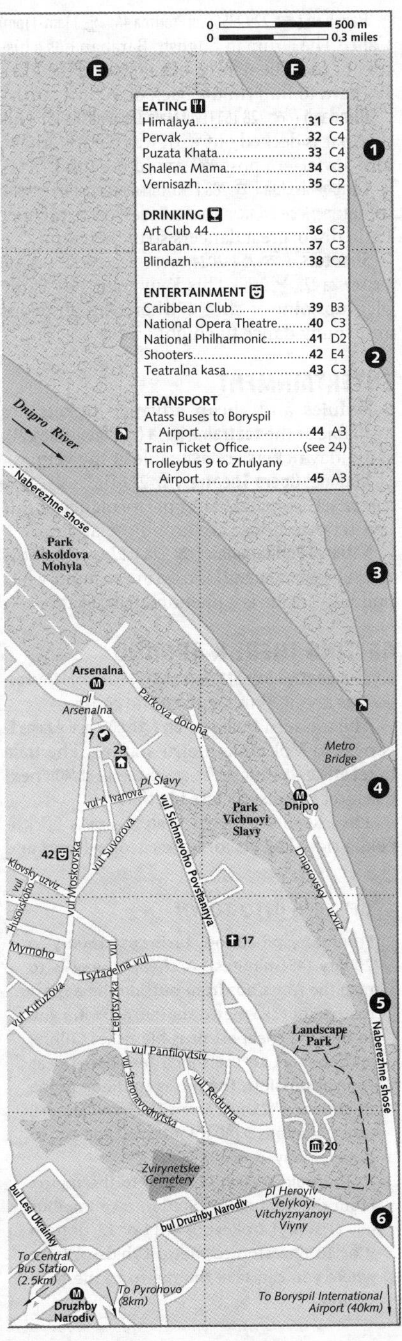

Andriyivsky uzviz 13; adult/student 5/3hry, obligatory excursion 12/6hry; 10am-5pm Thu-Tue) where the author of *The Master & Margarita* lived in the early 20th century. The **Museum of the Great Patriotic War** (☎ 285 9452; www.warmuseum.kiev.ua; vul Sichnevoho Povstannya 44; admission 4hry; 10am-4pm Tue-Sun) has triumphant displays of Soviet heroism. If you so much as approach the area, you'll soon see the 108m-tall metal Soviet woman that is 'Rodina Mat', or the **Defence of the Motherland Monument**. For decades, she has been affectionately known among expats as 'Tin Tits'.

SLEEPING

A good option in Kiev is to rent an apartment. Try **Teren Plus** (☎ 428 1010; www.teren.kiev.ua) and **UA Apartments** (☎ 205 9292; www.uaapartments.com).

IYH Kiev (☎ 481 3838; www.hihostels.com.ua; bldg 2, 5th fl, vul Artema 52A; dm 125hry). This place is hard to find, but it's centrally located behind the US consulate in the courtyard of Artema 52A. There's no kitchen, and bedrooms are basic but clean.

IYH Yaroslav (☎ 417 3189; www.hihostels.com.ua; vul Yaroslavska 10; dm/tw 140/300hry) Kyiv's other youth hostel is this tiny place in the residential district of Podil (go through the courtyard). Inside you'll find 10 beds and friendly, English-speaking staff.

St Petersburg Hotel (☎ 279 7364; www.s-peter.com.ua; bul Tarasa Shevchenka 4; s/d with private bathroom 430/580hry, s/d/tr with shared bathroom 180/290/450hry) The ornate facade of the St Petersburg belies the basic rooms inside, which have high ceilings but not much else to shout about. Breakfast included.

Sherborne Guest House (☎ 490 9693; www.sherbornehotel.com.ua; provulok Sichneviy 9; apt 450-1425hry)

SPLURGE

Sunflower B&B Hotel (☎ 279 3846; www.sunflowerhotel.kiev.ua; vul Kostolna 9-41; s/d 965/1100hry incl breakfast;) Within hearing range of St Michael's church bells, the Sunflower is the best midrange option in town. The yellow, Western-standard rooms are spacious and quiet, with light-wood floors and comfortable beds. You'll also get free internet access and continental breakfast delivered to your room. There are only a few rooms (all doubles, some with kitchens), so book in advance.

Awesome apartments make this good for small groups. On-site staff speak English. Book early.

Hotel Express (☎ 234 2113; www.expresskiev.com; bul Tarasa Shevchenka 38/40; s 450-600hry, d 698-990hry, ste 1500-1980hry, incl breakfast;) Rather better on the inside than you might expect from its gruesome exterior, the Express has been redone and rooms are now of a good standard, nearly all with balconies.

Hotel Ukraina (☎ 278 6675, 279 0347; www.ukraine-hotel.kiev.ua; vul Instytutska 4; s 490-610hry, d650-760hry) Location is the best reason to stay in this Stalinist behemoth overlooking maydan Nezalezhnosti. Rooms vary enormously, but all are clean and safe.

EATING

Puzata Khata (☎ 246 7245; vul Baseyna 1/2A; mains 5-15hry; 8am-11pm) This ubiquitous chain is cheap and offers cafeteria-style dining; the food isn't spectacular but it's reliably okay. It makes for an easy lunch stop.

Pervak (☎ 235 0952; vul Rognedynska 2; mains 30-80hry; 11am-last customer) Soviet style is superhip at Pervak, which serves high-quality Ukrainian food and has a popular and fun bar, as well as live music.

Shalena Mama (Crazy Mama; ☎ 234 1751; vul Tereshchenkivska 4A; mains 40-100hry; 24hr) This handy 24-hour diner with a Rolling Stones theme (each dish is a Stones anthem) features a range of Ukrainian and international dishes, from gazpacho to *deruni* (potato pancakes).

Vernisazh (☎ 425 2403; Andriyivsky uzviz 30; mains 50-90hry; 11am-11pm) This friendly and atmospheric eatery on Kyiv's most famous street is clad in local art and serves up decent meals despite the touristy nature of the area.

Himalaya (☎ 270 5437; vul Khreshchatyk 23; mains 50-100hry; 11.30am-11.30pm) A well-translated English menu and plenty of vegetarian options make Himalaya a firm favourite. It overlooks Kreshchatyk – go through the arch of number 23 and walk around to the right.

DRINKING & CLUBBING

Most clubs have a cover that varies (10hry to 50hry). Extensive lists of performances are featured in local magazine *What's On*, available in hotels, bars and restaurants around town.

Art Club 44 (☎ 279 4137; vul Khreshchatyk 44B; noon-last customer) This underground place has live music every night and is a good place to meet young locals.

Baraban (☎ 229 2355; vul Prorizna 4A; 11am-11pm) Called The Drum in English, Baraban has a history of cool clientele (journalists and the like). It's hard to find (in the back of a courtyard).

Blindazh (☎ 228 1511; vul Mala Zhytomirska 15) This dive bar is decked out with war paraphernalia and Soviet-era posters. Avoid the food.

Caribbean Club (☎ 288 1290; vul Kominternu 4; 4pm-last customer Mon-Fri, from 6pm Sat & Sun) Kyiv's premier Latin disco; great dancers strut their stuff.

Shooters (☎ 254 2024; www.shooters.kiev.ua; vul Moskovska 22; 24hr) This Kyiv mainstay is the pick-up joint of choice where the gorgeous and young dance the night away.

ENTERTAINMENT

Schedules and cheap advance tickets are available at the **teatralna kasa** (vul Khreshchatyk 21); same-day tickets are available at the venues.

National Opera Theatre (☎ 279 1169; www.opera.com.ua; vul Volodymyrska 50) A performance at this lavish opera house is a grandiose affair.

National Philharmonic (☎ 228 1697; www.filarmonia.com.ua; Volodymyrska uzviz) Housed in a beautiful white building. Inside is a phenomenal organ.

GETTING THERE & AROUND

Kyiv's **Central Bus Station** (☎ 265 0430; pl Moskovska 3) is about 3km south of the centre.

The modern **train station** (☎ 005; pl Vokzalna 2) is next to Vokzalna metro station. The **train ticket office** (☎ 050; bul Tarasa Shevchenka 38/40), next to Hotel Express, is less hectic.

The excellent metro system costs 50 kopeks a ride. Tickets for buses, trolleybuses and

GETTING INTO TOWN

From Boryspil airport, taxis cost 150hry to 200hry (45 minutes). A cheaper way is to take the Atass bus from outside the airport to Kharkhovska metro station, allowing you to buy the cheapest possible ticket (20hry) and connect to the much faster metro as soon as possible. The buses continue to the train station (25hry). From Zhulyany airport, take trolleybus 9 (40 minutes, 60 kopeks) to pl Peremohy; a taxi is 50hry.

The train station is linked to the metro. From the Central Bus Station take minibus 457 (1.50hry), trolleybus 4, 11 or 12, or tram 9 or 10 one stop to metro Lybidska, from where you can take the metro to the train station.

CONNECTIONS

Ukraine is well linked to its neighbours, particularly Russia and Belarus, with whom it shares the former Soviet rail system. Kyiv is connected by daily trains to Moscow, St Petersburg, Minsk, Warsaw and Budapest, as well as regular connections to other Eastern European capitals.

trams are 60 kopeks; minibuses are 1hry to 2hry – pay the driver.

Taxis are easy to find, but drivers rarely use their meter – set a price beforehand. By phone, try ☎ 200 0200. You can also flag down a private car and negotiate a price if you speak some basic Russian.

LVIV ЛЬВІВ

☎ **032 (7 digits), 0322 (6 digits) / pop 745,000**

Whether you're arriving from the east with its Soviet cities and concrete architecture, or from the west, where tourist numbers can feel out of control, you'll be extremely glad to have arrived in Lviv, Ukraine's most lovely city. This fabulous relic of Galicia's cosmopolitan past feels distinctly un-Soviet with its Central European flavour and charismatic population. Best of all, despite the extraordinary architectural wealth here, tourists remain a small minority even in the Unesco World Heritage–listed old town in midsummer.

INFORMATION

Budinok Knigi (☎ 722 550; pl Mitskevycha; ⏲ 10am-6pm Mon-Fri, to 3pm Sat) Lviv's oldest bookshop has maps, guides and some novels in English.

Internet Club (☎ 242 4210; vul Dudaeva 12; per hr 4-6hry; ⏲ 24hr) Twenty terminals, can connect laptops.

Internet Service (☎ 294 8204; vul Shevska 6; per hr 6hry; ⏲ 10am-9pm) Small internet cafe off the main square on 2nd floor of Litera Bookshop.

EMERGENCY NUMBERS

- Ambulance ☎ 03
- Fire ☎ 01
- Police ☎ 02

Tourist information centre (☎ 201 8666; www.tourinfo.lviv.ua; pl Rynok 2; ⏲ 10am-1pm & 2-6pm Mon-Fri) English-speaking staff are helpful and there's lots of information available.

SIGHTS

There are lots of museums in the old town, but nothing's signed in English. The main draw is exploring the meandering alleys lined with amazing architecture. Apart from wandering around the gorgeous **old town** and ogling the architecture, you can head to the **Vysoky Zamok** (High Castle) for hilltop views.

Lychakiv Cemetery (vul Mechinikova; adult/student 10/5hry; ⏲ 9am-5pm) is one of the most beautiful in Eastern Europe. If you get on tram 2 or 7 in the old town, you'll arrive right in front of the cemetery five stops later (if you get confused, ask for the *klad*-bee-sheh).

The **Pharmacy Museum** (☎ 722 041; vul Drukarska 2; adult/student 3/2hry; ⏲ 10am-7pm Mon-Fri, to 6pm Sat & Sun) is in the back of a functioning pharmacy that dates to 1735. Pay the pharmacists to open it for you, and walk into a world of containers, drawers and other gadgets for herbs, tinctures and salves. You can buy a small bottle of medicinal 'iron wine'.

SLEEPING

For apartments we recommend **In Lviv** (☎ 728 001; www.inlviv.info) and **Lviv Apartments** (☎ 067 672 5161; www.lviv-apartments.com) where prices start at around €25 per day per apartment.

Sun Hostel (☎ 291 1970; www.sun.lviv.ua; pr Shevchenko 12; dm/d from 50/100hry) This centrally located but rather chaotically run hostel has unbeatably low prices that include free wi-fi and access to a washing machine.

Kosmonaut Hostel (☎ 274 0274; www.thekosmonaut.com; vul Sichovykh Striltsiv 8; dm 70-90hry, s/d/apt 100/200/210hry; 💻) The Kosmonaut is great fun, with free guest wi-fi, a shared kitchen, four dorms, one apartment with private facilities and a twin room that can be booked as a single.

Hotel Lviv (☎ 423 555; hotel_lviv@svitonline.com; pr V Chornovola 7; s/d from 130/200hry) Just behind the opera house, this aging behemoth presents a number of options, from the very basic rooms with a basin and shared facilities to surprisingly spacious 'lux' rooms.

Hotel George (☎ 725 952; www.georgehotel.com.ua; pl Mitskevycha 1; s/tw with private bathroom 370/400hry, with shared bathroom 190/220hry) The George's colonnaded lobby gives this place an atmosphere that money alone just can't buy. The 'tourist class' rooms here are a great deal and share facilities on the corridor.

EATING & DRINKING

There are a few culinary gems in Lviv, although overall the city seems to run on coffee and cake far more than *haute cuisine*.

Puzata Khata (☎ 240 3265; vul Sichovykh Striltsiv; mains 5-15hry; 🕑 10am-10pm) This popular cafeteria-style chain serves up Ukrainian staples.

Korzo Pub (☎ 296 7092; vul Brativ Rohatyntsiv 10; mains 20-30hry; 🕑 noon-midnight Sun-Thu, to 2am Fri & Sat) This is the best pub in town, with a lovely wooden interior. There's a wide range of beers, decent food and a crowd of regulars.

Kabinet Café (vul Vynnychenka 12; mains 20-40hry; 🕑 10am-11pm) Kabinet serves up hot meals and cold bevies in a stylish library setting complete with billiards table.

Dzyha (☎ 297 5010; vul Virmenska 35; mains 25hry; 🕑 8am-11pm) This great option is a relaxed bar outside, with a decent yet informal restaurant inside. The place attracts an arty crowd, who order food from the newspaper-style menu.

Robert Doms (☎ 292 2593; vul Kleparivska 18; mains 25-50hry; 🕑 noon-midnight) Robert Doms is a converted beer storage vault once used by the neighbouring Lvivske brewery. There's great food and fresh brews.

GETTING THERE & AWAY

Lviv airport (☎ 298 112; www.avia.lviv.ua) is about 9km west of the centre. There are daily flights to/from Kyiv with budget airline **Wizzair** (www.wizzair.com).

The **train station** (☎ 005; pl Dvirtseva) is 1.75km west of the city centre and connected to town by trams 1 and 9. Tickets to Kyiv (70hry to 110hry, 6½ to 12 hours, six daily) can also be obtained from the **train ticket office** (☎ 226 5276; vul Hnatyuka 20; 🕑 8am-2pm & 3-8pm Mon-Sat, to 6pm Sun).

The **long-distance bus terminal** (Holovny Avtovokzal; ☎ 632 473; vul Stryska 271), about 8km south of the city centre (take minibus 71 or 180 from pl Svobody or trolleybus 5 from pl Petrushevycha) has buses to Kyiv (100hry, 11 hours, six daily).

Privately run **Autolux** (www.autolux.com.ua) operates from the long-distance terminal, sending nice, modern buses to Kyiv and other cities; see the website for details.

UKRAINE DIRECTORY

ACCOMMODATION

Book travel and accommodation well in advance during the 1 May holidays. Hostels are just starting up in Ukraine; check www.hihostels.com.ua/en for details.

Most budget hotels are unsightly Soviet monstrosities built in the '60s and '70s. Rooms are often well-worn, with outdated furniture, but are reasonably comfortable.

Midrange hotels or more expensive rooms in budget hotels may have more polite staff and remodelled, Western-style bathrooms.

BUSINESS HOURS

Official working hours are 9am (or 10am) to 5pm (or 6pm) Monday to Friday, with an hour-long break anywhere between noon and 3pm. Shops often open until about 8pm Monday to Friday and all day Saturday. Most bars and restaurants tend to open from 10am until 11pm or midnight; clubs stay open later.

EMBASSIES & CONSULATES

The following are in Kyiv unless otherwise noted:

Australia (Map pp1208-9; ☎ 044-246 4223; vul Kominternu 18/137)
Belarus (Map pp1208-9; ☎ 044-537 5200; www.belembassy.org.ua; vul Kotsyubynskoho 3)
Canada (Map pp1208-9; ☎ 044-590 3100; www.kyiv.gc.ca; vul Yaroslaviv Val 31)
France (Map pp1208-9; ☎ 044-590 3600; www.ambafrance-ua.org; vul Reitarska 39)
Germany (Map pp1208-9; ☎ 044-247 6800; www.german-embassy.kiev.ua; vul Bohdana Khmelnytskoho 25)
Moldova (Map pp1208-9; ☎ 044-280 7721; moldoukr@sovamua.com; vul Sichnevoho Povstannya 6)
Netherlands (Map pp1208-9; ☎ 044-490 8200; www.netherlands-embassy.com.ua; Kontraktova pl 7)
Romania (Map pp1208-9; ☎ 044-234 5261; www.kiev.mae.ro; vul M Kotsyubynskoho 8)
Russia (Map pp1208-9; ☎ 044-296 4504; www.embrus.org.ua; vul Kutuzova 8)
UK (Map pp1208-9; ☎ 044-490 3600; www.ukinukraine.fco.gov.uk; vul Desyatynna 9)
USA (Map pp1208-9; ☎ 044-490 0000/4000; www.usemb.kiev.ua; vul Yuriya Kotsyubynskoho 10)

FESTIVALS & EVENTS

International Labour Day (1 May) Always a big deal.
Independence Day (24 August) Sees each city in Ukraine hosts a festival and parade.

HOLIDAYS

New Year's Day 1 January
Orthodox Christmas 7 January
International Women's Day 8 March
Orthodox Easter (Paskha) April
Labour Day 1-2 May
Victory Day 9 May
Constitution Day 28 June
Independence Day 24 August
Catholic Christmas 25 December

MONEY

The hryvnia (hry) is divided into 100 units, called kopeks. Coins come in denominations of one, two, five, 10, 25 and 50 kopeks as well as one hryvnia, while there are one, two, five, 10, 20, 50, 100, 200 and 500 hryvnia notes.

Although many hotels give prices in US dollars or euros, you will be expected to pay in hryvnia.

POST

Normal-sized letters or postcards cost 3.50hry to anywhere outside Ukraine by ordinary mail or a bit more for express service. Domestic services take three days to a week; international takes a week to 10 days.

TELEPHONE

Every city and large town has a telephone centre (many open 24 hours), usually near the central post office. Pay in advance (you will get change for unused time). Public phones are a hassle.

When dialling Ukraine from abroad, dial ☎ 380, the city code (without the first zero) and then the number. To call overseas from Ukraine, dial ☎ 8 (wait for a tone), then 10, followed by the country code, city code and number.

For interstate calls within Ukraine, dial ☎ 8, wait for a tone, then the city code (with its first zero) and number – there should always be a 10-digit combination. If a telephone number has seven digits, use the first three digits of the area code, but if the telephone number has five/six digits use the first five/four digits of the area code.

Anyone with an unlocked GSM mobile phone can simply buy a Ukrainian SIM card from any dealer and slot it in their handset to make cheap calls locally.

To dial a local mobile-phone number within Ukraine, you must always prefix it with an ☎ 8, as if calling another town. Common codes for mobiles include ☎ 050 and ☎ 067.

VISAS

For stays of up to 90 days, visas are no longer required for EU, US, Swiss, Canadian and Japanese citizens. Australians and New Zealanders still need visas (and the visas should be obtained before you leave home; not in a neighbouring country). Point-of-entry visas are not issued. For more information see www.mfa.gov.ua/uk.

UKRAINE

Europe Directory

CONTENTS

Accommodation	1214
Activities	1217
Books	1218
Business Hours	1218
Climate	1218
Customs	1220
Dangers & Annoyances	1220
Discount Cards	1221
Discrimination	1222
Driving Licence	1222
Electricity	1222
Embassies & Consulates	1222
Festivals & Holidays	1222
Gay & Lesbian Travellers	1222
Insurance	1223
Internet Access	1223
Internet Resources	1223
Legal Matters	1223
Maps	1224
Media	1224
Money	1225
Passport	1227
Photography & DVD	1228
Post	1228
Studying	1228
Telephone	1228
Time	1229
Toilets	1229
Tourist Information	1229
Tours	1229
Travellers with Disabilities	1229
Visas	1229
Volunteering	1230
Women Travellers	1231
Working	1231

This chapter includes only general information about the region; for country-specific information refer to Directory in individual country chapters. Relevant cross-references have been added for your convenience.

ACCOMMODATION

Unless otherwise stated in individual reviews or in country directories, all hotels and hostels in this book include a private bathroom.

> **BOOK YOUR STAY ONLINE**
>
> For more accommodation reviews and recommendations by Lonely Planet authors, check out the online booking service at www.lonelyplanet.com/hotels. You'll find the true, insider low-down on the best places to stay. Reviews are thorough and independent. Best of all, you can book online.

Europe offers the fullest possible range of budget accommodation, from camping grounds, hostels and student dormitories to private rooms, guest houses and cheap hotels. Plus there are more novel options, such as farm-stays (opposite) and couch-surfing (p1216). Self-catering flats and cottages are also worth considering with a group, especially for longer stays.

Accommodation listings in this book are listed in cities and towns in ascending order of price, with worthwhile options for splurging also included. The hotels in this book generally range from no stars to two stars.

During peak holiday periods, particularly Easter, summer and Christmas – and any time of year in popular destinations such as London, Paris and Rome – it's wise to book ahead. Most places can now be reserved online. In general, always try to book directly with the establishment; this means you're paying just for your room and no surcharge is going to a middleman as with many hostel-booking websites.

Tourist offices often have extensive accommodation lists and the more helpful ones will go out of their way to find something suitable. There's usually a fee for this service, but it tends to be low; if accommodation is tight, it can save you hassle and potential language problems.

B&Bs, Guest houses & Hotels

Private rooms, guest houses (*pension, Gasthaus, chambre d'hôte* etc) and budget hotels offer greater comfort than hostels for a marginally higher price. Most are simple affairs, sometimes still with shared bathroom facilities.

In private rooms with a local family, or in a small guest house, you benefit from greater contact with locals. You'll still have a great deal of privacy and autonomy, but remember you won't be able to bring the party back to your place.

In some destinations, particularly in Eastern Europe, locals wait in train stations touting rented rooms. Just be sure such accommodation isn't in a far-flung suburb that requires an expensive taxi ride to and from town. Also check that both parties are clear on price beforehand, and remember that in these cases it's unwise to leave valuables in your room when you go out.

Many B&Bs (bed and breakfasts) in the UK and Ireland aren't budget accommodation at all. Even the lowliest tend to have midrange prices and a new generation of 'designer' B&Bs are positively top-end.

Be careful when choosing inexpensive hotels around the bus and train station areas. They can be convenient for late-night or early-morning arrivals and departures, but some hotels are unofficial brothels or just downright sleazy places where things go missing in the night.

If you can, check the room beforehand and make sure you're clear on price and what it covers.

Discounts for longer stays are usually possible and hotel owners in southern Europe *might* be open to a little bargaining if times are slack. In many countries, it's common for business hotels (usually more than two stars) to slash their rates by up to 40% on Friday and Saturday nights.

Look out for the following three budget hotel chains. All favour comfort and convenience over tasteful decoration and personality. However, they make useful boltholes if you need a break from hostels.

easyHotel (www.easyhotel.com) Only in the UK, Switzerland, Hungary and Cyprus.

Etap (www.etaphotel.com) Covering 10 European countries, including the UK, France and Germany

Formule 1 (www.hotelformule1.com) Operating in eight European countries, including expensive Sweden.

Camping

Camping is the cheapest option. It's newly trendy in parts of Europe, such as the UK (albeit with designer tents, eco tents and Airstream caravans; see, for example, www.coolcamping.co.uk). In other countries, such as the Czech Republic, Germany, the Netherlands and Poland, it has never gone out of fashion.

There's one drawback, though, and we don't mean having to carry your tent, sleeping bag and cooking equipment. In large European cities, most camping grounds are some distance from the centre, so you'll need your own transport. As not all budget travellers have that, this book lists easily accessible camping grounds only, or includes sites where it's common for travellers to bed down en masse under the stars (for example, on some Greek islands).

National tourist offices provide lists of camping grounds, and camping organisation contacts are also listed in some individual country directories of this book. At designated grounds, there will usually be a charge per tent or site, per person and per vehicle. In busy areas, in busy seasons, it's sometimes necessary to book.

Camping other than at designated grounds is difficult in Western Europe, because it's hard to find a suitably private spot. Camping is also illegal without the permission of the local authorities (the police or local council office) or the landowner. Don't be shy about asking; you might be pleasantly surprised.

In some countries, such as Austria, the UK, France and Germany, free camping is illegal on all but private land, and in Greece it's illegal altogether but not enforced. This doesn't prevent hikers from occasionally pitching their tent, and you'll usually get away with it if you have a small tent, are discreet, stay just one or two nights, decamp during the day and don't light a fire or leave rubbish. At worst, you'll be woken by the police and asked to move on.

In Eastern Europe, free camping is more widespread.

Farm stays

You needn't volunteer on a farm to sleep on it. In Switzerland and Germany, there's the opportunity for ordinary tourists to sleep in barns or 'hay hotels'. It saves you money and is a great experience. For further details, visit **Aventure sur la paille** (www.aventure-sur-la-paille.ch), **Abenteuer im Stroh** (www.abenteuer-stroh.ch) and **Hay Hotels** (www.heuhotel.de, in German). When their cows are out to pasture in summer or even after they've been brought in for the winter come early October, farmers charge travellers Sfr20 to Sfr30 per adult to sleep

STAY FOR FREE

Wish you had mates all over Europe so you could crash on their sofa when you were travelling? Don't we all? Luckily, with the new phenomenon of online hospitality clubs, you can make it a reality. **Couch Surfing** (www.couchsurfing.com) is the perfect example, linking travellers with more than 65,000 global residents who'll let you occupy their couch or spare room – and sometimes show you around town – all cost-free.

This club is unusual in not insisting you return the favour, by hosting other travellers at some point. Similar schemes, such as **Global Freeloaders** (www.globalfreeloaders.com) and **Hospitality Club** (www.hospitalityclub.org), tend to be stricter on that, although both are happy for you to first enjoy others' hospitality before reciprocating.

If you're worried about how safe this is, there are many security measures in place, with members verified and vouched for by others, and we've not heard any bad stories. However, at the very least always let friends and family know where you're staying and carry your mobile phone with you.

Female travellers might want to investigate the women-only, membership-based **5W** (www.womenwelcomewomen.org.uk).

on straw in their hay barns or lofts (listen to the jangle of cow or goat bells beneath your head!). Farmers provide cotton under-sheets (to avoid straw pricks) and woolly blankets for extra warmth, but guests need their own sleeping bags and pocket torch.

Hostels

HI HOSTELS

Hostels offer the cheapest (secure) roof over your head in Europe and you don't have to be a youngster to use them. Only southern German hostels enforce a strict age limit of 26 years. That said, if you're over 26, you'll frequently pay a small surcharge (usually about €3) to stay in an official hostel.

The hostels in this category are part of the national youth hostel association (YHA), which is affiliated to **Hostelling International** (HI; www.hihostels.com).

Most HI hostels have dorm rooms sleeping four to five people, although larger ones do exist. Hostel rules vary per facility and country, but some ask that guests vacate the rooms for cleaning purposes or impose a curfew. Most offer a complimentary breakfast, although the quality of this varies.

You need to be a YHA or HI member to use affiliated hostels, but nonmembers can stay by paying an extra charge of a few euros, which will then be set against future membership. After sufficient nights (usually six), you automatically become a member. To join, ask at any hostel or contact your national hostelling office, which you'll find on the HI website, where you can also make online bookings.

National hostelling associations across Europe are listed in the individual country directories of this book.

BACKPACKER HOSTELS

There are also many private hostelling organisations in Europe and hundreds of unaffiliated backpacker hostels. Private hostels have fewer rules (eg no curfew, no daytime lockout), more self-catering kitchens and a lower number of large, noisy school groups.

However, whereas HI hostels must meet minimum safety and cleanliness standards, facilities vary greatly in private hostels. Dorms in some private hostels, especially in Germanic countries, can be co-ed. If that makes you uncomfortable, be careful to ask.

Individual country chapters have reviews and the Directory sections list contact details for private hostel groups, where they exist.

University Accommodation

Some university towns rent out their student accommodation during the holiday periods. This is a popular practice in France, the UK and many Eastern European countries (see individual country chapters for more details). University accommodation will sometimes be in single rooms (although it's more commonly in doubles or triples) and might have cooking facilities. For details inquire at individual colleges or universities, at student information offices or local tourist offices.

ACTIVITIES

Europe offers countless sporting opportunities. The varied geography and climate support everything from hiking, mountaineering and skiing to windsurfing, diving and fishing. For further suggestions, see individual country chapters and A Year in Europe (p45).

Adventure Sports

New Zealand might boast it's the world's leading adventure-sports destination, but when it comes to bungee jumping, canyoning, ice-climbing, paragliding and skydiving, Interlaken (p1168) in Switzerland gives the Kiwis a thrill-per-minute run for their money. For operators see **Swissraft** (www.swissraft.ch) or the companies mentioned in the Switzerland chapter.

Another burgeoning, and more reasonably priced, adventure-sports destination is Bovec (p1040) in Slovenia. Parts of Bosnia and Macedonia also increasingly offer adventure-sports opportunities.

Of all these, Slovenia is the cheapest option, with prices in the region of €90 for paragliding or bungee jumping and €35 for rafting or canyoning. In Switzerland you'll pay the equivalent of €175 to go paragliding, €125 to €255 for a bungee jump, and €75 to €125 to go rafting or canyoning.

Cycling

For information on cycling in Europe, see p1236.

Diving

Ok, so it won't rival the Red Sea anytime soon, but Europe offers some surprisingly excellent diving opportunities. The Mediterranean is obviously a highlight – Sardinia, Malta and Sicily all regularly compete for title of the best dive destination on the continent with clear waters and dramatic scenery below the waves. If you want wreck diving, then Britain, with its colourful maritime history, offers some of the best in the world. For ancient wrecks, and even volcanoes, head to the waters of Greece and Turkey.

Hiking

Keen hikers could spend a lifetime exploring Europe's exciting trails. Probably the most spectacular are in the Alps and Italian Dolomites, which are criss-crossed with well-marked routes. In season, food and accommodation are available along the way.

The less-developed Pyrenees are equally sensational, especially as you pass through remote mountain villages. Even less well-known, but still stunning, hiking areas are found in Sardinia, northern Portugal, Turkey, Morocco, Slovakia, Poland, Romania and Bulgaria.

Ramblers' Association (www.ramblers.org.uk) promotes long-distance walking in the UK and can help with maps and information.

Snow Sports

In winter, thousands of Europeans head off skiing and snowboarding. Cross-country skiing is popular in some areas, and snowshoe hiking (walking on shoes shaped like tennis racquets) is the latest up-and-coming activity. A skiing holiday on the Continent usually works out to be twice as expensive as an equivalent summer holiday, by the time you've paid for ski lifts, accommodation, equipment hire and the inevitable après-ski drinking.

The well-equipped, long-standing resorts in the French and Swiss Alps are expensive. However, even in Western Europe you can get some cheap deals. Italy, Austria and the less-popular skiing regions of Germany (the Black Forest and Harz Mountains) are slightly cheaper. Even cheaper still are Andorra, the Pyrenees and the Sierra Nevada range in the south of Spain. Last-minute package deals can be surprisingly good value; look in newspaper travel sections or on booking sites.

For the best skiing bargains of all, head to Eastern Europe. Bulgaria, Romania, Slovakia, Czech Republic and Poland are all opening up as snow-sports destinations, although facilities are limited.

The skiing season used to last from early December to late March, but has become more unpredictable – which many attribute to global warming. In recent years, poor snowfall has meant a late start to the season (post-Christmas). Annual variations aside, January and February tend to be the best (and busiest) months.

At the Stubai Glacier (p98) in Austria, you can ski or snowboard all year.

Surfing & Windsurfing

Believe it or not, you can go surfing in Europe. There can be excellent waves, and an accompanying surfer scene, in southwest England (particularly Cornwall) and west Scotland (wetsuit advisable), along Ireland's northwest coast, on the Atlantic coast of France (particularly Biarritz) and Portugal, and along the north and southwest coasts of Spain. The area around Agadir, Morocco, also has great surf from late autumn to early spring.

After swimming and fishing, windsurfing could well be the most popular of Europe's many water sports. It's easy to rent sailboards in many tourist centres and courses are usually available for beginners.

BOOKS

This guide is tailored for travellers on a budget who wish to cover a lot of Europe, but Lonely Planet produces many other travel guides and books to complement the information here. These provide more in-depth information on specific areas and cater to a wider range of budgets.

As well as titles to Western, Mediterranean, Eastern, Central and Scandinavian Europe, and the Western Balkans, Lonely Planet has guides to most countries in this book, as well as to regions within some. We also publish city guides to various capitals (London, Paris, Rome, Berlin, Amsterdam etc) and various cycling and walking guides.

Travel Literature

Comic travel writing has been in vogue for a while, and three of the best examples recount pan-European journeys. In *Neither Here nor There: Travels in Europe,* Bill Bryson retraces his youthful 1970s European tour some 20 years later as an older, less agile, more sober adult. Tim Moore reaches further back into history with *Continental Drifter*. Here, he muses on the origins of the 17th-century European 'Grand Tour', by which well-to-do young Englishmen sought to educate themselves – all the while re-creating it himself, sleeping rough in a vintage Rolls Royce and (crumpled) velvet suit.

Peter Moore (no relation to Tim) makes life even more difficult for himself in *The Wrong Way Home*. The 'wrong way' turns out to be without a plane journey, from London to Sydney. Although the travelogue naturally ventures into Asia, it does have some sterling episodes in Europe.

For something perhaps more akin with your own experience, try *Rite of Passage: Tales of Backpacking 'round Europe.* Edited by Lisa Johnson, it's a group of stories by young travellers conquering the Continent for the first time. From crowded hostels to heated flings, this book taps into the seemingly insignificant events that fuel lifelong memories.

Classic European travel tales come from two leading authors. In *A Tramp Abroad,* Mark Twain chronicles, with his usual wit, a 15-month 'walking tour' (by train and coach) through central Europe and the Alps in the 19th century.

Meanwhile, Patrick Leigh Fermor's *A Time of Gifts* is widely regarded as a masterpiece of travel literature. Writing in 1977, Fermor looks back on the time when, as a teenager in 1934, he walked from the Hoek van Holland to Constantinople (present-day İstanbul), relying on the kindness of strangers to house and feed him. This book takes him as far as Hungary, where another book *Between the Woods and the Water* takes over.

BUSINESS HOURS

In most of Europe businesses are open 9am to 6pm Monday to Friday, and 9am to 1pm or 5pm on Saturday. In smaller towns there may be a one- to two-hour closure for lunch. Some shops close on Sunday. Businesses also close on national holidays and local feast days.

Banks have the shortest opening times, often closing between 3pm and 5pm, and occasionally even shutting for lunch. They only open during the week.

Restaurants typically open around noon until midnight and bars open around 6pm. Museums usually close on Monday or Tuesday.

CLIMATE

The climate in Western Europe is generally temperate and mild, except in mountainous areas. However, lately – some say as a result of global warming – there have been floods in the Alps and along the Danube in spring or summer, while other parts of the continent, particularly Portugal, have suffered drought.

The weather in Eastern Europe can be fairly extreme at times. However it's rarely enough to prevent travel, and during the icy winter the cities take on a magical frosty charm.

In the Mediterranean the weather is generally kinder. Summer is typically hot and sunny; in autumn it gets colder and rains,

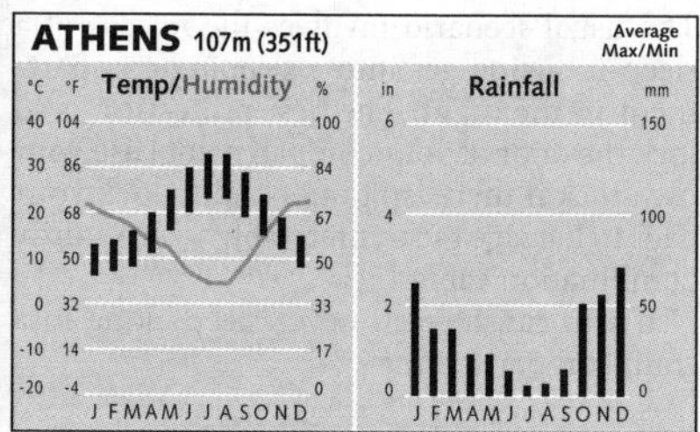
ATHENS 107m (351ft)
Average Max/Min
Temp/Humidity
Rainfall
°C °F %
in mm
40 104 100
30 86 84
20 68 67
10 50 50
0 32 33
-10 14 17
-20 -4 0
6 150
4 100
2 50
0 0
J F M A M J J A S O N D

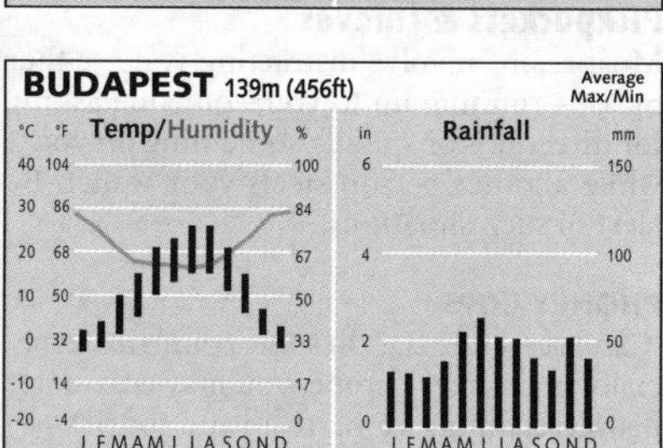
BUDAPEST 139m (456ft)
Average Max/Min
Temp/Humidity
Rainfall
°C °F %
in mm
J F M A M J J A S O N D

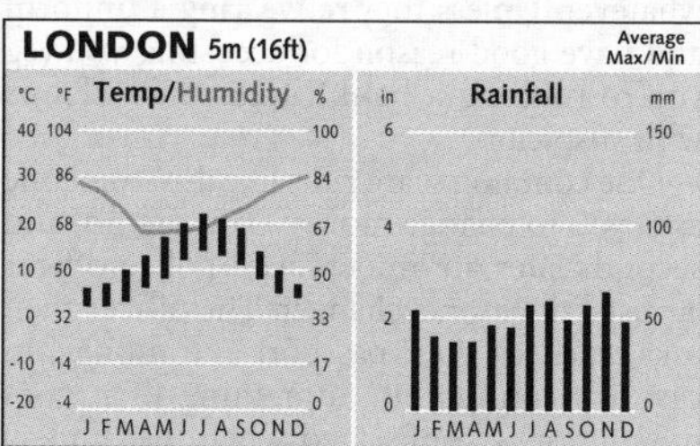
LONDON 5m (16ft)
Average Max/Min
Temp/Humidity
Rainfall
°C °F %
in mm
J F M A M J J A S O N D

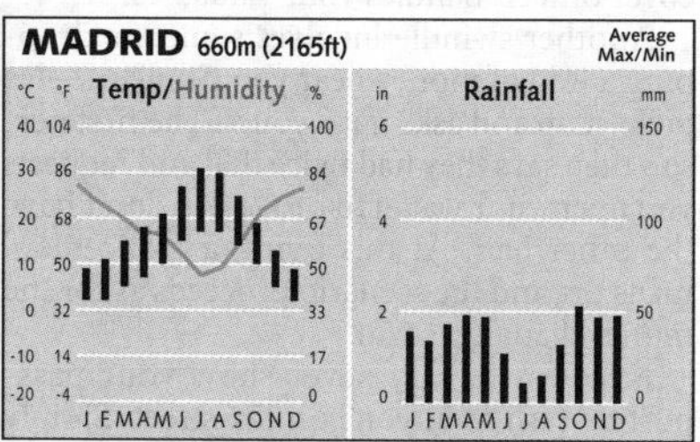
MADRID 660m (2165ft)
Average Max/Min
Temp/Humidity
Rainfall
°C °F %
in mm
J F M A M J J A S O N D

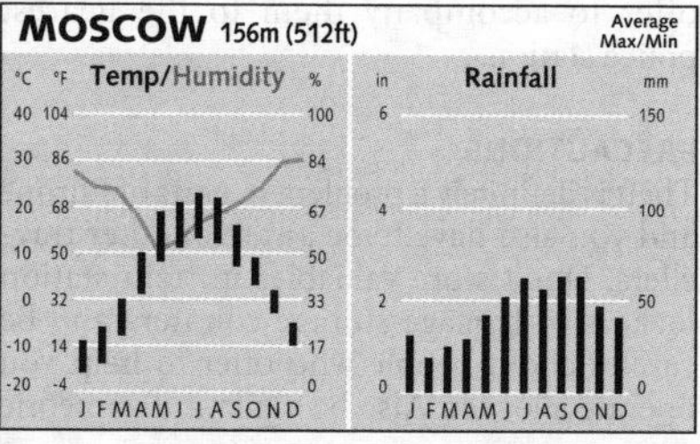
MOSCOW 156m (512ft)
Average Max/Min
Temp/Humidity
Rainfall
°C °F %
in mm
J F M A M J J A S O N D

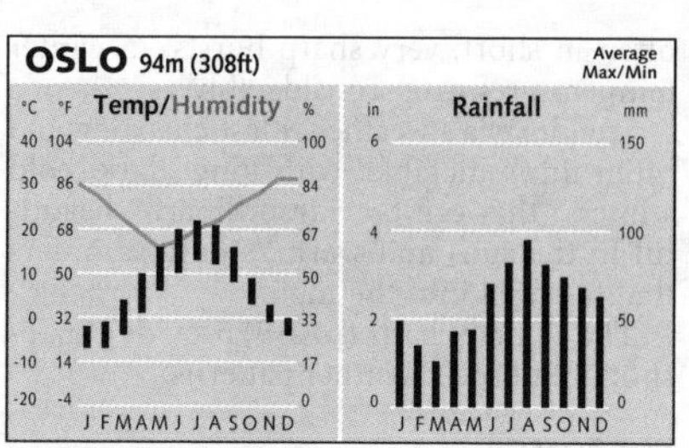
OSLO 94m (308ft)
Average Max/Min
Temp/Humidity
Rainfall
°C °F %
in mm
J F M A M J J A S O N D

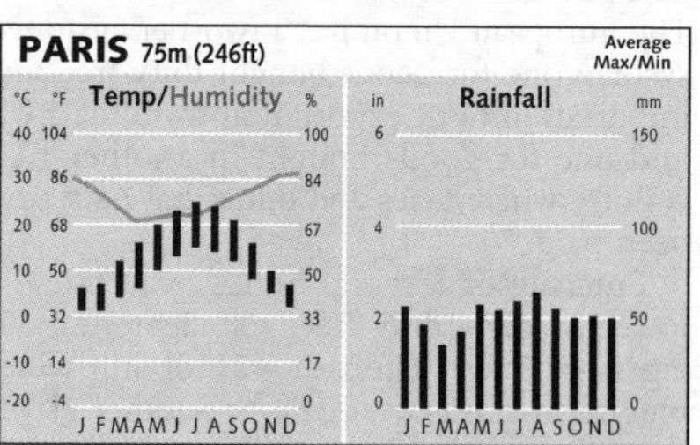
PARIS 75m (246ft)
Average Max/Min
Temp/Humidity
Rainfall
°C °F %
in mm
J F M A M J J A S O N D

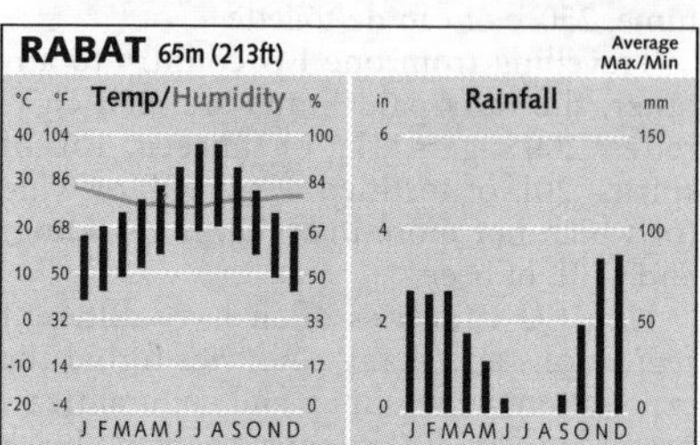
RABAT 65m (213ft)
Average Max/Min
Temp/Humidity
Rainfall
°C °F %
in mm
J F M A M J J A S O N D

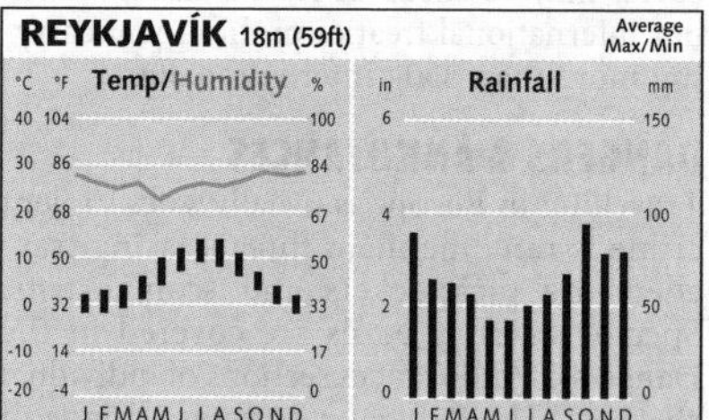
REYKJAVÍK 18m (59ft)
Average Max/Min
Temp/Humidity
Rainfall
°C °F %
in mm
J F M A M J J A S O N D

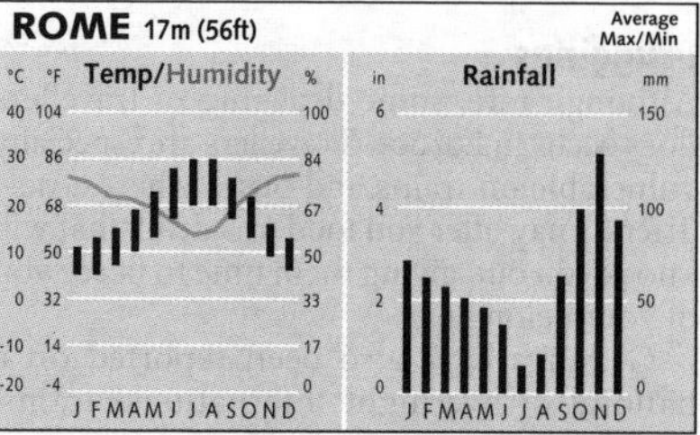
ROME 17m (56ft)
Average Max/Min
Temp/Humidity
Rainfall
°C °F %
in mm
J F M A M J J A S O N D

often in short, very sharp bursts; in winter temperatures drop considerably.

Scandinavia's weather is fast changing and often unpredictable, with long, dark, cold winters (that can be extraordinarily beautiful in the sun) and warm, sunny summers that last well into the night.

The climate charts (p1219) provide a snapshot of Europe's weather patterns.

CUSTOMS

The European Union has a two-tier customs system: one for goods bought duty-free for importation to or exportation from the EU, and one for goods bought in another EU country where taxes and duties have already been paid.

Entering or leaving the EU, you are allowed to carry duty-free: 200 cigarettes, 50 cigars or 250g of tobacco; 2L of still wine plus 1L of spirits over 22% or another 2L of wine (sparkling or otherwise); 50g of perfume, 250cc of eau de toilette.

Travelling from one EU country to another, the duty-paid limits are: 800 cigarettes, 200 cigars, 1kg of tobacco, 10L of spirits, 20L of fortified wine, 90L of wine (of which not more than 60L is sparkling) and 110L of beer.

Non-EU countries often have different regulations and many countries forbid the exportation of antiquities and cultural treasures; see individual country chapters. Black caviar may be cheap in Russia and Ukraine, but international treaties prohibit you carrying more than 250g internationally.

DANGERS & ANNOYANCES

Travelling in Europe is usually safe. Violent crime is rare; the main threats facing travellers are pickpockets and scam artists. Specific country perils are covered in the Dangers & Annoyances sections of individual chapters. The following outlines a range of general guidelines.

Druggings

Although rare, some drugging of travellers does occur in Europe. Travellers are especially vulnerable on trains and buses where a new 'friend' may offer you food or a drink that will knock you out, giving them time to fleece you of your belongings.

Gassings have also been reported on a handful of overnight international trains. The usual scenario involves the release of a sleep-inducing gas into a sleeping compartment in the night. The best protection is to lock the door of your compartment (use your own lock if there isn't one) and to lock your bags to luggage racks, preferably with a sturdy combination cable.

If you can help it, never sleep alone in a train compartment.

Pickpockets & Thieves

Most scams involve distracting you – either by kids running up to you, someone asking for directions or spilling something on you – while another person steals your wallet. Be alert in such situations.

PHONEY COPS

'Can I see some ID?' In some countries, especially in Eastern Europe, you may encounter people claiming to be from the tourist police, the special police, the super-secret police, whatever. Unless they're wearing a uniform and have good reason for accosting you (eg you're robbing a bank), treat their claims with suspicion.

One common scam runs like this: someone asks you to change money. You say no, and seconds later an 'undercover' police officer 'arrests' the moneychanger. The officer then asks to check your passport and money, in case it's counterfeit. Something then goes missing or is confiscated when the 'undercover officer' handles your valuables.

Another swindle involves someone dropping a wad of money near you. Someone else picks it up and asks if it's yours. The first person then says they had twice that and requests you open your wallet to prove you don't have the other half. At this point, a 'policeman' turns up, and the scenario proceeds as for the moneychanging scam.

Needless to say, never show your passport or cash to anyone on the street. Simply walk away. If someone flashes a badge, offer to accompany them to the nearest police station.

PRECAUTIONS

Theft is definitely a problem in parts of Europe and you also have to be aware of other travellers. Don't store valuables in train station lockers or luggage storage counters and be careful about people who offer to help you operate a locker. Also be vigilant if someone offers to carry your luggage: they might carry it away altogether.

Don't leave valuables lying around in your car, on train seats or in your room. When going out, don't flaunt cameras, portable CD players, MP3 players and other expensive electronic goods. Carry a small day-pack, as shoulder bags are an open invitation for snatch thieves and, for extra peace of mind, even use small zipper locks on your packs. Pickpockets are most active in dense crowds, especially in busy train stations and on public transport during peak hours. Be careful in these situations.

Experts suggest you spread valuables, cash and cards around your body or in different bags. Some travellers walk around with €100 in their shoe; others put €50 in their aspirin bottle. A money-belt with your essentials (passport, cash, credit cards, airline tickets) is usually a good idea. However, so you needn't delve into it in public, carry a wallet with a day's worth of cash. A dummy wallet, with fake 'credit' cards (eg library cards or video store cards) is also a good ploy.

Having your passport stolen is less of a disaster if you've recorded the number and issue date or, even better, photocopied the relevant data pages. You can also scan them and email them to yourself, if you're sure your webmail account is secure. Also record the serial numbers of travellers cheques and carry photocopies of your credit cards, airline tickets and other travel documents. If you do lose your passport, notify the police immediately to get a statement, and contact your nearest consulate.

If this all sounds a lot to absorb, remember it's basically common sense and rest assured there's no need to fret about theft constantly. Just be sensible with your possessions.

Scams

In some busy tourist centres, street hawkers will sometimes try to force you to buy their goods, by placing them in your hands or throwing them at you, so you reflexively catch. Simply put the object down (careful how you bend) and walk off.

Social Problems

Civil unrest and terrorist bombings are rare in Europe, but they do occur. Northern Ireland's IRA (Irish Republican Army), ETA (the Basque separatist group in Spain and France) and the Corsican National Liberation Front have all declared ceasefires – the IRA many years ago.

However, few will have missed the news of the al-Qaeda–linked Madrid bombings in March 2004 or the suicide attacks by British-raised Muslims on the London transport network in July 2005. These are, of course, part of a global phenomenon and fortunately so far remain isolated incidents. At the time of writing, attacks in Russia by Chechen rebels had tailed off, although tensions remain.

Likewise, tension continues across the Greek–Turkish divide in Cyprus, as well as in the Balkans (Bosnia and Hercegovina, Serbia, Montenegro, Albania and Macedonia). Northern Ireland still experiences continued turbulence in July (in particular around the 12th) during marching season.

Up-to-date travel advisories on individual countries are available from your own government or from the following:

Australian Department of Foreign Affairs & Trade (DFAT; www.smartraveller.gov.au)
UK Foreign & Commonwealth Office (FCO; www.fco.gov.uk)
US State Department (http://travel.state.gov)

DISCOUNT CARDS

Camping Cards

The Camping Card International (CCI; formerly the Camping Carnet) is camping-ground ID that can be used instead of a passport when checking into a camping ground and includes third-party insurance. Many camping grounds offer a small discount if you sign in with one. CCIs are issued by automobile associations, camping federations and, sometimes, at camping grounds.

Rail Passes

If you plan to visit more than a few countries, you might save money with a rail pass; see p1243.

Student Cards

The **International Student Travel Confederation** (ISTC; www.istc.org) issues three cards for students, teachers and under-26s, offering thousands of worldwide discounts on transport, museum entry, youth hostels and even some restaurants. These cards are: the International Student Identity Card (ISIC), the International Teacher Identity Card (ITIC) and the International Youth Travel

Card (IYTC). You can check the full list of discounts and where to apply for the cards on the ISTC website. Issuing offices include **STA Travel** (www.statravel.com).

For under-26s, there's also a specific European card, the **Euro<26** (www.euro26.org). Many countries have raised the age limit for this card to 30.

DISCRIMINATION

Divergent views about immigration, plus a small rump of anachronistic attitudes, mean that, in some parts of Europe, travellers of African, Arab or Asian descent might encounter unpleasant attitudes that are unrelated to them personally. In rural areas, travellers whose skin colour marks them out as foreigners might experience unwanted attention. Some travellers have reported negative encounters because locals mistook them for Roma.

Attitudes vary from country to country. People tend to be more accepting in cities than in the country. Race is also less of an issue in Western Europe than in parts of the former Eastern Bloc. For example, there has been a spate of fatal racist attacks in St Petersburg and other parts of Russia in recent years (see p995).

DRIVING LICENCE

Many non-European driving licences are valid in Europe, but an International Driving Permit (IDP) is always handy if you intend to drive. This document (basically a translation of the vehicle class and personal details noted on your home licence) can make life much more simple when hiring cars and motorcycles. An IDP is not valid unless accompanied by your original licence. One can be obtained for a small fee from your local automobile association – take a passport photo and a valid licence.

ELECTRICITY

Europe generally runs on 220V, 50Hz AC, but there are exceptions. The UK runs on 230/240V AC, and some old buildings in Italy and Spain have 125V (or even 110V in Spain). The Continent is moving towards a 230V standard. If your home country has a vastly different voltage you will need a transformer for delicate and important appliances.

The UK and Ireland use chunky, three-pin square plugs. Most of the Continent uses the 'europlug' with two round pins. Greece, Italy and Switzerland use a third round pin in a way that the two-pin plug usually – but not always in Italy and Switzerland – fits. The important thing is to buy an adapter before leaving home; those on sale in Europe generally go the other way.

EMBASSIES & CONSULATES

It's important to realise what your own embassy can and can't do to help you if you get into trouble.

Generally speaking, it won't be much help in emergencies if the trouble you're in is remotely your own fault. Remember, you're bound by the laws of the country you're in. Your embassy will not be sympathetic if you end up in jail after committing a crime locally, even if such actions are legal in your own country.

In genuine emergencies you might get some assistance, but only if other channels have been exhausted. For example, if you need to get home urgently, a free ticket is exceedingly unlikely – the embassy would expect you to have insurance. If you have all your money and documents stolen, it might assist with getting a new passport, but a loan for onward travel is out of the question.

See the individual country chapters for contact information for foreign embassies in Europe.

FESTIVALS & HOLIDAYS

See A Year in Europe (p45) for events of interest to backpackers, and the individual country chapters about holidays that could interfere with your plans.

If you want to know when European school holidays are, to avoid peak booking periods, the following offer a guide:

Calendrier Scolaire (www.education.gouv.fr, in French) For exact dates across France, click on 'Calendrier Scolaire' link.

Local Government Association (www.lga.gov.uk) Type 'standard school year' or 'school term database' into the search engine. Will give term dates and bank holidays for the current year.

Schulferien (www.schulferien.org) Time off for German students. Click on 'Ferienkalendar nach Jahren' for dates.

GAY & LESBIAN TRAVELLERS

In cosmopolitan centres, especially in Western Europe, you'll find very liberal attitudes towards homosexuality. Belgium, the Netherlands and Spain have all legalised full same-sex marriages, while Denmark, Finland, Iceland, Norway, Sweden and the UK offer civil partnerships granting all or most of the rights of marriage. Austria, Croatia, the Czech Republic, France, Germany, Luxembourg, Portugal, Slovenia and Switzerland offer limited-rights partnerships.

London, Paris, Berlin, Amsterdam, Madrid and Lisbon have thriving gay communities and pride events. The Greek islands of Mykonos and Lesvos are popular gay beach destinations. Gran Canaria and Ibiza in Spain are big centres for both gay clubbing and beach holidays.

Outside the big cities, attitudes become more conservative and discretion is advised, particularly in Morocco, Turkey and most parts of Eastern Europe. There is an absolute dearth of good gay travel websites, making it far better to consult websites specific to the country you're travelling to. See the individual country directories for these, where available.

Also see individual country chapters for gay and lesbian venues. For ages of consent, see p1224.

INSURANCE

It's foolhardy to travel without insurance to cover theft, loss and medical problems. There's a wide variety of policies, so check the small print. Some policies specifically exclude 'dangerous activities', which can include scuba diving, motorcycling, winter sports, adventure sports or even hiking. Some pay doctors or hospitals directly, but most require you to pay upfront, save the documentation and claim later. Some policies also ask you to call back (reverse charges) to a centre in your home country, where an immediate assessment of your problem is made. Check that the policy covers ambulances or an emergency flight home.

The policies handled by STA Travel and other student travel agencies are usually good value. In the UK, the website **Money Supermarket** (www.moneysupermarket.com) does an automated comparison of 450 partner policies and comes up with the best for your needs.

Worldwide cover to travellers from over 44 countries is available online at www.lonelyplanet.com/bookings/insurance.

For information on health insurance, see p1246; see p1240 for details on car insurance.

INTERNET ACCESS

You'll find internet cafes throughout Europe – and wi-fi in many hotels, should you need it. Apart from the cafes listed in country chapters, you might also find public internet access in banks, department stores, post offices, libraries, hostels, hotels and universities.

Access is generally straightforward, although a few tips are in order. If you can't find the @ symbol, try Alt Gr + 2, or Alt Gr + Q. Watch out for German and some Balkans keyboards, which reverse the Z and the Y positions. Using a French keyboard is an art unto itself (p444). Where necessary in relevant countries, click on the language prompt in the bottom right-hand corner of the screen or hit Ctrl + Shift to switch between the Cyrillic and Latin alphabets.

INTERNET RESOURCES

The internet is a rich resource for travellers and the following websites offer handy tips for those travelling in Europe. Travel booking websites are listed on p1232. Country-specific websites are in the relevant chapter.

Budget Traveller's Guide to Sleeping in Airports (www.sleepinginairports.net) Funny and useful resource for backpackers flying stand-by.

Currency Conversions (www.xe.net/ucc) Up-to-the-second exchange rates for hundreds of currencies.

Guide for Europe (www.guideforeurope.com) With a handy hostel review page posted by visitors.

Hostelworld (www.hostelworld.com) Also handy for other travellers' views on hostels.

Lonely Planet (www.lonelyplanet.com/thorntree) On Lonely Planet's message board you can usually get your travel questions answered by fellow travellers in a matter of hours.

Money Saving Expert (www.moneysavingexpert.com) Excellent tips on the best UK travel insurance, mobile phones and bank cards to use abroad. The Flightchecker facility shows the latest cheap flights available.

The Man in Seat 61 (www.seat61.com) A professional-standard personal website, dedicated to rail travel across Europe.

LEGAL MATTERS

Most European police are friendly and helpful, especially if you have been a victim of a crime. You are required by law to prove your identity if asked by police (although make sure they really are police, see p1220), so always carry your passport, or an identity card if you're an EU citizen.

Ages of Consent

The age of consent for heterosexual and homosexual intercourse is generally between 14 and 16 across Europe, although some countries such as Cyprus, Ireland and Northern Ireland have a higher age limit of 17 for certain types of sex. You can generally purchase alcohol (beer and wine) from between 16 and 18 (usually 18 for spirits), but if in doubt, ask. Although you can drive at 17 or 18, you might not be able to hire a car until you reach 25 years of age.

Illegal Drugs

Drugs are often quite openly available in Europe, but that doesn't mean they're legal. The Netherlands is most famed for its liberal attitudes, with 'coffee shops' openly selling cannabis. Yet this once famously relaxed drugs culture has been challenged in recent years, with local mayors objecting to 'drug tourism' and closing down coffee shops – particularly in Rotterdam and border towns. Elsewhere in the Netherlands possession of cannabis is only decriminalised not legalised (apart from its medicinal use). Don't take this relaxed attitude as an invitation to buy harder drugs; if you get caught, you'll be punished. Since 2008, magic mushrooms have been banned in the Netherlands.

Equally, in Belgium, the possession of up to 5g of cannabis is legal; but selling the drug isn't, so if you get caught at the point of sale, you could be in trouble. In Portugal, the possession of *all* drugs has been decriminalised. Once again, however, selling is illegal.

Britain downgraded cannabis from a Class B to a Class C drug several years back, but in 2009 it reverted to Class B status, meaning that if you're caught you may face arrest. Anyone caught smoking in public or in front of children is very likely to be arrested.

Switzerland has gone the other way. It was moving towards decriminalisation and then had a last-minute legal about-face. Some people still smoke pot openly, but if police decide to enforce the law, you'll face a fine of up to Sfr400 just for possession of cannabis.

Spain and Italy have also tightened their cannabis laws in recent years, so make sure you're careful there, too.

Getting caught with drugs in other parts of Europe, particularly countries such as Turkey, and Morocco, can also lead to imprisonment.

If in any doubt, err on the side of caution. For your own safety, don't even think about taking drugs across international borders.

Smoking

Cigarette smoking bans have been progressively introduced across Europe since 2004. Countries that now prohibit smoking in bars and restaurants include Austria, Croatia, Estonia, Finland, France, Greece, Hungary, Iceland, Ireland, Italy, Malta, the Netherlands, Norway, Sweden, Turkey and the UK. Many other countries will be passing similar laws in the near future, so with such change afoot, ask before lighting up.

MAPS

Good maps are easy to find in Europe and in good bookshops beforehand.

Road atlases are essential if you're driving or cycling. Leading brands are **Freytag & Berndt** (www.freytagberndt.com), **Hallwag, Kümmerly + Frey** (www.kuemmerly-frey.ch) and **Michelin** (www.michelin.com).

Maps published by European automobile associations such as Britain's **AA** (www.theaa.com) and Germany's **ADAC** (www.adac.de, in German) are usually excellent and sometimes free if membership of your local association gives you reciprocal rights.

Tourist offices are another good source for (usually free and fairly basic) maps.

MEDIA

Some UK newspapers, such as the *Guardian* and the *Financial Times* have international editions, which are circulated across large parts of Europe. Otherwise, the best-known English-language newspaper is the *International Herald Tribune,* produced in Paris by a US publisher, for expats. International newsweeklies such as the *Economist, Newsweek* and *Time* are also widely available.

In addition, many European capitals have their own English-language newspapers. The most famous are probably the *Prague Post* and *Moscow Times*. For others, see individual country chapters.

Serbia's **B92 radio station** (www.b92.net/english/) has an English-language website and **Radio Free Europe/Radio Liberty** (www.rferl.org), once an American Cold War–propaganda tool, survives across several countries in Eastern Europe as a station for locals and expats.

The **BBC World Service** (www.bbc.co.uk/worldservice) is available across Europe, although increasingly only in English as European language services have been slashed. See the website for how to tune in where you are. **BBC News** (http://news.bbc.co.uk) has a separate Europe section.

MONEY

A common currency, the euro, is used in 16 EU states: Austria, Belgium, Cyprus, France, Finland, Germany, Greece, Ireland, Italy, Luxembourg, Malta, the Netherlands, Portugal, Slovakia, Slovenia and Spain. A further eight EU member states in Eastern Europe are scheduled to join the 'euro zone' between 2010 and 2015. The euro is divided into 100 cents.

Denmark, the UK and Sweden have held out against adopting the euro for political reasons, while non-EU nations, such as Albania, Belarus, Iceland, Norway, Russia, Switzerland and Ukraine also have their own currencies. See individual country chapters for details.

For security and flexibility, diversify your source of funds. Carry an ATM card, credit card, cash and possibly travellers cheques. See p1220 for tips on carrying money safely.

Set up an internet banking account before you leave home, so you can track your spending. However, be very careful about logging off afterwards in internet cafes; after you've finished you really should erase the browser's history. Using Internet Explorer, go to the Tools menu, scroll down to Internet Options, click on History and Clear History.

ATMs

Every country in this book has international ATMs that allow you to withdraw cash directly from your home account, and this is the most common way European travellers now access their money. However, you should always have a back-up option, as some readers have reported glitches with ATMs in individual countries, even when their card worked elsewhere in Europe. In some remote villages, ATMs might be scarce, too.

Much of Western Europe now uses a chip-and-pin system for added security. You will have problems if you don't have a four-digit PIN number and might have difficulties if your card doesn't have a metallic chip. Check with your bank. Sometimes, too, the network will not recognise your card if it's very early in the morning back in your home country, when banks sometimes back-up their systems. If your card is rejected, try again in a

MINIMISING ATM CHARGES

When you withdraw cash from an ATM overseas, there are several ways you can get hit. Firstly, most banks add a hidden 2.75% loading to what's called the 'Visa/Mastercard wholesale' or 'interbank' exchange rate. In short, they're giving you a worse exchange rate than strictly necessary and you won't be aware of it unless you ask. Additionally, some banks charge their customers a cash withdrawal fee (usually 2% with a minimum €2 or more). If you're really unlucky, the bank at the foreign end might charge you as well. Triple whammy. If you use a credit card in ATMs, you'll also pay interest – usually quite high interest – on the cash withdrawn.

It doesn't have to be this way, however. Get the right plastic, and money-saving expert **Martin Lewis** (www.moneysavingexpert.com) estimates it can cut your costs by more than 6%. The undisputed global winner, recommended by many pundits, is the Nationwide Flex Account Visa Debit card, available in the UK, which has no exchange-rate loading and charges no withdrawal fees anywhere overseas.

We asked financial advisory body **Cannex** (www.cannex.com.au) about the best option coming from Australia to Europe and they pointed out that the Wizard Clear Advantage card doesn't put a premium on exchange rates or charge withdrawal fees. It is a credit card, though, so you would need to put money on it before leaving home, to avoid paying interest on cash withdrawn.

Travellers from the USA suggest investigating First Republic Bank in San Francisco (although you have to keep a balance of US$2500) or NetBank, an online bank.

Most crucially, banks can change their conditions at any time, so shop around a month before you leave. If you bank with HSBC, it's easy to open a local account in any country where you might be spending a good deal of time.

Most experts agree that having the right bankcard is still cheaper than exchanging cash directly. If your bank levies fees, larger, less frequent withdrawals are better.

few hours' time. Make sure you bring your bank's phone number and if your card fails again, call them. Also be aware that some banks automatically block foreign transactions until they are able to call the cardholder and confirm that they are abroad.

When you withdraw money from an ATM, the amounts are converted and dispensed in local currency. However, there will be fees (see p1225). If you're uncertain, ask your bank to explain.

Finally, always cover the keypad when entering your PIN and make sure there are no unusual devices attached to the machine, which can copy your card's details or cause it to stick in the machine. If your card disappears and the screen goes blank before you've even entered your PIN, don't enter it – especially if a 'helpful' bystander tells you to do so. If you can't retrieve your card, call your bank's emergency number, if you can, before leaving the ATM.

Black Market

Black-market (unauthorised) exchanges are rare in Europe. Changing money on the street is usually illegal and risky and you should be very suspicious of anyone offering the service as it's most likely a scam.

Cash

Nothing beats cash for convenience…or risk. If you lose it, it's gone forever and very few travel insurers will come to your rescue. Those that do will limit the amount to somewhere around €300.

It's still a good idea, though, to bring some local currency in cash, if only to cover yourself until you get to an exchange facility or find an ATM. The equivalent of €100 or €150 should usually be enough. Some extra cash in an easily exchanged currency is also a good idea, especially in Eastern Europe.

Credit Cards

Credit cards are handy for major purchases, such as air or rail tickets, and offer a lifeline in certain emergencies.

Visa and MasterCard/Eurocard are more widely accepted in Europe than Amex and Diners Club; Visa (sometimes called Carte Bleue) is particularly strong in France and Spain. There are, however, regional differences in the general acceptability of credit cards. In the UK, for example, you can usually flash your plastic in the most humble of budget restaurants; in Germany it's rare for restaurants to take credit cards. Cards are not widely accepted off the beaten track.

To reduce the risk of fraud, always keep your card in view when making transactions; for example, in restaurants that do accept cards, pay as you leave, following your card to the till. Keep transaction records and either check your statements when you return home, or set up an online login to manage your account while still on the road. Letting your credit-card company know roughly where you're going lessens the chance of fraud – or of your bank cutting off the card when it sees (your) unusual spending.

Debit Cards

Ticket machines in many European train stations and other places like car parks or free city-bike stands (eg in Vienna) frequently accept Maestro debit cards, sometimes exclusively. So when travelling to Europe, it's always worthwhile having a Maestro-compatible debit card, which differs from a credit card in deducting money straight from your bank account. Check with your bank or MasterCard (Maestro's parent) for compatibility.

Exchanging Money

In general, euros, US dollars and UK pounds are the easiest currencies to exchange in Europe. The major European currencies are fully convertible, but you may have trouble exchanging some lesser-known ones at small banks. The importation or exportation of certain currencies (eg Moroccan dirham) is restricted or banned, so try to get rid of any local currency before you leave such countries. The same goes for Latvian currency and small denominations of Czech crowns. Get rid of Scottish pounds before leaving the UK; nobody outside Britain will touch them.

Most airports, central train stations, big hotels and many border posts have banking facilities outside regular business hours, at times on a 24-hour basis. Post offices in Europe often perform banking tasks, tend to be open longer hours and outnumber banks in remote places. While they always exchange cash, they might baulk at handling travellers cheques not in the local currency.

The best exchange rates are usually at banks. *Bureaux de change* usually – but not always – offer worse rates or charge higher commissions. Hotels are almost always the worst places to change money.

International Transfers

International bank transfers are good for secure one-off movements of large amounts of money, but they might take three to five days and there will be a fee (about £25 in the UK, for example). Be sure to specify the name of the bank, plus the sort code and address of the branch where you'd like to pick up your money.

In an emergency, it's quicker and easier to have money wired via an **Amex office** (www.americanexpress.com), **Western Union** (www.westernunion.com) or **MoneyGram** (www.moneygram.com). All are quite costly.

Taxes & Refunds

Sales tax applies to many goods and services in Europe. Depending on the country and the product, it will add between 10% and 20% to the price of goods. Luckily, when non-EU residents spend more than a certain amount (around €75) they can usually reclaim that tax when leaving the country.

Making a tax-back claim is straightforward. First, make sure the shop offers duty-free sales. (Often a sign will be displayed reading 'Tax-Free Shopping'.) When making your purchase, ask the shop attendant for a tax-refund voucher, filled in with the correct amount and the date. This can be used to claim a refund directly at international airports, or stamped at ferry ports or border crossings and mailed back for a refund.

None of this applies to EU residents. Even an American citizen living in London is not entitled to rebate on items bought in Paris. Conversely, an EU passport holder living in New York is.

Tipping & Bargaining

Tipping has become more complicated, with 'service charges' increasingly added to bills. In theory, this means you're not obliged to tip. In practice, that money often doesn't go to the server and they might make it clear they still expect a gratuity.

Don't pay twice. If the service charge is optional, remove it from the bill and pay a tip. If the service charge is not optional, don't tip.

Generally, waiters in Western Europe tend to be paid decent wages. For more details on tipping, see the individual country chapters.

Bargaining is common in Turkey and Morocco; see those chapters for more information.

Travellers Cheques

As travellers cheques have been overtaken in popularity by international ATMs, it's become more difficult to find places that cash them. Certainly in parts of the former Soviet Union, only a few banks handle them, and the process can be quite bureaucratic and costly.

That said, having a few cheques is a good back-up. If they're stolen you can claim a refund, provided you have a record of cheque numbers, but it's vital to store these numbers away from the cheques themselves. Amex and Thomas Cook travellers cheques are reliable brands, while cheques in US dollars, British pounds or euros are the easiest to cash. When changing them, ask about fees and commissions as well as the exchange rate.

PASSPORT

Your most important travel document is your passport. Many countries require that it remain valid for at least six month after you *leave*. So if your passport is about to expire, renew it before you go. This might not be easy to do overseas.

Applying for or renewing a passport can take anything from a few days to several months, so don't leave it until the last minute. Check first what you need to take with you (passport photos, birth certificate, signed statements, exact payment in cash etc).

US citizens must apply in person (but may renew by mail) at a US Passport Agency office or at some courthouses and post offices. Australian citizens can apply at a post office or the passport office in their state capital, but anyone over 18 or married needs to attend an interview. Britons can pick up application forms from most post offices and the passport is issued by the regional passport office, although first-time applicants must now be interviewed. Canadians can apply at regional passport offices, and New Zealanders can apply at any district office of the Department of Internal Affairs.

Once you start travelling, carry your passport on your person at all times and guard it carefully. Camping grounds and hotels sometimes ask you to hand over your passport during your stay. If you're worried about this, a driving licence, HI membership card or Camping Card International usually suffices.

Some EU citizens and those from certain other European countries (eg Switzerland) don't need a valid passport to travel and around Europe; a national identity card is sufficient. If you want to exercise this option, check with the embassies of the countries you plan to visit.

See also the boxed text on p1230.

PHOTOGRAPHY & DVD

Film is still available in Europe, but most travellers shoot digital these days. So for the majority, the most important thing is to have enough memory to store pictures. Memory cards of up to 8GB are available, but if you do run out, some internet cafes will burn CDs.

DVDs each have a regional code (1 for North America, 2 for Europe and South Africa and 3 for Australasia). If you buy a disc in Europe, check that the code corresponds with your machine at home, or look for international discs coded 0. Additionally, you will have to check your DVD player is universally compatible and the TV systems work together too (which is NTSC in the USA and Japan, but PAL in Europe and Australasia).

The upshot of all this is that while DVDs bought in Europe frequently won't play on your TV back home, they will probably work on your computer. Universal players are more common in Europe, so DVDs brought here from elsewhere will probably (but not necessarily) work.

POST

From major European centres, airmail typically takes about five days to North America and about a week to Australasian destinations, although mail from such countries as Albania or Russia is much slower. See the individual country chapter for local costs.

Poste restante services, where friends and family can write to you care of the main post office, are still offered, but email has rendered these largely obsolete. Courier services such as **DHL** (www.dhl.com) are best for essential deliveries.

EMERGENCY NUMBERS

The phone number ☎ 112 can be dialled for emergencies in all EU states. See the individual country chapters for country-specific emergency numbers.

STUDYING

If your interests tend to be cerebral, Europe offers courses on anything from alternative medicine to zoology. Language learning is particularly popular, given you have the opportunity to immerse yourself in the local culture. Courses are available to foreigners through universities or private schools.

Otherwise, major language teaching institutes include the following:

Alliance Française (www.alliancefr.org) The Parisian school's website has details of all Alliances and locations worldwide.

Cactus Education (www.cactusworldwide.com) European courses in French, German, Italian or Spanish.

Goethe Institut (www.goethe.de) Learn *Deutsch* all across Europe, including in Germany itself.

Instituto Cervantes (www.cervantes.es) Click on your own language for a PDF guide or click on 'IC en el Mundo', then choose a country and city on the map.

Società Dante Alighieri (www.dantealighieri.com) This Siena-based Italian school specialises in Italian courses, though you can also take Italian cookery courses.

The best sources of information are the cultural institutes maintained by many European countries around the world or national tourist offices, embassies or student organisations.

TELEPHONE

You can ring abroad from almost any phone box in Europe. Public telephones accepting phonecards (available from post offices, telephone centres, newsstands or retail outlets) are virtually the norm now; in some countries, eg France, coin-operated phones are almost impossible to find.

Without a phonecard, you can ring from a telephone booth inside a post office or telephone centre and settle your bill at the counter. Reverse-charge (collect) calls are often possible, but not always. From many countries, however, the Country Direct system lets you phone home by billing the long-distance carrier you use at home. These numbers can often be dialled from public phones without even inserting a phonecard.

See individual country chapters for national and regional calling codes.

Mobile Phones

Europe uses the GSM 900 network, which also covers Australia and New Zealand, but is not compatible with the North American GSM 1900 or the totally different system in Japan.

However, some North American GSM 1900/900 phones do work here. If you have a GSM phone, check with your service provider about using it in Europe. You'll need international roaming, but this usually costs nothing to enable.

If you want to cut costs, it's usually well worth buying a prepaid local SIM in one European country. Even if you're not staying there long, calls across Europe will still be slightly cheaper if they're not routed via your home country and the prepaid card will enable you to keep a limit on your spending. In several countries you need your passport to buy a SIM card.

TIME

The standard international time measurements, GMT and UTC, are identical, and are both calibrated to the prime meridian, which passes through Greenwich in London.

At 9am in Britain (GMT/UTC) it's the following times:

US West Coast 1am (GMT/UTC minus eight hours)
US East Coast 4am (GMT/UTC minus five hours)
Paris & Prague 10am (GMT/UTC plus one hour, also called Central European Time)
Greece 11am (GMT/UTC plus two hours)
Sydney 7pm (GMT/UTC plus 10 hours)

In most European countries, clocks are put forward one hour for daylight-saving time on the last Sunday in March, and turned back again on the last Sunday in October. Thus, during daylight-saving time, Britain and Ireland are GMT/UTC plus one hour, Central European Time is GMT/UTC plus two hours and Greece is GMT/UTC plus three hours.

TOILETS

Many public toilets in Europe require a small fee either deposited in a box or given to the attendant.

TOURIST INFORMATION

Unless otherwise indicated in individual country chapters, tourist offices are common and widespread. Only in emerging tourist destinations might you have problems locating them.

TOURS

Don't dismiss package tours as universally too expensive. Some last-minute package holidays can be cheaper than getting there under your own steam. Check newspaper travel sections, travel agents and occasionally online booking sites, such as **lastminute.com** (www.lastminute.com).

Young revellers can party on Europe-wide bus tours. **Contiki** (www.contiki.com) and **Top Deck** (www.topdecktravel.co.uk) offer camping or hotel-based bus tours for 18- to 35-year-olds. Contiki's tours last from five to 46 days. Both companies have London offices plus offices or company representatives in Europe, North America, Australasia and South Africa.

TRAVELLERS WITH DISABILITIES

Cobbled medieval streets, 'classic' hotels, congested inner cities and underground metro systems make Europe a tricky destination for people with mobility impairments. However, the train facilities are good and some destinations boast new tram services or lifts to platforms. The following websites can help with specific details.

Accessible Europe (www.accessibleeurope.com) Specialist European tours with van transport. Prices start from as little as €240 for four days.

Lonely Planet (www.lonelyplanet.com/thorntree) Share experiences on the Travellers With Disabilities branch of the Thorn Tree message board.

Mobility International Schweiz (www.mis-ch.ch) Good site listing 'barrier-free' destinations in Switzerland and abroad, plus wheelchair-accessible hotels in Switzerland. Sadly it's only partly in English; address English emails to info@mis-ch.ch.

Mobility International USA (www.miusa.org) Publishes guides and advises travellers with disabilities on mobility issues.

Royal Association for Disability & Rehabilitation (www.radar.org.uk) Publishes a comprehensive annual guide, *Holidays in Britain & Ireland – A Guide for Disabled People*.

Society for the Advancement of Travelers with Handicaps (www.sath.org) Reams of information for travellers with disabilities.

VISAS

Citizens of the USA, Canada, Australia, New Zealand and the UK need only a valid passport to enter all countries of the EU. Two Eastern

THE SCHENGEN ZONE

Twenty-five European countries are signatories to the Schengen Agreement, which has effectively dismantled internal border controls between them. The countries in question are Austria, Belgium, Czech Republic, Denmark, Estonia, Finland, France, Germany, Greece, Iceland, Italy, Hungary, Latvia, Lithuania, Luxembourg, Malta, the Netherlands, Norway, Poland, Portugal, Slovenia, Slovakia, Spain, Sweden and Switzerland.

Citizens of the US, Australia, New Zealand, Canada and the UK only need a valid passport to enter these countries. However, other nationals, including South Africans, can apply for a single visa – a Schengen visa – when travelling throughout this region.

Non-EU visitors (with or without a Schengen visa) should expect to be questioned, however perfunctorily, when entering the region. However, later travel within the zone is much like a domestic trip, with no border controls. (Although some countries, such as France, have made noises about reimposing stricter internal Schengen checks since the bombings in Madrid and London.)

If you need a Schengen visa, you must apply at the consulate or embassy of the country that's your main destination, or your point of entry. You may then stay up to a maximum of 90 days in the entire Schengen area within a six-month period. Once your visa has expired, you must leave the zone and may only re-enter after three months abroad.

If you're a citizen of the US, Australia, New Zealand or Canada, you may stay visa-free a total of 90 days, during six months, within the *entire* Schengen region. Shop around when choosing your point of entry, as visa prices may differ from country to country.

If you're planning a longer trip, you need to inquire personally as to whether you need a visa or visas. Your country might have bilateral agreements with individual Schengen countries allowing you to stay there longer than 90 days without a visa. However, you will need to talk directly to the relevant embassies or consulates.

While the UK and Ireland are not part of the Schengen area, their citizens can stay indefinitely in other EU countries, only needing paperwork if they want to work long-term or take up residency.

See www.eurovisa.info for more information.

European countries, Belarus and Russia, require a prearranged visa before arrival and even an 'invitation' from (or booking with) a tour operator or hotel. Visas to these countries are seldom available at the border.

See the respective country chapters for specific information on travel visas and, because regulations can change, double-check with the relevant embassy or consulate.

Several types of visa exist, including tourist, transit and business permits. Transit visas are usually cheaper than tourist or business visas but they allow a very short stay (one to five days) and can be difficult to extend.

If you require a visa, remember it has a 'use-by' date and you'll be refused entry afterwards. It might not be checked when entering a country overland, but major problems can arise if it is requested during your stay or on departure and you can't produce it.

In some cases it's easier to get visas as you go along, rather than arranging them all beforehand. Carry spare passport photos (you may need from one to four every time you apply for a visa).

Visas to neighbouring countries are usually issued immediately by consulates in Eastern Europe, although some may levy a 50% to 100% surcharge for 'express service'. When regulations are confusing (say in Belarus or Russia) it's more simple and safer to obtain a visa before leaving home. Visas are often cheaper in your own country anyway.

Consulates are generally open weekday mornings (if there's both an embassy and a consulate, you want the consulate).

VOLUNTEERING

If you want to gain greater European insight, a short-term volunteer project might seem a good idea, say, teaching English in Poland or building a school in Turkey. However, most voluntary organisations levy high charges for airfares, food, lodging and recruitment (from about €250 to €800 per week) making such work impractical for most shoestringers.

One exception is **WWOOF International** (www.wwoof.org), which helps link volunteers with organic farms in Germany, Slovenia, Czech Republic, Denmark, the UK, Austria and Switzerland. A small membership fee (€10 to €30) is required to join the national chapter and occasionally an extra administration fee is charged to send you a list of farms looking for additional hands. In exchange for your labour, you'll receive free lodging and food.

WOMEN TRAVELLERS

Women might attract unwanted attention in rural Spain and southern Italy, especially Sicily, where many men view whistling and catcalling as flattery. Conservative dress can help to deter lascivious gazes and wolf-whistles; dark sunglasses help avoid unwanted eye contact. Marriage is highly respected in southern Europe, and a wedding ring can help, along with talk about 'my husband'. Women travelling with male friends or boyfriends might find that hotel operators in southern Europe would prefer to hear the couple is married. Hitchhiking alone is not recommended anywhere.

Female readers have reported assaults at Turkish hotels with shared bathrooms, so women travelling to Turkey might want to consider a more expensive room with private bathroom.

Journeywoman (www.journeywoman.com) maintains an online newsletter about solo female travels all over the world.

WORKING

Working in Europe is not always straightforward. Officially, an EU citizen is allowed to work in any other EU country, but the paperwork can be complicated for long-term employment. Other nationalities require special work permits that can be almost impossible to arrange, especially for temporary work.

However, that doesn't prevent enterprising travellers from topping up their funds by working in the hotel or restaurant trades at beach or ski resorts or teaching a little English – and they don't always have to do this illegally.

The UK, for example, issues special 'working holiday' visas to Commonwealth citizens who are aged between 17 and 30, valid for 12 months' work during two years (see www.ukvisas.gov.uk). Your national student-exchange organisation might be able to arrange temporary work permits to several countries.

If you have a grandparent or parent who was born in an EU country, you may have certain rights of residency or citizenship. Ask that country's embassy about dual citizenship and work permits. With citizenship, also ask about any obligations, such as military service and residency. Beware that your home country may not recognise dual citizenship.

Seasonal Work

Work Your Way Around the World, by Susan Griffith, gives practical advice, as does *Summer Jobs Abroad,* edited by David Woodworth.

Remember, if you find a temporary job, the pay might be less than that offered to locals. Typical tourist jobs (picking grapes in France, working at a bar in Greece) often come with board and lodging, and the pay is essentially pocket money, but you'll have a good time partying with other travellers.

Starting points include the following:

EuroJobs (www.eurojobs.com) Links to hundreds of organisations looking to employ both non-Europeans (with the correct work permits) and Europeans.

Jobs in the Alps (www.jobs-in-the-alps.com) Mainly service jobs, eg chambermaids, bar staff and porters. Some linguistic skills required.

Natives (www.natives.co.uk) Summer and winter resort jobs, and various tips.

Picking Jobs (www.pickingjobs.com) Includes some tourism jobs, too.

Season Workers (www.seasonworkers.com) Best for ski-resort work and summer jobs, although it also has some English-teaching jobs.

Busking is fairly common in major European cities such as Amsterdam and Paris. However, it's illegal in some parts of Switzerland and Austria. Even in Belgium and Germany, where it has been tolerated in the past, crackdowns are not unknown. Some other cities, including London, require permits and security checks. Make sure you talk to other buskers first.

Teaching English

Although teaching English is an option, most schools prefer a bachelor's degree and a TEFL (Teaching English as a Foreign Language) certificate. It is easier to find TEFL jobs in Eastern Europe than in Western or Central Europe. The **British Council** (www.britishcouncil.org) can provide advice about training and job searches.

Alternatively, try the big schools such as **Berlitz** (www.berlitz.com) and **Wall Street Institute International** (www.wallstreetinstitute.com).

Transport

CONTENTS

Getting There & Away	**1232**
Air	1232
Land	1234
Sea	1235
Getting Around	**1235**
Air	1235
Bicycle	1236
Boat	1237
Bus	1238
Car & Motorcycle	1238
Hitching	1242
Local Transport	1242
Taxi	1242
Train	1242

GETTING THERE & AWAY

Arriving from beyond the Continent is nearly always done by plane these days. While a few hardy souls do still arrive overland from Asia and the Middle East, or from North Africa by ferry, they are the small minority. This section covers all means of transport for getting to Europe from the rest of the world.

Flights, tours, rail tickets as well as insurance can be booked online at www.lonelyplanet.com/bookings/.

AIR

If travelling from another continent, your air ticket to Europe will be your single biggest expense. To save money, it's best to book off-season. This means, if possible, avoid mid-June to early September, Easter, Christmas and school holidays (see p1222).

Regardless of your ultimate destination, it's sometimes better to pick a recognised transport 'hub' as your initial port of entry, where high traffic volumes help keep prices down. The busiest, and therefore most obvious, airports are London Heathrow and Frankfurt; Barcelona, Paris and Shannon (Ireland) are other consistently cheaper destinations. Sometimes tickets to Amsterdam, Athens, Berlin, Rome and Vienna are worth investigating. Long-haul airfares to Eastern Europe are rarely a bargain; you're usually better flying to a Western European hub and taking an onward budget airline flight.

Most of the aforementioned gateway cities are also well serviced by low-cost carriers that fly to other parts of Europe. London gives the widest choice, but airlines are now spreading widely across the Continent; see p1235.

Few airlines still ask you to reconfirm onward or return bookings 72 hours before departure on international flights. If yours does, do.

Tickets

INTERNET BOOKING

Buying tickets to and within Europe is easily accomplished via the web. Individual airlines have exclusive online fares. However, checking a host of airline websites can soon become tedious and confusing, which is where the convenience of travel websites is unmatched. Lonely Planet's flight search engine compares lots of different flight websites to find you the best deal, see www.lonelyplanet.com/bookings/flights.do.

Some useful websites:

Ebookers (www.ebookers.com)
Expedia (www.expedia.com)
Hotwire (www.hotwire.com)
Kayak (www.kayak.com)
Opodo (www.opodo.com)
Orbitz (www.orbitz.com)
Travelocity (www.travelocity.com)

STUDENT & YOUTH FARES

Full-time students and people aged under 26 have access to better deals than other travellers. This might not mean cheaper fares, but could offer greater flexibility to change flights or routes or both. You have to show written proof of your date of birth or a valid International Student Identity Card (ISIC; see p1221) when buying your ticket and boarding the plane.

ROUND-THE-WORLD TICKETS

RTW tickets can work out to be as cheap as, or even cheaper than, an ordinary return ticket. Official RTW tickets are usually put together by a combination of two or more partner

THINGS CHANGE...

The information in this chapter is particularly vulnerable to change. Check directly with the airline or a travel agent to make sure you understand how a fare (and ticket you may buy) works and be aware of the security requirements for international travel. Shop carefully. The details given in this chapter should be regarded as pointers and are not a substitute for your own careful, up-to-date research.

airlines and permit you to fly anywhere you want on their route systems as long as you don't backtrack.

Two airline alliances dominate the global market: **Oneworld** (www.oneworld.com) and **Star Alliance** (www.staralliance.com), although there's also the smaller **Sky Team** (www.skyteam.com). Member airlines can piece together a journey using any of their partners' routes.

You cannot backtrack on your route with a RTW ticket, and other restrictions apply. You must (usually) book the first sector in advance and cancellation penalties will be levied. There might be restrictions on how many stops (or kilometres) you are permitted. Many RTW routes originate in the USA, stop in London and continue on to Southeast Asian destinations.

An alternative type of RTW ticket is one put together by a travel agent using a combination of discounted tickets. These can be much cheaper than the official ones, but usually carry a lot of restrictions.

Independent travellers' forum **BootsnAll** (www.bootsnall.com) publishes a regular 'RTW Ticket Watch' newsletter of current offers, and runs through the pros and cons of buying such a ticket.

OPEN-JAW TICKETS

So-called 'open-jaw' returns, where you land in one city and exit from another, are worth considering if you're pressed for time, but open-jaws can often work out to be more costly than simple returns. Most travel agents will sell multicity flights, but before paying up, compare the extra charge of the third city to the overland price of returning to your original destination. Open-jaws are especially convenient if you plan on traipsing across the Continent, say from London to İstanbul.

From Africa & Asia

Nairobi in Kenya and Johannesburg in South Africa are probably the best places in Africa to buy tickets to Europe, thanks to myriad discount shops and lively competition. Your first ports of call should be **Flight Centre** (☎ 0860-400 727; www.flightcentre.co.za) and **STA Travel** (☎ 0861-781 781; www.statravel.co.za).

Several West African countries, eg Senegal and The Gambia, offer cheap charter flights to France and Britain respectively. Charter and budget-airline fares from Morocco can also be quite cheap if you're able to find a seat.

Singapore and Bangkok are the discount-airfare capitals of Asia. Shop around and ask the advice of other travellers before handing over any money to ground-level travel agents. **STA Travel** (www.statravel.com) has branches in Asian cities, including Hong Kong, Tokyo, Singapore, Bangkok, Manila, Jakarta and Kuala Lumpur. Another resource in Japan is **No 1 Travel** (☎ 03 3205 6073; www.no1-travel.com); in Hong Kong try **Four Seas Tours** (☎ 2200 7777; www.fourseastravel.com).

In India, tickets may be even cheaper from the discount shops around Delhi's Connaught Pl. Check with other travellers about the current trustworthiness of these outlets.

From Australia & New Zealand

The cheapest flights from Australia and New Zealand to Europe generally go through Southeast Asian or Middle Eastern capitals, involving stopovers in Kuala Lumpur, Bangkok, Singapore or Dubai. Large Italian- and Greek-Australian communities also mean efficient services to Rome and Athens, as an alternative to London and Frankfurt. Some travellers on RTW tickets choose to fly via the USA.

Airlines such as Thai, Cathay Pacific, Malaysian, Qantas, Singapore and Emirates all have frequent promotional fares, so check the daily newspapers. Some travel agencies, particularly smaller ones, also advertise, so check the travel sections of weekend newspapers, such as the *Age* in Melbourne and the *Sydney Morning Herald*.

Flights from Perth are often a couple of hundred dollars cheaper than those originating in other Australian cities.

In Australia, the best-known agencies for cheap fares are, once again, **STA Travel** (☎ 134 782; www.statravel.com.au) and **Flight Centre** (☎ 133 133; www.flightcentre.com.au). Both have dozens of offices throughout the country.

CLIMATE CHANGE & TRAVEL

Climate change is a serious threat to the ecosystems that humans rely upon, and air travel is the fastest-growing contributor to the problem. Lonely Planet regards travel, overall, as a global benefit, but believes we all have a responsibility to limit our personal impact on global warming.

Flying & Climate Change

Pretty much every form of motor travel generates CO_2 (the main cause of human-induced climate change) but planes are far and away the worst offenders, not just because of the sheer distances they allow us to travel, but because they release greenhouse gases high into the atmosphere. The statistics are frightening: two people taking a return flight between Europe and the US will contribute as much to climate change as an average household's gas and electricity consumption over a whole year.

Carbon Offset Schemes

Climatecare.org and other websites use 'carbon calculators' that allow jetsetters to offset the greenhouse gases they are responsible for with contributions to energy-saving projects and other climate-friendly initiatives in the developing world – including projects in India, Honduras, Kazakhstan and Uganda.

Lonely Planet, together with Rough Guides and other concerned partners in the travel industry, supports the carbon offset scheme run by climatecare.org. Lonely Planet offsets all of its staff and author travel.

For more information check out our website: lonelyplanet.com.

TRANSPORT

These two operators are also based in New Zealand. For info there, contact **STA Travel** (☎ 0800 474 400; www.statravel.co.nz) or **Flight Centre** (☎ 0800 243 544; www.flightcentre.co.nz).

From the US & Canada

If you're flexible with your flight dates, contact discount travel agencies (known as consolidators) that serve as clearing houses for unsold seats on flights departing from major cities, including San Francisco, Los Angeles, New York, Montréal and Toronto. If you're adaptable with your destination city, scan major newspapers, such as the *New York Times, LA Times, Chicago Tribune, San Francisco Chronicle, Boston Globe, Globe & Mail, Toronto Star, Montreal Gazette* and *Vancouver Sun,* for seasonal sales. Several websites, including www.travelzoo.com, www.smarterliving.com and www.johnnyjet.com, post sales fares for large and small airlines.

STA Travel (☎ 800 781 4040; www.statravel.com) specialises in youth and student fares and has offices in major cities in the USA. **Travel CUTS** (☎ 866-246 9762; www.travelcuts.com) is Canada's national student travel agency and has offices in all major cities.

Web-based **Airhitch** (www.airhitch.org) sells stand-by tickets from US and Canadian cities to several European cities. Travel dates are not set but are based on availability of open seats. To reduce the time you spend waiting at the airport on stand-by, try to avoid travel during seasonal spikes, such as popular international events (the European Football Championship, Olympic Games etc).

Former courier agencies that now offer consolidated tickets include the **International Association of Air Travel Couriers** (IAATC; ☎ 402-218 1982; www.courier.org; PO Box 31279, Omaha, NE 68132, USA). Looking for a courier flight in the post-9/11 era is usually more trouble than it's worth.

Icelandair (☎ 800 223 5500; www.icelandair.us) flies from some North American cities via Reykjavík to several Scandinavian and Western European cities. All of its transatlantic flights stop over in Reykjavík, which is a great excuse to spend a few days in Iceland.

LAND

For details covering travel from Britain to Continental Europe, see p1238 and p1243 in Getting Around as well as the individual country chapters.

From Africa & Asia

Getting to Europe from Africa probably will involve a Mediterranean ferry crossing (see opposite). The only feasible overland route to

Europe is via Egypt, Jordan, Syria and on to Turkey. Most overland routes through Africa have all but closed down.

It is possible to get to Western Europe by train from Asia, though count on spending at least eight days doing it. You can choose from three main routes to Moscow:

Trans-Manchurian 9001km from Beijing
Trans-Mongolian 7860km from Beijing
Trans-Siberian 9297km from Vladivostok

Lonely Planet's *Trans-Siberian Railway* is a comprehensive guide to the route with details of costs, travel agencies that specialise in the trip, and highlights. There are countless travel options onwards between Moscow and the rest of Europe. Most people will opt for the train, usually to/from Berlin, Helsinki, Munich, Budapest or Vienna.

Elsewhere it is possible to travel from Pakistan, through Iran and on to Turkey. Travel from Central Asia, especially the former Soviet republics, is also feasible. For details on this very lightly travelled route, see Lonely Planet's *Central Asia*.

SEA

There are numerous ferry routes between Europe and Africa. For details on services within Europe, including the English Channel and the Baltic and North Seas, see p1237, as well as the individual country chapters.

Mediterranean Ferries

Ferries ply routes between Africa and Europe, including from Spain to Morocco, Italy and Malta to Tunisia, France to Morocco and France to Tunisia. Check out www.traghetti online.net for comprehensive information on all Mediterranean ferries. There are also ferries between Greece and Israel via Cyprus. Ferries are often filled to capacity in summer, especially to and from Tunisia, so book well in advance if you're taking a vehicle across.

Passenger Ships & Freighters

Regular long-distance passenger ships disappeared with the advent of cheap air travel and were replaced by a small number of luxury cruise ships. Even passenger freighters (typically carrying up to 12 passengers) aren't nearly as competitively priced as airlines. The journey also takes time; however, if you've got your heart set on a transatlantic journey, **Travltips Cruise & Freighter** (www.travltips.com) has a downloadable freighter directory.

GETTING AROUND

Travel within the EU, whether by air, rail or car, was made easier by the Schengen Agreement, which abolished border controls between most member states (see p1239).

In most European countries, the train is the best option for internal transport. Check the websites of national rail systems as they often offer fare specials and national passes that are significantly cheaper than point-to-point tickets.

AIR

Air Passes

Various travel agencies and airlines offer air passes for non-European citizens. Check with your travel agent for current promotions. The **Europebyair FlightPass** (www.europebyair.com) costs from US$99 per flight for hundreds of European cities. The most economical routes would be long hops from one region of Europe to another, such as St Petersburg to London, rather than shorter routes serviced by low-cost carriers (below).

BMI (☎ 800 788 0555; www.flybmi.com) offers a Discover Europe Pass (DEAP) available to US and Canadian residents for flights within its European network for US$80 to US$109.

Scandinavian Airline's **Visit Scandinavia/ Europe Air Pass** (☎ 08-797 0000 in Sweden; www.flysas .com) connects visitors to Scandinavian cities for US$60 to US$168 per flight.

Charter Flights

Charter flights, arranged by tour operators, typically fly from Britain, France, Germany and Italy to holiday destinations in Europe, Asia and the USA. Tour organisers typically sell spare seats to fill up the flight at discounts that can work out as a cheaper alternative to scheduled flights, especially if you are aged over 26 and not a student. Try contacting the airlines themselves – check out **TUIfly** (www .tuifly.com), **Monarch Airlines** (www.monarch.co.uk) and **Thomas Cook Airlines** (www.thomascookairlines.co.uk).

Low-Cost Airlines

In recent years low-cost carriers have revolutionised European transport, with some hour-long flights offered in the UK for as little as £30, £5 or even £1 (and €30, €5 and €2 fares on the Continent), plus taxes. Remember that most budget airlines have a similar pricing system – namely that ticket prices rise with the number of seats sold on each flight, so book as early as possible to get a decent fare.

Some low-cost carriers – Ryanair being the prime example – have made a habit of flying to smaller, less convenient airports on the outskirts of their destination city, or even at the airports of nearby cities, so check the airport out online before you book.

Departure and other taxes (often including extortionate booking fees, fees for having more than carry-on luggage and other surcharges) soon add up and are included in the final price of your ticket by the end of the online booking process – usually a lot more than you were hoping to pay! Departing from London, you'll pay anything from £15 to £65 extra; from many other European airports it's at least €20.

For a comprehensive overview of which low-cost carriers fly to or from which European cities, check out the excellent flycheapo.com. Some low-cost carriers:

Air Berlin (AB; www.airberlin.com) Well-respected German outfit. Flies to central airports, but you'll have to book early for good prices.

BMIBaby (WW; www.bmibaby.com) Cheap flights leaving from regional UK cities to Belgium, Czech Republic, France, Germany, Italy, Poland, Portugal, Spain and Switzerland.

easyJet (U2; www.easyjet.com) Award-winning low-cost airline flying to a large number of central airports. Main hubs in London, Paris, Madrid and Basel, but also has point-to-point services between Continental cities.

Flybe (BE; www.flybe.com) Cheap flights from regional UK cities within the UK and across Western Europe; much loved by business travellers.

German Wings (4U; www.germanwings.com) Another reputable German budget airline with an extraordinary number of flights to all corners of the Continent. Main hubs are Cologne-Bonn, Berlin Schönfeld and Stuttgart. Unusually, it has cheap flights to Russia.

Helvetic (2L; www.helvetic.com) Swiss operator with flights from its Zürich hub to Italy, Macedonia and Spain.

Ryanair (FR; www.ryanair.com) A truly pan-European airline, Ryanair's sheer number of routes is extraordinary. With nonreclining seats, incessant advertising throughout flights and tight leg room, you'll just have to grin and bear it if you get a good price – which, with all due credit – is all too often!

SkyEurope (NE; www.skyeurope.com) This Slovakia-based operator has a modern fleet and excellent coverage of Europe from its Bratislava, Prague and Vienna hubs.

Wizz Air (W6; www.wizzair.com) This recommended Hungarian operator has numerous bases in Poland as well as Budapest and London, and a vast array of flights across Europe. Wizz has the best links to Ukraine and Bulgaria from Western Europe.

National Airlines

In the face of competition from low-cost airlines, many national carriers have decided to drop their prices and/or offer special deals. Some, such as British Airways, have even adopted the low-cost model of online booking, where the customer can opt to buy just a one-way flight, or can piece together their own return journey from two one-way legs.

For details of national airlines, see individual country chapters.

BICYCLE

Much of Europe is ideally suited to cycling. In the northwest, the flat terrain ensures that bicycles are a popular form of everyday transport, though headwinds often spoil the fun. In the rest of the region, hills and mountains can make for tough going, but this is offset by the dense concentration of things to see. Cycling is a great way to explore many of the Mediterranean islands.

Popular cycling areas include the Belgian Ardennes, the west of Ireland, the upper reaches of the Danube in southern Germany and anywhere in northern Switzerland, Denmark or the south of France. Exploring the small villages of Turkey and Eastern Europe also provides up-close access to remoter areas.

A primary consideration on a cycling tour is to travel light, but you should take a few tools and spare parts, including a puncture-repair kit and an extra inner tube. Panniers are essential to balance your possessions on either side of the bike frame. The wearing of helmets is not compulsory but is certainly advised.

Michelin maps indicate scenic routes, which can help you plan good cycling itineraries. Seasoned cyclists can average 80km a day, but it depends on what you're carrying and your level of fitness.

Useful contacts and websites in English:

Cyclists' Touring Club (CTC; ☎ 0844 736 8450; www.ctc.org.uk, www.cyclingholidays.org) The national cycling association of the UK runs organised trips to Continental Europe.

Veloland European Cyclists' Federation (www.ecf.com) Has details of 'EuroVelo', the European cycle network of 12 pan-European cycle routes, plus tips for other tours.
Veloland Schweiz (www.cycling-in-switzerland.ch) Details of Swiss national routes and more.

Rental & Purchase

It is easy to hire bikes throughout most of Europe on an hourly, half-day, daily or weekly basis. Many train stations have bike-rental counters. It is sometimes possible to return the bike at a different outlet so you don't have to retrace your route. See individual country chapters for more details.

There are plenty of places to buy bikes in Europe (shops sell new and secondhand bicycles, or you can check local papers for private vendors), but you'll need a specialist bicycle shop for a bike capable of withstanding a European tour. Cycling is very popular in the Netherlands and Germany, and those countries are good places to pick up a well-equipped touring bicycle. European prices are quite high (certainly higher than in North America), however non-European resudents should be able to claim back VAT on the purchase.

Transporting a Bicycle

For major cycling tours, it's best to have a bike you're familiar with, so consider bringing your own rather than buying on arrival. If coming from outside Europe, ask about the airline's policy on transporting bikes before purchasing your ticket.

From the UK to the Continent, Eurostar (the train service through the Channel Tunnel) charges £20 to send a bike as registered luggage on its routes. You can also transport your bicycle with you on Eurotunnel through the Channel Tunnel. With a bit of tinkering and dismantling (eg removing wheels), you might be able to get your bike into a bag or sack and take it on a train as hand luggage.

Alternatively, the **European Bike Express** (☎ 014 3042 2111; www.bike-express.co.uk) is a coach service based in the UK where cyclists can travel with their bicycles to various cycling destinations on the Continent.

Once on the Continent, you can put your feet up on the train if you get tired of pedalling or simply want to skip a boring section. On slower trains, bikes can usually be transported as luggage, subject to a small supplementary fee. (Some cyclists have reported that Italian and French train attendants have refused bikes on slow trains, so be prepared for regulations to be interpreted differently by indifferent civil servants.) Fast trains can rarely accommodate bikes; they might need to be sent as registered luggage and may end up on a different train from the one you take. This is often the case in France and Spain.

BOAT

Several different ferry companies compete on the main ferry routes, resulting in a comprehensive but complicated service. The same ferry company can have a host of different prices for the same route, depending on the time of day or year, validity of the ticket and length of your vehicle. Vehicle tickets include the driver and often up to five passengers free of charge. It's worth planning (and booking) ahead where possible as there may be special reductions on off-peak crossings and advance-purchase tickets. On English Channel routes, apart from one-day or short-term excursion returns, there is little price advantage in buying a return ticket versus two singles.

Rail-pass holders are entitled to discounts or free travel on some lines. Food on ferries is often expensive (and lousy), so it is worth bringing your own. Also be aware that if you take your vehicle on board, you are usually denied access to it during the voyage.

Lake ferry services operate in many countries, Austria and Switzerland being just two. For more details, see the individual country chapters.

From the UK & Ireland

Britain is excellently connected with Western Europe and Scandinavia by ferry. Check out www.ferrybooker.com for information on all UK departures.

P&O Ferries (www.poferries.com) is one of the world's main ferry companies, serving Britain, Ireland, Scandinavia, the Netherlands, Poland and Spain. Ferries sail from England to France (Dover–Calais), to the Netherlands (Hull–Rotterdam), to Belgium (Hull–Zeebrugge), to Spain (Portsmouth–Bilbao) and to Ireland (Liverpool–Dublin), among many other routes.

Brittany Ferries (www.brittany-ferries.co.uk) operates services from England to France or Spain. You can also go by ferry from Ireland to France.

From Ireland it's possible to travel directly to mainland Europe with **Irish Ferries** (www.irishferries.com) on their routes to Roscoff and Cherbourg from Rosslare in Ireland.

From Germany

Northern German port towns such as Lübeck and Rostock are well connected by ferry to Scandinavia, the UK and the Baltics. For the full range of options visit:

Color Line (www.colorline.com)
Finnlines (www.finnlines.de)
Finnlines-Nordölink (www.nordoe-link.com)
Lisco (www.lisco-baltic-service.de)
Scandlines (www.scandlines.de)
Stena Line (www.stenaline.de)
TT-Line (www.ttline.de)

Mediterranean Ferries

Blue Star Ferries (www.bluestarferries.com) and **Hellenic Mediterranean** (www.hml.it) travel from Italy (Ancona, Brindisi or Bari) to Greece (Corfu, Igoumenitsa and Patras). The Greek Islands are connected to the mainland and each other by a spider web of routes; see p523 for more information.

BUS

International Buses

Buses are often cheaper than trains, sometimes substantially so, but also tend to be slower and less comfortable. While they are generally more expensive and take much longer than low-cost airlines (a double whammy), they do cover many routes low-cost airlines don't. In Portugal, Greece, parts of Spain and Turkey, buses are a better option than trains.

Europe's biggest organisation of international buses operates under the name **Eurolines** (www.eurolines.com). The various national companies that create this group can be accessed through this website.

The group's network covers cities as far afield as Edinburgh, Stockholm, Rīga, Bucharest, Rome and Madrid. A **Eurolines Pass** (www.eurolines-pass.com) is offered for extensive travel, allowing passengers to visit a choice 35 cities in 16 countries over 15 or 30 days. In the high season (mid-June to mid-September) the pass costs €279/359 for those aged under 26, or €329/439 for those 26 and over. It's cheaper in other periods.

Another popular option is **Busabout** (☎ 020-7950 1661; www.busabout.com; 258 Vauxhall Bridge Rd, Victoria, London SW1V 1BS), whose buses do circuits around Europe, stopping at major cities. You can 'hop off' at any scheduled stop, then 'hop on' a later bus. Buses are often oversubscribed, so book each sector to avoid being stranded. It departs every two days from April to the end of October (May to September for Spain and Portugal).

The circuits cover most countries in Continental Western Europe, plus the Czech Republic. Busabout's Flexipass allows you six city stops for £289/279 adult/student, after which you pay £25 for each supplementary stop. Myriad other options are available as well.

Another company offering a similar service is **Eastern Trekker** (www.easterntrekker.com), which covers Eastern Europe and offers everything from Dracula-themed castle tours of Romania to an eight-day sailing tour of Croatia.

National Buses

Domestic buses provide a viable alternative to trains in most countries. Again, they are usually slightly cheaper and somewhat slower. Buses are generally best for shorter hops, such as getting around cities and reaching remote villages and they are often the only option in mountainous regions. Reservations are rarely necessary. On many city buses you usually buy your ticket in advance from a kiosk or machine and validate it on entering the bus. See the individual country chapters for more details on local buses.

CAR & MOTORCYCLE

Travelling with your own vehicle gives flexibility and is the best way to reach remote places. However, the independence does sometimes isolate you from local life. Also, cars can be a target for theft and are often impractical in city centres, where traffic jams, parking problems and getting thoroughly lost can make it well worth ditching your vehicle and using public transport. Various car-carrying trains can help you avoid long, tiring drives.

Eurotunnel (☎ in Britain 087 0535 3535; www.eurotunnel.com) transports motor vehicles and bicycles between Folkestone in England and Coquelles in France (near Calais) through the Channel Tunnel. Services run up to every 15 minutes (up to two hourly from midnight to 6am). Fares are more advantageous for those going on day trips than for travellers on long jaunts, although you should keep an eye out for special deals. While a day return for a car and passengers normally costs £49 to £100, a one-way

BORDER CROSSINGS

Border formalities have been relaxed in most of the EU, but still exist in all their bureaucratic former glory in parts of Eastern Europe.

In line with the Schengen Agreement, there are officially no passport controls at the borders between Austria, Belgium, Czech Republic, Denmark, Estonia, Finland, France, Germany, Greece, Iceland, Italy, Hungary, Latvia, Lithuania, Luxembourg, Malta, the Netherlands, Norway, Poland, Portugal, Slovakia, Slovenia, Spain, Sweden and Switzerland. Sometimes, however, there are spot checks on trains crossing borders, so always have your passport. The UK, an EU country but a nonsignatory to Schengen, maintains border controls over traffic from other EU countries, although there is no Customs.

Most borders in Eastern Europe will be crossed via train, where border guards board the train and go through the compartments checking passengers' papers. It is rare to get hit up for bribes, but occasionally in Belarus you may face a difficulty that can only be overcome with a 'fine'. Travelling between Turkey and Bulgaria typically requires a change of trains and is subject to a lengthy border procedure. For information on visas, see p1229 and individual chapters.

ticket costs £145 to £199. An open-ended return can cost up to £398. The company takes a very dim view of passengers buying a day return and only using the outgoing leg, and has legal remedies open to it in such instances.

Campervan

One popular way to tour Europe is for a group of three or four people to band together and buy or rent a campervan. London is the usual embarkation point. Look at the advertisements in London's free magazine **TNT** (www.tntmagazine.com) if you wish to form or join a group. *TNT* is also a good source for purchasing a van, as is **Loot** (www.loot.com) newspaper.

Some second-hand dealers offer a 'buy-back' scheme for when you return from the Continent, but we've received warnings that some dealers don't fully honour their refund commitments. Buying and reselling privately should be more advantageous if you have time. In the UK, **Downunder Insurance** (☎ 020-7402 9211; www.duinsure.com) offers a camper-van policy.

Campervans usually feature a fixed high-top or elevating roof and two to five bunk beds. Apart from the essential camping gas cooker, you may get a sink, fridge and built-in cupboards. Prices vary considerably, and it's worth getting advice from a mechanic to determine whether you're being offered a fair price. Once on the road you should be able to keep budgets lower than backpackers using trains, but don't forget to set money aside for emergency repairs.

The main advantage of going by campervan is flexibility; with transport, eating and sleeping requirements all taken care of in one unit, you are tied to nobody's timetable but your own. It's also easier to set up at night than if you rely on a car and tent.

A disadvantage of campervans is that you are in a confined space for much of the time. Four adults in a small van can soon get on each other's nerves, particularly if the group has been formed at short notice. You might also miss out on experiences in the world outside your van. Other negatives are that vans are not very manoeuvrable around town, and you'll often have to leave your gear unattended inside (many people bolt extra locks onto the van). They're also expensive to buy in spring and hard to sell in autumn.

Fuel

Fuel prices can vary enormously (though fuel is always more expensive than in North America or Australia). Refuelling in Luxembourg or Andorra is about 30% cheaper than in neighbouring countries. The Netherlands, France and Italy have Europe's most expensive petrol; Gibraltar and Andorra are by far the cheapest in Western Europe. Greece, Spain and (surprisingly) Switzerland are also reasonable. The Baltics and Eastern European countries are cheaper still.

Petrol is unleaded only throughout much of Europe, but not in Romania, Albania, Slovakia, Serbia or Montenegro. Diesel is usually cheaper, though the difference is marginal in Britain, Ireland and Switzerland.

Ireland's Automobile Association maintains a webpage of European fuel prices at www.aaireland.ie/petrolprices.

Leasing

Leasing a vehicle involves fewer hassles than purchasing and can work out considerably cheaper than hiring for longer than 17 days. This program is limited to certain types of new cars, including Renault and Peugeot, but you save money because leasing is exempt from VAT, and inclusive insurance plans are cheaper than daily insurance rates. Leasing is also open to people as young as 18 years old. To lease a vehicle your permanent address must be outside the EU. In the USA, contact **Renault Eurodrive** (☎ 888 532 1221; www.renaultusa.com) for more information.

Motorcycle Touring

Europe is made for motorcycle touring, with quality winding roads, stunning scenery and an active motorcycling scene. Just make sure your wet-weather motorcycling gear is up to scratch.

Rider and passenger crash helmets are compulsory everywhere in Europe. Austria, Belgium, France, Germany, Luxembourg, Portugal and Spain also require that motorcyclists use headlights during the day; in other countries it is recommended.

On ferries, motorcyclists rarely have to book ahead as they can generally be squeezed on board.

Take note of the local custom about parking motorcycles on pavements (sidewalks). Though this is illegal in some countries, the police often turn a blind eye provided the vehicle doesn't obstruct pedestrians. Don't try to park your bike on the pavement in Britain, however.

Preparations

Always carry proof of ownership of your vehicle (Vehicle Registration Document for British-registered cars) when touring Europe. An EU driving licence is acceptable for those driving throughout Europe. If you have any other type of licence, you should obtain an International Driving Permit (IDP) from your motoring organisation. Check what type of licence is required in your destination prior to departure.

Third-party motor insurance is compulsory. Most UK policies automatically provide this for EU countries. Get your insurer to issue a Green Card (which may cost extra), an internationally recognised proof of insurance, and check that it lists all the countries you intend to visit. You'll need this in the event of an accident outside the country where the vehicle is insured. Also ask your insurer for a European Accident Statement form, which can simplify things if worst comes to worst. Never sign statements that you can't read or understand – insist on a translation and sign that only if it's acceptable. For non-EU countries, check the requirements with your insurer. Travellers from the UK can obtain additional advice and information from the **Association of British Insurers** (☎ 020 7600 3333; www.abi.org.uk).

Taking out a European motoring assistance policy – such as AA Five Star Service or RAC European Breakdown Assistance – is a good investment. Expect to pay about £50 for 14 days' coverage, with a 10% discount for association members. Non-Europeans might find it cheaper to arrange international coverage with their national motoring organisation before leaving home. Ask your motoring organisation for details about the free services offered by affiliated organisations around Europe.

Every vehicle that travels across an international border should display a sticker indicating its country of registration. A warning triangle, to be used in the event of breakdown, is compulsory almost everywhere. Some recommended accessories include a first-aid kit (compulsory in Austria, Slovenia, Croatia, Serbia, Montenegro and Greece), a spare bulb kit (compulsory in Spain), a reflective jacket for every person in the car (compulsory in France, Italy and Spain) and a fire extinguisher (compulsory in Greece and Turkey). Residents of the UK should contact the **RAC** (☎ 019 2272 7313; www.rac.co.uk) or the **AA** (☎ 0800 316 2456; www.theaa.com) for more information. In the USA, contact **AAA** (www.aaa.com).

Purchase

The purchase of vehicles in some European countries is illegal for non-nationals or non-EU residents. Britain is probably the best place to buy; second-hand prices are good and, whether buying privately or from a dealer, the absence of language difficulties will help you establish exactly what you are getting and what guarantees you can expect if you break down.

However, bear in mind that British cars have steering wheels on the right-hand side. If you wish to have left-hand drive and can afford to buy a new car, prices are generally reasonable in Greece, France, Germany, Belgium,

Luxembourg and the Netherlands. Paperwork can be tricky wherever you buy, and many countries have compulsory roadworthiness checks on older vehicles.

Rental

Renting a car is ideal for people who will need cars for 16 days or less. Anything more, it's better to lease; see opposite for more information. Big international rental firms will give you reliable service and good vehicles. Usually you will have the option of returning the car to a different outlet at the end of the rental period, but inquire about extra charges for noncircular itineraries. Book early for the lowest rates and make sure you compare rates in different cities. Prices in Brussels tend to be cheaper than in Paris. Taxes range from 15% to 20% and surcharges apply if rented from an airport.

One operator worth bearing in mind if you're renting a car in the UK, France, Greece, Ireland, Italy, Portugal, Spain or Switzerland is **Easycar** (www.easycar.com), which has rentals starting at rock-bottom rates.

Otherwise, check the sites of the following major operators, where you can make reservations online:

Alamo (www.alamo.com)
Avis (www.avis.com)
Budget (www.budget.com)
Europcar (www.europcar.com)
Hertz (www.hertz.com)

Note that if you rent a car in the EU you might not be able to take it outside the EU, and if you rent the car outside the EU, you will only be able to drive within the EU for eight days. Ask at the rental agencies for other such regulations.

Brokers can sometimes cut costs over quoted rates. In the UK **Holiday Autos** (☎ 087 1472 5229; www.holidayautos.com) has low rates and either offices or representatives in more than 20 countries. In the USA call **Kemwel Holiday Autos** (☎ 877 820 0668; www.kemwel.com).

If you want to rent a car and haven't booked ahead, look for national or local firms, which can often undercut the big companies by up to 40%. Nevertheless, you need to be wary of dodgy operations that take your money and point you towards some clapped-out wreck, or where the rental agreement is bad news if you have an accident or the car is stolen. Read before you sign.

No matter where you rent, make sure you understand what is included in the price (unlimited or paid kilometres, tax, injury insurance, collision damage waiver etc) and what your liabilities are. We recommend taking the collision damage waiver, though you can probably skip the injury insurance if you and your passengers have decent travel insurance. Ask in advance if you can drive a rented car across borders from a country where hire prices are low to another where they're high.

The minimum rental age is usually 21 years and frequently 25, and you'll need a credit card and to have held your licence for at least a year. Motorcycle and moped rental is common in some countries, such as Italy, Spain, Greece and southern France. Sadly, it's also common for inexperienced riders to leap on rented bikes and very quickly fall off them again, leaving a layer or two of skin on the road in the process.

Road Conditions & Road Rules

Conditions and types of roads vary across Europe. The fastest routes are generally four- or six-lane dual carriageways/highways (two or three lanes either side) called 'autoroutes', *autostrade, Autobahnen* etc. These tend to skirt cities and plough through the countryside in straight lines, often avoiding the most scenic bits. Some incur tolls, which are often quite hefty (especially in Italy, France and Spain), but there will always be an alternative route. Motorways and other primary routes are generally in good condition.

Road surfaces on minor routes are unreliable in some countries (eg Greece, Albania, Romania, Ireland, Morocco, Russia and Ukraine), although normally they will be more than adequate. These roads are narrower and progress is generally much slower. However, to compensate for this, you can expect much better scenery and plenty of interesting villages along the way.

Except in Britain, Ireland, Malta and Cyprus you should drive on the right. Vehicles brought to the Continent from any of these locales should have their headlights adjusted to avoid blinding oncoming traffic (a simple solution on older headlight lenses is to cover up a triangular section of the lens with tape). Priority is often given to traffic approaching from the right in countries that drive on the right-hand side.

Speed limits vary from country to country. You may be surprised at the apparent disregard for traffic regulations in some places (particularly in Italy and Greece), but as a visitor it is always best to be cautious. Many driving infringements are subject to an on-the-spot fine. Always ask for a receipt.

European drink-driving laws are particularly strict. The blood-alcohol concentration (BAC) limit when driving is usually between 0.05% and 0.08%, but in certain areas (such as Gibraltar and some Eastern European countries such as Bulgaria and Belarus) it can be zero.

HITCHING

Hitching is never entirely safe and we cannot recommend it. Travellers who decide to hitch should understand that they are taking a small but potentially serious risk. It will be safer if they travel in pairs and let someone know where they plan to go. A man and woman travelling together is probably the best combination. A woman hitching on her own is taking a larger than normal risk, particularly in parts of southern Europe.

Hitching in Western Europe can be simultaneously the most rewarding and yet frustrating way of getting around. You get to meet and interact with local people and can have unplanned detours that may yield unexpected highlights off-the-beaten track. But you might get stuck on the side of the road to nowhere with nowhere (or nowhere cheap) to stay. Then it begins to rain.

Don't try to hitch from city centres; take public transport to the suburban exit routes. Hitching is usually illegal on motorways (freeways) – stand on the slip roads, or approach drivers at petrol stations and truck stops. Look presentable and cheerful, and make a cardboard sign indicating your intended destination in the local language. Never hitch where drivers can't stop in good time or without causing an obstruction. At dusk, give up and find somewhere to stay.

It is sometimes possible to arrange a lift in advance: scan student notice boards in colleges, or check out www.hitchhikers.org. Car-sharing agencies (*Mitfahrzentrale;* see p451) are particularly popular in Germany.

In parts of Eastern Europe, the hitching situation is entirely different. In countries such as Russia and Ukraine, anyone with a car can be a taxi and it's quite usual to see locals stick their hands out (palm down) on the street, looking to hitch a lift. The difference with hitching here, however, is that you pay for the privilege. You will need to speak the local language to discuss your destination and negotiate a price.

LOCAL TRANSPORT

High-density populations mean European towns and cities have excellent local-transport systems, often encompassing trams as well as buses and metro/subway/underground rail networks. Be sure to remove your pack on public transport and hold it in front of you to avoid battering your neighbour and deter pickpockets. Also give up your seat to the elderly, infirm or pregnant women.

Most travellers will find European cities can be easily traversed by foot or bicycle. In Greece and Italy, travellers sometimes rent mopeds and motorcycles for scooting around a city or island.

TAXI

Taxis in Europe are metered and rates are usually high. There might also be supplements for things such as luggage, time of day, location of pick-up and extra passengers. Good bus, rail and underground-railway networks often render taxis unnecessary, but if you need one in a hurry, they can be found idling near train stations or outside big hotels. Lower fares make taxis more viable in some countries, such as Spain, Greece, Portugal and Turkey.

See also Hitching (left) for the situation in some Eastern European countries.

TRAIN

Comfortable, frequent and reliable, trains are *the* way of getting around Europe. Indeed, it's safe to say that Europe has some of the most efficient and comprehensive train services in the world, particularly in Switzerland, Austria and Germany. Trains are a great way to meet people, see the countryside, get into the heart of cities and to scribble furiously into that sacred journal.

If you plan to travel extensively by train, it is worth obtaining the *Thomas Cook European Timetable,* giving a complete listing of train schedules and indicating where supplementary fares apply or where reservations are necessary. It's available from **Thomas Cook** (www.thomascookpublishing.com) outlets and bookshops in the UK (online elsewhere in the world).

Many state railways now have interactive websites publishing their timetables and fares, including www.bahn.de (Germany) and www.rail.ch (Switzerland), which both have pages in English. The **Eurail** (www.eurail.com) website links to more than 20 national train companies in Europe (in the local language).

The very comprehensive, privately run website **The Man in Seat 61** (www.seat61.com) is a gem, while the US-based **Budget Europe Travel Service** (☎ 800 441 2387; www.budgeteuropetravel.com) can also help with tips.

Paris, Milan and Vienna are important hubs for international train connections. See the relevant city sections for details. Note that European trains sometimes split en route to service two destinations, so even if you're on the right train, make sure you're also in the correct carriage.

A train journey to almost every station in Europe can be booked via **Rail Europe** (☎ 084 4848 4064; www.raileurope.co.uk; 178 Piccadilly London W1), which also sells InterRail and other passes; see right. Note that train travel is often much more expensive than air travel in Europe, especially since the advent of the low-cost airlines. But aside from being infinitely more pleasurable, it's also far more environmentally friendly than taking flights everywhere.

Express Trains

Europeans are normally avid fliers, but they're unlikely to catch a plane between London and Paris or Brussels. That's because those routes are conveniently served by the high-speed passenger train service **Eurostar** (☎ in Britain 087 0518 6186, in France 08 92 35 35 39, in Belgium 02 528 28 28; www.eurostar.com).

Eurostar links London's St Pancras International station, via the Channel Tunnel, with Paris' Gare du Nord (2¼ hours, up to 25 a day) and Brussels' international terminal (one hour 50 mins, up to 12 a day). Some trains also stop at Lille and Calais in France. The train stations at St Pancras International, Paris and Brussels are all much more central than the cities' airports. So, overall, the journey takes as little time as the equivalent flight, with less hassle.

From London to Paris or Brussels, fares start at £59 for a return; to Calais or Lille it's £55. These fares are widely available, but at times you might pay a higher price (up to £298 return). A return fare is only valid for six months. If you're going for longer you'll need a single ticket, from £40 to £149.

Eurostar in London also sells tickets onward to some Continental destinations, although its list is much less comprehensive than Rail Europe's (see left). Holders of Eurail and InterRail passes are offered discounts on some Eurostar services; check when booking.

Within Europe, express trains are identified by the symbols 'EC' (EuroCity) or 'IC' (InterCity). The French TGV, Spanish AVE and German ICE trains are even faster, reaching up to 300km/h. Supplementary fares can apply on fast trains (which you often have to pay when travelling on a rail pass), and it is a good idea (sometimes obligatory) to reserve seats at peak times and on certain lines. The same applies for branded express trains, such as the Thalys (between Paris and Brussels, Bruges, Amsterdam and Cologne), and the Eurostar Italia (between Rome and Naples, Florence, Milan and Venice).

If you don't have a seat reservation, you can still obtain a seat that doesn't have a reservation ticket attached to it. Be sure to check which destination a seat is reserved for – you might be able to sit in it until the person who's booked it boards the train.

International Rail Passes

If you're covering lots of ground, you should get a rail pass. But do some price comparisons of point-to-point ticket charges and rail passes beforehand to make absolutely sure you'll break even. Also shop around for rail-pass prices as they do vary between outlets. When weighing up options, look into cheap deals that include advance-purchase reductions, one-off promotions or special circular-route tickets. Normal point-to-point tickets are valid for two months, and you can make as many stops as you like en route; make your intentions known when purchasing, and inform train conductors how far you're going before they punch your ticket.

Supplementary charges (eg for some express and overnight trains) and seat reservation fees (mandatory on some trains, a good idea on others) are not covered by rail passes. Always ask. Note that European rail passes also give reductions on Eurostar through the Channel Tunnel and on certain ferries.

Pass-holders must always carry their passport with them for identification purposes. The railways' policy is that passes cannot be replaced or refunded if lost or stolen. However, with some sales outlets (ie www.raileurope.co.uk)

you can buy insurance that will reimburse you for any days not used at the point a pass is stolen.

NON-EUROPEAN RESIDENTS

Eurail Passes

Eurail (www.eurail.com) passes vary in what they cover depending on how much you pay. The inaccurately named 'Global Pass' covers 21 countries, namely Austria (including Liechtenstein), Belgium, Croatia, Czech Republic, Denmark, Finland, France (including Monaco), Germany, Greece, Hungary, Ireland, Italy, Luxembourg, the Netherlands, Norway, Portugal, Romania, Slovenia, Spain, Sweden and Switzerland.

While the pass is valid on some private train lines in the region, if you plan to travel extensively in Switzerland, be warned that the many private rail networks and cable cars there, especially in the Jungfrau region around Interlaken, don't give Eurail discounts. A Swiss Pass or Half-Fare Card (see p1153) might be an alternative or necessary addition.

While the UK is not covered by any Eurail pass, you can use it on some Italy–Greece, Denmark–Sweden, Germany–Sweden and Sweden–Finland ferries. Reductions are given on some other ferry routes and on river/lake steamer services in various countries.

Eurail can be bought only by residents of non-European countries and should be purchased before arriving in Europe.

For those under 26 years of age, a continuous Eurail Youth pass will cost €332/429/535/755/933 for 15 days/21 days/one month/two months/three months. Holders of youth passes must travel in 2nd-class compartments.

Those aged 26 and over must purchase the full-fare Eurail pass. This costs €511/662/822/1161/1432 for the periods outlined above. However, this full-fare pass entitles you to travel 1st class.

Many permutations of the pass are available. With a Selectpass you nominate three, four or five countries in which you wish to travel, and then buy a pass allowing five, six, eight, 10 or 15 travel days in a two-month period. Prices start at €211/324 per youth/adult. The five- and six-day passes offer an attractive price break, but as the Selectpass continues up its pricing ladder, the continuous pass becomes better value.

A range of more than 15 Eurail Regional Passes covering two or three countries is also offered, but you might want to ensure that they are good value given your travel plans. Similarly, there are now Eurail National Passes for just one country at a time.

Two to five people travelling together can get a Saver version of all Eurail passes for a 15% to 25% discount.

EUROPEAN RESIDENTS

InterRail

Rail Europe (see p1243) sells InterRail passes to European residents for unlimited 2nd- and 3rd-class rail travel through 29 European and North African countries (excluding the pass-holder's country of residence). To qualify as a resident in this sense, you must have lived in a European country for six months.

InterRail Global Passes for five days of travel in 10 days cost £146/229 for under 26 years/26 and over; 10 days travel in 22 days costs £220/330; and a one-month continuous global pass with unlimited travel is £367/550.

While an InterRail pass will get you further than a Eurail pass along the private rail networks of Switzerland's Jungfrau region (near Interlaken), its benefits are limited. A Swiss Pass or Half-Fare Card (see p1153) might be a necessary addition if you plan to travel extensively in that region.

Railplus Card

For a small fee European residents can buy a Railplus Card, entitling the holder to a 25% discount on international train journeys. In most countries, it's sold only to those aged 60 and over. However, some national rail networks may make the Railplus Card available to young people or other travellers. It is available from counters in main train stations.

ALL NATIONALITIES

For purchase of and further information about the following passes, contact **Rail Europe** (www.raileurope.co.uk, www.raileurope.com) in your home country.

France Railpass

This pass offers unlimited travel for three days during a one-month period. Full fares are US$250 for three days and US$37 for each additional travel day within the same month-long period.

Eastern Europe Passes

Several other passes are available, especially if you're interested in travelling in the Continent's east. For example, the European East Pass provides five days of travel over a month in Austria, Czech Republic, Hungary, Poland and Slovakia for US$229/209 for 1st/2nd class. Meanwhile, a Balkans Flexipass provides five to 15 days of 1st-class train travel in a month throughout Bulgaria, Greece, Macedonia, Montenegro, Romania, Serbia and Turkey, starting at US$128/256 per youth/adult.

National Rail Passes

As well as the national rail passes offered by Rail Europe (see opposite), national rail operators might offer their own passes, or at least a discount card, offering substantial reductions on tickets purchased (eg the Bahn Card in Germany or the Half-Fare Card in Switzerland). Link to individual train operator sites via www.raileurope.co.uk to check. Such discount cards are usually only worth it if you're staying in the country a while and doing a lot of travelling.

Overnight Trains

Want to do the whirlwind tour without wasting a day? Use your sleeping hours to cover territory and save money you'd otherwise use on hotels. On overnight trains, there are usually two types of sleeping accommodation: dozing off upright in your seat or stretching out in a sleeper. Again, reservations are advisable, as sleeping options are allocated on a first-come, first-served basis.

Couchette bunks are comfortable enough, if lacking in privacy. There are four per compartment in 1st class, six in 2nd class. A bunk costs a fixed price of around US$20 for most international trains, irrespective of the length of the journey.

Sleepers are the most comfortable option, offering beds for one or two passengers in 1st class, or two or three passengers in 2nd class. Charges vary depending upon the journey, but they are significantly more costly than couchettes. Most long-distance trains have a dining (buffet) car or an attendant who wheels a snack trolley through carriages. Prices tend to be steep.

In the former Soviet Union countries explored in this guide, the most common options are either 2nd-class *kupeyny* compartments – which have four bunks – or the cheaper *platskartny,* which are open-plan compartments with reserved bunks. This 3rd-class equivalent is not great for those who value privacy, and theft might be a problem. Other options include the very basic bench seats in *obshchiy* (*zahalney* in Ukrainian) class and 1st-class, two-person sleeping carriages (*myagki* in Russian). In Ukrainian, this last option is known as *spalney,* but is usually abbreviated to CB in Cyrillic (pronounced *es-ve*). First class is not available on every Russian or Ukrainian train.

Security

Stories sometimes surface about passengers being gassed or drugged and then robbed, but bag snatching is much more of a worry. Sensible security measures include always keeping your bags in sight (especially at stations), chaining them to the luggage rack, locking compartment doors overnight and sleeping in compartments with other people. See individual country chapters for problem routes.

Health

CONTENTS

Before You Go	**1246**
Insurance	1246
Recommended Vaccinations	1246
Online Resources	1246
Further Reading	1247
In Transit	**1247**
Deep Vein Thrombosis (DVT)	1247
Jet Lag & Motion Sickness	1247
In Europe	**1247**
Availability of Health Care	1247
Infectious Diseases	1248
Traveller's Diarrhoea	1248
Environmental Hazards	1248
Sexual Health	1250
Women's Health	1250

Europe comes without any major health warnings, and common-sense prevention is the key to staying well here. Travellers who take the necessary precautions and adopt a sensible approach to their health usually suffer nothing more than a little diarrhoea (if that).

BEFORE YOU GO

Ensure that you bring medications in their original, clearly labelled containers. A signed and dated letter from your physician describing your medical conditions and medications, including generic names, is a good idea. If you are carrying syringes or needles – apart from in a sealed, sterile first-aid kit – it's also wise to have a physician's letter documenting their medical necessity.

INSURANCE

If you're a citizen of the EU, Iceland, Liechtenstein, Norway or Switzerland, the **European Health Insurance Card** (EHIC; www.ehic.org.uk) covers you for most medical care within most of that zone (although some restrictions apply for Icelandic, Liechtenstein, Norwegian and Swiss citizens). The form is available from health centres, online from national health authorities or, in the UK, post offices.

The EHIC will only cover you for emergencies or emergency repatriation, however. Citizens from other countries should find out if there is a reciprocal arrangement for free medical care between their country and the country visited.

If you do need health insurance, strongly consider a policy that covers you for the worst possible scenario, such as an accident requiring an emergency flight home. Find out in advance if your insurance plan will make payments directly to providers or reimburse you later for overseas health expenditures. The former option is generally preferable, as it doesn't require you to pay out of pocket in a foreign country.

RECOMMENDED VACCINATIONS

No jabs are necessary for Europe. However, the World Health Organization (WHO) recommends that all travellers should be covered for diphtheria, tetanus, measles, mumps, rubella and polio, regardless of their destination. Since most vaccines don't produce immunity until at least two weeks after they're given, visit a physician at least six weeks before departure.

ONLINE RESOURCES

There is a wealth of travel health advice on the internet. For further information, **Lonely Planet.com** (www.lonelyplanet.com) is a good place to start. The **World Health Organization** (www.who.int/ith/en) also publishes a superb book called *International Travel and Health,* which is revised annually and is available online at no cost. Another useful website is **MD Travel Health** (www.mdtravelhealth.com), which provides travel health recommendations for every country; information is updated daily.

It's usually a good idea to consult your government's website before departure, if one is available:

Australia www.smartraveller.gov.au
Canada www.travelhealth.gc.ca
UK www.dh.gov.uk
USA www.cdc.gov/travel

FURTHER READING

In the UK, *Health Advice for Travellers* is a leaflet updated annually by the **Department of Health** (www.dh.gov.uk) and available free in post offices. Also published online, it contains some general information, legally required and recommended vaccines for different countries, reciprocal health agreements and an EHIC application form.

Recommended references include *Traveller's Health* by Dr Richard Dawood and *The Traveller's Good Health Guide* by Ted Lankester.

IN TRANSIT

DEEP VEIN THROMBOSIS (DVT)

Blood clots may form in the legs during plane flights, chiefly because of prolonged immobility. The chief symptom of DVT is swelling or pain of the calf, usually but not always on just one side. If a blood clot travels to the lungs, it may cause chest pain and breathing difficulties. Travellers experiencing any of these symptoms should immediately seek medical attention.

To prevent the development of DVT on long flights you should walk about the cabin when possible, contract the leg muscles while sitting, drink plenty of fluids and avoid alcohol.

MEDICAL CHECKLIST

Most of these can easily be purchased almost anywhere in Europe, but for the cautious or for those travelling in remote or backward regions, this is a useful checklist.

- Acetaminophen/paracetamol or aspirin
- Adhesive or paper tape
- Antibacterial ointment (eg Bactroban) for cuts and abrasions
- Antihistamines (for hay fever and allergic reactions)
- Anti-inflammatory drugs (eg ibuprofen)
- Bandages, gauze, gauze rolls
- Insect repellent, containing DEET if entering tick-infested areas, and after-bite lotion
- Insect spray containing pyrethrin for clothing, and for tents and bed nets if camping
- Over-the-counter cortisone cream (for poison ivy and other allergic rashes)
- Pocket knife
- Scissors, safety pins, tweezers
- Sun block
- Thermometer

JET LAG & MOTION SICKNESS

To avoid jet lag (common when crossing more than five time zones), try to drink plenty of nonalcoholic fluids and eat light meals. Try to readjust your schedule for meals, sleep etc as soon as you board your flight, or even in the days before departure. Upon arrival, get exposure to natural sunlight.

Antihistamines such as dimenhydrinate (Dramamine) and meclizine (Antivert, Bonine) are usually the first choice for treating motion sickness. A herbal alternative is ginger.

IN EUROPE

AVAILABILITY OF HEALTH CARE

Good, sometimes excellent, health care is readily available in Western Europe and, for minor illnesses, pharmacists can give valuable advice and sell over-the-counter medication. They can also advise when more-specialised help is required and point you in the right direction. The standard of dental care is usually good.

In Eastern Europe, while the situation is improving all the time since the EU accession of many countries, medical care is not always readily available outside of major cities but embassies, consulates and five-star hotels can usually recommend doctors or clinics. In some cases, medical supplies required in hospital may need to be bought from a pharmacy and nursing care may be limited. Although many Eastern European hospitals now use disposable syringes, supply can be short, so it doesn't hurt to bring your own, in a sterilised first-aid kit. Otherwise, note that there can be an increased risk of hepatitis B and HIV transmission via poorly sterilised equipment.

INFECTIOUS DISEASES

Diphtheria

This bacterial infection of the throat, nose and tonsils is resurgent in parts of the former Soviet Union (FSU). The disease causes lesions in the infected area and in severe cases can cause swelling and fluid build-up in the neck, very occasionally leading to death. In many Western countries, diphtheria booster shots are recommended every 10 years. Travellers should ensure theirs is current before visiting the FSU.

Rabies

Rabies is spread through bites or licks on broken skin from an infected animal. It is always fatal unless treated promptly. Animal handlers should be vaccinated, as should those travelling to remote areas where a reliable source of postbite vaccine is not available within 24 hours. Three preventive injections are needed over a month. If you have not been vaccinated, you will need a course of five injections starting 24 hours or as soon as possible after the injury. If you have been vaccinated, you will need fewer injections and have more time to seek medical help.

Tickborne Encephalitis

Spread by tick bites, this is a serious infection of the brain. Some medical practitioners advise vaccination for those planning to spend time hiking in the Alps and Carpathians between April and August. The risk of getting bitten is quite low, however, so other clinics suggest prophylactic prevention – ie using DEET- and pyrethrin-based insect repellents to prevent tick bites – particularly for short-term visitors. In either case, check your body for ticks each evening.

Two doses of vaccine will give a year's protection, three doses up to three years. However, many doctors' surgeries have to order the vaccine in advance and the shots need to be given at certain intervals for maximum protection. Therefore, if you plan to have a series of shots, you should look at having the first injection about a month before departure.

Tuberculosis

Although travellers might be aware that strains of drug-resistant tuberculosis have reappeared in the FSU, you're at minimal risk of contracting this disease because you need prolonged contact with an infected individual. Some practitioners believe that childhood immunisation against normal strains of TB and being in good health also offer some natural immunity to rogue variants.

In any case, try to avoid spending a lot of time with someone with a persistent dry cough. If that's not possible, it's a sensible precaution to get a TB test on your return home.

Typhoid & Hepatitis A

These diseases are spread through contaminated food (particularly shellfish) and water. Typhoid can cause septicaemia; Hepatitis A causes liver inflammation and jaundice. Neither is usually fatal but recovery can be prolonged. Hepatitis A and typhoid immunisation is now routinely provided in a single vaccine. However, the first dose only lasts a year, after which you will need a booster to provide 10 years' coverage.

TRAVELLER'S DIARRHOEA

If you develop diarrhoea, be sure to drink plenty of fluids, preferably an oral rehydration solution such as Dioralyte. If diarrhoea is bloody, persists for more than 72 hours or is accompanied by a fever, shaking, chills or severe abdominal pain, you should seek medical attention.

ENVIRONMENTAL HAZARDS

Altitude Sickness

Lack of oxygen at high altitudes (typically over 3500m) affects most people to some extent, but European travellers really only need to be aware of it if climbing or taking train rides high up in the Alps or, at a pinch, the Pyrenees. The Continent's third main mountain range, the Carpathians, barely reaches 2500m.

Mild symptoms include headache, lethargy, dizziness, difficulty sleeping and loss of appetite. If you take a high-altitude train ride in Switzerland (specifically to Jungfraujoch; p1171), you might feel sleepy and lethargic, but just take it slowly.

However, the onset of Acute Mountain Sickness (AMS) may occur without warning and can be fatal. Severe symptoms include breathlessness, a dry, irritative cough (which may progress to the production of pink, frothy sputum), severe headache, lack of coordination and balance, confusion, irrational behaviour, vomiting, drowsiness and unconsciousness. If this happens, *immediate descent is necessary;* even 500m can help.

Beware that altitude sickness can sometimes occur as low as 2500m. For more details contact or visit the website of the **British Mountaineering Council** (www.thebmc.co.uk; 177-179 Burton Rd, West Didsbury, Manchester, M20 2BB).

Bites & Stings

As European mosquitoes do not carry malaria, you really only need an ordinary repellent against them, saving harsher DEET-based repellents to ward off ticks (see opposite).

Sand flies are found around the Mediterranean beaches. In Europe, they usually cause only a nasty itchy bite, but very, very occasionally they can carry a rare skin disorder called cutaneous leishmaniasis – a series of boils erupting weeks or months after you've been bitten.

Bees and wasps cause real problems only to those with a severe allergy (anaphylaxis). If you have a severe allergy to bee or wasp stings, carry an 'epipen' or similar adrenalin injection.

Bedbugs lead to very itchy, lumpy bites. Spraying the mattress with insect killer after changing bedding will get rid of them.

Scabies are tiny mites that live in the skin, particularly between the fingers. They cause an intensely itchy rash. Scabies is easily treated with lotion from a pharmacy; other members of the household also need treating to avoid spreading scabies between asymptomatic carriers.

Scorpions can also be found in a number of European countries but although their sting can be distressingly painful, it is not considered fatal.

Of the 28 types of snake found in Europe, only four are poisonous and only the two vipers ever kill – and then fairly rarely. Nevertheless, to avoid being bitten do not walk barefoot or stick your hand into holes or cracks. If bitten, do not panic. Immobilise the bitten limb, apply a bandage over the site firmly, similar to a bandage over a sprain, and apply a splint if possible. Do not apply a tourniquet, or cut or suck the bite. Get the victim to medical help as soon as possible so that antivenin can be given if necessary.

Different varieties of jellyfish can be found throughout southern European waters. However, they generally occur in large numbers or hardly at all, so it's fairly easy to know when not to go in the sea. Heed local warnings.

Heat Exhaustion & Heat Stroke

Heat exhaustion occurs following excessive fluid loss with inadequate replacement of fluids and salt. Symptoms include headache, dizziness and tiredness. Dehydration has already started by the time you're thirsty – aim to drink sufficient water to produce pale, diluted urine. Replace lost fluids by drinking water and/or fruit juice, and cool the body with cold water and fans. Treat salt loss with salty fluids such as soup or add a little more table salt to foods than usual.

Heat stroke is much more serious, resulting in irrational and hyperactive behaviour, and eventually loss of consciousness and death. Rapid cooling by spraying the body with water and fanning is ideal. Emergency fluid and electrolyte replacement by intravenous drip may be required.

Hypothermia

The weather in mountainous regions can be extremely changeable at any time of year. Proper preparation will reduce the risks of getting hypothermia. Even on a hot day the weather can change rapidly; carry waterproof garments and warm layers, and inform others of your route.

Hypothermia starts with shivering, loss of judgment and clumsiness. Unless rewarming occurs, the sufferer deteriorates into apathy, confusion and eventually coma. Prevent further heat loss by seeking shelter, warm dry clothing, hot sweet drinks and shared bodily warmth.

Water

Tap water is generally safe to drink in large parts of Western Europe. However, bottled water is recommended in most parts of Eastern Europe, and is a must in some countries including Russia (particularly St Petersburg) and Ukraine, where giardia can be a problem. Do not drink water from rivers or lakes as it may contain bacteria or viruses that can cause diarrhoea or vomiting.

WARNING

Codeine, which is commonly found in headache preparations, is banned in Greece; check labels carefully or risk prosecution. There are strict rules applying to the importation of medicines into Greece, so obtain a certificate from your doctor that outlines any medication you may have to carry into the country with you.

SEXUAL HEALTH

Condoms are widely available in Europe; however, emergency contraception may not be, so take the necessary precautions. The **International Planned Parent Federation** (www.ippf.org) can advise about the availability of contraception in different countries.

When buying condoms, look for a European CE mark, which means they have passed quality tests. Remember to keep them in a cool, dry place.

WOMEN'S HEALTH

Travelling during pregnancy is usually possible but always seek a medical check-up before planning your trip. The most risky times for travel are during the first 12 weeks of pregnancy and after 30 weeks.

Language

CONTENTS

Albanian	1255
Bulgarian	1256
Croatian & Serbian	1257
Czech	1259
Danish	1260
Dutch	1261
Estonian	1262
Finnish	1263
French	1265
German	1266
Greek	1267
Hungarian	1268
Icelandic	1270
Italian	1271
Latvian	1272
Lithuanian	1273
Macedonian	1274
Maltese	1275
Moroccan Arabic	1276
Norwegian	1278
Polish	1279
Portuguese	1280
Romanian	1282
Russian	1283
Slovak	1285
Slovene	1286
Spanish	1287
Swedish	1288
Turkish	1289

Don't let the language barrier get in the way of your travel experience. This language guide offers basic vocabulary and some pronunciation guidelines to help you negotiate your way through all the countries of Europe and beyond. For more extensive coverage of the languages we have included here, choose from Lonely Planet's extensive range of phrasebooks, which cover all of these languages in much greater detail.

You should be aware that many of the languages in this chapter use polite and informal modes of address (indicated by the abbreviations 'pol' and 'inf' respectively). Use the polite form when addressing older people, officials or service staff.

ALBANIAN

PRONUNCIATION

Written Albanian is phonetically consistent and pronunciation shouldn't pose too many problems for English speakers. The Albanian **rr** is rolled and each vowel in a diphthong is pronounced. However, Albanian possesses certain letters that are present in English but pronounced in a different way.

ë	often silent; at the beginning of a word it's like the 'a' in 'ago'
c	as the 'ts' in 'bits'
ç	as the 'ch' in 'church'
dh	as the 'th' in 'this'
gj	as the 'gy' in 'hogyard'
j	as the 'y' in 'yellow'
q	between 'ch' and 'ky', similar to the 'cu' in 'cure'
th	as in 'thistle'
x	as the 'dz' in 'adze'
xh	as the 'j' in 'jewel'

ACCOMMODATION

hotel	*hotel*
camping ground	*kamp pushimi*

Do you have any rooms available?
A keni ndonjë dhomë të lirë?
How much is it per night/per person?
Sa kushton për një natë/për një njeri?
Does it include breakfast?
A e përfshin edhe mëngjesin?

a single room	*një dhomë më një krevat*
a double room	*një dhomë më dy krevat*

CONVERSATION & ESSENTIALS

Hello.	*Tungjatjeta/Allo.*
Goodbye.	*Lamtumirë.* (pol) *Mirupafshim.* (inf)
Yes.	*Po.*
No.	*Jo.*
Please.	*Ju lutem.*
Thank you.	*Ju falem nderit.*
That's fine.	*Eshtë e mirë.*
You're welcome.	*S'ka përse.*
Excuse me.	*Me falni.*
Sorry.	*Më vjen keq* or *Më falni, ju lutem.*

EMERGENCIES – ALBANIAN

Help!	*Ndihmë!*
Call a doctor!	*Thirrni doktorin!*
Call the police!	*Thirrni policinë!*
Go away!	*Zhduku!/Largohuni!*
I'm lost.	*Kam humbur rrugë.*

Do you speak English? *A flisni anglisht?*
How much is it? *Sa kushton?*
What's your name? *Si quheni ju lutem?*
My name is ... *Unë quhem .../ Mua më quajnë ...*

SHOPPING & SERVICES

a bank *një bankë*
chemist/pharmacy *farmaci*
the ... embassy *... ambasadën*
my hotel *hotelin tim*
the market *pazarin*
newsagency *agjensia e lajmeve*
the post office *postën*
the telephone centre *centralin telefonik*
the tourist office *zyrën e informimeve turistike*

What time does it open/close?
Në ç'ore hapet/mbyllet?

TIME, DAYS & NUMBERS

What time is it? *Sa është ora?*
today *sot*
tomorrow *nesër*
yesterday *dje*
in the morning *në mëngjes*
in the afternoon *pas dreke*

Monday *e hënë*
Tuesday *e martë*
Wednesday *e mërkurë*
Thursday *e ënjte*
Friday *e premte*
Saturday *e shtunë*
Sunday *e diel*

1	*një*	**7**	*shtatë*
2	*dy*	**8**	*tetë*
3	*tre*	**9**	*nëntë*
4	*katër*	**10**	*dhjetë*
5	*pesë*	**100**	*njëqind*
6	*gjashtë*	**1000**	*njëmijë*

TRANSPORT & DIRECTIONS

I'd like ... *Dëshiroj ...*
a one-way ticket *një biletë vajtje*
a return ticket *një biletë kthimi*

What time does the ... leave/arrive? *Në ç'orë niset/arrin ...?*
boat *barka/lundra*
bus *autobusi*
tram *tramvaji*
train *treni*

1st/2nd class *klas i parë/i dytë*
timetable *orar*
bus stop *stacion autobusi*

Where is ...? *Ku është ...?*
Go straight ahead. *Shko drejt.*
Turn left. *Kthehu majtas.*
Turn right. *Kthehu djathtas.*
near/far *afër/larg*

SIGNS – ALBANIAN

Hyrje	Entrance
Dalje	Exit
Informim	Information
Hapur	Open
Mbyllur	Closed
E Ndaluar	Prohibited
Nevojtorja	Toilets
Burra	Men
Gra	Women

BULGARIAN

ALPHABET

Bulgarian uses the Cyrillic alphabet (see p1280), and it's worth familiarising yourself with it.

ACCOMMODATION

Do you have any rooms available?
imateh li svobodni stai?
How much is it?
kolko struva?
Does it include breakfast?
zakuskata vklyuchena li e?

camping ground *kâmpinguvane*
youth hostel *obshtezhitie*
guest house *pansion*
hotel *khotel*
private room *stoya v chastna kvartira*
single room *edinichna staya*
double room *dvoyna staya*

LANGUAGE

EMERGENCIES – BULGARIAN

Help!	*pomosh!*
Call a doctor!	*povikayte lekar!*
Call the police!	*povikayte politsiya!*
Go away!	*mahayte se!*
I'm lost.	*zagubih se*

CONVERSATION & ESSENTIALS

Hello.	*zdraveyte/zdrasti* (pol/inf)
Goodbye.	*dovizhdane/chao* (pol/inf)
Yes.	*da*
No.	*ne*
Please.	*molya*
Thank you.	*blagodarya/mersi* (pol/inf)
I'm sorry.	*sâzhalyavam*
Excuse me.	*izvinete me*
Do you speak English?	*govorite li angliski?*
I don't understand.	*az ne razbiram*
What's it called?	*kak se kazva tova?*
How much is it?	*kolko struva?*

SHOPPING & SERVICES

the bank	*bankata*
the hospital	*bolnitsata*
the market	*pazara*
the museum	*muzeya*
the post office	*poshtata*
the tourist office	*byuroto za turisticheska informatsiya*

TIME, DAYS & NUMBERS

What time is it?	*kolko e chasât?*
today	*dnes*
tonight	*dovechera*
tomorrow	*utre*
yesterday	*vchera*
in the morning	*sutrinta*
in the evening	*vecherta*

Monday	*ponedelnik*
Tuesday	*vtornik*
Wednesday	*sryada*
Thursday	*chetvârtâk*
Friday	*petâk*
Saturday	*sâbota*
Sunday	*nedelya*

1	*edno*	**7**	*sedem*
2	*dve*	**8**	*osem*
3	*tri*	**9**	*devet*
4	*chetiri*	**10**	*deset*
5	*pet*	**100**	*sto*
6	*shest*	**1000**	*hilyada*

TRANSPORT & DIRECTIONS

What time does the … leave/arrive?	*v kolko chasa zaminava/ pristiga …?*
city bus	*gradskiyat avtobus*
intercity bus	*mezhdugradskiyat avtobus*
plane	*samolehtât*
train	*vlakât*
tram	*tramvayat*
arrival	*pristigane*
departure	*zaminavane*
timetable	*razpisanie*

Where is the bus stop?
kâde e avtobusnata spirka?
Where is the train station?
kâde e zhelezopâtnata gara?
Where is the left-luggage room?
kâde e garderobât?
Please show me on the map.
molya pokazhete mi na kartata

straight ahead	*napravo*
left	*lyavo*
right	*dyasno*

SIGNS – BULGARIAN

Вход	Entrance
Изход	Exit
Информация	Information
Отворено	Open
Затворено	Closed
Забранено	Prohibited
Тоалетни	Toilets
Мъже	Men
Жени	Women

CROATIAN & SERBIAN

Serbian is written in both the Cyrillic and the Roman alphabet, and it's worth familiarising yourself with the former (see p1280). Croatian uses a Roman alphabet and many letters are pronounced as in English. Note the following exceptions:

c	as the 'ts' in 'cats'
ć	as the 'tch' sound in 'future'
č	as the 'ch' in 'chop'
đ	as the 'dy' sound in 'verdure'
dž	as the 'j' in 'just'
j	as the 'y' in 'young'
lj	as the 'lli' in 'million'
nj	as the 'ny' in 'canyon'

LANGUAGE

EMERGENCIES – CROATIAN & SERBIAN

Help!	*Upomoć!*
Call a doctor!	*Pozovite liječnika/lekara!* (C/S)
Call the police!	*Pozovite policiju!*
Go away!	*Idite!*
I'm lost.	*Izgubljen/Izgubljena sam.* (m/f)

š	as the 'sh' in 'hush'
ž	as the 's' in 'pleasure'

Croatian and Serbian are very similar and minor differences in pronunciation aren't marked in the following words and phrases, which are Croatian. You'll still be understood, even with a Croatian lilt to your language. Where significant differences occur, we've included both, with Croatian marked (C) and Serbian marked (S).

ACCOMMODATION

hotel	*hotel*
guest house	*privatno prenoćište*
youth hostel	*omladinsko prenoćište*
camping ground	*kamping*

Do you have any rooms available?
Imate li slobodne sobe?
How much is it per night/per person?
Koliko košta za jednu noć/po osobi?
Is breakfast included?
Da li je u cijenu uključen i doručak?
I'd like a (single/double) room.
Želim sobu sa (jednim/duplim) krevetom.

CONVERSATION & ESSENTIALS

Hello.	*Zdravo.*
Goodbye.	*Doviđenja.*
Yes.	*Da.*
No.	*Ne.*
Please.	*Molim.*
Thank you.	*Hvala.*
You're welcome.	*Nema na čemu.*
Excuse me.	*Pardon.*
Sorry.	*Oprostite.*
Do you speak English?	*Govorite li engleski?*
How much is it?	*Koliko košta?*

SHOPPING & SERVICES

I'm looking for ...	*Tražim ...*
a bank	*banku*
the ... embassy	*... ambasadu*
the market	*pijacu*
the post office	*poštu*
the tourist office	*turistički biro*

TIME, DAYS & NUMBERS

What time is it?	*Koliko je sati?*
today	*danas*
tomorrow	*sutra*
in the morning	*ujutro*
in the afternoon	*popodne*

Monday	*ponedeljak*
Tuesday	*utorak*
Wednesday	*srijeda*
Thursday	*četvrtak*
Friday	*petak*
Saturday	*subota*
Sunday	*nedjelja*

1	*jedan*	**7**	*sedam*
2	*dva*	**8**	*osam*
3	*tri*	**9**	*devet*
4	*četiri*	**10**	*deset*
5	*pet*	**100**	*sto*
6	*šest*	**1000**	*tisuću* (C)/*hiljada* (S)

SIGNS – CROATIAN & SERBIAN

Ulaz/Izlaz	**Улаз/Излаз**	Entrance/Exit
Informacije	**Информације**	Information
Otvoreno/Zatvoreno	**Отворено/Затворено**	Open/Closed
Zabranjeno	**Забрањено**	Prohibited
Toaleti/WC	**Тоалети/WC**	Toilets

TRANSPORT & DIRECTIONS

What time does the ... leave/arrive?	*Kada ... polazi/dolazi?*
boat	*brod*
city bus	*gradski autobus*
intercity bus	*međugradski autobus*
train	*vlak* (C)/*voz* (S)
tram	*tramvaj*

one-way ticket	*kartu u jednom pravcu*
return ticket	*povratnu kartu*
1st class	*prvu klasu*
2nd class	*drugu klasu*
near/far	*blizu/daleko*

Where is the bus/tram stop?
Gdje je autobuska/tramvajska postaja?
Can you show me (on the map)?
Možete li mi pokazati (na karti)?
Go straight ahead.
Idite pravo naprijed.
Turn left/right.
Skrenite lijevo/desno.

CZECH

PRONUNCIATION

Many Czech letters are pronounced as per their English counterparts. An accent over a vowel lengthens its pronunciation and the stress is always on the first syllable. Words are pronounced as written, so if you follow the guidelines below you should have no trouble being understood. When consulting indexes on Czech maps, be aware that **ch** comes after **h**.

c	as the 'ts' in 'bits'
č	as the 'ch' in 'church'
ch	as in Scottish *loch*
ď	as the 'd' in 'duty'
ě	as the 'ye' in 'yet'
j	as the 'y' in 'you'
ň	as the 'ni' in 'onion'
ř	as the sound 'rzh'
š	as the 'sh' in 'ship'
ť	as the 'te' in 'stew'
ž	as the 's' in 'pleasure'

ACCOMMODATION

hotel	*hotel*
guest house	*penzión*
youth hostel	*ubytovna*
camping ground	*kemping*
private room	*privát*
single room	*jednolůžkový pokoj*
double room	*dvoulůžkový pokoj*
Do you have any rooms available?	*Máte volné pokoje?*
How much is it?	*Kolik to je?*

CONVERSATION & ESSENTIALS

Hello/Good day.	*Dobrý den.* (pol)
Hi.	*Ahoj.* (inf)
Goodbye.	*Na shledanou.*
Yes.	*Ano.*
No.	*Ne.*
Please.	*Prosím.*
Thank you.	*Dekuji.*
That's fine/You're welcome.	*Není zač/Prosím.*
Excuse me/Sorry.	*Promiňte.*
Do you speak English?	*Mluvíte anglicky?*
I don't understand.	*Nerozumím.*
How much is it?	*Kolik to stojí?*

SHOPPING & SERVICES

Where is it?	*Kde je to?*
the bank	*banka*
the chemist	*lékárna*
the market	*trh*
the museum	*muzeum*
the post office	*pošta*
the tourist office	*turistické informační centrum (středisko)*

EMERGENCIES – CZECH

Help!	*Pomoc!*
Go away!	*Běžte pryč!*
I'm lost.	*Zabloudil jsem.* (m) *Zabloudila jsem.* (f)
Call ...!	*Zavolejte ...!*
a doctor	*doktora*
an ambulance	*sanitku*
the police	*policii*

TIME, DAYS & NUMBERS

What time is it?	*Kolik je hodin?*
today	*dnes*
tonight	*dnes večer*
tomorrow	*zítra*
in the morning	*ráno*
in the evening	*večer*
Monday	*pondělí*
Tuesday	*úterý*
Wednesday	*středa*
Thursday	*čtvrtek*
Friday	*pátek*
Saturday	*sobota*
Sunday	*neděle*

1	*jeden*	**7**	*sedm*
2	*dva*	**8**	*osm*
3	*tři*	**9**	*devět*
4	*čtyři*	**10**	*deset*
5	*pět*	**100**	*sto*
6	*šest*	**1000**	*tisíc*

TRANSPORT & DIRECTIONS

What time does the ... leave/arrive?	*Kdy odjíždí/přijíždí ...?*
boat	*loď*
city bus	*městský autobus*
intercity bus	*meziměstský autobus*
train	*vlak*
tram	*tramvaj*
arrival	*příjezdy*
departure	*odjezdy*
timetable	*jízdní řád*

SIGNS – CZECH	
Vchod	Entrance
Východ	Exit
Informace	Information
Otevřeno	Open
Zavřeno	Closed
Zakázáno	Prohibited
Telefon	Telephone
Záchody/WC/Toalety	Toilets

Where is the ...? *Kde je ...?*
bus stop *autobusová zastávka*
station *nádraží*
left-luggage room *úschovna zavazadel*

Please show me on the map. *Prosím, ukažte mi to na mapě.*
left/right *vlevo/vpravo*
straight ahead *rovně*

DANISH

PRONUNCIATION

a	as in 'father'
a/æ	as in 'act'
å/o/u(n)	a long rounded 'a' as in 'walk
e(g)	as in 'eye'
e, i	as the 'e' in 'bet'
i	as the 'e' in 'theme'
ø	as the 'er' in 'fern'
o, u	as the 'oo' in 'cool'
o	as in 'pot'
o(v)	as the 'ou' in 'out'
o(r)	as the 'or' in 'for' with less emphasis on the 'r'
u	as in 'pull'
y	say 'ee' while pursing your lips
c	as in 'celery'
(o)d	a flat 'dh' sound, as the 'th' in 'these'
j	as the 'y' in 'yet'
r	a rolling 'r' abruptly cut short
sj	as in 'ship'

ACCOMMODATION

hotel *hotel*
guest house *gæstgiveri*
hostel *vandrerhjem*
camping ground *campingplads*

Do you have any rooms available? *Har I ledige værelser?*

How much is it per night/person? *Hvor meget koster det per nat/person?*
one day/two days *en nat/to nætter*

I'd like ... *Jeg ønsker ...*
a single room *et enkeltværelse*
a double room *et dobbeltværelse*

CONVERSATION & ESSENTIALS

Hello. *Hallo.*
Hej. (informal)
Goodbye. *Farvel.*
Yes. *Ja.*
No. *Nej.*
Please. *Må jeg bede/Værsgo.*
Thank you. *Tak.*
You're welcome. *Selv tak.*
Excuse me/Sorry. *Undskyld.*
Do you speak English? *Taler De engelsk?*
How much is it? *Hvor meget koster det?*

EMERGENCIES – DANISH	
Help!	*Hjælp!*
Call a doctor!	*Ring efter en læge!*
Call the police!	*Ring efter politiet!*
Go away!	*Forsvind!*
I'm lost.	*Jeg har gået vild.*

SHOPPING & SERVICES

a bank *en bank*
a chemist/pharmacy *et apotek*
the ... embassy *den ... ambassade*
the market *ma rkedet*
a newsagent *en aviskiosk*
the post office *postkontoret*
the tourist office *turistinformationen*

What time does it open/close? *Hvornår åbner/lukker det?*

TIME, DAYS & NUMBERS

What time is it? *Hvad er klokken?*
today *i dag*
tomorrow *i morgen*
morning *morgenen*
afternoon *eftermiddagen*

Monday *mandag*
Tuesday *tirsdag*
Wednesday *onsdag*
Thursday *torsdag*
Friday *fredag*
Saturday *lørdag*
Sunday *søndag*

SIGNS – DANISH

Indgang	Entrance
Udgang	Exit
Information	Information
Åben	Open
Lukket	Closed
Forbudt	Prohibited
Toiletter	Toilets
Herrer	Men
Damer	Women

0	*nul*	**7**	*syv*
1	*en*	**8**	*otte*
2	*to*	**9**	*ni*
3	*tre*	**10**	*ti*
4	*fire*	**11**	*elve*
5	*fem*	**100**	*hundrede*
6	*seks*	**1000**	*tusind*

TRANSPORT & DIRECTIONS

What time does … leave/arrive?	*Hvornår går/ankommer …?*
the boat	*båden*
the bus (city)	*bussen*
the bus (intercity)	*rutebilen*
the tram	*sporvognen*
the train	*toget*
I'd like …	*Jeg vil gerne have …*
a one-way ticket	*en enkeltbillet*
a return ticket	*en tur-retur billet*
1st/2nd class	*første/anden klasse*
left-luggage office	*reisegodsoppbevaringen*
timetable	*køreplan*
bus stop	*bus holdeplads*
tram stop	*sporvogn holdeplads*
train station	*jernbanestation (banegård)*
Where can I hire a car/bicycle?	*Hvor kan jeg leje en bil/cykel?*
Where is …?	*Hvor er …?*
Go straight ahead.	*Gå ligefrem.*
Turn left/right.	*Drej til venstre/højre.*
near/far	*nær/fjern*

DUTCH

PRONUNCIATION

au/ou pronounced somewhere between the 'ow' in 'how' and the 'ow' in 'glow'

eu a tricky one; try saying 'eh' with rounded lips and the tongue forward, then slide the tongue back and down to make an 'oo' sound; it's similar to the 'eu' in French *couleur*

i/ie long, as the 'ee' in 'meet'

ij/ei as the 'ey' in 'they'

oe as the 'oo' in 'zoo'

ui a very tricky one; pronounced somewhere between au/ou and eu; it's similar to the 'eui' in French *fauteuil*, without the slide to the 'i'

ch/g in the north, a hard 'kh' sound as in the Scottish *loch*; in the south, a softer, lisping sound

j as the 'y' in 'yes'; also as the 'j' in 'jam' or 'zh' 'pleasure'

r in the south, a rolled sound; in the north it varies, often guttural

ACCOMMODATION

hotel	*hotel*
guest house	*pension*
youth hostel	*jeugdherberg*
camping ground	*camping*
Do you have any rooms available?	*Heeft u kamers vrij?*
single/double room	*eenpersoons/tweepersoons kamer*
one/two nights	*één nacht/twee nachten*
How much is it per night/ per person?	*Hoeveel is het per nacht/ per persoon?*

EMERGENCIES – DUTCH

Help!	*Help!*
Call a doctor!	*Haal een dokter!*
Call the police!	*Haal de politie!*
Go away!	*Ga weg!*
I'm lost.	*Ik ben de weg kwijt.*

CONVERSATION & ESSENTIALS

Hello.	*Dag/Hallo.*
Goodbye.	*Dag.*
Yes.	*Ja.*
No.	*Nee.*
Please.	*Alstublieft.(pol)/Alsjeblieft.(inf)*
Thank you.	*Dank u/je (wel).*
You're welcome.	*Geen dank.*
Excuse me.	*Pardon.*
Sorry.	*Sorry.*
Do you speak English?	*Spreekt u/spreek je Engels?*
How much is it?	*Hoeveel kost het?*

LANGUAGE

SHOPPING & SERVICES

a bank	*een bank*
the … embassy	*de … ambassade*
the market	*de markt*
the pharmacy	*de drogist*
the newsagent/ stationer	*de krantenwinkel/ kantoorboekhandel*
the post office	*het postkantoor*
the tourist office	*de VVV/het toeristenbureau*
What time does it open/close?	*Hoe laat opent/sluit het?*

TIME, DAYS & NUMBERS

What time is it?	*Hoe laat is het?*
today	*vandaag*
tomorrow	*morgen*
in the morning	*'smorgens*
in the afternoon	*'smiddags*

Monday	*maandag*
Tuesday	*dinsdag*
Wednesday	*woensdag*
Thursday	*donderdag*
Friday	*vrijdag*
Saturday	*zaterdag*
Sunday	*zondag*

0	*nul*	**7**	*zeven*
1	*één*	**8**	*acht*
2	*twee*	**9**	*negen*
3	*drie*	**10**	*tien*
4	*vier*	**11**	*elf*
5	*vijf*	**100**	*honderd*
6	*zes*	**1000**	*duizend*

TRANSPORT & DIRECTIONS

What time does the … leave/arrive?	*Hoe laat vertrekt/ arriveert de …?*
(next)	*(volgende)*
boat	*boot*
bus	*bus*
train	*trein*
tram	*tram*

I'd like to hire a car/bicycle.	*Ik wil graag een auto/fiets huren.*
I'd like a one-way/ return ticket.	*Ik wil graag een enkele reis/een retour.*
1st/2nd class	*eerste/tweede klas*
left-luggage locker	*bagagekluis*
bus/tram stop	*bushalte/tramhalte*
train station/ ferry terminal	*treinstation/veerhaven*

SIGNS – DUTCH

Ingang	Entrance
Uitgang	Exit
Informatie	Information
Open	Open
Gesloten	Closed
Verboden	Prohibited
WC/Toiletten	Toilets
Heren	Men
Dames	Women

Where is the …?	*Waar is de …?*
Go straight ahead.	*Ga rechtdoor.*
Turn left/right.	*Ga linksaf/rechtsaf.*
far/near	*ver/dichtbij*

ESTONIAN

ALPHABET & PRONUNCIATION

The letters of the Estonian alphabet are: **a b d e f g h i j k l m n o p r s š z ž t u v õ ä ö ü**.

a	as the 'u' in 'cut'
b	similar to English 'p'
g	similar to English 'k'
j	as the 'y' in 'yes'
š	as 'sh'
ž	as the 's' in 'pleasure'
õ	somewhere between the 'e' in 'bed' and the 'u' in 'fur'
ä	as the 'a' in 'cat'
ö	as the 'u' in 'fur' but with rounded lips
ü	as a short 'you'
ai	as the 'i' in 'pine'
ei	as in 'vein'
oo	as the 'a' in 'water'
uu	as the 'oo' in 'boot'
öö	as the 'u' in 'fur'

CONVERSATION & ESSENTIALS

Hello.	*Tere.*
Goodbye.	*Head aega/Nägemiseni.*
Yes.	*Jah.*
No.	*Ei.*
Excuse me.	*Vabandage.*
Please.	*Palun.*
Thank you.	*Tänan./Aitäh.*
Do you speak English?	*Kas te räägite inglise keelt?*

SHOPPING & SERVICES

bank	*pank*
chemist	*apteek*

currency exchange	*valuutavahetus*
market	*turg*
toilet	*tualett*

Where?	*Kus?*
How much?	*Kui palju?*

EMERGENCIES – ESTONIAN

Help!	*Appi!*
I'm ill.	*Ma olen haige.*
I'm lost.	*Ma olen eksinud.*
Go away!	*Minge ära!*
Call ...!	*Kutsuge ...!*
a doctor	*arst*
an ambulance	*kiirabi*
the police	*politsei*

TIME, DAYS & NUMBERS

today	*täna*
tomorrow	*homme*

Monday	*esmaspäev*
Tuesday	*teisipäev*
Wednesday	*kolmapäev*
Thursday	*neljapäev*
Friday	*reede*
Saturday	*laupäev*
Sunday	*pühapäev*

1	*üks*	**7**	*seitse*
2	*kaks*	**8**	*kaheksa*
3	*kolm*	**9**	*üheksa*
4	*neli*	**10**	*kümme*
5	*viis*	**100**	*sada*
6	*kuus*	**1000**	*tuhat*

SIGNS – ESTONIAN

Sissepääs	Entrance
Väljapääs	Exit
Avatud/Lahti	Open
Suletud/Kinni	Closed
Mitte Suitsetada	No Smoking
WC	Toilets
Naistele	Men
Meestele	Women

TRANSPORT & DIRECTIONS

airport	*lennujaam*
bus station	*bussijaam*
port	*sadam*
stop (eg bus stop)	*peatus*
train station	*raudteejaam*

bus	*buss*
taxi	*takso*
train	*rong*
tram	*tramm*
trolleybus	*trollibuss*

ticket	*pilet*
ticket office	*piletikassa/kassa*
soft class/deluxe	*luksus*
sleeping carriage	*magamisvagun*
compartment (class)	*kupee*

FINNISH

PRONUNCIATION

The final letters of the alphabet are **å**, **ä** and **ö** (important to know when looking for something in a telephone directory).

y	as the 'u' in 'pull' but with the lips stretched back (like the German 'ü')
å	as the 'oo' in 'poor'
ä	as the 'a' in 'act'
ö	as the 'e' in 'summer'
z	pronounced (and sometimes written) as 'ts'
v/w	as the 'v' in 'vain'
h	a weak sound, except at the end of a syllable, when it is almost like 'ch' in German *ich*
j	as the 'y' in 'yellow'
r	a rolled 'r'

ACCOMMODATION

hotel	*hotelli*
guest house	*matkustajakoti*
youth hostel	*retkeilymaja*
camping ground	*leirintäalue*

Do you have any rooms available?	*Onko teillä vapaata huonetta?*
one day	*yhden päivän*
two days	*kaksi päivää*

How much is it ...?	*Paljonko se on ...?*
per night	*yöltä*
per person	*hengeltä*

I'd like ...	*Haluaisin ...*
a single room	*yhden hengen huoneen*
a double room	*kahden hengen huoneen*

EMERGENCIES – FINNISH

Help!	*Apua!*
Call a doctor!	*Kutsukaa lääkäri!*
Call the police!	*Soittakaa poliisi!*
Go away!	*Mene pois! (Häivy!)*
I'm lost.	*Minä olen eksynyt.*

CONVERSATION & ESSENTIALS

Hello.	*Hei./Terve.*
	Moi. (inf)
Goodbye.	*Näkemiin./Moi.* (inf)
Yes.	*Kyllä/Joo.*
No.	*Ei.* (pronounced 'ay')
Please.	*Kiitos.*
Thank you.	*Kiitos.*
That's fine/You're welcome.	*Ole hyvä/Eipä kestä.* (inf)
Excuse me/Sorry.	*Anteeksi.*
Do you speak English?	*Puhutko englantia?*
How much is it?	*Paljonko se makasaa?*

SHOPPING & SERVICES

bank	*pankkia*
chemist/pharmacy	*apteekki*
... embassy	*... -n suurlähetystöä*
market	*toria*
newsagent	*lehtikioski*
post office	*postia*
tourist office	*matkailutoimistoa/ matkailutoimisto*

What time does it open/close?	*Milloin se aukeaan/sul jetaan?*

SIGNS – FINNISH

Sisään	Entrance
Ulos	Exit
Opastus	Information
Avoinna	Open
Suljettu	Closed
Kiellety	Prohibited
WC	Toilets
Miehet	Men
Naiset	Women

TIME, DAYS & NUMBERS

What time is it?	*Paljonko kello on?*
today	*tänään*
tomorrow	*huomenna*
morning	*aamulla*
afternoon	*iltapäivällä*
Monday	*maanantai*
Tuesday	*tiistai*
Wednesday	*keskiviikko*
Thursday	*torstai*
Friday	*perjantai*
Saturday	*lauantai*
Sunday	*sunnuntai*

0	*nolla*	**7**	*seitsemän*
1	*yksi*	**8**	*kahdeksan*
2	*kaksi*	**9**	*yhdeksän*
3	*kolme*	**10**	*kymmenen*
4	*neljä*	**11**	*yksitoista*
5	*viisi*	**100**	*sata*
6	*kuusi*	**1000**	*tuhat*

TRANSPORT & DIRECTIONS

What time does ... leave/arrive?	*Mihin aikaan ... lähtee/saapuu?*
the boat	*laiva*
the bus (city)	*bussi*
the bus (intercity)	*bussi/linja-auto*
the train	*juna*
the tram	*raitiovaunu/raitikka*

I'd like a one-way/return ticket.
Saanko menolipun/menopaluulipun.
Where can I hire a car?
Mistä mina voisin vuokrata auton?
Where can I hire a bicycle?
Mistä mina voin vuokrata polkupyörän?

1st class	*ensimmäinen luokka*
2nd class	*toinen luokka*
left luggage	*säilytys*
timetable	*aikataulu*
bus/tram stop	*pysäkki*
train station	*rautatieasema*
ferry terminal	*satamaterminaali*

Where is ...?	*Missä on ...?*
Go straight ahead.	*Kulje suoraan.*
Turn left.	*Käänny vasempaan.*
Turn right.	*Käänny oikeaan.*
near/far	*lähellä/kaukana*

FRENCH

ACCOMMODATION

the hotel	*l'hôtel*
the youth hostel	*l'auberge de jeunesse*
the camping ground	*le camping*

Do you have any rooms available?
Est-ce que vous avez des chambres libres?

for one person	*pour une personne*
for two people	*pour deux personnes*

How much is it ...?	*Quel est le prix ...?*
per night	*par nuit*
per person	*par personne*

CONVERSATION & ESSENTIALS

Hello.	*Bonjour.*
Goodbye.	*Au revoir.*
Yes.	*Oui.*
No.	*Non.*
Please.	*S'il vous plaît.*
Thank you.	*Merci.*
That's fine/You're welcome.	*Je vous en prie.*
Excuse me.	*Excusez-moi.*
Sorry.	*Pardon.*
Do you speak English?	*Parlez-vous anglais?*
How much is it?	*C'est combien?*

EMERGENCIES – FRENCH

Help!	*Au secours!*
Call a doctor!	*Appelez un médecin!*
Call the police!	*Appelez la police!*
Leave me alone!	*Fichez-moi la paix!*
I'm lost.	*Je me suis égaré/e.*

SHOPPING & SERVICES

a bank	*une banque*
the chemist/pharmacy	*la pharmacie*
the ... embassy	*l'ambassade de ...*
the market	*le marché*
the newsagent	*l'agence de presse*
the post office	*le bureau de poste*
the tourist office	*l'office de tourisme*

What time does it open/close?
Quelle est l'heure de ouverture/fermeture?

TIME, DAYS & NUMBERS

What time is it?	*Quelle heure est-il?*
today	*aujourd'hui*
tomorrow	*demain*
morning	*matin*
afternoon	*après-midi*

Monday	*lundi*
Tuesday	*mardi*
Wednesday	*mercredi*
Thursday	*jeudi*
Friday	*vendredi*

SIGNS – FRENCH

Entrée	Entrance
Sortie	Exit
Renseignements	Information
Ouvert	Open
Fermée	Closed
Interdit	Prohibited
Toilettes, WC	Toilets
Hommes	Men
Femmes	Women

Saturday	*samedi*
Sunday	*dimanche*

1	*un*	**7**	*sept*
2	*deux*	**8**	*huit*
3	*trois*	**9**	*neuf*
4	*quatre*	**10**	*dix*
5	*cinq*	**100**	*cent*
6	*six*	**1000**	*mille*

TRANSPORT & DIRECTIONS

When does the next ... leave/arrive?	*À quelle heure part/arrive le prochain ...?*
boat	*bateau*
bus (city)	*bus*
bus (intercity)	*car*
train	*train*
tram	*tramway*

left-luggage office	*consigne*
timetable	*horaire*
bus stop	*arrêt d'autobus*
tram stop	*arrêt de tramway*
train station	*gare*
ferry terminal	*gare maritime*

I'd like a ... ticket.	*Je voudrais un billet ...*
one-way	*aller simple*
return	*aller retour*
1st class	*de première classe*
2nd class	*de deuxième classe*

I'd like to hire a car/bicycle.	*Je voudrais louer une voiture/un vélo.*
Where is ...?	*Où est ...?*
Go straight ahead.	*Continuez tout droit.*
Turn left.	*Tournez à gauche.*
Turn right.	*Tournez à droite.*
near	*proche*
far	*loin*

GERMAN

PRONUNCIATION

Vowels

As a rule, German vowels are long before one consonant and short before two, eg the **o** is long in the word *Dom* (cathedral), but short in the word *doch* (after all).

au	as the 'ow' in 'vow'
ä	short, as in 'cat' or long, as in 'care'
äu	as the 'oy' in 'boy'
ei	as the 'ai' in 'aisle'
eu	as the 'oy' in 'boy'
ie	as in 'brief'
ö	as the 'er' in 'fern'
ü	similar to the 'u' in 'pull' but with lips stretched back

Consonants

The consonants **b**, **d** and **g** sound like 'p', 't' and 'k', respectively, when word-final.

ch	as in Scottish *loch*
j	as the 'y' in 'yet'
qu	as 'k' plus 'v'
r	can be rolled or guttural, depending on the region
s	as in 'sun'; as the 'z' in 'zoo' when followed by a vowel
sch	as the 'sh' in 'ship'
sp, **st**	as 'shp' and 'sht' when word-initial
tion	the 't' is pronounced as the 'ts' in 'its'
v	as the 'f' in 'fan'
w	as the 'v' in 'van'
z	as the 'ts' in 'its'

LANGUAGE

ACCOMMODATION

hotel	*Hotel*
guest house	*Pension, Gästehaus*
youth hostel	*Jugendherberge*
camping ground	*Campingplatz*
Do you have any rooms available?	*Haben Sie noch freie Zimmer?*
a single room	*ein Einzelzimmer*
a double room	*ein Doppelzimmer*

How much is it ...?	*Wieviel kostet es ...?*
per night	*pro Nacht*
per person	*pro Person*

CONVERSATION & ESSENTIALS

Good day.	*Guten Tag.*
Hello. (in Bavaria and Austria)	*Grüss Gott.*
Goodbye.	*Auf Wiedersehen.*
Bye.	*Tschüss.* (informal)
Yes.	*Ja.*
No.	*Nein.*
Please.	*Bitte.*
Thank you.	*Danke.*
You're welcome.	*Bitte sehr.*
Excuse me/Sorry.	*Entschuldigung.*
What's your name?	*Wie heissen Sie?*
My name is ...	*Ich heisse ...*
Do you speak English?	*Sprechen Sie Englisch?*
How much is it?	*Wieviel kostet es?*

EMERGENCIES – GERMAN

Help!	*Hilfe!*
Call a doctor!	*Holen Sie einen Arzt!*
Call the police!	*Rufen Sie die Polizei!*
Go away!	*Gehen Sie weg!*
I'm lost.	*Ich habe mich verirrt.*

SHOPPING & SERVICES

I'm looking for ...	*Ich suche ...*
a bank	*eine Bank*
the ... embassy	*die ... Botschaft*
the market	*der Markt*
the newsagency	*der Zeitungshändler*
the pharmacy	*die Apotheke*
the post office	*das Postamt*
the stationers	*der Schreibwarengeschäft*
the tourist office	*das Verkehrsamt*

What time does it open/close?
Um wieviel Uhr macht es auf/zu?

TIME, DAYS & NUMBERS

What time is it?	*Wie spät ist es?*
today	*heute*
tomorrow	*morgen*
in the morning	*morgens*
in the afternoon	*nachmittags*

Monday	*Montag*
Tuesday	*Dienstag*
Wednesday	*Mittwoch*
Thursday	*Donnerstag*
Friday	*Freitag*
Saturday	*Samstag/Sonnabend*
Sunday	*Sonntag*

SIGNS – GERMAN

Eingang	Entrance
Ausgang	Exit
Auskunft	Information
Offen	Open
Geschlossen	Closed
Verboten	Prohibited
Toiletten (WC)	Toilets
Herren	Men
Damen	Women

0	*null*	**8**	*acht*
1	*eins*	**9**	*neun*
2	*zwei/zwo*	**10**	*zehn*
3	*drei*	**11**	*elf*
4	*vier*	**12**	*zwölf*
5	*fünf*	**13**	*dreizehn*
6	*sechs*	**100**	*hundert*
7	*sieben*	**1000**	*tausend*

TRANSPORT & DIRECTIONS

What time does … leave/arrive? *Wann (fährt … ab/kommt … an)?*
- **the boat** *das Boot*
- **the (intercity) bus** *der (überland) Bus*
- **the train** *der Zug*
- **the tram** *die Strassenbahn*

I'd like to hire a car/bicycle. *Ich möchte ein Auto/Fahrrad mieten.*
I'd like a one-way/return ticket. *Ich möchte eine Einzelkarte/Rückfahrkarte.*

1st/2nd class *erste/zweite Klasse*
left-luggage lockers *Schliessfächer*
timetable *Fahrplan*
bus stop *Bushaltestelle*
tram stop *Strassenbahnhaltestelle*
train station *Bahnhof (Bf)*
ferry terminal *Fährhafen*

Where is the …? *Wo ist die … ?*
Go straight ahead. *Gehen Sie geradeaus.*
Turn left. *Biegen Sie links ab.*
Turn right. *Biegen Sie rechts ab.*
near/far *nahe/weit*

GREEK

ACCOMMODATION

a hotel *ena xenothohio*
a youth hostel *enas xenonas neoitos*
a camping ground *ena kamping*
I'd like a … room. *thelo ena dhomatio …*
- **single** *ya ena atomo*
- **double** *ya dhio atoma*

How much is it per night/person?
poso kostizi ya ena vradhi/atomo?

CONVERSATION & ESSENTIALS

Hello. *yasu* (informal)
yasas (polite/plural)
Goodbye. *andio*
Yes. *ne*
No. *okhi*
Please. *sas parakalo*
Thank you. *sas efharisto*
That's fine/You're welcome. *ine endaksi/parakalo*
Excuse me/Sorry. *signomi*
Do you speak English? *milate anglika?*
How much is it? *poso kani?*

EMERGENCIES – GREEK

Help!	*voithia!*
Call a doctor!	*fonakste ena yatro!*
Call the police!	*tilefoniste tin astinomia!*
Go away!	*fighe/dhromo!*
I'm lost.	*eho hathi*

SHOPPING & SERVICES

a bank *mia trapeza*
the … embassy *i … presvia*
the market *i aghora*
newsagent *efimeridhon*
pharmacy *farmakio*
the post office *to takhidhromio*
the tourist office *to ghrafio turistikon pliroforion*

What time does it open/close?
ti ora aniyi/klini?

TIME, DAYS & NUMBERS

What time is it? *ti ora ine?*
today *simera*
tomorrow *avrio*
in the morning *to proi*
in the afternoon *to apoyevma*

Monday *dheftera*
Tuesday *triti*
Wednesday *tetarti*
Thursday *pempti*
Friday *paraskevi*
Saturday *savato*
Sunday *kiryaki*

THE GREEK ALPHABET

Greek	English	Pronunciation
Α α	a	as in 'father'
Β β	v	as the 'v' in 'vine'
Γ γ	gh/y	like a rough 'g', or as the 'y' in 'yes'
Δ δ	dh	as the 'th' in 'then'
Ε ε	e	as in 'egg'
Ζ ζ	z	as in 'zoo'
Η η	i	as the 'ee' in 'feet'
Θ θ	th	as the 'th' in 'throw'
Ι ι	i	as the 'ee' in 'feet'
Κ κ	k	as in 'kite'
Λ λ	l	as in 'leg'
Μ μ	m	as in 'man'
Ν ν	n	as in 'net'
Ξ ξ	x	as in 'taxi'
Ο ο	o	as in 'hot'
Π π	p	as in 'pup'
Ρ ρ	r	slightly trilled 'r'
Σ σ/ς	s	as in 'sand' (ς at the end of a word)
Τ τ	t	as in 'to'
Υ υ	i	as the 'ee' in 'feet'
Φ φ	f	as in 'fee'
Χ χ	kh/h	as the 'ch' in Scottish *loch*, or as a rough 'h'
Ψ ψ	ps	as the 'ps' in 'lapse'
Ω ω	o	as in 'lot'

1	*ena*	**7**	*epta*
2	*dhio*	**8**	*okhto*
3	*tria*	**9**	*enea*
4	*tesera*	**10**	*dheka*
5	*pende*	**100**	*ekato*
6	*eksi*	**1000**	*khilya*

TRANSPORT & DIRECTIONS

What time does the … leave/arrive? *ti ora fevyi/apo horito …?*
- **boat** *to plio*
- **bus** (city/intercity) *to leoforio (ya tin boli/ya ta proastia)*
- **train** *to treno*
- **tram** *to tram*

I'd like a … ticket. *tha ithela isitirio …*
- **one-way** *horis epistrofi*
- **return** *met epistrois*
- **1st class** *proti thesi*
- **2nd class** *dhefteri thesi*

SIGNS – GREEK

Εισοδος	Entrance
Εξοδος	Exit
Πληροφοριες	Information
Ανοικτο	Open
Κλειστο	Closed
Απαγορευεται	Prohibited
Τουαλετες	Toilets
Ανδρων	Men
Γυναικων	Women

left luggage *horos aspokevon*
timetable *dhromologhio*
bus stop *i stasi tu leoforiu*

Go straight ahead. *pighenete efthia*
Turn left. *stripste aristera*
Turn right. *stripste dheksya*

HUNGARIAN

PRONUNCIATION

The letters **cs**, **dz**, **dzs**, **gy**, **ly**, **ny**, **sz**, **ty**, and **zs** (consonant clusters) are separate letters in Hungarian and appear that way in telephone books and other alphabetical listings, eg *cukor* (sugar) appears in the dictionary before *csak* (only).

c	as the 'ts' in 'hats'
cs	as the 'ch' in 'church'
dz	as in 'adze'
dzs	as the 'j' in 'jet'
gy	as the 'du' in 'endure'
j	as the 'y' in 'yes'
ly	as the 'y' in 'yes'
ny	as the 'ni' in 'onion'
r	like a slightly rolled Scottish 'r'
s	as the 'sh' in 'ship'
sz	as the 's' in 'set'
ty	as the 'tu' in British English 'tube'
w	as 'v' (found in foreign words only)
zs	as the 's' in 'pleasure'

The meaning of words with **a**, **e** or **o** with and without an accent mark can be quite marked. For example, *hát* means 'back' while *hat* means 'six'.

a	as the 'o' in hot
á	as in 'father'
e	a short 'e' as in 'set'

é	as the 'e' in 'they' with no 'y' sound
i	as in 'hit' but shorter
í	as the 'i' in 'police'
o	as in 'open'
ó	a longer version of **o** above
ö	as the 'ur' in 'fur'
ő	a longer version of **ö** above
u	as in 'pull'
ú	as the 'ue' in 'blue'
ü	similar to the 'u' in 'flute'; purse your lips tightly and say 'ee'
ű	a longer, breathier version of **ü** above

ACCOMMODATION

hotel *szálloda*
guest house *panzió*
youth hostel *ifjúsági szálló*
camping ground *kemping*
private room *fizetővendégszoba*

Do you have rooms available?
Van szabad szobájuk?

How much is it ...? *Mennyibe kerül ...?*
per night *éjszakánként*
per person *személyenként*

single room *egyágyas szoba*
double room *kétágyas szoba*

EMERGENCIES – HUNGARIAN

Help! *Segítség!*
Call a doctor! *Hívjon orvost!*
Call an ambulance! *Hívja a mentőket!*
Call the police! *Hívja a rendőrséget!*
Go away! *Menjen innen!*
I'm lost. *Eltévedtem.*

CONVERSATION & ESSENTIALS

Hello. *Jó napot kívánok.* (pol)
Szia./Szervusz. (inf)
Goodbye. *Viszontlátásra.* (pol)
Szia./Szervusz. (inf)
Yes. *Igen.*
No. *Nem.*
Please. *Kérem.*
Thank you. *Köszönöm.*
Excuse me. *Bocsánat.*
Sorry. *Elnézést.*
What's your name? *Mi a neve?/Mi a neved?* (pol/inf)
My name is ... *A nevem ...*
I don't understand. *Nem értem.*
Do you speak English? *Beszél angolul?*
How much is it? *Mennyibe kerül?*

SHOPPING & SERVICES

Where is ...? *Hol van ...?*
a bank *bank*
a chemist *gyógyszertár*
the market *a piac*
the museum *a múzeum*
the post office *a posta*
a tourist office *turistairoda*

What time does it (open/close)?
Mikor (nyit ki/zár be)?

TIME, DAYS & NUMBERS

What time is it? *Hány óra?*
today *ma*
tonight *ma este*
tomorrow *holnap*
in the morning *reggel*
in the evening *este*

Monday *hétfő*
Tuesday *kedd*
Wednesday *szerda*
Thursday *csütörtök*
Friday *péntek*
Saturday *szombat*
Sunday *vasárnap*

1	*egy*	**7**	*hét*
2	*kettő*	**8**	*nyolc*
3	*három*	**9**	*kilenc*
4	*négy*	**10**	*tíz*
5	*öt*	**100**	*száz*
6	*hat*	**1000**	*ezer*

TRANSPORT & DIRECTIONS

What time does the ... leave/arrive? *Mikor indul/érkezik a ...?*
boat/ferry *hajó/komp*
city bus *város*
intercity bus *varosközi*
plane *repülőgép*
train *vonat*
tram *villamos*

arrival *érkezés*
departure *indulás*
timetable *menetrend*

Where is ...? *Hol van ...?*
the bus stop *az autóbuszmegálló*
the station *az állomás*
the left-luggage office *a csomagmegőrző*

SIGNS – HUNGARIAN

Bejárat	Entrance
Kijárat	Exit
Információ	Information
Nyitva	Open
Zárva	Closed
Tilos	Prohibited
Toalett/WC	Toilets
Férfiak	Men
Nők	Women

Turn left.	*Forduljon balra.*
Turn right.	*Forduljon jobbra.*
Go straight ahead.	*Menyen egyenesen elore.*
near/far	*közel/messze*

ICELANDIC

PRONUNCIATION

i, y	as the 'e' in 'pretty'
í, ý	as the 'e' in 'evil'
ú	as the 'oo' in 'moon', or as the 'o' in 'woman'
ö	as the 'er' in 'fern'
á	as the 'ou' in 'out'
ei, ey	as the 'ay' in 'day'
ó	as the word 'owe'
æ	as the word 'eye'
au	as 'er' + 'ee' (as the 'eui' in French *fauteuil*)
é	as the 'y' in 'yet'
Ð, ð	as the 'th' in 'lather'
j	as the 'y' in 'yellow'
Þ, þ	as the 'th' in 'thin' or 'three'

ACCOMMODATION

hotel	*hótel*
guest house	*gistiheimili*
youth hostel	*farfuglaheimili*
camping ground	*tjaldsvæði*
one day	*einn dag*
two days	*tvo daga*

Do you have any rooms available?
Eru herbergi laus?
How much is it per night/per person?
Hvað kostar nóttin/fyrir manninn?

I'd like …	*Gæti ég fengið …*
a single room	*einstaklingsherbergi*
a double room	*tveggjamannaherbergi*

CONVERSATION & ESSENTIALS

Hello.	*Halló.*
Goodbye.	*Bless.*
Yes.	*Já.*
No.	*Nei.*
Please.	*Gjörðu svo vel.*
Thank you.	*Takk fyrir.*
That's fine/You're welcome.	*Allt í lagi/Ekkert að þakka.*
Excuse me/Sorry.	*Afsakið.*
Do you speak English?	*Talar þú ensku?*
How much is it?	*Hvað kostar tað*

EMERGENCIES – ICELANDIC

Help!	*Hjálp!*
Call a doctor!	*Náið í lækni!*
Call the police!	*Náið í lögregluna!*
Go away!	*Farðu!*
I'm lost	*Ég er villtur/villt.* (m/f)

SHOPPING & SERVICES

bank	*banka*
chemist/pharmacy	*apótek*
… embassy	*… sendiráðinu*
market	*markaðnum*
newsagent/stationer	*blaðasala/bókabúð*
post office	*pósthúsinu*
tourist office	*upplýsingaþjónustu fyrir ferðafólk*

TIME, DAYS & NUMBERS

What time is it?	*Hvað er klukkan?*
today	*í dag*
tomorrow	*á morgun*
yesterday	*í gær*
in the morning	*að morgni*
in the afternoon	*eftir hádegi*

Monday	*mánudagur*
Tuesday	*þriðjudagur*
Wednesday	*miðvikudagur*
Thursday	*fimmtudagur*
Friday	*föstudagur*
Saturday	*laugardagur*
Sunday	*sunnudagur*

0	*núll*	**7**	*sjö*
1	*einn*	**8**	*átta*
2	*tveir*	**9**	*níu*
3	*þrír*	**10**	*tíu*
4	*fjórir*	**20**	*tuttugu*
5	*fimm*	**100**	*eitt hundrað*
6	*sex*	**1000**	*eitt þúsund*

SIGNS – ICELANDIC

Inngangur/Inn	Entrance
Útgangur/Út	Exit
Upplýsingar	Information
Opið	Open
Lokað	Closed
Bannað	Prohibited
Snyrting	Toilets
Karlar	Men
Konur	Women

TRANSPORT & DIRECTIONS

What time does … leave/arrive?	*Hvenær fer/kemur …?*
the boat	*báturinn*
the bus (city)	*vagninn*
the tram	*sporvagninn*

I'd like …	*Gæti ég fengid …*
a one-way ticket	*miða/aðra leiðina*
a return ticket	*miða/báðar leiðir*
1st-class	*fyrsta farrými*
2nd-class	*annað farrými*

timetable	*tímaáætlun*
bus stop	*biðstöð*
ferry terminal	*ferjuhöfn*
I'd like to hire a car/bicycle.	*Ég vil leigia bíl/reiðhjól.*

Where is …?	*Hvar er …?*
Go straight ahead.	*Farðu beint af áfram.*
Turn left.	*Beygðu til vinstri.*
Turn right.	*Beygðu til hægri.*
near/far	*nálægt/langt í burtu*

ITALIAN

Many older Italians expect to be addressed in the second person formal – *Lei* instead of *tu*. It isn't polite to use *ciao* when addressing strangers, unless they use it first; use *buongiorno* and *arrivederci*.

PRONUNCIATION

c	as 'k' before **a**, **o** and **u**; as the 'ch' in 'choose' before **e** and **i**
ch	a hard 'k' sound
g	as in 'get' before **a**, **o** and **u**; as in 'gem' before **e** and **i**
gh	as in 'get'
gli	as the 'lli' in 'million'
gn	as the 'ny' in 'canyon'
h	always silent
r	a rolled 'r' sound
sc	as the 'sh' in 'sheep' before **e** and **i**; a hard sound as in 'school' before **h**, **a**, **o** and **u**
z	as the 'ts' in 'lights' or the 'ds' in 'beds'

ACCOMMODATION

hotel	*albergo*
guest house	*pensione*
youth hostel	*ostello per la gioventù*
camping ground	*campeggio*

Do you have any rooms available?
Avete delle camere libere/C'è una camera libera?
How much is it per (night/person)?
Quanto costa per (la notte/ciascuno)?

a single room	*una camera singola*
a twin room	*una camera doppia*
a double-bed room	*una camera matrimoniale*
for one night	*per una notte*
for two nights	*per due notti*

EMERGENCIES – ITALIAN

Help!	*Aiuto!*
Call a doctor!	*Chiama un dottore/medico!*
Call the police!	*Chiama la polizia!*
Go away!	*Vai via!*
I'm lost.	*Mi sono perso/a* (m/f)

CONVERSATION & ESSENTIALS

Hello.	*Buongiorno.* (pol) *Ciao.* (inf)
Goodbye.	*Arrivederci.* (pol) *Ciao.* (inf)
Yes.	*Sì.*
No.	*No.*
Please.	*Per favore/Per piacere.*
Thank you.	*Grazie.*
That's fine/You're welcome.	*Prego.*
Excuse me.	*Mi scusi.*
Sorry.	*Mi scusi/Mi perdoni.*
Do you speak English?	*Parla inglese?*
How much is it?	*Quanto costa?*

SHOPPING & SERVICES

a bank	*una banca*
the chemist/pharmacy	*la farmacia*

SIGNS – ITALIAN

Ingresso/Entrata	Entrance
Uscita	Exit
Informazione	Information
Aperto	Open
Chiuso	Closed
Proibito/Vietato	Prohibited
Gabinetti/Bagni	Toilets
Uomini	Men
Donne	Women

the market	*il mercato*
the newsagent	*l'edicola*
the post office	*la posta*
the tourist office	*l'ufficio di turismo*

What time does it open/close?
A che ora (si) apre/chiude?

TIME, DAYS & NUMBERS

What time is it?	*Che ora è?/Che ore sono?*
today	*oggi*
tomorrow	*domani*
morning	*mattina*
afternoon	*pomeriggio*

Monday	*lunedì*
Tuesday	*martedì*
Wednesday	*mercoledì*
Thursday	*giovedì*
Friday	*venerdì*
Saturday	*sabato*
Sunday	*domenica*

1	*uno*	**7**	*sette*
2	*due*	**8**	*otto*
3	*tre*	**9**	*nove*
4	*quattro*	**10**	*dieci*
5	*cinque*	**100**	*cento*
6	*sei*	**1000**	*mille*

TRANSPORT & DIRECTIONS

When does the ... leave/arrive?	*A che ora parte/ arriva ...?*
boat	*la barca*
bus	*l'autobus*
ferry	*il traghetto*
train	*il treno*

bus stop	*fermata dell'autobus*
train station	*stazione*
ferry terminal	*stazione marittima*
1st/2nd class	*prima/seconda classe*
left luggage	*deposito bagagli*
timetable	*orario*

I'd like a one-way/return ticket.
Vorrei un biglietto di solo andata/di andata e ritorno.
I'd like to hire a car/bicycle.
Vorrei noleggiare una macchina/bicicletta.

Where is ...?	*Dov'è ...?*
Go straight ahead.	*Si va sempre diritto.*
Turn left/right.	*Giri a sinistra/destra.*
far/near	*lontano/vicino*

LATVIAN

ALPHABET & PRONUNCIATION

The letters of the Latvian alphabet are: **a b c č d e f g ģ (Ģ) h i j k ķ l ļ m n ņ o p r s š t u v z ž**.

c	as the 'ts' in 'bits'
č	as the 'ch' in 'church'
ģ	as the 'j' in 'jet'
j	as the 'y' in 'yes'
ķ	as 'tu' in 'tune'
ļ	as the 'lli' in 'billiards'
ņ	as the 'ni' in 'onion'
o	as the 'a' in 'water'
š	as the 'sh' in 'ship'
ž	as the 's' in 'pleasure'
ai	as in 'aisle'
ei	as in 'vein'
aa	as the 'a' in 'barn'
ē	as the 'e' in 'where'
oo	as the 'oo' in 'boot'

CONVERSATION & ESSENTIALS

Hello.	*Labdien./Sveiki.*
Goodbye.	*Uz redzēšanos./Ataa.*
Yes.	*Jaa.*
No.	*Nē.*
Excuse me.	*Atvainojiet.*
Please.	*Loodzu.*
Thank you.	*Paldies.*
Do you speak English?	*Vai joos runaajat angliski?*

EMERGENCIES – LATVIAN

Help!	*Palīgā!*
I'm ill.	*Es esmu slims/slima.* (m/f)
I'm lost.	*Es esmu apmaldījies/ apmaldījusies.* (m/f)
Go away!	*Ejiet projam!*

LANGUAGE

SIGNS – LATVIAN

Ieeja	Entrance
Izeja	Exit
Informācija	Information
Atvērts	Open
Slēgts	Closed
Smēķet Aizliegts	No Smoking
Maksas Tualetes	Public Toilets
Vīriešu	Men
Sieviešu	Women

SHOPPING & SERVICES

bank	*banka*
chemist	*aptieka*
currency exchange	*valootas maiņa*
hotel	*viesneeca*
market	*tirgus*
post office	*pasts*
toilet	*tualete*
Where?	*Kur?*
How much?	*Cik?*

TIME, DAYS & NUMBERS

today	*šodien*
tomorrow	*reet*
Sunday	*svētdiena*
Monday	*pirmdiena*
Tuesday	*otrdiena*
Wednesday	*trešdiena*
Thursday	*ceturtdiena*
Friday	*piektdiena*
Saturday	*sestdiena*

1	*viens*	**7**	*septiņi*
2	*divi*	**8**	*astoņi*
3	*trees*	**9**	*deviņi*
4	*četri*	**10**	*desmit*
5	*pieci*	**100**	*simts*
6	*seši*	**1000**	*tookstots*

TRANSPORT & DIRECTIONS

airport	*lidosta*
train station	*dzelzceļa stacija*
train	*vilciens*
bus station	*autoosta*
bus	*autobuss*
port	*osta*
taxi	*taksometrs*
tram	*tramvajs*
stop (eg bus stop)	*pietura*
departure time	*atiešanas laiks*
arrival time	*pienaakšanas laiks*
ticket	*biļete*
ticket office	*kase*

LITHUANIAN

ALPHABET & PRONUNCIATION

The letters of the Lithuanian alphabet are: **a b c č d e f g h i/y j k l m n o p r s š t u v z ž**. The **i** and **y** are very similar.

c	as 'ts'
č	as 'ch'
y	between the 'i' in 'tin' and the 'ee' in 'feet'
j	as the 'y' in 'yes'
š	as 'sh'
ž	as the 's' in 'pleasure'
ei	as the 'ai' in 'pain'
ie	as the 'ye' in 'yet'
ui	as the 'wi' in 'win'

Accent marks above and below vowels (eg **aa**, **ė** and **į**) all have the general effect of lengthening the vowel:

aa	as the 'a' in 'father'
ę	as the 'ai' in 'air'
į	as the 'ee' in 'feet'
ų	as the 'oo' in 'boot'
oo	as the 'oo' in 'boot'
ė	as the 'a' in 'late'

CONVERSATION & ESSENTIALS

Hello.	*Labas./Sveikas.*
Goodbye.	*Sudie./Viso gero.*
Yes.	*Taip.*
No.	*Ne.*
Excuse me.	*Atsiprašau.*
Please.	*Prašau.*
Thank you.	*Ačioo.*
Do you speak English?	*Ar kalbate angliškai?*

EMERGENCIES – LITHUANIAN

Help!	*Gelėbkite!*
I'm ill.	*Aš sergu.*
I'm lost.	*Aš paklydęs/paklydusi.* (m/f)
Go away!	*Eik šalin!*
Call ...!	*Iššaukite ...!*
a doctor	*gydytoją*
an ambulance	*greitąją*
the police	*policiją*

LANGUAGE

SIGNS – LITHUANIAN

Įėjimas	Entrance
Išėjimas	Exit
Informacija	Information
Atidara	Open
Uždara	Closed
Nerūkoma	No Smoking
Patogumai	Public Toilets

SHOPPING & SERVICES

bank	*bankas*
chemist	*vaistinė*
currency exchange	*valiutos keitykla*
hotel	*viešbutis*
market	*turgus*
post office	*paštas*
toilet	*tualetas*
Where?	*Kur?*
How much?	*Kiek?*

TIME, DAYS & NUMBERS

today	*šiandien*
tomorrow	*rytoj*
yesterday	*vakar*

Monday	*pirmadienis*
Tuesday	*antradienis*
Wednesday	*trečiadienis*
Thursday	*ketvirtadienis*
Friday	*penktadienis*
Saturday	*šeštadienis*
Sunday	*sekmadienis*

1	*vienas*	**7**	*septyni*
2	*du*	**8**	*aštuoni*
3	*trys*	**9**	*devyni*
4	*keturi*	**10**	*dešimt*
5	*penki*	**100**	*šimtas*
6	*šeši*	**1000**	*tookstantis*

TRANSPORT & DIRECTIONS

airport	*oro uostas*
bus station	*autobusų stotis*
port	*uostas*
train station	*geležinkelio stotis*
stop (eg bus stop)	*stotelė*
bus	*autobusas*
taxi	*taksi*
train	*traukinys*
tram	*tramvajus*
departure time	*išvykimo laikas*
arrival time	*atvykimo laikas*
ticket	*bilietas*
ticket office	*kasa*

LANGUAGE

MACEDONIAN

PRONUNCIATION

There are 31 letters in the Macedonian Cyrillic alphabet (see p1280).

ACCOMMODATION

hotel	*hotel*
guest house	*privatno smetuvanje*
youth hostel	*mladinsko prenocjishte*
camping ground	*kamping*

Do you have any rooms available?
dali imate slobodni sobi?
How much is it per night/per person?
koja e cenata po nocj/po osoba?

a single room	*soba so eden krevet*
a double room	*soba so brachen krevet*
for one/two nights	*za edna/dva vecheri*

EMERGENCIES – MACEDONIAN

Help!	*pomoš!*
Call a doctor!	*povikajte lekar!*
Call the police!	*viknete policija!*
Go away!	*odete si!*
I'm lost.	*jas zaginav*

CONVERSATION & ESSENTIALS

Hello.	*zdravo*
Goodbye.	*priatno*
Yes.	*da*
No.	*ne*
Please.	*molam*
Thank you.	*blagodaram*
You're welcome.	*nema zoshto/milo mi e*
Excuse me.	*izvinete*
Sorry.	*oprostete ve molam*
Do you speak English?	*zboruvate li angliski?*
What's your name?	*kako se vikate?*
My name is ...	*jas se vikam ...*
How much is it?	*kolku chini toa?*

SHOPPING & SERVICES

bank	*banka*
chemist/pharmacy	*apteka*
my hotel	*mojot hotel*
market	*pazarot*
newsagent	*kiosk za vesnici*
post office	*poshtata*
tourist office	*turistichkoto biro*
What time does it open/close?	*koga se otvora/zatvora?*

SIGNS – MACEDONIAN

Влез	Entrance
Излез	Exit
Информации	Information
Отворено	Open
Затворено	Closed
Забранетo	Prohibited
Клозети	Toilets
Машки	Men
Женски	Women

TIME, DAYS & NUMBERS

What time is it?	*kolku e chasot?*
today	*denes*
tomorrow	*utre*
yesterday	*vchera*
morning	*utro*
afternoon	*popladne*

Monday	*ponedelnik*
Tuesday	*vtornik*
Wednesday	*sreda*
Thursday	*chetvrtok*
Friday	*petok*
Saturday	*sabota*
Sunday	*nedela*

1	*eden*	**7**	*sedum*
2	*dva*	**8**	*osum*
3	*tri*	**9**	*devet*
4	*chetiri*	**10**	*deset*
5	*pet*	**100**	*sto*
6	*shest*	**1000**	*hiljada*

TRANSPORT & DIRECTIONS

What time does the next … leave/arrive?	*koga doagja/zaminuva idniot …?*
boat	*brod*
city bus	*avtobus gradski*
intercity bus	*avtobus megjugradski*
train	*voz*
tram	*tramvaj*

I'd like …	*sakam …*
a one-way ticket	*bilet vo eden pravec*
a return ticket	*povraten bilet*
1st class	*prva klasa*
2nd class	*vtora klasa*

timetable	*vozen red*
bus stop	*avtobuska stanica*
train station	*zheleznichka stanica*
Where is …?	*kade je …?*
Go straight ahead.	*odete pravo napred*
Turn left/right.	*svrtete levo/desno*
near/far	*blisku/daleku*

I'd like to hire a car/bicycle.
sakam da iznajmam kola/tochak

MALTESE

PRONUNCIATION

ċ	as the 'ch' in 'child'
g	as in 'good'
ġ	as the 'j' in 'job'
għ	silent; lengthens the preceding or following vowel
h	silent, as in 'hour'
ħ	as the 'h' in 'hand'
j	as the 'y' in 'yellow'
ij	as the 'igh' in 'high'
ej	as the 'ay' in 'day'
q	a glottal stop; like the missing 't' between the two syllables in 'bottle'
x	as the 'sh' in 'shop'
z	as the 'ts' in 'bits'
ż	soft as in 'buzz'

ACCOMMODATION

Do you have a room available?
Ghandek kamra jekk jogħoġbok?
Do you have a room for one person/two people?
Ghandek kamra għal wieħed/tnejn?
Do you have a room for one/two nights?
Ghandek kamra ghal lejl/zewgt iljieli?

EMERGENCIES – MALTESE

Help!	*Ajjut!*
Call a doctor.	*Qibgħad ghat-tabib.*
Police!	*Pulizija!*
I'm lost.	*Ninsab mitluf.*
hospital	*sptar*
ambulance	*ambulans*

CONVERSATION & ESSENTIALS

Hello.	*Merħba.*
Good morning/day.	*Bonġu.*
Goodbye.	*Saħħa.*
Yes.	*Iva.*
No.	*Le.*
Please.	*Jekk jogħoġbok.*
Thank you.	*Grazzi.*
Excuse me.	*Skużani.*
Do you speak English?	*Titkellem bl-ingliż?*
How much is it?	*Kemm?*

SHOPPING & SERVICES

the bank	*il-bank*
chemist/pharmacy	*l-ispiżerija*
the … embassy	*l'ambaxxata …*
the market	*is-suq*
the post office	*il-posta*
shop	*ħanut*

What time does it open/close?
Fix'ħin jiftaħ/jagħlaq?

TIME, DAYS & NUMBERS

What's the time?	*X'ħin hu?*
today	*illum*
tomorrow	*għada*
morning	*fil-għodu*
afternoon	*nofs in-nhar*

Monday	*it-tnejn*
Tuesday	*it-tlieta*
Wednesday	*l-erbgħa*
Thursday	*il-ħamis*
Friday	*il-gimgħa*
Saturday	*is-sibt*
Sunday	*il-ħadd*

0	*xejn*	**7**	*sebgħa*
1	*wieħed*	**8**	*tmienja*
2	*tnejn*	**9**	*disgħa*
3	*tlieta*	**10**	*għaxra*
4	*erbgħa*	**11**	*ħdax*
5	*ħamsa*	**100**	*mija*
6	*sitta*	**1000**	*elf*

TRANSPORT & DIRECTIONS

When does the boat leave/arrive?
Meta jitlaq/jasal il-vapur?
When does the bus leave/arrive?
Meta titlaq/jasal il-karozza?
I'd like to hire a car/bicycle.
Nixtieq nikri karozza/rota.

I'd like a … ticket.	*Nixtieq biljett …*
one-way/return	*'one-way/return'*
1st-/2nd-class	*'1st/2nd class'*

left luggage	*hallejt il-bagalji*
bus/trolleybus stop	*xarabank/coach*

Where is a/the …?	*Fejn hu …?*
Go straight ahead.	*Mur dritt.*
Turn left.	*Dur fuq il-lemin.*
Turn right.	*Dur fuq ix-xellug.*
near/far	*il-viċin/-bogħod*

SIGNS – MALTESE

Dhul	Entrance
Hrug	Exit
Informazjoni	Information
Miftuh	Open
Maghluq	Closed
Tidholx	No Entry
Toilets	Toilets
Rgiel	Men
Nisa	Women

MOROCCAN ARABIC

PRONUNCIATION

a	as in 'had' (sometimes very short)
aa	as the 'a' in 'father'
e	as in 'bet' (sometimes very short)
ee	as in 'beet'
i	as in 'hit'
o	as in 'hot'
oo	as in 'cool'
u	as the 'oo' in 'book'
aw	as the 'ow' in 'how'
ai	as the 'i' in 'high'
ei/ay	as the 'a' in 'cake'
j	more or less as the 'j' in 'John'
H	a strongly whispered 'h', almost like a sigh of relief
q	a strong guttural 'k' sound
kh	a slightly gurgling sound, like the 'ch' in Scottish 'loch'
sh	as in 'she'
z	as the 's' in pleasure
gh	called 'ghayn', similar to the French 'r', but more guttural

GLOTTAL STOP (')

The glottal stop is the sound you hear between the vowels in the expression 'oh oh!'. When it occurs before a vowel (eg 'ayn), the vowel is 'growled' from the back of the throat. Before a consonant or at the end of a word, it sounds like a glottal stop.

ACCOMMODATION

hotel	*al-otēl*
youth hostel	*dar shabbab*
camp site	*mukhaym*

Is there a room available?
wash kayn shee beet xaweeya?
How much is this room per night?
bshaHal al-bayt liyal?

LANGUAGE

CONVERSATION & ESSENTIALS

Hello.	*as-salaam 'alaykum*
Goodbye.	*ma' as-salaama*
Yes.	*eeyeh*
No.	*la*
Please.	*'afak*
Thank you (very much).	*shukran (jazilan)*
You're welcome.	*la shukran, 'ala wajib*
Excuse me.	*smeH leeya*
Do you speak English?	*wash kat'ref negleezeeya?*
I understand.	*fhemt*
I don't understand.	*mafhemtsh*
How much (is it)?	*bish-hal?*

SHOPPING & SERVICES

the bank	*al-banka*
the embassy	*as-sifaara*
the market	*as-sooq*
the police station	*al-bolees*
the post office	*al-boosta/maktab al-bareed*
a toilet	*bayt al-ma/mirHad*

TIME, DATES & NUMBERS

What time is it?	*shHal fessa'a?*
today	*al-yoom*
tomorrow	*ghaddan*
yesterday	*al-bareh*
in the morning	*fis-sabaH*
in the evening	*fil-masa'*

Monday	*(nhar) al-itnēn*
Tuesday	*(nhar) at-talata*
Wednesday	*(nhar) al-arba'*
Thursday	*(nhar) al-khamees*
Friday	*(nhar) al-juma'*
Saturday	*(nhar) as-sabt*
Sunday	*(nhar) al-ahad*

1	*waaHid*	**7**	*saba'a*
2	*jooj/itneen*	**8**	*tamanya*
3	*talata*	**9**	*tissa'*
4	*arba'a*	**10**	*'ashara*
5	*khamsa*	**100**	*miyya*
6	*sitta*	**1000**	*alf*

TRANSPORT & DIRECTIONS

What time does the … leave/arrive?	*emta qiyam/wusool …*
boat	*al-baboor*
bus (city)	*al-otobees*
bus (intercity)	*al-kar*
train	*al-masheena*

EMERGENCIES – MOROCCAN ARABIC

Help!	*'teqnee!*
Call a doctor!	*'ayyet 'la shee tbeeb!*
Call the police!	*'ayyet 'la lboolees!*
Go away!	*seer fhalek!*

1st class	*ddarazha lloola*
2nd class	*ddarazha ttaneeya*
train station	*maHattat al-masheena/al-qitar*
bus stop	*mawqif al-otobis*

Where can I hire a car/bicycle?	*fein yimkin ana akra tomobeel/beshkleeta?*
Where is (the) …?	*fein …?*
Go straight ahead.	*seer neeshan*
Turn right.	*dor 'al leemen*
Turn left.	*dor 'al leeser*

NORWEGIAN

PRONUNCIATION

å	as the 'aw' in 'paw'
æ	as the 'a' in 'act'
ø	long, as the 'er' in 'fern'; short, as the 'a' in 'ago'
u, y	say 'ee' while pursing your lips
ai	as the word 'eye'
ei	as the 'ay' in 'day'
au	as the 'o' in 'note'
øy	as the 'oy' in 'toy'
d	at the end of a word, or between two vowels, it's often silent
g	as the 'g' in 'get'; as the 'y' in 'yard' before **ei, i, j, øy** and **y**
j	as the 'y' in 'yard'
k	as in 'kin'; as the 'ch' in 'chin' before **ei, i, j, øy** and **y**
r	a rolled 'r'
rs	as the 'sh' in 'fish'
s	as in 'so'; as the 'sh' in 'ship' before **ei, i, j, øy** and **y**

ACCOMMODATION

hotel	*hotell*
guest house	*gjestgiveri/pensionat*
youth hostel	*vandrerhjem*
camping ground	*kamping/leirplass*
one day/two days	*en dag/to dager*

Do you have any rooms available?
Har du ledige rom?
How much is it per night/person?
Hvor mye er det pr dag/person?

EMERGENCIES – NORWEGIAN	
Help!	*Hjelp!*
Call a doctor!	*Ring en lege!*
Call the police!	*Ring politiet!*
Go away!	*Forsvinn!*
I'm lost.	*Jeg har gått meg vill.*

I'd like ... *Jeg vil gjerne ha ...*
a single room *et enkeltrom*
a double room *et dobbeltrom*

CONVERSATION & ESSENTIALS

Hello. *Goddag.*
Goodbye. *Ha det.*
Yes. *Ja.*
No. *Nei.*
Please. *Vær så snill.*
Thank you. *Takk.*
That's fine/You're welcome. *Ingen årsak.*
Excuse me/Sorry. *Unnskyld.*
Do you speak English? *Snakker du engelsk?*
How much is it? *Hvor mye koster det?*

SIGNS – NORWEGIAN	
Inngang	Entrance
Utgang	Exit
Åpen	Open
Stengt	Closed
Forbudt	Prohibited
Toaletter	Toilets
Herrer	Men
Damer	Women

SHOPPING & SERVICES

bank *banken*
chemist/pharmacy *apotek*
... embassy *... ambassade*
market *torget*
newsagent *kiosk*
post office *postkontoret*
telephone centre *televerket*
tourist office *turistinformasjon*

TIME, DAYS & NUMBERS

What time is it? *Hva er klokka?*
today *i dag*
tomorrow *i morgen*
in the morning *om formiddagen*
in the afternoon *om ettermiddagen*

Monday *mandag*
Tuesday *tirsdag*
Wednesday *onsdag*
Thursday *torsdag*
Friday *fredag*
Saturday *lørdag*
Sunday *søndag*

0	*null*	**7**	*sju*
1	*en*	**8**	*åtte*
2	*to*	**9**	*ni*
3	*tre*	**10**	*ti*
4	*fire*	**11**	*elleve*
5	*fem*	**100**	*hundre*
6	*seks*	**1000**	*tusen*

TRANSPORT & DIRECTIONS

What time does ... leave/arrive? *Når går/kommer ...?*
the boat *båten*
the (city) bus *(by)bussen*
the intercity bus *linjebussen*
the tram *trikken*
the train *toget*

I'd like ... *Jeg vil gjerne ha ...*
a one-way ticket *enkeltbillett*
a return ticket *tur-retur*
1st class *første klasse*
2nd class *annen klasse*

left luggage *reisegods*
timetable *ruteplan*
bus stop *bussholdeplass*
tram stop *trikkholdeplass*
train station *jernbanestasjon*
ferry terminal *ferjeleiet*

Where can I rent a car/bicycle? *Hvor kan jeg leie en bil/sykkel?*
Where is ...? *Hvor er ...?*
Go straight ahead. *Det er rett fram.*
Turn left. *Ta til venstre.*
Turn right. *Ta til høyre.*
near/far *nær/langt*

POLISH

PRONUNCIATION

Written Polish is phonetically consistent, which means that the pronunciation of letters or clusters of letters doesn't vary from word to word. The stress almost always goes on the second-last syllable.

Vowels

a as the 'u' in 'cut'
e as in 'ten'
i as the 'ee' in 'feet' but shorter
o as in 'lot'
u as the 'oo' in 'book' but shorter
y similar to the 'i' in 'bit'

There are three vowels unique to Polish:

ą a nasal vowel sound like the French *un*, similar to 'own' in 'sown'
ę also nasalised, like the French *un*, but pronounced as 'e' when word-final
ó similar to Polish **u**

Consonants

In Polish, the consonants **b**, **d**, **f**, **k**, **l**, **m**, **n**, **p**, **t**, **v** and **z** are pronounced more or less as they are in English. The following consonants and clusters of consonants sound distinctly different to their English counterparts:

c as the 'ts' in 'its'
ch similar to the 'ch' in the Scottish *loch*
cz as the 'ch' in 'church'
ć much softer than Polish **c** (as 'tsi' before vowels)
dz as the 'ds' in 'suds' but shorter
dź a soft **dz** (as 'dzi' before vowels)
dż as the 'j' in 'jam'
g as in 'get'
h as **ch**
j as the 'y' in 'yet'
ł as the 'w' in 'wine'
ń as the 'ny' in 'canyon' (as 'ni' before vowels)
r always rolled
rz as the 's' in 'pleasure'
s as in 'set'
sz as the 'sh' in 'show'
ś as **s** but softer (as 'si' before vowels)
w as the 'v' in 'van'
ź softer version of **z** (as 'zi' before vowels)
ż as **rz**

ACCOMMODATION

hotel	*hotel*
youth hostel	*schronisko młodzieżowe*
camping ground	*kemping*
private room	*kwatera prywatna*
single room	*pokój jednoosobowy*
double room	*pokój dwuosobowy*

Do you have any rooms available?
Czy są wolne pokoje?
How much is it?
Ile to kosztuje?
Does it include breakfast?
Czy śniadanie jest wliczone?

CONVERSATION & ESSENTIALS

Hello/Good morning.	*Dzień dobry.*
Hello.	*Cześć.* (informal)
Goodbye.	*Do widzenia.*
Yes/No.	*Tak/Nie.*
Please.	*Proszę.*
Thank you.	*Dziękuję.*
Excuse me/Sorry.	*Przepraszam.*
Do you speak English?	*Czy pan/pani mówi po angielsku?* (m/f)
I don't understand.	*Nie rozumiem.*
What is it called?	*Jak to się nazywa?*
How much is it?	*Ile to kosztuje?*

EMERGENCIES – POLISH

Help!	*Pomocy!/Ratunku!*
Call a doctor!	*Proszę wezwać lekarza!*
Call the police!	*Proszę wezwać policję!*
I'm lost.	*Zgubiłem się.* (m) *Zgubiłam się.* (f)

SHOPPING & SERVICES

the bank	*bank*
the chemist	*apteka*
the church	*kościół*
the city centre	*centrum miasta*
the market	*targ/bazar*
the museum	*muzeum*
the post office	*poczta*
the tourist office	*informacja turystyczna*

What time does it open/close?
O której otwierają/zamykają?

TIME, DAYS & NUMBERS

What time is it?	*Która jest godzina?*
today	*dzisiaj*
tonight	*dzisiaj wieczorem*
tomorrow	*jutro*
in the morning	*rano*
in the evening	*wieczorem*
Monday	*poniedziałek*
Tuesday	*wtorek*
Wednesday	*środa*
Thursday	*czwartek*

SIGNS – POLISH

Wejście	Entrance
Wyjście	Exit
Informacja	Information
Otwarte	Open
Zamknięte	Closed
Wzbroniony	Prohibited
Toalety	Toilets
Panowie	Men
Panie	Women

Friday	*piątek*
Saturday	*sobota*
Sunday	*niedziela*

1	*jeden*	**7**	*siedem*
2	*dwa*	**8**	*osiem*
3	*trzy*	**9**	*dziewięć*
4	*cztery*	**10**	*dziesięć*
5	*pięć*	**100**	*sto*
6	*sześć*	**1000**	*tysiąc*

TRANSPORT & DIRECTIONS

What time does the … leave/arrive? *O której godzinie przychodzi/odchodzi …?*

plane	*samolot*
boat	*statek*
bus	*autobus*
train	*pociąg*
tram	*tramwaj*

arrival	*przyjazd*
departure	*odjazd*
timetable	*rozkład jazdy*

Where is the bus stop?
Gdzie jest przystanek autobusowy?
Where is the station?
Gdzie jest stacja kolejowa?
Where is the left-luggage office?
Gdzie jest przechowalnia bagażu?
Please show me on the map.
Proszę pokazać mi to na mapie.

straight ahead	*prosto*
left	*lewo*
right	*prawo*

PORTUGUESE

Note that Portugese uses masculine and feminine word endings, usually '-o' and '-a' respectively – to say 'thank you', a man will therefore use *obrigado*, a woman, *obrigada.*

PRONUNCIATION

Nasalisation is represented by an 'n' or an 'm' after the vowel, or by a tilde over it, eg **ã**. The nasal 'i' exists in English as the 'ing' in 'sing'.

ão	nasal 'ow' (owng)
ãe	nasal 'ay' (eing)
õe	nasal 'oy' (oing)
ui	similar to the 'uing' in 'ensuing'
é	short, as in 'bet'
ê	long, as the 'a' in 'gate'
ô	long, as in 'note'
c	as in 'cat' before **a**, **o** or **u**; as the 's' in 'sin' before **e** or **i**
ç	as the 'c' in 'celery'
g	as in 'go' before **a**, **o** or **u**; as the 's' in 'treasure' before **e** or **i**
h	never pronounced when word initial
nh	as the 'ni' in 'onion'
lh	as the 'lli' in 'million'
j	as the 's' in 'treasure'
m	not pronounced when word-final – it simply nasalises the previous vowel, eg *um* (oong), *bom* (bõ)
x	as the 'sh' in 'ship', as the 'z' in 'zeal', or as the 'x' in 'taxi'
z	as the 's' in 'treasure' before a consonant or at the end of a word

ACCOMMODATION

hotel	*hotel*
guest house	*pensão*
youth hostel	*pousada da juventude*
camping ground	*parque de campismo*

Do you have any rooms available?
Tem quartos livres?
How much is it per night/per person?
Quanto é por noite/por pessoa?

a single room	*um quarto individual*
a twin room	*um quarto duplo*
a double bed room	*um quarto de casal*
for one night	*para uma noite*
for two nights	*para duas noites*

CONVERSATION & ESSENTIALS

Hello.	*Olá.*
Goodbye.	*Adeus/Ciao.* (informal)
Yes.	*Sim.*
No.	*Não.*
Please.	*Se faz favor.*
Thank you.	*Obrigado/a.* (m/f)

You're welcome.	*De nada.*
Excuse me.	*Com licença.*
Sorry.	*Desculpe.*
Do you speak English?	*Fala Inglês?*
How much is it?	*Quanto custa?*

SHOPPING & SERVICES

a bank	*um banco*
the chemist/ pharmacy	*a farmácia*
the ... embassy	*a embaixada de ...*
the market	*o mercado*
the newsagent	*a papelaria*
the post office	*os correios*
the tourist office	*o (posto de) turismo*

What time does it open/close?
A que horas abre/fecha?

SIGNS – PORTUGUESE

Entrada	Entrance
Saída	Exit
Informações	Information
Aberto	Open
Fechado	Closed
Proíbido	Prohibited
Empurre/Puxe	Push/Pull
Lavabos/WC	Toilets
Homens	Men
Senhoras	Women

TIME, DAYS & NUMBERS

What time is it?	*Que horas são?*
today	*hoje*
tomorrow	*amanhã*
morning	*manhã*
afternoon	*tarde*

Monday	*segunda-feira*
Tuesday	*terça-feira*
Wednesday	*quarta-feira*
Thursday	*quinta-feira*
Friday	*sexta-feira*
Saturday	*sábado*
Sunday	*domingo*

0	*zero*	**7**	*sete*
1	*um/uma*	**8**	*oito*
2	*dois/duas*	**9**	*nove*
3	*três*	**10**	*dez*
4	*quatro*	**11**	*onze*
5	*cinco*	**100**	*cem*
6	*seis*	**1000**	*mil*

EMERGENCIES – PORTUGUESE

Help!	*Socorro!*
Call a doctor!	*Chame um médico!*
Call the police!	*Chame a polícia!*
Go away!	*Deixe-me em paz!* (pol)
	Vai-te embora! (inf)
I'm lost.	*Estou perdido/a.* (m/f)

TRANSPORT & DIRECTIONS

What time does the ... leave/arrive?	*A que horas parte/chega ...?*
boat	*o barco*
bus (city)	*o autocarro*
bus (intercity)	*a camioneta*
tram	*o eléctrico*
train	*o combóio*

bus stop	*paragem de autocarro*
train station	*estação ferroviária*
timetable	*horário*

I'd like a ... ticket.	*Queria um bilhete ...*
one-way	*simples/de ida*
return	*de ida e volta*
1st class	*de primeira classe*
2nd class	*de segunda classe*

I'd like to hire ...	*Queria alugar ...*
a car	*um carro*
a bicycle	*uma bicicleta*

Where is ...?	*Onde é ...?*
Go straight ahead.	*Siga sempre a direito/ Siga sempre em frente.*
Turn left.	*Vire à esquerda.*
Turn right.	*Vire à direita.*
near/far	*perto/longe*

ROMANIAN

PRONUNCIATION

Until the mid-19th century, Romanian was written in the Cyrillic script. Today Romanian employs 28 Latin letters, some of which bear accents. At the beginning of a word, **e** and **i** are pronounced 'ye' and 'yi', while at the end of a word **i** is almost silent. At the end of a word **ii** is pronounced 'ee'. Word stress usually falls on the penultimate syllable.

ă	as the 'er' in 'brother'
î	as the 'i' in 'river'
c	as 'k', except before **e** and **i**, when it's as the 'ch' in 'chip'
ch	always as the 'k' in 'king'
g	as in 'go', except before **e** and **i**, when it's as in 'gentle'
gh	always as the 'g' in 'get'
ş	as 'sh'
ţ	as the 'tz'in 'tzar'

ACCOMMODATION

hotel *hotel*
guest house *casa de oaspeţi*
youth hostel *camin studentesc*
camping ground *camping*
private room *cameră particulară*
single room *o cameră pentru o persoană*
double room *o cameră pentru două persoane*

Do you have any rooms available?
Aveţi camere libere?
How much is it?
Cît costă?
Does it include breakfast?
Include micul dejun?

CONVERSATION & ESSENTIALS

Hello. *Bună.*
Goodbye. *La revedere.*
Yes. *Da.*
No. *Nu.*
Please. *Vă rog.*
Thank you. *Mulţumesc.*
Excuse me. *Scuzaţi-mă.*
Sorry. *Iertaţi-mă.*
Do you speak English? *Vorbiţi engleza?*
I don't understand. *Nu înţeleg.*
What is it called? *Cum se cheamă?*
How much is it? *Cît costă?*

EMERGENCIES – ROMANIAN

Help! *Ajutor!*
Call a doctor! *Chemaţi un doctor!*
Call the police! *Chemaţi poliţia!*
Go away! *Du-te!/Pleacă!*
I'm lost. *Sînt pierdut.*

SHOPPING & SERVICES

the bank *banca*
the chemist/ pharmacy *farmacistul*
the city centre *centrum oraşului*
the … embassy *ambasada …*

SIGNS – ROMANIAN

Intrare Entrance
Ieşire Exit
Informaţii Information
Deschis Open
Inchis Closed
Nu Intraţi No Entry
Toaleta Toilets

the market *piaţa*
the museum *muzeu*
the post office *poşta*
the tourist office *birou de informatii turistice*

TIME, DAYS & NUMBERS

What time is it? *Ce oră este?*
today *azi*
tonight *deseară*
tomorrow *mîine*
in the morning *dimineaţa*
in the evening *seară*

Monday *luni*
Tuesday *marţi*
Wednesday *miercuri*
Thursday *joi*
Friday *vineri*
Saturday *sîmbătă*
Sunday *duminică*

1	*unu*	**7**	*şapte*
2	*doi*	**8**	*opt*
3	*trei*	**9**	*nouă*
4	*patru*	**10**	*zece*
5	*cinci*	**100**	*o sută*
6	*şase*	**1000**	*o mie*

TRANSPORT & DIRECTIONS

What time does the … leave/arrive? *La ce oră pleacă/soseşte …?*
boat *vaporul*
bus *autobusul*
train *trenul*
tram *tramvaiul*
plane *avionul*

arrival *sosire*
departure *plecare*
timetable *mersul/orar*

Where is the bus stop? *Unde este staţia de autobuz?*
Where is the station? *Unde este gară?*

LANGUAGE

Where is the left-luggage office?
Unde este biroul pentru bagaje de mînă?
Please show me on the map.
Vă rog arătaţi-mi pe hartă.

straight ahead	*drept înainte*
left	*stînga*
right	*dreapta*

RUSSIAN

Russian uses the Cyrillic alphabet. The table on p1280 shows all the characters used in the Cyrillic alphabets of Bulgarian, Macedonian, Russian and Serbian. It's well worth familiarising yourself with them.

ACCOMMODATION

hotel	*gastinitsa*
room	*nomer*
breakfast	*zaftrak*
How much is a room?	*skol'ka stoit nomer?*

CONVERSATION & ESSENTIALS

Hello.	*zdrastvuyte*
Good morning.	*dobraye utra*
Good afternoon.	*dobryy den'*
Good evening.	*dobryy vecher*
Goodbye.	*da svidaniya*
Bye!	*paka!* (inf)
How are you?	*kak dila?*
Yes.	*dat*
No.	*net*
Please.	*pazhalsta*
Thank you (very much).	*(bal'shoye) spasiba*
Pardon me.	*prastite/pazhalsta*
No problem/Never mind.	*nichevo* (literally, 'nothing')
Do you speak English?	*vy gavarite pa angliyski?*
What's your name?	*kak vas zavut?*
My name is …	*minya zavut …*
How much is it?	*skol'ka stoit?*

SHOPPING & SERVICES

bank	*bank*
market	*rynak*
pharmacy	*apteka*
post office	*pochta*
telephone booth	*tilifonnaya budka*
open	*otkryta*
closed	*zakryta*

EMERGENCIES – RUSSIAN

Help!	*na pomashch'!/pamagite!*
I'm sick.	*ya bolen/ya bal'na* (m/f)
I need a doctor.	*mne nuzhin vrach*
hospital	*bal'nitsa*
police	*militsiya*
I'm lost.	*ya zabludilsya* (m) *ya zabludilas'* (f)

TIME, DATE & NUMBERS

What time is it?	*katoryy chas*
today	*sivodnya*
tomorrow	*zaftra*
am/in the morning	*utra*
pm/in the afternoon	*dnya*
in the evening	*vechira*
Monday	*panidel'nik*
Tuesday	*ftornik*
Wednesday	*srida*
Thursday	*chitverk*
Friday	*pyatnitsa*
Saturday	*subota*
Sunday	*vaskrisen'e*

0	*nol'*	**7**	*sem'*
1	*adin*	**8**	*vosim'*
2	*dva*	**9**	*devit'*
3	*tri*	**10**	*desit'*
4	*chityri*	**11**	*adinatsat'*
5	*pyat'*	**100**	*sto*
6	*shest'*	**1000**	*tysyacha*

SIGNS – RUSSIAN

Вход	Entrance
Выход	Exit
Справки	Information
Мест Нет	No Vacancies
Открыто	Open
Закрыто	Closed
Касса	Ticket Office
Больница	Hospital
Туалет	Toilets
Мужской (М)	Men
Женский (Ж)	Women

TRANSPORT & DIRECTIONS

What time does the … leave?
f katoram chasu pribyvaet …?
What time does the … arrive?
f katoram chasu atpravlyaetsa …?

THE CYRILLIC ALPHABET

Cyrillic	Roman	Pronunciation
А а	**a**	as in 'father'; also as in 'ago' when unstressed in Russian
Б б	**b**	as in 'but'
В в	**v**	as in 'van'
Г г	**g**	as in 'go'
Ѓ ѓ	**gj**	as the 'gu' in 'legume' (Macedonian only)
Д д	**d**	as the 'd' in 'dog'
Е е	**ye**	as in 'yet' when stressed; as in 'year' when un stressed (Russian)
	e	as in 'bet' (Bulgarian); as in 'there' (Macedonian)
Ё ё	**yo**	as in 'yore' (Russian only)
Ж ж	**zh**	as the 's' in 'measure'
З з	**z**	as in 'zoo'
S s	**zj**	as the 'ds' in 'suds' (Macedonian only)
И и	**i**	as the 'ee' in 'meet'
Й й	**y**	as in 'boy'
J j	**j**	as the 'y' in 'young' (Macedonian only)
К к	**k**	as in 'kind'
Ќ ќ	**kj**	as the 'cu' in 'cure' (Macedonian only)
Л л	**l**	as in 'lamp'
Љ љ	**lj**	as the 'lli' in 'million' (Macedonian only)
М м	**m**	as in 'mat'
Н н	**n**	as in 'not'
Њ њ	**nj**	as the 'ny' in 'canyon' (Macedonian only)
О о	**o**	as the 'a' in 'water' when stressed; the 'a' in 'ago' when unstressed (Russian); as in 'hot' (Bulgarian & Macedonian)
П п	**p**	as in 'pick'
Р р	**r**	as in 'rub' (but rolled)
С с	**s**	as in 'sing'
Т т	**t**	as in 'ten'
У у	**u**	as in 'rule'
Ф ф	**f**	as in 'fan'
Х х	**kh**	as the 'ch' in 'Bach' (Russian)
	h	as in 'hot' (Macedonian)
Ц ц	**ts**	as in 'bits'
Џ џ	**dz**	as the 'j' in 'judge' (Macedonian only)
Ч ч	**ch**	as in 'chat'
Ш ш	**sh**	as in 'shop'
Щ щ	**shch**	as 'shch' in 'fresh chips' (Russian)
	sht	as the '-shed' in pushed' (Bulgarian)
Ъ ъ	**â**	as the 'a' in 'ago' (Bulgarian only)
ъ		'hard' sign (Russian only)
Ы ы	**y**	as the 'i' in 'ill' (Russian only)
ь		'soft' sign (Russian only)
Э э	**e**	as in 'end' (Russian only)
Ю ю	**yu**	as the word 'you'
Я я	**ya**	as in 'yard

bus *aftobus*
fixed-route minibus *marshrutnaye taksi*
steamship *parakhot*
train *poyezt*
tram *tramvay*
trolleybus *traleybus*
pier/quay *prichal/pristan'*
train station *zhilezna darozhnyy vagzal*
stop (bus/trolleybus/tram) *astanofka*
one-way ticket *bilet v adin kanets*
return ticket *bilet v oba kantsa*
two tickets *dva bilety*
soft/1st-class *myahkiy*
hard/2nd-class *kupeyny*
3rd-class *platskartny*

Where is ...? *gde ...?*
to (on) the left *naleva*
to (on) the right *naprava*
straight on *pryama*

SLOVAK

PRONUNCIATION

In words of three syllables or less the stress falls on the first syllable. Longer words generally also have a secondary accent on the third or fifth syllable. There are 13 vowels (**a**, **á**, **ä**, **e**, **é**, **i**, **í**, **o**, **ó**, **u**, **ú**, **y**, **ý**), three semivowels (**l**, **ľ**, **r**) and five diphthongs (**ia**, **ie**, **iu**, **ou**, **ô**).

c	as the 'ts' in 'its'
č	as the 'ch' in 'church'
dz	as the 'ds' in 'suds'
dž	as the 'j' in 'judge'
ia	as the 'yo' in 'yonder'
ie	as the 'ye' in 'yes'
iu	as the word 'you'
j	as the 'y' in 'yet'
ň	as the 'ni' in 'onion'
ô	as the 'wo' in 'won't'
ou	as the 'ow' in 'know'
š	as the 'sh' in 'show'
y	as the 'i' in 'machine'
ž	as the 'z' in 'azure'

ACCOMMODATION

hotel *hotel*
guest house *penzion*
youth hostel *mládežnícka ubytovňa*
camping ground *kemping*
private room *privat*

Do you have any rooms available?
Máte voľné izby?
How much is it?
Koľko to stojí?
Does it include breakfast?
Sú raňajky zahrnuté v cene?

single room *jednolôžková izba*
double room *dvojlôžková izba*

CONVERSATION & ESSENTIALS

Hello. *Ahoj.*
Goodbye. *Dovidenia.*
Yes. *Áno.*
No. *Nie.*
Please. *Prosím.*
Thank you. *D'akujem.*
Excuse me. *Prepáčte mi.*
Sorry. *Odpuste mi.*
Do you speak English? *Hovoríte anglicky?*
I don't understand. *Nerozumiem.*
What is it called? *Ako sa do volá?*
How much is it? *Koľko to stojí?*

EMERGENCIES – SLOVAK

Help! *Pomoc!*
Call a doctor! *Zavolajte doktora/lekára!*
Call an ambulance! *Zavolajte záchranku!*
Call the police! *Zavolajte políciu!*
Go away! *Chod preč!* (sg)/ *Chodte preč!* (pl)
I'm lost. *Nevyznám sa tu.*

SHOPPING & SERVICES

the bank *banka*
the chemist *lekárnik*
the market *trh*
the post office *pošta*
the telephone centre *telefónnu centrálu*
the tourist office *turistické informačné centrum*

TIME, DAYS & NUMBERS

What time is it? *Koľko je hodín?*
today *dnes*
tonight *dnes večer*
tomorrow *zajtra*
in the morning *ráno*
in the evening *večer*

Monday *pondelok*
Tuesday *utorok*
Wednesday *streda*
Thursday *štvrtok*
Friday *piatok*
Saturday *sobota*
Sunday *nedeľa*

1	*jeden*	**7**	*sedem*
2	*dva*	**8**	*osem*
3	*tri*	**9**	*deväť*
4	*štyri*	**10**	*desať*
5	*päť*	**100**	*sto*
6	*šesť*	**1000**	*tisíc*

TRANSPORT & DIRECTIONS

What time does the … leave/arrive? *Kedy odchádza/prichádza …?*
boat *loč*
city bus *mestský autobus*
intercity bus *medzimestský autobus*
plane *lietadlo*
train *vlak*
tram *električka*

arrival *príchod*
departure *odchod*
timetable *cestovný poriadok*

SIGNS – SLOVAK

Vchod Entrance
Východ Exit
Informácie Information
Otvorené Open
Zatvorené Closed
Zakázané Prohibited
Telefón Telephone
Záchody/WC/Toalety Toilets

Where is the bus stop?	*Kde je autobusová zastávka?*
Where is the station?	*Kde je vlaková stanica?*
Where is the left-luggage room?	*Kde je úschovňa batožín?*
Please show me on the map.	*Prosím, ukážte mi to na mape.*
left	*vľavo*
right	*vpravo*
straight ahead	*rovno*

SLOVENE

PRONUNCIATION

The letters **l** and **v** are both pronounced like the English 'w' when they occur at the end of syllables and before vowels. Though words like *trn* (thorn) look unpronounceable, most Slovenes (depending on dialect) add a short vowel like an 'a' or the German 'ö' in front of the 'r' to give a Scot's pronunciation of 'tern' or 'tarn'.

c	as the 'ts' in 'its'
č	as the 'ch' in 'church'
ê	as the 'a' in 'apple'
e	as the 'a' in 'ago' (when unstressed)
é	as the 'ay' in 'day'
j	as the 'y' in 'yellow'
ó	as the 'o' in 'more'
ò	as the 'o' in 'soft'
r	a rolled 'r' sound
š	as the 'sh' in 'ship'
u	as the 'oo' in 'good'
ž	as the 's' in 'treasure'

ACCOMMODATION

hotel	*hotel*
guest house	*gostišče*
camping ground	*kamping*

Do you have a ...?	*Ali imate prosto ...?*
bed	*posteljo*
cheap room	*poceni sobo*
single room	*enoposteljno sobo*
double room	*dvoposteljno sobo*

How much is it per night?	*Koliko stane za eno noč?*
How much is it per person?	*Koliko stane za eno osebo?*
for one/two nights	*za eno noč/za dve noči*
Is breakfast included?	*Ali je zajtrk vključen?*

CONVERSATION & ESSENTIALS

Hello.	*Pozdravljeni.* (pol)
	Zdravo/Živivio. (inf)
Good day.	*Dober dan!*
Goodbye.	*Nasvidenje!*
Yes.	*Da./Ja.* (inf)
No.	*Ne.*
Please.	*Prosim.*
Thank you (very much).	*Hvala (lepa).*
You're welcome.	*Prosim/Ni za kaj!*
Excuse me.	*Oprostite.*
Do you speak English?	*Govorite angleško?*
What's your name?	*Kako vam je ime?*
My name is ...	*Jaz sem ...*

EMERGENCIES – SLOVENE

Help!	*Na pomoč!*
Call a doctor!	*Pokličite zdravnika!*
Call the police!	*Pokličite policijo!*
Go away!	*Pojdite stran!*

SHOPPING & SERVICES

Where is the/a ...?	*Kje je ...?*
bank/exchange	*banka/menjalnica*
post office	*pošta*
telephone centre	*telefonska centrala*
tourist office	*turistični informacijski urad*

TIME, DAYS & NUMBERS

today	*danes*
tonight	*nocoj*
tomorrow	*jutri*
in the morning	*zjutraj*
in the evening	*zvečer*

Monday	*ponedeljek*
Tuesday	*torek*
Wednesday	*sreda*
Thursday	*četrtek*
Friday	*petek*
Saturday	*sobota*
Sunday	*nedelja*

1	*ena*	**7**	*sedem*
2	*dve*	**8**	*osem*
3	*tri*	**9**	*devet*
4	*štiri*	**10**	*deset*
5	*pet*	**100**	*sto*
6	*šest*	**1000**	*tisoč*

TRANSPORT & DIRECTIONS

What time does the ... leave/arrive?	*Kdaj odpelje/pripelje ...?*

SIGNS – SLOVENE

Vhod	Entrance
Izhod	Exit
Informacije	Information
Odprto	Open
Zaprto	Closed
Prepovedano	Prohibited
Stranišče	Toilets

boat/ferry	*ladja/trajekt*
bus	*avtobus*
train	*vlak*

timetable	*spored*
train station	*železniška postaja*
bus station	*avtobusno postajališče*
one-way ticket	*enosmerna vozovnica*
return ticket	*povratna vozovnica*

Can you show me on the map?	*A mi lahko pokažete na mapi?*

SPANISH

ACCOMMODATION

hotel	*hotel*
guest house	*pensión/casa de huéspedes*
youth hostel	*albergue juvenil*
camping ground	*camping*

Do you have any rooms available?
¿Tiene habitaciones libres?
How much is it per night/per person?
¿Cuánto cuesta por noche/por persona?

a single room	*una habitación individual*
a double room	*una habitación doble*
a room with a double bed	*una habitación con cama de matrimonio*
for one night	*para una noche*
for two nights	*para dos noches*

CONVERSATION & ESSENTIALS

Hello/Goodbye.	*Hola./Adiós.*
Yes.	*Sí.*
No.	*No.*
Please.	*Por favor.*
Thank you.	*Gracias.*
You're welcome.	*De nada.*
Excuse me.	*Perdón/Perdoneme.*
Sorry.	*Lo siento/Discúlpeme.*
Do you speak English?	*¿Habla inglés?*
How much is it?	*¿Cuánto cuesta/vale?*

EMERGENCIES – SPANISH

Help!	*¡Socorro!/¡Auxilio!*
Call a doctor!	*¡Llame a un doctor!*
Call the police!	*¡Llame a la policía!*
Go away!	*¡Váyase!*
I'm lost.	*Estoy perdido/a.* (m/f)

SHOPPING & SERVICES

a bank	*un banco*
the chemist	*la farmacia*
the … embassy	*la embajada …*
the market	*el mercado*
newsagent/stationer	*papelería*
the post office	*los correos*
the tourist office	*la oficina de turismo*

What time does it open/close?
¿A qué hora abren/cierran?

TIME, DAYS & NUMBERS

What time is it?	*¿Qué hora es?*
today	*hoy*
tomorrow	*mañana*
yesterday	*ayer*
morning	*mañana*
afternoon	*tarde*

Monday	*lunes*
Tuesday	*martes*
Wednesday	*miércoles*
Thursday	*jueves*
Friday	*viernes*
Saturday	*sábado*
Sunday	*domingo*

1	*uno/una*	**10**	*diez*
2	*dos*	**11**	*once*
3	*tres*	**12**	*doce*
4	*cuatro*	**13**	*trece*
5	*cinco*	**14**	*catorce*
6	*seis*	**15**	*quince*
7	*siete*	**16**	*dieciéis*
8	*ocho*	**100**	*cien/ciento*
9	*nueve*	**1000**	*mil*

TRANSPORT & DIRECTIONS

What time does the next … leave/arrive?	*¿A qué hora sale/llega el próximo …?*
boat	*barco*
bus (city)	*autobús, bus*
bus (intercity)	*autocar*
train	*tranvía*

SIGNS – SPANISH

Entrada	Entrance
Salida	Exit
Información	Information
Abierto	Open
Cerrado	Closed
Prohibido	Prohibited
Servicios/Aseos	Toilets
Hombres	Men
Mujeres	Women

I'd like a … ticket. *Quisiera un billete …*
one-way *sencillo/de sólo ida*
return *de ida y vuelta*
1st class *de primera clase*
2nd class *de segunda clase*

left luggage *consigna*
timetable *horario*
bus stop *parada de autobus*
train station *estación de ferrocarril*

I'd like to hire … *Quisiera alquilar …*
a car *un coche*
a bicycle *una bicicleta*

Where is …? *¿Dónde está …?*
Go straight ahead. *Siga/Vaya todo derecho.*
Turn left. *Gire a la izquierda.*
Turn right. *Gire a la derecha/recto.*
near/far *cerca/lejos*

SWEDISH

PRONUNCIATION

å long, as the word 'awe'; short as the 'o' in 'pot'
ä as the 'a' in 'act'
ö as the 'er' in 'fern'
y like 'ee' while pursing your lips
c as the 's' in 'sit'
ck as a double 'k'; shortens the preceding vowel
tj/rs as the 'sh' in 'ship'
sj/ch similar to the 'ch' in Scottish *loch*
g as in 'get', but also as the 'y' in 'yet'
lj as the 'y' in 'yet'

ACCOMMODATION

hotel *hotell*
guest house *gästhus*
youth hostel *vandrarhem*
camping ground *campingplats*

Do you have any rooms available?
Finns det några lediga rum?
How much is it per night/person?
Hur mycket kostar det per natt/person?

for one night *i en natt*
for two nights *i två nätter*

I'd like … *Jag skulle vilja ha …*
a single room *ett enkelrum*
a double room *ett dubbelrum*

EMERGENCIES – SWEDISH

Help!	*Hjälp!*
Call a doctor!	*Ring efter en doktor!*
Call the police!	*Ring polisen!*
Go away!	*Försvinn!*
I'm lost.	*Jag har gått vilse.*

CONVERSATION & ESSENTIALS

Hello. *Hej.*
Goodbye. *Adjö/Hej då.*
Yes. *Ja.*
No. *Nej.*
Please. *Snälla/Vänligen.*
Thank you. *Tack.*
That's fine/You're welcome. *Det är bra/Varsågod.*
Excuse me. *Ursäkta mig.*
Sorry. *Förlåt.*
Do you speak English? *Talar du engelska?*
How much is it? *Hur mycket kostar den?*

SIGNS – SWEDISH

Ingång	Entrance
Utgång	Exit
Öppet	Open
Stängt	Closed
Förbjudet	Prohibited
Toalett	Toilets
Herrar	Men
Damer	Women

TIME, DAYS & NUMBERS

What time is it? *Vad är klockan?*
today *idag*
tomorrow *imorgon*
morning *morgonen*
afternoon *efter middagen*

Monday	*måndag*
Tuesday	*tisdag*
Wednesday	*onsdag*
Thursday	*torsdag*
Friday	*fredag*
Saturday	*lördag*
Sunday	*söndag*

0	*noll*	**7**	*sju*
1	*ett*	**8**	*åtta*
2	*två*	**9**	*nio*
3	*tre*	**10**	*tio*
4	*fyra*	**11**	*elva*
5	*fem*	**100**	*ett hundra*
6	*sex*	**1000**	*ett tusen*

SHOPPING & SERVICES

bank	*bank*
chemist/pharmacy	*apotek*
… embassy	*… ambassaden*
market	*marknaden*
newsagent/ stationer	*nyhetsbyrå/ pappers handel*
post office	*postkontoret*
tourist office	*turistinformation*

What time does it open/close?	*När öppnar/stänger de?*

TRANSPORT & DIRECTIONS

What time does … leave/arrive?	*När avgår/kommer …?*
the boat	*båten*
the city bus	*stadsbussen*
the intercity bus	*landsortsbussen*
the tram	*spårvagnen*
the train	*tåget*

I'd like …	*Jag skulle vilja ha …*
a one-way ticket	*en enkelbiljett*
a return ticket	*en returbiljett*
1st class	*första klass*
2nd class	*andra klass*

left luggage	*effektförvaring*
timetable	*tidtabell*
bus stop	*busshållplats*
train station	*tågstation*

Where can I hire a car/bicycle?	*Var kan jag hyra en bil/cykel?*
Where is …?	*Var är …?*
Go straight ahead.	*Gå rakt fram.*
Turn left.	*Sväng till vänster.*
Turn right.	*Sväng till höger.*
near/far	*nära/långt*

TURKISH

PRONUNCIATION

A, a	as the 'a' in 'art' or 'bar'
E, e	as in 'fell'
İ, i	as 'ee'
I, ı	as 'uh'
O, o	as in 'hot'
U, u	as the 'oo' in 'moo'
Ö, ö	as the 'ur' in 'fur'
Ü, ü	as the 'ew' in 'few'

Note that both **ö** and **ü** are pronounced with pursed lips.

Ç, ç	as the 'ch' in 'church'
C, c	as English 'j'
Ğ, ğ	not pronounced; draws out the preceding vowel a bit – ignore it!
J, j	as the 's' in 'treasure'
S, s	hard, as in 'stress'
Ş, ş	as the 'sh' in 'shoe'
V, v	as the 'w' in 'weather'

ACCOMMODATION

hotel	*otel(i)*
guest house	*pansiyon*
student hostel	*öğrenci yurdu*
camping ground	*kampink*

Do you have any rooms available?
Boş oda var mı?
How much is it per night/per person?
Bir gecelik/Kişibaşına kaç para?

a single room	*tek kişilik oda*
a double room	*iki kişilik oda*

EMERGENCIES – TURKISH

Help!/Emergency!	*İmdat!*
Call a doctor!	*Doktor çağırın!*
Call the police!	*Polis çağırın!*
Go away!	*Gidin/Git!/Defol!*
I'm lost.	*Kayboldum.*

CONVERSATION & ESSENTIALS

Hello.	*Merhaba.*
Goodbye.	*Allahaısmarladık/Güle güle.*
Yes.	*Evet.*
No.	*Hayır.*
Please.	*Lütfen.*
Thank you.	*Teşekkür ederim.*

That's fine/You're welcome.	*Bir şey değil.*
Excuse me.	*Affedersiniz.*
Sorry/Pardon.	*Pardon.*
Do you speak English?	*İngilizce biliyor musunuz?*
How much is it?	*Ne kadar?*

SIGNS – TURKISH

Giriş	Entrance
Çikiş	Exit
Danişma	Information
Açik	Open
Kapali	Closed
Yasak(tir)	Prohibited
Tuvalet	Toilets

SHOPPING & SERVICES

a bank	*bir banka*
a chemist/pharmacy	*bir eczane*
the … embassy	*… büyükelçiliği*
the post office	*postane*
the market	*çarşı*
the tourist office	*turizm danışma bürosu*

What time does it open/close?
Ne zamam açılır/kapanır?

TIME, DAYS & NUMBERS

What time is it?	*Saat kaç?*
today	*bugün*
tomorrow	*yarın*
morning	*sabah*
afternoon	*öğleden sonra*

Monday	*Pazartesi*
Tuesday	*Salı*
Wednesday	*Çarşamba*
Thursday	*Perşembe*
Friday	*Cuma*
Saturday	*Cumartesi*
Sunday	*Pazar*

1	*bir*	**8**	*sekiz*
2	*iki*	**9**	*dokuz*
3	*üç*	**10**	*on*
4	*dört*	**11**	*on bir*
5	*beş*	**12**	*on iki*
6	*altı*	**100**	*yüz*
7	*yedi*	**1000**	*bin*

one million	*bir milyon*

TRANSPORT & DIRECTIONS

What time does the next … leave/arrive?	*Gelecek … ne zaman kalkar/gelir?*
ferry/boat	*feribot/vapur*
bus (city)	*şehir otobüsü*
bus (intercity)	*otobüs*
tram	*tramvay*
train	*tren*

I'd like …	*… istiyorum*
a one-way ticket	*gidiş bileti*
a return ticket	*gidiş-dönüş bileti*
1st/2nd class	*birinci/ikinci mevkii*

left luggage	*emanetçi*
timetable	*tarife*
bus/tram stop	*otobüs/tramvay durağı*
train station	*gar/istasyon*
boat/ship dock	*iskele*

I'd like to hire a car/bicycle.	*Araba/bisiklet kirala mak istiyorum.*
Where is a/the …?	*… nerede?*
Go straight ahead.	*Doğru gidin.*
Turn left.	*Sola dönün.*
Turn right.	*Sağa dönün.*
near/far	*yakın/uzak*

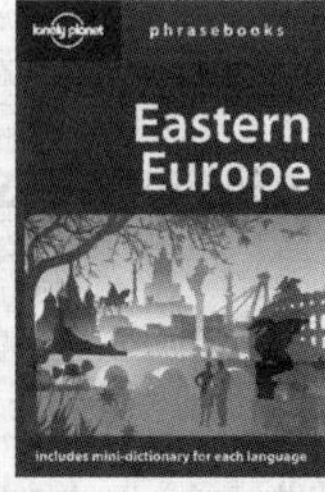

Also available from Lonely Planet: *Western Europe* and *Eastern Europe* phrasebooks

The Authors

TOM MASTERS

Coordinating Author, Belarus, Malta & Ukraine

Tom's first travel memory is long overnight drives to Nice every summer to stay at his grandparents' house. Having convinced his parents to diversify to camping in the Black Forest, and on one occasion even Switzerland, rather than always going back to the same place, he's never looked back. Two decades later he has been to nearly every country on the continent, but can never get enough of anywhere Slavic or Mediterranean. Tom works in London as a freelance writer and can be found online at www.mastersmafia.com

BRETT ATKINSON

Czech Republic

After visiting 60 countries Brett is sometimes tired of people asking 'So what's your favourite place?' When he's in the Czech Republic, the combination of a thrilling history, world-class beers and a darkly dry sense of humour, means the country is somewhere near the top of his personal list. When his passport is having a breather, Brett lives in Auckland, New Zealand with Carol. He's looking forward to finally sharing Bohemia and Moravia with her sometime in the near future.

CAROLYN BAIN

Estonia

Melbourne-based Carolyn studied European history and languages and has lived and studied in a few Euro hotspots. Lonely Planet has given her licence to further investigate great pockets of the continent – Greece, Malta, Sweden, Denmark, the Baltics – and there's still a huge buzz to be had in crossing the Arctic Circle or swimming in the Med in December, all in the name of work. For this book she ventured to the northeast, where Estonia combines the best of Eastern Europe and Scandinavia and delivers something heart-warmingly unique.

JAMES BAINBRIDGE

Turkey

Pictured on a hot-air balloon ride above Cappadocia's fairy chimneys, James is the coordinating author of Lonely Planet's guide to Turkey. He has contributed to Lonely Planet books ranging from *Africa* and *India* to *A Year of Festivals*, which features events such as Turkey's camel- and oil-wrestling festivals. When he's not charging around with a notebook in one hand, James lives in London – right on Green Lanes, the city's 'little Turkey'.

LONELY PLANET AUTHORS

Why is our travel information the best in the world? It's simple: our authors are passionate, dedicated travellers. They don't take freebies in exchange for positive coverage so you can be sure the advice you're given is impartial. They travel widely to all the popular spots, and off the beaten track. They don't research using just the internet or phone. They discover new places not included in any other guidebook. They personally visit thousands of hotels, restaurants, palaces, trails, galleries, temples and more. They speak with dozens of locals every day to make sure you get the kind of insider knowledge only a local could tell you. They take pride in getting all the details right, and in telling it how it is. Think you can do it? Find out how at **lonelyplanet.com**.

NEAL BEDFORD
Austria & Lithuania

Neal has been exploring the broad boulevards and back waters of central and eastern Europe since first arriving on the continent some 15 years ago. He has yet to wake up bored with the place or the people, but often misses the easy availability of Griffins Gingernuts. He has called Vienna home for the past eight years and has researched a number of guides across the globe for Lonely Planet and other travel publishers.

OLIVER BERRY
France

Oliver graduated with a degree in English from University College London and spent the next few years seeing what the rest of the world had to offer (quite a lot as it turned out). He now lives and works in Cornwall as a writer and photographer. His travels for Lonely Planet have carried him everywhere from Canada to the Cook Islands, but he always finds the best adventures have a French flavour. He has also worked on several editions of Lonely Planet's *France* guide.

PAUL CLAMMER
Morocco

As a student, Paul had his first solo backpacking experience when he took a bus from his Cambridgeshire home all the way to Casablanca. Morocco instantly enchanted him. After an interlude when he trained and worked as a molecular biologist, he eventually returned to work as a tour guide, trekking in the Atlas and trying not to lose passengers in the Fez medina. He returns on a regular basis both for recreation and as coordinating author for Lonely Planet's *Morocco* guidebook.

GEERT COLE
Belgium & Luxembourg

According to a local saying, Belgians are born with a brick in their stomach. Not Geert. He combed continents for years before finally realising that only one nation on earth is founded on beer, chocolate and chips – it's good to be back home! But discovering there is a small brick in one's stomach can be hard to digest. Luckily, that's when Lonely Planet stepped in and, 18 years later, Geert still loves life-on-the-road, whether it's in Belgium, Luxembourg or continents further afield.

JAYNE D'ARCY
Albania

Albania hit Jayne's radar in 2006 when she joined her first ever package tour, and while complaining about the herd-mentality of her fellow tourists, she was pretty stoked to get a new passport stamp and see some amazing ruins in relative peace. The changes in Albania since then are astonishing, and the similarities to the 'old Ireland' are huge (home-made spirits, dodgy roads). Apart from travel writing, Jayne writes features on design, people and the environment.

CHRIS DELISO
Macedonia

Originally from the US, Chris has been all over the Balkans as a professional writer and journalist for the better part of a decade. Since finishing a master's in Byzantine History at Oxford University, he has lived in Greece, Turkey and (since 2002) Macedonia, a country that still continues to surprise him on a daily basis. Over the past few years, he has contributed to several other guidebooks for Lonely Planet, including *Greece*, *Bulgaria*, *Western Balkans* and *Eastern Europe*.

PETER DRAGICEVICH

Montenegro

While it was family ties that first drew Peter to the Balkans, it's the history, natural beauty, convoluted politics, cheap *rakija* and intriguing people that keep bringing him back. His first Lonely Planet assignment was writing the Albania and Macedonia chapters for the previous edition of this book. Since then he's written about England, Wales, Vietnam, Australia, New Zealand, Samoa, American Samoa and Tokelau. He has also just completed Lonely Planet's first *Montenegro* guidebook.

LISA DUNFORD

Slovakia

Lisa first became hooked on globetrotting when she learned her grandfather came from a Carpathian region that was once Hungary, then Czechoslovakia and is now in Ukraine. She studied in Budapest during university and then worked at the US Agency for International Development in Bratislava. She learned the Slovak language, danced with the country on the night it became a nation and made life-long friends. Still travelling often, Lisa, her husband and their dogs call a riverfront in Texas home.

MARK ELLIOTT

Bosnia & Hercegovina

Mark was only 11 when he first stood on the Sarajevo street corner from which Gavrilo Princip shot Franz Ferdinand (no, not the band). He's since travelled all over BiH, supping fine Hercegovinian wines, philosophising with Serb monks, meeting Sufi mystics and overdosing on Bosnian coffee. His writing career began with the 1990s backpacker bible, *Asia Overland,* for which he spent three years crisscrossing that continent and being regularly interrogated by bemused KGB officers in the newly opened 'stans'.

DAVID ELSE

Britain

As a backpacker, David has travelled widely in Europe, Africa, India and beyond. As a writer, David has authored more than 20 guidebooks, including Lonely Planet's *Great Britain* and *England* guides. Originally from London, David's knowledge of Britain comes from a lifetime of travel around the country – often on foot or by bike – a passion dating from university years, when heading for the hills was always more attractive than visiting the library.

STEVE FALLON

Slovenia

Steve has been travelling to Slovenia since the early 1990s, when a travel publishing company initially refused his proposal to write a guidebook to the country because of 'the war going on' (it had ended two years before). Though he still hasn't reached the top of Triglav, Steve considers at least part of his soul Slovenian and returns to the country as often as he can for a glimpse of the Julian Alps, a dribble of *bučno olje*, and a dose of the dual.

DUNCAN GARWOOD

Italy

Duncan has been living in Italy since 1997 and has spent much of the last six years travelling up and down the country on behalf of Lonely Planet. His first taste of journalism came on a local paper in Slough, an experience which not surprisingly led to dreams of more exotic climes. Fortunately, it's worked out and he now gets to drink in crowded Sicilian bars and sunbathe on Sardinia's beaches and still say he's at work.

LEANNE LOGAN

Belgium & Luxembourg

Leanne first tasted Belgium and Luxembourg as a pre-puber in the '70s as part of a family campervan trip around Europe. You could feed pigeons on Brussels' Grand Place back then. A decade later, and now a journalist, she returned to find the pigeons gone but the country more vibrant then ever. A love of travel and writing led naturally to Lonely Planet – for the past two decades Leanne has combed not only Belgium and Luxembourg many times, but also Africa, Asia and the Pacific.

VESNA MARIC

Croatia & Cyprus

Vesna was born in Bosnia & Hercegovina while it was still a part of Yugoslavia, and she has never been able to see Croatia as a foreign country. A lifetime lover of Dalmatia's beaches, pine trees, food and wine, Vesna felt that researching this book was a true delight.

MARIKA MCADAM

Kosovo & Serbia

Marika is an Australian writer and lawyer currently based in Vienna. She has explored Europe as far north as Sweden, as far west as Spain and as far south as Italy, but the further east she goes the more at home she feels. This research trip reminded her that the similarities between people are far more important than their differences; Europe has no friendlier folk than Serbs and Kosovars.

CRAIG MCLACHLAN

Greece

An adventurous Kiwi, Craig enjoys nothing more than visiting the Greek Isles to down Mythos beer, ouzo and consume *gyros*. A self-described 'island nut' and 'freelance anything', he regularly leads hiking tours in Greece. Jobs have included stints as an author, pilot, hiking guide, interpreter and karate instructor. In his other life, Craig has an MBA from the University of Hawaii and resides in Queenstown, New Zealand where he runs an outdoor activity company. Check out www.craigmclachlan.com

BECKY OHLSEN

Sweden

Becky grew up with a thick book of Swedish fairy tales illustrated by John Bauer, so the deep, black forests of Norrland hold particular fascination for her. Hiking through them, she stays alert for *tomtes* and trolls (which, to the untrained eye, look just like big rocks). Though raised in Colorado, Becky has been a frequent explorer of Sweden since childhood, while visiting her grandparents in Stockholm and her great-aunt in Härnösand. She loves the extremes of light up north, its round-the-clock summer glare and near-total absence in winter.

FRAN PARNELL

Iceland

Fran updated the Iceland chapter. Her love of the country began while studying for a masters degree in Anglo-Saxon, Norse and Celtic, and has just kept on growing. It's hard not to fall for the cool, clean city of Reykjavík, with its Viking history, charming people, quirky cafes and thoughtful museums. A highlight of this research trip was scuba-diving in Lake Þingvellir. When not working on Lonely Planet's guides to Denmark, Sweden, Iceland and Reykjavík, Fran enjoys diving in southeast Asia.

LEIF PETTERSEN

Moldova & Romania

In 2003, Leif – originally from Minneapolis, Minnesota – was 'Kramered' into becoming a travel writer. His weakness for pretty girls first brought him to Romania in 2004, where he's lived and travelled for nearly two cumulative years. He's repeatedly visited every notable patch of grass in Romania and Moldova, making priceless friends, except for Romania's Neo-Nazi Party who publicly denounced him in 2008 as a 'slimeball' (yes, really). Leif writes an almost award-winning, 'slightly caustic' blog, KillingBatteries.com.

BRANDON PRESSER

Latvia

His wanderlust bigger than his wallet, Brandon earned his shoestringer stripes after an epic overland adventure from Morocco to Finland. He relished the opportunity to revisit Latvia and put his Harvard art history degree to good use while checking out Rīga's surplus of evocative art nouveau architecture. Brandon has contributed to a handful of Lonely Planet guides including *Estonia, Latvia & Lithuania,* and when he's not writing his way around the globe he enjoys crossword puzzles and scuba diving.

ROBERT REID

Bulgaria

Raised in Oklahoma and living in Brooklyn, Robert (www.reidontravel.com) has looked east since his lad days when he studied the Bulgarian alphabet in fashionably unhip Russian courses. Before his author days, he oversaw the shoestring series from Lonely Planet's London offices, and has since written the Bulgaria chapter for this book three times, as well as *Romania & Moldova* and *Trans-Siberian Railway*.

TIM RICHARDS

Hungary & Poland

Tim spent a year teaching English in Kraków in 1994–95, having transferred with an international teaching organisation from Egypt. He was fascinated by the postcommunism transition affecting every aspect of Polish life, and by surviving remnants of the Cold War days. He's since been delighted by his reacquaintance with this beautiful, complex country. When he's not on the road for Lonely Planet, Tim is a freelance journalist based in Melbourne, Australia. You can see more of his writing at www.iwriter.com.au.

SIMON RICHMOND

Russia

An award-winning writer and photographer, Simon first visited Russia in 1994 when he wandered goggle-eyed around gorgeous St Petersburg, and peeked at Lenin's mummified corpse in Red Square. He's since travelled the breadth of the nation from Kamchatka to Kaliningrad stopping off at many points between. Simon is the coauthor of the first and subsequent editions of Lonely Planet's *Trans-Siberian Railway* as well as several editions of *Russia*. Catch him online at www.simonrichmond.com.

MILES RODDIS

Andorra

Living in Valencia, on Spain's Mediterranean coast, Miles loses count of the times he's nipped up to Andorra for a skiing weekend or a summertime camping and walking break – though never, ever to shop. He has written or contributed to more than 30 Lonely Planet titles, including guides, both general and walking, about Spain and France, Andorra's immediate neighbours.

DAMIEN SIMONIS

Spain

The spark was lit on a trip over the Pyrenees to Barcelona during a summer jaunt in France. It was Damien's first taste of Spain and he found something irresistible about the place. He came back years later, living in medieval Toledo, frenetic Madrid and, finally, settling in Barcelona. He has ranged across the country, from the Picos de Europa to the Sierra Nevada, from Córdoba to Cáceres, slurping cider in Asturias and gin in the Balearic Islands. He has no plans to leave.

JOHN SPELMAN

Norway

John frequently travels to Norway to be overwhelmed by the world's most stunning landscape. He's embarked upon Arctic-Circle dog-sled rides and licked several glaciers. Otherwise, find him wandering between cafes in Oslo. He likes to spend a week in Paris before arriving in Norway, as the juxtaposition actually makes the City of Light seem inexpensive. John is a PhD candidate researching urban histories, some of them Norwegian. This is his sixth time covering Norway for a Lonely Planet title.

REGIS ST LOUIS

Portugal

A lover of wine, rugged coastlines and a bit of *bacalhau* (dried cod) now and again, Regis was destined for a romance with small, irresistible Portugal when he first explored the country some years back. Favourite memories of a recent trip include delving into Porto's bohemian side, sampling wines from Douro vineyards and hiking remote corners of the north. Regis has contributed to numerous other Lonely Planet guides, including Lonely Planet's recent *Portugal* guide. He lives in New York City.

ANDREW STONE

Denmark

Denmark's sense of history, the way distant epochs take on a compelling immediacy, still surprises Andrew on return visits. Copenhagen is his other abiding pleasure: its food, bars, shopping and sense of cultured ease. It might just be the perfect European city.

ANDY SYMINGTON

Finland

Andy first visited Finland many years ago more or less by accident, and walking on frozen lakes with the midday sun low in the sky made a quick and deep impression on him, even as fingers froze in the -30°C temperatures. Since then they can't keep him away, fuelled by a love of huskies, saunas, Finnish mustard, moody Suomi rock and metal, but above all of Finnish people and their beautiful country.

RYAN VER BERKMOES

Germany & the Netherlands

Ryan Ver Berkmoes once lived in Germany (three years in Frankfurt), during which time he edited a magazine until he got a chance for a new career with Lonely Planet. Later he worked on the first edition of Lonely Planet's *The Netherlands*, a country where they pronounce his name better than he can. These days he lives in Portland, Oregon. Learn more at ryanverberkmoes.com.

NICOLA WILLIAMS

Liechtenstein & Switzerland

Frontier life is tough for Nicola, who's never shaken off that uncanny feeling she's on holiday since bunking down in a village on the Swiss-French border, on the southern side of Lake Geneva. Must be the skiing... A garden tumbling towards Europe's largest alpine lake and Switzerland's mysterious Jura mountains beyond is her wake-up call. Nicola has lived and worked in France since 1997 and when not at her desk writing she's gadding around in Switzerland, Italy, France, Liechtenstein and Germany.

NEIL WILSON

Ireland

Neil's first backpacking trip was back in 1983, but despite living in Scotland he never made it to neighbouring Ireland till 1990. Trips to Northern Ireland followed in 1994, and his interest in the place intensified a few years later when he found out that most of his mum's ancestors were from Ulster. Neil is a full-time travel writer based in Edinburgh, Scotland, and has worked on more than 40 guidebooks for half a dozen publishers, including the last three editions of Lonely Planet's *Ireland* guide.

Behind the Scenes

THIS BOOK

Many people have helped to create this 6th edition of *Europe on a Shoestring,* which is part of Lonely Planet's Europe series. Other titles in the series include *Western Europe, Eastern Europe, Mediterranean Europe, Central Europe* and *Scandinavian Europe*. Lonely Planet also publishes phrasebooks to these regions. This guidebook was commissioned in Lonely Planet's London office, and produced by the following:

Commissioning Editors Fiona Buchan, Sally Schafer, Clifton Wilkinson
Coordinating Editor Barbara Delissen
Coordinating Cartographer Anita Banh
Coordinating Layout Designer Margaret Jung
Managing Editors Imogen Bannister, Katie Lynch
Managing Cartographers Mark Griffiths, Herman So
Managing Layout Designers Laura Jane, Indra Kilfoyle
Assisting Editors Susie Ashworth, Janet Austin, Nigel Chin, Jessica Crouch, Charlotte Harrison, Shawn Low, Rosie Nicholson, Katie O'Connell, Charlotte Orr, Kirsten Rawlings, Erin Richards, Tom Smallman, Angela Tinson
Assisting Cartographers Barbara Benson, Ildiko Bogdanovits, Csanad Csutoros, Tadhgh Knaggs, Alex Leung, Khanh Luu, Jolyon Philcox, Sophie Reed, James Regan, Brendan Streager, Tom Webster
Assisting Layout Designers Cara Smith, Carlos Solarte
Cover Image research provided by lonelyplanetimages.com
Colour Designer Vicki Beale
Project Manager Glenn van der Knijff

Thanks to Lucy Birchley, Sally Darmody, Janine Eberle, Ryan Evans, Will Gourlay, Robyn Loughnane, Lucy Monie, Wayne Murphy, Jacqueline Nguyen, Darren O'Connell, Trent Paton, Caroline Sieg, Sarah Sloane, Lyahna Spencer, Gina Tsarouhas, Branislava Vladisavljevic

THANKS

TOM MASTERS

An enormous shout out to all the writers who criss-crossed Europe for this book and to the fantastic team of editors and cartographers at Lonely Planet who turned the manuscript into a finished book. Thanks also to Will Gourlay who entrusted this book to me after a rocky start, and to Fee Buchan and Clifton Wilkinson who saw through the process from Lonely Planet's London offices. Many thanks to a host of people who helped me with the research for this book, but particularly to Gabriel Gatehouse in Ukraine and James Bridle in Malta.

BRETT ATKINSON

In the Czech Republic thanks to Greg, Francie, Tomáš, Oldřiška and Doug. In Lonely Planet-Ville thanks to coordinating author Tom Masters, Mark Griffiths and the cartography team for making sense of my multicoloured maps, and special thanks to the tireless Will Gourlay for his energy and passion for the region and for this book. Finally, thanks to Carol for actually recognising me when I (eventually) got home. I promise to take you to Prague next time, OK?

CAROLYN BAIN

A huge *aitäh* to Steve Kokker for his friendship, kindness and local wisdom. Others who helped out with tips and company around Estonia include Pille Petersoo, Liina Laar, Geli Lillemaa, Hugo and Tim, Maido Rüütli, Sergei Iarovenko, Malcolm Russell, Madis Mutso and Varje Papp. Heartfelt thanks to friends who shared with me the pleasure of their company on parts of this trip: Sally O'Brien and George Dunford for the memorable weekend in Tallinn; Brandon Presser and Neal Bedford for making work fun in Rīga and Vilnius; and Amanda Harding and Graham Harris for the incredible Baltic City Blitz.

JAMES BAINBRIDGE

Teşekkür ederim (thank you) to Padi and Hülya in İstanbul; to Jahid, Aziz and the Hemi posse in Sivas; to Pat, Süha, Ali, Mustafa, Maggie, Kaili, Crazy Ali and everyone who brought Cappadocia to life; to Mustafa in Boğazkale and Nazlı in Konya; to Ollagh in Kayseri and the Kurds in Çorum.

NEAL BEDFORD

Special thanks to Karin for all her support, love, and patience. Lithuania wouldn't have been so enjoyable without the help of Nicola Williams, Andrew Quested, Hans Bastian Hauck, Cornelis Oskamp, and Lena Björkenor, and Austria without the wonderful folk I've known over the past years. Thanks a bunch.

PAUL CLAMMER

At Lonely Planet thanks to Lucy Monie, who is always a delight to work with, and to my coauthors on the full Morocco guide: Anthony Sattin, Alison Bing and Paul Stiles. Special thanks also to Fez resident and fellow Lonely Planet author Helen Ranger, who smoothed several crooked medina pathways. Also in Fez, thanks to Mike, Max, Jess and the rest of the Café Clock crew, and again to Jen and Sebastian. *Mulţumesc* to Alexa Radulea. And of course, thanks and love to Jo, for looking after the home front.

JAYNE D'ARCY

Thanks to Sharik Billington for taking on Albania with me and my three-year-old, to Miles, for coping with all the cheek-pinching, to Will Gourlay for sending me up the Accursed Mountains in the first place, and to Orieta Gliozheni, Stavri Cifligu, Marius Qytyku, Yolanda Kebo and Edward Shehi and his Italian tourists. Thanks Dr Shannon Woodcock at La Trobe University, Australia, Mada at Sunrock, Corfu, and everyone along the way who had the keys and let us in.

CHRIS DELISO

So many people in Macedonia (locals and adopted locals alike) have helped me over the years that it would be impossible to mention them all. For the sections represented in this book, at least, special thanks are due to Igor at the Skopje tourism office, Jason Miko, Daniel Medaroski in Ohrid and Patrice Koerper in Bitola. Thanks too to all the good folks at Lonely Planet, especially Will Gourlay, Fiona Buchan, Mark Griffiths and coordinating author Tom Masters.

PETER DRAGICEVICH

A huge thanks to all the wonderful people who helped me along the way, especially my beloved Dragičević cousins, Hayley and Jack Delf, Goran and Jadranka Marković, Dragana Ostojić, Slavko Marjanović, Danica Ćeranić, Kirsi Hyvaerinen and David Mills. Extra special thanks to Milomir Jukanović and to my enthusiastic commissioning editor Will Gourlay.

LISA DUNFORD

Dearest Saša, I'm so glad to be part of your family; Fero, Šimi, Sari Petriska – thank you. I appreciate the help of everyone who made suggestions and helped me along my way, including Martin Latal, Karen and Matuš Sulek, Zuzana Bielikova, Jimbo Holden and the Monkey.

MARK ELLIOTT

Many thanks to the Lonely Planet team, to Edis Hodžić, Guillaume Martin, Olivier Janoschka, Snezhan in Trebinje, Vlaren at Tvrdoš Monastery, Semir in Blagaj, Narmina in Mostar and so many more. As ever my greatest thanks go to my endlessly inspiring wife Dani Systermans and to my unbeatable parents who, three decades ago, had the idea of driving me to Bosnia in the first place.

DAVID ELSE

As always, massive appreciation goes to my wife Corinne, for joining me on many research trips around Britain, and for not minding when I locked myself away for 12 hours at a time to write this chapter – and for bringing coffee when it got nearer 16 hours. Thanks also to coordinating author Tom, and the coauthors who worked on the original version of this Britain chapter: Belinda, Neil, Andy, David A, James, Nana, Neil, Fionn, Oliver, Etain and Peter. And finally, thanks to all the friendly faces in the commissioning, editorial, cartography and design departments at Lonely Planet who helped bring this book to final fruition.

STEVE FALLON

A number of people assisted in the research and writing of the Slovenia chapter, in particular my dear friends and fonts-of-all-knowledge at the Ljubljana Tourist Board: Verica Leskovar, Tatjana Radovič and Petra Stušek. Others to whom I'd like to say *najlepša hvala* for assistance, inspiration, sustenance and/or a few laughs along the way include the boys (Miha Anzelc, Luka Esenko and Tomaž Marič) of Židana Marela in Ljubljana; Brina Čehovin and Tina Križnar of the Slovenian Tourist Board, Ljubljana; Marino Fakin of Slovenian Railways, Ljubljana; Aleš and Tanja Hvala of the Hotel Hvala and Restavracija Topli Val, Kobarid; Lado Leskovar of Unicef based in Ljubljana; Tomaž Škofic of Adria Airways in Ljubljana; Robert Stan of Adventure Rafting Bled; and the staff at the Tourist Information Centre Ptuj for assistance (way beyond the call of duty) in helping me find an industrial-strength *klopotec* (wind rattle) on short notice as I whizzed in on a rainy morning from southwest Hungary. Goodbye pigeons!

As always, my efforts here are dedicated to my partner, Michael Rothschild, who is way overdue a visit to God's own country.

DUNCAN GARWOOD

As always thanks to all the helpful folk I met on the road. Tourist-office staff generally went out of their way to help, particularly Fabiana at Tivoli, Marilù Milo at Amalfi and Fabiola Fasulo at Sorrento. It was good to meet Giovanni, Palermo's most enthusiastic host and gourmet guide. Thanks also to Richard and Rebecca for lunch in Rome, and Sheena and Pasquale in Bari. Tim, wherever you are, thanks for helping me research Lipari. At Lonely Planet, a big thank you to Caroline Sieg for the commission, Clifton Wilkinson for his prompt responses, Mark Griffiths for his map help, and Virginia Maxwell for her great text. On the home front, a huge heartfelt hug to Lidia, without whom I couldn't do the job, to Nick and Ben for so ably taking my mind off work, and to my indefatigable in-laws Nicla and Aniello Salvati for their unquestioning support.

LEANNE LOGAN & GEERT COLE

Bedankt in Belgium to Roos and Bert Cole, Erik and An, and Katrien and Albert for your kind support. To our daughters Gwynevere and Eleonor, we thank you for being wonderful travelling companions. And to our buddies, Sixy and Bluey, thanks for always being there. Thanks too for the enthusiastic support of Jean-Claude Conter at the Luxembourg National Tourist Office, Helga Van Muylders at Toerisme Vlaanderen, Cathérine Langue at the Office de Promotion du Tourisme Wallonie-Bruxelles and Anousjka Schmidt at Brussels International and Anne De Meerleer at Toerisme Brugge in Bruges. To the readers and travellers who offered advice, insights and criticisms, thanks also. Lastly, *merci* to all those at Lonely Planet who were involved in this book's production.

VESNA MARIC

Hvala to Maja Gilja, my mother, Toni and Marina Ćavar, Ružica, Stipe, Ante, Dana and Loreta Barać. Also *hvala* to Kristina Hajduka, and Janica and Matej. Thanks to Gabriel and all the travellers I chatted to along the way. Thanks also to Anja Mutić and William Gourlay.

MARIKA MCADAM

As always, the folk I met on the road are what make this job the best one in the world. It was an honour to be among the army of authors assembled to put this book together, and a girl could have no finer colleague than a Lonely Planet commissioning editor. Thanks also to Lorina who was up for anything in Serbia and to Jo who came to Kosovo and always makes wherever he is my favourite place in the world.

CRAIG MCLACHLAN

A hearty thanks to all those who helped me out on the road, but most of all to my exceptionally beautiful wife Yuriko and our boys Riki and Ben.

BECKY OHLSEN

Thanks to Cristian Bonetto, who coauthored the *Sweden* guidebook with me; all the Scandinavian Europe coauthors; Lonely Planet commissioning editors Emma Gilmour, Fiona Buchan and Jo Potts; my frequent coexplorers Joel and Christina Ohlsen and Karl, Natalie and Clara Ohlsen; my would-be coexplorer RSE; Mormor Elisabeth Odeen, Moster Kristina Björholm and Captain Joe 'The Singing Sailor' Eriksson; Matt and Lindy in Tärnaby; Jannike Åhlund in Fårö; the awesome librarians in Rättvik; the commander of the paintball war in Härnösand who rescued us from certain discomfort; the bartender in Gävle who let me watch the MotoGP race on TV; and the cyclist who shared his breakfast at Björkvatten youth hostel.

FRAN PARNELL

Huge thanks to everyone who helped during the research and writing of the Iceland chapter: all the tourist-office staff; other travellers who shared their tips and comments; Ella, Julia and Guðni for great kindness; and Jón Trausti Sigurðarson at Grapevine for Reykjavík gossip. Thank you too to coordinating author Tom Masters for chilled-outness in the face of deadline stupidity, and to the Lonely Planet in-house crew: Mark Griffiths, Fee Buchan and Jo Potts for being such lovely people to work with.

LEIF PETTERSEN

Thanks goes to Gruia Badescu and Cristiana Groza who helped me find the oft-well-hid beauty in Bucharest. In Chişinău, Marina Waters and Vitale Eremia for follow-up fact checking. Monica Zavoianu for her Bucovina monastery expertise. Daniela and Florentina at the Info Litoral Tourist Information Centre in Mamaia for saving me hours of pavement pounding. Sebastian Muntean in Sibiu. In London, I'm indebted again to Will 'Power' Gourlay whose poised direction and advice are like an email valium every time.

BRANDON PRESSER

Paldies to Aleks Karlsons and Ellie Schilling, Ojars and Irma Kalnins, Inese Loce – you were lifesavers (literally!), Vaira Vīķe-Freiberga, Aleks Čakste, Jānis Jenzis, Māra Bergmane, Karlis Celms, Jānis Rutka, Richards Baerug and Richard Kalnins. A big thank you to all of my wonderful coauthors, especially Carolyn Bain and Neal Bedford, and thanks to the ab fab Lonely Planet production staff. Finally, I'd like to dedicate my chapter to Christine Otal who was there when it all began.

ROBERT REID

Thanks to the many countless Bulgarians who stopped to assist me along the way, particularly Assen and Ira in Sofia. I also appreciate Lonely Planet's Will Gourlay for sending me back to Bulgaria.

TIM RICHARDS

As always, I'm indebted to the professional staff of Poland's tourist offices, and the helpful staff at the Australian Embassy in Warsaw. I also give thanks to the national train company PKP. Much love to my Polish friends – particularly Ewa, Magda, Gosia and Andrzej – for your thoughts on Poland's history (and also for those tip-offs on local musicians). And a final thanks to all the waitresses who were amused by my dodgy Polish – there's plenty more where that came from!

SIMON RICHMOND

It's always a pleasure returning to St Petersburg and catching up with old friends such as Peter, Sasha and Andrey. Cheers also to Matt Brown, Jennifer Fell, Ilya Gurevich, Dr Dimitri Ozerkov, Andrei Dmitriev, Vyacheslav Bochkov, Valery Katsuba, Sergei Politovsky, marathon train traveller Ed Greig, Chris Hamilton, and Paul and Veronica at Express to Russia for assistance with my visa. In Kaliningrad my gratitude goes to Elmira Khaimourzina, Marina Drutman, Ksenia Prasolava and Irina Yegorava.

MILES RODDIS

As always, a packful of thanks to Ingrid, who shared the summer walks and, when the snow lay thick, regaled me daily with tales of her skiing exploits as I explored the inner recesses of Andorra's hotels and restaurant kitchens. Thanks too to tourist-office staff throughout the principality, especially those friendly folk in the Canillo branch.

DAMIEN SIMONIS

In Barcelona, countless folks keep me on my toes and make rediscovering the city as fun as it is challenging (they know who they are!). In Cantabria and Asturias, *gracias a* Ricardo, Begoña, Esperanza and Juan for a memorable last night of cider and *baile vaquiero*. In Mallorca, special thanks go to Roberto Fortea, Verónica García, Carlos García, Felipe Amorós, Miquel Àngel Part, Antonio Bauzá, Alessandra Natale, Verónica Carretero. In Ibiza, *mille mercis* to the multicultural Daraspe family.

JOHN SPELMAN

Thanks to Alv Gustavsen, Anja Lyngsmark and Therese Rustad for ceaseless hospitality and excellent guidance; to Solveig and Christian; to the depravity of M Gibson; to Jannicke Risjord, her friends and their observations; to Stig Arne Somby; to Black Metal specialist Megan Knight; and to Ariel Acosta's friendship and generosity. Thanks also to my comrades at Lonely Planet – Clifton Wilkinson, Tom Masters, Becky Ohlsen and Mark Griffiths – you make my life more interesting and my manuscripts less humiliating.

REGIS ST LOUIS

Thanks to all the helpful locals and travellers who helped along the way. *Muito obrigado* to my fellow *Portugal* guide colleagues, whose fine research contributed immeasurably to this title. Thanks to all the Lonely Planet staff whose hard work made this book shine. *Beijos* to Cassandra and Magdalena, who joined me in the journey across the north.

ANDREW STONE

I'm grateful to the many experts who spared their time and their expertise on Denmark's cultural quirks, environmental issues and everyday tips and fact checking. They include Erik Rimmer, Mads Flarup Christensen and Birgitta Capetillo. Thanks also to Linda Lerdorff, Anne Marie Barsøe and everyone at the Danish Tourist board for all their help with my many questions. Once more I owe Denmark expert Michael Booth and Lissen, his wonderful wife, a great debt for all their help and hospitality on this trip and all the others before it.

ANDY SYMINGTON

Many thanks to George Dunford for research on this project and to Jo Potts, Fiona Buchan and Ella O'Donnell for running it from the Lonely Planet end. Particular thanks for proofreading and Finnish support go to Riika Åkerlind, and to my family for their encouragement. I am indebted to numerous helpful people that I met along the way, particularly in tourist offices, and owe thanks to many Finnish friends for kindnesses and hospitality.

RYAN VER BERKMOES

If all politics is local, so is guidebook research. Harry Berg made me feel like a local in Den Haag. Sandra Bos and Dolf Pauw saved my bacon in Rotterdam, even though they'd just been sacked. Meanwhile in Germany, Angela Cullen was a dear as always and I'm happy to see she still prefers Harry over a chihuahua. It was good to get back on track with Alan Wissenburg. Thanks to Birgit Borowski and Dr Eva Missler, who showed me the highs and the very few lows of Stuttgart. Kudos to the various Munich folk who made me wish for 24-hour opening times. Thanks to Barbara Delissen who ensured these very words appeared and to Erin and Annah who always give me a home.

NICOLA WILLIAMS

Several friends recommended places to eat, not least my efficient army of Geneva-savvy volunteers:

SEND US YOUR FEEDBACK

We love to hear from travellers – your comments keep us on our toes and help make our books better. Our well-travelled team reads every word on what you loved or loathed about this book. Although we cannot reply individually to postal submissions, we always guarantee that your feedback goes straight to the appropriate authors, in time for the next edition. Each person who sends us information is thanked in the next edition – and the most useful submissions are rewarded with a free book.

To send us your updates – and find out about Lonely Planet events, newsletters and travel news – visit our award-winning website: **www.lonelyplanet.com/feedback.**

Note: we may edit, reproduce and incorporate your comments in Lonely Planet products such as guidebooks, websites and digital products, so let us know if you don't want your comments reproduced or your name acknowledged. For a copy of our privacy policy visit www.lonelyplanet.com/privacy.

Carine Benetti, Lena Hagelstein, Sophie Lux, Stéphanie Nassenstein, Juraj Ondrejkovic, Tessema Tesfachew and party gal Ciara Browne. Appreciation in equal measure to man-around-town Alan Turner and to Sarah Garner for putting me in touch; to temporary New Yorker Claudia Rosiny for Bern talk; Elizabeth and Nicolas at Ferme Montavon for Jurassic farm pleasures; Nana/Omi for domestic reinforcement; and Niko, Mischa and Matthias for always travelling so happily. Last but far from least, sincere thanks to Damien Simonis and Kerry Walker whose inspired Switzerland text formed the bulk of the Switzerland and Liechtenstein chapters.

NEIL WILSON

Thanks to the friendly and helpful tourist-office staff all over Ireland, to black cab tour guide Ken Harper, to the Bogside Artists, and to all those folk in pubs and on the road who offered advice and recommendations.

OUR READERS

Many thanks to the travellers who used the last edition and wrote to us with helpful hints, useful advice and interesting anecdotes:

A Gillian Abbott, Sharlene Abela, Halley Aelion, Bahman Ahmadbehbahani, Debbie Amos, Sine Arildskov **B** Richard Bergen, Gillian Billington, Iain Bisset, Angela Bolivar, Dana Boyd, Kris Brackx, Nate Budziszewski **C** Joao Caixeta, Steven Carrasco, Jocelyn Chan, Anna Chetwynd, Lozanka Cilindrova, Hamish Clark, Gordon Clouser, Angela Coleman, Vincent Cordero **D** Assen Davidov, Michael de Wildt, Faruk Demirciolu, Johan Deprez, Kristen Doyle **E** Michelle Earle, Suzanne Eddy, Renee Egyed, Harald Enoksson **F** Santiago Fajardo, Anna Ficek, Dennis Fischer, Amanda Fox, Jamie Fraser, Stef Fulford **G** Ben Gammans, Janet Glensor, Kevin Gordon, Gregory Green, Rick Green, Mario Guajardo, Marcos Guerra Lopes, Michael Guo, Richard Gustatus **H** Siri Haavimb, Ken Haley, Stuart Harper, Blaise Harvey, Joe Harwood, Lizzy Henry, Carlos Hernandez, Christine Hetley, Rebecca Horgan, Lauren Houpapa, Max Humphries, Martin Hunt **J** Linus Jonsson, Petra Josticova **K** Nikki Kirk, Arda Kocaman **L** Adele Lafrance, John Latham, Gloria Lee, Mariel Lødum, Heidi Lyss **M** Philip Mancini, Kieran Marks, Anna Mashman, Ninh McInnis, Lachlan McInnis, Kerryn McMahon, John Mitchinson, Chris Morey, Sophie Moussi **N** Michaela Newell **O** Tara O'Donvoan, James O'Neill **P** Trent Paton, Louisa Pennell, Binesh Perera, Mark Pettitt, Francesca Picon, Vivvi Pierce, John Pot, Warren Prestidge, Shrikant Pusalkar **Q** Lige Qiu **R** Nicole Ramsay, Kelly Reaston, Joe Reeder, Maurits Rehm, Agnes Reich, Raphael Richards, Rhiannon Riches, Katie Robinson, Ivor Roth **S** Paul Sayce, Gianrico Scarpa, Brian Scully, Paul Seaver, Siu Lam Seen, Stephen Shaw, Nolan Shulak, Alexander Smith, Barney Smith, Rachel Smith, Breeann St Onge, Astrid & Harry Stark, Daniel Stevens, Andrew Strudwick, Jackie Sweetman **T** Chelsea Toomey, Fernanda Torre **V** Jenny van Dertled, Paula Vandalen, Esther Veen, Meg Viezbicke, Kelly Vogel **W** Alex Walker, Kimberly Ward, Jesse Weil, Ralph Weinmann, Robert Wenzel, Simon Wilhelmsen, Amy Wooding, Brendan Woods **Z** Henry Zados

ACKNOWLEDGMENTS

Many thanks to the following for the use of their content:

Globe on title page ©Mountain High Maps 1993 Digital Wisdom, Inc.

Index

A

Å 886
Aachen 500-2
Aalborg 324-5
Abri du Cap Blanc 422
absinthe 469, 1149, 1157
accommodation 1214-16, *see also individual countries & cities*
  free accommodation 1216
Acropolis 526-7
activities 1217-18
Aegean Coast 1187-92
Aegean Islands 553-5
Aegina 539
Aeolian Islands 702-3
Agrigento 705
Aiguille du Midi 419
Aínsa 1106
air travel
  airfares 1232
  to/from Europe 1232-5
  within Europe 1235-6
airlines 1235-6
Aix-en-Provence 431
Ajaccio 440-1
Akamas Peninsula 279
Akdamar Island 1200
Akragas 705
Akrotiri 545
Aksaray 1199
Åland 361-2
Albania 50-61, **51**
  accommodation 60
  business hours 60
  culture 53
  embassies & consulates 60
  environment 53
  history 52-3
  language 50, 1251-2
  money 50, 61
  travel to/from 53-4
  travel within 54
  visas 50, 61
Alcázar 1065
Alcobaça 942
Ålesund 882-3

000 Map pages
000 Photograph pages

Algarve 937-9
Algeciras 1100
Alghero 707-8
Alhambra 1095
Alicante 1087-8
Alicudi 702-3
Aliki 542
Alkmaar 848
Almería 1098
Alonnisos 556
Alps 43, 1231, 8
  Austria 96, 100
  Bavaria 482-3
  France 419-20, 8
  Julian Alps 1037-40
Alsace 404-8
Altinkum 281
Amalfi Coast 697-8
Ambleside 204
Amboise 412-13
Amsterdam 46, 48, 841-7, **842**, 20
Åndalsnes 882
Andalucia 1088-102, 8
Andermatt 44
Andersen, Hans Christian 320
Andorra 62-70, **63**
  accommodation 69
  business hours 70
  culture 64
  embassies & consulates 70
  festivals & events 70
  history 64
  language 62
  money 62
  travel to/from 64
  travel within 64
  visas 62
Andorra la Vella 64-6, **66-7**
Aneto 1106
Angel of the North 208
animals 43-4
Ankara 1196-7, **1197**
Antalya 1195-6
Antwerp 120-3, **122**
Apollonia 58
Aragón 1105-6
Aran Islands 618-19
archaeological sites & ruins
  Albania 58, 59
  Britain 222
  Bulgaria 239
  Croatia 260, 262
  Cyprus 277, 279, 281
  France 425-6
  Greece 526-7, 539, 545, 5
  Ireland 609, 618-19
  Italy 637-41, 654, 663, 695, 699, 703, 704, 705, 706
  Latvia 729
  Malta 782
  Montenegro 802
  Morocco 822, 827, 830
  Poland 917
  Portugal 937, 938, 941, 943
  Spain 1065, 1080, 1092-3, 1104, 1111
  Turkey 1188, 1189, 1191, 1193, 1194, 1195, 1196
architecture, contemporary 24
  Arkitekturmuseet 1125
  Cogels-Osylei 121
  Croatian National Theatre 263
  Mediahafen 499-500
  Museo Guggenheim 1108
  Nederlands Architectuur Instituut 851
  Vila Tugendhat 302
Arctic Circle marker 366
Arctic fox 583
Areopoli 534
Århus 321-4, **322**
Arinsal 69
Arromanches 402
art 38-9
art nouveau
  Ålesund 882-3
  Brussels 118
  Košice 1023
  Rīga 724
  Sinaia 964
  Subotica 1008
Artà 1082
arts 38-41, *see also individual countries*
Assisi 689-90
Assmannshausen 492
Asturias 1110-12
Atatürk 1175, 1187, 1196
Athens 524-31, **525**, **526**
Atlantic Coast 421-5
ATMs 1225-6

Augsburg 478
Aurland 877
Auschwitz 905
Austria 71-102, **73**
accommodation 101
arts 72-4
business hours 101
culture 72
embassies & consulates 101-2
environment 74
festivals & events 80, 88, 93, 102
history 72
language 71, 102
money 71, 102
travel to/from 74-5
travel within 75-6
visas 71, 102
Autostadt 503
Avakas Gorge 279
Avebury 186
Avignon 431-4, **433**
Ávila 1062-3
Aya Sofya 1182, **9**
Azay-le-Rideau 411

B

B&Bs 1215
Bach, Johann Sebastian 468
Bacharach 492
Baden-Württemberg 483-90
Bahía de Santander 1110
Balchik 246
Balearic Islands 1080-6
Balestrand 881-2
Ballaghbeama Pass 615
Bamberg 479-80
Banat 971-2
Bar 802-3
Barcelona 1069-79, **1072-3**
accommodation 1076-7
attractions 1070-6
clubbing 1078
drinking 1078
entertainment 1078-9
food 1077
shopping 1079
travel to/from 1079
travel within 1070, 1079
Barcelos 950
Bardejov's 1024
Bardejovské Kúpele 1024
bargaining 1227
Bari 699
Basel 1171-2
Basque Country 1106-9
Bastenaken 131-2
Bastia 442-3
Bastille Day 48
Bastogne 131-2
Batalh 942
Bath 187-9, **188**
baths, *see* hamams
Battle of the Bulge 131-2, 759
Bavaria 472-82
Bavarian Alps 482-516
Bayeux 400-1
Bayeux Tapestry 400-1
beaches
Albania 59
Bulgaria 243, 246, 247
Croatia 260, 264, 266-8, **10**
Cyprus 279, 281
Denmark 325
Estonia 336, 342
France 404, 423, 444
Germany 510
Greece 540, 542, 545, 551, 552, 555
Hungary 575
Italy 702, 703, 706
itineraries 33
Macedonia 768
Malta 778-9, 783
Montenegro 802, 803
Netherlands 849, 856
Norway 869
Portugal 936, 937, 938, 942, 949
Russia 995
Spain 1080, 1083, 1085, 1086, 1087, 1098, 1099, 1101, 1106, 1110
Sweden 1137
Turkey 1192, 1193, 1194, 1195
Beatles 202
Beaune 414-15
Beddgelert 214
beer
Belgium 133
breweries 299, 477, 505, 605, 886, 887
Czech Republic 298, 299
festivals 47
Germany 477, 496, 514-15
museums 118, 298-9
beer gardens 477
beer halls 477
Beethoven, Ludwig van 39, 499
Belá Tatras 1022
Belarus 103-11, **104**
accommodation 110
business hours 110
culture 105
embassies & consulates 110
environment 105
festivals & events 110-11
history 104
language 103
money 103, 111
travel to/from 105
travel within 105
visas 103, 111
Belfast 620-5, **622**
Belgium 112-33, **113**, **23**
accommodation 132
arts 114
business hours 132
culture 114
embassies & consulates 132
environment 114-15
festivals & events 132-3
history 113-14
language 112, 114, 133
money 112, 133
travel to/from 115-16
travel within 116
visas 112, 133
Belgrade 1001-7, **1003**, **11**
Ben Nevis 223
Benasque 1106
Bendery 794
Berat 59
Berbers 832
Berchtesgaden 482-3
Bergama 1188-9
Bergen 877-81, **878**
Berlin 47, 452-63, **457**, **460**
accommodation 458-9
attractions 453-8
clubbing 462
drinking 461-2
entertainment 462-3
food 459-61
travel to/from 463
travel within 456, 463
Berlin Wall 457
Bern 1159-61, **1160**
Berner Oberland 1167-71
Betws-y-Coe 214
Biarritz 423-4
bicycle travel, *see* cycling
Bilbao 1108-9
birds 583
birdwatching
Britain 213
Ireland 627
Lithuania 750
Birkenau 905

Bitola 770-1
Black Forest 486-8
Black Madonna 906
Black Sea 243-7
Blaenau Ffestiniog 214
Blarney 613-14
Bled 1037-9, **1038**
Blenheim Palace 196
Blois 408-9
Bloody Sunday 625
Blue Lagoon 591, 782
Blue Mosque 1182
boat travel 1234-5, 1237-8
boat trips
 Austria 86-7, 93
 Britain 213
 Denmark 315
 Finland 359
 France 387
 Germany 466, 489, 497, 506
 Greece 555
 Hungary 575
 Netherlands 847, 851
 Norway 875
 Portugal 949
 Sweden 1144
 Turkey 1183, 1192, 1193, 1194, 1201
boating 1125
bobsledding 729
Boca do Inferno 936
Bodensee 489-90
Bodø 885
Bodrum 1191-2
bogwalking 343
Bohemia 297-301
Bohinj 1039-40
Bohinjska Bistrica 1039
Bologna 674-6
Bom Jesus do Monte 950
bombings 1221
Bonaparte, Napoléon 37, 440, 442
Bonifacio 441-2
Bonn 499
books 1218, *see also* literature
Boppard 492
Bordeaux 421-3
border crossings 1239
 Albania 54
 Austria 74
 Bulgaria 232
 Croatia 254
 Cyprus 280
 Kosovo 714
 Macedonia 763
 Moldova 788, 795
 Montenegro 799
 Poland 894
 Russia 978
 Serbia 1000
 Transdniestr 795
Borgå 358
Bornholm 319
Bosa 708
Bosnia & Hercegovina 134-48, **135**
 accommodation 147
 business hours 147
 culture 136
 embassies & consulates 147
 environment 136
 festivals & events 139
 history 135-6
 language 134
 money 134,148
 travel to/from 136-7
 travel within 137
 visas 134, 148
Bosphorus 1183
Bovec 1040
Bowness 204
Bøyabreen 882
Boyana 236
B-Parade 47, 458, 514
Braemar 49
Braga 949-50
Bran 967
Brandenburg Gate 453
Braşov 964-7, **966**
Bratislava 1015-19
Brecon 211-13
Brecon Beacons National Park 211
Bremen 504-5
Brest 109-10
Brest Fortress 109-10
Brighton 181-3, **182**
Brighton Pier 183
Bristol 189-90
Britain 42, 149-228, **151**
 accommodation 225-6
 arts 153-4
 business hours 226
 culture 153
 embassies & consulates 227
 environment 154
 festivals & events 48, 49, 169-70, 216, 227, 9
 history 150-3
 language 149
 money 149, 227-8
 travel to/from 154-6
 travel within 156-9
 visas 149, 228
British Museum 166
Brittany 402-4
Brno 302-3
Brocken's summit 504
Brú na Bóinne 609
Bruges 126-8, **127**
Brussels 116-20, **117**
Buçaco Forest 943-4
Bucegi Mountains 964
Bucharest 957-63
Buchenwald 471
Buckingham Palace 167
Bucovina 972
Budapest 564-73, **566**, **570**
 accommodation 568-9
 attractions 565-8
 clubbing 571-2
 drinking 571-2
 entertainment 572
 food 569-71
 travel to/from 572-3
 travel within 567, 573
budgets 27, 28, 29, 30
Budva 802
Bulgaria 229-48, **230-48**
 accommodation 247
 arts 231
 culture 231
 embassies & consulates 248
 environment 231
 festivals & events 243, 248
 history 231
 language 229, 232, 236, 248, 1252-3
 money 229, 248
 religion 231
 travel to/from 231-2
 travel within 232-3
 visas 229, 248
bullfighting
 France 426
 Portugal 934, 952
 Spain 1048, 1057, 1061, 1089, 1091
Bundoran 620
bungee jumping 1217
 Latvia 728, 729
 Switzerland 1168, 1172
bunkers 53

000 Map pages
000 Photograph pages

Buñol 48
Burano 670
Burgas 246-7
Burgos 1066-7
Burgundy 413-19
Burren 615-16
bus travel 1238
business hours 1218, *see also individual countries*
Butrint 59
Butterfly Valley 1193
Bygdøy 869

C

Cabo da Roca 936
Cabo de Gata 1098
Cabo de São Vicente 939
Cabril 950
Cáceres 1103-4
Cádiz 1100-1
Caen 402
Cagliari 706-7
Cahirciveen 615
Calais 398-9
Cambridge 198-200, **199**
Camp Nou 1079
campervans 1239
camping 1215
Çanakkale 1188
canal boats 126, 315, 847, 851
Canazei 677
Canillo 66-8
cannabis 834, 838-9, 846, 1114, 1224
Cannes 438-9
canoeing
  Czech Republic 300, 304
  Denmark 327
  Finland 364, 367, 368
  France 444
  Germany 506
  Greece 543
  Hungary 579
  Ireland 627
  Netherlands 848
  Poland 918
  Portugal 937, 939, 943, 951
  Slovenia 1039
  Sweden 1125
  Switzerland 1152
Cantabria 1110-12
Canterbury 179-80
Canterbury Cathedral 180
canyoning 1217
  Bosnia & Hercegovina 143, 144
  Portugal 935
  Slovenia 1043
  Switzerland 1168, 1172
Cape Kolka 727-8
Cappadocia 1198-200
Capri 696
car travel 1238-42
Carcassonne 425
Cardiff 209-11
carnival 46
  Venice Carnevale 24, **5**, **24**
Carpathian Mountains 908-9
Carrick-a-Rede Island 625
Carrowmore 619
Casablanca 816-19, **817**
Cascais 936
Castelo de Vide 941
Castilla y León 1062-7
Castilla-La Mancha 1067-9
Castle Howard 207
Catalonia 1069-80
Causeway Coast 625
caves, *see also* ice caves, sea caves
  Belgium 131
  Britain 198
  France 422, 424
  Greece 534, 552
  Italy 698
  Latvia 729
  Macedonia 768
  Moldova 793
  Netherlands 857
  Slovenia 1040
  Spain 1102
  Ukraine 1207
caving 198, 765, 768
cell phones 1229
cemeteries
  American Military Cemetery 402
  Bayeux war cemetery 401
  catacombes 381-4
  Cimetière du Père Lachaise 386
  Heroes' Cemetery 794
  Jardin des Enfeus 421
  Jewish Cemetery (Fez) 822
  Jewish Cemetery (Warsaw) 898
  Lychakiv Cemetery 1211
  megalithic cemetery 619
  Mirogoj graveyard 258
  Old Jewish Cemetery 292
  Tyne Cot Cemetery 129
  US Military Cemetery 755-7
  Vienna 80
Cerveteri 655
Cēsis 728
České Budějovice 299-300
Český Krumlov 300-1
Cetinje 803
Ceuta 814-15
Cézanne, Paul 431
Chamonix 419-20
Chartres 396-7
Château de Bourscheid 759
Château de Chambord 409
Château de Chaumont 409-10
Château de Chenonceau 411
Château de Cheverny 409
Château de Langeais 411
chateaux tours 410
Checkpoint Charlie 457
Chefchaouen 815-16
Chimaera 1195
Chipping Campden 196-7
Chişinău 788-92, **790**
chocolate
  museums 126, 496-7, 1162
  shops 118, 302, 412, 847, 1060
Chopin, Fryderyk 898
Chornobyl 1207
christmas markets 514
Churchill, Winston 196
Cinque Terre 657-8
Ciutadella 1085
Clervaux 758-9
Cliffs of Moher 616
climate 25, 38, 1218-20
clothes 28-9
Cluj-Napoca 969-71
coasteering 213, 226
Cochem 490
Coimbra 942-3
Cojuşna 793
Cold War 38
Cologne 496-9, **497**
Colosseum 637-41
Columbus, Christopher 655, 1071, 1100
Comino 782
concentration camps
  Auschwitz 905
  Birkenau 905
  Buchenwald 471
  Dachau 475
  Majdanek 906
  Paneriai 747
  Płaszów 902
  Sachsenhausen 464-5
Conimbriga 943
Constance 489-90
consulates 1222
Copenhagen 311-18, **312**

Copernicus 917
Córdoba 1092-4, **1093**
Corfu 556-7
Corinth 532-3
Cork 610-13, **612-13**
Corniglia 657-8
Corsica 440-3
Costa Blanca 1086
Costa de Almería 1098
costs 25, *see also* budgets, free stuff
Côte d'Azur 434-9
Cotswolds 196-7
courses 688
  diving 1194
  language 236, 970, 1228
  surfing 1218
Crete 546-9, **548-9**
credit cards 1226
Cricova 792-3
Crişana 971-2
Croatia 249-71, **250-1**
  accommodation 269-70
  arts 252
  business hours 270
  culture 252
  embassies & consulates 270
  environment 253
  festivals & events 260, 268, 270
  history 252
  language 249, 1253-4
  money 249, 271
  travel to/from 253
  travel within 253-4
  visas 249, 271
Cuenca 1069
culture 28-30, 38-41, *see also individual countries*
Curie, Marie 897
Curium 277
Curonian Spit 749-50
customs regulations 1220
Cyclades 540-6, **5**
cycling 43, 1217, 1236-7
  Albania 60
  Andorra 69
  Austria 91
  Belgium 131, 132
  Britain 213, 226
  Bulgaria 242, 247
  Cyprus 281
  Czech Republic 301, 304
  Denmark 327
  Estonia 337, 339, 343
  France 386, 444
  Germany 475, 489, 491, 513
  Hungary 579
  Italy 657, 709
  Liechtenstein 735
  Lithuania 750
  Netherlands 858
  Norway 881
  Poland 908, 918, 919
  Portugal 937, 938, 939, 949, 950, 951
  Romania 964, 973
  Slovakia 1025
  Slovenia 1039, 1043
  Spain 1112-13
  Sweden 1125, 1134
  Switzerland 1152
Cyprus 272-82, **273**
  accommodation 281
  arts 274
  business hours 281
  culture 274
  embassies & consulates 281
  environment 274
  festivals & events 281
  history 274
  language 272, 282
  money 272, 282
  travel to/from 274-5
  travel within 275
  visas 272, 282
Cyrillic alphabet 1280
Czech Republic 283-305, **285**
  accommodation 303-4
  arts 284
  business hours 304
  culture 284
  embassies & consulates 304
  environment 284
  festivals & events 46, 293, 304
  history 284
  language 283, 1255-6
  money 283, 305
  travel to/from 284-6
  travel within 286
  visas 283, 305
Częstochowa 906

D

Dachau 475
Dalí, Salvador 1079-80
Dalí Espace Montmartre 386, **6**
Dalmatia 261-9
Dalyan 1193
dance parades
  Berlin 47, 458, 514
  Zürich 48, 1166
  Rotterdam 859
Danube River 44
Danube Valley 86-8
d'Arc, Jeanne 399
Dartmoor National Park 191-2
Darwin, Charles 41
Datça 1192
David 681
D-Day 401, 402
debit cards 1226
Deià 1082-3
Delfshaven 852
Delft 850-1
Delos 540
Delta Project 848
Den Haag 849-50
Denmark 306-28, **308**
  accommodation 326-7
  arts 309
  business hours 327
  culture 307
  embassies & consulates 327
  environment 309
  festivals & events 315, 327
  history 307
  language 306, 1256-7
  money 306, 328
  travel to/from 309-10
  travel within 310-11
  visas 306, 328
Derinkuyu 1199
Derry 625-7
Descartes, René 39
Deventer 848
Devín Castle 1018
Dhërmi 59
Didyma 1190
Diekirch 759
Dijon 413-14
Dinkelsbühl 478
Diocletian's Palace 262
disabilities, travellers with 1229
discount cards 1221-2
  Bulgaria 248
  Croatia 255, 262
  Estonia 333
  Finland 351
  France 380
  Germany 453, 456, 472, 496, 506, 513
  Greece 524

000 Map pages
000 Photograph pages

Hungary 565
Iceland 584
Ireland 599, 600
Italy 664, 665-6, 673, 691
Latvia 721
Luxembourg 760
Netherlands 841, 851, 858
Norway 866
Portugal 925
Slovakia 1015
Sweden 1123
Switzerland 1153
discrimination 1222
Dodecanese 550-2
dogsledding 45, 364, 368, 886
Dolomites 676-7
dolphins 223, 556
dolphin-watching 593, 937, 1101, 1102
Dom (Cologne) 496
Dordogne 420-1
Douro River 948-9
Dover 180-1
Drâa Valley 833
Dracula 967, 968
Dragalevtsi 236
Dresden 465-7
drinks 41-2, *see also* absinthe, beer, wine
Belgium 133
Bosnia & Hercegovina 147
Finland 369
Germany 514-15
Hungary 580
Iceland 591
Italy 710
Montenegro 805
Serbia 1010
Slovenia 1044
Switzerland 1157
driving licence 1222
druggings 1220
drugs 1224, *see also* medication
cannabis 834, 838-9, 846, 1114, 1224
Denmark 328
LSD 1149
Morocco 834
Netherlands 838-9, 846, 859
Norway 889
Spain 1114
Drvengrad 1009
Drymades beach 59
Dublin 599-609, **602**
accommodation 605-6
attractions 601
clubbing 607-8
drinking 607-8
entertainment 608
food 606-7
travel to/from 608
travel within 609
Dubrovnik 266-9, **267, 268**
Duinen van Texel National Park 856
Dún Aengus 618
Dún Chonchúir 619
Dún Dúchathair 618
Dún Eochla 618
Duomo (Florence) 680
Duomo (Milan) 659-60
Dürer, Albrecht 481
Durham 207
Durmitor National Park 804-5
Durrës 58
Düsseldorf 499-500
DVDs 1228

E

Eagle's Nest 483
Easter 46
Echternach 759
Eckerö 362
ecotourism 556, *see also* sustainable travel
Eden Project 193
Edinburgh 45, 48, 214-18, **12**
Edinburgh Fringe Festival 48, 216, **9**
Eger 578-9
Eiffel Tower 380-1
Einstein, Albert 41, 1149, 1159
Eisenach 470
electricity 1222
Elsinore 318
embassies & consulates 1222, *see also individual countries*
emergencies 1228
England 159-209, **160**
Enlightenment 39
environment 43-4, 634, *see also individual countries*
sustainable travel 25-7, 864, 1152
environmental issues 44, 1234
Erfurt 469-70
Ermida 950
Escadaria do Bom Jesus 950
Essaouira 820-1
Estany de les Truites 69
Esterházy Palace 574
Estonia 329-44, **330**
accommodation 343
arts 331
culture 331
embassies & consulates 343
environment 331
festivals & events 47, 337, 343
history 331
language 329, 1258-9
money 329, 343-4
travel to/from 331-2
travel within 332
visas 329, 344
Estoril 936
Esztergom 574
etiquette 28, 810
Eton 179
EU 36-7
Eurotunnel 1238-9
Eurovision Song Contest 40
events, *see* festivals & events
Évora 940-1, **940**
exchanging money 1226-7
Exit Festival 47, 1008
Exmoor National Park 191

F

fado 928, 933
Falera 1163
Famagusta 280-1
farm stays 1215-16
Faro 937-8
FC Barcelona 1079
Feldberg 488
Ferrara 673-4
Festival d'Avignon 432
festivals & events 24, 45-9, 1222, *see also individual countries*, film festivals, music festivals
carnival 46, **5, 24**
Edinburgh Fringe Festival 48, 216, **9**
Exit Festival 47, 1008
Guy Fawkes Night 49
Il Palio 47
Khamoro Festival 46
La Tomatina 48
Las Fallas 24, 45, 1087
Notting Hill Carnival 48
Oktoberfest 24, 48, 475, 514
Õllesummer 47
Running of the Bulls 24, 47, 1109
Sanfermines 24, 47, 1109
St Patrick's Day 24, 45
Venice Carnevale 24, **5, 24**
Walpurgisnacht 46
Fethiye 1193-4
Fez 46, 821-6, **823, 825**

Figueres 1079-80
Filicudi 702-3
film festivals
  Amsterdam Fantastic Film Festival 858
  Black Nights Film Festival 337
  Cannes film festival 438
  Dublin International Film Festival 628
  Fantasporto 945
  International Astra Film Festival 969
  International Film Festival (Locarno) 1162
  International Film Festival – OSFAF 765
  International Film Festival Berlin 458
  Karlovy Vary International Film Festival 297, 304
  Krakow International Film Festival 902
  Pula Film Festival 260
  Sarajevo Film Festival 139
  Venice International Film Festival 671
  Warsaw Film Festival 898
films 29
Filoti 543
Finland 345-69, **347**
  accommodation 367
  arts 346-8
  business hours 368
  culture 346
  embassies & consulates 368
  environment 348
  festivals & events 354, 363, 368
  history 346
  language 345, 1259-60
  money 345, 369
  travel to/from 348-9
  travel within 349-50
  visas 345, 369
Finnhamn 1134
Finse 877
Fira 545
Fishguard 213
fishing
  Britain 213
  Czech Republic 301
  Hungary 574
  Ireland 619, 627
  Lithuania 748
  Norway 883, 885, 886, 888
  Poland 918
  Slovenia 1043
Fjærland 882
fjords 877-83, 885
Flåm 881
Flanders 120-9, **23**
Flatbreehytta 882
Flims-Laax 1163
Florence 677-84, **679**
flying fox 1171
Foča 147
food 41-2, *see also* chocolate
  Belgium 133
  Bosnia & Hercegovina 147
  Britain 42
  Finland 368-9
  France 42
  Germany 42, 502, 514
  Hungary 42, 580
  Iceland 591
  Italy 41-2, 710
  meals 29
  Montenegro 805
  Serbia 1009
  Slovenia 1044
  Spain 1107, **6**
football 43, **12**
  Britain 176, 201, 227
  Ireland 628
  Italy 633, 662
  Netherlands 846
  Portugal 934
  Slovakia 1013
  Spain 1048, 1061, 1079
  Sweden 1117
football stadiums
  Britain 176, 201
  Italy 662
  Netherlands 846
  Spain 1061, 1079
  Sweden 1143
Formentera 1084-5
Formula One 43, 440, 568, 633
Fornalutx 1082
Fornells 1085
Fort William 223-4
Fossa di Vulcano 702
France 42, 370-446, **371**, **8**
  accommodation 443-4
  arts 372-4
  business hours 444
  culture 372
  embassies & consulates 444-5
  environment 374
  festivals & events 426, 432, 445
  history 371-2
  language 370, 1260-1
  money 370, 446
  travel to/from 374-5
  travel within 375-6
  visas 370, 446
Frank, Anne 839, 843
Frankfurt-am-Main 492-6, **494**
Franz Josefs Höhe 100
Frederikshavn 325
free stuff 932
  accommodation 1216
  Albania 57
  Andorra 68
  Austria 84
  Britain 166
  Croatia 258
  Czech Republic 293
  Estonia 336
  France 385
  Germany 459, 475
  Greece 528
  Hungary 567
  Ireland 601
  Italy 634
  Latvia 725
  Luxembourg 755
  Macedonia 765
  Montenegro 800
  Norway 868
  Russia 980
  Slovakia 1019
  Spain 1054
  Sweden 1125
  Switzerland 1152, 1155
  Turkey 1177
Freiburg 488-90
French Alps 419-20, **8**
French Basque Country 421-5
Freudenstadt 487
Fribourg 1157
Friedrichshafen 489
Frösön 1144
Fruška Gora 1008
Funen 320
Fürstensteig 735
Füssen 482

G
Galicia 1110-12
Galilei, Galileo 41
Gallipoli 1187-8
Galway 616-18, **617**

000 Map pages
000 Photograph pages

Gap of Dunloe 614
Gateshead 208
Gaudí, Antoni 1071-5
Gauja National Park 728
gay & lesbian travellers 48, 554, 1222-3
  Albania 60
  Bosnia & Hercegovina 147
  Britain 177
  Bulgaria 248
  Czech Republic 304-5
  Denmark 328
  festivals 48, 458
  Germany 462, 515
  Greece 530, 540, 558
  Italy 710-11
  Netherlands 846, 859
  Norway 874
  Poland 920
  Slovenia 1044
  Spain 1060, 1078
  Sweden 1133
Gazimağusa 280-1
Gdańsk 913-16, **915**
Gefyra 534
Geilo 877
Gelemiş 1194
Gelibolu 1187-8
Geneva 1149, 1152-6, **1154**
Genoa 655-7
geography 43-4
geology 43, 546
Gerlachovský štít 1020
Germany 42, 447-516, **449**
  accommodation 512-13
  arts 450
  business hours 513
  culture 448-50
  embassies & consulates 513
  environment 450
  festivals & events 46, 458, 475, 514
  history 448
  language 447, 515, 1262-3
  money 447, 515
  travel to/from 450-1
  travel within 451-2
  visas 447, 516
Geysir 592
Ġgantija 782
Ghent 124-6, **125**, **23**
Giant's Causeway 625
Gibraltar 1102-3
Gimmelwald 1170
Girne 280
Girona 1079
Giverny 400
Gjirokastra 60
glaciers 43-4
  Gurschen Glacier 44
  Jostedalsbreen glacier 877, 882
  Marmolada glacier 677
  Mer de Glace 419
  Pasterze Glacier 100
  Stubai Glacier 98
  Switzerland 1169, 1171
glacier golf 1171
Glasgow 218-21, **220**
Glastonbury 191
Glastonbury Festival 22, 47, 191, 227
global warming 44
Goethe 471, 493
Golden Circle 592
golf 222, 1171
Goli Vrâh 236
gondolas 670-1
Göreme 1198-9
Gornergrat 1158
Goslar 504
Göteborg 1140-4, **1142**
Gotland 1135-6
Gouda 848
Gouveia 944
Gozo 781-2
Gračanica Monastery 716
Granada 1094-8, **1096**
Grandvalira 66
Grasmere 204
Grass, Günter 512
Graubünden 1163
Graz 88-91, **89**, **9**
Great Masurian Lakes 918-19
Great Plain 577-8
Greece 517-59, **520-1**, **5**
  accommodation 557
  arts 519
  business hours 558
  culture 518-19
  embassies & consulates 558
  environment 519
  festivals & events 528, 558
  history 518
  language 517, 1263-4
  money 517, 559
  religion 519
  travel to/from 519-22
  travel within 522-4
  visas 517, 559
  weather 518
Greek alphabet 1264
Greenwich 169
Grindelwald 1169
Groningen 855-6
Grossglockner 100
Grossglockner Hochalpenstrasse 100
Grotte de Font de Gaume 422
Grotte de Rouffignac 422
Grūto Parkas 748
Gryon 1158
Guarda 944
Gudhjem 319
guest houses 1214-15
Guimarães 950
Guinness Brewery 605
Gullfoss 592
Gura Humorului 972
Gurschen Glacier 44
Guy Fawkes Night 49
Gythio 534

H

Haarlem 848
Hadrian's Wall 209
Hafelekar peak 98
Hague, The 849-50
Hal Saflieni Hypogeum 779
Hall in Tirol 99
Hallstatt 95-6
hamams
  Cyprus 276, 277
  Greece 535
  Morocco 834
  Spain 1092
  Turkey 1186
Hamburg 506-11, **508-9**
Hamelin 503
hang-gliding 1168
Hania 548-9
Hanover 502-3
Han-sur-Lesse 131
Hardangerjøkulen 877
Hardangervidda 877
Harz Mountains 504
Hassan II Mosque 816
Hautes Fagnes Nature Reserve 130
health 1246-50
Heidelberg 485-6, **484**
Hellbrunn 95
Hellenic Wildlife Rehabilitation Centre 539
Helsingborg 1139-40
Helsingør 318
Helsinki 350-8, **352-3**
Hermitage 990, **11**
Hierapolis 1191

INDEX

High Atlas Mountains 832-3
High Tatras 1020-2, 4
Highland Games 49
hiking 1217, 8
  Andorra 67, 68, 69
  Austria 98, 101
  Belgium 131, 132
  Britain 209, 226
  Bulgaria 235, 241-2, 247
  Cyprus 278, 279, 281
  Czech Republic 301, 304
  Estonia 339
  Finland 368
  France 387, 419, 444
  Germany 492, 513
  Greece 549, 558
  Iceland 592
  Ireland 615, 627
  Italy 657, 709
  Liechtenstein 734-5
  Lithuania 750
  Luxembourg 759
  Macedonia 768, 771
  Morocco 832, 834
  Norway 869, 877, 879, 882, 886, 888
  Poland 908, 909, 918, 919
  Portugal 937, 944, 950
  Romania 964, 973-4
  Serbia 1009
  Slovakia 1020, 1021, 1022, 1025
  Slovenia 1038, 1043
  Spain 1113
  Sweden 1144, 1146
  Switzerland 1152, 1158, 1170, 1172
  Turkey 1193, 1201
Hill of Crosses 749
Hippocrates 551
Hirtshals 326
Hisarönü Peninsula 1192
history 37-8
hitching 1242
Hitler, Adolf 38, 448, 457, 481, 483, 918-19
hockey 43, 1013, 1018, 1117, 1143
Hofmann, Albert 1149
Hohe Tauern National Park 100
Hohenschwangau 482
Holocaust Memorial 453
horse riding
  Czech Republic 301
  Hungary 579

000 Map pages
000 Photograph pages

  Iceland 592
  Ireland 620, 627
  Lithuania 748
  Portugal 950
hostels 1216
hot-air ballooning 1199, 1201
hot springs, *see* springs
hotels 1215
Houses of Parliament 166
Hovedøya 869
Hrebienok 1021
Humor 972
Hungary 42, 560-80, **562**
  accommodation 579
  arts 561-3
  business hours 579
  culture 561
  embassies & consulates 580
  environment 563
  festivals & events 568, 580
  history 561
  language 560, 1264-6
  money 560, 580
  travel to/from 563-4
  travel within 564
  visas 560, 580
Hvar Island 263-4
Hydra 539

I

Ibiza 1083-4
ice caves 95, 96, 419
ice climbing 444, 1217
ice hockey 43, 1013, 1018, 1117, 1143
Ice Hotel 1145
Iceland 43, 581-93, **582**
  accommodation 592
  arts 583
  business hours 593
  culture 583
  embassies & consulates 593
  environment 583
  festivals & events 588, 593
  history 583
  language 581, 1266-7
  money 581, 584, 593
  travel to/from 583
  travel within 583-4
  visas 581, 593
ice-skating 49, 1125, 1169
Ieper 128-9
Igoumenitsa 538
Ihlara Valley 1199-200
Il Palio 47
Île Ste-Marguerite 439
Île St-Honorat 439
Îles de Lérins 439
Îles Lavezzi 441
Ilha de Tavira 938
Ilha Deserta 938
Inari 367
Inisheer 618-19
Inishmaan 618-19
Inishmór 618-19
in-line skating 1125, 1152
Innisfree 619
Innsbruck 96-9, **97**
insurance 1223, 1240, 1246
Interlaken 1168-9
internet access 1223
internet resources 1223
  air tickets 1232
  Andorra 70
  Bosnia & Hercegovina 148
  Bulgaria 248
  Croatia 271
  Cyprus 281-2
  Czech Republic 305
  Finland 369
  Greece 559
  health 1246-7
  Hungary 580
  Ireland 628
  Italy 711
  Latvia 730
  Lithuania 751
  Macedonia 771
  Malta 783
  Moldova 795
  Montenegro 805
  Morocco 835
  Norway 889
  Poland 920
  Slovakia 1025
  Sweden 1146
  Turkey 1202
Inverness 224-5
Ioannina 538
Ionian Islands 556-7
Ios 543-4, **544**
Iraklio 546-7
Ireland 594-629, **596**
  accommodation 627
  arts 597
  business hours 627-8
  culture 597
  embassies & consulates 628
  environment 597
  festivals & events 24, 45, 616, 628
  history 595-7

language 594
money 594, 628-9
religion 597
travel to/from 598-9
travel within 599
visas 594, 629
Isla de Santa Clara 1106
Islam 42
Isle of Mull 223
Isle of Skye 224
İstanbul 1179-87, **1180-1**, **1184**, **9**, **22**
Istria 260-1
Italy 630-711, **632**, **5**, **24**
accommodation 708-9
arts 633-4
business hours 709
culture 631
embassies & consulates 710
environment 634
festivals & events 24, 46, 47, 706, 710
history 631
language 630, 1267-8
money 630, 711
religion 633
travel to/from 634-5
travel within 635-6
visas 630, 711
itineraries 31-5
Ivan Kupalo 47
İzmir 1189

J
Jaanipäev 47
Jajce 143-4
Jasna Góra monastery 906
Javorovača 804
John O'Groats 225
Jomala 362
Jostedalsbreen 882
Joyce, James 607
Jukkasjärvi 1145
Julian Alps 1037-40
Jungfraujoch 1171
Jungfrau Region 1169-71
Juno Beach 402
Juodkrantė 750
Jura 1157
Jūrmala 727
Jutland 321-6

K
Kabelvåg 885-6
Kadifekale 1189
Kafka, Franz 289
Kahta 1200
Kaliakra Nature Reserve 246
Kaliningrad 992-5, **994**
Kant, Immanuel 39
Kantara 281
Karaite 747
Kardamyli 534
Karlovy Vary 297-8
Karlštejn 296
Karpas Peninsula 281
Kars 1201
Karst 1040-2
Kaş 1194
Käsmu 339
Kaunas 748-9
Kaunos 1192
kayaking
Albania 55
Bosnia & Hercegovina 144
Britain 198, 213
Estonia 343
Finland 368
France 429, 444
Italy 657
Netherlands 848
Portugal 938, 939, 951
Slovenia 1038, 1039
Sweden 1125
Switzerland 1168
Turkey 1194, 1201
Kayaköy 1193
Kaymaklı 1199
Kayseri 1200
Kazanlâk 240
Kecskemét 577-8
Kefallonia 557
Kemal, Mustafa 1175, 1187, 1196
Kerry Way 615
Keswick 204
Keszthely 575
Keukenhof Gardens 848
Khamoro Festival 46
kicksledding 343
Kilkenny 609-10
Killarney 614-15
Killarney National Park 614
Kinderdijk 853
Kiruna 1144-5
Kiskunság National Park 577
Kiten 247
kitesurfing 226, 327, 429, 558, 1101, 1113
Kitzbühel 99-100
Klagenfurt 91
Klaipėda 749
Klee, Paul 1160
Klein Matterhorn 1158
Knidos 1192
Knights Templar 942
Knivskjelodden 887
Knossos 547
Koblenz 490, 491-2
Köln 496-9
Kolossi Castle 278
Kolovesi 364
Konya 49, 1197-8
Koper 1041
Korčula Island 264-6
Kos 551-2
Košice 1023-4
Kosovo 36, 712-16, **713**
embassies & consulates 716
history 713
language 712
money 712, 716
travel to/from 713-14
travel within 714
visas 712, 716
Kotor 800-1, **801**
Kourion 277
Kraków 49, 901-5, **903**
Kravice Waterfalls 146-8
Kremlin 980-1
Krems an der Donau 87
Kristiansand 876-7
Kronborg Slot 318
Kruja 58
Ksamil 59
Kuldīga 728
Kuopio 363-4
Kurshskaya Kosa National Park 995
Kurzeme 727
Kuşadasi 1190-1
Kutná Hora 296-7
Kyiv 1206-11
Kykkos 278
Kyrenia 280

L
La Besurta 1106
La Tomatina 48
Laax 1163
Lagos 938-9
Lahemaa National Park 339
Lake Bled 49
Lake Constance 489-90
Lake District National Park 203-4
Lake Geneva 1152

Lake Köyceğiz 1193
Lake Malta 912
Lake Matka 768
Lake Morskie Oko 909
Lake Ohrid 768
Lake Śniardwy 918
Lakonian Mani 534
land mines 147
Land's End 193
Langøyene 869
language 36, 1251-86, *see also individual countries*
  courses 236, 970, 1228
  Cyrillic alphabet 1280
  Greek alphabet 1264
Languedoc-Roussillon 425-8
Larnaka 277
Las Fallas de San José 24, 45, 1087
Lascaux Caves 422
Latvia 717-30, **718**
  accommodation 729
  arts 719
  business hours 729
  culture 719
  embassies & consulates 729-30
  environment 719
  festivals & events 730
  history 719
  language 717, 1268-9
  money 717, 730
  travel to/from 719
  travel within 720
  visas 717, 730
Lausanne 1156-7
Lauterbrunnen 1170
Leaning Tower 684-5
Lecce 699-700
Lech 101
Leeds Castle 181
Lefkoşa 279-80
Lefkosia 275-7
legal matters 1223-4
Leiden 848-9
Leipzig 467-9
Lemesos 277-8
Lenin, Vladimir Ilich 360, 980
León 1066
Léopold II 121
lesbian travellers, *see* gay & lesbian travellers
Lesvos 553-5
Letoön 1194
Levoča 1022-3
Leysin 1158
Liechtenstein 731-5, **732**
  history 732
  language 731
  money 731, 735
  travel to/from 732
  travel within 732
  visas 731
Liège 129-30
Lienz 100
Liepāja 728
life expectancy, highest 66
Lille 397-8
Limasol 277-8
Lindau 489-90
Linnansaari 364
Linz 87-8
Lipari 702-3
Lisbon 925-35, **926-7**
  accomodation 929
  attractions 928-9
  clubbing 933-4
  drinking 932-3
  entertainment 934
  food 929-32
  travel to/from 934
  travel within 928, 934-5
Liseberg 1140
literature 40-1, 1218
  Albania 53
  Belarus 105
  Belgium 114
  Bosnia & Hercegovina 136
  Britain 153
  Bulgaria 231
  Croatia 252
  Cyprus 275
  Czech Republic 286
  Estonia 331
  France 372
  Germany 450
  Hungary 563
  Italy 633
  Kosovo 714
  Macedonia 763
  Malta 775
  Moldova 789
  Montenegro 799
  Netherlands 839
  Poland 893
  Romania 956
  Russia 978
  Sarajevo Haggadah 138
  Serbia 1000
  Slovakia 1014
  Slovenia 1028
  Spain 1049
  Turkey 1178
  travel 28
  Ukraine 1207
Lithuania 736-51, **738**
  accommodation 750
  business hours 750
  culture 737
  embassies & consulates 750-1
  environment 737
  festivals & events 749, 751
  history 737
  language 736, 1269-70
  money 736, 751
  travel to/from 737-9
  travel within 739
  visas 736, 751
Little Mermaid 315
Liverpool 202-3
Ljubljana 1031-7, **1032-3**
Llanberis 214
Locarno 1162
Loch Lomond & the Trossachs National Park 222
Loch Ness 224
Lofoten 885-6
Loire Valley 408-13
Loket 298
Lokrum Island 268
Loksa 339
Lomnický štít 1021
London 48, 49, 159-79, **162-3**, **172-3**, **10**
  accommodation 170-4
  attractions 164
  clubbing 175-6
  drinking 175
  entertainment 176-7
  festivals & events 169-70
  food 174-5
  shopping 177, 178
  tours 169
  travel to/from 177
  travel within 165, 168, 177-9
London Eye 168, **10**
Londonderry 625-7
Lorraine 404
Lourdes 424-5
Louvre 385
Loveparade, *see* B-Parade
Lower Saxony 502-3

000 Map pages
000 Photograph pages

LSD 1149
Lübeck 511-12
Lublin 906-7
Lucca 687-8
Lucerne 1167-8
Lugano 1162
luggage 26
Luik 129-30
Lund 1139
Lüneburg 503
Luso 943-4
Luxembourg 752-60, **753**
accommodation 760
business hours 760
culture 754
embassies & consulates 760
environment 754
festivals & events 760
history 753-4
language 752
money 752, 760
travel to/from 754
travel within 754
visas 752, 760
Luxembourg City 754-8, **756**
Lviv 1211-12
Lyon 415-19, **416**

M

Maastricht 856-7
Macedonia 761-72, **762**
accommodation 771
arts 763
business hours 771
culture 763
embassies & consulates 771
environment 763
festivals & events 765, 768
history 762-3
language 761, 1270-1
money 761, 771-2
travel to/from 763-4
travel within 764
visas 761, 772
Madrid 1051-62, **1052-3**
accommodation 1057-8
attractions 1055-7
clubbing 1060
drinking 1059-60
entertainment 1060-1
food 1058-9, 1060
shopping 1061-2
travel to/from 1062
travel within 1054, 1062
Madurodam 849
Magritte, René 118
Mainau Island 489
Mainz 491-2
Majdanek 906
Malá Fatra National Park 1020
Málaga 1099-100
Malbork Castle 917
Malbun 735
Mali Štuoc 804
Mallorca 1082-3
Malmö 1136-9, **1138**
Małopolska 901-8
Malta 773-84, **774**
accommodation 782
business hours 783
culture 775
embassies & consulates 783
environment 775
festivals & events 783
history 774
language 773, 1271-2
money 773, 783
travel to/from 775
travel within 775-6
visas 773, 784
Manarola 657-8
Manchester 200-2
Manchester United 201
Mani 534
Mann, Thomas 512
Mannerheim, CGE 354
Manteigas 944
Mantova 662
Maó 1085
maps 1224
Maribor 1041
Mariehamn 361-2
marijuana 834, 838-9, 846, 1114, 1224
Marmaris 1192-3
Marmolada glacier 677
Marpissa 542
Marrakesh 827-32, **828-9**
Marsalforn 781-2
Marseille 428-31
Marvão 941
Marx, Karl 491
Masuria 918-19
Matera 698-9
Matisse, Henri 435
Matterhorn 37, 1158
Mdina 781
medication 1250
medicine 41
Medina Azahara 1092
medinas 815, 818, 819, 822, 830
Meersburg 489
Megalo Papingo 538
Meissen 467
Meknès 826-7
Melk 87
Menhir of Outeiro 941
Menorca 1085-6
Mer de Glace 419
Mercedes-Benz Museum 483
Mérida 1104-5
Messinian Mani 534
Meteora 537
Mevlâna 49, 1198, 1202
Mevlevi 279
Međugorje 146
M'Hamid 833
Michelangelo 681
midsummer celebrations 47
Denmark 327
Estonia 343
Finland 368, 369
Iceland 593
Latvia 730
Lithuania 751
Spain 1076
Miffy 854
Mikołajki 918
Mikro Papingo 538
Milan 659-62, **7**
Mileştii Mici 793
Miletus 1190
mines 147
Minsk 105-9, **107**
Miró, Joan 1076, 1082
Mithymna 554-5
mobile phones 1229
Mobile Phone Throwing World Championships 363
Mokra Gora 1009
Moldova 785-96, **787**
accommodation 794
arts 786
business hours 794
culture 786
embassies & consulates 795
environment 788
festivals & events 795
history 786
language 785
money 785, 793, 795
travel to/from 788
travel within 788
visas 785, 796

INDEX

Moldoviţa 972
Monaco 439-40
Monemvasia 534
Monet, Claude 400
money 25, 1225-7, *see also individual countries*, discount cards, free stuff
  budgets 27, 28, 29, 30
Monodendri 538
Monsaraz 941
Mont Blanc 37
Mont St-Michel 401-2
Monte Igueldo 1107
Monte Toro 1085
Monte Urgull 1106
Montenegro 797-806, **798**
  accommodation 805
  business hours 805
  culture 799
  embassies & consulates 805
  environment 799
  history 798-9
  language 797, 805
  money 797, 805-6
  travel to/from 799-800
  travel within 800
  visas 797, 806
Monterosso 657-8
Montreux 1157
Moravia 302-3
Moreton-in-Marsh 196
Morocco 807-36, **809**
  accommodation 833-4
  business hours 834
  culture 808
  embassies & consulates 834
  environment 808-10
  etiquette 810
  festivals & events 821, 835
  history 808
  language 807, 1272-3
  money 807, 835
  religion 808
  travel to/from 810
  travel within 810-11
  visas 807, 836
Moscow 979-86, **7**
Moselle Valley 490-1, 759
Moskenesstraumen 886
mosquitoes 368
Mostar 48, 144-6, **145**
motorcycle travel 1238-42

000 Map pages
000 Photograph pages

Moulay Idriss 827
mountainbiking, *see* cycling
mountaineering
  Austria 101
  Britain 1249
  France 419, 444
  Germany 513
  Iceland 592
  Norway 885
  Switzerland 1158
movies 29
Mozart, Wolfgang Amadeus 93
Mt Elbrus 37
Mt Etna 704
Mt Fløyen 879
Mt Gubałówka 908, 909
Mt Kasprowy Wierch 909
Mt Kynthos 540
Mt Nemrut National Park 1200
Mt Olympus 537
Mt Vitosha 235
Mt Zeus 543
Mucha, Alfons 292
Munch, Eduard 868
Munich 48, 472-8, **473**
Murano 670
Murcia 1088
Mürren 45, 1170
Museo Guggenheim 1108
Museo Nacional del Prado 1055
music 39-40, 154
music festivals 22
  B-Parade 47
  Black Nights Film Festival 337
  Bratislava Jazz Days 1016
  Bratislava Music Festival 1016
  Celtic music festival 945
  Český Krumlov International Music Festival 304
  Copenhagen Jazz Festival 315, 327
  Donauinselfest 80
  Dragačevo Trumpet Festival 1009
  Dvořák Autumn 304
  Exit Festival 22, 47
  Fès Festival of World Sacred Music 822
  Fête de la Musique 22, 445
  Fez Festival 46
  Glastonbury Festival 22, 47, 191
  Gnaoua & World Music Festival 821
  Iceland Airwaves 22, 588
  Inferno Metal Festival 869
  International Festival of Street Musicians 1009
  International İstanbul Music Festival 1202
  International Organ Music Festival 914
  Jazz on the Odra International Festival 910
  Jazzkaar 337
  Kaliakra Rock Fest 248
  Karlovy Vary International Film Festival 304
  Musica Polonica Nova Festival 910
  Nice Jazz Festival 445
  North Sea Jazz Festival 859
  Õllesummer 337
  Oslo International Jazz Festival 869
  Øya Festival 869
  Poznań Jazz Festival 912
  Prague Autumn 304
  Prague Spring 304
  rock festival (Porto) 945
  Roskilde Rock festival 22, 47, 327
  Skanderborg Festival 327
  Skopje Jazz Festival 765
  Stockholm Jazz Festival 1129
  Street Parade 48
  United Islands 304
  Warsaw Autumn International Festival of Contemporary Music 898
Mycenae 533
Mykonos 540-1, **541**
Myrdal 877
Mystras 533
Mytilini 554

N

Nafplio 533
Nagy Alföld 577-8
Namen 130-1
Namur 130-1
Naoussa 542
Naples 690-5, **692-3**
National Archaeological Museum 528
National Marine Park of Alonnisos 556
national parks & reserves
  Brecon Beacons National Park 211
  Curonian Spit National Park 750
  Dartmoor National Park 191-2
  Duinen van Texel National Park 856
  Durmitor National Park 804-5
  Exmoor National Park 191
  Gauja National Park 728
  Hautes Fagnes Nature Reserve 130
  Hohe Tauern National Park 100
  Kaliakra nature reserve 246

Killarney National Park 614
Kiskunság National Park 577
Kolovesi 364
Kurshskaya Kosa National Park 995
Lahemaa National Park 339
Lake District National Park 203-4
Linnansaari 364
Loch Lomond & The Trossachs National Park 222
Malá Fatra National Park 1020
Mt Nemrut National Park 1200
National Marine Park of Alonnisos 556
Parco Nazionale delle Cinque Terre 657-8
Parque Nacional Da Peneda-Gerês 950-1
Parque Nacional de Ordesa y Monte Perdido 1106
Parque Natural de Serra da Estrela 944
Parque Natural Posets-Maladeta 1106
Peak District National Park 198
Pembrokeshire Coast National Park 213
Snowdonia National Park 213-14
Strandjha Nature Park 247
Sutjeska National Park 147-8
Tatra National Park 909, 1020
Trakai Historical National Park 748
Upper Rock Nature Reserve 1102-3
Þingvellir National Park 592

Navarra 1109
Naxos 542-3
Nazaré 942
Nea Kameni 545
Nesebâr 246
Netherlands 837-60, **838**
accommodation 857-8
arts 839
business hours 858
culture 839
embassies & consulates 858
environment 839
festivals & events 858-9
history 838-9
language 837, 1257-8
money 837, 859
travel to/from 839-40
travel within 840-1
visas 837, 860
Neuchâtel 1157
Neuschwanstein 482
Newcastle-upon-Tyne 207-9
Newquay 192
newspapers 1224
Newton, Isaac 41
Nice 434-8, **436-7**
Nida 750
Nîmes 425-6
Njeguši 805
Nordkapp 887
Normandy 399-402
North Cyprus 279-81
North Nicosia 279-80
Northern Ireland 620-7
northern lights 48
Norway 861-90, **863**
accommodation 887-8
arts 862-4
business hours 888
culture 862
embassies & consulates 888-9
environment 864
festivals & events 869, 889
history 862
language 861, 1273-4
money 861, 889
travel to/from 864-5
travel within 865-6
visas 861, 890
weather 888
Notre Dame 384
Notting Hill Carnival 48
Novi Sad 47, 1007-8, **1007**
nude sunbathing 474, 856
nudist beaches 264, 268
Nuraghe di Palmavera 708
Nuremberg 480-1

O

Oban 222-3
Oberwesel 492
Óbidos 941-2
Odense 320
Ohrid 767-70, **769**
Oia 545
Oktoberfest 24, 48, 475, 514
Olavinlinna 362
Old Trafford stadium 201
Õllesummer 47
Olomouc 303
Ölüdeniz 1193
Olympia 535
Olympos 1195
Omaha Beach 402
Omodos 278
Ordino 68
Orheiul Vechi 793
Ortisei 677
Ortygia 704
Oslo 866-75, **867, 870-1**
accommodation 869-72
attractions 867-9
clubbing 874
drinking 873-4
entertainment 874
food 872-3
shopping 874
travel to/from 874-5
travel within 875
Östersund 1144
Ostia Antica 654
Ostrog Monastery 804
Ostrožac Fortress 144
Oswald, Lee Harvey 108
Oświęcim 905-6
Oulu 364-6
Oxford 193-6, **194**

P

Paceville 778-81, **780**
packing 26
Padua 664-5
Pafos 278-9
painting 38-41
Pakleni Islands 264
Pal 69
Palau de Gel 67
Palermo 700-2
Palia Kameni 545
Palio 686
Palma 1082-3
Pamplona 47, 1109
Pamukkale 1191
Panarea 702-3
Paneriai 747
Pantheon 644
Paola 779
paragliding 1217
Cyprus 281
Slovenia 1043
Switzerland 1158, 1168, 1172
Turkey 1193
Parco Archeologico della Neapolis 704
Parco Nazionale delle Cinque Terre 657-8
Paris 48, 376-96, **378-9, 387, 6**
accommodation 388-90
attractions 380-6
clubbing 393
drinking 392-3
entertainment 393
food 390-2

Paris *continued*
shopping 387, 390
tours 386-7
travel to/from 393-4
travel within 381, 394-6
Pärnu 342
Paros 541-2
Parque Nacional Da Peneda-Gerês 950-1
Parque Nacional de Ordesa y Monte Perdido 1106
Parque Natural de Serra da Estrela 944
Parque Natural Posets-Maladeta 1106
Parthenon 527
passports 1227-8
Patara 1194
Patmos 552
Patra 532
Pāvilosta 728
Peak District National Park 198
Peć 716
Pécs 576-7
Peja 716
Peloponnese 532-5
Pembrokeshire Coast National Park 213
Penzance 193
Pergamum 1188
Perugia 688-9
phonecards 1228
photography 30, 1228
Piazza San Marco 667
Pic de Coma Pedrosa 69
Picasso, Pablo 39, 386, 1071, 1099
pickpockets 1220-1
Pınara 1193
Pinnerkreuz 490
pintxos 1107, 6
Piraeus 531-2
Piran 1042
Pisa 684-5
planning 25-30
itineraries 31-5
Płaszów Concentration Camp 902
Platres 278
Plovdiv 238-40
Plzeň 298-9
Počitelj 146
Pointe Helbronner 419
Poland 891-920, **892**
accommodation 919
arts 893
business hours 919
culture 893
embassies & consulates 919
environment 893
festivals & events 46, 898, 910, 912, 914
history 892-3
language 891, 1274-6
money 891, 920
travel to/from 893-4
travel within 895
visas 891, 920
Polis 279
Pollença 1082
Pomerania 913-18
Pompeii 695-6
Pont du Gard 426
Poprad 1022
population 36
Porsche Museum 483
Porto 944-8, **946-7**
Portsmouth 183-4
Portugal 921-52, **923**
accommodation 951
arts 922
business hours 951
culture 922
embassies & consulates 951-2
environment 922-4
festivals & events 945, 949, 952
history 922
language 921, 1276-7
money 921, 952
travel to/from 924
travel within 924-5
visas 921, 952
Porvoo 358
Positano 697-8
postal services 1228
Postojna 1040
Postojna Cave 1040
Potsdam 463-4
Poznań 912-13
Prague 46, 287-96, **289**, **290-1**
accommodation 293-4
attractions 288-92
clubbing 295
drinking 294-5
entertainment 295-6
food 294
travel to/from 288, 296
travel within 287, 296
Prague Castle 288-9, **289**
prehistoric paintings 422
Preikestolen 875
Priene 1190
Primorsko 247
Pristina 714-15, **715**
Prizren 716
Provence 428-34
Pula 260-1
Pythagoras 553
Pythagorio 553

Q

quad-biking 139
Quedlinburg 504
Quercy 420-1
Quimper 402-3

R

Rabat (Gozo) 781
Rabat (Morocco) 819-20
radio 1224-5
Radovan Karadzic 36
rafting 1217
Albania 55
Bosnia & Hercegovina 139, 143, 144, 147
Czech Republic 298, 300-1, 304
Estonia 343
France 444
Iceland 592
Montenegro 804
Portugal 935, 943, 951
Slovenia 1038, 1040, 1043
Switzerland 1163, 1168, 1172, 1217
Rambla 1070-1
Ramla Bay 782
Randstad 848-55
Râşnov 967
Ravenna 676
Real Madrid 1061
red-light districts
Amsterdam 843, 844
Basel 1172
Hamburg 507
Zürich 1166
Red Square 980
Regensburg 481-2
reindeer 348, 364, 422, 1144, 1145
reindeer-sledding 368
religion 30, 37, 42, *see also individual countries*
Rembrandt 843
Remich 759
Renaissance 38
Republic of Cyprus 275-9
Reşadiye Peninsula 1192
Rethymno 547-8

000 Map pages
000 Photograph pages

Reykjavík 584-91, **586-7**
Rheinschlucht 1163
Rhine Valley 491-2
Rhodes 550-1
Rhône Valley 413-19
Ribčev Laz 1039
Ribe 326
Rīga 720-7, **722-3**
Rijksmuseum 841-3
Rijsel 397-8
Rila Monastery 238
Ring of Kerry 615-16
Ring of Skellig 615
Riomaggiore 657-8
Rochefort 131
rock climbing 1217
  Andorra 67
  Bosnia & Hercegovina 144
  Britain 198, 213
  Bulgaria 242, 247
  France 444
  Greece 537
  Ireland 627
  Luxembourg 759
  Macedonia 768
  Norway 885
  Slovakia 1025
  Spain 1106
  Switzerland 1168
  Turkey 1195, 1199
Rodin, Auguste 381
Roman Forum 641
Romania 953-74, **954**
  accommodation 972-3
  arts 955
  culture 955
  embassies & consulates 973
  environment 956
  festivals & events 973
  history 955
  language 953, 1277-9
  money 953, 973-4
  travel to/from 956-7
  travel within 957
  visas 953, 974
Romantic Road 478
Rome 636-54, **638-9**, **640**
  accommodation 649-50
  attractions 637-49
  clubbing 652
  drinking 651-2
  entertainment 652
  foos 650-1
  travel to/from 652-3
  travel within 637, 653-4
Rops, Félicien 130-1
Røros 883
Rosenborg Slot 314
Roskilde 47, 318-19, 327
Rothenburg ob der Tauber 480
Rothorn 1158
Rotterdam 851-4, **852**
Rouen 399-400
Rousseau, Jean Jacques 39
Route du Vin 759
Rovaniemi 366-7
royal family of Luxembourg 758
Royal Shakespeare Company 197
Rubens, Pieter Paul 121
Rüdesheim 492
rugby 43, 153, 176
Rumi, Celaleddin 1198
Rundāle Palace 727
Running of the Bulls 24, 47, 1109
Russia 975-97, **977**
  accommodation 995
  arts 976
  business hours 995
  culture 976
  embassies & consulates 996
  environment 976-8
  history 976
  language 975, 1279-80
  money 975, 996
  travel to/from 978
  travel within 978-9
  visas 975, 997

S

Sachsenhausen Concentration Camp 464-5
safe travel 1220
  Albania 60
  Austria 101
  Bosnia & Hercegovina 147
  Britain 164, 226
  Czech Republic 304
  France 380, 429
  Germany 506, 513
  Italy 691
  Kosovo 716
  Macedonia 771
  Montenegro 805
  Morocco 822, 834
  Poland 919
  Romania 958
  Russia 995
  Serbia 1009
  Slovakia 1025
  Turkey 1202
Sagrada Família 1075
Sagres 939
Sahara 832-3
sailing
  Austria 80
  Germany 489
  Greece 543
  Hungary 575
  Ireland 627
  Lithuania 748
  Netherlands 858
  Sweden 1129
  Switzerland 1172
Saklıkent Gorge 1193
Salamanca 1063-5, **1063**
Salamis 281
Salina 702-3
Salisbury 185-6
Salzburg 91-5, **92**
Salzkammergut 95-6
Samaria Gorge 549
Sámi 364
Samos 553
San Gimignano 687
San José 1098
San Martino di Castrozza 677
San Sebastián 1106-8, **6**
Sanctuary of Apollon Ylatis 277
Sant Antoni 1084
Sant Julià de Lòria 69
Santa Claus Village 366
Santa Cristina 677
Santander 1110-11
Santiago Bernabéu Stadium 1061
Santiago de Compostela 1111-12
Santillana del Mar 1111
Santorini 544-6, **545**
Sappho 554
Sarajevo 137-43, **140-1**
Sarajevo Haggadah 138
Saranda 59-60
Sardinia 705-8
Sarlat-la-Canéda 420-1
Saronic Gulf Islands 539-40
sassi 698
saunas
  Andorra 68
  Britain 177
  Estonia 336
  Finland 354, 360, 363, 368
  Germany 501
  Russia 995
  Sweden 1137
Savin Kuk 804
Savonlinna 362-3

scams 1221
Schauinsland peak 488
Schengen Agreement 1230
Scheveningen 849
Schiltach 487
Schilthorn 1170
Schloss Hellbrunn 95
Schloss Schönbrunn 77-80
Schwaz 99
science 41
Scotland 49, 214-25, **215**
scuba diving 1217
  Croatia 261, 270
  Cyprus 281
  Estonia 343
  Greece 558
  Iceland 593
  Ireland 627
  Italy 657, 702-3
  Lithuania 748
  Malta 782-3
  Portugal 939
  Turkey 1191, 1194, 1201
sea caves 696, 698, 707
seals 326, 364, 519, 556
Segovia 1065-6
Seia 944
Selçuk 1189-90
Selime 1199
Selva 677
Serbia 998-1010, **999**
  accommodation 1009
  arts 1000
  business hours 1009
  culture 1000
  embassies & consulates 1009
  environment 1000
  festivals & events 47, 1008, 1009
  history 999-1000
  language 998, 1010, 1253-4
  money 998, 1010
  travel to/from 1000-1
  travel within 1001-10
  visas 998, 1010
Serra da Estrela 944
Setúbal 936-7
Seville 38, 1088-92, **1090**
Shakespeare, William 197, 318, 662
Shipka Pass 240
Šiauliai 749
Sibiu 968-9

000 Map pages
000 Photograph pages

Sicily 700-5
Siena 47, 685-7, **686**
Sighişoara 967-8
Sigulda 728-9
Silesia 909-11
Silves 939
Simenon, Georges 129-30
Simeonovo 236
Sinaia 963-4
Sinemorets 247
Sintra 935-6
Siófok 575-6
Sítio 942
Skagen 325-6
Skala 552
Skalnaté pleso 1021
Skåne 1136
Skellig Rocks 615
Skiathos 555
skiing 43, 45, 1217
  Andorra 66, 69
  Austria 98, 100-1
  Bosnia & Hercegovina 139, 147
  Bulgaria 235, 247
  Finland 368
  France 419, 444
  Germany 513
  Italy 676-7, 709
  Liechtenstein 735
  Montenegro 804
  Norway 869, 877, 886, 888
  Poland 908, 909
  Romania 964, 973
  Serbia 1009
  Slovakia 1020, 1025
  Slovenia 1043
  Spain 1113
  Sweden 1144, 1146
  Switzerland 1152, 1158, 1163, 1169, 1171, 1172
  Turkey 1201
Škocjan Caves 1040
Skopelos 555-6
Skopje 764-7, **766**
skydiving 729, 1168, 1170, 1217
Śląsk 909-11
Sliema 778-81, **780**
Sligo 619-20
Slovakia 1011-26, **1012**
  accommodation 1024
  arts 1013
  business hours 1025
  culture 1013
  embassies & consulates 1025
  environment 1013
  festivals & events 1016, 1025
  history 1013
  language 1011, 1280-2
  money 1011, 1025
  travel to/from 1013
  travel within 1014
  visas 1011, 1026
Slovenia 1027-45, **1029**
  accommodation 1043
  arts 1028
  business hours 1043
  culture 1028
  embassies & consulates 1043
  environment 1028
  festivals & events 1043-4
  history 1028
  language 1027, 1044, 1282-3
  money 1027, 1044-5
  travel to/from 1028-30
  travel within 1030-1
  visas 1027, 1045
Smiltynė 750
snorkelling
  Cyprus 281
  Greece 558
  Italy 657, 702
  Portugal 939
  Turkey 1191
snow disc 1171
snowboarding, *see* skiing
Snowdonia National Park 213-14
snowmobiling 368
snowshoeing 343
snowsurfing 1163
Soča Valley 1040
soccer, *see* football
Sofia 233-8, **234**
Sognefjorden 881-2
Soldeu 66-8
Sóller 1082-3
Sonkajärvi 365
Sopron 574-5
Sorrento 697
Sound of Music 93
Southern Bucovina 972
South Nicosia 275-7
Sozopol 247
Spa 130
Spain 1046-115, **1048**, **8**
  accommodation 1112
  arts 1048-9
  business hours 1113
  culture 1047
  embassies & consulates 1113
  environment 1049

festivals & events 24, 45, 47, 48, 1057, 1076, 1087, 1089, 1109, 1113-14
history 1047
language 1046, 1114, 1283-4
money 1046, 1114
travel to/from 1049-50
travel within 1050-1
visas 1046, 1115
Spanish Riding School 85
Spanish Steps 645
Sparta 533
spas, *see* springs
Spetses 539-40
Spišské Podhradie 1023
Split 261-3
Sporades 555-6
sport 43
springs
Andorra 68
Belgium 130
Czech Republic 297
Germany 501
Greece 555
Hungary 567, 579
Iceland 591
Macedonia 770
Portugal 944
Slovakia 1022, 1024
Turkey 1193
Sremski Karlovci 1008
St Andrews 221-2
St Anton am Arlberg 101
St Christoph 101
St Davids 213
St Goar 492
St Goarshausen 492
St Ives 192
St John 552, 1190
St Julian's 778-81, **780**
St Moritz 1163
St Patrick's Day 24, 45
St Paul's Cathedral 167
St Peter's Basilica 642
St Petersburg 46, 986-92, **988-9**, 11
Stamsund 886
Stara Fužina 1039
Stari Most 144
Starý Smokovec 1020
Stasi 458, 468
Stavanger 875-6
Stephansdom 77
Stirling 221
St-Malo 403-4
Stockholm 1123-34, **1126-8**
accommodation 1129-30
attractions 1124-5
clubbing 1132
drinking 1131-2
entertainment 1132-3
food 1130-1
shopping 1133
travel to/from 1133-4
travel within 1124, 1134
Stockholm Archipelago 1134
Stockhorn 1158
Stolac 146
Stonehenge 186
Stow-on-the-Wold 196
Strandjha Nature Park 247
Strasbourg 404-8, **406-7**
Stratford-upon-Avon 197-8
Strathdon 49
Štrbské Pleso 1020
Strokkur 592
Stromboli 702-3
Stubai Glacier 98
Stuben 101
Studor 1039
studying 1228
Stuttgart 483-5
Subotica 1008-9
Suceava 972
summer solstice, *see* midsummer celebrations
Sund 362
Suomenlinna 351
Supphellebreen 882
surfing 1217-18
Britain 192, 213, 226
Denmark 327
France 423, 444
Greece 542, 543, 558
Ireland 620, 627
Latvia 728
Morocco 834
Netherlands 858
Norway 875
Portugal 936, 937, 939, 951
Spain 1085, 1101, 1106, 1113
Switzerland 1172
sustainable travel 25-7, 864, 1152
Sutjeska National Park 147
Svaneke 319
Sveti Sava 1002
Sveti Stefan 802
Svolvær 885
Svolværgeita 885
Sweden 1116-47, **1118**
accommodation 1145
arts 1119
business hours 1146
culture 1117
embassies & consulates 1146
environment 1119
festivals & events 1129, 1136, 1146
history 1117
language 1116, 1284-5
money 1116, 1146-7
travel to/from 1119-22
travel within 1122-3
visas 1116, 1147
swimming, *see also* beaches
Albania 60
Estonia 336, 342
Finland 354
Iceland 593
Italy 697
Macedonia 771
Malta 782, 783
Norway 869, 879
Sweden 1134
Switzerland 1166, 1171
Vienna 80
Switzerland 1148-73, **1150**
accommodation 1152, 1172
business hours 1172
culture 1149-51
embassies & consulates 1172-3
environment 1151
festivals & events 46, 1155, 1160, 1162, 1166, 1167-8, 1173
history 1149
language 1148
money 1148, 1173
travel to/from 1151
travel within 1151-2
visas 1148, 1173
Syracuse 704-5
Szeged 578
Szentendre 573

T

Tallinn 47, 332-9, **334**
accommodation 337
attractions 333-6
clubbing 338
drinking 337
entertainment 338
food 337
shopping 338
travel to/from 338
travel within 335, 338-9

INDEX

Tampere 360-1
Tangier 811-14, **813**
Taormina 703-4
tapas 1059
Tara River 804
Tarifa 1101-2
Tarquinia 655
Tarragona 1080-1, **1081**
Tartu 339-42, **340**
Tatra Mountains 909
Tatra National Park 909, 1020
Tatranská Lomnica 1020
Tatras 1020
Tavira 938
taxes 1227
taxis 1242
Tekija 146
Telč 303
telephone services 1228-9
Telmessos 1193
tennis 43, 789
Terchová 1020
Teruel 1106
Texel 856
Thames 168
The Hague 849-50
theft 1220-1, 1245
thermal springs, *see* springs
Thessaloniki 535-7, **536**
Thira 544
Thirasia 545
Ticino 1162
time 1229
Timişoara 971-2
tipping 1227
Tirana 54-8, **56**
Tiraspol 793-4
Tirol 96-100
Titanic 621
Titisee 487-8
Tito, Josip Broz 1002
Tivoli (Denmark) 313-14
Tivoli (Italy) 654
Tlos 1193
toilets 166, 1229
Tokaj 579
Toledo 1067-9, **1068**
Tomar 942
Topkapı Palace 1183, **20**
Torcello 670
Torla 1106

000 Map pages
000 Photograph pages

Torre de Belém 928
Toruń 916-18
Toulouse 426-8
Tour de France 43
tourist information 1229
tours 410-11, 1229
Tower Bridge 167
Tower of London 167
Tragaea region 543
train travel 1235, 1242-5, **4**
  rail passes 1243-5
train trips 214
Trakai 747-8
Trakai Historical National Park 748
Transdniestr 793-4
Transylvania 963-71
travel to/from Europe 1232-5
travel within Europe 1235-45
travellers cheques 1227
Trebinje 146
Trenčín 1019-20
Treska Canyon 768
Trevi Fountain 645
Triberg 487
Trier 491
Triesenberg 734
Triglav 1037
Trinity College 601
Trollfjord 885
Trollveggen 882
Tromsø 45, 886-7
Trondheim 883-5
Troodos Massif 278
Trossachs National Park 222
Troy 1188
Trümmelbach Falls 1170
Tsarevets fortress 240-1
Tübingen 485
Turin 658-9
Turkey 1174-203, **1176-7**
  accommodation 1201
  business hours 1201
  culture 1175-6
  embassies & consulates 1202
  environment 1176
  festivals & events 1202
  history 1175
  language 1174, 1285-6
  money 1174, 1202-3
  travel to/from 1177-8
  travel within 1178-9
  visas 1174, 1203
Turku 358-60
turtles 279, 281, 519, 1193, 1194

U
Uçhisar's 1199
Uffizi Gallery 680
Ukraine 1204-13, **1206-7**
  accommodation 1212
  business hours 1212
  culture 1205
  embassies & consulates 1212
  environment 1205
  festivals & events 1212
  history 1205
  language 1204
  money 1204, 1213
  religion 1205
  travel to/fom 1205-6
  travel within 1206
  visas 1204, 1213
Ulcinj 803
Umeå 1144
Una Valley 144
university accommodation 1216
Uppsala 1135
Urbino 690
Utö 1134
Utrecht 854-5

V
vaccinations 1246
Vaduz 732-4, **734**
Valais 1158-9
Val de Travers 1157
Val Gardena 677
Valencia 45, 1086-7
Valentia Island 615
Valldemossa 1082
Valletta 776-8, **777**, **780**
Van 1200-1
Van Gogh, Vincent 843
Van Rijn, Rembrandt 843
Varna 243-6, **244**
Vatican City 641-4
Vatican Museums 643-4
Veliko Târnovo 240-3, **241**
Venice 665-73, **666**, **5**, **24**
Ventspils 728
Vermeer, Jan 850
Vernazza 657-8
Verona 662-4
Versailles 396
Vevčani 770
Viana do Castelo 949
Vianden 758
Victoria 781

Vienna 76-86, **78-9, 82-3**
accommodation 80-1
attractions 76-80
clubbing 85
drinking 81-5
entertainment 85
festivals 80
food 81
shopping 85-6
travel to/from 86
travel within 80, 86
Vienna Boys' Choir 85
Vikings
Britain 205
Denmark 307, 314, 318-19, 324, 326
Iceland 583, 585, 592
Norway 862, 869, 882, 883
restaurants 359
Sweden 1117, 1140
Vikos Gorge 538
Vila do Gerês 950
Vilarinho das Furnas 950
Villa Adriana 654
Villa d'Este 654
Vilnius 740-7, **742-5**
visas 1229-30, *see also individual countries*, passports
Visby 1136
Visegrád 574
Vojvodina 1007-9
volcanoes
Fossa di Vulcano 702
Mt Etna 704
Santorini 546
Stromboli 702
Volcano Show 585
Volubilis 827
volunteering 1230-1
Vorarlberg 100-1
Vorkuta 38
Voroneţ 972
Võsu 339
Vrátna Valley 1020
Vuelta a España 1112-13
Vulcano 702-3
Vyros Gorge 534

W
Wales 209-14, **212**
walking, *see* hiking
Wallonia 129-32
Walpurgisnacht 46
Warmia 918-19
Warsaw 895-901, **896**
Wartburg 470
waterfalls
Bosnia & Hercegovina 143, 146
Germany 487
Iceland 592
Latvia 728
Norway 869, 882
Waterloo 120
Wattens 99
Wawel Castle 902
Waxholmsbolaget 1134
weather 25, 38, 1218-20
Weimar 470-2
Wembley Stadium 176
Werfen 95
Westminster Abbey 166
whales 583, 862
whaling 583, 862
whale-watching
Britain 213
Iceland 585, 593
Spain 1101
whirling dervishes 49, 279, 1197-8
White Cliffs of Dover 180-1
Wielkopolska 912-13
Wife-Carrying World Championships 365
Winchester 184-5
wind tunnel 729
Windermere 204
windmills
Greece 540
Netherlands 848, 852, 853, 859
Windsor 179
Windsor Castle 179
windsurfing, *see* surfing
wine
Croatia 264
festivals 795
Germany 490, 492, 495, 515
Hungary 567, 578, 580
Italy 710
Luxembourg 759
Moldova 792-3
Montenegro 805
Portugal 937, 945, 949
Route du Vin 759
Slovenia 1044
Winter Palace 987, 11
Wolf's Lair 918
Wolfsburg 503
women travellers 1231, 1250
wooden churches 1024
work 1231
World Air Guitar Championships 365
Wörthersee 91
Wrocław 909-11
Würzburg 478-9
WWI 128, 129, 1187
WWII 38, 131-2
cemeteries 401-2, 755-7
concentration camps 464-5, 471, 475, 747, 902, 905-6, 906
D-Day 401, 402
Holocaust Memorial 453
museums 481, 483
WWOOF 1231

X
Xagħra 782
Xanthos 1194

Y
Yeats, WB 619
yodelling 1151, 1168
York 204-7, **206**
Ypres 128-9

Z
Žabljak 804
Zagora 833
Zagorohoria 538
Zagreb 254-9, **256-7**
Zakopane 908-9
Zamość 907-8
Zappa, Frank 741
Zaragoza 1105-6
Ždiar 1022
Zealand 318-19
Zermatt 1158-9
Zlatibor 1009
zorbing 1168
Zürich 48, 1163-7, **1164-5**
Zürs 101

Þ
Þingvellir National Park 592
Þórsmörk 592

INDEX

THE LONELY PLANET STORY

Fresh from an epic journey across Europe, Asia and Australia in 1972, Tony and Maureen Wheeler sat at their kitchen table stapling together notes. The first Lonely Planet guidebook, *Across Asia on the Cheap*, was born.

Travellers snapped up the guides. Inspired by their success, the Wheelers began publishing books to Southeast Asia, India and beyond. Demand was prodigious, and the Wheelers expanded the business rapidly to keep up. Over the years, Lonely Planet extended its coverage to every country and into the virtual world via lonelyplanet.com and the Thorn Tree message board.

As Lonely Planet became a globally loved brand, Tony and Maureen received several offers for the company. But it wasn't until 2007 that they found a partner whom they trusted to remain true to the company's principles of travelling widely, treading lightly and giving sustainably. In October of that year, BBC Worldwide acquired a 75% share in the company, pledging to uphold Lonely Planet's commitment to independent travel, trustworthy advice and editorial independence.

Today, Lonely Planet has offices in Melbourne, London and Oakland, with over 500 staff members and 300 authors. Tony and Maureen are still actively involved with Lonely Planet. They're travelling more often than ever, and they're devoting their spare time to charitable projects. And the company is still driven by the philosophy of *Across Asia on the Cheap*: 'All you've got to do is decide to go and the hardest part is over. So go!'

Published by Lonely Planet Publications Pty Ltd
ABN 36 005 607 983

© Lonely Planet Publications Pty Ltd 2009

© photographers as indicated 2009

Cover montage by Yukiyoshi Kamimura. Photographs by JerryPDX, iStockphoto and Lonely Planet Images: Bruce Bi, John Elk III, Richard I'Anson, Diana Mayfield, Gareth McCormack, Guy Moberly, Andrew Peacock, Craig Pershouse, Will Salter, Damien Simonis, David Tomlinson.

Many of the images in this guide are available for licensing from Lonely Planet Images: www.lonelyplanetimages.com.

All rights reserved. No part of this publication may be copied, stored in a retrieval system, or transmitted in any form by any means, electronic, mechanical, recording or otherwise, except brief extracts for the purpose of review, and no part of this publication may be sold or hired, without the written permission of the publisher.

Printed by Hang Tai Printing Company, Hong Kong. Printed in China.

Lonely Planet and the Lonely Planet logo are trademarks of Lonely Planet and are registered in the US Patent and Trademark Office and in other countries.

Lonely Planet does not allow its name or logo to be appropriated by commercial establishments, such as retailers, restaurants or hotels. Please let us know of any misuses: www.lonelyplanet.com/ip.

LONELY PLANET OFFICES

Australia
Head Office
Locked Bag 1, Footscray, Victoria 3011
☎ 03 8379 8000, fax 03 8379 8111
talk2us@lonelyplanet.com.au

USA
150 Linden St, Oakland, CA 94607
☎ 510 250 6400, toll free 800 275 8555
fax 510 893 8572
info@lonelyplanet.com

UK
2nd fl, 186 City Rd,
London EC1V 2NT
☎ 020 7106 2100, fax 020 7106 2101
go@lonelyplanet.co.uk

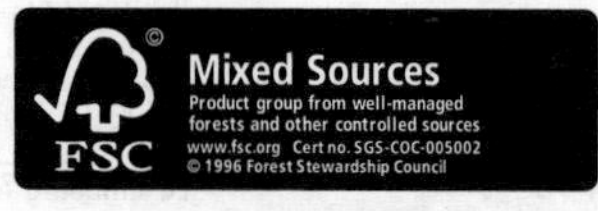

Although the authors and Lonely Planet have taken all reasonable care in preparing this book, we make no warranty about the accuracy or completeness of its content and, to the maximum extent permitted, disclaim all liability arising from its use.